dev.	development	GNP	Gross National Product	m	
dwt	dead weight tonnage	HEP	hydroelectric power	mi	
ECU	European Currency Unit	in	inches	NGC	
EMS	European Monetary System	kg	kilograms	NIC	
est	estimated	km	kilometers	PC	
°F	degrees Fahrenheit	km²	square kilometer	sq	
ft	feet	kw	kilowatts	TV	
g	grams	kwh	kilowatt hours	VCR	
GDP	Gross Domestic Product	LNG	liquefied natural gas		

D0842420

RESOURCES

Electricity generation: total per year in kilowatt hours (kwh), and total available capacity (kw)

Oil production: barrels per day (b/d); total oil reserves in billion barrels (bbl)

Estimated livestock resources

Main mineral resources

Fish catch per year (where fishing is a major industry)

ENVIRONMENT

Protected land as percentage of total land area

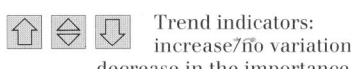 Trend indicators: increase/no variation/ decrease in the importance of environmental issues as a national concern

SIGNATORY TO THE FOLLOWING TREATIES

International Tropical Timber Agreement (ITTA) *Geneva, 1983*

Convention on the International Trade in Endangered Species of Wild Fauna and Flora (CITES) *Washington DC, 1973*

Convention on the Prevention of Marine Pollution by Dumping of Wastes and other Matter *London Dumping Convention, 1972*

1992 Amendment to Protocol on Substances that Deplete the Ozone Layer (Amendment to Montreal Protocol) *Copenhagen, 1992*

Convention on Biological Diversity *Earth Summit in Rio, 1992*

UN Convention on Climate Change *Earth Summit in Rio, 1992*

MEDIA

Media censorship assessment

Main national newspapers

Television stations: state-owned/independent

Radio stations: state-owned/ independent

Satellite TV availability

Cable TV availability

CRIME

Total prison population (where available)

 Crime trend indicators: increase/no variation/ decrease over previous year

EDUCATION

Literacy rate (percentage of total population)

Numbers in tertiary education and percentage enrolment among 20–24-year-olds

HEALTH

People per doctor

Major causes of death

WEALTH

Sample wage rates

MAP SYMBOLS AND LETTERING

ADMINISTRATION

International border

Disputed border (*de facto*)

Disputed border (territorial claim)

Undefined border

Cease-fire line

Internal administrative border

COMMUNICATIONS

International airport

Expressway/Highway

Major road

Secondary road

Unsurfaced road, track

Railroad

Canal

Tunnel

Mountain pass

HYDROGRAPHY

Major river

Minor river

Seasonal river

Lake

Seasonal lake

Wetland

Salt lake

Salt pan

Waterfall

Dam/reservoir

OTHER SYMBOLS

▲ Highest point in country

▲ High point

Site of interest (mentioned in text)

LETTERING

ECUADOR   Country name

DUBLIN   Capital city

San Francisco
Dover   } Cities and towns (type is graded according to population size and map scale)

QUEBEC   Administrative division

LANGUEDOC   Regional name

HIMALAYAS
Lake Baikal
Congo
Mt Fiji
Baffin Bay
SULU SEA   } Physical and hydrographic features

JULESBURG HIGH SCHOOL

THE DORLING KINDERSLEY

WORLD
REFERENCE
ATLAS

THE DORLING KINDERSLEY
WORLD
REFERENCE
ATLAS

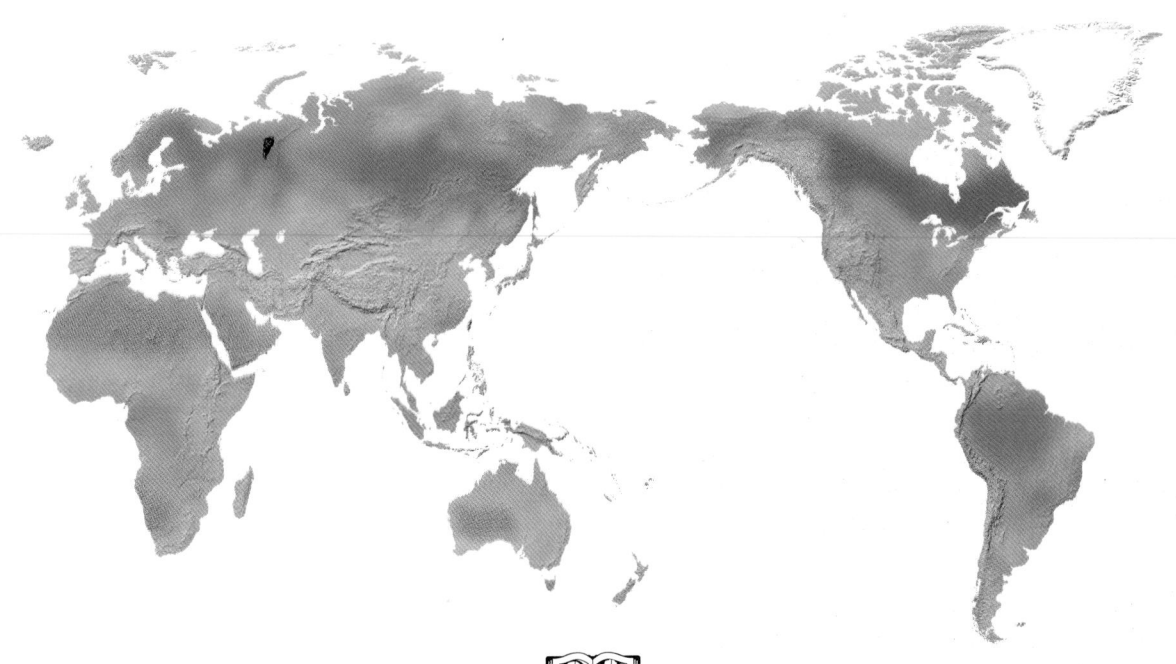

DORLING KINDERSLEY
LONDON • NEW YORK • STUTTGART • MOSCOW

A Dorling Kindersley Book

Managing Editor
Ian Castello-Cortes

Managing Art Editor
Philip Lord

Project Editors
Debra Clapson, Catherine Day,
Jo Edwards, Jane Oliver

Project Designers
Martin Biddulph, Scott David,
Yahya El-Droubie, Karen Gregory

Editors
Alastair Dougall, Ailsa Heritage,
Nicholas Kynaston, Susan Turner, Chris Whitwell,
Elizabeth Wyse

Designers
Rhonda Fisher,
Nicola Liddiard
Katy Wall

Project Cartographers
Caroline Bowie, Ruth Duxbury,
James Mills-Hicks, John Plumer,
Julie Turner

Cartographers
James Anderson, Roger Bullen, Tony Chambers,
Jan Clark, Martin Darlison, Claire Ellam, Julia Lunn,
Michael Martin, Peter Winfield, Claudine Zante

Additional Editorial Assistance
Louise Keane, Caroline Lucas,
Crispian Martin St. Valery,
Laura Porter, Ulrike Fritz-Weltz
Sally Wood

Additional Design Assistance
Paul Bayliss, Carol Ann Davis,
Adam Dobney, Kenny Laurenson

Picture Research
Alison McKittrick, Sarah Moule, Christine Rista

Readers
Jane Bruton, Reg Grant, Ann Kramer, Lesley Riley

Index Gazetteer
Margaret Hynes, Barbara Nash, Jayne Parsons, Janet Smy

Database Manager
Simon Lewis

Editorial Direction
Andrew Heritage, Louise Cavanagh

Art Director
Chez Picthall

Production
Hilary Stephens

Editorial update for second edition
CIRCA Research and Reference Information, Cambridge, UK

Published in the United States by Dorling Kindersley Publishing, Inc.,
95 Madison Avenue, New York, New York 10016
Visit us on the World Wide Web at http://www.dk.com

Reprinted with revisions 1995
Second American Edition 1996

A CIP catalog record for this book is available from the Library of Congress.
ISBN: 0-7894-1085-0
Text film output by Lyledale T/A Elements (London), Printed Word, UK, Colourpath, UK
Printed and bound by New Interlitho (Italy)

FOREWORD

THIS ATLAS is presented to the public in the full knowledge that the world is in a state of continual flux. Political fashions and personalities come and go, while the ebb and flow of peoples and ideas across the face of the planet create constant shifts in the cultural landscape. All the material assembled for this Atlas has been researched from the most up-to-date and authoritative sources; our team of consultants and contributors, designers, editors, and cartographers have endeavoured not only to explain the meaning of this material, to place it in a useful and clear context, but also to present it in a way which has a lasting value and relevance, regardless of the turmoil of daily events. This Second Edition has been entirely revised and updated, and includes a new country entry for Palau, the latest statistical data, several additional fields of information, and over forty new photographs.

The publishers would like to thank the many consultants and contributors whose diligence, perseverance and attention to detail made this book possible.

GENERAL CONSULTANTS
Anthony Goldstone, Senior Editor Asia-Pacific, *The Economist* Intelligence Unit, London
Professor Jack Spence, Director of Studies, The Royal Institute of International Affairs, London

REGIONAL CONSULTANTS

ASIA
Anthony Goldstone, London

USA
Michael Elliot, Diplomatic Editor, *Newsweek*, Washington DC

AFRICA
James Hammill, Lecturer in African Politics, University of Leicester
Kaye Whiteman, Editor-in-Chief, *West Africa Magazine*, London

EUROPE
John Ardagh, London
Rory Clarke, Senior Editor Europe, *The Economist* Intelligence Unit, London
Charles Powell, Centre for European Studies, St. Antony's College, Oxford

RUSSIA AND CIS
Martin McCauley, Senior Lecturer, School of Slavonic and East European Studies, University of London

MIDDLE EAST
John Whelan, Ex Editor-in-Chief, *Middle East Economic Digest*

CENTRAL AND SOUTH AMERICA
Nick Caistor, Producer, Latin American Section, BBC World Service

PACIFIC
Jim Boutilier, Professor in History, Royal Roads Military College, Victoria, Canada

CARIBBEAN
Canute James, *The Financial Times*, Kingston, Jamaica

CONTRIBUTORS
Janice Bell, School of Slavonic and East European Studies, University of London
Gerry Bourke, Asia Correspondent, *The Guardian*, Islamabad
Vincent Cable, Director, International Economics Program
P K Clark, MA, Former Chief Map Research Officer, Ministry of Defence
Ken Davies, Senior Editor, *The Economist* Intelligence Unit, London
Roger Dunn, Analyst, Control Risks Group, London
Aidan Foster-Carter, Senior Lecturer in Sociology, University of Leeds
Professor Murray Forsyth, Centre for Federal Studies, University of Leicester
Natasha Franklin, School of Slavonic and East European Studies, London
Adam Hannestad, *Blomberg Business News*, Copenhagen
Peter Holden, *The Economist* Research Department, London
Tim Jones, Knight Ritter, Brussels
Angella Johnstone, Home Affairs Correspondent, *The Guardian*, London
Oliver Keserü, International Chamber of Commerce, Paris
Robert Macdonald, *The Economist* Intelligence Unit
William Mader, Former Europe Bureau Chief, *Time Magazine*, Washington DC
Professor Brian Matthews, Institute of Commonwealth Studies, London
Nick Middleton, Oriel College, Oxford
Professor Mya Maung, Department of Finance, Boston College, Massachusetts
Judith Nordby, Leeds University
Simon Orme, London
Professor Richard Overy, Department of History, King's College, London
Steve Percy, East Asia Service, BBC World Service

Douglas Rimmer, Honorary Senior Research Fellow, Centre for West African Studies, University of Birmingham
Donna Rispoli, Linacre College, Oxford
Ian Rodger, *The Financial Times*, Zürich
The Royal Institute of International Affairs, London
Struan Simpson, St. James Research, London
Julie Smith, Brasenose College, Oxford
Elizabeth Spencer, London
Michiel Van Kuyen, Erasmus University, Rotterdam
Steven Whitefield, Pembroke College, Oxford
Georgina Wilde, Regional Director, Asia-Pacific, *The Economist* Intelligence Unit, London
H P Willmott, Visiting Professor, Dept. of Military Strategy & Operations, The National War College, Washington DC
Andrew Wilson, Sydney Sussex College, Cambridge
Tom Wingfield, *Reuters*, Bangkok
The World Conservation Monitoring Centre, Cambridge

Database research for Second Edition:
CIRCA Research and Reference Information Limited, Cambridge, UK
John Coggins, Roger East, Tanya Joseph, Stephen Lewis, Frances Nicholson, Darren Sagar, Farzana Shaikh. **Database research and project management:** Rosemary Payne, Philippa Youngman

CONTENTS

OVERSEAS TERRITORIES & DEPENDENCIES

3
GLOBAL ISSUES

4
INDEX ~ GAZETTEER

------ END PAPERS ------
KEY TO SYMBOLS, ICONS AND
ABBREVIATIONS USED IN THE ATLAS

HOW THE ATLAS WORKS

THIS ATLAS is divided into the four main sections detailed below. Each section has four main elements: maps, charts, icons and text. The opposite page explains how each of these are used in the book. The central section of the book is the Nations of the World which includes detailed mapping and encyclopedic information for every one of the world's 192 countries as defined by the UN.

1 THE WORLD TODAY: Ten double-page spreads examine the world and its continents. Regional maps highlight major physical features, with additional data about the continent's physical and political geography listed in the fact box. Introductory texts offer a concise view of each continent – its physical geography, people and resources, while illuminating cross-sections offer a different perspective.

A further eight double-page spreads are devoted to The Formation of the Modern World, which surveys world history over the last 500 years focusing on key dates and periods, starting with The Age of Discovery: 1492.

2 THE NATIONS OF THE WORLD: 567 pages of information broken down on a country-by-country basis, and listed alphabetically. For a detailed explanation of how this section works, refer to opposite page.

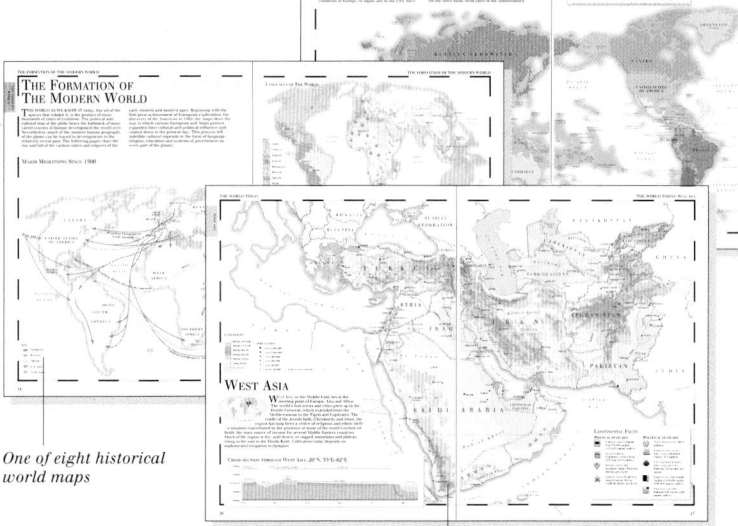

The political reference map of the world includes an inset map of the world's time zones

One of eight historical world maps

National coverage is presented across one, two, three or four double-page spreads

The eight continental and regional maps provide a detailed overview of the physical and political geography of each part of the world

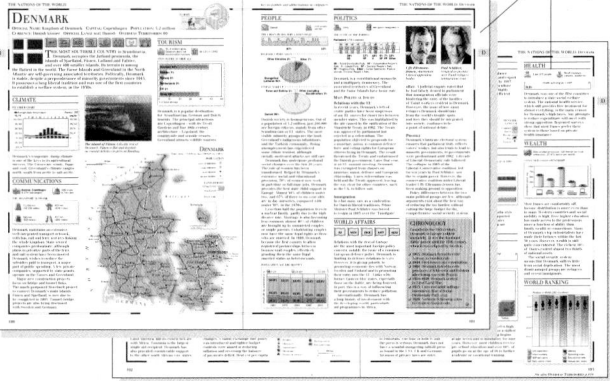

3 GLOBAL ISSUES: 18 pages of double-page spreads which examine major issues in the modern world, presented thematically on a global map supplemented by regional examples, diagrams, text and captions.

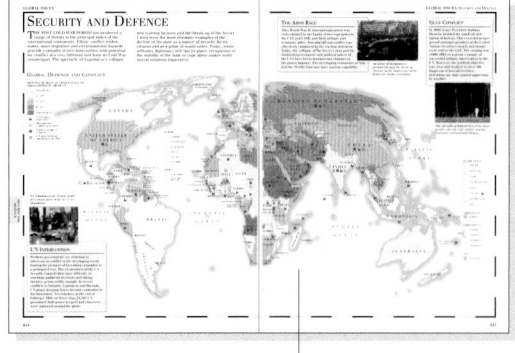

One of the nine Global Issues double-page spreads, which combines a world map with diagrams, illustrations and informative text

4 INDEX – GAZETTEER: 77 pages of index list all the names shown on the national maps. Cross-references are made to alternative place name forms and spellings. This section also includes a listing of international organizations.

THE NATIONS OF THE WORLD

THE NATIONS OF THE WORLD is the largest section in the Atlas. Countries are arranged alphabetically for ease of reference. Each country is mapped, has an introductory Country Profile Reference Panel and is analyzed under 18 consistent subject headings. See following pages for a complete listing.

The Atlas is designed so that every country entry is structured in the same way. The title headings are always arranged in the same sequence and all the information is comparable from one country to another.

This makes it very easy to find exactly what you want to read about in a particular country section. It also makes comparisons between countries much easier.

In addition to the explanations and definitions provided overleaf, both endpapers carry a detailed key to the icons, map symbols and abbreviations used in this section of the Atlas.

BUSINESS AND LAND USE MAPS

The world's 73 largest countries are also provided with business and land use maps to reflect the more complex nature of their economies. These give an instant idea of where major business sectors are located and the nature of the country's agriculture.

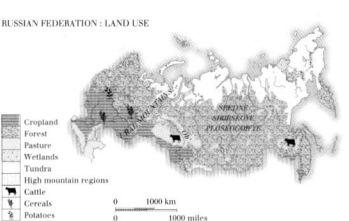

DENMARK : MAJOR BUSINESSES

RUSSIAN FEDERATION : LAND USE

NATIONAL FLAGS

The national flag of each country is shown in color and in its correct geometric proportions.

LOCATOR MAPS

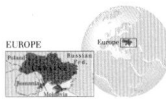

The locator maps are always found next to the country name. They provide both a world and regional location for each country.

COUNTRY MAPS

Each country is mapped in considerable detail. The maps show the national boundaries and neighboring countries, the major physical features, main road and railroad infrastructure, and populated and administrative centers. A key provides a breakdown of land height (in feet and meters) and of populated places.

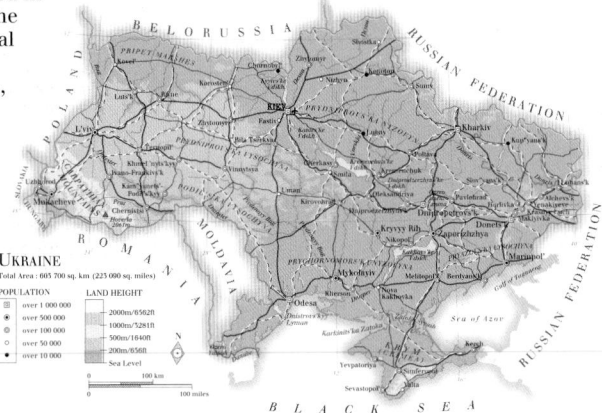

UKRAINE
Total Area : 603 700 sq. km (233 000 sq. miles)

REGIONAL MAPS

Regional maps are featured for 13 of the world's leading countries. The regions or cities are chosen to reflect national differences or because they are of particular economic importance. Each map has a full explanatory text.

CHARTS

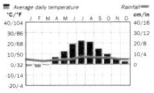

Charts are used to show each country's climate, social makeup and the economy. All countries have a standard set of charts.

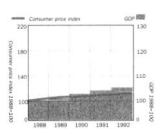

The top 73 countries have additional charts. This chart, for example, provides a guide to the country's economic performance.

This chart appears in the Defense, Education and Health sections. It shows how much major countries spend on each, as a proportion of Gross Domestic or National Product.

ICONS

Icons are a key feature of the book. The design of the icon gives an indication of the information being represented.

Icons are of three types. The icons appearing under the title give a ready reference to the political, economic and social status of the country.

Icons under section headings appear for all countries.

Grouped icons are mostly found in the world's top 73 countries.

Trend icons show whether the trend of their subject matter is increasing, decreasing or level.

TEXT

The text in the Atlas is intended to be highly accessible so that essential information can always be found quickly.

The larger countries are presented across more pages and thus have more text, reflecting their greater complexity. Longer text entries have, however, been broken down by introducing sub-headings to guide the reader to the subject of interest.

The text for larger countries has more detailed profiles of political and economic systems and reports on cities and/or regions of special interest.

KEY TO CHARTS AND ICONS

Icons and trend indicators vary. Not all variations are shown in the key below, but where they do occur the symbols have been "stacked."

COUNTRY PROFILE REFERENCE PANEL
These icons are coloured yellow when the information is applicable.

 1850 Date of independence, or date current borders set.

 Democratic system of election in use.

 Convertible national currency.

 International aid status: donor/recipient/neither.

Net energy importer/exporter.

 Compulsory military service.

 Death penalty currently in use.

Welfare provision: health and unemployment benefits

CLIMATE

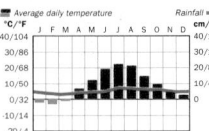 Statistics are given for the the national capital. They represent maximum summer and minimum winter averages.

TRANSPORTATION

 The country's principal international airport with annual passenger numbers.

 Total size of national merchant or cargo fleet.

THE TRANSPORT NETWORK
National communications infrastructure given in miles and kilometers.

Extent of national paved road network

Extent of expressways or major national highways

Extent of commercial railroad network

Extent of inland waterways navigable by commercial craft

TOURISM

Number of visitors per year, including business travelers.

Indicators showing trend in recent visitor numbers (up/level/down).

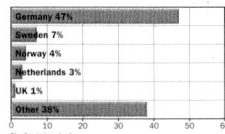 The state of each nation's tourism is explained, with reasons given when there is no significant tourist industry. The chart shows the percentage of total visitors by country of origin.

PEOPLE

 Main languages spoken, in descending order of importance.

 Population density. This is an average over the whole country.

 The pie chart proportions show the religious affiliations of those who profess a belief.

 This pie chart illustrates the ethnic origin of the country's population.

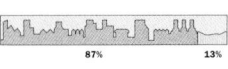 This graph represents the proportion of the population living in urban areas (grey) and rural areas (green).

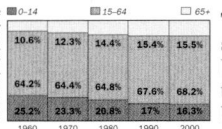 This chart shows the breakdown of the population by age groupings over a 40-year period, providing an interesting insight into the country's demography.

POLITICS

 Dates of last and next legislative elections for Upper (U.) and Lower (L.) Houses.

 Name of head of state. In many cases this is a nominal position and does not indicate that this is the country's most powerful person.

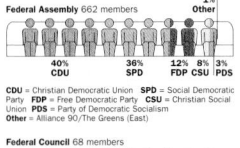
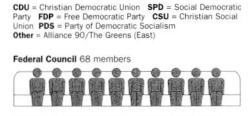

A graphic representation of the political makeup of the country's government, based on each party's showing at the last election. Where there are two houses, the most important elected body is shown first.

WORLD AFFAIRS

 Comm Abbreviations indicate membership of international organizations. UN membership is assumed.

 UN Signifies nonmembership of the UN

 Nonmembership of additional international organizations.

AID

 The amount of net international aid given or received is shown in US$. Undisclosed military aid is not included.

 Symbols indicate whether aid payments or receipts are rising, level or declining.

DEFENSE

 The defense budget, the country's annual expenditure (in US$) on arms and military personnel.

 Symbols indicate if the trend in defense spending is rising, level or declining.

Spending on arms is shown as a proportion of Gross Domestic Product (GDP). The general state of the country's defenses and the status of the military is discussed in the text.

THE ARMED FORCES
Icons represent the main branches of the national armed forces.

 Army: equipment and personnel

 Navy: equipment and personnel

 Airforce: equipment and personnel

 Nuclear capability: armaments

ECONOMICS

 Gross National Product (GNP) – the total value of goods and services produced by a country.

 Exchange rates against the US$ over the last year. Some currencies are too volatile for a useful figure to be given.

❏ World GNP Ranking	24th
❏ GNP per Capita	$24,388
❏ Balance of Payments	$2.2bn
❏ Inflation	5.6%
❏ Unemployment	10.6%

The score cards are intended to give a broad picture of the country's economy. Gross National Product (GNP), unlike GDP, includes income from investments and businesses held abroad. Balance of payments is the difference between a country's payments to and receipts from abroad.

 This graph shows year-on-year variations in GDP and consumer prices.

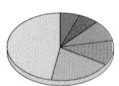 This pie chart gives a broad picture of the country's principal import trading partners.

This pie chart gives a broad picture of the country's principal export trading partners.

RESOURCES

 Electricity generation is expressed in kilowatt hours (kwh) per year, and total available capacity (kw).

 Oil produced in barrels per day (b/d). Refining capacity, oil reserves, and other fossil fuels are given where applicable.

 Estimated livestock resources.

 Main mineral reserves are listed in descending order of economic importance.

 Fish catch per year (where fishing is a major industry).

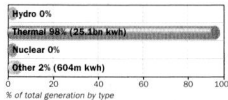

Hydro 0%	
Thermal 98% (25.1bn kwh)	
Nuclear 0%	
Other 2% (604m kwh)	

Percentages of the different energy sources used for the generation of electricity are represented graphically ("thermal" indicates the burning of fossil fuels, wood, etc.). An account of the country's resource base is given in the text.

ENVIRONMENT

 Percentage of land which is protected or conserved by law. Protection is often only theoretical.

 Symbols indicate a trend in the importance of environmental issues as a national concern.

ENVIRONMENTAL TREATIES
National signatory to international environmental treaties.

 ITTA: timber

 Montreal Protocol: CFC emissions

CITES: endangered species

 Biological Diversity Convention

 LDC: marine pollution

 Convention on Climate Change

MEDIA

 An assessment of political censorship in national media.

PUBLISHING AND BROADCAST MEDIA
National broadcast and print media, by size and ownership.

 Main national newspapers

Television stations: state-owned/independent

 Radio: state-owned/independent

 Satellite TV availability

 Cable TV availability

CRIME

 Prison population statistics (where available).

 Symbols show general trend in crime figures.

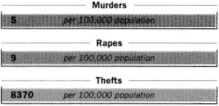

Murders		
5	*per 100,000 population*	
Rapes		
9	*per 100,000 population*	
Thefts		
8370	*per 100,000 population*	

This section records official crime figures only. Reported statistics are normally lower than the actual figures.

CHRONOLOGY

Beginning at a significant date in the recent history of the country, the outline chronology continues through to the present day, and highlights key dates and turning points.

EDUCATION

 Literacy rate. UNESCO defines as literate anyone who can read and write a short statement.

 The number of students in tertiary education, with the percentage enrolment among 20–24 year olds.

The state's total budget for education is shown as a proportion of its Gross National Product (GNP).

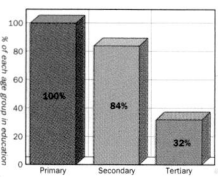 This graph shows the percentages of each age group in education. Primary is up to age 11; secondary is age 11–16/18; tertiary is expressed as a percentage of 20-24-year-olds.

HEALTH

 Ratio of doctors per head of population is given as a national average.

 Major causes of death are listed.

Health spending is shown as a proportion of the Gross Domestic Product (GDP).

WEALTH

 This section highlights wealth disparities by contrasting sample blue-collar and managerial salaries. Earnings are shown in local currency and in US$.

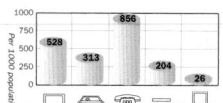 This graph shows the comparative ownership of consumer goods. Figures may reflect access to, rather than ability to purchase, high-value consumer durables.

WORLD RANKING

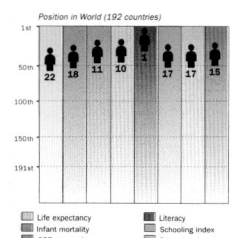 Schooling, educational attainment, and human development rankings are based on the UN Human Development Index (which covers 174 countries). Expert consultants have advised on various other indicators.

1

THE WORLD
TODAY

THE POLITICAL WORLD

THE PHYSICAL WORLD

• NORTH AMERICA • SOUTH AMERICA • EUROPE • AFRICA
• WEST ASIA • NORTH ASIA • SOUTH ASIA
• AUSTRALASIA & OCEANIA

THE FORMATION OF THE MODERN WORLD

• THE WORLD IN 1492 • THE AGE OF DISCOVERY 1492-1648
• THE AGE OF EXPANSION 1648-1789
• THE AGE OF REVOLUTION 1789-1830
• THE AGE OF EMPIRE 1830-1914
• THE AGE OF GLOBAL WAR 1914-1945
• THE MODERN AGE 1945-1996

THE POLITICAL WORLD

IN TODAY'S RAPIDLY EVOLVING WORLD, a political perspective on international boundaries is more important than ever before. The world currently comprises 192 independent states – more than at any previous time – and 57 dependencies. Antarctica is the only land area on the earth's surface which is not part of and does not belong to any one country.

A massive transformation has taken place since 1950, when the world comprised only 82 countries. In the decades following World War II, many states came into being as they achieved independence from their former colonial rulers. Most recently, the breakup of the Soviet Union in 1991, and Yugoslavia in 1992,

swelled the ranks of independent states. Generally, a worldwide trend towards fragmentation has been seen as nationalist aims have come to the fore. Civil wars and separatist campaigns are currently being waged in many parts of the world, including Afghanistan, Indonesia, Somalia, Sri Lanka, and Sudan. Within the former Soviet Union there is a civil war in Tajikistan, while in Russia itself the Chechen conflict is the most dramatic but not the only separatist threat.

The Russian Federation is the world's largest state; Vatican City is the smallest. In 1995, Palau became the most recent addition to the world map.

THE WORLD POLITICAL MAP

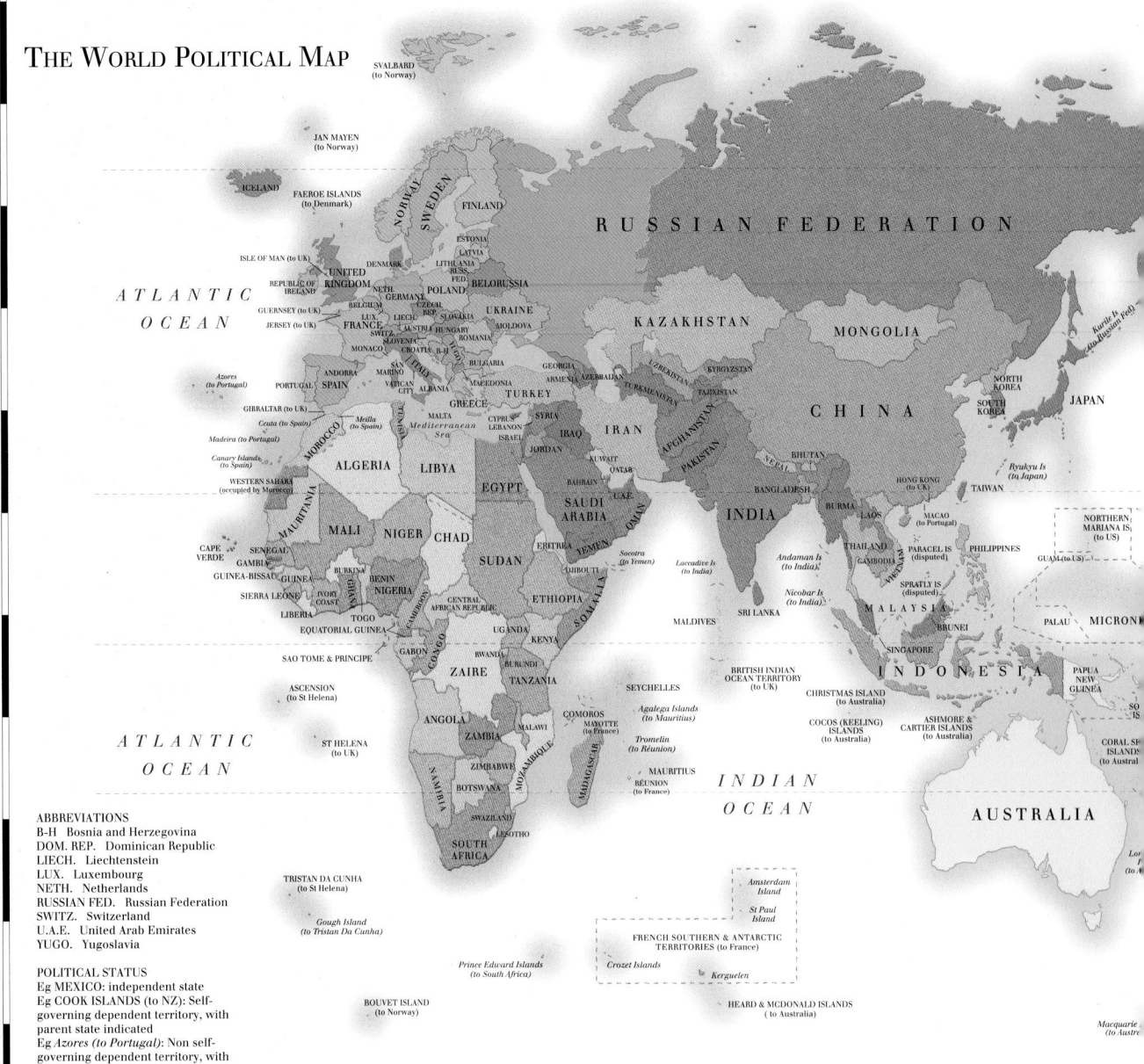

ABBREVIATIONS
B-H   Bosnia and Herzegovina
DOM. REP.   Dominican Republic
LIECH.   Liechtenstein
LUX.   Luxembourg
NETH.   Netherlands
RUSSIAN FED.   Russian Federation
SWITZ.   Switzerland
U.A.E.   United Arab Emirates
YUGO.   Yugoslavia

POLITICAL STATUS
Eg MEXICO: independent state
Eg COOK ISLANDS (to NZ): Self-
governing dependent territory, with
parent state indicated
Eg *Azores (to Portugal)*: Non self-
governing dependent territory, with
parent state indicated

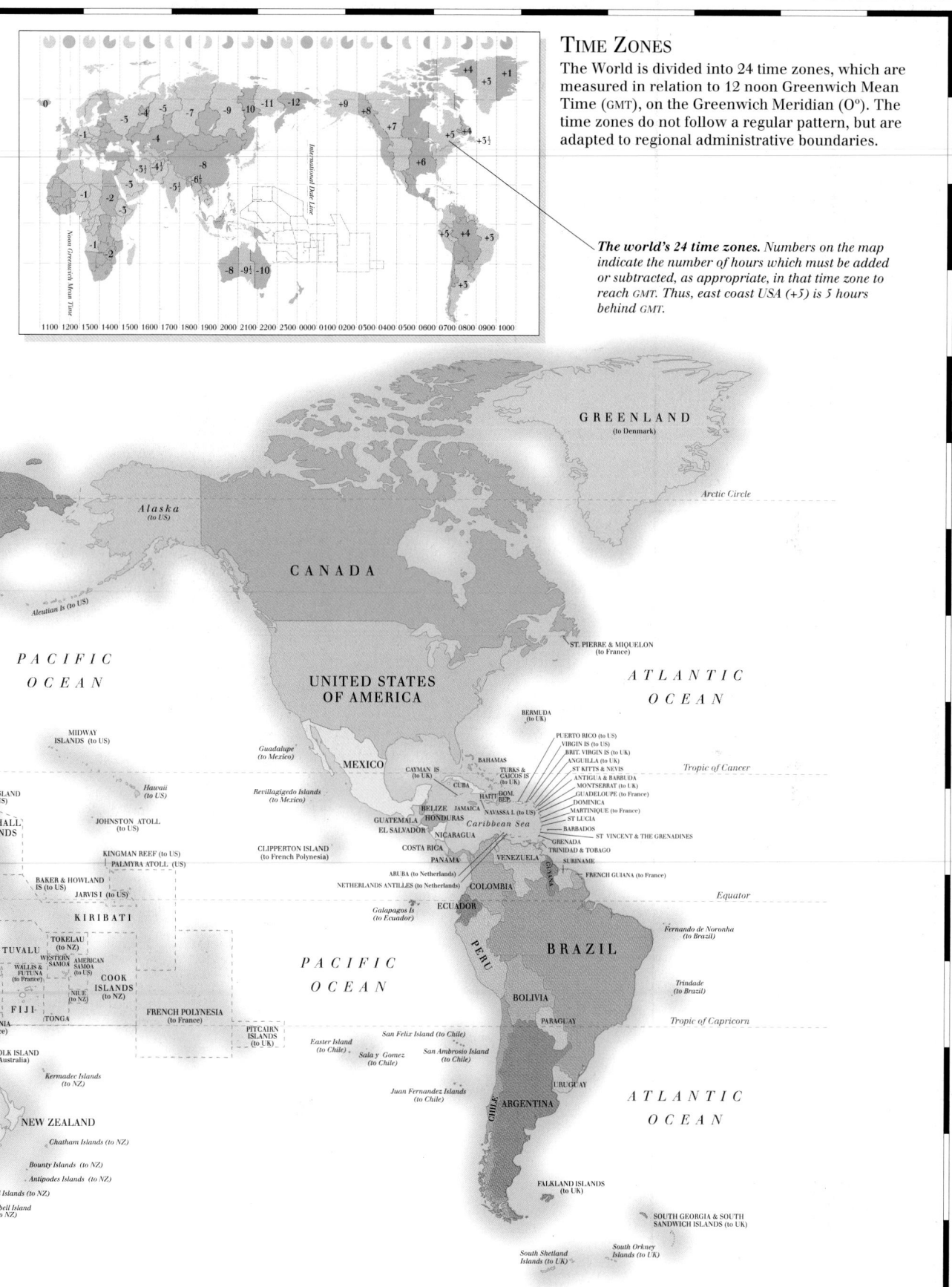

TIME ZONES

The World is divided into 24 time zones, which are measured in relation to 12 noon Greenwich Mean Time (GMT), on the Greenwich Meridian (0°). The time zones do not follow a regular pattern, but are adapted to regional administrative boundaries.

The world's 24 time zones. Numbers on the map indicate the number of hours which must be added or subtracted, as appropriate, in that time zone to reach GMT. Thus, east coast USA (+5) is 5 hours behind GMT.

THE PHYSICAL WORLD

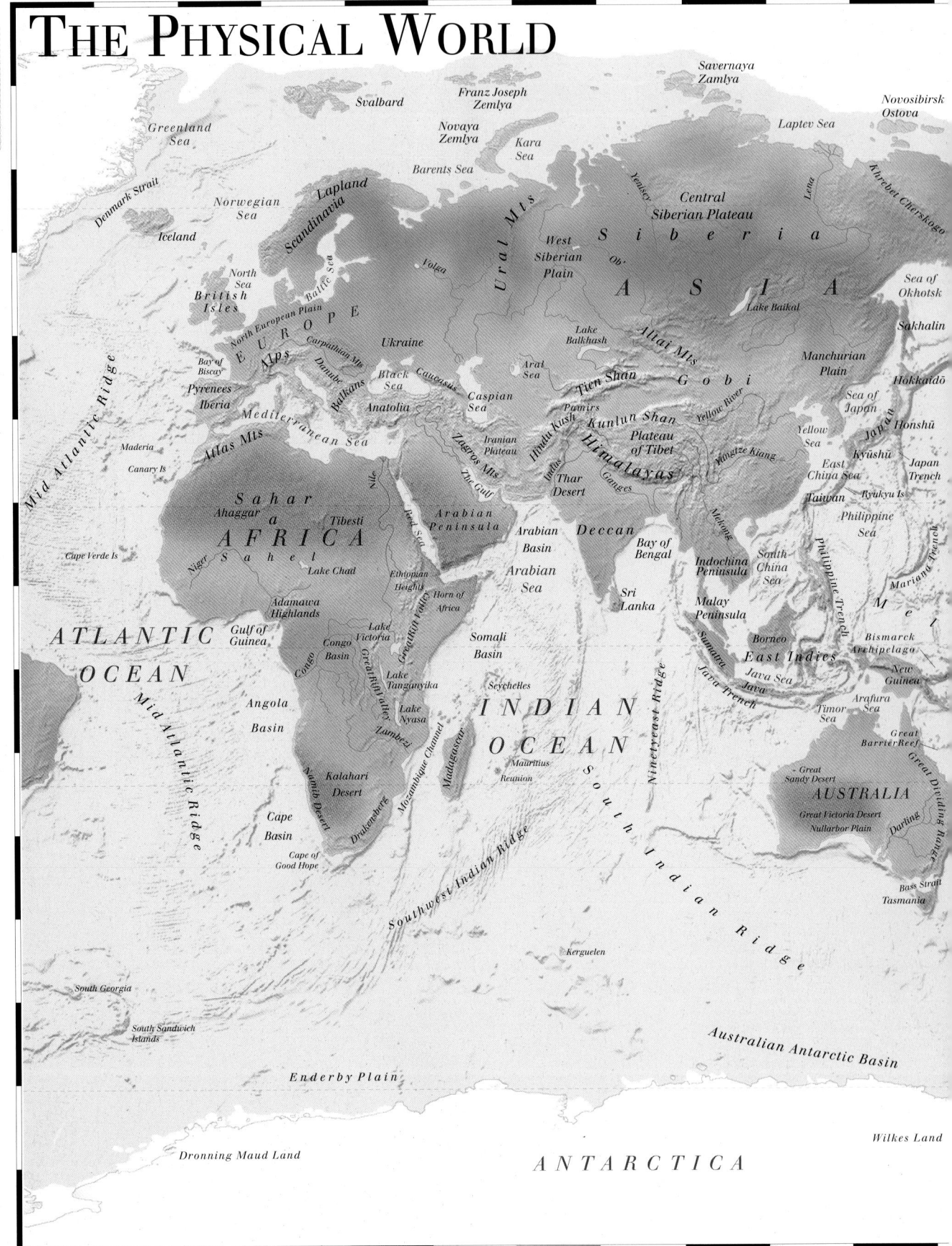

Greenland
Sea

Svalbard

Franz Joseph
Zemlya

Savernaya
Zamlya

Novaya
Zemlya

Laptev Sea

Novosibirsk
Ostova

Denmark Strait

Norwegian
Sea

Lapland

Scandinavia

Kara
Sea

Khrebet Cherskogo

Iceland

Baltic Sea

Barents Sea

Yenisey

Central
Siberian Plateau

Lena

North
Sea

Ukraine

West
Siberian
Plain

Siberia

Sea of
Okhotsk

British
Isles

North European Plain

EUROPE

Ob'

ASIA

Sakhalin

Bay of
Biscay

Alps

Carpathian Mts

Volga

Lake
Balkhash

Altai Mts

Lake Baikal

Manchurian
Plain

Hokkaidō

Pyrenees
Iberia

Danube

Black
Sea

Caucasus

Arat
Sea

Gobi

Sea of
Japan

Balkans

Anatolia

Caspian
Sea

Tien Shan

Pamirs

Kunlun Shan

Yellow River

Honshū

Japan

Maderia

Atlas Mts

Mediterranean Sea

Iranian
Plateau

Hindu Kush

Plateau
of Tibet

Yangtze Kiang

Yellow
Sea

Kyūshū

Japan
Trench

Canary Is

Zagros Mts

Himalayas

East
China Sea

Mid Atlantic Ridge

Nile

The Gulf

Indus

Ganges

Thar
Desert

Ryukyu Is

Taiwan

Sahara

Ahaggar

Tibesti

Arabian
Peninsula

Deccan

South
China
Sea

Philippine
Sea

AFRICA

Sahel

Arabian
Basin

Arabian
Sea

Bay of
Bengal

Indochina
Peninsula

Philippine Trench

Mariana Trench

Me

Cape Verde Is

Niger

Lake Chad

Red Sea

Ethiopian
Heights

Horn of
Africa

Sri
Lanka

Malay
Peninsula

Bismarck
Archipelago

Adamawa
Highlands

Great Rift Valley

Lake
Victoria

Somali
Basin

Borneo

East Indies

New
Guinea

ATLANTIC

OCEAN

Gulf of
Guinea

Congo
Basin

Congo

Lake
Tanganyika

Seychelles

Sumatra

Java Sea

Java

Arafura
Sea

Angola
Basin

Lake
Nyasa

INDIAN

Java Trench

Timor
Sea

Great
Barrier Reef

Zambezi

OCEAN

Great Dividing Range

Mid Atlantic Ridge

Madagascar

Mauritius
Reunion

Ninetyeast Ridge

Great
Sandy Desert

AUSTRALIA

Kalahari
Desert

Mozambique Channel

South Indian Ridge

Great Victoria Desert

Darling

Cape
Basin

Namib Desert

Drakensberg

Nullarbor Plain

Bass Strait

Cape of
Good Hope

Southwest Indian Ridge

Tasmania

South Georgia

Kerguelen

South Sandwich
Islands

Australian Antarctic Basin

Enderby Plain

Wilkes Land

Dronning Maud Land

ANTARCTICA

ARCTIC OCEAN

Ellesmere Island

Limit of permanent pack ice

Queen
Elizbeth
Islands

Baffin Bay

Greenland

Greenland
Sea

Siberian Sea

Chukchi Sea

Beaufort Sea

Baffin Island

Great Bear
Lake

Brooks Range

Yukon

Mackenzie

Great Slave
Lake

Hudson
Bay

Ungava
Peninsula

Labrador
Sea

Arctic Circle

Iceland

Bering Sea

Aleutian Basin

Aleutian Islands

Gulf of
Alaska

Canadian Shield

Mid Atlantic Ridge

Trench

Aleutian Trench

Rocky Mountains

Coast Mountains

Lake
Winnipeg

NORTH AMERICA

Grand
Bank

Vancouver I

Coast Ranges

Great Plains

Great Lakes

Azores

Emperor Seamount Chain

Mendocino Fracture Zone

Missouri

Appalachian Mountains

North America
Basin

ATLANTIC
OCEAN

Hawaiian Islands

Murray Fracture Zone

Baja California

Mississippi

Tropic of Cancer

Mld Pacific
Mountains

PACIFIC

OCEAN

Sierra Madre

Gulf of
Mexico

Yucatán
Peninsula

Guatemala Trench

West Indies

Greater Antilles

Caribbean
Sea

Lesser
Antilles

Polynesia

Micronesia

Tungaru

Line Islands

Guiana
Highlands

Phoenix Is

Galapagos
Islands

Amazon

Amozon Basin

SOUTH
AMERICA

Brazillian
Basin

Equator

Fiji

Tonga

Cook Is

Tuamotu
Islands

Andes

Peru-Chile Trench

Mato Grosso

Brazilian Highlands

Tonga Trench

Peru Basin

Paraná

Tropic of Capricorn

Kermadec Trench

East Pacific Ridge

sman
ea

North
Island

New
Zealand

Southwest

Pacific

Basin

Pampas

Argentine
Basin

Tristian
da Cunha

Mid Atlantic Ridge

Campbell
Plateau

Patagonia

Falkland Is

South Georgia

Tierra
del Fuego

Cape
Horn

Drake Passage

Antarctic
Peninsula

Antarctic Circle

Bellinghausen
Sea

Weddell Sea

Ross Sea

Byrd Land

Ronne Ice Shelf

ANTARCTIC

Ross Ice Shelf

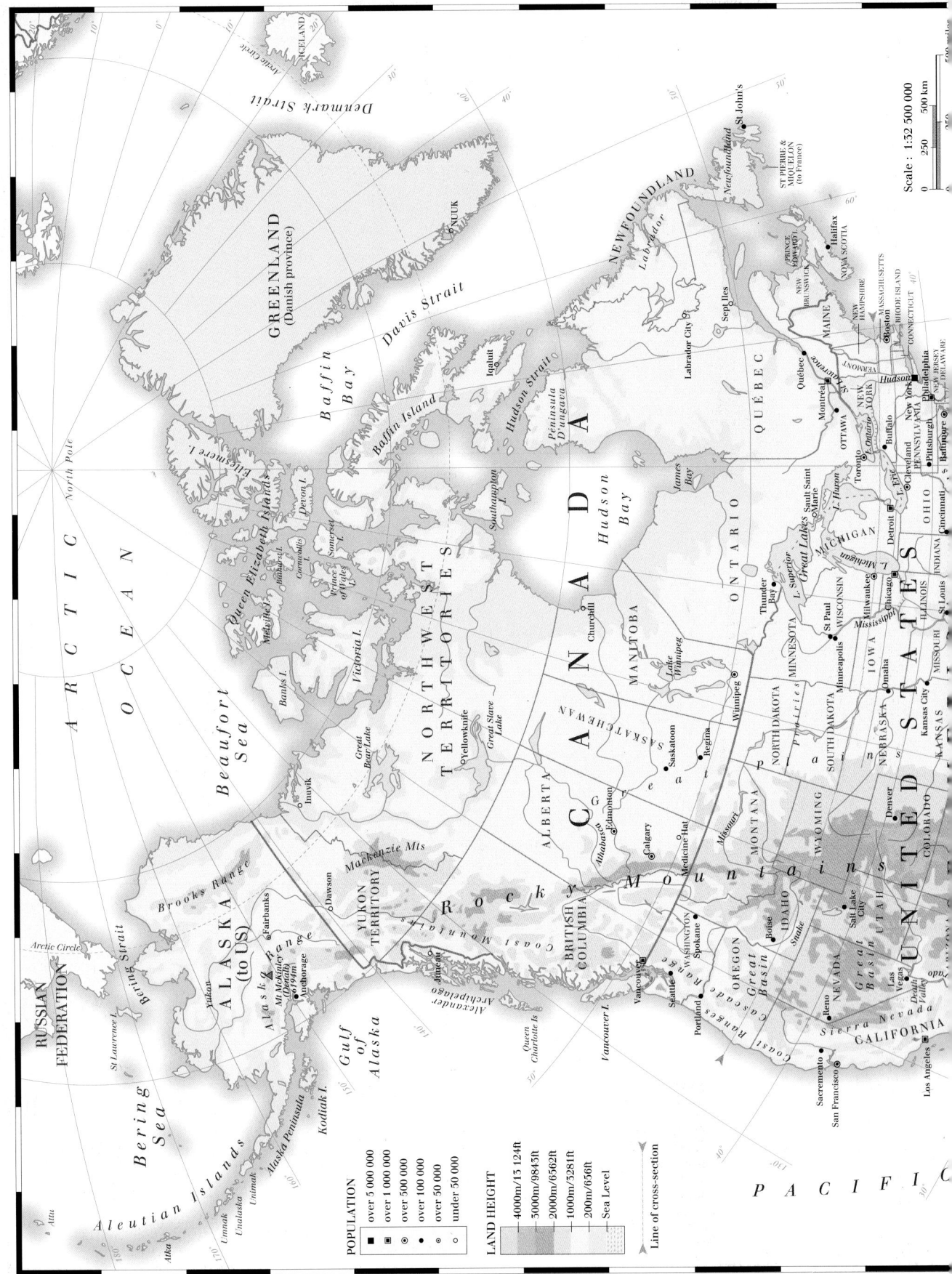

Scale : 1:32 500 000

0   250   500 km

GREENLAND
(Danish province)

CANADA

UNITED STATES

ALASKA
(to US)

RUSSIAN FEDERATION

ARCTIC OCEAN

Beaufort Sea

Bering Sea

Gulf of Alaska

PACIFIC

POPULATION
- over 5 000 000
- over 1 000 000
- over 500 000
- over 100 000
- over 50 000
- under 50 000

LAND HEIGHT
- 4000m/13 124ft
- 3000m/9845ft
- 2000m/6562ft
- 1000m/3281ft
- 200m/656ft
- Sea Level

Line of cross-section

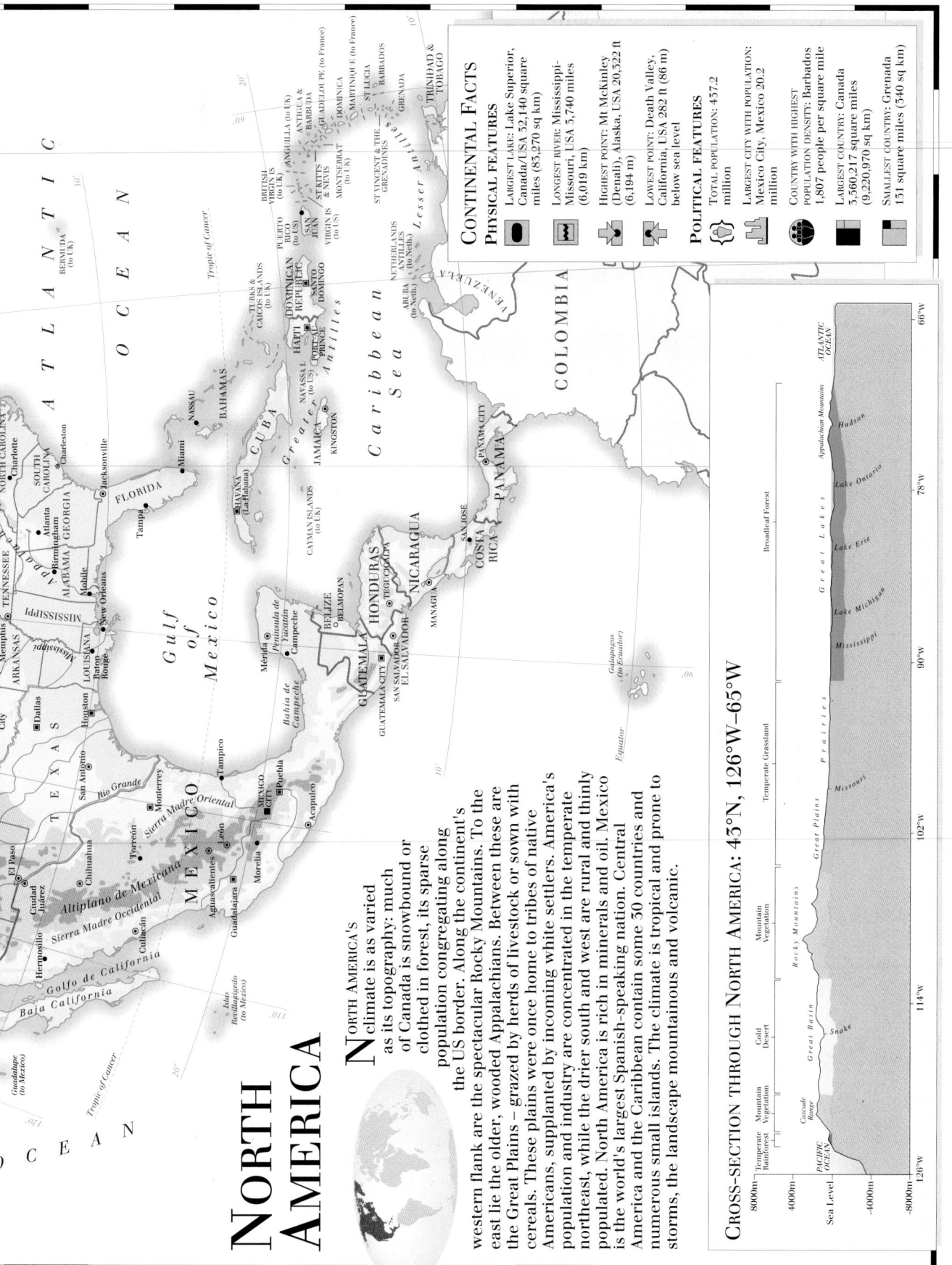

NORTH AMERICA

NORTH AMERICA'S climate is as varied as its topography: much of Canada is snowbound or clothed in forest, its sparse population congregating along the US border. Along the continent's western flank are the spectacular Rocky Mountains. To the east lie the older, wooded Appalachians. Between these are the Great Plains – grazed by herds of livestock or sown with cereals. These plains were once home to tribes of native Americans, supplanted by incoming white settlers. America's population and industry are concentrated in the temperate northeast, while the drier south and west are rural and thinly populated. North America is rich in minerals and oil. Mexico is the world's largest Spanish-speaking nation. Central America and the Caribbean contain some 30 countries and numerous small islands. The climate is tropical and prone to storms, the landscape mountainous and volcanic.

CONTINENTAL FACTS

PHYSICAL FEATURES

LARGEST LAKE: Lake Superior, Canada/USA 32,140 square miles (83,270 sq km)

LONGEST RIVER: Mississippi-Missouri, USA 3,740 miles (6,019 km)

HIGHEST POINT: Mt Mckinley (Denali), Alaska, USA 20,322 ft (6,194 m)

LOWEST POINT: Death Valley, California, USA 282 ft (86 m) below sea level

POLITICAL FEATURES

TOTAL POPULATION: 457.2 million

LARGEST CITY WITH POPULATION: Mexico City, Mexico 20.2 million

COUNTRY WITH HIGHEST POPULATION DENSITY: Barbados 1,807 people per square mile

LARGEST COUNTRY: Canada 3,560,217 square miles (9,220,970 sq km)

SMALLEST COUNTRY: Grenada 151 square miles (340 sq km)

CROSS-SECTION THROUGH NORTH AMERICA: 43°N, 126°W–65°W

SOUTH AMERICA

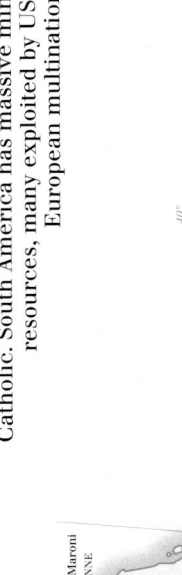

THE WORLD's fourth largest continent includes one of its most important resources – the Amazonian rain forest. It is a major source of oxygen and includes half of all known living species, while the Amazon – the world's second longest river – contains one fifth of the world's fresh water. The Andes mountain chain reaches down South America's western flank, sheltering the prairies of the Gran Chaco, the Pampas, and the wastes of the far south. Most South Americans are *mestizo* – of mixed European and Amerindian descent and live in the coastal regions. Spanish is the most widely-spoken language, and over 90% of South Americans are Roman Catholic. South America has massive mineral resources, many exploited by US and European multinationals.

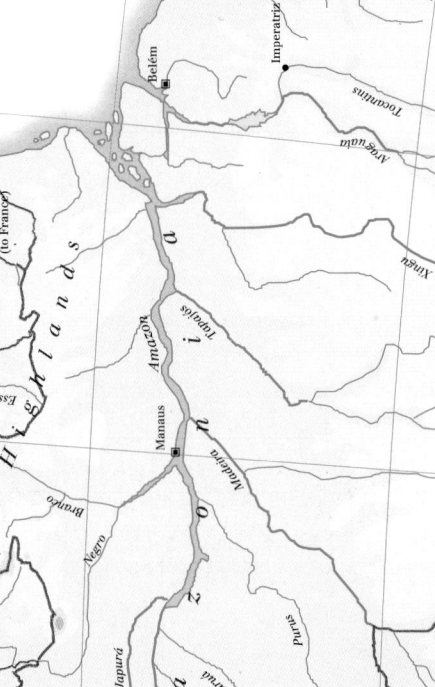

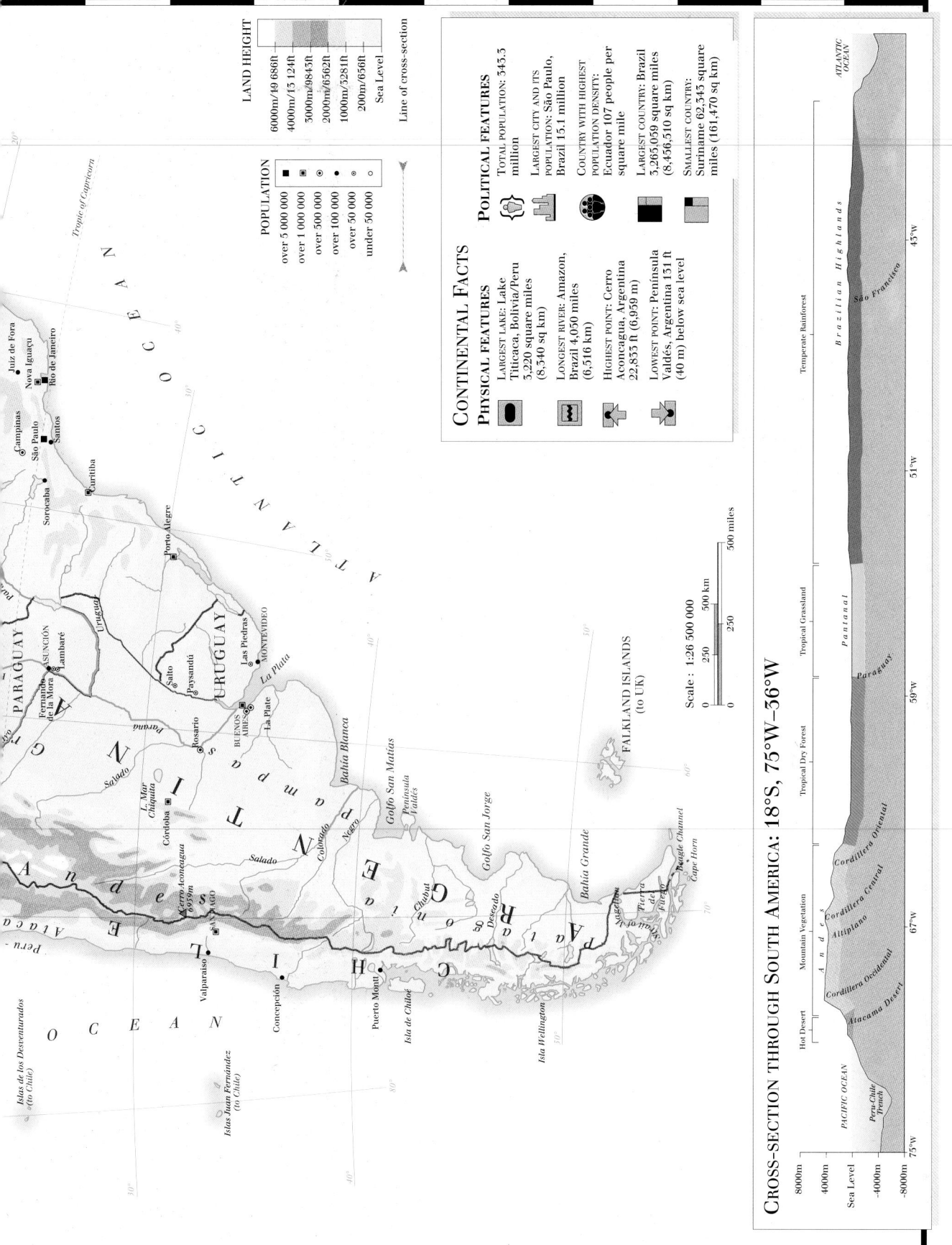

LAND HEIGHT

6000m/19 686ft
4000m/13 124ft
3000m/9845ft
2000m/6562ft
1000m/3281ft
200m/656ft
Sea Level

Line of cross-section

POPULATION

over 5 000 000
over 1 000 000
over 500 000
over 100 000
over 50 000
under 50 000

POLITICAL FEATURES

TOTAL POPULATION: 343.5 million

LARGEST CITY AND ITS POPULATION: São Paulo, Brazil 15.1 million

COUNTRY WITH HIGHEST POPULATION DENSITY: Ecuador 107 people per square mile

LARGEST COUNTRY: Brazil 3,265,059 square miles (8,456,510 sq km)

SMALLEST COUNTRY: Suriname 62,345 square miles (161,470 sq km)

CONTINENTAL FACTS

PHYSICAL FEATURES

LARGEST LAKE: Lake Titicaca, Bolivia/Peru 3,220 square miles (8,340 sq km)

LONGEST RIVER: Amazon, Brazil 4,050 miles (6,516 km)

HIGHEST POINT: Cerro Aconcagua, Argentina 22,835 ft (6,959 m)

LOWEST POINT: Península Valdés, Argentina 151 ft (40 m) below sea level

Scale : 1:26 500 000

500 km
250
0

500 miles
250
0

CROSS-SECTION THROUGH SOUTH AMERICA: 18°S, 75°W–36°W

8000m
4000m
Sea Level
-4000m
-8000m

75°W
67°W
59°W
51°W
43°W

PACIFIC OCEAN
Peru-Chile Trench
Hot Desert
Atacama Desert
Cordillera Occidental
Mountain Vegetation
A n d e s
Cordillera Central
Altiplano
Cordillera Oriental
Tropical Dry Forest
Tropical Grassland
Pantanal
Paraguay
Temperate Rainforest
Brazilian Highlands
São Francisco
ATLANTIC OCEAN

ATLANTIC OCEAN

P A C I F I C   O C E A N

Tropic of Capricorn

Islas de los Desventurados (to Chile)

Islas Juan Fernández (to Chile)

Juiz de Fora
Nova Iguaçu
Rio de Janeiro
Campinas
São Paulo
Santos
Sorocaba
Curitiba
Porto Alegre

PARAGUAY
ASUNCIÓN
Fernando de la Mora
Lambaré
Uruguay
Paraná
URUGUAY
Salto
Paysandú
Las Piedras
MONTEVIDEO
La Plata
BUENOS AIRES
La Plate
Rosario
Córdoba
L. Mar Chiquita
Salado
Cerro Aconcagua 6,959m
SANTIAGO
Valparaíso
Concepción
Puerto Montt
Isla de Chiloé
Isla Wellington

A R G E N T I N A
C H I L E
Atacama
Peru
A n d e s
Salado
Colorado
Negro
Chubut
Deseado
Golfo San Matías
Península Valdés
Bahía Blanca
Golfo San Jorge
Bahía Grande
P A T A G O N I A
Santa Cruz
Tierra del Fuego
Magallanes
Cabo de Hornos
Beagle Channel
Cape Horn

FALKLAND ISLANDS (to UK)

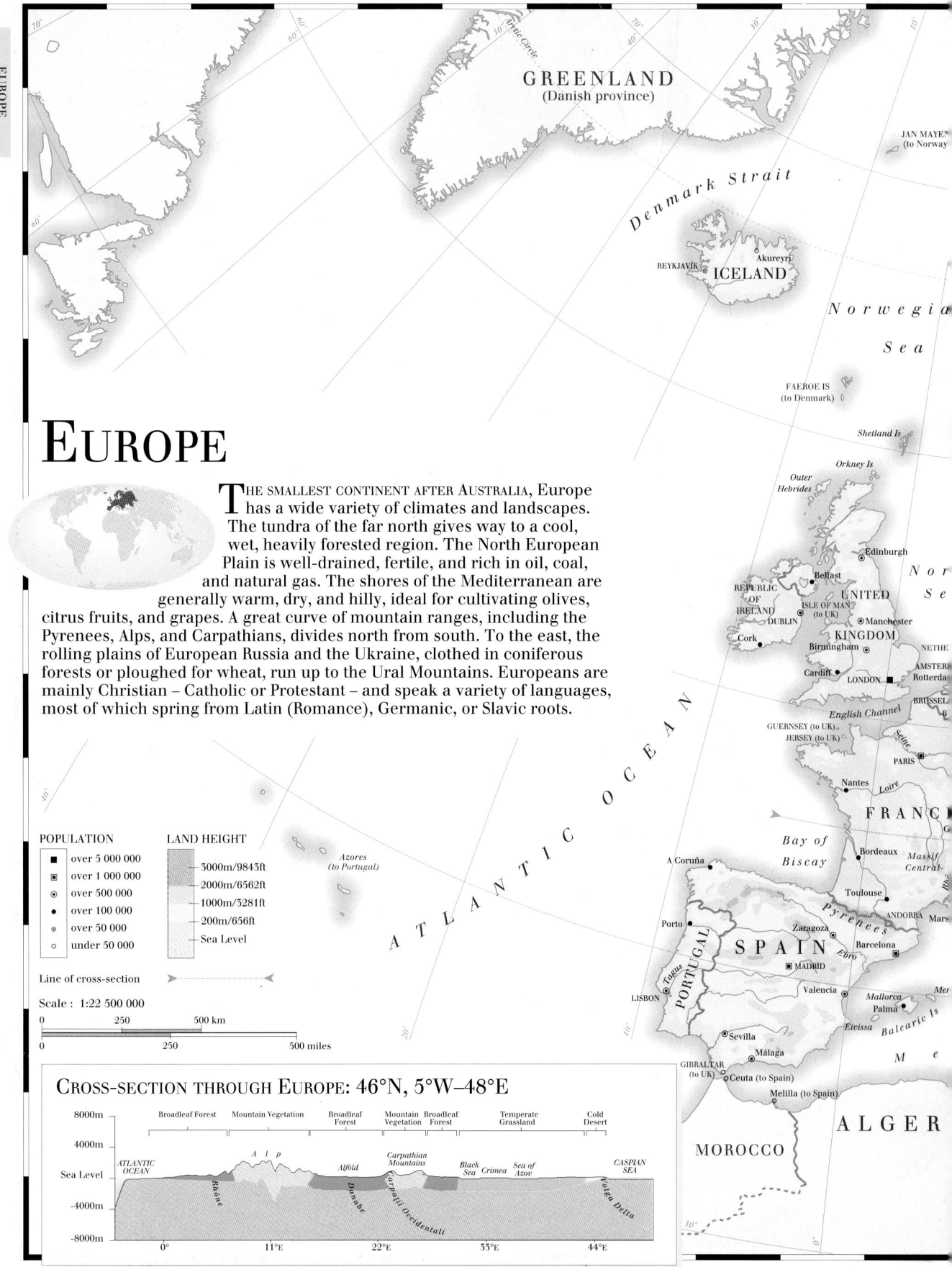

GREENLAND
(Danish province)

JAN MAYEN
(to Norway)

Denmark Strait

Akureyri
REYKJAVÍK · ICELAND

*N o r w e g i a
      S e a*

FAEROE IS 0
(to Denmark)

Shetland Is

Orkney Is

*Outer
Hebrides*

Edinburgh

*N o r
  S e*

Belfast

REPUBLIC · UNITED
OF   ISLE OF MAN
IRELAND   (to UK)   · Manchester
   DUBLIN

Cork   · Birmingham   NETHE

Cardiff   · AMSTER
         · LONDON   Rotterdam

English Channel   BRUSSEL

GUERNSEY (to UK) ·   *Seine*
JERSEY (to UK)   PARIS

Nantes   *Loire*

F R A N C

*Bay of
Biscay*   Bordeaux   *Massif
                        Central*

A Coruña   Toulouse
                        ANDORRA   Mars
            Pyrenees

Porto   Zaragoza   Barcelona
              · *Ebro*
S P A I N

    · MADRID   *Mer*
LISBON
       Valencia   *Mallorca*
                   Palma
Sevilla   *Eivissa*   *Balearic Is*
Málaga   *M   e*

GIBRALTAR
(to UK) · Ceuta (to Spain)
     Melilla (to Spain)

A L G E R

MOROCCO

EUROPE

T HE SMALLEST CONTINENT AFTER AUSTRALIA, Europe has a wide variety of climates and landscapes. The tundra of the far north gives way to a cool, wet, heavily forested region. The North European Plain is well-drained, fertile, and rich in oil, coal, and natural gas. The shores of the Mediterranean are generally warm, dry, and hilly, ideal for cultivating olives, citrus fruits, and grapes. A great curve of mountain ranges, including the Pyrenees, Alps, and Carpathians, divides north from south. To the east, the rolling plains of European Russia and the Ukraine, clothed in coniferous forests or ploughed for wheat, run up to the Ural Mountains. Europeans are mainly Christian – Catholic or Protestant – and speak a variety of languages, most of which spring from Latin (Romance), Germanic, or Slavic roots.

POPULATION

■ over 5 000 000
▣ over 1 000 000
◉ over 500 000
● over 100 000
◎ over 50 000
○ under 50 000

LAND HEIGHT

3000m/9843ft
2000m/6562ft
1000m/3281ft
200m/656ft
Sea Level

Line of cross-section

Scale : 1:22 500 000

0   250   500 km

0   250   500 miles

*Azores
(to Portugal)*

A T L A N T I C   O C E A N

CROSS-SECTION THROUGH EUROPE: 46°N, 5°W–48°E

| | Broadleaf Forest | Mountain Vegetation | Broadleaf Forest | Mountain Vegetation | Broadleaf Forest | Temperate Grassland | Cold Desert |

8000m

4000m

Sea Level

-4000m

-8000m

*ATLANTIC
OCEAN*   *A l p*   *Alföld*   *Carpathian
Mountains*   *Black   Crimea   Sea of
Sea   Azov*   *CASPIAN
SEA*

Rhône   *Danube*   *Carpatii Occidentali*   *Volga Delta*

0°   11°E   22°E   33°E   44°E

CONTINENTAL FACTS

PHYSICAL FEATURES

LARGEST LAKE: Ladoga, European Russia 7,100 square miles (18,390 sq km)

LONGEST RIVER: Volga, European Russia 2,290 miles (3,688 km)

HIGHEST POINT: El'brus, Caucasus Mts, European Russia 18,510 ft (5,642 m)

LOWEST POINT: Volga Delta, Caspian Sea, European Russia 92 ft (28 m) below sea level

POLITICAL FEATURES

TOTAL POPULATION: 678.2 million

COUNTRY WITH HIGHEST POPULATION DENSITY: Monaco 37,333 people per square mile

LARGEST CITY AND ITS POPULATION: Moscow, European Russia 8.9 million

LARGEST COUNTRY: European Russia 1,527,341 square miles (3,955,818 sq km)

SMALLEST COUNTRY: Vatican City, Italy 0.17 square miles (0.44 sq km)

23

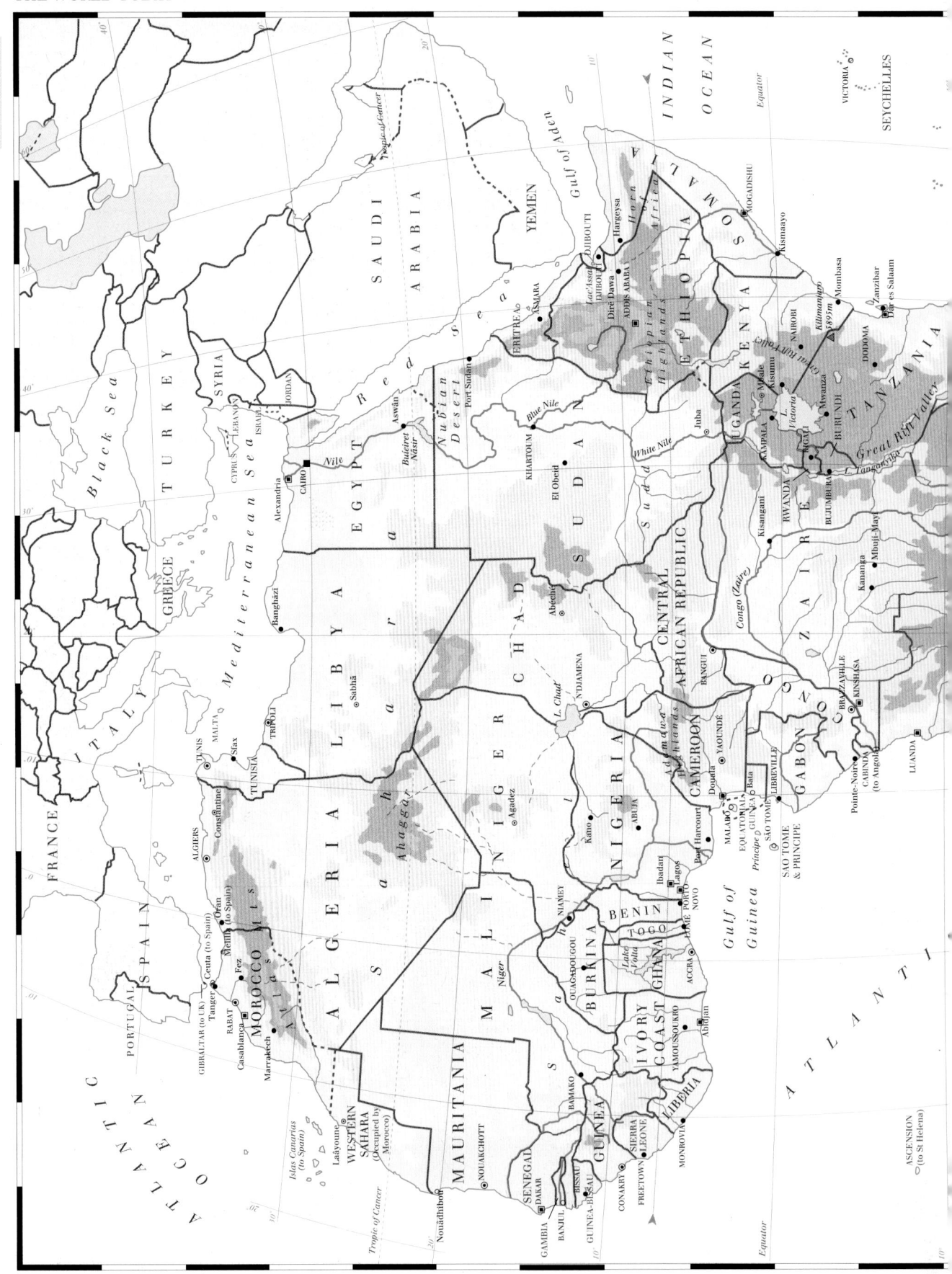

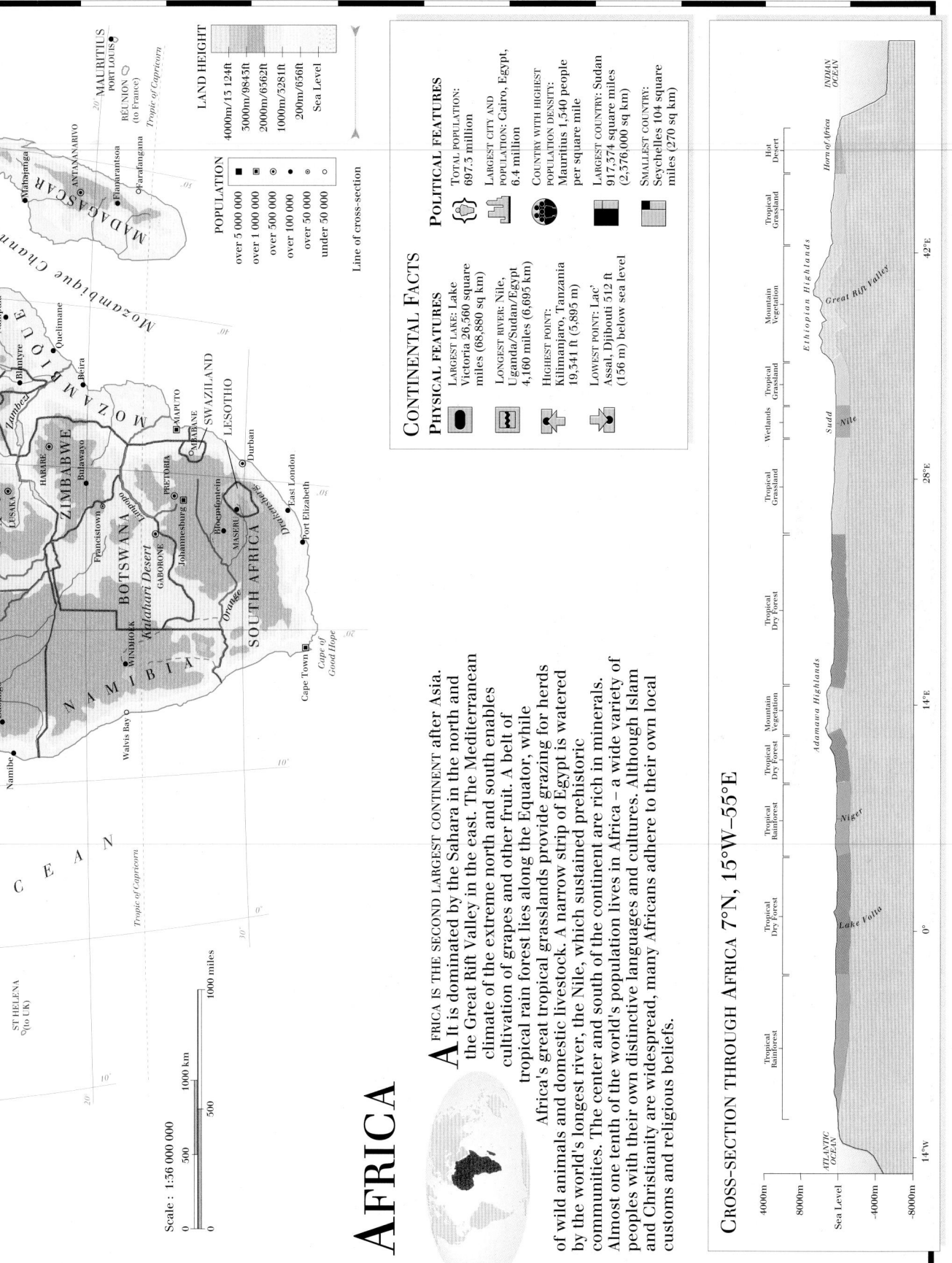

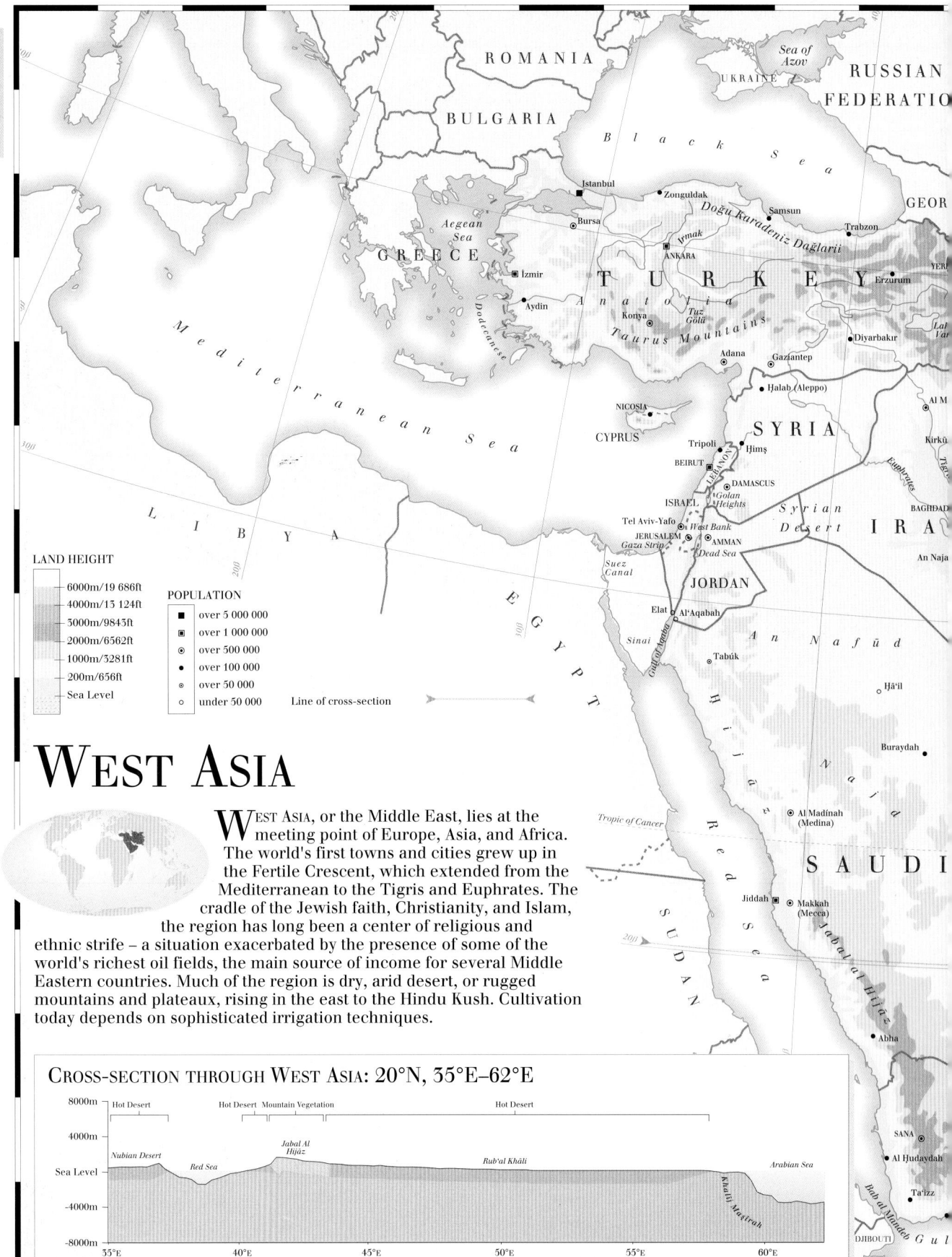

ROMANIA

BULGARIA

Black Sea

Sea of
Azov

UKRAINE

RUSSIAN
FEDERATIO

GREECE

*Aegean
Sea*

Istanbul

Bursa

Zonguldak

İzmir

Aydın

Samsun

Trabzon

GEOR

ANKARA

Irmak

Doğu Karadeniz Dağlarıı

Konya

*Tuz
Gölü*

T U R K E Y

Anatolia

Taurus Mountains

Erzurum

Diyarbakır

YER

Lat
Var

Dodecanese

M
e
d
i
t
e
r
r
a
n
e
a
n

S
e
a

Adana

Gaziantep

Ḥalab (Aleppo)

Al M

NICOSIA

CYPRUS

Tripoli

BEIRUT

LEBANON

Ḥimş

S Y R I A

Kirkū

Euphrates

BAGHDAD

IRA

DAMASCUS

*Golan
Heights*

*Syrian
Desert*

L   I   B   Y   A

ISRAEL

Tel Aviv-Yafo

JERUSALEM
Gaza Strip

West Bank

AMMAN

Dead Sea

An Naja

*Suez
Canal*

JORDAN

E   G   Y   P   T

Elat

Al'Aqabah

An   Nafūd

Sinai

Tabūk

Gulf of Aqaba

Ḥijāz

Ḥā'il

Buraydah

LAND HEIGHT

6000m/19 686ft
4000m/13 124ft
3000m/9843ft
2000m/6562ft
1000m/3281ft
200m/656ft
Sea Level

POPULATION

■ over 5 000 000
▣ over 1 000 000
◉ over 500 000
● over 100 000
◉ over 50 000
○ under 50 000

Line of cross-section

Tropic of Cancer

◉ Al Madínah
(Medina)

Najd

S A U D I

Red   Sea

Jiddah

Makkah
(Mecca)

SUDAN

Jabal al Ḥijāz

Abha

WEST ASIA

WEST ASIA, or the Middle East, lies at the
meeting point of Europe, Asia, and Africa.
The world's first towns and cities grew up in
the Fertile Crescent, which extended from the
Mediterranean to the Tigris and Euphrates. The
cradle of the Jewish faith, Christianity, and Islam,
the region has long been a center of religious and
ethnic strife – a situation exacerbated by the presence of some of the
world's richest oil fields, the main source of income for several Middle
Eastern countries. Much of the region is dry, arid desert, or rugged
mountains and plateaux, rising in the east to the Hindu Kush. Cultivation
today depends on sophisticated irrigation techniques.

CROSS-SECTION THROUGH WEST ASIA: 20°N, 35°E–62°E

Hot Desert   Hot Desert   Mountain Vegetation   Hot Desert

8000m

4000m

Sea Level

-4000m

-8000m

Nubian Desert   *Red Sea*

*Jabal Al
Hijāz*

Rub'al Khāli

Arabian Sea

Khalīj Maşīrah

35°E   40°E   45°E   50°E   55°E   60°E

SANA

Al Ḥudaydah

Ta'izz

Bab al Mandeb

Gul

DJIBOUTI

KAZAKHSTAN

Aral Sea

BISHKEK · Karakol
Ozero Issyk-Kul'

Kyzyl Kum

UZBEKISTAN

TASHKENT
Dashkhovuz · Urgench
Ozero Aydarkul' · Namangan
· Osh
KYRGYZSTAN
Khudzhand

CHINA

ERBAIJAN

BAKU · Krasnovodsk
· Nebitdag
· Lānkāran
· Basht

Caspian Sea

Karakumy · Samarkand · Karshi
TAJIKISTAN
· Chardzhev · Amu · DUSHANBE
· Kulyab · Khorog
· Kurgan-Tyube

Pamirs

Karakoram Range · Indus
K2 8611m

TURKMENISTAN

Khrebet Kopetdag · ASHGABAT
· Mary
· Gorgān

· Mazār-e-Sharīf
· Baghlān

Hindu Kush

KĀBUL · Jalālābād · Peshāwar · ISLĀMĀBĀD
· Rāwalpindi
· Gujrānwāla
· Lahore

riz
elt-ye eh
Basht

Reshteh-ye Kuhhā ye Alborz
Mashhad
TEHRĀN
· Hamadān · Qom
· Bākhtarān

Dasht-e-Kavīr

· Herāt

AFGHANISTAN

IRAN

Plateau of Iran
· Eşfahān

Hāmūn-e Şāberī

· Kandahār

· Faisalābād
· Multān

Helmand

· Quetta

· Ahvāz
şrah
· Ābādān

Zagros Mountains

· Shīrāz
· Kermān
· Zāhedān

PAKISTAN

INDIA

Thar Desert

Indus

· Sukkur

UWAIT
KUWAIT CITY

· Bandar-e 'Abbās

Persian Gulf

BAHRAIN
MANAMA
DOHA
Al Hufūf · QATAR
· ABU DHABI

· Dubai
· Sharjah

Strait of Hormuz

Gulf of Oman

· Hyderābād

· Karāchi

Arabian Sea

Tropic of Cancer

ADH

Ḩaraḑ

UNITED ARAB EMIRATES
· Suḩār
· MUSCAT
· Ar Rustāq
· Nazwā
· Şūr

OMAN

RABIA

b'al Khāli

Khalīj Maşīrah

EMEN

· Şalālah

Hadhramaut

· Al Mukallā

INDIAN OCEAN

Socotra (to Yemen)

Aden

CONTINENTAL FACTS

PHYSICAL FEATURES

LARGEST LAKE: Caspian Sea 143,205 square miles (371,000 sq km)

LONGEST RIVER: Euphrates, Syria/Iraq 1,750 miles (2,815 km)

HIGHEST POINT: K2, Kashmir, India/Pakistan 28,252 ft (8,611 m)

LOWEST POINT: Dead Sea, Israel/Jordan 1,286 ft (392 m) below sea level

POLITICAL FEATURES

TOTAL POPULATION: 401.5 million

LARGEST CITY AND ITS POPULATION: Istanbul, Turkey 6.5 million

COUNTRY WITH HIGHEST POPULATION DENSITY: Bahrain 2,290 people per square mile

LARGEST COUNTRY: Saudi Arabia 829,995 square miles (2,149,690 sq km)

SMALLEST COUNTRY: Bahrain 263 square miles (680 sq km)

CONTINENTAL FACTS

PHYSICAL FEATURES

LARGEST LAKE: Aral Sea, Asiatic Russia 25,700 square miles (66,500 sq km)

LONGEST RIVER: Chang Jiang (Yangtze), China 3,965 miles (6,380 km)

HIGHEST POINT: Xixabangma Feng, China 26,286 ft (8,012 m)

LOWEST POINT: Turpan Hami (Turfan Basin), China 505 ft (154 m) below sea level

POLITICAL FEATURES

TOTAL POPULATION: 1,432 million

LARGEST CITY AND ITS POPULATION: Tokyo, Japan 18.1 million

COUNTRY WITH HIGHEST POPULATION DENSITY: Taiwan 1,245 people per square mile

LARGEST COUNTRY: Asiatic Russia 5,065, 471 square miles (13,119,582 sq km)

SMALLEST COUNTRY: Taiwan 12,455 square miles (32,260 sq km)

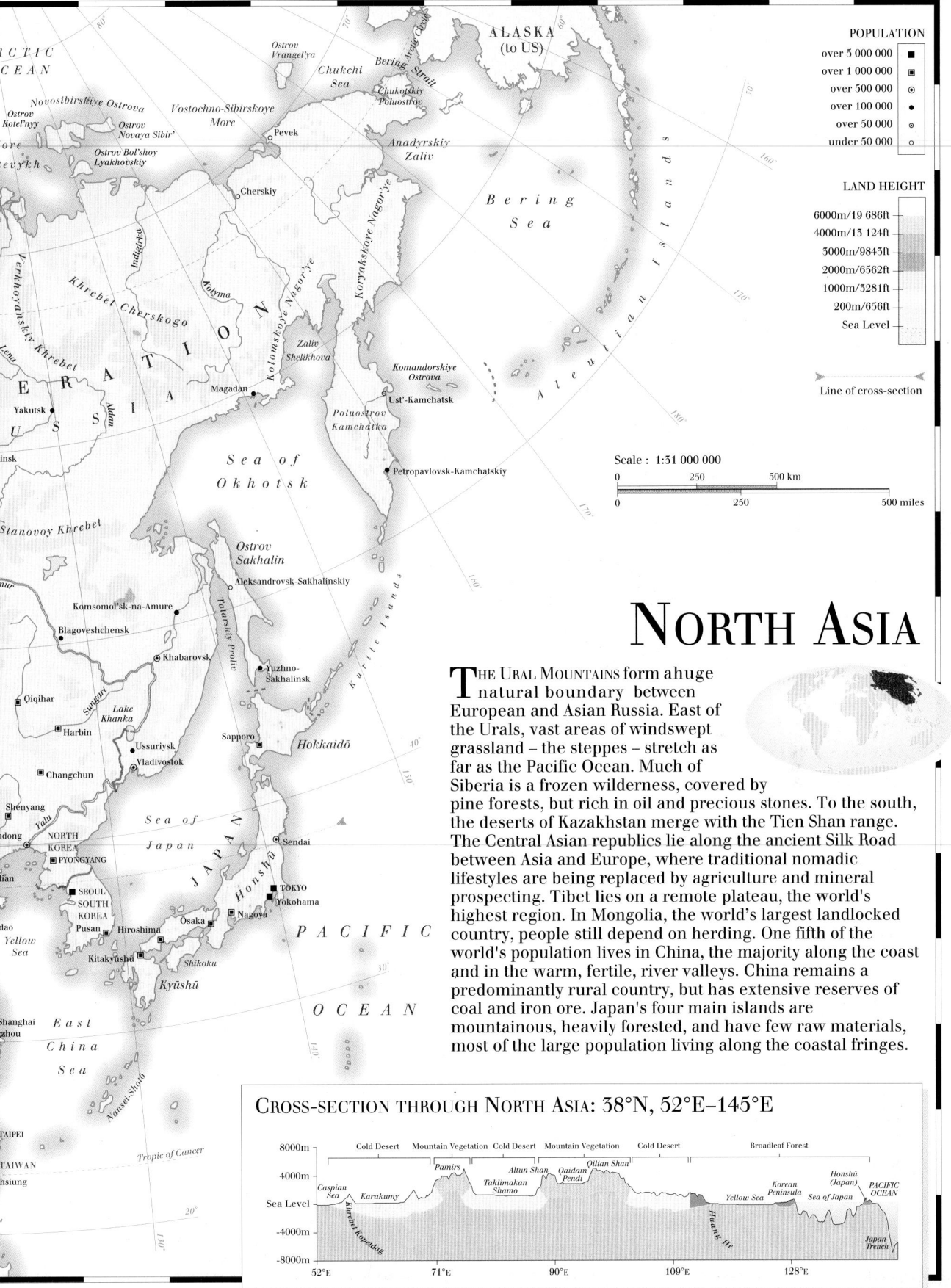

POPULATION

- ■ over 5 000 000
- ▣ over 1 000 000
- ◉ over 500 000
- • over 100 000
- ◦ over 50 000
- ○ under 50 000

LAND HEIGHT

- 6000m/19 686ft
- 4000m/13 124ft
- 3000m/9843ft
- 2000m/6562ft
- 1000m/3281ft
- 200m/656ft
- Sea Level

▶ Line of cross-section

Scale : 1:31 000 000

0 ... 250 ... 500 km
0 ... 250 ... 500 miles

NORTH ASIA

The URAL MOUNTAINS form a huge natural boundary between European and Asian Russia. East of the Urals, vast areas of windswept grassland – the steppes – stretch as far as the Pacific Ocean. Much of Siberia is a frozen wilderness, covered by pine forests, but rich in oil and precious stones. To the south, the deserts of Kazakhstan merge with the Tien Shan range. The Central Asian republics lie along the ancient Silk Road between Asia and Europe, where traditional nomadic lifestyles are being replaced by agriculture and mineral prospecting. Tibet lies on a remote plateau, the world's highest region. In Mongolia, the world's largest landlocked country, people still depend on herding. One fifth of the world's population lives in China, the majority along the coast and in the warm, fertile, river valleys. China remains a predominantly rural country, but has extensive reserves of coal and iron ore. Japan's four main islands are mountainous, heavily forested, and have few raw materials, most of the large population living along the coastal fringes.

CROSS-SECTION THROUGH NORTH ASIA: 38°N, 52°E–145°E

Cold Desert | Mountain Vegetation | Cold Desert | Mountain Vegetation | Cold Desert | Broadleaf Forest

8000m — 4000m — Sea Level — -4000m — -8000m

Caspian Sea · Karakumy · Khrebet Kopetdag · Pamirs · Taklimakan Shamo · Altun Shan · Qaidam Pendi · Qilian Shan · Yellow Sea · Huang He · Korean Peninsula · Sea of Japan · Honshū (Japan) · PACIFIC OCEAN · Japan Trench

52°E · 71°E · 90°E · 109°E · 128°E

29

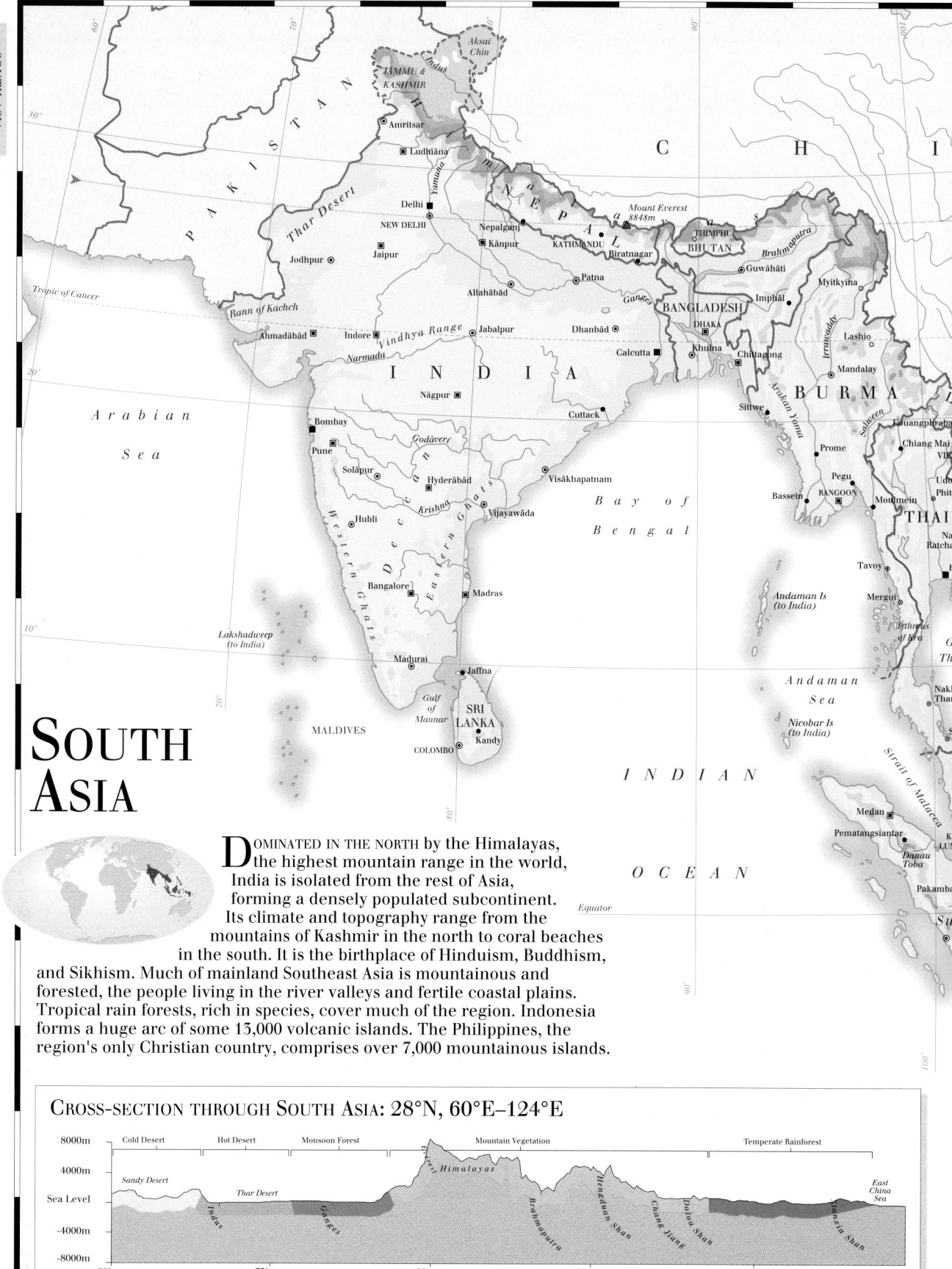

SOUTH ASIA

DOMINATED IN THE NORTH by the Himalayas, the highest mountain range in the world, India is isolated from the rest of Asia, forming a densely populated subcontinent. Its climate and topography range from the mountains of Kashmir in the north to coral beaches in the south. It is the birthplace of Hinduism, Buddhism, and Sikhism. Much of mainland Southeast Asia is mountainous and forested, the people living in the river valleys and fertile coastal plains. Tropical rain forests, rich in species, cover much of the region. Indonesia forms a huge arc of some 13,000 volcanic islands. The Philippines, the region's only Christian country, comprises over 7,000 mountainous islands.

CROSS-SECTION THROUGH SOUTH ASIA: 28°N, 60°E–124°E

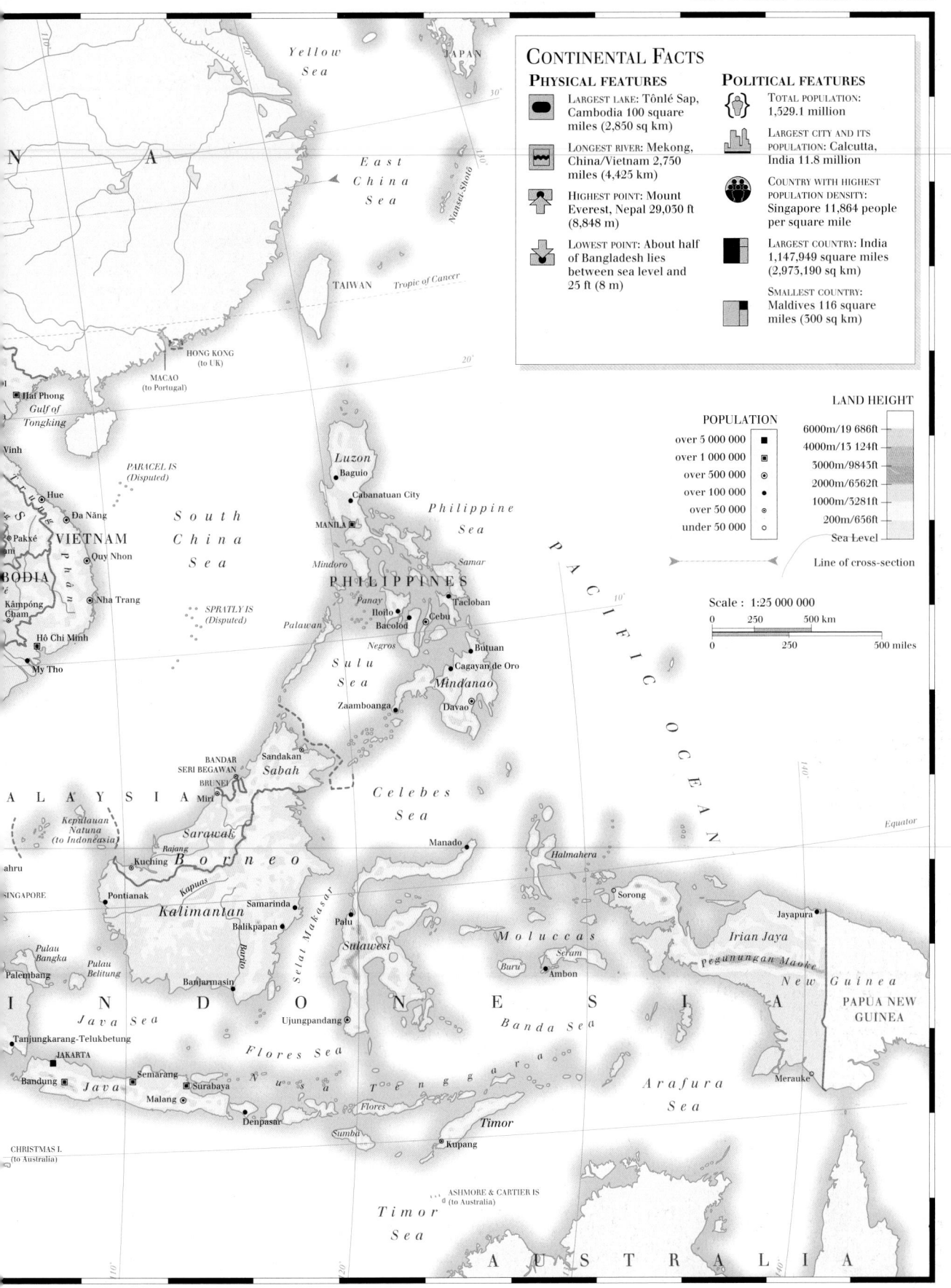

Yellow Sea

JAPAN

East China Sea

Nansei-Shotō

TAIWAN   *Tropic of Cancer*

HONG KONG
(to UK)

MACAO
(to Portugal)

■ Hai Phong
Gulf of Tongking

Vinh

PARACEL IS
(Disputed)

South China Sea

Luzon
● Baguio

● Cabanatuan City

Philippine Sea

MANILA ■

Hue
● Đa Nẵng

VIETNAM

Mindoro

Samar

Pakxé

BODIA

Quy Nhon

SPRATLY IS
(Disputed)

PHILIPPINES

● Tacloban

Panay
Iloilo ● Bacolod ● Cebu

Palawan

Negros

● Butuan

Kâmpóng
Cham

● Nha Trang

Sulu Sea

● Cagayan de Oro

Mindanao

Hô Chí Minh

Zaamboanga ●

● Davao

My Tho

Sandakan

BANDAR
SERI BEGAWAN
BRUNEI
● Miri

Sabah

Celebes Sea

ALAYSIA

*Kepulauan Natuna
(to Indonesia)*

Sarawak

Rajang

Kuching ●
Pontianak ●

Borneo

Kapuas

Kalimantan

Samarinda ●
Balikpapan ●

● Palu

● Manado

Halmahera

Sorong ●

● Jayapura

Irian Jaya

ahru

SINGAPORE

Sulawesi

Selat Makasar

Barito

Moluccas

Buru

Seram

● Ambon

Pegunungan Maoke

New Guinea

PAPUA NEW
GUINEA

Pulau Bangka

Pulau Belitung

Palembang

Banjarmasin ●

I   N   D   O   N   E   S   I   A

Java Sea

Tanjungkarang-Telukbetung ●

JAKARTA

Ujungpandang ⊙

Banda Sea

Arafura Sea

● Merauke

Bandung ●

Java

Semarang ●
■ Surabaya
Malang ●

Denpasar ●

Flores Sea

Flores

Sumba

● Kupang

Timor

CHRISTMAS I.
(to Australia)

ASHMORE & CARTIER IS
(to Australia)

Timor Sea

A   U   S   T   R   A   L   I   A

PACIFIC OCEAN

Equator

CONTINENTAL FACTS

PHYSICAL FEATURES

LARGEST LAKE: Tônlé Sap, Cambodia 100 square miles (2,850 sq km)

LONGEST RIVER: Mekong, China/Vietnam 2,750 miles (4,425 km)

HIGHEST POINT: Mount Everest, Nepal 29,030 ft (8,848 m)

LOWEST POINT: About half of Bangladesh lies between sea level and 25 ft (8 m)

POLITICAL FEATURES

TOTAL POPULATION: 1,529.1 million

LARGEST CITY AND ITS POPULATION: Calcutta, India 11.8 million

COUNTRY WITH HIGHEST POPULATION DENSITY: Singapore 11,864 people per square mile

LARGEST COUNTRY: India 1,147,949 square miles (2,973,190 sq km)

SMALLEST COUNTRY: Maldives 116 square miles (300 sq km)

POPULATION

over 5 000 000	■
over 1 000 000	▣
over 500 000	◉
over 100 000	●
over 50 000	⊙
under 50 000	○

LAND HEIGHT

6000m/19 686ft
4000m/13 124ft
3000m/9843ft
2000m/6562ft
1000m/3281ft
200m/656ft
Sea Level

Line of cross-section

Scale : 1:25 000 000

0   250   500 km

0   250   500 miles

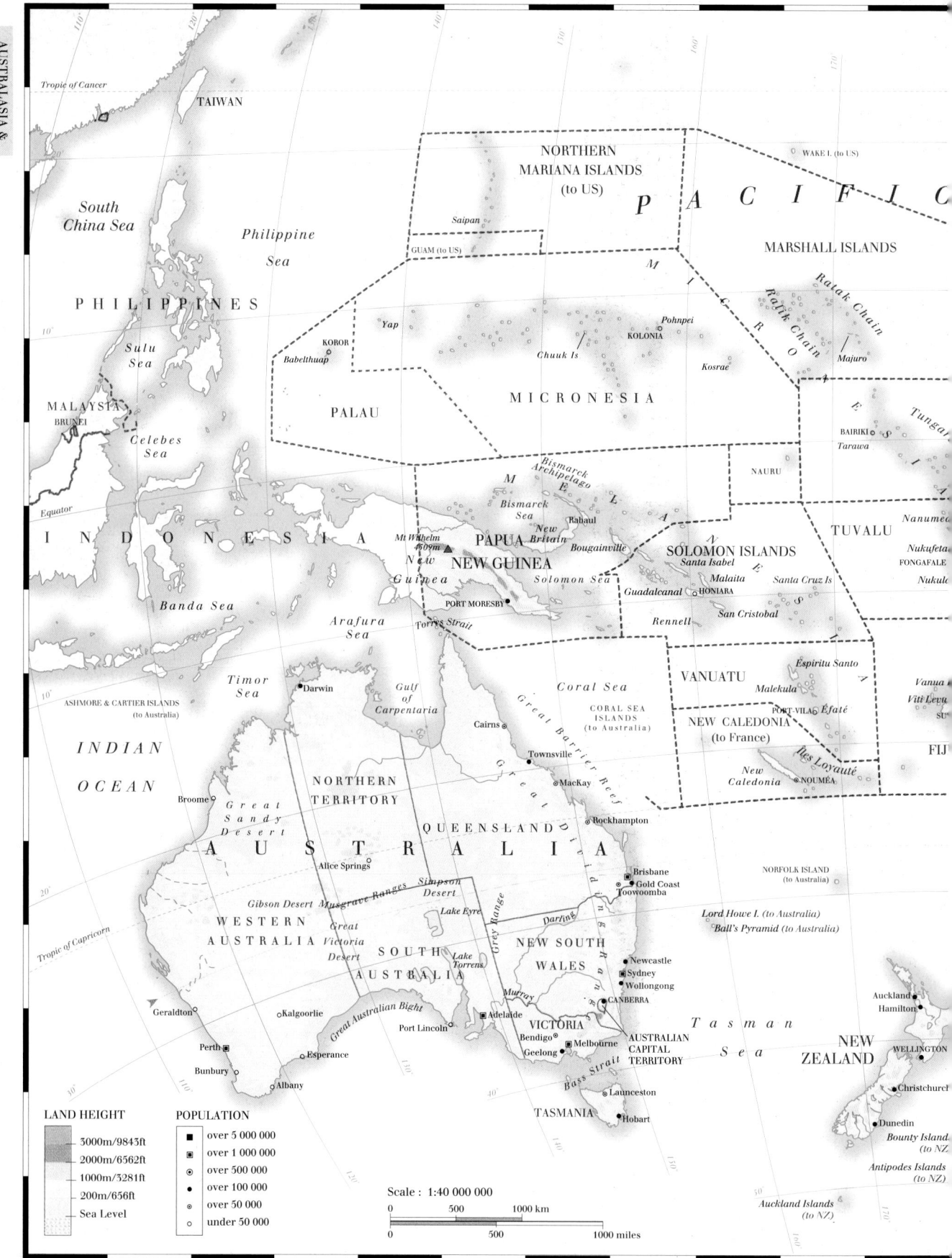

Tropic of Cancer

TAIWAN

*South
China Sea*

*Philippine
Sea*

NORTHERN
MARIANA ISLANDS
(to US)

WAKE I. (to US)

P A C I F I C

Saipan

GUAM (to US)

MARSHALL ISLANDS

PHILIPPINES

*Sulu
Sea*

MALAYSIA
BRUNEI

*Celebes
Sea*

Yap

KOROR
Babelthuap

PALAU

Pohnpei
KOLONIA

Chuuk Is

Kosrae

M I C R O N E S I A

Ratak Chain

Rafik Chain

Majuro

BAIRIKI
Tarawa

NAURU

Equator

I N D O N E S I A

Mt Wilhelm
4509m

Banda Sea

*New
Guinea*

PORT MORESBY

*Bismarck
Archipelago*

*Bismarck
Sea*

Rabaul

*New
Britain*

Bougainville

PAPUA
NEW GUINEA

Solomon Sea

SOLOMON ISLANDS

Santa Isabel

Malaita
HONIARA

Guadalcanal

Santa Cruz Is

San Cristobal

Rennell

TUVALU

Nanume

Nukufeta
FONGAFALE

Nukulo

*Arafura
Sea*

Torres Strait

*Timor
Sea*

Darwin

*Gulf
of
Carpentaria*

Coral Sea

CORAL SEA
ISLANDS
(to Australia)

VANUATU

Espiritu Santo

Malekula

PORT VILA *Éfaté*

Iles Loyauté

*Vanua
Viti Levu
SU*

FIJ

ASHMORE & CARTIER ISLANDS
(to Australia)

I N D I A N

O C E A N

Cairns

Townsville

MacKay

NEW CALEDONIA
(to France)

*New
Caledonia*
NOUMÉA

Broome

*Great
Sandy
Desert*

NORTHERN
TERRITORY

Rockhampton

QUEENSLAND

NORFOLK ISLAND
(to Australia)

A U S T R A L I A

Alice Springs

Brisbane
Gold Coast
Toowoomba

Lord Howe I. (to Australia)
Ball's Pyramid (to Australia)

Gibson Desert *Musgrave Ranges* *Simpson
Desert*

WESTERN
AUSTRALIA

*Great
Victoria
Desert*

SOUTH
AUSTRALIA

Lake Eyre

Lake
Torrens

Murray

NEW SOUTH
WALES

Darling

Newcastle
Sydney
Wollongong
CANBERRA

AUSTRALIAN
CAPITAL
TERRITORY

*Tasman
Sea*

Auckland
Hamilton

Kalgoorlie

Port Lincoln

Adelaide

Esperance

VICTORIA

Bendigo
Geelong

Melbourne

NEW
ZEALAND

WELLINGTON

Perth

Great Australian Bight

Bunbury

Albany

Bass Strait

Launceston

TASMANIA

Hobart

Christchurch

Dunedin

*Bounty Island
(to NZ)*

*Antipodes Islands
(to NZ)*

Tropic of Capricorn

Geraldton

Scale : 1 : 40 000 000

0   500   1000 km

0   500   1000 miles

*Auckland Islands
(to NZ)*

AUSTRALASIA & OCEANIA

OCEANIA EMBRACES THE WORLD'S smallest continent, Australia, large island groups such as New Zealand, Papua New Guinea, and Fiji, and the myriad volcanic and coral islands scattered across the Pacific Ocean, consisting of three main groups, Micronesia, Melanesia, and Polynesia. Australia, flat and dry, is sparsely populated, most people living along the coastal lowlands, especially in the southeast. The continent's first settlers, the Aboriginal peoples, retain some of their original lands in the interior, but later European and Asian settlers form most of the population. Owing to its isolation from other continents, Australia's flora and fauna have evolved many unique species. The continent is rich in minerals, such as gold, uranium, and iron ore, which are the basis of Australia's prosperity. Mountainous Papua New Guinea is covered in tropical rain forest, while New Zealand is temperate, rugged, and volcanic in the north. The peoples of Oceania colonized the Pacific by AD 1500, and the many insular farming and fishing communities have developed distinctive cultures, the Maoris of New Zealand being among the most notable.

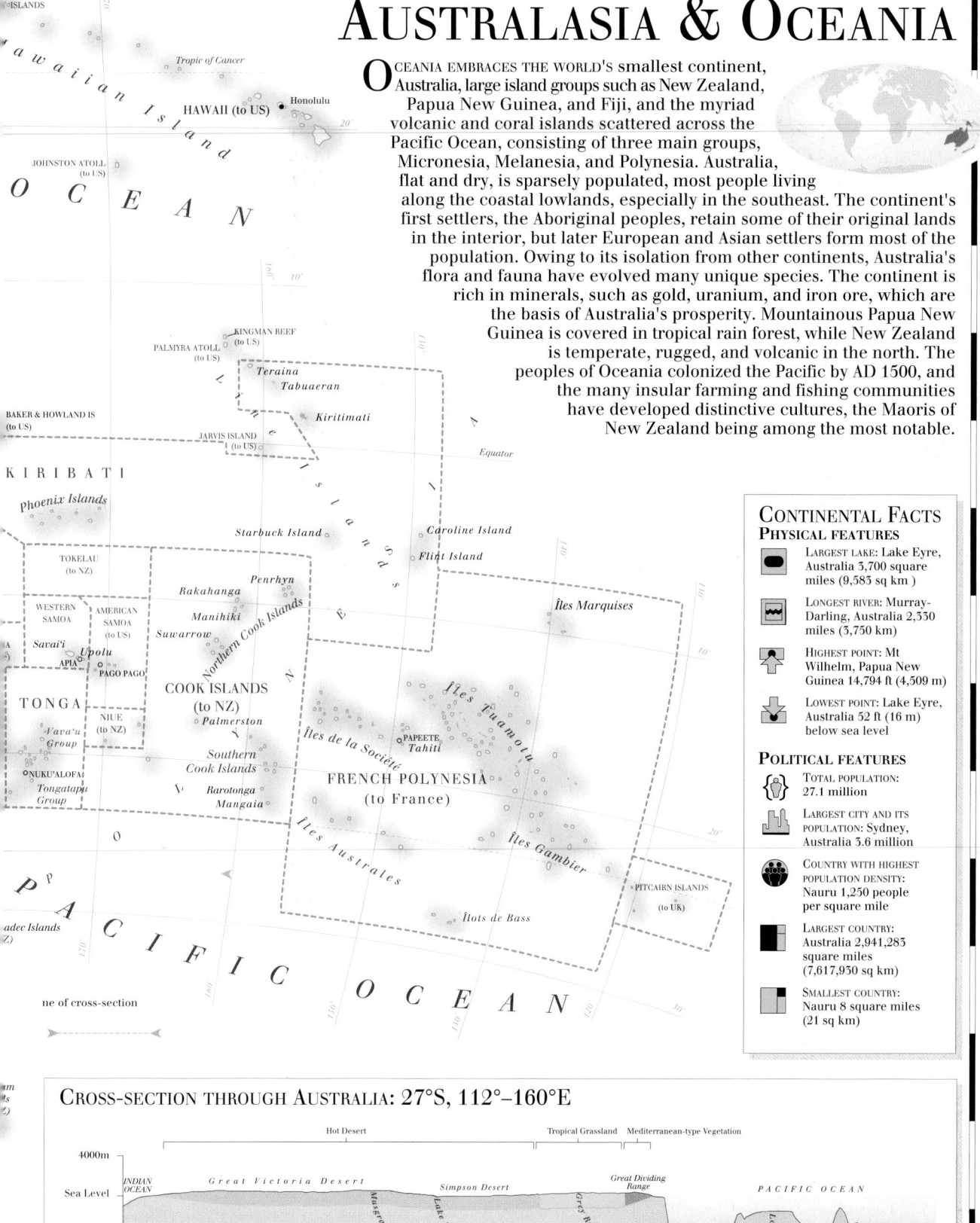

CONTINENTAL FACTS

PHYSICAL FEATURES

LARGEST LAKE: Lake Eyre, Australia 3,700 square miles (9,583 sq km)

LONGEST RIVER: Murray-Darling, Australia 2,330 miles (3,750 km)

HIGHEST POINT: Mt Wilhelm, Papua New Guinea 14,794 ft (4,509 m)

LOWEST POINT: Lake Eyre, Australia 52 ft (16 m) below sea level

POLITICAL FEATURES

TOTAL POPULATION: 27.1 million

LARGEST CITY AND ITS POPULATION: Sydney, Australia 3.6 million

COUNTRY WITH HIGHEST POPULATION DENSITY: Nauru 1,250 people per square mile

LARGEST COUNTRY: Australia 2,941,283 square miles (7,617,930 sq km)

SMALLEST COUNTRY: Nauru 8 square miles (21 sq km)

CROSS-SECTION THROUGH AUSTRALIA: 27°S, 112°–160°E

Hot Desert • Tropical Grassland • Mediterranean-type Vegetation

4000m · Sea Level · -4000m · -8000m

INDIAN OCEAN · Great Victoria Desert · Musgrave Ranges · Lake Eyre · Simpson Desert · Grey Range · Great Dividing Range · PACIFIC OCEAN · Lord Howe Rise · New Caledonia · South Fiji Basin

112°E · 125°E · 138°E · 151°E · 164°E

THE FORMATION OF THE MODERN WORLD

THE WORLD AS WE KNOW IT today, like all of the species that inhabit it, is the product of many thousands of years of evolution. The political and cultural map of the globe bears the hallmark of many varied courses of human development the world over. Nevertheless, much of the modern human geography of the planet can be traced to developments in the relatively recent past. The following pages chart the rise and fall of the various states and empires of the early modern and modern ages. Beginning with the first great achievement of European exploration, the discovery of the Americas in 1492, the maps show the way in which various European and Asian powers expanded their cultural and political influence and control down to the present day. This process left indelible cultural imprints in the form of language, religion, education, and systems of government on every part of the planet.

MAJOR MIGRATIONS SINCE 1500

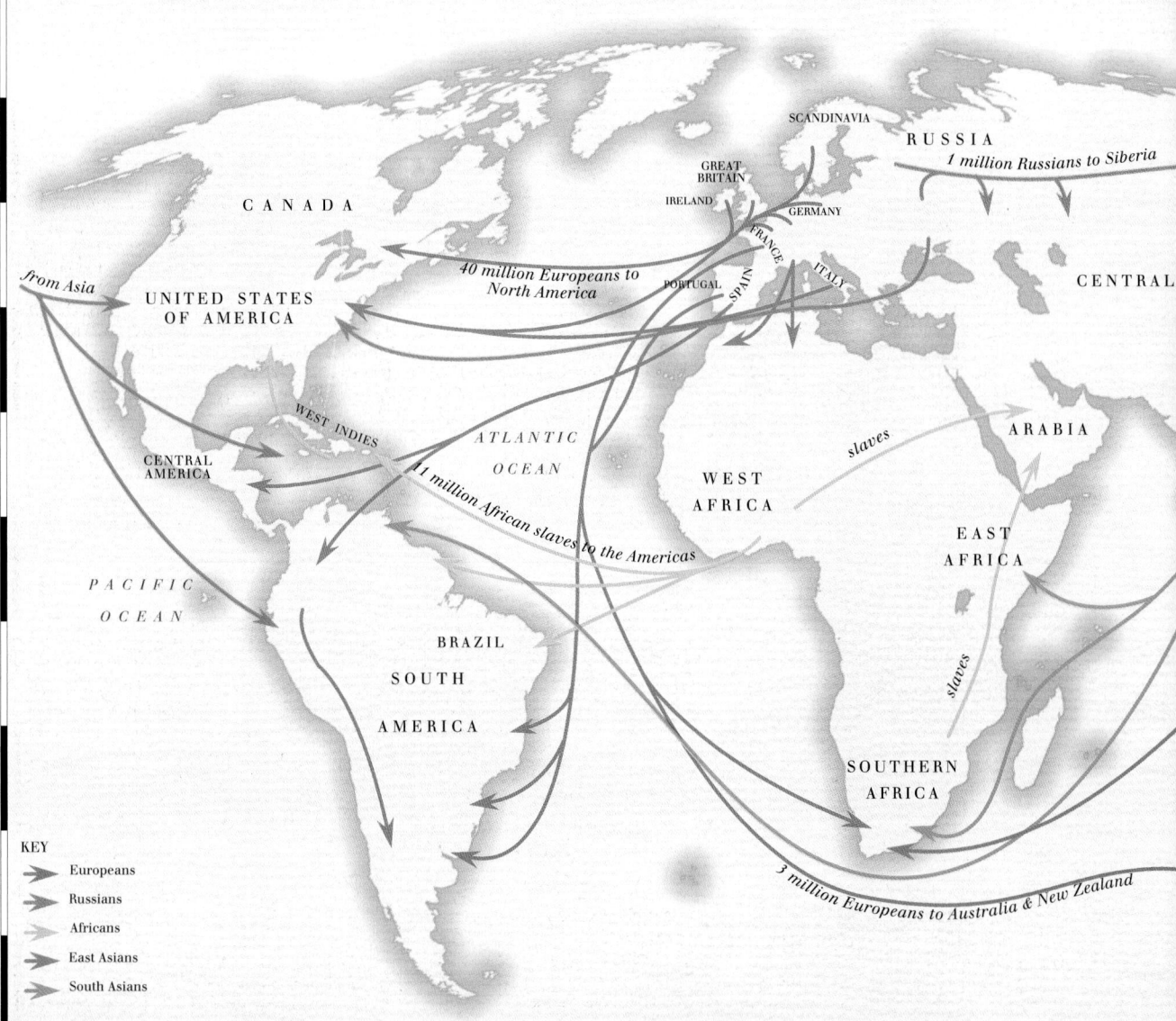

KEY
- Europeans
- Russians
- Africans
- East Asians
- South Asians

LANGUAGES OF THE WORLD

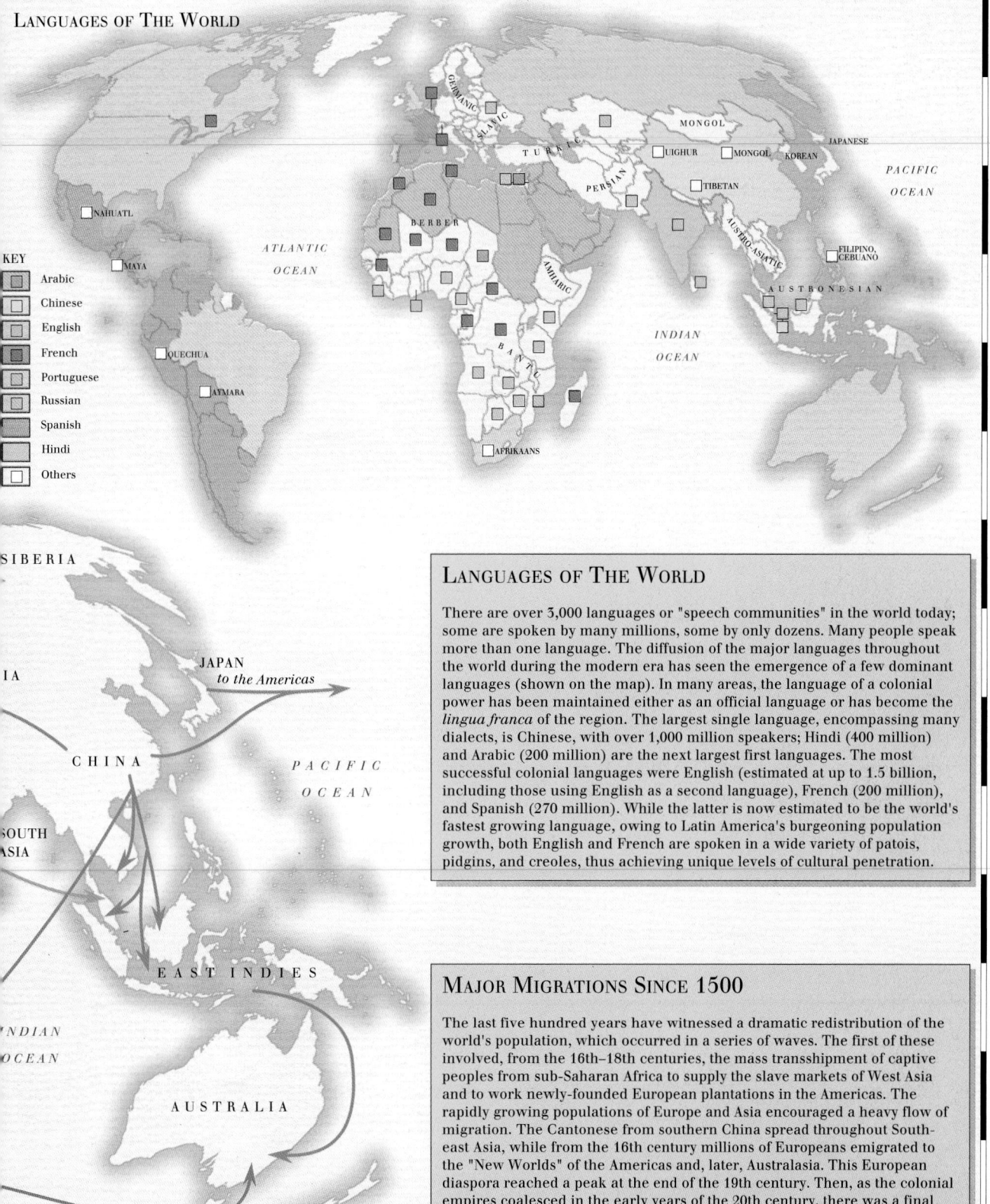

KEY

- Arabic
- Chinese
- English
- French
- Portuguese
- Russian
- Spanish
- Hindi
- Others

LANGUAGES OF THE WORLD

There are over 3,000 languages or "speech communities" in the world today; some are spoken by many millions, some by only dozens. Many people speak more than one language. The diffusion of the major languages throughout the world during the modern era has seen the emergence of a few dominant languages (shown on the map). In many areas, the language of a colonial power has been maintained either as an official language or has become the *lingua franca* of the region. The largest single language, encompassing many dialects, is Chinese, with over 1,000 million speakers; Hindi (400 million) and Arabic (200 million) are the next largest first languages. The most successful colonial languages were English (estimated at up to 1.5 billion, including those using English as a second language), French (200 million), and Spanish (270 million). While the latter is now estimated to be the world's fastest growing language, owing to Latin America's burgeoning population growth, both English and French are spoken in a wide variety of patois, pidgins, and creoles, thus achieving unique levels of cultural penetration.

MAJOR MIGRATIONS SINCE 1500

The last five hundred years have witnessed a dramatic redistribution of the world's population, which occurred in a series of waves. The first of these involved, from the 16th–18th centuries, the mass transshipment of captive peoples from sub-Saharan Africa to supply the slave markets of West Asia and to work newly-founded European plantations in the Americas. The rapidly growing populations of Europe and Asia encouraged a heavy flow of migration. The Cantonese from southern China spread throughout South-east Asia, while from the 16th century millions of Europeans emigrated to the "New Worlds" of the Americas and, later, Australasia. This European diaspora reached a peak at the end of the 19th century. Then, as the colonial empires coalesced in the early years of the 20th century, there was a final wave of global movement within them, when South and East Asians migrated to fill labor markets and exploit opportunities in Africa and the Americas. While homogenous societies have developed in North America and Australia, many diverse ethnic communities remain scattered across the world.

THE WORLD IN 1492

WHEN CHRISTOPHER COLUMBUS sailed west from Europe, seeking a quicker route to Asia, he launched a process of discovery that was eventually to bring the disparate regions of the world into closer contact, to form the global map we know today. The largest political entity in the world at that time was the Chinese Ming empire. Culturally, the Islamic faith had forged a bond of religious unity which extended in a broad swath from Southeast Asia to the Atlantic coast of North Africa. Europe was a mêlée of rival monarchies; sub-Saharan Africa a patchwork of trading kingdoms; the Americas, a separate world of rich tribal cultures, with empires established only in Central America and the central Andes.

GLOBAL STATES AND TERRITORIES

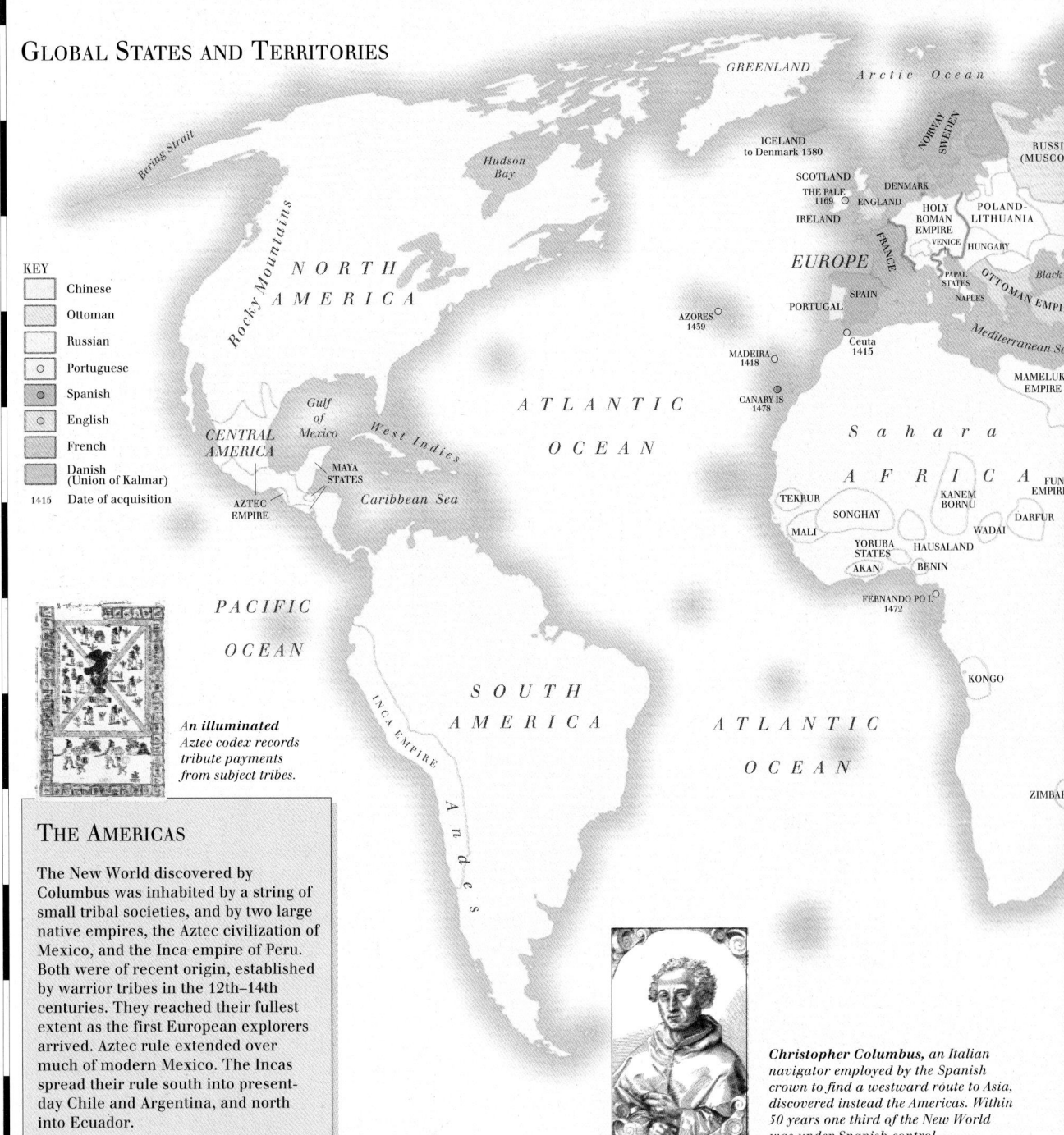

KEY

	Chinese
	Ottoman
	Russian
○	Portuguese
◉	Spanish
○	English
	French
	Danish (Union of Kalmar)
1415	Date of acquisition

An illuminated Aztec codex records tribute payments from subject tribes.

THE AMERICAS

The New World discovered by Columbus was inhabited by a string of small tribal societies, and by two large native empires, the Aztec civilization of Mexico, and the Inca empire of Peru. Both were of recent origin, established by warrior tribes in the 12th–14th centuries. They reached their fullest extent as the first European explorers arrived. Aztec rule extended over much of modern Mexico. The Incas spread their rule south into present-day Chile and Argentina, and north into Ecuador.

Christopher Columbus, an Italian navigator employed by the Spanish crown to find a westward route to Asia, discovered instead the Americas. Within 50 years one third of the New World was under Spanish control.

EUROPE

Though Christian Europe later transformed the exploration and settlement of the world, the Europe from which Columbus sailed was an unstable, violent continent, threatened by invaders from Asia to the east, and from the Ottoman Empire to the south. Civil wars and dynastic conflict resulted in shifting frontiers and small, militarily weak states. Only France, united by the late 15th century, Spain, a single monarchy from the 1490s, Portugal and England were close to their modern forms.

The Portuguese caravel, buoyant, sturdy and lateen-rigged, was an ideal ocean-going vessel.

EAST ASIA

The most powerful state in the world in 1492 was Ming China. Set up in 1386 after the collapse of Mongol power, the Ming dynasty ruled an area from Manchuria in the north to the borders of Vietnam in the south. Based on a traditional structure of bureaucratic control, the Ming emperors controlled their vast empire from Peking (Beijing), from where they launched punitive wars against the Mongols and Japanese pirates along the coast. Chinese culture and trade spread throughout East and Southeast Asia, and Chinese navigators reached the Red Sea and the East African coast.

Chinese junks plied the China seas, and traded as far as the East Indies, Ceylon, and East Africa.

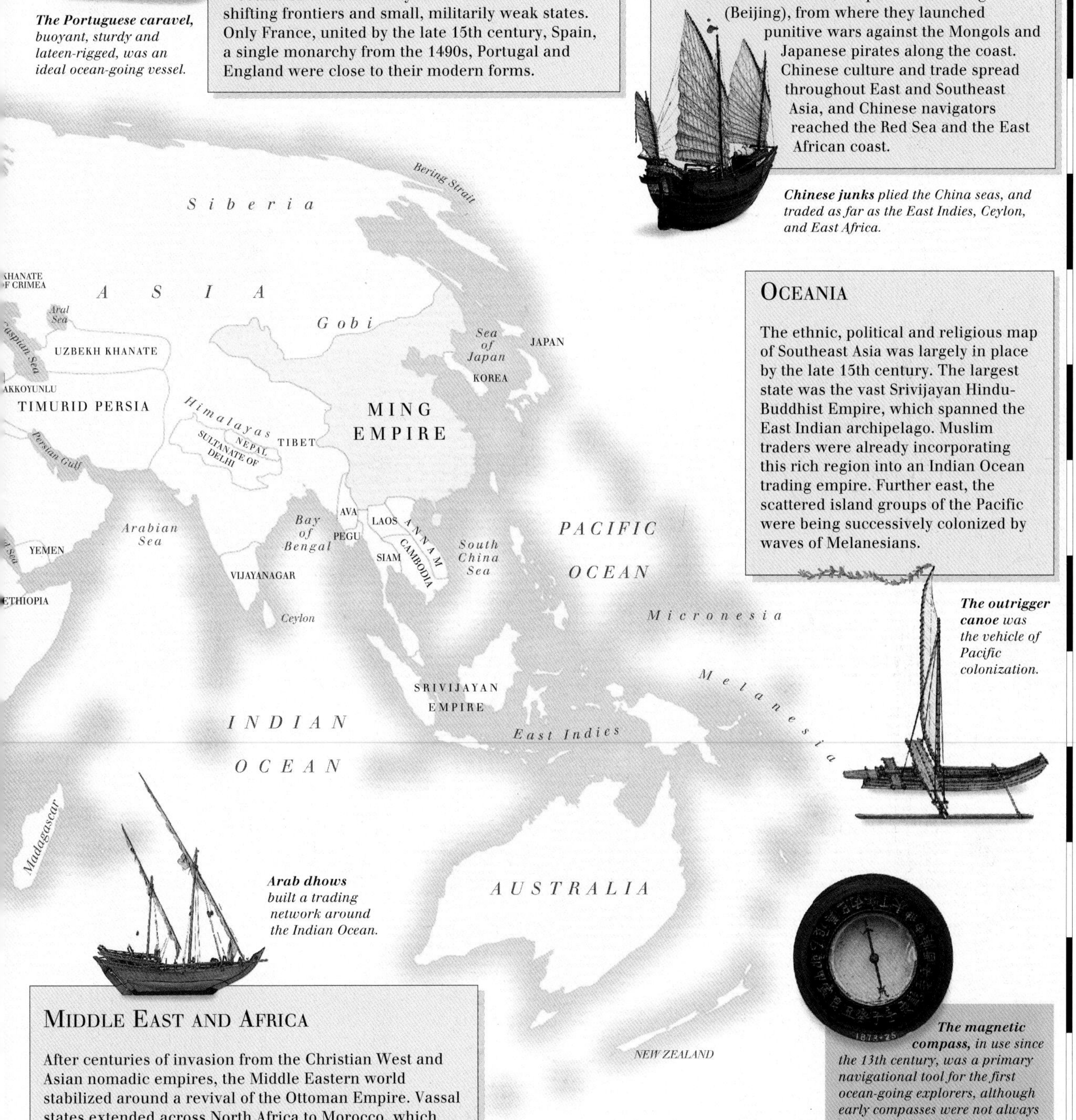

OCEANIA

The ethnic, political and religious map of Southeast Asia was largely in place by the late 15th century. The largest state was the vast Srivijayan Hindu-Buddhist Empire, which spanned the East Indian archipelago. Muslim traders were already incorporating this rich region into an Indian Ocean trading empire. Further east, the scattered island groups of the Pacific were being successively colonized by waves of Melanesians.

The outrigger canoe was the vehicle of Pacific colonization.

Arab dhows built a trading network around the Indian Ocean.

MIDDLE EAST AND AFRICA

After centuries of invasion from the Christian West and Asian nomadic empires, the Middle Eastern world stabilized around a revival of the Ottoman Empire. Vassal states extended across North Africa to Morocco, which linked the trading kingdoms of sub-Saharan Africa with the markets of Asia. The great cities of the Middle East surpassed those of Europe in wealth and learning.

The magnetic compass, in use since the 13th century, was a primary navigational tool for the first ocean-going explorers, although early compasses were not always reliable, and ships often went astray. Accurate navigation only came later with the invention of the chronometer.

Map labels: Siberia, Bering Strait, ASIA, KHANATE OF CRIMEA, Aral Sea, Gobi, Caspian Sea, UZBEKH KHANATE, Sea of Japan, JAPAN, AKKOYUNLU, TIMURID PERSIA, Himalayas, KOREA, Persian Gulf, NEPAL, TIBET, MING EMPIRE, SULTANATE OF DELHI, Arabian Sea, AVA, LAOS, ANNAM, PACIFIC OCEAN, YEMEN, Bay of Bengal, PEGU, CAMBODIA, South China Sea, ETHIOPIA, VIJAYANAGAR, SIAM, Ceylon, Micronesia, INDIAN OCEAN, Melanesia, SRIVIJAYAN EMPIRE, East Indies, Madagascar, AUSTRALIA, NEW ZEALAND

THE AGE OF DISCOVERY: 1492-1648

THE FIRST STATE to take advantage of the new age of exploration was Spain. By the middle of the 16th century, under the Emperor Charles V, Spain was established as the foremost European colonial power, and one of the richest and most powerful kingdoms in Europe. Spanish rule was extended over the whole of Central America, much of South America, Florida, and the Caribbean; in Asia, Spanish rule was established in the Philippines. Spain led the way in establishing European settler colonies overseas. By the middle of the 17th century, British, Dutch, and French colonists began to challenge Spanish dominance in the Americas and East Asia, while pirates around the world plundered Spain's wealthy merchant convoys.

GLOBAL STATES AND TERRITORIES

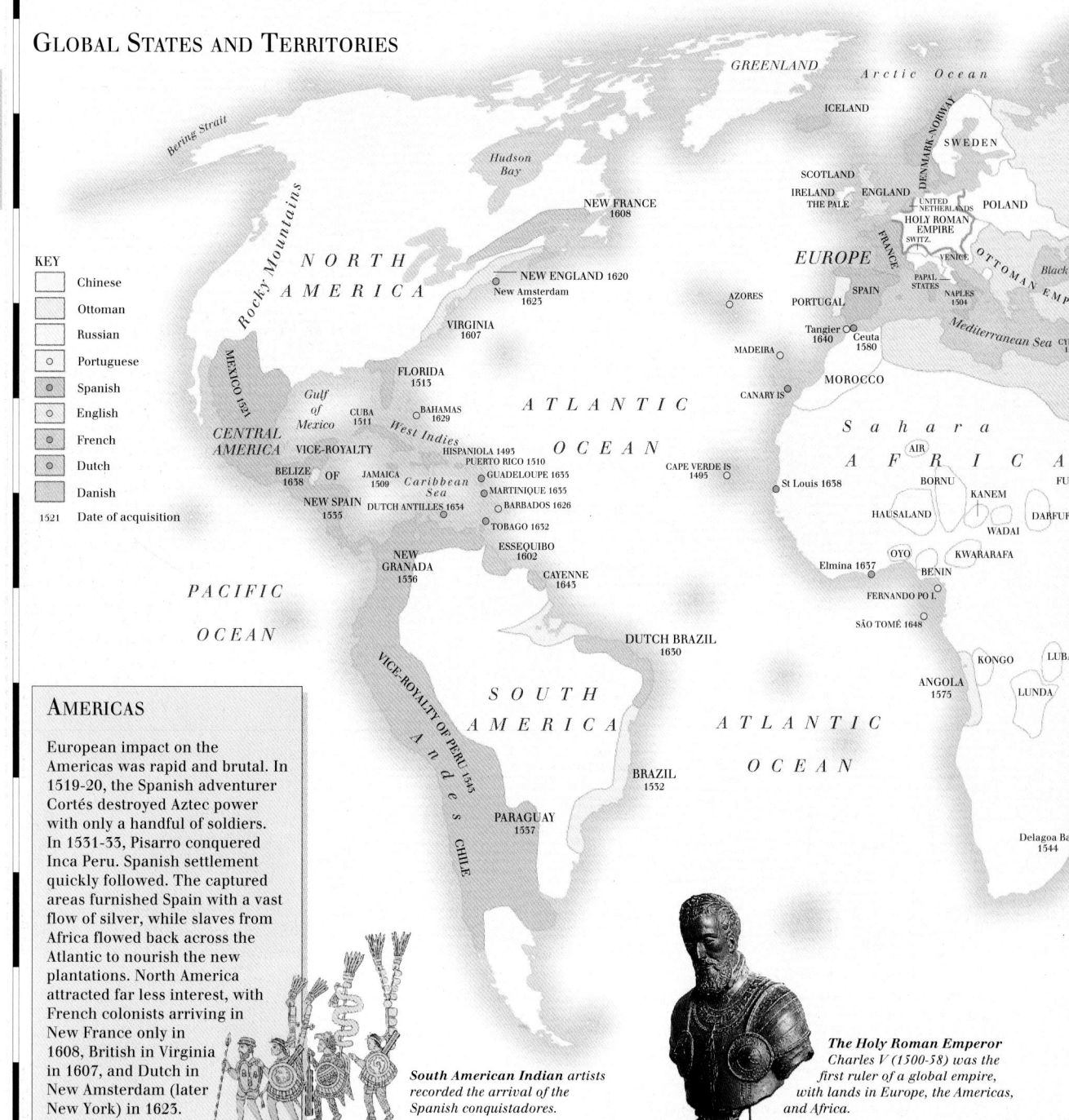

KEY

▢	Chinese
▢	Ottoman
▢	Russian
○	Portuguese
◉	Spanish
○	English
◉	French
○	Dutch
▢	Danish
1521	Date of acquisition

AMERICAS

European impact on the Americas was rapid and brutal. In 1519-20, the Spanish adventurer Cortés destroyed Aztec power with only a handful of soldiers. In 1531-33, Pisarro conquered Inca Peru. Spanish settlement quickly followed. The captured areas furnished Spain with a vast flow of silver, while slaves from Africa flowed back across the Atlantic to nourish the new plantations. North America attracted far less interest, with French colonists arriving in New France only in 1608, British in Virginia in 1607, and Dutch in New Amsterdam (later New York) in 1623.

South American Indian artists recorded the arrival of the Spanish conquistadores.

The Holy Roman Emperor Charles V (1500-58) was the first ruler of a global empire, with lands in Europe, the Americas, and Africa.

EUROPE

For more than a century after Martin Luther inspired the Protestant Reformation in the 1520s, Europe was torn by religious wars. Scandinavia, England, and Scotland adopted the new church but elsewhere bitter civil conflicts led to the prolonged warfare and persecution known as the Thirty Years' War. This ended in 1648; it destroyed wide areas of Central Europe and decimated the German population, but resulted in a religious settlement which carried down to the 20th century. The Dutch Republic and northern Germany became Protestant while southern Germany, Poland, and southwest Europe remained Catholic.

Printing, using movable type, was a key development in the dissemination of ideas, knowledge and commerce in early modern Europe.

ASIA

In 1480, the small principality of Muscovy (Moscow) threw off Mongol control, and proceeded to expand Muscovite power over the whole of the area from the Arctic Ocean to the Caspian Sea. In the 1550s, the conquest of Kazan brought Russian power to the Urals, and over the next century it spread across Siberia reaching the Pacific coast by 1649. Much of the area remained uninhabited, but to the south this new empire jostled uneasily with a string of Central Asian Muslim khanates, and with the newly-established Manchurian Ch'ing dynasty, which wrested control of China from the Ming in 1644.

European navigators and surveyors produced accurate maps and charts of their voyages.

The Indian Mughal ruler Shahjahan (1592-1648), builder of the Taj Mahal.

SOUTH ASIA AND OCEANIA

The Portuguese and the Spanish were the first European powers to open trade with the powerful Asian states of Mughal India and Ch'ing China, the Spanish opening trans-Pacific routes between Central America, the Philippines, and China. But the establishment of the Dutch and British East India companies in the early 17th century announced the advent of two new maritime powers.

RUSSIAN EMPIRE
Siberia

Bering Strait

KAZAKHSTAN
Aral Sea
KHWARIZM
KHOKAND KHANATE
KASHGAR KHANATE
UZBEKISTAN
Caspian Sea

A S I A

SAFAVID PERSIA
Himalayas
TIBET
NEPAL
MUGHAL EMPIRE
Hooghly 1640
Persian Gulf
OMAN 1508
Diu 1555
Surat 1608
Daman 1559
Bombay 1534
BURMA
ARAKAN
Bay of Bengal
LAOS
Arabian Sea
Goa 1510
Masulipatam 1611
Madras 1639
SIAM
ANNAM
CEYLON 1505
Galle 1640

MANCHU (CH'ING) EMPIRE
Sea of Japan
JAPAN
KOREA
Deshima 1641
Macao 1557
FORMOSA 1624
PHILIPPINES from 1565
South China Sea

PACIFIC OCEAN

Micronesia

MOLUCCAS from 1605

Melanesia

ETHIOPIA

PORTUGUESE EAST AFRICA from 1505

I N D I A N   O C E A N

Malacca 1641
Makassar 1607
Batavia 1619
East Indies
1610
TIMOR 1618

Madagascar

A U S T R A L I A

West African trading kingdoms produced artifacts such as this bronze Portuguese soldier from Benin.

AFRICA AND THE MIDDLE EAST

While Europe was divided by the Reformation, Islam experienced a remarkable resurgence in the 16th century. The revival of the Ottoman Empire brought Islamic rule over much of southeast Europe. Islam spread along trade routes to sub-Saharan Africa. In east Africa, it spread south along the coast. Further east, Muslim rulers established new imperial states in Persia (Iran) and India.

NEW ZEALAND

The sextant allowed navigators to take accurate measurements of heavenly bodies in relation to the horizon, thus allowing latitude to be calculated correctly. Early sextants had to be hand-held and were often used on shore rather than on board ship.

THE AGE OF EXPANSION: 1648-1789

THE YEARS FROM the middle of the 17th century to the end of the 18th century saw a massive consolidation of European discovery and exploration, which took the form of colonial settlement and political expansion. This period also witnessed the beginning of a sharp rise in European population and in its economic strength, accompanied by rapid developments in the arts and sciences. All these factors

powered European expansion – a process that would bring European culture to every part of the globe, gradually filling in the world map, and bringing it into often fatal contact with less robust indigenous cultures. By the last quarter of the 18th century, with Europe poised on the brink of political turmoil, only Africa and Australasia remained largely unmolested by European attentions.

GLOBAL STATES AND TERRITORIES

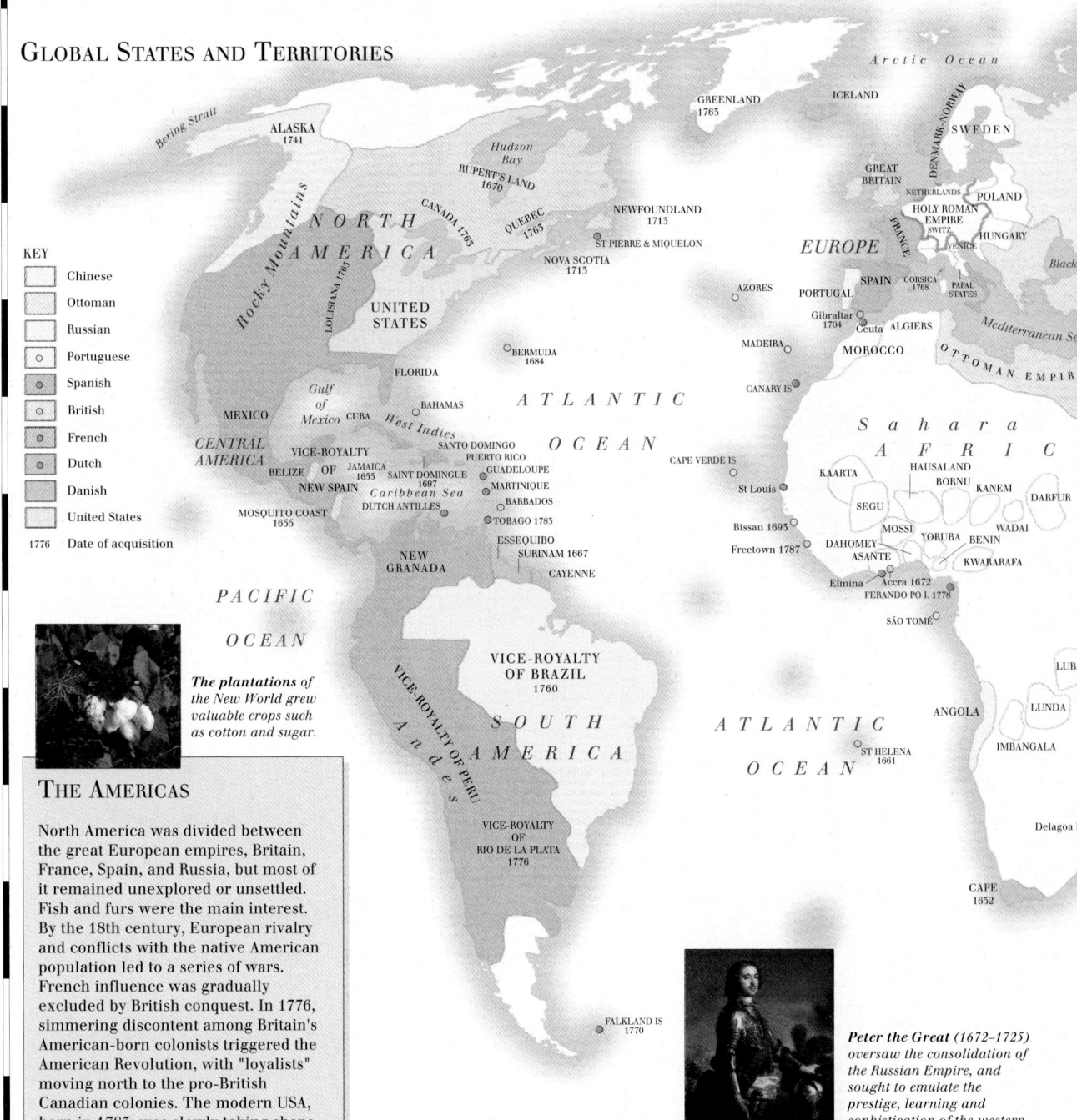

KEY

	Chinese
	Ottoman
	Russian
○	Portuguese
●	Spanish
○	British
●	French
○	Dutch
	Danish
	United States
1776	Date of acquisition

The plantations of the New World grew valuable crops such as cotton and sugar.

THE AMERICAS

North America was divided between the great European empires, Britain, France, Spain, and Russia, but most of it remained unexplored or unsettled. Fish and furs were the main interest. By the 18th century, European rivalry and conflicts with the native American population led to a series of wars. French influence was gradually excluded by British conquest. In 1776, simmering discontent among Britain's American-born colonists triggered the American Revolution, with "loyalists" moving north to the pro-British Canadian colonies. The modern USA, born in 1783, was slowly taking shape.

Peter the Great (1672–1725) oversaw the consolidation of the Russian Empire, and sought to emulate the prestige, learning and sophistication of the western European monarchies.

EUROPE

After the crisis of the Thirty Years' War, Europe began to develop a more settled state system as successful dynastic houses imposed more centralized rule. The Habsburgs acquired control over Hungary and much of Central Europe. Russia's frontiers pushed into Poland and the Ukraine. The French Bourbon monarchy became the most powerful in Europe. Its material wealth and culture made it a rival to the older empires of Asia. French became the common language of educated Europeans and French philosophy led to the intellectual "enlightenment."

Isaac Newton (1642-1727), the leading scientist of Europe's Age of Reason.

ASIA

The Ch'ing Dynasty forged the shape of modern China. By 1658 the whole of southern China was under Manchu control. Formosa (Taiwan) was occupied in 1683, outer Mongolia in 1697. A protectorate was established over Tibet in 1751. Over the course of this expansion, the population of China trebled and the economy boomed through trade in tea, porcelain, and silk with Russia and the West. Manchu China was powerful enough to resist incursions by the European empires, avoiding the fate of the crumbling Mughal Empire in India, where Britain and France competed for trade and territory.

Dutch and British East Indiamen carried the vast European trade with Asia.

Maori New Zealand was one of the few indigenous cultures to remain untouched by European contact until the 19th century.

OCEANIA

Southeast Asia and Oceania was an area of small, warring kingdoms, increasingly prey to the ambitions of European traders, first Spanish and Portuguese, then Dutch and British. Yet, by the late 18th century, there was still little formal colonization. Though first discovered by Tasman in 1692, most of Australasia was still unexplored and unsettled, except for a number of small penal colonies set up by the British in New South Wales (1788) and Tasmania (1804).

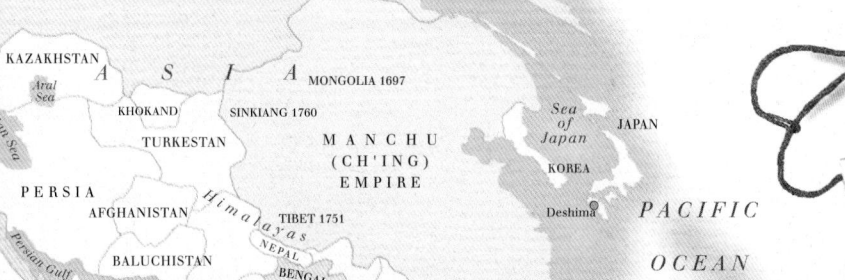

African slavers marched their human cargo from the interior to the coast for transshipment.

AFRICA

During the 17th and 18th centuries Africa was regarded by the rest of the world as a source of two things: gold and slaves. Some 13.5 million slaves were shipped in the 1700s, from the west coast and from Portuguese Angola. African dealers sold to European middlemen, who in turn sold on the surviving slaves. In northern and northeastern Africa, Arab slavers traded with the Ottoman Empire. But the rest of Africa remained isolated from the outside world.

Harrison's chronometer, invented in 1762, allowed navigators to measure time accurately, and thus calculate longitude correctly. This greatly reduced the risk of shipwreck and heralded the beginning of accurate mapping of the world.

Map labels:

RUSSIAN EMPIRE

KAZAKHSTAN
Aral Sea
KHOKAND
TURKESTAN
SINKIANG 1760
MONGOLIA 1697
A S I A
Sea of Japan
JAPAN
KOREA
Deshima
PACIFIC OCEAN
PERSIA
AFGHANISTAN
Himalayas
TIBET 1751
NEPAL
BALUCHISTAN
Persian Gulf
Arabian Sea
Surat
Diu
Daman
Bombay 1661
MARATHA CONFEDERACY
Goa
Mahé 1725
Karikal 1758
MADRAS
Pondicherry 1674
BENGAL 1757
Chandernagore
Bay of Bengal
BURMA 1688
NORTHERN CIRCARS 1756
ANDAMAN IS 1789
ANNAM
SIAM
South China Sea
FORMOSA 1685
Macao
PHILIPPINES
MARIANAS 1668
CAROLINE IS 1686
Micronesia
MALAYA
MOLUCCAS
Melanesia
Galle
CEYLON 1658
Penang 1786
INDIAN OCEAN
MANCHU (CH'ING) EMPIRE
PORTUGUESE EAST AFRICA
CHAGOS IS 1784
DUTCH EAST INDIES
TIMOR
ETHIOPIA
Madagascar
RÉUNION 1662
Fort Dauphin 1766
AUSTRALIA
LORD HOWE I. 1788
NEW SOUTH WALES 1788
NEW ZEALAND

THE AGE OF REVOLUTION: 1789-1830

IN 1789 ROYAL POWER was shattered by the French Revolution. The collapse of the most powerful monarchy in Europe reverberated worldwide. The revolutions in France and America ushered in the idea of the modern nation state, and of popular representative government. Revolutionary outbreaks occurred elsewhere in Europe, and overseas colonies in Latin America won their independence. At the same time, an industrial revolution was taking place in Europe, transforming the old trading economy into a manufacturing base which would require a global supply of raw materials and a global market to fuel it. The revolutionary years thus marked the beginning of the modern political and economic world order.

GLOBAL STATES AND TERRITORIES

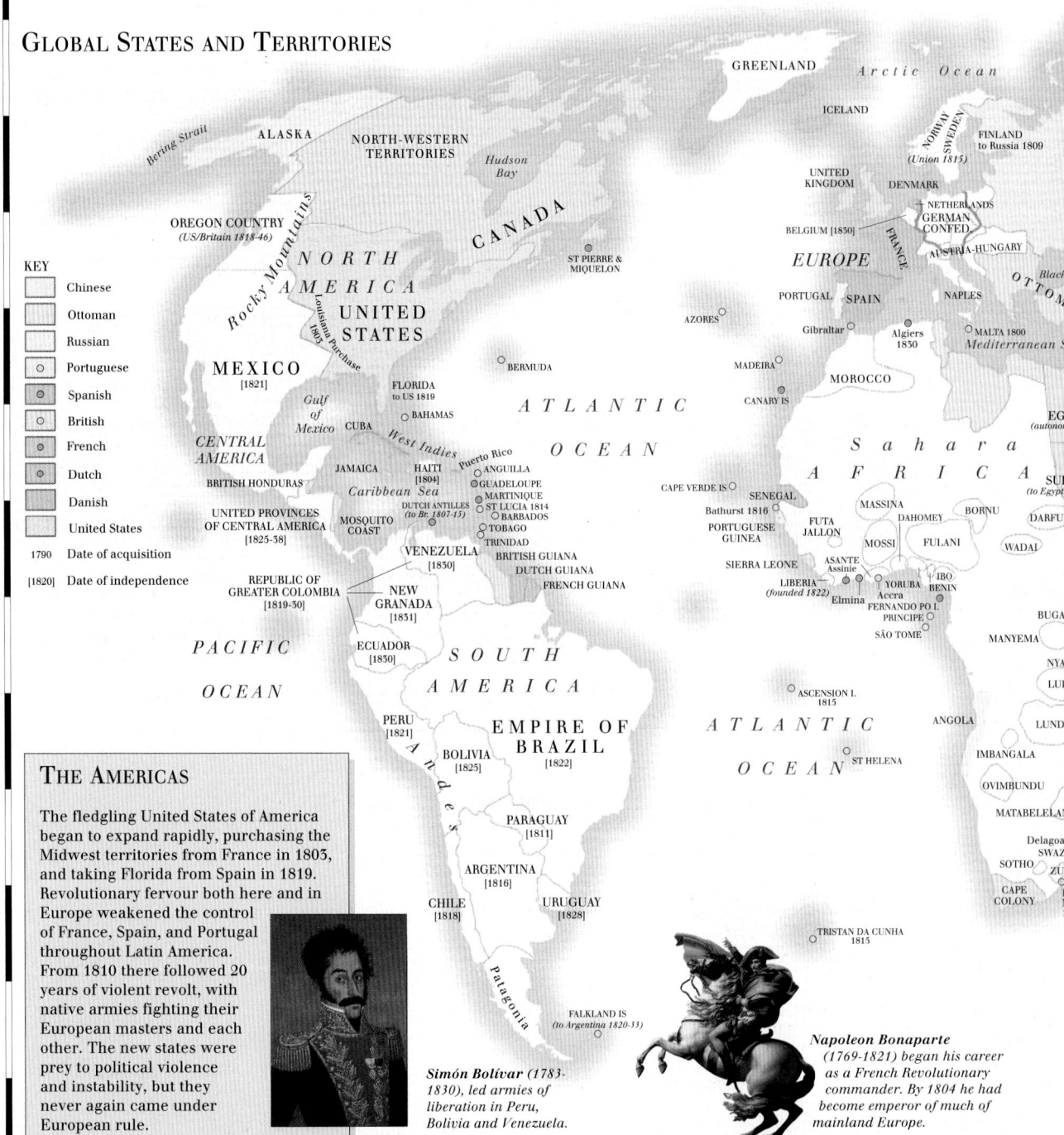

KEY

	Chinese
	Ottoman
	Russian
○	Portuguese
◉	Spanish
○	British
◉	French
◉	Dutch
	Danish
	United States
1790	Date of acquisition
[1820]	Date of independence

GREENLAND — *Arctic Ocean*
ICELAND
Bering Strait
ALASKA — NORTH-WESTERN TERRITORIES
Hudson Bay
NORWAY SWEDEN (Union 1815)
FINLAND to Russia 1809
UNITED KINGDOM — DENMARK
NETHERLANDS GERMAN CONFED
BELGIUM [1850] FRANCE
AUSTRIA-HUNGARY
EUROPE
OREGON COUNTRY (US/Britain 1818-46)
NORTH AMERICA
Rocky Mountains
CANADA
ST PIERRE & MIQUELON
PORTUGAL SPAIN
NAPLES
OTTOM...
Black
Louisiana Purchase 1804
UNITED STATES
Gibraltar
Algiers 1830
MALTA 1800
Mediterranean Se
MEXICO [1821]
Gulf of Mexico
FLORIDA to US 1819
BERMUDA
AZORES
MADEIRA
CANARY IS
MOROCCO
EGY (autonom
CUBA
BAHAMAS
ATLANTIC OCEAN
Sahara
AFRICA
SUD (to Egypt 1
CENTRAL AMERICA
West Indies
JAMAICA
HAITI [1804]
Puerto Rico ANGUILLA
GUADELOUPE
MARTINIQUE
MASSINA
DAHOMEY BORNU
DARFUR
BRITISH HONDURAS
Caribbean Sea
DUTCH ANTILLES (to Br. 1807-15)
ST LUCIA 1814
BARBADOS
CAPE VERDE IS
SENEGAL
Bathurst 1816
PORTUGUESE GUINEA
FUTA JALLON
MOSSI
FULANI
WADAI
UNITED PROVINCES OF CENTRAL AMERICA [1825-38]
MOSQUITO COAST
TOBAGO
TRINIDAD
SIERRA LEONE
ASANTE Assinie
LIBERIA (founded 1822)
Elmina
YORUBA IBO BENIN
Accra
FERNANDO PO I.
PRINCIPE
BUGAN
VENEZUELA [1850]
BRITISH GUIANA
DUTCH GUIANA
FRENCH GUIANA
REPUBLIC OF GREATER COLOMBIA [1819-30]
NEW GRANADA [1831]
SÃO TOME
MANYEMA
PACIFIC OCEAN
ECUADOR [1830]
SOUTH AMERICA
ANDES
ASCENSION I. 1815
ANGOLA
LUNDA
NYA
LUBA
PERU [1821]
EMPIRE OF BRAZIL [1822]
BOLIVIA [1825]
ATLANTIC OCEAN
ST HELENA
IMBANGALA
OVIMBUNDU
MATABELELANI
Delagoa I
SWAZI
SOTHO ZUL
CAPE COLONY
Po N 18
PARAGUAY [1811]
ARGENTINA [1816]
CHILE [1818]
URUGUAY [1828]
TRISTAN DA CUNHA 1815
Patagonia
FALKLAND IS (to Argentina 1820-33)

THE AMERICAS

The fledgling United States of America began to expand rapidly, purchasing the Midwest territories from France in 1803, and taking Florida from Spain in 1819. Revolutionary fervour both here and in Europe weakened the control of France, Spain, and Portugal throughout Latin America. From 1810 there followed 20 years of violent revolt, with native armies fighting their European masters and each other. The new states were prey to political violence and instability, but they never again came under European rule.

Simón Bolívar (1783-1830), led armies of liberation in Peru, Bolivia and Venezuela.

Napoleon Bonaparte (1769-1821) began his career as a French Revolutionary commander. By 1804 he had become emperor of much of mainland Europe.

EUROPE

Under the Revolutionary general, Napoleon Bonaparte, France conquered a large part of Europe and destroyed the old feudal order. Napoleon helped to shape the new nation states that emerged in 19th-century Europe – Belgium, Italy, and Germany. He gave much of Europe its modern legal code and systems of education and local government.

Steam-powered engines transformed the European industrial economy.

ASIA

The principal colonial power in Asia was Russia, whose consolidation of its empire in northern and central Asia continued throughout the 19th century. But now the Dutch began to extend their control of the East Indies, while a bitter struggle between the British and the French was conducted in and around the Indian Ocean. France was gradually forced to concede many of its footholds in India, where the British East India Company rapidly extended its interests by a mixture of diplomacy and military force. But the elusive key to Asia's largest markets remained the slumbering giant of Ch'ing China, whose Manchu rulers, like those of Japan, remained unimpressed by European overtures.

The spices of the East Indies, such as pepper, were among the most highly valued traded commodities from Asia.

James Cook (1728-1779) charted much of the Pacific between 1768 and 1779.

OCEANIA

Though Portuguese and Dutch explorers had confirmed the existence of Australasia in the 16th and 17th centuries, it was not until the voyages of Captain Cook in the 1770s that the geography of the Pacific was established, and the fertile eastern coast of Australia was explored and charted. Over the next 30 years, small settlements were established around the coast; by 1829, Britain had brought the whole continent under the British flag.

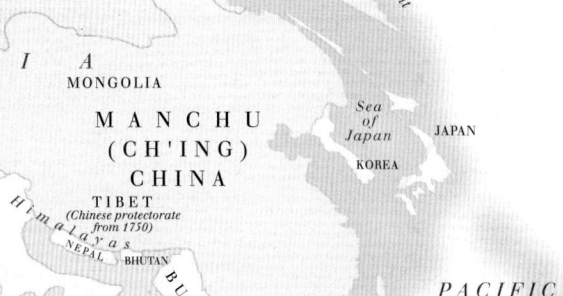

RUSSIAN EMPIRE

A   S   I   A

Aral Sea

Caspian Sea

MONGOLIA

Bering Strait

MANCHU (CH'ING) CHINA

Sea of Japan

JAPAN

KOREA

TIBET
(Chinese protectorate from 1750)

Himalayas

NEPAL

BHUTAN

PERSIA

Persian Gulf

AFGHAN-ISTAN

BURMA

ANNAM

Macao

FORMOSA

PACIFIC OCEAN

ARABIA

OMAN

Diu

Daman

INDIA

Arabian Sea

Goa

Bay of Bengal

SIAM

South China Sea

PHILIPPINES

MARIANAS

ETHIOPIA

Mahé

Pondicherry

LACCADIVE IS
1791

Karikal

TENASSERIM
1826

ANDAMAN IS

Ceylon

CAROLINE IS

Micronesia

MALDIVE IS
1887

MALAYA

Malacca 1824

SINGAPORE
1819

ZANZIBAR
(to Oman)

SEYCHELLES
1794

CHAGOS IS

DUTCH EAST INDIES

New Guinea

Melanesia

PORTUGUESE EAST AFRICA

INDIAN

Madagascar

Timor

HOVA KINGDOM

MAURITIUS
1810

RÉUNION

OCEAN

WESTERN AUSTRALIA
1829

NEW SOUTH WALES

AUSTRALIA

LORD HOWE I.

The first European migrants to Africa settled in Cape Colony.

NEW ZEALAND

CHATHAM IS
1791

AFRICA

The northern regions of Africa were part of the vast Islamic Ottoman Empire; from here Islam spread south to West Africa and the Horn of Africa. Holy wars (or *jihads*) late in the 18th and early 19th centuries completed the conversion to Islam of much of Saharan and sub-Saharan Africa. In the south, large tribal kingdoms flourished, in the Congo basin and southern Africa.

TASMANIA
(Van Diemen's Land)

AUCKLAND IS
1806

MACQUARIE IS
1811

The development during the European industrial revolution of mechanized manufacturing plant and machinery, such as power looms, gave Europe effective control of a booming global trade in raw materials and mass-manufactured commodities.

THE AGE OF EMPIRE: 1830-1914

THE NINETEENTH CENTURY was dominated by the spread of modern industry and transportation, and the expansion of European trade and influence world-wide. Industry made Europe rich and powerful; its capital cities were monuments to the self-confidence of the new European age. Railroads and steam ships revolutionized communications, bringing a stream of industrial goods, technical know-how, and European settlers across America, Africa, and Asia. Modern industry and weapons brought Europe to the summit of global influence. In these developments lay the origins of the division of the world into rich and poor regions; a developed, prosperous north, an under-developed, dependent south.

GLOBAL STATES AND TERRITORIES

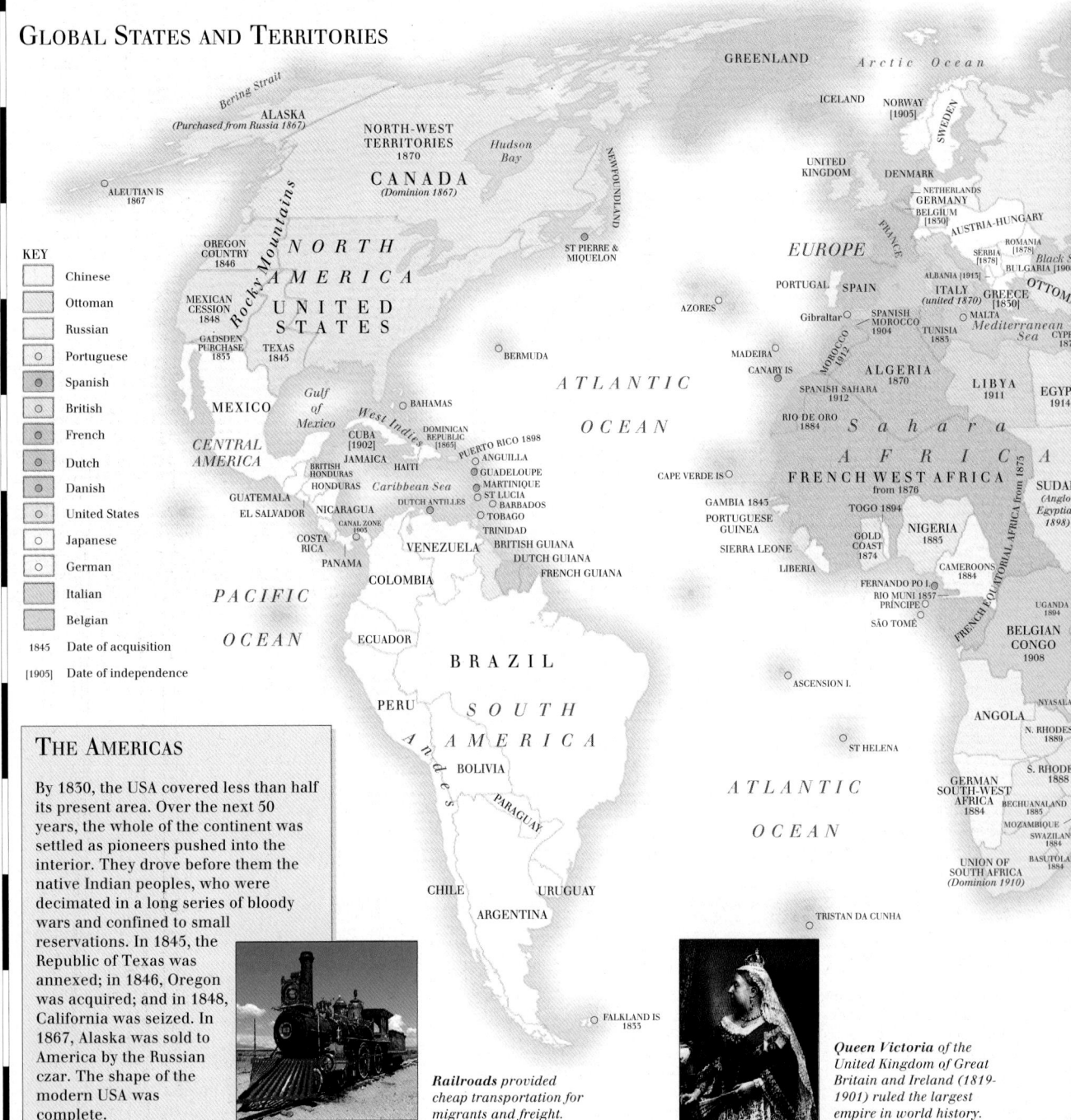

KEY

	Chinese
	Ottoman
	Russian
○	Portuguese
◉	Spanish
○	British
◉	French
◉	Dutch
○	Danish
○	United States
○	Japanese
○	German
	Italian
	Belgian

1845   Date of acquisition

[1905]   Date of independence

THE AMERICAS

By 1830, the USA covered less than half its present area. Over the next 50 years, the whole of the continent was settled as pioneers pushed into the interior. They drove before them the native Indian peoples, who were decimated in a long series of bloody wars and confined to small reservations. In 1845, the Republic of Texas was annexed; in 1846, Oregon was acquired; and in 1848, California was seized. In 1867, Alaska was sold to America by the Russian czar. The shape of the modern USA was complete.

Railroads provided cheap transportation for migrants and freight.

Queen Victoria of the United Kingdom of Great Britain and Ireland (1819-1901) ruled the largest empire in world history.

EUROPE

In the 19th century, Europe was transformed into an industrial economy. In the new industrial cities, pressure developed for liberal reforms and parliamentary politics. Nationalists created new states in Germany, Italy, Greece, Serbia, and Belgium. While the modern map of Europe gradually began to take shape, European imperialists brought still further areas of the world under their control.

Sailing ships carried most oceanic trade until 1900.

ASIA

Building on colonial interests that stretched back into the 18th century, Britain and France transformed the political world of South Asia. Britain extended its rule in India and, in 1885, Burma was brought under British control. The Vietnamese and Chinese Empires were pressured by Europeans anxious to trade and to spread Christianity: the Ch'ing Empire conceded areas of influence; the Vietnamese Empire resisted and was brought by force under French domination. By the 1890s the whole of southern Asia except for Siam was dominated by Europe, which created the modern state structure of the region.

The Japanese emperor Mutsuhito (1852-1912) opened Japan to Western trade and influence.

The colonization of Australia and New Zealand was based on sheep farming.

OCEANIA

During the 19th century, Australia and New Zealand remained closely tied to the British homeland. British settlers came to farm and later to prospect for gold and other valuable minerals. In 1840, New Zealand came under British rule and the native Maoris were forced off the land. Not until 1872 was the continent of Australia traversed, and not until 1901 was a single state, the Commonwealth of Australia, proclaimed.

RUSSIAN EMPIRE

Bering Strait

KAZAKHSTAN
1854
Aral Sea

MONGOLIA
(autonomous 1912)

MANCHURIA

AMUR 1858

SAKHALIN 1855 1905

USSURI 1860

KURILE IS 1875

Sea of Japan

JAPAN

Caspian Sea

TURKESTAN 1895

TURKMENISTAN 1885

BUKHARA 1868

A S I A

Port Arthur 1905

Weihaiwei 1898

Tsingtao 1898

KOREA 1905

AFGHANISTAN

TIBET [1912]

CHINA

RYUKYU IS 1874

PERSIA

Himalayas

NEPAL

BHUTAN †

BURMA

PACIFIC

OCEAN

EMPIRE

Persian Gulf

BAHRAIN 1861

ARABIA

OMAN

Chandernagore

Diu
Daman

INDIA

Macao

FORMOSA 1895

Hong Kong 1841

FRENCH INDO-CHINA 1887

Bay of Bengal

MARIANAS 1899

Arabian Sea

Goa

Mahé

Pondicherry

SIAM

South China Sea

PHILIPPINES 1898

GUAM 1898

ERITREA 1889

Aden 1859

HADHRAMAUT 1888

SOCOTRA 1886

LACCADIVE IS

Karikal

CEYLON

ANDAMAN IS

CAROLINE IS 1899

BRITISH SOMALILAND 1884

FRENCH SOMALILAND 1884

NICOBAR IS 1869

Micronesia

ETHIOPIA

ITALIAN SOMALILAND

MALDIVE IS

MALAYA

BRITISH NORTH BORNEO 1881

SARAWAK 1888

BISMARCK ARCHIPELAGO 1884

NAURU 1888

BRITISH EAST AFRICA 1888

ZANZIBAR 1890

SEYCHELLES

CHAGOS IS

DUTCH EAST INDIES

NEW GUINEA

PAPUA 1906

Melanesia

SOLOMON IS 1893

RMAN ST AFRICA 55

COMORO IS 1886

I N D I A N

O C E A N

CHRISTMAS I. 1888

COCOS IS 1857

TIMOR

MADAGASCAR 1882

MAURITIUS

RÉUNION

NEW CALEDONIA 1855

A U S T R A L I A
(Commonwealth 1901)

LORD HOWE I.

Quinine – the cure for malaria.

New medicines made the colonization of Africa possible.

NEW ZEALAND 1840
(Dominion 1907)

CHATHAM IS

AFRICA

The political structure of independent Africa was torn up by encroaching European empires. As native societies reacted violently to European intrusion, so European military and political power was increased to secure European interests. In 1884, in Berlin, the European powers divided Africa between them. The "Partition of Africa" established many states' modern frontiers.

TASMANIA

AUCKLAND IS

MACQUARIE IS

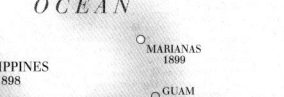

The Gatling gun, the most successful of the hand-driven machine guns of the 19th century.

The European imperial powers maintained control of their often far-flung colonies by military superiority. Native forces were rarely a match for the large, highly trained armies, powerful navies and technically advanced weaponry which the Europeans had at their disposal.

THE AGE OF GLOBAL WAR: 1914-45

IN 1914, IMPERIAL AND MILITARY rivalry in Europe provoked the first of two world wars, the largest and most destructive wars in human history. At the end of the first war, in 1918, the old international order was dead. The Russian Empire collapsed in revolution and was transformed by a communist minority into the Soviet Union. The German, Habsburg, and Ottoman empires were dismembered. A fragile peace ensued but the old equilibrium was gone. The rise of strident nationalism in Germany, Japan, and Italy destroyed the peace once again in 1939. The second war cost the lives of 50 million people and ravaged Europe and Asia. At its end, in 1945, the USA and the Soviet Union had emerged as the new superpowers.

GLOBAL STATES AND TERRITORIES

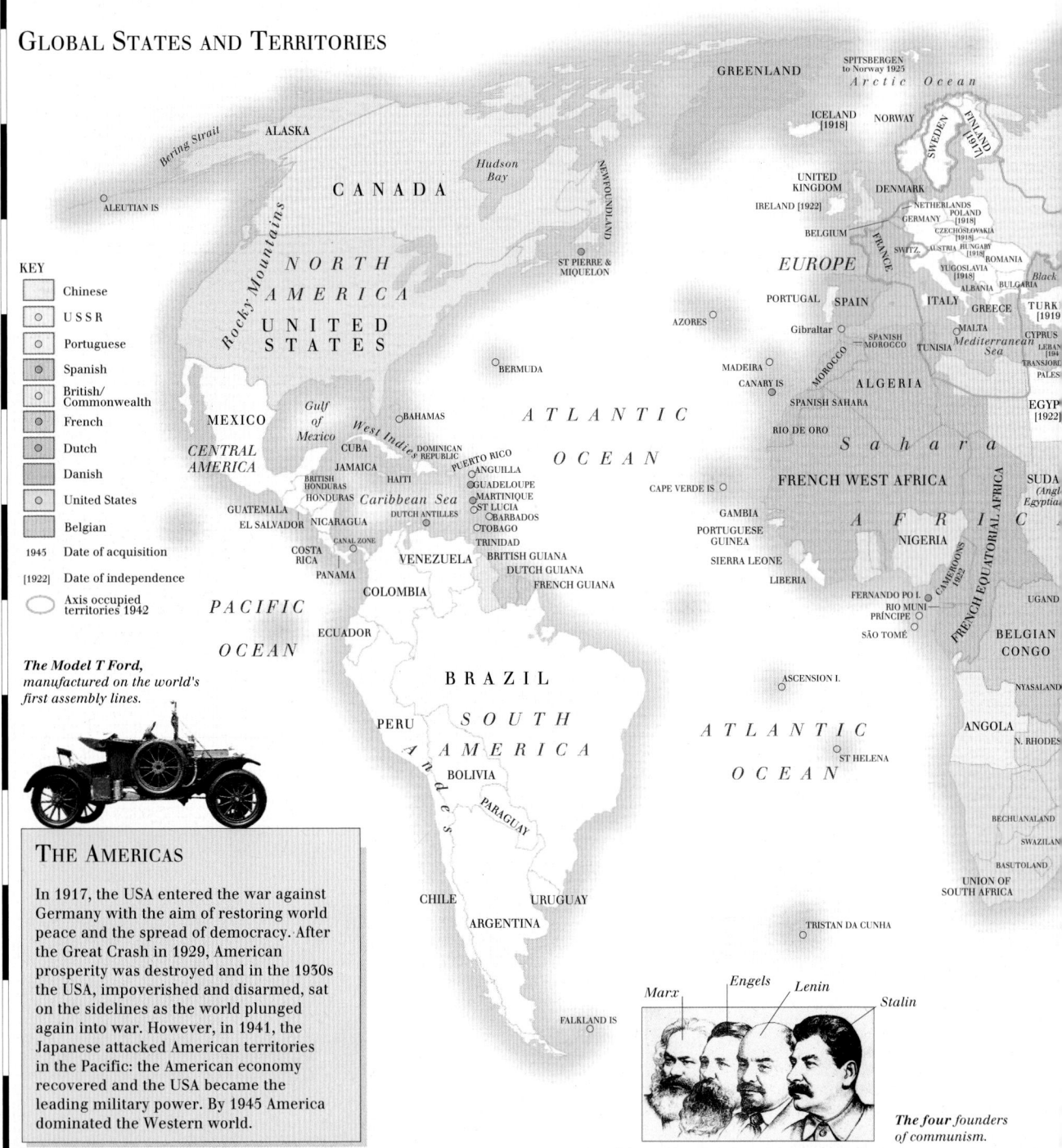

KEY

	Chinese
⊙	USSR
⊙	Portuguese
⊚	Spanish
⊙	British/Commonwealth
⊙	French
⊙	Dutch
	Danish
⊙	United States
	Belgian
1945	Date of acquisition
[1922]	Date of independence
⬭	Axis occupied territories 1942

The Model T Ford, *manufactured on the world's first assembly lines.*

THE AMERICAS

In 1917, the USA entered the war against Germany with the aim of restoring world peace and the spread of democracy. After the Great Crash in 1929, American prosperity was destroyed and in the 1930s the USA, impoverished and disarmed, sat on the sidelines as the world plunged again into war. However, in 1941, the Japanese attacked American territories in the Pacific: the American economy recovered and the USA became the leading military power. By 1945 America dominated the Western world.

Marx   Engels   Lenin   Stalin

The four *founders of communism.*

EUROPE

Both world wars had their origins in Europe. In 1914 Britain, France, and Russia combined to defeat Germany, with US help. In 1918 new nation states were established in Eastern Europe. But, by 1939, revived German nationalism started a second world war; much of Western Europe came under a German "New Order" until the Soviet Union, Britain, and the USA developed sufficient military strength to reconquer Europe and defeat Germany.

World War II was decided by mechanical and industrial superiority.

ASIA

The collapse of the Chinese Empire in 1911, followed in 1917 by the disappearance of the Russian Empire, produced instability across Asia. Full-scale war broke out between Japan and China in 1937, with Japan trying to conquer China. The Soviet Union was the victim of German aggression from 1941. Both Japan and Germany were held at bay by communist forces which eventually succeeded in imposing stable politics on Asia. By 1945, the Soviet Union had reconquered its lost territories and dominated Eastern Europe. In China, communist armies filled the vacuum left by the Japanese defeat.

Mahatma Gandhi (1868-1948) led India to independence through peaceful noncooperation and protest.

OCEANIA

For the only time in its history, Australia was faced with the very real prospect of invasion. In World War II, Japanese armies reached the island of New Guinea, and bombed towns in northern Australia. Japanese submarines attacked Sydney Harbour. The Battle of the Coral Sea, in May 1942, saved Australia, but it took almost three years to clear Japanese forces from the South Pacific, where they hung on grimly to the rich oil and mineral resources they had captured.

Japan promoted itself as the liberator of Asia from the chains of European colonialism.

MIDDLE EAST

In 1918, the Turkish Empire disappeared after 400 years of Ottoman rule. The modern map of North Africa and the Middle East was carved out of its ruins by the victors of World War I. After World War II, the foundation was laid for a new state of Israel, following the genocide of Europe's Jews by Nazi Germany. This led to conflict between native Arabs and Jewish migrants.

Haile Selassie (1892-1975), ruler of Ethiopia, the only independent empire in Africa.

A German Zeppelin airship of the 1930s.

The conquest of the air was the most important technological achievement of the period. It added a devastating dimension to warfare, in the form of bombing, while transforming civil transportation.

Map labels:

U S S R

Bering Strait

MONGOLIA [1924]

SAKHALIN 1945

KURILE IS 1945

Sea of Japan

JAPAN

KOREA [1945]

A S I A

Aral Sea

Caspian Sea

CHINA

AFGHANISTAN

TIBET

Himalayas

NEPAL

BHUTAN

IRAN (Persia)

IRAQ [1932]

Persian Gulf

RYUKYU IS 1945

PACIFIC OCEAN

BAHRAIN

Chandernagore

Macao

Hong Kong

TAIWAN (Formosa) 1945

SAUDI ARABIA [1952]

YEMEN [1918]

Diu

Daman

BURMA

FRENCH INDO CHINA

MARIANAS 1945

HADHRAMAUT

Arabian Sea

Goa

Bay of Bengal

THAILAND (Siam)

South China Sea

PHILIPPINES

Aden

Mahé

Pondicherry

GUAM

ERITREA 1941

OMAN

SOCOTRA

FRENCH SOMALILAND

LACCADIVE IS

Karikal

ANDAMAN IS

CAROLINE IS 1945

ETHIOPIA

CEYLON

NICOBAR IS

Micronesia

ITALIAN SOMALILAND

MALAYA

MALDIVE IS

NEW GUINEA

NAURU 1945

ZANZIBAR

SEYCHELLES

CHAGOS IS

DUTCH EAST INDIES

Melanesia

SOLOMON IS

MOZAMBIQUE

COMORO IS

INDIAN OCEAN

COCOS IS

CHRISTMAS I. 1888

TIMOR

MADAGASCAR

MAURITIUS

RÉUNION

NEW CALEDONIA

LORD HOWE I.

RISE OF ASIA

CHATHAM IS

TASMANIA

AUCKLAND IS

MACQUARIE IS

THE MODERN AGE: 1945-96

THE WARTIME ALLIANCE between the USA and the Soviet Union turned sour in efforts to reconstruct Europe and the Far East. The world became divided into two hostile camps; liberal-capitalism on the one hand, communism on the other. The two sides fought a "Cold War," each trying to contain and subvert the other. The main conflicts of the war occurred over small issues – Korea (1950-53), Cuba (1962), and Vietnam (1954-75). Larger wars were avoided because of the nuclear deterrent. With the crumbling of communist power in Russia and Eastern Europe, the stalemate of the Cold War was replaced by a less stable international order, dominated by economic uncertainty and revived nationalism.

GLOBAL STATES AND TERRITORIES

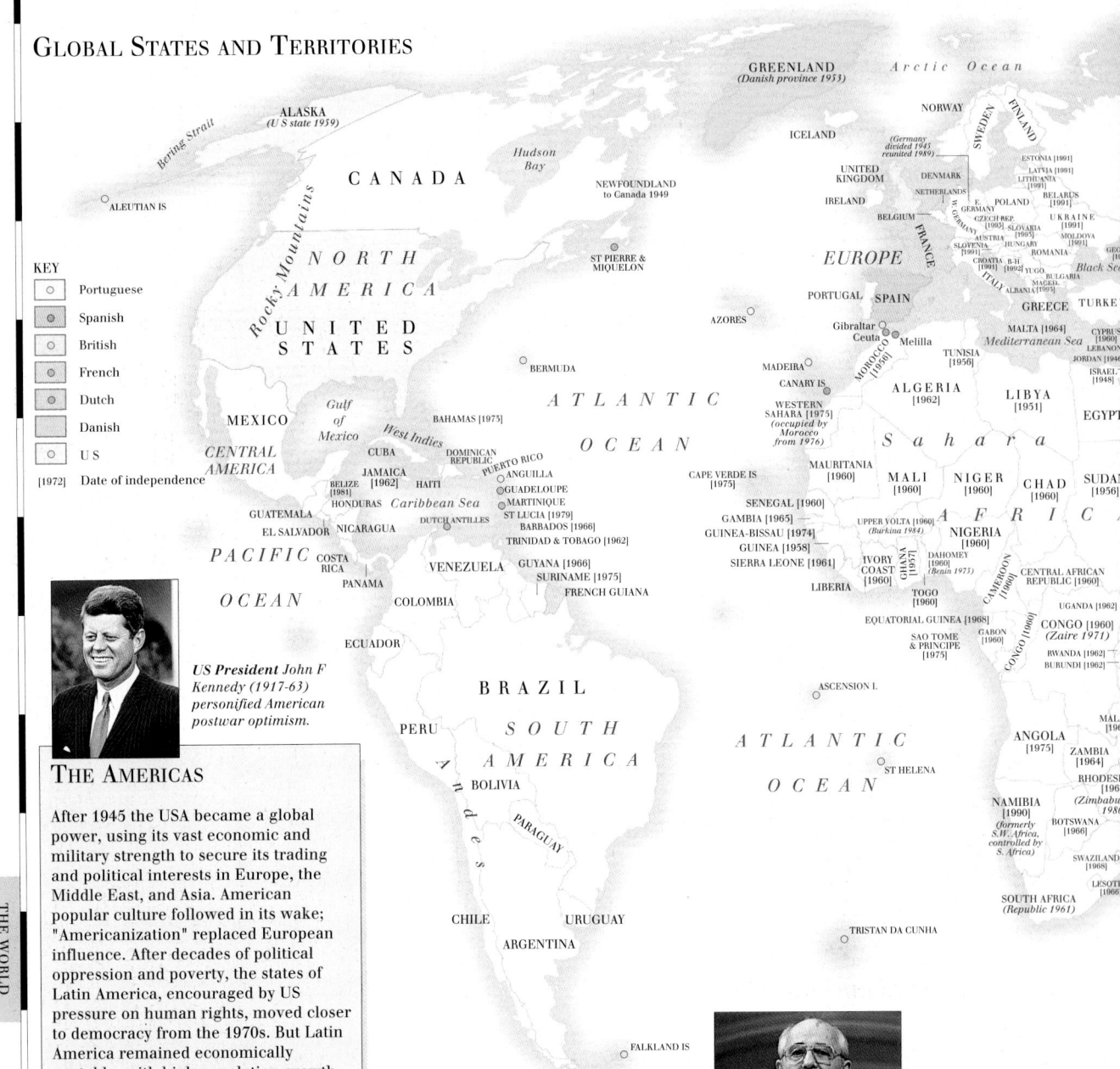

KEY

○	Portuguese
▣	Spanish
○	British
◉	French
◉	Dutch
▢	Danish
○	US
[1972]	Date of independence

US President John F Kennedy (1917-63) personified American postwar optimism.

THE AMERICAS

After 1945 the USA became a global power, using its vast economic and military strength to secure its trading and political interests in Europe, the Middle East, and Asia. American popular culture followed in its wake; "Americanization" replaced European influence. After decades of political oppression and poverty, the states of Latin America, encouraged by US pressure on human rights, moved closer to democracy from the 1970s. But Latin America remained economically unstable, with high population growth, chronic inflation, and international debt, and powerful criminal organizations producing Latin America's fastest growing export, drugs.

In 1985, the Soviet leader Mikhail Gorbachev launched a program of economic and political reform which brought Soviet communism to an end.

The Berlin Wall, symbol of the Cold War division of Europe, was demolished in 1989.

EUROPE

In 1945, Europe lay in ruins, but during the next 30 years, Western Europe experienced a long economic boom, restoring widespread prosperity and political stability. It progressed towards economic and political unity under the EC. In Eastern Europe development was overshadowed by Soviet communism until its collapse. As democracies many new nations now face an uncertain future.

ASIA

In southern Asia, popular nationalist movements came to power in India, Burma, Malaya, and Indonesia; in China and Indochina, power passed to native communist movements whose roots went back to the 1920s. After 1949, China under Mao Zedong became, with its vast population and large military forces, a second communist superpower. But the success story of modern Asia has been Japan. Defeated in 1945, its economy and cities laid waste by bombing, Japan began a program of economic rebuilding with American aid. By the 1980s Japan had emerged as one of the world's largest manufacturing economies.

Chinese communism, based on the mobilization of peasants and workers, has nevertheless recognized the need for economic reforms.

A treaty banning the testing of nuclear bombs in the Pacific was signed in 1986.

OCEANIA

The postwar economies of Japan, USA, and Australia had by the 1990s created a new industrial and trading network around the Pacific Rim. Cheap labor and low overheads drew younger states – South Korea, Taiwan, Singapore, and Indonesia – into the system and much of the world's manufacturing is now concentrated there, creating a consequent shift in the balance of the global economy.

Gamal Abdel Nasser (1918-70) of Egypt, galvanized the Arab states to resist the West.

AFRICA AND THE MIDDLE EAST

The colonial powers, weakened by war, faced an irresistible wave of demands for self-determination. Between 1958 and 1975, 41 African countries gained independence. In Rhodesia and South Africa, white rule survived independence. In North Africa and throughout the Middle East a new form of anti-imperialism emerged in the 1970s in the form of Islamic fundamentalism.

From the 1950s to the 1970s, superpower rivalry focused on space exploration. The Soviets put the first man in space in 1961, and the Americans landed on the moon in 1969. Since then both manned and unmanned missions have become almost everyday events.

RUSSIAN FEDERATION

KAZAKHSTAN [1991]
MONGOLIA
UZBEKISTAN [1991]
KYRGYZSTAN [1991]
TURKMENISTAN [1991]
TAJIKISTAN [1991]
AZERBAIJAN [1991]
ARMENIA [1991]
A S I A
CHINA
N. KOREA [1948]
Sea of Japan
JAPAN
S. KOREA [1948]
IRAN
AFGHANISTAN
Himalayas
TIBET (to China 1950)
RYUKYU IS (to Japan)
IRAQ
BAHRAIN [1971]
QATAR [1971]
PAKISTAN [1947]
NEPAL
BHUTAN
UNITED ARAB EMIRATES (formed 1971)
BANGLADESH [1971] (formerly E. Pakistan)
BURMA [1948]
Macao
NORTH VIETNAM [1954]
TAIWAN [1949]
Hong Kong
SAUDI ARABIA
ERITREA [1995]
NORTH YEMEN [1967]
SOUTH YEMEN (Yemen united 1990)
Arabian Sea
INDIA [1947]
Bay of Bengal
LAOS [1954]
(Vietnam united 1976)
PACIFIC OCEAN
MARIANAS
OMAN
THAILAND
South China Sea
PHILIPPINES [1946]
DJIBOUTI [1977]
LACCADIVE IS (to India)
CAMBODIA [1955]
SOUTH VIETNAM [1954]
GUAM
ETHIOPIA
ANDAMAN IS (to India)
MICRONESIA [1991]
SOMALIA [1960]
CEYLON [1948] (Sri Lanka 1972)
NICOBAR IS (to India)
MALAYA [1957]
BRUNEI [1984]
PALAU [1995]
MALDIVE IS [1965]
MALAYSIA (formed 1963)
KENYA [1963]
SINGAPORE [1965]
BISMARCK ARCHIPELAGO (to P N G)
NAURU [1968]
SEYCHELLES [1976]
CHAGOS IS
INDONESIA [1949]
Melanesia
PAPUA NEW GUINEA [1975]
SOLOMON IS [1978]
TANZANIA [1964]
COMOROS [1975]
MOZAMBIQUE [1975]
INDIAN OCEAN
CHRISTMAS I. (to Australia)
COCOS IS (to Australia)
E. TIMOR (to Indonesia)
MADAGASCAR [1960]
RÉUNION
MAURITIUS [1968]
NEW CALEDONIA
AUSTRALIA
LORD HOWE I. (to Australia)
NEW ZEALAND
CHATHAM IS (to N Z)
AUCKLAND IS (to N Z)
MACQUARIE IS (to Australia)
Bering Strait
Caspian Sea
Aral Sea
Persian Gulf
Red Sea
SOCOTRA (to S. Yemen)

2

THE NATIONS
OF THE
WORLD

THE NATIONS OF THE WORLD
• AFGHANISTAN ~ ZIMBABWE
OVERSEAS TERRITORIES & DEPENDENCIES

A

AFGHANISTAN

OFFICIAL NAME: Islamic State of Afghanistan **CAPITAL:** Kābul
POPULATION: 20.1 million **CURRENCY:** Afghani **OFFICIAL LANGUAGES:** Persian and Pashtu

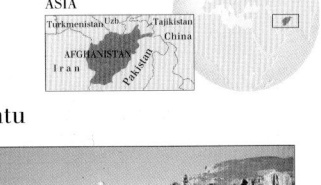
ASIA   Asia

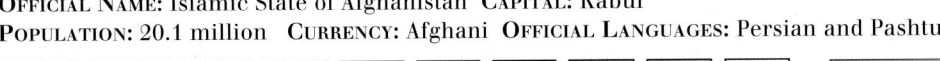
1919

LANDLOCKED IN southwestern Asia, Afghanistan is surrounded by Iran, Pakistan, China, Tajikistan and Turkmenistan. Approximately three-quarters of its territory is inaccessible terrain. Afghanistan effectively has no government, other than a fragile power-sharing arrangement between *mujahideen* leaders, whose factions have been fighting each other since the departure of Soviet invasion forces in 1989. Agriculture is the main economic activity, but less than two-thirds of farmland is cultivated. Since the April 1992 handover of power to the *mujahideen*, women have returned to wearing veils in public.

The Band-i-Amir River, in the Hindu Kush. Afghanistan is mountainous and arid. Many Afghans are nomadic sheep farmers.

CLIMATE

WEATHER CHART

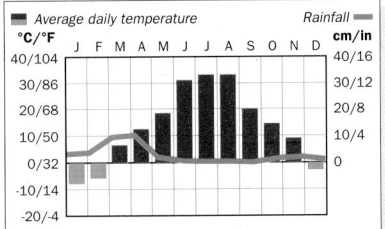

Afghanistan has a harsh continental climate and the severity of winter is accentuated by high altitudes. It has the widest temperature range in the world, with lows of –58°F and highs of 127°F.

TRANSPORTATION

 Kābul International   Has no fleet

THE TRANSPORTATION NETWORK

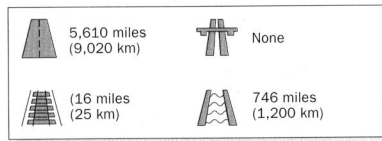

5,610 miles (9,020 km)	None
(16 miles (25 km)	746 miles (1,200 km)

The repair and reconstruction of war-damaged roads and the provision of a minimum of facilities to allow air traffic to function safely are the present priorities. Road rebuilding is usually carried out by local communities. However, neighboring Pakistan has undertaken to rebuild a number of key routes, including the Kābul–Torkam link, which will benefit its own trade with central Asia.

Obtaining and securing key supply routes is a crucial factor in intra-*mujahideen* feuding. The *Hezb-i-Islami* recently increased its stranglehold on the main eastern artery out of Kābul, and is also seeking to control the Salang Highway, the northern route out of the capital. Much of Afghanistan's outlying territory is sown with land mines.

TOURISM

 5,000 visitors   Down 17% in 1994

MAIN OVERSEAS ARRIVALS

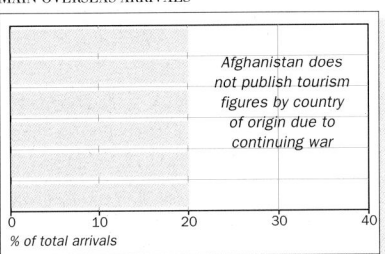

Afghanistan does not publish tourism figures by country of origin due to continuing war

% of total arrivals

Afghanistan is a war zone. There are virtually no visitors apart from occasional UN and aid agency personnel, and journalists. Few hotels or restaurants are open in Kābul. Travel is extremely dangerous due to mines as well as bandit activity. *Air Ariana*, the Afghan national airline, no longer flies from Kābul, but from Dushanbe in neighboring Tajikistan.

The lack of a formal economy means that Afghanistan gets few visits from businessmen, and any expatriates who were previously in Kābul have left.

PEOPLE

 Persian, Pashtu, Dari, Uzbek, Turkmen   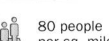 80 people per sq. mile

THE URBAN/RURAL POPULATION SPLIT

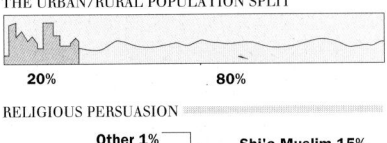

20%   80%

RELIGIOUS PERSUASION

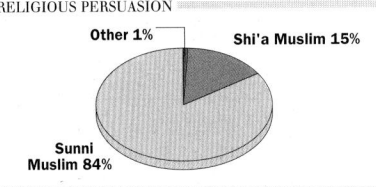

Other 1%   Shi'a Muslim 15%
Sunni Muslim 84%

ETHNIC MAKEUP

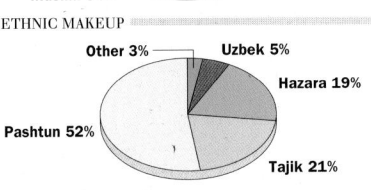

Other 3%   Uzbek 5%
Hazara 19%
Pashtun 52%
Tajik 21%

The Pashtuns are the largest ethnic group and traditional rulers of Afghanistan, making up 52% of the population; the main minorities are Tajiks, Hazaras and Uzbeks. It is these ethnic divisions which have largely, though not exclusively, determined the intra-*mujahideen* feuding that has plagued the country since April 1992. Assaults on Kābul by the *Hezb-i-Islami*

group and the extreme fundamentalist group, the *talibaan*, represent an attempt by the Pashtuns to regain control of the capital, currently under the precarious control of a Tajik–Uzbek alliance led by the predominantly Tajik *Jamiat-i-Islami*.

Some two million of the country's population were killed as a result of the 1979–1989 war, which followed invasion by the Soviet Union. As many again were maimed. A further six million were forced to flee to neighboring Pakistan and Iran; most have not yet been able to return. Women in Afghanistan have few rights in what is rapidly becoming a male-dominated Islamic fundamentalist society. They are officially discouraged from working and are largely confined to the home.

POPULATION AGE BREAKDOWN

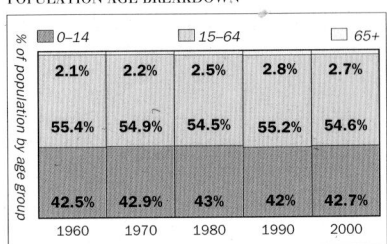

% of population by age group	☐ 0–14	☐ 15–64	☐ 65+		
65+	2.1%	2.2%	2.5%	2.8%	2.7%
15–64	55.4%	54.9%	54.5%	55.2%	54.6%
0–14	42.5%	42.9%	43%	42%	42.7%
	1960	1970	1980	1990	2000

A

POLITICS

 1988/Uncertain

 President
Burhanuddin Rabbani

THE STATE OF THE PARTIES

House of Representatives 234 members

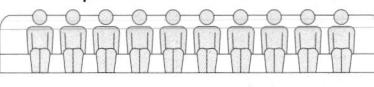

Following the downfall of Najibullah's regime in April 1992, both houses were dissolved and an interim *mujahideen* legislature formed

Senate 192 members

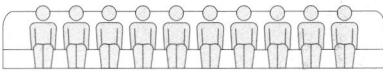

A power struggle between the *Hezb-i-Islami* and the *Jamiat-i-Islami*, which began in 1994, suspended Afghanistan's parliamentary system.

MAIN POLITICAL ISSUES
Elections
According to the March 7 1993 Islamabad peace accord, elections were to be held by the end of the year. However, they are still awaited as the civil war continues.

Control of Kābul
Kābul is at present in the hands of the *Jamiat-i-Islami*. Repeated attempts by the *Hezb-i-Islami* and, more recently, by *talibaan*, to enter the capital have been unsuccessful.

PROFILE
The political system has all but collapsed in Afghanistan. All the key players have their own private armies and make their influence felt militarily. The country has been under the control of rival *mujahideen* factions since April 1992, when President Najibullah, who had held power since the withdrawal of Soviet forces in 1989, stepped down. The main *mujahideen* leaders met in Islamabad in March 1993 and agreed a basis for government of the country until elections could be held and a constitution formulated. In January 1994 the agreement collapsed with the outbreak of fighting between followers of Prime Minister Golboddin Hekmatyar, head of the *Hezb-i-Islami*, and troops loyal to President Rabbani, leader of the *Jamiat-i-Islami*. Fighting escalated sharply with the involvement in early 1995 of the *talibaan*, a milita of hardline Sunni Muslims who have been assisted by Pakistan. They now control vast swaths of the country and are beseiging the government in Kābul. International mediators, led by the UN, are trying to negotiate a settlement between the rival *mujahideen* factions.

Burhanuddin Rabbani, *president since 1992.*

Prime Minister Hekmatyar, *the Pashtun leader.*

WORLD AFFAIRS

 CP ECO IBRD NAM OIC

At the end of 1992, 60,000 refugees, who opposed the neo-communist government in Dushanbe, fled from southern Tajikistan into Afghanistan. Northern Afghanistan faces cross-border bombardments by CIS forces based in Tajikistan. An estimated 3,500 CIS troops are stationed there in an attempt to stem the flow of weapons and militants from Afghanistan to Islamic groups in Tajikistan. Relations with Pakistan are important to secure overland transit and port facilities. However, allegations of Pakistan's support for the *talibaan*, opposed to the government of President Rabbani, threaten to weaken these links.

CHRONOLOGY
The foundations of an Afghan state of Pashtun peoples were laid in the mid-18th century, when Durrani Ahmad Shah became paramount chief of the Abdali Pashtun peoples.

❑ **1838–1842** First Anglo-Afghan war. Britain fails in attempt to install Shah Shura on throne.
❑ **1878** Second British invasion of Afghan territory.
❑ **1879** Under Treaty of Gandmak signed with Amir Yaqub Ali Khan, various Afghan areas annexed by Britain. Yaqub Ali Khan later exiled. New treaty signed with Amir Abdul Rahman, establishing the Durand line, a contentious boundary between Afghanistan and Pakistan.
❑ **1919** Declaration of Afghan independence as an autonomous state backed at Paris Peace Conference. Britain briefly declares war on Afghanistan. ➪

AFGHANISTAN
Total Land Area : 652 090 sq. km
(251 770 sq. miles)

LAND HEIGHT	POPULATION	
3000m/9845ft	over 1 000 000	▣
2000m/6562ft	over 100 000	◎
1000m/3281ft	over 50 000	○
500m/1640ft	over 10 000	●
200m/656ft	under 10 000	•

0   100 km
0   100 miles

CHRONOLOGY *continued*

- ❏ **1921** Treaty of friendship with Russia.
- ❏ **1933** Muhammed Zahir Shar in power.
- ❏ **1936** Mutual trade agreement signed with USSR.
- ❏ **1950** Pakistan closes its border with Afghanistan.
- ❏ **1953** Mohammed Daud Khan prime minister. Links with USSR developed.
- ❏ **1963** Daud resigns after king rejects his proposals for democratic reforms.
- ❏ **1965** Elections held, but monarchy still retains power. Marxist Party of Afghanistan (PDPA) formed and banned. PDPA splits into the *Parcham* and *Khalq* factions.
- ❏ **1973** Daud mounts a successful coup, abolishes monarchy and declares republic. *Mujahideen* rebellion begins. Thousands of refugees flee into Pakistan.
- ❏ **1978** Opposition to Daud from PDPA culminates in *Saur* revolution. Revolutionary Council under Mohammad Taraki takes power. Daud assassinated.
- ❏ **1979** Taraki ousted. Hafizullah Amin takes power. Amin killed in December coup backed by USSR. 80,000 Soviet Army troops invade Afghanistan. *Mujahideen* rebellion stepped up into full-scale guerrilla war, with US backing.
- ❏ **1980** Babrak Karmal, leader of *Parcham* PDPA, installed as head of Marxist regime. Fighting escalates.
- ❏ **1986** Najibullah replaces Karmal as head of government.
- ❏ **1989** Soviet Army withdraws. *Mujahideen* control limited to rural areas. Najibullah remains in power.
- ❏ **1991** Russia and USA stop arms supplies to competing factions.
- ❏ **1992** Najibullah hands over power to *mujahideen* factions. Pakistan stops supplying arms to its *mujahideen* groups.
- ❏ **1993** *Mujahideen* agree on formation of government.
- ❏ **1994** Power struggle between Rabbani and Hekmatyar rekindles civil war.
- ❏ **1995** Anti-government *talibaan* militia advance towards Kābul.

AID

 $224m (receipts)   Up 28% in 1994

The main official aid is emergency humanitarian assistance from the UN. Saudi Arabia, Iran and Pakistan have promised modest grants. Large-scale funding for reconstruction is conditional on the restoration of peace. Individual *mujahideen* factions receive aid from Islamic states, Muslim organizations and wealthy benefactors.

DEFENSE

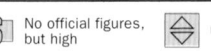

💲	No official figures, but high	⬡ Uncertain

0	Defense spending as % GDP	40
8.7%		

AFGHAN ARMED FORCES

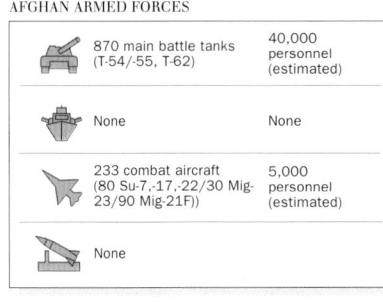

🔫	870 main battle tanks (T-54/-55, T-62)	40,000 personnel (estimated)
⛴	None	None
✈	233 combat aircraft (80 Su-7,-17,-22/30 Mig-23/90 Mig-21F))	5,000 personnel (estimated)
🚀	None	

In 1991, the US–Russian agreement to suspend military supplies to the Afghan groups marked the end of the superpowers' active involvement in Afghanistan. The Kābul communists, in particular, had been almost totally dependent on Moscow for arms, even after the Soviet withdrawal in 1989. In practice, Afghanistan has no formal defense arrangements, although there is a covert arms trade which has expanded since the resumption of the civil war in January 1994. The bulk of these arms originate in Eastern Europe and the former Soviet Union. Weapons dumps in no-man's-land on the border with Pakistan supply Golboddin Hekmatyar, the nominal prime minister.

Afghanistan still has approximately 300–400 of the 1,000 *Stinger* missiles given by the USA to the *mujahideen* in the 1980s. The USA, concerned that they may be used against civilian airliners, is offering $100,000 each to buy them back. To date, none has been returned.

ECONOMICS

📊 $2.7bn (est)	💲 3,460–4,750 afghanis	

SCORE CARD

- ❏ WORLD GNP RANKING.......................135th
- ❏ GNP PER CAPITA $695
- ❏ BALANCE OF PAYMENTS....................$–143m
- ❏ INFLATION ....*The formal economy*
- ❏ UNEMPLOYMENT........................*has collapsed*

EXPORTS

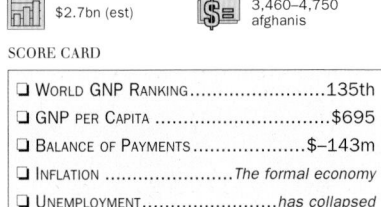

Germany 5% UK 5% India 6% Pakistan 8% Former Soviet Republics 58% Other 18%

IMPORTS

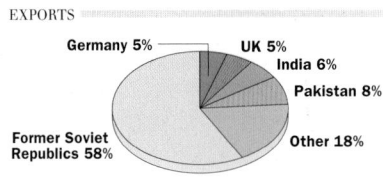

Germany 4% Hong Kong 3% Singapore 5% Japan 14% Former Soviet Republics 47% Other 27%

STRENGTHS
Very few, apart from illicit opium trade. Agriculture, still the largest sector, accounted for 45% of GDP in 1986–1987.

WEAKNESSES
Economy has collapsed. No end to factional fighting in sight. Damage to agriculture, with domino effect on industry. Inaccessible terrain and severed communications links.

PROFILE
Following ten years of war between the Soviet-backed Kābul government and *mujahideen* rebels and subsequent *mujahideen* in-fighting, Afghanistan is

ECONOMIC PERFORMANCE INDICATOR

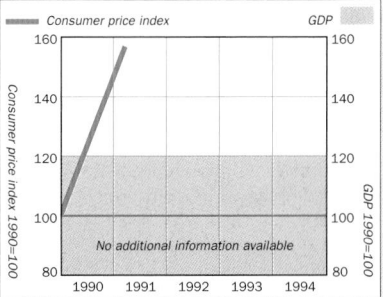

Consumer price index   GDP

No additional information available

one of the poorest and least developed countries in the world. Estimates suggest that $4 billion is needed to rebuild the country and that 80% of its infrastructure has been destroyed. Agricultural activity has fallen back from pre-1979 levels; the Soviets' "scorched earth" policy laid waste large areas and much of the rural population fled to the cities. Many farmers are now turning back to opium production. Afghanistan is regarded by the UN as the world's-largest opium producer. However, most profits are made by Pakistani middlemen.

Mujahideen *guerrillas, members of just one of the many factions vying for power in Afghanistan, prepare to launch a rocket attack.*

A

RESOURCES

	0.6bn kwh (capacity 494,000 kw)		Not an oil producer and has no refineries
	14.2m sheep, 1.5m cattle, 1.2m asses, 300,000 horses		Natural gas, salt, coal, copper, lapis lazuli, barytes, talc

ELECTRICITY GENERATION

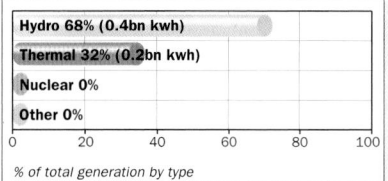

Hydro 68% (0.4bn kwh)
Thermal 32% (0.2bn kwh)
Nuclear 0%
Other 0%

% of total generation by type

Natural gas and coal are Afghanistan's most important strategic resources. Restoring the power generation system, which has suffered widespread deterioration and destruction, is a government priority. The construction

ENVIRONMENT

	0.3% (0.2% partially protected)		Civil war prevents any initiatives

ENVIRONMENTAL TREATIES

	No		Yes		No
	Yes		No		No

Environmental priorities are low given Afghanistan's anarchic civil war conditions. However, the country's relative lack of industry, even in Kābul, means that industrial pollution is minimal. The biggest problem facing Afghanistan is land mines: over ten million have been laid, and the UN estimates it will take 100 years to make the country safe for civilians.

MEDIA

Information is regulated by individual factions in the areas which they control

PUBLISHING AND BROADCAST MEDIA

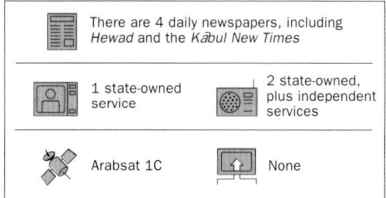

	There are 4 daily newspapers, including *Hewad* and the *Kābul New Times*
	1 state-owned service		2 state-owned, plus independent services
	Arabsat 1C		None

Most of the *mujahideen* factions run their own newspapers and radio stations, which follow the party line and denigrate rivals. The BBC, which broadcasts in Pashtu and Dari, is more popular than Radio Free Afghanistan, especially for its soap operas. These convey information on issues such as health care and the disposal of land mines.

of dams on the Kunar and Laghman rivers is being considered. Coal production has fallen from prewar levels and mines are also in urgent need of rehabilitation. Western technology is needed to rebuild the gas industry.

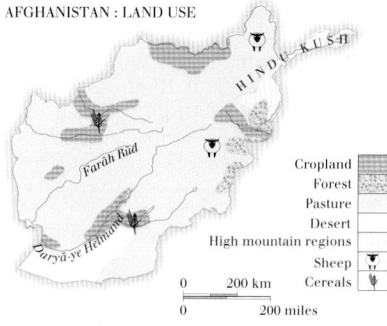

AFGHANISTAN : LAND USE

Cropland	
Forest	
Pasture	
Desert	
High mountain regions	
Sheep	
Cereals	

0   200 km
0   200 miles

CRIME

	Afghanistan does not publish prison figures		Levels of all crimes remain very high

CRIME RATES

No statistics for murders, rapes and thefts are published due to the war situation

Fear of looting in Kābul is stifling economic activity. Gun law operates in most parts of the country. Herāt, once an exception, has also experienced violence since falling to *talibaan* forces.

EDUCATION

	29%		24,333 students

0   Education spending as % GNP   25
2.0%

THE EDUCATION SYSTEM

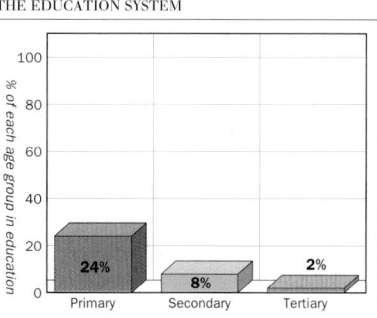

% of each age group in education

Primary	Secondary	Tertiary
24%	8%	2%

The education system has been destroyed by the war, and as a result illiteracy rates are high. However, some schools have responded to a mid-1993 government directive and reopened. Kābul University has been closed since the fall of the Najibullah regime.

HEALTH

	1 per 7,358 people		Infectious, parasitic, respiratory and digestive diseases

0   Health spending as % GDP   25
1.6%

The health service has collapsed completely and almost all medical professionals have left the country. Infant and maternal mortality rates are among the highest in the world, and life expectancy one of the lowest, at 42 years. Parasitic diseases and infections are a particular problem. The UN has organized a well-water chlorination program, following an outbreak of cholera in Kābul. The admission of women to hospital is strongly discouraged under increasingly prevalent Islamic laws of modesty.

WEALTH

	Faction leaders and arms dealers are the wealthiest groups

CONSUMER GOODS OWNERSHIP

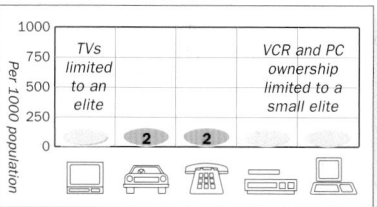

Per 1000 population

TVs limited to an elite   VCR and PC ownership limited to a small elite

2   2

The vast majority of Afghans live in conditions of extreme poverty. The country does not have the resources to feed its people at present – a situation likely to be exacerbated by the return of refugees from neighboring Pakistan and Iran – and is likely to be heavily dependent on outside assistance for its rehabilitation. However, a number of *mujahideen* leaders have accumulated personal fortunes during the war. These derive in part from the substantial foreign aid that was once available and, in some cases, from the trafficking of opium.

WORLD RANKING

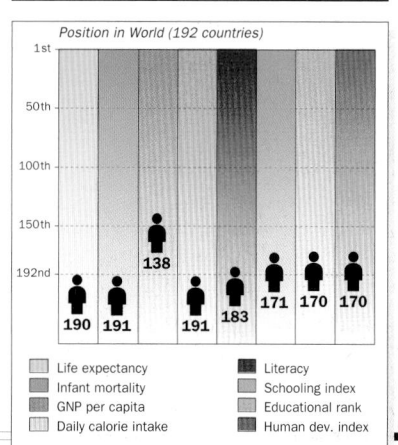

Position in World (192 countries)

1st	
50th	
100th	
150th	
192nd	

138

190   191   191   183   171   170   170

	Life expectancy		Literacy
	Infant mortality		Schooling index
	GNP per capita		Educational rank
	Daily calorie intake		Human dev. index

A

ALBANIA

OFFICIAL NAME: Republic of Albania   **CAPITAL:** Tiranë
POPULATION: 3.4 million   **CURRENCY:** New lek   **OFFICIAL LANGUAGE:** Albanian

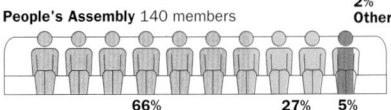

L YING AT THE southeastern end of the Adriatic Sea, opposite the heel of Italy, Albania is a mountainous country vulnerable to earthquakes. It achieved *de facto* independence from Turkey in 1913 and became a one-party communist state in 1944. Albania held its first multiparty elections in 1992. Its return to the international community has been delayed by its support for the ethnic Albanian insurrection in the Kosovo region of Serbia.

CLIMATE

WEATHER CHART

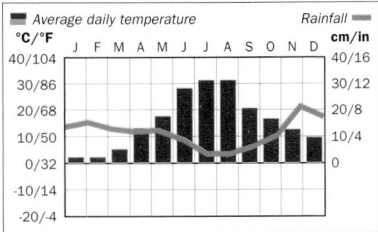

The coastal climate is Mediterranean, but rather wet in winter. Heavy rain or snow falls in winter in the mountains.

TRANSPORTATION

 Tiranë Rinas   20 ships 85,500 dwt

THE TRANSPORTATION NETWORK

1,770 miles (2,850 km)		None
425 miles (684 km)		28 miles (43 km)

Albania has Europe's least developed transportation network. Private cars were first allowed in 1991. The horse and cart is the main means of transportation.

TOURISM

 28,000 visitors   Down by 37% in 1994

MAIN OVERSEAS ARRIVALS

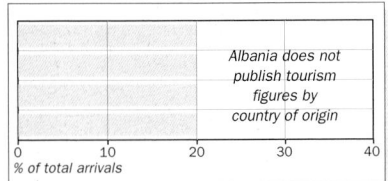

Albania does not publish tourism figures by country of origin

% of total arrivals

Tourism during the communist era was limited to small organized groups. The government has now begun to exploit Albania's scenic beauty.

PEOPLE

 Albanian, Greek    321 people per sq. mile

THE URBAN/RURAL POPULATION SPLIT

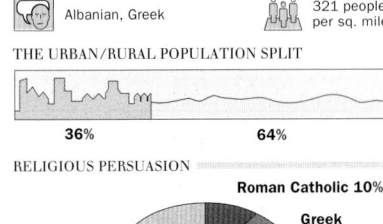

36%   64%

RELIGIOUS PERSUASION

Roman Catholic 10%
Greek Orthodox 20%
Muslim 70%

Official statistics admitted the existence of ethnic minorities in Albania only in 1989. The Greek minority strongly contests these statistics, which state that 98% of the population are Albanian. Located mainly in the south and identifying with Athens rather than Tiranë, the Greeks claim to make up 20% of the population. They suffer considerable discrimination. Many have sought refuge in northern Greece, but tensions between the two states have also led to a number of these refugees being sent back to Albania.

Under communism, Albania was the only officially atheist state in the world. Many Albanians maintained their beliefs in private – 70% are Muslim. Religious worship is now permitted and mosques have reopened. Society is traditional and male-dominated. The extended family remains strong.

City of a thousand windows. *Berat was preserved as a museum city whilst a new town was built further down the valley.*

POLITICS

 1992/1996   President Sali Berisha

THE STATE OF THE PARTIES

People's Assembly 140 members   2% Other

66% DPA   27% SPA   5% SDP

DPA = Democratic Party of Albania   **SPA** = Socialist Party of Albania   **SDP** = Social Democratic Party
Other = Union for Human Rights, Albanian Republican Party

Albania was dominated for more than 40 years by communist ruler Enver Hoxha, who died in 1985. At first, it seemed to resist the tide of change that swept through eastern Europe in 1989. However, by 1990, it became apparent that an upheaval in the one-party communist state could be delayed but not resisted. An increase in popular demonstrations gave reformers within the Party the upper hand and hardliners were forced to concede changes. A mass exodus of Albanians towards the end of 1991 finally persuaded Ramiz Alia, Enver Hoxha's successor, to call multiparty elections. These were held in 1992 and saw victory for the center-right DPA-led coalition. The Greek minority was forbidden to field candidates. The main issue in politics is the creation of a Western-style liberal economic state.

WORLD AFFAIRS

 BSEC   CE   OSCE   OIC   PfP

Ethnic tension in the region of Kosovo in Serbia dominates foreign policy. Rich in minerals and 90% ethnically Albanian, Kosovo was an autonomous republic in former Yugoslavia. In 1989, it was forcibly integrated into Serbia. Persecution of Albanians by Serbs has increased tension in the region. Tiranë is now suspected of supporting armed resistance groups in Kosovo.

AID

 $194m (receipts)   Down by 35% in 1993

The West replaced the Soviet Union as the main source of aid to Albania after 1991. Initially, most was humanitarian food aid. The largest proportion came from Italy, which wished to reduce the flow of economic migrants to its shores. Aid is now directed at infrastructure modernization projects.

DEFENSE

 $50.4m

 Up 14% in 1995

Officer ranks were reestablished in the Albanian armed forces in 1991. The ability of the under-resourced army to defend Albania's borders has been questioned. Albanians perform 18 months of mandatory military service.

ECONOMICS

 $1.2bn

 100.43–93.85 New leke

SCORE CARD

❑ WORLD GNP RANKING	150th
❑ GNP PER CAPITA	$360
❑ BALANCE OF PAYMENTS	$157m
❑ INFLATION	22.6%
❑ UNEMPLOYMENT	9.1%

STRENGTHS

Europe's highest growth rate in 1993. Growth in agricultural output. Oil and gas reserves.

WEAKNESSES

Rudimentary infrastructure. Low level of technical skills. Regional instability has discouraged foreign investment.

EXPORTS

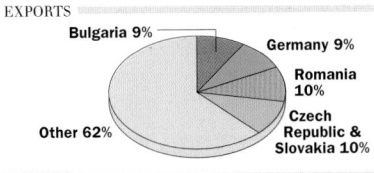

Bulgaria 9%
Germany 9%
Romania 10%
Czech Republic & Slovakia 10%
Other 62%

IMPORTS

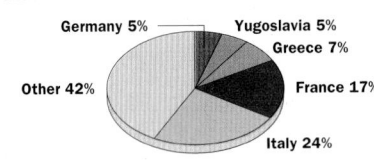

Germany 5%
Yugoslavia 5%
Greece 7%
Other 42%
France 17%
Italy 24%

ALBANIA

Total Land Area : 27 400 sq. km (10 579 sq. miles)

POPULATION	
◎	over 100 000
○	over 50 000
●	over 10 000
·	under 10 000

LAND HEIGHT	
	2000m/6562ft
	1000m/3281ft
	500m/1640ft
	200m/656ft
	Sea Level

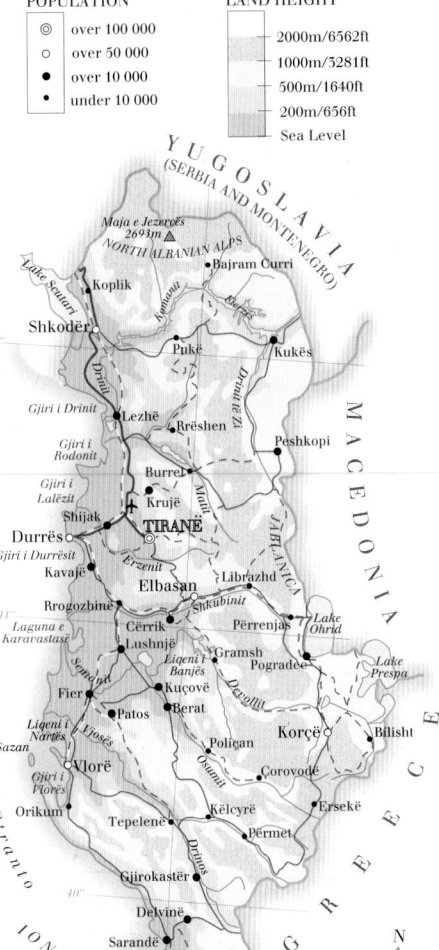

RESOURCES

 3.3bn kwh (capacity 780,000 kw)

 585,000 b/d (reserves 165,000,000 bbl)

 63,000 cattle, 1.9m sheep, 1.3m goats, 86,000 pigs

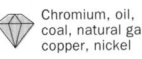 Chromium, oil, coal, natural gas, copper, nickel

Albania needs huge capital investment to develop its minerals and to create a modern electricity supply system.

ENVIRONMENT

 1.2% (0.8% partially protected)

 There is no money for environmental protection measures

Industry, which is underdeveloped, has little impact on the environment. Years of shortages in the economy mean that most materials are recycled.

MEDIA

 Since the fall of communism there has been no official censorship

PUBLISHING AND BROADCAST MEDIA

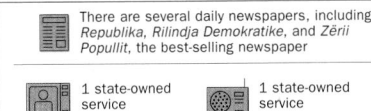

There are several daily newspapers, including *Republika, Rilindja Demokratike*, and *Zërii Popullit*, the best-selling newspaper

1 state-owned service

1 state-owned service

The leading paper, *Zërii Popullit*, is run by the SPA. Journalists opposing the government can suffer intimidation.

CRIME

 1,640 prisoners

 Crime levels are rising sharply

Most crimes are on the increase; tourists in Tiranë are targets for mugging. Cannabis is widely grown.

CHRONOLOGY

Albania gained independence for the first time in its history in 1913.

- ❑ **1924–1959** Ahmet Zogu, crowned King Zog in 1928, in power.
- ❑ **1939–1943** Occupied by Italy.
- ❑ **1944** Communist state; led by Enver Hoxha until 1985.
- ❑ **1948–1961** Pro-Soviet period.
- ❑ **1961–1978** Pro-Chinese period.
- ❑ **1981** Prime minister, Mehmet Shehu, shot dead.
- ❑ **1992** Democratic multiparty state.

EDUCATION

 72%

 122,835 students

The system is derived from the Soviet, Chinese and Italian models. Albania has four universities.

HEALTH

 1 per 735 people

Heart, respiratory and digestive diseases, cancers

The health service is rudimentary and dependent on Western aid for most drugs and medical supplies.

WEALTH

 Demand for imported luxury goods has increased

CONSUMER GOODS OWNERSHIP

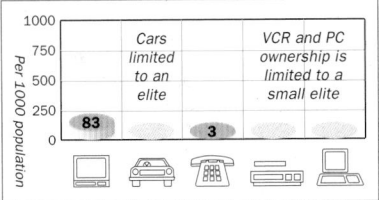

Cars limited to an elite

VCR and PC ownership is limited to a small elite

83

3

Wealth is limited to a small, slowly expanding group of private-sector entrepreneurs.

WORLD RANKING

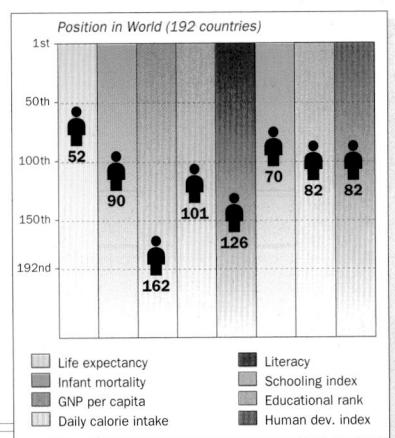

Position in World (192 countries)

52
90
101
126
162
70
82
82

☐ Life expectancy	☐ Literacy
☐ Infant mortality	☐ Schooling index
☐ GNP per capita	☐ Educational rank
☐ Daily calorie intake	☐ Human dev. index

A

ALGERIA

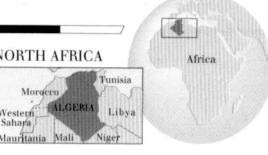

OFFICIAL NAME: Democratic and Popular Republic of Algeria   **CAPITAL:** Algiers
POPULATION: 27.9 million   **CURRENCY:** Algerian dinar   **OFFICIAL LANGUAGE:** Arabic

AFRICA'S SECOND-LARGEST COUNTRY, Algeria shares borders with Morocco, Mauritania, Mali, Niger, Libya and Tunisia. Algeria won independence from France in 1962. Today, the military-dominated government faces a severe challenge from Islamic fundamentalists. A founder-member of OPEC, Algeria has significant oil and gas reserves. The country also has one of the youngest populations, and highest birth-rates, in North Africa.

CLIMATE

WEATHER CHART

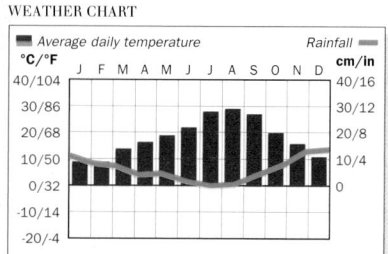

Coastal areas have a warm, temperate climate. The area to the south of the Atlas Mountains is hot desert.

TRANSPORTATION

Dar-el-Beida, Algiers 3.68m passengers	78 ships 1.08m dwt

THE TRANSPORTATION NETWORK

30,080 miles (48,400 km)	None
2,576 miles (4,146 km)	None

There are five international airports. Rail is the quickest way to travel between the main urban centers.

TOURISM

 0.81m visitors   Down 29% in 1994

MAIN OVERSEAS ARRIVALS

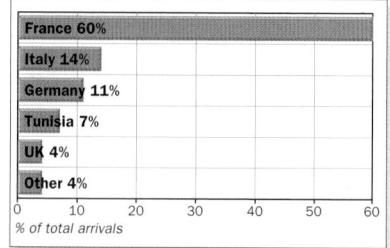

France 60%
Italy 14%
Germany 11%
Tunisia 7%
UK 4%
Other 4%

% of total arrivals

The once-popular desert safaris are now rare. Tourists are a target for militant Islamic groups.

PEOPLE

Arabic, Berber (Kabyle, Shawia, Tamashek), French	31 people per sq. mile

THE URBAN/RURAL POPULATION SPLIT

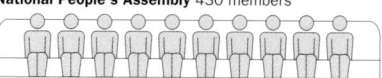

53%   47%

RELIGIOUS PERSUASION

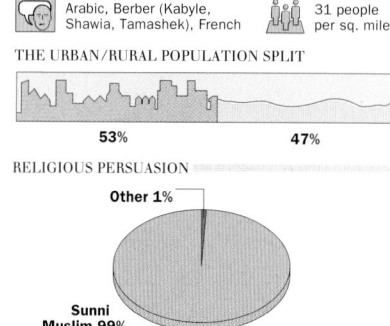

Other 1%
Sunni Muslim 99%

ETHNIC MAKEUP

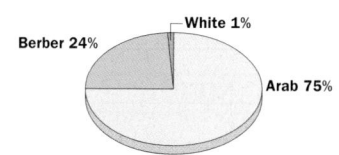

White 1%
Berber 24%
Arab 75%

Algeria's population is predominantly Arab, under 30 years of age and urban; about 20% are Berber. More than 85% of the population speak Arabic, the official language, and 99% are Sunni Muslim. Of the million or so French who settled in Algeria before independence, only about 6,000 remain. Most Berbers consider the mountainous Kabylia region to be their homeland. If the struggle between Islamic fundamentalists and the government intensifies, Kabylia may try to seek independence. As in the rest of North Africa, the mosque is an important provider of social and medical services.

POPULATION AGE BREAKDOWN

	0–14		15–64		65+

65+	3.9%	4.1%	3.9%	3.6%	3.3%
15–64	52.4%	47.5%	49.6%	52.8%	57.4%
0–14	43.7%	48.4%	46.5%	43.6%	39.3%
	1960	1970	1980	1990	2000

% of population by age group

POLITICS

1991/Uncertain   President Brig.-Gen. Liamine Zeroual

THE STATE OF THE PARTIES

National People's Assembly 430 members

The National People's Assembly was dissolved in 1992, following the first round of elections

Military rule ended in 1994. Presidential elections were held in 1995, although legislative elections are not scheduled.

MAIN POLITICAL ISSUES
Islamic fundamentalism
Nearly 50,000 Algerians are estimated to have died in political violence since 1992. The country's Islamic militants want to establish an Islamic theocracy. Its leading proponent is the Islamic Salvation Front (FIS), led by Abassi Mandani, which demonstrated its success in the 1991 general election by winning 188 of the 228 seats contested. The FIS was prevented from taking power after the second round of voting was annulled by a military government in 1992. This unleashed a wave of political violence, spearheaded mainly by the extremist Armed Islamic Group (GIA).

The market economy
In 1988, President Bendjedid decided to embark on market reforms to introduce competition into Algeria's large state-run economy. The policy, involving tough austerity measures, met with opposition from political parties which accused the government of bowing to Western pressure, and contributed to the FIS's strong showing in the 1991 polls. After a brief suspension following the army takeover the liberalization program was revived under pressure from the IMF and the World Bank.

PROFILE
Until 1988, Algeria was a Soviet-style regime. Following the collapse of the Soviet Union, the ruling elite adopted IMF privatization policies. This was fiercely opposed by the fundamentalists, who were prevented from taking power. President Zeroual was democratically elected in 1995 and has promised legislative elections. The fundamentalists have effective control of most areas outside the capital, but their political standing has been tarnished by their involvement in a brutal terrorist campaign.

WORLD AFFAIRS

Algeria's struggle for independence from France lasted from 1954 until 1962. Throughout the 1960s and 1970s, Algeria's success in rejecting a colonial power made it a champion for the developing world. It had a leading voice within the UN, the Arab League and the Organization for African Unity. However, relations with the West remained essentially stable. Algeria was increasingly seen by the diplomatic community as a useful bridge between the West and Iran.

In 1981, Algerian diplomats helped to secure the release of American hostages held in Tehran during the last days of US President Carter's term of office. Algeria also attempted to act in a mediating role during the 1980–1988 Iran–Iraq War.

Algeria's influence overseas has diminished as the country has become increasingly unstable politically. Throughout the 1990s, the government has been under severe pressure from the Islamic fundamentalist FIS. A victory for the FIS in Algeria would greatly encourage Islamic militants in neighboring Morocco and Tunisia, and further undermine Egypt's embattled government.

European governments are also concerned that an FIS takeover could trigger a wave of refugees seeking entry into France, Spain and Italy.

AID

 $352m (receipts)　　 Down 13% in 1993

As a major oil producer, Algeria receives only small quantities of aid. During the 1980s, its economy became dependent on eastern European manufactures, which were swapped for oil. The collapse of this trade in the 1990s led Algeria to turn to the West for loans. Oil revenues encouraged the West to offer export credits. The IMF provided loans to help Algeria meet payments on its debt, $29.5 billion at end-1994, on condition that it move toward a market-orientated economy. However, these sources are now threatened by Algeria's growing political instability.

ALGERIA

Total Land Area :
2 381 740 sq. km
(919 590 sq. miles)

POPULATION

over 500 000	◉
over 100 000	◎
over 50 000	○
over 10 000	●

LAND HEIGHT

2000m/6562ft
1000m/3281ft
500m/1640ft
200m/656ft
Sea Level

Saharan town, showing the wide range of Algeria's scenery, from lush, irrigated gardens near water sources to barren sand dunes beyond. 80% of Algeria is desert.

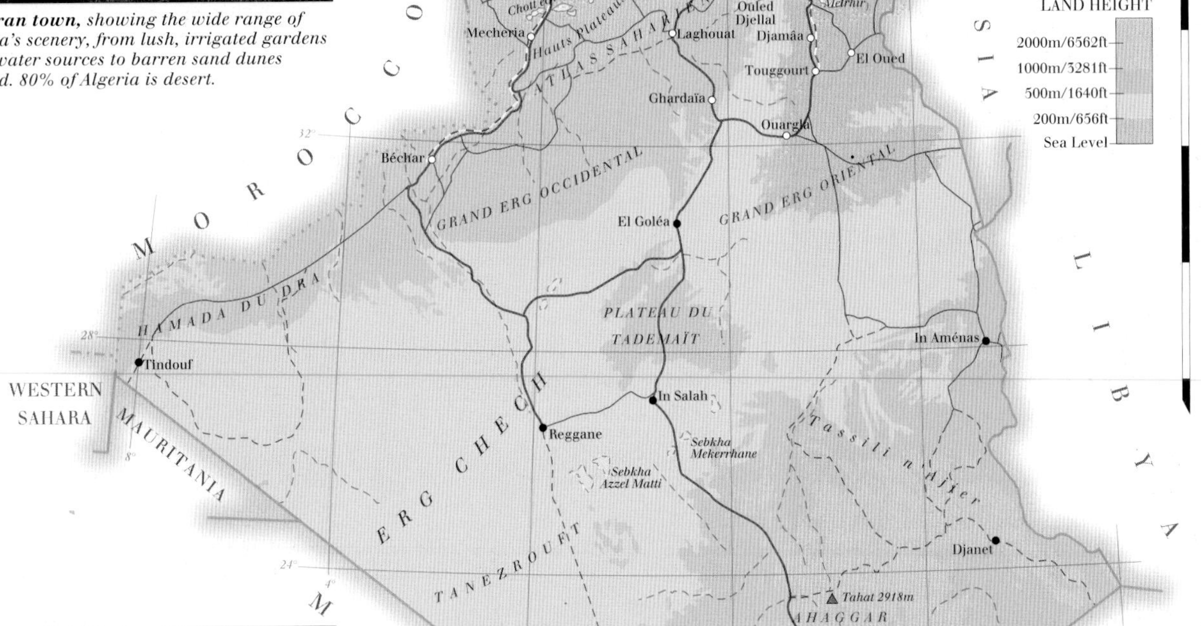

President Zeroual, democratically elected in the 1995 elections.

Abassi Madani, leader of the Islamic Salvation Front (FIS).

A

CHRONOLOGY

The conquest of Algeria by France began in 1830. By 1900, French settlers occupied most of the best land. In 1954, war was declared on the colonial administration by the National Liberation Front (FLN).

❏ **1962** Ceasefire reached, followed by declaration of independence and founding of Algerian republic.

❏ **1965** Military junta topples government of Ahmed Ben Bella. Revolutionary council set up.

❏ **1966** Judiciary "Algerianized." Tribunals try "economic crimes."

❏ **1971** Oil industry nationalized. Boumedienne continues with land reform, a national health service and "socialist" management.

❏ **1976** National Charter establishes a socialist state.

❏ **1979** Bendjedid Chadli sworn in as president.

❏ **1980** Ben Bella released after 15 years' detention. Agreement signed with France, whereby latter gives incentives for return home of 800,000 Algerian immigrants.

❏ **1981** Algeria helps to negotiate release of American hostages from the US embassy in Tehran, Iran.

❏ **1985** The two most popular Kabyle (Berber) singers are given 3-year jail sentences for opposing regime.

❏ **1987** Government introduces limited liberalization by giving private enterprise more freedom. Algeria signs cooperation agreement with Soviet Union.

❏ **1988** Violence directed at ruling party. State of emergency. Algeria negotiates release of Kuwaiti hostages held on aircraft by Shi'a gunmen. The hijackers escape unpunished.

❏ **1989** Constitutional reforms, which diminish power of FLN. New political parties are founded, including the Islamic Salvation Front (FIS). The Arab Maghreb Union is established by the leaders of Algeria, Libya, Morocco and Tunisia.

❏ **1990** Political exiles permitted to return home. FIS wins municipal elections.

❏ **1991** FIS leaders Abassi Madani and Ali Belhadj arrested. FIS wins large majority in National Assembly.

❏ **1992** Bendjedid overthrown by military. Second round of elections scrapped. President Boudiaf assassinated. Succeeded by Ali Kafi. FIS leaders Abassi Madani and Ali Belhadj given 12 years in jail.

❏ **1994** Political violence led by Armed Islamic Group.

❏ **1995** Democratic presidential elections. Zeroual sworn in as president.

DEFENSE

 $1330m

Up 18% in 1995

0	Defense spending as % GDP	40
2.7%		

The National Liberation Army (NLA), equipped with Russian weapons, is the dominant power in politics. There are fears that parts of the army will forge an alliance with Muslim militants. The extreme rebel Armed Islamic Group, which has split from the FIS, is led by former army officers.

ALGERIAN ARMED FORCES

	960 main battle tanks (330 T–54/–55, 330 T–62, 300 T–72)	105,000 personnel
	2 submarines, 3 frigates, 25 surface vessels and 8 patrol	6,700 personnel
	170 combat aircraft (10 Su-24, 40 MiG-23BN, 10 MiG-25,20, MiG-23B/E)	10,000 personnel
	None	

ECONOMICS

 $46.1bn

43.05–52.17 dinars

SCORE CARD

❏ World GNP Ranking	47th
❏ GNP per Capita	$1,690
❏ Balance of Payments	$2.4bn
❏ Inflation	31%
❏ Unemployment	30%

EXPORTS

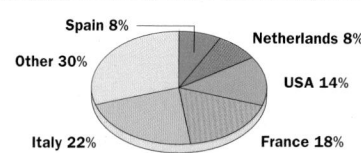

Spain 8%
Other 30%
Netherlands 8%
USA 14%
Italy 22%
France 18%

IMPORTS

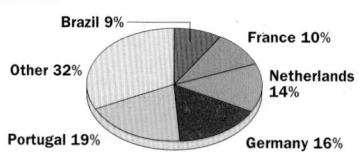

Brazil 9%
Other 32%
France 10%
Netherlands 14%
Portugal 19%
Germany 16%

ECONOMIC PERFORMANCE INDICATOR

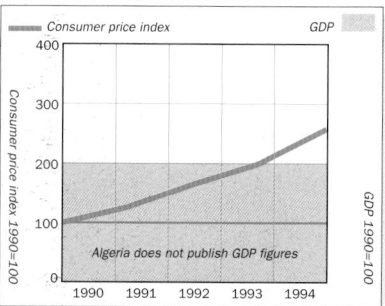

Consumer price index — GDP — Consumer price index 1990=100 — GDP 1990=100 — Algeria does not publish GDP figures — 1990 1991 1992 1993 1994

STRENGTHS

Oil and gas. Recent collaboration with Western oil companies should see improvements in productivity. Natural gas is supplied to Europe.

WEAKNESSES

Oil revenues yet to recover from the 1986 collapse in world prices. Political turmoil threatens many new projects and has led to an exodus of expatriate workers important to the economy. Lack of skilled labor plus high unemployment. Limited agriculture. Shortages of basic foodstuffs. A thriving black market.

PROFILE

Under the pro-Soviet National Liberation Front, the Algerian economy was dominated by centralized socialist planning. In the late 1980s, the economic collapse of the Soviet Union led to a change in policy, and the country began moving toward a market economy. These reforms were frozen after the military takeover in 1992,

though many have since restarted under pressure from the IMF and the World Bank. However, the majority of the economy's most productive sectors remain under state control.

Only the oil industry has encouraged private investment. A number of Western oil companies have signed exploration contracts with Algiers. Yet, Western levels of investment are likely to remain small as long as the political situation is unstable. Algeria is now importing more than half its grain, and long food lines are routine in the capital.

ALGERIA : MAJOR BUSINESSES

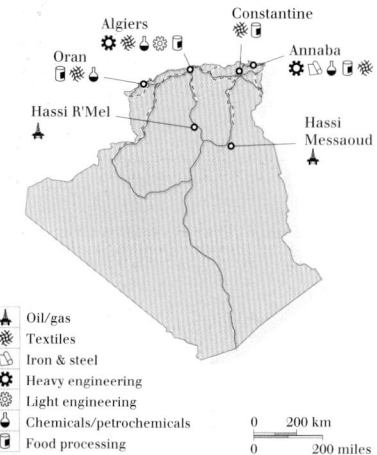

Constantine
Algiers
Oran
Annaba
Hassi R'Mel
Hassi Messaoud

⚓ Oil/gas
✳ Textiles
⬡ Iron & steel
✿ Heavy engineering
◉ Light engineering
⚗ Chemicals/petrochemicals
▯ Food processing

0		200 km
0		200 miles

A

RESOURCES

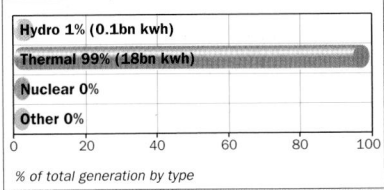

18.3bn kwh (capacity 4.66m kw)

766,000 b/d (reserves 9,200,000,000 bbl)

17.8m sheep, 2.8m goats, 1.4m cattle, 315,000 asses

Oil, natural gas, iron, phosphates, lead, zinc, silver, copper, tungsten

ELECTRICITY GENERATION

Hydro 1% (0.1bn kwh)

Thermal 99% (18bn kwh)

Nuclear 0%

Other 0%

% of total generation by type

Crude oil and natural gas, Algeria's main resources, were first produced in the 1950s. Algeria also has diverse minerals, including iron ore, zinc, silver, copper ore and phosphates. In the 1960s and 1970s, Algeria sought to become a manufacturing country, with investments in building materials, refined products and steel; none of these sectors is competitive on world markets. Although agriculture employs one-quarter of Algeria's work force, its importance to the economy is diminishing. State forests cover some 2% of Algeria's land. Most are brushwood, but some areas include cork oak trees, Aleppo pine, evergreen oak and cedar. Algeria has a large fishing fleet. Sardines, anchovies, tuna and shellfish are the major species caught commercially.

ENVIRONMENT

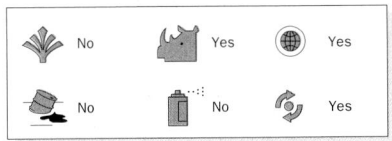

5% (0.1% partially protected)

Desertification owing to pressure on land

ENVIRONMENTAL TREATIES

No

Yes

Yes

No

No

Yes

Since most of Algeria is desert or semi-desert, over 90% of the population is forced to live on the remaining 20% of land. The desert is moving northward. Vegetation has been stripped for use as firewood and animal fodder, leaving fragile soils exposed which then require expensive specialist care in order to conserve them. Water purification techniques are below standard and rivers are increasingly being contaminated by untreated sewage, industrial effluent and wastes from petroleum refining.

MEDIA

 The media is under government control

PUBLISHING AND BROADCAST MEDIA

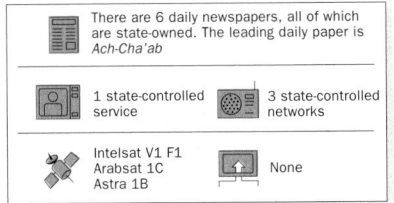

There are 6 daily newspapers, all of which are state-owned. The leading daily paper is *Ach-Cha'ab*

1 state-controlled service

3 state-controlled networks

Intelsat V1 F1 Arabsat 1C Astra 1B

None

Newspapers, TV and radio are state-controlled and permit no criticism of government actions. TV is broadcast in Arabic, French and Kabyle (Berber), but Algeria has only about 2 million TVs. The six daily newspapers have a combined circulation of 1.3 million. However, distribution is limited outside the main cities.

CRIME

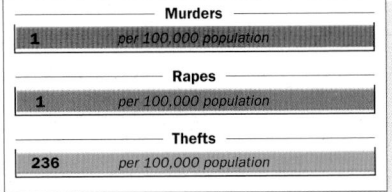

Algeria does not publish prison figures

Crime levels rising sharply

CRIME RATES

Murders

1 per 100,000 population

Rapes

1 per 100,000 population

Thefts

236 per 100,000 population

Thousands of people have been killed by the radical Islamists since 1992, while human rights groups have accused pro-government death squads of persecuting suspected Islamic militants.

EDUCATION

 57%

 298,117 students

0 — Education spending as % GNP — 25

5.7%

THE EDUCATION SYSTEM

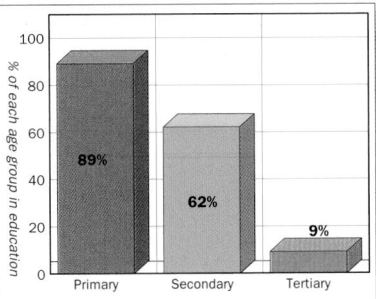

% of each age group in education

89% Primary

62% Secondary

9% Tertiary

Over three-quarters of the school-age population receive a formal education. The literacy rate is 57%. Since 1973, the curriculum has been Arabized and the teaching of French has diminished. Ten universities and seven polytechnics provide higher education to some 175,000 students.

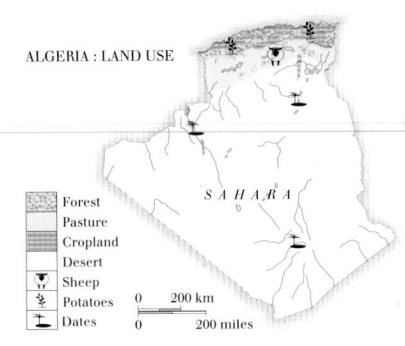

ALGERIA : LAND USE

Forest
Pasture
Cropland
Desert
Sheep
Potatoes
Dates

SAHARA

0 — 200 km
0 — 200 miles

HEALTH

 1 per 2,350 people

Respiratory, heart and cerebrovascular diseases, malaria

0 — Health spending as % GDP — 25

5.4%

Primary health care is rudimentary outside main cities. The infant mortality rate is 5.5%, well below the North African average of 7.3%. Life expectancy is just above the average for the region, at 66 years for men and 68 for women.

WEALTH

 Waiter, 2,282 dinars ($45); per month doctor, 5,802 ($116) dinars per month

CONSUMER GOODS OWNERSHIP

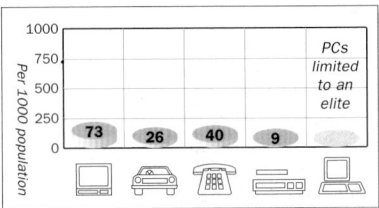

Per 1000 population

PCs limited to an elite

73   26   40   9

There is great disparity in wealth between the political elite and the rest of the population. Those connected to the military are the wealthiest. Most Algerians have had to contend with soaring prices for basic necessities.

WORLD RANKING

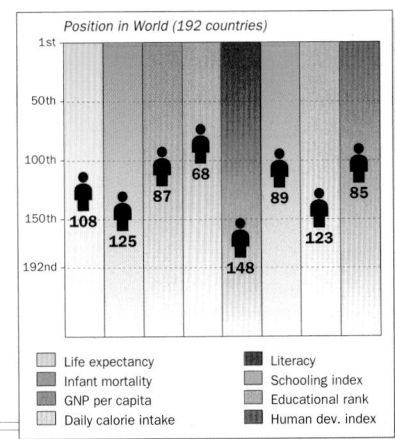

Position in World (192 countries)

1st
50th
100th
150th
192nd

108   125   87   68   148   89   123   85

Life expectancy
Infant mortality
GNP per capita
Daily calorie intake
Literacy
Schooling index
Educational rank
Human dev. index

A

ANDORRA

OFFICIAL NAME: Principality of Andorra **CAPITAL:** Andorra la Vella
POPULATION: 64,000 **CURRENCY:** French franc and Spanish peseta **OFFICIAL LANGUAGE:** Catalan

A TINY, LANDLOCKED principality between France and Spain, Andorra lies high in the eastern Pyrenees. From the 13th century, French and Spanish co-princes (today the President of France and the Bishop of Urgel) have governed Andorra. In December 1993, the principality held its first full elections. Andorra's spectacular scenery, alpine climate and duty-free shopping have made tourism, especially skiing, its main source of income.

Andorra's outstanding mountain scenery attracts 500,000 skiers a year.

CLIMATE

WEATHER CHART

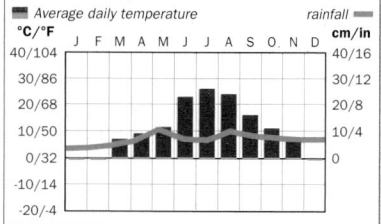

Springs are cool and wet; summers are dry and warm. Snowfalls in December and January lay the ground for good skiing up to March. Andorra's climate supports an abundance of wild flowers.

TRANSPORTATION

 None   🚢 Has no fleet

THE TRANSPORTATION NETWORK

🛣️ 60 miles (96 km)	🛤️ None	🚆 None	⛰️ None

The road from France to Spain climbs to 8,872 feet through one of the most dramatic mountain passes in Europe. During the summer months, the sheer number of day-trippers often brings traffic to a standstill around Andorra la Vella.

TOURISM

 12m visitors   ⬍ No change in 1993

MAIN OVERSEAS ARRIVALS

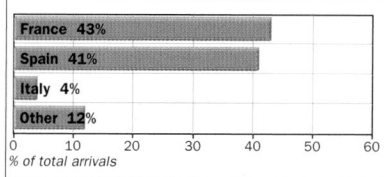

France	43%
Spain	41%
Italy	4%
Other	12%

% of total arrivals

Most tourists visit Andorra to ski or shop. However, the traditional trade in day-trippers from France and Spain, coming to shop in the many tax-free designer-label boutiques, is threatened by EU regulations seeking to end Andorra's beneficial tax regime. Five ski resorts receive over 500,000 visitors a year. In summer they cater for mountain hikers; Andorra's wild flowers attract many, but there is also much for the birdwatcher to see. Hunting of wild boar is popular, and the goat-like chamois can be hunted under special licence.

 EUROPE

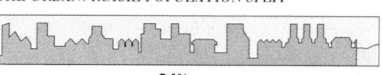

PEOPLE

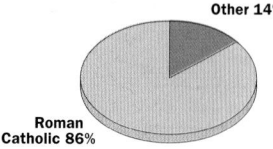

👤 Spanish, Catalan, French, Portuguese   👥 357 people per sq. mile

THE URBAN/RURAL POPULATION SPLIT

94%   6%

RELIGIOUS PERSUASION

Other 14%

Roman Catholic 86%

Immigration is strictly monitored and restricted by quota to French and Spanish nationals intending to work in Andorra. Divorce is illegal.

POLITICS

 1993/1997   👥 Co-Princes Jacques Chirac and Joan Martí Alanis

THE STATE OF THE PARTIES
General Council of the Valleys 28 members

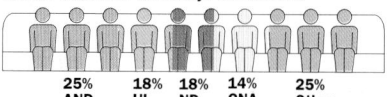

| 25% AND | 18% UL | 18% ND | 14% CNA | 25% Other |

AND = National Democratic Grouping **UL** = Liberal Union
ND = New Democracy **CNA** = National Andorran Coalition
Other = Canillo-Massana Grouping, Independents

14 members are elected on a national list and 14 are elected in 7 dual-member constituencies

Until recently, Andorra was a semi-feudal state. In March 1993, a referendum approved democratic measures which legalized political parties and the right to strike, and altered relations with the co-princes. Following elections in December 1993, an AND-led coalition government was formed.

ANDORRA

Total Land Area :
468 sq. km
(181 sq. miles)

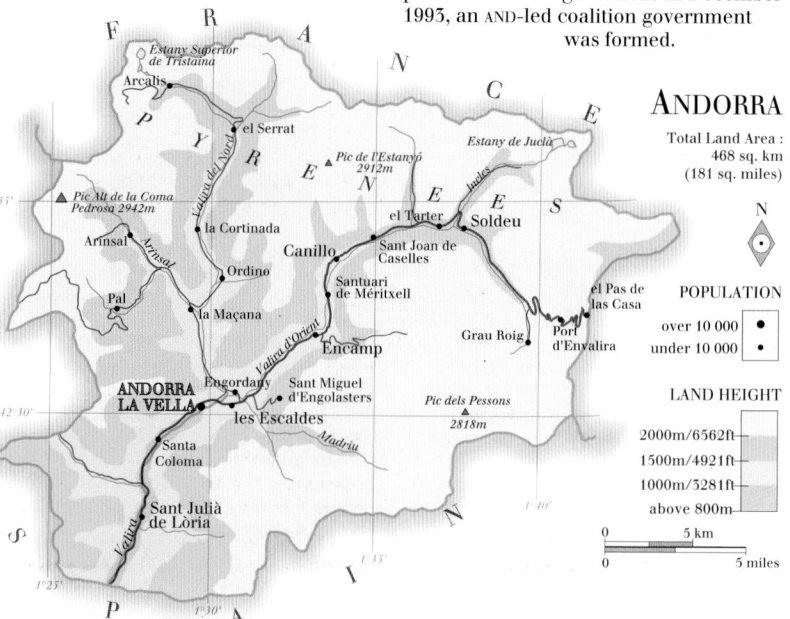

POPULATION

over 10 000 ●
under 10 000 ●

LAND HEIGHT

2000m/6562ft
1500m/4921ft
1000m/3281ft
above 800m

0   5 km
0   5 miles

WORLD AFFAIRS

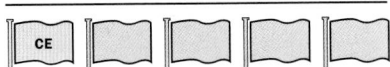

Andorra's limited membership of world bodies reflects its ambiguous status; it is not recognized by a number of nations. Since 1991, it has been a member of the EU customs union and has applied its external tariff and trade policy.

AID

 Andorra has no aid receipts or donations   Not applicable

The principality of Andorra neither receives nor provides aid, and has no plans to do so.

DEFENSE

 Andorra has no defense budget   Not applicable

Andorra has no defense budget; protection is provided by France and Spain. The French intervention of 1933 was the last military action on Andorran soil.

ECONOMICS

 $895m   4.89–5.34 francs 121.32–131.63 pesetas

SCORE CARD

❏ WORLD GNP RANKING	166th
❏ GNP PER CAPITA	$8,956
❏ BALANCE OF PAYMENTS	Included in Spanish total
❏ INFLATION	Not applicable
❏ UNEMPLOYMENT	0%

STRENGTHS
Tourism, the basis of the economy. Strict banking secrecy laws make Andorra an important tax haven; low consumer taxes have also encouraged a healthy luxury retail sector. Farming: cereals, potatoes and tobacco are the major products.

WEAKNESSES
France and Spain effectively decide economic policy. There is a dependence on imported food and raw materials.

EXPORTS

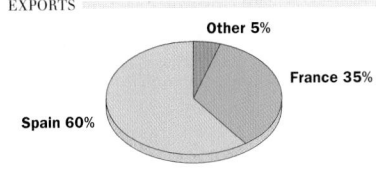

Other 5%
France 35%
Spain 60%

IMPORTS

Spain 27%
France 42%
Other 31%

RESOURCES

 115m kwh   Not an oil producer and has no refineries

 5,600 sheep, 1,700 cattle   None

Water is a major resource, hydropower providing most domestic energy needs. However, Andorra has to import twice as much electricity as it produces, and there are plans to increase capacity. A third of the country is designated forest.

ENVIRONMENT

 None   Desire for larger tourist revenues conflicts with nature conservation

Twelve million tourists a year have had an inevitably adverse impact over time on a country of 64,000 people. Concern is growing, at the moment chiefly among NGOs, about the scarring of Andorra's alpine landscape by hotel and ski developments, as well as about the future of its unique mountain flora. Hunting, notably of the Pyrenean chamois and the wild boar, is still a significant tourist attraction. However, restrictions are gradually being introduced to preserve certain animal species.

MEDIA

 No political censorship since 1993

PUBLISHING AND BROADCAST MEDIA

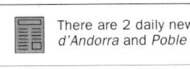 There are 2 daily newspapers, *Diari d'Andorra* and *Poble Andorra*

 1 independent station   1 independent station

Andorra receives most Spanish and French TV broadcasts. A private TV company in Spain broadcasts one hour a day of programs designed specifically for Andorra.

CRIME

 Andorra does not publish prison figures   Up 20% in 1992

Tourists are natural targets for thieves, most of whom are not Andorran. Thefts of expensive cars for resale in France and Spain are on the increase.
    Andorra has two criminal courts – the *Tribunals de Corts*.

EDUCATION

 100%   1659 students

There are 18 schools in Andorra, most of which teach in Spanish and French. Instruction in Catalan is available, but only in the elementary schools and one secondary school.

CHRONOLOGY

Since 1278, Andorra has been autonomous, ruled by French and Spanish co-princes.

- ❏ **1970** Women get the vote.
- ❏ **1982** First constitution enshrines popular sovereignty.
- ❏ **1983** General Council votes in favor of income tax.
- ❏ **1984** Government resigns over attempt to introduce indirect taxes.
- ❏ **1991** EC Customs Union comes into effect.
- ❏ **1992** Political demonstrations demanding constitutional reform. Government resigns.
- ❏ **1993** Referendum approves new constitution. General election.
- ❏ **1994** AND-led Government falls; replaced by administration of center-right LU.

HEALTH

 1 per 555 people   Heart and cerebrovascular diseases

Andorra has one public and one private hospital. Hot springs at les Escaldes are popular with rheumatism sufferers.

WEALTH

 Experienced waiter, 170,000 pesetas ($1400) per month; elementary school teacher, 220,000 pesetas ($1800) per month

CONSUMER GOODS OWNERSHIP

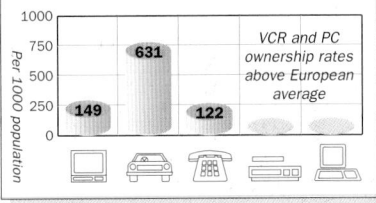

VCR and PC ownership rates above European average

631
149
122

Hotel owners are the wealthiest group in Andorran society; many choose to live across the border in Spain.

WORLD RANKING

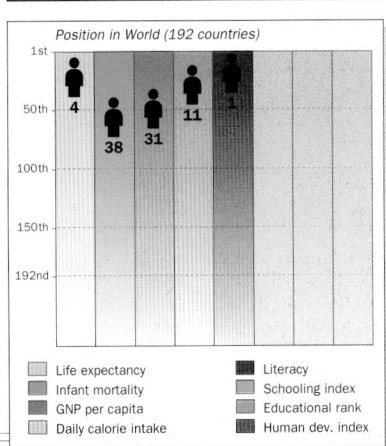

Position in World (192 countries)

4
38
31
11

- Life expectancy
- Infant mortality
- GNP per capita
- Daily calorie intake
- Literacy
- Schooling index
- Educational rank
- Human dev. index

ANGOLA

OFFICIAL NAME: Republic of Angola **CAPITAL:** Luanda
POPULATION: 11.1 million **CURRENCY:** Readjusted kwanza **OFFICIAL LANGUAGE:** Portuguese

A N OIL-RICH COUNTRY in southwest Africa, Angola has been in a state of almost permanent civil war since 1975 when the colonial power, Portugal, left. For many years it was a key Cold War frontier in Africa, with the West supporting UNITA against the Soviet-backed MPLA. A fragile UN-supervised peace process was consolidated by the signing of the 1994 Lusaka Protocol.

Angola's capital, Luanda. Founded in 1575 by the Portuguese, it became a transshipment point for slaves en route to Brazil.

CLIMATE

WEATHER CHART

 Average daily temperature   Rainfall

The climate varies from temperate to tropical. Rainfall decreases from north to south. The Benguela Current makes the coast unusually cool and dry.

TRANSPORTATION

 Luanda International
1.33m passengers

 29 ships
112,500 dwt

THE TRANSPORTATION NETWORK

11,282 miles (18,157 km) according to most recent figures. Much has been destroyed during civil war.

1,981 miles (3,189 km) according to most recent figures. Much has been destroyed during civil war.

The war has destroyed the transportation infrastructure and severely restricted the movement of goods and people. The UN peacekeepers have made the repair and reopening of roads, bridges and railroads, and the clearing of mines priorities. Both sides have also committed themselves to removing unauthorized checkpoints. Air travel remains the safest means of transportation. The war has led to a collapse in port traffic: Namibe handled 6 million tons in 1973, but just 171,000 tons by 1985.

TOURISM

 There are no tourists

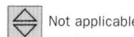 Not applicable

Most overseas visitors are Western journalists, or employees of the big oil multinationals in Cabinda. Angola, a disease-ridden war zone, where up to 500,000 people have died since October 1992, attracts no tourists.

PEOPLE

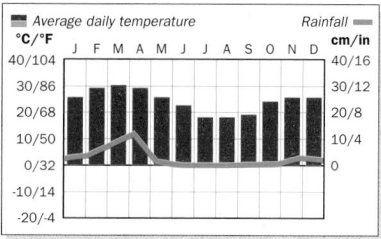

Portuguese, Umbundu, Kimbundu, Kongo

23 people per sq. mile

THE URBAN/RURAL POPULATION SPLIT

30%   70%

ETHNIC MAKEUP

Ovimbundu 37%
Bakongo 13%
Other 25%
Kimbundu 25%

Ethnic tensions in Angola are few. UNITA has cast itself as the sole representative of the Ovimbundu in order to attack the mainly urban-based and largely Kimbundu MPLA. Religion has undergone a revival since the 1980s as the MPLA has now abandoned its Marxist philosophy. Around 20% of the population are internal refugees.

POLITICS

 1992/1996

 President José Eduardo dos Santos

THE STATE OF THE PARTIES

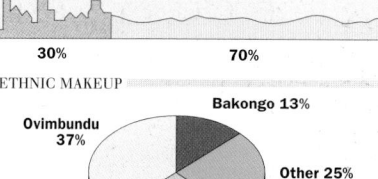

National Assembly 233 members

4% Other

59% MPLA   32% UNITA   3% PRS   2% FNLA

MPLA = People's Movement for the Liberation of Angola
UNITA = National Union for the Total Independence of Angola
PRS = Social Renewal Party FNLA = National Front for the Liberation of Angola Other = Democratic Liberal Party

Angola is dominated by two main groups, the MPLA and UNITA. In 1991, the MPLA, in power since 1975, decided to abandon Marxist one-party rule and embraced market capitalism. In 1992, democratic elections confirmed the MPLA in power, prompting Jonas Savimbi's UNITA to reopen the civil war. Numerous peace efforts culminated in the signing of a peace protocol in Lusaka, Zambia, in November 1994. However, the slow implementation of the peace, particularly the demobilization of UNITA guerrillas, has aroused the concern of the international community.

ANGOLA

Total Land Area :
1 124 670 sq. km
(434 255 sq. miles)

POPULATION

over 1 000 000
over 100 000
over 50 000
over 10 000
under 10 000

LAND HEIGHT

2000m/6562ft
1000m/3281ft
500m/1640ft
200m/656ft
Sea Level

0   200 km
0   200 miles

N

CONGO
CABINDA
Cabinda
Z A I R E
M'Banza Congo
Uíge
Ambriz
Caxito
LUANDA
Viana
'Dalatando
Dondo
Gabela
Sumbe
Lobito
Catumbela
Benguela
Cubal
Camabatela
Golungo Alto
Lucala
Malanje
Calandula
Lóvua
Cambulo
Lucapa
Saurimo
Uaco Cungo
Bailundo
Camacupa
Luena
Moço 2620m
Huambo
Caála
Kuito
PLANALTO DO BIE
Caconda
Cubango
Menongue
Lubango
Namibe
Tombua
N'Giva
Cunene
Cuito Cuanavale
Cuando
ATLANTIC OCEAN
NAMIBIA
Capriri Strip
BOTSWANA

A

WORLD AFFAIRS

Comesa | Lusoph | NAM | OAU | SADC

Angola was one of the key Cold War frontiers in Africa, with Soviet advisers and Cuban troops supporting the MPLA, and South Africa and the USA backing UNITA forces. Since the resumption of fighting in late 1992, UNITA has lost international support. At the same time, the MPLA government has won US recognition. Having brokered the 1991 peace deal, the USA, Russian Federation and Portugal remain key players, while since 1994 South Africa has played a prominent role in the peace process.

AID

 $300m (receipts)   Up 10% in 1993

Meeting in Brussels in late 1995, donors responded to the plea made jointly by President dos Santos and Jonas Savimbi for international financial assistance to rebuild the shattered economy by pledging a total of $1 billion in aid and reconstruction. Donors include the EU, the USA, the World Bank and Japan.

DEFENSE

 Precise figures not available but largest proportion of budget   Rose again in 1993, after 1992 fall

The 1994 peace agreement provides for the demobilization of both government and UNITA troops, and the integration of selected members into a new national army. Delays in this process have caused concern, with UNITA particularly criticized for failing to confine its troops. In 1996 the government halted its use of South African mercenaries.

ECONOMICS

 $3.5bn   25,000 readjusted kwanza

SCORE CARD

❑ WORLD GNP RANKING.....................	117th
❑ GNP PER CAPITA	$726
❑ BALANCE OF PAYMENTS....................	$–769m
❑ INFLATION	1737%
❑ UNEMPLOYMENT.................................	15%

STRENGTHS
Oil sector, which has been protected from the worst effects of war, earns important foreign exchange. Some of the richest mineral deposits in Africa.

WEAKNESSES
Civil war. Destruction of infrastructure. Ten million land mines laid nationwide. Lack of skilled manpower.

EXPORTS

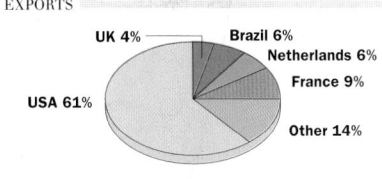

UK 4%   Brazil 6%
Netherlands 6%
France 9%
USA 61%   Other 14%

IMPORTS

France 10%   Portugal 19%
Brazil 9%
Germany 16%
Other 32%
Netherlands 14%

RESOURCES

 1.9bn kwh (capacity 620,000 kw)   521,300 b/d

3m cattle, 225,000 pigs, 255,000 sheep, 5000 asses   Oil, diamonds, iron, copper, lead, zinc, gold, manganese

Cabinda is the main oil-producing region. Angola has some of the richest alluvial diamond deposits in the world.

ENVIRONMENT

 2% (1% partially protected)   Ecological initiatives not a priority

The 1990 drought threatened three million Angolans with famine. Other ecological issues do not feature at all.

MEDIA

 The constitution recognizes freedom of speech.

PUBLISHING AND BROADCAST MEDIA

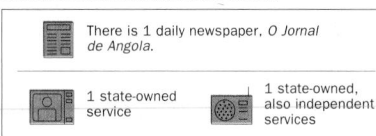

There is 1 daily newspaper, *O Jornal de Angola*.

1 state-owned service   1 state-owned, also independent services

The *Voice of the Resistance of the Black Cockerel*, UNITA's once clandestine radio station, now broadcasts legitimately.

CRIME

 Angola does not publish prison figures   Dramatic increase due to war

Murder, theft, corruption and diamond smuggling are commonplace in war-torn Angola. All areas outside main cities are effectively controlled by armed gangs. Both the MPLA and UNITA have poor human rights records.

EDUCATION

 42%   6534 students

The system has all but collapsed in most areas, although the university in Luanda still functions.

CHRONOLOGY
The Portuguese first established forts along the coast of present-day Angola in 1482.

- ❑ **1956** MPLA founded.
- ❑ **1961** Liberation struggle begins.
- ❑ **1975** Independence from Portugal. Civil war between Soviet and Cuban-backed MPLA and US and South African-backed UNITA.
- ❑ **1979** José Eduardo dos Santos (MPLA) becomes president.
- ❑ **1991** UN-brokered peace.
- ❑ **1992** MPLA election victory provoking UNITA to resume fighting.
- ❑ **1994** Lusaka peace agreement.

HEALTH

 1 per 14,300 people   Malaria, diarrheal and respiratory diseases, severe malnutrition

The system is in a state of collapse, unable to cope with the huge numbers of famine victims and the hundreds of thousands war-wounded. Angola has the highest infant mortality rate and the greatest number of amputees (caused by exploding mines) in the world.

WEALTH

 Formal employment has effectively collapsed in Angola

CONSUMER GOODS OWNERSHIP

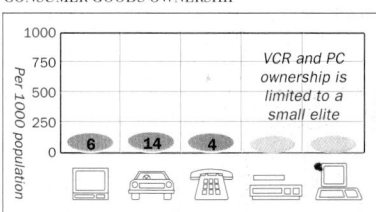

VCR and PC ownership is limited to a small elite

6   14   4

Higher-ranking state officials enjoy luxuries, such as access to cars and certain consumer goods. The majority of Angolans are struggling to survive.

WORLD RANKING

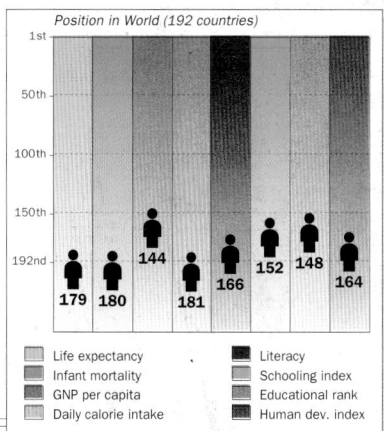

Position in World (192 countries)

179   180   144   181   166   152   148   164

Life expectancy   Literacy
Infant mortality   Schooling index
GNP per capita   Educational rank
Daily calorie intake   Human dev. index

A

ANTARCTICA

OFFICIAL NAME: Antarctica **CAPITAL:** *None*
POPULATION: 4000 **CURRENCY:** *None* **OFFICIAL LANGUAGE:** None

ANTARCTICA

T HE FIFTH-LARGEST CONTINENT, Antarctica is almost entirely covered by ice over 1 mile thick. The area sustains a varied wildlife, including seals, whales and penguins. The Antarctic Treaty, signed in 1959 and enforced in 1961, provides for international governance of Antarctica. To gain Consultative Status, countries have to set up a program of scientific research in the continent. Several countries support the proposal that Antarctica should become a world park.

CLIMATE

WEATHER CHART

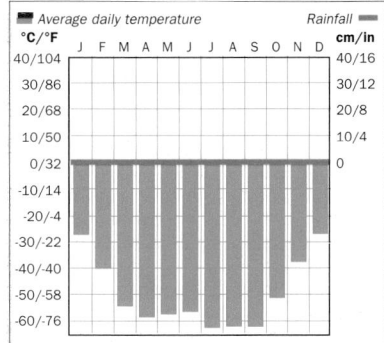

Antarctica is the windiest as well as the coldest continent. Powerful winds create a narrow storm belt around the continent, which brings cloud, fog and severe blizzards. Icebergs, which tend to be slab-shaped, barricade more than 90% of the coastline. Antarctica contains over 80% of the world's fresh water in the form of ice. The blood of polar fish contains anti-freeze agents.

TRANSPORTATION

Airstrips to some stations

Has no fleet

Ships are the main mode of transportation to Antarctica. They are also used for marine research projects. Air traffic from Chile is growing, and France and the UK are building new airstrips. Most planes have to be equipped with skis.

TOURISM

 3,000 visitors

Small increase from year to year

Tourism is mainly by cruise ship to the Antarctic Peninsula, Ross Sea and the sub-Antarctic islands. In 1983, the Chileans began flights to King George Island, where an 80-bed hotel has been built. Main attractions are the wildlife, skiing, and visits to scientific stations and historic huts. The growth of tourism has disrupted scientific programs and official regulation of tourism is now essential.

PEOPLE

English, Spanish, French, Norwegian, Chinese, Polish, Russian, German, Japanese

0 people per sq. mile

ETHNIC MAKEUP

Antarctica has a transient population of Americans, English, French, Norwegians, Argentinians, Chileans, Chinese, Russians, Poles and Japanese. Most are involved in research. Few stay more than two years.

Antarctica has no indigenous population. The people who live in the continent are scientists and logistical staff working at the 40 permanent, and as many as 100 temporary, research stations. Most stations are too far apart for direct contact between different nationalities. A few Chilean settler families are resident on King George Island.

ANTARCTICA

Total Land Area : 13 900 000 sq. km (5 366 790 sq. miles)

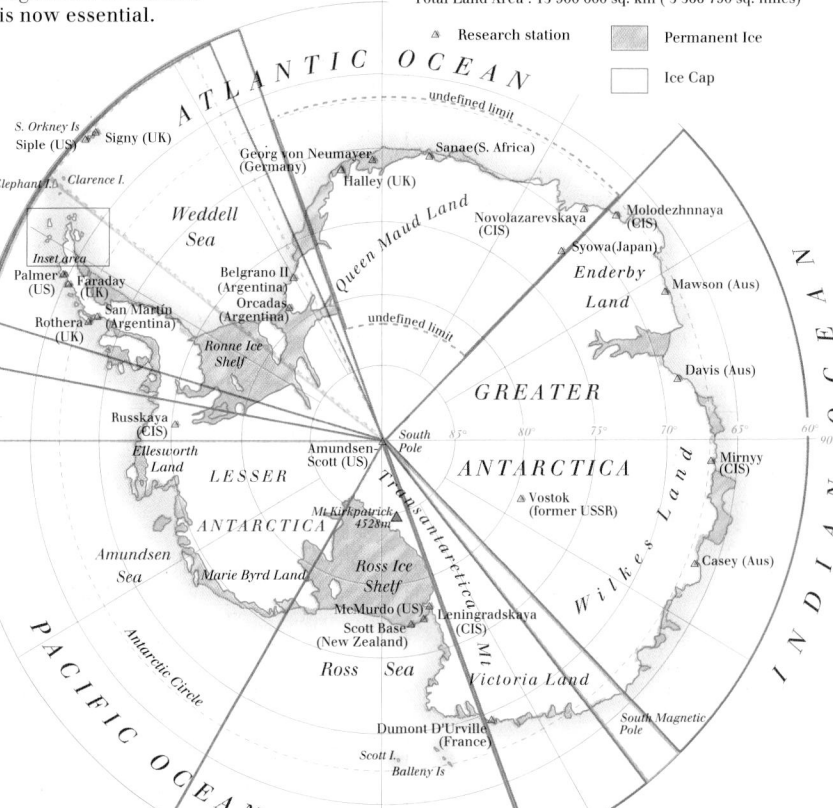

Research station

Permanent Ice

Ice Cap

TERRITORIAL CLAIMS

Australian claim   British claim   French claim   Norwegian claim

Argentinian claim   Chilean claim   New Zealand claim   Brazilian zone of interest

Antarctic Peninsula

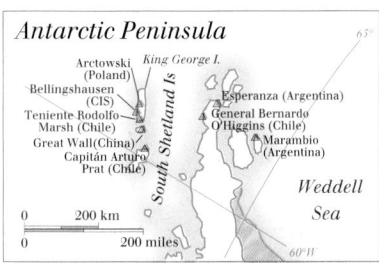

Neumayer Channel, Antarctica. Many states are pressing for the whole of Antarctica to be protected as an international park.

POLITICS

 Not applicable   Consultative Parties to Antarctic Treaty

THE STATE OF THE PARTIES

The Antarctic Treaty of 1959 was signed by 12 nations and acceded to by 26. Consultative meetings are held annually to discuss scientific, environmental and political matters

There are 26 signatories to the Antarctic Treaty and 14 nations with observer status. There are territorial claims by Australia, France, New Zealand and Norway, and overlapping claims in the Antarctic Peninsula by Argentina, Chile and the UK. Other states do not recognize these claims. Of main concern is the adoption of a wide range of environmental protection measures. Proposals include the monitoring of all scientific activities and prosecuting any country whose research would lead to detrimental global change.

WORLD AFFAIRS

    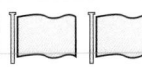

Rivalries exist between nations wishing to preserve Antarctica as a world park and those pursuing territorial claims.

AID

 Each country's research is government-funded   Subject to individual government budgets

Scientific programs in the Antarctic are almost entirely funded by government agencies in the home countries. Some funding is occasionally provided by scientific institutions and universities.

DEFENSE

 No defense force   Not applicable

Under the Antarctic Treaty, Antarctica can be used only for peaceful purposes. Any military personnel present perform purely scientific or logistical roles.

ECONOMICS

 Not applicable   Antarctica has no currency

Research is government-funded and therefore subject to cuts. The exploitation of marine stocks provides no income to Antarctica.

RESOURCES

 Each station has its own generator   Not an oil producer and has no refineries

 Included in national fish catch totals   Mineral extraction is banned

Antarctica's main resources are its marine stocks, including fin fish, seals and whales. A campaign by environmental groups, supported by Australia and France, to ban mining and declare Antarctica a world park was rewarded in 1991 with an agreement to impose a 50-year ban on mining, and in 1994 by the approval of a whale sanctuary. Prospects for alternative energy sources to fossil fuels, such as solar power and wind generators, are being explored.

ENVIRONMENT

 0.02%   1994 Antarctic whale sanctuary established

Antarctica is one of the last great wildernesses on Earth. Its layer of ice, 13,000 feet thick in places, has taken thousands of years to form. Its ecosystem is so fragile that even a footprint will leave its mark for years. Several species are unique to the continent, including King penguins. A major ecological concern in Antarctica is overfishing, particularly of krill, cod and squid. Also of concern is the depletion of the ozone layer over Antarctica, which may have adverse effects on phytoplankton, the foundation of the food chain for marine life. In 1994, the IWC agreed to a French proposal to create an Antarctic whale sanctuary. Together with the Indian Ocean sanctuary, this will protect the feeding grounds of 90% of the world's whales.

MEDIA

 There are no daily newspapers produced in Antarctica. Any papers would have to be brought in from the home countries

A few bases publish newsletters for local consumption. Local radio stations are found at some of the larger bases.

CRIME

 There are no prisons in Antarctica   Crime is negligible

Crime is negligible. Each person in Antarctica is subject to their national laws. Occasional petty theft from stations is linked to visits from tourists.

CHRONOLOGY

The Russian explorer, Thaddeus von Bellinghausen, was the first to sight Antarctica, in 1820. The South Pole was first reached by the Norwegian, Roald Amundsen, in December 1911.

❑ **1912** Scott leads UK expedition. All perish on return journey.
❑ **1957–1958** International Geophysical Year launches scientific exploration of Antarctica.
❑ **1959** Antarctic Treaty signed by 12 countries. Territorial claims frozen.
❑ **1978** Convention for the Conservation of Antarctic Seals.
❑ **1991** Agreement on 50-year ban on mineral extraction in Antarctica.
❑ **1994** Establishment of Antarctic whale sanctuary.

EDUCATION

 100%   None

Schoolhouses exist on the Chilean base, Villa Las Estrellas, and the Argentinian base, Esperanza. Teaching is geared to the relevant national system. Some researchers' studies contribute to higher degrees.

Antarctic-based research has resulted in a number of major scientific breakthroughs, including the discovery of ozone depletion.

HEALTH

 1 medical officer per station   Deaths are extremely rare in Antarctica

There is no central health system. Each station has its own medical officer who treats mostly minor complaints. Disease is rare as all personnel are medically screened. The problems usually associated with polar conditions, such as frostbite and snow blindness, are very rare. Serious illness cannot be treated locally, and patients have to be evacuated.

WEALTH

 Most Antarctic researchers draw salaries equivalent to their earnings at home

Wealth disparities reflect the different levels of funding received by each national base. The US bases are the best-funded. Most stations have a TV and video recorder. Telephone systems operate only within stations. PCs are supplied for scientific research. There are no cars.

WORLD RANKING

The UN Human Development Index conditions are not applicable to Antarctica.

A

ANTIGUA & BARBUDA

OFFICIAL NAME: Antigua and Barbuda   **CAPITAL:** St. John's
POPULATION: 65,000   **CURRENCY:** East Caribbean dollar   **OFFICIAL LANGUAGE:** English

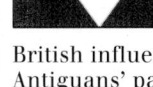

L OCATED BETWEEN THE Atlantic and the Caribbean, Antigua, one of the Leeward Islands, was in turn a Spanish, French and British colony. British influence is still strong, and most clearly revealed in the Antiguans' passion for cricket. Antigua has two remote dependencies: Barbuda, 30 miles to the northeast, sporting a magnificent beach; and Redonda, 25 miles southwest, an uninhabited rock with its own king.

CLIMATE

WEATHER CHART

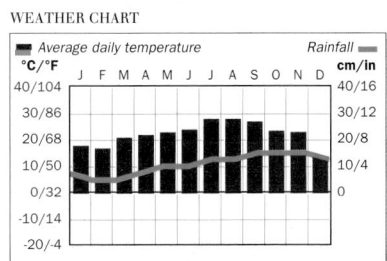

Antigua is less humid than other Caribbean islands. Year-round trade winds moderate the heat.

TRANSPORTATION

V C Bird International, St. John's
727,292 passengers

310 ships
1.21m dwt

THE TRANSPORTATION NETWORK

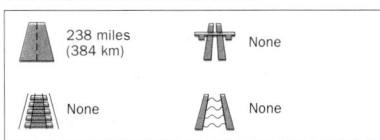

238 miles (384 km)	None
None	None

Encouraging tourism lies behind two recent projects: the improvement of the international airport and an extended pier at St. John's to take cruise ships.

TOURISM

255,000 visitors   Up 6% in 1995

MAIN OVERSEAS ARRIVALS

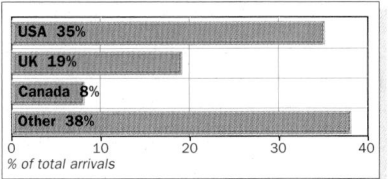

| USA 35% |
| UK 19% |
| Canada 8% |
| Other 38% |

% of total arrivals

Antigua is increasingly popular with US cruise-ship tourists and the yachting rich who attend the annual Sailing Week. The 18th-century Nelson's Dockyard at. St. John's is a major attraction.

PEOPLE

English, English patois

384 people per sq. mile

THE URBAN/RURAL POPULATION SPLIT

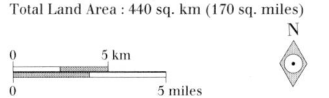

36%   64%

RELIGIOUS PERSUASION

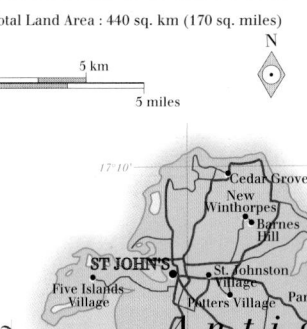

Other 3%
Roman Catholic 10%
Anglican 45%
Other Protestant 42%

Most of Antigua's population is descended from Africans, brought over between the 16th and 19th centuries. There are, in addition, a few Europeans and South Asians. Racial tensions are few. Life is based around the extended family. Since the 1960s, the status of women has risen as a result of their greater access to education, and many are now entering the legal, financial and medical professions. Unemployment is low and wealth disparities are small.

ANTIGUA & BARBUDA

Total Land Area : 440 sq. km (170 sq. miles)

POLITICS

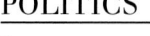
U. House 1994/1999
L. House 1994/1999
H.M. Queen Elizabeth II

THE STATE OF THE PARTIES

House of Representatives 17 members

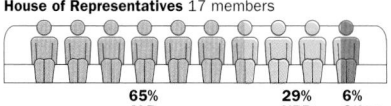

65% **ALP**   29% **UPP**   6% **Other**

ALP = Antigua Labour Party   **UPP** = United Progressive Party
BPM = Barbuda People's Movement

Senate 17 members

11 members chosen by the prime minister, 4 by the leader of the opposition, 1 by the governor-general and 1 by the Barbuda Council

Antigua's multiparty democracy has been dominated for the past 30 years by the Bird family. Vere Bird Sr., veteran prime minister and ALP leader, retired in 1993 and a battle between his two sons to succeed him was won by Lester Bird after Vere Jr. was barred from holding public office, having been accused of involvement in gun-running. Lester Bird won the 1994 general election and introduced stern measures to restructure the economy. New taxes provoked public protests in 1995.

POPULATION

● over 10 000
• under 10 000

LAND HEIGHT

200m/656ft
Sea Level

WORLD AFFAIRS

 ACS Caricom Comm OECS  OAS

Antigua backs US policy in the Caribbean, supporting both the US invasion of Grenada in 1983 and economic sanctions against Cuba.

AID

 $3m (receipts)   Down 40% in 1993

Donors, which include the USA, UK and France, have expressed concern that project development aid may have been misused by the Bird regime. The EU gives aid under the Lomé Convention.

DEFENSE

 $3.3m   No change in 1995

The USA and UK are the main suppliers of equipment and training to the small army and coastguard. The army is not involved in politics. Two military bases on Antigua are leased to the USA.

ECONOMICS

 $453m    2.69–2.70 East Caribbean dollars

SCORE CARD

❏ WORLD GNP RANKING	164th
❏ GNP PER CAPITA	$6,970
❏ BALANCE OF PAYMENTS	$–18m
❏ INFLATION	3.5%
❏ UNEMPLOYMENT	6%

STRENGTHS
Tourism is a growing business. The extension of the pier at St. John's has encouraged more cruise-ship trade. Sailing Week has proved a great success, attracting world-class competition every April.

WEAKNESSES
Very little diversification makes Antigua vulnerable to downturns in the world tourism market.

EXPORTS

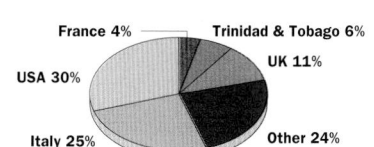

St Kitts & Nevis 3%
Dominica 3%
St Lucia 3%
Trinidad & Tobago 3%
Barbados 6%
Other 82%

IMPORTS

France 4%
Trinidad & Tobago 6%
UK 11%
USA 30%
Other 24%
Italy 25%

Nelson's Dockyard. *Luxury yachts fitted with 20th-century, state-of-the-art gadgetry contrast with the 18th-century St. John's harbor.*

RESOURCES

 95m kwh (capacity 30,000 kw)   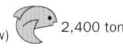 2,400 tons

 16,000 cattle, 13,000 sheep, 12,000 goats   None

Antigua has no strategic or commodity resources and has to import almost all its energy requirements.

ENVIRONMENT

 9%   Continuing state failure to control hotel development

Uncontrolled sewage disposal from beachfront hotels causes problems. In the 1990 McKinnon Swamp incident, untreated hotel effluent killed valuable inshore fish stocks. Antigua's mangrove systems are also threatened by hotel developments.

MEDIA

 Laws forbid political interference with the media, but the opposition press still faces suppression

PUBLISHING AND BROADCAST MEDIA

 There is 1 daily newspaper, the *Observer*. The leading paper is the weekly *Outlet*

 1 state-owned, 1 independent service   1 state-owned, 2 independent services

There is one independent newspaper in Antigua and Barbuda. Three of the weekly newspapers are published by political parties; the fourth is funded by the government.

CRIME

 Antigua and Barbuda does not publish prison figures   There are no particularly dangerous areas on the islands

Murder is rare on Antigua and Barbuda. Rape, armed robbery and burglary are the main local concerns.

EDUCATION

 96%   631 students

Education is based on the British selective 11-plus system. Students go on to the University of the West Indies, or to study in the UK or the USA.

HEALTH

  1 per 3,750 people   Heart and respiratory diseases, cancers

By Caribbean standards, Antigua and Barbuda's health system is extremely efficient, with easy access to the state-run clinics and hospitals.

WEALTH

 Minimum wage 4 East Caribbean dollars ($1.50) per hour

CONSUMER GOODS OWNERSHIP

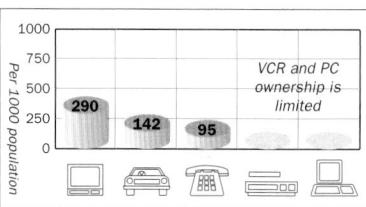

VCR and PC ownership is limited

Per 1000 population: 290, 142, 95

Antigua is fairly socially mobile. Wealthier Antiguans are involved in the tourist industry; Japanese cars, BMWs and satellite dishes are their favored status symbols.

WORLD RANKING

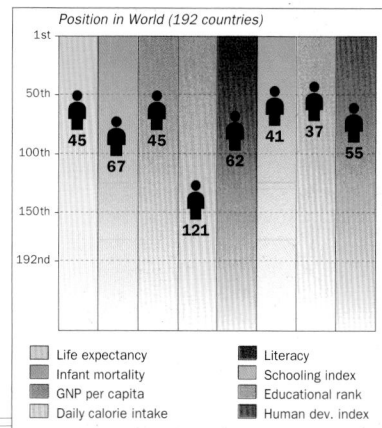

Position in World (192 countries)

45, 67, 45, 121, 62, 41, 37, 55

Life expectancy
Infant mortality
GNP per capita
Daily calorie intake
Literacy
Schooling index
Educational rank
Human dev. index

A

ARGENTINA

OFFICIAL NAME: Argentine Republic   **CAPITAL:** Buenos Aires
POPULATION: 34.6 million   **CURRENCY:** Argentine peso   **OFFICIAL LANGUAGE:** Spanish

SOUTH AMERICA

OCCUPYING MOST OF THE southern half of South America, Argentina extends 2,145 miles from Bolivia to Cape Horn. The Andes mountains in the west run north–south, forming a natural border with Chile. To the east they slope down to the fertile central pampas, the region known as Entre Ríos. Agriculture, especially beef, wheat and fruit, and energy resources are Argentina's main sources of wealth. Politics in Argentina has been characterized in the past by periods of military rule. In 1983, however, Argentina returned to multiparty democracy.

Herding cattle *in the northeast, near Corrientes. Beef, Argentina's first source of wealth, remains a major export.*

CLIMATE

WEATHER CHART

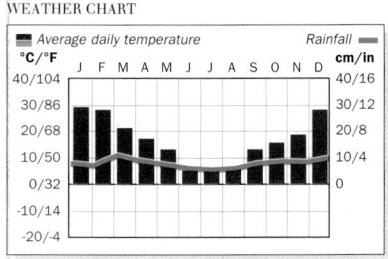

The northeast is near-tropical. The Andes are semi-arid in the north and snowy in the south. The western lowlands are desert, while the pampas have a mild climate with heavy summer rains.

TRANSPORTATION

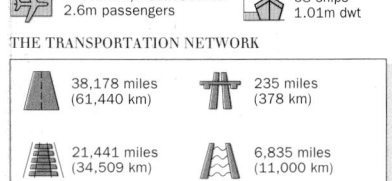

Ezeiza Intl, Buenos Aires
2.6m passengers

68 ships
1.01m dwt

THE TRANSPORTATION NETWORK

38,178 miles (61,440 km)	235 miles (378 km)
21,441 miles (34,509 km)	6,835 miles (11,000 km)

The government is seeking to privatize as much of the transportation network as possible. The state airline, *Aerolíneas Argentinas*, has been successfully sold off to the Spanish national carrier, *Iberia*. Argentina's antiquated rail system will be harder to sell, even in the proposed regional sections, which will end the notion of a national railroad. In 1993, virtually the whole system was temporarily closed down, threatening 20,000 jobs.

Private investment is also being sought for new toll roads and for a massive plan to link Buenos Aires to Uruguay and Brazil with a tunnel under the River Plate. Road deaths remain a major problem; Argentina has one of the worst fatality rates in the world.

TOURISM

3.87m visitors

Up 9% in 1994

MAIN OVERSEAS ARRIVALS

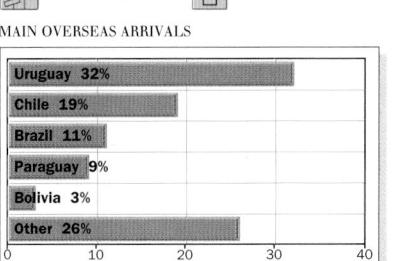

% of total arrivals

Although tourism is a significant export earner, Argentina is still on the fringe of the world tourism market as 80% of foreign visitors come from adjoining countries, attracted mainly by Buenos Aires' city life and the ski resorts. The resort of Mar del Plata on the coast and the ski stations in the Córdoba highlands have become mass tourism destinations. Wealthy Argentinians, however, are abandoning these in favor of foreign trips. The rash of privatization plans includes the very popular state-run casinos.

PEOPLE

Spanish, Italian, Indian languages

34 people per sq. mile

THE URBAN/RURAL POPULATION SPLIT

87%   13%

RELIGIOUS PERSUASION

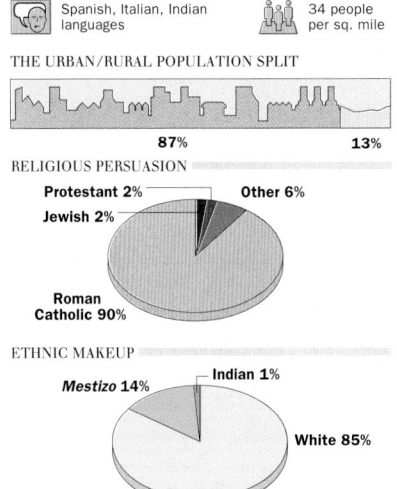

The large proportion of Argentinians of European descent are from recent 20th-century migrations; over one-third are of Italian origin. Indigenous peoples are now a minority, living mainly in Andean regions or in the *Gran Chaco*. Over 85% of Argentinians are urban dwellers, with 40% living in the capital, Buenos Aires. In general,

POPULATION AGE BREAKDOWN

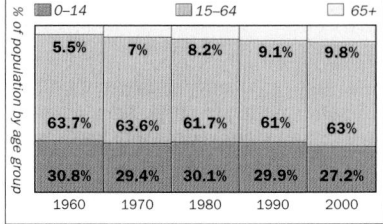

% of population by age group	1960	1970	1980	1990	2000
65+	5.5%	7%	8.2%	9.1%	9.8%
15–64	63.7%	63.6%	61.7%	61%	63%
0–14	30.8%	29.4%	30.1%	29.9%	27.2%

there is little ethnic tension. Bolivian and Paraguayan immigrants remain the poorest groups.

Catholicism and the extended family remain strong in Argentina, and social and religious reunions are common. The family also forms the basis of many successful businesses.

Women have a higher profile than in most Latin American countries. Argentinian women were enfranchised before their French counterparts received the vote. Today, many enter the professions and rise to positions of influence in service businesses such as the media. The exception is politics. Eva Perón, who inspired the musical *Evita*, did help to push women into a more active political role in the 1940s and 1950s, but this trend was reversed under military rule.

A

POLITICS

U. House 1992/1997
L. House 1995/1997

President Carlos
Saúl Menem

Argentina is a multiparty democracy; the president is head of state.

MAIN POLITICAL ISSUES
Restoring economic confidence
Carlos Menem's vigorous free-market and privatization policies lowered inflation from over 7,000% to 18% by 1992 and the currency was pegged to the dollar. The government now has to raise tax revenues while simultaneously restoring confidence after growth contracted by 2.5% in 1995, unemployment soared to 19% and $8 billion fled the country following the Mexican financial crisis.

Style of government
Menem called an election in 1994 to allow himself to amend the constitution so that he could stand again. Since being reelected in 1995 his increasing use of vetoes and decrees to secure his free-market policies has provoked resentment in the Congress and at large. Congress reluctantly approved his request for emergency powers in February 1996 to carry out a "second reform of the state."

The role of the military
Following the military's fall from power in 1983, officers were tried during Alfonsín's administration for the murder of thousands of "suspects." Menem later pardoned officers and in 1995 the Chiefs of Staff publicly admitted responsibility for past abuses. Many people remain suspicious of the military's political agenda.

THE STATE OF THE PARTIES

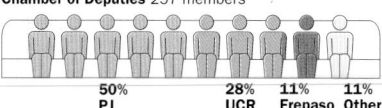

Chamber of Deputies 257 members

| 50% PJ | 28% UCR | 11% Frepaso | 11% Other |

PJ = Justicialist Party (Peronists)   **UCR** = Radical Civic Union
Frepaso = Front for a Country in Solidarity
Other = Movement for Dignity and Independence (Modin) and Union of the Democratic Center (UCeD)

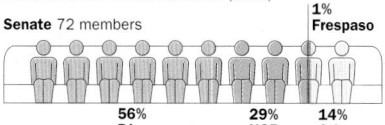

Senate 72 members   1% Frepaso

| 56% PJ | 29% UCR | 14% Other |

PROFILE
The Peronists have been the dominant civilian political force in Argentina since the 1940s. The party was founded on mass working-class and left-wing intellectual support inimical to the military which promoted its own interests and that of the right and mounted coups in 1955, 1966 and 1976. The UCR has tended to stay in opposition, except when the electorate wishes to register a protest vote, as in 1983. Carlos Menem won elections in 1989 on a populist, left-wing platform but quickly steered the Peronists to the right. His free-market policies attracted the support of conservatives and ended hyperinflation, important factors behind his reelection in 1995.

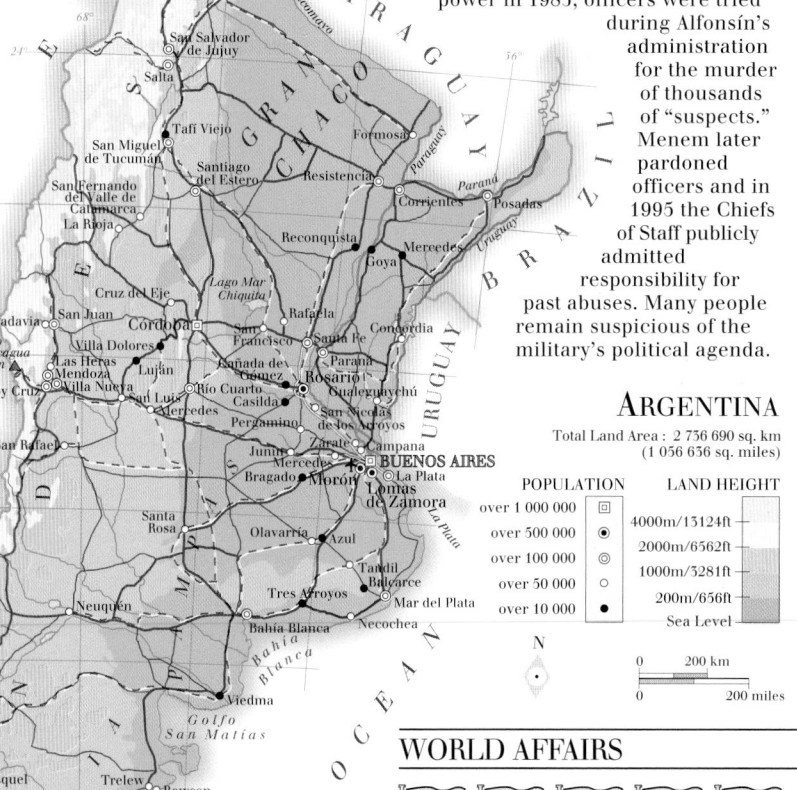

ARGENTINA

Total Land Area : 2 736 690 sq. km
(1 056 636 sq. miles)

POPULATION		LAND HEIGHT	
over 1 000 000	▣	4000m/13124ft	
over 500 000	◉	2000m/6562ft	
over 100 000	◎	1000m/3281ft	
over 50 000	○	200m/656ft	
over 10 000	●	Sea Level	

N

0   200 km

0   200 miles

Carlos Menem, Justicialist Party (Peronist) leader; president since 1989.

Domingo Cavallo, finance minister and architect of radical privatization.

WORLD AFFAIRS

 ALADI   Mercsr   OAS   RG   WTO

Argentina's claim to the Falkland Islands remains at the top of its foreign policy agenda. Following the failure to take the islands from the UK by military action in 1982–1983, the claim is now being pursued through diplomatic channels. Bilateral relations have improved to the point where both heads of state met in 1995; both sides continued talks on fisheries and signed a Falklands Islands oil exploration and production agreement.

Argentina is keen to move closer to the USA, which had traditionally been treated with suspicion by the Peronists. The main reason for the change in policy is Argentina's move away, under the Menem administration, from state-run businesses to American-style free-market economics, and the need to attract US investment. Trade relations with Brazil, Paraguay and Uruguay are being pursued vigorously. The four states formed a common market in 1995 geared to the gradual elimination of all trade tariffs.

Argentina is promoting itself as a member of the "first world." Making its forces available to the UN is part of this strategy, as is the idea of a South Atlantic Defense Alliance with South Africa.

AID

 $283m (receipts)   No significant change from year to year

Receipts, other than restructured loan arrangements with international bodies, are modest. A $7 billion IMF-led financial rescue plan was approved in 1995.

CHRONOLOGY

The Spanish first established settlements in the Andean foothills in 1543. The indigenous Indians, who had stopped any Inca advance into their territory, also prevented the Spaniards from settling in the east until the 1590s.

- ❑ 1816 United Provinces of Río de la Plata declare independence; 70 years of civil war follow between central government unitarists and provincial federalists.
- ❑ 1835–1852 Dictatorship of Juan Manuel Rosas.
- ❑ 1853 Federal system set up.
- ❑ 1857 Europeans start settling the pampas; six million by 1930. Most land is held by an oligarchy of 200 families.
- ❑ 1877 First refrigerated ship starts frozen beef trade to Europe.
- ❑ 1878–1883 War against the Pampas Indians almost exterminates them.
- ❑ 1916 Hipólito Yrigoyen wins first democratic presidential elections.
- ❑ 1930 Military coup upsets republican constitution.
- ❑ 1943 New military coup. Juan Perón organizes trade unions.
- ❑ 1946 General Juan Perón elected president, with backing of the military and organized labor.
- ❑ 1952 Eva Perón, wife of Juan Perón and charismatic champion of workers' welfare, dies of leukemia.
- ❑ 1955 Military coup ousts Perón. Inflation, strikes, unemployment.
- ❑ 1973 Perón returns from exile in Madrid and is reelected president.
- ❑ 1974 Perón dies; succeeded by his third wife "Isabelita," who is unable to control either left-wing Peronist or urban guerrilla violence.
- ❑ 1976 Military junta under General Videla seizes power. Political parties are banned. Brutal repression of Dirty War sees "disappearance" of over 10,000 "left-wing suspects."
- ❑ 1981 General Galtieri president.
- ❑ 1982 Galtieri orders invasion of Falkland Islands. UK retakes them.
- ❑ 1983 Pro-human rights candidate Raúl Alfonsín (UCR) becomes president in free multiparty elections. Hyperinflation.
- ❑ 1989–1992 Carlos Menem wins presidency. Inflation down to 18%.
- ❑ 1995 Menem reelected. Economy enters recession.

DEFENSE

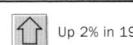 $3.1bn   ⬆ Up 2% in 1995

0	Defense spending as % GDP	40

1.7%

ARGENTINIAN ARMED FORCES

🪖	296 main battle tanks (96 M-4 *Sherman*, 200 TAM)	40,400 personnel
🚢	3 submarines, 6 destroyers, 7 frigates	18,000 personnel
✈	237 combat aircraft (42 *Mirage* IIIC/IIIEA/5P, 22 *Dagger Nesher*)	8,900 personnel
🚀	None	

Despite the military's fall from power in 1983, its influence remains strong. The amnesty to officers found guilty of human rights abuses during the military dictatorship was condemned by human rights groups who were not placated by the military's admissions of guilt in 1995.

Argentina has a well-developed arms industry, much of it built up with Israeli assistance. France was a major source of weapons – the role of *Mirage* fighters and *Exocet* missiles was well publicized during the Falklands war. Recently, the air force has been buying US fighter aircraft. Argentina, despite having signed the Nuclear Non-Proliferation Treaty, is suspected of being close to achieving an independent nuclear capability.

ECONOMICS

 $275.6bn    0.99–1.00 Argentine pesos

SCORE CARD

- ❑ WORLD GNP RANKING..........................17th
- ❑ GNP PER CAPITA $8,060
- ❑ BALANCE OF PAYMENTS...................$–7.4bn
- ❑ INFLATION 2.7%
- ❑ UNEMPLOYMENT...................................19%

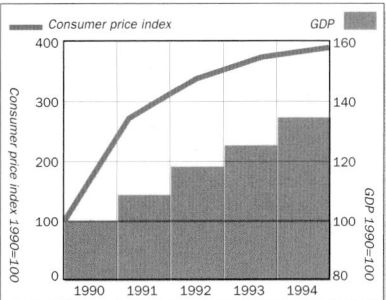

ECONOMIC PERFORMANCE INDICATOR

— Consumer price index   ▧ GDP

EXPORTS

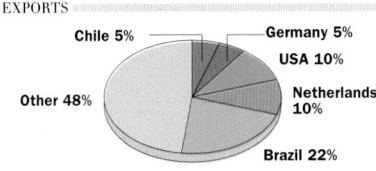

Chile 5%   Germany 5%   USA 10%   Netherlands 10%   Other 48%   Brazil 22%

IMPORTS

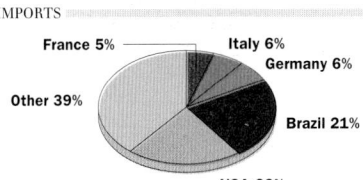

France 5%   Italy 6%   Germany 6%   Other 39%   Brazil 21%   USA 23%

STRENGTHS

A rich and varied agricultural base, powerful agribusiness (mainly beef, wheat, fruit, wine), a wealth of energy resources and a skilled labor force are major strengths. Economic reforms, in particular currency stabilization and the reduction in inflation, have attracted overseas investors.

WEAKNESSES

The recent history of hyperinflation still casts doubts over the longevity of low inflation. Regional nervousness about currency stability provoked capital flight of $8 billion in 1995. Privatization successes have added to record unemployment, while many major businesses still remain under highly inefficient state control. A long history of political instability remains a deterrent to long-term investment.

PROFILE

Hyperinflation during the 1980s made economic planning impossible. Menem's government was the first to tackle the problem head-on, by imposing wage freezes, refusing to print money to finance deficits and introducing a new stable currency, the peso. Inflation dropped, and the government began reversing Perón's major legacy, nationalization. The economy, however, remains vulnerable to external pressures.

ARGENTINA : MAJOR BUSINESSES

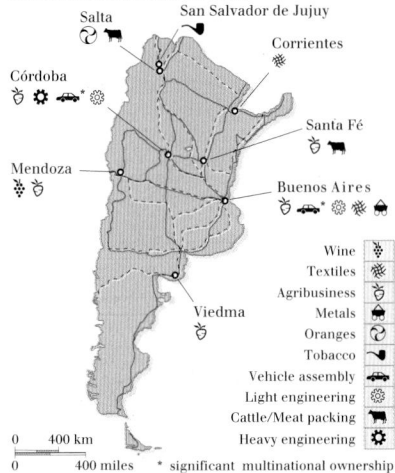

Wine	🍇
Textiles	✴
Agribusiness	🐂
Metals	♠
Oranges	🍊
Tobacco	🚬
Vehicle assembly	🚗
Light engineering	🔧
Cattle/Meat packing	🐄
Heavy engineering	⚙

0	400 km
0	400 miles

* significant multinational ownership

RESOURCES

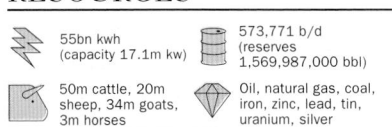

55bn kwh
(capacity 17.1m kw)

573,771 b/d
(reserves
1,569,987,000 bbl)

50m cattle, 20m
sheep, 34m goats,
3m horses

Oil, natural gas, coal,
iron, zinc, lead, tin,
uranium, silver

ELECTRICITY GENERATION

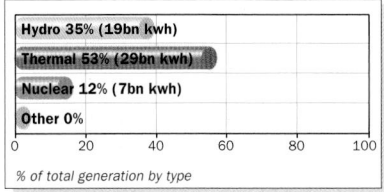

Hydro 35% (19bn kwh)

Thermal 53% (29bn kwh)

Nuclear 12% (7bn kwh)

Other 0%

% of total generation by type

Only one-third of Argentina has been properly surveyed for oil and other mineral resources. Important known

ENVIRONMENT

1.6% (2% partially
protected)

Increasing general
interest in
environmental issues

ENVIRONMENTAL TREATIES

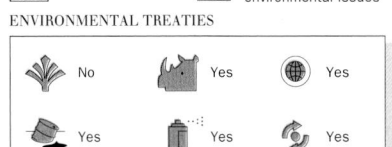

No

Yes

Yes

Yes

Yes

Yes

Nuclear power was encouraged by the military, which covered up leaks and accidents from the two main plants – Atocha I and II. Otherwise, the main concerns are the extreme pollution of rivers in Buenos Aires, the 50% depletion of the ozone layer in southern regions and the illegal export of rare birds, particularly from the north.

Environmental issues are of increasing interest to the electorate, but have yet to make a political impact. In 1993, however, residents in Tierra del Fuego succeeded in diverting an oil pipeline to save a colony of penguins.

MEDIA

Freedom guaranteed by the constitution, but media subject to government pressure in practice

PUBLISHING AND BROADCAST MEDIA

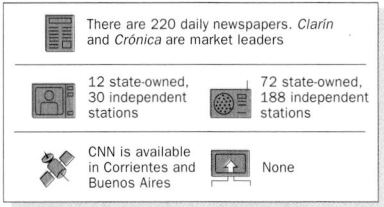

There are 220 daily newspapers. *Clarín* and *Crónica* are market leaders

12 state-owned,
30 independent
stations

72 state-owned,
188 independent
stations

CNN is available
in Corrientes and
Buenos Aires

None

The press in Argentina was liberated under the UCR (1983–1989). Many journalists were killed in the late 1970s for expressing their political beliefs. The Menem administration is once again applying pressure on the media, by withdrawing state advertising from newspapers critical of its policies.

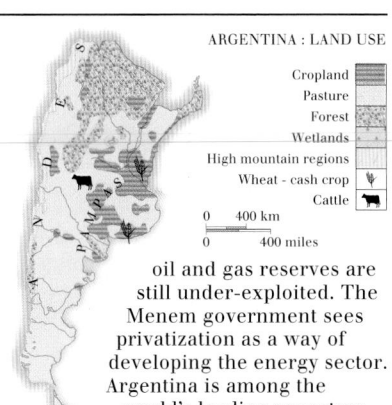

ARGENTINA : LAND USE

Cropland
Pasture
Forest
Wetlands
High mountain regions
Wheat - cash crop
Cattle

0　　400 km

0　　400 miles

oil and gas reserves are still under-exploited. The Menem government sees privatization as a way of developing the energy sector. Argentina is among the world's leading exporters of beef, wheat and fruit.

CRIME

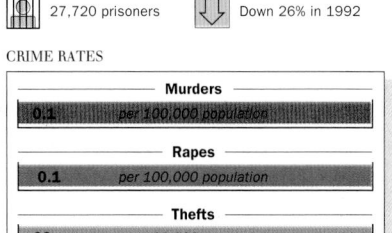

27,720 prisoners

Down 26% in 1992

CRIME RATES

Murders

0.1　*per 100,000 population*

Rapes

0.1　*per 100,000 population*

Thefts

63　*per 100,000 population*

Buenos Aires remains one of the safest cities in Latin America, apart from the shanty town areas, where crime is rising. Narcotics-money laundering is also a growing problem. The army has still not recovered respect following the human rights abuses of the 1970s.

EDUCATION

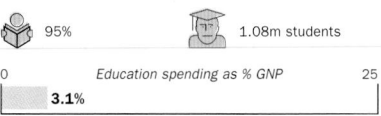

95%

1.08m students

0　*Education spending as % GNP*　25

3.1%

THE EDUCATION SYSTEM

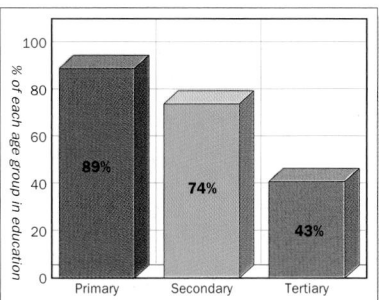

% of each age group in education

89%　Primary

74%　Secondary

43%　Tertiary

Schooling is effectively a mix of the French and US systems. Schools in the interior have the highest drop-out rate. Argentina has a strong tertiary sector, with most students attending free state universities.

HEALTH

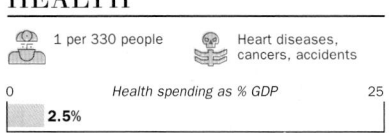

1 per 330 people

Heart diseases,
cancers, accidents

0　*Health spending as % GDP*　25

2.5%

Health care in Argentina is nationwide and Argentina has proportionally more doctors than the USA. Doctors charge, but most Argentinians are covered by insurance policies. High-technology equipment is concentrated in private Buenos Aires hospitals. A Worker's Health Plan system, introduced by the Menem administration, is nominally aimed at improving care for the poor.

WEALTH

Chambermaid, 80 Argentine pesos ($80) per month; company director, 5,000 Argentine pesos ($5,000) per month

CONSUMER GOODS OWNERSHIP

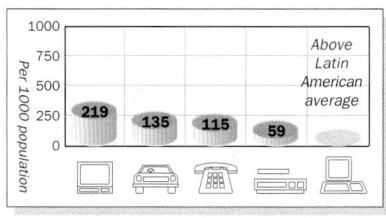

Per 1000 population

Above Latin American average

219　135　115　59

Considerable social mobility can still be achieved in Argentina. The wealthy travel in private jets to their *estancias* (country estates), holiday in Europe and the USA, and play polo and rugby. Argentina is a major market for designer labels – Rolex watches, BMW cars and Italian fashion are particularly favored. Middle-income groups travel to resorts such as Punta del Este in Uruguay or Copacabana in Brazil, and enjoy the European lifestyle of Buenos Aires, which boasts a world-class opera house. The standard of living of the underclass, most of whom are from poor rural interior provinces and trying to find work in Buenos Aires, has been falling since Menem took power.

WORLD RANKING

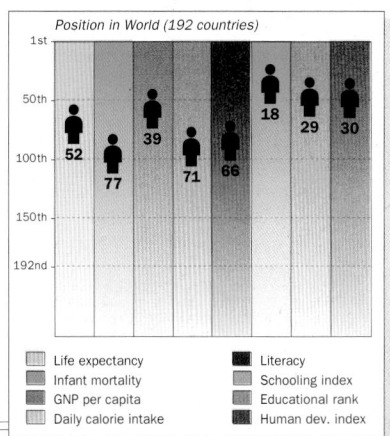

Position in World (192 countries)

1st

50th

100th

150th

192nd

52　77　39　71　66　18　29　30

Life expectancy

Infant mortality

GNP per capita

Daily calorie intake

Literacy

Schooling index

Educational rank

Human dev. index

A

ARMENIA

OFFICIAL NAME: Republic of Armenia **CAPITAL:** Yerevan
POPULATION: 3.6 million **CURRENCY:** Dram **OFFICIAL LANGUAGE:** Armenian

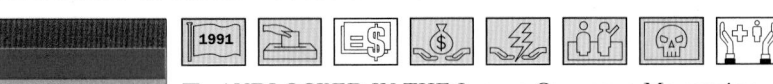

EUROPE

ANDLOCKED IN THE Lesser Caucasus Mountains, Armenia is the smallest of the former USSR's republics and was the first to adopt Christianity as its state religion. It is bordered by Muslim states to the south, east and west. Keen to develop links with the CIS, Armenia has kept to a path of radical economic reform including privatization. War with Azerbaijan over the enclave of Nagorno Karabakh has dominated national life since 1988.

Landscape near Yerevan. Armenia's very dry climate results in expanses of semi-desert. Its famous vineyards flourish in sheltered areas.

CLIMATE

WEATHER CHART

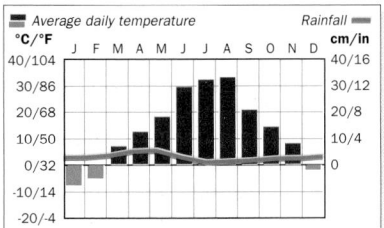

Armenia has a continental climate, with little rainfall in the lowlands. Winters can be very cold.

TRANSPORTATION

✈ Yerevan Intl   Has no fleet

THE TRANSPORTATION NETWORK

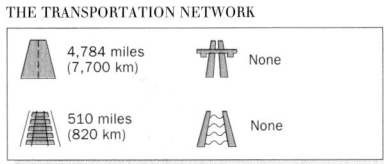

| 4,784 miles (7,700 km) | None |
| 510 miles (820 km) | None |

Public transportation has been badly hit by the war-induced fuel crisis, and the main road to Georgia is cut because it crosses Azerbaijani territory. The vital Aras bridge to Iran reopened in 1992.

TOURISM

Very few, due to war with Azerbaijan   Similar levels from year to year

MAIN OVERSEAS ARRIVALS

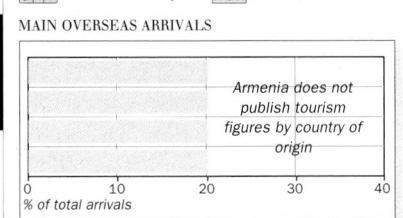

Armenia does not publish tourism figures by country of origin

0   10   20   30   40
% of total arrivals

War has discouraged visitors. Ancient churches and the cellar vaults of the cognac-producing regions are Armenia's main attractions.

PEOPLE

Armenian, Russian   314 people per sq. mile

THE URBAN/RURAL POPULATION SPLIT

68%   **32%**

ETHNIC MAKEUP

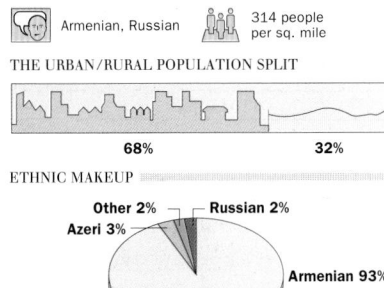

Other 2%   Russian 2%
Azeri 3%
                                    Armenian 93%

Minority nationalities are well integrated into the Armenian population. Very strong contacts are maintained with the large number of Armenian emigrants, estimated at some nine million in the USA, France and Syria. Some 100,000 Armenians who lived in Azerbaijan have been forced to return home since the outbreak of war.

POLITICS

1995/2000   President Levon Ter-Petrossian

THE STATE OF THE PARTIES

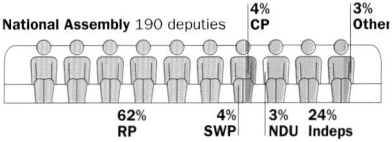

National Assembly 190 deputies   4% CP   3% Other

62% RP   4% SWP   3% NDU   24% Indeps

RP = Republican Bloc **SWP** = Shamiram Women's Party
CP = Communist Party **NDU** = National Democratic Union
Indeps = Independents

Armenia has been a multiparty democracy since 1991. The first parliamentary elections since independence to the newly created National Assembly, held in July 1995, resulted in the emergence of the Republican Bloc, of which the president's party, the Armenian Pan-National Movement was the major element. A referendum on a new constitution decided that Armenia should be a presidential republic. The current prime minister, who was appointed by President Ter-Petrossian, is Hrand Bagratian, a young radical economist. The war with Azerbaijan, over the issue of whether the Armenian enclave of Nagorno Karabakh inside Azerbaijan should become part of Armenia, dominates politics. Some nationalist-oriented opposition parties advocate the independence of Nagorno Karabakh.

ARMENIA

Total Land Area : 29 800 sq. km
(11 506 sq. miles)

POPULATION

▣ over 1 000 000
◉ over 100 000
○ over 50 000
● over 10 000
• under 10 000

LAND HEIGHT

3000m/9843ft
2000m/6562ft
1000m/3281ft
500m/1640ft

WORLD AFFAIRS

 BSEC　 CIS　 IBRD　 NACC　 OSCE

The war with Azerbaijan dominates the agenda. Efforts to improve traditionally sour relations with Turkey have failed

AID

 $35m (receipts)　 The trend in receipts is up

Most funds have come from Armenians living abroad. Armenia is seeking aid from the EU for the Medzamor nuclear power plant, reactivated in 1995.

DEFENSE

 $77m　 Up 8% in 1995

The success of the armed forces in the war with Azerbaijan has increased their political profile and their independence from civilian control. In 1993, peace overtures to the Azeris by Armenia's President Ter-Petrossian were ignored by the army, which mounted a further offensive into Nagorno Karabakh.

ECONOMICS

 $2.5bn　 403–406 dram

SCORE CARD

❑ WORLD GNP RANKING	129th
❑ GNP PER CAPITA	$670
❑ BALANCE OF PAYMENTS	$–106m
❑ INFLATION	5273%
❑ UNEMPLOYMENT	6.4%

STRENGTHS

Strong ties with Armenian emigrants. Major deposits of rare metals, as yet unexploited. Well-developed machine-building and manufacturing – includes textiles and bottling of mineral water.

WEAKNESSES

Dependent on imported energy, raw materials and semi-finished goods. Gas pipeline through Azerbaijani-controlled region of Georgia often sabotaged.

EXPORTS

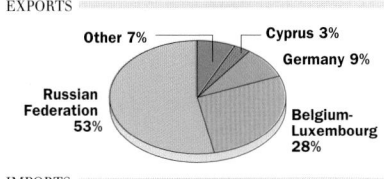

Other 7%
Cyprus 3%
Germany 9%
Russian Federation 53%
Belgium-Luxembourg 28%

IMPORTS

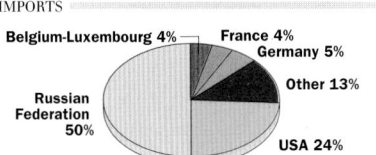

Belgium-Luxembourg 4%
France 4%
Germany 5%
Other 13%
Russian Federation 50%
USA 24%

---

following Armenia's military successes in Nagorno Karabakh. Relations with Iran have cooled as Azerbaijan has developed closer ties with Tehran. Moscow is less supportive of Armenia since Azerbaijan rejoined the CIS.

RESOURCES

 703m kwh　Minimal oil production

 4m poultry, 720,000 sheep, 502,000 cattle　Coal, oil, natural gas, rare metals

Armenia has negligible energy resources, but viable deposits of rare metals have been found. Arable land is scarce, producing mainly vegetables and grapes. Abundant sources of mineral water have given rise to a large bottling industry.

ENVIRONMENT

 7.2%　 War: all environmental measures on hold

The Medzamor nuclear power station was declared unsafe after the 1988 earthquake. It was reactivated in 1995, owing to the energy crisis, despite opposition from environmental groups. HEP generation near Lake Sevan has seriously reduced the lake's water level.

MEDIA

 Criticism of the government is not tolerated in practice

PUBLISHING AND BROADCAST MEDIA

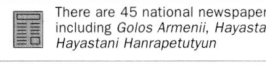

 There are 45 national newspapers, including *Golos Armenii*, *Hayastan* and *Hayastani Hanrapetutyun*

 1 state-controlled service　1 state-controlled service

There are many independent journals and newspapers, but government control of the paper industry gives it an effective censorship weapon.

CRIME

 Armenia does not publish prison figures　 Crime levels reasonably stable

Armenia's legal system survived within the Soviet system. Crime levels are lower than those of other ex-Soviet states. Amnesty International gives Armenia a clean bill of health.

EDUCATION

 99%　 67,019 students

The education system, previously conforming to that of the USSR, now emphasizes Armenian history and culture; 14% of the population have received higher education.

CHRONOLOGY

Armenia lost its autonomy in the 14th century. In 1639, Turkey took the west and Persia the east; Persia ceded its part to Russia in 1828.

- ❑ **1877–1878** Massacre of Armenians during Russo–Turkish war.
- ❑ **1915** Ottomans force 1.75 million Turkish Armenians into exile; most die.
- ❑ **1917–1918** Russian Armenia's anti-Bolshevik alliance with Georgia and Azerbaijan.
- ❑ **1920** Independence.
- ❑ **1922** Becomes a Soviet republic.
- ❑ **1988** Earthquake kills 25,000.
- ❑ **1990** Declares Nagorno Karabakh (in Azerbaijan) part of Armenia.
- ❑ **1991** Independence from USSR.
- ❑ **1995** First parliamentary elections.

HEALTH

 1 per 260 people　 Circulatory diseases, cancers, accidents, violence

Hospitals are suffering from the erratic electricity supply, while the breakdown in sewerage and other services has led to a rise in hepatitis and tuberculosis.

WEALTH

 Around 70% of the Armenian population live in poverty, as defined by the UN

CONSUMER GOODS OWNERSHIP

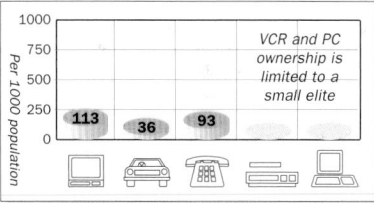

VCR and PC ownership is limited to a small elite

113　36　93

Per 1000 population

The richest Armenians are those living in the USA and France. The many refugees from Baku are the poorest.

WORLD RANKING

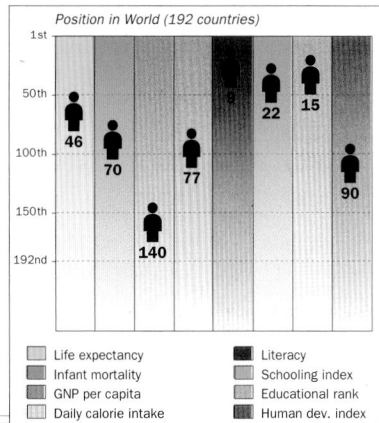

Position in World (192 countries)

46　70　140　77　22　15　90

Life expectancy
Infant mortality
GNP per capita
Daily calorie intake
Literacy
Schooling index
Educational rank
Human dev. index

A

AUSTRALIA

OFFICIAL NAME: Commonwealth of Australia   CAPITAL: Canberra
POPULATION: 17.8 million   CURRENCY: Australian dollar   OFFICIAL LANGUAGE: English   OVERSEAS TERRITORIES: 6

1901

THE WORLD'S SIXTH LARGEST COUNTRY, Australia is an island continent located between the Indian and Pacific oceans. Its six states and the Northern Territory have a variety of landscapes, including tropical rainforests, the deserts of the arid "red center," snow-capped mountains, rolling tracts of pastoral land and magnificent beaches. Famous natural features include Uluru (Ayers Rock) and the Great Barrier Reef. Most Australians live on the coast. All the state capitals, with the exception of Canberra, are coastal cities. The strip down the length of the eastern seaboard is the country's richest and most populous area. In 2000, Sydney will host the millennium Olympics.

Uluru (Ayers Rock), Northern Territory.
*The renaming of Ayers Rock reflects growing
Aboriginal influence in Australia.*

CLIMATE

WEATHER CHART

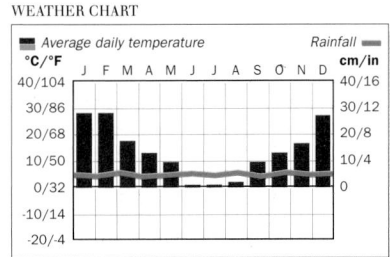

The interior, west and south are arid or semi-arid and very hot in summer; central desert temperatures can reach 120°F. The north, around Darwin and Cape York Peninsula, is hot all year and humid during the summer monsoon. Only the east and southeast within 250 miles of the coast, and the southwest around Perth are temperate. It is in these areas that most Australians live.

TRANSPORTATION

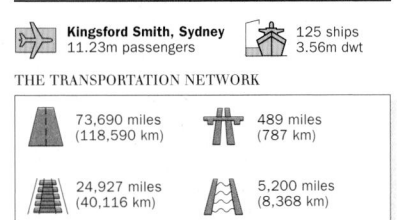

Kingsford Smith, Sydney
11.23m passengers

125 ships
3.56m dwt

THE TRANSPORTATION NETWORK

73,690 miles (118,590 km)	489 miles (787 km)
24,927 miles (40,116 km)	5,200 miles (8,368 km)

Air transportation is well developed and vital to Australia's sparsely populated center and west. Sydney suffers from air congestion; a third runway is being added to Kingsford Smith airport, and Sydney West airport is due to open in 1998. A high-speed train linking Sydney, Canberra and Melbourne is under discussion. Most freight in Australia travels in massive trucks known as "road trains." Improvements in urban transportation are a priority, particularly in Sydney, in the run-up to the 2000 Olympic Games.

TOURISM

3.3m visitors

Up 12% in 1994

MAIN OVERSEAS ARRIVALS

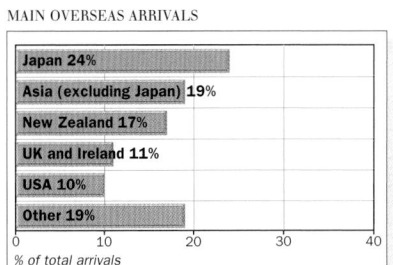

Tourism is now Australia's largest single foreign exchange earner, accounting for 10% of the total. Faster, cheaper air travel and highly successful government marketing campaigns draw tourists in increasing numbers, especially from Asia, which has been the focus of Australia's strategy to develop tourism's rich potential. The Japanese are now the largest single group of visitors, although many also come from Europe, North America and New Zealand. While Japanese tourists stay a shorter time – on average eight nights – they tend to spend more than other nationalities.

The country's attractions include wildlife, swimming and surfing off Pacific and Indian Ocean beaches, skin-diving along the Great Barrier Reef and skiing in the Australian Alps. Aboriginal culture and the town of Alice Springs are among the outback's attractions. The far north has tropical resorts, the northwest, pearl-fishing. The vineyards of the south and southeast attract many visitors, as do the cultural life of Melbourne and Sydney and the arts festivals held in state capitals. Sydney's hosting of the Olympic Games in 2000 will give the city a massive economic boost.

Growth, while still strong, is slowing from the phenomenal boom seen in the mid-1980s, when tourist arrivals rose by almost 200% in five years. One result of this is that the rush to invest has left many hotels, especially those at the luxury end of the market, struggling in the 1990s.

AUSTRALIA

Total Land Area : 7 617 930 sq. km (2 941 283 sq. miles)

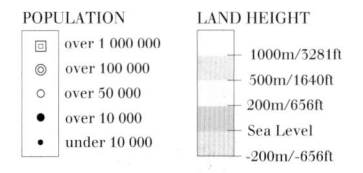

POPULATION

over 1 000 000
over 100 000
over 50 000
over 10 000
under 10 000

LAND HEIGHT

1000m/3281ft
500m/1640ft
200m/656ft
Sea Level
-200m/-656ft

PEOPLE

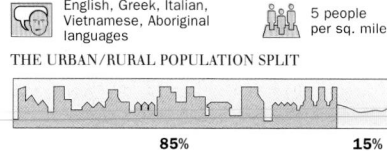

English, Greek, Italian, Vietnamese, Aboriginal languages

5 people per sq. mile

THE URBAN/RURAL POPULATION SPLIT

85%   15%

The first settlers arrived in Australia almost 100,000 years ago. Their modern descendants, the Aborigines, today make up less than 1% of the population. European settlement began in 1788 and was dominated by British and Irish immigrants – some of whom were convicts – until the gold rushes of the 1850s. Immigrants of other nationalities – including many Chinese – arrived to prospect for gold, then settled in the cities, especially Melbourne and Sydney. When the new federal government was installed in 1901, one of its first acts was to prevent further Chinese immigration. The act set out the "White Australia" policy, which conditioned attitudes to immigration for almost 70 years.

A massive immigration drive after World War II brought many more British settlers to Australia in the 1950s. Further government initiatives to "populate or perish" saw the arrival of large numbers of Italians and Greeks.

From the late 1960s, the "White Australia" policy was progressively wound down. It was officially ended during the 1972–1975 Whitlam administration. Ever since, up to 50% of immigrants each year have come from Asia, transforming Australia from an almost exclusively European enclave into a multicultural society, in which immigrant groups are encouraged to maintain connections with their own cultures and languages.

Aborigines are the exception in an otherwise integrated society. Numbering around 250,000, they remain marginalized economically and socially and still face considerable discrimination. Until the mid-1960s, they were not considered Australian citizens and were denied the vote, full social benefits and inclusion in the census. Aboriginal land had been occupied by settlers on the basis that it was *terra nullius* that belonged to no-one. Since the 1970s, Aborigines have made an increasingly organized stand over land rights and abuse of their civil rights. Government attempts to address the land rights issue initially foundered in the face of opposition by powerful mining companies and several state governments. However, the 1993 Native Title Act, rescinding the concept of *terra nullius*, has paved the way to a settlement of Aborigines' grievances.

During the 1950s and 1960s, Catholic–Protestant differences were a strong enough force to cause a rift in the Australian Labor Party (ALP). However, a subsequent policy encouraging mixed denomination schooling, coupled with a decline in religious observance, has largely neutralized the issue.

RELIGIOUS PERSUASION

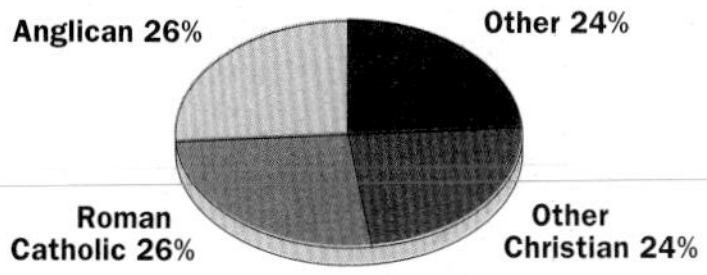

Anglican 26%

Other 24%

Roman Catholic 26%

Other Christian 24%

ETHNIC MAKEUP

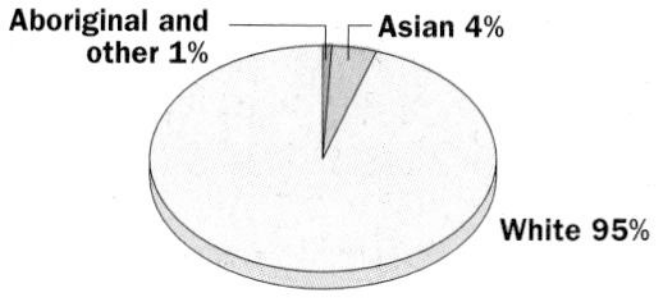

Aboriginal and other 1%

Asian 4%

White 95%

POPULATION AGE BREAKDOWN

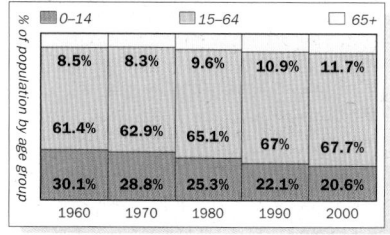

% of population by age group	■ 0–14	□ 15–64	□ 65+		
65+	8.5%	8.3%	9.6%	10.9%	11.7%
15–64	61.4%	62.9%	65.1%	67%	67.7%
0–14	30.1%	28.8%	25.3%	22.1%	20.6%
	1960	1970	1980	1990	2000

ARAFURA SEA

PAPUA NEW GUINEA

GREAT

Torres Strait
Bamaga Cape York

Melville Island

Bathurst Island

Darwin

Arnhem Land

Katherine

Groote Eylandt

Wessel Islands

Gulf of Carpentaria

Cape York Peninsula

B A R R I E R

C O R A L   S E A

Sir Edward Pellew Group

Wellesley Islands

Cooktown

Cairns

Karumba

Mitchell

TANAMI DESERT

Barkly Tableland

Tennant Creek

Flinders

NORTHERN

Mount Isa

Cloncurry

Hughenden

Townsville

R E E F

Winton

Mackay

TERRITORY

GREAT DIVIDING RANGE

Macdonnell Ranges

Alice Springs

QUEENSLAND

Longreach

Emerald

Rockhampton

SOUTH PACIFIC

Uluru (Ayers Rock)

Great Artesian Basin

SIMPSON DESERT

Birdsville

Cooper Creek

Bundaberg

Fraser I.

Maryborough

Gympie

SOUTH

Charleville

AUSTRALIA

Lake Eyre

Cunnamulla

Toowoomba

Brisbane

Ipswich

Gold Coast

VICTORIA DESERT

Lake Torrens

Lake Frome

Bourke

Darling

Moree

Lismore

Grafton

Armidale

Coffs Harbour

Nullarbor plain

Lake Gairdner

Flinders Ranges

Grey Range

Broken Hill

NEW SOUTH

Tamworth

Port Macquarie

Dubbo

Taree

Great Australian Bight

Port Augusta

Whyalla

Port Pirie

WALES

Orange

Maitland

Newcastle

Gosford

Eyre Peninsula

Elizabeth

Mildura

Murrumbidgee

Griffith

Bathurst

Lithgow

Sydney

Port Lincoln

Adelaide

Lachlan

Wagga Wagga

Goulburn

Wollongong

Queanbeyan

Kangaroo I.

VICTORIA

Shepparton

Albury

CANBERRA

Mount Kosciusko 2228m

AUST. CAPITAL TERRITORY

Horsham

Wangaratta

Australian Alps

Murray

Bendigo

TASMAN

Mount Gambier

Ballarat

Melbourne

Traralgon

Cape Howe

SEA

N

Warrnambool

Geelong

Sale

Morwell

0   400 km

0   400 miles

Bass Strait

King I.

Furneaux Group

Flinders I.

Burnie

Ulverstone

Devonport

Launceston

Hobart

A

CHRONOLOGY

Dutch, Portuguese, French and – decisively – British incursions throughout the 17th and 18th centuries signalled the end of 40,000 years of Aboriginal occupancy. Governor Arthur Phillip raised the Union Jack at Sydney Cove on January 26, 1788.

- ❏ **1901** Inauguration of the Commonwealth of Australia.
- ❏ **1915** Australian troops suffer heavy casualties at Gallipoli.
- ❏ **1929** Industrial upheaval and financial collapse: "The Great Depression."
- ❏ **1939** Prime Minister Menzies announces Australia will follow Britain into war with Germany.
- ❏ **1941** John Curtin becomes prime minister.
- ❏ **1942** Fall of Singapore to Japanese army. Japanese invasion of Australia seems imminent. Curtin turns to USA for help.
- ❏ **1950** Australian troops committed to UN–US Korean War against North Korean communists.
- ❏ **1962** Menzies government commits Australian aid to war in Vietnam.
- ❏ **1966** Adopts decimal currency.
- ❏ **1972** Election of Gough Whitlam government. Aid to South Vietnam ceases.
- ❏ **1975** Whitlam government dismissed by Governor-General Sir John Kerr. Malcolm Fraser forms Liberal–National Party coalition government.
- ❏ **1983** Fraser government defeated. Bob Hawke, having become leader of the Labor Party on the eve of the election, becomes prime minister.
- ❏ **1985** Corporate boom followed by deepening recession, termed "the recession we had to have" by Treasurer Paul Keating.
- ❏ **1992** Keating defeats Hawke in vote to become prime minister. He announces "Turning toward Asia" policy and places republican debate at top of political agenda. High Court's "Mabo Judgement" on Aboriginal land title paves the way for a settlement of Aborigines' grievances.
- ❏ **1993** Against most predictions, Keating ALP government reelected. Prime Minister Keating visits UK and outlines republican timetable to Queen Elizabeth II. Native Title Act recinds the concept of *terra nullius* and provides compensation for Aboriginal rights extinguished by existing land title.
- ❏ **1996** Defeat of Keating government. John Howard, LP leader, becomes prime minister.

POLITICS

 U. House 1996/1999
L. House 1996/1999   HM Queen Elizabeth II

THE STATE OF THE PARTIES

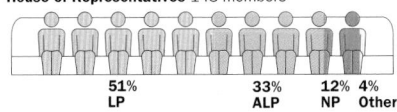

House of Representatives 148 members

| 51% LP | 33% ALP | 12% NP | 4% Other |

ALP = Australian Labor Party **LP** = Liberal Party
NP = National Party **AD** Australian Democrats
Other = Independent members

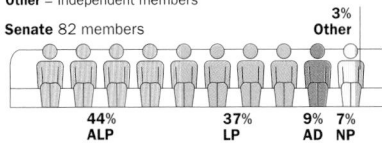

Senate 82 members

| 44% ALP | 37% LP | 9% AD | 7% NP | 3% Other |

Australia is a parliamentary democracy on the British model. There are six state governments, all but one (Queensland) bicameral. The Northern Territory became self-governing in 1978.

MAIN POLITICAL ISSUES
Aboriginal rights
The 1993 Native Title Act sought to harmonize recognition of Aboriginal claims to land with which they had a "close and continuing relationship" while leaving lawful European title land undisturbed. While the Act validated existing land titles, it provided for compensation if Aboriginal claims were deemed to have been extinguished as a result. A challenge to the Act by Western Australia (where up to 40% of claims were likely to be made) was rejected by the Australian High Court in March 1995. The majority of Australians generally support the Act, hoping that it will bury a conscience-pricking question and at the same time appease mining and agricultural interests.

Unemployment
Running at close to 10%, unemployment was expected to be the issue that would sink Prime Minister Keating's ALP government in the 1993 election. However, a skilful campaign helped to bring the ALP back to power. For most Australians though, unemployment remains a central concern. Now that the economy is showing signs of emerging from recession, there are hopes that the unemployment figures will begin to fall. Much new investment, however, is in high-tech, low-labor industries and commentators fear that unemployment will remain at around 10% for a number of years.

The Republic
Despite international press coverage, the republican issue is not of major

Vineyards in South Australia. Wine-making has been one of Australia's greatest agricultural success stories in recent years

importance to most Australians. The former ALP government played down the debate in order to avoid inflaming monarchist groups. Under the ALP, the replacement of the British monarch as head of state with an elected president before Australia celebrated its centenary in 2001 was envisaged. However, with the defeat of the ALP in 1996, the establishment of a republic in the immediate future has become less likely, although the eventual severance of ties with the monarchy is inevitable. In taking his oath of office, Prime Minister John Howard swore allegiance to Queen Elizabeth II, but not her successors.

PROFILE
The Labor (ALP), Liberal and National parties have dominated Australian politics since 1945. The Liberal and National parties are to the right of the political spectrum and work together in coalition. They broadly represent big business and agricultural interests. The ALP managed to remain in power for over a decade by attracting former traditional coalition supporters by, for example, adopting free-market policies. This brought a blurring of the differences between parties. However, in 1996 the ALP government fell to the LP in the general elections.

Paul Keating, *resigned as ALP leader after his 1996 election defeat.*

John Howard, *leader of the LP, was elected prime minister in 1996.*

Bill Hayden, *Governor-General of Australia.*

WORLD AFFAIRS

Australia's international focus has shifted from Europe and the USA toward Asia. Geopolitically it is in an ambiguous position. Having lost its place as a major trading partner for the UK when the latter joined the EEC, Australia has found that it is still regarded as a European outsider by the Asian nations with which it wishes to foster closer links. Australia has taken practical steps to redefine its role. It was the main backer of the 1989 Asia Pacific Economic Cooperation forum (APEC), an attempt to create a multilateral regional trading bloc, similar to the EU and NAFTA. After a faltering start, APEC began to get results. It was the first group to have China, Taiwan and Hong Kong sitting around the same table. The USA was a strong supporter, seeing APEC as a means of promoting free-market economics in Asia. Japan gave APEC its backing and now sees no conflict in belonging to APEC and leading ASEAN, the other key economic grouping. Australia's ambition is for APEC to become the leading association in the region.

Relations with the USA are tense on questions of trade. Australia objects to subsidized US wheat undercutting its own in Asia, particularly in the key Chinese market. It now sees the EU and USA as its main competitors in booming Southeast Asian economies.

However, on security issues Australia still supports the West. Against much public opposition, it sent troops to the 1991 Gulf War. Its commitment to the Pacific region also remains strong. The end of the Cold War, however, has meant that this is now expressed in terms of development aid rather than defense arrangements.

Within the Pacific region, fishing is a major issue. There have been a number of minor skirmishes with Indonesian and Japanese long-line fishing boats. Australia objects to this form of fishing as it kills large numbers of dolphins, and employs anti-submarine patrols to regulate the industry.

AID

 US$953 (donations) ⬆ Up 1% in 1993

Australia spends 0.36% of its GNP on aid programs. Most is spent in the Asia–Pacific region. Particular areas of focus are non-governmental organizations and HIV/AIDS programs. By far the greatest recipient, with A$335 million, is Papua New Guinea, where Australian companies such as Broken Hill Proprietary have major mining operations.

DEFENSE

 US$7.3bn   Down 1.6% in 1995

0   *Defense spending as % GDP*   40
2.3%

AUSTRALIAN ARMED FORCES

🛡	90 main battle tanks (90 *Leopard* 1A3)	23,700 personnel
⚓	4 submarines, 8 frigates, 3 destroyers and 16 patrol boats	15,000 personnel
✈	125 combat aircraft (17 F–111C, 15 F–1118, 52 F–18)	17,425 personnel
🚀	None	

Strategic ties with the USA remain an important element of defense policy. Australia has defense arrangements with the Philippines, Brunei and Thailand among others. Expenditure is designed to keep Australia self-reliant in defense and to encourage the participation of industry.

ECONOMICS

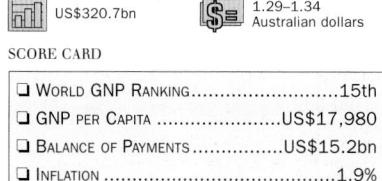 US$320.7bn   1.29–1.34 Australian dollars

SCORE CARD

❏ WORLD GNP RANKING	15th
❏ GNP PER CAPITA	US$17,980
❏ BALANCE OF PAYMENTS	US$15.2bn
❏ INFLATION	1.9%
❏ UNEMPLOYMENT	9.7%

EXPORTS

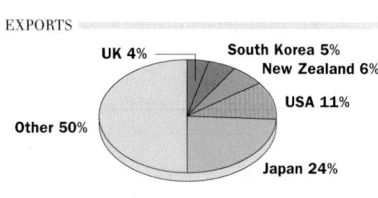

UK 4%
South Korea 5%
New Zealand 6%
USA 11%
Other 50%
Japan 24%

IMPORTS

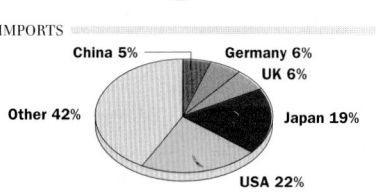

China 5%
Germany 6%
UK 6%
Other 42%
Japan 19%
USA 22%

ECONOMIC PERFORMANCE INDICATOR

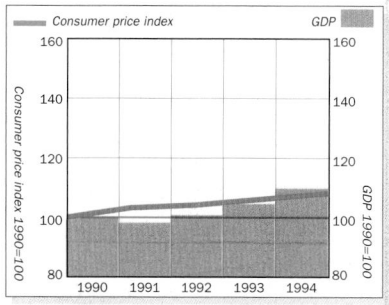

STRENGTHS

Efficient agricultural and mining industries. Vast mineral deposits. Highly profitable tourist industry with huge untapped potential. Successful investor in booming Southeast Asian economies such as Vietnam.

WEAKNESSES

May suffer from EU and NAFTA protectionist policies. Political instability in some export markets in Southeast Asia could dent exports. Competition from Asian economies with lower wage rates and poorer working conditions. Balance of payments deficit. Unemployment likely to remain high.

PROFILE

Australia's companies are concentrating on the growing Asian market. From accounting for a quarter of exports in 1960, Asia now accounts for 60% of the Australia's trade. Japan remains the country's most important trading partner.

In order to compete in Asia, Australia's economy has been undergoing massive structural adjustment. The former ALP government slowly removed the tariffs that had made Australia one of the most heavily protected economies within the OECD. Higher unemployment and the collapse of many businesses accompanied the change. In 1994, however, strong growth was seen.

AUSTRALIA : MAJOR BUSINESSES

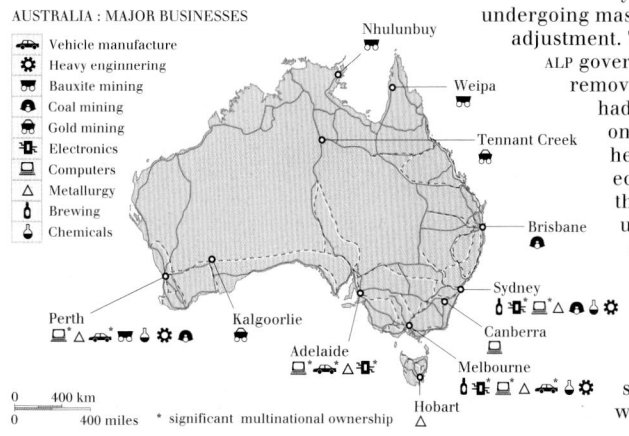

🚗 Vehicle manufacture
⚙ Heavy engineering
🚂 Bauxite mining
⬤ Coal mining
⬤ Gold mining
⚡ Electronics
💻 Computers
△ Metallurgy
⬤ Brewing
⚗ Chemicals

Nhulunbuy
Weipa
Tennant Creek
Brisbane
Sydney
Canberra
Perth
Kalgoorlie
Adelaide
Melbourne
Hobart

0   400 km
0   400 miles   * significant multinational ownership

A

RESOURCES

 159bn kwh
(capacity 33.9m kw)

 501,390 b/d
(reserves
1,767,900,000 bbl)

 132m sheep,
24.7m cattle,
2.7m pigs

Coal, iron, bauxite,
zinc, lead, copper,
nickel, opals, gold

ELECTRICITY GENERATION

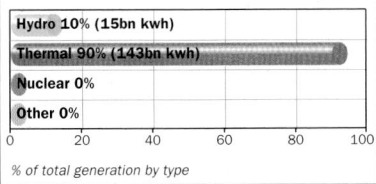

Hydro 10% (15bn kwh)		
Thermal 90% (143bn kwh)		
Nuclear 0%		
Other 0%		

0   20   40   60   80   100

% of total generation by type

Australia has one of the world's most important mining industries. It is a world leader in exports of coal, iron ore, gold, bauxite and copper. Minerals account for 9.4% of Australia's GDP and 53% of all of its merchandise export earnings. Since the first discoveries of coal in 1798, mineral production in Australia has risen every year. In the decade to 1992 it doubled. Even further growth is expected in the late 1990s. Eighty major new mining projects are already planned, worth some A$33 billion. Minerals' share of the total economy will continue to grow into the next century. The industry has benefited from Australia's location. Most increases in production go to the booming economies of Southeast Asia.

While minerals underpin much of Australia's wealth, there is growing concern at the environmental cost of extraction. In the past, many mining companies were concerned that Aborigines could lay claim to land holding valuable minerals, particularly after the "Mabo Judgement" of 1992. In 1993, Comalco threatened to halt expansion plans worth over $1 billion if Aboriginal claims over its bauxite leases were upheld. However, the 1993 Native Title Act has clarified the position, allowing existing title-holders to retain their holding, but providing for those with valid claims to be compensated.

AUSTRALIA : LAND USE

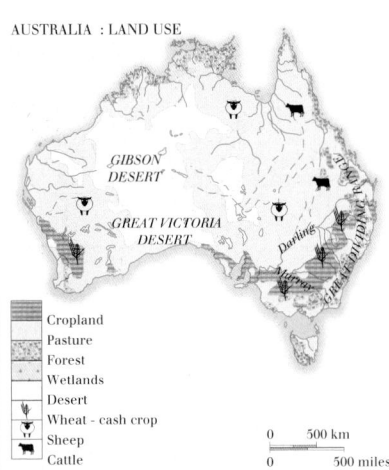

GIBSON DESERT

GREAT VICTORIA DESERT

Darling

Cropland
Pasture
Forest
Wetlands
Desert
Wheat - cash crop
Sheep
Cattle

0   500 km

0   500 miles

Green Island, *on the Great Barrier Reef Marine Park in the far north of Queensland. The reef stretches 1,240 miles down the coast.*

ENVIRONMENT

 12.1% (2% partially protected)

 Environmental issues are a priority

ENVIRONMENTAL TREATIES

Yes	Yes	Yes
Yes	Yes	Yes

Australia's voters are among the most environmentally conscious in the industrialized world. Green issues are dominated by the Australian Conservation Foundation (ACF) and the more radical Greenpeace. The ACF has concentrated on developing links with industry in cooperative conservation programs. Its endorsement of the ALP in 1993 helped the party to win the elections that year. The ACF has also been behind stricter laws to protect endangered species. Its major success, however, has been in persuading the government to adopt a nationwide policy making environmental concerns a key part of any planning decision.

MEDIA

 The press is free from government control

PUBLISHING AND BROADCAST MEDIA

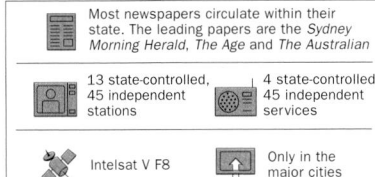

Most newspapers circulate within their state. The leading papers are the *Sydney Morning Herald*, *The Age* and *The Australian*	
13 state-controlled, 45 independent stations	4 state-controlled, 45 independent services
Intelsat V F8	Only in the major cities

The Australian press is firmly in the grip of press "barons" such as Rupert Murdoch, Kerry Packer and Conrad Black. In 1992, the ALP decided to begin deregulating media industries by auctioning satellite pay-TV. Public-sector broadcasting remains dominated by the politically neutral Australian Broadcasting Corporation (ABC), which receives complaints about its coverage from both main parties.

CRIME

 12,557 prisoners

 Significant increase in all types of crime

CRIME RATES

Murders	
2	per 100,000 population

Rapes	
44	per 100,000 population

Thefts	
3577	per 100,000 population

Crime is on the increase. Rising narcotics-related offenses are a major concern. Australia is active in narcotics control throughout Southeast Asia. In 1996, the federal government tightened Australia's gun laws in response to the massacre of 35 people in Tasmania.

Each state has its own police force and court system. Federal courts deal with disputes between states. The High Court and Family Court both have national jurisdiction. Since the 1970s, the legal system has been placing greater emphasis on the rights of the individual. The deaths of a number of Aborigines in custody have, however, led to calls for their greater protection.

EDUCATION

 99%

559,365 students

0   *Education spending as % GNP*   25

5.5%

THE EDUCATION SYSTEM

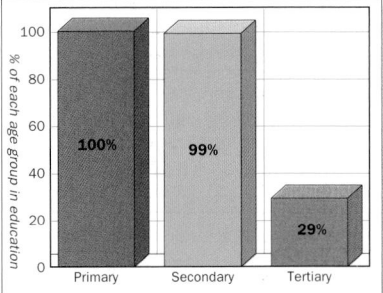

% of each age group in education

100   80   60   40   20   0

Primary 100%   Secondary 99%   Tertiary 29%

Education in Australia is a state responsibility, except in Canberra, where it is funded by the federal government. State education departments run the government schools and set the policies for educational practice and standards for all schools. Non-government schools, run by religious and other groups, exist in all states. Special provision is made for inaccessible outback areas. Schooling is compulsory from age 5–6 to age 15–16 in all states. Universities are independent of state control and are funded by the federal government. In 1990, education accounted for over 13% of government expenditure.

REGIONS

SYDNEY

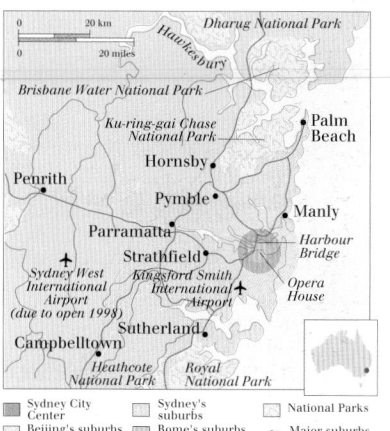

Sydney City Center · Sydney's suburbs · National Parks
Beijing's suburbs (to scale) · Rome's suburbs (to scale) · Major suburbs

SYDNEY IS Australia's largest and most famous city. Its success in winning the bid to host the 2000 Olympics will further raise its global profile. Since 1932, it has had one of the world's most recognizable structures – the Harbour Bridge, which spans Sydney's stunning harbor. In 1973, its new Opera House also became an instantly recognizable landmark. Sydney has the world's largest suburban area, a conurbation so vast that the city is twice as large as Beijing and six times the size of Rome.

As Australia changes its focus toward Asia, so Sydney will gain in importance as one of the key cities of the Pacific Rim.

QUEENSLAND

THE CLOSEST Australian state to the booming economies of Southeast Asia, Queensland's economy has been expanding. In recent years it has experienced a net migration from the southern states. Tourism has been a major beneficiary of closer links with Japan. Cairns, in particular, has seen rapid growth as the gateway to the Great Barrier Reef. Stretching for over 1,240 miles along the Queensland coast, it is the largest marine park in the world. Composed mostly of coral polyps, it is also the largest living organism on earth. Clear waters, sponges, algae and 1,500 species of fish make the reef a superb snorkelling and diving location.

National Park · △ Aboriginal communities · Tourism

WESTERN AUSTRALIA

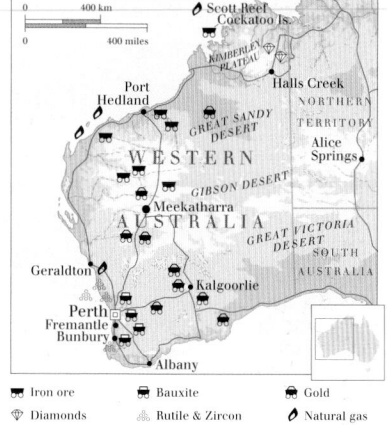

Iron ore · Bauxite · Gold
Diamonds · Rutile & Zircon · Natural gas

OCCUPYING ONE-THIRD of the Australian continent, and with a greater land area than Western Europe, Western Australia exports twice as much per capita as the national average. Its main economic strength is its mineral resources. The state produces 11% of the world's iron ore, 60% of Australia's gold, and is a major supplier of bauxite to the West. The northwest shelf includes one of the world's major deposits of natural gas and the largest known diamond deposits, accounting for one-third of global production.

Perth is the state capital. Australia's most isolated city, it is 2,500 miles from the eastern seaboard; it is quicker and cheaper to fly to Hong Kong from Perth than to Sydney. With a population of just over one million, Perth is Australia's fourth-largest city. The success of minerals industries has also made it the fastest-growing. The booming economy has brought high-rise steel and glass office blocks, which have transformed the Perth skyline.

HEALTH

 1 per 434 people

Heart, cerebrovascular and respiratory diseases, cancers

0 — Health spending as % GDP — 25
8.6%

Australia's extensive public health service has standards as high as any in the world. Hospital waiting lists are short. Outback areas are served by the efficient Royal Flying Doctor Service. While vigilance continues in the areas of hygiene, nutrition and general living standards, Australian health authorities have targeted Aboriginal health, heart disease, injury prevention, personal fitness and the prevention of cancers – particularly lung, cervical, breast and skin cancers – as contemporary priorities. Life expectancy is 81 years for women and 75 for men.

WEALTH

Industrial worker, A$20,000–23,000 (US$14,900–17,200) per year; industrial project engineer, A$45,000–50,000 (US$33,600–37,300) per year

CONSUMER GOODS OWNERSHIP

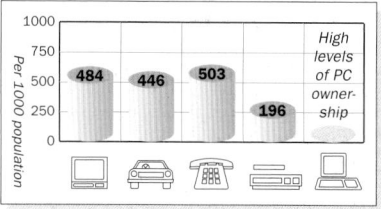

High levels of PC ownership

484 · 446 · 503 · 196

Australians enjoy reasonable equality of wealth. A large proportion of families own two cars and have relatively high disposable incomes. A benign climate helps most to live comfortably. However, high unemployment during the 1990s' recession has widened the gap between rich and poor, and Australia has slipped down the world standard of living list in recent years. The incidence of homelessness, critical poverty and child neglect due to poverty has increased slightly.

WORLD RANKING

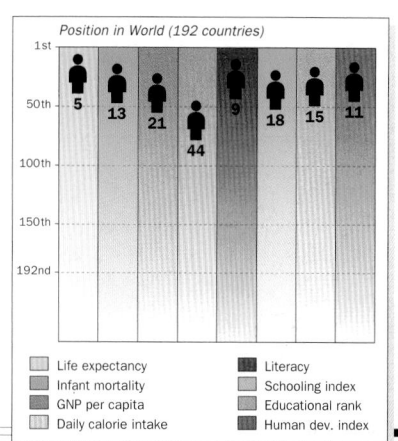

Position in World (192 countries)

5 · 13 · 21 · 44 · 9 · 18 · 15 · 11

Life expectancy · Literacy
Infant mortality · Schooling index
GNP per capita · Educational rank
Daily calorie intake · Human dev. index

A

AUSTRIA

EUROPE

OFFICIAL NAME: Republic of Austria   **CAPITAL:** Vienna
POPULATION: 8 million   **CURRENCY:** Austrian schilling   **OFFICIAL LANGUAGE:** German

LYING IN THE HEART OF EUROPE, Austria is dominated by the Alps in the west of the country, while fertile plains make up its eastern half. Created in 1920, after the collapse of the Habsburg empire, Austria was absorbed into Hitler's Germany in 1938. It gained independence again in 1955 after the departure of the last Soviet troops from the Allied Occupation Force. Austria's economy encompasses successful high-tech sectors, a tourist industry which attracts the wealthier end of the market and a strong agricultural base. In 1995 Austria joined the EU.

CLIMATE

WEATHER CHART

■ Average daily temperature   Rainfall

Austria has a temperate continental climate. Alpine areas experience colder temperatures and higher precipitation.

TRANSPORTATION

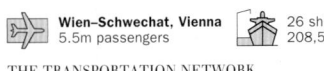

Wien–Schwechat, Vienna
5.5m passengers

26 ships
208,500 dwt

THE TRANSPORTATION NETWORK

66,059 miles (106,307 km)	899 miles (1,447 km)
3,495 miles (5,624 km)	277 miles (446 km)

Austria's central geographical position has encouraged the development of a sophisticated communications and transportation network.

TOURISM

 17.9m visitors    Down 2% in 1994

MAIN OVERSEAS ARRIVALS

Germany 56%	
Netherlands 7%	
Italy 6%	
France 4%	
UK 4%	
Other 23%	

% of total arrivals

The earnings of the Austrian tourist industry amount to more than 14% of GDP. The well-developed Alpine skiing and winter sports resorts account for almost one-third of the country's total tourist earnings. Many resorts, such as St. Anton and Kitzbühel, cater for the top end of the market. In the summer season, which peaks in July and August, tourists visit the scenic Tirol and the lakes around Bad Ischl. Vienna and Salzburg, the country's second city, are major attractions. The latter is internationally famous for its summer music festival and as the birthplace of the composer Mozart.

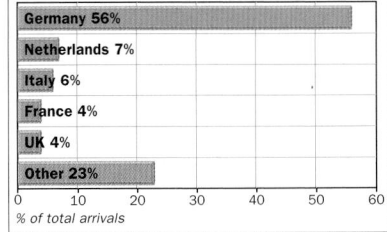

The Tirol is situated in the heart of Austria's Alps. It is the most mountainous region of all and attracts both winter and summer visitors.

AUSTRIA

Total Land Area : 82 730 sq. km (31 942 sq. miles)

LAND HEIGHT

- 3000m/9843ft
- 2000m/6562ft
- 1000m/3281ft
- 500m/1640ft
- 200m/656ft
- Sea Level

POPULATION

- over 1 000 000
- over 500 000
- over 100 000
- over 50 000
- over 10 000

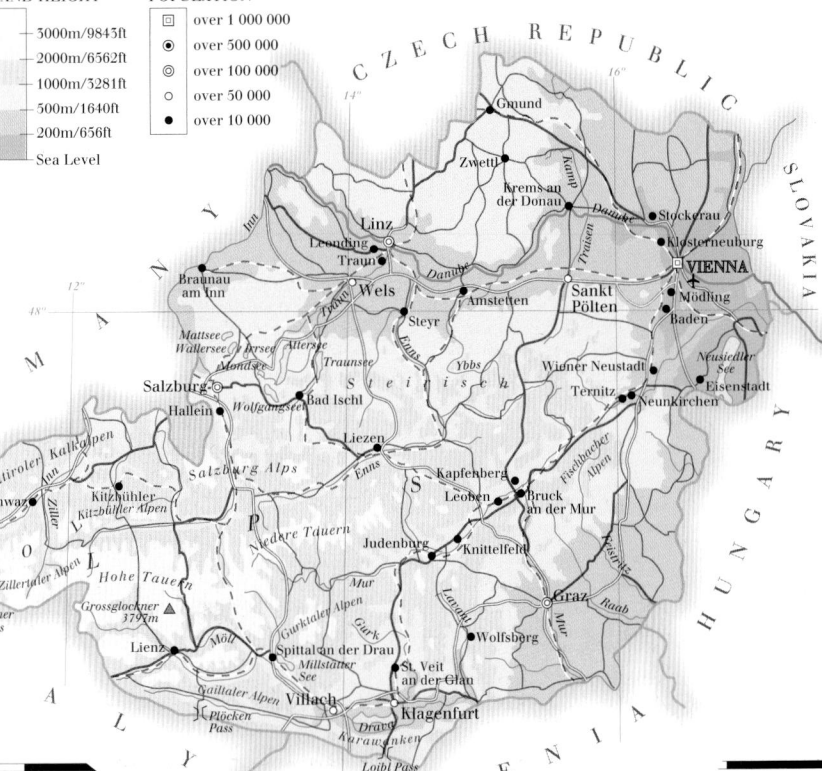

PEOPLE

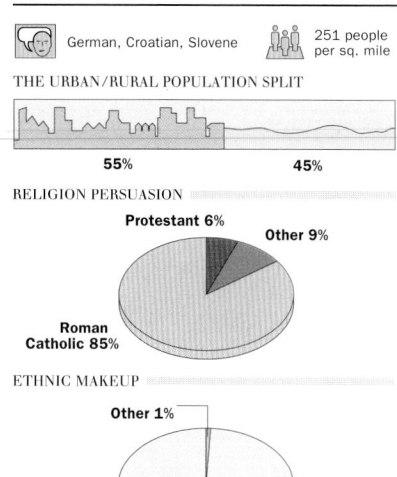

German, Croatian, Slovene

251 people per sq. mile

THE URBAN/RURAL POPULATION SPLIT

55%   45%

RELIGION PERSUASION

Protestant 6%   Other 9%

Roman Catholic 85%

ETHNIC MAKEUP

Other 1%

German 99%

Austrian society is homogeneous. Almost 99% of Austrians are German speakers. However, Austrians like to consider themselves ethnically distinct from Germans. Minorities are few; there are some ethnic Slovenes, Croats and Hungarians in the south and east, as well as some Gypsy communities. These minorities have been supplemented by large numbers of immigrants from eastern Europe and refugees from the conflict in former Yugoslavia. The result has been a perceptible increase in ethnic tension, particularly as the downturn in the economy has led some Austrians to claim that migrants are taking jobs from the local population.

The nuclear family is the norm in Austria. It is common for both parents to work. While sexual equality is enshrined in the constitution, in practice society is still strongly patriarchal. Compared to the rest of Europe, few women enter politics.

Young Austrians tend to live in their parental home until they marry. This reflects the long time taken to complete university degrees, for which students do not receive maintenance grants. Austrians marry younger than the European average. Nominally a Catholic country, Austria is a less conservative society than some German states.

POPULATION AGE BREAKDOWN

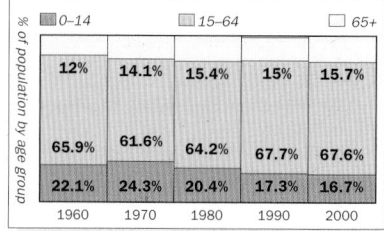

% of population by age group	0–14	15–64			65+
65+	12%	14.1%	15.4%	15%	15.7%
15–64	65.9%	61.6%	64.2%	67.7%	67.6%
0–14	22.1%	24.3%	20.4%	17.3%	16.7%
	1960	1970	1980	1990	2000

POLITICS

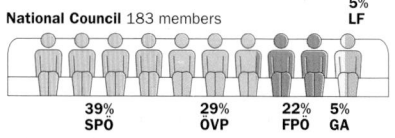

U. House 1995/1999
L. House 1995/1999

President Thomas Klestil

THE STATE OF THE PARTIES

National Council 183 members

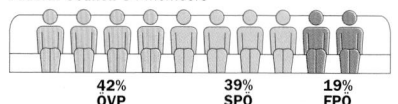

5% LF

39% SPÖ   29% ÖVP   22% FPÖ   5% GA

SPÖ = Social Democratic Party of Austria ÖVP = Austrian People's Party FPÖ = Freedom Party of Austria GA = Green Alternative LF = Liberal Forum

Federal Council 64 members

42% ÖVP   39% SPÖ   19% FPÖ

Austria is a federal, multiparty democracy. The chancellor (premier) holds real executive power.

MAIN POLITICAL ISSUES
Entry into the EU
Austria's population was divided over its entry into the EU, although the country voted in favor of joining in a referendum held in June 1994. There was an unexpectedly high "yes" vote of 66.4%, in an 81% turnout. Although Austrians have benefited from lower food prices and greater consumer choice, there are now fears that economic policy is being driven by the need to meet EU economic convergence criteria, and that membership is eroding national identity and independence. The farming lobby remains concerned that EU agricultural policy could endanger the livelihood of up to half of Austria's farmers. Some Austrians fear EU membership will increase German influence.

Economic decline
After stability in the 1970s and 1980s, industry has been exposed to recession in the neighboring countries of eastern Europe and Germany. As a result, export orders have fallen and unemployment has increased. In particular, the traditional methods of protectionism and subsidies have failed to work and this has been followed by growing social and political tension. However, recently there have been signs of significant economic revival.

PROFILE
A coalition headed by the SPÖ, with the ÖVP as the junior partner, has governed Austria since the 1950s. The left-of-center consensus is beginning to show signs of strain as the ÖVP is losing many of its working class voters to the right-wing FPÖ. The main reason is the decline in the economy and the perception that immigrant labor is taking jobs from Austrians, a perception exploited by the FPÖ's leader, Jörg Haider. The FPÖ's anti-EU stance had also attracted support. Local government is run by the nine provincial assemblies. Vienna is dominated by the SPÖ.

Dr. Thomas Klestil, *the ÖVP candidate, became Austria's president in 1992.*

Franz Vranitzky. *Elected chancellor in 1990, he leads an SPÖ-ÖVP coalition.*

WORLD AFFAIRS

| EU | CE | NAM | OECD | OSCE |

While Austria wants to be seen as independent of German influence, it cannot avoid the fact that Germany is its main trading partner and the most powerful state in the region. Relations with Germany are therefore Austria's major concern. However, there is a conscious policy to create a diplomatic distance from Bonn. Austria is keen to maintain its direct line to Washington. The fact that Austria supplies much of the US army's small arms helps to cement this relationship.

Like Germany, Austria supports the early entry to the EU of east European states. Austria has been exploiting its geo-political position to increase its influence in the region, and remains an important trading partner of many ex-COMECON states. Austria is a neutral state and its constitution bans its forces from serving abroad. It has, however, been a critic of the failure by the UN and EU to stop the conflict in former Yugoslavia. In April 1995, it signed the Schengen Convention abolishing border controls between most EU mainland countries.

AID

  $544m (donations)

  Small reduction in 1993

Austria is a major donor of aid to eastern Europe. Much aid is aimed at stemming a large influx of economic refugees from the former communist states. Aid donations to former Yugoslavia are likely to increase once peace is achieved. Austria was a major exporter to the region and will be seeking a key role in reconstruction.

A

CHRONOLOGY

Austria came under the control of the Habsburgs in 1273. In 1867, the Dual Monarchy of Austria–Hungary was formed under Habsburg rule. Defeat in World War I led to the abdication of the last Habsburg emperor, Charles and the breakup of the Austro-Hungarian empire in 1918.

- ❑ **1920** Republic of Austria formed.
- ❑ **1934** Chancellor Dollfuss dismisses parliament and starts imprisoning Social Democrats, communists and National Socialist Party (NAZI) members. NAZIs attempt coup.
- ❑ **1938** The Anschluss – Austria forcibly incorporated into Germany by Hitler.
- ❑ **1945** Austria occupied by Russian, British, US and French forces. Elections result in People's Party (ÖVP) and Socialist Party (SPÖ) coalition. Remains in power for most of the postwar period.
- ❑ **1950** Attempted coup by Communist Party fails. Marshall aid helps economic recovery. USSR resists calls from France, USA and UK for independent Austria.
- ❑ **1955** Soviet troops withdrawn. USSR recognizes Austria as a neutral sovereign state.
- ❑ **1971** SPÖ government formed under Federal Chancellor Bruno Kreisky who dominated Austrian politics for next 13 years.
- ❑ **1983** Socialists and the Freedom Party (FPÖ) form a coalition government under Fred Sinowatz.
- ❑ **1986** Dr. Kurt Waldheim, former UN secretary-general, elected president, despite war crimes allegations. Franz Vranitsky replaced Sinowatz as Federal Chancellor. Nationalist Jörg Haider succeeds more moderate Norbert Steger as FPÖ leader, prompting the SPÖ to pull out of the government. Elections produce stalemate. Return to "grand coalition" of SPÖ and ÖVP.
- ❑ **1990** ÖVP loses 17 seats in parliamentary elections.
- ❑ **1992** Thomas Klestil (ÖVP) elected president, replacing Waldheim. Elections confirm some traditional ÖVP supporters defecting to FPÖ.
- ❑ **1993** FPÖ splits into two. Breakaway Liberal Forum takes over five FPÖ seats. Liberal Forum voices opposition to FPÖ's nationalism.
- ❑ **1994** Austrians vote in favor of EU membership in referendum.
- ❑ **1995** Austria joins EU. Elections after disagreement within coalition over budget; both SPÖ and ÖVP increase their representation. "Grand coalition" re-forms in early 1996.

DEFENSE

 $2.0bn   ⬆ Up 9% in 1995

0   *Defense spending as % GDP*   40

0.9%

Under the terms of the 1955 State Treaty, which granted Austria its full independence, the country is neutral. Despite the small size of its defense forces, Austria's arms industry is thriving and meets most of the hardware needs of the army. It also exports arms to the USA and other countries.

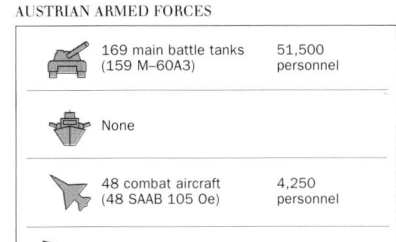

AUSTRIAN ARMED FORCES

🛡	169 main battle tanks (159 M–60A3)	51,500 personnel
🚢	None	
✈	48 combat aircraft (48 SAAB 105 Oe)	4,250 personnel
	None	

ECONOMICS

 $197.5bn   10.07–10.91 Austrian schillings

SCORE CARD

❑ WORLD GNP RANKING	22nd
❑ GNP PER CAPITA	$24,950
❑ BALANCE OF PAYMENTS	$–2,452m
❑ INFLATION	3%
❑ UNEMPLOYMENT	4.4%

EXPORTS

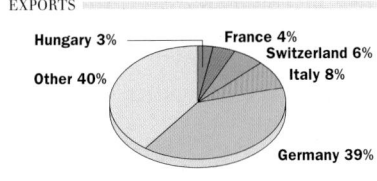

Hungary 3%   France 4%   Switzerland 6%   Other 40%   Italy 8%   Germany 39%

IMPORTS

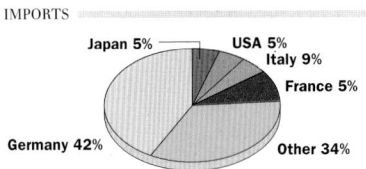

Japan 5%   USA 5%   Italy 9%   France 5%   Germany 42%   Other 34%

STRENGTHS

Large manufacturing base. Strong chemical and petrochemical industries. Electrical engineering sector, textiles and wood processing industries. Highly skilled labor force. Tourism an important foreign currency earner.

WEAKNESSES

Lacks natural resources. Reliant on imported raw materials, particularly oil and gas. High levels of subsidies to state-owned industry. Weak and overregulated banking system.

PROFILE

Austria's industrial and high-tech sector is highly developed and contributes around 25% to GDP. Some services, notably tourism, are highly sophisticated and profitable. However, the Austrian economy suffers from a weak banking sector. This is due in part to the high level of state subsidies to industry, which has in turn meant that there has been little demand for flexible private finance.

ECONOMIC PERFORMANCE INDICATOR

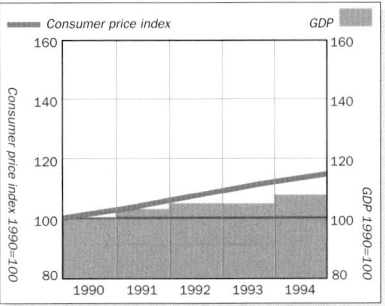

Consumer price index   GDP

Consumer price index 1990=100 / *GDP 1990=100* — 1990, 1991, 1992, 1993, 1994

The banking system is facing increased competition as a result of entering the EU, and this has led to a series of mergers by Austrian banks. There have been benefits from EU membership, however, as prices for many products, particularly food and books, have fallen. The Austrian labor market has also seen an influx of immigrant labor more willing to accept flexible working arrangements and lower wages. There has also been an increase in foreign investment, as more multinationals locate their headquarters for eastern European operations in Austria. Austrian companies are major investors in eastern Europe.

AUSTRIA : MAJOR BUSINESSES

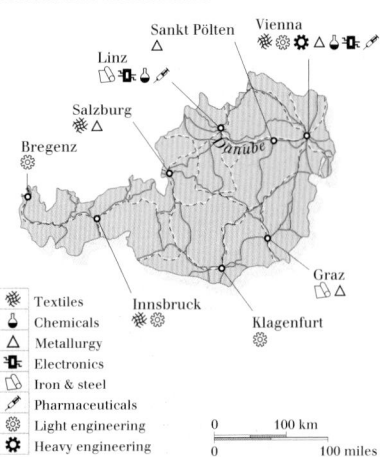

Sankt Pölten, Vienna, Linz, Salzburg, Bregenz, Danube, Innsbruck, Graz, Klagenfurt

❊	Textiles
⬡	Chemicals
△	Metallurgy
🔌	Electronics
◻	Iron & steel
✎	Pharmaceuticals
⚙	Light engineering
✿	Heavy engineering

0 — 100 km / 0 — 100 miles

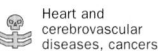

A

RESOURCES

51bn kwh
(capacity 16.8m kw)

23,700 b/d
(reserves
93,200,000 bbl)

324,000 sheep,
3.8m pigs,
2.4m cattle

Iron, coal, magnesite,
zinc, lead

ELECTRICITY GENERATION

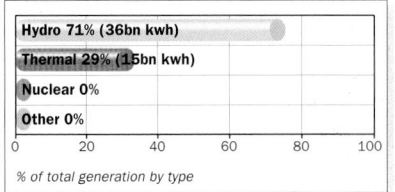

Hydro 71% (36bn kwh)

Thermal 29% (15bn kwh)

Nuclear 0%

Other 0%

% of total generation by type

Austria has few resources. It lacks significant oil, coal and gas deposits and has to import over $2.7 billion-worth of energy every year. Russia remains one of Austria's main energy suppliers. Gas is provided via pipelines running through the Czech and Slovak

ENVIRONMENT

24% partially
protected

Environment is an
increasingly
important issue

ENVIRONMENTAL TREATIES

Yes Yes Yes

Yes Yes Yes

Environmental awareness is high. Domestic waste has to be separated for recycling; heavy fines exist for those who fail to observe the regulations. Car emissions are increasingly controlled. New cars in Austria have catalytic converters and most drivers use lead-free gasoline. The safety of nuclear reactors in Slovakia is a major concern.

MEDIA

Media is, for the most part, independent of the government. It is relatively conservative

PUBLISHING AND BROADCAST MEDIA

There are 33 daily newspapers, including the leading *Die Presse*

2 state-owned services

1 state-owned service

Banned in large urban areas

Main cities

TV and radio are more tightly controlled than the press. They are operated by *Österreichischer Rundfunk* (ORF), under a politically appointed general director. Cable TV is carefully licensed by ORF, to prevent it taking viewers away from existing stations. Satellite dishes are banned in main cities. Some unlicensed radio stations broadcast from neighboring states.

republics. Oil is imported up the Danube. Russia and Germany are the major suppliers of iron ore and raw steel for Austria's industry.

AUSTRIA : LAND USE

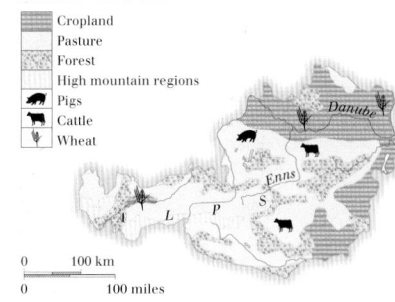

Cropland
Pasture
Forest
High mountain regions
Pigs
Cattle
Wheat

0   100 km
0   100 miles

CRIME

5,862 prisoners

Up 8% in 1990

CRIME RATES

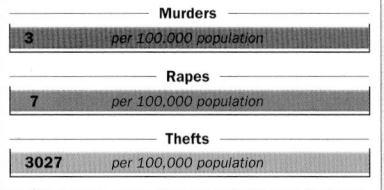

Murders
3 per 100,000 population

Rapes
7 per 100,000 population

Thefts
3027 per 100,000 population

Austria's crime rate is below Europe's average. However, the number of burglaries is rising. The arrival of the Russian mafia in Vienna has led to an increase in money laundering.

EDUCATION

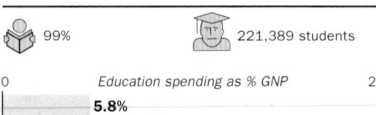
99%   221,389 students

0   Education spending as % GNP   25
5.8%

THE EDUCATION SYSTEM

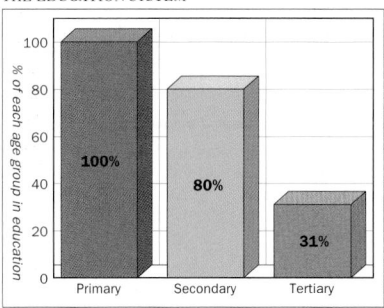

% of each age group in education

Primary 100% Secondary 80% Tertiary 31%

Children are streamed into two types of school according to their ability. Those in a *Gymnasium* (11–18) are entitled to enter university. However, children in a *Hauptschule* (11–15) are not. The universities are oversubscribed, with students taking six years or more to finish their first degrees.

HEALTH

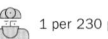
1 per 230 people

Heart and cerebrovascular diseases, cancers

0   Health spending as % GDP   25
8.5%

Austria has relatively high levels of spending on health. The ability of the state to continue to maintain the current level of service is being questioned. Many patients choose to use the expanding private health sector to avoid waiting lists for operations.

WEALTH

Agricultural worker, 78 Austrian schillings ($8) per hour; doctor, 33,279 Austrian schillings ($3305) per month

CONSUMER GOODS OWNERSHIP

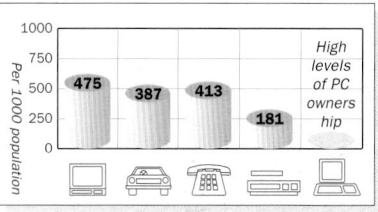

Per 1000 population

475   387   413   181

High levels of PC owners hip

Despite having had a centrist government for most of the last four decades, Austria has retained many of its traditional social divisions. Inherited wealth is still respected above earned wealth, and social mobility is somewhat less than in neighboring Germany. Austrians have the highest savings rate of any country in the OECD. Only about 4% of Austrians own stocks and shares, and limited amounts are invested in property. Austria is the only EU country which allows anonymous savings accounts, a system which, it has been argued, encourages money laundering and insider dealing. Government bonds offer low rates of interest and the property market is weak, with many people tending to rent rather than buy their apartments. The poorest group are the refugees from the conflict in the former Yugoslavia.

WORLD RANKING

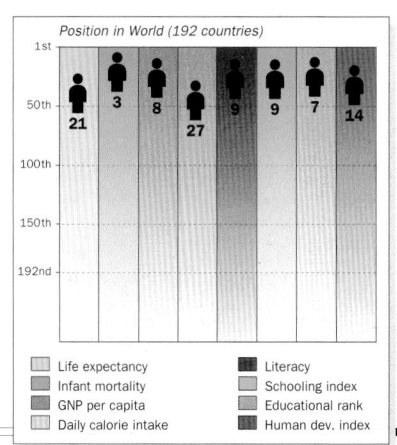

Position in World (192 countries)

1st

50th

21   3   8   27   9   9   7   14

100th

150th

192nd

Life expectancy
Infant mortality
GNP per capita
Daily calorie intake
Literacy
Schooling index
Educational rank
Human dev. index

A

AZERBAIJAN

OFFICIAL NAME: Republic of Azerbaijan CAPITAL: Baku
POPULATION: 7.6 million CURRENCY: Manat OFFICIAL LANGUAGE: Azerbaijani

SITUATED ON THE WESTERN COAST of the Caspian Sea, Azerbaijan was the first Soviet republic to declare independence, in 1991. The issue of the disputed enclave of Nagorno Karabakh, which Armenia seeks to annex, led to full-scale war in 1993 and has since dominated all other concerns in Azeri life. The war and an estimated 500,000 refugees have added to the problems of Azerbaijan's troubled economy. Its oil wealth, however, gives it long-term potential.

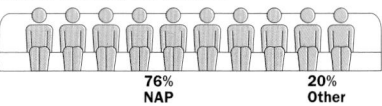

Landscape typical of the Lesser Caucasus mountains near Qazax in the extreme northwest of Azerbaijan.

CLIMATE

WEATHER CHART

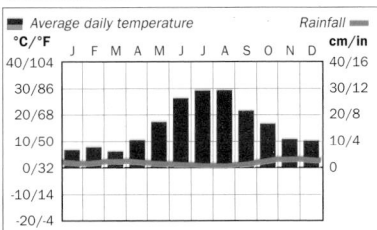

Coastal areas are subtropical, but bitter winters inland have become a life-or-death issue for thousands of refugees.

TRANSPORTATION

 Baku   Has no fleet

THE TRANSPORTATION NETWORK

36,640 miles) (58,960 km)		None
1,268 miles (2,040 km)		None

Improving links with Iran and Turkey to the south, rather than with Moscow, is the focus of transportation spending.

TOURISM

The only visitors are on business   No change from year to year

MAIN OVERSEAS ARRIVALS

Azerbaijan does not publish tourism figures by country of origin

0   1   2   3   4
% of total arrivals

Because of the war over Nagorno Karabakh, and strong anti-Western feelings (Azerbaijan interprets the West as taking the Armenian side in the conflict), there is only a tiny trickle of visitors, most of them on business.

PEOPLE

Azerbaijani, Russian   228 people per sq. mile

THE URBAN/RURAL POPULATION SPLIT

55%   45%

ETHNIC MAKEUP

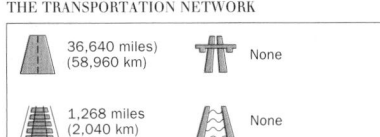

Daghestani 3%   Armenian 6%
Other 2%   Russian 6%
Azeri 83%

At the last census, held in 1989, Azeris made up 83% of the population. Today the proportion is even greater – thousands of Armenians, Jews and Russians have left as a result of rising nationalism among Azeris. Racial hostility against those that remain is increasing. Women, once prominent within the ruling party, have lost their position in political life, and their general status is also declining. The once effective social security system has collapsed.

POLITICS

 1995/2000   President Geidar Aliyev

THE STATE OF THE PARTIES

National Assembly 360 members

76% NAP   20% Other

NAP = New Azerbaijan Party **Other** = Popular Front of Azerbaijan (PFA), National Independence Party, Musvat Party, Dozkurt Party

The 1988 decision of Nagorno Karabakh's Armenian-dominated council to unite with Armenia led to war with Armenia in 1993, resulting in Armenian control over 20% of Azerbaijan's territory. A ceasefire was declared in 1994 while peace talks were mediated by the OSCE. The first legislative elections since independence held in 1995 returned a majority from the New Azerbaijan party (NAP), aligned with President Aliyev, which replaced the communists.

AZERBAIJAN

Total Land Area : 86 600 sq. km (33 436 sq. miles)

POPULATION
- ☑ over 1 000 000
- ◎ over 100 000
- ○ over 50 000
- ● over 10 000
- • under 10 000

LAND HEIGHT
- 4000m/13 124ft
- 3000m/9843ft
- 2000m/6562ft
- 1000m/3281ft
- 500m/1640ft
- 200m/656ft
- Sea Level

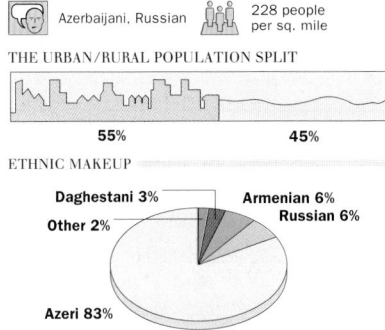

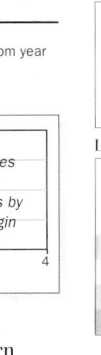

WORLD AFFAIRS

Russia's military withdrawal in 1993 ended the chances of a CIS-brokered settlement of the war with Armenia. Since 1992, peace talks between Armenia and Azerbaijan have continued under the auspices of the OSCE, although Azerbaijan is openly backed by Iran (which has a large Azeri population).

AID

 $14m (receipts)   Military aid is rising

Azerbaijan has been receiving covert military aid from Iran and Turkey, both vying for influence in Baku.

DEFENSE

 $109m   Down 17% in 1995

The 73,300-strong Azeri army has performed badly in the war with Armenia. Russia withdrew the last of its 62,000 troops in 1993.

ECONOMICS

 $3.7bn   4,168–4,440 manat

SCORE CARD

❑ WORLD GNP RANKING	112th
❑ GNP PER CAPITA	$500
❑ BALANCE OF PAYMENTS	$499m
❑ INFLATION	1664%
❑ UNEMPLOYMENT	0.8%

STRENGTHS
Oil and natural gas have considerable potential; a $7 billion oil deal has now been struck. The wine industry is efficient by regional standards.

WEAKNESSES
Years of antiquated practices in the oil industry are reflected in poor production efficiency. The war in Nagorno Karabakh remains an enormous drain on state resources.

EXPORTS

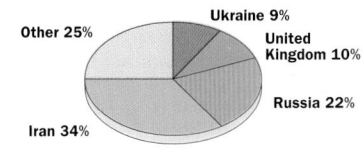

IMPORTS

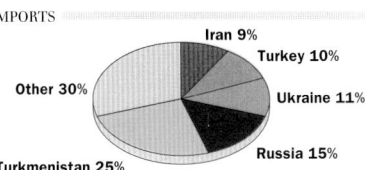

RESOURCES

 20bn kwh

 212,530 b/d (reserves 1,300,000,000 bbl)

 4.5m sheep and goats, 1.6m cattle

 Iron, bauxite, copper, lead, zinc, limestone, salt, oil, gas

The USSR did little to modernize Azerbaijan's oil fields, preferring to concentrate on Siberia; Azeri oil production fell from 8% of the USSR's total in 1965 to 0.6% by 1988. Major investment is now needed.

ENVIRONMENT

 2.2%   Environmental issues are not yet receiving state attention

Under the Soviet regime there was relatively unchecked oil pollution into the Caspian Sea and an overuse of pesticides in agriculture. Azeris are now far more conscious of the need to protect their environment.

MEDIA

 No press comment critical of the government is tolerated

PUBLISHING AND BROADCAST MEDIA

 There are 151 newspapers published, including 133 in Azerbaijani

 1 state-controlled service   1 state-controlled service

The new government has promised to restore media freedom restricted by the communists.

CRIME

 Azerbaijan does not publish prison figures   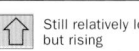 Still relatively low, but rising

The judicial system returned to political control in 1993. Levels of crime outside Nagorno Karabakh are relatively low. Within the enclave, however, there are frequent reports of human rights abuses by members of the armed forces.

EDUCATION

 97%   100,985 students

The return to power of the New Azerbaijan party is expected to reverse communist-control over education policy, which has been particularly noticeable in the teaching of history. Baku, the main university, specializes in Oriental studies.

HEALTH

 1 per 260 people   Heart, cerebrovascular and respiratory diseases, cancers

The already basic health system in Azerbaijan effectively collapsed as a result of shortages caused by the war.

CHRONOLOGY

Under consecutive Persian, Ottoman and Russian influence, Azerbaijan, one of the world's major oil producers in 1900, attained independence in 1917.

- ❑ **1920** Soviet Red Army invades. Soviet republic established.
- ❑ **1922** Incorporated in Transcaucasian Soviet Federative Socialist Republic (TSFSR).
- ❑ **1930** Forced collectivization of agriculture.
- ❑ **1936** TSFSR disbanded. Azerbaijan a full union republic (ASSR).
- ❑ **1945** Attempted annexation of Azeri region of Iran.
- ❑ **1985** President Gorbachev tackles corruption in CPA.
- ❑ **1988** Nagorno Karabakh seeks unification with Armenia.
- ❑ **1990** Nagorno Karabakh attempts secession. Soviet troops move in.
- ❑ **1991** Independence from Moscow.
- ❑ **1993** War with Armenia over Nagorno Karabakh.
- ❑ **1994** Declaration of ceasefire.
- ❑ **1995** General election returns New Azerbaijan party to power.

WEALTH

 A majority of Azeris live close to the breadline

CONSUMER GOODS OWNERSHIP

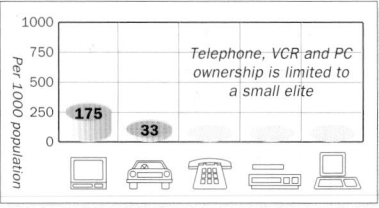

The old Communist Party executives, once more in control of the state economy, are the wealthiest group.

WORLD RANKING

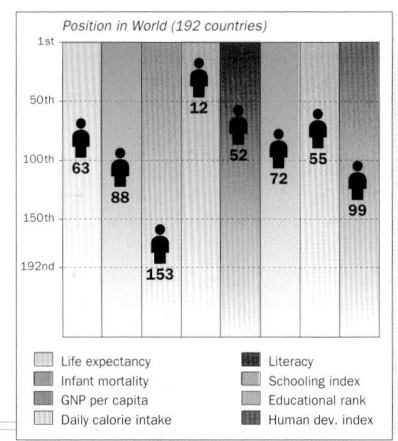

BAHAMAS

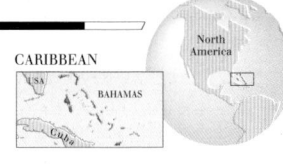

CARIBBEAN

OFFICIAL NAME: The Commonwealth of the Bahamas **CAPITAL:** Nassau
POPULATION: 300,000 **CURRENCY:** Bahamian dollar **OFFICIAL LANGUAGE:** English

B

 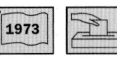

LOCATED OFF THE FLORIDA coast in the western Atlantic, the Bahamas comprises an archipelago of some 700 islands and 2,400 cays, of which 30 are inhabited. One of the first transatlantic tourist destinations, the Bahamas today is also a major offshore financial center. It has one of the world's largest open-registry fleets, but only 0.2% of the total tonage is owned by Bahamian nationals.

CLIMATE

WEATHER CHART

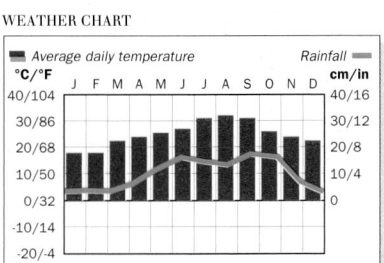

The whole of the Bahamas chain has a typically subtropical climate with consistently mild winters. Hurricanes may occur from July to December.

TRANSPORTATION

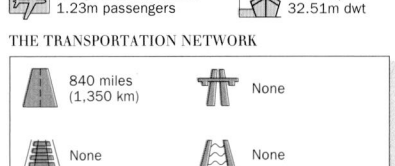

Freeport International
1.23m passengers

914 ships
32.51m dwt

THE TRANSPORTATION NETWORK

840 miles (1,350 km)	None
None	None

Getting around 700 islands spread over 100,300 square miles is a major problem. There are plans to increase the number of ferry and seaplane services.

TOURISM

 1.52m visitors   Up 2% in 1994

MAIN OVERSEAS ARRIVALS

USA **85%**	
Canada **6%**	
UK **3%**	
Other **6%**	

0 10 20 30 40 50 60 70 80 90 100
% of total arrivals

The casinos and beaches are major attractions. Charters from the USA, which arrive in the afternoon, allowing visitors to play the casinos and return home the next morning, are increasingly popular. The Bahamas is also one of the Caribbean's major cruise-ship centers.

PEOPLE

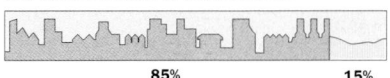

English, English Creole, French Creole

78 people per sq. mile

THE URBAN/RURAL POPULATION SPLIT

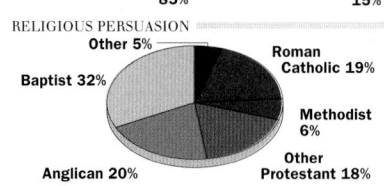

85%   15%

RELIGIOUS PERSUASION

Other 5%
Baptist 32%
Roman Catholic 19%
Methodist 6%
Other Protestant 18%
Anglican 20%

Africans first arrived as slaves in the 16th century; their descendants now make up most of the population, alongside a rich white minority. The nuclear family is the norm, although absentee fathers are fairly common, especially in outlying fishing communities. More women are entering the professions.

POLITICS

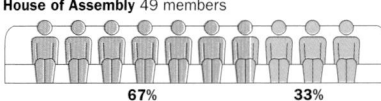

U. House 1992/1997
L. House 1992/1997

H.M. Queen Elizabeth II

THE STATE OF THE PARTIES

House of Assembly 49 members

67% FNM   33% PLP

FNM = Free National Movement **PLP** = Progressive Liberal Party

Senate 16 members

9 members chosen by the prime minister, 4 by the leader of the opposition and 3 by the prime minister after consultation with the leader of the opposition

The 1992 election defeat of Lynden Pindling, the result of increasing numbers of allegations of narcotics corruption against senior government members, ended a period of 25 years of continuous rule by his Progressive Liberal Party (PLP). Pindling was instrumental in steering the Bahamas to independence, ending the domination of the white elite "Bay Street Boys" in Bahamian politics and bringing blacks into the political process for the first time. Prime Minister Hubert Ingraham, leader of the FNM, has concentrated on tightening up ministerial accountability in government and in October 1995 introduced legislation to counter money laundering.

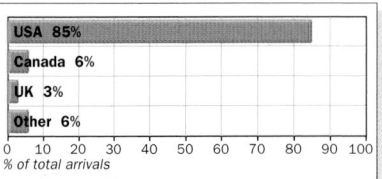

BAHAMAS

Total Land Area: 10 010 sq. km (3864 sq. miles)

POPULATION
- over 100 000
- over 10 000
- under 10 000

LAND HEIGHT
200 m/656ft
Sea level

0   100 km
0   100 miles

B

WORLD AFFAIRS

Dealing with Haitian refugees, 5,000 of whom were repatriated in 1995, and repairing relations with the USA, which considers the island a money-laundering risk, are the dominant issues.

AID

 US$2m (receipts)   Up in 1993

One of the healthiest economies in the Caribbean, the Bahamas receives negligible aid. The USA is the principal donor, mainly providing soft loans.

DEFENSE

 US$20m   Up 11% in 1995

The UK is the main trainer of and supplier for the 900-strong defense force and coastguard. Intercepting narcotics-smugglers and Haitian refugees are the main activities.

ECONOMICS

 US$3.2bn   1.00 Bahamian dollar

SCORE CARD

❏ WORLD GNP RANKING	119th
❏ GNP PER CAPITA	US$11,790
❏ BALANCE OF PAYMENTS	US$–113m
❏ INFLATION	2.6%
❏ UNEMPLOYMENT	13.1%

STRENGTHS

A major international financial services sector, including banking and insurance, which has benefited from political uncertainty in Hong Kong. Tourism and ship registration are also important.

WEAKNESSES

Growing competition in financial services from the Cayman Islands and Bermuda, and vulnerability of tourism to international recession.

EXPORTS

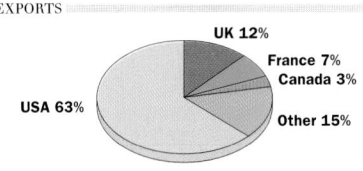

UK 12%
France 7%
Canada 3%
Other 15%
USA 63%

IMPORTS

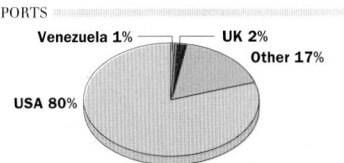

Venezuela 1%   UK 2%
Other 17%
USA 80%

Archetypal island paradise. Its natural beauty belies the fact that six tourists per inhabitant visit the Bahamas every year.

RESOURCES

 975m kwh (capacity 400,000 kw)   10,051 tons

 2m chickens, 40,000 sheep, 15,000 pigs   Salt, aragonite

The Bahamas has no strategic resources and all its energy requirements have to be imported.

ENVIRONMENT

 9%   Plans to increase numbers of protected sites

As in other Caribbean states, hotel overdevelopment is a major cause for concern. Environmental groups have also pointed out the potential for accidents posed by the Bahamas' enormous oil storage depots.

MEDIA

 No restrictions on political reporting

PUBLISHING AND BROADCAST MEDIA

There are 3 daily newspapers, the *Nassau Guardian*, the *Tribune* and the *Freeport News*

1 limited state-owned service   1 state-owned and 4 independent licensed services

The state-owned TV channel faces very stiff competition from Florida-based US broadcasters.

CRIME

 3789 prisoners   Up 8% in 1990

In the first quarter of 1995, 12 murders and 31 attempted murders were reported. The availability of illegal weapons is a major problem. Violent crime ranges from narcotics-related activity to serious vandalism by youths.

EDUCATION

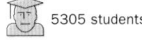 98%   5305 students

Education follows the standard pattern of other Caribbean states, with a British 11-plus selective system. Students go on to the University of the West Indies.

HEALTH

 1 per 692 people   Obstetric causes, heart diseases, cancers, crime, accidents

The Bahamian health service combines state and private systems. Access to care in the outlying islands is difficult, relying on unscheduled inter-island or privately owned boats.

WEALTH

Hotel cook, 13,000 Bahamian dollars (US$13,000) per year; professional nurse, 15,000–27,500 Bahamian dollars (US$15,000–27,500) per year

CONSUMER GOODS OWNERSHIP

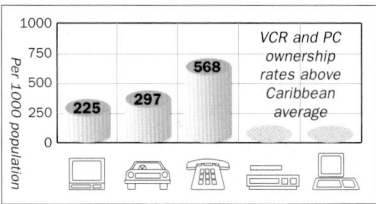

VCR and PC ownership rates above Caribbean average

225   297   568

There are marked wealth disparities between urban professionals working in the financial sector and poor fishermen from the outlying islands. Haitian refugees, who have no legal status, are the poorest group.

WORLD RANKING

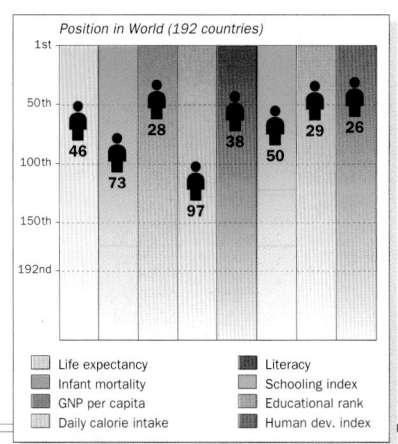

Position in World (192 countries)

46   73   28   97   38   50   29   26

Life expectancy
Infant mortality
GNP per capita
Daily calorie intake
Literacy
Schooling index
Educational rank
Human dev. index

B

BAHRAIN

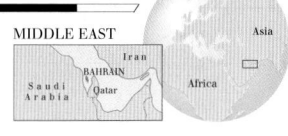
MIDDLE EAST

OFFICIAL NAME: State of Bahrain CAPITAL: Manama
POPULATION: 600,000 CURRENCY: Bahrain dinar OFFICIAL LANGUAGE: Arabic

 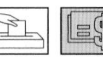

BAHRAIN IS AN ARCHIPELAGO of 33 islands between the Qatar peninsula and the Saudi Arabian mainland. Only three of the islands are inhabited. Bahrain Island is connected to Saudi Arabia's eastern province by a road causeway opened in 1986. Bahrain was the first Gulf emirate to export oil; its reserves are now almost depleted. Services such as offshore banking, insurance and tourism are major employment sectors for skilled Bahrainis.

CLIMATE

WEATHER CHART

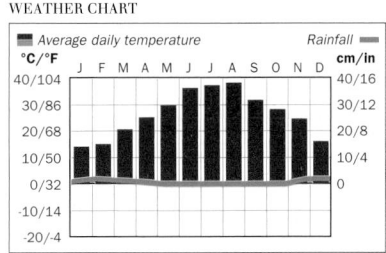

Temperatures soar to 105°F from June to September. Between December and March the weather is pleasantly warm.

TRANSPORTATION

Bahrain International, Muharraq
1.87m passengers

15 ships
158,700 dwt

THE TRANSPORTATION NETWORK

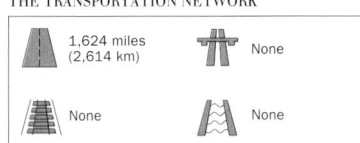

1,624 miles (2,614 km)	None
None	None

Saudi Arabia paid for the 15-mile-long causeway linking it with Bahrain; the four-lane road was completed in 1986.

TOURISM

 1.5m visitors

 Tourist levels have risen since 1991

MAIN OVERSEAS ARRIVALS

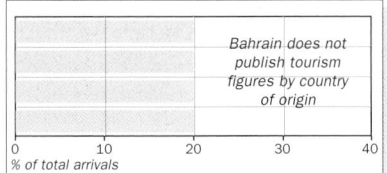
Bahrain does not publish tourism figures by country of origin

% of total arrivals

Bahrain's "liberal" lifestyle is reflected in Manama's bars and nightlife. Since the causeway opened in 1986, there has been a boom in weekend tourists from Saudi Arabia and other Gulf states. Bahrain is a business convention center.

PEOPLE

 Arabic

2,286 people per sq. mile

THE URBAN/RURAL POPULATION SPLIT

89%   11%

ETHNIC MAKEUP

Iranian 20%

Arab 80%

The key division in Bahrain is between Sunni and Shi'a Muslims, 30% and 70% of the population respectively. The ruling class is Sunni and they hold the best jobs in business and the bureaucracy. Shi'a Muslims tend to do menial work and have a lower standard of living. Tension between the two groups can spill over into violence, particularly during religious festivals.

Bahrain has a smaller expatriate population than many other Arab countries. The ruling Al-Khalifa family has responded to declining oil reserves by diversifying the economy to provide service industry jobs for Bahrainis.

Bahrain is the most "liberal" of the Gulf states. Women have access to education and the professions and are not obliged to wear veils. Arranged marriages, however, remain common.

The Grand Mosque, Manama. *It is the largest building in Bahrain and can accommodate 7,000 people.*

POLITICS

 Not applicable

Amir Sheikh Isa bin Sulman Al-Khalifa

THE STATE OF THE PARTIES

Bahrain is an absolute monarchy, ruled by the Amir through an appointed cabinet

The Al-Khalifa family has dominated Bahraini politics since 1783. Politics is effectively autocratic, and political dissent is not tolerated. Bahrain is one of the few Gulf states with political prisoners. Opponents of the regime – usually Shi'a fundamentalists – are frequently exiled and have their passports canceled. Iran has sought to encourage fundamentalists in Bahrain by distributing cassettes of Iranian mullahs' sermons preaching revolution. Radio broadcasts from Tehran also reach Bahrain. Whilst there is considerable Shi'a discontent at their low social status, there are few channels by which this can be expressed or organized.

The current Amir, Sheikh Isa bin Sulman Al-Khalifa, is a liberal in economic policy, encouraging private enterprise. Politically he is cautious of introducing democracy. An attempt at representative government in 1973 was suspended in 1975 on the grounds that it provoked instability. Political reform is the key demand of Shi'a activists behind the civil unrest which has shaken the country since late 1994.

WORLD AFFAIRS

 AL Damasc GCC OIC OAPEC

Bahrain holds to a staunchly independent line in foreign policy. It maintains good relations with the USA, the main guarantor of its security, yet has also called for relations with Iraq to be restored. Despite objecting to Bahrain's liberal social attitudes, Saudi Arabia finds the Al-Khalifas useful allies against Gulf fundamentalists.

AID

 $4m (receipts)

Down 94% in 1993

Bahrain receives low levels of aid, but takes the lion's share of the offshore oil field shared with Saudi Arabia, effectively a subsidy from the latter.

B

DEFENSE

 $253m   Up 2% in 1995

The 6,150-strong defense force includes a small but well-equipped air force. Bahrain has traditionally maintained close relations with the USA. US air bases on Bahrain were used in the 1990–1991 Gulf War. The small navy is hard-pressed to patrol the 33-island archipelago.

ECONOMICS

 $4.1bn   0.38 Bahrain dinars

SCORE CARD

- ❑ WORLD GNP RANKING........................107th
- ❑ GNP PER CAPITA $7,500
- ❑ BALANCE OF PAYMENTS...................$–993m
- ❑ INFLATION 0.8%
- ❑ UNEMPLOYMENT..................................15%

EXPORTS
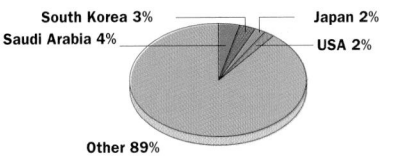
South Korea 3%   Japan 2%
Saudi Arabia 4%   USA 2%
Other 89%

IMPORTS
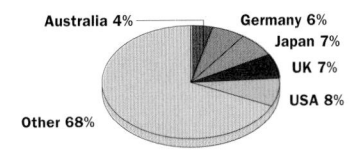
Australia 4%   Germany 6%
Japan 7%
UK 7%
USA 8%
Other 68%

STRENGTHS
Oil. Arab world's major offshore banking sector. Lack of restrictions encourages inward investment. Tourism.

WEAKNESSES
Depleted oil reserves and insufficient diversification could lead to future drop in currently high living standards. High levels of government borrowing.

RESOURCES

 3.5bn kwh (capacity 1.04m kw)

38,200 b/d (reserves 69,584,000 bbl)

 17,000 goats, 29,000 sheep, 16,000 cattle

Oil, natural gas

Bahrain remains dependent on its oil and gas production. Production of crude oil declined however, from 65,000 b/d in the 1970s to 38,200 b/d in 1994. Reserves will probably run out by 2010. As oil has declined, so gas has assumed greater importance. Most is used to supply local industries, particularly the aluminum plant established in 1972.

BAHRAIN

Total Land Area : 680 sq. km (263 sq. miles)

POPULATION
- ◎ over 100 000
- ○ over 50 000
- ● over 10 000
- • under 10 000

LAND HEIGHT
- 100m/328ft
- Sea Level

0   10 km
0   10 miles

ENVIRONMENT

 None   Environmental issues not a priority

Local marine life, particularly the dugong, is vulnerable to upstream oil pollution from the Gulf.

MEDIA

The information ministry is relatively liberal. However, the press is still semi-controlled

PUBLISHING AND BROADCAST MEDIA

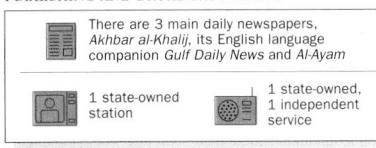
There are 3 main daily newspapers, *Akhbar al-Khalij*, its English language companion *Gulf Daily News* and *Al-Ayam*

1 state-owned station   1 state-owned, 1 independent service

Bahrain has the most liberal information policy in the Gulf. CNN and BBC satellite TV are freely available.

CRIME

 Bahrain does not publish prison figures   Down 57% in 1990

Crime is minimal and theft and muggings rare. Suspected political dissidents are monitored by the police.

CHRONOLOGY

Bahrain has been ruled since 1785 by the Al-Khalifa family.

- ❑ **1971** Independence from Britain.
- ❑ **1981** Founder-member of GCC. December, abortive coup backed by Iran. Bahrain gives backing to Iraq in Iran–Iraq war.
- ❑ **1991** Bahrain backs UN in expelling Iraq from Kuwait.
- ❑ **1994–1996** Shi'a unrest increases pressure for political reform.

EDUCATION

 84.1%   7,763 students

Female literacy rates are well above the Gulf average. Lack of funding has held up plans for a university.

HEALTH

 1 per 930 people   Circulatory diseases, perinatal deaths, injury, poisonings

The health service is extensive and run to world-class standards. Bahraini nationals receive free treatment. Some go abroad for advanced care.

WEALTH

 Agricultural worker, 196 Bahrain dinars ($519) per month; oil engineer, 698 Bahrain dinars ($1,851) per month

CONSUMER GOODS OWNERSHIP
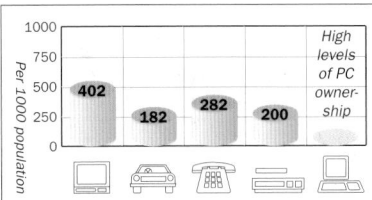
High levels of PC ownership
402   182   282   200

Beneficiaries of the Amir's extensive patronage are the wealthiest group. Shi'a Muslims are the poorest.

WORLD RANKING

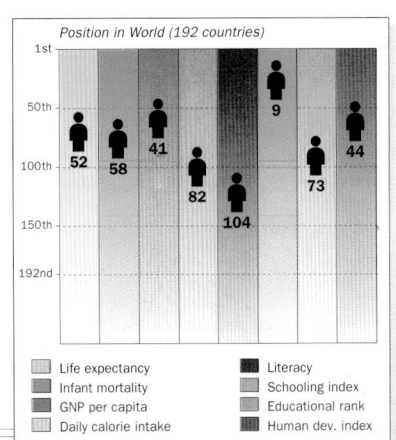
Position in World (192 countries)
52   58   41   82   104   9   73   44

- Life expectancy
- Infant mortality
- GNP per capita
- Daily calorie intake
- Literacy
- Schooling index
- Educational rank
- Human dev. index

B

BANGLADESH

OFFICIAL NAME: People's Republic of Bangladesh CAPITAL: Dhaka
POPULATION: 120.4 million CURRENCY: Taka OFFICIAL LANGUAGE: Bengali

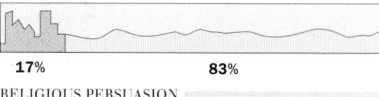

BANGLADESH LIES AT the north of the Bay of Bengal and shares borders with India and Burma. Most of the country is composed of fertile alluvial plains; the north and northeast are mountainous, as is the Chittagong region. Since its secession from Pakistan in 1971, Bangladesh has had a troubled history of political instability, with periods of emergency rule. Effective democracy was restored in 1991. Bangladesh's major economic sectors are jute production, textiles and agriculture. Its climate can wreak havoc. In 1991, a massive cyclone killed more than 140,000 people.

PEOPLE

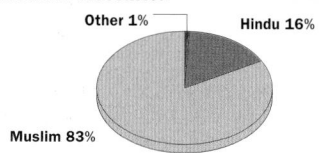

Bengali, Urdu, Chakma, Marma (Magh), Garo, Khasi, Santhali, Tripuri, Mro

2,330 people per sq. mile

THE URBAN/RURAL POPULATION SPLIT

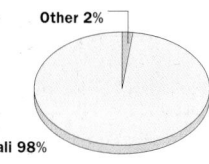

17%   83%

RELIGIOUS PERSUASION

Other 1%   Hindu 16%

Muslim 83%

ETHNIC MAKEUP

Other 2%

Bengali 98%

CLIMATE

WEATHER CHART

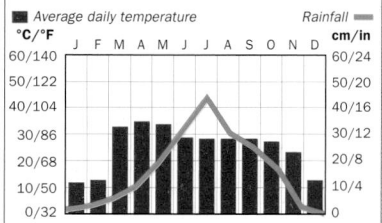

During the monsoon, the water level normally rises 20 feet above sea level, flooding two-thirds of the country. The floods are made much worse when the Ganges, Jamuna and Meghna rivers, which converge in a huge delta in Bangladesh, are swollen by the melting of the Himalayan snows, and heavy rain, in India. Cyclones regularly build up in the Bay of Bengal, with sometimes devastating effect on the flat coastal region.

TRANSPORTATION

 Zia International, Dhaka 1.19m passengers   172 ships 532,600 dwt

THE TRANSPORTATION NETWORK

 3,877 miles (6,240 km)   None

1,735 miles (2,792 km)   5,240 miles (8,433 km)

Most transportation in Bangladesh is by water, although government transportation policy is now concentrating on developing road and rail links. A major bridge is currently being built across the Jamuna River, which bisects Bangladesh from north to south. The $500-million project has suffered numerous delays and is now due to be completed in 1996. Bangladesh's two major ports, Mungla and Chittagong, are being upgraded to take advanced container ships.

Begum Khaleda Zia, *prime minister since February 1991.*

Shaikh Hasina Wajed, *leader of the Awami League.*

TOURISM

 140,000 visitors    Down 2% in 1992

MAIN OVERSEAS ARRIVALS

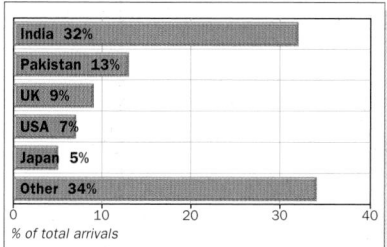

India 32%	
Pakistan 13%	
UK 9%	
USA 7%	
Japan 5%	
Other 34%	

0   10   20   30   40
% of total arrivals

Tourist earnings and numbers have been falling since the mid-1980s. Most visitors are Indian businessmen or Bangladeshis who live overseas returning to see their relatives. The mogul architecture in Dhaka and the Pala dynasty (7th–10th centuries) city of Sonargaon are major attractions.

Traders on the Meghna River, *which flows into the Padma. Bangladesh's flood-plains are among the most fertile in the world.*

Bangladesh is one of the most densely populated countries in the world, despite the fact that 83% of the population is rural. As in India, there is considerable Muslim–Hindu tension; the destruction of the Ayodhya mosque in northern India in 1992 incited violence in Bangladesh.

The most significant ethnic conflict occurs in the Chittagong Hill Tracts in the southeast, where 12 Buddhist tribes – the Chakma – demanding autonomy have waged a low-level guerrilla war since 1974. Until 1993 the south of the country also accommodated Muslim refugees from Burma, many of whom have since been repatriated.

Although about 55% of Bangladeshis, rural and urban, still live below the poverty line, there has been an improvement in living standards over the past decade.

The textile trade, by providing an independent income, has been one factor in the growing emancipation of Bangladeshi women. They are now included in official employment statistics and are the main customers of the most successful rural bank. Women lead both the government and opposition.

POPULATION AGE BREAKDOWN

% of population by age group	■ 0–14	▨ 15–64	□ 65+		
	3.7%	3.5%	3.4%	2.9%	3%
	55.4%	51.1%	50.4%	53.2%	58.2%
	40.9%	45.4%	46.2%	43.9%	38.8%
	1960	1970	1980	1990	2000

B

POLITICS

 1991/1996

 President Abdur Rahman Biswas

THE STATE OF THE PARTIES

National Assembly 330 members

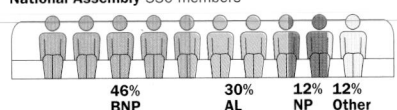

| 46% BNP | 30% AL | 12% NP | 12% Other |

BNP = Bangladesh National Party **AL** = Awami League
NP = National Party **Other** = Islamic Party of Bangladesh, Bangladesh Communist Party

Bangladesh returned to multiparty democracy in 1991, following a period of military rule.

MAIN POLITICAL ISSUES
The State sector
Bangladesh is coming under increasing pressure from multilateral lending institutions, which account for the vast majority of the country's capital inflows, to cut costs in the state sector. Simultaneously, state sector workers are demanding wage increases in line with inflation.

BANGLADESH

Total Land Area : 133 910 sq. km (51 703 sq. miles)

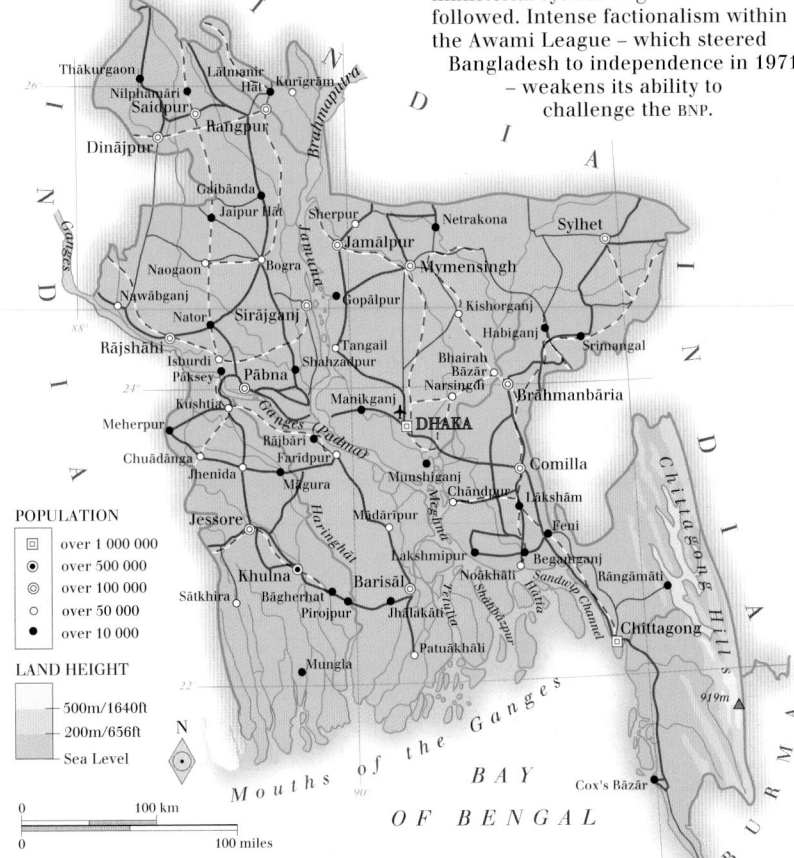

POPULATION

- ⊡ over 1 000 000
- ⊙ over 500 000
- ◎ over 100 000
- ○ over 50 000
- ● over 10 000

LAND HEIGHT

- 500m/1640ft
- 200m/656ft
- Sea Level

0   100 km

0   100 miles

The Chittagong Hill Tracts insurgency
Buddhist Mongol groups, the Chakma, have been waging a low-level guerrilla war since 1974 in support of greater autonomy. Despite an agreement with the government finalized in 1994, many Chakma continue to fear persecution by Bengali Muslim settlers.

Golam Azam
Golam Azam, leader of the Islamic Party, has been in custody since 1990, accused of war crimes during Bangladesh's struggle for independence from Pakistan. Opposition groups are campaigning for Azam to stand trial as a war criminal and be stripped of his Bangladeshi citizenship.

PROFILE
Between 1975 and 1990 the military was in power in Bangladesh. The overthrow of President Ershad in 1990 saw a return to multiparty politics; the army remains poised, however, to intervene in the event of a breakdown in law and order. Bangladesh's first woman prime minister, Begum Khaleda Zia, head of the ruling BNP, was elected in February 1991. A change from a presidential to a prime-ministerial system of government followed. Intense factionalism within the Awami League – which steered Bangladesh to independence in 1971 – weakens its ability to challenge the BNP.

WORLD AFFAIRS

 Comm   NAM   OIC   SAARC   WTO

Bangladesh concentrates mostly on maintaining good relations with the West, the main source of essential aid. Relations with Pakistan have slowly been improving since the low point of 1971. Pakistan finally agreed in 1991 to repatriate the 250,000 pro-Pakistani Bihari Muslims languishing in Bangladeshi refugee camps since 1971. Relations with India are strained. The effects of the Indian construction of the Farakka Dam across the Ganges have deprived Bangladeshi farmers of water for irrigation. The failure of Delhi to curb guerrilla groups operating out of India into the Chittagong region has also soured relations.

AID

 $1.4bn (receipts)   Down 20% in 1991

Aid disbursements to Bangladesh each year are over 1,000 times greater than the annual value of foreign investment in the country. Aid also finances more than 90% of state capital spending. The Bangladesh Development Aid Consortium meets annually to discuss aid spending under the auspices of the World Bank. One result of the level of aid is that Bangladesh has fallen into one of the traps of an aid-dependent economy: the large middle class has a vested interest in perpetuating a system which provides its members with lucrative contracts and access to external resources.

CHRONOLOGY
British rule in India began in Bengal (now Bangladesh), when Robert Clive, army head of the East India Company, defeated the ruler of Bengal at Plassey in 1765.

- ❏ **1905** Muslims persuade British rulers to partition state of Bengal, to create a Muslim-dominated East Bengal.
- ❏ **1906** Muslim League established in Dhaka.
- ❏ **1912** Partition of 1905 reversed.
- ❏ **1947** British withdrawal from India. Partition plans establish a largely Muslim state of East (present-day Bangladesh) and West Pakistan, separated by 992 miles of Indian, and largely Hindu, territory. The capital of the new, bisected state established at Islamabad in West Pakistan.
- ❏ **1949** Awami League founded to campaign for autonomy from West Pakistan.   ⇨

B

CHRONOLOGY *continued*

- ❏ **1968** General Yahya Khan heads government in Islamabad.
- ❏ **1970** Elections give Awami League, under Sheikh Mujibur Rahman, clear majority. Rioting and guerrilla warfare following Yahya Khan's refusal to convene assembly. The year ends with the worst recorded storms in Bangladesh's history – between 200,000 and 500,000 dead.
- ❏ **1971** Civil War, as Sheikh Mujibur and Awami League declare unilateral independence. Ten million Bangladeshis flee to India. Pakistani troops defeated in 12 days by *Mukhti Bahini* – the Bengal Liberation Army.
- ❏ **1972** Sheikh Mujibur prime minister. Nationalization program for the utilities and tea, jute and textiles industries introduced. Bangladesh achieves international recognition and joins Commonwealth. Pakistan withdraws in protest.
- ❏ **1974** Severe floods damage rice crop.
- ❏ **1975** Sheikh Mujibur assassinated. Military coups end with General Zia Rahman taking power. Institution of single-party state.
- ❏ **1976** Banning of trade union federations.
- ❏ **1977** General Zia assumes presidency. Islam adopted as first principle of the constitution.
- ❏ **1981** General Zia assassinated.
- ❏ **1982** General Ershad takes over.
- ❏ **1983** Democratic elections restored by Ershad; marred by political violence. Ershad assumes presidency.
- ❏ **1986** Elections again affected by intimidation and violence. Awami League and BNP fail to unseat Ershad.
- ❏ **1987** Ershad announces state of emergency following anti-government strikes.
- ❏ **1988** Islam becomes constitutional state religion.
- ❏ **1990** Ershad resigns following renewed demonstrations. Bangladeshis in Kuwait suffer loss of earnings due to Gulf War.
- ❏ **1991** Elections won by BNP. Khaleda Zia becomes prime minister. Ershad imprisoned. Role of the president reduced to ceremonial functions. Floods kill 150,000 people.
- ❏ **1994** Author Taslima Nasreen, who is accused of blasphemy, escapes to Sweden. Opposition parties intensify campaign for fresh elections.
- ❏ **1996** General election, boycotted by opposition parties, returns BNP to power.

DEFENSE

 $483m   Down in 1995

0   *Defense spending as % GDP*   40

1.8%

The military, which dominated politics between 1975 and 1990, continues to wield influence. However, spending on defense as a proportion of GDP has recently declined, with greater emphasis on poverty alleviation programs. The army, at 101,000 personnel, is also relatively small.

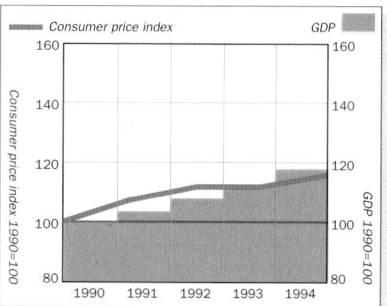

BANGLADESHI ARMED FORCES

140 main battle tanks (T-59/-69, T-54/-55)	101,000 personnel	
4 frigates and 40 patrol boats	8,000 personnel	
57 combat aircraft (17 J-7M/16 MiG-21M F/2 MiG-21U)	6,500 personnel	
None		

ECONOMICS

 $26.6bn   39.8–40.3 taka

SCORE CARD

❏ WORLD GNP RANKING	58th
❏ GNP PER CAPITA	$230
❏ BALANCE OF PAYMENTS	$197m
❏ INFLATION	3.6%
❏ UNEMPLOYMENT	1.9%

EXPORTS

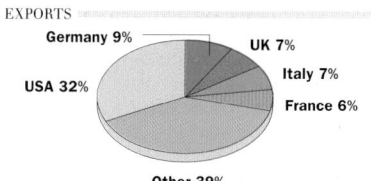

Germany 9%   UK 7%
Italy 7%
USA 32%   France 6%
Other 39%

IMPORTS

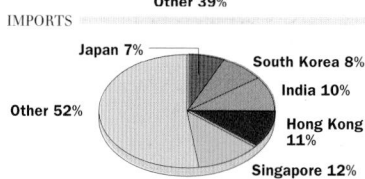

Japan 7%   South Korea 8%
India 10%
Other 52%   Hong Kong 11%
Singapore 12%

ECONOMIC PERFORMANCE INDICATOR

— Consumer price index   GDP ▨

Consumer price index 1990=100   *GDP 1990=100*

1990 1991 1992 1993 1994

STRENGTHS

Jute is the major industry: Bangladesh accounts for 80% of world jute fibre exports. Low wages ensure a competitive and expanding textile industry, which constitutes one-third of the small manufacturing sector.

WEAKNESSES

The agricultural sector, which employs 68% of Bangladeshis, is vulnerable to the violent and unpredictable climate.

PROFILE

Government ministers like to portray Bangladesh as an emerging NIC, but its economy is still overwhelmingly dependent on agriculture and large aid inflows. Agriculture, which provides the major export, jute, is productive; Bangladesh's soils, fed by the Ganges, Jamuna and Meghna rivers, are highly fertile. However, the effects of the weather can be devastating, frequently destroying a whole year's crop. Agricultural wages are among the lowest in the world.

The state sector, which owns large, inefficient and massively loss-making companies (such as the Bangladesh Jute Mills Corporation), is in difficulty. The World Bank, which channels most aid into the country, wishes to see loss-making concerns cut their work forces or close down.

Textiles and garments are currently the healthiest sectors. Economic zones (Export Processing Zones) with special concessions have attracted foreign investment, as well as helping to promote a small indigenous electronics industry. Bangladesh receives generous textile import quotas from the EU and NAFTA, but its economy is so weak that it fails to reach them.

BANGLADESH : MAJOR BUSINESSES

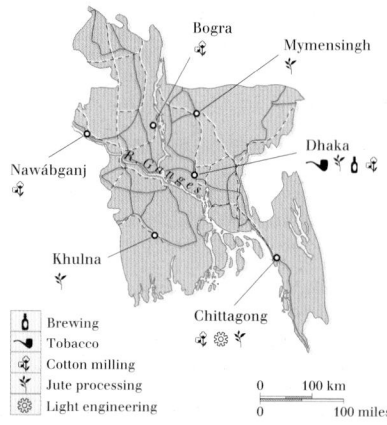

Bogra
Mymensingh
Dhaka
Nawábganj
Khulna
Chittagong

🍶	Brewing
	Tobacco
	Cotton milling
	Jute processing
	Light engineering

0   100 km
0   100 miles

RESOURCES

8.7bn kwh (capacity 2.52m kw)

Not an oil producer; refines 31,200 b/cd

24.1m cattle, 1.1m sheep, 25.9m goats

Salt, oil, natural gas, limestone

Bangladesh is the world's major jute producer, accounting for 80% of world jute fibre exports and about 50% of world jute manufactures exports. Natural gas from the Bay of Bengal, exploited by the state-owned Bangladesh Oil, Gas and Minerals Corporation, came on stream in 1988;

ELECTRICITY GENERATION

Hydro 8% (0.7bn kwh)
Thermal 92% (8bn kwh)
Nuclear 0%
Other 0%

0   20   40   60   80   100

% of total generation by type

production had increased to 6.5 billion cubic yards by 1991. Reserves are estimated at 200 years.

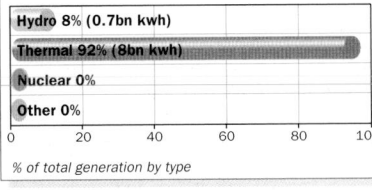

BANGLADESH : LAND USE

Cropland
Wetlands
Forest
Rice
Jute - cash crop

0   100 km
0   100 miles

ENVIRONMENT

0.7% partially protected

Protection measures being incorporated into donor programs

Bangladesh's climate, which is prone to devastating floods and cyclones, results in huge death tolls and substantial damage to crops. Bangladesh is too poor to finance environmental initiatives.

ENVIRONMENTAL TREATIES

No   Yes   Yes
No   Yes   No

HEALTH

1 per 5,220 people

Parasitic, diarrheal and communicable diseases

0   *Health spending as % GDP*   25

1.4%

Although primary health care in rural areas has improved over the last decade, Bangladesh's health problems remain severe and are exacerbated by a shortage of staff and facilities. The priority given to birth-control programs has reduced the population growth rate by 23% over the last 15 years, from 2.6% to 2% a year.

MEDIA

Political intervention in the media, which was greatly reduced in 1990, is on the rise.

PUBLISHING AND BROADCAST MEDIA

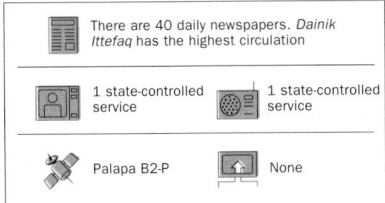

There are 40 daily newspapers. *Dainik Ittefaq* has the highest circulation

1 state-controlled service

1 state-controlled service

Palapa B2-P

None

Press freedom, which emerged after the fall of President Ershad in 1990, has tended to be steadily eroded under pressure from the ruling BNP. Of the daily newspapers, the 10 English-language titles appeal mainly to the urban elite. Among political weeklies, the most respected is called *Holiday* (originally a travel magazine whose name was retained by its new owners). Over 70% of TV programs are produced locally; about one-third are in black and white.

WEALTH

Machine cloth weaver, 950 taka ($24) per month; natural gas engineer, 2,850 taka ($71) per month

CONSUMER GOODS OWNERSHIP

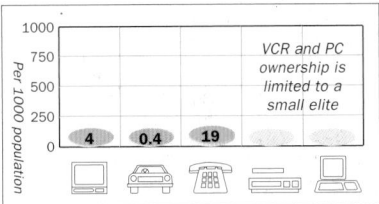

VCR and PC ownership is limited to a small elite

1000
750
500
250
0

Per 1000 population

4   0.4   19

Average incomes are very low, but wealth disparities are not as marked as in India or Pakistan. State officials tend to be among the better-off.

CRIME

31,192 prisoners

Up 6% in 1990

CRIME RATES

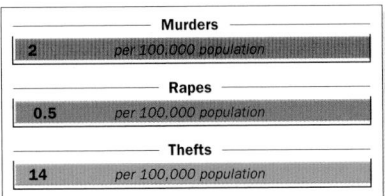

Murders
2 *per 100,000 population*

Rapes
0.5 *per 100,000 population*

Thefts
14 *per 100,000 population*

Rising levels of political and religious violence led the new government of 1991 to introduce a controversial anti-terrorism law, which offered swift (and many thought careless) justice with heavy penalties, including death. The Special Powers Act, which was used by Ershad to detain political opponents, is still in force. Deaths in Bangladeshi prisons are common and the army's human rights record, especially that of the paramilitary Bangladesh Rifles in the Chittagong Hills, has also been questioned by Amnesty International.

EDUCATION

35%

434,309 students

0   *Education spending as % GNP*   25

2.3%

THE EDUCATION SYSTEM

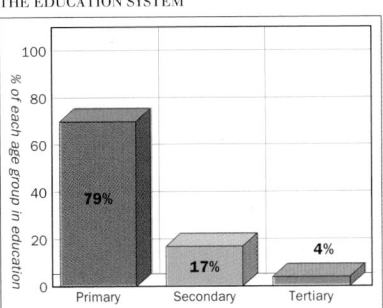

100
80
60
40
20
0

% of each age group in education

79%   17%   4%

Primary   Secondary   Tertiary

Education in Bangladeshi society has been poorly addressed, although recent increases in expenditure show a greater determination to combat the low literacy figure. The seven universities, frequently experience political violence.

WORLD RANKING

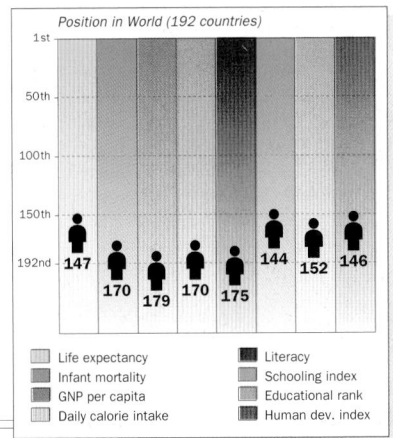

Position in World (192 countries)

1st
50th
100th
150th
192nd

147   170   179   170   175   144   152   146

Life expectancy
Infant mortality
GNP per capita
Daily calorie intake

Literacy
Schooling index
Educational rank
Human dev. index

BARBADOS

B

OFFICIAL NAME: Barbados **CAPITAL:** Bridgetown
POPULATION: 300,000 **CURRENCY:** Barbados dollar **OFFICIAL LANGUAGE:** English

CARIBBEAN

SITUATED TO THE NORTHEAST of Trinidad, Barbados is the most easterly of the West Indian Windward Islands. In the 16th century, the Portuguese became the first Europeans to reach the island, which was inhabited by Arawak Indians. However, Barbados was not colonized until the 1620s, when British settlers arrived. Popularly referred to by its neighbors as "little England," Barbados still retains a strong British influence.

CLIMATE

WEATHER CHART

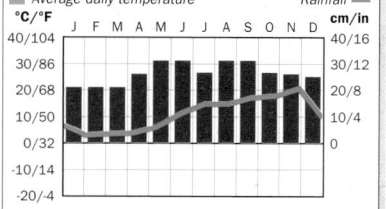

Barbados has a moderate tropical climate and is sunnier and drier than its more mountainous Caribbean neighbors. Hurricanes may occur in the rainy season.

TRANSPORTATION

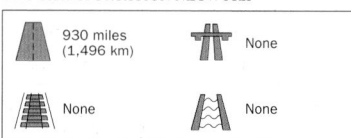

Grantley Adams International, Bridgetown
1.21m passengers

3 ships
79,900 dwt

THE TRANSPORTATION NETWORK

930 miles
(1,496 km)

None

None

None

Recent major construction projects have included the resurfacing of the runway at the international airport and the expansion of piers at Bridgetown's port. Upgrading the island's dense road network is a priority. Bus routes cover most of the island.

House of Assembly, Trafalgar Square, Bridgetown. Barbados's parliament, the third-oldest in the Commonwealth, dates from 1639.

TOURISM

447,000 visitors

Up 13% in 1994

MAIN OVERSEAS ARRIVALS

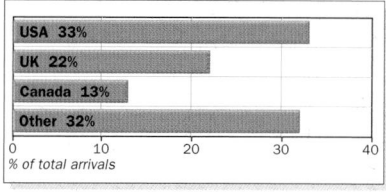

USA 33%
UK 22%
Canada 13%
Other 32%

% of total arrivals

The airport runway has been improved in an effort to encourage tourists. Visitors come mainly from North America and Europe. Cruise-ship traffic is on the increase.

PEOPLE

Bajan (Barbadian English), English

1,809 people per sq. mile

THE URBAN/RURAL POPULATION SPLIT

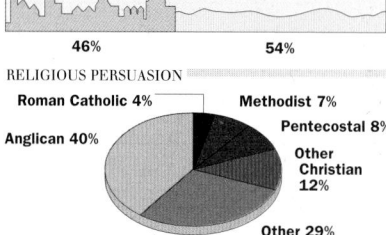

46%   54%

RELIGIOUS PERSUASION

Roman Catholic 4%
Methodist 7%
Pentecostal 8%
Other Christian 12%
Anglican 40%
Other 29%

Most Bajans are the descendants of Africans brought to the island between the 16th and 19th centuries; there are also small groups of South Asians and of Europeans, mainly expatriate Britons, many of whom take up residence on retirement. There is some latent tension between the white community, which controls most of the economy, and the majority black population, although this rarely spills over into violence. Increasing social mobility has allowed many black Bajans to move into the professions and the civil service. Barbados enjoys a higher standard of living than most Caribbean countries.

POLITICS

U. House 1994/1999
L. House 1994/1999

HM Queen Elizabeth II

THE STATE OF THE PARTIES

House of Assembly 28 members

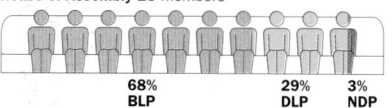

68% BLP   29% DLP   3% NDP

BLP = Barbados Labour Party **DLP** = Democratic Labour Party **NDP** = National Democratic Party

Senate 21 members

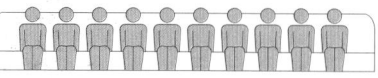

12 members chosen by the prime minister, 2 by the leader of the opposition and 7 by the governor-general

Barbados is a multiparty democracy. The main power brokers are a primarily European, affluent elite, who finance the parties and exert an indirect influence on government policy. The BLP swept to power in the 1994 elections. Owen Arthur, BLP leader and prime minister, has prioritized economic growth and international competitiveness. In 1995 he established an advisory commission on constitutional and institutional reform.

WORLD AFFAIRS

ACS   Comm   Caricom   NAM   OAS

Barbados is a strong supporter of US policy in the region, and was a staging post for the 1983 invasion of Grenada.

AID

US$1m (receipts)

Down 50% in 1993

Barbados receives the bulk of its aid from the USA, EU and UK, mainly in the form of development project loans and balance of payments support.

DEFENSE

US$14m

No change in 1995

The 1,000-strong Barbadian army and the constabulary benefit from financial support and training from the US and UK governments, which also supply equipment. The country is the headquarters of the Regional Security System, established in 1982 by the Windward and Leeward Islands, a body which acts as a multinational security force for its members.

ECONOMICS

 US$1.7bn

 2.01 Barbados dollars

SCORE CARD

❏ WORLD GNP RANKING	139th
❏ GNP PER CAPITA	US$6,530
❏ BALANCE OF PAYMENTS	US$64m
❏ INFLATION	0.1%
❏ UNEMPLOYMENT	24.2%

STRENGTHS

Well-developed tourism based on climate and accessibility. Sugar industries. Information processing and financial services are important new growth sectors.

WEAKNESSES

Narrow economic base, vulnerable to downturns in tourism, failures of sugar harvest and the latter's dependency on loans and secure markets. Relatively high manufacturing costs.

EXPORTS

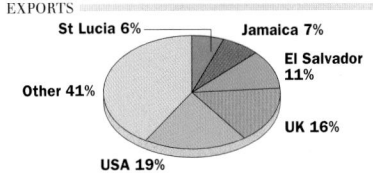

St Lucia 6%
Jamaica 7%
El Salvador 11%
Other 41%
UK 16%
USA 19%

IMPORTS

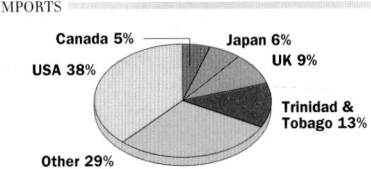

Canada 5%
Japan 6%
USA 38%
UK 9%
Trinidad & Tobago 13%
Other 29%

BARBADOS

Total Land Area : 430 sq. km (166 sq. miles)

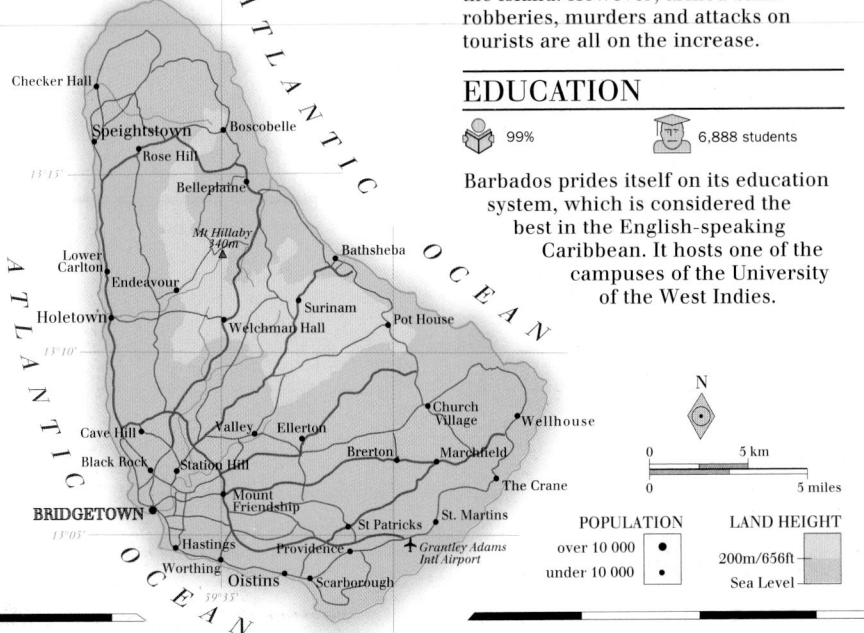

ATLANTIC OCEAN

Checker Hall
Speightstown · Boscobelle
Rose Hill
Belleplaine
Lower Carlton
Mt Hillaby 340m
Endeavour
Bathsheba
Holetown
Surinam
Welchman Hall · Pot House
Cave Hill
Valley · Ellerton
Church Village · Wellhouse
Black Rock
Brereton
Marchfield
Station Hill
BRIDGETOWN
Mount Friendship
St Patricks · St. Martins
The Crane
Hastings · Providence
Grantley Adams Intl Airport
Worthing · Oistins · Scarborough

N

0   5 km

0   5 miles

POPULATION
over 10 000 ●
under 10 000 ·

LAND HEIGHT
200m/656ft
Sea Level

RESOURCES

 537m kwh (capacity 140,000 kw)

 1,246 b/d (reserves 5,892,000 bbl)

 3m chickens, 41,000 sheep, 30,000 pigs

Oil, natural gas

Barbados has few strategic resources. The domestic petroleum industry provides about one-third of the country's energy requirements.

ENVIRONMENT

 1%

 The only mangrove swamp on Barbados is still unprotected

Oil slicks created by waste dumped from passing ships are polluting the encircling reef and adversely affecting the life cycle of the flying fish, Barbados's main fish stock.

MEDIA

 Freedom of expression guaranteed by the constitution. Defamation law restrictive to investigative journalism

PUBLISHING AND BROADCAST MEDIA

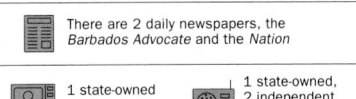

There are 2 daily newspapers, the *Barbados Advocate* and the *Nation*

1 state-owned service

1 state-owned, 2 independent services

There is no political interference in the media in Barbados. The two daily newspapers are privately owned, as are two of the radio stations.

CRIME

 260 prisoners

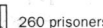 Up 9% in 1990

Compared with other Caribbean islands, Barbados still has a low crime rate. There are no "no-go" areas on the island. However, armed bank robberies, murders and attacks on tourists are all on the increase.

EDUCATION

99%

6,888 students

Barbados prides itself on its education system, which is considered the best in the English-speaking Caribbean. It hosts one of the campuses of the University of the West Indies.

HEALTH

 1 per 874 people

 Heart and cerebrovascular diseases, cancers

The health system is based on subsidized government-run clinics and hospitals, supplemented by more expensive private clinics and private doctors. Facilities are within easy reach of all Bajans.

WEALTH

 Plantation field worker, 4 Barbados dollars (US$2) per hour; oil refinery foreman, 564 Barbados dollars (US$280) per week (minimum)

CONSUMER GOODS OWNERSHIP

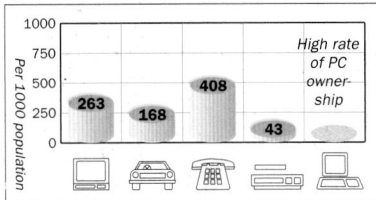

High rate of PC ownership

263   168   408   43

(Per 1000 population)

There is a significant disparity between most Bajans and a small affluent group, mostly of European origin, which owns and controls business and industry. Among the latter, status symbols include yachts and exclusive club membership.

WORLD RANKING

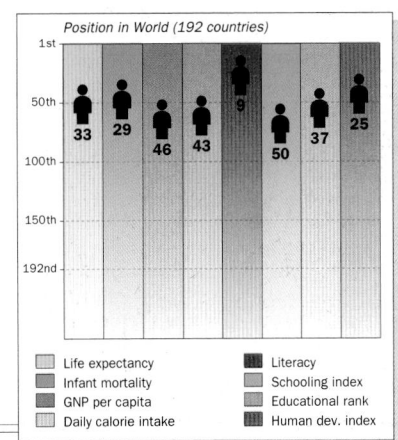

Position in World (192 countries)

33   29   46   43   9   50   37   25

Life expectancy
Infant mortality
GNP per capita
Daily calorie intake
Literacy
Schooling index
Educational rank
Human dev. index

BELGIUM

B

OFFICIAL NAME: Kingdom of Belgium **CAPITAL:** Brussels
POPULATION: 10.1 million **CURRENCY:** Belgian franc **OFFICIAL LANGUAGE:** Dutch, French and German

LOCATED BETWEEN GERMANY, France and the Netherlands, Belgium has a short coastline on the North Sea. The south includes the forested Ardennes region, while the north is dissected by canals. Belgium has been fought over many times in its history. It was occupied by Germany in both World Wars. Long-standing tensions have existed between the majority Flemish and minority French-speakers since the 1830s. These have been somewhat defused by Belgium's move to a federal structure and the national consensus on the benefits of EU membership.

CLIMATE

WEATHER CHART

Belgium has a typical maritime climate and is influenced by the Gulf Stream. Temperatures are mild with heavy cloud cover and much rain. The west coast climate can be disrupted by widely fluctuating weather conditions, caused by cyclonic disturbances. Summers tend to be short.

TRANSPORTATION

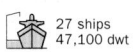

Zaventem International, Brussels
6.87m passengers

27 ships
47,100 dwt

THE TRANSPORTATION NETWORK

85,804 miles (138,080 km)

1,013 miles (1,631 km)

5,224 miles (8,408 km)

949 miles (1,528 km)

Belgium can be crossed within four hours by car or train, and access to France, Germany, the Netherlands and beyond is easy. Belgium's highway network is extensive and so well lit that, along with the Great Wall of China, it is the most distinctive sight from orbit. Although the railroad system has been reduced since 1970, it is still one of the world's densest networks. When new high-speed TGV (*train à grande vitesse*) lines open in 1996 and 1998, it will be possible to reach Paris in 1 hour 20 minutes and London via the Channel Tunnel in 2 hours 40 minutes. Antwerp, an old Hanseatic city, is Europe's second-largest port.

TOURISM

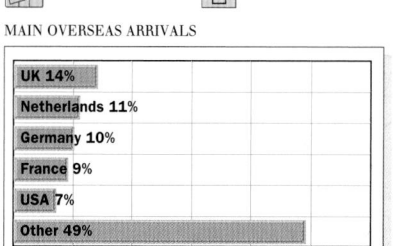

3.3m visitors

Up 0.6% in 1994

MAIN OVERSEAS ARRIVALS

UK	14%
Netherlands	11%
Germany	10%
France	9%
USA	7%
Other	49%

% of total arrivals

Belgium's main attractions are its historic cities and museums of Flemish art. Bruges, the capital of west Flanders, is often called the "Venice of the North." With unspoiled Renaissance architecture and a complex canal system, it has become a favored destination for British weekend visitors and Japanese honeymooners. In Brussels, the famous "Grand Place," a cluster of Gothic, Renaissance and Baroque buildings in a cobbled square, survived bombing during World War II. Much of the rest of the old city center, however, was destroyed. Belgium has 15 resorts on its 38-mile coastline, with a single tramline running its entire length. Forests in the Ardennes to the south attract hikers.

The Ardennes, in the southeast, are famous for their forests, cuisine and lakes. Rivers, such as the Meuse and Semois, dissect the region.

PEOPLE

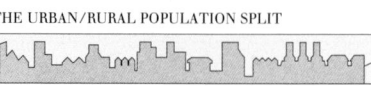

Flemish, French, German

798 people per sq. mile

THE URBAN/RURAL POPULATION SPLIT

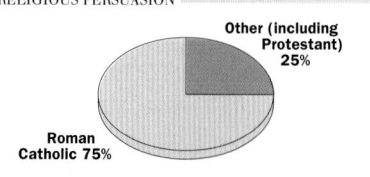

97% 3%

RELIGIOUS PERSUASION

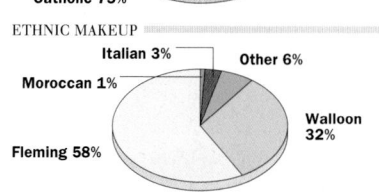

Other (including Protestant) 25%

Roman Catholic 75%

ETHNIC MAKEUP

Italian 3% Other 6%

Moroccan 1%

Walloon 32%

Fleming 58%

Belgian history has been marked by the divisions between its Flemish and French-speaking communities. Flemish speakers, who are a majority, are concentrated in Flanders. Wallonia is French-speaking and Brussels is 85% francophone. French-speakers were in the ascendancy for many years, as they controlled the profitable coal and steel industries in Wallonia. Their greater economic wealth was reinforced by a constitution which gave them political control. Tensions between French-speakers and Flemings occasionally erupted into violence. However, in the past two decades, the position of the two communities has been reversed. Wallonia's industries have declined and Flanders is now the wealthier region. In order to contain tensions, Belgium began to change in 1980, from being the most centralist to the most federal state in Europe; both communities now have their own governments and control most of their own affairs.

Belgium has a sizeable immigrant population. Women gained the vote in 1948. They earn, on average, 25% less than their male counterparts.

POPULATION AGE BREAKDOWN

% of population by age group	0–14	15–64	65+		
65+	12%	13.4%	14.3%	14.9%	16.5%
15–64	64.5%	63%	65.6%	67.2%	66.2%
0–14	23.5%	23.6%	20.1%	17.9%	17.3%
	1960	1970	1980	1990	2000

EUROPE

United Kingdom Netherlands

BELGIUM

Germany

France Lux.

Europe

BELGIUM

Total Land Area : 32 820 sq. km
(12 672 sq. miles)

POPULATION

⊡	over 1 000 000
◎	over 100 000
○	over 50 000
●	over 10 000

LAND HEIGHT

- 500m/1640ft
- 200m/656ft
- Sea Level

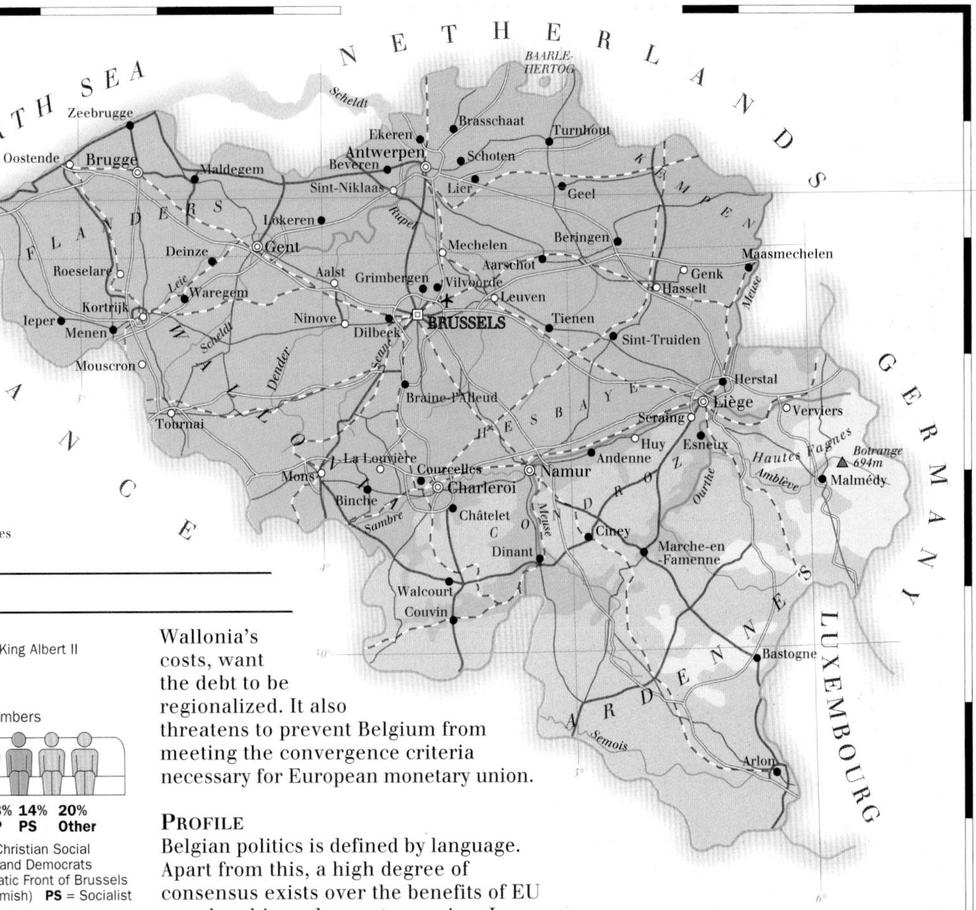

POLITICS

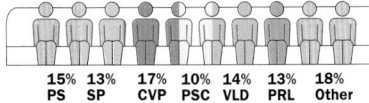

U. House 1995/1999
L. House 1995/1999

HM King Albert II

THE STATE OF THE PARTIES

Chamber of Representatives 150 members

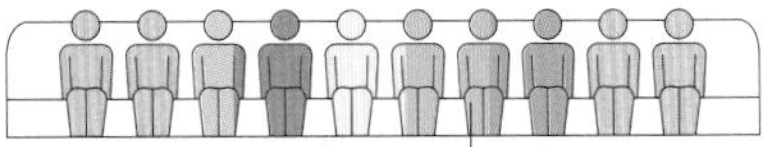

19% CVP	8% PSC	14% VLD	12% PRL-FDF	13% SP	14% PS	20% Other

CVP = Christian People's Party   **PSC** = Christian Social
Party (Walloon)   **VLD** = Flemish Liberals and Democrats
PRL-FDF = Liberal Reform Party -Democratic Front of Brussels
Francophones   **SP** = Socialist Party (Flemish)   **PS** = Socialist
Party (Walloon)

Senate 71 members

15% PS	13% SP	17% CVP	10% PSC	14% VLD	13% PRL	18% Other

The senate has 40 directly elected members and 31 co-
opted by the elected members and the heir to the throne

Until 1970, Belgium was a unitary state.
Tensions between language groups led
to four waves of federalist reforms
from 1980, which culminated in the
St. Michel Accords of 1993, confirming
the state as a federal monarchy.

MAIN POLITICAL ISSUES
Language
Tensions between the two language
groups are receding. However, the
divisions remain strong. Each
community has its own Socialist Party
(the PS in Wallonia, the SP in Flanders),
and the Christian Democrats are
split into the francophone PSC and
Flemish CVP. Under the premiership
of Jean-Luc Dehaene, the four parties
have worked in an uneasy coalition.

Debt
Belgium's debt is now greater than
its national income. The question of
how to deal with it dominates and
defines most political debate. Many
Flemings, who feel they are subsidizing
Wallonia's
costs, want
the debt to be
regionalized. It also
threatens to prevent Belgium from
meeting the convergence criteria
necessary for European monetary union.

PROFILE
Belgian politics is defined by language.
Apart from this, a high degree of
consensus exists over the benefits of EU
membership and monetary union. In
recent years, there has been an increase
in support for the racist *Vlaams Blok*,
which objects to Belgium's Turkish
and Moroccan minorities. *Vlaams Blok*
secured 27.6% of Antwerp's vote in 1995.

The current government is a centrist
coalition, composed of the Socialist
and Christian Democrat parties from
the Flemish and French-speaking
communities. Although the coalition
has a majority in parliament, it had
difficulty in securing the necessary two-
thirds majority for the constitutional
reform enacted in the St. Michel
Accords. These gave the three regional
governments, Flanders, Wallonia and
Brussels, significant powers under
a federal government. Most of the
population sees this as the best system
to cope with the country's diversities.

***King Albert II**, who
succeeded his father
King Baudouin who
died in 1993.*

***Jean-Luc Dehaene**,
premier and leader
of the Christian
People's Party (CVP).*

WORLD AFFAIRS

Benelux	CE	EU	OECD	OSCE

Belgium's key concern is its role in the
EU. It is a keen supporter of economic
and monetary union. As a frequent
victim of wars between France and
Germany, Belgium sees the EU as a
guarantor of western European peace.
The EU is also perceived as an important
foundation for Belgium's own federalist
structure, without which many fear
that Belgium could split into two.

Belgium has little in the way of an
independent foreign policy, but does
frequently contribute troops to UN
operations. Belgian soldiers have served
in Bosnia and Somalia in recent years
and a number were killed in Rwanda
in 1994 during ethnic violence.

AID

$808m (donations)   Up 2.9% in 1993

In 1993, overseas aid accounted for
about 0.7% of budgetary spending.
Between 1987 and 1993, most of the
aid program was spent on education
and agricultural projects in Africa.
The former colonies of Burundi and
Rwanda were the major beneficiaries.

B

CHRONOLOGY

Formerly ruled by the French dukes of Burgundy, Belgium became a Habsburg possession in 1477. It passed to the Austrian Habsburgs in 1700. Napoleon ended Austrian rule of the Low Countries in 1797.

❑ **1814–1815** Congress of Vienna; European powers decide to merge Belgium with the Netherlands under King William I of Orange.

❑ **1830** Revolt against Dutch. Provisional government declares independence.

❑ **1831** European powers place Leopold Saxe Coburg as king.

❑ **1865** Leopold II crowned king.

❑ **1885** After agreement by European powers, King Leopold given Congo basin as colony.

❑ **1914** German armies invade. Leopold II declares war on Germany. Germans occupy Belgium until 1918.

❑ **1921** Belgo–Luxembourg Economic Union formed. Luxembourg locks its currency to the Belgian franc.

❑ **1952** Flemish language accorded equal official status with French.

❑ **1936** Belgium declares neutrality.

❑ **1940** King Leopold III capitulates to Hitler. Belgium occupied until 1944.

❑ **1948** Forms customs union with Luxembourg and the Netherlands (BENELUX).

❑ **1950** King Leopold wins referendum but rumors over his collaboration during World War II persist. Abdicates in favor of his son, Baudouin.

❑ **1957** Signs Treaty of Rome with France, Germany, Italy, the Netherlands and Luxembourg.

❑ **1958** Treaty of Rome members form the EEC.

❑ **1992** Culmination of reforms transforming Belgium into federal state. Greater powers for regions and city governments.

❑ **1992** Christian-Democrat–Socialist government led by Jean-Luc Dehaene takes over federal government.

❑ **1993** Death of King Baudouin. Succeeded by Albert II. Belgian EU presidency advances moves toward monetary union agreed at Maastricht in 1992.

❑ **1995** Bribery scandal forces ministerial resignations and that of Willy Claes as NATO secretary.

❑ **1995** General election results in return to power of the Dehaene administration.

DEFENSE

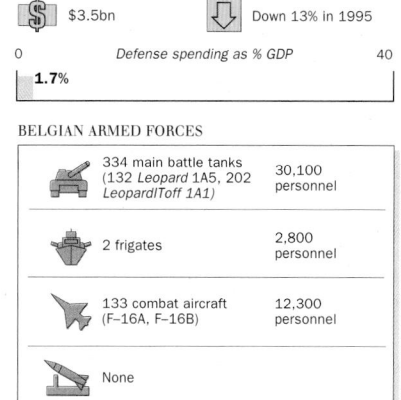

💲 $3.5bn   ⬇ Down 13% in 1995

0   Defense spending as % GDP   40

1.7%

BELGIAN ARMED FORCES

🪖	334 main battle tanks (132 *Leopard* 1A5, 202 *LeopardlToff 1A1*)	30,100 personnel
🚢	2 frigates	2,800 personnel
✈	133 combat aircraft (F–16A, F–16B)	12,300 personnel
🚀	None	

Belgium spends less on defense than the NATO average and over the next decade the defense budget will fall further. In 1994, as part of Belgium's program to reduce government debt, all three military services were targeted for cuts. The government abolished conscription and drastically cut troop levels. In addition, the defense budget was frozen for five years.

Spending on paratroopers and transportation planes has increased, however. The aim is to allow the country's forces to fulfil their role in NATO's new rapid reaction forces. It will also make Belgian forces more useful to the UN's worldwide operations.

ECONOMICS

📊 $231bn   💲 29.43–31.83 Belgian francs

SCORE CARD

❑ WORLD GNP RANKING.........................19th
❑ GNP PER CAPITA $22,920
❑ BALANCE OF PAYMENTS....................$12.8bn
❑ INFLATION 1.3%
❑ UNEMPLOYMENT................................9.7%

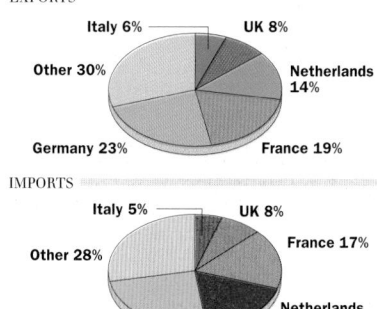

EXPORTS

Italy 6% — UK 8%
Other 30%
Netherlands 14%
Germany 23%
France 19%

IMPORTS

Italy 5% — UK 8%
Other 28%
France 17%
Netherlands 18%
Germany 24%

STRENGTHS

One of world's most efficient producers of metal products and textiles. Flanders is a world leader in new high-tech industries. Successful chemicals industry. Highly educated and motivated multilingual work force: estimates suggest productivity is 20% above that of Germany. Location makes Belgium an attractive location for US multi-nationals. Good sea outlets and access to Rhine inland waterway from Antwerp and Ghent.

WEAKNESSES

Highest public debt in the EU at 122% of GDP; costs 10% of public income per year to service. Rising unemployment. Large numbers of workers retire early, resulting in high state pension bill. Larger bureaucracy than European average.

ECONOMIC PERFORMANCE INDICATOR

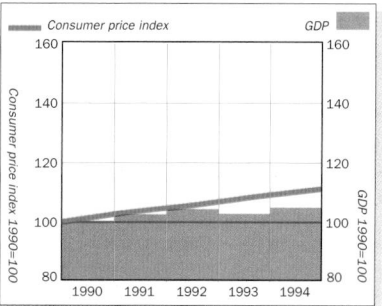

Consumer price index   GDP

(Consumer price index 1990=100 / GDP 1990=100)

1990 1991 1992 1993 1994

PROFILE

Belgium's economy went into recession with the rest of Europe in the early 1990s. Falling tax revenues coincided with rising unemployment, particularly in Wallonia, and a larger social security bill. In 1993, the Dehaene government introduced a scheme which encouraged work-sharing as a way of combating unemployment. Belgium aims to meet the criteria for monetary union but faces a considerable debt problem.

BELGIUM : MAJOR BUSINESSES

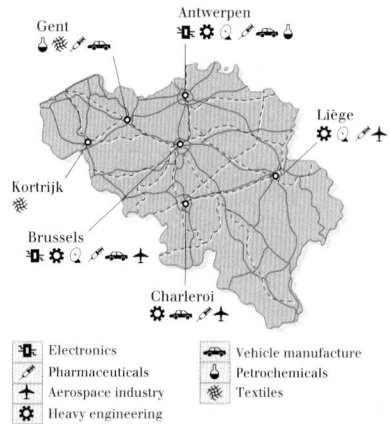

Gent
Antwerpen
Liège
Kortrijk
Brussels
Charleroi

⬛ Electronics   🚗 Vehicle manufacture
✒ Pharmaceuticals   🛢 Petrochemicals
✈ Aerospace industry   🧵 Textiles
⚙ Heavy engineering
📡 Telecommunications

0   50 km
0   50 miles

B

RESOURCES

71bn kwh (capacity 14.14m kw)

Not an oil producer; refines 607,000 b/cd

35m chickens, 6.9m pigs, 3.3m cattle

Coal, natural gas, shale, marble, sandstone, dolomite

ELECTRICITY GENERATION

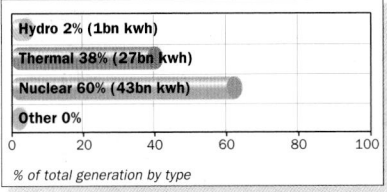

Hydro 2% (1bn kwh)
Thermal 38% (27bn kwh)
Nuclear 60% (43bn kwh)
Other 0%

% of total generation by type

Belgium has few natural resources and depends largely on the export of goods and services. The once-rich coal mines

ENVIRONMENT

 2.5%

 Government may introduce a green tax to help environment

ENVIRONMENTAL TREATIES

Yes   Yes   No
Yes   Yes   No

The regional government of Flanders is concerned about the pollution of its groundwater supplies through acid rain, heavy metals, fertilizers and pesticides. It is operating an environmental management plan to meet prescribed standards. Wallonia has initiated strict laws to prevent the illegal tipping of waste, and is also governing air quality and emissions. The population's growing awareness of environmental issues is reflected in the rise of the two Green Parties.

MEDIA

 Censorship is banned under the constitution. All types of media tend to be divided by language

PUBLISHING AND BROADCAST MEDIA

There are 33 daily newspapers; 18 in French, 14 in Dutch and 1 in German

3 state-owned, 2 independent services

3 state-owned, over 75 local stations

A mix of European satellite channels

Extensive use throughout the country

Newspapers tend to be regional and divided by language. Circulation is low, with the most widely read newspaper having a circulation of just 300,000. Over 80% of Belgians have cable TV, receiving as many as 30 channels from all over Europe. Commercial TV only began in 1989, with the Flemish *Station* VTM showing imported English-language programs and game shows.

of Wallonia are almost depleted. There is some deciduous and conifer forestry in the Ardennes region.

BELGIUM : LAND USE

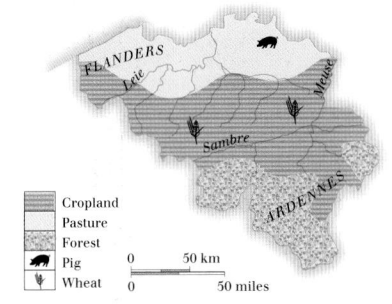

Cropland
Pasture
Forest
Pig
Wheat

0   50 km
0   50 miles

CRIME

 6,450 prisoners

 Down 1.3% in 1992

CRIME RATES

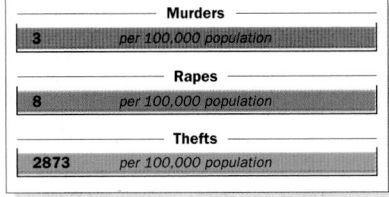

Murders
3   per 100,000 population
Rapes
8   per 100,000 population
Thefts
2873   per 100,000 population

Belgium's crime level is low compared with surrounding countries, although car theft has become more common. The majority of convicted offenses are for minor assaults and theft.

EDUCATION

 99%

 276,248 students

0   *Education spending as % GNP*   25
5.2%

THE EDUCATION SYSTEM

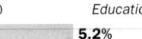
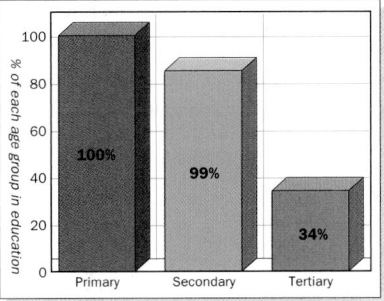

Primary 100%   Secondary 99%   Tertiary 34%

Since 1959 parents have been able to choose between secular and religious schooling. Since 1989 the system has been administered by the governments of the two main language groups. Education in Flanders is in Dutch, while Wallonia teaches in French. All universities are split by language.

HEALTH

 1 per 270 people

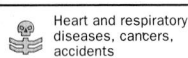 Heart and respiratory diseases, cancers, accidents

0   *Health spending as % GDP*   25
8.1%

The quality of health care in Belgium is among the best in the world. Belgium is a world leader in fertility treatment and heart and lung transplants. Treatment is not free, but Belgians hold insurance enabling them to claim back up to 75% of their costs. Car accidents are second only to heart disease as a cause of death; 62,000 accidents resulted in personal injury in 1990. In 1993, there were 1,600 registered AIDS patients.

WEALTH

 Baker, 305 Belgian francs ($10) per hour; bank employee, 43,009 Belgian francs ($1,430) per month

CONSUMER GOODS OWNERSHIP

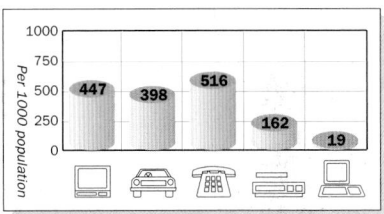

447   398   516   162   19

Per 1000 population

Despite high levels of state debt and the rundown of its traditional industries, Belgium remains one of the richest countries in Europe. GNP per head, at $22,920, is lower than Germany, but higher than the UK or Italy. The figure, however, masks considerable regional differences. Flanders, where most high-tech businesses are located, has an unemployment rate of 6%, while in Wallonia it is 11%; 25% of under-25s in Wallonia are unemployed. The presence of highly paid EU and international bank employees has made Brussels a distinctly wealthy city. In contrast to the state, Belgians are privately great savers. In 1993, they saved, on average, 20% of their income.

WORLD RANKING

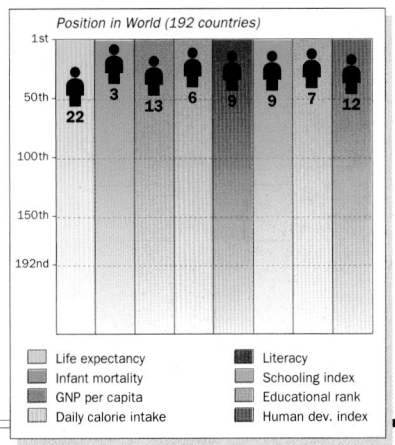

Position in World (192 countries)

22   3   13   6   9   9   7   12

Life expectancy
Infant mortality
GNP per capita
Daily calorie intake
Literacy
Schooling index
Educational rank
Human dev. index

BELIZE

OFFICIAL NAME: Belize   CAPITAL: Belmopan
POPULATION: 200,000   CURRENCY: Belizean dollar   OFFICIAL LANGUAGE: English

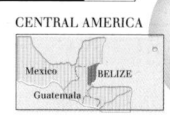
CENTRAL AMERICA
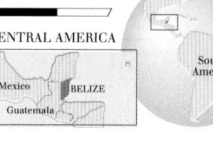

 1981

FORMERLY CALLED BRITISH HONDURAS, Belize was the last Central American country to gain its independence, in 1981. It lies on the eastern shore of the Yucatan peninsula and shares a border with Mexico along the River Hondo. Belize is Central America's least populous country, and almost one-half of its land area is still forested. Its swampy coastal plains are protected from flooding by the world's second-largest barrier reef.

Small fish market in Belize City. More than 500 tons of Caribbean spiny lobster, the main inshore species, are caught every year.

CLIMATE

WEATHER CHART

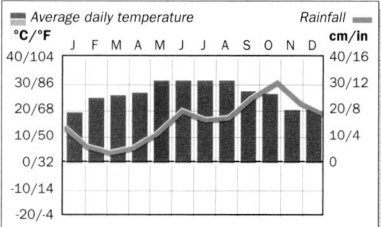

Conditions are hot and humid throughout the year. Coastal regions are affected by hurricanes.

TRANSPORTATION

Philip S W Goldson, Belize City
272,000 passengers

27 ships
48,300 dwt

THE TRANSPORTATION NETWORK

882 miles (1,419 km)	None
None	513 miles (825 km)

Rising prosperity has led to an increase in road traffic. Regular bus services operate between all main towns. A new terminal and runway extension were recently completed at the international airport near Belize City.

TOURISM

103,000 visitors

Up 1% in 1994

MAIN OVERSEAS ARRIVALS

USA 37%	
UK 5%	
Canada 3%	
Other 55%	

0 10 20 30 40 50 60
% of total arrivals

Very significant natural resources, Mayan ruins and nature reserves. Ecotourism is strongly promoted.

PEOPLE

English Creole, Spanish, English, Maya, Garifuna (Carib)

23 people per sq. mile

THE URBAN/RURAL POPULATION SPLIT

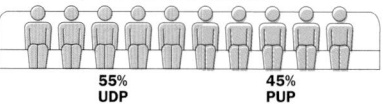

47%   53%

ETHNIC MAKEUP

South Asian 4%
Other 4%
Garifuna 7%
Maya 11%
Mestizo (European-Indian) 44%
Creole 30%

Spanish-speaking *mestizos* now outnumber black Creoles for the first time. The rest of the population is composed of Maya groups, black Caribs (Garifuna), and immigrants from Mexico, the Middle East and South Asia. Some self-contained communities of Swiss-descended Mennonites exist.

POLITICS

1993/1998

HM Queen Elizabeth II

House of Representatives 29 members

55% UDP   45% PUP

UDP = United Democratic Party   PUP = People's United Party

Senate 8 members

The members of the Senate are appointed by the governor-general

The desire for independence dominated politics until the 1980s. It was the PUP, under George Price, that negotiated this with the British in 1981. During the 1984–1989 UDP administration, the maintenance of a pro-US line and fears of communism in the region were the main concerns. In the absence of any major ideological or policy distinctions, the UDP won power back from the PUP in 1993. Austerity measures, "economic citizenship" programs and border tension with Guatemala remain key issues.

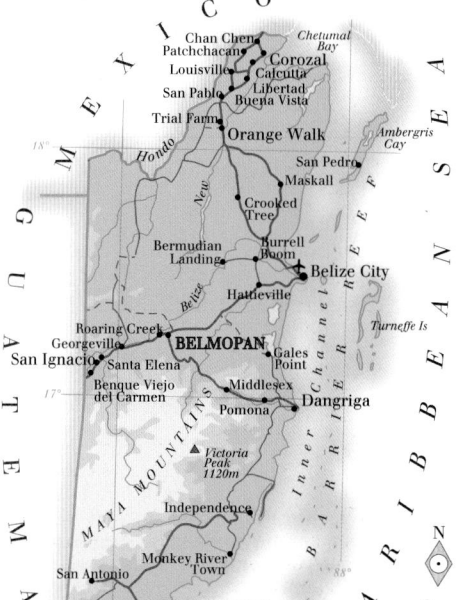

BELIZE

Total Land Area : 22 800 sq. km (8803 sq. miles)

POPULATION
● over 10 000
• under 10 000

LAND HEIGHT
1000m/3281ft
500m/1640ft
200m/656ft
Sea Level

0   50 km
0   50 miles

WORLD AFFAIRS

ACS Comm Carlcom NAM OAS

At the end of 1993, Guatemala officially recognized Belize as an independent state, thus ending a long period of uncertainty and fear of invasion.

AID

 US$28m (receipts)   Up 22% in 1993

Belize is one of the highest per capita recipients of US aid; its staunchly pro-US UDP administration, has led Belize to be seen as a useful anti-communist buttress in the region.

DEFENSE

 US$14m   Up 27% in 1995

The 555-strong Belize Defense Force includes two female platoons and is trained by the UK, the USA and Canada. As a result of Guatemala dropping its territorial claim, Britain withdrew its military garrison in 1994.

ECONOMICS

 US$535m   1.99–2.00 Belizean dollars

SCORE CARD

❏ WORLD GNP RANKING	161st
❏ GNP PER CAPITA	US$2,550
❏ BALANCE OF PAYMENTS	US$–49m
❏ INFLATION	2.4%
❏ UNEMPLOYMENT	10%

STRENGTHS
Sugar, textile manufacture, citrus fruits, bananas, cocoa and forestry. Small foreign debt, 90% of which is held by multilateral institutions on favorable concessionary terms.

WEAKNESSES
Heavy reliance on imports of processed foods. The economy's small size makes Belize vulnerable to even slight changes in external trading conditions.

EXPORTS

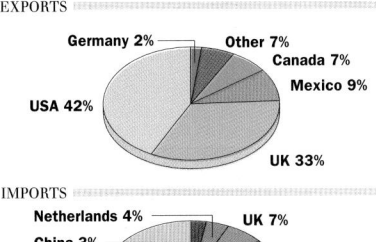

Germany 2% Other 7%
Canada 7%
Mexico 9%
USA 42%
UK 33%

IMPORTS

Netherlands 4% UK 7%
China 3%
Mexico 10%
USA 57% Other 19%

RESOURCES

 110m kwh (capacity 20,000 kw)   2,129 tons

 59,000 cattle, 26,000 pigs, 5,000 horses, 4,000 mules   None

Exploration for oil and gas, largely by US companies, is currently under way in the Corozal basin region.

ENVIRONMENT

 5% partially protected   Little protection for unique ecosystems

Uncontrolled logging threatens tropical forests and animal habitats. Mahogany was listed internationally as endangered in November 1995, meaning that all exports and transshipments now require a certificate of origin.

MEDIA

 Journalists have occasionally been detained for criticizing the government

PUBLISHING AND BROADCAST MEDIA

 There are no daily newspapers. The leading papers are the weekly *Belize Times*, the *People's Pulse* and the *Reporter*

 1 state-owned and 2 independent services   1 state-owned and 3 independent services

Belize has not suffered the degree of press interference experienced in neighboring states, but the government remains sensitive to even minor criticisms. In 1989, the PUP, newly returned to power, fulfilled its manifesto commitment by establishing a broadcasting corporation modeled on the British BBC, and by revoking the restrictive law of criminal libel. *Amandala* is the most politically independent newspaper, as well as the best for sports coverage.

CRIME

 89 prisoners   Increase in gun-related crime

Formerly a major regional exporter of marijuana until the US Drug Enforcement Agency destroyed the plantations, Belize is now an increasingly important transshipment point for Colombian cocaine to the USA. Since the 1980s, narcotics-related crime has risen sharply in Belize City, home to 11 highly organized gangs.

EDUCATION

 95%   9,457 students

Belize's schools are administered by its three main religious denominations: Roman Catholics, Anglicans and Methodists. University College of Belize maintains close links with the University of Michigan, USA.

HEALTH

 1 per 1,809 people   Respiratory, heart and cerebrovascular diseases

Around 75% of Belizeans have access to government health services, which include seven hospitals and numerous mobile clinics. Sanitation and water supplies are being improved; 62% of homes in Belmopan now have both.

WEALTH

 Skilled laborer, 700 Belizean dollars per month (US$350); general manager, 4,600 Belizean dollars (US$2,300) per month

CONSUMER GOODS OWNERSHIP

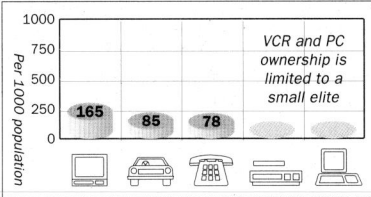

VCR and PC ownership is limited to a small elite

165 85 78

Per 1000 population

Wealth is more evenly distributed than in the rest of Central America. The narcotics trade is a source of wealth.

WORLD RANKING

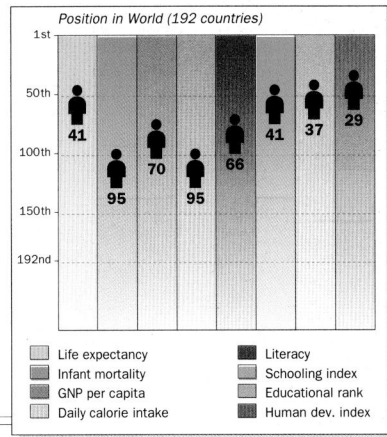

Position in World (192 countries)

1st
50th
100th
150th
192nd

41 95 70 95 66 41 37 29

❏ Life expectancy   ■ Literacy
❏ Infant mortality   ❏ Schooling index
■ GNP per capita   ■ Educational rank
❏ Daily calorie intake   ■ Human dev. index

B

BELORUSSIA (BELARUS)

OFFICIAL NAME: Republic of Belarus **CAPITAL:** Minsk
POPULATION: 10.1 million **CURRENCY:** Belorussian rouble **OFFICIAL LANGUAGE:** Belorussian

EUROPE

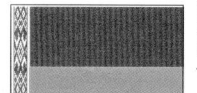 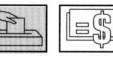
1991

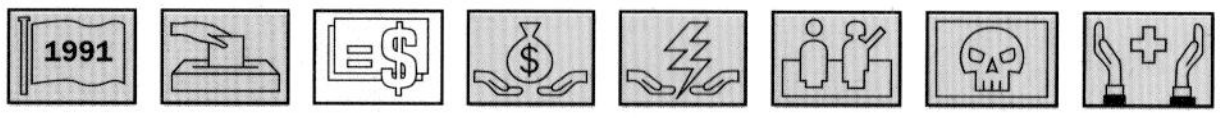

FORMERLY KNOWN AS White Russia, Belorussia is bordered by Lithuania and Latvia in the northwest, Ukraine in the south, and Poland and Russia in the west and east. The landlocked country, which reluctantly became independent of Moscow in 1991, has few resources other than agriculture. The Chernobyl' nuclear disaster in neighboring Ukraine in 1986 has had profound and lasting effects on the environment. The health of Belorussians has suffered severely and many areas are still contaminated.

CLIMATE

WEATHER CHART

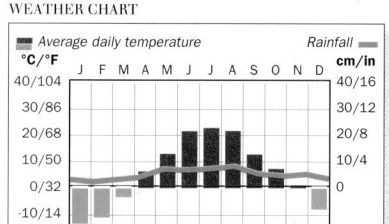

Belorussia has a continental climate. Temperatures in winter drop well below freezing, while in summer fairly high temperatures are reached.

Much of southern Belorussia is marshy and sparsely populated. It includes the vast Pripet Marshes and the Dnieper lowlands.

TRANSPORTATION

 Minsk International   Has no fleet

THE TRANSPORTATION NETWORK

 30,764 miles (49,510 km)   None

 3,474 miles (5,590 km)   Extensive canal and river systems

Belorussia has no direct access to the sea, but is close to the Baltic ports. Railroad communications are good.

TOURISM

Belorussia does not publish visitor figures   No significant change from year to year

MAIN OVERSEAS ARRIVALS

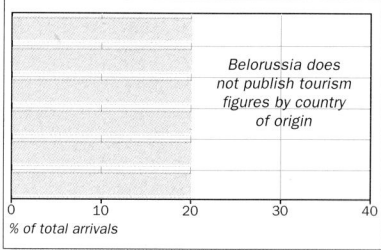
Belorussia does not publish tourism figures by country of origin

% of total arrivals

Belorussia has fewer tourists than its Slav and Baltic neighbours. Many of its historic buildings were destroyed during the Second World War. Minsk was completely flattened and is now characterized by Stalinist and high-rise buildings. There are few assets on which to build a tourist industry.

BELORUSSIA

Total Land Area : 207 600 sq. km
(80 154 sq. miles)

POPULATION

over 1 000 000	⊡
over 500 000	⊙
over 100 000	◎
over 50 000	○
over 10 000	●
under 10 000	•

LAND HEIGHT

200m/656ft
100m/328ft

(Map of Belorussia showing Latvia, Lithuania, Poland, Ukraine, and Russian Federation borders with cities including Braslaw, Navapolatsk, Polatsk, Vitsyebsk, Pastavy, Drysa, Hlybokaye, Lyepyel', Byahoml', Smarhon', Vilyeyka, Plyeshchanitsy, Orsha, Horki, Ashmyany, Maladzyechna, Zhodzina, Barysaw, Lida, MINSK, Hora Dzyarzhynskaya 345m, Byerazino, Mahilyow, Krychaw, Hrodna, Navahrudak, Cherikaw, Vawkavysk, Nyasvizh, Shyahchytsy, Asipovichy, Bykhaw, Kastsyukovichy, Baranavichy, Slonim, Slutsk, Babruysk, Rahachow, Ivatsevichy, Salihorsk, Zhlobin, Pruzhany, Byaroza, Svyetlahorsk, Homyel', Kobryn, Zhytkavichy, Rechytsa, Dobrush, Brest, Pinsk, Luninyets, Davyd-Haradok, Mazyr, Kalinkavichy, Yel'sk, Khoyniki)

N

0 — 100 km
0 — 100 miles

B

PEOPLE

 Belorussian, Russian

 127 people per sq. mile

THE URBAN/RURAL POPULATION SPLIT

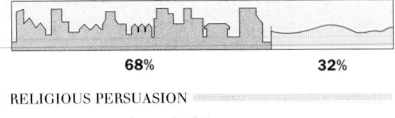

68%   32%

RELIGIOUS PERSUASION

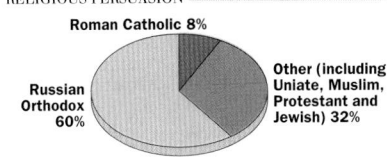

Roman Catholic 8%

Russian Orthodox 60%

Other (including Uniate, Muslim, Protestant and Jewish) 32%

ETHNIC MAKEUP

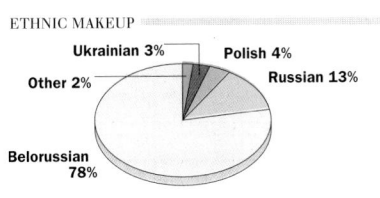

Ukrainian 3%   Polish 4%

Other 2%   Russian 13%

Belorussian 78%

Only 2% of the population is non-Slav and there is little ethnic tension. According to a law passed in late 1992, the entire population has an automatic right to Belorussian citizenship. Only 11% of the population, most of whom live in the countryside, are fluent in Belorussian. Attempts to boost the popularity of the official language in the early 1990s proved unsuccessful.

POPULATION AGE BREAKDOWN

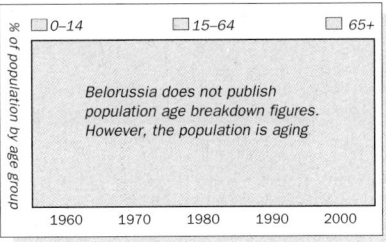

% of population by age group

☐ 0–14   ☐ 15–64   ☐ 65+

Belorussia does not publish population age breakdown figures. However, the population is aging

1960   1970   1980   1990   2000

POLITICS

 1995/1999

 President Aleksandr Lukashenka

THE STATE OF THE PARTIES

Supreme Council 260 seats

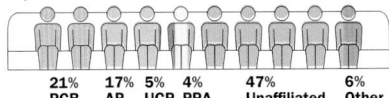

| 21% PCB | 17% AP | 5% UCP | 4% PPA | 47% Unaffiliated | 6% Other |

PCB = Party of Communists of Belorussia AP = Agrarian Party UCP = United Civic Party PPA = Party of People's Accord

Under the 1994 constitution, Belorussia is a multiparty democracy headed by a directly elected president.

MAIN POLITICAL ISSUES

Relationship with Russia

Belorussia's relationship with Russia is the key political issue. In April 1994 Belorussia signed a monetary union that effectively gives Moscow control of Belorussia's economic policy. In return, Russia will take on Belorussia's $1.5 billion debt. In July 1994 Aleksandr Lukashenka was elected president and has since sought ever-closer relations with Russia.

The environment

The 1986 Chernobyl' nuclear disaster continues to cast a shadow over life in Belorussia. The devastating effects of the accident are still being revealed in high incidences of leukaemia and cancers. Much of Belorussia's land and farm produce is still tainted with fallout radiation. The clean-up operation is slow and laborious and will take decades. It is a major drain on state finances. In 1993, 17% of government spending was set aside for this purpose.

PROFILE

Belorussia has struggled to find an identity since it achieved independence in 1991. It was by far the slowest of the ex-Soviet states to implement political reform. A post-Soviet constitution was not adopted until March 1994, and only at the end of 1995 was the first fully-fledged post-Soviet parliament elected, dominated by the PCB and its ally, the AP.

In a surprise victory, Aleksandr Lukashenka (chair of the parliamentary anti-corruption commission) was elected in mid-1994 as Belorussia's first president, replacing the former communist Mechislau Grib as head of state. Lukashenka defeated conservative prime minister Vyacheslau Kebich in the elections, after campaigning against corruption and for the restoration of ties with the former Soviet Union. Since his election, the fiery Lukashenka has made clear his commitment to political and economic integration with Russia. Much depends on events in Moscow. It does, however, appear likely that Russian president Boris Yeltsin will play on widespread public nostalgia for the old USSR during his 1996 election campaign.

President Aleksandr Lukashenka seeks closer ties with the Russian Federation.

Chairman Stanislau Shushkevich, ousted in a vote of no-confidence in 1993.

WORLD AFFAIRS

 CE   CIS   IAEA   NACC   OSCE

Relations with Russia are paramount. Numerous bilateral agreements have been signed since 1991. These ties are being strengthened now that the pro-Russian Aleksandr Lukashenka has been elected as president. However, relations could sour if the reformers in Moscow gain power. Many in Russia are opposed to closer links with Belorussia, believing it represents a drain on Moscow's resources for little strategic gain.

The good relations with the West developed by ex-chairman Stanislau Shushkevich have cooled. However, Belorussia retains its Most Favored Nation (MFN) trading status with the USA.

AID

 Receipts undisclosed

 Rising, particularly from Russia

In 1993, the World Bank and IMF granted Belorussia its first loans, on condition that the government carries out economic reforms. Under this package, $98 million was promised by the IMF and $120 million by the World Bank. The anti-reform stance of the current administration makes it unlikely that Belorussia will receive the full package.

The EU has extended some credits to Belorussia to assist in the conversion of the defense industry to non-military production. Belorussia still requires aid to combat the effects of radiation pollution in the wake of the Chernobyl' nuclear accident of 1986. Some help is being provided through the UK's Know-How Fund.

CHRONOLOGY

After forming part of medieval Kievan Rus, Belorussia experienced rule by three of its neighbours – Poland, Lithuania and Russia – before incorporation into the USSR.

❑ **1917** Nationalists and socialists try to gain autonomy within Russia.
❑ **1918** Belorussian Bolsheviks stage coup. Independence as Belorussian Soviet Socialist Republic.
❑ **1919** Invaded by Poland.
❑ **1920** Minsk retaken by Red Army. Eastern Belorussia reestablished as Soviet Socialist Republic (BSSR).
❑ **1921** Treaty of Riga – western Belorussia incorporated into Poland. New Economic Policy applied.
❑ **1922** BSSR merges with Russian Federation to form USSR.
❑ **1929** Stalin implements collectivization of agriculture. ⇨

B

- ❑ **1939** Western Belorussia reincorporated into USSR when Soviet Red Army invades Poland.
- ❑ **1941–1944** Belorussia under German occupation during World War II.
- ❑ **1945** Belorussia a founding member of the UN along with Ukraine and USSR.
- ❑ **1965** KT Mazurau, leader of Communist Party of Belorussia (PKB), becomes first deputy chair of USSR Council of Ministers.
- ❑ **1986** Accident at Chernobyl' nuclear power plant in Ukraine. Belorussia affected by 70% of plant's radioactive fallout.
- ❑ **1988** Archaeologist Zianon Pazniak reveals evidence of mass executions (over 300,000) by Soviet military between 1937 and 1941 in Kurapaty wood near Minsk. Popular outrage fuels formation of nationalist Belorussian Popular Front (BPF), with Pazniak as president. PKB authorities crush demonstration.
- ❑ **1989** Belorussian adopted as republic's official language.
- ❑ **1990** PKB prevents BPF participating in March elections to Supreme Soviet. BPF members join other opposition groups in Belorussian Democratic Bloc (BDB). BDB wins 25% of seats. July, PKB bows to opposition pressure and issues Declaration of the State Sovereignty of BSSR.
- ❑ **1991** March, 83% vote in referendum to preserve union with USSR. April, strikes against PKB and its economic policies. August, independence declared. Republic of Belarus adopted as official name. Stanislau Shushkevich elected chairman of Supreme Soviet. December, Belorussia, Russia and Ukraine establish CIS.
- ❑ **1992** Supreme Soviet announces Soviet nuclear weapons must be cleared from Belorussia by 1999. Help promised from USA.
- ❑ **1993** January, national army comes into existence. Ratification of START-1 and nuclear non-proliferation treaties by Belorussian parliament.
- ❑ **1994** Shushkevich ousted from post as chairman of Supreme Soviet. Replaced by pro-Russian former communist, Mechislau Grib. New presidential constitution approved. In a surprise victory, Aleksandr Lukashenka defeats conservative prime minister Vyachedlav Kebich in presidential elections. Monetary union (re-entry into rouble zone) agreed with Russia.
- ❑ **1995** First fully-fledged post-Soviet parliament elected.

DEFENSE

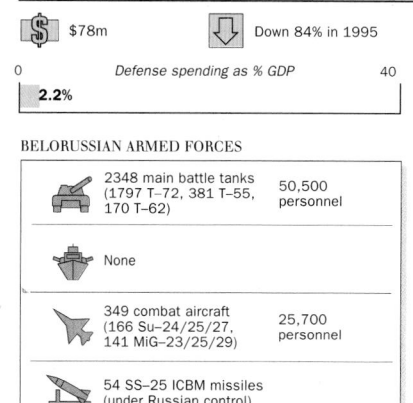

💲 $78m 　　　 ⬇ Down 84% in 1995

0 　　　 *Defense spending as % GDP* 　　　 40

2.2%

BELORUSSIAN ARMED FORCES

🛡	2348 main battle tanks (1797 T–72, 381 T–55, 170 T–62)	50,500 personnel
🚢	None	
✈	349 combat aircraft (166 Su–24/25/27, 141 MiG–23/25/29)	25,700 personnel
🚀	54 SS–25 ICBM missiles (under Russian control)	

Under Shushkevich, Belorussia was committed to a policy of neutrality. By mid-1993 all tactical nuclear weapons were removed and Belorussia announced its aim of removing all strategic nuclear weapons. It was also committed to the destruction of conventional weapons under the 1990 Conventional Forces In Europe Treaty, but in 1995 it suspended armaments destruction, claiming the cost of the program was prohibitive.

Stronger military ties with Moscow are being established and Belorussia now meets some of the costs of Russian troops stationed on its territory. However, Belorussia's large defense industry is hoping that the arrangement will mean an increase in orders from Russia.

ECONOMICS

📊 $21.9bn 　　　 💱 10,600–11,500 Belorussian roubles

SCORE CARD

- ❑ WORLD GNP RANKING 62nd
- ❑ GNP PER CAPITA $2160
- ❑ BALANCE OF PAYMENTS $104m
- ❑ INFLATION 2220%
- ❑ UNEMPLOYMENT.................................1.9%

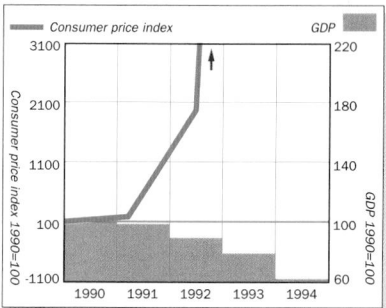

ECONOMIC PERFORMANCE INDICATOR

Consumer price index 　　　 GDP

EXPORTS

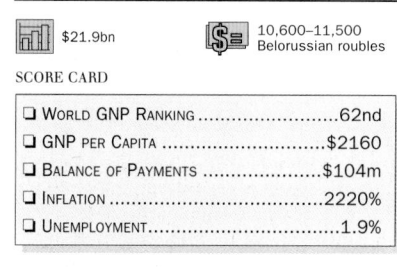

- Lithuania 3%
- USA 2%
- Russian Federation 66%
- Poland 5%
- Germany 10%
- Other 14%

IMPORTS

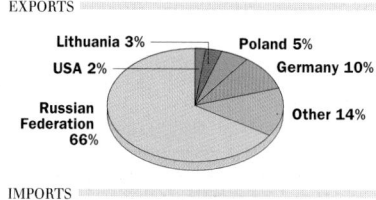

- Lithuania 3%
- Italy 1%
- Russian Federation 71%
- Poland 3%
- Germany 10%
- Other 12%

a market economy by the largely conservative parliament. Shortly after his election in July 1994, Lukashenka suspended a privatization program after allegations of corruption. The program was resumed in March 1995, but with little enthusiasm. It appears likely that traditional industries will continue to receive heavy subsidies. The small, pro-reform opposition fears the failure to reform will leave Belorussia impoverished.

STRENGTHS

Low unemployment rate: less than 2% of labor force (approximately 50,000). Better economic prospects than other CIS states. Monetary union with Russia aids currency stability. Potential of forestry and agriculture.

WEAKNESSES

Decision not to pursue economic reform will keep increasingly inefficient industries in business. Few natural resources. Dependence on Russia for energy. Clean-up costs of Chernobyl' drain government finances.

PROFILE

Following independence, Belorussia adopted a slower pace of economic reform than the other ex-Soviet states. Chairman Shushkevich was thwarted in his attempts to move more quickly to

BELORUSSIA : MAJOR BUSINESSES

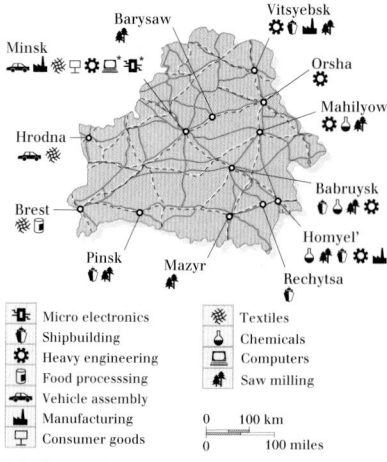

🔌	Micro electronics	※	Textiles
⚓	Shipbuilding	⚗	Chemicals
⚙	Heavy engineering	💻	Computers
🏭	Food processsing	🌲	Saw milling
🚗	Vehicle assembly		
🏭	Manufacturing	0 　 100 km	
🖥	Consumer goods	0 　 100 miles	

* significant multinational ownership

RESOURCES

37.6bn kwh (capacity 8.03m kw)

40,100 b/d

5.8m cattle, 4.7m pigs, 380,000 sheep

Natural gas, coal, rock salt

ELECTRICITY GENERATION

Hydro 0.1% (16m kwh)

Thermal 99.9% (37bn kwh)

Nuclear 0%

Other 0%

% of total generation by type

Belorussia has no significant strategic resources and is heavily dependent on the Russian Federation for fuel and energy supplies. Small quantities of oil and natural gas exist close to the Polish border.

BELORUSSIA : LAND USE

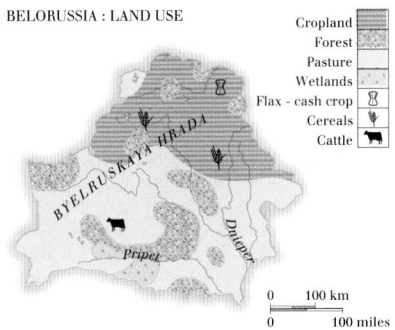

Cropland
Forest
Pasture
Wetlands
Flax - cash crop
Cereals
Cattle

0 100 km
0 100 miles

ENVIRONMENT

1.2%

Inadequate funds to deal with Chernobyl' clean-up

ENVIRONMENTAL TREATIES

No   Yes   Yes

Yes   Yes   No

In 1986 a massive leak from Ukraine's Chernobyl' nuclear reactor sent a huge cloud of radiation into Belorussia: 70% of the fallout fell on 40% of the country, including the capital Minsk; 2.3 million people were immediately affected. The government at the time kept the leak secret. Farmland, forests and water were all contaminated, including underwater streams feeding rivers in eastern Poland.

Cases of leukaemia and cancer are continuing to increase. Some areas in the fallout zone are still being farmed. Unscrupulous dealers are suspected of selling meat meant for destruction. A clean-up program is under way, swallowing 17% of government finances each year. Belorussia is seeking substantial Western aid to cope with the problem.

MEDIA

High level of state censorship

PUBLISHING AND BROADCAST MEDIA

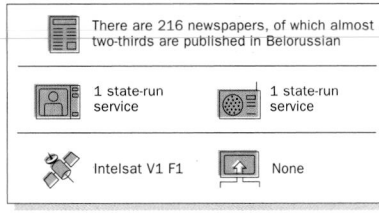

There are 216 newspapers, of which almost two-thirds are published in Belorussian

1 state-run service   1 state-run service

Intelsat V1 F1   None

The media is under central government control and is largely dependent on state subsidies. The one independent TV station was closed down in 1992.

CRIME

Belorussia does not publish prison figures   Rising

CRIME RATES

The rates of all categories of crime have increased since independence

As elsewhere in the former Soviet Union, economic hardship (although unemployment stands at less than 2%) and a general breakdown in law and order have resulted in a significant rise in crime. The murder rate increased by nearly 50% and muggings by nearly 60% in the first half of 1993. Belorussia has become a transshipment point for illegal narcotics destined for western Europe, while locally produced opium supplies the internal market.

EDUCATION

98%   187,700 students

0   Education spending as % GNP   25
5.3%

THE EDUCATION SYSTEM

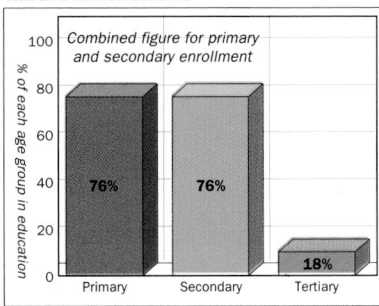

Combined figure for primary and secondary enrollment

Primary 76%   Secondary 76%   Tertiary 18%

Russian remains the main language of instruction in both secondary and tertiary establishments, despite attempts by some to promote Belorussian. University education is of a fairly high standard.

HEALTH

1 per 246 people

Heart attacks, cancers, accidents, violence

0   Health spending as % GDP   25
3.2%

Belorussia's good health service has been placed under enormous strain as a result of the Chernobyl' nuclear disaster. The number of cancer and leukaemia cases is currently 10,000 above the previous annual average. More wards and specialist units have had to be built. Under the Know-How Fund, many Belorussian doctors are being trained in the latest bone-marrow techniques in Europe and the USA.

WEALTH

Inflation is eroding the value of most salaries

CONSUMER GOODS OWNERSHIP

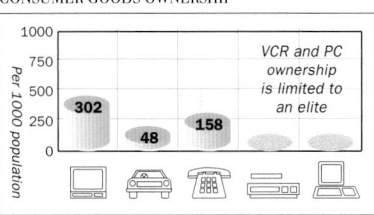

VCR and PC ownership is limited to an elite

302   48   158

The deteriorating economic situation has resulted in an overall drop in living standards. High inflation has particularly affected people on fixed incomes. Wealth is concentrated in the hands of a small, communist elite, which has been opposed to any market mechanisms. Now that they have the upper hand in parliament, they will strengthen their grip on the state's resources. Belorussia is unlikely to see the expansion of entrepreneurial activity to be found in Poland or the Russian Federation. However, the state's commitment to low unemployment will mean that the extreme social deprivation to be found in other former Soviet republics should be avoided.

WORLD RANKING

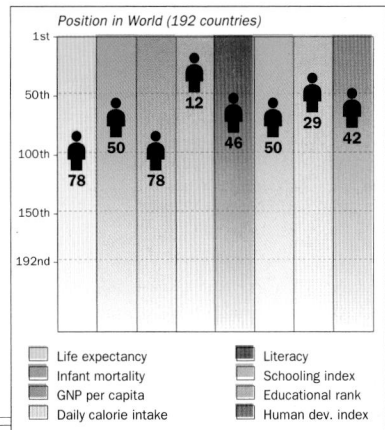

Position in World (192 countries)

78   50   78   12   46   50   29   42

Life expectancy   Literacy
Infant mortality   Schooling index
GNP per capita   Educational rank
Daily calorie intake   Human dev. index

BENIN

OFFICIAL NAME: Republic of Benin   CAPITAL: Porto-Novo
POPULATION: 5.4 million   CURRENCY: CFA franc   OFFICIAL LANGUAGE: French

BENIN STRETCHES NORTH from the West African coast, with a 62-mile shoreline on the Bight of Benin. Formerly the kingdom of Dahomey, Benin became a French protectorate and then a part of colonial French West Africa. It gained independence in 1960. In 1990, Benin became one of the pioneers of African multipartyism, ending 17 years of one-party Marxist–Leninist rule. Benin's economy is based on a well-diversified agricultural sector.

CLIMATE

WEATHER CHART

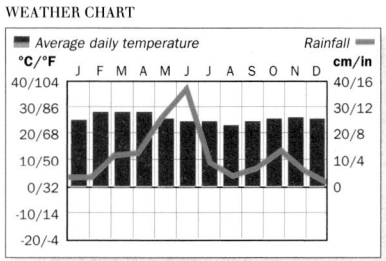

There are two rainy seasons. The hot, dusty *harmattan* wind characterizes the December to February dry season.

TRANSPORTATION

Cotonou Cadjehoun
123,331 passengers

Has no fleet

THE TRANSPORTATION NETWORK

760 miles (1,220 km)		None	
395 miles (635 km)		None	

The joint Benin–Niger railroad runs only as far as Parakou. Air travel through Cotonou is increasing rapidly.

TOURISM

142,000 visitors

Up 1% in 1994

MAIN OVERSEAS ARRIVALS

Europe 56%	
Africa 42%	
North and South America 1%	
Other 1%	

0   10   20   30   40   50   60
% of total arrivals

Tourism is not well developed, although there are plans to develop package tourism. There is some safari tourism in the north, particularly in the Atakora Mountains. Benin is popular as a weekend break for visitors to Nigeria.

PEOPLE

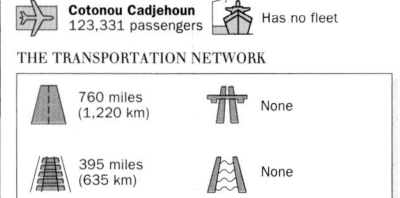

Fon, Bariba, Yoruba, Adja, Houeda, Somba, French

127 people per sq. mile

THE URBAN/RURAL POPULATION SPLIT

30%   70%

RELIGIOUS PERSUASION

Christian 15%

Muslim 15%

Indigenous beliefs 70%

Benin is politically dominated by the southern Fon people. There is some north–south tension, partly because the south is more developed, and partly reflecting a Muslim-Christian divide. Women hold positions of power in the retail trade.

BENIN

Total Land Area : 110 620 sq. km (42 710 sq. miles)

POPULATION

⊚ over 100 000
○ over 50 000
● over 10 000
· under 10 000

LAND HEIGHT

500m/1640ft
200m/656ft
Sea Level

0   100 km
0   100 miles

POLITICS

1995/1999

President Nicéphore Soglo

THE STATE OF THE PARTIES

National Assembly 83 seats

8% PSD

24% PRB	23% PRD	14% PTP	13% FARD	5% NCC	13% Other

PRB = Benin Renaissance Party   PRD = Parry of Democratic Renewal   PTP = Presidential Tendency parties
FARD = Action Front for Renewal and Development
PSD = Social Democrat Party   NCC = Our Common Cause

Benin has been at the forefront of African democratization. This process began at the National Conference of 1990, when General Kerekou agreed to hold multiparty elections after years of military one-party rule. Following elections in 1991, Kerekou became the first of the African one-party leaders to hand over power peacefully. Nicéphore Soglo, a former official of the World Bank and nephew of General Soglo who ruled from 1965 to 1967, took over the presidency. The former ruling party failed to gain any seats in the new parliament. The main political parties in Benin tend to be regionally based and depend on the leadership of individuals influential in local communities. Politics in Benin is characterized by constantly changing alliances. Soglo does not have an automatic majority in parliament, but has been forced to include opposition members in his government. The main political issue is the effect on the economy of Soglo's radical World Bank-style deregulation. Since 1993 he has twice had to force through controversial budgetary measures which have been against the will of parliament.

WORLD AFFAIRS

 Ecowas   OAU   OIC   FZ   UEMOA

Benin is largely dominated by its giant neighbor, Nigeria, by far the most powerful state in the region. President Soglo was recently chairman of ECOWAS and supports regional integration with neighboring countries. Continuing good relations with France, the main source of aid, is critical.

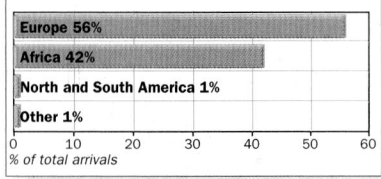

B

B

AID

 $267m (receipts)   Down 1% in 1993

Benin's poverty is such that the maintenance of aid is at the top of the political agenda. France, the main protector of Benin's independence since 1960, is the major aid donor. Other donors include the World Bank and IMF, the EU, Germany, Belgium, the Netherlands, Spain and the USA. Almost all development finance comes from aid, and some has been used to finance debt-servicing. There is the usual problem of finding suitable projects, although Benin has a large, well-educated (if top-heavy) civil service, making implementation easier than in many parts of Africa.

DEFENSE

 $25m   Down 4% in 1995

The 4800-strong army is actively involved in the attempt to curb smuggling on the border with Nigeria. In 1989 the army was employed internally against rioters.

ECONOMICS

 $2bn   533.68–489.05 CFA francs

SCORE CARD

❏ WORLD GNP RANKING	136th
❏ GNP PER CAPITA	$370
❏ BALANCE OF PAYMENTS	$36m
❏ INFLATION	38.6%
❏ UNEMPLOYMENT	Widespread underemployment

STRENGTHS
Agriculture-based economy, with good product diversification. Long-overdue devaluation of the CFA in 1994 made exports more competitive.

WEAKNESSES
Large-scale smuggling. High inflation had greatest impact on prices of essential goods and foodstuffs, forcing government to ban food exports. Top-heavy civil service.

EXPORTS
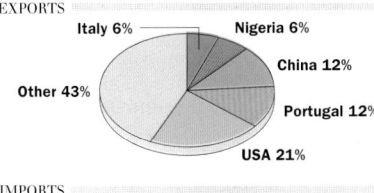
IMPORTS
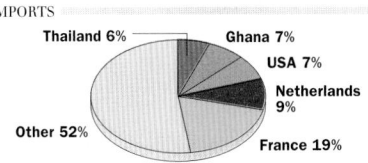

Flat landscape near Cotonou, characteristic of Benin's coastal region. Numerous lagoons lie behind its short, 62-mile coastline.

RESOURCES

 5m kwh (capacity 15,000 kw)   5975 b/d (reserves 19,900,000 bbl)

 1.2m cattle, 1.2m goats, 940,000 sheep   Oil, limestone, marble, gold

Since 1988 most electricity – which previously had to be imported from Ghana – is generated by the Nangbeto Dam on the River Mono.

ENVIRONMENT

 7%   New, environmentally aware rural development ministry

Desertification in the north is the major problem. Benin has been used in the past as a dumping ground for toxic waste.

MEDIA

 Although freedom of expression is guaranteed under the constitution, the press is quick to defend its rights

PUBLISHING AND BROADCAST MEDIA

 There are 2 daily newspapers, *L'Observateur* and *Le Soleil*

 1 state-owned service   1 state-owned service

The newly independent press faces economic difficulties. The biweekly *La Gazette du Golfe* has failed in its attempt to build a regional market.

CRIME

 Benin does not publish prison figures   Down 11% in 1992

Benin is relatively free of serious crime, though armed robbery is an increasing problem. There is also a very high level of smuggling, especially along the border with Nigeria.

EDUCATION

 23%   10,873 students

More is spent on education than on defense, and this is reinforced by Benin's active intellectual community, the "Latin Quarter of Africa." The university at Abomey-Calavi is rated highly in medicine and law.

CHRONOLOGY

In 1625 the Fon, indigenous slave traders, founded the kingdom of Dahomey. Dahomey in turn conquered the neighboring kingdoms of Dan, Allada and the coast around Porto Novo.

- ❏ **1857** French establish trading post at Grand-Popo.
- ❏ **1889** French defeat King Behanzin.
- ❏ **1892** French protectorate.
- ❏ **1904** Dahomey ruled as part of French West Africa.
- ❏ **1960** Independence from France.
- ❏ **1975** Renamed Benin.
- ❏ **1989** Marxism–Leninism abandoned as official ideology.
- ❏ **1991** Multiparty elections.
- ❏ **1994** 50% devaluation of CFA franc.

HEALTH

 1 per 14,300 people   Communicable and diarrheal diseases, malaria

Outside major towns, health services are scarce. Benin trains many doctors, but more of them work in France than in Benin.

WEALTH

 Railway ticket clerk, 35,000 CFA francs ($71) per month; oil industry engineer, 323,000 CFA francs ($660) per month

CONSUMER GOODS OWNERSHIP

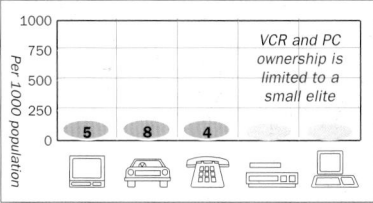

Substantial differences in wealth reflect the strongly hierarchical nature of society, especially in the south. French cars are considered status symbols.

WORLD RANKING

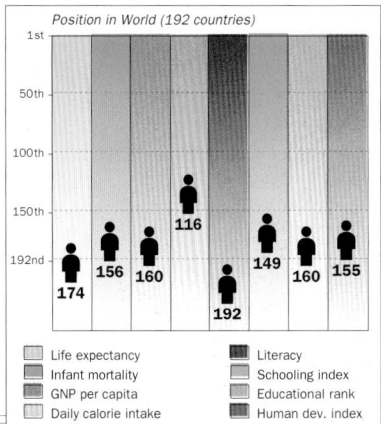

B

BHUTAN

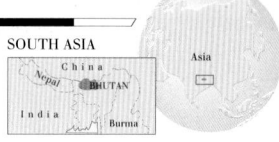
SOUTH ASIA

OFFICIAL NAME: Kingdom of Bhutan   **CAPITAL:** Thimphu
POPULATION: 1.6 million   **CURRENCY:** Ngultrum   **OFFICIAL LANGUAGE:** Dzongkha

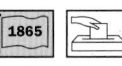

PERCHED IN THE HIMALAYAS between India and China, Bhutan is 70% forested. The land rises from the low, tropical southern strip, through the fertile central valleys, to the high Himalayas, inhabited by semi-nomadic yak herders. A formal Buddhist state where power is shared by the king and government, Bhutan began modernizing in the 1960s, but has chosen to do so gradually and remains largely closed to the outside world.

CLIMATE

WEATHER CHART

The south is tropical, the north alpine, cold and harsh. The central valleys are warmer in the east than in the west. The summer monsoon affects all parts.

TRANSPORTATION

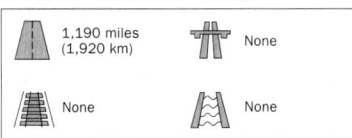

Paro International
19,939 passengers

Has no fleet

THE TRANSPORTATION NETWORK

1,190 miles (1,920 km)	None
None	None

The main surfaced road runs east–west across central Bhutan. Two others run south into India. Only the national airline, Druk Air, flies into Bhutan.

TOURISM

3,000 visitors

No change in 1994

MAIN OVERSEAS ARRIVALS

USA 30%	
Germany 19%	
UK 11%	
Other 40%	

% of total arrivals

The government's policy of allowing tourism to expand only very slowly aims to protect Bhutan's cultural values and natural environment. Most monasteries are closed to foreigners. Initial steps to privatize the industry were taken in 1991.

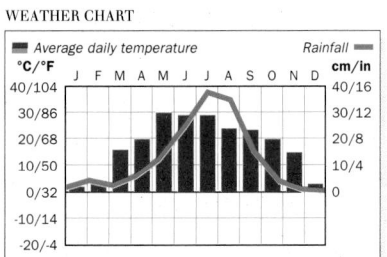

Less than 10% of Bhutan is arable, *but its fertility allows almost any crop to grow. The diversity of wild plant species inspired its old name: Southern Valleys of the Medicinal Herbs.*

PEOPLE

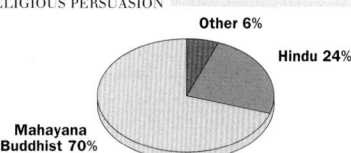

Dzongkha, Nepali, Assamese

88 people per sq. mile

THE URBAN/RURAL POPULATION SPLIT

6%   94%

RELIGIOUS PERSUASION

Other 6%
Hindu 24%
Mahayana Buddhist 70%

The majority of the population, the Drukpa peoples, originated from Tibet and are devoutly Buddhist. Twenty-four per cent are Hindu Nepalese, who settled in the south from 1910 to 1950. Many ethnic Nepalese have been deported as illegal immigrants, creating fierce ethnic tension. Bhutan has 20 languages. Dzongkha, the language of western Bhutan, native to just 16% of people, was made the official language in 1988.

POLITICS

Not applicable

HM *Druk Gyalpo* (Dragon King) Jigme Singye Wangchuck

THE STATE OF THE PARTIES

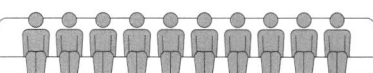

Bhutan is an absolute monarchy, ruled by the king together with the Council of Ministers, the National Assembly and the head of Bhutan's Buddhist monks

The present king is following his father's plans to modernize Bhutan. Until 1961, the country was run on feudal lines and closed to the outside world. The Drukpa-dominated government's policy of instilling a new sense of national identity has alienated the ethnic Nepalese in the south. It has also led directly to the foundation of the Bhutan People's Party. Banned in Bhutan, it has its headquarters in Kathmandu, Nepal.

BHUTAN

Total Land Area :
47 000 sq. km (18 147 sq. miles)

LAND HEIGHT

- 6000m/19686ft
- 4000m/13124ft
- 2000m/6562ft
- 1000m/3281ft
- 500m/1640ft
- 200m/656ft
- 160m/252ft

POPULATION

- over 10 000
- under 10 000

WORLD AFFAIRS

Bhutan's closest relations are with India. It also maintains cordial links with China and negotiations to settle the China–Bhutan border have been progressing since 1984. Relations with Nepal are cool owing to the Bhutan government's policy of sidelining its own ethnic Nepalese population.

AID

 $67m (receipts)   Up 6% in 1993

Bhutan relies on foreign aid for about half of its annual budget. The largest single donor is India.

DEFENSE

 Small army; India effectively guarantees security   Little change

Bhutan's 5,000-strong army, under the king's command, is trained by Indian military instructors. India provides *de facto* protection and would act to defend Bhutan against attack.

ECONOMICS

$272m 31.37–35.17 ngultrum

SCORE CARD

- ❑ WORLD GNP RANKING........................175th
- ❑ GNP PER CAPITA $400
- ❑ BALANCE OF PAYMENTS $9.4m
- ❑ INFLATION 8%
- ❑ UNEMPLOYMENT ....Low rate

STRENGTHS

New development of cash crops for Asian markets (cardamom, apples, oranges, apricots.) Hardwoods in south, especially teak, but exploitation so far tightly controlled. Large hydroelectric potential.

WEAKNESSES

Dependence on Indian workers for many public sector jobs from road-building to teaching. Around 90% of population dependent on agriculture. Just 6% of land cultivated – expansion difficult because of steep mountain slopes. Very little industry. Few mineral resources.

EXPORTS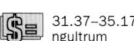

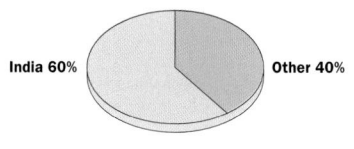

IMPORTS

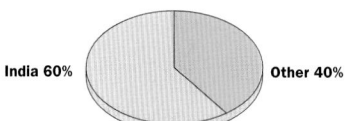

RESOURCES

 1.6bn kwh (capacity 350,000 kw)

75,000 pigs, 435,000 cattle, 59,000 sheep

 Not an oil producer and has no refineries

Talc, gypsum, coal, limestone, slate, dolomite

Bhutan's forests remain largely intact and logging is severely controlled. Hydroelectric potential is considerable, but few dams have been built. Power is sold to India from the Chhukha Dam, bringing in substantial foreign earnings.

ENVIRONMENT

 19% (18% partially protected) State is encouraging community tree-replanting projects

Bhutan's forests stabilize the steep mountainsides and supply 97% of all fuel needs. Road-building, which began in the 1960s, is the biggest cause of deforestation, which has led to topsoil erosion. The high northern pastures are at risk from overgrazing by yaks. Traditional Buddhist values instilling respect for nature and forbidding the killing of animals are still observed.

MEDIA

 All media is controlled by the government

PUBLISHING AND BROADCAST MEDIA

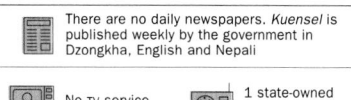

There are no daily newspapers. *Kuensel* is published weekly by the government in Dzongkha, English and Nepali

No TV service 1 state-owned service

Bhutan has never had a TV service. TV is banned on the grounds that it would dilute Bhutanese values.

CRIME

 Bhutan does not publish prison figures  Little variation from year to year

There is little violent crime and levels of theft are low. In 1991, *Driglam namzha*, an ancient code of conduct including the requirement to wear traditional dress, was revived, with fines or imprisonment for non-compliance.

EDUCATION

38% 519 students

Education is free, but not compulsory – 5% of children attend secondary school. Teaching is in English and Dzongkha. There are no universities.

The Drukpa, originally from Tibet, united Bhutan in 1656. It lost the Duars Strip to British India in 1865.

- ❑ **1907** Monarchy established.
- ❑ **1953** National Assembly set up.
- ❑ **1960** Chinese annexation of Tibet severs bilateral relations.
- ❑ **1964** First surfaced road finished.
- ❑ **1968** King forms first cabinet.
- ❑ **1971** Joins UN.
- ❑ **1978** New links with China.
- ❑ **1990** Southern Bhutanese stage campaign for minority rights.
- ❑ **1995** Southern Bhutanese refugees in Nepal renew rights campaign.

HEALTH

 1 per 10,900 people   Diarrheal, respiratory diseases, tuberculosis, malaria, infant deaths

Free clinics, and Thimphu's hospital, provide basic health care. Progress is being made in child immunization, and monks have recently been persuaded to teach hygiene. Infant mortality is high at 13.3% of live births. Bhutanese, Tibetan and Chinese traditional medicines are widely practised.

WEALTH

 Around 90% of people farm their own plots of land and herd cattle and yaks. Most live a subsistence existence

CONSUMER GOODS OWNERSHIP

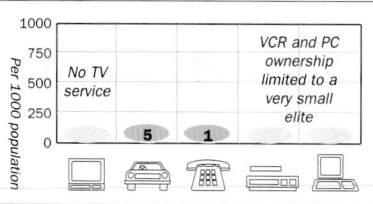

Most people are poor, but starvation is unknown. There is a small middle class of public employees and storekeepers.

WORLD RANKING

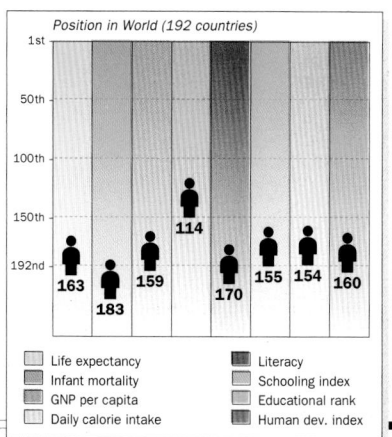

BOLIVIA

OFFICIAL NAME: Republic of Bolivia   **CAPITAL:** Sucre (official); La Paz (administrative)
POPULATION: 7.4 million   **CURRENCY:** Boliviano   **OFFICIAL LANGUAGES:** Spanish, Quechua and Aymará

SOUTH AMERICA

   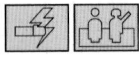

BOLIVIA LIES LANDLOCKED high in central South America. Over half of the population lives on the *altiplano*, the windswept plateau 11,484 ft. above sea level between two ranges of the Andes. La Paz is the highest capital city in the world and has spawned a neighboring large twin town. Bolivia has the world's highest golf course, ski run and soccer stadium. The lowland regions in the east are tropical and underdeveloped but are being rapidly colonized. Bolivia is the poorest nation in South America.

CLIMATE

WEATHER CHART

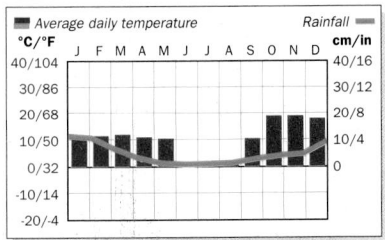

The Andean *altiplano* has an extreme tropical highland climate with frosts at night in winter. Annual rainfall in the west is only 10 inches. The hot eastern lowlands receive most rain in summer.

TRANSPORTATION

 El Alto, La Paz

 1 ship
15,800 dwt

THE TRANSPORTATION NETWORK

1,210 miles (1,940 km)		Pan-American Highway
2,269 miles (3,652 km)		8,699 miles (14,000 km)

Landlocked Bolivia is badly connected. Obtaining more port facilities on the Pacific coast from Chile and developing a Pacific–Atlantic waterway and railroad system, linking Bolivia with both seaboards, remain major aims.

Potato harvest on the altiplano.
The government is encouraging migration to the more fertile lands in the east.

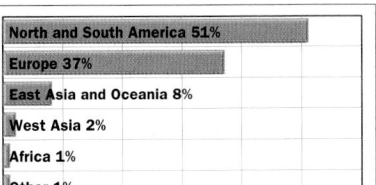

Copacabana on the shores of Lake Titicaca. It lies on a large headland owned by Bolivia on the Peruvian side of the lake.

TOURISM

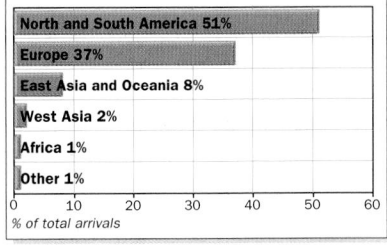 320,000 visitors   Up 19% in 1994

MAIN OVERSEAS ARRIVALS

North and South America 51%	
Europe 37%	
East Asia and Oceania 8%	
West Asia 2%	
Africa 1%	
Other 1%	

% of total arrivals

Foreign tourists are attracted mostly by the traditional festivals, especially the carnival in February or March, the variety of Bolivia's scenery and its Spanish colonial architecture. Major attractions include the Silver Mountain at Potosí, and Lake Titicaca, the highest navigable lake in the world, covering an area of 3,463 square miles. Recent political stability has encouraged some growth in tourism. The industry's potential is limited, however, by Bolivia's isolation, the rugged, inaccessible terrain and the limited infrastructure.

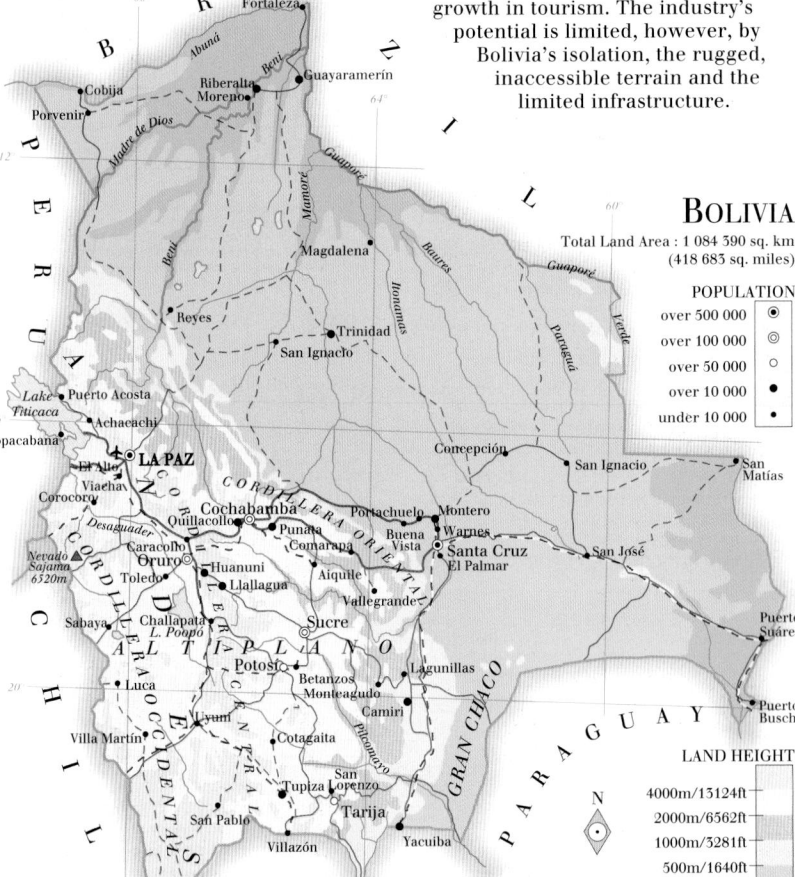

BOLIVIA

Total Land Area : 1 084 390 sq. km
(418 683 sq. miles)

POPULATION

over 500 000	◉
over 100 000	◎
over 50 000	○
over 10 000	•
under 10 000	·

LAND HEIGHT

4000m/13124ft
2000m/6562ft
1000m/3281ft
500m/1640ft
200m/656ft
Sea Level

PEOPLE

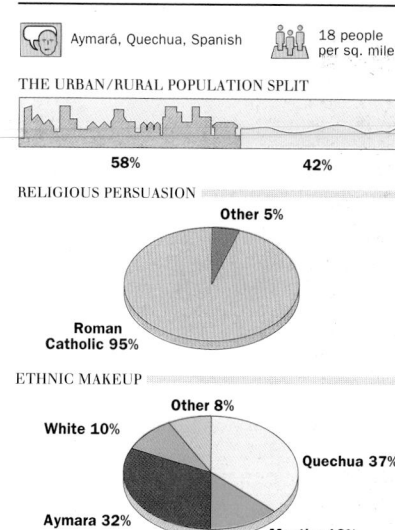

Aymará, Quechua, Spanish

18 people per sq. mile

THE URBAN/RURAL POPULATION SPLIT

58%   42%

RELIGIOUS PERSUASION

Other 5%

Roman Catholic 95%

ETHNIC MAKEUP

Other 8%

White 10%

Quechua 37%

Aymara 32%

Mestizo 13%

Two-thirds of Bolivia's population are indigenous, yet these groups suffer discrimination at most levels of society. The Aymará and Quechua lead an almost parallel existence and take little part in the political process or the formal economy, which remain under the control of a few wealthy city families. Most Bolivians are poor and government schemes, spontaneous colonization and the collapse of tin mining have been responsible for a large migration to lowland eastern regions in the last few decades. As well as Bolivians from the *altiplano*, Asians, South Africans and a few Mennonite communities have also migrated there.

Family life is close-knit; Roman Catholic influence and extended family ties among indigenous groups remain strong. Women have low status in Bolivia, particularly in Aymará and Quechua communities.

POPULATION AGE BREAKDOWN

% of population by age group	■0–14	□15–64	□ 65+		
	3.2%	3.3%	3.4%	3.6%	4.2%
	53.9%	53.8%	53.4%	55%	57.7%
	42.9%	42.9%	43.2%	41.4%	38.1%
	1960	1970	1980	1990	2000

POLITICS

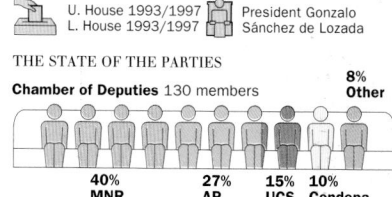

U. House 1993/1997
L. House 1993/1997

President Gonzalo
Sánchez de Lozada

THE STATE OF THE PARTIES

Chamber of Deputies 130 members

8% Other

40% MNR   27% AP   15% UCS   10% Condepa

MNR = National Revolutionary Movement   AP = Patriotic Accord (composed of: ADN = Democratic Nationalist Action, MIR = Movement of the Revolutionary Left)   UCS = Civic Solidarity Union   Condepa = Conscience of the Fatherland

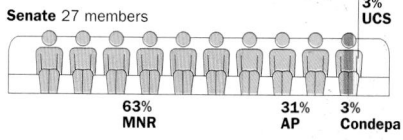

Senate 27 members

3% UCS

63% MNR   31% AP   3% Condepa

Bolivia is a multiparty democracy.

MAIN POLITICAL ISSUES
Privatization
Sánchez de Lozada's government is continuing the privatization and free-market economic policies of its predecessors, including the "capitalization" or part sale of 150 state-owned companies, and the privatization of the mining industry through joint ventures.

Cocaine
Cocaine barons are highly influential in Bolivia, the world's second-largest exporter, after Colombia, of refined cocaine. The government is trying to trim the drug barons' power by encouraging new cash crops to replace coca, but with limited success. Cocaine has become a significant, though illegal, foreign exchange earner for Bolivia.

PROFILE
Between independence from Spain in 1825 and the early 1980s, Bolivia experienced, on average, more than one armed coup a year. The cycle ended in 1982 when, unable to control a general strike, the military agreed to return power to a national congress. Full elections were delayed until 1985.

Behind the scenes, the military and the cocaine barons continue to enjoy influence. The latter, whose profits underpin the whole economy, are frequently implicated in political corruption scandals and have financed presidential campaigns. The pattern of politics remains one of similar parties competing for power in unstable coalitions. The main trade union federation (COB) and the Peasants' Union (CSUTCB) are frequently the focus of opposition to government.

The congressional elections of 1993 brought the right-wing MNR to power, replacing a coalition of left- and right-wing parties which enacted economic austerity policies. These continue to be applied, and the prospects for Bolivia's poor and underemployed remain bleak.

WORLD AFFAIRS

AG   Ama Pac   NAM   OAS   RG

Bolivia's main foreign policy concern is its attempt to negotiate an outlet to the Pacific with Peru and Chile. Relations with the USA are complicated. The USA is Bolivia's main source of aid, a key part of the national economy. Aid payments have, however, been made conditional on Bolivia taking measures to destroy the cocaine producing and trafficking industry, itself a major buttress of the Bolivian economy. The result to date has been a balancing act. The eradication of coca plantations, involving military attacks on peasant coca growers, has kept US aid flowing, yet Bolivia remains the world's second-largest producer of refined cocaine.

Bolivia is negotiating membership of the South American Common Market (MERCOSUR) with its neighbors Brazil, Argentina, Paraguay and Uruguay. As the most isolated and poorest economy in South America, it would be the major beneficiary of a tariff-free zone in the Andean region.

Left-wing MIR leader and president until 1993, Jaime Paz Zamora.

President Gonzalo Sánchez de Lozada, MNR leader, took power in 1993.

CHRONOLOGY
The Aymará civilization was conquered by the Incas in the late 1400s. Fifty years later, the Incas were defeated by the *conquistadores* and Upper Peru, as it became, was governed by Spain from Lima.

❑ 1545 Cerro Rico, the Silver Mountain, discovered at Potosí. Provides Spain with vast wealth.
❑ 1776 Upper Peru becomes part of Viceroyalty of Río de la Plata centered on Buenos Aires.
❑ 1809 Simón Bolívar inspires first revolutionary uprisings in Latin America at Chuquisaca (Sucre), La Paz and Cochabamba, but they fail.
❑ 1824 Spaniards suffer final defeat by Bolívar's general, José de Sucre.
❑ 1825 Independence.
❑ 1836–1839 Union with Peru fails under presidency of Andrés de Santa Cruz. Internal disorder ensues as wealthy local *caudillos* vie for power. ⇨

B

CHRONOLOGY continued

- **1864–1871** Mariano Melgarejo's ruthless rule. Three Indian revolts at seizure of ancestral lands.
- **1879–1883** War of the Pacific. Peru helps Bolivia against Chile, which had invaded nitrate-rich Atacama province. Chile wins. Bolivia is left landlocked.
- **1880–1930** Period of stable Liberal–Conservative governments. Exports from revived mining industry bring prosperity.
- **1903** Rubber-rich Acre province ceded to Brazil after conflict.
- **1920** Indian rebellion.
- **1923** Miners bloodily suppressed.
- **1932–1935** Chaco War with Paraguay. Bolivia loses three-quarters of Chaco. Rise of radicalism and labor movement.
- **1951** Víctor Paz Estenssoro of NMR elected president. Military coup.
- **1952** Revolution. Paz Estenssoro and NMR brought back. Land reforms improve Indians' status. Education reforms, universal suffrage, nationalization of tin mines.
- **1964** Military takes over in coup.
- **1967** Che Guevara killed while trying to mobilize Bolivian workers.
- **1969–1979** Military regimes rule with increasing severity. 1979 coup fails. Interim civilian rule.
- **1980** Indecisive elections. Military takes over again.
- **1982** President-elect Dr. Siles Zuazo finally heads leftist civilian MIR government. Inflation 24,000%.
- **1985** Paz Estenssoro's MNR wins elections. Austerity measures. Annual inflation down to 20%.
- **1986** Tin market collapses. 21,000 miners sacked.
- **1988** Anti-narcotics body set up.
- **1989** MIR takes power in close-run elections. President Paz Zamora makes pact with 1970s dictator Gen. Hugo Bánzer, head of ADN.
- **1990** 3.9m acres of rainforest recognized as Indian territory.
- **1993** MNR voted back to power.
- **1995** Seven-month State of Siege imposed by government.

AID

 $570m (receipts)    Down 16% in 1993

Large amounts of aid come from the USA, but depend on Bolivia making efforts to eradicate coca farms. Smaller amounts are given by Western European countries. Especially poor rural areas receive project aid from Western NGOs, charities and religious organizations. However, corruption and inefficiency hinder the implementation of many projects.

DEFENSE

 $136m   Up 5% in 1995

Defense spending as % GDP — 1.4% (0–40)

BOLIVIAN ARMED FORCES

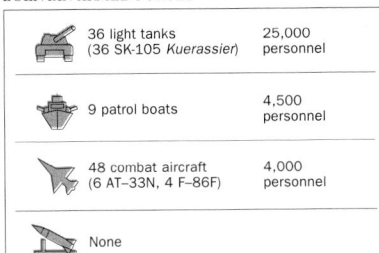

36 light tanks (36 SK-105 Kuerassier)	25,000 personnel
9 patrol boats	4,500 personnel
48 combat aircraft (6 AT–33N, 4 F–86F)	4,000 personnel
None	

The military has not interfered in politics for over a decade but is frequently used to quell internal dissent. The army is the main focus of defense spending, with weaponry bought almost entirely from the USA. The Bolivian navy consists mainly of gunboats on Lake Titicaca, which borders Peru, and on the Pilcomayo River. The army has worked with US forces against the cocaine business, although its integrity is questioned due to its past associations with narcotics-trafficking. The main ambition of the military is the unrealizable aim of recapturing territory that would allow Bolivia access to the Pacific. Military service lasts for one year.

ECONOMICS

 5.6bn    4.71–4.94 bolivianos

SCORE CARD

- ❑ WORLD GNP RANKING............................98th
- ❑ GNP PER CAPITA $770
- ❑ BALANCE OF PAYMENTS.....................$–218m
- ❑ INFLATION 9.5%
- ❑ UNEMPLOYMENT.................................5.4%

EXPORTS
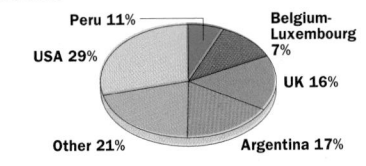
Peru 11%, Belgium-Luxembourg 7%, USA 29%, UK 16%, Argentina 17%, Other 21%

IMPORTS
Chile 8%, Argentina 10%, Other 36%, Japan 11%, Brazil 13%, USA 22%

STRENGTHS
Mineral riches: gold, silver, zinc and tin. Newly discovered oil and natural gas deposits.

WEAKNESSES
Bolivia's extreme poverty has created political instability. Although inflation has been reduced to around 10% annually, a history of hyperinflation – a severe problem until the late 1980s – still deters investors.

PROFILE
Traditionally, the state has used earnings from the public-owned mining sector to control the economy. However, since 1985 successive governments have sold off parts of state-owned companies and encouraged joint ventures and private investment in an attempt to modernize mining and other state sectors. The

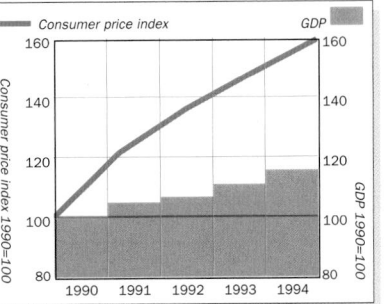
ECONOMIC PERFORMANCE INDICATOR

Consumer price index / GDP, 1990=100, 1990–1994

government hopes that the 50/50 sell-off of shares in state companies will kick-start the economy, reinvigorate public services and do something to alleviate extreme poverty. A decade of market reform has tamed inflation and brought modest growth. Bolivia's medium-term economic prospects have been boosted by the discovery of oil and gas fields, which should be a useful foreign exchange earner. However, there is little prospect of developing a significant industrial base.

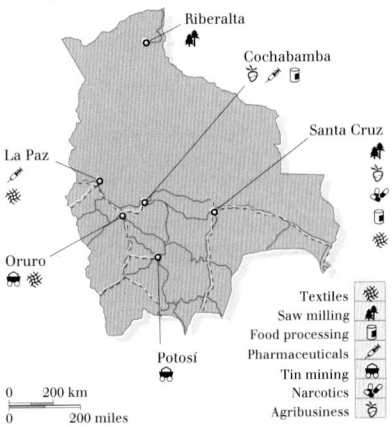
BOLIVIA : MAJOR BUSINESSES

Textiles, Saw milling, Food processing, Pharmaceuticals, Tin mining, Narcotics, Agribusiness

RESOURCES

2.3bn kwh (capacity 740,000 kw)

20,631 b/d (reserves 112,136,000 bbl)

8m sheep, 6m cattle, 2.3m pigs, 1.5m goats

Tin, natural gas, oil, zinc, tungsten, gold, antimony, silver, lead

ELECTRICITY GENERATION

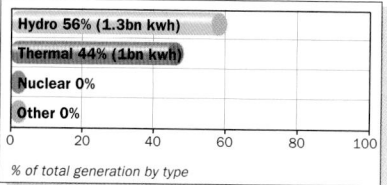

Hydro 56% (1.3bn kwh)
Thermal 44% (1bn kwh)
Nuclear 0%
Other 0%

% of total generation by type

Bolivia is the world's largest tin producer. The government is keen to allow foreign companies to prospect for more oil, and to increase sales of natural gas to Brazil and Argentina.

BOLIVIA : LAND USE

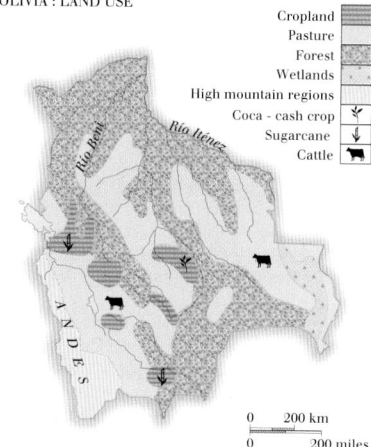

Cropland
Pasture
Forest
Wetlands
High mountain regions
Coca - cash crop
Sugarcane
Cattle

0   200 km
0   200 miles

ENVIRONMENT

8% (5% partially protected)

No effective controls on exports of rare species

ENVIRONMENTAL TREATIES

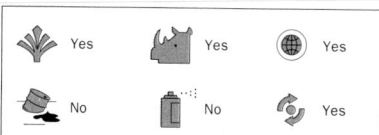

Yes   Yes   Yes
No   No   Yes

Deforestation is Bolivia's major ecological problem. Land clearances are occurring at the record rate of 4,900 acres a year. This is one of the world's highest annual depletion rates. Much of the cleared land is turned over to cattle ranching or the growing of coca. The overuse of pesticides and fertilizers in the coca business is also a concern. The industry is effectively uncontrolled and rivers in Amazonia have high pollution levels.

Pollution problems are compounded by waste chemicals used in minerals industries. Mercury, used in the extraction of silver, has been found in dangerous quantities in river systems.

MEDIA

Little formal censorship, but local journalists rarely comment on the narcotics business for fear of reprisals

PUBLISHING AND BROADCAST MEDIA

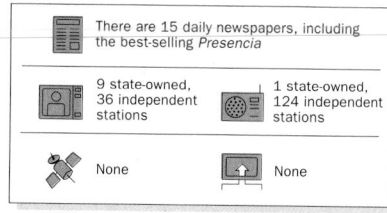

There are 15 daily newspapers, including the best-selling *Presencia*

9 state-owned, 36 independent stations

1 state-owned, 124 independent stations

None   None

Bolivia has the largest number of TV stations in South America. Political parties and cocaine barons frequently exert pressure on the media.

CRIME

Bolivia does not publish prison figures

Crime is rising in narcotics-trafficking centers

CRIME RATES

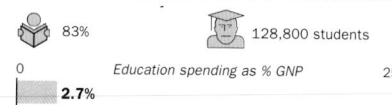

General crime levels are relatively low in urban areas. Bolivians are concerned about the increase in violence associated with the narcotics trade

Violent crime is centered on the narcotics-trafficking towns in the eastern lowlands, particularly Santa Cruz. However, the main cities are much safer for tourists, and have lower crime rates than cities in neighboring Peru, for example. The Bolivian police and army have a reputation for mistreating poor farmers and miners.

EDUCATION

83%   128,800 students

0   Education spending as % GNP   25
2.7%

THE EDUCATION SYSTEM

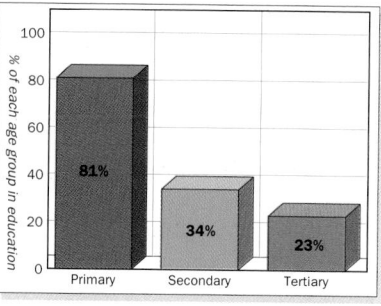

% of each age group in education

81%   Primary
34%   Secondary
23%   Tertiary

Education is based on a combination of the French and US systems. Although the majority of the population speaks indigenous languages, most teaching is in Spanish. Bolivia has one of the lowest literacy rates in South America. Only the 51% of the population who live in towns receive schooling.

HEALTH

1 per 1,971 people

Influenza, tuberculosis, other communicable diseases, malaria

0   Health spending as % GDP   25
2.4%

Bolivia has one of the lowest numbers of doctors per capita in the whole of Latin America. Only half the children under one year old are immunized, and diseases that are easily preventable by vaccination are a major cause of death. Approximately half of the population of Bolivia has safe drinking water. Rural areas are barely served by medicine, people there rely on traditional remedies.

WEALTH

Miner, 695 bolivianos ($140) per month; aircraft engine mechanic, 3,086 bolivianos ($625) per month

CONSUMER GOODS OWNERSHIP

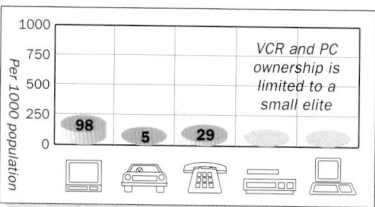

Per 1000 population

VCR and PC ownership is limited to a small elite

98   5   29

There is little social mobility in Bolivia; the main routes for advancement are the armed forces or the cocaine business. Generally, the indigenous peoples who form the rural poor are the worst off. The Andean highlands are extremely poor; economic growth is concentrated in the fertile, tropical, eastern lowlands, where the population density is lowest.

The small number of wealthy Bolivians holiday in Brazil or Miami. German luxury goods, and Mercedes cars in particular, are popular among Bolivians and the small German immigrant population. A recent reduction in tariff barriers has resulted in an increase in the import and sale of electronic goods.

WORLD RANKING

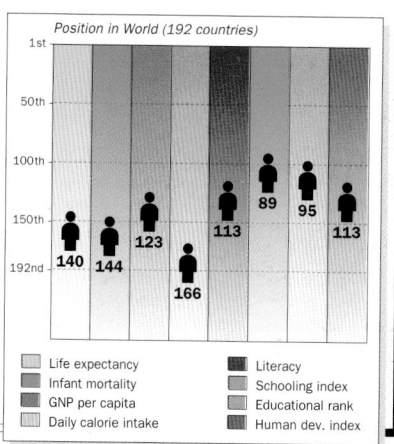

Position in World (192 countries)

1st
50th
100th
150th
192nd

140   144   123   166   113   89   95   113

Life expectancy
Infant mortality
GNP per capita
Daily calorie intake
Literacy
Schooling index
Educational rank
Human dev. index

BOSNIA & HERZEGOVINA

EUROPE

OFFICIAL NAME: The Republic of Bosnia and Herzegovina   CAPITAL: Sarajevo
POPULATION: 3.5 million   CURRENCY: Bosnian dinar   OFFICIAL LANGUAGE: Serbian and Croatian

B

A MOUNTAINOUS COUNTRY with a few miles of coast on the Adriatic Sea, Bosnia is bordered by Croatia, Serbia and Montenegro. Between 1943 and 1990, the Yugoslavian regime largely prevented conflict between Muslims, Croats and Serbs by allowing cultural freedom. Between mid-1992 and late 1995, however, the three main ethnic populations of the dissolved Yugoslavia fought over Bosnia. Tens of thousands died and many historic cities were destroyed.

CLIMATE

WEATHER CHART

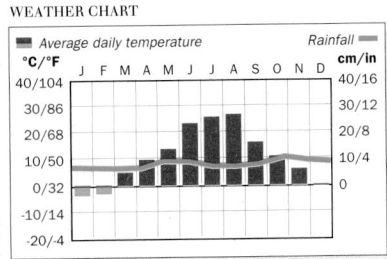

Bosnia has a continental climate with warm summers and bitterly cold winters, often with snow.

TRANSPORTATION

 Sarajevo Intl

 Has no fleet

THE TRANSPORTATION NETWORK

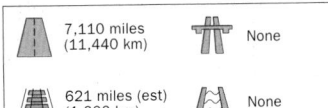

| 7,110 miles (11,440 km) | None |
| 621 miles (est) (1,000 km) | None |

War has severely damaged the transportation network, resulting in wrecked bridges, roads and railroads. The capital, Sarajevo, was formerly the focus for all national and international transportation networks.

TOURISM

None

No tourism likely until peace settlement

MAIN OVERSEAS ARRIVALS

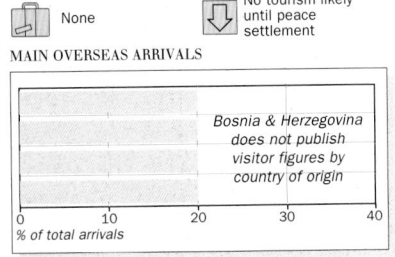

Bosnia & Herzegovina does not publish visitor figures by country of origin

% of total arrivals

Despite having hosted the 1984 Winter Olympics, Bosnia has not developed the infrastructure for a tourist industry.

PEOPLE

Serbian, Croatian

176 people per sq. mile

THE URBAN/RURAL POPULATION SPLIT

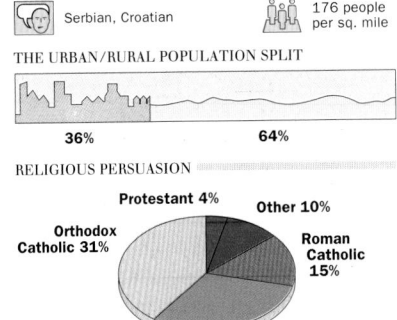

36%   64%

RELIGIOUS PERSUASION

Protestant 4%   Other 10%
Orthodox Catholic 31%   Roman Catholic 15%
Slavic Muslim 40%

Before the war, the population was 44% ethnic Bosnian (mostly Muslim), 31% Serb, 17% Croat and 8% originally from other parts of former Yugoslavia. Intermarriage was common and ethnic violence rare. Society was largely secular and materialistic. In the aftermath of secession, cultural differences became a basis for dividing society in order to lay claim to other ethnic groups' wealth.

BOSNIA & HERZEGOVINA

Total Land Area : 51 130 sq. km (19 741 sq. miles)

POPULATION

◎ over 100 000
○ over 50 000
● over 10 000
• under 10 000

LAND HEIGHT

2000m/6562ft
1000m/3281ft
500m/1640ft
200m/656ft
Sea Level

N

0   50 km
0   50 miles

POLITICS

1990/Uncertain

President Dr. Alija Izetbegovic

THE STATE OF THE PARTIES

National Assembly 240 members

8% LC/SA   5% ARF

36% PDA   30% SDP   18% CDU-BH   3% Other

PDA = Party for Democratic Action   SDP = Serbian Democratic Party   CDU-BH = Croatian Democratic Union of Bosnia-Herzegovina   LC/SA = League of Communists/Socialist Alliance   ARF = Alliance of Reform Forces

The Bosnian peace agreement, the so-called Dayton Accord, signed by the leaders of Bosnia, Serbia and Croatia in December 1995, provides for a single Bosnian state (with a democratically elected collective presidency and parliament) composed of two separate entities: some 51% of the territory to be controlled by a Muslim–Croat Federation and the remaining 49% by the Serbs. Hence, there are currently three distinct political structures in Bosnia: the Republic, with a head of state (Alia Izetbegovic), Assembly and government (headed by Hasan Muratovic); the nascent Federation, with a president (Kresimir Zubak), parliament and government (headed by Izudin Kapetanovic); and the Serb Republic, with indicted war criminal Radovan Karadzic as self-declared president, and a People's Assembly and government led by Rajko Kasagic.

B

WORLD AFFAIRS

The 1995 peace agreement sanctioned the entry into Bosnia of a 60,000-strong international Implementation Force (I-For), the biggest military initiative in Europe since World War II.

AID

 $696m (receipts) in first six months of 1994

 Will require massive amounts of reconstruction aid

Humanitarian aid has been crucial to the survival of many Bosnians, with the UN playing a vital role in distributing relief. Its Inter-Agency Appeal raised $696 million for the first half of 1994, chiefly for Bosnian Muslim refugees, but also for those in Serbia, Montenegro, Macedonia and Croatia.

DEFENSE

 Almost all state spending is on arms

 No likely change until full peace

It has been estimated that the Muslim government controls 60,000 lightly armed troops and 120,000 reservists. The "Serbian Republic of Bosnia" has 80,000 troops, backed by heavy weapons, and the Croats 50,000.

ECONOMICS

 $4bn (pre-war)

 751.22 Bosnian dinars

SCORE CARD

❑ WORLD GNP RANKING	120th
❑ GNP PER CAPITA	*The formal*
❑ BALANCE OF PAYMENTS	*economy now*
❑ INFLATION	*operates under*
❑ UNEMPLOYMENT	*war conditions*

STRENGTHS
Before 1991, Bosnia possessed five of former Yugoslavia's largest companies. Retail outlets were mostly privately operated and there was a sizeable thriving small-business sector. The country has the potential to become a thriving market economy, with a solid manufacturing base.

WEAKNESSES
According to the World Bank, the reconstruction of Bosnia's war-shattered infrastructure will cost around $5.1 million.

EXPORTS/IMPORTS

Bosnia & Herzegovina has no significant exports.
Most imports are in the form of UN aid and arms from the international market.
Oil imports are probably from the Middle East

RESOURCES

 Output down by 85% owing to war

 2,500 tons

 7m poultry, 600,000 sheep, 390,000 cattle, 223,000 pigs

 Coal, lignite, iron, bauxite, cement

Bosnia's land is not well suited to agriculture, but has mineral deposits, forests and hydroelectric potential.

ENVIRONMENT

 None owing to war

 No initiatives possible

Apart from war damage, Bosnia faces the effects of industrial pollution incurred during the communist regime.

MEDIA

 Censorship imposed owing to war

PUBLISHING AND BROADCAST MEDIA

	There are 2 daily newspapers. *Oslobodjenje* (Liberation) has appeared every day since the start of war
3 state-run, some independent services	3 state-run, some independent services

Between secession and war, Bosnia had an independent press with no censorship. The Muslim government engaged US PR firms to shape media coverage of the war.

CRIME

 Bosnia does not publish prison figures

 War crimes against civilians committed by all warring parties

All sides in the civil war, but especially the Serbs, have been accused of carrying out war crimes. "Ethnic cleansing" of towns and villages, whereby entire populations were forced to evacuate their homes to avoid murder, rape and torture, was common. Army officers exploited their power by running mafia-style operations.

EDUCATION

 93%

 40,000 students

Formerly obligatory for eight years, education at all levels has been disrupted or suspended by the war.

The Muslim town of Mostar. *Its 16th-century bridge at a strategic river crossing and much of the old town have been destroyed by war.*

CHRONOLOGY

In 1945 Bosnia Herzegovina became one of Yugoslavia's six republics.

- ❑ **1990** Nationalists defeat communists in multiparty elections. PDA leader Dr. Alija Izetbegovic president.
- ❑ **1991** Serbs declare "Autonomous regions." Parliament announces republican sovereignty.
- ❑ **1992** EC and USA recognize Bosnia. Serbs announce "Serbian Republic." Civil war between Muslims, Croats and Serbs begins. UN sends troops to guard aid convoys.
- ❑ **1995** NATO air strikes on Serbs; ceasefire; US-brokered peace agreement.
- ❑ **1996** NATO-led implementation of peace agreement begins.

HEALTH

 War has led to an exodus of doctors

 Cholera and diphtheria epidemics, violence, deaths from war-stress

War has placed an enormous strain on an underfunded service. Thousands have died for want of basic treatment.

WEALTH

 Most salaries have been eroded by hyperinflation. By 1995, two million people had been displaced by the war and one million had fled Bosnia

CONSUMER GOODS OWNERSHIP

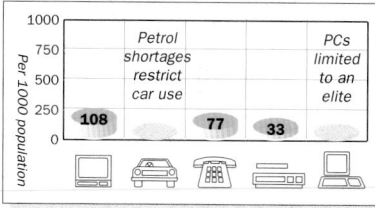

The only people currently acquiring wealth in Bosnia are those involved in profiteering and extortion.

WORLD RANKING

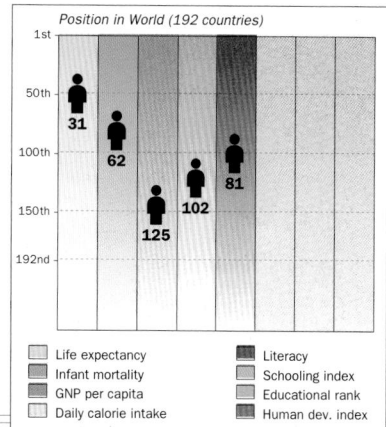

BOTSWANA

B

OFFICIAL NAME: Republic of Botswana CAPITAL: Gaborone
POPULATION: 1.5 million CURRENCY: Pula OFFICIAL LANGUAGE: English

   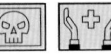

A RID AND LANDLOCKED, Botswana's central plateau separates the populous eastern grasslands from the Kalahari Desert and swamps of the Okavango Delta in the west. Botswana is a multiparty democracy, but the Botswana Democratic Party has won every election since independence. Diamonds provide the country with a prosperous economy, but rain is an even more precious resource, honored in the name of the currency, *pula*.

The Okavango Delta. Plans to draw water from it for irrigation were shelved in 1991 in the interests of wildlife conservation.

CLIMATE

WEATHER CHART

Botswana's subtropical climate is dry and prone to drought. Rainfall declines from 25 in. in the north to under 4 in. in the Kalahari Desert in the west.

TRANSPORTATION

Sir Seretse Khama Intl, Gaborone
168,000 passengers

Has no fleet

THE TRANSPORTATION NETWORK

1,560 miles (2,500 km)		None	
551 miles (887 km)		None	

The opening of the trans-Kalahari road to Namibia in 1998 will make Botswana less dependent on South African ports. Upgrading existing road and rail networks is now a priority.

TOURISM

637,000 visitors

Up 5% in 1994

MAIN OVERSEAS ARRIVALS

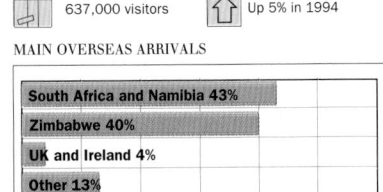

South Africa and Namibia 43%		
Zimbabwe 40%		
UK and Ireland 4%		
Other 13%		
% of total arrivals

Tourism is aimed at wealthy wildlife enthusiasts and focuses on safaris, especially to the Okavango Delta.

PEOPLE

Tswana, English, Shona, San, Khoikhoi, Ndebele

8 people per sq. mile

THE URBAN/RURAL POPULATION SPLIT

25%   75%

ETHNIC MAKEUP

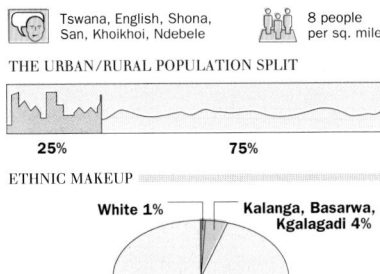

White 1%
Kalanga, Basarwa, Kgalagadi 4%
Tswana 95%

Botswana's stability reflects its ethnic homogeneity and the continuing importance of traditional forms of authority, notably the village *kgotla*, or parliament. The Tswana make up the vast majority of the population, with the Bamangwato forming the largest Tswana group. Botswana's first inhabitants, the San, have been marginalized. Whites continue to dominate the professions.

POLITICS

1994/1999

President Ketumile Joni Masire

THE STATE OF THE PARTIES

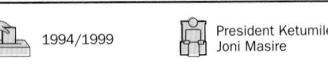

National Assembly 40 members

75% BDP   25% BNF

BDP = Botswana Democratic Party **BNF** = Botswana National Front

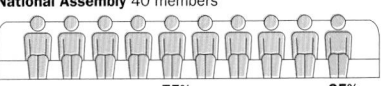

House of Chiefs 15 members

Comprises the chiefs of the 8 principal tribes, 4 sub-chiefs and 3 members elected by the other members of the House

Formally a multiparty democracy, Botswana has been ruled by a single elected party, the BDP, since independence. However, economic problems, corruption scandals and increasing urbanization have led to a decline in support for the BDP. This was reflected in the results of the 1994 elections, when the BNF made unexpected gains at the expense of the BDP, which nevertheless retained an absolute majority in parliament.

BOTSWANA

Total Land Area : 566 730 sq. km (218 814 sq. miles)

POPULATION

over 500 000	◉
over 50 000	○
over 10 000	•
under 10 000	·

LAND HEIGHT

1000m/3281ft
500m/1640ft

0   200 km
0   200 miles

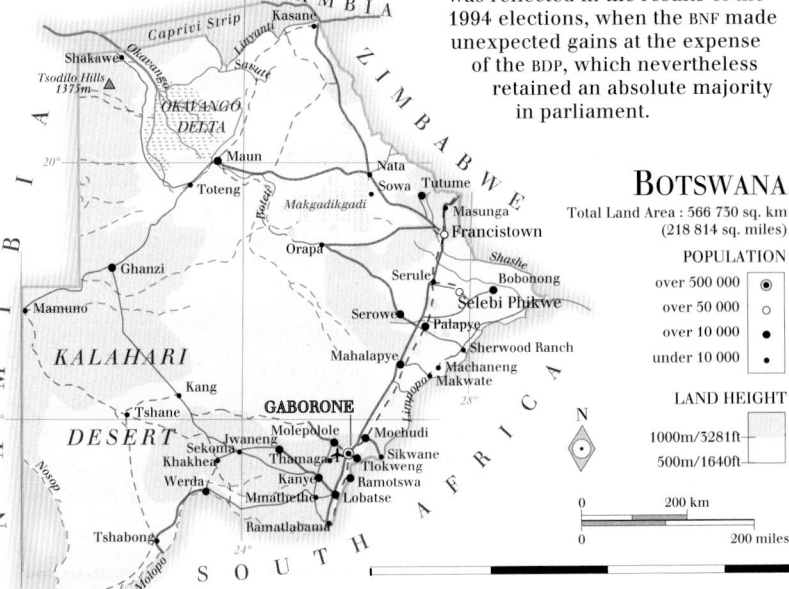

WORLD AFFAIRS

Having been at the receiving end of South African destabilization during the 1980s, Botswana's main concern is the establishment of a politically and economically stable post-apartheid state. Potential South African domination of the SADC is another fear. Internationally, relations with the UK and USA are important.

AID

 $127m (receipts)   Up 13% in 1993

Botswana's political and economic record has made it a favored aid recipient, notably from the EU, UK, USA and World Bank. Environmental projects trying to balance wildlife needs with rural development are the priority; 90% of EU aid is environment linked. Transportation is also an aid target.

DEFENSE

 $200m   Up 2% in 1995

Relatively large sums continue to be spent on defense, despite the reduction in regional tension following the political changes in South Africa.

ECONOMICS

 $4bn   2.73–2.82 pula

SCORE CARD

❑ WORLD GNP RANKING	108th
❑ GNP PER CAPITA	$2,800
❑ BALANCE OF PAYMENTS	$199m
❑ INFLATION	10.5%
❑ UNEMPLOYMENT	21%

STRENGTHS

Diamonds: transformed Botswana from subsistence to middle-income economy in 25 years; world's third-largest producer. High economic growth, averaging 11.3% a year in 1980s. Prudent economic management. Large financial reserves. Copper, nickel, beef.

WEAKNESSES

Overdependence on diamonds (80% of export earnings; 50% of GNP). Weak agriculture and industry. Small population, water shortages and drought add to diversification problems. Adverse impact of beef industry on environment. High transportation costs to coast.

EXPORTS

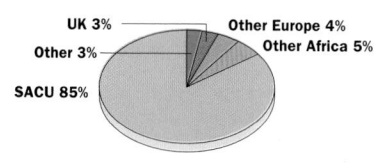

UK 3% — Other Europe 4%
Other 3% — Other Africa 5%
SACU 85%

IMPORTS

UK 3% — Europe (exc. UK) 5%
Other 2% — Rest of Africa 5%
SACU 85%

RESOURCES

 910m kwh   Not an oil producer and has no refineries

2.8m cattle, 2.5m goats, 344,000 sheep   Diamonds, copper, coal, nickel, soda ash, gold

Diamonds are mined by the 50% state-owned Debswana. Large coal deposits are the basis of power grid expansion. Water is Botswana's scarcest resource.

ENVIRONMENT

 18% (2% partially protected)   National Conservation Strategy regarded among world's best

Botswana is trying to reduce conflict between rural development and the environment by helping communities to earn a living from wildlife protection.

MEDIA

 There is no overt censorship

PUBLISHING AND BROADCAST MEDIA

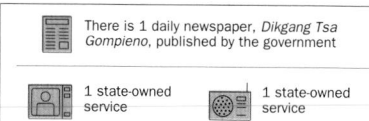

There is 1 daily newspaper, *Dikgang Tsa Gompieno*, published by the government

1 state-owned service   1 state-owned service

The government bias of the one daily paper and radio is offset in the many weekly and other journals. The 20,000 TVs also receive South African stations.

CRIME

 Botswana does not publish prison figures   Up 14% in 1992

Crime levels are generally low. Official corruption, diamond smuggling and robbery are the main concerns. Human rights are generally respected.

EDUCATION

 67%    6,409 students

Education is not compulsory. Elementary education is free. Enrolment drops from 90% to under 40% at secondary level. Adult literacy projects are well funded.

HEALTH

 1 per 5,150 people   Tuberculosis, heart diseases, pneumonia

The emphasis is on expanding primary health care services. The drought early warning system includes a national nutritional surveillance program.

WEALTH

 80% of the population live in rural areas and those with cattle are better off

CONSUMER GOODS OWNERSHIP

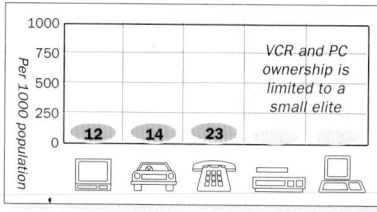

VCR and PC ownership is limited to a small elite

12   14   23

At $2,800, GNP per capita is among Africa's highest, but most people are poor. Wealth belongs to the urban elite.

WORLD RANKING

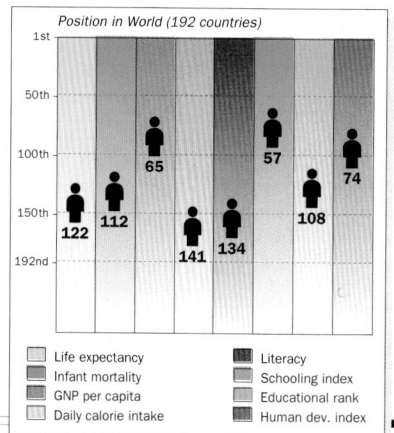

Position in World (192 countries)

122   112   65   141   134   57   108   74

Life expectancy	Literacy
Infant mortality	Schooling index
GNP per capita	Educational rank
Daily calorie intake	Human dev. index

BRAZIL

OFFICIAL NAME: Federative Republic of Brazil   **CAPITAL:** Brasília
POPULATION: 161.8 million   **CURRENCY:** Real   **OFFICIAL LANGUAGE:** Portuguese

THE LARGEST COUNTRY in South America, Brazil became independent of Portugal in 1822. Today, it is renowned as the site of the world's-largest tropical rainforest, the threat to which led to the UN's first international environmental conference being held at Rio de Janeiro in 1992. Covering one-third of Brazil's total land area, the rainforest grows around the massive Amazon River and its delta. Apart from the basin of the River Plate to the south, the rest of the country consists of highlands. The mountainous north is part forested and part desert. Brazil is the world's leading coffee producer and also has rich reserves of gold, diamonds, oil and iron ore. Cattle-ranching is an expanding industry. The city of São Paulo is the world's second-biggest conurbation, with 17 million inhabitants.

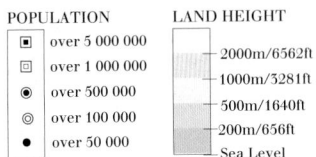

BRAZIL

Total Land Area : 8 456 510 sq. km
(3 265 059 sq. miles)

POPULATION	
▣	over 5 000 000
▢	over 1 000 000
◉	over 500 000
◎	over 100 000
●	over 50 000

LAND HEIGHT
2000m/6562ft
1000m/3281ft
500m/1640ft
200m/656ft
Sea Level

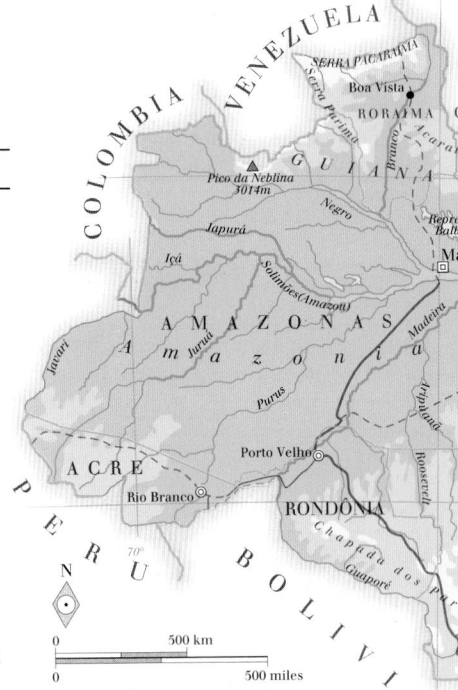

CLIMATE

WEATHER CHART

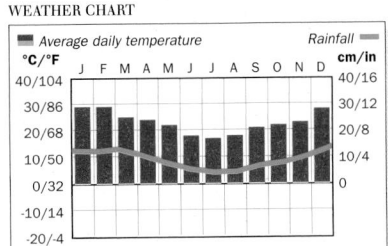

Brazil's share of the Amazon basin, occupying half of the country, has a model equatorial climate. The 59–79 inches of rain are spread throughout the year, although some periods are rather wetter than others according to region. Temperatures are high, with almost no seasonal variation, but scarcely ever rise above 100°F.

The Brazilian plateau, which occupies most of the rest of the country, has far greater temperature ranges. Rain falls mainly between October and April. However, the northeast, the least productive region of Brazil, is very dry and in recent years has been suffering from severe drought, which has compounded its problems. The southern states have hot summers and cool winters, when frost may occur.

TRANSPORTATION

Guarulhos Intl, São Paulo
5.78m passengers

277 ships
8.5m dwt

THE TRANSPORTATION NETWORK

139,440 miles (224,390 km)	Trans-Amazonian Highway 3,109 miles (5,000 km)
18,721 miles (30,129 km)	31,069 miles (50,000 km)

A vast road network is being built to link the main centers of Brazil, and five river systems are being harnessed for a total of 4,170 miles of waterways. São Paulo's subway is being extended to cope with the city's rapidly expanding population.

Parati, in Rio state, was one of Brazil's major gold exporting ports in the 17th century. Its colonial architecture is well preserved.

TOURISM

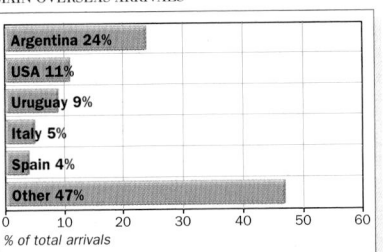

1.8m visitors

Up 9% in 1994

MAIN OVERSEAS ARRIVALS

Argentina 24%	
USA 11%	
Uruguay 9%	
Italy 5%	
Spain 4%	
Other 47%	

% of total arrivals

Its 1,243 miles of Atlantic beaches, the folklore and music of the northeast coast, and the annual *Mardi Gras* carnival in Rio de Janeiro are Brazil's major attractions. However, the increasingly affluent and international audience now controls the carnival.

The largely Afro-Brazilian residents of Rio's *favelas*, or shanty towns, can often no longer afford to take part in the parades that originate in their culture.

Brazil has targeted ecotourism as a major growth area. Foreign investment in tourist facilities in Amazonia is being encouraged by the government. However, Brazilians show little interest in ecotourism, preferring to visit Amazonia for the duty-free shopping zone in Manaus.

Brazil is still a relatively cheap destination for European and American tourists. Despite this, visitor numbers are declining, falling from 0.5% to 0.1% of the world market since 1970. Many visitors have been put off by the negative publicity generated by the conditions in the shanty towns and by Brazil's past human rights record.

Rio de Janeiro and Sugar Loaf Mountain seen from Corcovado (Hunchback) Peak. With a population of 11 million, the Rio conurbation is Brazil's largest after São Paulo.

PEOPLE

 Portuguese, German, Italian, Spanish, Polish, Japanese, Indian languages

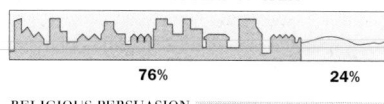 49 people per sq. mile

THE URBAN/RURAL POPULATION SPLIT

76%   24%

RELIGIOUS PERSUASION

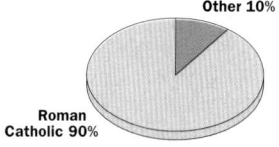

Other 10%

Roman Catholic 90%

ETHNIC MAKEUP

Black 6%

Other (including Portuguese, Italian, German & Indian) 56%

Mixed 38%

POPULATION AGE BREAKDOWN

% of population by age group	1960	1970	1980	1990	2000
0–14	43.6%	42.3%	37.7%	34.7%	29.1%
15–64	53.5%	54.3%	58.3%	60.6%	65.3%
65+	2.9%	3.4%	4%	4.7%	5.6%

Brazil's population is highly diverse. It includes indigenous Indian groups who have had little contact with the outside world, as well as the descendants of both its Portuguese colonizers and the Africans brought to work the sugar plantations in the 17th century. More recent immigrant groups include both Italians and Japanese. Indigenous Indians suffer prejudice from most other peoples in Brazil. Since 1900, 87 Indian groups have become extinct as a result of disease, starvation or the forceful taking of their land by miners, settlers and loggers. The Indian population today is estimated at just 220,000. Migrants from the poor northeast suffer considerable discrimination in the country's larger cities.

Brazil is a profoundly Catholic country with a traditional emphasis on the family. In the urban areas, however, family structures are under pressure. Migrants from the northeast often leave their families behind.

Women in Brazil have had the vote since 1934, but are still discriminated against in jobs and politics. A ministry for women has been established with the aim of defending and promoting their interests.

CHRONOLOGY

The first Portuguese, Pedro Alvares Cabral, arrived in Brazil in 1500. By the time Spain took control of the region, in 1580, it was a thriving colony drawing its wealth from sugar plantations in the northeast, worked by imported Africans, or Indians captured from further and further inland.

❏ **1637–1654** Dutch control sugar-growing areas.

❏ **1763** Rio becomes capital.

❏ **1788** *Inconfidência* rebellion, led by Tiradentes, fails.

❏ **1807** French invade Portugal. King João VI flees to Brazil with British naval escort. In return, Brazil's ports opened to foreign trade.

❏ **1821** King returns to Portugal. Son Pedro made regent of Brazil.

❏ **1822** Pedro declares independence and is made Emperor of Brazil.

❏ **1828** Brazil loses Uruguay.

❏ **1831** Military revolt after war with Argentina (1825–1828). Emperor abdicates. Five-year-old son succeeds him as Pedro II.

❏ **1835–1845** Rio Grande secedes.

❏ **1865–1870** Brazil wins war of Triple Alliance with Argentina and Uruguay against Paraguay.

❏ **1888** Pedro II abolishes slavery; landowners and military turn against him.

❏ **1889** First Republic established. Emperor goes into exile in Paris. Increasing prosperity as result of international demand for coffee.

❏ **1891** Federal constitution established.

❏ **1914–1918** World War I hits coffee exports.

❏ **1920s** Working class and intellectual movements call for end to oligarchical rule.

❏ **1930** Coffee prices collapse. Revolt led by Dr Getúlio Vargas, the "Father of the Poor," who becomes president. Fast industrial growth.

❏ **1937** Vargas's position as benevolent dictator formalized in "New State." based on fascist model. ⇨

CHRONOLOGY *continued*

- ❏ **1942** Declares war on Germany.
- ❏ **1945** Vargas forced out by military.
- ❏ **1951** Vargas reelected as leader of Labor Party.
- ❏ **1954** US opposes Vargas's socialist policies, including plans to double minimum wage. The right, backed by the military, demand his resignation. Commits suicide.
- ❏ **1956–1960** President Juscelino Kubitschek, backed by Brazilian Workers' Party (PTB), attracts foreign investment for new industries, especially from USA.
- ❏ **1960–1961** Conservative Jânio da Silva Quadros president. Tries to break dependence on US trade.
- ❏ **1961** Brasília, built in three years, becomes new capital. PTB leader, João Goulart, elected president.
- ❏ **1961–1964** President's powers briefly curtailed as right wing reacts to presidential policies.
- ❏ **1964** Bloodless military coup under army chief Gen. Castelo Branco.
- ❏ **1965** Branco assumes dictatorship. Bans existing political parties, but creates two official new ones. He is followed by a succession of military rulers. Fast-track economic development, the Brazilian Miracle, is counterbalanced by ruthless suppression of left-wing activists.
- ❏ **1974** World oil crisis marks end of economic boom. Brazil's foreign debt now largest in world.
- ❏ **1979** More political parties allowed.
- ❏ **1980** Huge migrations into Rondônia state begin.
- ❏ **1985** Civilian Senator Tancredo Neves wins presidential elections as candidate of new liberal alliance, but dies before taking office. Illiterate adults get the vote.
- ❏ **1987** Gold found on Yanomani lands in Roraima state; illegal diggers rush in by the thousand.
- ❏ **1988** New constitution promises massive social spending but fails to address land reform. Chico Mendes, rubber-tappers' union leader and environmentalist, murdered.
- ❏ **1989** Brazil's first environmental protection plan "Our Nature" drawn up. Inflation reaches 1,000% a year. First fully democratic presidential elections won by Fernando Collor de Mello of new PRN.
- ❏ **1990** Sweeping economic measures. New currency.
- ❏ **1992** Earth Summit held in Rio. President Collor de Mello resigns and is impeached for corruption.
- ❏ **1994–1995** Plan Real ends hyperinflation. Congress resists constitutional reforms, but key privatizations of state monopolies are passed.

POLITICS

 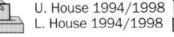
U. House 1994/1998
L. House 1994/1998
President Fernando Henrique Cardoso

THE STATE OF THE PARTIES

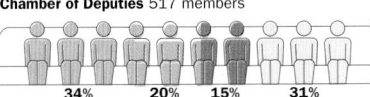

Chamber of Deputies 517 members

| 34% PSDB–PFL–PTB–PL | 20% PMDB | 15% PT | 31% Other |

PSDB–PFL–PTB–PL = Brazilian Social Democratic Party/Liberal Front Party/Brazilian Labor Party/Liberal Party
PMDB = Brazilian Democratic Movement Party
PT = Workers' Party

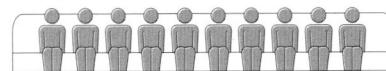

Federal Senate 81 members

3 members are elected by each of the 26 states and the Federal District

Brazil is a democratic federal republic with 27 regional parliaments and a national congress. In 1993, Brazilians voted to retain directly elected presidents.

MAIN POLITICAL ISSUES
Reducing the fiscal deficit
The reduction of the fiscal deficit, running at 4% of GDP in 1995, is a key objective. The government aims to dramatically reduce overstaffing at all levels of government, reduce social security payments and address the problem of the high level of interest rates.

Redrafting the constitution
The 1988 constitution, detailing promises for a better future, has proved to be unworkable in practice. The state cannot afford its social security, health and pension commitments. The proliferation of local governments, designed to check federal power, has led to a duplication of functions and is very expensive. The aim now is to develop a shorter and clearer constitution. Reformists want provisions to curb tax evasion, and were successful in 1995 in ending state monopolies and allowing foreign investment in telecommunications, oil, mining and shipping. Many also want to see changes in the electoral system in order to curb the increasing involvement of small parties in government.

Eradicating corruption
Former President Collor de Mello's 1992 impeachment for fraud underlines the depth of the problem of corruption. Many are demanding an end to parliamentary immunity: under the current system, elected officials cannot be prosecuted unless they have been suspended from office by a two-thirds vote.

PROFILE
Brazil's democracy is characterized by a weak party system, centered around

***President Fernando Cardoso**, who took office in January 1995.*

***Luís Ignacio da Silva, "Lula,"** former leader of the left-wing Workers' Party.*

***Former president Itamar Franco**, whose government introduced the real.*

personalities rather than parties. Parties do not have set ideological programs, but tend to form *ad hoc* coalitions to get legislation through Congress. The preponderance of small parties adds to the problems.

Politics has been further rocked by recent corruption scandals. Itamar Franco, who became president after Collor de Mello had been impeached for alleged fraud, was himself under investigation in 1993.

The dissatisfaction with the center-right has been a boost to the left. However, a victory for the left, led by the influential Luís da Silva – who came second to Collor de Mello in the 1989 presidential elections – could provoke fears of military intervention. This was a factor limiting the left's popular support in the run-up to the 1994 elections; Brazilians do not want a return to military rule.

The military, in power from 1964–1985, was responsible for human rights abuses, particularly against Amazon Indians. Its economic mismanagement left Brazil with a legacy of huge debts and inefficient state industries.

***Coffee plantation**, São Paulo state. Coffee was introduced into Brazil in the early 18th century. It is declining in importance and now accounts for less than 4% of export revenues.*

WORLD AFFAIRS

Brazil's main foreign policy concern is the working of MERCOSUR, a common market with Argentina, Paraguay and Uruguay, which in 1995 created an additional market of over 40 million for Brazil's relatively efficient producers. A successful outcome to negotiations with Chile and Peru for a Pacific port outlet would further boost Brazil's exports.

Beyond Latin America, relations with the USA and Japan, Brazil's main creditors, are critical for debt rescheduling. Brazil is campaigning for a seat in an enlarged UN Security Council. The 1992 Rio Earth Summit was a major boost to Brazil's international image. However, cases of continuing exploitation of Amazon Indian groups have recently come to light.

AID

 238m (receipts) 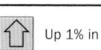 Up 1% in 1993

Brazil's main aid donors are the USA and the EU. The World Bank was to provide $2 billion in 1996 for environmental, basic sanitation, road building and anti-poverty projects. As well as official aid, much comes from NGOs, mainly for environmental and housing projects.

DEFENSE

 $7.2bn   Up 13% in 1995

0   *Defense spending as % GDP*   40

1.6%

BRAZILIAN ARMED FORCES

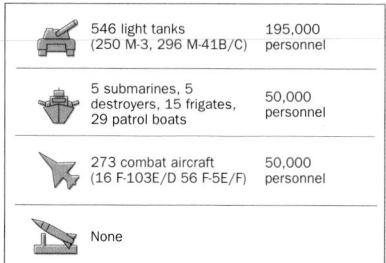

🔫	546 light tanks (250 M-3, 296 M-41B/C)	195,000 personnel
🚢	5 submarines, 5 destroyers, 15 frigates, 29 patrol boats	50,000 personnel
✈	273 combat aircraft (16 F-103E/D 56 F-5E/F)	50,000 personnel
	None	

Although it withdrew from direct participation in government in 1985, Brazil's military remains a powerful force in national political life. In 1989, it played a behind-the-scenes role in ensuring Collor de Mello's election. It controls the far north for national security reasons. Brazil has a large arms industry. Exports to Iraq, a major market, were hit by a UN embargo in 1991 following the Gulf War. Plans to develop nuclear weapons have now been abandoned by the military.

ECONOMICS

 $536.3bn   0.847–0.972 real

SCORE CARD

❏ WORLD GNP RANKING	9th
❏ GNP PER CAPITA	$3,370
❏ BALANCE OF PAYMENTS	$–1,153m
❏ INFLATION	33.4%
❏ UNEMPLOYMENT	5.3%

EXPORTS

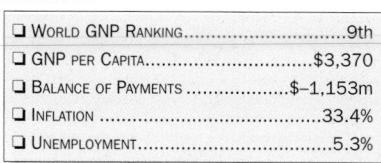

Germany 5% — Japan 6% — Netherlands 6% — Argentina 10% — Other 52% — USA 21%

IMPORTS

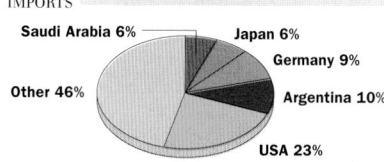

Saudi Arabia 6% — Japan 6% — Germany 9% — Other 46% — Argentina 10% — USA 23%

STRENGTHS

Local industry is well developed, making Brazil dominant in the region. Immense natural resources: the world's largest producer of coffee and soya beans and one of the largest sugar and orange juice exporters. Large deposits of gold, silver and iron. One of world's most important steel producers.

WEAKNESSES

Chaotic finances of the states threatens national economic stability. Foreign investment is deterred by corruption, the fragility of economic reforms and preferences given to national companies in the sale of state companies. Congressional opposition delays urgent tax and social security reforms and privatizations. Savings and investment rates are about half those of leading east Asian competitors.

PROFILE

Brazil has one of the world's major economies, but also one of the hardest to manage. During the 1960s and 1970s, GDP expanded by an average of 11% a year. The economy underwent major diversification and industrialization, and today Brazil is a significant producer of cars and computers. However, profligate spending during this period left Brazil saddled with a huge debt burden of over $116 billion, which dominated economic affairs in the 1980s.

Economic reform, initiated in 1990, enabled Brazil to reschedule its debts, but a steep recession followed in 1990–1992. The launching of the new currency, the real, in 1994 was the fifth attempt at monetary stabilization

ECONOMIC PERFORMANCE INDICATOR

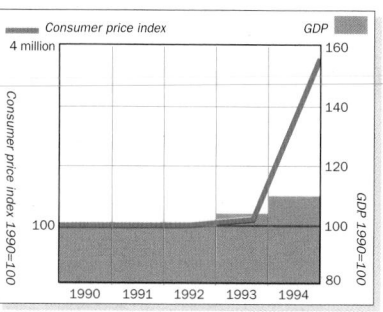

— Consumer price index — GDP

since 1986. It contributed to the dramatic reduction of inflation from 50% to as low as 2% a month in 1995, revived public trust in government and led to economic growth of 5.7% in 1994, the highest since 1986. This boosted regional confidence and facilitated the launch of MERCOSUR, the common market with neighboring Argentina, Paraguay and Uruguay. In 1995, a fractious Congress blocked constitutional reforms of the tax and social security system, but finally agreed to end state monopolies in such sectors as telecommunications and oil, thereby reviving the government's privatization program. Attempts to broaden the tax base, reform pensions and dismiss some one million public sector employees are expected to face stiff public opposition.

Despite enormous natural and economic resources, Brazil still has 32 million of its people living below the poverty line, and has not begun to tackle the problem of homelessness and street children in Rio, São Paulo and other large cities. An estimated one to five million families remain landless, while nearly 80% of farmland is owned by 10% of farmers.

BRAZIL : MAJOR BUSINESSES

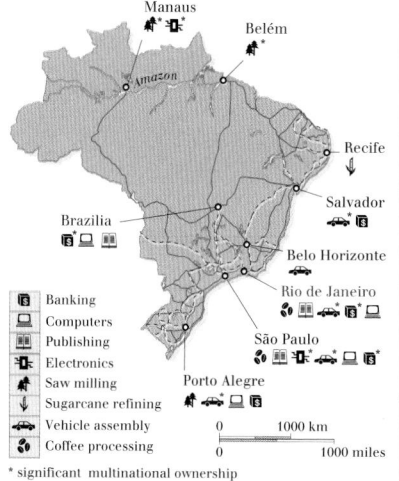

Manaus — Belém — Amazon — Recife — Salvador — Brasilia — Belo Horizonte — Rio de Janeiro — São Paulo — Porto Alegre

🏦 Banking
💻 Computers
📖 Publishing
⚡ Electronics
🪵 Saw milling
↓ Sugarcane refining
🚗 Vehicle assembly
☕ Coffee processing

0   1000 km
0   1000 miles

* significant multinational ownership

B

RESOURCES

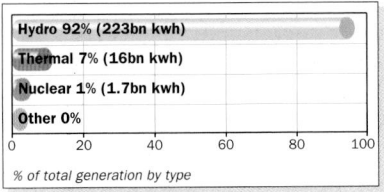

241.2bn kwh (capacity 52.9m kw)

630,732 b/d (reserves 3,030,000,000 bbl)

151.6m cattle, 30.5m pigs, 20.5m sheep

Iron, manganese, coal, bauxite, nickel, oil, tin, silver, diamonds, gold

ELECTRICITY GENERATION

Hydro 92% (223bn kwh)	
Thermal 7% (16bn kwh)	
Nuclear 1% (1.7bn kwh)	
Other 0%	

% of total generation by type

Under the military, Brazil commissioned several power stations from former West Germany. Energy from these has been more expensive than expected, but the construction of the Angra-2 nuclear station was approved in 1996. Hydropower has been more successful, accounting for 90% of electricity generation. An agreement to build a 1,367 miles pipeline from the Bolivian gas fields to Brazil's industrial south was signed in 1996 and put out to private tender. Ethanol is being made from sugar in an attempt to reduce gasoline imports. Within the agricultural sector, Brazil is the world's-largest producer of both coffee and soya beans.

BRAZIL : LAND USE

- Cropland
- Forest
- Pasture
- Cattle
- Coffee - cash crop
- Oranges

0 ____ 1000 km
0 ____ 1000 miles

Equatorial vegetation near Manaus *in the center of Amazonas state. The brown waters of the Rio Solimões and the black waters of the Rio Negro meet near Manaus.*

ENVIRONMENT

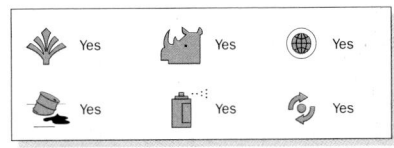

4% (1% partially protected)

Use of alcohol fuels for cars is reducing urban pollution

ENVIRONMENTAL TREATIES

Yes	Yes	Yes
Yes	Yes	Yes

Federal agencies charged with protecting the Amazon are underfunded, understaffed and accused of corruption.

The Amazon rainforest contains an estimated 90% of all the world's plants and animals and is the most complex ecosystem known. However, the demands of agriculture are leading to its destruction at a rate of 1.5 sq. miles per hour, or 13,513 square miles per year. As a result of such massive clearances, usually for conversion to cattle pasture, vital genetic diversity is being lost.

Brazil faces other environmental problems. Open-cast bauxite mining is polluting rivers and threatening the livelihoods of indigenous Indians. In the cities, widespread industrial pollution and untreated sewage are major problems.

MEDIA

 There has officially been freedom from censorship since the military withdrew from politics in 1985

PUBLISHING AND BROADCAST MEDIA

There are 293 daily newspapers. The leading newspapers include *A Folha de São Paulo*, *Jornal do Brasil* and *O Globo*

19 state-owned, 218 independent stations

1 state-owned, 2,000 independent services

Panamsat 1 Brazilsat

In some main cities

Although there is now no official censorship, TV and radio operating licenses are awarded as political favors, and state advertising is so extensive that it cannot fail to influence editorial policy. Media ownership is also highly concentrated. The *Globo* group, Brazil's only nationwide broadcasting company, was able to exclude the left from news reports and debates during the 1989 presidential elections, thus securing the victory of Collor de Mello.

CRIME

 87,053 prisoners

The rate is sharply up. More street children are being murdered

CRIME RATES

Murders	
2	per 100,000 population

Rapes	
3	per 100,000 population

Murders	
High levels of theft	

Urban life in Brazil can be violent. The incidence of armed robbery and narcotics-related crime is rising. Human rights abuses by the police are frequently reported. Death squads, uncontrolled by the government, target street children in particular, especially in Rio, São Paulo and Recife. Since 1985, the rate of street child murders has been rising. However, international condemnation of the crimes has led to action in some areas.

In the countryside, violent land disputes are common. Landless workers are repeatedly displaced and indigenous peoples driven from land to which the government has, in theory, guaranteed their rights. In Roraima state, the discovery of gold deposits has led to the homelands of Brazil's largest tribe, the Yanomani, being invaded by thousands of gun-toting prospectors, *garimpeiros*. The government halted their activities during the 1992 Earth Summit in Rio.

EDUCATION

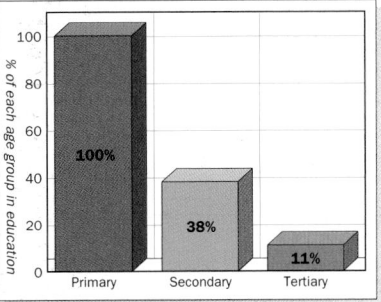 80%

1.56m students

0 ____ Education spending as % GNP ____ 25
4.6%

THE EDUCATION SYSTEM

% of each age group in education

- Primary 100%
- Secondary 38%
- Tertiary 11%

Education follows the French system with a *bachillerato* (*baccalauréat*) at the end of secondary schooling. State schools enjoyed a good reputation until the 1950s, but have declined since then. Most middle-class parents now send their children to private schools. The wealthy send theirs to Switzerland or France. Millions of the poor receive little education – especially those living in the northeast and Amazonia, and the urban poor. Brazil's three million street children have no schooling at all. Public degree courses work on credits, as in the USA. Of Brazil's 95 universities, 55 are administered by the state. São Paulo University is the most prestigious.

B

REGIONS
NORDESTE

Cattle ranchers in Pará state, where land reform is a major political issue.

NORDESTE, the northeast of Brazil, comprises nine states and is the country's most traditional region, but also its most backward. It was settled by the Portuguese, who brought Africans to work the sugar plantations. In the region's interior, the land is still divided into large ranches owned by a few families. This, and several years of drought that have made the land even more barren, have led to the emigration of millions of subsistence farmers to the more prosperous cities of the south, where they encounter great prejudice. The big landowners still hold a great deal of political power nationally, being heavily represented in the Congress, where they regularly obstruct attempts at land reform.

PANTANAL

THE PANTANAL, situated in the center-west of Brazil, bordering Paraguay and Bolivia, is the largest area of wetlands in the world. Flooded for seven months a year, it has some of the most diverse wildlife on the continent, with many thousands of species of birds, caymans (a type of alligator) and many varieties of snake. The inhabitants, or *pantaneros*, are indigenous groups who have adapted their way of life, which includes raising cattle and horses, to the regular flooding. The Pantanal is a great attraction for tourists and scientists who study wildlife behaviour. As with many regions in Brazil, it is now coming under pressure from cattle-ranchers and those who want to turn the area over to agriculture. However, its special climatic conditions

| National Park | Wetlands | Wildlife tourism |

act as a protection from any massive exploitation of its resources.

ESTADO DE SÃO PAULO

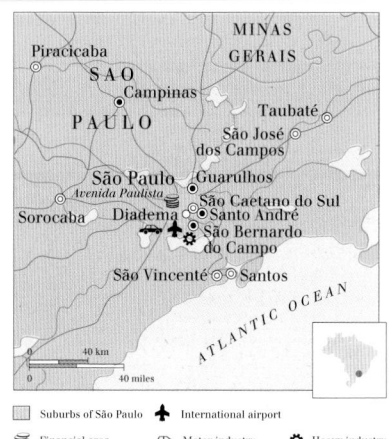

| Suburbs of São Paulo | International airport |
| Financial area | Motor industry | Heavy industry |

SÃO PAULO STATE, with almost 34 million inhabitants, is among the world's 20 most powerful economies.

At its center lies the city of São Paulo, which has over 10 million inhabitants and is the fastest growing city on the continent. Its population is mixed, including the *nordestinos* who have come in search of work, and a large Italo-Brazilian community who first helped the city to industrialize. The city is also home to almost two million Japanese descendants, the largest Japanese community outside Japan. The area of Avenida Paulista, once the home of coffee barons and São Paulo's wealthy citizens, is now Brazil's largest financial center. The urban area around São Paulo is the nucleus of Brazilian heavy industry, particularly the car and large-scale engineering industries. On the coast of São Paulo state is Brazil's largest port, Santos, which exports most of the country's coffee, as well as machinery and other heavy goods.

HEALTH

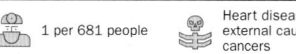

1 per 681 people

Heart diseases, external causes, cancers

Health spending as % GDP — 0 ... 25
2.8%

The public health system is limited. Less than 20% of hospitals are state-run and private care is very expensive. The World Bank has criticized the under-financing of preventive health care. On average, only 15% of the health budget is allocated to child health, immunization and other preventive programs. Reported malaria cases trebled between 1980 and 1990; 90% are in Amazonia, mainly in settler towns. Leprosy and parasitic skin infections are also becoming more common, again often affecting settlers.

WEALTH

A monthly national minimum wage of some $100 rises via a system of top-ups for those in the formal economy

CONSUMER GOODS OWNERSHIP

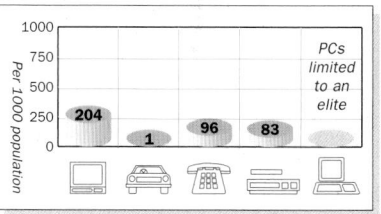

PCs limited to an elite

204   1   96   83

Brazil's large wealth disparities have been growing during the last decade. Relatively low levels of unemployment conceal large-scale underemployment, and the UN classifies over 50% of the population as suffering poverty. The large number of poor rural migrants to the cities live in the *favelas*, or shanty towns. *Favelas* are now also appearing in the countryside. The wealthy like to drive European cars, vacations in Paris or ski in Switzerland, where most of them keep their money to avoid scrutiny and interference in their accounts by the government.

WORLD RANKING

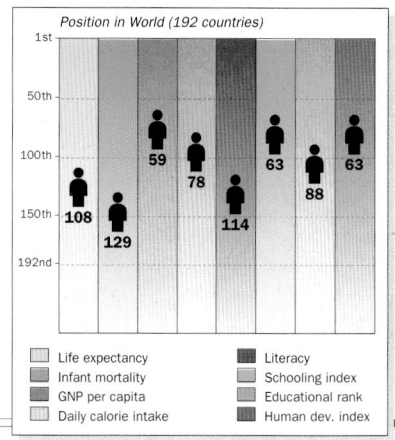

Position in World (192 countries)

108   129   59   78   114   63   88   63

- Life expectancy
- Infant mortality
- GNP per capita
- Daily calorie intake
- Literacy
- Schooling index
- Educational rank
- Human dev. index

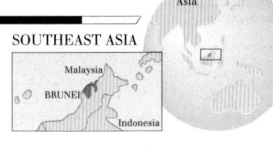

BRUNEI

OFFICIAL NAME: The Sultanate of Brunei   **CAPITAL:** Bandar Seri Begawan
POPULATION: 300,000   **CURRENCY:** Brunei dollar   **OFFICIAL LANGUAGE:** Malay

LYING ON THE NORTHWESTERN coast of the island of Borneo, Brunei is divided in two by a strip of the surrounding Malaysian state of Sarawak. The interior is mostly rainforest. Independent from the UK since 1984, Brunei is ruled by decree of the Sultan. It is undergoing increasing Islamicization. Oil and gas reserves have brought one of the world's highest standards of living.

CLIMATE

WEATHER CHART

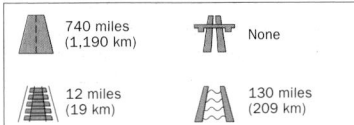

Just 298 miles north of the equator, Brunei has a six-month rainy season with extremely high humidity.

TRANSPORTATION

Brunei International, Bandar Seri Begawan | 10 ships 342,700 dwt

THE TRANSPORTATION NETWORK

| 740 miles (1,190 km) | None |
| 12 miles (19 km) | 130 miles (209 km) |

Interest-free loans for civil servants, subsidized gasoline and limited public transportation account for the high rates of car ownership.

TOURISM

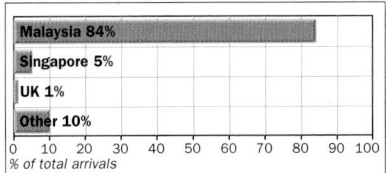

636,000 visitors   Up 8% in 1994

MAIN OVERSEAS ARRIVALS

| Malaysia 84% |
| Singapore 5% |
| UK 1% |
| Other 10% |

% of total arrivals

Although keen to protect Bruneians from Western influence, the government wants to develop quality tourism as part of its diversification program. Promoted as the "Gateway to Borneo," Brunei's rainforests could be developed for ecotourism. A former attraction was the Churchill Museum, founded by the late Sultan. This has now been superseded by the Museum of Royal Regalia.

PEOPLE

Malay, English, Chinese   148 people per sq. mile

THE URBAN/RURAL POPULATION SPLIT

58%   42%

ETHNIC MAKEUP

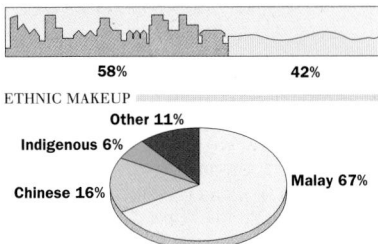

Other 11%
Indigenous 6%
Chinese 16%
Malay 67%

Malays benefit from positive discrimination; many in the Chinese community are either stateless or hold British protected person passports. Among indigenous groups, the Murut and Dusuns are favored over the Ibans. Women, less restricted than in some Muslim states, are obliged to wear headscarves but not veils. Many hold influential posts in the civil service.

POLITICS

 Not applicable   HM Sultan Haji Hassannal Bolkiah Mu'izzadin Waddaulah

THE STATE OF THE PARTIES

Council of Cabinet Ministers

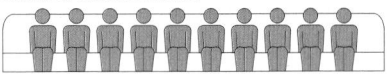

Brunei is an absolute monarchy. The Council of Cabinet Ministers is chosen by the Sultan. Political parties were banned in 1988

Since a failed rebellion in 1962, a state of emergency has been in force and the Sultan has ruled by decree. Hopes for democracy were dashed when political parties were banned in 1988. In 1990, "Malay Muslim Monarchy" was introduced, promoting Islamic values as the state ideology. This further alienated the large Chinese and expatriate communities. Power is closely tied to the royal family. Two of the Sultan's brothers hold the finance and foreign affairs portfolios; the Sultan himself looks after defense.

WORLD AFFAIRS

 APEC ASEAN Comm OIC  WTO

Brunei claims part of the Spratly Islands. Political exiles opposed to the government and based in Malaysia are a main concern. Relations with Britain, the ex-colonial power, are good.

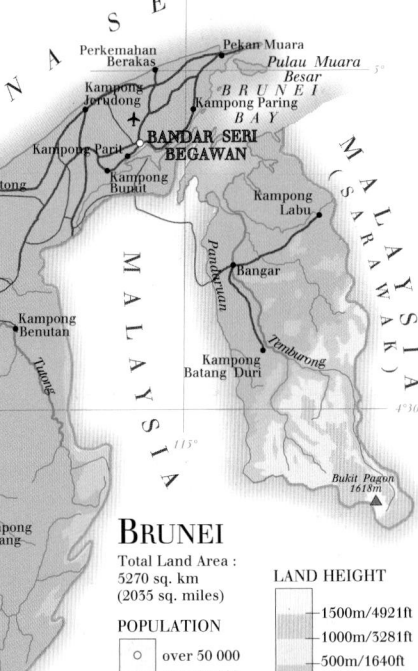

BRUNEI

Total Land Area :
5270 sq. km
(2035 sq. miles)

POPULATION
○ over 50 000
● over 10 000
• under 10 000

LAND HEIGHT
1500m/4921ft
1000m/3281ft
500m/1640ft
200m/656ft
Sea Level

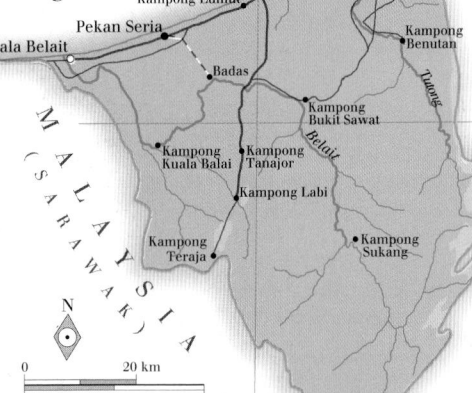

The magnificent Omar Ali Saifuddin *mosque is surrounded by an artificial lagoon.*

AID

 Ad hoc handouts of around US$150,000

 Increase or decrease depends on Sultan's decision

Aid spending is largely *ad hoc*. It has included donations to the Contras in Nicaragua, the Bosnian Muslims and the homeless of New York.

DEFENSE

 US$48m

 Down 80% in 1995

As well as being head of the 4,500-strong armed forces, the Sultan has a personal bodyguard of 2,000 UK-trained Gurkhas. The UK and Singapore are close defense allies.

ECONOMICS

 US$4bn

 1.41–1.46 Brunei dollars

SCORE CARD

❏ WORLD GNP RANKING	109th
❏ GNP PER CAPITA	US$14,240
❏ BALANCE OF PAYMENTS	US$83.8m
❏ INFLATION	2%
❏ UNEMPLOYMENT	4.7%

STRENGTHS
Twenty-five years of known oil reserves; 40 years of gas. Earnings from massive overseas investments, mainly in the USA and Europe, now exceed oil and gas revenues.

WEAKNESSES
Single-product economy. Failure of diversification programs could lead to problems in the future.

EXPORTS
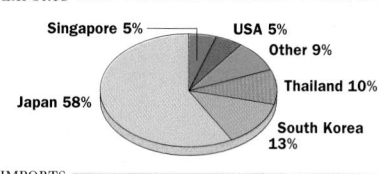
Singapore 5% — USA 5% — Other 9% — Thailand 10% — South Korea 13% — Japan 58%

IMPORTS
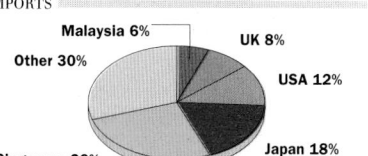
Malaysia 6% — UK 8% — Other 30% — USA 12% — Japan 18% — Singapore 26%

RESOURCES

 1.3bn kwh (capacity 380,000 kw)

 159,718 b/d (reserves 1,350,000,000 bbl)

 14,000 pigs, 10,000 buffaloes

Oil, natural gas

Oil and gas are the major resources, accounting for 0.5% and 9% of world production respectively. Energy policy now focuses on regulating output in order to conserve stocks.

ENVIRONMENT

 14% (5% partially protected)

 Little impetus behind legislation to protect forests

The Forest Strategic Plan aims to protect Brunei's forests (which account for 80% of its land area), but has yet to make specific areas of responsibility clear. The result is that rainforest is still under threat. Brunei's mangrove swamps, the largest in Borneo, remain unprotected.

MEDIA

 Extensive censorship, including foreign papers. Pictures deemed lewd or blasphemous by Religious Affairs Ministry are blacked out

PUBLISHING AND BROADCAST MEDIA

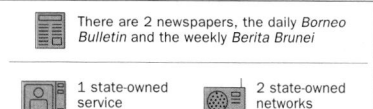
There are 2 newspapers, the daily *Borneo Bulletin* and the weekly *Berita Brunei*

1 state-owned service

2 state-owned networks

The state effectively controls all media. Brunei TV has recently increased its religious programing.

CRIME

 Brunei does not publish prison figures

 Down 12% in 1992

Crime levels are low. Most crime involves petty theft or is linked to alcohol and narcotics (both banned). A stolen car often makes TV news headlines. The state of emergency gives the government the power to detain without charge or trial for indefinitely renewable two-year periods.

EDUCATION

 89%

1,372 students

Free schooling is available to all the population, with the exception of stateless Chinese, who do not qualify. The University of Brunei Darussalam is undergoing Islamization.

HEALTH

 1 per 1,396 people

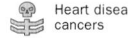 Heart diseases, cancers

The health service is free, although for major surgery Bruneians tend to travel to Singapore.

CHRONOLOGY

Under British control since 1841, Brunei became a formal British Protectorate in 1888.

- ❏ **1929** Oil extraction begins.
- ❏ **1941–1945** Occupied by Japan.
- ❏ **1959** First constitution enshrines Islam as state religion. Internal self-government.
- ❏ **1962** Pro-democracy rebellion crushed with help of British Gurkhas. State of emergency announced: Sultan rules by decree.
- ❏ **1984** Independence from Britain. Brunei joins ASEAN.
- ❏ **1990** Ideology of "Malay Muslim Monarchy" introduced.
- ❏ **1991** Imports of alcohol banned.
- ❏ **1992** Joins Non-Aligned Movement.

WEALTH

 Average manufacturing wage, 3.5 Brunei dollars (US$2.5) per hour

CONSUMER GOODS OWNERSHIP
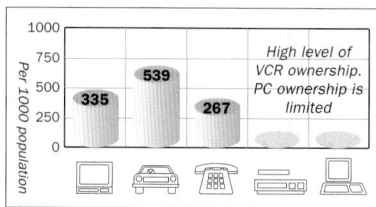
High level of VCR ownership. PC ownership is limited
335 — 539 — 267
Per 1000 population

The wealthy in Brunei are those close to the Sultan, the world's richest man according to *Forbes* magazine. A high general standard of living keeps discontent to a minimum. Promotion within the civil service and universal education allow some social mobility among Malays. Bruneians are major consumers of high-tech hi-fi and video equipment, label watches and Western designer clothes. Telephone lines, however, are difficult to install.

WORLD RANKING

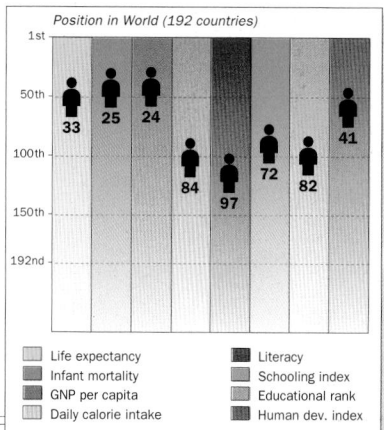
Position in World (192 countries)
33 — 25 — 24 — 84 — 97 — 72 — 82 — 41

Life expectancy — Literacy
Infant mortality — Schooling index
GNP per capita — Educational rank
Daily calorie intake — Human dev. index

BULGARIA

OFFICIAL NAME: Republic of Bulgaria **CAPITAL:** Sofia
POPULATION: 8.8 million **CURRENCY:** Lev **OFFICIAL LANGUAGE:** Bulgarian

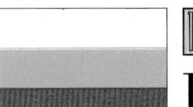

LOCATED IN SOUTHEASTERN EUROPE, Bulgaria is a mainly mountainous country. The River Danube forms the northern border, while the popular resorts of the Black Sea lie to the east. The most populated areas are around Sofia in the west, Plovdiv in the southeast, and along the Danube plain. Bulgaria was ruled by the Turks from 1396 until 1878. It became an independent kingdom in 1908, and was under communist rule from 1947 to 1989, the last 35 of those years under the leadership of Todor Zhivkov. The 1990s brought political instability as the country moved toward democracy.

Rila Monastery in the Rila Mountains. It is famous for its 1,200 National Revival Period frescoes dating from the mid-19th century.

CLIMATE

WEATHER CHART

The central valley and the lowlands have warm summers and cold, snowy winters, but hot or cold winds from Russia can bring spells of more extreme weather. The hotter summers on the Black Sea coast have encouraged the growth of tourist resorts. Snow may lie on the high mountain peaks until June.

TRANSPORTATION

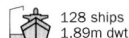 **Sofia International**

 128 ships 1.89m dwt

THE TRANSPORTATION NETWORK

21,070 miles (33,900 km)	165 miles (266 km)
2,617 miles (4,299 km)	292 miles (470 km)

The railroads are an integral part of the freight transportation system, but have become unsafe through lack of investment. North–south routes were intentionally left undeveloped under the Warsaw Pact. Ferries are used for most cross-Danube traffic – in 1989 there was only one bridge. Urban transportation is also lacking. Construction of a subway for Sofia began in 1979. The first section has yet to be completed.

TOURISM

 4.1m visitors

Up 3% in 1994

MAIN OVERSEAS ARRIVALS

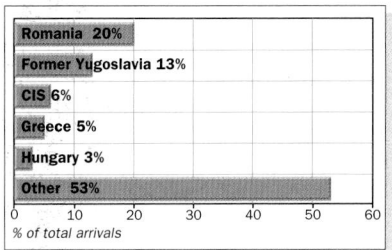

Romania	20%
Former Yugoslavia	13%
CIS	6%
Greece	5%
Hungary	3%
Other	53%

% of total arrivals

Under communism, Bulgaria's tourist industry catered for the East European mass market, which accounted for about two-thirds of visitors. In 1993, tourism showed unprecedented growth as the country found new popularity with Western visitors, attracted by low prices for ski resorts and beach vacations. Bulgaria is privatizing the industry, hoping to attract more upscale tourism by emphasizing its heritage.

BULGARIA

Total Land Area : 110 550 sq. km
(42 683 sq. miles)

POPULATION

over 1 000 000	▣
over 100 000	◉
over 50 000	○
over 10 000	●

LAND HEIGHT

2000m/6562ft	
1000m/3281ft	
500m/1640ft	
200m/656ft	
Sea Level	

PEOPLE

Bulgarian, Turkish, Macedonian, Romany, Armenian, Russian

207 people per sq. mile

THE URBAN/RURAL POPULATION SPLIT

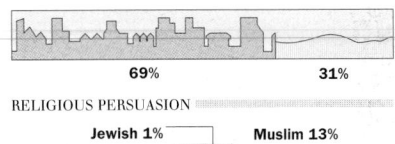

69%   31%

RELIGIOUS PERSUASION

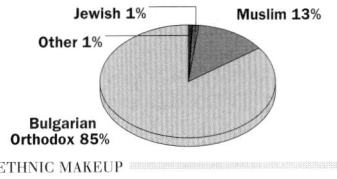

Jewish 1%   Muslim 13%
Other 1%
Bulgarian Orthodox 85%

ETHNIC MAKEUP

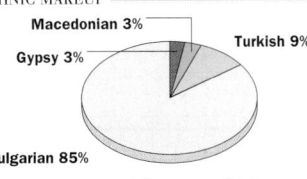

Macedonian 3%
Gypsy 3%   Turkish 9%
Bulgarian 85%

The government has sought to assimilate separate ethnic groups, thereby suppressing cultural identities. During the 1970s, Bulgarian Muslims, or *Pomaks*, had been forced to change Muslim names to Bulgarian ones. Bulgarian Turks were targeted in the 1980s. Despite the granting of linguistic and religious freedom in 1989, there was an exodus of ethnic Turks, when 300,000, or 40%, left for Turkey. Their farming skills have traditionally made an important contribution to the agricultural sector. Recent privatization programs left many Turks landless and provoked new emigration. The Turkish party, the MRF, which once held the balance of power in parliament, saw its seats reduced considerably following the 1994 elections. The Gypsy minority has no protection and suffers discrimination at all levels. Women, particularly Turkish women, have equal rights in theory but rarely in practice.

POPULATION AGE BREAKDOWN

	0–14	15–64	65+		
% of population by age group	7.5%	9.6%	11.9%	13%	15.6%
	66.4%	67.6%	66%	66.6%	65.3%
	26.1%	22.8%	22.1%	20.4%	19.1%
	1960	1970	1980	1990	2000

POLITICS

 1994/1999

President Zhelyu Zhelev

THE STATE OF THE PARTIES

National Assembly 240 members

53% BSP   29% UDF   18% Other

BSP = Bulgarian Socialist Party **UDF** = Union of Democratic Forces **Other** = Popular Union, Movement for Rights and Freedoms, Bulgarian Business Block

Bulgaria is a multiparty democracy.

MAIN POLITICAL ISSUES
Socialists return to power
Bulgaria has suffered from a succession of weak governments, each brought down by no-confidence votes, since its transition to democracy in 1990. In October 1992, the UDF, a broad anticommunist alliance, fell from office and was replaced by a non-party government led by an academic, Lyuben Berov, and supported by Bulgarian Socialist Party (BSP) votes. An early general election in December 1994 returned the BSP to power with an outright majority in parliament. Its leader Zhan Videnov became prime minister.

Political trials
After several years' delay, former communist officials are being prosecuted for abuses under the former regime. Ex-autocrat Todor Zhivkov has been sentenced to seven years' imprisonment, pending appeal. Parliament has decided temporarily to block access to the State Security archives. Even the suggestion of collaboration was sufficient to force the resignation of the UDF chair; open files would be much too destabilizing.

PROFILE
Bulgaria is one of several Eastern European countries in which former communists have returned to power. The ex-communist BSP, which won the 1994 general election, has resisted political and economic change. The result is one of the slowest privatization programs in Eastern Europe, with the old communist web of patronage still intact. The Movement of Rights and Freedom (MRF), which represents the Turks, has collaborated with its former communist oppressors, who have allowed the reversal of laws restricting the Turkish community.

Zhelyu Zhelev, *a founder-member of the UDF, and president since 1990.*

Zhan Videnov, *leader of the BSP and prime minister since 1995.*

WORLD AFFAIRS

 BSEC CE   IBRD   NACC   OSCE

Although maintaining good relations with Turkey is as important now as it was under communism, Bulgaria's new aims are to raise its profile in international organizations and gain greater trading access to the EU. Bulgaria has sent peacekeepers to Cambodia and has been conscientious in adhering to UN sanctions against former Yugoslavia, despite the costs of lost trade. Trade with former Soviet countries continues to supply important raw materials and spare parts.

AID

$192.8m

Down 49% in 1992

Aid, mainly from the IMF, World Bank, EU and EBRD, is granted mostly for infrastructure works. In 1993, IMF agreements were suspended because of a growing budget deficit. The absence of a modern banking and financial services industry hinders development. Western donors have agreed to reduce commercial bank debt by one-half.

CHRONOLOGY
Bulgaria was part of the Ottoman empire for five centuries until its independence in 1908. Under King Ferdinand, it took sides with Germany during World War I, and subsequently lost valuable territory to Greece and Serbia. Under King Boris, Bulgaria once again sided with Germany in World War II.

❑ **1943** King Boris dies.
❑ **1944** Allies fire bomb Sofia. Soviet army invades. Anti-fascist Fatherland Front coalition, including Agrarian Party and Bulgarian Communist Party (BCP), takes power in bloodless coup. Kimon Georgiev prime minister.
❑ **1946** September, referendum abolishes monarchy. Republic proclaimed. October, general election results in BCP majority.
❑ **1947** Prime Minister Georgi Dmitrov discredits Agrarian Party leader Nikola Petkov. Petkov arrested and sentenced to death. Dmitrov government receives international recognition. Soviet-style constitution adopted. One-party state established. Country renamed the People's Republic of Bulgaria. Nationalization of the economy begins.
❑ **1949** Dmitrov dies, succeeded as prime minister by Vasil Kolarov. ⟳

B

CHRONOLOGY *continued*

- ❏ **1950** Kolarov dies and is replaced by "Little Stalin" Vulko Chervenkov. He begins purge of BCP and collectivization.
- ❏ **1953** Stalin dies and the power of Chervenkov begins to wane.
- ❏ **1954** Chervenkov yields power to Todor Zhivkov. Zhivkov sets out to make Bulgaria an inseparable part of the Soviet Union.
- ❏ **1955–1960** Zhivkov exonerates victims of Chervenkov's purges.
- ❏ **1965** Plot to overthrow Zhivkov discovered by Soviet agents.
- ❏ **1968** Bulgarian troops aid Soviet army in invasion of Czechoslovakia.
- ❏ **1971** New constitution. Zhivkov becomes president of the State Council and resigns as premier.
- ❏ **1978** Purge of the BCP: 30,000 members expelled.
- ❏ **1984** Turkish minority forced to take Slavic names. Islamic rights curtailed; worldwide protests.
- ❏ **1989** June–August, exodus of 300,000 Bulgarian Turks. November, Zhivkov ousted as BCP leader and head of state. Replaced by Petur Mladenov. Mass demonstration in Sofia for democratic reform. December, Union of Democratic Forces formed.
- ❏ **1990** Economic collapse – food and fuel shortages. January, National Assembly votes to divest BCP of its constitutional right to be leading political party. Zhivkov arrested. April, BCP changes name to Bulgarian Socialist Party (BSP). June, election produces no overall result. August, Zhelyu Zhelev, UDF leader, becomes president. BSP in government. Country renamed The Republic of Bulgaria; communist symbols (grain sheaves and red star) removed from national flag.
- ❏ **1991** February, price controls abolished; steep price rises. July, new constitution adopted. October, UDF wins elections.
- ❏ **1992** Continued political and social unrest. October, UDF loses vote of confidence and resigns. December, the Movement for Rights and Freedoms (MRF) forms government. Lyuben Berov prime minister.
- ❏ **1993** Ambitious program to privatize economy begins. Berov survives no-confidence vote tabled by UDF.
- ❏ **1994** Todor Zhivkov begins prison sentence for corruption and human rights abuses. December, general election returns BSP to power.
- ❏ **1995** January, BSP leader, Zhan Videnov, becomes prime minister of a coalition government.
- ❏ **1996** Ethnic tension over political rights of Turkish minority.

DEFENSE

$364m   Up 30% in 1995

0   *Defense spending as % GDP*   40
2.5%

BULGARIAN ARMED FORCES

🚜	1,786 main battle tanks (177 T-34, 1276 T-55, 333 T-72)	51,600 personnel
🚢	2 submarines, 1 frigate and 23 patrol boats	3,000 personnel
✈	272 combat aircraft (39 Su-25, 212 Mig-21/23/29)	21,600 personnel
	None	

Economic difficulties have meant that Bulgaria has had to trim its defense spending. Moves to reorganize the army have caused serious disaffection in officer ranks. The government's defense priority is to ensure that Bulgaria can maintain national security without its old Soviet backing. It is therefore seeking new alliances. If the conflict in former Yugoslavia were to spread south, Bulgaria would probably join an anti-Serbian alliance. It also needs to decide whether to run down or expand the large arms industry of the communist era. Its main products were missiles, sub-machine guns, Kalashnikov rifles, ammunition and electronic equipment.

ECONOMICS

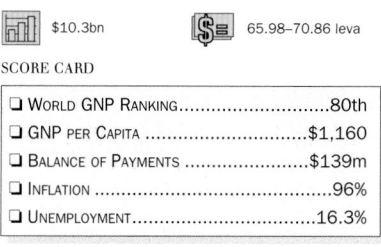

$10.3bn   65.98–70.86 leva

SCORE CARD

❏ WORLD GNP RANKING	80th
❏ GNP PER CAPITA	$1,160
❏ BALANCE OF PAYMENTS	$139m
❏ INFLATION	96%
❏ UNEMPLOYMENT	16.3%

ECONOMIC PERFORMANCE INDICATOR

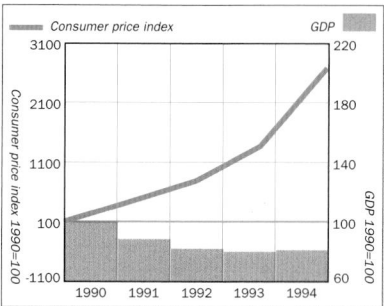

EXPORTS

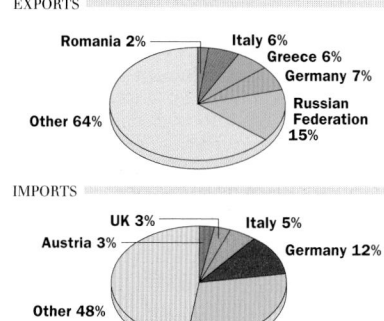

Romania 2%   Italy 6%   Greece 6%   Germany 7%   Russian Federation 15%   Other 64%

IMPORTS

UK 3%   Italy 5%   Austria 3%   Germany 12%   Other 48%   Russian Federation 30%

program appears to have lost momentum, although the current BSP-led government has responded to such criticism by injecting fresh vigor into its mass privatization schemes. Private and foreign investment is still negligible. Trade has shifted toward the EU, which accounts for an increasingly large share of foreign trade. While trade with the former USSR has fallen sharply, it is hoped economic relations will improve with Russia and the Ukraine.

STRENGTHS

Coal and natural gas. Good agricultural production, especially grapes for well-developed wine industry, and tobacco.

WEAKNESSES

Outdated equipment and outstanding debt throughout industry. Dependence on Russia for machinery and spare parts for existing factories. Location prevents easy access to rest of Europe.

PROFILE

Restructuring the economy is linked to privatization – a process that has been delayed for political and technical reasons. In 1980, joint ventures were approved permitting the transfer of state assets to privately owned companies. In 1992, new legislation allowed foreign firms to own companies outright. Since the mid-1990s, the privatization

BULGARIA : MAJOR BUSINESSES

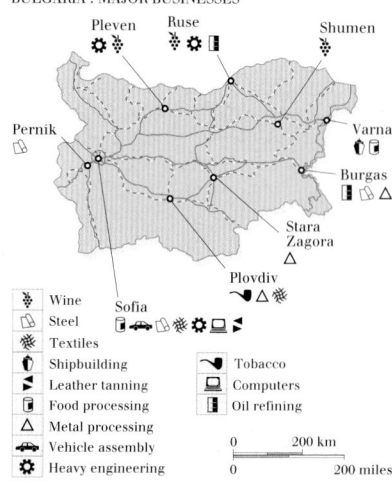

Pleven   Ruse   Shumen   Pernik   Varna   Burgas   Stara Zagora   Plovdiv   Sofia

- ✿ Wine
- ◻ Steel
- ✿ Textiles
- ◖ Shipbuilding
- ◢ Leather tanning
- ▤ Food processing
- △ Metal processing
- 🚗 Vehicle assembly
- ✿ Heavy engineering
- ◣ Tobacco
- ▢ Computers
- ▯ Oil refining

0   200 km
0   200 miles

RESOURCES

 34bn kwh (capacity 9.98m kw)

 Reserves of 15,000,000 bbl: refines 300,000 b/cd

 3.8m sheep, 2.1m pigs, 750,000 cattle, 676,000 goats

 Coal, iron, copper, lead, zinc, oil, natural gas

ELECTRICITY GENERATION

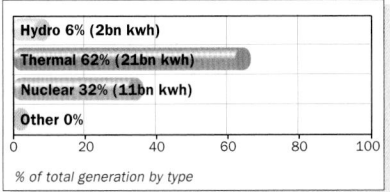

Hydro 6% (2bn kwh)
Thermal 62% (21bn kwh)
Nuclear 32% (11bn kwh)
Other 0%

% of total generation by type

Bulgaria has modest oil reserves and somewhat larger ones of coal and natural gas, but still has to import about 70% of its primary energy needs, much of it from the former Soviet Union. Unreliability of supplies in the past led to frequent winter power cuts. These have largely disappeared as decreased production in heavy industry and improved domestic supply from nuclear sources have lowered import demand. Bulgaria is partly reliant on nuclear power. Two of the four reactors at Kozloduy were upgraded after criticisms over safety measures, and in mid-1995 the government authorized the restart of the plant. The first generator at the Chaira Dam came into service in 1993 to boost hydroelectric supplies. Bulgaria must decide how many of its coal mines remain profitable.

ENVIRONMENT

 3%

 Several grassroots environmental pressure groups

ENVIRONMENTAL TREATIES

	No		Yes
	No		No

No / Yes

Serious environmental degradation in the 1980s led to the foundation of the party *Ecoglasnost* in 1989. It has been active in circulating information on pollution, health and nuclear waste dump locations and in bringing polluters to court. In October 1995, the government revived the operation of the Kozloduy nuclear plant despite concern among environmental groups about its poor safety standard. Bulgaria's main environmental problems are deforestation and air pollution.

MEDIA

 Nominally free press since 1989

PUBLISHING AND BROADCAST MEDIA

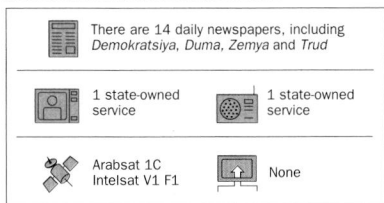

There are 14 daily newspapers, including *Demokratsiya*, *Duma*, *Zemya* and *Trud*

1 state-owned service

1 state-owned service

Arabsat 1C Intelsat V1 F1

None

The media was liberalized in 1989, although media freedom has come under pressure from the BSP-led government which, in 1995, ordered the dismissal of the top management of the Bulgarian Telegraph Agency for allegedly distorting the presentation of government policies. No paper is completely independent, as each is linked to some party or interest.

CRIME

 9,000 prisoners

 Up 27% in 1992

CRIME RATES

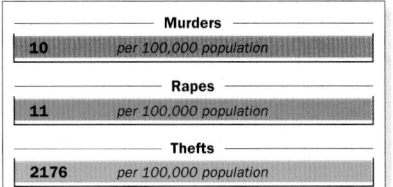

Murders	
10	per 100,000 population

Rapes	
11	per 100,000 population

Thefts	
2176	per 100,000 population

Police have been attempting to combat the increase in robberies and mugging. Tourists in the major vacation resorts are targets for muggers. In Sofia, the rise in organized crime is of growing concern. Violations of the Turkish minority's human rights are now a sensitive political issue.

EDUCATION

 98%

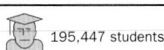 195,447 students

0	Education spending as % GNP	25
	6.4%	

THE EDUCATION SYSTEM

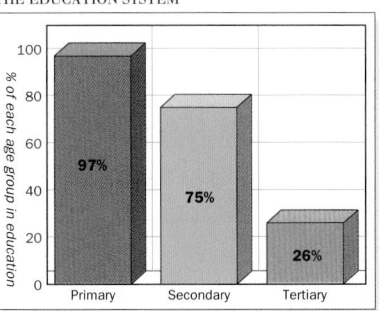

% of each age group in education

Primary 97%
Secondary 75%
Tertiary 26%

Bulgaria is changing its educational system from a Soviet-inspired to a European-style model. Teaching standards are lowest in the rural and Turkish communities.

BULGARIA : LAND USE

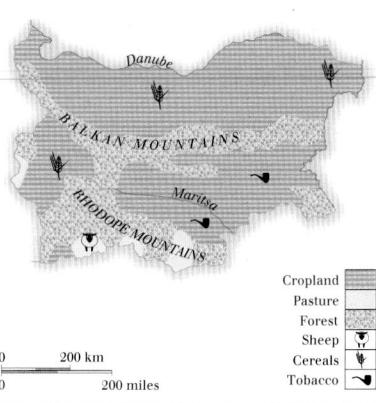

Danube

BALKAN MOUNTAINS

Maritsa

RHODOPE MOUNTAINS

0   200 km
0   200 miles

Cropland
Pasture
Forest
Sheep
Cereals
Tobacco

HEALTH

 1 per 297 people

Heart and cerebrovascular diseases, cancers

0	Health spending as % GDP	25
	5.4%	

Although hospital facilities have kept pace with population growth, the emigration of many doctors and nurses has lowered the standard of care. Shortages of medicines are widespread.

WEALTH

 Disparities in wealth are considerable

CONSUMER GOODS OWNERSHIP

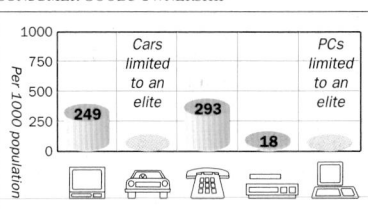

Per 1000 population

Cars limited to an elite

PCs limited to an elite

249   293   18

The former Communist Party elite is still the richest group; Turks and Gypsies are the poorest.

WORLD RANKING

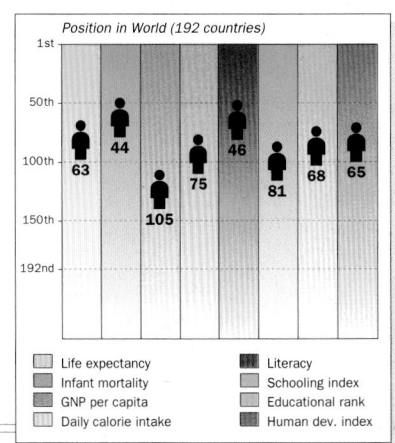

Position in World (192 countries)

1st
50th
100th
150th
192nd

63   44   105   75   46   81   68   65

Life expectancy
Infant mortality
GNP per capita
Daily calorie intake
Literacy
Schooling index
Educational rank
Human dev. index

BURKINA

B

OFFICIAL NAME: Burkina   CAPITAL: Ouagadougou
POPULATION: 10.3 million   CURRENCY: CFA franc   OFFICIAL LANGUAGE: French

WEST AFRICA

LANDLOCKED IN WEST AFRICA, Burkina (formerly Upper Volta) gained independence from France in 1960. The majority of Burkina lies in the arid fringe of the Sahara known as the Sahel. Ruled by military dictators for much of its post-independence history, Burkina became a multiparty state in 1991. However, much power still rests with President Blaise Compaoré. Burkina's economy remains largely based on agriculture.

CLIMATE

WEATHER CHART

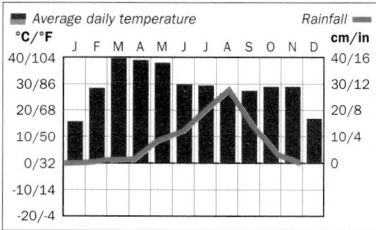

The tropical climate comprises two seasons – unreliable rains from June to October, and a long, dry season.

TRANSPORTATION

 **Ouagadougou Intl**
186,673 passengers

 Has no fleet

THE TRANSPORTATION NETWORK

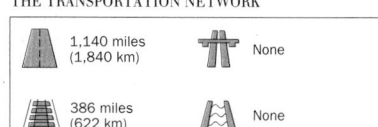

1,140 miles (1,840 km)	None
386 miles (622 km)	None

The railroad to the port of Abidjan in the Ivory Coast provides the main commercial route to the sea. Roads through Benin, Togo and Ghana provide alternative access.

TOURISM

 133,000 visitors   Up 20% in 1994

MAIN OVERSEAS ARRIVALS

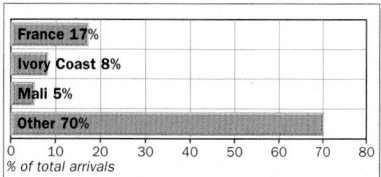

France 17%
Ivory Coast 8%
Mali 5%
Other 70%

0 10 20 30 40 50 60 70 80
% of total arrivals

Some potential exists for safari tourism, and the cities offer an attractive mix of colonial and African architecture. Big game hunting is allowed in some areas.

PEOPLE

Mossi, Fulani, French, Tuareg, Dyula, Songhai

98 people per sq. mile

THE URBAN/RURAL POPULATION SPLIT

22%   78%

RELIGIOUS PERSUASION

Christian (mainly Roman Catholic) 10%
Muslim 25%
Indigenous beliefs 65%

No ethnic group is dominant in Burkina, although the Mossi people who live in the area of their old empire around Ouagadougou have always played an important role in government. Burkina's first president, Maurice Yameogo, and the present leader, Blaise Compaoré, are both Mossi. The people from the west are much more ethnically mixed.

The extended family is important and reaches from the villages into the towns and cities. Extreme poverty has led to a strong sense of egalitarianism within society. The absence of women in public life belies their real power and influence, particularly within the traditional framework of the extended family. However, most women are still denied access to education and senior professional positions.

Camel plowing. Burkina's poor soils and frequent droughts lead many young men to emigrate seasonally in search of work.

POLITICS

 1992/1997

 President Blaise Compaoré

THE STATE OF THE PARTIES

Assembly of Popular Deputies 107 members

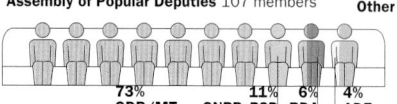

73% ODP/MT   11% CNPP–PSD   6% RDA   4% ADF   6% Other

OPT/MT = Organization for Popular Democracy/Labor Movement   **CNPP–PSD** = National Convention of Progressive Patriots – Social Democratic Party   **RDA** = African Democratic Assembly   **ADF** = Alliance for Democracy and Federation

A multiparty democracy in theory, Burkina is still dominated in practice by the former military dictator, Blaise Compaoré. He has been in power since the assassination in 1987 of Captain Thomas Sankara, Compaoré's former superior. Several of Compaoré's close military colleagues have also since been murdered.

Compaoré's grip on power in Burkina appears to be solid. In the National Assembly, the ODP/MT alliance offers total support. Most opposition leaders are still living in exile and real opposition within Burkina remains underground. Compaoré's military background also gives him the support of the army. While members of the military no longer holds ministerial posts – a measure which helps the country maintain its democratic image – it remains influential behind the scenes.

There are signs, however, that a small group within the ODP/MT will push for greater democracy once Compaoré retires from office.

WORLD AFFAIRS

 CILSS   Ecowas   OAU   OIC    FZ

Burkina's land locked position means good relations with countries to the south are a major foreign policy concern. However, Compaoré's relationship with other ECOWAS states is deteriorating over the war in Liberia.

AID

 $457m (receipts)   Up 3% in 1993

External aid, mostly from France and the EU, is important to Burkina's economy. The large number of NGOs has caused organizational problems; there is often difficulty in finding suitable projects for all the prospective donors.

BURKINA

Total Land Area : 273 800 sq. km
(105 714 sq. miles)

POPULATION

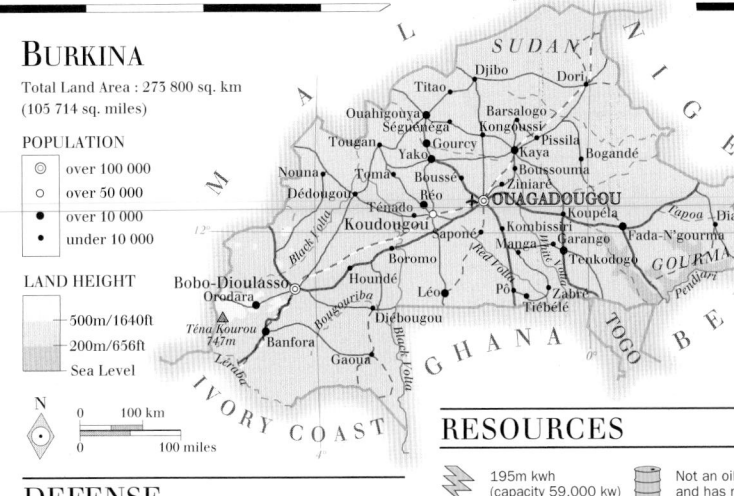

- ◎ over 100 000
- ○ over 50 000
- ● over 10 000
- • under 10 000

LAND HEIGHT

- 500m/1640ft
- 200m/656ft
- Sea Level

DEFENSE

 $61m   Up 42% in 1995

The army's main role has been maintaining internal security. Burkina is reliant on France for most equipment and training.

ECONOMICS

 $3bn    489.05–533.68 CFA francs

SCORE CARD

❏ WORLD GNP RANKING	126th
❏ GNP PER CAPITA	$300
❏ BALANCE OF PAYMENTS	$9m
❏ INFLATION	25.2%
❏ UNEMPLOYMENT	16%

STRENGTHS

Significant remittances from plantation workers in Ghana and the Ivory Coast – $100 million a year between 1980 and 1985. Low debt burden. Ability to attract foreign aid. Cotton growing. Gold is now leading non-agricultural export.

WEAKNESSES

Landlocked. Few economically viable natural resources. Prone to drought. Despite the benefits of foreign earnings, seasonal emigration has meant a decline in rural productivity.

EXPORTS

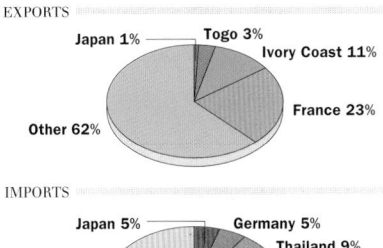

Japan 1% Togo 3% Ivory Coast 11% France 23% Other 62%

IMPORTS

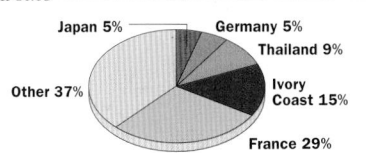

Japan 5% Germany 5% Thailand 9% Ivory Coast 15% France 29% Other 37%

RESOURCES

 195m kwh (capacity 59,000 kw)   Not an oil producer and has no refineries

7.4m goats, 5.7m sheep, 4.3m cattle   Gold, antimony, marble, manganese, silver, zinc

Burkina has considerable mineral wealth, including large manganese and silver deposits. However, the only metal ore being exploited is gold. Three dams to produce hydroelectric power will reduce dependence on thermal energy.

ENVIRONMENT

 10% (8% partially protected)   Droughts of 1973 and 1983 have aggravated desertification

Like other countries on the southern rim of the Sahara, desertification is the major ecological issue. The rate of tree cutting for fuel is on the increase.

MEDIA

 In spite of press freedom guarantees in the 1991 constitution, political censorship still exists in practice

PUBLISHING AND BROADCAST MEDIA

There are 3 daily newspapers, *Sidwaya*, *Le Pays* and *Observateur Paalga*

1 state-owned service   1 state-owned, 2 independent services

Limited press freedom since 1991 has seen the growth of a number of small independent newspapers funded by opposition parties.

CRIME

 Burkina does not publish prison figures   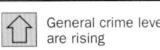 General crime levels are rising

Crime levels have traditionally been low. However, the urbanization of society and the increase in political violence have seen levels increase.

EDUCATION

 18%   5425 students

Education is based on the French system. Recently, practical subjects have received more emphasis.

HEALTH

 1 per 57,300 people   Malaria, diarrheal and respiratory diseases

The focus of the country's health spending is on primary health care and vaccination.

WEALTH

 Shop assistant, 30,250 CFA francs ($62) per month; dentist, 100,000 CFA francs ($204) per month

CONSUMER GOODS OWNERSHIP

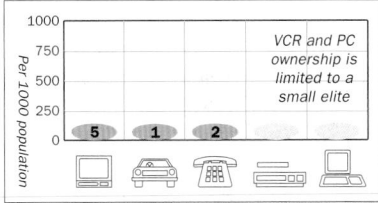

VCR and PC ownership is limited to a small elite

5   1   2

Burkina is a country of extreme, almost universal poverty. Displays of wealth are rare.

WORLD RANKING

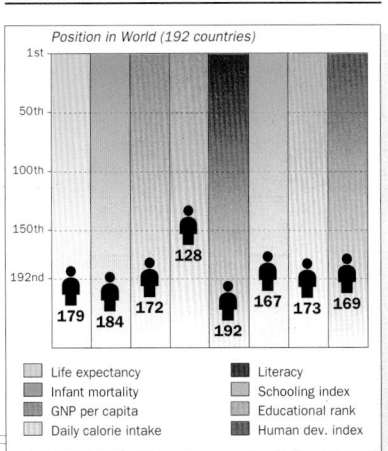

Position in World (192 countries): 179, 184, 172, 128, 192, 167, 173, 169

Life expectancy, Infant mortality, GNP per capita, Daily calorie intake, Literacy, Schooling index, Educational rank, Human dev. index

BURMA (MYANMAR)

OFFICIAL NAME: Union of Myanmar   **CAPITAL:** Rangoon (Yangon)
POPULATION: 46.5 million   **CURRENCY:** Kyat   **OFFICIAL LANGUAGE:** Burmese (Myanmar)

SOUTHEAST ASIA
Asia

FORMING THE EASTERN SHORES of the Bay of Bengal and the Andaman Sea in Southeast Asia, Burma is mountainous in the north, while the once-forested, fertile Irrawaddy basin occupies most of the country. Burma gained independence from British colonial control in 1948 and has recently suffered widespread political repression and ethnic conflict. In 1990, the National League for Democracy (NLD) gained a majority in free elections but was prevented from taking power by the military. Rich in natural resources, which include fisheries and teak forests, Burma's economy remains mostly agricultural.

Transporting timber *on the Irrawaddy River near Mandalay. Burma once had the world's largest reserves of teak.*

CLIMATE

WEATHER CHART

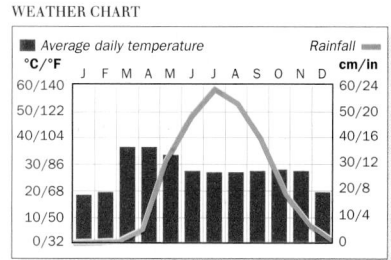

The tropical climate has three seasons: the wet season, when rainfall in the Irrawaddy delta and Tenasserim region can reach 195 in; summer, when northern Burma experiences 122°F and 100% humidity; and winter, when it is rarely cooler than 59°F, except in the northern mountains.

TRANSPORTATION

Mingaladon, Rangoon
580,000 passengers

72 ships
1.33m dwt

THE TRANSPORTATION NETWORK

5,550 miles (8,930 km)	None
2,801 miles (4,508 km)	1,988 miles (3,200 km)

Most current construction projects are linked to the booming China–Burma border trade, the majority of which was legalized in 1989. Old bridges and roads (including the famous Burma, Ledo and Silk Roads, all key routes into China) are being renewed and new ones built with Chinese aid. Although it will be easier to distribute key products, including opium, the motives for their construction are military as well as commercial. The state has recently relaxed its monopoly of transportation: since 1988, private bus companies have been given licenses to operate. Air and rail routes, however, remain under government control.

TOURISM

56,000 visitors   Up 2% in 1994

MAIN OVERSEAS ARRIVALS

Germany 18%	
USA 17%	
Italy 14%	
France 9%	
UK 6%	
Other 36%	

% of total arrivals

From 1962 until 1988, tourists were limited to one-week stays. Burma has recently adopted an open-door policy, designed to attract foreign exchange. Old hotels are now being renovated and new ones built in joint ventures with private companies. Much of the finance comes from Japan, Singapore, South Korea and Hong Kong. China is also helping to build an international airport at Mandalay. There have been widespread claims that the military junta has used forced labor to restore historic landmarks ahead of "visit Burma" year in 1996.

PEOPLE

Burmese, Karen, Shan, Chin, Kachin, Mon, Palaung, Wa

184 people per sq.mile

THE URBAN/RURAL POPULATION SPLIT

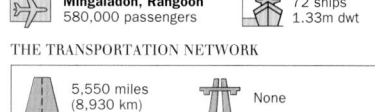

25%   75%

RELIGIOUS PERSUASION

Indigenous beliefs 1% — Other 2%
Roman Catholic 1% — Baptist 3%
— Muslim 4%
Buddhist 89%

ETHNIC MAKEUP

Rakhine 4%   Karen 6%
Shan 9%
Other 13%
Burman (Bamah) 68%

Burma suffers from considerable ethnic tension between the Burman majority and the smaller ethnic groups. At independence, the Shans, Karens, Kachins, Mons, Karennis and Chins all demanded their own state within a federation but were refused by the central government. All groups kept their demands alive with guerrilla activity against the state; in 1988 they united in a common cause against the military dictatorship, but almost all factions had signed peace treaties with the junta by early 1996.

A savage history, mainly of Burman repression of smaller groups, still plays a large part in the mistrust felt by the minorities for the Burman. Each group maintains a distinct cultural identity. While the Burman claim racial purity, in fact many of them are of mixed blood or ethnically Chinese.

Family life in Burma is still based around the extended family. Women have a prominent role, with access to education. Many run or own businesses in their own right. However, top jobs in government are still held almost exclusively by men.

POPULATION AGE BREAKDOWN

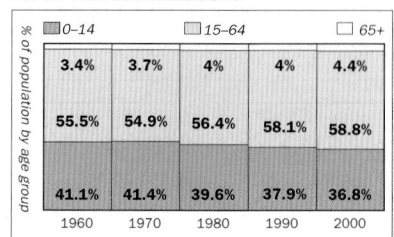

	0–14	15–64	65+		
65+	3.4%	3.7%	4%	4%	4.4%
15–64	55.5%	54.9%	56.4%	58.1%	58.8%
0–14	41.1%	41.4%	39.6%	37.9%	36.8%
	1960	1970	1980	1990	2000

% of population by age group

POLITICS

🗳 1990/uncertain   🏛 General Than Shwe

THE STATE OF THE PARTIES
Constituent Assembly 485 members

The National League for Democracy (NLD) won 81% of seats in the Assembly in elections in 1990. However, they were prevented from taking power by the State Law and Order Restoration Council (SLORC).

Burma has been ruled by the SLORC since 1988; the junta is dominated by Lt.-Gen. Khin Nyunt, chief of military intelligence.

MAIN POLITICAL ISSUES
Restoring democracy

The military rules Burma with little regard to human rights. Opposition is not tolerated and torture and killings are commonplace. Most of the ethnic rebel groups have agreed ceasefire terms with the regime. The focal point of opposition is Aung San Suu Kyi. Although freed from house arrest in 1995; the junta is wary of entering into official dialogue with her.

Refugees

Dislocated by the policies of the SLORC, around one million refugees are stranded along Burma's borders with Bangladesh, China, Thailand and India.

PROFILE

Demands for a return to democracy culminated in the student-led political uprisings of 1987–1988. The military seized power in 1988, ostensibly to maintain order until multiparty elections could be held. Instead, the State Law and Order Restoration Council (SLORC) was formed and all state bodies were abolished. Elections were held in 1990 and won by the

Aung San Suu Kyi,
figurehead of the pro-democracy movement.

General Ne Win,
Burma's leader 1964–1988.

BURMA

Total Land Area : 657 540 sq. km
(253 876 sq. miles)

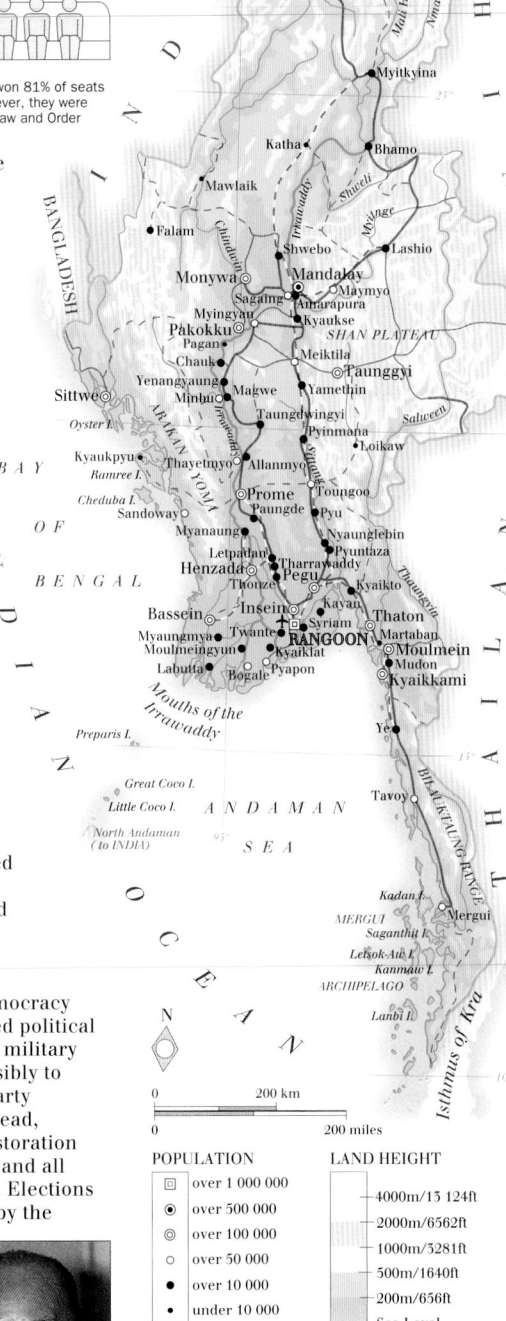

POPULATION
- ⊡ over 1 000 000
- ◉ over 500 000
- ◎ over 100 000
- ○ over 50 000
- ● over 10 000
- • under 10 000

LAND HEIGHT
- 4000m/13 124ft
- 2000m/6562ft
- 1000m/3281ft
- 500m/1640ft
- 200m/656ft
- Sea Level

National League for Democracy. However, the SLORC failed to relinquish power and pro-democracy opposition was brutally crushed. The junta has also largely succeded in surpressing the ethnic rebellion which had raged for decades in the borderlands.

WORLD AFFAIRS

CP   IAEA   IBRD   NAM   WTO

Burma's key relationship is with China. The latter has consistently backed the SLORC military regime and is a major supplier of weapons to the 350,000-strong Burmese army. The relationship is symbiotic, allowing China access to the Indian Ocean and giving it great influence over a regime partly dependent on its support. While Burma's neighbors regard the arrangement as one which is seriously destabilizing the whole of the Asia–Pacific region, many have adopted a controversial policy of "constructive engagement" with the SLORC.

Western governments have been active in the UN and EU in condemning the human rights abuses of the regime. In practice, however, they maintain an ambiguous relationship with the SLORC regime. Economic ties are growing stronger, particularly between the SLORC-owned state enterprises and Western multinationals. The latter are well represented in the increasingly profitable Burmese offshore oil and gas drilling industries.

CHRONOLOGY

From the 11th century, Burma's many ethnic groups came under the rule of three Tibeto–Burman dynasties, interspersed with periods of rule by the Mongols and the Mon. The Third Dynasty came into conflict with the British in India, sparking the Anglo–Burmese Wars of 1824, 1852 and 1885.

❏ **1886** Burma becomes a province of British India.
❏ **1906** Young Men's Buddhist Association founded to maintain cultural identity under British colonial influence.
❏ **1930–1931** Economic depression and slump in rice prices provokes uprising led by monk Saya San.
❏ **1937** Separation from India.
❏ **1942** Japan invades, receiving help from Burmese Independence Army (BIA) under "Thirty Comrades" previously trained in Japan.
❏ **1945** BIA swaps sides and, supported by Anti-Fascist People's Freedom League (AFPFL) led by Aung San, helps Allies reoccupy country.
❏ **1947** UK agrees to Burmese independence. Aung San wins elections, but is assassinated. ⇨

B

B

CHRONOLOGY *continued*

- ❑ **1948** Independence under new prime minister, U Nu, who initiates socialist policies. Revolts by ethnic separatists and communists, notably Karen liberation struggle.
- ❑ **1958** Ruling AFPFL splits into two. Shan liberation struggle begins.
- ❑ **1960** U Nu's faction wins elections.
- ❑ **1961** Kachin rebellion begins.
- ❑ **1962** Military coup led by Gen Ne Win. "New Order" policy of "Buddhist Socialism" – isolation from outside world. Mining and other industries nationalized. Free trade prohibited.
- ❑ **1964** Ne Win makes Socialist Program Party sole legal party.
- ❑ **1976** Social unrest. Attempted military coup; 40% of country now held by ethnic liberation groups.
- ❑ **1982** Non-indigenous people barred from public office.
- ❑ **1987** UN labels Burma a "least-developed nation." Ne Win accepts need to review economic policy.
- ❑ **1988** Student riots. Ne Win resigns. Martial law. More riots; 3,000–4,000 dead. Students and monks take control of many towns. NLD founded to form an alternative government by ex-premier U Nu, Aung San Suu Kyi, daughter of Gen. Aung San, and others. Gen. Saw Maung leads military coup. Students flee cities. SLORC takes power. National Democratic Front of ethnic resistance groups forms Democratic Alliance of Burma.
- ❑ **1989** Army arrests NLD leaders and steps up anti-rebel activity.
- ❑ **1990** Elections permitted. NLD landslide. SLORC, however, remains in power. More NLD leaders arrested.
- ❑ **1991** Aung San Suu Kyi, under house arrest, awarded Nobel Peace Prize. NLD expels her as result of SLORC pressure. Many parties deregistered.
- ❑ **1992** Gen. Than Shwe takes over as SLORC leader.
- ❑ **1995** Aung San Suu Kyi released from house arrest.

AID

 $102m (receipts)   On the increase, mostly from China

In 1988, Western nations, the World Bank and certain UN agencies such as the UNDP halted bilateral aid. The UN has, however, continued funding some development projects through its Drug Control Program and the World Health Organization. The largest bilateral donor is now China, which in 1990 struck an arms deal worth $1.4 billion and recently agreed a $6 million interest-free loan.

DEFENSE

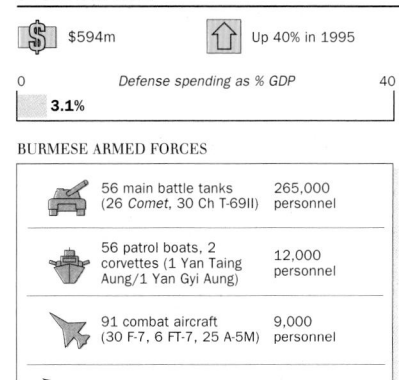

$594m   Up 40% in 1995

0   Defense spending as % GDP   40
3.1%

BURMESE ARMED FORCES

🪖	56 main battle tanks (26 *Comet*, 30 Ch T-69II)	265,000 personnel
🚢	56 patrol boats, 2 corvettes (1 Yan Taing Aung/1 Yan Gyi Aung)	12,000 personnel
✈️	91 combat aircraft (30 F-7, 6 FT-7, 25 A-5M)	9,000 personnel
🚀	None	

The SLORC has steadily obtained modern weapons and military technology from around the world, primarily from China but also from France, Germany, Sweden and former Yugoslavia. Since 1990, China alone has delivered $1.4 billion worth of arms to Burma, including tanks and jet fighters.

The army has managed to put down most ethnic insurgent campaigns by utilizing its military superiority, but also by cutting numerous deals with rebel leaders. In early 1996 troops took control of the headquarters of the notorious Shan drug warlord Khun Sa in what was widely seen as a negotiated takeover.

ECONOMICS

📊 $37.7bn   💵 5.87–5.71 kyats

SCORE CARD

- ❑ WORLD GNP RANKING...........................50th
- ❑ GNP PER CAPITA $863
- ❑ BALANCE OF PAYMENTS....................$–267m
- ❑ INFLATION 24.1%
- ❑ UNEMPLOYMENT......Widespread underemployment

EXPORTS

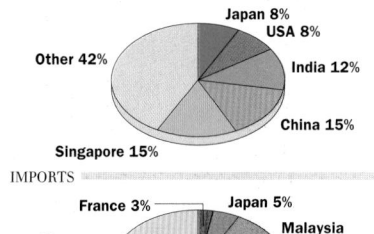

Japan 8%
USA 8%
Other 42%
India 12%
China 15%
Singapore 15%

IMPORTS

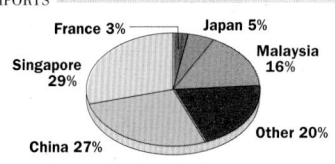

France 3%
Japan 5%
Singapore 29%
Malaysia 16%
China 27%
Other 20%

STRENGTHS

Very rich in natural resources: fertile soil, rich fisheries, timber including diminishing teak reserves, gems, offshore natural gas and oil.

WEAKNESSES

Shortage of skilled labor, managers and technicians. Rudimentary financial systems and institutions. Nationwide black market. Huge external debt. Dependence on imported manufactures.

PROFILE

Burma's economy is agriculture-based and functions mainly on a cash and barter system. Its key industries are controlled by 20 military-run state enterprises. Every aspect of economic life is permeated by a black market, on which prices are rocketing – a reaction to official price controls.

ECONOMIC PERFORMANCE INDICATOR

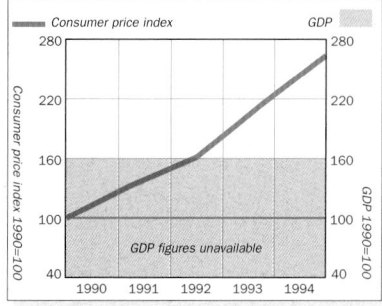

Consumer price index   GDP

GDP figures unavailable

Consumer price index 1990=100

GDP 1990=100

1990 1991 1992 1993 1994

Since 1989, the SLORC's open-door market-economy policy has brought a flood of foreign investment in oil and gas (by Western companies), and mining, forestry and tourism (by Asian companies). The recent boom in trade with China has turned less-developed Upper Burma into a thriving business center full of Chinese goods and foreign visitors. The junta is concentrating on developing the northeastern border states – the area which produces 200 tons of heroin a year, 60% of the world total. Few plans exist for the manufacturing sector, however, and an almost total dependence on imports will continue.

BURMA : MAJOR BUSINESSES

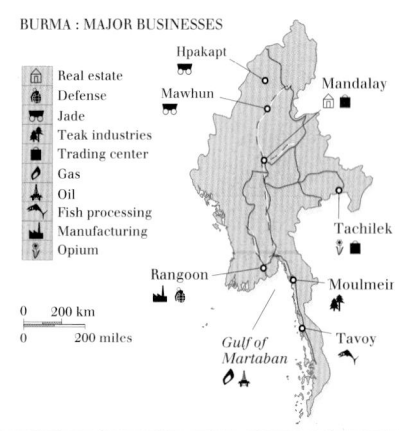

- 🏠 Real estate
- Defense
- Jade
- Teak industries
- Trading center
- Gas
- Oil
- Fish processing
- Manufacturing
- Opium

Hpakapt
Mandalay
Mawhun
Tachilek
Rangoon
Moulmein
Tavoy
Gulf of Martaban

0   200 km
0   200 miles

RESOURCES

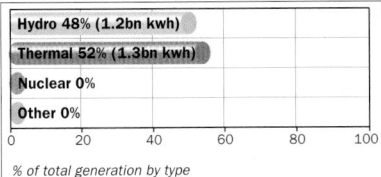

- 2.5bn kwh (capacity 1.12m kw)
- 15,037 b/d
- 9.7m cattle, 2.6m pigs, 1.1m goats
- Oil, natural gas, tin, antimony, zinc, copper, tungsten, lead, coal

ELECTRICITY GENERATION

- Hydro 48% (1.2bn kwh)
- Thermal 52% (1.3bn kwh)
- Nuclear 0%
- Other 0%

% of total generation by type

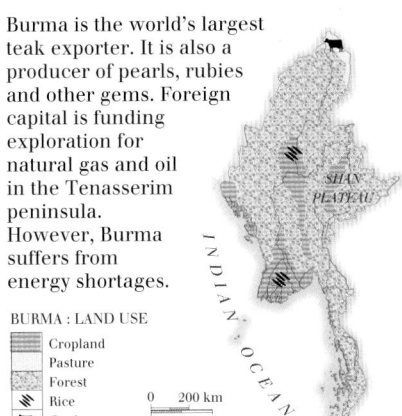

Burma is the world's largest teak exporter. It is also a producer of pearls, rubies and other gems. Foreign capital is funding exploration for natural gas and oil in the Tenasserim peninsula. However, Burma suffers from energy shortages.

BURMA : LAND USE
- Cropland
- Pasture
- Forest
- Rice
- Cattle

0   200 km
0   200 miles

ENVIRONMENT

 0.3%

New logging rights for Chinese companies

ENVIRONMENTAL TREATIES

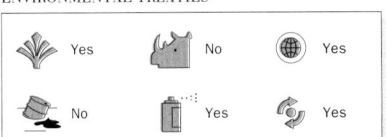

- Yes
- No
- Yes
- No
- Yes
- Yes

Deforestation is a major problem and has increased since the 1988 coup. Chinese companies have been given unrestricted logging concessions.

MEDIA

 No press freedom since 1962. All private periodicals and books have to be registered with, and approved by, the Ministry of Information

PUBLISHING AND BROADCAST MEDIA

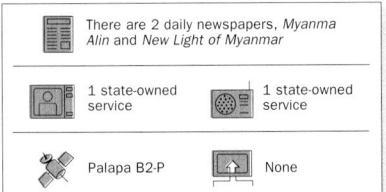

- There are 2 daily newspapers, *Myanma Alin* and *New Light of Myanmar*
- 1 state-owned service
- 1 state-owned service
- Palapa B2-P
- None

Political dissent of any kind is a criminal offense. An underground pro-democracy press produces anti-government material.

CRIME

 Burma does not publish prison figures

Down 0.3% in 1992

CRIME RATES

Murders
4 per 100,000 population

Rapes
2 per 100,000 population

Thefts
53 per 100,000 population

Levels of robbery, murder, bribery, corruption, embezzlement and black marketeering are high, compared to similar totalitarian regimes. The state is guilty of illegal activity. The UN reports regularly on human rights abuses against civilians, and the murder of innocent civilians including children, women, Buddhist monks, students, minorities and political dissidents.

There is a nominal civilian judicial system in Burma, but in practice all judges and lawyers are appointed by the junta and all legal functions executed by the SLORC. The most common charge is that of sedition against the state or the army under the 1975 "Law to Protect the State from Destructionists." Among the SLORC's frequent arbitrary "notices" is the Order 2/88 prohibiting assemblies of more than five persons. Most detainees have no legal rights of representation and are either jailed, used as forced labor or put under house arrest without public trial. Amnesty International is banned.

EDUCATION

 81%

260,300 students

0   Education spending as % GNP   25
2.4%

THE EDUCATION SYSTEM

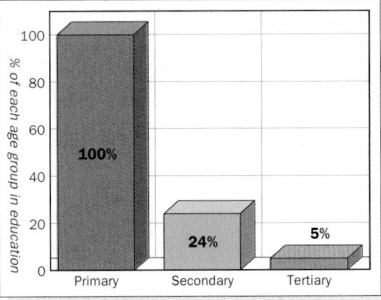

- Primary 100%
- Secondary 24%
- Tertiary 5%

% of each age group in education

The education system provides ten years of schooling. There are two universities, three medical schools and one technical institute. There is a general shortage of qualified teachers. Most foreign teachers, doctors and engineers have left or are in jail.

HEALTH

 1 per 12,900 people

Malaria, fevers, heart and diarrheal diseases

0   Health spending as % GDP   25
0.8%

Leprosy, although it affects relatively few people compared with other diseases, has a higher prevalence in Burma than in the rest of Asia. There has been an increase in the incidence of malaria in the last few years. The growing number of AIDS cases is largely due to migrant prostitution across the Thai–Burmese border.

WEALTH

 Forestry worker, 475 kyats ($83) per month; technical education secondary teacher, 1,000 kyats ($175) per month

CONSUMER GOODS OWNERSHIP

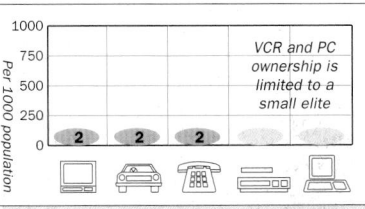

VCR and PC ownership is limited to a small elite

2   2   2

Per 1000 population

The state monopoly of the production and distribution of goods by rationing under General Ne Win's administration led to an increase in corruption and the rise of a nationwide black market, with huge disparities between official and unofficial prices. Only the military elite and their supporters could afford to live well. The situation has not changed significantly since 1988. Giant military enterprises grouped under a Defense Services holding company, whose capital amounts to 10% of GDP, now reap wealth and distribute privileges for a minority. Nevertheless, traditional social and economic mobility still exist. Climbing the socio-economic ladder is mainly a matter of loyalty to the military. Dissidents forced out of their jobs and hill tribes are the poorest groups.

WORLD RANKING

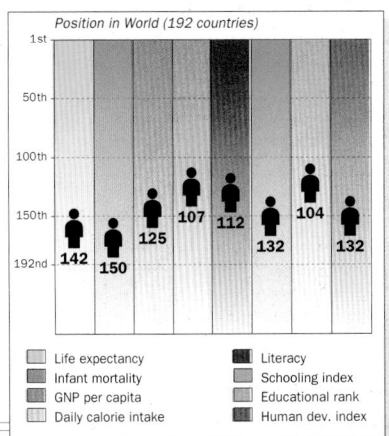

Position in World (192 countries)

142 150 125 107 112 132 104 132

- Life expectancy
- Infant mortality
- GNP per capita
- Daily calorie intake
- Literacy
- Schooling index
- Educational rank
- Human dev. index

BURUNDI

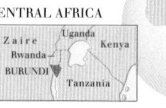

CENTRAL AFRICA

OFFICIAL NAME: Republic of Burundi **CAPITAL:** Bujumbura
POPULATION: 6.4 million **CURRENCY:** Burundi franc **OFFICIAL LANGUAGE:** French and Kirundi

   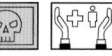

LANDLOCKED BURUNDI lies just south of the equator on the Nile–Congo watershed. Lake Tanganyika forms part of its border with Zaire. Tension between the Hutu majority and the dominant Tutsi minority remains the main factor in politics. The current political unrest dates from the assassination of the first-ever Hutu president in a coup by the Tutsi-dominated army in October 1993, which sparked terrible violence.

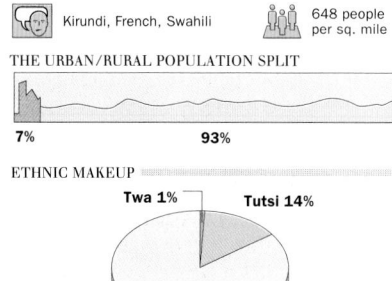

Pig farming and fish ponds. *The majority of Burundi's population depends on subsistence farming.*

CLIMATE

WEATHER CHART

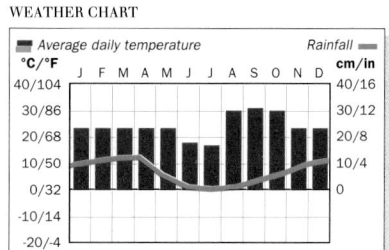

Burundi is temperate with high humidity, much cloud and frequent heavy rain. The highlands have frost.

TRANSPORTATION

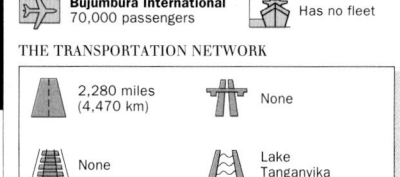

✈ **Bujumbura International**
70,000 passengers

Has no fleet

THE TRANSPORTATION NETWORK

2,280 miles (4,470 km)		None
None		Lake Tanganyika

The dense road network has been rehabilitated. There are plans to build a railroad linking Burundi with Rwanda, Uganda and Tanzania.

TOURISM

🧳 29,000 visitors

⬇ Down 61% in 1994

MAIN OVERSEAS ARRIVALS

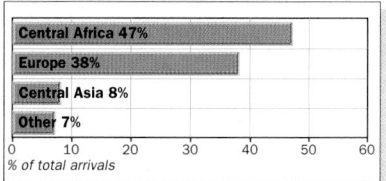

Central Africa 47%		
Europe 38%		
Central Asia 8%		
Other 7%		
0 10 20 30 40 50 60		
% of total arrivals		

A lack of basic infrastructure and violent political strife deter tourists. The industry has limited potential as Burundi lacks its neighbors' spectacular scenery and big game parks.

PEOPLE

Kirundi, French, Swahili

648 people per sq. mile

THE URBAN/RURAL POPULATION SPLIT

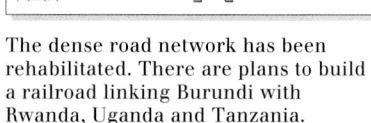

7%   93%

ETHNIC MAKEUP

Twa 1%   Tutsi 14%

Hutu 85%

Burundi's history has been marked by violent conflict between the majority Hutu and the Tutsi, formerly the political elite, who still control the army. Large-scale massacres have occurred repeatedly over the past two decades. Hundreds of thousands of people, mostly Hutu, have been killed in political and ethnic conflict since October 1993. The Twa pygmies do not suffer similar repression. Most Burundians are subsistence farmers; 78% are Roman Catholic.

POLITICS

1993/1998

President Sylvestre Ntibantunganya

THE STATE OF THE PARTIES

National Assembly 81 members

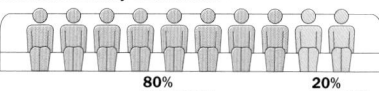

80% FRODEBU   20% UPRONA

FRODEBU = Front for Democracy in Burundi
UPRONA = Union for National Progress

Politics in Burundi remains divided sharply along ethnic lines, with the minority Tutsi seeking to control the majority Hutu population.

From 1966, the Tutsi UPRONA was the only legal party. Tutsi dominated the civil service, the judiciary and the army. The latter engaged in occasional mass slaughter of Hutu. In 1990, President Buyoya, a Tutsi, calling for greater unity, initiated the integration of Hutu into the political process. Opposition parties were legalized, and Burundi's first free presidential elections were held in June 1993. They were won by Melchior Ndadaye, a Hutu and leader of FRODEBU. However, Tutsi fears of Hutu dominance led to a coup in October and his assassination. Hundreds of thousands of Hutu were killed by the army. In 1994, Burundi's new president and his Rwandan counterpart died in an air crash. Since then, despite the formation of a coalition government, Burundi has edged towards civil war, with the Tutsi-dominated army constantly clashing with Hutu militias.

BURUNDI

Total Land Area : 25 650 sq. km
(9 903 sq. miles)

LAND HEIGHT

2000m/6562ft
1000m/3281ft
500m/1640ft

POPULATION

◎ over 100 000
○ over 50 000
● over 10 000
• under 10 000

0   50 km
0   50 miles

WORLD AFFAIRS

Since 1995, Burundi has rejected international proposals for UN/OAU military intervention to prevent further conflict.

AID

 $244m (receipts)   Down 23% in 1993

The fleeing of hundreds of thousands since 1993 has disrupted agriculture, making large (though now falling) numbers dependent on UN food aid.

DEFENSE

 $34m   Up 6% in 1995

The army is run by Tutsi. In line with the political changes taking place in Burundi, President Ndadaye proposed bringing Hutu into officer ranks. Tutsi resistance to this move was a major factor behind the October 1993 coup. Extremist Hutu have formed armed militia groups.

ECONOMICS

 $904m  247.99–254.47 Burundi francs

SCORE CARD

- ❑ WORLD GNP RANKING........................157th
- ❑ GNP PER CAPITA $150
- ❑ BALANCE OF PAYMENTS.....................$–25m
- ❑ INFLATION 14.8%
- ❑ UNEMPLOYMENT ......Widespread underemployment

STRENGTHS
Small quantities of gold and tungsten. Potential of massive nickel reserves and oil in Lake Tanganyika.

WEAKNESSES
Failure of democratic process to stem ethnic strife. Overwhelmingly agricultural economy (91% of labor force) under pressure from high birth-rate. Little prospect of political stability.

EXPORTS

IMPORTS

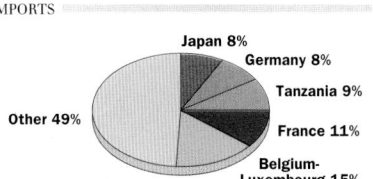

RESOURCES

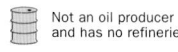

107m kwh (capacity 43,000 kw) Not an oil producer and has no refineries

850,000 goats, 380,000 cattle, 350,000 sheep Gold, tungsten, nickel, vanadium, uranium

Burundi has around 5% of the world's nickel reserves. Extraction, however, is not economically viable. There are also deposits of gold and vanadium. Surveys in the 1980s detected oil reserves below Lake Tanganyika, but production has yet to begin. Burundi imports gasoline from Iran and electricity from Zaire. However, once the HEP plants at Mugera and Rwegura are operational, they will meet most domestic electricity requirements.

ENVIRONMENT

 3%   Serious deforestation and soil impoverishment

Only 2% of Burundi is forest and even this is now under pressure from one of Africa's highest birth-rates. Burundi suffers from the problems associated with deforestation, particularly soil erosion. Some soils are also being exhausted from over-use. Several tree-planting programs have been introduced. UNESCO is also running ecological education initiatives at village level, aimed at women farmers.

MEDIA

 The media is state-controlled. General thaw in censorship since 1992 constitution in theory. Media has been regularly liberalized

PUBLISHING AND BROADCAST MEDIA

There is 1 daily newspaper, *Le Renouveau du Burundi*, published by the government.

1 state-owned service

1 state-owned, 1 independent service

Since 1994, pro-Hutu/anti-Tutsi radio stations have begun broadcasting. A private EU-funded radio station promoting peace began transmissions in 1996.

CRIME

 Burundi does not publish prison figures  Down 53% in 1990

Burundi has an appalling human rights record. There have been frequent massacres of Hutu by the Tutsi-dominated army. The worst pogroms occurred in 1972, 1988, 1993 and 1994.

EDUCATION

 50%   4,256 students

Elementary schooling begins at seven years of age and is compulsory. There are 67 elementary school children per teacher. The one university is located in the capital.

CHRONOLOGY

From the 16th century, Burundi was ruled by the minority Tutsi with the majority Hutu as their serfs. Merged with Rwanda, Burundi was controlled by Germany from 1884 and by Belgium from 1919.

- ❑ **1946** UN trust territory.
- ❑ **1959** Split from Rwanda.
- ❑ **1962** Independence.
- ❑ **1966** Army coup. Monarchy overthrown; becomes a republic.
- ❑ **1972** 150,000 Hutu massacred.
- ❑ **1993** June, first free elections. October, army coup; President Ndadaye assassinated.
- ❑ **1994** Establishment of four-year power-sharing government; violence continues.

HEALTH

 1 per 17,240 people   Communicable infections, parasitic diseases

2.1 million people have no access to health services. Only 7% of women use contraception; on average, women have seven children. Just 38% of Burundians have access to safe drinking water.

WEALTH

 Bus conductor, 63 Burundi francs (less than half of one US cent) per hour; bank accountant, 1,100 Burundi francs ($4.30) per hour

CONSUMER GOODS OWNERSHIP

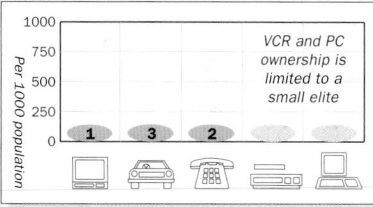

Wealth is concentrated within the Tutsi political and business elite. Most people live a subsistence existence.

WORLD RANKING

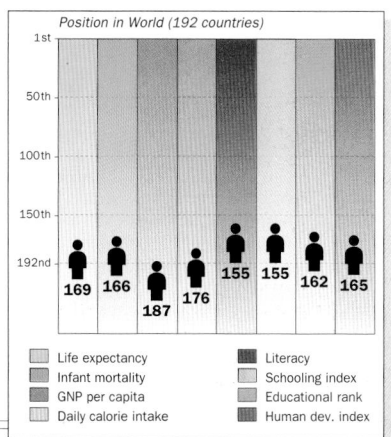

CAMBODIA

OFFICIAL NAME: State of Cambodia **CAPITAL:** Phnom Penh
POPULATION: 10.3 million **CURRENCY:** Riel **OFFICIAL LANGUAGE:** Khmer

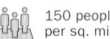
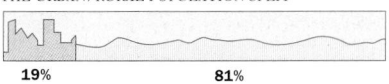
C

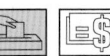

LOCATED IN THE INDOCHINESE PENINSULA in Southeast Asia, Cambodia has a coastline on the Gulf of Thailand and shares borders with Thailand, Laos and Vietnam. Its main topographical feature is the Tônlé Sap, or Great Lake, which drains into the Mekong River. Over three-quarters of Cambodia is forested, with mangroves lining the coast. Rice is the principal crop. Cambodia has emerged from two decades of civil war and invasion from Vietnam. The UN's biggest-ever peacekeeping operation resulted in free elections in 1993.

CLIMATE

WEATHER CHART

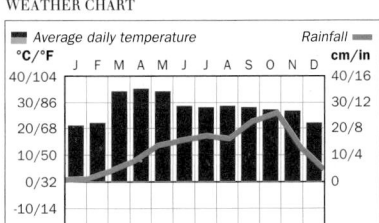

Cambodia has a more varied climate than neighboring Vietnam. Low-lying regions have moderate rainfall and the most consistent yearly temperatures. The wettest areas are the hillsides facing the Gulf of Thailand. The dry season lasts from December to April and is characterized by high temperatures and an average eight hours of sunshine a day. During the rainy season, Cambodia experiences high humidity and sultry heat. From May to September, winds are southeasterly, while from October to April they are north or northeasterly.

TRANSPORTATION

 Pochentong, Phnom Penh  1 ship 1,500 dwt

THE TRANSPORTATION NETWORK

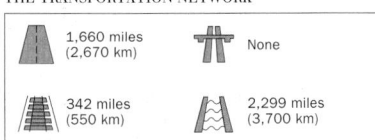

1,660 miles (2,670 km)	None
342 miles (550 km)	2,299 miles (3,700 km)

The civil war led to a near-collapse of Cambodia's road and rail system. Some parts of the network are still subject to attack by Khmer Rouge bandits. International aid is now being used to rehabilitate key routes, such as Highways 3 and 5, and to rebuild the Chroy Changba Bridge out of Phnom Penh. The bicycle and rickshaw are the main forms of urban transportation.

Angkor Wat *stands in the ruins of the ancient city of Angkor, once the capital of the Khmer empire. It is now one of Cambodia's leading tourist attractions.*

TOURISM

 176,000   Up 49% in 1994

MAIN OVERSEAS ARRIVALS

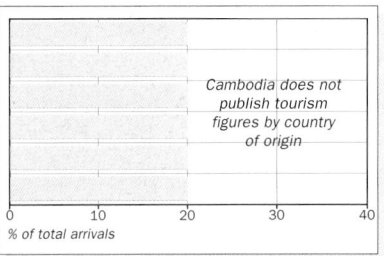

Cambodia does not publish tourism figures by country of origin

Cambodia, the center of the Khmer empire between 800 and 1400 AD, has some of the most impressive temples in Southeast Asia. The most famous is the extraordinary site at Angkor Wat, near Siĕmréab. Until recently it was controlled by the Khmer Rouge, who threatened any visitors with attack. Visitors are now allowed in small numbers; 3,000 visited the site in 1993.

Once basic infrastructure is in place and the political situation has stabilized, Cambodia has considerable tourism potential. It currently attracts adventurous, independent travelers. Tourists are occasionally kidnapped.

PEOPLE

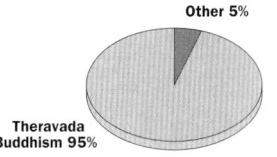 Khmer, French, Chinese, Vietnamese, Cham 150 people per sq. mile

THE URBAN/RURAL POPULATION SPLIT

19% 81%

RELIGIOUS PERSUASION

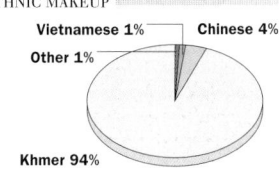

Other 5%

Theravada Buddhism 95%

ETHNIC MAKEUP

Vietnamese 1% Chinese 4%
Other 1%

Khmer 94%

Cambodian society underwent one of the 20th century's most horrific programs of social transformation between 1975 and 1979 under Pol Pot's Khmer Rouge regime. Over one million Cambodians, or one in eight, died from warfare, starvation, overwork or execution. Half a million more went into exile in Thailand. The Pol Pot regime's reforms led to the scrapping of money, possessions and hierarchy. Only peasants, soldiers of the revolution and some industrial workers were allowed to retain their pre-revolution status. Boys and girls of 13 and 14 were taken from their homes, indoctrinated in the tenets of revolution and allowed to kill those perceived to be guilty of bourgeois crimes. Violence at all levels was sanctioned in the name of revolution.

Pol Pot's regime ended with the Vietnamese invasion of 1979. Most professionals who had survived emigrated. The effects of revolution and subsequent civil war are still felt and reflected in the world's highest rate of orphans and widows.

POPULATION AGE BREAKDOWN

% of population by age group	0–14	15–64		65+
	2.7%	2.8%	2.5%	2.9%	3.5%
	54.8%	54%	64.6%	62.2%	57.9%
	42.5%	43.2%	32.9%	34.9%	38.6%
	1960	1970	1980	1990	2000

POLITICS

 1993/1998　　 King Norodom Sihanouk

THE STATE OF THE PARTIES

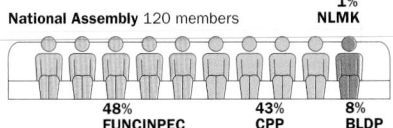

National Assembly 120 members

1%
NLMK

48%
FUNCINPEC

43%
CPP

8%
BLDP

FUNCINPEC = United National Front for an Independent, Neutral, Peaceful and Cooperative Cambodia
CPP = Cambodian People's Party　**BLDP** = Buddhist Liberal Democratic Party　**NLMK** = National Liberation Movement of Kampuchea

Cambodia held free multiparty elections under UN supervision in 1993.

MAIN POLITICAL ISSUES
Fledgling democracy
Since 1994 there has been growing evidence of the power struggles being fought between and within FUNCINPEC and the CPP. Allegations that the government has shifted from its free-market, liberal democratic platform have been highlighted by former finance minister Sam Rangsi, who formed a new opposition party in 1995.

The Khmer Rouge
The Khmer Rouge have continued to wage war in north and west Cambodia in support of their claim that the 1993 elections produced a Vietnamese "puppet" regime. Government military action and large-scale defections have weakened the group. However, it still controls much of the lucrative timber and gem border trades.

PROFILE
In 1975, the US-installed government was overthrown by the Maoist Khmer Rouge under Pol Pot. Pol Pot was in turn overthrown, following the Vietnamese invasion in 1979. The invasion united Cambodia's three main factions – the Khmer Rouge, the Sihanoukists and the Khmer Peoples' National Liberation Front (KPNLF) – in common cause against the Vietnamese. The coalition was recognized by the UN as the government of Democratic Kampuchea. Vietnam's decision to leave in 1989 led to peace talks in Paris and the signing of the October 1991 Paris Accords. The Paris Accords mandated the UN's UNTAC operation to steer the country to free democratic elections. The task involved imposing the ceasefire agreed, repatriating 370,000 refugees and overseeing the election campaign. Following FUNCINPEC's victory in the elections, Prince Sihanouk proposed a coalition government of national reconciliation. The Khmer Rouge refused to join, as they wanted a greater part in the government than their election results warranted. They have since continued armed resistance.

Saloth Sar, who assumed the name Pol Pot, still leads the Khmer Rouge.

King Norodom Sihanouk, the pivotal figure in Cambodian society and politics.

WORLD AFFAIRS

 Asean　 IAEA　 IBRD　 Mek Riv　 NAM

During the years of civil war that followed the Vietnamese invasion, the Phnom Penh government suffered the same isolation that was imposed on Vietnam. Recognized by few countries outside the Soviet bloc, it became an international pariah. The resistance movement that included the Khmer Rouge was allotted Cambodia's seat at the UN and gained the backing of an anti-Soviet, anti-Vietnamese alliance that included the USA and China.

Cambodia's new constitution talks of making the country once again a non-aligned "island of peace." While China and Thailand have disavowed their former support for the Khmer Rouge, the Thai military still provides arms, personnel and sanctuary for its troops, and China has supported King Sihanouk's call to bring the Khmer Rouge into the ruling coalition. By contrast, the USA has threatened to withdraw aid to the government if the Khmer Rouge is allowed to join the coalition. The government has to date been reluctant to fuel the historic animosity that exists with Vietnam.

AID

 $313m (receipts)　 Up 111% in 1993

Aid is the single most important part of the economy. It provides around 50% of government revenues. The government has benefited from large aid commitments from the International Committee for the Reconstruction of Cambodia. Disbursing aid is difficult.

CAMBODIA

Total Land Area : 176 520 sq. km (68 154 sq. miles)

POPULATION　　　　LAND HEIGHT

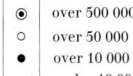
- ⊙ over 500 000
- ○ over 50 000
- ● over 10 000
- • under 10 000

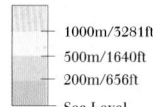
- 1000m/3281ft
- 500m/1640ft
- 200m/656ft
- Sea Level

C

CHRONOLOGY

A former French protectorate, Cambodia gained independence in 1953 as a constitutional monarchy with Norodom Sihanouk as king.

❑ **1955** Sihanouk abdicates to pursue political career.
❑ **1970** Right-wing coup led by Prime Minister Lon Nol deposes Sihanouk. Exiled Sihanouk forms Royal Government of National Union of Cambodia (GRUNC), backed by formerly hostile communist Khmer Rouge. Lon Nol proclaims Khmer Republic.
❑ **1974** GRUNC forces capture Phnom Penh. Prince Sihanouk head of state, Khmer Rouge assumes power. Hundreds of thousands die during radical social program.
❑ **1976** Country renamed Democratic Kampuchea. Elections. Sihanouk resigns; GRUNC dissolved. Khieu Samphan head of state; Pol Pot prime minister.
❑ **1978** Vietnam invades, supported by Cambodian communists opposed to Pol Pot.
❑ **1979** Vietnamese capture Phnom Penh. Khmer Rouge ousted by Kampuchean People's Revolutionary Party (KPRP), led by Pen Sovan. Khmer Rouge starts guerrilla war. Pol Pot held responsible for three million deaths and sentenced to death in absence. Vietnamese and DK (mostly Khmer Rouge) forces begin conflict on Thai border.
❑ **1980** Heng Samrin KPRP leader.
❑ **1982** Government-in-exile formed, including Khmer Rouge and Khmer People's National Liberation Front, headed by Prince Sihanouk; recognized by UN.
❑ **1988** Vietnam announces troop withdrawals. Khmer Rouge offensive. Khmer Rouge refuses to take part in peace talks.
❑ **1989** Vietnamese troops withdraw. Khmer Rouge forces make gains.
❑ **1990** UN Security Council approves plan for UN-monitored ceasefire and elections. Cambodian factions form Supreme National Council (SNC) but no agreement reached.
❑ **1991** SNC agree on elections. Factions sign accord. Sihanouk head of State of Cambodia. Khmer Rouge officials flee after attacks.
❑ **1992** Clashes between Cambodian troops and Khmer Rouge. UN ceasefire repeatedly violated.
❑ **1993** UN-supervised elections go ahead. UN peace operation leaves.
❑ **1994** Khmer Rouge refuses to join peace process.
❑ **1995** Former finance minister Sam Rangsi forms opposition party.

DEFENSE

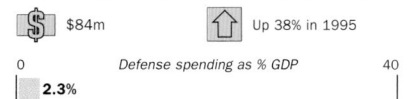

$84m   Up 38% in 1995

0   Defense spending as % GDP   40
2.3%

CAMBODIAN ARMED FORCES

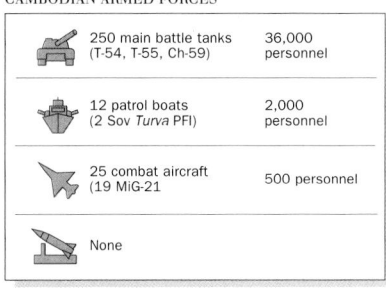

250 main battle tanks (T-54, T-55, Ch-59)	36,000 personnel
12 patrol boats (2 Sov *Turva* PFI)	2,000 personnel
25 combat aircraft (19 MiG-21	500 personnel
None	

The current government's defense priority is unifying the command structures of the three armies of the main coalition partners. This is essential to contain the continuing Khmer Rouge military struggle. The Khmer Rouge have so far rejected the terms of a "national reconciliation" advanced by the government, which they claim is dominated by pro-Vietnamese elements.

Despite the fact that the coalition's three armies (the Cambodian People's Armed Forces, FUNCINPEC's Armée Nationale Sihanoukiste and the KPNLF's Khmer People's National Liberation Armed Forces) number over 150,000 men, they continue to meet resistance from the Khmer Rouge's estimated 10,000 troops. The inability of the government's forces to inflict a final, fatal blow to the Khmer Rouge partly reflects low morale among government soldiers, who are poorly paid and have suffered heavily from disease.

ECONOMICS

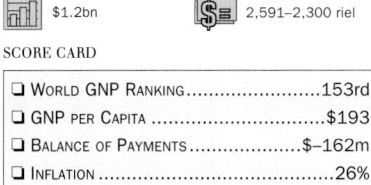

$1.2bn   2,591–2,300 riel

SCORE CARD

❑ WORLD GNP RANKING........................153rd
❑ GNP PER CAPITA $193
❑ BALANCE OF PAYMENTS....................$–162m
❑ INFLATION 26%
❑ UNEMPLOYMENT ....Widespread

EXPORTS

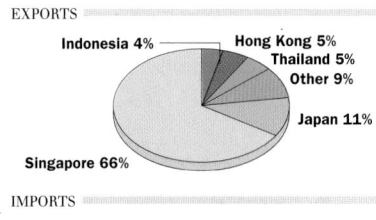

Indonesia 4%   Hong Kong 5%
                    Thailand 5%
                    Other 9%

                    Japan 11%

Singapore 66%

IMPORTS

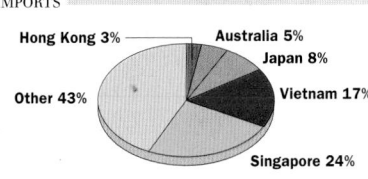

Hong Kong 3%   Australia 5%
                    Japan 8%

Other 43%   Vietnam 17%

                    Singapore 24%

STRENGTHS

Currently very few as economy is still recovering from civil war. Considerable future potential. Given the right conditions, Cambodia could achieve self-sufficiency in rice. Gems, especially sapphires. Possible offshore oil wealth. Timber trade to Thailand.

WEAKNESSES

Tiny tax base makes economic reform hard to implement. Dependence on overseas aid; corruption at most levels of government limits its effectiveness. Loss of skilled workers as result of Khmer Rouge anti-bourgeois atrocities in the 1970s.

ECONOMIC PERFORMANCE INDICATOR

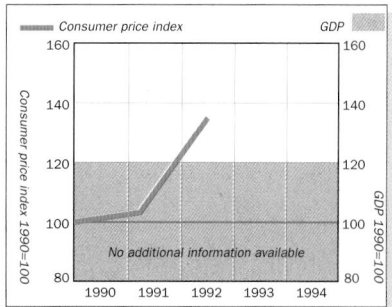

Consumer price index   GDP

No additional information available

1990 1991 1992 1993 1994

PROFILE

Cambodia's economy was devastated during the years Pol Pot was in power. The Vietnamese attempted some reconstruction based on central planning, then switched to policies encouraging the private sector. The presence of the UN has encouraged some limited development.

CAMBODIA : MAJOR BUSINESSES

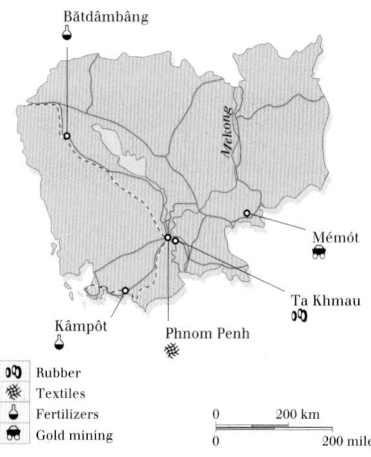

Bătdâmbâng

Mékôt

Ta Khmau

Kâmpôt   Phnom Penh

◗ Rubber
✳ Textiles
♨ Fertilizers
▦ Gold mining

0   200 km
0   200 miles

RESOURCES

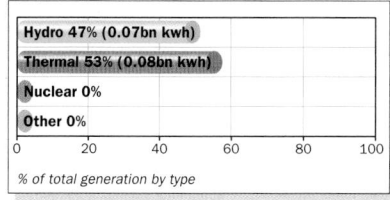

150m kwh (capacity 35,000 kw)

108,900 tonnes

2.6m cattle, 2.2m pigs, 829,000 buffaloes

Salt, phosphates

Tropical rainforest timber, particularly teak and rosewood, is Cambodia's most important resource. Most forests are located in the north and west.

ELECTRICITY GENERATION

Hydro 47% (0.07bn kwh)

Thermal 53% (0.08bn kwh)

Nuclear 0%

Other 0%

0	20	40	60	80	100

% of total generation by type

CAMBODIA : LAND USE

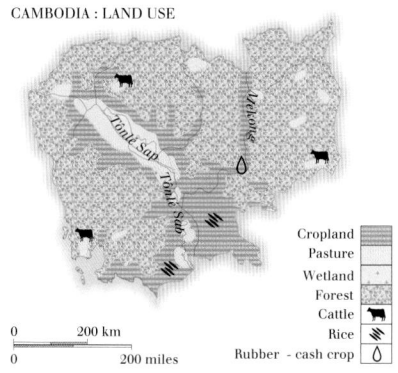

Cropland
Pasture
Wetland
Forest
Cattle
Rice
Rubber - cash crop

0   200 km
0   200 miles

ENVIRONMENT

None

Enforcement of any initiatives is impossible

ENVIRONMENTAL TREATIES

No	No	Yes
No	No	Yes

Deforestation is one of the most serious problems facing Cambodia. Timber, one of the country's most valuable assets, was sold in huge quantities by all Cambodian factions to finance their war efforts. According to the UN, in 1992 alone, more than 617,500 acres of forest were cleared. This provided over 1.3 million cubic yards of timber. A moratorium on logging was declared at the end of 1992, but was largely ignored. In many parts of the country logging is impossible to police and, at current rates, estimates suggest that what remains of Cambodia's forests will be cut down by 2000. The environmental consequences – topsoil erosion and increased risk of flooding – are enormous and will hold back Cambodia's reconstruction.

MEDIA

The government has extended its influence over the media

A 1995 press law provides for possible imprisonment for publishing material deemed to affect national security and political instability. During 1995, the government took at least seven newspapers to court, charging them with defamation and disinformation.

CRIME

Cambodia does not publish prison figures

Civilian crime rates are now fairly stable

CRIME RATES

Violence is increasing as more areas come under renewed attack by the Khmer Rouge

The UN-sponsored peace process and the successful elections in 1993 led to a dramatic drop in crime in Cambodia. Many areas are experiencing the first period of stability in two decades.

The exceptions are areas controlled by the Khmer Rouge, mostly in the west of the country. The regions around Pailĭn and Bătdâmbâng are particularly dangerous. Khmer Rouge guerrillas carry out frequent terror missions against villages. The lack of adequate policing has also led to a rise in banditry in these regions.

Allegations were made in 1995 that Cambodia was fast becoming Asia's new "narco-state." It was claimed that there was a proliferation of narcotics trading, money laundering and illegal banking operations.

EDUCATION

 35%

 43,302 students

0	*Education spending as % GNP*	25

Sufficient to send 80% of children to primary school

THE EDUCATION SYSTEM

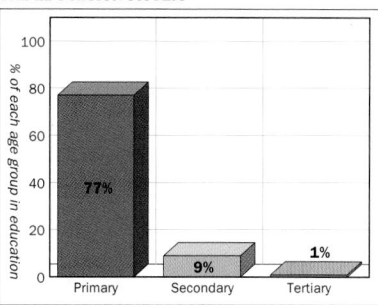

Primary	Secondary	Tertiary
77%	9%	1%

Only 5,000 of Cambodia's 20,000 teachers survived the Pol Pot period. The Vietnamese-installed government trained or retrained about 40,000.

PUBLISHING AND BROADCAST MEDIA

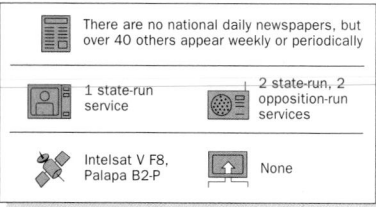

There are no national daily newspapers, but over 40 others appear weekly or periodically

1 state-run service

2 state-run, 2 opposition-run services

Intelsat V F8, Palapa B2-P

None

HEALTH

1 per 18,659 people

Circulatory and infectious diseases, cancers

0	*Health spending as % GNP*	25

Insufficient to provide comprehensive primary care

The Cambodian health system was effectively destroyed by the Khmer's period in power. Only 50 doctors survived the Pol Pot period. In the immediate aftermath of the Vietnamese invasion, Cambodia's health indicators were among the worst in the world. Over 25% of babies were dying before their first birthday.

Conditions have since improved. However, infant mortality remains high, and malaria and cholera are endemic.

WEALTH

Most Cambodians live a subsistence existence

CONSUMER GOODS OWNERSHIP

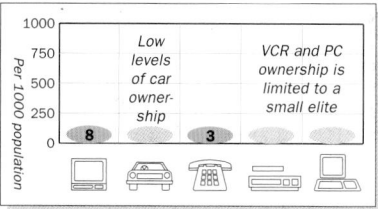

Low levels of car ownership

VCR and PC ownership is limited to a small elite

Per 1000 population

8

3

The opening up of the country's economy has led to an influx of capital. The benefits of new investment, however, are limited to those in power.

WORLD RANKING

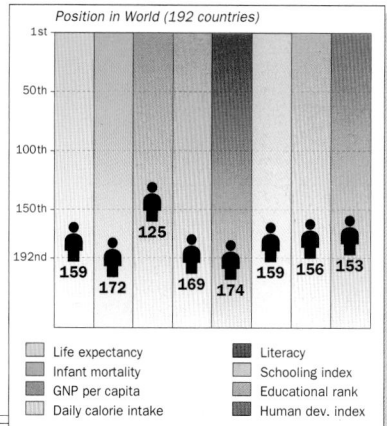

Position in World (192 countries)

| 1st | | 50th | | 100th | | 150th | | 192nd |

125
159   172   169   174   159   156   153

Life expectancy
Infant mortality
GNP per capita
Daily calorie intake

Literacy
Schooling index
Educational rank
Human dev. index

CAMEROON

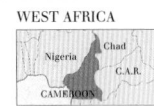
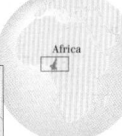

WEST AFRICA

Africa

OFFICIAL NAME: Republic of Cameroon **CAPITAL:** Yaoundé
POPULATION: 13.2 million **CURRENCY:** CFA franc **OFFICIAL LANGUAGES:** French and English

C

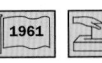
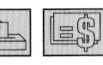

LOCATED ON THE CENTRAL WEST AFRICAN coast, over half of Cameroon is forested, with equatorial rainforest to the south, and evergreen forest and wooded savanna north of the Sanaga River. Most cities are located in the south, although there are densely populated areas around Mount Cameroon, a dormant volcano. For 30 years Cameroon was effectively a one-party state. Democratic elections in 1992 returned the former ruling party to power.

*Savanna landscape below **Mindif Pic** in Cameroon's far north. From here, the land slopes down to the hot, arid Lake Chad basin.*

CLIMATE

WEATHER CHART

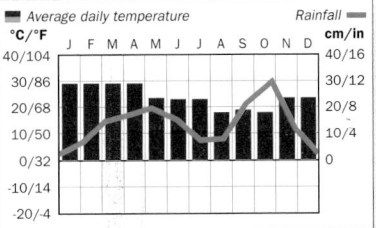

Climate varies from the equatorial south with 195 in. of rain a year to the drought-beset Sahel of the far north.

TRANSPORTATION

Douala International
436,000 passengers

2 ships
33,500 dwt

THE TRANSPORTATION NETWORK

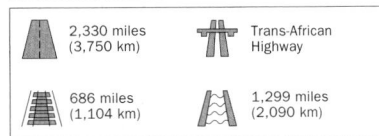

2,330 miles (3,750 km)	Trans-African Highway
686 miles (1,104 km)	1,299 miles (2,090 km)

Major projects are the east–west Trans-African Highway and realigning the Douala–Nkongsamba railroad.

TOURISM

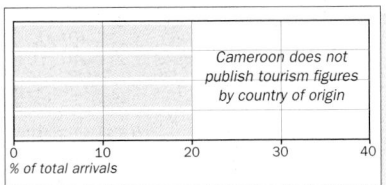

84,000 visitors   Up 4% in 1994

MAIN OVERSEAS ARRIVALS

Cameroon does not publish tourism figures by country of origin

% of total arrivals

In 1989, the first tourism minister was appointed to boost the still small industry. Some package tours visit the northern game parks. A new airport near Yaoundé will replace the present one. Beaches near Kribi have a small number of hotels.

PEOPLE

Fang, Bulu, Yaundé, Duala, Mbum, Fulani, Pidgin English, French, English

73 people per sq. mile

THE URBAN/RURAL POPULATION SPLIT

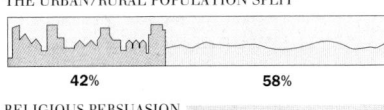

42%   58%

RELIGIOUS PERSUASION

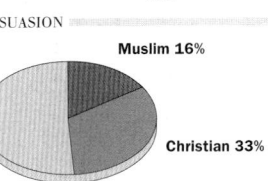

Muslim 16%
Indigenous beliefs 51%
Christian 33%

Cameroon is ethnically diverse – there are 230 groups although no single group is dominant. The largest is the Bamileke of the centre southwest, but this group has never held political power. When President Ahidjo, a northern Fulani, retired, he was replaced by Paul Biya of the southeastern Bulu-Beti group. The north–south enmity which affects other West African states is also present in Cameroon, although diminished by the great diversity of peoples. There is growing tension between the French- and English-speaking peoples, with sections of the latter demanding autonomy.

POLITICS

1992/1997   President Paul Biya

THE STATE OF THE PARTIES

National Assembly 180 members

| 49% RDPC | 38% UNDP | 10% UPC | 3% MDR |

RDPC = Cameroon People's Democratic Movement
UNDP = National Union for Democracy and Progress
UPC = Union of Peoples of Cameroon
MDR = Movement for the Defense of the Republic

Despite ruthless use of the security forces during demonstrations for change in 1990, multiparty elections were held in 1992. They were won by the RDPC. The following presidential elections were won by Paul Biya, though the results have been disputed; John Fru Ndi of the Social Democratic Front (SDF) claims to have defeated Biya. Despite being the most important opposition group, the SDF boycotted the parliamentary elections.

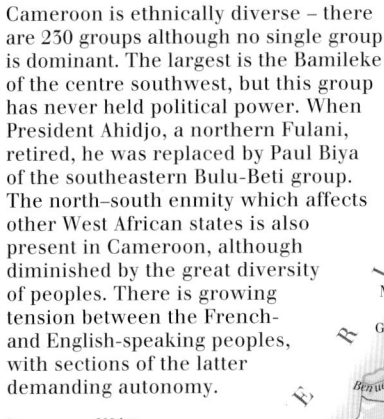

CAMEROON

Total Land Area :
465 400 sq. km
(179 691 sq. miles)

POPULATION

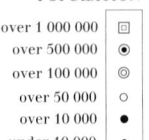

over 1 000 000	▣
over 500 000	◉
over 100 000	◎
over 50 000	○
over 10 000	●
under 10 000	•

LAND HEIGHT

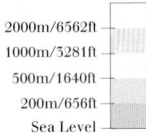

2000m/6562ft	
1000m/3281ft	
500m/1640ft	
200m/656ft	
Sea Level	

WORLD AFFAIRS

Cameroon's most important relationship has traditionally been with France, which gives considerable support.

However, its recent Commonwealth membership reflects the desire to strengthen other links. Care is taken to strike a balance in relations between the mainly French-owned and US-owned oil companies.

AID

 $547m (receipts)   Down 25% in 1993

France is by far the most important donor, even having twice paid Cameroon's back debts to the IMF to avoid it being blacklisted. Despite a poor economic performance, relations with the IMF are improving. Nevertheless, lack of funding has forced many development projects to be abandoned.

DEFENSE

 $105m   Up 2% in 1995

The military has been an active force in supporting the regime and keeping order in the face of democratic protests since before independence. The 13,000-strong army is equipped mainly from France. There is also a 9,000-member gendarmerie, which has been deployed to maintain public order.

ECONOMICS

 $8.7bn   489.05–533.68 CFA francs

SCORE CARD

- WORLD GNP RANKING 82nd
- GNP PER CAPITA $680
- BALANCE OF PAYMENTS ....$–512m
- INFLATION 12.7%
- UNEMPLOYMENT..................................25%

STRENGTHS
Moderate oil reserves. Very diversified agricultural economy (timber, cocoa, coffee, rubber) and food self-sufficiency preserved through oil boom. Historical liberalism. Private sector in relatively good state. Electricity is 95% HEP.

WEAKNESSES
Massive fuel smuggling from Nigeria affects refinery profits. Inflated civil service. Growing national debt owing to failure to adjust to fall in oil revenues.

EXPORTS

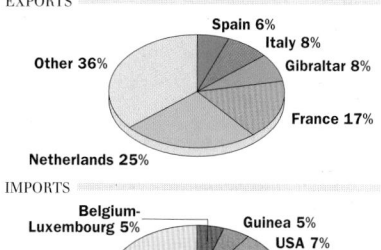

Spain 6%
Italy 8%
Gibraltar 8%
France 17%
Netherlands 25%
Other 36%

IMPORTS

Belgium-Luxembourg 5%
Guinea 5%
USA 7%
Germany 9%
France 27%
Other 47%

RESOURCES

 2.7bn kwh (capacity 627,000 kw)   140,710 b/d (reserves 400,000,000 bbl)

4.9m cattle, 3.8m sheep, 3.8m goats, 1.4m pigs   Oil, coal, tin, natural gas, bauxite, iron, uranium, gold

New oil discoveries may bolster declining extraction rates. In spite of large bauxite deposits, much is imported for the Edea smelter, which takes 50% of national electricity output.

ENVIRONMENT

 4% (2% partially protected)   Environment and forestry ministry ineffective

Conservation groups and official nature reserves are attempting to curb commercial timber felling. National parks are celebrated for their flora.

MEDIA

 Press censorship eased in 1990, but is still fairly severe

PUBLISHING AND BROADCAST MEDIA

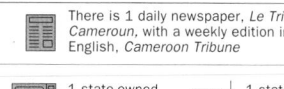
There is 1 daily newspaper, *Le Tribune du Cameroun*, with a weekly edition in English, *Cameroon Tribune*

1 state-owned service   1 state-owned service

There are often complaints of censorship, seizures and physical attacks on media workers. Journalists have demonstrated to highlight their grievances.

CRIME

 Cameroon does not publish prison figures   Up 76% in 1992

Armed robbery and burglary in Douala and Yaoundé are rising fast. The police are known to use torture.

EDUCATION

 54%    1817 students

The French-speaking majority has failed in its attempt to take over the bilingual system. In 1991, two new single-language universities were created.

CHRONOLOGY

One of the great trading emporia of West Africa, Cameroon was divided between the French and British in 1919, after 30 years of German rule.

- **1955** Revolt; French kill 10,000.
- **1960** French sector independent.
- **1961** British southern sector votes to join Cameroon; northern joins Nigeria. Federal system set up. Lasts 11 years – centralized in 1972.
- **1966** One-party state.
- **1982** Ahidjo dies. Paul Biya succeeds as president.
- **1983–1984** Coup attempts. Heavy casualties; 50 plotters executed.
- **1990** Demonstrations and strikes; declaration of multiparty state.
- **1991** Annexes nine Nigerian villages.
- **1992** Multiparty elections.

HEALTH

 1 per 12,000 people   Malaria, diarrheal and respiratory diseases

The sharp fall in government provision and financing means that more people are using the private health sector or traditional practitioners.

WEALTH

 Wealth disparities are marked

CONSUMER GOODS OWNERSHIP

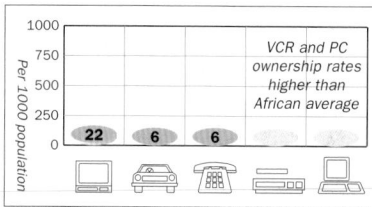

VCR and PC ownership rates higher than African average

22   6   6

The biggest African importer of French champagne in the oil boom, Cameroon still has a small but very wealthy sector.

WORLD RANKING

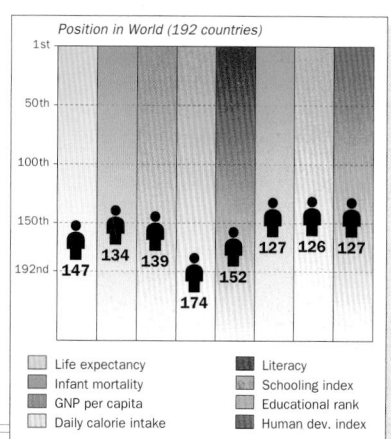

Position in World (192 countries)

147   134   139   174   152   127   126   127

- Life expectancy
- Infant mortality
- GNP per capita
- Daily calorie intake
- Literacy
- Schooling index
- Educational rank
- Human dev. index

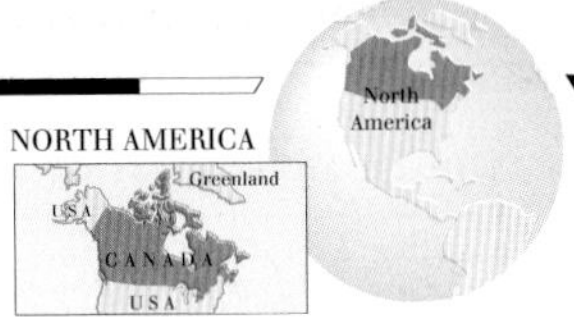

CANADA

OFFICIAL NAME: Canada **CAPITAL:** Ottawa **POPULATION:** 29.5 million
CURRENCY: Canadian dollar **OFFICIAL LANGUAGES:** English, French

C

STRETCHING FROM CAPE COLOMBIA on Ellesmere Island in the north to Middle Island in Lake Erie in the south, Canada is the world's second-largest country. It stretches across five time zones and is divided into ten provinces and two territories. The interior lowlands around Hudson Bay make up 80% of Canada's land area and include the vast Canadian Shield. West of the Shield, the plains of Saskatchewan and Manitoba include vast prairie lands. The St. Lawrence River and Great Lakes lowlands are the most populous areas. Canada's main rivers – the St. Lawrence, Yukon, Mackenzie and Fraser – are among the world's 40 largest. In recent years, the continued political relationship of French-speaking Québec with the rest of the country has been the key constitutional issue.

CLIMATE

WEATHER CHART

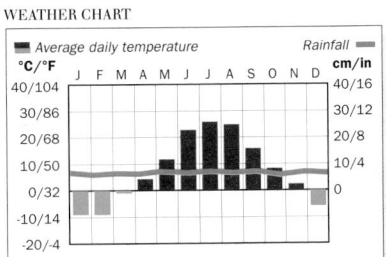

Canada's climate ranges from polar and sub-polar in the north, to cool in the south. Winters in the interior are colder and longer than on the coast, with temperatures well below freezing and deep snow; summers are hotter. The Pacific Coast around Vancouver has the warmest winters; temperatures rarely fall below zero.

TRANSPORTATION

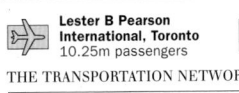 **Lester B Pearson International, Toronto** 10.25m passengers

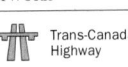 155 ships 515,800 dwt

THE TRANSPORTATION NETWORK

152,170 miles (244,880 km)	Trans-Canada Highway
120,546 miles (194,000 km)	1,864 miles (3,000 km)

Canada's size means the emergence of a national economy has depended on the development of an efficient system of transportation. The Trans-Canada Highway and two transcontinental rail systems are the focus of road and rail networks which reach into the far north. Air services are well-developed and expanding. However, easy access to the cheap water transportation of the Great Lakes–Saint Lawrence Seaway system has helped Ontario and Québec retain their dominance of the economy.

CANADA

Total Land Area : 9 220 970 sq. km (3 560 217 sq. miles)

POPULATION

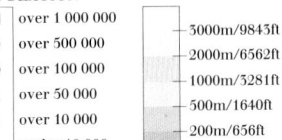

- over 1 000 000
- over 500 000
- over 100 000
- over 50 000
- over 10 000
- under 10 000

LAND HEIGHT

- 3000m/9843ft
- 2000m/6562ft
- 1000m/3281ft
- 500m/1640ft
- 200m/656ft
- Sea Level

TOURISM

 16m visitors

 Up 6% in 1994

MAIN OVERSEAS ARRIVALS

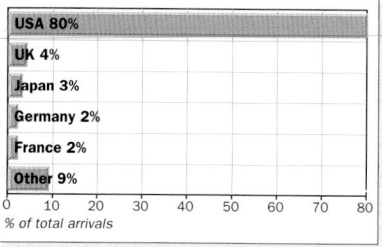

USA 80%	
UK 4%	
Japan 3%	
Germany 2%	
France 2%	
Other 9%	

% of total arrivals

The majority of tourists still come from the USA, despite efforts to attract more European visitors with campaigns emphasizing Canada's unpolluted natural beauty. An increasing number of tourists are Japanese, many on visits to *Anne of Green Gables'* Prince Edward Island home.

PEOPLE

 English, French, Chinese, Italian, German, Ukrainian, Portuguese, Inuktitut, Cree

8 people per sq. mile

THE URBAN/RURAL POPULATION SPLIT

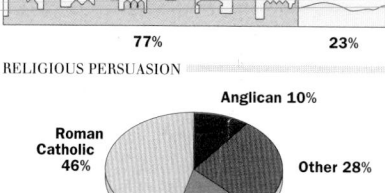

77%   23%

RELIGIOUS PERSUASION

Anglican 10%
Roman Catholic 46%
Other 28%
United Church 16%

ETHNIC MAKEUP

Indigenous Indian and Inuits 4%
Other 9%
British origin 40%
Other European 20%
French origin 27%

Relations between French-speaking Québécois and the English-speaking majority in Canada have been the dominant ethnic issue of the past 25 years. The Québécois feel distinct from the rest of Canada; their wish to preserve their culture and language from further anglicization has been reflected in the growth of secessionism. Support for pro-separatist parties has increased in the 1990s, mainly because of the failure of the provinces to deal with Québec's demand to be recognized as a "distinct society." In a provincial referendum in 1995, the electorate voted to remain within Canada;

A dude ranch in British Columbia. Many tourists are attracted by Canada's wide choice of outdoor pursuits.

POPULATION AGE BREAKDOWN

% of population by age group	■ 0–14	■ 15–64	□ 65+		
65+	7.5%	7.9%	9.5%	11.4%	12.7%
15–64	58.9%	61.9%	67.5%	67.7%	68.6%
0–14	33.6%	30.2%	23%	20.9%	18.7%
	1960	1970	1980	1990	2000

however, the result was so close that it did nothing to settle the issue.

More than 65% of the population still lives in the 5% of Canada taken up by the Great Lakes–St. Lawrence lowlands. However, Canada's ethnic mix has changed significantly in the past 20 years due to a move from a restrictive immigration policy to one which welcomes those with money or skills. Significant numbers of Asians have moved to Canada. The government promotes a policy which encourages each group to maintain its own culture. Canada is now officially a "Community of communities."

There is a long tradition of state welfare in Canada which is more akin to Scandinavia than the USA. Provisions for unemployment and health care, supported by high taxes, are still generous, despite recent cutbacks. The government has sought to end inequalities. Measures include the "pay-equity" laws which aim to specify pay rates for jobs done mainly by women – like receptionists – equivalent to similar skill jobs for men. Women are well represented at most levels of business and government.

Aboriginal Peoples of Canada account for around 4% of the country's population. There are some 50,000 Inuit, 213,000 Métis (French-Indian) and 800,000 Canadians of native Indian descent. Around 43,000 live in the north, in the Northwest and Yukon Territories. In 1992, the Inuit successfully settled their longstanding land claim with the Canadian government, paving the way for other indigenous groups. In 1999, the Inuit Nunavut area will become a territory, and the first part of Canada to be governed by Aboriginal Peoples of Canada in modern history.

Baffin Bay

Davis Strait

Baffin Island

Cumberland Peninsula

Hall Peninsula

Foxe Peninsula

Iqaluit

Meta Incognita Peninsula

Coral Harbour

Hudson Strait

Ivujivik

Péninsula D'ungava

Ungava Bay

Hudson Bay

Winisk

La Grande Rivière

James Bay

Moosonee

Albany

Timmins

Wawa

L. Superior

Sudbury

Sault Sainte Marie

North Bay

Peterborough

Oshawa

Toronto

Kitchener

Hamilton

St. Catherines

London

Windsor

L. Huron

L. Ontario

Niagara Falls

L. Erie

L. Michigan

LABRADOR SEA

NEWFOUNDLAND

Schefferville

Smallwood Res.

Happy Valley-Goose Bay

QUÉBEC

Belcher Is

Labrador City

LAURENTIAN HIGHLANDS

Corner Brook

Newfoundland

Sept-Îles

St. John's

Chicoutini

Jonquière

Québec

Trois-Rivières

Laval

Hull

Montréal

Verdun

OTTAWA

Kingston

St. Lawrence

Gulf of St. Lawrence

Péninsule de Gaspé

Prince Edward I.

Cabot Strait

Sydney

Cape Breton I.

NEW BRUNSWICK

Fredericton

Moncton

Charlottetown

Dartmouth

Halifax

Saint John

NOVA SCOTIA

Yarmouth

Sherbrooke

ATLANTIC OCEAN

C

CHRONOLOGY

Peopled for centuries by indigenous Inuits and Indians, Canada began to experience extensive European settlement following the landing of the English expedition led by John Cabot in 1497 and the French landing of Jacques Cartier in 1534.

- ❏ **1754** French and Indian War between Britain and France. France forced to relinquish St. Lawrence and Québec settlements to Britain.
- ❏ **1774** Act of Québec recognizes Roman Catholicism, French language, culture and traditions.
- ❏ **1775–1783** American War of Independence. Canada becomes refuge for loyalists to British Crown.
- ❏ **1885** Transcontinental railroad completed.
- ❏ **1897** Klondike gold rush begins.
- ❏ **1914–1918** Canadian troops fight in World War I.
- ❏ **1926** Commonwealth Conference. Principle of equal status with London in deciding foreign policy accepted.
- ❏ **1936** Reciprocity Treaty with the USA lays foundations for increased economic links.
- ❏ **1939–1945** Canadian troops fight in World War II.
- ❏ **1949** Founder member of NATO. Newfoundland joins Federation.
- ❏ **1968** Liberal Party under Pierre Trudeau in power. Québec Party (PQ) formed to demand complete separation from federal government.
- ❏ **1970s** Québec secessionist movement grows, accompanied by terrorist bombings and murders.
- ❏ **1976** PQ wins Québec elections. French made official language in Québec.
- ❏ **1980** Separation of Québec rejected at referendum. Pierre Trudeau prime minister again.
- ❏ **1982** UK transfers all powers relating to Canada in British law.
- ❏ **1984** Trudeau resigns. Elections won by Conservatives and Brian Mulroney.
- ❏ **1987** Meech Lake Accord.
- ❏ **1989** Canadian–USA Free Trade Agreement (NAFTA).
- ❏ **1992** Charlottetown Agreement rejected at referendum. Canada, Mexico, USA finalize NAFTA terms.
- ❏ **1993** Crushing election defeat of the PCP marks a watershed in Canadian history, with the rise of regional parties.
- ❏ **1994** PQ takes power in Québec. NAFTA takes effect.
- ❏ **1995** Narrow "no" vote in Québec sovereignty referendum. Dispute with the EU (led by Spain) about overfishing of Canada's waters.

POLITICS

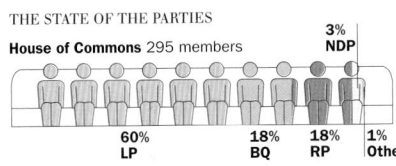

1993/1998   HM Queen Elizabeth II

THE STATE OF THE PARTIES

House of Commons 295 members

| 60% LP | 18% BQ | 18% RP | 1% Other | 3% NDP |

LP = Liberal Party   **BQ** = Québec Bloc   **RP** = Reform Party
NDP = New Democratic Party   **PCP** = Progressive Conservative Party

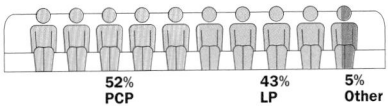

Senate 98 members

| 52% PCP | 43% LP | 5% Other |

The Senate's members are nominated

Canada is a federal multiparty democracy.

MAIN POLITICAL ISSUES
The unity of the state

Canada has been struggling to find a place for francophone Québec and its separatist tendencies almost since the foundation of the state. The issue rose to prominence again in 1976 when the separatist Québec Party (PQ) won power in the 1976 Québec provincial elections. The PQ at first advocated independence, then economic association. However, its proposals were rejected in a referendum in 1980 by 59.5% to 40.5%.

In 1990, a constitutional agreement, the Meech Lake Accord, recognized Québec as a distinct society within the Canadian Federation. The Accord also granted additional powers to other federal states. However, it was not ratified, as Newfoundland objected to its provisions. In 1992, another proposal, the Charlottetown Agreement, was put to referendum. This recognized Québec as a distinct society and granted the province a guaranteed 25% of seats in the National Assembly. This was turned down both in Québec and at national level. A second referendum in 1995 failed to settle the matter when a PQ proposal that Québec should leave the Canada federation was narrowly defeated by 50.6% to 49.4%, though Lucien Bouchard, who became the Quebec premier in 1996, continues to press the separatist cause.

NAFTA

The proposed North American Free Trade Agreement (NAFTA) dominated the Canadian elections of 1988. Many are still opposed to the agreement. There are fears that Canadian workers may suffer from competition from Mexico. Tensions between Canadian and US trades unions have also risen as Canadian workers have been forced to accept more flexible US working

The Niagara Falls *are situated between Lakes Erie and Ontario on the Canada–US border. The Horseshoe Falls, in Canada, are 160 feet high and 2,591 feet across.*

practices. Many sectors of business, particularly grains, oilseeds, textiles, oil and gas, and engineering services, have benefited from NAFTA.

PROFILE

Until recently, Canadian politics was dominated by three main parties. The PCP and LP had few ideological differences. The NDP advocated greater government intervention. Only the PCP and LP had held office.

Major political changes were seen in 1993. Brian Mulroney, the leader of the PCP, resigned in the wake the failure of the Charlottetown Agreement, economic recession and the unpopularity of a new sales tax. He was replaced by Kim Campbell as PCP leader. However, in elections in October 1993, nine years of PCP rule were brought to an end by a landslide LP victory led by Jean Chrétien. The change represented a rejection of mainstream politics by the electorate, who voted for parties representing regional interests, with the BQ establishing itself as the official opposition, and the RP, which represents the interests of the western provinces, increasing in influence.

Lucien Bouchard, *the separatist premier of Québec*

Brian Mulroney *resigned as PCP leader in 1993.*

Jean Chrétien, *prime minister since 1993*

WORLD AFFAIRS

Canada's most important relationship is with the USA, its main trading partner. There are tensions in the relationship, however. Canada has not managed to reach agreement on restricting pollution from US border plants, which

have been responsible for much of the acid rain affecting the country's forests. A US–Canadian commission recommended a $5 billion program, but did not suggest sources of funding. Minor maritime waters disputes exist with the USA over stretches of the Northwest Passage; the USA recognizes Canadian claims over the islands, but

not the waters. A dispute with France over the boundary of waters around St. Pierre et Miquelon, the French-controlled islands off Newfoundland's coast, was settled in 1993. Until 1993, Canada's trade with Mexico was just 1.6% of that with the USA. However, as trade increases under NAFTA, so relations will become more important.

AID

 $2.4bn (donations)   Up 6% in 1993

Canada's aid budget has been one of the first areas of government spending to be earmarked for cuts. While most Canadians support aid – Canada gives twice as much per capita as the USA – the issue is not politicized to the point where cuts have been reversed.

First to suffer have been the large number of NGOs which the Canadian International Development Agency (CIDA) supports. The regional focus of aid has shifted from traditional areas, such as francophone West Africa, to Southeast Asia. This reflects the growing importance of Canada's Asian minority trade links; Pacific trade is now 65% greater than that across the Atlantic. Aid now aims to provide know-how skills, rather than funding for large-scale development projects.

DEFENSE

 $8.1bn   Down 4% in 1995

0   Defense spending as % GDP   40
1.7%

CANADIAN ARMED FORCES

🛡	114 main battle tanks (*Leopard* C–1)	20,300 personnel
🚢	12 frigates, 3 submarines, 4 destroyers and 12 patrol boats	10,000 personnel
✈	140 combat aircraft (122 CF–18)	17,100 personnel
🚀	None	

Canada cooperates with the USA in the defense of North America. However, in response to the end of the Cold War in Europe, Canada withdrew its forces stationed there in 1992. As in other NATO states, defense spending has been cut significantly. Even so, many Canadians would like to see it cut even further. The focus of defense planning is now the creation of rapid reaction forces. In 1993 and 1994, Canadian troops were deployed in UN peacekeeping operations in Somalia and former Yugoslavia.

ECONOMICS

$569.9bn   1.36–1.40 Canadian dollars

SCORE CARD

❏ WORLD GNP RANKING	8th
❏ GNP PER CAPITA	$19,570
❏ BALANCE OF PAYMENTS	$–17.4bn
❏ INFLATION	2.4%
❏ UNEMPLOYMENT	10.3%

EXPORTS
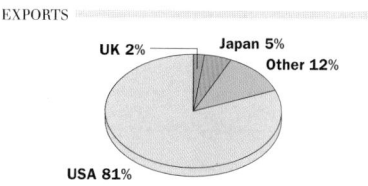

IMPORTS
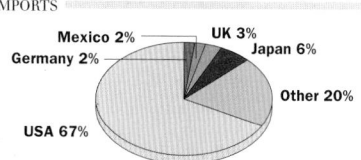

STRENGTHS

A broad and rich resource base. Provides exports, raw materials for manufacturing sector and massive cheap energy, notably HEP; also large oil and gas reserves. Agriculture and forestry contribute 3% of GDP; mining 4%. Successful manufacturing sector, contributes 17% of GDP; notably forestry products, transportation equipment and chemicals. Free access to huge US and Mexican markets through NAFTA.

WEAKNESSES

Increasingly uncompetitive; higher taxes, more regulations, lower productivity relative to most competitors. Political uncertainty over future of the federation dents business confidence. High federal and provincial budget deficits; slow recovery from early 1990s recession.

ECONOMIC PERFORMANCE INDICATOR
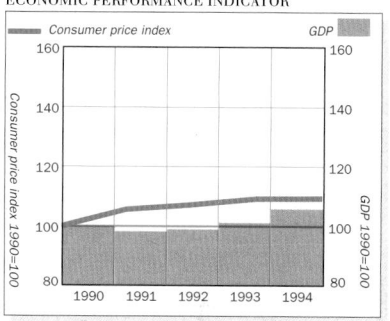

PROFILE

Canada's enormous resource base has delivered one of the OECD's highest standards of living since 1945. After the mid-1980s, however, its manufactured exports faced increasing competition, while prices for its primary exports fell. From 1980–1988, real growth averaged 3.5% a year. After 1989, it stagnated, while budget deficits rose – forcing restructuring at both federal and provincial levels. Many of Canada's welfare programs were cut back; the defense budget was sharply reduced. The end result was a marked drop in inflation from 4% to 1.3%, the lowest in the G7, and a resumption of growth after 1993. Another motivation for the changes was Canada's membership of NAFTA. Its firms have had to become more competitive to maintain exports. Most have been successful, but better productivity and a shift to high-tech has left unemployment at around 10%.

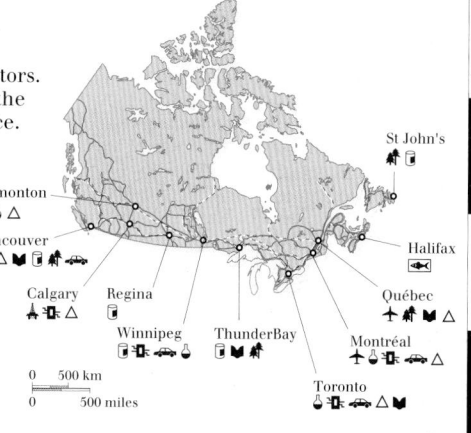

CANADA : MAJOR BUSINESSES

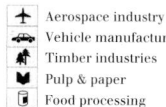 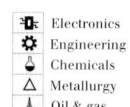

✈	Aerospace industry	🔲	Electronics
🚗	Vehicle manufacture	✿	Engineering
🌲	Timber industries	△	Chemicals
🌾	Pulp & paper	△	Metallurgy
🐟	Food processing	⚒	Oil & gas
🐟	Fish processing		

0   500 km
0   500 miles

RESOURCES

521bn kwh (capacity 104.14m kw)

1.6m b/d (reserves 5,291,630,000 bbl)

12.3m cattle, 11.2m pigs, 691,000 sheep

Coal, oil, natural gas, gold, zinc, uranium

ELECTRICITY GENERATION

Hydro 61% (316bn kwh)

Thermal 24% (123bn kwh)

Nuclear 15% (80bn kwh)

Other 0%

0   20   40   60   80   100

% of total generation by type

Canada is a country of enormous natural resources. It is the world's largest exporter of forest products and a top exporter of fish, furs and wheat. Minerals have played a key role in Canada's transformation into an urban–industrial economy. Alberta, British Columbia, Québec and Saskatchewan are the principal mining regions. Ontario and the Northwest (NWT) and Yukon Territories are also significant producers. Canada is the world's largest producer of zinc and uranium; the second-largest of

nickel, asbestos, potash and gypsum. Oil and gas are exploited in Alberta, off the Atlantic coast and in the NWT – huge additional reserves are thought to exist in the high Arctic. Most exports go to the USA. Canada is also one of the world's top hydroelectricity producers.

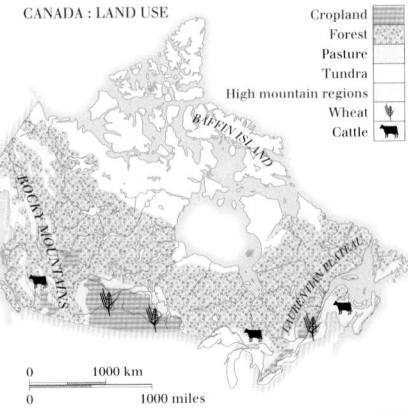

CANADA : LAND USE

Cropland
Forest
Pasture
Tundra
High mountain regions
Wheat
Cattle

0   1000 km
0   1000 miles

ENVIRONMENT

 8% (2% partially protected)

 State policies framed with sustainable development in mind

ENVIRONMENTAL TREATIES

Yes   Yes   Yes
Yes   Yes   Yes

With a population of 29.5 million living in the world's second-largest country, Canada does not suffer from the environmental pressures of more populated states. The country is justly renowned for vast tracts of wild countryside untroubled by industrial pollution or pollution caused by intensive farming methods.

Canadians have tighter pollution controls than the neighboring USA. However, Canada's rate of carbon-dioxide emissions is higher, at 4.1 tons per person per year, than the Soviet Union's (3.4), Japan's (2.1) or France's (1.7). Per capita production of hazardous waste is also higher than the European average. Environmental measures are now concentrating on bringing both measures up to the world's highest standards.

A particular concern to Canadians has been damage to the ozone layer caused by CFCs. Canada followed the US lead in 1978 by banning the use of CFCs for aerosols. In 1987, Montréal was the site of the international agreement to cut CFC use by half by the year 2000.

MEDIA

 No political censorship

PUBLISHING AND BROADCAST MEDIA

There are 110 daily newspapers, including the *Globe and Mail*, the *Toronto Star*, *Le Journal de Montréal* and *La Presse*

1 state-owned, 2 independent services

1 state-owned, also independent services

Galaxy 5

67% of homes are connected to a cable network

Two of the three national TV networks are run by the Canadian Broadcasting Corporation (CBC), one channel in English, the other in French. Canadian TV is renowned for its news and sports coverage. Over three-quarters of the country can receive broadcasts from the USA. Most cities now have cable TV, which usually offers at least one multi-lingual or ethnic channel. *La Presse* is the leading French-language daily.

Autumn in the tundra in northern Canada Trees such as the black spruce are subject to the effects of acid rain originating in the USA's northern industrial regions.

CRIME

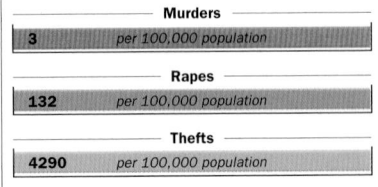 31,302 prisoners   Up 7% in 1991

CRIME RATES

Murders	
3	per 100,000 population

Rapes	
132	per 100,000 population

Thefts	
4290	per 100,000 population

Crime rates in Canada are much lower than in the USA. Canadians ascribe this to their far tighter gun control laws. In 1993, the regulations were made even stricter. Another factor has been the careful efforts to maintain the inner cities as crime-free zones. The ghetto problems of US inner cities have largely been avoided. However, Canada does have a rising narcotics problem. Youth crime is also growing, with over 22% of federal charges being laid against youths between the ages of 12 and 17 in 1991. However, only 0.04% of youth charges were murder-related.

EDUCATION

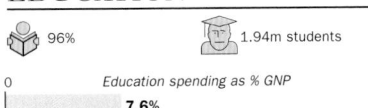 96%   1.94m students

0   Education spending as % GNP   25

7.6%

THE EDUCATION SYSTEM

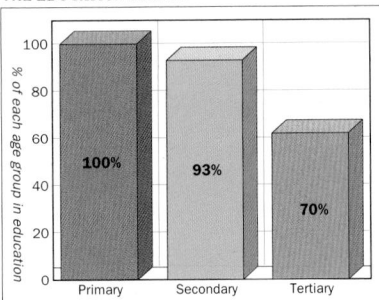

% of each age group in education

Primary 100%   Secondary 93%   Tertiary 70%

Education policy is a responsibility of the provinces. The period of free compulsory school attendance varies, but is a minimum of nine years. The prime medium of instruction is English in all provinces except francophone Québec. However, in several other provinces, French-speaking students are entitled to be taught in French.

Canada has 69 universities and 203 other higher education institutions. Over 75% of secondary level students go on to some form of higher education – the highest proportion in the industrialized world. The emphasis placed on education is also reflected in the fact that Canada's total education expenditure as a percentage of GDP also tops the league at over 7%.

REGIONS

QUÉBEC

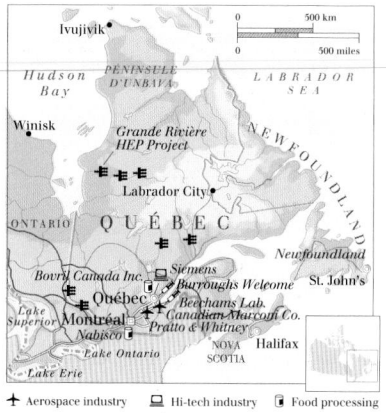

ALMOST ALL 6.9 MILLION Québécois live in the south of the province; 50% in Greater Montréal. The northern forests generate 20% of the world's pulp and paper. Québec is also the world's fourth-largest hydropower producer. Secession has long been an issue for the francophone majority. However, support for separatist parties in the early 1990s reflected discontent with traditional parties as much as a wish to go it alone. Separation could be costly, notably in jobs. Of Québec's exports, 90% go to the USA and the rest of Canada. To keep these NAFTA markets, Québec, at present highly protectionist, would have to embrace free trade.

✈ Aerospace industry   📱 Hi-tech industry   📦 Food processing
⊞ Hydroelectric power   🧪 Pharmaceuticals

TORONTO

TORONTO IS CANADA's largest, fastest-growing and most polyglot city. As the destination for 50% of immigrants and most of Canada's internal migrants, it is expected to almost double in size to five million by the year 2000. One in six housing-starts in Canada during the late 1980s were in Toronto. Like Ontario as a whole, it has a broad industrial base and excellent public services. Toronto is also the country's leading financial and services center – a role it took away from Montreal during the secession fears of the late 1970s. Like Montreal, it was hard hit by recession in the early 1990s. Unemployment rose and the city government had to impose unpopular budget cuts.

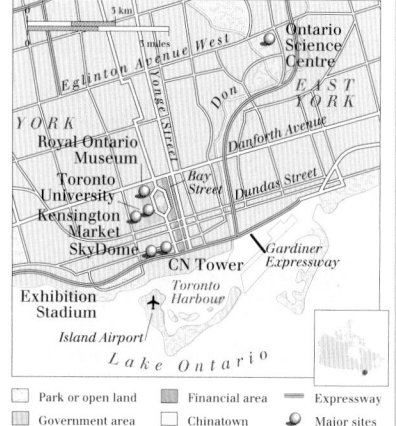

☐ Park or open land   ☐ Financial area   ➡ Expressway
☐ Government area   ☐ Chinatown   🔍 Major sites

NORTHWEST TERRITORIES

☐ Permanent ice sheet   ☐ Pack ice

THE NORTHWEST TERRITORIES covers 1.3m square miles, or one-third of Canada. However, its population is tiny – just 57,650 people. Over 60% are of indigenous descent, mostly Inuit, but also Dene and Métis Indians. The incomer minority work mainly in the mining industry, which has expanded rapidly since the discovery of gold in the 1930s. Zinc is the top export, but oil and gas and many other minerals are extracted. There are increasing concerns about the effects of mining on the NWT's environment, but the main casualties have been the Inuit. They have largely given up their nomadic, hunting lifestyle and today are amongst Canada's most marginalized and poorest people. However, the 1992 settlement of Inuit land claims in the high Arctic holds out hope of a better future. They have won title to 135,135 square miles of land and now have a say in how it is developed. In 1999, the area will become the self-governing Nunavut Territory, making the Inuit the first of the Aboriginal Peoples of Canada to gain self-determination.

HEALTH

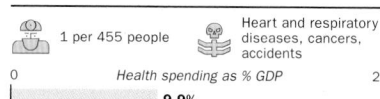

👤 1 per 455 people   ☠ Heart and respiratory diseases, cancers, accidents

0   *Health spending as % GDP*   25

9.9%

Canada's state health service, funded by a national insurance scheme, covers the whole population. However, about 25% use private health facilities. The government is under pressure to cut the budget deficit while facing a higher health bill. Rising costs are the result of an aging population and more expensive treatments. Surveys show, though, that most Canadians want to retain the present system.

WEALTH

💰 Similar wage levels to the USA

CONSUMER GOODS OWNERSHIP

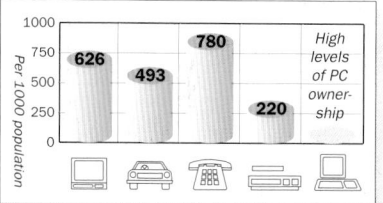

Despite the strains caused by recession during the early 1990s – including a rise in unemployment to over 10% – life for most Canadians remains very good. In fact, the UN ranks Canada as one of the best countries in the world in which to live. In its 1995 overall assessment of human development indicators, like income, education and life expectancy, Canada came in top, ahead of the USA.

However, disadvantaged groups do exist, in particular among Aboriginal Peoples of Canada. Unemployment, poor housing and mortality rates for Indians and Inuits are well above those for other Canadians. Those who live on the reserves are the poorest group.

WORLD RANKING

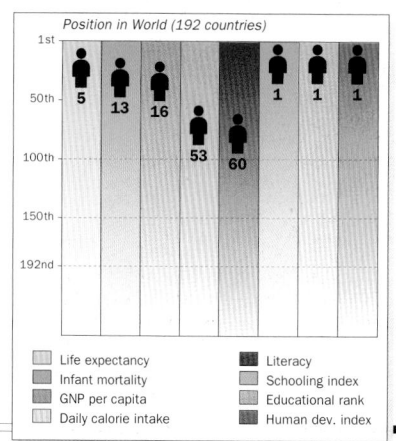

☐ Life expectancy   ☐ Literacy
☐ Infant mortality   ☐ Schooling index
☐ GNP per capita   ☐ Educational rank
☐ Daily calorie intake   ☐ Human dev. index

CAPE VERDE

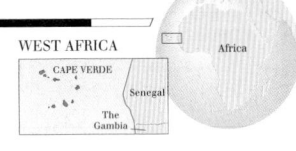

WEST AFRICA

OFFICIAL NAME: Republic of Cape Verde   **CAPITAL:** Praia
POPULATION: 400,000   **CURRENCY:** Cape Verde escudo   **OFFICIAL LANGUAGE:** Portuguese

THE CAPE VERDE ARCHIPELAGO off the west coast of Africa became independent of its colonial ruler, Portugal, in 1975. Following a period of single-party socialist rule, Cape Verde held its first multiparty elections in 1991. Most of the islands are mountainous and volcanic; the low-lying islands of Sal, Boa Vista and Maio have agricultural potential, though they are prone to debilitating droughts. Around 50% of the population lives on São Tiago.

CLIMATE

WEATHER CHART

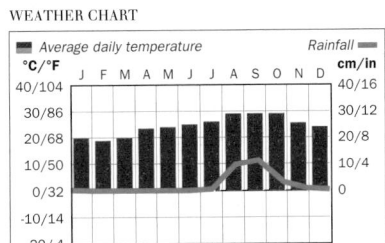

Cape Verde has a very dry climate, subject to droughts that sometimes last for years at a time.

TRANSPORTATION

Amilcar Cabral, Sal Island
156,000 passengers

17 ships
25,900 dwt

THE TRANSPORTATION NETWORK

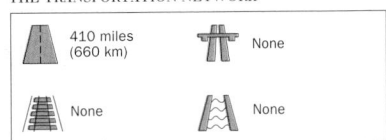

410 miles (660 km)		None
None		None

Cape Verde has a strategic position on international sea and air routes, which it is beginning to exploit.

TOURISM

32,000 visitors

Up 60% in 1994

MAIN OVERSEAS ARRIVALS

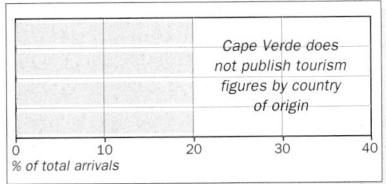

Cape Verde does not publish tourism figures by country of origin

% of total arrivals

Tourism has not been a government priority and is on a modest scale. The islands of São Tiago, Santo Antão, Fogo and Brava have tourist potential, offering a combination of mountain scenery and extensive beaches.

PEOPLE

Portuguese Creole, Portuguese

257 people per sq. mile

THE URBAN/RURAL POPULATION SPLIT

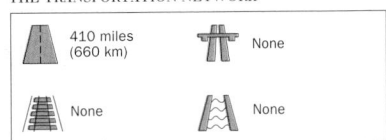

49%   51%

ETHNIC MAKEUP

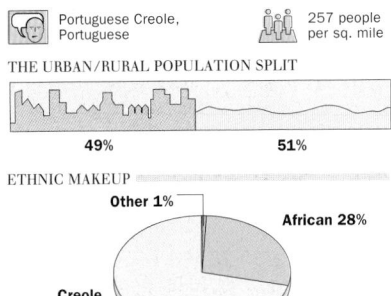

Other 1%
African 28%
Creole (*mestiço*) 71%

The majority of the population is Portuguese-African *mestiço*; the remainder is largely African, descended either from slaves or from more recent immigrants from the mainland. The Creolization of the culture has led to a relative lack of ethnic tension, though there is some bad feeling between islands. African traditions of the extended family and the Catholic Church have helped to ensure the vitality of family life. Women's role in public affairs is not prominent, in part due to the conservative Catholic influence.

POLITICS

1995/2000

President António Mascarenhas Monteiro

THE STATE OF THE PARTIES

National People's Assembly 72 members

69% MPD   30% PAICV   1% PCD

MPD = Movement for Democracy   **PAICV** = African Party for the Independence of Cape Verde   **PCD** = Democratic Convergence Party

Cape Verde experienced a peaceful transition to multipartyism in 1991, when elections brought the MPD to power. Although there had previously been a decade of single-party rule under the PAICV, it had in fact operated a liberal system in which opposition and dissent were tolerated. The large number of Cape Verdeans living and working abroad, who had remained in contact with the islands, helped to smooth the process as democracy was already widely understood and favored.

The most important issue for the government now, apart from preserving the present political consensus, is that of economic survival, particularly in periods of drought. An ideological debate is continuing over the extent of the successes and failures of the PAICV's period of rule.

WORLD AFFAIRS

CILSS   Ecowas   Lusoph   NAM   OAU

Cape Verde aims to diversify its international contacts in order to secure aid, while maintaining good relations with the former colonial power, Portugal, although it is not a major donor. Within the region, Cape Verde seeks to restore normal relations with Guinea-Bissau, after withdrawing from a proposed union in 1980, and is trying to develop contacts with nations on the African mainland, such as Senegal.

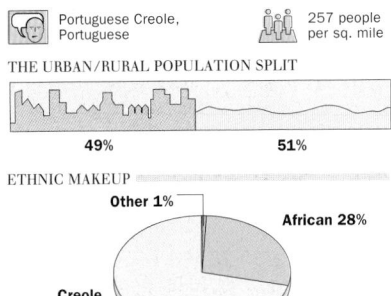

Chã da Igreja   Vila Maria Pia
Santo Antão   Ribeira Grande
Tarrafal   Janela
São Pedro   Mindelo   Calhau
São Vicente   Santa Luzia
Ilhéu Branco   Barril   Ribeira Funda
Ilhéu Raso   Preguiça   Vila de Brava
Castilhiano
São Nicolau

Sal
Palmeira   Pedra Lume
Santa Maria

ATLANTIC OCEAN

Derrubado
Sal Rei   Gata
Boa Vista
João Barrosa
Curral Velho

Ilhas de Barlavento

0   50 km
0   50 miles

N

Ilhas de Sotavento

Maio
Tarrafal   Santiago   Santo Antonio
Ribeira   Maior   Maio
da Barça
Ilhéus do Rombo   Fogo   Fajãzinha
Furna   Picodo do   Santiago (São Tiago)
Fajã   Cano 2829m   Cidade   PRAIA
São   Cova   Velha
Filipe   Figueira
Brava

CAPE VERDE

Total Land Area : 4030 sq. km (1556 sq. miles)

LAND HEIGHT

2000m/6562ft
1000m/3281ft
500m/1640ft
200m/656ft
Sea Level

POPULATION

over 50 000   ○
over 10 000   ●
under 10 000   ·

AID

 $116m (receipts)   Down 3% in 1993

The most important donor is the EU, which has provided substantial food aid in the wake of recent droughts, as well as funding aid programs. The World Bank is also a major source, as are the Netherlands, Sweden, Germany, France and Italy. Aid donations finance almost all development in Cape Verde, which is one of the least industrialized countries in the world.

DEFENSE

 $3.8m   Up 9% in 1995

After independence, small armed forces were established, now consisting of a 1,000-strong army, an air force of 100 and a naval coastguard of 50. They have never been called upon to play a political role; their main duties are to protect territorial waters against illegal fishing and to curb smuggling.

ECONOMICS

 $346m   82.91–82.97 Cape Verde escudos

SCORE CARD

❏ WORLD GNP RANKING	172nd
❏ GNP PER CAPITA	$910
❏ BALANCE OF PAYMENTS	$–4m
❏ INFLATION	4.6%
❏ UNEMPLOYMENT	26%

STRENGTHS

Strategic geographical position, off the westernmost tip of Africa, close to the mid-Atlantic where Africa is nearest to Latin America. This has military and economic advantages, including shipping maintenance and air travel. Low debt servicing costs.

WEAKNESSES

Permanent threat of drought and water supply problems, despite desalination plants. Lack of agricultural land and dependency on food aid. Difficulties of communications between islands.

EXPORTS

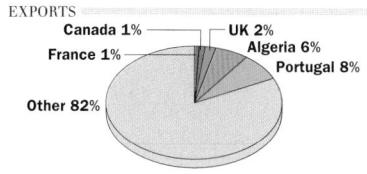

Canada 1% UK 2%
France 1% Algeria 6%
Portugal 8%
Other 82%

IMPORTS

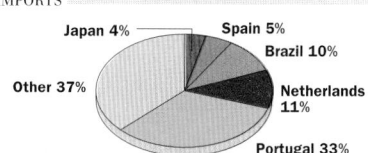

Japan 4% Spain 5%
Brazil 10%
Other 37%
Netherlands 11%
Portugal 33%

Portuguese colonial-style architecture on Fogo, one of the larger islands. The volcano in its center is the highest point in Cape Verde.

RESOURCES

 37m kwh (capacity 7000 kw)   7,130 tons

 137,000 goats, 111,000 pigs, 18,000 cattle   Salt, pozzolana

Cape Verde has no known strategic resources. With no oil and no possibility of hydroelectric power, it depends on imported gasoline for energy. However, experimental projects have been carried out to investigate the potential of windmills, wave power and biogas.

ENVIRONMENT

 None   Introduction of reforestation programs

Cape Verde has recently suffered several years of persistent drought, which has affected food production and reduced livestock herds. It is a very active member of CILSS, which struggles against drought in the Sahel region. Environmental initiatives include reforestation, soil conservation and a water resources program.

MEDIA

 Since multipartyism, virtually no censorship

PUBLISHING AND BROADCAST MEDIA

There are no daily newspapers. Weekly newspapers include *Voz do Povo*, published by the government

 1 state-owned service   1 state-owned service

For economic reasons, the press is limited to some extent, as it was under single-party rule. An experimental TV station was forced to close in the late 1980s, but French assistance has allowed both TV and radio to start broadcasting again.

CRIME

 Cape Verde does not publish prison figures   Little change from year to year

Crime is not a serious problem, even in urban centers, though smuggling is fairly widespread.

CHRONOLOGY

Cape Verde was a Portuguese colony from 1462 until 1975, and was ruled jointly with Guinea-Bissau.

- ❏ **1961** Joint struggle for liberation of Cape Verde and Guinea-Bissau (then Portuguese Guinea) begins.
- ❏ **1974** Guinea-Bissau independent.
- ❏ **1975** Independence, but with view to union with Guinea-Bissau.
- ❏ **1981** New constitution formalizes final split from Guinea-Bissau.
- ❏ **1990** Multipartyism legalized.

EDUCATION

 63%   Not available

At independence, education became a priority after years of neglect; 80% of children now attend elementary school.

HEALTH

 1 per 5,100 people   Heart disease, tuberculosis, typhoid and accidents

Health care has improved since the colonial era, yet there are still less than 100 doctors in the whole archipelago.

WEALTH

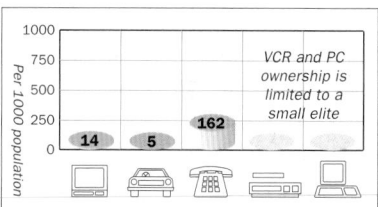 Most Cape Verdeans lead a subsistence existence

CONSUMER GOODS OWNERSHIP

VCR and PC ownership is limited to a small elite

14 5 162

Compared with the 90% of the population in primary production, the small business class in Praia is well-off.

WORLD RANKING

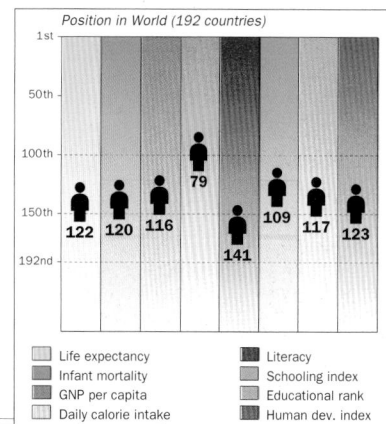

Position in World (192 countries)

122 120 116 79 141 109 117 123

Life expectancy Literacy
Infant mortality Schooling index
GNP per capita Educational rank
Daily calorie intake Human dev. index

CENTRAL AFRICAN REPUBLIC

CENTRAL AFRICA

OFFICIAL NAME: Central African Republic **CAPITAL:** Bangui
POPULATION: 3.3 million **CURRENCY:** CFA franc **OFFICIAL LANGUAGE:** French

 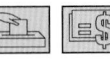

LANDLOCKED AT THE WESTERN end of the Sahel the Central African Republic (CAR) is a low plateau stretching north from one of Africa's great rivers, the Ubangi, which forms its border with Zaire. Most of the population lives in the equatorial, rainforested south. The arid north sustains less than 2% of the population. Emperor Bokassa's 14-year rule from 1965 to 1979 was followed by military dictatorship. Democracy was restored in 1993.

CLIMATE

WEATHER CHART

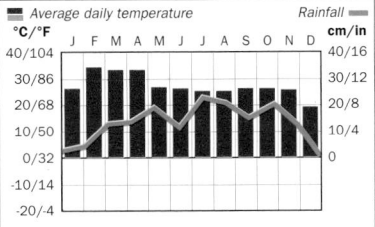

The south is equatorial, the north has a savanna-type climate, and the far north lies within the Sahel.

TRANSPORTATION

 Mpoko, Bangui   Has no fleet

THE TRANSPORTATION NETWORK

 270 miles (430 km)   Trans-African Highway

 None   497 miles (800 km)

The CAR has a limited transportation system, with dependence on the river link to Brazzaville, Congo, and rail from there to Pointe-Noire and Zaire's ports.

TOURISM

 6,000 visitors   No change in 1994

MAIN OVERSEAS ARRIVALS

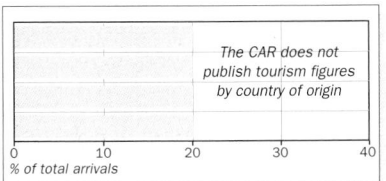
The CAR does not publish tourism figures by country of origin

0   10   20   30   40
% of total arrivals

Tourist promotion is small-scale, but since 1979 there has been a modest increase in national park safaris. Plans for a new runway in Bangui will permit air charters, chiefly from France.

PEOPLE

 Sango, Banda, Gbaya, French   13 people per sq. mile

THE URBAN/RURAL POPULATION SPLIT

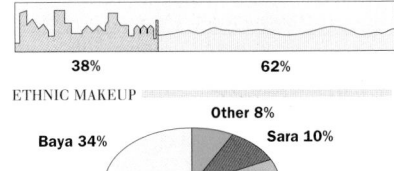

38%   62%

ETHNIC MAKEUP

Baya 34%
Banda 27%
Mandjia 21%
Sara 10%
Other 8%

Although the Baya and the Banda are the largest ethnic groups, the *lingua franca* is Sango. This is spoken by the southern riverine minorities, who provided the political leaders from independence (Presidents Dacko and Kolingba and Emperor Bokassa), until President Patasse, who comes from the interior. Resentment against the river peoples occasionally flares up, but ethnic diversity minimizes polarization. Women, as in other non-Muslim African countries, have considerable power. Elizabeth Domitien was prime minister from 1975–1976 and Ruth Rolland ran for president in 1993.

POLITICS

 1993/1998   President Ange-Félix Patasse

THE STATE OF THE PARTIES

National Assembly 85 members

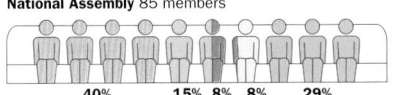

40% MPLC 15% RDC 8% FPP 8% PLD 29% Other

MPLC = Central African People's Liberation Party
RDC = Central African Democratic Rally **FPP** = Patriotic Front for Progress (part of the CFD = Consultative Group of Democratic Forces) **PLD** = Liberal Democratic Party

Economic and Regional Council

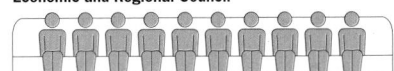

One half of the members are chosen by the president and the other half are elected by the National Assembly

WORLD AFFAIRS

 BDEAC   CEMAC FZ   LCBC  OAU

Apart from keeping up the momentum of its improving political image in international life, the CAR is anxious to continue good relations with France, whose financial help will be needed for some time, and with Cameroon and Congo – its main outlets to the sea. Otherwise, containing any spillover from the fighting in Chad and insulating itself from the problems in Sudan and Zaire are priorities.

AID

 $174m (receipts)   Down 3% in 1993

Almost all the CAR's development projects are funded from external aid. France, as the former colonial power, provides two-thirds of the total. The European Union (notably Belgium, Italy and Germany), Japan and, since 1989, the USA and Israel are the principal donors. It also receives assistance from the IMF and World Bank.

DEFENSE

 $21m   Down 13% in 1995

The 4,950-strong armed forces (2,500 army, 2,300 *gendarmerie* and 150 navy) are the subject of major spending and are very well equipped, mostly with French hardware. The French also provide important economic military aid and officers to fill key posts. Around 1,300 French troops are stationed in the country.

The return to democratic elections in 1993 after Gen. Kolingba's single-party rule brought in Ange-Félix Patasse as president. He was Bokassa's prime minister in the 1970s, but was jailed for dissent and subsequently went into exile in Paris. His party, the MPLC is the most important in the new parliament, but can govern only in coalition with others, including the PLD, the Alliance for Democracy and Progress. Balancing coalitions can be a problem in the CAR – it was the confusion of alliances in Dacko's government which led to Kolingba's coup in 1981. Serious economic problems, which have resulted in civil servants unpaid, are the major political concern.

CENTRAL AFRICAN REPUBLIC

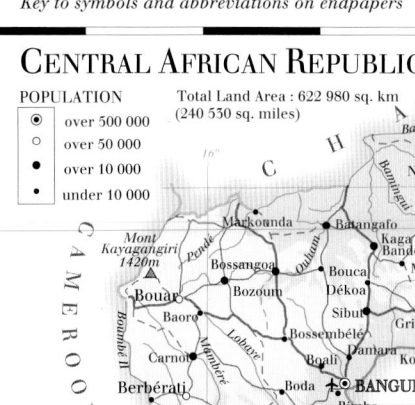

POPULATION

- ⊙ over 500 000
- ○ over 50 000
- ● over 10 000
- • under 10 000

Total Land Area : 622 980 sq. km
(240 550 sq. miles)

LAND HEIGHT

- 1000m/3281ft
- 500m/1640ft
- 200m/656ft

ECONOMICS

$1.2bn

489.05–533.68 CFA francs

SCORE CARD

- ❏ WORLD GNP RANKING.......................151st
- ❏ GNP PER CAPITA $370
- ❏ BALANCE OF PAYMENTS.....................$–25m
- ❏ INFLATION 24.5%
- ❏ UNEMPLOYMENT..................................30%

STRENGTHS

Self-sufficiency in food. Some diversity of export earnings (iron, cotton, timber, diamonds, coffee). Transit zone in central Africa. Trans-African Highway and waterways.

WEAKNESSES

Landlocked. Poor infrastructure. Not enough trained people to run economy.

EXPORTS

- Sudan 2%
- Spain 2%
- Switzerland 4%
- Other 5%
- Belgium-Luxembourg 52%
- France 35%

IMPORTS

- Zaire 4%
- Germany 5%
- Japan 8%
- Cameroon 9%
- France 43%
- Other 31%

RESOURCES

96m kwh (capacity 43,000 kw)

Not an oil producer and has no refineries

2.8m cattle, 1.3m goats, 480,000 pigs

Diamonds, gold, uranium, iron, copper, manganese

Cotton is one of the few major exports, but mineral resources are of potential importance.

ENVIRONMENT

10% (4% partially protected)

Unplanned devastation of tropical rainforest

There has been an attempt to impose a conservationist forest policy. Hunting of elephants was banned only in 1985; numbers fell from 80,000 in the mid-1970s to 13,000 in 1987.

MEDIA

Although an opposition press has developed, censorship can still be imposed

PUBLISHING AND BROADCAST MEDIA

There is 1 daily newspaper, *E Le Songo*

1 state-owned service

1 state-owned service

An opposition press has developed with multipartyism, but is inhibited by lack of resources and journalists. The Catholic Church maintained some independent media under Bokassa.

CRIME

CAR does not publish prison figures

Down 48% in 1989

Human rights abuses have decreased drastically since the excesses of the Bokassa years. The level of criminality is low and increasing urban robbery is regarded as the chief problem. The Muslims form too small a minority to influence the French-style legal system.

***Baskets of cotton**, Meme village. Cotton is one of the Central African Republic's most significant export crops.*

The French established the colony of Ubangi-Shari in 1905 and gave it autonomy as the CAR in 1958.

- ❏ **1960** Independence under David Dacko; sets up one-party state.
- ❏ **1965** Coup by Jean-Bédel Bokassa.
- ❏ **1976** Sets up Empire. In 1977, one quarter of GDP spent on coronation.
- ❏ **1979** French help reinstate Dacko.
- ❏ **1981** Gen. Kolingba ousts Dacko.
- ❏ **1990** Major pro-democracy riots.
- ❏ **1993** First multiparty elections.

EDUCATION

 38%

 3482 students

Schooling, on the French model, is compulsory, but in practice is only received by 68% of 6–14 year olds.

HEALTH

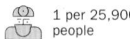 1 per 25,900 people

 Communicable and parasitic diseases, malnutrition

Colonial neglect and post-colonial maladministration have resulted in a poorly developed health system.

WEALTH

 Bricklayer, 35,000 CFA francs (US$72) per month; physiotherapist, 82,000 CFA francs (US$168) per month

CONSUMER GOODS OWNERSHIP

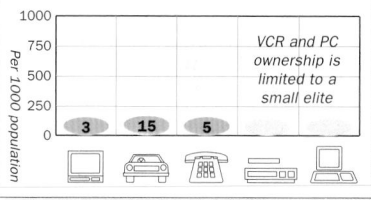

VCR and PC ownership is limited to a small elite

- 3
- 15
- 5

For the politico-military elite, which only arose after colonial days, Paris is the choice destination and style leader.

WORLD RANKING

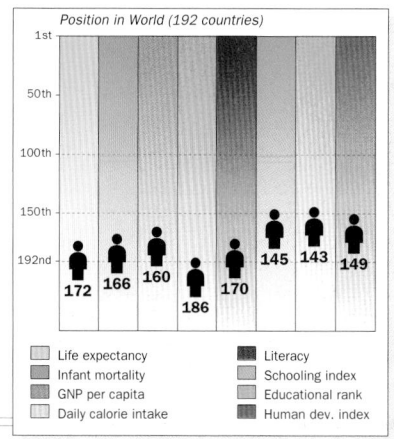

Position in World (192 countries)

- 172
- 166
- 160
- 186
- 170
- 145
- 143
- 149

- Life expectancy
- Infant mortality
- GNP per capita
- Daily calorie intake
- Literacy
- Schooling index
- Educational rank
- Human dev. index

C

CHAD

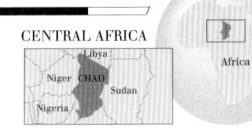

CENTRAL AFRICA

OFFICIAL NAME: Republic of Chad **CAPITAL:** N'Djamena **POPULATION:** 6.4 million
CURRENCY: CFA franc **OFFICIAL LANGUAGE:** French

 1960

LANDLOCKED IN NORTH central Africa, Chad has had a turbulent history since independence from France in 1960. Intermittent periods of civil war involving French and Libyan troops followed a military coup in 1975. In 1990, a transitional government was established to oversee the change to multipartyism. Chad remains one of the poorest countries in Africa. The tropical, cotton-producing south is the most populous region. The north is semi-arid desert.

CLIMATE

WEATHER CHART

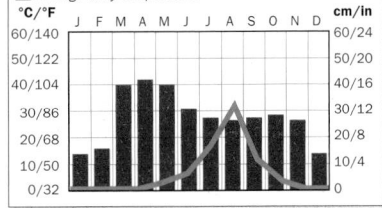

There are three distinct zones: the tropical south, the central semi-arid Sahelian belt and the desert north.

TRANSPORTATION

 **N'Djamena International** 7760 passengers 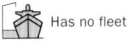 Has no fleet

THE TRANSPORTATION NETWORK

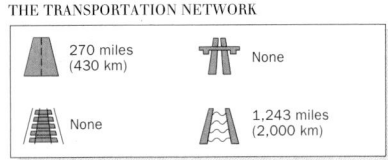

270 miles (430 km)	None
None	1,243 miles (2,000 km)

Chad has a limited transportation infrastructure. The nearest rail links are in Nigeria and Cameroon.

TOURISM

 22,000 visitors  Up 5% in 1994

MAIN OVERSEAS ARRIVALS

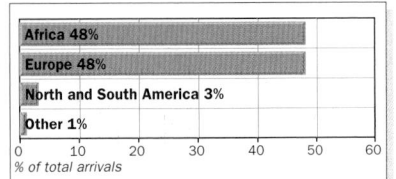

Africa 48%	
Europe 48%	
North and South America 3%	
Other 1%	

% of total arrivals
0 10 20 30 40 50 60

Tourism is now virtually non-existent. The national parks and game reserves are the main potential attractions. The prehistoric rock painting of the Tibesti plateau and the Muslim cities of central Chad attract the adventurous.

Watering hole at Oum Hadjer, a village on the Batha watercourse in central Chad, 90 miles east of Ati.

PEOPLE

 French, Sara, Arabic, Maba 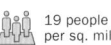 19 people per sq. mile

THE URBAN/RURAL POPULATION SPLIT

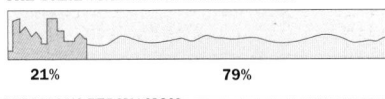

21%   79%

RELIGIOUS PERSUASION

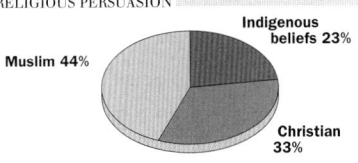

Muslim 44%

Indigenous beliefs 23%

Christian 33%

About half the population, mainly the Sara-speaking and related peoples, is concentrated in the south in one-fifth of the national territory. Most of the rest are located in the central sultanates. The northern third of Chad has a population of only 100,000 people, mainly nomadic Muslim Toubeu.

CHAD

Total Land Area : 1 259 200 sq. km (486 177 sq. miles)

POPULATION

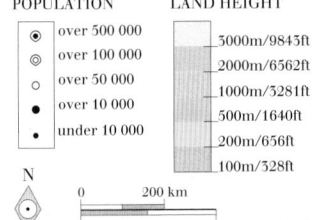

- ◉ over 500 000
- ◎ over 100 000
- ○ over 50 000
- ● over 10 000
- • under 10 000

LAND HEIGHT

3000m/9843ft
2000m/6562ft
1000m/3281ft
500m/1640ft
200m/656ft
100m/328ft

N

0   200 km

0   200 miles

POLITICS

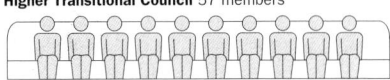

1996   President Idriss Deby

THE STATE OF THE PARTIES

Higher Transitional Council 57 members

Multiparty elections are scheduled for 1996

Following an invasion from Sudan, where he had been in exile since a previous coup attempt, Idriss Deby overthrew President Hissène Habré in 1990. He promised to bring multipartyism to Chad, and legalized political parties in 1992, the first time they had been allowed since the 1960s. However, this transition has been subject to delays. Instability has prevented progress on the drawing up of the constitution and the holding of presidential and parliamentary elections. Some opponents question whether President Deby and his backers, the Zaghawa tribesmen, want to give up power at all. Meanwhile, the government has sought to restore peace by making agreements with several rebel groups. However, some armed groups continue to operate.

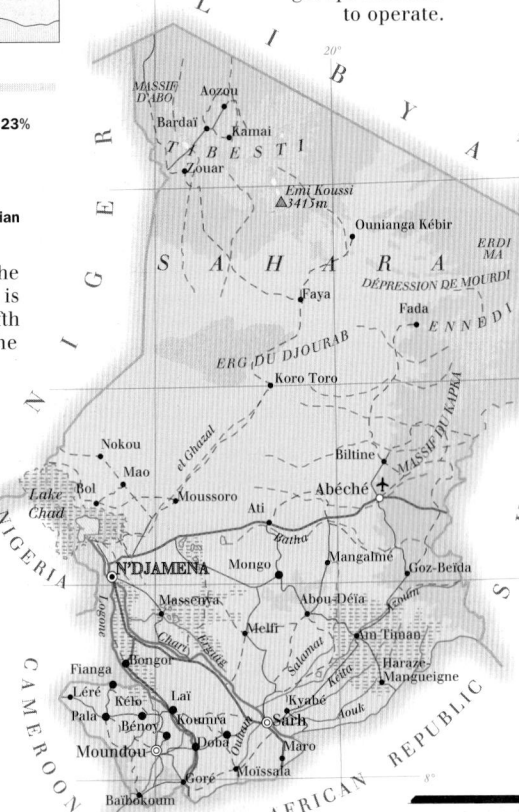

WORLD AFFAIRS

Chad has to balance relations with France and Libya, both of whom have been important influences.

AID

 $229m (receipts)　 Down 8% in 1993

France is by far the major donor. Other sources include Libya, the EU, USA, IMF and Arab funds, especially OPEC. Without assistance to cover civil servants' pay over recent years, the administration would have collapsed.

DEFENSE

 $26m　 Down 16% in 1995

On seizing power, Deby swelled the army with irregulars. This has now been reversed and the army reduced to 25,000. Former rebels are now integrated into the national army. France provides military aid and personnel.

ECONOMICS

 $1.2bn　 489.05–533.68 CFA francs

SCORE CARD

- ❏ WORLD GNP RANKING 152nd
- ❏ GNP PER CAPITA $190
- ❏ BALANCE OF PAYMENTS....................$–117m
- ❏ INFLATION 40.8%
- ❏ UNEMPLOYMENT......Widespread underemployment

STRENGTHS
Revenues from recent discovery of large oil deposits could transform Chad's poor financial position. Cotton industry; potential for other agriculture in south. Strategic trading location in heart of Africa.

WEAKNESSES
Underdevelopment and poverty. Lack of transportation infrastructure an obstacle to development. Frequent droughts.

EXPORTS

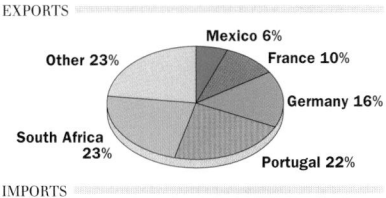

Mexico 6%, France 10%, Germany 16%, Portugal 22%, South Africa 23%, Other 23%

IMPORTS

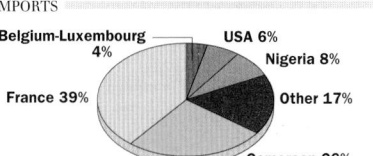

Belgium-Luxembourg 4%, USA 6%, Nigeria 8%, Other 17%, Cameroon 26%, France 39%

RESOURCES

 85m kwh (capacity 31,000 kw)

 Not an oil producer and has no refineries

 4.6m cattle, 3.2m goats, 2.2m sheep

 Natron, uranium, oil, kaolin, soda, rock salt

A consortium of ESSO, Shell and ELF has discovered large oil reserves in the south, mostly near Doba, which could make Chad a major African producer. Natron, found north of Lake Chad, is the only mineral currently exploited. Uranium exists in the Aozou strip.

ENVIRONMENT

 9%　 Transitional government has appointed environment ministry

The worst single environmental crisis Chad has had to face in recent years was the drought of 1983, which coincided with intensified fighting in the civil war. In a significant policy reversal, the transitional government regards the preservation of the environment as a political priority and has established an environment ministry.

MEDIA

 The government claims to support press freedom, but interference in editorial decisions has been reported

PUBLISHING AND BROADCAST MEDIA

 There is 1 daily newspaper, *Info-Tchad*, a daily bulletin produced by the government news agency

 1 state-owned service　 1 state-owned service

Since Deby came to power, the press has opened up and a number of outspoken independent publications have appeared. The best known is the weekly *N'Djamena-Hebdo*, produced by Saleh Kebzabo, a well-known journalist who was briefly a member of the transitional government.

CRIME

 Chad does not publish prison figures　 Crime is rising

Armed robbery and vandalism are problems, as well as traditional crimes such as smuggling. In N'Djamena and the south, the activities of a bandit group known as *les enturbannés*, "the turbanned ones," from President Deby's army, are widely feared.

EDUCATION

 45%　 2983 students

Education is based on the French model, although there are Koranic schools in the north. Recently, World Bank aid has been directed at elementary schooling. The literacy rate is among the lowest in Africa.

CHRONOLOGY

Chad gradually came under Arab domination. The French overthrew the last Arab ruler in 1900.

- ❏ **1960** Independence. N'Garta Tombalbaye's one-party state.
- ❏ **1966** Northern-based rebels start Libyan-backed insurgency.
- ❏ **1973** Libyans invade Aozou strip.
- ❏ **1975** Coup. Gen. Malloum comes to power. Receives French support.
- ❏ **1979–1982** Civil war between Christian south and Muslim north.
- ❏ **1980** Goukouni Weddeye in power.
- ❏ **1982** Hissène Habré (northerner) defeats Goukouni. France transfers military support to Habré.
- ❏ **1990** Idriss Deby invades from exile in Sudan. Defeats Habré.
- ❏ **1994** Libya gives up Aozou strip.

HEALTH

 1 per 29,410 people　 Diarrheal, parasitic and communicable diseases

There are few city hospitals and less than 300 smaller health centers; half are run by religious groups or charities.

WEALTH

 Butcher, 17,571 CFA francs ($36) per month; central government official, 76,487 CFA francs ($156) per month.

CONSUMER GOODS OWNERSHIP

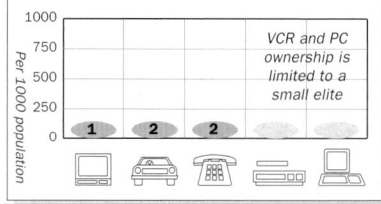

VCR and PC ownership is limited to a small elite

Poverty is almost universal; the middle class is very small. Individuals have been known to achieve wealth – Habré looted the treasury when he left power.

WORLD RANKING

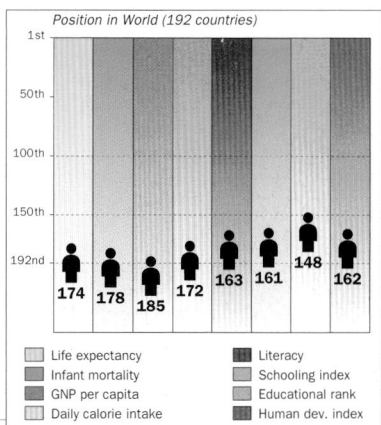

Position in World (192 countries)

Life expectancy 174, Infant mortality 178, GNP per capita 185, Daily calorie intake 172, Literacy 163, Schooling index 161, Educational rank 148, Human dev. index 162

CHILE

SOUTH AMERICA

OFFICIAL NAME: Republic of Chile **CAPITAL:** Santiago
POPULATION: 14.3 million **CURRENCY:** Chilean peso **OFFICIAL LANGUAGE:** Spanish

   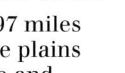

CHILE EXTENDS IN A NARROW RIBBON 2,697 miles down the Pacific coast of South America. The plains of the central pampa lie between a coastal range and the Andes; most of the population lives in the fertile heartland around Santiago. Glaciers are a prominent feature of the southern Andes, as are fjords, lakes and deep sea channels. In 1989, Chile returned to elected civilian rule, following a popular rejection of the Pinochet dictatorship. Today, the world's largest copper producer is enjoying economic growth which has averaged 5% a year.

General Pinochet, *a dictatorial president rejected by popular referendum in 1988.*

President Eduardo Frei. *He took office following elections in 1993.*

CLIMATE

WEATHER CHART

Chile has an immensely varied climate. The north, which includes the world's driest desert, the Atacama, is frequently cloudy and cool for its latitude. The central regions have an almost Mediterranean climate, with changeable winters and hot, dry summers. The higher reaches of the Andes have a typically alpine climate, with glaciers and year-round snow The south is the wettest region.

TRANSPORTATION

Comodoro Arturo Merino Benítez, Santiago
1.95m passengers

51 ships
735,900 dwt

THE TRANSPORTATION NETWORK

7,690 miles (12,370 km)

Pan-American Highway 2,146 miles (3,455 km)

5,086 miles (8,185 km)

451 miles (725 km)

Chile's unusual shape, 2,697 miles long and nowhere more than 112 miles wide, makes air travel indispensable. Internal air routes are well developed; some, including flights to the Juan Fernández Islands, are served by air taxis. The Pan-American Highway is Chile's only arterial road, crossing the Peruvian border and running down, via the capital Santiago, to Puerto Montt. Santiago is notorious in Latin America for its severe congestion. The launch of the first Chilean-made communications satellite is scheduled for 1996.

TOURISM

 1.6m visitors

 Up 15% in 1994

MAIN OVERSEAS ARRIVALS

Argentina 51%
Peru 10%
USA 7%
Bolivia 6%
Brazil 6%
Other 20%

% of total arrivals

The Pinochet years saw a dramatic decline in tourists from the USA and Western Europe. The number of visitors from neighboring Latin American states remained fairly constant; South Americans with a closer knowledge of Chile's political culture were aware that much of the violence was state-directed and aimed at Chileans, not tourists. Since 1988, tourists have returned and Chile has been making more of its stunning Andean scenery, its immensely long coastline and a number of exceptional sites, including Chuquicamata, the world's largest copper mine, the Elqui Valley wine-growing region, and the spectacular glaciers and fjords of southern Chile. Easter Island in the Pacific is another major attraction.

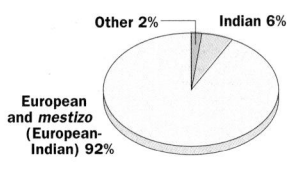

Peaks in the Paine range, southern Chile. *Fjords, glaciers and a myriad islands typify Chile's very wet, wild and stormy south.*

PEOPLE

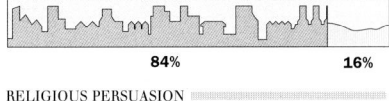

Spanish, Indian languages

49 people per sq. mile

THE URBAN/RURAL POPULATION SPLIT

84%   16%

RELIGIOUS PERSUASION

Protestant 11%
Roman Catholic 89%

ETHNIC MAKEUP

Other 2%   Indian 6%
European and *mestizo* (European-Indian) 92%

Chile is highly urbanized, with 86% of the population living in towns. Most people are of mixed Spanish-Indian descent. The estimated 800,000 Mapuche Indians live almost exclusively in the south. Santiago is home to one-third of the population. Large slum areas known as *callampas*, or mushrooms, have grown up around Santiago, and water and air pollution are major problems. Many Chileans, especially those in small enterprises, live on subsistence wages. Over 25% of working women are employed in domestic service.

POPULATION AGE BREAKDOWN

% of population by age group	☐ 0–14	☐ 15–64	☐ 65+		
	4.3%	4.7%	5.1%	5.6%	6%
	58.9%	55.9%	55.8%	61%	63.4%
	36.8%	39.4%	39.1%	33.4%	30.6%
	1950	1960	1970	1980	1990

Juan Fernández Is

I. Alejandro Selkirk
San Juan Bautista
I. Robinson Crusoe

0   100 km
0   100 miles

Easter I.

Terevaka

Hanga Roa

0   10 km
0   10 miles

CHILE

Total Land Area :
748 800 sq. km
(289 112 sq. miles)

POPULATION

over 1 000 000	▣
over 100 000	◎
over 50 000	○
over 10 000	●
under 10 000	●

LAND HEIGHT

4000m/13124ft	
2000m/6562ft	
1000m/3281ft	
200m/656ft	
Sea Level	

N

0   300 km
0   300 miles

POLITICS

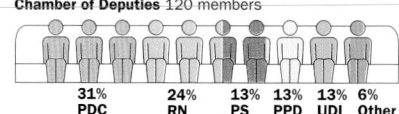

U. House 1993/1997
L. House 1993/1997

President Eduardo
Frei Ruiz-Tagle

THE STATE OF THE PARTIES

Chamber of Deputies 120 members

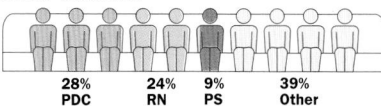

31%	24%	13%	13%	13%	6%
PDC	RN	PS	PPD	UDI	Other

PDC = Christian Democratic Party **RN** = National Renewal
PS = Socialist Party of Chile **PPD** = Party for Democracy
UDI = Independent Democratic Union **Other** = Radical Party

Senate 46 members

28%	24%	9%	39%
PDC	RN	PS	Other

38 members elected and 8 chosen by the outgoing
government and the Supreme Court

After 12 years of military rule under
Pinochet, Chile returned to multiparty
democracy in 1989.

MAIN POLITICAL ISSUES
Human rights abuse trials

Under a compromise 1995 bill, cases
against the military would only be
reopened if plaintiffs could submit
fresh evidence. Opponents demand
the automatic reopening of 542 pending
cases, which is resisted by the army,
still headed by Pinochet. To date,
only two officers have been imprisoned
for past abuses.

Poverty

Opposition groups point out that the
promised "trickle down" effect of
Pinochet's Chicago School economic
policies has not reached Chile's poor.
Many believe that the present Frei
administration cannot deliver improved
conditions for the poor and maintain
Pinochet's economic policies.

PROFILE

In 1988, Chile voted for political
change, effectively rejecting the system
instituted by the military dictator,
Pinochet, for a return to Chile's
once-strong democratic traditions.

Pinochet seized power in a chaotic
situation. The socialist Allende
government had been attempting the
wholesale nationalization of the
Chilean economy. His nationalization
of the largely US-owned copper mines
led the CIA – which had a specific budget
to overthrow the democratically elected
Allende – to back the Pinochet coup.

In 1973, the military stormed the
presidential palace; it is now accepted
that Allende committed suicide during
the attack. Subsequently, thousands
of Chileans were killed by the
military, an estimated 3,000 people
"disappeared" and 80,000 political
prisoners were taken.

Pinochet's politics – largely based on
a notion of the nation-state modeled
on Franco's Spain – replaced
democratic traditions and conflict.
His economic policy reversed Allende's,
and was one of the first experiments
in the free-market Chicago School
of monetarism which was later to be
influential in the West, particularly
in the UK under Margaret Thatcher.

Although opposition to the regime
was brutally suppressed by DINA, the
secret police, it also had considerable
support – particularly among Chile's
business and middle classes, which
prospered. Opposition came from the
Church, an embarrassment to
Pinochet, who saw himself as a
champion of Catholicism, and the
urban poor.

In 1988, Pinochet, seeking popular
legitimacy, held a plebiscite which,
given the military's control over the
country, he expected to win. Contrary
to his expectations, the vote turned
not on his economic record but on
whether Chile wished to continue
living under a military dictatorship.
On a turnout of 93%, 55% voted for
democracy and 43% for the *status
quo*. Pinochet stepped down, but
remained head of the army. Patricio
Aylwin won the presidential elections
held in 1989.

During Aylwin's presidency, Chilean
politics became more stable, in part
the result of a cross-party consensus
on economic policy. The economy
continued to grow and social measures,
which marginally increased protection
for workers, gave Aylwin the support
of the trade unions.

In elections at the end of 1993,
Eduardo Frei of the PDC was elected
president. He has continued the free-
market economic and social policies
of his predecessor, and is governing
a broad coalition of center-left parties.
The armed forces, however, retain a
strong role in politics. They, not the
president, appoint their own chief.

CHRONOLOGY

The Spanish first attempted the
conquest of Chile against the fierce
indigenous Araucanian people in
1535. Santiago was founded in 1541.
Chile was subject to Spanish rule
until independence in 1818.

❏ **1817–1818** Bernardo O'Higgins
leads the republican Army of the
Andes in victories against royalist
forces at the battles of Chacabuco
and Maipú.

❏ **1879–1883** War of the Pacific with
Bolivia and Peru. Chile gains
valuable nitrate regions. ⇨

CHRONOLOGY *continued*

- ❏ **1891–1924** Parliamentary republic ends with growing political chaos.
- ❏ **1936–1946** Communist, Radical and Socialist parties form influential Popular Front coalition.
- ❏ **1943** Chile backs USA in World War II.
- ❏ **1946–1964** Right-wing Chilean presidents follow US McCarthy policy and marginalize the left.
- ❏ **1964–1970** Social reforms of PDC government alienate the right.
- ❏ **1970** Salvador Allende elected. Reforms provoke strong reaction from the right.
- ❏ **1973** Allende dies in military coup. Brutal dictatorship of Gen. Pinochet continues as president.
- ❏ **1988** Referendum votes "no" to Pinochet continuing as president.
- ❏ **1989** Democracy peacefully restored; Pinochet steps down after Aylwin election victory.
- ❏ **1995** First military officers jailed for human rights abuses.

WORLD AFFAIRS

Chile's most important relationship remains with its main trading partner, the USA, which supplies 95% of materials for the critical copper industry. The relationship has not always been easy. Under Allende, the USA actively worked against the government, fearing that the spread of socialism would jeopardize its investments in Chile and the rest of Latin America. Pinochet's human rights record eventually became an embarrassment to the Reagan administration, which qualified its backing for him. Present relations are good; the Frei government concurs with US economic and regional policy in Latin America.

A territorial dispute with Argentina over islands in the Beagle Channel, which almost led to war in 1978, was finally settled in 1984 with Vatican mediation. Chile was awarded 12 islands including Picton, Nueva and Lennox. International arbitration settled ownership of the Laguna del Desierto region in October 1995. Border disputes continue with Bolivia and Peru.

AID

 $184m (receipts)    Up 34% in 1993

The majority of aid is in the form of debts rescheduled by the World Bank at the instigation of the USA.

DEFENSE

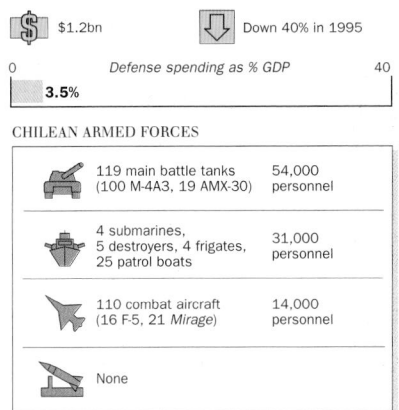

💲 $1.2bn   ⬇ Down 40% in 1995

0   *Defense spending as % GDP*   40
3.5%

CHILEAN ARMED FORCES

🛡	119 main battle tanks (100 M-4A3, 19 AMX-30)	54,000 personnel
⚓	4 submarines, 5 destroyers, 4 frigates, 25 patrol boats	31,000 personnel
✈	110 combat aircraft (16 F-5, 21 *Mirage*)	14,000 personnel
	None	

The military, and in particular the army, enjoyed preferential treatment under Pinochet. Its success in taking power in 1973 was a reflection of its cohesive command structure rather than of any right-wing ideological conviction. Pinochet exercised enormous influence in his position as commander-in-chief, but during his period in office worked with civilian rather than military advisers. The army's considerable influence is demonstrated by the failure of the Aylwin and Frei administrations to press human rights charges over atrocities committed during the Pinochet years. Much of its equipment is supplied by Chile's own CARDOENS munitions factories.

ECONOMICS

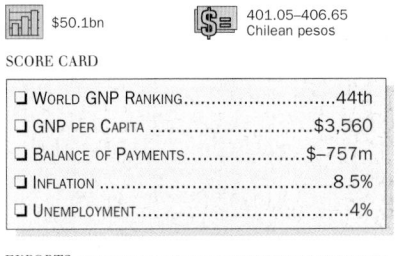

📊 $50.1bn   💲 401.05–406.65 Chilean pesos

SCORE CARD

- ❏ WORLD GNP RANKING............................44th
- ❏ GNP PER CAPITA $3,560
- ❏ BALANCE OF PAYMENTS......................$–757m
- ❏ INFLATION 8.5%
- ❏ UNEMPLOYMENT.......................................4%

EXPORTS

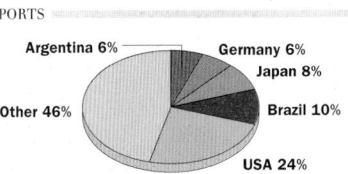

Germany 5%   UK 5%
Argentina 7%
Other 50%   USA 16%
Japan 17%

IMPORTS

Argentina 6%   Germany 6%
Japan 8%
Other 46%   Brazil 10%
USA 24%

STRENGTHS

The world's biggest copper producer. Political stability and free-market policies of the Aylwin government led to a massive inflow of investment, which has kept the economy growing at 5% a year since 1991. Continuing sell-off of the state sector – ruthlessly cut by Pinochet to leave it small and efficient – will attract further investment.

WEAKNESSES

Dependence on the USA as its largest single trading partner makes Chile vulnerable to changes in US trade policy. Copper revenues are vulnerable to shifts in world market prices.

PROFILE

Chile's economy has been a battle-ground for competing ideologies. Under Allende, socialist policies brought huge

ECONOMIC PERFORMANCE INDICATOR

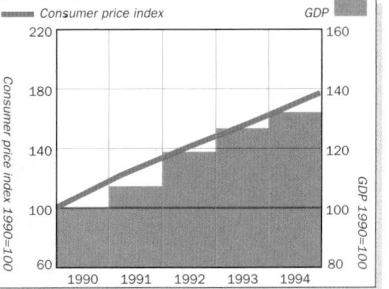

corporations into the state sector. The Pinochet dictatorship which overthrew him introduced radical monetarist policies. Drastic cutting of the state sector and the selling-off of state enterprises at below market value led to large profits for investors and speculators. Tough economic measures, irrespective of the social consequences, reduced Chile's inflation rate from 400% to 15%.

The Aylwin and Frei governments have continued the market-led approach to the economy with some success. In particular, exports are continuing to rise, helping to finance the capital goods imports which are vital to the modernization of Chile's industrial sector.

CHILE : MAJOR BUSINESSES

- 🛢 Oil
- 🛢 Oil refining
- ⛏ Copper mining
- 🏭 Manufacturing
- 💊 Pharmaceuticals
- ⚙ Heavy engineering
- 🐟 Fish processing
- 🌾 Agribusiness

Iquique
Chuquicamata
Vina del Mar ⚙
Santiago 🌾⚙💊⚙
Teniente ⛏
Talcahuano 🐟⚙
Concepción 🌾🛢
Punta Arenas 🛢
Straits of Magellan

0   300 km
0   300 miles

RESOURCES

22.4bn kwh
(capacity 4.1m kw)

14,697 b/d
(reserves
300,000,000 bbl)

4.6m sheep, 3.7m
cattle, 1.4m pigs,
600,000 goats

Coal, copper,
gold, silver, iron,
molybdenum, iodine

ELECTRICITY GENERATION

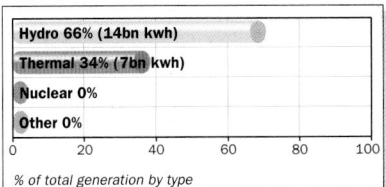

Hydro 66% (14bn kwh)
Thermal 34% (7bn kwh)
Nuclear 0%
Other 0%

% of total generation by type

Chile is the world's most
important copper producer.
The state-owned industry
was established in 1968 as a
joint venture with US
companies, but was fully
nationalized under
Allende. It accounts for
35% of Chile's GNP. New
investments in gold mining
will bring Chile into the
world's top ten producers.
It also leads the world in
fishmeal production and
has a flourishing
wine industry.

CHILE : LAND USE

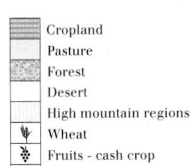

Cropland
Pasture
Forest
Desert
High mountain regions
Wheat
Fruits - cash crop
Sheep

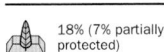
0　　500 km

0　　300 miles

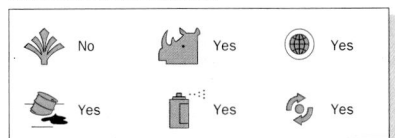

ENVIRONMENT

18% (7% partially
protected)

Felling of endangered
araucaria pines
recently banned

ENVIRONMENTAL TREATIES

No
Yes
Yes

Yes
Yes
Yes

Environmental concerns do not rank
highly on the political agenda.
Pinochet's constitution enshrined
the right to live in a pollution-free
environment, but bad smogs still cover
Santiago, due in part to diesel fumes
from the city's 14,500 buses. The chief
concern is logging in the south by
Japanese and other foreign companies.
The huge growth of the salmon
industry, which fences off sea lakes,
is resulting in dolphins losing their
natural habitats.

MEDIA

Many of the army's powers over the press imposed
during the Pinochet regime have yet to be repealed

PUBLISHING AND BROADCAST MEDIA

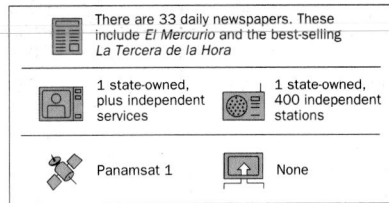

There are 33 daily newspapers. These
include *El Mercurio* and the best-selling
La Tercera de la Hora

1 state-owned,
plus independent
services

1 state-owned,
400 independent
stations

Panamsat 1

None

The media was brutally controlled by
Pinochet; journalists "disappeared" in
the early years of the regime. They are
now relatively free, but journalists can
still be tried under military justice for
slander or abuse of the armed forces.

CRIME

2,176 prisoners

Down 16% in 1992

CRIME RATES

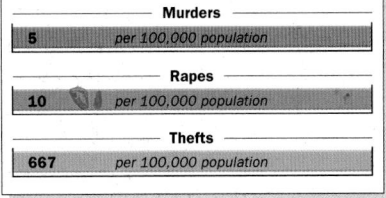

Murders
5　　per 100,000 population

Rapes
10　　per 100,000 population

Thefts
667　　per 100,000 population

The judiciary is still not independent and
is not pursuing the human rights cases
from the Pinochet regime, in spite of the
discovery in 1991 of the mass graves of
victims of the DINA (secret police).
Mapuche leaders were among those
who "disappeared."

EDUCATION

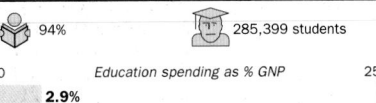
94%　　　　　285,399 students

0　　Education spending as % GNP　　25
2.9%

THE EDUCATION SYSTEM

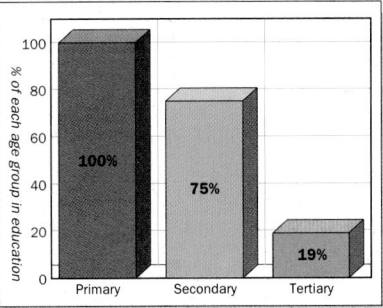

% of each age group in education

100%　Primary
75%　Secondary
19%　Tertiary

Recent years have seen many new
private universities operating for profit
and offering vocational courses.
Environmental issues and human rights
now appear on school curricula.

HEALTH

1 per 2,150 people

Heart diseases,
cancers, crime,
accidents

0　　Health spending as % GDP　　25
3.4%

The public health service covers
80% of the population, but medical
personnel are mostly concentrated in
urban areas. Pollution in Santiago
is so bad that it is noticeably affecting
its inhabitants' health.

WEALTH

Live-in maid, 80,000 Chilean pesos ($197) per
month; company secretary, 1m Chilean pesos
($2,460) per month

CONSUMER GOODS OWNERSHIP

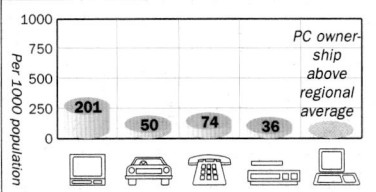

Per 1000 population

PC owner-
ship
above
regional
average

201　50　74　36

Chile's traditionally large middle
class did well under Pinochet and the
economic policies of the Chicago
School. The wealthiest sections
benefited considerably from the sale
of state assets at 40% to 50% of their
true market value. Five years into the
regime, wealth had become highly
concentrated, with just nine economic
conglomerates controlling the assets of
the top 250 businesses, 82% of banking
and 64% of all financial loans. The
regime's artificially high domestic
interest rates enabled those with access
to international finance to earn an
estimated $800 million between 1977
and 1980, simply by borrowing abroad
and lending at home. These groups
have retained their position.

The poor, by contrast, are 15% worse
off than in 1970, with an estimated four
million living just above the UN poverty
line and one million below it.

WORLD RANKING

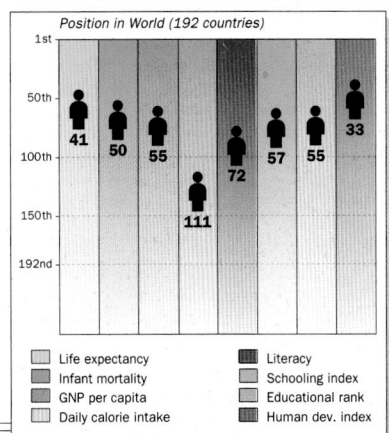

Position in World (192 countries)

41　50　55　72　111　57　55　33

Life expectancy
Infant mortality
GNP per capita
Daily calorie intake

Literacy
Schooling index
Educational rank
Human dev. index

C

CHINA

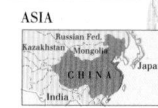
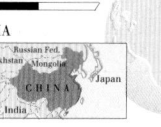

OFFICIAL NAME: People's Republic of China CAPITAL: Beijing
POPULATION: 1.2 billion CURRENCY: Yuan OFFICIAL LANGUAGE: Mandarin

C

COVERING A VAST AREA of eastern Asia, China is bordered by 14 countries; to the east it has a long Pacific coastline. Two-thirds of China is uplands. The southwestern mountains include the Tibetan Plateau. In the northwest, the Tien Shan Mountains separate the Tarim and Dzungarian basins. The low-lying east is home to two-thirds of the population. From the founding of the Communist People's Republic in 1949, until his death in 1976, China was dominated by Mao Zedong. Under Mao, China became an industrial and nuclear power, but also experienced the disasters of the 1950s Great Leap Forward and the 1960s Cultural Revolution. Today, China is rapidly moving toward a market-orientated economy. However, as the 1989 Tiananmen Square massacre tragically underlined, political reform is not on the agenda of China's aging leadership.

Li River, Guangxi, *China's most beautiful region. Its spectacular scenery has encouraged large-scale tourist development.*

CLIMATE

WEATHER CHART

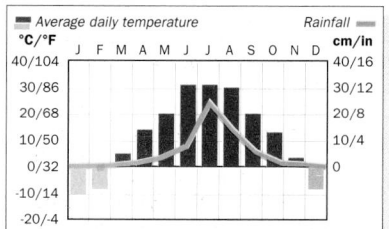

China is divided into two main climatic regions. The north and west are semi-arid or arid, with extreme temperature variations. The south and southeast are warmer and more humid, with year-round rainfall.

Winter temperatures vary with latitude and are warmest on the subtropical southeast coast, where they average about 60°F. Summer temperatures are more uniform, rising above 70°F throughout China. On the southeast coast, the July average is about 86°F. In the north and west, temperate summers contrast with harsh winters. In northern Manchuria, rivers freeze for five months and temperatures can fall to –13°F. In the deserts of Xinjiang province, temperatures range from –12°F in winter to 90°F in summer.

Summer and autumn are China's wettest seasons. Only the south and east have wet winters. The winter monsoon, which brings cold, dry air from Siberia, affects the rest of China. Moisture-laden winds from the Pacific during the summer monsoon bring rains to most of the country.

Droughts and floods are frequent. The 1960–1962 drought contributed to the famine which killed millions during the Great Leap Forward.

CHINA

Total Land Area : 9 326 410 sq. km
(3 600 927 sq. miles)

POPULATION

- ■ over 5 000 000
- ▣ over 1 000 000
- ◉ over 500 000
- ◎ over 100 000
- ○ over 50 000
- ● over 10 000

⎍⎍⎍ Great Wall of China

LAND HEIGHT

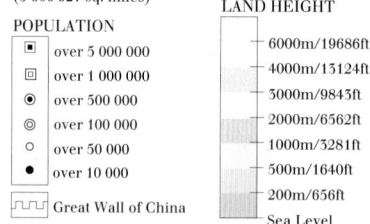

- 6000m/19686ft
- 4000m/13124ft
- 3000m/9843ft
- 2000m/6562ft
- 1000m/3281ft
- 500m/1640ft
- 200m/656ft
- Sea Level

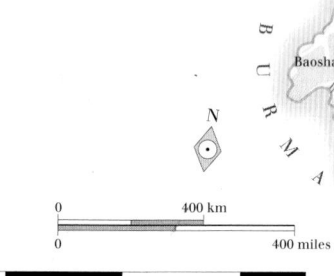

TOURISM

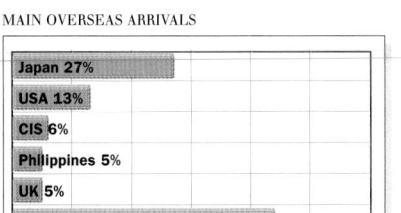

21.7m visitors   Up 111% in 1994

MAIN OVERSEAS ARRIVALS

Japan 27%	
USA 13%	
CIS 6%	
Philippines 5%	
UK 5%	
Other 44%	

% of total arrivals

Most visitors to China are overseas Chinese or business travelers, but an increasing number of tourists are also coming. The easing of restrictions since the 1980s has led to the rapid growth of all kinds of tourism, from luxury tours to back-packing. Most of China is now open to visitors. The Great Wall, the Forbidden City in Beijing and the terracotta warriors at Xi'an remain among the top attractions. The Chinese government has also begun to open up Tibet to tourists. Hong Kong is a major entry point for many visitors.

TRANSPORTATION

 Capital International Central, Beijing   1,577 ships 20.41m dwt

THE TRANSPORTATION NETWORK

575,700 miles (926,460 km)		None	
33,554 miles (54,000 km)		68,226 miles (109,800 km)	

Roads and railroads have been extended since 1949 to provide a basic national network. The aim now is to modernize and expand the transportation system to support the push for economic growth. Additions to the railroad system – all provinces but Tibet are connected to the system – have been concentrated in the west. However, the railroads, especially in the east, are still badly congested. Under the Ninth Five-Year Plan (1996–2000), 5,033 miles of new lines will be built, boosting the total railroad network to over 38,525 miles. Projected 1996 investment in the eastern region is $509 million to speed up construction.

Shanghai handled 1.5 million containers in 1995, one-third of the total handled by upgraded Chinese ports. Container shipping is increasing by 30% annually. Hong Kong has the best natural harbor and handles 40% of China's exports. The inland waterway system, which fell into a state of disrepair, is now being upgraded. Water transportation now accounts for about 33% of internal freight traffic. The Chang Jiang is navigable by ships of over 1,000 tons for more than 600 miles from the coast.

Many small airlines have sprung up since the state monopoly was ended in 1988. Air transportation is growing rapidly, like private car ownership, as wealth increases. However, the bicycle is still the ubiquitous mode of personal transportation in China.

Li River Valley. *Irrigation helps Chinese farmers to feed 20% of the world's people, using only 7% of the world's farmland.*

C

[map of China with labeled regions and cities: RUSSIAN FEDERATION, MANCHURIA, HEILONGJIANG, JILIN, LIAONING, NORTH KOREA, MONGOLIA, HEBEI, BEIJING (PEKING), Tianjin, SHANXI, SHANDONG, SHAANXI, GANSU, NINGXIA, HENAN, JIANGSU, ANHUI, HUBEI, ZHEJIANG, JIANGXI, HUNAN, GUIZHOU, FUJIAN, GUANGXI, GUANGDONG, HAINAN, VIETNAM, TAIWAN, and other cities and geographic features]

163

C

PEOPLE

 Mandarin, Wu, Cantonese, Hsiang, Min, Hakka, Kan

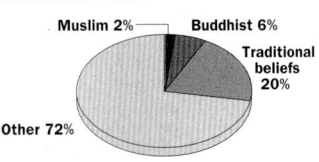 340 people per sq. mile

THE URBAN/RURAL POPULATION SPLIT

28%   72%

RELIGIOUS PERSUASION

Muslim 2%   Buddhist 6%
Traditional beliefs 20%
Other 72%

ETHNIC MAKEUP

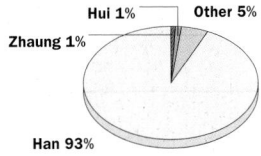

Hui 1%   Other 5%
Zhaung 1%
Han 93%

About 93% of China's population of 1.2 billion are Han Chinese. The remaining 92 million belong to one of 55 minority nationalities, or recognized ethnic groups. The minorities have disproportionate political significance because many, like the Mongolians, Tibetans, or Muslim Uygurs in Xinjiang, live in strategic border areas.

The policy of resettling Han Chinese in remote regions is deeply resented and has led to uprisings in Xinjiang and Tibet, all ruthlessly suppressed. Han Chinese are now a majority in Xinjiang and Nei Mongol Zizhiqu. Tibet, however, is gaining international support for its call for true autonomy.

The government has relaxed family planning controls for minorities, after some small groups were brought near to extinction by the one-child policy adopted in 1979. Most Han Chinese still face strict controls. Even so, the population will top 1.3 billion by 2000.

Chinese society is patriarchal in practice and several generations tend to live together. However, economic change is putting pressure on family life and breaking down the social controls of the Mao era. Divorce and unemployment are rising; materialism has replaced the puritanism of the past. A resurgence of religious belief is another response to the uncertainties of life in today's China.

POPULATION AGE BREAKDOWN

%	0–14	15–64		65+	
	4.8%	4.3%	4.7%	5.8%	7%
	56.3%	56%	59.8%	67.7%	66.4%
	38.9%	39.7%	35.5%	26.5%	26.6%
	1960	1970	1980	1990	2000

POLITICS

 1993/1998

 President Jiang Zemin

THE STATE OF THE PARTIES

National People's Congress 2938 members

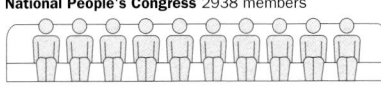

The members of the National People's Congress are elected by the provinces, municipalities and autonomous regions under the government, and by the armed forces. The Communist Party of China (CCP) has effective political control

China is a single-party state, dominated by the Communist Party (CCP), the world's largest political party. The National People's Congress, indirectly elected every five years, is theoretically the supreme organ of state power. It appoints the president and executive State Council, headed by the prime minister. The real focus of power, however, is the 22-member Politburo of the CCP and, in particular, its Standing Committee of six.

MAIN POLITICAL ISSUES
Reform and the authority of the CCP
Since the death of Mao Zedong in 1976, China has embarked on a process of economic reform which has led to divisions between reformers and conservatives within the CCP. Both sides want to secure the dominance of the party and avoid political reform. The reformers, headed by Deng Xiaoping, China's paramount leader, believe only a fast-track move to a "socialist market economy" will save the CCP. They look to South Korea and Taiwan as countries which have achieved high growth without political reform. The conservatives recognized the need for economic change, but wanted it to be slow and controlled by the center.

The pro-democracy protests of 1989, culminating in the Tiananmen Square massacre, enabled the conservatives under premier Li Peng to gain the upper hand for a while. Deng moved to restore the balance and his longevity has shifted the balance toward his heir apparent, President Jiang Zemin. Economic reform poses a real threat to the CCP's authority. The 22 provinces, particularly those in the southeast, are acting increasingly independently of

Nanjing Donglu (Nanking Road), *in central Shanghai, is one of China's most famous shopping streets. With a population of nearly eight million, Shanghai is China's largest city.*

Beijing. At a popular level, party authority is being challenged by growing rural discontent over widening wealth differentials.

The succession
The powerful governors of Guandong and Sichuan provinces have been replaced by supporters of Deng Xiaoping's heir apparent President Jiang Zemin, who in 1996 also promoted four army generals in an attempt to boost his standing with the military. Jiang, by attacking corruption and cultivating the military, has attempted to assert his own power base but premier Li Peng remains a powerful rival for the leadership. No formal structure for the transfer of power exists and who eventually comes to the fore will depend on the outcome of complex power brokering.

PROFILE
Politics is dominated by the last of the "Immortals" who took part with Mao Zedong in the 1934–1935 Long March. Deng Xiaoping, the architect of China's economic reforms and its paramount leader, has outlived myriad forecasts of his imminent death, but in everyday politics the post-Deng era has begun. He was the most prominent of the Immortals, but has worked hard behind the scenes forming alliances to promote his reformist ideas and followers. The succession and the effects of economic change are a challenge to the 52-million-strong CCP, but it faces no real opposition as yet.

Deng Xiaoping, *China's paramount leader, although he holds no official post.*

Jiang Zemin, CCP *leader and China's president since Deng resigned the post.*

Premier Li Peng, *urging economic reform, but keeping conservative values.*

Zhu Rongji, *vice-premier, reformer and a protégé of Deng Xiaoping.*

WORLD AFFAIRS

The push for economic modernization is a key determinant of foreign policy. Investment, technology and trade, rather than ideology, now tend to condition China's relationships. The other, often interlinked factor is the country's desire to secure regional stability.

Diplomatic links have been established with states of the former Soviet Union – trade and military contacts with Russia are strong. On the Korean peninsula, China has acted to restrain North Korea while deepening ties with Seoul. Relations with Vietnam have been normalized and links with Japan are growing, despite China's suspicions about Tokyo's intentions toward ASEAN. China staged major military exercises off Taiwan in 1996 to reinforce its claim to the island, as the first direct presidential elections were held there.

Relations with the West have improved markedly since the 1989 Tiananmen Square massacre but China resents its Most Favored Nation (MFN) status with the USA being renewed annually, after it has been assessed whether Beijing has made progress on human rights, nuclear and economic piracy issues. Relations with the UK are dominated by Hong Kong, and have been strained by London's plans, under Governor Chris Patten, to increase democracy in the colony before handing it back to China in 1997.

AID

 $3.3bn (receipts)　 Up 11% in 1993

Aid was an important part of Chinese diplomacy in the 1970s. Most went to Africa, but other communist and Southeast Asian states were also recipients. Aid flows outward have almost dried up since the late 1970s, as the economic reform process has turned China itself into a major aid recipient. Japan is the biggest bilateral donor to China, but the potential of the Chinese market means most developed states provide aid. A significant proportion of aid funding is used to finance high-tech imports. The 1989 Tiananmen Square massacre led to a temporary suspension of aid disbursements by the West.

DEFENSE

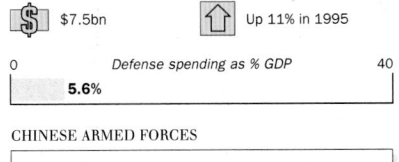 $7.5bn　Up 11% in 1995

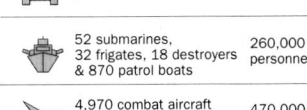

China's armed services are grouped in the People's Liberation Army (PLA), which has close links with the CCP. The army comprises one-third conscripts and two-thirds professional soldiers. It was announced in 1996 that its size was to be gradually cut from 3 to 2.5 million. From 1967, when it restored order after the chaos of the Cultural Revolution, to 1989, when it fired on civilians in Tiananmen Square, the PLA has been used to ensure the party's dominance. It is still used to suppress dissent in Tibet, though elements in the military reportedly want a less political role. China has a large weapons industry, including nuclear weapons, and is a significant arms exporter.

ECONOMICS

 $630bn　 8.32–8.45 yuan

SCORE CARD

- ❏ WORLD GNP RANKING..............................7th
- ❏ GNP PER CAPITA...................................$530
- ❏ BALANCE OF PAYMENTS $6.5bn
- ❏ INFLATION 17%
- ❏ UNEMPLOYMENT ....2.3% (official)

STRENGTHS

Domestic market of 1.2 billion. Self-sufficiency in food. Mineral reserves. Increasingly diversified industrial sector. Economic reforms which led to growth averaging 10% a year in 1980s, rapid rise in exports. Low wage costs.

ECONOMIC PERFORMANCE INDICATOR

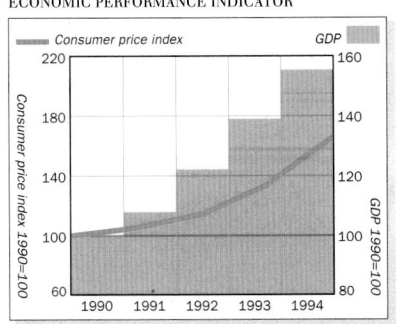

EXPORTS

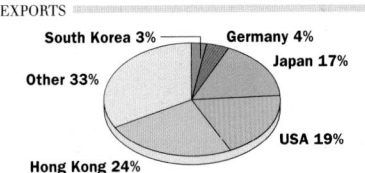

IMPORTS

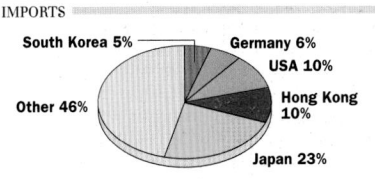

WEAKNESSES

Population growth. Massive underemployment. Poor transportation system. Delayed reform of weak state sector.

CHINA : MAJOR BUSINESSES

* significant multinational ownership

PROFILE

China's shift from a centrally planned to a market economy has steamed ahead since the 1980s, notably in the south, where liberalization has gone furthest. However, growth had to be curbed twice in the because of high inflation. Credit restrictions and price controls reduced inflation in 1995 as GDP grew by 10.2%. Under the Ninth Five-Year Plan (1996–2000) the government will retain strict controls and promote intensive rather than extensive growth. The modernization of industry and increased competition will be encouraged to reduce subsidies to both weak and efficient sectors. Stability in agriculture and in the prices of agricultural and associated products are also a priority in the long-term reduction of inflation.

C

REGIONS
BEIJING

☐ Builtup area	⛺ Economic development area	⟋ Canals
📷 Tourism	⚙ Light industry	⬢ Chemicals	✹ Textiles

WITH A COMBINED POPULATION of almost 19 million, the cities of Beijing and Tianjin have the status of provinces. Beijing (formerly Peking) is China's capital and the focus of political life. Together with its port of Tianjin, 87 miles away, it also forms a powerful industrial and commercial nexus which has attracted considerable foreign investment since 1980.

Both Beijing and Tianjin are leading producers of textiles, chemicals and light industrial goods. Beijing is also the country's most popular tourist destination. Approximately 9.23 million tourists visited the old imperial capital and its Forbidden City between 1991–1995.

In 1995, Beijing achieved growth of 12.6%, attracted $2.74 billion in foreign investment from Europe, the USA and Japan and approved the establishment of 1552 overseas-funded companies. Its foreign trade alone was worth $4.23 billion.

Tianjin, and especially its economic development area (TEDA), are thriving. Costs are lower than Beijing and city officials are less constrained by the watchful eye of central government. Tianjin is rapidly developing into China's leading gateway city. In 1995, it handled 34.408 million tons of cargo and the value of its foreign trade was put at $21,746 billion.

THE SOUTHEAST

THE SOUTHEASTERN COAST, especially Guangdong province, is the exemplar of modern market-oriented China. It was in Guangdong, and neighboring Fujian province, that the first Special Economic Zones were set up in 1980 to attract foreign investors. The target was the 30 million overseas Chinese, particularly those living in Hong Kong and Taiwan, who have their ancestral home in the two provinces.

Hong Kong and to a lesser extent Taiwan have been responsible for over half of all recent foreign investment into China. Most has been concentrated in Guangdong – notably the Pearl River delta to the south – a center of export-oriented light industry whose GDP was some

$65.5 billion in 1995, 140% higher than 1990. Income levels here are around ten times higher than the national average, millionaires flourish and residents have acquired the consumer aspirations of their Hong Kong counterparts.

Guangdong is on target to be Asia's largest industrial region within 20 years. However, explosive growth has also brought problems which threaten to undermine future development. Prime among these are rising wage and land costs, and escalating housing and power shortages. They are forcing out many of the low-cost industries which formed the basis of Guangdong's early growth and are deterring high-tech companies.

⬡ Special Economic Zones	💲 Stock exchange - opened 1990

SHANGHAI

⟋ Canals	⚱ Financial center	⚓ Major ports
⬢ Steelworks	⚘ Wheat	✹ Rice	⚘ Tea

SHANGHAI AND ITS SATELLITE cities in Jiangsu and Zhejiang provinces form China's economic heartland.

Shanghai, a city state of 12.5 million, is China's largest and most densely populated urban area. It was a focus of foreign settlement in the 19th century and of revolutionary activity in the 20th. In 1921, the Chinese Communist Party was founded there, and it was the base for the 1960s Cultural Revolution.

Despite relative stagnation after 1949, Shanghai remains China's foremost industrial and commercial city, and its leading financial center and port. With important political friends such as Vice-Premier Zhu Rongji and CCP Secretary-General Jiang Zemin, both former mayors, to promote its interests, it is beginning to undergo a revival. It registered 14% growth in 1995 and attracted over 100 million domestic and 1.4 million foreign tourists.

Shanghai is popular with foreign firms which like its workers – China's best educated and most highly skilled.

Its new development area will treble its size, with South Asian companies already investing $255 per square foot of land, the highest among the development regions. Shanghai's satellite cities of Nantong, Ningbo, Hangzhou and Suzhou are also a major focus for foreign investors, and have benefitted from infrastructure problems experienced by Shanghai.

Zhejiang province's foreign trade rose by 250% in 1991–1995 and the approval of 11,774 foreign-funded enterprises involved foreign investment of $17.02 billion. Over the last five years, Jiangsu province has approved 29,442 foreign-funded enterprises and 90 of the world's top 500 companies operate here. It attracted $5.3 billion in foreign investment in 1995 and exported goods worth $16.54 billion. In 1995, it launched an anti-poverty drive.

REGIONS

THE NORTHEAST

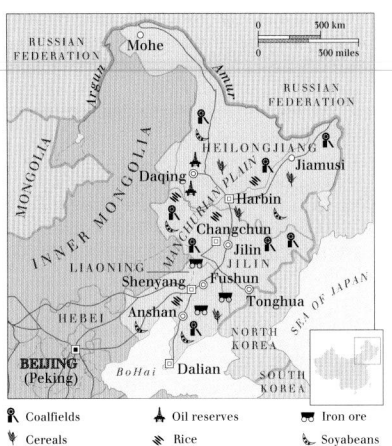

Coalfields **Oil reserves** **Iron ore**
Cereals **Rice** **Soyabeans**

CALLED DONGBEI by the Chinese, the northeast is a vast region of 300,000 square miles. It was once the territory of the Manchus, the founders of China's last dynasty. Today, it comprises Liaoning, Jilin and Heilongjiang provinces.

Except for Liaoning, the region is relatively sparsely populated, for the most part by the descendants of recent migrants. The fertile Manchurian plain has made the northeast a leading producer of grains and soybeans. It also has rich mineral resources. Heilongjiang has China's largest oilfield, at Daqing. Large coal and iron ore reserves have helped to make Liaoning China's second-largest producer of heavy industrial goods.

Growth in the northeast lagged behind most of China during the 1980s, principally due to central planning, but the non-state sector has recently rapidly expanded, as has cross-border trade with the Russian Federation. Heilongjiang experienced 9.5% growth in 1995 and attracted $940 million in foreign investment. Liaoning borders the Korean peninsula and investment from South Korea is strong, primarily in the port of Dalian. Proximity has also helped make Dalian the preferred target of Japanese investment in China. By 1993, 125 Japanese companies were operating in the city. Jilin province's light industry grew by 17.2% in 1994.

CENTRAL CHINA

THIS REGION FOCUSES on the inland provinces of Henan, Hubei, Hunan and Sichuan. It also includes Anhui and Jiangxi provinces to the east, and Shaanxi and Shanxi to the west. Travesed by the Chang Jiang and Huang He rivers, central China is the country's agricultural heartland. Henan, Hubei, Hunan and Sichuan are the leading producers of rice and wheat. Minerals, including coal, oil and tungsten, are also important to the region.

Sichuan is China's most populous province, with 10% of the population. Under the leadership of Zhao Ziyang, later China's premier, Sichuan was the testing ground in the late 1970s for the shift from communal to

individual farm production which marked the start of the present era of reform. It has also had success in developing rural enterprises to absorb surplus farm labor. Around 25% of the population is now employed by these.

Remoteness from the country's economic hub on the eastern seaboard means that Sichuan and most other central provinces, despite significant industrial bases, have been slow to benefit from China's "open door" foreign investment policy. Hebei province aims to become an economic giant by the year 2000. Its foreign trade exports amounted to $3.04 billion in 1995 and its capital, Wuhan, is a major inland port on the Chang Yiang. Foreign investment in Henan reached $918.8 million in 1995.

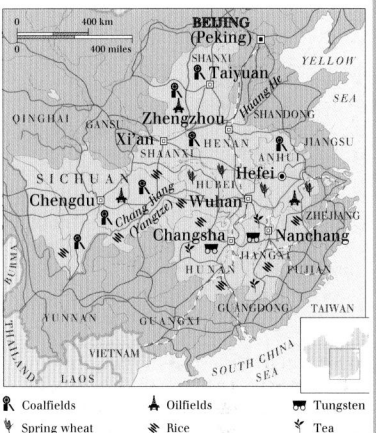

Coalfields **Oilfields** **Tungsten**
Spring wheat **Rice** **Tea**

TIBET

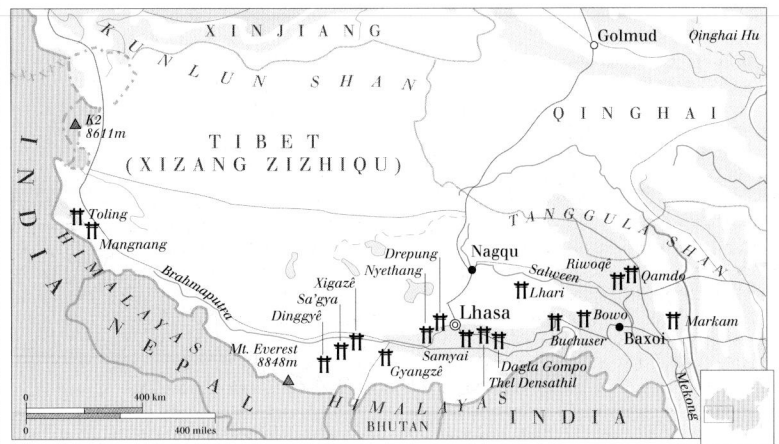

Monasteries

VAST, HIGH AND MOUNTAINOUS, Tibet has features in common with the other provinces and regions of

western China – Xinjiang, Qinghai, Gansu, Ningxia and Nei Mongol Zizhiqu. All are sparsely populated and ethnic

minorities make up a significant percentage of the population. Tibet has China's lowest population density. Despite strongly resented Han Chinese immigration, Tibetans are still just in a majority.

Another common feature is opposition to Beijing's centralist policies. Although part of the Manchu empire from the 18th century until 1911, Tibet exercised full control over most of its affairs under the rule of the Dalai Lama, spiritual head of Tibetan Buddhism. In 1950, China invaded Tibet, and ruthlessly crushed the 1959 independence uprising. The Dalai Lama fled to India and established a government in exile. In 1965, Tibet was made a region of China. Opponents of Chinese rule were imprisoned or executed. Clashes between nationalists and Chinese troops in 1987 led to a renewed clampdown on Tibetans.

C

CHRONOLOGY

China has the world's oldest continuous civilization. Its recorded history begins 4,000 years ago with the Shang dynasty, founded in the north in 1766 BC. Succeeding dynasties expanded China's boundaries; it reached its greatest extent under the Manchu (Qing) dynasty in the 18th century. Chinese isolationism frustrated Europe's attempts to expand into the empire until the 19th century, when China had fallen behind the industrializing West. For the previous 3,000 years, it had been one of the world's most advanced nations.

❑ **1839–1860** Opium Wars with Britain. China defeated; forced to open ports to foreigners.
❑ **1850–1873** Internal rebellions against Manchu empire.
❑ **1895** Defeat by Japan in war over Korean peninsula.
❑ **1900** Boxer Rebellion to expel all foreigners suppressed.
❑ **1911** Manchu empire overthrown by nationalists led by Sun Yat-sen. Republic of China declared.
❑ **1912** Sun Yat-sen creates National People's Party (Guomindang).
❑ **1916** Nationalists factionalize. Sun Yat-sen sets up government in Guangdong. Rest of China under control of rival warlords.
❑ **1921** Communist Party of China (CCP) founded in Shanghai.
❑ **1923** CCP joins Soviet-backed Guomindang to fight warlords.
❑ **1925** Chiang Kai-shek becomes Guomindang leader on death of Sun Yat-sen.
❑ **1927** Chiang turns on CCP. CCP leaders, including Mao Zedong, escape to rural south.
❑ **1930–1934** Mao formulates strategy of peasant-led revolution.
❑ **1931** Japan invades Manchuria.
❑ **1934** Chiang forces CCP out of its southern bases. Start of 7,500-mile Long March.
❑ **1935** Long March ends in Yanan, Shaanxi province. Mao becomes CCP leader.
❑ **1936** Chiang agrees to joint offensive with CCP against Japan.
❑ **1937–1945** War against Japan; CCP Red Army in north, Guomindang in south. Japan defeated.
❑ **1945–1949** War between Red Army and Guomindang. US-backed Guomindang retreats to Taiwan.
❑ **1949** October, Mao proclaims People's Republic of China.
❑ **1950** Invasion of Tibet. Mutual assistance treaty with USSR.
❑ **1950–1958** Land reform; culminates in setting up of communes. First Five-Year Plan (1953–1958) fails. ⇨

RESOURCES

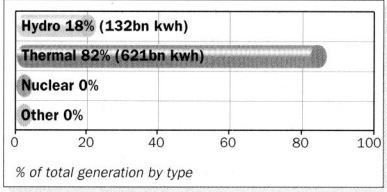

754bn kwh (capacity 98.6m kw)		2.8m b/d (reserves 24,000,000,000 bbl)	
402.8m pigs, 111.6m sheep, 105.9m goats		Coal, oil, natural gas, salt, iron, molybdenum, titanium, tungsten	

ELECTRICITY GENERATION

Hydro 18% (132bn kwh)	
Thermal 82% (621bn kwh)	
Nuclear 0%	
Other 0%	

% of total generation by type

China has commercial deposits of most minerals and probably the world's largest reserves of 17. These include molybdenum, titanium and tungsten, in which it dominates the world market.

China is the world's largest coal producer, with output of 1.28 billion tons in 1995 used mainly for power generation. Reserves are estimated at around 800 billion tons, primarily in the Shaanxi and Sichuan basins.

Power generation is lagging well behind demand. The first two nuclear plants opened in the early 1990s and four more are planned under the Ninth Five-Year Plan (1996–2000). The world's largest hydropower station,

known as the "Three Gorges" scheme, is being built at Santoup'ing on the Chang Jiang. The scheme has raised controversy over its proposed benefits and costs.

Crude oil production in 1995 was a record 140 million tons. Eastern oil fields are ageing and hopes for the future now center on the Tarim basin in the far west, which Western oil companies say could have Middle East-size reserves. Gas production exceeded 21 billion cubic yards in 1995.

CHINA : LAND USE

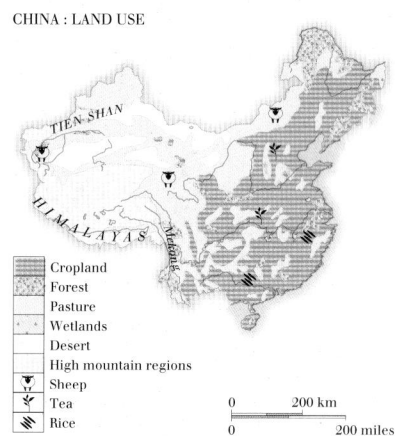

Cropland	
Forest	
Pasture	
Wetlands	
Desert	
High mountain regions	
Sheep	
Tea	
Rice	

0   200 km
0   200 miles

ENVIRONMENT

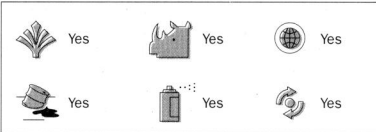

6%	Economic growth has precedence over ecological concerns

ENVIRONMENTAL TREATIES

Yes		Yes		Yes	
Yes		Yes		Yes	

Climate and geology mean that natural disasters are quite frequent in China. However, their impact is often made worse by human actions. Poor building standards helped push the death toll in the 1976 Tangshan earthquake to over 500,000. The economic policies of the 1950s turned drought into a famine, which is estimated to have killed up to 100 million between 1959 and 1961.

Economic growth is the priority of China's leaders, who tend to view Western pressure for environmental controls with suspicion. As a result, industrial pollution and environmental degradation, already widespread, are increasing. However, the environment appears to be a growing concern among educated Chinese. In 1992, they campaigned, albeit unsuccessfully, to stop the Three Gorges hydroelectric scheme which will lead to large-scale loss of wildlife habitats and could increase the risk of earthquakes.

MEDIA

 The government still attempts to enforce tight censorship, often by withdrawal of licenses

PUBLISHING AND BROADCAST MEDIA

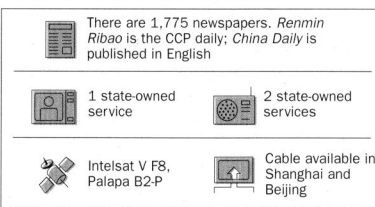

There are 1,775 newspapers. *Renmin Ribao* is the CCP daily; *China Daily* is published in English	
1 state-owned service	2 state-owned services
Intelsat V F8, Palapa B2-P	Cable available in Shanghai and Beijing

For China's leaders, one less welcome result of a more open, market-oriented economy has been people's increasing access to non-official sources of information. TV ownership is rising with living standards. Many sets, especially in the populous south and east, are tuned to Hong Kong stations. The growing number of satellite-dish owners have an even wider choice.

These changes have undermined but not ended censorship. In 1996, controls were imposed on electronic financial news services and access to the Internet. The printed media remain on a tight rein. Papers considered undesirable have their licenses removed in periodic clean-ups. Millions still buy, but few now read, the CCP-owned *Renmin Ribao* (People's Daily) with its editorials defending revolutionary purity.

CHRONOLOGY *continued*

- ❏ **1958** "Great Leap Forward" to boost production fails; contributes to millions of deaths during 1959–1961 famine. Mao resigns as CCP chairman; succeeded by Lui Saoqi.
- ❏ **1960** Sino–Soviet split.
- ❏ **1961–1965** More pragmatic economic approach led by Lui and Deng Xiaoping.
- ❏ **1966** Cultural Revolution initiated by Mao to restore his supreme power. Youthful Red Guards encouraged to attack all authority. Revolutionary Committee formed, including Mao's wife Jiang Qing. Mao rules with Military Commission under Lin Biao and State Council under premier Zhou Enlai.
- ❏ **1967** Army intervenes to restore some order amid countrywide chaos. Lui and Deng are purged from party.
- ❏ **1969** Mao regains chairmanship of CCP. Lin Biao designated his successor, but quickly comes under attack from Mao.
- ❏ **1971** Lin dies in plane crash.
- ❏ **1972** US President Nixon visits. More open foreign policy initiated by Zhou Enlai, a moderating force during Cultural Revolution.
- ❏ **1973** Jiang Qing, Zhang Chunquio and other "Gang of Four" members elected to Politburo. Deng Xiaoping rehabilitated as vice-premier.
- ❏ **1976** January, death of Zhou Enlai. April, mass demonstration of support for Zhou and moderates. Mao strips Deng of posts, confirms Hua Guo Feng as new premier. September, Mao dies. October, "Gang of Four" arrested.
- ❏ **1977** Deng regains party posts, begins to extend his power base.
- ❏ **1978** Decade of reform and economic modernization launched. Open door policy to foreign investment; farmers allowed to farm for profit.
- ❏ **1980** Deng emerges as China's paramount leader. Economic reform gathers pace, but hopes for political change suppressed.
- ❏ **1983–1984** Conservative elderly leaders attempt to slow pace of economic reform under Deng. Several subsequently forced to step down from Politburo.
- ❏ **1984** Industrial reforms announced; less successful than earlier agricultural changes.
- ❏ **1989** Demonstrations in Tiananmen Square demanding greater openness in government. Crushed by army; between 1,000 and 5,000 dead. Beijing under martial law.
- ❏ **1992–1995** Trials of pro-democracy activists continue. Plans for market economy accelerated.

CRIME

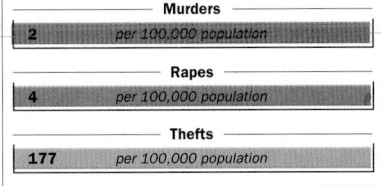

1.3m prisoners   Up 11% in 1990

CRIME RATES

Murders
2 *per 100,000 population*

Rapes
4 *per 100,000 population*

Thefts
177 *per 100,000 population*

China's legal system is a mix of custom and statute, and has a reputation for arbitrariness. Economic reform and the breakdown of social controls have been paralleled by a rise in corruption and violent crime. Many new economic crimes have been made capital offenses, leading to 1791 executions in 1994.

China has a poor human rights record and still holds thousands of political prisoners. The Tiananmen Square massacre brought human rights to the fore in China's relations with the USA and EU – some detainees have now been released. The Red Cross is negotiating with China to allow access to political prisoners.

EDUCATION

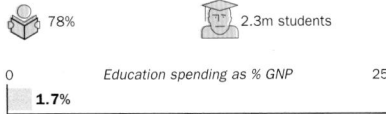

78%   2.3m students

0   *Education spending as % GNP*   25
1.7%

THE EDUCATION SYSTEM

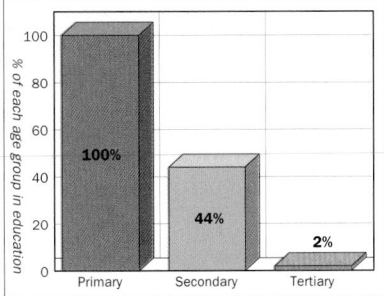

Despite the expansion of education since 1949, illiteracy and semi-literacy are still quite widespread. In part, this is due to the Cultural Revolution which left a generation with little education. It also reflects lower rural attendance and attitudes to women. In 1990, 38% of women and 16% of men were illiterate. To raise skill levels, the government has set a target of nine years of education for all. School attendance fell when fees were introduced in the 1980s, but is now nearing 90%. Higher education, which is also fee-paying, attracts only 2% of 20–24 year-olds. Today, however, selection is based on academic rather than political criteria.

HEALTH

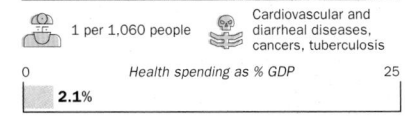

1 per 1,060 people   Cardiovascular and diarrheal diseases, cancers, tuberculosis

0   *Health spending as % GDP*   25
2.1%

Health care, combining traditional and Western medicine and based on an extensive primary care network, used to extend to the remotest regions. Life expectancy on a par with many richer nations is now threatened as the market-oriented economy has produced a two-tier system. A gaping divide exists between city and rural provision, fees are rising and fewer people are covered by the free care that goes with state employment.

WEALTH

Garment cutter, 215 yuan ($26) per month; doctor, 216 yuan ($26) per month

CONSUMER GOODS OWNERSHIP

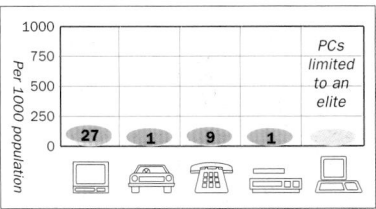

Economic change has led to improved living standards, seen in the growing demand for consumer goods, but also widening wealth disparities. The burgeoning small-business class and employees of companies with foreign investment have benefited most. They mainly live in the east, especially the southeast, which is home to a number of millionaires. The main losers are the 150 million "surplus" agricultural workers, many of whom have migrated to the cities in search of jobs. The majority of Chinese are still farmers. They initially benefited from reform, but their living standards are now threatened by rising production costs.

WORLD RANKING

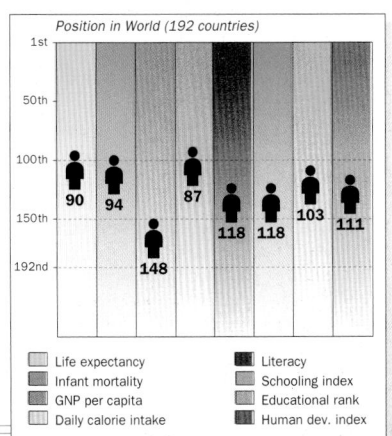

▢ Life expectancy	▮ Literacy
▨ Infant mortality	▢ Schooling index
▨ GNP per capita	▨ Educational rank
▢ Daily calorie intake	▮ Human dev. index

C

COLOMBIA

OFFICIAL NAME: Republic of Colombia   **CAPITAL:** Bogotá
POPULATION: 35.1 million   **CURRENCY:** Colombian peso   **OFFICIAL LANGUAGE:** Spanish

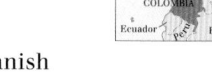
C

LYING IN NORTHWEST SOUTH AMERICA, Colombia has coastlines on both the Caribbean and the Pacific. The east of the country is densely forested and sparsely populated, and separated from the western coastal plains by the Andes Mountains. The Andes divide into three ranges (*cordilleras*) in Colombia. The eastern range is divided from the two western ranges by the densely populated Magdalena river valley. The Colombian lowlands are very wet, hot and fertile, supporting two harvests and allowing many crops to be planted at any time of year. A multiparty democracy since 1957, Colombia is noted for its coffee, emeralds, gold and narcotics-trafficking.

PEOPLE

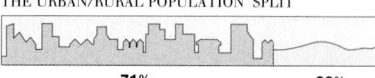

Spanish, Indian languages, English Creole

88 people per sq. mile

THE URBAN/RURAL POPULATION SPLIT

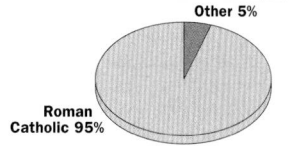

71%   29%

RELIGIOUS PERSUASION

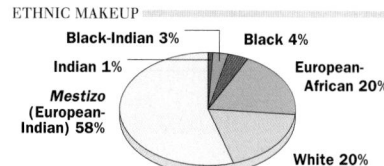

Other 5%
Roman Catholic 95%

ETHNIC MAKEUP

Black-Indian 3%   Black 4%
Indian 1%   European-African 20%
Mestizo (European-Indian) 58%
White 20%

CLIMATE

WEATHER CHART

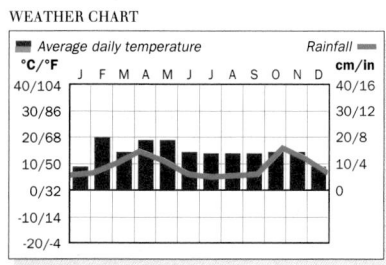

Most of Colombia is wet and the hot Pacific coastal areas receive up to 195 in. of rain a year. The Caribbean coast is a little drier. The Andes have three climatic regions: the *tierra caliente* (hot lowlands), *tierra templada* (temperate uplands), and *tierra fría* (cold highlands). A feature of the last is year-round spring-like conditions such as those found in Bogotá. The equatorial east has two wet seasons.

TRANSPORTATION

 Eldorado, Bogotá
4.66m passengers

 48 ships
385,300 dwt

THE TRANSPORTATION NETWORK

 7,940 miles (12,800 km)

 Caribbean Trunk Highway

 1,573 miles (2,532 km)

 8,886 miles (14,300 km)

Roads in the north are in reasonable condition. Those in the south and east tend to be rutted and badly affected by the frequent rains. Colombia's antiquated railroad system, which currently has few fast intercity services, is due to be privatized.

Rivers are an important means of transportation in Colombia; the Magdalena, Orinoco, Atrato and Amazon river systems are all extensively navigable. Plans exist to connect Colombia to the Pan-American Highway.

TOURISM

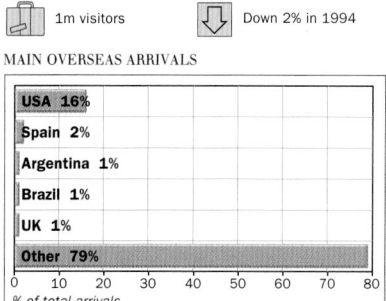

1m visitors   Down 2% in 1994

MAIN OVERSEAS ARRIVALS

USA 16%	
Spain 2%	
Argentina 1%	
Brazil 1%	
UK 1%	
Other 79%	

% of total arrivals

Tourism in Colombia is largely limited to the beaches of the Caribbean coast. Cartagena, Barranquilla and Santa Marta are the main resorts. Cartagena has also been developed as a major Latin American conference center.

Expansion of the tourist business has been limited by Colombia's political instability and the prevalence of narcotics-related crime. The well-publicized activities of drug cartels in Medellín and Cali, and instances of kidnappings in Bogotá, are major deterrents.

Limited infrastructure makes many regions of Colombia, particularly Amazonia to the east of the Andes, almost inaccessible. The Atlantic coast is also barely exploited.

Simón Bolívar and Cristóbal Colón, twin peaks with a height of over 19,030 feet in the heart of the Colombian Andes.

The majority of Colombians are people of mixed blood. An estimated 450,000 indigenous Indians are largely concentrated in the southwest and Amazonia, although some communities are scattered throughout the country. A small black population lives along both coasts, and especially in Chocó, Colombia's poorest region. Blacks are the most unrepresented group.

Some progress has been made in giving Indians a greater political voice. In 1991, constitutional reforms reserved two seats in the Senate for indigenous representatives, and Indian pressure groups are increasingly active. Harassment by landowners and narcotics-traffickers continues in Amazonia and very few investigations into suspected human rights violations against Indians have led to prosecutions.

Women in Colombia have a higher profile than in much of the rest of Latin America. Many are prominent in the professions, though few reach the top in politics. The traditional extended Catholic family is still the norm in Colombia. Regional identity is strong.

POPULATION AGE BREAKDOWN

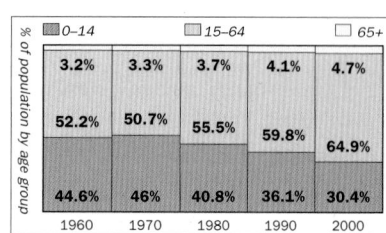

	0–14	15–64	65+
% of population by age group			

	1960	1970	1980	1990	2000
65+	3.2%	3.3%	3.7%	4.1%	4.7%
15–64	52.2%	50.7%	55.5%	59.8%	64.9%
0–14	44.6%	46%	40.8%	36.1%	30.4%

C

POLITICS

 U. House 1994/1998
L. House 1994/1995

 President Ernesto
Samper Pizano

Colombia is a presidential democracy. Presidents may not serve two consecutive terms.

MAIN POLITICAL ISSUES
Narcotics-related corruption
In 1996 President Ernesto Samper faced a congressional investigation, leading to possible impeachment and criminal proceedings, following charges that his 1994 presidential campaign received $6 million from the Cali drug cartel.

Guerrillas, paramilitaries and drug cartels
Left-wing guerrilla and right-wing paramilitary activity makes many regions ungovernable. In 1991, the former Gaviria government persuaded two of Colombia's four main guerrilla groups to accept an amnesty but the Armed Revolutionary Force of Colombia (FARC), the largest guerrilla group, and the National Liberation Army (ELN) which specializes in oil pipeline attacks, remain major sources of instability.

The Gaviria administration neutralized the Medellín cartel and its leader Pablo Escobar, who was shot dead by police after escaping jail. The rapid arrest of seven drug barons in 1995 raised speculation that the Samper government had reached an accommodation with the Cali drug cartel.

PROFILE
The Conservatives (PSC) and the Liberals (PL), have shared power for the past 40 years. Both have large numbers of followers. Official corruption both high and low, and the violence associated with drug cartels, guerrillas and paramilitaries, have seriously weakened public confidence in the government.

THE STATE OF THE PARTIES

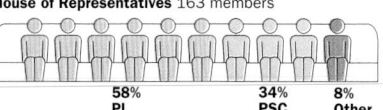
House of Representatives 163 members

58% PL	34% PSC	8% Other

PL = Liberal Party **PSC** = Social Conservative Party
NFD = New Democratic Force

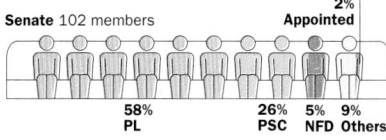
Senate 102 members — 2% Appointed

58% PL	26% PSC	5% NFD	9% Others

2 special representatives of the indigenous (Indian) communities are appointed to the Senate

Ernesto Samper Pizano, *elected president in 1994.*

Pablo Escobar, *cocaine king and leader of the Medellín cartel until 1993.*

WORLD AFFAIRS

 ACS   AG   G3   OAS RG

Colombia's most important foreign relations are with the USA, the major market for its exports and also its main source of aid. The USA has intervened directly to attack the narcotics business in Colombia, making its elimination a condition of aid, which it heavily restricted in 1996. Colombia has among other things refused US demands that narcotics-traffickers be extradited for trial in the USA.

Relations with neighboring states are fairly stable. A border dispute with Venezuela, Colombia's traditional enemy, is yet to be resolved, but the issue is unlikely to lead to major conflict. A dispute with Nicaragua over a common border in the Caribbean continues.

AID

 $109m (receipts)   Down 55% in 1993

The US, a provider of military aid to fight drug cartels, imposed economic and aid restrictions in 1996 after declaring Colombia an "uncooperative" nation in the fight against drugs.

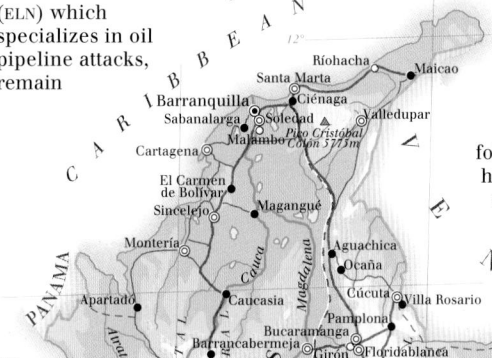

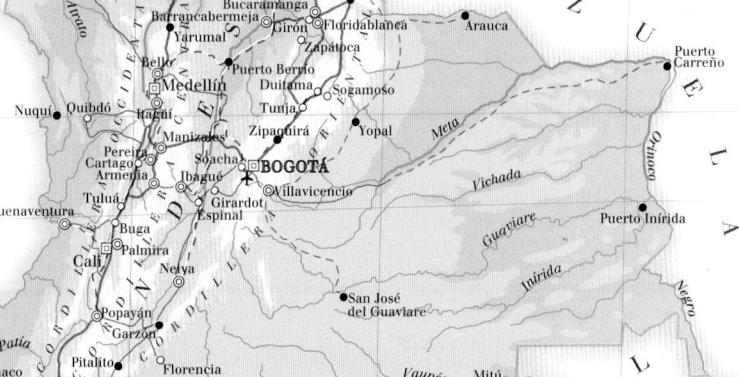

COLOMBIA

Total Land Area : 1 038 700 sq. km (401 042 sq. miles)

LAND HEIGHT

3000m/9843ft	
2000m/6562ft	
1000m/3281ft	
500m/1640ft	
Sea Level	

POPULATION

▣	over 1 000 000
◉	over 500 000
◎	over 100 000
○	over 50 000
●	over 10 000
•	under 10 000

0 — 200 km
0 — 200 miles

CHRONOLOGY

In 1525, Spain began the conquest of Colombia, which became its chief source of gold.

❏ **1819** Simón Bolívar defeats Spanish at Boyacá. Republic of Gran Colombia formed with Venezuela, Ecuador and Panama.
❏ **1830** Venezuela and Ecuador split away during revolts and civil wars.
❏ **1849** Conservative and Liberal parties established, the former with centralist and the latter with federalist tendencies.
❏ **1861–1886** Liberals hold monopoly on power.
❏ **1886–1930** Conservative rule.

➪

C

CHRONOLOGY *continued*

- ❏ **1899–1903** Liberal "War of 1,000 Days" revolt fails; 120,000 die.
- ❏ **1903** Panama secedes, but is not recognized by Colombia until 1921.
- ❏ **1930** Liberal President Olaya Herrera elected by coalition in first peaceful change of power.
- ❏ **1946** Conservatives take over.
- ❏ **1948** Shooting of Liberal mayor of Bogotá and riot known as *El Bogotazo* spark civil war, *La Violencia*, to 1957; 300,000 killed.
- ❏ **1953–1957** Military dictatorship of Rojas Pinilla.
- ❏ **1958** Conservatives and Liberals agree to alternate government in a National Front until 1974. Other parties banned.
- ❏ **1965** Left-wing guerrilla National Liberation Army and Maoist Popular Liberation Army founded.
- ❏ **1966** Pro-Soviet FARC guerrilla group formed.
- ❏ **1968** Constitutional reform allows new parties, but two-party parity continues. Guerrilla groups proliferate from now on.
- ❏ **1971** M-19 emerges as armed left-wing guerrilla group.
- ❏ **1984** Minister of Justice assassinated for attempting to enforce anti-drug campaign.
- ❏ **1985** M-19 guerrillas blast way into Ministry of Justice; 11 judges and 90 others killed. Patriotic Union (UP) party formed.
- ❏ **1986** Liberal Virgilio Barco Vargas wins presidential elections, so ending power-sharing. UP wins ten seats in parliament. Right-wing paramilitary start murder campaign against UP politicians. Violence by both left-wing groups and death squads run by drug cartels continues.
- ❏ **1989** M-19 reaches peace agreement with government, including the granting of a full pardon. Becomes legal party.
- ❏ **1990** UP and Liberal presidential candidates murdered during general and presidential elections. Liberal César Gaviria elected on anti-drug platform.
- ❏ **1991** New constitution legalizes divorce and prohibits extradition of Colombian nationals. Indigenous peoples' democratic rights guaranteed, but territorial claims not addressed.
- ❏ **1992** Six armed anti-terrorism units set up to combat rising violence.
- ❏ **1992–1993** Medellín drug cartel leader, Pablo Escobar, captured, escapes and is shot dead by police .
- ❏ **1995–1996** President Samper charged with receiving Cali cartel funds.

DEFENSE

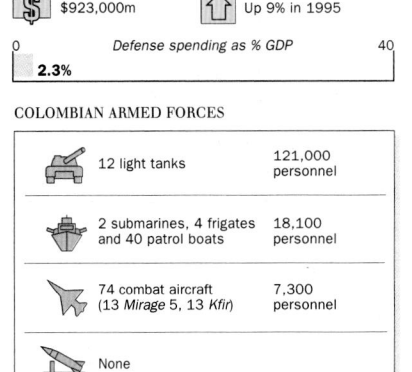

$923,000m   Up 9% in 1995

Defense spending as % GDP 0 — 40
2.3%

COLOMBIAN ARMED FORCES

12 light tanks	121,000 personnel
2 submarines, 4 frigates and 40 patrol boats	18,100 personnel
74 combat aircraft (13 *Mirage* 5, 13 *Kfir*)	7,300 personnel
None	

The Colombian military is powerful but rarely intervenes directly in politics. Human rights groups accuse the armed forces and paramilitary allies of gross and systematic abuses involving "disappearances" and torture, and operating with near impunity in its fight against guerrilla groups and narcotics-traffickers. Narcotics-related corruption in army ranks has dented the effectiveness of campaigns. Drug barons have their own armed forces, which are often better equipped than the state's.

Colombia participates in the joint Latin American Defense Force. Most arms are bought from the USA, although France supplies the Colombian Air Force.

ECONOMICS

$58.9bn   831.60–990.75 Colombian pesos

SCORE CARD

- ❏ WORLD GNP RANKING...........................42nd
- ❏ GNP PER CAPITA $1,620
- ❏ BALANCE OF PAYMENTS $912m
- ❏ INFLATION 21.3%
- ❏ UNEMPLOYMENT....................................8.7%

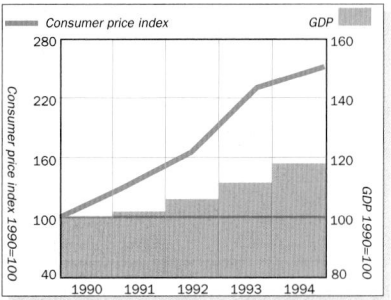

ECONOMIC PERFORMANCE INDICATOR

Consumer price index — GDP

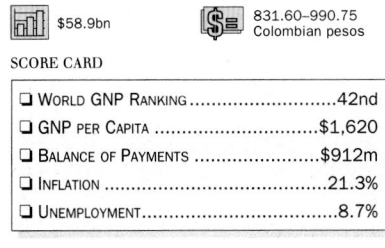

EXPORTS

Germany 8%
Venezuela 10%
USA 40%
Other 32%

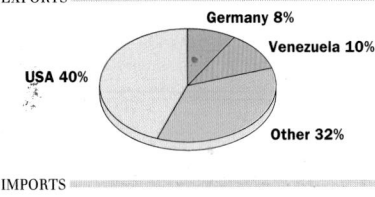

IMPORTS

Brazil 5%   Germany 6%
Other 35%   Venezuela 10%
Japan 11%
USA 33%

STRENGTHS

Substantial oil and coal deposits plus well-developed hydroelectric power makes Colombia almost self-sufficient in energy. Healthy and diversified export sector – especially coffee and coal. Light manufactures. Worldwide market for cocaine still growing.

WEAKNESSES

Narcotics-related violence and corruption discourages foreign investors. Industries serving local markets uncompetitive owing to decades of protection. High unemployment rate - officially 8.7% but, in reality, probably nearer 30%. Vulnerability of coffee to international price fluctuations.

PROFILE

Of all the Latin American economies, Colombia's is probably the closest to the

US model. The state has traditionally played a relatively minor role and Colombia has a successful private export sector. A program of privatization is reducing the state's involvement further.

Regional disparities remain marked. Most wealth is centered in the Bogotá, Medellín and Cali regions. Rural areas are largely underdeveloped. The main obstacle to growth is the instability caused by the narcotics business. Given stability and investment, Colombia's potential for growth is considerable.

COLOMBIA : MAJOR BUSINESSES

Pulp and paper
Narcotics
Steel
Chemicals
Vehicle assembly
Food processing
Textiles
Oil

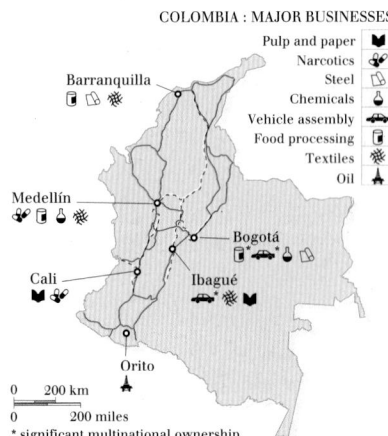

Barranquilla
Medellín
Cali
Bogotá
Ibagué
Orito

0 200 km
0 200 miles
* significant multinational ownership

RESOURCES

35.9bn kwh (capacity 9.41m kw)

444,508 b/d (reserves 1,935,200 bbl)

25.7m cattle, 2.6m pigs, 2.5m sheep, 2m horses

Oil, natural gas, coal, nickel, emeralds, gold

ELECTRICITY GENERATION

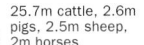

Hydro 62% (22bn kwh)

Thermal 38% (13.5bn kwh)

Nuclear 0%

Other 0%

0   20   40   60   80   100

% of total generation by type

Recent discoveries have made Colombia self-sufficient in oil. Coal surpluses are exported mainly to the UK and USA. Gold reserves are significant. Colombia also produces 60% of the world's emeralds.

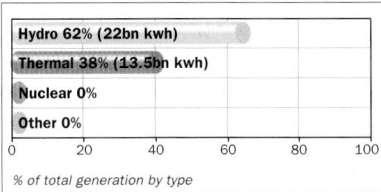

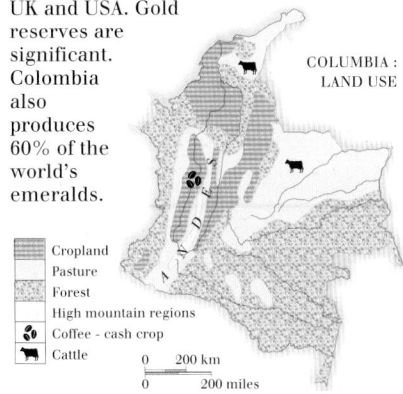

COLUMBIA : LAND USE

Cropland
Pasture
Forest
High mountain regions
Coffee - cash crop
Cattle

0   200 km
0   200 miles

ENVIRONMENT

8%

Rising pollution levels in the Magdalena River

ENVIRONMENTAL TREATIES

Yes	Yes	Yes
No	Yes	Yes

Cattle ranching, logging and coca growing have caused extensive soil degradation and loss of bird habitat.

MEDIA

In theory the press is free, but in practice there is some political censorship. Journalists tend to avoid criticizing drug cartels

PUBLISHING AND BROADCAST MEDIA

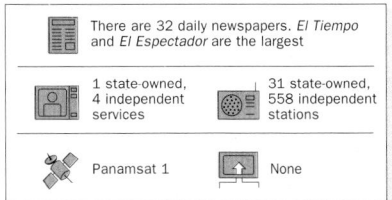

There are 32 daily newspapers. *El Tiempo* and *El Espectador* are the largest

1 state-owned, 4 independent services

31 state-owned, 558 independent stations

Panamsat 1

None

The independent press is small. The main papers are owned by corporations whose interests they promote.

CRIME

32,549 prisoners

Very high levels, but falling due to recent guerrilla amnesties

CRIME RATES

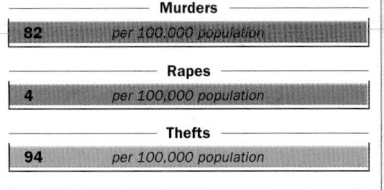

Murders

82   *per 100,000 population*

Rapes

4   *per 100,000 population*

Thefts

94   *per 100,000 population*

Colombia is the most violent society in Latin America and one of the most violent in the world. Violence and clashes with the military led to some 30,000 deaths in 1995. Homicide is the main cause of death among young men in cities; overall it is the most common cause of death after cancer. Most of the violence is narcotics-related and Cali and Medellín are the most dangerous cities. The frequency of urban armed robbery makes residents extremely security conscious. Wealthier Colombians employ several security guards.

The army and police have used intimidation and torture in the fight against both guerrillas and narcotics-traffickers, but have themselves also been accused of participating in the trade. A relatively new phenomenon is that of "social cleansing," the murder of street children and beggars by organized armed gangs. Some gangs in Bogotá are funded by local businesses.

Colombia's extensive gem deposits attract large numbers of illegal miners and smugglers. Around 15,000 were estimated to be active in Boyacá department in 1993.

EDUCATION

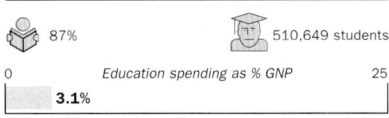

87%

510,649 students

0   *Education spending as % GNP*   25

3.1%

THE EDUCATION SYSTEM

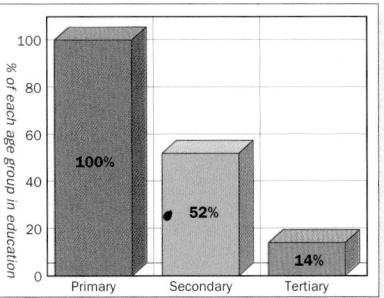

% of each age group in education

100%   Primary
52%   Secondary
14%   Tertiary

Colombia's education system is a mixture of the French and US models, with a *baccalauréat* exam at the end of secondary schooling. Educational provision in rural areas is uneven and increasing numbers of schools are being closed. The public universities (the main ones are in Bogotá, Medellín and Cali) are occasionally disrupted by political strikes and violence.

HEALTH

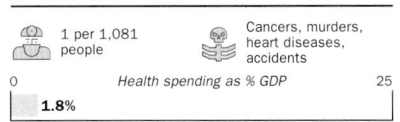

1 per 1,081 people

Cancers, murders, heart diseases, accidents

0   *Health spending as % GDP*   25

1.8%

Only 16% of Colombians benefit from any social security system, rather fewer than in most neighboring states. Rural areas have little health provision, as most doctors work in the larger cities. A polio vaccination campaign has largely eradicated the virus, except in coastal regions.

WEALTH

School teacher, 150,000 pesos ($152) per month; senior engineer, 500,000 pesos ($505) per month

CONSUMER GOODS OWNERSHIP

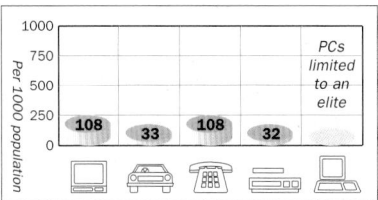

PCs limited to an elite

Per 1000 population

108   33   108   32

There is little social mobility in Colombia; the historically wealthy Spanish families still dominate political and business life. The rich favor BMWs or jeeps, weekend in Miami or Colombia's Caribbean islands, shop in Paris and Rome, and go to the USA for medical treatment. Their children are educated overseas. The rural poor are mostly landless. The inhabitants of the shanty towns of Cali, Barranquilla, Cartagena and Buenaventura are the poorest groups in Colombian society.

WORLD RANKING

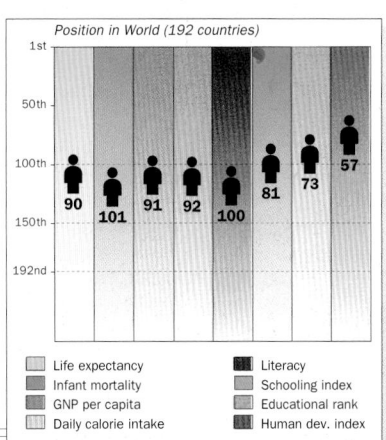

Position in World (192 countries)

1st
50th
100th
150th
192nd

90   101   91   92   100   81   73   57

Life expectancy
Infant mortality
GNP per capita
Daily calorie intake

Literacy
Schooling index
Educational rank
Human dev. index

C

COMOROS

OFFICIAL NAME: Federal Islamic Republic of the Comoros   **CAPITAL:** Moroni
POPULATION: 700,000   **CURRENCY:** Comorien franc   **OFFICIAL LANGUAGES:** Arabic and French

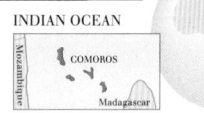

INDIAN OCEAN
COMOROS
Madagascar
Africa

THE ARCHIPELAGO REPUBLIC OF the Comoros lies between Mozambique and Madagascar and consists of three main islands and a number of islets. The region is poor, with most of the population engaged in subsistence farming. In 1975, the Comoros, with the exception of the island of Mayotte, became independent of France. Since then instability has plagued the political process, and there have been several coups and counter-coups.

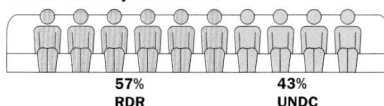

Moroni, the capital, on Njazidja. The Comoros islands are highly fertile and heavily forested. Many are ringed by coral reefs.

CLIMATE

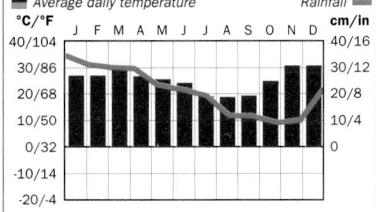

WEATHER CHART

The islands are tropical; it is hot and humid on the coasts and cooler higher up, notably on Mount Kartala.

TRANSPORTATION

Moroni-Hahaya, Njazidja | 3 ships / 2,300 dwt

THE TRANSPORTATION NETWORK

| 410 miles (650 km) | None |
| None | None |

Recent projects have included development of the port at Moroni and upgrading the international airport.

TOURISM

27,000 visitors | Up 13% in 1994

MAIN OVERSEAS ARRIVALS

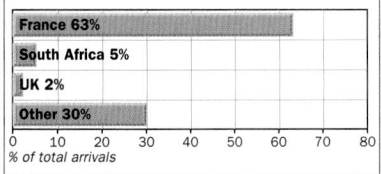

France 63%								
South Africa 5%								
UK 2%								
Other 30%								

0 10 20 30 40 50 60 70 80
% of total arrivals

In 1988, Sun International of South Africa joined a major project to build four hotels designed to attract 12,000 visitors a year from South Africa, France and Italy. Mauritius and the Seychelles provide tough competition.

PEOPLE

Arabic, Comoran, French | 814 people per sq. mile

THE URBAN/RURAL POPULATION SPLIT

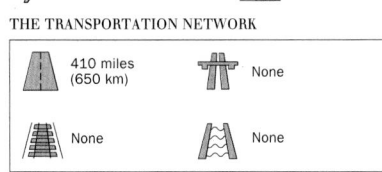

29%   71%

RELIGIOUS PERSUASION

Roman Catholic 14%
Muslim 86%

The Comoros has absorbed a diversity of Polynesians, Africans, Indonesians, Persians and Arabs over its history; in addition, there have also been Portuguese, Dutch, French and Indian immigrants. However, some sections of the community have retained their individual character; Mwali and Mayotte are still primarily African. Ethnic tension is rare, partly owing to the unifying force of the predominant religion, Islam.

POLITICS

U. House 1993/1997 | President Saïd
L. House 1993/1997 | Mohamed Djohar

THE STATE OF THE PARTIES

Federal Assembly 42 members

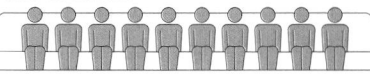

57% RDR   43% UNDC

RDR = Union for Democracy and Renovation
UNDC = National Union for Democratic Comoros

Senate 15 members

Five members chosen from each island by an electoral college

The Comoros has begun a transition from one-party rule to a democratic system. However, the country has been dogged by political instability. Frequent attempted coups (in 1990, 1991, 1992 and 1995, for example), together with a relatively immature party system based more on personalities than on policies and hence constantly changing party allegiances, have made the transition process long and at times uncertain. The 1995 coup attempt, once again led by veteran mercenary Bob Denard, resulted in President Djohar having to relinquish all executive power.

COMOROS

Total Land Area :
2230 sq. km
(861 sq. miles)

POPULATION

over 10 000 ●
under 10 000 ·

LAND HEIGHT

2000m/6562ft
1000m/3281ft
500m/1640ft
Sea Level

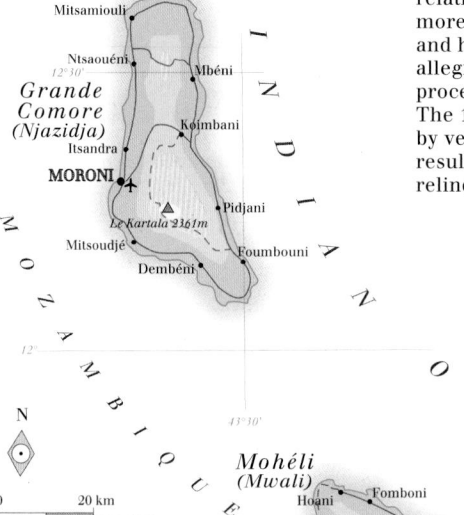

Mitsamiouli
Ntsaouéni
Mbéni
Grande Comore (Njazidja)
Koimbani
Itsandra
MORONI
Pidjani
Le Kartala 2361m
Mitsoudjé
Foumbouni
Dembéni

Mohéli (Mwali)
Fomboni
Hoani
Itsamia
Ndréméani

Anjouan (Nzwani)
Ouani
Moutsamoudou
Sima
Domoni
Moya
Mrémani

MOZAMBIQUE CHANNEL

INDIAN OCEAN

N

0 20 km
0 20 miles

C

WORLD AFFAIRS

The Comoros has a close relationship with France, its main benefactor. More recently, an economic link has been developed with South Africa, which used the islands for sanctions-busting purposes. In 1985, the Comoros became the fourth member of the Indian Ocean Commission (IOC), with the Seychelles, Mauritius and Madagascar.

AID

 $51m (receipts)   Up 6% in 1993

Foreign aid, mainly from France, accounts for over 40% of GDP, but even so has been insufficient to install the infrastructure necessary for economic development. Because of its Islamic links, the Comoros benefits from some Arab aid, as well as some from the EU, the World Bank and OPEC.

DEFENSE

 $3.1m   Little change from year to year

The influence of the military is small beyond the presidential guard, financed by France and South Africa, which has been involved in coups.

ECONOMICS

 $249m   367.09–401.08 Comoros francs

SCORE CARD

❏ WORLD GNP RANKING	178th
❏ GNP PER CAPITA	$510
❏ BALANCE OF PAYMENTS	$–9m
❏ INFLATION	25%
❏ UNEMPLOYMENT	16%

STRENGTHS
Vanilla, ylang-ylang and cloves are the main cash crops. Tourism is a potential growth area.

WEAKNESSES
Underdevelopment of agriculture; most production is at a subsistence level using traditional techniques. Over 50% of food requirements are imported. Lack of basic infrastructure, especially electricity and transportation.

EXPORTS

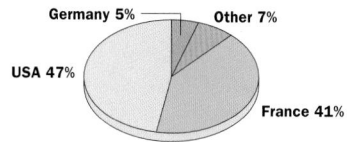

Germany 5%   Other 7%
USA 47%
France 41%

IMPORTS

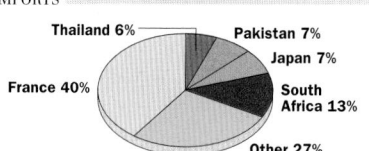

Thailand 6%   Pakistan 7%
Japan 7%
France 40%   South Africa 13%
Other 27%

RESOURCES

 16m kwh (capacity 5,000 kw)   7,000 tons

 128,000 goats, 50,000 cattle, 15,000 sheep   None

The Comoros has no strategic resources. An HEP plant is under construction on Nzwani, but there is no prospect of moving away from imports for the bulk of fuel requirements.

ENVIRONMENT

 None   The Comoros is too poor for any major initiatives

The environment is not a major priority in the Comoros; natural disasters, such as the volcanic eruption in 1977 which left 20,000 homeless, are of more immediate concern. The government is promoting tourism and recognizes the long-term commercial value of imposing environmental controls on new developments.

MEDIA

 The press had little political independence after the 1990 coup attempt, but since then the situation has slowly been improving

PUBLISHING AND BROADCAST MEDIA

 There are no daily newspapers. There are 2 weekly newspapers, the state-owned *Al Watany* and the independent *L'Archipel*

 No TV service   1 state-controlled service

There is currently a shift towards liberalization. The French government has announced that it will fund the establishment of a TV station.

CRIME

 The Comoros does not publish prison figures   The general trend is up

Although the judiciary can arbitrate where the government is accused of malpractice, some members of opposition groups have been arrested and imprisoned on political grounds.

EDUCATION

 48%   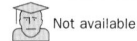 Not available

The education system does not extend beyond secondary level. Schools are equipped to teach only basic literacy, hygiene and agricultural techniques. Pupil–teacher ratios are high.

CHRONOLOGY

The Comoros was ruled by matrilineally inherited sultanates until shortly before becoming a French protectorate in 1886.

- ❏ **1912** Proclaimed a French colony.
- ❏ **1961** Internal self-government.
- ❏ **1975** Independence. Mayotte votes to remain French. President Abdallah overthrown in coup.
- ❏ **1978** Mercenaries led by Bob Denard restore Abdallah to power.
- ❏ **1989** Abdallah assassinated. Saïd Mohamed Djohar named interim president.
- ❏ **1990** Djohar elected president.
- ❏ **1993** Chaotic first multiparty elections.
- ❏ **1995** Attempted coup led by Denard leads to Djohar relinquishing executive power.

HEALTH

 1 per 12,300 people   Malaria, infectious intestinal and bacterial diseases

Health care is rudimentary; loans have been used to construct two maternity clinics and renovate 30 health centers.

WEALTH

 Virtually the whole population lives close to the poverty line

CONSUMER GOODS OWNERSHIP

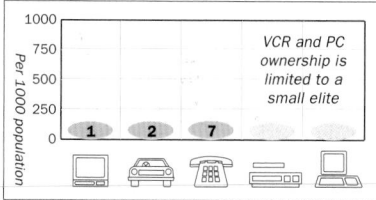

VCR and PC ownership is limited to a small elite

Per 1000 population

1   2   7

Wealth is concentrated among the political and business elite; most of the population lives at subsistence level.

WORLD RANKING

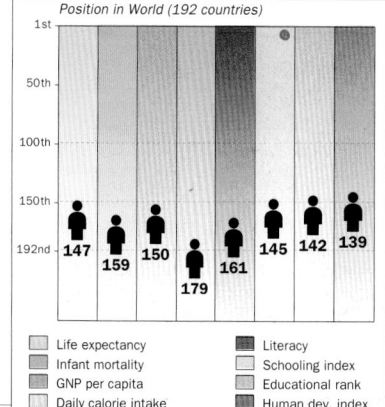

Position in World (192 countries)

1st — 50th — 100th — 150th — 192nd

147   159   150   179   161   145   142   139

- ▫ Life expectancy
- ▫ Infant mortality
- ▫ GNP per capita
- ▫ Daily calorie intake
- ▪ Literacy
- ▫ Schooling index
- ▪ Educational rank
- ▪ Human dev. index

CONGO

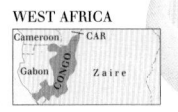

OFFICIAL NAME: The Republic of the Congo   **CAPITAL:** Brazzaville
POPULATION: 2.6 million   **CURRENCY:** CFA franc   **OFFICIAL LANGUAGE:** French

C

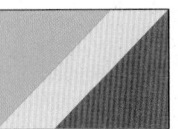

S TRADDLING THE EQUATOR in west central Africa, the area now covered by the Congo was first inhabited by Bantu-speaking peoples in the 15th century. In the 1880s it became a French colony, achieving independence in 1960. Rich in oil reserves, the Congo is now emerging from two decades of Marxist–Leninist rule.

CLIMATE

WEATHER CHART

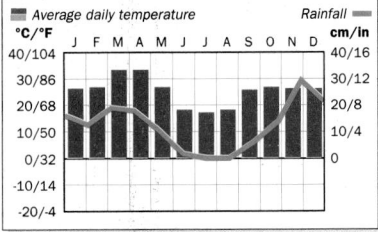

In most years there are two wet seasons and two dry seasons. Rainfall is heaviest in the coastal regions south of the equator.

TRANSPORTATION

 Brazzaville International   Has no fleet

THE TRANSPORTATION NETWORK

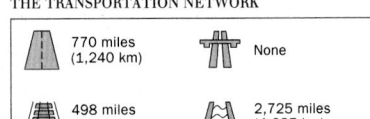

770 miles (1,240 km)		None	
498 miles (801 km)		2,725 miles (4,385 km)	

The Congo aims to maintain its entrepôt position linking the Central African Republic, Chad and Cameroon with the Atlantic coast. The Congo Ocean Railroad runs from Brazzaville to the major port of Pointe-Noire.

TOURISM

 30,000 visitors   Down 14% in 1994

MAIN OVERSEAS ARRIVALS

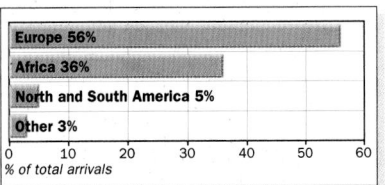

| Europe 56% |
| Africa 36% |
| North and South America 5% |
| Other 3% |

% of total arrivals

The Marxist–Leninist regime did not seek to develop tourism, and visitors, mostly on safaris and business-related trips, are still rare.

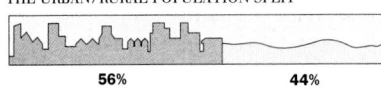

***The Loufoulakari Falls,** near Brazzaville. Swamps and mangroves border many of the rivers in the Congo's northern region.*

PEOPLE

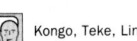 Kongo, Teke, Lingala, French   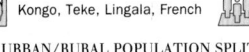 21 people per sq. mile

THE URBAN/RURAL POPULATION SPLIT

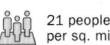

56%   44%

ETHNIC MAKEUP

Bakongo 48%
Mbochi 12%
Teke 17%
Sangha 20%
Other 3%

The Congo is one of the most tribally conscious countries in Africa. The main tensions are between the Bakongo, who live in the north, and the Mbochi, who are concentrated in the more prosperous south. Since the 1950s, women have achieved considerable emancipation.

POLITICS

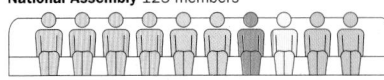

U. House 1995/1998
L. House 1993/1998
President Pascal Lissouba

THE STATE OF THE PARTIES

National Assembly 125 members

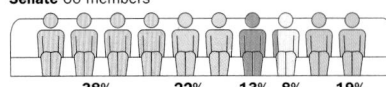

38% UPADS	22% MCDDI	12% CLP	8% RDPS	20% Other

UPADS = Pan-African Union for Social Democracy
MCDDI = Congolese Movement for Democracy and Integral Development   **CLP** = Congolese Labor Party   **RDPS** = Rally for Democratic and Social Progress   **RDD** = Rally for Democracy and Development

Senate 60 members

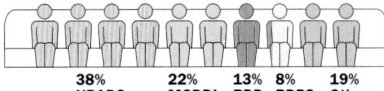

38% UPADS	22% MCDDI	13% RDD	8% RDPS	19% Other

In 1991, Congo renounced Marxism and a multiparty constitution was introduced. Elections held in 1992–1993 eventually resulted in victories for Lissouba and his UPADS party. However, the results were disputed by opposition parties, whose armed supporters have since frequently clashed with pro-Lissouba forces.

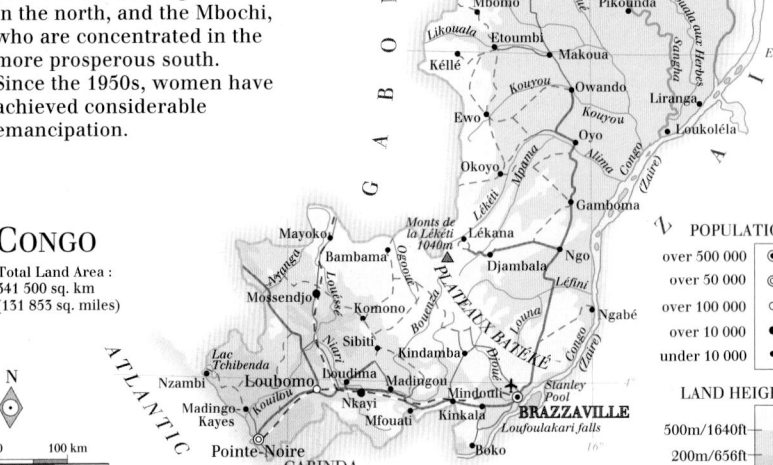

CONGO

Total Land Area :
341 500 sq. km
(131 853 sq. miles)

POPULATION
- over 500 000
- over 50 000
- over 100 000
- over 10 000
- under 10 000

LAND HEIGHT
500m/1640ft
200m/656ft
Sea Level

C

WORLD AFFAIRS

Carefully balancing its relations with France and the USA is a priority. Both wish to gain control of the oil industry.

The Congo is keen to maintain the ties developed during the 1970s and 1980s with what was then the communist world. Relations with eastern Europe, the former Soviet Union, Cuba and particularly China remain strong.

AID

 $129m (receipts)   Up 12% in 1993

Before 1990, the USSR, Cuba and China were the major donors. Most aid now comes from France. High levels of 1970s debt mean that, despite its oil, the Congo remains dependent on aid.

DEFENSE

 $50m   Up 4% in 1995

The militias of the various political forces are currently being integrated into the 10,000-strong army. Although relatively small, Congo's air force is very well equipped, with 20 MiG-17s and 12 MiG-21s.

ECONOMICS

 $1.6bn   533.68–489.05 CFA francs

SCORE CARD

- ❑ WORLD GNP RANKING.......................141st
- ❑ GNP PER CAPITA $640
- ❑ BALANCE OF PAYMENTS....................$–868m
- ❑ INFLATION 56.9%
- ❑ UNEMPLOYMENT ...Widespread underemployment

STRENGTHS

Oil has increased in importance, now providing 90% of export revenues compared with 5% in 1970. Significant timber supplies. Skilled and well-trained work force helps sustain substantial industrial base in the capital and Pointe-Noire.

WEAKNESSES

$4 billion debt by the late 1980s. Top-heavy bureaucracy inherited from Marxist years. Over-dependence on oil.

EXPORTS

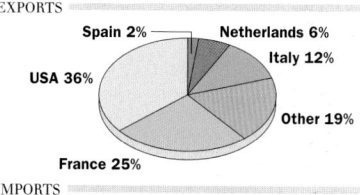

IMPORTS

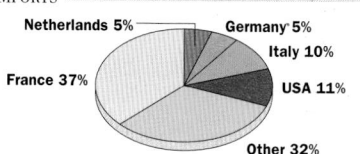

RESOURCES

428m kwh (capacity 149,000 kw)	173,513 b/d (reserves 830,000,000 bbl)
305,000 goats, 111,000 sheep, 68,000 cattle	Oil, natural gas, zinc, gold, copper

Oil is by far the Congo's most important resource. Natural gas reserves have yet to be exploited; the oil industry currently flares excess gas. Bauxite and iron ore reserves are not large enough to be profitably mined and phosphate production was abandoned in 1977. Chinese aid has helped build two hydroelectric dams, on the Bouenza and Djoué rivers. A third is currently being built on the Léfini at Imboulou.

ENVIRONMENT

 3%   Still no effective controls on deforestation

There is increasing concern at the uncontrolled exploitation of tropical timber. The Congo has also been used in the past as a dumping ground for dangerous toxic waste from the West.

MEDIA

 In theory, all censorship restrictions have been lifted. However, occasional acts of censorship and press intimidation are still reported

PUBLISHING AND BROADCAST MEDIA

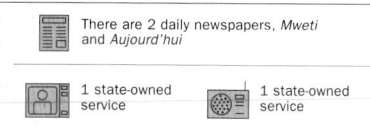

There are 2 daily newspapers, *Mweti* and *Aujourd'hui*	
1 state-owned service	1 state-owned service

During World War II, *Radio Brazzaville* was a vital organ of De Gaulle's Free French. Satellite links will mean *Canal France Internationale* TV will soon be available.

CRIME

 The Congo does not publish prison figures   Fairly constant in last 5 years

Armed robbery and smuggling remain the major problems. The state's human rights record has improved since the Marxist–Leninist secret police years.

EDUCATION

 57%  12,045 students

Originally pioneered by French Catholic missions, schools are still subject to inspection from Paris.

CHRONOLOGY

The kingdoms of Teke and Loango were incorporated as the Middle Congo (part of French Equatorial Africa) between 1880 and 1883.

- ❑ **1960** Independence. Former priest Fulbert Youlou president.
- ❑ **1964** Marxist–Leninist National Revolution Movement (MNR) becomes only legal party.
- ❑ **1977** President Ngoumbi assassinated. Martial law declared; Yhompi-Opango head of state.
- ❑ **1979** Col. Denis Sassou-Nguesso president.
- ❑ **1991** Return to multiparty democracy.
- ❑ **1992** Elections. Pascal Lissouba (former geneticist) president.
- ❑ **1993** In elections, Lissouba's UPADS party gains majority.

HEALTH

 1 per 8,300 people   Diarrheal, parasitic and respiratory diseases, malaria

The health service, established by French military doctors at the turn of the century, is considered effective.

WEALTH

 Wage rates among the Congo's middle class are higher than in most African countries

CONSUMER GOODS OWNERSHIP

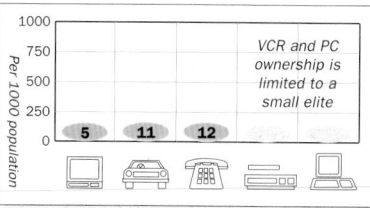

Oil has sustained an active and confident middle class. French label products are seen as status symbols.

WORLD RANKING

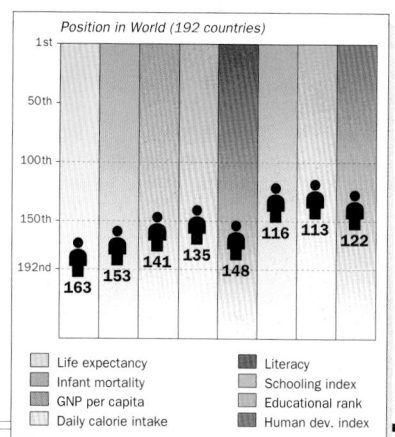

COSTA RICA

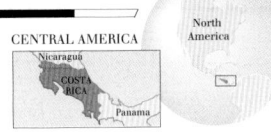

OFFICIAL NAME: The Republic of Costa Rica   **CAPITAL:** San José
POPULATION: 3.4 million   **CURRENCY:** Costa Rican colón   **OFFICIAL LANGUAGE:** Spanish

C

LOCATED IN CENTRAL AMERICA between Nicaragua and Panama, Costa Rica gained its independence from Spain in 1821. From 1948 until the end of the 1980s, it was the most developed welfare state in Central America. Costa Rica is nominally a multiparty democracy, but in practice two parties dominate. Its constitution is unique in the world as it contains a clause which forbids the formation of a national army; its own was abolished in 1949.

CLIMATE

WEATHER CHART

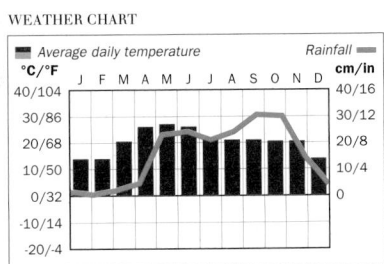

The Atlantic coast has heavy rainfall, while the Pacific coast is much drier. The central uplands are temperate.

TRANSPORTATION

Juan Santamaría, San José
988,000 passengers

4 ships
2,700 dwt

THE TRANSPORTATION NETWORK

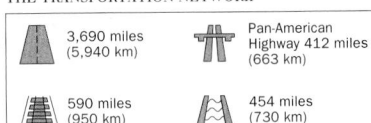

3,690 miles (5,940 km)	Pan-American Highway 412 miles (663 km)
590 miles (950 km)	454 miles (730 km)

The "Jungle Train" railroad is being revived. The rest of the network has closed; 80% of roads need repair.

TOURISM

722,000 visitors   Up 6% in 1994

MAIN OVERSEAS ARRIVALS

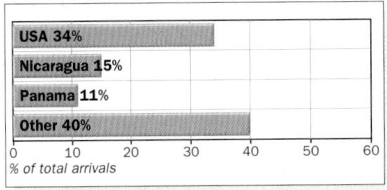

USA 34%
Nicaragua 15%
Panama 11%
Other 40%

% of total arrivals

Increased prices coupled with armed robberies on foreigners in 1995, including a $1 million ransom demand by kidnappers, led to a sharp fall in tourism and damaged the country's reputation as a safe destination.

PEOPLE

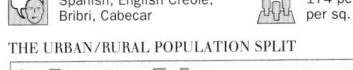

Spanish, English Creole, Bribri, Cabecar

174 people per sq. mile

THE URBAN/RURAL POPULATION SPLIT

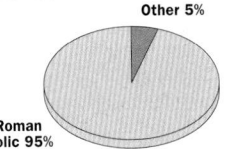

48%   52%

RELIGIOUS PERSUASION

Other 5%

Roman Catholic 95%

The majority of the population is *mestizo* of Spanish origin. One-third of people in the Puerto Limón area are black and often English-speaking. There are only about 5,000 indigenous Indians.

POLITICS

1994/1998

President José María Figueres

THE STATE OF THE PARTIES

Legislative Assembly 57 members

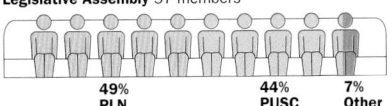

49% PLN   44% PUSC   7% Other

PLN = National Liberation Party   PUSC = Social Christian Unity Party   **Other** = General Union Party, Popular Front, Farmers of Cartaginesa Action

Employees of Costa Rica's extensive bureaucracy tend to belong to one of the two main parties – the PUSC or the PLN. Former president Luis Alberto Monge of the PLN, the Calderón family which supports the PUSC, and the major banana and coffee families are powerful behind the scenes, forming coalitions and shaping policies. Historically the USA has exercised a very powerful influence on politics. The PLN held power from 1982 until 1990, when President Rafael Calderón pursued austerity policies. In 1994, José María Figueres of the PLN won the presidency promising state intervention and a welfare state. In 1995, under pressure from international financial organizations to reduce the budget deficit, he reached a consensus with the PUSC and implemented harsh structural adjustment measures. This made him the most unpopular president in the country's history.

WORLD AFFAIRS

ACS   Geplac   NAM   OAS   San José

Costa Rica has always emphasized its neutrality in foreign affairs, but it maintains very strong ties with the USA. The protection of export prices for coffee and bananas is a major concern. Costa Rica has long-term aspirations to join NAFTA.

Pineapple plantation near Buenos Aires, *crossed by the Pan-American Highway which runs for 411 miles through Costa Rica.*

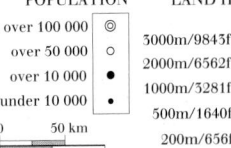

COSTA RICA

Total Land Area : 51 060 sq. km
(19 714 sq. miles)

POPULATION	
over 100 000	◎
over 50 000	○
over 10 000	●
under 10 000	•

LAND HEIGHT

3000m/9843ft
2000m/6562ft
1000m/3281ft
500m/1640ft
200m/656ft
Sea level

0   50 km
0   50 miles

AID

 $99m (receipts)   Down 27% in 1993

Aid mostly comes from the USA in the form of money for defense and drug-enforcement. The balance-of-payments support was sharply reduced in the early 1990s with the return of peace to the region, but the USA still sees Costa Rica as a useful base against potential left-wing insurgencies in neighboring El Salvador, Guatemala and Nicaragua.

DEFENSE

 No armed forces; anti-terrorist and security force exist   Not applicable

Costa Rica emerged from the 1948 civil war as a neutral, demilitarized modern state. A 7,500-strong Civil Guard is complemented by a highly-trained police force. Lack of a common command structure hinders the influence of the security forces but also renders them less accountable to public control. Spending on security is the lowest in the region. However, many right-wing paramilitary groups are known to exist.

ECONOMICS

 $7.9bn   164.19–191.76 colones

SCORE CARD

- ❏ WORLD GNP RANKING..........................85th
- ❏ GNP PER CAPITA $2,380
- ❏ BALANCE OF PAYMENTS....................$–463m
- ❏ INFLATION 22.3%
- ❏ UNEMPLOYMENT 4%

STRENGTHS

Traditional coffee industry still creates largest export revenues. Tourism has a long-term future because of general political stability. Government privatization program has lowered costs and encouraged competition.

WEAKNESSES

Main exports of coffee, beef and especially bananas have been hit by falling international prices. Political tensions threatening security of banana exports to EU. Dependent on imported oil. National economy too small to provide rapid growth; need for regional economic integration.

EXPORTS

Belgium-Luxembourg 4%
Italy 5%
Nicaragua 7%
Germany 10%
USA 48%
Other 26%

IMPORTS

Venezuela 4%
Guatemala 4%
Mexico 5%
Japan 6%
USA 50%
Other 31%

RESOURCES

 4.1bn kwh (capacity 933,000 kw)   Not an oil producer; refines 15,000 b/cd

 1.7m cattle, 252,000 pigs, 114,000 horses   Gold, bauxite, silver, manganese, mercury

Costa Rica has large bauxite deposits at Boruca – aluminum smelting is an important industry. Small quantities of gold, silver, manganese and mercury are also mined. Self-sufficiency in energy is being pursued through the development of hydroelectric power. Forests cover 34% of the country.

ENVIRONMENT

 13% (3% partially protected)   Monteverde Cloud Forest is an example of a well-run reserve

The remaining rainforests are slowly being cut down to make way for commercial agriculture. The government, however, is beginning to protect land by designating national parks. Ecotourism is being encouraged, as is the sensitive exploitation of natural resources.

MEDIA

 Journalists are supposed to join *Colegio*, a state-run trade union, effectively run by the government

PUBLISHING AND BROADCAST MEDIA

 There are 4 daily newspapers, *La Nación*, *La República*, *La Prensa Libre* and *Extra*

 1 state-owned, 4 independent stations   State-owned and independent stations

There are four private TV stations providing round-the-clock programing direct from the USA.

CRIME

 Costa Rica does not publish prison figures   Up 3% in 1990

Costa Rica is the least violent Central American country, but attacks on tourists have damaged its image. Colombian drugs cartels use the country to transfer cocaine to the USA. The police show some hostility towards refugees, most of whom are from from Nicaragua and El Salvador.

CHRONOLOGY

Costa Rica, ruled since the 16th century by Spain, gained independence in 1821.

- ❏ **1948** Disputed elections lead to civil war; ended by Social Democratic Party (later known as the PLN) forming provisional government under José Ferrer.
- ❏ **1949** Ferrer abolishes army.
- ❏ **1987** Central American Peace Plan initiated by President Arias.

EDUCATION

 93%   80,442 students

Schooling is based on the French system. The regional University of Central America is based in Costa Rica.

HEALTH

 1 per 1,205 people   Heart diseases, accidents, cancers, perinatal deaths

The public health system is one of the most developed in Latin America. The private system is noted as a regional center for plastic surgery.

WEALTH

 Agricultural worker, 16,661 colones ($87) per month; construction worker, 23,319 colones ($122) per month

CONSUMER GOODS OWNERSHIP

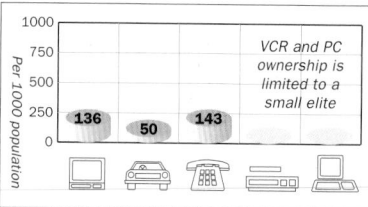

VCR and PC ownership is limited to a small elite

136   50   143

The plantation-owning families are the wealthiest group; the blacks on the Caribbean coast are the poorest.

WORLD RANKING

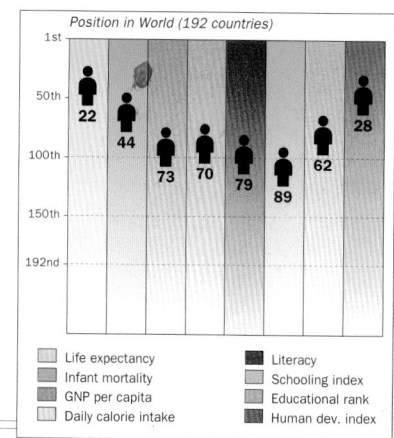

Position in World (192 countries)

22   44   73   70   79   89   62   28

- Life expectancy
- Infant mortality
- GNP per capita
- Daily calorie intake
- Literacy
- Schooling index
- Educational rank
- Human dev. index

CROATIA

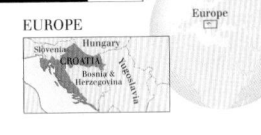

OFFICIAL NAME: Republic of Croatia **CAPITAL:** Zagreb
POPULATION: 4.5 million **CURRENCY:** Kuna **OFFICIAL LANGUAGE:** Croatian

LOCATED TO THE SOUTH OF Slovenia and west of Serbia, Croatia includes the historic regions of Istra, Dalmatia and Slavonia. Its Adriatic coast is important for tourism and shipping, which have played major roles the economy. Since the breakup of the Federal Republic of Yugoslavia, Croatia has been involved in warfare in Bosnia and in defending its own territory. Eastern Slavonia remains under Serbian control pending implementation of a 1995 peace accord.

CLIMATE

WEATHER CHART

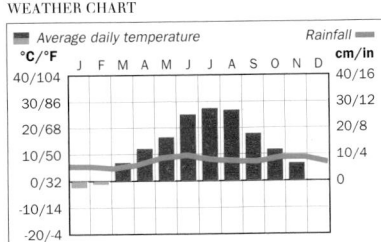

Northern Croatia has a temperate continental climate. Its Adriatic coast has a Mediterranean climate.

TRANSPORTATION

 Pleso International, Zagreb    85 ships 184,000 dwt

THE TRANSPORTATION NETWORK

 7,660 miles (12,330 km)   188 miles (302 km)

 1,507 miles (2,425 km)   Islands are linked to the mainland by ferries

Communications in western Slavonia and Krajina were affected by Croatian military operations which retook them in 1995. In 1993, Croats regained Maslenica Bridge, a vital link between northern Croatia and Dalmatia.

TOURISM

 2.3m visitors   Down 4% in 1994

MAIN OVERSEAS ARRIVALS

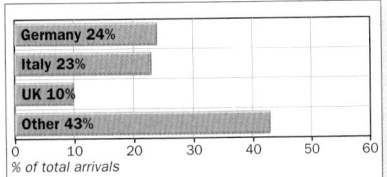

Germany 24%
Italy 23%
UK 10%
Other 43%

% of total arrivals

Croatia's seaside resorts, particularly in northern Istra, are leading a modest recovery of the tourist industry.

PEOPLE

 Croatian    207 people per sq.mile

THE URBAN/RURAL POPULATION SPLIT

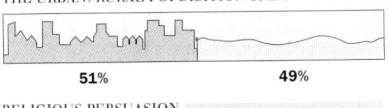

51%   49%

RELIGIOUS PERSUASION

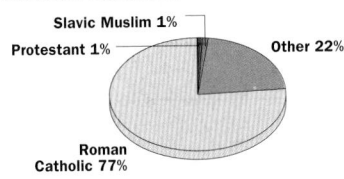

Slavic Muslim 1%
Protestant 1%
Other 22%
Roman Catholic 77%

Croats make up 80% of the population, Serbs 12%. In 1991, the Serbs, alienated by a climate of Croatian nationalism, proclaimed the Republic of Serbian Krajina, made up of the areas where they formed a majority, notably the Krajina, and western and eastern Slavonia. In 1995, Croatian forces retook western Slavonia and Krajina. After mediation from the UN, the Croatian government and rebel Croatian Serb leaders signed an agreement in November 1995 which provided for the eventual reintegration of eastern Slavonia into Croatia.

POLITICS

 1995/1999    President Dr. Franjo Tudjman

THE STATE OF THE PARTIES
Chamber of Deputies 127 members

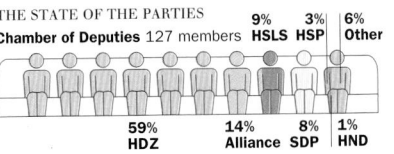

9% HSLS 3% HSP 6% Other
59% HDZ 14% Alliance 8% SDP 1% HND

HDZ = Croatian Democratic Union **HSLS** = Croatian Social Liberal Party **SDP** = Party of Democratic Change **HSP** = Croatian Party of Rights

Following the break-up of former Yugoslavia, the Croatian independence movement was led by the right-wing Croatian Democratic Union (HDZ) under Franjo Tudjman. Multiparty elections in 1995 consolidated the HDZ's

WORLD AFFAIRS

CE IAEA IBRD NAM OSCE

Croatia's major concern is with the implementation of the November 1995 agreement signed by the government and rebel Croatian Serbs providing for the reintegration of eastern Slavonia into Croatia. President Franjo Tudjman has made it clear that reintegration is a precondition for the normalization of relations between Croatia and Serbia. The signing of the December 1995 Bosnian peace agreement was widely recognized as a major foreign policy success for President Tudjman. Out of EU countries, Croatia maintains closest links with Germany.

AID

 $500m (est)   Aid levels have increased markedly since 1991

Croatia has been a major target of UNHCR and bilateral humanitarian aid. It has an estimated 526,000 refugees from Bosnia and Serb-held areas in Croatia. The main UNHCR warehouses are in Zagreb, Split and Rijeka.

DEFENSE

 $1.8bn   Up 60% in 1995

Croatia's defense forces comprises about 99,600 army, 1,100 navy and 300 air force personnel. In addition, the Croat Defense Association (HOS) has about 10,000 armed men in Bosnia; they will remain in place under the terms of the 1995 peace agreement. The army recaptured Serb-held western Slavonia and the Krajina in 1995.

and Tudjman's hold on power. The main political issues are the planned reintegration of eastern Slavonia, the last remaining sector of Serb-held territory within Croatia, and the implementation of the 1995 Bosnian peace agreement. Underpinning the agreement is the establishment of a workable Croat–Muslim Federation in Bosnia. Despite the creation of the Federation some doubts remain over the viability of the exercise. Ominously, problems arose in 1996 with the administration of the divided city of Mostar. The Muslims fear that the collapse of the Federation could lead to the division of Bosnia into Croat and Serb sectors.

C

ECONOMICS

 $12.1bn   5.63–5.33 kuna

SCORE CARD

- ❏ WORLD GNP RANKING..........................76th
- ❏ GNP PER CAPITA $510
- ❏ BALANCE OF PAYMENTS $625m
- ❏ INFLATION 2.1%
- ❏ UNEMPLOYMENT................................12.6%

STRENGTHS

Tourism recovering in safe areas. Exports to the West growing. Economy well placed to expand in peacetime.

WEAKNESSES

Economic reform held up by outdated infrastructure. Costs of repairing war damage. Refugees an economic strain.

EXPORTS/IMPORTS

> Before the conflict, Croatia's main trading partners were the former Yugoslavian republics, Italy and Germany

Dubrovnik, Dalmatia. *This historic city on the Adriatic coast was shelled and besieged by the Yugoslav federal army in 1991.*

RESOURCES

 8.9bn kwh   38,436 b/d

 14m poultry, 1.3m pigs, 519,000 cattle   Coal, bauxite, iron, oil, china clay, natural gas

Croatia generates half its energy needs from hydroelectric and half from thermal sources. It has few minerals, although it does have oil and gas fields. The rich fishing grounds off the Adriatic coast are a major resource.

ENVIRONMENT

 6%   Environmental issues not yet a priority following war

Croatia was the first Yugoslav republic to create reserves in order to protect endangered and unique wetlands.

MEDIA

 The government has extended its influence over the media. The HDZ effectively controls Hina, the national news agency

PUBLISHING AND BROADCAST MEDIA

 There are 9 daily newspapers, published locally, including *Vercenji List* in Zagreb and *Slobodna Dalmacija* in Split

 1 state-controlled service   1 state-controlled service

Inconsistencies in the official media line in war reporting led to enforced guidelines for presenting information.

CRIME

Croatia does not publish prison figures   Crime has risen since independence

The Croat militia in Bosnia, the HOS, is suspected of involvement in "ethnic cleansing." The UN has accused all sides in Bosnia of human rights abuses.

CHRONOLOGY

In 1945–1991 Croatia was a republic within the Yugoslav federation.

- ❏ **1991** Croatian independence. Rebel Serb Croatian republic proclaimed.
- ❏ **1992** UN and EU recognize Croatia.
- ❏ **1992–1995** Bosnian Croat involvement in Bosnian civil war.
- ❏ **1995** Croats retake Krajina from rebel Serbs, sign deal on reintegration of western Slavonia; Croatia signs Bosnian peace accord.

EDUCATION

 97%   77,689 students

Croatia has a well-developed education system. It has four universities, at Zagreb, Rijeka, Osijek and Split.

HEALTH

 1 per 435 people   Cerebrovascular and heart diseases, cancers

Most Croats are covered by a health insurance scheme. However, coping with refugees and war casualties poses an extra strain on already scarce funds.

WEALTH

 Standards of living are falling under the government's austerity program

CONSUMER GOODS OWNERSHIP

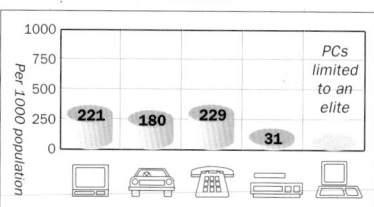

PCs limited to an elite

221   180   229   31

The net monthly wage in Croatia is equal to $149. Many Croatians are finding it difficult to meet basic needs.

WORLD RANKING

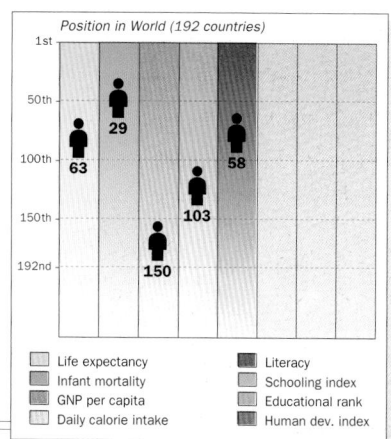

Position in World (192 countries)

- 63
- 29
- 150
- 103
- 58

- Life expectancy
- Infant mortality
- GNP per capita
- Daily calorie intake
- Literacy
- Schooling index
- Educational rank
- Human dev. index

Čakovec
Varaždin
H U N G A R Y
Koprivnica
Krapina   Križevci   Bilo Gora
S L O V E N I A
Samobor   Sesvete
Drava
ZAGREB   Velika Gorica
Virovitica
Beli Manastir
Karlovac
Sisak   Kutina
Podravska Slatina
Golfo di Venezia
Rijeka
Petrinja
Una
Sava
SLAVONIA
Papuk
Osijek
Borovo
Vukovar
Pazin   Ogulin
Glina
Slavonska Požega
Nova Gradiška
Đakovo
Vinkovci
Županja
ISTRA
Rovinj
Crikvenica
Krk
Seni
Slavonski Brod
Pula   Cres
Kvarner
D I N A R I C   A L P S
BOSNIA & HERZEGOVINA
Lošinj   Pag
Gospić
Rab
Zadar
Dugi Otok
Knin
Dinara 1831m
Dinaric Alps
Šibenik   Sinj
A D R I A T I C
Trogir
Solin
Split
Brač
Makarska
Hvar
Vis
Metković
Korčula
D A L M A T I A
Mljet
Dubrovnik
S E A
YUGOSLAVIA (SERBIA & MONTENEGRO)
YUGOSLAVIA (SERBIA & MONTENEGRO)

CROATIA

Total Land Area : 56 558 sq. km (21 829 sq. miles)

LAND HEIGHT

- 1000m/3281ft
- 500m/1640ft
- 200m/656ft
- Sea Level

POPULATION

- over 500 000 ⊙
- over 100 000 ◎
- over 50 000 ○
- over 10 000 ●
- under 10 000 •

N

0   50 km
0   50 miles

CUBA

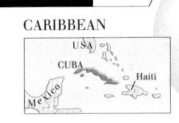

OFFICIAL NAME: Republic of Cuba   **CAPITAL:** Havana
POPULATION: 10.8 million   **CURRENCY:** Cuban peso   **OFFICIAL LANGUAGE:** Spanish

C

THE CARIBBEAN'S LARGEST ISLAND, Cuba has widely cultivated lowlands, which fall between three mountainous areas. The fertile soil of the lowlands supports the sugarcane, rice and coffee plantations. Sugar, the country's major export, is suffering from depressed world prices. A former Spanish colony, Cuba is the only communist state in the Caribbean. Since the collapse of communism in the Soviet Union, the USA sees Cuba as less of a threat, in marked contrast to 1962, when the Soviet nuclear missiles on the island brought the two superpowers close to war. Cuba is still subject to US sanctions and unable to afford oil imports.

Valle de Viñales, Pinar del Río province.
Cuba's undulating countryside is ideal for growing the main export crop, sugar.

CLIMATE

WEATHER CHART

		Rainfall
Average daily temperature		

°C/°F   J F M A M J J A S O N D   cm/in
40/104   40/16
30/86   30/12
20/68   20/8
10/50   10/4
0/32   0
-10/14
-20/-4

Cuba's subtropical climate is hot all year round and very hot in the summer. Rainfall is heaviest in the mountains, which receive up to 98 inches a year. Generally, the north is wetter than the south; the Guantánamo area receives only 8 inches of rainfall annually. In winter, the west is sometimes affected by cold air from the USA, but only for a day or two at a time.

TRANSPORTATION

José Martí, Havana
1.2m passengers

85 ships
711,300 dwt

THE TRANSPORTATION NETWORK

21,127 miles (34,000 km)		357 miles (575 km)	
9,022 miles (14,519 km)		149 miles (240 km)	

Public transportation has been extremely cheap in Cuba, although fuel shortages have made it increasingly erratic and unreliable. Cubans rely mostly on traditional black bicycles, which are imported by the thousand from China. Havana owes much of its charm to the number of 40-year-old Chevrolets and Oldsmobiles still being driven around. Although this is another result of sanctions, it keeps the many inventive local spare-parts workshops in business.

TOURISM

424,041 visitors

Up 25% in 1991

MAIN OVERSEAS ARRIVALS

Canada	19%
Germany	15%
Mexico	11%
Spain	9%
Italy	5%
Other	41%

0   10   20   30   40   50   60
% of total arrivals

Cuba, once a playground for wealthy Americans, reduced tourism after 1959 as being unfit for a socialist society. Recently the policy has changed. Although most tourist arrivals are from Canada, Germany, Mexico and Spain, some are Americans going via these destinations to skirt the US trade embargo – the Cuban authorities do not stamp US passport holders. About 2,000 affluent Latin American "health-tourists" visit Cuba annually for low-cost, advanced surgery, or to stay at sanatoria.

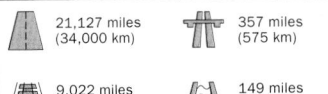

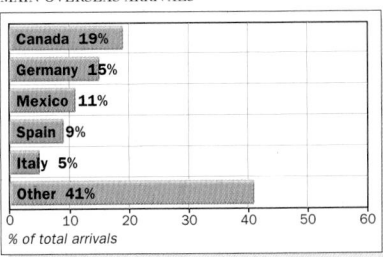

GULF OF MEXICO

Straits of Florida

Archipiélago de los Colorados

HAVANA (La Habana)   Guanabo   Matanzas   Varadero
Marianao   Cárdenas
Mariel   Guanabacoa
Guanajay   Jovellanos
Artemisa   Colón   Cifuentes
San Cristóbal   Perico   Sagua la Grande
Minas de Matahambre   Hanábana   Santo Domingo   Caibarién
Consolación del Sur   Santa Clara
Pinar del Río   Golfo de   Placetas
Batabanó   Cienfuegos   Cabaiguán   Chambas   Morón
La Fé   Juraguá   Sancti Spíritus   Taguasco
Nueva Gerona   Condado   Ciego de Ávila   Esmeralda
C. San Antonio   Céspedes
Isla de la   Florida   Nuevitas
Juventud   Santa Fé   Vertientes
Archipiélago de los Canarreos   Crucero   Camagüey
Cayo Largo   Contramaestre   Puerto Padre   Jesús Menén
Guáimaro   Las Tunas

ATLANTIC OCEAN

Archipiélago de Sabana
Cayo Sabinal
Cayo Romano
Archipiélago de Camagüey

Archipiélago de los Jardines de la Reina

Yucatan Channel

Santa Cruz del Sur   Salado
Golfo de   Bayamo   Jigu
Guacanayabo   Manzanillo   Palma Sor
Bartolomé   Masó   MAESTRA
Niquero   SIERRA   Pico Turquino   Sa
1994 m   S   E

Guanabo, 15 miles east of Havana, is a low-key holiday resort favored by Cubans. The most modern cars in Cuba are imported, along with computers, in exchange for sugar in a special trading deal with Japan.

CUBA

Total Land Area : 110 860 sq. km
(42 803 sq. miles)

POPULATION
▣ over 1 000 000
◉ over 500 000
◎ over 100 000
○ over 50 000
● over 10 000
• under 10 000

LAND HEIGHT
1000m/3281ft
500m/1640ft
200m/656ft
Sea Level

N

0   50 km
0   50 miles

PEOPLE

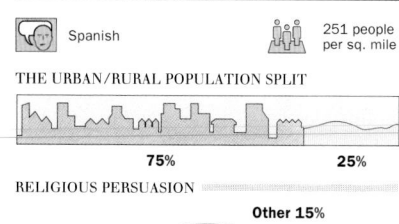

Spanish

251 people per sq. mile

THE URBAN/RURAL POPULATION SPLIT

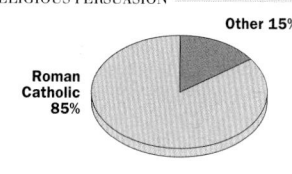

75%   25%

RELIGIOUS PERSUASION

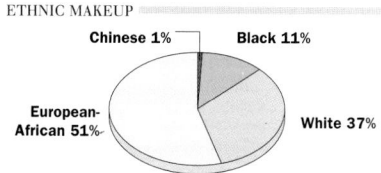

Other 15%

Roman Catholic 85%

ETHNIC MAKEUP

Chinese 1%   Black 11%

European-African 51%   White 37%

Ethnic tension in Cuba is minimal. About 70% of Cubans are of Spanish descent, mainly from the settlers who began arriving in Cuba in the 16th century, but also from the more recent influx of exiles from Franco's Spain. The black population is descended from the slaves and migrants from Cuba's neighboring states, in particular Jamaica.

Living standards in Cuba have fallen dramatically since the collapse of the East European communist bloc, previously its main trading partner. In 1991, further rationing was introduced for most basic foodstuffs; yet in Havana, exotic goods are easily available in the many exclusive dollar stores.

An increasing number of women are playing prominent roles in politics, the professions and the armed forces. Child-care facilities are freely available and there is a law requiring men to share equally in housework and child-rearing if a wife is working in "social production" – the state, however, does not check how well this law is observed.

POPULATION AGE BREAKDOWN

% of population by age group	0–14	15–64	65+		
	5%	6.1%	7.6%	8.5%	9.4%
	60.8%	56.9%	60.7%	68.8%	67.2%
	34.2%	37%	31.7%	22.7%	23.4%
	1960	1970	1980	1990	2000

POLITICS

1994/1998

President Fidel Castro Ruz

THE STATE OF THE PARTIES

National Assembly of People's Power 589 members

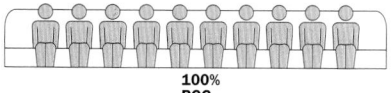

100% PCC

PCC = Cuban Communist Party

Fidel Castro has led Cuba since 1959 and was the founder of the one-party communist system, formalized in the 1976 constitution.

MAIN POLITICAL ISSUES
The succession
Castro has stated his wish to retire from the Council of State when his current term ends in 1998. Contenders for the leadership include his brother Raúl, current defense minister, Roberto Robaina, the foreign minister, and economic guru Carlos Lage. Castro, who has said that the Communist Party must be invigorated with younger minds, is thought to favor Robaina.

The economy
Cuba chose not to go down the capitalist route when its main patron and supplier, the former USSR, ended aid in 1991. The socialist economy remains in place, although it is increasingly short of supplies and subject to the disabling effects of the US trade embargo.

PROFILE
Cuban politics have always been dominated by the perceived US threat. The Party has reacted to the collapse of the USSR by strengthening its dominance, as illustrated by the 1992 imposition of death sentences on several Cuban dissidents. As the USA has tightened economic sanctions, as the surest way to end Castro's rule, so Castro has increased his powers. Constitutional changes in 1992 gave the president the right to declare a state of emergency and to take full command of the military.

Raúl Castro*, brother of Fidel and the Minister of Defense.*

Fidel Castro*, Cuba's leader since 1959. The USA is keen to oust his regime.*

Moa

yarí

Baracoa

El Salvador

Guantánamo

GUANTANAMO BAY (to US)

Windward Passage

WORLD AFFAIRS

| ACS | ALADI | SELA | NAM | OAS |

Since the 1962 stand-off, when Cuba accepted Russian missiles targeted at US cities, Cuba has been considered a danger by the USA and has been subject to diplomatic isolation from countries which support US policies in the Caribbean. The end of aid from Moscow after 1991, following the collapse of the USSR, made conditions in Cuba increasingly difficult. The USA increased pressure on the Castro administration by tightening the rules of the trade embargo, including an effective ban on ships docking in the USA which had been in a Cuban port. Cuba has mustered support in the UN, as well as EU backing, for a lifting of the US embargo, but without effect. The USA has vetoed any UN debate, and will not abandon its stand until Cuba adopts a multiparty democracy.

Iran and the Russian Federation now take most of Cuba's sugar, in exchange for badly needed oil supplies. Iran is now one of Cuba's few supporters worldwide. Trade between the two countries has grown as the Moscow alliance declines in importance.

AID

 $42m (receipts)   Up 45% in 1991

Cuba claims to receive no aid, but does receive donations from Spain. Sweden used to be an important donor, but withheld aid payments in 1993 in response to human rights violations by the Castro regime.

CHRONOLOGY
Originally inhabited by the Arawak people, Cuba was claimed by Columbus for Spain in 1492. Development of the sugar industry from the 18th century, using imported slave labor, made Cuba the world's third-largest producer by 1860.

❑ **1868** End of the slave trade.
❑ **1868–1878** Ten Years' War for independence from Spain.
❑ **1895** Second war of independence. Thousands die in Spanish concentration camps.
❑ **1898** USA declares war on Spain in support of Cuban rebels to protect strong American financial interests in Cuba.
❑ **1899** USA takes Cuba and installs military interim government.
❑ **1901** USA is granted intervention rights and military bases, including Guantanamo Bay naval base. ⇨

C

C

CHRONOLOGY *continued*

- ❏ **1902** Tomás Estrada Palma takes over as first Cuban president. USA leaves Cuba, but intervenes in 1906–1909 and 1919–1924.
- ❏ **1909** Liberal presidency of José Miguel Goméz. Economy prospers; US investment in tourism, gambling and sugar.
- ❏ **1925–1933** Dictatorship of President Gerardo Machado.
- ❏ **1933** Years of guerrilla activity end in revolution. Sergeant Fulgencio Batista takes over and leads military dictatorship.
- ❏ **1955** Fidel Castro exiled after two years imprisonment for subversion.
- ❏ **1956–1958** Castro returns to lead a guerrilla war in the Sierra Maestra.
- ❏ **1959** Batista flees. Castro takes over, his brother, Raúl, is deputy, Che Guevara third in rank. Wholesale nationalizations; Cuba reorganized on Soviet model.
- ❏ **1961** USA breaks off relations. US-backed, anti-Castro Cubans attempt invasion at Bay of Pigs. Fail. Cuba declares itself Marxist-Leninist.
- ❏ **1962** US economic and political blockade. Missile crisis: May, Khrushchev agrees to defend Cuba; October 14, US spy planes see nuclear missile on site; October 22, Kennedy orders seizure of weapons on Soviet ships in "quarantine zone." USA prepares for war; October 28, Khrushchev orders return of weapons; November 20, USA lifts "quarantine."
- ❏ **1965** Che Guevara resigns to pursue foreign liberation wars. One-party state formalized.
- ❏ **1972** Cuba joins COMECON.
- ❏ **1976** New socialist constitution. Cuban troops in Angola until 1991.
- ❏ **1977** Sends troops to Ethiopia.
- ❏ **1980** 125,000 Cubans, including "undesirables" (criminals or people with learning disabilities) flee to USA.
- ❏ **1982** USA tightens sanctions and bans flights and tourism to Cuba.
- ❏ **1983** US invasion of Grenada. Cuba involved in clashes with US forces.
- ❏ **1984** Agreement with USA on Cuban emigration and repatriation of "undesirables" is short-lived.
- ❏ **1986** Many government changes, but Soviet-style *glasnost* rejected.
- ❏ **1987** Cubans riot in US jails at new repatriation accord.
- ❏ **1988** UN's second veto of US attempt to accuse Cuba of human rights violations. Diplomatic relations established with EC.
- ❏ **1989** Senior military men executed for arms and drugs smuggling.
- ❏ **1991** Preferential trade agreement with USSR ends. Severe rationing.
- ❏ **1992** USA tightens blockade.
- ❏ **1993** All ex-Soviet military leave.

DEFENSE

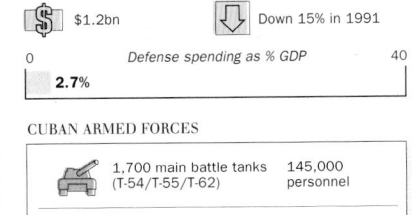

| 💲 $1.2bn | ⬇ Down 15% in 1991 |

0   *Defense spending as % GDP*   40

2.7%

CUBAN ARMED FORCES

🛡	1,700 main battle tanks (T-54/T-55/T-62)	145,000 personnel
🚢	3 submarines, 3 frigates and 28 patrol boats	12,000 personnel
✈	162 combat aircraft (146 MiG); also 200+ SAM launchers	7,000 personnel
🚀	None	

From 1959 to the 1980s, Cuba's efficient military was one of the achievements of the revolution. Under Castro's brother, Raúl, it succeeded in repelling the US-sponsored Bay of Pigs invasion in 1961, and saw effective action in Africa in the 1970s, preventing South Africa from taking control of Angola, and Somalia from occupying the Ogaden region. Today, with communist regimes collapsed around the world, it has lost much of its prestige. Russia is still the main supplier of arms and spares, but now has to be paid in increasingly scarce hard currency. In an effort to save money, compulsory military service has been cut from three years to two.

ECONOMICS

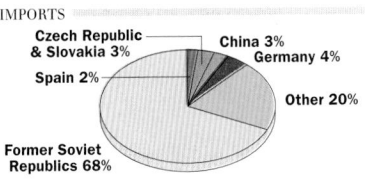

| 📊 $20.9bn | 💲 0.76 Cuban pesos |

SCORE CARD

- ❏ WORLD GNP RANKING..........................64th
- ❏ GNP PER CAPITA $1,935
- ❏ BALANCE OF PAYMENTS ....In deficit
- ❏ INFLATION..High
- ❏ UNEMPLOYMENT 6%

ECONOMIC PERFORMANCE INDICATOR

Consumer price index   *GDP*

Cuba does not publish Consumer price or GDP figures

Consumer price index 1988=100: 1000, 700, 400, 100, 0
GDP 1988=100: 160, 140, 120, 100, 0
1988 1989 1990 1991 1992

EXPORTS

- Czech Republic & Slovakia 3%
- Bulgaria 3%
- Former Soviet Republics 60%
- China 4%
- Germany 5%
- Other 25%

IMPORTS

- Czech Republic & Slovakia 3%
- Spain 2%
- Former Soviet Republics 68%
- China 3%
- Germany 4%
- Other 20%

STRENGTHS

A relatively broad base compared with other Caribbean states. Sugar is the main product, followed by nickel, citrus fruits, tobacco and, increasingly, tourism.

WEAKNESSES

US trade embargo robs Cuba of a major market and investment capital; Cuba was once second only to Venezuela in US overseas investment in Latin America. Non-convertible currency is an increasing liability as Russia demands payment for oil in dollars. Loss of ex-communist states as trading partners.

PROFILE

Since 1959, the nationalized economy has oscillated between concentration on sugar and attempts at industrialization. Following a brief experiment in market liberalization, the Castro regime went back to total state control in 1986 – although some moves toward a free market were made in 1993. Since then, the economy has been in recession and is suffering from an acute shortage of fuel, spare parts for the sugar industry and chemicals. Foreign capital is increasingly hard to come by, although Castro is beginning to allow some foreign investment in hotels and tourism. The government is also selling its first oil concessions to foreign companies. The USA is now relying on the regime to collapse with the economy. It is, therefore, unlikely to lift its trade embargo unless Cubans adopt a multiparty democracy and reject Castro.

CUBA : MAJOR BUSINESSES

Havana
Matahambre   Cardenas Bay
Ciego de Ávila
Cienfuegos
Pinar del Rio   Isla de la Juventud
Santiago de Cuba

🏭 Oil refining		🐀 Nickel mining
⚒ Manufacturing		🍊 Citrus fruits
🏭 Sugarcane refining		📜 Cigars
⚗ Pharmaceuticals		🛢 Oil

0   100 km
0   100 miles

RESOURCES

 13.2bn kwh (capacity 4m kw)

 15,000 b/d (reserves 100,000,000 bbl)

4.9m cattle, 1.9m pigs, 630,000 horses

Iron, nickel, cobalt, chromite, gold, manganese, oil

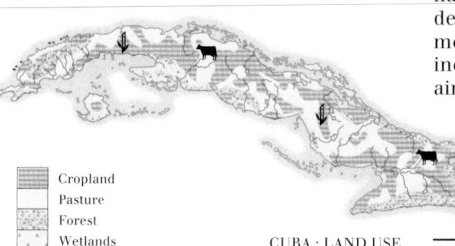

Cropland
Pasture
Forest
Wetlands
Sugarcane - cash crop
Cattle

CUBA : LAND USE

0   100 km
0   100 miles

ELECTRICITY GENERATION

Hydro 1% (0.08bn kwh)
Thermal 99% (12.4bn kwh)
Nuclear 0%
Other 0%

0   20   40   60   80   100

% of total generation by type

ENVIRONMENT

 6% (2% partially protected)

Deforestation rate remains lowest in Latin America

ENVIRONMENTAL TREATIES

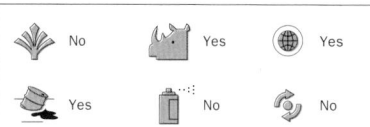

No
Yes
Yes
Yes
No
No

Before the revolution, Cuba had no environmental protection laws at all. At that time, only 14% of its forest cover remained, but a strong drive to replant has raised the tree cover level to 18%. There is concern about a nuclear reactor under construction at Juraguá.

MEDIA

 Government censorship; demand for more outspoken media is growing

PUBLISHING AND BROADCAST MEDIA

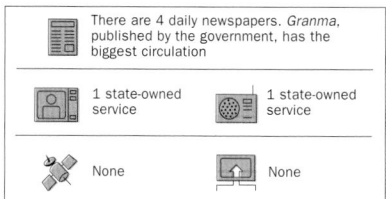

There are 4 daily newspapers. *Granma*, published by the government, has the biggest circulation

1 state-owned service
1 state-owned service
None
None

The Cuban media is state controlled. Two Florida-based stations, *Radio Martí* and *TV Martí* are financed by the US government; both make anti-Castro broadcasts.

Cuba's major resource is its sugar. Production is the fifth-largest in the world and helps to determine international prices. The island also has the world's fourth-largest nickel deposits, but lack of investment capital means they are under-exploited and inefficiently worked. Energy policy is aimed at encouraging foreign companies, through profit-sharing agreements, to exploit Cuba's known oil reserves. A Russian-built nuclear reactor was due to be completed in 1995.

CRIME

 Cuba does not publish prison figures

 Crime is rising

CRIME RATES

Cuba does not publish official statistics for murders, rapes or thefts

Cuba has a low crime rate. Murders are rare and there are few unsafe areas on the island. Political dissent, however, is not tolerated and human rights abuses by the military and police are frequently reported. Occasionally Cuba opens its jails. Petty criminals often flee to the USA as refugees. The Revolutionary Summary Tribunal deals with serious political crimes, as defined by the communist constitution.

EDUCATION

 94%   198,474 students

0   *Education spending as % GNP*   25
6.6%

THE EDUCATION SYSTEM

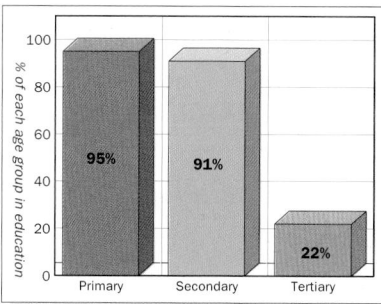

% of each age group in education

Primary 95%   Secondary 91%   Tertiary 22%

Education in Cuba combines academic with manual work, in line with Marxist-Leninist principles. The high priority given to education under Castro, which is reflected in the high literacy rate, is now being promoted to attract foreign investment in high-tech industries, particularly biotechnology.

HEALTH

 1 per 333 people

Heart disease, cancers, nutritional disorders

0   *Health spending as % GDP*   25
3.4%

Life expectancy in Cuba is 76 years, the highest in Latin America, which is a reflection of its efficient, countrywide health service. The US blockade has led to shortages of hospital equipment and raw materials for drugs. The latter are normally supplied by Havana's sizeable pharmaceuticals industry. Cuba's advanced eye surgery techniques attract patients from overseas.

WEALTH

 Factory worker, 220 Cuban pesos ($289) per month; engineer, 300 Cuban pesos ($395) per month

CONSUMER GOODS OWNERSHIP

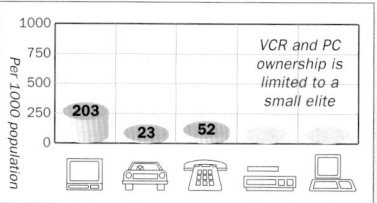

Per 1000 population

203   23   52

VCR and PC ownership is limited to a small elite

Under Batista, Cuba had huge wealth disparities, and was a playground for the rich. The 1959 revolution succeeded in reducing these, partly by taking over all businesses, from oil companies to barbershops, and partly by prescribing not only minimum but also maximum wages. Economic regulations have varied since then; for a brief period in 1985, different wage rates were allowed in an attempt to provide incentives for hard workers, but this decision was reversed in 1986. In the same year, a purge of old party hands on the grounds of corruption revealed the relatively high standard of living enjoyed by a few government officials. Generally, however, wealth is fairly evenly distributed.

WORLD RANKING

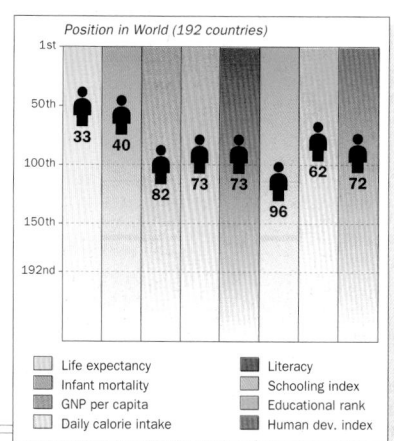

Position in World (192 countries)

1st
50th
100th
150th
192nd

33   40   82   73   73   96   62   72

Life expectancy
Infant mortality
GNP per capita
Daily calorie intake
Literacy
Schooling index
Educational rank
Human dev. index

CYPRUS

C

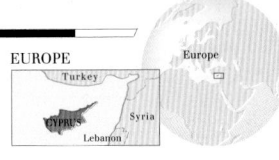

EUROPE

OFFICIAL NAME: Republic of Cyprus   **CAPITAL:** Nicosia   **POPULATION:** 700,000
CURRENCY: Cyprus pound (Turkish lira)   **OFFICIAL LANGUAGES:** Greek (Turkish)

THE ISLAND OF CYPRUS, which rises from a central plateau to a high point at Mount Olympus, lies south of Turkey in the eastern Mediterranean. Cyprus was partitioned in 1974, following an invasion by Turkish troops. The south of the island is the Greek Cypriot Republic of Cyprus (Cyprus); the self-proclaimed Turkish Republic of Northern Cyprus (TRNC) is recognized only by Turkey.

CLIMATE

WEATHER CHART

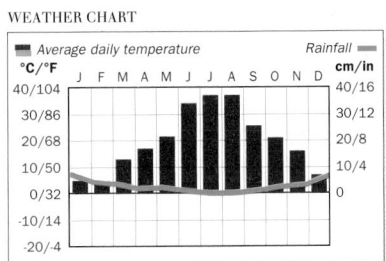

The climate is typically Mediterranean: summers are hot and dry and winters mild, though there is mountain snow.

TRANSPORTATION

 **Larnaka**
2.48m passengers

 1,384 ships
35.55m dwt

THE TRANSPORTATION NETWORK

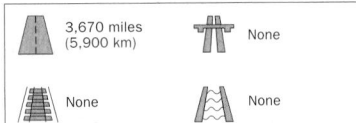

3,670 miles (5,900 km)		None
None		None

Travel between the two zones is impeded. The south regards the airport at Ercan as an illegal point of entry.

TOURISM

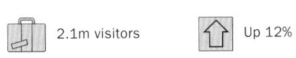 2.1m visitors

Up 12% in 1994

MAIN OVERSEAS ARRIVALS

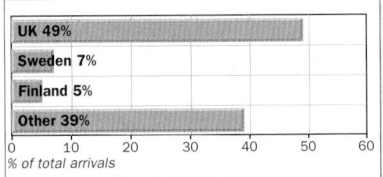

UK 49%
Sweden 7%
Finland 5%
Other 39%

0 10 20 30 40 50 60
% of total arrivals

Tourism in southern Cyprus expanded rapidly during the 1980s, and tourism in the north is also growing. The country has now become a popular destination for tourists from the former Soviet bloc. Ecotourism is being promoted in the Akamas peninsula.

PEOPLE

Greek, Turkish

197 people per sq. mile

THE URBAN/RURAL POPULATION SPLIT

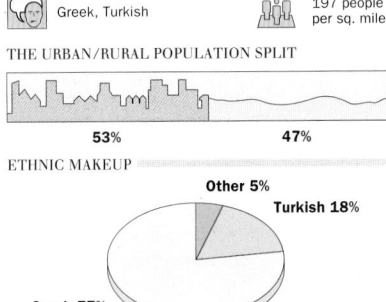

53%   47%

ETHNIC MAKEUP

Other 5%
Turkish 18%
Greek 77%

Cyprus's Greek majority, who make up 77% of the population, are Christian. The 18% Turkish minority are Muslim. Some are the descendants of Turks who settled on the island from the 16th century, under the rule of the Ottoman Empire. Turkish Cypriots have been isolated following the 1974 partitioning, since when the only country to recognize the self-styled republic has been Turkey, which has resettled thousands of mainland Turks on the island. Both communities have suffered enormous upheavals: in 1974, 180,000 Greek Cypriots were forced to flee to the south of the island, while 100,000 Turkish Cypriots fled in the other direction. Wage levels are on average four times higher in the south, where eastern European contract labor is brought in to staff the hotel industry. Levels of unemployment in the north, meanwhile, are rising.

The 2nd-century theater at the ruined city of Curium, 9 miles west of Limassol. Curium was a flourishing Mycenaean colony before 1100 BC.

POLITICS

 1991/1996 Cyprus
1993/1998 TRNC

President Glavkos Clerides (Cyprus) President Rauf Denktaş (TRNC)

THE STATE OF THE PARTIES

House of Representatives (Cyprus) 56 members

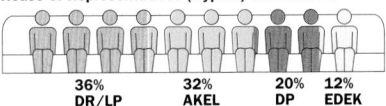

| 36% DR/LP | 32% AKEL | 20% DP | 12% EDEK |

DR/LP = Democratic Rally/Liberal Party **AKEL** = Progressive Party of the Working People (Communist Party) **DP** = Democratic Party **EDEK** = Cyprus National Democratic Union (Socialist Party)

Legislative Assembly (TRNC) 50 members

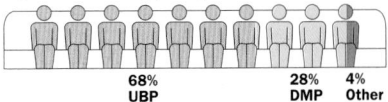

| 68% UBP | 28% DMP | 4% Other |

UBP = National Unity Party **DMP** = Democratic Struggle Party (composed of: CTP = Republican Turkish Party, TKP = Communal Liberation Party, YDP = New Dawn Party)

The UN-backed proposal of a two-zoned federation for Cyprus is supported by both the Greek and Turkish governments, eager to solve the dispute. Under this plan, each community would have its own territory but share a number of government functions and ministries. TRNC president Rauf Denktaş, mindful of the Greek Cypriots' suppression of the Turks prior to 1974, is unwilling to accept a plan that does not ensure full sovereignty and political equality for Turks. Greek Cypriots, in turn, fear the plan would lead to domination of their affairs by the small Turkish minority, who would be able to veto all government decisions.

WORLD AFFAIRS

| CE | Comm | IBRD | NAM | OSCE |

The permanent presence of 2,000 UN troops since 1974 manning the "Green Line" – only the Middle East and Kashmir have longer-standing peace-keeping forces – is estimated to cost in excess of $100 million a year. Cyprus's 1990 application for EU membership is still a source of contention.

AID

 $35m (receipts) (Cyprus)

 Up 30% in 1993 (Cyprus)

Cyprus receives aid from international agencies, as well as the UK and other EU countries. The TRNC is dependent on aid from Turkey of more than $60 million a year.

CYPRUS

Total Land Area :
9251 sq. km
(3572 sq. miles)

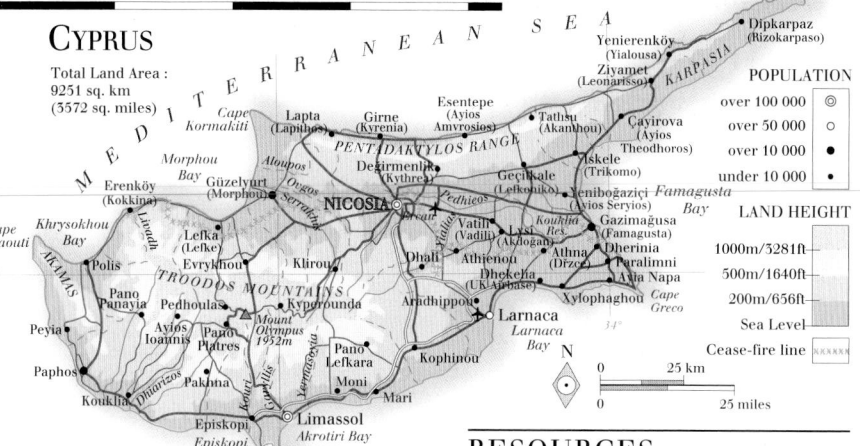

POPULATION

over 100 000 ◎
over 50 000 ○
over 10 000 ●
under 10 000 ·

LAND HEIGHT

1000m/3281ft
500m/1640ft
200m/656ft
Sea Level
Cease-fire line ✕✕✕✕

0   25 km

0   25 miles

CHRONOLOGY

Cyprus came, in turn, under the domination of Egypt, Greece, the Byzantines, the Ottomans and Britain.

- ❑ **1960** Independence from Britain.
- ❑ **1963** Following constitutional violation by Greeks, Turkish Cypriots abandon parliament.
- ❑ **1974** President Makarios deposed by Greek military junta. Turkey invades. Partition.
- ❑ **1983** Self-proclamation of TRNC.

DEFENSE

 $411m (Cyprus)   Up 12% in 1995 (Cyprus)

In addition to UN forces, there are Greek Cypriot, Turkish Cypriot, Greek and Turkish troops posted along the buffer zone that divides the island. Both the 10,000-strong Greek Cypriot and 4,000-strong Turkish Cypriot armies rely heavily on conscripts.

ECONOMICS

 $7.5bn (Cyprus)   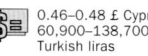 0.46–0.48 £ Cyprus 60,900–138,700 Turkish liras

SCORE CARD

- ❑ WORLD GNP RANKING.........................88th
- ❑ GNP PER CAPITA $8,956
- ❑ BALANCE OF PAYMENTS $44m
- ❑ INFLATION 2.7%
- ❑ UNEMPLOYMENT.................................2.3%

STRENGTHS

Tourism, the basis of the economy. Manufacturing sector and provision of services to Middle Eastern countries.

WEAKNESSES

Tourism damaged by effects of Gulf crisis. Economic stagnation and lack of foreign investment in TRNC. Collapse of Asil Nadir's manufacturing empire – employer of 12% of Turkish Cypriots.

EXPORTS

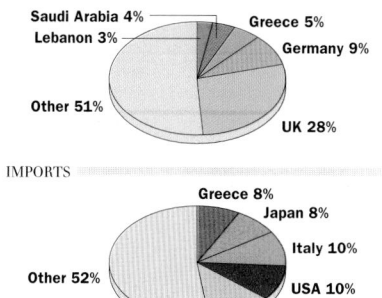

Saudi Arabia 4%
Lebanon 3%
Greece 5%
Germany 9%
Other 51%
UK 28%

IMPORTS

Greece 8%
Japan 8%
Italy 10%
USA 10%
Other 52%
UK 12%

RESOURCES

 2.4bn kwh (capacity 471,000 kw)   Not an oil producer; refines 18,600 b/cd

370,000 pigs, 285,000 sheep, 200,000 goats   Asbestos, gypsum, iron, bentonite, copper

Cyprus has continued to supply electricity to the TRNC, although it has not been paid for this. An oil refinery has been built in a project involving the Greek Cypriot government, BP, Mobil and a local company.

ENVIRONMENT

 0.2% partially protected   Increasing environmental awareness

The protection of the 60 square mile Akamas peninsula from the threat of hotel development by landholders, including the Orthodox Church, is a major project. This new national park is home to an unusual variety of plant and bird life, and contains the bay where the rare green turtle breeds.

MEDIA

 Freedom of speech is guaranteed in both Cyprus and the TRNC

PUBLISHING AND BROADCAST MEDIA

 There are 10 daily newspapers. The largest is *Fileleftheros* and others include *Charavgi*, *Simerini* and *Alithia*

1 state-controlled, 1 independent service   1 state-controlled, 9 independent stations

Cyprus's press is lively and tends to be highly politicized. The radio and TV services for British troops based in Cyprus are also popular.

CRIME

 219 prisoners   Up 3% in 1992

Crime, including ethnic violence, is not a major problem. Palestinian-linked terrorism has declined in recent years. The rape and murder of a Danish tourist by three British soldiers caused widespread outrage, and made Cypriots question the British military presence.

EDUCATION

 94%   6,263 students

Education is free and compulsory up to the age of 12 (15 in the TRNC). Many Greek Cypriots go to university abroad.

HEALTH

 1 per 750 people   Heart diseases, accidents, cancers

Health care is more advanced in the south; sophisticated surgery is carried out at Nicosia General Hospital.

WEALTH

 Wages in the south are 4 times those in the north

CONSUMER GOODS OWNERSHIP

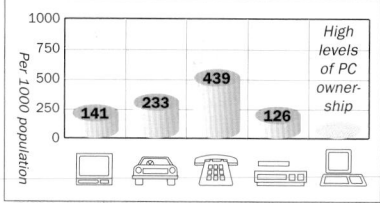

High levels of PC ownership

141   233   439   126

Income per capita in the south of the island is higher than in mainland Greece and is comparable to Spain.

WORLD RANKING

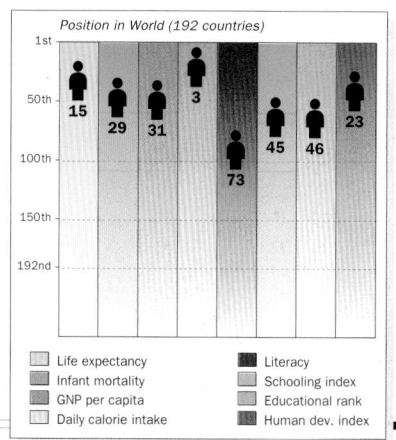

Position in World (192 countries)

15   29   31   3   73   45   46   23

- ☐ Life expectancy
- ☐ Infant mortality
- ☐ GNP per capita
- ☐ Daily calorie intake
- ☐ Literacy
- ☐ Schooling index
- ☐ Educational rank
- ☐ Human dev. index

CZECH REPUBLIC

OFFICIAL NAME: Czech Republic **CAPITAL:** Prague
POPULATION: 10.3 million **CURRENCY:** Czech koruna **OFFICIAL LANGUAGE:** Czech

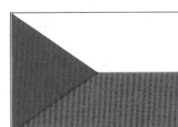

C

LANDLOCKED IN EASTERN Europe, the Czech Republic comprises the territories of Bohemia and Moravia and was formerly part of Czechoslovakia. Czechoslovakia's "Velvet Revolution" in 1989, led to the fall of the communist regime. Free elections followed in 1990. In 1993, the Czech Republic and Slovakia peacefully dissolved their federal union to become two independent states.

CLIMATE

WEATHER CHART

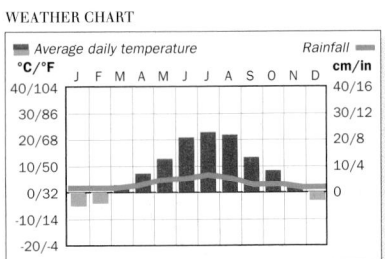

The Czech climate is more moderate than that of Slovakia, though easterly winds bring low temperatures in winter.

TRANSPORTATION

 **Ruzyně, Prague** 18 ships 443,155 dwt

THE TRANSPORTATION NETWORK

34,530 miles (55,560 km)	227 miles (366 km)
5,865 miles (9,439 km)	188 miles (303 km)

Rail links and highways to Germany are planned. Customs barriers have been installed on the border with Slovakia.

TOURISM

🧳 17m visitors ⬆ Up 50% in 1994

MAIN OVERSEAS ARRIVALS

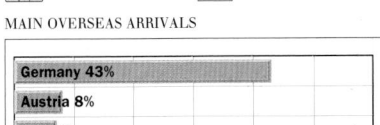

Germany 43%	
Austria 8%	
Italy 7%	
Other 42%	

% of total arrivals

Revenues from the expansion of tourism are an invaluable source of hard currency for the Czech economy. In 1994, 17 million tourists, mainly Germans, visited the country, with revenues from tourism reaching $2.6 billion in 1995. Prague is visited by most tourists. It has many fine buildings and rivals Paris as the most beautiful capital in Europe. Skiing in the Carpathian Mountains and the country's many spa towns are also very popular.

CZECH REPUBLIC

Total Land Area : 78 864 sq. km (30 449 sq. miles)

LAND HEIGHT	POPULATION
1000m/3281ft	over 1 000 000 ▣
500m/1640ft	over 500 000 ◉
200m/656ft	over 100 000 ◎
150m/492ft	over 50 000 ○
	over 10 000 ●
	under 10 000 ·

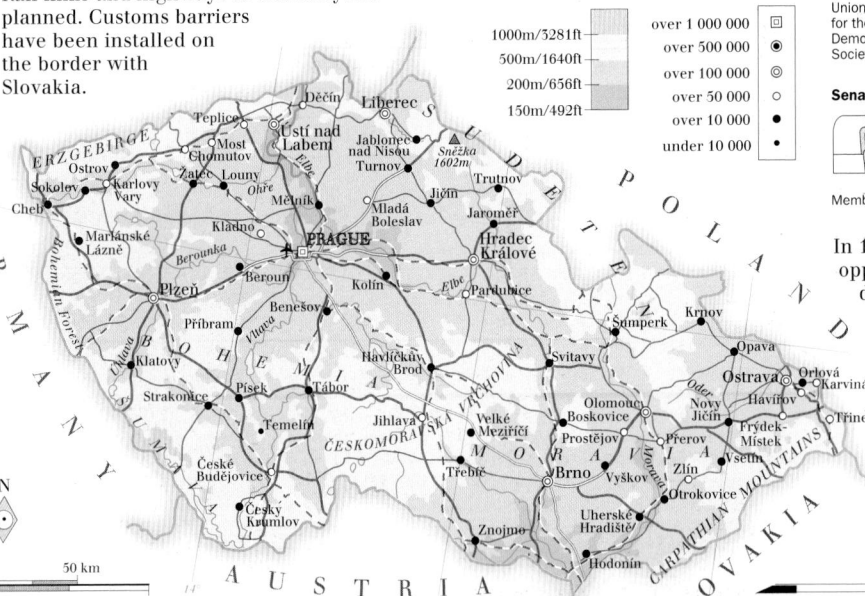

PEOPLE

 Czech, Slovak, Hungarian | 👥 339 people per sq. mile

THE URBAN/RURAL POPULATION SPLIT

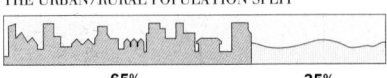

65% | 35%

RELIGIOUS PERSUASION

Other Catholic 2%
Protestant 20%
Roman Catholic 50%
Other 28%

Czechs make up 85% and Moravians 14% of the population. The 300,000 Slovaks left in the country after partition now form the largest single ethnic minority. Ethnic tensions are few, although there is some resentment against Romanian immigrants. A new commercial elite is emerging alongside ex-communist entrepreneurs. Divorce rates are high.

POLITICS

U. House 1992/1996
L. House 1992/1996 | President Václav Havel

THE STATE OF THE PARTIES

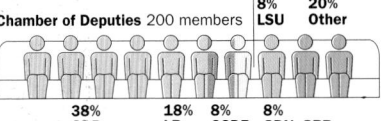

Chamber of Deputies 200 members

8% LSU | 20% Other

38% CDP | 18% LB | 8% CSDP | 8% CDU–CPP

CDP = Civic Democratic Party **LB** = Left Bloc
CSDP = Czechoslovak Social Democratic Party
LSU = Liberal Social Union **CDU–CPP** = Christian Democratic Union – Czechoslovak People's Party **Other** = Association for the Republic – Czechoslovak Republican Party, Civic Democratic Alliance, Movement for Autonomous Democracy – Society for Moravia and Silesia

Senate 81 members

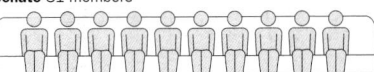

Members are elected for 6 years by universal adult suffrage

In 1990, the Civic Forum coalition of opposition groups won free elections and dissident playwright Václav Havel became president. By 1991, the Civic Forum had splintered and Václav Klaus's CDP, a major force behind the split from Slovakia in 1993, emerged as the dominant party. Among current political issues are the pace of economic liberalization and the extension of a law banning former intelligence officials from holding public office.

WORLD AFFAIRS

Good relations with Germany are a priority. However, the issue of property restitution for Germans ejected from the republic in 1945 is a source of friction. Germany has implied that the matter must be resolved before it will back Czech membership of the EU. The Czech Republic has downgraded relations with its v4 neighbors.

AID

 The Czech Republic is an aid recipient

 Aid donations are increasing steadily

Aid, mainly from the IMF and the EU, is crucial for modernizing infrastructure such as telecommunications.

DEFENSE

 $1bn

 Up 10% in 1995

The split with Slovakia left an army too large and expensive for the new Czech state. In 1994, plans to cut the military by 20,000 were approved. Professional soldiers with a communist past have been the first to go. The Czech Republic has a strong armaments and explosives industry. It is now seeking markets beyond the former Warsaw Pact.

ECONOMICS

 $33bn

 26.67–27.88 Czech koruny

SCORE CARD

- ❑ WORLD GNP RANKING............................53rd
- ❑ GNP PER CAPITA $3,210
- ❑ BALANCE OF PAYMENTS.......................$–81m
- ❑ INFLATION 8.7%
- ❑ UNEMPLOYMENT...................................3.3%

STRENGTHS

Skilled industrial labor force. Good industrial base. Speed of privatization of state industries. Attractive to German investors, including Volkswagen. Draw of Prague as tourist center.

WEAKNESSES

Lack of diversification in sectors likely to attract overseas investment. Limited restructuring. Unemployment, while relatively low, is rising.

EXPORTS

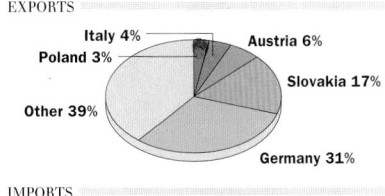

Italy 4%
Poland 3%
Austria 6%
Slovakia 17%
Other 39%
Germany 31%

IMPORTS

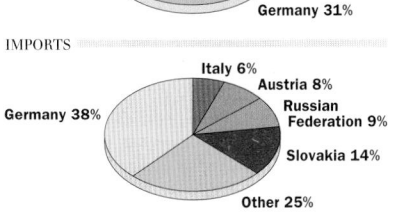

Italy 6%
Austria 8%
Russian Federation 9%
Germany 38%
Slovakia 14%
Other 25%

RESOURCES

 59bn kwh

1,644 b/d

4m pigs, 2.1m cattle, 196,000 sheep

Oil, natural gas, copper, lead, zinc, coal

Copper, lead, zinc and coal are the chief resources. The government is aiming to phase out the worst polluting coal-fired power stations. A 2,000-MW Soviet-designed nuclear power station at Temelin is due to come on stream in the late 1990s.

ENVIRONMENT

 14%

 Public awareness of environmental problems is rising

High pollution levels from the power, chemical and cement industries are the main environmental problem.

MEDIA

 No official censorship

PUBLISHING AND BROADCAST MEDIA

There are 9 daily newspapers. *Mladá Fronta Dnes* has the largest circulation

2 state-owned services

Several networks

Since the fall of communism, the Czech media has grown rapidly. Political debates are well covered in the press.

CRIME

 8,002 prisoners

 The crime rate has tripled since 1989

The republic is a transit point for Turkish narcotics destined for Germany. Narcotics trading, not possession, is illegal.

EDUCATION

 99%

 116,560 students

Schooling has reverted to the pre-1945 system. Charles University in Prague was founded in the 13th century.

HEALTH

 1 per 270 people

 Cancers, heart and cerebrovascular diseases, accidents

In the worst polluted towns, infant mortality reached levels found in the developing world. Rich Czechs travel to Germany for complex operations.

The Vltava River in Prague. Over 50 million tourists, mainly from Europe and the USA, now visit Prague each year.

CHRONOLOGY

Following the collapse of the Austro–Hungarian empire in 1918, the Republic of Czechoslovakia was established.

- ❑ **1968** "Prague Spring." Invasion by Warsaw Pact countries.
- ❑ **1989** Beginning of the "Velvet Revolution."
- ❑ **1990** Free legislative elections.
- ❑ **1993** Division into Czech Republic and Slovakia.
- ❑ **1996** Delineation of new borders with Slovakia.

WEALTH

 Entrepreneurs in the private sector have rapidly acquired wealth

CONSUMER GOODS OWNERSHIP

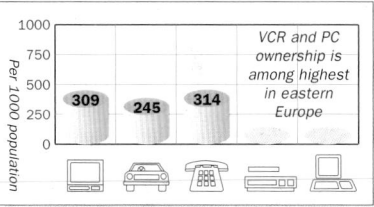

VCR and PC ownership is among highest in eastern Europe

309 245 314

Per 1000 population

Since 1989 a new entrepreneurial class has emerged. Almost all Czechs have shares in privatized enterprises.

WORLD RANKING

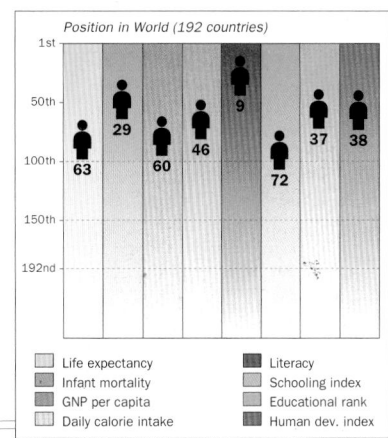

Position in World (192 countries)

63 29 60 46 9 72 37 38

Life expectancy
Infant mortality
GNP per capita
Daily calorie intake
Literacy
Schooling index
Educational rank
Human dev. index

C

DENMARK

OFFICIAL NAME: Kingdom of Denmark **CAPITAL:** Copenhagen **POPULATION:** 5.2 million
CURRENCY: Danish krone **OFFICIAL LANGUAGE:** Danish **OVERSEAS TERRITORIES:** 2

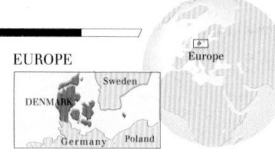

D

THE MOST SOUTHERLY COUNTRY in Scandinavia, Denmark occupies the Jutland peninsula, the islands of Sjælland, Fyn, Lolland and Falster, and over 400 smaller islands. Its terrain is among the flattest in the world. The Faeroe Islands and Greenland in the North Atlantic are self-governing associated territories. Politically, Denmark is stable, despite a preponderance of minority governments since 1945. It possesses a long liberal tradition and was one of the first countries to establish a welfare system, in the 1930s.

CLIMATE

WEATHER CHART

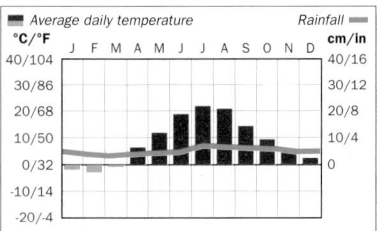

Denmark's temperate, damp climate is one of the keys to its agricultural success. The Faeroes are windy, foggy and cool. Greenland's climate ranges north–south from arctic to sub-arctic.

TRANSPORTATION

Kastrup, Copenhagen
9.27m passengers

499 ships
6.74m dwt

THE TRANSPORTATION NETWORK

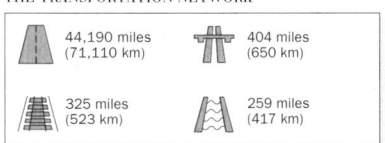

44,190 miles
(71,110 km)

404 miles
(650 km)

325 miles
(523 km)

259 miles
(417 km)

Denmark maintains an extensive, well-integrated transportation network, with bus, rail and ferry services linking the whole kingdom. State-owned companies predominate, though plans to privatize parts of the ferry and rail systems have been mooted. Denmark wants to reduce subsidies paid to transportation, a major part of public spending. Private companies, supported by the state operate in the Faeroes and Greenland.

Major new projects focus on bridge and tunnel links, like the Storebælt project to connect Denmark's main islands of Fyn and Sjælland. In 1991, Denmark and Sweden agreed to construct a 10 mile road and rail link by bridge and tunnel between them, although this has been delayed by ecological objections within Sweden.

The island of Fyn, like the rest of Denmark, is flat and depends on coastal defenses to prevent flooding by the sea.

TOURISM

 1.6m visitors

 Up 1% in 1994

MAIN OVERSEAS ARRIVALS

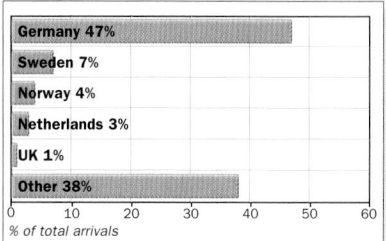

Germany 47%
Sweden 7%
Norway 4%
Netherlands 3%
UK 1%
Other 38%

% of total arrivals

Denmark is a popular destination for Scandinavian, German and Dutch tourists. The principal attractions are Copenhagen – with its Tivoli Gardens and fine 18th-century architecture – Legoland, the countryside and seaside resorts. Greenland attracts wildlife tourists.

DENMARK

Total Land Area : 45 070 sq. km
(16 629 sq. miles)

POPULATION

over 1 000 000
over 100 000
over 10 000
under 10 000

LAND HEIGHT

175m/574ft
Sea Level

Ferry link

PEOPLE

Danish

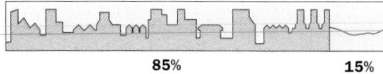 319 people per sq. mile

THE URBAN/RURAL POPULATION SPLIT

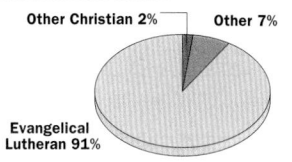

85%   15%

RELIGIOUS PERSUASION

Other Christian 2%   Other 7%

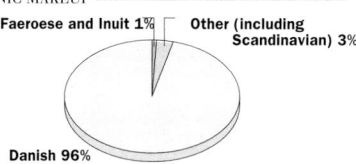

Evangelical Lutheran 91%

ETHNIC MAKEUP

Faeroese and Inuit 1%   Other (including Scandinavian) 3%

Danish 96%

Danish society is homogeneous. Out of a population of 5.2 million, just 200,000 are foreign citizens, mainly from other Scandinavian or EU states. The most visible minority groups are the Inuit, Greenland's indigenous inhabitants, and the Turkish community. Rising unemployment has engendered some ethnic tension, although racially motivated attacks are still rare.

Denmark has undergone profound social changes over the last 20 years. The role of women has been transformed. Helped by Denmark's extensive social and educational provision, 76% of women now work in part-time or full-time jobs. Denmark provides the best state child-support in Europe. Almost 50% of children under two, and 67% of three to six-year-olds are in day nurseries, compared with under 30% in the 1970s.

Less than half the population lives in a nuclear family, partly due to the high divorce rate. Marriage is also becoming less common; almost 40% of children are brought up by unmarried couples or single parents. Cohabiting couples now have the same legal rights as those who are married. In 1990, Denmark became the first country to allow registered partnerships between homosexual couples, effectively granting them the same legal married status as heterosexuals.

POPULATION AGE BREAKDOWN

%	0–14		15–64		65+
	10.6%	12.3%	14.4%	15.4%	15.5%
	64.2%	64.4%	64.8%	67.6%	68.2%
	25.2%	23.3%	20.8%	17%	16.3%
	1960	1970	1980	1990	2000

% of population by age group

POLITICS

 1994/1998

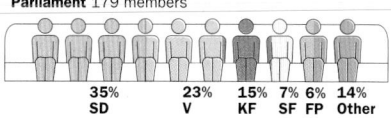 H.M. Queen Margrethe II

THE STATE OF THE PARTIES

Parliament 179 members

35% SD	23% V	15% KF	7% SF	6% FP	14% Other

SD = Social Democratic Party **V** = Liberal Party
KF = Conservative People's Party **SF** = Socialist People's Party **FP** = Progress Party **Other** = Radical Liberals, Unity List, Center Democrats, Christian People's Party

Denmark is a constitutional monarchy and a multiparty democracy. The associated territories of Greenland and the Faeroe Islands have home rule.

MAIN POLITICAL ISSUES
Relations with the EU

In recent years, Denmark's left-of-center parties have been suspicious of any EU moves for closer ties between member states. This was highlighted by the stir caused by the ratification of the Maastricht Treaty in 1992. The Treaty was approved by parliament but rejected in a referendum. The people objected to proposals for a monetary union, a common defense force and voting rights for European citizens living in Denmark. The result threatened the Treaty and embarrassed the government. Later that year, at an EU summit meeting, Denmark was exempted from clauses on monetary union, defense and European citizenship. A new referendum was held in 1993 and the Treaty approved, leaving the way clear for other countries, such as the UK, to ratify it.

Immigration

In what many saw as a vindication of Danish liberal traditions, Prime Minister Poul Schlüter was forced to resign in 1993 over the "Tamilgate"

WORLD AFFAIRS

 CE   EU   NATO   OECD   OSCE

Relations with the rest of Europe are the most important foreign policy concern, notably the issue of a common European defense policy. Denmark is limiting its defense relations to NATO. It is giving priority to promoting economic ties with Norway, Sweden and Finland. It is also intent on forging links with former Eastern Bloc states, especially those on the Baltic. In part, this is motivated by the desire to influence these governments to reduce pollution, a subject taken very seriously in Denmark.

Internationally, Denmark has a long history of involvement with the developing world, particularly aid programs in Africa.

Poul Nyrup Rasmussen, *prime minister and* SD *leader.*

Poul Schlüter, *resigned as premier over Tamil refugees immigration issue.*

affair. A judicial enquiry ruled that he had falsely denied in parliament that immigration officials were hindering the entry of the families of Tamil workers resident in Denmark. However, the issue of how many refugees Denmark should take from the world's trouble spots, and how they should be integrated into society, continues to be a point of national debate.

PROFILE

Denmark's intricately proportional electoral system ensures that parliament truly reflects voters' wishes, but also tends to lead to minority governments. SD governments were predominant until 1982. A decade of Conservative–Liberal rule under Prime Minister Poul Schlüter followed. In 1993, the SD regained power, at the head of a center-left coalition. Although the coalition lost ground in the 1994 elections, it has continued to form the government.

Policy differences between the two main political groups are few, although differences of opinion exist about the best way of reducing the tax burden without cutting the large budget for the comprehensive Danish social security system.

CHRONOLOGY

Founded in the 10th century, Denmark is Europe's oldest monarchy. It was the dominant Baltic power until the 17th century, when it was eclipsed by Sweden.

❑ **1815** Denmark forced to cede Norway to Swedish rule.
❑ **1849** First democratic constitution.
❑ **1864** Denmark forced to cede provinces of Schleswig and Holstein after losing war with Prussia.
❑ **1914–1918** Denmark neutral in World War I.
❑ **1915** Universal adult suffrage introduced. Rise of Social Democratic Party (SD).
❑ **1920** Northern Schleswig votes to return to Danish rule. ⇨

D

D

CHRONOLOGY *continued*

- ❏ **1929** First full SD government takes power under Thorvald Stauning.
- ❏ **1950s** Implementation of advanced social welfare legislation and other liberal reforms under SD.
- ❏ **1939** Outbreak of World War II; Denmark reaffirms neutrality.
- ❏ **1940** Nazi occupation. National coalition government formed.
- ❏ **1943** Danish Resistance successes lead Nazis to take full control.
- ❏ **1944** Iceland declares independence from Denmark.
- ❏ **1945** Denmark recognizes Icelandic independence. After defeat of Nazi Germany, SD leads post-war coalition governments.
- ❏ **1948** Faroe Islands given home rule.
- ❏ **1949** Founder member of NATO.
- ❏ **1952** Founder-member of Nordic Council.
- ❏ **1953** Constitution reformed; single-chamber, proportionately elected parliament created.
- ❏ **1959** Denmark joins the European Free Trade Association (EFTA).
- ❏ **1973** Denmark joins EC.
- ❏ **1979** Greenland granted home rule.
- ❏ **1975–1982** SD Anker Jorgensen heads series of coalitions; elections in 1977, 1979 and 1981. Final coalition collapses over economic policy differences.
- ❏ **1982** Poul Schlüter first KF prime minister since 1894.
- ❏ **1992** Maastricht Treaty on European Union rejected in referendum.
- ❏ **1993** Schlüter resigns over "Tamilgate" scandal. Center-left government led by Poul Nyrup Rasmussen. Danish voters ratify revised Maastricht Treaty. Result greeted with demonstrations.
- ❏ **1994** General election; SD-led coalition under Rasmussen returned to power without an overall majority.

AID

 $1.3bn (donations)   Up 4% in 1993

In GNP terms, Denmark is one of the world's leading aid donors, contributing an average 1% of its national income. It supports both economic and social development projects and policy reforms. Aid is an important political issue; the current debate is over its use as a tool to promote democracy.

Denmark provides aid to Asia and Latin America, but its closest ties are with Africa. Tanzania is the largest single aid recipient. Denmark has also provided considerable support to the other southern African SADC states.

DEFENSE

 $3.1bn   Up 13% in 1995

0   *Defense spending as % GDP*   40
1.9%

Denmark was neutral until 1945. Apart from its NATO commitments, defense has a low priority. Spending accounts for 2% of GDP. Its troops have joined UN forces on peacekeeping duties in the former Yugoslavia. Ten thousand of the army's troops are conscripts. Denmark does not have plans to join the WEU.

DANISH ARMED FORCES

411 main battle tanks (230 *Leopard* 1A5, 128 *Centurion*, 53 M-41)	19,100 personnel	
5 submarines, 3 frigates and 29 patrol boats	6,000 personnel	
106 combat aircraft (F-16A,-B/F35 *Draken*)	8,000 personnel	
None		

ECONOMICS

 $145bn   5.54–6.09 Danish kroner

SCORE CARD

- ❏ WORLD GNP RANKING.............................25th
- ❏ GNP PER CAPITA $28,110
- ❏ BALANCE OF PAYMENTS $2.7bn
- ❏ INFLATION 1.7%
- ❏ UNEMPLOYMENT................................12.1%

EXPORTS

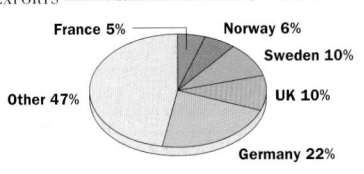

France 5%, Norway 6%, Sweden 10%, UK 10%, Germany 22%, Other 47%

IMPORTS

USA 6%, Netherlands 6%, UK 8%, Sweden 10%, Germany 23%, Other 47%

ECONOMIC PERFORMANCE INDICATOR

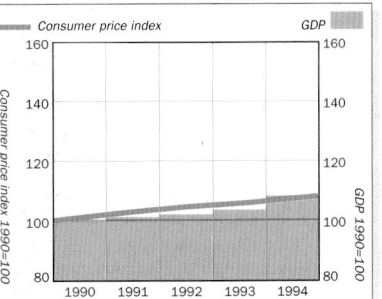

Consumer price index — GDP

Consumer price index 1990=100 / GDP 1990=100

1990 1991 1992 1993 1994

STRENGTHS

Successful high-tech, high-profit manufacturing industries. Low inflation and moderate budget deficit. Large gas and oil reserves. Skilled population. Large balance of payments surplus.

WEAKNESSES

Budget deficits, although falling since 1995, and heavy tax burden. High unemployment, currently over 12%. Sluggish GDP growth; reached 4.4% in 1994 but then fell back.

PROFILE

Denmark's mix of a large state sector and a private sector has been successful. At $28,110, GNP per capita is one of the highest among the OECD countries.

During the 1980s, the advent of a minority conservative government and the prospect of the wider European market led to a number of major policy changes. A stable exchange rate policy was introduced and tighter budget controls were aimed at reducing inflation and reversing the balance of payments deficit. Real GNP per capita grew by 2.1% a year from 1981–1991. The balance of payments went into surplus and inflation was cut to 2%. Denmark refused to join the EMU but was one of the few countries able to meet the convergence criteria.

After 1991, the recession in Europe led to slower growth. Denmark has emerged from this in better condition than many of its EU neighbors. The economic upturn since mid-1993 was initially led by private consumption, but subsequently it has been buoyed by strong export growth and increased business investment.

DENMARK : MAJOR BUSINESSES

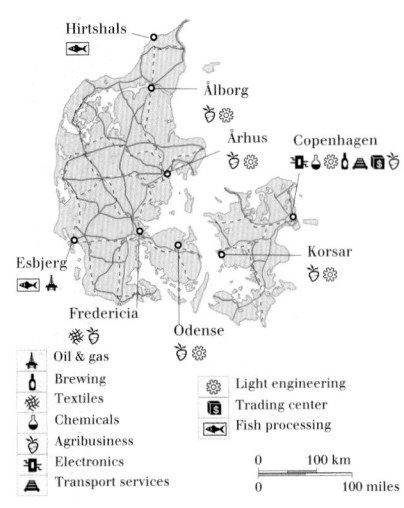

Hirtshals, Ålborg, Århus, Copenhagen, Esbjerg, Korsar, Frederica, Odense

🏭 Oil & gas
🍺 Brewing
Textiles
Chemicals
Agribusiness
Electronics
Transport services
Light engineering
Trading center
Fish processing

0   100 km
0   100 miles

RESOURCES

30bn kwh (capacity 9.13m kw)

10.9 pigs, 2m cattle, 82,000 sheep

155,508 b/d (reserves 729,618,000 bbl)

Natural gas, oil

ELECTRICITY GENERATION

Hydro 0.1% (0.03bn kwh)

Thermal 97% (29bn kwh)

Nuclear 0%

Other 2.9% (0.9bn kwh)

% of total generation by type

Although a net oil exporter since 1993, Denmark is still an overall importer of energy. The expansion of North Sea oil and gas output should balance import and export costs by 1997. Danish agriculture is very efficient.

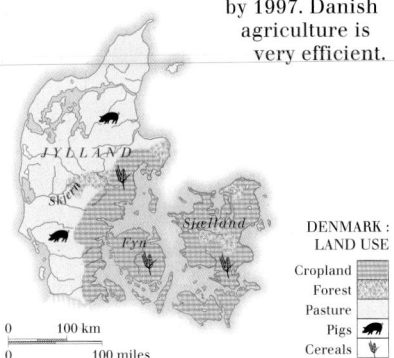

DENMARK : LAND USE

Cropland
Forest
Pasture
Pigs
Cereals

ENVIRONMENT

 32%

Very strict laws in Greenland to protect polar ecosystems

ENVIRONMENTAL TREATIES

Yes | Yes | Yes
Yes | Yes | Yes

The environment is of popular and governmental concern. Denmark's regulations, including those aimed at reducing ozone-destroying emissions and water pollution, are among the strictest in Europe. Fears that they may be eroded have been a key element in Danish ambivalence towards the EU. In 1993, Denmark was successful in persuading the EU to locate the Environmental Agency in Copenhagen. It hopes to extend its own standards to the rest of Europe.

MEDIA

 Media censorship is forbidden by the constitution

PUBLISHING AND BROADCAST MEDIA

There are 49 daily newspapers, including *BT, Politiken, Ekstra Bladet* and *Berlingske Tidende*

1 state-owned, 30 independent services

1 state-owned, 300 independent services

Thor, Astra 1B, Intelsat V1 F1

The cable network is growing

The media has a long history of political independence, and objectivity is prized. Most of the press has a political viewpoint, but expression of this is largely limited to editorials. The tone of both TV and the press is serious; Denmark does not have a scandal-mongering tabloid press as found in the USA, UK and Germany. Invasion of privacy laws are strict.

CRIME

3469 prisoners

Up 1% in 1992

CRIME RATES

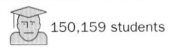

Murders

5 | per 100,000 population

Rapes

11 | per 100,000 population

Thefts

8495 | per 100,000 population

The main concern is that mafia-style organized crime could be imported from eastern Europe. Computer hacking and narcotics-trafficking are also problems.

EDUCATION

100%

150,159 students

0 | Education spending as % GNP | 25

7.4%

THE EDUCATION SYSTEM

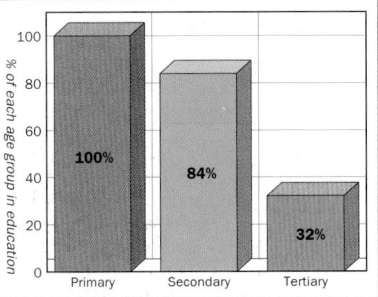

% of each age group in education

Primary 100%
Secondary 84%
Tertiary 32%

The average educational level is high, in part reflecting the need for a skilled work force. Formal schooling begins at age seven and is mandatory for nine years. However, most children receive pre-school education and over 90% of pupils go on at the age of 16 to further academic or vocational training.

HEALTH

1 per 357 people

Heart diseases, cancers, accidents

0 | Health spending as % GDP | 25

7%

Denmark was one of the first countries to introduce a state social welfare system. The national health service, which still provides free treatment for almost everything, is the main reason for Denmark's high taxes. Any attempts to reduce expenditure will meet with strong opposition. Repeated surveys show that most Danes prefer their system to those based on private health insurance.

WEALTH

Dairy product processor, 120 Danish kroner ($22) per hour; airline pilot, 27,671 Danish kroner ($4,990) per month

CONSUMER GOODS OWNERSHIP

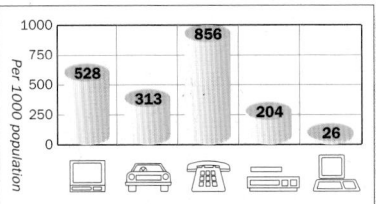

Per 1000 population

528 | 313 | 856 | 204 | 26

Most Danes are comfortably off. Income distribution is more even than in many Western countries and social mobility is high. Free higher education has made access to the professions more a question of ability than family wealth or connections. Many of Denmark's top industrialists have made their fortunes within the last 30 years. However, wealth is still quite concentrated. The richest 10% of Danes control almost two-thirds of national assets.

The extensive social security system means that Denmark suffers little from social deprivation. The groups that are most disadvantaged are refugees and recent immigrants.

WORLD RANKING

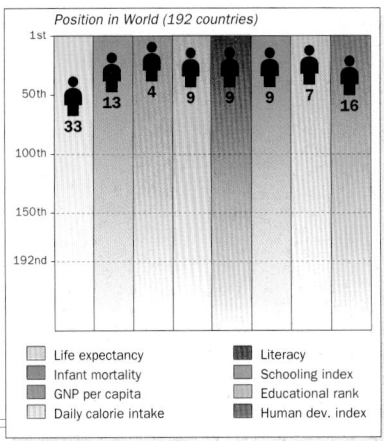

Position in World (192 countries)

33 | 13 | 4 | 9 | 9 | 9 | 7 | 16

Life expectancy
Infant mortality
GNP per capita
Daily calorie intake
Literacy
Schooling index
Educational rank
Human dev. index

See also OVERSEAS TERRITORIES *p.618*

DJIBOUTI

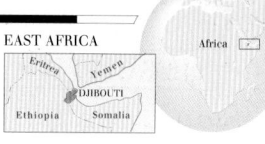

OFFICIAL NAME: Republic of Djibouti   **CAPITAL:** Djibouti
POPULATION: 600,000   **CURRENCY:** Djibouti franc   **OFFICIAL LANGUAGES:** Arabic and French

D

A CITY STATE WITH a desert hinterland, Djibouti lies in northeast Africa on the strait joining the Red Sea and the Indian Ocean. Known from 1967 as the French Territory of the Afars and Issas, Djibouti became independent in 1977. Its economy relies on the port, the railroad to Addis Ababa and French aid. A guerrilla war which erupted in 1991 as a result of tension between the Issas in the south and the Afars in the north has largely been resolved.

CLIMATE

WEATHER CHART

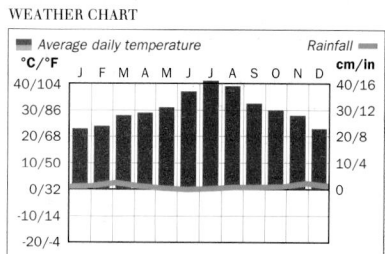

Despite extremely low rainfall, the monsoon season is characterized by very humid conditions. Even locals find the June to August heat unbearable.

TRANSPORTATION

Ambouli Intl, Djibouti

2 ships
2,300 dwt

THE TRANSPORTATION NETWORK

250 miles (400 km)		None
62 miles (100 km)		None

The key to Djibouti's livelihood is its port, created by the French in the 19th century and now a modern container facility. The railroad to Addis Ababa is one of Ethiopia's key links to the sea.

TOURISM

22,000 visitors   Down 12% in 1994

MAIN OVERSEAS ARRIVALS

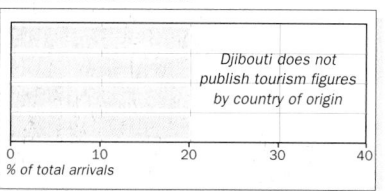

Djibouti does not publish tourism figures by country of origin

% of total arrivals

Most visitors are passing through on their way to Ethiopia, or coming to see relatives working in the port.

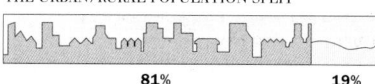
Nomadic Djiboutian village, *close to Balho near the Ethiopian border.*

PEOPLE

 Somali, Afar, French, Arabic   67 people per sq. mile

THE URBAN/RURAL POPULATION SPLIT

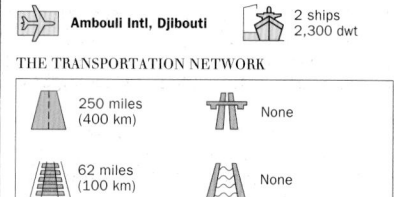

81%   19%

ETHNIC MAKEUP

Other 5%
Afar 35%
Issa 60%

The main ethnic groups are the Afars and Issas; tension between these groups developed into a guerrilla war in 1991. The population was swelled in 1992 by 20,000 Somali refugees. The rural people are mostly nomadic.

POPULATION
⊚ over 100 000
• under 10 000

LAND HEIGHT
1000m/3281ft
500m/1640ft
200m/656ft
Sea Level
-200m/656ft

POLITICS

 1992/1997

 President Hassan Gouled Aptidon

THE STATE OF THE PARTIES

National Assembly 65 members

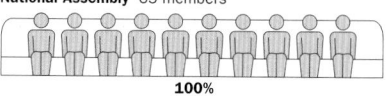

100%
RPP

RPP = People's Progress Party

Since independence, politics has been dominated by President Aptidon, an Issa, and a carefully chosen group of Issa and Afar politicians. Behind the scenes, French backing is essential to the ruling group. Afar fears of Issa domination erupted in 1991, when the Afar guerrilla group FRUD took control of much of the country against a background of similar ethnic conflicts in neighboring states. The French intervened militarily to keep Aptidon in power, but forced him to hold elections in 1992. These were won by the RPP, on a turnout of only 49%. In 1994, the government signed a peace agreement with a key FRUD faction and later brought two FRUD leaders into the cabinet.

DJIBOUTI

Total Land Area : 23 180 sq. km
(8950 sq. miles)

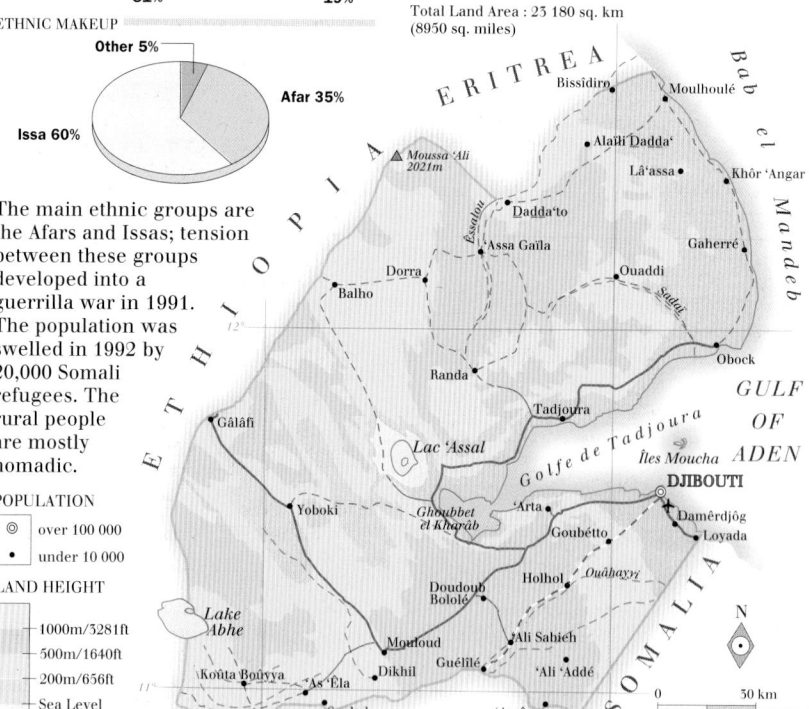

WORLD AFFAIRS

Relations with France, which wants to see faster moves to reform, have soured. Djibouti, Ethiopia and Eritrea all wish to contain Afar militancy; the ethnic group crosses national borders and has demanded its own state.

AID

 $131m (receipts)   Up 12% in 1993

France is the major donor, effectively financing one-third of government expenditure. Djibouti has also received aid from Saudi Arabia and Kuwait.

DEFENSE

 $24m    Down 4% in 1995

The size of the armed forces is a state secret but is estimated at 9,600 personnel; some 2,500 FRUD guerrillas are being integrated into the army. There is a 3,900-strong French garrison.

ECONOMICS

 $448m   160.00–177.61 Djibouti francs

SCORE CARD

❑ WORLD GNP RANKING	168th
❑ GNP PER CAPITA	$960
❑ BALANCE OF PAYMENTS	$–88m
❑ INFLATION	4%
❑ UNEMPLOYMENT	30%

STRENGTHS
Free port in key Red Sea location; made large profits from 1991 Gulf War and from 1992 US and UN intervention in Somalia. Development as container transshipment port continuing.

WEAKNESSES
Dependence on French aid and garrison. Civil war has delayed planned Saudi investment. Other ports on Red Sea now providing stiff competition.

EXPORTS

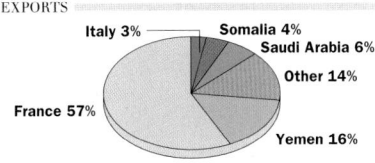

Italy 3%
Somalia 4%
Saudi Arabia 6%
Other 14%
France 57%
Yemen 16%

IMPORTS

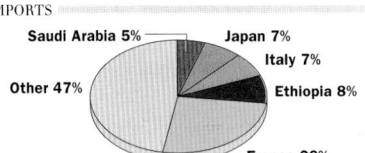

Saudi Arabia 5%
Japan 7%
Italy 7%
Other 47%
Ethiopia 8%
France 26%

RESOURCES

 180m kwh (capacity 38,000 kw)
 300 tons
507,000 goats, 470,000 sheep, 190,000 cattle
 Gypsum, mica, amethyst, sulfur

The few mineral resources are scarcely exploited. Geothermal energy is being developed and natural gas has recently been found. The war has delayed attempts to develop underground water supplies for agriculture.

ENVIRONMENT

 0.4%   Minimal industry presents no ecological threat

The concentration of business around Djibouti port means the inland desert areas are not threatened. Ecological issues are not a national concern.

MEDIA

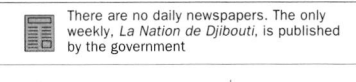 The press was freed from restrictions in 1992, but with little effect; most is still state-owned

PUBLISHING AND BROADCAST MEDIA

There are no daily newspapers. The only weekly, *La Nation de Djibouti*, is published by the government

1 state-owned service

1 state-owned service

Djibouti is a member of the Arab Satellite Communications Organization. It has two earth stations for radio, TV and telecommunications.

CRIME

 Djibouti does not publish prison figures   Up 9% in 1992

The government has accused FRUD of war atrocities, but its own human rights record has been criticized by Amnesty International. Livestock smuggling across the Red Sea is a problem.

EDUCATION

 43%   53 students

Schooling is mostly in French, although there has been a growing emphasis on Islamic teaching, particularly as Saudi Arabia has declared an interest in providing aid for education. Djibouti does not provide university education.

HEALTH

 1 per 4,200 people   Respiratory and heart diseases

AIDS is a growing problem in Djibouti port, with its large prostitute population. Estimates suggested 3,500 HIV-positive cases in 1992, as against government figures of 1,600. Small French-financed hospitals cater for the urban elite.

CHRONOLOGY

Formerly the Islamic state of Adal, the French made Djibouti the capital of French Somaliland in 1896.

- ❑ **1917** Railroad from Addis Ababa reaches Djibouti port.
- ❑ **1946** Given French Overseas Territory status.
- ❑ **1977** Independence.
- ❑ **1981** One-party state declared.
- ❑ **1989** Violence erupts between Afar and Issa groups.
- ❑ **1991** FRUD opposition formed. Launches armed insurrection.
- ❑ **1994** Peace agreement with FRUD.

WEALTH

 Minimum wage, 15,860 Djibouti francs ($99) per month; senior manager (not expatriate), 700,000 Djibouti francs ($4,375) per month

CONSUMER GOODS OWNERSHIP

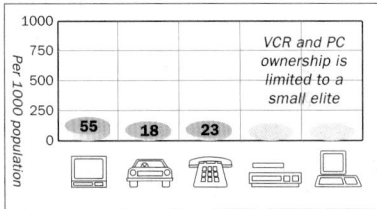

VCR and PC ownership is limited to a small elite

55   18   23

As in many African states, wealth is concentrated among those closest to government. Djiboutians working in the port also do well, although much port labor is expatriate. The war has had little effect on port life, as it is almost completely isolated from the rest of the country. The nomads of the interior are the poorest group.

Trade in the mild narcotic *qat*, grown in Ethiopia and shipped through Djibouti, is highly lucrative. The state is now taking its share of the profits, granting export licenses to only a few favored traders. In Djibouti, as in Yemen and Somalia, *qat* chewing is an age-old, if expensive, social ritual.

WORLD RANKING

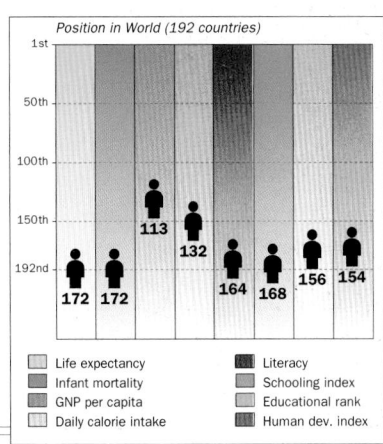

Position in World (192 countries)

Life expectancy
Infant mortality
GNP per capita
Daily calorie intake
Literacy
Schooling index
Educational rank
Human dev. index

DOMINICA

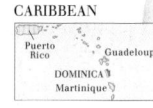
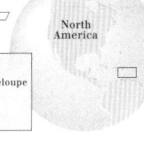

CARIBBEAN

North America

Puerto Rico • Guadeloupe
DOMINICA
Martinique

OFFICIAL NAME: Commonwealth of Dominica **CAPITAL:** Roseau
POPULATION: 71,000 **CURRENCY:** East Caribbean dollar **OFFICIAL LANGUAGE:** English

D

DOMINICA IS RENOWNED as the Caribbean island that resisted European colonization until the 18th century, when it was controlled first by the French then, from 1759, by the British. Known as the 'Nature Island' due to its spectacular, lush and abundant flora and fauna, which are protected by extensive national parks, Dominica is the most mountainous of the Lesser Antilles. Located between Guadeloupe and Martinique in the West Indian Windward Islands group, its volcanic origin has given it very fertile soils and the second largest boiling lake in the world.

CLIMATE

WEATHER CHART

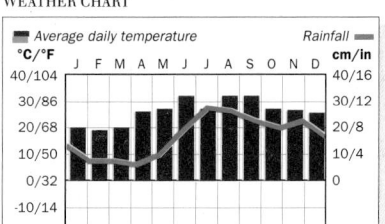

Part of the Windward Islands group in the eastern Caribbean, Dominica is subject to constant trade winds. The rainy season is in the summer, and tropical depressions and hurricanes are likely between June and November. Short, thundery showers in the late afternoon and evening are common all year round.

TRANSPORTATION

Canefield, Roseau
108,179 passengers

2 ships
1600 dwt

THE TRANSPORTATION NETWORK

229 miles (370 km)

None

None

None

The two airports can take only small propeller aircraft. Improving the road system is now a priority.

TOURISM

 57,000 visitors

 Up 10% in 1994

MAIN OVERSEAS ARRIVALS

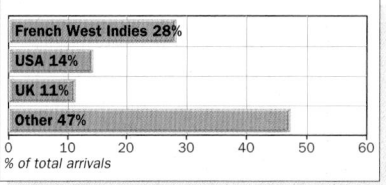

French West Indies 28%
USA 14%
UK 11%
Other 47%

% of total arrivals

The lack of an airport able to take commercial jetliners (visitors arrive on connecting flights from Barbados or Antigua) has made Dominica less accessible to mass-market tourism than its neighbors. Ecotourism is growing, with visitors coming to view the national parks with their rare indigenous birds, hot springs and sulfur pools.

PEOPLE

French Creole, English

246 people per sq. mile

THE URBAN/RURAL POPULATION SPLIT

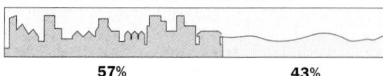

57%   43%

RELIGIOUS PERSUASION

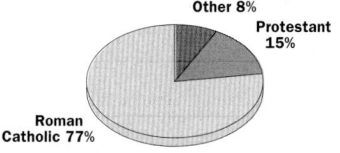

Other 8%
Protestant 15%
Roman Catholic 77%

The majority of Dominicans are descendants of Africans brought over to work the banana plantations. Family life is based around the extended family and in rural areas is often matriarchal.

POLITICS

 1995/2000

 President Crispin Sorhaindo

THE STATE OF THE PARTIES

House of Assembly 30 members

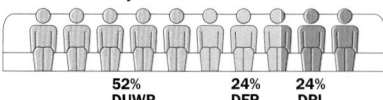

52% DUWP   24% DFP   24% DPL

DUWP = Dominica United Workers' Party **DFP** = Dominica Freedom Party **DPL** = Dominica Labour Party

Dominica's electoral system is based on the British model. Politicians tend to come from the professional classes – usually young lawyers and doctors. Occasionally the larger farmers, who provide most party funding, stand for elections. The center-left DUWP, led by Edison James, narrowly won the 1995 elections, ending 15 consecutive years of rule by the right-wing DFP. The dominant political issue is the proposal that Dominica join with the three other islands of the Windward group to form a political and economic union, leading to a single state. Any change would be subject to a referendum.

WORLD AFFAIRS

ACS   Comm   Caricom   OAS   OECS

A disagreement with Latin American states over banana exports to the EU is the dominant issue. Dominica wishes to maintain its preferential market share and has threatened to leave the Organization of American States.

Map

61°10'
Guadeloupe Passage
Peinville
Clifton
Guillet
Vieille Case
Thibaud
16°20'
Belmanier
Bense
Calibishie
Tarieu
Portsmouth
Prince Rupert Bay
Dos D'Ane
Glanvillia
Wesley
NORTHERN FOREST RESERVE
Melville Hall
Dublanc
Morne Diablotins 1447m
Marigot
Bataka
15°30'
Salbia
Colihaut
Coulibistri
Gaulette
Morne Raquette
Salisbury
Layou
Castle Bruce
St Joseph
Mahaut
Good Hope
Saint Sauveur
Petite Soufrière
Massacre
Morne Trois Pitons
Morne Aux Frégates
Rosalie
15°20'
Canefield Airport
Roger
Trafalgar
Laudat
La Plaine
ROSEAU
Giraudel
Boetica
Charlotte Ville
Bellevue
Chopin
Pichelin
Délices
Loubiere
Pointe Michel
Petite Savane
Soufrière
Fond St. Jean
Tête Morne
Berekua
Scotts Head Village
Martinique Passage
15°10'

ATLANTIC OCEAN
CARIBBEAN SEA

DOMINICA

Total Land Area : 750 sq. km (290 sq. miles)

LAND HEIGHT

1000m/3281ft
500m/1640ft
200m/656ft
Sea Level

POPULATION

over 10 000 •
under 10 000 ·

0   10 km
0   10 miles

Inshore fishing boats, *which mostly supply the domestic market, on a typical Dominican beach.*

AID

 US$10m (receipts)   Down 28% in 1993

The EU and UK are regular donors; France donated US$1 million in 1995 to help finance rebuilding following major hurricane damage.

DEFENSE

 Dominican Defense Force officially disbanded in 1981   Not applicable

Dominica has no armed forces, but it does participate in the US-sponsored Regional Security System.

ECONOMICS

 US$201m   2.69–2.70 East Caribbean dollars

SCORE CARD

❏ WORLD GNP RANKING........................183rd
❏ GNP PER CAPITA ....US$2830
❏ BALANCE OF PAYMENTS ....US$–36m
❏ INFLATION 1.6%
❏ UNEMPLOYMENT....................................15%

STRENGTHS

Bananas have proved a useful foreign currency earner, though this sector is now threatened.

WEAKNESSES

Dependence on preferential access to US and EU markets for its banana crop (70% of export earnings) highlighted by US moves to deregulate the banana trade. Dominica cannot compete with cheaper Latin American fruit.

EXPORTS

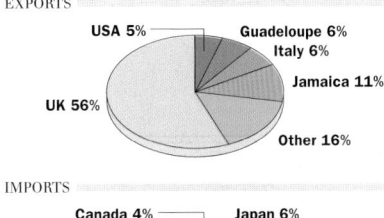

USA 5% Guadeloupe 6% Italy 6% Jamaica 11% UK 56% Other 16%

IMPORTS

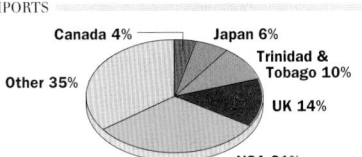

Canada 4% Japan 6% Trinidad & Tobago 10% Other 35% UK 14% USA 31%

RESOURCES

 31m kwh (capacity 8000 kw)   795 tons

 10,000 goats, 9,000 cattle, 8,000 sheep, 5,000 pigs None

Dominica has no natural resources and has to import almost all its energy. The development of hydroelectric power at Morne Trois Pitons has been proposed.

ENVIRONMENT

 9%   Hydropower plans threaten Morne Trois Pitons National Park

The expansion of both agriculture and timber harvesting is threatening Dominica's rainforest; already there is more land under cultivation than planned by the government. Tourism does not currently pose a threat, but this could change if the government succeeds in raising funds to expand the airports to take jets. Two species of parrot – the *Amazonia imperialis* and the Red Necked – are threatened, despite conservation orders. Turtles living on coral reefs off the island will soon be protected.

MEDIA

 Journalists accuse the government of placing them under pressure to reveal sources

PUBLISHING AND BROADCAST MEDIA

 There are no daily newspapers. The dominant newspaper is the bi-weekly *New Chronicle*, which takes a center-left editorial stance

 No TV service   1 state-owned station

Local franchises, offering cable TV with selected US networks, serve one-third of the island. Broadcasts from other Caribbean states can also be received. Dominica has one cinema.

CRIME

 Dominica does not publish prison figures   Up 62% between 1983 and 1986

Dominica has a lower crime rate than most of its Caribbean neighbors. Burglary and armed robbery are the major concerns; murders are rare. Justice is based on British common law and administered by the Eastern Caribbean Supreme Court, which is based in St. Lucia.

EDUCATION

 97%   658 students

Education is based on the British system, and retains the selective 11-plus exam for entrance to high school. Students go on to the University of the West Indies or, increasingly, to colleges in the USA and the UK.

CHRONOLOGY

First colonized by the French, Dominica came under British control in 1759.

- ❏ **1951** Universal suffrage.
- ❏ **1975** Morne Trois Pitons national park established.
- ❏ **1978** Independence from UK. Patrick John first prime minister.
- ❏ **1980** Eugenia Charles, the Caribbean's first woman prime minister, elected.
- ❏ **1981** Two coup attempts, backed by Patrick John, foiled.
- ❏ **1995** The opposition DUWP wins general election. Dame Eugenia Charles retires after 27 years in politics.

HEALTH

 1 per 1,947 people   Heart and respiratory diseases, cancers

There are 44 health centers, but difficult communications hamper emergency hospital access for people living in the interior.

WEALTH

 Agricultural field hand, 2 East Caribbean dollars (US$0.70) per hour; office manager, 9 East Caribbean dollars (US$3.40) per hour

CONSUMER GOODS OWNERSHIP

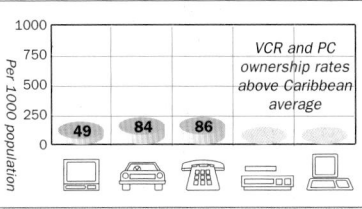

VCR and PC ownership rates above Caribbean average

49 84 86

Wealth disparities are not as marked as on the larger Caribbean islands. Dominica now has access to US cable shopping networks. New Japanese cars are particularly favored.

WORLD RANKING

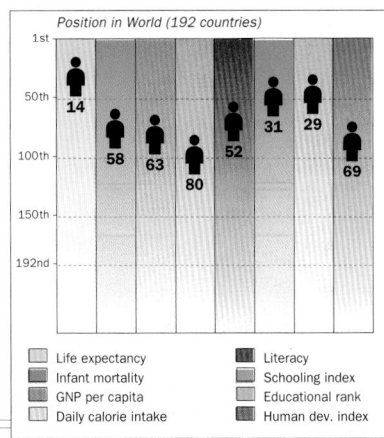

Position in World (192 countries)

14 58 63 80 52 31 29 69

- Life expectancy
- Infant mortality
- GNP per capita
- Daily calorie intake
- Literacy
- Schooling index
- Educational rank
- Human dev. index

DOMINICAN REPUBLIC

OFFICIAL NAME: Dominican Republic   **CAPITAL:** Santo Domingo
POPULATION: 7.8 million   **CURRENCY:** Dominican Republic peso   **OFFICIAL LANGUAGE:** Spanish

THE LARGEST TOURIST DESTINATION in the Caribbean, greatly favored by Germans and Italians, the Dominican Republic lies 603 miles southeast of Florida. Once ruled by Spain, it occupies the eastern two-thirds of the island of Hispaniola and boasts both the highest point (Pico Duarte, 10,417 feet) and the lowest point (Lake Enriquillo, 144 feet below sea level) in the West Indies. Frequent coups and a strong US influence mark its recent history.

View south from Pico Duarte along the fertile banks of the Río Yaque del Norte.

CLIMATE

WEATHER CHART

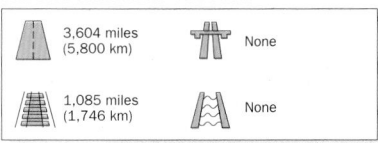

The trade winds blow all year round, providing relief from the tropical heat. The hurricane season runs from June until November.

TRANSPORTATION

✈ **Aeropuerto Intl de las Américas, Santo Domingo**
1.79m passengers

🚢 12 ships
12,500 dwt

THE TRANSPORTATION NETWORK

3,604 miles (5,800 km)

None

1,085 miles (1,746 km)

None

Road repair and expansion programs began in 1994; railroads are mainly for transporting sugarcane and ores. Santo Domingo's airport was improved in 1992 to boost tourism.

TOURISM

🧳 1.72m visitors

↑ Up 1.5% in 1994

MAIN OVERSEAS ARRIVALS

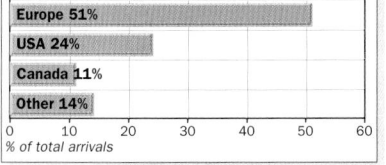

Europe 51%	
USA 24%	
Canada 11%	
Other 14%	

0 10 20 30 40 50 60
% of total arrivals

The Dominican Republic has good beaches and a hotel capacity of 30,000 rooms, the highest in the Caribbean.

PEOPLE

👤 Spanish, French Creole

👥 417 people per sq. mile

THE URBAN/RURAL POPULATION SPLIT

62%   38%

RELIGIOUS PERSUASION

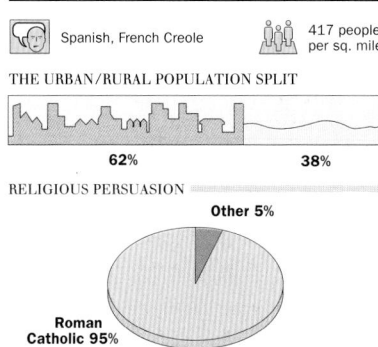

Other 5%

Roman Catholic 95%

The white population, primarily the descendants of Spanish settlers, still owns most of the land. The mixed race majority – about 73% – controls much of the republic's commerce, and forms the bulk of the professional middle classes. Blacks, the descendants of Africans, are mainly small-scale farmers and often the victims of latent racism, especially in business. Women in the black community work the farms; in the white and mixed-race communities women are starting to appear in the professions.

DOMINICAN REPUBLIC

Total Land Area : 48 730 sq. km (18 815 sq. miles)

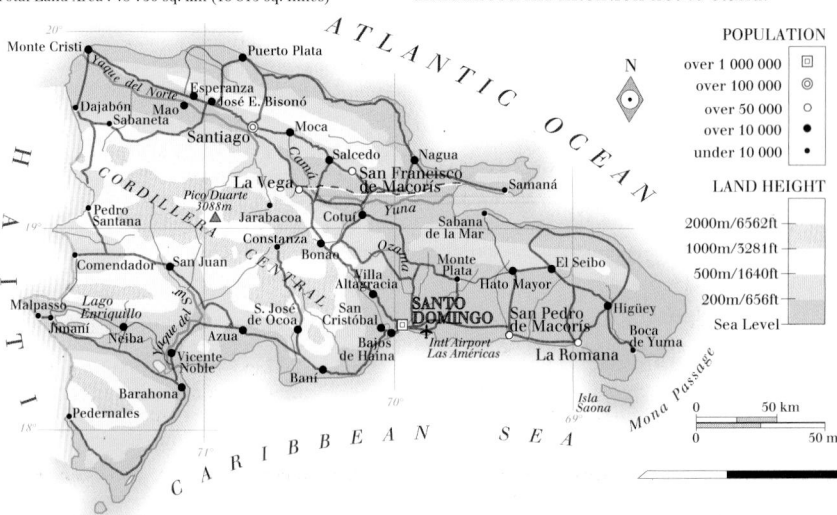

POPULATION

⊡ over 1 000 000
◉ over 100 000
○ over 50 000
● over 10 000
• under 10 000

LAND HEIGHT

2000m/6562ft
1000m/3281ft
500m/1640ft
200m/656ft
Sea Level

0   50 km
0   50 mi

POLITICS

U. House 1994/1996
L. House 1994/1996

President Joaquín Balaguer Ricardo

THE STATE OF THE PARTIES

Chamber of Deputies 120 members

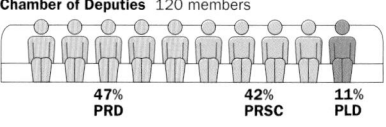

47% PRD   42% PRSC   11% PLD

PRSC = Christian Social Reform Party   **PLD** = Dominican Liberation Party   **PRD** = Dominican Revolutionary Party   **DU** = Democratic Union

Senate 30 members

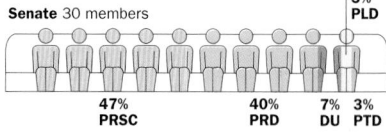

3% PLD

47% PRSC   40% PRD   7% DU   3% PTD

Historically, affluent white landowners and the military have wielded power behind the scenes and until recently there was little political difference between main parties. Octogenarian President Joaquín Balaguer of the right-wing PRSC, a political patriarch since the 1960s, was forced to agree to fresh elections in 1996 when the ascendant center-left PLD mobilized wide opposition to his fraudulent re-election in 1994. He subsequently announced his intention not to stand.

WORLD AFFAIRS

    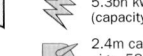

The Dominican Republic's main concerns are whether to join Caribbean or Central and South American economic organizations. It has uneasy relations with its neighbor Haiti.

AID

 $2m (receipts)　　　 Down 96% in 1993

Substantial foreign aid is received from the USA and, more recently, from the EU.

DEFENSE

 $78m　　　 Up 7% in 1995

The 25,000-strong military, apart from its interest in domestic politics, concentrates on preventing illegal immigration from Haiti. The main equipment supplier is the USA.

ECONOMICS

 $10.1bn　　　 13.22–13.31 Dominican Republic pesos

SCORE CARD

❏ WORLD GNP RANKING	91st
❏ GNP PER CAPITA	$1,320
❏ BALANCE OF PAYMENTS	$–161m
❏ INFLATION	8.3%
❏ UNEMPLOYMENT	30%

STRENGTHS

Dramatic growth in tourism in recent years. Mining – mainly of nickel and gold – and sugar are major sectors. Tobacco – most is sold to the USA. Large hidden economy based on transshipment of narcotics to the USA.

WEAKNESSES

Major sectors severely affected by fluctuating world prices and cutbacks in US import quotas. Failure to diversify, and loan repayments, are long-term problems.

EXPORTS

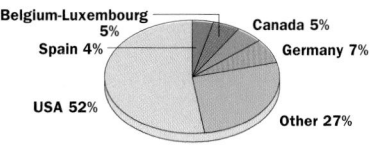

IMPORTS

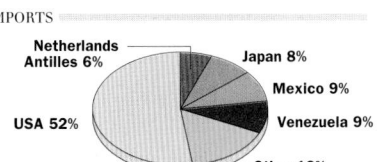

RESOURCES

5.3bn kwh (capacity 1.45m kw)　　14,144 tons

2.4m cattle, 900,000 pigs, 587,000 goats, 134,000 sheep　　Ferro-nickel, bauxite, copper, gold, silver

The government is investing $450 million in two new dams to produce HEP as power cuts remain a frequent occurence. Attempts at oil prospecting have not been successful. Under the terms of the San José Agreement, almost 2 million tons of oil are bought annually from Venezuela and Mexico at preferential terms (20% of the cost is converted into loans).

ENVIRONMENT

 21% (10% partially protected)　　 Inadequate legislation has not halted deforestation

The government is lax about enforcing existing laws protecting diminishing forests. Legislation is often conflicting: a 1931 hunting law effectively nullifies recent wildlife protection measures.

MEDIA

 No overt censorship laws, though many instances of newspapers caving in to state pressure

PUBLISHING AND BROADCAST MEDIA

 There are 12 daily newspapers, including *Listín Diario*, *Ultima Hora*, *El Nacional de Ahora* and *El Caribe*

 1 state-owned, 6 independent stations　　 10 state-owned, 140 independent stations

Television broadcasts from both Mexico and the USA can easily be received in the Dominican Republic.

CRIME

 Dominican Republic does not publish prison figures　　 Rape down 70% between 1985 and 1988

Recent increases in violent crime are mainly the result of narcotics-traffickers fighting for territory. The USA has accused government officials of complicity in the narcotics trade.

EDUCATION

 83%　　 123,748 students

Most schools operate a curriculum aimed at preparing pupils for graduate studies in the USA. However, wealthier Dominicans send their children to universities in Spain.

HEALTH

 1 per 930 people　　 Heart attacks, infectious and parasitic diseases

Wealthy Dominicans fly to Cuba rather than Florida for medical treatment. The poor rely on a rudimentary public service.

CHRONOLOGY

The 1697 Franco–Spanish partition of Hispaniola left Spain with the eastern two-thirds of the island, today the Dominican Republic.

- ❏ **1865** Independence from Spain.
- ❏ **1930–1961** Gen. Molina dictator.
- ❏ **1965** Civil war. US intervention.
- ❏ **1966–1978** Balaguer president.
- ❏ **1978–1982** Guzmán president; commits suicide in 1982.
- ❏ **1982–1986** Blanco president.
- ❏ **1986** Balaguer reelected president.
- ❏ **1994–1995** Balaguer reelection and price increases provoke serious civil unrest.

D

WEALTH

 Clothing worker, 333 Dominican Republic pesos ($25) per month; oil refinery worker, 2,594 Dominican Republic pesos ($196) per month

CONSUMER GOODS OWNERSHIP

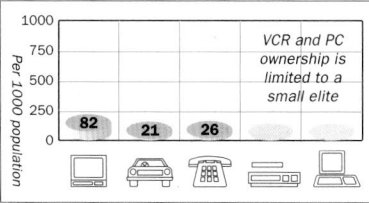

There are great disparities between rich and poor. Generations of governments have promised to close the gap, with few results. The most socially mobile group in the last 20 years has been those of mixed race, who have come to dominate the expanding professional sector. Black Dominicans remain at the bottom of the social ladder, accounting for the major proportion of small farmers. The old Spanish families are still the wealthiest, retaining their grip on the valuable estates; their younger members spend weekends at Puerto Plata or on shopping trips to Miami.

WORLD RANKING

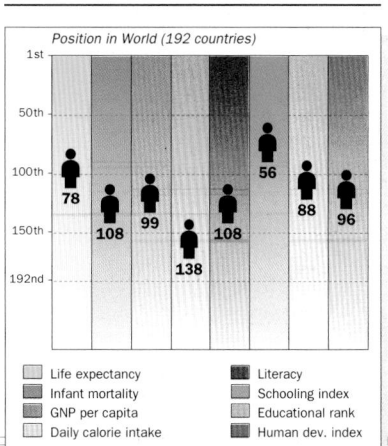

ECUADOR

OFFICIAL NAME: Republic of Ecuador **CAPITAL:** Quito
POPULATION: 11.5 million **CURRENCY:** Sucre **OFFICIAL LANGUAGE:** Spanish

 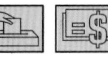

ONCE PART OF THE INCA heartland, Ecuador lies on the western coast of South America. It was ruled by Spain from 1533, when the last Inca emperor was executed, until independence in 1830. Most Ecuadorians live either in the lowland Costa region or in the Andean Sierra. The Amazonian Indians are now successfully pressing for their land rights to be recognized. Oil deposits have boosted the economy in recent years.

SOUTH AMERICA

South America

CLIMATE

WEATHER CHART

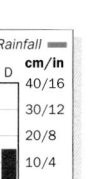

■ Average daily temperature	Rainfall ▬

Climate varies from hot equatorial in the Amazon forests, to dry heat in the south and "perpetual spring" in Quito.

TRANSPORTATION

Mariscal Sucre, Quito
1.71m passengers

55 ships
480,600 dwt

THE TRANSPORTATION NETWORK

5325 miles (8,570 km)	Pan-American Highway
600 miles (965 km)	932 miles (1,500 km)

Ecuador's extensive road network and antiquated rail system suffer from regular flooding.

TOURISM

482,000 visitors

Up 2% in 1994

MAIN OVERSEAS ARRIVALS

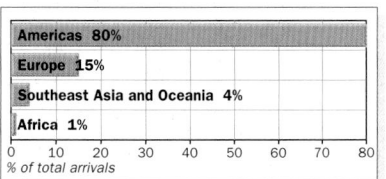

| Americas 80% |
| Europe 15% |
| Southeast Asia and Oceania 4% |
| Africa 1% |

0 10 20 30 40 50 60 70 80
% of total arrivals

Tourism is well developed. Quito, once the capital of the Inca empire, is having its Spanish imperial buildings, including 86 churches, restored. Access to the Galápagos is restricted to 40,000 visitors a year.

PEOPLE

Spanish, Quechua, other Indian languages

109 people per sq. mile

THE URBAN/RURAL POPULATION SPLIT

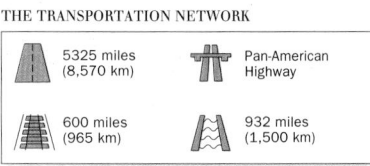

56%   44%

RELIGIOUS PERSUASION

Other 5%

Roman
Catholic 95%

Over half of the population is of Indian-Spanish extraction (*mestizo*). Black communities exist on the coast. The Indians, who make up about a quarter of the population, are currently pressing for Ecuador to be described as a pluri-national state, where different communities of Indians are recognized as distinct nationalities. The result is a strong and largely unified Indian movement.

POLITICS

1994/1996

President Sixto Durán Ballén

THE STATE OF THE PARTIES

National Congress 77 members

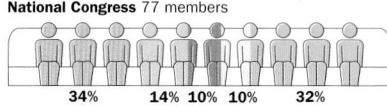

34%   14% 10% 10% 32%
PSC   PRE MPD ID   Other

PSC = Social Christian Party **PRE** = Ecuadorian Republican Party **MPD** = Popular Democratic Movement
ID = Democratic Left **Other** = Ecuadorian Conservative Party, Popular Democratic Party, United Republican Party

Durán Ballén's right-wing government has been plagued with corruption scandals – including the 1995 flight of the vice-president to Costa Rica following embezzlement allegations involving public funds. It is in a minority in the Congress, which has opposed constitutional reforms and, along with urban and rural labor, the government's austerity and privatization policies. The military has great influence, boosted by the 1995 border conflict with Peru which created temporary national unity.

WORLD AFFAIRS

 AG Ama Pac NAM OAS RG

Keeping preferential access to the US and EU markets for bananas is a major concern. Relations remain strained with Peru following the 1995 border conflict.

ECUADOR

Total Land Area : 276 840 sq. km
(106 888 sq. miles)

POPULATION

▣	over 1 000 000
◉	over 500 000
◎	over 100 000
○	over 50 000
●	over 10 000
•	under 10 000

LAND HEIGHT

4000m/13124ft
2000m/6562ft
500m/1640ft
Sea Level

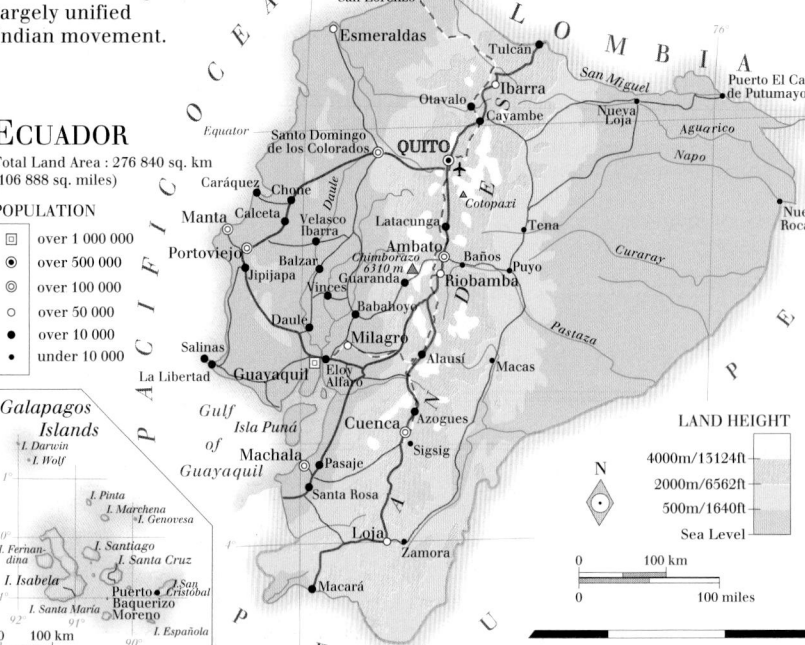

E

***Quito is the highest** capital in the world after La Paz in Bolivia. It lies in an Andean valley, lined by 30 volcanoes.*

AID

 $240m (receipts)   Down 4% in 1993

Aid is mostly from the USA and EU, and is essential in tackling foreign debt equal to 87% of GDP. The Galápagos receive generous grants from UNESCO.

DEFENSE

 $550m   Up 3% in 1995

The 58,000-strong military is trained by the USA. Narcotics gangs are the major concern. Since a brief period of military rule in the mid-1970s, the army has not been directly involved in politics.

ECONOMICS

 $14bn    2,272.00–2,919.00 sucres

SCORE CARD

❏ WORLD GNP RANKING	71st
❏ GNP PER CAPITA	$1,310
❏ BALANCE OF PAYMENTS	$–807m
❏ INFLATION	22%
❏ UNEMPLOYMENT	8.9%

STRENGTHS

Net oil exporter. World's biggest banana producer. Fishing industry. Hopes for Andean free-trade accords.

WEAKNESSES

Agricultural land has relatively low productivity. Banana crop vulnerable to new EU import regulation.

EXPORTS

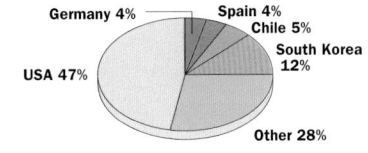

Germany 4%   Spain 4%   Chile 5%   South Korea 12%   USA 47%   Other 28%

IMPORTS

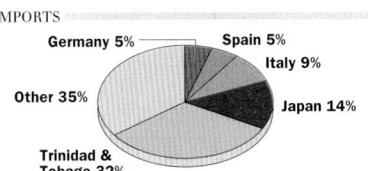

Germany 5%   Spain 5%   Italy 9%   Other 35%   Japan 14%   Trinidad & Tobago 32%

RESOURCES

 7.2bn kwh (capacity 1.66m kw)   335,957 b/d (reserves 1,599,793 bbl)

 4.9m cattle, 2.5m pigs, 1.7m sheep, 535,000 horses   Oil, natural gas, gold, silver, copper, zinc

The government is encouraging faster oil exploration and higher output. Ecuador left OPEC in 1992. Over-fishing is threatening mackerel and squid stocks.

ENVIRONMENT

 39%   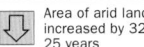 Area of arid land has increased by 32% in 25 years

The invasion of oil drillers to new areas of Amazonia could spell the end of the Waorani nomads, who have to date successfully avoided all contact with outsiders. In the offshore territory of the Galápagos Islands, the growth in legal and illegal tourism has upset the islands' delicate ecosystems; the land iguana has become sterile and black coral is being stolen in quantity for souvenirs.

MEDIA

 Freedom of speech is guaranteed

PUBLISHING AND BROADCAST MEDIA

  There are 36 daily newspapers. The most popular are *El Universo* and *El Comercio*

3 national independent networks   1 state-owned, 32 independent networks

Ecuador's press is largely independent and free of censorship. It is highly regionalized, based either in the Quito region or around Guayaquil on the coast. The latter is also a center for commercial radio stations.

CRIME

 Ecuador does not publish prison figures   Down 5% in 1992

Unlike its neighbors, Ecuador has not suffered from instability caused by left-wing guerrilla action. Minor groups, such as *Alfaro, Vive ¡Carajo!,* have joined the legal political process. Ecuador is classified by the USA as a "transit country" for narcotics, and receives modest anti-drug aid. Several aircraft have also been donated to help combat trafficking.

EDUCATION

 87%    206,541 students

Around 25% of Ecuadorians – a total of 200,000 students – receive higher education at 16 universities. In schools, teaching is often in Indian languages. Programs have been launched to combat the relatively high levels of adult illiteracy in the countryside.

E

HEALTH

 1 per 960 people   Intestinal infectious diseases, pneumonia, accidents, murders

Health care services are now being brought to poor urban districts, but are still unavailable in many rural areas. Between 1987 and 1990, 469 outpatient centers opened. Malaria and stomach cancer are significant health problems.

WEALTH

 Chauffeur, 200,000 sucres ($68) per month; junior company executive, 400,000 sucres ($137) per month

CONSUMER GOODS OWNERSHIP

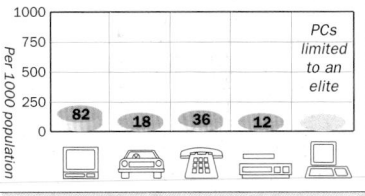

PCs limited to an elite

82   18   36   12

During the 1980s, income per capita dropped by 7.5%. An estimated 60% of the population live in poverty.

WORLD RANKING

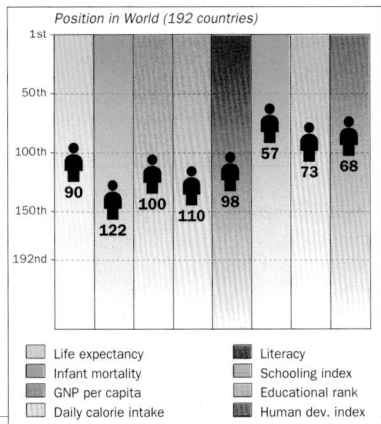

Position in World (192 countries)

90   122   100   110   98   57   73   68

- ☐ Life expectancy
- ☐ Infant mortality
- ☐ GNP per capita
- ☐ Daily calorie intake
- ☐ Literacy
- ☐ Schooling index
- ☐ Educational rank
- ☐ Human dev. index

EGYPT

OFFICIAL NAME: Arab Republic of Egypt   CAPITAL: Cairo
POPULATION: 62.9 million   CURRENCY: Egyptian pound   OFFICIAL LANGUAGE: Arabic

E

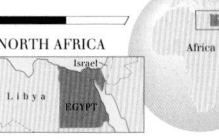

NORTH AFRICA

OCCUPYING THE NORTHEAST corner of Africa, Egypt is bisected by the highly fertile Nile valley which separates its arid western desert from the smaller semi-arid eastern desert. Egypt's 1979 peace treaty with Israel brought security, the return of the Sinai and large injections of US aid. Its essentially pro-Western military-backed regime is now being challenged by an increasingly influential Islamic fundamentalist movement.

18th-Dynasty Temple of Queen Hatshepsut dating from the Middle Kingdom, c 1480 BC. It is at Deir el-Bahri on the west bank of the Nile opposite Thebes, Egypt's capital at the time.

CLIMATE

WEATHER CHART

Summers are very hot, especially in the south, but winters are cooler. The only significant rain falls in winter along the Mediterranean coast.

TRANSPORTATION

Cairo International
5.62m passengers

205 ships
1.55m dwt

THE TRANSPORTATION NETWORK

11,180 miles
(18,000 km)

None

3,175 miles
(5,110 km)

Suez Canal
107 miles
(173 km)

Egypt's cities are linked by adequate roads, but railroads are the main transportation arteries. The Suez Canal is a vital international shipping lane. Cairo's subway opened in 1987.

TOURISM

2.3m visitors

Up 11.5% in 1994

MAIN OVERSEAS ARRIVALS

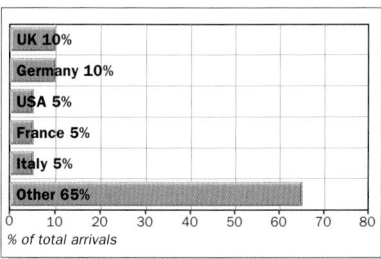

UK 10%	
Germany 10%	
USA 5%	
France 5%	
Italy 5%	
Other 65%	

% of total arrivals

Egypt's wealth of antiquities from its ancient civilizations have made it a key tourist destination since the 1880s. Today, it also offers Nile cruises and some of the world's best scuba diving, notably at the coral reefs near Hurghada on the Red Sea.

In the 1990s, however, the industry went into sharp decline. Islamic fundamentalists began attacking Western tourists. Their aim was to pressure the government into moving the state more toward Islam. The result was a sharp decline in the number of visitors and a major dent in foreign exchange earnings, although there has recently been some improvement. The business convention trade has been particularly affected.

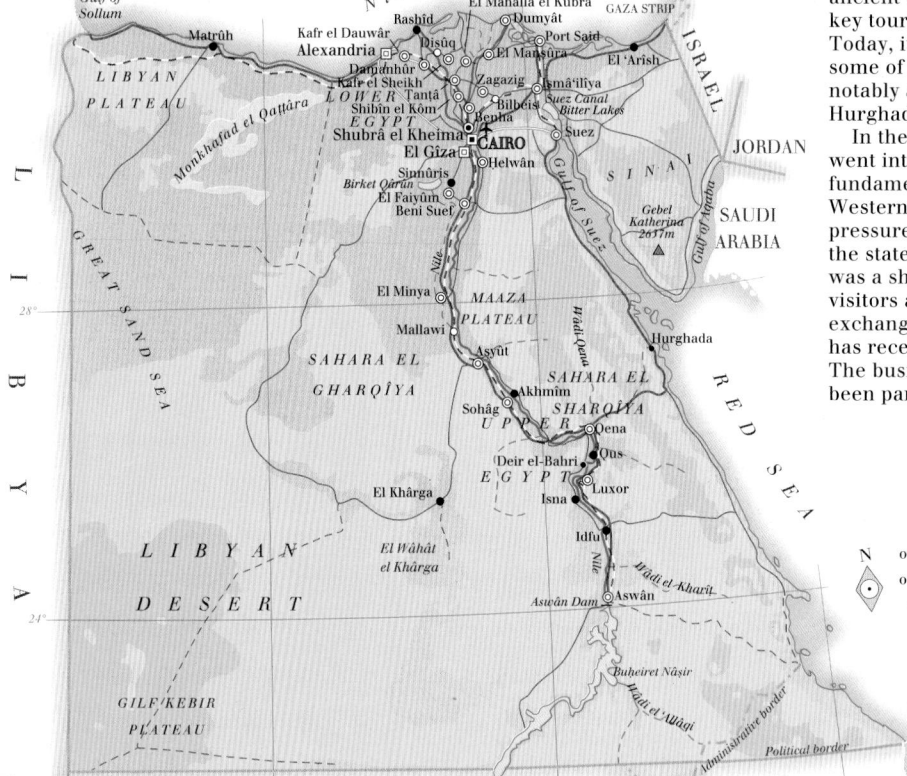

EGYPT

Total Land Area : 995 450 sq. km
(384 343 sq. miles)

POPULATION

over 5 000 000
over 1 000 000
over 500 000
over 100 000
over 50 000
over 10 000
under 10 000

LAND HEIGHT

2000m/6562ft
1000m/3281ft
500m/1640ft
200m/656ft
Sea Level
-200m/-656ft

0   200 km

0   200 miles

PEOPLE

 Arabic, French, English, Berber

 163 people per sq. mile

THE URBAN/RURAL POPULATION SPLIT

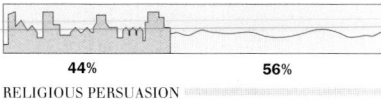

44%   **56%**

RELIGIOUS PERSUASION

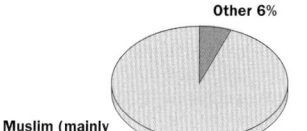

Other 6%

Muslim (mainly Sunni) 94 %

ETHNIC MAKEUP

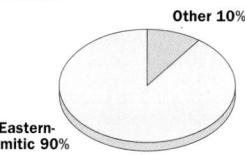

Other 10%

Eastern-Hamitic 90%

Egypt has a long tradition of ethnic and religious tolerance. Most Egyptians speak Arabic, though many also have French or English as a second language. There are Berber-speaking communities in the western oases. Small colonies of Greeks and Armenians live in the larger towns. Islam is the dominant religion, followed by Coptic Christianity. While many Jews left Egypt after the creation of Israel in 1948, a small Jewish community remains in Cairo.

Cairo is Africa's most populous city, and a key social question in Egypt is the high birth-rate. Aware of the demands this puts on the country's resources, economy and social services, in 1985 the government set up the National Population Council, which made birth control readily available. Since then, the birth-rate has dropped by 10%, but Egypt's population is still growing at a rate that will see it double in 30 years. The growing influence of Islamic fundamentalists, who are opposed to contraception, could see the rate accelerate once more.

Egyptian women have traditionally been among the most liberated in the Arab world, playing a full part in the education system, politics and the economy. The steady rise of Islamic fundamentalism, however, threatens their position, particularly in rural areas.

POPULATION AGE BREAKDOWN

% of population by age group	■ 0–14	▨ 15–64	□ 65+		
65+	3.3%	4.3%	4%	3.9%	4.4%
15–64	54.2%	54.3%	56.5%	56.7%	61%
0–14	42.5%	41.4%	39.5%	39.4%	34.6%
	1960	1970	1980	1990	2000

POLITICS

 1995/2000

 President Muhammad Hosni Mubarak

THE STATE OF THE PARTIES

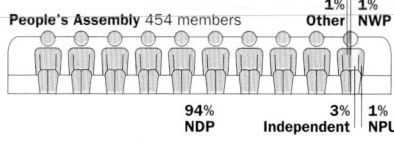

People's Assembly 454 members

1% Other   1% NWP

94% NDP   **3% Independent**   **1% NPU**

NDP = National Democratic Party **NPU** = National Progressive Unionist Party **NWP** = New Wafd Party

Egypt is a multiparty system in theory. In practice, the ruling NDP, backed by the military, runs a one-party state.

MAIN POLITICAL ISSUES
Islamic fundamentalism

The NDP government is engaged in a struggle against Islamic terrorist groups who are seeking to turn Egypt into a Muslim theocracy along Iranian lines. Extremists, led recently by the *Gamaat Islamiya* which advocates a more radical program of Islamic reform than the comparatively moderate Muslim Brotherhood, have been responsible for numerous attacks on police and tourists. The fundamentalist message, with promises of improved conditions, has proved attractive to both urban and rural poor. Mosques are often the main providers of education and health services that parallel the state's. The NDP's response has been to introduce draconian measures to counter the terrorist threat, while allowing religious organizations to pursue their social programs.

The state of emergency

The ruling NDP party in 1994 extended the national state of emergency in force since the assassination of President Sadat by Islamic terrorists in 1981. Emergency laws have been invoked to justify the ban on religious parties, especially the Muslim Brotherhood. In the last general election, held in 1995, opposition parties accused the NDP of using existing laws to ensure its electoral success. Human rights groups claim that emergency powers are routinely applied to silence the NDP's political opponents.

Hosni Mubarak, *president since the assassination of Anwar Sadat in 1981.*

Dr. Atif Sidki, *prime minister and minister for international cooperation since 1986.*

PROFILE

Egypt has been politically stable since World War II. Since the death of President Nasser in 1970, it has had just four presidents. Although Anwar Sadat was assassinated in 1981, he was immediately replaced by a man in the same mold, President Hosni Mubarak, who has been in power ever since. The NDP retains a tight grip on the political process through its use of the state of emergency. It has close links with the military (both Sadat and Mubarak were fighter pilots) and with Egypt's massive bureaucracy.

Under Nasser, Egypt promoted Arab socialism, influenced by the Soviet model. Since Sadat, the economy has been liberalized and private enterprise encouraged. However, no parallel liberalization has occurred in politics – one reason for the growing success of Islamic fundamentalists.

WORLD AFFAIRS

 AL NAM OAPEC   OAU   OIC

Following the 1979 peace treaty with Israel, Egypt has developed closer relations with the USA. Its political and military support for the US-led reaction to Iraq's invasion of Kuwait in 1990 was critical to the success of Operation Desert Storm in 1991. By having the backing of the most powerful state in the region, the Gulf states were able to avoid the charge that they were simply acting at the bidding of the USA. Egypt received massive economic reward from Saudi Arabia for its participation.

Relations with Iran are tense. Iran actively supports the Islamic groups operating against the NDP government, and characterizes Egypt as a corrupt nation under US influence. Egypt is concerned that the international boycott and air exclusion zones imposed on Iraq are simply allowing Iran to extend its power in the Middle East.

Egypt's diplomatic service is the Arab world's largest, and many Egyptians serve on international bodies. UN Secretary General Boutros Boutros Ghali is an ex-Minister of State for Egypt. Cairo hosts the headquarters of the Arab League.

AID

 $2.3bn (receipts)

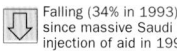 Falling (34% in 1993) since massive Saudi injection of aid in 1991

Since the Camp David peace accords of 1978, Egypt has received massive levels of US military aid; the aim was for Egypt to achieve parity with Israel in aid receipts. By 1991, this had almost been achieved.

E

E

CHRONOLOGY

Egypt's centuries-old Ottoman occupation ended in 1914 when the country came under British rule. It became fully independent in 1936. Army officers led by Lt.-Col. Nasser seized power in 1952.

- ❑ **1953** Political parties dissolved, monarchy abolished. Republic proclaimed with General Neguib as president.
- ❑ **1954** Nasser deposes Neguib to become president.
- ❑ **1956** Suez Crisis. British troops withdraw from Canal. Nasser orders nationalization of Suez Canal Company to raise revenue for Aswân Dam. Israeli, British and French forces invade, but withdraw after pressure from UN and USA.
- ❑ **1957** Suez Canal reopens after UN salvage fleet clears blockade.
- ❑ **1958** Egypt merges with Syria as United Arab Republic.
- ❑ **1960** Soviets begin work on the Aswân Dam.
- ❑ **1961** Syria breaks away from union with Egypt.
- ❑ **1967** Six Day War with Israel results in loss of Sinai.
- ❑ **1970** Nasser dies of heart attack. Succeeded by Anwar Sadat.
- ❑ **1971** Readopts the name Egypt. Islam becomes state religion.
- ❑ **1972** Soviet military advisers dismissed from Egypt.
- ❑ **1974–1975** USA brokers partial Israeli withdrawal from Sinai.
- ❑ **1977** Sadat visits Jerusalem for first-ever meeting with Israeli prime minister.
- ❑ **1978** Camp David peace accords brokered by US President Carter, signed by Egypt and Israel.
- ❑ **1979** Egypt and Israel sign peace treaty. Egypt is shunned by most Arab states.
- ❑ **1981** Sadat assassinated by Islamic extremists. Succeeded by Hosni Mubarak.
- ❑ **1982** Last Israeli troops leave Sinai.
- ❑ **1988** Novelist Naguib Mahfuz wins the Nobel Prize for Literature.
- ❑ **1989** After 12-year rift, Egypt and Syria resume diplomatic relations.
- ❑ **1990** Egypt participates in UN operation to liberate Kuwait.
- ❑ **1991** Damascus declaration provides for a defense pact among Egypt, Syria and Gulf cooperation countries against Iraq.
- ❑ **1994–1995** Islamic extremists launch campaign of terrorism killing scores of civilians and foreign tourists.

DEFENSE

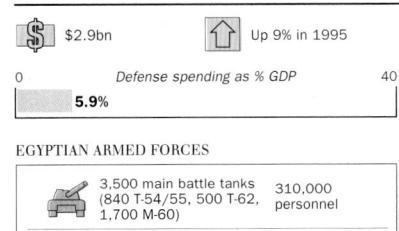

💲 $2.9bn   ⬆ Up 9% in 1995

0	Defense spending as % GDP	40
5.9%		

EGYPTIAN ARMED FORCES

🚙	3,500 main battle tanks (840 T-54/55, 500 T-62, 1,700 M-60)	310,000 personnel
🚢	4 submarines, 1 destroyer, 6 frigates and 43 patrol boats	16,000 personnel
✈	564 combat aircraft (42 *Alpha Jet*, 44 Ch J-6, 29 F-4E/143 F-16A/C)	30,000 personnel
🚀	None	

Egypt's armed forces, the largest in the Arab world, are battle-hardened from successive wars with Israel and from participation in Operation Desert Storm to liberate Kuwait in 1991. Over 500,000 reservists augment the regular troops.

After the 1978 Camp David accords with Israel, Egypt stopped buying Soviet weapons and aircraft in favor of Western suppliers. Cooperation with the USA has reaped dividends in the form of more sophisticated defense equipment and improved training. Egypt has a small arms industry and sells light weapons, notably a version of the AK-47 assault rifle, to other developing countries.

ECONOMICS

📊 $40.9bn   💲 3.403–3.407 Egyptian pounds

SCORE CARD

- ❑ WORLD GNP RANKING............................49th
- ❑ GNP PER CAPITA...............................$710
- ❑ BALANCE OF PAYMENTS $31m
- ❑ INFLATION....................................9.7%
- ❑ UNEMPLOYMENT...................................20%

EXPORTS

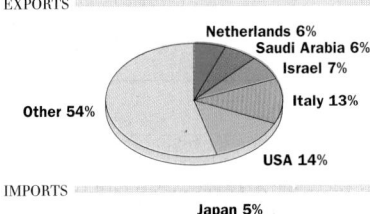

- Netherlands 6%
- Saudi Arabia 6%
- Israel 7%
- Italy 13%
- USA 14%
- Other 54%

IMPORTS

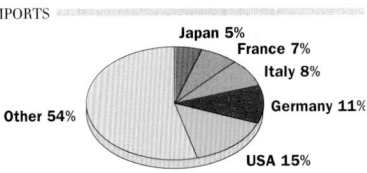

- Japan 5%
- France 7%
- Italy 8%
- Germany 11%
- USA 15%
- Other 54%

STRENGTHS

Oil and gas revenues. Tourist industry. Remittances from Egyptians working overseas. Suez Canal tolls. Agricultural produce, especially cotton. Light industry and manufacturing.

WEAKNESSES

Reduction in remittances from Egyptians working overseas owing to Gulf States' recession. Dependence on imported technology. High birth-rate.

PROFILE

Under President Nasser, Egypt followed an economic policy inspired by the Soviet model. Rigid and highly centralized, it gave Egypt one of the largest public sectors of all developing countries. Economic restrictions were first relaxed in 1974. President Sadat's open-door policy allowed joint ventures

ECONOMIC PERFORMANCE INDICATOR

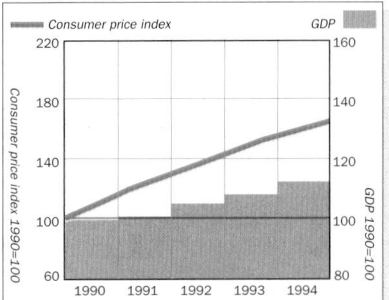

Consumer price index ▬▬   GDP ▒

with foreign partners for the first time, although the business classes were the only ones to profit. Most Egyptians suffered from new austerity measures.

Under President Mubarak, economic reform has quickened and policies are more sensitive to the high levels of unemployment and poverty. Priorities now are to reduce import dependence by encouraging manufacturing, and to sustain economic growth to keep up with the increase in population.

EGYPT : MAJOR BUSINESSES

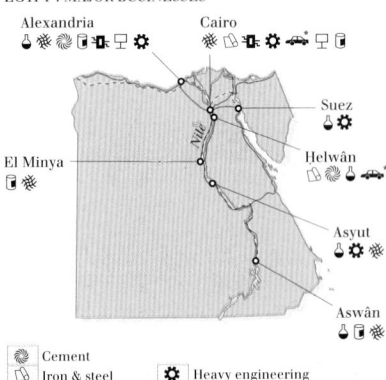

Cement		
Iron & steel	⚙	Heavy engineering
Food processing	🚐	Vehicle manufacture
Consumer goods	🧪	Chemicals
Electronics	※	Textiles

* significant multinational ownership

0 — 200 km
0 — 200 miles

RESOURCES

45bn kwh (capacity 11.7m kw)

870,000b/d (reserves 6,200,000,000 bbl)

3.3m sheep, 3.1m cattle, 3.2m goats, 190,000 camels

Natural gas, oil, phosphates, manganese, uranium

ELECTRICITY GENERATION

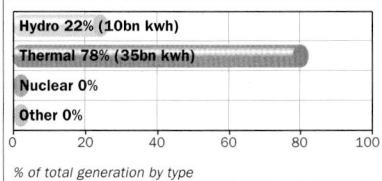

Hydro 22% (10bn kwh)

Thermal 78% (35bn kwh)

Nuclear 0%

Other 0%

% of total generation by type

Oil and gas are Egypt's most valuable resources. Most of the oil comes from its western desert, the Red Sea, Sinai and Upper Egypt. Oil multinationals are involved in new explorations, but Egypt is not as profitable a source as more competitive oil-rich countries, such as Algeria and Yemen; 55% of Egypt's oil production is consumed locally.

Most electricity is derived from hydroelectric power and coal. The massive Aswân Dam provides the bulk of hydroelectricity. Built between 1960 and 1970, the dam has a generating capacity of 10 billion kwh. By 1974, revenue from it had covered construction costs.

EGYPT : LAND USE

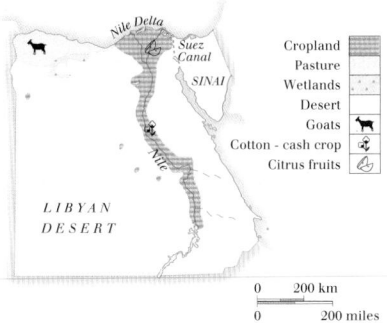

Cropland
Pasture
Wetlands
Desert
Goats
Cotton - cash crop
Citrus fruits

0   200 km
0   200 miles

ENVIRONMENT

0.8% (0.7% partially protected)

Population control and water are prime concerns

ENVIRONMENTAL TREATIES

Yes Yes Yes
Yes Yes No

Most of Egypt suffers from a chronic lack of water. The Nile is the only perennial source and is increasingly saline due to the Aswân Dam. The main cities suffer heavy industrial pollution, and environmental controls are few. In Cairo, the recent completion of a sewerage system has improved sanitary conditions.

MEDIA

Free press in theory, but government restrictions in practice

Once a center of Arab liberal journalism, Egypt is under siege from Islamic pressure groups and the government. While the media allocates more airtime to Islamic sermons, press legislation introduced in 1995 imposed draconian penalties for defamation and the publication of false information.

CRIME

Egypt does not publish prison figures

Up 11% in 1991

CRIME RATES

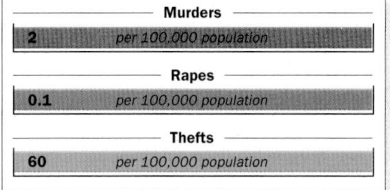

Murders
2   per 100,000 population

Rapes
0.1   per 100,000 population

Thefts
60   per 100,000 population

Terrorist attacks have tarnished Egypt's reputation as a law-abiding country; street crime and muggings were previously rare. Inter-community violence – particularly attacks by Muslims on Christians and *vice versa* – has become more common, as have attacks against Western tourists by Islamic extremists. Human rights groups have criticized the police for abusing current emergency laws, resulting in the routine torture and death in police custody of scores of political prisoners.

EDUCATION

48%   708,417 (19%)

0   Education spending as % GNP   25
5%

THE EDUCATION SYSTEM

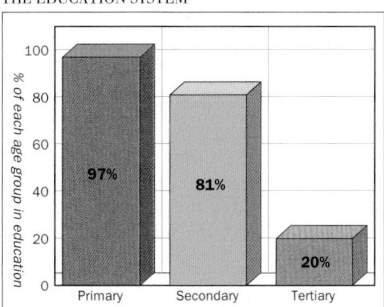

Primary 97%   Secondary 81%   Tertiary 20%

Education is free. Most Egyptians attend elementary school to the age of 11, but few complete secondary education, even though it is in theory compulsory until 15 years of age. The literacy rate is 62% for men and 34% for women. Egypt has 13 universities.

PUBLISHING AND BROADCAST MEDIA

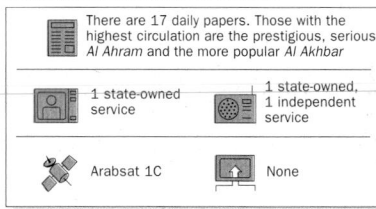

There are 17 daily papers. Those with the highest circulation are the prestigious, serious *Al Ahram* and the more popular *Al Akhbar*

1 state-owned service

1 state-owned, 1 independent service

Arabsat 1C

None

HEALTH

1 per 1,340 people

Digestive, respiratory and heart diseases, perinatal deaths

0   Health spending as % GDP   25
1%

Health care is rudimentary – there is only one hospital bed for every 500 people. Patient–doctor ratios are among the lowest in the Arab world. Islamic medical centers based on the mosque organization are spreading and replacing the state system.

WEALTH

Wealth heavily concentrated in Cairo

CONSUMER GOODS OWNERSHIP

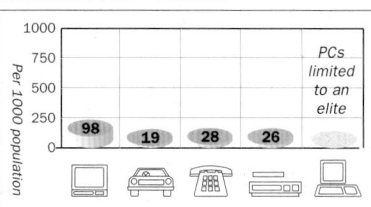

PCs limited to an elite

98   19   28   26

Wealth disparities are highly marked in Egypt. The largely urban Coptic Christian community is the group with the highest standard of living. Most Egyptians are subsistence farmers. The return of many workers from the Gulf states has further depressed employment conditions in the countryside.

WORLD RANKING

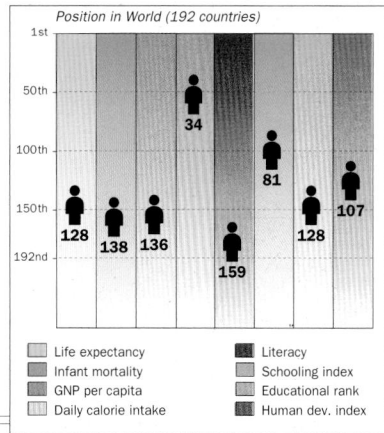

Position in World (192 countries)

34 81 128 138 136 159 128 107

Life expectancy
Infant mortality
GNP per capita
Daily calorie intake
Literacy
Schooling index
Educational rank
Human dev. index

EL SALVADOR

OFFICIAL NAME: Republic of El Salvador   **CAPITAL:** San Salvador
POPULATION: 5.8 million   **CURRENCY:** Colón   **OFFICIAL LANGUAGE:** Spanish

  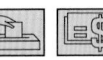

CENTRAL AMERICA
North America

THE SMALLEST AND MOST densely populated Central American republic, El Salvador won full independence in 1856. Located on the Pacific coast, it lies within a seismic zone. Between 1979 and 1991, El Salvador was ravaged by a civil war between US-backed right-wing governments and left-wing FMLN guerrillas. Since the UN-brokered peace agreement, the country has been concentrating on rebuilding its shattered economy.

***View over the capital, San Salvador.** It lies in a depression in the southern and higher of El Salvador's two mountain ranges, which is punctuated by more than 20 volcanoes.*

CLIMATE

WEATHER CHART

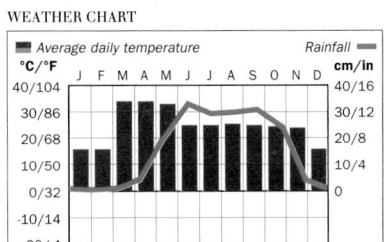

The tropical coastal *tierra caliente* is very hot, with seasonal rains. The low hills are cooler at night; the higher *tierra templada* is drier and also cooler.

TRANSPORTATION

 Cuscatlan, San Salvador 537,961 passengers   Has no fleet

THE TRANSPORTATION NETWORK

 1,270 miles (2,050 km)

1,270 miles (2,050 km)   Pan-American Highway 190 miles (306 km)

374 miles (602 km)   Rio Lempa

Infrastructure was badly affected by the civil war. Roads and bridges, natural FMLN targets, are gradually being repaired.

TOURISM

 181,000 visitors   Down 32% in 1994

MAIN OVERSEAS ARRIVALS

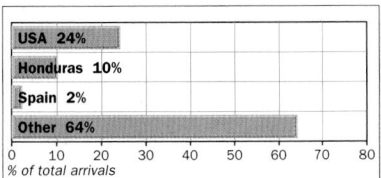

USA 24%
Honduras 10%
Spain 2%
Other 64%

0 10 20 30 40 50 60 70 80
% of total arrivals

The civil war effectively ended tourism. Peace has brought a few visitors back to the unspoilt beach resorts of El Salvador's Costa del Sol.

PEOPLE

 Spanish   726 people per sq. mile

THE URBAN/RURAL POPULATION SPLIT

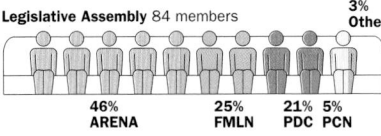

44%   56%

RELIGIOUS PERSUASION

Other (including Protestant) 25%
Roman Catholic 75%

Salvadoreans are largely a *mestizo* people with few ethnic tensions. The civil war was fought over economic disparities, which still exist.

POLITICS

 1994/1997   President Armando Calderón Sol

THE STATE OF THE PARTIES

Legislative Assembly 84 members

3% Other

46% ARENA   25% FMLN   21% PDC   5% PCN

ARENA = National Republican Alliance   **FMLN** = Farabundo Martí Liberation Front   **PDC** = Christian Democratic Party
PCN = National Conciliation Party   **Other** = Democratic Convergence, National United Movement

El Salvador has traditionally been dominated by two main parties, the centrist PDC and right-wing ARENA. The latter represents the interests of the 14 main coffee-growing families. However, in the 1994 elections, the left-wing FMLN, whose guerrillas at one time controlled one-third of El Salvadorean territory, won 25% of the vote. The elections marked the return of the left and center-left to the formal political system for the first time in 60 years. Apart from the huge task of rebuilding the shattered economy, the major problem is lack of progress in accomplishing judicial, electoral and land reforms.

WORLD AFFAIRS

 ACS   Geplac   NAM   OAS    San José

During the 1980s, El Salvador was renowned internationally for abuses of human rights by military death squads, allegedly controlled by ex-ARENA leader, Roberto D'Aubuisson. El Salvador's attempt to defend its record at the UN failed.

Today, conditions have improved and El Salvador seeks integration with its neighbors, reflecting US policy for the region. Dependence on US aid means that the US ambassador remains one of the most influential figures in El Salvador's external and internal affairs.

AID

 $405m (receipts)   Up 2% in 1993

In 1995, the USA was the main aid donor, followed by Japan. International organizations, including the IMF and EU, loaned $662 million and donated $3.9 million. The focus remains to secure peace and achieve national reconciliation by funding rebuilding and refugee resettlement programs. The World Bank and Inter-American Development Fund have also directed hundreds of millions of dollars into El Salvador.

DEFENSE

 $109m    Up 22% in 1995

Between 1979 and 1991, the military fought against the FMLN. Human rights were effectively suspended and governments that opposed the military overthrown. Its main backers were the USA which supplied over $1 billion-worth of arms, and Israel. The peace treaty reduced the army's size and established a civilian police force, but death squads still operate.

E

ECONOMICS

 $8.4bn

 8.760–8.764 colones

SCORE CARD

❑ WORLD GNP RANKING	83rd
❑ GNP PER CAPITA	$1,480
❑ BALANCE OF PAYMENTS	$–18m
❑ INFLATION	10.5%
❑ UNEMPLOYMENT	8.1%

STRENGTHS

Very few. Cheap labor. Increase in assembly plants for foreign goods.

WEAKNESSES

Civil war damage of $2 billion. Over-dependence on aid and coffee, which accounts for 90% of exports. Rural poor often landless; unofficial estimate of 60% unemployment.

EXPORTS

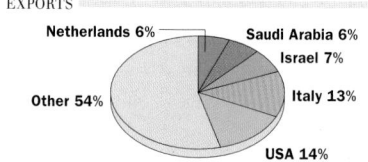

Netherlands 6%, Saudi Arabia 6%, Israel 7%, Italy 13%, Other 54%, USA 14%

IMPORTS

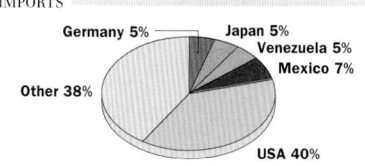

Germany 5%, Japan 5%, Venezuela 5%, Mexico 7%, Other 38%, USA 40%

RESOURCES

 2.5bn kwh (capacity 740,000 kw)

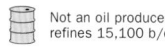 Not an oil producer; refines 15,100 b/cd

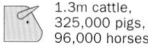 1.3m cattle, 325,000 pigs, 96,000 horses

Salt, limestone, gypsum

El Salvador has no significant resources. The restoration of the electricity system is a priority.

ENVIRONMENT

 1% (0.2% partially protected)

 20,235 hectares set aside for conservation

Most of the rainforest has been cut down for agriculture, leading to topsoil erosion and desertification. Pesticide poisoning of land is a major problem.

MEDIA

 Harassment of 11 community radio stations. The 4 independent TV stations have one owner

PUBLISHING AND BROADCAST MEDIA

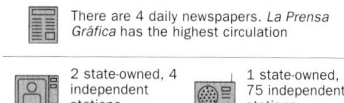

There are 4 daily newspapers. *La Prensa Gráfica* has the highest circulation

2 state-owned, 4 independent stations

1 state-owned, 75 independent stations

A pending constitutional amendment would outlaw press coverage of corruption cases of government officials.

CRIME

 El Salvador does not publish prison figures

 Rising

A weak and corrupt judiciary and police have been unable to deal with a postwar crime wave and narcotics trafficking. There is an unwillingness to investigate official corruption. Death squads have reappeared, and elements of the peace accords, particularly land transfers, have increased violence.

EDUCATION

 73%

 206,541 students

Education is based on the US system and is limited in rural areas. During the civil war, state universities were closed down by the military and replaced by private universities whose low standards provoked a 1995 reform bill which tried to address the negative impact of deregulation.

CHRONOLOGY

El Salvador was Spanish until 1821. Part of the United Provinces of Central America from 1823–1839, it became fully independent in 1856.

- ❑ **1952** Army crushes popular insurrection led by Farabundo Martí.
- ❑ **1944–1979** Army effectively rules through PCN.
- ❑ **1979** Reformist officers overthrow PCN government. Fail to curb rising army-backed political violence.
- ❑ **1981** Left-wing Farabundo Martí National Liberation Movement (FMLN) launches civil war.
- ❑ **1991** UN-brokered peace. FMLN recognized as a political party.
- ❑ **1992–1995** Escalating protests over delayed peace pledges.

HEALTH

 1 per 2,312 people

Accidents, violence, circulatory diseases, infections

Health spending almost halved during the civil war. Only the military hospitals are now adequately supplied.

WEALTH

 Machine assembler, 1,772 colones ($202) per month; insurance agent, 6,510 colones ($743) per month

CONSUMER GOODS OWNERSHIP

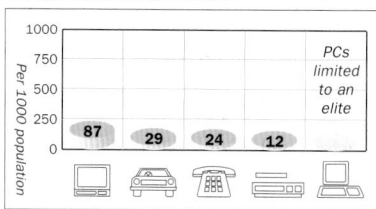

87, 29, 24, 12; PCs limited to an elite

El Salvador has considerable wealth disparities, with 20% owning 70% of national wealth. The rich favor bullet-proof cars and tend to own second homes in Los Angeles or Miami.

WORLD RANKING

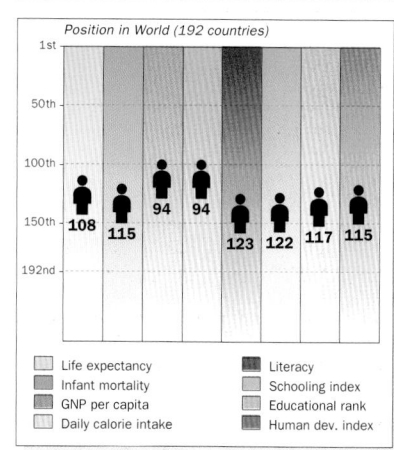

Position in World (192 countries)

108, 115, 94, 94, 123, 122, 117, 115

Life expectancy, Infant mortality, GNP per capita, Daily calorie intake, Literacy, Schooling index, Educational rank, Human dev. index

EL SALVADOR

Total Land Area : 20 720 sq. km (8000 sq. miles)

POPULATION
- over 500 000
- over 100 000
- over 50 000
- over 10 000
- under 10 000

LAND HEIGHT
- 2000m/6562ft
- 1000m/3281ft
- 500m/1640ft
- 200m/656ft
- Sea Level

E

207

EQUATORIAL GUINEA

OFFICIAL NAME: Republic of Equatorial Guinea **CAPITAL:** Malabo
POPULATION: 400,000 **CURRENCY:** CFA franc **OFFICIAL LANGUAGE:** Spanish

     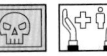

COMPRISING FIVE ISLANDS and the territory of Río Muni on the west coast of Africa, Equatorial Guinea lies just north of the equator. Mangrove swamps border the mainland coast. The republic gained its independence in 1968 after 190 years of Spanish rule. Multipartyism was accepted in 1991, but observers questioned the fairness of elections in 1993 and 1996.

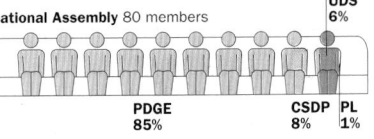

Bioko, formerly Fernando Po. Although the volcanic land is very fertile, cocoa production fell by 90% during the Macías years.

CLIMATE

WEATHER CHART

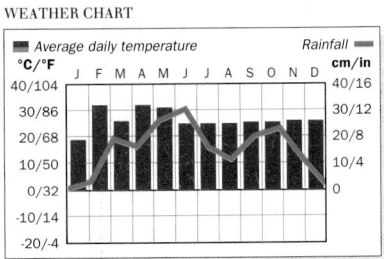

The island of Bioko is extremely wet and humid, with an annual rainfall of 78 inches, while the mainland is only marginally drier and cooler.

TRANSPORTATION

  Malabo   2 ships 6,700 dwt

THE TRANSPORTATION NETWORK

320 miles (510 km)		None	
None		None	

Apart from once- or twice-weekly *Iberia* flights, all airlinks are through neighboring countries. The Chinese financed the Ncue-Mongomo Highway project in the 1980s.

TOURISM

A few independent visitors	Numbers are unlikely to increase

MAIN OVERSEAS ARRIVALS

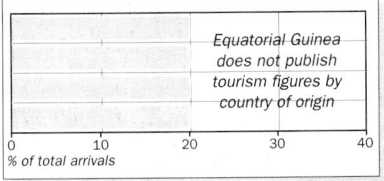

Equatorial Guinea does not publish tourism figures by country of origin

0 10 20 30 40
% of total arrivals

Equatorial Guinea is still very much a destination for the adventurous, independent tourist only, despite the potential attraction of Malabo's spectacular scenery and beaches.

PEOPLE

  Spanish, Fang, Bubi    36 people per sq. mile

THE URBAN/RURAL POPULATION SPLIT

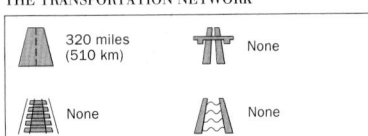

39%   61%

RELIGIOUS PERSUASION

Other 10%

Roman Catholic 90%

The mainland has a majority of Fang, a people who also inhabit Cameroon and northern Gabon. Bioko is populated by a majority of Bubi and a minority of Creoles, known as *Fernandinos*. The Macías dictatorship consolidated the power of the Fang, especially the Mongomo clan, from which both Macías and his successor Obiang come. The extended family is strong and maintained its solidarity despite disruptive social pressure during the Macías dictatorship.

EQUATORIAL GUINEA

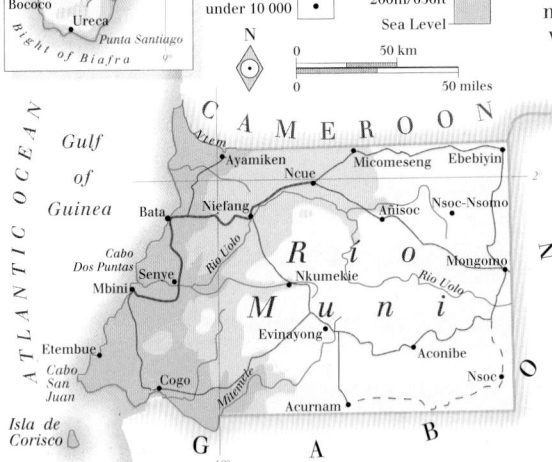

Total Land Area : 28 050 sq. km (10 830 sq. miles)

POPULATION
over 10 000 ●
under 10 000 •

LAND HEIGHT
2000m/6562ft
1000m/3281ft
500m/1640ft
200m/656ft
Sea Level

0 50 km
0 50 miles

POLITICS

1993/1998   President Brig.-Gen. Teodoro Obiang Nguema Mbasogo

THE STATE OF THE PARTIES

National Assembly 80 members

UDS 6%
PDGE 85%   CSDP 8%   PL 1%

PDGE = Democratic Party of Equatorial Guinea
CSDP = People's Social Democratic Convention
UDS = Social Democratic Union **PL** = Liberal Party

Despite officially being a multiparty state since 1991, some of the several exiled political parties have not yet found it safe to return – opposition leaders who publicize themselves tend to be arrested. The ruling PDGE was set up in 1987 by Teodoro Obiang Nguema Mbasogo, nephew of the dictator Francisco Macías Nguema, whom he overthrew in 1979. It replaced Macías' even more notional party, the National Workers' Party (PUNT), which in 1970 had forced a merger of the parties existing before independence. The PDGE benefits from heavy government patronage, receiving 3% of all salaries.

The movement toward multipartyism – which was initiated in 1988 following the first elections for 20 years – has been marked by instability. The 1993 parliamentary elections were boycotted by the main opposition parties, while the presidential poll in 1996 in which Obiang was the only candidate was declared farcical by foreign observers.

E

WORLD AFFAIRS

After a period of extreme isolation under the Macías dictatorship, Equatorial Guinea sought to rebuild links, especially its relationship with Spain, the former colonial power and traditionally a haven for political dissenters. However, the international community remains wary of the Obiang regime. Joining the Franc Zone in 1988 did not bring the expected benefits. Spain is suspicious of French commercial ambitions in the country.

AID

 $51m (receipts)   Down 19% in 1993

Equatorial Guinea is underdeveloped and aid is vital to get such projects as there are off the ground. Planning and implementation, however, have proved difficult owing to the lack of skilled labor, inefficiencies and instances of corruption.

The EU, especially France, Italy and Spain, the World Bank, IMF and Arab funds are all important sources of aid. However, the government's political record has threatened funding.

DEFENSE

 $2.5m   Up 4% in 1995

The main concern for the 1,320-man military and paramilitary force is internal security. Morocco has provided a 360-strong presidential guard since the early 1980s to guarantee Obiang's security. Nigeria, Cameroon and Gabon have interests in maintaining the autonomy of the Malabo and Río Muni regions.

ECONOMICS

 $167m   489.05–533.68 CFA francs

SCORE CARD

❏ WORLD GNP RANKING	186th
❏ GNP PER CAPITA	$430
❏ BALANCE OF PAYMENTS	$–22m
❏ INFLATION	40.6%
❏ UNEMPLOYMENT	5.9%

STRENGTHS

Fertile soils. Large tropical timber reserves. Cocoa and coffee. Extensive territorial waters, with potential for fisheries. Oil and natural gas reserves yet to be fully exploited.

WEAKNESSES

Lasting effects of economic regression under the Macías dictatorship. Maladministration and ideological

RESOURCES

 19m kwh (capacity 5,000 kw)   Reserves of 3,600,000 bbl

 36,000 sheep, 8,000 goats, 5,000 cattle   Oil, natural gas, gold

Offshore and mainland oil and gas reserves have yet to be fully exploited, but Mobil began pumping oil from a single field in 1996. Bata is served by a 3.2 MW hydropower station built by the Chinese in 1983.

ENVIRONMENT

 None   Government has no environmental protection expertise

The government has failed to take any serious measures to stop timber companies depleting the rainforest.

MEDIA

 Censorship is liable to be arbitrarily and suddenly imposed

PUBLISHING AND BROADCAST MEDIA

	There is no regular daily press. The formerly daily newspaper *Poto Poto* now appears irregularly
1 state-owned service	1 state-owned service

There has been very little sign of press liberalization, despite the adoption of multipartyism. Political parties produce a few tracts and broadsheets.

CRIME

 Equatorial Guinea does not publish prison figures   No measurable change from year to year

Levels of recorded crime are relatively low, although much does not get reported. Many human rights abuses still occur.

EXPORTS

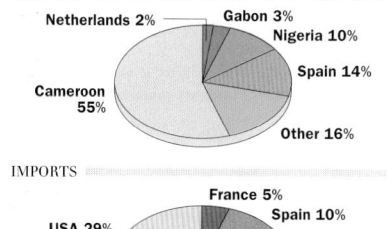

Netherlands 2%
Gabon 3%
Nigeria 10%
Spain 14%
Cameroon 55%
Other 16%

IMPORTS

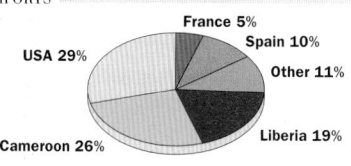

France 5%
Spain 10%
Other 11%
USA 29%
Liberia 19%
Cameroon 26%

attacks on the educated have restricted growth; during the Macías period, cocoa production slumped by 90%. Lack of a coherent, trained administration. Continuing problems with communications.

E

CHRONOLOGY

Equatorial Guinea remained a backwater of Spanish colonialism until development began after 1939.

❏ **1968** Independence. President Macías launches reign of terror. Puts own family in all top jobs.
❏ **1972** Attempt to stop mass exodus: people forbidden to leave country
❏ **1979** Coup puts nephew in power with Spanish approval.
❏ **1991** Multiparty constitution.

EDUCATION

 50%   578 students

Education declined in the Macías years, when attendance rates fell from 90% to 55%. Although declared the state's first priority, funding is poor.

HEALTH

 1 per 4,200 people   Diarrheal and respiratory diseases, malaria

Life expectancy has risen from 37 years in 1960 to 47 in 1990. Restoring basic health care is a priority.

WEALTH

 Most of the population leads a subsistence existence; a minority has formal employment

CONSUMER GOODS OWNERSHIP

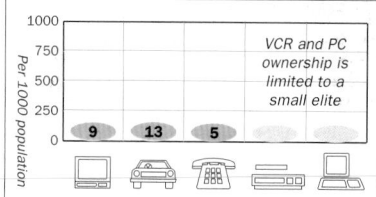

VCR and PC ownership is limited to a small elite

9   13   5

What wealth there is tends to be concentrated in the ruling clan. There is also a relic of Spanish plutocracy.

WORLD RANKING

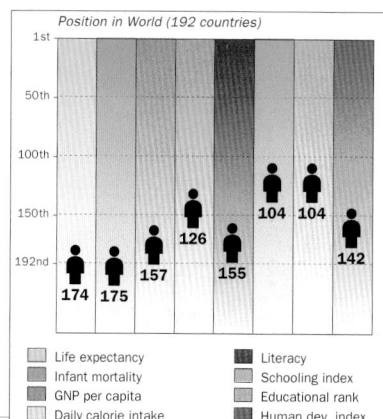

Position in World (192 countries)

1st
50th
100th
150th
192nd

174   175   157   126   155   104   104   142

▨ Life expectancy	▨ Literacy
▨ Infant mortality	▨ Schooling index
▨ GNP per capita	▨ Educational rank
▨ Daily calorie intake	▨ Human dev. index

ERITREA

EAST AFRICA

OFFICIAL NAME: State of Eritrea **CAPITAL:** Asmara
POPULATION: 3.5 million **CURRENCY:** Ethiopian birr **OFFICIAL LANGUAGES:** Tigrinya and Arabic

E

L YING ON THE SHORES of the Red Sea, Eritrea's
landscape is dominated by rugged mountains, bush
and the Danakil Desert. The country effectively seceded
from Ethiopia in 1991, after a 30-year war for independence that left much
of its infrastructure in ruins. A failure of the harvest in 1993 compounded
the new state's problems, placing 400,000 at risk of famine. The transitional
government is due to hold multiparty democratic elections in 1997.

CLIMATE

WEATHER CHART

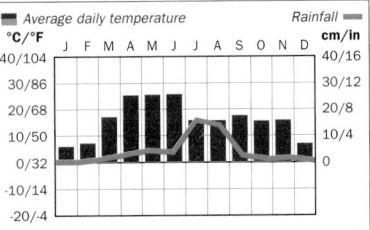

Eritrea's harvest is dependent on
rainfall in September. Droughts from
July onward are common.

TRANSPORTATION

 Yohannes IV, Asmara   Has no fleet

THE TRANSPORTATION NETWORK

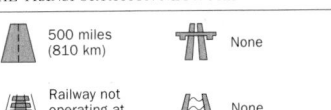

500 miles (810 km)	None
Railway not operating at present	None

All transportation systems need massive
investment. Eritrea will benefit as a
transit point for landlocked neighbors.

TOURISM

 Visitors limited to aid workers and business people   Government is encouraging the tourist sector

MAIN OVERSEAS ARRIVALS

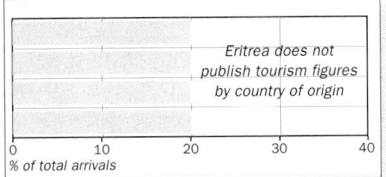

Eritrea does not
publish tourism figures
by country of origin

0   10   20   30   40
% of total arrivals

There is very little tourism; most
visitors are aid workers or on business.
Planners are keen to develop coastal
resorts for the regional Arab market.
However, the task of clearing beaches
of mines will take several years.

PEOPLE

 Tigrinya, Tigre, Afar, Arabic, Bilen, Kunama, Nara, Saho, Hadareb   96 people per sq. mile

THE URBAN/RURAL POPULATION SPLIT

22%   78%

RELIGIOUS PERSUASION

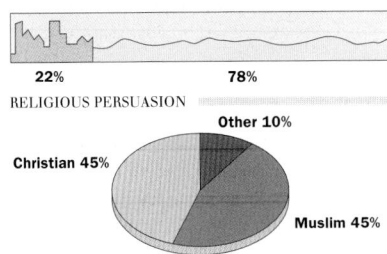

Other 10%
Christian 45%
Muslim 45%

Tigrinya-speakers form the largest of
Eritrea's nine main ethnic groups. A
strong sense of nationhood has been
forged by the 30-year struggle for
independence. Women played an
important role in the war. From 1973,
30,000 fought alongside men, some in
positions of command. Their claim to
equal rights is likely to be enshrined in
the new constitution. Over 80% of the
people are subsistence
farmers. Few live
beyond their
early fifties.

ERITREA

Total Land Area : 93 680 sq. km
(36 170 sq. miles)

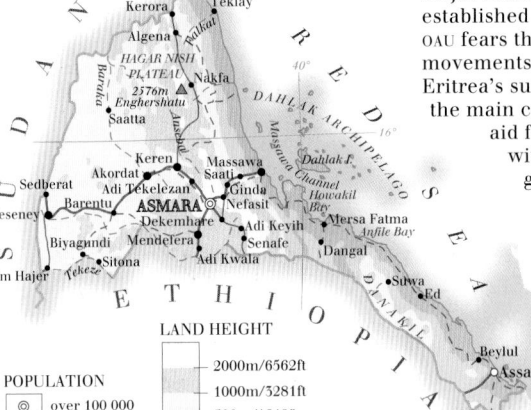

LAND HEIGHT

2000m/6562ft
1000m/3281ft
500m/1640ft
200m/656ft
Sea Level
-200m/-656ft

POPULATION

◎	over 100 000
○	over 50 000
●	over 10 000
•	under 10 000

POLITICS

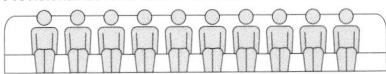

1997   President Issaias Afewerki

THE STATE OF THE PARTIES

Provisional Government of Eritrea

The transitional government will be in place until 1997

Eritrea became a region of Ethiopia
as a result of European power politics.
Formerly an Italian colony, it came
under British mandate in 1941. In
1952, London handed the region to
Addis Ababa. The long struggle for
independence began in the same year.
The Eritrean People's Liberation Front
(EPLF) finally drove out Ethiopian
troops in 1991. A referendum held
in May 1993 resulted in 99.8% of
voters on a 98.2% turnout voting
"yes" to independence.

Until multiparty elections are held
in 1997, the country is being run by
a core of former EPLF (now the People's
Front for Democracy and Justice (PFDJ))
leaders who conducted the military
campaign. A new constitution is
planned that will forbid parties based
on religious or ethnic affiliations.
Issaias Afewerki, a Christian, has
also been careful to include Muslims
in his transitional cabinet.

WORLD AFFAIRS

 Comesa   iBRD   IGADD   NAM   OAU

Eritrea's secession was significant
for African politics. It marked the first
major redrawing of the national borders
established by Africa's colonizers. The
OAU fears that other African secessionist
movements will be encouraged by
Eritrea's success. For Eritrea, however,
the main concern is attracting Western
aid for reconstruction. Relations
with Ethiopia's new
government, which also
fought the Mengistu
regime, are good. Eritrea
has a territorial dispute
with Yemen over the
Red Sea Hanish
Islands.

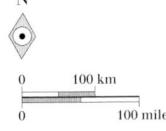

AID

 $67m (receipts)　　 Down 37% in 1993

Eritrea's economy is almost entirely aid-dependent. Food aid, on which 75% of the population survive, is the most pressing need given the vulnerability of the country to famine. The UN has frequently provided food aid. Western donors have been less generous with aid for the $2 billion reconstruction costs. Compared with Somalia, the country's aid receipts are tiny.

DEFENSE

 $40m　　 Up 3% in 1995

The 55,000-strong army (of whom about one-third are women) is currently being demobilized. As with other groups, troops are being reintegrated into the national economy on "food for work" schemes. In return for repairing the damage wrought by war on the environment and to the infrastructure, they receive basic rations.

ECONOMICS

 $393m (est)　　 5.42–5.80 Ethiopian birr

SCORE CARD

- ❏ WORLD GNP RANKING......................176th
- ❏ GNP PER CAPITA $120
- ❏ BALANCE OF PAYMENTS......................Deficit
- ❏ INFLATION 12%
- ❏ UNEMPLOYMENT ......Widespread underemployment

STRENGTHS

Strategically important position on Red Sea. Potential for developing a mining industry and for foreign earnings from oil exports. Government commitment to reducing dependence on food aid. Potential for tourism on Red Sea coast.

WEAKNESSES

Lack of basic information and equipment. Coherent economic policy still being formulated. Not an aid priority for Western donors. Legacy of disruption and destruction from civil war. Port of Massawa heavily bombed. Most of population living at subsistence level. Susceptibility to drought and famine. Expense of repatriating and supporting the 750,000 who fled abroad as refugees and have now returned.

EXPORTS/IMPORTS

Eritrea does not yet publish export or import figures

RESOURCES

 Electricity supply is prone to surges　　 Not an oil producer; oil refinery at Assab

 1.6m cattle, 1.5m sheep, 1.4m goats　　 Copper, potash, gold, iron, silver, zinc, oil, silica, granite, marble

Eritrea has substantial copper reserves, and lesser ones of silver, zinc and gold. High-quality silica, granite and marble deposits could be exploited. Onshore and offshore oil deposits are believed to exist. Concessionary exploration deals with Western companies have yet to be established.

ENVIRONMENT

 None at present　　 New government conscious of conservation needs

Deforestation and soil erosion are major problems. The Ethiopian army uprooted trees to destroy the cover they provided for Eritrean soldiers. Since 1991, 22 million seedlings have been grown in a replanting scheme. The Red Sea coast is a conservation priority.

MEDIA

 Most of the media is controlled by the government

PUBLISHING AND BROADCAST MEDIA

 New Eritrea, owned by the PFDJ, is published every 3 days in Tigrinya and Arabic

 1 state-controlled service　　 1 state-controlled service

The media is largely controlled by the PFDJ who run both the radio and TV services. Independent newspapers are not encouraged.

CRIME

 Eritrea does not publish prison figures　　 Crime levels remain low

Crime has not been a problem since independence. The judiciary and police answer to the PFDJ. There are a number of political prisoners.

EDUCATION

 20%　　 Not available

Very few schools functioned during the war. There is one university. In an attempt to reduce potential ethnic tension, all children above the age of 11 are being taught in English.

HEALTH

 1 per 48,000 people　　 Malaria. Potential risk of famine

The risk of famine overrides normal health concerns. Eritreans built their own hospitals during the independence struggle. Health provision is basic.

Seasonal river beds carry rain from the Ethiopian highlands into Eritrea, providing essential irrigation for agriculture.

E

CHRONOLOGY

British military rule replaced Italian colonial authority in 1941.

- ❏ **1952** Eritrea absorbed by Ethiopia.
- ❏ **1961** EPLF begins armed struggle.
- ❏ **1987** EPLF refuses offer of autonomy; fighting intensifies.
- ❏ **1991** EPLF takes control of Asmara. New EPRDF government in Addis Ababa effectively agrees to Eritrean secession.
- ❏ **1993** Formal independence.

WEALTH

 Demobilized soldier in Asmara, $325 per month; the 1 million refugees who fled to neighboring countries are destitute

CONSUMER GOODS OWNERSHIP

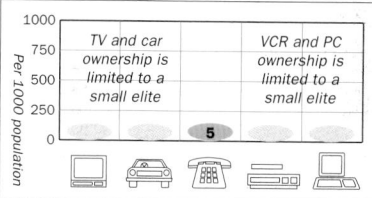

Over 80% of people are subsistence farmers. A few of the 150,000 refugees who fled to Arab and Western countries have built up some personal savings.

WORLD RANKING

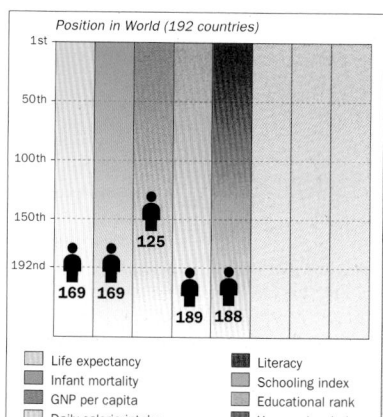

- Life expectancy
- Infant mortality
- GNP per capita
- Daily calorie intake
- Literacy
- Schooling index
- Educational rank
- Human dev. index

ESTONIA

OFFICIAL NAME: Republic of Estonia **CAPITAL:** Tallinn
POPULATION: 1.5 million **CURRENCY:** Kroon **OFFICIAL LANGUAGE:** Estonian

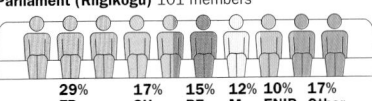

EUROPE

Europe

TRADITIONALLY THE MOST Western-oriented of the Baltic states, Estonia is bordered by Latvia and the Russian Federation. Its terrain is flat, boggy and partly wooded, and includes more than 1,500 islands. Estonia formally regained its independence as a multiparty democracy in 1991. In contrast to the peoples of the other Baltic states, Latvia and Lithuania, Estonians are Finno-Ugric and their language is similar to Finnish.

CLIMATE

WEATHER CHART

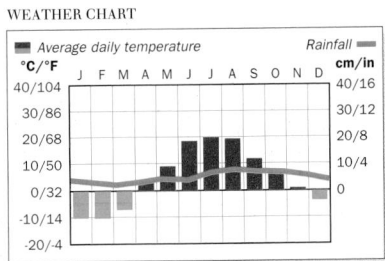

Estonia's coastal location gives it wet springs and cool summers. Winters are cold as the Baltic freezes.

TRANSPORTATION

✈ **Tallinn Ulemiste**

102 ships
587,800 dwt

THE TRANSPORTATION NETWORK

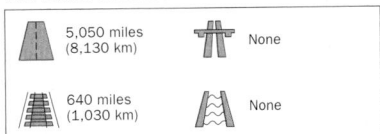

| 5,050 miles (8,130 km) | None |
| 640 miles (1,030 km) | None |

The transportation system is in need of modernization. Tallinn Airport is currently being upgraded.

TOURISM

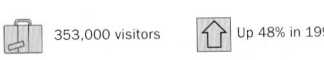

353,000 visitors

⬆ Up 48% in 1994

MAIN OVERSEAS ARRIVALS

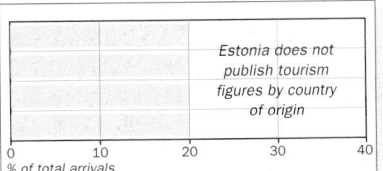

Estonia does not publish tourism figures by country of origin

% of total arrivals

Estonia is a popular destination for Scandinavians, in particular Finns. Tallinn's medieval center is a major attraction. The capital is also an important Baltic yachting center, with many summer regattas.

PEOPLE

💬 Estonian, Russian

👥 86 people per sq. mile

THE URBAN/RURAL POPULATION SPLIT

72% **28%**

ETHNIC MAKEUP

Other 8%

Russian 30%

Estonian 62%

Under Moscow's rule, Estonia underwent a process of enforced Sovietization. The immigration of a large Russian work force, many attracted by Estonia's higher living standards, reduced the proportion of Estonians from 90% to 62% of the population. Since 1991, Estonians have been reasserting their dominance. Non-Estonian Russian speakers are finding it harder to get jobs, and several thousand have left. Estonians are predominantly Protestant. Families are small; divorce rates are high.

POLITICS

🗳 1995/1999

🧑 President Lennart Meri

THE STATE OF THE PARTIES

Parliament (Riigikogu) 101 members

| **29%** FP | **17%** SH | **15%** PF | **12%** M | **10%** ENIP | **17%** Other |

FP = Fatherland Party **SH** = Secure Home
PF = Popular Front **M** = Moderates **ENIP** = Estonian
National Independence Party **Other** = Estonian Citizen,
Independent Royalists

The center-right coalition which had dominated Estonian politics since 1992 was heavily defeated in legislative elections in March 1995. It was replaced by a center-left coalition led by Tiit Vahi, but this collapsed in October 1995 in the face of a phone-tapping scandal. Vahi subsequently formed a center-right administration committed to market-led economic reform and privatizing ex-Soviet enterprises. The status of Russians is a major issue. A 1995 citizenship law extended the minimum period of residence required for naturalization applications from two to five years, a stipulation condemned by Moscow as designed to legitimize discrimination against the Russian minority.

ESTONIA

Total Land Area :
45 125 sq. km
(17 423 sq. miles)

LAND HEIGHT

200m/565ft
Sea Level

POPULATION

⊙ over 500 000
◎ over 100 000
○ over 50 000
● over 10 000
· under 10 000

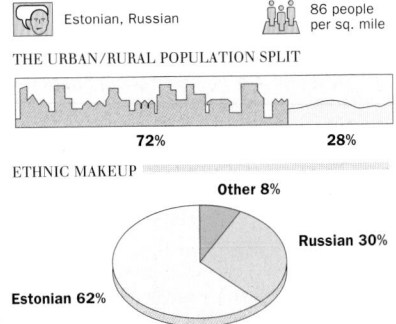

E

WORLD AFFAIRS

 CBS CE NACC OSCE WEU

Estonia wants to secure the return of territories ceded to Russia in the Soviet period. It is keen to obtain greater access to EU markets and signed an association agreement with the EU in 1995. The government has been criticized by the international community for its treatment of the ethnic Russian minority; the prospect of a Russian intervention is Estonia's main fear.

AID

 Estonia does not publish aid receipts Probably rising

Finland, Sweden, Germany, the EU and the IMF are major sources of aid, which is spent on infrastructure projects.

DEFENSE

 $33.4m Up 36% in 1995

Building up the military is a priority. The withdrawal of the 8,000 Russian troops from Estonian territory was completed in 1994. Estonia is developing a closer relationship with NATO under the Partnership for Peace program.

ECONOMICS

 $4.4bn 12.37–11.46 kroons

SCORE CARD

- ❏ WORLD GNP RANKING.......................105th
- ❏ GNP PER CAPITA $2,820
- ❏ BALANCE OF PAYMENTS...................$–171m
- ❏ INFLATION 47.7%
- ❏ UNEMPLOYMENT...............................1.8%

STRENGTHS

Oil shale and phosphorite reserves. Light industrial sector. Own stable currency, the kroon. Reduced dependence on Russia. Growing links with Finland and Germany.

WEAKNESSES

Antiquated industrial infrastructure in urgent need of investment. Poor raw materials base. Dependence on imported energy supplies.

EXPORTS

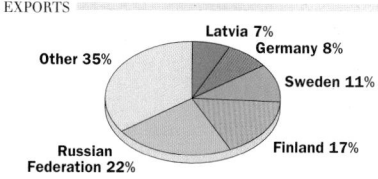

IMPORTS

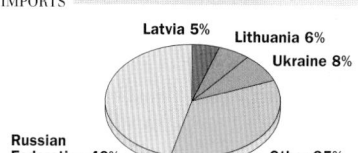

RESOURCES

 11.8bn kwh Oil figures not published

 3m poultry, 463,000 cattle, 424,000 pigs Oil shale, coal, phosphorite

The chief resources are oil shale and phosphorite. The latter is processed to make phosphates for agricultural use.

ENVIRONMENT

 10% Northern coniferous forests are suffering from acid rain

Environmental issues are prominent. Protests against Soviet plans to expand phosphorite mining in the northeast, the most polluted area, were part of the late 1980s independence movement.

MEDIA

 Little censorship for Estonians; Russian access to the media is decreasing

PUBLISHING AND BROADCAST MEDIA

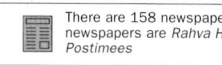 There are 158 newspapers. The main daily newspapers are *Rahva Hääl*, *Päevaleht* and *Postimees*

 1 state-owned service  1 state-owned service

The media are mostly pro-government. The number of Russian language programs is declining. Estonians have been able to receive Finnish satellite TV for some years.

CRIME

 Estonia does not publish prison figures Up 30% in 1992

Robbery and narcotics are the main crime problems. Generally, however, crime levels are still relatively low.

EDUCATION

 99%  24,768 students

Education is becoming increasingly Westernized. Six higher-education establishments have 25,000 students.

HEALTH

 1 per 260 people 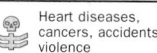 Heart diseases, cancers, accidents, violence

The health system, improved since the collapse of communism, is better than that of most former Soviet republics.

The Russian Orthodox convent of Pühtitsa at Kuremäe in Estonia's marshy north. Most of the population is Evangelical Lutheran.

E

CHRONOLOGY

After Swedish and then Russian rule, Estonia briefly enjoyed independence from 1921 until its incorporation into the Soviet Union in 1940.

- ❏ **1990** Unilateral declaration of independence.
- ❏ **1991** Independence recognized by Russia.
- ❏ **1992** Multiparty elections; center-right coalition government.
- ❏ **1995** General election results in center-left government, but this later collapses and is replaced by center-right coalition.

WEALTH

 Traders are the wealthiest group

CONSUMER GOODS OWNERSHIP

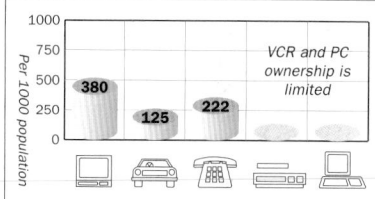

Growing Western economic ties have maintained Estonia's traditionally high standard of living.

WORLD RANKING

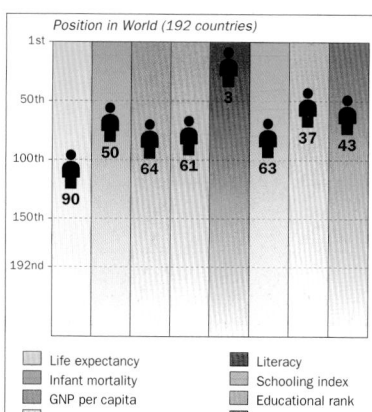

ETHIOPIA

OFFICIAL NAME: Ethiopia **CAPITAL:** Addis Ababa **POPULATION:** 55.1 million
CURRENCY: Ethiopian birr **OFFICIAL LANGUAGE:** Amharic

E

LOCATED IN NORTHEAST AFRICA, Ethiopia reverted to its historical landlocked status in 1993, when Eritrea, its coastal province on the Red Sea, regained its independence. Ethiopia is mountainous except for the desert lowlands in the northeast and southeast and is subject to devastating droughts and famines. Civil war began in the 1960s and ended in 1991 with the defeat of the Marxist military dictatorship that had ruled since 1974. In 1995, following a four-year transition period, a free-market, multiparty democracy was created. It provides for an unprecedented degree of regional autonomy and seeks to share power equally among Ethiopia's ethnic groups. In recent years, farming reforms and good rains have halved Ethiopia's need for food aid.

CLIMATE

WEATHER CHART

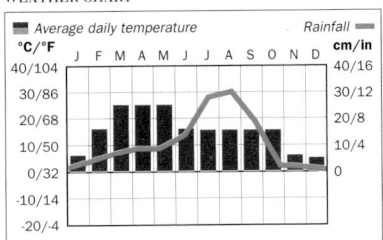

In general, the climate is moderate, except in the lowlands of the Danakil Desert and the Ogaden, which are hot all year round and can suffer severe drought. The highlands are warm, with night frost and snowfalls in the mountains. The single rainy season in the west brings twice as much rain as do the two wet seasons in the east. During these cloudy periods, thunderstorms occur almost daily.

TRANSPORTATION

 Bole Intl, Addis Ababa
480,000 passengers

 20 ships
87,000 dwt

THE TRANSPORTATION NETWORK

11,820 miles (19,020 km)	Trans-East Africa Highway
423 miles (681 km)	None

The single railroad links Addis Ababa with Djibouti, and the only all-weather roads are those between main business centers. Repairing war damage is a priority, with efforts concentrated on the roads through Eritrea to the Red Sea ports of Assab and Massawa. As ownership of motor vehicles of any kind is rare, pack donkeys and donkey carts are widely used, especially in the highlands.

TOURISM

 98,000 visitors   Up 5% in 1994

MAIN OVERSEAS ARRIVALS

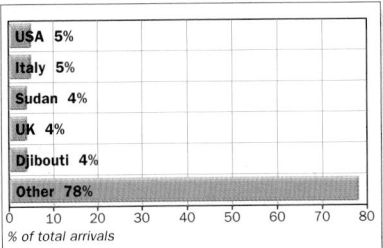

Tourism has always been on a small scale, although since 1991 there has been a moderate increase in the number of visitors. By 1994, the need for permits to travel within the country had been abolished. Several new hotels are being built. Most tourists go to Ethiopia on expensive organized tours, and Lake Gonder with its spectacular scenery is a popular destination. Ethiopia's ancient forts, churches and cities such as Āksum, the royal capital of the first Ethiopian kingdom, are now accessible. Some safari tours operate to the five national parks.

Lalibela, 75 miles northwest of Desē in Ethiopia's central highlands. An important pilgrimage center, it is famous for its ten 12th-century Christian churches.

PEOPLE

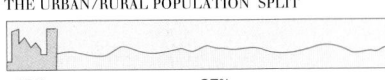 Amharic, Tigrinya, Galla, Sidamo, Somali, English, Arabic   130 people per sq. mile

THE URBAN/RURAL POPULATION SPLIT

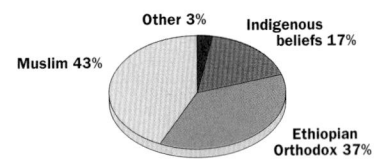

13%   87%

RELIGIOUS PERSUASION

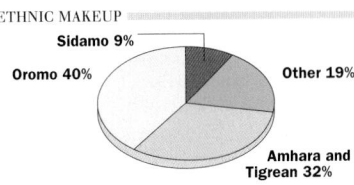

Other 3%
Indigenous beliefs 17%
Muslim 43%
Ethiopian Orthodox 37%

ETHNIC MAKEUP

Sidamo 9%
Oromo 40%
Other 19%
Amhara and Tigrean 32%

There are 76 nationalities in Ethiopia speaking 286 languages. Oromos form the largest group, followed by Amharas and Tigreans.

Civil war was sparked by fighting between different ethnic groups, but they later united in opposition to the Mengistu regime's centralist policies. Ethnic tensions are still near the surface, in spite of the new federal structure, and there have been reports of boundary disputes in several regions. The Oromos withdrew from the Tigrean-dominated government in 1992. Opposition to the transitional government has also been voiced by disaffected Amharas, who had held the reins of power for the last century, and by the Orthodox Church. Amnesty International has also expressed concern at the arrest of Amharan leaders.

No discrimination is shown toward minorities. Most of the small Jewish population was evacuated to Israel in 1991. The participation of women in rural organizations is increasing, reflecting the key role women played in the war.

POPULATION AGE BREAKDOWN

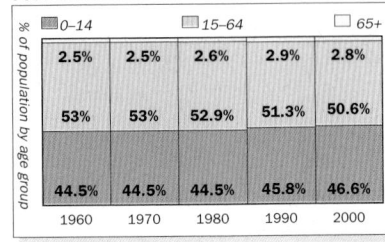

% of population by age group	0–14		15–64		65+
65+	2.5%	2.5%	2.6%	2.9%	2.8%
15–64	53%	53%	52.9%	51.3%	50.6%
0–14	44.5%	44.5%	44.5%	45.8%	46.6%
	1960	1970	1980	1990	2000

ETHIOPIA

Total Land Area :
1 101 000 sq. km
(425 096 sq. miles)

POPULATION

over 1 000 000	▣
over 100 000	◉
over 50 000	◎
over 10 000	○
under 10 000	•

LAND HEIGHT

4000m/13 124ft	
3000m/9843ft	
2000m/6562ft	
1000m/3281ft	
500m/1640ft	
200m/656ft	
Sea Level	
-200m/656ft	

0 ___ 200 km
0 ___ 200 miles

WORLD AFFAIRS

Landlocked Ethiopia has maintained cordial relations with Eritrea, ensuring that it has continued access to the Red Sea. These have been partly cemented in a number of recent bilateral accords, which allow for the harmonization of economic policy and the free movement of peoples.

Addis Ababa is the headquarters of the OAU and Ethiopia plays an active role in diplomacy in the region, including numerous attempts at brokering peace in Somalia.

During the Mengistu regime, Ethiopia's liberation movements supported dissidents in neighboring Sudan and Somalia. However, the government's official policy now is one of non-interference in the affairs of neighboring countries. Relations with Sudan have deteriorated significantly since the 1995 attempt on Egyptian President Hosni Mubarak's life in Addis Ababa, in which Sudan was implicated. Links with the USA, the main bilateral aid donor, and Israel have been strengthened.

POLITICS

 1995/2000   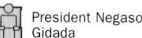 President Negaso Gidada

THE STATE OF THE PARTIES

Council of People's Representatives 548 members

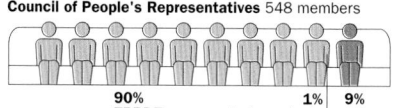

90% EPRDF	1% Independents	9% Other

EPRDF = Ethiopian People's Revolutionary Democratic Front

The transitional period which followed the collapse in 1991 of Mengistu Haile Mariam's military dictatorship ended in 1995 with mulitparty elections.

MAIN POLITICAL ISSUE
Ethnic representation
The 1994 constitution established a nine-state democratic federation. It grants the states considerable powers and gives them a large degree of autonomy, including the right of secession. Thus any or all of the states have the option to break away from the federation and form independent republics in the same way as Eritrea did in 1993. The Ethiopian People's Revolutionary Democratic Front (EPRDF) government believes this to be the best way to prevent secessionist conflict and to maintain a sense of national unity.

PROFILE
The current government elected in 1995, is the successor to that set up in 1991 by the EPRDF, the strongest of the liberation groups that fought Mengistu's Marxist regime and the faction chiefly responsible for winning the civil war. Prime Minister Meles Zenawi is the leader of the Tigrean People's Liberation Front, the largest group within the EPRDF. There is growing opposition to the dominance of Tigreans by the Oromos and Amharas, the two second-largest groups, notably since January 1994. The nine states are largely governed by elected governments dominated by local liberation movements, which helped to overthrow the Mengistu regime.

***Prime Minister Meles Zenawi**, leader of the EPRDF, which ousted the Mengistu regime.*

***Mengistu Haile Mariam**, who ran Ethiopia on Soviet lines from 1977–1991.*

CHRONOLOGY

After repelling a devastating Muslim invasion in 1523, Ethiopia developed as an isolated empire until Egyptian and Sudanese incursions in the 1850s led to its renewed political power under Emperor Theodor. His successor, Menelik II, doubled the empire southward and eastward.

❑ **1896** Italian invasion of Tigre defeated. Europeans recognize Ethiopia's independence.

❑ **1913** Menelik II dies.

❑ **1916** His son, Lij Iyasu, deposed for his conversion to Islam and proposed alliance with Turkey. Menelik's daughter, Zauditu, becomes empress with Ras Tafari as regent.

❑ **1923** Joins League of Nations.

❑ **1930** Zauditu dies. Ras Tafari crowned Emperor Haile Selassie.

❑ **1936** Italians occupy Ethiopia. Europe fails to react.

❑ **1941** Allies oust Italians and restore Haile Selassie, who sets up a constitution, parliament and cabinet, but retains personal power and the feudal system.

❑ **1952** Eritrea, formerly ruled first by the Italians then by the British, federated to Ethiopia.

⇨

E

E

CHRONOLOGY *continued*

- ❏ **1962** Unitary state created; Eritrea fully absorbed.
- ❏ **1972–1974** Famine kills 200,000.
- ❏ **1974** Strikes and army mutinies at Haile Selassie's autocratic rule and country's economic decline. Dergue (Military Committee) stages coup.
- ❏ **1975** Becomes socialist state. Nationalizations, worker cooperatives and health reforms.
- ❏ **1977** Col. Mengistu Haile Mariam takes over. Somali invasion of the Ogaden defeated with Soviet and Cuban help.
- ❏ **1978–1979** Thousands of political opponents killed or imprisoned.
- ❏ **1984** Workers' Party of Ethiopia (WPE) set up on Soviet model. Live Aid concert raises funds to relieve famine caused by war and three years' drought. One million die.
- ❏ **1986** Eritrean rebels now control the whole northeastern coast.
- ❏ **1987** People's Democratic Republic of Ethiopia declared with Mengistu as president. New serious drought.
- ❏ **1988** Eritrean and Tigrean People's Liberation Fronts (EPLF and TPLF) begin new offensives. Mengistu's budget is for "Everything to the War Front." Ethiopia agrees not to interfere in Somali factional fighting and resumes diplomatic relations severed in 1977.
- ❏ **1989** Military coup attempt fails. TPLF in control of most of Tigre. TPLF and Ethiopian People's Revolutionary Movement form alliance – the EPRDF.
- ❏ **1990** WPE renamed Ethiopian Democratic Unity Party and opened to non-Marxists. Moves toward market economy begin. Distribution of food aid for victims of new famine hampered by both government and rebel forces.
- ❏ **1991** Mengistu flees country in face of big advances by EPRDF and EPLF. EPRDF enters Addis Ababa and sets up provisional government, dividing country into 14 semi-autonomous regions and promising representation for all ethnic groups. However, fighting continues between the mainly Tigrean EPRDF troops and various opposing groups. EPLF enters Asmara, the Eritrean capital, and sets up government.
- ❏ **1993** Eritrean independence recognized.
- ❏ **1995** Transitional rule ends with multiparty democratic elections and the establishment of a new nine-state federation. Having won a landslide victory, the EPRDF forms the first democratic government.

AID

 $1.1bn (receipts)   Down 16% in 1993

The World Food Program and the EU are the largest sources of assistance, while the USA has taken over from Italy and the former Soviet Union as the major bilateral donor. Aid per capita is low by regional standards.

However, long-term development assistance and balance of payments support look set to continue their recent growth. Aid is now playing an increasingly important part in the economy. The emphasis is shifting from food aid toward credit for infrastructure development.

DEFENSE

 $19m   Down 83% in 1995

0   *Defense spending as % GDP*   40
2.6%

Ethiopia has no formal military alliances. A key issue is improving government control of the many ethnic and clan-based militias. A national army representing all ethnic groups is being formed. Much of the Mengistu regime's $6 billion arms debt to the former USSR is unpaid.

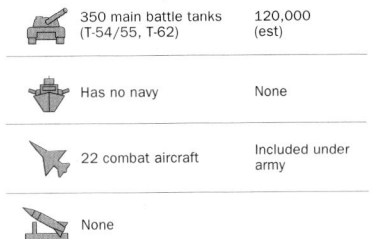

ETHIOPIAN ARMED FORCES

350 main battle tanks (T-54/55, T-62)	120,000 (est)
Has no navy	None
22 combat aircraft	Included under army
None	

ECONOMICS

 $6.9bn   5.42–5.80 Ethiopian birr

SCORE CARD

- ❏ WORLD GNP RANKING...........................91st
- ❏ GNP PER CAPITA $130
- ❏ BALANCE OF PAYMENTS.....................$–52m
- ❏ INFLATION 1.5%
- ❏ UNEMPLOYMENT.......Widespread underemployment

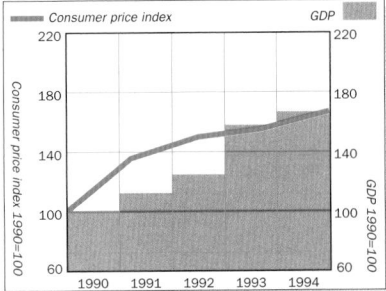

ECONOMIC PERFORMANCE INDICATOR

Consumer price index — GDP

EXPORTS

France 7%
Italy 7%
Saudi Arabia 8%
Germany 29%
Japan 23%
Other 26%

IMPORTS

France 7%   Italy 7%
Saudi Arabia 8%
Germany 29%
Japan 23%
Other 26%

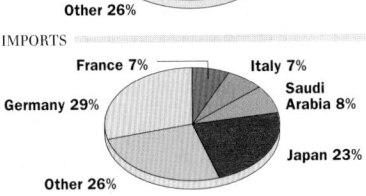

STRENGTHS
Peace and greater flow of economic aid. Dismantling of total state control. Coffee production.

WEAKNESSES
Overwhelming dependence upon agriculture – engages 75% of population, accounts for 80% of exports. Periodic serious droughts. War-damaged infrastructure. Huge displacement of population by war and drought. Small industrial base. Lack of skilled workers. Legacy of Mengistu regime's disastrous experiment in a centrally-planned economy.

PROFILE
Since the end of the civil war, Ethiopia has begun moving toward a market economy by encouraging foreign investment and reforming land tenure. Economic decline was reversed in 1993 as agricultural and industrial output grew. The latter was fueled by the purchase of parts and raw materials funded by foreign aid. Ethiopia is one of the world's poorest nations.

ETHIOPIA : MAJOR BUSINESSES

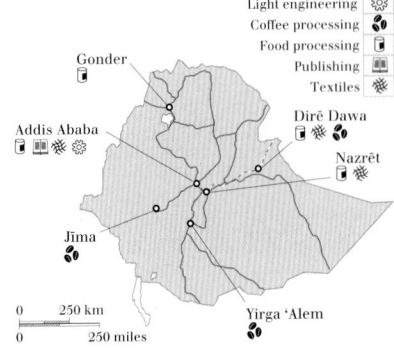

Light engineering
Coffee processing
Food processing
Publishing
Textiles

Gonder
Addis Ababa
Dirē Dawa
Nazrēt
Jīma
Yirga 'Alem

0   250 km
0   250 miles

E

RESOURCES

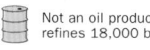

1.3bn kwh (capacity 400,000 kw)

Not an oil producer; refines 18,000 b/cd

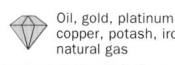

29m cattle, 22m sheep, 17m goats, 5m asses

Oil, gold, platinum, copper, potash, iron, natural gas

ELECTRICITY GENERATION

Hydro 88% (1.1bn khw)

Thermal 7% (90m khw)

Nuclear 0%

Other 5% (68m khw)

% of total generation by type

Manpower and financial constraints have prevented a systematic survey of mineral resources. At present, mining contributes less than 1% of GDP. Ethiopia has great potential for hydroelectric power which, in the long run, could offset a domestic reliance on fuelwood and also slow massive deforestation and soil erosion. Current exploration for oil and gas has revealed reserves in the Ogaden, but exploitation has not begun. When Eritrea seceded in 1993, Ethiopia lost other substantial oil reserves and many oil concessions.

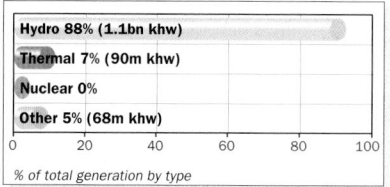

ETHIOPIA : LAND USE

Cropland
Forest
Pasture
Cattle
Coffee - cash crop
Cereals

0   250 km
0   250 miles

ENVIRONMENT

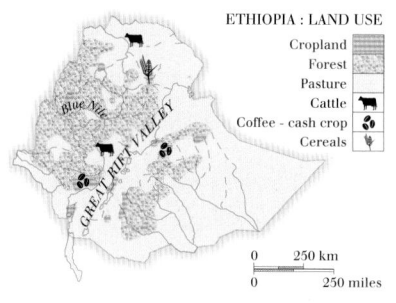

2.5%

Soil erosion due to deforestation is the biggest problem

ENVIRONMENTAL TREATIES

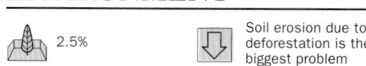

No   Yes   Yes

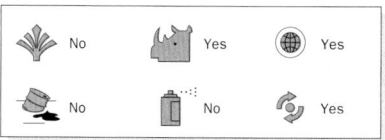

No   No   Yes

Deforestation for fuelwood and the resultant rapid soil erosion, particularly in the highlands, are serious problems. Forest cover has fallen from 40% in 1900 to only 2% today. Shortage of wood means that dung is increasingly being used for fuel. Its fertilizer value is put at $123 million a year, enough to increase annual grain harvests by up to 1.5 million tons. Local projects include terracing hillsides to prevent soil and water runoff – 22,320 miles of terraces were built in Tigray in 1992.

MEDIA

There is now considerable freedom of expression compared with the blanket censorship of the Mengistu years

The government remains uneasy about the post-Mengistu independent press, which has become prolific and critical. Legal action has been taken to silence several publications. A recent proliferation of pornographic magazines has also resulted in closures and government clampdowns.

PUBLISHING AND BROADCAST MEDIA

There are 3 daily newspapers, *Addis Zemen*, *Ethiopian Herald* and *Hibret*, all published by the government

1 state-owned service

1 state-owned, also independent services

Arabsat 1C
Palapa B2-P

None

CRIME

13,585 prisoners

Down 2% in 1988

CRIME RATES

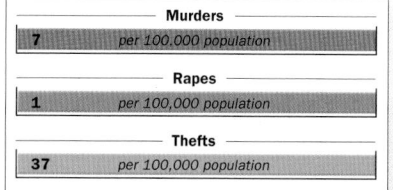

Murders
7   *per 100,000 population*

Rapes
1   *per 100,000 population*

Thefts
37   *per 100,000 population*

A number of human rights abuses by the transitional government have been documented by the independent Ethiopian Human Rights Council. These include detention without trial, "disappearances" and extra-judicial killings. There is some concern over indiscipline among EPRDF forces, who provide a *de facto* police force in many regions. In many rural areas, traditional clan justice has replaced the state system.

EDUCATION

24%

26,218 students

0   *Education spending as % GNP*   25
4.9%

THE EDUCATION SYSTEM

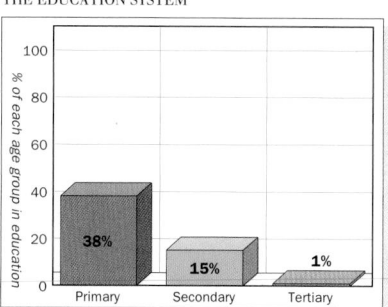

Primary 38%
Secondary 15%
Tertiary 1%

% of each age group in education

The education system was severely disrupted during the civil war. Addis Ababa University has been a center of political activity, usually anti-EPRDF, and is subject to periodic closures and the dismissal of its leading academics.

HEALTH

1 per 32,500 people

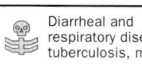

Diarrheal and respiratory diseases, tuberculosis, malaria

0   *Health spending as % GDP*   25
0.7%

Only about half of the population lives within 7 miles of a health unit. Hospital building, distribution of resources to rural areas, outpatient visits and referrals are all very slow. Skin and eye diseases are common. Church hospitals are of a reasonably high standard.

WEALTH

Most Ethiopians lead a subsistence existence

CONSUMER GOODS OWNERSHIP

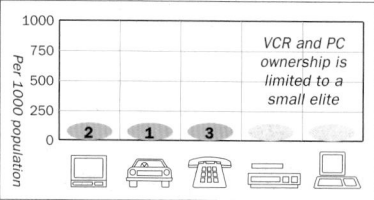

VCR and PC ownership is limited to a small elite

Per 1000 population

2   1   3

There is very little wealth in Ethiopia. The central plateau is historically the richest region. Average incomes fell by 8.5% in 1991, while prices rose by 25%. Corruption among public employees is rising again, owing to pressures on incomes. Ethiopian culture places more value on maintaining traditional social structures than on individual ambition.

WORLD RANKING

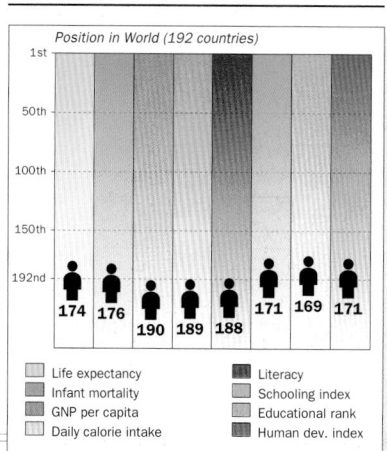

Position in World (192 countries)

1st
50th
100th
150th
192nd

174   176   190   189   188   171   169   171

Life expectancy
Infant mortality
GNP per capita
Daily calorie intake
Literacy
Schooling index
Educational rank
Human dev. index

FIJI

OFFICIAL NAME: Republic of Fiji   **CAPITAL:** Suva
POPULATION: 800,000   **CURRENCY:** Fiji dollar   **OFFICIAL LANGUAGE:** English

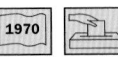

FIJI IS A VOLCANIC ARCHIPELAGO in the southern Pacific Ocean, comprising two large islands and 880 smaller islets. From 1874 to 1970, Fiji was a British colony. The British introduced Indian workers to the islands and by 1946 their descendants, the Indo-Fijians, outnumbered the Native Fijian population. In 1987, Native Fijians overthrew the democratically elected government. After the coups, thousands of Indo-Fijians left the country.

CLIMATE

WEATHER CHART

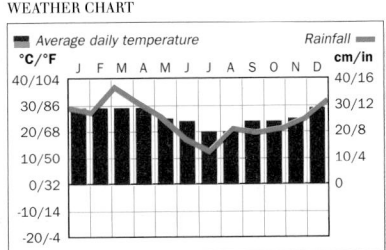

The eastern sides of the main islands are wettest, having more than twice the annual rainfall of the western flanks. Fiji lies in a cyclone path.

TRANSPORTATION

Nadi International
785,000 passengers

25 ships
62,900 dwt

THE TRANSPORTATION NETWORK

1,240 miles (1,990 km)	None
370 miles (595 km)	76 miles (122 km)

On the axis of Australian–US west coast air routes, Fiji is well served by international flights. It is promoting an increase in Pacific shipping routes.

TOURISM

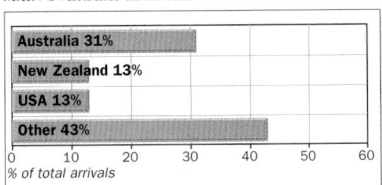

319,000 visitors   Up 11% in 1994

MAIN OVERSEAS ARRIVALS

Australia 31%	
New Zealand 13%	
USA 13%	
Other 43%	

0   10   20   30   40   50   60
% of total arrivals

Tourists – mainly from Australia, New Zealand and west coast USA – are returning, after a 76% drop in numbers following the 1987 coups.

PEOPLE

Fijian, English, Hindi, Urdu, Tamil, Telugu

114 people per sq. mile

THE URBAN/RURAL POPULATION SPLIT

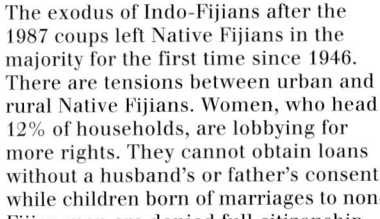

40%   60%

RELIGIOUS PERSUASION

Other 2%   Other Christian 6%
Hindu 38%   Muslim 8%
Roman Catholic 9%
Methodist 37%

The exodus of Indo-Fijians after the 1987 coups left Native Fijians in the majority for the first time since 1946. There are tensions between urban and rural Native Fijians. Women, who head 12% of households, are lobbying for more rights. They cannot obtain loans without a husband's or father's consent, while children born of marriages to non-Fijian men are denied full citizenship.

POLITICS

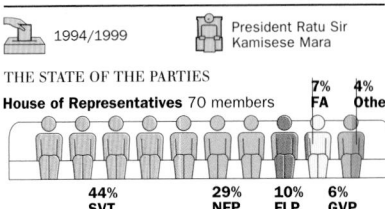

1994/1999

President Ratu Sir Kamisese Mara

THE STATE OF THE PARTIES

House of Representatives 70 members

44% SVT   29% NFP   10% FLP   6% GVP   7% FA   4% Other

SVT = Fijian Political Party   NFP = National Federation Party   FLP = Fiji Labour Party   FA = Fijian Association
GVP = General Voters' Party   Other = All Nationals Congress

Senate 34 members

24 members are chosen by the Great Council of Chiefs, 9 by the president and 1 by the Rotuma Island Council

The 1987 coups were justified as defending the land rights of Native Fijians. In practice, they were a move by Native Fijian chiefs to secure their power, which was being threatened both by the growing Indo-Fijian urban class, and by the increasingly Westernized younger Native Fijians. The 1990 constitution enshrining Native Fijian supremacy, although under reconsideration, is unlikely to be amended radically.

FIJI

Total Land Area : 18 270 sq. km (7054 sq. miles)

POPULATION

over 50 000   ○
over 10 000   ●
under 10 000 ·

LAND HEIGHT

1000m/3281ft
500m/1640ft
Sea Level

WORLD AFFAIRS

ACP   CP   IBRD   SPC   SPF

Fiji is still working to repair its international reputation following the coups of 1987, the subsequent discriminatory constitution and its expulsion from the Commonwealth.

AID

 $59m (receipts)   Down 6% in 1993

Fiji is one of the world's highest per capita aid recipients. Australia, Japan and the EU are the main donors.

DEFENSE

 $30m   Up 7% in 1995

Of the 3,900-strong, almost entirely Native-Fijian military, 1,200 are assigned to UN duties and have served in Lebanon and Egypt.

ECONOMICS

 $1.8bn    1.41–1.43 Fiji dollars

SCORE CARD

❏ WORLD GNP RANKING	137th
❏ GNP PER CAPITA	$2,320
❏ BALANCE OF PAYMENTS	$13m
❏ INFLATION	2.7%
❏ UNEMPLOYMENT	6%

STRENGTHS

Relatively well-diversified economy, with a growing tourist industry. Location on Pacific air routes an impetus to tourism; the many regional and international organizations located in Suva also bring benefits.

WEAKNESSES

Migration of many Indo-Fijian professionals and entrepreneurs following the coups. Major exports – sugar, copra and gold – subject to large fluctuations in world prices.

EXPORTS

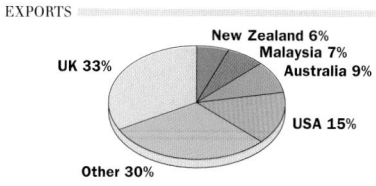

New Zealand 6%
Malaysia 7%
Australia 9%
USA 15%
UK 33%
Other 30%

IMPORTS

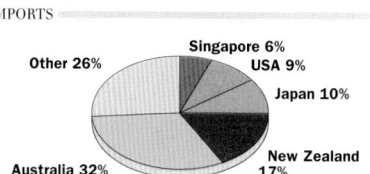

Singapore 6%
USA 9%
Japan 10%
New Zealand 17%
Australia 32%
Other 26%

Cane field on the west side of Viti Levu, between Nadi and Lautoka. Sugar accounts for about one-third of Fiji's exports.

RESOURCES

 477m kwh (capacity 200,000 kw)

 31,399 tons

334,000 cattle, 205,000 goats, 115,000 pigs

 Gold, silver

The varied terrain allows diversified agriculture. There are minerals and hydroelectric potential, which is partly developed in the Monasavu project.

ENVIRONMENT

 0.3%   Overuse of fertilizers

The government is environmentally aware; Fiji is downwind of France's Pacific nuclear test sites. Tourism is damaging the coral reefs.

MEDIA

 Under newly introduced restrictions, no aspersions may be cast on the Fijian leadership

PUBLISHING AND BROADCAST MEDIA

 There are 2 English-language dailies, the *Fiji Times* and the *Daily Post. Nai Lalakai* and *Shanti Dut* are the Fijian and Indian weeklies

 1 state-owned service   5 state-controlled, 2 independent stations

Newspapers and videotapes are the major source of information on the islands. Radios keep the many Fijians who are away from home in touch with news from their villages.

CRIME

 878 prisoners   Up 9% in 1992

Theft and drink-related violence top the crime list. Fiji also has one of the world's highest *crime passionel* rates.

EDUCATION

 87%    7,908 students

Education, originally modeled on the British system, is now mostly run by local committees and is increasingly racially segregated. Attendance, though high, is not compulsory.

F

CHRONOLOGY

The British decision to import Indian sugar workers between 1879 and 1916, many of whom settled, dramatically changed Fijian society.

- ❏ **1970** Independence from Britain.
- ❏ **1987** Indo-Fijian majority coalition wins power for first time. Two coups secure Native Fijian supremacy. Fiji ejected from Commonwealth.
- ❏ **1989** Mass Indo-Fijian emigration.
- ❏ **1990** Constitution discriminating against Indo-Fijians introduced.
- ❏ **1992** General election. Rabuka's SVT secures power as dominant partner in a coalition.
- ❏ **1994** General election; governing coalition returned to power.

HEALTH

 1 per 2,074 people   Cerebrovascular and heart diseases, cancers, accidents

People living in rural areas and on the outlying islands are served by 95 nursing stations. Fiji is free of almost all tropical diseases, including malaria.

WEALTH

 Agricultural worker, 12 Fiji dollars (US$17) per day; construction worker, 14 Fiji dollars (US$10) per day

CONSUMER GOODS OWNERSHIP

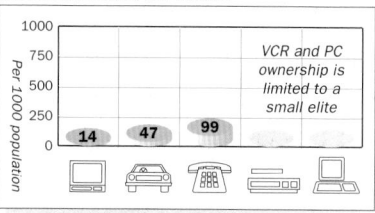

VCR and PC ownership is limited to a small elite

14   47   99

Per 1000 population

Ostentatious displays of wealth are rare; prestige derives from family and landholdings. The professional middle class, while still dominated by Indo-Fijians, is becoming more mixed.

WORLD RANKING

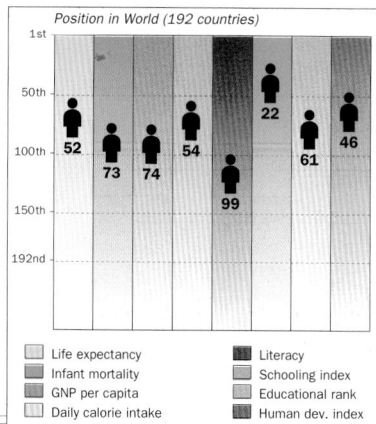

Position in World (192 countries)

52   73   74   54   99   22   61   46

- ☐ Life expectancy
- ☐ Infant mortality
- ☐ GNP per capita
- ☐ Daily calorie intake
- ☐ Literacy
- ☐ Schooling index
- ☐ Educational rank
- ☐ Human dev. index

FINLAND

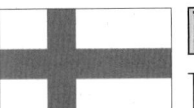

OFFICIAL NAME: Republic of Finland   **CAPITAL:** Helsinki
POPULATION: 5.1 million   **CURRENCY:** Markka   **OFFICIAL LANGUAGES:** Finnish and Swedish

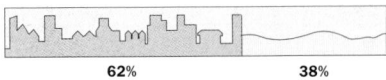

B ORDERED TO THE north and west by Norway and Sweden, and to the east by Russia, Finland is a low-lying country of forests and over 60,000 lakes. Politics is based on consensus and the country has been stable despite successive short-lived coalitions. Russia annexed Finland in 1809, ruling it until 1917, and subsequently Finland accepted a close relationship with the Soviet Union as the price of maintaining its independence. It joined the EU in 1995. Living standards are high, but the country is recovering from a recession which, in 1990, ended a decade of record growth.

CLIMATE

WEATHER CHART

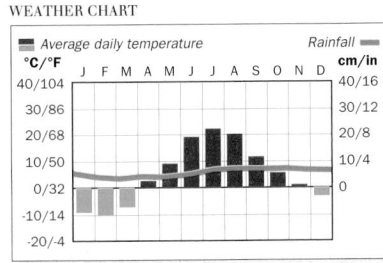

North of the Arctic Circle the climate is extreme. Temperatures fall to –22°F in the six-month winter and rise to 80°F during the 73 days of summer midnight sun. In the south, summers are mild and short, winters are cold. The annual average temperature in Helsinki is 41°F.

TRANSPORTATION

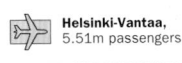 **Helsinki-Vantaa,** 5.51m passengers
 121 ships 1.02m dwt

THE TRANSPORTATION NETWORK

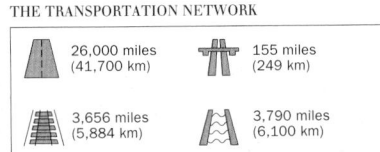

26,000 miles (41,700 km)	155 miles (249 km)
3,656 miles (5,884 km)	3,790 miles (6,100 km)

Finland has a well-integrated transportation system. The railroad connects with the Swedish and Russian networks. There are also frequent air services to most neighboring states. At present, links with the Baltic countries are being improved. Internal air travel is also important, particularly north of the Arctic Circle.

With over 60,000 lakes and rivers, Finland has Europe's largest inland waterway system. Although it still carries freight, its use today is mainly recreational. Finland's international ports handle around 60 million tons a year. Kotka is the chief port for exports. Helsinki, with its five specialized harbors, handles most imports.

TOURISM

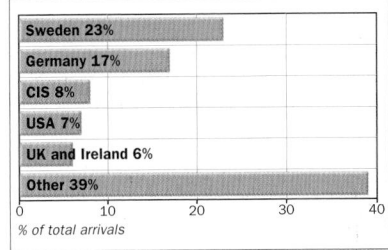

833,000 visitors   Up 4% in 1994

MAIN OVERSEAS ARRIVALS

- Sweden 23%
- Germany 17%
- CIS 8%
- USA 7%
- UK and Ireland 6%
- Other 39%

% of total arrivals

The scenery of the southern lakes and the vast forests of its Arctic north are Finland's main attractions. Helsinki is an important cultural center and hosts an annual arts festival. Its opera house has an international reputation and the capital has many first-class restaurants. Most tourists try a sauna, a Finnish invention, and the local vodka, which is reputedly among the world's finest.

Visitors come mostly from other Nordic countries and Germany. Since 1990, there has been an increase in visitors from the Baltic States and the Russian Federation. The depreciation of the markka since 1992 has helped to boost visitor numbers.

A summer's night at Kilpisjärvi, – "The Way of the Four Winds," which lies at the point where Finland, Sweden and Norway meet.

PEOPLE

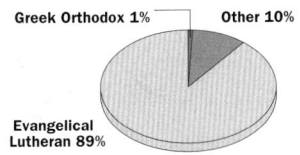 Finnish, Swedish, Lappish
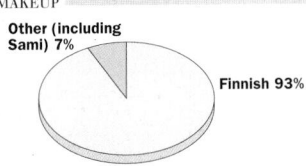 44 people per sq. mile

THE URBAN/RURAL POPULATION SPLIT

62%   38%

RELIGIOUS PERSUASION

- Greek Orthodox 1%
- Other 10%
- Evangelical Lutheran 89%

ETHNIC MAKEUP

- Other (including Sami) 7%
- Finnish 93%

Most Finns are of Scandinavian-Baltic extraction. Finnish belongs to the small Finno-Ugric linguistic group and is a legacy of the country's earliest invaders from Asia. Although they were later ousted by the ancestors of today's Finns, their language was retained. Lappish, also a Finno-Ugric language, is spoken by the small Sami (Lapp) population, who live above the Arctic Circle. Around 6% of the population live in the Åland Islands in the southwest and speak Swedish.

More than 50% of Finns live in the five southernmost districts around Helsinki. Families tend to be close-knit, although divorce rates are high. The sauna is an integral part of everyday life; there are 1.5 million saunas among five million Finns.

Finnish women have a long tradition of political and economic participation. They were the first in Europe to achieve suffrage in 1906, and the first in the world who were allowed to stand for seats in parliament. Almost 50% of women now have work outside the home and one-third of the Cabinet is female.

POPULATION AGE BREAKDOWN

%	0–14	15–64	65+		
	7.2%	9.2%	12%	13.2%	14.4%
	62.4%	66.2%	67.7%	67.5%	68.1%
	30.4%	24.6%	20.3%	19.3%	17.5%
	1960	1970	1980	1990	2000

POLITICS

 1995/1999

 President Martti Ahtisaari

THE STATE OF THE PARTIES

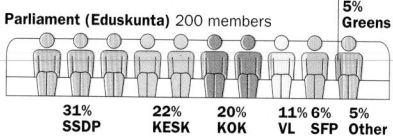

Parliament (Eduskunta) 200 members

| 31% SSDP | 22% KESK | 20% KOK | 11% VL | 6% SFP | 5% Other | 5% Greens |

SDP = Finnish Social Democratic Party   KESK = Center Party
KOK = National Coalition Party   VL = Left Wing Alliance
SFP = Swedish People's Party

President Martti Ahtisaari, who won the 1994 presidential election.

Prime Minister, Paavo Lipponen, leader of the SDP-led coalition.

Finland's constitution combines parliamentary government with a strong presidency. The external territory of the Åland Islands has internal self-government.

MAIN POLITICAL ISSUES
EU membership
In a national referendum held in October 1994, Finland voted to join the EU. Membership was a less contentious issue than in other Nordic countries and many Finns supported entry as a way of identifying with western Europe. However, the small but influential farming community was hostile to membership because it poses a threat to farm subsidies. Further opposition stemmed from fears that public spending cuts, in particular welfare cuts, would be required to meet the economic criteria for membership.

Unemployment
The victory of SDP candidate Martti Ahtisaari in the 1994 presidential election was a sign of discontent with the conservative KESK–KOK coalition led by Esko Aho. Its handling of the recession resulted in record unemployment levels and welfare cuts. The 1995 general election resulted in the return of an SDP-led coalition which has continued many of the previous government's austerity policies.

PROFILE
Proportional representation has led to government by coalition, usually dominated by the SDP or KESK. The emphasis on consensus, which has favored stability but resulted in slow decision-making, was undermined by the policies pursued by the Aho administration.

WORLD AFFAIRS

 CE   EU   OECD   OSCE   WEU

After carefully balancing its relations with the Soviet Union and the West during the Cold War, Finland has now decided that its national interest lies within western Europe. In addition to joining the EU, it also has observer status at the WEU. However, acknowledging historical and geographical realities, the government is also keen to maintain a special relationship with Russia.

AID

 $355m (donations)   Up 8% in 1993

Finland is one of the few donor countries to have achieved the UN target of allocating 0.7% of GDP to aid. The main recipients are countries in Southeast Asia and Africa.

CHRONOLOGY

Finland's history has been closely linked with the competing interests of Sweden and Russia.

❏ **1323** Treaty of Pähkinäsaari. Finland part of Swedish Kingdom.
❏ **1809** Treaty of Fredrikhamn, Sweden cedes Finland to Russia. Finland becomes a Grand Duchy enjoying considerable autonomy.
❏ **1812** Helsinki becomes capital.
❏ **1863** Finnish becomes an official language alongside Swedish.
❏ **1865** Grand Duchy acquires its own monetary system.
❏ **1879** Conscription law lays the foundation for a Finnish army.
❏ **1899** Tsar Nicholas II begins process of Russification. Labor Party founded.
❏ **1900** Gradual imposition of Russian as the official language begins.
❏ **1901** Finnish army disbanded, Finns ordered into Russian units. Disobedience campaign prevents men being drafted into the army.

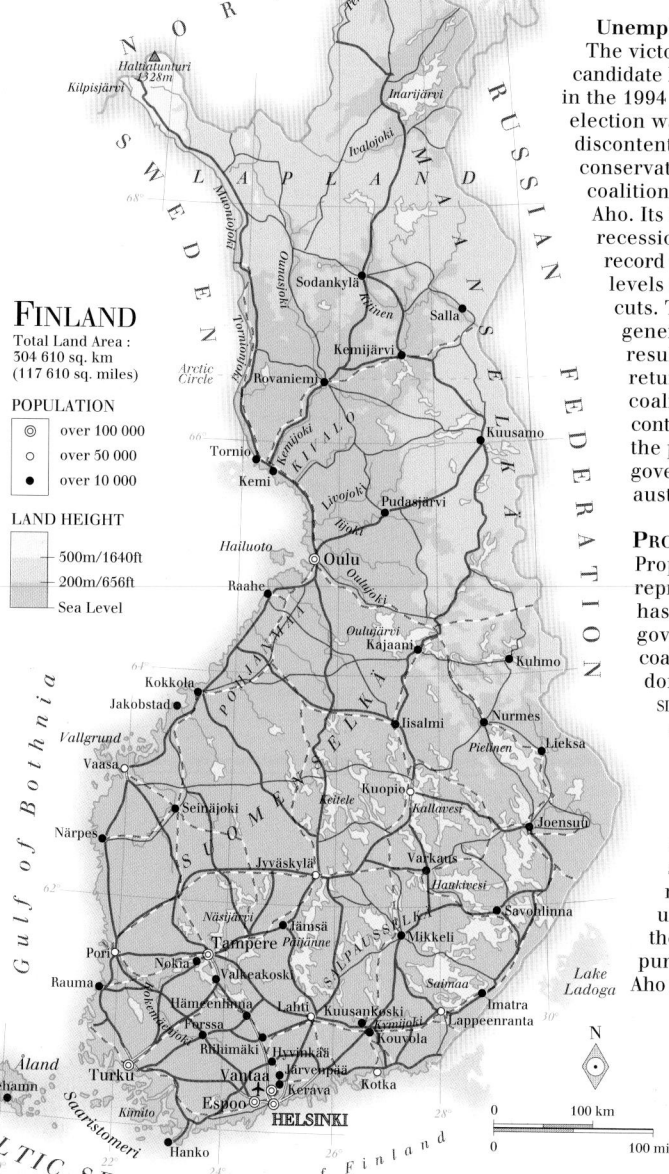

FINLAND

Total Land Area :
304 610 sq. km
(117 610 sq. miles)

POPULATION

◎ over 100 000
○ over 50 000
• over 10 000

LAND HEIGHT

500m/1640ft
200m/656ft
Sea Level

CHRONOLOGY *continued*

- ❑ **1903** Labor Party becomes the Social Democratic Party (SDP).
- ❑ **1905** National strike forces restoration of 1899 *status quo*.
- ❑ **1906** Parliamentary reform. Universal suffrage introduced.
- ❑ **1907** SDP main party in parliament.
- ❑ **1910** Responsibility for important legislation passed to Russian Duma.
- ❑ **1917** Russian revolution allows Finland to declare independence.
- ❑ **1918** Civil war between Bolsheviks and right-wing government. Gen. Mannerheim leads the government to victory at the Battle of Tampere.
- ❑ **1919** Finland becomes a republic. Kaarlo Ståhlberg elected president with wide political powers.
- ❑ **1920** Treaty of Tartu: Soviet Union recognizes Finland's borders.
- ❑ **1921** London Convention. Åland Islands become part of Finland.
- ❑ **1939** August, Hitler-Stalin non-aggression pact gives the USSR a free hand in Finland. November, Soviet invasion. Strong Finnish resistance in ensuing Winter War.
- ❑ **1940** Invaded by USSR. Treaty of Moscow. Finland cedes one-tenth of national territory.
- ❑ **1941** Finnish troops join Germany in its invasion of the USSR.
- ❑ **1944** June, Red Army invades. August, President Ryti resigns. September, Finland, led by Marshal Mannerheim, signs armistice.
- ❑ **1946** President Mannerheim resigns, Juho Paasikivi president.
- ❑ **1948** Signs friendship treaty with the USSR. Agrees to resist any attack on the USSR made through Finland by Germany or its allies.
- ❑ **1952** Payment of $570 million in war reparations completed.
- ❑ **1956** Uhro Kekkonen, leader of the Agrarian Party, becomes president.
- ❑ **1956–1991** A series of coalition governments involving the SDP and the Agrarians, renamed the Center Party (KESK) in 1965, hold power.
- ❑ **1981** President Kekkonen resigns.
- ❑ **1982** Dr. Mauno Koivisto president.
- ❑ **1989** USSR recognizes Finnish neutrality for the first time.
- ❑ **1991** Non-socialist government elected. Budget cut as part of austerity measures.
- ❑ **1992** January, signs ten-year agreement with Russia which, for the first time since World War II involves no military agreement.
- ❑ **1994** SDP candidate, Martti Ahtisaari, elected president in show of electoral dissatisfaction with the conservative government.
- ❑ **1995** Becomes member of EU. General election; return to power of SDP at head of five-party coalition.

DEFENSE

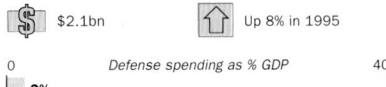

💲 $2.1bn   ⬆ Up 8% in 1995

0   *Defense spending as % GDP*   40
2%

The Finnish military is small, with 32,800 troops, but there are also 700,000 active reservists and a large border guard force. The Russian Federation's instability has reinforced concern about border security, the top defense issue. Finland has observer status in the WEU.

FINNISH ARMED FORCES

🪖	232 main battle tanks (70 T–55, 162 T–72)	25,700 personnel
🚤	21 patrol boats	2,500 personnel
✈	116 combat aircraft (MiG 21bis/Hawk Mk51/J–35)	2,900 personnel
🔪	None	

ECONOMICS

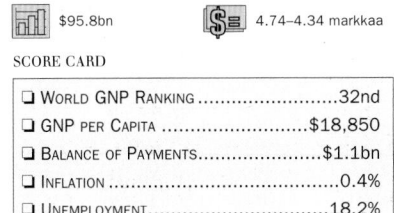

📊 $95.8bn   💲 4.74–4.34 markkaa

SCORE CARD

- ❑ WORLD GNP RANKING 32nd
- ❑ GNP PER CAPITA $18,850
- ❑ BALANCE OF PAYMENTS.....................$1.1bn
- ❑ INFLATION 0.4%
- ❑ UNEMPLOYMENT...............................18.2%

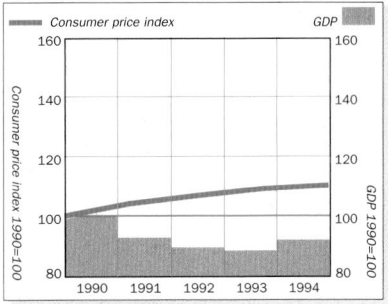

ECONOMIC PERFORMANCE INDICATOR

Consumer price index — GDP

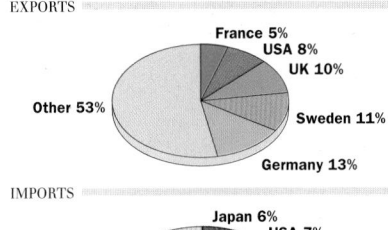

EXPORTS

France 5%
USA 8%
UK 10%
Other 53%
Sweden 11%
Germany 13%

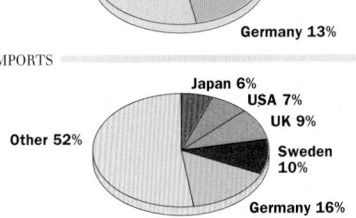

IMPORTS

Japan 6%
USA 7%
UK 9%
Other 52%
Sweden 10%
Germany 16%

STRENGTHS

Industry is export- and quality-orientated. Large high-tech sector. World leader in pulp and paper. Exports quick to recover from recession. Low inflation, now less than 2% a year. Improved foreign investment incentives. Gateway to Russian and Baltic economies.

WEAKNESSES

Severe recession following fast growth during 1980s; real GDP declined 15% during 1991–1993. High level of public sector and foreign debt, the latter 22% of GDP. Highest unemployment rate in Western Europe, 20% in 1993 and declining only slowly since then. Small domestic market and peripheral position in Europe.

PROFILE

Finland is a market economy and still a wealthy one, although just emerging from its worst recession in 60 years. The boom years of the 1980s, when GDP expanded by almost 4% a year, came

to an abrupt end in 1990. The collapse of the former Soviet Union, which had taken 28% of Finland's exports, was largely responsible for the downturn. A rapid rise in unemployment and business failures pushed up government spending. The floating of the markka in 1992 and austerity measures, including welfare benefit cuts, higher taxes and wage restraints, improved Finland's competitiveness. Exports have largely recovered. However, full recovery will take longer and unemployment is likely to stay above 15% for some years. With private investment remaining low, the economy will take time to recover.

FINLAND : MAJOR BUSINESSES

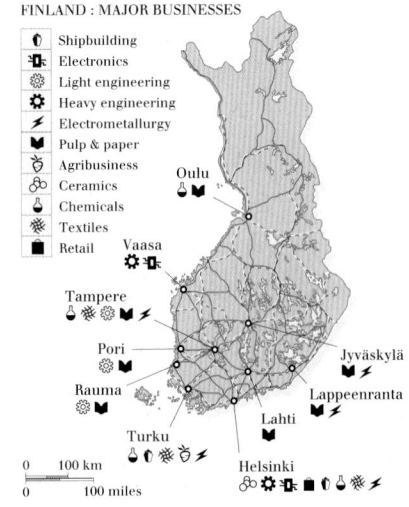

- ⛴ Shipbuilding
- ⚡ Electronics
- ⚙ Light engineering
- ✿ Heavy engineering
- ⚡ Electrometallurgy
- ♥ Pulp & paper
- 🐄 Agribusiness
- ⚗ Ceramics
- 🔬 Chemicals
- ✽ Textiles
- ■ Retail

Oulu
Vaasa
Tampere
Pori
Jyväskylä
Rauma
Lappeenranta
Turku
Lahti
Helsinki

0   100 km
0   100 miles

RESOURCES

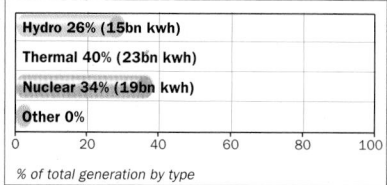

57.4bn kwh (capacity 13.2m kw)

Not an oil producer; refines 200,000 b/cd

1.3m pigs, 1.2m cattle, 79,000 sheep

Gold, copper, zinc, iron, lead, silver

ELECTRICITY GENERATION

| Hydro 26% (15bn kwh) |
| Thermal 40% (23bn kwh) |
| Nuclear 34% (19bn kwh) |
| Other 0% |

0   20   40   60   80   100

% of total generation by type

Finland's trees are its prime natural resource. Commercial forests cover 65% of the land and wood products account for 40% of exports. Finland has no oil, but has significant hydroelectric resources. Industry's high energy demands are met chiefly by thermal and nuclear power. A fifth nuclear power station is planned. Oil import costs have risen since 1990, when the collapse of the USSR ended a 42-year agreement on the exchange of Finnish manufactures for Soviet oil.

FINLAND : LAND USE

Cropland
Forest
Pasture
Reindeer
Barley

0   100 km
0   100 miles

ENVIRONMENT

8%

Very high degree of ecological consciousness

ENVIRONMENTAL TREATIES

| Yes | Yes | Yes |
| Yes | Yes | Yes |

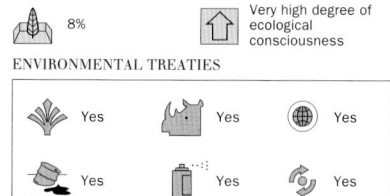

Finland has strict laws on industrial emissions. Energy efficiency is a priority; over 40% of homes are connected to district heating systems. Growing public concern about nuclear safety has led to opposition to the planned fifth nuclear plant and to proposals for the greater use of waste materials in energy generation. The government is funding nuclear safety programs in Russia. Rising levels of pollution in the Baltic are of concern.

MEDIA

There is no censorship of the media

PUBLISHING AND BROADCAST MEDIA

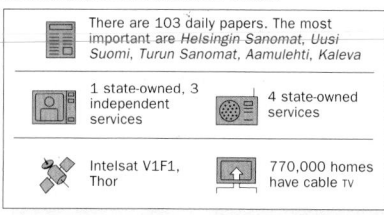

There are 103 daily papers. The most important are *Helsingin Sanomat, Uusi Suomi, Turun Sanomat, Aamulehti, Kaleva*

1 state-owned, 3 independent services

4 state-owned services

Intelsat V1F1, Thor

770,000 homes have cable TV

Nine out of ten Finns take a daily paper, the world's third-highest circulation to population ratio. Regional papers dominate; the only national is *Helsingin Sanomat*. There is no censorship, but the press shows restraint in criticizing the government.

CRIME

3,106 prisoners

Up 2% in 1992

CRIME RATES

| **Murders** |
| 1 *per 100,000 population* |

| **Rapes** |
| 7 *per 100,000 population* |

| **Thefts** |
| 2972 *per 100,000 population* |

The jump in unemployment, from 3.5% in 1990 to 20% in 1993, is one cause of rising crime. There is concern about links with organized crime in Russia.

EDUCATION

99%

188,162 students

0   *Education spending as % GNP*   25
7.4%

THE EDUCATION SYSTEM

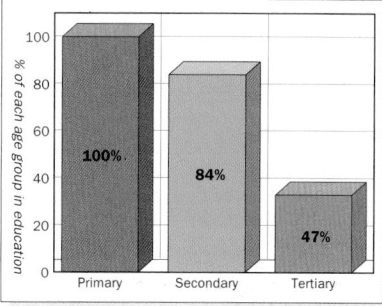

% of each age group in education

Primary 100% Secondary 84% Tertiary 47%

Compulsory education lasts from 7 to 16 years of age. Almost all children receive preschool education and go on to three years of upper secondary education. Tough examinations mean that only 35% of entrants qualify to attend one of the 20 universities.

HEALTH

1 per 385 people

Cerebrovascular and heart diseases, cancers, suicides

0   *Health spending as % GDP*   25
8.9%

Spending on Finland's well-developed health care system accounts for about 10% of the state budget. Every Finn is legally guaranteed access to a local health center staffed by up to four doctors, as well as nurses and a midwife. National health insurance covers most non-hospital medical costs, and hospital fees are moderate.

WEALTH

Paper machine operator, 58 markkaa ($13) per hour; general physician, 16,900 markkaa ($3,892) per month

CONSUMER GOODS OWNERSHIP

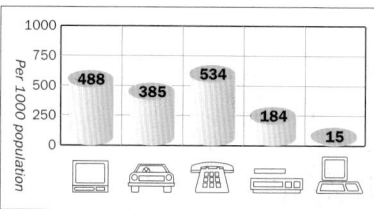

Per 1000 population

488   385   534   184   15

Income disparities are more marked in Finland than in the rest of Scandinavia. However, the economic boom and labor shortages of the 1980s led to a sharp rise in all living standards. Personal consumption reached Swedish levels and many families were able to take two holidays a year. Social security benefits were extended.

Since the recession began in 1990, this improvement has been reversed. Wealth disparities have also widened. Cuts in budgetary expenditure have resulted in a decline in social security benefits paid to the unemployed. Those in work have had to accept lower pay rises and higher taxes. Average real disposable income has dropped by more than 7% since 1991. Estonian immigrants form the poorest group.

WORLD RANKING

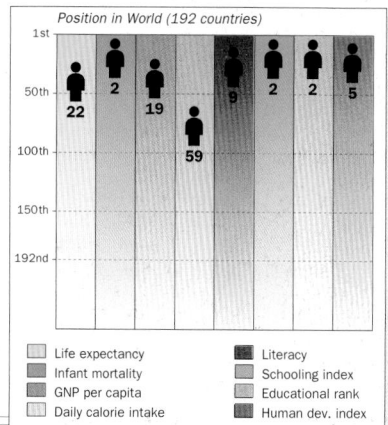

Position in World (192 countries)

22   2   19   59   9   2   2   5

Life expectancy
Infant mortality
GNP per capita
Daily calorie intake
Literacy
Schooling index
Educational rank
Human dev. index

F

FRANCE

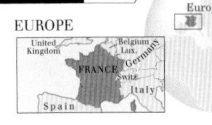

OFFICIAL NAME: The French Republic CAPITAL: Paris POPULATION: 58 million
CURRENCY: Franc OFFICIAL LANGUAGE: French OVERSEAS TERRITORIES: 10

S TRADDLING WESTERN EUROPE from the English Channel to the Mediterranean, France was Europe's first modern republic and possessed a colonial empire second only to Britain's. Today, it is one of the world's major industrial powers and its fourth-largest exporter. Industry is the leading economic sector, but the agricultural lobby remains powerful – French farmers are willing to mount the barricades in defense of their interests. Today, France's focus is very much toward Europe. Together with Germany it was a founder member of the European Economic Community, and following a referendum in 1992, France endorsed the Maastricht Treaty on European Union. Paris, the French capital, is generally considered one of the world's most beautiful cities. It has been home to some of the 20th century's most influential artists, writers and filmmakers.

Le Plessis-Bourré, Loire Valley. The region is famous for its many chateaux, which attract thousands of visitors every year

CLIMATE

WEATHER CHART

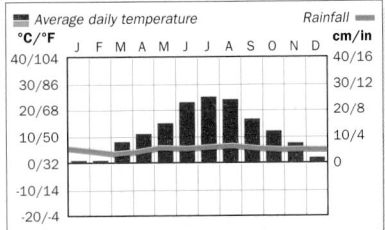

France has, in broad terms, three climates – Atlantic, Continental and Mediterranean. The northwest, in particular Brittany, is mild but damp. The east has hot summers and stormy winters. Summers in the south are dry and hot, and forest fires are common.

TRANSPORTATION

Charles de Gaulle, Paris
22.5m passengers

210 ships
5.56m dwt

THE TRANSPORTATION NETWORK

516,400 miles (831,000 km)	4,151 miles (6,680 km)
21,388 miles (34,421 km)	5,282 miles (8,500 km)

Once pioneers of aviation and cobuilders of Concorde, the French also led the world in high-speed train technology, with the TGV (*Train à Grande Vitesse*). The first TGV line, opened in 1983, does the 285-mile Paris to Lyon journey in two hours – faster, door-to-door, than air travel. TGV lines have since been built to the north and west as well as to the Channel Tunnel, which opened in 1994. It was the French, rather more than the British, who pressed for the tunnel to be built.

TOURISM

60.6m visitors

Up 1% in 1994

MAIN OVERSEAS ARRIVALS

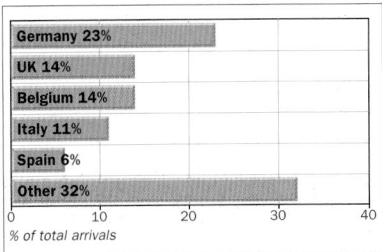

France is the world's leading tourist destination. It tops the list for the Germans and the British, and is the most popular European destination for the Japanese. Most French people prefer to spend their vacations in their own country, rather than traveling abroad.

Paris is Europe's most visited city. Its attractions include the Eiffel Tower, the Pompidou Center, Nôtre Dame cathedral and the Louvre, the world's largest and most popular museum.

Modern tourism was all but invented on the Côte d'Azur, when crowned heads and grandees flocked to fashionable resorts like Nice at the end of the 19th century. Today, Cannes hosts the world's leading film festival, and has a growing business convention trade, but most tourism is more populist, including camping vacations and package tours.

In 1992, EuroDisney opened east of Paris. Initially it was much less popular than the traditional French cultural attractions – in its first year it lost a great deal of money. However, after it was relaunched as Disneyland Paris in late 1994, it went into profit, attracting over 10 million visitors the following year.

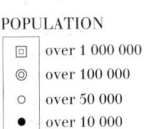

FRANCE

Total Land Area :
550 100 sq. km
(212 594 sq. miles)

POPULATION

▣	over 1 000 000
◎	over 100 000
○	over 50 000
●	over 10 000

LAND HEIGHT

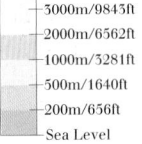

3000m/9843ft
2000m/6562ft
1000m/3281ft
500m/1640ft
200m/656ft
Sea Level

N

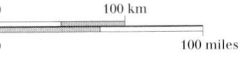

0   100 km
0   100 miles

PEOPLE

French, Provençal, German, Breton, Catalan, Basque

272 people per sq. mile

The French, despite their strong national identity, are a great mix of peoples. Bretons, Normans, Flemmings, Alsatians, Savoyards, Provençaux, Basques and Corsicans still maintain their traditions, although today local languages are little spoken. France has nearly 5 million foreign-born residents, a quarter of whom are now naturalized citizens, and the largest Jewish community in Europe outside Russia, numbering over 700,000.

From 1945 until the mid-1980s, France suffered relatively little from racism. Many Muslim

THE URBAN/RURAL POPULATION SPLIT

73%   27%

POPULATION AGE BREAKDOWN

% of population by age group	0–14	15–64	65+		
0–14	11.6%	12.9%	14%	13.8%	15.4%
15–64	62%	62.3%	63.7%	66.1%	65.2%
65+	26.4%	24.8%	22.3%	20.1%	19.4%
	1960	1970	1980	1990	2000

RELIGIOUS PERSUASION

Muslim 1% Protestant 2%
Jewish 1% Other 6%
Roman Catholic 90%

ETHNIC MAKEUP

German 2% Other 2%
Breton 1% North African 3%
French 92%

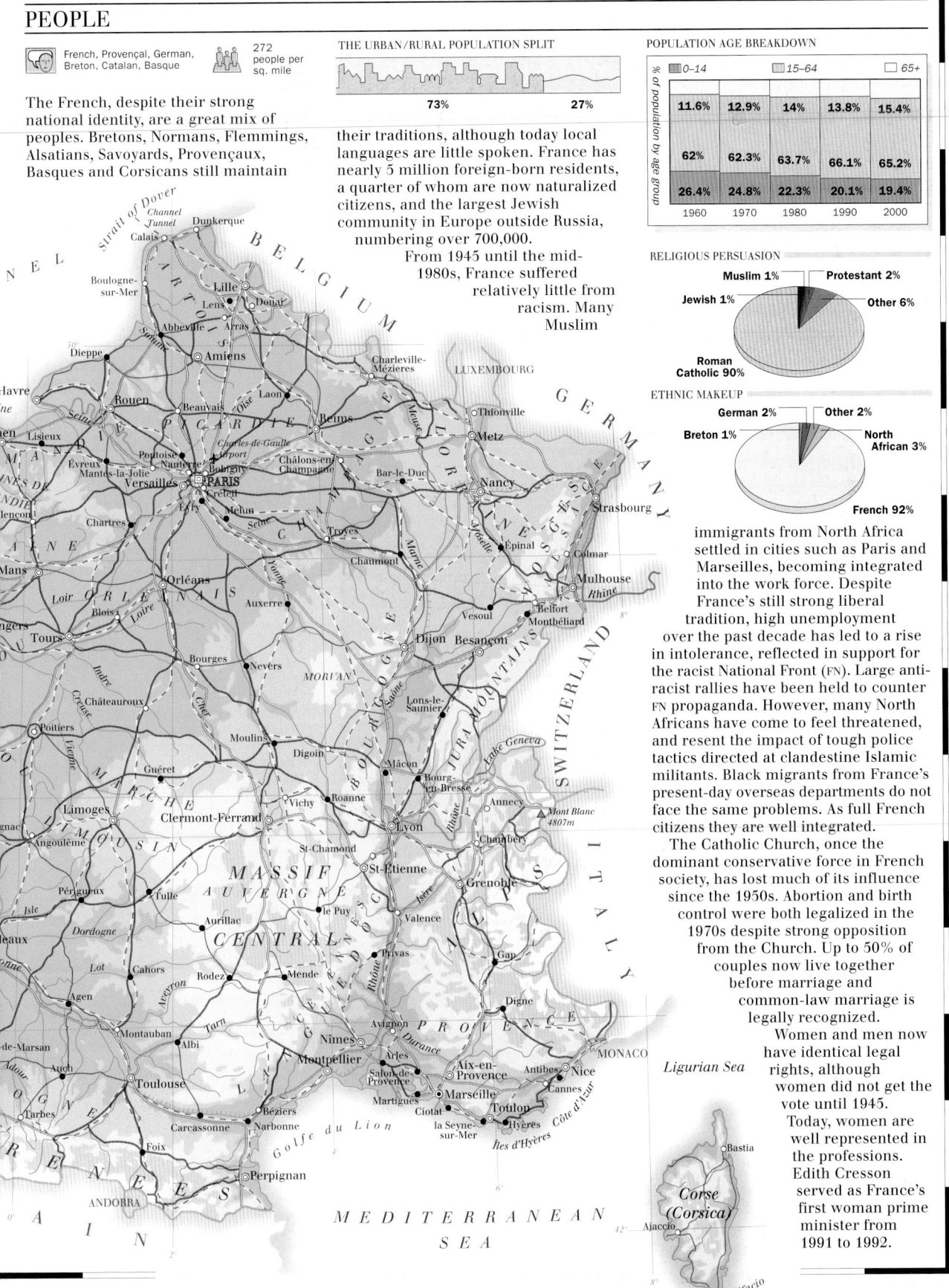

immigrants from North Africa settled in cities such as Paris and Marseilles, becoming integrated into the work force. Despite France's still strong liberal tradition, high unemployment over the past decade has led to a rise in intolerance, reflected in support for the racist National Front (FN). Large anti-racist rallies have been held to counter FN propaganda. However, many North Africans have come to feel threatened, and resent the impact of tough police tactics directed at clandestine Islamic militants. Black migrants from France's present-day overseas departments do not face the same problems. As full French citizens they are well integrated.

The Catholic Church, once the dominant conservative force in French society, has lost much of its influence since the 1950s. Abortion and birth control were both legalized in the 1970s despite strong opposition from the Church. Up to 50% of couples now live together before marriage and common-law marriage is legally recognized.

Women and men now have identical legal rights, although women did not get the vote until 1945.

Today, women are well represented in the professions. Edith Cresson served as France's first woman prime minister from 1991 to 1992.

F

F

CHRONOLOGY

The French Revolution of 1789 overthrew a monarchy that had lasted for more than 1,300 years. It ushered in a period of alternating republicanism, Napoleonic imperialism and monarchism, ending in 1870 when the founding of the Third Republic firmly established France in the republican tradition.

❏ **1914–1918** 1.4 million French killed in World War I.
❏ **1918–1939** Economic recession and political instability; 44 governments and 20 prime ministers.
❏ **1940** Capitulation to Germany. Marshal Pétain heads puppet Vichy regime. General de Gaulle leads "Free French" abroad.
❏ **1944** Liberation of France.
❏ **1946–1958** Fourth Republic. Political instability; 26 governments. Nationalizations. France takes leading role in EEC formation.
❏ **1958** Fifth Republic. De Gaulle becomes president with strong executive powers.
❏ **1960** Most French colonies gain independence.
❏ **1962** Algerian independence after bitter war with France.
❏ **1966** France withdraws from NATO military command.
❏ **1968** General strike and riots over education policy and low wages. National Assembly dissolved; Gaullist victory in June elections.
❏ **1969** De Gaulle resigns after defeat in referendum on regional reform; replaced by Georges Pompidou.
❏ **1974** Valéry Giscard d'Estaing elected president. Center-right coalition.
❏ **1981** PS victory in elections; François Mitterrand president.
❏ **1983–1986** Left-wing coalition changes course over handling economic recession, governs without PCF support.
❏ **1986** *Cohabitation* between socialist president and right-wing government after elections return right-wing coalition led by Jacques Chirac, who challenges presidential powers. Privatization program introduced.
❏ **1988** Mitterrand wins second term. PS-led coalition returns.
❏ **1991** Edith Cresson becomes first woman prime minister.
❏ **1993** Center-right coalition under Edouard Balladur wins elections.
❏ **1995** Jacques Chirac wins presidential election, confirming ascendancy of center-right.
❏ **1995–1996** Controversial series of Pacific nuclear tests, ending with Chirac's January 1996 promise of disarmament initiatives.

POLITICS

 U. House 1993/1998
L. House 1993/1998

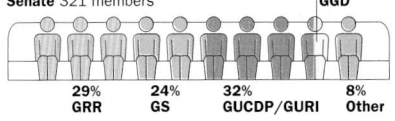

President Jacques Chirac

THE STATE OF THE PARTIES

National Assembly 577 members

43% RPR	37% UDF	9% PS	4% PCF	7% Other

RPR = Rally for the Republic (Gaullists) **UDF** = Union for French Democracy **PS** = Socialist Party **PCF** = French Communist Party **GRR** = Rally for the Republic Group **GS** = Socialist Group **GUCDP** = Central Union of Progressive Democrats Group **GURI** = Union of Republicans and Independents Group **GGD** = Democratic Left Group **Other** = Left Radical Movement, Communist Party

Senate 321 members

29% GRR	24% GS	32% GUCDP/GURI	7% GGD	8% Other

France is a multiparty democracy where the president rules in tandem with a prime minister and government chosen by the *Assemblée Nationale*. Both are elected separately and serve seven and five-year terms respectively. Occasionally this results in periods of *cohabitation*, where the president and *Assemblée* are of opposite political persuasions. Presidents tend to look after foreign policy and defense issues, while the *Assemblée* focuses on domestic and economic policy.

MAIN POLITICAL ISSUES
The presidential system
The experience since 1986 of two periods of *cohabitation*, between a Socialist President and a right-wing government, has effectively weakened the power of the presidential office. Many now argue that presidential and *Assemblée* terms should run concurrently and for the same duration.

Racism and "exclusion"
Rising unemployment has led to the growth of racist parties. There is also concern about the socially divisive "exclusion" of the unemployed and homeless, and inner city deprivation and violence. The major parties have not provided policies to combat these problems, despite President Chirac's 1995 campaign promises.

Reviving a strong opposition
Political scandals since 1989 have badly dented the image of politicians, especially the Socialist Party (PS), which took a beating at the polls in 1993 and lost the presidency in 1995.

Costs of European integration
Before German reunification in 1990, there was a clear consensus in France favoring European integration. Since then, however, support has cooled, amid fears about the increased power of Germany within Europe. Unpopular austerity measures in 1995, designed to prepare the economy for European monetary union, brought out huge protest demonstrations and strikes.

PROFILE
Between 1959 and 1981, France had right-of-center governments, firstly under the presidency of General de Gaulle, then Georges Pompidou and Valéry Giscard d'Estaing. The election in 1981 of François Mitterrand brought the left, including the French Communist Party (PCF), to the fore. The PS-led government nationalized many of France's most famous businesses, while local government was decentralized. However, the failure of its reflationary economic policy forced the PS to change course in 1983. Becoming a social democratic party, it adopted the monetarist policies then in vogue. All the major French parties have since moved toward the political center. The PS, however, badly tainted by scandal and loss of direction, faces a period in the political wilderness after its crushing electoral defeat in 1993 and the election of the right-of-center Gaullist President Chirac as Mitterrand's successor in 1995.

The fortunes of the far left have continued to decline. In 1945, the PCF had 25% of the vote. Today, it is nearer 9%. Some workers have switched allegiance to the racist FN. The FN's share of the vote has never been higher than the 15% which its leader Jean Marie Le Pen won in the 1995 presidential elections, but the party has had a disproportionate political impact, partly because of Le Pen's ability to attract publicity. One impact of the FN's rise has been that all the main parties now support tougher immigration laws.

François Mitterrand, the former president who died in 1996.

Jacques Chirac, elected president of France in 1995

Alain Juppé, prime minister of France

WORLD AFFAIRS

French foreign policy has followed two, apparently contradictory, strands since World War II – maintenance of a strongly independent line and furtherance of French interests within a united Europe. France's leading role within the EU meant that, until recently, it could combine the two. The reunification of Germany and its subsequent increased influence led many to question the wisdom of the "what is good for Europe is good for France" policy. In the Maastricht referendum in 1992, only 51% voted for the Treaty on European Union.

The keystone of foreign policy remains the containment of German power in Europe through political and monetary union. France supported a broadening of the EU to include Scandinavia, but opposes the early entry of eastern European states that would naturally fall within Germany's sphere of influence.

France also seeks to combat US dominance in both foreign affairs and culture. It left NATO's military command in 1966, maintains an independent nuclear deterrent (which it insisted on testing in the Pacific in 1995–1996, despite a wave of international criticism), and provides a balance to US influence in the Middle East and Africa.

AID

 $7.9bn (donations)   Down 1% in 1993

France is one of the world's major aid donors. Its motives are not simply commercial; it also wishes to maintain the influence of the French language, particularly in West Africa, which has been the main aid recipient. *Médecins sans Frontières* reflects a long French tradition of NGO aid agencies.

DEFENSE

 $40.5bn   Up 13% in 1995

0   *Defense spending as % GDP*   40
3.3%

FRENCH ARMED FORCES

	1,016 main battle tanks (974 AMX-30, 42 *Leclerc*)	241,000 personnel
	2 carriers, 18 submarines, 1 cruiser, 4 destroyers and 35 frigates	64,200 personnel
	682 combat aircraft (*Mirage* F-1B/1C/1CR/*Jaguar*, *Alpha Jet*)	89,200 personnel
	80 SLBM in 5 SSBN, 18 IRBM (SSBS S-3D/TN-61), 15 *Hades* SSM launchers	

France was a founder member of NATO, but left its military command structure in 1966 because of US domination of the alliance. France supports an EU-based defense force, and forms part of the *Eurocorps,* based on French and German troops. However, its defense policy is still effectively defined by NATO, which it has moved closer to in the 1990s.

The influence of the army, once very strong, is now much diminished due to the debacles of 1940 and of the 1962 Algerian war. President Chirac plans to phase out compulsory military service.

France has one of the world's largest and most export-oriented defense industries, producing its own tanks, *Mirage* jets and the new *Rafale* fighter.

ECONOMICS

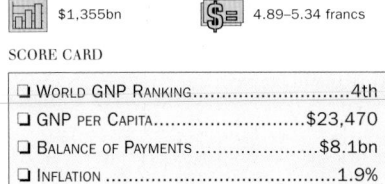 $1,355bn   4.89–5.34 francs

SCORE CARD

- ❏ WORLD GNP RANKING............................4th
- ❏ GNP PER CAPITA..........................$23,470
- ❏ BALANCE OF PAYMENTS $8.1bn
- ❏ INFLATION 1.9%
- ❏ UNEMPLOYMENT................................12.5%

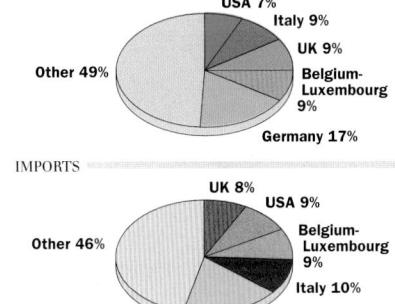

EXPORTS

- USA 7%
- Italy 9%
- UK 9%
- Belgium-Luxembourg 9%
- Germany 17%
- Other 49%

IMPORTS

- UK 8%
- USA 9%
- Belgium-Luxembourg 9%
- Italy 10%
- Germany 18%
- Other 46%

STRENGTHS

Engineering, reflected in the TGV and nuclear industries. Specializations like cars (Renault and Citroën) and telecommunications (Alcatel). Defense sector major exporter, with *Mirage* jets and *Exocet* missiles, but sales falling in mid-1990s. Strong technocratic traditions; unlike USA or UK, top graduates attracted into engineering. Luxury goods; world leader in cosmetics, perfume and wine. Agriculture well modernized. Docile trade unions; only 12% of work force unionized.

WEAKNESSES

High unemployment, currently around 12%. Many sectors of industry still failing to compete due to outmoded working practices, particularly in machine tools, electric consumer durables and some textiles. Some high-

tech industries, like telecommunications, partly run to further national pride, rather than on a strictly commercial basis. Still many small farms despite agricultural modernization.

PROFILE

Compared to other nations in Europe, especially Germany and the UK, France was slow to industrialize. In the 1950s and 1960s, protectionist France started competing in world markets and modernizing its industry, turning the country around to make it one of the world's top exporters. During the 1990s, its foreign trade balance has been in healthy surplus. France has a long tradition of state ownership; the railroads were nationalized in 1938, followed by Air France, Renault, the coal, electricity and gas industries, as well as large insurance companies and banks. Further nationalizations in 1981–1983 were abruptly halted, and the right-of center government of 1986–1988 pursued privatization with vigor. However, even after massive sell-offs, much of the economy still remains under state control. France is the EU's largest agricultural producer and its farmers are a powerful and very vocal political lobby.

ECONOMIC PERFORMANCE INDICATOR

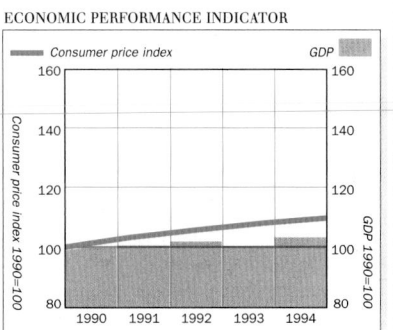

F

FRANCE : MAJOR BUSINESSES

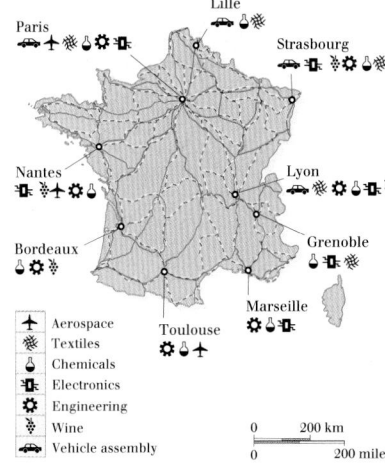

- ✈ Aerospace
- ✳ Textiles
- ⚗ Chemicals
- ▮▮ Electronics
- ⚙ Engineering
- ⚗ Wine
- 🚗 Vehicle assembly

0   200 km
0   200 miles

RESOURCES

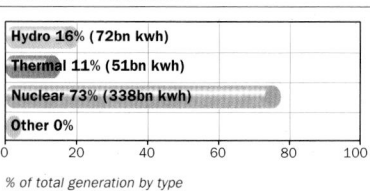

462bn kwh (capacity 103m kw)

57,463 b/d (reserves 177,434,000 bbl)

20.1m cattle, 13.4m pigs, 10.5m sheep, 1m goats

Coal, oil, natural gas, iron, zinc

ELECTRICITY GENERATION

Hydro 16% (72bn kwh)	
Thermal 11% (51bn kwh)	
Nuclear 73% (338bn kwh)	
Other 0%	

% of total generation by type

0 20 40 60 80 100

France is the world's most committed user of nuclear energy, which provides 73% of its electricity requirements. The policy reflects a desire for national energy self-sufficiency. Coal, once plentiful in the north and Lorraine, is now mostly exhausted, as are the gas fields off the southwest coast.

FRANCE : LAND USE

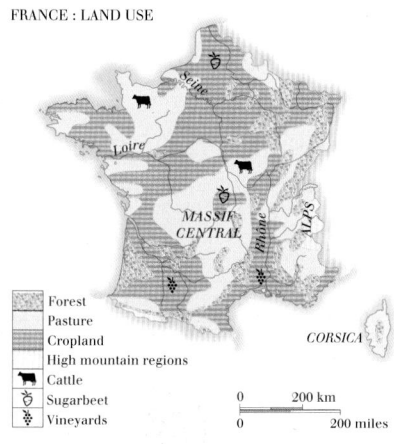

	Forest
	Pasture
	Cropland
	High mountain regions
🐄	Cattle
♀	Sugarbeet
🍇	Vineyards

0 200 km
0 200 miles

ENVIRONMENT

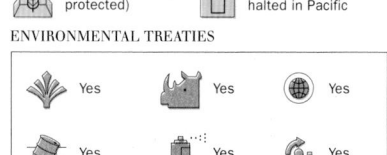

10% (9% partially protected)

Nuclear testing now halted in Pacific

ENVIRONMENTAL TREATIES

🌿	Yes	🦏	Yes	🌐	Yes
	Yes		Yes	♻	Yes

French "green" consciousness, in the past lower than that of Germans or Britons, has been rising. The Seine has been cleaned up, the size of buildings on the south coast is now restricted and, especially in Paris, controlling air pollution has become a major issue. The state policy of backing big projects (*gigantisme*) has been reversed. The exception is nuclear policy. France's latest series of nuclear weapons tests in the Pacific in 1995–1996 aroused strong international opposition.

REGIONS

THE NORD-PAS DE CALAIS REGION

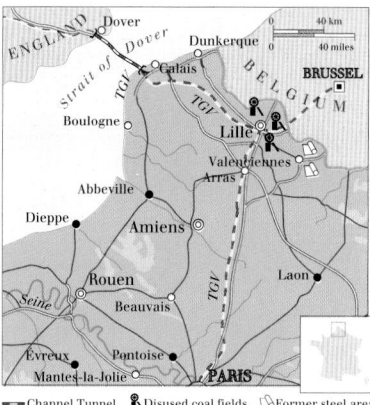

■━━ Channel Tunnel   ⚒ Disused coal fields   🏭 Former steel area

THE NORD-PAS DE CALAIS region has suffered mixed fortunes since the 1970s. Once a French industrial heartland, with Lille its foremost city, the region shed jobs and businesses at an alarming rate during the 1970s as traditional coalfields were worked out and the steel industry proved to be less competitive than its overseas rivals. By 1979, unemployment was 30% above the national average.

The arrival of the Channel Tunnel project dramatically changed the prospects for the region. French railroads (SNCF) built a TGV line to connect Paris to both London and Brussels in less than three hours, providing a new focus for the region.

PARIS

SINCE THE 1960s, the regeneration of Paris has been inextricably linked to national prestige. In 1961, to tackle congestion, five new towns were created within a 25-mile radius of the center. Meanwhile, government set out to make Paris the architectural, scientific and cultural envy of the world. The high-tech Pompidou arts center (1977) set the tone. Under Mitterrand, the process accelerated, resulting in numerous *Grands Projets*, such as the Arab World Institute, the Villette science center, the remodelling of the Louvre museum (including I M Pei's glass pyramid entrance), the new opera house at La Bastille and the futuristic La Defense commercial center.

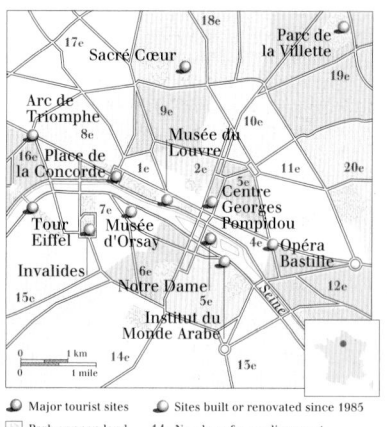

🔵 Major tourist sites   🔵 Sites built or renovated since 1985
◻ Park or open land   14e Number of arrondissement

LANGUEDOC

🎭 Cultural tourism   ⚓ Tourism   ⋯ Rhône-Montpellier canal
🦐 Fruit orchards   💻 Hi-tech industry   🍇 Vineyards

LANGUEDOC has benefited from several initiatives in recent years. The Rhône-Montpellier canal system, Europe's biggest postwar irrigation

network designed to improve yields, led to the replacement of much vine land with fruit orchards, but was not as wealth-creating as had been hoped due to cuts in EU fruit quotas.

Languedoc also has the biggest state-sponsored tourist development in history, the La Motte complex. Built to a master plan by architect George Candillis, a pupil of Le Corbusier, 280,000 new tourist beds were provided in massive resort complexes along a previously undeveloped mosquito-ridden coast. Visitor numbers have risen from 500,000 in 1965 to around four million today.

In the 1980s, Languedoc became France's leading high-tech region. IBM established its largest French manufacturing plant in Montpellier bringing in its wake many "sun-belt" companies. The new industries have also been a great boost to the town's university, the largest in the region.

F

MEDIA

 The media have been free of state control since the 1980s

PUBLISHING AND BROADCAST MEDIA

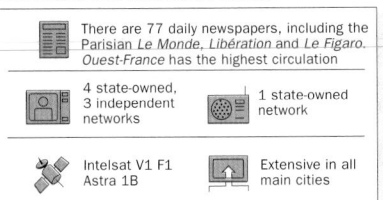

There are 77 daily newspapers, including the Parisian *Le Monde*, *Libération* and *Le Figaro*. *Ouest-France* has the highest circulation

4 state-owned, 3 independent networks

1 state-owned network

Intelsat V1 F1 Astra 1B

Extensive in all main cities

Formerly controlled and censored by the state and very timid, TV and radio were freed from direct state influence by the PS government in the 1980s. *TF1*, the primary TV network, is now privately owned and financed by advertising revenue. *France 2* is still owned by the state but is now fairly autonomous. In sharp contrast to its very strong cinema tradition which is assisted financially by the government, France has a weak TV service, with many bought-in US soaps.

Le Monde is the most prestigious of the seven national daily newspapers with circulations of over 100,000. Regional newspapers are strong.

EDUCATION

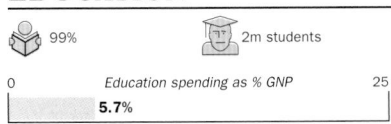 99%   2m students

0   *Education spending as % GNP*   25
5.7%

THE EDUCATION SYSTEM

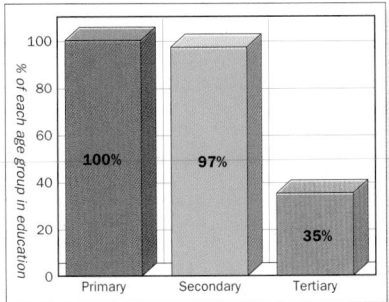

French education remains centralized, despite some relaxation of the system brought about by the student riots of 1968. The education ministry organizes the curriculum, exams and staffing, and most schools have little autonomous control over their affairs. Catholic Church schools, which account for 17% of the school population, are the exception. These are fee-paying but also receive large state subsidies. However, despite their relative independence, they are still obliged to follow the national curriculum.

The focus in teaching remains the acquisition of a broad range of knowledge, and classes are highly

CRIME

 46,423 prisoners   Up 1% in 1992

CRIME RATES

Murders
5 per 100,000 population

Rapes
9 per 100,000 population

Thefts
4487 per 100,000 population

The French legal system is based on Roman law codified by Napoleon. The *juge d'instruction* is arguably the most important figure, a magistrate who has considerable powers in examining witnesses and assessing evidence. The press are not restricted by *sub judice* rules in reporting trials and can speak freely of suspects. Political corruption cases attract much attention.

Petty crime and crimes of violence have risen sharply over recent years. Public concern about this helped return the right – with a law and order platform – to power in 1993. Narcotics-trafficking through the port of Marseilles remains a problem.

disciplined. French children tend to be better informed than their counterparts in other western European countries.

France has over 70 universities – 13 in Paris – and higher education bodies with 1.2 million students. Entry is not competitive, but based on passing the secondary-level exam, the *baccalauréat*. Most students attend their local university. The universities have not been given the funds or staff to cope with the huge increase in student numbers in recent years. The 150 *Grandes Écoles* are outside the university system and have just a few hundred carefully selected students each. The most influential tertiary institutions, they open the door to the top civil service and professional jobs.

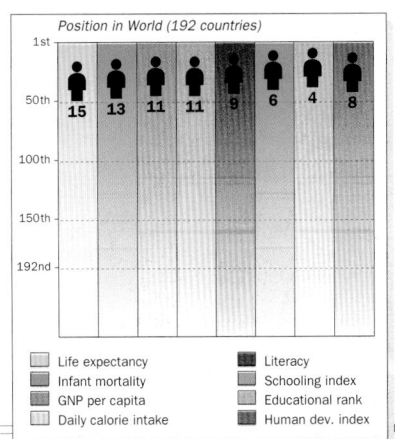

Massif Central, Auvergne. *The Massif's lonely granite plateaus and extinct volcanoes are France's oldest rock formations.*

HEALTH

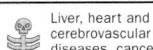 1 per 357 people   Liver, heart and cerebrovascular diseases, cancers

0   *Health spending as % GDP*   25
9.1%

Under the French national health system, patients pay for treatment, and get 70% to 80% of this reimbursed by an insurance company paid by the social services. The Juppé government launched a fiercely contested cost-cutting reform plan in 1995. Health awareness has recently risen, and the French still consume more medicines per capita than any other nation. A 1992 law banning smoking in public places is widely ignored. Alcoholism remains a problem, and cirrhosis of the liver is still the most common cause of death.

WEALTH

Blue-collar worker 101,000 francs ($20,000) per year; technical manager, 267,000 francs ($53,000) per year

CONSUMER GOODS OWNERSHIP

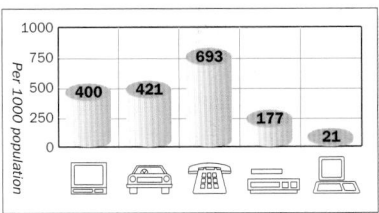

Wealth and income disparities in France are higher than in most OECD countries. The Socialists narrowed the gap a little with the introduction of the legal minimum wage (*le SMIC*). Most tax is indirect – a result of a long French tradition of income-tax evasion – which hits the poor and rich equally.

France has a fairly rigid class structure, although social mobility is increasing. The wealthy favor expensive French, German and British cars, and take exotic vacations to the Himalayas, the Andes and Polynesia.

WORLD RANKING

Position in World (192 countries)

15	13	11	11	9	6	4	8

Life expectancy
Infant mortality
GNP per capita
Daily calorie intake
Literacy
Schooling index
Educational rank
Human dev. index

F

GABON

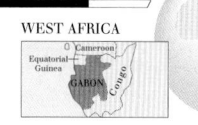
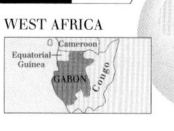

WEST AFRICA

Africa

OFFICIAL NAME: The Gabonese Republic   CAPITAL: Libreville
POPULATION: 1.3 million   CURRENCY: CFA franc   OFFICIAL LANGUAGE: French

AN EQUATORIAL COUNTRY on the west coast of Africa, Gabon's major economic activity is oil. Only a small area of Gabon is cultivated and more than two-thirds constitutes one of the world's finest virgin rainforests. Gabon became independent of France in 1960. A single-party state from 1968, it returned to multiparty democracy in 1990. Gabon's population is small and the government is encouraging its increase.

CLIMATE

WEATHER CHART

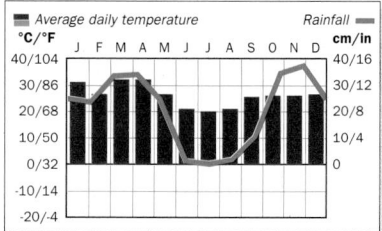

Gabon's climate is heavily equatorial, with very little distinction between seasons. The cold Benguela current lowers coastal temperatures.

TRANSPORTATION

Léon M'Ba , Libreville
611,000 passengers

7 ships
27,600 dwt

THE TRANSPORTATION NETWORK

380 miles (620 km)		None
404 miles (650 km)		994 miles (1,600 km)

The Trans-Gabon Railroad completed in 1986, from Owendo port near Libreville to Massoukou, is the key transportation link. Air transportation is well developed and most big companies have airstrips.

TOURISM

103,000 visitors

Down 10% in 1994

MAIN OVERSEAS ARRIVALS

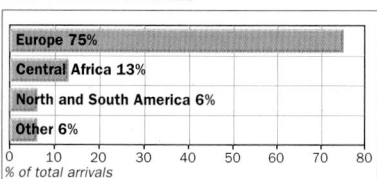

Europe 75%
Central Africa 13%
North and South America 6%
Other 6%

0 10 20 30 40 50 60 70 80
% of total arrivals

Despite Libreville's many hotels, Gabon has little tourism, in part a reflection of its lack of good beaches.

PEOPLE

Fang, French, Punu, Sira, Nzebi, Mpongwe

13 people per sq. mile

THE URBAN/RURAL POPULATION SPLIT

48%   52%

ETHNIC MAKEUP

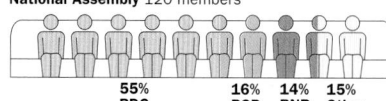

Other African and White 9%
French 2%
Fang 35%
Other Bantu 29%
Eshira 25%

The largest ethnic group in Gabon is the Fang, who live mainly in the north, but they have yet to gain control of government. President Omar Bongo, from a sub-group of the minority Bateke in the southeast, has artfully united the common interests of other ethnic groups to keep the Fang from power. The Myene group around Port-Gentil consider themselves to be the aristocrats of Gabonese society owing to their long-standing ex-colonial contacts. Oil wealth has led to the growth of a distinct bourgeoisie.

POLITICS

1990/1998

President Omar Bongo

THE STATE OF THE PARTIES

National Assembly 120 members

55% PDG   16% PGP   14% RNB   15% Other

PDG = Gabonese Democratic Party   PGP = Gabonese Progress Party   RNB = National Rally of Lumberjacks   Other = Association for Socialism in Gabon, Gabonese Socialist Union

Gabon has had a multiparty constitution since 1990, when a national conference paved the way for elections. The elections confirmed in power the only constitutional party of the previous 20 years – Omar Bongo's PDG. In part this was due to the divided opposition, which comprised over 30 distinct parties. In 1993, the opposition learned from the mistakes of 1990 and backed only one candidate to challenge Bongo in the presidential elections. Bongo was reelected, but disputes about the fairness of the poll have forced the government to concede to further democratic reforms, including early elections.

WORLD AFFAIRS

FZ   G24   OAU   OIC   OPEC

Gabon still maintains close links with France, although US companies are also making inroads into Gabon's oil-rich economy. In regional terms, Gabon remains influential in Francophone Africa, although relations further afield, particularly with OPEC (Gabon was president in 1993), are also important.

GABON

Total Land Area : 257 670 sq. km (99 486 sq. miles)

POPULATION

over 100 000
over 10 000
under 10 000

LAND HEIGHT

500m/1640ft
200m/656ft
Sea Level

0   100 km
0   100 miles

CAMEROON

EQUATORIAL GUINEA

Bitam   Minvoul
Cocobeach   Médouneu   Oyem
Mitzic   Mékambo
LIBREVILLE   Ntoum   Ovan   Alakokou
Foulenzem   Rango   Boué
Cap Lopez   Ndjolé   Equator   Aboumi
Lambaréné   Okondja   Onga
Port-Gentil   Fougamou   Iboundji   Lastoursville   Lékila
Ombooé   Koulamoutou   Mounana   Alténi
Mandji   Mimongo   Moanda   Ngouoni   Lékoni
Mouila   Mbigou   Pana   Bongoville
Guietsou   Mont Milondo 1020m   Bakoumba   Massoukou
Setté Cama   Moabi   Lébamba   Boumango
Gamba   Ndendé   Malinga
Mabanda
Nyanga   Tchibanga
Mayumba   Moulèngui Binza
Ndindi

ATLANTIC OCEAN

CONGO

AID

 $102m (receipts)   Up 48% in 1993

France is by far the major aid donor, providing two-thirds of total receipts. For a middle income country with one of the highest GNPs per capita in the developing world, Gabon has benefited from considerable aid. Its indebtedness is the result of excessive borrowing encouraged by Western banks in the 1970s. Much aid goes to servicing this debt.

DEFENSE

 $98m   Up 5% in 1995

President Bongo's background in the military is reflected in Gabon's large defense budget and prestige weaponry, which includes French *Mirage* jets.

Even the presidential guard has its own fleet of 12 aircraft. France guarantees Gabon's security and keeps a 600-strong garrison in Libreville; this last intervened in 1964 to suppress an attempted coup.

ECONOMICS

 $3.7bn   533.68–489.05 CFA francs

SCORE CARD

- ❏ WORLD GNP RANKING 114th
- ❏ GNP PER CAPITA $3,550
- ❏ BALANCE OF PAYMENTS $320m
- ❏ INFLATION 36.1%
- ❏ UNEMPLOYMENT ....High underemployment

STRENGTHS
Oil and a relatively small population give Gabon a high per capita GNP. Other abundant resources – including some of the world's best tropical hardwoods – are just beginning to be tapped.

WEAKNESSES
Large debt burden incurred in the 1970s. Continuing dependence on French technical assistance.

EXPORTS

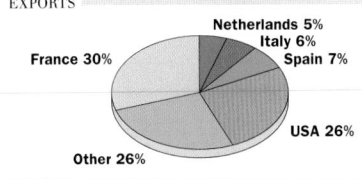

Netherlands 5%
Italy 6%
France 30%
Spain 7%
USA 26%
Other 26%

IMPORTS

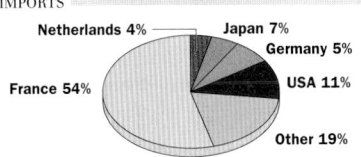

Netherlands 4%
Japan 7%
Germany 5%
France 54%
USA 11%
Other 19%

RESOURCES

 919m kwh (capacity 279,000 kw)   341,000 b/d (reserves 730,000,000 bbl)

 170,000 sheep, 165,000 pigs, 83,000 goats   Oil, manganese, uranium, gold, iron, natural gas

Oil is the major export earner. Gabon also has large deposits of uranium and over 100 years' reserves of manganese. The unexploited iron ore deposits at Bélinga are the world's largest.

ENVIRONMENT

 4%   Adoption of EU-funded pilot conservation project

The Trans-Gabon Railroad has sliced through one of the world's finest virgin rainforests and has opened the interior to indiscriminate exploitation of rare woods such as oleoirme. Gabon abandoned plans for nuclear power following the 1986 Chernobyl' disaster.

MEDIA

 No restrictions

PUBLISHING AND BROADCAST MEDIA

 There are 2 daily newspapers, *L'Union* and *Gabon-Matin*

 1 state-owned service   1 state-owned service

The media has become much more diverse since 1990 and Gabon now has an opposition press and *La Griffe*, a satirical weekly. *L'Union*, the state paper, carries occasional contributions from Omar Bongo, the president.

CRIME

 Gabon does not publish prison figures   Down 31% in 1992

Urban crime rates (Gabon is one of Africa's most urbanized nations) have been growing. Gabon's human rights record has improved in the last five years.

Albert Schweitzer Hospital, *Lambaréné, on the lower Ogooué River. Schweitzer won a Nobel Prize for his pioneering work in Africa.*

CHRONOLOGY

Gabon became a French colony in 1886, administered as part of French Equatorial Africa.

- ❏ **1960** Independence. Léon M'ba president.
- ❏ **1964** Military coup. French intervene to reinstate M'ba.
- ❏ **1967** Albert-Bernard (later Omar) Bongo president.
- ❏ **1968** Single-party state instituted.
- ❏ **1990** Multiparty democracy. Omar Bongo's PDG wins elections.

G

EDUCATION

 61%   4,007 students

Education follows the French system. Libreville University, founded in the 1970s, now has over 4,000 students.

HEALTH

 1 per 2,800 people   Heart and diarrheal diseases, pneumonia, accidents

Oil revenues have allowed substantial investment in the health service which is now among the best in Africa.

WEALTH

 Cabinet-maker, 86,000 CFA francs ($176) per month; electricity industry office clerk, 204,000 CFA francs ($417) per month

CONSUMER GOODS OWNERSHIP

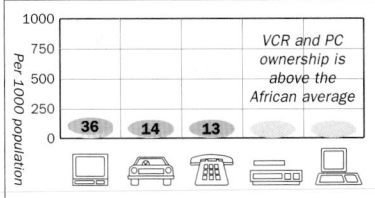

VCR and PC ownership is above the African average

36   14   13

Oil wealth has led to the growth of an affluent bourgeoisie. Menial jobs are done by immigrant workers.

WORLD RANKING

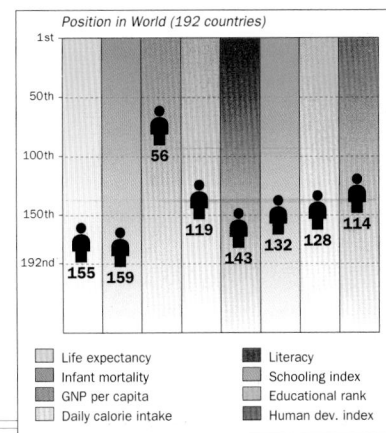

Position in World (192 countries)

56
119
143 132 128 114
155 159

- Life expectancy
- Infant mortality
- GNP per capita
- Daily calorie intake
- Literacy
- Schooling index
- Educational rank
- Human dev. index

GAMBIA

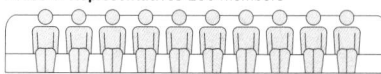

OFFICIAL NAME: Republic of The Gambia **CAPITAL:** Banjul
POPULATION: 1.1 million **CURRENCY:** Dalasi **OFFICIAL LANGUAGE:** English

A NARROW COUNTRY on the western coast of Africa, The Gambia had been renowned for its political stability until its government was overthrown in a coup in 1994. Agriculture accounts for 65% of its GDP, yet more Gambians are leaving rural areas for the towns, where average incomes are four times higher. Its position as an enclave within Senegal seems likely to endure following the failure of an experiment in federation in the 1980s.

CLIMATE

WEATHER CHART

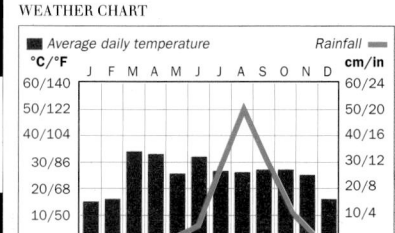

The subtropical and sunny dry season is punctuated by intermittent hot *harmattan* winds.

TRANSPORTATION

Yundum Intl, Banjul
220,156 passengers

Has no fleet

THE TRANSPORTATION NETWORK

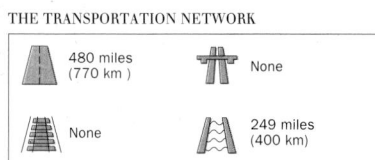

480 miles (770 km)	None
None	249 miles (400 km)

The River Gambia carries more traffic than the roads – ships of up to 3,000 tons can reach Georgetown. Yundum airport was upgraded by NASA in 1989 for US space shuttle emergency landings.

TOURISM

 82,000 visitors   Down 9% in 1994

MAIN OVERSEAS ARRIVALS

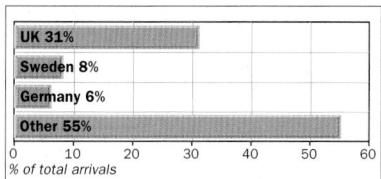

UK 31%
Sweden 8%
Germany 6%
Other 55%

% of total arrivals

The successful tourist industry offers sunshine, beaches and resort hotels. Most visitors are northern Europeans escaping winter.

PEOPLE

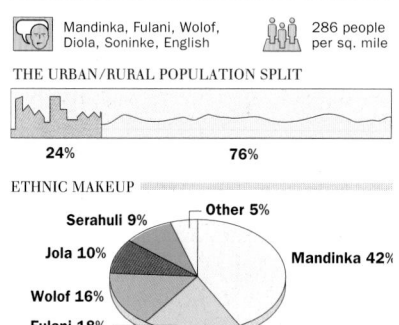

Mandinka, Fulani, Wolof, Diola, Soninke, English

286 people per sq. mile

THE URBAN/RURAL POPULATION SPLIT

24%   76%

ETHNIC MAKEUP

Serahuli 9%
Jola 10%
Wolof 16%
Fulani 18%
Other 5%
Mandinka 42%

If there is any ethnic tension in The Gambia, it has come from minority resentment of the Mandinka's domination of politics. The 1962–1994 Jawara administration had, however, sought to distribute political offices fairly according to ethnic origins. The Creole community, known as the Aku, is small but socially prominent. In the early years of the tourist industry, the presence of northern Europeans created some tension in a country that is essentially Muslim. About 85% of Gambians follow Islam although there is no official state religion. There is a yearly influx of seasonal immigrants, who come from Senegal, Guinea and Mali to grow groundnuts. The Gambia is still a very poor country, with 80% of the labor force engaged in agriculture. As elsewhere in West Africa, women are active as traders.

Fishing village. Overfishing in the waters off the Gambia and Senegal, mainly by distant nations, is a growing problem.

POLITICS

 1992/1996   Lt. Yahya Jameh

THE STATE OF THE PARTIES

House of Representatives 150 members

Legislative elections have been promised by Gambia's new leadership following its takeover of power in 1994

The PPP (People's Progressive Party) provided Gambia's government from 1962 until 1994, during which time the country was never a single-party state. The PPP was strongly backed by traditional rulers, especially in the Mandinka areas. The main opposition party, the NCP, was also Mandinka-led, but dependent on minority parties for support.

In 1994, however, President Jawara, leader of the PPP since 1962, was ousted in a coup led by members of the military. Sir Dawda Jawara, who had secured a fourth term of office in the 1992 presidential elections, left the country aboard a US warship. The coup's leaders claimed that it had been initiated in a bid to end corruption and pledged to preserve democracy. A new government was swiftly announced, in which several portfolios went to civil servants who had served in the former Jawara administration. The coup drew no active response from the potentially influential Senegal or Nigeria.

WORLD AFFAIRS

 CILSS Comm Ecowas OAU OIC

Relations with Senegal are crucial, especially since the collapse in 1989 of the Senegambian federation, which had been set up under pressure from the Senegalese after the attempted coup of 1981. Outside West Africa, ties remain chiefly with the Commonwealth; good relations with the UK, a major aid donor, are important.

AID

 $92m (receipts)   Down 21% in 1993

The Gambia's relative stability has enabled it to attract aid easily, notably from the World Bank, IMF, AfDB, the UK and Saudi Arabia. Italy and the Netherlands have given aid for health, and Japan for ferry services.

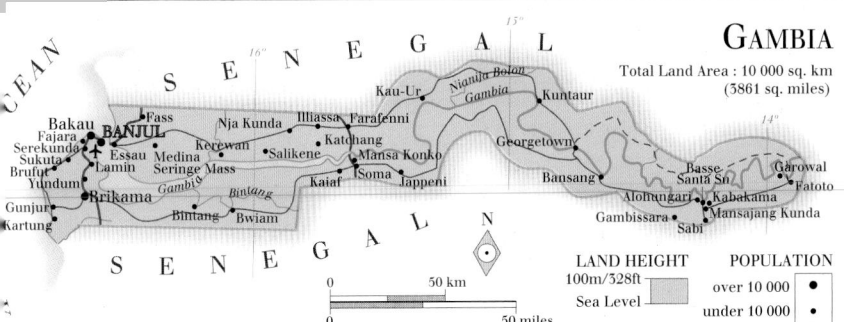

GAMBIA

Total Land Area : 10 000 sq. km
(3861 sq. miles)

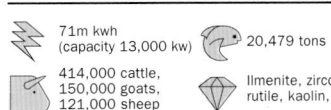

LAND HEIGHT
100m/328ft
Sea Level

POPULATION
over 10 000 •
under 10 000 ·

CHRONOLOGY

Mandinka traders brought Islam in the 13th century and were the main influence until the 18th century. The 1700s and 1800s saw colonial rivalry between Britain and France.

- ❑ **1888** British colony. Boundaries with France agreed in next year.
- ❑ **1959** Dawda Jawara founds PPP.
- ❑ **1962** Jawara prime minister.
- ❑ **1965** Independence.
- ❑ **1970** Republic; Jawara president.
- ❑ **1981** Senegalese troops help crush junior army officers' coup attempt.
- ❑ **1982–1989** Federated with Senegal.
- ❑ **1992** Jawara's fourth reelection.
- ❑ **1994** Jawara ousted in coup.

DEFENSE

 $15m    Up 7% in 1995

The Gambia National Army, with one infantry battalion, takes about half of the defense budget; the rest finances the 600-strong gendarmerie. Most arms are bought from the UK, although supplies are now increasingly coming from Nigeria too. A defense pact with Senegal collapsed with the federation in 1989.

ECONOMICS

 $384m    9.67–9.85 dalasi

SCORE CARD

❑ WORLD GNP RANKING	170th
❑ GNP PER CAPITA	$360
❑ BALANCE OF PAYMENTS	$8m
❑ INFLATION	1.7%
❑ UNEMPLOYMENT	Widespread underemployment

STRENGTHS

Low tariffs make the Gambia a focus of regional trade. Natural deep-water harbor at Banjul, one of the finest on the West African coast. Well-managed economy, favorably viewed by donors.

WEAKNESSES

Small size of country, and hence small size of market, sometimes inhibits investment. Smuggling deprives government of significant revenues. Lack of significant resources and little diversification in agriculture.

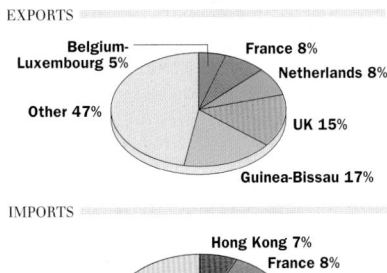

EXPORTS

Belgium-Luxembourg 5%
France 8%
Netherlands 8%
Other 47%
UK 15%
Guinea-Bissau 17%

IMPORTS

Hong Kong 7%
France 8%
Netherlands 11%
Other 46%
UK 13%
China 15%

RESOURCES

 71m kwh (capacity 13,000 kw)   20,479 tons

414,000 cattle, 150,000 goats, 121,000 sheep   Ilmenite, zirconium, rutile, kaolin, tin

The River Gambia is one of Africa's few good waterways, but is underused as it is separated from its natural hinterland by the Gambia–Senegal border. Irrigation is at present provided by a single dam; plans for further dams for power generation have met with opposition. Most mineral deposits have yet to be exploited.

ENVIRONMENT

 2%   Increasing awareness of environment by tourism ministry

The impact of tourism on the country's environment and overfishing in Gambian waters are major concerns.

MEDIA

 Increasingly restrictions are being imposed on the media

PUBLISHING AND BROADCAST MEDIA

There are no daily newspapers. *The Gambia Weekly* and *The Gambia Times* are prominent.

No television service   1 state-owned, 1 independent service

The Gambian press is independent. In 1996, the military government imposed restrictions, including the requirement of the payment of a $10,000 bond.

CRIME

 The Gambia does not publish prison figures    General crime levels are rising

Crime levels are relatively low in what is a peaceful society compared to many other states in the region.

EDUCATION

64%   1,489 students

The literacy rate is low for the level of school enrollment – 75% in elementary and 20% in secondary schools. Tertiary education is limited to teacher training.

HEALTH

 1 per 11,700 people   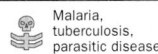 Malaria, tuberculosis, parasitic diseases

Most people have access to basic medicines, but these are no longer free. Advanced medical care in the public sector is limited. A quarter of state doctors work in the main hospital.

WEALTH

 The majority of the population is poor. Rising educational opportunities should result in greater social mobility.

CONSUMER GOODS OWNERSHIP

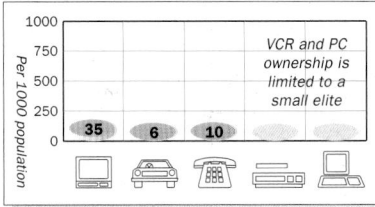

VCR and PC ownership is limited to a small elite

35   6   10

Public service and the professions have made some comfortably off, but great wealth is not a feature of Gambian life. Unemployed young men in Banjul are regarded as the underclass.

WORLD RANKING

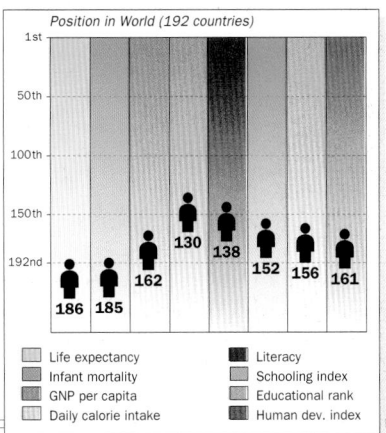

Position in World (192 countries)

186   185   162   130   138   152   156   161

- Life expectancy
- Infant mortality
- GNP per capita
- Daily calorie intake
- Literacy
- Schooling index
- Educational rank
- Human dev. index

GEORGIA

OFFICIAL NAME: Republic of Georgia   CAPITAL: Tbilisi
POPULATION: 5.5 million   CURRENCY: Lari   OFFICIAL LANGUAGE: Georgian

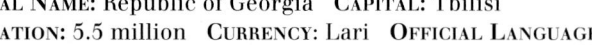

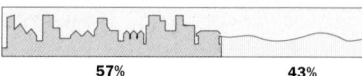

SITUATED ON THE EASTERN coast of the Black Sea, Georgia is largely mountainous. Its coastline stretches from Abkhazia in the north to Ajaria in the south. Georgia was one of the first republics to demand independence from Moscow, but has been plagued over recent years by civil war and ethnic disputes in Abkhazia and South Ossetia. The birthplace of Stalin, Georgia is primarily agricultural and is famous for its wine.

CLIMATE

WEATHER CHART

Georgia's climate is continental inland and subtropical along the coast, where grapes, citrus fruit and tea are grown.

Tbilisi, Georgia's capital since the 5th century AD. Its buildings rise in steep terraces from both banks of the River Kura.

TRANSPORTATION

Novo Alexeyevka, Tbilisi   47 ships
                                  1.01m dwt

THE TRANSPORTATION NETWORK

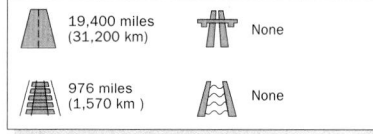

19,400 miles (31,200 km)	None
976 miles (1,570 km)	None

Civil war has caused the near collapse of the transportation system. The autonomous republic of Ajaria maintains good communications with Turkey.

TOURISM

 Flourishing Black Sea tourist trade before civil war   Sharp fall since start of civil war

MAIN OVERSEAS ARRIVALS

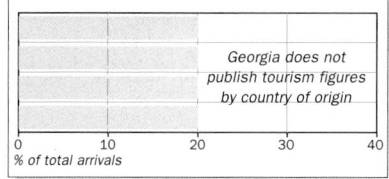

Georgia does not publish tourism figures by country of origin

0   10   20   30   40
% of total arrivals

The volatility of the current political situation has discouraged tourism, although Georgia was previously a popular destination.

PEOPLE

Georgian, Russian   206 people per sq. mile

THE URBAN/RURAL POPULATION SPLIT

57%   43%

ETHNIC MAKEUP

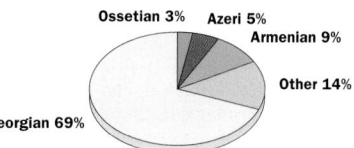

Ossetian 3%   Azeri 5%
              Armenian 9%
              Other 14%
Georgian 69%

Georgia is a paternalistic society, with strong family and cultural traditions. The proportion of Georgians, who currently make up 69% of the population, is gradually increasing. Minority groups include Armenians, Russians, Azeris, Ossetians, Greeks and Abkhazians.

POLITICS

 1995/1999   President Eduard Shevardnadze

THE STATE OF THE PARTIES

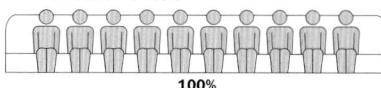

Parliament 235 members

100%
CUG

CUG = Citizens' Union of Georgia

Politics in Georgia remains in a state of flux. President Eduard Shevardnadze, the former Soviet foreign minister, narrowly escaped an assassination attempt in mid-1995. An uneasy truce has followed the 1990–1993 civil war between the supporters of ex-president Zviad Gamsakhurdia, who committed suicide while under fire at the end of 1993, and troops loyal to the government. Russian military intervention on the government's side brought the fighting to an end.

In the province of Abkhazia, another civil war is being fought as ethnic Abkhazians attempt to secede from Georgia. Georgians are being expelled from the region.

GEORGIA

Total Land Area :
69 700 sq. km
(26 911 sq. miles)

POPULATION

☐ over 1 000 000
◎ over 100 000
○ over 50 000
● over 10 000
• under 10 000

LAND HEIGHT

3000m/9843ft
2000m/6562ft
1000m/3281ft
500m/1640ft
200m/656ft
Sea Level

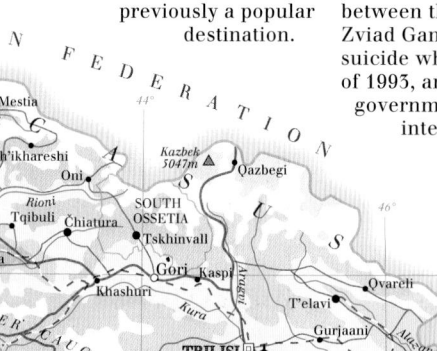

WORLD AFFAIRS

Georgia joined the CIS in 1993 in order to secure Russian military support against Gamsakhurdia.

AID

 $28m (receipts)   No obvious increase

In 1996, the IMF awarded the government a $246 million loan to support its reform program.

DEFENSE

 $56m   Up 19% in 1995

Georgia's military strength has been boosted by the presence of Russian troops in the country since it joined the CIS in October 1993. The Abkhazian conflict now dominates the agenda for the Georgian army. Training for the government security forces is provided by the CIA.

ECONOMICS

 $3bn    1.25 lari

SCORE CARD

❏ World GNP Ranking	123rd
❏ GNP per Capita	$725(est)
❏ Balance of Payment	$–23.7m
❏ Inflation	7,380%
❏ Unemployment	8.4%

STRENGTHS
Potential gateway to West for Azeri oil through pipelines over Georgian territory. Ports on the Black Sea. Award of IMF loan in 1996.

WEAKNESSES
Breakdown of economy due to war and severance of links with other ex-Soviet republics. Hyperinflation following introduction of first the coupon and then the lari. Influence of powerful economic mafias.

EXPORTS

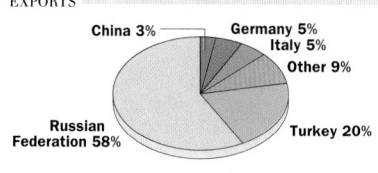

IMPORTS

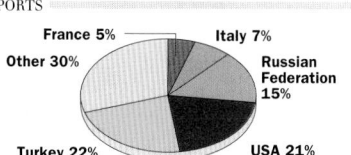

RESOURCES

 9.3bn kwh (capacity 4.9m kw)   2,005 b/d

17m poultry, 1.3m sheep, 1m cattle, 650,000 pigs   Manganese, coal, oil, natural gas, zinc, cobalt, vanadium

Known oil reserves are as yet undeveloped and Georgia is dependent on Russia for much of its gasoline and electricity supply. Cobalt and vanadium are being mined, although only in small quantities which are not easy to sell on the world market. Georgia is a predominantly agricultural country and food processing and wine production are the major industries.

ENVIRONMENT

 3%   No resources for environmental initiatives

Pollution of the Black Sea is a major concern. The protection of upland pastures and hill farms from soil erosion is another key issue.

MEDIA

 Government censorship is widespread

PUBLISHING AND BROADCAST MEDIA

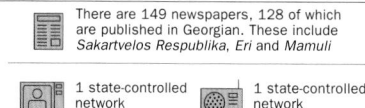 There are 149 newspapers, 128 of which are published in Georgian. These include *Sakartvelos Respublika*, *Eri* and *Mamuli*

1 state-controlled network   1 state-controlled network

There is little press freedom as the media survives on government subsidies. All TV broadcasting is controlled by the state.

CRIME

 Georgia does not publish prison figures   Levels of all crime, especially organized crime, are rising

Organized crime under the control of mafia-style groups has flourished since independence in 1991. The judicial system currently favors Shevardnadze and his supporters.

EDUCATION

 99%   103,900 students

All levels of education are now seriously underfunded. The University of Tbilisi was formerly of a high standard, with a particular reputation for the arts and economics.

HEALTH

 1 per 180 people   Circulatory and respiratory diseases, cancers, accidents

The health system was limited under the Soviet Union. Internal strife and a lack of resources have prevented any recent investment.

CHRONOLOGY

A Russian protectorate from 1763, Georgia was absorbed into the Russian empire in 1801. It was established as an independent state under a Menshevik socialist government in 1918.

- ❏ **1879** Stalin born in Gori.
- ❏ **1920** Recognized as an independent state by Soviet Russia.
- ❏ **1921** Soviet Red Army invades. Effectively part of USSR.
- ❏ **1922** Incorporated into the Transcaucasian Soviet Federative Socialist Republic (TSFSR).
- ❏ **1936** TSFSR dissolved.
- ❏ **1989** Pro-independence riots in Tbilisi put down by Soviet troops.
- ❏ **1990** Declares sovereignty. Shevardnadze resigns as Soviet foreign minister.
- ❏ **1991** Independence. Gamsakhurdia elected president.
- ❏ **1992** Gamsakhurdia flees Tbilisi. Shevardnadze elected chairman of Supreme Soviet and State Council.
- ❏ **1995** Shevardnadze survives an assassination attempt and is subsequently elected president.

G

WEALTH

 Wealth is concentrated in Tbilisi

CONSUMER GOODS OWNERSHIP

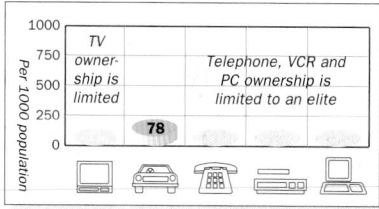

At least 80% of the population live in poverty. There is a small wealthy and extravagant elite.

WORLD RANKING

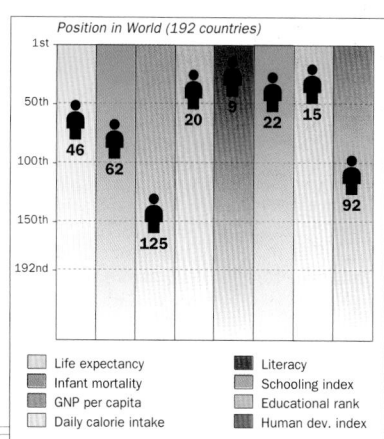

GERMANY

OFFICIAL NAME: Federal Republic of Germany **CAPITAL:** Berlin
POPULATION: 81.6 million **CURRENCY:** Deutsche Mark **OFFICIAL LANGUAGE:** German

WITH COASTLINES on both the Baltic and North Seas, Germany is bordered by nine states. The north is characterized by plains and rolling hills; the south by more mountainous terrain. The most populous country in Europe after Russia, Germany is also its foremost industrial power and, after Japan, the world's second-biggest exporter. United in the 1870s, it was divided following the defeat of the Nazi regime in 1945. The western part became a free-market democracy aligned with the West; the east became a communist-ruled state in the Soviet bloc. The collapse of the East German regime in 1989 paved the way for political reunification in 1990. Tensions created by the wealth differences between east and west have been exacerbated by a lengthy economic recession, and rising unemployment has also created a groundswell of anti-immigrant feeling.

CLIMATE

WEATHER CHART

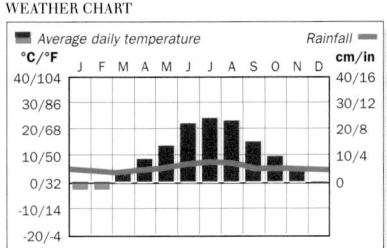

Germany has a broad climatic range. The upper Rhine Valley is very mild and suitable for wine-making. The Bavarian Alps, the Harz Mountains and the Black Forest are by contrast cold, with heavy falls of snow in winter.

TRANSPORTATION

 **Frankfurt/Main International**
28.7m passengers

 720 ships
6.21m dwt

THE TRANSPORTATION NETWORK

309,000 miles (496,000 km)	5,482 miles (8,822 km)
26,098 miles (42,000 km)	4,163 miles (6,700 km)

Germany virtually invented the modern expressway with its 1930s *Autobahnen*, built by the Nazis primarily for military purposes. Today, the country has Europe's most elaborate expressway network. Most *Autobahnen* still have no speed limit, despite the strong environmental lobby and strict standards on vehicle emissions. German railroads are mostly state-owned and efficient. Its ICE lost the high-speed train race to the French TGV. Germany is now planning a 217 miles-per-hour MAGLEV train to run between Berlin and Hamburg.

TOURISM

 14.5m visitors   Up 1% in 1994

MAIN OVERSEAS ARRIVALS

Austria	21%
Spain	16%
Italy	14%
Hungary	8%
Switzerland	8%
Other	33%

% of total arrivals

Northerly beaches and a colder climate make Germany less of a tourist draw than France or Italy. Skiing in the Bavarian Alps, the historic castles of the Rhine Valley and the Black Forest are all major attractions. Even before German reunification in 1990, Berlin attracted many tourists with its rich cultural life and its Wall separating West and communist East. Now once more the capital of Germany, it has a huge reconstruction program and a dynamic and vibrant atmosphere.

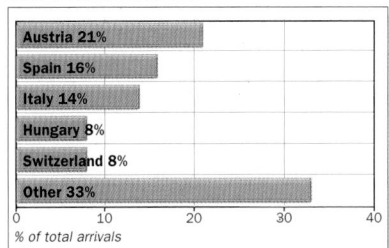

The Stillach Valley, Allgäu Alps, Bayern (Bavaria). *Germany's forests, which are found mainly in its mountain regions, are suffering badly from the effects of acid rain.*

GERMANY

Total Land Area : 349 520 sq. km
(134 910 sq. miles)

POPULATION

⊡	over 1 000 000
◉	over 500 000
◎	over 100 000
○	over 10 000

LAND HEIGHT

- 2000m/6562ft
- 1000m/3281ft
- 500m/1640ft
- 200m/656ft
- Sea Level

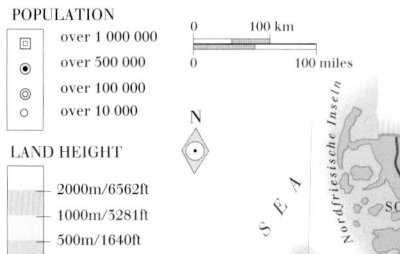

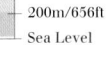

PEOPLE

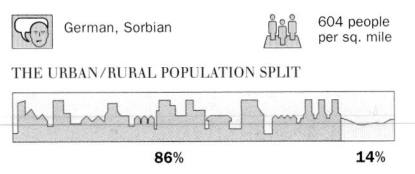

German, Sorbian

604 people per sq. mile

THE URBAN/RURAL POPULATION SPLIT

86%   14%

RELIGIOUS PERSUASION

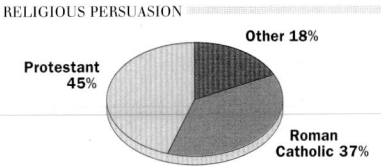

Other 18%

Protestant 45%

Roman Catholic 37%

ETHNIC MAKEUP

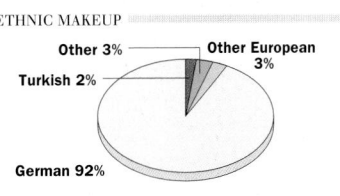

Other 3%   Other European 3%

Turkish 2%

German 92%

Germans share a common language, but they speak it with a variety of dialects, reflecting a strong sense of regionalism. Some German-speaking peoples live in neighboring Austria, France and Switzerland, but most now live in Germany. The north is still largely Protestant, while the south and southwest, particularly Bayern (Bavaria), have strong Catholic traditions.

A large immigrant population, now some seven million people, provided much of the labor on which former West Germany's economic recovery was built. Known as *Gastarbeiter* (guest workers), they cannot easily claim full German nationality and so do not have equal rights. The 1.9 million Turks are the largest single group. Germany's once liberal asylum laws were tightened in 1993 in response to domestic tension over the huge influx of ethnic Germans and "economic" refugees from Russia and eastern Europe following the collapse of communism. Unemployment and disappointed expectations, particularly among young Germans, has helped extreme right-wing parties win a significant, but still limited following. While their racism targets non-Germans, recently the main influx has been of ethnic Germans with automatic rights to nationality, who are increasingly resented as unemployment grows.

POPULATION AGE BREAKDOWN

% of population by age group	0–14	15–64		65+	
	11.5%	13.7%	15.6%	14.6%	15.4%
	67.2%	63.1%	65.9%	68.7%	67.7%
	21.3%	23.2%	18.5%	16.7%	16.9%
	1960	1970	1980	1990	2000

Family ties in Germany are little different from those in the USA or UK. Millions of couples live together in common-law arrangements, and while this is frowned on by the Catholic Church, it is largely in rural districts in Bayern (Bavaria) that traditional habits are still observed. The birth-rate is one of Europe's lowest and the population would be falling were it not for the influx of immigrants since the 1950s.

Women have full rights under the law and play a bigger role in politics than in most other European countries. In 1994, they formed one-sixth of the *Bundestag* (Federal Assembly). They are less well represented, however, in top jobs in business and industry. Germany has a tradition of strong feminism. Abortion remains a charged issue. Women in former East Germany had wanted to keep their right to abortion on demand, but the constitutional court, after strong Catholic lobbying, overruled a relatively liberal 1992 compromise for the whole country. Under a law eventually passed in mid-1995, women can arrange abortions (but only after counseling) within three months of conception.

Despite their liberal reputation, Germans retain relatively formal social habits, with clear distinctions drawn between acquaintances and friends. This is reflected in the still widespread use of the formal *Sie* rather than the more familiar *du* as a form of address.

G

CHRONOLOGY

German unification in the 19th century brought together a mosaic of states with a common linguistic but varied political heritage.

❑ **1815** German Confederation under nominal Austrian leadership.

❑ **1834** Zollverein Customs Union of 18 states, including Prussia.

❑ **1862** Otto von Bismarck appointed Prussian chancellor.

❑ **1864–1870** Prussia defeats Danes, Austrians and French; north German states under Prussian control.

❑ **1871** Southern states join Prussian-led unified German Empire under William I.

❑ **1870s** Rapid industrialization.

❑ **1890** Kaiser Wilhelm II accedes with aspirations for German world role. Bismarck sacked.

❑ **1914–1918** World War I.

❑ **1918** Germany signs armistice; Weimar Republic created.

❑ **1919** Treaty of Versailles: colonies lost and payment of reparations. Rhineland demilitarized. ➪

G

The Messeturm, Frankfurt, the tallest office building in Europe. Frankfurt is Germany's financial services center and home to many of its leading companies.

POLITICS

L. House 1994/1998   President Roman Herzog

THE STATE OF THE PARTIES

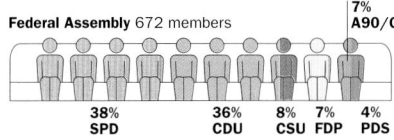

Federal Assembly 672 members

38% SPD	36% CDU	8% CSU	7% FDP	4% PDS	7% A90/G

SPD = Social Democratic Party **CDU** = Christian Democratic Union **CSU** = Christian Social Union **FDP** = Free Democratic Party **A90/G** = Alliance 90/Greens **PDS** = Party of Democratic Socialism

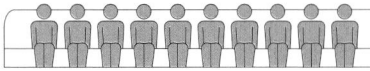

Federal Council 68 members

Between 3 and 6 members represent each of 16 states *(Länder)*

Germany is a federal democratic republic of 16 states, or *Länder*. The government is led by the chancellor, who is elected by the *Bundestag* (Federal Assembly). The president's role is largely ceremonial. The "Basic Law" of West Germany, drawn up in 1948, became the 1990 federal constitution of reunified Germany.

MAIN POLITICAL ISSUES
Reunification
Although the overwhelming majority of Germans supported reunification in 1990, the general rejoicing which had greeted the fall of the Berlin Wall at the end of 1989 quickly soured as the true costs of the process became clear. Unemployment in the east rose to 30% with the collapse of inefficient industries, and the "solidarity surcharge" on income tax became a semi-permanent feature, although in 1996 the government pledged to cut it from 7.5% to 5.5% in 1997.

The recession
Germans, used to constant growth since the 1950s, were shocked by recession in 1991, doubly painful because it coincided with the enormous costs of reunification. Economic recovery faltered in 1995, with the government reining in public spending to meet targets for European monetary union, and unemployment topped four million at the end of that year.

Nationalism
Increasing unemployment has led to anti-immigrant attacks and support for far-right parties. Some Germans fear that foreigners are taking "their" jobs, and foreign workers, particularly Turks, and asylum-seekers have been subject to shocking attacks, the worst in Rostock and Mölln in 1992, Magdeburg in 1994 and Ulm in 1995. The problem of racism, even if no worse than in many other European states, is more sensitive given Germany's history.

PROFILE
Germany's politics remain strongly democratic and essentially stable, with a long tradition of federative association. Before unification in 1871, Germany was a mass of separate principalities, kingdoms and city states, a tradition in many ways maintained by Bismarck in his unification constitution. The 1933–1945 Nazi period, during which the federal system was abolished, was very much a hiatus. The Allies reestablished the system in West Germany in 1949; in the east, the *Länder* were restored after reunification in 1990. In many ways, the *Länder* are at the heart of German political life. Each *Land* has its own elected parliament and largely controls its own finances. In addition, German cities have larger budgets than their European counterparts and city mayors wield considerable power. By general consensus the system delivers efficient and commercially astute government.

Nationally, the conservative CDU dominated the *Bundestag* from 1949 to 1966 and headed a "grand coalition" in 1966–1969 with the SPD, hitherto the main opposition party. An SPD–FPD coalition, with Willy Brandt and Helmut Schmidt as chancellors, held power for the next 13 years. Since then, a conservative government has again been in power, led by Chancellor Helmut Kohl. In practice, at least in domestic policy, there have been few major differences between CDU-led and SPD-led coalitions. Their economic policies, based on low inflation, stable growth and an independent central bank, are almost identical. All parties support the *Sozialmarktwirtschaft*, the social market economy, on which West Germany's prosperity was built.

Dr. Helmut Kohl, *federal chancellor and CDU chairman.*

Dr. Klaus Kinkel *took over as foreign minister in 1992.*

Oskar Lafontaine, *became the SPD leader in 1995.*

WORLD AFFAIRS

Before reunification, Germany played only a modest part in international politics. The focus of West Germany was the creation of the EU and the policy of *Ostpolitik* – improving relations with Moscow, which had 400,000 troops stationed in East Germany.

Since 1990, the emphasis has changed and a united Germany is starting to voice foreign policy which reflects its position as the most economically powerful country in Europe. On the world stage, this has raised the possibility of Germany becoming a permanent member of the UN Security Council. The country is the biggest investor in the ex-COMECON economies, bringing the region once again under its influence. Germany remains a leading proponent of European Union, encouraged by France as its closest ally.

AID

 $6.9bn (donations)   No change in 1993

Unlike the USA, the UK and France, Germany's aid programs are not directly motivated by its desire for political influence in the world's poorer regions. Most are multilateral, although there is also a strong tradition of direct aid. Much comes directly from Church organizations such as the Protestant *Brot für die Welt*. Many German volunteers and missionaries work overseas on aid programs.

DEFENSE

 $34bn   Up 17% in 1995

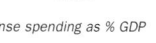

Germany's army is Europe's largest. US and UK troop numbers in western Germany are being gradually being reduced. The constitutional court ruled in 1994 that army units could participate in UN, NATO or WEU collective defense activities abroad, such as in the former Yugoslavia.

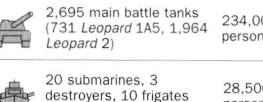

GERMAN ARMED FORCES

	2,695 main battle tanks (731 *Leopard* 1A5, 1,964 *Leopard* 2)	234,000 personnel
	20 submarines, 3 destroyers, 10 frigates and 36 patrol boats	28,500 personnel
	488 combat aircraft (157 F-4, 273 *Tornado*, 24 MiG-29, 34 *Alpha*)	75,300 personnel
	None	

G

ECONOMICS

 $2075bn  1.43–1.55 Deutsche Marks

SCORE CARD

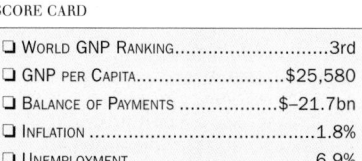
- ❑ WORLD GNP RANKING..........................3rd
- ❑ GNP PER CAPITA.........................$25,580
- ❑ BALANCE OF PAYMENTS ....$–21.7bn
- ❑ INFLATION 1.8%
- ❑ UNEMPLOYMENT................................6.9%

EXPORTS
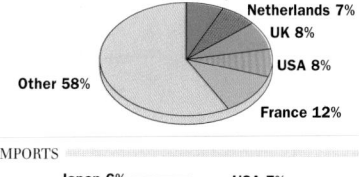
Italy 7%, Netherlands 7%, UK 8%, USA 8%, France 12%, Other 58%

IMPORTS
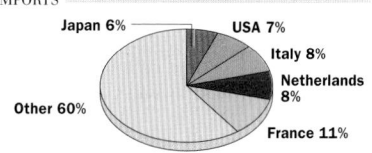
Japan 6%, USA 7%, Italy 8%, Netherlands 8%, France 11%, Other 60%

ECONOMIC PERFORMANCE INDICATOR
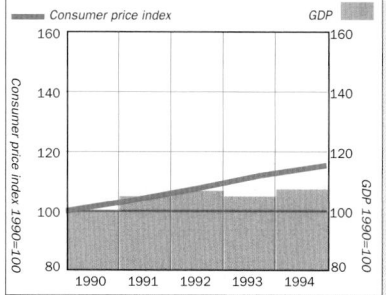

STRENGTHS
Europe's major industrial power and, until now, most successful economy. Very efficient industry benefits from Germany's low inflation environment. German workers and managers live up to their reputation for hard work, thoroughness and discipline. Strongest sectors are cars, heavy engineering, electronics and chemicals; all have massive export success.

WEAKNESSES
The east: costs of incorporating out-of-date and massively inefficient ex-communist economy underestimated.

High social security costs, including unemployment, and pension obligations with an aging population. Growing competition from increasingly efficient, low-wage Asian economies.

PROFILE
West Germany's postwar recovery, to become the world's third-strongest economy, was based on the concept of a social market economy. This charged the state with providing welfare and ensuring workers' rights, while leaving the economy in private hands. Germany has developed little of the coordinated state and regional planning found in France. Major banks and businesses are in private hands. One exception is Volkswagen, which is partly state-owned. The central bank, which sets interest rates and is responsible for controlling inflation, enjoys a large measure of independence from the government. The strong currency is a key symbol of German success, which many would regret abandoning in favor of the proposed common European currency, the Euro.

GERMANY : MAJOR BUSINESSES
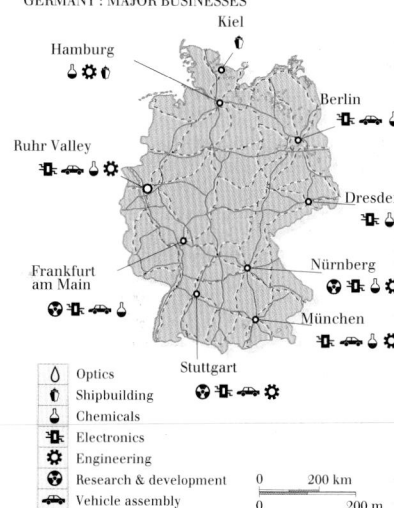

The greatest challenge for Germany remains rebuilding the east. The state privatization agency, the *Treuhand*, has now sold off all of the former East German state-owned concerns.

Friedrichstrasse, East Berlin. *Berlin was redesignated Germany's capital city in 1991. Redevelopment of its center has been planned.*

RESOURCES

- 536bn kwh (capacity 123m kw)
- 65,744 b/d (reserves 449,814,000 bbl)
- 26m pigs, 15.9m cattle, 2.4m sheep, 530,000 horses
- Coal, oil, natural gas, copper, salt, potash, tin, nickel

ELECTRICITY GENERATION

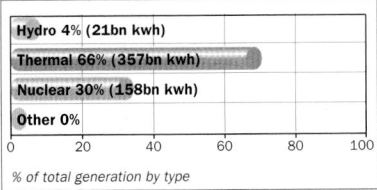

Hydro 4% (21bn kwh)
Thermal 66% (357bn kwh)
Nuclear 30% (158bn kwh)
Other 0%

% of total generation by type

Germany has relatively few natural resources. It imports over 50% of its energy needs. Coal, the basis of its industrialization, has diminished in importance, accounting for less than 20% of energy today, compared with 51% 30 years ago. Unlike France, the former West Germany did not invest heavily in nuclear power; the accident at Chernobyl' in the Ukraine strengthened the anti-nuclear lobby's case. In eastern Germany, all the Soviet-built nuclear power stations have been shut down. Germany's energy conservation program is generally considered to be the most successful in Europe.

ENVIRONMENT

- 26%
- Successful energy conservation and recycling programs

ENVIRONMENTAL TREATIES

Yes — Yes — Yes
Yes — Yes — Yes

Germans are among the world's most environmentally conscious people. Led by the Green Party, which emerged as a powerful political force in the 1980s, environmental campaigns have had a major influence on the policies of all the major parties. At national level, the Greens hold 49 seats in the *Bundestag*, and they are strongly represented in *Land* parliaments and local councils.

Germany has some of the strictest pollution controls in the world, adding extra costs to businesses and forcing them to become even more efficient. Germans recycle 47% of their waste paper, reprocess 70% of their used tires and sort 75% of their glass according to color, to aid recycling.

Apart from the nuclear debate, which has been vigorously fought and won by the Greens, the main concern is Germany's forests. Acid rain from car fumes and industrial pollution was suspected to be killing trees in all parts of the country. Official estimates in 1986 suggesting that up to 50% of trees were sick or dying resulted in Germany becoming the first European country to insist that new cars be fitted with catalytic converters.

The east had particular problems, including the highest per capita rate of sulphur emissions in the world. These have been reduced by the shut-down of industrial plants and the elimination of the noxious Trabant cars, replaced with Western ones.

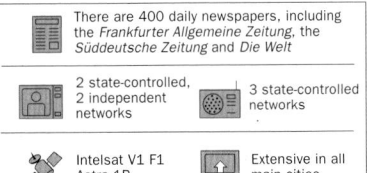

GERMANY : LAND USE

- Cropland
- Forest
- Pasture
- Vineyards
- Pigs
- Cattle

0   200 km
0   200 miles

MEDIA

No political censorship

PUBLISHING AND BROADCAST MEDIA

There are 400 daily newspapers, including the *Frankfurter Allgemeine Zeitung*, the *Süddeutsche Zeitung* and *Die Welt*

2 state-controlled, 2 independent networks

3 state-controlled networks

Intelsat V1 F1 Astra 1B

Extensive in all main cities

German TV is carefully supervised by the political parties to ensure a balance of views. The main channels, ARD and ZDF, have a reputation for safe programing, but the arrival of satellite and cable TV and competition has begun to make TV more lively. Newspapers are mostly regional and serious. An exception is *Bild Zeitung*, the right-wing, sensationalist tabloid, which sells four million copies daily.

Neuschwanstein Castle, Bayern (Bavaria), one of Germany's major tourist attractions. It was built for the eccentric King Ludwig II.

EDUCATION

99%

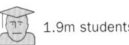
1.9m students

0   Education spending as % GNP   25

4%

THE EDUCATION SYSTEM

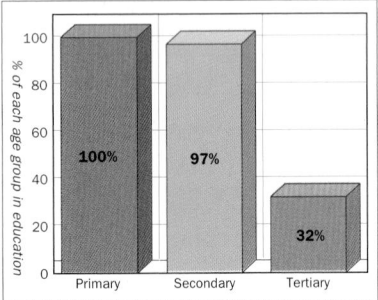

Primary 100%
Secondary 97%
Tertiary 32%

% of each age group in education

Education in Germany is run by the separate *Länder*. They coordinate their teaching policies, but have full autonomy within their own borders. The German approach to education stresses academic efficiency and discipline, with few sporting or cultural activities.

Those who wish to go to university attend the upper-secondary *Gymnasien* to prepare for the essential *Abitur*. Since this set of examinations was made easier, thousands more have exercised their right to attend university, leading to strains on resources. Students frequently take eight years or more to complete their degrees. Research is done as much by companies such as Siemens, as by the universities.

CRIME

52,076 prisoners

Up 18% in 1992

CRIME RATES

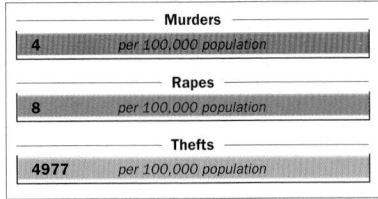

Murders
4   per 100,000 population

Rapes
8   per 100,000 population

Thefts
4977   per 100,000 population

Crime rates in Germany are lower than in most other European countries. This is largely the result of a genuine respect for the law, coupled with a strong police force. Recently, however, rising unemployment has led to an increase in petty theft and a wave of violence, notably against immigrants.

German politics, once with an enviably clean reputation, has suffered several corruption scandals. Civil service corruption remains rare. People convicted under environmental laws will face ten-year jail sentences.

G

REGIONS

BERLIN

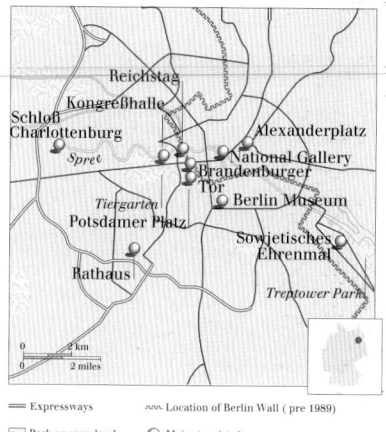

Expressways | ∧∧∧ Location of Berlin Wall (pre 1989)
Park or open land | Major tourist sites

THE PROCESS OF REBUILDING Berlin as the capital of Germany began after reunification in 1990. The transformation of the city is based on planning by an international team of architects led by Norman Foster. Much of Berlin was destroyed during the war. In the Cold War years, it was split into US, UK, French and Soviet occupation zones. The first three were separated from the fourth by the notorious Berlin Wall. Many people were shot trying to cross the Wall to the western sector, which itself was an enclave within East Germany. In 1989, the almost spontaneous demolition of the Berlin Wall became a potent symbol of German reunification.

BADEN-WÜRTTEMBERG

BADEN-WÜRTTEMBERG has a long industrial tradition. It was here that Benz and Daimler invented the motor car. Its capital, Stuttgart, remains home to both Porsche and Daimler-Benz, as well as to Bosch and IBM's main European plants.

Baden-Württemberg is also a center for medium-sized precision manufacturing firms. It has emerged as a center of excellence for new technologies, including robotics and molecular industries. Lothar Späth, prime minister from 1978–1991, was largely responsible for initiatives to establish 30 new research institutes and ten science parks, encouraging links between Stuttgart University and local industry.

Expressways | Park or open land | Major tourist sites
Motor industry | Hi-tech industry | Electronics industry

BAYERN

Expressways | Park or open land | Motor industry
Major tourist sites | Hi-tech industry | Aerospace industry

THE LARGEST OF the *Länder*, Bayern (Bavaria) has a reputation for conservatism. It was one of the *Länder*

to maintain its monarchy until 1918. Catholicism is stronger here than elsewhere in Germany; after a long legal battle in 1995, state schools continue to display crucifixes in their classrooms. Liberal social and sexual habits are still frowned upon in Bayern's rural districts. In its heavily agricultural economy, small farms have suffered as subsidies provided by the EU have become less generous.

Other parts of Bayern's economy are prosperous and it has been developing new high-tech industries. It is often referred to, along with Baden-Württemberg, as Germany's sunbelt. Its major firms – BMW, Siemens and Audi – have also been growing.

Munich, Bayern's capital, is the center for the German fashion, film and advertising industries. Its multipurpose arts center, the *Gasteig*, opened in 1983.

HEALTH

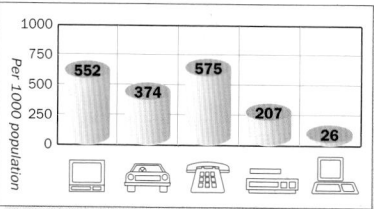

1 per 313 people | Heart and cerebro-vascular diseases, cancers, accidents

Health spending as % GDP
0 — **9.1%** — 25

The German social security system, first pioneered by Bismarck, is one of the most comprehensive in the world. Health insurance is compulsory, and employer and employee contributions are high. Although most hospitals are run by the *Länder*, some are still owned by Germany's wealthy churches.

Germans are increasingly health-conscious, paying great attention to diet. Millions go on cures every year to the country's 200-plus spas. In the east, many are still suffering from lung diseases caused by pollution.

WEALTH

Car mechanic, 18 Deutsche Marks ($13) per hour; government official, 8,314 Deutsche Marks ($5,809) per month

CONSUMER GOODS OWNERSHIP

Per 1000 population
1000 — 750 — 500 — 250 — 0
552 | 374 | 575 | 207 | 26

The effects of the Nazi period, which discredited many of Germany's ruling class, and the destruction of the property of millions of families in the war, account for the relatively classless nature of German society. Status is now more closely linked to wealth than to birth. In the west, disparities are less than in most of Europe; workers are generally well paid and social security is generous. East German wages, however, are still pegged well below western rates, and there are a disproportionate number of unemployed living on welfare benefit.

WORLD RANKING

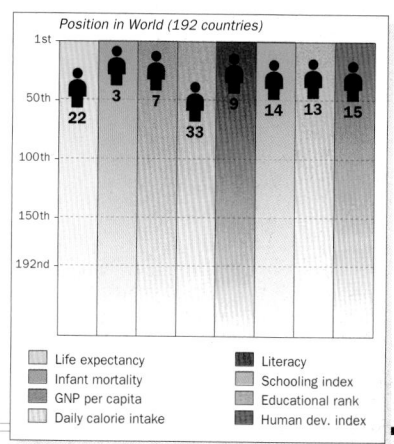

Position in World (192 countries)
1st — 50th — 100th — 150th — 192nd
22 | 3 | 7 | 33 | 9 | 14 | 13 | 15

Life expectancy | Literacy
Infant mortality | Schooling index
GNP per capita | Educational rank
Daily calorie intake | Human dev. index

G

GHANA

WEST AFRICA

OFFICIAL NAME: Republic of Ghana CAPITAL: Accra
POPULATION: 17.5 million CURRENCY: Cedi OFFICIAL LANGUAGE: English

THE HEARTLAND OF THE ancient Ashanti kingdom, modern Ghana is a union of the former British colony of the Gold Coast and the British-administered part of the UN Trust Territory of Togoland. Ghana gained independence in 1957, the first British colony to do so. Its recent history has been one of intermittent military rule; the embracing of multiparty democracy in 1992 confirmed former military leader Jerry Rawlings in power.

G

CLIMATE

WEATHER CHART

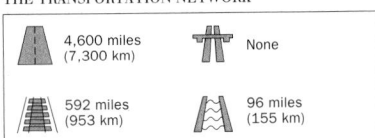

Southern Ghana has two rainy seasons: from April to July and September to November. The drier north has just one, from April to September.

TRANSPORTATION

 Kotoka Intl, Accra
467,000 passengers

 11 ships
83,400 dwt

THE TRANSPORTATION NETWORK

4,600 miles
(7,300 km)

None

592 miles
(953 km)

96 miles
(155 km)

In 1983, work began to restore Ghana's roads, which had fallen into disrepair in the 1960s and 1970s; the network is now improving.

TOURISM

248,000 visitors

Up 6% in 1994

MAIN OVERSEAS ARRIVALS

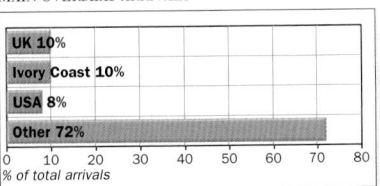

UK 10%								
Ivory Coast 10%								
USA 8%								
Other 72%								

0 10 20 30 40 50 60 70 80
% of total arrivals

Tourism is still small-scale; most visitors come from Africa, the UK and the USA. Good beaches and old coastal forts are the major attractions.

PEOPLE

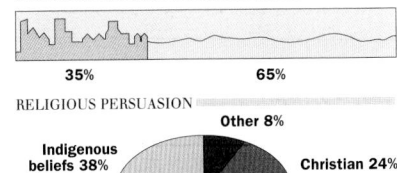

Twi, Fanti, Ewe, Ga, Adangbe, Gurma, Dagomba (Dagbani)

197 people per sq. mile

THE URBAN/RURAL POPULATION SPLIT

35%   65%

RELIGIOUS PERSUASION

Other 8%
Indigenous beliefs 38%
Christian 24%
Muslim 30%

Ghana contains various cultural-linguistic groups. The largest is the Akan, who include the Ashanti and Fanti peoples. Other important groups are the Mole-Dagbani in the north, Ga-Adangbe around Accra and Ewe in the southeast. There are few tribal tensions. Family ties are strong.

POLITICS

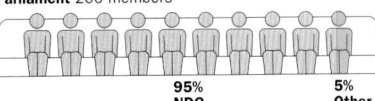

1992/1996

President Jerry Rawlings

THE STATE OF THE PARTIES

Parliament 200 members

95% NDC   5% Other

NDC = National Democratic Congress (closely linked to the former PNDC) Other = National Convention Party, Independent Party, Egle Party

Ghana's return to multiparty rule in 1992 marked the effective legitimization of the military government which had previously resisted the call for greater democracy. Jerry Rawlings, a flight-lieutenant of Ewe–Scottish descent and one of the great survivors of African politics, staged coups in 1979 and 1981, and led the 1981–1992 Provisional National Defense Council (PNDC) military government. Rawlings emerged as a late candidate for the NDC and won 58% of the vote in the 1992 presidential elections. Opposition parties claimed malpractice and refused to contest the parliamentary elections the following month. The NDC swept the board. Opposition is still effectively outside parliament; the difference is that since 1992 political dissent is accepted.

WORLD AFFAIRS

Comm	Ecowas	G24	IAEA	OAU

Good relations with the West, which provides the bulk of Ghana's military and development aid, are a priority. Ghana has played a significant part in UN peacekeeping operations. After Nigeria, it is also the main contributor to the ECOWAS forces (ECOMOG) stationed in war-torn Liberia since 1990. In 1993, the Ghanaian government called unsuccessfully for ECOWAS to intervene to suppress civil unrest in Togo.

GHANA

Total Land Area :
238 540 sq. km (92 100 sq. miles)

LAND HEIGHT

500m/1640ft
200m/656ft
Sea Level

POPULATION

over 500 000
over 100 000
over 50 000
over 10 000
under 10 000

0 100 km
0 100 miles

AID

 $633m (receipts)   Up 1% in 1993

In 1983, the PNDC began a largely successful economic recovery program backed by World Bank and IMF aid. Between 1984 and 1989, Ghana received $3.5 billion, the third-largest recipient of World Bank aid after India and China.

DEFENSE

 $53m   Down 30% in 1995

In 1966, 1972, 1979 and 1981, the military mounted successful coups. There have also been frequent unsuccessful coups, many mounted by disaffected officers against both military and civilian governments. Outside the country, the army has mainly been deployed in UN and ECOWAS operations.

ECONOMICS

 $7.3bn  1,036–1,438 cedis

SCORE CARD

❏ WORLD GNP RANKING	89th
❏ GNP PER CAPITA	$430
❏ BALANCE OF PAYMENTS	$–264m
❏ INFLATION	24.9%
❏ UNEMPLOYMENT	10%

STRENGTHS

Cocoa, the main export crop, is cheap to produce and accounts for 15% of the world total. 1993 gold exports totaled 1 million fine ounces; the main source is the Ashanti goldfields. Bauxite – with some processed alumina – is a major export. Since 1983, economic recovery policies have raised GNP 5% a year.

WEAKNESSES

High budget deficits and debt repayments: the cedi was devalued in 1983 and has since tended to float downward. Foreign investors generally invest solely in gold mining. Many loss-making state enterprises.

EXPORTS

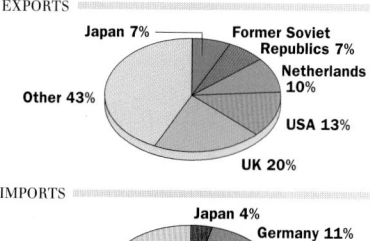

Japan 7% — Former Soviet Republics 7% — Netherlands 10% — USA 13% — UK 20% — Other 43%

IMPORTS

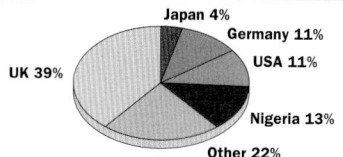

Japan 4% — Germany 11% — USA 11% — UK 39% — Nigeria 13% — Other 22%

Dixcove harbor, close to Ghana's most southerly cape. The majority of Ghanaians lead a traditional subsistence existence.

RESOURCES

 6.1bn kwh (capacity 1.12m kw)   Reserves of 500,000 bbl; refines 26,600 b/cd

 3.3m goats, 3.2m sheep, 1.7m cattle, 595,000 pigs   Gold, diamonds, bauxite, manganese

Over the last ten years, gold production has expanded; in 1993, gold was the major export. Diamonds, bauxite and manganese are also exported. Surplus hydropower from the Volta Dam, completed in the early 1960s, is exported to Togo and Benin.

ENVIRONMENT

 5%   Very low public awareness of ecological issues

Cutting of wood for fuel, timber and farming has destroyed 70% of forests. Mining has devastated the surrounding land and caused serious pollution.

MEDIA

 Self-censorship by press. Overt criticism of government is not tolerated

PUBLISHING AND BROADCAST MEDIA

 There are 3 daily newspapers, the *Ghanaian Times*, the *People's Daily Graphic* and the *Pioneer*

 1 state-controlled service   1 state-controlled service

New independent weeklies reflect the increase in private press ownership. Radio and TV tend to follow government reporting guidelines.

CRIME

 Ghana does not publish prison figures   Up 4% in 1990

The judiciary has little independence and the government often resorts to *ad hoc* "people's tribunals." Corruption is less of a problem than in recent years.

EDUCATION

 61%   9,609 students

All sectors of the education system are over-subscribed. There are a few high-quality boarding schools and four universities.

CHRONOLOGY

Finding the Ashanti uncompliant with their demands, the British sacked Kumasi, their capital, in 1874 and created the Gold Coast colony.

- ❏ **1957** Independence under authoritarian Kwame Nkrumah.
- ❏ **1964** Single-party state.
- ❏ **1966** Economy founders. Bloodless army coup.
- ❏ **1972–1979** Corrupt "kleptocracy" of Gen. Acheampong. Executed 1979.
- ❏ **1979** Flt.-Lt. Jerry Rawlings' coup. Civilian Dr. Limann wins elections.
- ❏ **1981** Rawlings takes power again.
- ❏ **1992** Rawlings' NDC wins elections – boycott by four opposition parties.

G

HEALTH

 1 per 23,000 people   Malaria, diarrheal diseases, tuberculosis

The health of most of the population has benefited more from improvements in public hygiene than improvements in medical care.

WEALTH

 The many Ghanaians who emigrated in search of better jobs remit $300 million a year – a substantial contribution to Ghana's economy

CONSUMER GOODS OWNERSHIP

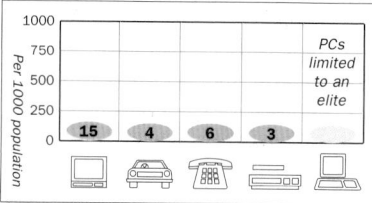

PCs limited to an elite

15   4   6   3

Political uncertainty brought few opportunities for advancement and many Ghanaians emigrated, but the situation is now improving. The key disparity is still between the poorer north and richer, more urban, south.

WORLD RANKING

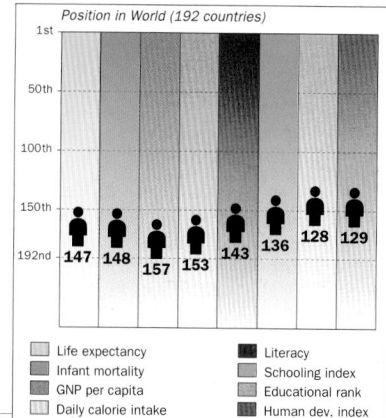

Position in World (192 countries)

147 148 157 153 143 136 128 129

- ☐ Life expectancy
- ☐ Infant mortality
- ☐ GNP per capita
- ☐ Daily calorie intake
- ☐ Literacy
- ☐ Schooling index
- ☐ Educational rank
- ☐ Human dev. index

GREECE

OFFICIAL NAME: Hellenic Republic **CAPITAL:** Athens
POPULATION: 10.5 million **CURRENCY:** Drachma **OFFICIAL LANGUAGE:** Greek

THE SOUTHERNMOST NATION of the Balkans, Greece is surrounded by the Aegean, Ionian and Cretan seas. Its mainly mountainous territory includes over 2,000 islands. Only one-third of the land is cultivated. Greece has a strong seafaring tradition and some of the world's biggest ship-owners. Greece is rich in minerals, including rare minerals like chromium. Greek concern about the potential claim of the Former Yugoslav Republic of Macedonia over the Greek province of Macedonia has recently been overshadowed by the revival of ancient Greek territorial disputes with Turkey.

CLIMATE

WEATHER CHART

The climate varies from region to region. The northwest is alpine, while parts of Crete border on the subtropical. The large central plain experiences high summer temperatures. Water is a problem as many rivers have been diverted underground by earthquakes.

TRANSPORTATION

Athinai, Athens
6.3m passengers

1,407 ships
46.35m dwt

THE TRANSPORTATION NETWORK

17,950 miles (28,890 km)

57 miles (91 km)

1,544 miles (2,484 km)

Corinth Canal

The easiest and cheapest method of transportation between the islands and the mainland is by boat or Russian-built hovercraft. Greece has a total of 444 ports, of which 123 are large enough to handle passenger or freight traffic. Of the 37 civilian airports in Greece, two-thirds are located on the islands and are also used by the military. Although the rail system is undeveloped, an inter-urban bus system and fleet of air-conditioned tourist Pullmans offer a more extensive service. In general, Greece has a good, if increasingly congested, road network; the number of motor vehicles is three million and rising. Piraeus is the country's main port.

TOURISM

10.1m visitors

Up 7% in 1994

MAIN OVERSEAS ARRIVALS

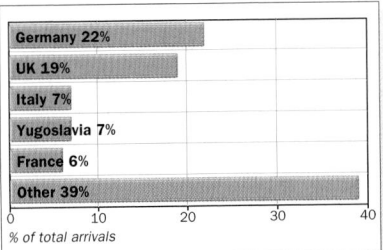

Germany 22%
UK 19%
Italy 7%
Yugoslavia 7%
France 6%
Other 39%

% of total arrivals

Tourism is a mainstay of the Greek economy and a major source of foreign exchange. Until recently, the government gave grants for hotel development. As a result, many third-grade hotels were built, especially on Crete and Rhodes. Smaller islands also tried to encourage tourism, but few have reliable water supplies or enough sandy beaches to attract visitors. Recently, tourism has declined as many people have opted for cheaper holidays elsewhere. The breakup of former Yugoslavia has also deterred visitors. The Greek tourist industry is now trying to encourage visitors by upgrading its image to include sailing and conference tourism. Thessaloníki will be the European City of Culture in 1997.

Roman ruins, Dodona. Classical sites such as this amphitheatre in northwestern Greece, have helped to make tourism one of Greece's most important industries.

PEOPLE

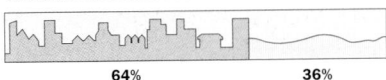

Greek, Turkish, Macedonian, Albanian

207 people per sq. mile

THE URBAN/RURAL POPULATION SPLIT

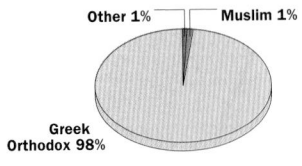

64%   36%

RELIGIOUS PERSUASION

Other 1%   Muslim 1%

Greek Orthodox 98%

ETHNIC MAKEUP

Other 2%

Greek 98%

Greece was for many centuries a largely agrarian and seafaring nation. The German occupation during World War II, and the civil war that followed, destroyed much of the fabric of rural life and there was rapid urbanization after the 1950s. There was also extensive emigration during the 1950s and 1960s to northern Europe, Australia, the USA, Canada and southern Africa. However, many people returned to Greece in the 1980s, putting pressure on the labor market. The socialist PASOK governments of 1981–1989 spent large sums, mostly from EU sources, on developing the infrastructure and business life of the rural regions with a view to halting emigration to the cities. The policy was mostly successful, but over half the population still lives in the capital, Athens, and the main northern city, Thessaloníki.

Christianity is the main religion; 98% of the population belong to the Greek Orthodox Church. Civil marriage and divorce only became legal in 1982. There are small minorities of Muslims, Catholics and Jews.

POPULATION AGE BREAKDOWN

%	☐ 0–14	☐ 15–64		☐ 65+	
65+	8.3%	11.1%	13.1%	13.7%	16.9%
15–64	65.2%	64%	64.1%	66.6%	65.9%
0–14	26.5%	24.9%	22.8%	19.7%	17.2%
	1960	1970	1980	1990	2000

POLITICS

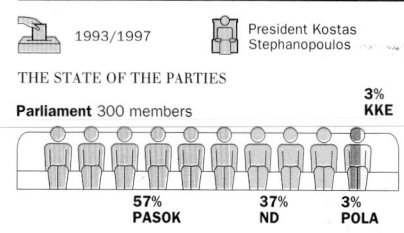

1993/1997

President Kostas Stephanopoulos

THE STATE OF THE PARTIES

Parliament 300 members

57% PASOK **37% ND** **3% POLA** **3% KKE**

PASOK = Panhellenic Socialist Movement **ND** = New Democracy Party **POLA** = Political Spring **KKE** = Communist Party of Greece

Greece is a multiparty democracy. A military government was in power between 1967 and 1974.

MAIN POLITICAL ISSUES
Terrorism
During the 1990s, left-wing groups, notably November 17, staged a number of "anti-capitalist" attacks against US companies and the conservative ND party. A 1990 law banning the publication of the views of alleged terrorists was abolished in 1993.

Relations with Macedonia
In 1995, Greece finally recognized the sovereignty of the Former Yugoslav Republic of Macedonia. The recognition followed an agreement under which Macedonia undertook to remove from its national flag the "Vergina Sun" which was claimed by Greece as a part of its cultural heritage.

Albanian refugees
Large numbers of Albanians of Greek descent have been entering Greece illegally since 1990. Willing to work for very low wages, they have swelled the already thriving black economy. Tough border controls were introduced in 1994, as a result of which more than 30,000 Albanians were said to have been deported.

PROFILE
The 1993 elections returned PASOK to power. Economic realities forced PASOK to continue with the conservative economic policies of the preceding ND government.

Kostas Simitis, prime minister since January 1996.

Andreas Papandreou, former leader of PASOK 1981–1989, 1993–1996.

In early 1996, Andreas Papandreou resigned as prime minister; he was succeeded by Kostas Simitis.

G

WORLD AFFAIRS

EU · NATO · OECD · OSCE · WEU

Throughout the Cold War, Greece was closely allied to the West, although there are strong sympathies between the Greeks, Russians and Serbs because of their shared Orthodox heritage. Greece withdrew from the military command of NATO in 1974 in protest at the failure of the Alliance to prevent the Turkish invasion of Cyprus. It has since rejoined under a formula to negotiate with Turkey new command and control arrangements over the Aegean. These regional security issues, however, remain unresolved.

AID

$44m (receipts) Up 13% in 1993

Greece gives relatively little aid. It is, however, a large net receiver of regional development assistance from the EU. Total EU aid could reach $19 billion by the end of the decade. In particular, it is a major beneficiary of the EU's structural and cohesion funds. The allocation of cohesion funds for Greece are estimated to amount to around $3.5 billion over the 1993–1999 period. Some of the money has been used to reverse the decline of northeast Greece – the EU's least developed region. EU funds make up 70% of a $370 million program to upgrade the region's road network and expand its port facilities.

GREECE

Total Land Area : 130 850 sq. km
(50 521 sq. miles)

POPULATION
- ▣ over 1 000 000
- ⊙ over 500 000
- ◎ over 100 000
- ○ over 50 000
- • over 10 000

LAND HEIGHT
- 2000m/6562ft
- 1000m/3281ft
- 500m/1640ft
- 200m/656ft
- Sea Level

G

CHRONOLOGY

Greece was occupied by Nazi Germany between 1941 and 1944. After liberation by the Allies, communists and royalists fought a five-year civil war. This ended with communist defeat, and King Paul became the constitutional monarch.

- ❑ **1964** King Paul dies. Succeeded by son, King Constantine.
- ❑ **1967** Military coup. King in exile. Colonel Papadopoulos premier.
- ❑ **1973** Greece declared a republic, with Papadopoulos as president. Papadopoulos overthrown in military coup. Lt.-Gen. Ghizikis becomes president with Adamantios Androutsopoulos as prime minister.
- ❑ **1974** Greece leaves NATO in protest at Turkish occupation of northern Cyprus. "Colonels regime" falls. Constantinos Karamanlis becomes premier and his ND party wins subsequent elections.
- ❑ **1975** Konstantinos Tsatsou becomes president.
- ❑ **1977** Elections. ND reelected.
- ❑ **1980** Karamanlis president. Georgios Rallis prime minister. Greece rejoins NATO.
- ❑ **1981** Socialist PASOK party wins elections. Andreas Papandreou first-ever socialist premier. Greek accession to EC.
- ❑ **1985** Proposals to limit power of president. Karamanlis resigns. Christos Sartzetakis president. Greece and Albania re-open borders, closed since 1940.
- ❑ **1985–1989** Civil unrest caused by economic austerity program.
- ❑ **1988** Cabinet implicated in financial scandal. Several leading members resign.
- ❑ **1989** Defense agreement with the USA. After inconclusive elections, Left coalition forms government. Charilaos Florakis president. ND join Left coalition in government. Further election inconclusive. All-party coalition.
- ❑ **1990** Coalition government collapses. ND party wins elections. Mitsotakis prime minister; Karamanlis president.
- ❑ **1990–1992** Strikes against economic reform.
- ❑ **1992** EC persuaded to withhold recognition of Republic of Macedonia (FYRM). Maastricht Treaty on European union ratified.
- ❑ **1993** PASOK wins general election; Andreas Papandreou premier.
- ❑ **1995** Kostas Stephanopoulos elected president; recognition of Macedonian sovereignty.
- ❑ **1996** Andreas Papandreou resigns as prime minister and is succeeded by Kostas Simitis.

DEFENSE

 $3.4bn   ⬆ Up 11% in 1995

0	Defense spending as % GDP	40

5.7%

Greece spends a higher percentage of GDP on defense than any other NATO country. Its main concern is the perceived threat from Turkey. Greece is seeking full membership to the Western European Union, although this is being blocked because of disputes with Turkey.

GREEK ARMED FORCES

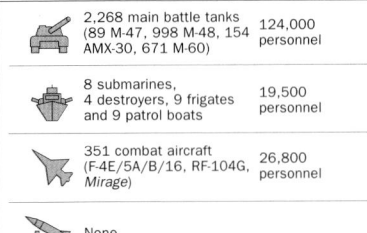

2,268 main battle tanks (89 M-47, 998 M-48, 154 AMX-30, 671 M-60)	124,000 personnel
8 submarines, 4 destroyers, 9 frigates and 9 patrol boats	19,500 personnel
351 combat aircraft (F-4E/5A/B/16, RF-104G, Mirage)	26,800 personnel
None	

ECONOMICS

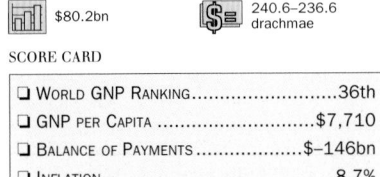 $80.2bn   240.6–236.6 drachmae

SCORE CARD

- ❑ WORLD GNP RANKING.........................36th
- ❑ GNP PER CAPITA $7,710
- ❑ BALANCE OF PAYMENTS..................$–146bn
- ❑ INFLATION 8.7%
- ❑ UNEMPLOYMENT..................................9.6%

EXPORTS

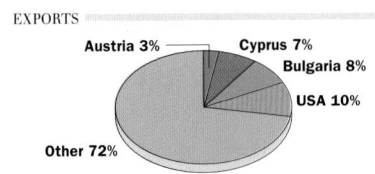

Austria 3%   Cyprus 7%   Bulgaria 8%   USA 10%   Other 72%

IMPORTS

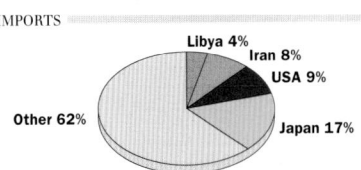

Libya 4%   Iran 8%   USA 9%   Japan 17%   Other 62%

STRENGTHS

One of the major tourist destinations in Europe. Efficient agricultural exporter. Shipping: the world's largest beneficially owned fleet.

WEAKNESSES

High levels of public debt. High interest rates and bureaucratic banking system discourage private initiative. State involved in almost 70% of businesses. High levels of tax evasion. Black economy accounts for 30%–50% of GDP.

PROFILE

Greece took longer than most other northern European countries to recover from World War II, owing to years of civil strife. It was not until the 1960s that any substantial investment occurred. The Colonels' dictatorship curbed inflationary pressures by the introduction of a wage freeze. When civilian government was restored in 1974, a spate of high wage settlements and the oil price shocks of 1973 and 1979 drove inflation

ECONOMIC PERFORMANCE INDICATOR

Consumer price index   GDP

to above 20%, a level at which it hovered for some years. From 1982–1986, Greece's largest companies reported substantial losses. There was a modest return to profitability following the socialists' austerity program of 1986–1987.

In general, the return on capital has persistently been a fraction of the rate of inflation. However, economic reforms in the late 1980s led to a resurgence of interest in the Stock Exchange, which also attracts investment from the black economy.

GREECE : MAJOR BUSINESSES

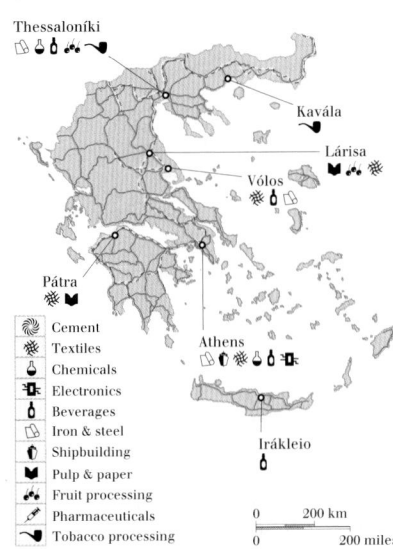

Thessaloníki   Kavála   Lárisa   Vólos   Pátra   Athens   Irákleio

- 🌀 Cement
- ✳ Textiles
- ⚗ Chemicals
- ⚡ Electronics
- 🍶 Beverages
- ⬟ Iron & steel
- ⚓ Shipbuilding
- Ⓜ Pulp & paper
- ⚜ Fruit processing
- ✐ Pharmaceuticals
- Ⓛ Tobacco processing

0		200 km
0		200 miles

RESOURCES

 37bn kwh (capacity 8.5m kw)
 13,092 b/d (reserves 41,000,000 bbl)
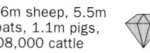 9.6m sheep, 5.5m goats, 1.1m pigs, 608,000 cattle
 Coal, iron, bauxite, marble, nickel, magnesite

ELECTRICITY GENERATION

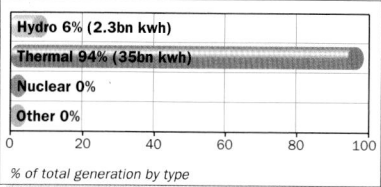

Hydro 6% (2.3bn kwh)
Thermal 94% (35bn kwh)
Nuclear 0%
Other 0%

% of total generation by type

Greece has an oil and gas field off the coast of Thásos island. Reserves may be available in its eastern waters, ownership of which is contested by Turkey. Coal, iron and other mining contributes less than 2% to GDP. Greece is a leading producer of marble.

ENVIRONMENT

 1.7% (0.2% partially protected)
 Economic growth has precedence over ecological concerns

ENVIRONMENTAL TREATIES

Yes / Yes / Yes / Yes / Yes / Yes

Local fishing interests have formed a highly successful anti-pollution organization known as *Helmepa*. Athens is plagued with smog known as *nefos*, which is irritating to the eyes and throat. It is also highly damaging to Greece's ancient monuments. The Parthenon in Athens has suffered more erosion in the last two decades than in the previous 2,000 years.

MEDIA

 The press are free from government interference; however, the state broadcasting services are under strong government control

PUBLISHING AND BROADCAST MEDIA

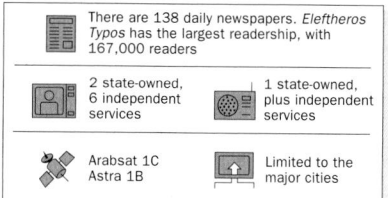

There are 138 daily newspapers. *Eleftheros Typos* has the largest readership, with 167,000 readers

2 state-owned, 6 independent services
1 state-owned, plus independent services
Arabsat 1C Astra 1B
Limited to the major cities

The state had a monopoly on radio and TV until 1989. Commercial broadcasting has made politicians far more answerable to the electorate than ever before. It has also had a cultural impact with the import of more foreign, particularly US, programing. There are eight legal TV networks and many pirate stations.

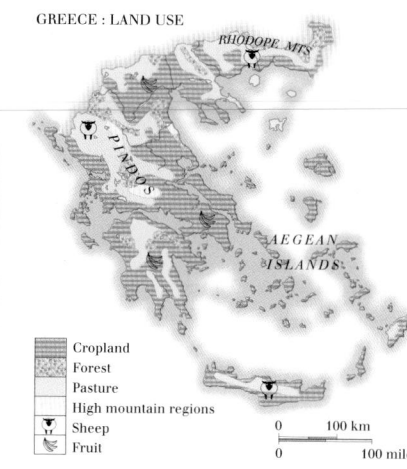
GREECE : LAND USE

RHODOPE MTS
PINDOS
AEGEAN ISLANDS

Cropland
Forest
Pasture
High mountain regions
Sheep
Fruit

0   100 km
0   100 miles

CRIME

 5,008 prisoners   Up 3% in 1992

CRIME RATES

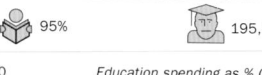

Murders — 2 per 100,000 population
Rapes — 2 per 100,000 population
Thefts — 534 per 100,000 population

An influx of refugees from eastern Europe, North Africa and the Far East has seen an increase in violent crime. The terrorist group November 17 has assassinated wealthy citizens.

EDUCATION

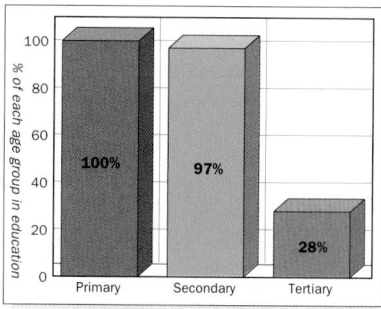 95%   195,213 students

0   Education spending as % GNP   25
3.1%

THE EDUCATION SYSTEM

% of each age group in education
Primary 100%
Secondary 97%
Tertiary 28%

Teachers are poorly paid and qualifications are low. University places are limited and many students go abroad for tertiary education. Technical courses, funded by the EU, have increased since the 1990s.

HEALTH

 1 per 263 people   Heart and cerebrovascular diseases, cancers

0   Health spending as % GDP   25
4.8%

The socialists (PASOK) introduced a National Health Service and a national pharmaceuticals industry. However, the service is short of staff and families have to perform many of the services normally expected of nurses. The New Democracy (ND) government tried to upgrade private medicine and incorporate its activities with those in state hospitals. Many Greeks requiring major surgery travel to Germany, Switzerland or the UK for treatment.

WEALTH

 Teacher, 120,000 drachmas ($500) per month; doctor, 230,000 drachmas ($970) per month

CONSUMER GOODS OWNERSHIP

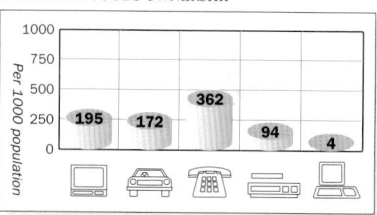
Per 1000 population: 195, 172, 362, 94, 4

Greek society changed dramatically in the postwar period. Formerly a largely isolated agricultural community, rapid urbanization in the 1950s led to many former agricultural workers making fortunes. Many grabbed opportunities presented by the shipping industry. Among these were the prominent Niarchos and Onassis families.

The advent of the republic in 1973 reflected social changes which had occurred since the war. New wealth and success became more admired than aristocratic birth or prestige. Greece is now a socially mobile society. Living standards have improved throughout society since the 1950s.

WORLD RANKING

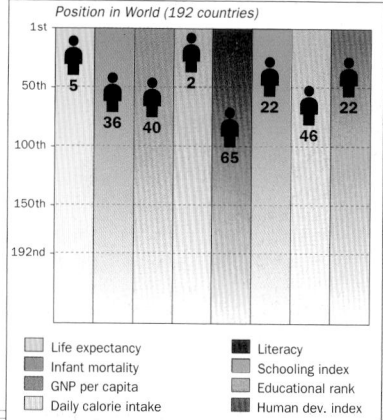
Position in World (192 countries)
5, 36, 40, 2, 65, 22, 46, 22

Life expectancy / Literacy
Infant mortality / Schooling index
GNP per capita / Educational rank
Daily calorie intake / Human dev. index

G

GRENADA

OFFICIAL NAME: Grenada **CAPITAL:** St. George's
POPULATION: 92,000 **CURRENCY:** East Caribbean dollar **OFFICIAL LANGUAGE:** English

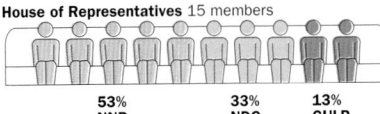

THE MOST SOUTHERLY of the Windward Islands, Grenada also includes the islands of Carriacou and Petite Martinique. It is the world's second-largest nutmeg producer. Grenada became a focus of attention in 1983 when the USA, with token backing from several Caribbean states, mounted an invasion to sever its growing links with Castro's Cuba. Grenada is discussing a political union with St. Lucia, Dominica, and St. Vincent and the Grenadines.

CLIMATE

WEATHER CHART

■ Average daily temperature   Rainfall ▬

Annual rainfall ranges from 59 in. on the coast to 117 inches in the mountains. Hurricanes occur in the rainy season.

TRANSPORTATION

Point Salines, St. George's 206,000 passengers

Has no fleet

THE TRANSPORTATION NETWORK

372 miles (600 km)		None	
None		None	

Mountain roads are frequently washed away in the rains. US aid helped to finance the international airport.

TOURISM

317,645 visitors   Up 6% in 1995

MAIN OVERSEAS ARRIVALS

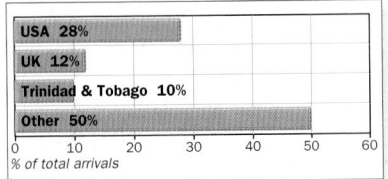

USA 28%
UK 12%
Trinidad & Tobago 10%
Other 50%

% of total arrivals

Tourism has developed since the restoration of democracy and the completion of the international airport in 1984. Large resort projects have caused serious beach erosion, in turn requiring costly coastal defenses.

PEOPLE

English, English Creole

705 people per sq. mile

THE URBAN/RURAL POPULATION SPLIT

17%   83%

RELIGIOUS PERSUASION

Other 15%
Anglican 17%
Roman Catholic 68%

Most Grenadians are descendants of Africans, brought over to work sugar plantations between the 16th and 19th centuries. Intermarriage between this group and the small numbers of Europeans and indigenous Indians has meant that there is little racial tension. As in other Caribbean states, extended families with absentee fathers are not uncommon.

GRENADA

Total Land Area : 340 sq. km (131 sq. miles)

POPULATION
● over 10 000
• under 10 000

LAND HEIGHT
500m/1640ft
200m/656ft
Sea Level

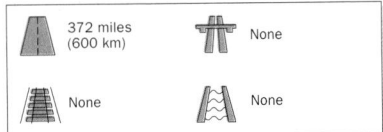

POLITICS

1995/2000   H.M. Queen Elizabeth II

THE STATE OF THE PARTIES

House of Representatives 15 members

53% NNP   33% NDC   13% GULP

NNP = New National Party **NDC** = National Democratic Congress **GULP** = Grenada United Labor Party

House of Chiefs 13 members

10 members chosen by the prime minister (3 after consulting various interests) and 3 by the leader of the opposition

The past 20 years have seen Grenada move toward a position of political isolation to integration with the rest of the region. Former prime minister Sir. Eric Gairy was as well known for his eccentric requests to the UN Security Council – he once asked it to investigate UFOs on the island – as for his intimidation of political opponents with organized gangs. Gairy was overthrown in 1979 by armed militants of the New Jewel Movement led by Maurice Bishop, a charismatic socialist who in turn was deposed and executed by former allies in 1983. This coup was the pretext for the US invasion, the primary motive of which was to end the perceived Cuban influence in Grenada. A new government was elected in 1984 and the US provided large amounts of aid. Politics has since been center-right and ideologically there is little to choose between the four main parties, the latest elected being the New National Party, led by Keith Mitchell, in 1995. The dominant political issue is the proposed federation between Grenada and its neighbors in the Windward Islands: St. Lucia, Dominica, and St. Vincent and the Grenadines.

WORLD AFFAIRS

ACS · Caricom · NAM · OAS · OECS

Priorities are the proposed federation with the rest of the Windward Islands group, preferential access to the EU for bananas and strategies with Indonesia aimed at steadying world nutmeg prices. Since 1983, US policy in the Caribbean has been supported.

AID

 $9m (receipts)　 Down 25% in 1993

The main aid sources are the UK, the EU, the USA and Japan. Cuba, before the 1983 invasion, helped build the airport at Point Salines.

DEFENSE

 Minimal receipts　 Defense spending is falling

The People's Revolutionary Army, created by Maurice Bishop in the wake of his 1979 coup, was replaced in 1983 by a paramilitary defense unit trained by the USA and the UK.

ECONOMICS

 $241m　 2.70 East Caribbean dollars

SCORE CARD

- ❏ WORLD GNP RANKING.....................179th
- ❏ GNP PER CAPITA $2,620
- ❏ BALANCE OF PAYMENTS.....................$–33m
- ❏ INFLATION 2.6%
- ❏ UNEMPLOYMENT.................................25%

STRENGTHS
Second largest producer of nutmeg after Indonesia, with 23% of the world market. Important sectors are tourism, bananas, financial services.

WEAKNESSES
Weak tax base, opposition to privatizations, lack of diversification. Labor productivity levels are the lowest in the East Caribbean.

EXPORTS

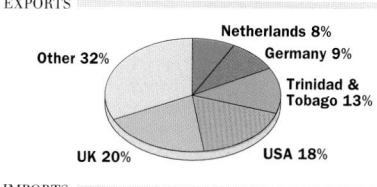
Netherlands 8%
Germany 9%
Trinidad & Tobago 13%
USA 18%
UK 20%
Other 32%

IMPORTS

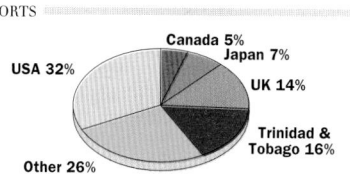
Canada 5%
Japan 7%
UK 14%
Trinidad & Tobago 16%
Other 26%
USA 32%

RESOURCES

 62m kwh (capacity 9,000 kw)　 2,000 tons

 12,000 sheep, 3,000 pigs, 11,000 goats, 4,000 cattle　None

Grenada has no strategic resources and has to import most of its energy. Its major asset is the nutmeg industry, which accounts for almost one-quarter of total world production.

ENVIRONMENT

 None　 National parks legislation still inadequate

The government has recently become aware of the potential value of ecotourism, but has failed to protect some key environmental sites. The best remnant of rainforest, near Epping Forest, has not been included within an ecological protection zone.

MEDIA

 Freedom of expression guaranteed under the constitution. Little government censorship

PUBLISHING AND BROADCAST MEDIA

 There are no daily newspapers. The *Grenadian Voice* and the *Grenada Guardian* are published weekly

 1 state-owned service　 1 state-owned station

The press in Grenada is privately owned and is free from overt political interference.

CRIME

 Grenada does not publish prison figures　 Rising

The doubling of poverty over the last eight years and a marked increase in unemployment are associated with a rise in the crime rate. Narcotics-trafficking in particular is a growing problem.

EDUCATION

 98%　 535 students

Education follows the former British selective 11-plus system. Most students go on to the University of the West Indies, or to college in the USA.

HEALTH

 1 per 1,693 people　 Heart diseases, cancers, nutritional disorders

After Maurice Bishop's takeover in 1979, Cuban physicians provided a basic health care system, which did not include any dental treatment. Subsidized state hospitals now cover most areas fairly efficiently, matching the Caribbean average.

St. George's Harbor. The newest hotel developments are on the beaches to the south of the capital.

CHRONOLOGY

A French colony from 1650, Grenada was captured by the British in 1762.

- ❏ **1951** Universal suffrage introduced.
- ❏ **1967** Internal self-government. Labour Party wins elections and campaigns for independence. Eric Gairy prime minister
- ❏ **1974** Full independence from UK.
- ❏ **1979** Coup. Maurice Bishop prime minister. Growing links with Cuba.
- ❏ **1983–84** US invasion establishes pro-US administration.

WEALTH

 The disparities which existed between a few rich farmers and the majority of laborers have been reduced

CONSUMER GOODS OWNERSHIP

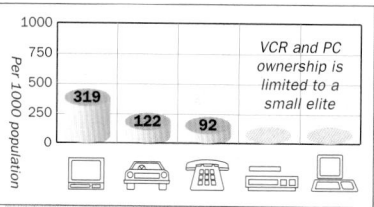
VCR and PC ownership is limited to a small elite
Per 1000 population
1000
750
500
319
250
122
92
0

Wealth disparities on Grenada are less marked than in most Caribbean states. The wealthiest groups control the nutmeg trade.

WORLD RANKING

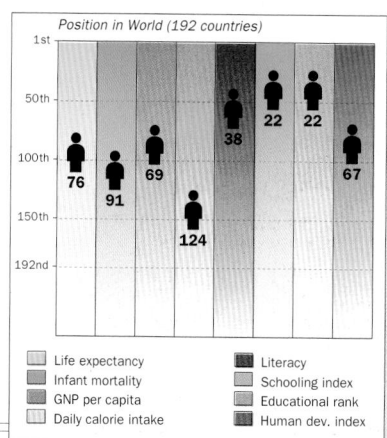
Position in World (192 countries)
1st
50th
22　22
38
100th
76　69　67
91
124
150th
192nd

- Life expectancy
- Infant mortality
- GNP per capita
- Daily calorie intake
- Literacy
- Schooling index
- Educational rank
- Human dev. index

G

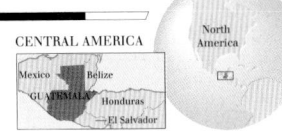
CENTRAL AMERICA

GUATEMALA

OFFICIAL NAME: Republic of Guatemala   CAPITAL: Guatemala City
POPULATION: 10.6 million   CURRENCY: Quetzal   OFFICIAL LANGUAGE: Spanish

L ARGEST AND MOST POPULOUS of the states of the
Central American isthmus, Guatemala was home to
the ancient Maya civilization. Its fertile Pacific and Caribbean coastal
lowlands give way to the highlands which dominate the country.
Independent since 1838, Guatemala's history since 1954 has been one
of military rule. Civilian rule returned in 1986, but 90% of people still
live below the poverty line.

G

CLIMATE

WEATHER CHART

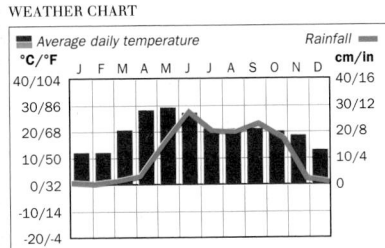

The climate varies with altitude.
Daytime temperatures average 82°F in
the tropical coastal regions and 68°F in
the more temperate central highlands.

TRANSPORTATION

 La Aurora, Guatemala City
939,000 passengers

 Has no fleet

THE TRANSPORTATION NETWORK

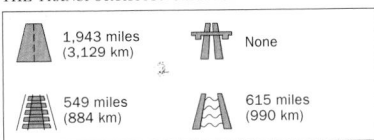

| 1,943 miles (3,129 km) | None |
| 549 miles (884 km) | 615 miles (990 km) |

Good roads link the towns, but volcanic
ash surfaces elsewhere are difficult in
the wet. There are almost 400 airstrips.

TOURISM

 537,000 visitors

 Down 4% in 1994

MAIN OVERSEAS ARRIVALS

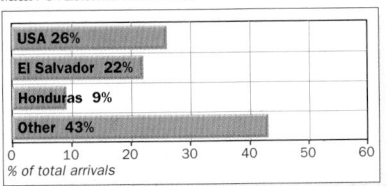

| USA 26% |
| El Salvador 22% |
| Honduras 9% |
| Other 43% |

% of total arrivals

Tourism rapidly revived after the
military excesses in the 1980s but dipped
in 1994–1995 following general instability
and attacks on foreigners. The Maya
ruins are the top attractions.

PEOPLE

Quiché, Mam, Cakchiquel,
Kekchí, Spanish

255 people
per sq. mile

THE URBAN/RURAL POPULATION SPLIT

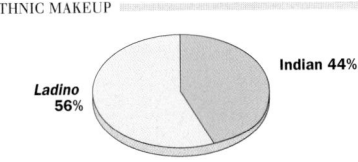

40%   60%

ETHNIC MAKEUP

Ladino 56%   Indian 44%

About 44% of Guatemalans are Indians,
descendants of the founders of the
Maya civilization. Culture and language
distinguish them from *ladino*, non-
Indian, groups. *Ladinos* include a white
elite, a large mixed race group, and
now also Indians who have rejected
traditional dress and language
to escape oppression and
marginalization. Political power
and 65% of land are in
the hands of a few *ladino*
families. Indians mainly
live in the highlands,
by subsistence farming.
Women are legally as
well as traditionally
discriminated against.

GUATEMALA

Total Land Area : 108 430 sq. km
(41 865 sq. miles)

POPULATION
☐ over 1 000 000
◎ over 100 000
○ over 50 000
• over 10 000

LAND HEIGHT
3000m/9843ft
2000m/6562ft
1000m/3281ft
500m/1640ft
200m/656ft
Sea Level

POLITICS

 1995/1999

 President Alvaro
Arzú Irigoyen

THE STATE OF THE PARTIES

National Congress 80 members

| 53% PAN | 26% FRG | 6% FNDG | 15% Other |

PAN = National Advancement Party   FRG = Guatemalan
Republican Front   FNDG = Guatemalan Democratic Front

In 1954, the military, with US-backing,
toppled a democratic government
pledged to land and social reforms. Its
32-year rule was based on the violent
suppression of all opposition. The huge
increase in death-squad murders and
the scorched-earth campaigns against
highland Indians from 1979 to 1984
led to the suspension of US support.
International criticism and the wishes
of moderate army factions helped bring
back civilian rule in 1986. President
Serrano's attempted "self coup" in 1993
was defeated by a combination of
popular resistance and military
hesitancy. His successor, former human
rights ombudsman Ramiro de León
Carpio, relied on the military and did
little to initiate reforms. President Arzú,
inaugurated in January 1996, promises
national reconciliation.

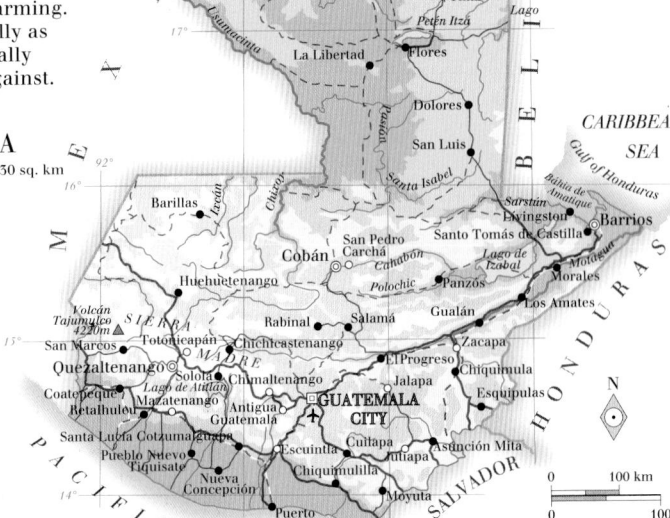

CARIBBEAN SEA

PACIFIC OCEAN

WORLD AFFAIRS

Relations with the USA and regional integration are priorities, as is the honoring of a 1991 accord renouncing a claim to Belize.

AID

 $212m (receipts)　　 Up 1% in 1993

The USA was the major donor in the 1980s, but human rights concerns and changing policy in the region have led to cuts in military and economic aid in the 1990s. A 1995 IMF stamp of approval opened the way for increased aid.

DEFENSE

 $120m　　 Up 9% in 1993

The army acts with near impunity and its latest massacre of peasants in October 1995 forced the Defense Minister to resign. Death squads also operate. The URNG guerrillas have been the main armed opposition since the 1980s.

ECONOMICS

 $12.2bn　　 5.61–5.95 quetzales

SCORE CARD

- ❑ WORLD GNP RANKING..........................75th
- ❑ GNP PER CAPITA $1,190
- ❑ BALANCE OF PAYMENTS....................$–625m
- ❑ INFLATION 10.9%
- ❑ UNEMPLOYMENT.................................5.5%

STRENGTHS

Central America's largest economy. Agriculture key sector. Coffee, sugar, bananas, beef, cardamom top exports.

WEAKNESSES

Low GDP growth and investment. Persistent trade deficit. Extreme inequalities in land and wealth distribution limit domestic market and agriculture modernization.

EXPORTS

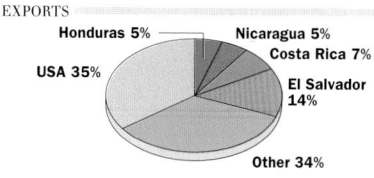

Honduras 5%　Nicaragua 5%
USA 35%　Costa Rica 7%
El Salvador 14%
Other 34%

IMPORTS

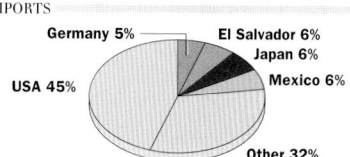

Germany 5%　El Salvador 6%
Japan 6%
USA 45%　Mexico 6%
Other 32%

North Acropolis, Tikal, Petén. *One of the largest lowland Maya cities, Tikal was virtually abandoned by about AD 900.*

RESOURCES

 2.3bn kwh (capacity 700,000 kw)　 6,135 b/d (reserves of 27,000,000 bbl)

2.2m cattle, 720,000 pigs, 440,000 sheep　　Oil, antimony, lead, tungsten, nickel, copper

Agriculture provides 25% of GDP and about 70% of export earnings. Guerrilla activity has hindered exploitation of oil reserves. Chixoy hydroplant generates 65% of power but was closed by low rainfall during during the early 1990s.

ENVIRONMENT

 8% (0.5% partially protected)　 Environmental laws have been enacted but had little effect

Guatemala means "land of trees," but its rich biodiversity is endangered. Forest cover has been halved to 35% since 1954. The quetzal, the national bird, is one of 133 near-extinct species. Urban pollution and erosion are problems.

MEDIA

 The media is ostensibly free, but journalists are still subjected to beatings and death threats, despite the return to civilian rule

PUBLISHING AND BROADCAST MEDIA

 There are 8 daily newspapers, including *Prensa Libre, Siglo Veintiuno, El Gráfico* and the state *Diario de Centroamerica*

1 state-owned, 4 independent stations　　 5 state-owned, 140 independent stations

Intimidation, coupled with low pay, explain the lack of critical and investigative reporting of both human rights abuses and the government.

CRIME

 Guatemala does not publish prison figures　 All types of crime are increasing

A rapid escalation in violent crime is overshadowing concern, locally, about continuing human rights abuses.

EDUCATION

 54%　　 51,860 students

The capital takes 70% of an education budget of under 2% of GDP. As a result, Guatemala has 75% rural illiteracy, the worst record in Latin America.

G

HEALTH

 1 per 2,270 people　　Heart disease, violence, tuberculosis, accidents

Mortality rates are the highest, while health spending is the lowest, in Central America; 70% of funding goes to the capital, where 80% of doctors work. Most deaths are poverty linked.

WEALTH

 The majority of the population lives a subsistence existence

CONSUMER GOODS OWNERSHIP

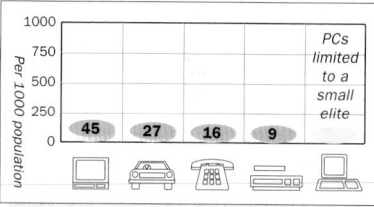

PCs limited to a small elite

45　27　16　9

Poverty has risen since 1980: 90% now live below the poverty line. The rich 10% control 45% of national wealth.

WORLD RANKING

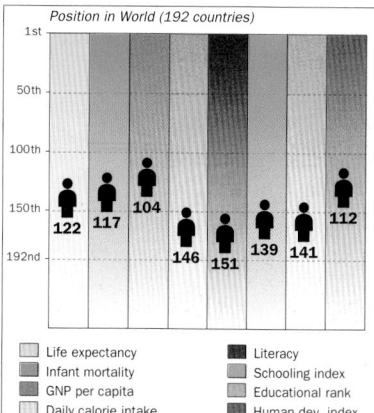

Position in World (192 countries)

122　117　104　146　151　139　141　112

- ☐ Life expectancy
- ☐ Infant mortality
- ☐ GNP per capita
- ☐ Daily calorie intake
- ■ Literacy
- ☐ Schooling index
- ☐ Educational rank
- ■ Human dev. index

GUINEA

OFFICIAL NAME: Republic of Guinea **CAPITAL:** Conakry
POPULATION: 6.7 million **CURRENCY:** Guinea franc **OFFICIAL LANGUAGE:** French

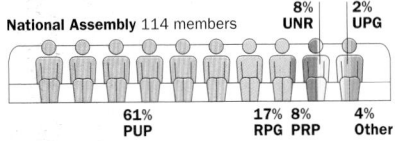

WEST AFRICA   Africa

 1958

GUINEA LIES ON the western coast of Africa. Coastal plains and swamps in the west rise to densely forested or savanna highlands before sloping down to the semi-desert of the north. Military rule, established in 1984, ended with legislative elections in 1995; however, the results were disputed.

CLIMATE

WEATHER CHART

Conakry, Guinea's capital, receives particularly heavy rainfall, with an average of 51 inches in July alone

130/51

■ Average daily temperature   Rainfall ▬
°C/°F   cm/in

Guinea's climate is similar to that of Sierra Leone; the rainy season lasts from April to September.

TRANSPORTATION

 Conakry-Gbessia    1 ship
100 dwt

THE TRANSPORTATION NETWORK

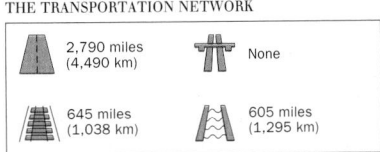

2,790 miles (4,490 km)	None
645 miles (1,038 km)	605 miles (1,295 km)

Major roads and rail lines are being rebuilt with World Bank and French aid. Much of the rail network is exclusively for the use of the bauxite industry.

A small mosque in Conakry. *Muslims make up 85% of the population; 8% are Christian. The remainder follow traditional beliefs.*

TOURISM

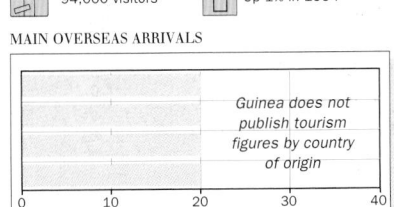 94,000 visitors   ⬆ Up 1% in 1994

MAIN OVERSEAS ARRIVALS

Guinea does not publish tourism figures by country of origin

% of total arrivals

Limited infrastructure means that Guinea cannot exploit the tourist potential of its beaches, scenery and rich culture.

PEOPLE

 Fulani, Malinke, Soussou, French   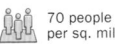 70 people per sq. mile

THE URBAN/RURAL POPULATION SPLIT

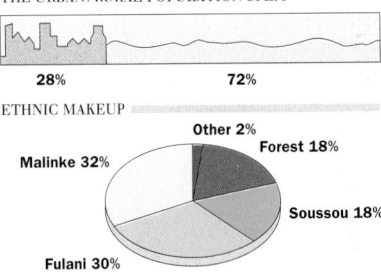

28%   72%

ETHNIC MAKEUP

- Other 2%
- Forest 18%
- Soussou 18%
- Fulani 30%
- Malinke 32%

Guinea has a population of almost seven million people consisting of a number of ethnic groups. Since 1984, and the death of the Marxist dictator Sekou Touré, traditional rivalries have re-emerged. The largest ethnic group, the Malinke, lost the power they held under Touré, and have suffered reprisals. Today, the coastal peoples, including the Soussou, are dominant, benefiting from renewed rivalry between the two major groups – Malinke and Fulani, the latter based in the western highland region of Fouta Djallon.

Daily life in Guinea revolves around the extended family, which survived the climate of suspicion generated by paid informers under Touré. Women acquired influence within Touré's Marxist party, but a Muslim revival since 1984 has reversed this trend.

POLITICS

 1995/2000   President Maj.-Gen. Lansana Conté

THE STATE OF THE PARTIES

National Assembly 114 members   8% UNR   2% UPG

61% PUP   17% RPG   8% PRP   4% Other

PUP = Party of Unity and Progress **RG** = Rally of the Guinean People **PRP** = Party of Renewal and Progress
UNR = Union for the New Republic **UPG** = Union for the Prosperity of Guinea

There has been a fragile start to multiparty democracy. In 1984, Sekou Touré died, having headed the Marxist single-party regime of the Guinea Democratic Party since 1958. This opened the way for the military to intervene, with promises of multiparty elections to come. In 1990, a referendum overwhelmingly approved the changes, but the military appointed a Transitional Committee to run the country.

When presidential elections were finally held in late 1993, the incumbent, Gen. Lansana Conté, won with 52% of the votes. His closest rival, the Malinke leader Alpha Condé received 20% of the votes. This was contested by opposition parties, which alleged the elections had been rigged. Serious violence broke out after the result was announced. The results of legislative elections in 1995, which gave Condé's PUP victory, were also disputed by opposition parties who claimed there had been substantial malpractice.

WORLD AFFAIRS

 Ecowas   Franc   OAU OIC  OMVG

Guinea is an important financial backer of ECOWAS and contributes to its multinational force in neighboring Liberia. A growing concern is balancing the interests of its two major aid donors, France and the USA.

AID

 $414m (receipts)   Down 11% in 1993

In 1969, the World Bank funded the Boké bauxite project, one of its most ambitious projects at that time. Western aid dried up during the Touré years but, since 1986, it has returned in full force, now financing more than 85% of all Guinea's development projects.

G

GUINEA

Total Land Area :
245 860 sq. km
(94 926 sq. miles)

POPULATION

 over 500 000
○ over 50 000
● over 10 000
· under 10 000

LAND HEIGHT

1000m/3281ft
500m/1640ft
200m/656ft
Sea Level

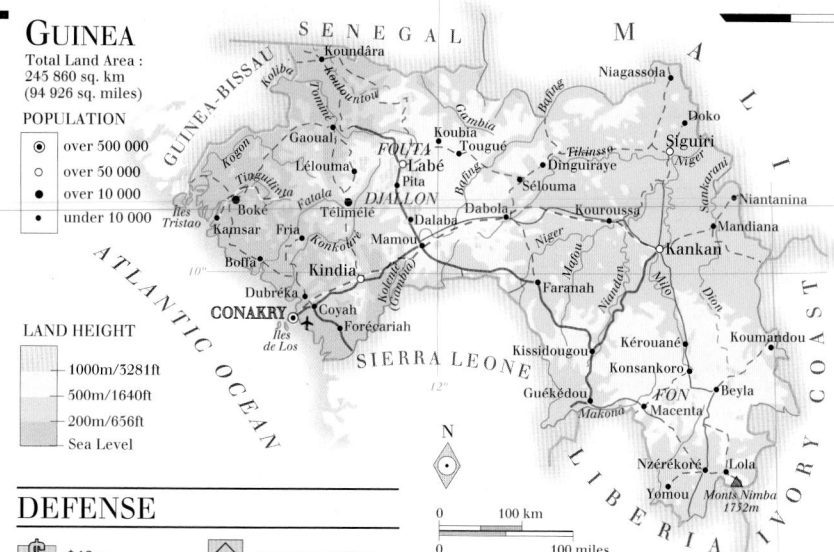

G

CHRONOLOGY

France made Guinea a colony in 1890, strongly opposed by the Fulani Muslim empire of Fouta Djallon.

- ❑ **1958** Full independence under Sekou Touré. France ends support.
- ❑ **1984** Touré dies. Army coup.
- ❑ **1993** Disputed presidential elections.
- ❑ **1995** Multiparty legislative elections ushering in civilian rule.

DEFENSE

 $43m

 No change in 1995

Defense forces consist of an 8,500-strong army and 7,000-strong militia, which have been partly merged since the 1984 coup. China, North Korea and the Eastern bloc used to be the main arms procurement markets. Most weaponry is now supplied by France and the USA.

ECONOMICS

 $3.3bn

997.00– 1,001 Guinea francs

SCORE CARD

❑ WORLD GNP RANKING	118th
❑ GNP PER CAPITA	$510
❑ BALANCE OF PAYMENTS	$65m
❑ INFLATION	4.1%
❑ UNEMPLOYMENT	Widespread underemployment

STRENGTHS

Wide range of natural resources, including bauxite, gold, diamonds. Major iron ore deposits at Mount Nimba. Good soil and climate lead to high cash-crop yields and allow Guinea the prospect of self-sufficiency in food.

WEAKNESSES

Years of confused state control under Touré make IMF and World Bank reforms hard to implement. Limited and antiquated infrastructures.

EXPORTS

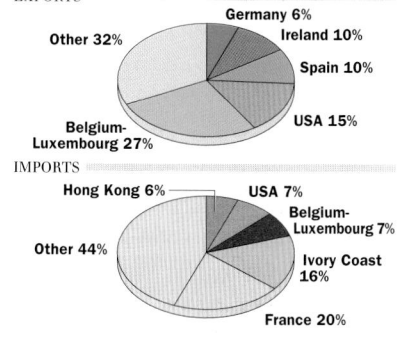

Other 32%
Germany 6%
Ireland 10%
Spain 10%
USA 15%
Belgium-Luxembourg 27%

IMPORTS

Hong Kong 6%
USA 7%
Belgium-Luxembourg 7%
Ivory Coast 16%
Other 44%
France 20%

RESOURCES

 531m kwh (capacity 176,000 kw)

1.7m cattle, 435,000 sheep, 33,000 pigs

 40,000 tons

Bauxite, diamonds, gold, iron

Bauxite accounts for over 90% of export earnings. Guinea, with 30% of known world reserves, is the world's largest producer after Australia. Demand for electricity for bauxite processing is high. Aid from former Yugoslavia funded the dam on the Bafing River.

ENVIRONMENT

 0.7%

 Droughts, as in 1973 and 1983, seriously affect savanna areas

Uncontrolled deforestation, particularly of rainforest areas, is the major long-term problem.

MEDIA

 Although there has been a relaxation of strict censorship, political parties are still communicating through pamphlets

PUBLISHING AND BROADCAST MEDIA

There is 1 daily newspaper, *Fonike*

1 state-owned service

1 state-owned service

For a country of almost seven million, Guinea has limited media. There has been a relaxation in censorship. *Horoya*, the main newspaper, is a weekly.

CRIME

 Guinea does not publish prison figures

 Up 20% in 1992

The state's human rights record has not improved since 1984 and there has been an increase in political violence. Diamond smuggling is commonplace.

EDUCATION

 33%

 5,923 students

French was readopted as the main teaching language in 1984, after Touré's decolonizing teaching experiments.

HEALTH

 1 per 11,650 people

 Malaria, diarrheal and respiratory diseases, tuberculosis

Health provision is very poor, reflected in an infant mortality rate of 132 per 1,000 live births and an average life expectancy of 45 years.

WEALTH

 Manual worker, 150,000 Guinea francs ($150) per month; secretary, 300,000 Guinea francs ($300) per month

CONSUMER GOODS OWNERSHIP

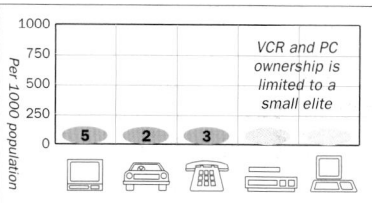

VCR and PC ownership is limited to a small elite

Per 1000 population

5   2   3

Poverty is endemic, but private enterprise has brought with it a new business class and some wealthy exiles. French and American canned foods are highly favored by the well-off.

WORLD RANKING

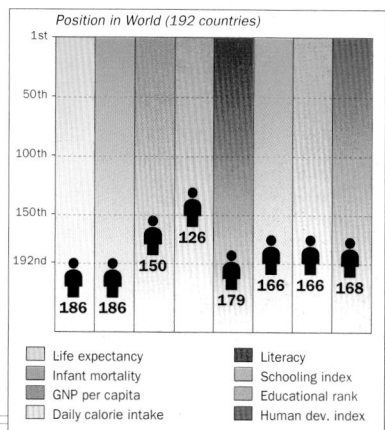

Position in World (192 countries)

186 186 150 126 179 166 166 168

Life expectancy
Infant mortality
GNP per capita
Daily calorie intake
Literacy
Schooling index
Educational rank
Human dev. index

GUINEA-BISSAU

OFFICIAL NAME: Republic of Guinea-Bissau **CAPITAL:** Bissau
POPULATION: 1.1 million **CURRENCY:** Guinea peso **OFFICIAL LANGUAGE:** Portuguese

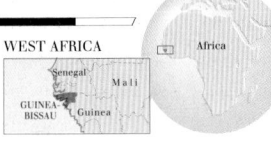

WEST AFRICA

LYING ON AFRICA'S west coast, Guinea-Bissau is bordered by Senegal to the north and Guinea to the south and east. Apart from savanna highlands in the northeast, the country is low-lying. In 1974, it was the first Portuguese colony to gain independence. The ruling PAIGC initiated a process of change to multiparty democracy in 1990, as a result of which elections were held in 1994. Guinea-Bissau is one of the world's poorest countries.

CLIMATE

WEATHER CHART

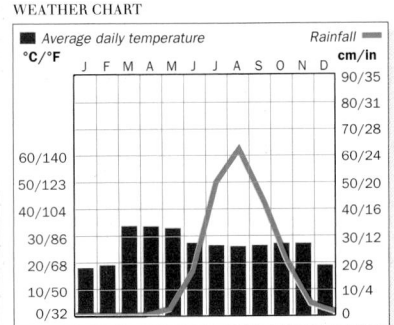

The climate is tropical. The north is affected by the Sahel, the wetter south by the Atlantic. Droughts can occur.

TRANSPORTATION

Bissalanca International, Bissau

Has no fleet

THE TRANSPORTATION NETWORK

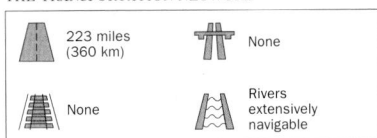

223 miles (360 km)	None
None	Rivers extensively navigable

The many rivers and estuaries mean water transportation is as important as the roads. Both are being improved.

TOURISM

A small number of visitors

No significant change from year to year

MAIN OVERSEAS ARRIVALS

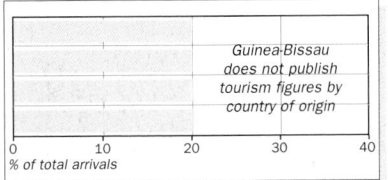

Guinea-Bissau does not publish tourism figures by country of origin

% of total arrivals

Guinea-Bissau's lack of tourist facilities means it remains a destination for only the most independent of travelers.

PEOPLE

Portuguese Creole, Balante, Fulani, Malinke, Portuguese

102 people per sq. mile

THE URBAN/RURAL POPULATION SPLIT

21%   79%

RELIGIOUS PERSUASION

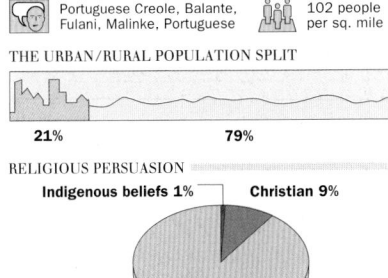

Indigenous beliefs 1%
Christian 9%
Muslim 90%

About 98% of Guinea-Bissau's people come from indigenous ethnic groups. The largest is the southern Balante, who form almost one-third of the population. Mixed-race *mestiço* and European minorities make up just 2% of the population. Although small in number, the *mestiços* – many of whom derive from Cape Verde, Portugal's other former West African colony – still dominate the bureaucracy and the top ranks of the PAIGC. Resentment at this, especially among the Balante who provided most of the PAIGC troops in the independence war, was one cause of the 1980 coup. The majority of the population live and work on small family farms, grouped in self-contained villages. The bulk of the urban population live in the capital, Bissau.

POLITICS

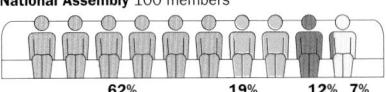

1994/1998

President Brig.-Gen. João Bernardo Vieira

THE STATE OF THE PARTIES

National Assembly 100 members

62% PAIGC   19% PRGB-MB   12% PRS   7% Other

PAIGC = African Party for the Independence of Guinea-Bissau and Cape Verde **PRGB-MB** = Guinea-Bissau Resistance Party - Bafata Movement **PRS** = Party for Social Renovation

Council of State 15 members

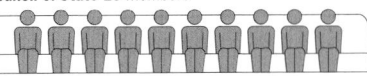

Members are elected by the National People's Assembly from among their own number

Guinea-Bissau has been ruled by the PAIGC since independence in 1974. Since 1990, it has been moving slowly toward multiparty democracy. The country's first multiparty elections were eventually held in 1994, after repeated postponements. The elections, which were declared free and fair by international observers, saw the PAIGC returned to power with an absolute majority. The opposition disputed the result and declared its intention not to participate in the new government, but predicted political instability has yet to materialize.

WORLD AFFAIRS

Ecowas   Lusoph   NAM   OAU   OIC

Guinea-Bissau's foreign policy is non-aligned. It trades mainly with India and the West. A maritime border dispute with Senegal has recently been resolved. However, relations with Senegal remain tense as a result of Casamance separatist bases in north Guinea-Bissau.

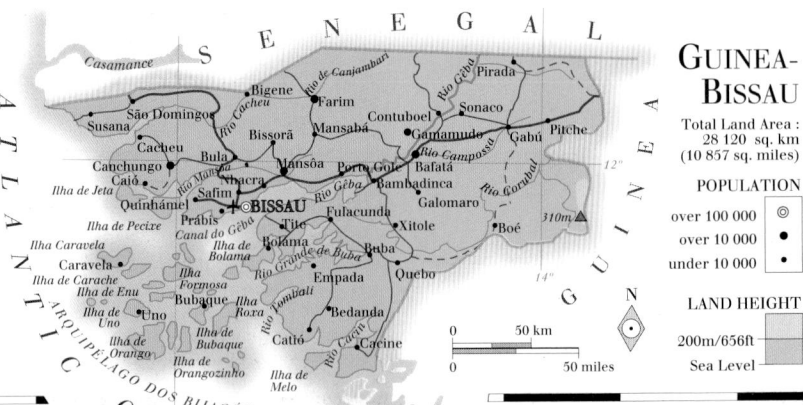

GUINEA-BISSAU

Total Land Area :
28 120 sq. km
(10 857 sq. miles)

POPULATION

over 100 000
over 10 000
under 10 000

LAND HEIGHT

200m/656ft
Sea Level

AID

 $97m (receipts)   Down 9% in 1993

Portugal is Guinea-Bissau's largest aid donor. Balance of payments support is critical to the economy. Export earnings rarely top $20 million and import and debt service costs are over $100 million. Despite the freezing of donor support in 1991 because of Guinea-Bissau's World Bank arrears, the government pushed ahead with economic reforms begun in the mid-1980s. Donor support is now beginning to be restored. The infrastructure, education and health care are the main targets of project aid.

DEFENSE

 $8m   Down 2% in 1995

The lower ranks of the 9,200-strong armed forces are mainly Balante from the south. Resentment at their lack of promotion and the predominance of *mestiços* in the senior ranks was a cause of the 1980 coup. Troops serve with the UN in Angola and Mozambique.

ECONOMICS

 $253m   13,560–18,036 Guinea pesos

SCORE CARD

- ❏ WORLD GNP RANKING......................177th
- ❏ GNP PER CAPITA $240
- ❏ BALANCE OF PAYMENTS.....................$–62m
- ❏ INFLATION 15%
- ❏ UNEMPLOYMENT....Widespread underemployment

STRENGTHS

Minimal at present, but good potential in fisheries and timber. Both are barely exploited. Offshore oil potential.

WEAKNESSES

Lack of sufficiency in rice staple. Few exports, mainly cashew nuts and groundnuts. Minimal industry. Lack of an entrepreneurial business class. High illiteracy. Poor state economic management.

EXPORTS

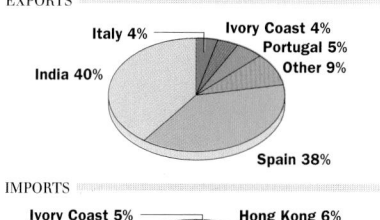

Italy 4%   Ivory Coast 4%
            Portugal 5%
India 40%   Other 9%

Spain 38%

IMPORTS

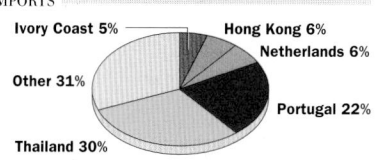

Ivory Coast 5%   Hong Kong 6%
                  Netherlands 6%
Other 31%

                  Portugal 22%
Thailand 30%

Bafatá, the chief town in central Guinea-Bissau. It lies on the Gêba River and is also an important inland port.

RESOURCES

 41m kwh (capacity 7,000 kw)   5,350 tons

494,000 cattle, 312,000 pigs, 263,000 sheep,   Bauxite, phosphate

Fish and timber are the main natural resources, but local exploitation is only 10% of the sustainable levels of 250,000 tons and 100,000 tons a year. Guinea Bissau's considerable hydropower potential is also under-exploited.

ENVIRONMENT

 None    Economic growth has precedence over ecological concerns

Drought and locust plagues are serious natural hazards. A small population and minimal industry mean there are few serious environmental problems.

MEDIA

 Censorship is still strong, but press freedom has increased markedly since 1991

PUBLISHING AND BROADCAST MEDIA

 There are 2 daily newspapers, *Voz da Guiné* and *Nô Printcha*, published by the government

 1 state-owned service    1 state-owned service

Only one newspaper, *Baguerra*, and one magazine, *Expresso-Bissau*, are not state-owned. Portugal helps to fund the TV service, started in 1989.

CRIME

 Guinea-Bissau does not publish prison figures   Up 66% in 1992

The death penalty was abolished in 1993. Reform of the legal system is in progress to make it more independent of the PAIGC. The government has been criticized for human rights abuses.

EDUCATION

 36%    404 students

Around 60% of children attend the rudimentary education service. Guinea-Bissau has no university.

CHRONOLOGY

The Portuguese explored the area in the 15th century. In 1879, Portuguese Guinea became a colony. A war of independence began in the 1960s, led by the PAIGC.

- ❏ **1974** Independence. PAIGC led by Luis Cabral takes power.
- ❏ **1980** Coup. João Vieira replaces Cabral.
- ❏ **1990** Vieira accepts principle of multiparty politics.
- ❏ **1991–1992** Opposition parties formed; election postponed.
- ❏ **1993** Coup attempt.
- ❏ **1994** Multiparty elections won by PAIGC.

G

HEALTH

 1 per 7,250 people   Parasitic, diarrheal and communicable diseases, malaria

Guinea-Bissau's health statistics are among the world's worst, due partly to the minimal medical facilities. Average life expectancy is just 44 years; infant mortality is 138 per 1,000 live births; the maternal death rate is high.

WEALTH

 Most of the population lives in poverty

CONSUMER GOODS OWNERSHIP

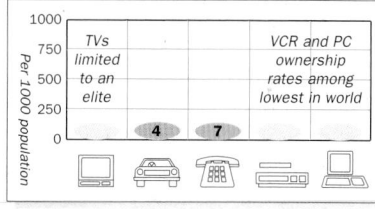

Living conditions for the majority of people are extremely poor; over 70% are unable to meet their basic needs. The tiny elite is mainly *mestiço*.

WORLD RANKING

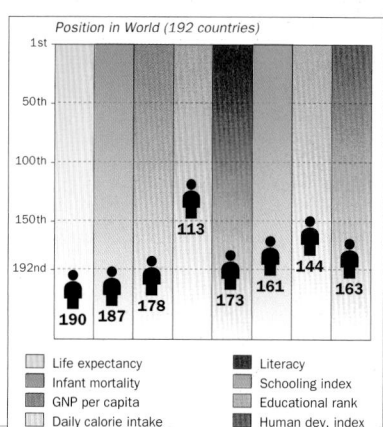

Position in World (192 countries)

Life expectancy — 190
Infant mortality — 187
GNP per capita — 178
Daily calorie intake — 113
Literacy — 173
Schooling index — 161
Educational rank — 144
Human dev. index — 163

GUYANA

OFFICIAL NAME: Co-operative Republic of Guyana **CAPITAL:** Georgetown
POPULATION: 800,000 **CURRENCY:** Guyana dollar **OFFICIAL LANGUAGE:** English

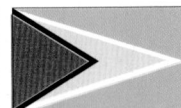
      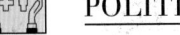  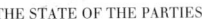

GUYANA LIES ON the northeast coast of South America, bordered by Venezuela and Brazil to the west and Suriname to the east. Dense interior rainforest covers 85% of its territory. Independence from Britain came in 1966. The export of four key products, bauxite, gold, rice and sugar, sustains the economy. The vast majority of Guyana's population lives on the narrow coastal plain, which is partially reclaimed from the sea.

CLIMATE

WEATHER CHART

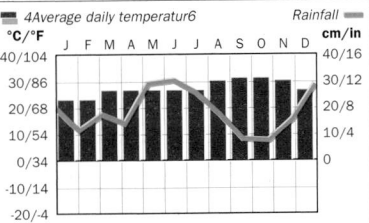

The lowlands are very humid with a constant temperature. The highlands are a little cooler, especially at night.

TRANSPORTATION

Timehri Intl, Georgetown 270,500 passengers

11 ships 7600 dwt

THE TRANSPORTATION NETWORK

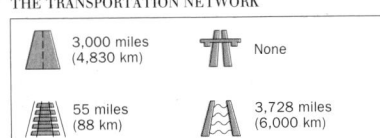

3,000 miles (4,830 km)

None

55 miles (88 km)

3,728 miles (6,000 km)

Reliable travel into the interior is by air or river; ferries link coastal roads. The only international airport is Timehri.

TOURISM

108,000 visitors

Up 1% in 1994

MAIN OVERSEAS ARRIVALS

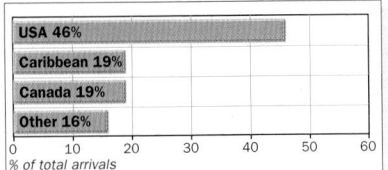

USA 46%
Caribbean 19%
Canada 19%
Other 16%
% of total arrivals

The government is keen to develop ecotourism using private investment. Guyana means Land of Many Waters; the Kaieteur Falls are among the world's most impressive. Old Dutch wooden architecture characterizes Georgetown.

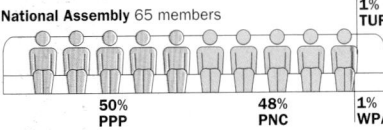

Modest homes, Georgetown. Most buildings there are of wood. The cathedral is one of the world's tallest freestanding wooden buildings.

PEOPLE

English Creole, Hindi, Tamil, Indian languages, English

10 people per sq. mile

THE URBAN/RURAL POPULATION SPLIT

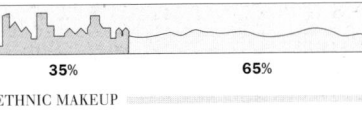

35% 65%

ETHNIC MAKEUP

Indian 4% Other 4%
White & Chinese 2%
Black 38%
South Asian 52%

Tension exists between Afro-Guyanese, who are descended from Africans brought over between the 17th and 19th centuries, and Indo-Guyanese, descendants of South Asian laborers brought from India in the 19th century. There were a number of instances of discrimination against Indo-Guyanese during the PNC's rule.

GUYANA

Total Land Area : 196 850 sq. km (76 004 sq. miles)

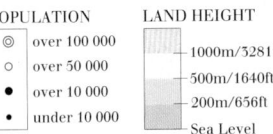

POPULATION
◎ over 100 000
○ over 50 000
● over 10 000
• under 10 000

LAND HEIGHT
1000m/3281ft
500m/1640ft
200m/656ft
Sea Level

POLITICS

1992/1997

President Cheddi Jagan

THE STATE OF THE PARTIES

National Assembly 65 members

50% PPP 48% PNC 1% WPA 1% TUF

PPP = People's Progressive Party PNC = People's National Congress WPA = Working People's Alliance
TUF = The United Force

The main power brokers in Guyana's multiparty democracy are the urban businessmen and professionals who fund the political parties. The 29-year rule of the PNC was characterized by favoritism towards the Afro-Guyanese. This was reversed with the election of the Indian-dominated PPP in 1992, in what international observers – and many Guyanese – saw as the first fair election since independence. As leader of the PPP, Cheddi Jagan's switch from avowed Marxism in the 1970s to free-market economics in the 1990s proved a success with voters.

WORLD AFFAIRS

Rescheduling debt with western creditor nations is paramount. Other concerns include the long-standing border dispute with Venezuela and closer integration with Caribbean states.

AID

 $85m (receipts)   Down 11% in 1993

The majority of Guyana's aid comes from the USA, EU and UK. Most aid has been in the form of development assistance and project loans.

DEFENSE

 $7m   No change in 1995

The security forces, which include a 1,400-strong army, benefit from financial support and training provided by the US and UK governments.

ECONOMICS

 $434m    139.50–141.91 Guyana dollars

SCORE CARD

❏ World GNP Ranking	169th
❏ GNP per Capita	$530
❏ Balance of Payments	$–97m
❏ Inflation	14%
❏ Unemployment	12%

STRENGTHS
Widespread deregulation of the economy. Bauxite, gold, rice, sugar and diamond production. Sugar production has already increased. Overseas investment in rice and gold will see the further development of both sectors.

WEAKNESSES
High per capita foreign debt. Narrow economic base. Weakness of state-owned bauxite industry. Exchange rate fluctuations. Dependence on imports.

EXPORTS
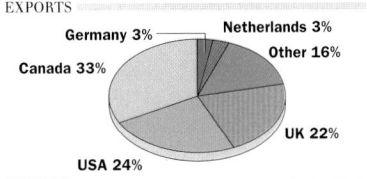

Germany 3%, Netherlands 3%, Other 16%, Canada 33%, UK 22%, USA 24%

IMPORTS
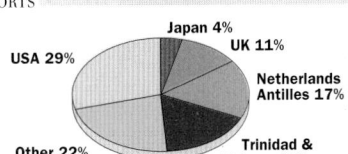

Japan 4%, UK 11%, USA 29%, Netherlands Antilles 17%, Other 22%, Trinidad & Tobago 17%

RESOURCES

 235m kwh (capacity 110,000 kw)
 190,000 cattle, 131,000 sheep, 79,000 goats

 40,000 tons
Bauxite, gold, diamonds, gemstones, oil, manganese, uranium

Gold and bauxite are the main strategic resources in Guyana. However, several companies are prospecting offshore and onshore for oil, amid reports that commercially exploitable deposits have been located. Hydroelectric power plants are planned on the many rivers.

ENVIRONMENT

 0.05%   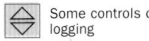 Some controls on logging

Disrepair of the 18th-century sea defense system threatens the urbanized coastline that lies below sea level. There is growing concern about the impact of commercial logging on the rainforest. In 1995 there was massive cyanide pollution of the Essequibo river by the Omai gold mine.

MEDIA

 A relaxation of government pressure on the media has been seen in recent years

PUBLISHING AND BROADCAST MEDIA

There is 1 daily newspaper, the *Guyana Chronicle*, published by the government

1 state-owned, 2 independent services

1 state-owned service

With the liberalization of the economy, which started with the Hoyte administration, there has been a relaxation of pressure on the media.

CRIME

 Guyana does not publish prison figures   Rising

The poorer neighborhoods of most major towns are considered unsafe to walk in by locals, especially at night. The police are strongly criticized for ineffectiveness in the face of rising crime.

EDUCATION

 98%    4,665 students

Education is based on the British system. Entry to high-schools is by 11-plus examination. Guyana has a state-financed university, although many students go to the USA or UK.

HEALTH

 1 per 3,360 people   Heart diseases, violence, accidents, cancers, tuberculosis

Around 95% of the population have access to Guyana's mainly state-run health service. The referral system is relatively good.

CHRONOLOGY

During the 17th and 18th centuries, the Dutch founded three colonies, Essequibo, Demerara and Berbice, in the region. In 1814, these came under British control, and were later combined to form the colony of British Guiana.

- ❏ **1953** First universal elections won by PPP under leadership of Dr. Cheddi Jagan; parliament later suspended by Britain.
- ❏ **1957** Forbes Burnham founds PNC.
- ❏ **1964** PNC becomes leading force in coalition government.
- ❏ **1966** Independence from Britain.
- ❏ **1973** PPP boycotts parliament, accusing PNC of electoral fraud.
- ❏ **1985** Burnham dies. Replaced by Desmond Hoyte as PNC leader.
- ❏ **1989** Foreign aid suspended; renewed calls for reform.
- ❏ **1992** Fair elections won by PPP.

G

WEALTH

 Wealth is concentrated among a few Georgetown families

CONSUMER GOODS OWNERSHIP

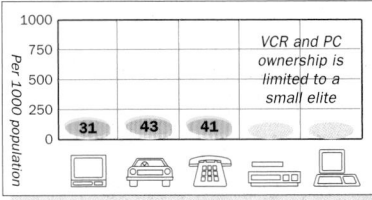

VCR and PC ownership is limited to a small elite

31   43   41

Most Guyanese enjoy a relatively similar standard of living, although there are a few very affluent urban families whose wealth is derived from business and farming. Large air-conditioned four-wheel-drive vehicles and fine whiskies are the major status symbols. The poorest group are Indian subsistence farmers.

WORLD RANKING

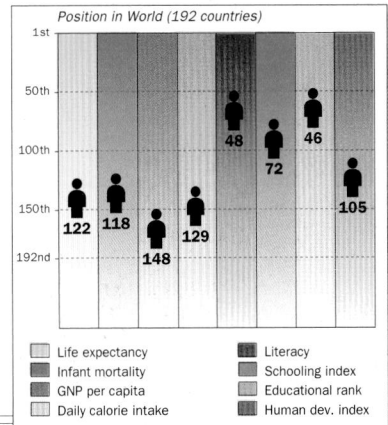

Position in World (192 countries)

122, 118, 148, 129, 48, 72, 46, 105

- Life expectancy
- Infant mortality
- GNP per capita
- Daily calorie intake
- Literacy
- Schooling index
- Educational rank
- Human dev. index

HAITI

OFFICIAL NAME: Republic of Haiti   **CAPITAL:** Port-au-Prince   **POPULATION:** 7.2 million
CURRENCY: Gourde   **OFFICIAL LANGUAGES:** French and French Creole

HAITI OCCUPIES the western third of the Caribbean island of Hispaniola. Formerly a French colony, it was the first Caribbean state to achieve independence, in 1804, and has been in a state of political chaos virtually ever since. Democracy did not materialize with the exile of the dictator Jean-Claude Duvalier in 1986. Elections were held in 1990, but by 1991 the military were back in power and were only ousted in 1994 through US intervention.

CLIMATE

WEATHER CHART

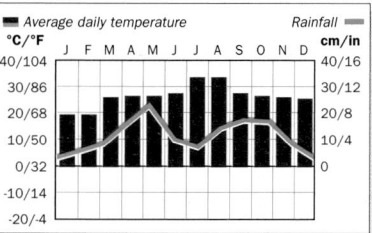

Haiti lies mostly in the rain shadow of the central mountains so is slightly less humid than average for the Caribbean.

TRANSPORTATION

Port-au-Prince
545,000 passengers   Has no fleet

THE TRANSPORTATION NETWORK

370 miles (600 km)		None
25 miles (40 km)		62 miles (100 km)

By regional standards, Haiti has a poor road system. Ferries provide transportation to the southern peninsula.

TOURISM

70,000 visitors   Down 42% in 1994

MAIN OVERSEAS ARRIVALS

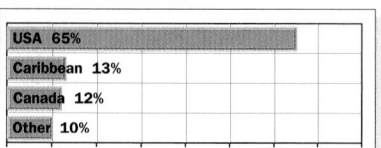

USA 65%
Caribbean 13%
Canada 12%
Other 10%
% of total arrivals

Haiti's location, history and culture provided much of its attraction for tourists in the 1960s and 1970s. The resurgence of political instability and violence in the 1980s, however, led to the industry's near collapse.

PEOPLE

French Creole, French   679 people per sq. mile

THE URBAN/RURAL POPULATION SPLIT

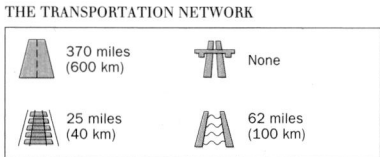

30%   70%

RELIGIOUS PERSUASION

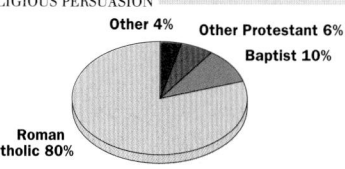

Other 4%   Other Protestant 6%   Baptist 10%   Roman Catholic 80%

Most Haitians are the descendants of Africans; a few have European roots, primarily French. The majority of the population lives in extreme poverty: Haiti is the poorest country in the Americas; Port-au-Prince has the worst slums in the Caribbean. Social tensions run high, and focus on class rather than race. In recent years, the combination of political repression and a collapsing economy led many to emigrate illegally to the USA, or across the border to the neighboring Dominican Republic.

HAITI

Total Land Area : 27 560 sq. km (10 641 sq. miles)

POPULATION
- over 1 000 000
- over 500 000
- over 10 000
- under 10 000

LAND HEIGHT
1000m/3281ft
500m/1640ft
200m/656ft
Sea Level

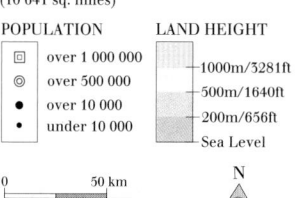
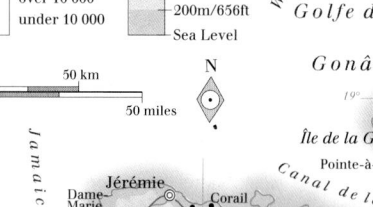

POLITICS

U. House 1995/1999
L. House 1995/1999   President René Préval

THE STATE OF THE PARTIES

Chamber of Deputies 83 members

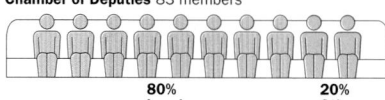

80% Lavalas   20% Other

Senate 27 members

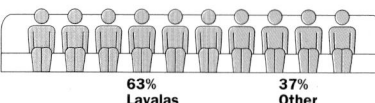

63% Lavalas   37% Other

Haiti's politics has long been directly managed by the wealthy businessmen who live in palatial style above Port-au-Prince. It was this group, backed by the military, that supported the popularly detested Duvalier regime. The same group has, since the overthrow of "Baby Doc" Duvalier in 1986, financed regular coups to ensure that the 1987 democratic constitution cannot be implemented.

The military last intervened in 1991, following the 1990 election of Jean-Bertrand Aristide on a populist platform. Aristide was exiled by the army and his supporters suppressed. The UN imposed sanctions and the US government intervened militarily to restore Aristide to office in 1994, primarily to stem the flood of refugees. Aristide's left-wing Lavalas Party won the legislative and presidential elections in 1995 and René Préval was inaugurated as the new president in 1996. His administration is under strong US pressure to impose free-market policies.

WORLD AFFAIRS

Following three years of sanctions, Haiti's economic links with the outside world have been restored. A UN force is scheduled to remain in the country until late 1996.

AID

 $128m (receipts)   Up 21% in 1993

In 1995 the USA made $134 million in aid conditional on a program of privatization. It has pledged $5 million for police training. The IMF is setting stiff conditions for loan support.

DEFENSE

 $47m   Up 34% in 1995

In 1994, the military were ousted and democracy was restored. The armed forces and police were disbanded and an interim public security force of 3,000 formed. A new national police force of some 4,000 personnel is being funded and trained by the USA.

ECONOMICS

 $1.5bn   19.08–19.00 gourdes

SCORE CARD

❏ WORLD GNP RANKING	143rd
❏ GNP PER CAPITA	$220
❏ BALANCE OF PAYMENTS	$4m
❏ INFLATION	42.6%
❏ UNEMPLOYMENT	50%

STRENGTHS
Few, though outlook improved with lifting of sanctions. Income from coffee and from Haitians living abroad. Large profits from the transportation of narcotics to the USA.

WEAKNESSES
Political instability. Manufacturing collapsed following sanctions in 1991.

EXPORTS

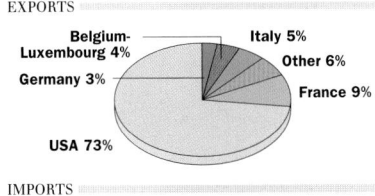

IMPORTS

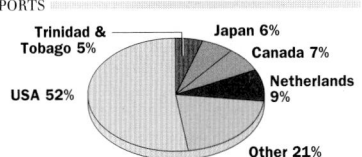

Haiti: the poorest country in the Americas. *In remote villages, most houses are made of earth and have no windows.*

RESOURCES

 430m kwh (capacity 150,000 kw)   5,600 tons

 1.6m cattle 950,000 pigs 432,000 horses   Marble, limestone, clay, silver, gold, natural asphalt

Haiti has no strategic resources. Under the recent economic sanctions, it had to find unofficial sources of oil; much was imported from Europe.

ENVIRONMENT

 0.4%   Ecological initiatives hijacked for political purposes

Haiti's ecological problems receive little attention. It is one of the most environmentally degraded countries in the world; one-third of its soil is seriously eroded.

MEDIA

 Radio stations shut down by the military have reopened. Newspapers, almost exclusively in French, are not accessible to most Creoles

PUBLISHING AND BROADCAST MEDIA

 There are 5 daily newspapers, *Le Nouveau Monde, L'Union, Le Nouvelliste, Le Matin* and *Panorama*

 1 state-owned service   1 state-owned service; several private

The media was largely controlled through intimidation under the military. The transition to democracy has produced a more open press.

CRIME

 Haiti does not publish prison figures   Crime is rising

Gun possession is widespread in Haiti and crime levels are high. The UN agreed in February 1996 that its multinational force would remain for an extra six months in the absence of a fully trained police force.

EDUCATION

 35%    6,288 students

Education, run by the state and the Roman Catholic and missionary churches, is based on the French system. The wealthy are often educated abroad.

CHRONOLOGY

In 1697, Spain ceded the west of Hispaniola to France. Ex-slave Toussaint l'Ouverture's rebellion in 1791 led to independence in 1804.

❏ **1915–1954** US occupation.
❏ **1957–1971** François "Papa Doc" Duvalier's brutal dictatorship.
❏ **1971** Son Jean-Claude, "Baby Doc," takes over. Slight liberalization.
❏ **1986** Flees. Gen. Namphy steps in.
❏ **1987** Elections abandoned.
❏ **1988** Lt.-Gen. Avril takes power.
❏ **1990** Jean-Bertrand Aristide elected, but exiled in 1991 coup.
❏ **1994–1995** US forces oust military. Aristide reinstated and election held.

HEALTH

 1 per 7,040 people   Malaria, other parasitic diseases, tuberculosis

Most Haitians cannot afford health care. In rural areas, help is often sought from voodoo priests.

WEALTH

 One million Haitians work as cheap labor in the Dominican Republic, many effectively as slaves on the state-owned sugarcane plantations

CONSUMER GOODS OWNERSHIP

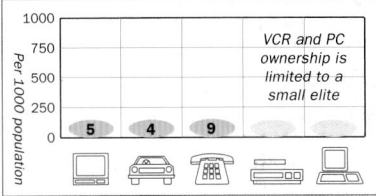

Haiti's rigid class structure maintains extreme disparities of wealth between the mass of the population, who live in slums without running water or proper sanitation, and a few affluent families. These enjoy a luxurious way of life and educate their children in France.

WORLD RANKING

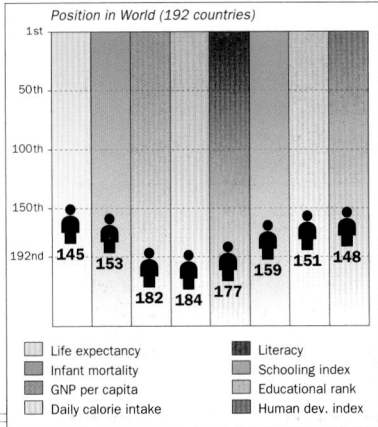

HONDURAS

OFFICIAL NAME: Republic of Honduras **CAPITAL:** Tegucigalpa
POPULATION: 5.7 million **CURRENCY:** Lempira **OFFICIAL LANGUAGE:** Spanish

STRADDLING THE Central American isthmus, Honduras has only a short Pacific coast. Its long Caribbean shoreline includes the virtually uninhabited Mosquito Coast, while most of the rest of the country is mountainous. Honduras declared independence from Spain in 1821 and returned to full civilian rule in 1984 after a succession of military governments. Honduras is one of the world's leading banana producers, but is very poor and dependent on aid.

CLIMATE

WEATHER CHART

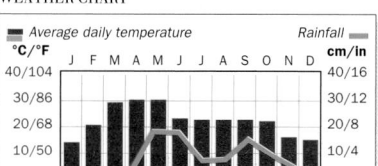

The Honduran Caribbean coast is extremely hot. The central highlands are much cooler.

TRANSPORTATION

Toncontín, Tegucigalpa
404,000 passengers

572 ships
1.41m dwt

THE TRANSPORTATION NETWORK

1,580 miles (2,540 km)		None	
593 miles (955 km)		289 miles (465 km)	

The government plans to close down the remaining railroads and improve the road system with US aid.

TOURISM

196,000 visitors

Down 13% in 1994

MAIN OVERSEAS ARRIVALS

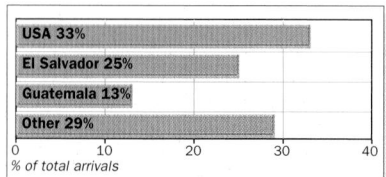

| USA 33% |
| El Salvador 25% |
| Guatemala 13% |
| Other 29% |

0   10   20   30   40
% of total arrivals

Ecotourism plans include building hotels on the virgin coastline of the Bay of Tela and lodges in the remote region inland from the Mosquito Coast. Jungle river rafting is a growing sport among wealthy locals and foreigners.

PEOPLE

Spanish, Black Carib, English Creole

133 people per sq. mile

THE URBAN/RURAL POPULATION SPLIT

42%   58%

ETHNIC MAKEUP

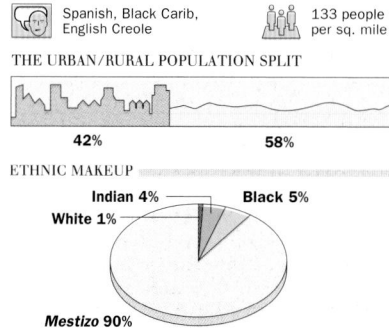

Indian 4%   Black 5%
White 1%
Mestizo 90%

As in most of Central America, very few pure indigenous groups remain. There are an estimated 45,000 Miskito Indians, and an English-speaking black population on the Caribbean coast. Poverty is the root cause of social tension; whites still have the best opportunities.

Honduras has one of the most unequal societies in the region: 4% of people own 60% of the land. Rural poverty and strong Roman Catholicism (93% are Roman Catholic) mean that the family is a powerful unifying force. Women's status is low; many work in domestic service.

POLITICS

1993/1997

President Carlos Roberto Reina Idiaquez

THE STATE OF THE PARTIES

National Assembly 128 members

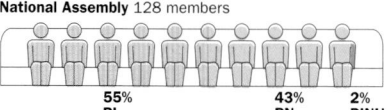

55% PL   43% PN   2% PINU

PL = Liberal Party **PN** = National Party **PINU** = Innovation and Unity Party

The main brokers in political power today are the military, the US embassy and the United Fruit Company, the biggest banana producers in Honduras.

The military held power intermittently from 1956 until 1984, when, under pressure from US President Jimmy Carter, it allowed a return to multiparty democratic civilian rule. The National and Liberal parties, with few real ideological differences, have since alternated in power. Presidents have tended to be weak because they can serve only one four-year term.

During the 1980s, US President Ronald Reagan effectively converted the country into a US "aircraft carrier" to counter a perceived communist threat from El Salvador and Nicaragua. The end of hostilities in these countries meant a reduction in the amount of US aid. In 1994, the center-right government of President Reina promised reforms, but a shortage of development funds and harsh austerity policies means that unemployment, agrarian reform and the state of the landless rural poor remain unresolved issues.

HONDURAS

Total Land Area : 111 890 sq. km
(43 201 sq. miles)

LAND HEIGHT

2000m/6562ft
1000m/3281ft
500m/1640ft
200m/656ft
Sea Level

POPULATION

over 500 000
over 100 000
over 50 000
over 10 000
under 10 000

WORLD AFFAIRS

The major issues are the settlement of border disputes with El Salvador and Nicaragua, close ties with the USA and further regional economic integration.

AID

 $324m (receipts)　　 Down 9% in 1993

The World Bank and Inter-American Development Bank disbursed $220 million in 1995 to support a government modernization plan. US aid has fallen.

DEFENSE

 $49m　　 Up 11% in 1995

During the 1980s, the military repressed internal dissent, backed right-wing Contras, and still cooperates with US forces. It successfully resists human rights charges and vigorously promotes its burgeoning economic interests.

ECONOMICS

 $3.2bn　　 9.30–10.09 lempiras

SCORE CARD

- ❏ WORLD GNP RANKING 122nd
- ❏ GNP PER CAPITA $580
- ❏ BALANCE OF PAYMENTS....................$–271m
- ❏ INFLATION 26.6%
- ❏ UNEMPLOYMENT................................5.9%

STRENGTHS
Unexploited mineral deposits. Hardwoods. Bananas. Diversification into non-traditional, high-earning agriculture such as flowers and fruit.

WEAKNESSES
Servicing of $4.9 billion foreign debt. Corruption. Industry only 13% of GDP. Vulnerability of banana exports. Massive underemployment. Lack of land reform. Decline in US investment since end of regional hostilities.

EXPORTS

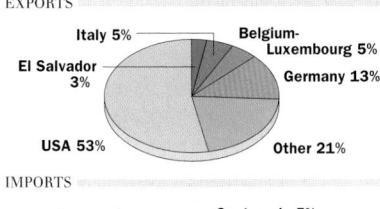

IMPORTS

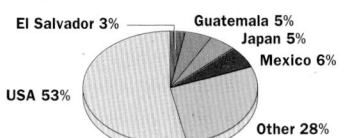

Tobacco field. *Tobacco accounts for 1% of export revenues. Honduras' biggest earners are bananas, almost 40%, and coffee, 20%.*

RESOURCES

 2.3bn kwh (capacity 290,000 kw)　　 Not an oil producer; refines 14,000 b/cd

 2.3m cattle, 603,000 pigs, 177,000 horses　　Lead, zinc, silver, gold, copper, iron, tin, coal

Offshore oil exploration has begun in the north. An HEP dam at El Cajón now allows Honduras to export electricity

ENVIRONMENT

 8%　　 US company wants to exploit 2.5m acres of rainforest for woodchip

Environmental groups are active, but have to face opposition from multi-national commercial interests.

MEDIA

 Although the media is officially free, some journalists will accept bribes to misreport. Left-wing publications may receive death threats

PUBLISHING AND BROADCAST MEDIA

 There are 4 daily newspapers, *La Prensa*, *El Heraldo*, *La Tribuna* and *El Tiempo*

 9 independent stations　　 1 state-owned, 280 independent stations

Honduran TV and radio programs are mostly sourced from the USA. As a result, local coverage remains limited.

CRIME

 Honduras does not publish prison figures　　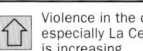 Violence in the cities, especially La Ceiba, is increasing

Narcotics-related crime is a major problem. Occasional human rights abuses by the military are reported.

EDUCATION

 71%　　 44,849 students

State-run education follows the US system, although the drop-out rate from secondary schools is high.

HEALTH

 1 per 2,330 people　　 Circulatory, infectious and parasitic diseases, malaria

Only 66% of people have easy access to health services, although most infants receive basic care.

CHRONOLOGY

Honduras was a Spanish possession until 1821. In 1823, it joined the United Provinces of Central America with four neighboring nations.

- ❏ **1838** Declares full independence.
- ❏ **1890s** US banana companies set up extensive plantations.
- ❏ **1932–1949** Dictatorship of Gen. Tiburcio Carías Andino of PN.
- ❏ **1954** Elected PL president Dr. Villeda Morales deposed.
- ❏ **1957** Villeda reelected.
- ❏ **1963** Military coup.
- ❏ **1969** 13-day Football War with El Salvador sparked by World Cup.
- ❏ **1980** PL wins elections but Gen. Alvarez holds real power. Military manoeuvres initiated with USA.
- ❏ **1982–1983** Alvarez arrests trades unionists; death squads operate.
- ❏ **1984** Return to democracy.
- ❏ **1988** 12,000 Contra rebels forced out of Nicaragua into Honduras.
- ❏ **1990** Contra troops leave.
- ❏ **1995** Military defies human rights charges.

WEALTH

 Plantation worker, 175 lempiras ($17) per week; high school science teacher, 415 lempiras ($41) per week

CONSUMER GOODS OWNERSHIP

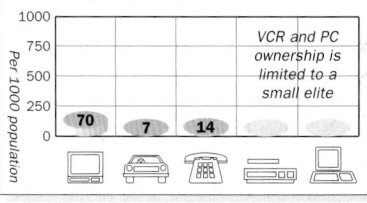

Two-thirds of the rural population live in absolute poverty. The best chance of social mobility is to join the military. Salvadorean immigrants suffer low social status.

WORLD RANKING

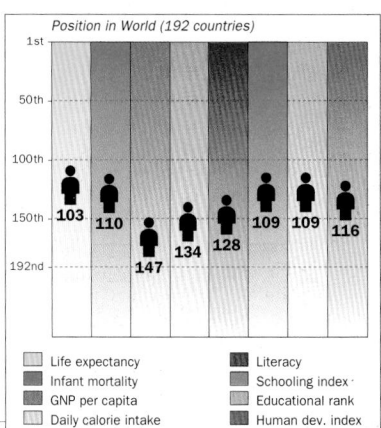

H

HONG KONG

OFFICIAL NAME: Hong Kong   **CAPITAL:** Victoria   **POPULATION:** 5.9 million
CURRENCY: Hong Kong dollar   **OFFICIAL LANGUAGES:** English and Cantonese

H ONG KONG COMPRISES Hong Kong Island, lying off the southeastern coast of China, Kowloon and the New Territories on the mainland, and adjacent islets. Its strategic position has made it one of the world's leading trade and financial centers. In 1997, Hong Kong will revert to China, when the UK's 99-year lease on the New Territories expires. The degree of future Beijing interference in its political and economic affairs is the dominant political issue.

CLIMATE

WEATHER CHART

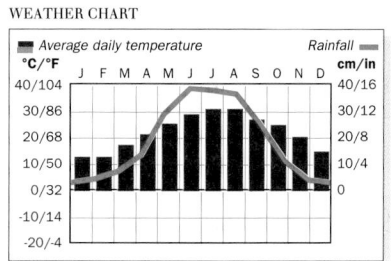

Hong Kong's climate is subtropical; it feels hotter and more humid on the streets due to the number of people.

TRANSPORTATION

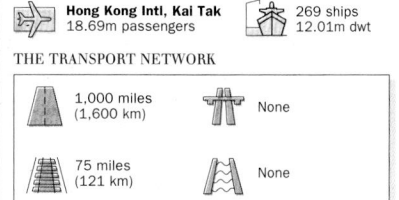

Hong Kong Intl, Kai Tak
18.69m passengers

269 ships
12.01m dwt

THE TRANSPORT NETWORK

1,000 miles (1,600 km)	None
75 miles (121 km)	None

The underground Mass Transit Railroad is efficient, clean and safe. The Chek Lap Kok airport/rail project, set to open in April 1998, will reduce congestion.

TOURISM

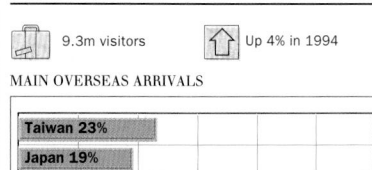

9.3m visitors   Up 4% in 1994

MAIN OVERSEAS ARRIVALS

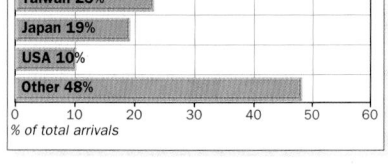

| Taiwan 23% |
| Japan 19% |
| USA 10% |
| Other 48% |

% of total arrivals

The "Manhattan of the Orient" attracts tourists with its shopping, its food and as a gateway to China and other parts of Asia. Tourism is now the third largest foreign exchange earner.

Hong Kong harbor and city skyline, looking across to the mainland, viewed from Victoria Peak on Hong Kong Island.

PEOPLE

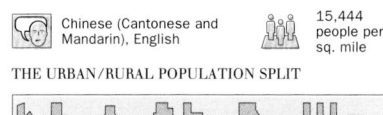

Chinese (Cantonese and Mandarin), English

15,444 people per sq. mile

THE URBAN/RURAL POPULATION SPLIT

94%   6%

RELIGIOUS PERSUASION

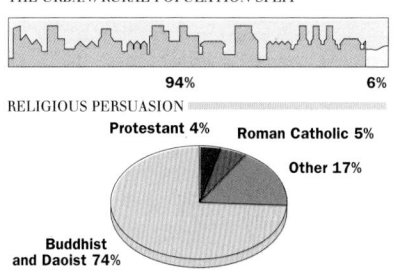

Protestant 4%   Roman Catholic 5%

Other 17%

Buddhist and Daoist 74%

Ethnic tension is not a problem because of the homogeneity of the Han (Chinese) population, over 60% of whom were born in Hong Kong. Many wealthy citizens are planning to emigrate before 1997.

HONG KONG

Total Land Area : 990 sq. km (382 sq. miles)

Urban Areas

Harbour road tunnels

LAND HEIGHT

500m/1640ft
200m/656ft
Sea Level

0   10 km

0   10 miles

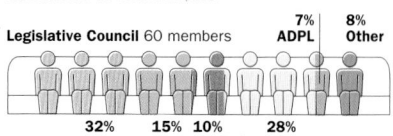

POLITICS

1995/1999   HM Queen Elizabeth II

THE STATE OF THE PARTIES

Legislative Council 60 members

7% ADPL   8% Other

32% DP   15% LP   10% DABHK   28% Independents

DP = Democratic Party   **LP** = Liberal Party
DABHK = Democratic Alliance for Betterment of Hong Kong
ADPL = Association for Democracy and People's Livelihood

At present a British Crown colony, Hong Kong will revert to Chinese sovereignty in 1997, when it will become a Special Administrative Region (SAR) of China. The British and Chinese governments fundamentally disagree about the interpretation of the 1985 Sino-British agreement and the Basic Law (Hong Kong's post-1997 constitution). Britain wants to push Hong Kong further toward elective democracy. However, Governor Chris Patten's policy is being undermined by his failure to conclude a deal with China, which strongly opposes any change in the *status quo*. Protracted talks have failed to resolve the dispute.

Prompted by Patten's political reforms, democratic candidates capitalized on concerns over the transfer to defeat pro-Beijing parties in the 1995 elections to the first all-elected Legislative Council. China redressed the balance by appointing pro-Chinese politicians and business leaders to its Preparatory Committee charged with overseeing the transfer of sovereignty to the SAR. Martin Lee, the leader of the UDHK, and the British colonial and administrative elites were excluded.

WORLD AFFAIRS

As a Crown colony, Hong Kong's foreign policy is controlled by the UK. Diplomatic and economic links with other countries are, however, extensive. Future Chinese rule and free access to the UK post-1997 are major concerns.

AID

 $30m (receipts)　　 Down 19% in 1993

Hong Kong provides some aid to Vietnam to ease the repatriation of Vietnamese "economic" refugees.

DEFENSE

 UK responsible for weaponry　　 Not applicable

Hong Kong bears the manpower cost of its 10,000-strong tri-national army, which is made up of Gurkhas, Hong Kong Chinese and UK personnel.

ECONOMICS

 $126.3bn　　 7.73–7.74 Hong Kong dollars

SCORE CARD

❏ WORLD GNP RANKING	28th
❏ GNP PER CAPITA	$21,650
❏ BALANCE OF PAYMENTS	$2bn
❏ INFLATION	6.6%
❏ UNEMPLOYMENT	3.2%

STRENGTHS
World's busiest port is hub of East and Southeast Asian trade. Sophisticated service center. Position in time zone makes it a key global financial market.

WEAKNESSES
Dependence on Chinese economic performance and resources. Sensitivity to international price fluctuations. Dependence on trade, especially US–China trade. Unskilled labor. Uncertainties of future Chinese rule deterring some investors.

EXPORTS
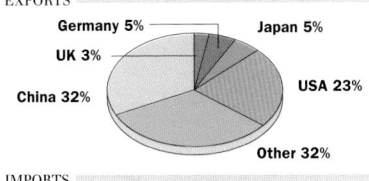

IMPORTS
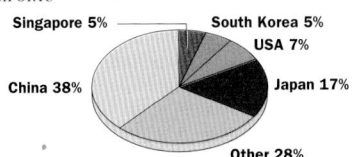

RESOURCES

 34.9bn kwh (capacity 8.3m kw)　　 226,843 tons

97,000 pigs, 2000 cattle, 1000 horses　　Kaolin, felspar

Hong Kong lacks strategic resources. Energy and water have to be imported from China. Coal is imported from the Guangdong province of China in return for the export of electricity by Hong Kong's China Light and Power Company.

ENVIRONMENT

 36% partially protected　　 Few controls on pollution levels

Growth and urbanization have brought serious water and air pollution. The construction of the Daya Bay nuclear power station has been the focus of much public concern.

MEDIA

 Some self-censorship has reportedly been exercised in the run-up to 1997. China has an aversion to freely distributed information

PUBLISHING AND BROADCAST MEDIA

 41 daily newspapers, 31 in Chinese and 2 in English, prior to a 1995 price war

 1 state-controlled, 3 independent networks　　 1 state-controlled, 3 independent networks

The press is divided into pro-Chinese and independent camps. Satellite broadcasting to the whole of Asia is carried out by one of Hong Kong's largest conglomerates – Hutchvision Hong Kong, which opened five Star-TV channels in 1991.

CRIME

 12,095 prisoners　　 Down 6% in 1992

Crime is rising and becoming more violent. This is partly due to growing links with organized crime and Triad activity in China. Corruption among the elite is increasingly an issue.

EDUCATION

 91%　　 88,950 students

Elementary schools are oversubscribed and most can offer only two half-day sessions a week. There are three universities, where the emphasis is now on science and technology.

HEALTH

 1 per 789 people　　 Heart and cerebrovascular diseases, cancers

Mother and child care, and emergency services, are free. Subsidies from the government keep charges for medical treatment and hospital care low.

CHRONOLOGY

Under the Treaty of Nanking in 1842, Hong Kong was ceded in perpetuity to Britain. The UK also acquired the Kowloon peninsula in 1860, and the New Territories, under a 99-year lease, in 1898.

- ❏ **1941–1945** Japanese occupation.
- ❏ **1985** Sino–British Joint Declaration. China to regain Hong Kong sovereignty in 1997; its present social and economic systems to remain unchanged for 50 years.
- ❏ **1989** Demonstrations following Beijing Tiananmen Square massacre.
- ❏ **1992** Governor Chris Patten announces democracy plans.
- ❏ **1995** China rejects elections to first all-elected Hong Kong Legislative Council (Legco).

H

WEALTH

 Shoe sewer, 170 Hong Kong dollars (US$22) per day; clerk of works, 11,738 Hong Kong dollars (US$1,518) per month

CONSUMER GOODS OWNERSHIP

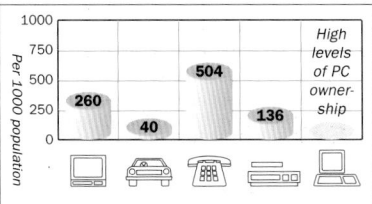

Social mobility is rapid, as exemplified by the rise to great wealth of families whose heads came to Hong Kong to escape communist China. Hong Kong consumers are highly status conscious and will pay over the odds for fashionable goods; attempts to curb car ownership by taxation have had little effect. Rich families have been able to buy citizenship overseas, allowing them to relocate, if necessary, in 1997.

WORLD RANKING

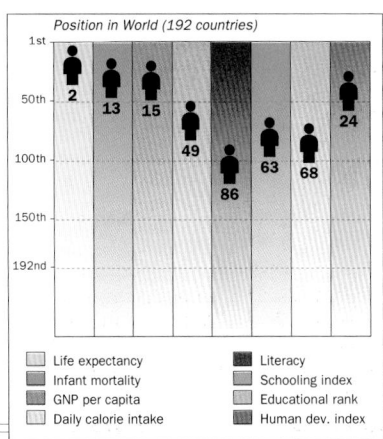

HUNGARY

OFFICIAL NAME: Republic of Hungary   CAPITAL: Budapest
POPULATION: 10.1 million   CURRENCY: Forint   OFFICIAL LANGUAGE: Hungarian (Magyar)

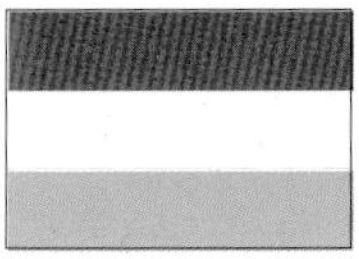

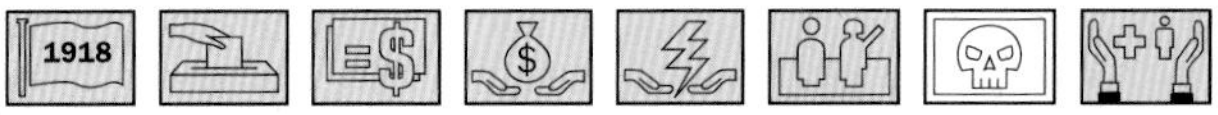

L YING AT THE HEART of Central Europe, Hungary is landlocked and has borders with seven states. Historically, Hungary has been a cosmopolitan cultural center, and during its years of market socialism was more prosperous than the other Eastern Bloc countries. Hungary's economic and political reforms have brought it closer to the EU. It now receives the lion's share of overseas investment in the former COMECON states. The treatment of the Hungarian minority in Romanian Transylvania, Serbian Kosovo and Slovakia is a major foreign policy concern.

TOURISM

21.4m visitors   Down 6% in 1994

MAIN OVERSEAS ARRIVALS

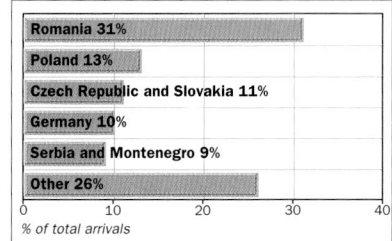

Tourism is an important source of hard currency earnings, which totaled $1.2 billion in 1993. Visitors come mainly from eastern Europe, Germany and Austria. Since 1989, Hungary has invested heavily in tourism. The number of travel agents and hotels has risen dramatically. Lake Balaton is the traditional summer destination. In the capital city, Budapest, the baths, some of which date from the Ottoman period, are among the most popular tourist attractions. Budapest is also promoting itself as an international business convention center.

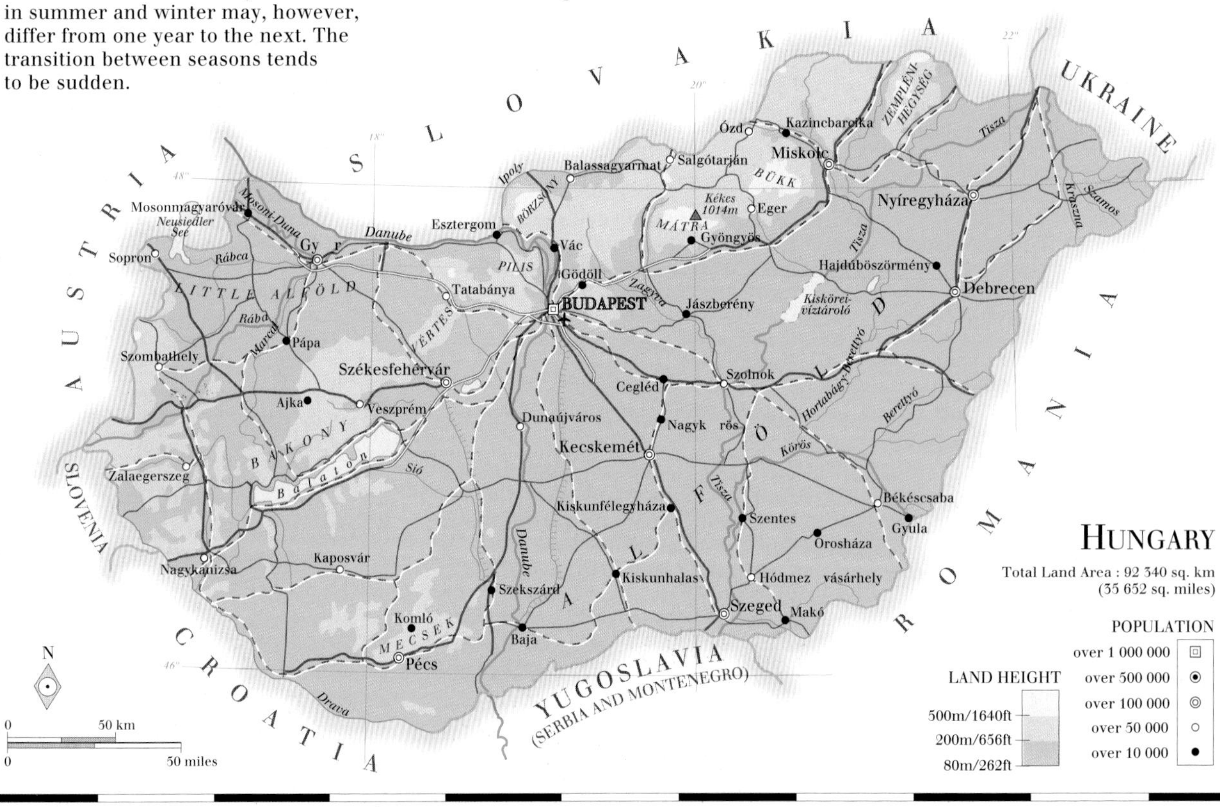

CLIMATE

WEATHER CHART

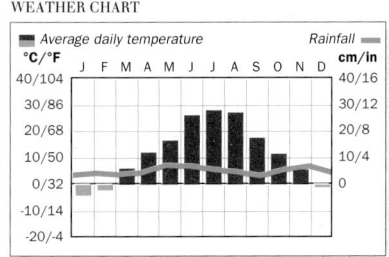

Hungary has a continental climate, with wet springs, late summers and cold, cloudy winters. There are no great differences of weather and climate within the country. Conditions in summer and winter may, however, differ from one year to the next. The transition between seasons tends to be sudden.

TRANSPORTATION

Budapest Ferihegy
2.46m passengers

14 ships
133,000 dwt

THE TRANSPORTATION NETWORK

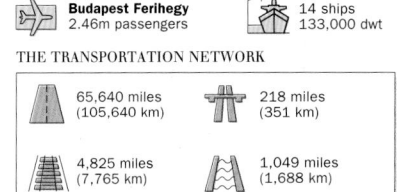

65,640 miles
(105,640 km)

218 miles
(351 km)

4,825 miles
(7,765 km)

1,049 miles
(1,688 km)

Freight travels mainly via the rail link from Budapest to the Austrian border. Most foreign investment is located along this corridor. Good roads link Hungary with Germany and Austria while elsewhere the road system continues to improve.

HUNGARY

Total Land Area : 92 340 sq. km
(35 652 sq. miles)

POPULATION

over 1 000 000
over 500 000
over 100 000
over 50 000
over 10 000

LAND HEIGHT

500m/1640ft
200m/656ft
80m/262ft

PEOPLE

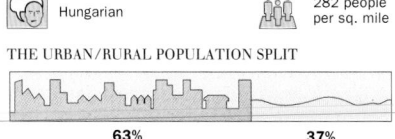

Hungarian

282 people per sq. mile

THE URBAN/RURAL POPULATION SPLIT

63%   37%

RELIGIOUS PERSUASION

Lutheran 5%
Other 7%
Calvinist 20%
Roman Catholic 68%

ETHNIC MAKEUP

Slovak 2%
Other 6%
German 2%
Hungarian 90%

Hungary is ethnically homogeneous. There are also small minorities of Germans, Slovaks, Gypsies, Serbs, Croats and Romanians. There is little ethnic tension at home, although there is considerable concern about the treatment of Hungarian minorities in neighboring states. In terms of religion, the country is more diversified. A small Jewish community in Budapest has sometimes been the target of isolated outbursts of anti-semitism, although prevailing opinion in Hungary remains tolerant.

Hungary suffers from a severe housing shortage. Most family homes are overcrowded, a factor that may contribute to the high rate of stress-related health disorders. Since 1989, a bourgeois class which is benefiting from the market economy has emerged. Life for the unskilled and unemployed is tougher, however, than under communism. Hungary has the highest suicide rate in the world.

POPULATION AGE BREAKDOWN

% of population by age group	☐ 0–14		☐ 15–64		☐ 65+
	9%	11.6%	13.4%	13.4%	14.8%
	65.7%	67.6%	64.7%	66.7%	70.6%
	25.3%	20.8%	21.9%	19.9%	14.6%
	1960	1970	1980	1990	2000

The Hungarian parliament buildings in Budapest, viewed across the Danube from the castle area of the city.

WORLD AFFAIRS

CE   CEFTA   IBRD   NACC   OSCE

Hungary was disappointed to have its application to join NATO rejected, but joined NATO's Partnership for Peace program in 1994; the same year it was also granted associate status by the WEU. Hungary signed an association agreement with the EU in early 1994 and soon afterwards applied for membership. A treaty of cooperation and friendship has been signed with Russia, but relations have been strained by Hungary's open courting of the West.

The most problematic relations are with Romania. For centuries, the two nations have disputed the status of the Hungarian minority in Transylvania. Hungary's relations with Slovakia are also tense.

POLITICS

1994/1998

President Árpád Göncz

THE STATE OF THE PARTIES

National Assembly 386 members

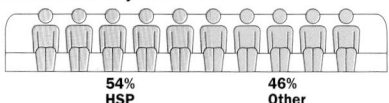

54% HSP   46% Other

HSP = Hungarian Socialist Party (formerly HWSP = Hungarian Workers' Socialist Party) **Other** = Hungarian Democratic Forum, Alliance of Free Democrats, Independent Smallholders' Party, Federation of Young Democrats, Christian Democratic People's Party

Hungary has been a multiparty democracy since 1990.

MAIN POLITICAL ISSUES
The HSP's election promises
Following their unexpected victory in the general elections of 1994, the ex-communists (the HSP) promised voters a softer landing to the market economy. However, they failed to curb the rising tide of social and political protest prompted by the introduction in 1994–1995 of austerity measures and radical cuts in social security demanded by the IMF to trim the inflated state sector.

Hungarian minorities abroad
Between 1989 and 1991, 50,000 ethnic Hungarians living abroad returned home. Many complained of poor treatment from nationalistic neighboring states. The issue has achieved prominence, particularly as Hungarians are wary of the effects of any additional competition for jobs in a tight labor market.

PROFILE
The HDF government of József Antall was installed following the elections of 1990. Until his death in 1993, Antall was a symbol of stability in Hungarian democratic politics. However, party disintegrations and the lack of an economic upturn led to an increase in apathy and disillusionment among voters. In a 1993 poll, only 6% of Hungarians considered life to be better than under the communists.

In the May 1994 general election, voters rejected the MDF's Christian nationalist stance and voted ex-communists back into power. The victorious HSP, under Gyula Horn, pledged to work in coalition in order to ease the passage of economic and social reforms through parliament.

President Árpád Göncz was elected in 1990 and is head of the armed forces.

Gyula Horn, ex-communist foreign minister and leader of the HSP.

H

CHRONOLOGY
The region today occupied by Hungary was first settled by the Finno–Ugrian Magyar peoples from the 8th century. In the 16th and 17th centuries, it came under Austrian domination, lasting until 1867, when Austria–Hungary was formed.

❑ **1918** Hungarian Republic created as successor state to Austria-Hungary.
❑ **1919** Béla Kún leads a short-lived communist government. Romania intervenes militarily and hands power to Admiral Horthy.
❑ **1938–1941** Hungary gains territory from Czechoslovakia, Yugoslavia and Romania in return for supporting Nazi Germany.
❑ **1941** Hungary drawn into World War II on Axis side when Hitler attacks Soviet Union.
❑ **1944** Nazi Germany preempts Soviet advance on Hungary by invading. Deportation of Hungarian Jews and Gypsies to extermination camps begins. Soviet Red Army enters in October. Horthy forced to resign. ➪

H

CHRONOLOGY *continued*

- ❑ **1945** Liberated by Red Army. Soviet-formed provisional government installed. Imre Nagy introduces land reform.
- ❑ **1947** Communists emerge as largest party in second postwar election.
- ❑ **1948** Forcible merger of Social Democrats with communists to establish Hungarian Socialist Workers' Party (HSWP) in 1956.
- ❑ **1949** New constitution; formally becomes People's Republic.
- ❑ **1950–1951** First Secretary Rákosi uses authoritarian powers to collectivize agriculture and industrialize the economy.
- ❑ **1953** Imre Nagy, Rákosi's rival, becomes premier and reduces political terror.
- ❑ **1955** Nagy deposed by Rákosi.
- ❑ **1956** Rákosi out. Student demonstrations demanding withdrawal of Soviet troops and Nagy's return become popular uprising. Nagy becomes premier; Kádár becomes First Secretary. Nagy announces Hungary will leave Warsaw Pact. Three days later, Soviet forces suppress protests. Approximately 25,000 killed in resistance. Kádár becomes premier.
- ❑ **1958** Nagy executed.
- ❑ **1968** Kádár introduces New Economic Mechanism to bring market elements to socialism.
- ❑ **1986** Commemoration of the 1956 uprising broken up by police. Democratic opposition demands Kádár's resignation.
- ❑ **1987** Party reformers establish HDF as a political movement.
- ❑ **1988** Kádár ousted. Environmental protests force suspension of plans for controversial Nagymaros Dam on the Danube.
- ❑ **1989** Parliament votes to allow independent parties. Nagy rehabilitated posthumously and given full state funeral. First opposition candidate since 1947 elected in by-election. Round-table talks between HWSP and opposition.
- ❑ **1990** Multiparty elections held. HDF wins decisively and Antall's government is sworn in. Speed of economic reform hotly debated.
- ❑ **1991** Warsaw Pact dissolved. Last Soviet troops leave.
- ❑ **1993** József Antall dies. Peter Boross elected prime minister.
- ❑ **1994** Hungary joins NATO Partnership for Peace program. HSP wins general election.
- ❑ **1994–1995** Government austerity program prompts widespread public protests.

AID

 $1bn (receipts)   Aid is increasing

Hungary has received substantial assistance from the World Bank since 1982. The EU is also an important source of assistance. Hungary has credit lines with the World Bank's International Finance Corporation and the EBRD. Loans are mainly used for infrastructure and energy projects.

DEFENSE

 $641m   Up 15% in 1995

0	*Defense spending as % GDP*	40
1.6%		

Real defense spending has been halved from its 1989 level. Troop numbers have been slashed. Conventional arms and the military hierarchy have been updated to meet NATO standards. Hungary has been improving its rapid reaction forces with MIGs bought in debt-for-arms deals with Russia.

HUNGARIAN ARMED FORCES

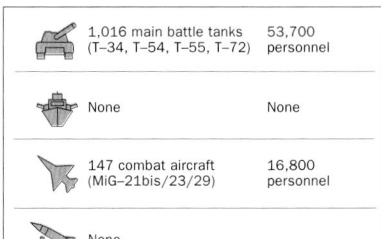

🛡	1,016 main battle tanks (T–34, T–54, T–55, T–72)	53,700 personnel
	None	None
✈	147 combat aircraft (MiG–21bis/23/29)	16,800 personnel
	None	

ECONOMICS

 $39bn   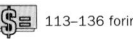 113–136 forint

SCORE CARD

- ❑ WORLD GNP RANKING 51st
- ❑ GNP PER CAPITA $3,840
- ❑ BALANCE OF PAYMENTS ....$–4bn
- ❑ INFLATION 18.9%
- ❑ UNEMPLOYMENT...............................11.3%

EXPORTS

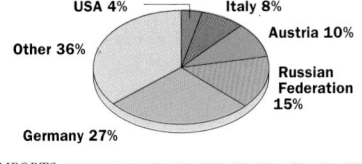

USA 4%   Italy 8%
Austria 10%
Other 36%
Russian Federation 15%
Germany 27%

IMPORTS

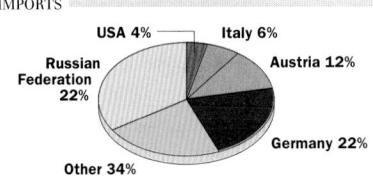

USA 4%   Italy 6%
Russian Federation 22%   Austria 12%
Germany 22%
Other 34%

ECONOMIC PERFORMANCE INDICATOR

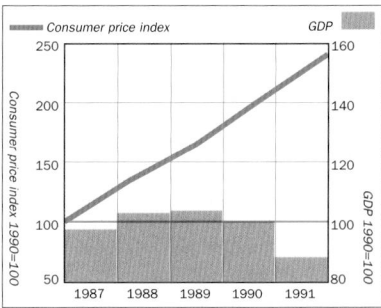

— Consumer price index   GDP

PROFILE

The costs of Hungary's transition to a market economy have been higher than expected. The collapse of COMECON trade caused a reorientation of trade toward western Europe, and Hungary's economic recovery now depends largely on trade with the EU. High tax rates make privatized assets less attractive to foreign investors.

STRENGTHS

Openness to foreign direct investment. By 1995, Hungary had attracted half of the foreign investment coming to eastern Europe: $5 billion. Favorable tax regime, streamlined bureaucracy and new legislation permitting fully owned subsidiaries help to attract international business.

WEAKNESSES

Lending by the banks to borrowers regardless of creditworthiness triggered a banking crisis. In mid-1994, the privatization program ground to a halt but was revived by the HSP government under a 1995 law which increased the pace of privatization.

HUNGARY : MAJOR BUSINESSES

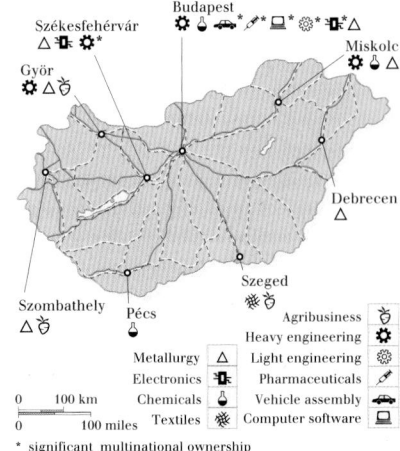

Budapest
Székesfehérvár
Győr
Miskolc
Debrecen
Szeged
Szombathely   Pécs

Agribusiness	Heavy engineering	Light engineering
Metallurgy	Electronics	Pharmaceuticals
Chemicals	Textiles	Vehicle assembly
		Computer software

0   100 km
0   100 miles

* significant multinational ownership

RESOURCES

- 30.1bn kwh (capacity 6.6m kw)
- 5m pigs, 1.3m sheep, 1m cattle
- 36,591 b/d (reserves 146,956,000 bbl)
- Bauxite, coal, oil, natural gas

ELECTRICITY GENERATION

Hydro 0.5% (0.1bn kwh)	
Thermal 55.5% (17bn kwh)	
Nuclear 44% (13bn kwh)	
Other 0%	

| 0 | 20 | 40 | 60 | 80 | 100 |

% of total generation by type

Hungary has bauxite, coal and fertile farmlands. Electricity companies are currently being privatized. The state holding company will retain 50% of shares, with foreign companies acquiring controlling rights with 30% or more of shares.

ENVIRONMENT

- 6% (5% partially protected)
- Greater awareness of environmental problems

ENVIRONMENTAL TREATIES

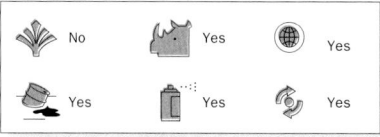

No		Yes		Yes	
Yes		Yes		Yes	

Hungary's oil reserves have a high sulfur content, which exacerbates the already serious air pollution in the industrial zones. It is estimated that 40% of Hungarians live in severely polluted areas.

Opposition by Hungary on environmental grounds has caused the Gabcikovo-Nagymaros twin-dam project on the Danube frontier with Slovakia, involving extensive destruction of wetlands, to be scaled down.

MEDIA

Little government censorship of the press

PUBLISHING AND BROADCAST MEDIA

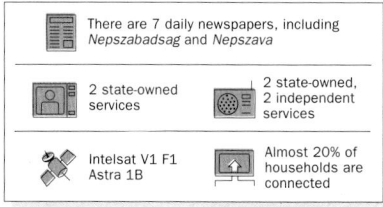

- There are 7 daily newspapers, including *Nepszabadsag* and *Nepszava*
- 2 state-owned services
- 2 state-owned, 2 independent services
- Intelsat V1 F1 Astra 1B
- Almost 20% of households are connected

Following the end of official censorship in 1988–1989, the number of newspapers and magazines has soared. Some are foreign-owned; most are fiercely independent and critical of government policy. The TV broadcasting service is nominally independent, but in practice the state controls its news coverage. However, in 1994 the Constitutional Court declared state interference in the media unlawful.

HUNGARY : LAND USE

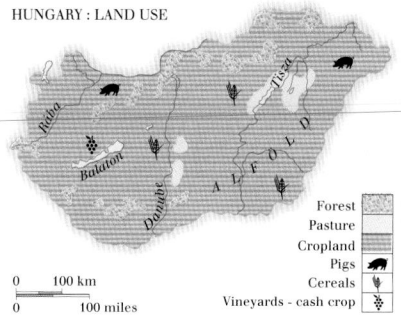

| 0 | 100 km |
| 0 | 100 miles |

Forest
Pasture
Cropland
Pigs
Cereals
Vineyards - cash crop

CRIME

- 12,373 prisoners
- Up 2% in 1992

CRIME RATES

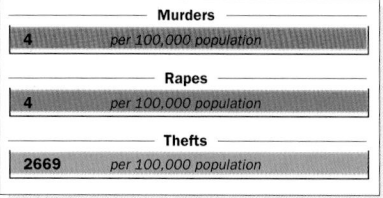

Murders	
4	*per 100,000 population*

Rapes	
4	*per 100,000 population*

Thefts	
2669	*per 100,000 population*

There were 288 murders in 1993. A growing proportion of these were a settling of business scores. Organized crime is also rising, and Hungary has become a money-laundering center.

EDUCATION

 99%

 117,460 students

| 0 | *Education spending as % GNP* | 25 |

7.2%

THE EDUCATION SYSTEM

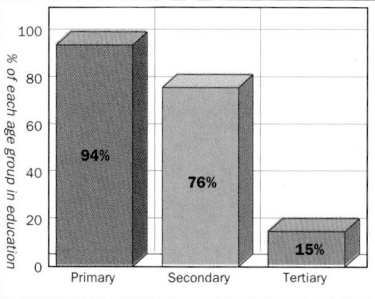

% of each age group in education

Primary	Secondary	Tertiary
94%	76%	15%

Education is free and compulsory from the ages of six to 16. Bilingual schools are being established to provide education in the language of Hungary's ethnic minorities. There are 77 higher education institutions – including ten universities – from which over 20,000 students graduated in 1992.

HEALTH

1 per 336 people

Heart diseases, cancers, accidents, suicides

| 0 | *Health spending as % GDP* | 25 |

6%

Medical treatment in Hungary is free of charge to all patients, although there is a 15% charge toward the cost of prescriptions. The health service is currently underfunded and suffers from a lack of supplies. In order to jump waiting lists or to obtain better care, it is common for patients in the state health system to offer doctors gifts or bribes. The state provides sickness benefit at 75% of wages.

WEALTH

Transportation worker, 16,403 forint ($120) per month; teacher, 21,928 forint ($160) per month

CONSUMER GOODS OWNERSHIP

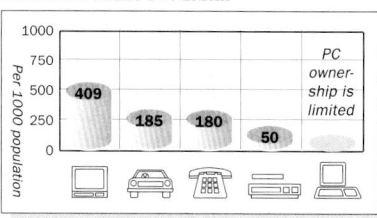

Per 1000 population

| 1000 | 750 | 500 | 250 | 0 |

409   185   180   50

PC ownership is limited

Hungary currently enjoys a higher standard of living than the other ex-COMECON countries. Around 90% of households have refrigerators, washing machines and TVs. Demand for luxury goods is rising. In 1992, Hungary was the second-biggest market after Germany for BMW cars.

Real wages fell less in Hungary than in other eastern European states. However, Hungarians have to work longer hours to pay for basic consumer goods than their western European counterparts. Per capita GDP is still lower than that in the poorest EU state. There is also a growing sense of inequality between those working in the state and private sectors.

WORLD RANKING

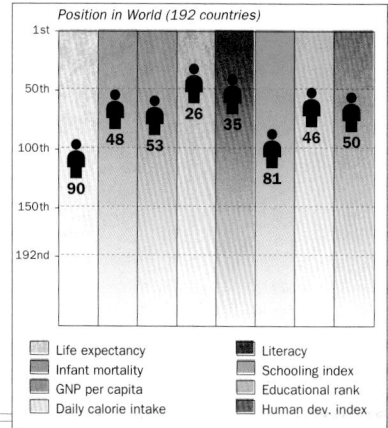

Position in World (192 countries)

| 1st | 50th | 100th | 150th | 192nd |

90   48   53   26   35   81   46   50

- Life expectancy
- Infant mortality
- GNP per capita
- Daily calorie intake
- Literacy
- Schooling index
- Educational rank
- Human dev. index

H

ICELAND

OFFICIAL NAME: Republic of Iceland **CAPITAL:** Reykjavík
POPULATION: 300,000 **CURRENCY:** New Icelandic króna **OFFICIAL LANGUAGE:** Icelandic

EUROPE

EUROPE'S WESTERNMOST COUNTRY, Iceland has a strategic location in the North Atlantic, just south of the Arctic Circle. Its position, on the rift where the North American and European continental plates are pulling apart, accounts for its 200 volcanoes and its numerous geysers and solfataras. Previously a Danish possession, Iceland became fully independent in 1944. Most settlements are along the coast, where ports remain ice-free in winter.

CLIMATE

WEATHER CHART

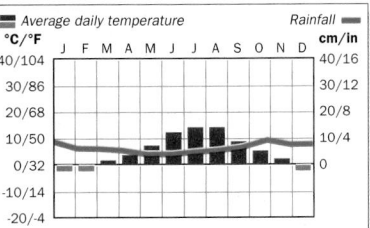

Iceland sits in the Gulf Stream. Winters are consequently mild. Summers are cool, with fine, long sunny days.

TRANSPORTATION

 Keflavík Intl, Reykjavík
557,000 passengers

 18 ships
55,300 dwt

THE TRANSPORTATION NETWORK

2,530 miles (4,070 km)	None
None	None

Icelanders rely entirely on cars, and ownership rates are among the world's highest. Most freight moves by sea. The only main road is the island ring road.

TOURISM

 179,000 visitors   Up 14% in 1994

MAIN OVERSEAS ARRIVALS

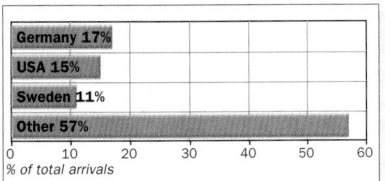

Germany 17%
USA 15%
Sweden 11%
Other 57%

0 10 20 30 40 50 60
% of total arrivals

Iceland is promoting itself, especially in Japan, as an up-market destination for ecotourists, attracted by its spectacular scenery, glaciers, green valleys, fjords and hot springs.

PEOPLE

Icelandic

8 people per sq. mile

THE URBAN/RURAL POPULATION SPLIT

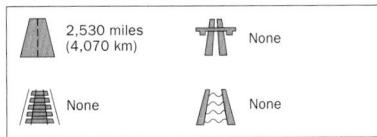

91%   9%

RELIGIOUS PERSUASION

Other 1%   Other Christian 3%

Evangelical Lutheran 96%

Descended from Norwegians and Celts, Icelanders form an ethnically homogeneous society; there are only 4,700 foreign residents. Most people follow the Evangelical Lutheran Church. Living standards are high and there are few social tensions. The predominant cultural influence is from the USA.

POLITICS

 1995/1999

President Vigdís Finnbogadóttir

THE STATE OF THE PARTIES

Parliament 63 members

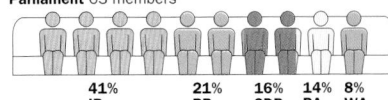

41% IP   21% PP   16% SDP   14% PA   8% WA

IP = Independence Party **PP** = Progressive Party
SDP = Social Democratic Party **PA** = People's Alliance
WA = Women's Alliance

From independence, Iceland was ruled by coalitions. However, in the 1980s the traditional four-party system began to splinter. After the 1991 election, a new IP/SDP coalition promoted market-led reforms. The coalition collapsed after the 1995 election, when both parties had lost support, and was replaced by a center-right government led by the IP, with David Oddsson as prime minister.

The main political issues are the economic downturn and how best to manage Iceland's uneasy dependence on its major source of wealth: fish. Arguments over whether or not to join the EU were defused in 1992 with the successful negotiation of the EEA, giving Iceland access to the key EU market.

ICELAND

Total Land Area : 100 250 sq. km
(38 707 sq. miles)

POPULATION
○ over 50 000
● over 10 000
· under 10 000

LAND HEIGHT
1000m/3281ft
500m/1640ft
200m/656ft
Sea Level
Ice Cap

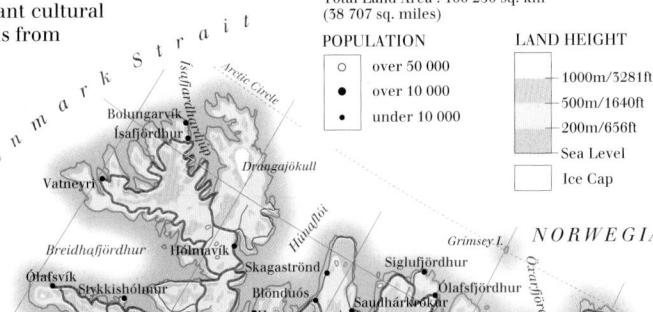

WORLD AFFAIRS

Iceland has traditionally maintained an arm's length relationship with the EU and USA, while seeking to ensure access to both their markets. Its major disputes have been over the extension of its fishing waters. Agreements were ratified with the EEA in 1993, and with the International Whaling Commission over Iceland's wish to continue whaling.

AID

 $5.3m (donations)   No significant change

Aid donations are modest, and form a smaller proportion of the budget than in other Scandinavian states.

DEFENSE

 Coastguard of 130 personnel only   Not applicable

Iceland has no armed forces, but is a member of NATO. The USA has 3,000 troops based at Keflavík.

ECONOMICS

 $6.5bn    68.57–65.23 new Icelandic krónur

SCORE CARD

- ❑ WORLD GNP RANKING..........................94th
- ❑ GNP PER CAPITA $24,590
- ❑ BALANCE OF PAYMENTS $125m
- ❑ INFLATION 1.8%
- ❑ UNEMPLOYMENT.................................4.7%

STRENGTHS

High-tech fishing industry and exclusive access to prime fishing grounds place Iceland in an almost unique position to supply EU and US markets. Very cheap geothermal power.

WEAKNESSES

Dependence on fish for 75% of export earnings. Attempts to diversify have been delayed by world recession.

EXPORTS

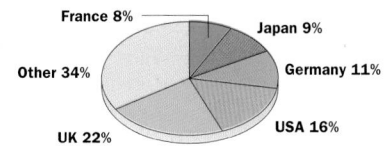

France 8%
Japan 9%
Other 34%
Germany 11%
UK 22%
USA 16%

IMPORTS

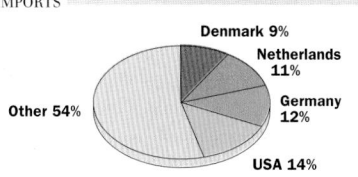

Denmark 9%
Netherlands 11%
Germany 12%
Other 54%
USA 14%

Lava Towers, *near Lake Mӯvatn in northern Iceland, a region of grassy lowlands. The center consists of cold lava desert and glaciers.*

RESOURCES

 4.5bn kwh (capacity 957,000 kw)   1.7m tons

500,000 sheep, 82,000 horses, 77,000 cattle   Diatomite

Iceland has virtually no minerals. All energy needs are met by geothermal and hydroelectric sources. It has implemented measures to try to restore its once abundant fish stocks.

ENVIRONMENT

 9% (7% partially protected)    Iceland has the largest bird sanctuary in Europe

Iceland has no nuclear or coal-fired power stations. The end of Soviet and US submarine operations in the Arctic Circle has removed an environmental threat. Believing that Minke whales eat valuable cod stocks, Iceland decided to resume whale hunting in 1992.

MEDIA

 Freedom of expression is guaranteed

PUBLISHING AND BROADCAST MEDIA

 There are six daily newspapers – most support the views of one political party. *Morgunbladid* has the largest circulation

 1 state-owned, 1 independent service   1 state-owned, 1 independent service

Iceland is renowned for having one of the highest per capita newspaper circulations in the world.

CRIME

 89 prisoners   Crime rates are fairly stable

Crime rates are comparatively low. The rate of alcohol-related murders is higher than the European average.

EDUCATION

 100%    6,161 students

Icelanders buy more books per capita than any other nation. Education is state-run; 25% of school students go on to university at Reykjavík or Akureyri or to colleges in the USA.

CHRONOLOGY

Settled in the 9th century by Norwegians, Iceland was ruled by Denmark from 1380–1944, becoming fully self-governing in 1918.

- ❑ **1940–1945** Occupied by UK and USA.
- ❑ **1944** Independence as a republic.
- ❑ **1949** Founder-member of NATO.
- ❑ **1951** US air base built at Keflavík despite strong local opposition.
- ❑ **1972–1976** Extends fishing limits to 50 miles; two "cod wars" with UK.
- ❑ **1975** Sets 200-mile fishing limit.
- ❑ **1980** Vigdís Finnbogadóttir world's first elected woman head of state.
- ❑ **1985** Declares nuclear-free status.
- ❑ **1995** General election leads to formation of center-right coalition government.

HEALTH

 1 per 333 people   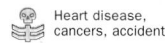 Heart disease, cancers, accidents

The state health system is free to all Icelanders. Iceland has the lowest infant mortality rate, and one of the highest longevity rates, in the world.

WEALTH

 Meat packer, 387 new Icelandic krónur ($6) per hour; bookkeeper, 638 new Icelandic krónur ($10) per hour

CONSUMER GOODS OWNERSHIP

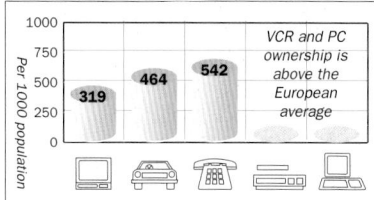

319
464
542

VCR and PC ownership is above the European average

Wealth distribution is comparatively even and social mobility is high. Domestic heating, from geothermal sources, is almost free.

WORLD RANKING

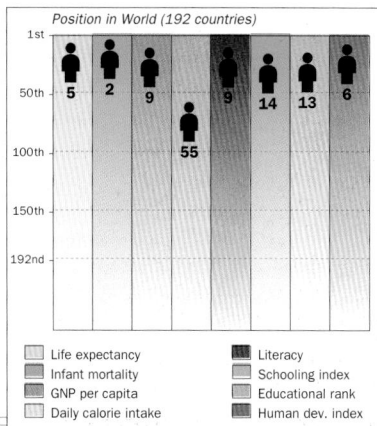

Position in World (192 countries)

5   2   9   55   9   14   13   6

- Life expectancy
- Infant mortality
- GNP per capita
- Daily calorie intake
- Literacy
- Schooling index
- Educational rank
- Human dev. index

I

INDIA

OFFICIAL NAME: Republic of India **CAPITAL:** New Delhi
POPULATION: 935.7 million **CURRENCY:** Rupee **OFFICIAL LANGUAGE:** Hindi and English

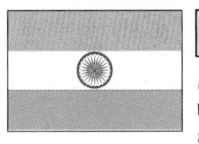 

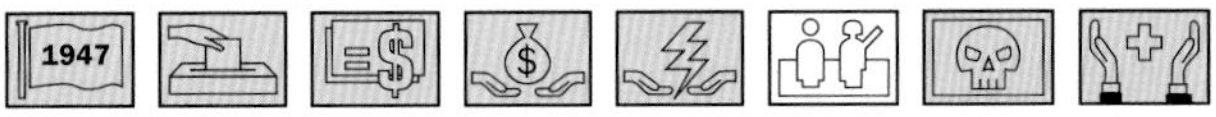

SEPARATED FROM THE REST of Asia by the Himalaya mountain range, India forms a subcontinent. Besides the Himalayas, there are two other main geographical regions, the Indo-Gangetic plain, which lies between the foothills of the Himalayas and the Vindhya Mountains, and the central-southern plateau. India is the world's largest democracy and second most populous country after China. The birth-rate has recently been falling, but even at its current level India's population will probably overtake China's by 2030. After years of protectionism, India is opening up its economy to the outside world. The hope is that the free market will go some way to alleviating one of the country's major problems, poverty.

I

CLIMATE

WEATHER CHART

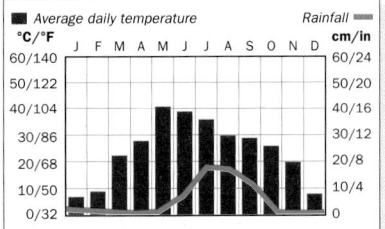

During the hot season, temperatures in the north can reach 104°F. The monsoon breaks in June and peters out in September or October. In the cool season, average temperatures are 50°F–59°F in the north and the weather is mainly dry. However, the south has a less variable climate. Madras is always hot. Average temperatures range from 75°F in January to 90°F in May and June.

TRANSPORTATION

 **Bombay International**
4.05m passengers

 347 ships
1m dwt

THE TRANSPORTATION NETWORK

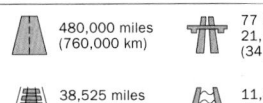

480,000 miles (760,000 km)	77 highways totaling 21,163 miles (34,058 km)
38,525 miles (62,000 km)	11,896 miles (19,145 km)

India's state-owned railroad system spans all the major cities. Rail carries 40% of passenger traffic and 65% of freight. Some routes still use steam locomotives. Intercity highways are narrow, poorly maintained and congested. Scooter and cycle rickshaws are common in urban centers. Calcutta still has rickshaws pulled by hand.

INDIA

Total Land Area : 2 973 190 sq. km
(1 147 949 sq. miles)

POPULATION

- ■ over 5 000 000
- ◉ over 1 000 000
- ◎ over 500 000
- ⊙ over 100 000
- • over 10 000

LAND HEIGHT

- 5000m/16 405ft
- 4000m/13 124ft
- 3000m/9843ft
- 2000m/6562ft
- 1000m/3281ft
- 500m/1640ft
- 200m/656ft
- Sea Level

A religious festival. Such festivals are a frequent occurrence and form an important part of Hindu culture.

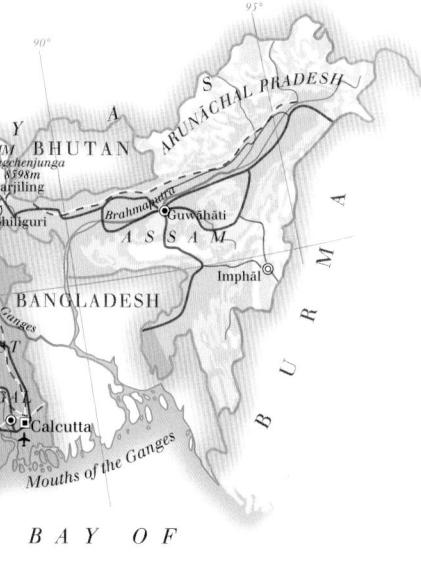

BAY OF
BENGAL

TOURISM

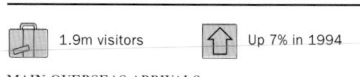

1.9m visitors   Up 7% in 1994

MAIN OVERSEAS ARRIVALS

UK 14%	
Bangladesh 13%	
Pakistan 9%	
USA 7%	
Sri Lanka 1%	
Other 56%	

0   10   20   30   40   50   60
% of total arrivals

Tourism is India's sixth-largest foreign exchange earner. More luxury hotels are now being built, and wildlife and adventure tourism are being developed. However, India still has only a small share of the world tourism market – 0.3% of the world's tourists and 1% of revenue – and is keen to expand this source of revenue and take in 2.5 million visitors by the late 1990s.

PEOPLE

 Hindi, Urdu, Bengali, Marathi, Telugu, Tamil, Bihari, Gujarati, Kanarese   816 people per sq. mile

THE URBAN/RURAL POPULATION SPLIT

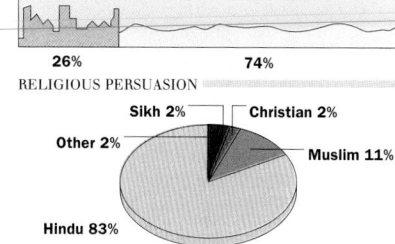

26%   74%

RELIGIOUS PERSUASION

Sikh 2%   Christian 2%
Other 2%   Muslim 11%
Hindu 83%

ETHNIC MAKEUP

Mongoloid and other 3%
Dravidian 25%
Indo-Aryan 72%

The world's second most populous country after China, India is home to 16% of the global population. Despite a major birth-control program, population growth has decreased only slightly from 2.1% a year in the mid-1980s to 2% in 1990–1991. Nationwide awareness campaigns aim to promote the idea of smaller families. India's planners consider the rise in the population the most significant brake on development. Cultural and religious pressures encourage large families, however, and the extended family is seen as an essential security for old age.

The fertile rice-growing areas of the Gangetic plain and delta are very densely populated. The northern state of Uttar Pradesh has the largest population, at 139 million, followed by neighboring Bihār and the western state of Mahārāshtra. Mahārāshtra is also the most urbanized state, with 55% of its people living in towns or cities. Elsewhere, most Indians live in rural areas, although poverty continues to drive many to the swelling cities.

Some 83% of the population are Hindus. Each Hindu belongs to one of thousands of castes and sub-castes. Hindus are born into their caste and caste determines whom they marry and their future status and occupation. Various attempts to reform the system have met with violent opposition.

POPULATION AGE BREAKDOWN

%	■ 0–14	□ 15–64	□ 65+		
	3.4%	3.7%	4%	4.5%	5.1%
	56.8%	55.9%	57.5%	59%	60.4%
	39.8%	40.4%	38.5%	36.5%	34.5%
	1960	1970	1980	1990	2000

% of population by age group

CHRONOLOGY

The origins of an Indus valley civilization may be traced back to the third millennium BC. By the 3rd century BC, the Mauryan kingdom under Ashoka encompassed most of modern India. Following the Battle of Plassey in 1757, British rule – through the East India Company – was consolidated.

❑ **1885** Indian National Congress formed to press for political reform.
❑ **1919** Act of parliament for "responsible government."
❑ **1920–1922** Mahatma Gandhi's first civil disobedience campaign.
❑ **1930–1933** Further civil disobedience action.
❑ **1935** Government of India act.
❑ **1936** First elections under new constitution.
❑ **1942–1943** "Quit India" movement.
❑ **1947** August, independence and partition into India and Pakistan. Jawarhalal Nehru becomes first prime minister.
❑ **1948** Assassination of Mahatma Gandhi. War with Pakistan over Kashmir. India becomes a republic.
❑ **1951–1952** First general election won by Congress party.
❑ **1957** Second elections won by Congress. First elected communist government anywhere installed in Kerala.
❑ **1960** Bombay divided into states of Gujarat and Mahārāshtra.
❑ **1962** Congress party reelected. Border war with China.
❑ **1964** Death of Nehru. Lal Bahadur Shastri becomes prime minister.
❑ **1965** Second war with Pakistan over Kashmir.
❑ **1966** Shastri dies; Indira Gandhi (daughter of Jawarhalal Nehru) becomes prime minister.
❑ **1967** Opposition takes control of several states following general election.
❑ **1969** Split of Congress party into two factions, the larger of which is led by Indira Gandhi.
❑ **1971** Indira Gandhi's Congress party wins elections. Third war with Pakistan over creation of Bangladesh.
❑ **1972** Simla (peace) Agreement signed with Pakistan.
❑ **1974** Explosion of first nuclear device in underground test.
❑ **1975–1977** Imposition of state of emergency.
❑ **1977** Congress loses general election. People's Party (JD) takes power at the center.
❑ **1978** New political group, Congress (Indira) – Congress (I) – formally established.
❑ **1980** Indira Gandhi's C(I) wins general election. ⇨

I

CHRONOLOGY *continued*

- ❏ **1984** Storming of Sikh Golden Temple of Amritsar by Indian troops. Assassination of Indira Gandhi by Sikh bodyguard; her son Rajiv becomes prime minister. Gas explosion at US-owned Union Carbide Corporation plant in Bhopāl kills 2,000 people, becoming the country's worst-ever environmental disaster.
- ❏ **1985** Peace accords with militant separatists in Assam and Punjab.
- ❏ **1987** Indian peacekeeping force deployed in northern Sri Lanka to combat Tamil terrorists.
- ❏ **1988** Punjab unrest continues. Golden Temple in Amritsar again stormed by army.
- ❏ **1989** General election results in electoral setback for C(I) which is implicated in Bofors arms scandal. National Front forms minority government with BJP support.
- ❏ **1990** Withdrawal of peacekeeping troops from Sri Lanka. BJP leader Lal Advant arrested. No-confidence motion in parliament; Chandra Shekhar prime minister of minority government.
- ❏ **1991** February, C(I) led by Rajiv Gandhi, Indira's son, ousts minority government. May, Rajiv Gandhi assassinated during polling in general elections. His successor, P. V. Narasimha Rao, becomes prime minister of a C(I) minority government. Program of economic liberalization and reform is initiated. Government removes trade barriers and encourages foreign and private investment.
- ❏ **1992** Major financial scandal involving Bombay Stock Exchange. Demolition of the Babri Masjid mosque at Ayodhya by Hindu extremists causes widespread violence leaving 1,200 people dead.
- ❏ **1993** Resurgence of Hindu–Muslim riots leaves over 500 dead in Bombay. Bomb explosions rock Bombay. Border troop agreement with China.
- ❏ **1994** Protests against the government's privatization plans. Rupee made fully convertible. Outbreak of pneumonic plague. C(I) routed in key state elections amid allegations of growing corruption in the ruling party.
- ❏ **1995** C(I) suffers electoral setback in further state elections, triggering a party split as dissidents accuse Prime Minister Rao of condoning political corruption. Punjab Chief Minister is assassinated by Sikh extremists.
- ❏ **1996** Corruption scandal triggers huge political crisis and a string of ministerial resignations.

POLITICS

 L. House 1996/2001   President Shankar Dayal Sharma

THE STATE OF THE PARTIES

House of the People (*Lok Sabha*) 543 members

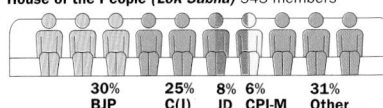

30% BJP	25% C(I)	8% JD	6% CPI-M	31% Other

BJP = Indian People's Party **C (I)** = Congress (I)
JD = People's Party **CPI-M** = Communist Party of India – Marxist **Other** = Communist Party of India, Telugu Nation

Council of States (*Rajya Sabha*) 245 members

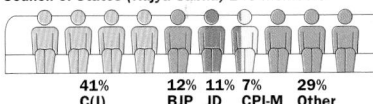

41% C(I)	12% BJP	11% JD	7% CPI-M	29% Other

India is a multiparty democracy. The *Lok Sabha* (lower house) is directly elected by universal adult suffrage, while the *Rajya Sabha* (upper house) is indirectly elected by the state assemblies. There are 25 self-governing states. Of the seven union territories, Delhi and Pondicherry have their own assemblies.

MAIN POLITICAL ISSUES
Political corruption
Allegations of political corruption have recently dominated the Indian political scene. In 1989, the political reputation of the C(I) prime minister Rajiv Gandhi was tarnished after he was accused of receiving payments from the Swedish arms company, Bofors, in return for an arms contract. Another financial scandal involving the C(I) that erupted in May 1992 renewed charges of corruption against the party. Fears of widespread corruption across the political spectrum were confirmed in early 1996, when several C(I) ministers and leaders of the main opposition BJP were charged with receiving bribes from a businessman.

Hindu militancy
The right-wing nationalist BJP, supported mainly by the middle classes and upper castes, has consolidated its position as a credible alternative to the C(I). In the 1989 general election, it surprised analysts by winning 86 seats, and two years later, with its ally the *Shiv Sena,* raised its tally to 123. It also gained control of five states, including Uttar Pradesh. Despite the BJP's alleged involvement in the country's biggest political scandal, which erupted early in 1996, it emerged as the largest party in the *Lok Sabha* after the 1996 elections though its minority government lasted only ten days.

The free market
Economic liberalization and the signing of the GATT agreement has led to widespread public protest in Delhi and other parts of the country. The government's critics contend that GATT will undermine local production and lead to higher prices, while liberalization policies will encourage investment by foreign multinational companies to the detriment of the national economy. Recognizing the potential impact of these claims, the C(I) in 1994 increased spending on rural development programs – a trend reinforced in the latest 1996–1997 budget.

PROFILE
Narasimha Rao, prime minister from 1991 to 1996, became leader of the C(I) after Rajiv Gandhi's assassination. He was only the second leader of India's main party not to be related the Nehru dynasty. In the state elections of 1993, he consolidated his rule as the C(I) recaptured Madhya Pradesh and the Himalayan state of Himachal Pradesh, the first reversal since the early 1980s for the Hindu nationalist BJP. Defeat in the 1996 general election, however, left Rao's political future in doubt.

The 1996 general election was a major setback for C(I). The dominant political force for five decades, it originated in the 1930s as an umbrella group with a left of center stance fighting for independence. Rao reshaped the party's philosophy, offering a "new vision" of the market-led open economy. The general election results reflect the advances made in recent years by the BJP, the regional parties, and parties representing lower castes.

Now India faces a period of political uncertainty, in which the loose center-left coalition must present a united front in order to stave off moves by the BJP to call another general election.

P. V. Narasimha Rao, prime minister from 1991–1996.

President Shankar Dayal Sharma, who took office in July 1992.

Manmohan Singh, architect of India's liberalization.

WORLD AFFAIRS

 Comm **G15** **G24** **NAM** **SAARC**

Delhi's overriding preoccupation in foreign policy is the divided territory of Kashmir. Disputes with Pakistan sparked two bloody wars, in 1948 and 1965. Pakistan wishes to annex largely Muslim Kashmir, and believes it would receive the support of the Kashmiri population. India is unwilling to hold a referendum or to cede any territory. The USA sees Kashmir as a potential nuclear flashpoint. It is promoting a settlement on the basis that both states limit their nuclear arsenals. However, India will not discuss nuclear weapons. It regards the Nuclear Non-proliferation Treaty as an instance of First World discrimination. Indo–US relations have recently been strained following Washington's delivery of nearly 40 F-16 jets to Pakistan, in return for a cap on its nuclear program. Relations with Beijing are now cordial.

AID

 $1.5bn (receipts)   Down 36% in 1993

India receives aid, but, unlike other countries in the region, is not dependent on it. Receipts have largely been spent on building infrastructure. The World Bank recently pulled out of the Narmada Dam project following a long campaign by environmentalists.

DEFENSE

 $8.1bn   Up 11% in 1995

0   *Defense spending as % GDP*   40

2.8%

INDIAN ARMED FORCES

2,400 main battle tanks (500 T–55, 1,100 T–72, 800 *Vijayanta*)	980,000 personnel
15 submarines, 2 carriers, 5 destroyers, 18 frigates and 41 patrol boats	55,000 personnel
844 combat aircraft (97 *Jaguar* S(I), MiG–21/23/27/29)	110,000 personnel
Nuclear capability	

India has an army of almost one million men, making it the fourth-largest in the world. Included in its arsenal is the recently displayed *Prithvi* missile. However, cuts in defense are forecast as the defense budget is squeezed. Much of India's foreign weaponry is outdated. Aging MiG-21s, which form a central part of the air force, are unlikely to be replaced. India produces its own *Arjun* battle tank.

ECONOMICS

 $279bn    31.36–35.17 Indian rupees

SCORE CARD

❏ WORLD GNP RANKING	16th
❏ GNP PER CAPITA	$310
❏ BALANCE OF PAYMENTS	$–7bn
❏ INFLATION	10.2%
❏ UNEMPLOYMENT	Widespread underemployment

EXPORTS

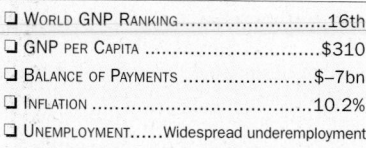

United Arab Emirates 4% — UK 7% — Germany 8% — Japan 8% — USA 19% — Other 54%

IMPORTS

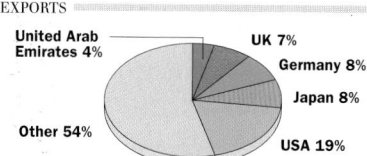

UK 9% — Germany 9% — Japan 9% — USA 11% — Other 62%

STRENGTHS

Massive home market of over 800 million people. Cheap labor. Some of the work force possess skills for new high-tech industries such as software programing. Highly efficient textile sector and garment manufacturers. Growing competitiveness on world market reflected in high export growth – up 20% in 1993. Competition is encouraging firms to manufacture to international standards.

There has been a massive rise in foreign direct investment as the economy is opened up to foreign competition; $5 billion worth of investment has been approved by government since 1991, including $3 billion in 1993. Much of this will go into the power sector. Large multinationals, such as Coca-Cola and IBM, are returning after leaving the country despite protests from some opposition groups who are hostile to the growing presence of foreign businesses in the country.

WEAKNESSES

A large budget deficit continues to dog India's economy. In 1995–1996, the budget deficit reached 5.9% of GDP, exceeding the set target of 5.5% of GDP. Cuts in industrial and food subsidies, aimed at reducing the budget deficit have fueled inflation, which stood at over 10% in 1995. Poor roads, ports and telecommunications systems, coupled with power shortages have all acted as a brake on economic growth. Mass unemployment and underemployment – urban unemployed estimated to be in the region of 37 million.

ECONOMIC PERFORMANCE INDICATOR

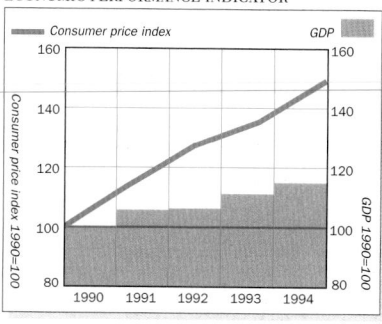

Consumer price index — GDP

Consumer price index 1990=100 / GDP 1990=100

1990 1991 1992 1993 1994

PROFILE

India's economy is undergoing radical changes. India has converted from a highly protectionist mixed economy, which built the basis of a modern industrial state, to a free-market economy. It is now entering the global marketplace. A series of wide-ranging reforms, from lowering trade barriers to attracting foreign investment, have been put in place. Despite objections from opposition parties, India ratified the GATT world trade agreement in 1995.

INDIA : MAJOR BUSINESSES

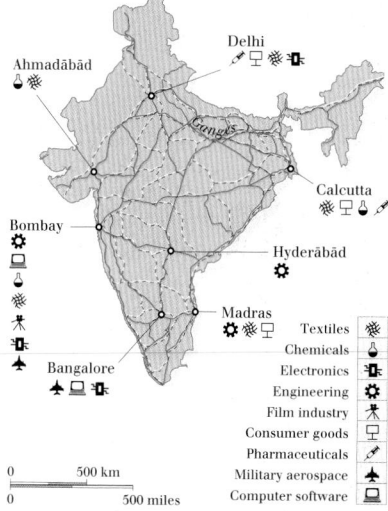

Delhi — Ahmadābād — Bombay — Bangalore — Calcutta — Hyderābād — Madras

Textiles — Chemicals — Electronics — Engineering — Film industry — Consumer goods — Pharmaceuticals — Military aerospace — Computer software

0   500 km
0   500 miles

Hillside monastery in Ladakh, Kashmir, northern India. *The Ladakhi Buddhists maintain their traditional farming existence and are known for their friendliness.*

I

I

RESOURCES

326bn kwh
(capacity 75.9m kw)

549,109 b/d
(reserves
6,049,068,000 bbl)

193m cattle, 118m
goats, 44.8m sheep

Iron, diamonds, coal,
limestone, zinc, lead

ELECTRICITY GENERATION

Hydro 21% (69bn kwh)

Thermal 77% (251bn kwh)

Nuclear 2% (6bn kwh)

Other 0%

% of total generation by type

ENVIRONMENT

4% (3% partially
protected)

Forestry programs
are largely funded
through foreign aid

ENVIRONMENTAL TREATIES

Yes	Yes	Yes
No	Yes	Yes

Deforestation is one of India's most pressing environmental problems. Unplanned industrial development and the pressure for more agricultural land have felled once lush tree cover and less than 11% of original forest cover remains. The effect has been a sharp rise in soil erosion, the silting up of dams, and landslides. India experienced its worst environmental accident in 1984, when an explosion at the Union Carbide plant in Bhopāl led to an escape of lethal gases. Over 2,000 died.

MEDIA

 Some censorship of the press. Western TV soaps and films widely considered unsuitable

PUBLISHING AND BROADCAST MEDIA

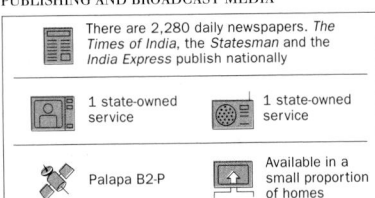

There are 2,280 daily newspapers. *The Times of India*, the *Statesman* and the *India Express* publish nationally

1 state-owned
service

1 state-owned
service

Palapa B2-P

Available in a
small proportion
of homes

Satellite TV is increasingly popular in India. Services range from the BBC World Service to CNN, Hindi language Zee TV and MTV, and one state-run channel. More than seven million households are estimated to have acquired dishes. State-run terrestrial TV has suffered as a result. Critics fear a Western onslaught on Indian values. Recent newspaper launches include the *Asian Age*, which is simultaneously published in London by satellite and claims to be India's first truly international paper.

India's most significant mineral exports are iron ore and cut diamonds. There are, in addition, large coal reserves. The steel industry has recently been opened up in line with the free market reforms. Steel imports are now subject to lower duties, but the industry has so far withstood external competition, and exports have increased. However, production, which consumes up to twice as much energy as that used by some foreign competitors, is inefficient by international standards.

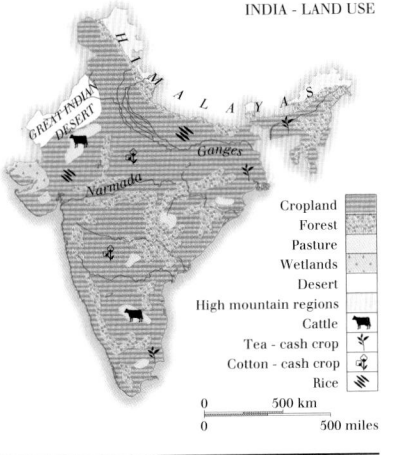

INDIA - LAND USE

	Cropland
	Forest
	Pasture
	Wetlands
	Desert
	High mountain regions
	Cattle
	Tea - cash crop
	Cotton - cash crop
	Rice

0   500 km
0   500 miles

CRIME

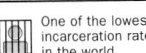 One of the lowest incarceration rates in the world

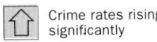 Crime rates rising significantly

CRIME RATES

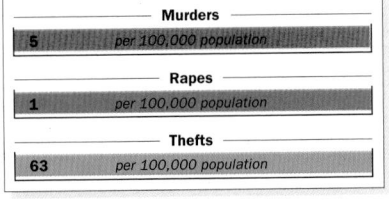

Murders
5   per 100,000 population

Rapes
1   per 100,000 population

Thefts
63   per 100,000 population

Violent crime is on the increase in India, particularly in the big cities. Theft has risen sharply as consumer spending increases.

Many of the violent criminal gangs operating in major cities such as Bombay have made vast profits from smuggling, prostitution, narcotics, protection and extortion rackets, together with forcibly taking land from the poor. Bombay's gangs have strong connections with Dubai and the Middle East; they are also said to have contacts among politicians and the police.

In large areas of central India and particularly in the region around Gwalior, *dacoits* still operate. Modeled on the *thugee* gangs of the 19th century, they are outlaws who live by highway robbery and terrorizing small rural communities.

The state is currently unable to meet the country's demand for electricity. Petroleum and coal are the main sources of energy generation although these are imported. There are plans to increase capacity by another 31,000 MW by 1997. However, a recent scheme in Mahārāshtra to increase output by attracting investment from the US-led consortium, Enron, was mired in controversy when the BJP state government temporarily suspended negotiations to appease nationalist groups opposed to foreign businesses.

EDUCATION

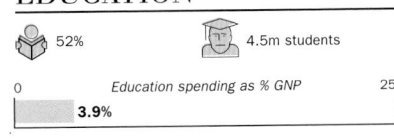

52%

4.5m students

0   Education spending as % GNP   25

3.9%

THE EDUCATION SYSTEM

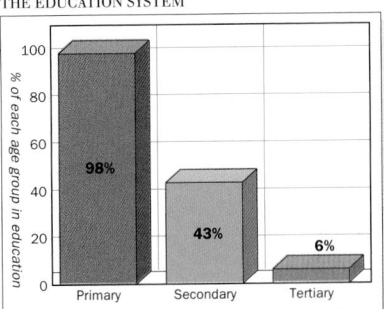

% of each age group in education

100
80
60
40
20
0

Primary 98%   Secondary 43%   Tertiary 6%

There is now an elementary school in every village across the subcontinent. However, many children drop out of school to provide supplementary income for their families. There are 50 million students at secondary level, and some 10 million graduates from nearly 200 universities. Women make up 9% of those enrolled in higher education, a high percentage for a low-income economy. India has one of the largest pools of science graduates anywhere in the world. However, the 48% illiteracy rate among adults is a significant brake on development.

Corn cultivation in terraced fields in central India. *In addition to rice, wheat, sorghum, corn, millet and barley are also important cereal crops.*

REGIONS

WEST BENGAL

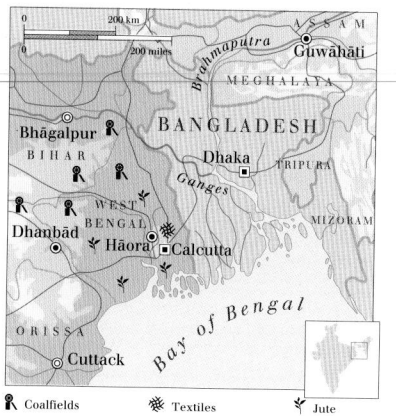

Coalfields   Textiles   Jute

WEST BENGAL is the only region in the world with a freely elected communist government. The communists have ruled the state since 1978. Once home to 80% of the country's industry, West Bengal then became synonymous with economic decline and stagnation. However, the government has now revolutionized its economic policy, welcoming once-hated multinationals in key sectors.

Calcutta, the capital of the British Raj until 1911, has been in slow decline ever since. Over 20% of the city's 12 million people live in appalling slum conditions. Mother Theresa runs her famous mission in the city.

KARNATAKA

BANGALORE, THE CAPITAL of Karnataka, has earned itself the name of the "silicon plateau." Reputed to be South Asia's fastest growing city, it is the home of a burgeoning electronics industry. A large pool of skilled engineering staff and comparatively low wage rates have attracted many foreign, particularly US, firms to the city.

The rich forest areas of Karnataka, particularly in the Western Ghats, include rare tracts of moist tropical deciduous forest. Vast acreages of eucalyptus trees have been planted, but most of these have been used for industrial purposes rather than to alleviate the fuelwood crisis faced by the rural poor.

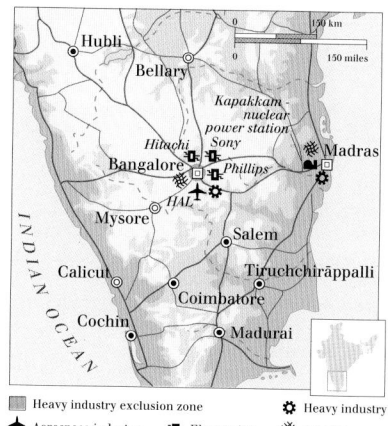

Heavy industry exclusion zone   Heavy industry
Aerospace industry   Electronics   Textiles

BOMBAY

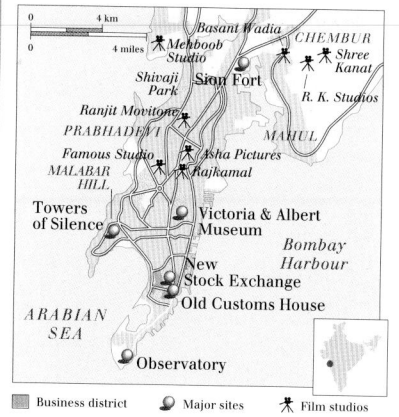

Business district   Major sites   Film studios

BOMBAY, RENAMED MUMBAI, in 1995, is the symbol of 1990s India, with a reputation for making people rich, legally or illegally. Fast moving and cosmopolitan, it is the country's commercial capital. Central Bombay, a mixture of skyscrapers and English colonial architecture, boasts some of the highest real estate prices in the world. Dalal Street is home to the Bombay Stock Exchange, which was established in 1875. One of the city's folk heroes is Harshad Mehta, who made a fortune selling stocks and shares in the early 1990s, before being exposed as the man behind India's biggest-ever financial fraud.

Bombay is the center of India's film industry, which is the world's biggest producer of feature films. Indian films are exported to over 100 countries. The stars of what is known as "Bollywood," India's Hollywood, live in the affluent Malabar Hills neighborhood. Close by there is mass poverty. A 2.8 mile sprawl of shanties known as Dharavi in central Bombay is reputed to be the world's biggest slum.

HEALTH

1 per 2,157 people

Respiratory, nutritional and diarrheal diseases, malaria

0   Health spending as % GDP   25
1.3%

Malnutrition is common among the poor, and infant mortality stands at 80 per 1,000 live births. Much of this is due to preventable diseases such as diarrhea. AIDS began to spread in the mid-1980s and is now accelerating. HIV infection rates among prostitutes have increased twentyfold in seven years. An unusual outbreak of pneumonic plague in 1995 was estimated to have killed more than 100 people.

WEALTH

Field crop worker, 7–33 Indian rupees ($0.2–0.9) per day; office clerk, 380–875 Indian rupees ($11–25) per month

CONSUMER GOODS OWNERSHIP

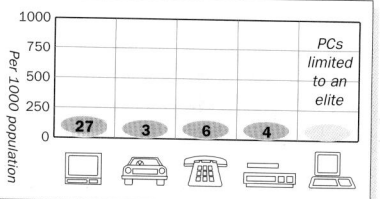

PCs limited to an elite

27   3   6   4

According to the government, 240 million people (30% of the population), mostly in rural areas, were living below the poverty line in the late 1980s. Recent studies dispute whether this figure is rising or falling. Extremes of wealth, particularly with the opening up of the economy, are frequently seen alongside extremes of poverty. The middle class, who number some 150–200 million, have an exceedingly comfortable lifestyle, with servants and plush housing. Many of the slums in cities such as Bombay and Calcutta have five to nine people living in one room; few slum houses have sanitation. In Bombay alone, over 100,000 people live on the sidewalks.

WORLD RANKING

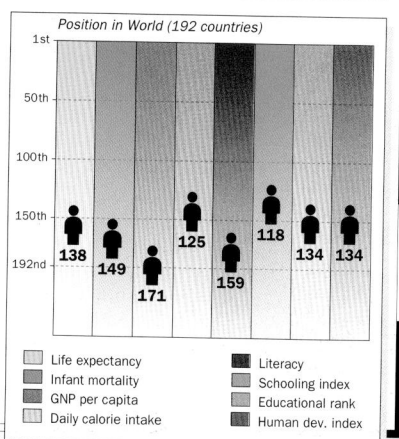

Position in World (192 countries)

1st   50th   100th   150th   192nd

138   149   171   125   159   118   134   134

Life expectancy   Literacy
Infant mortality   Schooling index
GNP per capita   Educational rank
Daily calorie intake   Human dev. index

INDONESIA

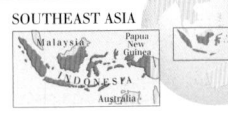

SOUTHEAST ASIA

OFFICIAL NAME: Republic of Indonesia **CAPITAL:** Jakarta
POPULATION: 197.6 million **CURRENCY:** Rupiah **OFFICIAL LANGUAGE:** Bahasa Indonesia

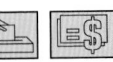

THE WORLD'S LARGEST ARCHIPELAGO, Indonesia's myriad islands stretch 3,107 miles eastwards across the Pacific, from the Malay Peninsula to New Guinea. The main islands of Sumatra, Java, Kalimantan, Irian Jaya and Sulawesi are mountainous, volcanic and densely forested. Formerly the Dutch East Indies, Indonesia achieved independence in 1949. Politics has since been dominated by the military. Demands for greater autonomy on outlying islands and for liberation by East Timor, annexed in 1975, have been forcefully opposed.

Rice terraces on Bali, one of Indonesia's 13,677 islands and its most popular tourist destination. Rice is the staple food crop.

CLIMATE

WEATHER CHART

Indonesia's climate is predominantly tropical monsoon. Variations relate mainly to differences in latitude and physical structure, but hilly areas are cooler overall. Rain falls throughout the year, often in thunderstorms, but there is a relatively dry season from June to September. December to March is the wettest period, except in the Moluccas, which receive the bulk of their rain between June and September. Rainfall averages between 59 inches and 157 inches a year.

TRANSPORTATION

 Sukarno-Hatta, Jakarta
7.53m passengers

 810 ships
2.96m dwt

THE TRANSPORTATION NETWORK

85,170 miles (137,000 km)		125 miles (200 km)	
4,168 miles (6,708 km)		13,409 miles (21,579 km)	

With 13,677 islands spread across nearly 3,107 miles and three time zones, communications are an obvious government priority. Indonesia was an early entrant into satellite communications and a countrywide, satellite-based telephone system is being installed.

Indonesia's road and shipping infrastructure is also being improved. Ports are being extended and expressway projects include the recently completed Jakarta–Bandung link. The toll roads around Jakarta are contracted to President Suharto's daughter, Siti.

TOURISM

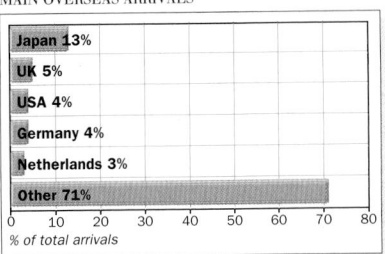

4m visitors

Up 18% in 1994

MAIN OVERSEAS ARRIVALS

Japan	13%
UK	5%
USA	4%
Germany	4%
Netherlands	3%
Other	71%

% of total arrivals

Tourism has taken off since the mid-1980s. The number of visitors increased steadily by an average 24% a year between 1986 and 1992, to over three million. Bali, Java and Sumatra are the most popular destinations. The expansion has been underpinned by several factors, including a major investment in hotels and the opening of Bali to airlines other than the national carrier, *Garuda Indonesia.*

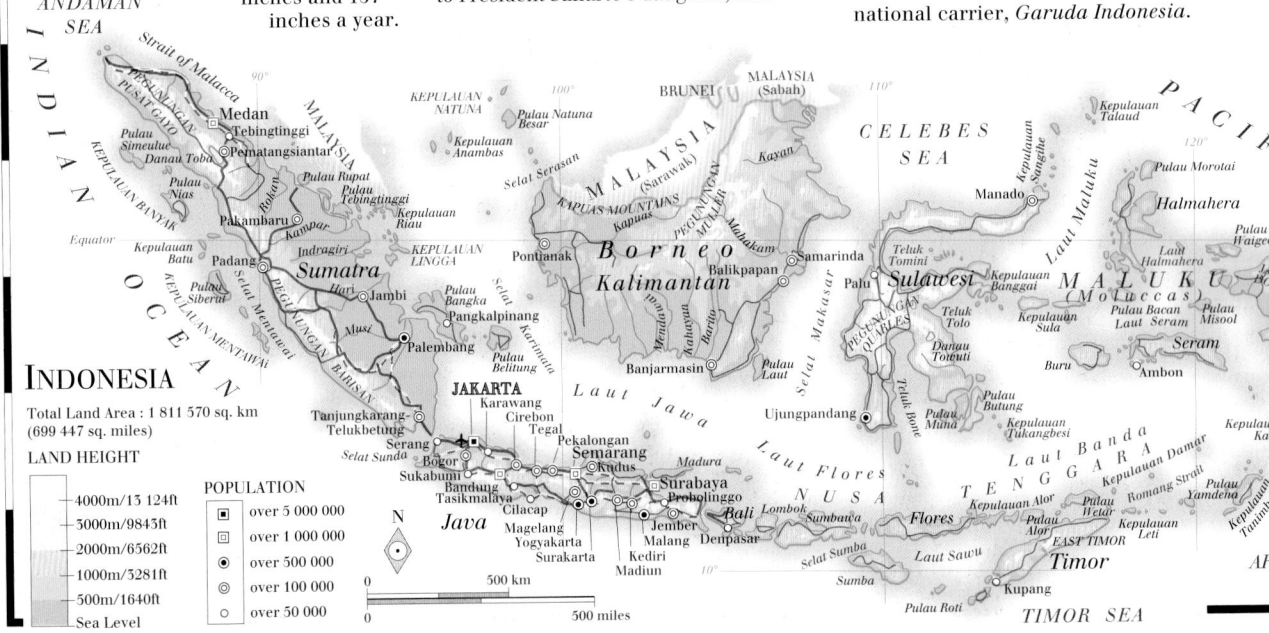

INDONESIA

Total Land Area : 1 811 570 sq. km
(699 447 sq. miles)

LAND HEIGHT

- 4000m/13 124ft
- 3000m/9843ft
- 2000m/6562ft
- 1000m/3281ft
- 500m/1640ft
- Sea Level

POPULATION

- ■ over 5 000 000
- ⊡ over 1 000 000
- ◉ over 500 000
- ◎ over 100 000
- ○ over 50 000

500 km

500 miles

PEOPLE

 Javanese, Madurese, Sundanese, Bahasa Indonesia, Dutch

 282 people per sq. mile

THE URBAN/RURAL POPULATION SPLIT

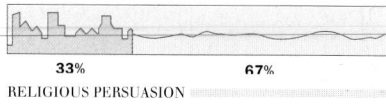

33%   67%

RELIGIOUS PERSUASION

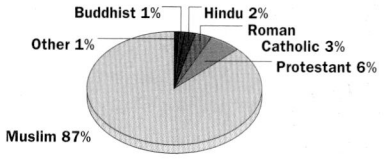

Buddhist 1% | Hindu 2%
Roman Catholic 3%
Other 1%
Protestant 6%
Muslim 87%

ETHNIC MAKEUP

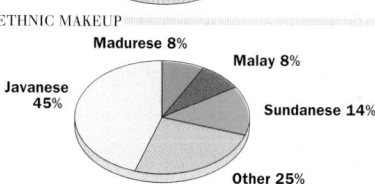

Madurese 8%
Malay 8%
Javanese 45%
Sundanese 14%
Other 25%

Indonesia's basic Melanesian–Malay ethnic division disguises a very diverse society. At least 250 languages or dialects are spoken. Urbanization and the national language, Bahasa Indonesia, have acted as unifying factors. The Javanese-dominated central government, however, has caused much resentment by attempting to suppress local culture and politics in order to create a national identity. The East Timoreans, the Aceh of northern Sumatra and the Papuans of Irian Jaya, denied autonomy, are all in conflict with the government.

Discrimination against the Chinese community, which has included a ban on Chinese script, has not undermined its dominance of big business.

The traditional extended family is breaking down in urban areas. There is legal sexual equality, and women are taking an increasingly active economic role – led by President Suharto's wife and daughter, both engaged in business.

POPULATION AGE BREAKDOWN

% of population by age group	0–14	15–64	65+

	1960	1970	1980	1990	2000
65+	3.3%	3.1%	3.3%	3.9%	5.1%
15–64	56.6%	54.7%	55.7%	60.4%	63.6%
0–14	40.1%	42.2%	41%	35.7%	31.3%

POLITICS

 U. House 1992/1997
L. House 1992/1997

President Gen. Suharto

THE STATE OF THE PARTIES

House of Representatives 500 members

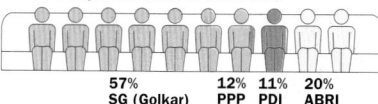

57% SG (Golkar) | 12% PPP | 11% PDI | 20% ABRI

SG = Joint Secretariat of Functional Groups **PPP** = United Development Party **PDI** = Indonesian Democratic Party **ABRI** = Indonesian Armed Forces (appointed members)

People's Consultative Assembly 1000 members

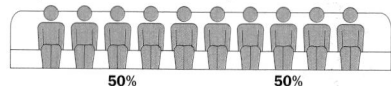

50% House of Representatives | 50% Other

500 members of House of Representatives and 500 further members, including delegates from regional assemblies and representatives of political organizations

Indonesia is a highly controlled semi-democracy, headed by General Suharto, who was returned for his sixth consecutive term as president in 1993.

MAIN POLITICAL ISSUE
The succession
President Suharto will be almost 77 by the next elections. Although he is under some pressure to relinquish power, it appears likely that Asia's longest-serving leader is heading for a seventh five-year term. A key factor in his decision is expected to be the protection of his children – and their extensive economic interests.

PROFILE
Golkar – a loose federation of groups representing sectional interests – is the dominant political organization. Its main function is to provide a civilian base for Suharto's "New Order" regime. The army remains the ultimate source of political power. The two legal opposition parties – the PPP and the PDI – effectively serve as "partners" of government. However, the election of former president Sukarno's daughter as PDI chair raised the party's profile. Opposition to Jakarta's centralist politics has fueled secessionist movements in Sumatra and Irian Jaya and a liberation movement on East Timor, annexed by Indonesia in 1975.

General Suharto, ex-army chief of staff. President since 1968.

Sukarno, first president and "Father of Independence."

WORLD AFFAIRS

 APEC ASEAN G15 NAM OPEC

Indonesia's foreign policy under General Suharto has been one of non-alignment – it became NAM chairman in 1992 – tempered by the need to retain good relations with the West.

Foreign policy concerns include a continuing suspicion of China, despite the restoration of diplomatic ties in 1990. Indonesia and Australia signed a ground-breaking security cooperation agreement in late 1995.

Internationally, the government is coming under pressure, particularly from the USA, to improve its human rights record, especially with regard to East Timor.

AID

 $2bn (receipts)   Down 3% in 1993

Indonesia relies on aid to cover its current account deficit. Japan accounts for 75% of bilateral aid; the World Bank for 58% of multilateral. Almost 30% of all aid is affected by "leakage," including project delays and corruption.

CHRONOLOGY

On the trade route between India and China, the Indonesian archipelago has long attracted outside interest – Hindu, Buddhist, Islamic, then, from the 16th century, European. The Dutch were victors in the rivalry to exploit its strategic position, valuable spices and oil. Colonization began in the 17th century on Java. By 1910, the Dutch East Indies encompassed the whole of present-day Indonesia, except East Timor.

❑ **1901** Dutch introduce "ethical policy" giving limited educational and administrative opportunities to indigenous population; encourages growth of intellectual class with nationalist aspirations.

❑ **1912** Sarekat Islam party formed.

❑ **1920** Indonesian Communist Party (PKI) formed; leads revolts in West Java, 1926; Sumatra, 1927.

❑ **1927** Indonesian National Party formed under Dr. Sukarno.

❑ **1930s** Dutch repression.

❑ **1942–1945** Japanese occupation. Promise of autonomy in "Greater East Asia." Sukarno works with Japanese while promoting independence.

❑ **1945** August, three days after Japanese surrender, Sukarno declares Indonesia independent from the Netherlands. ➪

I

DEFENSE

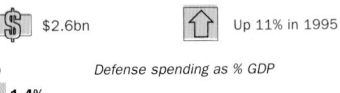

$2.6bn | Up 11% in 1995

0 — Defense spending as % GDP — 40
1.4%

INDONESIAN ARMED FORCES

331 light tanks (275 AMX-13, 30 PT-76, 26 *Scorpion*)	214,000 personnel
2 submarines, 13 frigates, 34 patrol boats	40,500 personnel
73 combat aircraft (24 A-4, 11 F-16, 14 I HAWK Mk 53)	20,000 personnel
None	

The constitution enshrines the military's political role, and it remains a key influence in Indonesia. The recent "civilianization" of political parties, the bureaucracy and state companies has reduced the presence of the military in these areas, if not their influence. This was also apparent in the appointment of former supreme commander Try Sutrisno as vice-president, and thus a leading candidate to succeed Suharto. Defense spending is low by regional standards. However, "off-budget funds" often supplement official allocations. The main defense issues are currently internal security and the perceived Chinese threat.

ECONOMICS

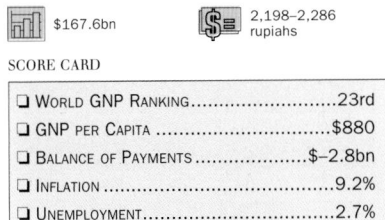

$167.6bn | 2,198–2,286 rupiahs

SCORE CARD

❏ WORLD GNP RANKING............................23rd
❏ GNP PER CAPITA $880
❏ BALANCE OF PAYMENTS ....$–2.8bn
❏ INFLATION 9.2%
❏ UNEMPLOYMENT..................................2.7%

ECONOMIC PERFORMANCE INDICATOR

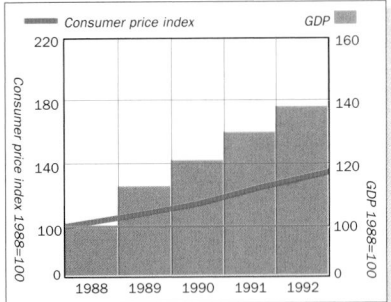

Consumer price index / GDP

EXPORTS

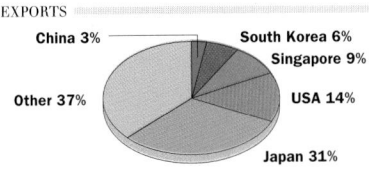

China 3% | South Korea 6%
Singapore 9%
Other 37% | USA 14%
Japan 31%

IMPORTS

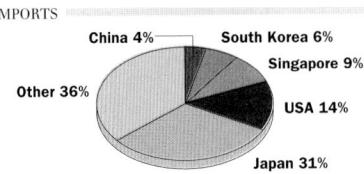

China 4% | South Korea 6%
Singapore 9%
Other 36% | USA 14%
Japan 31%

STRENGTHS

Varied resources, especially energy. Expansion of manufacturing, including high-tech. Growth of nearly 7% a year. Cheap and plentiful labor.

WEAKNESSES

Red tape; corruption. State control of economy. Competition for investment from China and Vietnam. $95 billion debt burden.

PROFILE

Under Suharto's firm guidance, the economy has grown rapidly during the past 30 years, thanks largely to oil. State-owned corporations play a significant role in the economy, which is protected against foreign competition. Non-oil exports, especially manufactures, are rapidly diversifying and expanding, but there is concern about the future. Oil revenues are set to decline and competition for investment from Vietnam and China is growing. However, the debt burden eats up 32% of export earnings. Government promises to cut red tape and privatize have yet to be fulfilled, reflecting conflict between advocates of deregulation and the "technologists" who argue that, in the short term, industrialization is more important than profitable state concerns.

INDONESIA : MAJOR BUSINESSES

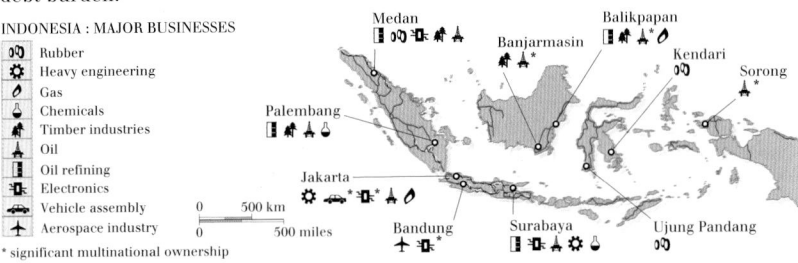

🧵	Rubber
⚙	Heavy engineering
◊	Gas
⌂	Chemicals
♣	Timber industries
⬆	Oil
⬛	Oil refining
⚡	Electronics
🚗	Vehicle assembly
✈	Aerospace industry

0 ____ 500 km
0 ____ 500 miles

* significant multinational ownership

RESOURCES

 44.2bn kwh (capacity 11.48m kw)

 1.4m b/d (reserves 5,779,000,000 bbl)

 12.3m goats, 11.6m cattle, 8.7m sheep

 Oil, natural gas, tin, bauxite, nickel, copper, gold, coal

ELECTRICITY GENERATION

Hydro 19% (8bn kwh)
Thermal 80.5% (36bn kwh)
Nuclear 0%
Other 0.5% (0.2bn kwh)

% of total generation by type

INDONESIA : LAND USE

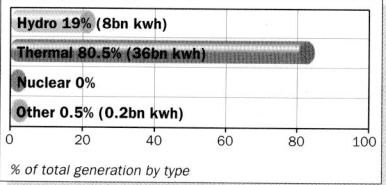

- Cropland
- Forest
- Pasture
- Wetlands
- Rice
- Nutmeg - cash crop
- Cattle

0   500 km
0   500 miles

Indonesia is rich in energy sources. Oil, which financed rapid industrialization, and liquefied natural gas – the country is the world's-largest LNG exporter – are the main export earners. However, oil output remains static, at about 1.5m b/d, set to fall to 1m b/d by 2000. Combined with rapid growth in domestic energy demand, this could turn Indonesia into an oil importer in the next decade. The government is therefore encouraging the extension of exploration into remote regions. It is also considering developing geothermal and nuclear energy sources. Indonesia's other main resources are coal, bauxite and nickel, and agricultural products such as rubber and palm oil. With 75% of the land classified as forest, timber production is also significant.

ENVIRONMENT

 10% (3% partially protected)

 Few active restrictions on logging

ENVIRONMENTAL TREATIES

Yes — Yes — Yes
No — Yes — Yes

Environmental legislation is badly policed and often ignored. The worst problem relates to the protection of Indonesia's rich tropical forests, which are threatened by excessive logging. Some predict the forests could be gone in 30 years. Frequent oil spillages in the Malacca Strait are a major hazard.

MEDIA

 The government maintains tight control of all media outlets

PUBLISHING AND BROADCAST MEDIA

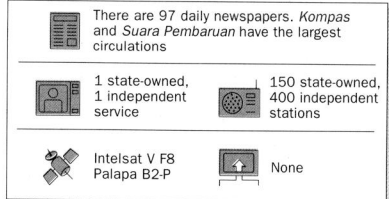

There are 97 daily newspapers. *Kompas* and *Suara Pembaruan* have the largest circulations

1 state-owned, 1 independent service

150 state-owned, 400 independent stations

Intelsat V F8 Palapa B2-P

None

Media self-censorship encourages a rich rumour-mongering tradition. The government closed three popular news magazines in 1994, in the most severe crackdown on the press in recent years. Suharto's children were quick to take advantage of the 1987 decision to open TV to the private sector.

CRIME

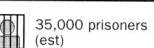 35,000 prisoners (est)

Down 22% in 1992

CRIME RATES

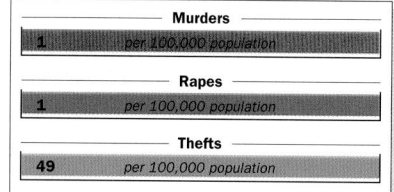

Murders
1   per 100,000 population

Rapes
1   per 100,000 population

Thefts
49   per 100,000 population

Human rights agencies are concerned at the government's violent reaction to demands for autonomy.

EDUCATION

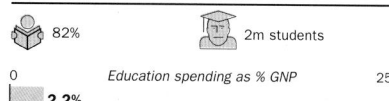 82%   2m students

0   Education spending as % GNP   25
2.2%

THE EDUCATION SYSTEM

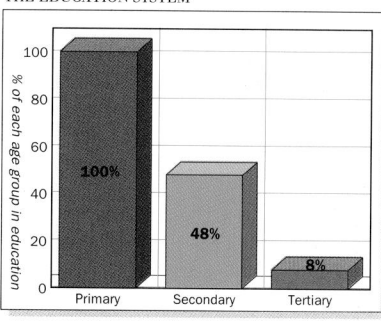

% of each age group in education

Primary 100%
Secondary 48%
Tertiary 8%

Elementary education is compulsory. Secondary schooling is expanding, but is still limited in rural areas.

HEALTH

 1 per 6,956 people   Lower respiratory and diarrheal diseases

0   Health spending as % GDP   25
0.7%

Indonesia has relatively few hospitals; about half are privately administered. However, the extensive network of clinics, down to village level, means access to health care is reasonable. As a result, health indicators have improved significantly over the past 20 years. The death rate declined from 20 per 1,000 in 1965 to 9 per 1,000 in 1990, helping to increase life expectancy to 62 years. Infant mortality more than halved, from 128 to 61 per 1,000 live births, over the same period.

WEALTH

 Agricultural worker, 100,000 rupiahs ($44) per month; engineer, 1.5m rupiahs ($656) per month

CONSUMER GOODS OWNERSHIP

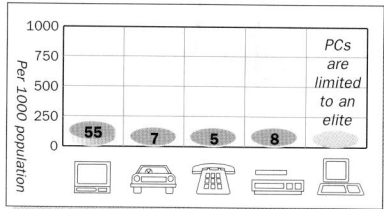

Per 1000 population

PCs are limited to an elite

55   7   5   8

Despite its oil wealth and the rapid industrialization and improvements in agricultural productivity of the past 30 years, Indonesia is still grouped among the low-income economies by the World Bank. Health and education have improved, but many Indonesians live in relative poverty, and those on the peripheral islands, notably Irian Jaya, northern Sumatra and East Timor, live in real poverty. This reflects both a concentration of wealth in the hands of a limited number of key political and business figures, and the concentration of development and investment on the main islands, particularly on Java.

I

WORLD RANKING

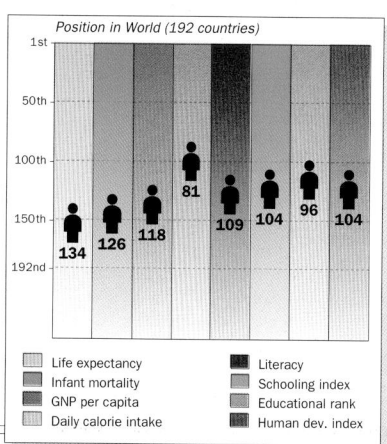

Position in World (192 countries)

1st
50th
100th
150th
192nd

134   126   118   81   109   104   96   104

- Life expectancy
- Infant mortality
- GNP per capita
- Daily calorie intake
- Literacy
- Schooling index
- Educational rank
- Human dev. index

IRAN

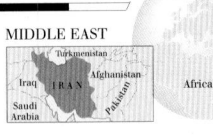

MIDDLE EAST

Asia

Africa

OFFICIAL NAME: Islamic Republic of Iran CAPITAL: Tehran
POPULATION: 67.3 million CURRENCY: Iranian rial OFFICIAL LANGUAGE: Farsi

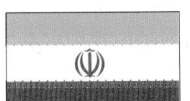   

IRAN IS SURROUNDED by powerful neighbors, with republics of the former Soviet Union to the north, Afghanistan and Pakistan to the east, and Iraq and Turkey to the west. The south faces the Persian Gulf and the Gulf of Oman. Since 1979, when a revolution led by Ayatollah Khomeini deposed the Shah, Iran has become the world's largest theocracy and the leading center for militant Shi'a Islam. Iran's active support for Islamic fundamentalist movements has led to strained relations with Central Asian, Middle Eastern and North African nations, as well as the USA.

The Reshteh-ye Kuhhā-ye Alborz (Elburz Mountains). Their Caspian Sea slopes are rainy and forested; the southern slopes are dry.

CLIMATE

WEATHER CHART

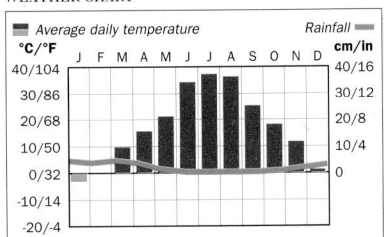

The area bordering the Caspian Sea is Iran's most temperate region. Most of the country has a desert climate.

TRANSPORTATION

 Mehrabad International, Tehran
1.16m passengers

184 ships
828,700 dwt

THE TRANSPORTATION NETWORK

32,200 miles (51,810 km)	304 miles (490 km)
2,859 miles (4,601 km)	81 miles (130 km)

Adequate roads link main towns, but rural areas are less well served. Most freight travels by rail. A ferry runs from Bandar-e 'Abbās to the UAE.

TOURISM

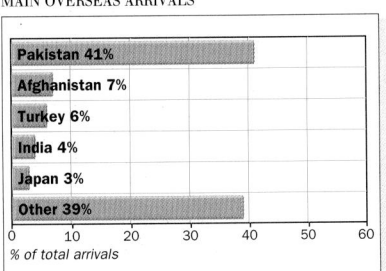 362,000 visitors Up 77% in 1994

MAIN OVERSEAS ARRIVALS

Pakistan 41%	
Afghanistan 7%	
Turkey 6%	
India 4%	
Japan 3%	
Other 39%	

0   10   20   30   40   50   60
% of total arrivals

Iran's impressive historical heritage, mosques and bazaars formerly attracted sizeable numbers of tourists. This flow was cut off by the 1979 revolution. Since then, adverse publicity for the regime has deterred visitors, especially from the West. In the 1990s, however, the number of business people visiting Iran has risen as the regime shows clear signs of wishing to improve its international relations. Procedures at Tehran's Mehrabad airport have been greatly speeded up and the capital's hotels have undergone some restoration.

PEOPLE

Farsi (Persian), Azerbaijani, Gilaki, Mazanderani, Kurdish, Baluchi, Arabic, Turkmen

106 people per sq. mile

THE URBAN/RURAL POPULATION SPLIT

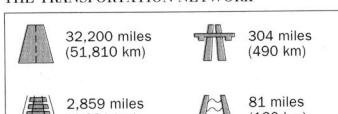

57%   43%

RELIGIOUS PERSUASION

Other 1%   Sunni Muslim 4%

Shi'a Muslim 95%

ETHNIC MAKEUP

Arab 2%   Kurd 8%
Lur & Bakhtiari 10%
Persian 50%
Other 10%
Azeri 20%

The population comprises several ethnic groups. The people of the north and center – about half of all Iranians – speak Farsi (Persian), while a further 25% speak related languages, including Kurdish in the west and Baluchi in the southeast. About a quarter of the population speaks Turkic languages, primarily the Azeris in the northwest

and the Turkmen in the northeast. Smaller groups, such as the Circassians and Georgians, are found in the northern provinces.

Until the 16th century, much of Iran followed the Sunni interpretation of Islam, but since then the Shi'a sect has been dominant. Religious minorities, accounting for just 1% of the population, include followers of the Bahai faith, who suffer discrimination, Zoroastrians, Jews and Christians. The regime has a remarkably liberal attitude to refugees of the Muslim faith. Nearly three million Afghan refugees were received during the height of the Afghan civil war although many have since been repatriated. In Khorosan province in the east, refugees account for around 23% of the population, and near the Turkish border the figure rises to 50%. Many are young, resulting in intense competition with Iranians for jobs and consequent ethnic tensions.

One of the prime aims of the 1979 Islamic revolution was to reverse the policy of female emancipation, introduced during the Shah's rule. The revolution restricted the public role of women and enforced a strict dress code, obliging women to wear the ankle-length *hijab* and keep their heads covered with a scarf. More liberal attitudes have appeared gradually, notably the appointment in 1995 of the first woman minister since the 1979 revolution.

POPULATION AGE BREAKDOWN

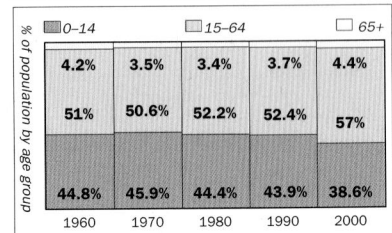

% of population by age group	0–14	15–64	65+		
65+	4.2%	3.5%	3.4%	3.7%	4.4%
15–64	51%	50.6%	52.2%	52.4%	57%
0–14	44.8%	45.9%	44.4%	43.9%	38.6%
	1960	1970	1980	1990	2000

I

POLITICS

 1992/1996

 President Ali Akbar
Hashemi Rafsanjani

THE STATE OF THE PARTIES

Consultative Assembly (*Majlis*) 270 members

All members are elected on a non-party basis

Iran is a theocracy. An uneasy relationship exists between the mullahs (their leader exercises supreme authority, in theory) and the secular authorities, headed by an elected president.

MAIN POLITICAL ISSUE
Mosque versus secular state

The precise division of power between the mullahs and the secular state remains ill-defined. Edicts contradicting secular policy are often issued. The result is a tussle over how to run a modern economy between the conservative clergy on the one hand,

Ayatollah Khamenei, *who became spiritual leader after the death of Ayatollah Khomeini.*

Hashemi Rafsanjani, *who was elected president in 1989.*

and members of the assembly (*Majlis*) and reformist politicians, led by President Rafsanjani, on the other.

The mullahs remain less concerned about the effects of stagnation than the secular authorities, believing that the people's adherence to religious values is more important than their economic or material welfare. President Rafsanjani has sought to modernize the economy gradually. However, with mullahs objecting to the use of borrowed money and the import of "corrupt" Western technology, economic growth in Iran has become rather erratic.

PROFILE

Iran's religious revolution, which brought down the monarchy, was fueled by an underprivileged people outraged at the corruption, repression and inequalities of the Shah's regime. Ayatollah Khomeini proved an effective leader of Iranian dissatisfaction. Iran's government is based on the notion that the clergy have a religious duty to establish a just social system. Accordingly, the legislature, the executive and the judiciary may, in theory, be overruled by the religious leadership. President Rafsanjani's moderate policies, which seek to break Iran's international isolation, are questioned by radical clergymen who advocate "permanent revolution" and allegedly support Muslim terrorism abroad. Although popular among many Iranians, the mullahs' failure to offer solutions to ease the country's chronic economic problems have eroded their political standing.

WORLD AFFAIRS

 ECO   G24   NAM   OIC   OPEC

Following the Khomeini revolution, Iran assumed international significance as the voice of militant Shi'a Islam. This was exemplified by the 1989 Salman Rushdie affair, in which Khomeini issued a *fatwa* (edict) demanding the death of the British novelist for blasphemy. Iran is accused of fostering unrest among Shias in Saudi Arabia and Bahrain, as well as in Sudan, Algeria, Egypt, Lebanon and the Muslim republics of the former Soviet Union. Recently Iran has also been charged with backing terrorist activity by the radical Palestinian group, *Hamas*. The West views Iran's export of Islamic revolution with anxiety, and in 1995 the USA took action by imposing sanctions against Iran.

Iran's relations with the Gulf states were strained in 1970 when it seized the islands of Abu Musa and the Tumbs from the UAE. Iran's main preoccupation is Iraq, which allows *mujahideen* guerrillas to mount attacks on Iran from its territory.

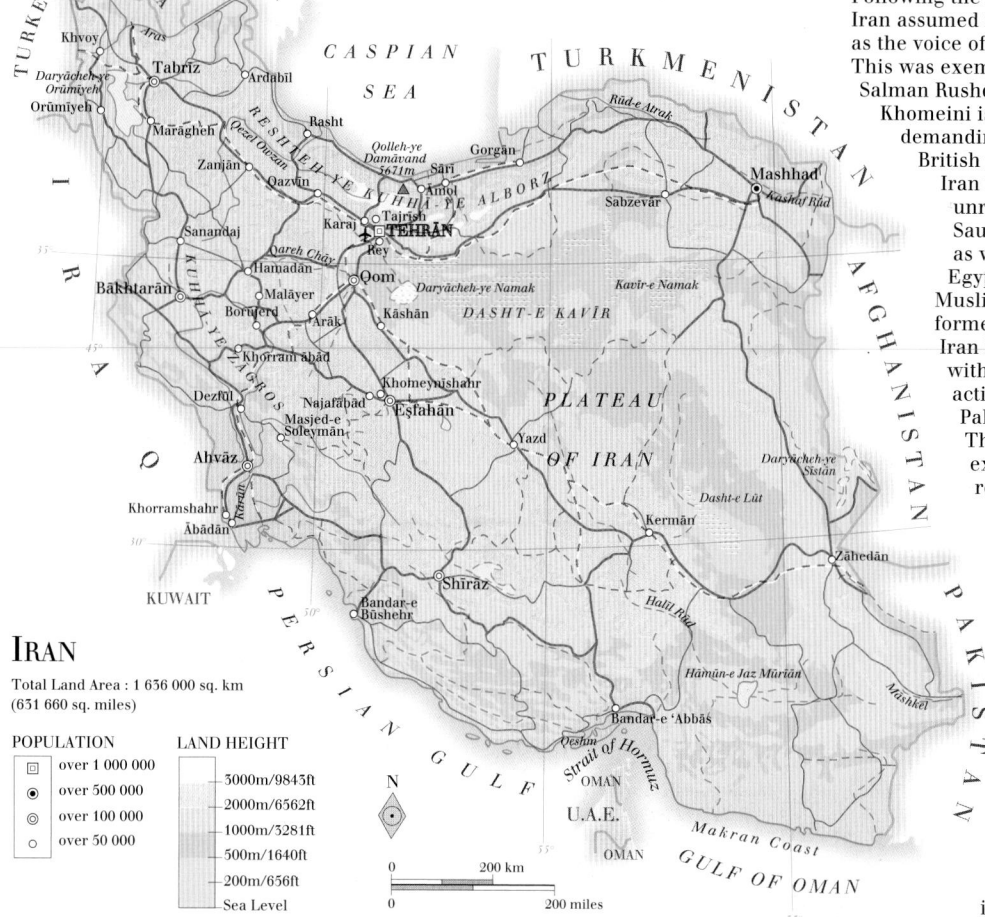

IRAN

Total Land Area : 1 636 000 sq. km
(631 660 sq. miles)

POPULATION
- ⊡ over 1 000 000
- ⊙ over 500 000
- ◎ over 100 000
- ○ over 50 000

LAND HEIGHT
- 3000m/9843ft
- 2000m/6562ft
- 1000m/3281ft
- 500m/1640ft
- 200m/656ft
- Sea Level

0   200 km

0   200 miles

I

CHRONOLOGY

Iran (Persia) was ruled by the Shahs as an absolute monarchy until 1906 when the first constitution was approved. The Pahlavis took power in 1925 and changed the country's name to Iran in 1935.

❏ **1957** SAVAK, Shah's secret police, established to control opposition.
❏ **1964** Ayatollah Khomeini exiled for criticisms of secular state.
❏ **1971** Shah celebrates 2,500th anniversary of Persian monarchy.
❏ **1975** Long-running dispute over access to Shatt Al Arab waterway settled with Iraq.
❏ **1977** Khomeini's son dies. Anti-Shah demonstrations during mourning.
❏ **1978** Riots and strikes. Khomeini exiled from Iraq to Paris.
❏ **1979** January, rising discontent; Shah goes into exile. February, Ayatollah Khomeini returns in triumph from exile in France. Islamic Revolutionary Council takes power. April, Iran declared Islamic republic. November, students seize 63 hostages at US Embassy in Tehran.
❏ **1980** Shah dies in exile. Start of eight-year Iran–Iraq war. Iraq invades, annulling 1975 Shatt Al Arab waterway agreement.
❏ **1981** US hostages released. Hojatoleslam Ali Khamenei elected president by huge majority.
❏ **1984** Iran captures part of marshlands around southern Iraqi island of Majnoun.
❏ **1985** Khamenei reelected.
❏ **1986** UN Security Council blames Iraq for war with Iran.
❏ **1987** Around 275 Iranian pilgrims killed in riots in Mecca.
❏ **1988** July, *USS Vincennes* shoots down Iranian airliner; 290 killed. August, Iran–Iraq war ends with UN-arranged ceasefire.
❏ **1989** February, Khomeini issues *fatwa* condemning Salman Rushdie to death for blasphemy in his novel *The Satanic Verses*. June, Khomeini dies. President Ali Khamenei appointed Supreme Religious Leader. Hashemi Rafsanjani elected president.
❏ **1990** Earthquake hits northern provinces, killing 45,000 people. Gulf War – Iran remains neutral.
❏ **1991** Iranian diplomacy helps free Western hostages in Lebanon.
❏ **1992** *Majlis* elections result in two-thirds support for president.
❏ **1993** Rafsanjani reelected president.
❏ **1995** Imposition of US sanctions.
❏ **1996** *Majlis* elections.

AID

 $141m (receipts)   Down 17% in 1993

As an oil exporter, Iran does not qualify for much aid. Hardliners also oppose Western aid – even when faced with disasters such as the 1990 earthquake. However, Iran receives some UN aid for its millions of mainly Afghan and Iraqi refugees. In 1994, the World Bank suspended loans amid international concern over Iranian support for Muslim terrorism abroad. In 1995, the USA imposed economic sanctions ending bilateral trade and aid.

DEFENSE

 $2.5bn   Up 7% in 1995

0 ————— Defense spending as % GDP ————— 40
3.8%

With more than half a million men under arms, including the Revolutionary Guard Corps (*Pasdaran*), and battle experience from the war with Iraq, Iran is regarded by neighboring states as a serious military threat. The *Pasdaran* form one-third of personnel and also serve to safeguard moral and behavioral standards set by the mullahs. They were used in mass frontal assaults during the Iran–Iraq war. Clashes with Iraq and the USA have weakened the navy. Two years' military service is compulsory.

IRANIAN ARMED FORCES

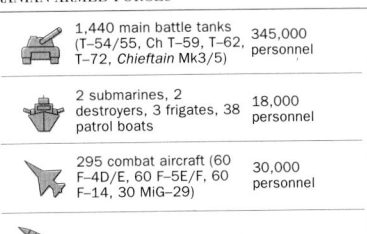

1,440 main battle tanks (T–54/55, Ch T–59, T–62, T–72, *Chieftain* Mk3/5)	345,000 personnel
2 submarines, 2 destroyers, 3 frigates, 38 patrol boats	18,000 personnel
295 combat aircraft (60 F–4D/E, 60 F–5E/F, 60 F–14, 30 MiG–29)	30,000 personnel
None	

ECONOMICS

 $125bn   1,729–3,000 Iranian rials

SCORE CARD

❏ WORLD GNP RANKING...........................30th
❏ GNP PER CAPITA $2,068
❏ BALANCE OF PAYMENTS.....................$–6.5bn
❏ INFLATION 52.1%
❏ UNEMPLOYMENT................................15.2%

EXPORTS

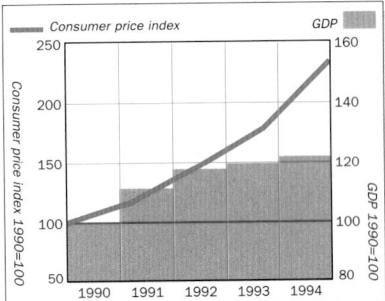

France 5%
Italy 5%
Other 66%
Netherlands 5%
South Korea 6%
Japan 13%

IMPORTS

Italy 7%
France 8%
Japan 8%
United Arab Emirates 9%
Germany 14%
Other 54%

ECONOMIC PERFORMANCE INDICATOR

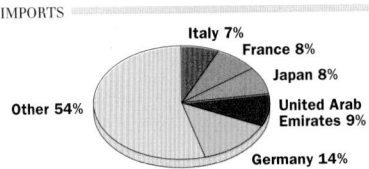

— Consumer price index   GDP

Consumer price index 1990=100 (left axis: 50–250)
GDP 1990=100 (right axis: 80–160)
1990 1991 1992 1993 1994

PROFILE

Iran has few industries other than oil. The chronic shortage of foreign exchange and the costs of the long war with Iraq have accelerated a decline in living standards in the past decade.

IRAN : MAJOR BUSINESSES

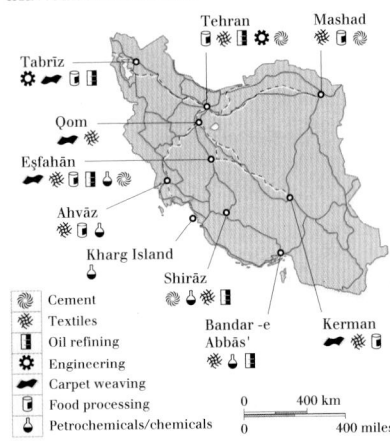

Tehran
Mashad
Tabrīz
Qom
Eşfahān
Ahvāz
Kharg Island
Shirāz
Bandar -e Abbās'
Kerman

Cement
Textiles
Oil refining
Engineering
Carpet weaving
Food processing
Petrochemicals/chemicals

0 ——— 400 km
0 ——— 400 miles

STRENGTHS

OPEC's second-biggest oil producer. Potential for related industries and increased production of traditional exports: carpets, pistachio nuts and caviar.

WEAKNESSES

Theocratic government restricts contact with West, and access to technology. High unemployment and inflation. Excessive foreign debts. Sharp decline in oil revenues following US sanctions in 1995.

RESOURCES

52bn kwh
(capacity 17.5m kw)

3.6m b/d
(reserves
92,860,000,000 bbl)

45.4m sheep,
23.5m goats,
7.1m cattle

Iron, copper, lead, oil,
zinc, chromite, coal,
manganese, gypsum

ELECTRICITY GENERATION

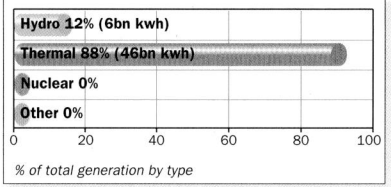

Hydro 12% (6bn kwh)

Thermal 88% (46bn kwh)

Nuclear 0%

Other 0%

% of total generation by type

Iran has substantial oil reserves. It also has metal, coal and salt deposits, but these are relatively undeveloped. The agricultural sector is an important part of Iran's economy. Principal crops are wheat, barley, rice, sugar beet, tobacco and pistachio nuts.

Iran was once an opium exporter, but its cultivation and use has since been banned. The vodka industry has also been closed down. Enough wool is produced to supply the carpet weaving industry. Iran has insufficient livestock to supply the domestic meat market and has to import large quantities. The Caspian Sea fisheries are controlled by the state, which sells caviar for export.

IRAN : LAND USE

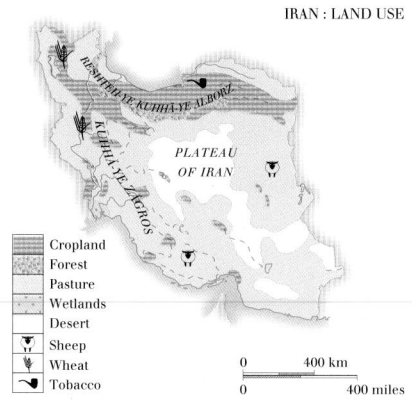

RESHTEH-YE KUHHA-YE ALBORZ

KUHHA-YE ZAGROS

PLATEAU
OF IRAN

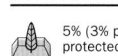

Cropland
Forest
Pasture
Wetlands
Desert
Sheep
Wheat
Tobacco

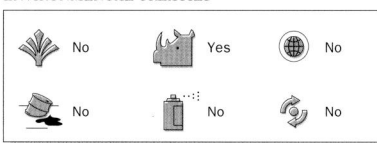

0   400 km

0   400 miles

ENVIRONMENT

5% (3% partially
protected)

Environmental
protection is not of
state concern

ENVIRONMENTAL TREATIES

No   Yes   No

No   No   No

War damage to southern Iran, especially at Bandar Khomeini, the tanker terminal at Kharg Island and the refinery at Ābādān, has caused significant environmental damage. Environmental issues are not of concern to the religious leadership.

MEDIA

Censorship was introduced by the stringent
Press Law of 1979. Infringement is treated as
a criminal offense

PUBLISHING AND BROADCAST MEDIA

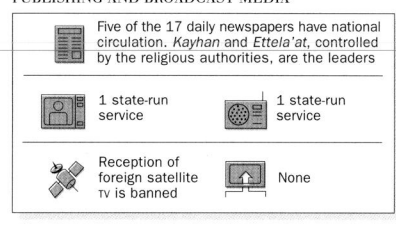

Five of the 17 daily newspapers have national
circulation. *Kayhan* and *Ettela'at*, controlled
by the religious authorities, are the leaders

1 state-run
service

1 state-run
service

Reception of
foreign satellite
TV is banned

None

There is virtually no press freedom. Rafsanjani's attempts to liberalize the media are opposed by the mullahs. Satellite dishes receiving Western programs are banned.

CRIME

Iran does not publish
prison figures

Little change from
year to year

CRIME RATES

Iran does not publish crime statistics.
However, general crime rates are
relatively low

Revolutionary guards enforce law and order. More than a hundred offenses carry the death sentence. However, moves to extend the death penalty to economic crimes were rejected by the *Majlis* in 1995. Executions, of both men and women, are common for political "crimes." Iran is accused by Western governments of international terrorism by Muslim extremists abroad.

EDUCATION

72%

636,255 students

0   Education spending as % GNP   25

4.6%

THE EDUCATION SYSTEM

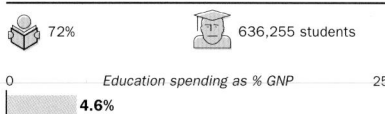

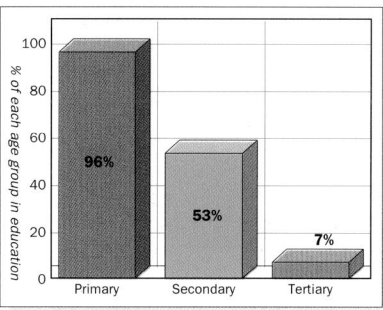

% of each age group in education

100

80

60

40

20

0

96%

53%

7%

Primary   Secondary   Tertiary

Over half the population is literate. Education in state elementary schools and universities is free. Pupils pay small fees for secondary education. There are insufficient teachers to cope with rising student numbers. Most schools have been made single-sex since 1979.

HEALTH

1 per 2,538 people

Heart and respiratory
diseases, injuries,
neonatal deaths

0   Health spending as % GDP   25

1.5%

Although an adequate system of primary health care exists in the cities, conditions in rural areas are basic. The major problem facing the nation's health is the fast-growing population. Under Khomeini, producing children became a political and religious duty. The government has now introduced sterilization and contraception programs. Almost 40% of children under five are malnourished.

WEALTH

The acquisition of private wealth is discouraged

CONSUMER GOODS OWNERSHIP

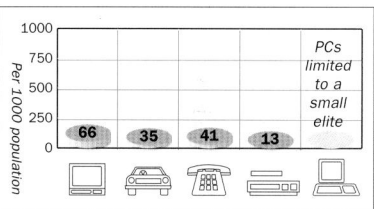

1000

750

500

250

0

Per 1000 population

PCs
limited
to a
small
elite

66   35   41   13

Since the 1979 revolution, living standards have declined markedly. A shortage of foreign exchange has stifled imports of consumer goods. Rationing, brought in during the war with Iraq, is still partly in force and smuggling from the Arab Gulf states is rife. Unemployment is high, with few Iranians able to gain access to modern technology such as telephones. Official figures for income per head do not relate to conditions on the ground. In reality, oil wealth fails to reach the economically deprived. Private businesses, although discouraged by the mullahs, have gradually emerged with the launch in 1994 of the country's first private savings and loans associations.

WORLD RANKING

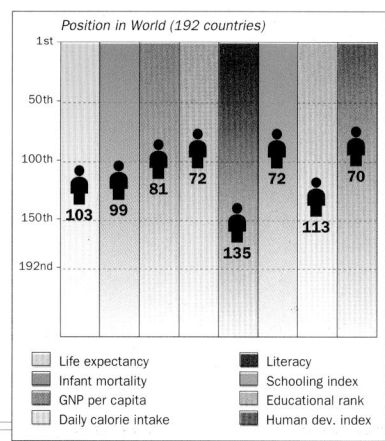

Position in World (192 countries)

1st

50th

100th

150th

192nd

103   99   81   72   135   72   113   70

Life expectancy
Infant mortality
GNP per capita
Daily calorie intake

Literacy
Schooling index
Educational rank
Human dev. index

I

IRAQ

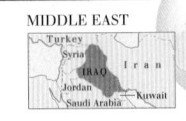

MIDDLE EAST

OFFICIAL NAME: Republic of Iraq   **CAPITAL:** Baghdad   **POPULATION:** 20.4 million
CURRENCY: Iraqi dinar   **OFFICIAL LANGUAGE:** Arabic

1932

Oil-RICH IRAQ shares borders with Iran, Turkey, Syria, Jordan, Saudi Arabia and Kuwait. The Tigris and Euphrates rivers flow across the country; as they approach the Gulf their fertile valleys broaden into marshlands, but most of the country is desert or mountains. Iraq was the site of the ancient civilization of Babylon. Today, its borders encompass Shi'a Muslim holy shrines. Since the removal of the monarchy in 1958, Iraq has experienced considerable political turmoil. The current regime stays in power through repression.

Golden Mosque at *Sāmarrā' on the Tigris. Among the extensive remains of its ancient city are those of the Great Mosque built in AD 847.*

CLIMATE

WEATHER CHART

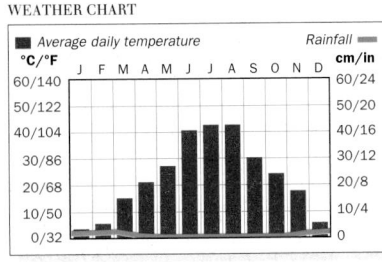

The weather is dry and rainfall is low and unreliable, except in the northeast. Iraq experiences a wide range of temperatures. The south has a desert climate, with hot, dry summers and mild winters. The summers are also dry in the north but in mountainous Iranian and Turkish border regions winters can be harsh, with frost and heavy falls of snow. Sudden hot spells are a unique feature of winter in the center and north of the country.

TRANSPORTATION

 Saddam International, Baghdad

 33 ships 136,870 dwt

THE TRANSPORTATION NETWORK

22,640 miles (36,440 km)	None
1,262 miles (2,032 km)	81 miles (130 km)

Adequate roads link main cities. Railroads provide vital arteries for the movement of goods. The land route to the Gulf states via Kuwait is closed.

TOURISM

 33,000 visitors

 Down 18% in 1994

MAIN OVERSEAS ARRIVALS

West Asia 69%	
Africa 13%	
Europe 7%	*Pre 1991 Gulf War figures*
South Asia 4%	
South East Asia and Oceania 1%	
Other 6%	

0 10 20 30 40 50 60 70 80
% of total arrivals

The Shi'a holy shrines in the south attract thousands of pilgrims each year. Iraq is effectively closed to Western tourists, who once visited its many archaeological sites. In particular, the ruins of Babylon, with its fabled hanging gardens, was once a major tourist attractions. Westerners also used to journey to the marshlands close to the Shaṭṭ al 'Arab waterway. However, this area of ecological importance is now being drained as part of a campaign to suppress the Marsh Arabs.

IRAQ

Total Land Area : 437 370 sq. km
(168 869 sq. miles)

POPULATION

⊡	over 1 000 000
◉	over 500 000
◎	over 100 000
○	over 50 000
●	over 10 000

LAND HEIGHT

3000m/9843ft
2000m/6562ft
1000m/3281ft
500m/1640ft
200m/656ft
Sea Level

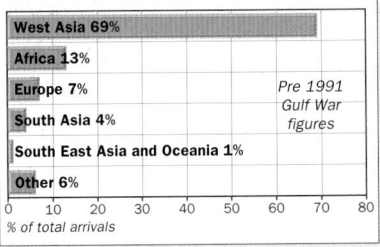

0   100 km
0   100 miles

PEOPLE

 Arabic, Kurdish, Armenian, Assyrian

 122 people per sq. mile

THE URBAN/RURAL POPULATION SPLIT

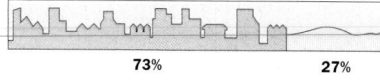

73%   **27%**

RELIGIOUS PERSUASION

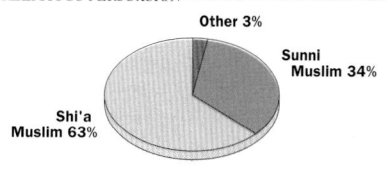

Other 3%

Sunni Muslim 34%

Shi'a Muslim 63%

ETHNIC MAKEUP

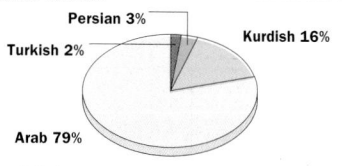

Persian 3%

Turkish 2%

Kurdish 16%

Arab 79%

In addition to the Arab and Kurdish populations, Iraq has a small number of minority groups, such as the Turks and Persians. Over 90% of the population is Muslim, while the rest comprises a variety of Christian sects. Since the creation of Israel, most Iraqi Jews have emigrated. The Arab Muslims are divided into Sunni and Shi'a sects. The Shi'a form the largest single religious group; however, Shi'a divines do not have as intimate a connection with the people as they do in Iran and their influence on government is limited.

Since the mid-1970s, many Iraqis have moved, or been forced to move, to the cities, where some 70% of the population now live.

In the marshes of the extreme south, communities of Marsh Arabs survive. In the wake of the 1991 Gulf War, some of these attempted a rebellion against the state, which is now draining the marshes in order to destroy both the people and their culture.

POPULATION AGE BREAKDOWN

%	☐ 0–14	☐ 15–64		☐ 65+	
	2.4%	2.4%	2.6%	2.7%	3%
	51.5%	51%	50.4%	50.9%	52.9%
	46.1%	46.6%	47%	46.4%	44.1%
	1960	1970	1980	1990	2000

WORLD AFFAIRS

 AL   NAM   OAPEC   OIC   OPEC

In 1990, Saddam Hussain embarked on a grand plan to show himself as the undisputed leader of the Arab world: the invasion of Kuwait. Saddam was counting on the West responding with sanctions rather than arms, and on Syria and Egypt not joining an Arab coalition to oppose him.

As a result of the Gulf War that followed, Iraq was economically and diplomatically isolated. Iraq was ousted from Kuwait, and sanctions were imposed. Relations with the West are now deadlocked. Iraq is effectively neutralized as a power in the region, but remains unwilling to allow UN inspection of its arsenal. No major Western state has restored diplomatic relations, although economic links have resumed with some countries, especially France. Among Arab states, Sudan alone is a close ally.

Relations with Iran are tense. Iranian guerrillas working against the regime in Tehran continue to use Iraq as a base for their operations.

I

POLITICS

 1989/1996

 President Saddam Hussain

THE STATE OF THE PARTIES

National Assembly 250 members

The National Assembly operates under the supervision of the Revolutionary Command Council. It is composed of Ba'athists and their supporters

Revolutionary Command Council

Members are appointed by the president

President Saddam Hussain has dominated Iraqi politics since overthrowing his predecessor in 1979. In theory, the highest state authority rests with the nine-member Revolutionary Command Council.

MAIN POLITICAL ISSUES
Sanctions
Iraq's invasion of Kuwait in 1990 led to UN sanctions being imposed. In 1991, Iraq was forced to withdraw from Kuwait following its military defeat by a US-led international coalition. However, sanctions against Iraq have continued pending its full compliance with UN Security Council resolutions on the destruction of banned weapons. In 1994, Iraq recognized Kuwait but failed to secure an end to sanctions because of its repeated defiance of UN attempts to monitor its weapons programs. Sanctions have wrought economic devastation although the Iraqi regime determinedly pursues a program of reconstruction.

Threats to the regime
There is little unity among opposition groups, most of which are based abroad. The most significant groups are the Tehran-based Supreme Council for the Islamic Revolution in Iraq, and the Iraqi National Congress operating from London. The defection to Jordan in 1995 of General Hussain Kamil, a senior minister and relation of Saddam Hussain, failed to mobilize any opposition; Kamil was assassinated after returning to Iraq in early 1996.

The separatist Kurdish minority in the north, which has waged its struggle against the regime since 1962, is hindered by the reluctance even of Iraq's enemies to endorse the state's territorial dismemberment.

PROFILE
Iraq's regime – the most autocratic in the Arab world – is dominated by President Saddam Hussain and his lieutenants, mainly trusted members of his family. However, the defection in 1995 of Saddam Hussain's son-in-law, General Hussain Kamil, suggested growing dissent within the ruling inner circle.

***Tarek Aziz,** deputy prime minister and mediator between Iraq and the UN.*

***Saddam Hussain,** Iraq's dictatorial leader since he seized power in 1979.*

Saddam Hussain has promoted his own extreme personality cult. In a typical political broadcast, his name is mentioned 30 to 50 times an hour. The streets of Baghdad grind to a halt when the president leaves his palace. The regime stays in force through terror and the military's backing. A vast secret service network ensure that opposition groups cannot organize a challenge.

AID

 $170m (receipts)   Down 9% in 1993

Before its invasion of Kuwait, Iraq received economic aid from neighboring Gulf states. Under UN sanctions, Iraq is entitled only to humanitarian aid, but there is mounting evidence of covert trade, especially through Jordan.

CHRONOLOGY

Iraq became independent in 1932. In 1958, the Hashemite dynasty was overthrown when King Faisal died in a coup led by the military under Brigadier Kassem. He was initially supported by the Iraqi Ba'ath Party.

❑ **1961** Kurdish rebellion erupts in northern Iraq. Iraq claims sovereignty over Kuwait on the eve of Kuwait's independence.

❑ **1963** Kassem overthrown. Colonel Abd as-Salem Muhammad Aref takes power. Kuwait's sovereignty recognized.

❑ **1964** Ayatollah Khomeini, future leader of Iran, takes refuge at Najaf in Iraq.

❑ **1966** Aref is succeeded by his brother, Abd ar-Rahman.

❑ **1968** Ba'athists under Ahmad Hassan Al-Bakr take power.

❑ **1970** Revolutionary Command Council agrees manifesto on Kurdish autonomy with Kurdish leader Mulla Mustafa Barzani.

❑ **1972** Nationalization of Iraq Petroleum Company, owned by Western interests.

❑ **1978** Iraq and Syria sign charter for economic and political union. Ayatollah Khomeini leaves Iraq for Paris.

❑ **1979** Saddam Hussein replaces President Al-Bakr.

❑ **1980** Outbreak of Iraq–Iran war.

❑ **1982** President Saddam Hussein withdraws troops from Iran. Iran occupies parts of southern Iraq. Shi'a leader Mohammed Baqir Al-Hakim, exiled in Tehran, forms Supreme Council of the Islamic Revolution in Iraq.

❑ **1988** Iraq and Iran agree ceasefire. Iraqi troops alleged to be using chemical weapons in bomb attacks on Kurdish villages.

❑ **1990** British journalist Farzad Bazoft hanged for spying. Iraq and Iran restore diplomatic relations. Iraq invades Kuwait, annexing emirate as its 19th province. UN imposes trade sanctions.

❑ **1991** Western allies launch successful 100-hour campaign to liberate Kuwait. Shi'a rebellion in southern Iraq put down.

❑ **1992** USA, UK, France and Russia proclaim air exclusion zone over southern Iraq.

❑ **1993** Iraqi attempts to recover military equipment from Kuwait provoke Western air attacks.

❑ **1994** Iraq recognizes Kuwaiti sovereignty.

❑ **1995** Government minister General Hussain Kamil defects to Jordan; he is murdered on his return to Iraq in January 1996.

DEFENSE

💲 $8.6bn   ⬍ Fairly consistent since Gulf War

0   *Defense spending as % GDP*   40
                    14.6%

IRAQI ARMED FORCES

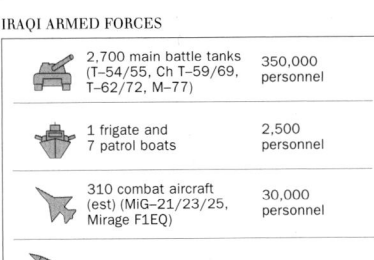

🛡	2,700 main battle tanks (T–54/55, Ch T–59/69, T–62/72, M–77)	350,000 personnel
⚓	1 frigate and 7 patrol boats	2,500 personnel
✈	310 combat aircraft (est) (MiG–21/23/25, Mirage F1EQ)	30,000 personnel
🚀	None	

Iraq's military defeat by the US-led coalition in 1991 led to the destruction of much of its arsenal. Since then, UN Security Council resolutions have ensured the elimination of the bulk of Iraq's weapons of mass destruction. There is a shortage of high-tech weaponry that could match the kind acquired by Kuwait and Saudi Arabia from US and other Western suppliers since the Gulf War. The army is large, but poorly trained and equipped. The military relies on tanks and aircraft from the former Soviet Union and China. The air force, the most prestigious service, has some French *Mirage* fighters and US helicopters.

ECONOMICS

💲 $20bn (est)   💲 0.31–0.56 Iraqi dinars

SCORE CARD

❑ WORLD GNP RANKING...........................64th
❑ GNP PER CAPITA $1,036
❑ BALANCE OF PAYMENTS $3,149m
❑ INFLATION 60%
❑ UNEMPLOYMENT................................5.1%

EXPORTS

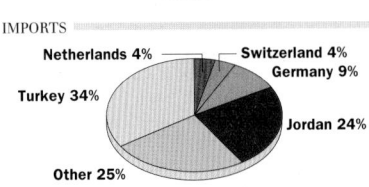

Other 2% — Greece 5% — Turkey 7% — Jordan 86%

IMPORTS

Netherlands 4% — Switzerland 4% — Germany 9% — Turkey 34% — Jordan 24% — Other 25%

STRENGTHS

Second largest crude oil and natural gas reserves in OPEC. Large labor force.

WEAKNESSES

Inability to sell oil on the international market; UN sanctions have halved the country's gross national product. Once-thriving agricultural sector devastated by war.

PROFILE

Before 1990, Iraq was the world's third-largest oil supplier. Today, oil is being produced only for domestic consumption. Assuming an end to sanctions, however, the potential for Iraq's oil industry is massive.

Sanctions have hit Iraq hard. The severance of almost all trade has stifled the economy, although the recent resumption of informal economic links

ECONOMIC PERFORMANCE INDICATOR

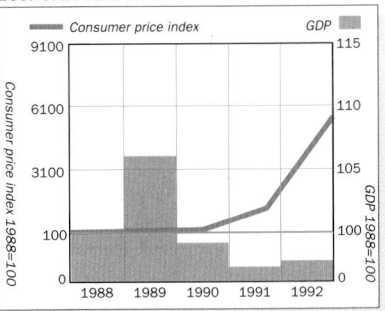

with France and Russia may lead to some improvement. Iraq was formerly rich in agriculture, but the sector was badly affected by war. Plans to liberalize the economy are on hold while the state seeks to avert an economic catastrophe. However, even the introduction of draconian penalties, including the death sentence, have failed to curb the thriving black market and the sharp depreciation in the value of the dinar.

IRAQ : MAJOR BUSINESSES

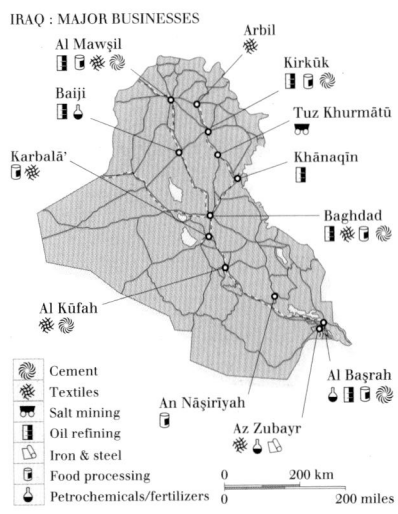

🌀 Cement
✳ Textiles
⛏ Salt mining
🛢 Oil refining
🔩 Iron & steel
🍴 Food processing
⚗ Petrochemicals/fertilizers

0   200 km
0   200 miles

RESOURCES

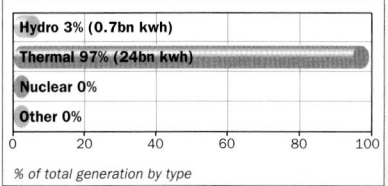

24.7bn kwh (capacity 9m kw)

6.3m sheep, 1.1m cattle, 1m goats

600,000 b/d (reserves 100,000,000,000 bbl)

Oil, natural gas, sulfur

ELECTRICITY GENERATION

Hydro 3% (0.7bn kwh)

Thermal 97% (24bn kwh)

Nuclear 0%

Other 0%

% of total generation by type

Iraq has huge reserves of oil and gas. The oil industry is controlled by the Iraqi National Oil Company. In 1990, proven reserves were conservatively estimated at 100,000 million barrels – sufficient for 97 years' production at 1989 levels of 4.5 million b/d.

Total gas reserves, three-quarters of which are associated with oil, are estimated at 3.52 billion cubic yards. Hydroelectric power is the main source of energy, though there is also a single oil-fired power station.

Before the invasion of Kuwait and subsequent war, Iraq was supplying 80% of the world's trade in dates. Production is now sharply down. Foods are now produced simply for domestic consumption. Iraq has, however, achieved a degree of self-sufficiency in crops such as wheat, rice and sugar.

ENVIRONMENT

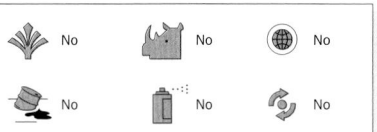

None

Destruction of marshlands in south

ENVIRONMENTAL TREATIES

No　No　No

No　No　No

Wars with Iran and with the UN coalition over the Kuwait occupation led to massive environmental damage. Hundreds of thousands of land mines remain in the Kuwait border regions, posing lethal hazards to farmers, livestock and wild animals. The north has been affected by chemical weapons, used by the regime against the Kurds. In the south, an entire wetland ecosystem is being destroyed by an engineering program aimed at draining the marshes for largely political reasons.

MEDIA

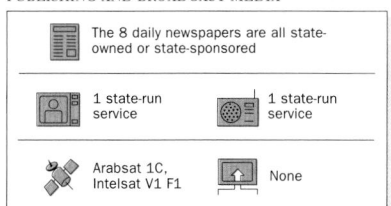

Tight government censorship

PUBLISHING AND BROADCAST MEDIA

The 8 daily newspapers are all state-owned or state-sponsored

1 state-run service

1 state-run service

Arabsat 1C, Intelsat V1 F1

None

The media is strictly controlled though rebel groups circulate clandestine newspapers. Baghdad has four daily newspapers, one of which, the *Baghdad Observer*, is in English. Saddam Hussein's son, *Uday*, controls the influential Arabic newspaper, *Babil*, which favors Iraq's defiance of UN Gulf War resolutions. Foreign journalists are carefully vetted and their reports censored.

CRIME

Iraq does not publish prison figures

Up 28% in 1992

CRIME RATES

Murders

7 per 100,000 population

Rapes

not available

Thefts

63 per 100,000 population

Iraq was formerly a law-abiding society, but economic collapse has sent crime rates soaring, especially in cities. Theft has been made a capital offense – encouraging thieves to murder in order to escape detection.

EDUCATION

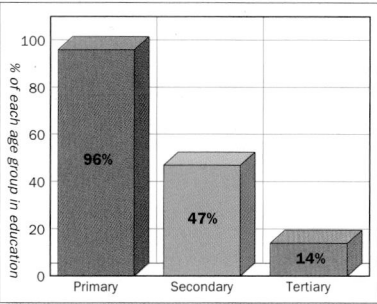

60%

209,818 students

0　Education spending as % GNP　25

5.1%

THE EDUCATION SYSTEM

Primary 96%
Secondary 47%
Tertiary 14%

% of each age group in education

Elementary and secondary education are free and universal, except in remote rural areas. There are six universities. Academics from Iraq authorized the organized plunder of antiquities and university equipment from Kuwait during the 1990 occupation.

IRAQ : LAND USE

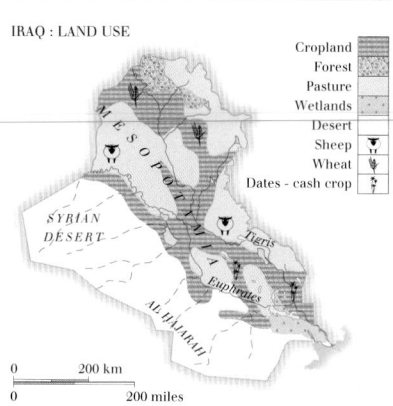

Cropland
Forest
Pasture
Wetlands
Desert
Sheep
Wheat
Dates - cash crop

0　200 km
0　200 miles

HEALTH

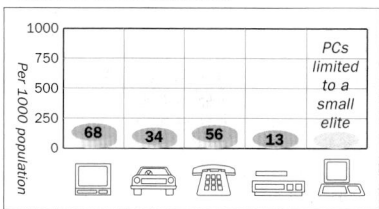

1 per 1,810 people

Pneumonia, influenza, cancers, heart diseases

0　Health spending as % GNP　25

0.8%

Iraqi doctors claim that the welfare of children, the sick and the elderly has suffered because of the UN embargo. Child mortality is high and the standard of hospital equipment and facilities low.

WEALTH

Few opportunities for enrichment

CONSUMER GOODS OWNERSHIP

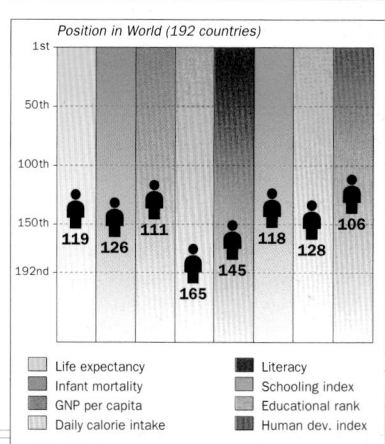

PCs limited to a small elite

Per 1000 population

68　34　56　13

Many middle-class Iraqis and traders have taken advantage of the open border with Jordan to relocate from Baghdad to Amman.

WORLD RANKING

Position in World (192 countries)

1st
50th
100th
150th
192nd

119　126　111　165　145　118　128　106

Life expectancy
Infant mortality
GNP per capita
Daily calorie intake
Literacy
Schooling index
Educational rank
Human dev. index

IRELAND

OFFICIAL NAME: Republic of Ireland   **CAPITAL:** Dublin   **POPULATION:** 3.6 million
CURRENCY: Irish Pound   **OFFICIAL LANGUAGES:** Irish, English

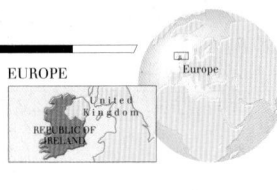

EUROPE

 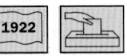    

L YING IN THE ATLANTIC OCEAN, off the west coast of Britain, the Irish Republic occupies about 85% of the island of Ireland. Surrounded by low coastal mountain ranges, the central basin is punctuated by lakes, undulating hills and peat bogs. Centuries of struggle against English colonialism led to the formation of the Irish Free State in 1922 and full sovereignty in 1937. The resolution of the Northern Ireland conflict is a major concern.

CLIMATE

WEATHER CHART

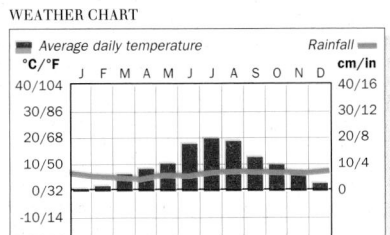

Moderated by the Gulf Stream, the Irish climate is mild, equable and wet. The mean annual temperature is 54°F.

TRANSPORTATION

   Dublin International

   62 ships
189,400 dwt

THE TRANSPORTATION NETWORK

53,930 miles (86,790 km)		5 miles (8 km)	
1,210 miles (1,947 km)		267 miles (429 km)	

Over 40 road improvement projects are being funded by the EU. Dublin suffers from severe truck congestion.

TOURISM

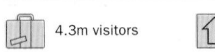   4.3m visitors   Up 13% in 1994

MAIN OVERSEAS ARRIVALS

UK 64%	
USA 11%	
France 5%	
Other 20%	

0 10 20 30 40 50 60 70 80
% of total arrivals

Intensive promotional campaigns have helped Ireland widen its tourist base, notably in Germany and Scandinavia. Its attractions include its scenery and "clean" environmental image, and its relaxed lifestyle.

PEOPLE

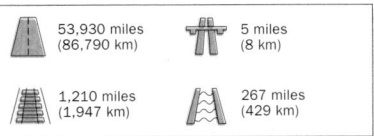   English, Irish Gaelic   135 people per sq. mile

THE URBAN/RURAL POPULATION SPLIT

57%   **43%**

RELIGIOUS PERSUASION

Anglican 3%   Other 4%

Roman Catholic 93%

The population is 95% ethnic Irish. The Catholic Church has a huge influence, opposing abortion and birth control. Many Irish still emigrate to find jobs.

POLITICS

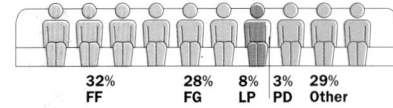

U. House 1993/1997
L. House 1992/1997

President Mary Robinson

THE STATE OF THE PARTIES

House of Representatives 166 members

4% Other

| **41% FF** | **27% FG** | **20% LP** | **6% PD** | **2% DL** |

FF = Fianna Fáil (Soldiers of Destiny)   FG = Fine Gael (United Ireland Party)   LP = Labour Party   PD = Progressive Democrats   DL = Democratic Left

Senate 60 members

| **32% FF** | **28% FG** | **8% LP** | **3% PD** | **29% Other** |

In 1973, an FG–LP coalition took power, which saw the end of the FF as the traditional party of government – a role it had held since 1932. FF and FG–LP governments since have tended to be short-lived and, since 1989, the FF has needed PD support to govern. In 1994, the FF–LP government fell once more and was replaced by an FG–LP–DL coalition, led by FG leader John Bruton. The new government's priority has been to sustain the Northern Ireland peace process.

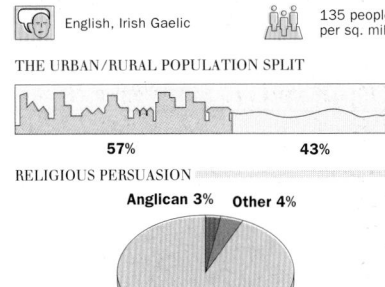

REPUBLIC OF IRELAND

Total Land Area :
68 890 sq. km
(26 598 sq. miles)

POPULATION

over 500 000	◉
over 100 000	◎
over 50 000	○
over 10 000	●
under 10 000	∙

LAND HEIGHT

1000m/3281ft
500m/1640ft
200m/656ft
Sea Level

WORLD AFFAIRS

The Northern Ireland peace process is the main issue, prompting considerable contact with the UK as well as the USA.

AID

 $81m (donations)   Down 17% in 1993

Africa is the main target of Irish aid. As one of the poorer European states, Ireland is a major recipient of EU aid.

DEFENSE

 $700m   Up 14% in 1991

Ireland is determined to maintain its traditional neutrality, notwithstanding provisions within the Maastricht Treaty for a common European defense policy.

ECONOMICS

 $48.3bn    0.65–0.62 Irish pounds

SCORE CARD

❏ WORLD GNP RANKING	45th
❏ GNP PER CAPITA	$13,630
❏ BALANCE OF PAYMENTS	$3.2bn
❏ INFLATION	2.3%
❏ UNEMPLOYMENT	14.7%

STRENGTHS

One of Europe's fastest-growing economies: real GDP rose 3.5% a year in 1980–1990 and 5.5% in 1995. Trade surplus. Low inflation. Efficient agriculture, food processing industries. Rapidly expanding high-tech sector; electronics account for 25% of exports. Large recipient of EU infrastructure funding. Highly educated work force.

WEAKNESSES

Many key sectors owned by overseas multinationals. One of EU's highest unemployment rates: 14.7% overall, higher among youths. High interest rates slow investment.

EXPORTS

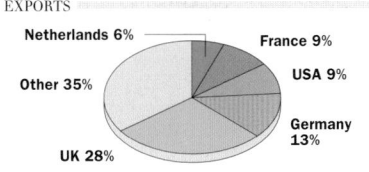

Netherlands 6%   France 9%   USA 9%   Germany 13%   UK 28%   Other 35%

IMPORTS

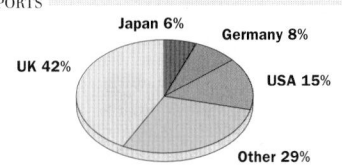

Japan 6%   Germany 8%   USA 15%   UK 42%   Other 29%

RESOURCES

 16bn kwh (capacity 3.8m kw)

 6.3m cattle, 5.9m sheep, 1.5m pigs

 Not an oil producer; refines 56,000 b/cd

 Lead, zinc, natural gas, silver, coal

Oil has been found off the southern coast. Studies suggest this may be in commercially exploitable quantities.

ENVIRONMENT

 0.7%   Recent anti-pollution legislation

The main environmental concerns are over-exploitation of the country's peat bogs for fuel and the recent expansion of conifer plantations. While Ireland's levels of forest cover will increase in the next few years, most new planting is of conifers. Controls on pollution were extended in 1994 with the introduction of stringent new laws.

MEDIA

 There is no official censorship, but there can be self-censorship on moral issues

PUBLISHING AND BROADCAST MEDIA

 There are 7 daily newspapers. These include the *Irish Times* and the *Irish Independent*

 1 state-owned, 1 independent service   1 state-owned, 1 independent service

Censorship of media coverage of Sinn Féin was lifted in 1994. There is wide access to British papers, TV and radio.

CRIME

 1953 prisoners   Up 1% in 1992

Rural Ireland has the EU's lowest crime rate. Urban crime is growing and drug abuse is a problem in Dublin and Cork.

EDUCATION

 99%   101,108 students

The Catholic Church runs many schools. Trinity College, Dublin, is the most prestigious of four universities.

Clew Bay in County Mayo, on the western coast of Ireland, viewed from the slopes of *neighboring Croagh Patrick.*

CHRONOLOGY

English colonization, which began in 1167, was reinforced after 1558 by oppressive anti-Catholic legislation and the settlement of Scottish Protestants in the north.

- ❏ **1845–1855** Famine. One million die, 1.5 million emigrate.
- ❏ **1919–1921** Anglo–Irish war after republican Sinn Féin proclaims Irish independence.
- ❏ **1922** Irish Free State set up.
- ❏ **1949** Ireland becomes a republic.
- ❏ **1973** FG–LP win elections.
- ❏ **1992** Resignation of FF Premier Charles Haughey.
- ❏ **1994** Irish–UK talks on Northern Ireland; London Declaration.
- ❏ **1995** Referendum in favor of divorce.

I

HEALTH

 1 per 588 people   Heart diseases, cancers, accidents

Free care is means tested. One-third of the population relies on health care insurance. Ireland has the EU's lowest per capita consumption of alcohol.

WEALTH

 Fork lift truck driver, 285 Irish pounds ($457) per week; junior manager, 450 Irish pounds ($721) per week

CONSUMER GOODS OWNERSHIP

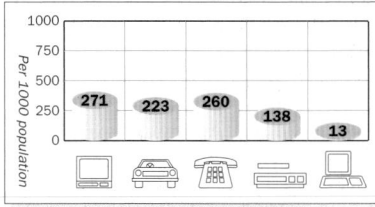

271   223   260   138   13

Living standards for those in jobs are rising steadily. Unemployment has, however, forced more onto welfare.

WORLD RANKING

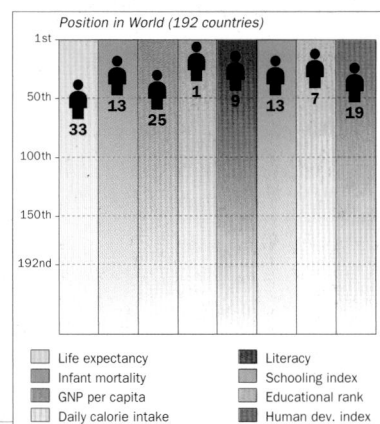

Position in World (192 countries)

33   13   25   1   9   13   7   19

Life expectancy	Literacy
Infant mortality	Schooling index
GNP per capita	Educational rank
Daily calorie intake	Human dev. index

ISRAEL

OFFICIAL NAME: State of Israel CAPITAL: Jerusalem
POPULATION: 5.6 million CURRENCY: New shekel OFFICIAL LANGUAGE: Hebrew

CREATED AS A NEW STATE IN 1948 with the backing of the USA and other Allied powers, Israel is bordered by Egypt, Jordan, Syria and Lebanon. Its topography varies from the HaNegev Desert in the south to the Dead Sea, the lowest point on the Earth's surface. Following wars with its Arab neighbors, Israel has unilaterally extended its original boundaries to control the West Bank, Gaza Strip, East Jerusalem and the Golan Heights.

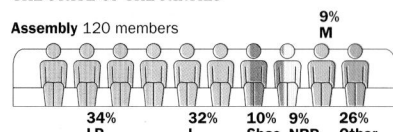
MIDDLE EAST

CLIMATE

WEATHER CHART

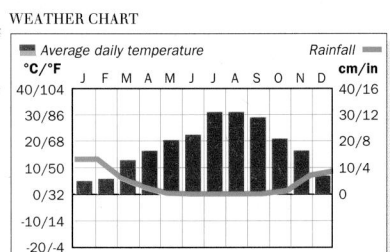

Summers are hot and dry. The wet season is between November and March, when the weather is mild.

TRANSPORTATION

Ben-Gurion Intl, Tel Aviv-Yafo 3.5m passengers

36 ships
820,000 dwt

THE TRANSPORTATION NETWORK

8,190 miles
(13,180 km)

None

329 miles
(530 km)

None

Excellent roads link all Israeli towns. Railroads are being extended, and there are three commercial ports.

TOURISM

1.6m visitors

Down 1% in 1994

MAIN OVERSEAS ARRIVALS

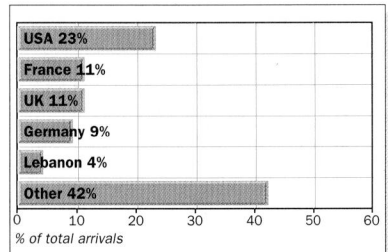

USA 23%					
France 11%					
UK 11%					
Germany 9%					
Lebanon 4%					
Other 42%					

0 10 20 30 40 50 60
% of total arrivals

Jerusalem is the major tourist destination. Elat and the Dead Sea have been developed as beach resorts.

PEOPLE

Hebrew, Arabic, Yiddish, German, Russian, Polish, Romanian, Persian

713 people per sq. mile

THE URBAN/RURAL POPULATION SPLIT

91%   9%

RELIGIOUS PERSUASION

Christian 2%
Other 2%
Muslim (mainly Sunni) 14%
Jewish 82%

ETHNIC MAKEUP

Other (mostly Arab) 17%
Jewish 83%

Large numbers of Jewish immigrants settled in Palestine before Israel was founded in 1948. After World War II, there was a massive increase in immigration. Sephardic Jews from the Middle East and Mediterranean are now in the majority, but Ashkenazi Jews, mostly of central European origin, still dominate politics, business and social life. Thousands of Russian Jews have emigrated since 1989. Israel's Palestinian population totals some 800,000. While many take part in the democratic process, they remain sidelined in Israeli life. Those in occupied territories decline Israeli citizenship.

POPULATION AGE BREAKDOWN

	0–14	15–64	65+		
65+	4.9%	6.7%	8.6%	8.8%	8.6%
15–64	59%	60.2%	58.2%	59.9%	63.3%
0–14	36.1%	33.1%	33.2%	31.3%	28.1%
	1960	1970	1980	1990	2000

% of population by age group

POLITICS

1996/2000

President Ezer Weizmann

THE STATE OF THE PARTIES

Assembly 120 members

9% M
34% LP   32% L   10% Shas   9% NRP   26% Other

LP = Labor Party L = Likud (Consolidation)
NRP = National Religious Party M = Meretz (composed of Ratz, Shinui, United Workers' Party) Other = Yisrael Ba'aliya, Hadash, United Torah Judaism, The Third Way, United Arab List, Moledet

Israel is a multiparty democracy. The prime minister and his cabinet wield executive power under the president.

MAIN POLITICAL ISSUES
Peace with the PLO
This issue is explained on page 292.

Elections
Following the assassination of Prime Minister Yitzhak Rabin in November 1995, his successor Shimon Peres called an early general election in May 1996. Likud leader Binyamin Netanyahu became prime minister, beating Peres by the narrowest of margins. His election caused fears that a more conservative, hard-line approach would be taken by Israel in dealings with its Arab neighbors.

Peace with Syria
Peres made clear his commitment to concluding a peace deal with Syria, the key to an all-encompassing Middle East agreement. However Netanyahu's position is more hard-line, and he is likely to want to concede less to Syria to secure peace agreement.

PROFILE
Elected by proportional representation, Israeli governments tend to depend on minor parties for survival. Political tensions are increased by friction between Orthodox and secular Jews, and settlers and Arabs in the West Bank.

Yitzhak Rabin, the prime minister was assassinated in November 1995.

Yasser Arafat, the militant-turned-moderate leader of the PLO.

WORLD AFFAIRS

| CERN | IAEA | IBRD | WTO | |

Israel remains technically at war with all Arab states except Egypt and Jordan. A comprehensive Middle East peace agreement is dependent upon an Israeli-Syrian deal on the Golan Heights. Israel has a close relationship with the USA.

AID

 $1.3bn (receipts)   ⬇ Down 39% in 1993

Israel receives massive military and economic aid from the USA. Large *ad hoc* donations are also received from Jewish NGOs.

ISRAEL

Total Land Area : 20 330 sq. km (7849 sq. miles)

POPULATION

◎ over 100 000
○ over 50 000
● over 10 000

LAND HEIGHT

1000m/3281ft
500m/1640ft
200m/656ft
Sea Level
-200m/-656ft

DEFENSE

 $6.9bn   ⬆ Up 3% in 1995

0   *Defense spending as % GDP*   40
9.5%

The only Middle Eastern country with a nuclear deterrent, Israel has a small regular defense force which can be boosted by nearly 600,000 reservists. Equipped with some of the latest US technology, the Israeli forces' firepower is vastly superior to that of its Arab neighbors.

ISRAELI ARMED FORCES

	4,095 main battle tanks (1,080 *Centurion*, 325 M-48A5, 800 M-60)	134,000 personnel
	2 submarines and 55 patrol boats	6,000 personnel
	449 combat aircraft (50 F-4E, 63 F-15, 205 F-16, 20 *Kfir* C7)	32,000 personnel
	Widely believed that Israel has a nuclear capacity with up to 100 warheads. Delivery via *Jericho* 1 and *Jericho* 2 missiles	

ECONOMICS

 $78.1bn   3.02–3.14 new shekels

STRENGTHS

Government commitment to economic reform. Huge potential of agriculture, manufacturing and industrial products. Important banking sector. Prospect of peace in region. Sizeable aid from US government and international Jewish organizations.

WEAKNESSES

High unemployment and inflation. Large defense budget. History of regional and internal instability inhibits foreign investment. Little trade with Arab neighbors.

PROFILE

Progress in the peace negotiations with Syria would be a huge boost to the economy. The government is seeking ways to reduce state spending, which accounts for two-thirds of GNP. The state owns 90% of all land and controls over 20% of all industries and services. Public companies are being privatized and there are plans to end restrictive labor practices. Agriculture is highly specialized and profitable. The state is now aiming to boost the service sector.

Despite a world recession, Israel's economy has continued to expand in the 1990s. The engine of this continued

SCORE CARD

❏ WORLD GNP RANKING	37th
❏ GNP PER CAPITA	$14,410
❏ BALANCE OF PAYMENTS	$–4bn
❏ INFLATION	8.9%
❏ UNEMPLOYMENT	10%

EXPORTS

Japan 5%
Germany 5%
Other 48%
Belgium-Luxembourg 5%
UK 6%
USA 31%

IMPORTS

UK 9%
Other 39%
Switzerland 9%
Germany 12%
Belgium-Luxembourg 13%
USA 18%

growth has been the mass immigration of Jews, many highly educated, from the former Soviet Union. Although unemployment levels have risen as a result of immigration, new skills and contacts have also helped the Israeli economy toward sustained export-led growth.

ISRAEL : MAJOR BUSINESSES

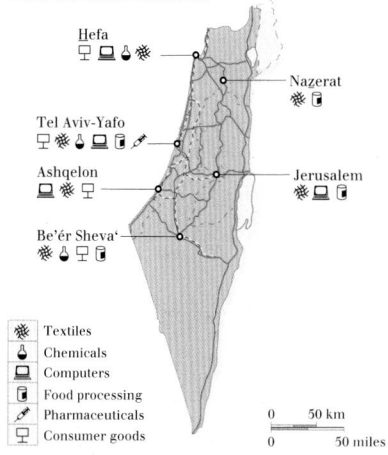

Hefa
Nazerat
Tel Aviv-Yafo
Ashqelon
Jerusalem
Be'ér Sheva'

❋ Textiles
🜁 Chemicals
🖳 Computers
🗄 Food processing
✒ Pharmaceuticals
🖵 Consumer goods

0   50 km
0   50 miles

ECONOMIC PERFORMANCE INDICATOR

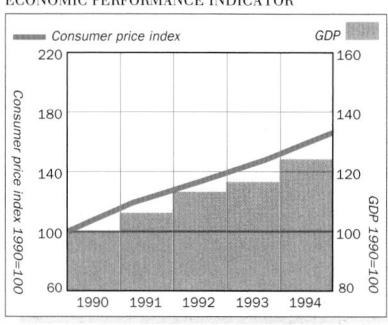

Consumer price index   GDP

0   50 km
0   50 miles

N

THE WEST BANK & GAZA STRIP

OCCUPIED BY ISRAELI TROOPS in the Six Day War in 1967, the West Bank and Gaza Strip were administered by Israel until 1994. The West Bank, with a land area of 2,278 square miles, has a population of 859,000, of whom 97% are Palestinian Arabs. Israeli settlers have encroached on much of the best land. The Gaza Strip covers only about 386 square miles but has a population of almost 600,000 Palestinian Arabs. Both territories rely on agriculture and remittances from work in Israel. Following negotiations between Israel and the PLO in 1993–1995, agreement was reached allowing limited autonomy for the Palestinians in Gaza and in much of the West Bank pending "final status" talks.

HISTORY

Israeli settlement of the West Bank began soon after the area's conquest in 1967. The Gaza Strip, the most turbulent region, was not formally incorporated into Israel until 1973.

After Egypt's President Sadat visited Israel in 1977, progress on Palestinian autonomy seemed possible. The framework agreed at Camp David in 1978, however, failed to materialize and Israeli attitudes appeared to harden, with proposals for more Jewish settlements. By 1985, Israel had direct control of most of the West Bank. Attempts to bring peace to the region by allowing Palestinians an independent state were blocked by the PLO's refusal to recognize Israel's right to exist and Israel's refusal to negotiate with what it regarded as a terrorist group.

The frequency and violence of Arab anti-Israeli demonstrations in the Occupied Territories intensified, culminating, in January 1988, in an *intifada* (uprising) involving a strike by 120,000 Palestinians with jobs in Israel. The Israeli cabinet endorsed an "iron fist" approach by the security forces, but was divided as to long-term solutions. That year, King Hussein of Jordan abandoned links with the West Bank, allowing the PLO to declare an independent Palestinian state. The PLO also endorsed UN Resolution 242 and thus Israel's right to exist. However, only after the Rabin-led Labor coalition came to power in Israel in 1992 was progress made toward peace. At the same time, the Islamic militant group *Hamas*, opposed to any deal with Israel, was gaining support in the Occupied Territories.

KEY ISSUES

With the annexation of the West Bank and Gaza Strip, Israel was faced with the dilemma of whether to grant the Arab population citizenship or to exclude it from the democratic process. Although some right-wing Israeli leaders advocated retaining the territories, the growing power of *Hamas* demonstrated that incorporating the West Bank and Gaza into Israel was fraught with difficulty.

Much of the population in the West Bank and Gaza supports the PLO, although the organization's ranks are split. Hardliners disagree with PLO leader Yasser Arafat's moderate demands on Israel. The challenge for Israel is to maintain law and order and contain the extremists, while working to implement the 1993 Oslo Accords. The problem for Arafat and his backers in the PLO is to keep a grip on the territories and to eclipse the influence of *Hamas*.

SETTLEMENT

An Israeli–PLO agreement signed in September 1995 (the so-called Oslo B agreement) extended the rule of the Palestine National Authority (PNA), confined since May 1994 to the Gaza Strip and the West Bank town of Jericho. As of the end of 1995, PNA civilian rule was extended to six other main West Bank towns. In January 1996, a Palestinian Legislature was elected, with Arafat as "president" of the body's executive council. The transfer of PNA control to Hebron, scheduled for early 1996, was temporarily halted when rogue *Hamas*

WEST BANK

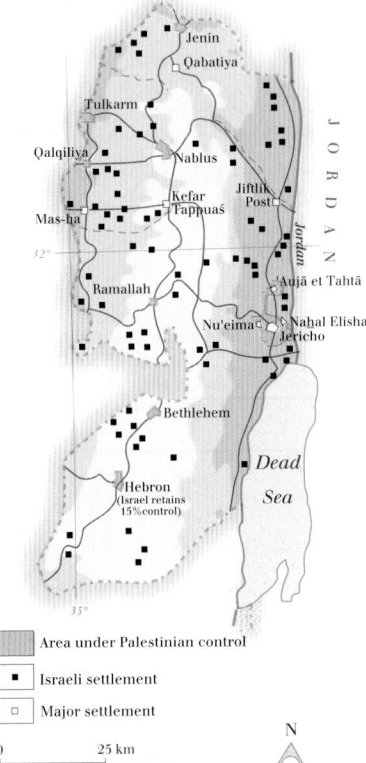

▨ Area under Palestinian control

■ Israeli settlement

□ Major settlement

guerrillas carried out a series of devastating suicide bomb attacks in Israel in February–March 1996. The attacks, carried out in retaliation for Israel's assassination of *Hamas*'s leading bomb-maker, appeared to place in jeopardy the start of "final status" talks aimed at tackling contentious issues such as Jerusalem and refugees and scheduled to start in mid-1996. The attacks also increased pressure on the Israeli government to "seal" and "cantonize" the Palestinian autonomous areas to prevent further atrocities.

***Bethlehem**, situated in the troubled West Bank, is just one of the many holy places that remain a principal attraction for visitors.*

GAZA STRIP

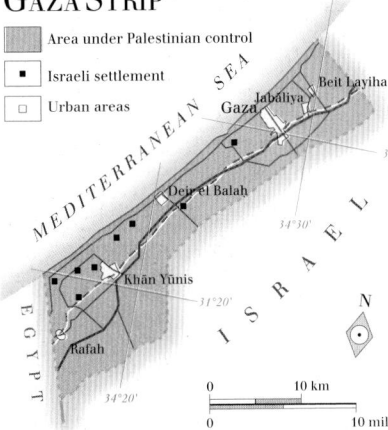

▨ Area under Palestinian control

■ Israeli settlement

□ Urban areas

RESOURCES

24.5bn kwh
(capacity 4.1m kw)

180 b/d
refines 221,000 b/cd

362,000 cattle,
330,000 sheep,
100,000 pigs

Natural gas, oil,
potash, bromine,
magnesium, salt

ELECTRICITY GENERATION

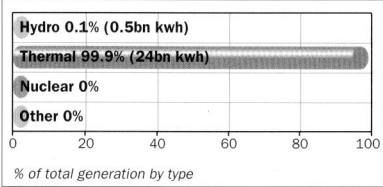

Hydro 0.1% (0.5bn kwh)	
Thermal 99.9% (24bn kwh)	
Nuclear 0%	
Other 0%	

0 20 40 60 80 100

% of total generation by type

The country's most valuable deposits of minerals are potash, bromine (of which Israel is the world's largest exporter) and other salts mined near the Dead Sea. Reserves of copper ore and gold were discovered in 1988. In the coastal plain, mixed farming, vineyards and citrus groves are plentiful. Former desert areas now have extensive irrigation systems supporting specialized agriculture.

Israel's most critical resource is its water. Shortages have forced the country to buy water, transported in plastic bags, from Turkey.

Dead Sea

Jordan

HANAGEV

ISRAEL : LAND USE

Cropland
Forest
Pasture
Desert
Sheep
Citrus fruit - cash crop

0   50 km
0   50 miles

ENVIRONMENT

  15%

Consistently high standards from year to year

The government declared 1993–1994 Environment Year. It aimed to promote recycling schemes, the clean-up of rivers and improvements in Israel's urban environment.

ENVIRONMENTAL TREATIES

No	Yes		Yes
No	Yes		No

MEDIA

Foreign journalists are monitored. The media is constrained by extensive military and security censorship and other administrative restrictions

PUBLISHING AND BROADCAST MEDIA

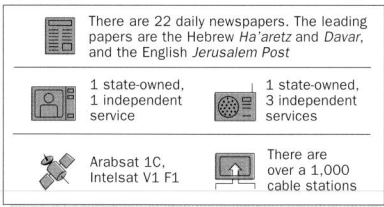

There are 22 daily newspapers. The leading papers are the Hebrew *Ha'aretz* and *Davar*, and the English *Jerusalem Post*	
1 state-owned, 1 independent service	1 state-owned, 3 independent services
Arabsat 1C, Intelsat V1 F1	There are over a 1,000 cable stations

The largely centrist to left-wing press has been at the forefront of support for the Arab–Israeli peace process.

CRIME

  43,900 prisoners

  Up 13% in 1992

CRIME RATES

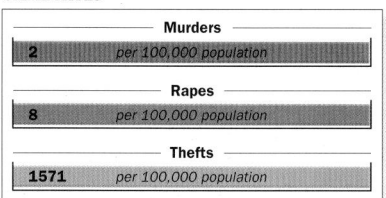

Murders	
2	*per 100,000 population*
Rapes	
8	*per 100,000 population*
Thefts	
1571	*per 100,000 population*

Terrorism by Arab, Islamic and Jewish extremists is the major problem. The army has been accused of abuses.

EDUCATION

  95%

  119,124 students

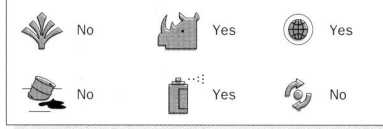

0   *Education spending as % GNP*   25
5.8%

THE EDUCATION SYSTEM

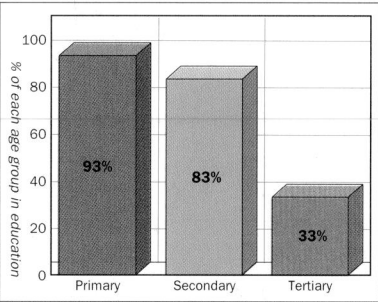

% of each age group in education

Primary 93%
Secondary 83%
Tertiary 33%

Education is free and compulsory for all between five and 16. There are both secular and religious universities. Many students study in the USA.

HEALTH

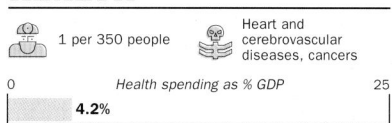 1 per 350 people

Heart and cerebrovascular diseases, cancers

0   *Health spending as % GDP*   25
4.2%

Primary health care reaches all communities. Israel's hospitals have pioneered many innovative treatments.

CHRONOLOGY

The creation of Israel in Palestine in 1948 realized the Zionist dream of a Jewish homeland.

❑ **1967** The Six Day War with Arab states. Israel seizes the Gaza Strip, Sinai, the Golan Heights and the West Bank of the Jordan River. The UN Security Council calls for Israeli withdrawal.

❑ **1973** Egypt and Syria attack Israel and fight inconclusive 18-day war.

❑ **1977** Egypt's President Sadat's Jerusalem visit signals accord.

❑ **1979** Peace treaty signed with Egypt.

❑ **1982** Withdrawal from Sinai; invasion of Lebanon.

❑ **1993** Oslo Accords signed with PLO; PLO recognition of Israel in return for autonomy for Palestinians in Gaza Strip and Jericho.

❑ **1995** Palestinian autonomy extended to much of West Bank. Prime minister Rabin assassinated; replaced by Shimon Peres.

❑ **1996** Palestinian elections. First direct elections for post of prime minister. Binyamin Netanyahu (Likud) defeats Peres (Labor).

I

WEALTH

Social worker, $800 ($255) per monthπ; army officer, $1,500 ($478) per month

CONSUMER GOODS OWNERSHIP

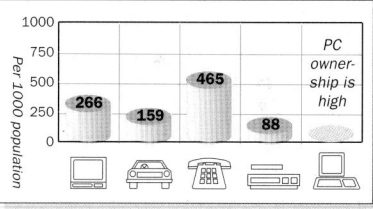

Per 1000 population

266   159   465   88

PC ownership is high

Income per head is high, but taxation is heavy. Some Israelis live in communes and eschew personal material wealth.

WORLD RANKING

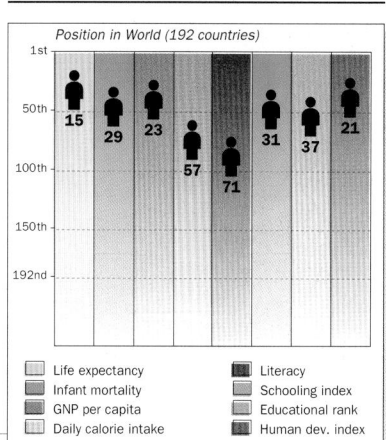

Position in World (192 countries)

1st
50th
100th
150th
192nd

15   29   23   57   71   31   37   21

Life expectancy	Literacy
Infant mortality	Schooling index
GNP per capita	Educational rank
Daily calorie intake	Human dev. index

ITALY

OFFICIAL NAME: Italian Republic   **CAPITAL:** Rome
POPULATION: 57.2 million   **CURRENCY:** Italian lira   **OFFICIAL LANGUAGE:** Italian

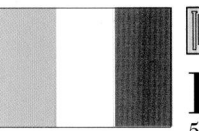     

LYING IN SOUTHERN EUROPE, Italy comprises the famous boot-shaped peninsula stretching 500 miles into the Mediterranean and a number of islands – Sicily and Sardinia being the largest. The Alps form a natural boundary to the north, while the Apennine Mountains run the length of the peninsula. The south is an area of seismic activity, epitomized by the volcanoes of Mounts Etna and Vesuvius. United under ancient Roman rule, Italy subsequently developed into a series of competing kingdoms and states, not fully reunited until 1870. Italian politics was dominated by the Christian Democrats (CD) from 1945 to 1992 under a system of political patronage and a succession of short-lived governments. Investigations into corruption from 1992 led to the demise of this system in the elections of 1994.

CLIMATE

WEATHER CHART

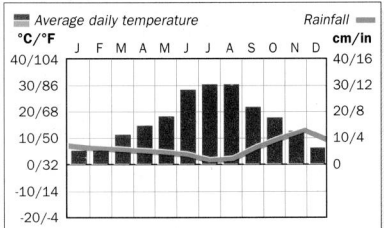

Southern Italy has a Mediterranean climate; the north is more temperate. Summers are hot and dry, especially in the south. Temperatures range from around 75°F to over 81°F in Sardinia and Sicily. Southern winters are mild; northern ones are cooler and wetter. The mountains usually experience heavy snow. The Adriatic coast suffers from cold winds such as the *bora*.

TRANSPORTATION

 Leonardo da Vinci (Fiumicino), Rome
15.55m passengers

 791 ships
10.13m dwt

THE TRANSPORTATION NETWORK

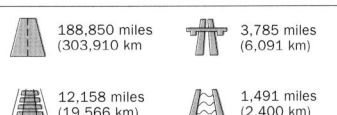

188,850 miles (303,910 km)	3,785 miles (6,091 km)
12,158 miles (19,566 km)	1,491 miles (2,400 km)

Many of Italy's key routes are congested. The trans-Apennine *autostrada* (expressway) from Bologna to Florence is being doubled in size. A high-speed train program (*treno ad alta velocità* – TAV) is planned to link Turin, Milan, Venice, Bologna, Florence and Naples to Rome. Most of Italy's exports travel by road, via Switzerland and Austria. Only 16% goes by sea.

TOURISM

 27.5m visitors   Up 4% in 1994

MAIN OVERSEAS ARRIVALS

Germany 30%	
France 10%	
USA 9%	
UK 6%	
Austria 5%	
Other 40%	

% of total arrivals

Italy has been a tourist destination since the 16th century and probably invented the concept. Roman Popes consciously aimed to make their city the most beautiful in the world to attract travelers. In the 18th century, Italy was the focus of any Grand Tour. Today, its many unspoilt centers of Renaissance culture continue to make Italy one of the world's major tourism destinations. The industry accounts for 3% of Italy's GDP, and hotels and restaurants employ one million out of a working population of 21 million.

Most visitors travel to the northern half of the country, to cities such as Rome, Florence, Venice and Padova. Many are increasingly traveling to the northern lakes. Beach resorts such as Rimini attract a large, youthful crowd in summer. Italy is also growing in popularity as a skiing destination.

Fears have been expressed that tourism may be having a detrimental impact on Italy's environment. The pressure of visitors to Venice, in particular, is such that in summer one-way systems for pedestrians have to be introduced and day-trippers are often turned away.

Tuscan landscape. *Chianti wine is produced in this region, where many northern Europeans own vacation homes.*

ITALY

Total Land Area : 294 060 sq. km
(301 270 sq. miles)

POPULATION

over 1 000 000	▣
over 500 000	◉
over 100 000	◎
over 50 000	○
over 10 000	●

LAND HEIGHT

3000m/9843ft	
2000m/6562ft	
1000m/3281ft	
500m/1640ft	
200m/656ft	
Sea Level	

PEOPLE

Italian, German, French, Rhaeto–Romanic, Sardinian

505 people per sq. mile

THE URBAN/RURAL POPULATION SPLIT

67%   **33%**

RELIGIOUS PERSUASION

Roman Catholic 100%

ETHNIC MAKEUP

Sardinian 2%   Other 4%

Italian 94%

Italy is a remarkably homogenous society. Most Italians are Roman Catholics and Italy has far fewer ethnic minorities than its EU neighbors. Most are fairly recent immigrants from Ethiopia, the Philippines and Egypt. A sharp rise in illegal immigration in the 1980s and 1990s, from North and West Africa, Turkey and Albania, generated a right-wing backlash and tighter controls. It became a major election issue in 1993 and a factor in the rise of the federalist

Northern League. Further stringent measures against illegal immigrants were introduced in 1995.

Difficult economic conditions caused many Italians to emigrate in the 1950s and 1960s. There are now five million Italians living abroad. About half live in other EU countries, the rest mainly in the USA, South America and Australia. Most migrants then, as now, are from the poorer south – the *Mezzogiorno*. Within Italy, prejudice still exists in the north against southern Italians.

Italians do not have a strong sense of national identity – except when it comes to sport. State institutions are viewed as inefficient and corrupt. Allegiance is to Europe, the region or community, above all to the family. The extended family remains Italy's key social and economic support system. Most Italians live at home before marriage. Marriage rates are among the highest in Europe and divorce rates the lowest. Catholicism, however, has not stopped Italy having the lowest birth-rate and one of the highest abortion rates in the EU.

Italians have long had a reputation of being world-leaders in the fields of fashion and design. Their preoccupation with style reflects the traditional importance of *bella figura* – image, cutting a dash – in Italian life as much as the high living standards which most now enjoy.

POPULATION AGE BREAKDOWN

% of population by age group	0–14	15–64	65+
	9.3%	10.9%	13.1%	14.3%	16.9%
	65.9%	64.6%	64.6%	69%	67.6%
	24.8%	24.5%	22.3%	16.7%	15.5%
	1960	1970	1980	1990	2000

CHRONOLOGY

A collection of independent monarchies, dukedoms and city states, Italy became a unified independent nation in 1871.

❏ **1922** Mussolini asked to form government by king.
❏ **1928** One-party rule by Fascists.
❏ **1929** Lateran Treaties with Vatican recognize sovereignty of Holy See.
❏ **1936–1937** Axis formed with Nazi Germany. Ethiopia conquered.
❏ **1939** Albania annexed.
❏ **1940** Italy enters World War II on German side.
❏ **1945** Invaded by Allies. Mussolini imprisoned by Victor Emmanuel III. Armistice concluded with Allies. Italy declares war on Germany. ⇨

I

0   100 km
0   100 miles

I

CHRONOLOGY *continued*

- ❑ **1944** Christian Democratic Party (CD) formed.
- ❑ **1945** Mussolini released. Establishes puppet regime in north. Executed by Italian partisans.
- ❑ **1946** Referendum votes in favor of Italy becoming a republic.
- ❑ **1947** Italy signs peace treaty with Allies. Cedes border areas to France and Yugoslavia, Dodecanese to Greece and gives up colonies.
- ❑ **1948** Elections. CD under De Gaspieri forms coalition with left-of-center PSDI, PLI and PRI.
- ❑ **1949** Italy a founder member of NATO.
- ❑ **1950** Agreement with USA on US bases in Italy.
- ❑ **1951** Joins European Coal and Steel Community.
- ❑ **1957** Founder-member of European Economic Community. Aided by EEC funds and Marshall Aid, industrial growth accelerates.
- ❑ **1964** CD government under Aldo Moro forms coalition with PSI.
- ❑ **1969** Red Brigades, extreme left terrorist group, formed.
- ❑ **1972** Support for extreme right reaches postwar peak (9%). Rise in extreme left and right urban terrorism.
- ❑ **1976** PCI support reaches a peak of 34% under Enrico Berlinguer's Eurocommunist philosophy.
- ❑ **1978** CD president Aldo Moro abducted and murdered by Red Brigades.
- ❑ **1980** Extreme right group plants bomb in Bologna railroad station, killing 84 and wounding 200.
- ❑ **1983** Center-left coalition under Bettino Craxi governs until 1987.
- ❑ **1990** Northern League, a coalition of regionalist parties, attacks government's immigration policies and subsidies to southern Italy.
- ❑ **1992** Corruption scandal, involving the acceptance of bribes in return for public contracts, uncovered in Milan. Government members accused.
- ❑ **1994** General elections held. CD collapses. Coalition between *Forza Italia* and left and right-wing parties led by Silvio Berlusconi forms government. December, collapses following resignation of NL ministers.
- ❑ **1995** Government of technocrats headed by Lamberto Dini tackles budget, pensions, media and regional issues before resigning in January 1996.
- ❑ **1996** April elections lead to historic victory for center-left *L'Ulivio* (Olive Tree) alliance headed by Romano Prodi.

POLITICS

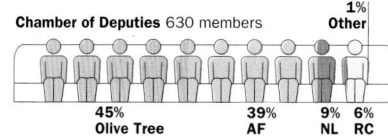

U. House 1996/1999
L. House 1996/1999

President Oscar
Luigi Scalfaro

THE STATE OF THE PARTIES

Chamber of Deputies 630 members

1%
Other

45% Olive Tree   39% AF   9% NL   6% RC

RC = Communist Refoundation   **Olive Tree** = center-left bloc (composed of PDS = Democratic Party of the Left, Greens, PPI = Popular Party, RI = Italian Renewal)   **NL** = Northern League   **AF** = Freedom Alliance (composed of FI = Forza Italia, AN = National Alliance, CD = Christian Democrats)

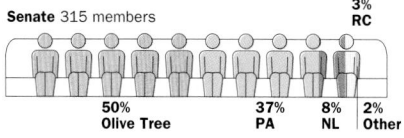

Senate 315 members

3%
RC

50% Olive Tree   37% PA   8% NL   2% Other

Italy is a multiparty democracy.

MAIN POLITICAL ISSUES
Corruption

The *Mani pulite*, "Clean Hands," investigations, precipitated by the 1992 revelations of illegal party financing in Milan, have revealed a network of institutionalized corruption linking the traditional parties and business. By 1994, over 4,500 people had been arrested, many of them public figures. Several, like Carlo de Benedetti, head of one of Italy's most prestigious firms, Olivetti, have been imprisoned. The issue, which has destroyed the old political order, will remain prominent for some years owing to the enormous backlog of cases still to be tried. Former prime minister Silvio Berlusconi faced charges in 1996 concerning bribe payments, and former prime minister Giulio Andreotti is charged with links to the Mafia.

Lamberto Dini, caretaker prime minister of Italy until April 1996.

Umberto Bossi, leader of the regionalist Northern League.

Silvio Berlusconi, former prime minister and leader of Forza Italia.

The church of Santa Maria della Salute marks the entrance to Venice. The city state managed to retain its independence until Napoleon Bonaparte's invasion of Italy.

Institutional Reform

The main center-left and center-right political blocs in 1996 failed to agree on key constitutional and electoral reforms for stable government. Both sides agreed on a French-style system, but the far-right insisted on a strong presidency whereas the left preferred a stronger role for parliament.

PROFILE

In 1993, Italy experienced its worst political crisis since 1945. *Mani pulite* investigations revealed a dense network of institutionalized corruption and discredited a whole political class – in particular the Christian Democrats (CD) and Socialists (SP). Electoral reform by an interim government, after a positive referendum on the issue, meant that in the elections in March 1994, 75% of seats were chosen by a simple majority.

The left-wing alliance headed by the PDS, the reformed communists, were early favorites before millionaire businessman Silvio Berlusconi entered the race. His *Forza Italia* went into coalition with the secessionist NL and neo-fascist MSI/NA, to keep the left out. The PS and CD collapsed into factions. The CD was not only disgraced, it also lost the justification for its political dominance since 1945 – keeping from power Italy's once-large Communist Party.

Berlusconi's Alliance for Freedom coalition won the election but its period in office was turbulent and it collapsed in December 1994 when the NL decided to withdraw. Berlusconi, facing defeat in a no-confidence debate in parliament, resigned. A technocratic government, led by Lamberto Dini, lasted until January 1996. Dini stayed on as caretaker prime minister after the failure of parties to agree on urgent constitutional and electoral reforms. Early April 1996 elections resulted in a historic victory for the center-left *L'Ulivio* (Olive Tree) alliance whose leader, Romano Prodi, promised a period of new political stability.

WORLD AFFAIRS

 EU G10 NATO OECD OSCE

Since World War II, Italy has pursued a strongly Atlanticist foreign policy. Italy has also been one of the most committed members of the EU. Its strategic position in the Mediterranean has made Italy a central member of NATO since its foundation in 1949. NATO's South European Command is based in Naples.

Since the end of the Cold War, Italy's major concern has been unrest in the Balkans. The fear that thousands of Bosnian war refugees would seek entry to Italy proved unfounded, however. The rise of Islamic fundamentalism in Algeria and UN sanctions against Libya are of concern since Italy is highly dependent on the two North African states for its energy supplies.

AID

 $3bn   Up 26% in 1993

Italy has been targeting aid at the Balkan states and Albania. Its aim is to prevent a flood of "economic" migrants. Around 750 military personnel continue to operate relief in Albania; their stay has been extended indefinitely. Africa receives the bulk of development aid.

DEFENSE

 $16bn   Down 1% in 1995

0	Defense spending as % GDP	40
2.1%		

ITALIAN ARMED FORCES

	1,319 main battle tanks (167 M-60A1, 910 *Leopard*, 242 *Centauro*)	175,000 personnel
	9 submarines, 1 carrier, 1 cruiser, 4 destroyers, 26 frigates, 6 patrol boats	44,000 personnel
	369 combat aircraft (82 *Tornado*, 112 F-104S, 58 G-91)	67,800 personnel
	None	

The breakup of the Soviet Union and civil war in parts of former Yugoslavia refocused Italy's defense priorities. The "New Model Defense" announced in 1992 will lead to a 23% reduction in all armed forces. The army is being remodeled for a rapid-intervention role for NATO's southern flank. The navy will be cut to fulfil Mediterranean coastal roles rather than maintaining its current ocean-going capabilities. An estimated 45% of Italy's weapons systems need to be replaced before the year 2000.

ECONOMICS

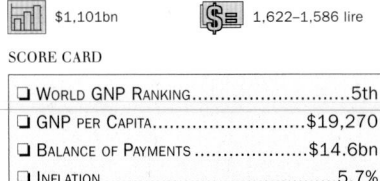 $1,101bn   1,622–1,586 lire

SCORE CARD

❏ WORLD GNP RANKING	5th
❏ GNP PER CAPITA	$19,270
❏ BALANCE OF PAYMENTS	$14.6bn
❏ INFLATION	5.7%
❏ UNEMPLOYMENT	12%

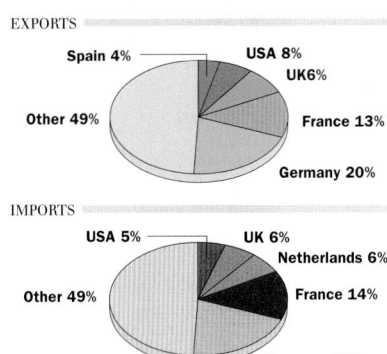

EXPORTS

Spain 4% · USA 8% · UK 6% · France 13% · Germany 20% · Other 49%

IMPORTS

USA 5% · UK 6% · Netherlands 6% · France 14% · Germany 20% · Other 49%

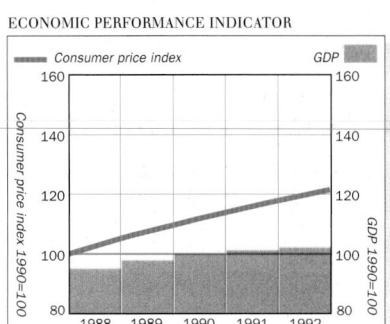

ECONOMIC PERFORMANCE INDICATOR

Consumer price index — GDP

STRENGTHS

Highly competitive, innovative small to medium-size business sector. World leader in industrial and product design, textiles and household appliances. Several highly innovative firms include Fiat (cars), Montedison (plastics), Olivetti (computers) and Benetton (fashion). Strong tourism and agriculture sectors. Weak lira a boost to exports.

WEAKNESSES

Huge public deficit and government debt; over 100% of GDP. Large and inefficient public sector. Uneven wealth distribution: northern Italy far richer than the south, which suffers from high unemployment and where organized crime deters investment. Relatively small companies could find competing in a free international market hard. Heavy dependence on imported energy.

PROFILE

Since World War II, Italy has developed from a mainly agricultural society into a world industrial power, with a GDP greater than the UK's. The economy is characterized by a large state sector, a mass of family-owned businesses, relatively high levels of protectionism and strong regional differences. Compared to the other G7 economies, Italy also has relatively few multinationals.

State businesses are run mainly by two holding companies, the Institute for Industrial Reconstruction (IRI) and the National Hydrocarbons Group (ENI). IRI owns major electronics, steel, telecommunications, engineering, shipbuilding and aerospace companies. ENI is one of the world's top players in

the energy and chemicals sectors.

Family-owned businesses are the backbone of Italy's private sector. They include Fiat, whose interests include aero-engines, telecommunications and bioengineering, as well as cars. Similar businesses tend to congregate. This geographical specialization encourages local competition which has translated into national success.

The *Mezzogiorno* remains the exception. It has 35% of Italy's population, but contributes only 24% of GDP. State attempts to attract new investment have met with success in areas immediately south of Rome. Elsewhere, organized crime has deterred investors and siphoned off state funds. Industrial production has stagnated and unemployment soared. Anger at the misuse of state funds in the south has been a powerful factor in the growth of the Northern League with its demands for autonomy from Rome. One-third of Italian tax revenue is generated in Italy's industrial heartland of Milan.

I

ITALY : MAJOR BUSINESSES

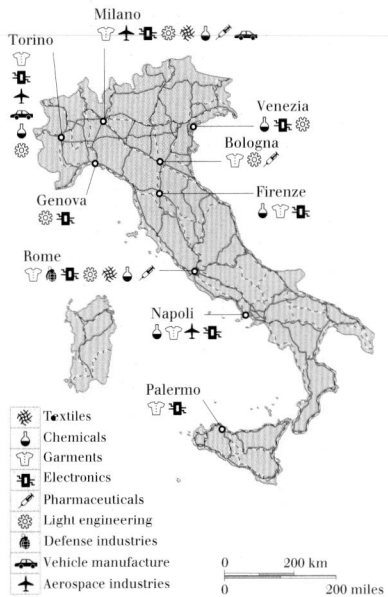

Milano · Torino · Venezia · Bologna · Genova · Firenze · Rome · Napoli · Palermo

❋ Textiles
⚗ Chemicals
👕 Garments
💡 Electronics
✒ Pharmaceuticals
⚙ Light engineering
🛡 Defense industries
🚗 Vehicle manufacture
✈ Aerospace industries

0   200 km
0   200 miles

Remains of the Greek theater *at Taormina, eastern Sicily. It was rebuilt by the Romans in the 2nd century AD. Today, the theater is the venue for an annual arts festival.*

RESOURCES

 226.2bn kwh (capacity 56.5m kw)

 89,804 b/d (reserves 746,977,000 bbl)

10.4m sheep, 8.2m pigs, 7.7m cattle, 1.3m goats

Coal, oil, lignite, pyrites, fluorspar, barytes, bauxite

ELECTRICITY GENERATION

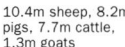

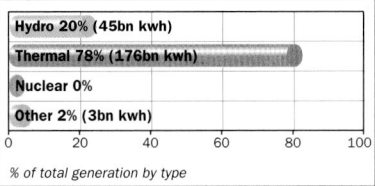

Hydro 20% (45bn kwh)
Thermal 78% (176bn kwh)
Nuclear 0%
Other 2% (3bn kwh)

0   20   40   60   80   100
% of total generation by type

Italy has very few natural resources. It produces just 1% of its oil needs and is highly vulnerable to both fluctuations in world prices and political instability in its North African suppliers. It has reduced its exposure since 1973, when oil accounted for 71% of its needs. Even so, oil still accounts for 56% of energy consumption. Some power is generated from hydro and geothermal sources. Nuclear power was rejected in a 1987 referendum and development has effectively been abandoned. Italy's mineral assets are small and the sector contributes little to national wealth.

ITALY : LAND USE

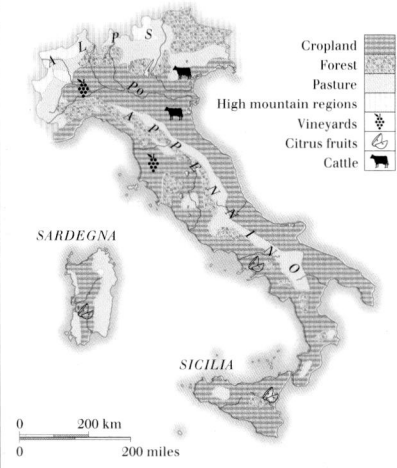

Cropland
Forest
Pasture
High mountain regions
Vineyards
Citrus fruits
Cattle

SARDEGNA

SICILIA

0   200 km
0   200 miles

ENVIRONMENT

 8%

 Environmental concerns not a priority

ENVIRONMENTAL TREATIES

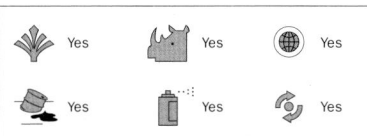

Yes   Yes   Yes
Yes   Yes   Yes

Italy has extensive environmental legislation but, compared to other EU states, has faced problems in enforcing directives. Under the Amato administration, new measures such as energy taxes and waste recycling laws were considered. However, the government of Silvio Berlusconi was less keen to introduce environmental laws which might have restricted business competitiveness.

Pollution in cities such as Naples and Rome is a major concern. Bans on traffic for up to seven hours during windless days are not uncommon. Air pollution and acid rain have also been damaging forests; 10% of trees are affected. Concern has also been expressed at the hunting of migrant birds, a popular sport in Italy, and the use by some in the fishing industry of drift nets in the Ionian Sea. Sometimes up to 19 miles long, these nets catch dolphins and turtles as well as fish. Under EU law, all drift nets over 1.6 miles long are illegal.

MEDIA

 No censorship restrictions

PUBLISHING AND BROADCAST MEDIA

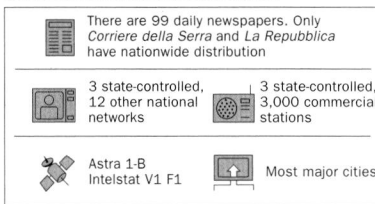

There are 99 daily newspapers. Only *Corriere della Serra* and *La Repubblica* have nationwide distribution

3 state-controlled, 12 other national networks

3 state-controlled, 3,000 commercial stations

Astra 1-B Intelstat V1 F1

Most major cities

Italy's media is dominated by a few conglomerates, notably the Fininvest Group owned by Silvio Berlusconi and Carlo de Benedetti's Ferruzzi group. It has traditionally been highly politicized. Until the exposures of the post-1992 corruption investigations brought reform, this was particularly true of the state TV RAI channels. Like the rest of the state sector, they were apportioned between the main parties: RAI 1 to the Christian Democrats, RAI 2 to the Socialists and RAI 3 to the former Communist Party. All the media reflect the Italian love of sport, especially soccer. *La Gazzetta dello Sport* has one of the largest circulations of the national dailies.

CRIME

 Italy does not publish prison figures

 No change in 1992

CRIME RATES

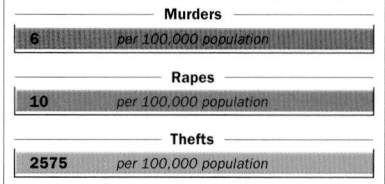

Murders
6   per 100,000 population

Rapes
10   per 100,000 population

Thefts
2575   per 100,000 population

Organized crime remains Italy's most significant problem. The Mafias of Sicily, Naples and Calabria – the *Cosa Nostra, Camorra* and *'ndrangheta* – control wholesale agricultural markets and much of the narcotics trade, bleed businesses of protection money, and manipulate public works contracts and politics. Journalists and public officials delving too deeply into their activities are killed. Giovanni Falcone, the most successful anti-Mafia magistrate, was assassinated in Sicily in 1992. Estimates suggest Mafia businesses are worth $1 billion–$10 billion a year, on a par with US multinationals ITT and Exxon.

EDUCATION

 97%

 1.6m students

0   Defense spending as % GDP   40
2.1%

THE EDUCATION SYSTEM

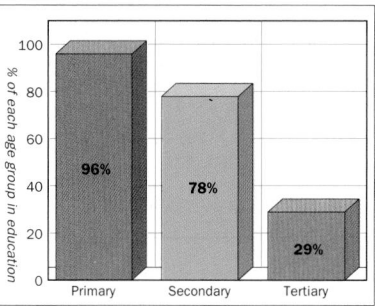

% of each age group in education

100
80
60
40
20
0

Primary 96%   Secondary 78%   Tertiary 29%

Italy's schooling is almost entirely state-run, apart from a few religious schools and elite private institutions. The pupil–teacher ratio is one of the best in Europe. In 1993, the school leaving age was raised from 14 to 16 years, bringing Italy in line with the rest of Europe. The intention was to cut the high drop-out rate in schools, which in Sicily is as high as 50%.

Universities in Italy are over-subscribed. Rome has 180,000 students, only 30% of whom gain a degree. Many Italian educationalists wish to restrict entry. Another concern is the fact that Italy devotes only 1.4% of its GNP to research, compared to the European average of 2.5%.

REGIONS

MILAN

Milan

- Builtup area
- Park or open land
- Old City
- Major sites
- Hi-tech industry
- Electronics
- Motor industry
- Food processing
- Fashion
- Finance

ITALY'S SECOND CITY is also its prime industrial and commercial center. The focus of the fashion, finance and publishing industries, among others, Milan and its province contribute 12% of national GDP. Its inhabitants are among the wealthiest in Europe. Since the 1970s, there has been a shift from manufacturing towards the service and high-tech sectors which now employ 50% of the population. Many major firms have their head offices in Milan, but its economy depends on small, highly innovative businesses. The city's pride in its efficiency took a knock in 1992 when it became a focus of investigations into corruption in the awarding of public contracts.

TUSCANY

MIDWAY BETWEEN MILAN and Rome, Tuscany in many ways epitomizes Italy – certainly to the thousands of foreigners who have made it their home and the millions of tourists attracted by its beaches, hill towns and the artistic glories of its capital, Florence. It is also quintessentially Italian in that its economy depends on a myriad of small firms clustered around particular centers – such as Prato for textiles and Santa Croce for leather. Over the past 40 years, these family-run concerns have transformed Tuscany from a mainly agricultural society into a major industrial area and one of Italy's richest regions.

- Etruscan/classical sites
- Renaissance sites

CALABRIA

- Areas of agricultural reform
- Areas of industrial reform
- Tourism
- Vegetable oil
- Citrus fruits
- Wine

OCCUPYING THE FOOT of the Italian "boot," Calabria is a region of harsh mountains. It has poor soils, virtually no industry and Italy's highest rate of unemployment. The Calabrians are Italy's poorest people, and among the poorest in Europe. To other Italians, the region is a world apart. Southern Calabria, home of the notorious 'ndrangheta Mafia, has Europe's highest murder rate. A few Mafia-dominated communities like Natile, San Luca and Plati have grown relatively wealthy extorting money from northern industrialists. The area is the kidnap capital of Italy. State development funds have been siphoned off by Mafia clans who control 90% of building and public works contracts. Investors, including state industries like IRI – used as pump primers in other parts of the south – have stayed away. Virtually abandoned by the state, which has made little attempt to control the 'ndrangheta, many Calabrians have emigrated. In the years after 1945, up to one-third of Calabria's population emigrated to Australia.

HEALTH

 1 per 909 people

 Heart and cerebrovascular diseases, cancers

0	Health spending as % GDP	25
	8.3%	

Italy's current state-run health system was introduced in the 1970s. Standards vary as services are run by the regions, but few Italians rate their hospitals very highly. Initially free at point of use, charges were introduced in 1988. In addition to some dental and prescription costs, patients have to pay a daily hospital charge and a yearly health fee. AIDS patients are exempt.

WEALTH

 Waiter, 1,533,871 Italian lire ($967) per month; journalist, 2,855,655 Italian lire ($1,800) per month

CONSUMER GOODS OWNERSHIP

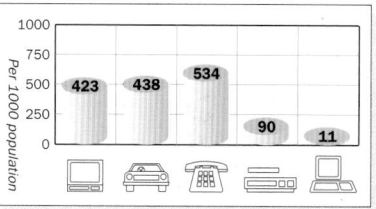

Italians, particularly in the north, are today among the world's wealthiest people in terms of disposable income. This is a result not only of economic growth, but also of the structure of Italian society.

Many Italians have more than one job. The extended families in which most people still live often have access to more than one income. Few people have mortgages, and savings and tax avoidance levels are high.

The main exceptions are in parts of the south. In places like Calabria and Naples, where investment has been lowest and unemployment is highest, many people live in poverty. For those who do not emigrate, organized crime is often the only way to make money.

WORLD RANKING

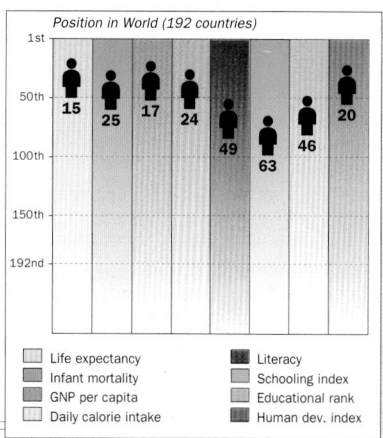

- Life expectancy
- Infant mortality
- GNP per capita
- Daily calorie intake
- Literacy
- Schooling index
- Educational rank
- Human dev. index

IVORY COAST

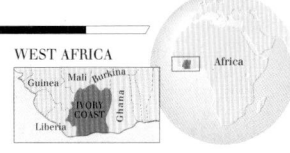

OFFICIAL NAME: Republic of Côte d'Ivoire   **CAPITAL:** Yamoussoukro
POPULATION: 14.3 million   **CURRENCY:** CFA franc   **OFFICIAL LANGUAGE:** French

ONE OF THE LARGER of the West African coastal nations, the Ivory Coast – officially Côte d'Ivoire – remains under the powerful influence of its former colonial ruler, France. Most of its population lives along the sandy coastal strip. The forested interior, apart from the capital, is sparsely populated. Between independence in 1960 and his death in 1993, the Ivory Coast was ruled by President Houphouët-Boigny.

CLIMATE

WEATHER CHART

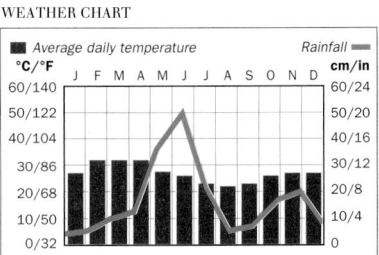

The south's four seasons – two rainy and two dry – merge in the north into a single wet season with lower rainfall.

TRANSPORTATION

Abidjan–Port-Bouët
849,000 passengers

 8 ships
93,300 dwt

THE TRANSPORTATION NETWORK

3,290 miles (5,290 km)		96 miles (155 km)	
396 miles (638 km)		609 miles (980 km)	

The relatively good transportation system focuses on Abidjan, the premier port of francophone West Africa.

TOURISM

 230,000 visitors   Up 15% in 1988

MAIN OVERSEAS ARRIVALS

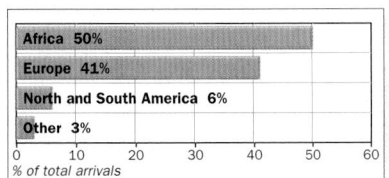

Africa 50%
Europe 41%
North and South America 6%
Other 3%
% of total arrivals

Ambitious plans for an "African Riviera" east of Abidjan and the opening of an hotel by the French *Club Méditerranée* did not boost tourism as expected. The giant Christian basilica built at Yamoussoukro is a major attraction.

PEOPLE

 Akan, French, Kru, Voltaic   117 people per sq. mile

THE URBAN/RURAL POPULATION SPLIT

42%   58%

RELIGIOUS PERSUASION

Christian 12%
Muslim 25%
Indigenous beliefs 63%

Although there are more than 60 ethnic groups, the key ones are the Baoule in the center, the Agri in the east, the Senufo in the north, the Dioula in the northwest and west, the Bété in the center-west and the Dan–Yacouba in the west. Houphouët-Boigny promoted his own group, the Baoule, who number only 23% of the population. The succession of Konan Bedic, another Baoule, has annoyed many groups, the Bété in particular. The extended family is an important force in the shanty towns of Abidjan and connects migrants with their villages. As a result of improved education, women now hold many top jobs.

POLITICS

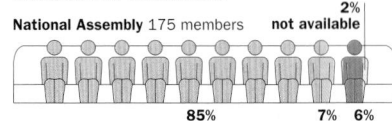

1995/2000   President Konan Bedic

THE STATE OF THE PARTIES

National Assembly 175 members   2% not available

85% PDCI   7% RDR   6% FPI

PDCI = Democratic Party of Ivory Coast   **RDR** = Rally of the Republicans   **FPI** = Ivorian Popular Front

The death of President Houphouët-Boigny in 1993 threw the Ivory Coast's politics into turmoil. No clear successor had been identified by the man who had run the Ivory Coast since independence. Under his rule, the Democratic Party of the Ivory Coast (PDCI) developed a monopoly on patronage which permeated all ranks of the civil service, one reason for the opposition FPI's poor showing in the country's first multiparty elections in 1990. France (the main aid donor), the business community and party barons all maintained their influence under the rule of Houphouët-Boigny, who carefully balanced competing demands. The power vacuum that followed his death left all parties with an influence in politics in a state of uncertainty, at a time when the Ivory Coast had pressing economic problems to deal with. However, the transition has been relatively smooth and Konan Bedic now has firm control.

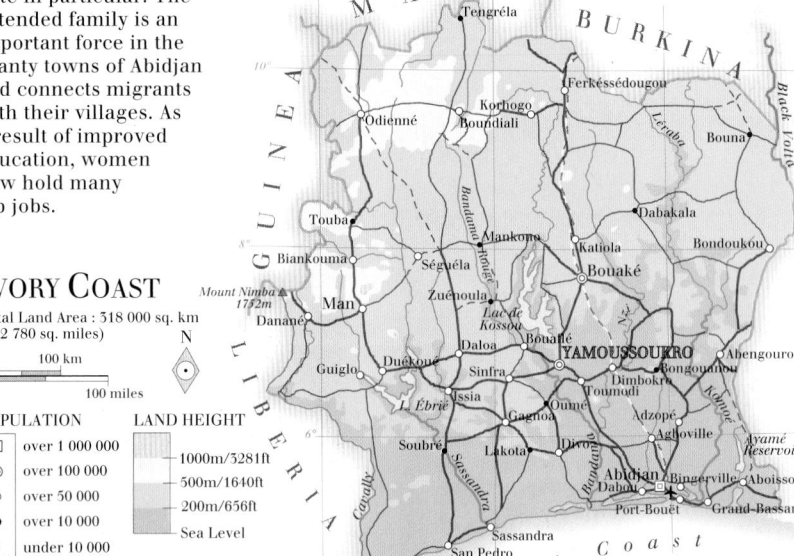

IVORY COAST

Total Land Area : 318 000 sq. km
(122 780 sq. miles)

N

0   100 km
0   100 miles

POPULATION

◫ over 1 000 000
◎ over 100 000
○ over 50 000
● over 10 000
· under 10 000

LAND HEIGHT

1000m/3281ft
500m/1640ft
200m/656ft
Sea Level

WORLD AFFAIRS

The Ivory Coast fears that the civil war in neighboring Liberia could affect its own stability. However, its main concern is balancing the demands and interests of its creditors: the US-dominated World Bank on the one hand and France on the other. Within ECOWAS, the Ivory Coast's most important relationship is with Nigeria.

AID

 $766m (receipts)　　 Up 0.4% in 1991

France donates most overall aid. Structural adjustment loans from the World Bank have been particularly important in easing the acute debt problem. The Ivory Coast gives aid to poorer West African countries.

DEFENSE

 $75m　　 Up 23% in 1995

Since independence, a defense accord has existed with France, the main supplier of equipment and trainer of officers for the 6,800-strong army. The greatest security threat is along the border with war-torn Liberia.

ECONOMICS

 $7.1bn　　 489– 553 CFA francs

SCORE CARD

- ❏ WORLD GNP RANKING.........................90th
- ❏ GNP PER CAPITA $630
- ❏ BALANCE OF PAYMENTS $13m
- ❏ INFLATION 26%
- ❏ UNEMPLOYMENT...................................14%

STRENGTHS
Diversified nature of the agricultural sector. Relatively good infrastructure. Benefits of early liberalism and attractiveness to investors.

WEAKNESSES
Major debt from over-borrowing for projects such as the Kossou Dam. Overproduction of some commodities. Political patronage system of the ruling party, which exploits farmers.

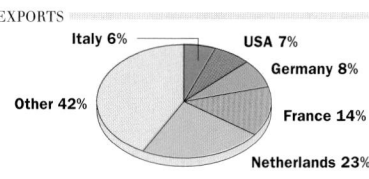

EXPORTS

Italy 6%　USA 7%　Germany 8%　France 14%　Netherlands 23%　Other 42%

IMPORTS

Germany 5%　Italy 5%　Netherlands 5%　Nigeria 16%　France 29%　Other 40%

RESOURCES

 1.9bn kwh (capacity 1.17m kw)　　Reserves of 100,000,000 bbl; refines 6,516 b/d

 1.3m sheep, 1.2m cattle, 1m pigs, 305,000 goats　　 Oil, diamonds, cobalt, gold, iron, manganese, nickel

Oil reserves have failed to meet expectations; negotiations are under way on offshore gas development.

ENVIRONMENT

 6% (0.3% partially protected)　　 Ban on timber exports imposed 1995

The government imposed a ban on unprocessed timber exports in 1995 to protect the Ivory Coast's forests.

MEDIA

 Despite reduction in censorship since 1990, the press is still subject to controls

PUBLISHING AND BROADCAST MEDIA

There are 2 daily newspapers, *Fraternité-Matin* and *Ivoir 'Soir*, both published by the government

 1 state-owned service　　 1 state-owned, 1 independent service

The heavy censorship of the past 30 years is easing, but serious government harassment of media continues.

EDUCATION

 54%　　 23,642 students

A high percentage of students fail the *baccalauréat*. As expenditure has been cut, student agitation has grown.

CRIME

Ivory Coast does not publish prison figures　　Up 300% in 1992

Crime levels are low in rural areas. However, armed robbery and violent crime are on the increase in Abidjan.

The basilica, Yamoussoukro. *Built in the new capital, President Houphouët-Boigny's birthplace, it is modeled on St. Peter's, Rome.*

I

HEALTH

 1 per 16,650 people　　 Malaria, communicable diseases, neonatal deaths

Health improved notably in the 1980s, with many more paramedical workers. Infant mortality rates are high.

WEALTH

 Metalworking machine setter, 181,900 CFA francs ($372) per month; dentist, 288,250 CFA francs ($590) per month

CONSUMER GOODS OWNERSHIP

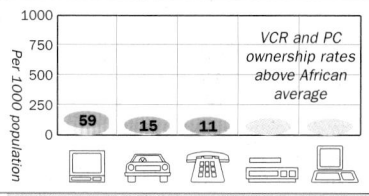

VCR and PC ownership rates above African average

59　15　11

A large bourgeoisie grew rich in the boom years. Urban living standards are better than in many African countries.

WORLD RANKING

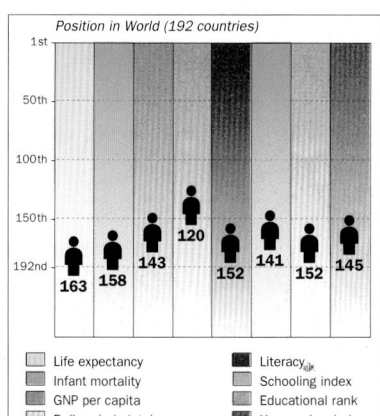

Position in World (192 countries)

163　158　143　120　152　141　152　145

- Life expectancy
- Infant mortality
- GNP per capita
- Daily calorie intake
- Literacy
- Schooling index
- Educational rank
- Human dev. index

JAMAICA

OFFICIAL NAME: Jamaica   CAPITAL: Kingston
POPULATION: 2.4 million   CURRENCY: Jamaican dollar   OFFICIAL LANGUAGE: English

CARIBBEAN

FIRST COLONIZED BY THE SPANISH and then, from 1655, by the English, Jamaica is located in the Caribbean, south of Cuba. It was the first of the Caribbean island nations to become independent from colonial control in the postwar years, and remains an influential force in Caribbean politics. Jamaica is also influential on the world music scene: *reggae* and *ragga* (or *dancehall*) developed in the tough conditions of Kingston's poor districts.

CLIMATE

WEATHER CHART

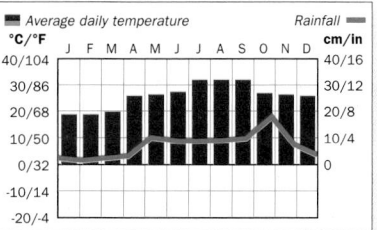

Hurricanes are likely between June and November. The hills above Kingston are the coolest spot during hot summers.

TRANSPORTATION

 Norman Manley International, Kingston   4 ships 16,200 dwt

THE TRANSPORTATION NETWORK

 7,830 miles (12,600 km)   None

 211 miles (339 km)   None

In 1996, US$10 million was to be spent on 300 new buses for Kingston. Its harbor is also being deepened and widened for bigger ships.

TOURISM

 977,000 visitors   Down 0.2% in 1994

MAIN OVERSEAS ARRIVALS

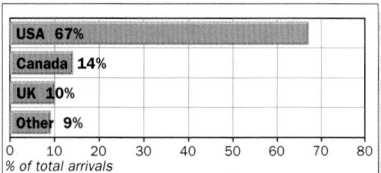

USA	67%
Canada	14%
UK	10%
Other	9%

0   10   20   30   40   50   60   70   80
% of total arrivals

Tourism is a major industry in Jamaica. Most tourists stay in large, enclosed beach resorts. Ocho Rios and Montego Bay have the best beaches.

PEOPLE

 English Creole, English   577 people per sq. mile

THE URBAN/RURAL POPULATION SPLIT

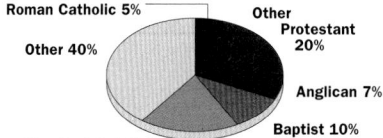

52%   48%

RELIGIOUS PERSUASION

Roman Catholic 5%   Other Protestant 20%
Other 40%
Anglican 7%
Baptist 10%
Church of God 18%

Jamaica has a broad ethnic mix. Most Jamaicans are the descendants of Africans brought to the island between the 16th and 19th centuries, but there are also minorities of Europeans, Arabs, Indians and Chinese. Jamaica is also home to the Rastafarians, worshippers of the former Emperor of Ethiopia.

Most social tension is the result of the marked disparities in wealth. The Caribbean women's rights movement arrived first in Jamaica, and today many women hold senior positions in economic and political life.

Although life revolves around the family, absentee fathers are common. Many career women are single parents by choice. Life in the ghettos of Kingston is often violent and based largely on gun law. Kingston slums have their own patois.

Bauxite mine and terminal, *Runway Bay. Bauxite – from which aluminum is made – is the main source of foreign income.*

POLITICS

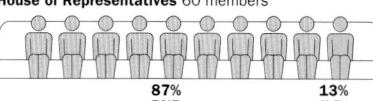

 1993/1998   HM Queen Elizabeth II

THE STATE OF THE PARTIES

Senate 21 members

13 members chosen by the prime minister and 8 by the leader of the opposition

House of Representatives 60 members

87% PNP   13% JLP

PNP = People's National Party   **JLP** = Jamaica Labour Party

Political and economic life is dominated by a few long-established and wealthy families, who fund the parties. Elections are often characterized by violence, and even the murder of candidates.

The country's political complexion changed markedly in the late 1980s, as the ideologies of the once-socialist PNP and the conservative JLP converged towards a moderate free-market economic approach.

In 1996, the ruling PNP proposed a social contract in an effort to stem strong opposition to its austerity policies. The JLP and new National Democratic Movement party claimed the initiative placed the onus for economic stability on the private sector and labor.

WORLD AFFAIRS

 ACS   Caricom   Geplac   NAM   OAS

The USA is the focus of foreign policy. Jamaica liaises with US agencies in anti-narcotics programs.

AID

 $109m (receipts)   Down 13% in 1993

Most aid comes from the USA, the EU and the UK. It includes both project loans and balance of payments support.

DEFENSE

 $29m    Up 7% in 1995

Jamaica's 3,320-strong defense force buys its arms from the USA, but is trained by the UK. Today, the defense force is used against narcotics smugglers and to break up violence during elections.

J

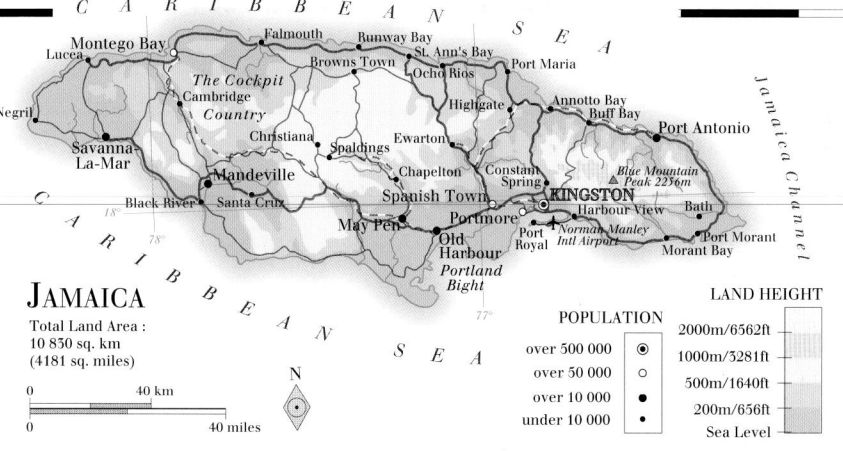

JAMAICA

Total Land Area :
10 850 sq. km
(4181 sq. miles)

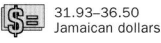

POPULATION		LAND HEIGHT
over 500 000	◉	2000m/6562ft
over 50 000	○	1000m/3281ft
over 10 000	●	500m/1640ft
under 10 000	•	200m/656ft
		Sea Level

CHRONOLOGY

Spain occupied the island in 1510, wiping out the indigenous Arawak population. Britain seized the island in 1655.

- ❑ **1938** JLP founded.
- ❑ **1958–1961** West Indies Federation.
- ❑ **1962** Independence under JLP.
- ❑ **1972** PNP elected. Social and economic reforms fail; street violence begins.
- ❑ **1980** Unpopular IMF austerity measures lead to JLP election win.
- ❑ **1991–1995** PNP returned and austerity measures continued.

ECONOMICS

$3.6bn

31.93–36.50 Jamaican dollars

SCORE CARD

WORLD GNP RANKING	115th
❑ GNP PER CAPITA	$1,420
❑ BALANCE OF PAYMENTS	$48m
❑ INFLATION	35.1%
❑ UNEMPLOYMENT	15.7%

STRENGTHS

A relatively broadly based economy. Mining and refining of bauxite for aluminum. Successful tourism industry. Agriculture, including sugar, bananas, rum and coffee. Light manufacturing and data-processing for US companies are growing sectors.

WEAKNESSES

Most products are dependent on protected markets, which are under threat in both the USA and the EU.

EXPORTS

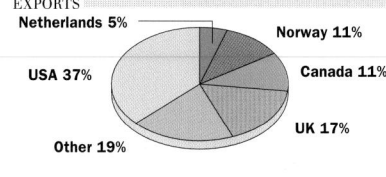

Netherlands 5%
Norway 11%
USA 37%
Canada 11%
UK 17%
Other 19%

IMPORTS

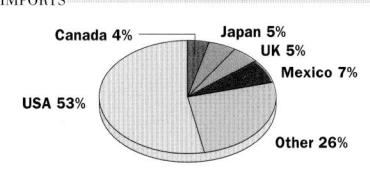

Canada 4%
Japan 5%
UK 5%
Mexico 7%
USA 53%
Other 26%

RESOURCES

2.2bn (capacity 730,000 kw)

Not an oil producer; refines 32,000 b/cd

442,000 goats, 335,000 cattle, 180,000 pigs

Bauxite, marble, gypsum, silica, clay

Jamaica is the world's third-largest producer of bauxite, accounting for 11% of total global output.

ENVIRONMENT

 0.1%

Beach pollution from Kingston's inadequate sewerage

Acidic dust which is a by-product from bauxite processing, the biggest heavy industry in Jamaica, is the major problem. Pollution of Kingston Bay.

MEDIA

 Freedom of expression is guaranteed under the constitution

PUBLISHING AND BROADCAST MEDIA

 There are 3 daily newspapers, the *Daily Gleaner*, the *Daily Star* and the *Jamaica Herald*

1 state-owned, 1 independent service

6 independent services

The government is in the process of loosening its hold on broadcasting. The Jamaican press is one of the most influential in the Caribbean.

CRIME

 4,350 prisoners

 Down 1% in 1992

Armed crime is a major problem. Many murders are the result of armed robberies linked to narcotics gangs competing for territory. Much of the world crack trade is still controlled from Jamaica. Large areas of Kingston are ruled by *Dons*, gang leaders who administer their own violent justice. The armed police are also frequently accused of the peremptory shooting of suspects.

The British Privy Council is the last court of appeal; in 1993, 80 men on death row for more than five years were reprieved in a landmark decision.

EDUCATION

 98%

 23,220 students

Education is based on the former British 11-plus selection system. Jamaica hosts the largest of the three campuses of the University of the West Indies.

HEALTH

 1 per 6,276 people

 Cerebrovascular and heart diseases, cancers, diabetes

The once-efficient state health service is now seriously underfunded. There are fewer doctors and nurses than in the 1980s and hospitals generally have a shortage of drugs and rudimentary medical equipment.

WEALTH

 Miner, 1,139 Jamaican dollars (US$31) per week; metal manufacturing worker, 2,840 Jamaican dollars (US$78) per week

CONSUMER GOODS OWNERSHIP

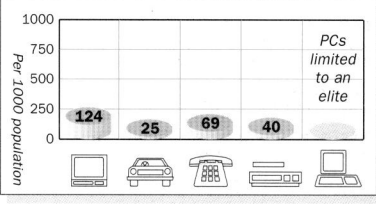

PCs limited to an elite

124 25 69 40

Wealth disparities are highly marked in Jamaica, although better education has seen an increase in the number of black Jamaicans taking more lucrative, white-collar jobs. The poorest in Jamaica, mostly migrants from rural areas, live in the slums of Kingston.

WORLD RANKING

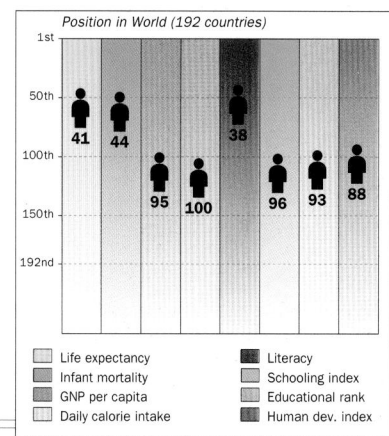

Position in World (192 countries)

41 44 95 100 38 96 93 88

▨ Life expectancy	▨ Literacy
▨ Infant mortality	▨ Schooling index
▨ GNP per capita	▨ Educational rank
▨ Daily calorie intake	▨ Human dev. index

J

JAPAN

OFFICIAL NAME: Japan   CAPITAL: Tokyo
POPULATION: 125.1 million   CURRENCY: Yen   OFFICIAL LANGUAGE: Japanese

A CONSTITUTIONAL MONARCHY, with an emperor as head of state, Japan is located off the east Asian coast in the north Pacific. It comprises four principal islands, and over 3,000 smaller islands. Sovereignty over the most southerly islands in the Kurile chain is disputed with the Russian Federation. Japan's terrain is mostly mountainous, with fertile coastal plains; over two-thirds is woodland. The Pacific coast is vulnerable to *tsunamis* – tidal waves triggered by submarine earthquakes. Most cities are located by the sea; the Kanto plain around Tokyo, Kawasaki and Yokohama is the most populous and heavily industrialized. To the north, Hokkaido is the most rural of the main islands. Japan is the world's most powerful economy, with a current trade balance of over $100 billion per annum, and overseas investments of $240 billion.

Traditional paddy field *in Hokkaido. Rice farming is among the most protected sectors of the Japanese economy.*

CLIMATE

WEATHER CHART

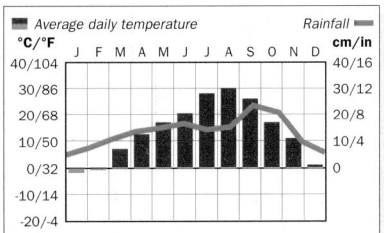

The Sea of Japan has a moderating influence on Japan's climate. Winters are less cold than on the Asian mainland. Japan also has much higher rainfall. Spring is perhaps the most pleasant season, with warm, sunny days but without the sultry, oppressive heat and rainfall of the summer. The freak storms and floods of August 1992 were the worst for 120 years.

TRANSPORTATION

 **Narita, Tokyo**
32m passengers

 3,792 ships
36.34m dwt

THE TRANSPORTATION NETWORK

 485,960 miles
(782,050 km)

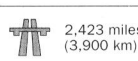 2,423 miles
(3,900 km)

 16,980 miles
(27,327 km)

 1,099 miles
(1,770 km)

Railroads are the most important means of transportation in Japan. The *Shinkansen*, known in the West as the bullet train, is the second-fastest in the world. It is renowned as much for its reliability as its speed. The Tokyo–Chitose air route, with six million passengers a year, is the busiest in the world.

JAPAN

Total Land Area : 376 520 sq. km
(145 574 sq. miles)

POPULATION

- ▣ over 5 000 000
- ▢ over 1 000 000
- ◉ over 500 000
- ◎ over 100 000
- ○ over 50 000
- ● over 10 000

LAND HEIGHT

- 1500m/4921ft
- 1000m/3281ft
- 500m/1640ft
- Sea Level

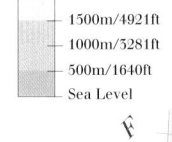
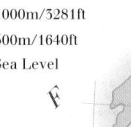

J

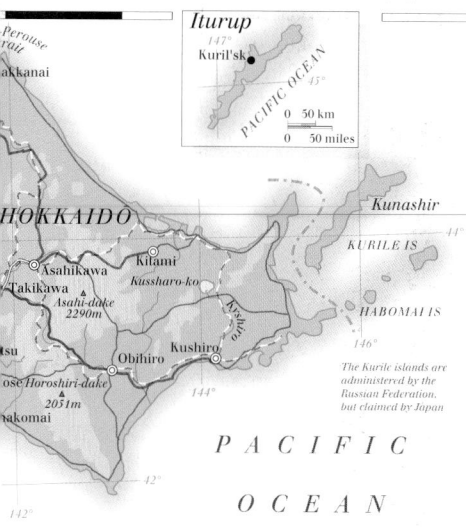

 Iturup
147°
Kuril'sk

Kunashir

HOKKAIDO

KURILE IS

44°

HABOMAI IS

146°

The Kurile islands are administered by the Russian Federation, but claimed by Japan

Asahikawa
Kitami
Takikawa
Asahi-dake
2290m
Kussharo-ko
Obihiro
Kushiro
ose Horoshiri-dake
2051m
akomai
144°
42°

P A C I F I C

O C E A N

142°

TOURISM

1.9m visitors   Down 1% in 1994

MAIN OVERSEAS ARRIVALS

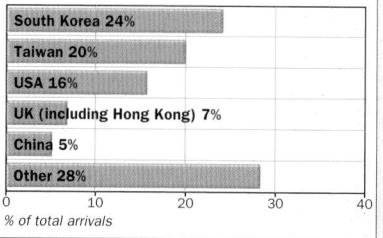

| South Korea 24% |
| Taiwan 20% |
| USA 16% |
| UK (including Hong Kong) 7% |
| China 5% |
| Other 28% |

0   10   20   30   40
% of total arrivals

The high value of the yen makes Japan an expensive tourist destination. Attractions include the extraordinary variety of energetic high-tech urban living in Tokyo and Osaka. By contrast, rural areas such as Hokkaido are highly traditional.

A new trend in Japan is ecotourism. Over three million people a year come to look at whales. Sightseeing boats leave from former whaling villages such as Ogata. The ancient imperial capital, Kyoto, remains the most popular tourist destination. Over 35 million people visit it every year.

High Street, Ginza District, Tokyo at night. Japan's well-policed cities are among the safest in the world.

PEOPLE

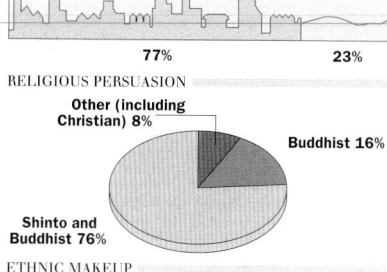

Japanese, Korean, Chinese   834 people per sq. mile

THE URBAN/RURAL POPULATION SPLIT

77%   23%

RELIGIOUS PERSUASION

Other (including Christian) 8%

Buddhist 16%

Shinto and Buddhist 76%

ETHNIC MAKEUP

Other (mainly Korean) 1%

Japanese 99%

Japan is one of the most racially homogeneous societies in the world. Its sense of order is reflected in the phenomenon of the lifetime employer. Many Japanese men define themselves by the company they work for rather than the job they do. An employer's influence stretches to commanding employees' social time, and even to encouraging and approving marriages.

Women mostly play a traditional role, running the home and supervising the all-important education of their children. They tend to work until the age of 26, when many will marry and continue to work part-time. Some Japanese women are, however, beginning to follow independent, long-term careers. More are entering the medical and legal professions. Japan saw its first female party leader – Takako Doi – in 1991.

There is little tradition of teenage rebellion in Japan. While the young still tend to follow their parents' lifestyles, some are questioning established attitudes. They are less likely to want to work for the same company for life, and less willing to give up evenings and weekends to entertaining company clients.

Social form remains extremely important in Japanese society. Respect for elders and social and business superiors is still strong.

POPULATION AGE BREAKDOWN

%	0–14	15–64	65+		
	1960	1970	1980	1990	2000
65+	6%	7%	9%	12%	16%
15–64	64%	69%	67%	70%	68%
0–14	30%	24%	24%	18%	16%

% of population by age group

CHRONOLOGY

Japan's tendency to limit its contacts with the outside world ended in 1853, when a US naval squadron coerced trading concessions from the last of the Tokugawa shoguns.

❑ **1868** Meiji Restoration; overthrow of Tokugawa regime and restoration of imperial power.

❑ **1872** Modernization along Western lines. Japan's strong military tradition becomes state-directed.

❑ **1889** Constitution modelled on Bismarck's Germany adopted.

❑ **1894–1895** War with China; ends in Japanese victory.

❑ **1904–1905** War with Russia; ends in Japanese victory. Formosa and Korea annexed.

❑ **1914** Japan joins World War I on Allied side. Sees limited naval action.

❑ **1919** Versailles peace conference gives Japan limited territorial gains in the Pacific.

❑ **1923** Yokohama earthquake kills 140,000.

❑ **1927** Japan enters period of radical nationalism, and introduces the notion of a "co-prosperity sphere" in Southeast Asia under Japanese control. Interpreted in the USA as a threat to its Pacific interests.

❑ **1931** Manchuria invaded, placed under Japanese control and renamed Manchukuo.

❑ **1937** Japan launches full-scale invasion of China.

❑ **1958** All political parties placed under one common banner; Japan effectively ruled by militarists.

❑ **1959** Undeclared border war with Soviet Union results in Japanese defeat.

❑ **1940** Fall of France in Europe; Japan occupies French Indo–China.

❑ **1941** USA imposes total trade embargo, including oil, on Japan thereby threatening to stifle its military machine. Japan responds in December by launching attack on US fleet at Pearl Harbor and invading US, British and Dutch possessions in the Pacific.

❑ **1942** Japan loses decisive naval battle of Midway. Thereafter the tide of war turns as Japanese forces are driven back toward their home islands.

❑ **1945** Huge US bombing campaign culminates in atomic bombing of Hiroshima and Nagasaki. Soviet Union declares war on Japan. Emperor Hirohito surrenders, gives up divine status. Japan placed under US military government with Gen. MacArthur installed as supreme commander of Allied Powers in Japan.

J

J

POLITICS

 U. House 1995/1998
L. House 1993/1997

 Emperor Tsegu no Miya Akihito

THE STATE OF THE PARTIES

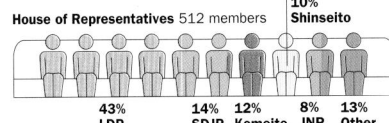

House of Representatives 512 members

| 43% LDP | 14% SDJP | 12% Komeito | 8% JNP | 10% Shinseito | 13% Other |

LDP = Liberal Democratic Party **SDJP** = Social Democratic Party of Japan **Komeito** = Clean Government Party **Shinseito** = Japan Renewal Party **JNP** = Japan New Party **Other** = Japan Communist Party, New Harbinger Party, Democratic Socialist Party and vacant seats

House of Councillors 252 members

| 43% LPD | 27% SDJP | 10% Komeito | 20% Other |

Japan is a multiparty democracy. The Emperor has a non-political role.

MAIN POLITICAL ISSUES
Reform

Japanese politics was dominated for 38 years by a system of patronage, which linked big business, the bureaucracy and the ruling LDP. After numerous scandals, public dissaffection was demonstrated by the ousting of the LDP from government in July 1993. Far-reaching electoral reform was adopted in 1994, and the opposition parties were unified by the creation of *Shinshinto* by Ichiro Ozawa. Although the process of realignment is not yet complete, there is now an incipient two-party system based on center-right parties.

The key aspect of Japan's electoral reform has been the replacement of multi-member constituencies which, by encouraging competition by candidates from the same party,

Morihiro Hosokawa, *prime minister 1993–1994, whose coalition ousted the LDP.*

Ichiro Ozawa *founder and leader of united opposition party* Shinshinto.

Ryutaro Hashimoto, *prime minister and head of the current LDP/SDJP coalition.*

Emperor Tsegu no Miya Akihito. *He acceded in 1989 on the death of his father, Hirohito.*

had been the foundation of the system of LDP factions, the financing of which had fueled the system of "money politics."

The role of the military

The Japanese constitution enshrines the principle of pacifism by forever renouncing war as a sovereign right and "the threat or use of force as a means of settling international disputes." The degree to which this prohibition remains desirable is a matter of debate within Japan, highlighted by the controversial 1993 decision to send armed forces abroad for the first time since 1945 by participating in the UN peacekeeping operation in Cambodia.

PROFILE

In 1993, 38 years of LDP rule in Japan came to an end. Morihiro Hosokawa took over as prime minister, helped by the fact that he was not associated with the tainted world of Tokyo politics. He headed a fragile seven-party coalition.

A string of corruption scandals had led to the LDP's fall from power. Four LDP prime ministers – Takeshita, Uno, Kaifu and Miyazawa – were forced to resign because they were implicated in scandals, or had failed to stamp out corruption. Hosokawa's period in office was brief. He was accused of financial irregularities and forced to resign in 1994. However, his government laid the basis for electoral reform, apologized for Japan's war crimes and began the process of institutional deregulation. Tsutomu Hata took over in April 1994, but the government collapsed in June after the withdrawal of the SDPJ which then joined a coalition including the LDP. In January 1996, LDP leader Ryutaro Hashimoto became prime minister. With the opposition parties having been amalgamated into a new party grouping called *Shinshinto*, formed in December 1994 by Ichiro Ozawa, the next Japanese election will be essentially a two-party contest.

WORLD AFFAIRS

APEC   G5   IAEA   IWC   OECD

After years of limiting its role on the world stage to that of a minor power rather than that of one of the world's most powerful economies, Japan is starting to make its influence felt. Its eventual aim is a seat on the UN Security Council, which would be in keeping with its economic influence. Tentative moves were made in 1993, with Japanese forces joining UN peace-keepers in Cambodia. The lobby that fears a resurgence of Japanese militarism is still strong, however, and wishes to avoid foreign entanglements. In Asia, Japan remains burdened by the legacy of distrust arising from its military expansion and harsh colonial exploitation of its neighbors in the first half of the 20th century.

AID

 11.3bn (donations)   Down 1% in 1993

Japan is the world's largest aid donor. Most aid is spent in Asia and the Pacific, particularly in the expanding economies of Thailand, Vietnam and Cambodia. Polynesian islands are beneficiaries of Japanese aid. Tokyo effectively supports their main livelihood, fishing.

DEFENSE

 $53.8bn   Up 17% in 1995

0   *Defense spending as % GDP*   40
| 1%

JAPANESE ARMED FORCES

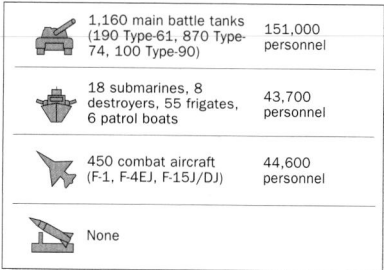

	1,160 main battle tanks (190 Type-61, 870 Type-74, 100 Type-90)	151,000 personnel
	18 submarines, 8 destroyers, 55 frigates, 6 patrol boats	43,700 personnel
	450 combat aircraft (F-1, F-4EJ, F-15J/DJ)	44,600 personnel
	None	

The defense establishment in Japan has not recovered from the effects of the 1941–1945 war. Any signs of military activity – even the UN peace-keeping duties which Japan undertook in Cambodia in 1993 – arouse fierce debate among pacifists. Japan's constitution forbids the use of military force, and defense spending has been limited to around 1% of GNP. However, Japan's economic success has allowed its Self-Defense Forces to become relatively large in world terms.

ECONOMICS

 $4,321.14bn   99.77-103.16 yen

ECONOMIC PERFORMANCE INDICATOR

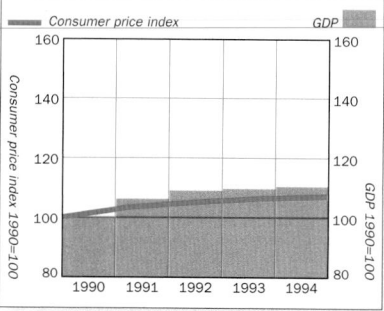

SCORE CARD

❑ WORLD GNP RANKING	2nd
❑ GNP PER CAPITA	$34,630
❑ BALANCE OF PAYMENTS	$129.2bn
❑ INFLATION	1.9%
❑ UNEMPLOYMENT	2.9%

STRENGTHS

The world's most competitive producer of high-tech electronic products and cars. Commitment to long-term research and development. Talent for developing ideas from EU and USA. Global spread of business, including plants in key markets of EU and USA. Revolutionary management and production techniques continue to lead the world. *Keiretsu* – vertically integrated families of companies who agree to cooperate in business – keep non-Japanese companies out of Japanese markets.

WEAKNESSES

Heavy dependence on imported oil. Enormous trade surplus a source of international tension. Financial system burdened by high level of bad debts.

PROFILE

The Tokyo stock market crash in 1990, and particularly the collapse of the sky-high property market, ended a period of exponential growth in the Japanese economy. Industrial production fell by 8% in 1992, the sharpest drop since 1975. Corporate profits were also sharply down. The contraction in demand saw the flow of imports – particularly of European luxury products – stemmed.

However, through this slowdown, the economy continued to grow at a rate of 2% a year. Companies did not shed great amounts of labor, and research and development spending went up. The government stepped in with a five-year economic plan ($60 billion in the first year) of infrastructure spending. The decline in imports saw Japan's trade surplus climb to $100 billion a year by 1993.

Policy is now shifting away from an almost total concentration on export-led growth, to stimulating the domestic economy. Japan is also aware that it has to relax its regulatory framework and allow in

more imports, if relations with the USA and EU are not to be irreparably damaged.

Future growth is expected from new products, from wall-hung flat-screen TV sets, to digital video recorders and high-speed trains. Long overdue improvements to Japanese housing will further stimulate the home economy.

EXPORTS

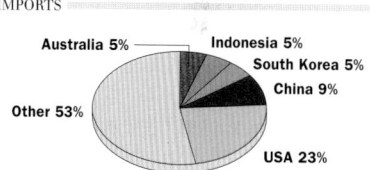

China 5% / Germany 5% / Other 49% / South Korea 5% / Hong Kong 6% / USA 30%

IMPORTS

Australia 5% / Indonesia 5% / South Korea 5% / China 9% / Other 53% / USA 23%

Japan's economic supremacy is likely to continue for some time. Analysts have predicted that, by 2010, Japanese GNP per capita could be over twice that of the USA.

JAPAN : MAJOR BUSINESSES

- Research & development
- Vehicle manufacture
- Heavy engineering
- Consumer goods
- Shipbuilding
- Iron & steel
- Electronics
- Chemicals
- Brewing
- Textiles
- Optics

RESOURCES

 893bn kwh
(capacity
194.76 bn kw)

 17,183 b/d
(reserves
59,850,000 bbl)

 10.6m pigs,
5m cattle,
31,000 goats

 Limestone,
sulfur, coal

ELECTRICITY GENERATION

Hydro 10% (89bn kwh)

Thermal 64.8% (580bn kwh)

Nuclear 25% (223bn kwh)

Other 0.2% (1bn kwh)

0   20   40   60   80   100

% of total generation by type

Japan has few commercially exploitable resources. Production costs make coal extraction uneconomical, and Japan has become the world's largest coal importer. In an attempt to reduce dependence on imported fuels, Japan has developed alternative sources of energy. It is now the world's fourth-biggest generator of nuclear power. However, environmentalists strongly oppose any expansion of this sector.

ENVIRONMENT

 7%

 Japan wishes to resume minke whale hunting

ENVIRONMENTAL TREATIES

Yes   Yes   Yes

Yes   Yes   Yes

Japanese governments have seen environmental issues as a way of making an impact on the world stage. First steps were taken in 1992 to set up an International Environmental Foundation, with a budget of $12 billion for grants to encourage environmentally friendly expansion in developing countries.

Respect for nature is deeply embedded in Japan's psyche, and reflected in a long history of highly sophisticated garden design. This attitude forms the bedrock of a vigorous grass-roots ecological movement, which has succeeded in preventing development at Tokyo's Narita airport for 20 years. It also continues effective opposition to nuclear expansion. Japan supports the hunting of minke whales. It argues that there are enough for this not to threaten the species.

Datsetsusan National Park, Hokkaido. Japan's northerly island is the least populous of the main group.

HOKKAIDŌ

HONSHŪ

CHŪGOKU SANCHI

SHIKOKŪ

ŪSHŪ

JAPAN : LAND USE

Cropland
Forest
Pasture
Sheep
Fruits
Rice

0   300 km

0   300 miles

MEDIA

 No political restrictions

PUBLISHING AND BROADCAST MEDIA

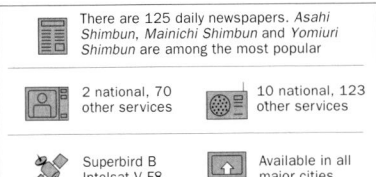

There are 125 daily newspapers. *Asahi Shimbun, Mainichi Shimbun* and *Yomiuri Shimbun* are among the most popular

2 national, 70 other services

10 national, 123 other services

Superbird B Intelsat V F8

Available in all major cities

The Japanese are among the world's most avid newspaper readers. Most dailies carry serious news and are owned by large media groups who also have TV and cable interests. Weekly newspapers carry more tabloid journalism. The magazine market is huge. Over 36 billion magazines are sold in Japan every year. *Non Non*, a women's magazine, is the best-selling title. Lifestyle magazines, encouraging the Japanese to make more use of their limited leisure time, are a growing sector of the market.

Japan is, in dollar terms, the world's second largest film-maker after the USA. It is also Hollywood's major export market.

Japan has redefined much of the world's media. It invented the personal stereo and created the huge computer games market. In the past five years, this market has seen exponential growth. Nintendo, a leading games company, is one of the most profitable in Japan, rivalling long-established corporate giants such as Matsushita.

EDUCATION

 99%

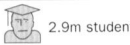 2.9m students

0   *Education spending as % GNP*   25

4.7%

THE EDUCATION SYSTEM

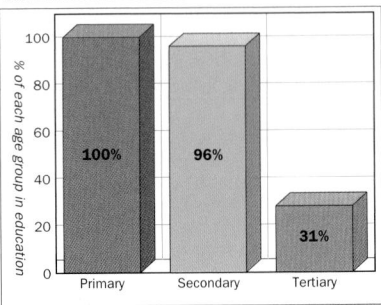

100%   96%   31%

Primary   Secondary   Tertiary

% of each age group in education

One of the key dividing lines in Japanese society is between university graduates, who get the coveted white-collar jobs for life, and non-graduates. The latter have difficulty reaching management level. The result is that the Japanese education system is highly pressurized. Competition for university places is intense, and starts with the choice of kindergarten, which the Japanese attend from the age of four. Once at university, students tend to relax – the important thing is getting in. Tokyo, Kyoto, Waseda and Keio are the most prestigious universities. Their graduates have access to top civil service and business jobs. The system succeeds in producing a uniform, and thoroughly educated, work force.

CRIME

 51,829 prisoners

 Up 1% in 1992

CRIME RATE

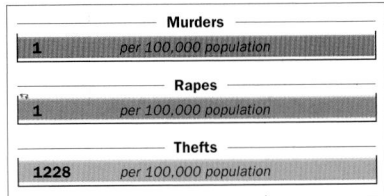

Murders
1   *per 100,000 population*

Rapes
1   *per 100,000 population*

Thefts
1228   *per 100,000 population*

Japan has one of the lowest crime rates in the world. This is in part the result of an efficient police system. Cities are safe, with police kiosks at frequent intervals on street corners.

The major crime problem is fraud and the activities of the *kumi*, organized mafia-style syndicates whose members are known as *yakuza*. The authorities show little enthusiasm in challenging these groups, seeking to contain rather than eradicate their activities. *Kumi* are suspected of having connections with the extreme right in Japanese politics.

J

REGIONS

HOKKAIDO

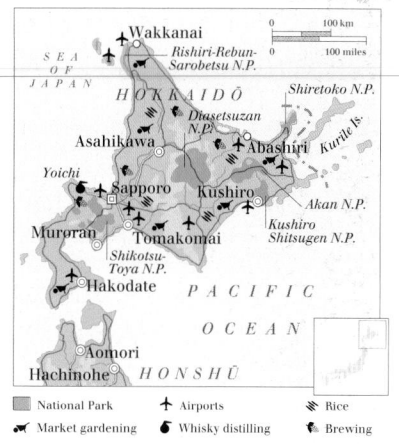

▨ National Park	✈ Airports	🌾 Rice
🐄 Market gardening	🍶 Whisky distilling	🍺 Brewing

THE SECOND-LARGEST and most northerly of the four main islands, Hokkaido is Japan's biggest and most productive farming region. Its open terrain and climate is similar to the US Midwest. US advisors established wheat production here in the 1860s, and Hokkaido now produces over half of Japan's cereal needs. German Americans, from Milwaukee, also established Japan's first brewery, which produces the world-famous *Sapporo* beer.

Recent government investment has encouraged high-tech industries on Hokkaido. Japan's first magnetic train (MAGLEV) test track is being developed on the island.

TOKYO AND DISTRICT

THE IMMENSE CONCENTRATION of Japanese wealth in Tokyo was reflected in 1988, when the value of one square mile of prime real estate in the capital was estimated to be greater than the whole of California. Unplanned expansion since 1945 has resulted in a large conurbation, merging Tokyo with neighboring Yokohama and Kawasaki. During the 1980s, the demands on office space resulted in a rash of new office buildings, crammed into every available piece of land. The lack of vistas – Tokyo has few parks – gives Tokyo's architecture a rather uniform feeling. Notable exceptions to this include two office buildings by the French designer Philippe Starck.

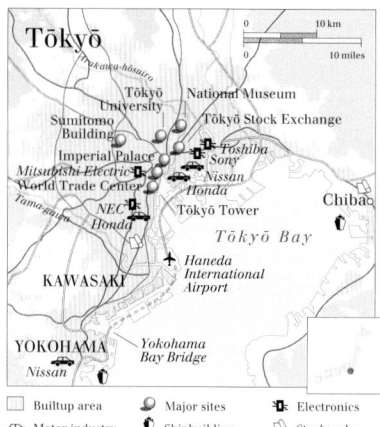

▢ Builtup area	🏛 Major sites	⚡ Electronics
🚗 Motor industry	⚓ Shipbuilding	🏭 Steelworks

KANSAI REGION

🚗 Motor industry	⚡ Electronics

COMPRISING THE SIX PREFECTURES Osaka, Hyogo, Kyoto, Shiga, Nara and Wakayama, Kansai has always had a strong regional identity. In recent years, support for a Kansai federation, with greater independence from Tokyo, has increased. Some 20 million people live here, producing 20% of Japan's textiles, 25% of its steel and 23% of its machine tools. Kansai's share of Japan's GNP exceeds the total GNP of Canada. Its industries have long been renowned for their creativity. Kansai developed the world's first desktop calculator and the first automatic ticket barrier. It is home to world-famous companies such as Matsushita, Sanyo and Sharp.

A healthy rivalry has grown up between Osaka – Kansai's main business city – and Tokyo. Osaka has sought to develop its own fashion and design industries in emulation of Tokyo. Kyoto, with its 1,400 temples and shrines, is Japan's favorite tourist destination. Kansai International, currently being built off Kobe, will be Japan's first 24-hour international airport. It is the 20th century's biggest engineering project.

HEALTH

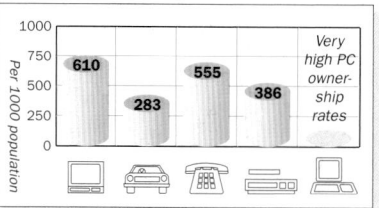

👤 1 per 588 people	Heart and circulatory diseases, cancers, tuberculosis

0   *Health spending as % GDP*   25
6.8%

Japan has a world-class health system, which has delivered some of the highest longevity and lowest infant mortality rates in the world. Most Japanese contribute towards health costs through a national insurance scheme, with premiums calculated on earnings. The poorest in society receive free treatment. Japan's rapidly aging population presents a major future funding challenge.

WEALTH

💲 Machine general worker, 339,524 yen ($3,291) per month; factory manager, 596,665 yen ($5,784) per month

CONSUMER GOODS OWNERSHIP

[Bar chart: Per 1000 population — 610, 283, 555, 386. *Very high PC ownership rates*]

Measured in consumer goods, the Japanese are wealthy; highly restrictive city parking restrictions account for the low rates of car ownership. The yen's high value makes foreign vacations, for those who can afford to take time off, relatively inexpensive. However, living costs are high – a recent survey judged Tokyo more than twice as costly as New York. This means that most Japanese do not live near their place of work and must commute – an often long, cramped journey. It is 18–25-year-old girls who do best – receiving large cash donations from their fathers – by avoiding the pitfalls and living at home. As a group they are reputed to have the highest disposable income in Japan.

WORLD RANKING

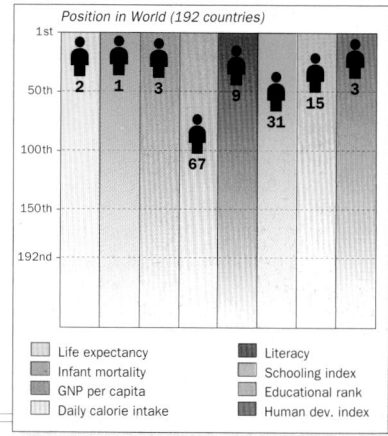

Position in World (192 countries)

[Chart values: 2, 1, 3, 67, 9, 31, 15, 3]

▨ Life expectancy	▨ Literacy
▨ Infant mortality	▨ Schooling index
▨ GNP per capita	▨ Educational rank
▨ Daily calorie intake	▨ Human dev. index

J

JORDAN

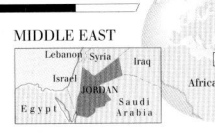

MIDDLE EAST

OFFICIAL NAME: Hashemite Kingdom of Jordan   CAPITAL: Amman
POPULATION: 5.4 million   CURRENCY: Jordanian dinar   OFFICIAL LANGUAGE: Arabic

S HARING BORDERS WITH Iraq, Syria, Israel and Saudi Arabia, Jordan has just 16 miles of coastline on the Gulf of Aqaba. Jordanian territory legally includes the West Bank of the Jordan River and east Jerusalem, but Israel has occupied these areas since 1967. Jordan ceded its claim to the West Bank to the PLO in 1988. Phosphates and tourism associated with important historical sites such as Petra are the mainstays of the economy.

CLIMATE

WEATHER CHART

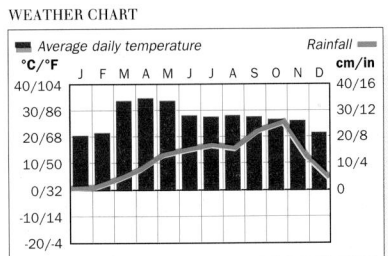

Summers are hot and dry, winters cool and wet. Areas below sea level are very hot in summer and warm in winter.

TRANSPORTATION

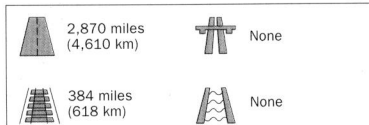

Queen Alia Intl, Amman 1.71m passengers		2 ships 113,600 dwt	

THE TRANSPORTATION NETWORK

2,870 miles (4,610 km)		None
384 miles (618 km)		None

Adequate roads link main cities. A railroad links the port of Al 'Aqabah with the Syrian capital, Damascus.

TOURISM

844,000 visitors   Up 10% in 1994

MAIN OVERSEAS ARRIVALS

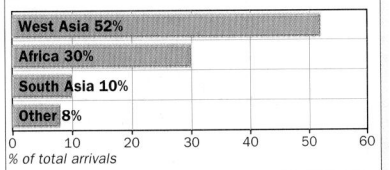

West Asia 52%		
Africa 30%		
South Asia 10%		
Other 8%		

% of total arrivals

Al 'Aqabah offers fine beaches, water sports and subaqua diving, while the ancient city of Petra attracts visitors interested in Roman remains. Amman is developing as a center for Arabic culture and the arts.

PEOPLE

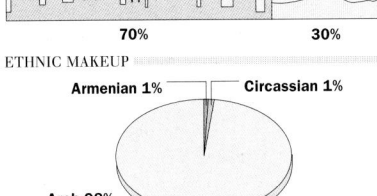

Arabic   159 people per sq. mile

THE URBAN/RURAL POPULATION SPLIT

70%   30%

ETHNIC MAKEUP

Armenian 1%   Circassian 1%

Arab 98% (49% Palestinian)

Jordan is a predominantly Muslim country drawn from Bedouin roots, with a Christian minority and a large Palestinian population. The monarchy's power base lies among the rural tribes, which also provide the backbone of the military. National identity is strong.

POLITICS

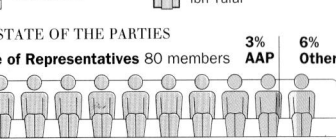

1993/1997   King Hussein ibn Talal

THE STATE OF THE PARTIES

House of Representatives 80 members   3% AAP   6% Other

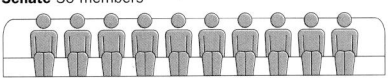

68% Independent   20% IAF   3% JADP

Independent = Centrist (55%), Islamicist (8%) and Leftist (5%)   **IAF** = Islamic Action Front   **JADP** = Jordan Arab Democratic Party   **AAP** = Al Ahd Party

Senate 30 members

The members of the Senate are appointed by the King

King Hussein, the longest-reigning Arab ruler, retains a strong grip on government. In 1965, he eliminated any doubts over the succession by naming his technocrat brother, Hassan, as Crown Prince. Hussein has sought to promote a strong nationalism based on Jordan's tribal structure. He is also careful not to alienate Jordan's other constituencies. In 1993, he responded to calls for greater democracy by agreeing to multiparty elections. Contrary to expectations, gains were not made by fundamentalists.

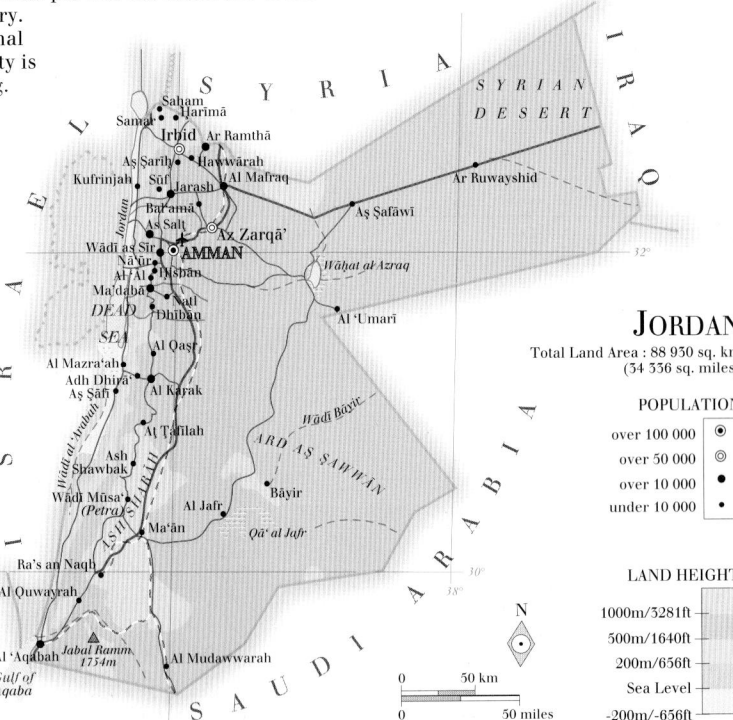

JORDAN

Total Land Area : 88 930 sq. km
(34 336 sq. miles)

POPULATION

- over 100 000
- over 50 000
- over 10 000
- under 10 000

LAND HEIGHT

1000m/3281ft
500m/1640ft
200m/656ft
Sea Level
-200m/-656ft

WORLD AFFAIRS

Jordan's role as a key player in Middle East politics was enhanced by the signing of a peace treaty with Israel in October 1994. Relations with the PLO are often tense and the precise nature of the relationship between Jordan and the newly emerging Palestinian state remains uncertain. Relations with the Gulf states and the West deteriorated during the 1991 Gulf War after King Hussein remained loyal to Baghdad. He finally distanced himself from Saddam Hussein's Iraqi regime in 1995.

AID

 $245m (receipts)   Down 35% in 1993

The Gulf states are set to restore aid to Jordan after King Hussein moved to distance himself from Iraq in 1995.

DEFENSE

 $448m   Up 3% in 1995

Jordanian forces played no part in the 1991 Gulf War. The armed forces are loyal to the monarchy. They have a reputation for thorough training and professionalism. The forces are dependent on Western support for credit in purchasing advanced arms and equipment.

ECONOMICS

 $5.8bn    0.70–0.71 Jordanian dinars

SCORE CARD

- ❏ World GNP Ranking..........................97th
- ❏ GNP per Capita $1,390
- ❏ Balance of Payments....................$–398m
- ❏ Inflation 2.7%
- ❏ Unemployment.................................16%

Strengths

Positive impact of 1994 peace treaty with Israel. Major exporter of phosphates. Skilled and adaptable work force.

Weaknesses

Reliant on imports to satisfy energy requirements. Unemployment owing to influx of Jordanians and Palestinians expelled from Kuwait. Tourism yet to recover from 1991 Gulf crisis.

EXPORTS

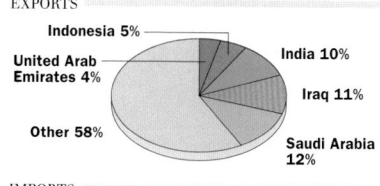

Indonesia 5%
United Arab Emirates 4%
India 10%
Iraq 11%
Saudi Arabia 12%
Other 58%

IMPORTS

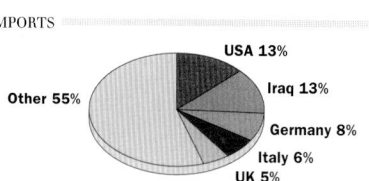

USA 13%
Iraq 13%
Germany 8%
Italy 6%
UK 5%
Other 55%

RESOURCES

 4.4bn kwh (capacity 1m kw)   60 b/d (reserves 4,000,000 bbl)

 77m poultry, 2.1m sheep, 555,000 goats   Oil, phosphates, potash

Oil deposits have been discovered. Phosphates, livestock and crops such as tomatoes, wheat, olives and vegetables are the main resources.

ENVIRONMENT

 3%   Government is pursuing vigorous conservation programs

Conservation is a government priority. Rare animals are protected and species that became extinct in the wild in the 1950s are being reintroduced into controlled environments.

MEDIA

 Widespread self-censorship of the press, in accordance with government guidelines

PUBLISHING AND BROADCAST MEDIA

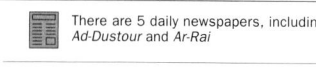

There are 5 daily newspapers, including *Ad-Dustour* and *Ar-Rai*

1 state-owned service   1 state-owned service

Radio and TV are controlled by the state. Private and publicly owned newspapers follow the government line.

CRIME

 Jordan does not publish prison figures   Up 11% in 1992

Jordan is largely peaceful. Crime levels are generally low, although theft in urban areas is rising.

EDUCATION

 83%   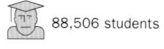 88,506 students

Men and women receive the same education. Jordanian teachers work all over the Middle East.

HEALTH

  1 per 770 people   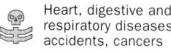 Heart, digestive and respiratory diseases, accidents, cancers

Health care is subsidized by the government. Hospitals are distributed throughout the country.

CHRONOLOGY

King Hussein succeeded to the throne in 1952 after his father was deposed owing to mental illness.

- ❏ **1958** Iraqi revolution ends Jordan's federation with Iraq.
- ❏ **1967** Israel seizes West Bank territories placed under Jordanian rule in 1949.
- ❏ **1988** King Hussein cedes claims to West Bank to PLO.
- ❏ **1994** Jordan signs full peace treaty with Israel.

The King's Highway, *seen from the castle at Al Karak. This strategic fortress was built by Crusader knights in the 12th century.*

WEALTH

 The wealthiest are those closest to the king

CONSUMER GOODS OWNERSHIP

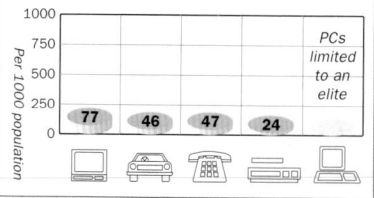

PCs limited to an elite

77   46   47   24

Per 1000 population

The wealthiest Jordanians are Amman-based entrepreneurs, bankers and engineers. Poverty is relatively rare.

WORLD RANKING

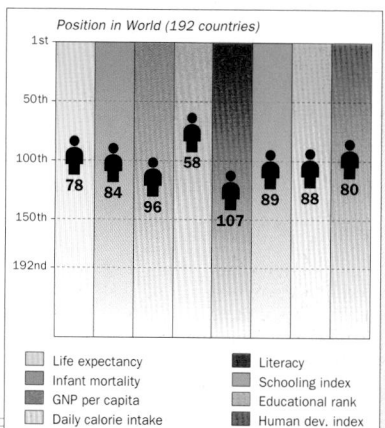

Position in World (192 countries)

1st
50th
100th
150th
192nd

78   84   96   58   107   89   88   80

- ▢ Life expectancy
- ▢ Infant mortality
- ▢ GNP per capita
- ▢ Daily calorie intake
- ▢ Literacy
- ▢ Schooling index
- ▢ Educational rank
- ▢ Human dev. index

J

KAZAKHSTAN

OFFICIAL NAME: Republic of Kazakhstan **CAPITAL:** Almaty
POPULATION: 17.1 million **CURRENCY:** Tenge **OFFICIAL LANGUAGE:** Kazakh

     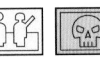

THE SECOND-LARGEST of the former Soviet republics, Kazakhstan extends almost 1,240 miles from the Caspian Sea in the west to the Altai Mountains in the east, and 806 miles north to south. It borders Russia to the north and China to the east. Kazakhstan was the last Soviet republic to declare its independence, in 1991. In 1994, elections confirmed the former-communist Nursultan Nazarbayev and his supporters in power. Kazakhstan is mineral-rich and has considerable economic potential. Many Western companies are seeking to exploit its natural resources.

The Altai Mountains, eastern Kazakhstan.
Subject to harsh continental winters, the Altai range is a cold, inhospitable place. Rivers carry meltwater down onto the vast steppe.

CLIMATE

WEATHER CHART

Kazakhstan has a continental climate with large temperature variations between summer and winter. Average January temperatures range from 0°F on the northern Kazakh steppe to 27°F in the deserts 806 miles to the south. July temperatures average 66°F and 86°F respectively. As the Caspian Sea never freezes, winters are mildest on Kazakhstan's southwestern coast.

TRANSPORTATION

 Almaty

Small Caspian Sea merchant fleet

THE TRANSPORTATION NETWORK

51,310 miles (82,570 km)

None

8,985 miles (14,460 km)

Caspian Sea provides access to four countries

Transportation networks focus on the north and east, the key economic areas. The railroads link into the Russian system and most international flights go via Moscow. Extending the network and reducing dependence on Russia are priorities. There are now direct flights to Germany. A rail link with China was opened in 1992. Kazakhstan has access to Caspian Sea ports.

TOURISM

Visitors still largely limited to business people

Increased since the breakup of the USSR

MAIN OVERSEAS ARRIVALS

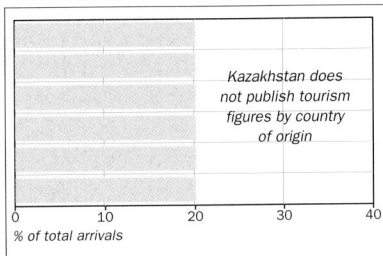

Kazakhstan does not publish tourism figures by country of origin

0   10   20   30   40
% of total arrivals

The number of visitors to Kazakhstan is increasing, but very few come solely as tourists. The majority are business travelers and a dense web of contacts with foreign companies has evolved. Of the Central Asian states, Kazakhstan has cultivated the closest links with the West. There is now a large community of foreign businesspeople living in Almaty.

KAZAKHSTAN

Total Land Area : 2 717 300 sq. km
(1 049 150 sq. miles)

POPULATION

over 500 000 ◉
over 100 000 ◎
over 50 000 ○
over 10 000 ●
under 10 000 ·

LAND HEIGHT

3000m/9843ft
2000m/6562ft
1000m/3281ft
500m/1640ft
200m/656ft
Sea Level
-200m/-656ft

K

PEOPLE

 Kazakh, Russian, German, Uigur

 16 people per sq. mile

THE URBAN/RURAL POPULATION SPLIT

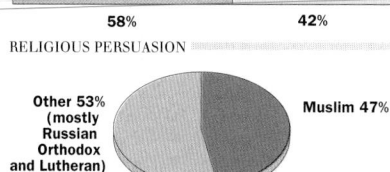

58%   **42%**

RELIGIOUS PERSUASION

Other 53% (mostly Russian Orthodox and Lutheran)

Muslim 47%

ETHNIC MAKEUP

German 6%   Ukrainian 6%

Kazakh 40%   Other 10%

Russian 38%

Kazakhstan's ethnic diversity is a product of the forced settlement of Germans, Tatars and others during the Soviet era. Russian settlement began in the 19th century, but peaked after 1920. By 1959, ethnic Russians outnumbered Kazakhs. The balance has recently

POPULATION AGE BREAKDOWN

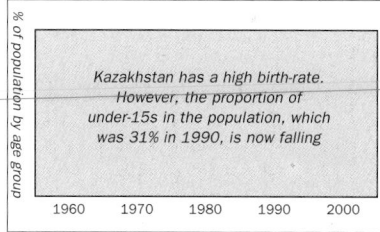

% of population by age group

Kazakhstan has a high birth-rate. However, the proportion of under-15s in the population, which was 31% in 1990, is now falling

1960   1970   1980   1990   2000

been redressed by the immigration of ethnic Kazakhs from neighboring states.

Tension between Kazakhs and ethnic Russians has grown steadily. In 1995, ethnic Russians criticized the country's new constitution for preventing dual citizenship with Russia and refusing to recognize Russian as an official language. President Nazarbayev has reinforced central control over ethnic Russians with plans to shift to a new capital, Akmola, in northern Kazakhstan – where the majority of ethnic Russians currently reside – by 2000.

Only a minority of Kazakhs retain their traditional nomadic life. However, commitment to Islam and loyalty to the clan remain strong.

POLITICS

 U. House 1995/1999
L. House 1995/1999

 President Nursultan Nazarbayev

THE STATE OF THE PARTIES

Parliament 67 members

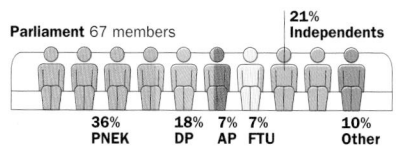

21% **Independents**

| 36% PNEK | 18% DP | 7% AP | 7% FTU | 10% Other |

PNEK = Party of People's Unity of Kazakhstan   **DP** = Democratic Party   **AP** = Agrarian Party   **FTU** = Federation of Trade Unions

Senate 47 members

2 members elected by each of 20 districts, and 7 nominated by the President. In December 1995 only 49 candidates stood for the the 40 vacancies.

Legislative authority is vested in the 114-member bicameral Supreme *Kenges*. The president, who must be fluent in Kazakh, has supreme executive power.

MAIN POLITICAL ISSUE
Presidential powers
The growing powers of President Nazarbayev are the focus of political controversy. In early 1995, Nazarbayev, who was due to face reelection in 1996, announced a referendum on extending his term of office until 2000. The resulting vote in Nazarbayev's favor and additional powers granted to him under the 1995 constitution, prompted his

critics to accuse Nazarbayev of developing a personality cult. The subsequent creation of a Constitutional Council whose decisions were subject to a presidential veto gave Nazarbayev undivided power.

PROFILE
Despite a democratic government, the president enjoys political dominance, and the patronage of the Kazakh clans is still important. Since coming to power Nazarbayev has concentrated on market reforms designed to attract more private and foreign investment. However, his political credibility was badly shaken in 1994 when allegations of widespread electoral fraud led to the annulment of legislative elections. Although new elections were held in 1995, Nazarbayev currently faces mounting domestic and international criticism of his attempts to expand the scope of presidential powers.

President Nursultan Nazarbayev, *who steered Kazakhstan to independence.*

Foreign Minister *Toleubai Suleimenov, the first professional diplomat in the post.*

WORLD AFFAIRS

CIS   ECO   NACC   OIC   OSCE

Maintaining close ties with other former Soviet republics is a priority. Relations with Russia, although strained at times by Moscow's concern over Kazakhstan's ethnic Russians, have been cemented by a 25-year cooperation treaty. The question of the rights of Kazakhstan's ethnic German minority has renewed interest in closer relations with Germany.

Kazakhstan's rich mineral resources have generated wider economic links with potential investors from Europe, the USA and Asia. Ties with South Korea are growing particularly fast, partly reflecting President Nazarbayev's interest in that country's model of economic development. Relations with China remain strained, however, as Beijing has territorial claims to parts of eastern Kazakhstan.

AID

 $14m (receipts)

 Up 40% in 1993

Kazakhstan joined the IMF and World Bank in 1992, and is also a member of the EBRD. Both multilateral and bilateral aid tend to be directed at supporting economic reform and providing know-how and training. The government is seeking to link the dismantling of nuclear warheads to aid payments from the West.

CHRONOLOGY

Once part of the Mongol Empire, Kazakhstan was absorbed by the Russian Empire in the 19th century. Ethnic Russians began to settle on land used by nomadic Kazakhs. Russian settlement intensified after the 1917 revolution and Kazakhstan was subjected to intensive industrial and agricultural development.

❑ **1916** Rebellion against the Russian rule brutally repressed.

❑ **1917** Russian Revolution inspires civil war in Kazakhstan between Bolsheviks, anti-Bolsheviks and Kazakh nationalists.

❑ **1918** Kazakh nationalists set up autonomous republic.

❑ **1920** Bolsheviks take control. Kirghiz Autonomous Soviet Socialist Republic (ASSR) set up within Russian Soviet Federative Socialist Republic.

❑ **1925** Kirghiz ASSR renamed Kazakh ASSR.

❑ **1936** Kazakhstan becomes full union republic of the USSR as Kazakh SSR.

K

CHRONOLOGY *continued*

- **1950s** Stalin's collectivization program leads to increase in Russian settlement and the deaths of an estimated one million Kazakhs forced to abandon their nomadic lifestyle.
- **1941–1945** Large-scale deportations of Germans, Jews, Crimean Tatars and others to Kazakhstan during World War II.
- **1950s** Intensification of heavy industry development begun in 1920s. Nuclear test site set up at Semipalatinsk in the east; 500 nuclear explosions follow before testing ends in 1991.
- **1954–1960** Khrushchev's policy to plow "Virgin Lands" for grain most vigorously followed in Kazakhstan. Russian settlement reaches a peak.
- **1986** Riots in Almaty after an ethnic Russian, Gennadi Kolbin, appointed head of Kazakhstan Communist Party (CPK) to replace Kazakh, Dinmukhamed Kunyev.
- **1989** June, Kolbin replaced by Nursultan Nazarbayev, an ethnic Kazakh and chair of Council of Ministers. September, political and administrative system reformed.
- **1990** March, elections to Supreme Soviet. Overwhelming CPK majority. April, Nazarbayev appointed first president of Kazakhstan. October, Kazakhstan declares sovereignty.
- **1991** March, referendum on future of USSR in nine republics. Kazakhstan votes to preserve USSR as union of sovereign states. USSR authorities hand control of enterprises in Kazakhstan to Kazakh government. August, CPK ordered to cease activities in official bodies following abortive August coup in Moscow. CPK restructures itself as Socialist Party of Kazakhstan (SPK). December, independence of Republic of Kazakhstan declared. Joins CIS.
- **1992** Opposition demonstrations against continuing dominance of reformed communists in Supreme Soviet, now Supreme *Kenges*. Leading nationalist groups unite to form Republican Party, *Azat*.
- **1993** January, new constitution adopted. Guarantees equal rights for all groups. December, Kazakh currency, the tenge, introduced.
- **1994** Legislative elections annulled after proof of widespread voting irregularities.
- **1995** Referendum extends Nazarbayev's term until 2000; adoption of new constitution extending presidential powers; legislative elections.

DEFENSE

 $297m    Down 28% in 1995

0   Defense spending as % GDP   40

3.5%

KAZAKH ARMED FORCES

	624 main battle tanks (T-62, T-72)	25,000 personnel
	None	None
	133 combat aircraft (MiG-23/27/29, Su-24)	15,000 personnel
	48 ICBM (SS-18 *Satan*) (all nuclear warheads returned to Russia)	

Kazakhstan, as the largest of the five former Soviet Central Asian republics, is a potential guarantor of regional peace. Kazakhstan ratified the Start I nuclear reduction treaty in 1992 and the NPT in 1993, but the process of disarmament has been delayed due mainly to financial problems. In 1993, the USA agreed to provide Kazakhstan with $84 million to dismantle its nuclear weapons. In May 1995, Kazakhstan announced that all its nuclear weapons had been transferred to Russia or destroyed. Military relations with Russia were sealed with a landmark agreement in 1995 under which Kazakh and Russian armed forces were to be unified within a year.

ECONOMICS

 $18.9bn   54.00–63.76 tenge

SCORE CARD

- WORLD GNP RANKING..........................65th
- GNP PER CAPITA $1,110
- BALANCE OF PAYMENTS ....$–2.1bn
- INFLATION 1,879%
- UNEMPLOYMENT................................0.8%

EXPORTS

- Poland 4%
- Italy 4%
- Germany 5%
- UK 5%
- Other 15%
- Russian Federation 67%

IMPORTS

- China 4%
- Turkey 4%
- USA 3%
- Germany 13%
- Other 17%
- Russian Federation 59%

STRENGTHS

Vast mineral resources, notably oil, gas, coal, gold, silver and uranium. Also bismuth and cadmium, used in electronics industry. Foreign investors attracted by liberal investment laws. Joint oil and gas ventures recently concluded with US and Western companies. Mass privatization program launched in 1994 aimed to privatize 30% of the economy by 1995.

WEAKNESSES

Collapse of former Soviet economic and trading system. Heavy reliance on imported consumer goods. Rapid introduction of the tenge in 1993 increased economic instability and fueled sharp price rises of basic commodities, especially bread. Inefficient industrial plants.

ECONOMIC PERFORMANCE INDICATOR

Consumer prices have risen sharply since 1991. GDP is likely to rise following new foreign investment

PROFILE

Under Nazarbayev, Kazakhstan has moved faster than other former Soviet republics to establish a market economy. It was the first to introduce free economic zones, investment incentives and privatization. Prices have been freed, foreign trade largely decontrolled and the tax system reformed. Despite these reforms, growth has been elusive. Unemployment and inflation have risen sharply, due in large part to the impact of the collapse of the wider Soviet economy.

However, by the end of 1993, $9 billion had already been committed in foreign direct investment, mainly in the energy sector. Outdated equipment and inadequate distribution networks mean that Kazakhstan, surprisingly, has to import energy. It hopes to become self-sufficient by 2000.

KAZAKHSTAN : MAJOR BUSINESSES

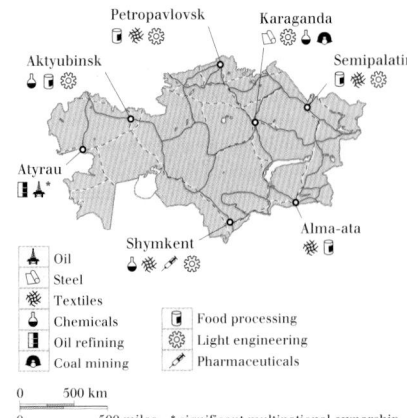

- Oil
- Steel
- Textiles
- Chemicals
- Oil refining
- Coal mining
- Food processing
- Light engineering
- Pharmaceuticals

0   500 km

0   500 miles   * significant multinational ownership

RESOURCES

81.3bn kwh (capacity 19.1m kw)

435,907 b/d Massive new oil reserves confirmed

33.5m sheep, 9.3m cattle, 2.4m pigs

Oil, gas, manganese, gold, silver, coal, iron, tungsten, chromite

ELECTRICITY GENERATION

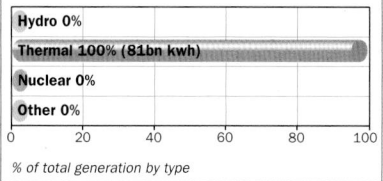

Hydro 0%	
Thermal 100% (81bn kwh)	
Nuclear 0%	
Other 0%	

% of total generation by type

Mining is the single most important industry in Kazakhstan. In 1993, the US company Chevron signed a deal to

ENVIRONMENT

0.3%

Western pressure on government may cause improvement

ENVIRONMENTAL TREATIES

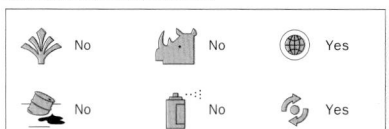

| | No | | No | | Yes |
| | No | | No | | Yes |

The environmental damage caused by intensive industrial and agricultural development is a major concern. The eastern cities are heavily polluted and farmlands are being eroded. The Aral Sea has been polluted by the overuse of fertilizers and has shrunk by 40% owing to the diversion of rivers for irrigation.

In 1991, environmental pressure groups succeeded in ending 42 years of nuclear testing at Semipalatinsk in the northeast. The green lobby is now pressing for tighter pollution controls.

MEDIA

Censorship exists. Neither direct criticism of the president nor the incitement of ethnic tension is tolerated

PUBLISHING AND BROADCAST MEDIA

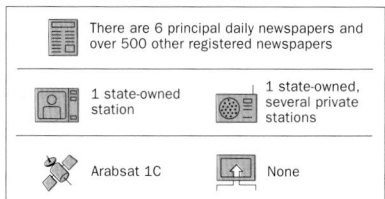

There are 6 principal daily newspapers and over 500 other registered newspapers

1 state-owned station

1 state-owned, several private stations

Arabsat 1C

None

The state-owned media compete with independent publications and privately owned radio stations. However, the government strictly controls all reports pertaining to ethnic minorities, and in 1995 jailed the prominent ethnic Russian journalist, Boris Suprunyuk, for inciting inter-ethnic hatred. There are over 500 registered newspapers, about 40% of them in Kazakh.

develop the huge Tengiz oilfield, and in 1995 Russia agreed to a joint venture with Kazakhstan on the exploitation of the substantial oil and gas reserves in the Caspian Sea. Kazakhstan also holds vast iron ore reserves and one of the biggest goldfields.

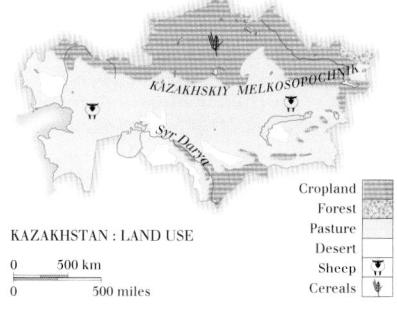

KAZAKHSTAN : LAND USE

0   500 km
0   500 miles

Cropland
Forest
Pasture
Desert
Sheep
Cereals

CRIME

Kazakhstan does not publish prison figures

Crime levels are rising

CRIME RATES

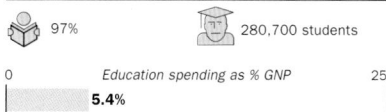

Theft is rising more sharply than other crime

Rural people are starting to grow drug crops, mainly opium poppies, to offset falling incomes. The government has appealed for UN help to combat the problem. General crime rates are low.

EDUCATION

97%

280,700 students

0   *Education spending as % GNP*   25

5.4%

THE EDUCATION SYSTEM

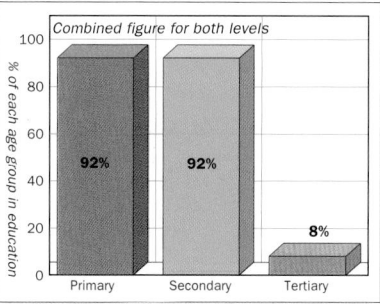

Combined figure for both levels

% of each age group in education

| Primary | Secondary | Tertiary |
| 92% | 92% | 8% |

Education is based on the Soviet model. Much teaching is still in Russian, despite the adoption of Kazakh as the state language. Kazakh textbooks and Kazakh-speaking teachers are in short supply. Literacy levels are relatively low. There are 63 higher-education institutions and 53 medical schools.

HEALTH

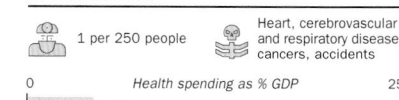
1 per 250 people

Heart, cerebrovascular and respiratory diseases, cancers, accidents

0   *Health spending as % GDP*   25

4.4%

The health system is limited in terms of both facilities and coverage. Rural people have minimal access to clinics. As a result, Kazakhstan has the highest infant mortality rate in Central Asia. The country's size means that extending coverage and improving the quality of care will be costly. Attempts are therefore being made to attract foreign investment into the health sector. Many doctors have emigrated to Russia.

WEALTH

The living standards of many Kazakhs have declined since independence from the USSR

CONSUMER GOODS OWNERSHIP

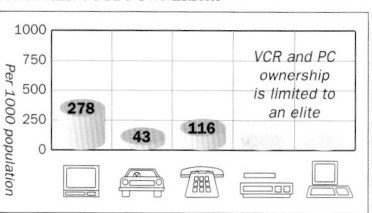

Per 1000 population

1000
750
500
250
0

VCR and PC ownership is limited to an elite

278   43   116

Life for the majority of Kazakhs has always been hard, and has grown even more difficult since 1989. Living standards have deteriorated and unemployment has risen as a result of market-oriented reforms within Kazakhstan. The liberalization of the economy also fueled sharp price rises of essential commodities during 1995.

The rural population, the poorest group, has been badly affected. The small wealthy elite is made up mainly of former officials within the CPK, many of whom have benefited from privatization, or belong to President Nazarbayev's clan. In 1995, the government banned all foreign currency transactions by Kazakhs.

WORLD RANKING

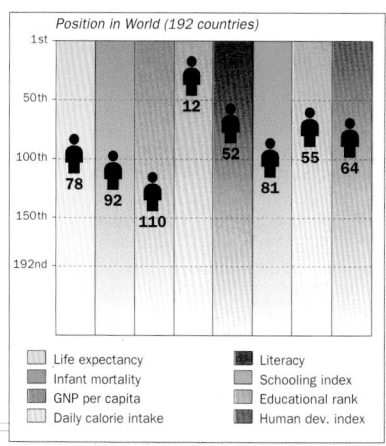

Position in World (192 countries)

1st
50th
100th
150th
192nd

78   92   110   12   52   81   55   64

Life expectancy
Infant mortality
GNP per capita
Daily calorie intake

Literacy
Schooling index
Educational rank
Human dev. index

K

KENYA

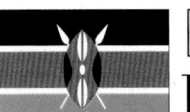

OFFICIAL NAME: Republic of Kenya   **CAPITAL:** Nairobi
POPULATION: 28.3 million   **CURRENCY:** Kenya shilling   **OFFICIAL LANGUAGE:** Swahili

KENYA STRADDLES THE EQUATOR on Africa's east coast. Its central plateau is bisected by the Great Rift Valley. The land to the north is desert, while to the east lies a fertile coastal belt. After gaining independence from Britain in 1963, politics was dominated by Jomo Kenyatta. He was succeeded in 1978 by President Moi, who easily survived a return to multiparty elections in 1992. Ethnic violence is now the main political issue. The economic mainstays are tourism and agriculture, notably coffee and tea. Very high population growth is a key constraint on economic growth.

Kenyatta Conference Center, Nairobi. The modern skyline of the business center contrasts sharply with the slums on the city's outskirts.

CLIMATE

WEATHER CHART

The coast and Great Rift Valley are hot and humid, the plateau interior is temperate and the northeastern desert hot and dry. Rain generally falls from April to May and October to November.

TRANSPORTATION

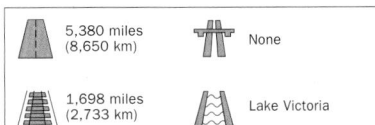

Jomo Kenyatta, Nairobi
1.52m passengers

6 ships
9,900 dwt

THE TRANSPORTATION NETWORK

5,380 miles (8,650 km)		None
1,698 miles (2,733 km)		Lake Victoria

Kenya's railroad, ports and main airport are being upgraded, a reflection of the importance of tourism and Kenya's role as an outlet for landlocked neighbors.

Great Rift Valley, Kenya. This huge crack in the Earth's crust runs from the River Jordan right through Africa to the Zambezi River.

TOURISM

863,000 visitors

Up 4% in 1994

Tourism, which is mainly beach and safari-oriented, is vital to the economy and a key foreign-exchange earner. However, despite moving into the package vacation market during the 1980s, Kenya has seen visitor numbers decline since 1990. The main factors are world recession and the well-publicized murder of several tourists.

MAIN OVERSEAS ARRIVALS

Germany 18%
UK 15%
Tanzania 11%
USA 9%
Italy 6%
Other 41%

% of total arrivals

KENYA

Total Land Area :
566 970 sq. km
(218 907 sq. miles)

POPULATION

over 1 000 000
over 500 000
over 100 000
over 50 000
over 10 000
under 10 000

LAND HEIGHT

3000m/9843ft
2000m/6562ft
1000m/3281ft
500m/1640ft
200m/656ft
Sea Level

PEOPLE

 Swahili, English, Kikuyu, Luo, Kamba

 130 people per sq. mile

THE URBAN/RURAL POPULATION SPLIT

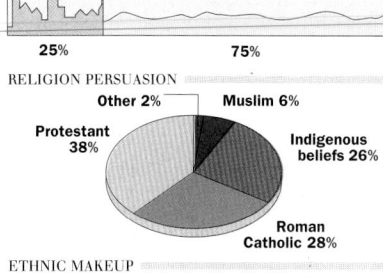

25% **75%**

RELIGION PERSUASION

Other 2% Muslim 6%
Protestant 38%
Indigenous beliefs 26%
Roman Catholic 28%

ETHNIC MAKEUP

Kalenjin 11%
Other 30%
Kamba 11%
Luo 13%
Kikuyu 21%
Luhya 14%

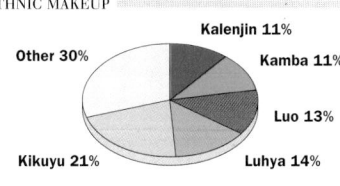

Kenya's ethnic diversity, with about 70 different groups, reflects its past as a focus of population movements. Asians, Europeans and Arabs form 1% of the population. The rural majority retains strong clan and extended family links, although these are being weakened by urban migration. Poverty and one of the world's highest population growth rates (3.5% a year) are the root causes of the land hunger which has recently been fueling a surge in ethnic violence. Much is concentrated in western Kenya, where Kikuyu are the main targets of violent attacks by Kalenjin, Masai and Pokor groups. Over 300,000 Kikuyu have also been displaced from their villages by a form of organized ethnic cleansing known as *majimboism*.

POPULATION AGE BREAKDOWN

	0–14	15–64		65+	
65+	4.1%	3.9%	3.4%	3%	2.9%
15–64	50.3%	47.9%	46.5%	47.9%	50.9%
0–14	45.6%	48.2%	50.1%	49.1%	46.2%
	1960	1970	1980	1990	2000

WORLD AFFAIRS

 Comm   Comesa IAEA   IGADD OAU

Relations with neighboring states and with key Western donors, notably the USA, are Kenya's priorities. In 1991, human rights concerns were partly responsible for a suspension of aid. Payments were restored in 1993, but made subject to an improved record. The main regional concern is the

resurrection, with Uganda and Tanzania, of the East African Community, an economic zone which collapsed in 1977. The northern border dispute with Sudan over the Elemi Triangle is unresolved. Kenya lays claim to this arid piece of land which has a concentration of Christian refugees fleeing Sudanese government repression. The conflict in Somalia has also spilt over into northeast Kenya.

POLITICS

 1992/1997

 President Daniel arap Moi

THE STATE OF THE PARTIES

National Assembly 202 members **15% FORD-K** **8% Other**

51% KANU **15% FORD-A** **11% DP**

KANU = Kenya African National Union
FORD-A = Forum for the Restoration of Democracy – Asili
FORD-K = Forum for the Restoration of Democracy – Kenya
DP = Democratic Party
Other = Kenya Social Congress, Kenya National Congress

Kenya became a multiparty democracy in 1992 and has been led by President Daniel arap Moi since 1978.

MAIN POLITICAL ISSUE
Ethnic violence
The ethnic polarization of political parties in Kenya and rising poverty are fueling ethnic violence. Determined to ensure KANU dominance, President Moi, a Kalenjin, is turning the party into an alliance of smaller ethnic groups opposed to the Kikuyu. The latter are the largest ethnic group, the main victims of violence and the main supporters of the opposition. Rift Valley, Nyanga and western provinces – those with most seats in parliament – are focuses of anti-Kikuyu ethnic cleansing.

PROFILE
Kenya's status following independence as a *de facto* one-party state was formalized in 1982. President Moi's subsequent efforts to entrench KANU's power further provoked demands at home for the introduction of multiparty politics, and condemnation abroad of human rights abuses. Forced in 1992 to concede free elections, Moi helped ensure KANU's victory by curtailing the campaign period. He has since been condemned again by the international community for manipulating ethnic conflict, part of his strategy to entrench KANU's power.

Opposition groups remain divided, although popular pressure for reform is growing. Many are also critical of Moi's failure to improve the economy and to control corruption in the bureaucracy.

President Daniel arap Moi, *Kenya's leader since 1978.*

Richard Leakey, *palaeontologist turned politician.*

AID

 $894m (receipts) Up 15% in 1993

Kenya has been a major recipient of aid from donors – such as the UK, Japan, the EU, the World Bank and the IMF – who are keen to support its free-market approach. Little, however, has trickled down to the majority of the population, who continue to live in poverty. This is partly because of the high proportion of aid tied to construction projects and donor-country firms, and partly because of mismanagement and official corruption. Concern over both this and human rights abuses led to a freeze on aid from 1991 to 1993.

K

CHRONOLOGY

From the 10th century, Arab coastal settlers mixed with indigenous peoples in the region. Britain's need for a route to landlocked Uganda led to the formation in 1895 of the British East African Protectorate in the coastal region.

- ❏ **1900–1918** White settlement of interior; removal of local peoples from land.
- ❏ **1920** Interior becomes a British colony; coast remains protectorate.
- ❏ **1930** Jomo Kenyatta goes to UK; stays 14 years.
- ❏ **1944** Kenyan African Union (KAU) formed; Kenyatta returns to lead it.
- ❏ **1952–1956** Mau Mau, Kikuyu-led violent campaign to restore African lands. State of emergency; 13,000 people killed.
- ❏ **1953** KAU banned. Kenyatta jailed.
- ❏ **1960** State of emergency ends. Tom Mboya and Oginga Odinga form KANU.
- ❏ **1961** Kenyatta freed; takes up presidency of KANU.
- ❏ **1963** KANU wins elections. Kenyatta prime minister. Full independence declared.
- ❏ **1964** Republic of Kenya formed with Kenyatta as president and Odinga as vice-president. ➪

K

DEFENCE

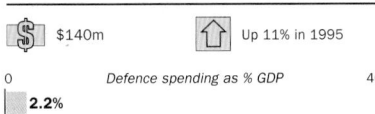

$140m   Up 11% in 1995

| 0 | Defence spending as % GDP | 40 |

2.2%

KENYAN ARMED FORCES

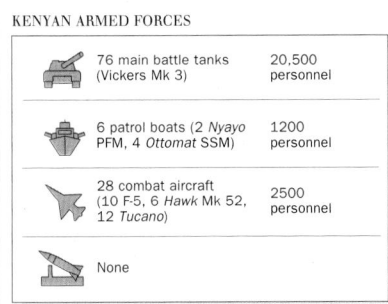

76 main battle tanks (Vickers Mk 3)	20,500 personnel	
6 patrol boats (2 *Nyayo* PFM, 4 *Ottomat* SSM)	1200 personnel	
28 combat aircraft (10 F-5, 6 *Hawk* Mk 52, 12 *Tucano*)	2500 personnel	
None		

Destabilization of the northeastern border by the Somali civil war is the main defence issue. The military plays little part in politics.

ECONOMICS

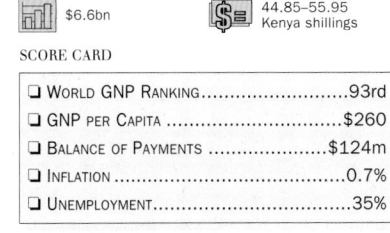

$6.6bn   44.85–55.95 Kenya shillings

SCORE CARD

- ❏ WORLD GNP RANKING..........................93rd
- ❏ GNP PER CAPITA $260
- ❏ BALANCE OF PAYMENTS $124m
- ❏ INFLATION 0.7%
- ❏ UNEMPLOYMENT...................................35%

EXPORTS

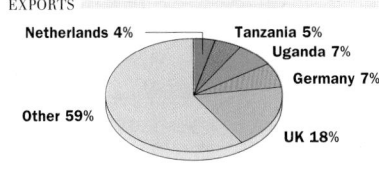

- Netherlands 4%
- Tanzania 5%
- Uganda 7%
- Germany 7%
- UK 18%
- Other 59%

IMPORTS

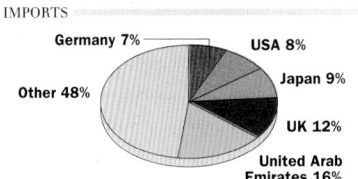

- Germany 7%
- USA 8%
- Japan 9%
- UK 12%
- United Arab Emirates 16%
- Other 48%

STRENGTHS

Tourism, which is the largest foreign exchange earner. Broad agricultural base, especially cash crops such as coffee and tea. East Africa's largest, most diversified manufacturing sector.

WEAKNESSES

Susceptibility of tourism, coffee and tea to fluctuating world prices. Poor recent GDP growth. High population growth of 3.5% a year. Land shortage, leading to subdivision of plots into uneconomical small units.

PROFILE

Kenya has been hailed as an example to the rest of Africa of the benefits of a mainly free-market economy. Government involvement has been relatively limited, and recently further reduced by privatization. Foreign investment has been encouraged, with some success. Tourism has developed into the leading foreign exchange earner over the past 20 years. Manufacturing now accounts for 21% of GDP, and is the most diversified sector in East Africa. However, it employs only 200,000 in formal jobs and needs to expand rapidly to provide more urban employment.

Economic growth was good by African standards during the 1980s, averaging over 4% a year. However, it was not good enough to compensate for one of the world's highest population growth rates. GDP per capita stagnated and too few jobs were created to make much impact on unemployment. The problem was exacerbated by urban migration and the yearly influx of thousands of school leavers onto the

ECONOMIC PERFORMANCE INDICATOR

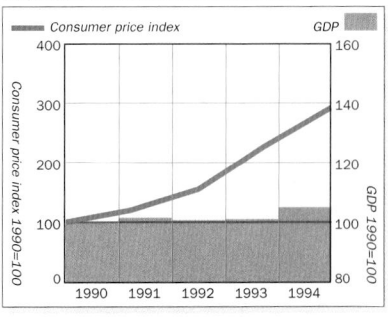

- Consumer price index
- GDP

labour market. For the majority of Kenyans, farming ever-smaller landholdings or earning a living in the informal sector, life has recently become harsher.

Other problems, including inflation, a heavy debt burden (now $7.5 billion), and growing dependence on balance of payments support came to a head in the early 1990s, when economic growth gave way to recession. Real GDP growth fell to 0.4% in 1992 and was negative in 1993. The rise in poverty-linked violence and political unrest hit tourism; earnings fell by 15% in 1992 and again in 1993. Agricultural and manufacturing output have both fallen in the past three years.

Partly as a response to pressure from donors, including the 1991–1993 freeze on balance of payments support, the government has implemented some economic liberalization measures. These include floating the Kenya shilling, raising interest rates and giving exporters direct access to their hard currency earnings. However, real growth is likely to remain elusive until Kenya overcomes two fundamental problems – the official corruption which drains vital resources, including foreign aid, and its high rate of population growth.

KENYA : MAJOR BUSINESSES

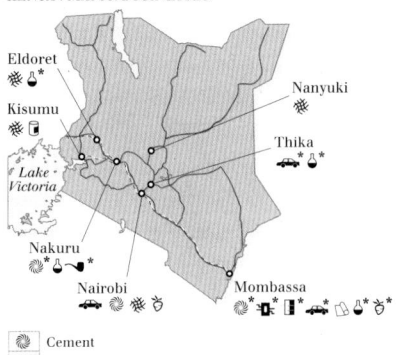

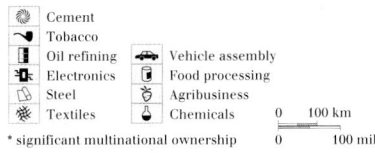

- Cement
- Tobacco
- Oil refining
- Electronics
- Steel
- Textiles
- Vehicle assembly
- Food processing
- Agribusiness
- Chemicals

0   100 km
0   100 miles

* significant multinational ownership

RESOURCES

2.1bn kwh (capacity 723,000 kw)

Not an oil producer; refines 90,000 b/cd

11m cattle, 7.4m goats, 5.5m sheep

Soda ash, fluorspar, limestone, rubies, gold, vermiculite

ELECTRICITY GENERATION

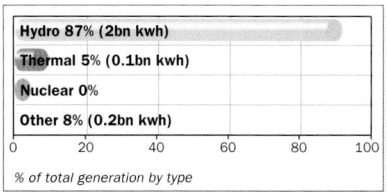

Hydro 87% (2bn kwh)
Thermal 5% (0.1bn kwh)
Nuclear 0%
Other 8% (0.2bn kwh)

0   20   40   60   80   100

% of total generation by type

Agriculture underpins Kenya's economy and is still the largest sector, accounting for 27% of GDP. Kenya's varied topography means tropical, subtropical and temperate crops may be grown. Coffee and tea, the main export crops, have been affected by falling world prices. Efforts to reduce dependence on these crops have led to the growth of a successful export-oriented horticultural industry.

Kenya has few mineral resources and mining accounts for only 0.2% of GDP. Hydroelectric and geothermal sources are being developed to reduce energy imports – currently 70% of total requirements. Oil exploration in the Great Rift Valley and the northeast has revealed deposits in Turkana District.

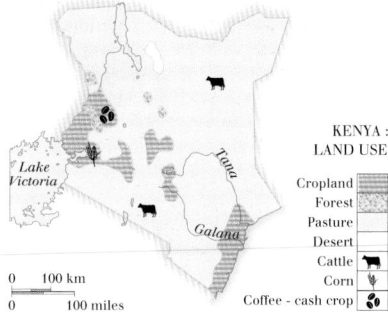

KENYA : LAND USE

Cropland
Forest
Pasture
Desert
Cattle
Corn
Coffee - cash crop

0   100 km
0   100 miles

ENVIRONMENT

6%

Tourist numbers pose threat to safari park ecosystems

ENVIRONMENTAL TREATIES

No   Yes   Yes
Yes   No   Yes

The government recognizes the importance of wildlife conservation to the tourist industry, and recent elephant protection schemes have been a success. However, initiatives to set up national reserves are competing with agriculture for land. The effect of dams on the Tana River is another concern.

MEDIA

Criticism of the government is not tolerated in practice

PUBLISHING AND BROADCAST MEDIA

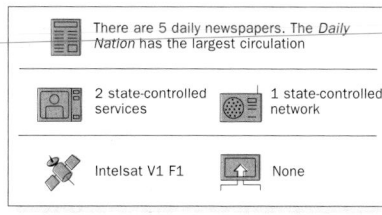

There are 5 daily newspapers. The *Daily Nation* has the largest circulation

2 state-controlled services

1 state-controlled network

Intelsat V1 F1   None

Government intolerance of criticism is long-standing and includes plays and novels as well as the media. Ngugi wa Thiongo, Kenya's most famous novelist, was exiled for his criticism of KANU.

CRIME

Kenya does not publish prison figures

Up 15% in 1992

CRIME RATES

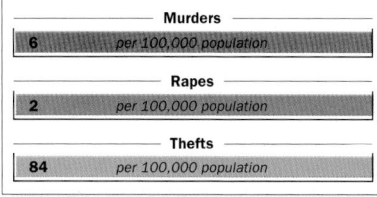

Murders
6   *per 100,000 population*

Rapes
2   *per 100,000 population*

Thefts
84   *per 100,000 population*

Nairobi's high crime levels are spreading countrywide, as a result of worsening poverty, ethnic violence and rising banditry in the northeast. An increase in the use of guns underlies the rapid increase in violent crime.

EDUCATION

69%

31,287 students

0   *Education spending as % GNP*   25
            7%

THE EDUCATION SYSTEM

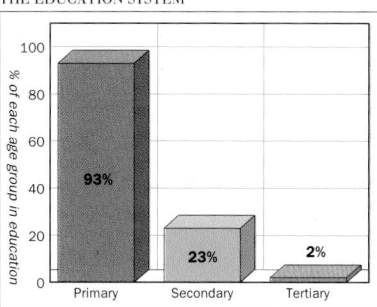

100
% of each age group in education
80
60
40   93%
20   23%   2%
0
Primary Secondary Tertiary

The education system is loosely based on the British model. Schooling is not compulsory, but free elementary education means most children attend; the drop-out rate at secondary level is high. In higher education, the emphasis is on vocational training.

HEALTH

1 per 10,150 people

Respiratory and diarrheal diseases, malaria

0   *Health spending as % GDP*   25
      2.7%

The health system is a mix of state and private facilities, the latter mainly run by charities and missions. The state system has been hit by recession, worsening the already limited access of the rural majority. Poverty-related illnesses are increasing, particularly among children and women. HIV and AIDS are a growing problem among some sections of the community.

WEALTH

The majority of Kenya's rising number of poor live outside the formal economy

CONSUMER GOODS OWNERSHIP

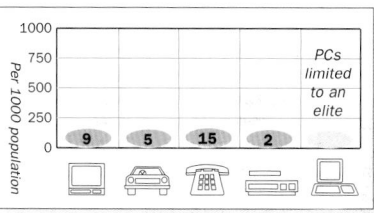

1000
Per 1000 population
750
500   PCs limited to an elite
250
0   9   5   15   2

Wealth disparities in Kenya are large and growing, exacerbated by land hunger and migration to the cities, where jobs are few and existence depends on the informal economy. The slum dwellers of Nairobi's Amarthi Valley are among Africa's poorest, worst-nourished people. Their lives contrast with those of the country's elite – top government officials with access to patronage; white Kenyans, who derive their wealth largely from agricultural estates; and the largely Asian business community. Among these groups, Mercedes and the latest four-wheel-drive cars are popular, as are designer-label clothes. Wealthy Kenyans often send their children abroad for higher education.

WORLD RANKING

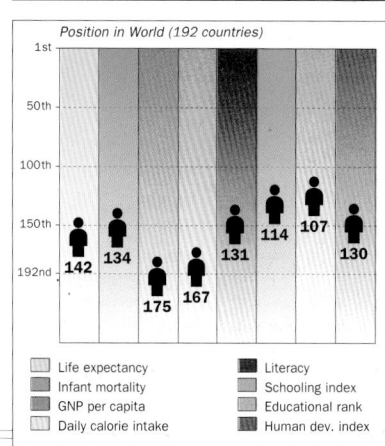

Position in World (192 countries)

1st
50th
100th
150th
192nd

142   134   175   167   131   114   107   130

Life expectancy   Literacy
Infant mortality   Schooling index
GNP per capita   Educational rank
Daily calorie intake   Human dev. index

K

KIRIBATI

OFFICIAL NAME: Republic of Kiribati **CAPITAL:** Bairiki
POPULATION: 77,000 **CURRENCY:** Australian dollar **OFFICIAL LANGUAGE:** English

FORMERLY PART OF THE British colony of the Gilbert and Ellice Islands, the Gilberts became independent in 1979 and adopted the name Kiribati (pronounced Kiribass). British interest in the Gilberts rested solely on the exploitation of the phosphate deposits on Banaba; these ran out in 1980. In 1981, Kiribati won damages (but not the costs of litigation) from the British for decades of phosphate exploitation.

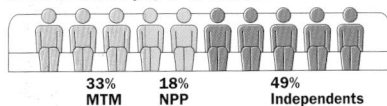

Banreaba Island, Tarawa atoll. *None of the atolls is more than 26 feet high except Banaba, the main source of phosphates.*

CLIMATE

WEATHER CHART

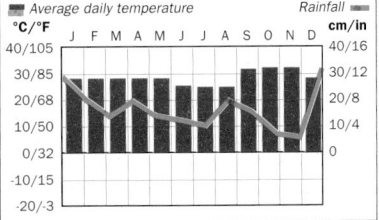

Kiribati's small land area in the vast Pacific means it often goes for months without rain. In the 1950s, a serious drought led to the resettlement of Gilbertese to the Solomon Islands.

TRANSPORTATION

 Bonriki Intl, Tarawa
51,000 passengers (est)

 5 ships
2,700 dwt

THE TRANSPORTATION NETWORK

398 miles (640 km)		None
None		3 miles (5 km)

Kiribati has a limited air link with Fiji. Small-scale shipping and good satellite communications also keep it in touch with the outside world.

TOURISM

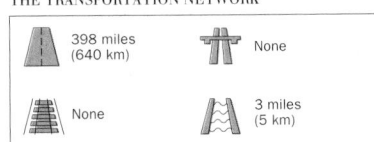 5,000 visitors   No change in 1994

MAIN OVERSEAS ARRIVALS

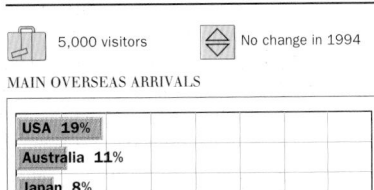

USA	19%
Australia	11%
Japan	8%
Other	62%

% of total arrivals

Kiritimati, which has a weekly air service to Honolulu, has been singled out for tourist development.

PEOPLE

 English, Micronesian dialect

 281 people per sq. mile

THE URBAN/RURAL POPULATION SPLIT

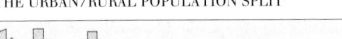

36% **64%**

RELIGIOUS PERSUASION

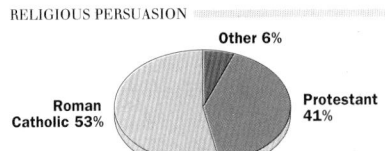

Roman Catholic 53%
Protestant 41%
Other 6%

Locals still refer to themselves as Gilbertese. Apart from the inhabitants of Banaba, who employed anthropologists to establish their racial distinction, almost all Gilbertese are Micronesian. Tension with the Banabans is intense, but mostly fueled by the historic value of Banaba's phosphate deposits. Most Gilbertese are poor. Many go to Nauru as guest workers, living in barrack-room conditions, or work as merchant shipping crew. Those who stay at home go through a circular migration from the outlying islands to Tarawa, returning to see relatives. Women play a prominent role, especially on outlying islands, where they run most of the farms.

POLITICS

 1994/1998   President Teburoro Tito

THE STATE OF THE PARTIES

House of Assembly up to 41 members

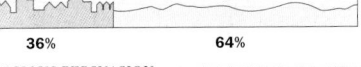

33% **18%** **49%**
MTM NPP Independents

MTM = Maneaban Te Mauri   **NPP** = National Progressive Party

The traditional chiefs still effectively rule Kiribati, through a party system on the British model. The main concern is the economy, which is extremely vulnerable to any fluctuations in world demand for coconuts. The overpopulation of Tarawa is the other major issue. Possible restrictions on travel to the island have been discussed. In part, the problem of migration is caused by the poverty and lack of opportunity on the outer islands. Plans for a wealth distribution program to reduce migration exist, but they have yet to become policy. Victory for the TMP in the 1994 elections ended 15 years of rule by the NPP.

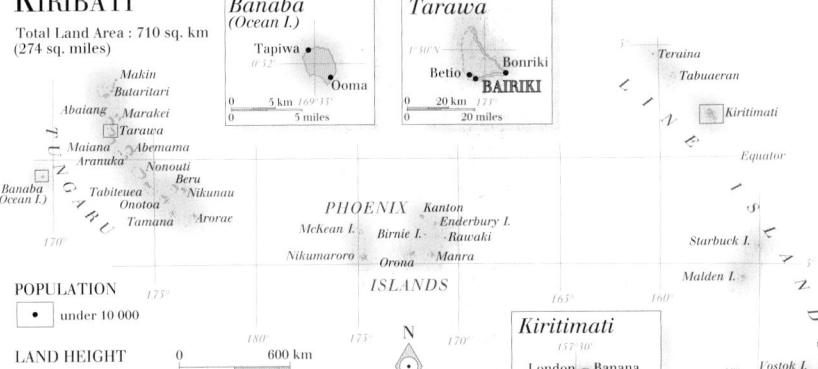

KIRIBATI

Total Land Area : 710 sq. km
(274 sq. miles)

Banaba (Ocean I.)

Tapiwa
Ooma

Tarawa

Betio
Bonriki
BAIRIKI

Makin
Butaritari
Abaiang   Marakei
Maiana   Abemama
Aranuka   Nonouti
Banaba (Ocean I.)
Tabiteuea   Beru
Onotoa   Nikunau
Tamana   Arorae

Teraina
Tabuaeran

Kiritimati

Equator

PHOENIX   Kanton
McKean I.   Enderbury I.
Birnie I.   Rawaki
Nikumaroro   Orona   Manra
ISLANDS

Starbuck I.

Malden I.

POPULATION
• under 10 000

LAND HEIGHT
under 100m

0   600 km
0   600 miles

N

Kiritimati

London   Banana
Paris

Vostok I.   Caroli
Flint I.

0   20 km
0   20 miles

K

WORLD AFFAIRS

ACP Comm SPC SPF UN

Kiribati has little impact internationally because of its tiny size and remote location, but is able to make its voice heard regionally through the South Pacific Forum. In 1986, Kiribati was a signatory to a deal between the USA and a number of Pacific Island states that resulted in the USA paying US$60 million, in return for access to Pacific fishing grounds. Kiribati used to play the USSR off against the USA as the USSR was happy to pay US$1.5 million for fishing leases which allowed it to spy on US nuclear testing on the neighboring Kwajalein atoll in the Marshall Islands.

AID

 $15m (receipts)   Up 14% in 1993

Aid is mostly for small infrastructure projects. The causeway linking Tarawa to the airport on Bonriki, a nearby atoll, was built with Japanese aid.

DEFENSE

 Kiribati has no defense budget   Not applicable

Australia and New Zealand provide *de facto* protection, with regular anti-submarine patrols.

ECONOMICS

 $56m   1.29–1.34 Australian dollars

SCORE CARD

❑ WORLD GNP RANKING 192nd
❑ GNP PER CAPITA ....US$730
❑ BALANCE OF PAYMENTS ....US$12m
❑ INFLATION 4%
❑ UNEMPLOYMENT 2%

STRENGTHS
Subsistence economy has survived, and Kiribati has no need to import food. Coconuts provide some export income: the EU is the biggest market. Fisheries have limited potential.

WEAKNESSES
Banaba's phosphate deposits ran out in 1980. Isolation, and large distances between islands. Heavy dependence on international aid. Almost no economic potential.

EXPORTS
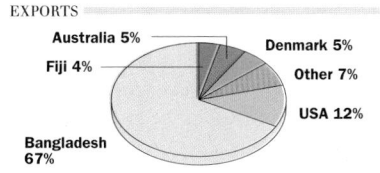

IMPORTS
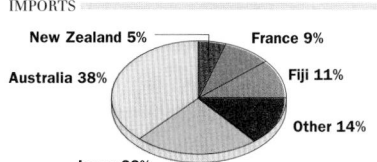

RESOURCES

 7m kwh (capacity 2,000 kw)   29,295 tons
9,000 pigs   None

Phosphate deposits on Banaba ran out in 1980. All energy supplies have to be imported. Underwater agriculture is being developed.

ENVIRONMENT

 39% (including marine and semi-protected areas)   Refusal to allow Western toxic waste dumping

Overpopulation on Tarawa is the cause of major problems. The coral reef, which protects Tarawa from the sea and which holds important inshore fish stocks in the lagoon, is threatened by untreated effluent. Approaches have been made by international – mainly US – companies seeking to dump industrial waste into the lagoons.

MEDIA

 No restrictions on political reporting

PUBLISHING AND BROADCAST MEDIA

 There are no daily newspapers. There are 2 weekly newspapers, *Atoll Pioneer* and *Te Uekera*

 No TV service   1 independent service

The main sources of news and information on Kiribati are *Pacific Islands Monthly* and *Islands' Business* magazines.

CRIME

 77 prisoners   Down 46% in 1990

Crime, apart from brawls resulting from drunkenness, is minimal. The judicial system is based on the British model.

EDUCATION

 98%   Not applicable

Education is British-inspired. The best students go to King George V School, and on to university in Fiji.

CHRONOLOGY

The British established the phosphate-producing colony of the Gilbert and Ellice Islands in 1892.

❑ **1957** First British nuclear tests take place near Kiritimati.
❑ **1979** Independence as two states, Kiribati (The Gilberts) and Tuvalu (The Ellice Islands).
❑ **1981** British agree to pay damages for almost total destruction of Banaba by phosphate mining.
❑ **1986** Kiribati–US fishing deal.
❑ **1994** Election ousts those who had governed since independence.

HEALTH

 1 per 1,939 people   Heart diseases, diabetes

Most Gilbertese are healthy, thanks to the home-grown diet. Those on Tarawa are starting to import canned food, due to a lack of agricultural land, and vitamin A deficiency is becoming a problem.

WEALTH

The state is the only formal employer. Remittances from Gilbertese working in Nauru are an important source of national income

CONSUMER GOODS OWNERSHIP

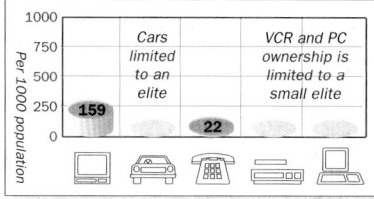

Life in Kiribati is modest. Civil servants in the capital, Bairiki, are the wealthiest group. There is a handful of cars on Tarawa, and these are confined to the single 18-mile stretch of road, from Tarawa to the airport. Most Gilbertese live by subsistence farming.

WORLD RANKING

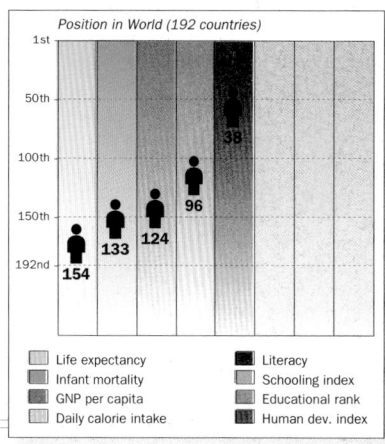

K

321

KUWAIT

OFFICIAL NAME: State of Kuwait **CAPITAL:** Kuwait City
POPULATION: 1.5 million **CURRENCY:** Kuwaiti dinar **OFFICIAL LANGUAGE:** Arabic

MIDDLE EAST

 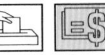

A T THE NORTHWEST EXTREME of the Persian Gulf, Kuwait is dwarfed by its neighbors Iraq, Iran and Saudi Arabia. The flat, almost featureless landscape conceals huge oil and gas reserves, which made Kuwait the world's first oil-rich state. In 1990, Iraq invaded, claiming Kuwait as its 19th province. A US-led alliance, under the aegis of the UN, expelled Iraqi forces following a short war in 1991. Since its liberation, Kuwait has built a wall separating its territory from Iraq.

Saffar Towers in the business center of Kuwait City. The postwar cost of rebuilding Kuwait's economy is put at $25 billion.

CLIMATE

WEATHER CHART

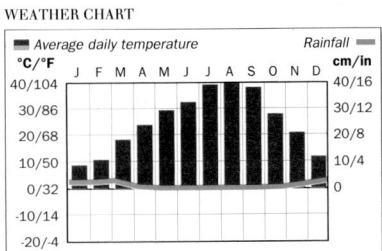

Summer temperatures can soar to over 104°F, but winters can be cold with frost at night.

TRANSPORTATION

 Kuwait International,
Kuwait City
1.41m passengers

 62 ships
3.79m dwt

THE TRANSPORTATION NETWORK

940 miles (1,520 km)		174 miles (280 km)
None		None

Kuwait has a system of radial highways around the capital and good connecting roads to Saudi Arabia.

TOURISM

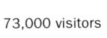 73,000 visitors No change in 1994

MAIN OVERSEAS ARRIVALS

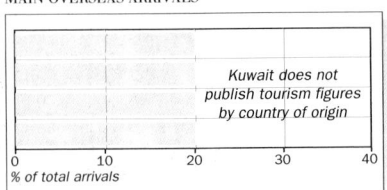
Kuwait does not publish tourism figures by country of origin

0   10   20   30   40
% of total arrivals

Most Western visitors to Kuwait go specifically to see relatives working in the oil industry. The limited tourism from neighboring Arab states, notably Saudi Arabia, has not recovered since the 1990–1991 Gulf War.

PEOPLE

 Arabic, English

 218 people per sq. mile

THE URBAN/RURAL POPULATION SPLIT

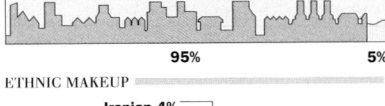
95%   5%

ETHNIC MAKEUP

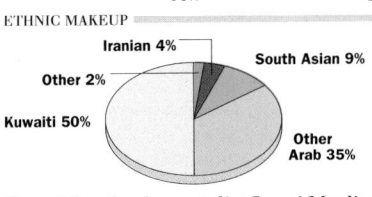
Iranian 4%
Other 2%
South Asian 9%
Kuwaiti 50%
Other Arab 35%

Kuwait is a fundamentalist Sunni Muslim society. Women have considerable freedom, but are not allowed to vote.

Kuwait's oil wealth has drawn in thousands of workers from India, Pakistan and other Arab countries. Before the Iraqi invasion in 1990, Kuwait had the largest Palestinian population in the Arabian peninsula. The PLO's support for Iraq's invasion led to most Palestinians being driven out. After the war, Kuwaitis vowed never again to become a minority in their own country. In 1995, native Kuwaitis only just outnumbered resident foreign nationals.

POLITICS

 1992/1996

Amir HH Sheikh Jaber al–Ahmad alñJaber as–Sabah

THE STATE OF THE PARTIES

National Assembly 50 members

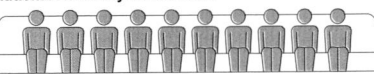

Political parties are not allowed. The members of the National Assembly are elected for a 4-year term by all literate Kuwaiti males over the age of 21, except servicemen and police

In 1992, Kuwait's ruler, Amir Sheikh Jaber, restored the National Assembly and allowed a general election to take place. The franchise was restricted to male Kuwaiti nationals. Islamic and independent candidates were elected, and six deputies with opposing views to those of the government were given cabinet posts in order to create a new sense of national unity.

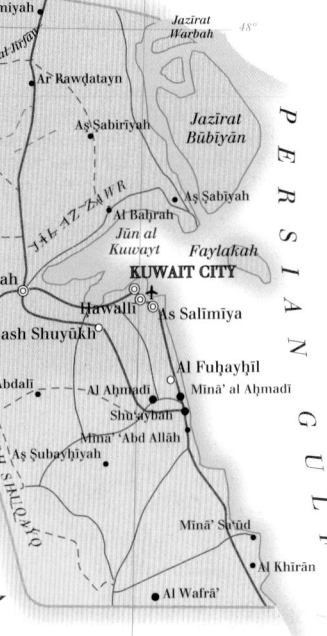

KUWAIT

Total Land Area :
17 820 sq. km
(6880 sq. miles)

POPULATION

◎	over 100 000
○	over 50 000
●	over 10 000
•	under 10 000

LAND HEIGHT

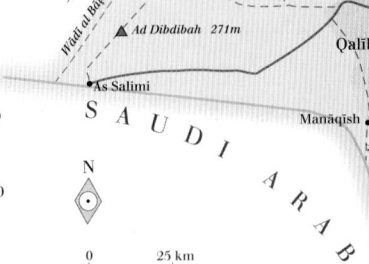

200m/656ft
Sea Level

0   25 km
0   25 miles

WORLD AFFAIRS

Kuwait's strategic importance is as a major exporter of crude oil and natural gas. As such, it has always maintained very close links with the West. Since the war with Iraq, its foreign policy has become even more pro-Western. It therefore depends on its neighbor Saudi Arabia and on Western allies for its future security.

AID

 $395m   Up 95% in 1993

The Kuwait Fund for Arab Economic Development continued to give aid even during the invasion crisis.

DEFENSE

 $2.9bn   Down 6% in 1995

Kuwait's 11,000-strong, partly volunteer army was easily overrun by vastly superior Iraqi forces in August 1990. Since the liberation, defense pacts have been signed with the USA, the UK, France and Russia. Kuwait is rearming fast, with weapons purchased from major Western suppliers.

ECONOMICS

 $31.4bn   0.29–0.30 Kuwaiti dinars

SCORE CARD

❏ WORLD GNP RANKING	54th
❏ GNP PER CAPITA	$19,040
❏ BALANCE OF PAYMENTS	$3bn
❏ INFLATION	4.7%
❏ UNEMPLOYMENT	0%

STRENGTHS
Production of oil and gas has been restored to pre-invasion levels. Large overseas investments.

WEAKNESSES
Economy devastated by Iraqi scorched-earth policy, when oil installations were destroyed. Vulnerability to Iraqi attack deters Western industrial investment. Skilled labor, food and raw materials have to be imported.

EXPORTS

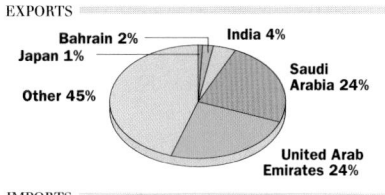

Bahrain 2%
Japan 1%
India 4%
Other 45%
Saudi Arabia 24%
United Arab Emirates 24%

IMPORTS

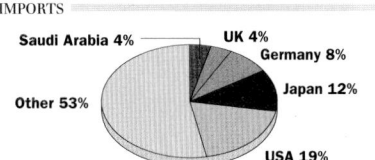

Saudi Arabia 4%
UK 4%
Germany 8%
Japan 12%
Other 53%
USA 19%

RESOURCES

11.2bn kwh (capacity 6.8m kw)

150,000 sheep, 15,000 goats, 12,000 cattle

2.1bn b/d (reserves 94,000 million bbl)

Oil, natural gas, salt

The oil industry is Kuwait's most profitable sector, accounting for over 80% of export earnings. It was badly hit as a result of the Gulf War, when large numbers of oil wells were deliberately fired, but with foreign assistance it has been quickly rehabilitated. Kuwait also possesses valuable reserves of natural gas.

ENVIRONMENT

 1.5%   Rapid clean-up in 1991 following end of Gulf War

The Iraqi invasion and the subsequent war caused an ecological disaster. Although the effects of this did not prove as grave as some observers first feared, marine life has been damaged and many thousands of acres of cultivated land have been obliterated. Millions of land mines still litter Kuwait's border areas.

MEDIA

 There is officially no press censorship. However, the government acts swiftly against publishers who breach informal guidelines

PUBLISHING AND BROADCAST MEDIA

 There are 7 daily newspapers, the largest of which is *Al-Qabas*

1 state-controlled service   3 state-controlled services

Radio and TV are state-controlled, but satellite TV is freely available. Press freedom exists in theory.

CRIME

 500 prisoners    Up 900% in 1992

Isolated acts of terrorism related to the war still occur. There have been reports of human rights abuses.

EDUCATION

 73%   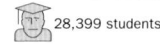 28,399 students

Kuwaiti citizens receive free education from nursery to university. Since liberation, more emphasis has been placed on technology in the curriculum.

CHRONOLOGY

Kuwait traces its independence to 1710, but was under British rule from the late 18th century until 1961. The government denies any historical link with Iraq.

- ❏ **1961** Independence from the UK. Iraqi claims against its sovereignty.
- ❏ **1976** The Amir suspends the National Assembly.
- ❏ **1990** Iraq invades Kuwait. The Amir flees to Saudi Arabia.
- ❏ **1991** Operation Desert Storm liberates Kuwait.
- ❏ **1992** National Assembly elections.

HEALTH

 1 per 585 people   Heart diseases, accidents, cancers, perinatal deaths

Despite theft of equipment during the Iraqi invasion, Kuwait has restored its Western-standard health care service. Nationals receive free treatment.

WEALTH

 Most Kuwaitis have total financial security

CONSUMER GOODS OWNERSHIP

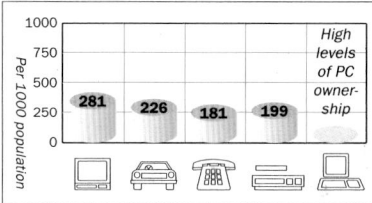

281   226   181   199

High levels of PC ownership

Kuwaitis enjoy high incomes and the government has repeatedly rescued citizens who have suffered stock market or other financial losses. School and university leavers are guaranteed jobs. Capital is easily transferred abroad and there are effectively no exchange controls.

WORLD RANKING

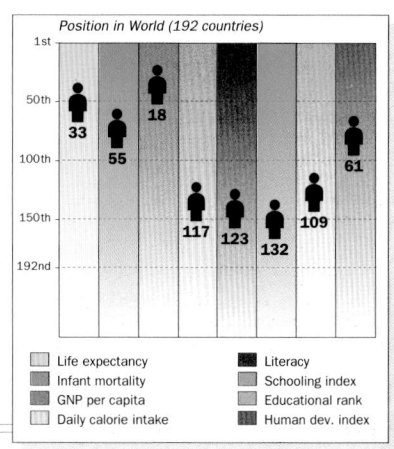

Position in World (192 countries)

33   55   18   117   123   132   109   61

- ▢ Life expectancy
- ▢ Infant mortality
- ▢ GNP per capita
- ▢ Daily calorie intake
- ▣ Literacy
- ▢ Schooling index
- ▢ Educational rank
- ▣ Human dev. index

K

KYRGYZSTAN

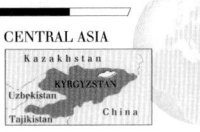

CENTRAL ASIA

OFFICIAL NAME: Kyrgyz Republic CAPITAL: Bishkek
POPULATION: 4.7 million CURRENCY: Som OFFICIAL LANGUAGES: Kyrgyz, Russian

KYRGYZSTAN IS A SMALL and very mountainous nation in central Asia. It is the least urbanized of the ex-Soviet republics (the rural population is growing faster than the towns) and was among the last to develop its own cultural nationalism. Its moderate government is treading uncertainly between Kyrgyz nationalist pressures, and ensuring that the minority Russians are not alienated as they tend to possess the skills necessary to run a market-based economy.

CLIMATE

WEATHER CHART

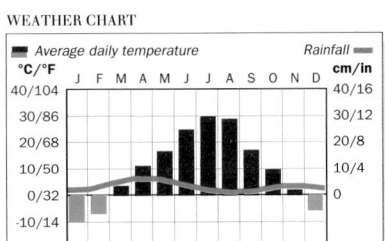

Conditions vary from permanent snow and cold deserts at altitude to hot deserts in low regions. Intermediate slopes and valleys receive some rain.

TRANSPORTATION

 Bishkek International   Has no fleet

THE TRANSPORTATION NETWORK

 13,920 miles (22,400 km) None

230 miles (370 km)   373 miles (600 km)

Kyrgyzstan does not have the funds to improve its poor mountain road network.

TOURISM

 Mainly business visitors   Little change from year to year

MAIN OVERSEAS ARRIVALS

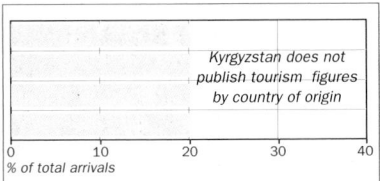

Kyrgyzstan does not publish tourism figures by country of origin

0   10   20   30   40
% of total arrivals

The tourist industry is undeveloped. Most visitors to Kyrgyzstan are people on business from Turkey and China in search of new contracts, or working on multilateral aid agency projects.

PEOPLE

Kyrgyz, Russian 62 people per sq. mile

THE URBAN/RURAL POPULATION SPLIT

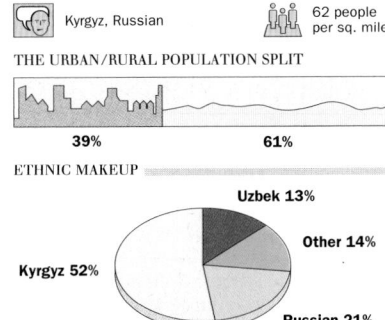

39%   61%

ETHNIC MAKEUP

Uzbek 13%
Other 14%
Kyrgyz 52%
Russian 21%

Despite claims to the contrary, Kyrgyzstan suffers from a forceful nationalism similar to that in other ex-Soviet republics. There is considerable tension between the Kyrgyz and other minorities, particularly Uzbeks. The preference given to Kyrgyz in the political system and in particular in the land laws, which exclude all others from full title, has aggravated tensions. The trend in politics is toward greater Islamicization, which is linking religion and race issues more closely and adding pressure on "foreigners," particularly Russians, to leave.

Since 1989 their high birth-rate has enabled the Kyrgyz to resume their position as the dominant ethnic group replacing the Russian community which until recently controlled the economy. In 1994, however, the government moved to stem the tide of Russian emigration by declaring Russian an official language.

Loess landscape, Naryn valley. Kyrgyzstan is dominated by the ice-capped Tien Shan Mountains, but valleys are green and fertile.

POLITICS

 1995/2000 President Askar Akayev

THE STATE OF THE PARTIES

Supreme Soviet 105 members

Legislative elections were held for the first time since independence in February 1995. Party affiliations were declared for only 15 of the 105 members elected.

Kyrgyzstan has gone further than most ex-Soviet republics in embracing political change. As the first republic to denounce the attempted coup in Moscow in 1991, it swiftly banned the Communist Party, which was, however, revived in 1992 and renamed the Communists of the Republic of Kyrgyzstan.

Akayev, the academic picked as a reformist president by the Supreme Soviet in 1990, has steered a precarious course by seeking to accommodate the demands of nationalist Kyrgyz and important minorities like the Uzbeks who were involved in fierce ethnic clashes in the city of Osh in 1990. Akayev's economic policies, with their emphasis on market-led reforms, have shown few tangible results.

Criticism of Akayev's government is compounded by allegations that he wished to foster a personality cult. In 1995, parliament rejected a proposal for a referendum to extend Akayev's tenure until 2001. Later that year, Akayev was reelected president for a second five-year term, having held the post since 1990.

WORLD AFFAIRS

 CIS   ECO OIC   OSCE   NACC

Relations with Russia are good, though Kyrgyzstan is working to reduce its dependence on it. Turkey, the second country to establish a mission in Bishkek after the USA, is developing close links aimed at restraining Iranian fundamentalist influence in the region. Relations with Uzbekistan, which supports anti-democratic forces in Kyrgyzstan, are tense.

AID

 $94m (receipts)  Up 2,250% in 1993

Major donors include the USA and Japan. In 1995, the World Bank promised credits totaling $680 million.

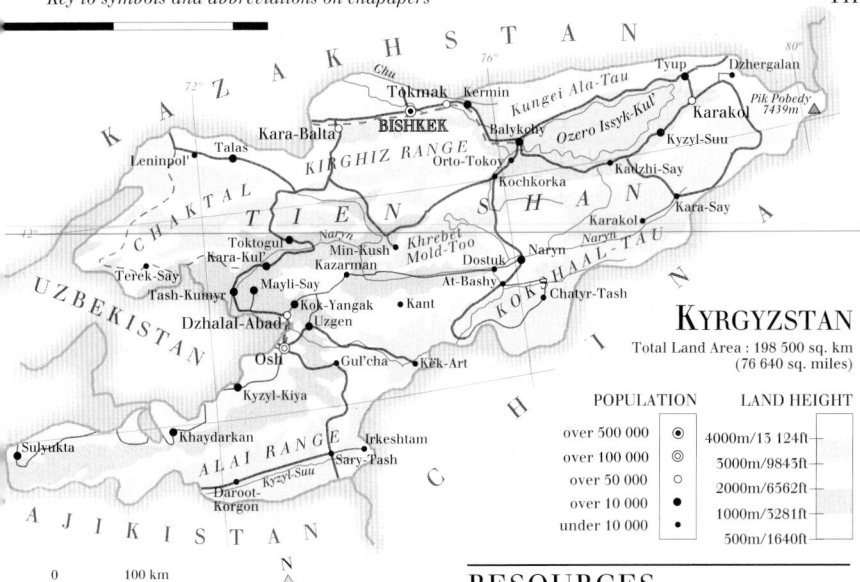

CHRONOLOGY

The Kyrgyz first developed a recognizable ethnic conciousness in the late 18th century.

- ❑ **1860s** Expansion of Russian Empire into Kyrgyz lands.
- ❑ **1916** Kyrgyz resistance to call-up to Tsar's armies fighting Germany; 120,000 Kyrgyz die in uprisings.
- ❑ **1924** Incorporated in USSR.
- ❑ **1991** Independence from USSR.

KYRGYZSTAN

Total Land Area : 198 500 sq. km
(76 640 sq. miles)

POPULATION		LAND HEIGHT	
over 500 000	◉	4000m/13 124ft	
over 100 000	◎	3000m/9843ft	
over 50 000	○	2000m/6562ft	
over 10 000	•	1000m/3281ft	
under 10 000	•	500m/1640ft	

EDUCATION

 97%    55,229 students

Replacing Russian as the main teaching language is proving an enormous task. Russian is likely to survive at tertiary level, as the Kyrgyz language lacks key technical and scientific terms.

K

DEFENSE

 $13m    Down 73% in 1995

The small army, composed of the Kyrgyz remnants of the former CIS force, is weak and not influential in politics. Recruitment to a 7,000-strong National Guard was set up in 1992. Kyrgyzstan looks to its alliance with the CIS, particularly Russia, for its security.

ECONOMICS

 $2.8bn    10.50–11.15 som

SCORE CARD

- ❑ World GNP Ranking........................128th
- ❑ GNP per Capita $610
- ❑ Balance of Payments.................$–100.8m
- ❑ Inflation 278%
- ❑ Unemployment...................................0.4%

STRENGTHS

Agricultural self-sufficiency. Minerals, especially gold and mercury for export. Large hydroelectric power potential.

WEAKNESSES

Agriculture-based economy. Economy still dominated by the state and the mentality of collective farming. Sharp economic decline since 1991 breakup of USSR, on which it depended totally for trade and supplies. Hyperinflation running at 278% in 1996.

EXPORTS/IMPORTS

Trade is overwhelmingly with the Russian Federation. A smaller proportion is with other states of the former Soviet Union

RESOURCES

 11.9bn kwh (capacity 4.1m kw)   2,266 b/d

 7m sheep, 1.1m cattle, 300,000 horses   Coal, antimony, gas, oil, tin, mercury, iron, uranium, zinc, gold

Kyrgyzstan has small quantities of commercially exploitable coal, oil and gas and great hydroelectric power potential. Energy policy, which relies on Western aid and technology, is primarily aimed at developing these further in order to reduce dependence on supplies from Russia, and eventually to achieve self-sufficiency in energy.

ENVIRONMENT

 1.4%   No funds for major initiatives

The major problem is the salination of the soil caused by excessive irrigation of cotton. Kyrgyzstan has a poor record in limiting industrial pollution.

MEDIA

 There is no censorship

PUBLISHING AND BROADCAST MEDIA

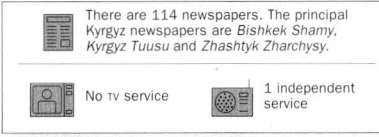

There are 114 newspapers. The principal Kyrgyz newspapers are *Bishkek Shamy, Kyrgyz Tuusu* and *Zhashtyk Zharchysy.*

No TV service   1 independent service

TV programing is mostly from Russia. The Kyrgyz press is the most liberal in Central Asia.

CRIME

 Kyrgyzstan does not publish prison figures   The crime rate is soaring

Outbreaks of violence are often the result of ethnic tensions. Economic decline is encouraging farmers to grow opium for the illegal narcotics trade.

HEALTH

 1 per 310 people   Heart diseases, cancers, accidents, violence, tuberculosis

Kyrgyzstan had one of the Soviet Union's least developed public health systems. Infant mortality remains high.

WEALTH

 Inflation is eroding the value of most salaries

CONSUMER GOODS OWNERSHIP

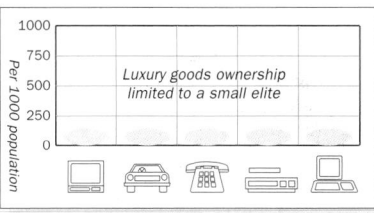

Luxury goods ownership limited to a small elite

The old Communist Party *nomenklatura*, using their contacts in trade, are still the wealthiest group.

WORLD RANKING

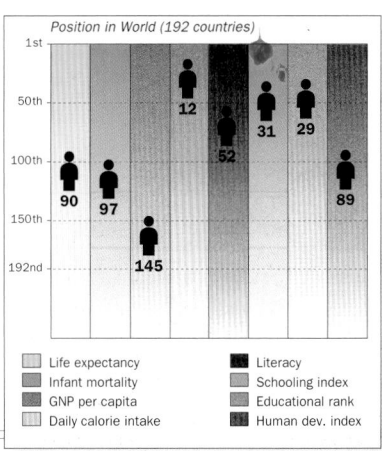

Position in World (192 countries)

☐ Life expectancy	■ Literacy
☐ Infant mortality	☐ Schooling index
☐ GNP per capita	☐ Educational rank
☐ Daily calorie intake	■ Human dev. index

LAOS

OFFICIAL NAME: Lao People's Democratic Republic
CAPITAL: Vientiane **POPULATION:** 4.9 million **CURRENCY:** New kip **OFFICIAL LANGUAGE:** Lao

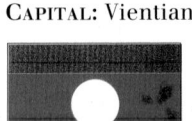

L

LAOS IS A LANDLOCKED country surrounded by Vietnam, Cambodia, Thailand, Burma and China. The Mekong River forms its main thoroughfare and feeds the fertile lowlands of the Mekong valley. Laos became independent of France in 1953. It was heavily bombed by US aircraft during the Vietnam War. The communist Lao People's Revolutionary Party (LPRP) has held power since 1975. The government began introducing market-oriented reforms in 1986. A transfer of power took place in 1992 following the death of party leader, Kaysone Phomvihane.

Farm in northeastern Laos. *The only lowlands are along the Mekong River. Three quarters of Laotians are subsistence farmers.*

CLIMATE

WEATHER CHART

The tropical southerly monsoon brings heavy rains from May to September. For the rest of the year Laos has dry northerly winds and sunny skies.

TRANSPORTATION

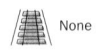

Wattay, Vientiane 165,000 passengers	1 ship 1500 dwt

THE TRANSPORTATION NETWORK

1,410 miles (2,261 km)	None
None	2,858 miles (4,600 km)

In 1994, a bridge was opened over the Mekong at Vientiane, creating the first road link between Thailand and Laos. Foreigners may enter Laos only via this route or by air to Vientiane. Other roads lead into Vietnam and Cambodia.

PEOPLE

Lao, Miao, Yao, Vietnamese, Chinese, French	54 people per sq. mile

THE URBAN/RURAL POPULATION SPLIT

20%   80%

RELIGIOUS PERSUASION

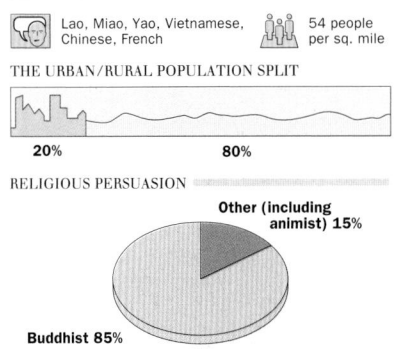

Other (including animist) 15%

Buddhist 85%

ETHNIC MAKEUP

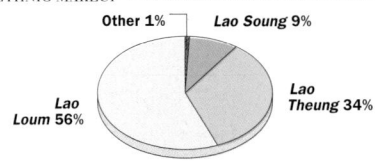

Other 1%   Lao Soung 9%

Lao Loum 56%   Lao Theung 34%

There are more than 60 ethnic groups in Laos and this considerable diversity has hindered national integration. Society is broadly divided by altitude rather than by region.

The lowland Laotians (*Lao Loum*), who make up the majority of the population and are mostly ethnic Lao, reside in the river valleys along the Mekong River and practise wet rice agriculture. The upland Laotians (*Lao Theung*) live in the hills above the valleys and practise slash-and-burn agriculture. Efforts by the government in Vientiane to alter this traditional form of farming, which can destroy forests and watersheds, have been resisted by the people.

Similarly, the mountain-top Laotians (*Lao Soung*), who include the Hmong, Yao and Man groups, have resisted government efforts to introduce substitutes for traditional cash crops such as opium. The Hmong, in particular, are distanced from the Vientiane leadership. Tens of thousands fled to Thailand when the LPRP took power in 1975. Today, the government continues to face small pockets of Hmong resistance.

Two-thirds of the population speak Lao, and a large number of tribal dialects are also spoken. Buddhism is the main religion, but there are some Christians and animists.

POPULATION AGE BREAKDOWN

% of population by age group	0–14	15–64		65+
	2.4%	2.6%	2.8%	3%	3%
	55.5%	55.1%	55.2%	53.4%	52.6%
	42.1%	42.3%	42%	43.6%	44.4%
	1960	1970	1980	1990	2000

TOURISM

25,000 visitors	No change in 1994

Tourists were first allowed into Laos in 1989. The government is shunning mass-market development, encouraging expensive package tours in small groups. Hotels are few, and travel outside the Vientiane area is difficult as passes must be obtained for each province. Thai entrepreneurs are funding some new hotels.

MAIN OVERSEAS ARRIVALS

Laos does not publish tourism figures by country of origin. Most tourists come to Laos on day trips from Thailand

0   10   20   30   40
% of total arrivals

President Nouhak Phoumsavan, *who took office in November 1992.*

General Khamtay Siphandon, *prime minister and head of the armed forces.*

POLITICS

 1992/1997

 President Nouhak Phoumsavan

THE STATE OF THE PARTIES

National Assembly 85 members

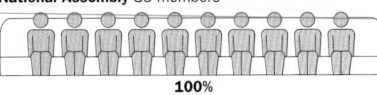

100%
LPRP

LPRP = Lao People's Revolutionary Party
Many candidates ran as independents, but all were
effectively approved by the LPRP

Laos is a communist, one-party state under the direct control and administration of the LPRP.

MAIN POLITICAL ISSUES
Political reform
Reforms are currently being introduced to modernize key state functions. The country's first written constitution was adopted in 1991, and a modern legal infrastructure has been introduced.

The LPRP has begun to relax its total hold on power. The executive branch of government appears to be asserting its authority, although it still relies on the Party for broad guidelines. The legislative branch is also taking more initiative and the National Assembly is no longer simply a rubber stamp for Party edicts.

Central control
Tensions continue to be felt between the communist government in the capital Vientiane and the rural areas, where the rank and file of the LPRP and the military have their roots. There is particular resistance to central attempts to alter traditional farming methods.

PROFILE
Laos has been ruled by the same circle of communist revolutionaries since 1975. They have proved to be one of the world's most durable and closely knit hierarchies.

The vacuum left by the death of long-time Party leader, Kaysone Phomvihane, in 1992 was quickly filled by his protégés, who show no sign of deviating from the path he laid down. The military, the Party and the executive branch remain closely intertwined. Despite limited moves toward political reform, the LPRP, which is modeled on the Communist Party of Vietnam, continues to dominate political life at every level.

The long-standing problem of corruption, sometimes at a high level, has become a matter of concern as Laos has opened to foreign investors. Concern that this may lead to a loss of faith has led to government crackdowns.

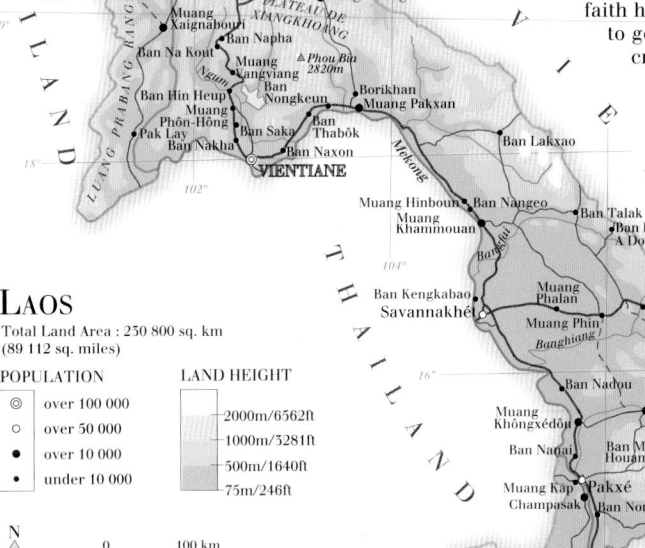

LAOS
Total Land Area : 230 800 sq. km
(89 112 sq. miles)

POPULATION
- ◎ over 100 000
- ○ over 50 000
- ● over 10 000
- • under 10 000

LAND HEIGHT
- 2000m/6562ft
- 1000m/3281ft
- 500m/1640ft
- 75m/246ft

N
0   100 km
0   100 miles

WORLD AFFAIRS

 ASEAN CP IBRD Mek Riv NAM

Throughout the 1960s and 1970s, Vietnam was Laos's most important ally. In the 1980s, after many years of political isolation, the party leadership in Vientiane began to seek improved relations with the outside world, the West in particular. Closer ties with Japan and rapprochement with both Thailand and with former enemies, the USA and France, were secured. The motivation was mainly the need for foreign aid.

Following the collapse of communism in eastern Europe, Laos turned to its northern neighbor, China, for ideological support and to counterbalance the growing influence of Thailand. At the same time, the government was careful not to jeopardize links with Vietnam.

In July 1992, Laos acceded to the Treaty of Amity and Concord of the Association of Southeast Asian Nations (ASEAN), marking a watershed in relations with its former adversaries in the region.

L

CHRONOLOGY
In the late 19th century, France established control over the three small kingdoms of Champasak, Louangphrabang and Vientiane.

- ❏ **1893** Franco-Siamese treaty establishes French control over all territory east of the Mekong.
- ❏ **1899** Creation of a unified Laos under the French.
- ❏ **1941** Japanese seize power from Vichy French in Indo–China.
- ❏ **1946** French rule resumed.
- ❏ **1950** Lao Patriotic Front, LPF, set up to oppose French rule. Gains support of newly formed communist Lao People's Party (LPP).
- ❏ **1953** Independence as a constitutional monarchy backed by France and the USA.
- ❏ **1963** LPF begins armed struggle against royal government through its armed wing, the Pathet Lao.
- ❏ **1964** US bombing of North Vietnamese sanctuaries in Laos; later escalated along the Ho Chi Minh trail.
- ❏ **1973** LPRP (formerly known as LPF) and royal government form a coalition after withdrawal of US forces from Indochina.
- ❏ **1975** LPRP seizes power, abolishes monarchy and proclaims Lao People's Democratic Republic. Premier Kaysone Phomvihane adopts policies for "socialist transformation" of economy. ➪

CHRONOLOGY *continued*

- ❏ **1977** The Treaty of Friendship and Cooperation, providing for mutual assistance in national security, signed with Vietnam. Relations with China begin to cool.
- ❏ **1978** Resistance to collectivization. Series of natural disasters leads to rice shortages. After increasing internal dissent, the former king and crown prince are arrested and die in captivity. Almost 50,000 Laotians flee to Thailand.
- ❏ **1979** Softer economic line adopted and the speed of "socialist transformation" slows.
- ❏ **1983** Thirty-two state officials are convicted of corruption and anti-state activities.
- ❏ **1986** Fourth Party Congress makes market-oriented reforms.
- ❏ **1988** Brief border war fought with Thailand. Diplomatic relations restored with China.
- ❏ **1989** National elections held. All candidates approved by LPRP. Rapprochement with Thailand.
- ❏ **1990** Counter-offensives against right-wing, largely Hmong, guerrilla bases located in the outer provinces. Most agricultural collectives and state farms disbanded. Arrest of three former government officials for promoting multiparty democracy.
- ❏ **1991** A constitution providing for a National Assembly, confirming the leading role of the LPRP and enshrining the right of private ownership, is promulgated. Kaysone steps down as prime minister and takes up post of president. Khamtay Siphandon becomes prime minister.
- ❏ **1992** Death of President Kaysone. Khamtay becomes head of the LPRP. Laos accedes to the Treaty of Amity and Concord of the ASEAN countries.
- ❏ **1994** Thai–Laos bridge opens over Mekong – first ever direct road link between the two countries.
- ❏ **1995** Former President Souphanouvong, the "Red Prince" dies.

AID

 $199m (receipts)   Up 15% in 1993

Laos has one of the highest per capita aid inflows in the developing world. However, severe problems have been encountered in the implementation of aid programs. In the 1980s, Laos was heavily dependent on the USSR and Vietnam for aid. Today, donors include the IMF, the World Bank, the Asian Development Bank, France, Sweden, Australia and Japan.

DEFENSE

 $121m   ⬆ Up 6% in 1995

0   *Defense spending as % GDP*   40
7.9%

The armed forces are estimated by the West to number over 30,000 personnel. This total is further swelled by a paramilitary militia. Military service is compulsory for all Laotian males for 18 months.

The military and the ruling LPRP have close links. The prime minister, Khamtay Siphandon, has long been considered the army's chief supporter in the politburo and served as defense minister from 1975 to 1991. In 1977,

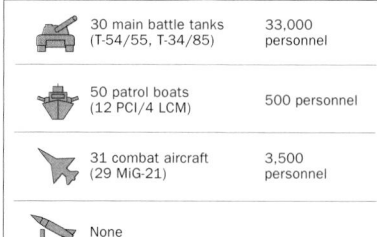

LAOTIAN ARMED FORCES

30 main battle tanks (T-54/55, T-34/85)	33,000 personnel
50 patrol boats (12 PCI/4 LCM)	500 personnel
31 combat aircraft (29 MiG-21)	3,500 personnel
None	

Laos signed a treaty with Vietnam, providing for mutual assistance in the event of a threat to national security.

ECONOMICS

📊 $1.5bn   💲 721–920 new kips

SCORE CARD

- ❏ WORLD GNP RANKING.......................145th
- ❏ GNP PER CAPITA $320
- ❏ BALANCE OF PAYMENTS.....................$–93m
- ❏ INFLATION 6.8%
- ❏ UNEMPLOYMENT...................................21%

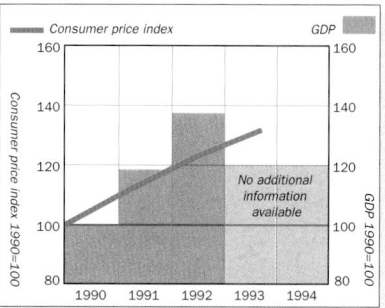

ECONOMIC PERFORMANCE INDICATOR

No additional information available

EXPORTS

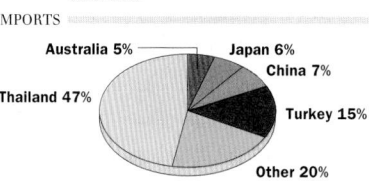

France 5%
Germany 6%
Japan 8%
Turkey 41%
Thailand 20%
Other 20%

IMPORTS

Australia 5%
Japan 6%
China 7%
Thailand 47%
Turkey 15%
Other 20%

STRENGTHS
Rising levels of overseas (mostly Thai) investment. Potential of garment manufacturing, mining, timber plantations, wood processing, tourism, banking and aviation. Minerals and possible oil and gas deposits.

WEAKNESSES
One of the world's 20 least-developed countries. Lack of technical expertise, a major constraint to further development. Imbalance in sources of foreign investment – most is Thai. Problems in targeting aid efficiently.

PROFILE
The LPRP began introducing market-oriented reforms in 1986. The collapse of the Soviet Union, and the subsequent loss of Soviet aid and markets in eastern Europe, speeded up this process in the early 1990s. The reforms

began by removing price controls on rice and other crops. This encouraged farmers to plant more and helped establish a degree of food self-sufficiency.

In recent years, the currency has been floated, interest rates eased and trade freed from restrictions. Laos has also opened its doors to foreign investment – the first country in Indochina to do so. However, most foreign interest has been confined to sectors that offer quick returns, such as services, and natural resource exploitation such as logging and mining. A number of state-owned companies, including the highly profitable national brewery, have recently been privatized.

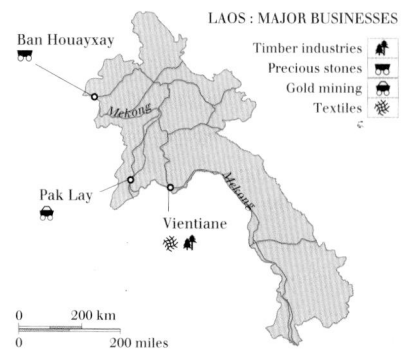

LAOS : MAJOR BUSINESSES

Timber industries
Precious stones
Gold mining
Textiles

Ban Houayxay
Mekong
Pak Lay
Vientiane

0   200 km
0   200 miles

RESOURCES

 910m kwh

 30,500 tons

 1.6m pigs,
1.1m cattle,
153,000 goats

Tin, gypsum, iron,
copper, potash, lead,
limestone, antimony

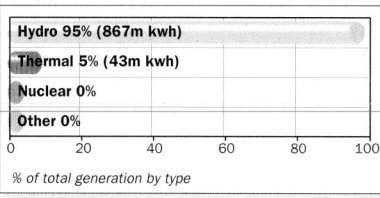

ELECTRICITY GENERATION

Hydro 95% (867m kwh)

Thermal 5% (43m kwh)

Nuclear 0%

Other 0%

% of total generation by type

Laos's most important agricultural resources are timber and coffee. The country is rich in minerals. Important deposits include tin and gypsum (which are also exported), iron ore, copper, potash, limestone, antimony, coal, manganese, lead and salt. An increasing number of foreign companies have been awarded concessions to mine for gold and precious stones. Two oil and gas exploration agreements with oil multinationals were also negotiated between 1990 and 1991. Laos's principal source of electricity is hydroelectric power. Surpluses are exported to Thailand.

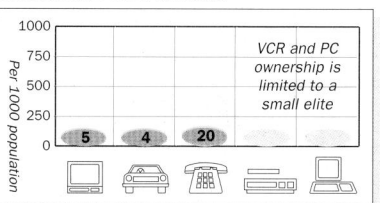

LAOS : LAND USE

Cropland
Forest
Pasture
Coffee - cash crop
Rice
Pigs

0 ——— 200 km
0 ——— 200 miles

ENVIRONMENT

 10%

 Building of more HEP dams will further reduce forest cover

Bombing and the use of defoliants in the Vietnam War did serious ecological damage. Slash-and-burn farming and illegal logging are destroying forests.

ENVIRONMENTAL TREATIES

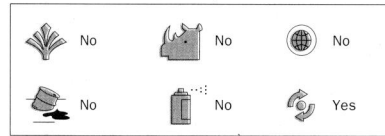

No　No　No
No　No　Yes

MEDIA

 Tight government control of media

PUBLISHING AND BROADCAST MEDIA

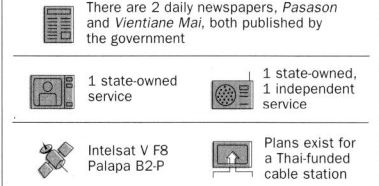

There are 2 daily newspapers, *Pasason* and *Vientiane Mai*, both published by the government

1 state-owned service

1 state-owned, 1 independent service

Intelsat V F8 Palapa B2-P

Plans exist for a Thai-funded cable station

Newspapers are owned and controlled by the LPRP. Revelations of corruption by state officials are not uncommon, but criticism of the party and its leaders remains taboo. In 1990, the illegal Radio Station of the Government for the Liberation of the Lao Nation began broadcasting anti-government propaganda for four hours per day.

CRIME

 Laos does not publish prison figures

 Rising overall, particularly corruption

CRIME RATES

> Most crime is rising. However the trend in mountain regions is hard to establish

Laos is the world's third largest opium producer. Since 1990, attempts have been made to combat the production and trafficking of illegal drugs. The USA is providing funds to substitute cash crops for poppies in the mountainous northeastern provinces.

EDUCATION

 57%

 4730 students

0　　*Education spending as % GNP*　　25

1.2%

THE EDUCATION SYSTEM

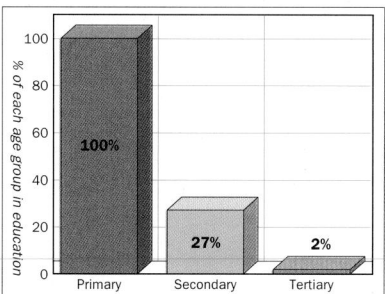

Primary 100%
Secondary 27%
Tertiary 2%

% of each age group in education

Literacy rates in Laos remain low, at 44% for women and 69% for men. However, adult education is currently being expanded and new schools are being built.

HEALTH

 1 per 4450 people

 Diarrheal, respiratory and parasitic diseases, malaria, influenza

0　　*Health spending as % GDP*　　25

1%

Poor sanitation and nutrition levels in most of rural Laos are reflected in the standard indicators of health and longevity. Infant mortality is over 10% and life expectancy is only 50 years. Malaria and hemorrhagic fever are on the increase.

WEALTH

 Middle and high level state officials, $20–$40 per month; trishaw drivers in Vientiane can earn nearly five times that amount

CONSUMER GOODS OWNERSHIP

VCR and PC ownership is limited to a small elite

5　4　20

Per 1000 population

There are large inequalities of wealth in Laos. A rapidly expanding group of Laotian entrepreneurs is profiting from the liberalization of the economy. The elite live in French-style villas. Mercedes are not uncommon in the capital and the number of motorcycles has doubled in the past few years.

Development is unevenly spread around the country. Many in the highlands and mountainous regions lead a subsistence existence, while farmers in the fertile Mekong valley are relatively well-off. Most homes along the Mekong have TV sets which can receive broadcasts from Thai stations. Bribes are a key part of most bureaucrats' incomes.

WORLD RANKING

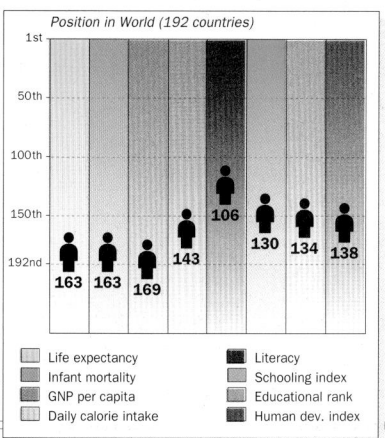

Position in World (192 countries)

1st
50th
100th
150th
192nd

163　163　169　143　106　130　134　138

Life expectancy
Infant mortality
GNP per capita
Daily calorie intake
Literacy
Schooling index
Educational rank
Human dev. index

L

LATVIA

OFFICIAL NAME: Republic of Latvia   **CAPITAL:** Riga
POPULATION: 2.6 million   **CURRENCY:** Lats   **OFFICIAL LANGUAGE:** Latvian

LYING BETWEEN ESTONIA and Lithuania, Latvia is situated on the eastern coast of the Baltic Sea. To the east it borders the Russian Federation and Belorussia. The whole country is a low-lying plain, that does not rise above 984 feet. Latvia's independence was recognized by Moscow in 1991. Defense-related industries and agriculture play an important role in the economy. Only 52% of the population are ethnic Latvians.

CLIMATE

WEATHER CHART

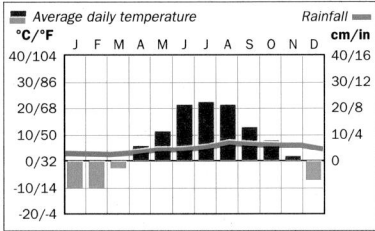

Latvia's coastal position means that the climate is temperate, with cold winters and cool summers.

TRANSPORTATION

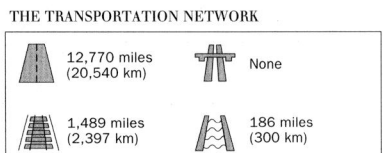

Riga International 491,000 passengers	130 ships 1.34m dwt

THE TRANSPORTATION NETWORK

12,770 miles (20,540 km)		None	
1,489 miles (2,397 km)		186 miles (300 km)	

The planned Finland–Poland road will run through Latvia. Ports are being upgraded, particularly Ventspils and Liepāja. The EBRD is spending 10 million ECU on improvements at Riga airport.

LATVIA

Total Land Area :
64 589 sq. km
(24 938 sq. miles)

POPULATION
- ◉ over 500 000
- ◎ over 100 000
- ○ over 50 000
- • over 10 000
- • under 10 000

LAND HEIGHT
- 200m/656ft
- Sea Level

The Russian Orthodox Cathedral in Riga. Used as a planetarium during the Soviet era, its interior is now being restored.

TOURISM

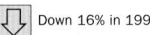

1.6m visitors	Down 16% in 1995

MAIN OVERSEAS ARRIVALS

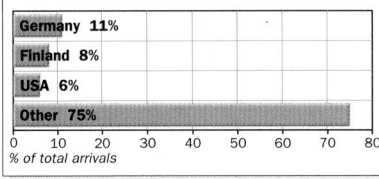

Germany	11%
Finland	8%
USA	6%
Other	75%

% of total arrivals (0 10 20 30 40 50 60 70 80)

Riga is the main tourist destination, with many hotels and restaurants. Its medieval center is being restored.

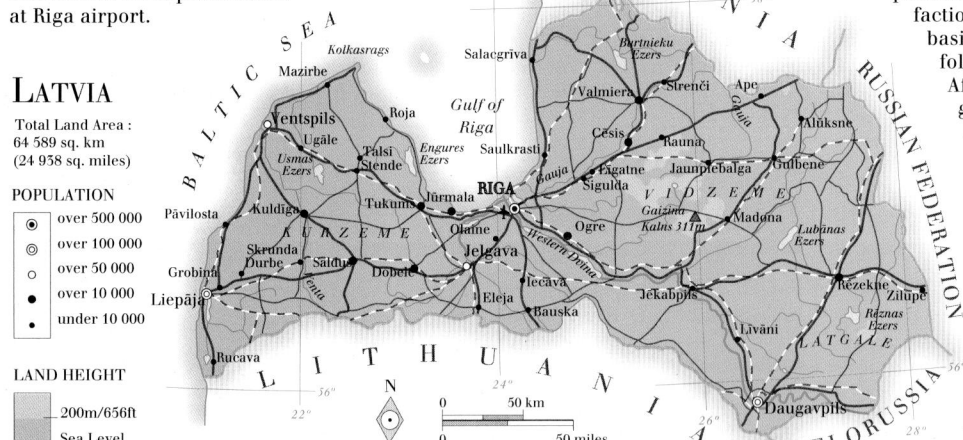

PEOPLE

Latvian, Russian	104 people per sq. mile

THE URBAN/RURAL POPULATION SPLIT

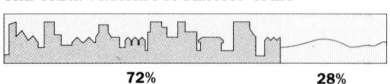

72%   28%

ETHNIC MAKEUP

- Other 5%
- Ukrainian 4%
- Latvian 52%
- Belorussian 5%
- Russian 34%

Latvians make up only 52% of the population, compared with 34% of Russians, and are a minority in the capital, Riga. Although some Latvians fear a potential cultural dilution, there is little tension between the various ethnic groups. Nevertheless, it is difficult for most ethnic Russians to become Latvian citizens. The status of women is on a par with that in western Europe. The divorce rate is high.

POLITICS

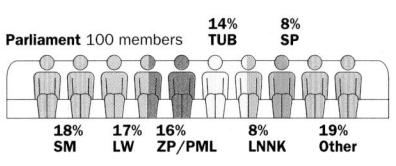

1995/1998	President Guntis Ulmanis

THE STATE OF THE PARTIES

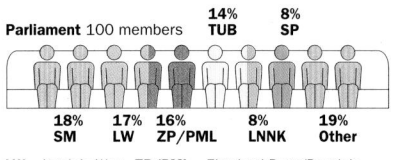

Parliament 100 members   14% TUB   8% SP

18% SM   17% LW   16% ZP/PML   8% LNNK   19% Other

LW = Latvia's Way   **ZP/PML** = Zigerists' Party/People's Movement for Latvia   **TUB** = Union for the Fatherland and Freedom   **LNNK** = National Conservative Party   **SP** = Unity Party   **SM** = Saimnieks

The LW is the strongest grouping in a political system plagued by factional instability, and was the basis of coalition government following the 1993 election. After an inconclusive general election in 1995 and several attempts to form a government, the LW again featured in a coalition led by Andris Skele. The question of citizenship remains a contentious one; full rights have only been granted to those with families resident in Latvia before 1940, thus disenfranchising two-thirds of the Russian minority.

WORLD AFFAIRS

Latvia signed an association agreement with the EU in June 1995 and applied for full membership later that year. It is also keen to revive its pre-Soviet status as a country with close Western cultural and trading connections. Relations with Russia have recently cooled; Moscow's increasingly nationalistic foreign policy is the main cause.

AID

 Latvia does not publish aid receipts   The trend is up

Aid to Latvia comes mainly from the World Bank, the IMF and the EU. The majority of it goes towards improving the country's infrastructure.

DEFENSE

 $65m   Up 2% in 1995

Building up the military is a priority. The withdrawal of Russian troops from Latvian territory was completed in 1994. Stationed ostensibly to secure the rights of ethnic Russians, they were seen as a threat to security. Latvia is seeking closer links with Western forces and hopes to join NATO.

ECONOMICS

 $5.9bn   0.54–0.55 lati

SCORE CARD

- ❏ WORLD GNP RANKING..........................96th
- ❏ GNP PER CAPITA $2290
- ❏ BALANCE OF PAYMENTS $201m
- ❏ INFLATION 22.7%
- ❏ UNEMPLOYMENT................................6.3%

STRENGTHS
Well-developed industrial base, especially for defense-related industries. Numerous port facilities. Agricultural surplus.

WEAKNESSES
Lack of raw materials. Dependence on Russia for supplies of oil and natural gas. Slump in demand for Latvian exports from former Soviet and eastern European trading partners.

EXPORTS
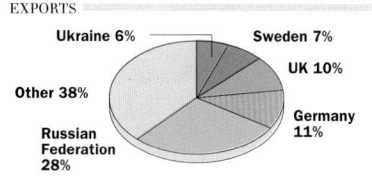

IMPORTS
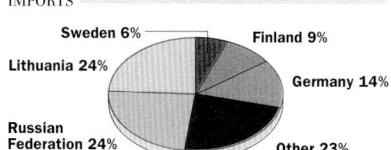

RESOURCES

 3.8bn kwh   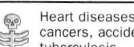 142,229 tons

 995,000 cattle, 737,000 pigs, 133,000 sheep   Amber, dolomite, gravel, gypsum, limestone, peat, sand

Latvia has no strategic resources and is dependent on imports to meet its energy requirements. In 1991, these represented almost one-third of total imports. Electricity supplies come chiefly from Lithuania and Estonia, while oil is imported from Russia and Lithuania. New infrastructure is being built to broaden the supply network.

ENVIRONMENT

 12%   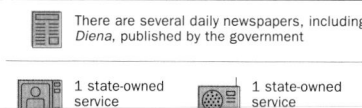 Environmental issues' role in independence movement

Peat extraction – Latvia is 5% bog – has damaged the environment. Pollution of the Baltic Sea and general air and water quality are also of concern. Environmental awareness is strong. In the run-up to independence green issues had a high profile.

MEDIA

 Officially none. Russians have restricted access to the media

PUBLISHING AND BROADCAST MEDIA

There are several daily newspapers, including *Diena*, published by the government

1 state-owned service   1 state-owned service

The press is now relatively free from state interference. Previously, the media were predominantly in Russian. Since 1991, the state, aiming to broaden the use of the official language, has actively promoted Latvian publications.

CRIME

 Latvia does not publish prison figures    Crime levels are rising slightly

Levels of crime are lower than in other ex-Soviet republics. However, organized crime is a growing problem.

EDUCATION

99%   41,138 students

Education in Latvia is now following the German model. There are over 40,000 students in higher education.

HEALTH

 1 per 280 people   Heart diseases, cancers, accidents, tuberculosis

The state-run health system is beset by shortages of medicines and equipment. Standards have improved little since the demise of communism.

WEALTH

Secretary, 30–40 lati ($56–$74) per month; dentist, 80 lati ($149) per month

CONSUMER GOODS OWNERSHIP
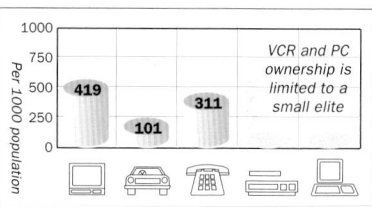

The old bureaucracy has retained its privileged status and contacts, and remains the wealthiest group.

WORLD RANKING

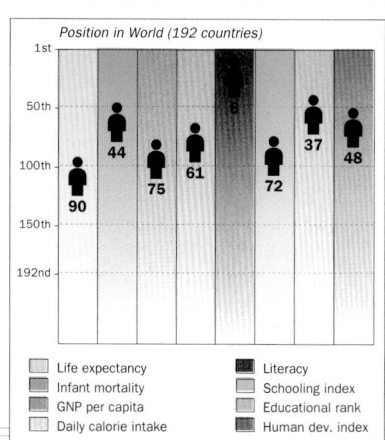

LEBANON

OFFICIAL NAME: Republic of Lebanon   **CAPITAL:** Beirut
POPULATION: 3 million   **CURRENCY:** Lebanese pound   **OFFICIAL LANGUAGE:** Arabic

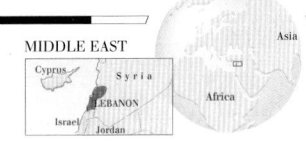

MIDDLE EAST

L EBANON IS DWARFED BY its two powerful neighbors, Syria and Israel. The country's coastal strip is fertile and the hinterland mountainous. Although in the minority, Maronite Christians have traditionally ruled Lebanon. A civil war between Muslim and Christian factional groups began in 1975 and threatened to lead to the breakup of the state. However, Saudi Arabia brokered a peace agreement in 1989. Elections were held in 1992.

POLITICS

 1992/1996   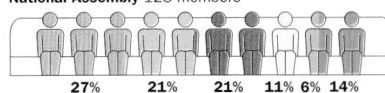 President Elias Hrawi

THE STATE OF THE PARTIES

National Assembly 128 members

| 27% MC | 21% Su M | 21% Sh M | 11% GO | 6% D | 14% Other |

MC = Maronite Catholics   **Su M** = Sunni Muslims
Sh M = Shi'a Muslims   **GO** = Greek Orthodox
D = Druzes (religious sect linked to Islam)

The president must be a Maronite Christian and the prime minister a Sunni Muslim

Civil war broke out in 1975. The main cause was the breakdown in the Muslim–Christian consensus over the constitution, which gave Christians a disproportionate political voice. The presence of independent factions, each with its own grievances, added to the complexity of the war. Lebanon was close to fragmentation when the various factions agreed terms for peace in 1989, ending 14 years of civil war and effectively giving the Muslims more power. The elections held in 1992 were the first for 20 years. Under Prime Minister Rafiq Al-Hariri, Lebanon has achieved relative stability. Syria remains the main power-broker in Lebanon.

CLIMATE

WEATHER CHART

Winters are mild and summers hot, with high humidity on the coast. Snow falls on high ground in the winter.

TRANSPORTATION

 Beirut International, Khaldeh   139 ships 428,800 dwt

THE TRANSPORTATION NETWORK

| 3,860 miles (6,200 km) | None |
| 138 miles (222 km) | None |

The redevelopment of Beirut could see it regain its position as one of the Middle East's major entrepôts.

TOURISM

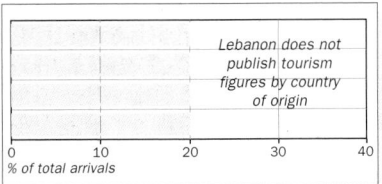 335,000   The number of tourists is rising

MAIN OVERSEAS ARRIVALS

Lebanon does not publish tourism figures by country of origin

% of total arrivals

Once the playground of the Arab world where East met West, Beirut was devastated by the civil war, ruining its profitable tourist industry. Formerly, over two million people a year visited its fine beaches and historical sites.

PEOPLE

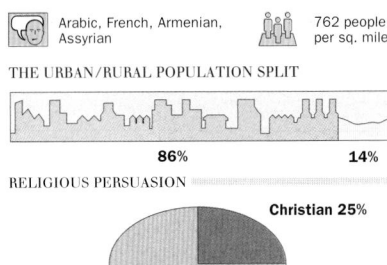

Arabic, French, Armenian, Assyrian   762 people per sq. mile

THE URBAN/RURAL POPULATION SPLIT

86%   14%

RELIGIOUS PERSUASION

Christian 25%

Muslim 75%

The Lebanese population is fragmented religiously into sub-sects of Christians and Muslims, but retains a strong sense of national identity. There has been a large Palestinian refugee population in the country since 1948. Islamic fundamentalism is influential among poorer Shi'a Muslims.

LEBANON

Total Land Area : 10 230 sq. km (3950 sq. miles)

LAND HEIGHT

3000m/9843ft
2000m/6562ft
1000m/3281ft
500m/1640ft
200m/656ft
Sea Level

POPULATION

over 1 000 000
over 100 000
over 10 000
under 10 000

WORLD AFFAIRS

The civil war, hijackings, the Israeli invasion of 1982 and the Western hostage crisis brought Lebanon to the top of the international agenda in the 1980s. A 1989 Arab solution ended internal strife. More intractable is the Arab–Israeli dispute, in which Lebanon closely follows the Syrian line. The Iranian-backed *Hezbollah* militia, aided by Syria, and Israeli forces still frequently clash in southern Lebanon.

AID

 $132m (receipts)   Up 63% in 1993

The government is seeking billions of dollars to rebuild the center of Beirut and restore the shattered infrastructure.

DEFENSE

 $343m   Up 11% in 1995

Under the terms of the Taif Agreement, 40,000 Syrian troops are stationed in Lebanon. Lebanon's own army has 43,000 troops. The south is controlled by the Israeli-backed South Lebanon Army. All the political factions maintain armed militias. A UN force attempts to police the border with Israel.

ECONOMICS

 $2.9bn  1,647–1,596 Lebanese pounds

SCORE CARD

- ❑ World GNP Ranking.......................127th
- ❑ GNP per Capita $2,107
- ❑ Balance of Payments.................$–2,561m
- ❑ Inflation 6.8%
- ❑ Unemployment...................................35%

Strengths

Peace will allow Lebanon to regain its position as an Arab center for banking and services. Potentially a major producer of wine and fruit.

Weaknesses

Dependent on imported oil and gas. Infrastructure – especially in Beirut – wrecked by civil war. Agriculture still at 40% of prewar levels. High public debt and inflation.

EXPORTS

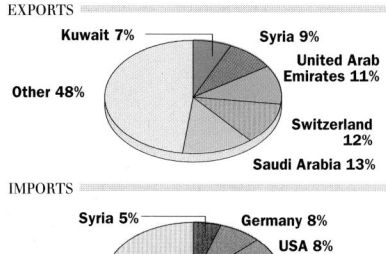

Kuwait 7%
Syria 9%
United Arab Emirates 11%
Other 48%
Switzerland 12%
Saudi Arabia 13%

IMPORTS

Syria 5%
Germany 8%
USA 8%
Other 56%
France 9%
Italy 14%

RESOURCES

 25bn kwh (capacity 603,000 kw)
 456,000 goats, 258,000 sheep, 80,000 cattle

 Not an oil producer; refines 37,500 b/cd
 Lignite, iron ore

Wine, cotton, fruit and vegetables are the main crops. Thermal power stations are fuelled by imported gasoline.

ENVIRONMENT

 0.3%   Initiatives will have to await reconstruction

Rebuilding Beirut's basic infrastructure and ridding the country of mines are the government's priorities.

MEDIA

 The press has greater freedom than in any other country in the Arab world

PUBLISHING AND BROADCAST MEDIA

 There are 40 daily newspapers, including *Al-Anwar*, *An-Nahar*, and its French companion, *L'Orient-Le Jour*

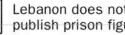 1 state-owned service   1 state-owned, 20 independent stations

Beirut could once again become a center for Arab media. However, in 1994 private TV stations were banned.

CRIME

 Lebanon does not publish prison figures   Crime is sharply down since 1989

The kidnapping of hostages and the breakdown of law during the civil war made Beirut a dangerous city for Western visitors.

Politically motivated violence has recently declined, though the risk of urban terrorism remains. Rural areas untouched by the conflict have low levels of crime.

The Corniche, Beirut, due to be rebuilt by US consultant engineers and architects in a privately financed scheme.

CHRONOLOGY

Lebanon became independent, after 20 years of French mandate, in 1944.

- ❑ **1975** Civil war erupts, stirred by Palestinian guerrillas evacuated from Jordan in 1970.
- ❑ **1982** Israel invades Lebanon.
- ❑ **1989** Taif Agreement brokered. Civil war ends.
- ❑ **1991** Release of most Western hostages secured.
- ❑ **1992** Elections held. Rafiq Al-Hariri appointed prime minister.

EDUCATION

 91% 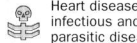 85,495 students

Lebanon has the highest literacy rate in the Arab world. However, education was severely disrupted by the war.

HEALTH

 1 per 670 people Heart diseases, infectious and parasitic diseases

An adequate system of primary health care exists. Hospital staffing is returning to prewar levels.

WEALTH

Minimum wage, 90 Lebanese pounds per month ($0.06)

CONSUMER GOODS OWNERSHIP

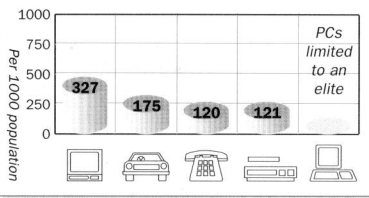

PCs limited to an elite

327 175 120 121

Average income per capita is low. A huge gulf exists between the poor and a small, massively rich elite.

WORLD RANKING

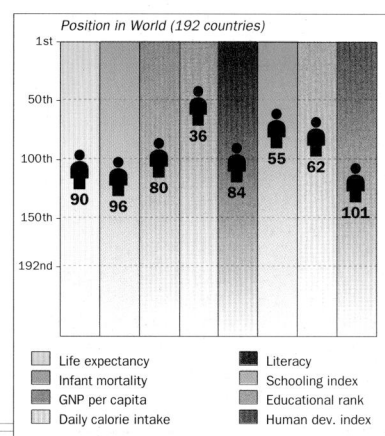

Position in World (192 countries)

90 96 80 36 84 55 62 101

- Life expectancy
- Infant mortality
- GNP per capita
- Daily calorie intake
- Literacy
- Schooling index
- Educational rank
- Human dev. index

L

LESOTHO

OFFICIAL NAME: Kingdom of Lesotho   **CAPITAL:** Maseru
POPULATION: 2.1 million   **CURRENCY:** Loti   **OFFICIAL LANGUAGES:** English and Sesotho

A MOUNTAINOUS AND landlocked country, Lesotho is entirely surrounded by South Africa. It is economically dependent on its larger neighbor, which provides all land transportation links with the outside world. The completion of the Highlands Water Scheme should bring major energy export revenues. Democratic elections in 1993 ended a period of military rule. About 38% of the male labor force are migrant workers in South Africa.

CLIMATE

WEATHER CHART

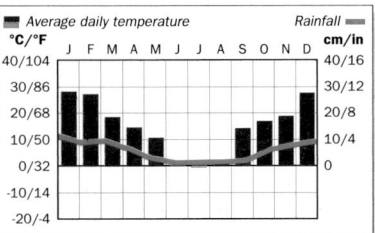

Drought is often followed by torrential rain storms. Snow is frequent in winter in the mountains.

TRANSPORTATION

 **Moshoeshoe Intl, Maseru** 43,000 passengers   Has no fleet

THE TRANSPORTATION NETWORK

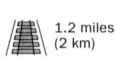 800 miles (500 km)		None
1.2 miles (2 km)		None

Lesotho relies on South African road and rail outlets. New roads have been constructed to service the Highlands Water Scheme.

TOURISM

 78,000 visitors   Down 40% in 1994

MAIN OVERSEAS ARRIVALS

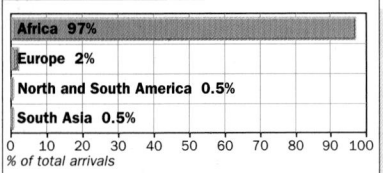

Africa 97%	
Europe 2%	
North and South America 0.5%	
South Asia 0.5%	

% of total arrivals

Tourism, largely based on Lesotho's spectacular mountain scenery, should benefit from South Africa's new political situation. Lakes created by Lesotho's HEP scheme will provide watersports.

PEOPLE

 English, Sesotho, Zulu   10 people per sq. mile

THE URBAN/RURAL POPULATION SPLIT

21%   79%

ETHNIC MAKEUP

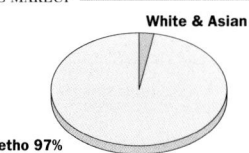

White & Asian 3%
Setho 97%

The overwhelming majority of the population are Basotho, though there are also Europeans and some South Asians and Chinese. Ethnic homogeneity and a strong sense of national identity have tended to minimize ethnic tension. However, South Asian and Chinese storekeepers, whose control of business is resented, came under attack in riots in 1991. The export of male contract labor to South African mines means that women head 72% of households; they also run farming, regarded by Lesotho men as "women's work."

POLITICS

 1993/1998   HM Letsie III

THE STATE OF THE PARTIES

National Assembly 65 members

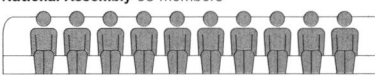

100% BCP

BCP = Basotho Congress Party
Senate 33 members

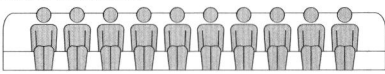

22 members are principal Chiefs and 11 are chosen by the King

The armed forces have been the key political players in Lesotho since 1986, when, following a South African blockade, Chief Jonathan's Basotho National Party (BNP) government was deposed and a military council assumed power. Colonel Elias Ramaema took over as chairman of the military council in a bloodless coup in 1991 and shortly afterwards lifted the prohibition on political parties. Direct military rule ended in 1993, when free and peaceful general elections resulted in a sweeping victory for the BCP. However, a new constitutional clause gives the army precedence over the government in matters of national security, ensuring its continuing influence in politics. Military resentment at the BCP election victory and the integration of former BCP guerrillas into the army provoked serious unrest in 1994, with mutinous troops killing the deputy prime minister.

LESOTHO

Total Land Area : 30 350 sq. km (11 718 sq. miles)

POPULATION

over 100 000 ◎
under 10 000 •

LAND HEIGHT

3000m/9843ft
2000m/6562ft
1000m/3281ft

WORLD AFFAIRS

Foreign policy is dominated by the nature of Lesotho's relationship with South Africa. Lesotho currently has duty-free access for most manufactured goods to the EU and preferential access to US and Scandinavian markets.

AID

 $128m (receipts)   Down 10% in 1993

Aid, over 50% of which comes from the Southern Africa Customs Union (SACU), is crucial to development, and accounts for 26% of Lesotho's GNP. Most is concentrated in land yield projects, with the aim of making Lesotho self-sufficient in food.

DEFENSE

 $28m   Up 56% in 1995

Many in the BCP are questioning the need for a 2,000-strong army, which poses a potential coup threat.

ECONOMICS

 $1.4bn    3.54–3.65 maloti

SCORE CARD

❏ WORLD GNP RANKING	146th
❏ GNP PER CAPITA	$700
❏ BALANCE OF PAYMENTS	$108m
❏ INFLATION	9.5%
❏ UNEMPLOYMENT	35%

STRENGTHS
Membership of Southern African Customs Union. Highlands Water Scheme, which will be a major revenue earner and employer.

WEAKNESSES
Economic over-dependence on South Africa. Weak agricultural sector, although it is the principal occupation. Lack of industrial development.

EXPORTS
Taiwan 4%, Other 13%, SACU 83%

IMPORTS
Hong Kong 3%, Taiwan 4%, Other 10%, SACU 83%

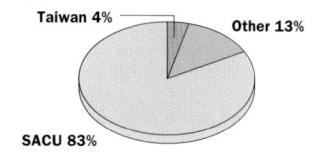

Landscape near Mohales Hoek in Lesotho's lowest lands, which are over 4,265 ft. above sea level. This spiral aloe grows only in Lesotho.

RESOURCES

 Over 90% of energy imported from South Africa   Not an oil producer and has no refineries

1.7m sheep, 1m goats, 663,000 cattle   Diamonds

The hugely ambitious Highlands Water hydroelectric scheme will supply all of Lesotho's energy requirements; it will also supply 16,722 gallons of water per second for South African use. Diamonds are mined in the northeast.

ENVIRONMENT

 0.2%   Government sensitive to environmental questions

Lesotho's land is seriously eroded due to the climate and overgrazing. There is also concern over the effects of the Highlands Water Scheme. The project's pylons are, however, bird-friendly, and there are schemes to protect the Maluti mountain minnow in its reservoirs.

MEDIA

 Censorship has reduced since the previous military regime, under which the editor of the *Mirror* was deported to Kenya

PUBLISHING AND BROADCAST MEDIA

There are no daily newspapers. *Leselinyana la Lesotho* and *Moetetsi oa Basotho* are popular religious periodicals

 1 state-owned service   1 state-owned service

The *Mirror* is the only independent paper in Lesotho. Radio and TV broadcasts are in Sesotho and English.

CRIME

 Lesotho does not publish prison figures   Up 1% in 1992

Crime levels are much lower than in South Africa. Robbery and corruption are problems in urban areas.

EDUCATION

 69%   5359 students

Lesotho has very high school enrollment levels and one of the highest literacy rates in Africa.

CHRONOLOGY

King Moshoeshoe I created a strong kingdom, but sought British help after defeat by the Boers in 1843.

- ❏ 1884 British Crown colony.
- ❏ 1966 Independent kingdom.
- ❏ 1970 Chief Jonathan of BNP annuls elections and bans parties.
- ❏ 1974 BCP, which had in effect won the elections, attempts coup.
- ❏ 1986 Maj.-Gen. Lekhanya leads successful military coup.
- ❏ 1990 King disagrees with military council. Exiled. Son elected king.
- ❏ 1991 Col. Ramaema seizes power.
- ❏ 1993 Free elections – BCP wins.

HEALTH

 1 per 18,600 people   Tuberculosis, parasitic diseases, nutritional disorders

Private health organizations and NGOs are responsible for about half of all health services and are regulated by the Ministry of Health. Although the government operates a flying-doctor service, the highlands are still not adequately covered. The main endemic disease is tuberculosis.

WEALTH

 Welder, 260 maloti ($71) per month; professional nurse, 531 maloti ($145) per month

CONSUMER GOODS OWNERSHIP

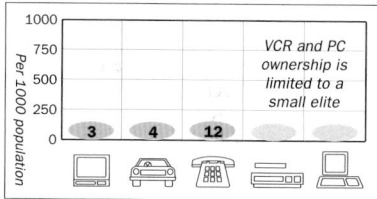
VCR and PC ownership is limited to a small elite
3 4 12

Social mobility is limited in Lesotho; the ruling elite keeps a tight control on power and wealth. Over 90% of the population live below the poverty line.

WORLD RANKING

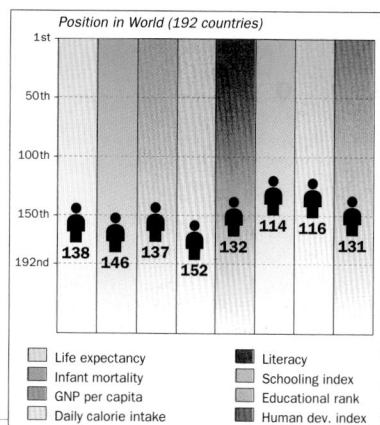
Position in World (192 countries)
138, 146, 137, 152, 132, 114, 116, 131

Life expectancy, Infant mortality, GNP per capita, Daily calorie intake, Literacy, Schooling index, Educational rank, Human dev. index

L

LIBERIA

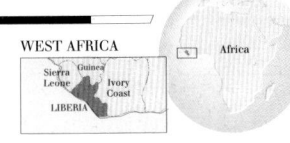

WEST AFRICA

Africa

OFFICIAL NAME: The Republic of Liberia   CAPITAL: Monrovia
POPULATION: 3 million   CURRENCY: Liberian dollar   OFFICIAL LANGUAGE: English

NAMED AFTER PEOPLE LIBERATED from slavery who began returning from the USA in 1816, Liberia is struggling to recover from a civil war which reduced it to a state of anarchy. Facing the Atlantic in equatorial West Africa, most of its coastline is characterized by lagoons and mangrove swamps. Inland, a grassland plateau supports the limited agriculture (just 1% of land is arable). Liberia has the world's largest flag of convenience merchant fleet.

L

CLIMATE

WEATHER CHART

Except in the extreme southeast there is only one rainy season, from May to October. Temperatures are consistently high. During the October to March dry season when the dust-laden *harmattan* wind blows, they rise even higher inland.

TRANSPORTATION

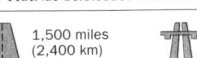 Roberts Field Intl, Monrovia

 1,548 ships 95.9m dwt

THE TRANSPORTATION NETWORK

1,500 miles (2,400 km)		None
304 miles (490 km)		None

Most roads in Liberia are unpaved. The 304-mile railroad was built to transport iron ore and carries little other traffic. Roberts Field airport was built by the USA during World War II.

TOURISM

 No tourists owing to war

 Not applicable

MAIN OVERSEAS ARRIVALS

Liberia does not publish tourism figures by country of origin

Effectively still a war zone, few tourists visited the country before the war, and tourism has now ceased.

PEOPLE

 Kpelle, Vai, Bassa, Kru, Grebo, Kissi, Gola, Loma, English

80 people per sq. mile

THE URBAN/RURAL POPULATION SPLIT

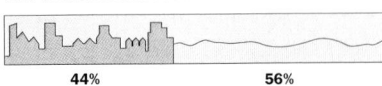

44%   56%

ETHNIC MAKEUP

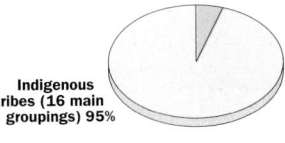

Americo-Liberian 5%

Indigenous tribes (16 main groupings) 95%

A key distinction in Liberia has been between Americo-Liberians, the descendants of those freed from slavery (known as 'civilized persons'), and the majority indigenous 'tribals'. The latter were long held in contempt by the Americos, but intermarriage and political assimilation since 1944 have softened attitudes. Inter-tribal tension is now a more serious problem. Conflict erupted during the 1990 invasion, when Samuel Doe's Krahn tribe exacted retribution from the Gio and Mano groups.

POLITICS

 1985/1996

Wilton Sankawulo

THE STATE OF THE PARTIES

Interim Legislative Assembly

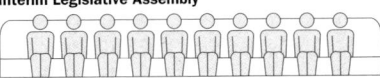

Liberia is in a state of chaos and its unelected parliament controls only the Monrovian region

Liberian politics effectively collapsed in 1990 into a chaotic, bloody and many-sided conflict, where the simple aim was the seizure of the spoils of office. The long period of Americo-Liberian rule had ended in 1980 when army sergeant Samuel Doe seized power. Doe executed the existing government and then succeeded in getting US backing. A series of armed invasions from neighboring states followed, prompting ECOWAS to send a peace-keeping force (ECOMOG) in 1990. ECOMOG turned aside from its role as peacekeeper in 1993 and launched an offensive to capture territory from the most successful of the armed groups, the National Patriotic Front of Liberia (NPFL) led by Charles Taylor. Negotiations finally resulted in 1995 in the signing of a peace agreement by the six main warring factions which provided for a transitional power-sharing government.

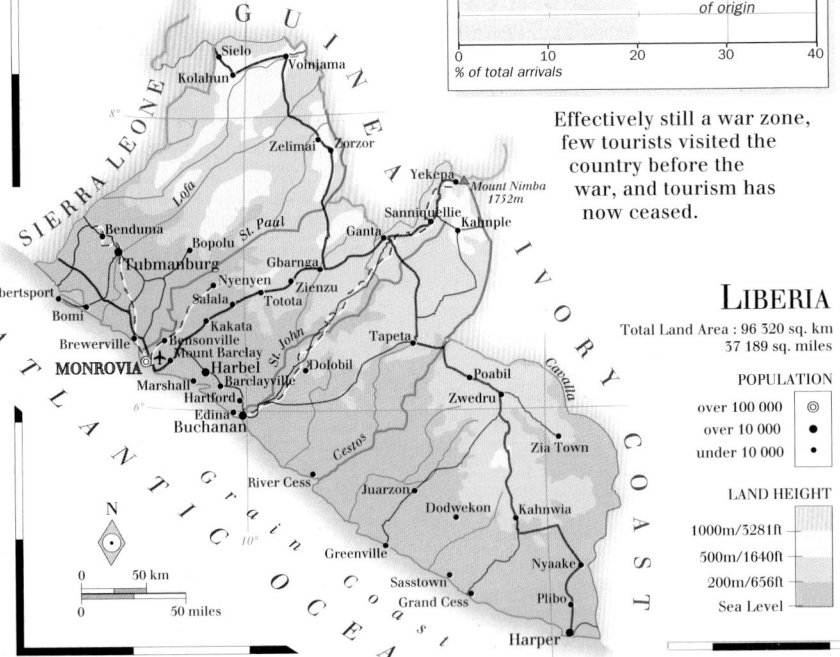

LIBERIA

Total Land Area : 96 320 sq. km
37 189 sq. miles

POPULATION

over 100 000	◎
over 10 000	●
under 10 000	•

LAND HEIGHT

1000m/3281ft	
500m/1640ft	
200m/656ft	
Sea Level	

WORLD AFFAIRS

 ACP Ecowas IAEA NAM  OAU

The USA was the main foreign influence in Liberia until the arrival of ECOMOG (the army formed by Liberia's neighbors in ECOWAS), backed chiefly by Nigeria and Ghana, both of which played key roles in brokering the peace agreement. Burkina, Ivory Coast and Libya were suspected of backing the NPFL. In 1993, the UN refused a request to become involved.

AID

 $121m (receipts)   Up 3% in 1993

International agencies stopped providing aid in 1986. The USA continued giving aid to the Doe regime until 1990, despite his apparent misuse of funds.

DEFENSE

 $37.62m   Up 34% in 1989

The 1995 peace agreement provides for the demobilization of the various warring factions and the formation of a single national army.

ECONOMICS

 $1.2 bn    1.00 Liberian dollar

SCORE CARD

- ❏ WORLD GNP RANKING........................156th
- ❏ GNP PER CAPITA $430
- ❏ BALANCE OF PAYMENTS...................$–145m
- ❏ INFLATION 10%
- ❏ UNEMPLOYMENT....................................43%

STRENGTHS
Very few. Peace could bring revival of operations of the Firestone rubber plantation and LAMCO iron ore mine. Tropical timber, but reserves declining.

WEAKNESSES
Little commercial activity. State of anarchy since 1990 has led to collapse of the economy.

EXPORTS
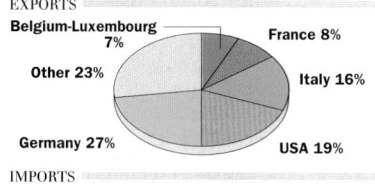
Belgium-Luxembourg 7%, France 8%, Other 23%, Italy 16%, Germany 27%, USA 19%

IMPORTS
UK 5%, Belgium-Luxembourg 6%, Netherlands 5%, Germany 15%, Other 48%, USA 21%

Village near Gbarnga. *The Kpelle, the largest of Liberia's 16 indigenous ethnic groups, are concentrated in this part of Liberia.*

RESOURCES

 460m kwh (capacity 0.33m kw)   Not an oil producer; refines 15,000 b/cd

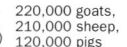 220,000 goats, 210,000 sheep, 120,000 pigs   Iron ore, diamonds, gold, barytes, kyanite, columbite, manganese

Liberia has an estimated one billion tons of iron ore reserves at Mount Nimba. Even when peaceful conditions return, the current state of world demand would not justify exploitation.

ENVIRONMENT

 1%   Civil war made environmental initiatives impossible

The NPFL, and other armed groups, cut down tropical forests to finance their armies.

MEDIA

 Criticism of the government in the press was dangerous from 1980 until the fall of the Doe regime in 1991

PUBLISHING AND BROADCAST MEDIA

 There are 2 daily newspapers, the independent *Daily Observer* and *The News*, published by the government

 1 state-owned service   2 state-owned, 1 independent service

The Monrovia press has been freer since the fall of Doe, but distribution problems in a state of war lessened the impact of newspapers.

CRIME

 Liberia does not publish prison figures   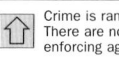 Crime is rampant. There are no enforcing agencies

Human rights have figured little in Liberian life, and since 1990 have disappeared altogether. The warring factions regularly massacred civilians, press-ganged armies and displaced thousands into seeking refuge in neighboring states.

EDUCATION

 39%    5095 students

Originally based on the US model, the education system effectively collapsed during the civil war.

CHRONOLOGY

Between 1816 and 1892, 22,000 people liberated from slavery, most from the USA, resettled in Liberia.

- ❏ **1847** Established as an independent republic.
- ❏ **1926** US Firestone Rubber Company granted 405,000-hectare concession.
- ❏ **1980** Coup. Tolbert assassinated by Master Sergeant Samuel Doe.
- ❏ **1990** Civil war grips whole country
- ❏ **1991** Fall of Doe government.
- ❏ **1995** Peace agreement and installation of power-sharing government.

HEALTH

 1 per 9,350 people   Communicable, diarrheal, parasitic and heart diseases

Only the Americo-Liberian community had ready access to health care before the current state of war. Adequate care is now limited to the military.

WEALTH

 The underclass was composed of rural dwellers, but as a consequence of the war it has encompassed most of the population

CONSUMER GOODS OWNERSHIP

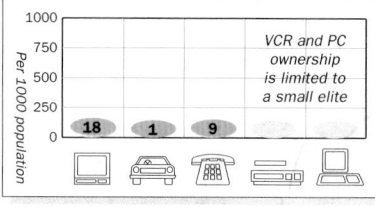
VCR and PC ownership is limited to a small elite 18, 1, 9

Power and wealth have a very direct connection in Liberia. Both the Americo-Liberian regimes, and Doe who replaced them, saw the state as a source of plunder in the form of well-paid jobs and kick-backs from contracts. The warring factions sought similar power.

WORLD RANKING

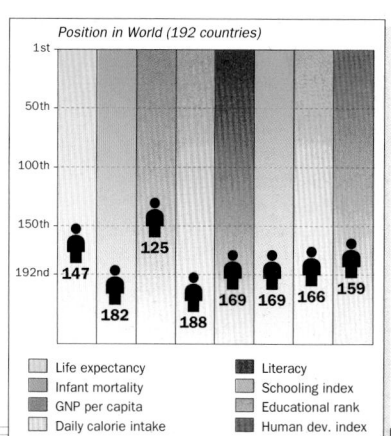
Position in World (192 countries)
147, 182, 125, 188, 169, 169, 166, 159

Life expectancy, Infant mortality, GNP per capita, Daily calorie intake, Literacy, Schooling index, Educational rank, Human dev. index

L

LIBYA

OFFICIAL NAME: The Great Socialist People's Libyan Arab Jamahiriya
CAPITAL: Tripoli **POPULATION:** 5.4 million **CURRENCY:** Libyan dinar **OFFICIAL LANGUAGE:** Arabic

L
IBYA IS SITUATED between Egypt and Algeria on the Mediterranean coast of North Africa, with Chad and Niger on its southern borders. Apart from the coastal strip and the mountains in the south, the country is desert or semi-desert. Libya's strategic position in North Africa and abundant oil and gas resources made it an important trading partner for European nations. However, it has been politically marginalized by the West for its past links with terrorist groups. Libya is also under UN sanctions for refusing to extradite two men suspected of the 1988 Lockerbie bombing.

Roman amphitheatre, Sabrātah. Libya's impressive Classical heritage testifies to its importance in ancient times.

CLIMATE

WEATHER CHART

The coastal region has a warm, temperate climate, with mild, wet winters and hot, dry summers.

TRANSPORTATION

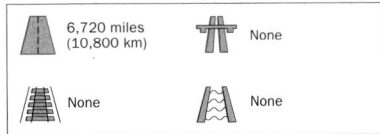

Tripoli International   42 ships 1.21m dwt

THE TRANSPORTATION NETWORK

6,720 miles (10,800 km)	None
None	None

The National Coast Road runs 1,134 miles from the Tunisian to the Egyptian borders linking the principal urban centers. There are no railroads, though some are planned. Owing to UN sanctions on international flights, the major transit point is through Tunisia.

Al Kufrah Oasis. As 90% of Libya is arid rock and sand, oases provide essential agricultural land, besides being tourist attractions.

TOURISM

 62,000 visitors   Down 2% in 1994

Libya possesses a rich Roman and Greek heritage, centered on the ancient Roman coastal towns of Labdah (Leptis Magna) and Sabrātah near Tripoli, and Shaḥḥāt (Cyrene) further east. There are fine beaches at Tripoli, which is also famous for its annual International Fair. However, UN sanctions on air links with Libya have effectively closed the country to Western tourists.

MAIN OVERSEAS ARRIVALS

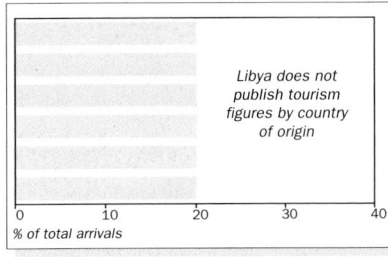

Libya does not publish tourism figures by country of origin

% of total arrivals

PEOPLE

 Arabic, Tuareg   8 people per sq. mile

THE URBAN/RURAL POPULATION SPLIT

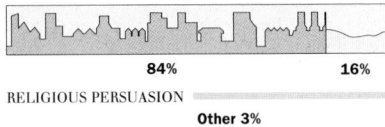

84%   16%

RELIGIOUS PERSUASION

Other 3%

Sunni Muslim 97%

ETHNIC MAKEUP

Other 3%

Berber and Arab 97%

POPULATION AGE BREAKDOWN

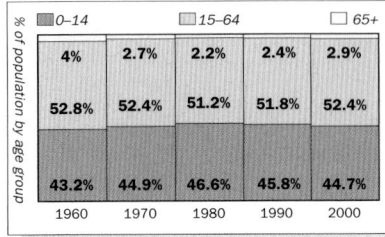

% of population by age group	0–14	15–64	65+
	4%	2.7%	2.2%	2.4%	2.9%
	52.8%	52.4%	51.2%	51.8%	52.4%
	43.2%	44.9%	46.6%	45.8%	44.7%
	1960	1970	1980	1990	2000

Ninety-seven per cent of Libyans are of Arab and Berber origin, split into many tribal groupings. They were artificially brought together when Libya was created in 1951 by the unification of the three historic provinces of Tripolitania, Cyrenaica and the Fazzān. The pro-Western monarchy, which was set up under King Idris, perpetuated the dominance of Cyrenaican tribes and the Sanusi religious order.

The revolution of 1969 brought to the fore Arab nationalist Colonel Gaddafi, who embodied the character and aspirations of the rural Sirtica tribes from Fazzān: fierce independence, deep Islamic convictions, belief in a communal lifestyle and hatred for the urban rich. His revolution wiped out private enterprise and the middle classes, banished European settlers and Jews, undermined the function of the religious Muslim establishment and imposed a form of popular democracy through the *jamahiriya* (state of the masses). However, resentment of the regime increased as it became clear that power now lay mainly with the Sirtica tribes, especially Gaddafi's own clan, the Qadhadhfa.

The years since the revolution have seen Libya change from being largely a nation of nomads and livestock herders to a society where 70% are city-dwellers.

POLITICS

 Not applicable
 Col. Muammar al-Gaddafi

THE STATE OF THE PARTIES

General People's Congress 1112 members

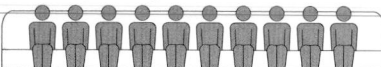

The only authorized political party is the Arab Socialist Union (ASU), from which the members of the Congress are appointed.

Executive power is exercised by the General People's Committee. The General People's Congress elects the head of state, the Revolutionary Leader.

MAIN POLITICAL ISSUES
Repression
Political dissidents, including Islamist militants, have been violently suppressed. Public executions are routine, while the murder of Libyan dissidents abroad, allegedly by government agents, is not unusual. Political parties were banned in 1971 but opposition groups, the Libyan Democratic Movement and the National Front for the Salvation of Libya, are active in Egypt and Sudan.

The regime's public image
In the past few years, the regime has made a deliberate effort to improve its international image. Measures have included freeing some political prisoners, allowing exiles to visit the country and permitting foreign travel.

PROFILE
In 1977, a new form of direct democracy was promulgated, through which some 2000 People's Congresses sought to involve every adult in policy-making. In theory, their wishes are carried out by popular committees. In practice, ultimate control rests with Colonel Gaddafi and his collaborators, many of whom date from the 1969 revolution. Recently some are believed to have been alienated from the regime. These include Gaddafi's deputy, Major Abdessalem Jalloud, who in 1994 was reportedly marginalized after expressing differences with Gaddafi. In 1995, another of Gaddafi's close associates, Khoueldi Hamidi, a defense commander, was also said to have become disillusioned with Gaddafi. Gaddafi is now believed to rely on members of his own tribal clan.

Colonel Gaddafi, *Libya's leader since 1969, rejects all official titles.*

Aby Zayd Omar *Durdah,* Secretary *of the General People's Committee.*

WORLD AFFAIRS

 AL   AMU   NAM   OIC   OPEC

Libya's international standing, already compromised by its ill-concealed support for terrorist groups, was finally undermined by allegations of Libyan complicity in the bombing of a US airliner over Lockerbie, Scotland, in 1988. Libya's refusal to hand over for trial in the West two men suspected of the bombing, resulted in UN sanctions against Libya in 1992. The sanctions, including a ban on air links and arms sales, remain in force. In 1995, Libya applied unsuccessfully for one of the UN Security Council's five non-permanent seats. Relations with the USA and the UK continue to be hostile, while regional states have distanced themselves from Libya's strong opposition to the ongoing Middle East peace process.

L

CHRONOLOGY
Italy occupied Libya and expelled the Turks in 1911. Britain and France agreed to a UN plan for an independent monarchy in 1951.

❑ **1969** King Idris deposed in coup by Revolutionary Command Council led by Colonel Gaddafi. Tripoli Charter sets up revolutionary alliance with Egypt and Sudan.

❑ **1970** UK and US military ordered out. Property belonging to Italians and Jews confiscated. Western oil company assets nationalized – a process completed in 1973.

❑ **1973** Libya forms abortive union with Egypt. Gaddafi launches Cultural Revolution. Libya occupies Aozou Strip in Chad.

❑ **1974** Libya forms union of Libya and Tunisia.

❑ **1977** Official name changed to The Great Socialist People's Libyan Arab *Jamahiriya.*

❑ **1979** Members of Revolution Command Council replaced by elected officials. Gaddafi remains Leader of the Revolution. ⇨

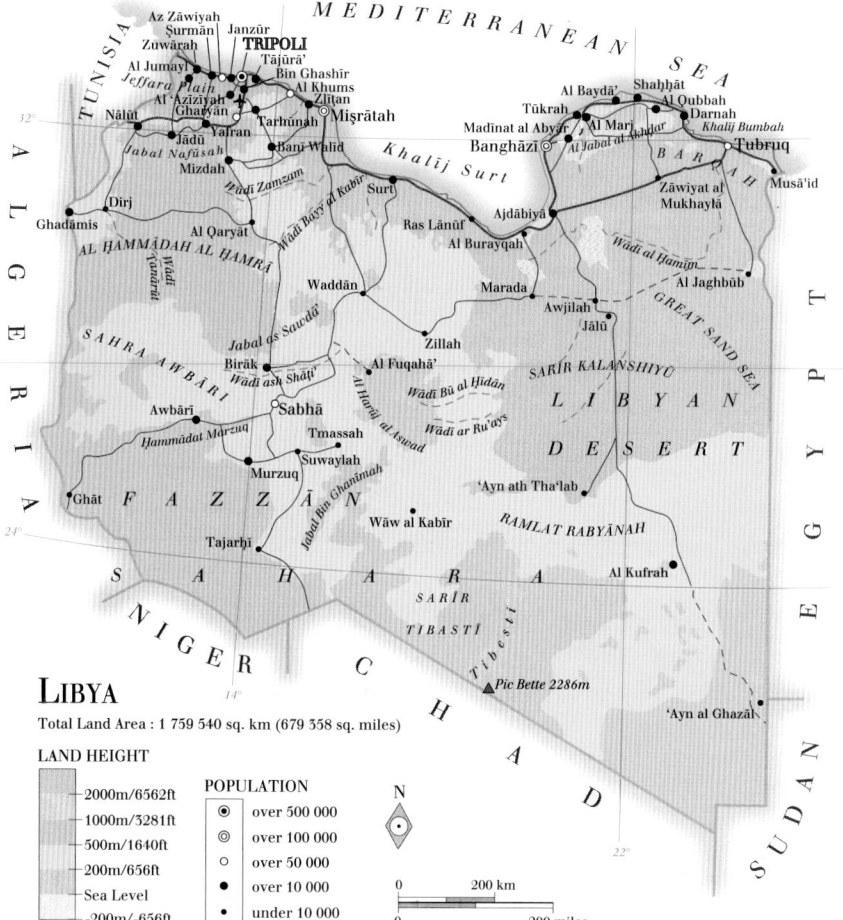

LIBYA

Total Land Area : 1 759 540 sq. km (679 358 sq. miles)

LAND HEIGHT

- 2000m/6562ft
- 1000m/3281ft
- 500m/1640ft
- 200m/656ft
- Sea Level
- -200m/-656ft

POPULATION

- ⊙ over 500 000
- ◎ over 100 000
- ○ over 50 000
- ● over 10 000
- • under 10 000

N

0   200 km

0   200 miles

L

CHRONOLOGY *continued*

❏ **1981** USA shoots down two Libyan aircraft over Gulf of Sirte.

❏ **1984** Gunman at Libyan embassy in London kills British policewoman; UK severs diplomatic relations with Libya. Libya signs Oudja Accord with Morocco for an Arab Africa Federation.

❏ **1985** Libya expels 30,000 foreign workers. Tunisia cuts diplomatic links.

❏ **1986** US aircraft bomb Libya, killing 101 people and destroying Gaddafi's residence.

❏ **1988** Army and police abolished. Pan-Am airliner explodes over Lockerbie, Scotland. Allegations of Libyan complicity.

❏ **1989** Arab Maghreb Union established with Algeria, Morocco, Mauritania and Tunisia. Libya and Chad ceasefire in Aozou Strip.

❏ **1990** Libya expels Palestinian splinter group led by Abu Abbas.

❏ **1991** Opening of first branch of the Great Man-Made River project.

❏ **1992** UN sanctions imposed as Libya fails to hand over Lockerbie suspects.

❏ **1993** Imposition of stricter UN sanctions.

❏ **1994** Religious leaders obtain the right to issue decrees (*fatwas*) for first time since 1969. Return of Aozou strip to Chad.

❏ **1995** US intelligence report claiming Iranian involvement in Lockerbie casts doubts over Libyan complicity in the bombing. Gaddafi expels an estimated 30,000 Palestinians who are ordered to go "home" to Palestine – he later revokes the order.

AID

 $6m (receipts)   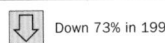 Down 73% in 1993

As an oil exporting nation, Libya fails to qualify for any international aid, despite its being a developing country. During the 1970s, Colonel Gaddafi aided several well-established African liberation movements, such as FROLINAT in Chad, as well as helping dissidents by giving them training in his Pan-African legion. He has also provided finance to the PLO in the Middle East, the IRA in Northern Ireland, the Moros in the southern Philippines, and the Basques in Spain, Corsicans and other ethnic causes in Europe. In 1993, Libya granted aid totaling $27 million despite UN sanctions and a lack of surplus resources.

DEFENSE

 $960m   Down 1% in 1995

0   Defense spending as % GDP   40

3.7%

LIBYAN ARMED FORCES

2210 main battle tanks (1600 T-54/55, 350 T-62, 260 T-72)	50,000 personnel	
4 submarines, 2 frigates and 36 patrol boats	8000 personnel	
417 combat aircraft (6 Tu-22, 40 MiG-23BN, 15 MiG-23U, 58 *Mirage*)	22,000 personnel	
None		

The armed forces suffered a blow in 1987 with the loss of thousands of men and equipment worth $1.4 billion in the Chad Civil War. The cost of Libya's border war with Chad ended in 1994 with the return of the Aozou Strip to Chad. In 1989, the armed forces were replaced by 'the Armed People'. Attempts to depoliticize the army received a setback following confirmation of an abortive military coup in 1993. UN sanctions have resulted in the concentration of military hardware that is outdated. In 1995, Libya was reportedly engaged in the construction of a chemical weapons plant with assistance from German companies.

ECONOMICS

$29.2bn   0.36 Libyan dinars

SCORE CARD

❏ WORLD GNP RANKING.........................159th
❏ GNP PER CAPITA $4755
❏ BALANCE OF PAYMENTS.......................$2.2bn
❏ INFLATION 30%
❏ UNEMPLOYMENT 2%

ECONOMIC PERFORMANCE INDICATOR

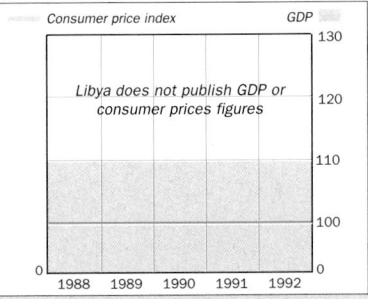

Consumer price index   GDP

Libya does not publish GDP or consumer prices figures

EXPORTS

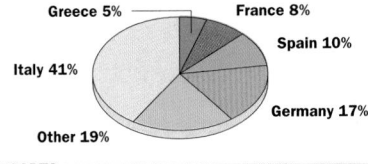

Greece 5%   France 8%
Spain 10%
Italy 41%
Germany 17%
Other 19%

IMPORTS

Turkey 6%   France 6%
UK 8%
Other 45%
Germany 13%
Italy 22%

STRENGTHS
Oil and gas production. High investment in downstream industries – petrochemicals, refineries, fertilizers and aluminum smelting.

WEAKNESSES
Single-resource economy subject to oil-market fluctuations. Most food is imported. Reliance on foreign labor. Lack of water for agriculture. History of international unreliability.

PROFILE
Western oil companies had close business ties with Libya until the imposition of UN sanctions over the Lockerbie affair in April 1992. In 1993, Gaddafi called for the program of privatization, authorized by the General People's Congress in late 1992, to be revived but there have been few

tangible results. An ambitious program of industrialization was launched in the 1970s, concentrating on sectors such as building materials and processed food. Gaddafi's most controversial economic project has been the Great Man-Made River. Started in 1984 and engineered by European and Korean companies, this scheme will bring underground water from the Sahara to the coast.

LIBYA : MAJOR BUSINESSES

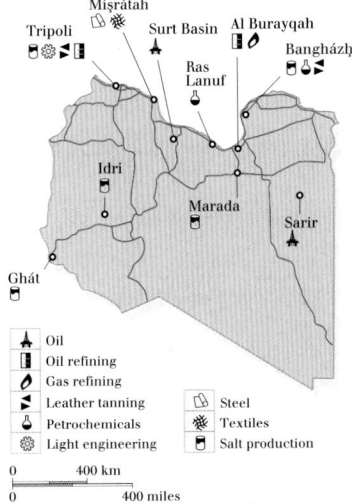

Mişrátah
Tripoli   Surt Basin   Al Burayqah
                                  Bangházĥ
                 Ras Lanuf
Idri
          Marada
                        Sarir
Ghát

⚒ Oil
🛢 Oil refining
⬧ Gas refining
◀ Leather tanning   ◻ Steel
⚙ Petrochemicals   ✳ Textiles
⚙ Light engineering   🛢 Salt production

0   400 km
0   400 miles

RESOURCES

 16bn kwh (capacity 4.1m kw)

 1.4bn b/d (reserves 22,800,000,000 bbl)

 3.5m sheep, 600,000 goats, 120,000 camels

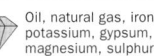 Oil, natural gas, iron, potassium, gypsum, magnesium, sulphur

ELECTRICITY GENERATION

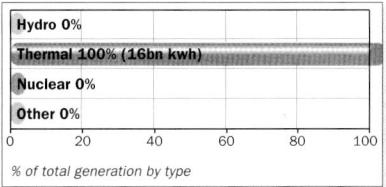

Hydro 0%

Thermal 100% (16bn kwh)

Nuclear 0%

Other 0%

% of total generation by type

With considerable crude oil reserves, Libya is likely to remain an oil exporting country well into the next century. Natural gas potential is more limited but, provided links are developed with other North African states, the future is assured. Libya also has reserves of iron ore, potassium, sulphur, magnesium and gypsum. With the Great Man-Made River project now on stream, the area of irrigated land has been increased, but 90% of Libya is desert. Animal husbandry is the basis of farming, but some cereal crops are grown, as well as dates, olives and citrus fruits. Cement production is sufficient to meet national demand and relies on local raw materials. Most other manufacturing inputs must be imported at considerable cost owing to UN sanctions.

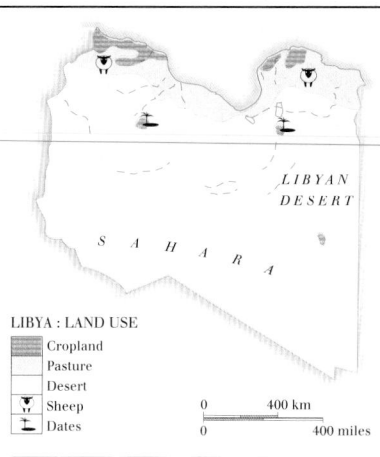

LIBYAN DESERT

SAHARA

LIBYA : LAND USE

- Cropland
- Pasture
- Desert
- Sheep
- Dates

0   400 km

0   400 miles

ENVIRONMENT

 0.1% partially protected

 Tapping desert water may shift rather than solve problems

ENVIRONMENTAL TREATIES

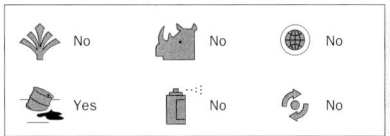

No	No	No
Yes	No	No

The UN Development Program has described Libya as more than 90% "wasteland." Both nature and man have conspired against the environment. Apart from two coastal strips – the Jafara Plain and the Al Jabal al-Akhḍar in Cyrenaica – together with the Fazzān Oasis, most of Libya is desert. Much of the irrigated area is saline because of unwise use of naturally occurring water from artesian wells. Seawater has penetrated the water table as far as 12 miles inland near Tripoli.

MEDIA

 The media are under strict government control

PUBLISHING AND BROADCAST MEDIA

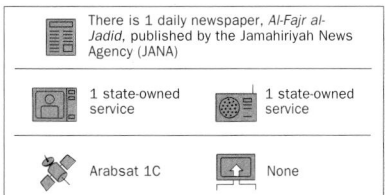

There is 1 daily newspaper, *Al-Fajr al-Jadid*, published by the Jamahiriyah News Agency (JANA)	
1 state-owned service	1 state-owned service
Arabsat 1C	None

Libya's press and TV are a mouthpiece for the leadership. The official news agency has voiced criticism of the wealthy elite for living in closed villas sprouting with satellite dishes. The only daily newspaper is published in Arabic and has a circulation of 40,000 readers. The TV station broadcasts mainly in Arabic, with some programs in Italian, French and English.

CRIME

 Libya does not publish prison figures

 Up 1% in 1992

CRIME RATES

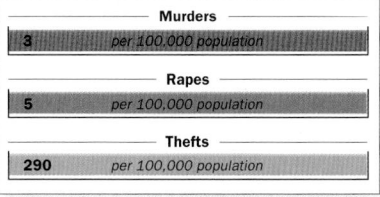

Murders

3   *per 100,000 population*

Rapes

5   *per 100,000 population*

Thefts

290   *per 100,000 population*

Policing is often in the hands of gangs appointed by Gaddafi's lieutenants to root out student protesters and other dissidents. Hit squads allegedly operate abroad against Libyan exiles.

EDUCATION

 64%

 72,899 students

0   *Education spending as % GNP*   25

9.6%

THE EDUCATION SYSTEM

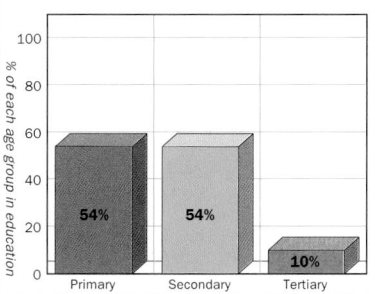

% of each age group in education

Primary	Secondary	Tertiary
54%	54%	10%

Some one million Libyans receive formal education. It is compulsory between the ages of six and 15, but varies in quality and is rudimentary in rural areas. There are universities, in Tripoli, Banghāzī and Sabhā. The literacy rate has improved from 39% in 1970 to 64% today.

HEALTH

 1 per 700 people

Pneumonia, diarrheal diseases, accidents, cancers

0   *Health spending as % GNP*   25

3.2%

An adequate system of primary health care exists except in remote areas. Hospitals lack equipment.

WEALTH

 Most Libyans have benefited little from oil wealth

CONSUMER GOODS OWNERSHIP

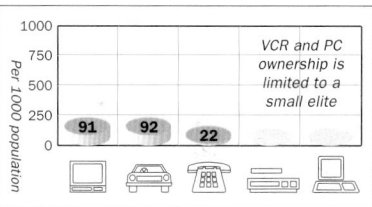

Per 1000 population

VCR and PC ownership is limited to a small elite

91   92   22

There is widespread poverty after years of import constraints. UN sanctions have worsened the situation. In 1994, Gaddafi promised to distribute oil earnings to low-income families.

WORLD RANKING

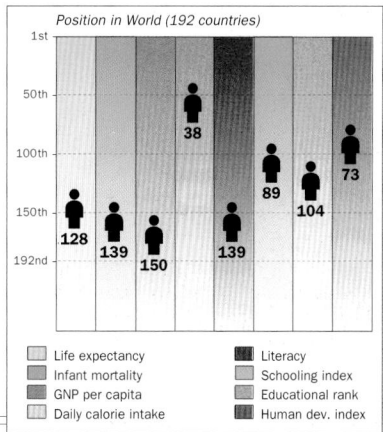

Position in World (192 countries)

1st

50th

100th

150th

192nd

38

89

104

73

128

139

150

139

- Life expectancy
- Infant mortality
- GNP per capita
- Daily calorie intake
- Literacy
- Schooling index
- Educational rank
- Human dev. index

L

LIECHTENSTEIN

OFFICIAL NAME: Principality of Liechtenstein **CAPITAL:** Vaduz
POPULATION: 30,630 **CURRENCY:** Swiss franc **OFFICIAL LANGUAGE:** German

PERCHED IN THE ALPS between Switzerland and Austria, Liechtenstein is rare among small states in having both a thriving banking sector and a well-diversified manufacturing economy. It is closely allied to Switzerland, which handles its foreign relations and defense. Life in Liechtenstein is stable and conservative. Its banking secrecy laws and low taxes make it home to many overseas trusts, banks and investment companies.

CLIMATE

WEATHER CHART

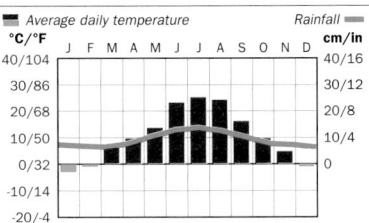

Climate varies with altitude. Excellent skiing conditions are the result of heavy settling snow from December to March. Summers are warm and dry.

TRANSPORTATION

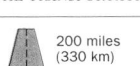 None   Has no fleet

THE TRANSPORTATION NETWORK

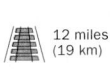

200 miles (330 km)	None
12 miles (19 km)	None

Public transportation in Liechtenstein is mostly by the postal bus network. The single-track railroad has few stops. Zurich, a two-hour drive away, is the nearest airport.

TOURISM

62,000 visitors    Down 5% in 1994

MAIN OVERSEAS ARRIVALS

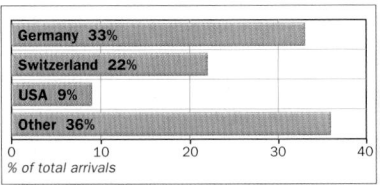

Germany 33%	
Switzerland 22%	
USA 9%	
Other 36%	

% of total arrivals

Liechtenstein's alpine scenery attracts skiers in the winter, and climbers and hikers in the summer.

PEOPLE

 German, Alemannish dialect, Italian   495 people per sq. mile

THE URBAN/RURAL POPULATION SPLIT

87%   **13%**

RELIGIOUS PERSUASION

Other 5%   Protestant 8%
Roman Catholic 87%

Liechtenstein's role as a financial center accounts for the many foreign residents (over 35% of the population), of whom half are Swiss and the rest mostly German. The high standard of living results in few ethnic or social tensions. Family life is highly traditional; women received the vote only in 1984, after much controversy. A proposal the following year that equal rights for women be enshrined in the constitution was rejected in a referendum by a large majority.

POLITICS

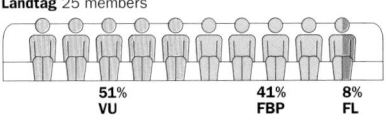 1993/1997   Prince Hans-Adam II

THE STATE OF THE PARTIES

Landtag 25 members

51% VU	41% FBP	8% FL

VU = Patriotic Party **FBP =** Progressive Citizens' Party
FL = Free List

Historically, the VU and the FBP have alternated as coalition leaders. However, the VU has been the leading party since 1978, except for a few brief months in 1993. An increasing use has been made of referenda to decide policy issues, such as the 1992 proposal to reduce the voting age from 20 to 18, rejected by 56% of voters.

WORLD AFFAIRS

CE	EEA	EFTA	OSCE	WTO

Liechtenstein effectively gave up control of its external relations when it signed the 1924 Customs Union Treaty with Switzerland. This requires Swiss approval for any treaty arrangements between Liechtenstein and a third state. The country became a member of the UN only in 1990. It joined EFTA in 1991, and has been a participant in the EEA since 1995. However, Switzerland's rejection of EU membership in a 1992 referendum effectively ended any prospect of Liechtenstein joining the EU within the foreseeable future.

AID

 Donor, but does not publish figures   Not applicable

Although overseas aid donations are small and aid issues have little political importance, Liechtenstein has helped to fund shelter and reconstruction projects in former Yugoslavia and local development projects in Bulgaria.

LIECHTENSTEIN

Total Land Area : 160 sq. km (62 sq. miles)

POPULATION
under 10 000 •

LAND HEIGHT
2000m/6562ft
1500m/4921ft
1000m/3281ft
500m/1640ft
400m/1312ft

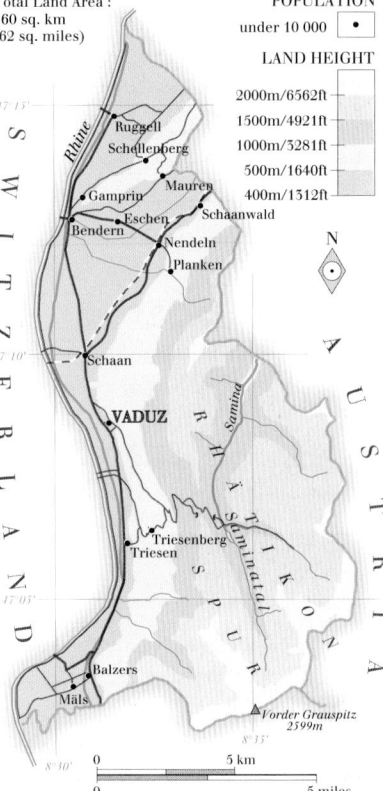

Alpine scenery near Vaduz. The state budget includes 2% allocated to restoring mountain vegetation and coordinating land use.

DEFENSE

 Police force of 56 men and 22 auxiliaries

 Not applicable

There has been no standing army since 1868 and there is only a small police force. *De facto* protection is provided by Switzerland. In theory, any male under 60 is liable for military service during a national emergency, although this law has never been invoked.

ECONOMICS

 $900m (est)

 1.15–1.31 Swiss francs

SCORE CARD

- ❏ World GNP Ranking........................165th
- ❏ GNP per Capita $31,000
- ❏ Balance of Payments.....Included in Swiss total
- ❏ Inflation 5.4%
- ❏ Unemployment................................1.5%

STRENGTHS

Stability and customs union with Switzerland make Liechtenstein a favored tax haven; its lack of EU membership makes the banking sector less vulnerable to future changes in EU banking laws. The economy is well diversified; chemicals, furniture and the manufacture of ceramic dentures and precision instruments are all thriving sectors.

WEAKNESSES

Very few. Liechtenstein might suffer if the EU restricts imports from EFTA countries in future.

EXPORTS

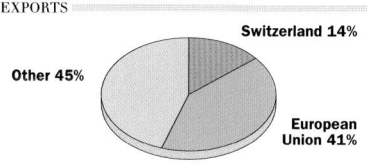

Switzerland 14%

Other 45%

European Union 41%

IMPORTS

With a limited domestic market, Liechtenstein's industry is export-oriented. Liechtenstein has a customs union with Switzerland and does not publish separate import figures.

RESOURCES

 94% of energy requirements imported

 Not an oil producer and has no refineries

 6,000 cattle, 3,000 pigs, 3,000 sheep

None

Liechtenstein has to import most of its energy. Almost all of its electricity comes from German power stations.

ENVIRONMENT

 38% partially protected

 Greens won two seats in parliament in 1993

Protection of Liechtenstein's alpine scenery is high enough on the political agenda for one of the five councillors, or ministers, to have responsibility for the environment. As in Switzerland, the greatest worry is the effect of through traffic and high rates of car ownership. However, the 1988 experiment in providing free public bus transportation proved a failure, as Liechtensteiners remained firmly wedded to their cars.

MEDIA

 No restrictions

PUBLISHING AND BROADCAST MEDIA

There are 2 daily newspapers, *Liechtensteiner Vaterland* and *Liechtensteiner Volksblatt*

No TV service

1 radio service

The two newspapers, although free of formal state control, are both run by political parties: the *Vaterland* by the VU; the *Volksblatt* by the FBP. Both have circulations of about 8,000.

CRIME

 Liechtenstein does not publish prison figures

 Crime does not pose any great problems

Crime is a minor problem, a result of the relatively even distribution of wealth and high average living standard. Liechtenstein has also taken great care to protect its tax-haven status by careful regulation of its financial sector. There have been no major scandals, such as the BCCI collapse which tainted the reputation of its main competitor, Luxembourg.

EDUCATION

 100%

Not available

Education, modeled on the German system, includes two types of school at secondary level – the grammar-style *Gymnasium* and the *Realschule*. Liechtenstein has no university; students go on to colleges in Austria, Switzerland and Germany, and to business schools in the USA.

HEALTH

 1 per 948 people

 Heart and respiratory diseases, cancers

Although clinics and hospitals are few, the health system provides advanced care. Many Liechtensteiners have private health insurance arrangements, which also give them access to Swiss medical expertise. Rabies remains a significant problem.

WEALTH

 Experienced carpenter, 4,700 Swiss francs ($4,084) per month; elementary school teacher, 4,800–7,490 Swiss francs ($4,171–$6,509) per month

CONSUMER GOODS OWNERSHIP

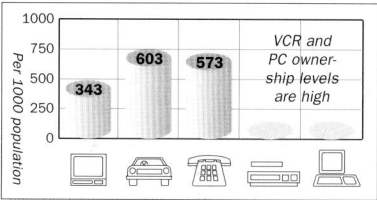

VCR and PC ownership levels are high

343   603   573

Per 1000 population

Most Liechtensteiners have a high standard of living, similar to that of the Swiss. Unlike other tax havens, such as Monaco, it does not attract the jet-set rich and private deposit accounts are not a key part of its banking business. The state welfare system is generous.

WORLD RANKING

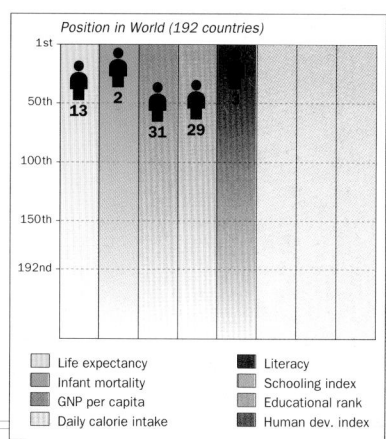

Position in World (192 countries)

13   2   31   29

- Life expectancy
- Infant mortality
- GNP per capita
- Daily calorie intake
- Literacy
- Schooling index
- Educational rank
- Human dev. index

 L

LITHUANIA

OFFICIAL NAME: Republic of Lithuania   CAPITAL: Vilnius
POPULATION: 3.7 million   CURRENCY: Litas   OFFICIAL LANGUAGE: Lithuanian

LYING ON THE EASTERN COAST of the Baltic Sea, Lithuania is bordered by Latvia, Belorussia, Poland and the Kaliningrad area of the Russian Federation. Its terrain is mostly flat with many lakes, moors and bogs. Now a multiparty democracy, Lithuania achieved independence from the former USSR in 1991. Industrial production and agriculture are the mainstays of the economy. Russia finally withdrew all its troops from Lithuania in 1993.

CLIMATE

WEATHER CHART

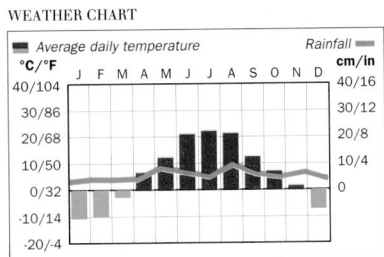

Lithuania's coastal position moderates an otherwise continental-type climate. Summers are cool.

TRANSPORTATION

 Vilnius Intl

 69 ships
467,800 dwt

THE TRANSPORTATION NETWORK

| 26,230 miles (42,210 km) | None |
| 1,885 miles (3,033 km) | River Neman |

Lithuania has an efficient rail service. Plans exist to upgrade the Soviet-built road network and port facilities.

TOURISM

 222,000   Up 217% in 1994

MAIN OVERSEAS ARRIVALS

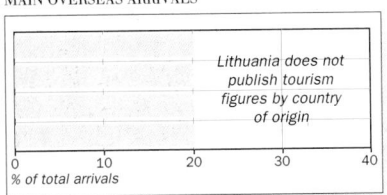

Lithuania does not publish tourism figures by country of origin

Tourism has expanded rapidly in recent years. Vilnius is well preserved: its historic center survived German and Russian occupation. Trakai, the capital of the Grand Duchy in the 16th century, is also popular.

PEOPLE

 Lithuanian, Russian

 148 people per sq. mile

THE URBAN/RURAL POPULATION SPLIT

70%   30%

ETHNIC MAKEUP

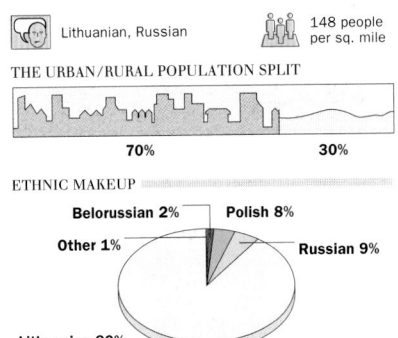

Belorussian 2%   Polish 8%
Other 1%
Russian 9%
Lithuanian 80%

The population is made up of an 80% majority of Lithuanians, together with small groups of Russians, Poles and Belorussians. Citizenship is not a political issue in Lithuania as it is in the other Baltic states. Ethnic relations are relatively good and inter-ethnic marriages are fairly common. Lithuania is strongly Catholic, in contrast to Protestant Latvia and Estonia. Divorce rates are high.

POLITICS

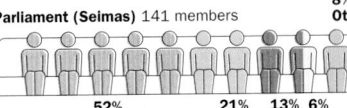

1992/1996

President Algirdas Brazauskas

THE STATE OF THE PARTIES

Parliament (Seimas) 141 members

8% Other

52% LDLP   21% SP   13% CDP   6% SDP

LDLP = Lithuanian Democratic Labour Party   **SP** = Sajudis Party   **CDP** = Christian Democratic Party   **SDP** = Social Democratic Party   **Other** = Union of Lithuanian Political Prisoners and Refugees, Lithuanian Democratic Party

The 1992 election saw a return to the pre-independence leadership, with the victory of the ex-communist LDLP and the election as president of Algirdas Brazauskas in 1993. Brazauska's non nationalist background won him support from the non-Lithuanain community. This marked the end of rule by the SP, under Vytautas Landsbergis, which had held office at independence in 1991. However, the LDLP has pursued free-market and privatization policies. In 1996 Adolfas Slezevicius was forced to resign as prime minister as a result of his role in a major banking crisis.

Lithuania is the most politically stable of the Baltic republics. In 1993, Russian troops left its territory, reducing fears of intervention from Moscow. However, the banking crisis of 1995–1996, and the conduct of the prime minister who withdrew his savings before the suspension of banking operations, caused the worst political crisis in the country's post-independence history.

LITHUANIA

Total Land Area :
65 200 sq. km
(25 174 sq. miles)

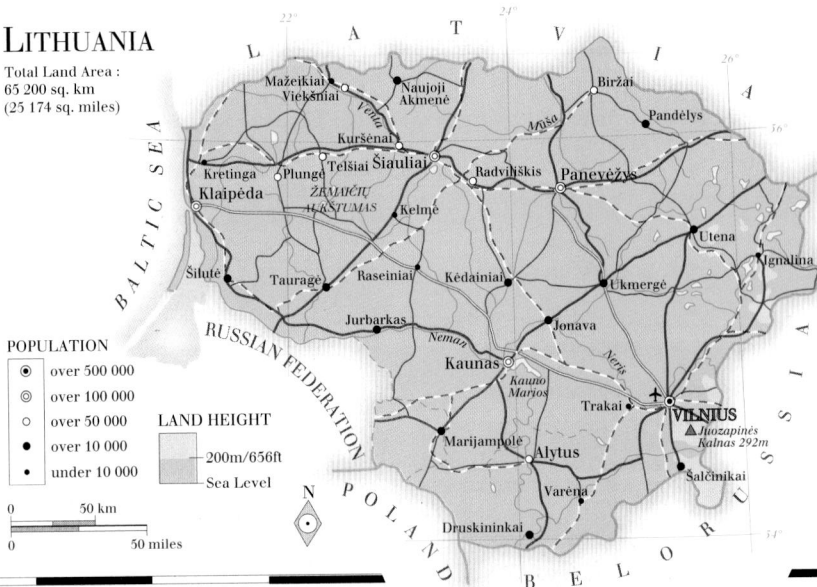

POPULATION
⊙ over 500 000
◎ over 100 000
○ over 50 000
● over 10 000
• under 10 000

LAND HEIGHT
200m/656ft
Sea Level

0   50 km
0   50 miles

WORLD AFFAIRS

CE | CBS | NACC | OSCE | WEU

In 1993, Russia withdrew its troops from Lithuanian soil. Lithuania signed an association agreement with the EU in June 1995 and applied for membership in December 1995.

AID

 Lithuania does not publish aid receipts   Probably rising

Aid, mostly from the IMF and EU, is used for infrastructure projects and to promote private enterprise.

DEFENSE

 $116m   Up 23% in 1995

Lithuania's security is in the hands of its army and a National Guard formed to patrol its frontiers. However, it would be unable to defend itself against Russian attack. Most of the Russian troops who left in 1993 were relocated in neighboring Kaliningrad.

ECONOMICS

 $5bn  3.99–4.00 litas

SCORE CARD

- ❑ WORLD GNP RANKING........................100th
- ❑ GNP PER CAPITA $1,350
- ❑ BALANCE OF PAYMENTS......................$–91m
- ❑ INFLATION 36.1%
- ❑ UNEMPLOYMENT..................................1.6%

STRENGTHS

Occasional agricultural surpluses. Some exports of peat, amber, linen and light industrial goods.

WEAKNESSES

Poor raw material base. Need to import oil, natural gas and industrial products from Russia. Uncompetitive, outdated industry. Difficulty in attracting significant foreign investment. The weakest Baltic state economically.

EXPORTS

IMPORTS

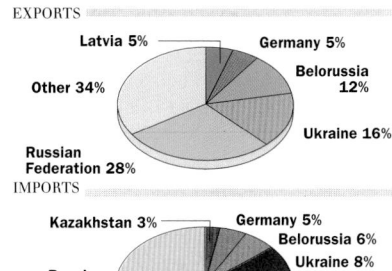

One of Lithuania's 3,000 lakes. The entire country is low-lying. Its coast, fringed by sand dunes and pine forests, is famous for amber.

RESOURCES

 18.7bn kwh   119,852 tons

1.7m cattle, 1.2m pigs, 78,000 horses Sand, gravel, clay, limestone, gypsum

Lithuania has no strategic resources. Nuclear power is a major source of energy. Most of the country's oil still comes from Russia, as the supply infrastructure is in place. However, Lithuania is seeking other suppliers.

ENVIRONMENT

 10%   Pollution in Baltic Sea

The Ignalina nuclear plant, which came on stream in the mid-1980s, has experienced leakage problems. Water and air pollution levels are high. Lithuania's Baltic coast has been polluted by oil spillages.

MEDIA

 No restrictions on political reporting

PUBLISHING AND BROADCAST MEDIA

 There are several daily newspapers, including *Lietuvos Rytas* and *Respublika*

 1 state-owned service  1 state-owned service

The mainstream media, Russian under communism, now publish and broadcast mainly in Lithuanian.

CRIME

 Lithuania does not publish prison figures  Crime levels are rising slightly

Levels of crime are low compared to other parts of the former USSR. Robbery is a growing problem.

EDUCATION

  98% 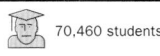 70,460 students

Teaching at all levels is in Lithuanian, making access to higher education harder for minorities; 8% of the population are graduates.

HEALTH

 1 per 230 people   Heart diseases, cancers, accidents, tuberculosis

Reforms to Lithuania's health system began in 1990 and include the legalization of private medicine.

WEALTH

 Traders in Vilnius are the wealthiest group

CONSUMER GOODS OWNERSHIP

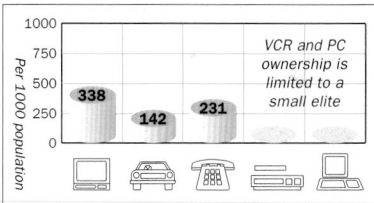

Western cars and designer goods are popular status symbols among an increasingly prosperous elite.

WORLD RANKING

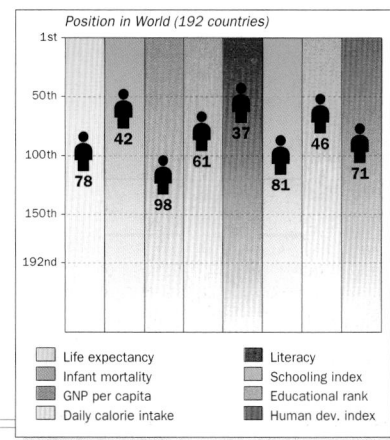

L

LUXEMBOURG

OFFICIAL NAME: Grand Duchy of Luxembourg **CAPITAL:** Luxembourg
POPULATION: 400,000 **CURRENCY:** Luxembourg franc **OFFICIAL LANGUAGE:** Letzeburgish

L UXEMBOURG SHARES BORDERS with the industrial regions of Germany, France and Belgium and has the highest per capita income in the EU. Making up part of the plateau of the Ardennes, its countryside is undulating and forested. Its prosperity was once based on steel; before World War II it produced more per capita than the USA. Today, it is known as a tax haven and banking center, and as the headquarters of key EU institutions.

CLIMATE

WEATHER CHART

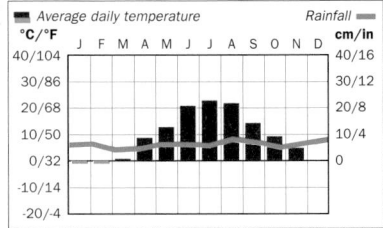

The south, where vines grow, is the warmest area. Winter is cold and snowy, especially in the Ardennes.

TRANSPORTATION

 **Findel, Luxembourg-Ville** 932,000 passengers 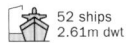 52 ships 2.61m dwt

THE TRANSPORTATION NETWORK

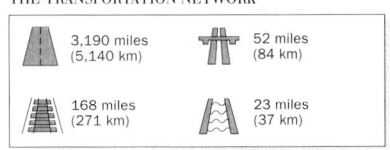

3,190 miles (5,140 km)	52 miles (84 km)
168 miles (271 km)	23 miles (37 km)

There is an excellent road network, though congestion is a problem. Rail and bus services are integrated.

TOURISM

 799,000 visitors Down 4% in 1994

MAIN OVERSEAS ARRIVALS

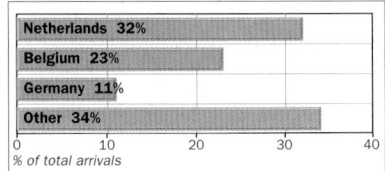

Netherlands	32%
Belgium	23%
Germany	11%
Other	34%

% of total arrivals

The mountains and forests, and 76 castles, many recently re-roofed, are the main attractions. The government has begun an initiative to teach foreign hotel workers the history, language and culture of the Duchy.

PEOPLE

 Letzeburgish, German, French 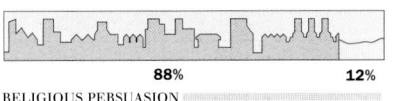 403 people per sq. mile

THE URBAN/RURAL POPULATION SPLIT

88% **12%**

RELIGIOUS PERSUASION

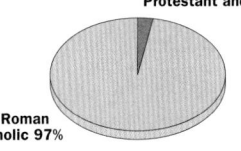

Protestant and Jewish 3%

Roman Catholic 97%

Nearly a third of Luxembourg's residents and half of its workers are foreigners. Integration has been straightforward; most are fellow western Europeans and Catholics, mainly from Italy and Portugal. Life in Luxembourg is comfortable. Salaries are high, unemployment very low and social tensions few.

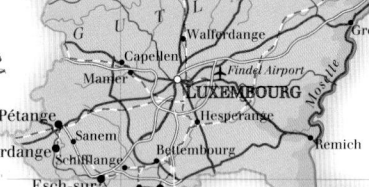

POLITICS

 1994/1999 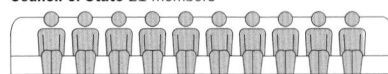 HRH Grand Duke Jean d'Aviano

THE STATE OF THE PARTIES

Council of State 21 members

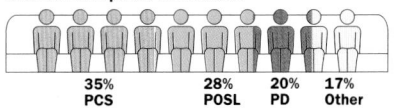

The members of the Council of State are appointed for life by the Grand Duke

Chamber of Deputies 60 members

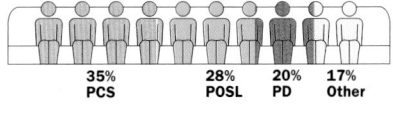

| **35%** PCS | **28%** POSL | **20%** PD | **17%** Other |

PCS = Christian Social Party **POSL** = Luxembourg Socialist Workers' Party **PD** = Democratic Party **Other** = Action Committee for Democracy and Justice, Green Alternative Party

Luxembourg's politics has achieved remarkable consensus, and is characterized by coalitions and long-serving prime ministers. The main political issues are now economic – raising taxes and trimming spending to cope with the economic slow-down.

WORLD AFFAIRS

 Benelux EU NATO OECD OSCE

Luxembourg has long been the keenest member of the EU. It was during its EU presidency that the Maastricht agreement for closer European union was brokered; Luxembourg was not only the first member state to meet all the economic, financial and legal requirements of union under Maastricht, but it also did so a year early. This commitment to the EU reflects the tremendous benefits Luxembourg has gained from membership. It is home to both the Secretariat of the European Parliament and the Court of Justice, and its citizens enjoy the high, tax-free salaries that work in these organizations brings. In 1995, Prime Minister Jacques Santer left office to become President of the European Commission.

LUXEMBOURG

Total Land Area : 2585 sq. km (998 sq. miles)

| 0 | 10 km |
| 0 | 10 miles |

LAND HEIGHT

500m/1640ft
200m/656ft
Sea Level

POPULATION

○ over 50 000
● over 10 000
● under 10 000

Charlotte Bridge, Luxembourg.
The modern road system provides excellent communications with the rest of Europe.

AID

 $50m (donations)   Down 39% in 1993

Luxembourg's aid donations, equal to only 0.35% of GNP, are largely directed towards sub-Saharan Africa.

DEFENSE

 $114m   Up 3% in 1995

Luxembourg's army numbers 800 full-time soldiers. Spending is 1.2% of GDP and has risen slightly in recent years.

ECONOMICS

 $16bn    31.83–29.43 Luxembourg francs

SCORE CARD

❏ WORLD GNP RANKING	67th
❏ GNP PER CAPITA	$39,850
❏ BALANCE OF PAYMENTS	Included in Belgian total
❏ INFLATION	1.8%
❏ UNEMPLOYMENT	2.7%

STRENGTHS

Site of EU institutions. Banking secrecy and expertise make the capital home to over 980 investment funds and 192 banks – more than in any other city in the world.

WEAKNESSES

International service industries account for 65% of GNP, making Luxembourg vulnerable to changing conditions overseas. Downturn in steel market.

EXPORTS

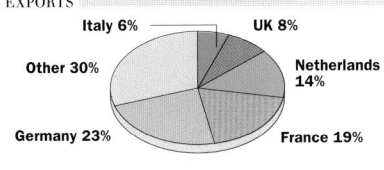

Italy 6%   UK 8%
Other 30%   Netherlands 14%
Germany 23%   France 19%

IMPORTS

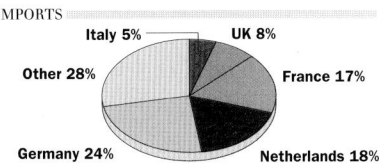

Italy 5%   UK 8%
Other 28%   France 17%
Germany 24%   Netherlands 18%

RESOURCES

 1.2bn kwh (capacity 1.24m kw)   Not an oil producer and has no refineries

 Cattle, deer, wild boar, sheep   Iron

Luxembourg can meet few of its own energy needs; it produces only a small amount of hydroelectricity. The steel industry accounts for 10% of GDP.

ENVIRONMENT

 None   One of few nations active in transfrontier pollution control

Acid rain from European industry has affected about 19% of Luxembourg's trees and, in the worst cases, 30% of trees in mature stands. The Duchy is a member of an international committee on decreasing pollution of the Rhine.

MEDIA

 Freedom of expression is guaranteed by law

PUBLISHING AND BROADCAST MEDIA

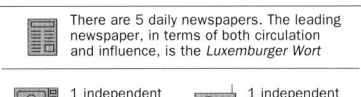

There are 5 daily newspapers. The leading newspaper, in terms of both circulation and influence, is the *Luxemburger Wort*

1 independent service   1 independent service

Broadcasting is dominated by RTL (*Radio-Television Luxembourg*), one of the largest media groups in Europe, which exports programs in a variety of languages.

CRIME

 352 prisoners   Up 4% in 1992

Luxembourg's stringent banking secrecy rules can provide a cover for both tax evasion and – as in the case of the collapsed BCCI bank, which was registered in Luxembourg – fraud.

EDUCATION

 99%   759 students

Teaching is mainly in German at elementary and French at secondary level. Higher education is limited and many students go on to universities in other European countries. Training given by Luxembourg banks is reputed to be the best in Europe.

HEALTH

1 per 476 people   Heart and cerebrovascular diseases, cancers

There are no private commercial hospitals in Luxembourg; they are run either by the state or by nuns. The fees paid by patients are refunded from the *Caisse de Maladie* (state sickness fund).

CHRONOLOGY

Throughout its history, Luxembourg has been ruled by a succession of neighboring European powers.

- ❏ **1890** Separates from Netherlands.
- ❏ **1921** Economic union with Belgium. End of German ties.
- ❏ **1940–1944** Occupation by German forces.
- ❏ **1948** Benelux treaty creating a customs union comes into effect.
- ❏ **1960** Economic Union Treaty, signed by Benelux countries, removes internal frontiers.
- ❏ **1991** Luxembourg first country to ratify Maastricht Treaty.
- ❏ **1995** Prime Minister Jacques Santer becomes President of the European Commission.

WEALTH

 Junior salesperson, 10,000 Luxembourg francs ($340) per month; sales representative, 500,000 Luxembourg francs ($16,989) per month

CONSUMER GOODS OWNERSHIP

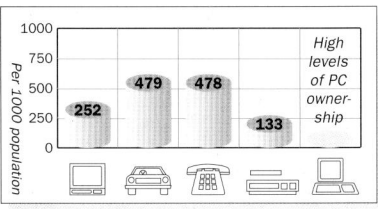

With the highest per capita income in the EU, Luxembourgers enjoy a comfortable lifestyle. In recent years, the government has been able to hand back 5% of GDP in tax relief, while simultaneously increasing public spending. Very low unemployment has led to the influx of a large number of foreign workers, mainly from other EU countries such as Portugal and Italy, to take less well-paid jobs. Financing the aging population is likely to be a burden in the future.

WORLD RANKING

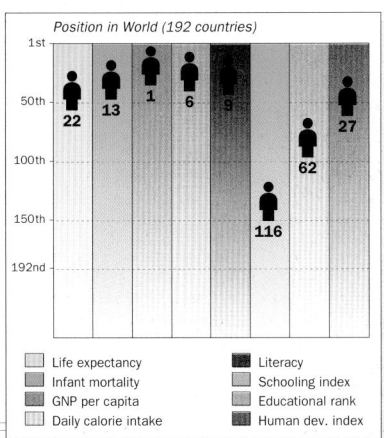

L

MACEDONIA

OFFICIAL NAME: Former Yugoslav Republic of Macedonia   **CAPITAL:** Skopje
POPULATION: 2.2 million   **CURRENCY:** Macedonian denar   **OFFICIAL LANGUAGE:** None

 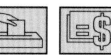   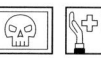

THE FORMER YUGOSLAV REPUBLIC of Macedonia (FYRM) is landlocked in southeastern Europe. The lifting of the economic blockade of Serbia and Montenegro in 1996 was a boost to the flagging FYRM economy. Despite the signing of an accord in 1995, Greece remains hostile to the FYRM because it suspects that the country may try to absorb a province in northern Greece – also called Macedonia – in a "Greater Macedonia."

*A **fisherman's hut** on Lake Dojran, which lies on the border with Greece in southeastern Macedonia and is shared by the two countries.*

M

CLIMATE

WEATHER CHART

(Average daily temperature / Rainfall)
°C/°F — cm/in
40/104 — 40/16
30/86 — 30/12
20/68 — 20/8
10/50 — 10/4
0/32 — 0
-10/14
-20/-4
J F M A M J J A S O N D

The FYRM has a continental climate, with dry autumns and wet springs. Winter snow supports skiing.

TRANSPORTATION

 Skopje Intl    Has no fleet

THE TRANSPORTATION NETWORK

| 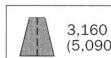 3,160 miles (5,090 km) | None |
| 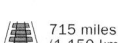 715 miles (1,150 km) | None |

Germany has suspended the Munich–Athens rail link, the last service linking Skopje to western Europe.

TOURISM

 185,000 visitors   Up 53% in 1994

MAIN OVERSEAS ARRIVALS

The FYRM does not publish tourism figures by country of origin

0   10   20   30   40
% of total arrivals

Tourism is a traditionally important income source. Lake resorts and skiing in the Śara mountains are among the attractions. However, regional political problems have reduced the number of tourists going to the FYRM.

PEOPLE

 Macedonian, Serbian, Croatian   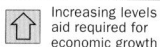 223 people per sq. mile

THE URBAN/RURAL POPULATION SPLIT
59%   41%

ETHNIC MAKEUP

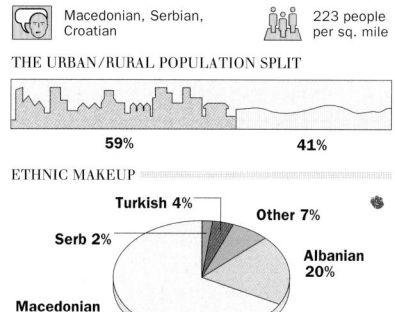

Turkish 4%   Other 7%
Serb 2%   Albanian 20%
Macedonian 67%

Around two-thirds of the population are ethnically Slav Macedonians. Officially 20% are Albanian, although Albanians themselves claim they account for 40%. Unlike the more publicized tensions between Serbs and Albanians in Kosovo, Slav Macedonian–Albanian stress has so far been restrained. Most Macedonians are Eastern Orthodox, but there are also a substantial number of Slavic Muslims, whose ancestors converted to Islam during the Ottoman occupation. Ethnic Albanians are mostly Muslim. There are also Roman Catholic and Jewish groups.

POLITICS

 1994/1998   President (acting) Stojan Andov

THE STATE OF THE PARTIES

Assembly of the Republic 120 members

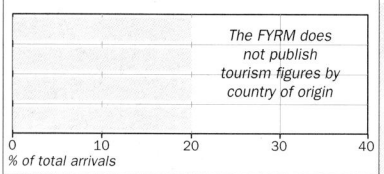

| 48% SDSM | 24% LP | 7% SPM | 8% PDP | 13% Other |

SDSM = Social Democratic Alliance of Macedonia
LP = Liberal Party   **SPM** = Socialist Party of Macedonia
PDP = Party of Democratic Prosperity

All political issues are overshadowed by the dispute with Greece over the state's name. An interim accord on relations signed by Macedonia and Greece in 1995 provided for both countries to respect the sovereignty, territorial integrity and political independence of the other, and confirmed their common existing frontier as an inviolable international border. Negotiations continue on the more intractable dispute over the name of Macedonia.

Politics in the FYRM is fragmented along nationalist lines, and is heavily influenced by tensions in neighboring states. Although the Slav Macedonian and Albanian Macedonian communities have acted with restraint, tensions still remain. Ethnic Albanian parties are now pursuing recognition as a constituent nation within the FYRM.

WORLD AFFAIRS

CE   IAEA   IBRD

In a major breakthrough, Macedonia and Greece signed a UN-brokered accord on relations in 1995. Negotiations are set to continue on the dispute over the name Macedonia.

AID

$ Over $100m   ⬆ Increasing levels of aid required for economic growth

The FYRM joined the World Bank in 1993 and a $40 million loan followed. The IDA has also extended $40 million in concessional lending. A $25 million grant from the Soros Foundation has boosted foreign exchange reserves.

DEFENSE

$ $34m   ⬆ Up 13% in 1995

The army is dominated by officers who resigned from the Yugoslav army in 1992. The USA has stationed 400 troops in the country in an effort to deter Serbian expansionism.

ECONOMICS

 $1.7bn

 39.0–39.3
Macedonian denars

SCORE CARD

❑ WORLD GNP RANKING	140th
❑ GNP PER CAPITA	$790
❑ BALANCE OF PAYMENTS	$–374m
❑ INFLATION	55%
❑ UNEMPLOYMENT	19%

EXPORTS

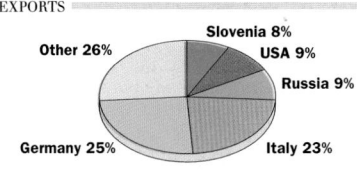

Slovenia 8%
USA 9%
Russia 9%
Italy 23%
Germany 25%
Other 26%

IMPORTS

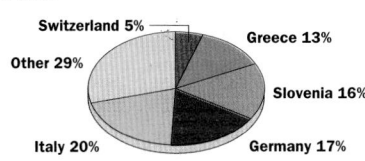

Switzerland 5%
Greece 13%
Other 29%
Slovenia 16%
Germany 17%
Italy 20%

STRENGTHS

Strong growth in private sector. Creation of Skopje stock exchange in 1996. Lifting of Greek economic embargo. Increased market supply – lifting of UN sanctions against Serbia and Montenegro.

WEAKNESSES

Technologically backward. Dependence upon outside sources for oil, gas and machinery.

FORMER YUGOSLAV REPUBLIC OF MACEDONIA

Total Land Area :
25 715 sq. km
(9929 sq. miles)

LAND HEIGHT

2000m/6562ft
1000m/3281ft
500m/1640ft
50m/164ft

POPULATION

⊙	over 500 000
◎	over 100 000
○	over 50 000
●	over 10 000
•	under 10 000

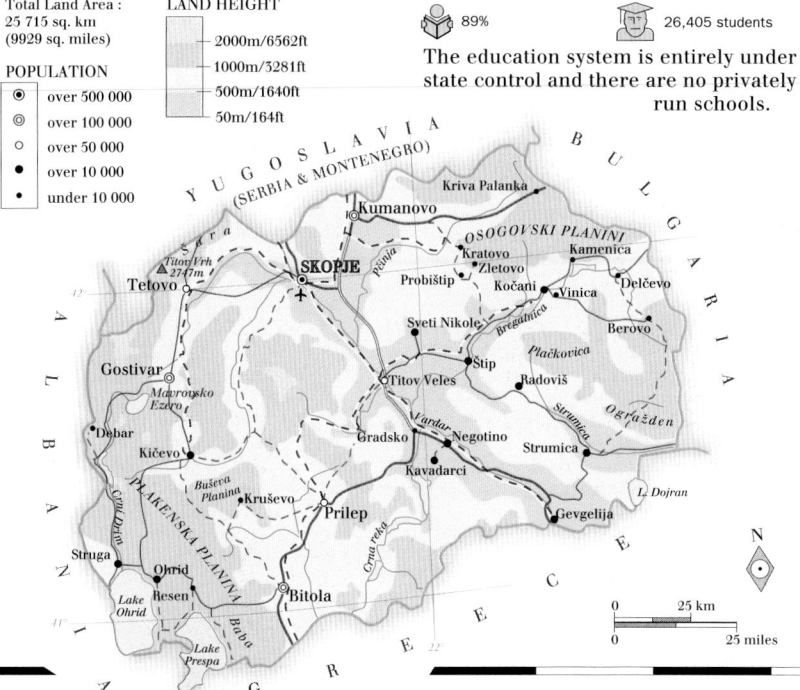

RESOURCES

 5.1bn kwh

 1,384 tons

2.4m sheep, 276,000 cattle, 181,000 pigs

Coal, copper, bauxite, iron, antimony, chromium, lead, zinc

Macedonia is self-sufficient in electricity production. Plants are thermal and fueled by coal.

ENVIRONMENT

 8%

Environmental concerns not a priority

City air pollution is a serious problem. The completion of a sewage works has reduced pollution in Lake Ohrid.

MEDIA

 No censorship restrictions

PUBLISHING AND BROADCAST MEDIA

 Newspapers include the Albanian *Flaka e Vellazerimit* and the Turkish *Birlik*, both of which are funded by the government

1 state-owned, 1 independent service

 1 state-owned, also independent services

The free and often critical press includes the influential *Nova Makedonija* and *Vecer*.

CRIME

 Macedonia does not publish prison figures

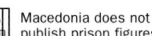 Illegal labor market increasing rapidly

The local Albanian mafia controls the illegal trade in cigarettes, narcotics, hard currencies and arms in Skopje.

EDUCATION

 89%

 26,405 students

The education system is entirely under state control and there are no privately run schools.

CHRONOLOGY

Following the Balkan wars, Macedonia was partitioned between Greece and Serbia in 1912–1913.

- ❑ **1944** Tito establishes Republic of Macedonia and consolidates national identity, partly to counteract Bulgarian influence.
- ❑ **1945** Adoption of standardized Macedonian language.
- ❑ **1989** Communists concede multiparty elections.
- ❑ **1990** Nationalists victorious in multiparty elections.
- ❑ **1991** Independence declared. EC recognition delayed by Greeks.
- ❑ **1995** Accord on relations with Greece. President survives assassination attempt.

HEALTH

 1 per 430 people

Heart and cerebrovascular diseases, cancers

In theory, the state guarantees universal health care, but effective and speedy treatment is increasingly only available in the private sector. Most pharmacies have also been privatized.

WEALTH

 The effects of recent war and UN sanctions have contributed to a sizable fall in living standards since 1991

CONSUMER GOODS OWNERSHIP

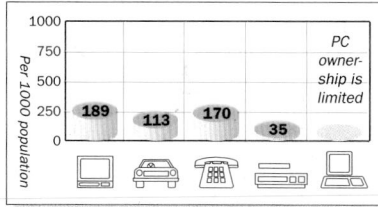

PC ownership is limited

189   113   170   35

On average, basic food accounts for 40% of household expenditure. Most houses and apartments are privately owned.

WORLD RANKING

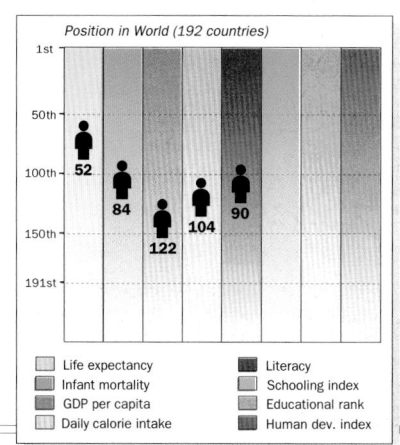

Position in World (192 countries)

52   84   122   104   90

Life expectancy
Infant mortality
GDP per capita
Daily calorie intake
Literacy
Schooling index
Educational rank
Human dev. index

M

MADAGASCAR

OFFICIAL NAME: Republic of Madagascar   **CAPITAL:** Antananarivo
POPULATION: 14.8 million   **CURRENCY:** Malagasy franc   **OFFICIAL LANGUAGES:** Malagasy and French

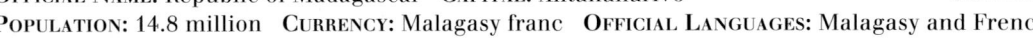

 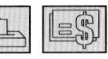

LYING IN THE INDIAN Ocean, Madagascar is the world's fourth-largest island. Its isolation means it is home to a host of unique wildlife and plants. To the east, the large central plateau drops precipitously through forested cliffs to the coast. In the west, gentler gradients give way to fertile plains. A former French colony, it became independent in 1960. After 18 years of radical socialism under Didier Ratsiraka, Madagascar is now a multiparty democracy struggling to rebuild an agriculturally based economy.

CLIMATE

WEATHER CHART

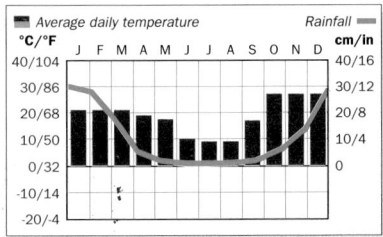

Madagascar is tropical and often hit by cyclones. The coastal lowlands are hot and humid. Rainfall averages 78 in. a year in the east, but under 30 in. in the southwest. The central plateau is cooler, with 40–60 in. of rain a year.

TRANSPORTATION

 Ivato, Antananarivo
340,000 passengers (est)

 18 ships
46,300 dwt

THE TRANSPORT NETWORK

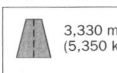
3,330 miles (5,350 km)

 None

559 miles (899 km)

268 miles (432 km)

The extensive domestic air network is a response to the inadequacies of the road and rail systems. Many roads are impassable during the rains; the rail network is very limited. Toamasina port handles about 70% of total traffic.

TOURISM

 65,000 visitors

 Up 18% in 1994

MAIN OVERSEAS ARRIVALS

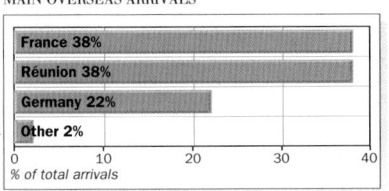

France 38%			
Réunion 38%			
Germany 22%			
Other 2%			

0   10   20   30   40
% of total arrivals

With 3,000 miles of unspoilt tropical beaches and unique flora and fauna, Madagascar has great tourism potential. However, while the sector is now an important foreign exchange earner, it is underdeveloped. After a marked decline in 1991, tourist arrivals reached a new peak of 65,000 in 1993.

PEOPLE

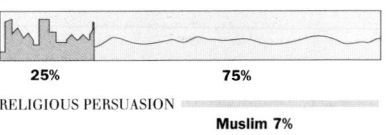

Malagasy, French

65 people per sq. mile

THE URBAN/RURAL POPULATION SPLIT

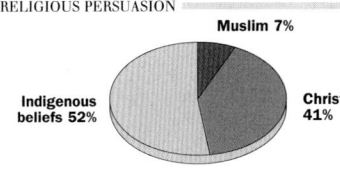

25%   75%

RELIGIOUS PERSUASION

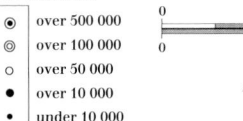

Muslim 7%
Indigenous beliefs 52%
Christian 41%

The people of Madagascar, like their language, Malagasy, are essentially Malay–Indonesian in origin. Their ancestors migrated across the Indian Ocean in successive waves from the 1st century AD. Later migrants from the African mainland intermixed and provided the many African words in Malagasy. The main ethnic division is between the central plateau and *côtier* (coastal) peoples. Of more pronounced Malay extraction, the plateau Merina were Madagascar's historic rulers. They remain the social elite and largely run the government – to the resentment of the poorer *côtier* groups. Former president Didier Ratsiraka owed much of his political longevity to the fact that he is a *côtier*. The extended family is the focus of social life for the rural majority.

POLITICS

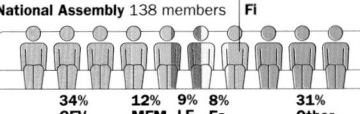

1993/1997

President Albert Zafy

THE STATE OF THE PARTIES

National Assembly 138 members   6% Fi

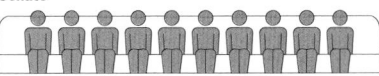

34% CFV   12% MFM   9% LF   8% Fa   31% Other

CFV = Forces Vives Coalition   **MFM** = Movement for Proletarian Power (coalition)   **LF** = Leader-Familo
Fa = Famima   **Fi** = Fihaonana

Senate

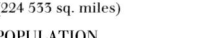

Two-thirds of members are selected by an electoral college and the remainder appointed by the president.

In 1993, 18-year *de facto* one-party rule ended with election victory for the *Forces Vives* opposition coalition. Rebuilding the economy is now the priority.

MADAGASCAR

Total Land Area : 581 540 sq. km (224 533 sq. miles)

POPULATION

- ⊙ over 500 000
- ◎ over 100 000
- ○ over 50 000
- ● over 10 000
- • under 10 000

LAND HEIGHT

- 2000m/6562ft
- 1000m/3281ft
- 500m/1640ft
- 200m/656ft
- Sea Level

0   200 km
0   200 miles

WORLD AFFAIRS

 Comesa Franc IAEA IOC OAU

Once-close ties with Moscow and North Korea have waned since the late 1980s, as Madagascar has improved relations with its main Western trading partners, especially France and the USA. It has also increased regional links, re-establishing ties with South Africa and, in 1994, joining the Common Market for Eastern and Southern Africa (COMESA).

AID

 $370m (receipts)   Up 3% in 1993

France is the top bilateral donor. The main multilateral donors are the EU and the World Bank. Most aid is now tied to economic reforms.

DEFENSE

 $29m   Down 24% in 1995

A key political force, the army's priority is to maintain a stable, unitary state. In 1992, it acted against federalist *côtiers*.

ECONOMICS

 $3.06bn   3,637.67–4,095.00 Malagasy francs

SCORE CARD

- ❏ WORLD GNP RANKING.......................124th
- ❏ GNP PER CAPITA $230
- ❏ BALANCE OF PAYMENTS...................$–197m
- ❏ INFLATION 38.9%
- ❏ UNEMPLOYMENT...   Widespread underemployment

STRENGTHS

Varied agricultural base; vanilla, coffee and clove exports. Offshore oil and gas. Prawns. Tourism.

WEAKNESSES

Losing out to cheaper vanilla exporters. Vulnerability to drought. Government slow to reform economy by cutting central controls and budget deficit. Not self-sufficient in rice, the food staple.

EXPORTS

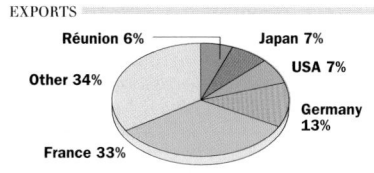

Réunion 6%
Japan 7%
USA 7%
Other 34%
Germany 13%
France 33%

IMPORTS

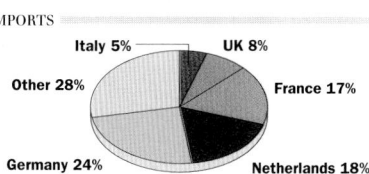

Italy 5%
UK 8%
Other 28%
France 17%
Germany 24%
Netherlands 18%

Tôlañaro (also known as Fort Dauphin), a port on the southeast coast. This was the area first settled by the French in the 16th century.

RESOURCES

 569m kwh (capacity 220,000 kw)   Not an oil producer; refines 16,350 b/cd

 10.3m cattle, 1.6m pigs, 1.3m goats   Chromite, graphite, mica, iron, bitumen, gemstones, marble

Madagascar is the world's largest vanilla exporter. Electricity is hydro-generated. Oil is imported, although offshore oil and gas have been found.

ENVIRONMENT

 2% (1% partially protected)   Serious deforestation and soil erosion

Madagascar's environment is a unique resource; 80% of its plant and many animal species, such as the lemur, are found nowhere else. Aid donors are providing funds to fight deforestation.

MEDIA

 Censorship exists, but is limited

PUBLISHING AND BROADCAST MEDIA

There are 4 daily newspapers, including the *Madagascar Tribune* and *Midi-Madagasikara*

1 state-owned service   1 state-owned service

Even before the return of multiparty democracy in 1993, there was a flourishing opposition press, including the Catholic-sponsored *La Croix*.

CRIME

 33,280 prisoners   Crime is rising

Urban crime levels are starting to rise. The army has been criticized for human rights abuses, including the shooting of federalists in 1993.

EDUCATION

 81%    42,681 students

Elementary education is universal. About 40% of children attend secondary school; 4% go on to higher education. Elementary education is to become French-based instead of Malagasy-based.

HEALTH

 1 per 8,100 people   Malaria, enteric and respiratory diseases

Private health care was legalized in 1993. State care is free but inadequate. Malaria is at epidemic levels. There are outbreaks of bubonic plague.

WEALTH

 Minimum wage in manufacturing, 22,000 Malagasy francs ($5) per month

CONSUMER GOODS OWNERSHIP

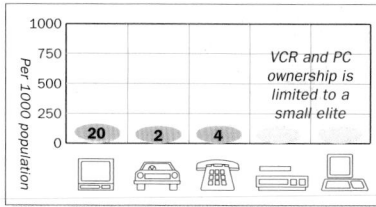

VCR and PC ownership is limited to a small elite

20   2   4

Most people are poor. However, central plateau dwellers are richer than the *côtier* farmers and fishermen.

WORLD RANKING

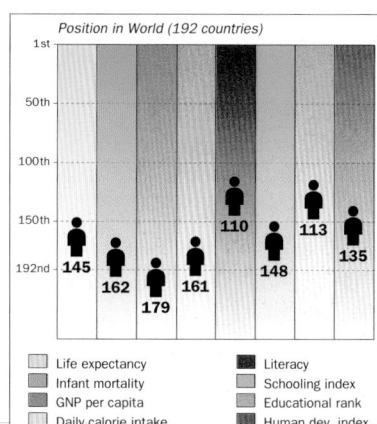

Position in World (192 countries)

145   162   179   161   110   148   113   135

- Life expectancy
- Infant mortality
- GNP per capita
- Daily calorie intake
- Literacy
- Schooling index
- Educational rank
- Human dev. index

M

MALAWI

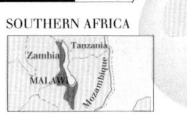

SOUTHERN AFRICA

OFFICIAL NAME: Republic of Malawi   CAPITAL: Lilongwe   POPULATION: 11.1 million
CURRENCY: Malawian kwacha   OFFICIAL LANGUAGES: Chewa and English

LANDLOCKED IN SOUTHEAST AFRICA, Malawi occupies a plateau bordering the Great Rift Valley. Lake Malawi, which is 352 miles in length and takes up one-fifth of the country, is among Africa's largest lakes and supports a sizable fishing industry. Mount Mulanje is the highest mountain in East Africa. In 1994 Malawi, a former British colony, successfully underwent the transition to democracy following three decades of one-party rule.

CLIMATE

WEATHER CHART

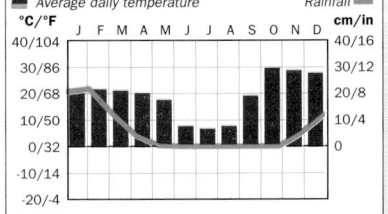

The south is hot and humid. The rest of Malawi is warm and very sunny in the dry season, but cooler in the highlands.

TRANSPORTATION

Kamuzu Intl, Lilongwe
232,000 passengers

 Has no fleet

THE TRANSPORTATION NETWORK

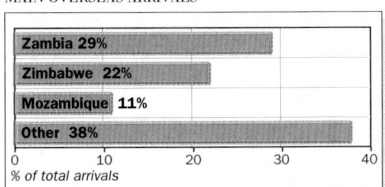

| | 1,650 miles (2,660 km) | | None |
| 490 miles (789 km) | | Lake Malawi, Shire River |

Access from rural areas to the good main road system is limited. The Kamuzu Highway, a key north–south link, is currently being upgraded.

TOURISM

 138,000 visitors   Up 1% in 1994

MAIN OVERSEAS ARRIVALS

Zambia	29%
Zimbabwe	22%
Mozambique	11%
Other	38%

% of total arrivals

The waters of Lake Malawi, with its 500 species of fish, attract angling, wildlife and water sports enthusiasts. The national parks and mountain lodges are also popular.

PEOPLE

 Chewa, Lomwe, Yao, Ngoni, English

307 people per sq. mile

THE URBAN/RURAL POPULATION SPLIT

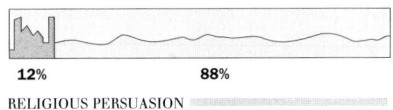

12%   88%

RELIGIOUS PERSUASION

Indigenous beliefs 5%
Muslim 20%
Protestant 55%
Roman Catholic 20%

Ethnic tensions are few in Malawi as most of the population share a common Bantu origin. The main ethnic groupings are the Chewa, Yao, Chieoka, Tonga, Tumbuka, Ngoni and Nyanja. Ethnicity has not been exploited for political ends to the extent that it has in neighboring states. Under the Banda regime northerners became increasingly disaffected at their lack of representation in politics. The new government has endeavoured to reduce these tensions.

Many of the Muslim Asians are involved in the retail trade. The discrimination that they suffered from the Banda regime has effectively ended. Former president Banda, a member of the Scottish Presbyterian Church, promoted the expansion of Protestantism in Malawi.

Fruit and vegetable sellers on the Mozambican border. The south of the country is intensively cultivated.

POLITICS

 1994/1999   President Bakili Muluzi

THE STATE OF THE PARTIES
National Assembly 177 members

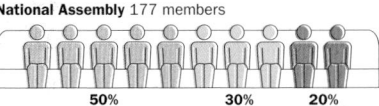

| 50% UDF | 30% MCP | 20% Aford |

UDF = United Democratic Front   MCP = Malawi Congress Party   Aford = Alliance for Democracy

From independence in 1964, Malawi fell under the personalized rule of Dr. Hastings Banda. Under a single-party regime, instituted in 1966, dissent was not tolerated and torture and imprisonment without trial were common. In 1992, international aid was suspended because of the regime's poor human rights record. A referendum was held in 1993 and Banda agreed to the introduction of multiparty politics. In 1994, presidential and legislative elections were held. The United Democratic Front (UDF), which draws most of its support from the south, scored a dramatic victory in the parliamentary elections. The UDF leader, Bakili Muluzi, also won the presidential election, bringing to an end one of the world's longest dictatorships. President Muluzi, a wealthy businessman and a former secretary-general of the MCP, recruited a number of prominent MCP politicians to the UDF, one reason for the party's good showing in the central region – a traditional MCP stronghold.

WORLD AFFAIRS

 Comm   Comesa   NAM   OAU   SADC

Malawi's principal concerns have been protecting its restored status as a recipient of Western aid and retaining a pragmatic relationship with South Africa. Malawi is the only black African country to have maintained full diplomatic relations with South Africa since 1967. One in ten Mozambicans fled to Malawi as refugees in the 1980s.

AID

 $503m (receipts)   Down 3% in 1993

Since the advent of multiparty politics, non-humanitarian aid has now been resumed. Its suspension was a significant factor in propelling Malawi to hold a referendum on whether to become a democracy in 1993.

M

Key to symbols and abbreviations on endpapers

DEFENSE

 $20m    No change in 1995

The new government is confident of the loyalty of the 8,200-strong military. In the last days of Banda rule, the military lost confidence in the ruling party, forcing the pace of democratization. In 1993, it disarmed the Young Pioneers, a militarized section of the MCP.

ECONOMICS

 $1.6bn   15.39–15.60 kwacha

SCORE CARD

❏ World GNP Ranking	142nd
❏ GNP per Capita	$140
❏ Balance of Payments	$–274m
❏ Inflation	34.7%
❏ Unemployment	Widespread underemployment

STRENGTHS
Tobacco, accounting for 76% of foreign exchange earnings. Tea and sugar production. Unexploited reserves of bauxite, asbestos and coal.

WEAKNESSES
Agriculture, accounting for 80% of GDP, often hit by drought. Only 14% of GDP from industry. Small domestic market. Shortage of skilled personnel. Regional instability and refugee problem.

EXPORTS

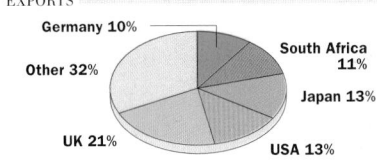

Germany 10%
Other 32%
South Africa 11%
Japan 13%
UK 21%
USA 13%

IMPORTS

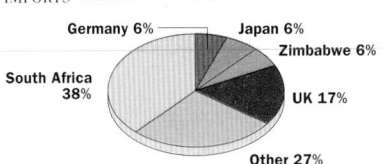

Germany 6%
South Africa 38%
Japan 6%
Zimbabwe 6%
UK 17%
Other 27%

RESOURCES

 792m kwh (capacity 190,000 kw)

980,000 cattle, 890,000 goats, 245,000 pigs

 65,000 tons

Coal, limestone, gemstones, bauxite, graphite, uranium

Malawi has few strategic resources. Three hydropower plants account for 85% of electricity generating capacity, but only 3% of total energy use. Over 90% of energy needs are met from fuel-wood as most Malawians do not have access to electricity. Malawi has reserves of bauxite and uranium, but not in commercially exploitable quantities. A deep-seam coal mine recently began production at Rumphi.

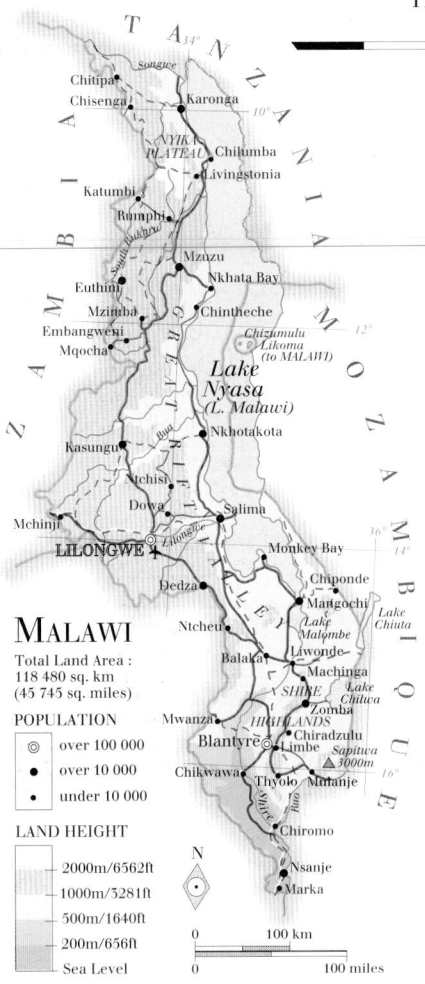

MALAWI

Total Land Area :
118 480 sq. km
(45 745 sq. miles)

POPULATION

 over 100 000
● over 10 000
· under 10 000

LAND HEIGHT

2000m/6562ft
1000m/3281ft
500m/1640ft
200m/656ft
Sea Level

 N

0   100 km
0   100 miles

ENVIRONMENT

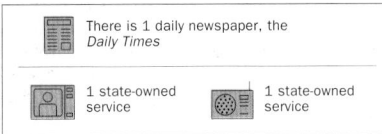 10%   Few environmental initiatives

Drought eclipses all other problems. Agricultural production fell by 25% in 1992 owing to its effects.

MEDIA

The media, formerly under tight government control, is now free

PUBLISHING AND BROADCAST MEDIA

 There is 1 daily newspaper, the Daily Times

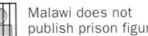 1 state-owned service   1 state-owned service

The first television company, launched in 1995, was expected to begin broadcasting in late 1996.

CRIME

Malawi does not publish prison figures   Up 10% in 1990

Urban crime is on the increase. The proliferation of weapons, especially guns, is contributing to a rise in armed robbery.

CHRONOLOGY

After strong Scottish missionary activity, Malawi came under British rule as Nyasaland in 1891.

- ❏ **1964** Independence under Dr. Hastings Banda.
- ❏ **1966** One-party state.
- ❏ **1992** Anti-government riots. Illegal pro-democracy groups unite.
- ❏ **1995** Referendum: 63% in favor of multipartyism.
- ❏ **1994** Banda and MCP defeated in multiparty elections.

EDUCATION

 49%    5,594 students

Elementary level education is widespread, with 73% of boys and 60% of girls attending school regularly.

HEALTH

 1 per 50,360 people   Infectious, parasitic and respiratory diseases

Access to health services is difficult and preventive care is viewed as a priority. Most doctors train abroad.

WEALTH

 Most Malawians lead a subsistence existence

CONSUMER GOODS OWNERSHIP

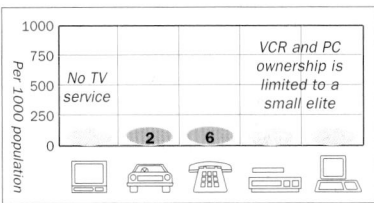

No TV service
VCR and PC ownership is limited to a small elite
2   6

The MCP elite formerly enjoyed considerable wealth. The government is investigating allegations that Banda stole huge sums of public money.

WORLD RANKING

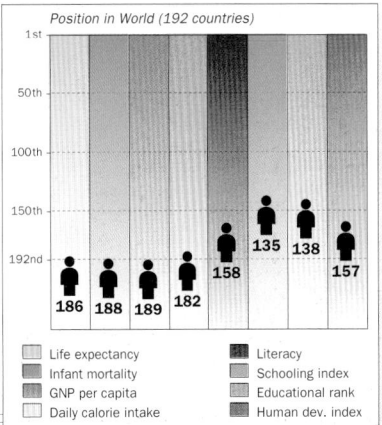

Position in World (192 countries)

186 188 189 182 158 135 138 157

Life expectancy
Infant mortality
GNP per capita
Daily calorie intake
Literacy
Schooling index
Educational rank
Human dev. index

M

MALAYSIA

OFFICIAL NAME: Malaysia **CAPITAL:** Kuala Lumpur
POPULATION: 20.1 million **CURRENCY:** Ringgit **OFFICIAL LANGUAGE:** Malay

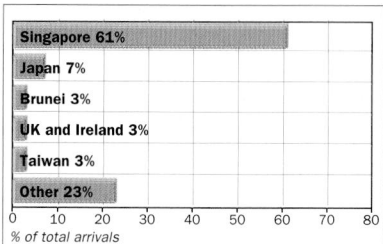

COMPRISING THE THREE separate territories of Malaya, Sarawak and Sabah, Malaysia stretches over 1,243 miles from Peninsular Malaysia to the northeastern end of the island of Borneo. It shares borders with Thailand, Indonesia and the enclave states of Singapore and Brunei. A central mountain chain divides Malaya, separating fertile western plains from a narrow eastern coastal belt. Sarawak and Sabah are characterized by swampy coastal plains rising to mountains on the border with Indonesia. Since 1987, Malaysia has been experiencing average economic growth rates of 8% a year.

CLIMATE

WEATHER CHART

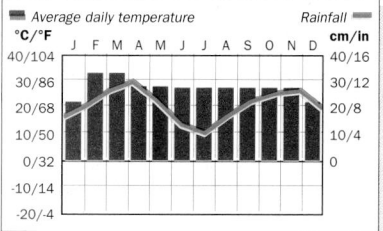

The whole of Malaysia has an equatorial climate. The country has rainfall throughout the year; it falls on between 150 and 200 days almost everywhere. However, there are two distinct rainy seasons, when the heaviest rain falls – from March to May and from September to November. Coastal areas are also subject to the alternating southwest and northeast monsoon winds.

Tea plantation in the Cameron Highlands, in central-western Malaya. This region also contains one of Asia's most popular mountain resorts.

TRANSPORTATION

 **Subang Intl,
Kuala Lumpur**
4.46m passengers

 310 ships
2.91m dwt

THE TRANSPORTATION NETWORK

| 43,130 miles (69,410 km) | None |
| 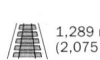 1,289 miles (2,075 km) | 1,994 miles (3,209 km) |

A major north–south highway is being built and in Kuala Lumpur a new mass transit system is being constructed to extend to its outer suburbs. Malaysia's "national car," the Proton, has been a success; since 1985, national car ownership has trebled. Several ports are being updated to reduce Malaysia's current dependence on Singapore.

TOURISM

7.2m visitors Up 10% in 1994

MAIN OVERSEAS ARRIVALS

Singapore 61%	
Japan 7%	
Brunei 3%	
UK and Ireland 3%	
Taiwan 3%	
Other 23%	

% of total arrivals

Malaysia is Southeast Asia's major tourist destination, with over seven million visitors a year. Most tourists come for the excellent tropical beaches on the east coast, to hike in the Cameron Highlands or to trek in the world's oldest rainforests in Borneo. There has recently been an increase in the international business convention trade.

By 1990, when the government ran the Visit Malaysia Year campaign, tourism had become Malaysia's third-biggest foreign exchange earner. There is still untapped potential for growth. Over half of visitors to Malaysia are short-stay trippers from Singapore, and tourists' spending per day is less than half of that in Thailand. A second Visit Malaysia Year was launched in 1994, and a third is planned to coincide with the holding of the Commonwealth Games in Malaysia in 1998. Hotel capacity is currently growing at 10% a year and 70 new beach resorts are planned before 2000.

MALAYSIA

Total Land Area : 328 550 sq. km (126 855 sq. miles)

POPULATION

- ◉ over 500 000
- ◎ over 100 000
- ○ over 50 000
- ● over 10 000
- · under 10 000

LAND HEIGHT

- 2000m/6562ft
- 1000m/3281ft
- 500m/1640ft
- 200m/656ft
- Sea Level

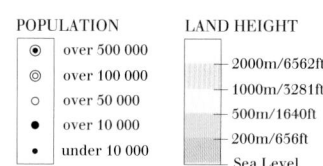

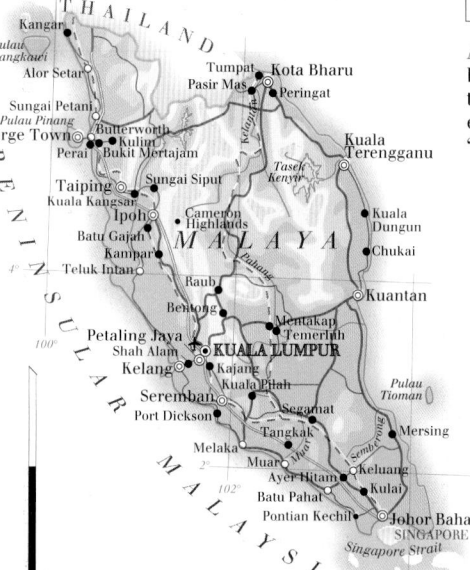

M

PEOPLE

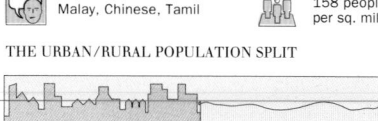

Malay, Chinese, Tamil   158 people per sq. mile

THE URBAN/RURAL POPULATION SPLIT

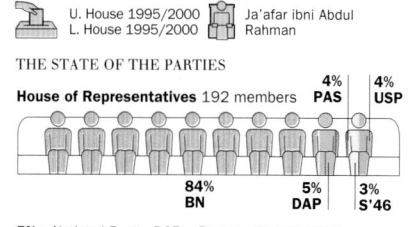

51%   49%

RELIGIOUS PERSUASION

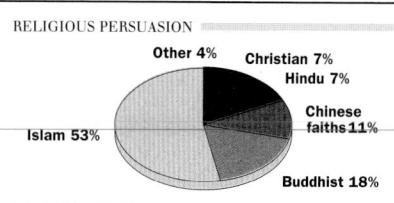

Other 4%
Christian 7%
Hindu 7%
Chinese faiths 11%
Islam 53%
Buddhist 18%

ETHNIC MAKEUP

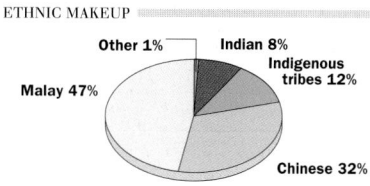

Other 1%
Indian 8%
Indigenous tribes 12%
Malay 47%
Chinese 32%

POPULATION AGE BREAKDOWN

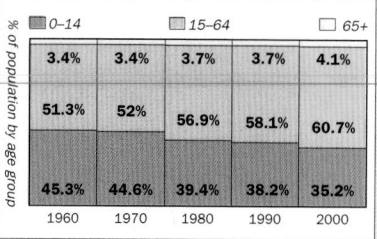

% of population by age group	0–14	15–64		65+	
65+	3.4%	3.4%	3.7%	3.7%	4.1%
15–64	51.3%	52%	56.9%	58.1%	60.7%
0–14	45.3%	44.6%	39.4%	38.2%	35.2%
	1960	1970	1980	1990	2000

The key distinction in Malaysian society is between the indigenous Malays, termed the "Bumiputras" (literally, sons of the soil), and the Chinese. The Malays form the largest group, accounting for 47% of the population. However, the smaller Chinese population (32%) has traditionally controlled most business activity. The New Economic Policy (NEP), introduced in the 1970s, was designed to address this imbalance by offering positive opportunities to the Malays through the education system and by making jobs available to them in both the state and private sectors. There are estimated to be more than one million Indonesian and Filipino immigrants in Malaysia, attracted by the country's labor shortages and a dearth of employment in their own countries. In addition, over 200,000 Vietnamese refugees were offered asylum in Malaysia in the last decade; most have now been resettled, but around 6,000 remain in the country. In an attempt to promote Islamic tradition, Muslim Malay women have been encouraged to wear veils.

POLITICS

U. House 1995/2000
L. House 1995/2000
Ja'afar ibni Abdul Rahman

THE STATE OF THE PARTIES

House of Representatives 192 members

4% PAS   4% USP
84% BN   5% DAP   3% S'46

BN = National Front   **DAP** = Democratic Action Party
PAS = Pan-Malaysian Islamic Party   **S'46** = Spirit of '46
USP = United Sabah Party

Senate 70 members

30 members elected – 2 from each of 13 State Legislative Assemblies and 2 Federal Territotories – and 40 members chosen by the Head of State

Supreme power rests with the monarch, who acts on the advice of parliament. Opposition parties, while legal, are under tight control.

MAIN POLITICAL ISSUE
Malay superiority
While the current administration of Dr. Mahathir has declared that it no longer wishes to discriminate positively in favor of Malays, the Chinese community is feeling increasingly isolated. They have accused the government of corruption and uncompetitive practices, declaring that Malays are still favored in the placing of government contracts. In 1993, investment in the domestic economy by indigenous Chinese fell by an estimated 30%. The pro-Malay policy is also expressed in a more restrictive Islamic society, which further alienates the Chinese community.

PROFILE
Malaysia has been dominated by the UMNO since independence from Britain in 1947. In 1970, it introduced a policy of favoring Malays over the Chinese and other minorities. The party is heavily involved in business and controls a huge network of both political and economic patronage. The latter gives it and its Malay supporters a significant and growing control of the economy. The semblance of a working democracy is maintained by staged grass-roots political debate. An opposition exists, but its effectiveness is limited by the UMNO's policy of cutting funding to constituencies who vote against the party.

The success of the UMNO, and of its leader Dr. Mahathir, has been to deliver consistent economic growth and prosperity. As long as this continues, few challengers will emerge to question Mahathir's pre-eminent position in Malay political life.

WORLD AFFAIRS

APEC   ASEAN   Comm   G15   OIC

Dr. Mahathir sees himself as one of the developing world's leading voices. He maintains a strongly anti-US line in his public speeches and has chastized the West for its failure to resolve the conflict in Bosnia. Mahathir's strong pro-Malay policies have caused tensions in the past with Singapore, which are exacerbated by the fact that Singapore is dependent on Malaysia for water.

AID

 $100m (receipts)   Down 53% in 1993

Malaysia has received soft loans from the West for large infrastructure projects. In recent years, it has also made donations. It has given aid to Bosnian Muslims and offered to take Bosnian refugees. Technical assistance has been made available to Vietnam.

Sultan Azlan Shah, *head of state from 1989–1994.*

Dr. Mahathir Mohamad, *prime minister since 1981.*

M

CHRONOLOGY

The former British protectorate of Malaya, made up of 11 states, gained independence in 1957. The federation of Malaysia, incorporating Singapore, Sarawak and Sabah, was founded in 1963.

❑ **1965** Singapore leaves federation, reducing Malaysian states to 13.

❑ **1970** Malay–Chinese ethnic tension results in resignation of Prime Minister Tunku Abdul Rahman. Tun Abdul Razak, new prime minister, creates national coalition, the BN.

❑ **1976–1978** Guerrilla attacks by banned Communist Party of Malaya (CPM), based in southern Thailand. Cooperation between Malaysian and Thai governments leads to eventual reduction in CPM activity.

❑ **1976** Tun Abdul Razak dies. Succeeded by his deputy.

❑ **1977** Unrest in Kelantan following expulsion of its chief minister from Pan-Malaysian Islamic Party (PAS). National emergency declared. PAS expelled from BN.

❑ **1978** Elections consolidate BN power. PAS marginalized. Flare-up of ethnic and religious tension over government rejection of Chinese university.

❑ **1978–1989** Unrestricted asylum given to Vietnamese refugees.

❑ **1981** Dr. Mahathir Mohamad becomes prime minister.

❑ **1982** General elections return BN with increased majority.

❑ **1985** In Sabah state elections, BN defeated by PBS. Legality of PBS victory questioned.

❑ **1986** PBS wins new election and joins BN coalition. Dispute between Dr. Mahathir and his deputy, Dakuk Musa, triggers general election. BN wins, but criticism of leadership continues. Tensions increase between Malays and Chinese.

❑ **1987** 106 politicians from all parties suspected of Chinese sympathies detained without trial. Media censored.

❑ **1989** Disaffected UMNO members join PAS. Screening of Vietnamese refugees introduced. CPM sign peace agreement with Malaysian and Thai governments.

❑ **1990** General election. PBS leaves BN. BN wins with reduced majority.

❑ **1993** Assembly votes for reduction in powers, including loss of legal immunity, for the nine sultans.

❑ **1994** Chief minister of Sabah found guilty of corruption.

❑ **1995** BN wins landslide victory in the country's ninth general election.

M

DEFENSE

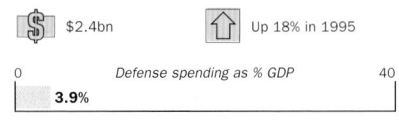

$2.4bn   Up 18% in 1995

Defense spending as % GDP   3.9%

MALAYSIAN ARMED FORCES

26 light tanks (*Scorpion* (90mm))		90,000 personnel
4 frigates and 29 patrol boats		12,000 personnel
120 combat aircraft (30 A-4PTM, 10 HAWK 108, 5 TA-4, 11 F-5E)		12,000 personnel
None		

The military is entirely composed of Malays. Defense spending currently accounts for 4% of GDP. There are plans to raise it to 6%, in line with neighboring Singapore. Malaysia is an important market for Western arms suppliers. However, in 1994 Malaysia signed an agreement to buy Russian MiG-29 fighter aircraft. The deal meant that Malaysia became the first non-communist state in Southeast Asia to operate Russian military equipment. The main defense concerns are Singapore's large and highly mechanized army and growing Chinese influence in the South China Sea. Patrolling East and West Malaysia is a key function of the navy, which is large by regional standards.

ECONOMICS

$68.7bn   2.99–2.54 ringgits

SCORE CARD

❑ WORLD GNP RANKING...........................38th
❑ GNP PER CAPITA $3,520
❑ BALANCE OF PAYMENTS....................$–4.1bn
❑ INFLATION 3.6%
❑ UNEMPLOYMENT 3%

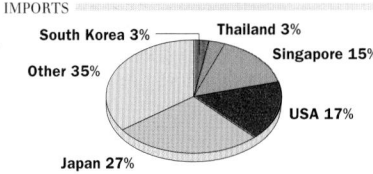

EXPORTS

Hong Kong 4% — Thailand 4%
Japan 13%
Other 37%
USA 20%
Singapore 22%

IMPORTS

South Korea 3% — Thailand 3%
Singapore 15%
Other 35%
USA 17%
Japan 27%

STRENGTHS

Electronics: the world's biggest producer of disk drives. Proton car a national and international success. Heavy industries such as steel. Latex and rubber industries.

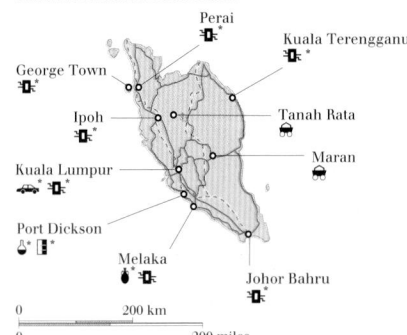

MALAYSIA : MAJOR BUSINESSES

Perai
Kuala Terengganu
George Town
Ipoh
Tanah Rata
Kuala Lumpur
Maran
Port Dickson
Melaka
Johor Bahru

0   200 km
0   200 miles

ECONOMIC PERFORMANCE INDICATOR

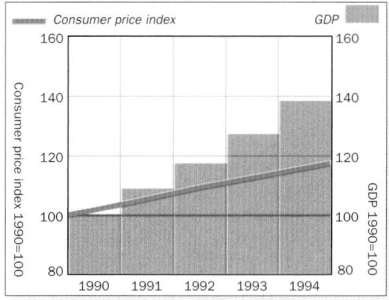

Consumer price index   GDP

1990 1991 1992 1993 1994

WEAKNESSES

Shortage of skilled labor. High interest rates deter private investors. High government budget spending. Competition from new NICs.

PROFILE

Growth in the economy took off in 1987. Since then, Malaysia has been expanding faster than any other Southeast Asian nation, at an average yearly rate of 8%. Much of the growth has been state-directed. In 1987, the government made a concerted push for foreign investment, which rose to a peak of 17.6 billion ringgits in 1990. The privatization of state assets was also stepped up. Goals have been set for full industrialization in a plan known as "Vision 2020."

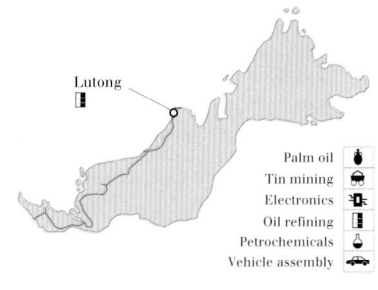

Lutong

Palm oil
Tin mining
Electronics
Oil refining
Petrochemicals
Vehicle assembly

* significant multinational ownership

RESOURCES

 32bn kwh (capacity 5.04m kw)

  627,404 b/d (reserves 3,700,000,000 bbl)

3.1m pigs, 686,000 cattle, 356,000 goats

Natural gas, oil, tin, bauxite, copper, iron, coal

ELECTRICITY GENERATION

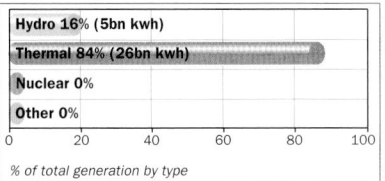

Hydro 16% (5bn kwh)

Thermal 84% (26bn kwh)

Nuclear 0%

Other 0%

% of total generation by type

Thailand has overtaken Malaysia as the world's major rubber producer. Palm oil, of which Malaysia is the world's largest producer, is now a more important export product. Malaysia is a significant exporter of oil and natural gas. Oil reserves are offshore from Sabah and Sarawak. The good quality of the oil means that most is exported, while crude imports are

MALAYSIA : LAND USE

Cropland
Forest
Pigs
Rubber
Palm oil

SABAH

SARAWAK

PENINSULAR MALAYSIA

0   200 km

0   200 miles

refined. Malaysia accounts for nearly half of world timber exports, most of which come from Sarawak.

ENVIRONMENT

 5%

 Deforestation remains a serious problem

ENVIRONMENTAL TREATIES

Yes   Yes   Yes

No   Yes   Yes

Logging remains the overwhelming environmental concern of groups such as Sahabat Alam Malaysia (Friends of the Earth, Malaysia). Unprocessed log exports from Sarawak rose from 3.4 million cubic feet in 1980 to 8 million cubic feet in 1991. World Bank estimates suggest that trees are being cut down at four times the sustainable rate. Indigenous forest communities such as the Penan are being destroyed and some species of wood such as Ramin are near extinction. In 1992, the state of Sarawak began to take action to diversify the economy. There is great pressure to maintain growth, however, and the profits from logging are hard to resist.

MEDIA

 All news bulletins for radio and TV by Department of Broadcasting

PUBLISHING AND BROADCAST MEDIA

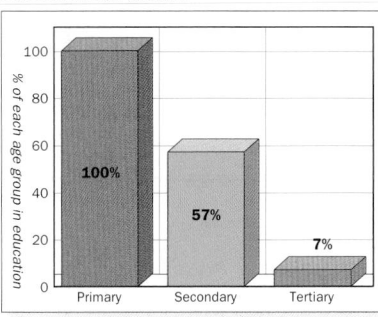

There are 42 daily newspapers. The most influential of these are the *New Straits Times*, *Utusan Malaysia* and *Xingzhou Ribao*

2 state-controlled, 1 independent service

1 state-controlled network

Palapa B2-P Intelsat V F8

None

Almost all newspapers in Malaysia are controlled by the UMNO, the dominant political party. The party owns the *Straits* group, which includes the most influential press. Radio and TV are also strictly controlled, under the 1987 Broadcasting Act, and Western commercials are banned. Singaporean TV can be received in the south.

CRIME

 22,832 prisoners

 Up 3% in 1992

CRIME RATES

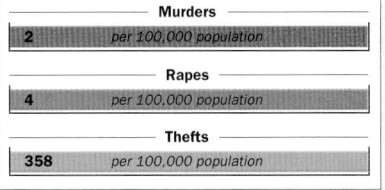

Murders
2   per 100,000 population

Rapes
4   per 100,000 population

Thefts
358   per 100,000 population

The judiciary and the ruling UMNO maintain close links. The death sentence for possession of narcotics is mandatory. Kelantan state has attempted to implement the Islamic penal code, including stoning for adulterers and amputation for thieves.

EDUCATION

 78%

 136,000 students

0   Education spending as % GNP   25
5.5%

THE EDUCATION SYSTEM

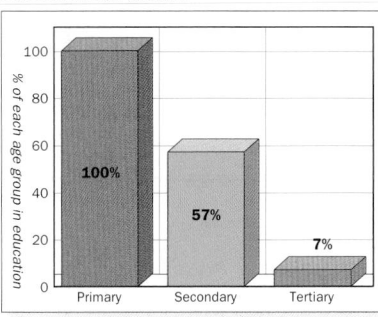

% of each age group in education

100%   (Primary)
57%   (Secondary)
7%   (Tertiary)

Malays are favored above other communities at tertiary level by a quota system which gives them preference for places. The Chinese community has its own schools. An attempt by some Chinese to establish their own, private university was vetoed by the government. Many students, particularly the Chinese, complete their studies in the UK or USA.

HEALTH

 1 per 2,410 people

Heart diseases, cancers

0   Health spending as % GDP   25
1.3%

There is a sharp distinction between care in cities and the traditional medicine practised in outlying areas.

WEALTH

Rubber tapper, 14.1 ringgits ($6) per day ; electronic technician, 1,000 ringgits ($394) per month

CONSUMER GOODS OWNERSHIP

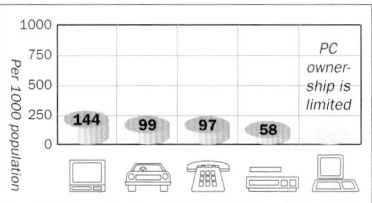

Per 1000 population

144   99   97   58

PC ownership is limited

The Chinese remain the wealthiest community in Malaysia. However, following riots in 1970, the UMNO government embarked on a deliberate program of achieving 30% Malay ownership of the corporate sector. Many Malays earned quick profits from preferential privatization share allocations in the early 1990s.

WORLD RANKING

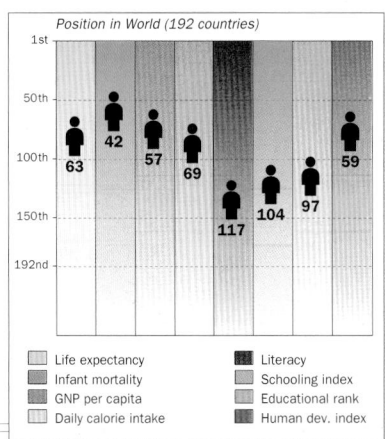

Position in World (192 countries)

1st
50th
100th
150th
192nd

63   42   57   69   117   104   97   59

Life expectancy
Infant mortality
GNP per capita
Daily calorie intake
Literacy
Schooling index
Educational rank
Human dev. index

M

MALDIVES

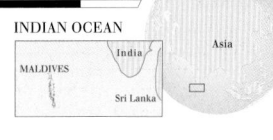

INDIAN OCEAN

OFFICIAL NAME: Republic of Maldives CAPITAL: Male'
POPULATION: 300,000 CURRENCY: Rufiyaa OFFICIAL LANGUAGE: Dhivehi

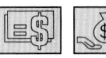

THE MALDIVES IS AN archipelago of 1,190 small coral islands set in the Indian Ocean west of Sri Lanka. The islands, none of which rise above 6 feet, are protected by encircling reefs or *faros*. Only 200 are inhabited. Tourism has grown in recent years, though holiday islands are separate from settler islands. In 1993, President Maumoon Abdul Gayoom, who has survived three coup attempts, was elected for a fourth term in office.

Traditional Maldivian trading yacht. The 1,190 coral islands are grouped in natural atolls, derived from the Maldivian word "atolu."

CLIMATE

WEATHER CHART

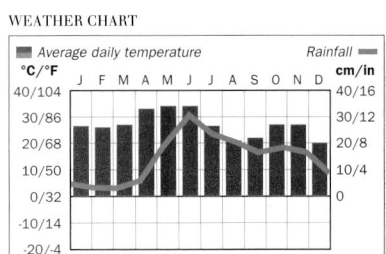

The Maldives has a tropical climate with abundant rainfall and high temperatures throughout the year. The northern islands are occasionally affected by violent storms caused by tropical cyclones. Most rain falls in the southern islands, from November to March.

TRANSPORTATION

Male' Intl, Hulule Island
486,000 passengers

28 ships
74,000 dwt

THE TRANSPORTATION NETWORK

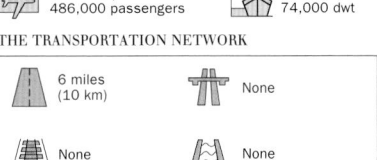

6 miles (10 km)	None
None	None

It is possible to walk across Male' island in 20 minutes. Inter-island travel is mostly by ferry and traditional *dhoni*.

TOURISM

280,000 visitors

Up 16% in 1994

MAIN OVERSEAS ARRIVALS

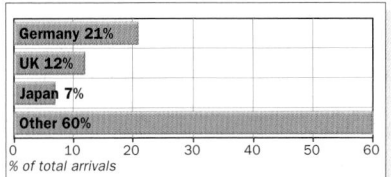

Germany 21%
UK 12%
Japan 7%
Other 60%

% of total arrivals

Tourism is the largest source of foreign exchange. The first resort was opened in 1972. Luxury hotels, financed by local and foreign capital, have been built on the uninhabited islands. The sea, with its many varieties of tropical fish, is a big attraction for divers.

POLITICS

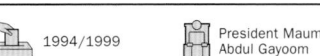

1994/1999

President Maumoon Abdul Gayoom

THE STATE OF THE PARTIES

Citizen's Council 48 members

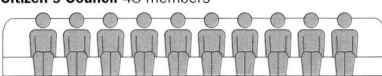

There are no political parties. 40 members are elected, 2 from Male' and 2 from each of the 19 administrative atolls. 8 members are chosen by the president.

Politics in the Maldives is in practice restricted to a small group of influential families. Most were already dominant under the Sultanate. Politics is not based on formal parties with ideological objectives; it is organized around family and clan loyalties.

A few figures have dominated politics since independence. Former president Ibrahim Nasir was responsible for abolishing the premiership in 1975, making the presidency even more powerful. Ilyas Ibrahim, exiled to an outlying island for 15 years, and Maumoon Abdul Gayoom, a wealthy businessman, are now the main figures. Gayoom was almost defeated by Ibrahim in the 1993 presidential elections. A new young elite, who have tasted democracy abroad, are pressing for a more liberal political system.

PEOPLE

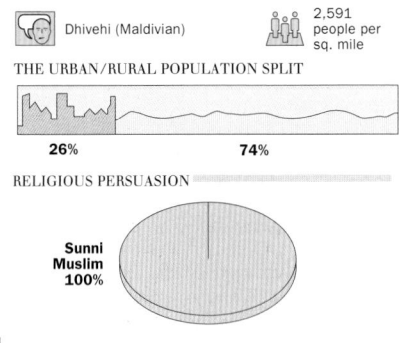

Dhivehi (Maldivian)

2,591 people per sq. mile

THE URBAN/RURAL POPULATION SPLIT

26%   74%

RELIGIOUS PERSUASION

Sunni Muslim 100%

It is believed the islands were first inhabited as early as 1500 BC. Aryan immigrants arrived around 500 BC. The islands were then discovered by Arab traders. The people, who are all Sunni Muslims, live on only 200 of the 1,190 islands. About 25% of the total population live on the island capital of Male'. It is estimated that 12,000 guest workers from neighboring Sri Lanka and India work in the Maldives. The country's new-found prosperity has seen the emergence of a commercial elite.

MALDIVES

Eight Degree Channel

Ihavandippolhu Atoll

Thiladhunmathi Atoll

Makunudhoo Atoll

North Miladummadulu Atoll

South Miladummadulu Atoll

North Maalhosmadulu Atoll

South Maalhosmadulu Atoll

Faadhippolhu Atoll

Horsburgh Atoll

Rasdu Atoll

Male' Atoll

Ari Atoll

Felidhu Atoll

North Nilandhe Atoll

South Nilandhe Atoll

Mulaku Atoll

Kolhumadulu Atoll

Hadhdhunmathi Atoll

One and Half Degree Channel

North Huvadhu Atoll

South Huvadhu Atoll

Equatorial Channel — Equator

Fuammulah

Addu Atoll
Gan

• MALE'

I N D I A N   O C E A N

Total Land Area : 300 sq. km (116 sq. miles)

POPULATION
over 10 000   •
under 10 000   •

LAND HEIGHT
100m/328ft
Sea Level

N

0   100 km
0   100 miles

M

WORLD AFFAIRS

The Maldives is a long-standing member of the Non-Aligned Movement. The government continues to support NAM and rejects the criticism that it does not have a role to play in the post-Cold War world. The Maldives' international standing was enhanced in 1990, when it hosted the fifth SAARC summit meeting, held in Male'.

CHRONOLOGY

The Maldives was a British protectorate from 1887 and gained its independence in 1965.

❑ **1932** First written constitution.
❑ **1968** Sultanate abolished. Declared a republic. Ibrahim Nasir elected as first president.
❑ **1988** Coup attempt. Suppressed by Indian troops sent over on request.
❑ **1993** President Gayoom reelected for fourth five-year term.

AID

 $31m (receipts)   Down 21% in 1993

Aid has helped to finance development of port and airport facilities. Japan is the most important bilateral aid donor, contributing 25% of total assistance in 1991. Relief aid, principally from India, Pakistan and the USA, was given after the storms of 1991 which caused $30 million worth of damage.

DEFENSE

 Paramilitary police force only   Not applicable

The British military presence ended in 1975, when troops were withdrawn from the staging post on Gan in the Addu atoll. The Maldives follows a policy of non-alignment but in 1988 called on India for military assistance to help suppress a coup attempt.

ECONOMICS

 $221m   11.76–11.77 rufiyaa

SCORE CARD

❑ WORLD GNP RANKING.........................181st
❑ GNP PER CAPITA $900
❑ BALANCE OF PAYMENTS......................$–48m
❑ INFLATION 16.5%
❑ UNEMPLOYMENT.................................0.1%

STRENGTHS
Growth of tourism. Fishing, especially tuna; mostly exported to the UK and Sri Lanka. Shipping. Clothing. Coconut production. Financial and commercial reforms as economy expands.

WEAKNESSES
Too dependent on fluctuating tourist industry. Growing trade deficit. Shortage of skilled labor. Small manufacturing base. Cottage industries employ 25% of work force; little scope for expansion.

EXPORTS

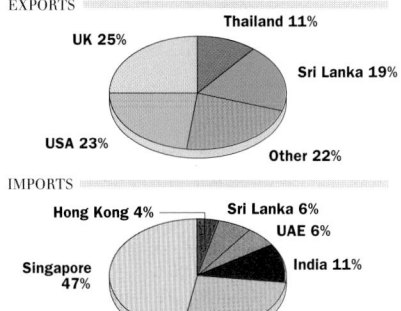

IMPORTS

RESOURCES

 30m kwh (capacity 5,000 kw)    90,012 tons

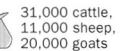 31,000 cattle, 11,000 sheep, 20,000 goats   None

Natural resources include abundant stocks of fish, particularly tuna. Fishing, still carried out by the traditional pole and line method to help conserve stocks, employs over 20% of the working population. Coconut production is also important. All oil products and virtually all staple foods are imported.

ENVIRONMENT

 None   Turtles are protected by law

It is believed global warming, climatic change and the rise of the sea level are threatening to submerge the islands, which have an average height of just 5.2 feet. A sea wall has been built around the capital island. Other environmental concerns are sewerage, waste disposal and the mining of coral for building.

MEDIA

 New libel laws are being implemented by the government against journalists

PUBLISHING AND BROADCAST MEDIA

There are 2 daily newspapers, *Haveeru* and *Aafathis*, published in Dhivehi and English

 1 state-owned service   1 state-owned service

There is a marked degree of press censorship. In the past, journalists and satirists have been imprisoned. There are only two newspapers.

CRIME

 The Maldives does not publish prison figures   Up 3% in 1990

The Maldives is a strict Islamic society. Narcotics crimes are heavily punished. Political prisoners are banished to outer islands. The judiciary and executive are closely linked.

EDUCATION

 91%   Not available

Elementary education has been improved. Secondary education is less developed in the outer islands; the first school outside Male' was opened in 1992.

HEALTH

 1 per 6,595 people   Infectious and parasitic diseases

There is a lack of general equipment and facilities. Health care is less developed on the outlying islands.

WEALTH

 Private-sector secretary, 2,868 rufiyaa ($244) per month; government minister, 5,975 rufiyaa ($508) per month

CONSUMER GOODS OWNERSHIP

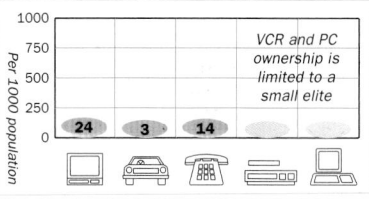

Great disparities exist between the people who live in Male' and those who live on the outer islands.

WORLD RANKING

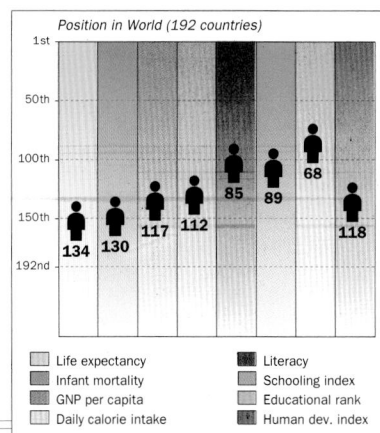

M

MALI

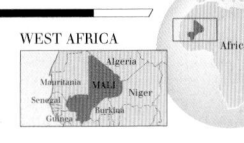

WEST AFRICA

OFFICIAL NAME: Republic of Mali   CAPITAL: Bamako
POPULATION: 10.8 million   CURRENCY: CFA franc   OFFICIAL LANGUAGE: French

 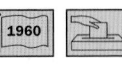 

MALI IS LANDLOCKED in the heart of West Africa. Its mostly flat terrain comprises virtually uninhabited Saharan plains in the north and more fertile savanna land in the south, where most of the population live. The River Niger irrigates the central and southwestern regions of the country. Following independence in 1960, Mali experienced a long period of largely single-party rule. It became a multiparty democracy in 1992.

CLIMATE

WEATHER CHART

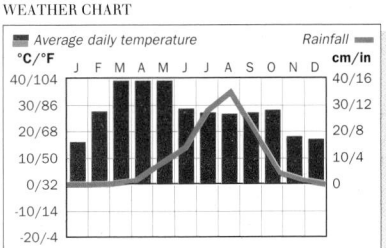

In the south, intensely hot, dry weather precedes the westerly rains. Mali's northern half is almost rainless.

TRANSPORTATION

✈ Bamako-Senou   🚢 Has no fleet

THE TRANSPORTATION NETWORK

1,240 miles (2,000 km)		None	
399 miles (642 km)		1,128 miles (1,815 km)	

Mali is linked by rail with the port of Dakar in Senegal, and by good roads to the port of Abidjan in Ivory Coast.

TOURISM

🧳 16,000 visitors   ⬇ Down 33% in 1994

MAIN OVERSEAS ARRIVALS

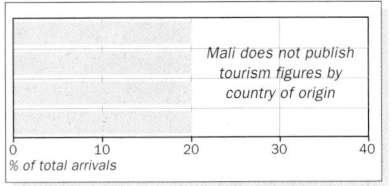

Mali does not publish tourism figures by country of origin

% of total arrivals

Tourism is largely safari-oriented, although the historic cities of Djénné, Gao and Mopti, lying on the banks of the River Niger, also attract visitors. A national domestic airline began operating in 1990.

PEOPLE

👤 Bambara, Fulani, Senufo, Soninke, French   👥 24 people per sq. mile

THE URBAN/RURAL POPULATION SPLIT

25%   75%

RELIGIOUS PERSUASION

Christian 1%   Indigenous beliefs 9%

Muslim 90%

Mali's most significant ethnic group, the Bambara, is also politically dominant. The Bambara speak the *lingua franca* of the River Niger, which is shared with other groups including the Malinke. The relationship between the Bambara–Malinke majority and the Tuareg nomads of the Saharan north is often tense and sometimes violent. As with elsewhere in Africa, the extended family, often based around the village, is a vital social security system and a link between the urban and rural poor. There are a few powerful women in Mali but, in general, women have little status.

POLITICS

🗳 1992/1997   President Alpha Oumar Konaré

THE STATE OF THE PARTIES

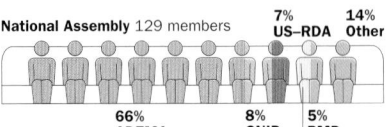

National Assembly 129 members

7% US–RDA
14% Other
66% ADEMA
8% CNID
5% PMD

ADEMA = Alliance for Democracy in Mali   CNID = National Committee for Democratic Initiative   US–RDA = Sudanese Union – African Democratic Rally   PMD = Popular Movement for the Development of West Africa   Other = Rally for Democracy and Progress, Union for Democracy and Development

The successful transition to multiparty politics in 1992 followed the overthrow in the previous year of Moussa Traoré, Mali's dictator for 23 years. The army's role was crucial in leading the coup, while Colonel Touré, who acted as interim president, was responsible for the swift return to civilian rule in less than a year. The change marks Mali's first experience of multipartyism. Maintaining good relations with the Tuaregs, after a peace agreement in 1991, is a key issue. However, the main challenge facing President Alpha Oumar Konaré's government is to alleviate poverty while placating the opposition, which feels that the luxury of multipartyism is something that Mali cannot afford. As Konaré's austerity measures have begun to take effect, opposition to his policies has increased.

MALI

Total Land Area : 1 220 190 sq. km (471 115 sq. miles)

POPULATION

◎	over 100 000
○	over 50 000
●	over 10 000
•	under 10 000

LAND HEIGHT

500m/1640ft
200m/656ft
over 100m/328ft

M

WORLD AFFAIRS

Mali concentrates on maintaining good relations with a wide variety of African neighbors, from the ECOWAS countries to its south, to its northern neighbors such as Algeria. Relations with Libya, which is suspected of fomenting Tuareg revolt, are tense. Good relations with Western aid-providers are crucial.

AID

 $360m (receipts)   Down 18% in 1993

Mali is highly dependent on foreign aid, which comes from France, the EU, China, a few Arab states, the USA and international lending institutions.

DEFENSE

  $47m   Up 4% in 1995

Mali has traditionally had a strong army. In 1985, the air force played an important role in the war with Burkina.

ECONOMICS

 $2.4bn   533.68–489.05 CFA francs

SCORE CARD

- ❏ WORLD GNP RANKING........................131st
- ❏ GNP PER CAPITA $250
- ❏ BALANCE OF PAYMENTS....................$–164m
- ❏ INFLATION 22.9%
- ❏ UNEMPLOYMENT...Widespread underemployment

STRENGTHS

Business opportunities arising from strategic location in heart of West Africa. Niger and Senegal rivers have irrigation and HEP potential.

WEAKNESSES

Endemic poverty. Underdevelopment – landlocked status and country's vast size present considerable problems of transportation and communications. Drought-prone climate.

EXPORTS

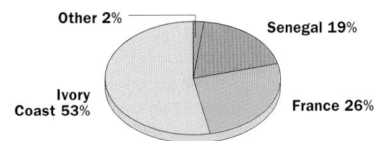

Other 2% | Senegal 19%
Ivory Coast 53% | France 26%

IMPORTS

USA 5% | Germany 6%
Other 39% | Senegal 9%
| Ivory Coast 18%
France 23%

Village near Bandiagara. *These low, broken hills typical of the east and southeast of Mali are the homeland of the Dogon people.*

RESOURCES

 324m kwh (capacity 90,000 kw)   64,352 tons

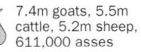 7.4m goats, 5.5m cattle, 5.2m sheep, 611,000 asses   Gold, salt, marble, phosphate, diamonds, tungsten, oil

Gold deposits are now being mined, and prospecting is under way for tungsten, diamonds and oil. The exploitation of other natural resources is hampered by Mali's poor infrastructure and landlocked situation. Almost all electricity is generated by hydroelectric power from the Selingue Dam on the Niger. When a second dam comes into operation, there should be a surplus.

ENVIRONMENT

 3%   New government takes environmental matters seriously

The 1983 drought destroyed herds and accelerated desertification and deforestation. The Selingue Dam seriously affects the levels of the Niger River, even in years of good rainfall.

MEDIA

 The constitution of 1992 guarantees freedom of expression. There are no restrictions on political reporting

PUBLISHING AND BROADCAST MEDIA

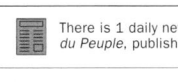 There is 1 daily newspaper, *L'Essor – La Voix du Peuple*, published by the government

 1 state-owned service    1 state-owned service

Even before the coup, previously rigid controls had begun to be relaxed. The militant campaigning of the privately owned press in early 1991 was a significant factor in the overthrow of the Traoré regime.

CRIME

 Mali does not publish prison figures   Crime is rising slowly

Crime is not particularly prevalent compared with some other countries in the region, owing to strong family ties and the relative lack of urbanization. In towns, robbery, juvenile delinquency and smuggling are problems.

CHRONOLOGY

Mali was a major trans-Saharan trading empire. The French colonized the area between 1881 and 1895.

- ❏ **1960** Independence under anti-French socialist Modibo Keita.
- ❏ **1968** Armed coup; single-party state under Gen. Traoré.
- ❏ **1985** Six-day war with Burkina. ICJ splits disputed land equally.
- ❏ **1990** Democracy demonstrations.
- ❏ **1991** Traoré arrested.
- ❏ **1992** Free multiparty elections.

EDUCATION

 32%   6,703 students

Education in Mali is based on the French system. Only 25% of children attend elementary school and just 7% receive secondary education.

HEALTH

 1 per 21,180 people   Malaria, pneumonia, parasitic and diarrheal diseases

Health provision is poor. Infant mortality is 130 per 1,000 live births and average life expectancy 48.

WEALTH

 Kindergarten teacher, 27,500 CFA francs ($56) per month; electrician, 101,500 CFA francs ($208) per month

CONSUMER GOODS OWNERSHIP

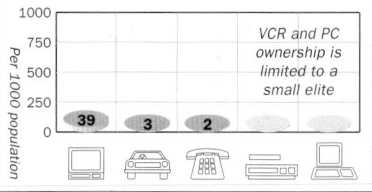

VCR and PC ownership is limited to a small elite

39   3   2

Poverty is widespread. Malians disapprove of flaunted wealth and public ostentation is rare.

WORLD RANKING

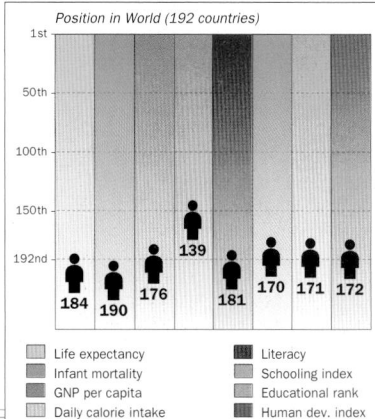

Position in World (192 countries)

- Life expectancy
- Infant mortality
- GNP per capita
- Daily calorie intake
- Literacy
- Schooling index
- Educational rank
- Human dev. index

M

MALTA

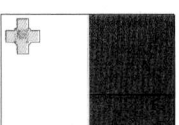

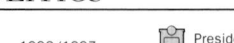
OFFICIAL NAME: Republic of Malta   **CAPITAL:** Valletta
POPULATION: 400,000   **CURRENCY:** Maltese lira   **OFFICIAL LANGUAGES:** Maltese and English

T HE MALTESE ARCHIPELAGO is strategically located, lying midway between Europe and North Africa. Controlled throughout its history by successive colonial powers, Malta gained independence from the UK in 1964. The islands are mainly low-lying, with rocky coastlines; only Malta, Gozo and Kemmuna are inhabited. Tourism is Malta's chief source of income, with an influx of tourists each year over two times the islands' population.

M

CLIMATE

WEATHER CHART

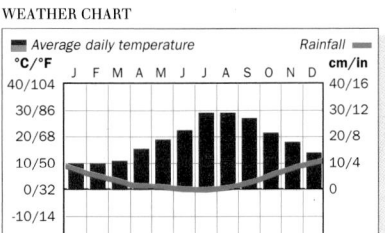

The climate is very similar to that of Greece – with at least six hours of sunshine a day, even in winter.

TRANSPORTATION

 **Luqa Intl, Valletta** 1.9m passengers

 837 ships 17.93m dwt

THE TRANSPORTATION NETWORK

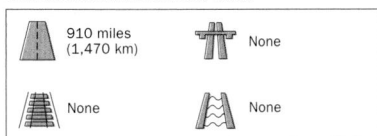

910 miles (1,470 km)	None
None	None

A new terminal with an annual capacity of 2.5 million passengers was recently opened at Luqa airport. The main external sea route is to Sicily. In summer, there is a five-minute helicopter link between the islands of Malta and Gozo, in addition to regular ferry and hovercraft services. There are regular buses on both islands.

Traditionally painted **luzzus** *at St Julian's harbor. The fish caught are now only for domestic and tourist consumption.*

TOURISM

1.2m visitors   Up 11% in 1994

MAIN OVERSEAS ARRIVALS

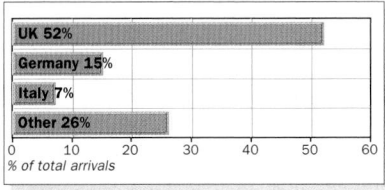

UK 52%	
Germany 15%	
Italy 7%	
Other 26%	

% of total arrivals

Tourism in Malta is a booming industry, accounting for 30% of GNP. In addition to Malta's beaches and scenery, the government is keen to promote the historical attractions of Mdina and Valletta. Development on the quieter island of Gozo is being limited to luxury-grade hotels.

PEOPLE

 Maltese, English

3,239 people per sq. mile

THE URBAN/RURAL POPULATION SPLIT

88%   12%

RELIGIOUS PERSUASION

Other 2%

Roman Catholic 98%

Malta's population has been subject over the centuries to diverse Arabic, Sicilian, Norman, Spanish, English and Italian influences. Today, many young Maltese go abroad to find work, especially to the USA and Australia; opportunities for them on the islands are few.

The Maltese are staunch Roman Catholics, on a percentage basis more so than virtually any other nation. The remainder are mainly Anglicans, who are included within the diocese of Gibraltar. Divorce is illegal.

POLITICS

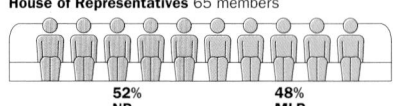

1992/1997   President Ugo Mifsud-Bonnici

THE STATE OF THE PARTIES

House of Representatives 65 members

52% NP	48% MLP

NP = Nationalist Party   **MLP** Malta Labour Party

The Nationalists, led by Dr. Fenech Adami, came to power in 1987 after 16 years of Labour rule. Adami's subsequent reelection to a second term of office in 1992 was largely due to a rise in living standards and economic growth. The Maltese were also reluctant to return to the divisive politics of the past.

Under Labour, politics was shaped by the leadership of the charismatic Dom Mintoff, who championed state control of industry and a strategy of international non-alignment. The Nationalists retained the non-aligned policy and wrote it into the constitution. In 1990, they succeeded in sealing a three-way accord between government, unions and businesses, under which wages are agreed in line with inflation.

The opposition is now led by Dr. Alfred Sant, a leading Maltese writer and Harvard MBA, and Labour's traditional links with the unions have been diluted. The main current political issue is Malta's application for membership of the EU.

WORLD AFFAIRS

CE	Comm	IBRD	NAM	OSCE

Malta is optimistic that it will gain entry into the EU; a formal application was made in 1990. All legislation is now drafted to EU regulations and old measures are being updated in accordance with them. Membership is expected to bring significant economic benefits; already, an estimated 75% of trade is with EU nations.

Closer links with Europe have to be balanced with Malta's traditional association with the Arab world and North Africa. Relations with Libya and the Gaddafi regime are good, though not as close as under the Labour government of Prime Minister Mintoff in the 1970s. However, a friendship treaty was recently signed between the two countries. Malta also maintains close commercial links with the CIS and China.

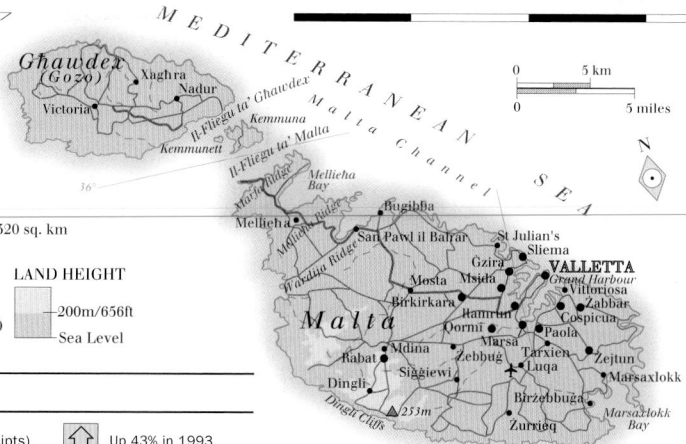

MALTA

Total Land Area : 320 sq. km
(124 sq. miles)

POPULATION	LAND HEIGHT
● over 10 000	200m/656ft
• under 10 000	Sea Level

AID

💲 $30m (receipts)   ⬆ Up 43% in 1993

Malta receives economic assistance under an agreement with the EU. The UK is the main bilateral source of aid.

DEFENSE

💲 $30m   ⬆ Up 10% in 1995

The 1,850-strong Maltese army, advised by the Libyans in the 1980s, now receives training and equipment from Italy, Germany and the UK.

ECONOMICS

📊 $2.6bn   💲 0.37–0.35 Maltese liri

SCORE CARD

❑ WORLD GNP RANKING	138th
❑ GNP PER CAPITA	$7,298
❑ BALANCE OF PAYMENTS	$–86m
❑ INFLATION	3.7%
❑ UNEMPLOYMENT	4.5%

STRENGTHS

Tourism and naval dockyards. Schemes to attract foreign high-tech industry. Offshore banking potential. Strategic position between Europe and Africa, on the main Mediterranean shipping lines.

WEAKNESSES

Lack of diversification at present. Cut-price competition from Africa and Asia in traditional textile industry. Need to import almost all requirements.

EXPORTS

UK 7% USA 6%
France 9%
Italy 41%
Germany 14%
Other 23%

IMPORTS

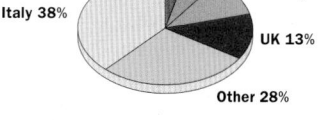

Japan 4% France 6%
Germany 11%
Italy 38%
UK 13%
Other 28%

RESOURCES

⚡ 1.1bn kwh (capacity 250,000 kw)
🐟 5,560 tons
🐷 111,000 pigs, 20,000 cattle, 6,000 sheep
💎 Stone, sand

Electrical generating capacity is due to increase with the completion of a new 360 MW-capacity power station in 1997. Malta is dependent on desalination plants for most of its water supply. All oil has to be imported.

ENVIRONMENT

🚀 None   ⬆ Controls on hotel developments

The main environmental concern is linked to the tourist industry. A lack of planning controls in the 1970s was responsible for unsightly beach developments. These are now tightly controlled, particularly on Gozo.

MEDIA

❌ Freedom of expression guaranteed under constitution

PUBLISHING AND BROADCAST MEDIA

📰 There are 3 daily newspapers, *In-Nazzjon Taghna*, *L-Orizzont* and *The Times*	
📺 1 state-owned service	📡 2 state-owned stations
🛰 Intelsat V1 F1 Astra 1B	📺 1 cable TV network in operation

The Maltese press is largely politically oriented. Two of the three main press groups are affiliated to the NP and MLP; one is independent.

CRIME

🏢 221 prisoners   ⬆ Up 3% in 1992

Crime rates are low compared to those on the European mainland. There has, however, been an increase in narcotics transshipment and associated crimes.

EDUCATION

👤 86%   🎓 3,123 students

Spending on education is equal to 4.6% of GNP. There are 3,123 full-time students at the University of Malta in Valletta.

HEALTH

🏥 1 per 406 people   💀 Cerebrovascular and heart diseases, cancers

Malta has six state-run hospitals. Around 7% of government expenditure is allocated to health services.

WEALTH

💰 Income per capita is below the European average

CONSUMER GOODS OWNERSHIP

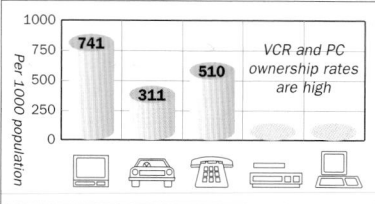

VCR and PC ownership rates are high

741 311 510

Per 1000 population

Remittances from Maltese working abroad are an important source of income for many island families.

WORLD RANKING

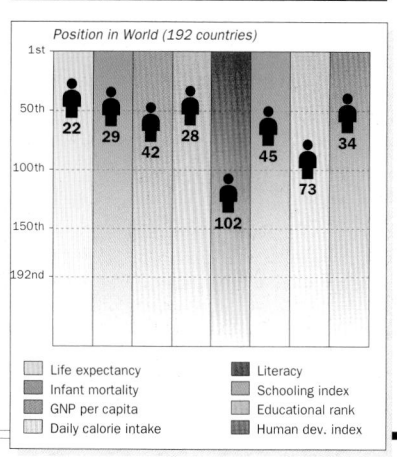

Position in World (192 countries)

22 29 42 28 102 45 73 34

▫ Life expectancy	▪ Literacy
▪ Infant mortality	▫ Schooling index
▪ GNP per capita	▪ Educational rank
▫ Daily calorie intake	▪ Human dev. index

M

MARSHALL ISLANDS

PACIFIC OCEAN

Pacific Ocean

Northern Marianas Islands — MARSHALL ISLANDS

Micronesia

OFFICIAL NAME: Republic of the Marshall Islands **CAPITAL:** Majuro
POPULATION: 52,000 **CURRENCY:** US dollar **OFFICIAL LANGUAGES:** English and Marshallese

THE MARSHALL ISLANDS comprise a group of 34 widely scattered atolls in the central Pacific Ocean. They were formerly under US rule as part of the UN Trust Territory of the Pacific Islands; an agreement which granted internal sovereignty in free association with the US became operational in 1986, and the Trust was formally dissolved in 1990. The economy is almost entirely dependent on US aid and rent for the US missile base on Kwajalein atoll.

Ebeye Island in the Marshalls. Population pressures have led to the disappearance of most tree and grass cover on the island.

CLIMATE

WEATHER CHART

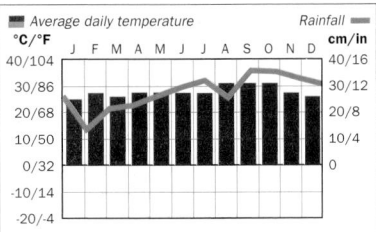

The climate is tropical oceanic. Temperatures show little seasonal variation, averaging around 86°F.

TRANSPORTATION

 Majuro Intl    Has no fleet

THE TRANSPORTATION NETWORK

| Surfaced roads only on larger islands | None |
| None | None |

The transportation system is limited, although there is some inter-island shipping. Regular scheduled flights connect ten of the atolls.

TOURISM

 6,000 visitors   Up 20% in 1994

MAIN OVERSEAS ARRIVALS

The Marshall Islands does not publish tourism figures by country of origin

0   10   20   30   40
% of total arrivals

There are few hotels or amenities for tourists, though outlying islands have the potential of unspoilt beaches. Those who visit are mainly Japanese and American; many are war veterans.

PEOPLE

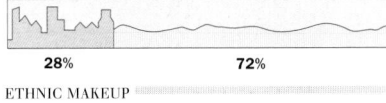 Marshallese, English, Japanese, German   744 people per sq. mile

THE URBAN/RURAL POPULATION SPLIT

28%   72%

ETHNIC MAKEUP

Other 3%

Micronesian 97%

Of the 34 atolls making up the Marshall Islands, 24 are inhabited. Majuro, the capital and commercial center, is home to almost half of the population, many of whom live in its overcrowded slums. The other main center of population is Ebeye, where tensions are high due to poor living conditions. Most of Ebeye's inhabitants were forcefully relocated from Kwajalein in 1947 to make way for a US missile tracking, testing and interception base; many still travel back to Kwajalein daily to work at the base. Life on the outlying islands is still centered around subsistence agriculture and fishing. Society is traditionally matrilineal.

MARSHALL ISLANDS

Total Land Area : 181 sq. km (70 sq. miles)

LAND HEIGHT

100m/328ft

Sea Level

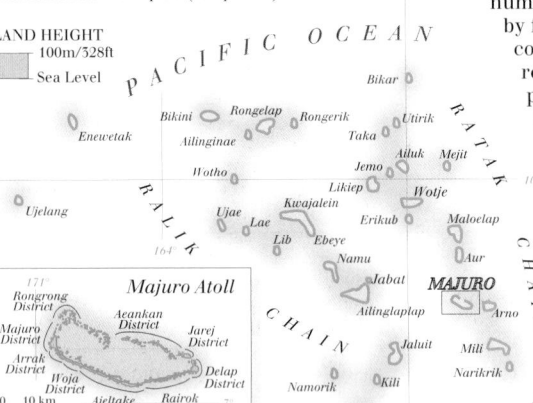

PACIFIC OCEAN

Bokak

Bikar

Bikini   Rongelap   Rongerik

Enewetak   Ailinginae   Taka

Wotho   Jemo   Ailuk   Mejit

Ujelang   Likiep   Wotje

Ujae   Kwajalein   Erikub   Maloelap

Lae   Lib   Ebeye

Namu   Aur

Jabat

MAJURO   Arno

Ailinglaplap

Jaluit   Mili

Namorik   Kili   Narikrik

Ebon

RALIK CHAIN   RATAK CHAIN

Utirik

Majuro Atoll

Rongrong District
Aeankan District
Majuro District   Jarej District
Arrak District   Delap District
Woja District
Ajeltake District   Rairok District

0   10 km
0   10 miles

N

0   200 km
0   200 miles

POLITICS

1995/1999   President Amata Kabua

THE STATE OF THE PARTIES

Parliament (Nitijela) 33 members

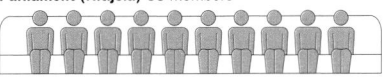

The 33 members are elected from 25 districts

Council of Chiefs 12 members

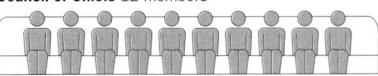

All 12 members are high chiefs

Politics is traditionally dominated by chiefs. President Amata Kabua, who has been in power since self-government began in 1979, is the islands' high chief. Members of his family hold several important government posts. There are two main political groupings, the ruling RMI and the opposition Ralik-Ratak Democratic Party. The main political issue is the islands' continuing inability to achieve financial self-sufficiency.

Their economy is almost totally dependent on US aid. Discussion has centered recently on a number of projects proposed by foreign states, which could bring in additional revenue. These include a proposal for a plant to generate electricity by burning used tyres and a project to use toxic waste to build a causeway on Kwajalein. The likely environmental impact of such projects is an important issue.

M

WORLD AFFAIRS

From 1947, the islands were controlled by the USA as part of the Trust Territory of the Pacific Islands. Under the terms of the Compact of Free Association signed in 1982 and operational from 1986, the USA is to pay $1 billion in aid over 15 years. In return, it has control of Kwajalein, and determines foreign and defense policies. In addition, no further claims for compensation by victims of US nuclear testing between 1946 and 1958 will be considered.

AID

 $32m (receipts)   Up 300% in 1993

Aid from the USA accounts for around two-thirds of the islands' revenue. Australia and Taiwan also provide some assistance.

DEFENSE

 USA responsible for defense   Not applicable

There is no defense force. All defense is provided by the USA under the terms of the Compact of Free Association. The USA does not have offensive weapons sited in the Marshalls, but its navy regularly patrols the region.

ECONOMICS

 $88m   US dollar

SCORE CARD

- ❏ World GNP Ranking........................189th
- ❏ GNP per Capita $1,680
- ❏ Balance of Payments......................$–59m
- ❏ Inflation 2.8%
- ❏ Unemployment.................................16%

STRENGTHS
Aid from the USA, on which the islands are almost totally dependent. Strategic refusal by US to allow impoverishment, so that no other foreign power can gain influence. Copra.

WEAKNESSES
Dependence on imports, which are 11 times greater than exports. All fuel has to be imported. Vulnerability to storm damage. Large state sector employing 75% of workers.

EXPORTS/IMPORTS

The Marshall Islands' main trading partners are the USA and Japan

RESOURCES

 Electricity is provided by small diesel generators   Not an oil producer and has no refineries

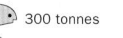 300 tonnes    Phosphates

There are very few known strategic resources. Exploratory tests have revealed some high-grade phosphate deposits, but not in economically viable quantities. Small diesel generators are used for electricity production.

ENVIRONMENT

 None   Plans for toxic waste dump

Between 1946 and 1958, Bikini and Enewetak atolls were the site of a series of US nuclear military tests. Islanders were exposed to radiation and both atolls were rendered uninhabitable. The residents of Enewetak were allowed to return in 1980, following some decontamination of the land. The USA has now paid out over $101 million to victims of nuclear testing. In recent years, the Marshall Islands have been proposed as a potential toxic waste dump by both the USA and Japan. Discussions have also taken place on creating landfill sites, to take US household refuse.

MEDIA

 The media is generally free of censorship

PUBLISHING AND BROADCAST MEDIA

 There are no daily newspapers. The one weekly newspaper, the *Marshall Islands Journal*, is privately owned

 1 independent service   1 state-controlled, 1 independent station

Radio is the main source of information in the Marshalls. There is also a subscription-only TV service. The US personnel stationed on Kwajalein have their own TV and radio stations.

CRIME

 The Marshalls does not publish prison figures   Little change from year to year

Crime levels are generally low; however, the rate is up on Ebeye. Outlying islands are crime-free.

EDUCATION

 91%   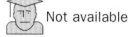 Not available

Education is based on the US model. The number of secondary school graduates exceeds the availability of suitable employment in the Marshall Islands. Many go on to university in the USA. Small church institutions in the USA often subsidize students.

CHRONOLOGY

After a period under Spanish rule, the Marshall Islands became a German protectorate in 1885; Japan took possession at the start of World War I. The islands were transferred to US control in 1945.

- ❏ **1946** US government begins a program of nuclear testing.
- ❏ **1947** UN Trust Territory of the Pacific established.
- ❏ **1961** Kwajalein becomes US army missile range, the target for ICBMs fired from California.
- ❏ **1979** Constitution approved in referendum. Government set up.
- ❏ **1986** Compact of Free Association with US operational.
- ❏ **1990** Trust terminated by UN Security Council.

HEALTH

 1 per 2,137 people   Respiratory, heart and diarrheal diseases

Medical facilities are rudimentary. Complex operations are performed in hospitals on Hawaii. Levels of malnutrition are high.

WEALTH

 Most Marshall Islanders live a subsistence existence

CONSUMER GOODS OWNERSHIP

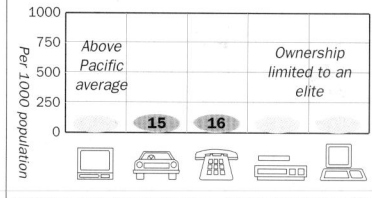

Wealth disparities are small. Very few citizens can afford luxuries such as air conditioning or cars.

WORLD RANKING

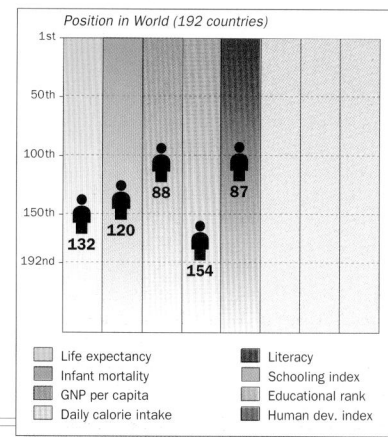

M

MAURITANIA

OFFICIAL NAME: Islamic Republic of Mauritania **CAPITAL:** Nouakchott
POPULATION: 2.3 million **CURRENCY:** Ouguiya **OFFICIAL LANGUAGE:** French

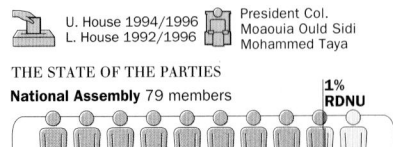

NORTH AFRICA

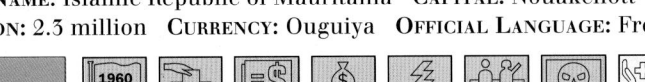

1960

LOCATED IN NORTHWEST AFRICA, Mauritania is a member of both the OAU and the Arab League. Formerly a French colony, the country has taken a strongly Arab direction since 1964; today, it is the Maures who control political life and dominate the minority black population. The Sahara extends across two-thirds of Mauritania's territory. The only productive land is that drained by the Senegal River in the south and southwest.

CLIMATE

WEATHER CHART

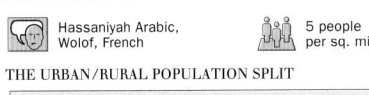

| Average daily temperature | | Rainfall |
| °C/°F | | cm/in |

The dusty Saharan *harmattan* wind often aggravates the very hot, dry conditions. Some rain falls in the south.

TRANSPORTATION

Nouakchott

2 ships
3,000 dwt

THE TRANSPORTATION NETWORK

1,050 miles (1,690 km)		None	
441 miles (710 km)		River Senegal	

The transportation system is limited and unevenly developed. There are two major roads, but shifting sands mean they require constant maintenance.

TOURISM

13,000 visitors

No change in 1994

MAIN OVERSEAS ARRIVALS

Mauritania does not publish tourism figures by country of origin

0	10	20	30	40

% of total arrivals

There are few tourists apart from desert safari enthusiasts. The more mountainous areas are especially dramatic, but access is difficult. Nouakchott has some hotels.

PEOPLE

Hassaniyah Arabic, Wolof, French

5 people per sq. mile

THE URBAN/RURAL POPULATION SPLIT

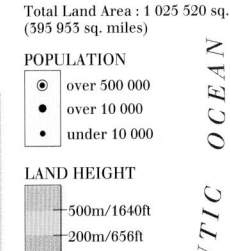

50%   50%

RELIGIOUS PERSUASION

Muslim 100%

The politically dominant Maures make up about one-third of the population. The black population is composed of the Havalin, the Senegalese peoples and the Tukolor, Peulh and Wolof groups. Ethnic tension centers on the oppression of blacks by Maures. The old black bourgeoisie has now been superseded by a Maurish class; tens of thousands of blacks are estimated to be in slavery. Ethnic tension came to a head in 1989, when 200,000 Maures fled from Senegal. There were attacks on Senegalese in Mauritania and many fled or were deported to refugee camps along the Senegal River. Family solidarity among nomads is particularly strong.

MAURITANIA

Total Land Area : 1 025 520 sq. km
(395 953 sq. miles)

POPULATION
- ◉ over 500 000
- ● over 10 000
- • under 10 000

LAND HEIGHT
- 500m/1640ft
- 200m/656ft
- Sea Level

0 ___ 200 km
0 ___ 200 miles

POLITICS

U. House 1994/1996
L. House 1992/1996

President Col. Moaouia Ould Sidi Mohammed Taya

THE STATE OF THE PARTIES

National Assembly 79 members

1% RDNU
85% DSRP
1% MPR
10% Other

DSRP = Democratic and Social Republican Party
MPR = Mauritanian Party for Renewal **RDNU** = Rally for Democracy and National Unity
Senate 56 members

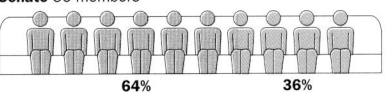

64% DSRP
36% Other

3 members are chosen to represent the interests of Mauritanians abroad

In 1991, partly because of pressure from Western aid donors, Mauritania officially returned to multiparty democracy. However, the 1992 presidential elections simply returned the incumbent military ruler, President Moaouia Ould Taya, to power. General elections were held but were boycotted by the opposition parties. These are mainly Maure-led; the blacks of the south support exiled parties, such as the Dakar-based liberation group FLAM. The issue of ethnic relations is the central political problem, especially since a 1987 coup plot, which caused the blacks' base in the army to collapse.

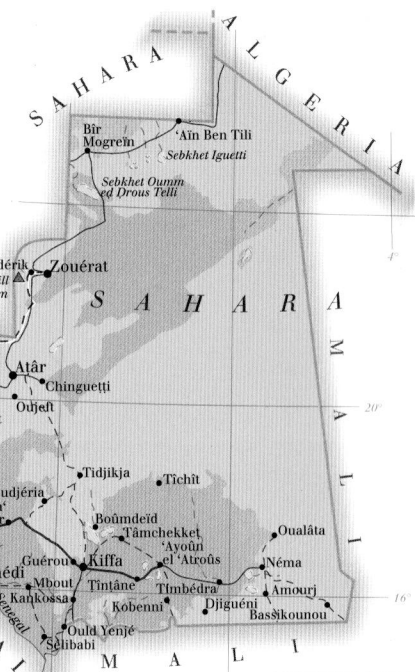

WORLD AFFAIRS

Mauritania has to maintain a delicate balance in relations with sub-Saharan Africa and the Arab world; as a result, it belongs to both ECOWAS and the Arab Maghreb Union. Relations with neighboring Senegal have improved since the conflicts of 1989.

AID

 $331m (receipts)   Up 58% in 1993

France, Germany, the IMF, OPEC and Iraq are all donors. Most aid is used for development projects, such as the EU-funded Trans-Mauritanian Highway.

DEFENSE

 $37m   Up 3% in 1995

The 15,000-strong military is a strain on Mauritania's limited budget. Much arms procurement is still from France, but some is now from the Arab world.

ECONOMICS

 $1.1bn   122–135 ouguiyas

SCORE CARD

- ❏ WORLD GNP RANKING........................154th
- ❏ GNP PER CAPITA $480
- ❏ BALANCE OF PAYMENTS....................$–139m
- ❏ INFLATION 4.1%
- ❏ UNEMPLOYMENT.................................20%

STRENGTHS

Iron from the Cominor mine at Zouérat. Largest gypsum deposits in the world. Copper, yet to be properly exploited. Offshore fishing among the best in West Africa.

WEAKNESSES

"Debt-distressed," with a debt of nearly $2 billion – a legacy of its move to leave the Franc Zone. Poor land – two-thirds is desert. Very hot, dry climate.

EXPORTS

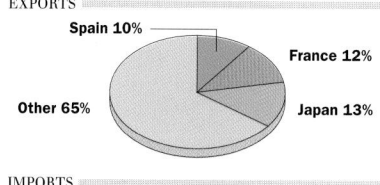

Spain 10%
France 12%
Japan 13%
Other 65%

IMPORTS

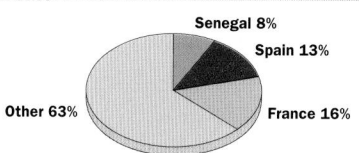

Senegal 8%
Spain 13%
France 16%
Other 63%

Mauritania's extreme aridity means that only 1% of the land is arable. Two-thirds of the country is part of the Sahara desert; sparse vegetation over the rest supports some livestock.

RESOURCES

 146m kwh (capacity 110,000 kw)   92,800 tons

 4.8m sheep, 3.1m goats, 1m cattle   Iron, gypsum, copper, gold, phosphates, yttrium

Iron, which in the 1960s brought economic profitability, continues to be exploited, despite low prices on the world market. Electricity generation has expanded rapidly since the late 1960s, from 38.4m kwh in 1967 to 146m kwh in 1992, reflecting the growing needs of the minerals industries. Phosphates have been found near the Senegal River.

ENVIRONMENT

 2% (0.2% partially protected)   Desertification is the major problem

The chief environmental problem in Mauritania is that of the encroaching Sahara desert, a situation worsened by the droughts of 1973 and 1983, which caused widespread loss of grazing land. The consequent exodus of people away from the land has led to Nouakchott's population increasing from 20,000 in 1960 to over 500,000 today.

MEDIA

 There are still instances of censorship

PUBLISHING AND BROADCAST MEDIA

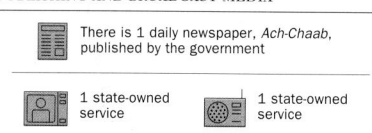

There is 1 daily newspaper, *Ach-Chaab*, published by the government

1 state-owned service   1 state-owned service

French-language press and radio are increasingly under pressure from militant Maures, who are eager to promote the use of Arabic.

CRIME

 Mauritania does not publish prison figures   Up 53% in 1992

The main problems are smuggling and robbery. Levels of violence are lower than the West African average.

EDUCATION

 34%   5,850 students

Arabic has been compulsory in all schools since 1988, though this has met resistance from blacks. Around 55% of children attend elementary school.

HEALTH

 1 per 11,900 people   Diarrheal and respiratory diseases, influenza, tuberculosis

Historic regional inequalities persist and the best facilities are in the capital. The overall level of care is on a par with neighboring states.

WEALTH

 Slavery officially became illegal in 1980, but much *de facto* slavery survives

CONSUMER GOODS OWNERSHIP

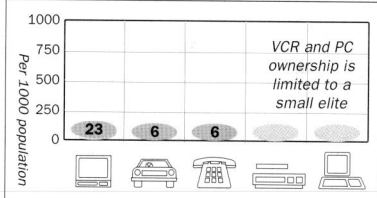

VCR and PC ownership is limited to a small elite

23   6   6

The ruling Maures form the wealthiest sector. Wealthy Maures travel to Mecca to perform the *haj* (Muslim pilgrimage).

WORLD RANKING

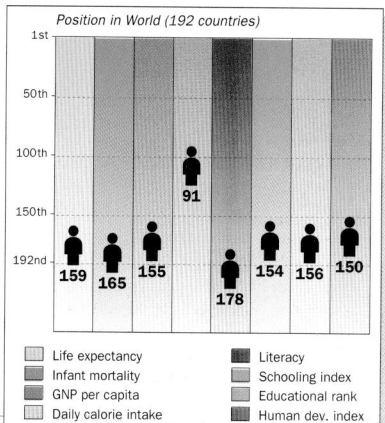

Position in World (192 countries)

91
159   165   155   178   154   156   150

- ❏ Life expectancy
- ❏ Infant mortality
- ❏ GNP per capita
- ❏ Daily calorie intake
- ❏ Literacy
- ❏ Schooling index
- ❏ Educational rank
- ❏ Human dev. index

M

MAURITIUS

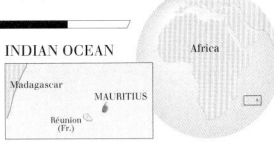

INDIAN OCEAN

OFFICIAL NAME: Mauritius **CAPITAL:** Port Louis
POPULATION: 1.1 million **CURRENCY:** Mauritian rupee **OFFICIAL LANGUAGE:** English

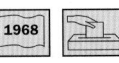 

THE ISLANDS THAT MAKE up Mauritius lie in the Indian Ocean east of Madagascar. The principal island, from which the country takes its name, is of volcanic origin and surrounded by coral reefs. The outer islands, 311 mi. to the north, are Rodrigues, the Agalega Islands and the Cargados Carajos Shoals. Mauritius has enjoyed considerable economic success following recent industrial diversification and the expansion of its tourist industry.

CLIMATE

WEATHER CHART

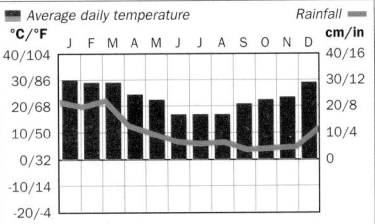

The climate is subtropical and humid. December to March are the hottest and wettest months. Tropical cyclones are an occasional threat at this time.

TRANSPORTATION

Sir Seewoosagur Ramgoolam Intl
870,000 passengers

8 ships
166,600 dwt

THE TRANSPORTATION NETWORK

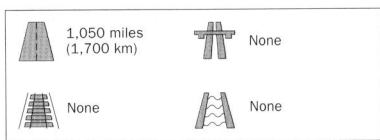

| 1,050 miles (1,700 km) | None |
| None | None |

Roads are extensive, but often congested. Plans exist for a monorail link between Port Louis and Curepipe.

TOURISM

401,000 visitors

Up 7% in 1994

MAIN OVERSEAS ARRIVALS

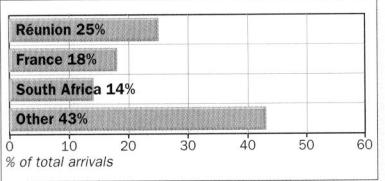

Réunion 25%
France 18%
South Africa 14%
Other 43%

0 10 20 30 40 50 60
% of total arrivals

Tourism has expanded rapidly in the past decade. Spectacular beaches, water sports and big game fishing are major attractions. However, many new hotels are usually only half full.

PEOPLE

French Creole, Hindi, Urdu, Tamil, Chinese, English, French

1,542 people per sq. mile

THE URBAN/RURAL POPULATION SPLIT

41%   59%

RELIGIOUS PERSUASION

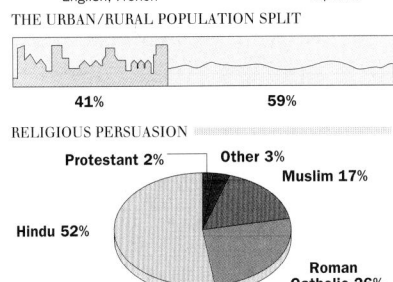

Protestant 2%   Other 3%
Muslim 17%
Hindu 52%
Roman Catholic 26%

The majority of the population are the descendants of indentured laborers brought over from India in the 19th century. Creoles make up 27% of the population, while 3% are of Chinese origin. The wealthiest group is the small minority of Mauritians of French descent, who control much of business, including the sugarcane industry.

POLITICS

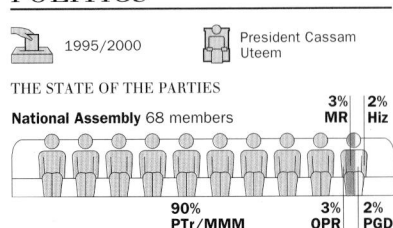

1995/2000

President Cassam Uteem

THE STATE OF THE PARTIES

National Assembly 68 members

90% PTr/MMM   3% OPR   3% MR   2% Hiz   2% PGD

PTr/MMM = Labour Party/Mauritius Militant Movement
OPR = Organization of the People of Rodrigues
MR = Rodrigues Movement Party **PGD** = Gaetan Duval Party
Hiz = Hizbullah Party

Mauritius became a republic in 1992. Politics are characterized by coalition governments, and are largely based around personalities. There is relatively little ideological difference between the main parties. Elections at the end of 1995 saw the PTr/MMM alliance inflict a humiliating defeat on Prime Minister Sir Aneerood Jugnauth, who had led the country since 1982. His MSM lost all its seats in parliament. The new prime minister is Navin Ramgoolam.

WORLD AFFAIRS

Comm   Comesa   IOC   OAU   SADC

Mauritius is a member of the Commonwealth, but it is also seeking to develop relations with French-speaking countries. In 1993, it hosted the fifth annual summit of francophone nations. Links with South Africa are also important.

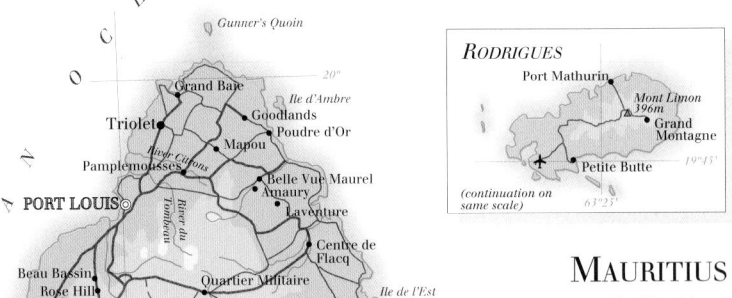

Round Island
Flat Island
Ilot Gabriel
Gunner's Quoin

Grand Baie
Ile d'Ambre
Triolet
Goodlands
Poudre d'Or
Mapou
Pamplemousses
Belle Vue Maurel
Amaury
Laventure
PORT LOUIS
Centre de Flacq
Beau Bassin
Rose Hill
Quartier Militaire
Ile de l'Est
Quatre Bornes
Phoenix
Ile aux Cerfs
Vacoas
Floréal
Tamarin
Curepipe
Grande River South East
Piton de la Petite Rivière Noire 828m
Nouvelle France
Mahebourg
Ile aux Bénitiers
Rose Belle
Sir Seewoosagur Ramgoolam Intl
Chamouny
Chemin Grenier
Rivière des Anguilles
Bel Ombre
Surinam
Souillac

RODRIGUES
Port Mathurin
Mont Limon 396m
Grand Montagne
Petite Butte
(continuation on same scale)

MAURITIUS

Total Land Area :
1860 sq. km (718 sq. miles)

LAND HEIGHT
500m/1640ft
200m/656ft
Sea Level

POPULATION
over 100 000
over 50 000
over 10 000
under 10 000

0   10 km
0   10 miles

AID

 $27m (receipts)   Down 43% in 1993

Aid is predominantly bilateral, with France and the UK as the main donors. Mauritius also receives aid from the EU, under the Lomé Convention, and other international organizations. A five-year conservation program was initiated in 1990 with assistance from the World Bank. The Bank has also promised $53 million toward the development of Port Louis as a free port.

DEFENSE

 $13.2m   Up 17% in 1995

Mauritius has no defense forces. There is, however, a special police unit to ensure internal security. Expenditure on policing accounts for 0.4% of total government spending.

ECONOMICS

 $3.5bn    18.05–18.21 Mauritian rupees

SCORE CARD

❏ World GNP Ranking	116th
❏ GNP per Capita	$3,180
❏ Balance of Payments	$–230m
❏ Inflation	7.3%
❏ Unemployment	2.4%

STRENGTHS

Economic growth averaging 6% a year over last decade. Sugar industry, which accounts for 30% of export earnings. Export Processing Zone (EPZ), especially for clothing manufacture. Tourism, the third-largest foreign exchange earner. Highly educated work force. Potential as offshore financial center now being developed.

WEAKNESSES

Vulnerability to fluctuations in world prices for sugar. 75% of food requirements imported. Occasional cyclones mean few crops other than sugar can be grown. Remoteness. Lack of strategic resources.

EXPORTS
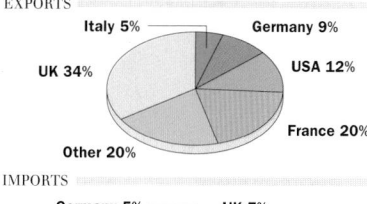
Italy 5%   Germany 9%
UK 34%   USA 12%
France 20%
Other 20%

IMPORTS
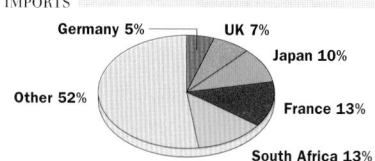
Germany 5%   UK 7%
Japan 10%
Other 52%   France 13%
South Africa 13%

Villagers at a water source in the center of Mauritius island. Mauritius' main rivers are used for hydropower generation.

RESOURCES

 925m kwh (capacity 313,000 kw)   92,800 tons

 95,000 goats, 34,000 cattle, 17,000 pigs   None

Mauritius is heavily dependent on imported oil supplies. The government has put considerable investment into developing alternative energy schemes, including hydroelectric power generation. Power stations fueled by bagasse (a by-product of the sugar industry) are now also in operation.

ENVIRONMENT

 2% (0.1% partially protected)   New government measures to restrict development

Rapid industrialization and unchecked hotel building have caused environmental problems. Coral reefs are under threat from both coral sand mining and the discharging of untreated sewage into the sea.

MEDIA

 Freedom of expression is guaranteed under the constitution. Foreign satellite TV broadcasts are subject to government approval

 There are 8 daily newspapers. *The Sun, L'Express* and *Le Mauricien* have the largest circulations

 2 independent stations   2 independent stations

Mauritius has an active press, subject to few regulations and with a wide readership. Newspapers are published in English, French, Creole, Hindi, Chinese and Tamil. However, opposition parties complain that TV and radio broadcasts are consistently biased toward the government.

CRIME

 2,145 prisoners   Up 9% in 1992

Crime rates on the main island are fairly low. There has been a small increase in thefts in the towns. Outlying islands are virtually crime-free.

CHRONOLOGY

Originally colonized by the Dutch in the 17th century, Mauritius later came under French rule. In 1810, it was captured by the British.

- ❏ **1959** First full elections.
- ❏ **1968** Independence as part of the Commonwealth. Seewoosagur Ramgoolam prime minister. Riots between Creoles and Muslims.
- ❏ **1969** MMM formed under Bérenger.
- ❏ **1992** Becomes a republic.

EDUCATION

 79%    2,179 students

Educational provision is good and the literacy rate for Mauritians under the age of 30 is 91%. The University of Mauritius has about 2,000 students.

HEALTH

 1 per 1,200 people   Circulatory and heart diseases, cancers, accidents

Free health care is universally available. There are 14 state hospitals and six private clinics.

WEALTH

 Sugar plantation worker, 13 Mauritian rupees ($0.7) per hour; journalist, 7,045 Mauritian rupees ($387) per month

CONSUMER GOODS OWNERSHIP

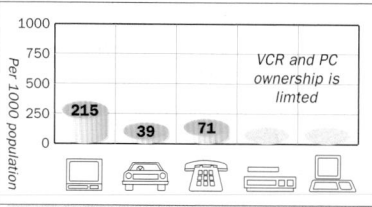

VCR and PC ownership is limted

215   39   71

French-descended hotel and plantation owners are the wealthiest group. Government employees are well paid.

WORLD RANKING

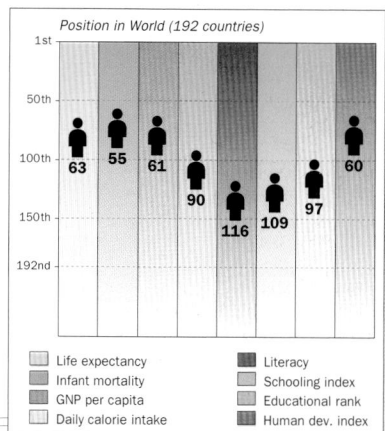

Position in World (192 countries)

63   55   61   90   116   109   97   60

- Life expectancy
- Infant mortality
- GNP per capita
- Daily calorie intake
- Literacy
- Schooling index
- Educational rank
- Human dev. index

MEXICO

OFFICIAL NAME: United States of Mexico **CAPITAL:** Mexico City
POPULATION: 93.7 million **CURRENCY:** Mexican new peso **OFFICIAL LANGUAGE:** Spanish

INCREASINGLY CONSIDERED a part of North rather than Central America, Mexico straddles the southern end of the continent. Coastal plains along its Pacific and Atlantic seaboards rise into an arid central plateau, which includes the world's biggest conurbation, Mexico City, built on the site of the Aztec capital, Tenochtitlán. Colonized by the Spanish for its silver mines, Mexico achieved independence in 1836. In the "Epic Revolution" of 1910–1920, in which 250,000 died, much of modern Mexico's structure was established. In 1994, Mexico signed the North American Free Trade Agreement (NAFTA).

The cathedral of Santa Prisca at Taxco in Cuernavaca. It was built in Spanish Churriguera style between 1748 and 1758.

CLIMATE

WEATHER CHART

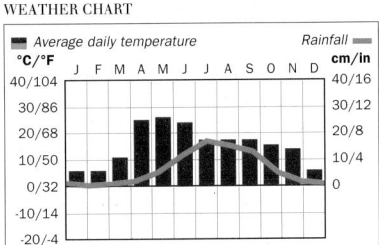

The plateau and high mountains are warm for much of the year. The Pacific coast has a tropical climate.

TRANSPORTATION

Benito Juárez International, Mexico City
3.83m passengers

79 ships
1.19m dwt

THE TRANSPORTATION NETWORK

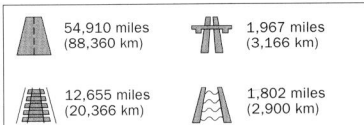

54,910 miles (88,360 km)	1,967 miles (3,166 km)
12,655 miles (20,366 km)	1,802 miles (2,900 km)

A privately financed $14 billion road network, some 2,317 miles of toll roads built under the previous Salinas government, is underused and a commercial failure. The construction of another 2,317 miles before the year 2000 is halted, further delaying integration into NAFTA. Tolls are being lowered to attract more traffic. The government hopes to privatize the extensive rail network in 1996.

TOURISM

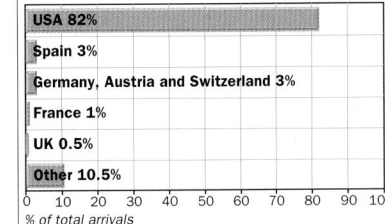

17.1m visitors

Up 4% in 1994

MAIN OVERSEAS ARRIVALS

USA 82%	
Spain 3%	
Germany, Austria and Switzerland 3%	
France 1%	
UK 0.5%	
Other 10.5%	

% of total arrivals

Tourism is now probably the largest employment sector in Mexico. Visitors are drawn to excellent beach resorts like Acapulco on the Pacific, and the new resorts of the Peninsula de Yucatán on the Atlantic Coast. Mexico also has many Aztec and Maya World Heritage archaeological sites. Other major tourist attractions include the many Spanish colonial cities, like Morelia and Guadalajara, which have remained virtually intact since the time of the Spanish conquest. In 1995 the Zedillo government announced an "Alliance for Tourism" program to promote the sector.

M

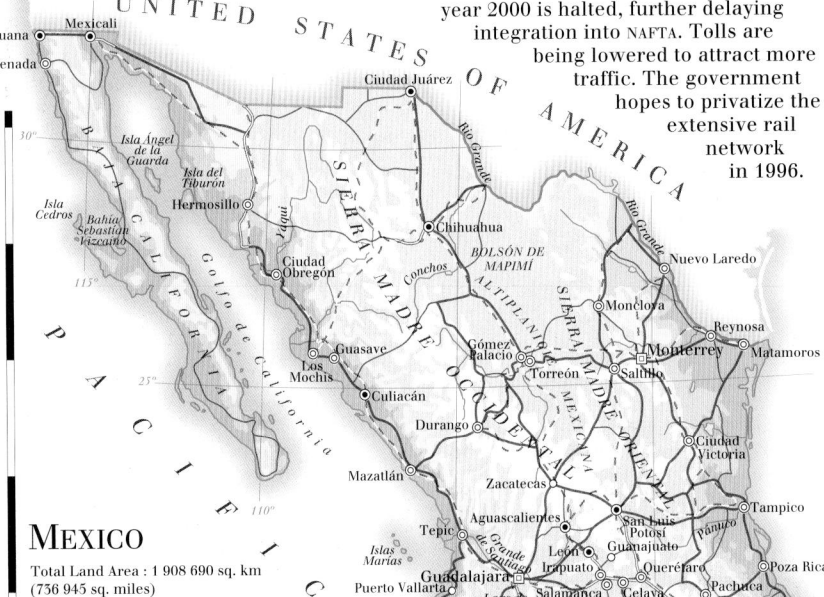

MEXICO

Total Land Area : 1 908 690 sq. km
(736 945 sq. miles)

LAND HEIGHT

3000m/9843ft
2000m/6562ft
1000m/3281ft
500m/1640ft
200m/656ft
Sea Level

POPULATION

over 5 000 000
over 1 000 000
over 500 000
over 100 000
over 50 000

0   200 km
0   200 miles

PEOPLE

 Spanish, Nahuatl, Maya, Zapotec, Mixtec, Otomi, Totonac, Tzotzil, Tzeltal

127 people per sq. mile

THE URBAN/RURAL POPULATION SPLIT

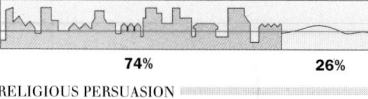

74%   26%

RELIGIOUS PERSUASION

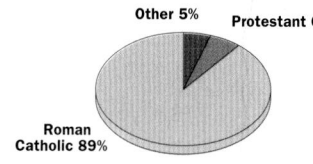

Other 5%   Protestant 6%

Roman Catholic 89%

ETHNIC MAKEUP

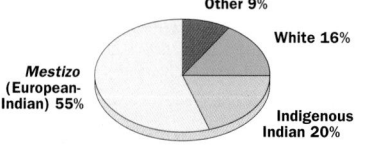

Other 9%

White 16%

Mestizo (European-Indian) 55%

Indigenous Indian 20%

While most Mexicans are *mestizo*, it is Mexico's Indian culture which is promoted by the state. This obscures the fact that rural Indians are largely segregated from Hispanic society. The situation dates back to the Spanish colonial period and is accepted by both

POPULATION AGE BREAKDOWN

%	1960	1970	1980	1990	2000
65+	3.3%	3.4%	3.5%	3.8%	4.6%
15–64	51.3%	49.7%	52.4%	59%	62.6%
0–14	45.4%	46.9%	44.1%	37.2%	32.8%

groups. The small black community, which is concentrated mainly along the eastern coast, is well integrated.

Several hundred thousand refugees fled to Mexico to escape Central American civil wars. They were mainly housed in camps, which were set apart from Mexican society. Many have now returned home.

The most pressing problem in Mexico is poverty. The 1994 Chiapas *Zapatista* guerrilla rebellion was instigated by landless Indians who had little to lose by rebelling against the state.

As in much of Latin America, men retain their dominance in business and relatively few women take part in the political process.

POLITICS

 U. House 1994/1997
L. House 1994/2000

President Ernesto Zedillo Ponce de León

THE STATE OF THE PARTIES

Federal Chamber of Deputies 500 members

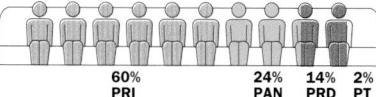

60% PRI	24% PAN	14% PRD	2% PT

PRI = Institutional Revolutionary Party   **PAN** = National Action Party   **PRD** = Party of Democratic Revolution
PT = Labor Party

Senate 64 members

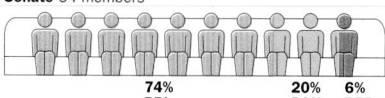

74% PRI	20% PAN	6% PRD

Mexico is a multiparty democracy in name. In practice, the PRI retains power by tampering with elections. The PRI has its own intelligence service.

MAIN POLITICAL ISSUES

NAFTA

The North American Free Trade Agreement (NAFTA) came into force in 1994. The transition to a tariff-free zone will take 15 years. US and Canadian firms will be free to set up factories in Mexico, and Mexican firms will no longer be protected by high tariffs. There will be tough competition from US products. The USA's 1995 decision to postpone Mexican cross-border truck transportations, increased opposition to NAFTA.

Corruption

There is endemic corruption at federal and state level. Raúl Salinas, brother of the former president, awaits trial on charges of murder and embezzling $100 million.

Poverty

Over 16% of Mexico's population are classified as living in "extreme poverty." The Chiapas rebellion of 1994, led by the charismatic *Zapatista* leader Sub-commander Marcos, highlighted the poverty and landlessness of many rural Indian communities.

PROFILE

The PRI has dominated Mexican political life at every level since 1929, checked only by large private industrial groups or multinationals operating in Mexico. Multiparty agreements promise reform of the flawed electoral system.

Ernesto Zedillo Ponce de León, *elected Mexican president in 1994.*

Sub-commander Marcos, *leader of the* Zapatista *National Liberation Army.*

WORLD AFFAIRS

G3	NAFTA	OECD	OAS	RG

The signing of the NAFTA pact has effectively bound together the economies of Mexico and the USA and threatens to become a political liability for both sides. The 1994 collapse of Mexico's currency, the peso, turned a US trade surplus with Mexico into a deficit and in 1995 the US Clinton administration began to side-step key NAFTA provisions to avert some of the painful consequences of falling trade barriers in politically sensitive states such as California, Texas and Florida. NAFTA has brought low-paid jobs to US-financed *maquiladoras*, assembly plants along the border, but fails to benefit the majority of the population. Illegal migration to the USA remains a major issue.

As a counter-balance, Mexico seeks a trade alliance with the South American Common Market (MERCOSUR – Brazil, Argentina, Paraguay, Uruguay), and stronger links with the EU. Trade links with Central America remain important.

AID

 $402m (receipts)   Up 27% in 1993

Mexico receives modest aid. Some European and US NGOs provide help, particularly for literacy campaigns in poorer areas.

CHRONOLOGY

The Aztec kingdom of Montezuma II was defeated in war with the Spaniard, Hernán Cortés, in 1521. By 1546, the Spaniards had discovered major silver mines at Zacatecas. Mexico, then known as New Spain, became a key part of the Spanish colonial empire.

- ❑ **1808** Napoleon invades Spain.
- ❑ **1810** Fr. Miguel Hidalgo leads abortive rising against Spanish.
- ❑ **1821** Spanish viceroy forced to leave by Agustín de Iturbide.
- ❑ **1822** Federal Republic established.
- ❑ **1823** Texas opened to US immigration.
- ❑ **1829** Spanish military expedition fails to regain control.
- ❑ **1836** The USA is the first country to recognize Mexico's independence. Spain then follows suit. Texas declares its independence from Mexico.
- ❑ **1846** War breaks out between Mexico and the USA.
- ❑ **1848** Treaty of Guadalupe Hidalgo. Mexico forced to cede almost half of its territory to the USA. ➡

M

M

DEFENSE

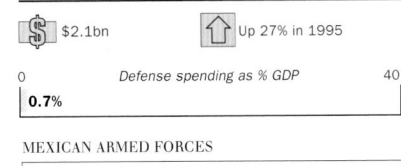

$2.1bn   Up 27% in 1995

0   *Defense spending as % GDP*   40

0.7%

MEXICAN ARMED FORCES

350 light tanks	130,000 personnel
3 destroyers, 2 frigates, 105 patrol boats	37,000 personnel
101 combat aircraft (9 F–5E)	8,000 personnel
None	

The Mexican military has, on the whole, kept out of politics. Although large in regional terms, Mexico has no ambitions beyond its borders and the army acts to defend internal security. Most arms procurement is from the USA and France. Some members of the military are worried that the PRI's current privatization policies could target the military for cutbacks. In 1994, the role of controlling the border with the USA was handed over to the police.

The rebellion in Chiapas in 1994 was swiftly put down by the army, acting on PRI orders. Concern was expressed by Mexicans at the brutality of the action in which 100 *Zapatistas* died.

ECONOMICS

$368.7bn   4.93–7.71 Mexican new pesos

SCORE CARD

- ❏ WORLD GNP RANKING.........................12th
- ❏ GNP PER CAPITA $4,101
- ❏ BALANCE OF PAYMENTS.................$28.8bn
- ❏ INFLATION 41.6%
- ❏ UNEMPLOYMENT................................3.4%

EXPORTS

Canada 3%   Spain 2%
France 1%   Other 10%
Japan 1%
USA 83%

IMPORTS

Brazil 2%   Germany 4%
Canada 2%   Japan 6%
Other 16%
USA 70%

ECONOMIC PERFORMANCE INDICATOR

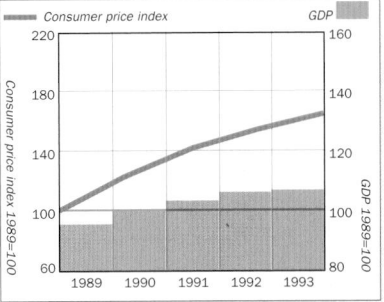

Consumer price index   GDP

Consumer price index 1989=100 / *GDP 1989=100*

1989 1990 1991 1992 1993

STRENGTHS
One of the world's largest oil producers, with substantial reserves. Extensive mineral resources – perhaps only 5% exploited to date. Low wages.

WEAKNESSES
High unemployment. Weak agriculture, with rural peoples lacking basic foodstuffs. Lack of development and investment may reduce Mexico under NAFTA to a cheap assembler of US products. High inflation. Instability of currency. Corruption.

PROFILE
Economic development is even. Traditionally the PRI ran almost every sector of the Mexican economy – around 160 major concerns. The debt crisis of the 1980s, however, forced privatization programs. The current new wave of

sell-offs includes assets of PEMEX, the state oil company and potent symbol of Mexican patriotism. The Zedillo government plans to push through pension and tax reforms and speed up privatizations to induce an economic recovery in the wake of the December 1994 peso crisis. This necessitated a USA-led $20 billion international bailout and propelled the economy into the worst slump in living memory. Currency and stock market recovery in early 1996 failed to dispel doubts about the weakness of the real economy.

MEXICO : MAJOR BUSINESSES

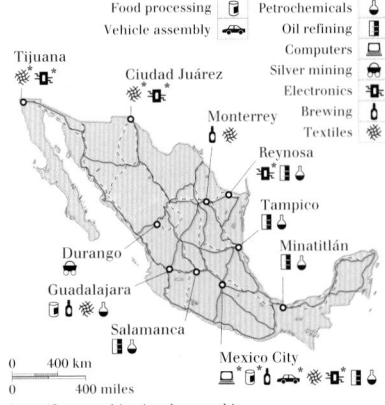

Food processing   Petrochemicals
Vehicle assembly   Oil refining
Computers
Tijuana   Silver mining
Ciudad Juárez   Electronics
Monterrey   Brewing
Reynosa   Textiles
Tampico
Durango   Minatitlán
Guadalajara
Salamanca
Mexico City

0   400 km
0   400 miles

* significant multinational ownership

RESOURCES

 121.8bn kwh (capacity 29.3m kw)

 2.79m b/d (reserves 51,298,000,000 bbl)

 30.7m cattle, 18m pigs, 10.5m goats

Oil, gas, gold, silver, copper, coal, fluorite, mercury, antimony

ELECTRICITY GENERATION

Hydro 17% (21bn kwh)	
Thermal 75% (91bn kwh)	
Nuclear 3% (4bn kwh)	
Other 5% (5bn kwh)	

0 20 40 60 80 100

% of total generation by type

Mexico is one of the largest oil exporters outside the OPEC cartel. Most of the country's oil production comes from offshore drilling platforms in the Gulf of Mexico. The industry was state-owned and state-run by PEMEX, the world's fifth-largest oil company, employing 120,000. The decision to

ENVIRONMENT

 5% (4% partially protected)

NAFTA's green measures might improve poor record

ENVIRONMENTAL TREATIES

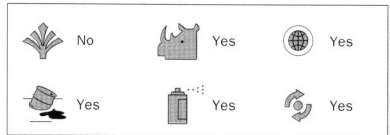

No	Yes		Yes
Yes	Yes		Yes

The largely unplanned conurbation of Mexico City struggles to accommodate 20.2 million inhabitants as the absence of environmental controls on factories contributes to perhaps the world's worst air quality levels. PEMEX stands accused of massive pollution.

Conditions along the Mexican border are a problem. *Maquiladoras* have no effective environmental controls (making them much cheaper than in the USA) and are usually surrounded by unsanitized slums. The few remaining tropical forests in the southwest are fast disappearing.

MEDIA

 Free in practice, but power of government advertising a strong incentive against criticism. Several critical journalists have been murdered

PUBLISHING AND BROADCAST MEDIA

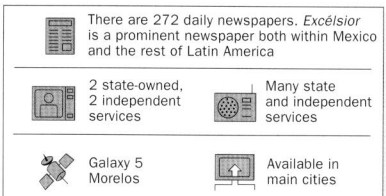

There are 272 daily newspapers. *Excélsior* is a prominent newspaper both within Mexico and the rest of Latin America	
2 state-owned, 2 independent services	Many state and independent services
Galaxy 5 Morelos	Available in main cities

The state retains a tight grip on the media, frequently paying the press to run favorable front page stories.

MEXICO : LAND USE

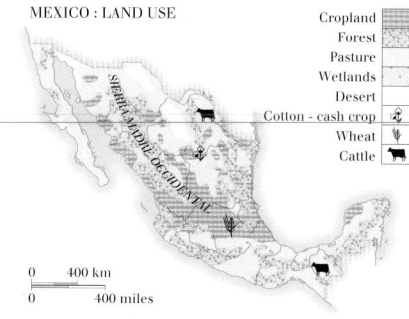

Cropland	
Forest	
Pasture	
Wetlands	
Desert	
Cotton - cash crop	
Wheat	
Cattle	

0 400 km
0 400 miles

privatize 61 petrochemical plants provoked serious social unrest in 1995–1996 from oil workers and Chontal Maya Indians who claimed compensation for years of environmental pollution. Despite its large oil reserves, Mexico has embarked on a nuclear power program. Its first plant was built at Laguna Verde.

CRIME

 Mexico does not publish prison figures

 Down 2% in 1987

CRIME RATES

Mexico does not publish murder, theft or rape statistics

Northern Mexico is a center for narcotics transshipments to the USA. Guns are rife and minor incidents often end in shootings. Petty offences are usually settled by bribing the police. Mexico also has a relatively high rate of petty violence which accompanies crimes such as robbery, car theft and burglary.

EDUCATION

 89%

 1.3m students

0 *Education spending as % GNP* 25
5.2%

THE EDUCATION SYSTEM

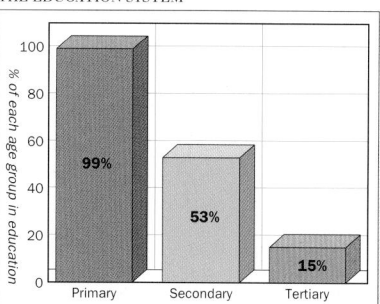

% of each age group in education

100
80
60
40
20
0

Primary 99% Secondary 53% Tertiary 15%

The system is a mixture of the French and US models. The public university system is well developed.

HEALTH

 1 per 1,000 people

Heart diseases, accidents, cancers, violence, tuberculosis

0 *Health spending as % GDP* 25
1.6%

Mexico's national health care system is rudimentary. Those in employment who pay social security receive slightly better care. Mexico has a good reputation for surgery and dentistry, but this is mostly in the private sector.

WEALTH

 Plantation worker, 1,746 Mexican new pesos ($227) per day; university science professor, 3,516 Mexican new pesos ($457) per day

CONSUMER GOODS OWNERSHIP

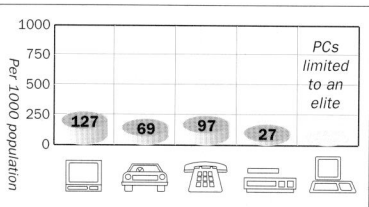

Per 1000 population

1000
750
500
250
0

PCs limited to an elite

127 69 97 27

Mexico has enormous wealth disparities, from the twelve dollar-billionaires to the 16% who live in extreme poverty. In the past, the wealthy did not generally pay taxes and often benefited from the large state machine. Tax reform is now a priority. There is little social mobility; the old Spanish families have retained their hold on government offices.

Rural Indians are probably the most disadvantaged group in society. In the last decade, poverty has forced them into city slums to work in factories or *maquiladoras* – assembly plants for foreign, usually US goods. Working conditions are usually so poor that there is a very high turnover in the work force. The 1994 Chiapas rebellion was fed by these conditions as well as demands for more land and more assistance in farming it. The flow of poor rural migrants to the USA stems from the need to subsidize families at home.

WORLD RANKING

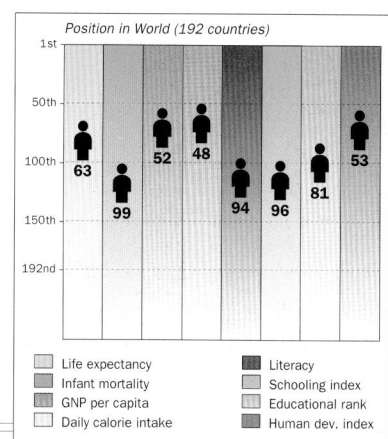

Position in World (192 countries)

1st
50th
100th
150th
192nd

63 99 52 48 94 96 81 53

Life expectancy	Literacy
Infant mortality	Schooling index
GNP per capita	Educational rank
Daily calorie intake	Human dev. index

M

MICRONESIA

OFFICIAL NAME: Federated States of Micronesia   **CAPITAL:** Palikir
POPULATION: 107,000   **CURRENCY:** US dollar   **OFFICIAL LANGUAGE:** English

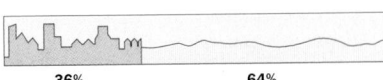
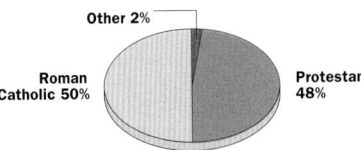
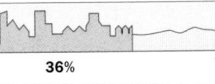

THE FEDERATED STATES of Micronesia (FSM), situated in the Pacific Ocean, encompasses all the Caroline Islands except Palau. It is composed of four main island cluster states: Pohnpei, Kosrae, Chuuk and Yap. The FSM was formerly under US rule as part of the UN Trust Territory of the Pacific Islands; an agreement which granted internal sovereignty in free association with the US became operational in 1986, and the Trust was formally dissolved in 1990. The islands continue to receive considerable aid from the USA.

CLIMATE

WEATHER CHART

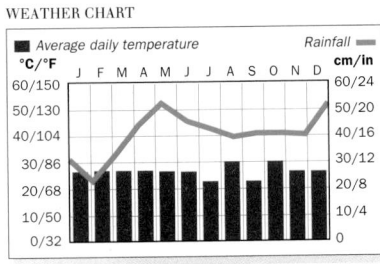

The islands are humid and fairly hot all year round, and the daily temperature range is small. Rainfall is abundant.

TRANSPORTATION

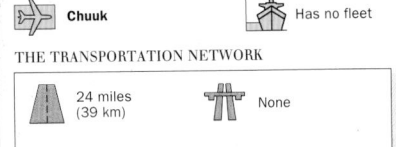

Chuuk   Has no fleet

THE TRANSPORTATION NETWORK

24 miles (39 km)	None
None	None

Fairly regular flights are available between the main islands. Local shipping is mainly used to transport bulk cargoes and copra.

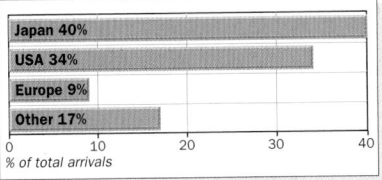

Micronesia, aerial view of rock islands. Like many Pacific states, Micronesia fears rising sea levels as a result of global warming.

TOURISM

 11,000 visitors    Down 79% in 1994

MAIN OVERSEAS ARRIVALS

Tourism is undeveloped. Chuuk's underwater war wreckage attracts visitors and Kosrae has good beaches. The outlying islands remain unspoilt.

PEOPLE

 Trukese, Pohnpeian, Mortlockese, Losrean, English

 394 people per sq. mile

THE URBAN/RURAL POPULATION SPLIT

36%   64%

RELIGIOUS PERSUASION

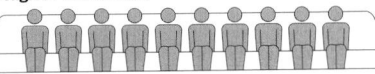

Other 2%
Roman Catholic 50%
Protestant 48%

Increasing numbers of Melanesians, especially Filipino laborers, threaten to swamp the resident Micronesian population. Most islanders live without electricity or running water and many are effectively recipients of US welfare. Society is traditionally matrilineal on most of the islands.

POLITICS

1995/1997   President Bailey Olter

THE STATE OF THE PARTIES

Congress 14 members

There are no political parties. The 14 senators are elected as independents, 10 for 2 years and 4 at-large senators – 1 for each state – for 4 years.

Under the federal structure, the president and vice-presidents are elected from among the four "at-large" senators (one from each state) by the federal legislature. However, the power of the traditional chiefs in politics remains very strong. Increasing Micronesia's economic independence is the key political issue, as at present it remains heavily dependent on aid received from the USA under the Compact of Free Association.

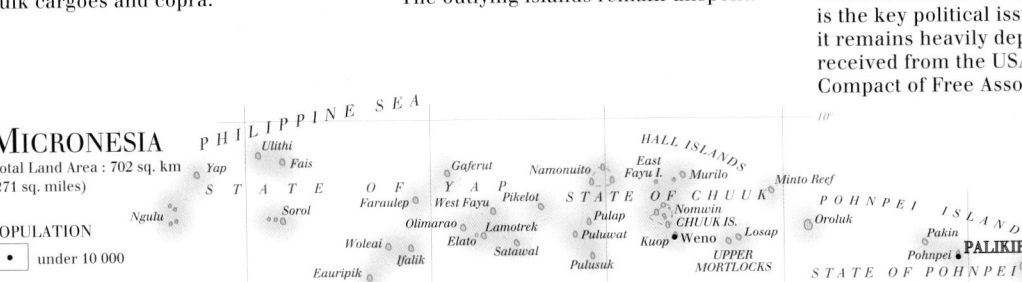

MICRONESIA

Total Land Area : 702 sq. km (271 sq. miles)

POPULATION
• under 10 000

LAND HEIGHT
■ 100m/328ft
Sea Level

0   200 km
0   200 miles

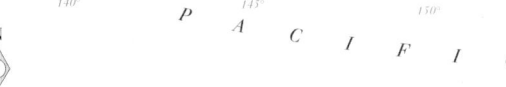

M

WORLD AFFAIRS

Micronesia's most important relationship is with the USA, which administered the islands from 1947 as part of the Trust Territory of the Pacific Islands. Under the Compact of Free Association, the USA has exclusive control over the FSM's foreign and defense policies. Japan is also important, with the Tokyo government providing aid; some of the older generation of FSM residents are still fluent in Japanese as a result of the Japanese administration of the islands. Recently, the FSM has also cultivated strong links with China.

AID

 $64m (receipts)   Up 400% in 1993

The USA is the principal donor of aid, which funds hospitals, schools, food stamps and construction projects.

DEFENSE

 USA responsible for defense   Not applicable

Defense is entirely in the hands of the USA. Airstrips in the FSM were used by the USA in the Vietnam War.

ECONOMICS

 $202m   US dollar

SCORE CARD

❏ WORLD GNP RANKING	182nd
❏ GNP PER CAPITA	$1,890
❏ BALANCE OF PAYMENTS	$–77.6m
❏ INFLATION	5%
❏ UNEMPLOYMENT	13.5%

STRENGTHS

Access to US economy, especially for garment manufacture through preferential trading rights. Construction industry is the largest private-sector activity. Tourism, fishing and copra production. US strategic interest in Micronesia and US budget subsidies.

WEAKNESSES

Dependence on USA for imports, especially for fuel. $30 million debt. Acute shortage of water limits development potential. High levels of underemployment.

EXPORTS

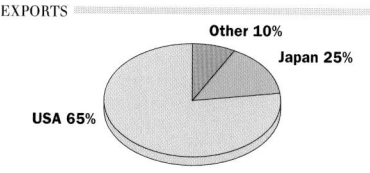

Other 10%
Japan 25%
USA 65%

IMPORTS

The majority of imports are from the USA

RESOURCES

 Most electricity is produced by small diesel generators   Not an oil producer and has no refineries

 1,555 tons   None

The FSM is entirely dependent on external sources for its energy supply. Almost all electricity is produced by small diesel generators. The main resources are copra and valuable fish stocks, especially tuna.

ENVIRONMENT

 None   No funds for environmental initiatives

The FSM does not face pollution on the scale of that in the neighboring Marshall Islands. However, Chuuk suffers serious droughts; occasionally water rationing has had to be introduced for short periods. In 1992, the US government used naval vessels to transport water from Guam to alleviate a severe water shortage.

MEDIA

 No political restrictions

PUBLISHING AND BROADCAST MEDIA

There is only one national newspaper, *The National Union*

1 state-owned, 1 independent service	1 state-owned service

TV, which previously consisted of reruns of US programs, can now be received by satellite.

CRIME

 Micronesia does not publish prison figures   Little change from year to year

On Chuuk, assault, especially alcohol-related cases, is increasing. The outlying islands are crime-free.

EDUCATION

 90%   861 students

Education is compulsory between the ages of six and 14 years. The USA provides grants for some students to attend US universities.

HEALTH

 1 per 3,294 people   Heart, cerebrovascular and intestinal diseases

Basic health care is accessible to all, but outlying islands may not have access to qualified doctors. Diabetes and drug abuse are growing problems.

WEALTH

 Minimum wage on Pohnpei, $1.35 per hour

CONSUMER GOODS OWNERSHIP

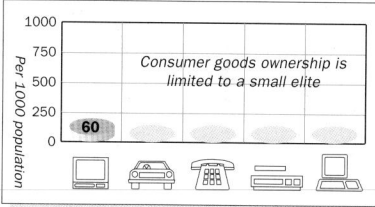

Consumer goods ownership is limited to a small elite

60

The gap between rich and poor is increasing as businessmen and local officials exploit US aid donations.

WORLD RANKING

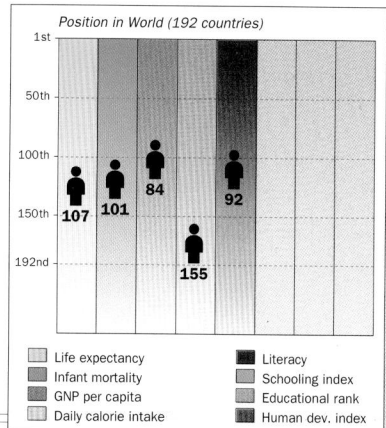

Position in World (192 countries)

107   101   84   92   155

Life expectancy	Literacy
Infant mortality	Schooling index
GNP per capita	Educational rank
Daily calorie intake	Human dev. index

M

MOLDOVA

EUROPE

OFFICIAL NAME: Republic of Moldova **CAPITAL:** Chişinău
POPULATION: 4.4 million **CURRENCY:** Moldovan leu **OFFICIAL LANGUAGE:** Moldovan

O NCE A PART OF ROMANIA, Moldova was incorporated into the Soviet Union in 1940. Independence in 1991 brought with it the expectation that Moldova would be reunited with Romania. At elections in 1993, however, Moldovans voted against the proposal. Moldova is mostly undulating steppe country. It is the smallest and most densely populated of the ex-Soviet republics. Most of its population is engaged in intensive agriculture.

Agricultural landscape. *Warm summers and even rainfall are ideal for cereal and fruit farming. Moldova is famous for its wine.*

CLIMATE

WEATHER CHART

Warm summers, mild winters and moderate rainfall give Moldova an ideal climate for cultivation.

TRANSPORTATION

 Chişinău International

Small Black Sea fleet

THE TRANSPORTATION NETWORK

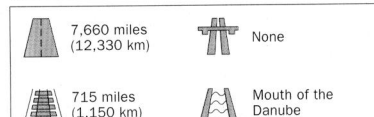

| 7,660 miles (12,330 km) | None |
| 715 miles (1,150 km) | Mouth of the Danube |

Moldova plans to build port facilities on the 2,953 feet of the Danube River which are its international waters.

TOURISM

Business people make up the majority of visitors

Moldova has seen no significant change in tourism arrivals

MAIN OVERSEAS ARRIVALS

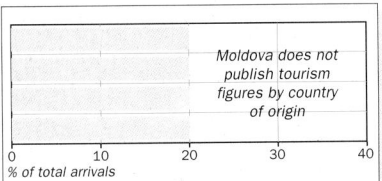

Moldova does not publish tourism figures by country of origin

0 10 20 30 40
% of total arrivals

Few tourists visit Moldova. However, its relatively well-developed infrastructure could allow some expansion of tourism in future. The vineyards and underground wine vault "streets" are the main attractions.

PEOPLE

Moldovan, Romanian, Russian

339 people per sq. mile

THE URBAN/RURAL POPULATION SPLIT

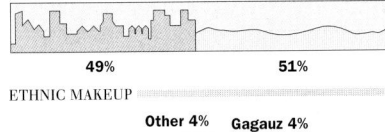

49% 51%

ETHNIC MAKEUP

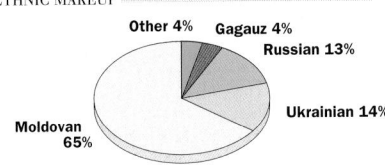

Other 4% Gagauz 4%
Russian 13%
Ukrainian 14%
Moldovan 65%

Moldovans are of the same ethnic grouping as Romanians. The southern Gagauzi (Orthodox Christian Turks), and the population of mixed Russian–Moldovan–Ukrainian parentage on the eastern bank of the Dniester, declared themselves separate republics in 1990.

POLITICS

 1993/1999

President Mircea Ion Snegur

THE STATE OF THE PARTIES

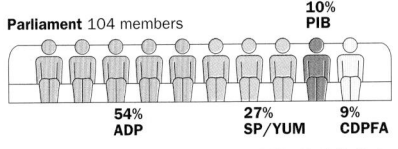

Parliament 104 members

10% PIB
54% ADP
27% SP/YUM
9% CDPFA

ADP = Agrarian Democratic Party **SP/YUM** = Socialist Party and Yedinstvo Unity Movement **PIB** = Peasants and Intellectuals Party **CDPFA** = Christian Democratic People's Front Alliance

Moldova declared itself a multiparty democracy in 1991, but initially kept the transitional administration appointed by the last Soviet in 1990. Elections were held in 1993 and the Agrarian Democratic Party (ADP) emerged as the largest party in parliament. A new constitution came into effect in 1994. The first post-independence question was whether or not Moldova should seek union with neighboring Romania. In a national plebiscite held in 1994, Moldovans overwhelmingly rejected the idea of possible unification with Romania.

The secessionist republic of Transnistria (on the eastern bank of the River Dniester) is seeking full independence and its leaders have rejected offers of "autonomous territory" status within Moldova. Furthermore, the 153,000 Gagauzi minority are still hoping for independence.

M

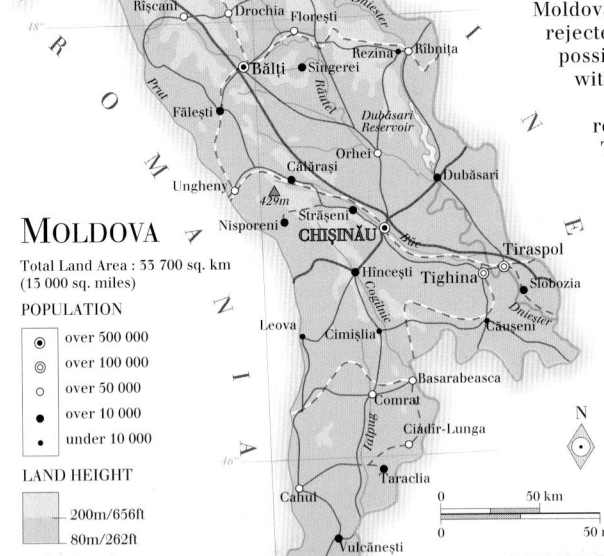

MOLDOVA

Total Land Area : 33 700 sq. km (13 000 sq. miles)

POPULATION

- ⊙ over 500 000
- ◎ over 100 000
- ○ over 50 000
- • over 10 000
- • under 10 000

LAND HEIGHT

200m/656ft
80m/262ft

Edineţ, Rişcani, Drochia, Floreşti, Soroca, Rezina, Râbniţa, Bălţi, Singerei, Dubăsari Reservoir, Fălești, Orhei, Dubăsari, Călăraşi, Ungheny, Nisporeni, Strășeni, CHIŞINĂU, Tiraspol, Hânceşti, Tighina, Slobozia, Leova, Cimişlia, Căuşeni, Basarabeasca, Comrat, Ciadir-Lunga, Cahul, Taraclia, Vulcăneşti

0 50 km
0 50 miles

N

WORLD AFFAIRS

   NACC OSCE

Ties with nations in the Black Sea Economic Zone are being developed. Relations with Romania have been diluted now that reunification is no longer an issue. Links with Russia are now paramount. Economic pressure from Russia persuaded Moldova to rejoin the CIS at the end of 1993. Russia still has troops stationed in Moldova.

AID

 Moldova is a net receiver of aid | Aid receipts have risen since independence

The IMF and World Bank are supporting economic reforms. The EU, Romania, Turkey and Bulgaria are Moldova's next most important aid providers.

DEFENSE

 $13m | Up 86% in 1995

Former officers of the Soviet army are helping Transnistrian rebels. The dismissal of Defense Minister Pavel Creanga in March 1996 raised fears of a coup.

ECONOMICS

 $3.8bn |  4.28–4.50 Moldovan leu

SCORE CARD

❏ World GNP Ranking	111th
❏ GNP per Capita	$870
❏ Balance of Payments	$–177m
❏ Inflation	111%
❏ Unemployment	0.9%

STRENGTHS

Agriculture – notably wine, tobacco and cotton – and food processing. Light manufacturing. Good progress made in establishing markets for exports, and earning foreign exchange.

WEAKNESSES

Dependent on Russian raw materials and fuel. Most electricity imported. Isolated location and weak transportation communications. Legacy of inefficient former Soviet state-run businesses. Shrinking economy as a result of privatization policies.

EXPORTS

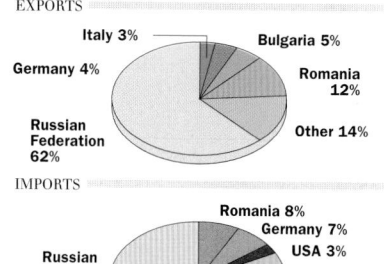

Italy 3%
Bulgaria 5%
Germany 4%
Romania 12%
Russian Federation 62%
Other 14%

IMPORTS

Romania 8%
Germany 7%
USA 3%
Russian Federation 67%
Italy 15%

RESOURCES

 11.3bn kwh (capacity 3.1m kw) | Oil and gas reserves not exploited

 15m poultry, 1.2m pigs, 1.4m sheep, 916,000 cattle | Lignite, phosphate, gypsum, oil, natural gas

Moldova has few mineral resources. It has to import all its fuel requirements and most of its electricity.

ENVIRONMENT

 0.2% | Economic growth has precedence over ecological concerns

Northern Moldova is still experiencing fallout from the Chernobyl nuclear accident in 1986. Over-use of pesticides on tobacco farms is a serious problem.

MEDIA

 Media is relatively free from state control

PUBLISHING AND BROADCAST MEDIA

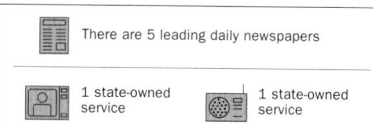

There are 5 leading daily newspapers

1 state-owned service | 1 state-owned service

The press was privatized in 1993. The many new publications represent widely differing interest groups.

CRIME

 Moldova does not publish prison figures | Crime levels remain at a relatively low level

Moldova still awaits a new legal system to accompany its constitution. Crime levels are generally low, but armed gangs have appeared in the south and west, and violence affects the two separatist republics.

EDUCATION

 96% |  72,986 students

Haphazard attempts have been made to switch from a Soviet to a Romanian (French-inspired) system. Engineering is the largest university faculty.

HEALTH

 1 per 250 people |  Circulatory diseases, cancers, accidents

The centralized health service is poor by regional standards, with its basic equipment and poorly trained doctors.

Modern Moldova corresponds roughly to the eastern part of the Romanian principality of Moldova, which existed for 500 years from 1359. Most of it was annexed by Russia in 1812 as Bessarabia.

- ❏ **1918** Bessarabia joins Romania.
- ❏ **1924** Moldovan Autonomous Soviet Republic formed within the USSR.
- ❏ **1940** Romania cedes Bessarabia to Ukrainian and Moldovan SSRs.
- ❏ **1941–1945** Bessarabia again under Romanian control.
- ❏ **1945** Returns to Soviet control.
- ❏ **1990** Declares sovereignty. Reunification with Romania mooted.
- ❏ **1991** Independence. Joins CIS, but then fails to ratify CIS treaty – adopts observer status.
- ❏ **1993** General election results in defeat for pro-unification parties. Moldova rejoins CIS.

WEALTH

 Increasing disparity in wealth between former-communist officials and the rest of the population

CONSUMER GOODS OWNERSHIP

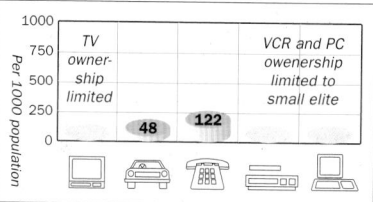

TV ownership limited | VCR and PC ownership limited to small elite

48   122

Per 1000 population

Former Communist Party officials have benefited most from the advent of capitalism. Counterfeit Turkish Napoleon brandy and Marlboro cigarettes are highly favored. The ethnic Gagauzi (Orthodox Christian Turks) form the poorest group.

WORLD RANKING

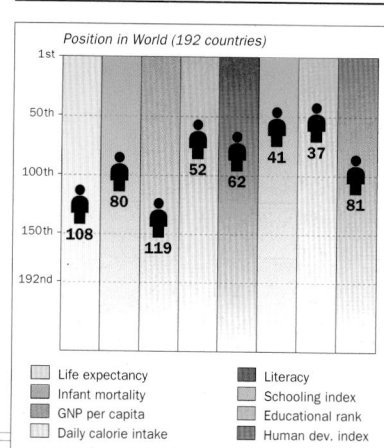

Position in World (192 countries)

108 80 119 52 62 41 37 81

- Life expectancy
- Infant mortality
- GNP per capita
- Daily calorie intake
- Literacy
- Schooling index
- Educational rank
- Human dev. index

M

MONACO

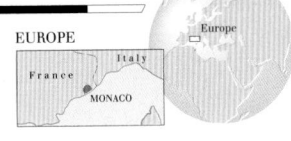
EUROPE

OFFICIAL NAME: Principality of Monaco **CAPITAL:** Monaco
POPULATION: 31,000 **CURRENCY:** French franc **OFFICIAL LANGUAGE:** French

MONACO IS A TINY ENCLAVE on the Côte d'Azur in southeastern France. Its destiny changed radically in 1863 when Prince Charles III, after whom Monte Carlo is named, opened the casino. Today, Monaco is a lucrative banking and services center, as well as a tourist destination. Prince Rainier's marriage to film star Grace Kelly, and some astute management of the economy, successfully transformed Monaco into a center for the international jet-set. In 1962, the prince's absolute authority was abolished in a new, democratic constitution.

PEOPLE

French, Italian, Monégasque, English

41,332 people per sq. mile

THE URBAN/RURAL POPULATION SPLIT

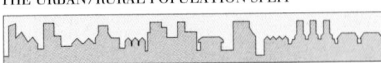

100%

RELIGIOUS PERSUASION

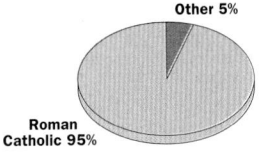

Other 5%

Roman Catholic 95%

Less than one-tenth of Monaco's residents are Monégasque. Over half are French, the rest Italian, American, British and Belgian. Monégasques enjoy considerable privileges, including housing subsidies to protect them from Monaco's high property prices, and the right of first refusal before a job can be offered to a foreigner. Women have equal status, but only acquired the vote in the constitutional changes of 1962.

CLIMATE

WEATHER CHART

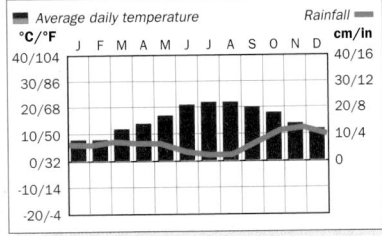

Summers are hot and dry; days with 12 hours of sunshine are not uncommon. Winters are mild and sunny.

TRANSPORTATION

None

Has no fleet

THE TRANSPORTATION NETWORK

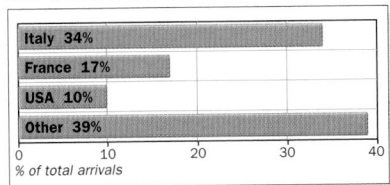

31 miles (50 km)

None

1 mile (1.6 km)

None

The one mile of main-line track is run by French state railroad. A helicopter shuttle links Fontvieille with Nice, the nearest airport. There are about 31 miles of major roads. Monaco is an easy drive from northern Italy, the source of most of its private banking trade.

TOURISM

217,000 visitors

Up 4% in 1994

MAIN OVERSEAS ARRIVALS

Italy 34%		
France 17%		
USA 10%		
Other 39%		

0 10 20 30 40
% of total arrivals

A nation of only 31,000 people, Monaco attracts huge numbers of tourists, mainly from France and Italy. Almost all are day-trippers, drawn by gambling and Monaco's high life. Efforts are being made to entice tourists and business travelers to spend more time. A new conference center has opened and exhibition facilities are being built. Monaco is a favorite destination of the rich, especially northern Italians, although their numbers have declined since the collapse of the lira in 1992. Spring is a key time for jet-set visitors, with several major social and sporting events: the Rose Ball (March), the Tennis Open (April) and the Grand Prix (May).

POLITICS

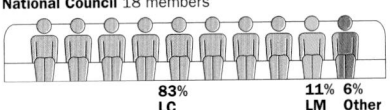

1993/1998

HSH Prince Rainier III

THE STATE OF THE PARTIES

National Council 18 members

83% LC   **11%** LM   **6%** Other

LC = Campora List   **LM** = Médecin List
There are no political parties, but candidates generally enter their names through an organization.

The Grimaldi princes (Rainier since 1949) have been hereditary rulers of Monaco for 700 years. The prince renounced absolute rule in the 1962 constitutional reforms. He still has considerable power and appoints the four-member executive. There are no political parties; National Council elections are based on personalities.

WORLD AFFAIRS

FZ   IAEA   IWC   OSCE

Monaco's key concern is to protect both banking secrecy and the liberal tax regime from EU regulation. French citizens are banned from banking in Monaco, a 1962 decision enforced by President de Gaulle, who sent troops to the border.

Hospitalier Grace

Lycée de l'Annonciade

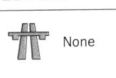
Musée Nation
Larvotto

Railway Station

La Condamine

Centre de la Culture et d'Expositions

Monte-Carlo Sporting Club d'Eté

Casino

MONACO

Total Land Area : 1.95 sq. km (0.75 sq. miles)

Places of Interest
Parks and Gardens
Grand Prix Circuit

0   500 m
0   656 ft

Centre de Congrès
Monte-Carlo

Palais du Prince

Stade Louis II

Port de Monaco

Ministère d'Etat

Palais de Justice

Cathédrale **MONACO**

Fontvieille

Musée Océanographique

Heliport

M

Monte Carlo *with its luxury hotels and yacht harbor. The only space for new development is on land reclaimed from the sea.*

AID

 Monaco has no aid receipts or donations Not applicable

Monaco neither receives nor gives aid, and the issue is not of concern to Monégasques.

DEFENSE

 France responsible for defense Not applicable

Monaco has no armed forces and no defense budget. France, as the protecting power, bears responsibility for the defense of the principality.

ECONOMICS

 $475m (est) 4.89–5.34 French francs

SCORE CARD

❑ WORLD GNP RANKING	173rd
❑ GNP PER CAPITA	$11,000
❑ BALANCE OF PAYMENTS	Included in French total
❑ INFLATION	Included in French total
❑ UNEMPLOYMENT	0%

STRENGTHS
Banking secrecy laws which made Monaco vulnerable to money-laundering were revised under a 1994 accord with France – banks are now obliged to furnish information about suspicious accounts. Prevailing code of strict banking confidentiality and low taxes, however, still attracts billions of dollars of overseas deposits. Strong tourism sector. Services, including property management and overseas shipping, account for 40% of economic turnover.

WEAKNESSES
Monaco remains vulnerable to money-laundering. Some EU states wish to further curtail Monaco's privileged tax and banking status. Strong influence of France on its affairs. Lack of natural resources has led to total dependence upon imports. No agricultural land.

EXPORTS/IMPORTS

Monaco has a full customs union with France

RESOURCES

 Included within French total Not an oil producer and has no refineries

 3 tons None

Monaco has no strategic resources and imports all its energy from France. It has no agricultural land.

ENVIRONMENT

 None Environmental issues not paramount

Environmental questions do not feature highly in political life, except where they might affect profitability. The quality of the built environment around the harbor occasionally arouses local passions. The important populations of red coral are under threat from land reclamation and pollution.

MEDIA

 Freedom of expression guaranteed under constitution

PUBLISHING AND BROADCAST MEDIA

 There are no daily newspapers published in Monaco. *Nice-Matin*, a regional French newspaper, publishes a Monaco edition

 1 independent service 1 service (controlled by French state)

In addition to its domestic radio and TV, Monaco receives all the mainstream French and Italian channels.

CRIME

 Monaco does not publish prison figures Down 12% in 1992

Monaco prides itself on its relatively low crime rates. It is quite safe for the rich to sport their furs and jewelry in public. However, money-laundering has fueled some criminal activity.

EDUCATION

 99% Not available

The education system is essentially the same as that of France, with students studying for the *baccalauréat* exam. Most go on to university in France, but then return to claim good jobs in Monaco. The Catholic Church exerts considerable influence and is still responsible for elementary schooling.

HEALTH

 1 per 373 people Heart and cerebrovascular diseases, cancers

Medical care is provided by a system of private health insurance. Doctors train in France. The Princess Grace Hospital can serve 60,000 people and thus caters for patients from outside Monaco.

WEALTH

 Owing to the high cost of living in Monaco, salaries have a premium of 5% over rates of pay in the neighboring area of the Alpes-Maritimes, France

CONSUMER GOODS OWNERSHIP

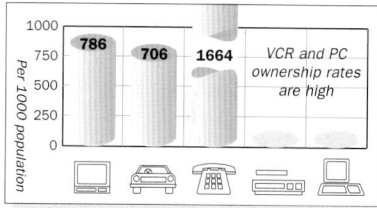

Monaco's image abroad has changed dramatically since Prince Rainier acceded in 1949. From being considered a simple gambling spot, it is now ranked as one of the world's most glamorous international jet-set destinations. In part, this was the result of Rainier's wedding to Grace Kelly, then a leading Hollywood star, which brought Monaco to the attention of US high society. More important was Rainier's work in turning Monaco into a major tax haven and an up-market resort, by making the most of its Mediterranean coastal location. Today, many tax exiles are resident, among them the Wall Street investment guru Bob Beckman.

WORLD RANKING

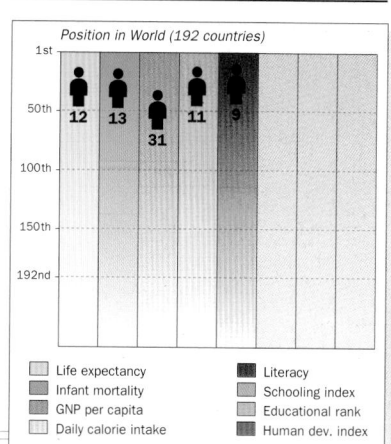

M

MONGOLIA

OFFICIAL NAME: Mongolia **CAPITAL:** Ulan Bator **POPULATION:** 2.4 million
CURRENCY: Tughrik **OFFICIAL LANGUAGE:** Khalkha Mongolian

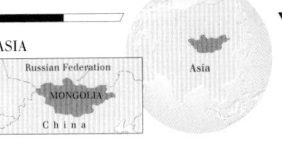

ASIA

LANDLOCKED BETWEEN Russia and China, Mongolia rises from the semi-arid Gobi Desert to mountainous steppe. It was unified by Genghis Khan in 1206 and became part of Manchu China in 1697. Independent in 1924, Mongolia became a communist state, and was officially aligned with the USSR from 1936. In 1990, it became the first Asian nation to abandon communist rule; in 1992 the ex-communists were voted back into power, but fell to a democratic coalition in 1996.

CLIMATE

WEATHER CHART

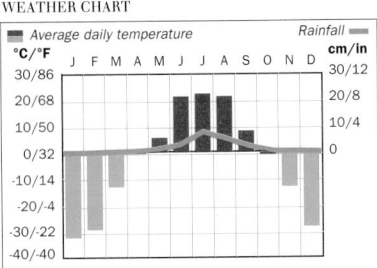

Temperatures occasionally drop to –20°F but can rise to 107°F. Sudden cold periods in early spring, known as *zud*, can kill many young livestock.

TRANSPORTATION

 Buyant-Ukhaa, Ulan Bator   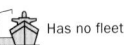 Has no fleet

THE TRANSPORTATION NETWORK

750 miles (1,200 km)   None

1,123 miles (1,807 km)   247 miles (397 km)

The focus of state transportation policy is shifting away from Moscow toward improved links with China and access to a Pacific port facility. Gasoline shortages have meant a large increase in the use of draft-animals.

MONGOLIA

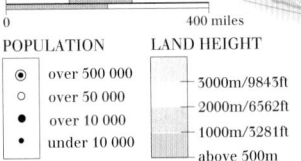

Total Land Area : 1 565 000 sq. km (604 247 sq. miles)

POPULATION
- ◉ over 500 000
- ○ over 50 000
- ● over 10 000
- • under 10 000

LAND HEIGHT
- 3000m/9843ft
- 2000m/6562ft
- 1000m/3281ft
- above 500m

***Traditional* gers in the Gobi Desert.**
Most Mongolians still choose to pursue a nomadic lifestyle, living in felt tents called gers.

TOURISM

 151,000 visitors    Up 1% in 1994

MAIN OVERSEAS ARRIVALS

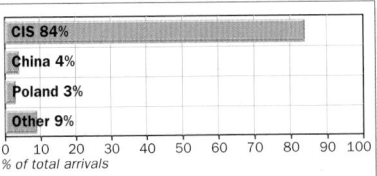

CIS 84%	
China 4%	
Poland 3%	
Other 9%	

% of total arrivals

Tourism has expanded since the easing of visa restrictions in 1991. Under communism, all travel was arranged through the state agency, *Zhuuichin*, but private companies are now entering the market.

PEOPLE

 Khalkha Mongolian, Turkic, Chinese, Russian   5 people per sq. mile

THE URBAN/RURAL POPULATION SPLIT

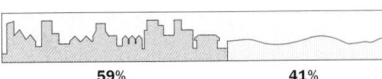

59%   41%

ETHNIC MAKEUP

- Russian 2%
- Chinese 2%
- Other 2%
- Kazakh 4%
- Khalkh Mongol 90%

Khalkh Mongols are the dominant ethnic group. The Kazakhs, who live in the northwest and speak a Turkic language, form the largest non-Mongol group. Since the collapse of the USSR, many Kazakhs have been emigrating to Kazakhstan. There is little indigenous ethnic tension, although there is considerable antagonism toward Chinese and Russian minorities.

POLITICS

 1996/2000    President Punsalmaagiyn Ochirbat

THE STATE OF THE PARTIES

Great Hural 76 members

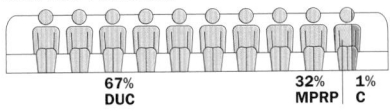

67% DUC   32% MPRP   1% C

DUC = Democratic Union Coalition (Mongolian Democratic Party MNDP, Mongolian Social Democratic Party MSDP, Independents) **MPRP** = Mongolian People's Revolutionary Party **C** = Conservative

After over 50 years of Soviet-style communist rule, the advent of democracy in 1990 revolutionized Mongolian politics. Political activity now functions on a constituency system. In 1992, the economy shrank by 16% and Mongolians began to look back to the guaranteed housing and jobs of the communist past, sweeping the MNDP from power and returning the communists (MPRP) with a large majority. However in the 1996 elections, a coalition of the two main democratic parties (the MNDP and MSDP) was voted into power and the communist vote fell dramatically.

M

WORLD AFFAIRS

IAEA IBRD NAM

Since 1990, Mongolia has tried to balance China's influence with that of Japan and other east Asian states. Mongolia is seeking to improve economic and political relations with China, but there is a fear of Chinese designs on its sovereignty. Mongolia is trying to ensure its security by joining international organizations.

AID

 $113m (receipts)   Up 8% in 1993

Aid is vital to the Mongolian economy. The main donors are now the USA and Japan.

DEFENSE

 $130m   Reduction since 1992

The last Soviet forces left in 1992 after the collapse of communism in Russia. The Mongolian forces have been drastically reduced and have barely any equipment. Video surveillance is being used to monitor the Chinese border.

ECONOMICS

 $801m  410.17–460.18 tughriks

SCORE CARD

- ❏ WORLD GNP RANKING........................159th
- ❏ GNP PER CAPITA $340
- ❏ BALANCE OF PAYMENTS $31m
- ❏ INFLATION 87.6%
- ❏ UNEMPLOYMENT................................8.5%

STRENGTHS
Coal and oil, though most remains untapped. Traditional farming economy still strong and supports the population efficiently in a harsh climate.

WEAKNESSES
Distance between centers. Limited infrastructure. Little manufacturing.

EXPORTS

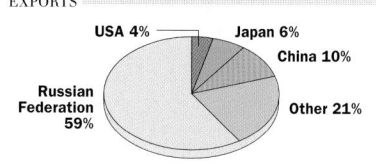

USA 4% Japan 6% China 10% Russian Federation 59% Other 21%

IMPORTS

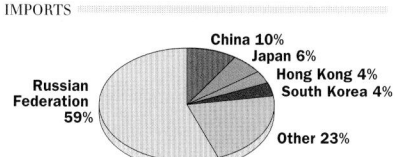

China 10% Japan 6% Hong Kong 4% South Korea 4% Russian Federation 59% Other 23%

RESOURCES

 3.3bn kwh (capacity 900,000 kw)
 Contracts have recently been signed with oil prospectors
 14.4m sheep, 6.5m goats, 2.8m cattle, 2.1m horses
 Oil, coal, copper, lead, fluorspar, tungsten, tin, gold, uranium

Mongolia is rich in oil and many other minerals. Under communism, Mongolia's vast mineral resources were barely exploited, and prospecting has only recently begun in earnest. Known oil reserves indicate that Mongolia should meet most of its future domestic needs. Mongolia is establishing a uranium-mining joint venture with Russia.

ENVIRONMENT

 4%   Traditional Buddhist values instil respect for nature

Industrial pollution around Ulan Bator is a concern; prevailing winds carry power station emissions over residential areas and there is a high incidence of respiratory diseases. The level of pollution in Lake Hövsgöl is also a serious problem.

MEDIA

 All restrictions on reporting have been removed

PUBLISHING AND BROADCAST MEDIA

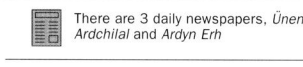
There are 3 daily newspapers, *Ünen, Ardchilal* and *Ardyn Erh*

1 state-owned service   1 state-owned service

Highly restricted under communism, Mongolia's press is now strongly outspoken; there are no slander or libel laws. However, limited supplies of ink and paper restrict publications. Fuel shortages are also a problem, making distribution into remote regions prohibitively expensive.

CRIME

 Mongolia does not publish prison figures   Crime, especially theft, is rising

Crime has risen rapidly since 1990, particularly organized crime and muggings by knife gangs. Ulan Bator is the most dangerous area, especially for foreigners; Russians, Chinese and dollar-carrying US tourists are the main targets.

EDUCATION

 81%  28,209 students

Education is modeled on the former Soviet system. The majority of teachers are women on low salaries. Private-sector schools emphasizing Mongol culture are beginning to open.

HEALTH

 1 per 360 people   Heart, parasitic and respiratory diseases

Shortages of drugs and equipment have renewed interest in traditional Mongolian herbal medicine. As well as the state-run system, some Buddhist monasteries provide health care.

WEALTH

 Street cleaner, 4,000 tughriks ($9) per month; hospital doctor, 8,000 tughriks ($18) per month

CONSUMER GOODS OWNERSHIP

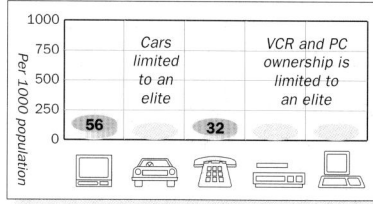

Cars limited to an elite   VCR and PC ownership is limited to an elite

56   32

The poorest Mongolians cannot even afford to buy bread. The wealthy are those with access to dollars, often spent on shopping expeditions to China. Russian cars are favored as parts are readily available.

WORLD RANKING

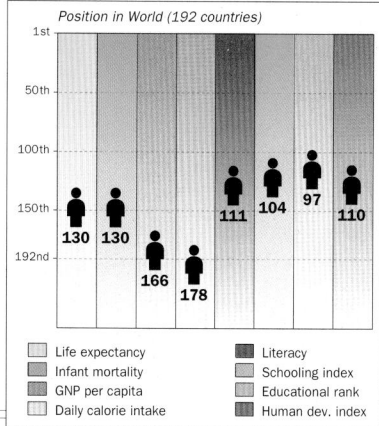

Position in World (192 countries)

130 130 166 178 111 104 97 110

- Life expectancy
- Infant mortality
- GNP per capita
- Daily calorie intake
- Literacy
- Schooling index
- Educational rank
- Human dev. index

M

MOROCCO

OFFICIAL NAME: Kingdom of Morocco   **CAPITAL:** Rabat
POPULATION: 27 million   **CURRENCY:** Moroccan dirham   **OFFICIAL LANGUAGE:** Arabic

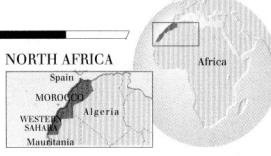

NORTH AFRICA

 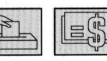

MOROCCO IS SITUATED in northern Africa and bordered by Algeria and the Western Sahara, the future of which is to be determined by a UN-supervised referendum. Its northern regions have a Mediterranean climate, while the south comprises semi-arid desert. King Hassan's international prestige has given Morocco status out of proportion to its wealth. The main issues the country faces are the unresolved fate of the Western Sahara and the internal threat of Islamic militancy. Tourism, phosphate production and agriculture are key economic strengths.

TOURISM

3.5m visitors   Down 13% in 1994

MAIN OVERSEAS ARRIVALS

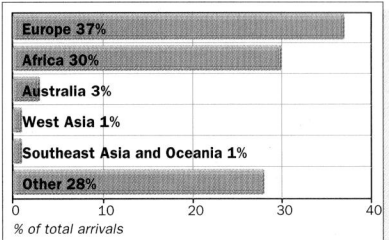

Europe 37%	
Africa 30%	
Australia 3%	
West Asia 1%	
Southeast Asia and Oceania 1%	
Other 28%	

% of total arrivals

Tourism is vital to the Moroccan economy. Good beaches abound; Agadir has 300 days of sunshine a year. Fès and Marrakech offer cultural interest, while the Atlas mountains attract walkers and skiers. Desert safaris are offered in the Sahara. Most Western tourists come from France, Germany and Spain.

CLIMATE

WEATHER CHART

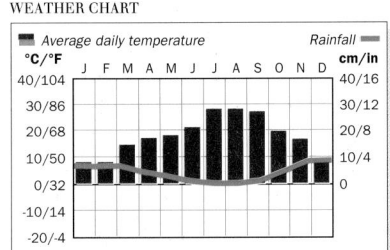

The climate ranges from warm and temperate in the north to semi-arid in the south, but temperatures are cooler in the mountains, especially in the high Atlas. During the summer, the effect of the *sirocco* and *chergui*, hot winds from the Sahara, are felt.

TRANSPORTATION

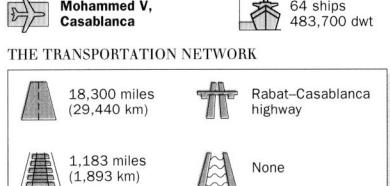

Mohammed V, Casablanca   64 ships
                                483,700 dwt

THE TRANSPORTATION NETWORK

18,300 miles (29,440 km)	Rabat–Casablanca highway
1,183 miles (1,893 km)	None

Morocco has six international airports. A highway links the cities of Rabat and Casablanca; however, roads tend to peter out in the rural areas. The railroad service is cheap, although its routes are limited.

M

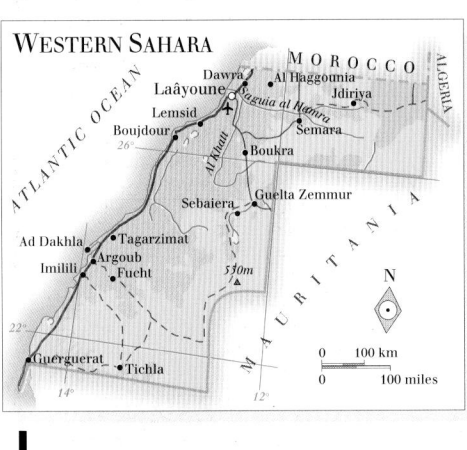

WESTERN SAHARA

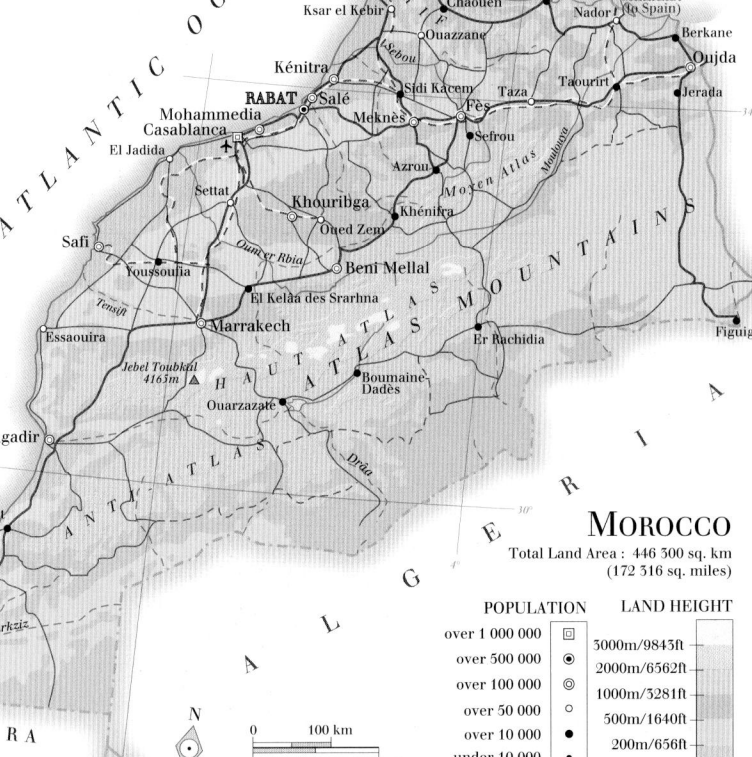

MOROCCO

Total Land Area : 446 300 sq. km
(172 316 sq. miles)

POPULATION | LAND HEIGHT

over 1 000 000	3000m/9843ft
over 500 000	2000m/6562ft
over 100 000	1000m/3281ft
over 50 000	500m/1640ft
over 10 000	200m/656ft
under 10 000	Sea Level

PEOPLE

 Arabic, Berber (Shluh, Tamazight, Riffian), French, Spanish

 155 people per sq. mile

THE URBAN/RURAL POPULATION SPLIT

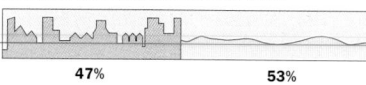

47%　　　　　53%

RELIGIOUS PERSUASION

Other 1%

Muslim 99%

ETHNIC MAKEUP

European 1%

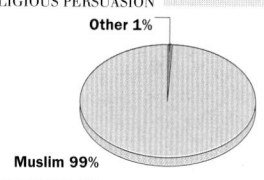

Arab and Berber 99%

Morocco, the westernmost of the Maghreb states, is the last refuge for descendants of the original Berber inhabitants of northwest Africa. About 35% of Moroccans are Berber-speaking. They live mainly in mountain villages, while the Arab majority inhabit the lowlands. Before independence from France, 450,000 Europeans lived in Morocco; numbers have since greatly diminished. Some 45,000 Jews enjoy religious freedom and full civil rights – a role in society unique among Arab countries. Most people speak Arabic, and French is also spoken in urban areas. Sunni Muslim is the religion of the majority of the population. King Hassan is the spiritual leader through his position as Commander of the Faithful. The emancipation of women was slow to take root in Morocco despite advances in education and increasing freedom of social integration between the sexes.

POPULATION AGE BREAKDOWN

	0–14	15–64		65+
4%	4%	4.1%	3.6%	4%
2.6%	4.2%			
47.4%	48.2%	52.7%	55.9%	59.1%
44.8%	47.6%	43.2%	40.5%	36.9%
1960	1970	1980	1990	2000

(% of population by age group)

POLITICS

 1993/1999

 HM King Hassan II

THE STATE OF THE PARTIES

Chamber of Representatives 333 members

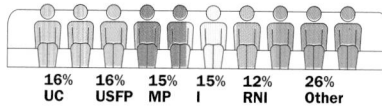

16% UC	16% USFP	15% MP	15% I	12% RNI	26% Other

UC = Constitutional Union USFP = Socialist Union of Popular Force MP = Popular Movement I = Independence Party (Istiqlal) RNI = National Assembly of Independents

Morocco is a constitutional monarchy with a single assembly, to which members are elected every six years.

MAIN POLITICAL ISSUES
The succession
King Hassan is only 67 and in good health, but the power of the monarchy is such that the succession is a major concern for the wealthy business and political elite. Crown Prince Sidi Mohammad will be the next head of state, but is a less dominating figure than his father and may wield less power. Most Moroccans accept that, for the next few years, the country has need of a strong, unifying force and, as a result, King Hassan is not challenged.

Islamic militancy
The government deals ruthlessly with Islamic militants. All Islamist groups are banned, while the death penalty applies to those defying the law; 14 Islamic Youth members received death sentences in 1985. However, popular support for Islamic fundamentalism is fueled by the fear that Morocco is losing its identity as an Arab, Islamic nation, and is becoming too influenced by Europe.

PROFILE
During his long reign, King Hassan has adopted a policy of divide and rule in his relationship with political parties. Although the constitution now allows the majority party in parliament to choose the government, the king reserves the right to appoint or dismiss the prime minister. Following the 1993 elections, Hassan appointed a government after the main center-right party refused his invitation to do so. In 1995, he chose a new center-right government led by Abdellatif Filali after the collapse of his talks with the left-wing opposition.

King Hassan II*, who acceded to the throne on the death of his father in 1961.*

Abdellatif Filali *prime minister of Morocco since 1995.*

 AL   AMU   IBRD   NAM   OIC

*The town of **Boumaine-Dadès** lies in the southern foothills of the Atlas Mountains. The region's outstanding scenery makes it one of Morocco's major tourist attractions.*

WORLD AFFAIRS

Morocco's important role in the quest for lasting peace in the Middle East was underlined by Israeli Prime Minister Yitzhak Rabin's visit to the capital Rabat following the signing of the 1993 peace accord with the Palestine Liberation Organization in Washington. King Hassan's foreign policy is ambiguous, for while he has negotiated with Israel he also heads the Jerusalem Committee of the Islamic Conference Organization. Generally more pro-Western than other Arab states, Morocco has also earned respect by protecting its Jewish minority. International condemnation has focused on Morocco's occupation of the former Spanish colony of Western Sahara in 1975 when King Hassan encouraged mass settlement by ordering the Green March of 350,000 people. Resistance by Polisario Front guerrillas, fighting for an independent Western Sahara, commenced in 1983 and continued, despite a UN-brokered peace plan in 1991. In 1994, the UN approved plans for a voter identification process and other arrangements designed to facilitate a referendum on self-determination in Western Sahara. These arrangements have yet to be completed. Relations with the EU have been strengthened with the signing of an association agreement in late 1995, which envisages free trade in industrial goods within 12 years. However, a fisheries dispute with the EU involving Portuguese and Spanish fishing rights off the Moroccan coast remains to be finally resolved.

AID

 $751m (receipts)   Down 25% in 1993

Saudi Arabia wrote off $2.7 billion of Moroccan debt after the Gulf War. The World Bank has given help to Morocco, but the country receives little aid.

M

CHRONOLOGY

Independence from France in 1956 was only the first step in ending colonial rule for the oldest kingdom in the Arab world, even though the present Alaoui dynasty has been in power for three centuries.

- ❏ **1956** France recognizes Moroccan independence under Sultan Mohammed Ibn Yousif. Morocco joins UN. Spain renounces control over its territories, except the enclaves of Ceuta, Melilla and Ifni and territories in the south.
- ❏ **1957** Sultan Mohammed king.
- ❏ **1961** Crown Prince Hassan becomes king on father's death.
- ❏ **1967** Morocco backs Arab cause in Six-Day War with Israel.
- ❏ **1969** Spain returns the enclave of Ifni to Morocco.
- ❏ **1971** Right-wing army officers stage abortive coup.
- ❏ **1972** King Hassan survives assassination attempt.
- ❏ **1975** International Court of Justice grants self-determination to Western Saharan people. King Hassan orders Moroccan forces to seize Saharan capital.
- ❏ **1976** Morocco and Mauritania partition Western Sahara.
- ❏ **1979** Mauritania renounces claim to part of Western Sahara, which is added to Morocco's territory.
- ❏ **1984** King Hassan and Colonel Gaddafi of Libya sign Oujda Treaty as first step toward a Maghreb union. Morocco withdraws from OAU after criticism of its role in Western Sahara.
- ❏ **1986** Morocco annuls Oujda Treaty.
- ❏ **1987** Defensive wall around Western Sahara.
- ❏ **1989** Arab Maghreb Union (AMU) creates no-tariff zone between Morocco, Algeria, Tunisia, Libya and Mauritania. Hassan first AMU president.
- ❏ **1990** Morocco condemns Iraq's invasion of Kuwait.
- ❏ **1991** Morocco accepts UN plan for referendum in Western Sahara.
- ❏ **1992** New constitution grants majority party in parliament right to choose the government.
- ❏ **1993** First general election for nine years. After major parties refuse his invitation, king appoints non-party government.
- ❏ **1994** King Hassan dismisses veteran prime minister Karim Lamrani. He is replaced by Abdellatif Filali.
- ❏ **1995** King Hassan appoints a new Cabinet headed by Filali. Islamist opposition leader Mohamed Basri returns to Morocco after 28 years of exile in France.

M

DEFENSE

💲 $1.2bn   ⬇ Down 2% in 1995

0	Defense spending as % GDP	40
4.3%		

MOROCCAN ARMED FORCES

🪖	524 main battle tanks (224 M–48A5, 300 M–60 A1/A3)	175,000 personnel
🚢	1 frigate, 29 patrol boats	7,000 personnel
✈	99 combat aircraft (16 F–5E, 14 *Mirage* F-1EH, 15 Mirage F–1CH)	13,500 personnel
🚀	None	

Morocco's long struggle in the Western Sahara against Polisario Front guerrillas has given the kingdom's forces a strong reputation. Moroccans have also fought as mercenaries in the Gulf. In the 1980s, Moroccan sappers constructed a 1,550-mile defensive wall to cordon off Western Sahara in an attempt to prevent incursions from Polisario guerrillas based in Algeria.

Morocco's pro-Western stance has allowed its forces access to sophisticated weapons and training from the West, particularly the USA – unlike neighboring North African states, which are dependent on the former Soviet bloc.

The air force was formed in 1956 and flies US and European aircraft, notably *Mirage* interceptors. The navy uses Western-supplied ships, but is insignificant in regional terms.

Some 6% of national income is spent on defense – a relatively, but not prohibitively, high figure for a developing country. Military service is compulsory for 18 months.

ECONOMICS

📊 $30.3bn   💱 8.47–8.91 Moroccan dirhams

SCORE CARD

- ❏ WORLD GNP RANKING..........................55th
- ❏ GNP PER CAPITA $1,150
- ❏ BALANCE OF PAYMENTS...................$–720m
- ❏ INFLATION 6%
- ❏ UNEMPLOYMENT....................................16%

EXPORTS

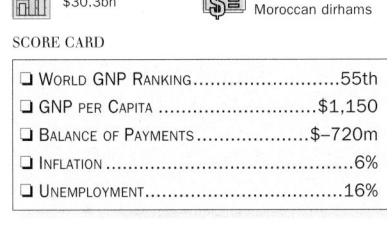

Germany 4% — Italy 5%
Japan 6%
Spain 9%
Other 43%
France 33%

IMPORTS

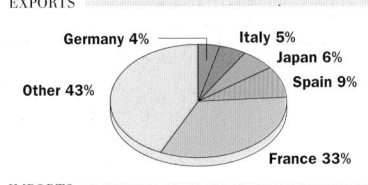

Germany 6% — Italy 6%
USA 10%
Other 44%
Spain 11%
France 23%

STRENGTHS

Pro-business policies and abundant labor attract foreign investment. Low inflation. Tourist industry, phosphates and agriculture all have great potential.

WEAKNESSES

High unemployment and population growth. Dirham not fully convertible. Droughts have hit agriculture. Cannabis production (30% of Europe's supply) complicates closer EU links.

PROFILE

The government embarked on a privatization program in 1992 designed to attract investment – particularly

ECONOMIC PERFORMANCE INDICATOR

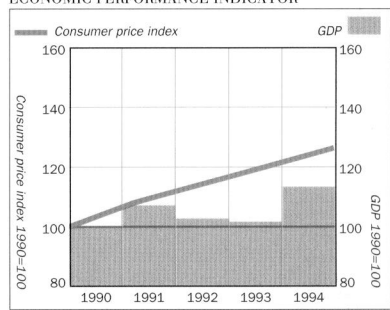

Consumer price index ▬▬   GDP ▓

from Europe. It raised $250 million (including $100 million from Spain) in 1993 and there are plans to sell companies worth a further $2 billion by 1995. These measures are opposed by trade unions, which have organized strikes over rising prices and deteriorating working conditions.

MOROCCO : MAJOR BUSINESSES

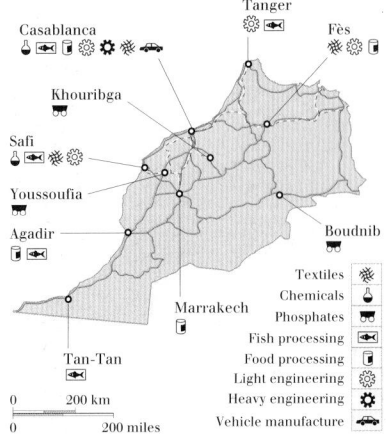

Textiles	🌸
Chemicals	🧪
Phosphates	🚜
Fish processing	🐟
Food processing	🍴
Light engineering	⚙
Heavy engineering	✿
Vehicle manufacture	🚗

0   200 km
0   200 miles

RESOURCES

 9.9bn kwh (capacity 2.36m kw)

 221 b/d refines 154,600 b/cd

 15.6m sheep, 4.4m goats, 2.4m cattle, 880,000 asses

Phosphates, oil, gas, coal, iron, barite, lead, copper, zinc

ELECTRICITY GENERATION

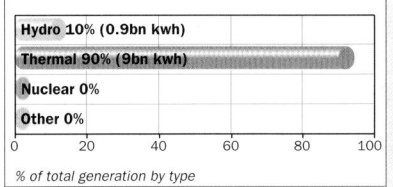

Hydro 10% (0.9bn kwh)

Thermal 90% (9bn kwh)

Nuclear 0%

Other 0%

% of total generation by type

Morocco possesses 75% of the world's phosphate reserves. Other minerals include anthracite and iron ore.

ENVIRONMENT

 0.8% (0.7% partially protected)

Ecological issues are not a high priority

ENVIRONMENTAL TREATIES

No　　Yes　　Yes

Yes　　No　　Yes

Morocco's wealth of plant and animal life has suffered severely from long periods of drought, most recently in the early 1980s and early 1990s. The unplanned development of tourist resorts is posing a threat to fragile coastal ecosystems.

MEDIA

 Criticism of the king is not allowed

PUBLISHING AND BROADCAST MEDIA

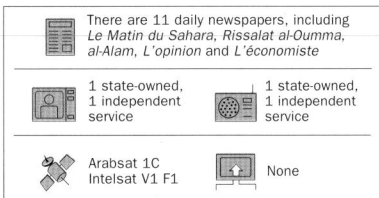

There are 11 daily newspapers, including *Le Matin du Sahara, Rissalat al-Oumma, al-Alam, L'opinion* and *L'économiste*

1 state-owned, 1 independent service

1 state-owned, 1 independent service

Arabsat 1C Intelsat V1 F1

None

The media is careful to avoid criticism of King Hassan, and the reporting of current affairs tends to be cautious. The sports pages, especially the soccer reports, are the most dynamic sections of the press – and may also contain implicit criticisms of the establishment. Newspapers are published both in Arabic and French. *L'Économiste* supplies the most authoritative economic information. State-owned TV began transmissions in Arabic and French in 1962. Radio broadcasts are in Arabic, Berber, French, Spanish and English from Rabat and Tangier.

Forestry is carried out in the mountains. Crops include grain, fruit, peppers, tomatoes and cut flowers.

MOROCCO : LAND USE

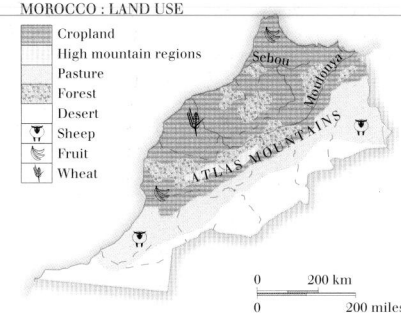

Cropland
High mountain regions
Pasture
Forest
Desert
Sheep
Fruit
Wheat

0　　200 km
0　　200 miles

CRIME

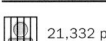 21,332 prisoners

 Up 26% in 1986

CRIME RATES

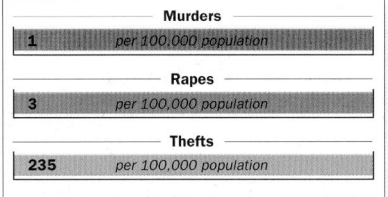

Murders

1　*per 100,000 population*

Rapes

3　*per 100,000 population*

Thefts

235　*per 100,000 population*

Urban crime is increasing, but muggings are rare. Apart from a 1990 strike that led to 40 deaths in Fès, Morocco has seen little civil unrest. Police watch Islamic militant activists.

EDUCATION

 44%

221,217 students

0　　*Education spending as % GNP*　　25

5.8%

THE EDUCATION SYSTEM

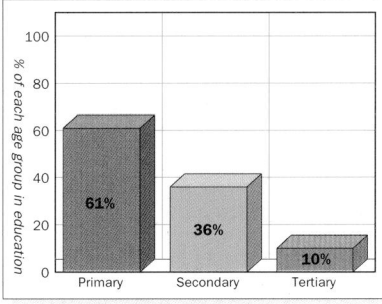

% of each age group in education

61% Primary

36% Secondary

10% Tertiary

Only 14% of Morocco's rural population is literate, as opposed to 50% in the cities. The literacy level and elementary school enrollment rates are well below the average for countries with similar standards of living. There are six universities which have a combined total of 100,000 students.

HEALTH

 1 per 4,850 people

 Neonatal causes, cerebrovascular and heart diseases

0　　*Health spending as % GDP*　　25

0.9%

Despite recent progress, child mortality and nutritional standards for the poorest Moroccans remain well below average for countries which are at a similar stage of development. There is one doctor for every 4,850 Moroccans and one hospital bed for every 1,000 people. Outside the cities, primary health care is virtually non-existent, with the result that people depend on traditional remedies for illnesses.

WEALTH

 Factory foreman, 4,950 Moroccan dirhams ($584) per month; executive engineer, 10,981 Moroccan dirhams ($1,296) per month

CONSUMER GOODS OWNERSHIP

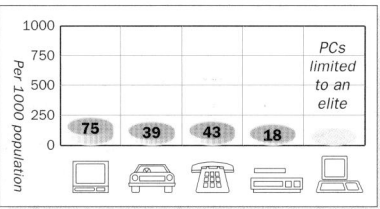

Per 1000 population

PCs limited to an elite

75　39　43　18

Income per head is considerably lower than in neighboring Algeria and Tunisia. One in seven Moroccans still live below the poverty line – an improvement, however, on the 1985 figure, which was one in five. About 45% of the population live in rural areas and the rural–urban gap in wealth is considerable. Drought in the 1990s accelerated the urban drift.

Unrest has largely been avoided owing to Morocco's thriving informal sector. Apart from the illegal hashish trade and the smuggling of alcohol and Western goods, this provides jobs in clothes manufacturing, food processing, goods transportation, and the hotel and building trades.

WORLD RANKING

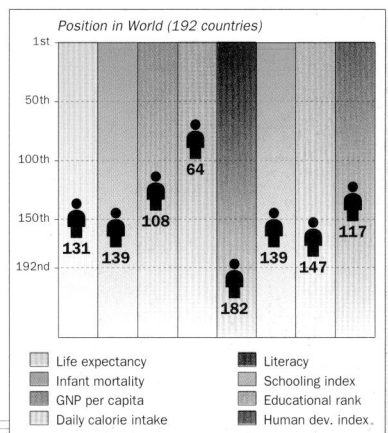

Position in World (192 countries)

1st
50th
100th
150th
192nd

64
108
131
139
182
139
147
117

Life expectancy
Infant mortality
GNP per capita
Daily calorie intake
Literacy
Schooling index
Educational rank
Human dev. index

M

MOZAMBIQUE

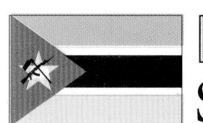

OFFICIAL NAME: Republic of Mozambique   **CAPITAL:** Maputo
POPULATION: 16 million   **CURRENCY:** Metical   **OFFICIAL LANGUAGE:** Portuguese

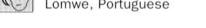

SOUTHERN AFRICA

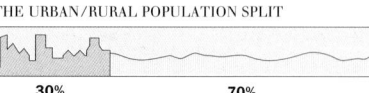

Situated on the southeast African coast, Mozambique is bisected from east to west by the Zambezi River, which is dammed at Cahora Bassa. South of the Zambezi lies a semi-arid savanna lowland. The north-central delta provinces around Tete are the most fertile and it is here that the bulk of Mozambique's racially mixed population lives. After independence from Portugal in 1975, Mozambique was torn apart by a savage and devastating civil war between the (then Marxist) FRELIMO government and the South African-backed Mozambique National Resistance (RENAMO). The conflict finally ended in 1992 by the signing of UN-brokered peace agreement. Subsequent multiparty elections returned FRELIMO to government.

PEOPLE

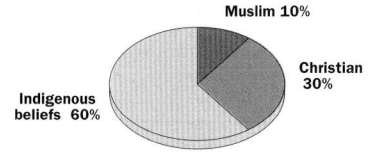

Makua, Tsonga, Sena, Lomwe, Portuguese

135 people per sq. mile

THE URBAN/RURAL POPULATION SPLIT

30%   70%

RELIGIOUS PERSUASION

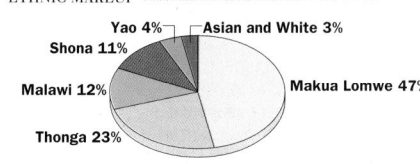

Muslim 10%

Christian 30%

Indigenous beliefs 60%

ETHNIC MAKEUP

Yao 4% — Asian and White 3%
Shona 11%
Malawi 12%
Thonga 23%
Makua Lomwe 47%

CLIMATE

WEATHER CHART

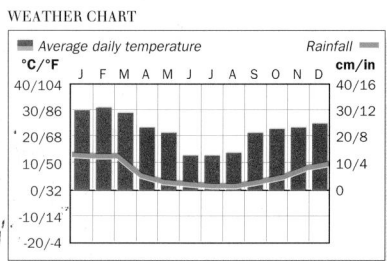

In theory, Mozambique has a rainy and a dry season. However, in the 1980s, frequent failure of the rains contributed to two disastrous famines: in 1982–1984 (when 100,000 died) and in 1986–1987. The coast south of Beira and the highlands adjoining Malawi and Zimbabwe are the wettest areas. The northern coast is dry because the moist trade winds are blocked by Madagascar. The Zambezi valley is the driest region.

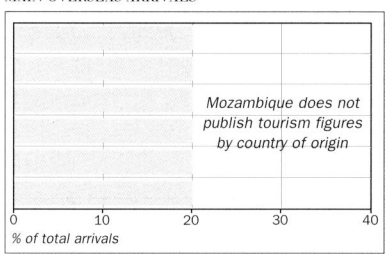

Tea picking. *Other important cash crops are cashew nuts, cotton, sugar, copra and citrus fruits. Agriculture employs 85% of workers.*

TOURISM

 Tourism has still not recovered after war
 No change due to effects of war

MAIN OVERSEAS ARRIVALS

Mozambique does not publish tourism figures by country of origin

0   10   20   30   40
% of total arrivals

The tourist industry, which regularly used to attract around 300,000 South Africans and Rhodesians in the 1970s, was destroyed by the civil war and is only slowly being rebuilt. The land mines planted throughout the country continue to make travel outside the capital hazardous, while food shortages and the still poor infrastructure are added obstacles.

If political stability can be maintained, however, Mozambique will be free to exploit its excellent beaches and game reserves, which include the Gorongosa Game Park. There is a proposal to incorporate game reserves on the Mozambican side of the border into South Africa's much-visited Kruger Park.

TRANSPORTATION

 Mavalane Intl, Maputo 409,000 passengers

 15 ships 24,100 dwt

THE TRANSPORTATION NETWORK

2,920 miles (4,690 km)	None
1,946 miles (3,131 km)	2,330 miles (3,750 km)

One of the biggest problems facing Mozambique is the estimated three million mines left over from the civil war, which prevent free access to many parts of the country. The hundreds of bridges destroyed in the war are slowly being rebuilt. Major improvements to road and rail links can be undertaken now the political situation is more stable. Much of Mozambique's intercontinental trade continues to pass through South African ports.

Mozambique is racially very mixed. The tensions that exist in society, however, are not between the different groups but between northerners and southerners. The government has consistently been accused of favoring the south over the north, while RENAMO enjoys most support in the north and central regions. Anti-white feelings are growing as certain "Africanist" groups are trying to use the claim of excessive white influence in government as a means of gaining popular support.

Life in Mozambique is based around the extended family. In some provinces, most notably Zambezia, Cabo Delgado and Tete, this is matriarchal. Polygamy is fairly widespread among those who are wealthy enough to afford second wives. Under FRELIMO, women's rights have been given particular attention. Women, who played an active part in FRELIMO armies, are now much better protected by divorce, child-custody and husband-desertion laws. The Mozambican Women's Organization encourages participation in political life.

POPULATION AGE BREAKDOWN

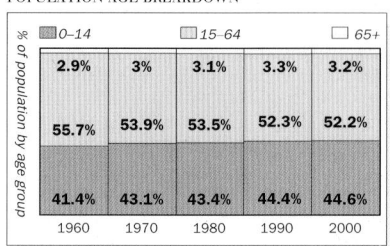

	0–14	15–64	65+		
65+	2.9%	3%	3.1%	3.3%	3.2%
15–64	55.7%	53.9%	53.5%	52.3%	52.2%
0–14	41.4%	43.1%	43.4%	44.4%	44.6%
	1960	1970	1980	1990	2000

M

POLITICS

 1994/1999

 President Joaquim Alberto Chissano

THE STATE OF THE PARTIES

Assembly of the Republic 250 members

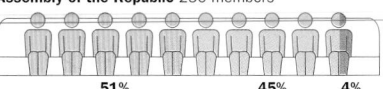

51%	45%	4%
FRELIMO	**RENAMO**	**UD**

FRELIMO = Mozambican Liberation Front **RENAMO** = Mozambique National Resistance **UD** = Democratic Union

MAIN POLITICAL ISSUES
The move to democracy
In 1993, the UN secured, with difficulty, the $260 million and the 7,500 multinational forces required both to demobilize Mozambique's warring factions and to stage the country's first democratic elections.

In 1994, elections were held, despite a last-minute withdrawal threat by RENAMO and returned FRELIMO to power. However, support for RENAMO proved to be stronger than anticipated. The former guerrillas won 112 of the 250 seats in the new parliament and their leader, Afonso Dhlakama, polled 33% of the votes cast in the presidential election.

Reconstruction
The government now faces the enormous task of rebuilding a country which has been ravaged by civil war – with its toll of 900,000 dead, one million refugees and an estimated 90% of the remaining population living below the poverty line.

Joaquim Chissano, president since 1986, has pushed toward political pluralism.

RENAMO leader, Afonso Dhlakama, now turning from militarism to politics.

PROFILE
Between 1977 and 1990, Mozambique was a one-party state ruled by the Soviet-backed FRELIMO, which had campaigned for independence from the colonial power, Portugal, in the 1960s. The RENAMO rebel group, who were backed by the government in Rhodesia and the apartheid regime in South Africa, conducted a civil war to limit Soviet influence, under the guise of seeking democracy. The changing political mood on the international scene led in 1990 to FRELIMO adopting a democratic constitution and to RENAMO losing its international sponsors. The key issue now is to ensure the survival of the fragile new democracy. Although FRELIMO is the largest party in the new parliament RENAMO is also clearly a popular force and will wish to receive some benefits from 15 years of struggle. New groups, such as the anti-white PALMO, COINMO and UNAMO, are now also starting to emerge.

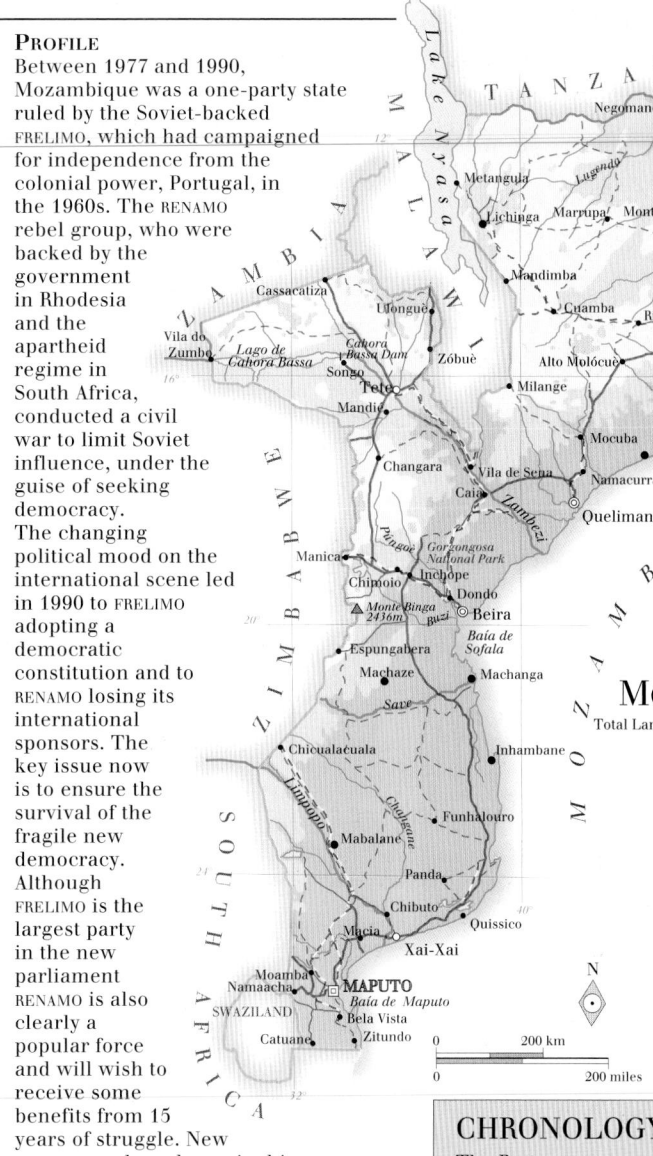

MOZAMBIQUE
Total Land Area : 784 090 sq. km (302 757 sq. miles)

POPULATION
over 1 000 000	▣
over 100 000	◉
over 50 000	○
over 10 000	●
under 10 000	•

LAND HEIGHT
2000m/6562ft	
1000m/3281ft	
500m/1640ft	
200m/656ft	
Sea Level	

M

WORLD AFFAIRS

 Comm   Lusoph   OAU   OIC   SADC

During the Cold War Mozambique was a key battleground in the conflict between Soviet-backed Marxism, and capitalism sponsored by the USA and South Africa. The result was a civil war, which devastated the country between 1977 and 1992.

A shift in the FRELIMO government's position had, however, already become apparent in the early 1980s, as Soviet aid levels became erratic. President Samora Machel then sought a reconciliation with the West, which saw the USA lifting its ban on economic assistance in 1984 and Britain agreeing to provide military training for FRELIMO's forces in 1987. Despite a 1984 pledge, South Africa continued to support RENAMO until at least 1990. Zimbabwean troops assisting the government in guarding the strategically important Beira and Limpopo corridors withdrew in 1993.

In 1995, the UN, having brokered the peace agreement and financed the transition to democracy, withdrew its 6,000 peacekeepers. Mozambique joined the Commonwealth despite having no formal links with the former British Empire.

CHRONOLOGY
The Portuguese tapped the local trade in slaves, gold and ivory in the 16th century and made Mozambique a colony in 1752. Large areas were run by private companies until 1929.

- ❑ **1962** FRELIMO founded.
- ❑ **1964** Starts war of liberation.
- ❑ **1975** Independence. Marxist FRELIMO leader Samora Machel is president. 230,000 of the 250,000 Portuguese leave, but destroy much transport and machinery.
- ❑ **1976** Resistance movement RENAMO set up inside Mozambique by Rhodesians.
- ❑ **1976–1980** Mozambique closes Rhodesian border, imposes economic sanctions, and supports Zimbabwean freedom fighters. Destructive reprisals by RENAMO. ⇨

M

CHRONOLOGY *continued*

- ❏ **1980** South Africa takes over backing of RENAMO.
- ❏ **1982** Zimbabwean troops arrive to guard Mutare–Beira oil pipeline and road–rail route.
- ❏ **1984** Nkomati Accord: South Africa agrees to stop support for RENAMO, and Mozambique for ANC. Ineffectual. Fighting continues.
- ❏ **1986** RENAMO declares war on Zimbabwe. Tanzania sends troops and military aid to FRELIMO. President Machel dies in mystery air crash in South Africa. Joaquim Chissano replaces him.
- ❏ **1988** Nkomati Accord reactivated. Mozambicans allowed back to work in South African mines.
- ❏ **1989** Civil war estimated to have killed 600,000 and caused 405,000 children to die of malnutrition. FRELIMO drops Marxism–Leninism.
- ❏ **1990** Multipartyism and free-market economy written into new constitution. RENAMO fails to recognize it or keep ceasefire.
- ❏ **1992** Chissano and RENAMO's leader, Afonso Dhlakama, meet for first time for peace talks. Peace agreement signed in October.
- ❏ **1994** Democratic elections return FRELIMO to power.

AID

 $1.2bn (receipts)   Down 17% in 1993

The economic situation left by the war has led Mozambique to launch a global campaign for assistance. Seven million Mozambicans are entirely dependent on food aid, and even the most basic economic activity relies on some form of aid. The main donor nations are Italy, the UK, the USA, Sweden, the Netherlands, Norway and, recently, South Africa – whose outlook has influenced Mozambique's turn toward a market economy. Debts from aid provided by the USSR in the late 1970s and early 1980s have been written off.

DEFENSE

 $89m   Down 14% in 1995

0   *Defense spending as % GDP*   40

7.1%

MOZAMBICAN ARMED FORCES

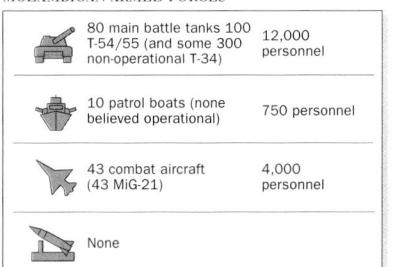

80 main battle tanks 100 T-54/55 (and some 300 non-operational T-34)	12,000 personnel	
10 patrol boats (none believed operational)	750 personnel	
43 combat aircraft (43 MiG-21)	4,000 personnel	
None		

Not surprisingly during the civil war, the armed forces had a dominant role in Mozambique's affairs, swallowing on average 40% of state income. Military figures were also prominent in the FRELIMO government. However, peace has stripped the military of political influence.

Between 1982 and 1993, Zimbabwe also deployed forces to secure the Beira and Limpopo railroad and transportation routes against RENAMO attack.

The 1992 peace agreement provided for the establishment of a new national army made up of former government and RENAMO troops. The new force, whose officers received British training, was formally inaugurated in August 1994 in advance of the elections. When fully deployed, the new army will number 30,000. A key issue now is the reintegration into civilian life and retraining of around 75,000 soldiers, whose demobilization pay was to end in mid-1996.

ECONOMICS

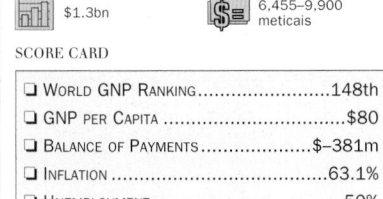 $1.3bn   6,455–9,900 meticais

SCORE CARD

- ❏ WORLD GNP RANKING.........................148th
- ❏ GNP PER CAPITA $80
- ❏ BALANCE OF PAYMENTS....................$–381m
- ❏ INFLATION 63.1%
- ❏ UNEMPLOYMENT.................................50%

EXPORTS

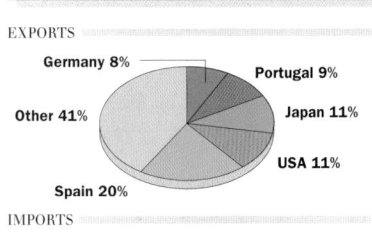

Germany 8%
Portugal 9%
Other 41%
Japan 11%
USA 11%
Spain 20%

IMPORTS

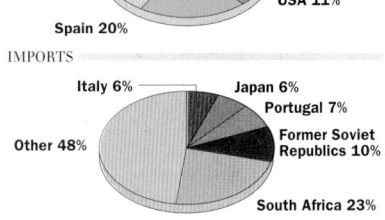

Italy 6%
Japan 6%
Portugal 7%
Other 48%
Former Soviet Republics 10%
South Africa 23%

STRENGTHS

Still struggling to come to terms with the ravages of the civil war, Mozambique's economy has few strengths to speak of and is almost entirely dependent on foreign aid. The government has begun to develop the agricultural sector, which employs 85% of the work force. The fisheries industry has great potential. Mozambique also has Africa's second-largest harbor, Maputo. Modernized in 1989, it is well placed to service southern Africa's landlocked regions.

WEAKNESSES

Mozambique is susceptible to drought and cyclones. A war-shattered infrastructure has left the economy in a condition where overseas aid is essential to prevent at least half the population starving. Destroyed transportation links make it extremely difficult to exploit resources such as iron ore and bauxite. Skilled workers have sought employment in other countries and their absence has delayed the return to normal economic activity.

ECONOMIC PERFORMANCE INDICATOR

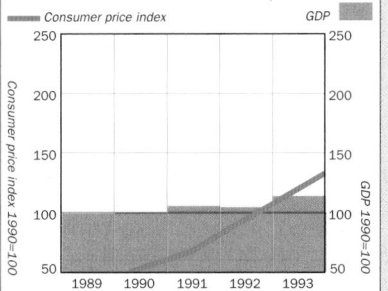

Consumer price index   GDP

1989 1990 1991 1992 1993

PROFILE

Mozambique's enormous problems are further exacerbated by the failure of the socialist model in the country's industry and agriculture. However, with peace assured and buoyed by aid pledges of $780 million, the government in 1995 produced an optimistic plan, based on World Bank recommendations, to eradicate poverty and raise annual GDP growth to 8–9% by 2000.

MOZAMBIQUE : MAJOR BUSINESSES

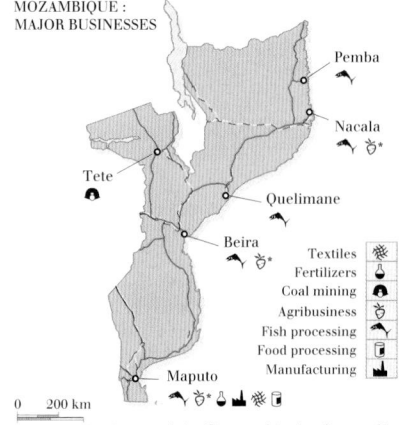

Pemba
Nacala
Tete
Quelimane
Beira
Maputo

Textiles
Fertilizers
Coal mining
Agribusiness
Fish processing
Food processing
Manufacturing

0   200 km
0   200 miles

* significant multinational ownership

RESOURCES

 900m kwh (capacity 2.36m kw)

 Not an oil producer and has no refineries

 1.3m cattle, 389,000 goats, 174,000 pigs

 Coal, iron, tantalite, uranium, gold, diamonds, copper,

ELECTRICITY GENERATION

Hydro 10% (0.05bn kwh)
Thermal 90% (0.4bn kwh)
Nuclear 0%
Other 0%

0   20   40   60   80   100

% of total generation by type

Mozambique's mineral reserves are modest and, due to the lack of useful transportation links, currently

unexploited. Fishing is the most important sector (shrimps accounted for 36% of all export revenue in 1989). The government is concentrating on restoring electricity supplies.

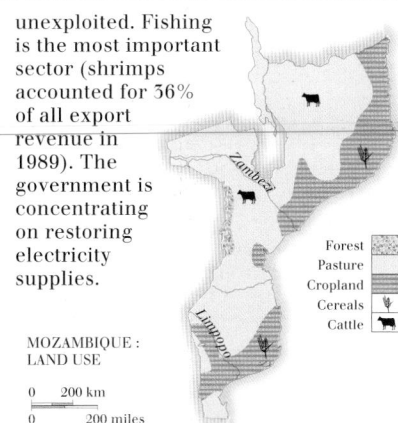

MOZAMBIQUE : LAND USE

0   200 km
0   200 miles

Forest
Pasture
Cropland
Cereals
Cattle

ENVIRONMENT

 None

 Peace has eased environmental pressures

ENVIRONMENTAL TREATIES

No | Yes | Yes
No | No | Yes

The devastating effects of perennial floods followed by droughts are Mozambique's major concern. A three-year drought between 1982 and 1984 resulted in the deaths of 100,000 and left four million close to starvation. The drought was followed in 1984 by massive flooding, which left 50,000 homeless and destroyed much of the harvest. Other ecological concerns are some way down the political agenda in the aftermath of recent conflict. An estimated 50,000 elephants were slaughtered for ivory in order to help fund RENAMO's war effort.

MEDIA

 The press is now free

PUBLISHING AND BROADCAST MEDIA

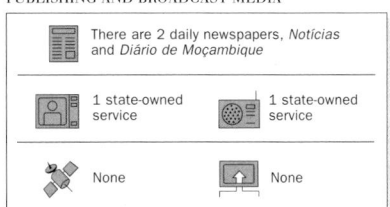

There are 2 daily newspapers, *Notícias* and *Diário de Moçambique*

1 state-owned service | 1 state-owned service
None | None

The press, traditionally a FRELIMO publicity machine, was freed from restrictions by the terms of the 1990 constitution and has become more active since the multiparty elections. With just 3 TV sets per 1,000 people in Mozambique, the political impact of television is minimal.

CRIME

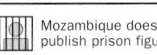 Mozambique does not publish prison figures

 Crime levels are very high and rising

CRIME RATES

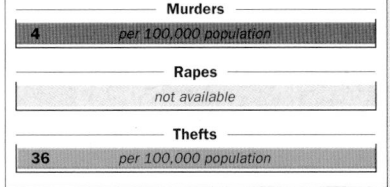

Murders
4 | per 100,000 population

Rapes
not available

Thefts
36 | per 100,000 population

Mozambique is awash with weapons. Banditry, often carried out by former soldiers, is endemic. All areas outside the main urban centers are highly dangerous and road travel is unsafe.

EDUCATION

 33%   5,250 students

0   Education spending as % GNP   25
6.2%

THE EDUCATION SYSTEM

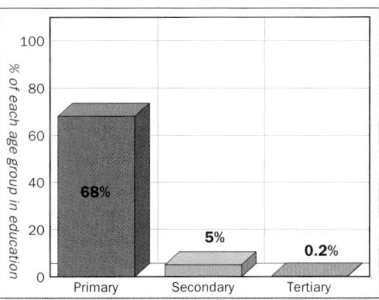

% of each age group in education

100
80
60 — 68% (Primary)
40
20 — 5% (Secondary)
0 — 0.2% (Tertiary)

Over 3,000 schools closed between 1983 and 1990 as a result of the war. The government is committed to ensuring that by 2000 at least 86% of school-age children should attend school. Currently around 63% of children attend elementary school with just 8% going on to secondary education.

HEALTH

 1 per 50,000 people

 Tuberculosis, gastroenteric infections, pneumonia

0   Health spending as % GDP   25
4.4%

Treatment of the victims of the savage war, including a huge number of people who have lost limbs as a result of anti-personnel mines, is the major priority. Since the ending of the war, there has been an improvement in the health service. Preventive medicines and pre-natal care are provided free and doctors serve a mandatory two-year period in rural areas. In 1987 private clinics were allowed, previously they had been banned by FRELIMO as unsocialist.

WEALTH

 Agricultural laborer, 24,310 meticais ($2) per month (minimum); medical consultant, 146,000 meticais ($15) per month

CONSUMER GOODS OWNERSHIP

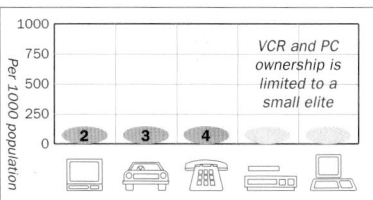

1000
750
500
250
0

Per 1000 population

2   3   4

VCR and PC ownership is limited to a small elite

Mozambique is one of the world's poorest countries with GNP per capita estimated at just $80. Society is hardly stratified as over 90% of the people live in similar breadline conditions. Measures linked to the provision of Western aid have made conditions tougher, raising the price of rice by 600%. Only the higher echelons of FRELIMO, RENAMO and the other political parties have luxuries such as cars, air-conditioning and brick-built apartments. The slow introduction of free-market reforms will, however, increase access to consumer goods in the longer term.

WORLD RANKING

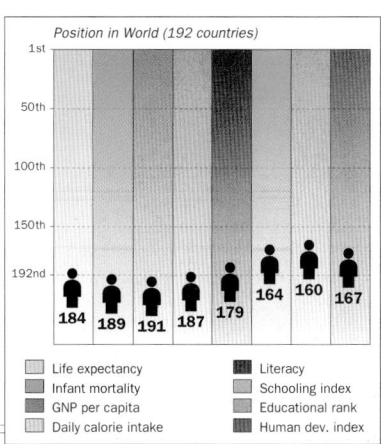

Position in World (192 countries)

1st
50th
100th
150th
192nd

184 189 191 187 179 164 160 167

Life expectancy
Infant mortality
GNP per capita
Daily calorie intake
Literacy
Schooling index
Educational rank
Human dev. index

M

NAMIBIA

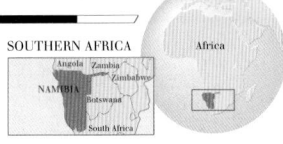

SOUTHERN AFRICA

OFFICIAL NAME: The Republic of Namibia   CAPITAL: Windhoek
POPULATION: 1.5 million   CURRENCY: Namibian dollar   OFFICIAL LANGUAGE: English

L OCATED IN SOUTHWESTERN AFRICA, Namibia has an arid coastal strip formed by the Namib Desert. After many years of guerrilla warfare, Namibia achieved independence from South Africa in 1990. Despite the move away from apartheid, Namibia's economy remains reliant on the expertise of the small white population, a legacy of the previously poor education for blacks. Namibia is Africa's fourth-largest minerals producer.

CLIMATE

WEATHER CHART

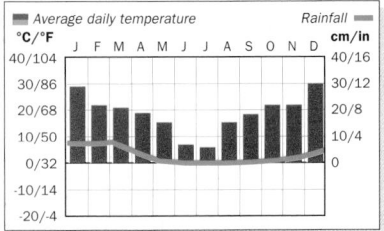

Namibia is almost rainless. The coast is usually shrouded in thick, cold fog unless the hot, very dry *berg* blows.

TRANSPORTATION

 Windhoek Intl
258,373 passengers   Has no fleet

THE TRANSPORTATION NETWORK

3,110 miles (5,010 km)	None
1,480 miles (2,382 km)	None

Large-scale industry is well served by road and rail. Plans exist to build a new harbor at Walvis Bay.

TOURISM

288,000 visitors   Up 35% in 1993

MAIN OVERSEAS ARRIVALS

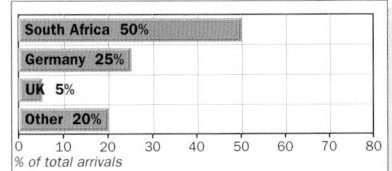

South Africa 50%
Germany 25%
UK 5%
Other 20%
% of total arrivals

Tourists make a very limited contribution to GDP. A quarter are German, many of whom come to visit Windhoek's German sector. There are plans to limit tourists to 300,000 a year to preserve Namibia's fragile desert ecology.

Spitzkoppe, west of Karibib. *Unique scenery such as this is attracting increasing numbers of ecotourists to Namibia.*

PEOPLE

 Ovambo, Kavango, English, Bergdama, German   5 people per sq. mile

THE URBAN/RURAL POPULATION SPLIT

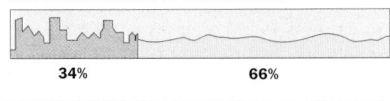

34%   66%

ETHNIC MAKEUP

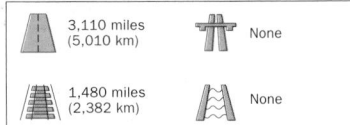

Whites and Mixed 6%   Damara 8%
                             Herero 8%
Ovambo 50%   Kavango 9%
                             Other tribes 19%

The largest ethnic group, the Ovambo, lives mostly in the north of the country. Whites – 60% of whom are Afrikaans-speakers – live mostly in Windhoek, which includes a large German community, living in comfortable, bourgeois, turn-of-the-century German houses. The strife between rival ethnic groups predicted at the time of independence in 1990 has not materialized, and Namibia has adapted well to a multiracial existence. Blacks, who are mostly subsistence farmers, have largely accepted the greater wealth of the white community.

Families are large in Namibia, and among the black community women have, on average, 6.5 children. The constitution supports sexual equality and positive discrimination in favor of women; few, however, have official jobs or own property.

POLITICS

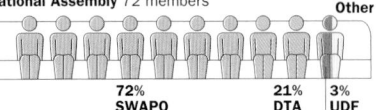 1994/1999   President Samuel Daniel Nujoma

THE STATE OF THE PARTIES

National Assembly 72 members

4% Other

72% SWAPO   21% DTA   3% UDF

SWAPO = South West Africa People's Organization of Namibia   **DTA** = Democratic Turnhalle Alliance   **UDF** = United Democratic Front

National Council 26 members

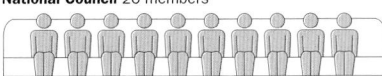

2 members are elected from among the members of each of the 13 regional councils

At independence from South Africa in 1990, Namibia switched from a system of apartheid based on ten separate homelands, to a state-wide, multiparty democracy. Since 1990, SWAPO, whose guerrilla wing fought for and won independence, has had control of the National Assembly. The Ovambo community in the north is SWAPO's main backer, although its center-left stance also gives it the support of large numbers of state employees.

SWAPO has been criticized for not moving swiftly enough to end wealth inequalities. The land reform promised in 1990 has not materialized, and whites remain in control of most areas of the economy, while unemployment among blacks is high. SWAPO's main opposition comes from the center-right DTA, a coalition of 11 parties which favors a free-market approach.

WORLD AFFAIRS

 Comm   Comesa   NAM   OAU   SADC

Namibia joined the UN, Commonwealth and OAU shortly after independence. In 1992, agreement was reached on the disputed southern border with South Africa and in 1994, South Africa relinquished control of the enclave of Walvis Bay – Namibia's only deep-water port. South Africa has also written off Namibia's pre-independence debts.

AID

 US$154m (receipts)   Up 10% in 1993

The UN provides most aid. Germany is the main unilateral donor. Around one-third of aid is spent on education.

N

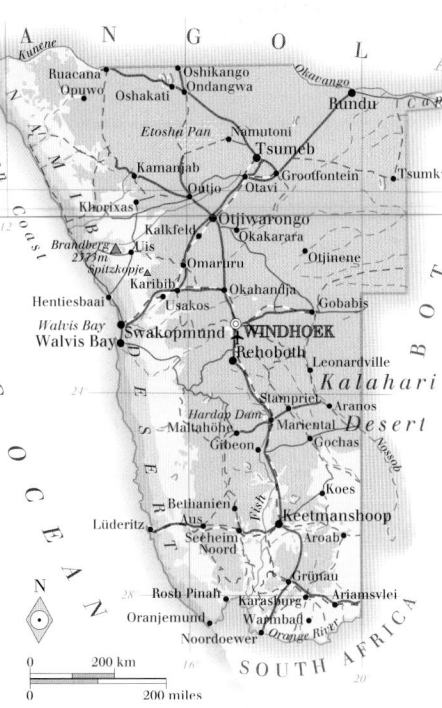

NAMIBIA

Total Land Area :
824 290 sq. km
(318 260 sq. miles)

LAND HEIGHT

2000m/6562ft
1000m/3281ft
500m/1640ft
200m/656ft
Sea Level

POPULATION

over 100 000 ◎
over 10 000 ●
under 10 000 ·

CHRONOLOGY

In 1915, South Africa took over the former German colony as a League of Nations' mandate known as South West Africa.

- ❏ **1950** South Africa refuses to give up the territory to the UN.
- ❏ **1966** Apartheid laws imposed. SWAPO begins armed struggle.
- ❏ **1968** Renamed Namibia.
- ❏ **1973** UN recognizes SWAPO.
- ❏ **1990** Independence.
- ❏ **1994** South Africa relinquishes Walvis Bay.

RESOURCES

 New hydroelectric station will ensure self-sufficiency

 329,790 tons

2.6m sheep, 2m cattle, 1.6m goats

 Uranium, lead, gold, diamonds, copper, zinc, silver, cadmium

Namibia has the world's largest uranium mine, is the world's second-largest lead producer and the third-largest producer of cadmium. Hydroelectric power has enormous potential; the Okavango River system carries a higher volume of water than all South Africa's rivers combined.

ENVIRONMENT

 12%

 More national parks planned

Illegal poaching and anthrax deposits are threatening the unique Namibian desert-adapted elephant (less than 50 remain) and black rhino. Namibia has a unique, but fragile, desert ecosystem, much of which is protected.

Government policy is generally sensitive to environmental issues (the annual seal-cull to protect fish stocks is an exception) and wishes to promote ecotourists rather than mass-market developments.

MEDIA

 Since 1990, press freedom has been guaranteed under the constitution

PUBLISHING AND BROADCAST MEDIA

There are 6 daily newspapers. The *Namibian* has the largest circulation

1 independent service

1 independent service

The Namibian Broadcasting Corporation transmits in 11 languages, including German and English.

CRIME

 Namibia does not publish prison figures

 Crime is rising, particularly in urban areas

Burglary and theft are rising, particularly in urban areas. Ostrich smuggling to the USA is common.

EDUCATION

 40%

 4,157 students

High illiteracy rates among black adults, a legacy of apartheid, is the education system's main challenge.

HEALTH

 1 per 4,320 people

Respiratory, heart and intestinal diseases

A new health ministry is trying to restructure the health service. Most areas lack safe water.

WEALTH

 Whites still earn, on average, 20 times more than blacks

CONSUMER GOODS OWNERSHIP

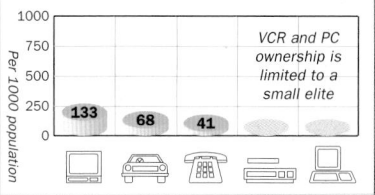

VCR and PC ownership is limited to a small elite

133 68 41

Although income levels have risen, wealth disparities remain. Mercedes are the most desirable status symbol.

WORLD RANKING

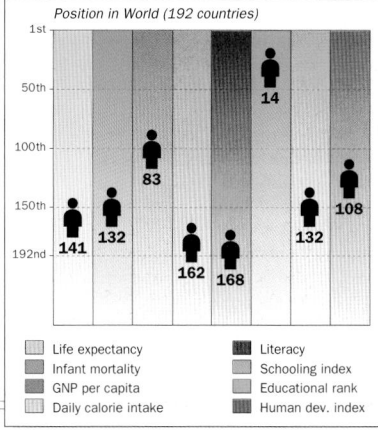

DEFENSE

 US$60m

 Up 18% in 1995

Patrolling fishing stocks, which are frequently raided by Spanish and South African trawlers, is the main activity.

ECONOMICS

 US$3bn

 3.54–3.65 Namibian dollars

SCORE CARD

- ❏ WORLD GNP RANKING........................125th
- ❏ GNP PER CAPITA ....US$1,900
- ❏ BALANCE OF PAYMENTS ....US$190m
- ❏ INFLATION 10.8%
- ❏ UNEMPLOYMENT..................................35%

STRENGTHS

Varied mineral resources make Namibia the third-wealthiest country in sub-Saharan Africa. Namibian waters encompass one of the world's richest offshore fishing grounds. Potential of Walvis Bay as transit point for Namibia's landlocked neighbors.

WEAKNESSES

Almost all manufactured goods have to be imported. Sensitivity to fluctuations in mineral prices. Lack of skilled labor; only 25% of Namibians participate in commercial economy.

IMPORTS/EXPORTS

Namibia has yet to publish official trade figures. South Africa remains the major source of imports and destination for exports

N

NAURU

OFFICIAL NAME: The Republic of Nauru **CAPITAL:** *No official capital*
POPULATION: 10,000 **CURRENCY:** Australian dollar **OFFICIAL LANGUAGE:** Nauruan

NAURU LIES IN the Pacific Ocean, 2,480 miles northeast of Australia. Formerly a British colony, Nauru was exploited for its phosphate deposits by the UK, Australia and New Zealand. Since independence in 1968, the phosphates industry has made Nauruan citizens among the wealthiest in the world. However, reserves are due to run out before the year 2000 and in the future, the proceeds of overseas investments will form the bulk of Nauru's income.

CLIMATE

WEATHER CHART

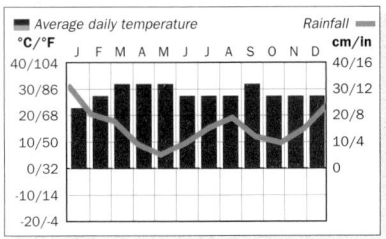

Nauru's tiny size means that rain clouds often miss the island; at times years pass without rain.

TRANSPORTATION

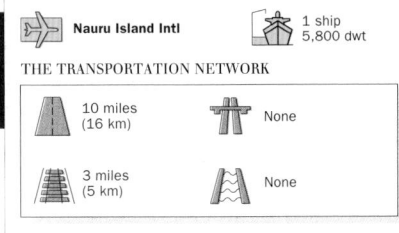

Nauru operates its own airline with Boeing 737s piloted by Australians. The Nauru Steamship Line is Nauru's main link with the outside world. However, all external travel is very expensive. Nauru has no harbor, so ships taking phosphates aboard dock with engines still running on huge concrete caissons floating out at sea. Most Nauruans can afford cars. The single circular road is often littered with abandoned cars, such as Mercedes, as it is much cheaper for Nauruans to import new vehicles than attempt to repair existing ones. The number of car accident fatalities is one of the highest in the South Pacific.

TOURISM

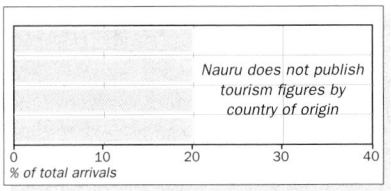

Even if Nauru had any conventional tourist attractions, the enormous cost of getting there would dissuade most tourists from making the journey. The main feature of interest on the island is the bizarre lunar landscape created by over 80 years of phosphate extraction. There are no beaches on Nauru and only a few basic hotels.

NAURU

Total Land Area : 21.2 sq. km (8.2 sq. miles)

LAND HEIGHT

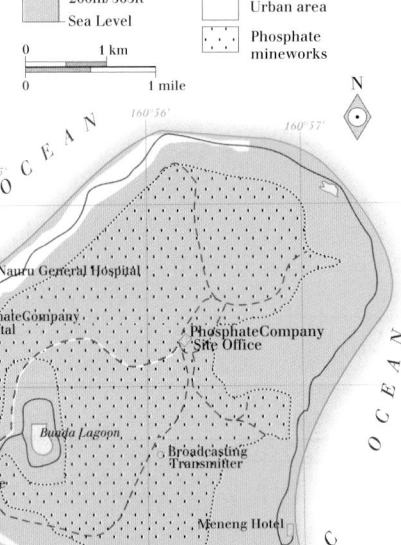

PEOPLE

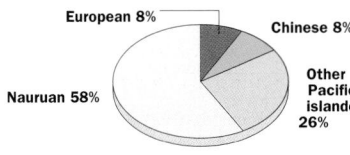

Nauruan, Kiribati, Chinese, Tuvaluan, English

1,233 people per sq. mile

THE URBAN/RURAL POPULATION SPLIT

> Nauru is 100% semi-urban

ETHNIC MAKEUP

European 8%
Chinese 8%
Nauruan 58%
Other Pacific islanders 26%

Indigenous Nauruans are a homogenous group. They do little of the tough work on the island, which is left to an imported labor force, mainly from Kiribati, who live in enclaves of male-only barracks and have few rights.

A society of just 9,400, Nauru is mostly self-regulating. There is some generational tension between younger Nauruans, who go to Australia to study, but have little incentive to do well, and their parents, who fought hard for independence. As the phosphate runs out, an increasing feeling of pointlessness is gripping the young. Many see their future in Australia or New Zealand, but are wary of a drop in living standards and of losing the luxury of sovereignty. It was the latter which led Nauruans to reject the offer of resettlement on an island off the Australian Queensland coast.

POLITICS

 1995/1998

President Lagumot Harris

THE STATE OF THE PARTIES

Parliament 18 members

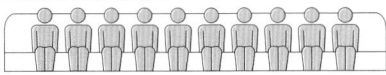

All members are elected as independents

Parliament is based on the British Westminster model, but traditional chiefly leaders are still the dominant political figures. Members of the legislature often switch between temporary, unstable groupings based on personalities rather than ideologies. Hammer DeRoburt became the island's first president in 1968, and dominated the political structure until a vote of no confidence forced him to resign in 1989. Following a general election in 1995, Lagumot Harris was chosen as president.

N

WORLD AFFAIRS

The case for compensation for phosphate exploitation brought by Nauru against the UK government was rejected in 1992 after the longest suit in British legal history. However, an Australian settlement in 1993 brought an immediate payment and a longer-term contribution totaling A$107 million Australian dollars. Nauru's main concern is participation in the South Pacific Forum and the management of trust funds to support Nauruans when phosphate deposits run out.

AID

 $2m (receipts)   Up in 1994

Nauru receives most of its aid through Western (non-US) countries and the South Pacific Forum.

DEFENSE

 Australia responsible for defense   Not applicable

Nauru, which faces no outside threats, has no defense force. Australia, under a *de facto* arrangement, is responsible for the island's security.

ECONOMICS

 $80m   1.29–1.34 Australian dollars

SCORE CARD

❏ WORLD GNP RANKING	190th
❏ GNP PER CAPITA	$8,070
❏ BALANCE OF PAYMENTS	$83.7m
❏ INFLATION	Low inflation rate
❏ UNEMPLOYMENT	Minimal unemployment

STRENGTHS
Considerable investments in Australian and Hawaiian property and hotels. Possible future as a tax haven.

WEAKNESSES
Phosphate, the only resource, is due to run out by the year 2000 and past mining has left 80% of the island uninhabitable and uncultivable. Nauru has been prone to poor investments, such as backing the flop London musical *Leonardo* in 1993. Nauru's flagship Melbourne skyscraper, Nauru House, has developed "concrete cancer" which is costing millions of dollars to repair.

IMPORT/EXPORTS

Nauru's only export commodity is phosphates, in which it trades with Australia and New Zealand. Almost all food, drinking water and manufactured goods are imported, mostly from Australia, New Zealand, the UK and Japan

RESOURCES

 30m kwh (capacity 10,000 kw)   500 tons

 3,000 pigs   Guano (phosphates)

Since 1888 Nauru has been exploited by the Germans, British, Australians, New Zealanders and recently by Nauruans themselves, for its valuable phosphate reserves. Extraction has destroyed 80% of the island, and the deposits are due to run out before the year 2000. Nauru has no other resources. The island is entirely dependent on outside energy supplies and the cost of oil is 50% higher than the Pacific average as Nauru does not lie on any shipping routes. Most electricity is produced by small diesel generators.

ENVIRONMENT

 None   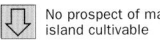 No prospect of making island cultivable

The main concern is possible fall-out from French nuclear test sites in the Pacific: Nauru lies downwind of these. Otherwise, ecological awareness is minimal. Nauruans accept that their source of wealth has effectively destroyed their island.

MEDIA

 Freedom of speech is protected by law

PUBLISHING AND BROADCAST MEDIA

 There are no daily newspapers. *The Bulletin*, the *Young Post* and *The Observer* are published weekly

 No TV service   1 state-owned service

Nauru has no national TV broadcasting service; some overseas programs are made available on video.

CRIME

 Nauru does not publish prison figures   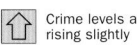 Crime levels are rising slightly

Theft is almost non-existent. Assaults and dangerous driving as a result of drunkenness are the major problems.

Nauru is almost circular with a single, 12-mile ring road. The overcrowded coastal strip is the sole habitable land.

EDUCATION

 99%   Not available

Many Nauruans attend boarding school in Australia from a young age. Few go on to university.

HEALTH

 1 per 700 people   Tuberculosis, vitamin deficiencies, diabetes

A diet of processed imported foods and widespread obesity are the major problems. One-third of the population suffers from non-insulin-dependent diabetes. Industrial accidents are treated in Australia.

WEALTH

 Average white-collar worker, 16,000 Australian dollars ($11,902) per year

CONSUMER GOODS OWNERSHIP

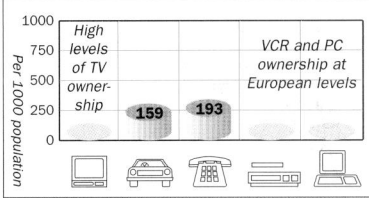

Nauru has one of the highest per capita incomes in the world. Wealth is fairly evenly distributed. Most Nauruans live in simple traditional houses and spend their money on luxury cars.

WORLD RANKING

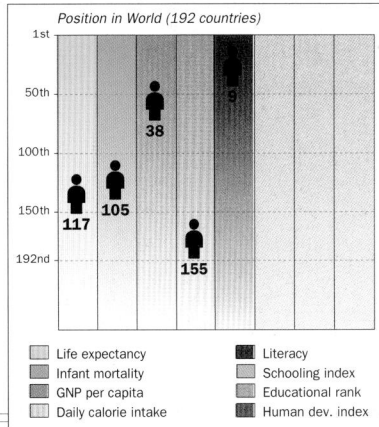

▢ Life expectancy	▨ Literacy
▢ Infant mortality	▨ Schooling index
▢ GNP per capita	▨ Educational rank
▢ Daily calorie intake	▨ Human dev. index

N

NEPAL

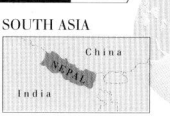

SOUTH ASIA

OFFICIAL NAME: Kingdom of Nepal   **CAPITAL:** Kathmandu
POPULATION: 21.4 million   **CURRENCY:** Nepalese rupee   **OFFICIAL LANGUAGE:** Nepali

ON THE SHOULDER OF the southern Himalayas, Nepal is surrounded by India and China. One of the world's poorest countries, its largely agricultural economy is dependent on the prompt arrival of the monsoon. New sources of income are being developed, including hydroelectric power and tourism. In 1991, elections were held for the first time since 1959, ending a period of absolute rule by the king.

CLIMATE

WEATHER CHART

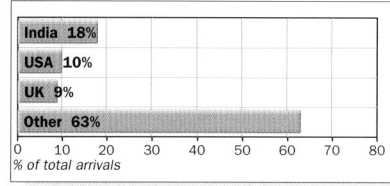

The warm July to October monsoon affects the whole country, causing flooding in the hot Terai plain, but generally decreases northward and westward. The rest of the year is dry, sunny and mild, except in the Himalayas, where valley temperatures in winter may average 14°F.

TRANSPORTATION

Tribhuvan International, Kathmandu
800,000 passengers

Has no fleet

THE TRANSPORTATION NETWORK

2,140 miles (3,440 km)		None
32 miles (52 km)		None

Domestic flights link the main towns. There are paved roads in the south and in the Kathmandu valley; only one runs north to China. Two short stretches of railroad cross into India.

Himalayan harvest. *The steep mountainsides and easily eroded soils mean that most fields are terraced. 90% of Nepalese are farmers.*

TOURISM

327,000 visitors   Up 12% in 1994

MAIN OVERSEAS ARRIVALS

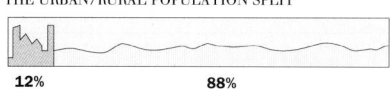

India	18%
USA	10%
UK	9%
Other	63%

% of total arrivals

A serious conflict exists between the wish to preserve the environment and the desire for tourist revenue. Areas in the northwest were opened up to tourists in 1989, but degradation caused by 72,000 hikers a year on popular routes forced the government to set up the Annapurna Conservation Project. Fuelwood cutting for tourists is said to have increased deforestation, and hence soil erosion, by 10%.

PEOPLE

 Nepali, Maithilli, Bhojpuri   404 people per sq. mile

THE URBAN/RURAL POPULATION SPLIT

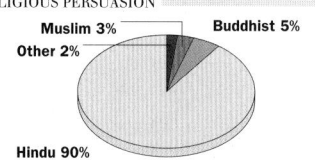

12%   88%

RELIGIOUS PERSUASION

Muslim 3%   Buddhist 5%
Other 2%

Hindu 90%

There are few tensions among different ethnic groups such as the Sherpas in the north, the inhabitants of the Terai in the south and the Newars of the Kathmandu valley. Hindu women are more restricted than Sherpas and Buddhists. Polygamy is practised in the hills. Since 1990, thousands of ethnic Nepalese refugees from Bhutan have settled in the country.

POLITICS

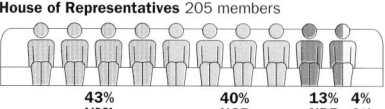

U. House 1995/1997   HM King Birendra Bir
L. House 1994/1999   Bikram Shah Deva

THE STATE OF THE PARTIES

House of Representatives 205 members

43% UML   40% NCP   13% NDP   4% Other

UML = Unified Marxist–Leninist Party **NCP** = Nepali Congress Party **NDP** = National Democratic Party **Other** = Nepali Sadbhavana, Nepal Workers' and Peasants' Party

National Council 60 members

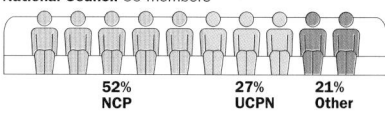

52% NCP   27% UCPN   21% Other

35 members elected by the House of Representatives, 15 chosen from the country's development zones, and 10 chosen by King Birendra

The end of absolute monarchy and the partyless *panchayat* system in 1990 led to general elections in 1991, which were won by the NCP. Divisions within the NCP forced fresh elections in 1994, which were won by the communist Unified Marxist–Leninist Party (UML). In 1995, the NCP returned to power after the UML lost a parliamentary vote of confidence. The NCP has since resumed its liberal economic policies.

WORLD AFFAIRS

 CP   IMF   NAM   SAARC

Nepal's security relations with India were under review by the pro-Chinese UML government. The NCP government has revived close links with India, on which Nepal depends for its external trade. Relations with Bhutan are strained over the issue of Bhutanese refugees in Nepal.

AID

 $364m (receipts)   Down 22% in 1993

Nepal's strategic position has made it a focus for powerful donors, including the USA, China, India, Japan and member states of the CIS.

DEFENSE

 $42.9m   Up 1% in 1995

The army is small at 35,000 men. It has no tanks, combat aircraft or armed helicopters. The limited weaponry comes from the UK and India.

N

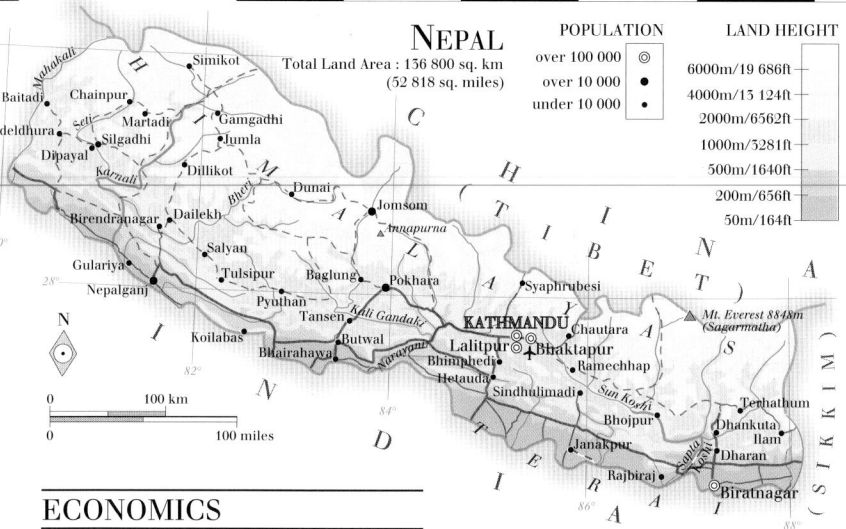

NEPAL

Total Land Area : 136 800 sq. km
(52 818 sq. miles)

POPULATION
over 100 000 ◎
over 10 000 ●
under 10 000 ·

LAND HEIGHT
6000m/19 686ft
4000m/13 124ft
2000m/6562ft
1000m/3281ft
500m/1640ft
200m/656ft
50m/164ft

CHRONOLOGY

The foundations of the Nepalese state were laid in 1769, when King Prithvi Narayan Shah conquered the region.

❏ **1816–1923** Establishment of quasi-British protectorate.
❏ **1959** First multiparty constitution.
❏ **1960** King Mahendra bans all political parties and suspends the constitution.
❏ **1962** *Panchayat* system launched.
❏ **1991** Multiparty elections.
❏ **1994** Election of first UML communist government.
❏ **1995** UML government loses vote of confidence. NCP is returned to power.

ECONOMICS

 $4.2bn   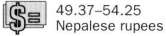 49.37–54.25 Nepalese rupees

SCORE CARD

❏ WORLD GNP RANKING.........................106th
❏ GNP PER CAPITA $200
❏ BALANCE OF PAYMENTS....................$-352m
❏ INFLATION 9.1%
❏ UNEMPLOYMENT 5%

STRENGTHS
Self-sufficiency in grain most years. Economic liberalization under NCP government. Potential for hydroelectric power generation. Low debt level.

WEAKNESSES
Agricultural dependency; only 10% of GDP from manufacturing. Landlocked status. Low savings rate. Absence of active entrepreneurial class.

EXPORTS
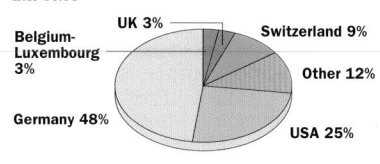
UK 3%, Belgium-Luxembourg 3%, Switzerland 9%, Other 12%, Germany 48%, USA 25%

IMPORTS
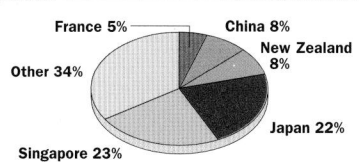
France 5%, China 8%, New Zealand 8%, Other 34%, Japan 22%, Singapore 23%

RESOURCES

 901m kwh (capacity 230,000 kw)   16,852 tons
6.5m cattle, 5.5m goats, 914,000 sheep, 612,000 pigs   Mica, lignite, copper, cobalt, iron

The Mahakali River project, developed under an agreement signed with India in 1996, will boost hydro-resources.

ENVIRONMENT

 8% (1% partially protected)   Two national parks threatened by large-scale HEP projects

Deforestation and soil erosion are serious problems. The native tiger is fast disappearing. In 1995, the World Bank canceled funding for the Arun III hydroelectric project, east of Kathmandu, on environmental grounds.

MEDIA

 Press freedom is guaranteed under the new constitution

PUBLISHING AND BROADCAST MEDIA

 There are 59 daily newspapers, including the leading *Gorkhapatra* and *Rising Nepal*

 1 limited state-owned service    1 state-owned service

The Nepal TV service began broadcasting in 1985 and 18% of the country now receives it. The press is mainly Kathmandu-based with low circulations. The *Sunday Despatch* is the paper most critical of government.

CRIME

 Nepal does not publish prison figures   Up 16% in 1992

Petty theft and smuggling are the main problems. The legal provision for detention without trial is used and police suppression of demonstrations is often brutal.

EDUCATION

 26%   103,800 students

Over 80% of boys attend school in Nepal, but still only a minority of girls. Nepal's literacy rate is among the lowest in the world.

HEALTH

 1 per 16,110 people   Respiratory and diarrheal diseases, maternal deaths

There are about 100 *dharmi-jhankri* (faith healers) for every health worker. Maternal mortality is high, the result of harmful traditional birth practices; a reeducation program for midwives has been established.

WEALTH

 Sawmill sawyer, 800 Nepalese rupees ($15) per month; yarn spinner, 2,500–6,000 Nepalese rupees ($46–$111) per month

CONSUMER GOODS OWNERSHIP
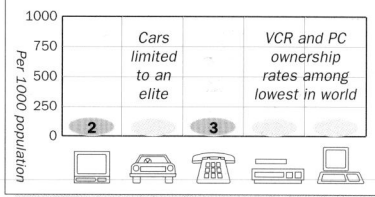
Cars limited to an elite. VCR and PC ownership rates among lowest in world

Nepal is one of the poorest countries in the world. Income per head is only $200 a year. There is little wealth.

WORLD RANKING

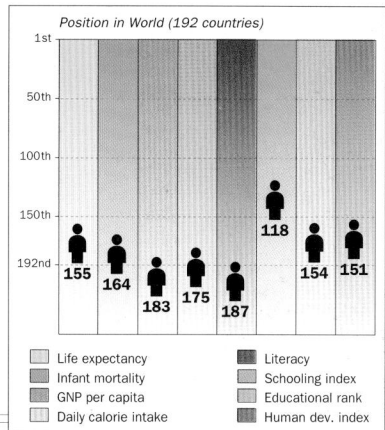

NETHERLANDS

OFFICIAL NAME: Kingdom of the Netherlands   CAPITALS: Amsterdam, The Hague
POPULATION: 15.5 million   CURRENCY: Netherlands guilder   OFFICIAL LANGUAGE: Dutch   OVERSEAS TERRITORIES: 2

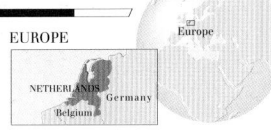

 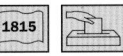    

THE NETHERLANDS IS LOCATED at the delta of five major rivers in northwest Europe. The few hills in the eastern and southern part of the country fall into a flat coastal area, bordered by the North Sea to the north and west. This is protected by a giant infrastructure of dunes, dikes and canals, as 27% of the coast is below sea level. The Netherlands became one of the world's first confederative republics after Spain recognized its independence in 1648. Its highly successful economy has a long trading tradition and Rotterdam, its main port, is also the world's largest.

CLIMATE

WEATHER CHART

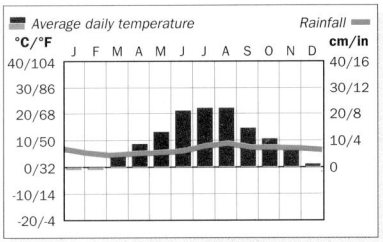

The Netherlands has a temperate climate, which is characterized by mild winters and cool summers. The country's coastal areas have the mildest climate, although northerly gales are fairly frequent, particularly in autumn and winter.

TOURISM

 6.2m visitors   Up 7% in 1994

MAIN OVERSEAS ARRIVALS

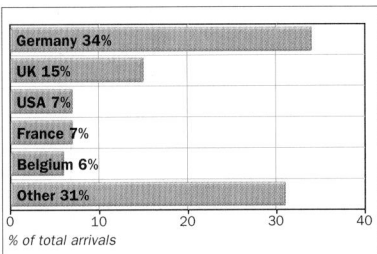

Germany 34%	
UK 15%	
USA 7%	
France 7%	
Belgium 6%	
Other 31%	

% of total arrivals

Tourism is a major business in the Netherlands. Visitors go mainly to Amsterdam, although cities such as Groningen and Maastricht are growing in popularity. Amsterdam caters for a diverse tourism market. Its world-famous museums include the Rijksmuseum, with its collection of Vermeers and Rembrandts. Amsterdam is also renowned as the sex capital of Europe. Its liberal traditions and red-light district draw millions every year.

TRANSPORTATION

Schipol, Amsterdam
14.9m passengers

515 ships
4.51m dwt

THE TRANSPORTATION NETWORK

57,190 miles (92,040 km)	1,271 miles (2,045 km)
1,757 miles (2,828 km)	3,002 miles (4,832 km)

Rotterdam, the key transshipment port for northern Europe, is also the world's largest. It is currently expanding its container capacity. The government is also expanding Schipol airport; $15 billion has been committed to make it a hub of transportation in Europe. There are plans to construct new high-speed track to allow the French TGV train to run from Brussels to Amsterdam.

In the past decade, the city has also become a center for the European gay community. A thriving club scene and liberal drug laws have brought an increase in ravers from neighboring countries. Rave trains from Brussels to the IT club carry thousands every week during the summer.

In spring and summer, the tulip fields and North Sea beaches attract large numbers of visitors.

Windmill at Baambrugge, near Amsterdam. A century ago there were 10,000 in the country compared with today's 1,000. A protective ring of 900 mills kept Amsterdam from flooding.

PEOPLE

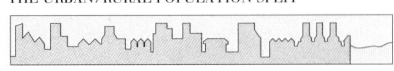 Dutch, Frisian

1,188 people per sq. mile

THE URBAN/RURAL POPULATION SPLIT

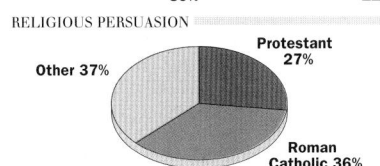

89%   11%

RELIGIOUS PERSUASION

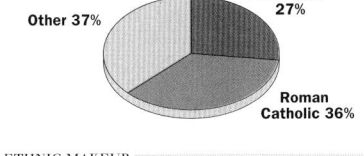

Other 37%
Protestant 27%
Roman Catholic 36%

ETHNIC MAKEUP

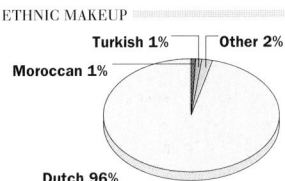

Turkish 1%   Other 2%
Moroccan 1%
Dutch 96%

The Dutch see their country as the most tolerant in Europe. This reflects a long history of welcoming refugees seeking religious and political asylum. In the 20th century, immigrants from former colonies have settled in the Netherlands and are fully accepted as citizens. The first wave came from Indonesia, followed by settlers from the Dutch colonies in the Caribbean and South America, Suriname and the Netherlands Antilles. The small Turkish community, however, does not enjoy full citizenship, but has guest worker status as in Germany.

The tradition of tolerance is also reflected in liberal attitudes to sexuality. Dutch homosexuals have the same rights, including the same age of consent, as heterosexuals.

The state does not try to impose a particular morality on its citizens. Drug taking is seen in the Netherlands as a matter of personal choice, as is euthanasia.

Women enjoy equal rights but they are not well-represented at boardroom level.

POPULATION AGE BREAKDOWN

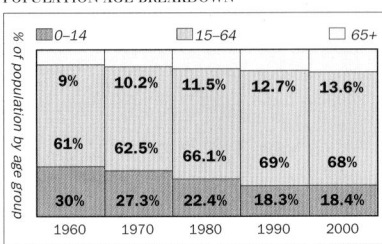

% of population by age group	0–14	15–64	65+		
65+	9%	10.2%	11.5%	12.7%	13.6%
15–64	61%	62.5%	66.1%	69%	68%
0–14	30%	27.3%	22.4%	18.3%	18.4%
	1960	1970	1980	1990	2000

POLITICS

 U. House 1995/1999
L. House 1994/1998

 H.M. Queen Beatrix
Wilhelmina Armgard

THE STATE OF THE PARTIES

Second Chamber 150 members

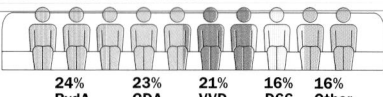

24% PvdA	23% CDA	21% VVD	16% D66	16% Other

PvdA = Labor Party   **CDA** = Christian Democratic Appeal
VVD = People's Party for Freedom and Democracy
D66 = Democrats 66

First Chamber 75 members

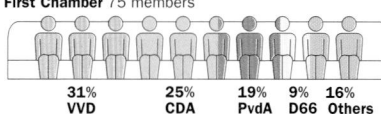

31% VVD	25% CDA	19% PvdA	9% D66	16% Others

The Netherlands is a constitutional monarchy. Legislative power is vested in parliament. The monarch has only nominal power.

MAIN POLITICAL ISSUES
The future of social welfare
Even after the cutbacks of the 1980s, the Dutch still have one of the most generous welfare systems in Europe. Most political parties now accept that current levels of provision cannot be maintained indefinitely. The debate is not whether to

Queen Beatrix, who acceded in 1980 and rebuilt support for the Dutch monarchy.

Wim Kok, won the 1994 elections and is the first labor prime minister since 1977.

cut welfare benefits, but by how much and in which areas. The right-wing Liberal party is advocating a minimal level of provision, and the PVDA has suggested cutbacks totaling $4 billion.

Political refugees
In recent years, a rising number of people have sought political asylum in the Netherlands. Increasingly this has led to concerns over the costs involved, and worries that this trend might lead to a rise in support for extreme right-wing nationalist parties. In 1994, immigration laws in the Netherlands were tightened, as in neighboring countries.

The fight against crime
The Dutch electorate has identified rising crime as a major concern. The prison system can no longer cope with the growing number of detainees, and many convicted criminals are being released for want of space. None of the parties has a program for reversing the trend.

PROFILE
Dutch politics is characterized by coalitions and a high degree of consensus. Most Dutch agree on the social function of government and readily accept relatively high taxes and a generous social security system. Political debate is more a question of the stress and focus of policy than of ideology. The CDA has traditionally led two-party coalition governments, either with the left-of-center PVDA or with the right-wing VVD. However, the PVDA won the 1994 elections, although both it and the CDA lost a significant number of seats.

WORLD AFFAIRS

The Netherlands has long been one of the main advocates of the EU. It supports both political and monetary integration, but failed in its attempt to rush through legislation enabling both during its EU presidency in 1992. In 1995, the Netherlands was one of seven EU countries to abolish internal borders under the Schengen Convention. Internationally, the Netherlands traditionally supports UK and US foreign policy, and is a member of NATO.

AID

$2.5bn (donations)   Up 8% in 1993

As a result of tight fiscal policies, Dutch foreign aid has slightly contracted over the past few years. The Dutch government actively pursues a policy to link foreign aid and human rights. This led to a clash with Indonesia which, as a former colony, was one of the biggest receivers of Dutch support. In 1993, Indonesia turned down all Dutch aid, accusing the Netherlands of interfering in its internal affairs.

NETHERLANDS

Total Land Area :
33 920 sq. km
(13 097 sq. miles)

POPULATION

over 1 000 000	▣
over 500 000	◉
over 100 000	◎
over 50 000	○
over 10 000	●

LAND HEIGHT
100m/328ft
Sea Level
-100m/-328ft

N

CHRONOLOGY

Suppression of Protestantism by the ruling Spanish Habsburgs led to the revolt of the Netherlands and the independence of the northern provinces as a republic in 1581.

❏ **1813** Dutch oust French after 30 years of French rule and choose to become a constitutional monarchy.
❏ **1815** United Kingdom of Netherlands formed to include Belgium and Luxembourg.
❏ **1830** Catholic southern provinces secede as Belgium.
❏ **1848** New constitution – ministers to be accountable to parliament.
❏ **1897–1901** Wide-ranging social legislation enacted. Development of strong trade unions.
❏ **1898** Wilhelmina succeeds to throne, so ending union with Luxembourg, where Salic Law is in force.
❏ **1914–1918** Dutch neutrality respected in World War I.
❏ **1922** Women fully enfranchised.
❏ **1940** Dutch attempt to maintain neutrality, but Germany invades. Fierce Dutch resistance.
❏ **1942** Japan invades Dutch East Indies.
❏ **1944–1945** "Winter of starvation."
❏ **1945** Liberation. International Court of Justice set up in The Hague.
❏ **1946** PvdA formed.
❏ **1946–1958** PvdA leads center-left coalitions with CVP. Marshall Aid from USA speeds reconstruction.
❏ **1948** Queen Juliana takes throne.
❏ **1949** Joins NATO. Most of East Indies colonies gain independence as Indonesia.
❏ **1957** Founder-member of EEC.
❏ **1960** Economic union with Belgium and Luxembourg comes into effect.
❏ **1973** PvdA wins power after 15 years spent mainly in opposition. Center-left coalition, first ever majority of left-wing ministers.
❏ **1980** Two main opposition Protestant parties unite in CDA. Queen Beatrix accedes to throne.
❏ **1977–1981** CDA–VVD coalition.
❏ **1982** PvdA rejects deployment of US Cruise missiles in Netherlands. CDA–VVD center-right coalition under Ruud Lubbers.
❏ **1989** VVD refuses to support finance for 20-year National Environment Policy (NEP). Elections. Lubbers' CDA–PvdA center-left coalition.
❏ **1990** NEP introduced.
❏ **1992** Licensed brothels and euthanasia legalized.
❏ **1994** Elections. PvdA heads new coalition under Wim Kok. Politically conservative VVD holds balance of power.

N

DEFENSE

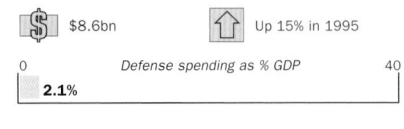

💲 $8.6bn   ⬆ Up 15% in 1995

0	Defense spending as % GDP	40
2.1%		

DUTCH ARMED FORCES

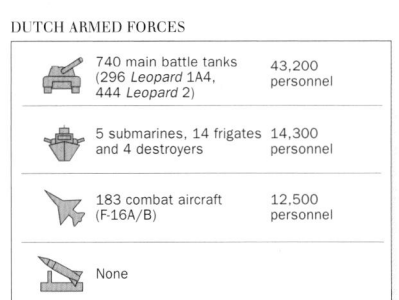

🛡	740 main battle tanks (296 *Leopard* 1A4, 444 *Leopard* 2)	43,200 personnel
🚢	5 submarines, 14 frigates and 4 destroyers	14,300 personnel
✈	183 combat aircraft (F-16A/B)	12,500 personnel
🚀	None	

The Dutch military, which is part of NATO, is currently undergoing major restructuring. By the year 2000, it will have been transformed from an organization focusing on an anti-Soviet defense role into a rapidly deployable, more flexible military force. The plans include a 44% reduction in personnel and the abolition of compulsory military service. Most of the reforms affect the army, which will be reduced from three to two divisions. In 1995, a joint Dutch–German army corps numbering 28,000 was inaugurated. The Netherlands also has a large defense industry which specializes in submarines, weapons systems and aircraft.

ECONOMICS

📊 $338.1bn   💱 1.60–1.74 guilders

SCORE CARD

❏ World GNP Ranking	14th
❏ GNP per Capita	$21,970
❏ Balance of Payments	$11.5bn
❏ Inflation	1.5%
❏ Unemployment	7.2%

EXPORTS

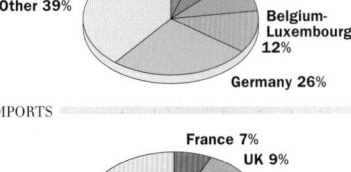

Italy 5%   UK 8%
Other 39%   France 10%
Belgium-Luxembourg 12%
Germany 26%

IMPORTS

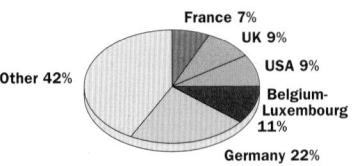

France 7%
UK 9%
USA 9%
Other 42%   Belgium-Luxembourg 11%
Germany 22%

ECONOMIC PERFORMANCE INDICATOR

— Consumer price index   GDP ▨

(Consumer price index 1990=100; GDP 1990=100; years 1990, 1991, 1992, 1993, 1994)

account for over 50% of GDP. Most goods travel through Rotterdam, the world's biggest port. In addition to high-tech sectors such as electronics, telecommunications and chemicals, the Netherlands has a successful agricultural industry. Productivity rates are high and agricultural products such as cheese, vegetables, meat and flowers are significant export earners.

STRENGTHS

Highly skilled and educated work force. Sophisticated infrastructure. Large number of blue-chip multinationals, including Philips and Shell. Strong currency, linked to the German Deutsche Mark. Low inflation. Tradition of high-tech innovation, including development of the music cassette and CD.

WEAKNESSES

Costly welfare system, resulting in high taxes and social insurance premiums; one-third of national income spent on social security. High labor costs.

PROFILE

The Dutch economy is one of the most successful in Europe. Since the 16th century, trade has been of great importance. Today, imports and exports

NETHERLANDS : MAJOR BUSINESSES

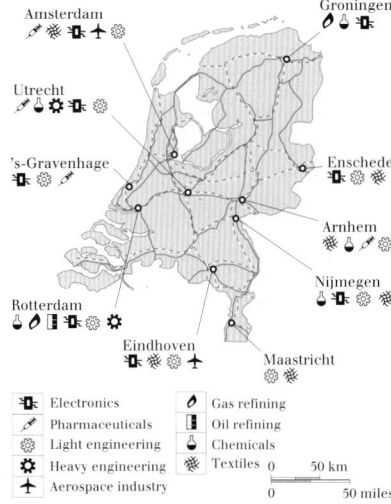

Amsterdam   Groningen
Utrecht
's-Gravenhage   Enschede
Arnhem
Nijmegen
Rotterdam
Eindhoven   Maastricht

🔌	Electronics	🌢	Gas refining
⚗	Pharmaceuticals	▮	Oil refining
⚙	Light engineering		Chemicals
✿	Heavy engineering	❋	Textiles
✈	Aerospace industry		

0   50 km
0   50 miles

RESOURCES

77.5bn kwh
(capacity 17.4m kw)

57,042 b/d
(reserves
144,650,000 bbl)

14m pigs, 4.6m
cattle, 2.2m sheep,
66,000 horses

Natural gas, oil

ELECTRICITY GENERATION

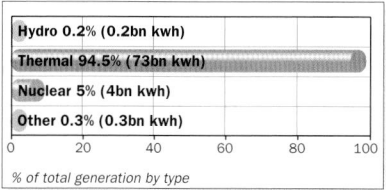

Hydro 0.2% (0.2bn kwh)

Thermal 94.5% (73bn kwh)

Nuclear 5% (4bn kwh)

Other 0.3% (0.3bn kwh)

0   20   40   60   80   100

% of total generation by type

There are large natural gas reserves in
the north. There is some oil production
from offshore drilling in the North Sea.

ENVIRONMENT

10%

National Environment
Policy adopted in
1990

ENVIRONMENTAL TREATIES

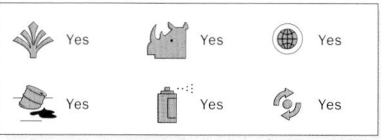

Yes		Yes		Yes	
Yes		Yes		Yes	

The Netherlands has a strong
environmental tradition, a legacy in
part of living in one of the most densely
populated states in the world. NGOs
such as Greenpeace are well supported
and the Green Party is well represented
in parliament. The Dutch recycle their
domestic trash and have a good record
of energy conservation.

The main concerns are halting
expressway building, and the proposed
high-speed TGV train. The government
plans that this will cross the green
heartland of the Netherlands, an area
known as the Randstad. It is being
strongly opposed by environmentalists,
who succeeded in halting a second
airport north of Rotterdam.

MEDIA

Freedom of press is guaranteed by the
constitution. The Netherlands has Europe's
most liberal laws on censorship

PUBLISHING AND BROADCAST MEDIA

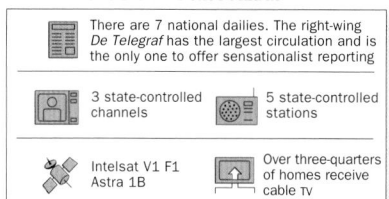

There are 7 national dailies. The right-wing
De Telegraf has the largest circulation and is
the only one to offer sensationalist reporting

3 state-controlled
channels

5 state-controlled
stations

Intelsat V1 F1
Astra 1B

Over three-quarters
of homes receive
cable TV

The media represent the whole social
and political spectrum. Newspapers are
aimed at the family and there is little
sensationalist reporting. Access to cable
TV is the highest in the world.

NETHERLANDS : LAND USE

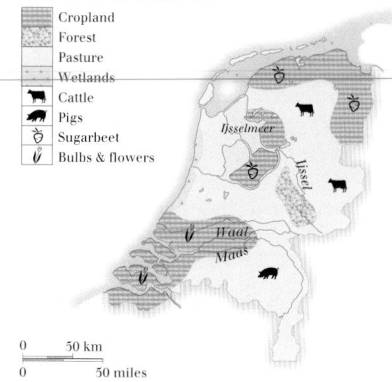

Cropland
Forest
Pasture
Wetlands
Cattle
Pigs
Sugarbeet
Bulbs & flowers

0   50 km
0   50 miles

CRIME

5,827 prisoners

Up 30% in 1992

CRIME RATES

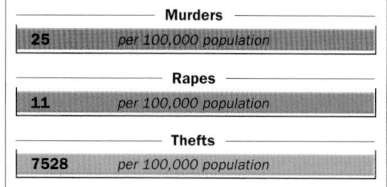

Murders	
25	per 100,000 population

Rapes	
11	per 100,000 population

Thefts	
7528	per 100,000 population

Liberal drug laws make the
Netherlands a gateway for the
narcotics trade. Several politicians
have suggested decriminalizing the
trade in order to reduce the crime
generated by the huge profits from the
business. However, such a policy faces
opposition from fellow participants in
the Schengen Convention.

EDUCATION

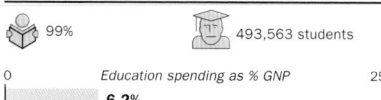
99%

493,563 students

0   Education spending as % GNP   25
6.2%

THE EDUCATION SYSTEM

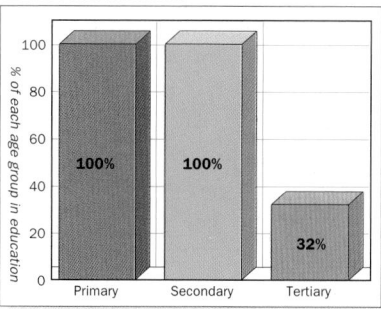

100
% of each age group in education
80

60

40

20

0

Primary 100%   Secondary 100%   Tertiary 32%

Apart from a few religious schools,
all education is state-run. Corporate
funding plays an important part in
university research.

HEALTH

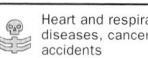
1 per 400 people

Heart and respiratory
diseases, cancers,
accidents

0   Health spending as % GDP   25
8.7%

Dutch health care is almost entirely
funded by the state. High spending
ensures that it is among the best in the
world. However, there are fears that
the Dutch may have to accept lower
standards in future, particularly as the
population is aging. Major health
problems are similar to those in the
rest of western Europe. There is a
higher incidence of AIDS. The Dutch
are active in research in this field.

WEALTH

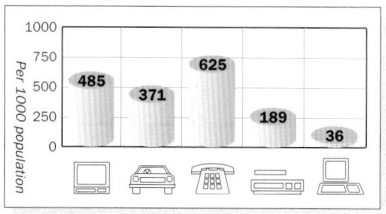
Electronic fitter, 2,248–2,387 guilders ($1,405–
$1,491) per month; journalist, 30,251–48,868
guilders ($18,907–$30,543) per year

CONSUMER GOODS OWNERSHIP

1000
Per 1000 population
750

500   485   371   625

250   189

0   36

The Netherlands is, per capita, one
of the richest nations in the world.
The wealthiest group are oil
executives, stock-market traders and
businessmen. A progressive taxation
system and extensive social welfare
mean that wealth is quite evenly
distributed. There is a small elite
who have considerable inherited
wealth, but extravagant displays of
wealth are rare.

Class does not play a big part in
Dutch society. Most citizens would
consider themselves middle class.
Immigrant communities are the
exception; they often live on the
edges of towns in deprived areas.
The poorest are the illegal immigrants.

WORLD RANKING

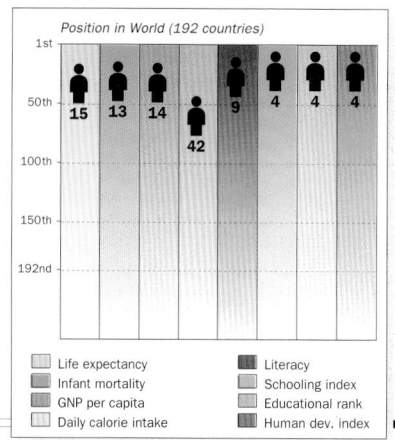

Position in World (192 countries)
1st

50th   15   13   14   9   4   4   4

42

100th

150th

192nd

Life expectancy   Literacy
Infant mortality   Schooling index
GNP per capita   Educational rank
Daily calorie intake   Human dev. index

N

NEW ZEALAND

OFFICIAL NAME: The Dominion of New Zealand **CAPITAL:** Wellington
POPULATION: 3.6 million **CURRENCY:** New Zealand dollar **OFFICIAL LANGUAGE:** English **OVERSEAS TERRITORIES:** 3

L YING IN THE SOUTH PACIFIC, 990 miles southeast of Australia, New Zealand comprises the main North and South Islands, separated by the Cook Strait, and numerous smaller islands. South Island is the more mountainous; North Island contains hot springs and geysers, and the bulk of the population. The political tradition is liberal and egalitarian, and has been dominated by the National and Labour parties. Radical, and often unpopular, reforms since 1984 have restored economic growth, speeded up economic diversification and strengthened New Zealand's position within the Pacific Rim countries.

CLIMATE

WEATHER CHART

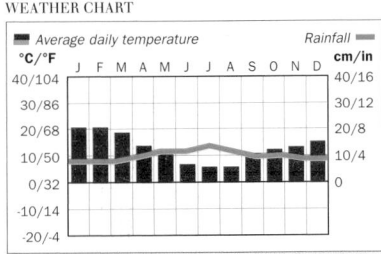

New Zealand's climate is generally temperate and damp, with an average temperature of 54°F. However, there are differences between the islands, which extend north–south nearly 1,240 miles. The extreme north is almost subtropical; southern winters are cold. New Zealand is windy. Wellington is particularly known for bouts of blustery weather that can last for days.

TRANSPORTATION

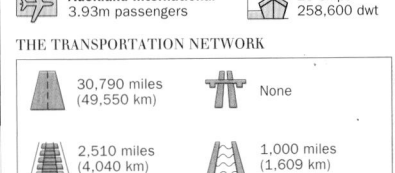

Although both New Zealand's major islands are well served by transportation services, the more populous North Island has a more extensive road and rail network than the South. Air and ferry services complement the land networks and provide links between the North and South Islands, as well as with the numerous smaller islands. Cargo ferry services are particularly important for remote populations in the Ross Dependency. Links with the Cook Islands, Niue and the Tokelau atolls, New Zealand's associated territories, are being improved.

TOURISM

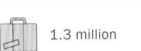 1.3 million    Up 14% in 1994

MAIN OVERSEAS ARRIVALS

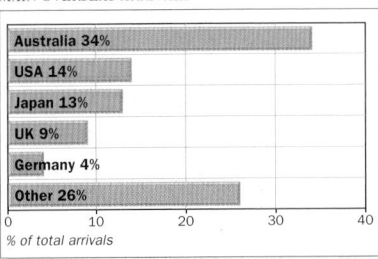

New Zealand's prime attraction is its scenery. Unspoilt and, relative to the country's size, the most varied in the world, it offers mountains, fjords and lakes, glaciers, rainforests, beaches, boiling mud pools and geysers. Other attractions are the Maori culture, and outdoor activities such as river rafting, fishing, skiing, whale watching and bungee jumping, a local invention.

Tourists come mainly from the USA, Australia, the UK, Japan and Germany. Low-cost charter flights have helped boost visitor numbers to over one million a year. Tourism is now the largest single foreign-exchange earner, generating US$3 billion yearly. A new state tourist board has embarked on a high-profile campaign to treble visitors to three million by the year 2000.

Mount Egmont, *an extinct volcano, is one of the numerous popular natural attractions of New Zealand's North Island.*

PEOPLE

 English, Maori    34 people per sq. mile

THE URBAN/RURAL POPULATION SPLIT

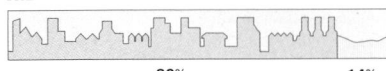

86%   14%

RELIGIOUS PERSUASION

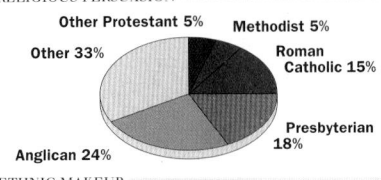

Other Protestant 5%   Methodist 5%
Other 33%   Roman Catholic 15%
Anglican 24%   Presbyterian 18%

ETHNIC MAKEUP

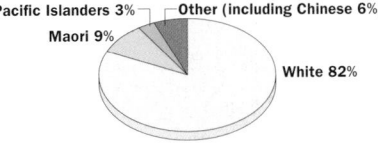

Pacific Islanders 3%   Other (including Chinese 6%)
Maori 9%
White 82%

New Zealand is a country of migrants. The islands were first settled about 1,200 years ago by the Maoris, as part of the Polynesian seaborne migrations. Today's majority European population is descended mainly from British migrants who settled after 1840. The Maoris ceded sovereignty to the British through the 1840 Treaty of Waitangi. Recent migrants have included Asians from Hong Kong and Malaysia, and those who left Fiji following the 1987 coup.

Maoris today comprise 9% of the population. Their living and education standards are generally lower, and rates of unemployment higher, than average. Relations with the European-descended majority have been tense in recent years as the Maoris have campaigned for compensation for land taken by the Europeans. In an effort to improve relations, the government reached a settlement of fishing claims with Maori leaders in 1992, and proposed a comprehensive land compensation package in 1994 which remains the subject of negotiation.

POPULATION AGE BREAKDOWN

% of population by age group	0–14	15–64	65+		
65+	8.6%	8.5%	10%	10.9%	11.3%
15–64	58.5%	59.8%	63.2%	66.4%	65.3%
0–14	32.9%	31.7%	26.8%	22.7%	23.4%
	1960	1970	1980	1990	2000

N

POLITICS

 1993/1996    HM Queen Elizabeth II

THE STATE OF THE PARTIES

House of Representatives 99 members

			2% NZ 1st

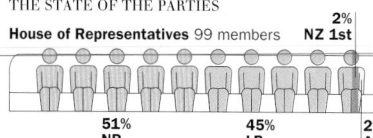

51% NP	45% LP	2% All.

NP = National Party **LP** = Labour Party **All.** = Alliance
NZ 1st = New Zealand First Party

*James Bolger, NP
leader, and prime
minister since 1990.*

*Roger Douglas,
the creator of
"Rogernomics."*

New Zealand is a single-chamber
parliamentary democracy within the
Commonwealth. The Cook Islands and
Niue are self-governing territories.

MAIN POLITICAL ISSUES
Electoral reform

New Zealand is to shift to a system of
proportional representation at the next
general election, due in 1996. Popular
endorsement of electoral reform in a
referendum in 1993 reflects widespread
disillusionment with the NP and LP.
The new German-style system, of
constituency candidates and those
drawn from party lists, will give a
much greater role to the smaller
parties which have proliferated since
the reforms were adopted, and is likely
to produce coalition governments.

PROFILE

Politics has been dominated by the NP
and the LP under the first-past-the-post
system. The period since 1984 has
been one of radical reform. The LP
deregulated the economy and
restructured it on a *laissez-faire*
basis, while the NP has, since
1990, imposed massive
cuts in the country's
comprehensive welfare
system. The ensuing
popular disaffection
with the two main
parties, even before
the switch to
proportional
representation,
had produced a
significant rise in
popularity of the
minor parties, which
took almost 30% of the
vote in the 1993 election.

WORLD AFFAIRS

ANZUS	APEC	OECD	SPF	SPC

Many New Zealanders remain strongly
committed to the British crown and the
Commonwealth, but the importance of
the UK has diminished.
The UK's involvement
in the EU has forced
New Zealand to
reorient its trade and
foreign policy toward its
Pacific Rim neighbors,
especially Australia. The
1983 Closer Economic
Relationship (CER) treaty freed
trade between the two states.
Australia is now New Zealand's
largest trading partner, and even
closer links have been mooted in
the form of an eventual political
union. Relations with Asia are
growing in importance. Exports
to Japan are now second to
those to Australia and trading
relationships with other Asian
states are being secured.
Relations with the USA are
improving after a low point
when New Zealand's anti-
nuclear stance led to its
exclusion from the ANZUS
pact. Relations with
France are still
recovering from the
1985 bombing of the
Greenpeace ship
Rainbow Warrior
by French
agents in
Auckland
harbor.

AID

 $98m (donations)   ⬇ Down 1% in 1993

Over half of New Zealand's overseas
aid is bilateral. Particular areas of focus
are the Pacific states and Pacific-wide
organizations. New Zealand is a major
supporter of the South Pacific Forum,
the University of the South Pacific
and the Pacific Environment
Program. It also offers
scholarships allowing
overseas students to
study or train in
New Zealand.

Chatham Is

Petre Bay   *Chatham I.*
Waitangi
Pitt Strait
Pitt I.
(continuation on same scale)

NEW ZEALAND

Total Land Area : 268 670 sq. km
(105 733 sq. miles)

LAND HEIGHT	POPULATION
2000m/6562ft	over 500 000 ◉
1000m/3281ft	over 100 000 ◎
500m/1640ft	over 50 000 ○
200m/656ft	over 10 000 ●
Sea Level	under 10 000 ·

0   100 km

0   100 miles

CHRONOLOGY

A former British colony, New Zealand became a dominion in 1907 and fully independent in 1947.

- ❏ **1962** Western Samoa gains independence.
- ❏ **1965** The Cook Islands become self-governing.
- ❏ **1975** Elections won by conservative NP party. Prime Minister Robert Muldoon introduces program of economic austerity.
- ❏ **1976** Immigration cut by over 80%.
- ❏ **1984** Election of LP; David Lange becomes prime minister. Waitangi Tribunal restores Auckland harbor headland to Maori people.
- ❏ **1985** New Zealand government prohibits nuclear vessels from its ports and waters. French agents sink Greenpeace ship *Rainbow Warrior* in Auckland harbor.
- ❏ **1986** USA suspends military obligations under ANZUS Treaty in protest over nuclear vessel ban.
- ❏ **1987** Elections won by LP. Controversial privatization program introduced. Nuclear ban enshrined in legislation.
- ❏ **1989** Cabinet split. Lange resigns. Succeeded by Geoffrey Palmer.
- ❏ **1990** Palmer resigns because of unpopularity in polls. LP defeated by NP in elections. James Bolger prime minister.
- ❏ **1991** Widespread protest at spending cuts.
- ❏ **1992** August, Waitangi Tribunal awards South Island fishing rights to Maoris. September, majority vote for electoral reform in referendum.
- ❏ **1993** May, *Jacques Cartier* first French naval ship to dock since 1985. November, elections. NP party returned with one-seat majority. As a result of referendum, proportional representation introduced for future elections.
- ❏ **1994** January, US announces restoration of senior-level contacts. December, government offers NZ$1,000 million over ten-year period to settle all outstanding Maori compensation claims. US announces that it will not send nuclear-armed ships to New Zealand ports.
- ❏ **1995** February, National Day celebrations abandoned after being disrupted by Maori protests. May, land compensation agreement signed with largest Maori tribal federation. June, resumption of visits by UK warships.
- ❏ **1996** February, ongoing process of fragmentation among the country's political parties results in the NP moving into a formal coalition to preserve overall legislative majority.

DEFENSE

💲 $599m	⬆ Up 10% in 1995

0   *Defense spending as % GDP*   40
1.1%

NEW ZEALAND ARMED FORCES

🛡	26 light tanks (26 *Scorpion*)	4,500 personnel
🚢	4 frigates and 4 patrol boats	2,200 personnel
✈	37 combat aircraft (15 A-4K, 5 TA-4K)	3,350 personnel
☢	None	

The security pact between Australia, New Zealand and the USA (ANZUS), the focus of New Zealand's defense policy since 1951, has been strained by New Zealand's refusal, since 1985, to allow nuclear warships into its ports. The USA suspended joint military exercises, forcing New Zealand to seek closer links with Australia. Senior-level contacts were resumed in 1994 and the US announced that it would not send nuclear-armed warships to New Zealand ports. Since then, the UK has also resumed naval visits.

Defense takes about 4.8% of government spending. The armed forces number 10,900 troops with an additional 8,500 reserves.

ECONOMICS

📊 $46.6bn	💲 1.53–1.56 New Zealand dollars

SCORE CARD

- ❏ WORLD GNP RANKING..........................46th
- ❏ GNP PER CAPITA ....US$13,190
- ❏ BALANCE OF PAYMENTS...................US$–2bn
- ❏ INFLATION 1.7%
- ❏ UNEMPLOYMENT..................................8.1%

EXPORTS

South Korea 5%
UK 6%
USA 12%
Other 43%
Japan 15%
Australia 19%

IMPORTS

Germany 4%
UK 6%
Japan 16%
Other 35%
USA 18%
Australia 21%

ECONOMIC PERFORMANCE INDICATOR

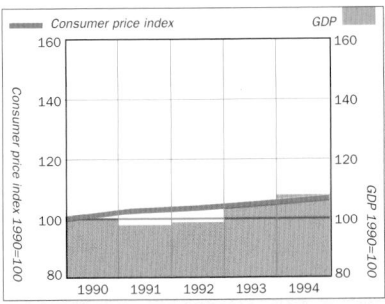

Consumer price index   GDP

(Consumer price index 1990=100; GDP 1990=100; years 1990 1991 1992 1993 1994)

"Rogernomics" after their initiator, LP Finance Minister Roger Douglas, helped to restore growth, cut inflation to 1.7% and encourage diversification into new markets and products. High public debt and poor levels of private investment, however, continue to constitute a problem for future development.

STRENGTHS

Modern agricultural sector; world's biggest exporter of wool, cheese, butter and meat. Rapidly expanding tourist sector. Manufacturing growing, with emphasis on high-tech. One of the world's most open economies. Rapidly expanding trade links within Pacific Rim.

WEAKNESSES

A high but falling level of public debt; one of highest levels outside developing world. Continuing reliance on imported manufactured goods.

PROFILE

Since 1984, New Zealand has changed from being one of the most regulated to one of the most open economies in the world. Radical reforms, dubbed

NEW ZEALAND : MAJOR BUSINESSES

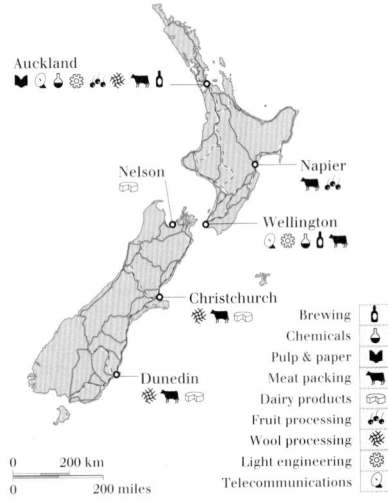

Auckland
Nelson
Napier
Wellington
Christchurch
Dunedin

0   200 km
0   200 miles

Brewing
Chemicals
Pulp & paper
Meat packing
Dairy products
Fruit processing
Wool processing
Light engineering
Telecommunications

RESOURCES

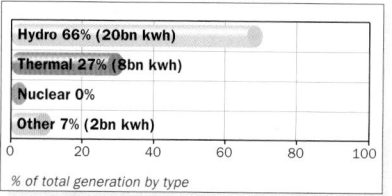

31.3bn kwh (capacity 7.5m kw)

34,546 b/d (reserves 169,670,000 bbl)

50.1m sheep, 8.6m cattle, 484,000 goats, 430,000 pigs

Coal, oil, natural gas, iron, gold, silica sand

ELECTRICITY GENERATION

Hydro 66% (20bn kwh)

Thermal 27% (8bn kwh)

Nuclear 0%

Other 7% (2bn kwh)

% of total generation by type

New Zealand's rich pastures, a result of even rainfall throughout the year, have traditionally been its key resource. The sheep, wool and dairy products on which the country's wealth was built are still important, but farmers are also moving into new areas. The kiwi fruit is now a thriving export. Fisheries are a growth area.

New Zealand is well endowed with energy resources. It has coal, oil, natural gas and huge hydroelectric potential.

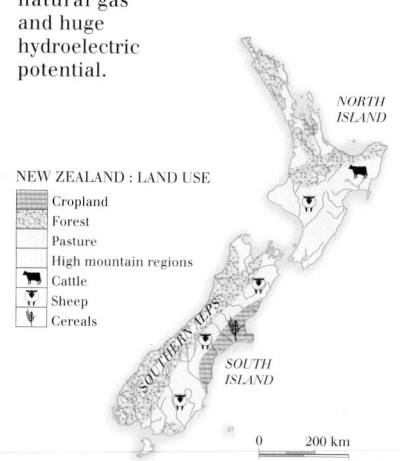

NEW ZEALAND : LAND USE

- Cropland
- Forest
- Pasture
- High mountain regions
- Cattle
- Sheep
- Cereals

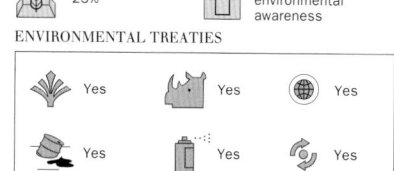

ENVIRONMENT

23%

Generally high environmental awareness

ENVIRONMENTAL TREATIES

Yes — Yes — Yes
Yes — Yes — Yes

New Zealand's isolation, small population and limited industry have helped to keep it one of the world's most pollution-free countries. Ozone depletion over Antarctica competes with nuclear power as the top domestic concern. New Zealand has been a leading opponent of French nuclear testing in the Pacific and has banned nuclear vessels from its ports.

MEDIA

 There is no censorship of the media

PUBLISHING AND BROADCAST MEDIA

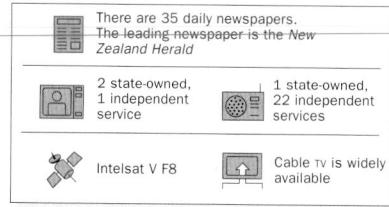

There are 35 daily newspapers. The leading newspaper is the *New Zealand Herald*

2 state-owned, 1 independent service

1 state-owned, 22 independent services

Intelsat V F8

Cable TV is widely available

The Auckland-based *New Zealand Herald* is the only daily with a national circulation; the others are primarily local papers. A third state-owned TV station is being considered.

CRIME

 3,736 prisoners

 Up 3% in 1992

CRIME RATES

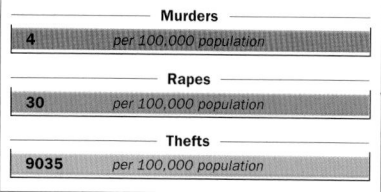

Murders
4 per 100,000 population

Rapes
30 per 100,000 population

Thefts
9035 per 100,000 population

Crime rates in New Zealand's urban areas have increased in recent years. However, overall, the country remains one of the world's safest and most peaceful places to live.

EDUCATION

 99%

146,215 students

0 Education spending as % GNP 25
7.2%

THE EDUCATION SYSTEM

Primary 100%
Secondary 88%
Tertiary 41%

% of each age group in education

Education is compulsory between the ages of six and 16. Nearly 77% of 16-year-olds stay in full-time education. About 4% of pupils attend independent schools. The free state system is in the process of change: the government plans to give schools direct control over their finances.

HEALTH

 1 per 504 people

Heart disease, cancers, accidents

0 Health spending as % GDP 25
7.7%

New Zealand has been a world leader in the provision of public health services. In 1936, it was the first country to introduce a full welfare state. Government efforts since 1991 to impose UK-style market systems on the health service have been very unpopular. Highly controversial charges for hospital beds had to be abolished in 1993 after widespread public protests.

WEALTH

 Truck parts dealer, 20,000 New Zealand dollars (US$13,333) per year; computer sales manager, 100,000 New Zealand dollars (US$66,665) per year

CONSUMER GOODS OWNERSHIP

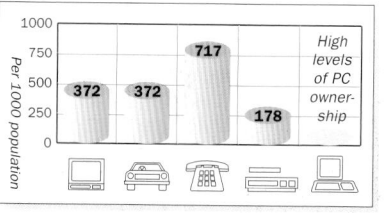

372 372 717 178

High levels of PC ownership

Per 1000 population

The years since 1984 have been very difficult for New Zealanders, who are used to affluence within a generous welfare state. A rash of economic and social reforms has held back wages, raised unemployment and cut welfare benefits. Even so, average living standards are still high, and a strong egalitarian tradition means that wealth remains quite evenly distributed.

New Zealanders also enjoy one of the world's best qualities of life, in terms of access to basic necessities, and a pure, healthy, urban and rural environment. Social mobility is fairly high. Wealthier people tend to spend their money on houses close to the water. Yachts are a major status symbol.

WORLD RANKING

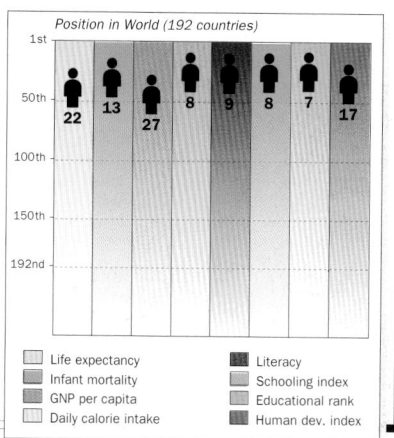

Position in World (192 countries)

1st
50th — 22 — 13 — 27 — 8 — 9 — 8 — 7 — 17
100th
150th
192nd

- Life expectancy
- Infant mortality
- GNP per capita
- Daily calorie intake
- Literacy
- Schooling index
- Educational rank
- Human dev. index

N

NICARAGUA

OFFICIAL NAME: Republic of Nicaragua **CAPITAL:** Managua
POPULATION: 4.4 million **CURRENCY:** Córdoba oro **OFFICIAL LANGUAGE:** Spanish

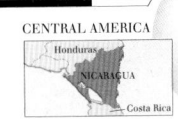

BOUNDED BY THE Pacific Ocean to the west and the Caribbean Sea to the east, Nicaragua lies at the heart of Central America. After more than 40 years of dictatorship, the Sandinista revolution in 1978 provoked 11 years of civil war, which almost destroyed the economy. The Sandinistas unexpectedly lost elections in 1990 and, like the ruling right-wing UNO, have experienced a split as moderates broke away to contest the political center ground in the 1996 poll.

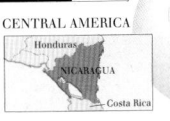

Oil refinery at Bluefields, on the Atlantic coast. Under the Sandinistas, most crude oil came from the former USSR, via Cuba.

CLIMATE

WEATHER CHART

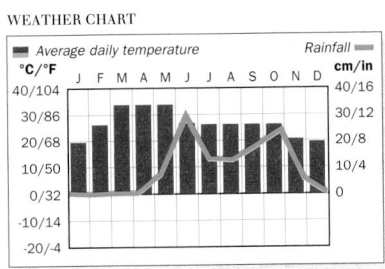

Nicaragua's climate is tropical and often violent. Hurricanes and earthquakes are an occasional threat.

TRANSPORTATION

Augusto C Sandino Intl, Managua
225,725 passengers

1 ship
1,200 dwt

THE TRANSPORTATION NETWORK

1,000 miles (1,600 km)	Pan-American Highway 239 miles (384 km)
199 miles (321 km)	1,380 miles (2,220 km)

Most roads are in the Pacific region and in poor condition. The Pan-American Highway is a key external link.

TOURISM

238,000 visitors

Up 20% in 1994

MAIN OVERSEAS ARRIVALS

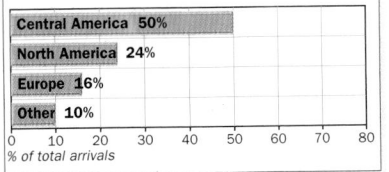

Central America	50%
North America	24%
Europe	16%
Other	10%

% of total arrivals

Historically modest tourism is slowly recovering. The civil war caused its near total collapse, although up to 100,000 "political tourists" visited the country every year to observe the effects of Sandinista reforms.

PEOPLE

Spanish, English Creole, Miskito

96 people per sq. mile

THE URBAN/RURAL POPULATION SPLIT

 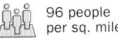

62%   38%

ETHNIC MAKEUP

Indian 5%
Black 9%
White 17%
Mestizo (European-Indian) 69%

The Atlantic regions, which in 1987 achieved limited independence, are isolated from the more populous Pacific regions. The indigenous Miskito tribes and the descendants of Africans, brought over by Spanish colonists in the 18th century to work the plantations, are concentrated along the Atlantic coast, where English Creole is widely spoken. Almost 80% of the population live in poverty. Of these, some 20% are defined by the UN as extremely poor; between 1991 and 1992, Nicaragua's GDP per capita fell below Haiti's, normally the world's lowest. Half the population has no permanent employment and poverty has forced many women into prostitution.

POLITICS

1990/1996

President Violeta Barrios de Chamorro

THE STATE OF THE PARTIES

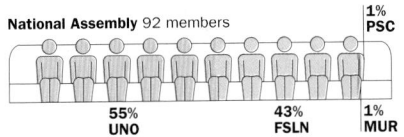

National Assembly 92 members

1% PSC

55% UNO   43% FSLN   1% MUR

UNO = National Opposition Union **FSLN** = Sandinista National Liberation Front **MUR** = Revolutionary Unity Movement **PSC** = Social Christian Party

Politics, once caught in the vice between right-wing pro-US parties and the Sandinistas, shifted in 1995 as moderate splitoffs from both sides competed for the center ground in the run-up to the 1996 presidential and legislative elections. Future governability and stability were enhanced by the successful resolution of a constitutional crisis. Multilateral agencies criticize the UNO's failure to meet structural adjustment targets to revive the economy.

NICARAGUA

Total Land Area : 118 750 sq. km
(45 849 sq. miles)

POPULATION

- ⊙ over 500 000
- ◎ over 100 000
- ○ over 50 000
- • over 10 000
- · under 10 000

LAND HEIGHT

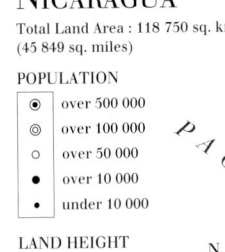

1000m/3281ft
500m/1640ft
200m/656ft
Sea Level

100 km
100 miles

WORLD AFFAIRS

ACS | Geplac | NAM | OAS | San José

The USA has used aid to pressurize Chamorro to reduce the perceived influence of the Sandinistas over political, economic and miltary matters and to guarantee the return of the property of US citizens seized by them. Debt renegotiations with the Russian Federation, Germany, Brazil and Central America are critical. Border disputes exist with Honduras, Costa Rica and Colombia.

AID

 $323m (receipts)   Down 51% in 1993

The USA is the largest donor and generally places political and economic conditions on aid. Donations from the EU, particularly Germany, are less troublesome and the World Bank and Inter-American Bank make development loans, sometimes as part of debt restructuring packages.

DEFENSE

 $37m   Down 5% in 1995

Sandinista forces that overthrew the Somoza regime were the basis of the army which expanded to some 134,000 troops during the war with the Contras. Chamorro reduced its size to 10,000 by 1995, and under USA pressure removed its Commander-in-Chief General Humberto Ortega, a former Sandinista. Some demobilized right-wing Contras and Sandinistas operate in gangs.

ECONOMICS

 $1.4bn   7.06–7.96 córdobas oro

SCORE CARD

- ❏ World GNP Ranking.......................147th
- ❏ GNP per Capita $330
- ❏ Balance of Payments....................$–694m
- ❏ Inflation 7.7%
- ❏ Unemployment................................21.8%

STRENGTHS

Very few. Coffee is the major export crop. Signs of cross-party support for an economic recovery program.

WEAKNESSES

$11 billion foreign debt. Reliance on aid. Mass unemployment, poor infrastructure and energy sector. Lack of investment and diversification. Opposition to privatization. World prices for Nicaragua's main exports have all fallen sharply in recent years. Banana quotas with the EU are threatened by the GATT proposals.

EXPORTS

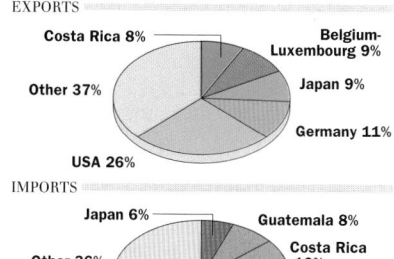

Costa Rica 8%
Belgium-Luxembourg 9%
Japan 9%
Germany 11%
USA 26%
Other 37%

IMPORTS

Japan 6%
Guatemala 8%
Costa Rica 10%
Venezuela 14%
USA 26%
Other 36%

RESOURCES

 1.6bn kwh (capacity 400,000 kw)

 Not an oil producer; refines 16,000 b/cd

 1.7m cattle, 535,000 pigs, 247,000 horses

Gold, silver, lead, zinc, copper, tungsten, salt

Nicaragua has no significant mineral resources and no oil. Lack of spare generator parts has led to longer and more frequent power cuts in Managua.

ENVIRONMENT

 7%   No efforts to check deforestation

Deforestation, particularly on the East Coast, and the widespread use of pesticides, are major problems.

MEDIA

 The press is now relatively outspoken

PUBLISHING AND BROADCAST MEDIA

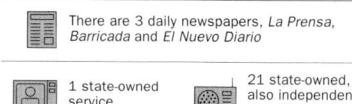

There are 3 daily newspapers, *La Prensa*, *Barricada* and *El Nuevo Diario*

1 state-owned service

21 state-owned, also independent stations

Radio is the most important medium. *Radio Mujer*, Central America's first station for women, went on air in 1992. *La Prensa*, the main daily newspaper, is owned by the Chamorro family.

CRIME

 Nicaragua does not publish prison figures   No official statistics, but the trend is up

Gun law still prevails in parts of the north, where gangs of ex-Contras and ex-Sandinistas remain active.

CHRONOLOGY

Nicaragua became independent in 1838. Guerrilla forces, led by Gen. Sandino, opposed the US marine presence in the early 1930s.

- ❏ **1935–1979** Somoza family in power.
- ❏ **1978** Sandinista revolution overthrows Anastasio Somoza II.
- ❏ **1979–1990** Civil war between Sandinistas and US-backed Contras.

EDUCATION

 65%   31,499 students

The Sandinista "Literacy Crusade," which achieved dramatic results in the 1980s, has long since died away. Poverty prevented some one-third of children starting school in 1994.

HEALTH

 1 per 1,490 people   Diarrheal and heart diseases, accidents, violence, tuberculosis

Life expectancy in Nicaragua rose from 50 to 64 years between 1960 and 1988. Real spending on health, however, fell by 71% between 1988 and 1993, with a consequent 15% rise in child mortality.

WEALTH

 Farm laborer, 300 córdobas oro ($38) per month, plus meals and accommodation; top executive, 6000–12,000 córdobas oro ($759–$1519) per month

CONSUMER GOODS OWNERSHIP

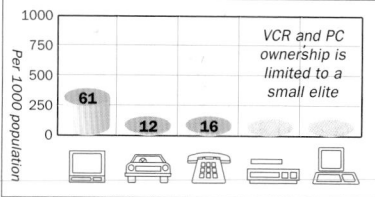

VCR and PC ownership is limited to a small elite

61   12   16

Wealthy Nicaraguans are based mainly in Miami. Some have returned under Chamorro as the "new entrepreneurs."

WORLD RANKING

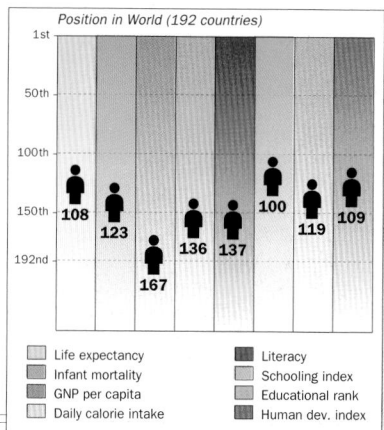

Position in World (192 countries)

108   123   167   136   137   100   119   109

- Life expectancy
- Infant mortality
- GNP per capita
- Daily calorie intake
- Literacy
- Schooling index
- Educational rank
- Human dev. index

NIGER

OFFICIAL NAME: Republic of Niger **CAPITAL:** Niamey
POPULATION: 9.2 million **CURRENCY:** CFA franc **OFFICIAL LANGUAGE:** French

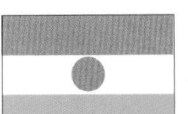    

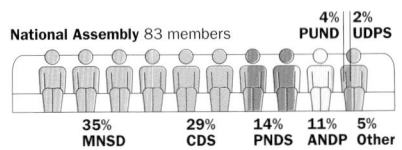
WEST AFRICA

L ANDLOCKED IN THE WEST of Africa, Niger is linked to the sea by the River Niger. The northern regions, the area around the Aïr mountains and particularly the vast uninhabited northeast have Saharan conditions. Niger was ruled by successive one-party or military regimes until 1992, when a multiparty constitution was introduced. The democratic process was, however, disrupted by a military coup in January 1996.

CLIMATE

WEATHER CHART

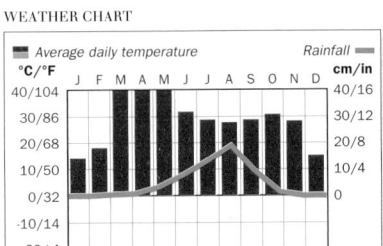

The Saharan north is virtually rainless. The south, in the Sahel belt, has an unreliable rainy season, preceded by a period of extreme daytime heat.

TRANSPORTATION

 Niamey International
74,319 passengers

 Has no fleet

THE TRANSPORTATION NETWORK

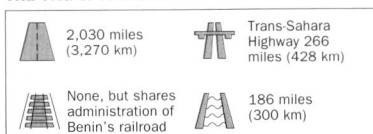

2,030 miles (3,270 km)	Trans-Sahara Highway 266 miles (428 km)
None, but shares administration of Benin's railroad	186 miles (300 km)

Plans to extend the railroad to Niamey from Parakou in Benin have been shelved. A bridge over the Niger, the country's second, is being built at Gaya.

TOURISM

 11,000 visitors   No change in 1994

MAIN OVERSEAS ARRIVALS

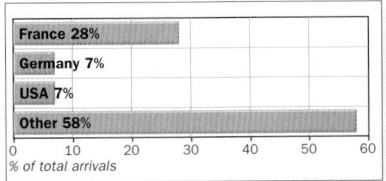

France 28%
Germany 7%
USA 7%
Other 58%
% of total arrivals

The Aïr mountains, southern Hausa cities and Saharan Tuareg culture attract some tourists in spite of Niger's limited infrastructure and instability.

PEOPLE

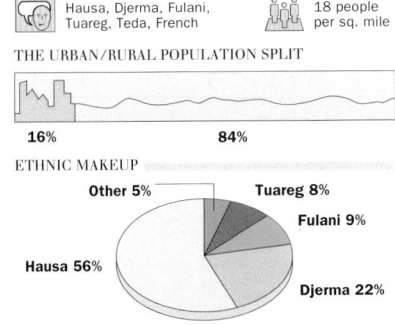

Hausa, Djerma, Fulani, Tuareg, Teda, French

18 people per sq. mile

THE URBAN/RURAL POPULATION SPLIT

16%   84%

ETHNIC MAKEUP

Other 5%
Tuareg 8%
Fulani 9%
Djerma 22%
Hausa 56%

Considerable tensions exist between the Tuaregs in the north and the southern groups. The Tuaregs' sense of alienation from mainstream Nigerien politics has increased since the 1973 and 1983 droughts. Their herds decimated, many Tuaregs were forced away from their nomadic way of life to the towns. Northern Tuaregs responded to these pressures by mounting a low-key revolt.

A more subtle antagonism exists between the Djerma and Hausa groups. Until recently, the Djerma elite from the southwest dominated politics in Niger. Since 1993, however, control has passed to the Hausa majority.

Niger is essentially an Islamic society, having an 80% Muslim majority. Women have, on the whole, only limited rights and restricted access to education.

Testing boating poles in the market at Ayorou on the River Niger, the country's only major permanent watercourse.

POLITICS

 1995/1996   Col. Ibrahim Barre

THE STATE OF THE PARTIES

National Assembly 83 members

35% MNSD	29% CDS	14% PNDS	11% ANDP	5% Other	4% PUND	2% UDPS

MNSD = National Movement for Development Society **PNDS** = Niger Party for Democracy and Socialism Tarayya Alliance of the forces of Change coalition comprises: **CDS** = Social Democratic Convention **ANDP** = Niger Alliance for Democracy and Social Progress **PUND** = Party or National Unity and Development Salama **UDPS** = Union for Democracy and Social Progress

The death of the military dictator, President Seyni Kountché, in 1987, opened the way for the pro-democracy protests of 1990 leading to multiparty elections in 1993. Early legislative elections in 1995 saw the defeat of the Alliance of the Forces of Change (AFC), and the beginning of an uneasy cohabitation between President Mahame Ousmane and new Prime Minister Hama Amadou. Their power struggle ultimately provoked the military to intervene. Colonel Ibrahim Barre, however, promised an early return to civilian rule with fresh elections scheduled for September 1996.

WORLD AFFAIRS

 CILSS   Ecowas   FZ   OAU   OIC

Relations with Libya and Algeria are sensitive, as Niger suspects they may be giving the Tuaregs support. French military and civilian cooperation, suspended following the 1996 coup, was restored within two months to support the military's commitment to a rapid return to civilian rule.

AID

 $347m (receipts)   Down 4% in 1993

Almost all development is aid-funded. France is the principal donor, followed by the IMF and Arab funds, and a little from Ivory Coast and Nigeria.

DEFENSE

 $22m    Up 10% in 1995

The military dramatically reentered politics in January 1996, claiming to be intervening only to protect democracy.

N

NIGER

Total Land Area : 1 266 700 sq. km
(489 073 sq. miles)

POPULATION   LAND HEIGHT

◎	over 100 000	1000m/3281ft
○	over 50 000	500m/1640ft
●	over 10 000	200m/656ft
·	under 10 000	150m/492ft

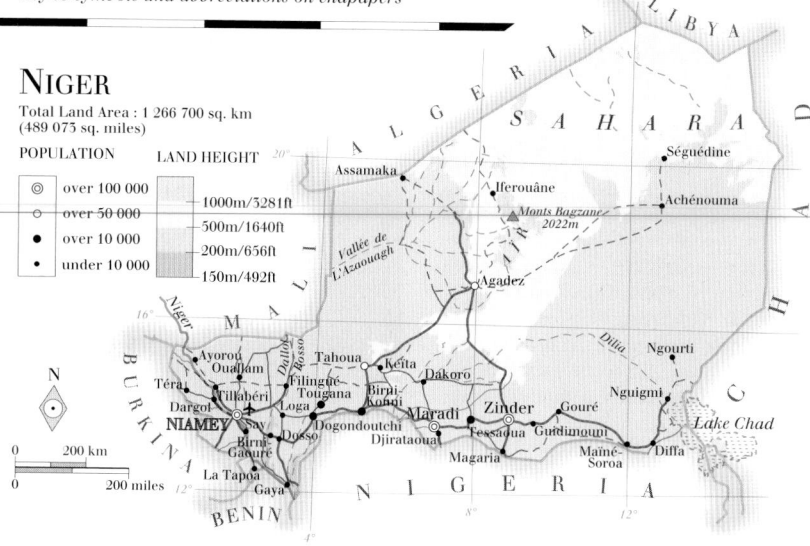

CHRONOLOGY

The powerful Islamic Sokoto Empire dissolved as the French took Niger over between 1883 and 1901.

- ❏ **1958** Autonomous republic within French community.
- ❏ **1960** Independence. Hamani Diori's one-party PPN state.
- ❏ **1968** French open uranium mines.
- ❏ **1973** Drought; 60% of livestock die; no harvest for two years.
- ❏ **1974** Military coup. Gen. Kountché bans political parties.
- ❏ **1984** New drought; River Niger dries up for first time in history. Uranium boom ends.
- ❏ **1987** Kountché dies. Gen. Saibou eases transition to democracy.
- ❏ **1992** New constitution drawn up. Tuareg rebellion becomes serious.
- ❏ **1993** Democratic elections.
- ❏ **1996** Military coup.

ECONOMICS

 $2bn    533.68–489.05 CFA francs

SCORE CARD

❏ WORLD GNP RANKING	134th
❏ GNP PER CAPITA	$230
❏ BALANCE OF PAYMENTS	$–78m
❏ INFLATION	7.5%
❏ UNEMPLOYMENT	47%

STRENGTHS

Vast uranium deposits; a few other minerals. Traditional Sahelian sense of community.

WEAKNESSES

Aid-dependent. Collapse of uranium prices in 1980s created large debt burden. Few other important minerals. Only 3% of land is cultivable. Crops are low in value. Frequent droughts.

EXPORTS

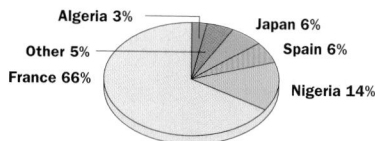

Algeria 3%
Japan 6%
Other 5%
Spain 6%
France 66%
Nigeria 14%

IMPORTS

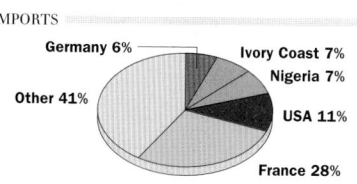

Germany 6%
Ivory Coast 7%
Nigeria 7%
Other 41%
USA 11%
France 28%

RESOURCES

 171m kwh (capacity 600,000 kw)

 2,172 tons

 5.9m goats, 3.7m sheep, 2m cattle

 Uranium, tin, gypsum, coal, salt, tungsten, irophosphates

During the 1970s, Niger's uranium mines boomed, but output collapsed in

ENVIRONMENT

 7%   Donor-funded afforestation programs

Serious droughts are increasing the rate of desertification, the problem that overrides all others in Niger.

MEDIA

 The 1992 constitution guaranteed freedom of expression; there is an official press

PUBLISHING AND BROADCAST MEDIA

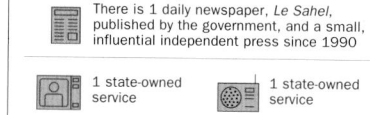

There is 1 daily newspaper, Le Sahel, published by the government, and a small, influential independent press since 1990

1 state-owned service   1 state-owned service

The BBC World Service's Hausa programing is more influential than local French short-wave radio.

CRIME

 Niger does not publish prison figures   Crime levels are fairly constant from year to year

Crime levels are low, though drought and Tuareg unrest have led to banditry. Smuggling to and from Nigeria is seen simply as part of the informal economy.

EDUCATION

 28%   4,506 students

Local languages are emphasized more strongly than in most Francophone states. School attendance is only 30%.

the 1980s when world prices slumped. Other mining is small-scale and oil reserves are not commercially viable. The uranium boom quadrupled electricity needs, half of which are now met by Nigeria's Kainji Dam on the River Niger.

HEALTH

 1 per 35,140 people   Malaria, tuberculosis, meningitis, measles, malnutrition

In spite of progress in rural health care, immunization, malaria control and child nutrition are still limited.

WEALTH

The Tuaregs are the lowest-paid social group

CONSUMER GOODS OWNERSHIP

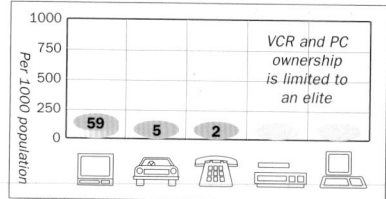

VCR and PC ownership is limited to an elite

59   5   2

Traditional egalitarianism in Sahelian life works against private enrichment, but uranium wealth is altering values.

WORLD RANKING

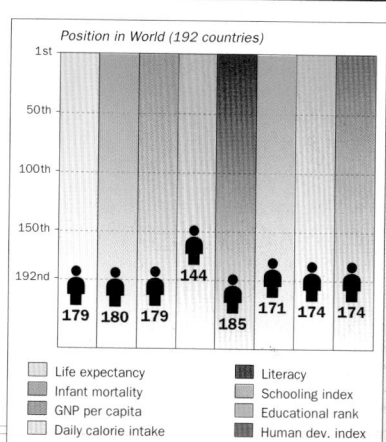

Position in World (192 countries)

179 180 179 144 185 171 174 174

☐ Life expectancy	☐ Literacy
☐ Infant mortality	☐ Schooling index
☐ GNP per capita	☐ Educational rank
☐ Daily calorie intake	☐ Human dev. index

NIGERIA

OFFICIAL NAME: Federal Republic of Nigeria **CAPITAL:** Abuja
POPULATION: 111.7 million **CURRENCY:** Naira **OFFICIAL LANGUAGE:** English

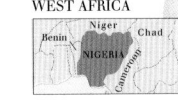

A FRICA'S MOST POPULOUS state, Nigeria gained its independence from Britain in 1960. Bordered by Benin, Niger, Chad and Cameroon, its terrain varies from tropical rainforest and swamps in the south to savanna in the north. Nigeria has been dominated by military governments since 1966. A promised return to civilian rule was aborted in 1993 when the army refused to accept the results of presidential elections. Nigeria is OPEC's fourth-largest oil producer, but it has experienced a fall in living standards since the 1970s, when it saw itself as the most dynamic African economy.

Village beneath Tengele Peak in Bauchi State. A large proportion of Nigerians live from subsistence agriculture.

CLIMATE

WEATHER CHART

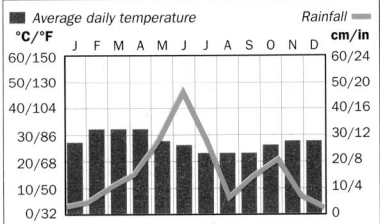

The south is hot, rainy and humid for most of the year. The arid north experiences only one, uncomfortably humid, rainy season from May to September. Its very hot dry season is marked by the dust-laden *harmattan* wind. The Jos Plateau and the eastern highlands are cooler than the rest of Nigeria. Forcados in the Niger delta gets most rain with 148 in. a year.

TRANSPORTATION

 **Murtala Muhammed, Lagos** 2.05m passengers

 48 ships 698,300 dwt

THE TRANSPORTATION NETWORK

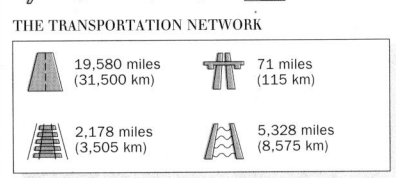

19,580 miles (31,500 km)

71 miles (115 km)

2,178 miles (3,505 km)

5,328 miles (8,575 km)

Nigeria relies almost entirely on road transportation. During the oil-boom years of the 1970s, new long-distance road links were built. Now that revenues have shrunk, maintenance is the major problem. The road accident rate is among the worst in the world. The small rail system, built for the once thriving bulk trade, is today very slow and badly maintained. Nigerian Airways' international operations have been privatized as a new corporation named Air Nigeria. The internal air market has shrunk since the prosperous years of the 1970s.

TOURISM

193,000 visitors

Up 1% in 1994

Nigeria has attempted to build a tourist industry, but with little success. Year-round tropical temperatures and poor infrastructure have limited its growth. The major deterrent to visitors, however, is crime. Travel can be hazardous, and Lagos has one of the world's highest crime rates.

MAIN OVERSEAS ARRIVALS

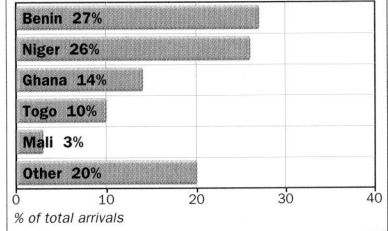

Benin 27%
Niger 26%
Ghana 14%
Togo 10%
Mali 3%
Other 20%
% of total arrivals

NIGERIA

Total Land Area : 910 770 sq. km (351 648 sq. miles)

POPULATION
over 1 000 000
over 500 000
over 100 000
over 50 000
over 10 000
under 10 000

LAND HEIGHT
2000m/6562ft
1000m/3281ft
500m/1640ft
200m/656ft
Sea Level

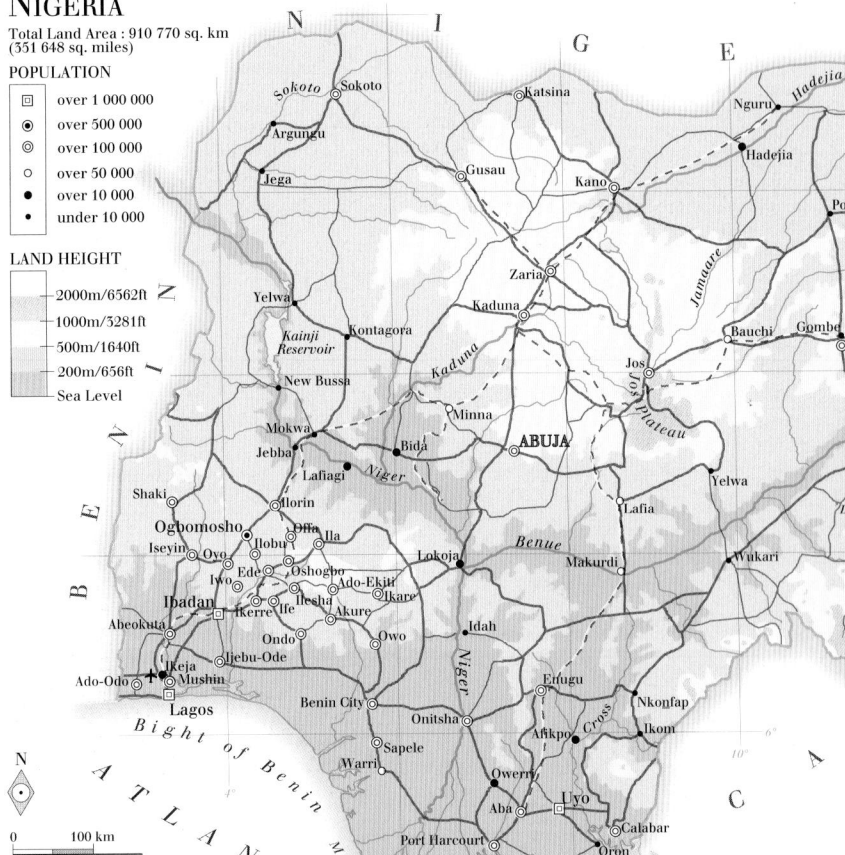

PEOPLE

 Hausa, English Creole, Yoruba, Ibo, English

 319 people per sq. mile

THE URBAN/RURAL POPULATION SPLIT

37%   63%

RELIGIOUS PERSUASION

Indigenous beliefs 10%

Muslim 50%

Christian 40%

ETHNIC MAKEUP

Yoruba 21%

Other 29%

Hausa 21%

Fulani 11%

Ibo 18%

In recent years, Nigeria has largely managed to contain the passions generated by the ethnic, religious and language differences that characterize its people. There is intense rivalry between the four main ethnic groups, as well as among the 245 smaller ones. Members of one group tend to blame those of another for their problems, rather than the broader political system. Religion is a particular source of tension. Outbreaks of communal violence, particularly in the north, are frequently attributable to clashes between Muslim fundamentalists and Christian proselytizers. Except in the Islamic north, women have traditionally possessed independent economic status. In recent years they have, however, been subjected to some prejudice in professional circles.

POPULATION AGE BREAKDOWN

%	☐ 0–14	☐ 15–64		☐ 65+	
2.3%	2.4%	2.5%	2.5%	2.7%
52.3%	51.3%	50.9%	50.1%	51.3%
45.4%	46.3%	46.6%	47.4%	46%
1960	1970	1980	1990	2000

(% of population by age group)

POLITICS

 1998

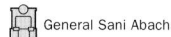 General Sani Abacha

THE STATE OF THE PARTIES
Provisional Ruling Council

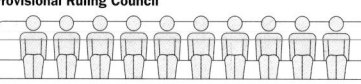

The National Assembly was dissolved in November 1993 after the resumption of military rule. Government is now by a Provisional Ruling Council of senior military figures

Nigeria is a federation, currently of 30 states, controlled by a military dictatorship. The present regime assumed formal control in November 1993 – in the wake of the aborted July elections – after dissolving the National Assembly.

MAIN POLITICAL ISSUES
Corruption
International agencies have identified corruption as a major cause of Nigeria's debt levels. Bureaucrats commonly regard holding office as a source of lucrative kickbacks from the granting of contracts. This attitude is raising anti-government feeling.

Instability
There are fears, particularly among the Western-dominated business community, that popular resentment at the military's apparent determination to cling to power will create serious long-term political instability.

PROFILE
A program to restore civilian government began in 1987 under President Babangida, but came to a halt in 1993 when he annulled the results of the presidential election. Protests abroad and strikes at home persuaded Babangida to give up the presidency and relinquish control to a "civilian" interim government.

However, the military soon resumed control under General Sani Abacha. The interim government was swept away, along with the two political parties set up to fight the elections. General Abacha set up a Provisional Ruling Council and sacked state governors, replacing them with military officers. Political activity was banned.

Moshood Abiola, presumed winner of 1993 elections, but detained since 1994.

Gen. Sani Abacha. Head of state since November 1993.

CHRONOLOGY

Before formal colonization by the British, begun only in 1861, Nigeria was a collection of African states owing their considerable wealth to trans-Saharan and transatlantic trade. During the 18th century the principal commodity was slaves: over 15,000 people were exported annually from the Bight of Benin and another 15,000 from the Bight of Biafra.

❑ **1885** George Goldie's Royal Niger Company given official responsibility for British sphere of influence along Niger and Benue rivers. British armed forces coerce local rulers into accepting British rule.

❑ **1897** West Africa Frontier Force (WAFF) established; subjugation of the north begins.

❑ **1898** The Royal Niger Company's charter revoked.

❑ **1900** British Protectorate of Northern Nigeria established.

❑ **1906** Lagos incorporated into the Protectorate of Southern Nigeria.

❑ **1914** Protectorates of Northern and Southern Nigeria joined to form colony of Nigeria.

❑ **1954** New constitution establishes federal system of government.

❑ **1960** Independence. Nigeria established as a federation.

❑ **1961** Northern part of UK-administered UN Trust Territory of the Cameroons incorporated as part of Nigeria's Northern Region.

❑ **1966** January, first military coup, led by Maj.-Gen. Ironsi. July, counter-coup mounted by group of northern army officers. Ironsi murdered. Thousands of Ibo in Northern Region massacred. Gen. Gowon in control of north and west.

❑ **1967–1970** Civil war. Lt.-Col. Ojukwu calls for secession of oil-rich east under the new name Biafra. Over one million Nigerians die before secessionists defeated by federal forces.

❑ **1970** Gowon in power.

❑ **1975** Gowon toppled in bloodless coup. Brig. Murtala Mohammed takes power.

❑ **1976** Murtala Mohammed murdered in abortive coup.

❑ **1978** Political parties legalized, on condition they represent national, not tribal, interests.

❑ **1979** Elections won by Alhaji Shehu Shagari and National Party of Nigeria (NPN), marking return to civilian government.

❑ **1983** Military coup. Maj.-Gen. Mohammed Buhari heads Supreme Military Council.

N

CHRONOLOGY *continued*

❑ **1985** Maj.-Gen. Ibrahim Babangida takes over in bloodless coup, promising a return to democracy.

❑ **1993** August, Babangida annuls presidential election thought to have been won by Moshood Abiola. International protest and strikes. Babangida resigns presidency; military sets up Interim National Government (ING) headed by Chief Adegunle Shonekan. November, ING dissolved. Military, headed by Gen. Sani Abacha, takes over.

❑ **1994** Abiola arrested; opposition harassed.

❑ **1995** Ban on political parties lifted, but military regime increasingly isolated following conviction by a military tribunal of former head of state Gen. Olusegun Obasango and 39 others for plotting a coup. Relations with Commonwealth and other individual states breached following execution of Ken Saro-Wiwa and eight other Ogoni activists.

WORLD AFFAIRS

Nigeria's overseas ambitions have expanded and contracted with its oil revenues. Successive governments have regarded Nigeria as Africa's leading voice. It is a keen sponsor of ECOWAS, playing a key role in the force deployed in war-torn Liberia. It also took the lead in planning for an African Common Market. Strongly opposed to apartheid, Nigeria's relations with South Africa were only restored following the 1994 democratic elections there. The country has one of the non-permanent African seats on the UN Security Council.

The current regime's reluctance to restore democracy and its violation of human rights (demonstrated by the execution of Ken Saro-Wiwa and eight other Ogoni activists in 1995) have angered the international community, prompting UN condemnation and suspension from the Commonwealth.

AID

 $284m (receipts)   Up 7% in 1993

Nigeria's debt rocketed with the 1981 drop in world oil prices and turned Nigeria from an aid donor into a major receiver of World Bank assistance. However, international assistance has largely been halted since the execution of Ken Saro-Wiwa and others in late 1995.

DEFENSE

 $319m   ⬇ Down 73% in 1995

0	*Defense spending as % GDP*	40
3.1%		

NIGERIAN ARMED FORCES

🛡	210 main battle tanks (60 T-55, 150 Vickers Mk 3)	62,000 personnel
🚢	1 frigate, 53 patrol boats (2 *Exocet* missiles)	5,600 personnel
✈	92 combat aircraft (20 *Alpha Jet*, 22 MiG, 15 *Jaguar*)	9,500 personnel
🚀	None	

The defense establishment in Nigeria suffers from problems caused by corruption. During Babangida's rule (1985–1993), most of the air force's prestige jets were grounded as money for spare parts was diverted into senior officers' bank accounts. Soldiers' salaries have been steadily declining in real terms in recent years, barrack conditions have deteriorated and morale is low. However, the November 1993 restoration of military government by the then Defense Minister General Sani Abacha – a key player in both the 1983 and 1985 coups – has encouraged expectations of improved conditions among the army rank and file.

ECONOMICS

📊 $30bn   💲 22 naira

SCORE CARD

❑ WORLD GNP RANKING.........................57th
❑ GNP PER CAPITA $280
❑ BALANCE OF PAYMENTS ....$–2.13bn
❑ INFLATION 57%
❑ UNEMPLOYMENT..................................28%

EXPORTS

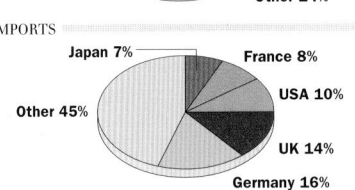

Germany 5%   Italy 6%
Netherlands 6%
USA 45%   Spain 14%
Other 24%

IMPORTS

Japan 7%   France 8%
USA 10%
Other 45%   UK 14%
Germany 16%

STRENGTHS

One of world's top oil producers at 1.9 million b/d. Vast reserves of natural gas, still only partly exploited. Almost self-sufficient in food. Strong entrepreneurial class. Large domestic market of over 111 million people.

WEAKNESSES

Over-dependence since the 1970s on oil, which accounts for 90% of export earnings and 80% of government revenue, and encourages massive state inefficiency. Advantages of a large domestic market mitigated by low per capita purchasing power and high unit transportation costs. Entrepreneurs focus on trade rather than production. Only cocoa remains of Nigeria's traditional agricultural exports; it was once a major producer of tropical vegetables and fruit.

ECONOMIC PERFORMANCE INDICATOR

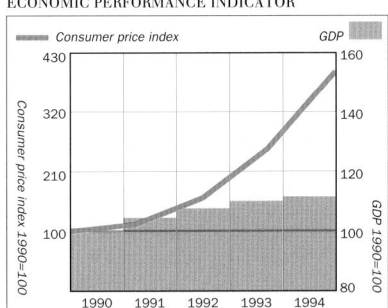

PROFILE

The economy has been characterized by massive government spending and the running up of debts which could not be serviced after the 1981 oil price fall. Led by the IMF, creditors want major cuts in spending – especially on loss-making public sector companies – and subsidies. Gasoline subsidies alone are estimated to have cost $2.4 billion a year. Such changes are politically fraught, however. When gasoline prices were raised 400% in 1993, there were nationwide strikes.

NIGERIA : MAJOR BUSINESSES

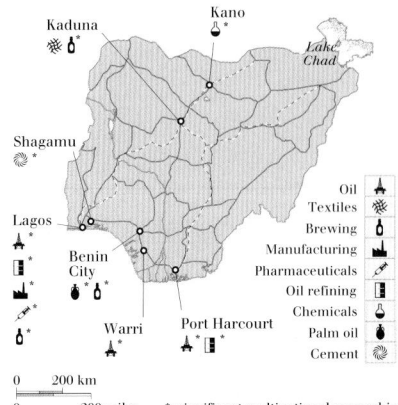

RESOURCES

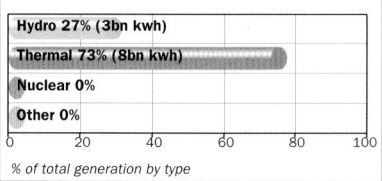

11bn kwh (capacity 4m kw)

1.9m b/d (reserves 17,899,820,000 bbl)

25.5m goats, 16.7m cattle, 14.5m sheep, 6.9m pigs

Oil, natural gas, coal, tin, iron, bauxite, columbite, lead

ELECTRICITY GENERATION

Hydro 27% (3bn kwh)	
Thermal 73% (8bn kwh)	
Nuclear 0%	
Other 0%	

% of total generation by type

Oil has been Nigeria's main resource since the 1970s. Government policy is to increase output from 1.9 million b/d (7.5% of OPEC output) to 2.5 million b/d. Domestic demand is 300,000 b/d, much of it smuggled to neighboring countries. Nigeria's vast gas deposits are still under-exploited. The state retains 60% control of the oil and gas industry. Shell is the main foreign shareholder, but most oil multinationals are represented.

Nigeria has sizeable iron ore deposits. These are not yet utilized in the state-run steel industry; imported ore is used instead. Bauxite deposits are also currently under-exploited. There are, however, plans for establishing an aluminum industry.

NIGERIA : LAND USE

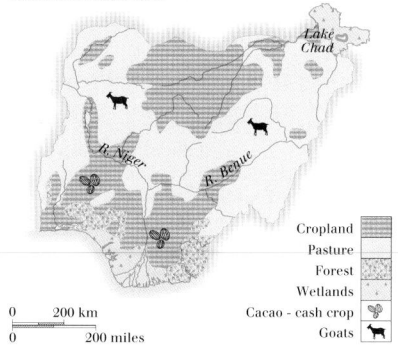

Lake Chad

R. Niger

R. Benue

0   200 km
0   200 miles

Cropland
Pasture
Forest
Wetlands
Cacao - cash crop
Goats

ENVIRONMENT

3% (1% partially protected)

No progress in controlling oilfield pollution

ENVIRONMENTAL TREATIES

 No		Yes		Yes
Yes		No		Yes

Oil industry pollution in the Niger delta is a major local concern, coming to international attention in 1995. Shell has been particularly condemned. Before the discovery of a highly toxic cargo in Lagos in 1988, Nigeria was a dumping ground for European chemical waste.

MEDIA

 Foreign journalists have been expelled for questioning corruption in government

Nigerians are avid newspaper readers and the press is traditionally one of Africa's liveliest. However, the new military regime has made clear its unwillingness to tolerate criticism. There are over 20 English-language current-affairs periodicals.

CRIME

Nigeria does not publish prison figures

Rising. One of the highest crime rates in the world

CRIME RATES

Murders	
94	*per 100,000 population*

Rapes	
	Above regional average

Thefts	
1256	*per 100,000 population*

The military government frequently uses *ad hoc* tribunals for politically sensitive cases. Nigeria has one of the highest crime rates in the world. Murder often accompanies even minor burglaries. Corruption pervades the bureaucracy; the provision of kickbacks to supporters is considered routine rather than a crime. Rich Nigerians live in high-security compounds, equipped with electric fencing and patrolled by armed guards.

EDUCATION

53%

335,824 students

0   *Education spending as % GNP*   25
1.7%

THE EDUCATION SYSTEM

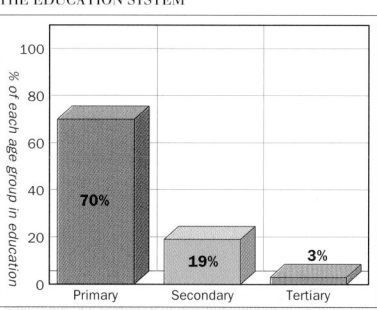

Education has suffered from the government's massive debt repayment burden. During the oil-boom years, Nigeria concentrated on creating 31 universities with prestigious medical and scientific schools. However, standards in elementary education, which has not received the same level of investment, have fallen since the 1970s.

	There are 35 daily newspapers. The largest is the *Daily Times*, published by the government
1 state-controlled service	1 state-controlled service
Intelsat V1 F1	None

HEALTH

1 per 66,650 people

Yellow fever, malaria, trachoma, yaws

0   *Health spending as % GDP*   25
1.2%

The health service is concentrated in urban areas and mostly aimed at richer Nigerians. Modern medicine is not available to those living in rural areas. Health provision, with other public services, has suffered from the crisis in government revenues.

WEALTH

International company finance officer, 200,000 naira ($9,090) per year; polytechnic principal lecturer, 24,000–41,000 naira ($1,090–$1,863) per year

CONSUMER GOODS OWNERSHIP

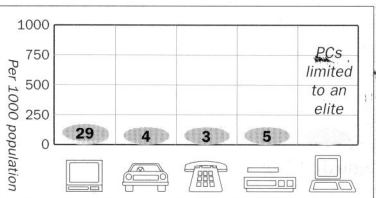

PCs limited to an elite

29   4   3   5

Nigerians with access to the rich pickings of political office spent on a massive scale during the oil-boom – on Maseratis, Mercedes and overseas education for their children. Much was financed by government loans. Habits have not changed with the fall in oil revenues: borrowing has simply grown.

WORLD RANKING

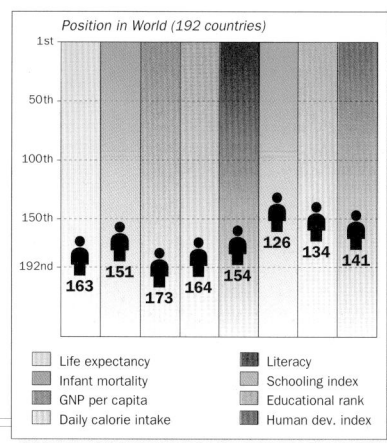

Position in World (192 countries)

1st
50th
100th
150th
192nd

163   151   173   164   154   126   134   141

Life expectancy
Infant mortality
GNP per capita
Daily calorie intake
Literacy
Schooling index
Educational rank
Human dev. index

N

411

NORTH KOREA

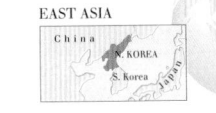

OFFICIAL NAME: Democratic People's Republic of Korea **CAPITAL:** Pyongyang
POPULATION: 23.9 million **CURRENCY:** Won **OFFICIAL LANGUAGE:** Korean

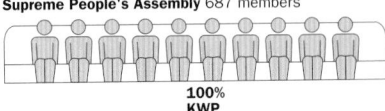

NORTH KOREA COMPRISES the northern half of the Korean peninsula and is separated from the US-dominated South close to the 38th parallel. Much of the country is mountainous; the Chaeryŏng and Pyongyang plains in the southwest are the most fertile regions. Established as an independent communist republic in 1948, North Korea remains largely isolated from the outside world. Its economy, starved of development capital, is now facing severe difficulties.

CLIMATE

WEATHER CHART

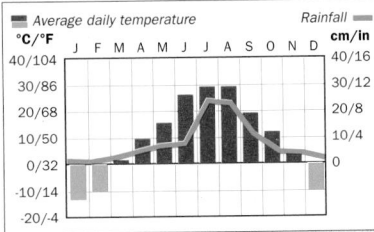

North Korea has a typically continental climate. Winters in the north can be extreme, with several months of snow.

TRANSPORTATION

 **Sunan, Pyongyang**

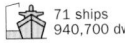 71 ships 940,700 dwt

THE TRANSPORTATION NETWORK

1,150 miles (1,860 km)	220 miles (354 km)
3,135 miles (5,045 km)	1,400 miles (2,253 km)

North Korea relies heavily on the antiquated railroad network built by the Japanese during their occupation. The Pyongyang–Kaesŏng highway, completed in 1992, is open only to very limited, officially approved traffic.

TOURISM

 126,000

 Up 26% in 1994

MAIN OVERSEAS ARRIVALS

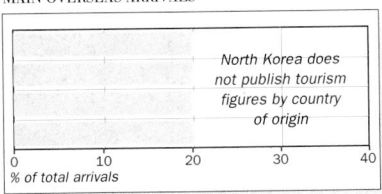

North Korea does not publish tourism figures by country of origin

% of total arrivals

The need to earn hard currency has forced an attempt to develop tourism, which remains strictly controlled.

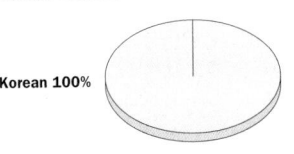

Rice paddy-field. *The hot, wet summers are ideal for rice growing. Most farms are run as cooperatives.*

PEOPLE

 Korean, Chinese

 515 people per sq.mile

THE URBAN/RURAL POPULATION SPLIT

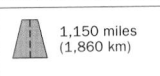

60%   40%

ETHNIC MAKEUP

Korean 100%

North Korea operates a strict "estates" system, by which the population is classed according to three categories: loyal, wavering and hostile. Inclusion in the first category is a prerequisite for advancement. Those deemed hostile – usually Christians and the children of landlords or of Koreans who fled to the South – have barely any rights. People live severely regulated lives. Divorce is non-existent and extra-marital sex highly frowned upon. Women form 57% of the work force, but are also expected to run the home; it is not uncommon for them to rise at 4 am, and end their working day at 7 pm. From an early age, children are looked after by an extensive system of state-run crèches. The privileged lifestyle of the political elite – numbering only about 200,000 – is a source of considerable popular resentment.

POLITICS

 Not applicable

 Vacant

THE STATE OF THE PARTIES

Supreme People's Assembly 687 members

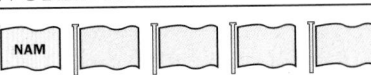

100%
KWP

KWP = Korean Workers' Party

The 3 million-strong KWP is the only legal party; membership is essential for individual advancement. Kim Il Sung, the subject of a lavish personality cult, died in 1994 after almost 50 years as leader. Since then, the key question has been how his son and chosen successor, Kim Jong Il, will handle the leadership. The fact that he has still not yet formally been installed as head of state or party, together with his few public appearances, has given rise to speculation that he is ill and that his succession is opposed by the military. Although the army appears loyal to the regime, the younger Kim lacks the military authority of his father.

WORLD AFFAIRS

NAM

The worldwide collapse of communism isolated North Korea by destroying its framework of traditional allies. Although it joined the UN in 1991, North Korea has since been involved in a protracted dispute with the International Atomic Energy Agency over its refusal to allow international inspection of its nuclear industry, which the US government believed was geared towards the development of nuclear weapons. In 1994, a deal was signed with the USA whereby North Korea froze its nuclear program in return for assistance in replacing its reactors with models less suited to the manufacture of weapons. Despite desultory talks over reunification, North and South Korean forces remain in a state of alert across the border.

AID

 $15m (receipts)

 Up 25% in 1993

Vital aid from the Soviet Union ended in 1991 and China ceased "friendship supplies" in 1993. Despite official denials, the aid-dependent economy has suffered badly.

NORTH KOREA

Total Land Area : 120 410 sq. km (46 490 sq. miles)

POPULATION

over 1 000 000
over 100 000
over 50 000
over 10 000

LAND HEIGHT

1500m/4920ft
1000m/3281ft
500m/1640ft
200m/656ft
Sea Level

CHRONOLOGY

The peninsula was divided at the 38th parallel in 1945; North Korea was created as an independent state in 1948.

 1950–53 Korean War, as North Korea invades the South. UN troops occupy North Korea but are driven back by Chinese intervention.
❑ **1994** Withdrawal from IAEA. Kim Il Sung dies.

EDUCATION

 99%   390,000 students

North Korea claims to have created over one million "intellectuals." Kim Il Sung, Pyongyang, is the only university.

HEALTH

1 per 370 people — Heart diseases, cancers, digestive diseases

The free health service has raised life expectancy. The showpiece Pyongyang Maternity Hospital appears unused.

WEALTH

 The 20% or so of the population classified as "hostile" live in remote areas, do the worst jobs and have little prospect of social advancement

CONSUMER GOODS OWNERSHIP

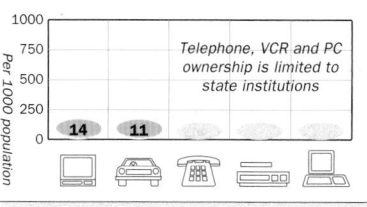

Telephone, VCR and PC ownership is limited to state institutions

14   11

An elite within the KWP lives well, with access to specialist shops and consumer goods such as VCRs. Both private car and telephone ownership are forbidden.

RESOURCES

 38bn kwh (capacity 9.5m kw) — Not an oil producer; refines 42,000 b/cd

 3.4m pigs, 1.3m cattle, 396,000 sheep — Coal, iron, lead, copper, zinc, tin, silver, gold, uranium

A shortage of electricity (blackouts are frequent) remains a major problem. Under the 1994 agreement with the USA, two new reactors are to be built with outside assistance. North Korea is relatively rich in metals and also ranks as the world's ninth-largest silver producer.

ENVIRONMENT

 0.5% (0.1% partially protected) — No access to state environmental information

Excessive use of fertilizers and unchecked pollution from heavy industry are the major problems.

MEDIA

Total censorship. No foreign publications permitted. Radios have fixed dials

PUBLISHING AND BROADCAST MEDIA

There are 5 daily newspapers, including the leading *Rodong Shinmun*, the party newspaper, and *Minju Choson*

1 limited state-owned service   2 state-owned services

North Korean TV consists mostly of musical shows praising the qualities of Kim Il Sung and Kim Jong Il.

CRIME

North Korea does not publish prison figures — Low level of violent street crime

Corruption at all levels in dealings with the state is the major problem. The criminal code is weighted to protect the state against "subversion", rather than the rights of the individual. North Korea has a very poor human rights record and a *gulag* of over 100,000 "subversives," where whole families are sent along with those accused and where torture is routine.

DEFENSE

 $2.2bn — No change in 1995

North Korea may have clandestinely manufactured a small number of nuclear weapons prior to the 1994 freeze on its nuclear program.

ECONOMICS

$29.7bn   2.15 won

SCORE CARD

❑ WORLD GNP RANKING..........................56th
❑ GNP PER CAPITA $1,390
❑ BALANCE OF PAYMENTS ....Closed economy;
❑ INFLATION ....does not publish
❑ UNEMPLOYMENT ....any figures

STRENGTHS
Other than minerals, strengths are now few.

WEAKNESSES
GNP has been declining by 5% a year since 1990. The economy has been starved of foreign capital and technology, and is now in dire shape.

EXPORTS/IMPORTS

North Korea's main trading partners are Russia, China and Japan

WORLD RANKING

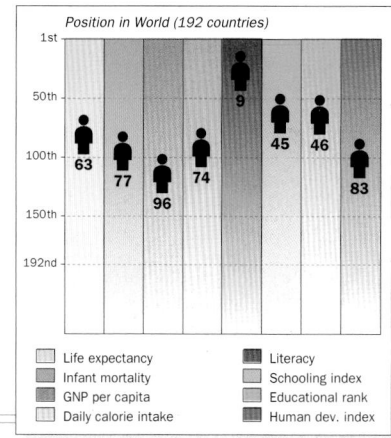

Position in World (192 countries)

63 77 96 74 9 45 46 83

- Life expectancy
- Infant mortality
- GNP per capita
- Daily calorie intake
- Literacy
- Schooling index
- Educational rank
- Human dev. index

NORWAY

OFFICIAL NAME: Kingdom of Norway **CAPITAL:** Oslo **POPULATION:** 4.3 million
CURRENCY: Norwegian krone **OFFICIAL LANGUAGE:** Norwegian **OVERSEAS TERRITORIES:** 3

OCCUPYING THE WESTERN PART of Scandinavia, Norway borders Sweden, Finland and Russia to its east; its western coastline is characterized by numerous fjords and islands. Large oil and gas revenues have brought moderate prosperity. Gro Harlem Brundtland became the country's first woman prime minister in 1981. Despite the Europe-wide recession, Norway has managed to keep its unemployment rate below 6%. The duty of government to create conditions that enable every person to find work is enshrined in the constitution.

The village of Reine on Moskenesøya, 99 mi. inside the Arctic Circle in the Lofoten Islands. It is a popular destination for summer visitors.

CLIMATE

WEATHER CHART

The whole of Norway's west coast is kept ice-free by the warm Gulf Stream. It receives much more precipitation than the rest of the country; Bergen has a yearly average of 88 in. Norway enjoys the highest mean temperatures in Scandinavia, but in winter the temperature in Oslo can drop to –13°F.

NORWAY

Total Land Area : 306 850 sq. km
(118 467 sq. miles)

LAND HEIGHT

2000m/6562ft
1000m/3281ft
500m/1640ft
200m/656ft
Sea Level

POPULATION

over 100 000   ◎
over 50 000   ○
over 10 000   •
under 10 000   ·

TRANSPORTATION

Fornebu Intl, Oslo
6.3m passengers

1,194 ships
36.52m dwt

THE TRANSPORTATION NETWORK

38,130 miles (61,360 km)	272 miles (437 km)
2,624 miles (4,223 km)	980 miles (1,577 km)

It has been impossible to extend rail links further than Bodø, inside the Arctic Circle. To reach Lofoten or Narvik and beyond, the most common form of transportation is air. In 1988, Scandinavian Airlines Systems agreed that British Midland would take over some of its UK–Norway direct routes.

The royal palace, Oslo. This is situated near the national theater, at one end of the Karl Johanisgate, the city's main thoroughfare.

TOURISM

 2.8m visitors   Up 11% in 1994

Norway is a popular destination with visitors from Sweden, Germany, Denmark, the UK and the USA. Its winter tourism industry is based on skiing and has been boosted by the location of the 1994 Winter Olympics in Lillehammer. Cruising along the fjords is popular with summer visitors. Areas within the Arctic Circle are a particular attraction in June, when tourists go in search of the midnight sun. Oslo has a reputation for good classical music and jazz. However, the strength of the

MAIN OVERSEAS ARRIVALS

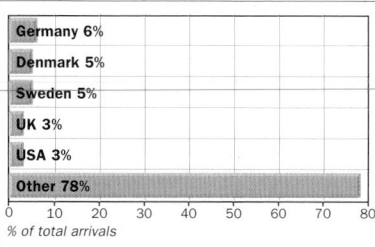

Germany 6%	
Denmark 5%	
Sweden 5%	
UK 3%	
USA 3%	
Other 78%	

% of total arrivals

krone and the high cost of living make Norway expensive.

PEOPLE

 Norwegian (*Bokmål* "book language" and *Nynorsk* "new Norsk"), Lappish

 36 people per sq. mile

THE URBAN/RURAL POPULATION SPLIT

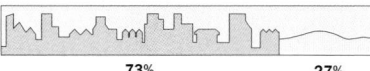

73%   27%

RELIGIOUS PERSUASION

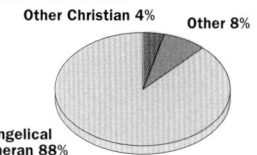

Other Christian 4%   Other 8%

Evangelical Lutheran 88%

ETHNIC MAKEUP

Lapp 1%   Other 4%

Norwegian 95%

Norway has a minimal immigrant population. Over the last few years there has been a small influx of European refugees; they have reportedly suffered some violent attacks from right-wing groups.

The family is traditionally close and nuclear. Men are expected to share responsibility for raising children.

Children frequently attend day schools from below the age of two years. Women in Norway enjoy considerable power and freedom. The prime minister is a woman, as are many other leading politicians.

Over half of marriages in Norway now end in divorce.

POPULATION AGE BREAKDOWN

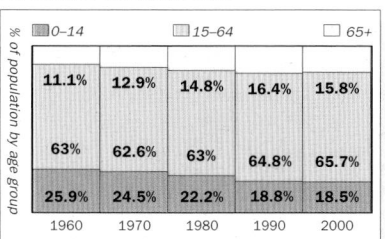

% of population by age group	■ 0–14	▨ 15–64	□ 65+		
	11.1%	12.9%	14.8%	16.4%	15.8%
	63%	62.6%	63%	64.8%	65.7%
	25.9%	24.5%	22.2%	18.8%	18.5%
	1960	1970	1980	1990	2000

POLITICS

 1993/1997   King Harald V

THE STATE OF THE PARTIES

Parliament 165 members

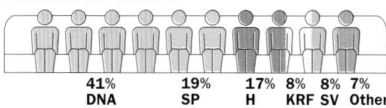

41% DNA	19% SP	17% H	8% KRF	8% SV	7% Other

DNA = Norwegian Labor Party **SP** = Center Party
H = Conservative Party **KRF** = Christian Democratic Party
SV = Socialist Left Party **Other** = Progress Party, Liberal Party, Red Electoral Alliance

Norway is a constitutional monarchy, with a king as head of state and an elected parliament.

MAIN POLITICAL ISSUE
Membership of the EU
In 1994, terms for Norway's accession to the EU were agreed. The issue was divisive; over 60% of the electorate were opposed to membership on the grounds that it would lead to a loss of control of national resources, notably fisheries and the offshore oil sector. However, government and industry supported the move. In a referendum held in November 1994, 52% voted against membership of the EU.

PROFILE
Political decisions are based on a process of consensus-building between the government, parliament and the strong trade unions. The SP, which was against joining the EU, more than doubled its representation in the elections of September 1993, whereas the pro-EU Conservatives slipped badly, becoming the third party in parliament.

Gro Harlem Brundtland's DNA has retained power since 1990, after a decade of short-lived governments. Part of the reason is the personal respect she commands among most of the population. Her pro-whaling stance, which has damaged her international image, has been popular at home.

WORLD AFFAIRS

 CE   NATO   OECD   OSCE WEU

Norway was a participant in the creation of the European Economic Area (EEA) in 1994, but its possible membership of the EU remains under debate. The other major foreign policy issue is ensuring the continuing security of its borders. As a member of NATO, Norway is concerned at the withdrawal of US military forces from Europe. To strengthen its security, Norway became an associate member of the WEU in November 1992.

Norway has played peacebroker in a number of major international conflicts, notably in helping to progress toward a resolution of the Palestinian-Israeli dispute.

The government is exasperated at its inability to control the ecological effects of acid rain, which is destroying its forests, and blames lax pollution controls in the UK, Germany and Russia for the problem. Representatives of 25 European countries and Canada met in Oslo in 1994 and signed a UN protocol on reducing sulfur emissions.

King Harald V, who succeeded his father King Olaf V in 1991.

Gro Harlem Brundtland, prime minister since 1990.

N

CHRONOLOGY

Norway gained independence from the Swedish crown in 1905 and elected its own king, Håkon VII.

❑ **1935** DNA forms government.
❑ **1940–1945** Nazi occupation. Puppet regime led by Vidkun Quisling.
❑ **1945** DNA resumes power.
❑ **1949** Norway joins NATO.
❑ **1957** King Håkon dies. Succeeded by son, Olaf V.
❑ **1960** Norway member of EFTA.
❑ **1962** Norway unsuccessfully applies for EC membership.
❑ **1965** DNA electoral defeat by SP coalition led by Per Borten.
❑ **1967** Norway makes second bid for EC membership.
❑ **1971** Prime Minister Per Borten resigns following disclosure of secret negotiations to join EC. DNA government, led by Trygve Bratteli. ⇨

CHRONOLOGY *continued*

- ❑ **1972** EC membership rejected by the people in referendum by 3% majority. Bratteli resigns. Center coalition government takes power. Lars Korvald prime minister.
- ❑ **1973** Elections. Bratteli returns to power as prime minister.
- ❑ **1976** Bratteli succeeded by Odvar Nordli.
- ❑ **1981** Nordli resigns owing to ill health. Gro Harlem Brundtland becomes Norway's first woman prime minister. Elections bring to power Norway's first Conservative Party (H) government for 53 years. Kare Willoch prime minister.
- ❑ **1983** H forms coalition with SP and KRF.
- ❑ **1985** Election. Willoch's H–SP–KRF coalition returned. Norway agrees to suspend commercial whaling.
- ❑ **1986** Industrial unrest involving over 100,000 workers over better pay and reduction in working week. Parliament rejects tax increase on gasoline. Willoch resigns. Minority DNA government takes power with Brundtland as prime minister. Currency devalued by 12%.
- ❑ **1989** Brundtland's government resigns. H–KRF coalition in power. USSR agrees exchange of information after fires on Soviet nuclear submarines stationed off Norwegian coast.
- ❑ **1990** H–KRF coalition breaks up over closer ties with EU. Brundtland and DNA in power.
- ❑ **1991** Olaf V dies and is succeeded by son, King Harald V.
- ❑ **1993** Reelection of government.
- ❑ **1994** EEA comes into effect. Norwegians vote against EU membership in referendum.

AID

 $1bn (donations)   Up 17% in 1993

Norway has been paying more than the UN development target of 0.7% of GNP in aid every year since 1975. Although Norway's ratio of aid to GNP declined from 1.17% to 1.14% in 1991, it remains the highest in the world.

The vast majority of Norway's bilateral aid donations goes to the least developed countries of southeastern Africa, southern Asia and Central America. The Norwegian government also allocates funds to various multilateral assistance programs. In 1991, some 20% of multilateral aid donations went through the UN and 34% through international development banks.

DEFENSE

 $3.8bn   ⬆ Up 12% in 1995

0   *Defense spending as % GDP*   40
3.1%

Norway spends just over 3% of GDP on defense, most of it on its conscript army of 14,700. It has been a full member of NATO since 1949, unlike its neighbors, Sweden and Finland. Norway's single overriding defense issue is the stability of Russia and the security of their common border.

NORWEGIAN ARMED FORCES

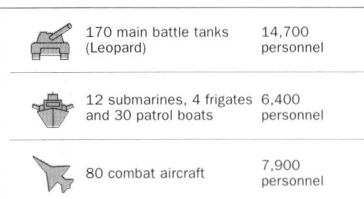

170 main battle tanks (Leopard)	14,700 personnel	
12 submarines, 4 frigates and 30 patrol boats	6,400 personnel	
80 combat aircraft	7,900 personnel	
None		

ECONOMICS

 $114.3bn   💲 6.76–6.32 Norwegian kroner

SCORE CARD

- ❑ WORLD GNP RANKING..........................31st
- ❑ GNP PER CAPITA $26,480
- ❑ BALANCE OF PAYMENTS.....................$3.6bn
- ❑ INFLATION 2.2%
- ❑ UNEMPLOYMENT.................................5.4%

ECONOMIC PERFORMANCE INDICATOR

Consumer price index   GDP

EXPORTS

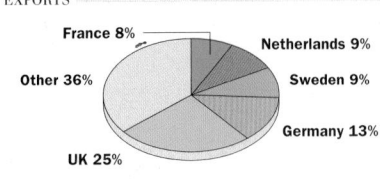

- France 8%
- Netherlands 9%
- Sweden 9%
- Germany 13%
- Other 36%
- UK 25%

IMPORTS

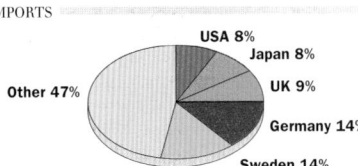

- USA 8%
- Japan 8%
- UK 9%
- Germany 14%
- Sweden 14%
- Other 47%

STRENGTHS

Western Europe's biggest producer and exporter of oil and natural gas. Mineral reserves. Hydroelectric power satisfies much of country's energy demands, allowing most oil to be exported. Large merchant-shipping fleet. Balance of payments surplus. Low inflation (2.2%) and unemployment compared to rest of Europe.

WEAKNESSES

Investment is still almost entirely directed at the oil industry. Over-dependence on oil revenue. Small home market and inaccessible geographical location. Harsh climate limits agriculture.

PROFILE

The state is interventionist by nature. In 1991, it stepped in to rescue most of the main commercial banks, which had been hit by bad loans. It began returning them to the private sector in 1994. The state also manages the distribution of offshore oil and gas

licenses, and maintains control of over 50% of these through its own company, Statoil.

Norway's immediate future prosperity is guaranteed by its lucrative offshore sector. However, despite a government jobs creation program, unemployment is likely to remain higher than is traditionally acceptable. Continuing the strong regional policy of redirecting resources from the more prosperous south to the isolated north is likely to remain a priority, both for social and strategic reasons.

NORWAY : MAJOR BUSINESSES

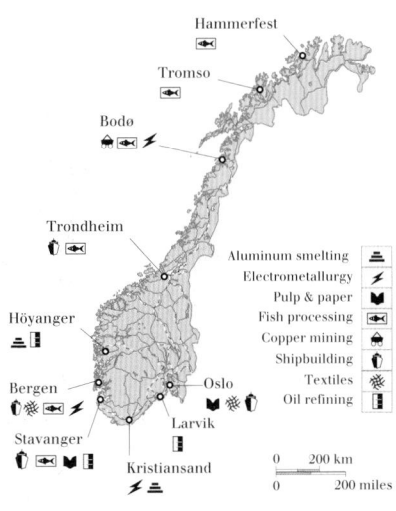

- Hammerfest
- Tromso
- Bodø
- Trondheim
- Höyanger
- Bergen
- Stavanger
- Larvik
- Oslo
- Kristiansand

Aluminum smelting	⬛
Electrometallurgy	⚡
Pulp & paper	🌲
Fish processing	🐟
Copper mining	⛏
Shipbuilding	⚓
Textiles	✳
Oil refining	🛢

0   200 km
0   200 miles

RESOURCES

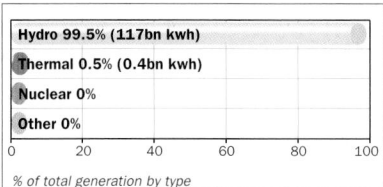

117.7bn kwh (capacity 27.2m kw)

2.1m b/d (reserves 8,805,734,000 bbl)

2.3m sheep, 1m cattle, 745,000 pigs, 89,000 goats

Oil, natural gas, iron, coal, copper, lead, zinc

ELECTRICITY GENERATION

Hydro 99.5% (117bn kwh)

Thermal 0.5% (0.4bn kwh)

Nuclear 0%

Other 0%

% of total generation by type

Norway is Europe's largest oil producer, with an output of some 2.1 million b/d; it also has sizable gas reserves. Most of Norway's electricity is produced by hydropower. In summer, the HEP surplus is exported. Fish and forestry are traditionally significant sectors. With agriculture, they account for only 6% of the work force and 3% of GDP, but to many Norwegians they are important enough to merit the rejection of EU membership. Salmon farms are especially efficient.

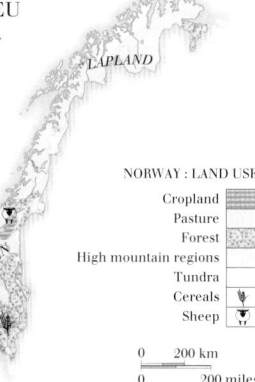

NORWAY : LAND USE

Cropland
Pasture
Forest
High mountain regions
Tundra
Cereals
Sheep

0   200 km
0   200 miles

ENVIRONMENT

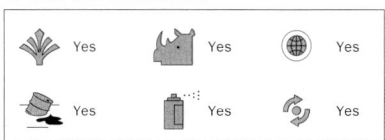

17%

Decision to lift ban on whaling

ENVIRONMENTAL TREATIES

Yes	Yes	Yes
Yes	Yes	Yes

The government devotes considerable attention to preventing oil spills at sea, but is virtually powerless to halt the harmful effects of acid rain, which is damaging Norway's extensive forests. The UK, Germany and Russia have been identified as the main polluters. The north of Norway has suffered from radioactive contamination caused by the 1986 Chernobyl' nuclear disaster. In 1993, Norway decided to lift a ban against fishing minke whales, arguing that the species was not threatened.

MEDIA

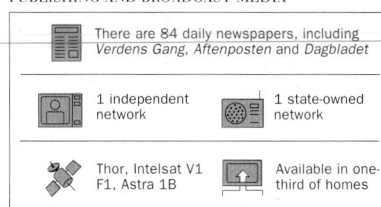

No government censorship

PUBLISHING AND BROADCAST MEDIA

There are 84 daily newspapers, including *Verdens Gang*, *Aftenposten* and *Dagbladet*

1 independent network

1 state-owned network

Thor, Intelsat V1 F1, Astra 1B

Available in one-third of homes

Norway has a diverse press. There are over 80 daily newspapers, with a combined circulation of over two million. *Verdens Gang* is the leading daily with a circulation of 377,000.

CRIME

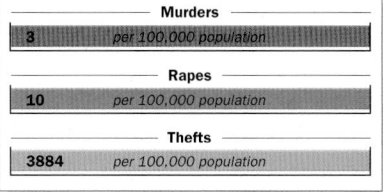

2,041 prisoners

Up 5% in 1992

CRIME RATES

Murders
3 *per 100,000 population*

Rapes
10 *per 100,000 population*

Thefts
3884 *per 100,000 population*

Norway has low levels of crime, even by Scandinavian standards. Violent crime barely exists – the murder rate is a quarter of that of Finland or Sweden, and there are considerably fewer assaults and robberies.

EDUCATION

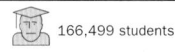

99%

166,499 students

0   *Education spending as % GNP*   25
8.7%

THE EDUCATION SYSTEM

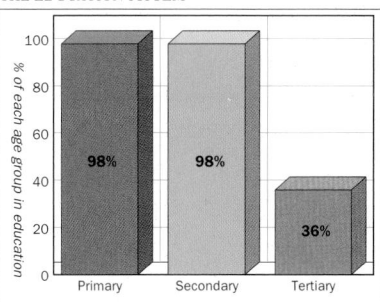

Most schools are run by the municipalities. Norway has a modern university system, with some 80,000 students attending higher education. There are four universities; specialized colleges include the Nordic College of Fisheries.

HEALTH

1 per 313 people

Heart and cerebrovascular diseases, cancers

0   *Health spending as % GDP*   25
8.4%

Norway's infant mortality rate is one of the lowest in the world and its life expectancy at birth one of the highest. Public health expenditure is, however, no higher than the OECD average, and it has a third of the number of hospital beds of neighboring Finland.

Telemedicine (on-line remote audio and image diagnosis) began in 1988 and is developing fast. It allows remote northern hospitals to obtain specialist consultations without having to send patients to the regional hospital.

WEALTH

Carpenter, 90 Norwegian kroner ($14) per hour; bank teller, 14,824 Norwegian kroner ($2,353) per month

CONSUMER GOODS OWNERSHIP

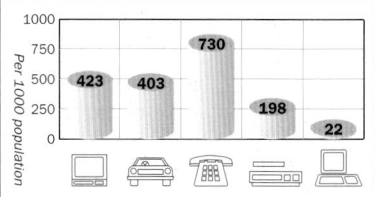

In terms of income distribution, the Nordic countries are the most egalitarian in the world. The top 10% of Norway's population owns 21% of its wealth. (In Switzerland the comparable proportion of wealth would be 30%.) Homelessness and social deprivation are very rare. Recent refugees from the Bosnian conflict are the most disadvantaged group.

The discrepancy between men's and women's pay is greater than in either Sweden or Finland, although still well below the European average. Social provision was maintained even through the recession. Benefits are generous.

WORLD RANKING

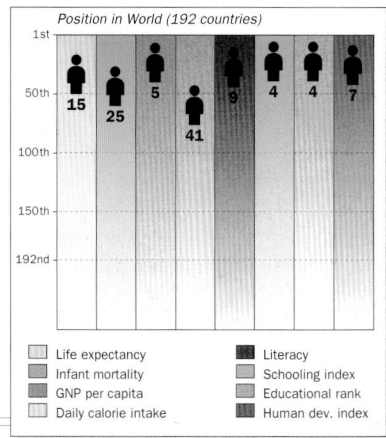

Position in World (192 countries)

15   25   5   41   9   4   4   7

Life expectancy
Infant mortality
GNP per capita
Daily calorie intake
Literacy
Schooling index
Educational rank
Human dev. index

See also OVERSEAS TERRITORIES *p.618*

OMAN

OFFICIAL NAME: Sultanate of Oman **CAPITAL:** Muscat
POPULATION: 2.2 million **CURRENCY:** Omani rial **OFFICIAL LANGUAGE:** Arabic

SHARING BORDERS WITH YEMEN, the United Arab Emirates and Saudi Arabia, Oman is the second-largest country in the Arabian peninsula. It is the least developed of the Gulf states. The most densely populated areas are the northern coast and the southern Şalālah plain. Oil exports have given Oman modest prosperity under a paternalistic sultan, who defeated a Marxist-led insurgency in the 1970s.

CLIMATE

WEATHER CHART

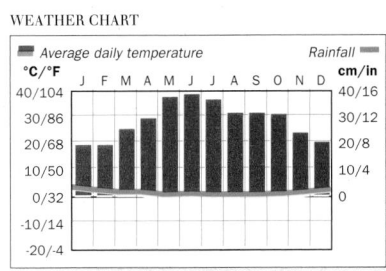

The north blisters under temperatures that often climb above 100°F in summer. The south has a monsoon climate.

TRANSPORTATION

 Seeb Intl, Muscat
1.34m passengers

 4 ships
8,100 dwt

THE TRANSPORTATION NETWORK

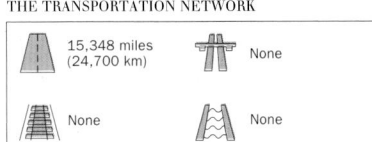

15,348 miles (24,700 km)	None
None	None

There are good roads to neighboring Gulf states, yet Oman's north–south road was only completed in 1982.

TOURISM

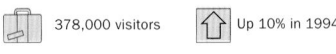 378,000 visitors   Up 10% in 1994

MAIN OVERSEAS ARRIVALS

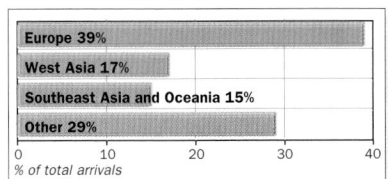

Europe 39%			
West Asia 17%			
Southeast Asia and Oceania 15%			
Other 29%			

| 0 | 10 | 20 | 30 | 40 |

% of total arrivals

Until the late 1980s, Oman was closed to all but business or official visitors. The sultanate's rich cultural heritage, fine beaches and luxury hotels are now enjoyed by thousands of Western visitors a year.

PEOPLE

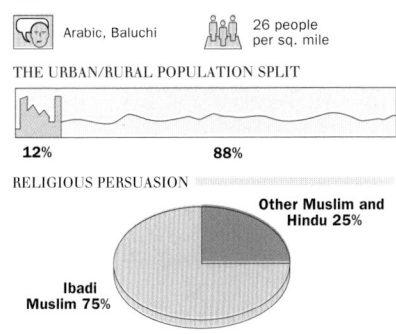

Arabic, Baluchi   26 people per sq. mile

THE URBAN/RURAL POPULATION SPLIT

12%   **88%**

RELIGIOUS PERSUASION

Other Muslim and Hindu 25%
Ibadi Muslim 75%

Native Omanis, who include Arab refugees who fled Zanzibar in the 1960s, make up three-quarters of the population. Baluchis are the largest foreign grouping. Expatriates pose no threat to the regime and Westerners enjoy considerable freedom. Although urban drift has taken place, most Omanis still live on the land, especially in the south. Oman has a number of distinct minorities; the most numerous are the Jebalis in Dhofar – nomadic herdsmen who speak a language which resembles Ethiopian. Many Dhofaris supported the Marxist-led insurgents in the 1970s, but they are now considered loyal. Most Omanis are Ibadi Muslims who follow an appointed leader, called the Imam. Ibadism is not opposed to freedom for women, and a few women enjoy positions of authority.

POLITICS

Not applicable   Sultan Qaboos bin Said

THE STATE OF THE PARTIES

Consultative Council 60 members

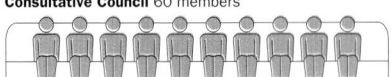

The Sultan rules by decree on the advice of the cabinet and the Consultative Council. The members of the Consultative Council, one for each of the 59 districts and a speaker, are chosen by the Sultan

Sultan Qaboos is an authoritarian but paternalistic monarch, whose dynasty traces its roots to the 18th century. In addition to being head of state, he is prime minister and minister for foreign affairs, defense and finance. The regime faces no serious challenge, although Qaboos keeps a careful eye on the religious right-wing. In 1991, he took the step of creating the Consultative Council (*majlis al-shura*), which gives a semblance of democracy. The main political issues include the planned privatization of medium-sized government projects, and the question of Oman's self-defense capability.

OMAN

Total Land Area : 212 460 sq. km
(82 030 sq. miles)

POPULATION
over 50 000 ○
over 10 000 ●
under 10 000 •

LAND HEIGHT
2000m/6562ft
1000m/3281ft
500m/1640ft
200m/656ft
Sea Level

0 100 km
0 100 miles

WORLD AFFAIRS

 AL AMF Dam Dec GCC OIC

Sultan Qaboos has built up relatively close relations with Israel in recent years. Oman is firmly pro-Western, but does not subscribe to Western anxieties about the region, maintaining good ties with Iran and calling for an easing of sanctions against Iraq.

A watchtower above an oasis. Most of Oman is gravelly desert. The only large area of cultivation is the 12-mile-wide Al Bāṭnah plain.

AID

 $1bn (receipts)   Up 1,883% in 1993

Oman is a recipient of World Bank, US and UK overseas assistance. Agencies face difficulty in allocating aid to Oman as it has yet to hold a census. Oman itself donated aid to anti-communist causes in the 1970s.

DEFENSE

 $1.6bn   Down 16% in 1995

The defense forces and internal security together absorb 30–40% of government spending. The UK is the main supplier of equipment. During the 1991 Gulf War, Oman provided services and communications to US and UK forces. The army relies on Baluchi mercenaries to maintain full strength.

ECONOMICS

 $10.8bn   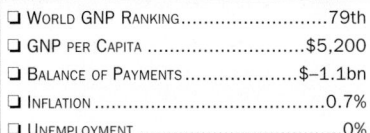 0.38 Omani rials

SCORE CARD

- ❑ WORLD GNP RANKING..........................79th
- ❑ GNP PER CAPITA $5,200
- ❑ BALANCE OF PAYMENTS....................$–1.1bn
- ❑ INFLATION 0.7%
- ❑ UNEMPLOYMENT 0%

STRENGTHS

Oil industry, led by Royal Dutch Shell. Oman has benefited from staying out of OPEC and selling oil at spot prices without quotas. Rich waters off the Indian Ocean coast, with potential for sizable fishing industry.

WEAKNESSES

Over-dependence on oil (90% of GNP); oil reserves, at some 4.5 billion barrels, are finite. Services sector less well-developed than in the United Arab Emirates. Reliance on foreign workers in all sectors of the economy.

EXPORTS

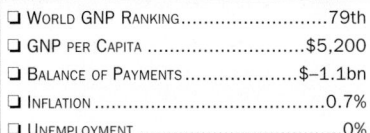

USA 4%
Tanzania 4%
Iran 11%
United Arab Emirates 44%
Hong Kong 12%
Other 25%

IMPORTS

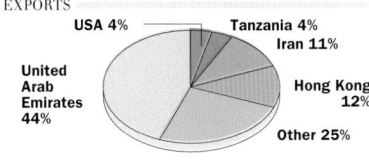

Germany 5%
USA 8%
Other 30%
UK 9%
Japan 21%
United Arab Emirates 27%

RESOURCES

 6.2bn kwh (capacity 1.53m kw)   737,980 b/d (reserves 4,483,000,000 bbl)

 739,000 goats, 149,000 sheep, 96,000 camels   Oil, natural gas, copper, chromite, marble, gypsum

Oman's policy of limiting oil production to conserve resources was abandoned in 1993 following a number of exploration successes.

ENVIRONMENT

 18%   Reintroduction of Arabian oryx into wild

The over-pumping of ground water is becoming a pervasive problem; sea water is seeping into coastal aquifers in traditional irrigation areas.

MEDIA

 There is no public expression of criticism of the government as all press is censored

PUBLISHING AND BROADCAST MEDIA

There are 4 daily newspapers, *Al-'Uman*, its English language companion the *Oman Daily Observer, Al-Watan* and the *Times of Oman*

2 state-controlled networks   1 state-controlled service

Nothing critical of the government may be published in Oman. Foreign press is censored for the Omani market.

CRIME

Oman does not publish prison figures   Crime levels are fairly constant

Reckless driving by young Omani males is a problem. A "flying court" serves remote communities.

CHRONOLOGY

The present Albusaidi dynasty has ruled in Oman since 1749.

- ❑ **1932** Sultan bin Taimur in power.
- ❑ **1950s** Saudi-backed uprising in interior quashed.
- ❑ **1970** Sultan Qaboos bin Said seizes power from his father. Oil revenues increase.
- ❑ **1975** Dhofar revolt overcome.
- ❑ **1991** Consultative Council set up.

EDUCATION

 44%   7,322 students

Education has improved since Sultan Qaboos came to power, though rural illiteracy rates are still high.

HEALTH

 1 per 857 people   Heart and cerebrovascular diseases, accidents

Muscat and Ṣalālah now have hospitals of a high standard. Rural areas are served by clinics.

WEALTH

 Many Omanis live off the land; some emigrate to seek work in other Gulf states

CONSUMER GOODS OWNERSHIP

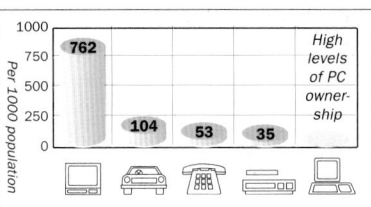

High levels of PC ownership

762   104   53   35

Omanis in urban areas enjoy the same high living standards as are found in other Gulf states. Among the rich, hunting trips to Pakistan are popular and a *khanjar*, a curved dagger, is a status symbol

WORLD RANKING

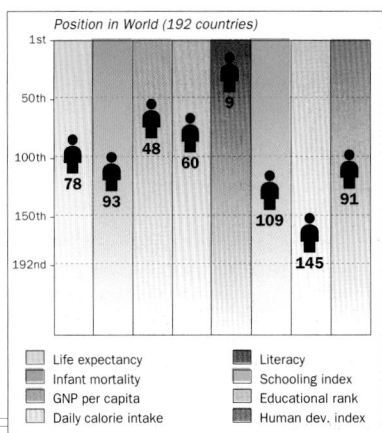

Position in World (192 countries)

78   93   48   60   9   109   145   91

Life expectancy
Infant mortality
GNP per capita
Daily calorie intake
Literacy
Schooling index
Educational rank
Human dev. index

PAKISTAN

OFFICIAL NAME: Islamic Republic of Pakistan **CAPITAL:** Islamabad
POPULATION: 140.5 million **CURRENCY:** Pakistani rupee **OFFICIAL LANGUAGE:** Urdu

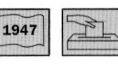

ONCE A PART OF BRITISH INDIA, Pakistan was created in 1947 to answer the need for an independent and largely Muslim Indian state. Initially the new nation included East Pakistan, present-day Bangladesh, which became independent of Islamabad in 1971. Eastern and southern Pakistan, the flood plain of the River Indus, is highly fertile and produces cotton, the basis of the large textile industry.

Barren landscape in Kachhi, Baluchistan.
This area of Pakistan has some of the highest May-to-September temperatures in the world.

CLIMATE

WEATHER CHART

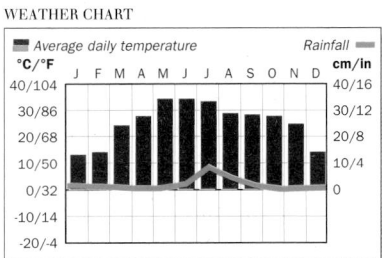

Temperatures can soar to 122°F in Sind and Baluchistan and fall to –4°F in the northern mountains.

TRANSPORTATION

Karáchi International
4.94m passengers

29 ships
491,100 dwt

THE TRANSPORTATION NETWORK

53,960 miles (86,840 km)	211 miles (340 km)
7,842 miles (12,620 km)	None

Basic infrastructure is to be given more priority, with less highway building and more farm-to-market roads.

TOURISM

441,000 visitors

Up 16% in 1994

MAIN OVERSEAS ARRIVALS

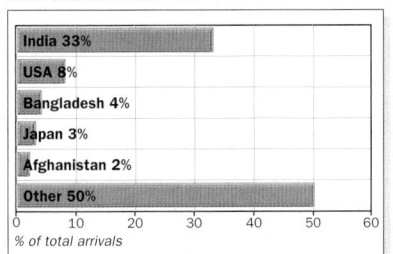

India 33%
USA 8%
Bangladesh 4%
Japan 3%
Afghanistan 2%
Other 50%

% of total arrivals

Relatively few tourists visit Pakistan, despite its rich cultural heritage and unspoilt natural beauty.

PEOPLE

Punjabi, Sindhi, Pashto, Urdu, Baluchi, Brahui

472 people per sq. mile

THE URBAN/RURAL POPULATION SPLIT

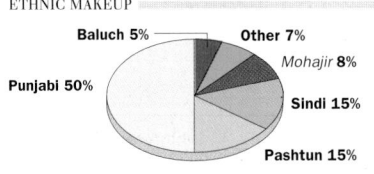

33% 67%

RELIGIOUS PERSUASION

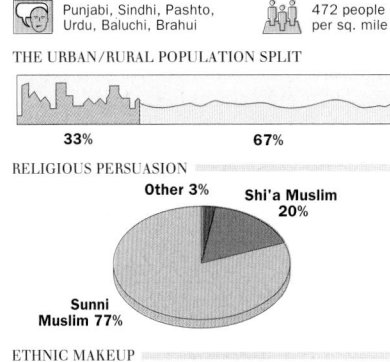

Other 3%
Shi'a Muslim 20%
Sunni Muslim 77%

ETHNIC MAKEUP

Baluch 5%
Other 7%
Mohajir 8%
Punjabi 50%
Sindi 15%
Pashtun 15%

Punjabis account for 50% of the population, while Sindhis, Pathans and Baluch are also prominent. *Mohajirs* – Urdu-speaking immigrants from India at the time of partition – predominate in Karáchi and Hyderábád, Sind's main urban centers. Punjabi dominance of the army and bureaucracy, and the central government's distance from the smaller provinces, has spawned many separatist and autonomy movements. Pathans have frequently threatened to establish a homeland with ethnic kinsfolk over the border in Afghanistan. Tensions between the Baluch and Pathan refugees from Afghanistan sporadically erupt into violence, as do those between native Sindhis and immigrant *Mohajirs*.

The gap between rich and poor, as exemplified by the "feudal" landowning class which dominates the ruling elite and their serfs, is considerable. Barring a massive education drive or an even less likely social revolution, it will not close. There is an expanding middle class of small-scale traders and manufacturers.

There has been a marked increase in Islamic militancy, accompanied by

POPULATION AGE BREAKDOWN

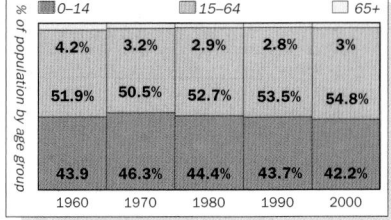

% of population by age group	0–14	15–64	65+		
65+	4.2%	3.2%	2.9%	2.8%	3%
15–64	51.9%	50.5%	52.7%	53.5%	54.8%
0–14	43.9	46.3%	44.4%	43.7%	42.2%
	1960	1970	1980	1990	2000

growing discrimination against religious minorities. In 1995, a controversial blasphemy law which carries a mandatory death sentence caused international outrage when it was used to convict a Christian child; he was subsequently acquitted.

The extended family is an enduring institution and ties between its members are strong, reflected in the dynastic and nepotistic nature of the political system. Although some women hold prominent positions, such as Prime Minister Benazir Bhutto, relatively few are allowed out to work by their religiously conservative menfolk. Pakistan has one of the world's lowest ratios of females to males, implying widespread neglect and some female infanticide. Women's rights groups exist – however, they are mainly urban-based and have made little impact.

POLITICS

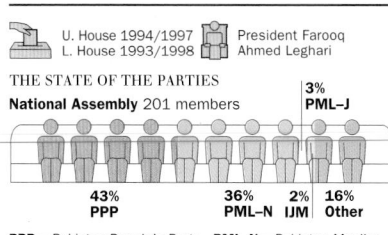

U. House 1994/1997
L. House 1993/1998

President Farooq
Ahmed Leghari

THE STATE OF THE PARTIES

National Assembly 201 members

3%
PML–J

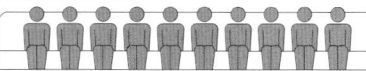

43%
PPP

36%
PML–N

2%
IJM

16%
Other

PPP = Pakistan People's Party **PML–N** = Pakistan Muslim League (Nawaz) **PML–J** = Pakistan Muslim League (Junejo)
IJM = Islami Jamhoori Mahaz **Other** = Awami National Party, Pakistan Islamic Front

Senate 87 members

The 87 members are elected by the 4 provincial legislatures

Pakistan is a multiparty democracy, with a president as head of state. The president has considerable power.

MAIN POLITICAL ISSUES
The army
Redefining the army's role is a major problem. The army has frequently intervened in politics, adding to instability. In 1995, dozens of army officers were arrested for allegedly planning a coup to enforce strict Islamic law.

Corruption
Corrupt governments have produced a deeply cynical electorate. Whatever the prospects of political parties with clean images, however, legislation alone is unlikely to stamp out pervasive corruption in Pakistan.

Ethnic violence
Escalating violence in Sind between Sindhis and Urdu-speaking *Mohajirs* has killed thousands of people. *Mohajirs* are demanding a separate province.

PROFILE
Pakistan is a weak democracy. The ruling parties tend to be fragile coalitions, forced to rule in cooperation with the president and the army, both of whom regularly intervene in politics. A large bureaucracy contributes to inefficient government. Although Islamic parties fared poorly in the 1993 elections, Islamic groups are active. Sectarian violence between Sunnis and minority Shias has risen sharply since 1994.

Benazir Bhutto, *serving a second term as prime minister.*

Nawaz Sharif, *PML–N leader and former prime minister.*

WORLD AFFAIRS

Comm   ECO   NAM   OIC   SAARC

Pakistan's major concern is to avoid a fourth war with India over Kashmir. Pakistan supports the idea of a plebiscite to allow the largely Muslim Kashmiris the right to self-determination. India, which fears losing, opposes it. Hostility with India has intensified with the recent emergence of a violent Muslim separatist movement which Pakistan is alleged to be financing in Kashmir. The USA regards the region as a potential nuclear flashpoint, and in 1990 cut aid to Pakistan because of suspicions that it was developing nuclear weapons. Pakistan denies possessing nuclear weapons. Bhutto's return to power in 1993 improved Pakistan's relations with the USA, which is currently considering lifting sanctions, apparently to support the government against the rising tide of Islamic fundamentalism. China, traditionally an ally, continues to provide substantial military assistance to Pakistan.

P

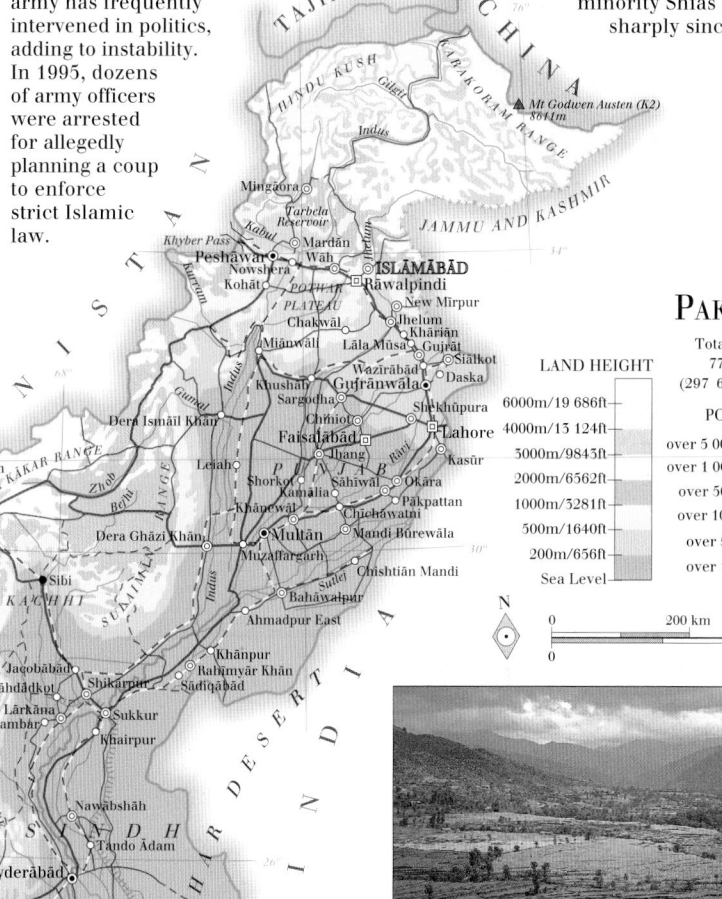

PAKISTAN

Total Land Area :
770 880 sq. km
(297 637 sq. miles)

LAND HEIGHT

6000m/19 686ft
4000m/13 124ft
3000m/9843ft
2000m/6562ft
1000m/3281ft
500m/1640ft
200m/656ft
Sea Level

POPULATION

over 5 000 000   ◼
over 1 000 000   ▢
over 500 000   ◉
over 100 000   ◎
over 50 000   ○
over 10 000   ●

N

0   200 km

0   200 miles

Rice paddy fields, with monsoon rains threatening from the Himalayas. Rice is Pakistan's second most valuable agricultural export after cotton.

CHRONOLOGY

From the 8th to the 16th centuries, Islamic rule extended to northwest and northeast India. The British East India Company annexed Punjab and Sind in the 1850s. They were ceded to the British Raj in 1857.

❑ **1906** Muslim League founded to demand independent Muslim state.
❑ **1947** Partition of India creating Muslim East and West Pakistan, divided by 992 mi. of largely Hindu Indian territory, is accompanied by violence and large-scale migration of Muslims and Hindus. Ali Jinnah appointed first governor-general.
❑ **1947–1949** Conflict with India over ownership of Kashmir.
❑ **1949** Awami League (AL) founded. Seeks autonomy for East Pakistan.
❑ **1951** Liaqat Ali Khan, successor to Ali Jinnah, assassinated.
❑ **1956** Constitution establishes Pakistan as an Islamic republic.

CHRONOLOGY *continued*

- **1958** Martial law. Gen. Muhammad Ayubb Khan takes over.
- **1960** Ayubb Khan elected president.
- **1970** Ayubb Khan resigns. Gen. Agha Yahya Khan takes over. First direct elections. AL, led by Sheikh Mujibur Rahman, wins. West rejects East-led government. Civil war – India supports East.
- **1971** East secedes as Bangladesh. Zulfikar Ali Bhutto, leader of Pakistan People's Party (PPP) holding majority in the West, becomes Pakistan's president.
- **1972** Ceasefire line in Kashmir agreed with India.
- **1973** End of martial law. New constitution; Bhutto, now as executive prime minister, initiates "Islamic socialism."
- **1977** Riots after alleged electoral rigging. Military coup led by Gen. Zia ul-Haq.
- **1979** Bhutto executed. Zia gets US backing as USSR invades Afghanistan.
- **1985** PPP boycotts non-party elections while Zia retains real power.
- **1986** Bhutto's daughter, Benazir, returns from exile to co-lead PPP.
- **1988** Zia killed in air crash. Benazir Bhutto wins general elections.
- **1990** Ethnic violence in Sind. President dismisses Bhutto government alleging corruption. Nawaz Sharif becomes premier.
- **1991** Muslim *sharia* law incorporated in legal code.
- **1992** Violence worsens in Sind.
- **1993** Benazir Bhutto returns to power.
- **1994** Political violence in Sind escalates as *Mohajirs* demand to be recognized as a fifth nationality.
- **1995** Talks between government and *Mohajir* representatives breakdown. Coup attempt.

AID

 $1.1bn (receipts)   Down 9% in 1993

Pakistan is heavily dependent on aid, although the government has a long history of misdirecting aid payments. Aid intended for major projects has regularly been used to fund the current account deficit. In 1995, the IMF suspended a three-year loan facility after Pakistan failed to meet budget deficit targets which it had set. In 1990, the USA cut off aid in response to concern over Pakistan's alleged nuclear program. In the absence of the USA, Japan and Germany are currently the main bilateral donors. Other donors are the World Bank and the ADP.

DEFENSE

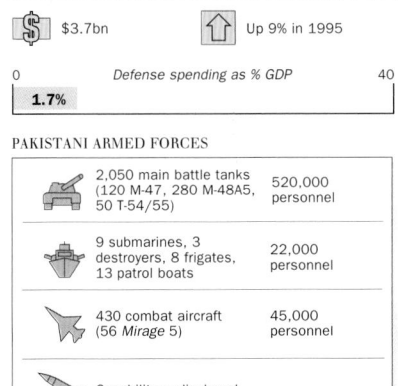

$3.7bn   Up 9% in 1995

Defense spending as % GDP — 1.7%

PAKISTANI ARMED FORCES

2,050 main battle tanks (120 M-47, 280 M-48A5, 50 T-54/55) — 520,000 personnel

9 submarines, 3 destroyers, 8 frigates, 13 patrol boats — 22,000 personnel

430 combat aircraft (56 *Mirage* 5) — 45,000 personnel

Capability undisclosed

Defense spending ranks high in the government's priorities despite a slight reduction in recent years. In 1994–1995 and again in 1995–1996, debt servicing overtook defense as the largest single item of expenditure. Nevertheless, defense spending currently accounts for more than 25% of all expenditure. The USA was the main arms supplier, until the severance of aid in 1990; military supplies may be partially resumed. Pakistan's other defense procurements are from France, the UK and China. The army is politically significant with indications of some links with Islamic groups. In 1995, several army officers were arrested on charges of plotting a coup to install a strict Islamic government.

ECONOMICS

$55.6bn   30.77–34.22 Pakistani rupees

SCORE CARD
- WORLD GNP RANKING.........................43rd
- GNP PER CAPITA $440
- BALANCE OF PAYMENTS...................$–2.9bn
- INFLATION 13%
- UNEMPLOYMENT................................5.8%

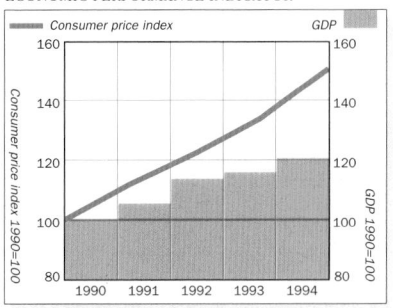

ECONOMIC PERFORMANCE INDICATOR

EXPORTS
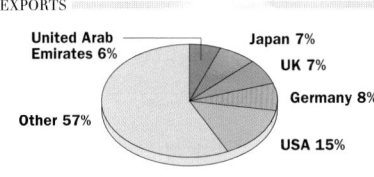
United Arab Emirates 6%, Other 57%, Japan 7%, UK 7%, Germany 8%, USA 15%

IMPORTS
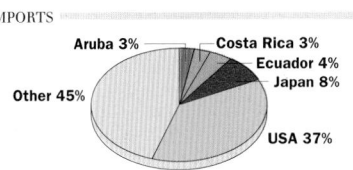
Aruba 3%, Other 45%, Costa Rica 3%, Ecuador 4%, Japan 8%, USA 37%

STRENGTHS
Gas, water, coal, oil. Substantial untapped natural resources. Low labor costs. Potentially huge market. One of the world's leading producers of cotton and a major exporter of rice.

WEAKNESSES
Weather conditions cause considerable variation in annual production and sales of cotton and rice. Inefficient and haphazard government economic policies. Weak and overstretched infrastructure.

PROFILE
Pakistan has recently begun to tackle its considerable economic problems. Successive governments have reversed the nationalization policies instituted in the 1970s by Prime Minister Zulfikar Ali Bhutto. Under ex-prime minister Sharif,

inefficiencies such as the lengthy procedure to license even small investment decisions began to be tackled. Private capital has been brought into previously state-only sectors such as banking, water and other utilities. However, a disproportionately large share of the state budget is still allocated to military spending, which remains a rein on development.

Despite its considerable economic potential, much of Pakistan's population lives below the poverty line.

PAKISTAN : MAJOR BUSINESSES

Light engineering, Carpet weaving, Chemicals, Electronics, Vehicle assembly, Textiles, Shipbuilding, Leather tanning, Food processing, Tobacco, Steel

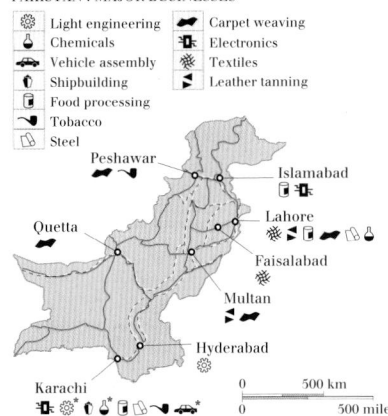

Peshawar, Islamabad, Quetta, Lahore, Faisalabad, Multan, Hyderabad, Karachi

0 — 500 km
0 — 500 miles

* significant multinational ownership

RESOURCES

 50.4bn kwh (capacity 9.14m kw)

 74,626 b/d (reserves 412,000,000 bbl)

41.3m goats, 29m sheep, 18m cattle, 4m asses

Oil, limestone, salt, gypsum, silica sand, natural gas, coal

ELECTRICITY GENERATION

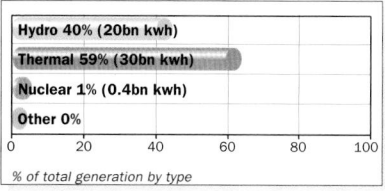

Hydro 40% (20bn kwh)
Thermal 59% (30bn kwh)
Nuclear 1% (0.4bn kwh)
Other 0%

% of total generation by type

Apart from cotton and rice, Pakistan's major resources are oil, coal, gas and water. The state hopes that the privatization of the utilities industries will reduce energy imports and shortages – peak electricity demand, for example, exceeds supply by 20%. Steps are being taken to attract more foreign investment in oil and gas exploration, extraction and distribution. Pakistan's current refining capacity of 150,000 b/d cannot meet the present 280,000 b/d demand, let alone the projected demand for 385,000 b/d by 1996.

PAKISTAN : LAND USE

Cropland, Pasture, Forest, Desert, Wetlands, High mountain regions, Sugarcane, Wheat, Cattle

ENVIRONMENT

 5% (3% partially protected)

2-year ban on logging

ENVIRONMENTAL TREATIES

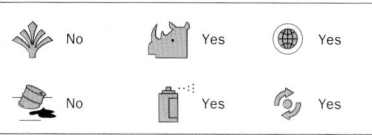

No / Yes / Yes / No / Yes / Yes

Revelations about large-scale illegal logging has led to a brief two-year ban. Green issues get little coverage; most concern is voiced by foreign NGOs

MEDIA

 No political censorship in theory

PUBLISHING AND BROADCAST MEDIA

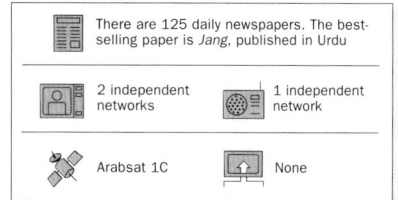

There are 125 daily newspapers. The best-selling paper is *Jang*, published in Urdu

2 independent networks / 1 independent network

Arabsat 1C / None

A ban on six Urdu newspapers in 1995 was revoked after strong protests from journalists.

EDUCATION

 38%

758,000 students

Education spending as % GNP
2.7%

THE EDUCATION SYSTEM

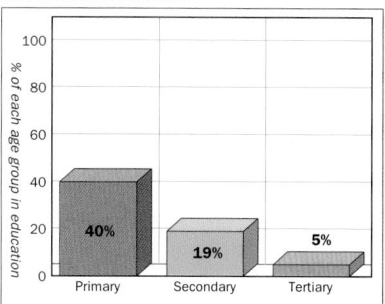

40% Primary / 19% Secondary / 5% Tertiary

The Pakistani education system is heavily Islamicized, and weighted toward educating males. Of the 8.9 million children enrolled in elementary schools in 1990, more than 5.8 million were boys. The 23 universities, 99 professional colleges and 675 arts and sciences colleges all have a heavy preponderance of arts students. Wealthy parents frequently choose to send their children abroad for higher education, mainly to colleges in the UK or USA.

HEALTH

 1 per 1,918 people

Malaria, tuberculosis, diarrheal diseases

Health spending as % GDP
1.8%

The availability of doctors and hospital beds is among the lowest in the world. In addition, there is a shortage of equipment and medicines, and uncontrolled counterfeit drugs are common. Pakistan has a high incidence of heroin addicts.

WEALTH

The *Peshgi* system of bonded labor traps millions in virtual slavery – 5 million in the notorious brick industry. Debt often passes down the generations

CONSUMER GOODS OWNERSHIP

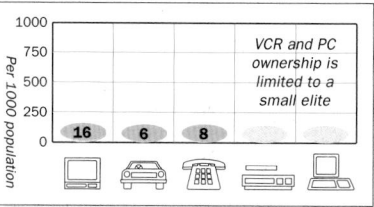

VCR and PC ownership is limited to a small elite
16 / 6 / 8

Members of the bureaucratic and political elite tend to be extremely rich, the top military less so. Bonded laborers, often Christians or recent converts to Islam, form the underclass.

CRIME

 44,640 prisoners

Crime levels at similarly high levels from year to year

CRIME RATES

Murders
78 per 100,000 population

Rapes
Pakistan does not publish rape statistics

Thefts
18 per 100,000 population

Compared to similar Islamic states, Pakistan has a high incidence of murder, kidnapping, rape, robbery and narcotics-trafficking. Corruption and the abuse of women (the latter usually unreported) are the main causes for concern. Torture of prisoners and deaths in custody are frequent, as is the rape of women prisoners in police lockups. The most dangerous area is Sind province, where the Mohajir Quami Movement has terrorized Karachi's residents since the army withdrew in 1994 after having been deployed since mid-1992. Heavily armed *dacoits* (bandits) still hold sway in the interior. Pressure from Islamic parties has forced the government in the North West Frontier Province to replace British-based civil law by the rulings of *sharia* courts.

WORLD RANKING

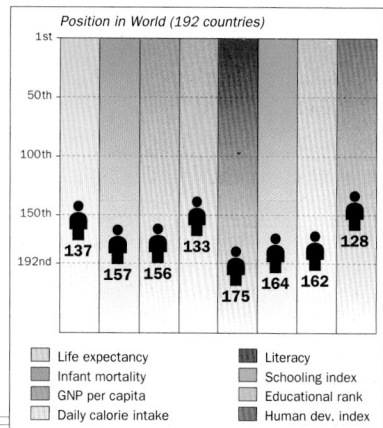

Position in World (192 countries)
137 / 157 / 156 / 133 / 175 / 164 / 162 / 128

Life expectancy / Infant mortality / GNP per capita / Daily calorie intake / Literacy / Schooling index / Educational rank / Human dev. index

PALAU

OFFICIAL NAME: Palau   CAPITAL: Koror   POPULATION: 16,200
CURRENCY: US dollar   OFFICIAL LANGUAGE: *No official language*

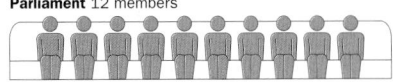

PACIFIC OCEAN

T HE REPUBLIC OF PALAU (also known as Belau) is situated in the western Pacific and comprises more than 200 islands in the Caroline Islands archipelago. Formerly a part of the US-administered Trust Territory of the Pacific Islands, Palau became independent in association with the USA in 1994, but continues to be heavily dependent on US aid.

CLIMATE

WEATHER CHART

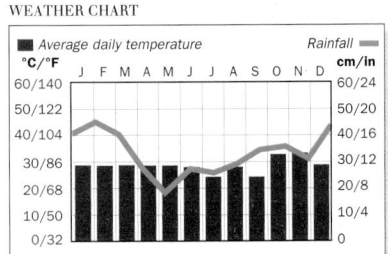

The islands are hot and humid and have a mean temperature of 81°F. Heavy rainfall occurs during two distinct wet seasons in July–August and December–January.

TRANSPORTATION

THE TRANSPORTATION NETWORK

22 miles (36 km)	None
None	None

Limited air links connect the islands, and local shipping is available for tourist and freight transportation.

TOURISM

MAIN OVERSEAS ARRIVALS

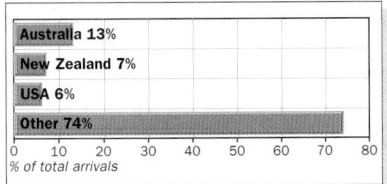

Australia 13%
New Zealand 7%
USA 6%
Other 74%
% of total arrivals

Tourism is growing, but remains underdeveloped because of poor communications and a lack of funding. Several islands have battle sites from the Pacific War. The outlying islands remain unspoilt.

PEOPLE

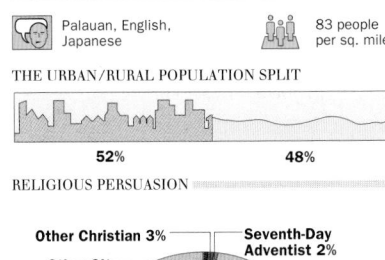

Palauan, English, Japanese

83 people per sq. mile

THE URBAN/RURAL POPULATION SPLIT

52%   48%

RELIGIOUS PERSUASION

Other Christian 3%
Seventh-Day Adventist 2%
Other 2%
Protestant 25%
Traditional 27%
Roman Catholic 41%

Palau, like other islands in the Pacific, is thought to have been originally settled by voyagers from Southeast Asia. More specifically, native Palauans are of Micronesian descent and, as inhabitants of the Caroline Islands, they are closely related to the people of the Federated States of Micronesia. Within Palau there are some ethnic and linguistic differences, with those in the most southerly islands speaking a separate language. Colonization by Spain, Germany, Japan and finally the US has also led to limited immigration to the islands from outside the region. Culturally, the population has been heavily Americanized by the years of US administration, although in the more remote islands people maintain a more traditional way of life and living conditions remain somewhat basic.

Palau's islands *have many idyllic beaches,* *but tourism remains underdeveloped due to a* *lack of resources and the country's remoteness.*

POLITICS

1992/1996

President Kuniwo Nakamura

THE STATE OF THE PARTIES

Parliament 12 members

There are no political parties. All members are independent candidates

Palau has a president who is directly elected for a four-year term and a bicameral National Congress. The power of the traditional chiefs is recognized through an advisory body to the president which is composed of the paramount chiefs of each of the country's 16 separate states. The Compact of Free Association, signed in 1982 – under which the USA granted internal sovereignty and aid in return for continuing control of the country's defense and foreign policies – has been the most important political issue of recent years.

WORLD AFFAIRS

SPC

Palau's most important relationship continues to be with the USA, which until 1994 administered the islands as part of the UN Trust Territory of the Pacific Islands. Under the conditions of the Compact of Free Association, the USA has exclusive control over the the country's foreign affairs as well as its defense policies.

AID

 $202m (receipts)
 Steady aid receipts

Palau's ecomomy is heavily dependent upon US aid. Those in the forefront of the campaign to amend the constitution stressed the importance of aid receipts in order to gain popular approval for the Compact. This protracted campaign was ultimately successful when the issue was approved by the Palau parliament.

DEFENSE

 There are no armed forces
 Not applicable

Under the Compact of Free Association, the USA is responsible for all Palau's defense measures.

P

ECONOMICS

 $81.8m

$ US dollar

SCORE CARD

- ❏ WORLD GNP RANKING........................191st
- ❏ GNP PER CAPITA $5,000
- ❏ BALANCE OF PAYMENTS...................$–24.6m
- ❏ INFLATION ....*Not available*
- ❏ UNEMPLOYMENT....................................20%

STRENGTHS

Access to US economy through preferential trading rights. Potential for expanding the tourism sector. Fishing and copra production. Some minerals (especially gold).

WEAKNESSES

Heavy dependence on US aid. High

RESOURCES

 22m kwh

 Not an oil producer and has no refineries

 Figures not available

 Gold, copra

On some islands the soil is highly fertile, although the terrain of the larger islands makes farming extremely difficult. Some islands are densely forested. Palau has some copra deposits, and possible reserves of unexploited seabed minerals. There are small quantities of gold. There is also a small fishing industry (of which shrimps are the main catch) which is considerably underdeveloped.

PALAU

Total Land Area : 508 sq. km
(196 sq. miles)

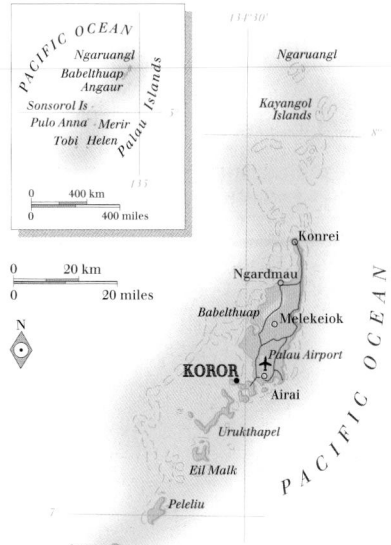

EXPORTS

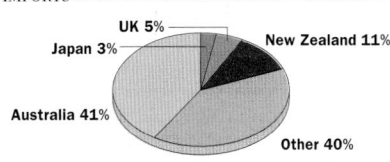

Palau does not publish export figures by country

IMPORTS

New Zealand 11%
UK 5%
Japan 3%
Australia 41%
Other 40%

levels of underemployment. Remote location. Limited resources for education. Aid dependent culture. Few natural resources. Reliance on exported goods.

ENVIRONMENT

 None

 Environmental issues not paramount

Palau suffers from inadequate facilities for the disposal of solid waste. There is also a significant threat to the marine ecosystem posed by sand and coral dredging, and by the illegal use of dynamite to catch fish. Typhoons sometimes cause severe damage to the inadequetely protected buildings in the main population centers, especially between June and December.

MEDIA

 No political restrictions

PUBLISHING AND BROADCAST MEDIA

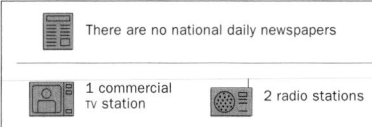

There are no national daily newspapers

1 commercial TV station

2 radio stations

The country's TV and radio stations tend to use material which is largely derived from the USA.

CRIME

 Palau does not publish prison figures

 Little change from year to year

There is a little alcohol-related crime, but much of the country, particularly the outlying islands, is crime-free.

EDUCATION

 92%

 305 students

Education is and compulsory between the ages of six and 14 years. The USA provides grants for students to attend US universities. There are no tertiary education facilities on the islands.

HEALTH

 83 per 1,000 people

 Heart, cerebrovascular and intestinal diseases

Basic health care is available, but most of the outlying islands do not have easy access to qualified doctors and often rely on nurses or traditional health remedies. Expatriates sometimes fly back to their home country for treatment.

WEALTH

 Small wealth disparities

CONSUMER GOODS OWNERSHIP

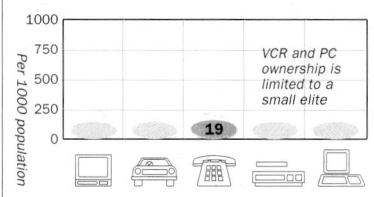

VCR and PC ownership is limited to a small elite

19

The gap between rich and poor is now becoming more marked as entrepreneurs and government officials exploit US aid and develop the tourist industry. Many Palauans lead a very basic, simple existence.

WORLD RANKING

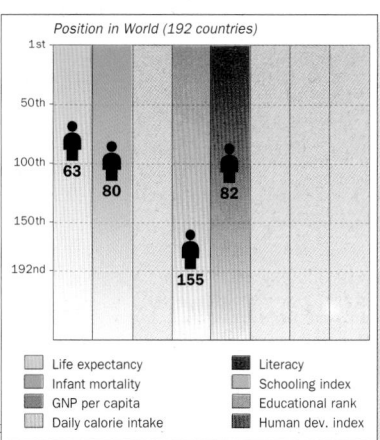

Position in World (192 countries)

63
80
82
155

- Life expectancy
- Infant mortality
- GNP per capita
- Daily calorie intake
- Literacy
- Schooling index
- Educational rank
- Human dev. index

P

PANAMA

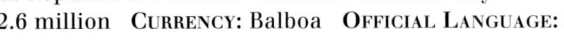

OFFICIAL NAME: Republic of Panama   CAPITAL: Panama City
POPULATION: 2.6 million   CURRENCY: Balboa   OFFICIAL LANGUAGE: Spanish

PANAMA IS THE SOUTHERNMOST of the seven countries occupying the isthmus that joins North and South America. The rainforests of the Darien peninsula are some of the wildest areas left in the Americas. Elected governments have held power since the US invasion of 1989. Panama's traditional economic strength is its banking sector. The USA is due to return control of the Panama Canal Zone to Panama in 2000.

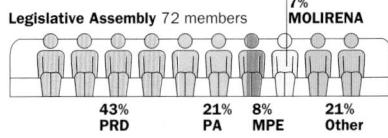

Cruise liner on the Panama Canal. The canal takes 2,976 miles off the otherwise shortest sea route from the east coast of the USA to Japan.

CLIMATE

WEATHER CHART

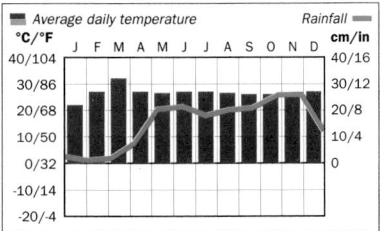

Panama has a humid tropical climate; rainfall is twice as heavy on the Caribbean coast as on the Pacific coast.

TRANSPORTATION

Tocumen Intl, Panama City
898,000 passengers

3,820 ships
79.31m dwt

THE TRANSPORTATION NETWORK

2,060 miles (3320 km)	Pan-American Highway 339 miles (545 km)
443 miles (737 km)	497 miles (800 km)

In tonnage, Panama has the world's second-largest merchant fleet, 40% of it owned by the Japanese. The 50-mile Panama Canal remains a key international waterway. Some 1,504 miles of roads need urgent repair.

TOURISM

 319,000 visitors    Up 7% in 1994

MAIN OVERSEAS ARRIVALS

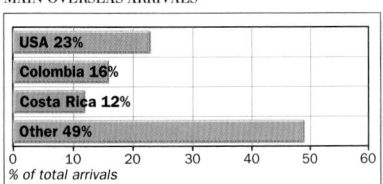

USA 23%	
Colombia 16%	
Costa Rica 12%	
Other 49%	

0 10 20 30 40 50 60
% of total arrivals

The bulk of tourism is from ships stopping at ports on the canal. A few ecotourists visit the rainforests.

PEOPLE

 Spanish, English Creole, Amerindian languages, Chibchan

88 people per sq. mile

THE URBAN/RURAL POPULATION SPLIT

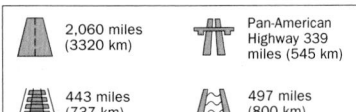

52%   48%

ETHNIC MAKEUP

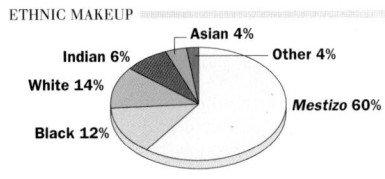

Asian 4%
Indian 6%
Other 4%
White 14%
Mestizo 60%
Black 12%

The northwest coast has a large black community, mostly descended from African immigrants who worked the plantations. The majority speak English Creole rather than Spanish. About 6% of the population are Indians from three main tribes, the Kunas, Guaymies and Chocoes. Roman Catholicism and the extended family remain strong, although the canal and US military bases have given society a more cosmopolitan outlook.

PANAMA

Total Land Area : 75 990 sq. km   (29 340 sq. miles)

POPULATION
⊙ over 500 000
◎ over 100 000
○ over 50 000
● over 10 000
· under 10 000

LAND HEIGHT
2000m/6562ft
1000m/3281ft
500m/1640ft
200m/656ft
Sea Level

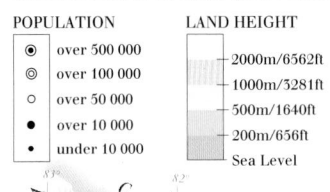

POLITICS

1994/1999

President Ernesto
Pérez Balladares

THE STATE OF THE PARTIES

Legislative Assembly 72 members

7% MOLIRENA

43% PRD   21% PA   8% MPE   21% Other

PRD = Democratic Revolutionary Party   PA = Arnulfista Party
MPE = Papa Egoro Movement   MOLIRENA = Nationalist Republican Liberal Movement

In 1989, the USA sent 23,000 troops into Panama and arrested its ruler, General Manuel Noriega, for narcotics smuggling. US forces seized power from the military and gave it to civilian politicians. Noriega was arrested and is now serving a life sentence in the USA. The government of President Endara, installed in 1989, was criticized for its failure to halt corruption. The 1994 presidential and congressional elections were won by Ernesto Balladares and the PRD, with the help of the British public relations firm, Saatchi and Saatchi. However, the PRD, Manuel Noriega's old party, fell short of a congressional majority. During the election campaign, the PRD toned down its previously anti-US views and now embraces free-market policies.

WORLD AFFAIRS

 ALADI Geplac NAM OAS San José

The possible extension of the US military presence after the Canal Zone reverts to Panama on December 31, 1999, to minimize the economic impact of a withdrawal, is a priority. Also important are canal-related investment, especially by Japan; cooperation with the US drugs policy; foreign debt reduction; WTO membership; regional trade.

AID

 $79m (receipts)   Down 50% in 1993

The USA is the largest donor. After the overthrow of Noriega in 1989, it provided a $480 million aid package.

DEFENSE

 $91m   Up 6% in 1995

The National Guard and defense forces were disbanded following the 1989 US invasion and were replaced by police numbering 11,800 in 1995. Panama is allied militarily to the USA and the main defense issue is the benefit to Panama of a possible permanent US military presence in the Canal Zone.

ECONOMICS

 $6.9bn   1.00 balboas

SCORE CARD

- ❏ World GNP Ranking 92nd
- ❏ GNP per Capita $2,670
- ❏ Balance of Payments ....$–1,209m
- ❏ Inflation 1.2%
- ❏ Unemployment................................12.5%

STRENGTHS

Banking institutions, providing secrecy for investors. Financial, insurance and other services built around this sector. Banana, shrimp exports and Colón Free Trade Zone. Merchant shipping payments for sailing under the Panamanian flag.

WEAKNESSES

History of political instability and corruption deters long-term investment. Large foreign debt, high unemployment, underemployment; poor infrastructure.

EXPORTS

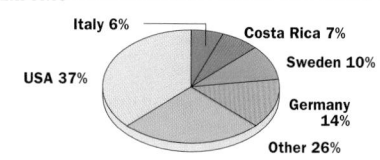

Italy 6%
Costa Rica 7%
Sweden 10%
USA 37%
Germany 14%
Other 26%

IMPORTS

Costa Rica 3%
Aruba 3%
Ecuador 4%
Japan 8%
Other 45%
USA 37%

ENVIRONMENT

 18%   More state concern over debt problems than the environment

The wholesale destruction of Panama's rainforests is proceeding at an increasingly rapid rate, resulting in widespread soil erosion. The Panama Canal is silting up with soil washed down from deforested areas. In addition, large numbers of rare bird and animal species are under threat. There are international protests over plans for the expansion of the massive Cerro Colorado copper mine.

RESOURCES

 3bn kwh (capacity 990,000 kw)   Not an oil producer; refines 100,000 b/cd

 1.4m cattle, 295,000 pigs, 150,000 horses   Copper, coal, gold, silver, manganese, salt, clay

Large copper deposits at Cerro Colorado have yet to be fully exploited. The government has stepped up hydroelectric production to reduce the country's dependence on oil imports; it claims 90% of power needs are now met in this way. Tropical hardwoods are being cut down at an alarming rate.

MEDIA

 The Inter-American Press Society in 1995 removed Panama from its list of countries respecting total press freedom

PUBLISHING AND BROADCAST MEDIA

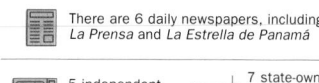

There are 6 daily newspapers, including *La Prensa* and *La Estrella de Panamá*

5 independent stations

7 state-owned, 89 independent stations

A more independent press has flourished since Noriega's overthrow. The US forces' TV network is popular.

CRIME

 Panama does not publish prison figures   Up 300% between 1989 and 1993

Panama City and Colón in particular are notorious for high levels of violence and muggings.

EDUCATION

 91%   63,288 students

Schooling is based on the US model. Provision for the urban poor, blacks and indigenous people is limited.

CHRONOLOGY

On independence from Spain in 1821, Panama was incorporated into Gran Colombia. Panama gained independence from Colombia with US support in 1903.

- ❏ **1903** USA buys concession for the construction of the Panama Canal.
- ❏ **1914** Canal opens to traffic.
- ❏ **1939** US protectorate status ended.
- ❏ **1968–1981** Administration of Colonel Torrijos Herrera.
- ❏ **1985** General Noriega indicted in USA on drugs-trafficking charges.
- ❏ **1989** Noriega annuls presidential elections and remains in power. US invasion. Endara, thought to have won elections, made president.
- ❏ **1994** The PRD's Ernesto Balladares wins presidential election. PRD largest party in parliament.

HEALTH

 1 per 845 people   Heart diseases, cancers, violence, accidents

Primary health care is accessible to around two-thirds of the rural population. The isolation of many villages hinders efforts to improve the system.

WEALTH

 Just under half the population live in poverty

CONSUMER GOODS OWNERSHIP

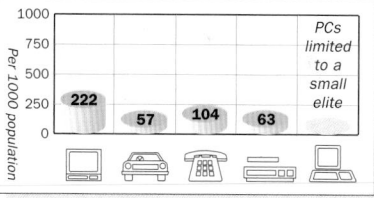

PCs limited to a small elite

222   57   104   63

The wealthier members of society tend to be bureaucrats. Poverty is centered in the cities rather than rural areas.

WORLD RANKING

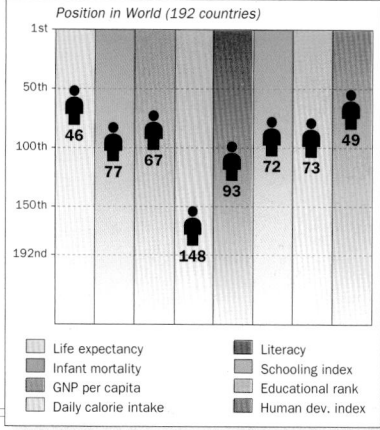

Position in World (192 countries)

46   77   67   93   72   73   49   148

- Life expectancy
- Infant mortality
- GNP per capita
- Daily calorie intake
- Literacy
- Schooling index
- Educational rank
- Human dev. index

PAPUA NEW GUINEA

OFFICIAL NAME: The Independent State of Papua New Guinea **CAPITAL:** Port Moresby
POPULATION: 4.3 million **CURRENCY:** Kina **OFFICIAL LANGUAGES:** Pidgin English and Motu

THE MOST LINGUISTICALLY diverse country in the world, where approximately 750 languages are spoken, Papua New Guinea (PNG) achieved independence from Australia in 1975. The country occupies the eastern end of the island of New Guinea, and several other groups of islands. Much of the country is still isolated; the majority of the rural population have the most basic of living conditions.

CLIMATE

WEATHER CHART

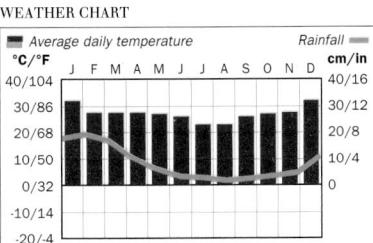

The unvarying heat of the lowlands decreases to snowfields on Mount Victoria. Rainfall is 78–195 in. a year.

TRANSPORTATION

 Jacksons, Port Moresby 745,000 passengers
 39 ships 47,100 dwt

THE TRANSPORTATION NETWORK

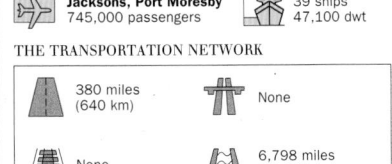

380 miles (640 km)	None
None	6,798 miles (10,940 km)

Plans exist to build a key road link between Port Moresby and the Lae–Mount Hagen road.

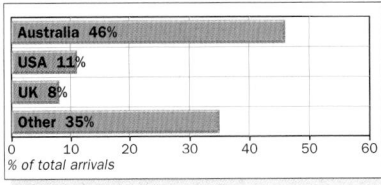

Volcano. Papua New Guinea's 600 or so outer islands are mainly high, volcanic islands with fringing coral reefs.

TOURISM

 39,000 visitors Down 3% in 1994

MAIN OVERSEAS ARRIVALS

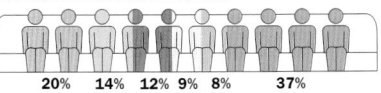

Australia 46%	
USA 11%	
UK 8%	
Other 35%	

% of total arrivals

Tourism is hampered by violent crime in urban centers. In more remote areas, native peoples are often pressured into performing for tourist groups.

PEOPLE

 Pidgin English, Papuan, English, Motu, 750 (est) native languages
23 people per sq. mile

THE URBAN/RURAL POPULATION SPLIT

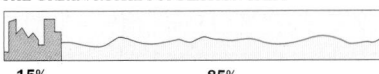

15% 85%

RELIGIOUS PERSUASION

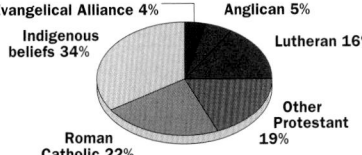

- Evangelical Alliance 4%
- Anglican 5%
- Indigenous beliefs 34%
- Lutheran 16%
- Other Protestant 19%
- Roman Catholic 22%

PNG has an extraordinary diversity of peoples, with around 750 different language groups and even more tribes. The key distinction is between the lowlanders, who have frequent contacts with the outside world, and the very isolated highlanders. Great tensions exist between highland tribes; anyone who is not a *wontok* (of one's tribe) is seen as potentially hostile. Vendettas can often last several generations and there are not infrequent tribal battles.

POLITICS

1992/1997 HM Queen Elizabeth II

THE STATE OF THE PARTIES

National Parliament 109 members

20% PP	14% PDM	12% PAP	9% PPP	8% MA	37% Other

PP = Pangu (Papua New Guinea Unity) Pati **PDM** = People's Democratic Movement **PAP** = People's Action Party **PPP** = People's Progress Party **MA** = Melanesian Alliance **Other** = League of National Advancement, National Party

PNG has a multiplicity of political parties, but in most cases they lack clear ideological foundations. Allegiance is to individuals and no coalition government has yet managed to complete a full term in office since independence. The patronage required to maintain these groupings greatly encourages corruption, as does the need to provide inducements for parties to enter and remain within governing coalitions. The main political issues include local government, land rights and resource exploitation. Strong local traditions and communications problems make greater centralization difficult to implement.

PAPUA NEW GUINEA

Total Land Area : 452 860 sq. km (174 849 sq. miles)

POPULATION

- ◎ over 100 000
- ○ over 50 000
- ● over 10 000
- • under 10 000

LAND HEIGHT

- 3000m/9843ft
- 2000m/6562ft
- 1000m/3281ft
- 500m/1640ft
- 200m/656ft
- Sea Level

0 200 km
0 200 miles

P

WORLD AFFAIRS

| APEC | Comm | NAM | SPC | SPF |

The main concern is the status of Bougainville, where secessionist rebels are active. Bougainvillians are bitter that they benefit little from Panguna, the world's largest copper mine, and have been waging a guerrilla war since 1988.

AID

 $303m (receipts)   Down 37% in 1993

Australian aid accounts for 20% of the PNG state budget. Japan has provided technical assistance.

DEFENSE

 $47.4m   Down 13% in 1995

Australia runs anti-submarine patrols throughout PNG's territorial waters and maintains military airfields inland.

ECONOMICS

 $4.9bn   1.18–1.33 kina

SCORE CARD

❑ WORLD GNP RANKING	103rd
❑ GNP PER CAPITA	$1,160
BALANCE OF PAYMENTS	$569m
❑ INFLATION	2.9%
❑ UNEMPLOYMENT	5%

STRENGTHS
Extensive copper resources, mainly controlled by the Australian Broken Hill group. Significant quantities of gold and other resources. Oil and gas reserves, now coming on-stream, and new gas discoveries, which have been made in the highlands.

WEAKNESSES
Copper production disrupted by rebels. Lack of economies of scale in cash-crop markets such as coffee and copra. Political instability. Impenetrable nature of much of the country's terrain.

EXPORTS

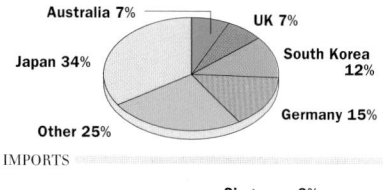

- Australia 7%
- UK 7%
- Japan 34%
- South Korea 12%
- Germany 15%
- Other 25%

IMPORTS

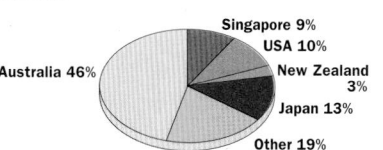

- Singapore 9%
- USA 10%
- Australia 46%
- New Zealand 3%
- Japan 13%
- Other 19%

RESOURCES

 1.8bn kwh (capacity 490,000 kw)

 Reserves of 340,000,000 bbl

 1m pigs, 105,000 cattle, 4,000 sheep, 2,000 horses

 Copper, gold, silver, natural gas, oil, chromite, cobalt

The world's largest copper mine, Panguna on Bougainville, has reserves of over 950 million tons. Ok Tedi in the Star Mountains is now the most productive copper mine. Porgera gold mine is one of the world's largest. Prospecting has revealed extensive oil and natural gas reserves.

ENVIRONMENT

 0.2%    Logging is on the increase

Some protection against development is provided by traditional PNG land laws, which attach a spiritual value to the land. Only 2% of land – mostly government-owned – is excluded from this system. The greatest problems are logging and heavy-metal pollution from the large mines.

MEDIA

 Freedom of speech is protected by law; the Bougainville uprising prompted limited censorship

PUBLISHING AND BROADCAST MEDIA

There are 2 daily newspapers, the *Papua New Guinea Post-Courier* and the *Niugini Nius*

2 independent services   1 state-owned service

Most villages have access to radio. Australian satellite TV can be received in Port Moresby and other major population centers.

CRIME

 PNG does not publish prison figures   Up 22% in 1992

Violent crime, by gangs known as "Rascals," is very common. Foreigners live amid tight security.

EDUCATION

 72%   6,397 students

Until 1975, all education was from religious missions. It is now state-funded with a university at Port Moresby.

HEALTH

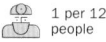 1 per 12,750 people   Malaria, pneumonia, diarrheal diseases

Hospital services are only available in Port Moresby. The barefoot doctor scheme, mostly run by women, has extended the net of state health care. However, the health system has suffered badly from recent cutbacks.

CHRONOLOGY

The British annexed the southeast and the Germans the southwest of the island of New Guinea in 1884.

- ❑ **1904** Australia takes over British sector; renamed Papua in 1906.
- ❑ **1914** German sector occupied by Australia.
- ❑ **1942–1945** Japanese occupation followed by Australian liberation.
- ❑ **1964** House of Assembly created, with elected indigenous majority.
- ❑ **1971** Renamed Papua New Guinea.
- ❑ **1975** Independence under Michael Somare, leader since 1972.
- ❑ **1985** State of emergency declared in Port Moresby as a result of ethnic unrest.
- ❑ **1988** Secessionist Bougainville Revolutionary Army (BRA) begins guerrilla campaign.
- ❑ **1994** The coalition government which had emerged from the 1992 general election is replaced by new coalition led by Sir Julius Chan.

WEALTH

 Water board administration manager, 18,000 kina ($13,482) per year

CONSUMER GOODS OWNERSHIP

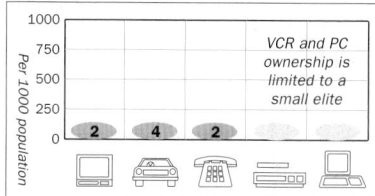

VCR and PC ownership is limited to a small elite

Per 1000 population: 2, 4, 2

Most Papua New Guineans are poor. There is little notion of individual wealth and those who make money in the mines and on plantations tend to divide their wealth among their tribes. PNG has few cars; Japanese motorbikes and pickups are favored.

WORLD RANKING

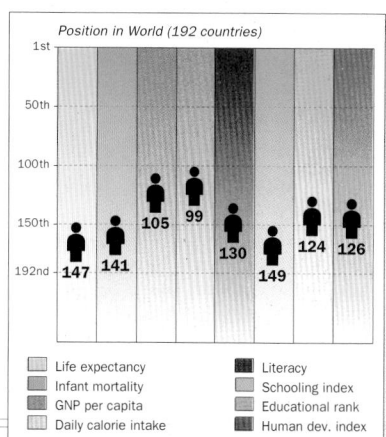

Position in World (192 countries)

147, 141, 105, 99, 130, 149, 124, 126

- Life expectancy
- Infant mortality
- GNP per capita
- Daily calorie intake
- Literacy
- Schooling index
- Educational rank
- Human dev. index

P

PARAGUAY

SOUTH AMERICA

OFFICIAL NAME: Republic of Paraguay   **CAPITAL:** Asunción
POPULATION: 5 million   **CURRENCY:** Guaraní   **OFFICIAL LANGUAGES:** Spanish and Guaraní

LANDLOCKED IN CENTRAL South America and a Spanish possession until 1811, Paraguay won large tracts of land from Bolivia in 1835. From then until the overthrow in 1989 of General Stroessner, South America's longest-surviving dictator, it experienced periods of anarchy and military rule. The River Paraguay divides the eastern hills and fertile plains, where 90% of people live, from the almost uninhabited Chaco in the west. Paraguay's economy is largely agricultural.

CLIMATE

WEATHER CHART

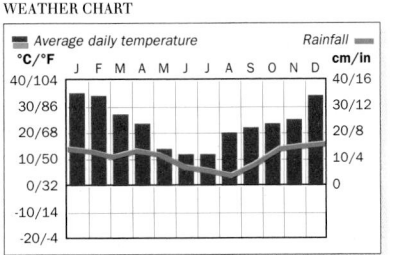

Paraguay is subtropical with all parts experiencing floods and droughts, but the Chaco is generally drier and hotter.

TRANSPORTATION

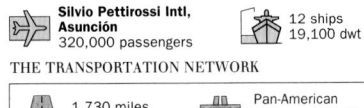

THE TRANSPORTATION NETWORK

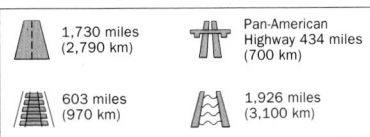

The state airline was privatized in 1994. Foreign investment is sought to upgrade roads and the antiquated railroads.

TOURISM

MAIN OVERSEAS ARRIVALS

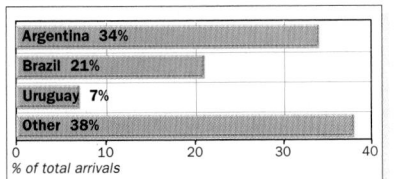

Tourism is low-level, except for large numbers of cross-border day-trippers from Brazil and Argentina, who flock to Ciudad del Este to buy cheap, mainly Far Eastern electrical goods. It is hoped the Chaco will entice ecotourists.

PEOPLE

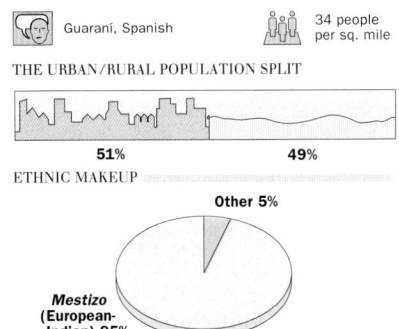

Guaraní, Spanish

34 people per sq. mile

THE URBAN/RURAL POPULATION SPLIT

51%   49%

ETHNIC MAKEUP

Other 5%

Mestizo (European-Indian) 95%

Tensions are few as most Paraguayans are of combined Spanish and native Guaraní origin. The majority are bilingual, although outside the large cities Guaraní is spoken almost exclusively. The vast Chaco is home to two-thirds of the small number of indigenous Indians. Many of the Indians have been deprived of their ancestral lands.

POLITICS

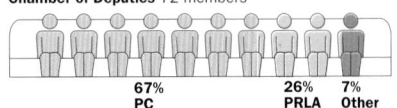

U. House 1993/1998
L. House 1993/1998
President Juan Carlos Wasmosy

THE STATE OF THE PARTIES

Chamber of Deputies 72 members

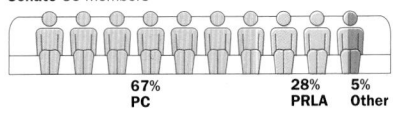

67% PC   26% PRLA   7% Other

PC = Colorado Party   **PRLA** = Authentic Radical Liberal Party
Other = Revolutionary Febrerista Party, Radical Liberal Party, Christian Democrat Party

Senate 36 members

67% PC   28% PRLA   5% Other

Disputes among the military elite about the succession, and economic discontent brought General Rodríguez to power in 1989 in a one-night coup that ended General Stroessner's 34-year military dictatorship. Rodríguez's promise to bring in democracy was fulfilled in 1993 in the first free elections in 60 years of military rule. The PC, Stroessner's old ruling party, although badly split, benefited from opposition complacency and used its extensive networks to retain power. President Wasmosy promised to strengthen democracy but bowed to military pressure on several occasions. He faces calls from peasants for land reform, and opposition to his privatization and free-market policies.

PARAGUAY

Total Land Area : 397 300 sq. km
(153 398 sq. miles)

POPULATION
◎ over 100 000
○ over 50 000
● over 10 000
• under 10 000

LAND HEIGHT
1000m/3281ft
500m/1640ft
200m/656ft
Sea Level

P

WORLD AFFAIRS

Main aims are integration in the MERCOSUR common market and improving relations with the USA and Europe.

AID

 $137m (receipts)   Up 38% in 1993

The World Bank gives development aid; the IMF conditional loans. NGO charities run small programs in rural areas.

DEFENSE

 $107m   Up 29% in 1995

Under Stroessner, the military controlled political and economic life. In 1994–1995, Congress tried to limit its powers but its political and institutional role has been endorsed by the actions of President Wasmosy. Military strongman General Lino Oviedo seems more intent on the presidency in 1998 than a coup.

ECONOMICS

 $7.6bn   1,913.77–1,962.50 guaranies

SCORE CARD

❑ WORLD GNP RANKING..........................87th
❑ GNP PER CAPITA $1,570
❑ BALANCE OF PAYMENTS...................$–749m
❑ INFLATION 20.6%
❑ UNEMPLOYMENT.................................5.1%

STRENGTHS
Electricity exporter – earnings cover oil imports. Self-sufficiency in wheat and other staple foodstuffs. Cotton, oilseeds, notably soy, exports.

WEAKNESSES
Very high reliance on agriculture – 30% of GDP, 90% of exports, 45% of labor force. Has virtually no minerals. Landlocked and remote. Slow growth. Dependent on growth sustained in neighboring countries.

EXPORTS
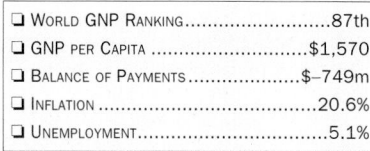

IMPORTS
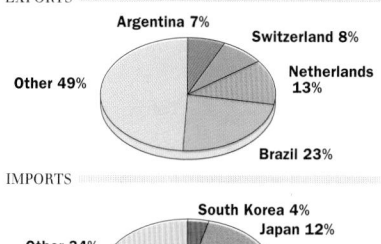

The Iguaçu Falls, *on the border with Brazil and Argentina, are composed of over 20 cataracts, separated by rocks and tree-covered islands.*

RESOURCES

 27.1bn kwh (capacity 5.8m kw)   Not an oil producer; refines 7,500 b/cd

 8m cattle, 3.3m pigs, 386,000 sheep, 370,000 horses   Gypsum, marble, clay, kaolin, iron, manganese, uranium

The joint Paraguay–Brazil Itaipú HEP project has the world's largest generating capacity. Paraguay now has an exportable electricity surplus.

ENVIRONMENT

 4%   Government has no environmental safeguard policies yet

Apart from the destruction of forests for farming, the chief ecological worry is the smuggling abroad of endangered species, particularly parrots.

MEDIA

 The press is free in theory and banned newspapers have reopened, but there have been some recent instances of shootings and beatings of journalists

PUBLISHING AND BROADCAST MEDIA

 There are 6 daily newspapers, including *ABC Color, Hoy, La Tribuna* and *Ultima Hora*

5 independent services   1 state-owned, 4 independent services

The media is generally sponsored by political parties. It flourished after the fall of Stroessner, publishing details of corruption and human rights abuses, but no longer concentrate on investigative reporting.

CRIME

 Paraguay does not publish prison figures   Up 2% in 1992

Paraguay is the contraband capital of Latin America, with trade in everything from cars to cocaine. Jungle airstrips near Brazil provide a route for narcotics.

EDUCATION

 92%    30,373 students

In 1992, 98% of children attended elementary school, but only 28% secondary school. Provision is limited in remote rural areas.

CHRONOLOGY

Paraguay was controlled by Spain from 1536 until 1811.

- ❑ **1864–1870** Loses War of the Triple Alliance against Argentina, Brazil and Uruguay; bloodiest ever in Latin America.
- ❑ **1928–1935** Two Chaco Wars against Bolivia; Paraguay wins most of the disputed land.
- ❑ **1954** Gen. Alfredo Stroessner seizes power; repressive military regime.
- ❑ **1984** Opposition demonstrations.
- ❑ **1989** Stroessner deposed by Gen. Andrés Rodríguez; democracy promised.
- ❑ **1991–1993** Brazil fails to pay Itaipú electricity royalties; in 1992 alone, these were to provide 25% of national budget.
- ❑ **1993** First democratic elections.

HEALTH

 1 per 1,260 people   Heart disease, cancers, obstetric causes, tuberculosis

Only one-third of the population has safe drinking water. Half of the country's hospital beds are located in Asunción.

WEALTH

 Kitchen assistant, 300,000 guaranies ($153) per month

CONSUMER GOODS OWNERSHIP

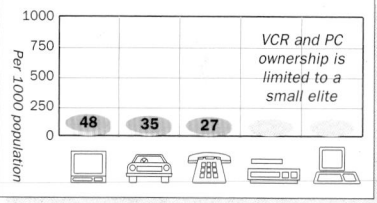

After having monopolized lucrative state contracts for 60 years, the top ranks of the military still control wealth.

WORLD RANKING

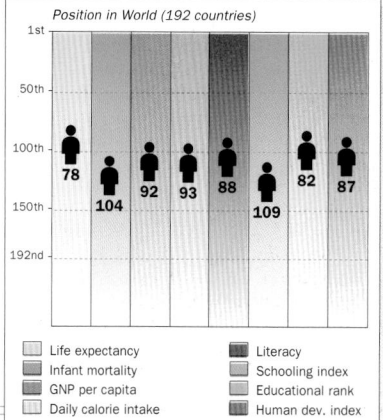

P

PERU

OFFICIAL NAME: Republic of Peru **CAPITAL:** Lima **POPULATION:** 23.8 million
CURRENCY: New sol **OFFICIAL LANGUAGES:** Spanish, Quechua and Aymará

LYING JUST SOUTH OF the equator, on the Pacific coast of South America, Peru became independent of Spain in 1824. It rises from an arid coastal strip to the Andes, dominated in the south by volcanoes; about half of the country's population live in mountain regions. Its border with Bolivia to the south runs through Lake Titicaca, the highest navigable lake in the world. In 1995, Peru was involved in a brief border war with its northern neighbor, Ecuador.

CLIMATE

WEATHER CHART

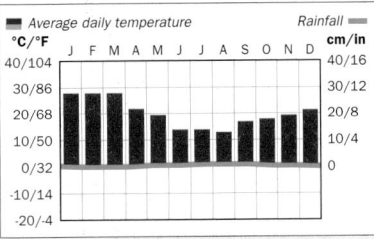

Peru has several distinct climatic regions. The arid or desert coastal region experiences the *garúa*, persistent low cloud and fog, giving Lima cool winters even though it is close to the equator. The temperate slopes of the Andes have large daily temperature ranges and one rainy season, while the tropical Amazon Basin receives year-round rains.

TRANSPORTATION

Jorge Chávez International, Lima
2.57m passengers

35 ships
519,900 dwt

THE TRANSPORTATION NETWORK

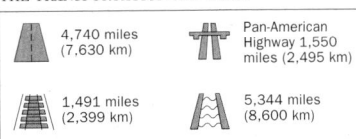

4,740 miles (7,630 km)

Pan-American Highway 1,550 miles (2,495 km)

1,491 miles (2,399 km)

5,344 miles (8,600 km)

The government is resurfacing some of the road network (most is unpaved and subject to landslides during the rains), and rebuilding bridges destroyed in the guerrilla war with *Sendero Luminoso*. Work has begun on a transcontinental highway from Ilo, a free port on the Pacific, via Puerto Suárez in Bolivia, to the port of Portos in Brazil. The two rail networks, the Central and Southern, are as yet unconnected. The La Oroya–Huancayo line is the world's highest stretch of standard-gauge railroad. River transportation provides major access to Iquitos in Amazonia. There are over 130 airports.

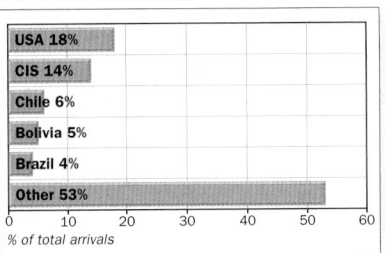

Spanish colonial church near Urubamba. The River Urubamba with its deep gorges was known as the Sacred Valley to the Incas.

TOURISM

 295,000 visitors  Up 8% in 1994

MAIN OVERSEAS ARRIVALS

USA 18%	
CIS 14%	
Chile 6%	
Bolivia 5%	
Brazil 4%	
Other 53%	

% of total arrivals

Tourism, plunged into crisis in the early 1990s by guerrilla activity, crime and cholera fears, is gradually recovering but the heavily indebted industry is unable to take full advantage of new investment opportunities. Visitors face poor infrastructure and accommodation to see incomparable sites such as Machu Picchu, the world-famous Inca city ruins in the Andes at the end of the 20-mile *Camino Inca*. Ecotourism to the Amazon is also growing, but some environmentalists object that indigenous families are being forced to work, dance and produce handicrafts for tourists. The pre-Colombian areas cleared in patterns in the desert by the Nazca civilization (known as the Nazca lines), dating from the 2nd century BC, are another major attraction.

PEOPLE

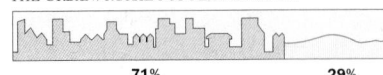 Spanish, Quechua, Aymará

49 people per sq. mile

THE URBAN/RURAL POPULATION SPLIT

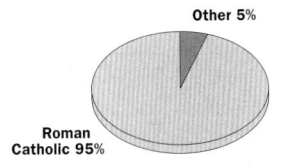

71%   29%

RELIGIOUS PERSUASION

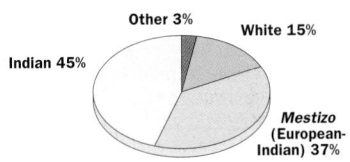

Other 5%
Roman Catholic 95%

ETHNIC MAKEUP

Other 3% White 15%
Indian 45%
Mestizo (European-Indian) 37%

The majority of Peruvians are Indian or *mestizo*. The small elite of Spanish descendants retain a strong hold on the economy, power and social standing. A few Chinese and Japanese live in the northern cities.

Previously remote Andean Indians are now increasingly informed of developments in Lima and the coastal strip by ethnic radio and relatives in urban slums. This has compensated for the problems associated with the marginalization of their native Quechua and Aymará languages in a Spanish-speaking culture. A further 250,000 Amazonian Indians live in the eastern lowlands. Together with the small community of blacks (descendants of plantation workers), they tend to suffer the worst discrimination in towns.

The extended family remains strong. A part of traditional native Indian traditions, its role as a social bond was strengthened by Catholicism. In recent years, economic difficulties have raised its profile as the key social support system for most Peruvians.

POPULATION AGE BREAKDOWN

% of population by age group	0–14	15–64	65+
65+	3.5%	3.4%	3.5%	3.6%	3.8%
15–64	54.9%	53.3%	52.5%	64.6%	58.6%
0–14	41.6%	43.3%	44%	31.8%	37.6%
	1950	1960	1970	1980	1990

POLITICS

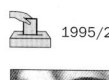 1995/2000

 President Alberto Keinya Fujimori

President Fujimori. *His dismissal of parliament was widely approved.*

Former UN Secretary General *Pérez de Cuéllar, presidential candidate in 1995.*

THE STATE OF THE PARTIES

National Congress 120 members

| 56% NM–C90 | 14% UPP | 7% APRA | 5% FIM | 18% Other |

NM–C90 = New Majority–Change-90   **UPP** = Union for Peru
APRA = American Popular Revolutonary Alliance
FIM = Independent Moralizing Front

Peru is nominally a multiparty democracy in which the president holds executive power.

MAIN POLITICAL ISSUES
Sendero Luminoso
The Maoist *Sendero Luminoso* (Shining Path) embarked on a guerrilla war in 1980 which has claimed over 30,000 lives. A fierce military response and the capture in 1992 of Abimael Guzmán, Sendero's leader, appear to have defeated the guerrillas militarily and politically. The group is badly split and only some 500 remain active, mostly in remote Andean and Amazonian areas. Lack of democracy, corruption, massive social and economic inequalities, and human rights abuses by the military could lead to a *Sendero* revival.

Democracy
In April 1992, President Fujimori, backed by the army, dismissed parliament, replacing it with an unelected Constituent Congress. He also introduced a new constitution allowing him to run again for election in 1995. Most Peruvians initially accepted his coup as being necessary for strong government and the fight against *Sendero* terrorism, but a submissive Congress, docile judiciary and state-managed media have increased opposition to Fujimori's concentration of power.

Debt and privatization
Modernization and investment hinge on the successful completion of negotiations with foreign creditors to reschedule Peru's $30 billion total foreign debt and the continuation of the government's privatization program, opposition to which is growing. Important sections of the military oppose the sale of the strategic state oil company Petroperu.

PROFILE
President Fujimori ended the tradition of large parties dominating politics by winning the 1990 presidential elections with a loose coalition. His 1992 "self-coup" closed Congress and the judiciary. After international protests, a new constitution created a compliant legislature and allowed his reelection in 1995. His defeat of hyperinflation and his onslaught on the *Sendero Luminoso* boosted his popularity, but his standing has since plummeted as he has tightened his control on power. Few checks on the executive remain as Fujimori's alliance of convenience with the military continues to marginalize the political parties, the discredited judiciary, local government and the trade unions.

CHRONOLOGY
Francisco Pizarro's arrival in 1532 during a war of succession between two Inca rulers marked the beginning of the Spanish colonization of Peru, and the end of the Inca empire.

❑ **1821** Independence proclaimed in Lima after its capture by the Argentine liberator, José de San Martín, who had just freed Chile.

❑ **1824** Spain suffers final defeats at battles of Junín and Ayacucho by Simón Bolívar and Gen Sucre, Venezuela and Colombia's liberators.

❑ **1836–1839** Peru and Bolivia joined in short-lived confederation.

❑ **1866** Peruvian–Spanish War.

❑ **1879–1884** War of the Pacific. Chile defeats Peru and Bolivia. Peru loses territory in south.

❑ **1908** Augusto Leguía y Salcedo's dictatorial rule.

❑ **1924** Dr. Víctor Raúl Haya de la Torre founds left-wing nationalist American Revolutionary Popular Alliance (APRA) in exile in Mexico.

❑ **1930** Leguía ousted. APRA moves to Peru as first political party.

❑ **1931–1945** APRA banned.

❑ **1939–1945** Moderate, pro-US civilian government.

❑ **1948–1956** Gen. Manuel Odría in power. APRA banned again.

❑ **1956–1962** Civilian government.

❑ **1962–1963** Two military coups.

❑ **1963** Election of Fernando Belaúnde Terry. Land reform, but military used to suppress communist-inspired insurgency. ➡

PERU

Total Land Area : 1 280 000 sq. km (494 208 sq. miles)

POPULATION
- ⊡ over 1 000 000
- ⊙ over 500 000
- ◎ over 100 000
- ○ over 50 000
- • under 50 000

LAND HEIGHT
- 4000m/13124ft
- 2000m/6562ft
- 500m/1640ft
- Sea Level

P

P

CHRONOLOGY *continued*

- ❑ **1968** Military junta takes over. Attempts to alleviate poverty. Large-scale nationalizations.
- ❑ **1975–1978** New right-wing junta.
- ❑ **1980** Belaúnde reelected. Popular Action (AP) wins majority. Maoist guerrilla organization, *Sendero Luminoso* (Shining Path), begins armed struggle.
- ❑ **1981** Border war with Ecuador over Cordillera del Cóndor, which a 1942 protocol had given to Peru. Ecuador wants access to Amazon.
- ❑ **1982** Deaths and "disappearances" start to escalate as army cracks down on guerrillas and narcotics.
- ❑ **1985** Electoral win for left-wing APRA under Alán García Pérez.
- ❑ **1987** Peru bankrupt. Guzmán's plans to nationalize banks blocked by new *Libertad* (Freedom) movement led by writer Mario Vargas Llosa.
- ❑ **1990** Over 3,000 political murders. Alberto Fujimori, an independent, is elected president on anti-corruption platform. Economic austerity program sends some food prices up 600%.
- ❑ **1991** Cholera epidemic.
- ❑ **1992** President Fujimori suspends democracy in a "self coup" – *auto golpe* – and establishes Constituent Congress. New constitution.
- ❑ **1995** Fujimori reelected.

WORLD AFFAIRS

 AG | Ama Pac | NAM | OAC | RG

Development is tied to the *imprimatur* and funds of multilateral financial institutions. Cooperation with the USA, the main source of aid, extends to the war on cocaine, although Peru remains the world's largest producer of coca. Peru seeks to strengthen its regional links, those with countries on the Pacific Rim, especially Japan, and with the EU. A border dispute with Ecuador, which led to war in 1995, remains unresolved.

AID

💲 $560m (receipts) ⬆ Up 34% in 1993

Aid provided by the USA has been mostly to help combat narcotics. The World Bank and Japan grant significant aid for infrastructure and food production projects. NGOs and Catholic charities have been active on a small scale in rural areas.

DEFENSE

💲 $784m   ⬆ Up 5% in 1995

0   *Defense spending as % GDP*   40
1.8%

PERUVIAN ARMED FORCES

🛡	300 main battle tanks (T-54/T-55)	75,000 personnel
⚓	6 submarines, 5 destroyers, 4 frigates, 7 patrol boats	25,000 personnel
✈	90 combat aircraft (15 *Canberra*, 20 *Mirage*)	15,000 personnel
	None	

The military, in power from 1968 to 1980, supported President Fujimori's 1992 presidential coup. It continues to exert a powerful influence in politics and currently holds sway in the quarter of the national territory which remains under a state of emergency. Fujimori's control over promotions and the National Intelligence Service (SIN) guarantees a loyal armed forces leadership, as does his 1995 amnesty law which protects the military from human rights charges. Spending curbs, the removal of the military from anti-narcotics efforts owing to corruption, and Chilean interest in the sale of the strategic Petroperu have caused widespread bitterness.

ECONOMICS

📊 $44.1bn   💲 2.18–2.30 new soles

SCORE CARD

- ❑ WORLD GNP RANKING..........................48th
- ❑ GNP PER CAPITA $1,890
- ❑ BALANCE OF PAYMENTS....................$–2.3bn
- ❑ INFLATION 10.5%
- ❑ UNEMPLOYMENT...................................10%

EXPORTS

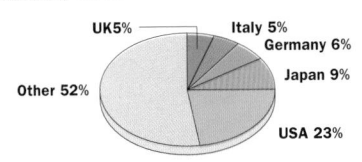

- UK 5%
- Italy 5%
- Germany 6%
- Japan 9%
- USA 23%
- Other 52%

IMPORTS

- Brazil 6%
- Colombia 6%
- Argentina 7%
- Japan 8%
- USA 30%
- Other 43%

STRENGTHS

Abundant mineral resources, including oil. Rich fish stocks in the Pacific. Wide variety of climates allowing diverse and productive agriculture; cotton and coffee are important. Well-developed textile industry.

WEAKNESSES

Dependency in the medium-term on international loans. High debt service. Corrupt judiciary, lack of modernization of armed forces and poor infrastructure deter investment. High levels of poverty.

PROFILE

Wealth and economic activity in Peru are largely confined to the cities of the coastal plain. The inhabitants of the Andean uplands are subsistence farmers or coca producers.

ECONOMIC PERFORMANCE INDICATOR

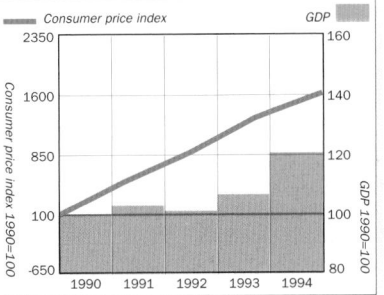

Consumer price index   GDP

Since Peru's bankruptcy under the center-left APRA administration of Alan García, the Fujimori government, under a severe IMF-sponsored austerity program, has ended hyperinflation and promoted the fastest rate of economic growth in Latin America. Privatization of state assets has raised $5 billion since 1991 and a $1 billion target is set for 1996. However, the country remains one of the most in debt in Latin America and macroeconomic policy is virtually dictated by the IMF.

PERU : MAJOR BUSINESSES

- 🛢 Oil
- Oil refining
- Textiles
- Mining
- Fish processing
- Food processing
- Vehicle assembly

0   400 km
0   400 miles

* significant multinational ownership

RESOURCES

 12bn kwh (capacity 4.1m kw)

 124,290 b/d (reserves 380,866,000 bbl)

11.6m sheep, 4m cattle, 2.4m pigs, 1.7m goats

 Oil, coal, lead, zinc, silver, iron, gold, copper

ELECTRICITY GENERATION

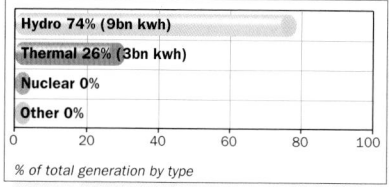

Hydro 74% (9bn kwh)
Thermal 26% (3bn kwh)
Nuclear 0%
Other 0%

% of total generation by type

Peru is an important exporter of copper and lead. Further exploration is required to establish the true extent of its large oil reserves. The state oil concern, Petroperu, is being privatized to attract new investment into the industry. The further development of hydroelectric power is a priority.

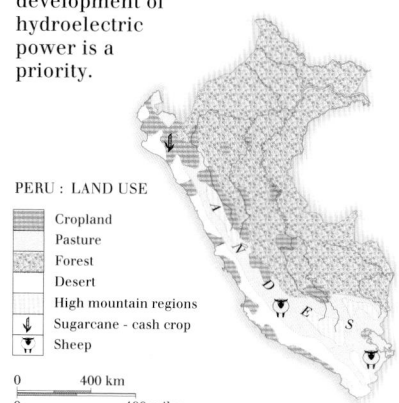

PERU : LAND USE

Cropland
Pasture
Forest
Desert
High mountain regions
Sugarcane - cash crop
Sheep

0   400 km
0   400 miles

ENVIRONMENT

 3%

 Unacceptable levels of coastal and Andean region pollution

ENVIRONMENTAL TREATIES

Yes   Yes   Yes
No   Yes   Yes

Environmentalists have long been concerned about coastal industrial pollution and the activities of its fishing industry. Overfishing of anchovies almost resulted in their extinction in the 1970s. Today, attention has switched to the rise in the number of dolphins being caught in drift nets. Dolphin meat is being sold as a cheap alternative to pork and beef in Peruvian markets.

Environmentalists fear that Peru's and the USA's policy of using air-sprayed herbicides to destroy the coca crops is adding to river pollution in the Andes, where mining also causes severe environmental problems.

MEDIA

 Press freedom is theoretically guaranteed. In practice, the media is expected to denounce terrorists and keep silent on human rights abuses

PUBLISHING AND BROADCAST MEDIA

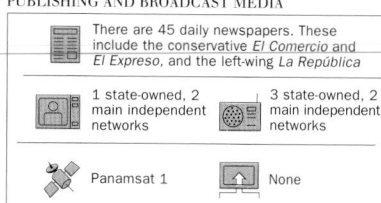

There are 45 daily newspapers. These include the conservative *El Comercio* and *El Expreso*, and the left-wing *La República*

1 state-owned, 2 main independent networks

3 state-owned, 2 main independent networks

Panamsat 1

None

Media freedom is severely restricted. Journalists and newspaper editors regularly receive death threats.

CRIME

 17,368 prisoners

 Up 15% in 1992

CRIME RATES

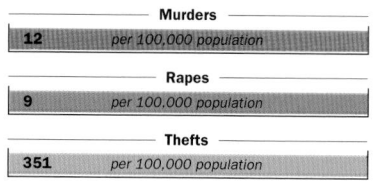

Murders
12   *per 100,000 population*

Rapes
9   *per 100,000 population*

Thefts
351   *per 100,000 population*

Random bombings, kidnappings and shoot-outs with security forces remain problems in Peru. Main cities still have curfews and those who can afford it protect themselves with high-security homes and armed guards.

In the Andes, where *Sendero Luminoso* has been active, military law has suspended normal rights. Since 1980, over 30,000 have died as a result of guerrilla and army violence.

EDUCATION

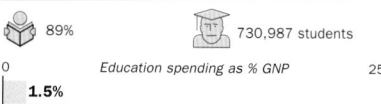 89%   730,987 students

0   Education spending as % GNP   25
1.5%

THE EDUCATION SYSTEM

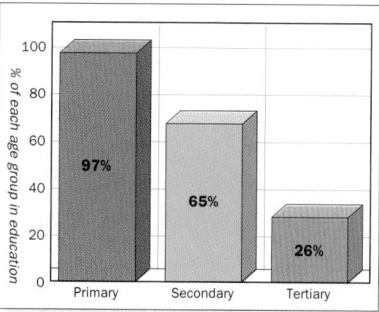

% of each age group in education

Primary 97%
Secondary 65%
Tertiary 26%

Education is based on the US system. Spending has been declining. The state and private university system is accessible to a small minority.

HEALTH

 1 per 940 people

 Respiratory, heart, infectious and parasitic diseases

0   Health spending as % GDP   25
1.9%

Peru's public health system virtually collapsed in the late 1980s. In many areas primary care is now non-existent. Advanced treatment is available only to private patients in city clinics. Goiter, a thyroid abnormality, is widespread, with a 38% prevalence among children in mountain areas; in some regions the incidence may be as high as 90%. Infant mortality is rising, the result of increasing social deprivation, diarrheal diseases and tuberculosis. Malaria is once again widespread, and cholera returned in 1991, reaching epidemic proportions by 1994.

WEALTH

 Chemical industry machine operator, 45 new soles ($20) per week; journalist, 377 new soles ($164) per month

CONSUMER GOODS OWNERSHIP

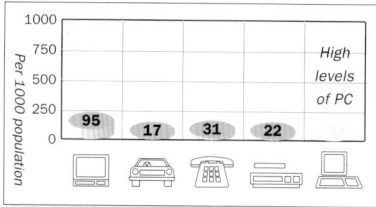

Per 1000 population

High levels of PC

95   17   31   22

Most wealth and power in Peru is still held by old Spanish families. Indigenous peoples remain excluded from both. The wealthy in Peru live in a state of siege; a key status symbol is the number of armed guards and security cameras protecting family property. German cars – Mercedes or BMWs – are now more fashionable than American ones, while San Francisco and Miami have replaced Paris and Rome as fashionable destinations. The UN estimates that over 30% of Peruvians live below the poverty line.

WORLD RANKING

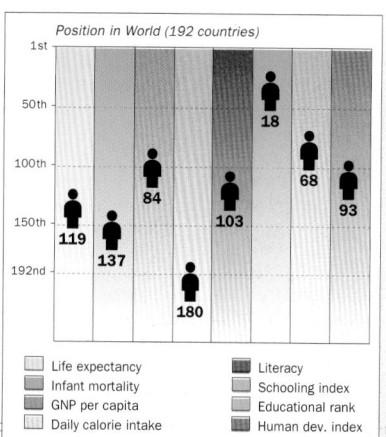

Position in World (192 countries)

1st
50th
100th
150th
192nd

119   137   84   180   103   18   68   93

Life expectancy
Infant mortality
GNP per capita
Daily calorie intake
Literacy
Schooling index
Educational rank
Human dev. index

P

PHILIPPINES

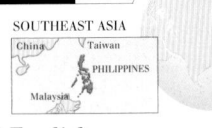

SOUTHEAST ASIA
China · Taiwan
PHILIPPINES
Malaysia
Asia

OFFICIAL NAME: Republic of the Philippines **CAPITAL:** Manila
POPULATION: 67.6 million **CURRENCY:** Philippine peso **OFFICIAL LANGUAGES:** Pilipino and English

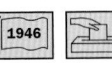

LYING IN THE WESTERN Pacific Ocean, the Philippines is the world's second-largest archipelago after Indonesia. It comprises 7,107 islands, of which 4,600 are named and 1,000 inhabited. There are three main island groupings: the Luzon group, the Visayan group, and the Mindanao and Sulu islands. Located on the Pacific "ring of fire," the Philippines is subject to frequent earthquakes and volcanic activity. Since 1992, President Fidel Ramos has worked hard to bring political stability to the country. However, economic expansion continues to fall short of the Philippines' population growth rate.

Bohol Island has over 1,000 of these famous mounds, also known as "the chocolate hills."

CLIMATE

WEATHER CHART

■ Average daily temperature   Rainfall

°C/°F   J F M A M J J A S O N D   cm/in
60/140   60/24
50/122   50/20
40/104   40/16
30/86   30/12
20/68   20/8
10/50   10/4
0/32   0

The Philippines is warm and humid all year round. The rainy season lasts from June to October. Humidity is 85% in September, falling to 71% in March.

TRANSPORTATION

 Nino Aquino Intl, Pasay City 6.44m passengers

 834 ships 13.67m dwt

THE TRANSPORTATION NETWORK

13,980 miles (22,490 km)		None	
500 miles (805 km)		2,000 miles (3,219 km)	

Spending on transportation infrastructure has fallen by over 40% since 1984. As a result, many main roads are in need of repair. Traffic jams in Manila are a growing problem and are holding back economic growth. Air transportation is the only means of getting around the islands quickly.

In 1992, the state airline, Philippines Airlines, was privatized. It is planning to buy $1.2 billion-worth of new aircraft and to add to its regional route network. Subic Bay, the USA's largest overseas base until 1992, when the US navy decided to leave, has a prime strategic location, which the government is now exploiting. Opening onto the South China Sea, its deep natural harbor is being developed as a free port and enterprise zone. The Taiwanese are the biggest investors in this project.

TOURISM

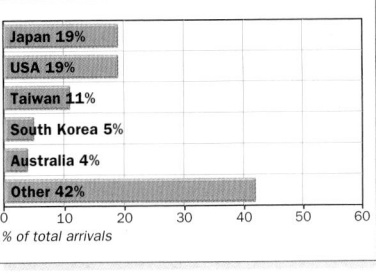 1.4m visitors   Up 13% in 1994

MAIN OVERSEAS ARRIVALS

Japan 19%	
USA 19%	
Taiwan 11%	
South Korea 5%	
Australia 4%	
Other 42%	

0   10   20   30   40   50   60
% of total arrivals

Tourism remains a smaller business in the Philippines than in the NICs of Southeast Asia. The industry is still largely based around sex-tourism, though this received a setback when an Australian law banning its citizens from sex-tourism holidays came into effect. Many of the islands have tourism potential. Palawan retains most of its tropical rainforest and coral lagoons.

The rice terraces of northern Luzon are another attraction.

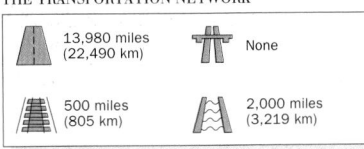

PHILIPPINES

Total Area : 500 000 sq. km (777 001 sq. miles)

POPULATION
⊡ over 1 000 000
◉ over 500 000
◎ over 100 000

LAND HEIGHT
2000m/6562ft
1000m/3281ft
500m/1640ft
200m/656ft
Sea Level

Batan Is
Babuyan Is
Babuyan Channel
Cordillera Central
Cagayan
Sierra Madre
Lingayen Gulf
Dagupan
Baguio
San Carlos
Tarlac
Luzon
Angeles
Cabanatuan City
San Fernando
Olongapo
Malolos
Subic Bay
San Juan del Monte
Polillo Is
Calagua Is
MANILA
Laguna de Bay
Muntinlupa
Lucena
San Pablo
Batangas
Lipa
Lubang I.
Naga
Catanduanes I.
Mindoro Strait
Marinduque I.
Burias I.
Legaspi
Mindoro
Busuanga I.
Calamian Group
Tablas I.
Sibuyan I.
Culion I.
Semirara Is
Jintotolo Channel
Masbate
Quiniluban Group
Panay
Biliran I.
Visayan Sea
Samar
Cuyo Is
Cuyo West Passage
Iloilo
Cadiz
Ormoc
Tacloban
Palawan
Silay
Sagay
Leyte Gulf
Bacolod
Toledo
Leyte
Bago
Mandaue
Dinagat I.
Panay Gulf
Cebu
Siargao I.
Puerto Princesa
San Carlos City
Cebu
Bohol
Cagayan Is
Negros
Bohol Sea
Butuan
Cagayan de Oro
Balabac I.
SULU SEA
Iligan
Lake Lanao
Mindanao
Agusan
Mindanao Mountains
Davao
Balabac Strait
Moro Gulf
Zamboanga
Basilan I.
Mount Apo 2054m
Pangutaran Group
Pilas Group
Tapiantana Group
Davao Gulf
Jolo I.
Jolo Group
Samales Group
General Santos
Tawi-Tawi
Tapul Group
Sarangani I.
Tawi-Tawi Group
SULU ARCHIPELAGO
(BORNEO)
CELEBES SEA

SOUTH CHINA SEA
PHILIPPINE SEA

N
200 km
0   200 miles

PEOPLE

Pilipino, Cebuano, Hiligaynon, Samaran, Ilocano, Bikol, English

588 people per sq. mile

THE URBAN/RURAL POPULATION SPLIT

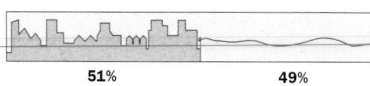

51%   49%

The Philippines encompasses over 100 distinct ethnic groups. The majority of Filipinos are of Malay origin, and Christian. Most Christians belong to the Tagalog, Cebuano, Llocan, Longgo, Bicolano, Waray, Pampangueno or Pangasinense ethnic groups. They are concentrated on the main island, Luzon, and are a majority on Mindanao. Most Muslims also live on Mindanao, but many are also found in the Sulu archipelago. The Chinese minority, which was well established by 1603, has remained significant in business and trade. Over 120 Chinese schools have ensured that it has retained a distinct identity.

There are also a number of cultural minorities who practise animist

RELIGIOUS PERSUASION

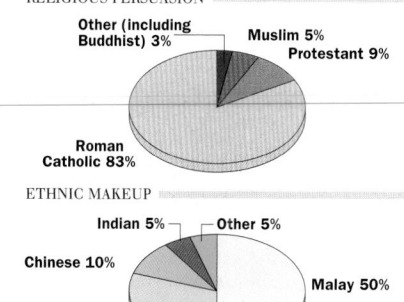

Other (including Buddhist) 3%
Muslim 5%
Protestant 9%
Roman Catholic 83%

ETHNIC MAKEUP

Indian 5%
Other 5%
Chinese 10%
Malay 50%
Indonesian and Polynesian 30%

religions. They include the Ifugaos, Bontocks, Kalingas and Ibalois on Luzon, the Manobo and Bukidnon on Mindanao and the Mangyans on Palawan. Many of these groups speak Malayo–Polynesian dialects. Limited intermarriage with other peoples has meant that groups in the more remote regions have managed to retain their traditional ways of life.

POPULATION AGE BREAKDOWN

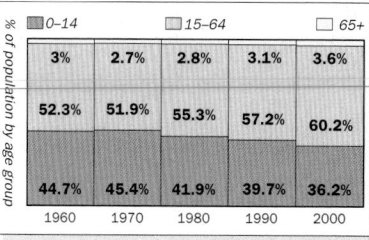

% of population by age group	0–14	15–64	65+
	1960	1970	1980	1990	2000
65+	3%	2.7%	2.8%	3.1%	3.6%
15–64	52.3%	51.9%	55.3%	57.2%	60.2%
0–14	44.7%	45.4%	41.9%	39.7%	36.2%

The Philippines is the only Christian state in Asia; over 80% of Filipinos are Roman Catholics and the Church is the dominant cultural force in the country. It opposes state-sponsored family planning programs, designed to curb accelerating population growth, currently at 2% a year.

Women have traditionally played a prominent part in Philippine life. Inheritance laws give them equal rights to men. Many go into politics, banking and business, and in several professions women form a majority.

POLITICS

U. House 1995/1998
L. House 1995/1998
President Gen. Fidel Ramos

THE STATE OF THE PARTIES

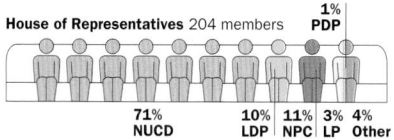

House of Representatives 204 members
1% PDP
71% NUCD | 10% LDP | 11% NPC | 3% LP | 4% Other

NUCD = Lakas - National Union of Christian Democrats
LDP = People's Power Movement of the Democratic Philippines   NPC = National People's Coalition   LP = Liberal Party   PDP-Laban = Filipino Democratic Party - Laban
PRP = People's Reform Party

Senate 24 members
4% NPC
63% LDP | 25% NUCD | 8% PRP

The Philippines is a multiparty democracy.

MAIN POLITICAL ISSUES
Power cuts
The 1986–1992 Aquino administration neglected investment in power stations. As a result, the Philippines suffers from widespread power cuts; in 1992 these occurred in 258 out of 297 working days. This disrupts business and deters foreign investment. Under the Electric Power Crisis Law of 1993, President Ramos was given extra powers to deal with the problem. New power station projects will no longer be subject to planning controls and the president is free to raise electricity prices by dictat.

Communist and Muslim separatists
Manila governments have been fighting communist and Muslim separatists for over 25 years. Ten thousand armed confrontations with rebels have been recorded by the army during this period. Much of the support for secession has been fueled by the failure of successive governments to curb poverty.

Since 1992, the Ramos government has been pursuing a peace process with all armed groups. The most powerful, the communist New People's Army (NPA), is in decline. Once regarded as a heroic army of the oppressed and as an alternative to traditional politics, it has split into factions. The Ramos government is involved in negotiations with the Moro National Liberation Front (MNLF), the main organization representing the secessionist Muslim rebels active in Mindanao. In 1995, a militant MNLF breakaway faction – the Muslim Islamic Liberation Front – emerged as a new threat when clashes with troops forced the government to abandon a massive irrigation project.

PROFILE
Democracy was restored to the Philippines in 1986. Ferdinand Marcos, in power since 1965, was effectively deposed by an army coup headed by Fidel Ramos and Marcos's defense minister, Juan Ponce Enrile. Although Marcos claimed victory, both Ramos and Enrile declared Corazon Aquino the true winner of the 1986 elections and the USA decided to remove its

General Fidel Ramos was elected president in 1992.

Imelda Marcos, wife of the former dictator Ferdinand Marcos.

backing for Marcos. Corazon Aquino's government succeeded in handing over power through fair elections in 1992, having survived seven coup attempts. Fidel Ramos, winner of the elections, is concentrating on achieving stability and economic growth. However, Ramos was elected on just 23% of the vote and is dependent on loose coalition arrangements in Congress. These arrangements have proved difficult to maintain and have threatened the government's economic liberalization program.

WORLD AFFAIRS

APEC   ASEAN   G24   NAM   WTO

Regional relationships are now paramount. The Philippines is keen to attract investment from booming ASEAN economies. The state took over US bases in 1992. US ships, however, still have right of access to military installations in the country. Manila has established a claim to the Spratlys.

P

CHRONOLOGY

Ceded to the USA by Spain in 1898, the Philippines became self-governing in 1935. After Japanese occupation during World War II, the Philippines became an independent republic in 1946.

❏ **1965** Ferdinand Marcos, NP candidate, becomes president.

❏ **1969–1972** Marcos reelected amid malpractice allegations.

❏ **1972** Marcos declares martial law. Opposition leaders arrested, National Assembly suspended, press censored.

❏ **1977** Ex-LP leader Benigno Aquino sentenced to death. Criticism forces Marcos to delay execution.

❏ **1978** Elections won by Marcos's new party, New Society (KBL). Marcos president and prime minister.

❏ **1980** Aquino allowed to travel to USA for medical help.

❏ **1981** Martial law ends. Marcos reelected president by referendum. Malpractice alleged by opposition.

❏ **1983** Benigno Aquino shot dead at Manila airport on return from USA. Inquiry blames military conspiracy.

❏ **1986** USA forces Marcos to call a presidential election. Result disputed. Army rebels led by General Fidel Ramos, and public demonstrations, bring widow of Benigno Aquino, Corazon, to power. Marcos exiled to USA. Two coups crushed by troops loyal to Aquino.

❏ **1987** New constitution. Aquino-led coalition wins Congress elections. Coup crushed by Aquino's troops.

❏ **1988** Marcos and wife, Imelda, indicted on $100 million charge for embezzlement and racketeering.

❏ **1989** Marcos dies in the USA. Coup attempt fails.

❏ **1990** Imelda Marcos acquitted of fraud charges in the USA. Earthquake in Baguio City leaves 1,600 dead.

❏ **1991** Mt. Pinatubo erupts. USA leaves Clark Air Base. Imelda Marcos returns to the Philippines.

❏ **1992** General Fidel Ramos wins presidential election. US navy leaves its bases in the Philippines.

AID

 $1.5bn (receipts)   Down 14% in 1993

The Philippines' main bilateral aid donors are the USA and Japan. Large remittances are also received from Filipinos working overseas. In 1975, there were 40,000 OCWs (Overseas Contract Workers). By 1994, this had risen to 680,000. Many NGOs operate in the outlying islands.

P

DEFENSE

 $1bn   Up 14% in 1995

0   Defense spending as % GDP   40

1.4%

Subic Bay was the largest US base outside America and was used in both the Vietnam War and the 1991 Gulf War. The USA left Clark base in 1991, following the eruption of Mt. Pinatubo, and Subic Bay in 1992. The military retains considerable political influence; Fidel Ramos is a former army general.

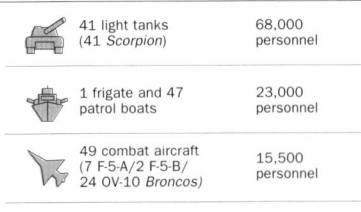

PHILIPPINE ARMED FORCES

🔫	41 light tanks (41 *Scorpion*)	68,000 personnel
⚓	1 frigate and 47 patrol boats	23,000 personnel
✈	49 combat aircraft (7 F-5-A/2 F-5-B/ 24 OV-10 *Broncos*)	15,500 personnel
🚀	None	

ECONOMICS

 $63.3bn   24.40–26.23 Philippine pesos

SCORE CARD

❏ WORLD GNP RANKING	40th
❏ GNP PER CAPITA	$960
❏ BALANCE OF PAYMENTS	$–3.3bn
❏ INFLATION	8.4%
❏ UNEMPLOYMENT	8.6%

EXPORTS

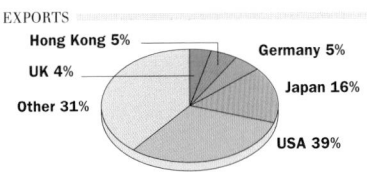

Hong Kong 5%
UK 4%
Other 31%
Germany 5%
Japan 16%
USA 39%

IMPORTS

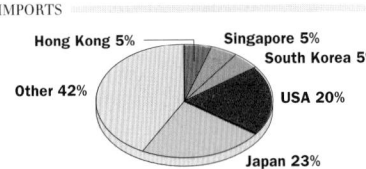

Hong Kong 5%
Other 42%
Singapore 5%
South Korea 5%
USA 20%
Japan 23%

STRENGTHS

Economy now fully open to outside investment. Agricultural productivity rising. Remittances from Filipinos working overseas, estimated at $2 billion. Well-equipped ex-US military installations with economic potential, such as Subic Bay.

WEAKNESSES

Power failures limit scope for expansion. Rudimentary infrastructure, particularly transportation. Low domestic savings rates make Philippines reliant on foreign finance. $30-billion debt.

PROFILE

In the 1950s, the Philippines was one of the strongest economies in Asia. Since then, it has fallen behind once much poorer nations such as Thailand, Malaysia and South Korea. Around 50% of the population live on the poverty line. It is this poverty that has fueled many of the secessionist movements that have threatened the stability of successive governments.

ECONOMIC PERFORMANCE INDICATOR

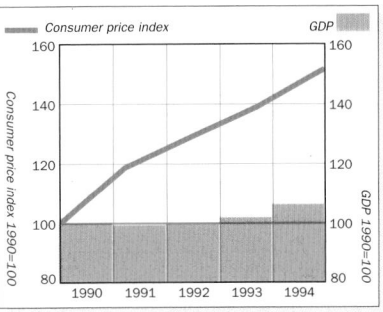

The economy is undergoing slow reform. The Ramos administration aims to emulate the success of the other Southeast Asian NICs. Backed by the IMF, it is deregulating the economy to encourage foreign investment. It is also trying to trim the power of some of the large privately run monopolies; a few families still control a major part of the economy. Long-term goals are to raise economic growth to double figures by 1998 and to reduce those affected by poverty to 30% of the population. The aim of raising per capita income to $1,000 has almost been achieved.

PHILIPPINES : MAJOR BUSINESSES

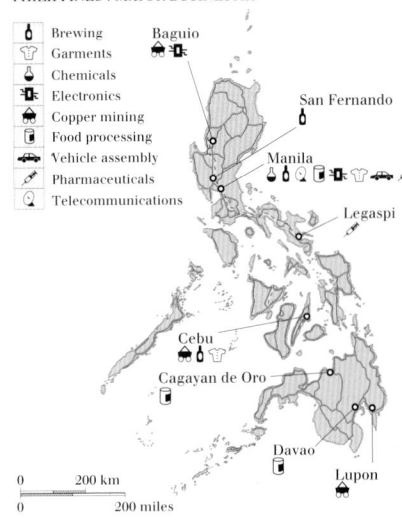

🍺 Brewing
👕 Garments
⚗ Chemicals
🔌 Electronics
⛏ Copper mining
🍴 Food processing
🚗 Vehicle assembly
💉 Pharmaceuticals
📞 Telecommunications

RESOURCES

 21bn kwh (capacity 6.87m kw)

 8,380 b/d (reserves 147,540,000 bbl)

 8.2m pigs, 2.8m goats, 1.8m cattle, 210,000 horses

 Coal, copper, nickel, chromium, silver, manganese, gold

ELECTRICITY GENERATION

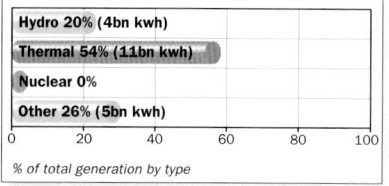

Hydro 20% (4bn kwh)
Thermal 54% (11bn kwh)
Nuclear 0%
Other 26% (5bn kwh)

% of total generation by type

The Philippines is the world's-biggest supplier of refractory chrome. Copper is also a significant export. Many areas of the country have yet to be surveyed and estimates suggest 90% of mineral potential remains undeveloped. Oil production off Palawan began in 1979. The Philippines is the world's second-biggest user of geothermal power after the USA. Almost 25% of electricity on Luzon is provided by this method. In 1989, timber exports were halted. However, illegal logging and slash and burn farming still cause deforestation.

ENVIRONMENT

 2% (1% partially protected)

 Economic growth has precedence over ecological concerns

ENVIRONMENTAL TREATIES

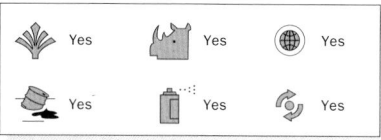

Yes   Yes   Yes
Yes   Yes   Yes

The environment has become a major issue in the Philippines. Most of the tropical rainforest has been destroyed, except for pockets such as the island of Palawan. Fishermen have dynamited unique coral habitats, and continue to use cyanide and muro-ami techniques to increase the size of their catches.

The government has recognized the costs of environmental damage. Soil run-off is silting rivers and reducing the power generated by hydroelectric dams. Fast-depleting coral habitats reduce the Philippines' attraction for tourists.

Logging has been banned, but enforcement is difficult; many loggers have their own private armies. In addition, continued use of slash and burn farming has aided deforestation.

MEDIA

 The media practises self-censorship and is inclined to be deferential to the government in power

PUBLISHING AND BROADCAST MEDIA

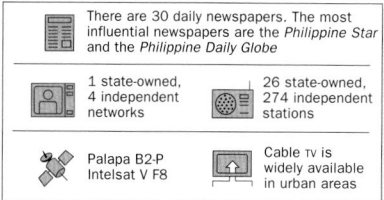

There are 30 daily newspapers. The most influential newspapers are the *Philippine Star* and the *Philippine Daily Globe*

1 state-owned, 4 independent networks

26 state-owned, 274 independent stations

Palapa B2-P Intelsat V F8

Cable TV is widely available in urban areas

The lifting of censorship following the election of Corazon Aquino in 1986 led to a burgeoning of the media. In addition to the national press, there are over 250 regional newspapers in local dialects. State TV broadcasts in English and Pilipino. Four independent television stations serve Metro Manila.

CRIME

 14,525 prisoners   Down 8% in 1990

CRIME RATES

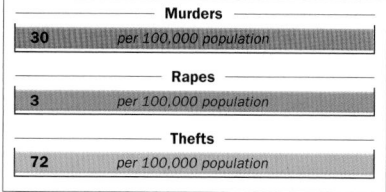

Murders
30 per 100,000 population

Rapes
3 per 100,000 population

Thefts
72 per 100,000 population

Crime rates are relatively high. Many shops have armed guards. Kidnapping of Chinese businessmen for ransom is a growing problem.

EDUCATION

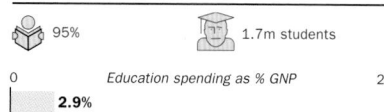 95%   1.7m students

0   Education spending as % GNP   25
2.9%

THE EDUCATION SYSTEM

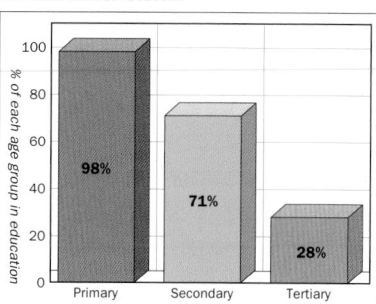

% of each age group in education

Primary 98%
Secondary 71%
Tertiary 28%

The Philippines has one of the highest literacy rates among developing countries. The education system is based on the US model, but characterized by many private schools. Sectarianism in education is common; the Chinese community has its own schools. Most colleges and universities are also run privately. The universities of San Carlos in Cebu city and Santo Tomas in Manila are Spanish colonial foundations, dating from 1595 and 1611 respectively.

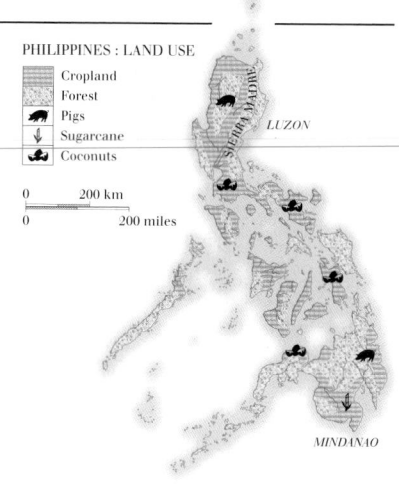

PHILIPPINES : LAND USE

Cropland
Forest
Pigs
Sugarcane
Coconuts

0   200 km
0   200 miles

LUZON
SIERRA MADRE
MINDANAO

HEALTH

 1 per 6,104 people   Pneumonia, tuberculosis, typhoid

0   Health spending as % GDP   25
1%

Most general hospitals are privately run. Malaria, once a major problem, has been eradicated in all but remote areas.

WEALTH

 Miner, 2,986 Philippine pesos ($114) per month; teacher, 3,121 Philippine pesos ($119) per month

CONSUMER GOODS OWNERSHIP

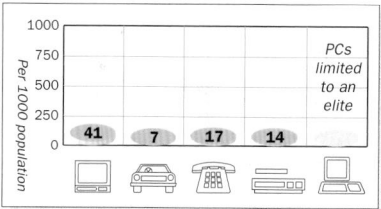

Per 1000 population

41   7   17   14

PCs limited to an elite

Around 50% of Filipinos live on the poverty line. Wealth remains highly concentrated in a few Manila-based business families.

WORLD RANKING

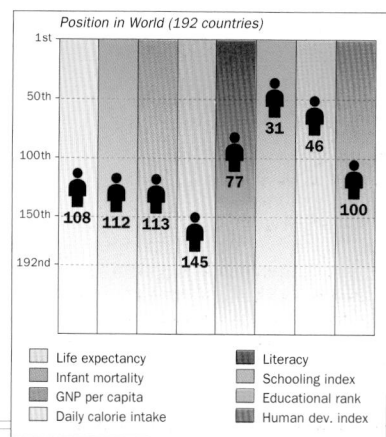

Position in World (192 countries)

1st
50th
100th
150th
192nd

108   112   113   145   77   31   46   100

Life expectancy
Infant mortality
GNP per capita
Daily calorie intake
Literacy
Schooling index
Educational rank
Human dev. index

P

POLAND

OFFICIAL NAME: Republic of Poland   **CAPITAL:** Warsaw
POPULATION: 38.4 million   **CURRENCY:** Zloty   **OFFICIAL LANGUAGE:** Polish

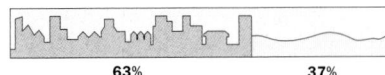

LOCATED IN THE HEART OF EUROPE, Poland's low-lying plains extend from the Baltic shore in the north to the Tatry Mountains on its southern border with the Czech Republic and Slovakia. Since the Round Table Agreement of 1989, which led to the fall of the communist regime, Poland has undergone massive social, economic and political change. It is currently experiencing rapid economic growth. Its size and strategic location between western and eastern Europe and its developing market economy could make it a major player in European politics in the future.

CLIMATE

WEATHER CHART

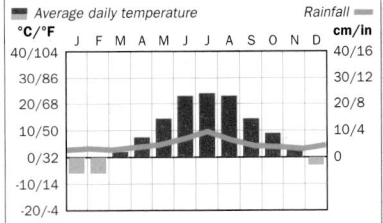

Most of the country experiences a similar climate. Summers are hot, with heavy rainfall often accompanied by thunder. Winters are severe, with snow covering the ground on the southern mountains and for as much as 60–70 days in the east.

TRANSPORTATION

 Okecie Intl, Warsaw   251 ships 4.08m dwt

THE TRANSPORTATION NETWORK

108,220 miles (174,160 km)	160 miles (257 km)
16,298 miles (26,228 km)	2,484 miles (3,997 km)

Polish communications are in need of widespread upgrading to facilitate closer links with western Europe. Poland is uniquely located to capture east–west and north–south trading routes. The Gdańsk–Gdynia port complex is poised to become the center of cross-Baltic trade and the Polish government is planning to build two east–west expressways. A new international airport has been built near Warsaw.

A much-needed improvement of the telecommunications network is beginning, with multinationals and Polish companies forming joint ventures to bring an optical fibre network to 125,000 households in southern Poland.

The medieval administrative center of Lublin lies in Poland's southeastern agricultural heartland.

TOURISM

 18.8m visitors   Up 110% in 1994

MAIN OVERSEAS ARRIVALS

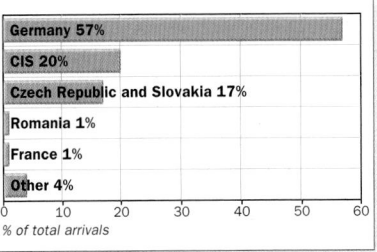

Germany 57%	
CIS 20%	
Czech Republic and Slovakia 17%	
Romania 1%	
France 1%	
Other 4%	

% of total arrivals

Tourism in Poland has, until recently, been targeted toward domestic or eastern European tourists. Since 1989, however, some of the most visible signs of foreign investment have been in the hotel industry.

Despite considerable environmental problems, Poland is renowned for its skiing and hiking, especially in the Tatry Mountains. Kraków's medieval core has been preserved, while Toruń has restored its historic German Hanseatic buildings. Warsaw's historic center has been meticulously reconstructed following its destruction in 1944.

Poznań has exploited its location between Warsaw and Berlin to create an international exhibition and business convention industry.

PEOPLE

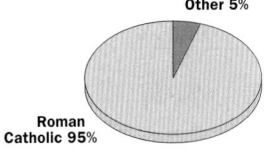 Polish   327 people per sq. mile

THE URBAN/RURAL POPULATION SPLIT

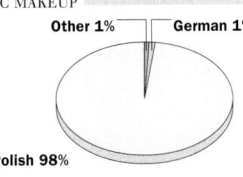

63%   37%

RELIGIOUS PERSUASION

Other 5%
Roman Catholic 95%

ETHNIC MAKEUP

Other 1%   German 1%
Polish 98%

As a result of the readjustment of its borders agreed at the Yalta Conference in 1945, Poland has few ethnic minorities. The ethnic German minority in Silesia is becoming more self-assertive, and now has representation in parliament. The Ukrainian minority form only 0.7% of the population. Residual anti-Semitism is a problem in public life. In 1995, Henryk Kankowski, an adviser to former president Lech Walęsa, apologized for anti-Semitic remarks made during a sermon.

The main social conflict in democratic Poland is between liberal, secular tendencies, and the opposing influence of the Catholic Church which exerts more influence than in any other European state (except the Vatican).

Wealth disparities are small although the growing wealth of the entrepreneurial class is causing tension. Opinion is divided between support for the free market and the socialist model.

Women are prominent policy makers. Hanna Suchocka was prime minister from 1992–1993.

POPULATION AGE BREAKDOWN

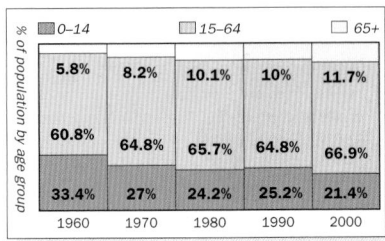

% of population by age group	0–14	15–64			65+
	5.8%	8.2%	10.1%	10%	11.7%
	60.8%	64.8%	65.7%	64.8%	66.9%
	33.4%	27%	24.2%	25.2%	21.4%
	1960	1970	1980	1990	2000

POLITICS

U. House 1993/1997
L. House 1993/1997

President Aleksander Kwasniewski

THE STATE OF THE PARTIES

Parliament (*Sejm*) 460 members

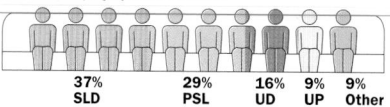

| 37% SLD | 29% PSL | 16% UD | 9% UP | 9% Other |

SLD = Democratic Left Alliance   **PSL** = Polish Peasant Party
UD = Democratic Union   **UP** = Labor Union   **S** = Solidarity
Other = Confederation for an Independent Poland, Non-party Bloc in Support of Reforms, German minority organizations

Senate 100 members

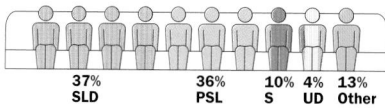

| 37% SLD | 36% PSL | 10% S | 4% UD | 13% Other |

Since 1989, Poland has been a multiparty parliamentary democracy.

MAIN POLITICAL ISSUES
Coalition rule
Poland's emerging party system has been hindered by a superfluity of political factions and sustaining coalitions has proved difficult.

POLAND

Total Land Area : 304 460 sq. km
(117 552 sq. miles)

Parties are required to have at least 5% of the vote in order to gain a seat and 8% to be eligible to join a coalition government.

Church–state relations
Building on the legitimization of its authority in the martial law years, the Catholic Church has been outspoken in its views on social and political policy. Recent debates over abortion, worship in schools and values in the media have fueled a heated dialogue over the proper role of the Church in public and private life.

PROFILE
A new post-socialist constitution has yet to be drafted and government is currently operating under a revised version of the 1952 constitution. Under its provisions, the president has considerable power; this has led to a number of battles with the *Sejm* (parliament) over ultimate control. Frequent government changes have occurred since 1989.

The 1993 elections led to the formation of a coalition government headed by reformed communists from the SLD and the PSL. In 1995, Prime Minister Waldemar Pawlak of the PSL was forced

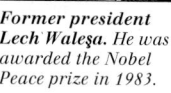

Former president Lech Wałęsa. *He was awarded the Nobel Peace prize in 1983.*

President Aleksander Kwasniewski, *leader of the SLD, who was elected in 1995.*

to resign amid sharp political differences with the then president, Lech Wałęsa. Pawlak was succeeded by Jozef Oleksy of the SLD. In 1996, Oleksy also resigned after facing charges of espionage. His successor, current Prime Minister Wlodsimierz Cimoszewicz who was nominated by the SLD, has promised to continue the economic reform program initiated by the ruling coalition. His chances of success may be ensured by President Aleksander Kwasniewski, leader of the SLD, who was elected in 1995.

WORLD AFFAIRS

| CE | CEFTA | IBRD | NACC | OSCE |

Poland has sought to expand its economic and security ties, especially with Europe. One of Poland's first acts as an independent nation was to apply for membership of the IMF, and in 1994 Poland became the first of two former communist states (with Hungary) to apply for membership of the EU. Poland is also developing closer links with the Baltics, Belorussia and the Ukraine.

CHRONOLOGY
Poland has Europe's second-oldest written constitution. In 1795, it was partitioned between Austria–Hungary, Germany and Russia.

- ❏ **1918** Polish state recreated.
- ❏ **1921** Democratic constitution.
- ❏ **1926–1935** Pilsudski heads military coup. Nine years of authoritarian rule.
- ❏ **1939** Molotov–Ribbentrop pact. September, Germany invades and divides Poland with Russians.
- ❏ **1941** First concentration camps built on Polish soil.
- ❏ **1944** Warsaw Uprising: 200,000 killed in last stand against Nazis.
- ❏ **1945** Potsdam and Yalta Conferences set present borders and determine political allegiance to Soviet Union.

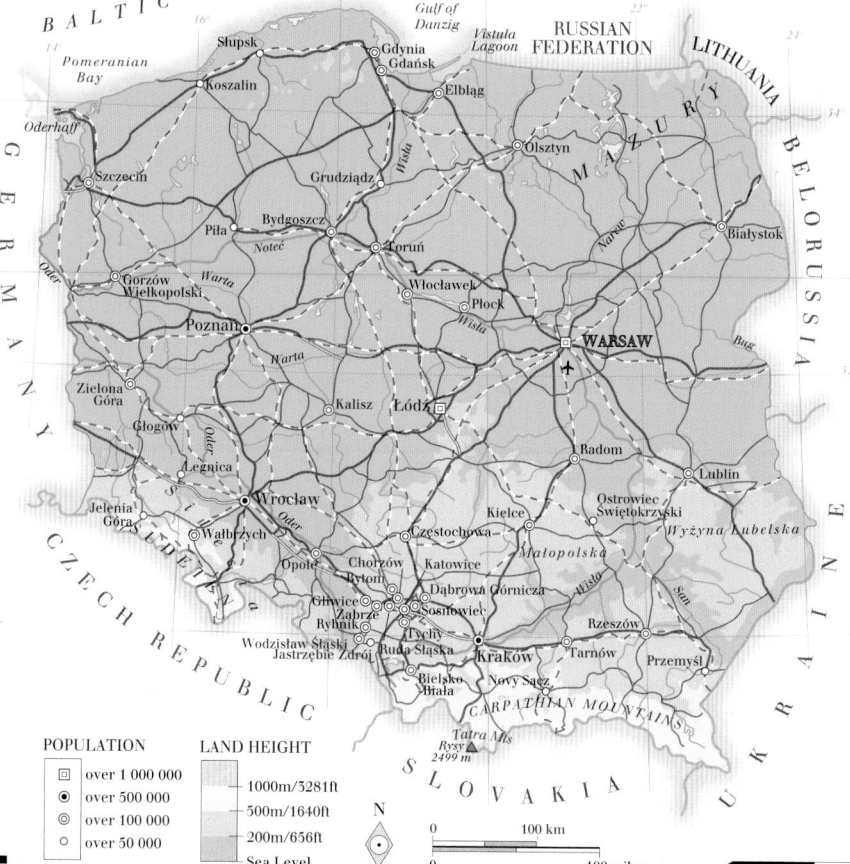

POPULATION
- ▣ over 1 000 000
- ⊙ over 500 000
- ◎ over 100 000
- ○ over 50 000

LAND HEIGHT
- 1000m/3281ft
- 500m/1640ft
- 200m/656ft
- Sea Level

N

0   100 km
0   100 miles

P

441

CHRONOLOGY *continued*

- ❑ **1947** Communists manipulate elections to gain power. Opposition dissolved and exiled.
- ❑ **1949** **The Communist Party** absorbs socialist coalition partners and forms Polish United Workers' Party.
- ❑ **1956** Protests in Poznaú erupt into riots. More than 50 killed.
- ❑ **1970** Food price increases lead to strikes and riots in the Baltic port cities. Hundreds are killed.
- ❑ **1979** Pope John Paul II elected.
- ❑ **1980** A series of strikes forces the government to negotiate with Solidarity. Resulting Gdańsk Accords grant the right to strike and to form free trade unions.
- ❑ **1981** General Wojciech Jaruzelski becomes prime minister.
- ❑ **1981–1983** Martial law. Solidarity forced into underground existence. Many of its leaders, including Waleşa, are interned.
- ❑ **1983** Waleşa awarded Nobel Peace Prize.
- ❑ **1986** Amnesty for political prisoners.
- ❑ **1987** Referendum rejects government austerity program.
- ❑ **1988** Industrial unrest leads to inconclusive government–Solidarity negotiations.
- ❑ **1989** PUWP agrees to hold talks with Solidarity, which is relegalized. Partially free elections are held. First postwar non-communist government formed.
- ❑ **1990** Launch of market reforms. Waleşa elected president.
- ❑ **1991** Free elections lead to fragmented parliament.
- ❑ **1992** Last Russian troops leave.
- ❑ **1993** Reformed communists form coalition government after elections.
- ❑ **1994** Launch of mass privatization.
- ❑ **1995** February,Waldemar Pawlak resigns as prime minister after differences with Waleşa March, Jozef Oleksy becomes premier. November, Aleksander Kwasiewski is elected president.
- ❑ **1996** Oleksy resigns over spying allegations; Wlodsimierz becomes prime minister.

AID

 $8bn promised by the 24 top industrial nations

 Aid is rising

Saddled with an enormous debt from the 1980s, Poland's most important foreign assistance was the cancellation of half of its debt by the Paris Club. A London Club agreement for commercial debt is still outstanding. The IMF, EBRD and EU have all taken an active role in supporting Poland's pioneering stabilization and reform program.

DEFENSE

 $2.6bn   ⬆ Up 12% in 1995

0   *Defense spending as % GDP*   40
2.5%

Since the demise of the Warsaw Pact, Poland has repeatedly stated its wish to join NATO, despite the West's hesitation. It recently signed the NATO-backed Partnership for Peace program. Russia is a source for cut-price armaments and equipment for Poland's standing army, the largest in Europe after Russia's.

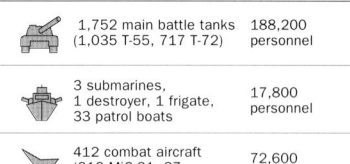

POLISH ARMED FORCES

🛡	1,752 main battle tanks (1,035 T-55, 717 T-72)	188,200 personnel
🚢	3 submarines, 1 destroyer, 1 frigate, 33 patrol boats	17,800 personnel
✈	412 combat aircraft (216 MiG-21, 37 MiG-23, 103 Su-22)	72,600 personnel
🚀	None	

ECONOMICS

 $94.6bn   💲 2.47–24,370 zlotys

SCORE CARD

- ❑ WORLD GNP RANKING..........................33rd
- ❑ GNP PER CAPITA $2,470
- ❑ BALANCE OF PAYMENTS....................$–2.5bn
- ❑ INFLATION 26.2%
- ❑ UNEMPLOYMENT................................16.4%

EXPORTS

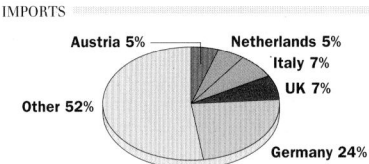

UK 4%
Czech Republic & Slovakia 4%
Other 49%
Italy 6%
Netherlands 6%
Germany 31%

IMPORTS

Austria 5%
Other 52%
Netherlands 5%
Italy 7%
UK 7%
Germany 24%

STRENGTHS
Fastest economic growth in Europe in 1993. Steadfast implementation of economic reform since 1989 has encouraged growth of private sector. Ability to attract foreign investment. Mass privatization scheme, including the 600 largest state-owned industries, launched in 1994.

WEAKNESSES
Persistent high inflation. Outdated production plants. Need to compete for foreign investment with other former COMECON states.

PROFILE
Poland entered deep economic crisis in the 1980s, fueled in part by high foreign debt levels. Following the change of government in January 1990, Finance Minister Leszek Balcerowicz implemented the Big Bang plan to bring about a swift transition to a market economy. Most prices were freed, trade was opened and the zloty was made convertible.

ECONOMIC PERFORMANCE INDICATOR

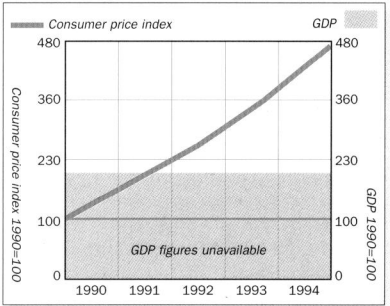

— Consumer price index   GDP ▦
Consumer price index 1990=100
GDP 1990=100
480 ... 360 ... 230 ... 100 ... 0
GDP figures unavailable
1990 1991 1992 1993 1994

Although 40 years of communism have left considerable distortions in the economy, the framework necessary for a market economy is now being developed. The private sector now accounts for half of GNP and employs 60% of workers. Small businesses are flourishing in the previously neglected services sector. Stock and credit markets have opened and bankruptcy laws have been established. Share prices rose 900% in 1993.

Poland's economic growth and its 39 million domestic market make it attractive to foreign investors, which include companies such as Fiat, McDonalds and Proctor & Gamble.

POLAND : MAJOR BUSINESSES

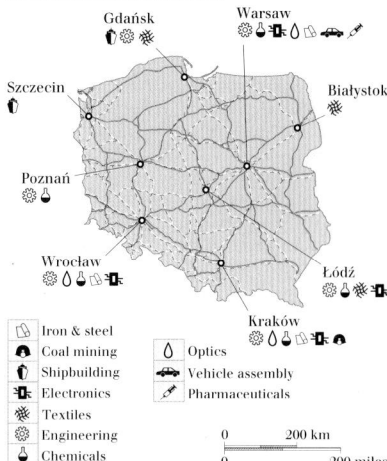

Gdańsk
Warsaw
Szczecin
Białystok
Poznań
Wrocław
Łódź
Kraków

🏭 Iron & steel		◊ Optics	
Coal mining		🚗 Vehicle assembly	
Shipbuilding		Pharmaceuticals	
Electronics			
❈ Textiles			
Engineering	0 200 km		
Chemicals	0 200 miles		

RESOURCES

132bn kwh (capacity 30.7m kw)

3,990 b/d (reserves of 42,208,000 bbl)

19.5m pigs, 7.7m cattle, 870,000 sheep

Coal, copper, silver, sulphur, natural gas, lead, salt, iron

ELECTRICITY GENERATION

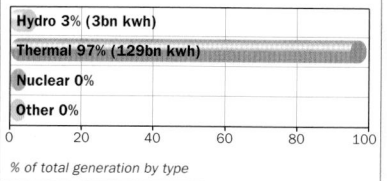

Hydro 3% (3bn kwh)

Thermal 97% (129bn kwh)

Nuclear 0%

Other 0%

% of total generation by type

Poland has significant quantities of coal, sulphur, copper, natural gas, silver, lead and salt. With the availability of cheap fuel from Russia at an end, Poland aims to reach self-sufficiency and eventually to export fuels. Coal supplies two-thirds of electricity generation. The amounts of copper ores mined are too small to affect world markets.

POLAND : LAND USE

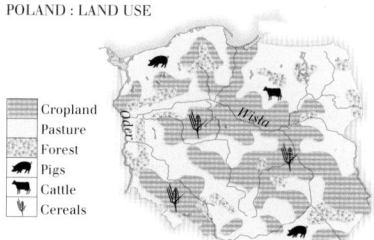

Cropland
Pasture
Forest
Pigs
Cattle
Cereals

0   200 km

0   200 miles

ENVIRONMENT

10%

Environmental initiatives too expensive

ENVIRONMENTAL TREATIES

No   Yes   Yes

No   No   Yes

Poland faces serious pollution problems arising from heavy industrialization. A third of Poles live in areas regarded as extremely polluted. In the southern region of Silesia, air, water and vegetation pollution are especially severe.

The metallurgical industry and thermal electric power stations are significant sources of air pollution. Sulphur dioxide readings in Kraków can exceed legal limits by 800 times.

Only 4% of Poland's river water is fit for human consumption; 75% had been declared biologically dead by the late 1980s. Neighboring western states are funding a clean-up operation.

MEDIA

Free, but broadcast media must by law reflect Christian values

Under martial law, Poland had a vigorous underground press and this energy has survived into democracy. The leading daily, *Gazeta Wyborcza*, began as Solidarity's paper. *Nie*, a satirical weekly, is edited by the former Communist Party spokesman, Jerzy Urban.

CRIME

40,321 prisoners

Down 1% in 1992

CRIME RATES

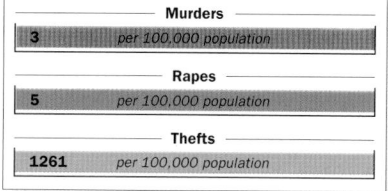

Murders
3   *per 100,000 population*

Rapes
5   *per 100,000 population*

Thefts
1261   *per 100,000 population*

Smuggling is seen as the most significant crime problem. Warsaw is a main route for illicit as well as legal trade. Expensive cars are transferred eastward to Russia and drugs westward to Berlin. Smuggling is mostly undertaken by Poles and other eastern Europeans. In 1993, customs seized goods worth over $660,000.

EDUCATION

99%

 584,177 students

0   *Education spending as % GNP*   25

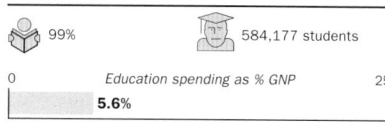
5.6%

THE EDUCATION SYSTEM

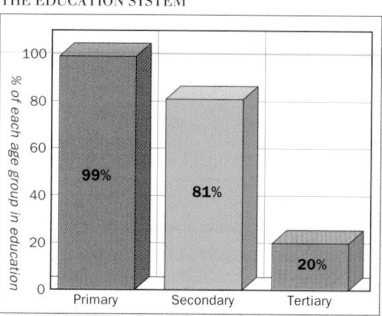

% of each age group in education

99%   81%   20%

Primary   Secondary   Tertiary

The most contentious change is the expanded influence of the Catholic Church. Religious education is mandatory in all schools, and Church-run schools are now allowed. Traditionally based on the Russian system, Polish schools are reorienting themselves towards the French model.

Universities are of a high standard, especially in mathematics and philosophy. Business schools are training badly needed managers.

MEDIA

PUBLISHING AND BROADCAST MEDIA

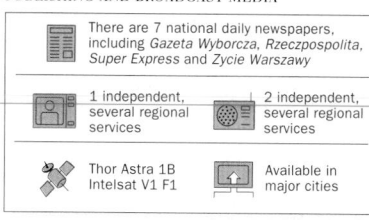

There are 7 national daily newspapers, including *Gazeta Wyborcza*, *Rzeczpospolita*, *Super Express* and *Zycie Warszawy*.

1 independent, several regional services

2 independent, several regional services

Thor Astra 1B Intelsat V1 F1

Available in major cities

HEALTH

1 per 450 people

Arteriosclerosis, heart disease, cancers, accidents, violence

0   *Health spending as % GDP*   25

5.1%

Medical care is provided free for workers and rural residents. Reform of the health system is being considered as the quality of health care is regarded as inadequate. Private health care is increasingly available in cities for those who can afford it.

WEALTH

State employees are significantly worse off than those in the private sector

CONSUMER GOODS OWNERSHIP

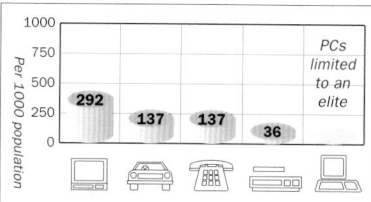

Per 1000 population

PCs limited to an elite

292   137   137   36

Poland began its transition to a market economy with an extremely equitable distribution of income. After 1990, real wages in industry and agriculture fell from artificially high levels and the entrepreneurial class visibly increased its wealth. Growing wealth disparities have led to resentment from those who have not benefited from reforms.

P

WORLD RANKING

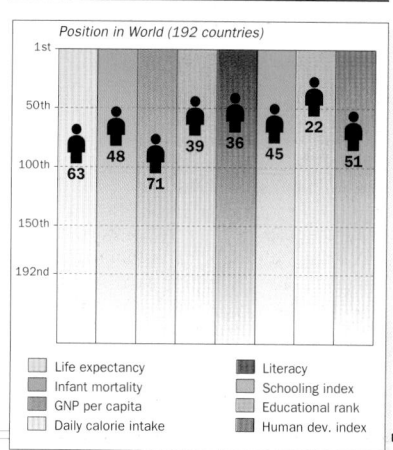

Position in World (192 countries)

1st
50th
100th
150th
192nd

63   48   71   39   36   45   22   51

Life expectancy
Infant mortality
GNP per capita
Daily calorie intake

Literacy
Schooling index
Educational rank
Human dev. index

PORTUGAL

OFFICIAL NAME: Republic of Portugal   **CAPITAL:** Lisbon   **POPULATION:** 9.8 million
CURRENCY: Escudo   **OFFICIAL LANGUAGE:** Portuguese   **OVERSEAS TERRITORIES:** 1

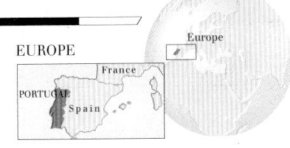

EUROPE

PORTUGAL, WITH ITS long Atlantic coast, lies on the western side of the Iberian peninsular. The River Tagus divides the more mountainous north from the lower, undulating terrain to the south. In 1974, a bloodless military coup overthrew a long-standing conservative dictatorship. Democratic elections were held in 1975 and the armed forces withdrew from politics thereafter. The 1980s witnessed the implementation of a substantial program of socio-economic modernization. Membership of the EU since 1986 has helped underpin this process.

Santa Marta de Penanguiao, a small village in the heart of Portugal's wine-producing region, which is centered on the Douro valley.

CLIMATE

WEATHER CHART

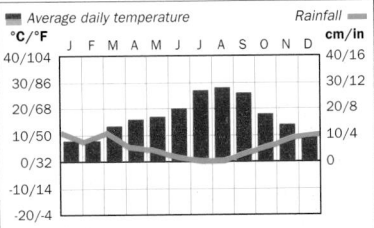

Portugal has a mild, Mediterranean climate, which is moderated by the influence of the Atlantic. Summers are hot and humid, while winters are relatively mild. Inland areas have more variable weather than coastal regions. Rainfall is generally higher in the mountainous north, while the central areas are more temperate. The southern Algarve region is predominantly dry and sunny.

TRANSPORTATION

Portela de Sacavem, Lisbon
4.98m passengers

69 ships
897,200 dwt

THE TRANSPORTATION NETWORK

37,500 miles (60,350 km)	132 miles (243 km)
2,205 miles (3,549 km)	510 miles (820 km)

The Portuguese road system, which was formerly one of the least developed in Europe, has been extensively improved in recent years with grants from the EU. However, road links with Spain remain limited, despite a number of modernization schemes. Lisbon, the densely populated capital, continues to suffer from very heavy traffic congestion, which only a major new beltway will alleviate. The railroad system is small but efficient. The national airline, TAP, is currently in economic difficulties.

TOURISM

9.1m visitors   Up 8% in 1994

MAIN OVERSEAS ARRIVALS

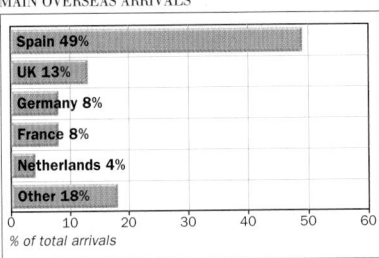

Spain 49%	
UK 13%	
Germany 8%	
France 8%	
Netherlands 4%	
Other 18%	

% of total arrivals

Since the 1960s, Portugal's popularity as a tourist destination has been linked to qualities which reflected its relatively poor economic development, such as low prices and little crime. Substantial economic growth has eroded some of its appeal, but tourism is likely to remain a major income-earner. The most popular destination is the Algarve, Portugal's southernmost province, followed by the western resorts of Figueira da Foz and the Tróia Peninsula. Visitors are also attracted by Portugal's architecture, notably that dating from the Manueline period (1490–1520), and handicrafts, such as ceramics, lace and tapestries. Portugal has some of Europe's finest golf courses.

PORTUGAL

Total Land Area : 91 950 sq. km (35 502 sq. miles)

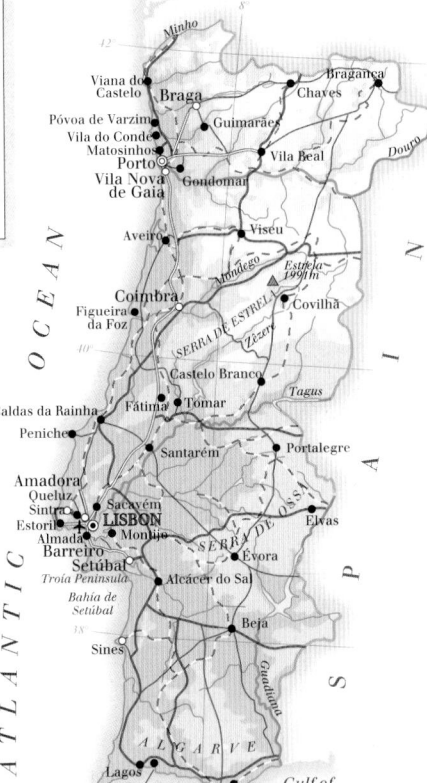

Azores

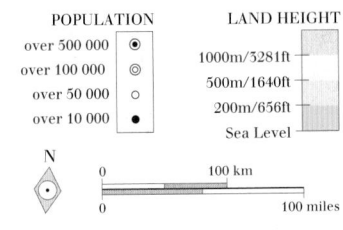

Madeira Is

POPULATION
over 500 000
over 100 000
over 50 000
over 10 000

LAND HEIGHT
1000m/3281ft
500m/1640ft
200m/656ft
Sea Level

PEOPLE

 Portuguese

 277 people per sq. mile

THE URBAN/RURAL POPULATION SPLIT

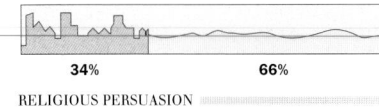

34%   66%

RELIGIOUS PERSUASION

Protestant 1%   Other 2%

Roman Catholic 97%

ETHNIC MAKEUP

African 1%

Portuguese 99%

Portuguese society, once regarded as rather inward-looking, is now becoming increasingly integrated into the rest of western Europe. Ethnic and religious tensions are limited. African immigrants, who come mainly from the former colonies, such as Angola, Mozambique and Guinea, have been assimilated into mainstream society with considerable ease.

As is true of other predominantly Catholic countries, the Church has lost some of its social influence in recent decades, a fact borne out by falling birth-rates and more liberal attitudes to abortion and divorce. Nevertheless, with the exception of large urban areas, the north remains devoutly Catholic.

Family ties remain all-important. Women now have greater access to business and media jobs. Overall, democracy and rapid socio-economic change have tended to produce a more egalitarian society.

POPULATION AGE BREAKDOWN

% of population by age group	■ 0–14	□ 15–64	□ 65+		
65+	8%	9.2%	10.5%	12.9%	14.4%
15–64	62.9%	62%	63.5%	65.8%	66.3%
0–14	29.1%	28.8%	26%	21.3%	19.3%
	1960	1970	1980	1990	2000

POLITICS

 1995/1999

 President Mário Alberto Nobre Lopes Soares

THE STATE OF THE PARTIES

Assembly of the Republic 230 members

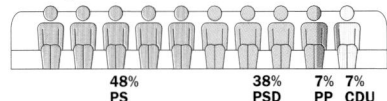

48% PS   38% PSD   7% PP   7% CDU

PS = Socialist Party   PSD = Social Democratic Party
PP = People's Party   CDU = United Democratic Coalition

Portugal is a multiparty democracy.

MAIN POLITICAL ISSUES
Limiting pay rises
The government wishes to improve the state's weak financial position by keeping public sector pay rises below inflation. It proposed limiting wage rises to 2% – a cut in real terms. In 1994, the unions responded with a number of one-day strikes. The threat of rising unemployment, however, will limit demands for wage rises in the private sector.

PROFILE
A decade of center-right government was brought to an end by the legislative elections of 1995 when the PSD was ousted from power by the PS. The PS polled almost 44% of the vote and its leader, Antonio Guterres, replaced Cavaco Silva as prime minister at the head of a minority government. Having fought the election on a platform of social reform, within weeks of the PS victory Finance Minister Antonio Sousa Franco warned that the administration's first priority would be to reduce the budget deficit by cutting public spending and that two years of economic stringency were required before the election pledges could be redeemed.

Presidential election
The 1995 election also ended a ten-year period in which the presidency and the government had been controlled by opposing parties, a situation which had encouraged conflict and obstruction. This position was maintained by the presidential election of February 1996 when former PS leader Jorge Sampaio defeated Silva in the contest to succeed President Mário Soares, whose term in office expired in March.

Dr Mário Soares, *Portugal's socialist president since 1986, reelected in 1991.*

Aníbal Cavaco Silva, *prime minister and leader of the center-right PSD.*

WORLD AFFAIRS

 EU   CE   NATO   OECD   OSCE

Since 1986, Portugal's foreign policy has dealt almost exclusively with the consequences of membership of the EU, from which the country has greatly benefited. It is a committed member of NATO, though its relative strategic importance has declined as a result of Spanish membership. Relations with the former African colonies are occasionally turbulent and remain a high priority, as do those with Brazil. Relations with China over the return of Macao to the latter in 1999 are cordial.

AID

 $246m (donations)   Up 19% in 1993

Portugal became an aid donor only in the early 1980s. It currently earmarks just under 0.2% of its GDP for aid to developing countries, mainly its former colonies in Africa. It has also offered $110 million to rebuild war-damaged power lines to the massive Cahora Bassa Dam in Mozambique.

CHRONOLOGY

Portugal has existed as a nation state since the 11th century, although this was frequently challenged by Spain. Portugal reached its zenith in the 16th century, after which it entered a period of decline.

❑ **1755** Earthquake destroys Lisbon.
❑ **1703** Joins coalition against revolutionary France.
❑ **1807** France invades; royal family flees to Brazil.
❑ **1808** British troops arrive under Wellington. Start of Peninsular War.
❑ **1810** French leave Portugal.
❑ **1820** Liberal revolution.
❑ **1822** King John VI returns and accepts first Portuguese constitution. His son Dom Pedro declares independence of Brazil.
❑ **1834** Dom Pedro returns to Portugal to end civil war and installs his daughter as Queen Mary II.
❑ **1875–1876** Republican and Socialist parties founded.
❑ **1890** British ultimatum ends the land connection between Angola and Mozambique.
❑ **1891** Republican uprising in Porto.
❑ **1908** Assassination of King Carlos I and heir to the throne.
❑ **1910** Abdication of Manuel II and proclamation of the Republic. Church and state separated.
❑ **1916** Portugal joins allied side in the World War I. ⇨

P

DEFENSE

$1.6bn   Up 6% in 1995

0   *Defense spending as % GDP*   40

2.6%

Portugal, a member of NATO since 1949, has a small but relatively modern navy. The army and air force are smaller and less efficient. Mounting opposition to military service is causing strains on these already semi-professional bodies. The USA is the major arms supplier. It has a strategic air base in the Azores.

PORTUGUESE ARMED FORCES

198 main battle tanks (24 M-47, 86 M-48A5)	29,700 personnel
3 submarines, 11 frigates, 29 patrol boats	12,500 personnel
97 combat aircraft (77 *Alpha Jet*)	7,300 personnel
None	

ECONOMICS

$92.1bn   149–159 escudos

SCORE CARD

❏ WORLD GNP RANKING	34th
❏ GNP PER CAPITA	$9,370
❏ BALANCE OF PAYMENTS	$-1bn
❏ INFLATION	4%
❏ UNEMPLOYMENT	6.8%

ECONOMIC PERFORMANCE INDICATOR

Consumer price index — GDP

(Consumer price index 1988=100; GDP 1990=100; years 1988, 1989, 1990, 1991, 1992)

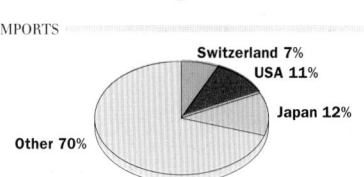

EXPORTS

- Spain 1%
- Angola 9%
- Sweden 10%
- USA 18%
- Other 62%

IMPORTS

- Switzerland 7%
- USA 11%
- Japan 12%
- Other 70%

STRENGTHS

Relatively low, though rapidly rising, labor costs. High rate of domestic and direct foreign investment. Strong banking and tourism sectors. Tourism makes up 6% of GDP, the highest ratio in the EU; potential for further growth. Fast-track improvement of transportation infrastructure under way. Good deep-water port at Lisbon. Wine, especially port. Citrus fruits, cork, sardines. Strong clothing and shoe manufacturing sectors.

WEAKNESSES

Large agricultural sector (5% of GDP, 10% of work force) is most inefficient in EU. Outdated farming methods, small landholdings, low crop yields. Farm products outpriced by Spain. Large, but falling, budget deficit (anticipated at 5.3% of GDP in 1995). Inflation higher than EU average. Rigid labor market. High dependence on imported oil.

PROFILE

EU membership in 1986 brought a sharp increase in foreign investment to Portugal. Its exports rose dramatically, until the economy went into recession in 1991.

Despite its improved economy, the country still has some way to go to achieve convergence with its EU partners. With an inflation rate which is 3% greater than the EU average, monetary union is a distant prospect. The new socialist government has stated its determination to reduce the size of the budget deficit by adopting a two-year program of austerity measures centered on cutting public expenditure. Under the plan, the deficit was to be reduced from an anticipated 5.3% in 1995, to 4% in 1996 and 3% in 1997.

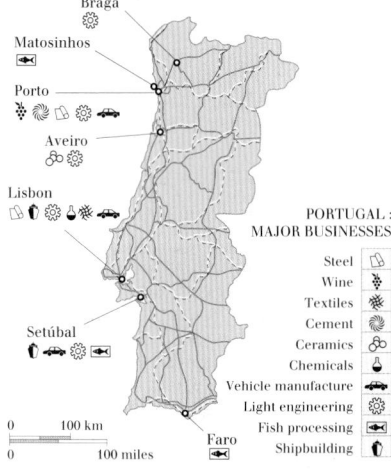

PORTUGAL : MAJOR BUSINESSES

- Braga
- Matosinhos
- Porto
- Aveiro
- Lisbon
- Setúbal
- Faro

Steel, Wine, Textiles, Cement, Ceramics, Chemicals, Vehicle manufacture, Light engineering, Fish processing, Shipbuilding

0   100 km
0   100 miles

P

RESOURCES

 30bn kwh (capacity 7.4m kw)

 Not an oil producer; refines 294,000 b/cd

 6m sheep, 1.5m pigs, 1.3m cattle, 836,000 goats

 Coal, limestone, granite, marble, copper

ELECTRICITY GENERATION

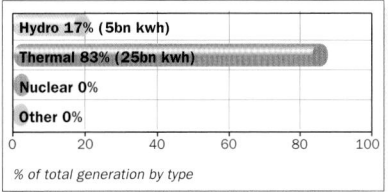

Hydro 17% (5bn kwh)
Thermal 83% (25bn kwh)
Nuclear 0%
Other 0%

% of total generation by type

Portugal has been plagued by a lack of natural resources, including water. Mining has historically been important, notably for tungsten, copper and tin. Industry has relied on small coal deposits and large oil imports. Portugal hopes to build HEP stations, and began piping natural gas from Algeria in 1996.

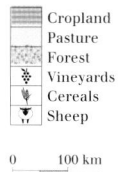

PORTUGAL : LAND USE

Cropland
Pasture
Forest
Vineyards
Cereals
Sheep

0   100 km
0   100 miles

ENVIRONMENT

 6%

 Fast modernization balanced by new conservation concern

ENVIRONMENTAL TREATIES

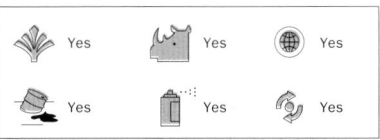

Yes   Yes   Yes
Yes   Yes   Yes

The unrestricted development of tourist resorts in the Algarve and the huge investment in new harbor, road and bridge developments are having detrimental effects on natural habitats. EU agricultural grants for projects such as draining meadows, and monoculture afforestation, notably of *Eucalyptus* and *Pinus*, are degrading biodiversity. Much toxic waste is dumped on any available land as few official controls or infill sites exist. New waste management regulations are being planned.

MEDIA

 There is full freedom from censorship and the press is entirely independent

PUBLISHING AND BROADCAST MEDIA

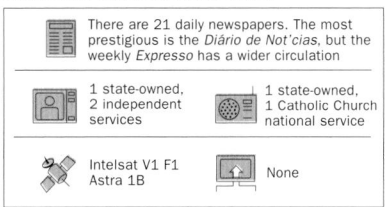

There are 21 daily newspapers. The most prestigious is the *Diário de Notícias*, but the weekly *Expresso* has a wider circulation.

1 state-owned, 2 independent services

1 state-owned, 1 Catholic Church national service

Intelsat V1 F1 Astra 1B

None

Newspaper circulation figures are among the lowest in Europe and most papers have regional rather than national distribution. Radio and TV are therefore the main source of news, in part reflecting Portugal's low literacy rate. In 1992, two independent TV stations began broadcasting, breaking the state's monopoly. Most English-language footage is not dubbed.

CRIME

 8,181 prisoners

Down 2% in 1992

CRIME RATES

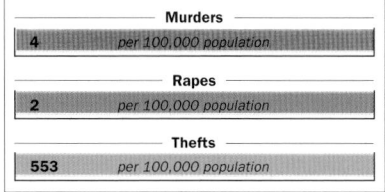

Murders
4   per 100,000 population

Rapes
2   per 100,000 population

Thefts
553   per 100,000 population

Compared to most western European countries, Portugal still enjoys a remarkably low crime rate. However, narcotics-trafficking and related offenses are rising.

EDUCATION

 86%

 190,856 students

0   Education spending as % GNP   25
4.8%

THE EDUCATION SYSTEM

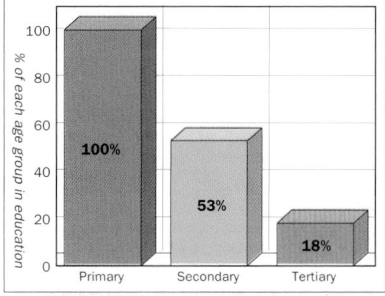

% of each age group in education

100% Primary
53%   Secondary
18%   Tertiary

Free state education is available to all pupils between the ages of three and 15, although the pre-school stage up to the age of six is not compulsory. Middle class parents rely heavily on the private sector. State universities are large and oversubscribed. There are several prestigious private universities.

HEALTH

 1 per 345 people

Heart and cerebrovascular diseases, cancers

0   Health spending as % GDP   25
6.2%

The public health system is free, but it suffers from underfunding. However, Portugal's larger urban hospitals are modern and well equipped.

Private health care schemes are both affordable and good value for money. Over 40% of the population use the private system. In spite of high tobacco and wine consumption, the Portuguese are a healthy nation, with similar life expectancy rates to neighboring Spain.

WEALTH

 Shop assistant, 1.7m escudos ($11,380) per year; managing director, 11.3m escudos ($75,640) per year

CONSUMER GOODS OWNERSHIP

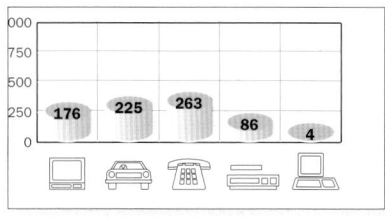

176   225   263   86   4

Wealth differentials in Portugal are smaller than in most EU countries. The bloodless military coup of 1974 led to many wealthy families transferring their assets abroad, or leaving Portugal altogether. The 1976 constitution enshrined socialist goals, and subsequent governments introduced limited wealth redistribution measures.

Many long-standing Portuguese families have seen the value of their assets fall with the dramatic drop in land prices since 1986. However, those with land with tourist development potential, such as golf courses, have made large profits. Much wealth generated by new businesses leaves Portugal, as most are foreign-owned.

WORLD RANKING

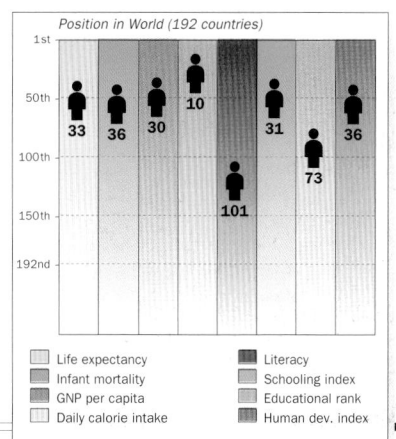

Position in World (192 countries)

33   36   30   10   31   36
101   73

Life expectancy   Literacy
Infant mortality   Schooling index
GNP per capita   Educational rank
Daily calorie intake   Human dev. index

P

QATAR

OFFICIAL NAME: State of Qatar   CAPITAL: Doha
POPULATION: 600,000   CURRENCY: Qatar riyal   OFFICIAL LANGUAGE: Arabic

MIDDLE EAST
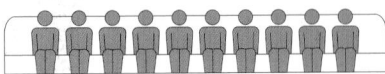

PROJECTING NORTH FROM the Arabian peninsula into the Persian Gulf, Qatar has land borders with Saudi Arabia and the United Arab Emirates, and a disputed sea border with Bahrain. Most of the country is flat, semi-arid desert. Qatar is a founder-member of OPEC and its plentiful oil and natural gas reserves make it one of the wealthiest states in the region. The country enjoys political stability under the rule of the 15,000-strong Al Thani clan.

CLIMATE

WEATHER CHART

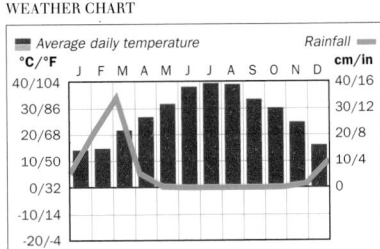

The climate is hot and humid with midsummer temperatures reaching 111°F. Rainfall is rare.

TRANSPORTATION

THE TRANSPORTATION NETWORK

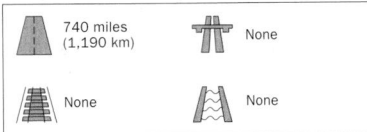

A good road network links Qatar to its neighbors. A new international airport in Doha is scheduled for 1997.

TOURISM

MAIN OVERSEAS ARRIVALS

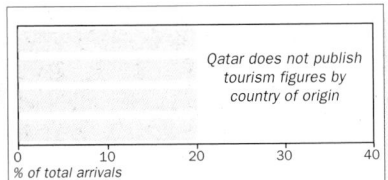

Qatar attracts mainly European visitors, who enjoy the country's unspoilt beaches, duty-free shopping, modern hotels and the desert hinterland. Alcohol is permitted in five-star hotels for non-Muslims.

PEOPLE

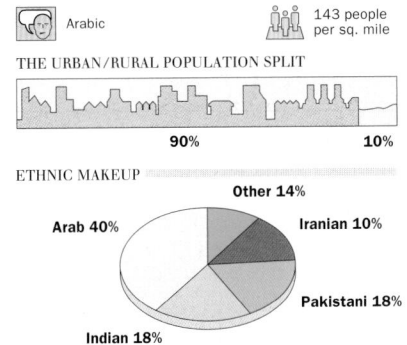

THE URBAN/RURAL POPULATION SPLIT

ETHNIC MAKEUP

Other 14%
Arab 40%
Iranian 10%
Pakistani 18%
Indian 18%

Only one in five Qataris is native-born. Most of the population are guest workers from the Indian subcontinent, Iran and the north African countries. Expatriates enjoy a high standard of living and take no part in politics.

Qataris are followers of the Wahhabi interpretation of Sunni Islam and espouse conservative religious views. However, women are not obliged to wear veil and can hold drivers' licenses. Expatriate Christians are allowed freedom to worship but not to promote Christianity.

Since the advent of oil wealth, the Qataris, who were formerly nomadic Bedouins, have become a nation of city-dwellers. Almost 90% of the population now inhabit the capital, Doha, and its suburbs. As a result, northern Qatar is dotted with depopulated and abandoned villages.

Doha, the capital. *Although desert covers the whole country, Qatar now grows most of its own vegetables by tapping ground water.*

POLITICS

Not applicable. Absolute rule by an Amir

Amir Sheikh Hamad bin Khalifa al Thani

THE STATE OF THE PARTIES

Qatar is an absolute monarchy and has no legislature. The Amir rules with the assistance of the Council of Ministers and the Advisory Council.

Qatar is a traditional emirate. Its government and religious establishment is dominated by Amir Sheikh Hamad, who took power from his father, Sheikh Khalifa, in a bloodless coup in 1995. A failed coup against Hamad in early 1996 was linked with efforts to regain power by Khalifa, who is now based in the United Arab Emirates. He reportedly has control of Qatari reserves which are worth over $3 billion. The largely middle-class, pro-democracy movement has called for reform of the 35-member Advisory Council. Sheikh Hamad's response to this has been to announce plans for the establishment of elected municipal councils.

WORLD AFFAIRS

AL   Dam Dec   GCC   OAPEC   OPEC

Qatar is a founder-member of the Gulf Cooperation Council (GCC), established in 1981. Since assuming power in mid-1995, Sheikh Hamad has caused some consternation within GCC ranks by adopting an independent, and at times belligerent, stance. Hamad boycotted part of the Council's annual summit in 1995 in protest at the appointment of a Saudi official. Relations with Bahrain are strained over a disputed Gulf island. Qatar has agreed to supply liquefied natural gas (LNG) to Israel. The Amir is keen to retain strong links with Western states, notably the UK and the USA – a ten-year defense agreement has been signed with the USA. Within the quotas set by OPEC, Qatar has supported a moderate oil price.

AID

 $3m (receipts)   Up 50% in 1993

Qatar was a generous aid donor to developing countries during the 1970s and early 1980s, but has in recent years effectively ceased to donate.

Q

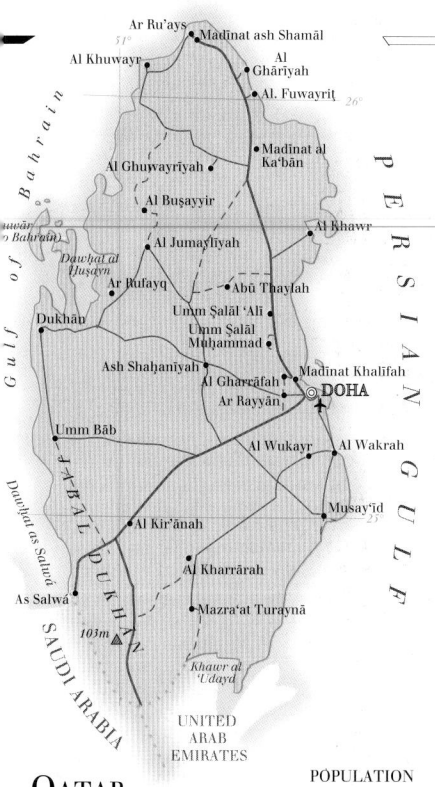

QATAR

Total Land Area : 11 000 sq. km
(4247 sq. miles)

POPULATION

over 100 000 ◎
under 10 000 •

```
0        50 km
0        30 miles
```

N

LAND HEIGHT

200m/1640ft

Sea Level

DEFENSE

 $326m

⬆ Up 8% in 1995

The 11,100-strong armed forces are too small to play a significant role in Qatari affairs, even in the event of political turmoil. A ten-year defense agreement with the USA provides for joint exercises, the stockpiling of American equipment and US access to bases.

ECONOMICS

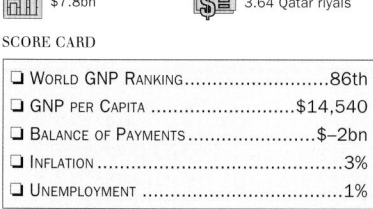 $7.8bn

3.64 Qatar riyals

SCORE CARD

❑ WORLD GNP RANKING.......................86th
❑ GNP PER CAPITA $14,540
❑ BALANCE OF PAYMENTS....................$-2bn
❑ INFLATION 3%
❑ UNEMPLOYMENT 1%

STRENGTHS

A steady supply of crude oil and huge gas reserves, plus related industries. Modern infrastructure.

WEAKNESSES

Dependence on foreign work force. All raw materials, and most food imported. Nearly all water has to be desalinated. Government has large foreign reserves,

RESOURCES

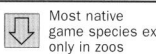

4.7bn kwh (capacity 1.41m kw)

448,000 b/d (reserves 3,729,000,000 bbl)

3m chickens, 170,000 sheep 43,000 camels

Oil, natural gas

Qatar has the third-smallest reserves of crude oil within OPEC but abundant reserves of gas, including the world's largest non-associated gas field, known as North Field.

ENVIRONMENT

None

Most native game species exist only in zoos

The desert hinterland supports little plant or animal life. Oil pollution has damaged marine life. On land, game has been hunted out and most native species are extinct in the wild.

MEDIA

 The press is subject to censorship

PUBLISHING AND BROADCAST MEDIA

There are 4 daily newspapers, *Ar-Rayah* and its English companion *Gulf Times*, *Al-'Arab* and *Ash-Sharq*

1 state-owned service

2 state-owned networks

There is total political censorship. The foreign media is also censored for good taste. Satellite TV channels are freely available.

CRIME

6,285 prisoners

⬆ Up 8% in 1992

Traditional Islamic punishments have deterred crime. However, narcotics-trafficking is on the increase. The incidence of street crime is low.

EXPORTS

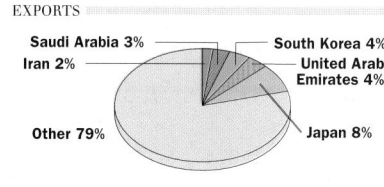

Saudi Arabia 3%
Iran 2%
South Korea 4%
United Arab Emirates 4%
Other 79%
Japan 8%

IMPORTS

Italy 7%
Germany 7%
USA 11%
Other 48%
UK 11%
Japan 16%

but new industries depend on cementing agreements with foreign partners. Potential threat to security from Iraq and Iran makes some multinationals wary of investment.

EDUCATION

 79%

7,283 students

Education is free from primary to university level. The government finances students to study overseas.

HEALTH

1 per 471 people

Heart, circulatory and infectious diseases, cancers

Primary health care is free to Qataris. Hospitals operate to Western standards of care and the government also funds treatment abroad.

WEALTH

 Poverty is very rare in Qatar

CONSUMER GOODS OWNERSHIP

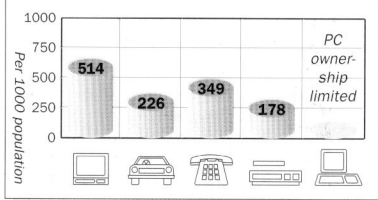

PC ownership limited

514
226
349
178

Qataris have a very high income per capita. There is no income tax, public services are free and the government guarantees jobs for school-leavers. There are no exchange controls.

WORLD RANKING

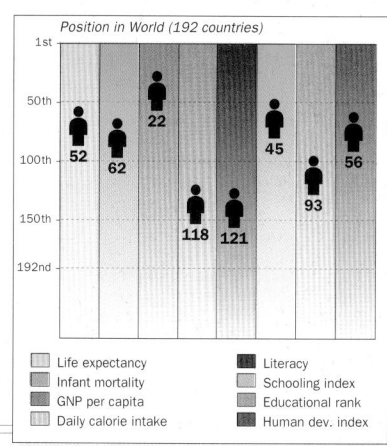

Position in World (192 countries)

52
62
22
118
121
93
45
56

Life expectancy
Infant mortality
GNP per capita
Daily calorie intake
Literacy
Schooling index
Educational rank
Human dev. index

Q

ROMANIA

OFFICIAL NAME: Romania **CAPITAL:** Bucharest
POPULATION: 22.8 million **CURRENCY:** Leu **OFFICIAL LANGUAGE:** Romanian

  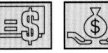

ROMANIA LIES ON THE Black Sea coast, with the Danube as its southern border. The eastern Carpathian Mountains form an arc across the country, curving around the upland basin of Transylvania. Long dominated by the Ottoman, Russian and Habsburg empires, Romania became an independent monarchy in 1878. After World War II, the monarchy was supplanted by a communist People's Republic, headed by Nicolae Ceaușescu from 1965. A coup in 1989 resulted in his execution. Romania is now a limited democracy, converting slowly to a free-market economy.

Village in northeastern Romania, in the foothills of the Carpathian Mountains, close to the border with Ukraine. Corn and wheat are Romania's main crops.

CLIMATE

WEATHER CHART

- Average daily temperature
- Rainfall

Romania has a continental climate with two growing seasons. Rainfall is generally moderate, with most falling in spring and early summer. Very heavy spring rains occasionally destroy new crops. Snow is frequent in winter, which can be bitterly cold.

TRANSPORTATION

Bucharest-Otopeni Intl
1m passengers

261 ships
4.13m dwt

THE TRANSPORTATION NETWORK

146,380 miles (235,560 km)	70 miles (113 km)
6,914 miles (11,127 km)	1,071 miles (1,724 km)

Outdated infrastructure is a major obstacle to Romania's development. Work on a subway for Bucharest, on new expressways and on the almost-complete Danube–Black Sea Canal was stopped in 1989. US interests have proposed increasing the regional role of the port of Constanța.

TOURISM

2.8m visitors

Down 4% in 1994

MAIN OVERSEAS ARRIVALS

CIS 36%	
Bulgaria 17%	
Hungary 13%	
Yugoslavia 13%	
Turkey 3%	
Other 18%	

% of total arrivals

The Black Sea, Danube delta and Carpathian Mountains are the primary natural attractions, while Transylvania has a rich historical heritage. However, tourist facilities are generally poor. Under Ceaușescu, the need for foreign currency meant that tourists came before Romanians in accommodation priorities. Today, privatization of property and an acute housing shortage have reduced accommodation available to visitors. By 1992, tourism was no longer a net foreign exchange earner for Romania.

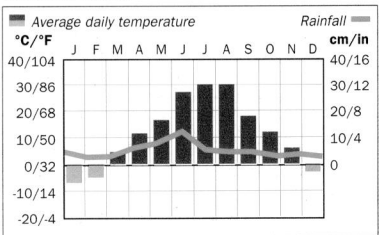

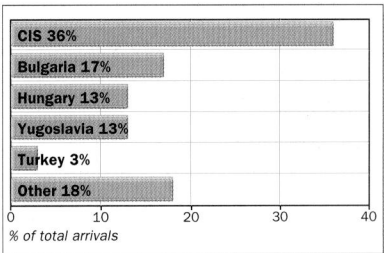

ROMANIA

Total Land Area: 230 340 sq. km
(88 954 sq. miles)

POPULATION

- over 1 000 000
- over 100 000
- over 50 000

LAND HEIGHT

- 2000m/6562ft
- 1000m/3281ft
- 500m/1640ft
- 200m/656ft
- Sea Level

PEOPLE

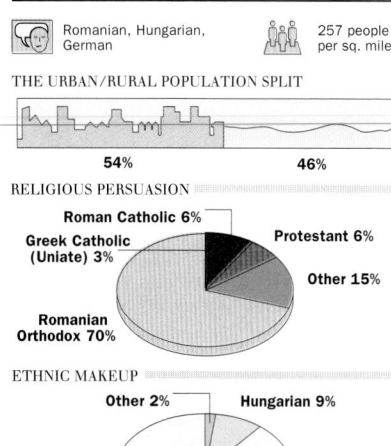

Romanian, Hungarian, German

257 people per sq. mile

THE URBAN/RURAL POPULATION SPLIT

54%   46%

RELIGIOUS PERSUASION

- Roman Catholic 6%
- Greek Catholic (Uniate) 3%
- Protestant 6%
- Other 15%
- Romanian Orthodox 70%

ETHNIC MAKEUP

- Other 2%
- Hungarian 9%
- Romanian 89%

Since 1989, there has been a rise in Romanian nationalism, aggravated by the hardships brought by the austerity measures of economic reform. The incidence of ethnic violence has also risen, particularly toward Gypsies and Hungarians. Ethnic Hungarians form the largest minority group in Romania. They are partly protected by the influence of the Hungarian state, whereas the Gypsies do not have any similar support and tend to suffer greater discrimination.

Romania's population is currently decreasing. This is due to rising emigration since 1989, mainly for economic reasons, and to a falling birth-rate since the early 1990s. The latter trend is in sharp contrast to the 1980s, when the Ceaușescu regime enforced a "pro-natalist" policy, banning abortion and contraception. The government also imposed taxes on childless adults or on those with fewer than four children and obliged married women to have monthly fertility examinations. The birth-rate accordingly rose. However, the population as a whole did not rise significantly due to an increase in Romania's mortality rate. Abortion was legalized in 1989; maternal death rates have recently declined.

POPULATION AGE BREAKDOWN

% of population by age group	0–14	15–64	65+		
	6.7%	8.6%	10.3%	10.3%	12.6%
	65.2%	65.4%	63.1%	66.3%	66.2%
	28.1%	26%	26.6%	23.4%	21.2%
	1960	1970	1980	1990	2000

WORLD AFFAIRS

| BSEC | CE | NACC | OSCE | WEU |

While making efforts to remain on good terms with the former Soviet states, Romania is building closer links with Western Europe. In 1993, it signed an association agreement with the EU, applying for membership in 1995.

Relations with Hungary are tense, Romania having resisted the demands of the Hungarian minority in Transylvania for greater autonomy.

After 1989, unification with Moldova was a distinct possibility as Romanians are of the same ethnic group as Moldovans. However, the issue was quashed in 1993 when Moldova voted for closer links with the CIS. Romania adhered to UN sanctions against Yugoslavia despite the negative effects on its own economy.

AID

Main donor is EBRD

Increasing aid from EBRD and IMF

The IMF, World Bank, EBRD and the EU approved loans totaling $774 million in 1994 to support the government's economic reform program. Aid is being directed chiefly into mechanizing the privatized, agricultural sector and improving telecommunications.

POLITICS

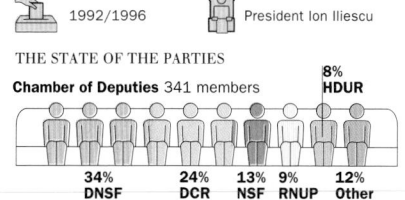

1992/1996

President Ion Iliescu

THE STATE OF THE PARTIES

Chamber of Deputies 341 members

| 34% DNSF | 24% DCR | 13% NSF | 9% RNUP | 12% Other | 8% HDUR |

DNSF = Democratic National Salvation Front
DCR = Democratic Convention of Romania (composed of: Christian Democrat National Peasants' Party, Party of the Civic Alliance, National Liberal Party – Democratic Convention, National Liberal Party – Youth Wing, Romanian Social Democratic Party, Romanian Ecology Party)
NSF = National Salvation Front **RNUP** = Romanian National Union Party **HDUR** = Hungarian Democratic Union of Romania **Other** = Greater Romania Party, Socialist Labor Party, Agrarian Democratic Party of Romania

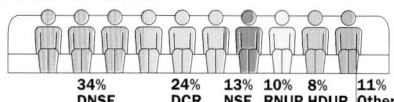

Senate 143 members

| 34% DNSF | 24% DCR | 13% NSF | 10% RNUP | 8% HDUR | 11% Other |

In a 1991 referendum, Romanians approved a new constitution establishing a multiparty democracy headed by a directly elected president.

MAIN POLITICAL ISSUES
Economic performance
The poor performance of the economy has exerted pressure on the minority government. General strikes in early 1994 expressed popular discontent with falling living standards, and the seeming inability of the government to develop a coherent economic policy.

Ethnic tensions
Ethnic tensions are rising in Romania. The far right has made political gains and nationalism is increasingly accepted. In 1993, elements of the extreme right were advocating labor camps for ethnic minorities. Gypsies are becoming victims of violent, racially motivated attacks.

PROFILE
Romania's 1989 "revolution" – in effect a coup – left an old communist elite in power. Unlike Poland, Hungary and Czechoslovakia, Romania did not have an organized group ready to introduce real democracy and with the skills necessary to create a vibrant market economy. Democracy is in place on the surface but political intimidation and ballot-rigging remain commonplace.

While many state assets have been privatized, most have remained in the hands of people tied to the ruling clique. The DNSF government retains the support of conservative groups, such as miners and rural workers.

President Ion Iliescu. He succeeded Ceaușescu and was reelected in 1992.

Nikolae Vacaroiu, an economist who became prime minister in 1992.

R

CHRONOLOGY

Many of Romania's foreign policy tensions are the legacy of its long history of redrawn borders. Former territories are resisting reunification, not least on economic grounds.

- ❏ **1859** Unification of Moldova and Wallachia forms basis of future Romania.
- ❏ **1878** Independence, but at cost of losing Bessarabia to Russia.
- ❏ **1916–1918** Enters World War I on Allied side. At end of war, gains substantial territory, including Transylvania from Hungary. ➡

R

DEFENSE

💲 $928m   ⬆ Up 22% in 1995

0   *Defense spending as % GDP*   40

2.9%

The military received limited funding under the Ceaușescu regime and troops were routinely deployed as cheap labor. Since the demise of the Warsaw Pact, Romania has not sought close ties with NATO. The weak economy means that military expenditure may fall in future.

ROMANIAN ARMED FORCES

🪖	1,843 main battle tanks (146 T-34, 822 T-55, 30 T-72, 620 TR-85, 225 TR-580)	128,800 personnel
🚢	1 submarine, 5 frigates, 1 destroyer and 77 patrol boats	19,000 personnel
✈	402 combat aircraft (10 MiG-17, 75 IAR-93, 120 MiG-21, 38 MiG-23)	54,000 personnel
	None	

ECONOMICS

📊 $27.9bn   💱 1,774.37–2,630.00 lei

SCORE CARD

- ❏ WORLD GNP RANKING............................61st
- ❏ GNP PER CAPITA $1,230
- ❏ BALANCE OF PAYMENTS....................$–259m
- ❏ INFLATION 28.2%
- ❏ UNEMPLOYMENT..................................11%

EXPORTS

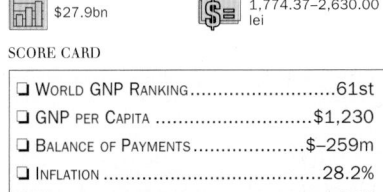

France 5%   Turkey 6%
Italy 8%
China 9%
Other 58%
Germany 14%

IMPORTS

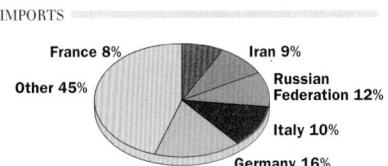

France 8%   Iran 9%
Russian Federation 12%
Other 45%
Italy 10%
Germany 16%

STRENGTHS

Large number of foreign joint ventures. Tourism potential.

WEAKNESSES

Slow transition from centrally planned to market economy. Delays in implementing economic reform. Low foreign investment levels. Large bureaucracy.

PROFILE

Few economic reforms have been undertaken in Romania compared with other former communist Eastern European states. While all have suffered recession in the reform process, Romania's has been the most severe, and there appears to be little prospect of improvement in the near future. Pressure for reform is strongest in the chemical, petrochemical, metal, transportation and food industries.

Only a small minority are doing well economically. Real wages have also fallen since the change of regime, and are continuing to do so. Farming began

ECONOMIC PERFORMANCE INDICATOR

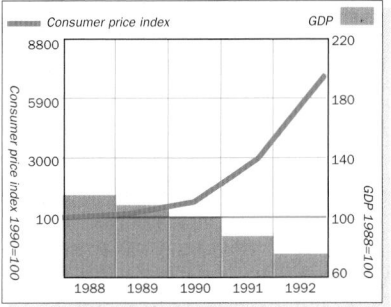

Consumer price index   GDP

to be privatized in 1989 and by 1994, 80% of farmland was in private hands. It remains severely undermechanized. Agricultural processing is still under state control, and output levels have fallen, notably in meat products.

Romania was the first Eastern European country to open its economy to foreign investment, allowing 100% foreign ownership from 1990. The number of joint ventures, 21,000, is the highest in Eastern Europe, but most are small-scale. Foreign investment is hindered by bureaucracy and doubts about the country's stability. In 1995, the government published a list of nearly 4,000 state-owned enterprises which were due for privatization.

ROMANIA : MAJOR BUSINESSES

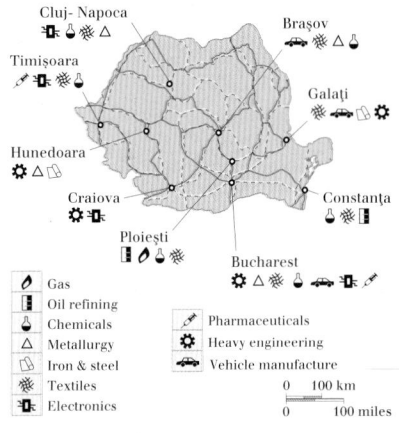

RESOURCES

 54.2bn kwh (capacity 22.9m kw)

 132,631 b/d (reserves 1,588,754,000 bbl)

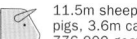 11.5m sheep, 9.2m pigs, 3.6m cattle, 776,000 goats

Coal, salt, iron, natural gas, methane, bauxite, copper, lead, zinc, oil

ELECTRICITY GENERATION

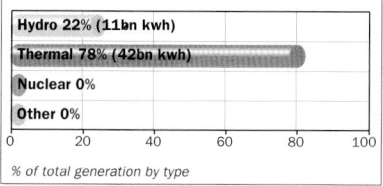

Hydro 22% (11bn kwh)

Thermal 78% (42bn kwh)

Nuclear 0%

Other 0%

% of total generation by type

Romania has oil and gas reserves, but production is insufficient to meet domestic demand. Production from onshore fields fell during the 1980s as reserves were depleted and oil imports have risen substantially since 1989. Efforts are being concentrated on developing offshore reserves in the Black Sea and several drilling platforms are now in operation. Romania has opened up exploration and processing to foreign investors, including Middle Eastern and CIS companies.

The electricity supply is outdated and has been insufficient to meet national demand for the last 20 years. The development of a nuclear power industry has been scrapped because of the lack of available funds.

Deposits of other minerals are small and contribute little to export earnings.

ENVIRONMENT

 5% (4% partially protected)

Rising public awareness, but no funds available

ENVIRONMENTAL TREATIES

No	Yes	Yes
No	Yes	Yes

The south is the region with the most serious pollution problems. Cement plant and power-station emissions have been linked to respiratory diseases. The incidence of birth defects has risen in the vicinity of the artificial fiber plant at Suceava. Industrial water pollution is also a major problem, and aggravated by insufficient purification facilities. However, nature conservation is currently receiving more attention. The Danube delta has been identified as a site for a biosphere reserve.

MEDIA

 In 1994, the government reimposed political reporting restrictions, which had been lifted in 1989

PUBLISHING AND BROADCAST MEDIA

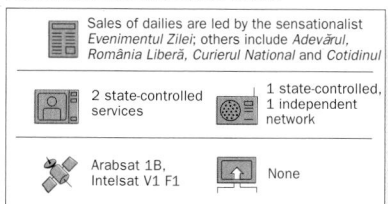

Sales of dailies are led by the sensationalist *Evenimentul Zilei*; others include *Adevărul*, *România Liberă*, *Curierul National* and *Cotidinul*

2 state-controlled services

1 state-controlled, 1 independent network

Arabsat 1B, Intelsat V1 F1

None

The number of newspapers rose to 1,600 after 1989, but many are now closing as rising prices mean that people can no longer afford them. The government reimposed political censorship in 1994 and in practice now also controls the national independent TV service. A new amateur TV station broadcasting from a Bucharest flat is unlikely to survive. The main opposition paper is *Cotidinul*.

CRIME

 41,300 prisoners

 Up 4% in 1992

CRIME RATES

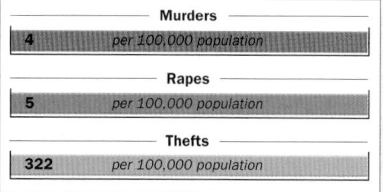

Murders

4 per 100,000 population

Rapes

5 per 100,000 population

Thefts

322 per 100,000 population

The black economy is the primary source of income for a third of the population. Levels of tax evasion are estimated to be among the highest in the world.

EDUCATION

 97%

235,669 students

0 Education spending as % GNP 25

3.6%

THE EDUCATION SYSTEM

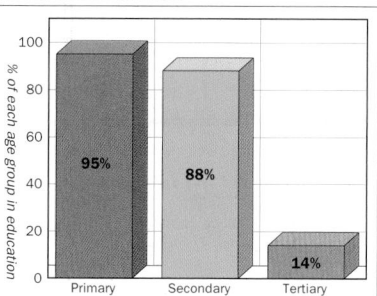

% of each age group in education

Primary 95%
Secondary 88%
Tertiary 14%

Attendance at elementary and secondary schools is far below the European average – in 1994, 100,000 children had no schooling. As university enrollment is no longer restricted, the number of tertiary students has risen by 30% since 1989, temporarily reducing high unemployment among young adults.

ROMANIA : LAND USE

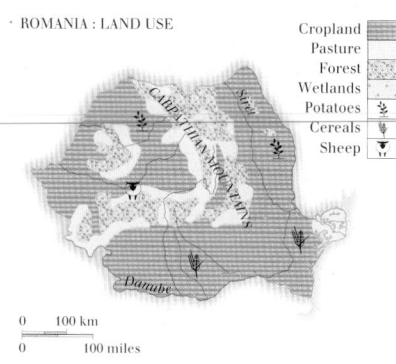

Cropland	
Pasture	
Forest	
Wetlands	
Potatoes	
Cereals	
Sheep	

0 100 km

0 100 miles

HEALTH

 1 per 540 people

Heart & cerebrovascular diseases, cancers, tuberculosis

0 Health spending as % GDP 25

3.9%

Romania's life expectancy is, jointly with Albania's, the lowest in Europe, at 70 years; in the worst polluted parts of Transylvania it is 61 years. Its TB rate is also the highest in Europe.

WEALTH

Coal miner, 19,349 lei ($7) per month ; senior electronics engineer, 85,000 lei ($32) per month

CONSUMER GOODS OWNERSHIP

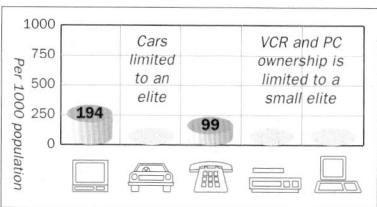

Per 1000 population

Cars limited to an elite — 194

VCR and PC ownership is limited to a small elite — 99

Wealth distribution has changed little since the fall of the Ceaușescu regime in 1989. The ruling ex-communist clique are still the richest group and determined to maintain their economic as well as political position.

WORLD RANKING

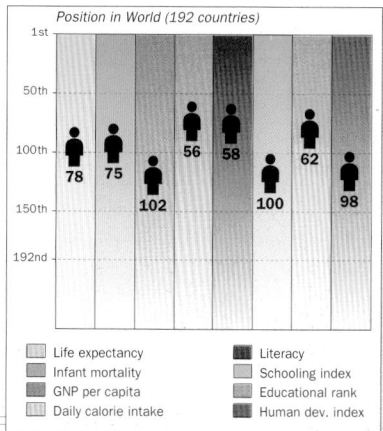

Position in World (192 countries)

1st
50th
100th
150th
192nd

78 75 102 56 58 62 100 98

Life expectancy	Literacy
Infant mortality	Schooling index
GNP per capita	Educational rank
Daily calorie intake	Human dev. index

R

453

RUSSIAN FEDERATION

OFFICIAL NAME: Russian Federation   **CAPITAL:** Moscow
POPULATION: 147 million   **CURRENCY:** Rouble   **OFFICIAL LANGUAGE:** Russian

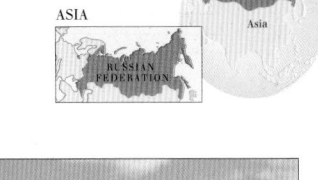

ASIA

W ITH A TERRITORY of 6 million sq. miles Russia is the world's largest state, almost twice as big as either the USA or China. Bounded by the Arctic and Pacific Oceans on its northern and eastern coasts, it also has land boundaries with 13 countries. With the formal dissolution of the USSR in 1991, Russia became an independent sovereign state. Within the CIS, it maintains a traditionally dominant role in Central Asia and Eurasia. Ethnic Russians make up 80% of the population, but there are around 150 smaller ethnic groups, many with their own national territories within Russia's borders. The growth of regionalism is a major political issue. The situation is complicated by the fact that many of these territories are rich in key resources such as oil, gas, gold and diamonds.

The Kremlin, Moscow. *Rebuilt in 1475 by Ivan the Great, who commissioned architects from Pskov and Italy, it is enclosed by walls 1.5 miles long and lies on the Moscow River.*

CLIMATE

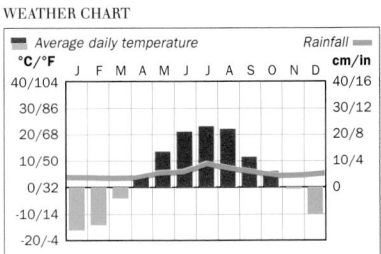

WEATHER CHART

Russia has a cold continental climate, characterized by two, widely divergent main seasons. Spring and autumn are very brief periods of transition between warm summers and freezing winters. The country is open to the influences of the Arctic and Atlantic to the north and west. However, mountains to the south and east prevent any warming effects from the Indian and Pacific Oceans filtering across. Severe winters characterize most regions. Winter temperatures vary surprisingly little from north to south, but fall sharply in eastern regions. The January temperature of –94°F recorded at Verkhoyansk in Siberia is the world record low outside Antarctica.

Housing in Moscow. *Living conditions in major cities are cramped, with two families often sharing one small flat.*

RUSSIAN FEDERATION

Total Land Area :
17 075 400 sq. km
(6 592 812 sq. miles)

POPULATION

- ■ over 5 000 000
- ▣ over 1 000 000
- ◉ over 500 000
- ◎ over 100 000
- ○ over 50 000
- ● over 10 000

LAND HEIGHT

- 3000m/9843ft
- 2000m/6562ft
- 1000m/3281ft
- 500m/1640ft
- 200m/656ft
- Sea Level
- –200m/-656ft

R

TRANSPORTATION

Sheremetyevo, Moscow
9.31m passengers

1,662 ships
13.98m dwt

THE TRANSPORTATION NETWORK

405,470 miles (652,500 km)		None	
54,115 miles (87,090 km)		76,865 miles (123,700 km)	

Russia has a comprehensive transportation network. Cities are served by good tram and bus systems and Moscow has one of the most impressive subway systems in the world. In rural areas, car ownership is still low and the population relies on an extensive bus service. However, since 1991, all systems have seen some decline. The railroads, which were already declining in the Soviet era, are now seriously overburdened and accidents and delays are occuring more frequently. About 20% of the railroad track should be renewed every year owing to frost and other damage. A shortage of funds means this is no longer done. Roads are also deteriorating, especially in major cities, but inter-urban highways are also affected. Crime is growing on railroads – notably the Trans-Siberian – and roads.

Since 1991, many new airlines have been set up as routes are privatized. However, Aeroflot, the former state monopoly airline, is still the largest. Now called Russian International Airlines on overseas routes, it uses Boeing aircraft on flights from Moscow to London, Paris, Frankfurt, New York and Tokyo.

Standards on international routes are generally high. However, the safety record of internal routes is declining.

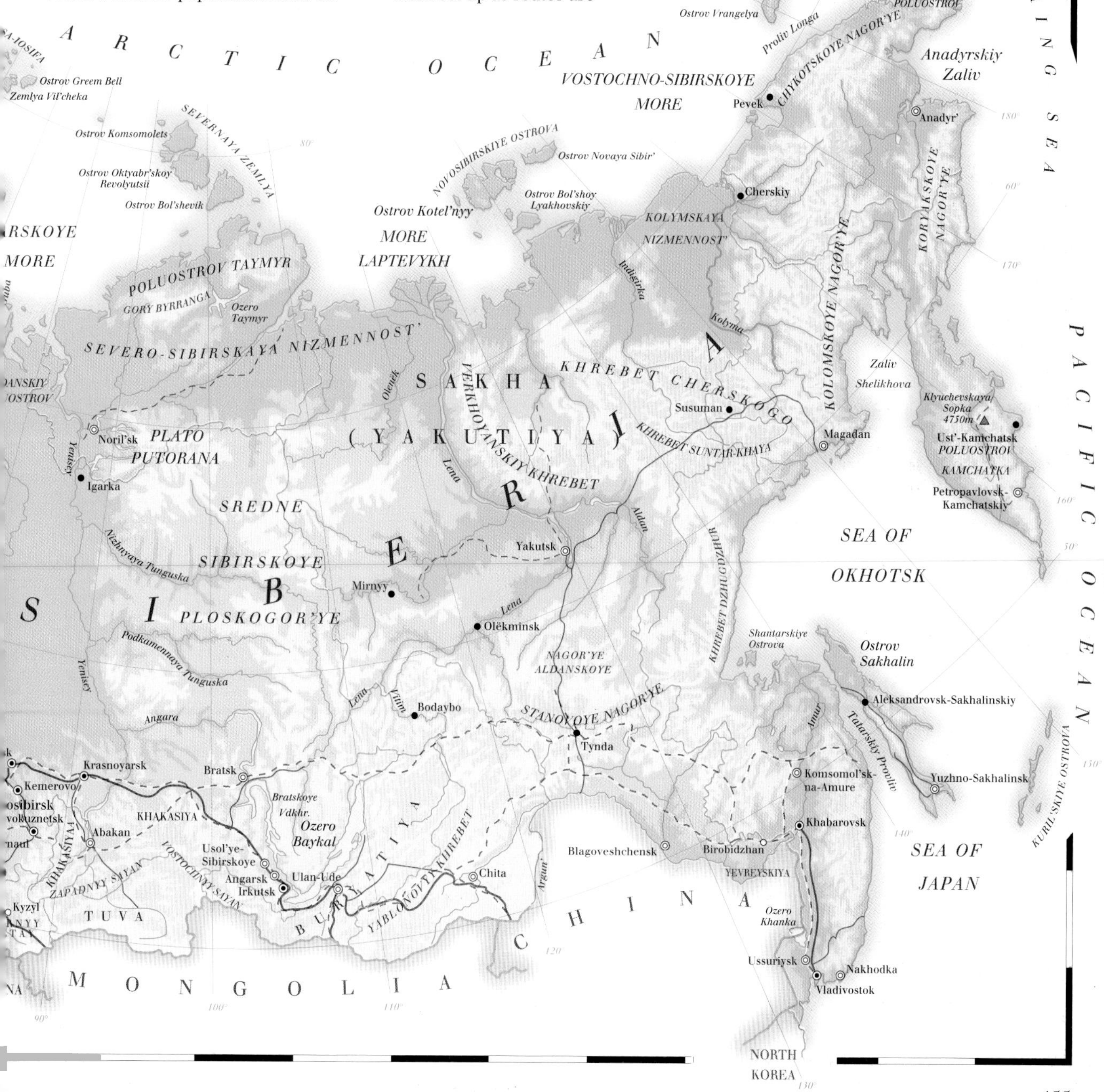

ARCTIC OCEAN

Ostrov Iosifa
Ostrov Greem Bell
Zemlya Vil'cheka
Ostrov Komsomolets
SEVERNAYA ZEMLYA
Ostrov Oktyabr'skoy Revolyutsii
Ostrov Bol'shevik

RSKOYE
MORE

ANSKIY
OSTROV

POLUOSTROV TAYMYR
GORY BYRRANGA
Ozero Taymyr
SEVERO-SIBIRSKAYA NIZMENNOST'

Noril'sk
PLATO PUTORANA
Igarka
SREDNE
SIBIRSKOYE
S I B E PLOSKOGOR'YE
Nizhnyaya Tunguska
S Podkamennaya Tunguska
Angara
Yenisey

Krasnoyarsk
Kemerovo
osibirsk
vokuznetsk
naul
Abakan
KHAKASIYA
VOSTOCHNYY SAYAN
Usol'ye-Sibirskoye
Kyzyl NNYY Angarsk
KNYY Irkutsk
TUVA
ZAPADNYY SAYAN
NA
M O N G O L I A

Bratsk
Bratskoye Vdkhr.
Ozero Baykal
Ulan-Ude
B U R Y A T I Y A
YABLONOVYY KHREBET

CHUKCHI SEA
Bering Strait
B E R I N G   S E A

CHUKOTSKIY POLUOSTROV
CHUKOTSKOYE NAGOR'YE
Proliv Longa
Anadyrskiy Zaliv
Anadyr'

VOSTOCHNO-SIBIRSKOYE MORE
Pevek

NOVOSIBIRSKIYE OSTROVA
Ostrov Novaya Sibir'
Ostrov Bol'shoy Lyakhovskiy
Ostrov Kotel'nyy
MORE LAPTEVYKH

Cherskiy
KOLYMSKAYA NIZMENNOST'
KOLYMSKOYE NAGOR'YE
KORYAKSKOYE NAGOR'YE

Kolyma
Indigirka
KHREBET CHERSKOGO
Susuman
Magadan
Zaliv Shelikhova
Klyuchevskaya Sopka 4750m
Ust'-Kamchatsk
POLUOSTROV KAMCHATKA
Petropavlovsk-Kamchatskiy

S A K H A
(Y A K U T I Y A)
VERKHOYANSKIY KHREBET
Olenëk
Lena
Yakutsk
Aldan
KHREBET SUNTAR-KHAYA
KHREBET DZHUGDZHUR

Mirnyy
Lena
Olëkminsk
NAGOR'YE ALDANSKOYE
Bodaybo
STANOVOYE NAGOR'YE
Tynda
Vitim

SEA OF OKHOTSK

Shantarskiye Ostrova
Ostrov Sakhalin
Aleksandrovsk-Sakhalinskiy
Tatarskiy Proliv
Komsomol'sk-na-Amure
Yuzhno-Sakhalinsk
KURIL'SKIYE OSTROVA

Chita
Argun'
Blagoveshchensk
Birobidzhan
YEVREYSKIYA
Amur
Khabarovsk
Ozero Khanka
Ussuriysk
Nakhodka
Vladivostok

SEA OF JAPAN

C H I N A

NORTH KOREA

P A C I F I C   O C E A N
R

TOURISM

 4.6m visitors   Down 41% in 1994

MAIN OVERSEAS ARRIVALS

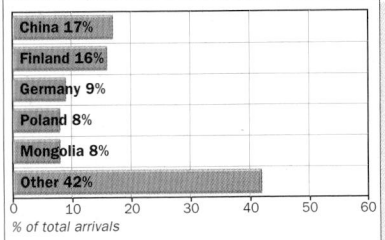

China 17%
Finland 16%
Germany 9%
Poland 8%
Mongolia 8%
Other 42%

% of total arrivals

The privatization and breakup of *Intourist*, the former monopoly tourist agency, has led to a vast expansion of tourism opportunities in Russia; each region is keen to earn hard currency and to attract rich visitors. At the luxury end of the market, trips from St. Petersburg to Tashkent are now available on former president Brezhnev's official train. River trips down the Volga and visits to medieval monasteries are increasingly popular. Tourists can also experience life in a Russian forest, or fish for salmon in the Kola peninsula. The defense sector has opened up to tourism and now offers flights in MiG jets, or drives in T-84 Russian tanks.

Moscow and St. Petersburg remain favorite destinations. Hotels in both cities tend either to cater for the well-off visitor, or to be of a basic standard. The St. Petersburg region is also increasingly explored. Novgorod has many fine churches and the Pskov area is celebrated as the setting for many of Pushkin's works, including *Eugene Onegin* and *Boris Godunov*.

Many parts of Russia remain inaccessible to most tourists. The communist ban on foreigners visiting the Urals has only recently been lifted, but the area still has very few facilities. However, resorts such as Sochi on the Black Sea have experienced a building boom, including the 2,500-room *Dagomys* Acapulco-style hotel complex.

PEOPLE

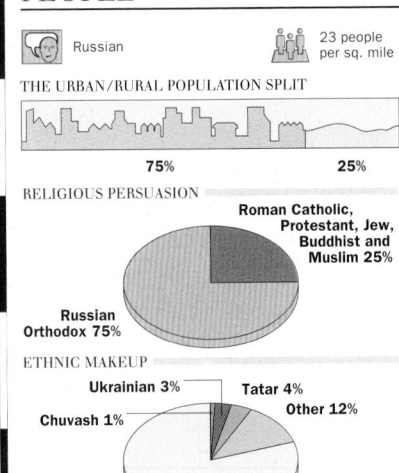

Russian   23 people per sq. mile

THE URBAN/RURAL POPULATION SPLIT

75%   25%

RELIGIOUS PERSUASION

Roman Catholic, Protestant, Jew, Buddhist and Muslim 25%

Russian Orthodox 75%

ETHNIC MAKEUP

Ukrainian 3%   Tatar 4%
Chuvash 1%   Other 12%

Russian 80%

In the former Soviet Union, Russians accounted for just over 50% of the population, but in Russia they are an overwhelming majority. Significant numbers of Russians still live in some of the neighboring republics, notably in Ukraine and Latvia. However, a rise in nationalism throughout the former USSR has persuaded many Russians to return to the Russian Federation.

Within Russia there has also been some increase in ethnic tension. There are 57 nationalities with their own territories within the federation and 95 nationalities without a territory (although these groups make up only 6% of the population).

Social life in Russia has not changed significantly since the demise of communism. However, with the lifting of censorship, there has been a greater expression of sexuality as well as of political and religious views. While there has been some increase in the availability of pornography and prostitution, this is mostly confined to major urban centers. There has been some revival of both the Russian Orthodox and Muslim faiths. However, Church attendance is still below Western levels. One marked change of which Russians speak is the growing importance attached to money. The mutual support systems of extended friendships are now in decline.

The position of women has changed little since the fall of communism. Many have suffered from the rise in unemployment, but this reflects the demise of many part-time or badly paid jobs, rather than a gender-motivated change in Russian society. Most Russians' very modest living standards have been maintained and retail sales in Russia are rising. Compared with the West, unemployment remains low at an official figure of 1.7% of the population.

POPULATION AGE BREAKDOWN

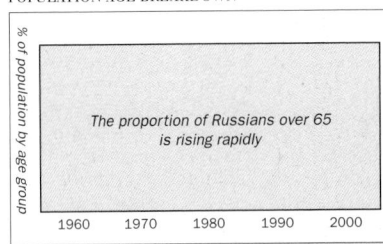

% of population by age group

The proportion of Russians over 65 is rising rapidly

1960   1970   1980   1990   2000

POLITICS

 U. House 1995/1999
L. House 1995/1999   President
Boris N. Yeltsin

THE STATE OF THE PARTIES

State Duma 450 members

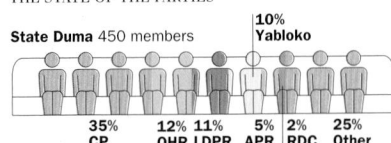

10% Yabloko

35% CP   12% OHR   11% LDPR   5% APR   2% RDC   25% Other

CP = Communist Party   OHR = Our Home is Russia   LDPR = Liberal Democratic Party of Russia   APR = Agrarian Party of Russia   RDC = Russia's Democratic Choice

Federal Council 178 deputies

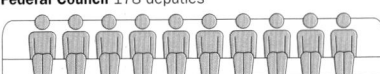

2 members are elected to represent each of 89 regions and republics

Russia has a democratically elected parliament under the leadership of an executive president.

MAIN POLITICAL ISSUES
Living standards
Russians are disillusioned at the failure of politicians to improve their living standards. The securities which used to underpin life – long-term employment, guaranteed housing and a basic diet – have been swept away. The decline has hit certain vulnerable groups – particularly the old – the hardest.

While 1995 was a watershed in Russia's transition to a market economy, there was a complete absence of any appreciable economic "feel-good" factor for most people.

Crime
Crime has risen alarmingly since the collapse of the Soviet Union. It is no longer safe to walk the streets in some parts of St. Petersburg or Moscow after dark. Bureaucratic corruption is now open and rising – officials demand payment for most services. Vladimir Zhirinovsky's promise to crush crime is a major reason behind his electoral success, particularly from the newly emerging middle class.

Disaffection with reform
Many Russians are disappointed with President Yeltsin's period in power and

President Yeltsin *backed the reformers who lost heavily in the 1993 elections.*

Vladimir Zhirinovsky, *leader of the ultra-right Liberal Party.*

R

POLITICS *continued*

his attempts at reform. Mindful of the changing popular mood, parties no longer use the word "reform" but speak of "stabilization."

Russia's loss of Great Power status

Under the Soviet Union, Russians took a great pride in their country's role in the world. The collapse of the economy and Russia's withdrawal from a global role have badly dented this pride. For many Russians, accepting Western aid and technology is a reminder of Russia's loss of status. Mindful of this, in early 1996 Yeltsin appointed as foreign minister Yevgeny Primakov, who pledged to institute policy befitting a "Great Power."

PROFILE

The elections of 1995 resulted in a victory for the Communist Party, which emerged as the single largest party in the *Duma*. Although President Yeltsin had appealed to the electorate not to "allow the forces of the past to seize power again," in the aftermath of the election he attempted to downplay the significance of the Communist Party's success. Nevertheless, Yeltsin responded to the result in early 1996 by dropping a number of high-profile reformers – including Anatoly Chubais – from his administration, thereby making the government less vulnerable to communist and nationalist criticism. The dismissal of Chubais – the leading advocate of economic reform – appeared to place a much-needed IMF loan in jeopardy. However, the loan was secured in March 1996 and was seen as a massive boost for Yeltsin ahead of the June presidential elections.

Yeltsin and the Communist Party leader Gennady Zyuganov both announced in February 1996 their intention to run in the election. Zyuganov and the communists are powerful because they have preserved a highly effective organization which proved – in the *Duma* elections – its ability to channel popular discontent with the downside of reform into votes. But for all the communists' natural advantages of a nostalgic and angry populace and an efficient organization,

Yeltsin's popularity has been steadily rising in the opinion polls.

There had been some speculation that Yeltsin would not run. He was hospitalized twice in 1995 because of a heart problem and many commentators thought that he could not win the election while Russian troops were fighting in Chechnya. Yeltsin accepted that the Chechen problem was a major obstacle to his reelection and in May 1996 he signed a settlement plan with the rebel leaders, which, it was hoped, would lay the foundations for peace in the region.

While many reformers, including Chubais, had backed Yeltsin as the only means of stopping a Zyuganov victory, others said they would support Grigory Yavlinsky, leader of the pro-reform Yabloko. Another dark horse was Vladimir Zhirinovsky, Russia's flamboyant ultra-nationalist. In the event, Yeltsin won a comfortable victory.

WORLD AFFAIRS

During 1992 and 1993, Russia displayed little independent initiative in foreign affairs and allied itself closely to the USA. Its weak economy and a need for regular infusions of hard currency put it in no position to antagonize the Western powers and Japan.

However, since 1993, Russia has developed a more independent foreign policy, a trend which looks set to continue.

In early 1996, Andrei Kosyrev resigned as foreign minister – a post he had held since 1990 – and was replaced by Yevgeny Primakov. Kosyrev had been heavily criticized by nationalists and communists for his relatively soft line on Bosnia. Primakov is regarded as more sceptical of Western intentions toward Russia and is expected to adopt a tough line on major issues, including NATO's eastward expansion. A Middle Eastern expert, Primakov is also expected to pursue a more independent Russian line on the various regional peace processes.

Russia remains the overwhelmingly dominant partner in the CIS. It regards the successor states of the USSR as the "near abroad" and maintains troops in most of them. The policy is motivated in part by the need to protect the many Russians living in these states. Many of the CIS regimes are run by ex-communists with close links with Moscow. The CIS states – with the exception of Belorussia which openly courts closer integration with Russia – expressed serious alarm at a non-binding *Duma* resolution passed in March 1996 which effectively called for the reformation of the USSR.

St. Basil's Cathedral, Moscow. It was built in 1555-1561 to celebrate Ivan the Terrible's capture of the Tatar stronghold of Kazan. The exterior domes were decorated in the 1670s.

AID

 $16bn   Aid is rising

Russia received about $16 billion from the IMF in 1995–1996 in support of its economic reform program. The EBRD has offered $300 million of credit; loans of up to $30,000 are on offer to small concerns. A similar fund invests in equities of newly privatized companies.

DEFENSE

 $63bn   Down 20% in 1995

0	Defense spending as % GDP	40
9.6%		

RUSSIAN ARMED FORCES

 19,000 main battle tanks (T-54/-55, T-62, T-64A, T-72, T-80/-M9) — 670,000 personnel

 183 submarines, 1 carrier, 22 destroyers, 102 frigates, 143 patrol boats — 130,000 personnel

 2,150 combat aircraft (MiG 29, MiG 27, MiG 25, MiG-23, Su-27, Su-24) — 200,000 personnel

 928 ICBM, 45 SSBN, 100 ABM

In 1991, Russia inherited armed forces of 2.7 million men, of whom 2.1 million were within its borders. However, it proved incapable of affording such a large army. By 1995, the forces had fallen to 1 million. Draft dodging has also increased. In 1992, the army lost 35,000 officers and another 16,000 resigned in the first four months of 1993. Defense budgets have also been reduced. Spending on strategic nuclear forces is now limited to the physical protection of warheads. Early warning and space programs have also been sharply reduced. The navy has been the worst affected, and Russia's northern and Pacific fleets are inactive and deteriorating fast. No agreement has yet been reached with the Ukraine over who owns the Black Sea fleet. The air force suffers from fuel shortages.

Yegor Gaidar, one of the leading reformers in the Russian parliament.

Defense Minister Grachev, effectively controls the Russian Army.

REGIONS

MOSCOW

M OSCOW, RUSSIA'S CAPITAL, administrative center and the seat of parliament, has a population of 8,801,500. It is now the most Westernized of Russia's cities. In practice, it functions almost like an independent city state. Market reforms have proceeded faster in Moscow than in any other Russian city and, in the December 1993 local elections, Russia's Choice, the pro-reform party, won a majority in the city *Duma.* Privatization of housing, stores and enterprises has been swift, but this has led to a rapid increase in corruption and crime. According to its forceful mayor, Yury Luzhkov, the city is almost bankrupt as the Russian government has failed to pay Moscow 250 billion roubles in central grants. A new tax of 0.1% of turnover in the Moscow Inter-Bank Currency Exchange has been imposed to raise revenue, much to the annoyance of businessmen.

CHECHNYA

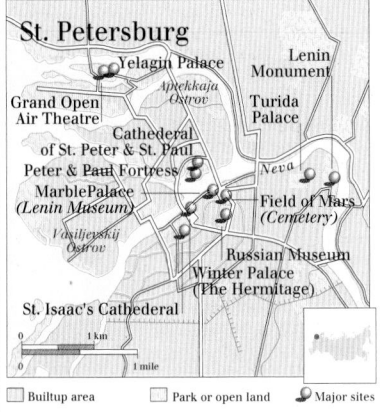

L OCATED IN THE SOUTHWEST of Russia, Chechnya region is dominated by the Chechens, the largest of the North Caucasian nationalities. In 1991, Chechnya declared itself independent of Russian rule and appointed its own president and government. An attempt to overthrow President Gen. Dzhokar Dudayev and replace him with a Moscow-approved leader failed and in 1994 President Yeltsin, despite much political opposition, launched a military offensive against rebel forces. Dudayev was killed in April 1996, as fighting in the region continued. However it was hoped that the signing in May 1996 of a peace plan between Yeltsin and rebels leaders would put an end to hostilities.

ST. PETERSBURG

B UILT BY PETER THE GREAT in the 18th century to emulate European capitals, St. Petersburg is still considered one of the most beautiful cities in Russia. Its magnificent Versailles-influenced architecture includes The Hermitage, home to one of the world's greatest art collections. It was the storming of its Winter Palace in 1917 which marked the start of the Revolution.

The city's various name changes reflect key periods in Russian history. In 1914, anti-German sentiment resulted in the more Slavic name of Petrograd. In 1924, the city became Leningrad, as a tribute to Lenin who died that year. In 1991, the restoration of St. Petersburg was a snub to Russia's years under the Communist Party.

St. Petersburg has faced greater problems than Moscow during its transition to a market economy. Its industry is dominated by companies supplying the defense sector.

KRASNOYARSK KRAY

C OVERING 14% of Russian territory, but with a population of only 3.1 million, Krasnoyarsk Kray is seeking greater autonomy from Moscow. The region has huge hydrocarbon and mineral reserves and wishes to establish greater control over the wealth that they produce. Over 60% of Siberia's oil and gas and a quarter of all Russian coal is found in the region. Krasnoyarsk Kray also accounts for most of Russia's nickel exports. Agriculture is a strong sector. With 8.1 million acres of fertile arable land, the region is a net exporter of farming produce and has 18% of Russia's huge timber reserves.

Over 100 distinct nationalities live in Krasnoyarsk Kray. The majority are Russian. Nearly a third of the population lives in the capital, Krasnoyarsk, which began expanding in the 19th century following the discovery of gold in the region. The arrival of the Trans-Siberian railroad and the relocation of industries to the city during World War II were a further boost.

In 1989, protests by the Krasnoyarsk residents managed to prevent the construction of the world's largest nuclear waste dump, which threatened to pollute the Yenisey River.

TYUMEN

L OCATED IN WESTERN SIBERIA, Tyumen Oblast (region) has considerable economic potential. In October 1993, the region produced 19.2 million tons of oil, bucking the Russian trend for declining oil output. Natural gas output is also increasing.

Deutsche Bank has extended the region a DM1 billion ($650 million) credit package. The region planned to export one million tons of oil annually to Germany between 1993 and 1995. The credit was also to be used to develop consumer goods and agribusiness in the region. A further DM1 billion credit to develop the oil and gas industry is being negotiated.

Tyumen also possesses the huge Yamal peninsula gas deposits. Much of its production is already exported to Western Europe through pipelines. Another pipeline (via Poland) is currently being built.

As Tyumen realizes its economic potential, so secession will become an increasingly popular prospect for the region. The state government is already in conflict with Moscow over how much of its economic and resource wealth must be delivered to the national treasury.

Trans-Siberian railroad · Northern limit of wooded country
— Gas pipeline · Natural gas · Oilfields
Coalfields · Nickel · Timber

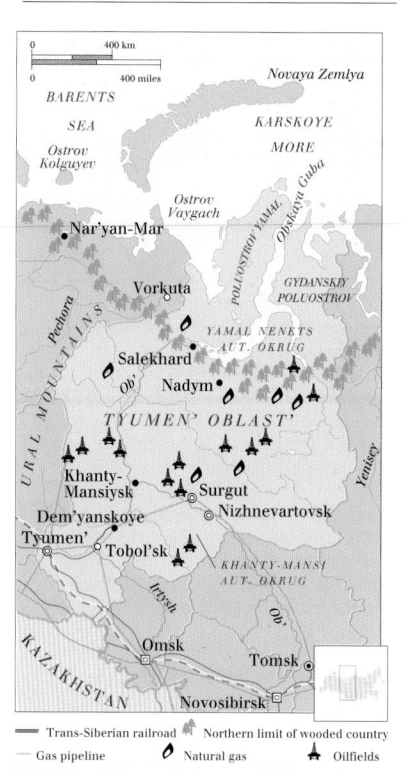

Trans-Siberian railroad · Northern limit of wooded country
— Gas pipeline · Natural gas · Oilfields

ECONOMICS

$392.5bn

0.64–1.04 roubles
(official rate)

SCORE CARD

- WORLD GNP RANKING.........................11th
- GNP PER CAPITA............................$2650
- BALANCE OF PAYMENTS.....................$5.1bn
- INFLATION 302%
- UNEMPLOYMENT................................1.7%

EXPORTS

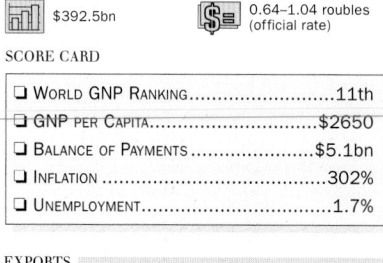

UK 6%
Switzerland 6%
USA 6%
Germany 9%
Ukraine 11%
Other 62%

IMPORTS

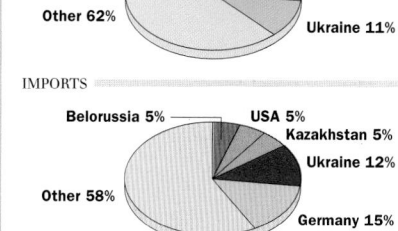

Belorussia 5%
USA 5%
Kazakhstan 5%
Ukraine 12%
Germany 15%
Other 58%

STRENGTHS

Huge natural resources; in particular hydrocarbons, precious metals, fuel, timber. Enormous engineering and scientific base. Some dynamic small joint-stock enterprises. Huge potential for oil and natural gas. IMF backing for reforms. Revival of industrial production after years of contraction. Reduction in budget deficit.

WEAKNESSES

Many company directors are asset-stripping privatized companies. Most are adjusting to a market economy unwillingly. Public disillusion over recent "shares for loans" privatization scheme. Many of the skills developed under communism are not relevant in an increasingly competitive economy. Lack of adequate legal infrastructure making establishing property rights

ECONOMIC PERFORMANCE INDICATOR

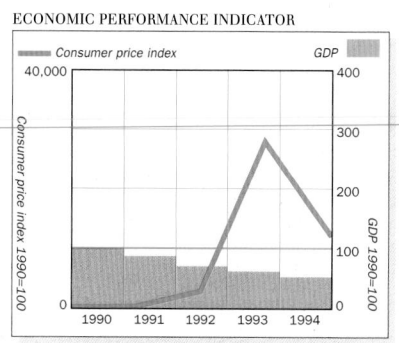

Consumer price index
GDP
40,000
Consumer price index 1990=100
GDP 1990=100
400
300
200
100
0
1990 1991 1992 1993 1994

and trading transactions difficult. Primitive and punitive tax code. Russian companies have an estimated $32 billion in Western bank accounts and the outflow of capital is estimated at $1 billion monthly.

PROFILE

The Yeltsin administration took major steps toward entrenching Russia's nascent market economy in 1995 and early 1996. The collapse of industrial production, which began with Gorbachev's introduction of market principles to the command economy in the late 1980s, finally appeared to bottom out. A tight monetary squeeze cut the rate of inflation to the lowest level since reforms began, the budget deficit was reduced and the value of the rouble was defended through the introduction of a currency "corridor." Yeltsin's stabilization program was backed by the international community and the IMF, which provided loans of over $16 billion in 1995–1996.

These achievements, however, were painfully won and the average Russian worker appears to have become disillusioned with the absence of state control over economic activities. This disillusion, combined with the communist success in the 1995 elections, prompted Yeltsin to drop some key reformers from his administration.

R

RUSSIAN FEDERATION : MAJOR BUSINESSES

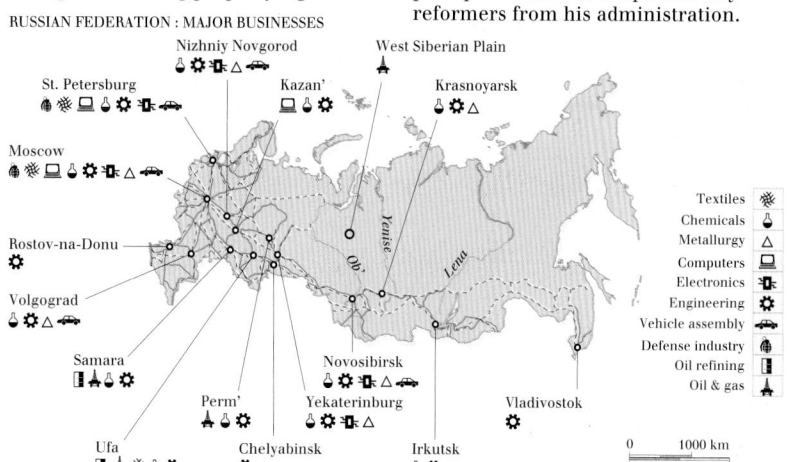

Nizhniy Novgorod
West Siberian Plain
St. Petersburg
Kazan'
Krasnoyarsk
Moscow
Rostov-na-Donu
Volgograd
Samara
Novosibirsk
Perm'
Yekaterinburg
Vladivostok
Ufa
Chelyabinsk
Irkutsk

Textiles
Chemicals
Metallurgy
Computers
Electronics
Engineering
Vehicle assembly
Defense industry
Oil refining
Oil & gas

0   1000 km
0   1000 miles

CHRONOLOGY

The first Russian state (Rus) was in present-day Ukraine. Occupation by the Tatars (1240–1480) left a mark on the Russian language and character. From the 17th century, rule was under the Romanovs.

❏ **1904–1905** Russian war against Japan; ends in defeat for Russia.

❏ **1905** Revolution.

❏ **1909–1914** Rapid expansion of economy.

❏ **1914** Enters World War I against Germany.

❏ **1917** February Revolution; abdication of Nicholas II. October Revolution; Bolsheviks take over with Lenin as leader.

❏ **1918** July, Nicholas II and family murdered.

❏ **1918–1920** Civil war.

❏ **1921** New Economic Policy; retreat from socialism.

❏ **1922** USSR established.

❏ **1924** Lenin dies. Struggle for leadership, eventually won by Stalin, follows.

❏ **1928** First Five-Year Plan begins; forced industrialization and collectivization.

❏ **1929** Trotsky is first banished to Kazakhstan, then deported to Turkey.

❏ **1936–1938** Show trials and campaigns against actual and suspect members of opposition. Millions sent to *gulags* in Siberia and elsewhere. Purges widespread.

❏ **1939** Hitler–Stalin pact gives USSR Baltic states, eastern Poland and Bessarabia.

❏ **1941** Germany attacks USSR. Stalin unprepared. December, Battle of Moscow is first German defeat.

❏ **1943** February, great Soviet victory at Stalingrad.

❏ **1944–1945** Soviet offensive penetrates Balkans.

❏ **1945** January, Yalta agreement recognizes eastern and southeastern Europe as Soviet zone of influence; four-power occupation of Germany. August, Potsdam agreement; intends Germany to be ruled as whole, but it quickly breaks up into east and west. USSR dominant European power.

❏ **1947** Cold War begins; Stalin on defensive and fears ideological penetration of Western and capitalist values.

❏ **1953** Stalin dies.

❏ **1956** Hungarian uprising against Soviet occupation. Moscow crushes uprising and reinstates Imre Nagy as prime minister. Krushchev's "secret speech" attacking Stalin at Party congress. ⇨

RESOURCES

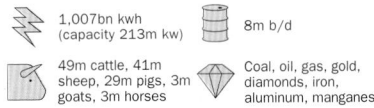

1,007bn kwh (capacity 213m kw)

8m b/d

49m cattle, 41m sheep, 29m pigs, 3m goats, 3m horses

Coal, oil, gas, gold, diamonds, iron, aluminum, manganese

ELECTRICITY GENERATION

Hydro 17% (172bn kwh)
Thermal 71% (716bn kwh)
Nuclear 12% (119bn kwh)
Other 0%

% of total generation by type

RUSSIAN FEDERATION : LAND USE

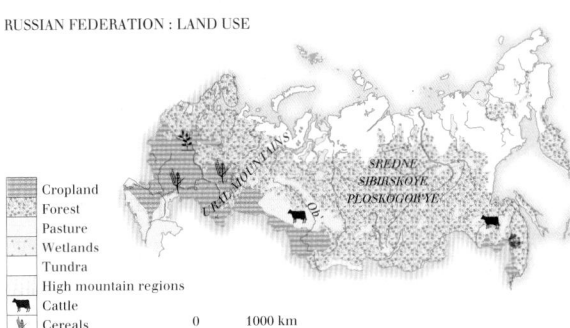

Cropland
Forest
Pasture
Wetlands
Tundra
High mountain regions
Cattle
Cereals
Potatoes

0   1000 km
0   1000 miles

Russia is a leading world producer of oil, natural gas and electricity, among other resources. Confirmed reserves make Russia the world's leading country in terms of hydrocarbons, gold, precious metals, diamonds and timber.

Unlike some of the other republics of the former Soviet Union, Russia has not opened its resources up to foreign concerns. It does not wish to lose any control to Western multinationals. They are consequently still under-exploited owing to a lack of investment and technology.

Most of the major resources are also located in national territories such as Tatarstan and Sakha Yakutia in Siberia. The regions' desire for greater autonomy from Moscow has turned the ownership of these resources into a delicate political issue.

ENVIRONMENT

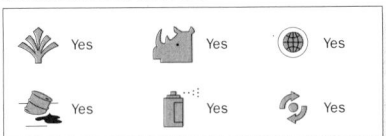

4%

Few environmental protection laws are being passed

ENVIRONMENTAL TREATIES

Yes   Yes   Yes
Yes   Yes   Yes

Awareness of Russia's environmental problems has risen sharply since the demise of communism. However, the resources, political will and know-how to tackle them are still lacking. While Russia now has an active green movement, it did not gain significant support at the 1995 general elections.

Each region has its own particular problems. The north suffers from the effects of nuclear dumping in the Barents Sea. Over 17,000 contaminated containers were dumped there by the Russian navy, including the old nuclear reactor from the icebreaker *Lenin*. Thousands of tons of chemical weapons have been dumped in the Baltic, although their exact location has not been revealed. The River Volga in Central Russia is so polluted and diverted by dam-building that many fish species are now extinct. The worst problems are probably in the Urals and the cities of European Russia. Chemical and heavy industrial plants still lack adequate protection. Most do not treat their effluents at all.

MEDIA

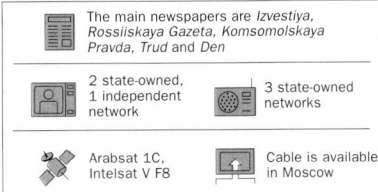

No political restrictions, though temporary censorship may occur

PUBLISHING AND BROADCAST MEDIA

The main newspapers are *Izvestiya, Rossiiskaya Gazeta, Komsomolskaya Pravda, Trud* and *Den*

2 state-owned, 1 independent network

3 state-owned networks

Arabsat 1C, Intelsat V F8

Cable is available in Moscow

Russians have traditionally been avid newspaper readers. This is reflected in the number of titles. In 1990, there were 4,808 daily newspapers with a total circulation of 166 million copies compared to a population of 146 million. Since then, however, the number of titles has fallen dramatically, largely due to a rise in the cost of paper. The old state daily, *Pravda*, is barely surviving and is partly dependent on subsidies from the Greek Communist Party. After the October 1993 right-wing coup attempt, many newspapers were banned. Most are now reappearing although often under new names. The regional and local press is also growing in importance. State TV is now the most important news source and less biased than under communism. It remains under the control of supporters of President Yeltsin. Many Russians now have satellite dishes and tune in to CNN and other Western channels.

Tundra in Russia's far east. *Russia has some of the largest uninhabited tracts of land in the world.*

CRIME

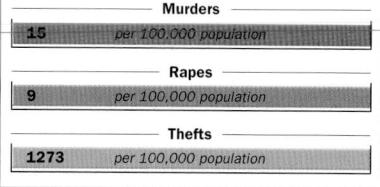

Russia does not publish prison figures

Up 27% in 1992

CRIME RATES

Murders	
15	*per 100,000 population*

Rapes	
9	*per 100,000 population*

Thefts	
1273	*per 100,000 population*

Crime is now a formidable problem in Russia, and the police cannot keep up with its rise. Reported murders have risen dramatically in recent years. Most murders are the result of inter-gang violence. Muggings and street crime in the larger cities are also sharply up.

Corruption and mafia-style activity are widespread. Protection rackets, prostitution, smuggling operations and narcotics are the Russian mafia's main sources of profit.

The rise in crime has become a major issue for most Russians. Parties such as Vladimir Zhirinovsky's LDPR, who are promising to stamp crime out, are gaining popular support for their hardline stance.

EDUCATION

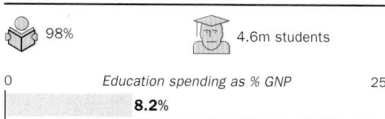

98%   4.6m students

0   *Education spending as % GNP*   25

8.2%

THE EDUCATION SYSTEM

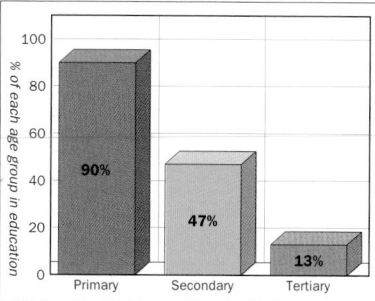

Russian education still follows the Soviet model. While there has been some attempt at historical revisionism, this has been hampered by a lack of funds to pay for new books. Many private *lycées* have sprung up – such as those run by the Orthodox Church – often offering courses in English and German. German, in particular, has made a comeback in Moscow as a key commercial language. Higher education is now underfunded. Prestigious institutions such as the Academy of Sciences have cut staff and research. Most academics now have to rely on extramural earnings.

HEALTH

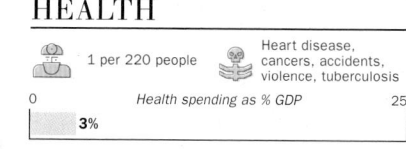

1 per 220 people

Heart disease, cancers, accidents, violence, tuberculosis

0   *Health spending as % GDP*   25

3%

Until 1991, state enterprises provided considerable health care for their employees. This is now disappearing as companies are privatized and seek to cut costs. Local authorities have few resources to take over these responsibilities. Bribing medical staff to obtain treatment is commonplace and there is a lack of pharmaceutical products and drugs. Hospital patients are normally fed by their relatives.

WEALTH

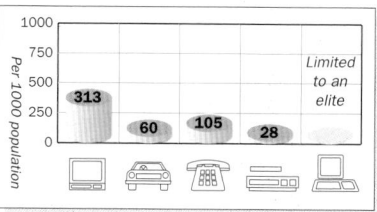

It is estimated that 35% of the population now live below the poverty line

CONSUMER GOODS OWNERSHIP

313   60   105   28   *Limited to an elite*

Wealth disparities in Russia are increasing rapidly. A small minority of the population has made huge profits from marketization. About 10% are thought to have benefited in some way.

There is a growing number of dollar millionaires who flaunt their wealth, especially in Moscow. Russia is now the biggest buyer of Rolls Royce cars, while BMWs, Mercedes and Volvos are relatively common in Moscow and St. Petersburg. A considerable amount of wealth is now deposited abroad, however. There are now thousands of Russian offshore bank accounts; Northern Cyprus is a favorite location. The bosses of organized crime are Russian society's wealthiest group.

WORLD RANKING

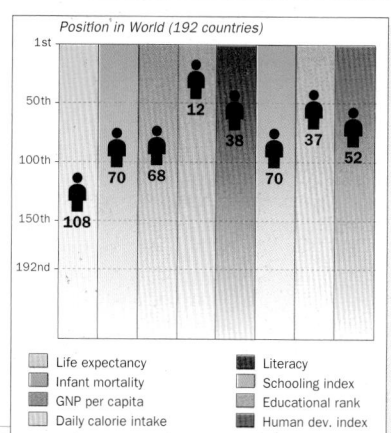

Position in World (192 countries)

1st — 50th — 100th — 150th — 192nd

108   70   68   12   38   70   37   52

- Life expectancy
- Infant mortality
- GNP per capita
- Daily calorie intake
- Literacy
- Schooling index
- Educational rank
- Human dev. index

R

RWANDA

CENTRAL AFRICA

OFFICIAL NAME: Republic of Rwanda **CAPITAL:** Kigali
POPULATION: 8 million **CURRENCY:** Rwanda franc **OFFICIAL LANGUAGES:** Kinyarwanda, French, English

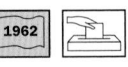 

LYING JUST SOUTH OF THE EQUATOR in east-central Africa, Rwanda is 992 miles from the nearest port. Since independence in 1962, ethnic tensions have dominated politics. In 1994, the death of the president in a plane crash led to an outbreak of political and ethnic violence in which an estimated 500,000 Rwandans died. Over half of the surviving population were displaced; many sheltering in refugee camps in neighboring countries.

CLIMATE

WEATHER CHART

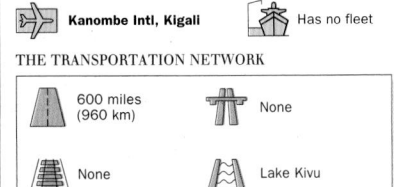

Rwanda's climate is tropical, tempered by altitude. Two wet seasons allow for two harvests each year.

TRANSPORTATION

✈ **Kanombe Intl, Kigali**   Has no fleet

THE TRANSPORTATION NETWORK

600 miles (960 km)	None
None	Lake Kivu

The road network is well developed. The international airport near Kigali was completed in 1986.

TOURISM

Aid workers and journalists are the only visitors   No tourism due to recent conflict

MAIN OVERSEAS ARRIVALS

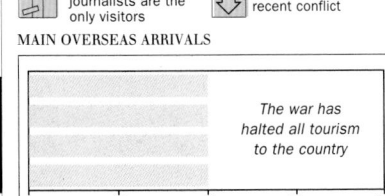

The war has halted all tourism to the country

0 10 20 30 40
% of total arrivals

All tourism has ceased as a result of the civil war. When peace is secured, Rwanda may be able to regain its status as a destination for wealthy wildlife enthusiasts. Top attractions are the mountain gorillas and Lake Kivu.

PEOPLE

Kinyarwanda, French, Kiswahili, English   788 people per sq. mile

THE URBAN/RURAL POPULATION SPLIT

6%   94%

ETHNIC MAKEUP

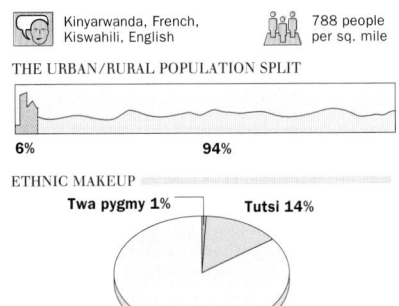

Twa pygmy 1%   Tutsi 14%
Hutu 85%

The Hutu and Tutsi are the main groups; the Twa pygmies, the original inhabitants, have been marginalized. For over 500 years, the cattle-owning Tutsi were politically dominant, oppressing the land-owning Hutu majority. In 1959, violent revolt led to a reversal of the roles. The two groups have since been waging a spasmodic war. It is estimated that 500,000 have been killed in the recent upsurge of violence, the majority Tutsi victims of Hutu massacres. Under the new government, many Tutsi in exile since 1959 are returning to Rwanda.

POLITICS

1988/1999   President Pasteur Bizimungu

THE STATE OF THE PARTIES

Parliament

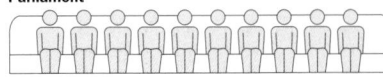

There are no plans for elections following the recent conflict. The 5 parties represented in the transitional legislature also form a governing coalition dominated by the FPR.

After 14 years of one-party rule under the MRND, Rwanda adopted a multiparty system in 1991. A peace accord to end the rebellion launched in 1990 by the Tutsi-dominated Rwandan Patriotic Front (FPR) was signed in 1993. However, the fragile peace process was halted in 1994 by the death of the president in a plane crash. Genocidal violence was unleashed between the predominantly Hutu supporters of the old regime and its mainly, but not exclusively, Tutsi opponents. An estimated 500,000 died and millions fled the conflict to the neighboring countries of Zaire, Burundi and Tanzania. The FPR eventually gained control of the country. Hutu have been allocated most of the key posts in the new government, including the presidency. The government's priorities are ensuring the resettlement of the displaced population and bringing the perpetrators of the genocide to justice.

RWANDA

Total Land Area : 24 950 sq. km (9633 sq. miles)

POPULATION
◎ over 100 000
● over 10 000
• under 10 000

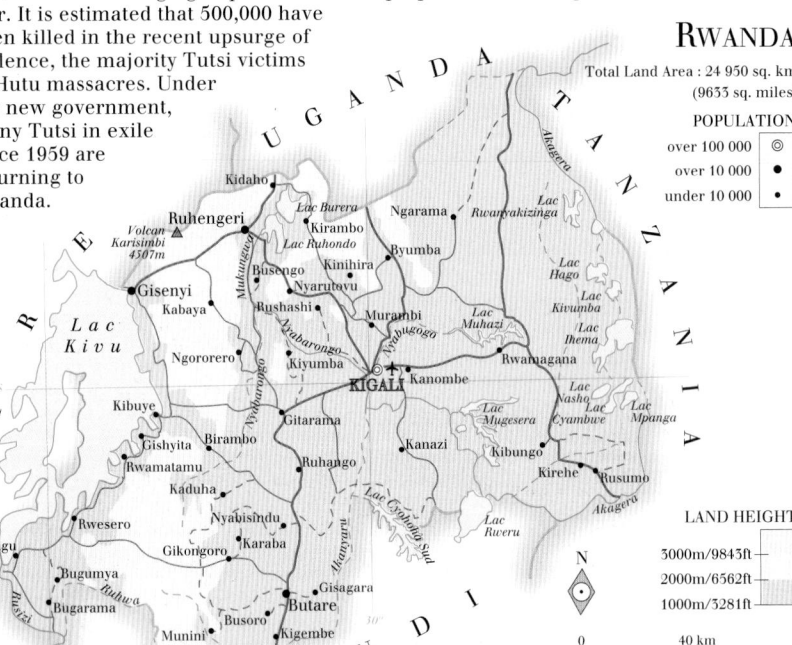

LAND HEIGHT
3000m/9843ft
2000m/6562ft
1000m/3281ft

N

0 40 km
0 40 miles

WORLD AFFAIRS

The international community was accused of abandoning Rwanda in 1994. Since then, UN efforts have included the establishment of a war crimes tribunal. Huge numbers of Rwandan refugees in Zaire have strained relations.

AID

 $361m (receipts)   Up 3% in 1993

Large amounts of aid are required, particularly in the agriculture sector, which was severely disrupted by the war. Humanitarian agencies active in the refugee camps face the dilemma of assisting the perpetrators of violence.

DEFENSE

 $116m   Up 3% in 1994

The former Rwandan army, and militia groups like the *Interahamwe* have regrouped in Zaire and are regarded as a threat.

ECONOMICS

 $1.5bn    138.38–220.00 Rwanda francs

SCORE CARD

- ❏ WORLD GNP RANKING......................144th
- ❏ GNP PER CAPITA $213
- ❏ BALANCE OF PAYMENTS.....................$–85m
- ❏ INFLATION 64%
- ❏ UNEMPLOYMENT.......Few have formal employment

STRENGTHS

Currently none. Assuming stability, Rwanda produces coffee. Possible oil and gas reserves.

WEAKNESSES

Economic activity ceased as a result of the 1994 violence. The long journey to both Kenyan and Tanzanian ports imposes high transportation costs. Rwanda has few resources.

EXPORTS

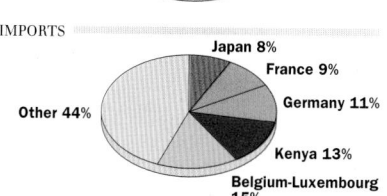

Italy 1%
UK 1%
Other 75%
USA 1%
Uganda 1%
Belgium-Luxembourg 21%

IMPORTS

Japan 8%
France 9%
Germany 11%
Kenya 13%
Belgium-Luxembourg 15%
Other 44%

Terraced hillside. *Before the war, Rwanda was the most densely populated country in Africa and its land was intensively cultivated.*

RESOURCES

 185m kwh (capacity 60,000 kw)   3,553 tons

610,000 cattle, 400,000 sheep, 130,000 pigs   Tin, tungsten, gold, columbo-tantalite, methane gas

Gas deposits in Lake Kivu are likely to be explored with Zaire. Only 20% of urban homes are on the national power grid.

ENVIRONMENT

 12%   Environmental concerns are not a priority

Soil erosion and forest loss are the major environmental problems, the effects of war aside. The tourist industry underpinned the preservation of the mountain gorilla.

MEDIA

 Under the MRND-led government there were many instances of opposition journalists being harassed and arrested

PUBLISHING AND BROADCAST MEDIA

 There are no daily newspapers. The weekly *Imvaho* and *La Relève* are published in Kinyarwanda and French respectively

 1 state-controlled service   1 state-controlled service, 2 operated by UN

The media has been used as an important propaganda tool by both sides in the conflict.

CRIME

 Rwanda does not publish prison figures   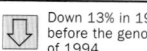 Down 13% in 1992, before the genocide of 1994

Previously benefiting from a low crime rate, an orgy of violence broke out in 1994, with thousands murdered and raped. Around 47,000 suspects are being held in relation to these crimes.

EDUCATION

 61%    3,389 students

Schools are run by the state and Christian missions. Elementary education is officially compulsory, but only 71% of children attended in 1991; just 8% go on to secondary schooling.

CHRONOLOGY

The Hutu majority began to arrive in the 14th century; the warrior Tutsi in the 15th. From 1890, German and then Belgian colonizers acted to reinforce Tutsi dominance.

- ❏ **1962** Independence under Hutu-led government.
- ❏ **1960s** Tutsi revolt; massacres by Hutu; thousands of Tutsi in exile.
- ❏ **1973** Habyarimana seizes power.
- ❏ **1975** One-party state under MRNDD.
- ❏ **1990** Invasion by FPR.
- ❏ **1992–1993** Transitional coalition.
- ❏ **1994** April, President Habyarimana dies in plane crash. Outbreak of genocidal violence. August, FPR-dominated government takes office.
- ❏ **1995** UN war crimes tribunal begins sitting.

HEALTH

 1 per 40,600 people   Malaria, measles, diarrheal diseases, violence

Rwanda has a network of 34 hospitals and 188 health centers. This should mean the majority have access to care, although treatment is rarely free.

WEALTH

 Most Rwandans live a subsistence existence

CONSUMER GOODS OWNERSHIP

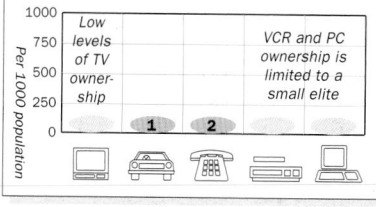

Low levels of TV owner-ship

VCR and PC ownership is limited to a small elite

Wealth is limited to the political elite. Most Rwandans are poor farmers; Twa pygmies and refugees are poorer still.

WORLD RANKING

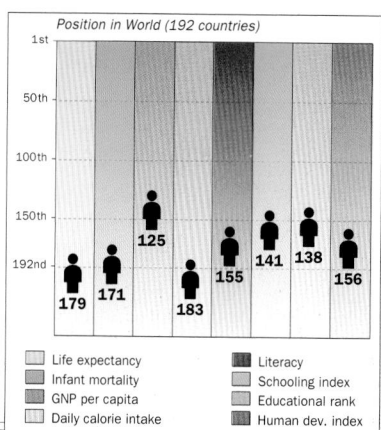

Position in World (192 countries)

179 171 125 183 155 141 138 156

- ☐ Life expectancy
- ☐ Infant mortality
- ☐ GNP per capita
- ☐ Daily calorie intake
- ☐ Literacy
- ☐ Schooling index
- ☐ Educational rank
- ☐ Human dev. index

R

ST. KITTS & NEVIS

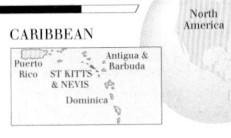

OFFICIAL NAME: Federation of Saint Christopher and Nevis **CAPITAL:** Basseterre
POPULATION: 41,000 **CURRENCY:** East Caribbean dollar **OFFICIAL LANGUAGE:** English

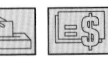

ONE OF THE CARIBBEAN'S most popular tourist destinations, St. Kitts and Nevis, a former British colony, lies at the northern end of the Leeward Islands chain. St. Kitts is of volcanic origin; Mount Liamuiga, a dormant volcano with a crater 745 feet deep, is the highest point on the island. Nevis is separated from St. Kitts by a 2-mile-wide channel and is the lusher but less-developed of the two islands. In the 18th century, its renowned hot and cold springs gave Nevis a reputation as "the Spa of the Caribbean."

CLIMATE

WEATHER CHART

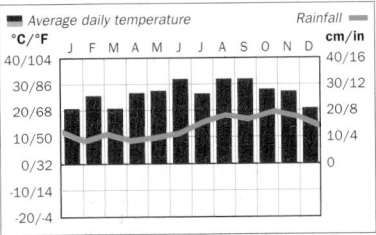

A combination of high temperatures, trade breezes, and moderate rainfall in summer account for St. Kitts' typically Caribbean climate.

TRANSPORTATION

 Golden Rock Intl, Basseterre

  1 ship 600 dwt

THE TRANSPORTATION NETWORK

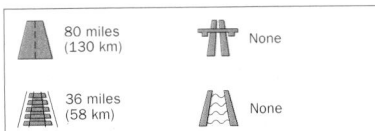

80 miles (130 km)		None
36 miles (58 km)		None

Most roads on the islands skirt the coast, with just a few crossing through the interior. The government is planning to build a road to the isolated southern tip of St. Kitts. The airport on St. Kitts takes large jets; Nevis airport accepts only small propeller aircraft. Regular ferries connect both islands.

The southeastern peninsula of St. Kitts, looking across to Nevis in the background, on a typical December evening.

TOURISM

 96,000 visitors
 Up 8% in 1994

MAIN OVERSEAS ARRIVALS

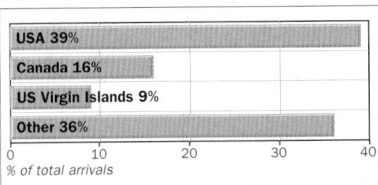

USA 39%	
Canada 16%	
US Virgin Islands 9%	
Other 36%	

% of total arrivals

Over the past 20 years, St. Kitts has targeted the US mass tourism market. With improvements in communications, in particular plans to open up the southern peninsula of St. Kitts island, the industry should continue to grow. Most visitors come for the beaches, the sun and the Caribbean mood, although in recent years safaris to see local wildlife and mineral springs have operated from isolated hotels in the hills. On St. Kitts, the old Brimstone Hill fortress has been converted into a museum, as has the Nevis birthplace of Alexander Hamilton, one of the architects of the US constitution.

ST. KITTS & NEVIS

Total Land Area: 360 sq. km (139 sq. miles)

LAND HEIGHT

1000m/3281ft
500m/1640ft
200m/656ft
Sea Level

POPULATION

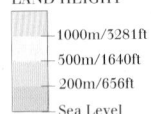

• over 10 000
• under 10 000

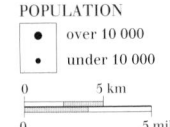

PEOPLE

 English, English Creole

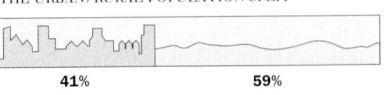 295 people per sq. mile

THE URBAN/RURAL POPULATION SPLIT

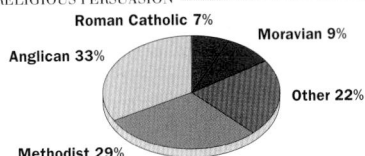

41%   59%

RELIGIOUS PERSUASION

Roman Catholic 7%
Moravian 9%
Anglican 33%
Other 22%
Methodist 29%

Most of the population is descended from Africans brought over in the 17th century; intermarriage has blurred other racial lines. There is opposition to government plans to grant citizenship to 3,000 Hong Kong business executives in exchange for investment in the islands.

POLITICS

 1995/2000
HM Queen Elizabeth II

THE STATE OF THE PARTIES

National Assembly 11 members

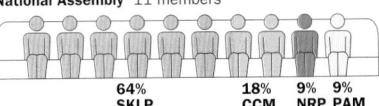

64% SKLP	18% CCM	9% NRP	9% PAM

SKLP = St Kitts Labour Party **CCM** = Concerned Citizens' Movement **NRP** = Nevis Reformation Party **PAM** = People's Action Movement

The center-left LP ended 15 years of rule by the right-wing PAM in the 1995 general election. This was held three years ahead of schedule due to political instability. Politics tends to focus on style rather than policies, except for occasional calls for greater autonomy from the NRP.

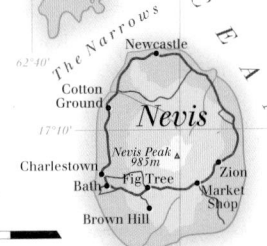

Map labels: CARIBBEAN; Dieppe Bay Town; Parson's Ground; Sadlers; St. Paul's; Tabernacle; Newton Ground; Mansion; Mt Liamuiga 1156m; Molineux; Lodge; Phillips; Cayon; Sandy Point Town; Brimstone Hill; St. Kitts; Middle Island; Parry's; Upper Conaree; Old Town Road; St. Peter's; Golden Rock Airport; Challengers; Stoddart's; Kittian Village; Boyd's; BASSETERRE; CARIBBEAN SEA; ATLANTIC OCEAN; Great Salt Pond; The Narrows; Newcastle; Cotton Ground; Nevis; Nevis Peak 985m; Charlestown; Fig Tree; Zion; Bath; Market Shop; Brown Hill

S

WORLD AFFAIRS

Maintaining preferential access to EU and US markets for its sugar is the main concern. The ruling center-left LP's foreign policy differs little from its right-wing predecessor's.

AID

 US$11m (receipts)   Up 57% in 1993

Aid, mostly from the USA, the EU and the UK, is very important, particularly project aid – such as the funding of the road to St. Kitts' southern peninsula. Donors are also providing support for economic diversification.

DEFENSE

 Army duties under-taken by Volunteer Defense Force   Not applicable

An army existed for six years before it was disbanded to cut government expenditure in 1981. A small paramilitary unit remains within the police; it made a token appearance with US forces during the 1983 invasion of Grenada.

ECONOMICS

 US$195m   2.70 East Caribbean dollars

SCORE CARD

❑ WORLD GNP RANKING	184th
❑ GNP PER CAPITA	US$4,760
❑ BALANCE OF PAYMENTS	US$–26m
❑ INFLATION	2.6%
❑ UNEMPLOYMENT	12.2%

STRENGTHS
Sugar industry, currently UK-managed, with preferential access to US and EU markets. Tourism, the source of recent growth, is set to expand further.

WEAKNESSES
Dependence on sugarcane industry, which is sensitive to fluctuating world market prices.

EXPORTS

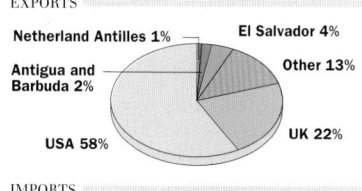

Netherland Antilles 1%
El Salvador 4%
Antigua and Barbuda 2%
Other 13%
USA 58%
UK 22%

IMPORTS

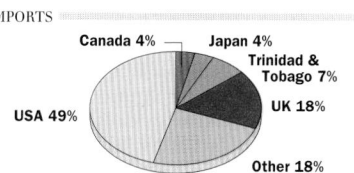

Canada 4%   Japan 4%
Trinidad & Tobago 7%
USA 49%
UK 18%
Other 18%

RESOURCES

 40m kwh (capacity 15,000 kw)
14,000 sheep, 10,000 goats, 5000 cattle, 2,000 pigs
 1,700 tons
None

St. Kitts has no strategic resources. Almost all energy has to be imported, mainly oil from Venezuela and Mexico. Sugar output is insignificant in world terms. New crops, such as Sea Island cotton on Nevis, are being introduced. Offshore fishing has potential.

ENVIRONMENT

 10%   New laws protecting monkeys

The greatest environmental threat to the islands is that of hurricanes. Hurricane Luis caused extensive damage to sugar crops, housing and infrastructure in 1995. As in the rest of the Caribbean, benefits from encouraging tourism must be set against potential ecological damage. The government has shown sensitivity, with strict preservation orders on the remaining rainforest and on indigenous monkeys.

MEDIA

 No political restrictions

PUBLISHING AND BROADCAST MEDIA

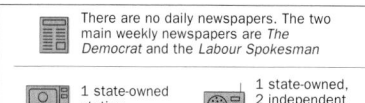

There are no daily newspapers. The two main weekly newspapers are *The Democrat* and the *Labour Spokesman*

1 state-owned station   1 state-owned, 2 independent stations

The media has little political independence, but this is not due to government interference. The funding for the two main weekly newspapers is provided by the political parties.

CRIME

 St. Kitts does not publish prison figures   Slight increase

The judicial system is based on British common law. The police force is trained by officers from London's Scotland Yard. Rape, burglary and armed robbery are the main concerns, and narcotics-related murders are on the increase. Parties have accused each other of intimidation and electoral irregularities.

EDUCATION

 97%    394 students

Education is based on the British 11-plus selective system and is mostly state-run. Students attend the regional University of the West Indies, or go on to colleges in the USA and UK.

CHRONOLOGY

A British colony since 1783 and part of the Leeward Islands Federation until 1956, St. Kitts and Nevis achieved independence in 1983.

- ❑ **1932** St. Kitts–Nevis–Anguilla Labour Party formed to campaign for independence.
- ❑ **1967** Internal self-government.
- ❑ **1980** Anguilla formally separates from St. Kitts & Nevis.
- ❑ **1983** Independence from UK.
- ❑ **1995** Opposition Labour Party wins election.

HEALTH

 1 per 2,180 people   Heart and respiratory diseases, cancers

The government-run health service provides rudimentary care on both St. Kitts and Nevis. Doctors and other medical specialists train at the University of the West Indies. Some of the better-off use private doctors and health clinics for treatment.

WEALTH

 There is no great disparity of wealth on the islands, although urban professionals enjoy a higher standard of living than rural cane farmers

CONSUMER GOODS OWNERSHIP

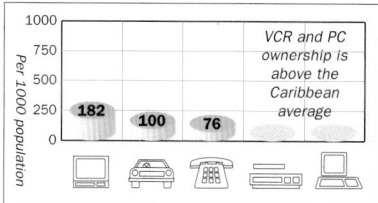

VCR and PC ownership is above the Caribbean average

182   100   76

Native professionals have replaced expatriates over the past 20 years. They are now the best-paid group, but there are no great extremes of income. Status symbols include Japanese cars and satellite dishes.

S

WORLD RANKING

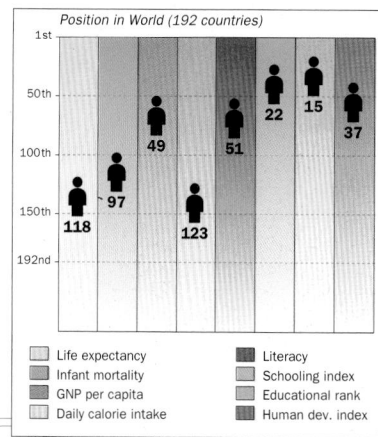

Position in World (192 countries)

1st
50th — 49, 22, 15, 37
100th — 97, 51
150th — 118, 123
192nd

- ❑ Life expectancy
- ❑ Infant mortality
- ❑ GNP per capita
- ❑ Daily calorie intake
- ❑ Literacy
- ❑ Schooling index
- ❑ Educational rank
- ❑ Human dev. index

ST. LUCIA

OFFICIAL NAME: Saint Lucia **CAPITAL:** Castries
POPULATION: 145,000 **CURRENCY:** East Caribbean dollar **OFFICIAL LANGUAGE:** English

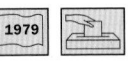

S**T. LUCIA IS ONE OF THE MOST BEAUTIFUL** islands of the Windward group of the Antilles. The twin Pitons, south of Soufrière, are among the most striking natural features in the Caribbean. Ruled by the French and British at different times in its past, St. Lucia retains the character of both. A multiparty democracy, it lives by banana-growing and beach and cruise-ship tourism. Its unspoilt rainforest makes it a popular ecotourist destination.

CLIMATE

WEATHER CHART

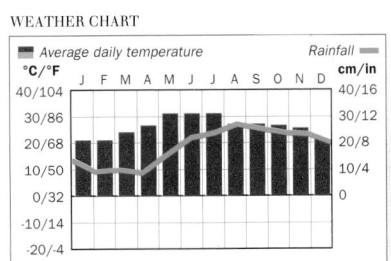

The dry season, from January to April, brings intense heat to sheltered parts of St. Lucia. During the rainy season, short warm showers can be expected daily. Rainfall is highest in the mountains.

TRANSPORTATION

 Hewanorra Intl, Vieux Fort
245,000 passengers

 2 ships
900 dwt

THE TRANSPORTATION NETWORK

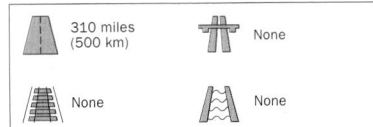

310 miles (500 km) | None
None | None

There are no railroads, and roads are confined to the west and southeast coasts, making the mountainous interior inaccessible except on foot or mule. The main airport (Hewanorra International) accepts jumbo jets.

One of the twin Pitons south of Soufrière, marking the entrance to the Jalousie Plantation harbor.

TOURISM

 210,000 visitors  Up 4% in 1994

MAIN OVERSEAS ARRIVALS

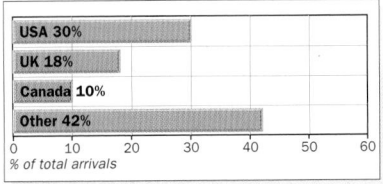

USA 30%
UK 18%
Canada 10%
Other 42%

% of total arrivals

Tropical beaches and typical Caribbean towns, such as Soufrière, have long made St. Lucia a favorite Caribbean tourist destination. Ecotourism into the island's rainforest and volcanic interior is growing, and with it local resistance to the over-development of the island.

PEOPLE

 English, French Creole   617 people per sq. mile

THE URBAN/RURAL POPULATION SPLIT

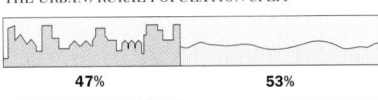

47% | 53%

RELIGIOUS PERSUASION

Anglican 3%   Other Protestant 7%
Roman Catholic 90%

St. Lucia now has a rich, tension-free racial mix of descendants of Africans, South Asians and European settlers. Despite relaxed attitudes, family life is still important to most St. Lucians, many of whom are practising Roman Catholics. The nuclear family is the norm, but in rural districts, where women run many of the farms, absentee fathers are fairly common. In recent years, women have had greater access to university education and are moving into the legal, medical and financial professions.

POLITICS

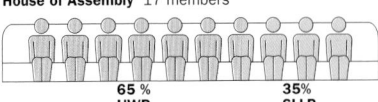 1992/1997   HM Queen Elizabeth II

THE STATE OF THE PARTIES
House of Assembly 17 members

65 % UWP | 35% SLLP

UWP = United Workers' Party
SLLP = Saint Lucia Labour Party

Senate 11 members

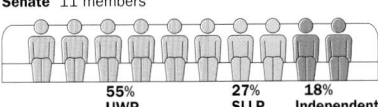

55% UWP | 27% SLLP | 18% Independent

11 members appointed by the governor-general, including 6 appointed with the advice of the prime minister and 3 with the advice of the leader of the opposition

Politics is dominated by two brothers-in-law: Prime Minister John Compton, of the UWP, and Julian Hunte, leader of the SLLP. The UWP favors the planned Windward Islands Federation. The SLLP opposes federation on the grounds that Compton will use it to retain power.

WORLD AFFAIRS

 ACS | Comm | Caricom | OECS | OAS

St. Lucia has traditionally backed US policy against left-wing regimes in the Caribbean, and it openly supported the US invasion of Grenada in 1983. Relations with Washington have recently soured, however, following US pressure on the EU to remove its preferential treatment of bananas from the Caribbean. St. Lucia cannot compete with cheaper fruit from South America. The other main issue is a proposed Windward Islands Federation with Dominica, Grenada and St. Vincent, which will require ratification.

AID

 US$27m (receipts)   Up 286% in 1993

The US, the EU, and, in particular, the UK are the main donors. Most aid is in the form of project loans.

DEFENSE

 Police force has special service unit for defense purposes   Not applicable

A police force of 500 is supported by a small paramilitary unit. Training is provided by the USA and the UK.

St. Lucia

Total Land Area : 620 sq. km (259 sq. miles)

POPULATION
- over 10 000
- under 10 000

LAND HEIGHT
- 500m/1640ft
- 200m/656ft
- Sea Level

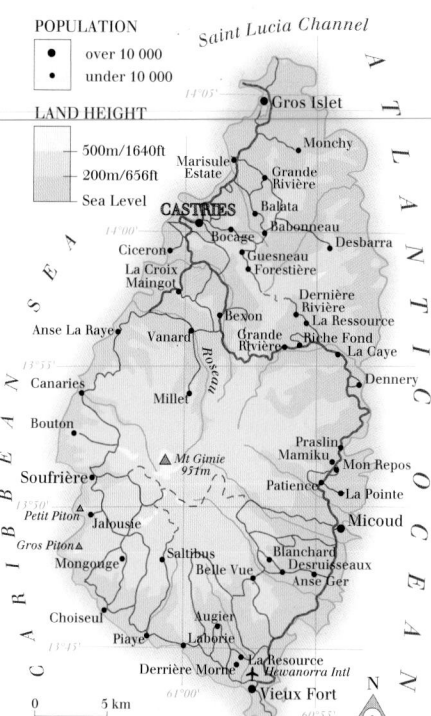

ECONOMICS

 US$501m

 2.70 East Caribbean dollars

SCORE CARD

- ❏ World GNP Ranking 162nd
- ❏ GNP per Capita ....US$3,450
- ❏ Balance of Payments..................US$–65m
- ❏ Inflation 2.2%
- ❏ Unemployment....................................25%

Strengths
Banana crop, currently with preferential access to EU, and tourism.

Weaknesses
Most tourist resorts foreign-owned; profits do not directly benefit St. Lucia.

EXPORTS

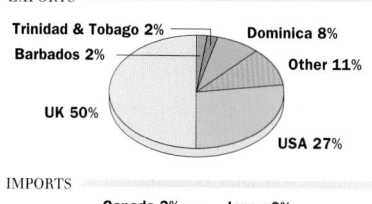

IMPORTS

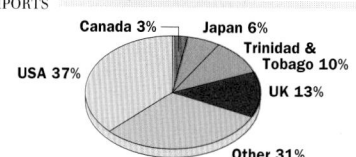

RESOURCES

107m kwh (capacity 22,000 kw)

1,114 tons

16,000 sheep, 13,000 pigs, 12,000 cattle

None

St. Lucia has no mineral resources and imports most of its energy. Plans exist to develop geothermal energy from the hot springs in the volcanic interior.

ENVIRONMENT

2% partially protected

Decision to allow development on Jalousie Plantation

St. Lucians are proud of their island and environmental questions arouse fierce debate. In recent years, the greatest controversy has surrounded the decision to allow a luxury hotel development on the ecologically important Jalousie Plantation, which encompasses the extraordinary twin Pitons and includes an important Indian archaeological site. The issue illustrates a key problem in St. Lucia, where business pressures to develop tourism can outweigh vital environmental concerns. One notable conservation success has been the St. Lucian parrot. In 1978, there were 150 birds; strict laws against the trade in parrots ensured that by 1992 numbers had risen to 400.

MEDIA

Generally free, although some government sensitivity about phone-in radio programs

PUBLISHING AND BROADCAST MEDIA

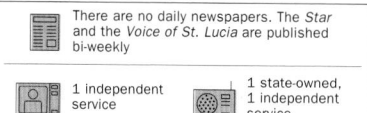

There are no daily newspapers. The *Star* and the *Voice of St. Lucia* are published bi-weekly

1 independent service

1 state-owned, 1 independent service

The privately owned press is free from government intervention. It is possible to receive TV programs from US, Mexican and some Caribbean stations.

CRIME

1,016 prisoners

Up 17% between 1985 and 1989

There are no particularly dangerous areas on the island. Murder is rare and burglary is regarded by the locals as a major crime. The police force is trained by the UK and the USA.

EDUCATION

93%

389 students

Education is based on the British system. St. Lucia has the most Nobel laureates per capita in the world – Sir Arthur Lewis (economics) and Derek Walcott (literature) are both St. Lucians.

CHRONOLOGY

In the 17th and 18th centuries, St. Lucia, which provided an excellent naval raiding base in the Caribbean, was fought over by France and Britain. Ownership alternated between the two before it was finally ceded to Britain in 1814. French influence survives in St. Lucian patois and the local cuisine.

- ❏ **1958** Joins West Indies Federation.
- ❏ **1964** Sugar growing ceases.
- ❏ **1967** Gains internal autonomy.
- ❏ **1979** Gains independence and joins Commonwealth.
- ❏ **1990** Anti-drugs force established.
- ❏ **1990** Establishes body with Dominica, Grenada and St. Vincent to discuss forming a Windward Islands Federation.

HEALTH

1 per 3,830 people

Heart and respiratory diseases, cancers

Health care has improved since the 1960s. State hospitals are supplemented by private clinics.

WEALTH

Factory worker, 99 East Caribbean dollars (US$37) per week ; communications office worker, 380 East Caribbean dollars (US$141) per week

CONSUMER GOODS OWNERSHIP

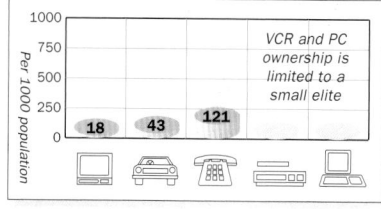

The big banana growers and hotel owners are the richest members of St. Lucian society. Japanese cars are particularly favored.

WORLD RANKING

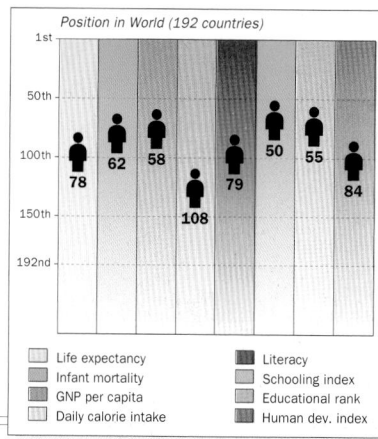

S

ST. VINCENT & THE GRENADINES

CARIBBEAN

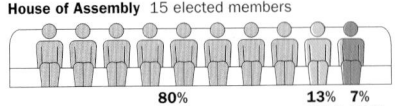

OFFICIAL NAME: Saint Vincent and the Grenadines   **CAPITAL:** Kingstown
POPULATION: 111,000   **CURRENCY:** East Caribbean dollar   **OFFICIAL LANGUAGE:** English

AMONG THE MOST ATTRACTIVE of the Windward Islands group, St. Vincent and the Grenadines is renowned as the Caribbean playground of the international jet-set. Tourism and bananas are the economic mainstays, and St. Vincent is also the world's largest arrowroot producer. St. Vincent is mostly volcanic; the one remaining active volcano, La Soufrière, last erupted in 1979. The Grenadines are flat, mainly bare coral reefs.

CLIMATE

WEATHER CHART

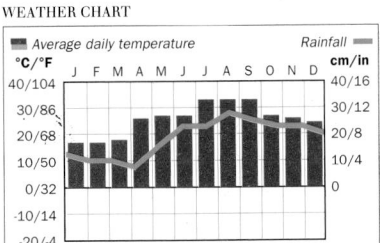

Constant trade winds moderate St. Vincent's tropical climate. Rainfall is heaviest during the summer months. Tropical depressions and hurricanes are likely between June and November.

TRANSPORTATION

 Arnos Vale, Kingstown   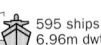 595 ships 6.96m dwt

THE TRANSPORTATION NETWORK

300 miles (490 km)		None	
None		None	

Over $50 million was spent on road development between 1991 and 1994. Principal paved roads encompass most of the coastal perimeter. Port improvements have been undertaken in recent years. In 1992, an airport taking executive jets was completed on Bequia.

Aerial view of Union Island in the Grenadines chain. The government is developing the island as a major yachting center.

TOURISM

🧳 55,000 visitors   ⬇ Down 4% in 1994

MAIN OVERSEAS ARRIVALS

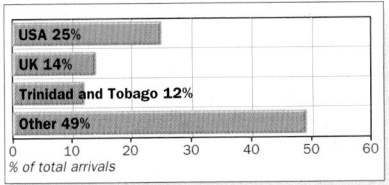

USA 25%
UK 14%
Trinidad and Tobago 12%
Other 49%

% of total arrivals

Tourism is targeted at the jet-set and cruise-ship rather than the mass market, and is concentrated on the Grenadines. Mustique, the most famous destination, has been frequented by Mick Jagger and Princess Margaret among others. Union Island is developing as a playground for the yachting rich. On St. Vincent, the pre-Columbian Indian petroglyphs at Layou are a major archaeological attraction.

PEOPLE

 English, English Creole    845 people per sq. mile

THE URBAN/RURAL POPULATION SPLIT

43%   57%

RELIGIOUS PERSUASION

Other 19%
Anglican 42%
Roman Catholic 19%
Methodist 20%

Family life on St. Vincent is heavily influenced by the Anglican Church. Racial tensions are few, and intermarriage has meant that the original communities of descendants of African slaves, Europeans and the few indigenous Carib Indians can no longer be distinguished. Many locals fear that the traditional St. Vincent way of life is being threatened by the expanding tourist industry.

POLITICS

🗳 1994/1999   HM Queen Elizabeth II

THE STATE OF THE PARTIES

House of Assembly 15 elected members

80% NDP   13% SVLP   7% MNU

NDP = New Democratic Party   **SVLP** = Saint Vincent Labour Party   **MNU** = Movement for National Unity

Prime Minister James Mitchell's NDP won a third consecutive term in the 1994 elections despite an appreciable drop in support. The previously weak and underfunded opposition show signs of revival. The top banana growers support the NDP. A major issue is the proposed Windward Islands Federation, which Mitchell favors, reportedly because he coverts the federal presidency.

ST. VINCENT & THE GRENADINES

Total Land Area : 340 sq. km (131 sq. miles)

POPULATION
● over 10 000
• under 10 000

LAND HEIGHT
1000m/3281ft
500m/1640ft
200m/656ft
Sea Level

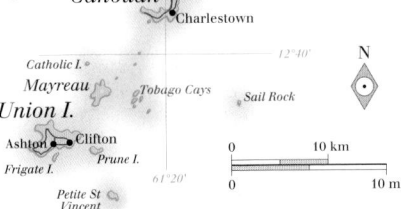

0   10 km
0   10 miles

WORLD AFFAIRS

ACS | Comm | Caricom | OAS | OECS

Usually excellent relations with Washington – St. Vincent supported the US invasion of Grenada in 1983 – have been put under strain by the USA's efforts to pressurize the EU into deregulating its trade, which currently favors Caribbean banana growers.

AID

 US$14m (receipts)   Down 50% in 1993

Aid is important in helping to stabilize the country's external finances. The USA and the EU are the main providers of project loans, the UK of grant aid.

DEFENSE

 US$3.2m   No significant change from year to year

St. Vincent has no army. A 500-strong police force, trained by the USA and UK, is part of the Windward and Leeward Islands' Regional Security System.

ECONOMICS

 US$235m   2.70 East Caribbean dollars

SCORE CARD

- ❏ World GNP Ranking........................180th
- ❏ GNP per Capita ....US$2,120
- ❏ Balance of Payments..................US$–61m
- ❏ Inflation 1%
- ❏ Unemployment...................................40%

STRENGTHS

Bananas, with preferential access to EU markets. Excellent underdeveloped tourist potential. Stable currency. Leading producer of arrowroot starch. Improving infrastructure.

WEAKNESSES

Little diversification. Vulnerability to US moves to deregulate the world banana market.

EXPORTS

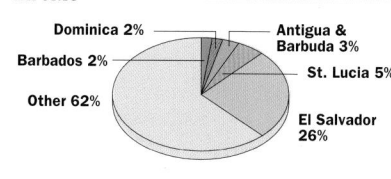

Dominica 2% | Antigua & Barbuda 3%
Barbados 2% | St. Lucia 5%
Other 62% | El Salvador 26%

IMPORTS

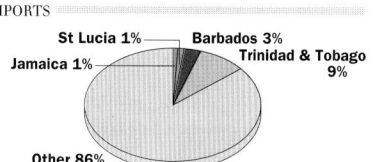

St Lucia 1% | Barbados 3%
Jamaica 1% | Trinidad & Tobago 9%
Other 86%

RESOURCES

 51m kwh (capacity 14,000 kw)   1,781 tons

 12,000 sheep, 9,000 pigs, 6,000 cattle   None

There is a hydroelectric plant on the Cumberland River. Virtually all other energy requirements have to be imported. Some of the Grenadines have no fresh water sources.

ENVIRONMENT

 21% (including marine and semi-protected areas)   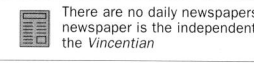 New airport on Bequia

Hurricanes are the main environmental threat; Hurricane Emily destroyed 70% of the banana crop in 1987. For years the inaccessibility of St. Vincent and the Grenadines meant that tourism was a minor environmental threat. The attraction of islands such as Mustique was based on their untouched, idyllic landscape. Mustique remains well protected – building has been restricted to 30 houses and further development is limited as fresh water has to be shipped in. On Bequia, the new airport and the associated increase in visitors are seen as a mixed blessing. Commercial whaling is a contentious issue.

MEDIA

 Journalists and radio news editors have been subjected to government intimidation

PUBLISHING AND BROADCAST MEDIA

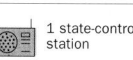 There are no daily newspapers. The main newspaper is the independent weekly, the *Vincentian*

1 independent service   1 state-controlled station

Only one of the four weekly papers is privately owned; the rest are published by political parties. Freedom of the press is written into the constitution.

CRIME

 281 prisoners   Down 9% in 1990

The judicial system on St. Vincent is based on British common law. Rape and robbery are the main local concerns, although on the outlying islands both incidents are very rare.

EDUCATION

 84%    677 students

State schools follow the British 11-plus selective system. There are a few private schools. University students go on to the regional University of the West Indies in Jamaica, although increasing numbers are also studying in the USA and the UK.

CHRONOLOGY

In 1795, the local Carib population staged a revolt against the British, who deported them, leaving a largely black African population.

- ❏ **1951** Universal suffrage.
- ❏ **1969** Internal self-government.
- ❏ **1972** James Mitchell premier; holds balance of power between People's Political Party (PPP) and St. Vincent Labour Party (SVLP).
- ❏ **1974** Coalition of PPP and SVLP.
- ❏ **1979** Milton Cato, head of coalition; leads St. Vincent to full independence from Britain. La Soufrière volcano erupts.
- ❏ **1994** General election; NDP, founded by James Mitchell in 1975, wins third term.

HEALTH

 1 per 3,760 people   Heart and respiratory diseases, cancers

Doctors train at the University of the West Indies. The system is a mixture of state and private hospitals and clinics; facilities are scarcer on the Grenadines.

WEALTH

 Wealth is quite evenly dispersed, although large banana growers and established urban professionals tend to be more affluent

CONSUMER GOODS OWNERSHIP

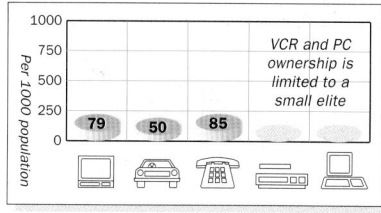

VCR and PC ownership is limited to a small elite

Per 1000 population: 79 | 50 | 85

Jet-set wealth is very much in evidence in the Grenadines, particularly on Union Island and Mustique. The local rich favor Jeeps and motor yachts.

S

WORLD RANKING

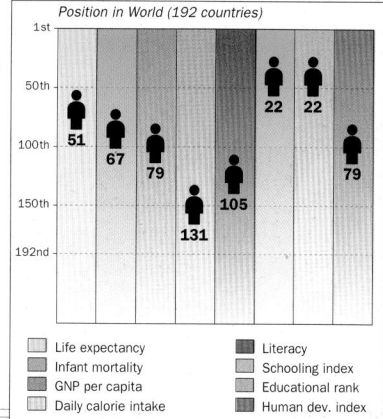

Position in World (192 countries)

51 | 67 | 79 | 131 | 105 | 22 | 22 | 79

- Life expectancy
- Infant mortality
- GNP per capita
- Daily calorie intake
- Literacy
- Schooling index
- Educational rank
- Human dev. index

SAN MARINO

OFFICIAL NAME: Republic of San Marino   **CAPITAL:** San Marino
POPULATION: 24,000   **CURRENCY:** Italian lira   **OFFICIAL LANGUAGE:** Italian

    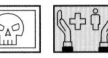

PERCHED ON THE SLOPES of Mount Titano in the Italian Appennines, San Marino is, after Nauru, the world's smallest republic. It has maintained its independence since the 4th century AD. The territory is divided into nine castles, or districts. One-third of Sanmarinesi live in the northern town of Serravalle. Today San Marino lives by agriculture, tourism and limited industry. Italy effectively controls most of its affairs.

San Marino's second fortress, the Cesta, built in the 13th century, dominates the republic from its highest pinnacle, 2,447 ft. above sea level.

CLIMATE

WEATHER CHART

San Marino's Mediterranean climate is moderated by cool sea breezes and its height above sea level. In summer temperatures can reach 80°F, while in winter they fall to 20°F. Rainfall is more common in the winter months.

TRANSPORTATION

✈ None   ⚓ Has no fleet

THE TRANSPORTATION NETWORK

140 miles (220 km)	None
None	None

The 15-mile highway to Rimini, which has the closest airport, is San Marino's most important link. Congestion is a major problem, particularly during the annual *Mille Miglia* car rally. A funicular railroad climbs the east side of Mount Titano. The railroad to Rimini, closed since 1945, is being rebuilt.

PEOPLE

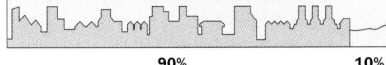

Italian   1,018 people per sq. mile

THE URBAN/RURAL POPULATION SPLIT

90%   **10%**

RELIGIOUS PERSUASION

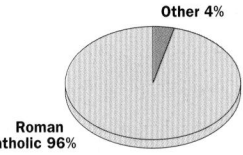

Other 4%

Roman Catholic 96%

San Marino is a tightly-knit society. Foreigners must have resided in the republic for at least 30 years to gain citizenship. Women gained the vote in 1960, but were able to stand for public office only in 1973. Twenty thousand San Marino citizens are resident abroad, mainly in Italy.

TOURISM

 533,000 visitors   Down 9% in 1994

Tourism is the mainstay of San Marino's economy. It contributes 60% of government revenue, and employs around 20% of the work force. Half a million visitors annually (and an additional 2.5 million day-trippers from Italy) come to sample the country's folklore and museums, and to explore the fortifications of Mount Titano.

The Titano fortresses of *la Rocca*, *la Cesta* and *Montale*, built during the Middle Ages, command superb views and are the main attractions. The Republic's tourist industry is

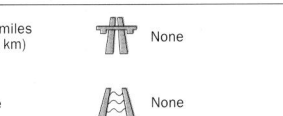

MAIN OVERSEAS ARRIVALS

73% of visitors to San Marino are Italian

% of total arrivals

boosted by the close proximity of two international airports, in Rimini and Pisa.

Efforts have been made to attract business meetings and conferences with extensive publicity in the Italian media. There are plans for a new high-tech conference hotel.

The San Marino tourist bureau is also attracting thousands of sports enthusiasts to the republic by hosting a series of top international sporting events. In March, both the Rimini–San Marino marathon and the *Mille Miglia* veteran car meeting are held. May heralds the San Marino Grand Prix, when thousands of Formula One fans descend on the country. June, meanwhile, attracts more motor-racing fans for the World Motocross Championships.

Religious procession. The official state religion of San Marino is Roman Catholicism, in contrast to Italy, which has no state religion.

SAN MARINO

Total Land Area : 61 sq. km (24 sq. miles)

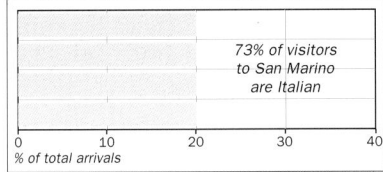

LAND HEIGHT

500m/1640ft
200m/656ft
above 175m/574ft

POPULATION

● under 10 000

Falciano
Dogana
Serravalle
Fiorina
Ventoso   Cailungo
Gualdicciolo
Acquaviva   Borgo   Domagnano
Maggiore
SAN MARINO
Monte Titano 739 m
Faetano
Murata
Chiesanuova   Montegiardino

ITALY   APPENNINES

0   4 km
0   4 miles

POLITICS

 1993/1998

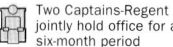 Two Captains-Regent jointly hold office for a six-month period

San Marino is a parliamentary democracy. The party system is parallel to Italy's, with regular coalition governments. The PDCS holds the majority of seats in the Great and General Council and governs in coalition with the PSS. The communists have been in decline since 1957.

THE STATE OF THE PARTIES

Great and General Council 60 members

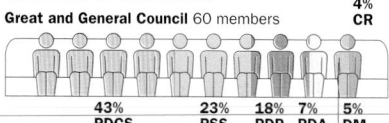

43% PDCS   23% PSS   18% PDP   7% PDA   5% DM   4% CR

PDCS = San Marino Christian Democrat Party
PSS = San Marino Socialist Party **PDP** = Democratic Progress Party **PDA** = Popular Democratic Alliance
DM = Democratic Movement **CR** = Communist Reformation

WORLD AFFAIRS

CE   NAM   OSCE

Foreign affairs are effectively decided by Italy, on which San Marino is entirely dependent. In 1992, San Marino acquired a seat at the UN.

AID

 Neither an aid donor nor receiver

 Not applicable

San Marino does not receive aid. However, annual subsidies from Italy and free access to the Italian market are essential to the economy.

DEFENSE

 Combined Voluntary Military Forces

 Not applicable

San Marino has a small territorial army and fortification guards. There is no compulsory military service, but males aged 16–55 may be called up in a national emergency.

ECONOMICS

 $188m

 1,622.25–1,586.45 Italian lira

SCORE CARD

❏ WORLD GNP RANKING	191st
❏ GNP PER CAPITA	$8,545
❏ BALANCE OF PAYMENTS	Within Italian total
❏ INFLATION	6.1%
❏ UNEMPLOYMENT	4.9%

STRENGTHS
Tourism, providing 60% of government revenue. Light industry, notably mechanical engineering and clothing, with emphasis on sportswear and high-quality prestige lines.

WEAKNESSES
Need to import all raw materials.

EXPORTS/IMPORTS

Does not publish independent trade statistics; trade movements are included in the Italian totals

RESOURCES

 No electricity generation

 Not an oil producer and has no refineries

 Small numbers of cattle, pigs, sheep and horses

None

San Marino has to import all its energy from Italy. It has no exploitable mineral resources now that the stone quarry on Mount Titano has been exhausted.

ENVIRONMENT

 None

 Farming demands threatening remaining indigenous woodland

Mount Titano is a unique limestone outcrop in the surrounding Italian plain and so has a very localized ecosystem.

MEDIA

 There is full freedom of expression

PUBLISHING AND BROADCAST MEDIA

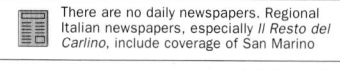

There are no daily newspapers. Regional Italian newspapers, especially *Il Resto del Carlino*, include coverage of San Marino

1 state-owned service

1 state-owned, 1 independent service

In 1993, a local TV station, *San Marino RTV*, began broadcasting. Sanmarinesi can also receive Italian TV.

CRIME

 San Marino does not publish prison figures

 Little change from year to year

San Marino has a low crime rate. Justice, except in minor civil cases, is administered by the Italian legal system.

EDUCATION

 96%

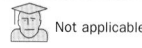 Not applicable

The government spends 13% of the budget on education. Secondary school pupils can go on to Italian universities.

HEALTH

 1 per 375 people

 Heart diseases, cancers, accidents

San Marino's hospital provides a limited health service. Those people requiring difficult operations are normally taken to Rimini for treatment.

WEALTH

 Similar wealth levels to those in northern Italy

CONSUMER GOODS OWNERSHIP

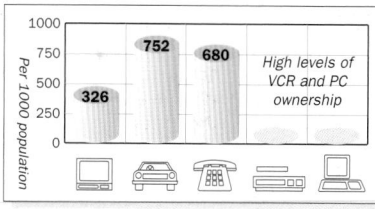

326   752   680   *High levels of VCR and PC ownership*

Per 1000 population

Living standards are similar to those of northern Italy. The unemployment rate of 4.9% is below the Italian average.

WORLD RANKING

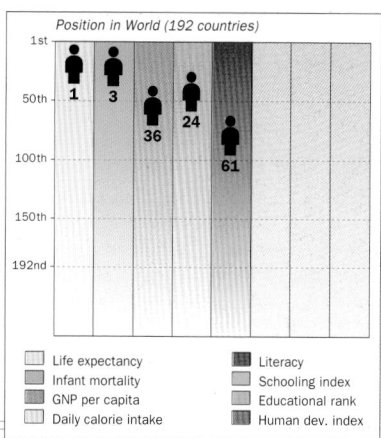

Position in World (192 countries)

1   3   36   24   61

- ☐ Life expectancy
- ☐ Infant mortality
- ☐ GNP per capita
- ☐ Daily calorie intake
- ▨ Literacy
- ☐ Schooling index
- ☐ Educational rank
- ☐ Human dev. index

S

SAO TOME & PRINCIPE

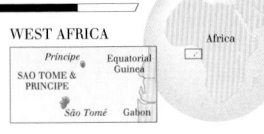

OFFICIAL NAME: Democratic Republic of Sao Tome and Principe   **CAPITAL:** São Tomé
POPULATION: 125,000   **CURRENCY:** Dobra   **OFFICIAL LANGUAGE:** Portuguese

COMPOSED OF the main islands of São Tomé and Príncipe and surrounding islets, the republic of Sao Tome and Principe is situated off the western coast of Africa. In 1975, a classic Marxist single-party regime was established following independence from Portugal, but a referendum in 1990 resulted in a 72% vote in favor of democracy. Sao Tome's main concerns are to rebuild relations with Portugal and to seek closer ties with the EU and the USA.

CLIMATE

WEATHER CHART

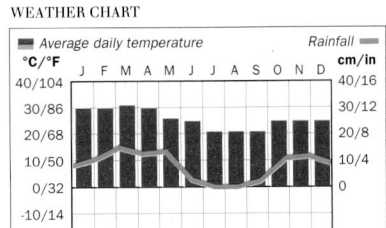

The hot, humid islands straddle the equator. Annual rainfall is 195 in. in the southwest and 39 in. in the north.

TRANSPORTATION

 São Tomé Intl
23,000 passengers (est)

 2 ships
1,300 dwt

THE TRANSPORTATION NETWORK

160 miles (250 km)		None	
None		None	

After years of neglect, road repairs and the upgrading of São Tomé's airport began in the late 1980s.

TOURISM

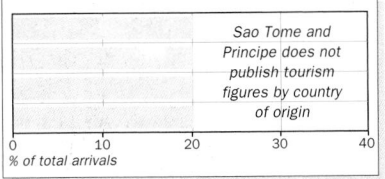 5,000 visitors   Up 67% in 1994

MAIN OVERSEAS ARRIVALS

Sao Tome and Principe does not publish tourism figures by country of origin

0   10   20   30   40
% of total arrivals

Tourism is still small-scale, attracting wealthy Gabonese and Europeans. Despite recent foreign investment, tourism on a sizeable scale will take decades to realize. The country's first modern hotel opened in 1986.

PEOPLE

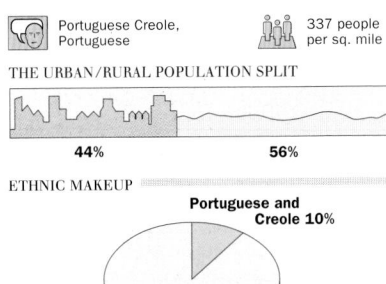 Portuguese Creole, Portuguese   337 people per sq. mile

THE URBAN/RURAL POPULATION SPLIT

44%   56%

ETHNIC MAKEUP

Portuguese and Creole 10%

Black 90%

The population is entirely descended from immigrants as the islands were uninhabited when the Portuguese arrived in 1470. As the Portuguese settled, they imported Africans as slaves to work the sugar and cocoa plantations. The abolition of slavery in the 19th century, and the departure of 4,000 Portuguese at independence, has resulted in a population which is 10% Portuguese and Creole and 90% black African, although Portuguese culture predominates. Blacks run the political parties. Society is well integrated and free of racial prejudice. The main conflicts relate to class or differing ideologies. The extended family still offers the best, if not the only, form of social security. Women have a higher status than in most other African countries; many have attained prominent positions in the professions.

Lush vegetation on São Tomé. The tropical climate is slightly moderated by the cool Benguela current.

POLITICS

 1994/1998   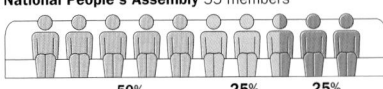 President Miguel dos Anjos da Cunha Lisboa Trovoada

THE STATE OF THE PARTIES

National People's Assembly 55 members

50%	25%	25%
MLSTP–PSD	PCD/GR	ADI

MLSTP–PSD = Sao Tome and Principe Liberation Movement – Social Democratic Party   **PCD/GR** = Democratic Convergence Party   **ADI** = Independent Democratic Action

In 1990, a new multiparty constitution swept away the Marxist single-party state that had existed since independence in 1975. Most parties are now grouped around personalities. Former leader Pinto da Costa steered the way to multipartyism. However, he withdrew from the 1990 presidential elections, leaving as sole candidate Miguel Trovoada, who returned from 11 years' exile to stand successfully as an independent. While the opposition PCD was swept to victory in 1991, early elections in 1994 saw a return to power of the MLSTP–PSD, the former ruling party, whose new name reflects its change of ideology. The most important pressure groups in politics now are the Roman Catholic Church (harassed under Marxism) and the trade unions. The main political concerns are to uphold the multiparty system and stimulate growth in the economy.

WORLD AFFAIRS

 ACP   CEEAC   Lusoph   NAM   OAU

Sao Tome has achieved rapprochement with Portugal and seeks to maintain links with other ex-Portuguese colonies, notably Angola. It has always had close ties with Gabon and, while not dropping its ex-communist links, is seeking closer relations with other CEEAC countries, France and the USA.

AID

$48m (receipts)   Down 11% in 1993

Sao Tome has one of the highest aid-to-population ratios in Africa. Joining the Lomé convention in the 1970s has meant that Sao Tome has found new sources of aid fairly easily since the demise of communism worldwide. The World Bank and IMF are the main donors.

S

DEFENSE

 Defense budget not disclosed   Probably constant from year to year

Since independence, the armed forces have figured prominently in national life. They have put down several attempted coups, notably in 1978, after which 2,000 Angolan troops plus Soviet and Cuban advisers were invited in, and in 1988. In 1995, a group of army officers seized temporary control of the country. The national armed forces are still believed to number 2,000. With the collapse of the Eastern Bloc, Sao Tome now receives military assistance from the USA.

ECONOMICS

 $31m   949.28–1,768.76 dobras

SCORE CARD

❏ WORLD GNP RANKING	193rd
❏ GNP PER CAPITA	$250
❏ BALANCE OF PAYMENTS	$–12m
❏ INFLATION	37.7%
❏ UNEMPLOYMENT	Widespread

EXPORTS

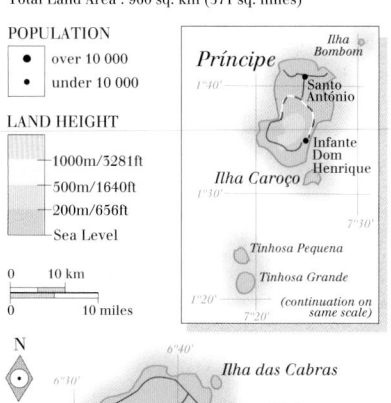

Cameroon 3%
Other 3%
Germany 51%
Portugal 13%
Netherlands 30%

SÃO TOME & PRINCIPE

Total Land Area : 960 sq. km (371 sq. miles)

POPULATION

● over 10 000
• under 10 000

LAND HEIGHT

1000m/3281ft
500m/1640ft
200m/656ft
Sea Level

0   10 km
0   10 miles

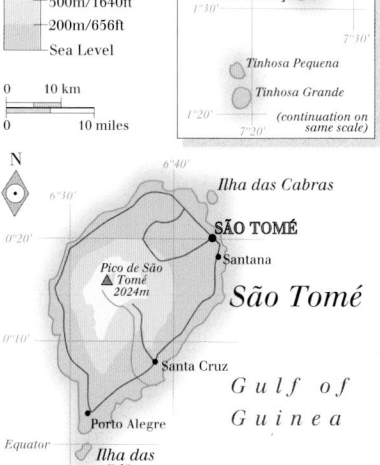

Príncipe
Ilha Bombom
Santo António
Infante Dom Henrique
Ilha Caroço
Tinhosa Pequena
Tinhosa Grande
(continuation on same scale)

N
Ilha das Cabras
SÃO TOMÉ
Santana
Pico de São Tomé ▲ 2024m
São Tomé
Santa Cruz
Gulf of Guinea
Porto Alegre
Equator
Ilha das Rôlas

RESOURCES

 15m kwh (capacity 6,000 kw)   2,200 tons

5,000 goats, 4,000 cattle, 2,000 sheep   None

Sao Tome has no mineral resources, although oil prospecting began in 1990. Almost all energy needs, apart from firewood, are met by oil imported from Angola. São Tomé is very fertile; cocoa estates are finally back to pre-1975 productivity and crop diversification is now a priority. Príncipe has better ports, but its wild scenery makes it more suitable for tourism than farming.

IMPORTS

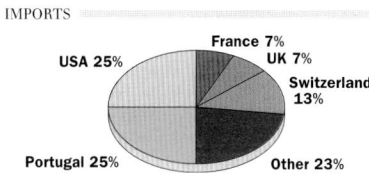

France 7%
UK 7%
Switzerland 13%
USA 25%
Portugal 25%
Other 23%

STRENGTHS

Legacy of Portuguese-built infrastructure. Potential for tourism, agricultural and fisheries development. Ability to attract substantial aid.

WEAKNESSES

Cocoa 90% of export earnings. Skilful diplomacy has attracted high levels of aid, but mismanagement of these funds has resulted in severe debt. Weak currency.

ENVIRONMENT

 None   No attempt to curb deforestation and soil erosion

Fish conservation, deforestation for fuel-wood and potential tourism expansion are the major issues.

MEDIA

 The press was strictly controlled until 1988, but censorship rules have now been relaxed

PUBLISHING AND BROADCAST MEDIA

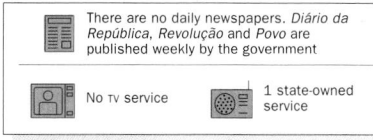

There are no daily newspapers. *Diário da República*, *Revolução* and *Povo* are published weekly by the government

No TV service   1 state-owned service

The strict censorship of the Marxist regime has been relaxed since 1988. Radio ownership is high for Africa.

CRIME

 Sao Tome does not publish prison figures   Down 20% in 1988

Crime levels are fairly low owing to the tightly knit nature of the community. Urban robbery is a problem.

EDUCATION

 57%   Not available

Education is compulsory for 7–14 year-olds. All staff at the one technical and three secondary schools are foreigners.

HEALTH

 1 per 1,950 people   Respiratory, diarrheal and parasitic diseases

Although health care is not free, Sao Tome has a better system of basic care than other ex-colonial African countries.

WEALTH

 Workers on the cocoa plantations form the poorest group

CONSUMER GOODS OWNERSHIP

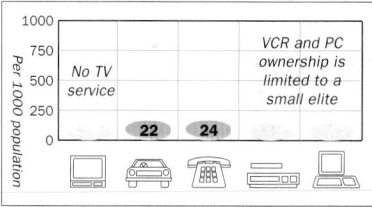

No TV service
VCR and PC ownership is limited to a small elite
22   24

Wealth disparities are not conspicuous. There is a growing business class. Cocoa workers are the poorest group.

WORLD RANKING

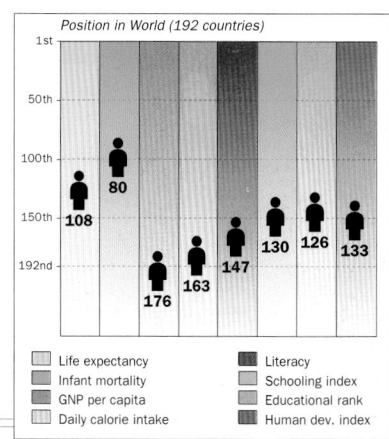

Position in World (192 countries)

108
80
176
163
147
130
126
133

■ Life expectancy
■ Infant mortality
■ GNP per capita
■ Daily calorie intake
■ Literacy
■ Schooling index
■ Educational rank
■ Human dev. index

S

SAUDI ARABIA

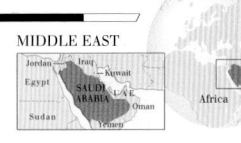

OFFICIAL NAME: Kingdom of Saudi Arabia   **CAPITAL:** Riyadh
POPULATION: 17.9 million   **CURRENCY:** Saudi riyal   **OFFICIAL LANGUAGE:** Arabic

OCCUPYING MOST OF THE Arabian peninsula, Saudi Arabia covers an area as large as Western Europe. Over 95% of its land is desert, with the most arid part, known as the "Empty Quarter" or Rub al Khali, in the southeast. Saudi Arabia has the world's-largest oil and gas reserves and major refining and petrochemicals industries. It includes Islam's holiest cities, Medina and Mecca, visited each year by two million Muslims performing the pilgrimage known as the *haj*. The Al-Sa'ud family have been Saudi Arabia's absolutist rulers since 1932.

TOURISM

 1m pilgrims    Up 2% in 1994

MAIN OVERSEAS ARRIVALS

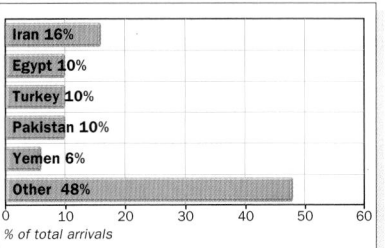

Iran 16%	
Egypt 10%	
Turkey 10%	
Pakistan 10%	
Yemen 6%	
Other 48%	

% of total arrivals

CLIMATE

WEATHER CHART

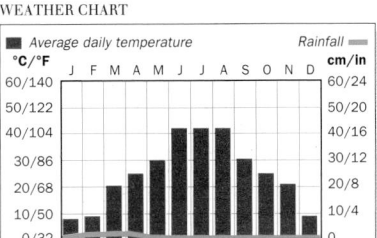

■ Average daily temperature   Rainfall ▬
°C/°F   J F M A M J J A S O N D   cm/in
60/140 .... 60/24
50/122 .... 50/20
40/104 .... 40/16
30/86 .... 30/12
20/68 .... 20/8
10/50 .... 10/4
0/32 0

The kingdom's only reliable rainfall is in the southern Asir province, which makes agriculture there viable. The central plateau requires deep artesian wells to water crops. Inland, summer temperatures often soar above 118°F, but in winter, especially in the northwest, they may fall to freezing point.

SAUDI ARABIA

Total Land Area : 2 149 690 sq. km
(829 995 sq. miles)

POPULATION
- ▣ over 1 000 000
- ◉ over 500 000
- ◎ over 100 000
- ○ over 50 000
- ● over 10 000
- · under 10 000

LAND HEIGHT
- 3000m/9843ft
- 2000m/6562ft
- 1000m/3281ft
- 500m/1640ft
- Sea Level

TRANSPORTATION

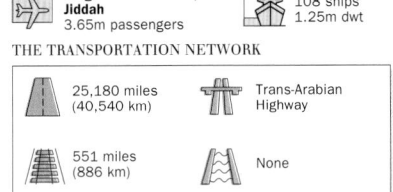

King Abd al-Aziz Intl, Jiddah
3.65m passengers

108 ships
1.25m dwt

THE TRANSPORTATION NETWORK

🛣	25,180 miles (40,540 km)	Trans-Arabian Highway	
🚂	551 miles (886 km)	None	

Since the advent of oil wealth in the 1970s, a modern transportation infrastructure has been created, linking the main centers of population to the Gulf States, Jordan and Egypt.

Saudi Arabia does not encourage foreign tourism. Only Muslim pilgrims, business people and foreign workers are permitted entry. Non-Muslims are banned from the holy cities. Over two million Muslims perform the *haj* (pilgrimage) in the twelfth month of the Arabic year. Muslims are expected to carry out the *haj* at least once in their life, and strict quotas have had to be imposed to avoid massive overcrowding. Many choose Jiddah as a base from which to begin the pilgrimage. The *umra*, or little pilgrimage, has also become popular as it can be made at any time of year. The royal family has spent $2.5 billion in recent years on improving facilities at Medina and Mecca. Excellent scuba diving exists on the Red Sea, especially at Jīzān in the south of the country.

S

[Map of Saudi Arabia showing JORDAN, EGYPT, IRAQ, KUWAIT, BAHRAIN, QATAR, UNITED ARAB EMIRATES, OMAN, YEMEN, Persian Gulf, Red Sea, and cities including Turayf, Sakākah, Al Jawf, Rafḥā, Tabūk, AN NAFŪD, Taymā', Hā'il, Al Wajh, Al 'Ula, Buraydah, Az Zilfī, Unayzah, Al Majma'ah, Shaqrā', Al Mubarraz, Al Hufūf, Al Jubayl, Ras Tannūrah, Ad Dammām, Al Khubar, Az Zahrān, Hafar al Bāţin, RIYADH, Yanbu' al Baḥr, Al Madīnah (Medina), Ḥaraḍ, Rābigh, Zalim, Laylā, Makkah (Mecca), Jiddah, Aţ Ţā'if, Qal'at Bishah, As Sulayyil, Tathlīth, Jabal Sawdā' 3133m, Khamīs-Mushayţ, Al Birk, Abhā, Zahrān, Jīzān, Najrān, Wuday 'ah, RUB AL KHALĪ]

0   200 km
0   200 miles

Network of modern road junctions spread out across the landscape near Mecca.

PEOPLE

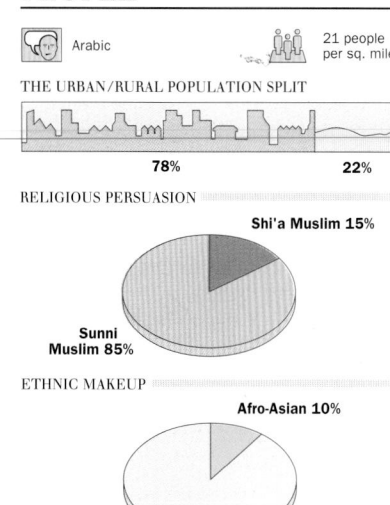

Arabic

21 people per sq. mile

THE URBAN/RURAL POPULATION SPLIT

78%　22%

RELIGIOUS PERSUASION

Shi'a Muslim 15%

Sunni Muslim 85%

ETHNIC MAKEUP

Afro-Asian 10%

Arab 90%

The Saudis take their name from the ruling Al-Sa'ud family. They were united by conquest between 1902 and 1932 by King Abdul-Aziz (ibn Sa'ud), who expelled the Turks.

The vast majority of Saudis are Sunni Muslims who follow the *wahhabi* (puritan) interpretation of Islam and embrace *sharia* (Muslim) law in their daily lives.

The politically dominant Nejadi tribes from the central plateau around Riyadh are Bedouin in origin. The Hejazi tribes from southern and western Saudi Arabia, who have a more cosmopolitan, mercantile background, have largely been displaced from politics. In the eastern province there is a Shi'a minority of some 300,000, many of whom are employed in the oilfields.

Women are obliged to wear veils, cannot hold driving licenses and have no role in public life. They are effectively barred from the workplace except as teachers and nurses.

POPULATION AGE BREAKDOWN

% of population by age group	■ 0–14	☐ 15–64			☐ 65+
	3.3%	3.2%	2.8%	2.6%	2.6%
	53.4%	52.3%	53%	52.1%	51.7%
	43.3%	44.5%	44.2%	45.3%	45.7%
	1960	1970	1980	1990	2000

POLITICS

Not applicable

King Fahd ibn Abdul Aziz

THE STATE OF THE PARTIES

Saudi Arabia is an absolute monarchy. The King rules with the assistance of an appointed Council of Ministers

Saudi Arabia is an absolute monarchy. A 60-man Consultative Assembly *(majlis ashoura)* is appointed by the king.

MAIN POLITICAL ISSUES
Questioning the ruling family

Following the 1991 Gulf War, a civil rights campaign emerged to challenge the authority of the ruling family, demanding closer adherence to Islamic values. The movement objected to the presence of US troops on Saudi territory and the consequent exposure to "corrupt" Western culture – particular outrage was felt at the presence of women soldiers. The Sa'uds moved swiftly to quash the protest, but exiled opponents have continued their activities using fax machines and e-mail.

The succession issue

The question of succession and the possibility of a future power struggle emerged as major issues in early 1996 when King Fahd, suffering the effects of a stroke, formally ceded the management of the kingdom's day-to-day affairs to his half-brother, Crown Prince Abdullah. A few weeks later, Fahd resumed control. It was a move which few doubted had its roots in rivalries which are endemic to the House of Sa'ud.

PROFILE

The royal family rules by carefully manipulating appointments in all sectors of government. Frequent changes of personnel within the armed forces ensure that officers do not build up personal followings. All influential cabinet portfolios, apart from those of oil and religious affairs, are held by princes.

Absolutist rule means that domestic politics are virtually non-existent. The regime retains feudal elements: weekly *majlis*, or councils, are held where citizens can present petitions or grievances to leading members of the royal family. Large cash sums are often dispensed at these meetings.

The legitimacy of the regime is built on its adherence to Islamic values, and the backing of the *ulema* (theologians). It is the stress on Islam that colours Saudi life most. The 5,000-strong *mutawa* (religious police) enforce the five-times-a-day call to prayer when businesses must close. During Ramadan the *mutawa* are especially active.

WORLD AFFAIRS

AL　Dam Dec　GCC　OIC　OPEC

Saudi Arabia's strategic importance is derived entirely from its oil reserves and worldwide investments. The Kingdom of Saudi Arabia is among the top ten trading partners of nearly every industrialized country in the world. Relations with the USA are particularly close. Although foreign reserves have fallen because of the cost of liberating Kuwait in 1991, the Saudis remain important institutional investors with significant amounts invested in the West.

The Saudi reaction to Iraq's invasion of Kuwait in 1990 demonstrated the Sa'uds' determination to maintain the current *status quo* in the Middle East. Saudi Arabia helped to persuade other Arab states of the need to evict Iraq from Kuwait. It gave sanctuary to the Kuwaiti royal family and offered its military bases to the Western allies. More Saudis fought in the UN's Operation Desert Storm than did troops from any other Arab country.

The guardian of Mecca, Saudi Arabia has immense importance as the spiritual center for more than a billion Muslims all over the world.

AID

$539m

Up 23% in 1993

Through the Saudi Fund for Development, the kingdom makes generous loans and grants to other Arab and developing countries, mainly for infrastructure projects. Saudi Arabia promotes Islam through charitable foundations, especially in Africa, Asia and the former Soviet Union. The royal purse also supports scientific and medical research. Since the liberation of Kuwait in 1991, Saudi Arabia has given large sums to countries that supported the Allies, notably Egypt, Syria, Morocco and Turkey. In addition, the Saudi government substantially reimbursed the USA and UK for the cost of their expeditionary forces, as well as favoring companies from the Allied powers for reconstruction contracts.

***King Fahd ibn Abdul Aziz** acceded to the Saudi throne in 1982.*

***Crown Prince Abdullah ibn Abdul Aziz**, Commander of the National Guard.*

S

CHRONOLOGY

The unification of Saudi Arabia under King Abdul Aziz (ibn Sa'ud) was achieved in 1932. The kingdom remains the only country in the world which is named after its royal family.

❏ **1937** Oil reserves discovered near Riyadh.

❏ **1939** Ceremonial start of oil production at Az Zahran.

❏ **1945** Abdul Aziz meets US President Roosevelt on USS *Quincy* in the Red Sea.

❏ **1953** King Sa'ud succeeds on the death of his father Abdul Aziz.

❏ **1964** King Sa'ud abdicates in favor of his brother Faisal.

❏ **1967** Saudi forces join with those of Jordan and Iraq against Israel during Six Day War.

❏ **1969** Air Force officers stage an abortive coup against King Faisal.

❏ **1973** Saudi Arabia imposes an oil embargo on Western supporters of Israel.

❏ **1975** King Faisal assassinated by a deranged nephew and is succeeded by his brother Khalid.

❏ **1979** Muslim fundamentalists led by Juhaiman ibn Seif al-Otaibi seize the Grand Mosque in Mecca and proclaim a *Mahdi* (messiah) on the first day of the Islamic year 1400.

❏ **1981** Formation of Gulf Co-operation Council, with secretariat in Riyadh.

❏ **1982** King Fahd succeeds on the death of his brother King Khalid. Promises to create consultative assembly.

❏ **1986** Opening of King Fahd Causeway to Bahrain. Sheikh Yamani sacked as oil minister.

❏ **1987** Diplomatic relations with Iran deteriorate after 402 people die in riots involving Islamic fundamentalists at Mecca during the *haj* (pilgrimage).

❏ **1989** Saudi Arabia signs non-aggression pact with Iraq. Saudi Arabia brokers political settlement to Lebanese civil war.

❏ **1990** Kuwaiti royals seek sanctuary in Taif after Iraqi invasion.

❏ **1990–1991** US, UK, French, Egyptian and Syrian forces assemble in Saudi Arabia for Operation Desert Storm. Public executions are halted.

❏ **1991** Iraqis seize border town of Al Khafji, but are driven out by Saudi, US and Qatari forces.

❏ **1993** King Fahd appoints 60-man Consultative Assembly.

❏ **1996** King Fahd briefly relinquishes control of national affairs to Crown Prince Abdullah.

DEFENSE

$13.2bn   Down 8% in 1995

0	Defence spending as % GDP	40
	11.2%	

SAUDI ARABIAN ARMED FORCES

🛡	910 main battle tanks (315 M-1A2, 145 AMX–30, 450 M60A3)	70,000 personnel
🚢	8 frigates, 29 patrol boats	13,500 personnel
✈	295 combat aircraft (56 F–5E, 42 *Tornado* IDS, 24 *Tornado* ADV)	18,000 personnel
🚀	None	

The liberation of Kuwait increased the armed forces' prestige. Military equipment is purchased mostly from the USA, UK and France. Weapons systems are advanced and include *Patriot* missiles and AWACS early warning radar. However, skilled foreign personnel operate many of these: 1,000 US Air Force troops are employed to keep AWACS flying. The air force is the elite branch of the military. It had one brief period of politicization in 1969 when officers attempted a coup. The paramilitary National Guard is drawn from tribal supporters of the Al-Sa'ud regime. Its commander-in-chief is the Crown Prince rather than the defense minister.

ECONOMICS

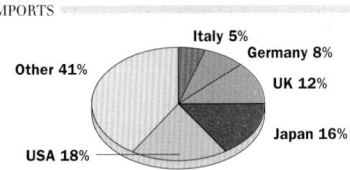

$126.6bn   3.75 Saudi riyals

SCORE CARD

❏ WORLD GNP RANKING	27th
❏ GNP PER CAPITA	$7,240
❏ BALANCE OF PAYMENTS	$–9.1bn
❏ INFLATION	4.8%
❏ UNEMPLOYMENT	6.5%

EXPORTS

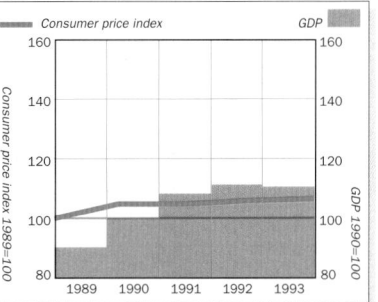

Netherlands 4%
Brazil 3%
Other 53%
Bahrain 5%
Japan 15%
USA 20%

IMPORTS

Italy 5%
Germany 8%
Other 41%
UK 12%
Japan 16%
USA 18%

ECONOMIC PERFORMANCE INDICATOR

Consumer price index — GDP

Consumer price index 1989=100 / GDP 1990=100

1989 1990 1991 1992 1993

financial markets are poorly developed, however, owing to religious inhibitions about paying or receiving interest. Saudi Aramco, the Middle East's largest employer, controls the national oil industry and has ambitious plans for new exploration. Large sums have been spent on giving Saudi Arabia a US-standard infrastructure, with the aim of providing the basis for a manufacturing economy. The economy, however, remains dependent on foreign workers.

STRENGTHS

Vast oil and gas reserves. World-class associated industries. Accumulated surpluses and steady current income. Large income from two million annual pilgrims to Mecca.

WEAKNESSES

Lack of skilled workers. Food production requires heavy subsidy. Most consumer items and industrial raw materials imported.

PROFILE

Since the 1970s, strenuous efforts have been made to shift the economy away from its dependence on oil exports and to provide employment for young Saudis. While most investment in oil is from the government, Saudi entrepreneurs have become more involved in secondary industries. Saudi

SAUDI ARABIA : MAJOR BUSINESSES

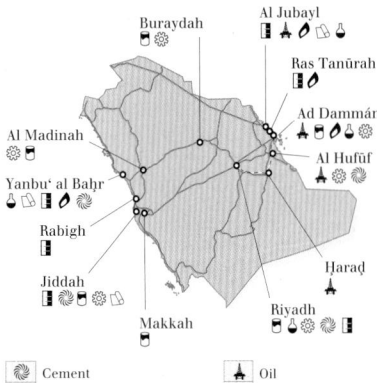

Buraydah
Al Jubayl
Ras Tanūrah
Ad Dammān
Al Madinah
Al Hufūf
Yanbu' al Bahr
Rabigh
Harad
Jiddah
Riyadh
Makkah

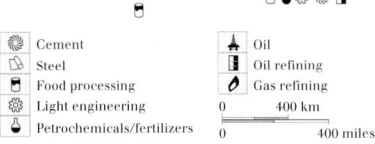

🌀 Cement		⚓	Oil
Steel			Oil refining
Food processing		◗	Gas refining
Light engineering		0	400 km
Petrochemicals/fertilizers		0	400 miles

S

RESOURCES

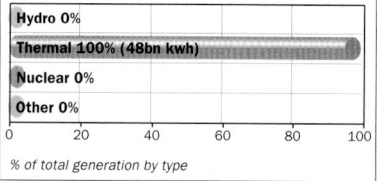

48bn kwh (capacity 18.5m kw)

8.23m b/d (reserves 257,842,000,000 bbl)

7.3m sheep, 4.2m goats, 415,000 camels

Oil, natural gas, limestone, gypsum, marble, clay, salt

ELECTRICITY GENERATION

Hydro 0%

Thermal 100% (48bn kwh)

Nuclear 0%

Other 0%

0   20   40   60   80   100

% of total generation by type

Home to the world's biggest oil and gas reserves, Saudi Arabia plays a key role in the global economy and

ENVIRONMENT

3%

Little environmental legislation

ENVIRONMENTAL TREATIES

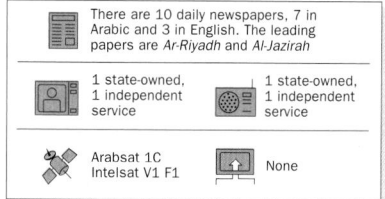

No   No   No

No   Yes   Yes

Pollution in the Gulf and Red Sea has threatened some wildlife and their habitats, as have hunters using high-velocity rifles and off-road vehicles. The government has taken steps to confine manufacturing to industrial estates. Environmental legislation is, nevertheless, poorly developed, although planning controls apply in the major cities.

MEDIA

Control of the media is achieved through the Ministry of Information, which controls the national news agency and the broadcasting services

PUBLISHING AND BROADCAST MEDIA

There are 10 daily newspapers, 7 in Arabic and 3 in English. The leading papers are *Ar-Riyadh* and *Al-Jazirah*

1 state-owned, 1 independent service

1 state-owned, 1 independent service

Arabsat 1C Intelsat V1 F1

None

The government imposes total censorship and insists on strict morality in the Saudi press. In 1994, private citizens were banned from owning satellite dishes, reflecting the state's wish to keep CNN out of Saudi homes. Saudi publishers play a leading role in the Arabic media, however. *Sharq Al Awsat* (The Middle East) published in Saudi Arabia is considered one of the leading Arabic dailies. Saudi investors have bought the influential press agency United Press International.

is among the top ten traders of all the world's major industrialized nations.

SAUDI ARABIA : LAND USE

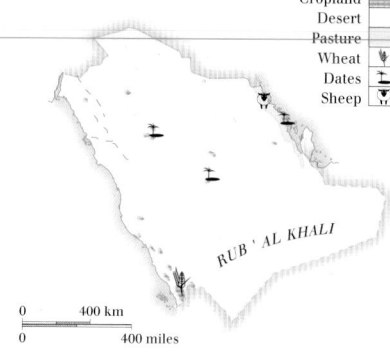

Cropland
Desert
Pasture
Wheat
Dates
Sheep

RUB ' AL KHALI

0   400 km

0   400 miles

CRIME

Saudi Arabia does not publish prison figures

Up 15% in 1992

CRIME RATES

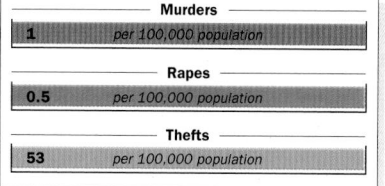

Murders

1   *per 100,000 population*

Rapes

0.5   *per 100,000 population*

Thefts

53   *per 100,000 population*

Strict Islamic punishments – stoning for adultery, amputation for stealing and beheading for murder – deter crime. Amnesty International has condemned the high number of public executions.

EDUCATION

63%

163,732 students

0   *Education spending as % GNP*   25

6.8%

THE EDUCATION SYSTEM

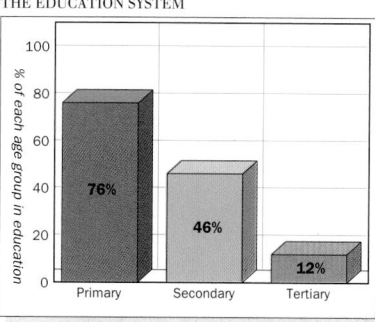

100

80

% of each age group in education

60

40

20

0

76%   Primary

46%   Secondary

12%   Tertiary

In the 1950s, the then Crown Prince Faisal persuaded the religious establishment to give women equal opportunities in education. Much government money has gone into higher education and Islamic universities, though many Saudis still travel abroad to complete their studies.

HEALTH

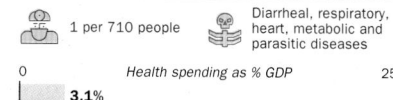

1 per 710 people

Diarrheal, respiratory, heart, metabolic and parasitic diseases

0   *Health spending as % GDP*   25

3.1%

In the 1970s, resources were committed to building a network of modern hospitals at the expense of primary health care. Large sums have been spent on Western expertise. The private sector has also been encouraged. Many Saudis are still sent overseas for treatment by the government, especially for transplant operations, which pose some ethical problems for religious leaders.

WEALTH

Top US surgeon (on contract), 267,023 Saudi riyals ($71,206) per year

CONSUMER GOODS OWNERSHIP

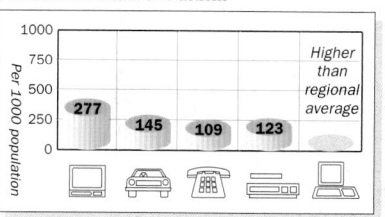

1000

750

Per 1000 population

500

250

0

277   145   109   123

Higher than regional average

Saudi citizens are among the most prosperous in the world. The Al-Sa'uds have used their wealth to create a cradle to the grave welfare system. Ownership of TVs, telephones and VCRs is among the region's highest. The distribution of wealth is carefully controlled by the royal family through the *majlis* system. Petitioners attend weekly assemblies held by prominent royals and beg favors, which are usually granted. There is no stock market, although shares in public companies are traded privately. Many Saudis refuse to accept interest on deposits with banks, but Islamic banks offer profit-sharing investment schemes as an alternative.

S

WORLD RANKING

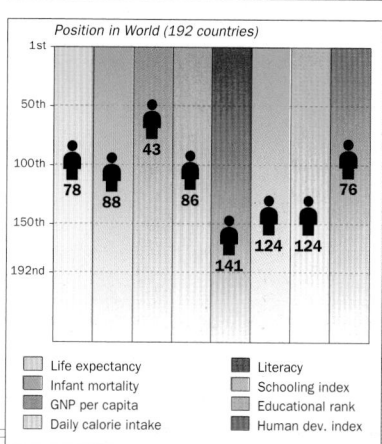

Position in World (192 countries)

1st
50th
100th
150th
192nd

78   88   43   86   141   124   124   76

Life expectancy
Infant mortality
GNP per capita
Daily calorie intake

Literacy
Schooling index
Educational rank
Human dev. index

SENEGAL

WEST AFRICA

OFFICIAL NAME: Republic of Senegal   **CAPITAL:** Dakar
POPULATION: 8.3 million   **CURRENCY:** CFA franc   **OFFICIAL LANGUAGE:** French

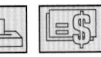

SENEGAL'S CAPITAL DAKAR lies on the westernmost cape of Africa. The country is mostly low, with open savanna and semi-desert in the north and thicker savanna in the south. After independence from France in 1960, Senegal was ruled for 20 years by its first president, Léopold Senghor, who maintained a system of virtual single-party rule. Full multipartyism was introduced in the 1980s. Fishing and tourism are important industries.

CLIMATE

WEATHER CHART

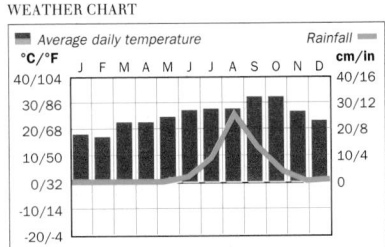

The coastal regions, which project into the path of the northern trade winds, are remarkably cool given their latitude.

TRANSPORTATION

Dakar-Yoff Intl
772,719 passengers

6 ships
18,500 dwt

THE TRANSPORTATION NETWORK

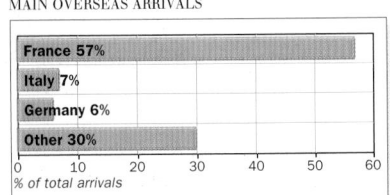

2,420 miles (3,900 km)

None

737 miles (1,186 km)

559 miles (900 km)

Dakar is too large a port for Senegal alone. It also serves the hinterland of Mali, southern Mauritania and Guinea. The key rail link to Bamako, Mali's capital, was built in the 1920s.

TOURISM

240,000 visitors

Up 43% in 1994

MAIN OVERSEAS ARRIVALS

France 57%					
Italy 7%					
Germany 6%					
Other 30%					

0   10   20   30   40   50   60
% of total arrivals

In addition to French package tours to coastal resorts, tours for African-Americans to Gorée, an old slave island, are increasingly popular.

PEOPLE

Wolof, Fulani, Serer, Diola, Malinke, Soninke, Arabic, French

111 people per sq. mile

THE URBAN/RURAL POPULATION SPLIT

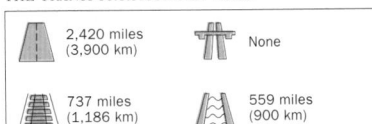

41%   59%

RELIGIOUS PERSUASION

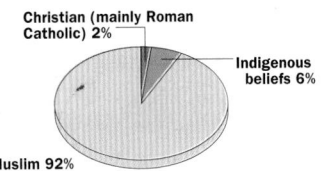

Christian (mainly Roman Catholic) 2%

Indigenous beliefs 6%

Muslim 92%

Senegal has a fairly well-developed sense of nationhood, and intermarriage between groups has reduced ethnic tensions. Groups can still be identified regionally, however. Dakar is a Wolof area, the Senegal River is dominated by the Toucouleur, the Malinke mostly live in the east and the Diola in Casamance. The Diola have felt excluded from the political process, and this has led to unrest in Casamance. A French-influenced class system is still prevalent and has become increasingly apparent in recent years.

POLITICS

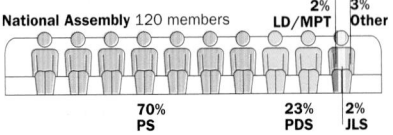

1993/1998

President Abdou Diouf

THE STATE OF THE PARTIES

National Assembly 120 members

2% LD/MPT   3% Other

70% PS   23% PDS   2% JLS

PS = Senegalese Socialist Party   **PDS** = Senegalese Democratic Party   **LD/MPT** = Democratic League/Movement for the Labor Party   **JLS** = "Let Us Unite" coalition   **Other** = Independence and Labor Party, Senegalese Democratic Union – Renovation

Senegal is a multiparty democracy and freedom of association is respected. However, the PS has been in power since the 1950s, albeit under different names, and has spread its influence deep into the civil service, judiciary and local government, making opposition difficult. The main issue is the economy which is still recovering from the 1994 CFA franc devaluation. A cautious privatization process has been initiated. Other problems include the separatist movement in anti-Islamic Casamance, and discontent in the northeast, where drought and refugees from Mauritania have led to tension.

WORLD AFFAIRS

CILSS	Ecowas	FZ	OIC	OMVS

Senegal's most important relationship is with France, which provides high levels of aid; whether these will be maintained is Senegal's major concern. Relations with Mauritania have improved since tension was caused by the expulsion of 200,000 Mauritanians in 1989. A border dispute with Guinea-Bissau remains unresolved. Relations with the USA are good.

SENEGAL

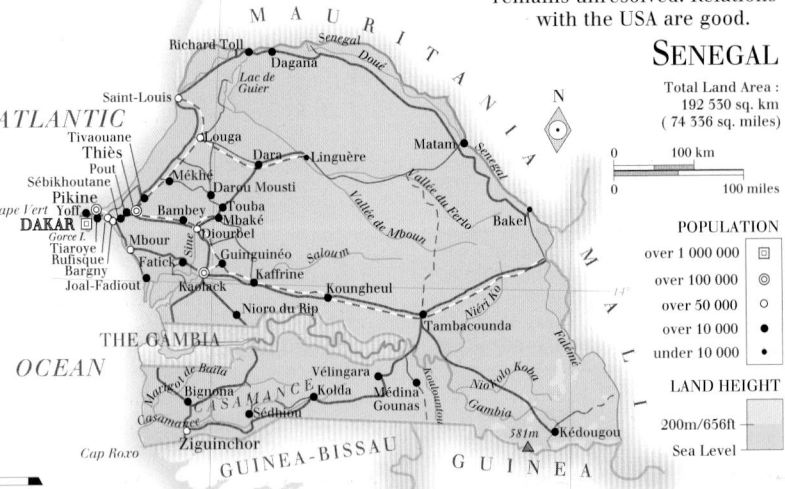

Total Land Area :
192 530 sq. km
(74 336 sq. miles)

0   100 km
0   100 miles

POPULATION

over 1 000 000
over 100 000
over 50 000
over 10 000
under 10 000

LAND HEIGHT

200m/656ft
Sea Level

AID

 $508m (receipts)   Down 25% in 1993

Senegal is one of the highest recipients of aid per capita in Africa, mostly from France, the EU and the World Bank. Aid receipts are used to import 400,000 tons of rice annually, but are also absorbed in administration costs, helping to finance the sizeable civil service. Senegal has given small aid donations to African liberation movements, including the ANC.

The mosque in Touba, religious capital of the Muslim Mouride sect, which was founded in 1887 in Senegal's groundnut-growing district.

DEFENSE

 $76m   Down 16% in 1995

Senegal receives protection from France, which maintains an important naval base at Dakar. By African standards the defense budget is small, and the army is not heavily involved in politics – Senegal has never had a coup. Senegal sent troops to Operation Desert Storm in 1991. Preventing assistance from Guinea-Bissau to Casamance separatists is the main current concern.

ECONOMICS

 $4.95bn   533.68–489.05 CFA francs

SCORE CARD

❏ WORLD GNP RANKING	101st
❏ GNP PER CAPITA	$610
❏ BALANCE OF PAYMENTS	$222m
❏ INFLATION	32.3%
❏ UNEMPLOYMENT	Widespread underemployment

STRENGTHS
Skilled work force is highly educated and motivated. Dakar port linked to the interior by good French-built infrastructure. Also a conference venue.

WEAKNESSES
Few natural resources are exploited, other than groundnuts, phosphates and

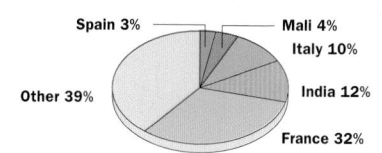

EXPORTS

Spain 3%   Mali 4%
Italy 10%
Other 39%   India 12%
France 32%

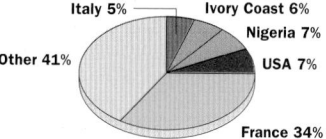

IMPORTS

Italy 5%   Ivory Coast 6%
Nigeria 7%
Other 41%   USA 7%
France 34%

fish. The Gambia River remains unbridged, making access to the oil-rich Casamance region difficult.

RESOURCES

 762m kwh (capacity 231,000 kw)   Not an oil producer; refines 22,600 b/cd

4.6m sheep, 3.2m goats, 2.8m cattle   Phosphates, bauxite, salt, natural gas, marble, iron, copper

Senegal's electricity capacity is largely dependent on imported fuel; cheaper supplies are expected to become available soon from the Manantali dam in Mali. Initial explorations suggest oil reserves may exist off Casamance.

ENVIRONMENT

 11% (6% partially protected)   Damming of the Senegal River

The damming of the Senegal River has caused concern that traditional farming practices, which rely on seasonal floods, may be disrupted. Two major droughts in 1973 and 1983 led to the advance of the Sahara in the west of the country.

MEDIA

 Opposition parties have limited access to the TV station. Together they are permitted 50% of viewing time; the rest goes to the ruling party

PUBLISHING AND BROADCAST MEDIA

📰	There are 3 daily newspapers, *Le Soleil*, *Wal Fadjiri* and *Réveil de l'Afrique Noire*
📺	1 state-owned service
📻	1 state-owned service

The independent media flourished with multipartyism. Senegal had the first satirical journal in Africa with the founding of *Le Politicien* in 1978.

CRIME

 Senegal does not publish prison figures   Up 31% in 1992

Senegal has comparatively low crime rates, though levels are on the increase in Dakar and the surrounding shanty towns, where gangs are based.

CHRONOLOGY

France colonized Senegal, a major entrepôt from the 15th century, in 1890. Dakar was the capital of French West Africa.

- ❏ **1885** Gambia split off as British enclave within Senegal.
- ❏ **1960** Independence under socialist president Léopold Sédar Senghor.
- ❏ **1966** One-party state.
- ❏ **1976** Three-party system.
- ❏ **1981** Abdou Diouf president. Full multipartyism restored.

EDUCATION

 33%   21,562 students

Illiteracy is the major challenge faced by the system. There are universities at Dakar and St-Louis.

HEALTH

1 per 17,650 people   Malaria, diarrheal diseases

Senegal's state health system is rudimentary. Rich Senegalese are well served by private clinics.

WEALTH

The majority of Senegalese lead a subsistence existence

CONSUMER GOODS OWNERSHIP

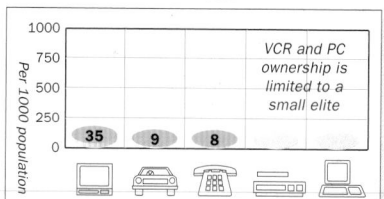

VCR and PC ownership is limited to a small elite

35   9   8

Wealth disparities are considerable and poverty widespread. Those close to the government are the wealthiest group.

WORLD RANKING

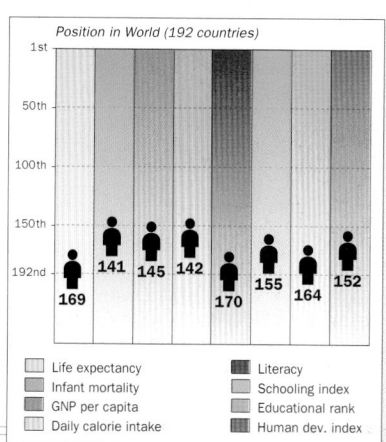

Position in World (192 countries)

169	
141	
145	
142	
170	
155	
164	
152	

Life expectancy   Literacy
Infant mortality   Schooling index
GNP per capita   Educational rank
Daily calorie intake   Human dev. index

S

SEYCHELLES

OFFICIAL NAME: Republic of the Seychelles **CAPITAL:** Victoria
POPULATION: 73,000 **CURRENCY:** Seychelles rupee **OFFICIAL LANGUAGE:** Creole

 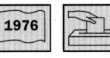 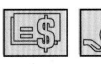 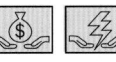

THE 115 ISLANDS of the Seychelles, lying in the Indian Ocean, support unique flora and fauna, including the giant tortoise and the world's largest seed, the *coco-de-mer*. Formerly a UK colony and then under one-party rule for 16 years, the Seychelles became a multiparty democracy in 1993. The economy is reliant on tourism.

CLIMATE

WEATHER CHART

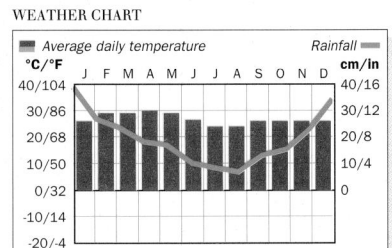

The islands have a tropical oceanic climate, with very little variation in temperature.

TRANSPORTATION

Pointe Larue Intl, Mahé
155,000 passengers

Has no fleet

THE TRANSPORTATION NETWORK

120 miles (190 km)		None
None		None

Transportation policy focuses on building airstrips – nine islands now have them, improving roads on tourist islands and renewing the public transportation fleet.

TOURISM

110,000 visitors

Down 5% in 1994

MAIN OVERSEAS ARRIVALS

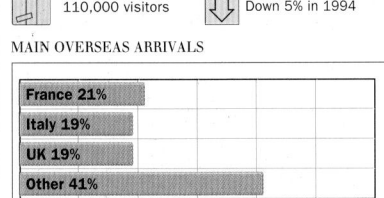

France 21%
Italy 19%
UK 19%
Other 41%
% of total arrivals

The opening of an international airport on Mahé in 1971 made tourism the mainstay of the economy. New hotels are now being built with private foreign investment, but development must comply with strict laws to protect the islands' beauty and unique wildlife.

PEOPLE

French Creole, English, French

700 people per sq. mile

THE URBAN/RURAL POPULATION SPLIT

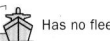

52%   48%

RELIGIOUS PERSUASION

Other 2%   Anglican 8%
Roman Catholic 90%

The Seychelles islands were uninhabited before French settlers arrived in the 1770s. Today, the population is markedly homogeneous as a result of intermarriage between different ethnic groups. The Creoles are the descendants of the French settlers and of the Africans who were settled in the islands by British administrators.

There are small Chinese and Indian minorities. Almost 90% of Seychellois live on Mahé. Population growth has been very low, as about 1,000 people a year have been emigrating. The new democracy may reverse this trend.

POLITICS

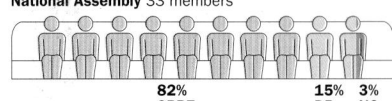

1993/1998

President France-Albert René

THE STATE OF THE PARTIES

National Assembly 33 members

82% SPPF   15% DP   3% UO

SPPF = Seychelles People's Progressive Front
DP = Democratic Party   **UO** = United Opposition

In 1993, the Seychelles returned to multiparty democracy after 16 years of one-party socialist rule under President René. As prime minister, he had seized complete power in a coup just one year after independence. Divisions within the opposition in the 1993 elections resulted in René being confirmed as president. His old party, renamed the SPPF, received the majority vote. In a major change of ideology and policy, the government has made wide-ranging social and economic reforms, including privatizations and the legalization of trade unions.

WORLD AFFAIRS

ACP   Comm   IOC   NAM   OAU

The Seychelles has pursued a policy of non-alignment. However, its strategic location in the Indian Ocean has encouraged competing world powers to seek its friendship. Trade accords exist with other Indian Ocean states.

SEYCHELLES

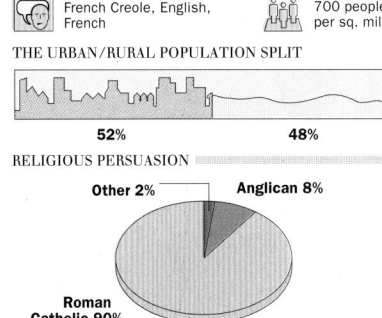

Total Land Area : 270 sq. km (104 sq. miles)

POPULATION
● over 10 000
• under 10 000

LAND HEIGHT
500m/1640ft
200m/656ft
Sea Level

AID

 $10m (receipts)　　 Down 50% in 1993

There is growing support for a range of development projects from multilateral agencies, notably the EU and the Arab Development Fund. Bilateral aid, which used to be the main type of assistance, comes mostly from France and the USA. The UK, Australia and Japan are also sizeable donors.

DEFENSE

 $9.6m　　 Up 3% in 1995

The Seychelles has a 300-strong army, and a paramilitary guard of 1,500. The latter includes a small coast guard made up of air and sea forces. The army, set up in 1977, was initially trained by Tanzania and Tanzanian troops were brought in for three years after a coup attempt in 1981. North Korea provided advisers until 1989.

ECONOMICS

 $453m　　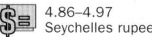 4.86–4.97 Seychelles rupees

SCORE CARD

- ❏ World GNP Ranking.......................167th
- ❏ GNP per Capita $6,210
- ❏ Balance of Payments.....................$–2m
- ❏ Inflation 0.7%
- ❏ Unemployment 9%

Strengths
Tourism. Fishing, especially shrimps and tuna: the latter is canned for export. Profitable re-export trade. Copra. Cinnamon. Tea.

Weaknesses
Growing trade and budget deficits in 1990s owing to drop in tourism following 1991 Gulf War, spending on hosting 1993 Indian Ocean Games and cost of four recent elections. High debt servicing costs. Reliance on food imports, especially for tourist industry. Copra production declining. Significant reliance on expatriate labor.

EXPORTS

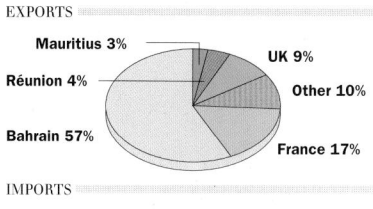

- Mauritius 3%
- Réunion 4%
- Bahrain 57%
- UK 9%
- Other 10%
- France 17%

IMPORTS

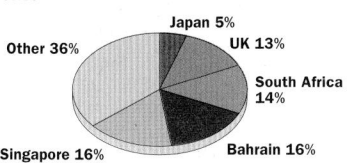

- Japan 5%
- Other 36%
- UK 13%
- South Africa 14%
- Singapore 16%
- Bahrain 16%

One of the 40 central islands. *These are mostly mountainous, with lush vegetation, and are the only granitic islands in the world.*

RESOURCES

 109m kwh (capacity 22,000 kw)　　7,000 tons

18,000 pigs, 5,000 goats, 2,000 cattle　　Phosphates (guano), salt, granite, natural gas

The Seychelles has virtually no mineral resources. All mineral fuel is imported. It is used to generate the power on the three islands which have an electricity supply system. Natural gas finds have spurred oil exploration.

ENVIRONMENT

 95%　　 Strict state controls to conserve land and marine ecosystems

The Seychelles has been praised for its commitment to conservation. It is the sole country to possess two natural World Heritage sites.

MEDIA

 Freedom of expression has been permitted since 1992

PUBLISHING AND BROADCAST MEDIA

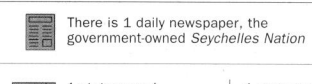

There is 1 daily newspaper, the government-owned *Seychelles Nation*

1 state-owned service　　1 state-owned service

The state broadcasting company has been reorganized and is now ostensibly free of government control. Private periodicals are now permitted.

CRIME

 1,060 prisoners　　 Up 13% in 1992

Violent crime is rare in the Seychelles. The main concern is the increasing rate of petty theft.

EDUCATION

 58%　　 1,682 students

Private schools have been allowed since 1993. National Youth Service has been reduced from two years to one, but is still mandatory for entry to higher education.

HEALTH

 1 per 2,150 people　　Heart and cerebrovascular diseases, cancers

State health care is free. Private medicine is now allowed for the first time under the government's new social legislation.

WEALTH

 Plantation worker, 2,000 Seychelles rupees ($400) per month; dentist, 9,000 Seychelles rupees ($1,800) per month

CONSUMER GOODS OWNERSHIP

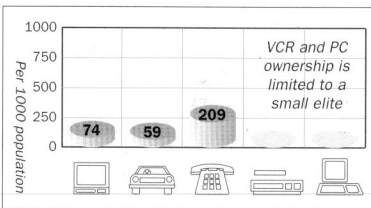

VCR and PC ownership is limited to a small elite

Per 1000 population: 74　59　209

Living standards are the highest among OAU nations. There are no slums and the welfare system caters for all.

WORLD RANKING

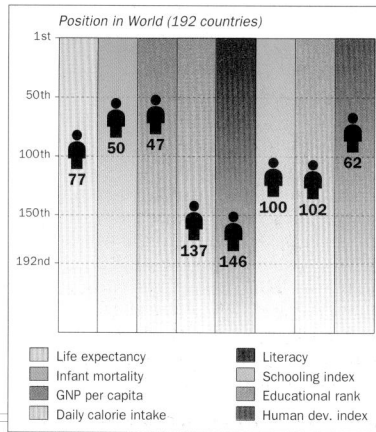

Position in World (192 countries)

- 77
- 50
- 47
- 137
- 146
- 100
- 102
- 62

- Life expectancy
- Infant mortality
- GNP per capita
- Daily calorie intake
- Literacy
- Schooling index
- Educational rank
- Human dev. index

S

SIERRA LEONE

OFFICIAL NAME: Republic of Sierra Leone **CAPITAL:** Freetown
POPULATION: 4.5 million **CURRENCY:** Leone **OFFICIAL LANGUAGE:** English

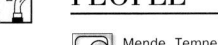

THE WEST AFRICAN STATE of Sierra Leone was first colonized by the British in 1787 as a settlement for Africans freed from slavery. Bordered by Guinea and Liberia, its terrain rises from flat, coastal lowlands to mountains in the northeast. A democratically elected government took office in 1996 ending 19 years of one-party or military rule. Its top priority is restoration of peace after five years of conflict with the RUF.

PEOPLE

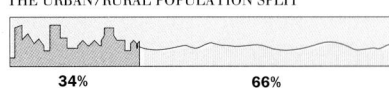

Mende, Temne, Krio, English

163 people per sq. mile

THE URBAN/RURAL POPULATION SPLIT

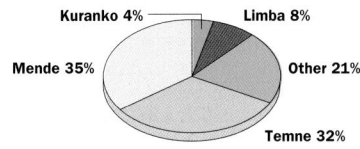

34%   66%

ETHNIC MAKEUP

Kuranko 4%   Limba 8%
Mende 35%   Other 21%
   Temne 32%

Freetown, as its name suggests, was founded as a settlement for people freed from slavery. Its citizens' British and North American origins account for Sierra Leone's strongly anglicized Creole culture. Indigenous groups gained political control in 1951.

CLIMATE

WEATHER CHART

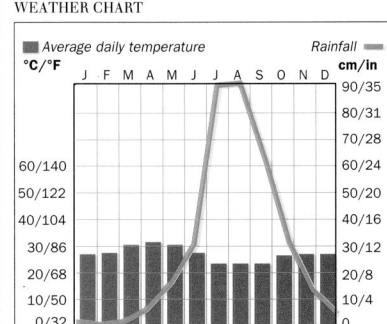

Rainfall on the coast can be as high as 195 inches a year, making Sierra Leone one of the wettest places in coastal West Africa. Humidity is consistently high – about 80% – during the rainy season. The dusty, northeasterly *harmattan* wind often blows during the hotter dry season from November to April. The northeastern savannas are drier, with 74–98 inches of rain a year, but are one of the hottest areas.

TOURISM

72,000 visitors   Down 21% in 1994

MAIN OVERSEAS ARRIVALS

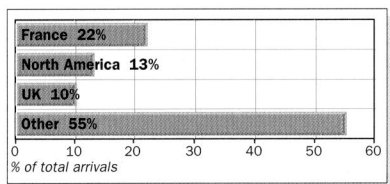

France 22%
North America 13%
UK 10%
Other 55%
% of total arrivals

Sierra Leone attracts few tourists, apart from occasional cruise-ship calls. Internal turmoil and instability mean that plans to develop tourism cannot progress at the moment. Among the chief potential attractions are the beaches along the Freetown peninsula, at present virtually undeveloped.

POLITICS

 1996/2001   Ahmad Tejan Kabbah

THE STATE OF THE PARTIES

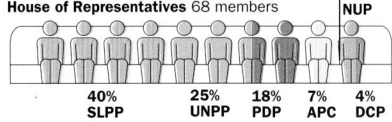

House of Representatives 68 members   6% NUP

40% SLPP   25% UNPP   18% PDP   7% APC   4% DCP

SLPP = Sierra Leone People's Party **UNPP** = United People's Party **PDP** = People's Democratic Party
APC = All People's Congress **NUP** = National Unity Party
DCP = Democratic Center Party

Army chief Gen. Momoh succeeded President Siaka Stevens on his retirement in 1985 and made moves to end the one-party system. However, a coup of junior army officers led by Capt. Valentine Strasser halted the process. In 1996, Strasser himself was replaced by former associate, Brig.-Gen. Julius Bio. Two months later, Bio handed over to an elected civilian government. Government energy has been aimed at controlling the guerrilla activities of the rebel Revolutionary United Front (RUF).

TRANSPORTATION

Lungi Intl, Freetown
84,547 passengers

6, ships
4500 dwt

THE TRANSPORTATION NETWORK

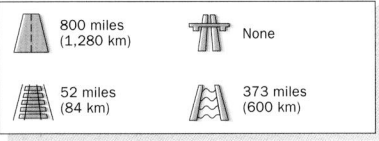

800 miles (1,280 km)   None
52 miles (84 km)   373 miles (600 km)

Little progress has been made in improving Sierra Leone's roads. The 186-mile narrow-gauge railroad was abandoned in 1971 as uneconomic, although 52 miles of track still runs to the closed iron ore mines at Marampa. Having failed in 1987, Sierra Leone's national airline resumed flights – to Paris only – in 1991. The airport is across the estuary from the capital. The only link between the two is a limited ferry service.

SIERRA LEONE

Total Land Area : 71 620 sq. km (27 652 sq. miles)

LAND HEIGHT

1000m/3281ft
500m/1640ft
200m/656ft
Sea Level

POPULATION

◎ over 100 000
● over 10 000
• under 10 000

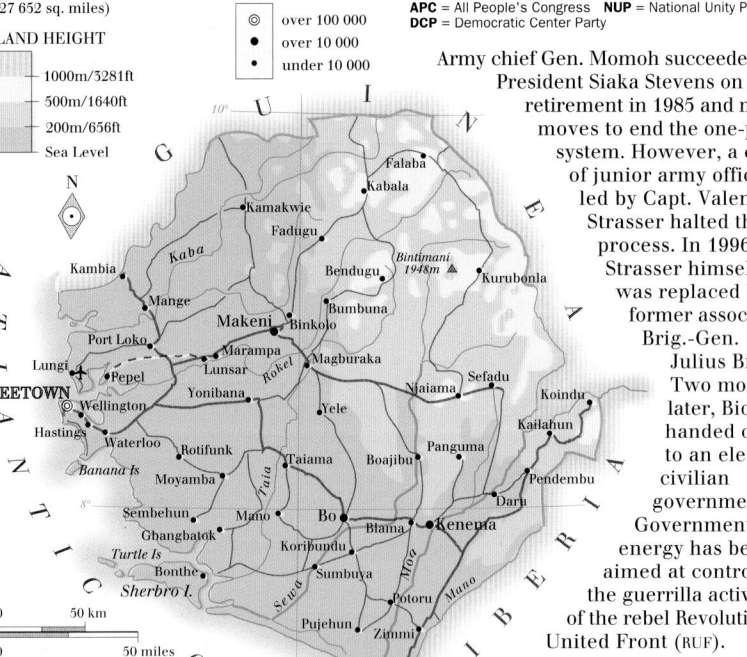

WORLD AFFAIRS

| Comm | Ecowas | MRU | OAU | OIC |

The main concern is that the conflict in neighboring Liberia will create increasing instability in Sierra Leone.

AID

 $1.2bn (receipts)　　 Up 592% in 1993

Sierra Leone has not been able to fulfil the terms of the aid package agreed with the IMF in 1989. Instead, funds have been diverted to cope with refugees from Liberia, internal migrants fleeing the rebellion in the southeast, and the near collapse of public services.

DEFENSE

 $27m　　 Up 13% in 1995

After its last intervention in politics in 1968, the army resumed a central role in the 1992 coup. It has little credibility, however, as a fighting force.

ECONOMICS

 $698m　　 594.62–910.00 leones

SCORE CARD

❏ WORLD GNP RANKING	160th
❏ GNP PER CAPITA	$150
❏ BALANCE OF PAYMENTS	$–58m
❏ INFLATION	27.9%
❏ UNEMPLOYMENT	Endemic

STRENGTHS
Diamonds, although much of the output is smuggled out. Some bauxite and rutile production. The new democratic government is committed to restoring peace and pursuing a more dynamic economic approach.

WEAKNESSES
Rebel fighting affects the most productive areas of the country, including diamond fields.

EXPORTS

Netherlands 7%
UK 10%
USA 15%
Other 68%

IMPORTS

Netherlands 9%
Nigeria 9%
Germany 10%
USA 10%
UK 13%
Other 49%

RESOURCES

 230m kwh (capacity 130,000 kw)　　 Not an oil producer; refines 10,000 b/cd

 362,000 cattle, 302,000 sheep, 168,000 goats　　 Diamonds, rutile, bauxite, gold, titanium

The large diamond deposits need fresh investment as areas currently being mined are becoming depleted. The southeast is the most fertile region.

ENVIRONMENT

 1%　　 Attempt to establish university conservation course

Strain is being placed on the land and on other natural resources to support the growing population.

MEDIA

 Relaxation of restrictions has been promised. Journalists have sometimes been imprisoned

PUBLISHING AND BROADCAST MEDIA

 There are no daily newspapers. The *New Breed*, published by the government, has the largest circulation of the 11 weeklies

 1 state-owned service　　 1 state-owned service

Freetown's Creole population is well served by the broad range of periodicals published there. The new government has promised press freedom.

CRIME

 Sierra Leone does not publish prison figures　　 Crime is rising

Illegal diamond mining and smuggling is one of the most lucrative crimes, in which several government members have been implicated. Sierra Leoneans do not have confidence in the legal system. In December 1992, 26 people were executed for allegedly planning a coup, despite the fact that some were in jail at the time.

EDUCATION

  31%　　 4,742 students

Freetown has a long tradition of education and its university, Fourahbay College, became affiliated with Durham University in the UK in 1876. In recent times, its students have often been active in political dissent. Educational provision has deteriorated with the economic situation over the last decade.

HEALTH

 1 per 14,300 people　　 Communicable diseases, malaria, malnutrition

Only traditional health care is available outside the capital. Average life expectancy is 43 years; only three other countries share such a low figure.

The main street, Kabala. *In 1993, Sierra Leone was second from bottom of the UN's Human Development Index.*

CHRONOLOGY

Freetown was founded in 1787 and became a British colony in 1808; the interior was annexed in 1896.

- ❏ **1961** Independence.
- ❏ **1978** Single-party republic under Siaka Stevens. National bankruptcy.
- ❏ **1991** Liberian rebels invade Sierra Leone in protest at its participation in ECOWAS force in Liberia. Sierra Leonean rebels join the fighting.
- ❏ **1992** Army coup installs Capt. Strasser.
- ❏ **1996** Multiparty democratic elections.

WEALTH

 Most of the population lead a subsistence existence

CONSUMER GOODS OWNERSHIP

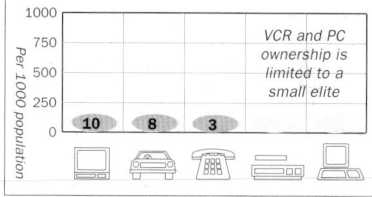

VCR and PC ownership is limited to a small elite

10　8　3

Most of the population is impoverished. Wealth is almost exclusively associated with political power and influence.

S

WORLD RANKING

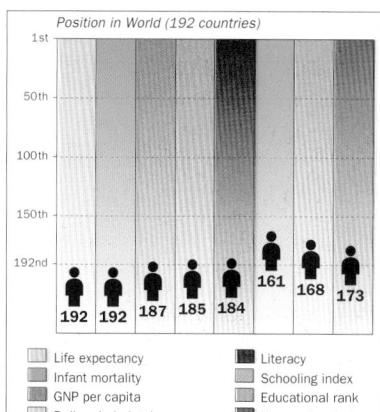

Position in World (192 countries)

192　192　187　185　184　161　168　173

Life expectancy	Literacy
Infant mortality	Schooling index
GNP per capita	Educational rank
Daily calorie intake	Human dev. index

SINGAPORE

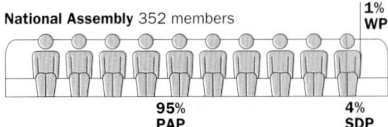

OFFICIAL NAME: Republic of Singapore   **CAPITAL:** Singapore City
POPULATION: 2.8 million   **CURRENCY:** Singapore dollar   **OFFICIAL LANGUAGES:** Malay, Chinese, Tamil and English

 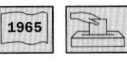 

AN ISLAND STATE linked to the southernmost tip of the Malay peninsula by a causeway, Singapore was largely uninhabited between the 14th and 18th centuries. In 1819, an official of the British East India Company, Stamford Raffles, recognized the island's strategic position on key trade routes and established Singapore as a trading settlement. Today, Singapore is still one of the most important entrepôts in Asia.

CLIMATE

WEATHER CHART

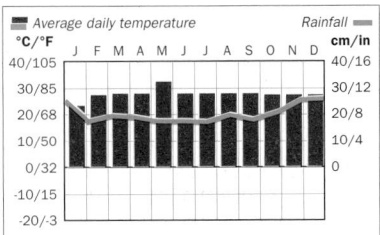

The only variations in the hot, wet and humid climate are the airless months of September and March, when the trade winds change direction.

TRANSPORTATION

 Changi International 1.49m passengers   600 ships 15.45m dwt

THE TRANSPORTATION NETWORK

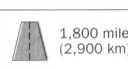 1,800 miles (2,900 km)   63 miles (102 km)

 16 miles (26 km)    None

The Mass Rapid Transit System (subway), completed in 1991, is among the world's most efficient. Space for new roads has run out and monthly auctions are held to sell certificates entitling people to buy from a quota of new cars. The massive port at Pasir Panjang is being expanded on reclaimed land.

The financial center. More than a quarter of Singapore's GDP is generated by financial and business services.

TOURISM

 7.1m visitors    Up 24% in 1994

MAIN OVERSEAS ARRIVALS

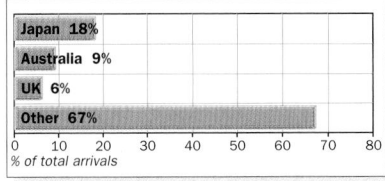

Japan 18%
Australia 9%
UK 6%
Other 67%
% of total arrivals

The Chinatown district is recognized as a picturesque tourist asset and its buildings are being restored. The other main attractions are shopping and golf; Singapore has one of the highest densities of golf courses in the world.

PEOPLE

  Chinese, Malay, Tamil, English   11,894 people per sq. mile

THE URBAN/RURAL POPULATION SPLIT

100%

ETHNIC MAKEUP

Other 2%   South Asian 7%
Malay 15%
Chinese 76%

Singapore is dominated by the Chinese, who make up 76% of the community; the old English-speaking Straits Chinese and newer Mandarin-speakers are now well integrated. Indigenous Malays are generally the poorest group. Serious race riots erupted in the 1950s, but today there is little overt ethnic tension. There is a significant foreign work force in Singapore; a recent labor shortage has forced the government to try to attract scientists from the CIS, Eastern Europe and Hong Kong. Society is highly regulated and government campaigns to improve public behavior are frequent.

POLITICS

 1991/1996   President Ong Teng Cheong

THE STATE OF THE PARTIES

National Assembly 352 members

1% WP
95% PAP
4% SDP

PAP = People's Action Party   **SDP** = Singapore Democratic Party   **WP** = Workers' Party

Singapore is a multiparty democracy, although the ruling People's Action Party (PAP) effectively controls all parts of the political process and much of the economy. Following a constitutional amendment in 1993, Ong Teng Cheong became the first president to be directly elected by the people of Singapore.

The government promotes the development of Singapore on the basis of a strong free-market economy, while continuing to place emphasis on social welfare. There are plans to create a national ideology ("shared values") based on Confucian traditions.

The PAP saw its share of the vote fall from 84% in 1968 to 61% in 1991, and there were signs that the party had lost support among the Chinese working class, its traditional backer. However, it is unlikely that the party, which has given Singaporeans one of the highest living standards in the world, will lose its grip on power.

WORLD AFFAIRS

APEC   ASEAN   Comm   NAM   WTO

Singapore has established diplomatic relations with China while continuing to maintain close economic ties with Taiwan. After 15 years of talks, Singapore and Malaysia in 1995 finally established their territorial water boundary.

AID

 US$24m (receipts)   Up 20% in 1993

Aid is not an important issue in Singapore. The state does not provide aid to any states in Southeast Asia.

DEFENSE

 US$4bn   Up 38% in 1995

Singapore is the most heavily armed state in the region. Defense accounts for 22% of government expenditure.

S

ECONOMICS

 $65.8bn   1.41–1.46 Singapore dollars

SCORE CARD

❏ WORLD GNP RANKING...........................39th
❏ GNP PER CAPITA ....US$23,360
❏ BALANCE OF PAYMENTS ....US$12bn
❏ INFLATION 1.3%
❏ UNEMPLOYMENT................................2.7%

STRENGTHS

Massive accumulated wealth – reserves are over US$60 billion – derived from success as an entrepôt and center of high-tech industries. Huge state enterprises, such as TAMESEK, with over 450 companies, have proved highly flexible in responding to market conditions. Singapore produces 50% of the world's computer disk drives. The world leader in new biotechnologies.

RESOURCES

 17.5bn kwh (capacity 3.4m kw)   Not an oil producer; refines 1.03m b/cd

 11,654 tons   Granite

Singapore has no strategic resources and has to import almost all the energy and food it needs. Its main resources, on which its wealth as a center of commerce has been built, are its strategic position and its people.

ENVIRONMENT

 5%   New clean city initiatives

There is a small green belt around the causeway. Singapore sees itself as a world leader in providing the perfect urban environment. There is no litter, thanks to instant heavy fines; chewing gum is banned by law.

SINGAPORE

Total Land Area : 610 sq. km (236 sq. miles)

Urban Areas
Open Areas
Nature Reserve

EXPORTS

Thailand 6%
Japan 8%
Hong Kong 9%
Other 43%
Malaysia 14%
USA 20%

IMPORTS

Saudi Arabia 4%
Thailand 4%
Other 37%
USA 16%
Malaysia 17%
Japan 22%

WEAKNESSES

Dependence on Malaysia for water. All food and energy has to be imported. Skills shortages in some key areas, especially engineering. Lack of land restraining further development.

MEDIA

 The press is completely regulated

PUBLISHING AND BROADCAST MEDIA

 There are 9 daily newspapers, including the leading *Straits Times* and *Business Times*

 1 state-owned service   1 state-owned service

The government is very sensitive to any criticism that might reflect badly on Singapore. The successful prosecutions of two libel suits against the *International Herald Tribune* in 1995 focused debate on the country's stringent media laws.

CRIME

6,470 prisoners   Down 4% in 1992

Crime is limited and punishment can be severe. The Triads are no longer a problem; the main issue is intellectual piracy.

EDUCATION

 91%   73,650 students

Education is not compulsory, but attendance at both elementary and secondary schools is high. There are two universities and five colleges.

HEALTH

 1 per 693 people   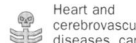 Heart and cerebrovascular diseases, cancers

Singapore has an efficient modern health system. Incentives exist aimed at preserving the extended family, so that the elderly are cared for at home.

WEALTH

 Live-in maid, 500 Singapore dollars (US$353) per month; experienced secretary, 5,000 Singapore dollars (US$3,535) per month

CONSUMER GOODS OWNERSHIP

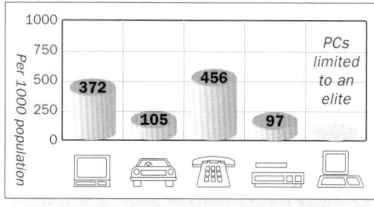

Per 1000 population

PCs limited to an elite

372
105
456
97

The Chinese and Indians live very well, although their party-allocated flats are not luxurious by Western standards. The Malays are the poorest group.

WORLD RANKING

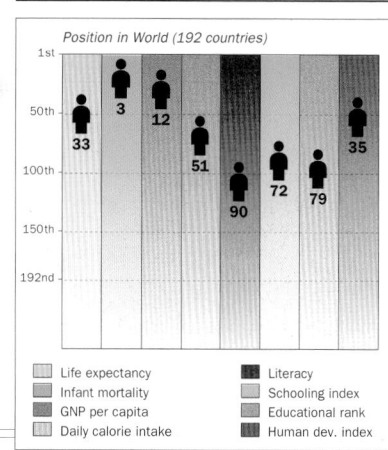

Position in World (192 countries)

33
3
12
51
90
72
79
35

Life expectancy
Infant mortality
GNP per capita
Daily calorie intake
Literacy
Schooling index
Educational rank
Human dev. index

S

SLOVAKIA

OFFICAL NAME: Slovak Republic **CAPITAL:** Bratislava
POPULATION: 5.4 million **CURRENCY:** Slovak koruna **OFFICAL LANGUAGE:** Slovak

SLOVAKIA IS BORDERED BY the Czech Republic, Austria, Poland, Hungary and the Ukraine. Southern lowlands contrast with the Carpathian mountain range, which extends along the Polish border. An independent democracy since 1993, Slovakia is the less-developed half of the former Czechoslovakia. It is facing difficulties in making its industry-based economy efficient.

Levoča, in northeastern Slovakia, dates from the 13th century and still retains its medieval street plan and town walls.

CLIMATE

WEATHER CHART

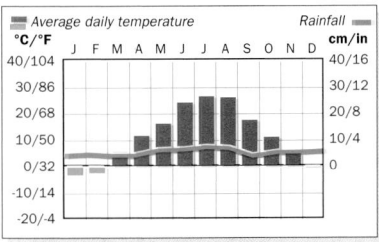

Slovakia has a continental climate. Snowfalls are heavy in winter, while summers are moderately warm.

TRANSPORTATION

 Milan Rastislav Stefanik, Bratislava   Has no fleet

THE TRANSPORTATION NETWORK

 11,020 miles (17,740 km)   119 miles (191 km)

 2,275 miles (3,661 km)   107 miles (172 km)

Establishing transportation links with Austria, the main route to Central and Western Europe, is vital. The horse and cart is still used in rural areas.

S

TOURISM

 902,000 visitors  Up 39% in 1994

MAIN OVERSEAS ARRIVALS

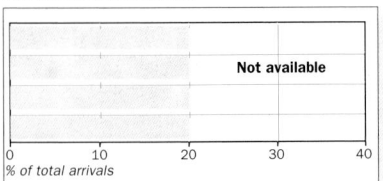

The Tatra Mountains are popular with skiers, hikers and cavers. Most of the tourist industry has been privatized, but the government plans to retain partial control of Slovakia's many thermal-spring health spas.

PEOPLE

 Slovak, Hungarian, Czech 285 people per sq. mile

THE URBAN/RURAL POPULATION SPLIT

 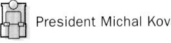
57% 43%

RELIGIOUS PERSUASION

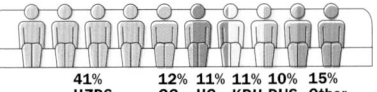
Orthodox Catholic 2%
Protestant 20%
Roman Catholic 50%
Other 28%

POLITICS

 1994/1998   President Michal Kováč

THE STATE OF THE PARTIES

National Council of the Slovak Republic 150 members

41% HZDS 12% CC 11% HC 11% KDH 10% DUS 15% Other

HZDS = Movement for a Democratic Slovakia
CC = Common Choice bloc **HC** = Hungarian Coalition
KDH = Christian Democratic Movement **DUS** = Democratic Union of Slovakia **Other** = Association of Workers of Slovakia, Slovak National Party

The move to independence in 1993 was more a result of Czech than Slovak policies. Václav Klaus, the Czech leader, offered Slovakia continued membership of the federation on Czech terms, or separation. Slovak leader Vladimír Mečiar, while apparently in favor of greater power within a federation, was also tempted by independence as this enhanced his own power base.

Slovakian politics are in flux. In 1994, Mečiar, who had been ousted from the premiership in a no-confidence vote, returned to power. An ongoing power struggle involving Mečiar and President Michal Kováč, both members of the HZDS, has also added to political uncertainty. The Hungarian minority has its own parties, but the 300,000 Gypsies have no official representation.

Slovaks dominate society, but 9% of the population is Hungarian, and there is a large Gypsy minority which faces discrimination and attacks. Tension has increased between the Slovaks and Hungarians, particularly over the directive that Hungarians should adopt Slovak name endings. Few Slovaks resident in the Czech Republic have returned to help structure the new Slovakia. Roman Catholicism remains a powerful social force.

WORLD AFFAIRS

 CE CEFTA IBRD NACC OSCE

Relations with Hungary are strained over Slovakia's unilateral decision to complete the Gabcikovo Nagymaros Dam, and the treatment of the Hungarian minority in Slovakia. Slovakia is working to raise its international profile.

AID

 Significant receipts   Little change in trends

Aid is of particular importance due to the lack of inward foreign investment. The IMF and EU are the main donors.

DEFENSE

 403.1m  Up 30% in 1995

A new Slovak army, one-third of the former Czechoslovak army, has been formed. Slovakia recently acquired some weapons from Russia, but lack of finance remains a major problem.

RESOURCES

 22.5bn kwh   1,403 b/d

 12m chickens, 2.2m pigs, 916,000 cattle, 397,000 sheep   Coal, lignite, gas, oil, antimony, copper, iron, mercury, zinc

Slovakia is planning to export power from the massive Gabcikovo Nagymaros Dam on the River Danube.

SLOVAKIA

Total Land Area : 49 036 sq. km
(18 933 sq. miles)

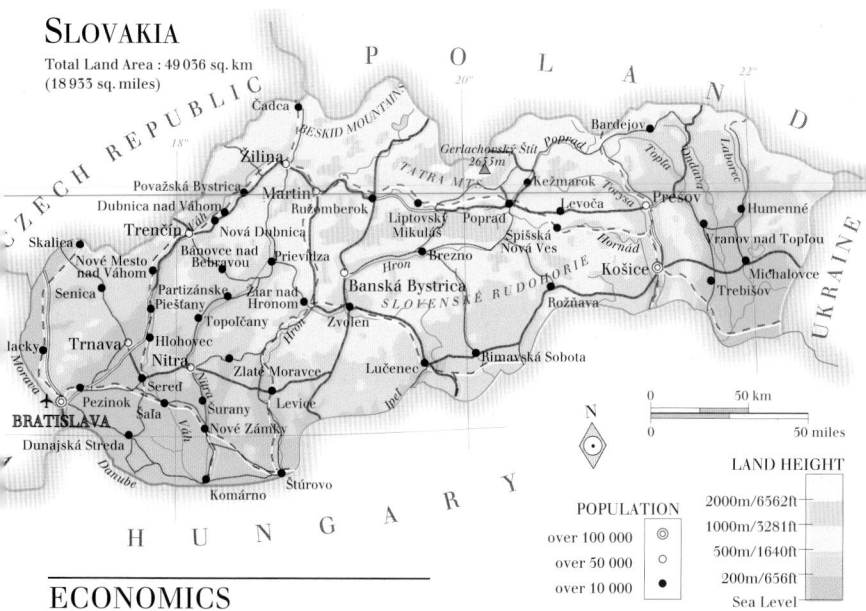

POPULATION

◎	over 100 000
○	over 50 000
●	over 10 000

LAND HEIGHT

2000m/6562ft
1000m/3281ft
500m/1640ft
200m/656ft
Sea Level

ECONOMICS

 $11.9bn   29.63–31.07 Slovak koruny

SCORE CARD

❏ WORLD GNP RANKING	77th
❏ GNP PER CAPITA	$2,230
❏ BALANCE OF PAYMENTS	$719m
❏ INFLATION	10.2%
❏ UNEMPLOYMENT	14.6%

STRENGTHS

Potential for tourism, particularly skiing in the Tatras, once hotel infrastructure is upgraded.

WEAKNESSES

Legacy of status as less-developed part of Czechoslovakia. Loss of subsidies from Czech Republic. Narrow emphasis of economy on heavy engineering and arms manufacture; collapse of COMECON markets for these have hit Slovakia very hard. Unemployment high, since Slovak economy is not competitive in European markets. Lack of foreign investors. Many skilled Slovaks in areas such as banking and policy-making have remained in the Czech Republic.

EXPORTS

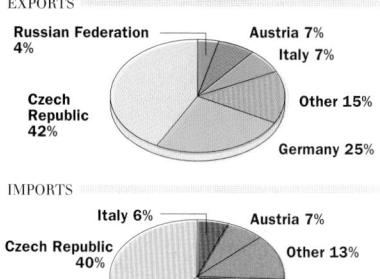

Russian Federation 4%
Austria 7%
Italy 7%
Other 15%
Czech Republic 42%
Germany 25%

IMPORTS

Italy 6%
Austria 7%
Czech Republic 40%
Other 13%
Russian Federation 13%
Germany 21%

ENVIRONMENT

 21%   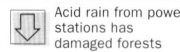 Acid rain from power stations has damaged forests

Levels of industrialization are not as great, and pollution not as serious, as in the neighboring Czech Republic.

MEDIA

 Press freedom is generally assured, though access is limited for minorities

PUBLISHING AND BROADCAST MEDIA

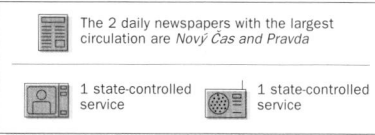

The 2 daily newspapers with the largest circulation are *Nový Čas* and *Pravda*

1 state-controlled service   1 state-controlled service

There are demands for greater press freedom and media coverage, especially for the Hungarian minority. Gypsies have practically no media coverage.

CRIME

 Slovakia does not publish prison figures   Up 33% in 1993

The state has taken steps to prevent Slovakia being used as a route to smuggle nuclear materials from the former Soviet Union. There is some politically motivated crime, including the abduction in 1995 of the son of President Kováč.

EDUCATION

 99%    66,002 students

Schooling is reverting to the pre-1939 Slovakian traditions. Rural areas tend to be failed by the education system. There is a modern university in Bratislava.

HEALTH

 1 per 290 people   Cancers, heart and cerebrovascular diseases, accidents

The health service is limited, although of a higher standard than in most of the ex-COMECON states.

WEALTH

 Secretary, 4,000 Slovak koruny ($140) per month; lawyer, 20,000 Slovak koruny ($675) per month

CONSUMER GOODS OWNERSHIP

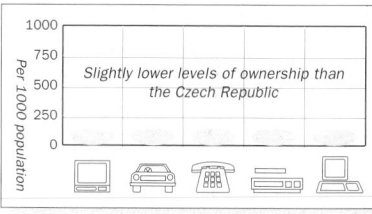

Slightly lower levels of ownership than the Czech Republic

A new elite is emerging that is keen on Western goods. Rural workers and Gypsies are the poorest groups.

WORLD RANKING

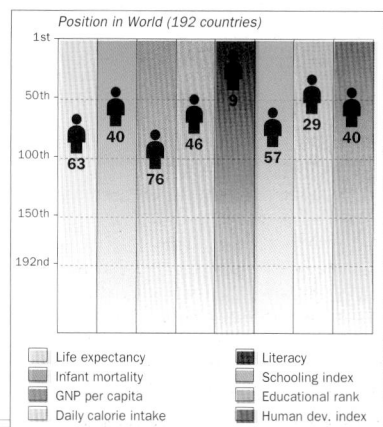

Position in World (192 countries)

☐ Life expectancy		☐ Literacy
☐ Infant mortality		☐ Schooling index
☐ GNP per capita		☐ Educational rank
☐ Daily calorie intake		☐ Human dev. index

S

SLOVENIA

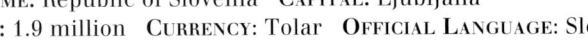

OFFICIAL NAME: Republic of Slovenia   **CAPITAL:** Ljubljana
POPULATION: 1.9 million   **CURRENCY:** Tolar   **OFFICIAL LANGUAGE:** Slovene

O F ALL THE FORMER Yugoslav republics, Slovenia has the closest links with Western Europe. Located at the northeastern end of the Adriatic Sea, this small, alpine country controls some of Europe's major transit routes. Its economy has been badly affected by the collapse of Yugoslavia, and it has struggled to develop economic ties with the West. Slovenia's transition to independence in 1991 avoided the violence associated with the breakup of Yugoslavia.

CLIMATE

WEATHER CHART

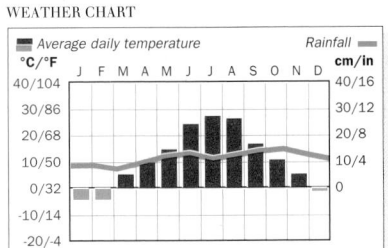

Slovenia's interior has a continental climate. Its small coastal region has a mild Mediterranean climate.

TRANSPORTATION

Brnik Intl, Ljubljana

2 ships
200 dwt

THE TRANSPORTATION NETWORK

8,270 miles (13,320 km)	50 miles (81 km)
743 miles (1,196 km)	None

Slovenia is strategically situated at some of Europe's major crossroads. In addition, its Adriatic ports provide Austria with its main maritime outlet.

TOURISM

748,000 visitors   Up 20% in 1994

MAIN OVERSEAS ARRIVALS

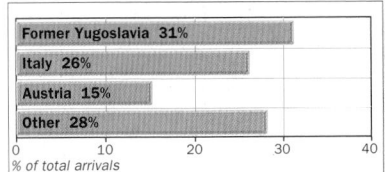

Former Yugoslavia	31%
Italy	26%
Austria	15%
Other	28%

% of total arrivals

Slovenia hopes "village tourism" will bring visitors to rural towns and farms, as well as to its mountains and beaches. However, large numbers of tourists are still put off by the uncertainty in Bosnia.

PEOPLE

Slovene, Serbian, Croatian

244 people
per sq. mile

THE URBAN/RURAL POPULATION SPLIT

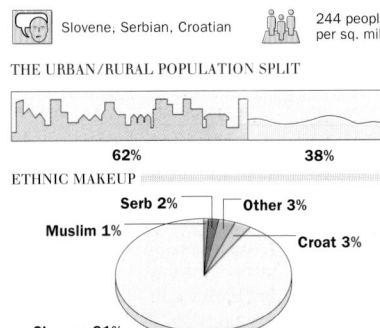

62%   38%

ETHNIC MAKEUP

- Serb 2%
- Other 3%
- Muslim 1%
- Croat 3%
- Slovene 91%

Slovenia is ethnically homogeneous; 91% are Slovene. There are also small communities of Italians and Hungarians. The Slovene language is sufficiently different from Serbian and Croatian to foster a separate identity from its Yugoslav neighbors. Slovenia has traditionally identified more with the alpine countries to the west than its Balkan neighbors. Access to Italy and Austria in the 1970s and 1980s fostered a separatist movement. These factors, and a well-developed economy, aided Slovenia's relatively peaceful secession from the former Yugoslavia in 1991.

SLOVENIA

Total Land Area : 20 250 sq. km
(7820 sq. miles)

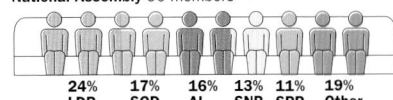

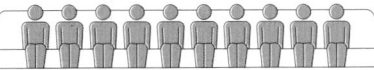

POPULATION

◎	over 100 000
○	over 50 000
●	over 10 000
•	under 10 000

LAND HEIGHT

1000m/3281ft
500m/1640ft
200m/656ft
Sea Level

POLITICS

 1992/1996    President Milan Kučan

THE STATE OF THE PARTIES

National Assembly 90 members

24% LDP	17% SCD	16% AL	13% SNP	11% SPP	19% Other

LDP = Liberal Democratic Party   **SCD** = Slovenian Christian Democrats   **AL** = Associated List   **SNP** = Slovenian National Party   **SPP** = Slovenian People's Party   **Other** = Democratic Party of Slovenia, Greens of Slovenia, Social Democratic Party of Slovenia

National Council 40 members

22 members are elected and 18 are chosen by an electoral college to represent various interests

Slovenia has been a force for stability in the war-torn former Yugoslavia. Nonetheless, the government of Janez Drnovsek is facing increasing tension, with a general election scheduled for 1996. Drnovsek's coalition lost its absolute majority in the National Assembly in early 1996 when the United List of Social Democrats became the main party of opposition. Strains over economic policy led to the departure of the United List, which was a successor to the Communist Party. Nevertheless Drnovsek remains confident that the votes of independents will sustain his government for the remainder of its term. However, it is far from clear what alliance will emerge after the election.

WORLD AFFAIRS

 CE NAM OSCE PfP WTO

Slovenia is planning to apply for full EU membership in 1996. At the start of 1996, it became a full member of CEFTA.

AID

 Attraction of aid is a major government concern

 Aid receipts have risen since independence

Recent agreements with the EU and the IMF have set up lines of credit. Aid is being targeted at infrastructural improvements and education projects.

DEFENSE

 $298m

 Up 56% in 1995

Slovene troops successfully held off federal Yugoslav army attacks following secession in 1991. A small air force is being developed.

ECONOMICS

 $14.2bn

 128–129 tolar

SCORE CARD

- ❏ World GNP Ranking..........................73rd
- ❏ GNP per Capita $7,140
- ❏ Balance of Payments $457m
- ❏ Inflation 11.1%
- ❏ Unemployment...............................14.4%

EXPORTS

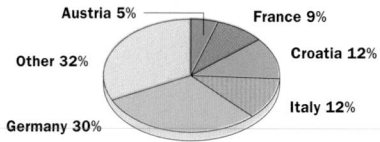

Austria 5%
France 9%
Other 32%
Croatia 12%
Italy 12%
Germany 30%

IMPORTS

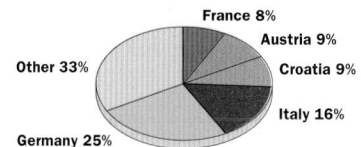

France 8%
Austria 9%
Other 33%
Croatia 9%
Italy 16%
Germany 25%

STRENGTHS

Competitive manufacturing industry. Prospects for growth in electronics industry. Well-developed tourist sector. Czech demand for Slovenia's consumer goods exports. Well placed to supply ex-Yugoslavia now sanctions have been lifted.

WEAKNESSES

Landmark deal on share of Yugoslav debt is being challenged by Serbia. Competitiveness is being undermined by rising costs and the strength of the Slovenian currency, the tolar.

Lake Bled in the Julian Alps, *which lie astride the Slovenian–Italian border. The lake is a popular tourist destination.*

RESOURCES

 12bn kwh

 40 b/d, refines 14,700 b/cd

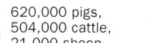 620,000 pigs, 504,000 cattle, 21,000 sheep

Coal, lignite, lead, zinc, uranium, silver, mercury

Slovenia has come under pressure from Austria to close the nuclear plant at Krško, which provides one-third of Slovenia's power. It has deposits of brown coal and lignite, but they are difficult to extract and of poor quality.

ENVIRONMENT

 5%

 Some industrial pollution

Slovenes were in the vanguard of former Yugoslavia's environmental movement. Protecting the country's alpine ecology is a priority.

MEDIA

 The media is free from government interference

PUBLISHING AND BROADCAST MEDIA

There are 3 daily newspapers. The weekly magazine *Mladina* offers independent reporting and commentary

1 state-run service

1 state-run service

The Slovene media actively worked to undermine Yugoslav institutions during the secession crisis, reinforcing the sense of national identity.

CRIME

 Slovenia does not publish prison figures

 Up 28% in 1992

Slovenia has traditionally been a transit point for drug-smuggling into Western Europe. The trade declined when the UN imposed sanctions on Serbia.

EDUCATION

 99%

 40,239 students

School is compulsory from 7 to 15 years, and standards are high. In 1993, there were over 40,000 students in tertiary education. The university at Ljubljana was founded in 1595.

CHRONOLOGY

Slovenia was part of the Austro-Hungarian empire until 1918. It was the first republic to secede from the Federal Republic of Yugoslavia.

- ❏ **1918** Slovenia joins Yugoslav kingdom.
- ❏ **1949** Tito's break with Moscow. Opens borders with the West.
- ❏ **1989** Parliament confirms right to secede. Calls multiparty elections.
- ❏ **1990** Control over army asserted, referendum approves secession.
- ❏ **1991** Independence declared. Yugoslav federal army attacks held off. EU-brokered ceasefire.
- ❏ **1992** EU recognizes Slovenia. First multiparty elections held. Milan Kučan elected president.
- ❏ **1993** Member of IMF and IBRD.

HEALTH

 1 per 1,449 people

 Cerebrovascular and heart diseases, cancers, accidents

National health care in Slovenia uses health centers and outpatient clinics to increase accessibility for patients.

WEALTH

 Slovenia has the highest wages among the former Yugoslav republics

CONSUMER GOODS OWNERSHIP

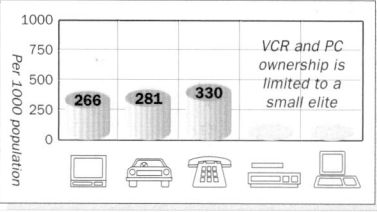

VCR and PC ownership is limited to a small elite

266 281 330

Per 1000 population

Slovenia was the most advanced and highly industrialized of the six Yugoslav republics. Average net monthly wages in 1993 were equivalent to $400.

S

WORLD RANKING

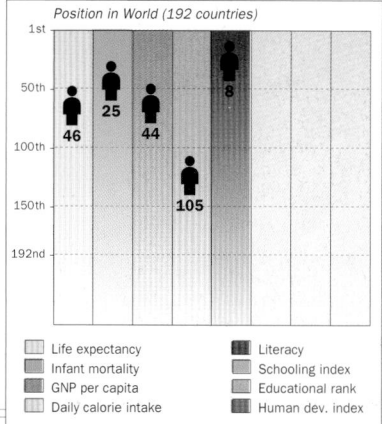

Position in World (192 countries)

46 25 44 8 105

- Life expectancy
- Infant mortality
- GNP per capita
- Daily calorie intake
- Literacy
- Schooling index
- Educational rank
- Human dev. index

SOLOMON ISLANDS

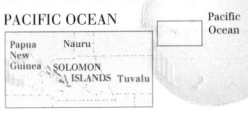

PACIFIC OCEAN

OFFICIAL NAME: Solomon Islands **CAPITAL:** Honiara
POPULATION: 400,000 **CURRENCY:** Solomon Islands dollar **OFFICIAL LANGUAGE:** English

SCATTERED OVER 289,000 sq. miles, the Solomons archipelago consists of several hundred islands. Most of the population live on the six largest islands – Guadalcanal, Malaita, New Georgia, Makira, Santa Isabel and Choiseul. The Solomons have been settled since at least 1000 BC and the Spanish reached the islands in 1568. They gained independence from Britain in 1978. Most of the Solomons are coral reefs. Just 1% of the islands' land area is cultivable.

CLIMATE

WEATHER CHART

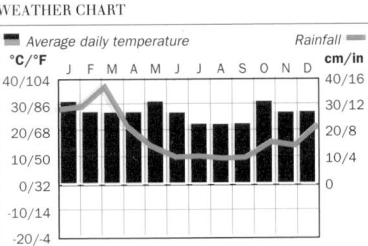

There is little variation in the humid, hot subtropical climate, but ferocious cyclones can occur in the rainy season.

TRANSPORTATION

 Henderson, Honiara 22,000 passengers

 2 ships 600 dwt

THE TRANSPORTATION NETWORK

20 miles (30 km)	None
None	None

The airport on Guadalcanal was begun by the Japanese and completed by the USA during World War II. Most airfields are simple grass strips.

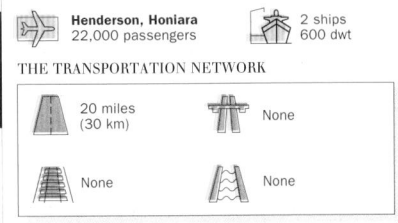

Unloading seed coconuts near Munda on New Georgia in the Solomons' southern chain of islands. Coconuts are by far the largest and most commercially important crop.

TOURISM

12,000 visitors   No change in 1994

MAIN OVERSEAS ARRIVALS

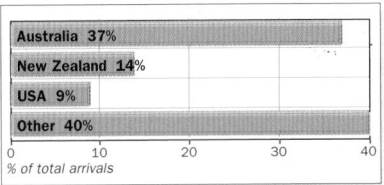

Australia 37%
New Zealand 14%
USA 9%
Other 40%

% of total arrivals

More tourists are expected now that Boeing 747 jets can land at the main airport. Guadalcanal, a key battle site of World War II in the Pacific, has seen a decline in visitors in recent years. Outlying islands cater for visitors wishing to "get away from it all."

PEOPLE

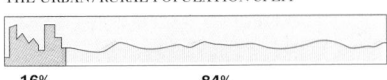

English, Pidgin English, Melanesian Pidgin   36 people per sq. mile

THE URBAN/RURAL POPULATION SPLIT

16%   84%

RELIGIOUS PERSUASION

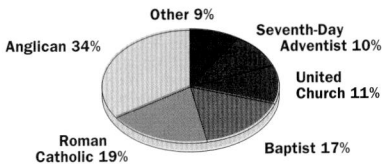

Other 9%
Seventh-Day Adventist 10%
Anglican 34%
United Church 11%
Roman Catholic 19%
Baptist 17%

Almost all Solomon Islanders are Melanesian. In 1957, large numbers of Gilbertese were resettled in the Solomons following a hurricane; a few stayed on and today form a small, distinct community. Over 50 dialects are spoken in the Solomons, a state of 326,000 people spread over 1,000 miles. As in other Melanesian island states, villagers are expected to share their wealth with their *wontoks*, or clan. Almost all islanders are nominally Christian. Most also maintain their traditional animist beliefs.

POLITICS

 1993/1997    HM Queen Elizabeth II

THE STATE OF THE PARTIES

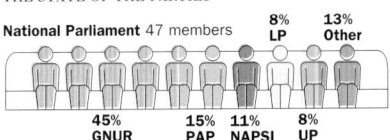

National Parliament 47 members

8% LP   13% Other
45% GNUR   15% PAP   11% NAPSI   8% UP

GNUR = Group for National Union and Reconciliation
PAP = People's Alliance Party **NAPSI** = National Action Party of the Solomon Islands **LP** = Labour Party **UP** = United Party

The Solomons' parliament is based on the Westminster model. Unlike other Pacific states, there is no one class of chiefs which dominates the political process. It is prominent figures in village life – known locally as "big men" – who stand as candidates. Legislators are often in parliament for just one term, as elections tend to result in a large turnover of members. Party arrangements within parliament are fluid and coalitions unstable. Women do not take part in the political process. How to reverse the decline in the economy is the main political issue.

SOLOMON ISLANDS

Total Land Area : 289 000 sq. km (11 158 sq. miles)

POPULATION	
over 10 000	●
under 10 000	●

LAND HEIGHT	
1000m/3280ft	
500m/1640ft	
Sea Level	

PAPUA NEW GUINEA (Bougainville I.)

SOUTH PACIFIC OCEAN

Ontong Java Atoll

Shortland Is
Shortland I.
Treasury Is
Vella Lavella
Ranongga
Gizo
Kolombangara
Munda
New Georgia
Rendova
Tetepare
NEW GEORGIA ISLANDS
Vangunu
Nggatokae
San Jorge
Pavuvu
Russell Is
SOLOMON SEA
Choiseul
Kia
Santa Isabel
Dai I.
Buala
Malaita
Auki
Florida Is
Fulaghi
Guadalcanal
HONIARA
Maramasike
Ulawa I.
Uki I.
SANTA CRUZ
Duff Is
Nupani
Swallow Is
Kirakira
San Cristobal
Lata
Nendö
ISLANDS
Rennell
Utupua
Vanikolo
Anuta
Fatutaka
Tikopia

GUADALCANAL
Visale
Arulihu
Aruligo
Maravovo
Lambi
Tangarare
HONIARA
Tenavatu
Ruavatu
Aola
Rere
Manikaraku
Mount Popomanaseu 2330m
Nduindui
Inakona
Mbalo
Avuavu

0 30 km
0 30 miles

0 200 km
0 200 miles

WORLD AFFAIRS

 ACP Comm IBRD SPC SPF

The main issue is the status of Bougainville in neighboring Papua New Guinea (PNG). Geographically part of the Solomons, Bougainville, which includes the world's largest copper mine, became part of PNG as a result of an Anglo–German colonial deal. Honiara gives tacit support to the Bougainvillian secessionist movement.

AID

 $64m (receipts)   Up 45% in 1993

The refocusing of Australian aid payments away from the Pacific islands toward Asia has already affected the Solomons' economy. However, Australia has provided cyclone relief and helped restore airfields. Australian NGOs are active. Japan gives technical aid related to the fishing industry.

DEFENSE

 Australia responsible for defense   Not applicable

The Solomons has no armed forces. Australia provides *de facto* protection and two fast patrol boats which are used to protect fisheries from Taiwanese and Okinawan poachers. However, the huge distances which have to be covered mean that their effectiveness is limited.

ECONOMICS

 $291m   3.29–3.44 Solomon Islands dollars

SCORE CARD

❑ WORLD GNP RANKING	174th
❑ GNP PER CAPITA	$800
❑ BALANCE OF PAYMENTS	$1m
❑ INFLATION	13.6%
❑ UNEMPLOYMENT	Some underemployment

EXPORTS

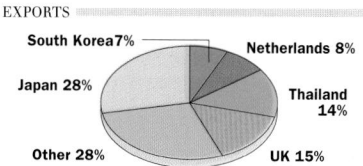

South Korea 7%
Netherlands 8%
Japan 28%
Thailand 14%
Other 28%
UK 15%

IMPORTS

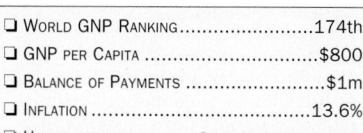

USA 6%
New Zealand 8%
Singapore 11%
Australia 36%
Other 19%
Japan 20%

STRENGTHS
Copra and timber. Survival of subsistence agriculture; Solomon Islanders are self-sufficient in food. Modest diversification of economy into oil palm and cocoa.

WEAKNESSES
Copra industry increasingly unproductive. Opposition to over-exploitation of timber. Dependence on imported energy. Location away from main Pacific sea and air routes.

RESOURCES

 30m kwh (capacity 10,000 kw)    45,406 tons

 55,000 pigs, 13,000 cattle   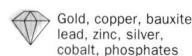 Gold, copper, bauxite, lead, zinc, silver, cobalt, phosphates

Bauxite deposits have been discovered on Rennett Island. In addition, there are traces of gold and copper on Guadalcanal, but not in commercially exploitable quantities. Most energy has to be imported.

ENVIRONMENT

 None    Successful environmental campaigns

The environmental movement is strong in the Solomons. It persuaded the government that exploiting bauxite on Rennett would destroy the island. It is currently mounting a fierce campaign against the tropical timber industry.

MEDIA

 Minimal government interference

PUBLISHING AND BROADCAST MEDIA

There are no daily newspapers. The *Solomon Star*, *Solomons Toktok*, *Solomons Voice* and *Solomon Nius* are published weekly

 No TV service   1 independent service

The one radio station broadcasts in English and Pidgin. Islanders oppose TV as it would dilute their culture.

CRIME

Solomon Islands does not publish prison figures   Crime rate rising

There has been a small increase in crime on Honiara. Most offenses are drink-related.

EDUCATION

 24%    Not available

Education is modeled on the British system. Tertiary students go to the University of the South Pacific in Fiji.

HEALTH

 1 per 8,719 people    Not available

The main hospital is in Honiara. Known as "Number 9," it was built as a military hospital by the US army during World War II.

WEALTH

 Most islanders are subsistence farmers

CONSUMER GOODS OWNERSHIP

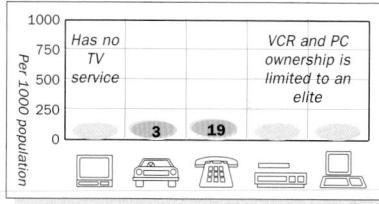

Has no TV service   VCR and PC ownership is limited to an elite

3   19

Solomon Islanders in government jobs are the wealthiest group. Outlying islands are extremely poor.

WORLD RANKING

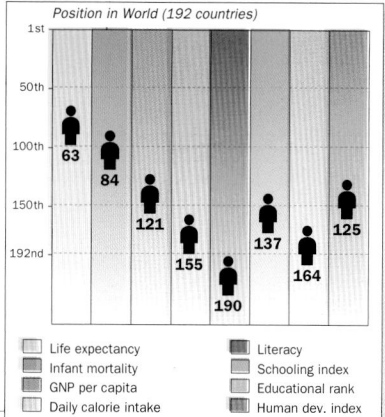

Position in World (192 countries)

63
84
121
155
190
137
164
125

Life expectancy   Literacy
Infant mortality   Schooling index
GNP per capita   Educational rank
Daily calorie intake   Human dev. index

S

SOMALIA

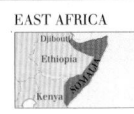

EAST AFRICA

OFFICIAL NAME: Somali Democratic Republic   CAPITAL: Mogadishu
POPULATION: 9.3 million   CURRENCY: Somali shilling   OFFICIAL LANGUAGES: Somali and Arabic

OCCUPYING THE HORN of Africa, Italian Somaliland and British Somaliland were united in 1960 to form an independent Somalia. The land is semi-arid, except in the more fertile south. Years of clan-based civil war have resulted in the collapse of central government. By 1992, drought and the conflict had created the worst mass starvation and refugee crisis ever to face the UN.

CLIMATE

WEATHER CHART

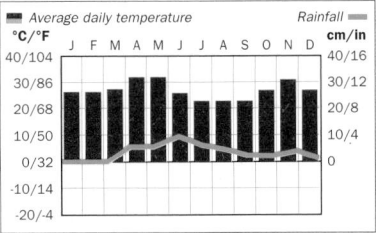

Somalia is very dry. The northern coast is very hot and humid, the eastern less so. The interior has some of the world's highest mean yearly temperatures.

TRANSPORTATION

✈ Mogadishu International   🚢 5 ships 12,800 dwt

THE TRANSPORTATION NETWORK

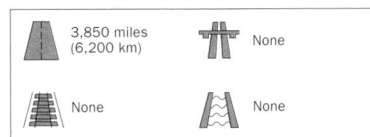

| 🛣 3,850 miles (6,200 km) | 🛤 None |
| None | None |

About 50% of Somalis are nomads for whom the camel is the principal means of transportation. In 1990, the IDA agreed to repair the road network, but by 1996 no work had started on the seven-year project.

TOURISM

Urban and rural instability deters tourism   Not applicable

MAIN OVERSEAS ARRIVALS

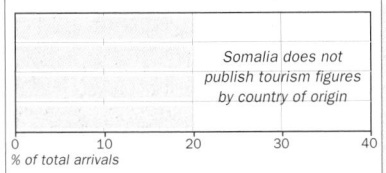

Somalia does not publish tourism figures by country of origin

0   10   20   30   40
% of total arrivals

Aid workers and foreign journalists are the only visitors. Land mines are a hazard.

Baydhabo market. *Subsistence farming supports most people despite chaos created by the fighting.*

PEOPLE

 Somali, Arabic, English, Italian   39 people per sq. mile

THE URBAN/RURAL POPULATION SPLIT

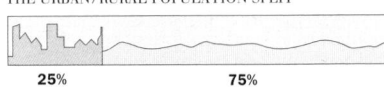

25%   75%

RELIGIOUS PERSUASION

Sunni Muslim 100%

The clan system is at the root of all social, political and commercial issues in Somalia. Shifting allegiances characterize its structure – a tendency stifled by Siad Barre's dictatorship but revived after his fall in 1991. His undermining of the traditional brokers of justice, the elders, contributed to the present power vacuum, while his persecution of the Issaqs led to Somaliland's declaration of secession in 1991. However, the entire population is ethnic Somali and national identity remains strong, reflected in the widespread opposition to the UN peacekeeping force.

POLITICS

1984/Uncertain   No internationally recognized head of state

THE STATE OF THE PARTIES

National Assembly 123 members

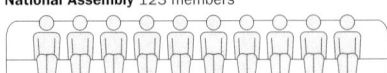

There has been no prospect of organizing new elections since the overthrow of Siad Barre, although an attempt has been made to draft a new democratic constitution

Somalia is no longer the undivided republic it was under its dictator, President Siad Barre. Civil war started in the north in the 1980s and spread as other opposition groups took up arms against his regime. He eventually fled the capital in early 1991. The subsequent civil war in the south, and the self-proclaimed independence of Somaliland in the north in May that year have meant that the unitary state has effectively ceased to exist. Despite the deployment of US-led UN peacekeepers in 1992, southern Somalia remained in the grip of warring clan factions and opportunist warlords. Anarchy has persisted after the UN withdrawal in 1995. The chief protagonists are General Aideed, who was instrumental in ousting Siad Barre, and Ali Mahdi, both of whom style themselves president. Now that fighting has stopped in Somaliland, the region awaits international recognition.

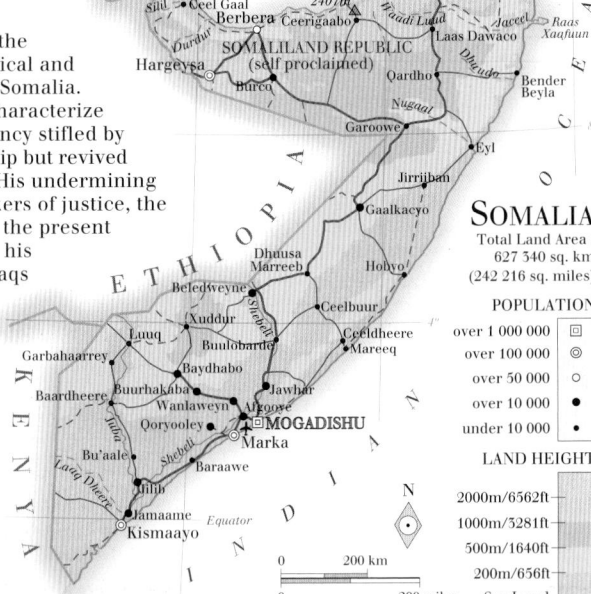

SOMALIA

Total Land Area :
627 340 sq. km
(242 216 sq. miles)

POPULATION

over 1 000 000	▣
over 100 000	◎
over 50 000	○
over 10 000	●
under 10 000	·

LAND HEIGHT

2000m/6562ft
1000m/3281ft
500m/1640ft
200m/656ft
Sea Level

S

WORLD AFFAIRS

Following the withdrawal of the controversial UN force, whose success was limited to alleviating starvation, the international community appears to have abandoned Somalia. Self-declared Somaliland is pressing for international recognition, with borders of former British Somaliland. Even though fighting has stopped there, no help other than emergency aid is being provided because the region lacks official status.

AID

 $881m (receipts)   Up 53% in 1993

Mass starvation among the Somali population in 1991 finally prompted the UN to launch a large-scale humanitarian aid effort. In this the UN was largely effective, averting widescale starvation and restoring food security.

DEFENSE

 None in 1995   Not applicable

Somalia is awash with weapons supplied by both the USA and the former USSR during the Cold War.

ECONOMICS

 $835m    2,618.33–2,620.00 Somali shillings

SCORE CARD

- ❏ WORLD GNP RANKING.......................158th
- ❏ GNP PER CAPITA $100
- ❏ BALANCE OF PAYMENTS.................*The formal*
- ❏ INFLATION ....*economy has*
- ❏ UNEMPLOYMENT ....*collapsed*

STRENGHTS
Very few. Export of livestock to Arabian peninsula resumed in the north. Inflow of money from Somalis living abroad. Growing market in stolen food aid.

WEAKNESSES
Every commodity, except arms, in extremely short supply. The south has little economic potential. Effects of drought include death of nomads' livestock herds.

EXPORTS
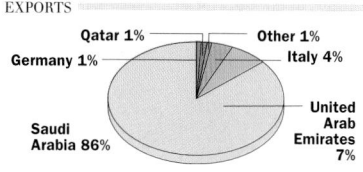

IMPORTS
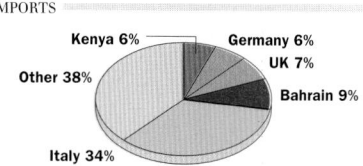

RESOURCES

 258m kwh (capacity 60,000 kw)   Not an oil producer; refines 10,000 b/cd

 13m sheep, 12m goats, 5m cattle, 6m camels   Salt, tin, zinc, copper, gypsum, manganese, uranium, iron

Commercially exploitable minerals remain untapped. Oil experts are confident of discovering large offshore reserves in the north.

ENVIRONMENT

 0.3% (partially protected)   Nomadic lifestyle by definition in tune with the environment

Human deprivation and starvation caused by the effects of drought and war on land and livestock outweigh all other ecological considerations.

MEDIA

 Following the overthrow of the Siad Barre regime, independent newspapers have been established

PUBLISHING AND BROADCAST MEDIA

 There are no daily newspapers

 No TV service    3 independent services

There are three radio stations in Mogadishu which are run by Ali Mahdi, General Aideed and a former ally of Aideed. There are few newspapers as paper is currently in very short supply.

CRIME

 Somalia does not publish prison figures   Widespread breakdown in law and order since 1991

Armed clan factions (some, in remoter regions, engaged in family feuds rather than the war) and bandits rule large areas. Police forces exist in some cities but, with few resources, dare not risk confrontation with warlords. Muslim *sharia* law, now the *de facto* system, is run in a makeshift fashion by elders.

EDUCATION

 24%    15,672 students

The system collapsed during the civil war. There were reports of improvised open-air schools starting up again in urban areas in 1993. Somali has been a written language only since 1972.

CHRONOLOGY

The lands of the Somalis became UK and Italian colonies in the 1880s.

- ❏ **1941–1950** UK rules both areas.
- ❏ **1960** Unification at independence.
- ❏ **1964** Somalia's claims to Ogaden leads to war with Ethiopia.
- ❏ **1969** Gen. Siad Barre seizes power.
- ❏ **1977–1978** Attack on Ethiopia fails.
- ❏ **1981** Two opposition groups based in Ethiopia begin guerrilla war.
- ❏ **1987** Reconciliation with Ethiopia induces Somali National Movement group to occupy north.
- ❏ **1991** Siad Barre ousted. War degenerates into clan chaos. Mass starvation. Somaliland secedes.
- ❏ **1992** Warlords plunder food aid. US sends in military with UN backing.
- ❏ **1995** UN force withdrawn.

HEALTH

 1 per 14,300 people   Diarrheal, communicable and parasitic diseases

The state-run system has collapsed entirely. A few very rudimentary facilities are run by foreign workers.

WEALTH

 The subsistence existence of the nomads (the bulk of the population) contrasts with the Somali warlords' wealth, won by armed force

CONSUMER GOODS OWNERSHIP

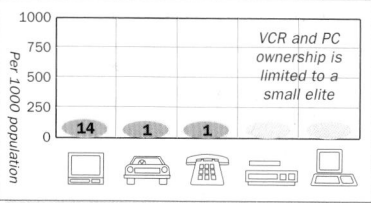

Rich pickings are available for bandits and warlords in the aid-stealing racket. In Somaliland, ministers survive from money sent by relatives living overseas.

WORLD RANKING

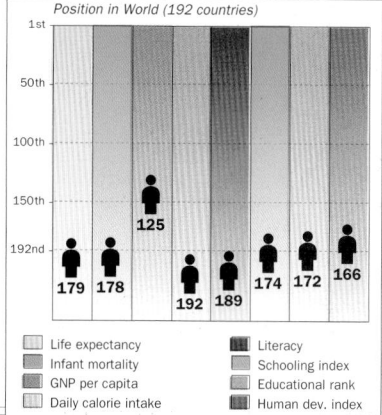

SOUTH AFRICA

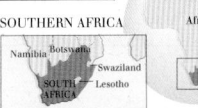

SOUTHERN AFRICA Africa

OFFICIAL NAME: Republic of South Africa **CAPITALS:** Pretoria, Cape Town, Bloemfontein
POPULATION: 41.5 million **CURRENCY:** Rand **OFFICIAL LANGUAGES:** 9 African languages, English, Afrikaans

RICH IN NATURAL RESOURCES, South Africa comprises a central plateau, or *veld*, bordered to the south and east by the Drakensberg Mountains. After eight decades of white minority rule, and racial segregation under the apartheid policy since 1948, South Africa held its first multiracial, multiparty elections in 1994. The revolution in South Africa's politics began in 1990, when President F. W. de Klerk legalized black freedom groups and began dismantling apartheid. The African National Congress (ANC), under Nelson Mandela, is now the leading political movement.

Nelson Mandela, who became president of South Africa in April 1994.

F. W. De Klerk. He dismantled apartheid legislation during his presidency.

CLIMATE

WEATHER CHART

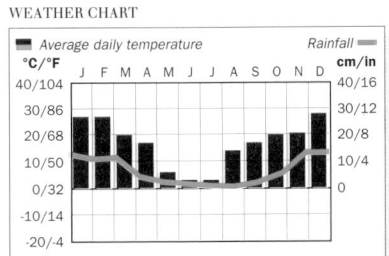

Despite the moderating effects of oceans on three sides, South Africa's warm temperate climate is dry; 65% of the country has less than 20 inches of rain a year. Drought is a periodic hazard.

TRANSPORTATION

Jan Smuts International, Johannesburg
4.5m passengers

6 ships
200,500 dwt

THE TRANSPORTATION NETWORK

34,450 miles (55,430 km)	1,268 miles (2,040 km)
13,201 miles (21,244 km)	None

The further expansion of port capacity is a priority. Improvements to the road network are aimed in part at reducing accidents: South Africa has one of the world's worst road death rates.

Vineyard backed by the dramatic mountains of Cape Province. The lifting of trade sanctions provided a major boost to the South African wine industry.

TOURISM

3.8m visitors   Up 16% in 1994

MAIN OVERSEAS ARRIVALS

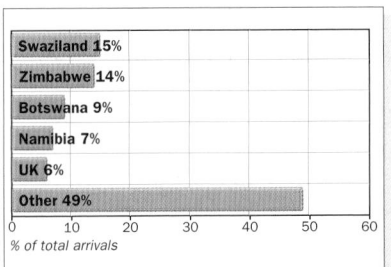

Swaziland 15%
Zimbabwe 14%
Botswana 9%
Namibia 7%
UK 6%
Other 49%

% of total arrivals

South Africa has a huge potential for tourism. Its attractions range from beaches to mountains, from prize-winning vineyards to internationally renowned wildlife reserves. The enormous Kruger National Park is perhaps the most diverse in the world, with 137 species of mammal and 450 species of bird. This potential, however, has yet to be fully realized. South Africa's isolation during the apartheid era kept tourist numbers down. Today, the key constraint on efforts to expand tourism is the rising level of violent crime.

PEOPLE

English, Afrikaans, Zulu, Xhosa, Ndebele, Setswana, Siswati, North Sotho, South Sotho, Tsongo, Venda

88 people per sq. mile

THE URBAN/RURAL POPULATION SPLIT

50%   50%

RELIGIOUS PERSUASION

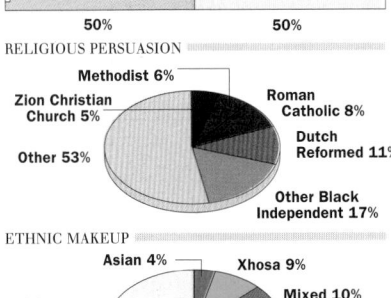

Methodist 6%
Zion Christian Church 5%
Roman Catholic 8%
Dutch Reformed 11%
Other 53%
Other Black Independent 17%

ETHNIC MAKEUP

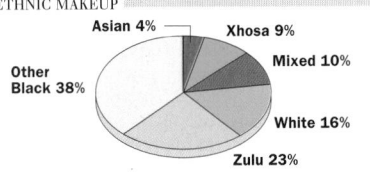

Asian 4%
Xhosa 9%
Other Black 38%
Mixed 10%
White 16%
Zulu 23%

Under apartheid, South Africans were divided into racial categories: whites (Afrikaners and English-speakers), and three black groups (coloreds, people whose descent was deemed mixed; Asians, mainly Indians; and Africans). Each category had different political, economic and social rights, with whites enjoying the most privileges and

Africans the fewest. While blacks now dominate politics, English-speaking whites continue to control the economy.

The extended family has been undermined by regulations forcing men to migrate for work, leaving their wives and children in the rural areas. A small black middle class has grown up, but most black South Africans are underemployed.

The expected post-apartheid ethnic conflict failed to materialize, although *Inkatha* has exploited feelings of Zulu identity in its quest for greater political power. However, demands for a white homeland have faded.

Many women are now taking prominent roles in public life. The new constitution guarantees equality of the sexes.

POPULATION AGE BREAKDOWN

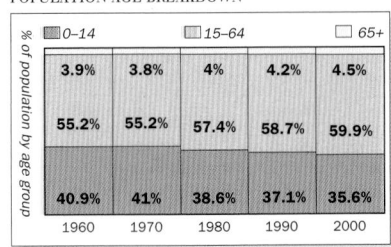

% of population by age group	■ 0–14		▨ 15–64		□ 65+
65+	3.9%	3.8%	4%	4.2%	4.5%
15–64	55.2%	55.2%	57.4%	58.7%	59.9%
0–14	40.9%	41%	38.6%	37.1%	35.6%
	1960	1970	1980	1990	2000

S

POLITICS

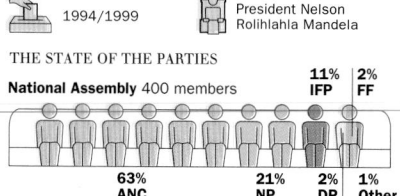

1994/1999

President Nelson
Rolihlahla Mandela

THE STATE OF THE PARTIES

National Assembly 400 members

| 63% ANC | 21% NP | 2% DP | 1% Other | 11% IFP | 2% FF |

ANC = African National Congress **NP** = National Party
IFP = Inkatha Freedom Party **DP** = Democratic Party
FF = Freedom Front **Other** = Pan African Congress (PAC),
African Christian Democratic Party

Senate 90 members

10 members elected by each of 9 regional legislatures

South Africa became a multiparty
democracy following elections in 1994.

MAIN POLITICAL ISSUES
Maintaining unity
In April 1994, South Africa confounded
the proponents of violence and ethnic
division by holding peaceful elections
which brought its first multiracial
government to power. The challenge
facing the new ANC-dominated
administration is to ensure that, while
pursuing the aspirations of the black
majority, it does not marginalize
South Africa's minorities. It is
following a cautious policy

of national reconciliation. The main
threat to stability is Chief Buthelezi's
demand for greater autonomy for
Kwazulu-Natal.

Reconstruction and development
The government instituted a costly
Reconstruction and Development
Program (RDP) aimed at improving
health, housing and education, and
promoting economic growth to boost
employment. However, implementation
has been slow and the government is
under pressure to deliver the benefits
of democratic rule to the black majority.

PROFILE
The 1994 elections put an end to over
45 years of white rule by the NP. Its
leader, F. W. De Klerk, played a central
role with ANC leader Nelson Mandela in
the transition to multiracial democracy.
The NP came second in the polls, well
behind the ANC, which just missed the
two-thirds majority it needed to govern
alone. After the signing of the new South
African constitution in 1996, the NP
withdrew their support and went into
opposition. The government's main
challenge will be to reconcile the
demands of its activists for jobs
and better living standards,
while encouraging
foreign investment.

WORLD AFFAIRS

| Comm | OAU | NAM | OAU | SADC |

After decades of political isolation and
economic sanctions, South Africa has
been welcomed back to the international
fold, reflected in its return to the UN
and the Commonwealth. Its priority
now is to attract new international
investors and to encourage the return
of the many who disinvested during
the 1980s. The end of apartheid
brought an end to hostility from its
neighbors. Improving relations with
them and with the non-aligned
countries is also important. South
Africa has taken on the role of Africa's
leading voice, with the government
intervening to help resolve disputes
and settle conflict. It has joined the
Southern African Development
Community (SADC), reassuring existing
members who had been concerned
about South Africa's regional
economic domination. A regional
security alliance has also been mooted.

SOUTH AFRICA

Total Land Area : 1 221 040 sq. km
(471 443 sq. miles)

POPULATION

over 1 000 000
over 500 000
over 100 000
over 50 000
over 10 000

LAND HEIGHT

2000m/6562ft
1000m/3281ft
500m/1640ft
Sea Level

AID

 $193m (receipts)

 Increasing with end of political isolation

South Africa was cut off from almost all aid, particularly from the World Bank and IMF, during the apartheid years. It is now trying to persuade donors to provide the massive financial aid needed to support reconstruction, in particular for job creation and social infrastructure programs.

CHRONOLOGY

Until 1652, South Africa was peopled by Bantu-speaking groups and Bushmen. Then Dutch settlers arrived. British colonizers followed in the 18th century.

- ❑ **1899–1902** Boer War with Britain.
- ❑ **1910** Union of South Africa set up as British dominion; white monopoly of power formalized.
- ❑ **1912** ANC formed.
- ❑ **1934** Independence.
- ❑ **1948** NP takes power; apartheid segregationist policy introduced.
- ❑ **1958–1966** Dr. Hendrik Verwoerd prime minister. "Grand Apartheid" policy implemented.
- ❑ **1959** Pan African Congress (PAC) formed in split from ANC.
- ❑ **1960** Sharpeville massacre. ANC, PAC banned. South Africa becomes republic; leaves Commonwealth.
- ❑ **1964** Nelson Mandela, a senior leader of the ANC, jailed.
- ❑ **1976** Soweto uprisings sparked by attempts to force black schools to teach Afrikaans; hundreds killed.
- ❑ **1978** P. W. Botha prime minister.
- ❑ **1984** New constitution: Indians and coloreds get some representation. Growing black opposition.
- ❑ **1985** State of emergency introduced. International sanctions.
- ❑ **1989** F. W. De Klerk replaces P. W. Botha as president. Elections underline white conservative hostility to change.
- ❑ **1990** De Klerk legalizes ANC and PAC; frees Nelson Mandela.
- ❑ **1990–1993** International sanctions gradually withdrawn.
- ❑ **1991** Multiparty Convention for a Democratic South Africa (CODESA) begins negotiating new political structure.
- ❑ **1992** De Klerk wins whites-only referendum; ANC breaks off talks over government veto on CODESA. September, talks resume.
- ❑ **1993** Transitional timetable takes shape. Mandela and De Klerk win Nobel Peace Prize.
- ❑ **1994** First multiracial elections won by ANC.
- ❑ **1996** New South African constitution signed.

DEFENSE

 $2.9bn

⬇ Down 16% in 1995

Defense spending as % GDP — 0 ... 40
3.3%

SOUTH AFRICAN ARMED FORCES

250 main battle tanks (*Oilfant* 1A/B)	121,500 personnel	
3 submarines, 12 patrol boats	4,500 personnel	
243 combat aircraft (75 *Impala* II, 11 *Cheetah*, 29 *Mirage* F-1AZ)	9,000 personnel	
None		

The discredited apartheid army has been replaced by a new national defense force comprising members of the former army, members of the armed wings of the ANC and other liberation groups. There have been cuts in defense spending, an end to the military's policy-making role and changes in top personnel. A security alliance with South Africa's former opponents in the region has been raised. The trial of the former defense minister and senior members of the former army on charges relating to the killing of anti-apartheid activists began in March 1996. Sanctions encouraged a major arms industry. South Africa is now the world's twelfth-leading arms exporter.

ECONOMICS

 $125.2bn

4.07–3.65 rand

SCORE CARD

- ❑ WORLD GNP RANKING 29th
- ❑ GNP PER CAPITA $3,010
- ❑ BALANCE OF PAYMENTS .... $–573m
- ❑ INFLATION 7.3%
- ❑ UNEMPLOYMENT 32.6%

ECONOMIC PERFORMANCE INDICATOR

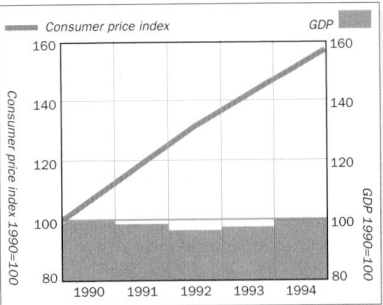

Consumer price index — GDP

EXPORTS

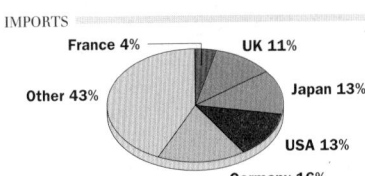

Germany 4% / Japan 6% / UK 6% / USA 7% / Switzerland 10% / Other 68%

IMPORTS

France 4% / UK 11% / Japan 13% / USA 13% / Germany 16% / Other 43%

forced the government to play a central economic role through state corporations in the 1980s. This is now being reduced in a series of privatizations. The ANC has declared its intention to work with big business in order to revivify the economy and develop the townships.

STRENGTHS

Africa's largest and most developed economy; highly diversified with modern infrastructure. Strong financial sector for mobilizing investment. Growing manufacturing sector, at present accounting for 23% of GDP. Varied resource base, particularly of strategically important minerals.

WEAKNESSES

Fears of political instability deter foreign investment. Growth too low to provide resources to overcome deprivation among black majority. Black unemployment growing by 2.5% a year. High population growth.

PROFILE

South Africa has a large and diverse private sector, much of it controlled by multinationals. International sanctions

SOUTH AFRICA : MAJOR BUSINESSES

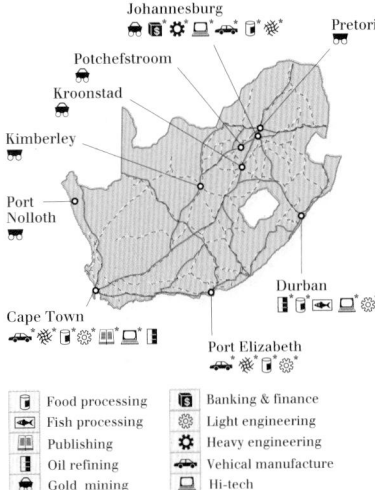

Food processing		Banking & finance	
Fish processing		Light engineering	
Publishing		Heavy engineering	
Oil refining		Vehical manufacture	
Gold mining		Hi-tech	
Diamond mining		Textiles	

* significant multinational ownership

0 ... 500 km
0 ... 500 miles

RESOURCES

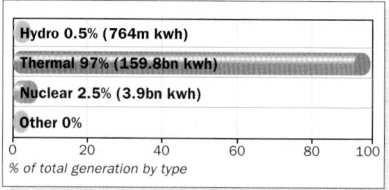

167.8bn kwh
(capacity 25.9m kw)

Not an oil producer;
refines 430,500 b/cd

29.1m sheep,
12.6m cattle,
6.4m goats

Gold, coal, vanadium,
vermiciline, diamonds,
chromium, manganese

ELECTRICITY GENERATION

Hydro 0.5% (764m kwh)

Thermal 97% (159.8bn kwh)

Nuclear 2.5% (3.9bn kwh)

Other 0%

0   20   40   60   80   100

% of total generation by type

South Africa has some of the continent's richest natural resources, in particular minerals. Its dominance of the world market in gold and diamonds was central to its survival of sanctions during apartheid. Over the past century, 47% of the world's gold has come from South Africa. Today's output of 600 tons a year accounts for 30% of the world total. South Africa is the single-largest producer of manganese metal, chrome ore, vanadium and vermiciline.

South Africa lacks oil reserves and sanctions-busting was costly. Its huge coal reserves are used to generate 87% of electricity and to make oil. The priority is to bring the 80% of black homes without electricity into the national grid. Agriculture is varied.

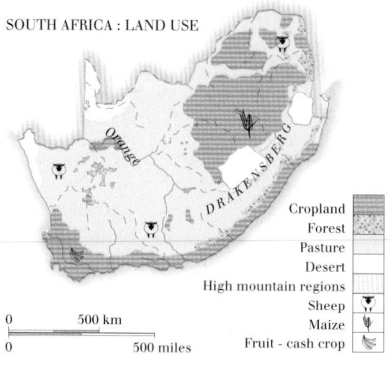

SOUTH AFRICA : LAND USE

Cropland	
Forest	
Pasture	
Desert	
High mountain regions	
Sheep	
Maize	
Fruit - cash crop	

0   500 km
0   500 miles

ENVIRONMENT

6% (4% partially protected)

Environmental legislation not a priority

ENVIRONMENTAL TREATIES

	No		Yes		Yes
	Yes		Yes		No

Natural disasters, notably floods and drought, are a hazard. The main concern is protecting rich and varied animal species. Environmental measures could conflict in future with the demands of economic growth.

MEDIA

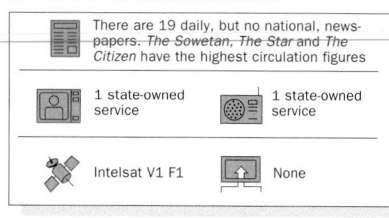

Censorship regulations imposed under apartheid have been dismantled

PUBLISHING AND BROADCAST MEDIA

There are 19 daily, but no national, news-papers. *The Sowetan, The Star* and *The Citizen* have the highest circulation figures

1 state-owned service

1 state-owned service

Intelsat V1 F1

None

The end of censorship is reflected in the press, which ranges from far-left to extreme-right. TV programing is now more balanced and diverse.

CRIME

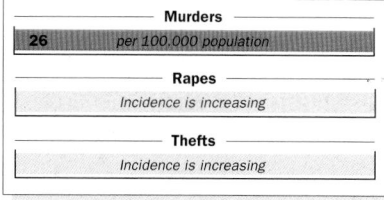

11,000 prisoners

Rapid rise in violent crime

CRIME RATES

Murders

26   per 100,000 population

Rapes

Incidence is increasing

Thefts

Incidence is increasing

South Africa is the world's most dangerous country (besides war zones), with a murder every 29 minutes. Despite its high profile, political violence accounts for only 10% of the total. The rise in levels of murder, armed robbery and muggings has led to a boom in the personal security industry.

EDUCATION

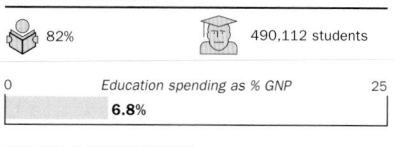

82%

490,112 students

0   Education spending as % GNP   25

6.8%

THE EDUCATION SYSTEM

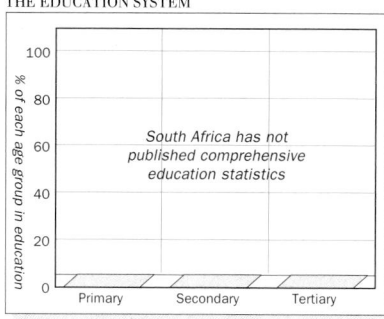

South Africa has not published comprehensive education statistics

% of each age group in education

100
80
60
40
20
0

Primary   Secondary   Tertiary

Education has now been desegregated, but most black children are still restricted to underfunded schools. Upgrading education is a priority if employment prospects for blacks are to meet their requirements.

HEALTH

1 per 1,750 people

Heart, respiratory and diarrheal diseases, cancers, road deaths

0   Health spending as % GDP   25

3.2%

Health services were desegregated in 1990, but have yet to be restructured and expanded to give all people equal access to care. The per capita figures on provision of medical facilities hide a strong bias towards whites and urban areas, where 80% of doctors work. The limited provision for rural black South Africans, in particular, is reflected in mortality figures. Out of every 1,000 black children, 200 die before the age of five, compared with the sub-Saharan average of 165 per 1,000.

WEALTH

Salaries among whites are substantially higher than among blacks

CONSUMER GOODS OWNERSHIP

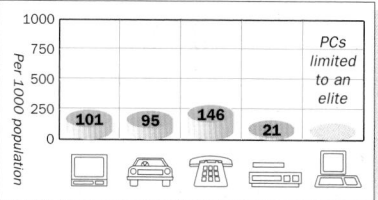

PCs limited to an elite

Per 1000 population

1000
750
500
250
0

101   95   146   21

In South Africa, the black majority is the poorest group. Wealth disparities are marked. At the top, the white elite enjoys one of the world's highest living standards on a par with that of California. In contrast, blacks are among Africa's poorest. Half of black adults are unemployed. Most blacks have been deprived of decent housing, education and health facilities. In between are the mixed race and Indian communities, given relatively more privileges under apartheid's strict racial hierarchy, and a very small black middle class. Reducing these disparities is the new government's priority.

S

WORLD RANKING

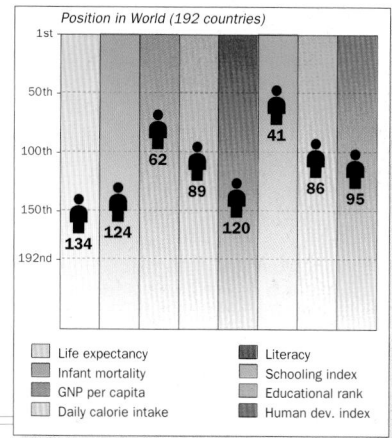

Position in World (192 countries)

1st
50th
100th
150th
192nd

62   41   89   86   95   120   134   124

Life expectancy	Literacy
Infant mortality	Schooling index
GNP per capita	Educational rank
Daily calorie intake	Human dev. index

SOUTH KOREA

OFFICIAL NAME: Republic of Korea **CAPITAL:** Seoul
POPULATION: 45 million **CURRENCY:** Won **OFFICIAL LANGUAGE:** Korean

SOUTH KOREA OCCUPIES the southern half of the Korean peninsula in East Asia. Over 80% of its terrain is mountainous and two-thirds is forested. Rice is the major agricultural product, grown by over 85% of South Korea's three million farmers. Most of the urban population lives along the coastal plains. Under US sponsorship, South Korea was separated from the communist North after World War II. Although the two states have discussed reunification, the legacy of hostility arising from the 1950–1953 Korean war remains a major obstacle.

CLIMATE

WEATHER CHART

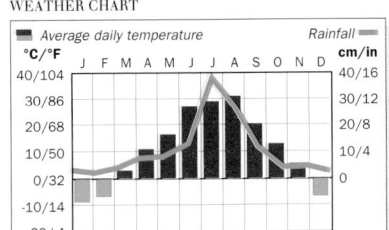

South Korea has four distinct seasons. Winters are dry and can be bitterly cold. Summers are hot and humid. The island of Cheju-do has a tropical climate.

TRANSPORTATION

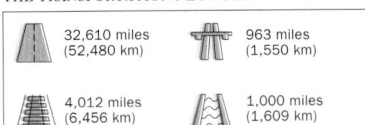

Kimpo Intl, Seoul
21.33m passengers

645 ships
1.34m dwt

THE TRANSPORTATION NETWORK

32,610 miles (52,480 km)		963 miles (1,550 km)	
4,012 miles (6,456 km)		1,000 miles (1,609 km)	

South Korea has a highly integrated transportation policy. Massive investments have been made in all aspects of communications. In 1968, a nationwide motor expressway network was inaugurated. Mainly toll-based, it now joins most major urban centers. Air travel, an easy way to get around the mountainous interior, has expanded rapidly. Competition for Korean Air (KAL) has come with the licensing of a second airline, Asiana. The increase in air traffic has also brought forward plans to replace Kimpo International with a new airport.

South Korea's public transportation system is possibly the world's best. Buses, trains, boats and planes are integrated in one timetable. All systems have a reputation for punctuality. A $14-billion high-speed rail link is being built between Seoul and Pusan.

TOURISM

3.4m visitors   Up 7% in 1994

MAIN OVERSEAS ARRIVALS

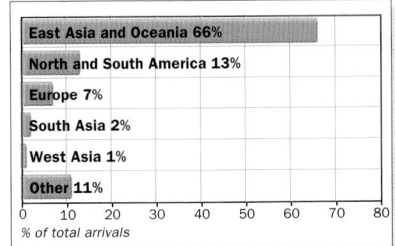

East Asia and Oceania 66%
North and South America 13%
Europe 7%
South Asia 2%
West Asia 1%
Other 11%
% of total arrivals

Overseas tourism to South Korea has increased tenfold since 1969. Most visitors are Japanese, who come for the golf and Seoul's nightlife. Cheju-do is a favored honeymoon destination. Whereas once visiting relations of US army personnel made up 13% of all tourists, today Los Angeles-based Korean-Americans make up the greatest proportion of visitors. However, despite the publicity generated by the 1988 Olympics, and the decision to make 1994 "Visit Korea Year," South Korea is still not seen in the West as a prime tourist destination.

SOUTH KOREA

Total Land Area : 98 750 sq. km
(38 120 sq. miles)

POPULATION

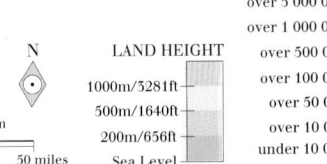

over 5 000 000
over 1 000 000
over 500 000
over 100 000
over 50 000
over 10 000
under 10 000

LAND HEIGHT
1000m/3281ft
500m/1640ft
200m/656ft
Sea Level

PEOPLE

 Korean, Chinese

 1,182 people per sq. mile

THE URBAN/RURAL POPULATION SPLIT

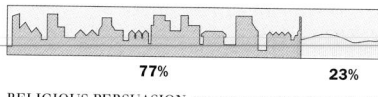

77%   23%

RELIGIOUS PERSUASION

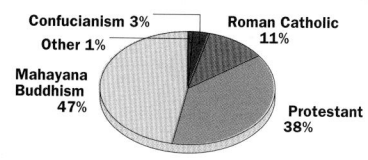

Confucianism 3%
Other 1%
Mahayana Buddhism 47%
Roman Catholic 11%
Protestant 38%

ETHNIC MAKEUP

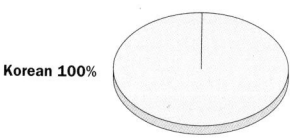

Korean 100%

South Korea, like the North, is unusual in having been inhabited by one ethnic group for the last 2,000 years. There is a tiny Chinese community, but this is diminishing as most emigrate to Taiwan. One result of economic growth has been

an increase in illegal immigrants from the poorer Asian countries who take menial jobs that Koreans now refuse. Family life is a central and clearly defined part of Korean society. Most Koreans can trace their ancestry back thousands of years. This is significant as those of the same surname group (rather than the same surname – 60% of Koreans are called Lee, Kim or Park) may not marry. Pressure on housing has led to an increase in nuclear families, as city-center apartments do not have room for the traditional household of three generations. Women play a traditional role in society: it is still not respectable for those who are married to have a job.

POPULATION AGE BREAKDOWN

% of population by age group	0–14	15–64	65+		
65+	3.3%	3.3%	3.8%	4.8%	6.4%
15–64	54.8%	54.7%	62.2%	69.5%	71.6%
0–14	41.9%	42%	34%	25.7%	22%
	1960	1970	1980	1990	2000

POLITICS

 1992/1996

 Kim Young-Sam

THE STATE OF THE PARTIES

National Assembly 299 members

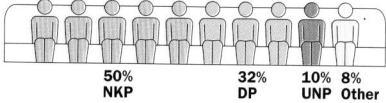

50% NKP   32% DP   10% UNP   8% Other

NKP = New Korea Party **DP** = Democratic Party
UNP = Unification National Party **Other** = New Political Reform Party

Officially a democracy since its inception, in practice South Korea was ruled by military dictators until 1987, when the Sixth Republic established multiparty democratic politics.

MAIN POLITICAL ISSUES
Corruption
President Kim Young-Sam's anti-corruption program has been popular with voters, and has succeeded in purging his enemies. The culmination of this process has been the legal action initiated in 1995–1996 against his two predecessors as president.

The economy
South Korea's growth slowed to 4.8% in 1992. However, the country's economic record remains one of the most impressive in the world.

Faction-led parties
South Korea's political parties are

highly factionalized and fragmented, and regroup often. Voters are beginning to demand unified parties that represent clearer ideological positions.

PROFILE
South Korea's politics changed radically in 1987 when President Roh Tae-Woo instituted a genuine transition to democracy, including, for the first time, direct elections for presidents, a parliament with enhanced powers and a free press.

In 1993, the first non-military leader in 30 years, Kim Young-Sam, became president. He quickly appointed a new head of the army staff, thereby establishing his independence from the military. A reform drive in 1994 was aimed at rooting out malpractice in all areas of government, and legal action has even been taken against Kim's two predecessors as president.

Kim Young-Sam, veteran democratic activist and president since 1993.

Roh Tae-Woo, a former general and president between 1988 and 1993.

WORLD AFFAIRS

 EU   NATO   OECD   OAS   OSCE

Since the 1950s, relations with North Korea have been the major concern of foreign policy. These remain unresolved. North Korea has indicated a willingness to consider reunification and, under US pressure, has dismantled its suspected nuclear-weapons program. However, hostility and suspicion continue to characterize the relations between the two Korean states. South Korea is also concerned that the North Korean economy may be about to collapse, thereby seriously increasing the social and economic costs of union. Relations with China, once an important ally of North Korea, have improved. Japan is also a major trading partner, although South Koreans harbor resentment over the 1910–1945 Japanese colonization.

AID

 $965m (donations)   Up 1600% in 1993

Once a massive recipient of US aid, and then from 1965 of Japanese war reparations, South Korea has in recent years become an aid donor. Aid is primarily used to further foreign policy, particularly in cultivating relations with former communist-bloc allies of North Korea.

CHRONOLOGY

The Yi dynasty, founded in Seoul in 1392, ruled the kingdom of Korea until 1910. However, Korea became a vassal state of China in 1644.

❑ **1860** Korea reacts to French and British occupation of Peking by preventing Western influence.
❑ **1864–1907** Taewon'gun's rule. Korea remains the "Hermit Kingdom."
❑ **1904–1905** Russo–Japanese War. Japan conquers Korea.
❑ **1910** Japan annexes Korea.
❑ **1919** Independence protests all over Korea violently suppressed.
❑ **1945** US and Soviet armies arrive. Korea split at 38°N. South comes under *de facto* US rule.
❑ **1948** Republic of South Korea created; Dr. Syngman Rhee becomes president at head of an increasingly authoritarian regime.
❑ **1950** Hostilities between North and South, each aspiring to rule a united Korea. North invades South sparking Korean War. US, with UN backing, enters on South's side. China unofficially assists the North. In 1951 the fighting stabilizes in the vicinity of the 38th parallel. ⇨

S

CHRONOLOGY *continued*

- ❏ **1953** Armistice ends the fighting and establishes a *de facto* border at the ceasefire line which lies close to 38th parallel.
- ❏ **1960** Syngman Rhee resigns in face of popular revolt.
- ❏ **1961** Military coup leads to authoritarian junta led by Park Chung-Hee.
- ❏ **1963** Pressure for civilian government. Park reelected as president (also in 1967 and 1971). Massive economic development in 1960s–1970s. All mineral resources in North Korea, so South concentrates on manufactures and huge export drive.
- ❏ **1965** Links restored with Japan.
- ❏ **1966** Sends 45,000 troops to fight for South Vietnam.
- ❏ **1972** Martial law stifles political opposition. New constitution with greater presidential powers.
- ❏ **1979** Park assassinated. Gen. Chun Doo Huan, intelligence chief, leads coup. Kim Young-Sam, opposition leader, expelled from parliament.
- ❏ **1980** Chun chosen as president. Kim Dae-Jong and other opposition leaders arrested.
- ❏ **1987** Domestic and international pressure for democracy. Roh Tae-Woo, Chun's chosen successor, elected president.
- ❏ **1988** Inauguration of Sixth Republic which includes genuine multiparty democracy. Olympic Games held in Seoul. Restrictions on foreign travel lifted.
- ❏ **1990** Government party and two opposition parties, including Kim Young-Sam's, merge to form DLP.
- ❏ **1991** Joins UN. Reunification discussions with North.
- ❏ **1992** Links with China established.
- ❏ **1993** Kim Young-Sam, having been elected president in December 1992, is inaugurated as Roh's successor.
- ❏ **1995** DLP renamed New Korea Party. Unprecedented charges brought against Chun and Roh for past crimes.

Seoul lit up at night. *The city is home to more than 10.5 million people – one-quarter of South Korea's population. Seoul means "capital."*

DEFENSE

 $14.4bn   ⬆ Up 6% in 1995

0   *Defense spending as % GDP*   40
1.6%

SOUTH KOREAN ARMED FORCES

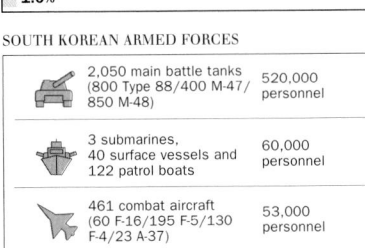

🛡	2,050 main battle tanks (800 Type 88/400 M-47/ 850 M-48)	520,000 personnel
🚢	3 submarines, 40 surface vessels and 122 patrol boats	60,000 personnel
✈	461 combat aircraft (60 F-16/195 F-5/130 F-4/23 A-37)	53,000 personnel
	None	

Since Kim Young-Sam came to power, the role of the military has been sharply downgraded. A campaign to root out corruption in arms procurement and investigations into past military involvement in politics have forced 40 generals to retire.

The main defense concern is the North Korean regime. South Korea has fewer troops, tanks, artillery and aircraft than the North, but it claims parity in having superior technology and the presence of 35,000 US troops permanently based on its territory. However, recent US computer simulations have questioned whether South Korea can resist an invasion by the North's one-million-strong army.

ECONOMICS

 $366.5bn   788.50–775.75 won

SCORE CARD

- ❏ WORLD GNP RANKING...........................13th
- ❏ GNP PER CAPITA $8,220
- ❏ BALANCE OF PAYMENTS ....$–3.9bn
- ❏ INFLATION 3.5%
- ❏ UNEMPLOYMENT..................................2.8%

EXPORTS

Germany 4% | China 6% | Hong Kong 8% | Japan 14% | USA 22% | Other 45%

IMPORTS

Germany 4% | China 6% | Hong Kong 8% | Japan 14% | USA 22% | Other 46%

STRENGTHS

The world's most successful shipbuilder, with 45% of the market. Continuing benefits of highly valued yen which make Korean exports more competitive than Japan's. Strong demand from China for Korean goods, particularly cars.

WEAKNESSES

Work force beginning to demand better working conditions. State sector is still a burden on the economy. Japanese plants in other Southeast Asian countries, particularly Indonesia, offering strong competition.

PROFILE

The first decades of the South Korean economic miracle were the result of centralized planning. Conglomerates known as *chaebol*, such as Samsung,

ECONOMIC PERFORMANCE INDICATOR

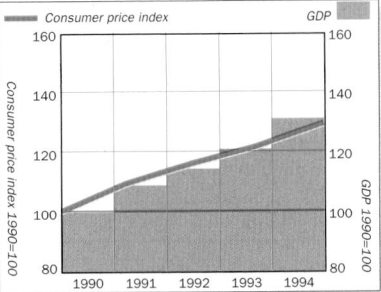

achieved impressive growth rates in strategic industries such as car manufacture, shipbuilding and semi-conductors. The three largest *chaebol* had sales of $180 billion. South Korea's work force, well-educated but cheaper than Japan's, and cheap state credit, gave Korea a competitive edge. The government now aims to encourage foreign investment and to concentrate on smaller industries, which it sees as the key to maintaining current growth.

SOUTH KOREA : MAJOR BUSINESSES

Garments
Chemicals
Electronics
Iron & steel
Shipbuilding
Fish processing
Vehicle assembly
Telecommunications

0   50 km
0   50 miles

S

RESOURCES

 147.8bn kwh (capacity 24.1m kw)

 Not an oil producer; refines 1.15m b/cd

 6.3m pigs, 3.2m cattle, 520,000 goats

 Coal, iron, lead, zinc, tungsten, gold, graphite, fluorite

ELECTRICITY GENERATION

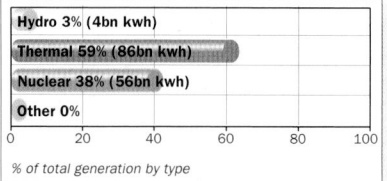

Hydro 3% (4bn kwh)

Thermal 59% (86bn kwh)

Nuclear 38% (56bn kwh)

Other 0%

% of total generation by type

South Korea has few natural resources. It has to import all of its oil and has built a series of nuclear reactors for generating electricity. Under the terms of the 1994 agreement between North Korean and the USA, two South Korean reactors are also to be built in North Korea which, in the event of reunification, will be connected to the national grid.

Agriculture remains a highly protected sector. Plans announced in 1994 to open up the rice market led to massive demonstrations in Seoul.

ENVIRONMENT

 7%

 Environmental protection is not yet of primary concern

ENVIRONMENTAL TREATIES

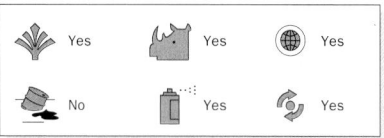

Yes   Yes   Yes

No   Yes   Yes

Environmental groups in Southeast Asia have expressed concern at South Korea's fast-track nuclear power program. The country's rapid industrialization and modernization have resulted in a number of environmental problems. Urban areas, particularly the capital Seoul, suffer from air pollution owing to the widespread use of low-grade coal for heating and industry. In rural parts, many rivers have been polluted by fertilizers and chemicals.

MEDIA

 The media is free of direct governmental interference

PUBLISHING AND BROADCAST MEDIA

There are 65 daily newspapers. *Tong-A Ilbo* is the leading paper

1 state-owned, also independent services

1 state-owned, 100 independent services

Superbird B Intelsat V F8

Available in major cities

South Korea's media has been freed of most restrictions since the advent of full multiparty democracy. However, criticisms of the armed forces are still frowned upon and journalists tend to avoid the subject of the role of the military in society altogether. Caution also has to be exercised in reporting facts about North Korea. In the past, South Korean journalists who have made favorable mention of President Kim Il Sung's communist regime in North Korea have suffered harassment and intimidation.

CRIME

 52,371 prisoners

 Down 84% in 1992

CRIME RATES

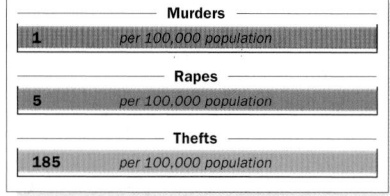

Murders

1 *per 100,000 population*

Rapes

5 *per 100,000 population*

Thefts

185 *per 100,000 population*

The government has begun to treat corruption as a crime. Otherwise, crime rates are relatively low and cases of violent crime uncommon. Since 1987, the internal security forces' operations have been restricted, although left-wing activists are still harassed. Striking workers and student demonstrators are subjected to tear gas and other methods of crowd control.

EDUCATION

 97%

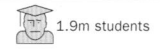 1.9m students

0   *Education spending as % GNP*   25

4.4%

THE EDUCATION SYSTEM

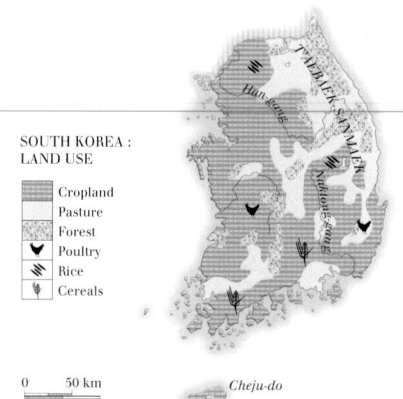

% of each age group in education

100% Primary   86% Secondary   46% Tertiary

South Korea embarked on a concentrated education program in the 1950s. The high priority given to education contributed greatly to South Korea's subsequent economic success. Tertiary enrollment is 46%, one of the highest rates in the world.

SOUTH KOREA : LAND USE

Cropland
Pasture
Forest
Poultry
Rice
Cereals

Cheju-do

0   50 km
0   50 miles

HEALTH

 1 per 950 people

Heart and cerebrovascular diseases, cancers

0   *Health spending as % GDP*   25

2.7%

The health service has improved in line with economic growth and now offers most advanced treatments. Health indicators such as infant mortality and longevity have improved accordingly.

WEALTH

Secretary, 800,000 won ($1,031) per month; dentist, 3m won ($3,867) per month

CONSUMER GOODS OWNERSHIP

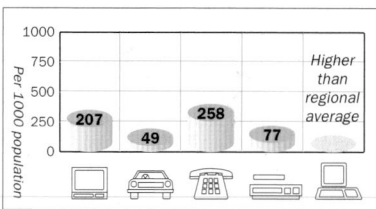

Per 1000 population

207   49   258   77

Higher than regional average

Most South Koreans have benefited from economic growth. However, the Cholla region remains the poorest.

WORLD RANKING

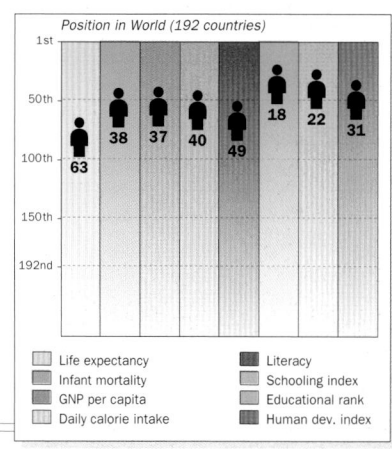

Position in World (192 countries)

1st
50th   38   37   40   18   22   31
100th   63   49
150th
192nd

Life expectancy   Literacy
Infant mortality   Schooling index
GNP per capita   Educational rank
Daily calorie intake   Human dev. index

S

SPAIN

OFFICIAL NAME: Kingdom of Spain **CAPITAL:** Madrid **POPULATION:** 39.6 million
CURRENCY: Peseta **OFFICIAL LANGUAGES:** Spanish, Galician, Basque and Catalan

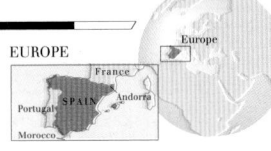
EUROPE

SITUATED IN SOUTHWESTERN EUROPE, Spain
has a wet Atlantic and a dry Mediterranean coast.
It is dominated by a central plateau drained by the
Duero, Tagus and Guadiana rivers. Since the death of General Franco
in 1975, Spain has managed a rapid and relatively peaceful transition
from dictatorship to democracy under the supervision of King Juan
Carlos I who was able to succeed to the throne on Franco's death.
Since joining the EC in 1986, there has been an increasing devolution
of power to the regions.

Alcaudete, Jaén Province, in the Andalusian
mountains between Granada and the River
Guadalquivir. The ruined castle is Moorish.

CLIMATE

WEATHER CHART

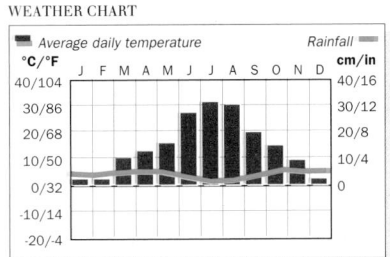

The central plateau, or *meseta*, endures
an extreme climate. Coastal areas
are milder, and wetter in the north
than in the south.

TRANSPORTATION

Barajas, Madrid
15.87m passengers

322 ships
3.98m dwt

THE TRANSPORTATION NETWORK

204,220 miles (328,640 km)	1,420 miles (2,286 km)
9,588 miles (15,430 km)	649 miles (1,045 km)

Modern transportation include the
AVE, a high-speed train linking Madrid
and Seville. Significant highway
construction is under way in Galicia.

TOURISM

43.2m visitors

Up 8% in 1994

MAIN OVERSEAS ARRIVALS

France 21%	
Portugal 21%	
Germany 14%	
UK 12%	
Netherlands 4%	
Other 28%	

% of total arrivals

Tourism accounts for some 10% of
GDP and employs more than 10% of the
work force. Spain thrives on the vacation
package sector despite government
marketing strategies to boost additional
cultural, historical and environmental
tourism. The cut-price vacation sector
is poised to benefit from an emerging
market in Central and Eastern Europe
and has been boosted by political
turbulence in potential competitor
countries in the Mediterranean.
Rising German unemployment
threatens resort occupancy.

PEOPLE

Spanish, Catalan, Galician,
Basque

205 people
per sq. mile

THE URBAN/RURAL POPULATION SPLIT

76%   24%

RELIGIOUS PERSUASION

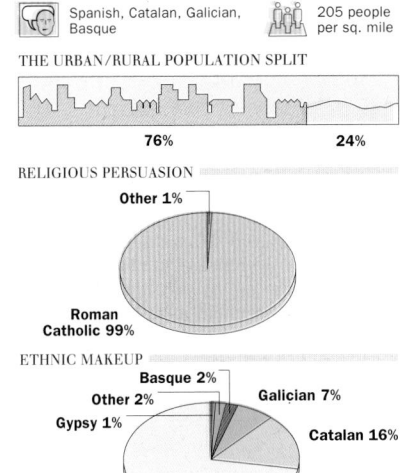

Other 1%

Roman
Catholic 99%

ETHNIC MAKEUP

Basque 2%   Galician 7%
Other 2%
Gypsy 1%   Catalan 16%

Castilian
Spanish 72%

A vigorous ethnic regionalism in Spain,
suppressed under Franco, now flourishes.
Despite a high-profile terror campaign,
ETA separatists fighting for independence
remain in a minority in the Basque
region. Spain today has one of the
lowest birth-rates in Europe and the
influence of the Catholic Church on
personal behavior has declined.
However, many traditional features of

POPULATION AGE BREAKDOWN

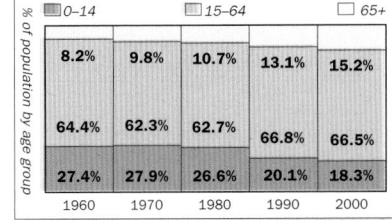

	0–14	15–64		65+
	8.2%	9.8%	10.7%	13.1%	15.2%
	64.4%	62.3%	62.7%	66.8%	66.5%
	27.4%	27.9%	26.6%	20.1%	18.3%
	1960	1970	1980	1990	2000

Spanish life remain.
While attitudes to
sexuality are
now relaxed,
church-going
remains
popular. The
divorce rate
is low and
family ties
remain
strong, with
many living at
home until their
late 20s.

Economic growth from
the 1970s led to a change
in the composition of
society. Migration from
rural regions to the coast
was associated with the
arrival of substantial
numbers of job-seeking
immigrants, mainly
from Latin America
and North Africa.
Economic downturn in
the 1990s led to a rise
in racial tensions.

Spanish women are
becoming increasingly
emancipated and more
influential in politics,
making up 15% of the
Spanish Congress in the
early 1990s, a higher
proportion than in any other
Western European country.

S

POLITICS

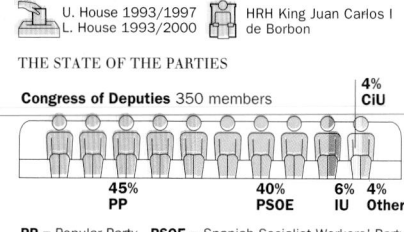

U. House 1993/1997
L. House 1993/2000

HRH King Juan Carlos I de Borbon

THE STATE OF THE PARTIES

Congress of Deputies 350 members

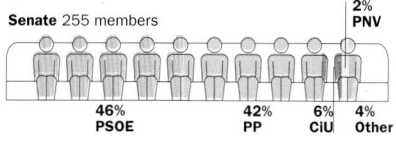

4% CiU

45% PP	40% PSOE	6% IU	4% Other

PP = Popular Party   **PSOE** = Spanish Socialist Workers' Party
IU = United Left   **CiU** = Convergence and Union
PNV = Basque National Party   **Other** = Canary Islands Coalition, National Galician Bloc, United People, Catalan Republican Left, Basque Solidarity, Valencian Union

Senate 255 members

2% PNV

46% PSOE	42% PP	6% CiU	4% Other

Since 1978, Spain has been a semi-federal multiparty parliamentary monarchy.

MAIN POLITICAL ISSUES
Clean government
Recent years saw the PSOE government discredited by a stream of corruption scandals and damaging allegations that ministers masterminded an undercover campaign of shootings and kidnappings of ETA Basque separatists in the 1980s.

The minority PP government led by José María Aznar faces the task of living up to its 1996 election promises and restoring public confidence in clean and honest government.

Increasing regionalism
Spain has 17 autonomous regions, all vying for greater funds or independence from Madrid. Many have bypassed central government to borrow their own funds on the international money markets and have been close to breaching their legal debt limits. Lacking a majority in the *Cortes* (parliament), the PP government has the problem of establishing a new model of financing for the autonomous regions while retaining the support of one or more nationalist parties in order to keep its legislative program on course.

PROFILE
Spain has been dominated for the past 13 years by Felipe González's PSOE, which was defeated in 1996. Such a long period in power, however, has blurred the boundaries between party and state. The *Cortes* has failed to check executive power, and political disputes are often left to the judiciary. Ideological issues no longer sharply divide the main parties, and they hold similar views on economic policy and EU membership. Political corruption – related to the financing of parties and cover-ups – has undermined voters' faith in Spain's political system.

King Juan Carlos, *who became head of state on the death of Gen. Franco in 1975.*

Felipe González Márquez, *prime minister from 1982–1996.*

WORLD AFFAIRS

GATT   NATO   WEU   CSCE

Spain remains an enthusiastic member of the EU but has been wary of enlarging the union to include Scandinavia or Central Europe, which it sees as a threat to its direct financial benefit. Elsewhere, Spain has sponsored an Ibero–American Community of Nations (a Hispanic Commonwealth), which held its fifth summit meeting in Argentina in 1995. Anxious to establish itself as a major international player, a Spaniard was appointed NATO Secretary-General in 1995 and Spain has contributed troops to the UN peacekeeping force in the former Yugoslavia, and aspires to a seat on the UN Security Council.

CHRONOLOGY
United under Ferdinand and Isabella in 1492, Spain became a dominant force in Europe. A long period of economic and political decline followed, however. By the mid-19th century, Spain lagged behind many other European countries in stability and prosperity.

- ❏ **1874** Constitutional monarchy restored under Alfonso XII.
- ❏ **1879** Spanish Socialist Workers' Party (PSOE) founded.
- ❏ **1881** Trade unions legalized.
- ❏ **1885** Death of Alfonso XII.
- ❏ **1898** Defeat in war with USA results in loss of Cuba, Puerto Rico and the Philippines.
- ❏ **1909** Barcelona's "tragic week" of anti-clerical riots.
- ❏ **1914–1918** Spain neutral in World War I.
- ❏ **1921** Spanish army routed by Berbers in Spanish Morocco.
- ❏ **1923** Coup by General Primo de Rivera accepted by King Alfonso XIII. Military dictatorship.
- ❏ **1930** General Primo de Rivera dismissed by monarchy.

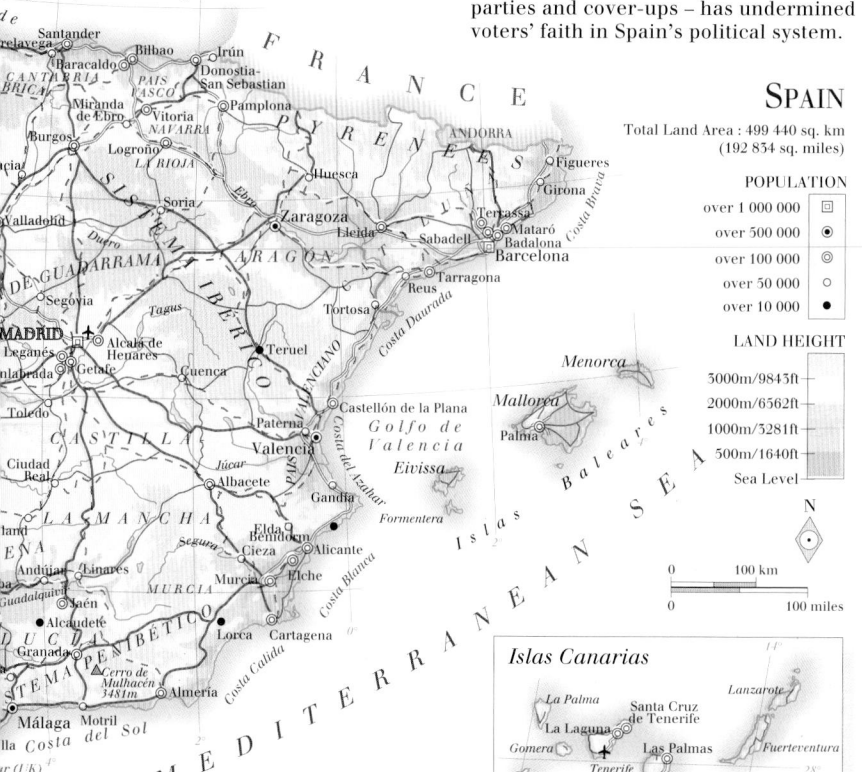

SPAIN
Total Land Area : 499 440 sq. km
(192 854 sq. miles)

POPULATION
over 1 000 000	▣
over 500 000	◉
over 100 000	◎
over 50 000	○
over 10 000	●

LAND HEIGHT
3000m/9843ft	
2000m/6562ft	
1000m/3281ft	
500m/1640ft	
Sea Level	

Islas Canarias

CHRONOLOGY *continued*

- ❑ **1931** Second Republic proclaimed. Alfonso XIII flees Spain.
- ❑ **1933** Center-right coalition wins general election.
- ❑ **1934** Asturias uprising quashed by army. Failure of attempt to form Catalan state.
- ❑ **1936** Popular Front wins elections. Right-wing military uprising against the Republic. Gen. Franco subsequently appointed leader.
- ❑ **1939** Franco wins civil war which claims 300,000 lives.
- ❑ **1940** Franco meets Hitler, but does not enter World War II.
- ❑ **1946** UN condemns Franco regime.
- ❑ **1948** Spain excluded from Marshall Plan.
- ❑ **1950** UN lifts veto.
- ❑ **1953** Concordat with Vatican. Spain grants USA military bases.
- ❑ **1955** Spain joins UN.
- ❑ **1959** Adoption of Stabilization Plan, prelude to rapid economic growth in the 1960s.
- ❑ **1962** Franco government applies for eventual membership of EEC.
- ❑ **1969** Gen. Franco names Juan Carlos, grandson of Alfonso XIII, his successor.
- ❑ **1970** Spain signs preferential trade agreement with EEC.
- ❑ **1973** Prime Minister Carrero Blanco assassinated by Basque separatists. Succeeded by Arias Navarro.
- ❑ **1975** Death of Gen. Franco. Proclamation of King Juan Carlos I.
- ❑ **1976** King replaces Arias Navarro with Adolfo Suárez.
- ❑ **1977** First democratic elections since 1936 won by Suárez's Democratic Center Union.
- ❑ **1978** New constitution declares Spain a parliamentary monarchy.
- ❑ **1981** Leopoldo Calvo Sotelo replaces Suárez. King foils military coup. Spain joins NATO.
- ❑ **1982** Felipe González wins landslide victory for PSOE.
- ❑ **1986** January, Spain joins EC. March, González wins referendum on keeping Spain in NATO.
- ❑ **1992** Olympic Games held in Barcelona, Expo '92 in Seville.
- ❑ **1996** PSOE loses general elections. José María Aznar prime minister.

AID

 $1.2bn   Up 25% in 1993

Spain's aid to Third World countries is often more conditional on the acquisition of goods and services than that of most other OECD countries. Aid in 1995 represented 0.31–0.35% of GDP.

DEFENSE

 $6.6bn   Up 6% in 1995

0   *Defense spending as % GDP*   40
| **1.6%** |

Spain has a substantial, largely state-owned defense industry, which is unviable commercially and is subsidized by the government for strategic reasons. Defense ambitions include the launch of a Spanish-built rocket by 1998. Compulsory national service is due to end in 2001.

SPANISH ARMED FORCES

668 main battle tanks (210 AMX-30, 164 M-48A5E, 294 M-60)	144,700 personnel
1 carrier, 8 submarines 17 frigates and 31 patrol boats	31,900 personnel
161 combat aircraft (EF-18 *Hornet*, RF-4C *Mirage* III/EE,-ED)	29,400 personnel
None	

ECONOMICS

 $525.3bn   131.63–121.32 pesetas

SCORE CARD

❑ WORLD GNP RANKING	10th
❑ GNP PER CAPITA	$13,280
❑ BALANCE OF PAYMENTS	-$6.4bn
❑ INFLATION	4.3%
❑ UNEMPLOYMENT	23.8%

EXPORTS

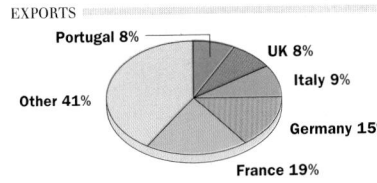

Portugal 8% UK 8% Italy 9% Germany 15% France 19% Other 41%

IMPORTS

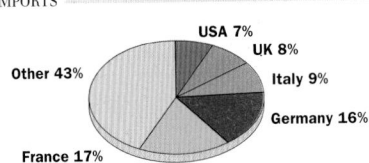

USA 7% UK 8% Italy 9% Germany 16% France 17% Other 43%

STRENGTHS

Spain's labor force is well qualified, has relatively low labor costs and is free of past trade union restrictions. Improvements in transportation and communications will continue to attract foreign investment. Potential for domestic growth is Spain's major asset.

WEAKNESSES

The massive foreign penetration of the Spanish economy and absence of any Spanish multinationals pose long-term problems. Low investment in research and development, a concentration in declining industries and low productivity – notably in agriculture – are major weaknesses. The percentage of people in Spain who are active economically is lower than in the rest of the EU.

PROFILE

Real convergence with the major European economies seemed possible between 1986–1991 as Spain posted the highest investment-led output growth

ECONOMIC PERFORMANCE INDICATOR

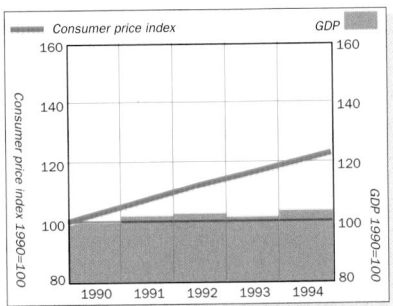

Consumer price index   GDP

in the OECD. By 1991, GDP per capita stood at almost 80% of the EC average. In 1992, however, Spain plunged into recession along with its major trading partners. In 1992–1993, three devaluations of the peseta, by a total of 18%, just managed to keep it within the ERM. Economic recovery produced growth of 3% by 1995, including strong domestic demand, but at 24%, unemployment remains twice the EU average. Priorities are to maintain low inflation and to halve the public sector deficit from 5.9% to 3% of GDP to meet the criteria for the European single currency.

SPAIN : MAJOR BUSINESSES

La Coruña Bilbao Zaragoza Barcelona Vigo Madrid Huelva Valencia Sevilla Málaga Cartagena

※ Textiles		✿ Heavy engineering	
🌾 Agribusiness		⚙ Light engineering	
Chemicals		Fish processing	
Shipbuilding			
Vehicle manufacture		0 200 km	
* significant multinational ownership		0 200 miles	

RESOURCES

- 156bn kwh (capacity 43.3m kw)
- 23.8m sheep, 18.1m pigs, 5m cattle
- 21,514 b/d (reserves 22,518,000 bbl)
- Coal, oil, iron, uranium, mercury, fluorspar, gypsum

ELECTRICITY GENERATION

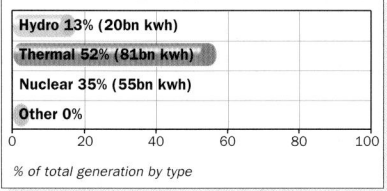

Hydro 13% (20bn kwh)
Thermal 52% (81bn kwh)
Nuclear 35% (55bn kwh)
Other 0%

% of total generation by type

Spain lacks natural resources, especially water, and is heavily dependent on imported oil and gas. Contrary to popular belief, food products such as fruit and vegetables constitute only 13% of its exports. Spain has one of the world's largest fishing fleets, but EU restrictions cut catches by some 120,000 tons in 1991–1994.

SPAIN : LAND USE

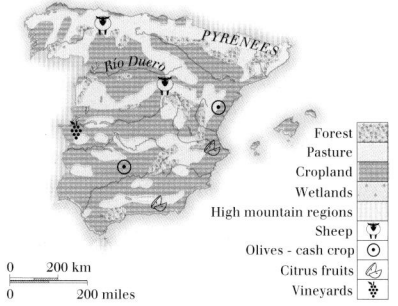

- Forest
- Pasture
- Cropland
- Wetlands
- High mountain regions
- Sheep
- Olives - cash crop
- Citrus fruits
- Vineyards

ENVIRONMENT

- 8%
- Consciousness is rising. Highly active green NGOs

ENVIRONMENTAL TREATIES

Yes		Yes		Yes	
Yes		Yes		Yes	

Although Spain paid little attention to environmental matters until very recently, public opinion is becoming increasingly demanding. A national tree-planting scheme has been initiated to reduce soil erosion, but its benefits have been offset by losses from increasingly frequent intentional forest fires. Spain has more land with national park status than any other country in Europe and there are plans to double the number. However, rising visitor numbers and tourist developments inside the parks, as in the Coto Doñana wetlands in the south, are damaging their integrity. A large new dam project is threatening the habitat and hence the survival of Spain's last brown bears.

MEDIA

Freedom of expression, though TV is vulnerable to government pressure

PUBLISHING AND BROADCAST MEDIA

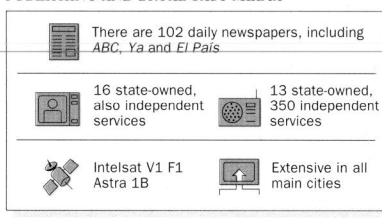

There are 102 daily newspapers, including *ABC, Ya* and *El País*

16 state-owned, also independent services

13 state-owned, 350 independent services

Intelsat V1 F1 Astra 1B

Extensive in all main cities

Despite the large number of daily newspapers, readership is among the lowest in Europe. Both public and private TV are popular. Radio is of a generally high standard.

CRIME

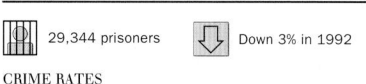

29,344 prisoners

Down 3% in 1992

CRIME RATES

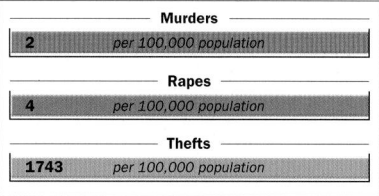

Murders
2 per 100,000 population

Rapes
4 per 100,000 population

Thefts
1743 per 100,000 population

Spain is a major crossroads in the world narcotics trade and narcotics-related crime is rising. Rape is increasing (or reported more often), as is property-related crime.

EDUCATION

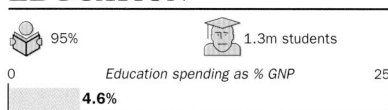

95%

1.3m students

0 *Education spending as % GNP* 25

4.6%

THE EDUCATION SYSTEM

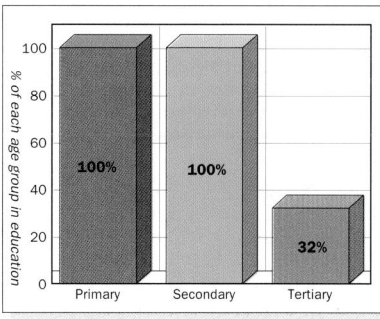

% of each age group in education

- Primary 100%
- Secondary 100%
- Tertiary 32%

Some 35% of elementary and secondary schooling is private. Compulsory secondary education remains a major political priority. Most teaching in over-subscribed universities is lecture-based. Students with parental funding and good English are increasingly completing their education abroad, often in the USA.

HEALTH

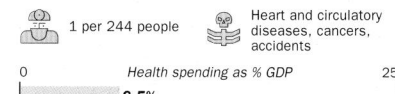

1 per 244 people

Heart and circulatory diseases, cancers, accidents

0 *Health spending as % GDP* 25

6.5%

Public health care is high-quality and readily available, and public hospitals are generally considered to be better than private ones. In spite of very high tobacco and alcohol consumption, Spain has a healthy population, possibly due to its Mediterranean diet. The incidence of AIDS, however, is the second-highest in Europe.

WEALTH

Cleaner, 100,000 pesetas ($824) per month; company director, 1m pesetas ($8,243) per month

CONSUMER GOODS OWNERSHIP

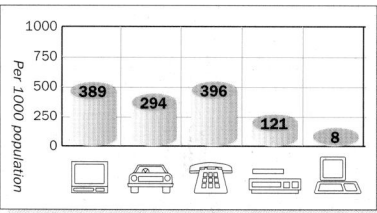

Per 1000 population

389 294 396 121 8

In the late 1980s, it became fashionable in Spain to compete openly, make money and consume. The country's rapid economic growth at this time greatly enriched the professional and managerial classes. The latter became the best-paid, in real terms, in Europe. Some, such as the now disgraced banker, Mario Conde of Banesto, became media celebrities, rivaling soccer players in popularity. In spite of high taxes, the rich became richer and more ostentatious. Spain quickly developed into an important market for luxury cars and yachts; a personal bodyguard also became a status symbol.

The recession of the early 1990s, however, changed attitudes, as Spain was afflicted with one of the highest unemployment rates in Europe.

S

WORLD RANKING

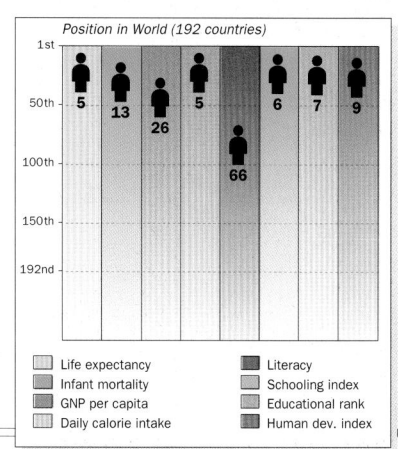

Position in World (192 countries)

5 13 26 5 66 6 7 9

- Life expectancy
- Infant mortality
- GNP per capita
- Daily calorie intake
- Literacy
- Schooling index
- Educational rank
- Human dev. index

SRI LANKA

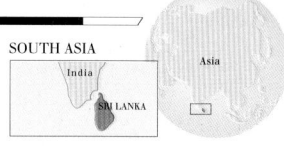

SOUTH ASIA

OFFICIAL NAME: Democratic Socialist Republic of Sri Lanka **CAPITAL:** Colombo
POPULATION: 18.4 million **CURRENCY:** Sri Lanka rupee **OFFICIAL LANGUAGE:** Sinhalese

SEPARATED FROM INDIA by the Palk Strait, Sri Lanka comprises one large island and several coral islets to the northwest known as Adam's Bridge. The main island is dominated by rugged central uplands. The fertile plains to the north are dissected by rivers and bordered to the southeast by the Mahaweli Ganga River. Sri Lankan affairs are dominated by the conflict between the government and the Tamils, who are fighting for an independent state.

CLIMATE

WEATHER CHART

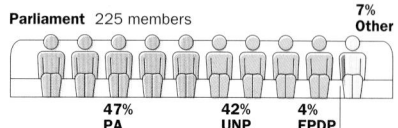

The climate is tropical, with afternoon breezes on the coast and cooler air in the highlands. The northeast is driest.

TRANSPORTATION

Katunayake, Colombo
1.52m passengers

32 ships
438,200 dwt

THE TRANSPORTATION NETWORK

17,180 miles (27,640 km)		None	
1,208 miles (1,944 km)		267 miles (430 km)	

Main roads are crowded and slow, but those to resorts are being improved. Air Lanka now flies non-stop to Europe.

TOURISM

408,000 visitors

Up 4% in 1994

MAIN OVERSEAS ARRIVALS

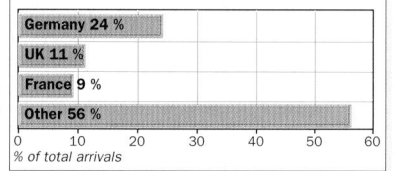

Germany 24 %
UK 11 %
France 9 %
Other 56 %

0 10 20 30 40 50 60
% of total arrivals

Sri Lanka's badly damaged tourist industry suffered further setbacks during 1995 and 1996 when Colombo became the target of Tamil bomb attacks. This instability impedes the development of mass tourism.

PEOPLE

Sinhalese, Tamil, Sinhalese-Tamil, English

736 people per sq. mile

THE URBAN/RURAL POPULATION SPLIT

22% 78%

ETHNIC MAKEUP

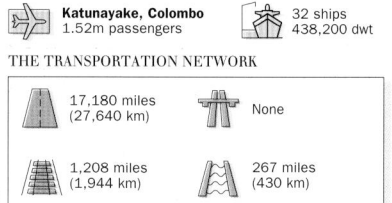

Burgher, Malay and Veddha 1% Moor 7%
Tamil 18%
Sinhalese 74%

Ethnic tensions between the minority Tamils and majority Sinhalese erupted into civil war in 1983. The Tamils were the minority group favored by the British colonists. When the British left, laws were passed to redress the balance by favoring the Sinhalese. The effect has been to make Tamils feel sidelined, and support for secessionism has grown. The conflict also has a religious dimension. Most Sinhalese are Buddhist, while Tamils are mostly Muslim or Hindu.

SRI LANKA

Total Land Area : 64 740 sq. km (24 996 sq. miles)

POPULATION
⊙ over 500 000
◎ over 100 000
○ over 50 000
● over 10 000
• under 10 000

LAND HEIGHT
2000m/6562ft
1000m/3281ft
500m/1640ft
200m/656ft
Sea Level

0   50 km
0   100 miles

N

POLITICS

1994/2000

President Chandrika Bandaranaike Kumaratunga

THE STATE OF THE PARTIES

Parliament 225 members

7% Other

47% PA   42% UNP   4% EPDP

PA = People's Alliance (of which main party is SLFP = Sri Lankan Freedom Party) **UNP** = United National Party **EPDP** = Eelam People's Democratic Party **Other** = Sri Lankan Muslim Congress, Tamil United Liberation Front, Democratic People's Liberation Front

The Tamil-Sinhalese conflict colours all political debate. In 1983, civil war erupted between the Liberation Tigers of Tamil Eelam (LTTE or Tamil Tigers) and the government. The LTTE wants an independent state in the north and east. The government is committed to keeping Sri Lanka unified, although it is considering plans for greater regional autonomy. However, attempts at a political settlement have been frustrated, most recently by the collapse of peace talks in April 1995. Since then a massive army operation and the resumption a civilian bombing campaign by the LTTE have hardened attitudes on both sides.

Map labels

India, Palk Strait, Mannar I., Kayts, Punkudutivu, Delft, Kankesanturai, Jaffna, Jaffna Lagoon, Bay of Bengal, Pooneryn, Kilinochchi, Nanthi Kadal Lagoon, Mullaittivu, Karaitivu, Mankulam, Adam's Bridge, Mannar, Palladi, Vavuniya, Gulf of Mannar, Medawachchiya, Horowupotana, Trincomalee, Koddiyar Bay, Anuradhapura, Upaar Lagoon, Puttalam Lagoon, Habarana, Polonnaruwa, Puttalam, Dambulla, Mundal Lagoon, Chenkaladi, Dedura, Batticaloa, Chilaw, Matale, Mahiyangana, Ampara, Kurunegala, Senanayake Samudra, Akkarai, Negombo, Kegalla, Kandy, Pidurutalagala 2524m, Badulla, Gampaha, COLOMBO, Talawakele, Namunukula, Dehiwala-Mount Lavinia, Sri Jayawardenapura, Nuwara Eliya, Monaragala, Moratuwa, Beragala, Panadura, Ratnapura, Wellawaya, Pottuvil, Kalu, Pelmadulla, Kalutara, Elpitiya, Ambalangoda, Hambantota, Galle, Weligama, Matara, INDIAN OCEAN

WORLD AFFAIRS

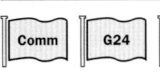

Comm | G24 | NAM | SAARC | WTO

Relations with India are paramount. The 1987 Indo–Sri Lankan accords led to Indian troops playing a peace-keeping role. They became embroiled in fighting the LTTE, however, and were forced to pull out. The LTTE is suspected of being behind the assassination of Indian president Rajiv Gandhi in 1992.

AID

 $551m (receipts)   Down 16% in 1993

The president responded positively to Western aid donors seeking improvements in Sri Lanka's human rights record.

DEFENSE

 $605m   Up 17% in 1995

Defeating the LTTE is the overwhelming concern. The collapse of peace talks in 1995 prompted the government to seek greater military assistance from abroad.

ECONOMICS

 $11.6bn    49.67–53.50 Sri Lanka rupees

SCORE CARD

- ❏ WORLD GNP RANKING..........................78th
- ❏ GNP PER CAPITA $640
- ❏ BALANCE OF PAYMENTS....................$–546m
- ❏ INFLATION 8.6%
- ❏ UNEMPLOYMENT...............................14.1%

STRENGTHS
The world's largest tea exporter. Export Processing Zones and state privatization programs attracting foreign investment. The left-wing government of President Kumaratunga has continued the sale of state assets.

WEAKNESSES
Civil war a drain on government funds and deters investors and many tourists. Poor infrastructure.

EXPORTS

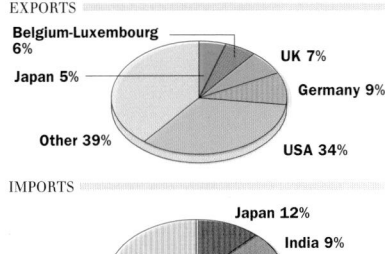

IMPORTS

RESOURCES

 3.5bn kwh (capacity 1.29m kw)   Not an oil producer; refines 50,000 b/cd

1.6m cattle, 500,000 goats, 90,000 pigs   Gemstones, graphite, iron, monazite, uranium, ilmenite, clay

Sri Lanka has to import all its oil. Hydro-power supplies 75% of electricity; droughts are frequent and supplies can be erratic. Sri Lanka is keen to diversify power sources and is turning to coal-powered generation.

ENVIRONMENT

 12% (4% partially protected)   Deforestation is under control

Sri Lanka has successfully promoted national parks. The government is keenly aware of the benefits to tourism of a protected environment.

MEDIA

 Little press freedom due to Tamil–Sinhalese conflict. Government is able to enact emergency controls

PUBLISHING AND BROADCAST MEDIA

There are 16 daily newspapers, including the *Daily News*, *Davasa*, *Irida Lankadipa* and *Dinapathi*

2 state-owned services   1 state-owned service

The government of President Chandrika Kumaratunga faced criticism after it imposed press censorship in late-1995 in an attempt to control war reporting.

CRIME

 14,128 prisoners   Up 0.3% in 1992

Both the army and the LTTE have been accused of human rights abuses. The civil war has claimed at least 30,000 lives since 1983. LTTE members carry cyanide capsules in case of arrest.

EDUCATION

 90%    61,628 students

Sri Lanka has the highest literacy rate of any developing nation. Many Sri Lankans attend US universities.

A peak in central Sri Lanka, close to the country's highest mountain, Pidurutalagala, which reaches 8,281 feet.

CHRONOLOGY

Sri Lanka has been inhabited by the Tamils and Sinhalese since before the 6th century. Named Ceylon under the British Empire, the island became independent in 1948.

- ❏ **1948** Indian Tamil workers stripped of suffrage and citizenship rights.
- ❏ **1956** SLFP wins election on platform to make Sinhalese the sole language.
- ❏ **1972** Name changed to Sri Lanka.
- ❏ **1983** Civil war erupts between Tamil LTTE and Sinhalese.
- ❏ **1990** Failed peace talks.
- ❏ **1993** President Premadasa murdered.
- ❏ **1994** August, left-wing People's Alliance wins general election. November, Chandrika Kumaratunga is elected president.
- ❏ **1995** Civil war continues after peace talks collapse.

HEALTH

 1 per 5,888 people   Suicide, heart attacks, cancers, pneumonia, strokes

Years of high spending on health have resulted in an accessible, fee-free system. Ayurvedic medicine is popular.

WEALTH

 Plantation worker, 6 Sri Lanka rupees ($0.10) per hour; hotel receptionist, 16 Sri Lanka rupees ($0.30) per hour

CONSUMER GOODS OWNERSHIP

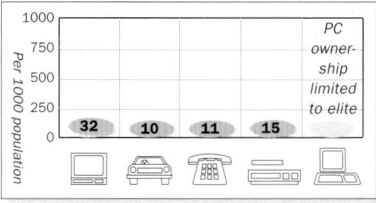

Economic growth has created a new class of wealthy Sinhalese. Tamil tea workers are the poorest group.

S

WORLD RANKING

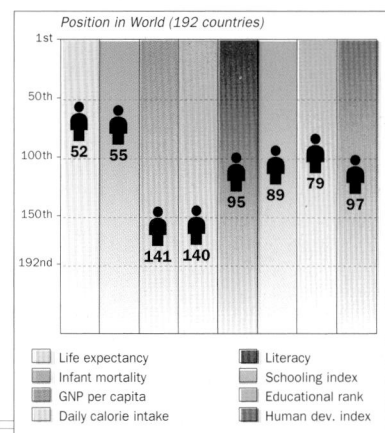

SUDAN

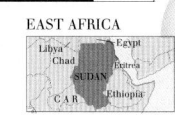

OFFICIAL NAME: Republic of Sudan   **CAPITAL:** Khartoum
POPULATION: 28.1 million   **CURRENCY:** Sudanese dinar   **OFFICIAL LANGUAGE:** Arabic

BORDERING THE RED SEA, Sudan is the largest country in Africa. Its landscape changes from desert in the north to lush tropical in the south, with grassy plains and swamps in the center. Tensions between the Arab north and African south have led to two civil wars since independence from British and Egyptian rule in 1956. The second of these conflicts remains unresolved. In 1989, an army coup installed a military Islamic fundamentalist regime.

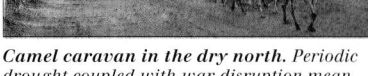
Camel caravan in the dry north. *Periodic drought coupled with war disruption mean that Sudan requires large amounts of food aid.*

CLIMATE

WEATHER CHART

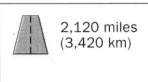

Sudan's northern half is hot arid desert with constant dry winds. The rest has a rainy season varying from two months in the center to eight in the south.

TRANSPORTATION

✈ **Khartoum International**	⚓	7 ships 62,100 dwt

THE TRANSPORTATION NETWORK

🛣 2,120 miles (3,420 km)	🛤 None	
🛤 2,936 miles (4,725 km)	🚢 2,528 miles (4,068 km)	

The Port Sudan–Khartoum railroad and road are Sudan's most important links. There are few other roads, but Iran is financing a Rabak–Malakal highway. Civil war has stopped all Nile shipping.

TOURISM

 12,000 visitors    Down 20% in 1994

MAIN OVERSEAS ARRIVALS

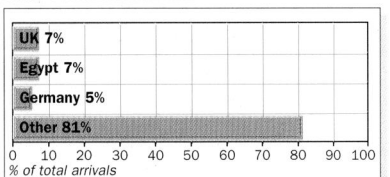

UK	7%
Egypt	7%
Germany	5%
Other	81%

0 10 20 30 40 50 60 70 80 90 100
% of total arrivals

Tourism has now almost ceased owing to political unrest and civil war. Visitors are mostly aid workers or on business.

PEOPLE

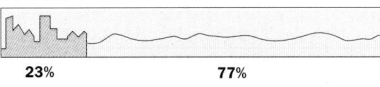

Arabic, Dinka, Nuer, Nubian, Beja, Zande, Bari, Fur, Shilluk, Lotuko

31 people per sq. mile

THE URBAN/RURAL POPULATION SPLIT

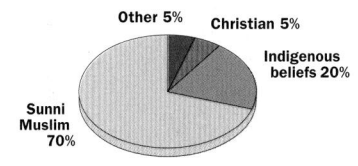

23%   77%

RELIGIOUS PERSUASION

Other 5%   Christian 5%
Indigenous beliefs 20%
Sunni Muslim 70%

Sudan has a large number of ethnic and linguistic groups. About two million Sudanese are nomads. The major social division, however, is between the Arabized Muslims in the north and the mostly African, largely animist or Christian population in the south. Attempts to impose Arab and Islamic values throughout Sudan have been the root cause of the civil war that has ravaged the south since 1983. However, the rebels have now split into two factions, pitting southern Sudan's small ethnic groups against the Dinka, the south's largest tribe. There are some non-Arab groups in the north and the densely populated Darfur region. Women not wearing Islamic dress can suffer harassment or even public flogging.

SUDAN

Total Land Area : 2 376 000 sq. km
(917 374 sq. miles)

0	400 km
0	400 miles

LAND HEIGHT

2000m/6562ft	
1000m/3281ft	
500m/1640ft	
200m/656ft	
Sea Level	

POPULATION

◉	over 500 000
◎	over 100 000
○	over 50 000
●	over 10 000
•	under 10 000

POLITICS

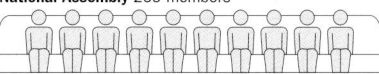

1992/2000   Lt.-Gen. Omar Hassan Ahmad al-Bashir

THE STATE OF THE PARTIES

National Assembly 269 members

The new non-party National Assembly is to draft a new constitution. It is dominated by NIF supporters.

The military regime headed by Gen. Bashir took over in a coup in 1989. It banned all political parties except the National Islamic Front (NIF), which emerged as the force behind the coup. After the non-party 1996 elections, NIF leader Hassan al-Tourabi, Sudan's most influential figure, became president of the National Assembly. A strict policy of Islamicization, including *sharia* law, has been imposed, but is ineffective in the southern areas held by non-Muslim rebels. Dissent elsewhere has been violently crushed. Many opposition leaders are in exile.

WORLD AFFAIRS

Sudan's support for Iraq in the Gulf War and belief that it sponsors terrorism have led to increasing isolation from the West and the Arab world. Only Iran, Yemen and Libya maintain friendly relations.

AID

 $485m (receipts)   Down 20% in 1993

Sudan's only substantial bilateral aid comes from Iran. IMF funding ceased in 1990. Sudan depends on food aid.

DEFENSE

 $134m   Down 56% in 1995

The NIF controls the military and police and has its own paramilitary militia. Sudan's 116,800-strong army is engaged in fighting the two factions of the southern Sudanese People's Liberation Army, numbering up to 100,000 men.

ECONOMICS

 $6.4bn    31.08–82.50 Sudanese dinars

SCORE CARD

- ❏ WORLD GNP RANKING..........................95th
- ❏ GNP PER CAPITA $269
- ❏ BALANCE OF PAYMENTS...................$–506m
- ❏ INFLATION 102%
- ❏ UNEMPLOYMENT...................................30%

STRENGTHS
Cotton, gum arabic, sesame, sugar. Some gold mining.

WEAKNESSES
Low industrialization. Lack of foreign exchange for importing energy and spare parts for industry. Little transportation infrastructure. Huge distances between towns. Exploitation of oil prevented by civil war. Drought. Alienation of Arab donors and investors.

EXPORTS

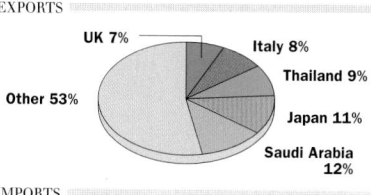

UK 7% | Italy 8% | Thailand 9% | Japan 11% | Saudi Arabia 12% | Other 53%

IMPORTS

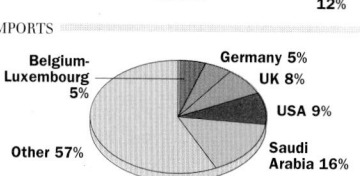

Belgium-Luxembourg 5% | Germany 5% | UK 8% | USA 9% | Saudi Arabia 16% | Other 57%

RESOURCES

 1.3bn kwh (capacity 500,000 kw)

 Reserves of 300m bbl; refines 21,700 b/cd

 22.9m sheep, 21.8m cattle, 16.4m goats, 2.9m camels

 Oil, gas, gold, copper, gypsum, marble, mica, silver, chromium, zinc

Large oil and gas reserves were found in the south in the 1980s, but civil war has prevented their exploitation. The half-thermal, half-hydroelectric generating capacity is insufficient and week-long power cuts are frequent. Gold mining has expansion potential.

ENVIRONMENT

 4% (0.3% partially protected)

 Desertification is increasing

Work on the Jonglei canal to straighten the White Nile was halted in 1986. If completed, environmentalists believe the world's-largest swamp in the Sudd Plain would dry up, destroying wildlife and intensifying desertification.

MEDIA

 Tight government control of the media

PUBLISHING AND BROADCAST MEDIA

 There are 3 daily newspapers, *Al-Engaz al-Watan*, *As-Sudan al-Hadith* and *Al-Nasr*

1 state-controlled service

1 state-controlled, 1 rebel-controlled service

The media was relatively free from 1985 to 1989, but is now controlled by the government or the army.

CRIME

 Sudan does not publish prison figures

 Up 26% in 1992

Anti-government dissent is often suppressed by violence, and torture by the security forces is widespread. The UN has condemned Sudan's poor human rights record, most recently in 1996.

EDUCATION

 46%   60,134 students

In 1991, measures were introduced to Islamicize education. Elementary school children must have two years of Islamic religious instruction, and men wishing to enter university must first serve a year in the NIF's People's Militia.

HEALTH

 1 per 11,100 people

 Infectious and parasitic diseases, malnutrition

As most health funds are tied to urban hospitals, health service standards in rural areas are basic. The civil war has led to an increase in communicable diseases, especially leishmaniasis.

CHRONOLOGY

Northern Sudan was taken by Egypt in 1821, the south by Britain in 1877.

- ❏ **1882** British invade Egypt.
- ❏ **1883** Muslim revolt in Sudan led by Muhammad Ahmed, the Mahdi.
- ❏ **1898** Mahdists defeated. Anglo-Egyptian condominium set up.
- ❏ **1955** Rebellion in south starts 17 years of civil war.
- ❏ **1956** Independence as republic.
- ❏ **1958–1964** Army runs Sudan.
- ❏ **1965** Civilian revolution, elections.
- ❏ **1969** Army coup led by Col. Nimeri.
- ❏ **1972** South gets limited autonomy.
- ❏ **1973** Sudanese Socialist Union (former communist) sole party.
- ❏ **1978** Supports Egypt–Israel peace.
- ❏ **1983** Southern rebellion resumes. *Sharia* law imposed. Nimeri's proposal that Sudan become a formal Islamic state is rejected.
- ❏ **1986** Army coup restores civilian government.
- ❏ **1989** Gen. al-Bashir takes over.
- ❏ **1991** *Sharia* penal code instituted. Sudan backs Iraq in Gulf War.
- ❏ **1996** Presidential and legislative elections.

WEALTH

 Most of the population lives a subsistence existence

CONSUMER GOODS OWNERSHIP

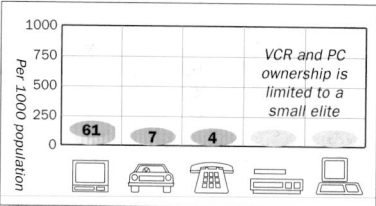

VCR and PC ownership is limited to a small elite

61 | 7 | 4

Wealth is limited to the NIF and southern rebel elites. Most of the population struggles to survive.

WORLD RANKING

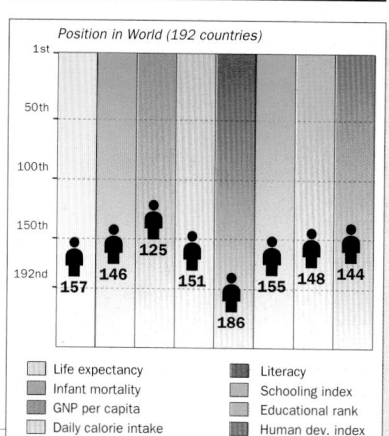

Position in World (192 countries)

157 | 146 | 125 | 151 | 186 | 155 | 148 | 144

- Life expectancy
- Infant mortality
- GNP per capita
- Daily calorie intake
- Literacy
- Schooling index
- Educational rank
- Human dev. index

S

SURINAME

SOUTH AMERICA

OFFICIAL NAME: Republic of Suriname   CAPITAL: Paramaribo
POPULATION: 400,000   CURRENCY: Suriname guilder   OFFICIAL LANGUAGE: Dutch

1975

LOCATED ON THE NORTH COAST of South America, Suriname is bordered by Guyana, French Guyana and Brazil. The interior is rainforested highlands; most people live near the coast. In 1975, after almost 300 years of Dutch rule, Suriname became independent. The Netherlands is still its main aid supplier, and home to one-third of Surinamese. Multiparty democracy was restored in 1991, after almost eleven years of military rule.

Congested street in Paramaribo. It boasts 18th and 19th century Dutch architecture and the Caribbean's largest mosque.

CLIMATE

WEATHER CHART

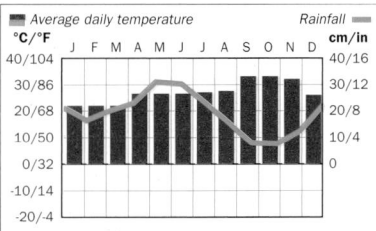

Suriname's tropical climate is cooled by the trade winds. The temperature averages 80°F. Rainfall varies from 59 to 118 inches between coast and interior.

TRANSPORTATION

Johann Pengel Intl, Paramaribo
175,000 passengers

7 ships
14,300 dwt

THE TRANSPORTATION NETWORK

1,480 miles (2,380 km)	None
98 miles (157 km)	3,125 miles (5,029 km)

The road network runs east–west and focuses on the coast and its immediate hinterland. Rivers provide the main north–south links. The vast interior relies on water or air transportation.

TOURISM

30,000 visitors

No change in 1994

MAIN OVERSEAS ARRIVALS

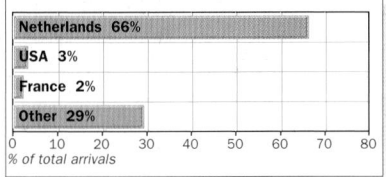

Netherlands 66%
USA 3%
France 2%
Other 29%

0 10 20 30 40 50 60 70 80
% of total arrivals

Tourism is undeveloped. Travelers outside Paramaribo are advised to carry their own hammock and food.

PEOPLE

Pidgin English (Taki-Taki), Dutch, Hindi, Javanese, Saramacca, Carib

5 people per sq. mile

THE URBAN/RURAL POPULATION SPLIT

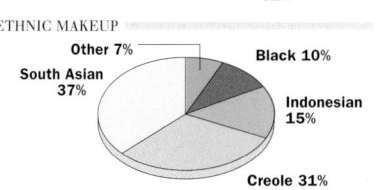

49%   51%

ETHNIC MAKEUP

Other 7%
South Asian 37%
Black 10%
Indonesian 15%
Creole 31%

About 200,000 Surinamese, one-third of the ethnically diverse population, have emigrated since 1975. Of those still in Suriname, 90% live near the coast. The rest live in very scattered rainforest communities. About 7,000 are Indians. The remainder are *bosnegers* (bush negros), the descendants of runaway African slaves. They fought the Creole-dominated government in the 1980s. Many South Asians and Indonesians work in farming.

POLITICS

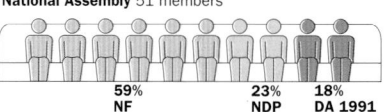

1991/1996

President Ronald R. Venetiaan

THE STATE OF THE PARTIES

National Assembly 51 members

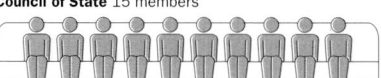

59% NF   23% NDP   18% DA 1991

NF = New Front (composed of: NPS = Suriname National Party, VHP = Progressive Reform Party, KTPI = Party for National Unity and Solidarity, SPA = Suriname Labor Party) **NDP** = National Democratic Party **DA 1991** = Democratic Alternative 1991

Council of State 15 members

Representatives of trade unions, armed forces and elected political parties

The democratically elected coalition that took power in 1991 is dominated by traditional, ethnically based parties: the Creole NPS, the South Asian VHP and the Indonesian KTPI. The opposition NDP is led by Desi Bouterse, former head of the military regime that ruled from 1980 to 1988. Bouterse was also the force behind the 1990 coup, which ended Suriname's first attempt to return to democracy, and is still a key political player.

SURINAME

Total Land Area : 161 470 sq. km (62 344 sq. miles)

LAND HEIGHT

1000m/3281ft
500m/1640ft
200m/1640ft
Sea Level

POPULATION

over 100 0
over 10 0
under 10 0

Map:

A T L A N T I C   O C E A N

PARAMARIBO

Nieuw Nickerie · Totness · Groningen · Calcutta · Nieuw Amsterdam · Galibi
Wageningen · Boskamp · Jenny · Lelydorp · Onverwacht · Moengo · Albina
Republiek · Paranam · Pilgrimkondre
Apoera · Bitagron · Kwakoegron · Zanderij
Kaaimanston · Berg en Dal · Joden Savanne · Brokopondo
Brownsweg · Afobaka · Langatabbetje
Njoeng Jacobkondre
Kabalebo Reservoir · Pokigron · W.J. van Blommesteinmeer · Stoelmanseiland
Boti-Pasi · Ladoewani
Asidonhopo · Pocketi
Juliana Top 1230m · Gran · Cottica
Teboe Top
Intelewa
Appikalo

GUYANA
FRENCH GUIANA
B R A Z I L

0 50 km
0 50 miles

S

WORLD AFFAIRS

ACS | Ama Pac | Caricom | NAM | OAS

Relations with the Netherlands and the USA, Suriname's key aid and trading partners, have eased since the return to democracy in 1991. Both stopped aid in the 1980s in response to the military regime's human rights abuses. Integration into the Caribbean region and relations with Mexico, Colombia, Venezuela and the EU are priorities.

AID

 $82m (receipts)   Up 4% in 1993

The Netherlands is the largest donor. Suriname's economy was badly hit by aid suspensions from 1982 to 1988 over human rights abuses and after the 1990 coup. Humanitarian aid resumed in 1992.

DEFENSE

 $12m   Up 9% in 1995

Under Colonel Desi Bouterse, the army has played a dominant political role since 1980. Bouterse resigned as army head in 1992, but military intervention remains a threat. A six-year civil war against *bosneger* rebels ended in 1992.

ECONOMICS

 $364m    330.29–420.00 Suriname guilders

SCORE CARD

❏ WORLD GNP RANKING	171st
❏ GNP PER CAPITA	$870
❏ BALANCE OF PAYMENTS	$59m
❏ INFLATION	368.5%
❏ UNEMPLOYMENT	16.5%

STRENGTHS

Bauxite. Rainforest potential, notably timber. Oil. Agricultural exports: rice, bananas, citrus fruits. Shrimp exports.

WEAKNESSES

Over-dependence on declining bauxite reserves and Dutch aid. Government failure to reform monetary system. Continued budget deficit is extending aid freeze and exacerbating associated economic recession. Net food importer.

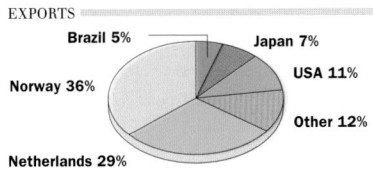

EXPORTS

Brazil 5% — Japan 7% — USA 11% — Other 12% — Netherlands 29% — Norway 36%

IMPORTS

Netherlands Antilles 5% — Brazil 4% — Trinidad and Tobago 9% — Other 17% — Netherlands 24% — USA 41%

RESOURCES

 1.4bn kwh (capacity 420,000 kw)   Not an oil producer; refines 4700 b/cd

 98,000 cattle, 37,000 pigs, 9,000 sheep   Bauxite, iron, manganese, copper, nickel, platinum, gold

Suriname is the world's sixth-largest bauxite producer. Aluminum and bauxite account for 74% of export earnings, but the sector has been hit by civil war and poor world prices. Oil production started in 1982, near Paramaribo. Exploitation of Suriname's rainforests has barely begun. Rice and fruit are the key agricultural products.

ENVIRONMENT

 4% partially protected   Economic growth has precedence over ecological concerns

Many of the 13 nature reserves were damaged in the civil war. *Bosneger* and Indian rainforest communities are becoming more militant in demanding control over their lands as commercial interest in the forests' potential grows.

MEDIA

 Censorship has eased since the return to democratic government in 1991

PUBLISHING AND BROADCAST MEDIA

 There are 2 daily newspapers, *De Ware Tijd* and *De West*

 2 state-owned services   2 state-owned, 6 independent services

The radio stations broadcast in a number of languages. Dutch is used by the daily newspapers and TV stations.

CRIME

 Suriname does not publish prison figures   Relatively high crime levels from year to year

The human rights abuses associated with the military regime have largely ended. President Venetiaan has also tried to clamp down on cocaine and illegal arms smuggling, which became a major problem during the 1980s.

EDUCATION

 93%   4,319 students

Education is free and includes adult literacy programs. There is a long tradition of higher education, but most graduates now live in the Netherlands.

HEALTH

 1 per 1,208 people   Heart attacks, cancers, malaria, malnutrition

Urban medical facilities are relatively good. In the interior, they are basic and provided largely by mission stations.

WEALTH

 A chemical industry foreman earns approximately 5 times the wage of a deep sea fisherman (wages have not kept pace with inflation)

CONSUMER GOODS OWNERSHIP

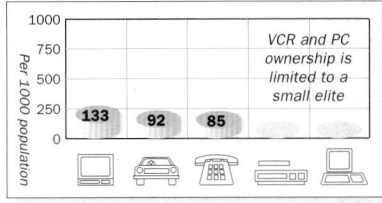

VCR and PC ownership is limited to a small elite

133   92   85

Per 1000 population

Living standards have fallen since 1982, due to the effects of aid suspension and civil war. Urban Creoles dominate the rich elite. Indians and *bosnegers* are the poorest groups.

WORLD RANKING

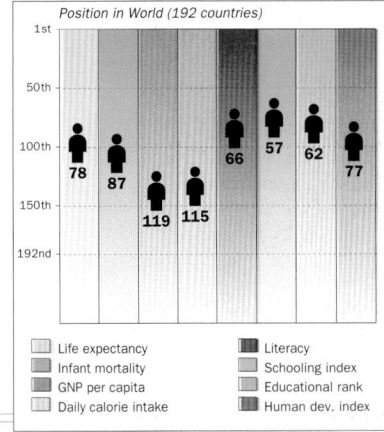

Position in World (192 countries)

78   87   119   115   66   57   62   77

- Life expectancy
- Infant mortality
- GNP per capita
- Daily calorie intake
- Literacy
- Schooling index
- Educational rank
- Human dev. index

S

SWAZILAND

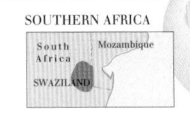

SOUTHERN AFRICA

OFFICIAL NAME: Kingdom of Swaziland   **CAPITAL:** Mbabane
POPULATION: 900,000   **CURRENCY:** Lilangeni   **OFFICIAL LANGUAGES:** Siswati and English

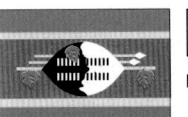

THE TINY SOUTHERN AFRICAN kingdom of Swaziland, bordered on three sides by South Africa and to the east by Mozambique, comprises mainly upland plateaux and mountains. Governed by a strong hereditary monarch, Swaziland is a country in which tradition is being challenged by demands for modern multiparty government. King Mswati III, crowned in 1986, has overhauled the electoral process, but has still to legalize party politics.

POLITICS

   1993/1998   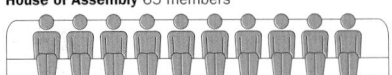 H.M. King Mswati III

THE STATE OF THE PARTIES

House of Assembly 65 members

55 members are elected by traditional communities, or Tinkhundla, from candidates nominated by the chiefs. 10 are appointed by the King

Senate 30 members

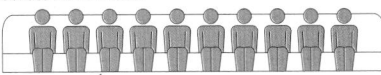

10 members are selected by the House of Assembly from among its own members, and 20 are appointed by the King

Politics is dominated by a strong executive monarchy, and rivalries within the royal Dlamini clan. The King's traditional advisers act as a counter to the Cabinet. Constitutional reform introduced direct elections to the House of Assembly in 1993. There is growing pressure for the King to legalize political parties and move toward multiparty democracy.

CLIMATE

WEATHER CHART

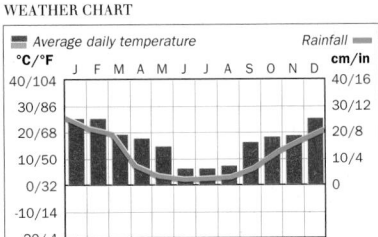

Swaziland is temperate. Temperatures rise and rainfall declines as the land descends eastward, from high to low *veld*. The Low Veld is prone to drought.

TRANSPORTATION

 Matsapha, Manzini
93,000 passengers

 Has no fleet

THE TRANSPORTATION NETWORK

500 miles (800 km)		None
230 miles (370 km)		None

A sharp rise in road traffic has led to a focus on road improvement schemes. The railroad, which runs to Mozambique and South Africa, mainly carries exports.

TOURISM

298,000 visitors   Up 5% in 1994

MAIN OVERSEAS ARRIVALS

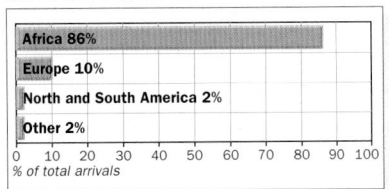

Africa 86%	
Europe 10%	
North and South America 2%	
Other 2%	

0 10 20 30 40 50 60 70 80 90 100
% of total arrivals

Swaziland's attractions are its game reserves, mountain scenery and, for the South Africans who make up more than 70% of tourists, its casinos.

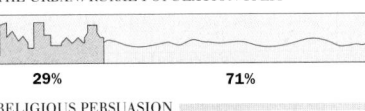

The outskirts of Mbabane. It lies on the High Veld, where traditional cattle farming has become more difficult owing to overgrazing.

PEOPLE

 Siswati, English, Zulu   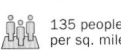 135 people per sq. mile

THE URBAN/RURAL POPULATION SPLIT

29%   **71%**

RELIGIOUS PERSUASION

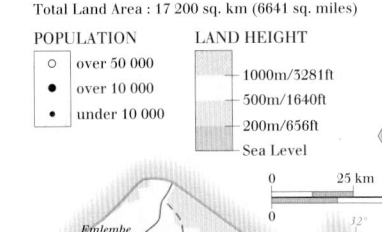

Indigenous beliefs 40%

Christian 60%

Over 95% of the population belong to the Swazi ethnic group, making Swaziland one of Africa's most homogeneous states. It is also one of the most conservative, although it is now coming under pressure from urban-based modernizers. Its political system actively promotes Swazi tradition and is dominated by a powerful monarchy. Society is patriarchal and focused around the clan and chiefs. Both are also politically important. Polygamy is tolerated. Women farm and may vote, but have little economic or political power. The exception is the Queen Mother, the "Great She Elephant," whose influence was demonstrated during the interregnum of the mid-1980s.

SWAZILAND

Total Land Area : 17 200 sq. km (6641 sq. miles)

POPULATION
○ over 50 000
● over 10 000
• under 10 000

LAND HEIGHT
1000m/3281ft
500m/1640ft
200m/656ft
Sea Level

WORLD AFFAIRS

 ACP Comm NAM OAU SADC

Economic dependence on South Africa led to the maintaining of relations with the apartheid government; the election of an ANC-dominated government there was welcomed. However, Mswati has expressed concern over South African support for Swazi pro-democracy campaigners. Peace in Mozambique has meant the return of 134,000 refugees.

AID

 $56m (receipts)   Up 14% in 1993

Balance of payments aid is important. Project aid has been targeted at the development of the Matsapha industrial estate, roads and social projects. Donors have generally looked favorably on Swaziland. The EU, Germany, the USA, the UK and the World Bank are important donors.

DEFENSE

 $12.68m   Up 12% in 1992

The Swaziland Defense Force numbers just 3,000 troops. Although it does not play an overt political role, its loyalty is to the monarch and the *status quo*.

ECONOMICS

 $1bn    3.54–3.65 emalangeni

SCORE CARD

❏ WORLD GNP RANKING	155th
❏ GNP PER CAPITA	$1,160
❏ BALANCE OF PAYMENTS	$24m
❏ INFLATION	14.8%
❏ UNEMPLOYMENT	15%

STRENGTHS
Economy quite diversified and buoyant; grew 4.5% a year during 1980s. Manufacturing 32% of GDP. Investment rules attractive. Sugar 33% of export earnings. Wood pulp. Debt service low: only 3.8% of export earnings in 1993. Risk to exports because of regional instability has diminished.

WEAKNESSES
Sugar vulnerable to changes in world prices. Dependence on South Africa for jobs, revenue, investment, electricity. Small plots of land and lack of land title hinder farm modernization. High population growth.

EXPORTS
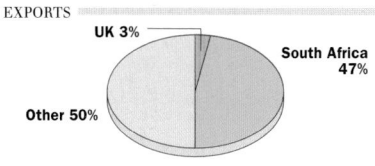

IMPORTS
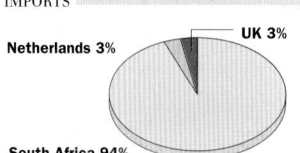

RESOURCES

 419m kwh   Not an oil producer and has no refineries

620,000 cattle, 434,000 goats, 32,000 pigs   Coal, diamonds, gold, asbestos, cassiterite, iron, tin

Swaziland's main export is sugarcane. Wood pulp, coal and asbestos are also exported. The HEP station at Lupholo-Ezulwim, completed in the 1980s, will reduce energy imports from South Africa.

ENVIRONMENT

 3% (partially protected)    Recognized as important for tourism

The main threat is land pressure owing to high population growth. In an effort to combat the problem, family planning programs are being introduced.

MEDIA

 The media is strictly controlled. Editors must get permission before publishing sensitive articles

PUBLISHING AND BROADCAST MEDIA

There are 3 daily newspapers, *The Times of Swaziland, Tikhatsi Temaswati* and the *Swaziland Observer*

1 state-owned service   1 state-owned, 3 independent services

The Times of Swaziland and *Swaziland Observer* are independent, but the press is generally respectful of the monarch and the royal Dlamini clan.

CRIME

 Swaziland does not publish prison figures   Up 17% in 1992

The crime rate is low but rising. An influx of illegal weapons brought in by refugees has boosted armed crime.

EDUCATION

 77%    3,023 students

Education is compulsory. Parents pay fees at all levels. Even so, elementary enrollment is about 93%. Drop-out rates at secondary level are high.

HEALTH

 1 per 18,800 people   Diarrheal and respiratory diseases

There is no national health service and the network of facilities is rudimentary. Health takes 8% of government spending.

WEALTH

Half the population lives below the UN poverty line

CONSUMER GOODS OWNERSHIP
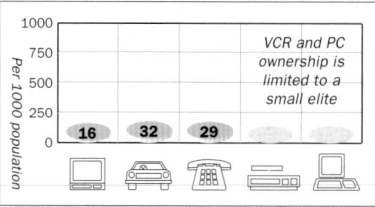

About 50% of Swazis live below the UN poverty line. The royal Dlamini clan enjoys Western luxuries and travel.

WORLD RANKING
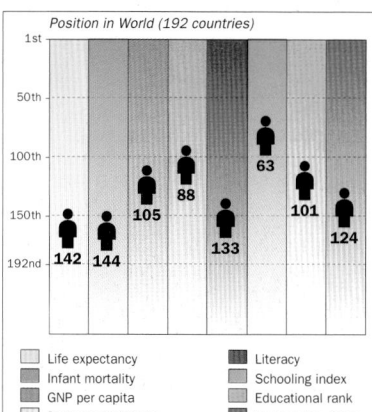

S

513

SWEDEN

OFFICIAL NAME: Kingdom of Sweden   **CAPITAL:** Stockholm
POPULATION: 8.8 million   **CURRENCY:** Swedish krona   **OFFICIAL LANGUAGE:** Swedish

SITUATED ON THE Scandinavian peninsula, between Norway and Finland, Sweden is a densely forested country with numerous lakes. The north of Sweden falls within the Arctic Circle. Much of the south is fertile and widely cultivated. Sweden has one of the most extensive welfare systems in the world, and is among the world's leading proponents of equal rights for women. Its economic strengths include high-tech industries and car production, including Volvo and Saab. It joined the EU in January 1995, along with Finland and Austria but not neighboring Norway.

CLIMATE

WEATHER CHART

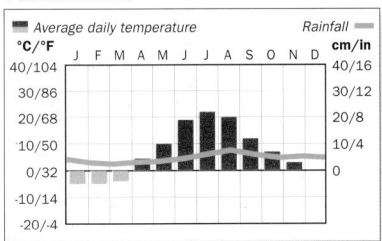

Sweden has a largely continental climate. The Baltic Sea often freezes in winter, making the east coast much colder than the west. Summers are cool everywhere, with temperatures varying surprisingly little between northern and southern regions.

TRANSPORTATION

 Arlanda, Stockholm
14.82m passengers

 273 ships
3.35m dwt

THE TRANSPORTATION NETWORK

83,060 miles (133,673 km)	582 miles (936 km)
6,961 miles (11,202 km)	1,275 miles (2,052 km)

Maintaining and improving transportation links in Europe's fourth-largest country is a key issue. Swedish governments have traditionally spent large sums on infrastructure. Transportation spending is also seen as a way of boosting the economy as a whole. A new $20 billion program was recently announced which will finance road, rail and port development.

Sweden's biggest single transportation project is a $5 billion bridge across The Sound. This will provide a road link to Denmark, and hence to the rest of Europe. A new rail link between Arlanda airport and Stockholm is also planned. By law, cars must travel with their headlights on at all times.

TOURISM

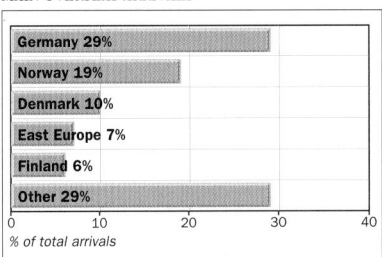

6.1m overnights. Sweden does not record visitor numbers

Up 3% in 1993

MAIN OVERSEAS ARRIVALS

Germany 29%	
Norway 19%	
Denmark 10%	
East Europe 7%	
Finland 6%	
Other 29%	

% of total arrivals

Sweden expanded rapidly as a tourist destination in the 1970s and 1980s. Stockholm, the capital, is renowned for its palaces. The international success of Abba in the 1970s boosted its vibrant nightlife. Visitors to the capital are typically young and affluent.

Although Sweden has fewer lakes than Finland, and lacks Norway's dramatic scenery, it still has a variety of natural attractions. The mountains of the "Midnight Sun" lie north of the Arctic Circle, while the southern coast has many white sandy beaches. Visitors have also been attracted by the vast tracts of deserted landscape and the simple country communal living. Despite the relatively high cost of travel to Sweden, tourism now accounts for 5% of GDP.

A crofter's holding in Darlana, Central Sweden, an area which is over 50% forested. The timber and paper industries account for almost 20% of Sweden's exports.

PEOPLE

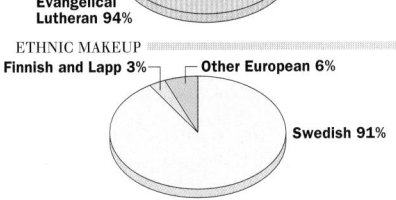

Swedish, Finnish, Lappish

50 people per sq. mile

THE URBAN/RURAL POPULATION SPLIT

83%   17%

RELIGIOUS PERSUASION

Pentecostal 1%
Roman Catholic 2%
Other 3%
Evangelical Lutheran 94%

ETHNIC MAKEUP

Finnish and Lapp 3%
Other European 6%
Swedish 91%

As in all of Scandinavia, the nuclear family forms the basis of society. The birth-rate is low with, on average, less than two children per family. Marriage is declining, and cohabitation outside marriage is common.

Swedish society has an egalitarian tradition. The role of the state is seen as the provision of conditions allowing each individual, male or female, to gain economic independence through employment. Sweden's welfare system is also one of the most extensive in the world. However, in the early 1990s, recession reduced benefits, and mothers in particular face increasing difficulties with the closure of childcare facilities. Women make up nearly half of the work force, one of the highest proportions in Europe.

While Sweden has generous asylum laws, immigration is tightly controlled. A 15,000-strong minority of Sami (or Lapps) live in northern Sweden. Their traditional way of life is protected.

In 1995, the Evangelical Lutheran church agreed that it should be disestablished from January 2000.

POPULATION AGE BREAKDOWN

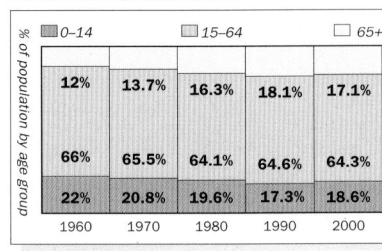

%	0–14	15–64	65+		
	12%	13.7%	16.3%	18.1%	17.1%
	66%	65.5%	64.1%	64.6%	64.3%
	22%	20.8%	19.6%	17.3%	18.6%
	1960	1970	1980	1990	2000

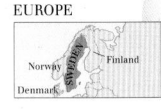

S

POLITICS

 1994/1998

 King Carl XVI Gustaf

THE STATE OF THE PARTIES

Parliament (Riksdag) 349 members

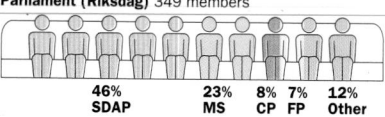

| 46% SDAP | 23% MS | 8% CP | 7% FP | 12% Other |

SDAP = Social Democratic Labor Party
MS = Moderate Party   CP = Center Party   FP = Liberal Party
Other = Green Party, Left Party, Christian Democratic Party

Sweden is a constitutional monarchy with an elected parliament under the leadership of the prime minister.

MAIN POLITICAL ISSUES
EU membership
In March 1994, Sweden agreed terms to join the EU. A referendum was held in November that year in which 52% voted in favor of membership, and the country became a member in 1995.

High cost of the welfare state
The cost of Sweden's welfare system has brought about an enormous budget deficit, equivalent to 15% of GDP in 1993. The government has to steer a difficult course between raising taxes and cutting benefits.

PROFILE
Swedish politics has traditionally been split between the monolithic Social Democrats (SDAP) and trade unions on the left, and a host of moderate center and right-wing parties. Since the 1930s, the Social Democrats have governed every term

with the exception of 1976–1982 and 1991–1994. The marked shift to the right in Swedish politics seen in 1991 was reversed in the 1994 elections, although the Social Democrats failed to gain an absolute majority in parliament. Ingvar Carlsson, SDAP leader, formed a minority government but resigned in 1996 and was replaced by Goran Persson.

Carl XVI Gustaf, ascended the throne in 1973. His role is purely ceremonial.

Carl Bildt, leader of the Moderate Party, was prime minister from 1991 to 1994.

WORLD AFFAIRS

 EU   CE   NAM   OECD   OSCE

Sweden's main recent foreign policy concern has been obtaining membership of the EU. Since the collapse of the Soviet Union, Sweden has also altered its traditionally neutral stance. It now has links with the Western European Union and even NATO membership is being considered. This contrasts sharply with Prime Minister Olof Palme's period in office in the 1980s, when Sweden was a vociferous critic of the USA's antagonistic policy toward the USSR. In 1993–1994, Sweden participated in the UN peacekeeping force in former Yugoslavia.

AID

 $1.8bn

 Up 28% in 1993

Sweden runs a very active development aid program, to which 1% of GDP is allocated. The majority of bilateral aid goes to African countries.

SWEDEN

Total Land Area : 411 620 sq. km (158 926 sq. miles)

POPULATION

▣	over 1 000 000
◉	over 100 000
○	over 50 000
●	over 10 000

LAND HEIGHT

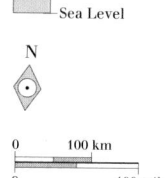

1000m/3281ft
500m/1640ft
200m/656ft
Sea Level

N

CHRONOLOGY

Sweden's history has been closely linked to the control of the Baltic Sea and its highly profitable trade routes. Under the house of Vasa, Sweden became a major power, controlling much of the Baltic region. By the 18th century, however, Sweden's position had been eroded by its regional rivals, particularly Russia.

❑ **1814–1815** Congress of Vienna. Sweden cedes territory to Russia and Denmark. Period of 180 years of unbroken peace begins.

❑ **1865–1866** Minister of Justice Louis De Greer reforms the Riksdag into a bicameral parliament.

❑ **1905** Norway gains independence from Sweden.

❑ **1911** First Liberal government.

❑ **1914** Government resigns over defense policy.

❑ **1914–1917** Sweden remains neutral though it supplies Germany.

S

DEFENSE

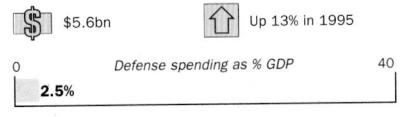

💲 $5.6bn ⬆ Up 13% in 1995

| 0 | Defense spending as % GDP | 40 |
| **2.5%** | | |

SWEDISH ARMED FORCES

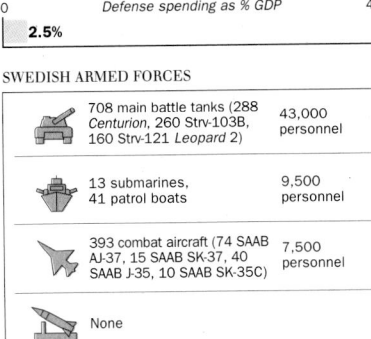

708 main battle tanks (288 *Centurion*, 260 Strv-103B, 160 Strv-121 *Leopard* 2)	43,000 personnel
13 submarines, 41 patrol boats	9,500 personnel
393 combat aircraft (74 SAAB AJ-37, 15 SAAB SK-37, 40 SAAB J-35, 10 SAAB SK-35C)	7,500 personnel
None	

Sweden maintains a sophisticated and powerful military force. Spending is concentrated on defense, reflecting Sweden's traditional need to protect its neutrality. Most weaponry, including Saab fighter jets and Boforsanti-aircraft guns, is supplied by its advanced home defense industry. Regular anti-submarine patrols are maintained in the Baltic and North Seas.

With the end of the Cold War, strategic priorities have changed. Sweden feels less bound to its neutral stance and has developed links with the Western European Union and is even considering NATO membership. Mutual security cooperation agreements are also being discussed with the Baltic States.

ECONOMICS

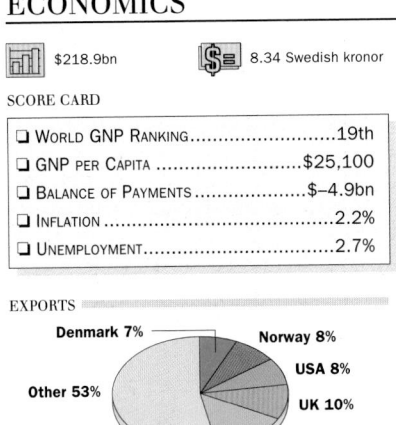

📊 $218.9bn   💲 8.34 Swedish kronor

SCORE CARD

- ❏ WORLD GNP RANKING..........................19th
- ❏ GNP PER CAPITA $25,100
- ❏ BALANCE OF PAYMENTS ....$–4.9bn
- ❏ INFLATION 2.2%
- ❏ UNEMPLOYMENT................................2.7%

EXPORTS

Denmark 7% Norway 8% USA 8% UK 10% Germany 14% Other 53%

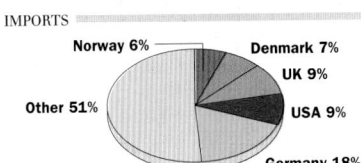

IMPORTS

Norway 6% Denmark 7% UK 9% USA 9% Germany 18% Other 51%

STRENGTHS

Companies of global importance, including Ericsson, Saab, Volvo, Electrolux and SKF, the world's biggest roller bearing manufacturer. Highly developed and constantly updated infrastructure. Sophisticated technology. Skilled labor force is virtually bilingual in English.

WEAKNESSES

Uncompetitive labor costs, although this is beginning to change slowly. Highest taxation in the OECD, accounting for over 60% of GDP. Peripheral location, raising costs for producers and exporters.

PROFILE

The state plays a significant role in the economy, but tends to restrict its role to services and infrastructure. Sweden's industrial giants have mostly been

ECONOMIC PERFORMANCE INDICATOR

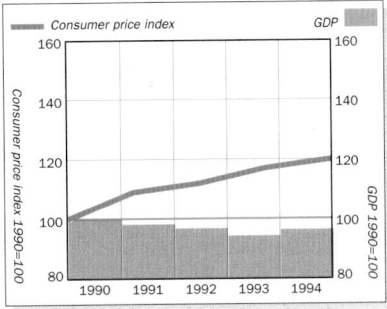

private-sector companies.

The early 1990s saw a shift in government economic policy. Some elements of the postwar consensus on the social role of government were abandoned in favor of measures designed to help business. However, the hoped-for result of greater growth was not achieved, and unemployment and the overall cost of welfare rose. Sweden's balance of payments deficit is now the highest in the OECD. Although Sweden has recently begun to emerge from recession, the deficit remains a significant problem.

SWEDEN : MAJOR BUSINESSES

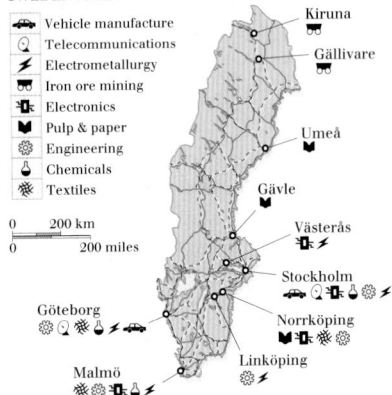

🚗 Vehicle manufacture
☎ Telecommunications
⚡ Electrometallurgy
⛏ Iron ore mining
🔌 Electronics
📦 Pulp & paper
⚙ Engineering
🧪 Chemicals
🧵 Textiles

| 0 | 200 km |
| 0 | 200 miles |

Kiruna, Gällivare, Umeå, Gävle, Västerås, Stockholm, Norrköping, Linköping, Göteborg, Malmö

RESOURCES

 144bn kwh (capacity 34.2m kw)

 Not an oil producer; refines 427,500 b/cd

2.3m pigs, 1.7m cattle, 401,000 sheep

Iron, uranium, copper, lead, zinc, silver

ELECTRICITY GENERATION

Hydro 51% (74bn kwh)

Thermal 5% (7bn kwh)

Nuclear 44% (63bn kwh)

Other 0%

0   20   40   60   80   100

% of total generation by type

Sweden is rich in minerals, pig iron, copper and silver. While mining and quarrying account for only 0.3% of GDP, they underpin other industrial sectors. Despite its abundant uranium deposits, making up 80% of the European total,

ENVIRONMENT

 6% (5% partially protected)

Environmental policy is a high priority

ENVIRONMENTAL TREATIES

Yes | Yes | Yes
No | Yes | Yes

Since the Environment Protection Act of 1969, investment in environmental protection measures has totaled 20 billion kronor. Sweden has blamed the considerable acid-rain damage to forests and lakes on airborne sulfur dioxide from factories in Western Europe. Swedish nuclear reactors are said to be very safe, with filtered venting systems designed to retain 90% of all radioactivity released in the event of a core meltdown.

MEDIA

 Government censorship is non-existent

PUBLISHING AND BROADCAST MEDIA

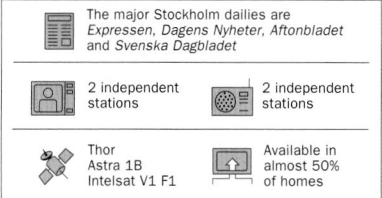

The major Stockholm dailies are *Expressen, Dagens Nyheter, Aftonbladet* and *Svenska Dagbladet*

2 independent stations | 2 independent stations

Thor Astra 1B Intelsat V1 F1 | Available in almost 50% of homes

Radical viewpoints are rarely expressed in the Swedish press. The influence of the major daily newspapers is largely confined to Stockholm, as the provinces have a strong press of their own. Six companies control almost all of Sweden's magazines. Political parties finance many newspapers.

Sweden has only four nuclear power stations. It is government policy that nuclear power should be abandoned by the year 2010. As a result, Sweden is importing energy from Germany, some of which is sourced from nuclear reactors.

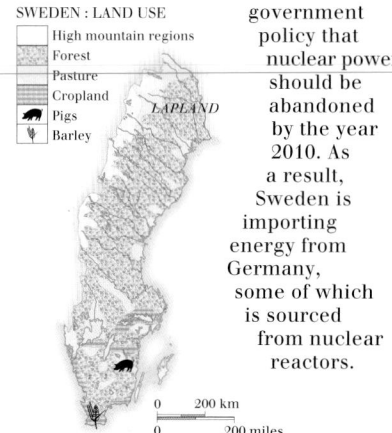

SWEDEN : LAND USE

High mountain regions
Forest
Pasture
Cropland
Pigs
Barley

LAPLAND

0   200 km
0   200 miles

CRIME

 4,716 prisoners

Up 6% in 1990

CRIME RATES

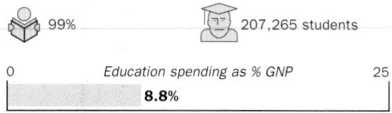

Murders
8 | per 100,000 population

Rapes
19 | per 100,000 population

Thefts
8419 | per 100,000 population

Crime rates are below the European average, although they are the highest among Scandinavian countries. Assault, rape and theft are growing problems, especially in the cities.

EDUCATION

99% | 207,265 students

0   Education spending as % GNP   25
8.8%

THE EDUCATION SYSTEM

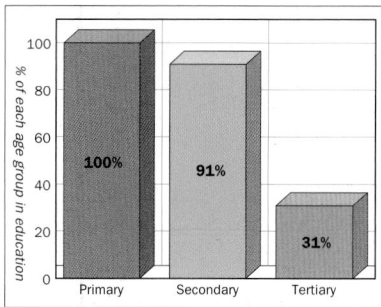

Primary 100% | Secondary 91% | Tertiary 31%

% of each age group in education

Coeducational comprehensive schools are the norm. The higher education system is freely available to most of the population, and many adults return to college to do further courses.

HEALTH

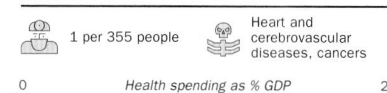 1 per 355 people

Heart and cerebrovascular diseases, cancers

0   Health spending as % GDP   25
8.8%

Sweden's health care system is comprehensive and of a universally high standard. Since 1991, it has been under review in an attempt to cut government spending. Almost 25% of surgical beds have been closed and 30,000 jobs cut. Sweden is now among the lowest spenders on health as a proportion of GNP in the OECD. Reforms in 1994 gave individuals the right to choose their own doctor, and allowed doctors and specialists to set up private practices.

WEALTH

 Sawmill sawyer, 86 kronor per hour; accountant, 21,649 kronor per month

CONSUMER GOODS OWNERSHIP

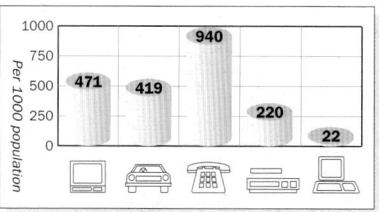

471 | 419 | 940 | 220 | 22

Per 1000 population

Sweden has limited income disparities and Swedish executives are generally paid less than their counterparts in France, Germany and Italy. Social competition and a sense of hierarchy are limited compared to other European states or the USA. Despite some cuts in services, the welfare system still provides some of the best health, unemployment, and pension provision in Europe.

Swedes are keen overseas property buyers, particularly of villas in Italy and the south of France. Net overseas per capita investment remains among the highest in the world.

WORLD RANKING

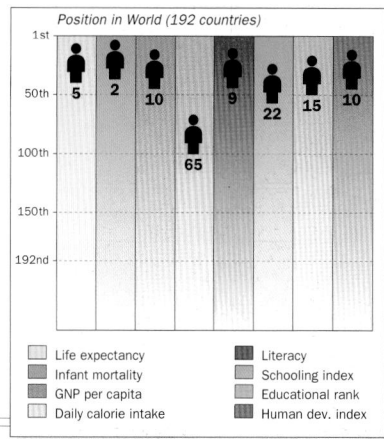

Position in World (192 countries)

5 | 2 | 10 | 65 | 9 | 22 | 15 | 10

Life expectancy | Literacy
Infant mortality | Schooling index
GNP per capita | Educational rank
Daily calorie intake | Human dev. index

SWITZERLAND

EUROPE

OFFICIAL NAME: Swiss Confederation **CAPITAL:** Bern
POPULATION: 7.2 million **CURRENCY:** Swiss franc **OFFICIAL LANGUAGES:** German, French and Italian

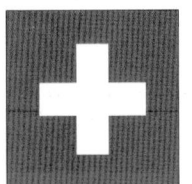

SWITZERLAND LIES AT THE center of western Europe geographically, but outside it politically. Sometimes called Europe's water tower, it is the source of Western Europe's largest rivers: the Po, the Rhine, the Rhône and the Inn-Danube. Switzerland has managed to retain its neutral status through every major European conflict since 1815. It has also built one of the world's most prosperous economies. Whether or not to join the process of greater European political and economic integration is a central issue.

The Eiger in the Berner Oberland. In 1994, a referendum voted to ban all truck transit traffic from the Swiss Alps from 2004.

CLIMATE

WEATHER CHART

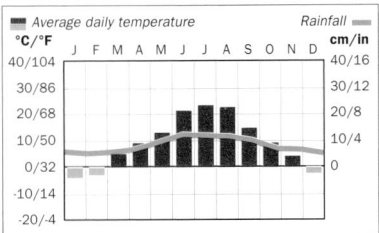

Temperature and weather vary enormously, not only with the seasons, but also because of the huge variations in altitude, and the country's location in the center of Europe. On the plateau north of the Alps, where most of the population live, summers are warm and winters dry, cool and often foggy. South of the Alps, it is considerably warmer and sunnier. Strong southerly winds, or *föhn*, can bring summer-like weather even in winter.

TRANSPORTATION

Kloten, Zürich
12.28m passengers

24 ships
604,800 dwt

THE TRANSPORTATION NETWORK

44,190 miles (71,120 km)	941 miles (1,515 km)
3,236 miles (5,208 km)	751 miles (1,208 km)

Switzerland is a major European freight transit route. Pollution caused by trucks is a major concern. The NEAT project, approved in 1992, will provide two new high-speed rail lines linking Basel and Milan, on which trucks will be carried on trains. Estimates suggest it will cost three times as much to build as the Channel Tunnel.

TOURISM

12.2m visitors

Down 2% in 1994

MAIN OVERSEAS ARRIVALS

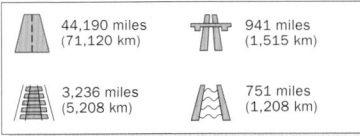

Germany 35%
UK 9%
USA 8%
France 7%
Italy 7%
Other 34%

% of total arrivals

Tourism is Switzerland's third-largest industry. About 350,000 Swiss earn their living from it, and in 1993 tourism accounted for 3% of GNP. The Alps are the main attraction, drawing winter and summer tourists from around the world. However, several factors have led to the recent downturn in the industry. Warmer winters have resulted in a shorter skiing season. The rise in value of the Swiss franc has made Switzerland an expensive destination and Austria is offering tough competition.

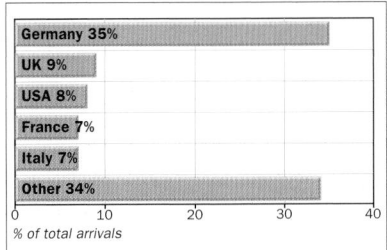

SWITZERLAND

Total Land Area : 39 770 sq. km
(15 355 sq. miles)

POPULATION

- over 100 000
- over 50 000
- over 10 000

LAND HEIGHT

3000m/9843ft
2000m/6562ft
1000m/3281ft
500m/1640ft
200m/656ft

PEOPLE

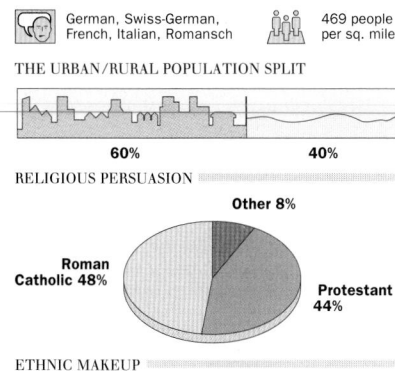

German, Swiss-German, French, Italian, Romansch

469 people per sq. mile

THE URBAN/RURAL POPULATION SPLIT

60%   **40%**

RELIGIOUS PERSUASION

Other 8%

Roman Catholic 48%

Protestant 44%

ETHNIC MAKEUP

Romansch 1%   Other 6%

Italian 10%

French 18%

German 65%

Switzerland is composed of distinct Swiss-Italian, Swiss-French and Swiss-German linguistic groups. About 40,000 in the canton of Grisons speak Romansch. The Swiss-Germans are in the majority. They are a tightly knit community, with a dialect that is impenetrable to most outsiders. In recent years, the three groups have grown further apart. The Swiss-French, in favor of joining the EU, are opposed by the Swiss-Germans. In Ticino, originally an Swiss-Italian canton, a political party has emerged to champion Swiss-Italian interests. There has also been a rise in tension between Swiss and guest workers. The fear that the Swiss are losing jobs to recent immigrants is commonly cited. Swiss society retains strong conservative elements. Two half-cantons granted women the vote at regional level only in 1989 and 1990. Marriage rates are high and divorce less common than in most other European states.

POPULATION AGE BREAKDOWN

% of population by age group	▣ 0–14	▢ 15–64		□ 65+	
65+	10.1%	12.6%	13.8%	15%	16.3%
15–64	65.7%	63.6%	66.5%	68.6%	66.9%
0–14	24.2%	23.8%	19.7%	16.4%	16.8%
	1960	1970	1980	1990	2000

POLITICS

U. House 1995/1999
L. House 1995/1999

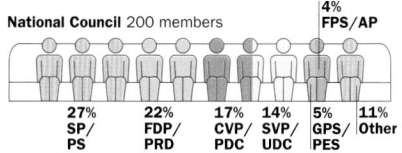
One of 7 Federal Council members annually made president

THE STATE OF THE PARTIES

National Council 200 members

4% FPS/AP

27% SP/ PS	22% FDP/ PRD	17% CVP/ PDC	14% SVP/ UDC	5% GPS/ PES	11% Other

SP/PS = Social Democratic Party **FDP/PRD** = Radical Democratic Party **CVP/PDC** = Christian Democratic People's Party **SVP/UDC** = Swiss People's Party **GPS/PES** = Green Party **FPS/AP** = Freedom Party of Switzerland/Automobile Party

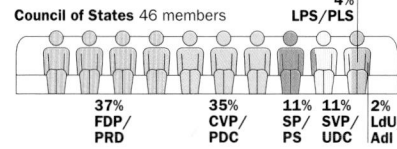

Council of States 46 members

4% LPS/PLS

37% FDP/ PRD	35% CVP/ PDC	11% SP/ PS	11% SVP/ UDC	2% LdU/ AdI

Switzerland is a federal democratic republic with 26 autonomous cantons.

MAIN POLITICAL ISSUES
Hard drugs
Public anxiety has been growing over the rise in narcotics-related crime; Zürich, where most addicts and dealers congregate, has one of the biggest open drugs scenes in Europe. At its center was the *Platsitz*, known as "needle park," which was cleared by police in 1995. To the dismay of civil rights activists, tough new measures limiting the rights of asylum seekers were introduced. The aim was to make it harder for narcotics dealers from eastern Europe to do business in Switzerland.

European integration
Almost all of the country's prominent politicians and business leaders favor joining the EU, but voters remain sharply divided. The Swiss are strongly attached to their decentralized style of government and fear that this would be lost within the EU. There are also fears that in a barrier-free Europe, Switzerland's high standards of living would fall because of a large influx of immigrants.

PROFILE
The same four-party coalition has been in power in Switzerland since 1959. This explains the consistency of the country's domestic and foreign policies and the slow rate of political change. Politics has recently become more contentious, however, with voting patterns becoming more polarized. Divisive issues are those of drug abuse and membership of the EU. Both right-wing and green minority parties have recently gained more seats in parliament.

Switzerland's political system is unique in Europe. Important decisions are all made on the results of referenda. A petition of more than 100,000 signatures can also force a referendum on any issue.

WORLD AFFAIRS

| CE | G10 | OECD | OSCE | UN |

The basis of Switzerland's foreign policy remains its neutrality. Geneva has retained its position as a center for many international organizations. The UN has its European headquarters there, and it is also home to the International Red Cross. The city is often chosen as a site for diplomatic negotiations: the Camp David accords, START nuclear reduction treaties and attempts to resolve the conflict in former Yugoslavia were all negotiated in Geneva.

Switzerland has chosen not to join the process for closer European integration. It turned down membership of the EEA and voted at referendum in 1992 against joining the EU. Many believe, however, that the economic case for joining the union will become overwhelming now that Switzerland's EFTA partners – Austria and the Scandinavian states – have become members. Opponents of integration argue that Switzerland's seeming isolation will enhance its role as an international tax haven.

Jean-Pascal Delamuraz, of the FDP/PRD, president of Switzerland for 1996.

Kaspar Villiger, of the FDP/PRD, was president in 1995.

CHRONOLOGY
The autonomy of the Swiss cantons was curtailed by the Habsburg Empire in the 11th century. In 1291, the three cantons of Unterwalden, Schwyz and Uri set up the Perpetual League to pursue Swiss liberty. Joined by other cantons, they succeeded in 1499 in gaining virtual independence. The Habsburgs retained a titular role.

❑ **1648** Peace of Westphalia ending 30 Years' War, in which Switzerland played no active part, recognizes full Swiss independence.
❑ **1798** Invaded by French.
❑ **1815** Congress of Vienna after Napoleon's defeat confirms Swiss independence and establishes its neutrality. Geneva and Valais join Swiss Confederation. ⇨

S

AID

 $793m   Up 30% in 1993

Switzerland ranks fairly high among developed countries as an aid donor, with total disbursements amounting to 0.5% of the country's GDP in 1992. However, a large part, some 40%, of its aid is conditional on the recipients buying Swiss goods and services.

DEFENSE

 $5.2bn   Up 20% in 1995

0   Defense spending as % GDP   40
1.7%

SWISS ARMED FORCES

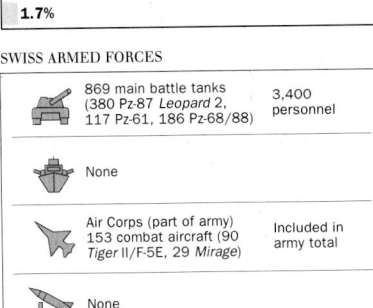

- 869 main battle tanks (380 Pz-87 *Leopard 2*, 117 Pz-61, 186 Pz-68/88)   3,400 personnel
- None
- Air Corps (part of army) 153 combat aircraft (90 *Tiger* II/F-5E, 29 *Mirage*)   Included in army total
- None

Switzerland has one of the largest reserve forces in Europe. Military service and further training at intervals is compulsory for males, up to 50. The army is organized so 400,000 reserves can be called up and armed in a few hours. The army still uses skis, bicycles and horses to protect the Alps. Bridges and tunnels are mined with explosives in accordance with a defense strategy drafted earlier this century. However, as in the rest of Europe, numbers are being cut in response to the end of the Cold War. In 1995, parliament approved legislation allowing civilian service in place of military service. Switzerland is also considering allowing its troops to join UN peacekeeping operations.

ECONOMICS

 $265bn    1.15–1.31 Swiss francs

SCORE CARD

- WORLD GNP RANKING..........................18th
- GNP PER CAPITA $37,180
- BALANCE OF PAYMENTS....................$18.5bn
- INFLATION 2%
- UNEMPLOYMENT..................................3.8%

EXPORTS
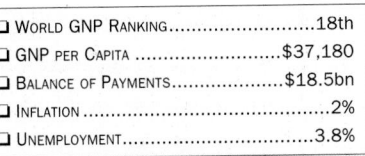
UK 7% | Italy 8% | France 9% | USA 9% | Germany 23% | Other 44%

IMPORTS
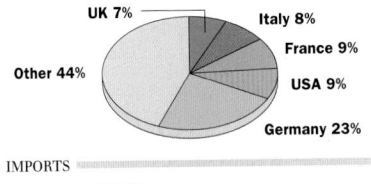
UK 7% | USA 6% | Italy 10% | France 11% | Germany 33% | Other 33%

STRENGTHS
Highly skilled work force. Reliable provider of services; key to strength of banking sector. Strong machine tools and precision engineering. Powerful chemical, pharmaceutical and banking multinationals; banking secrecy laws attract foreign capital. Ability to innovate to capture mass markets, typified by Swatch watch and proposed Swatch car.

WEAKNESSES
Protected cartels result in many over-priced goods. Highly subsidized agricultural sector. Withholding tax at 35% on income earned in Switzerland by non-residents stifles direct foreign investment in business.

PROFILE
The Swiss economy is widely diversified, with 61% of GDP coming

ECONOMIC PERFORMANCE INDICATOR
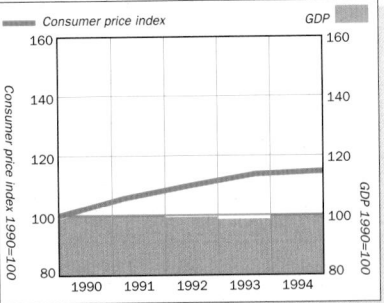

from services and 26% from industry. The country has an outsized banking sector, thanks to its outstanding success in attracting capital for investment. Almost half of the world's investment capital placed outside the investor's own country is in Switzerland. It is also home to some large multinational enterprises.

SWITZERLAND : MAJOR BUSINESSES
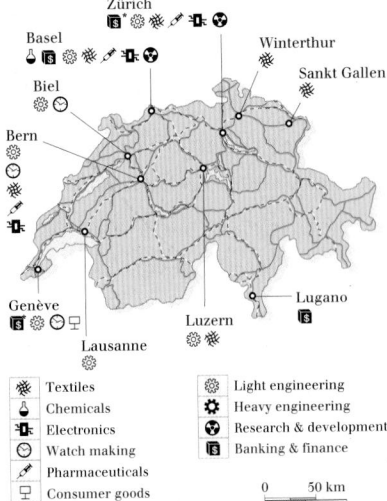

RESOURCES

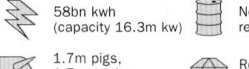

58bn kwh (capacity 16.3m kw)

Not an oil producer; refines 132,000 b/cd

1.7m pigs, 1.7m cattle, 425,000 sheep

Rock salt, marble, gypsum

ELECTRICITY GENERATION

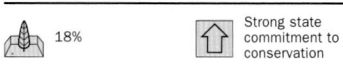

Hydro 57% (34bn kwh)

Thermal 3% (1bn kwh)

Nuclear 40% (23bn kwh)

Other 0%

% of total generation by type

Switzerland is poor in natural resources, having no valuable minerals in commercially exploitable quantities. Over half of its electricity comes from hydropower, while five nuclear plants supply most of the rest. This allows spending on imported oil and coal to be kept to a minimum – they account for less than 4% of the total import bill. The Chernobyl' accident inspired large-scale anti-nuclear-power demonstrations and a sixth plant was canceled. However, a referendum approved continued use of existing plants.

SWITZERLAND : LAND USE

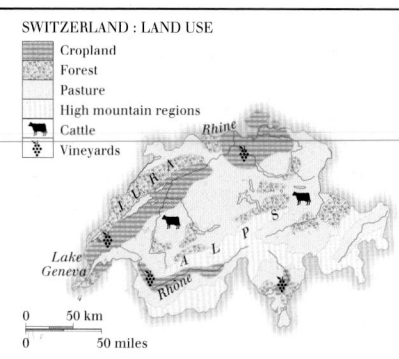

Cropland
Forest
Pasture
High mountain regions
Cattle
Vineyards

0   50 km
0   50 miles

ENVIRONMENT

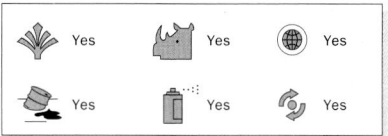

18%

Strong state commitment to conservation

ENVIRONMENTAL TREATIES

Yes   Yes   Yes

Yes   Yes   Yes

The Swiss are among the most environmentally conscious people in the world and are willing to back their convictions with money: the Basle–Milan tunnel plan was approved at referendum, despite the estimated $13.3bn cost. The planners aim to achieve a total ban on truck transit traffic by 2004, although some argue that a ban will not be necessary as trucks traveling on trains will cut two hours off the Basle–Milan journey. The Swiss are keen recyclers – in some cantons there is a tax on refuse sacks to encourage people to recycle as much as possible.

MEDIA

 Freedom of expression is guaranteed

PUBLISHING AND BROADCAST MEDIA

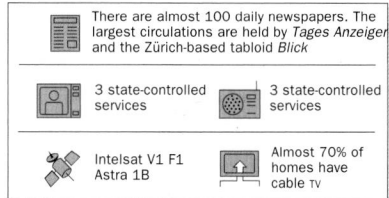

There are almost 100 daily newspapers. The largest circulations are held by *Tages Anzeiger* and the Zürich-based tabloid *Blick*

3 state-controlled services

3 state-controlled services

Intelsat V1 F1 Astra 1B

Almost 70% of homes have cable TV

The Swiss media are broadly organized along regional lines and reflect the country's linguistic divisions. The state-owned German, French and Italian language TV and radio stations tend to focus on the interests of their specific communities. German, Italian and French satellite TV are widely available. Few newspapers have national coverage. *Tribune de Genève* and *Neue Zürcher Zeitung* are the exceptions.

CRIME

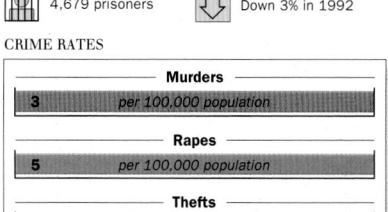

4,679 prisoners   Down 3% in 1992

CRIME RATES

Murders
3   *per 100,000 population*

Rapes
5   *per 100,000 population*

Thefts
4527   *per 100,000 population*

Crime rates are low by international standards. Reported crime fell in 1993 and 1994, although the long-term trends show muggings and burglaries on the increase. Much of the growth is narcotics related.

EDUCATION

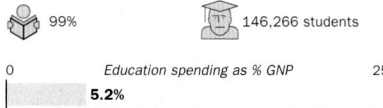

99%   146,266 students

0   *Education spending as % GNP*   25
5.2%

THE EDUCATION SYSTEM

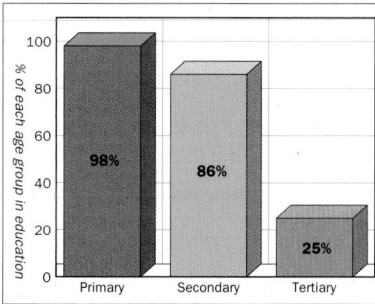

% of each age group in education

98%   86%   25%

Primary   Secondary   Tertiary

Most students after the age of 16 are encouraged to take up vocational studies. Training is thorough and is usually combined with three or four years' apprenticeship in the student's chosen field. The higher education institutions have the funds to attract top European academics. Zürich's Federal Technological Institute has gained an international reputation for its computer programming research.

HEALTH

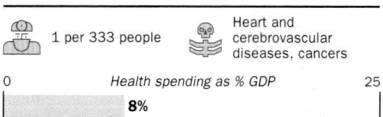

1 per 333 people

Heart and cerebrovascular diseases, cancers

0   *Health spending as % GDP*   25
8%

The health system is among the most efficient and pioneering in the world. Health costs are covered by compulsory insurance schemes.

WEALTH

Chambermaid, 2,875 Swiss francs ($2,498) per month; top chef, 12,000 Swiss francs ($10,428) per month

CONSUMER GOODS OWNERSHIP

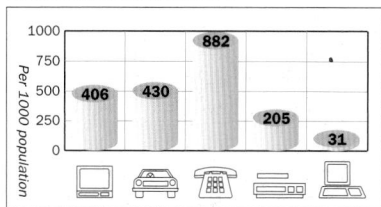

Per 1000 population

406   430   882   205   31

Switzerland is the world's wealthiest country – its per capita income is more than $37,000. Wages are relatively high although the cost of living is also well above the European average. Many workers choose to live in France and commute across the border. The land market is highly regulated.

S

WORLD RANKING

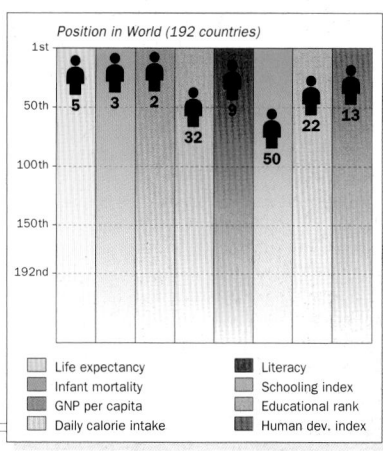

Position in World (192 countries)

1st   50th   100th   150th   192nd

5   3   2   32   9   50   22   13

Life expectancy   Literacy
Infant mortality   Schooling index
GNP per capita   Educational rank
Daily calorie intake   Human dev. index

SYRIA

OFFICIAL NAME: Syrian Arab Republic   **CAPITAL:** Damascus
POPULATION: 14.7 million   **CURRENCY:** Syrian pound   **OFFICIAL LANGUAGE:** Arabic

S YRIA SHARES BORDERS with Lebanon, Israel, Jordan, Iraq and Turkey. Many Syrians regard their country as an artificial creation of French colonial rule, which lasted from 1920 to 1946. They identify instead with a Greater Syria encompassing Lebanon, Jordan and Palestine. Since independence, Syria's foreign relations have been turbulent, although President Assad's authoritarian Ba'athist regime has brought a measure of internal stability.

MIDDLE EAST

CLIMATE

WEATHER CHART

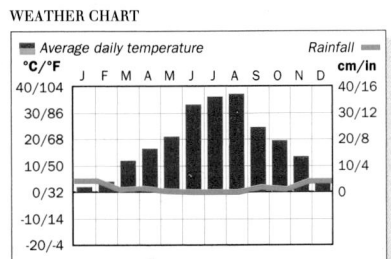

The coastal climate is Mediterranean, with mild, wet winters and dry, hot summers. Away from the coast, the country is increasingly arid, with some desert areas. In the mountains, snow is common in winter. Most of the country receives less than 10 inches of rainfall a year and, away from the coast, rainfall is very unpredictable.

TOURISM

 718,000 visitors   Up 2% in 1994

MAIN OVERSEAS ARRIVALS

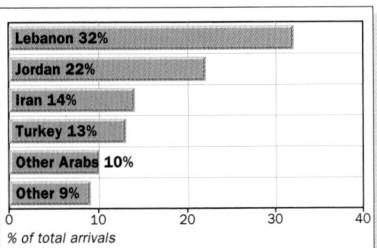

Lebanon 32%	
Jordan 22%	
Iran 14%	
Turkey 13%	
Other Arabs 10%	
Other 9%	

% of total arrivals

Years of political turbulence, allegations of human rights abuses committed by the Assad government and strict, complex, travel regulations retarded the development of tourism. However, just before the 1990–1991 Gulf War, Syria began to compete in popularity as a vacation destination with other Middle Eastern states. Modern hotels were built in most main cities and facilities improved to cater for growing numbers of Western visitors. Following the war, tourist numbers dropped sharply, but

TRANSPORTATION

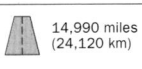 **Damascus International** 1.5m passengers    94 ships 231,000 dwt

THE TRANSPORTATION NETWORK

14,990 miles (24,120 km)	442 miles (712 km)
1,192 miles (1,918 km)	418 miles (672 km)

The road network is adequate in the cities, but unreliable in rural areas, especially during the winter wet season. State-run and privately owned bus services operate from Damascus and Aleppo to most towns. Roads are integrated with the railroads, which carry over four million passengers a year and are vital to freight transportation. Damascus is the main international airport and Latakia the main port.

they are now gradually recovering. Syria's main attractions are the antiquities of Damascus – the oldest inhabited city in the world – and Aleppo and Palmyra, with their covered markets (*soukhs*), mosques and baths. Syria has a wealth of castles dating back to the Crusades and sites associated with the advent of Islam. In addition, there are as many as 3,500 as yet unexcavated archaeological sites. Syria's Mediterranean coastline has fine beaches, and there are mountain resorts in Latakia.

The ancient city of Palmyra, in Syria's central region, possesses some of the Middle East's finest Classical monuments.

PEOPLE

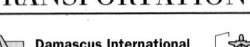 Arabic, French, Kurdish, Armenian, Circassian, Turkmen, Assyrian, Aramaic   207 people per sq. mile

THE URBAN/RURAL POPULATION SPLIT

51%   49%

RELIGIOUS PERSUASION

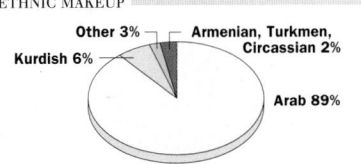

Christian 10%
Other Muslim 16%
Sunni Muslim 74%

ETHNIC MAKEUP

Other 3%   Armenian, Turkmen, Circassian 2%
Kurdish 6%
Arab 89%

Most Syrians live within 60 miles of the coast, where the largest cities are sited. About 90% are Muslim. They include the politically dominant Alawis, based in Latakia and Tartous provinces. There is also a sizeable Christian minority. In the west and north a mosaic of groups exists, including Kurds, Turkish-speaking communities and Armenians, the latter based in cities. Damascus, Al Qamishli and Aleppo have small Jewish communities, and there are three villages where Aramaic is spoken. In addition, some 300,000 Palestinian refugees have settled in Syria. Minorities were initially attracted to the ruling Ba'ath Party because of its emphasis on the state over sectarian interests. However, disputes between factions led to the Shi'a Muslim Alawis taking control, fostering resentment among the Sunni Muslim majority.

The emancipation of women, promoted by the Ba'ath regime in the late 1960s, has been carried forward under President Assad. His first woman cabinet minister was appointed in 1976.

POPULATION AGE BREAKDOWN

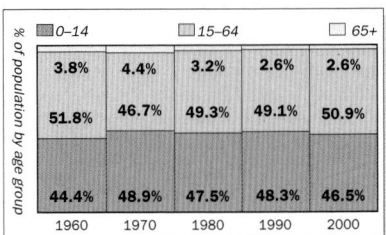

% of population by age group	0–14	15–64	65+		
65+	3.8%	4.4%	3.2%	2.6%	2.6%
15–64	51.8%	46.7%	49.3%	49.1%	50.9%
0–14	44.4%	48.9%	47.5%	48.3%	46.5%
	1960	1970	1980	1990	2000

S

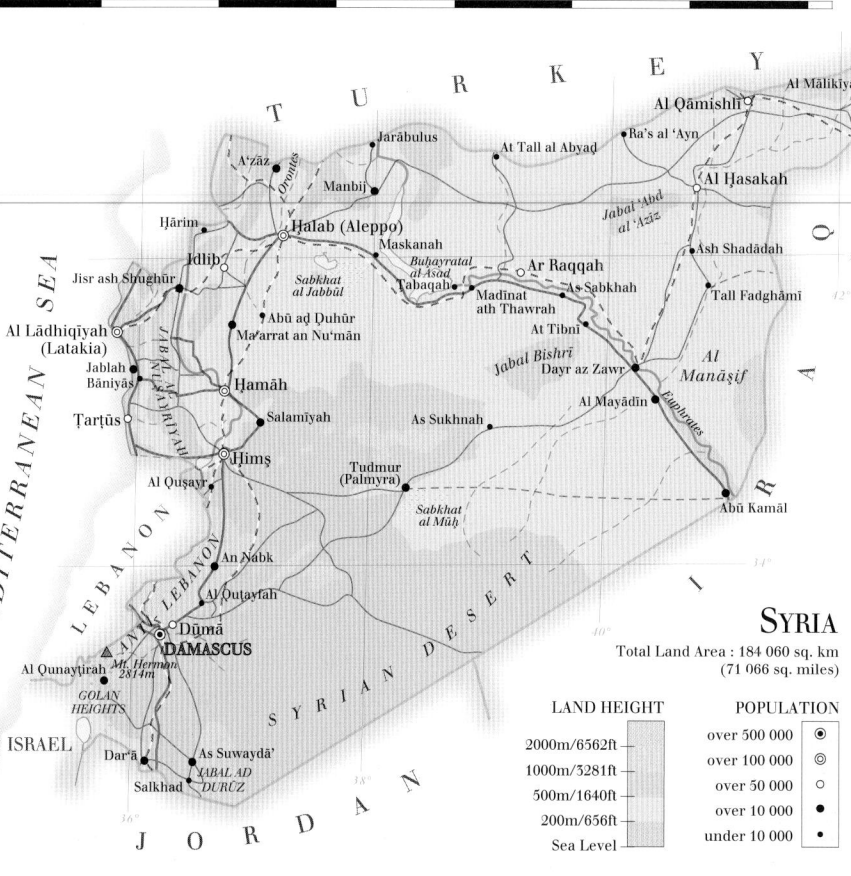

SYRIA

Total Land Area : 184 060 sq. km
(71 066 sq. miles)

LAND HEIGHT		POPULATION	
2000m/6562ft		over 500 000	◉
1000m/3281ft		over 100 000	◎
500m/1640ft		over 50 000	○
200m/656ft		over 10 000	●
Sea Level		under 10 000	·

WORLD AFFAIRS

AL	Damas	G24	NAM	OIC

Following Egypt's 1979 accord with Israel, Syria sees itself as the major barrier to Israel's regional dominance. Syria has extended its influence over Lebanon (where it has achieved a high degree of control) and radical Palestinian factions as well as seeking alliances with North African states. The biggest single issue between Syria and Israel remains the occupation of the strategically vital Golan Heights, seized by Israel during the Six Day War in 1967. Peace negotiations with Israel have made little concrete progress on the central issue of security arrangements in the event of an Israeli withdrawal from the Golan. Syria faced international isolation in the 1980s because of the Assad government's alleged backing of terrorists. It regained a measure of respect in 1990 by securing the release of Western hostages in Lebanon from Shi'a militants. Assad followed up this diplomatic triumph by backing the Western allies in the 1990–1991 Gulf War, contributing troops to liberate Kuwait from Iraqi forces. Syria's involvement in the Gulf War was vital in legitimizing the action in the eyes of the Arab world. Syria has now emerged as a major ally of the West in containing Iraqi expansionism.

AID

 $168m (receipts)   Up 3% in 1993

Syria has historically received little aid owing to its human rights record and substantial oil income. However, one-off payments totaling $2 billion in 1992 and $1.2 billion in 1993 were received after the Gulf War, mainly from Saudi Arabia and the Gulf states, but with contributions from the West and Japan.

President Assad, *who was elected for a fourth term of office in 1992.*

Mahmoud az-Zoubi, *who became prime minister of Syria in 1990.*

POLITICS

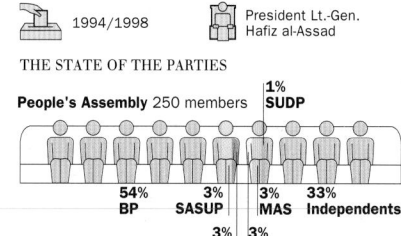

1994/1998

President Lt.-Gen. Hafiz al-Assad

THE STATE OF THE PARTIES

People's Assembly 250 members
1% SUDP

54% BP   3% SASUP   3% ASUP   3% CPSP   3% MAS   33% Independents

BP = Ba'ath Party   **CPSP** = Communist Party of Syria
SASUP = Syrian Arab Socialist Union Party   **ASUP** = Arab Socialist Unionist Party   **MAS** = Movement of Arab Socialists
SUDP = Socialist Unionist Democratic Party

Syria is, in practice, a single-party, national socialist state. Its military-backed leader since 1971 has been President Assad, a lifelong Ba'ath Party militant, dedicated to its campaign for Arab revival.

MAIN POLITICAL ISSUES
Human rights
The regime has improved its human rights record in recent years. Many political prisoners have been released and in 1994 all members of the Jewish minority were granted exit visas to travel abroad. The regime is alleged to maintain links with a number of international terrorist groups including the Palestinian Islamic militants *Hamas*.

Political pluralism
President Assad remains the dominant political figure and he and his military-backed regime, drawn mainly from the Shi'a Alawi grouping, keep a tight hold on power. Under international pressure, Assad has made promises to permit more political parties, but they remain unfulfilled. Assad was sworn in for another seven-year term in 1992.

PROFILE
The Ba'athist military swept to power in 1963 with a vision of uniting all Arab nations under one Syrian-dominated socialist system. The coup ended the power of city elites and promoted citizens from rural areas. The state became the main employer.

When Assad came to power in 1971, he consolidated the Ba'ath Party as the major political force. Unrest among Islamic militants was crushed, and Assad focused on foreign affairs in a bid to make Syria a major power.

Syria initially found a Ba'athist ally in Iraq, and the two countries embarked on a plan for union in 1978. Relations soon foundered amid mutual charges over interference in each other's internal affairs – to the extent that, alone among Arab nations, Syria backed Iran in the Iran–Iraq War.

CHRONOLOGY

Complete independence from France was achieved in 1946. From 1958–1961, Syria merged with Egypt to form the United Arab Republic.

❑ **1963** Ba'athist military junta, the National Council of the Revolutionary Command, seizes power. Maj.-Gen. Amin al-Hafiz president.

❑ **1966** Hafiz is ousted by military coup supported by radical Ba'ath Party members.

❑ **1967** Israel overruns Syrian positions above Lake Tiberias, seizes Golan Heights and occupies Quneitra. Syria boycotts Arab Summit and rejects compromise with Israel.

❑ **1970** Hafiz al-Assad seizes power in "corrective coup."

❑ **1971** Assad elected president for seven-year term.

❑ **1973** New constitution approved by plebiscite confirming Ba'ath Party as dominant force. War launched with Egypt against Israel to regain territory lost in 1967. Further territory lost to Israel.

❑ **1976** Syria intervenes militarily to quell fighting in Lebanon with a peacekeeping mandate from the Arab League.

❑ **1977** Relations broken off with Egypt after President Sadat's visit to Jerusalem.

❑ **1978** National charter signed with Iraq for union. President Assad returned for second term.

❑ **1980** Membership of Muslim Brotherhood made capital offense. Treaty of Friendship with USSR.

❑ **1981** Israel formally annexes Golan Heights. Charter with Iraq collapses.

❑ **1982** Islamic extremist uprising in Hama crushed; thousands killed. Israel invades Lebanon; Syrian missiles in Bekaa Valley destroyed.

❑ **1985** Assad reelected president. USA claims Syrian links to airport bombings at Rome and Vienna.

❑ **1986** Syrian complicity alleged in planting of bomb aboard Israeli airliner in London. EU, except for Greece, imposes sanctions.

❑ **1989** Diplomatic relations re-established with Egypt.

❑ **1990** Troops take part in Operation Desert Storm to liberate Kuwait from Iraqi forces. UK restores diplomatic relations after Syrian help in freeing Western hostages in Lebanon.

❑ **1991** Damascus Declaration aid and defense pact signed with Egypt, Saudi Arabia, Kuwait, the UAE, Qatar, Bahrain and Oman.

❑ **1992** Assad reelected president.

DEFENSE

💲 $2.6bn   ⬆ Up 7% in 1995

Defense spending as % GDP
0 — 40
8.6%

Having fought four wars against Israel since 1948, Syria is the Arab world's strongest military power after Egypt. There is no political mechanism to challenge the dominance of the military. With more than 400,000 troops and nearly 50% of government income spent on weapons, Syria is a formidable power. The military is mostly equipped with weapons obtained from the former Soviet Union.

During the 1980s, Syrian forces fought off a series of Israeli

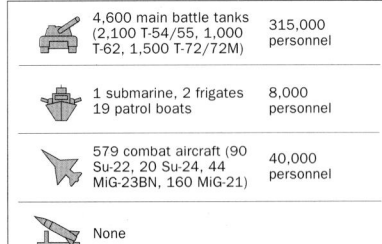

SYRIAN ARMED FORCES

🛡	4,600 main battle tanks (2,100 T-54/55, 1,000 T-62, 1,500 T-72/72M)	315,000 personnel
🚢	1 submarine, 2 frigates 19 patrol boats	8,000 personnel
✈	579 combat aircraft (90 Su-22, 20 Su-24, 44 MiG-23BN, 160 MiG-21)	40,000 personnel
	None	

encroachments in the region, and also foiled Israeli attempts to control Lebanon. Syria remains the power Israel fears most.

ECONOMICS

📊 $15.8bn   💱 22.72–41.90 Syrian pounds

SCORE CARD

❑ WORLD GNP RANKING..........................69th
❑ GNP PER CAPITA $1,218
❑ BALANCE OF PAYMENTS....................$–636m
❑ INFLATION 9.2%
❑ UNEMPLOYMENT....................................7.5%

EXPORTS

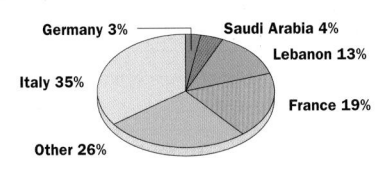

Germany 3%   Saudi Arabia 4%
Lebanon 13%
Italy 35%   France 19%
Other 26%

IMPORTS

France 6%   USA 6%
Italy 8%
Germany 10%
Other 60%
Japan 10%

ECONOMIC PERFORMANCE INDICATOR

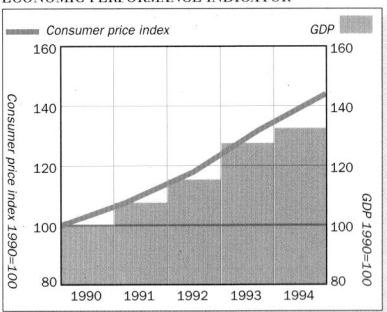

Consumer price index   GDP
(chart, 1990–1994, Consumer price index 1990=100, GDP 1990=100)

STRENGTHS

Exporter of crude oil – production increasing as a result of new oil strikes. Manufacturing base has grown. Thriving agricultural sector.

WEAKNESSES

High defense spending is a major drain on economy. Large black market. High inflation. Economy dominated by inefficient state-run companies. Autocratic regime deters foreign investment. High population growth.

PROFILE

Billions of dollars flowed into the Syrian economy from the USA, Japan, the EU, Saudi Arabia and other Gulf states following the 1990–1991 Gulf War. This cash injection, along with increased oil revenue, led to rapid growth. Also, a decision to divert water from the River Euphrates toward fertile plains, rather than using it to irrigate poorer land, led to a rise in agricultural output. However, long-term economic prospects remain uncertain. The large public sector, which employs 20% of the work force, makes little contribution to the economy. State controls have inhibited private enterprise and investment and created a booming black market. Turkey's plans to draw water from the Euphrates threaten farming in Syria.

SYRIA : MAJOR BUSINESSES

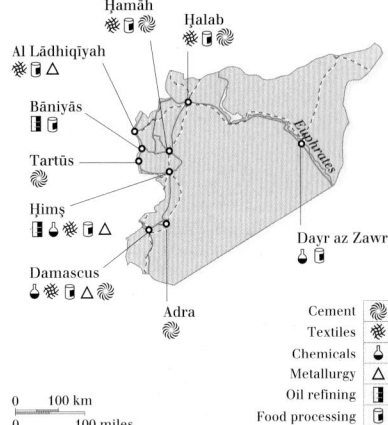

Ḥamāh
Ḥalab
Al Lādhiqīyah
Bāniyās
Tartūs
Ḥimṣ
Dayr az Zawr
Damascus
Adra

Cement
Textiles
Chemicals
Metallurgy
Oil refining
Food processing

0   100 km
0   100 miles

RESOURCES

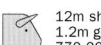

13bn kwh
(capacity 3.7m kw)

516,287 b/d
(reserves
1,700,000,000 bbl)

12m sheep,
1.2m goats,
770,000 cattle

Phosphate,
oil, natural gas,
iron ore

ELECTRICITY GENERATION

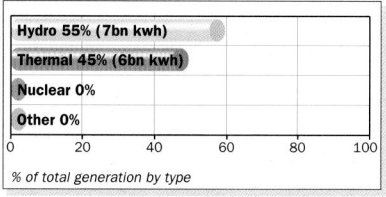

Hydro 55% (7bn kwh)

Thermal 45% (6bn kwh)

Nuclear 0%

Other 0%

0   20   40   60   80   100

% of total generation by type

Syria has large supplies of oil, mostly good quality light crude, which was discovered along the Euphrates in the 1980s. Gas was found in substantial quantities near Palmyra. Syria's other important minerals are phosphates and iron ore. Hydroelectric power satisfies most energy requirements. The manufacturing base is largely made up of oil-derived industries, including plastics and chemicals, textiles and food products. Cotton is the main cash crop, but fruit and vegetables are also grown. Livestock, especially sheep and goats, supports the rural economy.

SYRIA : LAND USE

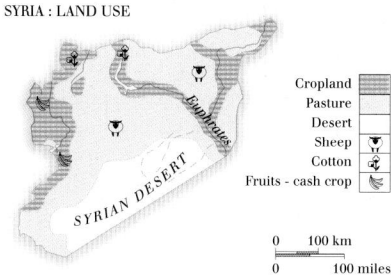

Cropland
Pasture
Desert
Sheep
Cotton
Fruits - cash crop

0   100 km
0   100 miles

ENVIRONMENT

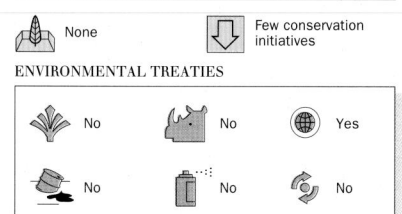

None

Few conservation initiatives

ENVIRONMENTAL TREATIES

No   No   Yes

No   No   No

The Assad regime's most expensive and controversial environmental project has been the Euphrates Dam, power station and irrigation network at Tabaqah. The dam's vast man-made reservoir, Lake Buhayratal al Asad, engulfed some 300 villages and destroyed 62,000 acres of fertile farmland. Syria's industrial program has on occasion damaged the environment. A giant cement factory, built by the East Germans at Tartus in the mid-1970s, has been held responsible for polluting a valuable stretch of Mediterranean coastline.

MEDIA

  The media is under strict government control

Virtually all daily newspapers, which include the English language *Syria Times*, are state-owned or have government affiliations. Radio and TV, the news agency SANA, press distribution and advertising companies are also controlled by the regime. There is no freedom of information.

CRIME

  Syria does not publish prison figures   Down 1% in 1992

CRIME RATES

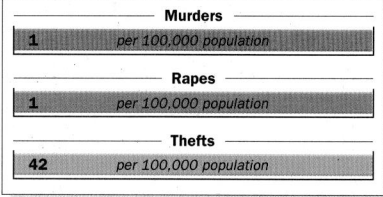

Murders
1   per 100,000 population

Rapes
1   per 100,000 population

Thefts
42   per 100,000 population

There is no truly independent judiciary. The powerful security services exercise arbitrary powers of arrest and detention. There are widespread reports of torture in custody. Most politicians overthrown by President Assad in the 1970s have recently been released from prison in Damascus.

EDUCATION

71%   194,371 students

0   Education spending as % GNP   25
4.2%

THE EDUCATION SYSTEM

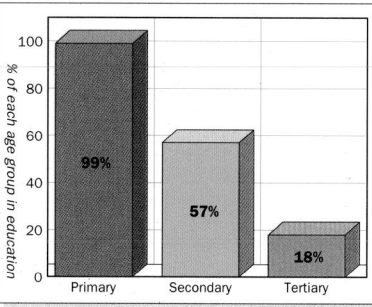

% of each age group in education

100
80
60
40
20
0

99%   Primary
57%   Secondary
18%   Tertiary

A free and compulsory system of elementary education for all was a priority of the Ba'ath Party when it came to power. Under Assad, co-education for boys and girls began in the cities and spread to rural areas. Higher education is provided by seven universities, notably at Damascus, Aleppo, Tishrin and Ḥimṣ. There are over 130,000 university students. Education ranks second – though by a considerable margin – to defense in government expenditure.

MEDIA

PUBLISHING AND BROADCAST MEDIA

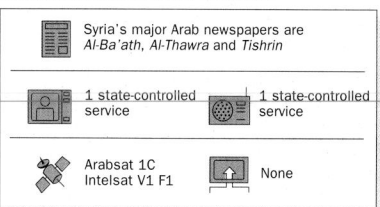

Syria's major Arab newspapers are *Al-Ba'ath*, *Al-Thawra* and *Tishrin*

1 state-controlled service   1 state-controlled service

Arabsat 1C
Intelsat V1 F1   None

HEALTH

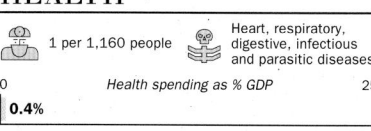

1 per 1,160 people   Heart, respiratory, digestive, infectious and parasitic diseases

0   Health spending as % GDP   25
0.4%

An adequate system of primary health care has been set up since the Ba'ath Party came to power. Treatment is free for those unable to pay. However, hospitals often lack modern equipment and medical services are in need of further investment.

WEALTH

  Very large gap between rich and poor

CONSUMER GOODS OWNERSHIP

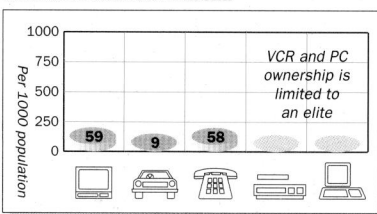

1000
750
500
250
0

Per 1000 population

VCR and PC ownership is limited to an elite

59   9   58

Syria is far from the equitable society that early Ba'ath Party thinkers envisioned. The gulf between rich and poor is widening. Syria's political elite, many of whom live in the West Malki suburb of Damascus, is more numerous and richer than ever before. Palestinian refugees and the urban unemployed make up the poorest groups.

S

WORLD RANKING

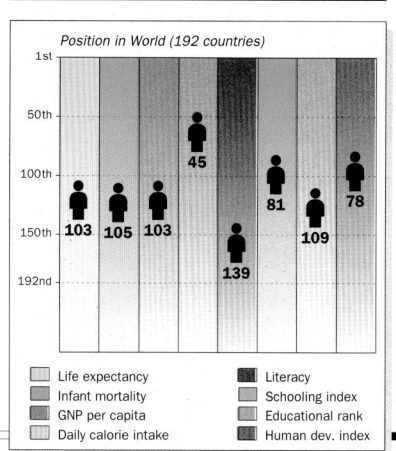

Position in World (192 countries)

1st
50th
100th
150th
192nd

103   105   103   45   81   109   78   139

Life expectancy   Literacy
Infant mortality   Schooling index
GNP per capita   Educational rank
Daily calorie intake   Human dev. index

TAIWAN

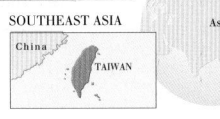

OFFICIAL NAME: Republic of China (Taiwan)   **CAPITAL:** Taipei
POPULATION: 20.9 million   **CURRENCY:** New Taiwan dollar   **OFFICIAL LANGUAGE:** Northern Chinese (Mandarin)

THE ISLAND REPUBLIC of Taiwan lies 80 miles off the southeast coast of mainland China. Formerly known as Formosa, the Republic of China was established in 1949 by Chiang Kai-Shek's Kuomintang (KMT), expelled from government in Beijing (then Peking) by the communists under Mao. Beijing still considers Taiwan a renegade province and Chinese claims of sovereignty are officially accepted by all but a few countries. Taiwan is dominated by a mountain region which runs north to south and covers two-thirds of the island. The lowlands are highly fertile, cultivated mostly with rice, and densely populated. In 1986, Taiwan adopted democracy in place of *de facto* military rule. The KMT has been in power since 1949.

Wen Wu Temple, on the shores of Sun Moon Lake in the mountains of central Taiwan – a region famous for its many temples.

CLIMATE

WEATHER CHART

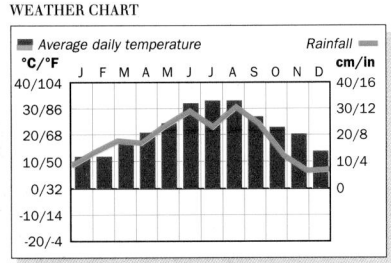

Taiwan has a tropical monsoon climate similar to that of the southern Chinese mainland. Typhoons from the South China Sea between July and September bring the heaviest rains.

TRANSPORTATION

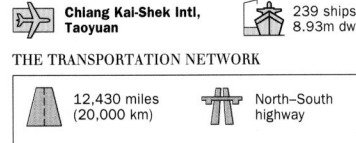

Chiang Kai-Shek Intl, Taoyuan

239 ships 8.93m dwt

THE TRANSPORTATION NETWORK

12,430 miles (20,000 km)	North–South highway
2,858 miles (4,600 km)	None

Taiwan is implementing several major new transportation infrastructure projects as part of the latest six-year economic plan. Metro and rapid transit systems are being built in Taipei and Kao-hsiung. Several new roads are planned, including north–south and east–west cross-island highways. The plan is motivated by the fear that congestion will restrain future growth. Most urban Taiwanese currently ride motor scooters, but transportation planners anticipate a sharp increase in car ownership over the next decade. The bicycle is not as popular in Taiwan as in mainland China. However, Taiwan is the world's biggest bicycle producer, exporting mostly to Europe and the USA.

TOURISM

2.1m visitors   Up 15% in 1994

MAIN OVERSEAS ARRIVALS

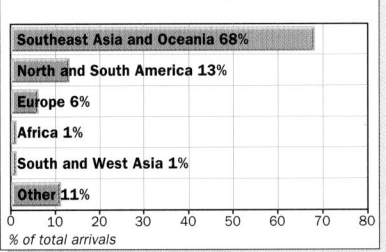

Southeast Asia and Oceania 68%	
North and South America 13%	
Europe 6%	
Africa 1%	
South and West Asia 1%	
Other 11%	

% of total arrivals

Taiwan is not a major tourist destination and has only recently begun to target tourists in the USA and Japan. As part of the most recent Six-Year Plan, hotels are being upgraded and tourist facilities at international airports are being improved. The major attraction is the Palace Museum in Taipei, which includes the massive treasure looted by the Nationalists from Beijing. Only 5% can be shown at any one time. Sex tourism is an important business in Taipei, which is second only to Bangkok. Sex establishments masquerade as barbers' shops.

PEOPLE

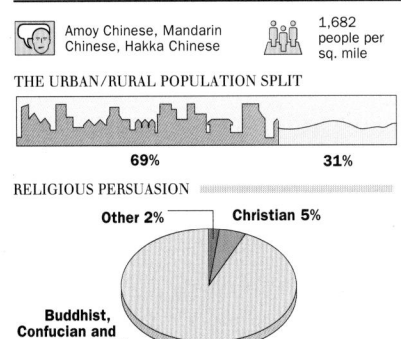

Amoy Chinese, Mandarin Chinese, Hakka Chinese

1,682 people per sq. mile

THE URBAN/RURAL POPULATION SPLIT

69%   31%

RELIGIOUS PERSUASION

Other 2%   Christian 5%
Buddhist, Confucian and Taoist 93%

ETHNIC MAKEUP

Aborigine 2%   Mainland Chinese 14%
Indigenous Chinese 84%

Most Taiwanese are Han Chinese, descendants of the 1644 migration of the Ming dynasty from mainland China. The 100,000 Nationalists who arrived in 1949 established themselves as a ruling class and monopolized the most prestigious jobs in the civil service.

This led to resentment from the local inhabitants, but as the generation elected on the mainland in 1947 have aged, so local Taiwanese have entered the political process.

There is little ethnic tension in Taiwan, although the indigenous minorities who live in the eastern hills do suffer considerable discrimination.

As in the rest of Southeast Asia, the extended family is still important and provides a social security net for the elderly. However, the trend is towards European-style nuclear families, a result partly of housing shortages. Women are not well represented in the political process, but are prominent in business and the civil service.

POPULATION AGE BREAKDOWN

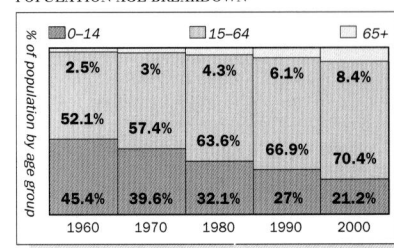

	1960	1970	1980	1990	2000
65+	2.5%	3%	4.3%	6.1%	8.4%
15–64	52.1%	57.4%	63.6%	66.9%	70.4%
0–14	45.4%	39.6%	32.1%	27%	21.2%

POLITICS

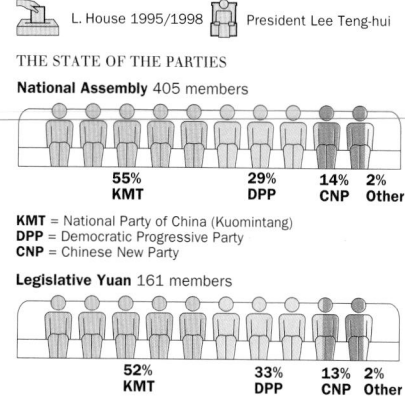

L. House 1995/1998   President Lee Teng-hui

THE STATE OF THE PARTIES

National Assembly 405 members

| 55% KMT | 29% DPP | 14% CNP | 2% Other |

KMT = National Party of China (Kuomintang)
DPP = Democratic Progressive Party
CNP = Chinese New Party

Legislative Yuan 161 members

| 52% KMT | 33% DPP | 13% CNP | 2% Other |

Until 1986, Taiwan was effectively a one-party state. Today, it is a fully functioning multiparty democracy.

MAIN POLITICAL ISSUES
Relations with China

Relations with China have a significant influence on domestic politics. The main opposition DPP claims independence from China but the ruling KMT favors eventual reunification if China changes dramatically and agrees to parity in terms of democracy, economic development and prosperity. The New Party advocates a non-confrontationist stance and reunification with the mainland. China mounted provocative military exercises in 1995 and 1996 ahead of the legislative and presidential elections which it denounced – this caused jitters in Taiwan, but did little to stifle the democratic process. Despite this, each depends on the other economically. China is currently Taiwan's single largest investment destination and Taiwan is the second-largest foreign investor in China after Hong Kong.

Lin Yang-kang,
*leading KMT
dissident.*

Lee Teng-hui,
*president since 1988,
reelected in 1996.*

Political stability

In the 1995 legislative elections, the ruling KMT posted its worst-ever result and now has a narrow majority in the legislature. The pro-independence opposition DPP and the New Party, which favors reunification with China, increased their strength. This places the onus on KMT President Lee to placate both sides, including hardline opponents in his own party. The preservation of political and economic stability will be essential as China intensifies its sovereignty claims on Taiwan after the return of Hong Kong in 1997.

PROFILE

Between 1949 and 1986, Chiang Kai-Shek's KMT monopolized political power and ruled by strict martial law. In 1986, Gen Chiang Ching-Kuo, Chiang Kai-Shek's son and successor, decided to pave the way for democracy. Free multiparty elections were first held in 1986. The president was directly elected for the first time in March 1996.

WORLD AFFAIRS

APEC   BCIE   UN

Nations wishing to do business with China cannot have formal relations with Taiwan. China rejects its sovereignty claims and regards it as a renegade province, so Taipei conducts its overseas relations via trade delegations rather than embassies. It cannot gain representation at the UN.

Official relations with the USA have been problematic since it recognized China at the UN in 1972. Taiwan effectively lost its status as a US client state, and the US 6th fleet was removed from the Taiwan Strait. US security guarantees to Taiwan have since been ambiguous and a strong US naval presence in early 1996 was a symbolic riposte to provocative Chinese military exercises. In practice, however, strong bilateral ties exist with the USA and Japan, and the higher ranks of government and industry are replete with officials and personnel who studied in both countries.

TAIWAN

Total Land Area : 32 260 sq. km (12 456 sq. miles)

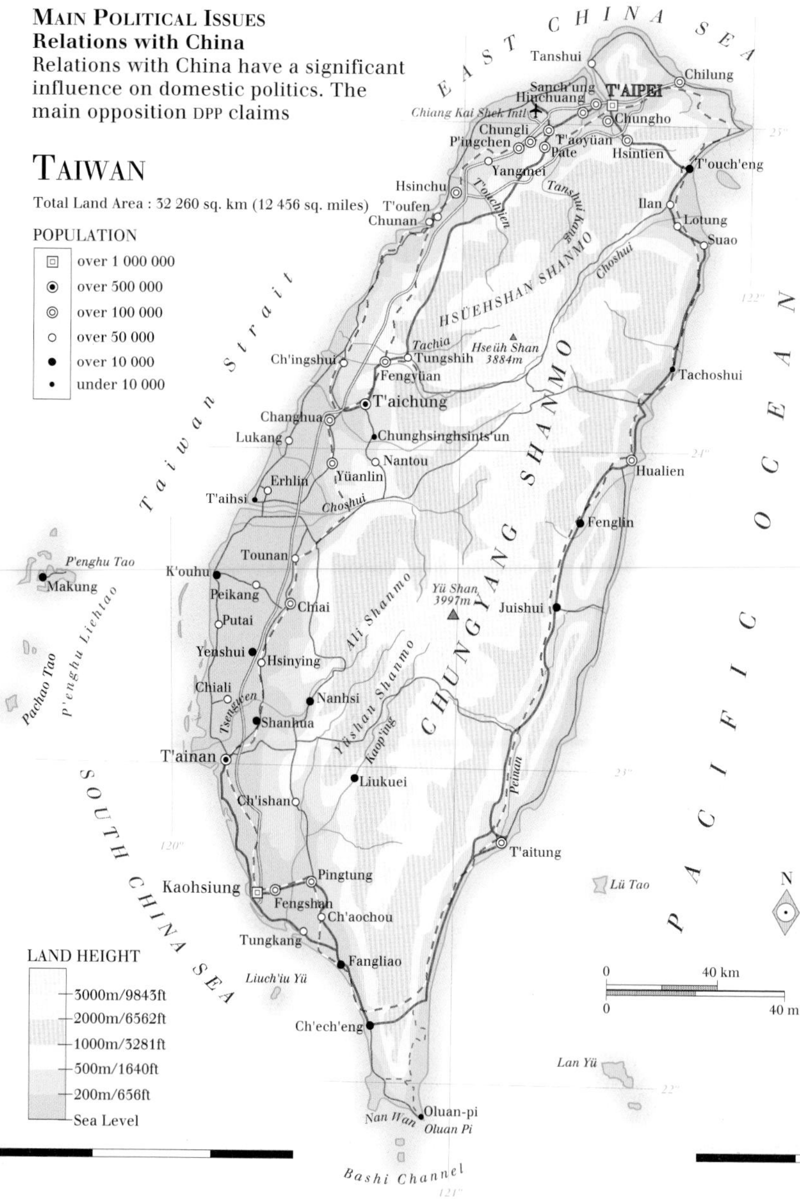

POPULATION

⊡	over 1 000 000
⊙	over 500 000
◎	over 100 000
○	over 50 000
●	over 10 000
·	under 10 000

LAND HEIGHT

| | |
| 3000m/9843ft |
| 2000m/6562ft |
| 1000m/3281ft |
| 500m/1640ft |
| 200m/656ft |
| Sea Level |

EAST CHINA SEA

Tanshui
Chilung
Sanch'ung
Hsinchuang
T'AIPEI
Chiang Kai Shek Intl
Chungho
Chungli
Taoyuan
P'ingchen
Pate
Hsintien
Yangmei
T'ouch'eng
Hsinchu
Touchien
Ilan
T'oufen
Lotung
Chunan
Suao

HSÜEHSHAN SHANMO

Ch'ingshui
Tachia
Hseüh Shan 3884m
Tungshih
Fengyüan
Tachoshui
T'aichung
Changhua
Lukang
Chunghsinghsints'un
Nantou
Erhlin
Yüanlin
Hualien
T'aihsi
Choshui
Tounan
Fenglin
K'ouhu
P'enghu Tao
Makung
Peikang
Yü Shan 3997m
Putai
Chiai
Juishui
Yenshui
Hsinying
Chiali
Nanhsi
Shanhua
T'ainan
Liukuei
Ch'ishan
T'aitung
Kaohsiung
Pingtung
Fengshan
Ch'aochou
Tungkang
Liuch'iu Yü
Fangliao
Ch'ech'eng
Nan Wan
Oluan-pi
Oluan Pi

Taiwan Strait
Pachiao Tao
P'enghu Liehtao
SOUTH CHINA SEA
CHUNGYANG SHANMO
Ali Shan mo
Yüshan Shanmo
Tsengwen
Kaoping
PACIFIC OCEAN
Lü Tao
Lan Yü
Bashi Channel
Choshui
Tanshui Ho

0   40 km
0   40 miles

N

T

AID

 US$7m (donations)   Up 40% in 1993

Taiwan has a substantial aid fund which is devoted to the small states which have offered it diplomatic recognition. These include the Pacific island of Kiribati, Tuvalu and Tonga, which have represented Taiwan's interests in the UN since 1972, when it lost its seat following the US recognition of China. Senegal decided to recognize Taiwan's sovereignty in 1996.

CHRONOLOGY

Following the 1949 communist revolution in China, Gen. Chiang Kai-Shek's nationalist KMT party sought refuge in the island province of Taiwan. The KMT saw the revolution as illegal and itself as the sole rightful Chinese government.

❑ **1971** People's Republic of China replaces Taiwan at UN and on UN Security Council.

❑ **1973** Taipei's KMT regime rejects Beijing's offer of secret talks on reunification of China.

❑ **1975** President Chiang Kai-Shek dies. His son Gen. Chiang Ching-Kuo becomes KMT leader. Dr. Yen Chia-kan president.

❑ **1979** USA severs relations with Taiwan in favor of People's Republic of China. However, arms sales to Taiwan continue.

❑ **1981** Beijing's terms for reunification rejected.

❑ **1984** President Chiang reelected.

❑ **1986** Political reforms: KMT allows other political parties in Taiwan, ends martial law and permits visits to China for "humanitarian" purposes for first time for 38 years. In 1988, Chinese are allowed to visit Taiwan on same basis.

❑ **1988** Lee Teng-hui becomes president.

❑ **1989** April, KMT considers reconciliation with Beijing under the formula of "one China, two governments." Ruthless suppression of student dissent by communist regime ends rapprochement.

❑ **1990** Lee Teng-hui reelected president. KMT formally ends state of war with People's Republic.

❑ **1991** DPP draft constitution for Taiwan independence opposed by ruling KMT and Beijing. KMT reelected with large majority.

❑ **1995** KMT majority sharply reduced in legislative elections.

❑ **1996** Chinese military exercises off Taiwanese coast. Lee Teng-hui elected in first direct vote for KMT president.

DEFENSE

 US$9.6bn Down 15% in 1995

0	Defense spending as % GDP	40

5.0%

Taiwan has the fifth-largest army in the world to face a possible Chinese invasion. Worries about US loyalty have led to purchase of French *Mirage* fighters in addition to US fighters. The AIDC defense research development body agreed in 1996 to a stake in the production of 700 helicopters with the US Sikorsky company.

TAIWANESE ARMED FORCES

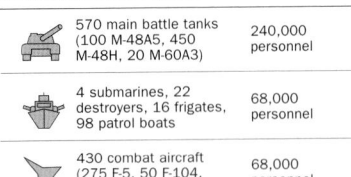

570 main battle tanks (100 M-48A5, 450 M-48H, 20 M-60A3)	240,000 personnel
4 submarines, 22 destroyers, 16 frigates, 98 patrol boats	68,000 personnel
430 combat aircraft (275 F-5, 50 F-104, 40 *Chung-Kuo*)	68,000 personnel
None	

ECONOMICS

 US$218.1bn  26.29-27.29 New Taiwan dollars

SCORE CARD

❑ WORLD GNP RANKING...........................20th
❑ GNP PER CAPITA ....US$10,479
❑ BALANCE OF PAYMENTS ....US$5.8bn
❑ INFLATION 4%
❑ UNEMPLOYMENT....................................1.6%

EXPORTS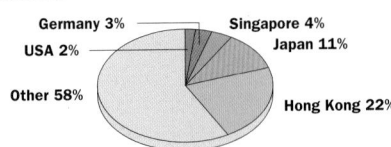

Germany 3%
USA 2%
Other 58%
Singapore 4%
Japan 11%
Hong Kong 22%

IMPORTS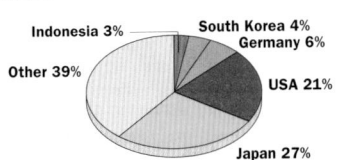

Indonesia 3%
Other 39%
South Korea 4%
Germany 6%
USA 21%
Japan 27%

STRENGTHS

Highly educated and ambitious work force, many US-trained and educated, with an inside knowledge of the US market. Manufacturing economy based on small companies which have proved extremely adaptable to changing market conditions. Strong track record of capturing major markets. Taiwan was successively the world's-biggest TV producer, watch producer, PC producer and track shoe manufacturer. Economy in strong surplus, allowing it to invest in burgeoning Southeast Asian economies.

WEAKNESSES

Taiwan's small economic units lack the muscle of Japanese and Western multinationals; they are consequently unable to follow predatory pricing policies. Weak research and development: the economy has no tradition of coming up with new products or creating new markets. Unresponsive banking system.

ECONOMIC PERFORMANCE INDICATOR

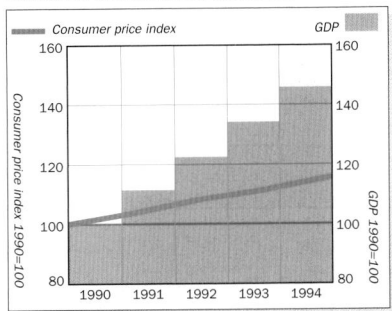

Consumer price index — GDP

PROFILE

Taiwan has one of the world's most successful economies. However, double digit growth is now over and more modest levels (6.5% in 1995) are forecast. The country now faces competition from underdeveloped countries with low production costs, which is likely to entail moving from labor-intensive to capital- and technology-intensive industries. Comprehensive six-year plans reflect a strong element of state direction. Heavy investment abroad includes over 60% of inward investment into China since 1990.

TAIWAN : MAJOR BUSINESSES

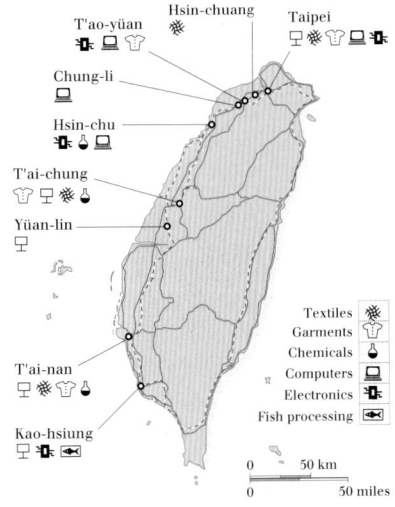

Textiles
Garments
Chemicals
Computers
Electronics
Fish processing

| 0 | 50 km |
| 0 | 50 miles |

T

RESOURCES

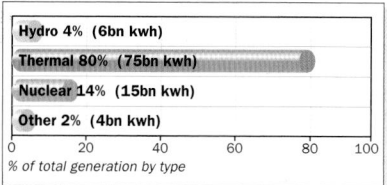

89bn kwh

Not an oil producer; refines 542,500 b/cd

77m chickens, 10.6m ducks, 8.6m pigs

Coal, copper, marble, dolomite, gold, silver

ELECTRICITY GENERATION

Hydro 4% (6bn kwh)

Thermal 80% (75bn kwh)

Nuclear 14% (15bn kwh)

Other 2% (4bn kwh)

0   20   40   60   80   100
% of total generation by type

Taiwan has few strategic resources and its minerals industry is not a significant foreign exchange earner; oil is imported. The country is a major buyer of South African uranium, but heavy reliance on nuclear power is now politically unfeasible due to serious safety and waste disposal problems. Hydroelectric power has been largely exploited and thermal power remains a controversial option. Fishing is highly successful and Taiwan is a major supplier to the huge Japanese market. The Taiwanese fishing fleet is often accused of plundering Atlantic stocks.

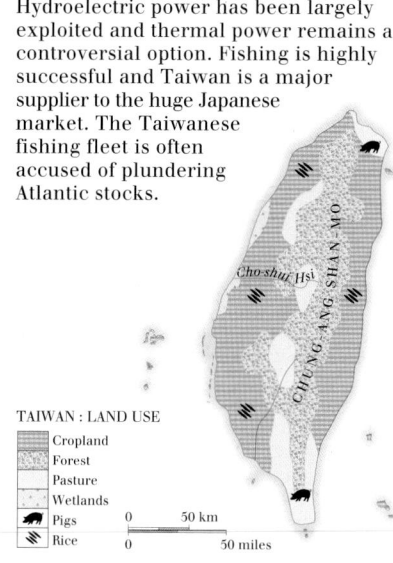

Cho-shui Hsi

CHUNG-YANG SHAN-MO

TAIWAN : LAND USE

- Cropland
- Forest
- Pasture
- Wetlands
- Pigs
- Rice

0   50 km
0   50 miles

ENVIRONMENT

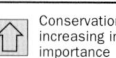

8% (3% partially protected)

Conservation increasing in importance

ENVIRONMENTAL TREATIES

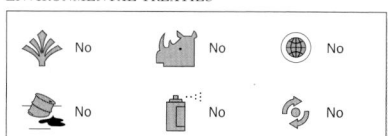

No   No   No
No   No   No

The dash for growth meant the absence of city planning or pollution laws. An increasingly aware public now opposes a fourth nuclear power station and is wary of coal-fired thermal power. Taiwan's fishing industry has been criticized for using long-line techniques which trap dolphins, and for plundering other nations' fishing grounds without regard to stock levels.

MEDIA

Criticism of the government is discouraged

PUBLISHING AND BROADCAST MEDIA

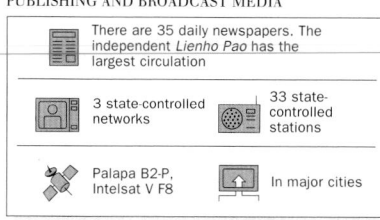

There are 35 daily newspapers. The independent *Lienho Pao* has the largest circulation

3 state-controlled networks

33 state-controlled stations

Palapa B2-P, Intelsat V F8

In major cities

The rigid state control which used to exist over the media has been relaxed. Opposition parties now have access to the state media. Before the 1990s, press with simplified Chinese characters was banned, thus excluding all publications from the mainland. Taiwan has a large domestic TV and film industry.

CRIME

Taiwan does not publish prison figures

Little change from year to year

CRIME RATES

Most Taiwanese are highly conscious of crime. However rates are low by US or European standards

Since the end of martial law in 1986, most political prisoners have been released. Taiwan does not suffer from organized crime to the extent found in Hong Kong or Japan. Multimedia pirating is a major problem.

EDUCATION

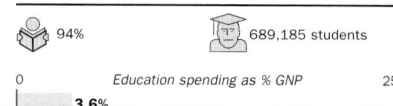

94%

689,185 students

0   *Education spending as % GNP*   25
3.6%

THE EDUCATION SYSTEM

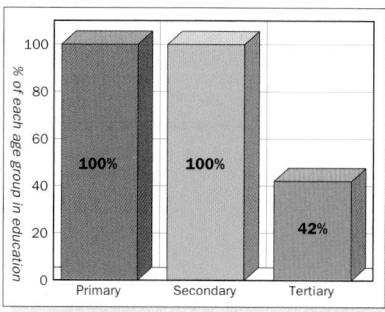

100% (Primary)   100% (Secondary)   42% (Tertiary)

% of each age group in education

The education system is the same as that found on the mainland and inspired by 1922 reforms suggested to Beijing by Bertrand Russell and John Dewey. Attendance at tertiary level is one of the highest in the world. Schools have good facilities and equipment. Many Taiwanese study in the USA.

HEALTH

1 per 894 people

Cerebrovascular and heart diseases, hypertension

0   *Health spending as % GDP*   25
Higher than regional average

Most health provision in Taiwan is in the private sector. Taiwanese take out elaborate health insurance schemes and it is essential to prove cover before treatment is provided. Health facilities are some of the best in the world and Taiwanese enjoy a high life expectancy, similar to that in Sweden or Japan. The incidence of AIDS is in line with the Southeast Asian average.

WEALTH

Most Taiwanese are comfortably off

CONSUMER GOODS OWNERSHIP

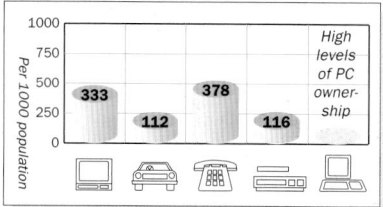

High levels of PC ownership

333   112   378   116

Per 1000 population

Until 1987, Taiwan had the largest cash reserves of any nation in the world. This reflected the closed nature of its markets and the success of the export economy. Taiwanese have shared in much of this wealth. Inequalities of income distribution are comparatively small, and a high degree of social cohesion has been achieved. In part, this is the result of the land reforms of the 1950s, which gave agricultural workers control of the land while compensating landowners and encouraging them to set up business in the cities. Today, most Taiwanese would describe themselves as middle class. Taiwan is perhaps the most consumerist society on earth; conspicuous consumption is celebrated.

WORLD RANKING

T

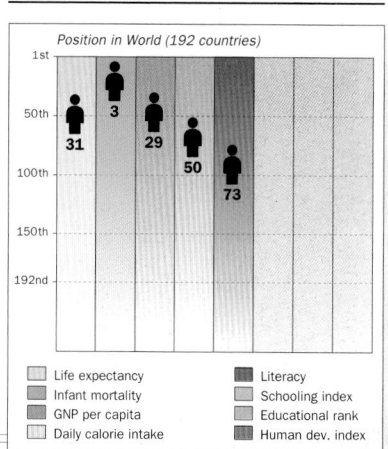

Position in World (192 countries)

1st   50th   100th   150th   192nd

3   31   29   50   73

- Life expectancy
- Infant mortality
- GNP per capita
- Daily calorie intake
- Literacy
- Schooling index
- Educational rank
- Human dev. index

TAJIKISTAN

OFFICIAL NAME: Republic of Tajikistan   **CAPITAL:** Dushanbe
POPULATION: 6.1 million   **CURRENCY:** Tajik rouble   **OFFICIAL LANGUAGE:** Tajik

 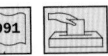   

CENTRAL ASIA

TAJIKISTAN LIES ON the western slopes of the Pamirs in Central Asia. The Tajiks' language and traditions are similar to those of Iran rather than of Turkic Uzbekistan. Tajikistan decided on independence only when neighboring Soviet republics declared theirs in late 1991. The republic has since been riven by armed conflict between the communist government, backed by Russia and the Uzbeks, and Tajik Islamic rebels.

The Varzob Gorge, north of Dushanbe. Half of the country is over 9,864 feet above sea level.

CLIMATE

WEATHER CHART

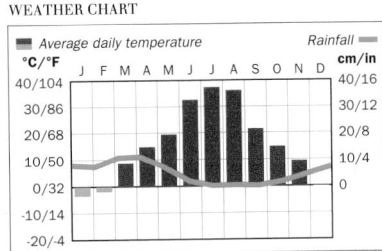

Rainfall is low in the valleys. In the mountainous areas, winter temperatures can fall below –45°C.

TRANSPORTATION

Dushanbe Intl   Has no fleet

THE TRANSPORTATION NETWORK

13,300 miles (21,400 km)		None	
298 miles (480 km)		124 miles (200 km)	

Tajikistan has good cross-border roads and well-maintained airfields, the result of its use as a staging post by Soviet forces during the Afghan War. The best way to visit the mountainous interior is by air.

TOURISM

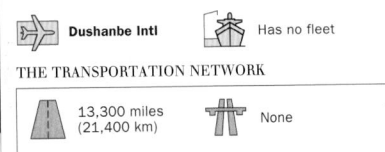

Almost no tourists   Little change from year to year

MAIN OVERSEAS ARRIVALS

Tajikistan does not publish tourism figures by country of origin

0   10   20   30   40
% of total arrivals

The conflict in Tajikistan makes travel almost impossible. Journalists from the West are often attacked.

PEOPLE

Tajik, Russian   111 people per sq. mile

THE URBAN/RURAL POPULATION SPLIT

32%   68%

RELIGIOUS PERSUASION

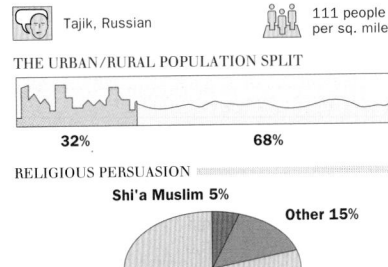

Shi'a Muslim 5%
Other 15%
Sunni Muslim 80%

The main ethnic conflict in Tajikistan is between the Tajiks and Uzbeks – peoples of Persian and Turkic origin respectively. As in neighboring Uzbekistan, however, Russians are discriminated against and their ranks have thinned from 400,000 in 1989 to around 200,000 today. By 1990, the 35,000-strong German minority had left. The struggle between Dushanbe-based communists and the Islamic militants in the central and eastern regions has displaced over 60,000 refugees into Afghanistan, whose own Tajik population numbers over one million. Attempts to repatriate the refugees in 1993 failed.

POLITICS

 1995/2000   Acting President Imamoli Rakhmanov

THE STATE OF THE PARTIES

Supreme Assembly 181 members

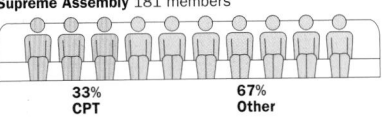

33% CPT   67% Other

CPT = Communist Party of Tajikistan
Genuine opposition was banned at the elections of 1990. Other main parties are the Democratic Party of Tajikistan, the Islamic Renaissance Party (IRP) and Rebirth

The lull in fighting between government forces and Islamic rebels, aided by a 1994 ceasefire and continuing peace talks, has consolidated the regime of former communists led by President Rakhmanov. In legislative elections held in 1995, a third of the deputies returned were communists. The powers of President Rakhmanov were also enhanced with the adoption of a presidential constitution in November 1994. However, Islamic and democratic opposition parties continue to accuse Rakhmanov of widespread political repression.

TAJIKISTAN

Total Land Area : 143 100 sq. km (55 251 sq. miles)

POPULATION
- ⊙ over 500 000
- ◎ over 100 000
- ○ over 50 000
- ● over 10 000
- • under 10 000

LAND HEIGHT
- 4000m/13 124ft
- 3000m/9843ft
- 2000m/6562ft
- 1000m/3281ft
- 500m/1640ft
- 200m/656ft

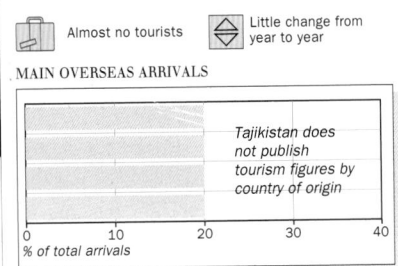

WORLD AFFAIRS

CIS ECO NACC OIC OSCE

Tajikistan is heavily dependent on Russia for economic and military assistance. In 1993, Tajikistan was the only Central Asian state to submit to Russia's conditions for membership of the rouble zone, thereby ceding considerable sovereignty on economic policy to Russia. This was partially reversed with the introduction in 1995 of the Tajik rouble. However, Russia shares the Tajik government's concern to limit the influence of Islamic fundamentalism, and lends military support to further this objective.

AID

 $29m (receipts) Up 141% in 1993

The government in Dushanbe is reliant on Russian and Uzbek military aid in its fight with the Afghan-based rebels.

DEFENSE

 $67m Down 1% in 1995

The Tajik armed forces are dependent on CIS peacekeeping forces to contain Tajik rebels, who are active in the Gorno Badakhshan region bordering Afghanistan. They are kept at bay by government forces assisted by Russian border guards.

ECONOMICS

 $2.1bn Official: 0.59 Russian roubles, Black market: 1,770 Russian roubles

SCORE CARD

- WORLD GNP RANKING........................133rd
- GNP PER CAPITA $350
- BALANCE OF PAYMENTS ....No formal economy
- INFLATION 350.4%
- UNEMPLOYMENT.................................1.5%

STRENGTHS
Few, although Tajikistan has 14% of known world uranium reserves. Hydroelectric power has considerable potential. Carpet-making.

WEAKNESSES
Formal economy on verge of collapse. Dependence on barter economy. No central planning. Little diversification in agriculture; only 6% of land is arable. Skilled Russians leaving. Production in all sectors in decline.

EXPORTS

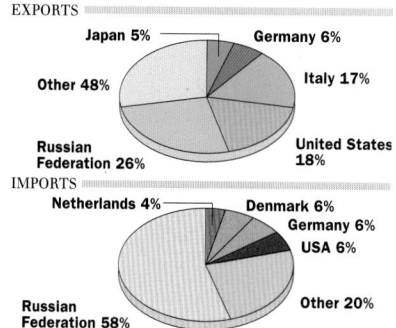

Japan 5% | Germany 6%
Other 48% | Italy 17%
Russian Federation 26% | United States 18%

IMPORTS

Netherlands 4% | Denmark 6%
Germany 6%
USA 6%
Russian Federation 58% | Other 20%

RESOURCES

 16.8bn kwh 2005 b/d

 2m sheep, 1.3m cattle, 845,000 goats, 50,000 horses Uranium, gold, iron, coal, lead, mercury, tin

Tajikistan has one key resource – uranium – which accounted for 30% of the USSR's total production before 1990. The end of the nuclear arms race has reduced its value, however. Most of Tajikistan is bare mountain and just 6% of the land can be used for agriculture. Industry is concentrated in the Fergana Valley, close to the Uzbek border.

ENVIRONMENT

 1% No resources for environmental measures

Landslides are a problem, frequently cutting off villages. Excessive irrigation for cotton production has led to salination of the soil, with consequent reduced crop yields.

MEDIA

 Journalists who criticize the government may be risking their lives

PUBLISHING AND BROADCAST MEDIA

 There are 74 newspapers, 66 of which are published in Tajik, including *Djavononi Todjikiston*, *Sadoi mardum* and *Tochikistoni*

 1 state-controlled service 1 state-controlled service

Communist control over the media was tightened in early 1994 with the takeover by President Rakhmonov of the press and broadcast media.

CRIME

 Tajikistan does not publish prison figures Crime has been rising dramatically

Only remote areas escape the violence perpetrated by armed gangs. In 1995, clashes between rival gangs killed 350 people in Kurgan-Tyube in the southwest.

EDUCATION

 98% 69,844 students

The university at Dushanbe has been weakened by the departure of its Russian academics.

HEALTH

 1 per 430 people Heart, cerebrovascular, respiratory, infectious and parasitic diseases

Tajikistan's health service has always been poor. The infant mortality rate before 1990 was one of the highest in the USSR.

WEALTH

 A minority are formally employed. Most Tajiks live by herding cattle

CONSUMER GOODS OWNERSHIP

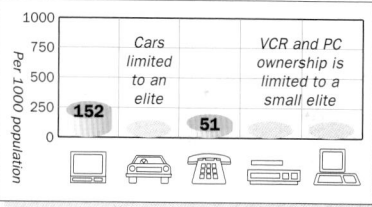

Cars limited to an elite | VCR and PC ownership is limited to a small elite
152 | 51

Around 87% of Tajiks live below the UN-defined poverty line. The war has made conditions even harder. The old communist bureaucrats are still the wealthiest group.

WORLD RANKING

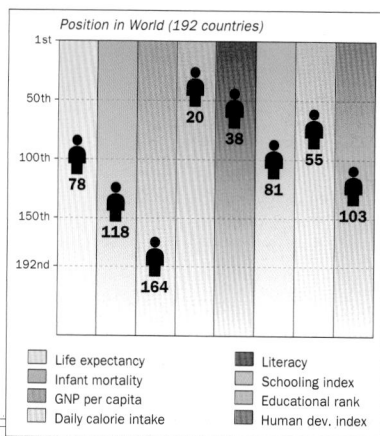

Position in World (192 countries)

Life expectancy 78 | Infant mortality 118 | GNP per capita 164 | Daily calorie intake 20 | Literacy 38 | Schooling index 81 | Educational rank 55 | Human dev. index 103

- Life expectancy
- Infant mortality
- GNP per capita
- Daily calorie intake
- Literacy
- Schooling index
- Educational rank
- Human dev. index

T

TANZANIA

OFFICIAL NAME: United Republic of Tanzania **CAPITAL:** Dodoma
POPULATION: 29.7 million **CURRENCY:** Tanzanian shilling **OFFICIAL LANGUAGES:** English and Swahili

TANZANIA LIES BETWEEN KENYA and Mozambique on the East African coast. Formed by the union of Tanganyika and Zanzibar and other islands, Tanzania comprises a coastal lowland, volcanic highlands and the Great Rift Valley. It includes Mount Kilimanjaro, Africa's highest peak. Tanzania was led by the socialist Julius Nyerere from 1962 until 1985. The Revolutionary Party of Tanzania (CCM) was returned in multiparty elections in 1995.

Arusha National Park. *Lying within the Ngurdoto volcanic crater, the park has herds of buffaloes, rhinos, elephants and giraffes.*

CLIMATE

WEATHER CHART

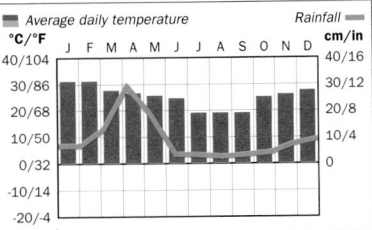

The coast and Zanzibar are tropical. The central plateau is semi-arid and the highlands are semi-temperate.

TRANSPORTATION

Dar es Salaam Intl
453,000 passengers

15 ships
45,200 dwt

THE TRANSPORTATION NETWORK

2,190 miles (3,520 km)		None
2,486 miles (4,000 km)		Lakes Tanganyika, Victoria, Nyasa

The roads, railroads and ports are being upgraded. An $870-million program to improve 70% of Tanzania's trunk roads is due for completion in 1996.

TOURISM

234,000 visitors

Up 2% in 1994

MAIN OVERSEAS ARRIVALS

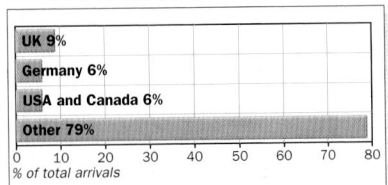

UK 9%
Germany 6%
USA and Canada 6%
Other 79%

% of total arrivals

One-third of Tanzania is national park or game reserve. The Ngorongoro Crater and the Serengeti Plain are top attractions. Tourist numbers have risen sharply since 1990.

PEOPLE

Swahili, Sukuma, Chagga, Nyamwezi, Hehe, Makonde, Yao, Sandawe, English

88 people per sq. mile

THE URBAN/RURAL POPULATION SPLIT

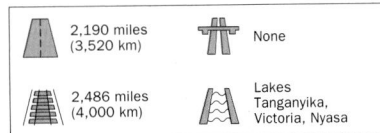

22%   78%

RELIGIOUS PERSUASION

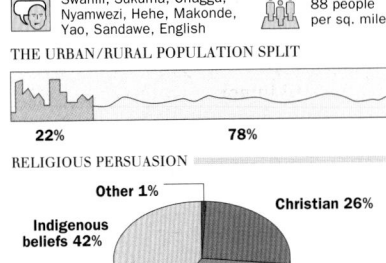

Christian 26%
Muslim 31%
Indigenous beliefs 42%
Other 1%

For many Tanzanians the family is the focus of traditional rural life. About 99% belong to one of 120 small ethnic Bantu groups. The remaining 1% comprises Arab, Asian and European minorities. The use of Swahili as a *lingua franca* has helped make ethnic rivalries almost non-existent.

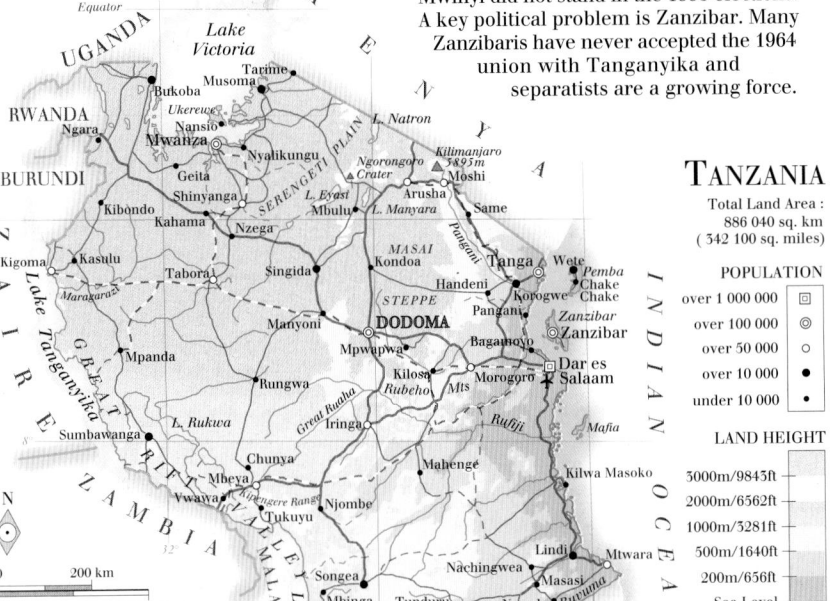

POLITICS

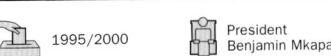

1995/2000

President
Benjamin Mkapa

THE STATE OF THE PARTIES

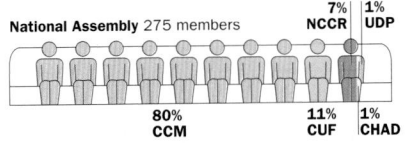

National Assembly 275 members

7% NCCR   1% UDP
80% CCM   11% CUF   1% CHAD

CCM = Revolutionary Party of Tanzania **CUF** = Civic United Front **NCCR-Madeuzi** = National Convention for Reconstruction and Reform-Mageuzi **CHADEMA** = Chama cha Democrasia na Maendeleo **UDP** = United Democratic Party of Tanzania

Now retired, Julius Nyerere was the dominant force in Tanzanian politics for 21 years. His brand of African socialism guided Tanzania's development. Ali Hassan Mwinyi succeeded him in 1985, and oversaw a relaxation of socialist policies, and the transition to multiparty democracy. Having served two terms, Mwinyi did not stand in the 1995 elections. A key political problem is Zanzibar. Many Zanzibaris have never accepted the 1964 union with Tanganyika and separatists are a growing force.

TANZANIA

Total Land Area :
886 040 sq. km
(342 100 sq. miles)

POPULATION

over 1 000 000
over 100 000
over 50 000
over 10 000
under 10 000

LAND HEIGHT

3000m/9843ft
2000m/6562ft
1000m/3281ft
500m/1640ft
200m/656ft
Sea Level

T

WORLD AFFAIRS

 Comm G15   NAM OAU   SADC

Tanzania plays a role in both eastern and southern Africa. An active member of the SADC, it was a base for the ANC during its liberation struggle. Relations with Kenya and Uganda have warmed since 1985, prompting efforts to revive the East African Community. A large influx of refugees has strained links with Burundi and Rwanda.

AID

 $949m (receipts)   Down 29% in 1993

Tanzania is heavily dependent on aid to help offset a severe balance-of-payments deficit. Most aid is now linked to an IMF-backed economic reform program. Infrastructure projects and the agricultural sector are the main recipients of aid.

DEFENSE

 $114m   Up 8% in 1995

Defense accounts for 3.5% of budget spending. The armed forces are closely linked with the ruling CCM. There is an 80,000-strong citizens' reserve force.

ECONOMICS

 $2.5bn 523.66–550.00 Tanzanian shillings

SCORE CARD

- ❏ WORLD GNP RANKING........................130th
- ❏ GNP PER CAPITA $90
- ❏ BALANCE OF PAYMENTS....................$–408m
- ❏ INFLATION 34.1%
- ❏ UNEMPLOYMENT.................................25%

STRENGTHS

Coffee, cotton, sisal, tea. Cloves from Zanzibar, the world's third-largest producer. Diamonds. State commitment to reforms which have cut inflation and the budget deficit. Rise in inward investment. A return to positive growth.

WEAKNESSES

Growth still too low to increase per capita income. Shortage of foreign exchange. Poor credit and equipment limit agricultural development.

EXPORTS

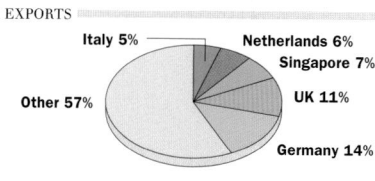

Italy 5% | Netherlands 6% | Singapore 7% | UK 11% | Germany 14% | Other 57%

IMPORTS

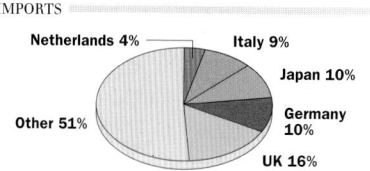

Netherlands 4% | Italy 9% | Japan 10% | Germany 10% | UK 16% | Other 51%

RESOURCES

 901m kwh   Not an oil producer; refines 17,000 b/cd

 13.3m cattle, 9.7m goats, 3.9m sheep   Natural gas, oil, iron, diamonds, gold, salt, phosphates, coal, gypsum, kaolin, tin

Agriculture, including livestock and forestry, is the key economic resource. It accounts for 60% of GDP and 80% of employment and exports. Forests cover 50% of Tanzania. More than 90% of energy demand is met from wood and charcoal. Hydropower provides 70% of electricity and is being expanded. To reduce oil imports, which take 40% of export earnings, Tanzania is starting to exploit offshore gas at Songo Songo. Oil has been discovered off Pemba Island.

ENVIRONMENT

 15%   Growth in tourism poses long-term threat

The demand for fuel-wood is a threat to forests. Tourism's demands have to be carefully balanced with those of delicate wildlife environments, like the Ngorongoro Crater and the Serengeti.

MEDIA

 Censorship is now minimal. There has been a great increase in the number of independent publishers

PUBLISHING AND BROADCAST MEDIA

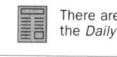 There are 3 daily newspapers, the *Daily News*, *Uhuru* and *Kipanga*

 Several limited independent services   1 state-owned, 1 independent service

Independent TV services operate in Zanzibar, Dar es Salaam and major towns. The daily press is state-owned.

CRIME

 Tanzania does not publish prison figures   Up 4% in 1990

Crime levels are low, although theft in Dar es Salaam has risen. Tanzania's human rights record is good.

EDUCATION

 68%  5,254 students

Elementary education is free; secondary students pay fees – 70% of children attend elementary and 5% secondary school. Adult literacy campaigns maintain average levels of literacy.

CHRONOLOGY

The mainland became the German colony of Tanganyika in 1884. The Sultanate of Zanzibar became a British protectorate in 1890.

- ❏ **1918** Tanganyika British mandate.
- ❏ **1961** Tanganyika independent.
- ❏ **1962** Nyerere becomes president.
- ❏ **1963** Zanzibar independent.
- ❏ **1964** Zanzibar signs union with Tanganyika to form Tanzania.
- ❏ **1977** One-party state. Mainland and Zanzibari parties form CCM.
- ❏ **1985** Nyerere resigns as president. President Mwinyi, former vice-president, begins relaxation of Nyerere's socialist policies.
- ❏ **1990** Mwinyi succeeds Nyerere as CCM chair.
- ❏ **1992** Political parties allowed.
- ❏ **1995** Multiparty elections.

HEALTH

 1 per 25,000 people   Diarrheal and respiratory diseases, malaria

Basic medical care is provided by the state and Christian missions. Rural areas are served by local clinics.

WEALTH

 Most Tanzanians lead a subsistence existence

CONSUMER GOODS OWNERSHIP

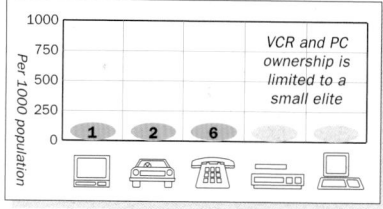

VCR and PC ownership is limited to a small elite

1 | 2 | 6

The majority of Tanzanians are subsistence farmers. The wealthy elite is small, composed mainly of Asian and Arab business families.

WORLD RANKING

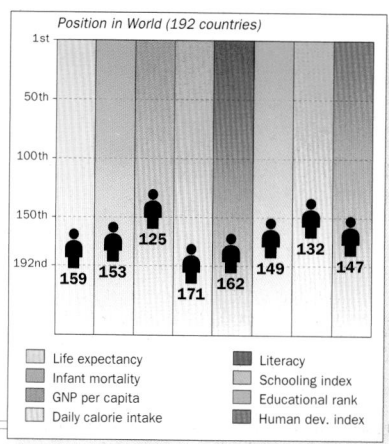

Position in World (192 countries)

159 | 153 | 125 | 171 | 162 | 149 | 132 | 147

- Life expectancy
- Infant mortality
- GNP per capita
- Daily calorie intake
- Literacy
- Schooling index
- Educational rank
- Human dev. index

THAILAND

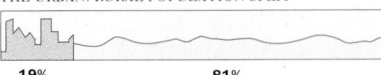

OFFICIAL NAME: Kingdom of Thailand **CAPITAL:** Bangkok
POPULATION: 58.8 million **CURRENCY:** Baht **OFFICIAL LANGUAGE:** Thai

 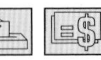

THAILAND LIES BETWEEN the Indian and Pacific Oceans in Southeast Asia. The north, the western border with Burma and the long Isthmus of Kra are mountainous. The central plain is the most fertile and densely populated area, while the low northeastern plateau is the poorest region. Thailand has been an independent kingdom for most of its history and, since 1932, a constitutional monarchy with alternating military and civilian governments. Continuing rapid industrialization is resulting in massive congestion in Bangkok and a serious depletion of natural resources.

CLIMATE

WEATHER CHART

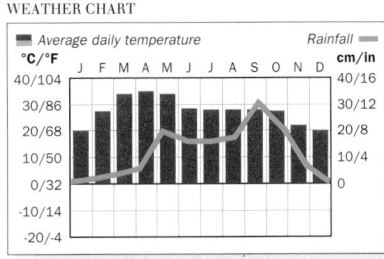

Thailand's tropical monsoon climate has three seasons – a hot sultry period, rains from May to October, and a dry, cooler season from November to March.

TRANSPORTATION

 Don Muang International, Bangkok 14.33m passengers

 283 ships 1.28m dwt

THE TRANSPORTATION NETWORK

 33,390 miles (53,740 km)

None

2,333 miles (3,755 km)

2,300 miles (3,701 km)

Bangkok suffers from huge traffic jams. An exclusively private funding package for Bangkok's first mass transit system was approved in 1996. Good US-built roads run to the north and east. The Chao Phraya River carries most freight.

Island in the Andaman Sea. *The over-development of Thailand's best-known resorts is pushing tourism into new, remoter locations.*

TOURISM

 6.2m visitors

Up 7% in 1994

MAIN OVERSEAS ARRIVALS

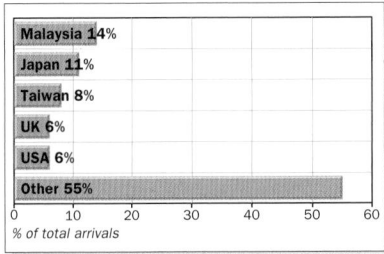

	% of total arrivals
Malaysia	14%
Japan	11%
Taiwan	8%
UK	6%
USA	6%
Other	55%

Tourism is an important contributor to the Thai economy. Tourist numbers fell in the early 1990s as a result of both the worldwide recession and local over-development during the 1980s boom. Although the number of arrivals has since recovered, visitors are tending to seek the less developed resorts. Bangkok's hotel occupancy rates are still falling as yet more hotels are built. Pattaya beach resort has seen such uncontrolled development that sea pollution is now a serious problem, while opposition to the intrusion of large numbers of tourists is growing among northern hill tribes.

Although prostitution is illegal, Bangkok and Pattaya are centers for sex tourism, which thrives despite the state's embarrassment at its effect on Thailand's image. Japanese and German men are among the main clients, while Burmese girls are increasingly recruited as prostitutes. Child prostitution is also a major problem.

There has been a boom in golf tourism, especially among the Japanese. The large number of new golf courses which are under construction will make Thailand the largest golf destination in Asia. The vast amounts of water needed to maintain the courses is aggravating Thailand's serious water shortage.

PEOPLE

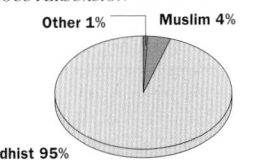 Thai, Chinese, Malay, Khmer, Mon, Karen, Miao

298 people per sq. mile

THE URBAN/RURAL POPULATION SPLIT

19%   81%

RELIGIOUS PERSUASION

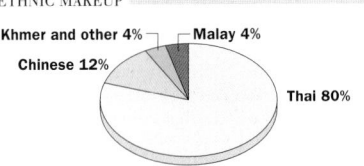

Other 1%   Muslim 4%

Buddhist 95%

ETHNIC MAKEUP

Khmer and other 4%   Malay 4%
Chinese 12%
Thai 80%

There is little ethnic tension in Thailand and Buddhism is a great binding force. The majority of Thais follow Theravada Buddhism, although the reformist Asoke Santi Buddhist sect, which advocates a new moral austerity, is gaining influence. Its principles have been espoused by one of the leading government parties, the Palang Dharma (PD), which seeks to clean up politics.

The far north and northeast are home to about 600,000 hill tribespeople with their own languages, and to permanently settled refugees from Laos, mostly of the Hmong tribal group.

The large Chinese community is the most assimilated in Southeast Asia. Sino-Thais are particularly dominant in agricultural marketing. Most of Thailand's one million Muslim Malays live in southern Thailand, bordering Malaysia. They feel a stronger affinity with Muslims in Malaysia than with Thai culture, and this has given rise to a secessionist movement.

Women are important in business, but their involvement in national politics is limited.

POPULATION AGE BREAKDOWN

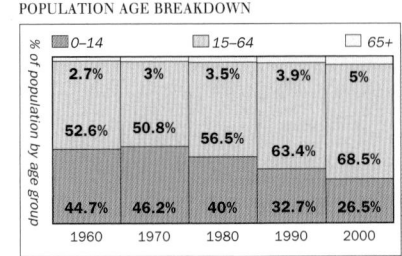

% of population by age group	0–14	15–64	65+
65+	2.7%	3%	3.5%	3.9%	5%
15–64	52.6%	50.8%	56.5%	63.4%	68.5%
0–14	44.7%	46.2%	40%	32.7%	26.5%
	1960	1970	1980	1990	2000

POLITICS

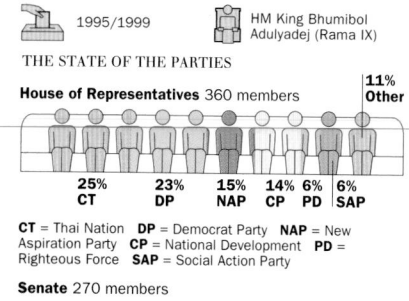

1995/1999

HM King Bhumibol
Adulyadej (Rama IX)

THE STATE OF THE PARTIES

House of Representatives 360 members

11% Other

25% CT	23% DP	15% NAP	14% CP	6% PD	6% SAP

CT = Thai Nation   DP = Democrat Party   NAP = New
Aspiration Party   CP = National Development   PD =
Righteous Force   SAP = Social Action Party

Senate 270 members

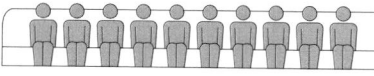

The members of the Senate are appointed by the Head
of State

Thailand is a parliamentary democracy.
The King is head of state. Despite his
position as a constitutional monarch,
he has immense personal prestige.
Criticism of the King is not tolerated.

MAIN POLITICAL ISSUES
The military–democratic cycle
Thailand has been ruled by alternating
military and civilian governments since
1932. When pro-military parties chose
an unelected army general as prime
minister in 1992, there were large
demonstrations in Bangkok. The army's
attempts to suppress them led to the
King's personal intervention. He ordered
General Suchinda to step down and the
constitution was amended. It now states
that any prime minister must be an
elected member of parliament. Since
then, the military has been subdued. The
right-wing Chart Thai (CT) and its allies
won the elections in 1995, prompting
hopes that the military–civilian cycle
has been broken.

Congestion in Bangkok
A major issue is the
concentration of
industry and
commerce in
the area
around
Bangkok.
Uncontrolled
development
has left it
with traffic
congestion
which is
among the
world's
worst and a
serious hindrance to economic
activity. Bangkok is also one of the
world's few major cities not to
have a mass transit system.
However, agreement on funding
for an elevated rail line for the
city was finally reached in
early 1996.
In 1993, the government
began offering incentives
for relocating industry to the
provinces. This is also intended
to help distribute wealth more
evenly – up to 60% of GDP is
generated in the Bangkok area.

***HM King Bhumibol
Adulyadej.** He stepped
in to resolve the
political crisis in 1992.*

***Banharn Silpa-
archa,** prime minister
and leader of the
Chart Thai Party.*

Water
The national water shortage, caused by
rapid industrialization, is so acute that
it is affecting industrial and farm output.

PROFILE
The Thai political process is highly
personalized. Parties are focused on
individuals, who dispense patronage or
represent business interest groups, and
seldom have strong ideologies. Their
large number means that it is rare for
one party to achieve a parliamentary
majority. Personality clashes are
common and often make coalitions
unstable. Lack of coordination between
coalition partners hinders major policy
decisions, notably on improvements
to Bangkok's transportation.
A large number of officers were
removed from the traditionally pro-
military Senate in 1996; nevertheless,
the military remain prominent in most
political parties. Communists are no
longer a political force. The only internal
threat, barring a new military coup, is
from southern Muslim separatists.

WORLD AFFAIRS

APEC   ASEAN   Mek Riv   NAM   WTO

Thailand has friendly relations with
China and Burma. Many Thai logging
concerns, often run by the military,
have been active in Burma since
Thailand's 1988 logging ban at home.
Following border disputes, relations
with Laos and Cambodia are improving,
as are those, more tentatively, with the
traditional enemy, Vietnam. Thailand
supported Khmer Rouge guerrilla
resistance to the Vietnamese regime
in Cambodia in the 1980s.
Thailand, Indonesia and Malaysia
have begun liberalizing trade to
promote development in southern
Thailand, Sumatra and northern
Malaysia – regions all distant from their
respective capitals.
Thailand maintains close relations
with the USA, despite some tension
over intellectual property rights and
minor trade issues, but no longer has
any US military bases on its territory.

THAILAND
Total Land Area : 510 890 sq. km (197 255 sq. miles)

LAND HEIGHT	POPULATION	
	over 5 000 000	■
2000m/6562ft	over 1 000 000	▣
1000m/3281ft	over 100 000	◉
500m/1640ft	over 50 000	○
200m/656ft	over 10 000	●
Sea Level		

0   200 km

0   200 miles

(Map of Thailand showing: Doi Inthanon 2594m, Chiang Mai, Nan, Lampang, Phrae, Uttaradit, Loei, Nong Khai, Nakhon Phanom, Udon Thani, Sakon Nakhon, Tak, Phitsanulok, Lom Sak, Kalasin, Khon Kaen, Maha Sarakham, Nakhon Sawan, Chaiyaphum, Roi Et, Ubon Ratchathani, Buriram, Lop Buri, Nakhon Ratchasima, Surin, Sara Buri, Ayutthaya, Thon Buri, Nakhon Pathom, BANGKOK, Chachoengsao, Samut Sakhon, Samut Prakan, Chon Buri, Phetchaburi, Ao Krung Thep, Ban Hua Hin, Rayong, Chanthaburi, Ko Chang, Chumphon, Ko Phangan, Ko Samui, Surat Thani, Nakhon Si Thammarat, Ko Phuket, Phuket, Trang, Songkhla, Hat Yai, Pattani, Yala, Narathiwat; regions: LAOS, BURMA, CAMBODIA, TANESSERIM RANGE, KORAT PLATEAU, Chao Phraya, Mekong, Mae Nam Ping, Salween, Bilauktaung, Ratchaburi Range, Phanom Dang Raek, Gulf of Thailand, Isthmus of Kra, ANDAMAN SEA, MALAY PENINSULA, MALAYSIA)

T

AID

 $614m (receipts)    Down 22% in 1993

The World Bank and Japan are the largest aid donors. Thailand has imposed a ceiling on foreign borrowing to keep its debt stable.

CHRONOLOGY

Thailand emerged as a kingdom in the 13th century and by the late 17th century its capital, then Ayudhya, was the largest city in Southeast Asia. In 1767, Burmese invaders destroyed the city. In 1782, the present Chakri dynasty and a new capital, Bangkok, were founded.

❏ **1855** King Mongut signs Bowring trade treaty with British – Thailand never colonized by Europeans.
❏ **1868–1910** King Chulalongkorn westernizes Thailand. Laos and Cambodia, taken by Thailand 1824–1851, ceded to France.
❏ **1925** King Prajadhipok begins absolute rule.
❏ **1932** Bloodless military–civilian coup. Constitutional monarchy.
❏ **1933** Military takes full control.
❏ **1941** Japanese invade. Government collaborates. Free-Thai movement aids Allies.
❏ **1944** Pro-Japanese prime minister Phibun voted out of office.
❏ **1945** Exiled King Ananda returns.
❏ **1946** Ananda assassinated. King Bhumibol accedes.
❏ **1947** Military coup. Phibun back.
❏ **1957** New military coup. Constitution abolished.
❏ **1965** Allows USA to use Thai bases in Vietnam War. Start of foreign investment and industrialization.
❏ **1969** Military leaders allow new constitution and elected parliament.
❏ **1971** Army suspends constitution.
❏ **1973–1976** Student riots lead to interlude of democracy.
❏ **1976** New military takeover.
❏ **1979** Vietnam invades Cambodia. Thailand backs Khmer resistance.
❏ **1980–1988** Gen. Prem. Tinsulanond prime minister. Partial democracy restored. Center-right coalition.
❏ **1988** Elections. Gen. Chatichai Choonhaven, right-wing CT leader, is prime minister.
❏ **1991** Military accuses government of corruption and takes over in coup. Civilian Anand Panyarachun is caretaker premier.
❏ **1992** Elections. Gen. Suchinda named premier. Widespread public demonstrations. King forces Suchinda to step down and reinstalls Anand. September, moderates win new elections.
❏ **1995** CT win general election.

DEFENSE

 $4bn   ⬆ Up 11% in 1995

0	Defense spending as % GDP	40
2.6%		

THAI ARMED FORCES

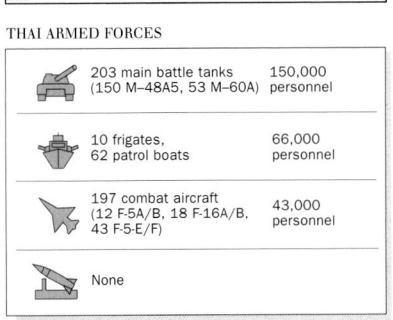

203 main battle tanks (150 M–48A5, 53 M–60A)	150,000 personnel	
10 frigates, 62 patrol boats	66,000 personnel	
197 combat aircraft (12 F-5A/B, 18 F-16A/B, 43 F-5-E/F)	43,000 personnel	
None		

The military has either ruled Thailand, or played a prominent role in politics, since 1932. Its last intervention was its takeover of power in 1991. In 1996, its role in the appointed Senate – hitherto a military stronghold – was reduced. Retired military figures are, however, prominent in the major political parties.

Since 1986, spending has focused on the navy and air force. China, Germany and Spain are supplying naval vessels, the UK, USA and Russia, aircraft.

The main defense concerns are border disputes with Cambodia, Burma and Laos, the Muslim secessionist movement in the south, and piracy and fishing disputes in the South China Sea.

ECONOMICS

📊 $129.9bn   💲 25.11–25.19 baht

SCORE CARD

❏ WORLD GNP RANKING...........................26th
❏ GNP PER CAPITA $2,210
❏ BALANCE OF PAYMENTS ....$–8.4bn
❏ INFLATION 4.7%
❏ UNEMPLOYMENT.................................1.4%

EXPORTS

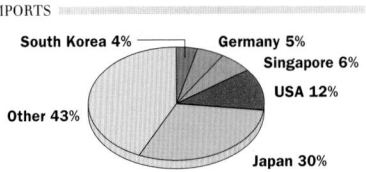

Germany 4%   Hong Kong 5%
Singapore 12%
Other 40%
Japan 17%
USA 22%

IMPORTS

South Korea 4%   Germany 5%
Singapore 6%
USA 12%
Other 43%
Japan 30%

STRENGTHS

Success of export-based and import-substituting manufacturing. Rapid economic growth. Natural gas. Tourism. Chief world exporter of rice and rubber.

WEAKNESSES

Concentration of economic activity in Bangkok area. Severe lack of transportation infrastructure there. Inadequate water storage facilities affecting agricultural output and industrial development. 60% of population in low-profit farming.

PROFILE

Thailand's economy has been growing at over 9% a year since 1988, driven by a combination of a steady rise in manufacturing and rising levels of overseas investment in industry, especially from Japanese companies.

ECONOMIC PERFORMANCE INDICATOR

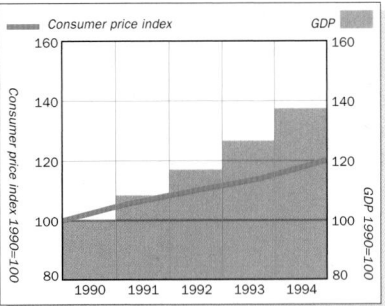

Consumer price index   GDP

Economic policy is concentrating on further industrialization, and expanding the finance and service sectors. A big problem is that as wages rise, Thailand is facing ever stiffer competition from China and Vietnam where labor is cheaper. However, not enough Thais have the skills to let the country move into high technology on a large scale, though it is a big producer of integrated circuits and electronic goods.

THAILAND : MAJOR BUSINESSES

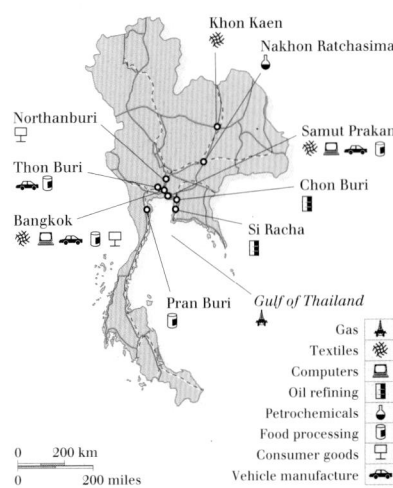

Khon Kaen
Nakhon Ratchasima
Northanburi
Samut Prakan
Thon Buri
Chon Buri
Bangkok
Si Racha
Pran Buri   Gulf of Thailand

Gas
Textiles
Computers
Oil refining
Petrochemicals
Food processing
Consumer goods
Vehicle manufacture

0   200 km
0   200 miles

T

RESOURCES

 59.7bn kwh (capacity 9.72m kw)

 26,406 b/d (reserves 241,900,000 bbl)

7.6m cattle, 4.9m pigs, 162,000 horses

Tin, lignite, gas, gems, oil, tungsten, lead, zinc, antimony, coal

ELECTRICITY GENERATION

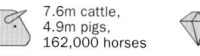

Hydro 7% (4bn kwh)

Thermal 93% (55bn kwh)

Nuclear 0%

Other 0%

% of total generation by type

Thailand has minimal crude oil and has rejected the nuclear option in favor of speeding up development of its large natural gas fields. It also has significant lignite deposits for power generation. World demand for Thailand's tin has declined, but recent gold and copper finds offer new potential. Thailand has valuable gemstone deposits. It is also the world's biggest shrimp producer.

THAILAND : LAND USE

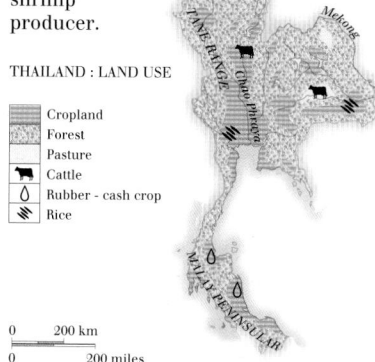

Cropland
Forest
Pasture
Cattle
Rubber - cash crop
Rice

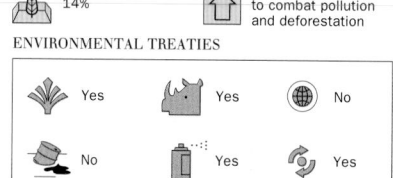

0   200 km
0   200 miles

ENVIRONMENT

 14%

Increasing efforts to combat pollution and deforestation

ENVIRONMENTAL TREATIES

Yes   Yes   No

No   Yes   Yes

Deforestation, especially of the watersheds in the north, has led to the increasing severity of both floods and droughts. Particularly serious flooding in the south resulted in a total logging ban in 1988. Illegal logging still continues, however. Reafforestation projects, some criticized for using single quick-growing species, will not solve the national water shortage. There is evidence of growing official concern at pollution levels. The worst polluting factories are being forced to move out of Bangkok and no new factories may use CFCs.

MEDIA

 Criticism of the King is not tolerated

PUBLISHING AND BROADCAST MEDIA

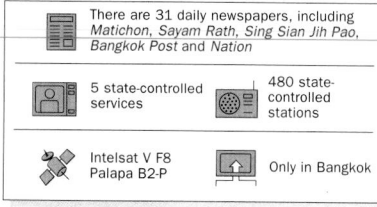

There are 31 daily newspapers, including *Matichon, Sayam Rath, Sing Sian Jih Pao, Bangkok Post* and *Nation*

5 state-controlled services

480 state-controlled stations

Intelsat V F8 Palapa B2-P

Only in Bangkok

Newspapers now enjoy a high level of freedom in political reporting. Two of the five TV stations are run by the military. A fast expansion of cable-TV networks is planned.

CRIME

 73,296 prisoners   Down 2% in 1992

CRIME RATES

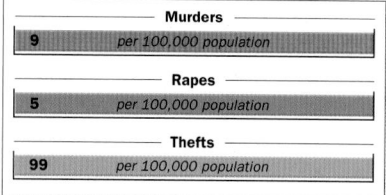

Murders

9   per 100,000 population

Rapes

5   per 100,000 population

Thefts

99   per 100,000 population

Political imprisonment has been almost non-existent since the early 1980s. There is some police involvement in crime, however, and extra-judicial killings and ill-treatment of prisoners in police detention are quite common.

The King has inspired an opium-substitution crop program. The government has cracked down on music, software and video piracy.

EDUCATION

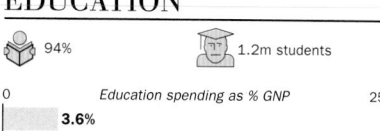 94%   1.2m students

0   Education spending as % GNP   25

3.6%

THE EDUCATION SYSTEM

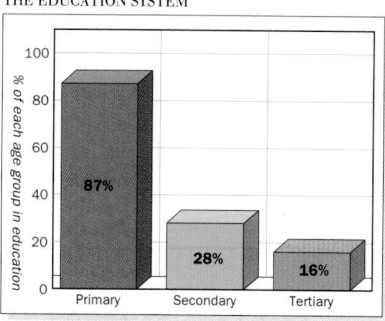

87%   28%   16%

Primary   Secondary   Tertiary

In 1993, the first steps were taken to make schooling compulsory for nine years instead of six.

HEALTH

 1 per 4,420 people   Heart diseases, gastroenteritis

0   Health spending as % GDP   25

1.1%

High-quality health care is heavily concentrated in Bangkok. Most of the 75% of the population who live in rural areas have access to primary health care. Trained personnel are aided by village health volunteers, monks, teachers and traditional healers. In 1993, the decision was taken to improve the skills of primary health workers, rather than increase the number of fully-trained doctors, as a means to improve rural health care.

The government operates a system whereby the poor can apply annually for a certificate entitling them to free health care. However, estimates suggest 30% of users can afford to pay.

High-profile family planning programs are slowing population growth, and sex education programs among prostitutes are aimed at combating the spread of AIDS.

WEALTH

 Employment of child labor is widespread

CONSUMER GOODS OWNERSHIP

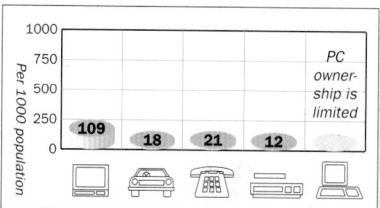

PC ownership is limited

109   18   21   12

The government is trying to spread the great concentration of people and wealth from Bangkok to the provinces. The northeast in particular is very poor. The gap between rich and poor is greater in Thailand than in other industrializing Southeast Asian states.

WORLD RANKING

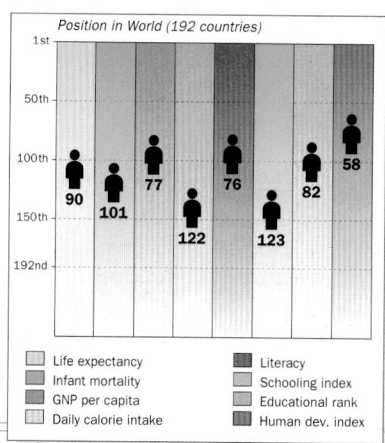

Position in World (192 countries)

1st
50th
100th
150th
192nd

90   101   77   76   82   58

122   123

Life expectancy   Literacy
Infant mortality   Schooling index
GNP per capita   Educational rank
Daily calorie intake   Human dev. index

T

TOGO

OFFICIAL NAME: Togolese Republic   **CAPITAL:** Lomé
POPULATION: 4.1 million   **CURRENCY:** CFA franc   **OFFICIAL LANGUAGES:** French, Kabye and Ewe

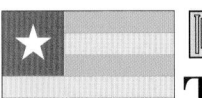  

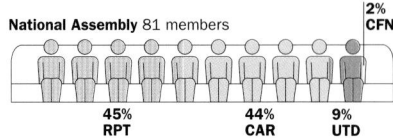

TOGO IS SANDWICHED between Ghana and Benin in West Africa. A central forested region is bounded by savanna to the north and south. Togo exploits its position, and the port at Lomé, to act as an entrepôt for West African trade. Multiparty elections – the first since independence – were held in 1993 and 1994.

CLIMATE

WEATHER CHART

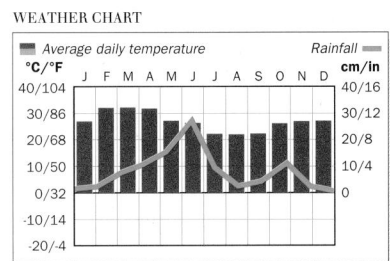

Togo has a typical Gulf of Guinea climate – very hot and humid on the coast and drier inland.

TRANSPORTATION

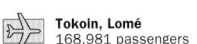 

Tokoin, Lomé
168,981 passengers

21 ships
20,600 dwt

THE TRANSPORTATION NETWORK

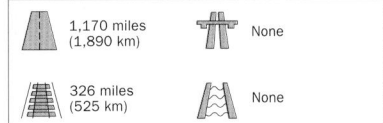

1,170 miles (1,890 km)	None
326 miles (525 km)	None

Improving the already good road network and Lomé's port facilities are priorities, given Togo's role as an entrepôt. The only railroad runs from Lomé to Kpalimé.

TOURISM

44,000 visitors   Up 83% in 1994

MAIN OVERSEAS ARRIVALS

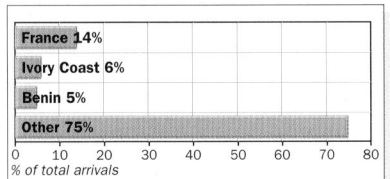

France 14%
Ivory Coast 6%
Benin 5%
Other 75%

% of total arrivals

There is some package tourism to coastal tourist villages and hotels built during the expansion program of the 1980s. Tourists, deterred by the political uncertainty after 1990, have begun to return.

PEOPLE

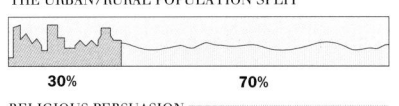

Ewe, Kabye, Gurma, French

195 people per sq. mile

THE URBAN/RURAL POPULATION SPLIT

30%   70%

RELIGIOUS PERSUASION

Muslim 10%

Christian 20%

Indigenous beliefs 70%

A bitter divide has existed between north and south since before independence. Most southern resentment is directed toward a minority in the north, the Kabye people from the Kabye plateau, because of their domination of the military. The Kabye and other northerners in turn resent their own underdevelopment in contrast to the high development, especially educationally, of all southerners. The dominant southern group is the Ewe, who make up more than 40% of the population.

As elsewhere in Africa, the extended family is important and tribalism and nepotism are key factors in everyday life. Some Togolese ethnic groups, such as the Mina, have matriarchal societies. The "Nana Benz," the market-women of Lomé market, who control the retail trade, have considerable private money. Politics, however, remains a male preserve.

Kabye cultivations near Kara, *in northern Togo. The main food crops grown are cassava, yams and corn.*

POLITICS

1994/1999

President Gen. Gnassingbe Eyadéma

THE STATE OF THE PARTIES

National Assembly 81 members

2% CFN

45% RPT   44% CAR   9% UTD

CAR = Action Committee for Renewal   **RPT** = Rally of the Togolese People   **UTD** = Togolese Union for Democracy
CFN = New Force Coordination

Politics has been dominated for two decades by General Gnassingbe Eyadéma, who took power at the head of a military government in 1967. The army is the main power broker, notably the small group of officers from Pya on the Kabye plateau.

A democracy movement has been gathering momentum since 1990, when serious rioting occurred in Lomé. Many unofficial parties sprang up and were legitimized early in 1991. Multiparty presidential elections held in 1993 confirmed Eyadéma in power. However, these were boycotted by some opposition candidates in protest at the exclusion from the elections of Gilchrist Olympio, an arch-opponent of Eyadéma and son of a former president. Controversial legislative elections in 1994 saw a close contest between the CAR and RPT which ultimately emerged as the largest party after the CAR was stripped of three seats. Eyadéma also successfully split the opposition drawing the UTD into the governing coalition. A CAR parliamentary boycott ended in 1995.

WORLD AFFAIRS

 BOAD   Ecowas   FZ   OAU   UEMOA

The priority now is maintaining traditional links, especially with France, in spite of the crisis. For the past two years, Eyadéma's foreign policy has competed with that of the democratic forces seeking allies in Europe, the USA and West Africa.

AID

$101m (receipts)   Down 55% in 1993

Development projects have suffered from recent aid suspensions by donors including the USA and the EU. Prior to this, Togo had a good record in project implementation, despite occasional cases of political interference.

T

TOGO

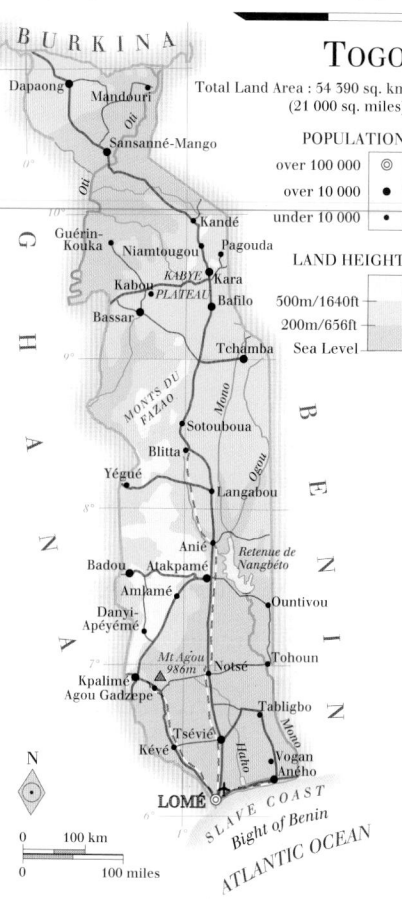

Total Land Area : 54 390 sq. km
(21 000 sq. miles)

POPULATION

over 100 000	◎
over 10 000	●
under 10 000	•

LAND HEIGHT

500m/1640ft
200m/656ft
Sea Level

 0   100 km

 0   100 miles

DEFENSE

 $29m

 Down 3% in 1995

The military has an important role in Togo, and spending on defense is high. Modern equipment is supplied mainly by France, Germany and the USA. Potential intervention by Ghana is regarded as a main defense issue. France guarantees Togo's security through a defense accord.

ECONOMICS

 $1.3bn

489.05–533.68 CFA francs

SCORE CARD

❑ WORLD GNP RANKING	149th
❑ GNP PER CAPITA	$320
❑ BALANCE OF PAYMENTS	$–98m
❑ INFLATION	41%
❑ UNEMPLOYMENT	2%

STRENGTHS

Efficient civil service. Ideal location for role as entrepôt, based on Lomé port. Proceeds of widespread smuggling. Resourcefulness of entrepreneurs, notably market-women. Phosphate deposits have the world's highest mineral content. Self-sufficient in basic foodstuffs. Diverse range of food crops.

RESOURCES

 60m kwh (capacity 34,000 kw)

 16,988 tons

 1.3m sheep, 2m goats, 934,000 pigs, 250,000 cattle

 Phosphates, iron, chromite, bauxite, marble, dolomite

Phosphates are Togo's most important resource. Exploration for oil is under way, but none has yet been found. The Nangbeto Dam, constructed jointly with Benin and opened in 1988, has reduced dependence on Ghana for energy.

ENVIRONMENT

 11%

Few ecological initiatives taken

Ecologists have been critical of the transformation of nature reserves into hunting grounds for the military elite. Other problems include coastal erosion around Aneho and desertification.

MEDIA

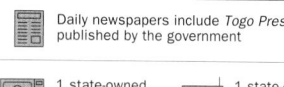 The total censorship which existed prior to 1990 has eased. However, the new independent press is subject to severe intimidation

PUBLISHING AND BROADCAST MEDIA

Daily newspapers include *Togo Presse*, published by the government

1 state-owned service

1 state-owned service

With the arrival of the democracy movement, a number of privately owned newspapers have sprung up.

CRIME

 Togo does not publish prison figures

Theft on increase in the capital

Togo is normally relatively peaceable. However, crime inevitably intensified during the recent periods of unrest. Robberies, in particular, are increasing in the capital.

EXPORTS

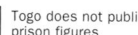

Philippines 5%
Italy 4%
Other 66%
France 7%
Spain 7%
Canada 11%

IMPORTS

Germany 4%
USA 6%
Japan 7%
Netherlands 8%
Other 42%
France 33%

WEAKNESSES

Smuggling-dependent economy could easily be disrupted by border closure with Ghana. Limited internal market due to size of country. Lack of natural resources.

CHRONOLOGY

After colonization by Germany in 1894, Togoland was divided between France and the UK in 1914.

- ❑ **1960** French part independent as Togo (UK part joined to Ghana).
- ❑ **1967** Eyadéma's bloodless coup.
- ❑ **1969** One-party state.
- ❑ **1993** Presidential elections.
- ❑ **1994** RPT wins controversial elections.

EDUCATION

 52%

 7,826 students

Schooling is based on the French model. The university in Lomé has over 4,000 students.

HEALTH

 1 per 12,500 people

 Malaria, diarrheal, infectious and parasitic diseases

Togo's relatively well-structured health care system is a reflection of its being a favored target of foreign aid.

WEALTH

 Agricultural worker, 16,500 CFA francs ($34) per month; bank employee, 57,964 CFA francs ($119) per month

CONSUMER GOODS OWNERSHIP

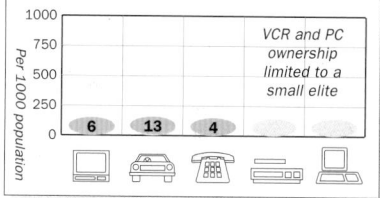

VCR and PC ownership limited to a small elite

6   13   4

Considerable wealth disparities exist between the political and business classes, and Togolese who work the land. Between these extremes, the urban class is relatively prosperous.

WORLD RANKING

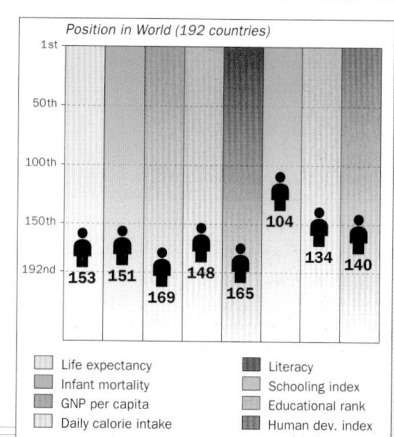

Position in World (192 countries)

153   151   169   148   165   104   134   140

Life expectancy	Literacy
Infant mortality	Schooling index
GNP per capita	Educational rank
Daily calorie intake	Human dev. index

T

TONGA

OFFICIAL NAME: Kingdom of Tonga   CAPITAL: Nuku'alofa
POPULATION: 98,000   CURRENCY: Pa'anga   OFFICIAL LANGUAGE: Tongan

LOCATED IN THE SOUTH PACIFIC northeast of New Zealand, Tonga is an archipelago of 170 islands. These are divided into three main groups, Vava'u, Ha'apai and Tongatapu. Tonga's easterly islands are generally low and fertile. Those in the west are higher and volcanic in origin. Tonga's economy is based on agriculture, especially coconut, cassava and passion fruit production. Politics is effectively controlled by the King.

CLIMATE

WEATHER CHART

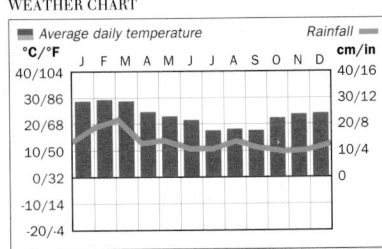

Tonga has a tropical oceanic climate, with year-round temperatures ranging between 68°F and 86°F.

TRANSPORTATION

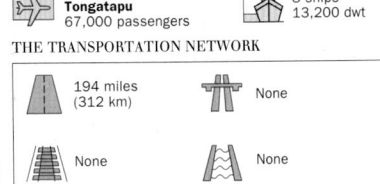

Fua'amotu International, Tongatapu
67,000 passengers

8 ships
13,200 dwt

THE TRANSPORTATION NETWORK

194 miles (312 km)   None

None   None

Japanese and other foreign aid is currently financing a major port development at Nuku'alofa.

TOURISM

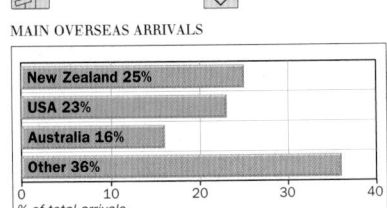

20,917 visitors   Down 1% in 1990

MAIN OVERSEAS ARRIVALS

New Zealand 25%
USA 23%
Australia 16%
Other 36%

% of total arrivals

Tonga's main attractions are its tropical beaches. Tourist arrivals, mainly from New Zealand and the USA, are expanding slowly. However, fears have been expressed that too many visitors may erode traditional Tongan culture.

Mountainous scenery typical of Tonga's westerly islands. Tonga's 170 islands are scattered over a wide expanse of the South Pacific. Only 45 are inhabited.

TONGA

Total Land Area : 720 sq. km (278 sq. miles)

POPULATION
• over 10 000
• under 10 000

LAND HEIGHT
200m/656ft
Sea Level

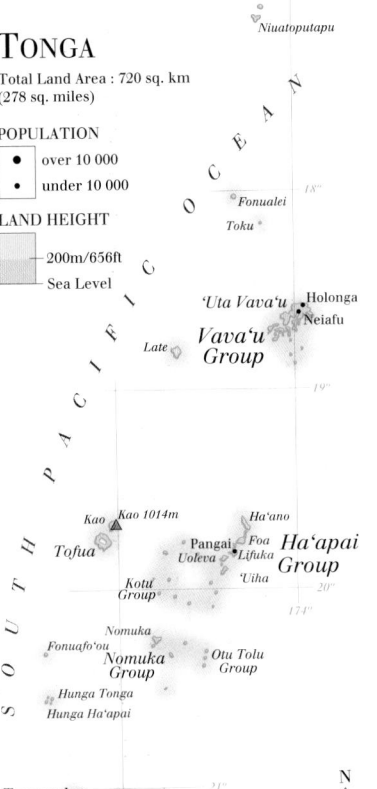

PACIFIC OCEAN
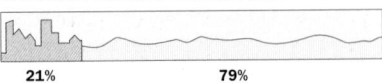

PEOPLE

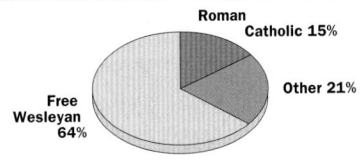

English, Tongan   352 people per sq. mile

THE URBAN/RURAL POPULATION SPLIT

21%   79%

RELIGIOUS PERSUASION

Roman Catholic 15%
Other 21%
Free Wesleyan 64%

Tonga has strong ethnic ties with eastern Fiji and there has traditionally been considerable population movement between the two states. Tongans tend to see themselves as unique among Pacific islanders as they were never fully colonized and retain their monarchy.

Respect for traditional values and institutions remains high. Tongans are strong church-goers; the Wesleyan, Roman Catholic and Mormon churches are influential and often fund education. However, a new generation of Western-educated Tongans is querying some traditional attitudes.

POLITICS

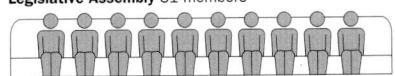

1996/1999   HM King Taufa'ahau Tupou IV

THE STATE OF THE PARTIES

Legislative Assembly 31 members

The Legislative Assembly comprises the King, the 12 members of the Privy Council, 9 hereditary nobles chosen by their peers and 9 elected members

The main power brokers in Tongan politics are the King, the noble establishment and the landowners. King Tupou IV effectively heads his government, frequently exercising kingly powers. The legislative assembly defers to his judgement and the King has taken the initiative in instigating several development projects which have been undertaken without reference to the government.

Younger westernized Tongans are now increasingly questioning the role of the monarchy and there is a growing movement in support of democratic change. When the current King dies, pressure for reform is likely to accelerate.

T

WORLD AFFAIRS

Tonga is firmly pro-Western in international affairs, and historically has come within New Zealand's sphere of influence. It is a member of the South Pacific Forum, but is one of the few states in the region not to endorse the South Pacific Nuclear Free Zone.

AID

 $30m   Up 57% in 1993

Aid finances major infrastructure projects; Australia, the USA, New Zealand, the EU and the ADB are major donors. Significant amounts were recently ploughed into oil exploration, but without success.

DEFENSE

 $2m   Little variation from year to year

Tonga has a small defense force, which includes both regulars and reserves; 5% of the state budget is currently allocated to defense.

ECONOMICS

 $160m    1.29–1.34 pa'anga

SCORE CARD

❏ WORLD GNP RANKING	188th
❏ GNP PER CAPITA	$1,640
❏ BALANCE OF PAYMENTS	$–6m
❏ INFLATION	1%
❏ UNEMPLOYMENT	4.1%

STRENGTHS

Range of subsistence agriculture. Commercial production of coconut, cassava and passion fruit.

WEAKNESSES

Off main shipping routes. Exports in direct competition with rest of South Pacific region. Many productive Tongans live abroad.

EXPORTS

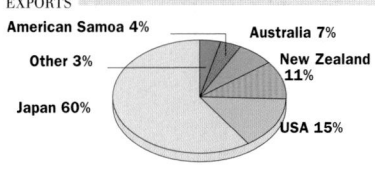

American Samoa 4%   Australia 7%
Other 3%   New Zealand 11%
Japan 60%   USA 15%

IMPORTS

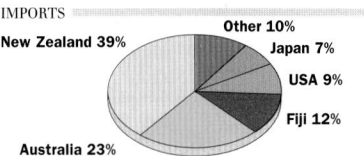

Other 10%
New Zealand 39%   Japan 7%
USA 9%
Fiji 12%
Australia 23%

RESOURCES

 27m kwh (capacity 7,000 kw)   2,481 tons

94,000 pigs, 16,000 goats, 11,000 horses   None

Tonga has no strategic or mineral resources. Electricity is generated from imported fuel, which is brought ashore in uneconomical 44-gallon units. Recent exploration has failed to identify any oil reserves.

ENVIRONMENT

 None   Environmental issues not of particular concern

Tonga does not suffer from serious environmental problems, although it is occasionally afflicted by natural disasters, such as the 1982 typhoon. Commercial activity has made little impact on the environment.

MEDIA

 Censorship tends to be self-imposed. Outspoken slander or attacks on the King are not acceptable

PUBLISHING AND BROADCAST MEDIA

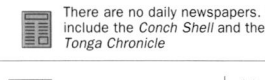

There are no daily newspapers. Weeklies include the *Conch Shell* and the *Tonga Chronicle*

No TV service   1 independent service

There are five main newspapers. The *Conch Shell* has a circulation of around 10,000. The *Tonga Chronicle* is published by the government.

CRIME

 58 prisoners   Rising levels of theft

Crime rates are generally low, partly due to the strong influence of the family. However, offenses such as breaking and entering have increased with rising unemployment levels among young Tongans.

EDUCATION

 99%    705 students

Education is based on the Australian and New Zealand models and church participation in schools is high. The 'Atenisi Institute offers university level courses. A few students go on to the University of the South Pacific in Fiji.

HEALTH

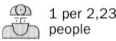 1 per 2,235 people   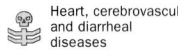 Heart, cerebrovascular and diarrheal diseases

Tonga has some modern health care facilities. However, patients have to be flown out to Australia or New Zealand for sophisticated surgery.

CHRONOLOGY

Originally discovered by the Polynesians, Tonga was visited by the Dutch in the 17th century and Captain Cook in the 18th. In the latter half of the 19th century the islands became a unified state after a period of civil war.

❏ **1875** First constitution established by King George Tupou I.
❏ **1900** Concern over German ambitions in region leads to signing of Treaty of Friendship and Protection with UK.
❏ **1918–1965** Reign of Queen Salote Tupou III.
❏ **1958** Greater autonomy from UK enshrined in Friendship Treaty.
❏ **1965** King Taufa'ahau Tupou IV accedes on mother's death.
❏ **1970** Independence within British Commonwealth.
❏ **1988** Treaty allowing US nuclear warships right of transit through Tongan waters signed.
❏ **1996** General election sees strong showing by pro-democracy candidates in the minority of seats decided by universal suffrage.

WEALTH

 Remittances from Tongans living overseas are important for the local economy

CONSUMER GOODS OWNERSHIP

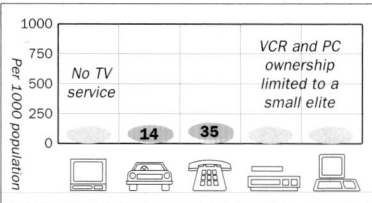

No TV service   VCR and PC ownership limited to a small elite
Per 1000 population: 14   35

Tongans indulge in few ostentatious displays of wealth. The well-off provide financial support for relatives.

WORLD RANKING

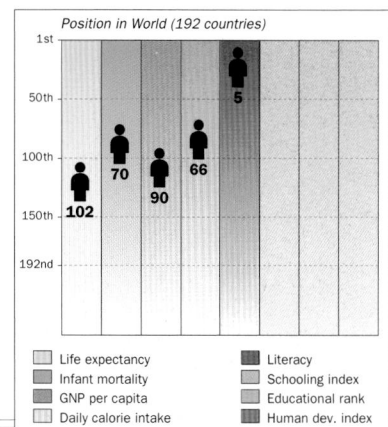

Position in World (192 countries)
102   70   90   66   5

Life expectancy
Infant mortality
GNP per capita
Daily calorie intake
Literacy
Schooling index
Educational rank
Human dev. index

T

TRINIDAD & TOBAGO

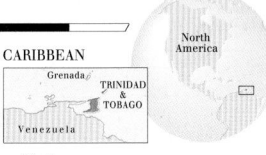

OFFICIAL NAME: Republic of Trinidad and Tobago **CAPITAL:** Port-of-Spain
CURRENCY: Trinidad and Tobago dollar **POPULATION:** 1.3 million **OFFICIAL LANGUAGE:** English

THE TWO ISLANDS of Trinidad and Tobago are the most southerly of the Caribbean Windward Islands and lie just 9 miles off the Venezuelan coast. They gained joint independence from Britain in 1962 and Tobago was given internal autonomy in 1987. The spectacular mountain ranges and large swamps are rich in tropical flora and fauna. Pitch Lake in Trinidad is the world's largest natural reservoir of asphalt.

CLIMATE

WEATHER CHART

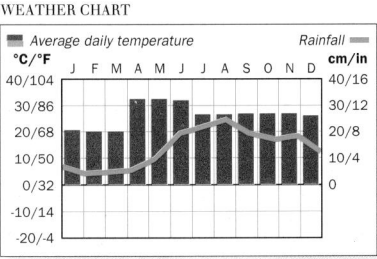

The islands are a little warmer than others in the Caribbean and escape the hurricanes, which pass by to the north.

TRANSPORTATION

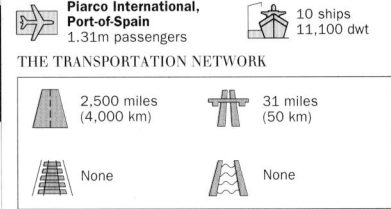

Piarco International, Port-of-Spain — 1.31m passengers

10 ships 11,100 dwt

THE TRANSPORTATION NETWORK

2,500 miles (4,000 km)

31 miles (50 km)

None

None

The road network is well developed. Most Trinidadians rely on private taxis or minibuses with set routes. The majority disinvestment of the BWIA state airline was completed in 1995.

TOURISM

266,000 visitors   Up 18% in 1994

MAIN OVERSEAS ARRIVALS

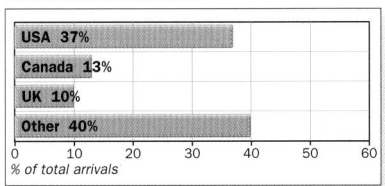

USA 37%
Canada 13%
UK 10%
Other 40%
% of total arrivals

Trinidad's concentration on the oil sector meant that it was one of the last Caribbean states to develop its tourism potential. Tourism is concentrated on Tobago (said to be the model for the island in *Robinson Crusoe*) renowned for its wildlife, including over 500 species of butterfly.

TRINIDAD & TOBAGO

Total Area : 5130 sq. km (1981 sq. miles)

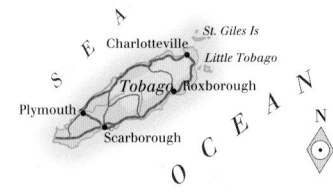

LAND HEIGHT
500m/1640ft
200m/656ft
Sea Level

POPULATION
over 50 000
over 10 000
under 10 000

PEOPLE

English Creole, English, Hindi, French, Spanish

656 people per sq. mile

THE URBAN/RURAL POPULATION SPLIT

70%   30%

ETHNIC MAKEUP

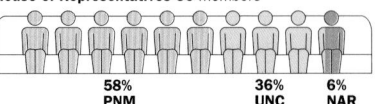

Other 2%
Mixed 14%
Chinese 1%
Black 43%
South Asian 40%

Trinidad's South Asian community is the largest in the Caribbean, and holds on to its Muslim and Hindu inheritance. The open discussion of racial issues in Trinidad has gone some way to dissipating latent tensions that exist between black and South Asian Trinidadians.

POLITICS

1995/2000

President Noor Mohammed Hassanali

THE STATE OF THE PARTIES

House of Representatives 36 members

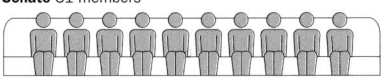

58% PNM   36% UNC   6% NAR

PNM = People's National Movement **UNC** = United National Congress **NAR** = National Alliance for Reconstruction

Senate 31 members

16 members chosen by the prime minister, 6 by the leader of the opposition, and 9 by the president

Trinidad has lacked a major political figure since the death of Eric Williams, the autocratic leader of the PNM, who presided over independence in 1962. Decades of increasingly right-wing PNM rule, interrupted in the mid-1980s, saw political fragmentation and the 1990 coup attempt by a Black-Muslim sect. The UNC's Basdeo Panday, the first ever South Asian prime minister in 1995, heads a coalition government committed to reducing unemployment, crime and racial discrimination.

Tobago's white sand beaches, verdant landscape and natural anchorages have enabled it to develop a thriving tourist industry.

WORLD AFFAIRS

 ACS Caricom Comm NAM OAS

Trinidad wishes to improve economic ties with the Group of Three: Venezuela, Colombia and Mexico. It is interested in future membership of or association with NAFTA but also seeks to consolidate its ties with the EU. Disputes with Venezuela over sea boundaries, important for establishing both fishing and marine oil rights, are ongoing.

AID

 $3m (receipts)   Down 63% in 1993

Aid is modest: in 1995 the World Bank approved a US$6.5 million environment protection loan.

DEFENSE

 $82m   Down 1% in 1995

Defense forces comprise a 2,100-strong army and coastguard. The latter is used to patrol fishing grounds.

ECONOMICS

 $4.8bn   5.67–5.71 Trinidad and Tobago dollars

SCORE CARD

❏ WORLD GNP RANKING	104th
❏ GNP PER CAPITA	$3,740
❏ BALANCE OF PAYMENTS	$218m
❏ INFLATION	8.8%
❏ UNEMPLOYMENT	20.3%

STRENGTHS

Oil, which accounts for 70% of export earnings. Gas is increasingly being exploited to support new industries, such as nitrogenous fertilizer manufacture. Tourism, particularly on Tobago, is being developed.

WEAKNESSES

Insufficiently diversified economy highly sensitive to world oil price movements. High unemployment.

EXPORTS

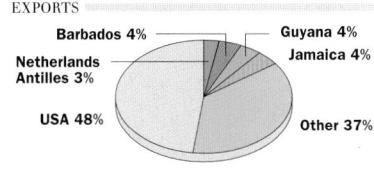

Barbados 4%
Guyana 4%
Jamaica 4%
Netherlands Antilles 3%
USA 48%
Other 37%

IMPORTS

Germany 4%
Singapore 5%
Hong Kong 3%
Japan 14%
Former Soviet Republic 47%
Other 27%

RESOURCES

 3.9bn kwh (capacity 990,000 kw)
 140,530 b/d (reserves 572,600,000 bbl)

55,000 cattle, 52,000 goats, 48,000 pigs
Oil, natural gas, asphalt, coal, gypsum, iron, fluorspar

Oil and gas are Trinidad's major resources. Government policy is to continue increasing both production and refinery output.

ENVIRONMENT

 3%   Greater environmental consciousness

Spillages from oil tankers, which pose a serious threat to coastal conservation areas such as the Caroni Swamp with its 500 species of butterflies, are the major concern. Oil spills are also threatening some tourist beaches.

MEDIA

 No restrictions on political reporting

PUBLISHING AND BROADCAST MEDIA

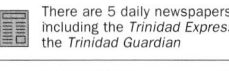 There are 5 daily newspapers, including the *Trinidad Express* and the *Trinidad Guardian*

 1 state-owned, 1 independent service
 1 state-owned, 1 independent service

New TV and radio stations have sprung up since broadcasting license rules were relaxed in 1992. Most TV programing is from US networks.

CRIME

 2,387 prisoners   Down 1% in 1992

Crime, especially narcotics-related, is higher than in most of the Caribbean. In 1994, there were 144 recorded murders compared to 100 in 1993. Locals oppose the abolition of the death penalty.

EDUCATION

 98%   7,161 students

Education is based on the British 11-plus system. Most students go on to the University of the West Indies; Trinidad hosts the St. Augustine campus. However, wealthy Trinidadians go to universities in the USA.

HEALTH

 1 per 1,541 people
 Heart disease, cancers, diabetes, accidents, violence

Oil wealth has given Trinidad a better public health service than most Caribbean states, and more private clinics, mainly serving the expatriate community. However, treatment delays are seen as a growing problem. 98% of the population have safe water.

CHRONOLOGY

Britain seized Trinidad from Spain in 1797 and Tobago from France in 1802. They were unified in 1888.

- ❏ **1956** Dr. Eric Williams founds PNM and wins general election: main support from blacks. Indian population supports opposition.
- ❏ **1961** Leaves West Indian Federation (joined 1958).
- ❏ **1962** Independence.
- ❏ **1970** Black Power demonstrations cause brief state of emergency.
- ❏ **1980** Tobago gets own House of Assembly; internal autonomy 1987.
- ❏ **1986** NAR coalition wins elections, but fails to halt economic decline.
- ❏ **1990–1991** Premier taken hostage in failed fundamentalist coup. PNM returned to power.
- ❏ **1995** UNC's Basdeo Panday becomes first Asian prime minister.

WEALTH

 Welder, 16 Trinidad and Tobago dollars (US$3) per hour; government computer programer, 2,640 Trinidad and Tobago dollars (US$462) per month

CONSUMER GOODS OWNERSHIP

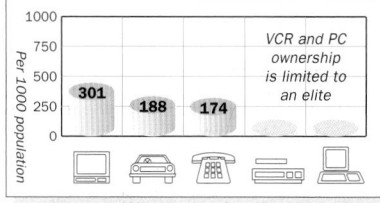

VCR and PC ownership is limited to an elite

Per 1000 population: 301   188   174

Wealth disparities between the affluent oil-rich business elite, many of whom are expatriate, and farm laborers are marked in Trinidad. During the oil-boom years of the 1970s, Trinidad was proportionately the world's biggest importer of Scotch whiskey. Today, rural poverty in the interior, particularly among South Asian Trinidadian farmers, is a growing problem.

WORLD RANKING

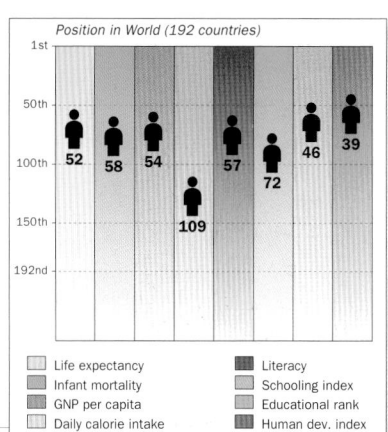

Position in World (192 countries)

52 58 54 109 57 72 46 39

- ☐ Life expectancy
- ☐ Infant mortality
- ☐ GNP per capita
- ☐ Daily calorie intake
- ☐ Literacy
- ☐ Schooling index
- ☐ Educational rank
- ☐ Human dev. index

T

TUNISIA

OFFICIAL NAME: Republic of Tunisia **CAPITAL:** Tunis
POPULATION: 8.9 million **CURRENCY:** Tunisian dinar **OFFICIAL LANGUAGE:** Arabic

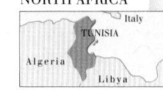

NORTH AFRICA

 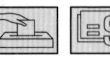 

NORTH AFRICA'S SMALLEST country, Tunisia lies sandwiched between Libya and Algeria. The populous north is mountainous, fertile in places and has a long Mediterranean coastline. The south is largely desert. Habib Bourguiba ruled the country from independence in 1956 until a bloodless coup in 1987. Under President Ben Ali, the government has moved toward multiparty democracy, but faces a challenge from Islamic fundamentalists. Ties with the EU, Tunisia's main trading partner, were strengthened at the first Euro–Mediterranean conference, held in 1995. Manufacturing and tourism are expanding.

TOURISM

 4m visitors   Up 8% in 1994

MAIN OVERSEAS ARRIVALS

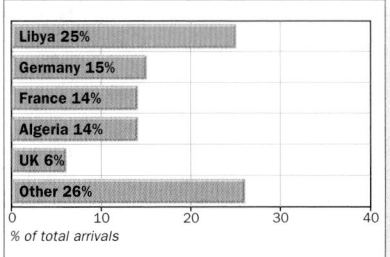

Libya 25%
Germany 15%
France 14%
Algeria 14%
UK 6%
Other 26%

% of total arrivals

CLIMATE

WEATHER CHART

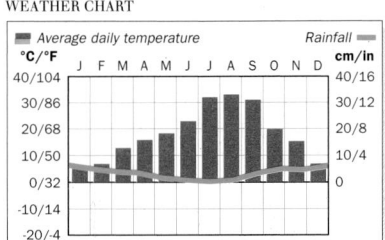

Tunisia is hot in summer. The north is often wet and windy in winter. The far south is arid. The spring brings the dry, dusty *chili* wind from the Sahara.

TRANSPORTATION

 **Habib Bourguiba, Monastir**
1.72m passengers

 28 ships
227,900 dwt

THE TRANSPORTATION NETWORK

10,880 miles
(17,510 km)

Highway from Tunis to Carthage airport

1,367 miles
(2,200 km)

 None

Tunisia has six international airports. A highway from Tunis to Carthage Airport opened in 1993. A light subway in Tunis and a rail link from Gafsa to Gabès are being built. The southern third of the country has few roads.

Tourists have flocked to Tunisia since the 1960s, attracted by its winter sunshine, beaches, desert and Roman remains. One of the Mediterranean's cheapest package destinations, Tunisia attracts almost two million European visitors a year. However, numbers were hit in 1990–1991 by the Gulf War and the fear of attacks by Islamic militants. Tourism employs more than 200,000 people and is a focus of investment. Capacity is set to top 200,000 beds by the year 2000. However, concern about its environmental impact is growing.

PEOPLE

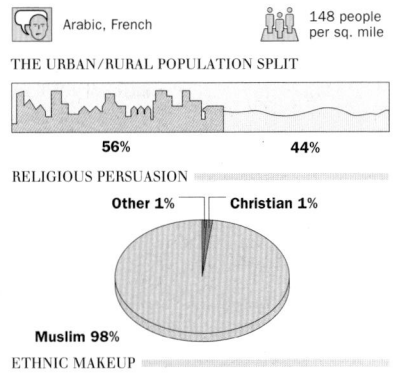 Arabic, French

148 people per sq. mile

THE URBAN/RURAL POPULATION SPLIT

56%   44%

RELIGIOUS PERSUASION

Other 1%   Christian 1%

Muslim 98%

ETHNIC MAKEUP

Other 1%   European 1%

Arab and Berber 98%

The population is almost entirely of Arab and Berber descent, although there are Jewish and Christian minorities. Many Tunisians still live in extended family groups, in which three or four generations are represented.

Tunisia has traditionally been one of the most liberal Arab states. The 1956 Personal Statutes Code of President Bourguiba gave women better rights than in any other Arab country. Further legislation has since given women the right to custody of children in divorce cases, made family violence against women punishable by law and helped divorced women to get alimony. Family planning and contraception have been freely available since the early 1960s. Now Tunisia's population grows by only 16,000 a year. Women make up 25% of the total work force and 35% of the industrial work force. Company ownership by women is steadily increasing; politics, however, remains exclusively a male preserve.

These freedoms are threatened by the growth in recent years of Islamic fundamentalism, which also worries the mainly French-speaking political and business elite who wish to strengthen links with Europe.

The Ben Ali regime, although not as repressive as its predecessor, has been criticized for its actions against Islamic activists, in particular the banned *Al-Nahda* party. Amnesty International has detailed a number of human rights abuses, mainly against female members of *Al-Nahda*.

POPULATION AGE BREAKDOWN

% of population by age group	0–14	15–64	65+

	1960	1970	1980	1990	2000
65+	4.2%	3.8%	3.8%	4%	4.8%
15–64	52.5%	49.9%	54.5%	58%	62.2%
0–14	43.3%	46.3%	41.7%	38%	33%

Roman remains at the village of La-Kesra *in Tozeur region, a low-lying area of oases in western central Tunisia.*

T

POLITICS

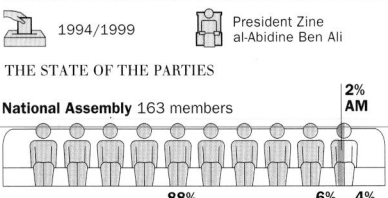

1994/1999

President Zine al-Abidine Ben Ali

THE STATE OF THE PARTIES

National Assembly 163 members

**2%
AM**

**88%
RCD**

**6%
MDS**

**4%
Other**

RCD = Constitutional Democratic Assembly **MDS** = Social Democratic Party **AM** = *Attajdid* Movement **Other** = Democratic Union, Popular Unity Party

President Ben Ali
*became head of
state in 1987.*

Dr. Hamed Karoui,
*was appointed prime
minister in 1988.*

Legally a multiparty democracy since 1988, Tunisia is still dominated by the RCD and President Ben Ali.

MAIN POLITICAL ISSUES
Fundamentalism
The RCD has clamped down on Islamic fundamentalists, particularly the outlawed *Al-Nahda*, or Renewal Party. In 1991, 500 *Al-Nahda* members were arrested following a failed coup, thought to be inspired by fundamentalists. Its leader, Rachid Gannouchi, is now in exile.

Human Rights
The RCD has been under increasing attack over its human rights record. In 1995, Amnesty International claimed that the torture of detainees had become "common currency" in Tunisia. The RCD is committed to promoting women's rights.

PROFILE
President Ben Ali has made efforts to liberalize the political system. The life presidency has been abolished, and political parties and press freedom are encouraged. The 1994 general election aimed at a national coalition against the growing trend of Islamic fundamentalism. However, a complex proportional representation system ensured that there was an overwhelming victory for the RCD, while allowing for a degree of political plurality. Since 1994, there has been evidence of a renewed crackdown against the left-wing opposition.

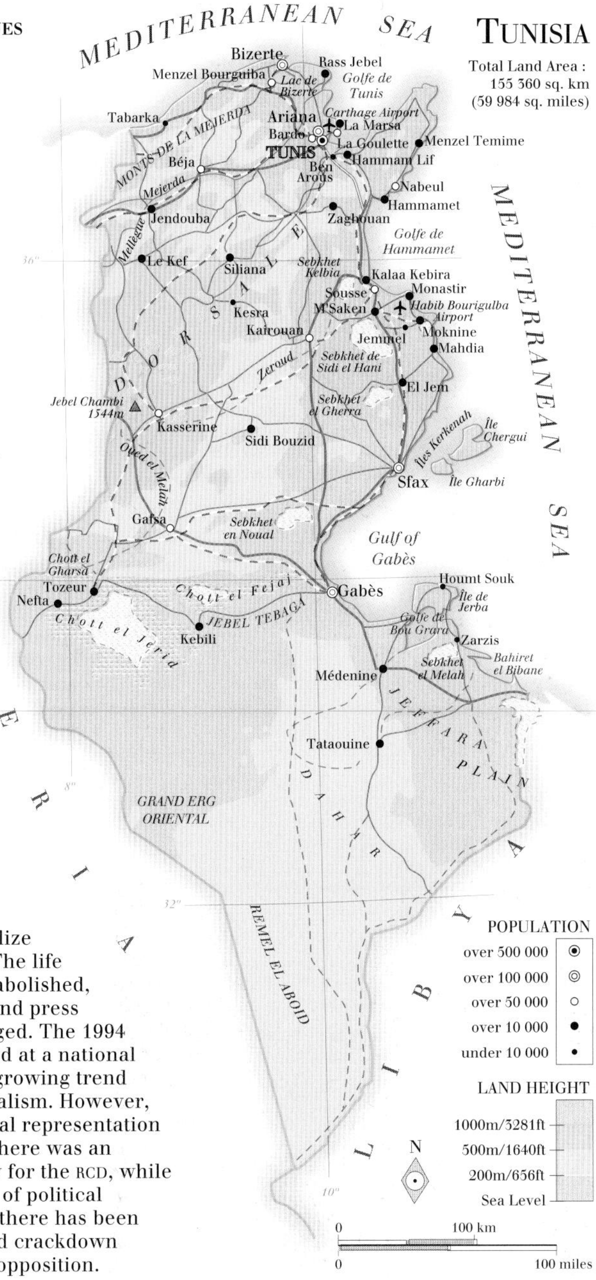

WORLD AFFAIRS

| AL | AMU | IBRD | NAM | OIC |

A foreign policy priority is to strengthen contacts with the West, which have generally been good because of Tunisia's liberal economic and social policies. Attention is focused on the EU, Tunisia's main export market, and Tunisia played an important role in the first Euro–Mediterranean conference, held in 1995.

Tunis has been host to the PLO since the organization was expelled from the Lebanon. Relations with other Arab states, particularly Kuwait and Saudi Arabia, were soured by Tunisia's support for Iraq during the Gulf War. The government regards the political success of Islamic fundamentalism in neighboring Algeria with some concern. Relations with Libya are improving, helped by the fact that Tunisia has been turning a blind eye to sanction-busters operating through its territory.

CHRONOLOGY

Tunisia has been home to the Zenata Berbers since earliest times and its history is linked to the rise and fall of the Mediterranean-centered empires. Carthage (near present-day Tunis), founded in the 9th century, became the hub of a 1,000-year Phoenician trading empire which linked European and African trading networks. Tunisia was then incorporated into the Roman, Byzantine, Arab, Ottoman and, finally, French empires.

❑ **1883** La Marsa Treaty makes Tunisia a French protectorate, ending its semi-independence. Bey of Tunis remains monarch.
❑ **1900** Influx of French and Italian settlers.
❑ **1920** *Destour* (Constitution) Party formed; calls for self-government.
❑ **1935** Habib Bourguiba forms *Neo-Destour* (New Constitution) Party.
❑ **1943** Defeat of Axis powers by British troops restores French rule.
❑ **1955** Internal autonomy. Bourguiba returns from exile.
❑ **1956** Independence. Bourguiba elected prime minister. Personal Statutes Code gives rights to women. Family planning introduced.
❑ **1957** The Bey is deposed. Tunisia becomes a republic with Bourguiba as first president.
❑ **1964** *Neo-Destour* becomes the only legal political party; changes its name to *Destour Socialist Party* (PSD). Moderate socialist economic program is introduced. ⇨

TUNISIA

Total Land Area :
155 360 sq. km
(59 984 sq. miles)

MEDITERRANEAN SEA

MONTS DE LA MEJERDA

Bizerte
Menzel Bourguiba
Rass Jebel
Lac de Bizerte
Golfe de Tunis
Tabarka
Ariana
Carthage Airport
Bardo
La Marsa
TUNIS
La Goulette
Menzel Temime
Béja
Ben Arous
Hammam Lif
Mejerda
Nabeul
Jendouba
Zaghouan
Hammamet
Le Kef
Golfe de Hammamet
Siliana
Sebkhet Kelbia
Kalaa Kebira
Kesra
Sousse
Monastir
M'Saken
Habib Bourigulba Airport
Kairouan
Jemmel
Moknine
Zeroud
Sebkhet de Sidi el Hani
Mahdia
Jebel Chambi 1544m
Sebkhet el Gherra
El Jem
Kasserine
Sidi Bouzid
Îles Kerkenah
Île Chergui
Sfax
Île Gharbi
Gafsa
Sebkhet en Noual
Gulf of Gabès
Chott el Gharsa
Tozeur
Nefta
Chott el Fejaj
Gabès
Houmt Souk
Île de Jerba
JEBEL TEBAGA
Golfe de Bou Grara
Kebili
Zarzis
Chott el Jerid
Bahiret el Bibane
Médenine
Sebkhet el Melah
JEFFARA PLAIN
Tataouine
DAHAR
GRAND ERG ORIENTAL
A L G E R I A
L I B Y A
REMEL EL ABIOD

N

POPULATION

over 500 000 ◉
over 100 000 ◎
over 50 000 ○
over 10 000 ●
under 10 000 ·

LAND HEIGHT

1000m/3281ft
500m/1640ft
200m/656ft
Sea Level

0   100 km

0   100 miles

T

CHRONOLOGY *continued*

- ❏ **1969** Agricultural collectivization program, begun 1964, abandoned.
- ❏ **1974** Bourguiba becomes president for life.
- ❏ **1974–1976** Hundreds imprisoned for belonging to "illegal organizations."
- ❏ **1978** Trade union movement, UGTT, holds 24-hour general strike; over 50 killed in clashes. UGTT leadership replaced with PSD loyalists.
- ❏ **1980** New prime minister Muhammed Mazli ushers in greater political tolerance.
- ❏ **1981** Elections. Opposition groups allege electoral malpractice.
- ❏ **1984** Widespread riots after food price increases.
- ❏ **1986** General Zine al-Abidine Ben Ali becomes interior minister. Four Muslim fundamentalists sentenced to death.
- ❏ **1987** Fundamentalist leader Rachid Gannouchi arrested. Ben Ali becomes prime minister; takes over presidency after doctors certify Bourguiba senile. PSD becomes the RCD.
- ❏ **1988** Most political prisoners released. Constitutional reforms introduce multiparty system and abolish the position of life president. Two opposition parties legalized.
- ❏ **1989** Elections. RCD wins all seats. Ben Ali president. Fundamentalists take 13% of vote.
- ❏ **1990** Tunisia backs Iraq over invasion of Kuwait. Clampdown on fundamentalists intensifies.
- ❏ **1991** Abortive coup blamed on *Al-Nahda*; over 500 arrests.
- ❏ **1993** Agreement on electoral reform paves way for opposition parties to participate equally with RCD in 1994 elections.
- ❏ **1994** Presidential and legislative elections. Ben Ali, the sole candidate, is reelected president. Ruling RCD wins all elected seats; opposition parties gain 19 reserved seats.

AID

 $250m (receipts) Down 39% in 1993

France is the largest single donor, providing almost a quarter of bilateral aid. Italy, Germany, the World Bank and the African Development Bank are other important sources of assistance for Tunisia. Oil-rich Arab states, including Saudi Arabia and Kuwait, have suspended their aid programs to the country since 1990 because of its pro-Iraq stance during the Gulf War. Tunisia's total external debt is estimated to be 60% of GNP.

DEFENSE

 $262m  Up 16% in 1995

0	Defense spending as % GDP	40

3.2%

Despite its small size – 35,500 troops, 26,400 of them conscripts – the military is an important political force, armed mainly with US weapons. Border security with Algeria was tightened in 1995 after Algerian Islamists attacked Tunisian border guards in protest against Tunisian support for Algerian security forces.

TUNISIAN ARMED FORCES

🛡	84 main battle tanks (54 M–60A3, 30 M–60A1)	27,000 personnel
🚢	23 patrol boats	5,000 personnel
✈	32 combat aircraft (15 F–5E/F)	3,500 personnel
🚀	None	

ECONOMICS

📊 $15.9bn 💵 0.95–0.99 dinars

SCORE CARD

- ❏ WORLD GNP RANKING 68th
- ❏ GNP PER CAPITA $1,800
- ❏ BALANCE OF PAYMENTS...................$–304m
- ❏ INFLATION 6.8%
- ❏ UNEMPLOYMENT..............................16.2%

EXPORTS

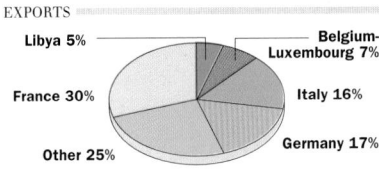

Libya 5%
Belgium-Luxembourg 7%
France 30%
Italy 16%
Germany 17%
Other 25%

IMPORTS

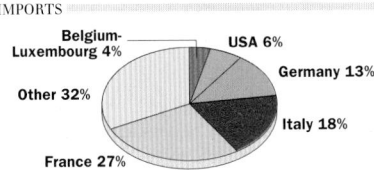

Belgium-Luxembourg 4%
USA 6%
Other 32%
Germany 13%
Italy 18%
France 27%

STRENGTHS

A well-diversified economy, despite limited resources. Tourism. Oil and gas exports. Manufacturing is expanding. European investment.

WEAKNESSES

Dependence on growth of drought-prone agricultural sector. Growing domestic energy demand on oil and gas resources.

PROFILE

Since it began a process of structural adjustment in 1988, supported by the IMF and World Bank, Tunisia has become an increasingly open, market-oriented economy. Real GDP growth has averaged 5% since 1987 and is poised to expand to 6%–7% in 1995–1996. However, the budget deficit rose to 4% of GDP in 1994, after being reduced to 2% of GDP in 1993. Prices have been freed, most state companies privatized and barriers against imports reduced.

The government has also begun a search for foreign investment, which

ECONOMIC PERFORMANCE INDICATOR

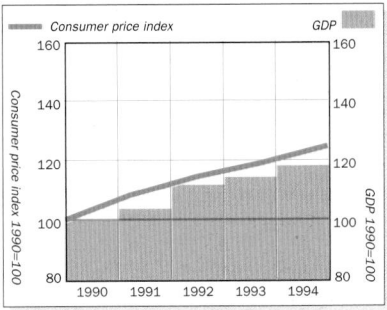

is targeted to treble by 1996. High investment levels are essential if the country is to reach its goal of providing an extra 313,000 jobs for young people over the next two years, and to cut the overall 16% unemployment rate. Another problem is the balance of payments, which relies on fluctuating receipts from the tourism industry to offset a trade deficit. The government must also balance the demands of growth with those of Tunisia's expanding middle class for better social provisions. Negotiations to increase trading opportunities with the EU, already Tunisia's main trading partner, are underway.

TUNISIA : MAJOR BUSINESSES

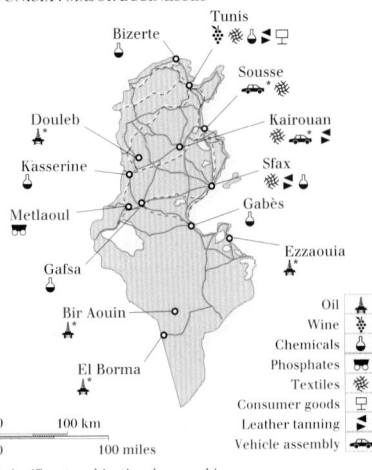

🛢	Oil
🍷	Wine
⚗	Chemicals
	Phosphates
	Textiles
🖥	Consumer goods
	Leather tanning
🚗	Vehicle assembly

* significant multinational ownership

RESOURCES

5.9bn kwh (capacity 1.52m kw)

100,651 b/d (reserves 1,700,000,000 bbl)

7.1m sheep, 1.4m goats, 660,000 cattle

Phosphates, iron, zinc, lead, salt, oil, gas

ELECTRICITY GENERATION

Hydro 2% 0.9bn kwh)	
Thermal 98% (5bn kwh)	
Nuclear 0%	
Other 0%	

% of total generation by type

Tunisia is one of the world's leading producers of phosphates for fertilizers, mainly from mines near Gafsa. Oil and

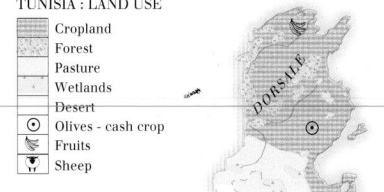

TUNISIA : LAND USE

Cropland
Forest
Pasture
Wetlands
Desert
Olives - cash crop
Fruits
Sheep

0   100 km
0   100 miles

gas are important exports, but growing domestic energy demands mean Tunisia may be a net energy importer by 2000. Electricity is mainly thermal, with some hydropower.

ENVIRONMENT

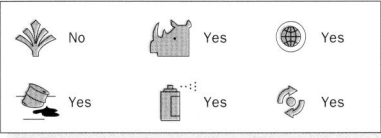

0.3%

Mass tourism is an ecological threat

ENVIRONMENTAL TREATIES

No		Yes		Yes	
Yes		Yes		Yes	

Desertification is a serious problem in the largely arid central and southern regions. However, the dominant environmental issue is the rapid expansion of tourism since the 1980s. Large, insensitively designed hotel and resort developments, which do not fit in with the local architecture, are spoiling coastal areas such as the Isle of Jerba and Hammamet. Tourism is also making an impact on the fragile desert ecology of the south, previously protected by its isolated position.

MEDIA

The press has enjoyed considerable freedom since 1987, but government still interferes at times

PUBLISHING AND BROADCAST MEDIA

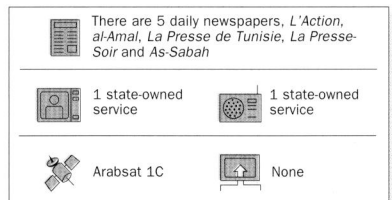

There are 5 daily newspapers, *L'Action, al-Amal, La Presse de Tunisie, La Presse-Soir* and *As-Sabah*

1 state-owned service

1 state-owned service

Arabsat 1C

None

Reforms since the late 1980s have in theory increased press freedom in Tunisia, a country traditionally considered a source of liberal ideas in the Arab world. In practice, government restrictions remain. The foreign press is also occasionally banned, as in 1994–1995, but the arrival of satellite TV from Europe has enabled people to receive a wide range of programs.

CRIME

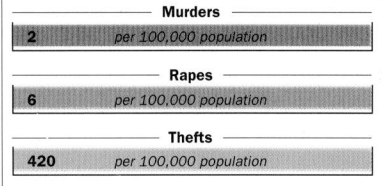

Tunisia does not publish crime figures

Down 1% in 1992

CRIME RATES

Murders	
2	per 100,000 population

Rapes	
6	per 100,000 population

Thefts	
420	per 100,000 population

Street crime is unusual. However, Tunisia's controversial human rights record has prompted criticism of its maltreatment of political and other detainees. Arbitrary arrests and torture while in police custody, especially of suspected Islamic activists, are routine.

EDUCATION

67%

87,780 students

0   Education spending as % GNP   25

4%

THE EDUCATION SYSTEM

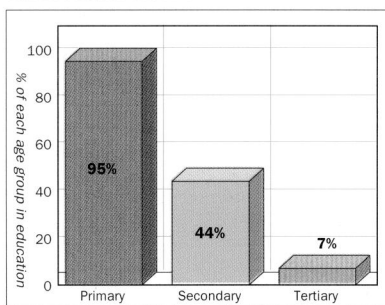

% of each age group in education

- Primary: 95%
- Secondary: 44%
- Tertiary: 7%

Schooling is not compulsory, but about 80% of school-age children attend school. French is taught from the second year of elementary school and is used almost exclusively in higher education. There are two universities.

HEALTH

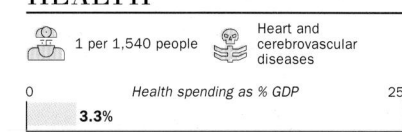

1 per 1,540 people

Heart and cerebrovascular diseases

0   Health spending as % GDP   25

3.3%

Well-developed family planning facilities have almost halved Tunisia's birth-rate over the past 30 years. The population growth rate has dropped from 3.2% to 1.9% – the lowest in the region. The mortality rate has been halved, to 6.4 per 1,000 population a year, reflecting the extension of free medical services to over 70% of the population. Services lack sophistication, but an umbrella of primary care facilities covers all but the most isolated rural communities.

WEALTH

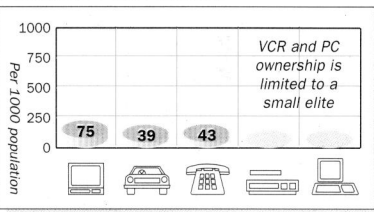

Waiter, 0.8 dinars ($1) per hour ; journalist, 1.7 dinars ($2) per hour

CONSUMER GOODS OWNERSHIP

Per 1000 population

VCR and PC ownership is limited to a small elite

75   39   43

Today 7% of Tunisians are estimated to live in absolute poverty. In 1970, it was 30%. The poorest tend to live in the urban shanty towns, or *bidonvilles*. The Western-oriented elite has links to government and business. Social security covers sickness, old age and maternity, but not unemployment, currently at 16%. The government is concerned that unemployment is encouraging the spread of Islamic fundamentalism. Economic growth is its medium-term solution to the problem. Special projects are being set up in the most deprived urban areas to offset the worst effects of poverty.

WORLD RANKING

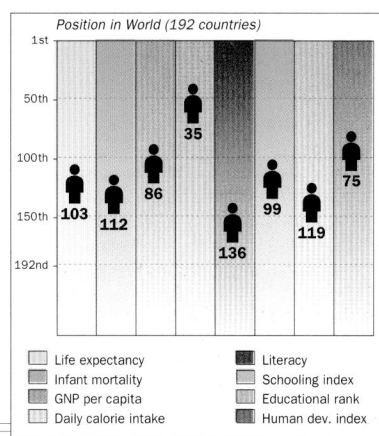

Position in World (192 countries)

- 103
- 112
- 86
- 35
- 136
- 99
- 119
- 75

Life expectancy	Literacy
Infant mortality	Schooling index
GNP per capita	Educational rank
Daily calorie intake	Human dev. index

T

TURKEY

OFFICIAL NAME: Republic of Turkey **CAPITAL:** Ankara
POPULATION: 61.9 million **CURRENCY:** Turkish lira **OFFICIAL LANGUAGE:** Turkish

A SECULAR ISLAMIC STATE, Turkey occupies the peninsula of Asia Minor and the region of Eastern Thrace in Europe. It thus controls the entrance to the Black Sea, which is straddled by Turkey's largest city, Istanbul. The majority of Turks live in the western half of the country. The eastern and southeastern reaches of the Anatolia Plateau are Kurdish regions. Turkey's strategic location gives it significant influence in the Mediterranean, Black Sea and Middle East. Since the breakup of the USSR, Turkey has also been developing trading links with Central Asia.

The island of Akdamar, eastern Anatolia. Surrounded by Lake Van, the island is the site of the 10th-century Church of the Holy Cross.

CLIMATE

WEATHER CHART

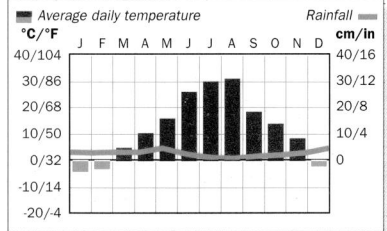

Coastal regions have a Mediterranean climate. The interior has cold, snowy winters and hot, dry summers.

TRANSPORTATION

 Atatürk Intl, Istanbul
7.1m passengers

703 ships
6.88m dwt

THE TRANSPORTATION NETWORK

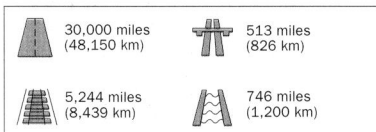

30,000 miles (48,150 km)	513 miles (826 km)
5,244 miles (8,439 km)	746 miles (1,200 km)

The rail system is well developed. Plans exist for a $4 billion rail tunnel under the Boğazi, and for a high-speed link between Istanbul and Ankara. More expressways are planned, including a road bridge across the Dardanelles.

TOURISM

 6m visitors

 Up 2% in 1994

Tourism suffered a setback in 1994 with increasing attacks on foreign tourists by Kurdish militants. However, tourism remains a major foreign currency earner. Visitors are attracted by Turkey's fine beaches, classical sites such as Ephesus and Troy, and antiquities of both the Ottoman and Byzantine periods. Istanbul is a magnet for shoppers.

PEOPLE

Turkish, Kurdish, Arabic, Circassian, Armenian, Greek, Georgian, Ladino

207 people per sq. mile

THE URBAN/RURAL POPULATION SPLIT

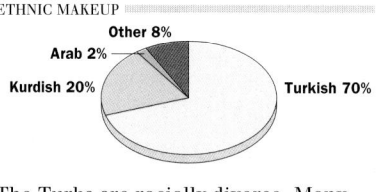

64% 36%

RELIGIOUS PERSUASION

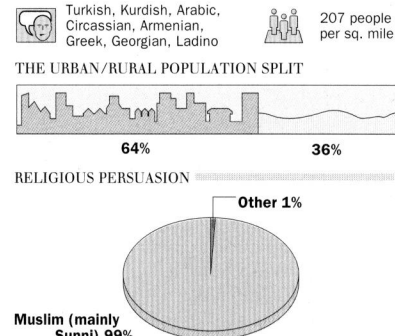

Other 1%
Muslim (mainly Sunni) 99%

ETHNIC MAKEUP

Other 8%
Arab 2%
Kurdish 20%
Turkish 70%

The Turks are racially diverse. Many are the descendants of refugees, often from the Balkans. However, the sense of national identity is strong, rooted in a shared language and religion. The majority are Sunni Muslim although there is a fast-growing Shi'a community, including the heterodox Alawite sect which has been the target of recent attacks by militant Sunnis. The largest minority are the Kurds, while there are some 500,000 Arabic speakers. Women have equal rights with men. Tansu Çiller became Turkey's first woman prime minister in 1993.

POPULATION AGE BREAKDOWN

	1960	1970	1980	1990	2000
65+	3.5%	4.4%	4.7%	4.2%	5.6%
15–64	55.2%	54.5%	56.1%	61.2%	62.6%
0–14	41.3%	41.1%	39.2%	34.6%	31.8%

% of population by age group

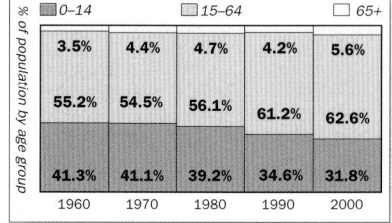

MAIN OVERSEAS ARRIVALS

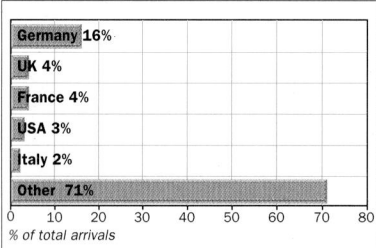

Germany	16%
UK	4%
France	4%
USA	3%
Italy	2%
Other	71%

% of total arrivals

POLITICS

 1995/2000    President Süleyman Demirel

THE STATE OF THE PARTIES

National Assembly 550 members

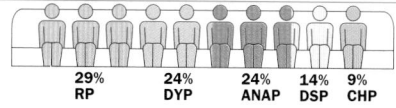

| 29% RP | 24% DYP | 24% ANAP | 14% DSP | 9% CHP |

RP = Welfare Party **DYP** = True Path Party **ANAP** = Motherland Party **DSP** = Democratic Left Party **CHP** = People's Republican Party

By the 1982 constitution, Turkey is a multiparty republic with a national assembly elected every five years. The president serves a seven-year term and appoints the prime minister.

MAIN POLITICAL ISSUES
Islamic fundamentalism
In the general election of 1995, the pro-Islamic RP took 21.38% of the vote, making it the largest party. However, the lack of support from secular parties prevented it from forming a government. The RP is backed mainly by the urban poor who are opposed to the secular model advocated by Kemal Atatürk. The growing political appeal of Islamic fundamentalism has made its containment a central issue in Turkish politics.

Kurdish separatists
Turkey's southeastern region has been the scene of a bitter civil war since 1984. Kurdish secessionists are led by the Kurdistan Workers Party (PKK). Thousands have died in conflict with the Turkish army. The PKK agreed a ceasefire in 1993 and declared that they no longer wished for secession, but for recognition of Kurdish rights within Turkey. There is pressure on the government to reach a settlement.

Human rights
Turkey's human rights record has been subject to intense international criticism. Although democratic reforms introduced in late 1995 lifted a number of restrictions on civil liberties written into the 1982 constitution, concerns remain over the high number of disappearances, illegal executions and the treatment of the Kurdish minority.

PROFILE
Turkish politics are characterized by a wide range of political parties, divided more by personalities than policies.

The ruling center-right coalition, led by Mesut Yilmaz of ANAP and Tansu Çiller of the DYP, took office in March 1996 after the pro-Islamic RP, which had emerged as the largest party in the 1995 general election, failed to form a government. The DYP represents small businesses. ANAP is backed by Istanbul's metropolitan interests.

Strong personal differences divide the leadership of ANAP and the DYP. These were thought to have been resolved by the system of a rotating prime ministership – however it did not stop the two parties from publicly squabbling. By May the long-term survival of the coalition looked highly unlikely.

Tansu Çiller, leader of the DYP and prime minister from 1993–1995.   *Turgut Özal, who died in 1993, presided over several years of prosperity.*

WORLD AFFAIRS

 CE   NATO   OECD   OIC   OSCE

With the end of the Cold War, Turkey's strategic value as NATO's first Western line of defense against the USSR has diminished. Turkey is now seeking closer ties with neighboring states. In 1992, Turkey joined the Black Sea Economic Cooperation Project, and tried to mediate in the war between Armenia and Azerbaijan. Turkey helped the Gulf War allies against Iraq in 1991, and has cordial relations with Arab states although there was tension with Saudi Arabia over its decision to execute eight Turkish nationals found guilty of narcotics-smuggling in 1995. Membership of the EU remains problematic. Greece will oppose Ankara's membership as long as Turkey occupies northern Cyprus, while Turkey's human rights record still causes concern among other EU members. However, trading links with the EU were strengthened with Turkey's entry into the EU customs union in 1995.

AID

 $461m (receipts)   Up 43% in 1993

Turkey has a foreign debt of over $68 billion and is a net recipient of aid. The government received over $4 billion in aid from Gulf War allies. In 1994, the USA threatened to suspend aid unless Turkey improved its human rights record. As a donor Turkey has pledged financial assistance to the West Bank.

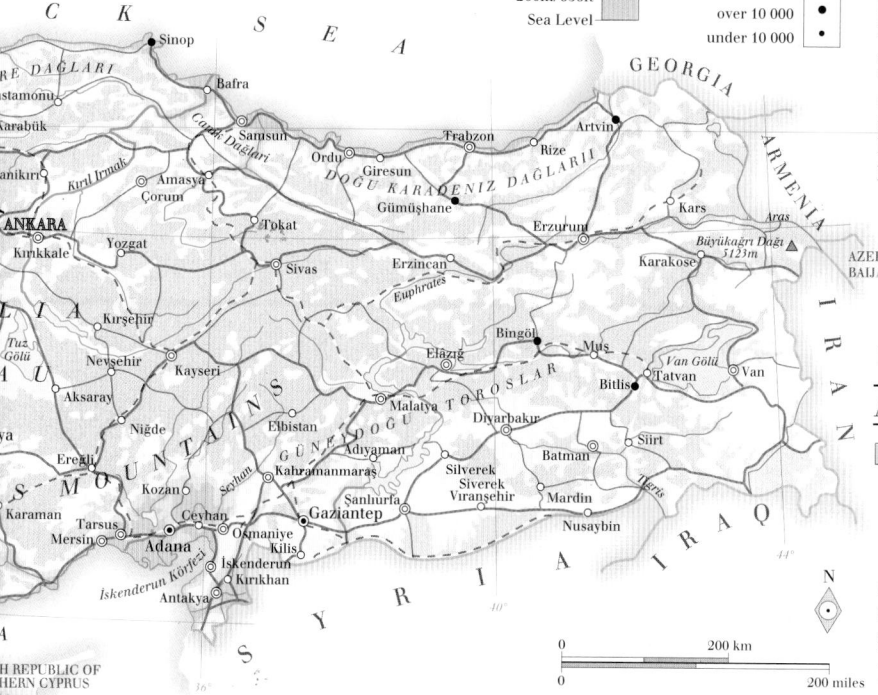

TURKEY
Total Land Area : 769 630 sq. km(297 154 sq. miles)

LAND HEIGHT	POPULATION
3000m/9843ft	over 5 000 000
2000m/6562ft	over 1 000 000
1000m/3281ft	over 500 000
500m/1640ft	over 100 000
200m/656ft	over 50 000
Sea Level	over 10 000
	under 10 000

CHRONOLOGY

Following the collapse of the Ottoman Empire and Turkey's defeat in World War I, nationalist Mustafa Kemal Atatürk deposed the ruling sultan in 1922, declaring Turkey a republic in 1923.

- ❑ **1924** Religious courts abolished.
- ❑ **1928** Islam no longer the state religion.
- ❑ **1934** Women given the vote.
- ❑ **1938** President Atatürk dies. Succeeded by Ismet Inonu.
- ❑ **1945** Turkey declares war on Germany and joins UN.
- ❑ **1952** Turkey admitted to Council of Europe and NATO.
- ❑ **1960** Army stages coup against ruling Democratic Party and suspends National Assembly.
- ❑ **1961** New constitution.
- ❑ **1963** Association agreement signed with EEC.
- ❑ **1974** Turkey invades northern Cyprus.
- ❑ **1980** Military coup. Imposition of martial law.
- ❑ **1982** New constitution.
- ❑ **1983** General election won by Turgut Özal's Motherland Party.
- ❑ **1984** Turkey recognizes "Turkish Republic of Northern Cyprus." Kurdish separatist PKK launch guerrilla war in southeast provinces.
- ❑ **1987** Turkey applies for full membership of EC.
- ❑ **1990** Turkey grants permission to US-led coalition against Iraq to launch air strikes from Turkish bases.
- ❑ **1991** Elections won by DYP. Süleyman Demirel becomes premier.
- ❑ **1992** Turkey joins Black Sea alliance.
- ❑ **1993** Demirel elected president. Tansu Çiller becomes DYP leader and prime minister of DYP–SHP coalition government. Ceasefire with PKK breaks down, conflict resumes.
- ❑ **1994** Çiller introduces austerity measures to control economic crisis. Mounting international pressure to improve Turkey's human rights record.
- ❑ **1995** March, major anti-Kurdish offensive. August, democratic reforms lower voting age from 21 to 18. September, collapse of coalition government; Çiller appointed caretaker premier. December, pro-Islamic RP emerges as the largest party in the general election but lacks support to form a government. Entry into customs union with EU.
- ❑ **1996** February, DYP and Motherland Party form center-right coalition government based on a rotating prime ministership. Mesut Yilmaz of the Motherland Party is first to take office of prime minister.

DEFENSE

💲 $6.2bn   ⬆ Up 16% in 1995

0   *Defense spending as % GDP*   40
▮ **3.1%**

TURKISH ARMED FORCES

🛡	4,280 main battle tanks (75 M-47, 2,876 M-48, 932 M-60, 397 *Leopard*)	400,000 personnel
🚢	16 submarines, 5 destroyers, 16 frigates and 44 patrol boats	51,000 personnel
✈	447 combat aircraft (F-16C/D, F-5, F-4E)	56,800 personnel
🚀	None	

The army has, on occasion, intervened in Turkish politics (the last time was the 1980 military coup). With 18 months' service compulsory for all males at the age of 20, Turkey is a sizeable military power. However, defense spending is slightly below average. Due to NATO membership, Turkey has had easy access to Western arms suppliers, although Germany was prompted in 1994 to threaten a ban on arms sales claiming that they were being used to suppress the Kurdish minority. Over 20,000 troops have been deployed to fight Kurdish separatists who are based in northern Iraq and in Turkey's own southeastern provinces.

ECONOMICS

📊 $149bn   💲 38,700–60,900 Turkish lira

SCORE CARD

- ❑ World GNP Ranking..........................24th
- ❑ GNP per Capita $2,450
- ❑ Balance of Payments.....................$2.6bn
- ❑ Inflation 90%
- ❑ Unemployment................................10.9%

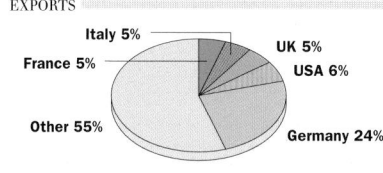

EXPORTS

Italy 5%
France 5%
Other 55%
UK 5%
USA 6%
Germany 24%

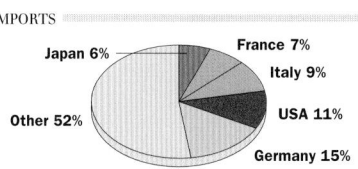

IMPORTS

Japan 6%
Other 52%
France 7%
Italy 9%
USA 11%
Germany 15%

ECONOMIC PERFORMANCE INDICATOR

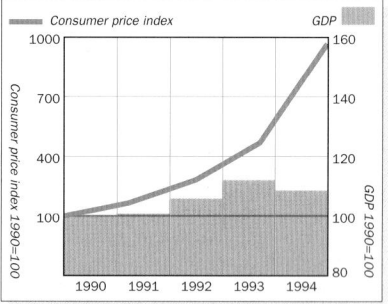

— Consumer price index   ▮ GDP

Consumer price index 1990=100 (left axis: 100, 400, 700, 1000)
GDP 1990=100 (right axis: 80, 100, 120, 140, 160)
1990 1991 1992 1993 1994

The cost of rapid expansion triggered high inflation, while high government spending led to a doubling of the budget deficit. The Çiller government brought in tough austerity measures and an ambitious privatization program to reduce the burden on public finances. However, the lack of political consensus on the measures forced Çiller in 1995 to call an early general election to seek a new mandate.

STRENGTHS

Liberalized economy resulted in highest growth rate in the OECD in early 1990s. Self-sufficient in agriculture. Textiles, manufacturing and construction sectors competitive on world markets. A 1994 privatization law aims to sell an estimated 100 state-owned companies. Companies more competitive now not protected by high tariff barriers, following Turkey's membership of the EU customs union in 1995. Tourism industry.

WEAKNESSES

High inflation and unemployment. Rocketing budget deficit. Shortage of investment capital. High costs of civil war with Kurds.

PROFILE

Turkey's once-buoyant economy declined sharply towards the mid-1990s.

TURKEY : MAJOR BUSINESSES

Istanbul   Ankara
Bursa   İzmit   Kırıkkale   Erzurum
Sivas
İsparta   Adana   Diyarbakır
İzmir   Mersin

- 🌀 Cement
- ✳ Textiles
- 🧪 Chemicals
- ⚡ Electronics
- 🛢 Oil refining
- ◰ Iron & steel
- 🍴 Food processing
- 🚗 Vehicle manufacture

0   200 km
0   200 miles

* significant multinational ownership

T

RESOURCES

 67.3bn kwh (capacity 16.3m kw)

 85,734 b/d (reserves 474,761,000 bbl)

 37.5m sheep, 11.9m cattle, 10m goats

Chromium, oil, copper, borax, coal, gas, bauxite, iron

ELECTRICITY GENERATION

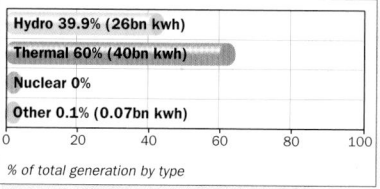

Hydro 39.9% (26bn kwh)

Thermal 60% (40bn kwh)

Nuclear 0%

Other 0.1% (0.07bn kwh)

% of total generation by type

In 1994, the Sanliurfa irrigation canal was inaugurated, marking a key stage in the Southeastern Anatolian Projects launched in the mid-1980s. Aimed at harnessing the waters of the Euphrates and Tigris rivers, the massive dams will allow the irrigation of 4.2 million acres of land.

Turkey produces oil in Garcan and Raman. The eastern Asian provinces are rich in minerals, such as chromium, of which Turkey is the world's largest producer.

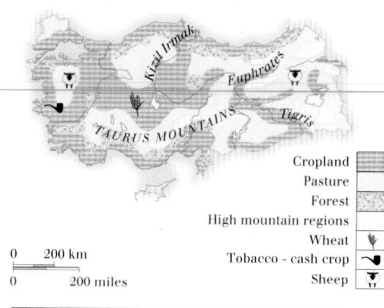

TURKEY : LAND USE

Cropland
Pasture
Forest
High mountain regions
Wheat
Tobacco - cash crop
Sheep

0   200 km
0   200 miles

ENVIRONMENT

 1%

 Yacht-tourism threat to marine ecosystems in south and west

ENVIRONMENTAL TREATIES

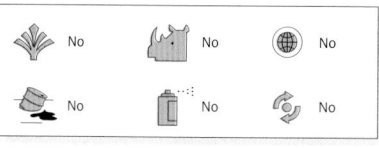

No   No   No

No   No   No

Turkey's program of dam-building on the Tigris and Euphrates has met with international condemnation, particularly from Syria and Iraq, whose rivers will suffer reduced flow rates as a result. Concern has also been expressed at plans to build a nuclear power plant. Much of the western coast has been spoilt by lack of planning and by uncontrolled tourist developments.

CRIME

 51,800 prisoners

 Up 10% in 1992

CRIME RATES

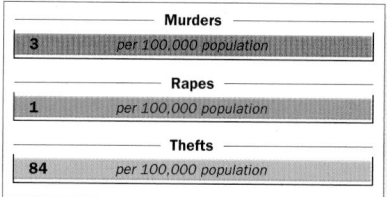

Murders
3 | per 100,000 population

Rapes
1 | per 100,000 population

Thefts
84 | per 100,000 population

Crime levels have risen since 1992, especially narcotics-related crime. Routine torture of prisoners by the police continues to cause concern. In 1994–1995, terrorism by Kurdish militants increased in Istanbul and other major tourist resorts.

HEALTH

 1 per 980 people

Heart, cerebrovascular, respiratory and digestive diseases

0   Health spending as % GDP   25

1.5%

Turkey possesses an adequate national system of primary health care. By Western standards, however, hospitals are under-equipped.

WEALTH

 Tanner, 4,535 Turkish lira ($0.07) per hour; chemical engineer, 2.53m Turkish lira ($42) per month

CONSUMER GOODS OWNERSHIP

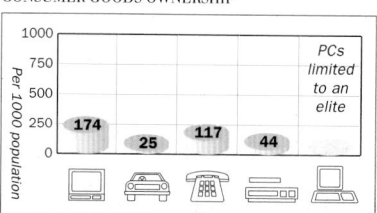

PCs limited to an elite

174   25   117   44

The economic expansion of the 1980s created a new class of wealthy entrepreneurs. High inflation in the last decade has eroded the earnings of those on fixed incomes. Many Turks take jobs abroad as *Gastarbeiter* (guest workers) in Germany and the Netherlands.

MEDIA

 Harsh laws inhibit freedom of expression

PUBLISHING AND BROADCAST MEDIA

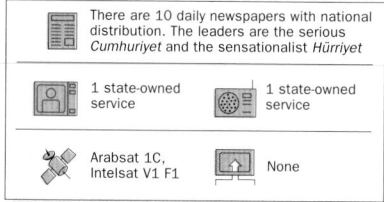

There are 10 daily newspapers with national distribution. The leaders are the serious *Cumhuriyet* and the sensationalist *Hürriyet*

1 state-owned service

1 state-owned service

Arabsat 1C, Intelsat V1 F1

None

The Turkish press is diverse, vigorous and largely privately owned. In 1995, the National Assembly amended censorship laws dating back to the 1980 military coup, easing restrictions on the propagation of Kurdish rights. Although Islam is the dominant religion, the media is not subject to the moral censorship found in the Gulf states. Almost all Istanbul newspapers are printed in Ankara and Izmir on the same day. As an addition to programing offered by the state-owned Turkish Radio and Television Corporation, many Turks are now buying satellite dishes to receive foreign broadcasts.

EDUCATION

 82%

 915,765 students

0   Education spending as % GNP   25

1.8%

THE EDUCATION SYSTEM

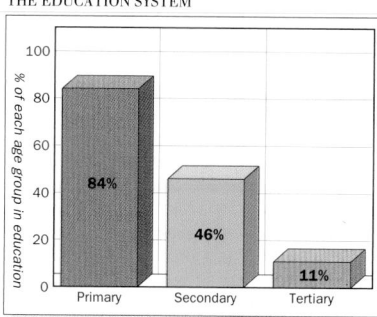

% of each age group in education

100
80
60
40
20
0

84%   46%   11%

Primary   Secondary   Tertiary

Upon the formation of the Turkish republic, all educational establishments were nationalized. In 1928, a Turkish alphabet was introduced which used Latin characters. Turkey spends around 10% of its state budget on education – a relatively high figure. Engineering is usually the strongest faculty in Turkey's many universities.

WORLD RANKING

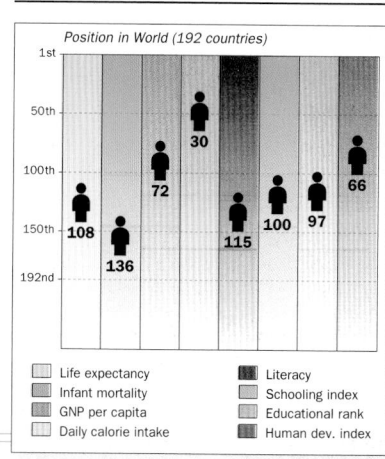

Position in World (192 countries)

1st
50th
100th
150th
192nd

30
72
108   136   115   100   97   66

Life expectancy
Infant mortality
GNP per capita
Daily calorie intake

Literacy
Schooling index
Educational rank
Human dev. index

T

TURKMENISTAN

OFFICIAL NAME: Republic of Turkmenistan **CAPITAL:** Ashgabat
POPULATION: 4.1 million **CURRENCY:** Manat **OFFICIAL LANGUAGE:** Turkmen

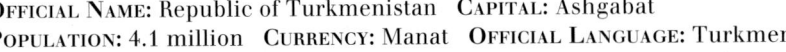

ORIGINALLY THE POOREST state among the former Soviet republics, Turkmenistan has adjusted better than most to independence, exploiting the market value of its abundant natural gas supplies. A largely Sunni Muslim area, Turkmenistan is part of the former Turkestan, the last expanse of Central Asia incorporated into Tsarist Russia. Much of life is still based on tribal relationships. Turkmenistan is isolated – telephones are rare and TV barely available.

CLIMATE

WEATHER CHART

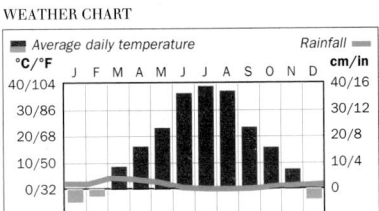

Most of Turkmenistan is arid desert. Only 2% of the total land area is suitable for agriculture.

TRANSPORTATION

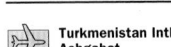 **Turkmenistan Intl, Ashgabat**    Has no fleet

THE TRANSPORTATION NETWORK

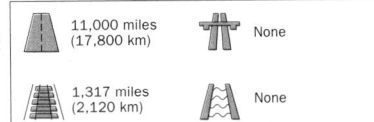

11,000 miles (17,800 km)	None
1,317 miles (2,120 km)	None

The road and rail links to Teheran will be the first to be upgraded. There are plans to modernize Ashgabat airport.

TOURISM

 Levels of tourist arrivals low    Slight increase

MAIN OVERSEAS ARRIVALS

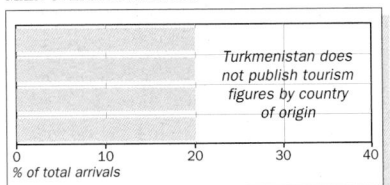

Turkmenistan does not publish tourism figures by country of origin

0   10   20   30   40
% of total arrivals

Most visitors are businessmen attracted by Turkmenistan's stability under President Niyazov. Turkmenistan may become a popular tourist destination in future; traditional Turkmen Muslim monuments are slowly being restored.

Kara Kum Canal zone: salt flats and the Kopetdag mountains on the Iranian border. The Kara Kum is Turkmenistan's largest desert.

PEOPLE

 Turkmen, Uzbek, Russian   21 people per sq. mile

THE URBAN/RURAL POPULATION SPLIT

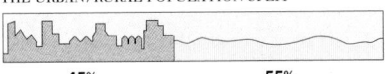

45%   55%

RELIGIOUS PERSUASION

Other 5%   Eastern Orthodox 10%
Muslim 85%

Before Tsarist Russia annexed Turkmenistan in 1884, the Turkmen were a largely nomadic tribal people. The tribal unit remains strong – the largest tribes are the Tekke in the center, the Ersary on the eastern Afghan border and the Yomud in the west. It is tribal conflicts among the Turkmen, rather than tensions with the two main minorities – Russians and Uzbeks – that are a source of strife. Paradoxically, this has meant that since independence from Moscow there has been less virulent nationalism than in other ex-Soviet republics. Since 1989, Turkmenistan has been rehabilitating its traditional language and culture, as well as reassessing its history. Islam is again central to the Turkmen, although few make the *haj* (pilgrimage) to Mecca and many continue to maintain a cult of ancestors.

POLITICS

 1994/1999   President Gen. Saparmurad Niyazov

THE STATE OF THE PARTIES

Parliament 50 members

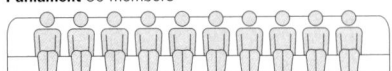

Elections were held on 11 December 1994. All candidates were returned unopposed – most belonged to the one permitted political party, The Democratic Party of Turkmenistan (the former Communist Party).

People's Council

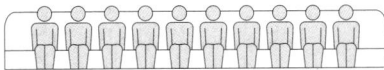

Comprises 60 elected members, the members of the Council of Ministers and others.

Officially, Turkmenistan became a multiparty democracy in 1990. As in other ex-Soviet states, however, former communists – regrouped since 1991 as the Democratic Party of Turkmenistan (DPT) – still dominate the political process. The DPT harbors the traditional communist suspicion of Islamic fundamentalism. President Niyazov has encouraged a personality cult, exemplified by the observance for the first time in 1995 of an official holiday to mark his birthday. The provision of free electricity and water guarantee his popularity.

The main political concern is to prevent the social and nationalistic conflicts which have blighted other former Soviet republics. Russian remains the bureaucratic language, and gas revenues are still used to subsidize inefficient industry and agriculture.

WORLD AFFAIRS

 CIS   ECO   NACC   OIC    OSCE

Turkmenistan is concentrating on establishing good relations with Iran and Turkey. It needs investment from both countries, but is wary of Islamic fundamentalism. President Niyazov opposes economic union with the CIS, and has also expressed caution about closer political union with other Turkic-speaking central Asian republics.

AID

 $25m (receipts)   Up 400% in 1993

Aid is mostly concentrated in the oil and gas industries and comes from Turkey, Iran, Switzerland and Germany.

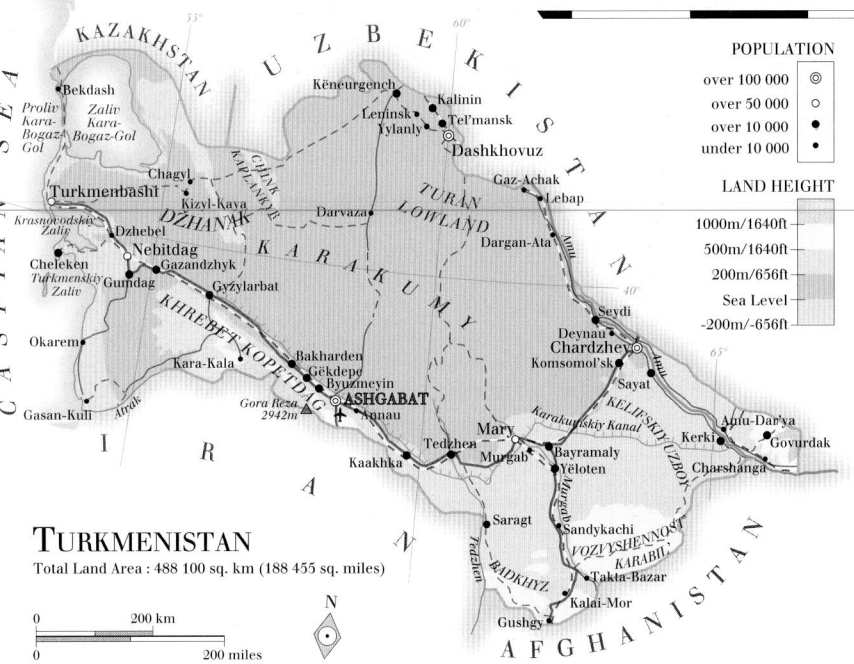

TURKMENISTAN
Total Land Area : 488 100 sq. km (188 455 sq. miles)

POPULATION

over 100 000	◎
over 50 000	○
over 10 000	●
under 10 000	•

LAND HEIGHT

1000m/1640ft
500m/1640ft
200m/656ft
Sea Level
-200m/-656ft

CHRONOLOGY
The nomadic peoples of Western Turkestan came under Russian imperial control from the 1850s.

❑ **1906** Mass colonization starts.
❑ **1924** Turkestan divided into five republics, including Turkmenistan.
❑ **1940** Cyrillic script imposed.
❑ **1991** Independence from USSR.
❑ **1992** Niyazov reelected president.
❑ **1994** Former communists win general election.

EDUCATION
 98%   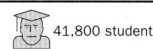 41,800 students

The Turkmen language and literature (banned until 1987) are now on the syllabus. However, Russian schools still have the highest standards.

HEALTH
 1 per 280 people   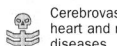 Cerebrovascular, heart and respiratory diseases

Highly polluted water is a major health hazard; only 35% of the population have treated water supply.

WEALTH
 The unemployed and the old form the poorest group. The extended family system and subsidies often prevent absolute poverty

CONSUMER GOODS OWNERSHIP

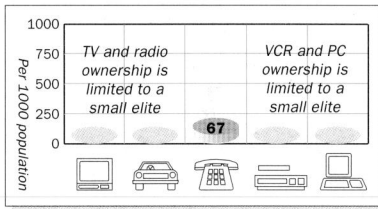

The ex-communist bureaucrats are still the richest group. They favor Japanese and Korean luxury goods.

DEFENSE
 $61m   Down 5% in 1995

Compared to other states in the region, Turkmenistan is reasonably stable. Its army is under joint control with Russia, on whom it is dependent for defense.

ECONOMICS
 $6.4bn   10 manats

SCORE CARD

❑ WORLD GNP RANKING	102nd
❑ GNP PER CAPITA	$1,650
❑ BALANCE OF PAYMENTS	$927m
❑ INFLATION	2611%
❑ UNEMPLOYMENT	2.4%

STRENGTHS
Cotton and gas. Turkmenistan was the USSR's major supplier of cotton and supplied 12% of gas. Hard currency trading allows real prices to be paid for these commodities. Abolition of collective farms is gradually encouraging private initiative and investment.

WEAKNESSES
Cotton monoculture has forced rising food imports. A thriving black market virtually wiped out the value of the manat in 1995.

EXPORTS/IMPORTS

Most imports and exports are still from and to Russia and other CIS republics. However, Turkmenistan is beginning to establish a wide range of Western contacts

RESOURCES
 13.1bn kwh   96,240 b/d

 6m sheep, 1.1m cattle, 314,000 goats   Oil, natural gas, potassium, sulfur, sodium sulfate

During the Soviet years most Turkmen agriculture was turned over to cotton – seen by Moscow as a strategic crop.

ENVIRONMENT
 2.3%   Greater awareness of environmental problems

The building of the Kara Kum Canal, hailed as a progressive move by Moscow in 1958, has drained 35% of the Aral Sea's water, leading to an increase in unproductive salinated soil.

MEDIA
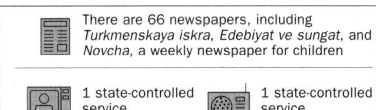 The government controls all media. Censorship is widespread

PUBLISHING AND BROADCAST MEDIA

There are 66 newspapers, including *Turkmenskaya iskra*, *Edebiyat ve sungat*, and *Novcha*, a weekly newspaper for children

 1 state-controlled service   1 state-controlled service

Iranian and Afghan radio stations, beaming in Islamic programs, are popular. TV is only available in cities.

CRIME
Turkmenistan does not publish prison figures   Increasing levels of theft

Levels of crime are low compared with neighboring ex-Soviet republics. Theft, however, is on the increase.

WORLD RANKING

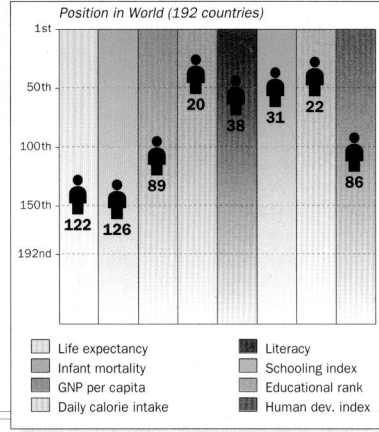

☐ Life expectancy	☐ Literacy
☐ Infant mortality	☐ Schooling index
☐ GNP per capita	☐ Educational rank
☐ Daily calorie intake	☐ Human dev. index

T

TUVALU

OFFICIAL NAME: Tuvalu   **CAPITAL:** Funafuti   **POPULATION:** 9,000
CURRENCIES: Australian dollar, Tuvaluan dollar   **OFFICIAL LANGUAGE:** *No official language*

 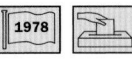

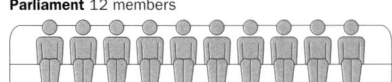
PACIFIC OCEAN

ONE OF THE WORLD'S SMALLEST, most isolated states, Tuvalu lies 650 miles north of Fiji in the central Pacific. A chain of nine coral atolls, 360 miles long, it has a land area of just 10 square miles. As the Ellice Islands, it was linked to the Gilbert Islands as a British colony until independence in 1978. Politically and socially conservative, Tuvaluans live by subsistence farming and fishing.

CLIMATE

WEATHER CHART

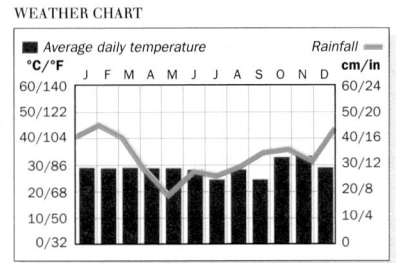

Although average humidity exceeds 90%, the climate is pleasantly warm. The mean annual temperature is 84°F. The October–March hurricane season brings many violent storms.

TRANSPORTATION

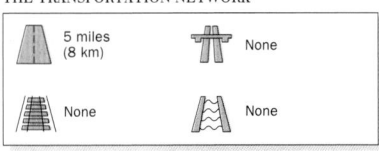

There is an airstrip on Funafuti atoll

5 ships 15,800 dwt

THE TRANSPORTATION NETWORK

5 miles (8 km)		None
None		None

A ferry links the atolls. There are air links with Kiribati and Fiji. Funafuti and Nukufetau have deep-water berths.

TOURISM

 1000 visitors   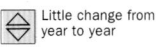 Little change from year to year

MAIN OVERSEAS ARRIVALS

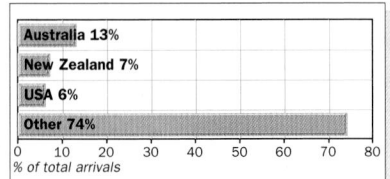

Australia 13%
New Zealand 7%
USA 6%
Other 74%

0 10 20 30 40 50 60 70 80
% of total arrivals

Unspoiled and lapped by some of the world's warmest waters, these remote coral atolls have few visitors. Tourism plans focus around the recently paved airstrip, and Taiwanese investment in Tuvalu's only hotel, on Funafuti.

PEOPLE

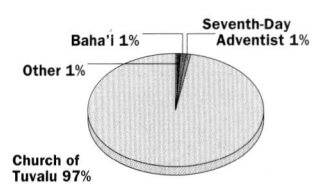 Tuvaluan, Kiribati, English   997 people per sq. mile

THE URBAN/RURAL POPULATION SPLIT

31%   69%

RELIGIOUS PERSUASION

Baha'i 1%   Seventh-Day Adventist 1%
Other 1%
Church of Tuvalu 97%

Around 95% of Tuvaluans are Polynesian. Their ancestors came from Tonga and Samoa 2,000 years ago. Nui atoll has Micronesian influences. There is an I-Kiribati community on Funafuti; many Tuvaluans who worked in Kiribati took local wives. Over 40% of the population now live on Funafuti, pushing its population density to almost 4,000 per sq. mile. Life is still communal, traditional and hard. Droughts are common and fresh water is precious. About 80% of people depend on subsistence farming, digging special pits out of the coral to grow most of the islands' limited range of crops. Fishing is also important, and Tuvaluans have a reputation as excellent sailors. Some 2,000 Tuvaluans work overseas, many in Nauru's phosphate mines, others as merchant seamen.

Tuvalu's soil is porous, but sufficiently fertile to support coconut palms, pandanus and salt-tolerant plants. Fresh water supply is limited.

POLITICS

1993/1997   HM Queen Elizabeth II

THE STATE OF THE PARTIES
Parliament 12 members

There are no political parties. All members are Independent candidates

The 12 MPs, elected every four years, are independents who work in loose political associations. The prime minister, an MP elected by parliament, works with a cabinet of up to four other MPs. After the 1993 elections, MPs were evenly divided between the two men who had dominated politics for most of the post-independence period, Tomasi Puapua and Bikenibeu Paeniu. After a second general election, Puapua pulled out of the premiership contest. Paeniu was then defeated by Kamuta Laatasi, BP Oil's manager in Tuvalu. Day-to-day administration is in the hands of elected councils on each island.

WORLD AFFAIRS

 ACP   Comm   SPC   SPF   UN

Agreements have been signed with Taiwan, Korea and the USA allowing their boats to exploit Tuvalu's fish-rich 3.2 million square mile Exclusive Economic Zone in return for licensing fees. British criticism of the government's economic policy and Tuvaluan attacks on the pace of UK aid disbursements have strained relations with the former colonial power since 1990.

AID

 US$4m (receipts)   Down 34% in 1993

With import costs over 400 times export earnings, aid is crucial to Tuvalu. Most importantly, in 1987 a trust fund was set up, with $A41 million in grants from Australia, New Zealand and the UK, to provide a regular income for Tuvalu. The first two are still major donors. The UK is reducing its aid as support from Taiwan and Japan grows.

DEFENSE

 There are no armed forces   Not applicable

Tuvalu has no military. Internal security is the responsibility of the small police force.

T

ECONOMICS

 US$3m

 1.29–1.34 Australian dollars

SCORE CARD

- ❏ WORLD GNP RANKING.......................194th
- ❏ GNP PER CAPITA ....US$326
- ❏ BALANCE OF PAYMENTS......................Deficit
- ❏ INFLATION 3.8%
- ❏ UNEMPLOYMENT ....Low

STRENGTHS

Exclusive Economic Zone: a source of jobs, and income through fishing license fees. Possible mineral potential. Regular income from trust fund. Sustainable subsistence economy.

WEAKNESSES

World's smallest economy. Physical

RESOURCES

 3m kwh

1,460 tons

13,000 pigs

None

Tuvalu's resource potential lies solely in the waters of its 3.2 million square mile Exclusive Economic Zone (EEZ). Its rich fish stocks are being exploited mainly by foreign boats in return for licensing fees. However, Japan has donated fishing boats to Tuvalu and deep-water fishing is being developed. Hopes of valuable mineral reserves have been raised by the discovery of an undersea mountain in the EEZ. Solar energy is being developed to cut the use of gasoline for power generation. Fuel accounts for about 14% of import costs.

TUVALU

Total Land Area : 26 sq. km (10 sq. miles)

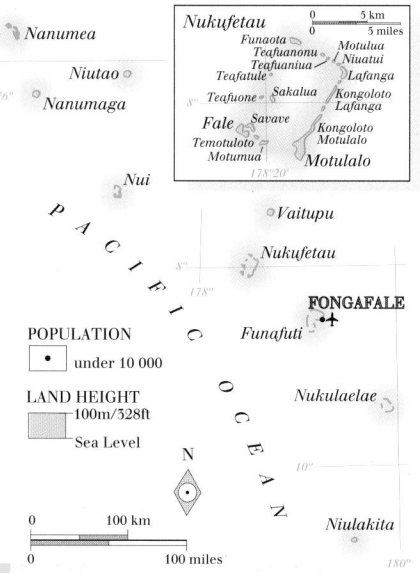

POPULATION
- under 10 000

LAND HEIGHT
100m/328ft
Sea Level

0   100 km
0   100 miles

EXPORTS

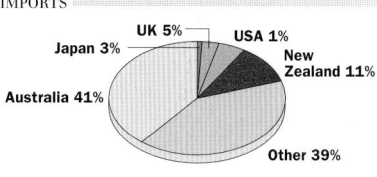

Tuvalu does not publish export figures by country of destination

IMPORTS

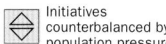

UK 5%   USA 1%
Japan 3%   New Zealand 11%
Australia 41%
Other 39%

isolation. Few exports: copra, stamps, garments. Few potential new income sources. Dependence on imports and aid. Remittances set to fall as Nauru phosphate mines nearly worked out.

ENVIRONMENT

 None

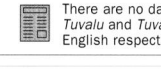 Initiatives counterbalanced by population pressure

Efforts to protect the environmentally fragile atolls include reafforestation and solar energy projects. On Funafuti, population pressure is leading to overfishing in the atoll lagoon. The "greenhouse effect" is a major concern since climate changes attributed to it are blamed for a steep rise in cyclone frequency. Any rise in sea levels induced by global warming would quickly submerge the atolls.

MEDIA

 There is no censorship of the media

PUBLISHING AND BROADCAST MEDIA

There are no daily newspapers. *Sikuleo o Tuvalu* and *Tuvalu Echoes*, in Tuvaluan and English respectively, are published biweekly

No TV service

1 independent service

Two biweekly papers and a religious monthly, *Te Lama*, are the only publications.

CRIME

 Tuvalu does not publish prison figures

 Little change from year to year

Crime is minimal and the result mainly of alcohol-related violence, particularly at the weekends.

EDUCATION

 95%

 20 students

Each island has an elementary school. A secondary school and a marine training school are based on Funafuti. There are 20 state-funded students at the University of the South Pacific.

CHRONOLOGY

The former Ellice Islands, together with the Gilbert Islands, were annexed by the UK in 1892.

- ❏ **1974** Islanders vote to separate from Micronesian Gilbertese.
- ❏ **1978** Ellice Islands become independent Tuvalu.
- ❏ **1987** Tuvalu Trust Fund set up.
- ❏ **1993** MPs fail to agree on prime minister after September elections. Second elections called. Kamuta Laatasi becomes prime minister.

HEALTH

 1 per 2,767 people

 Malaria, diarrheal, infectious and parasitic diseases

Concerted efforts since independence to improve health care facilities and programs have cut the incidence of communicable diseases. However, infant mortality rates remain high and life expectancy, at 59 years, is still well below the Pacific average of 71 years.

WEALTH

 Small wealth disparities

CONSUMER GOODS OWNERSHIP

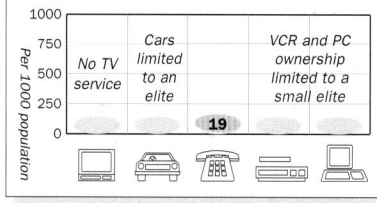

Although living standards are very low, traditional social support systems mean extreme poverty is rare. Most people rely on subsistence agriculture and fishing, supplemented by remittances from expatriate Tuvaluans.

WORLD RANKING

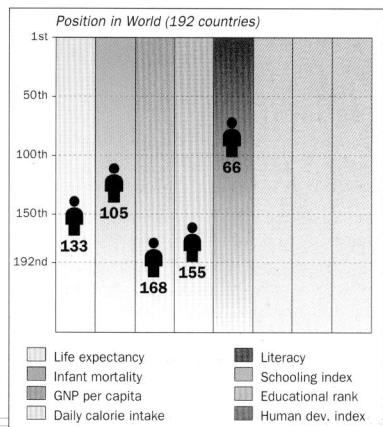

Position in World (192 countries)

- Life expectancy
- Infant mortality
- GNP per capita
- Daily calorie intake
- Literacy
- Schooling index
- Educational rank
- Human dev. index

T

UGANDA

EAST AFRICA

OFFICIAL NAME: Republic of Uganda   **CAPITAL:** Kampala
POPULATION: 21.3 million   **CURRENCY:** New Uganda shilling   **OFFICIAL LANGUAGE:** English

 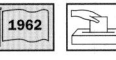

AN EAST AFRICAN COUNTRY of fertile upland plateaus and mountains, Uganda has outlets to the sea through Kenya and Tanzania. Its history from independence in 1962 until 1986 was one of ethnic strife. Since 1986, under President Museveni, peace has been restored and steps taken to rebuild the economy and democracy.

Kampala, Uganda's capital. It has 774,000 inhabitants, but only 25,000 of the city's households are supplied with running water.

CLIMATE

WEATHER CHART

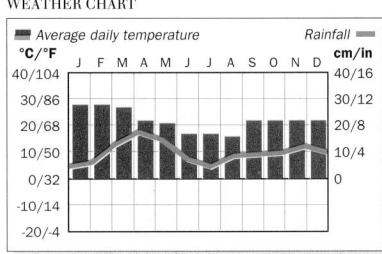

Altitude and the influence of Lake Victoria moderate Uganda's equatorial climate. Spring is the wettest period.

TRANSPORTATION

 Entebbe International
122,000 passengers

2 ships
5,900 dwt

THE TRANSPORTATION NETWORK

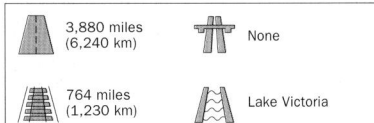

3,880 miles (6,240 km)	None
764 miles (1,230 km)	Lake Victoria

The government is rebuilding the transportation infrastructure with the help of international aid.

TOURISM

 150,000 visitors    Up 103% in 1994

MAIN OVERSEAS ARRIVALS

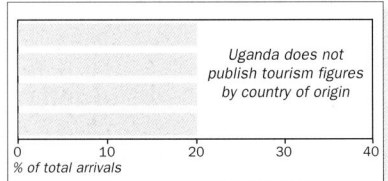

Uganda does not publish tourism figures by country of origin

% of total arrivals

The tourist industry is now recovering with the return of stability. Visitors are mainly high-spending independent travelers. The major attractions are Uganda's lakes and mountains, most notably the rugged Ruwenzori range, better known as the Mountains of the Moon.

PEOPLE

Luganda, Nkole, Chiga, Lango, Acholi, Teso, Lugbara, English

277 people per sq. mile

THE URBAN/RURAL POPULATION SPLIT

12%   88%

RELIGIOUS PERSUASION

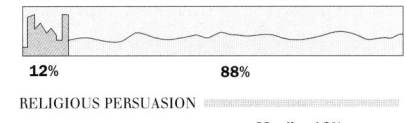

Roman Catholic 33%
Muslim 16%
Indigenous beliefs 18%
Protestant 33%

The predominantly rural population consists of 13 main ethnic groups. Traditional animosities, which were manipulated by ex-presidents Idi Amin and Milton Obote, underlie the ethnic conflict which has marred Uganda's history. Since 1986, President Museveni has worked hard for national reconciliation. In 1993, he allowed the restoration of Uganda's four historical monarchies.

UGANDA

Total Land Area : 199 550 sq. km
(77 046 sq. miles)

POPULATION

◎	over 100 000
○	over 50 000
●	over 10 000
•	under 10 000

LAND HEIGHT

3000m/9843ft
2000m/6562ft
1000m/3281ft
500m/1640ft

POLITICS

1989/Uncertain

President Lt.-Gen. Yoweri Kaguta Museveni

THE STATE OF THE PARTIES

National Resistance Council 278 members

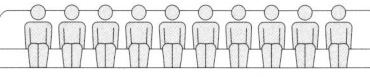

The National Resistance Council is to remain as the legislative body until elections take place, following the expected drafting of a new constitution

Since 1986, President Museveni has run a "no-party democracy," with political parties represented in a broadly based government, but banned from campaigning. Overcoming ethnic tension is now the main issue. In the 1970s and 1980s, ethnic conflict destroyed the economy and resulted in the death of almost one million Ugandans. A constitution promulgated in 1995 gave the 38 districts direct access to funds, but did not satisfy federalists' demands. The new constitution maintained the ban on political parties campaigning although it allows for a referendum on whether Uganda should return to full multipartyism in 1999. Museveni was elected President in May 1996.

WORLD AFFAIRS

 Comm Comesa IGADD NAM  OIC

Relations with Sudan and Rwanda are strained. Internal conflicts in both countries have resulted in a large influx of refugees into Uganda. Occasional border tensions have led to incursions by the Zairean military. Relations with Tanzania and Kenya are improving; the three nations are discussing reforming the former East African Community.

AID

 $616m (receipts)   Down 14% in 1993

Aid receipts, mainly from the World Bank and the IMF, rose in the late 1980s, encouraged by Uganda's adoption of economic liberalization and private sector investment policies. Aid has focused on balance of payments support and the rehabilitation of the key transportation sector.

DEFENSE

 $94m   Up 77% in 1995

Since 1986, the military's political role has been downgraded. The National Resistance Army, the official armed force, is being reduced in size and its ethnic base broadened. The pre-1986 army, dominated by northern Acholi and Langi groups, was responsible for many atrocities under Amin's rule. Security in border areas is the priority.

ECONOMICS

 $3.7bn   917.41–1,005.00 new Uganda shillings

SCORE CARD

- ❏ WORLD GNP RANKING........................113th
- ❏ GNP PER CAPITA $200
- ❏ BALANCE OF PAYMENTS....................$–153m
- ❏ INFLATION 9.7%
- ❏ UNEMPLOYMENT ....Widespread

STRENGTHS
Agriculture. Coffee brings in 93% of export earnings. Potential for more export crops. Road system is being repaired. Pro-investment policies.

WEAKNESSES
Recent ethnic conflict has left a generation lacking skills. Coffee vulnerable to world price fluctuations. High transportation costs.

EXPORTS
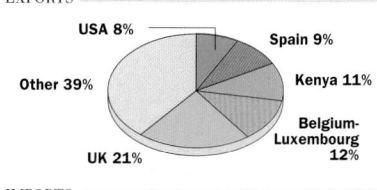

IMPORTS
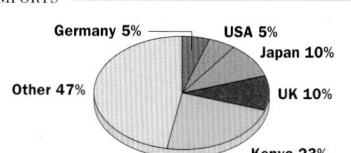

RESOURCES

 786m kwh (capacity 162,000 kw)   Not an oil producer and no refineries

 5.1m cattle, 3.4m goats, 2m sheep,   Copper, cobalt, tin, apatite, magnetite, tungsten, gold

Mineral resources are varied but barely exploited. Uganda has sizeable copper deposits. The mines, closed under Obote, are now being reopened. Gold and cobalt mining is also due to resume and oil exploration is under way. Hydroelectric output is being expanded, notably at Owen Falls, with the aim of replacing 50% of oil imports.

ENVIRONMENT

 8% (4% partially protected)   Rising environmental awareness

Uganda's priority is economic reconstruction but ecological issues are not ignored. Construction of a huge hydroelectric power station at the Murchison Falls was canceled recently, following strong local environmental objections to the choice of site.

MEDIA

 The press has been free since 1986. Comment likely to cause ethnic tension is banned

PUBLISHING AND BROADCAST MEDIA

The dailies include *New Vision, The Star, Munno* and *Taifa Uganda Empya*

1 state-controlled service   1 state-controlled service

The 13 daily and weekly papers cover the political and religious spectrum; eight are published in English. Only the *New Vision* is government-controlled.

CRIME

 10,080 prisoners   Up 35% in 1992

Crime levels are far lower than in neighboring Kenya, although theft in Kampala is a growing problem. Uganda now has one of the best human rights records in Africa.

CHRONOLOGY

Uganda's ancient kingdoms were combined in a British protectorate from 1893 until it achieved independence in 1962.

- ❏ **1962–1971** Milton Obote in power.
- ❏ **1971–1986** Ethnic strife. Economic collapse first under Idi Amin, then from 1980 under Obote.
- ❏ **1986** President Museveni in power. Ethnic strife ends. Moves toward democracy.

EDUCATION

 62%   21,489 students

Education is not compulsory and all schools charge fees. Only 11% of pupils go on to secondary school.

HEALTH

1 per 25,000 people   Malaria, respiratory and diarrheal diseases, measles

The health system, badly hit by war and the loss of foreign personnel, is slowly being rebuilt. AIDS-related illness is a major problem in some areas.

WEALTH

 Most Ugandans live a subsistence existence

CONSUMER GOODS OWNERSHIP

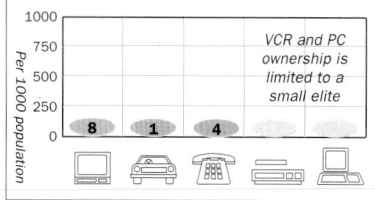

Uganda has a small but growing middle class. Those close to the government form the wealthiest group.

WORLD RANKING

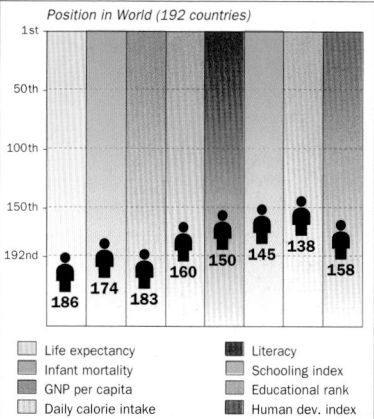

UKRAINE

OFFICIAL NAME: Ukraine   **CAPITAL:** Kiev
POPULATION: 51.4 million   **CURRENCY:** Karbovanets   **OFFICIAL LANGUAGE:** Ukrainian

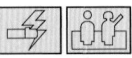

UKRAINE IS BORDERED by seven states; to the south it lies on the Black Sea and the Sea of Azov. An independent Ukrainian state was established in 1918, but was overrun in the same year by Soviet forces from the east and Polish forces from the west. In 1991, Ukraine again became an independent state. The country has historically been divided between the nationally conscious and Ukrainian-speaking west (which was not under Russian occupation until World War II) and the east, which has a large ethnic Russian population.

View toward the Cathedral of the *Assumption in Kharkiv. Many Ukrainian cities are equipped with elaborate trolley networks.*

CLIMATE

WEATHER CHART

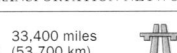

Ukraine has a continental climate, with the exception of the southern coast of Crimea, which has a Mediterranean climate. There are four distinct seasons.

TRANSPORTATION

 Boryspiel Intl, Kiev

2 ships
4,800 dwt

THE TRANSPORTATION NETWORK

33,400 miles (53,700 km)	None
14,124 miles (22,730 km)	2,734 miles (4,400 km)

Transportation within major cities includes Soviet-style subway systems and trolley networks. There are plans to improve the main highway linking Kiev and L'vov. The rail system is in need of extensive upgrading.

TOURISM

650,000 visitors

Tourist figures are increasing

MAIN OVERSEAS ARRIVALS

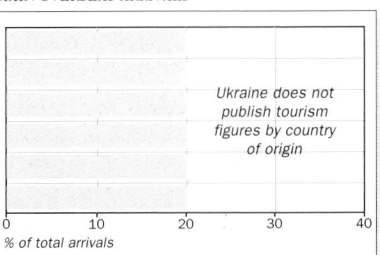

Ukraine does not publish tourism figures by country of origin

Among potential tourist attractions are warm resort areas in Crimea and the south, and the Carpathian Mountains. The government has maintained a highly regulated system of managing tourism. Western visitors are deterred by the expensive Soviet-style hotels they are required to use.

UKRAINE

Total Land Area :
603 700 sq. km (223 090 sq. miles)

POPULATION
- ⊡ over 1 000 000
- ◉ over 500 000
- ◎ over 100 000
- ○ over 50 000
- ● over 10 000

LAND HEIGHT
- 2000m/6562ft
- 1000m/3281ft
- 500m/1640ft
- 200m/656ft
- Sea Level

0   100 km

0   100 miles

U

PEOPLE

 Ukrainian, Russian, Tatar   220 people per sq. mile

THE URBAN/RURAL POPULATION SPLIT

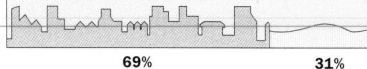

69%   31%

RELIGIOUS PERSUASION

Ukrainian Orthodox is the dominant religion of the Ukraine. It has three branches, those under the Moscow and Kiev Patriarchates and the Autocephalous branch. There are also small Catholic, Protestant and Jewish groups

ETHNIC MAKEUP

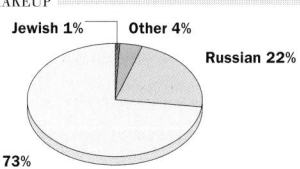

Jewish 1%   Other 4%
Russian 22%
Ukrainian 73%

In the cities and countryside of western Ukraine, Ukrainians make up over 90% of the population. However, in several of the large cities of the east and south, Russians form a majority. The large Russian population in these areas is a legacy of 19th-century industrialization, and more recent migration during the Soviet-era. At independence, most Russians accepted Ukrainian sovereignty. However, tensions are now rising as both groups adopt more extremist nationalist policies.

In Crimea, relations between Russians, ethnic Ukrainians and Tatars are becoming increasingly tense. Crimea has a majority Russian population, but is also home to the Tatars, a Turkic-speaking people. The Tatars were deported *en masse* to the eastern USSR under Stalin in 1945. They have been returning to the region since 1990 and now compose roughly 10% of its population.

POPULATION AGE BREAKDOWN

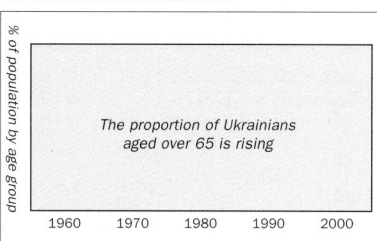

% of population by age group

The proportion of Ukrainians aged over 65 is rising

1960   1970   1980   1990   2000

Leonid Plyushch, *chairman of the Ukrainian parliament.*

Leonid Kravchuk, *president 1991–1994. He tried to postpone democratic elections.*

WORLD AFFAIRS

 BSEC   CE   CIS   IAEA   OSCE

Attitudes toward Russia, once the main foreign policy threat, are undergoing a change aided by a greater understanding of the benefits of closer bilateral cooperation. Ties have been strengthened since mid-1994 by the election as president of Leonid Kuchma who supports closer ties with Moscow.

However, Ukraine's internal instability and the hostility of some nationalist Russians toward it remains a source of concern. Ukrainians fear that if the pro-Russian regions in Ukraine demand unification with Russia, it could spark a civil war and encourage Russian intervention. Alternatively, should Russian nationalists, such as Vladimir Zhirinovsky, seize power in Moscow, they would seek to incorporate Ukraine into Russia. This scenario would be resisted by the USA and some European states, which regard Ukraine as a buffer to Russia.

POLITICS

 1994/1999    President Leonid Kuchma

THE STATE OF THE PARTIES

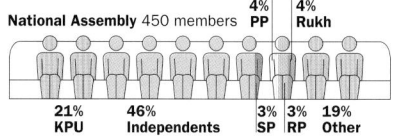

National Assembly 450 members   4% PP   4% Rukh

21% KPU   46% Independents   3% SP   3% RP   19% Other

KPU = Ukrainian Communist Party **PP** = Peasants' Party
SP = Socialist Party
RP = Republican Party Congress of Ukrainian Nationalists
Rukh = Ukrainian People's Movement

Ukraine's first multiparty elections took place in 1994.

MAIN POLITICAL ISSUES
Economic reform
Western and central Ukraine are generally in favor of greater economic reform, while the eastern regions are not. In 1994, Leonid Kuchma was elected president on a platform of greater economic reform, and in 1995 a reformist prime minister, Yevhenii Matchuk, replaced a conservative one.

Relations with Russia
Western Ukrainians are vehement in their opposition to closer ties with Russia, while such ties are strongly supported by their eastern counterparts. In a referendum in 1994, citizens in the Donets'k region voted for closer links with the CIS, and in favor of introducing Russian as a joint official language. Likewise in Crimea voters have demanded dual Russian–Ukrainian citizenship as well as closer economic integration.

Potential destabilization
Some commentators fear that the growing antagonism between nationalist and anti-nationalist groups could spark off a civil war. Conflict could also arise in Crimea, which is dominated by ethnic Russians. In 1994, the Crimean parliament issued another declaration of independence from Kiev. Kiev responded with an ultimatum, but so far has failed to act on its threat. The situation remains unresolved. Tension is increasing perceptibly in other regions with large Russian minorities, such as the Donbass.

PROFILE
Ukraine has yet to develop a strong democratic party system. Individuals – generally local potentates, such as enterprise directors or collective farm chairmen – are very influential. Around 30 parties competed in the 1994 elections, while more than half of the candidates ran as independents. The dominant figure in politics from 1990 to 1994 was Leonid Kravchuk. He became president at independence in 1991, but was subsequently ousted in the 1994 presidential elections by Leonid Kuchma.

CHRONOLOGY
In 1240, Kiev was conquered by the Mongols. The Ukrainian Cossacks later came under the domination of Lithuania, Poland and Russia.

❏ **1918** Independent Ukrainian state established in the aftermath of the collapse of Russian and Austrian empires. Brest-Litovsk Treaty signed with Germany.
❏ **1919** Red Army invades. Ukrainian Soviet Socialist Republic is proclaimed.
❏ **1920** Poland invades. Western Ukraine comes under Polish occupation.
❏ **1922** USSR founded; Ukrainian SSR is one of founder-members.
❏ **1922–1930** Cultural revival results from "Ukrainianization" policy adopted by Lenin to pacify national sentiment.

U

CHRONOLOGY *continued*

- ❑ **1932–1933** "Ukrainianization" policy reversed. Stalin's government induces man-made famine to eliminate Ukraine as source of opposition to his regime. Seven million die.
- ❑ **1939** Carpatho-Ukraine declares its independence from Slovakia. Soviet Union invades Poland and incorporates ethnic Ukrainian territories of Poland into the Ukrainian SSR.
- ❑ **1941** Germany invades USSR. Activities of Ukrainian nationalists suppressed by Germans. Seven and a half million Ukrainians die by end of World War II.
- ❑ **1942** Nationalists form Ukrainian Insurgent Army, which wages war against both Germans and Soviets.
- ❑ **1954** Crimea ceded to Ukrainian SSR.
- ❑ **1972** Widespread arrests of intellectuals and dissidents by Soviet state. Shcherbitsky, a Brezhnevite, replaces moderate reformer Shelest as head of Communist Party of Ukraine (CPU).
- ❑ **1986** World's worst nuclear disaster takes place at Chornobyl' nuclear power station north of Kiev.
- ❑ **1989** First major coalminers' strike in Donbass. Pro-Gorbachev Ivashko becomes head of CPU.
- ❑ **1990** July, Ukrainian parliament declares the Ukrainian SSR to be a sovereign state. Leonid Kravchuk replaces Ivashko as leader.
- ❑ **1991** January, Crimea declared an autonomous republic within Ukrainian SSR. August, government declares full independence, conditional on approval by referendum. December, over 90% of population approve move in referendum. CPU banned.
- ❑ **1993** Major strike in Donbass results in costly settlement, which exacerbates budget deficit and stimulates inflation. Karbovanets enters hyperinflation. CPU re-established at congress in Donetsk.
- ❑ **1994** First president of Crimea, Yuri Meshkov, elected on platform of Crimean independence and closer ties with Russia. March–April, first democratic elections in independent Ukraine take place.

AID

 Further aid is dependent on economic reform

 No significant change

Ukraine has received assistance from Western countries in training a new administrative elite, and in the modernization of its telecommunications infrastructure.

DEFENSE

💲 $850m   ⬇ Down 4% in 1995

0   *Defense spending as % GDP*   40
1.5%

UKRAINIAN ARMED FORCES

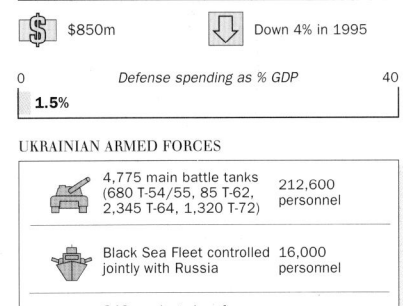

🔫	4,775 main battle tanks (680 T-54/55, 85 T-62, 2,345 T-64, 1,320 T-72)	212,600 personnel
🚢	Black Sea Fleet controlled jointly with Russia	16,000 personnel
✈	846 combat aircraft (MiG-21, MiG-23, MiG-25, MiG-27, MiG-29, Su-24)	151,000 personnel
🚀	136 ICBMs	

Ukraine is still a member of the CIS, but is consolidating its own forces because of fear about rising Russian willingness to intervene in other ex-Soviet republics. The main focus of defense spending is the modernization of weaponry. Ukraine has recently brought out a new version of the Soviet T-72 tank and is planning to update its fleet.

In late 1993, the Ukrainian parliament agreed to ratify the START-1 nuclear disarmament treaty. In 1994, Ukraine transferred a number of nuclear warheads to Russia, in accordance with the agreement.

The long-smouldering dispute between Ukraine and Russia over control of the Black Sea Fleet has still not been decisively resolved. Ukraine now seems likely to reverse its previous decision to keep the Fleet and give up ownership in return for debt relief from Russia. Negotiations are continuing.

ECONOMICS

📊 $80.9bn   💲 104,133–179,400 karbovanets

SCORE CARD

- ❑ WORLD GNP RANKING..........................35th
- ❑ GNP PER CAPITA $1,570
- ❑ BALANCE OF PAYMENTS...................$–168m
- ❑ INFLATION 891%
- ❑ UNEMPLOYMENT................................0.4%

EXPORTS

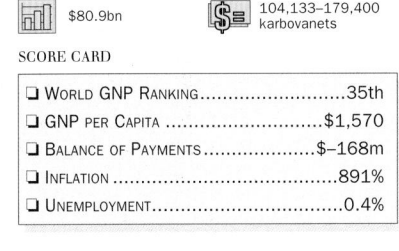

Italy 2% — Poland 3%
United States 2% — Germany 11%
Other 19%
Russian Federation 63%

IMPORTS

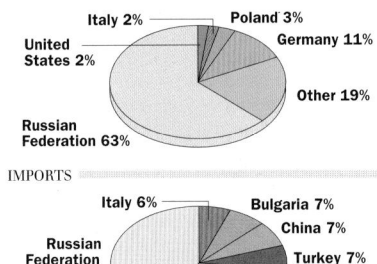

Italy 6% — Bulgaria 7%
Russian Federation 43% — China 7%
Turkey 7%
Other 30%

STRENGTHS

Well-educated work force. Good public transportation infrastructure within cities. Technological potential, especially in aerospace and computers; many research institutes in these areas. Long-term potential for extensive grain and food export. Minerals.

WEAKNESSES

Failure to reform centrally planned economy following collapse of Soviet Union. Hyperinflation. Anti-reform political elites. Inefficient, subsidized manufacturing industries. Corruption.

PROFILE

While privatization of large enterprises

ECONOMIC PERFORMANCE INDICATOR

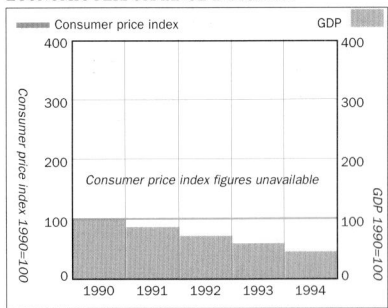

Consumer price index   GDP

Consumer price index figures unavailable

400 — 400
300 — 300
200 — 200
100 — 100
0 — 0
1990 1991 1992 1993 1994

has scarcely begun, there has been some privatization of small industries in the larger cities. Many traders and street vendors have sprung up in Kiev and other major cities. Agriculture, however, is still hindered by an entrenched collective farm system.

UKRAINE : MAJOR BUSINESSES

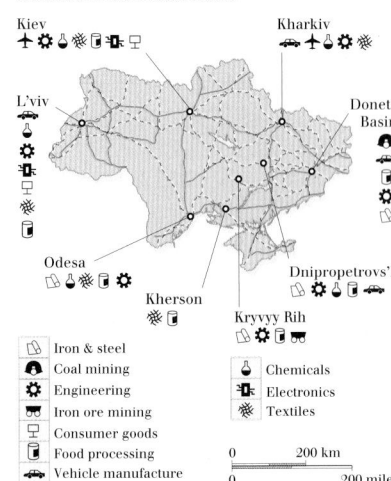

Kiev
Kharkiv
L'viv
Donets Basin
Odesa
Dnipropetrovs'k
Kherson
Kryvyy Rih

🗝 Iron & steel
⛏ Coal mining
⚙ Engineering
🚜 Iron ore mining
🖥 Consumer goods
🥫 Food processing
🚗 Vehicle manufacture
🧴 Chemicals
⚡ Electronics
❋ Textiles

0   200 km
0   200 miles

U

RESOURCES

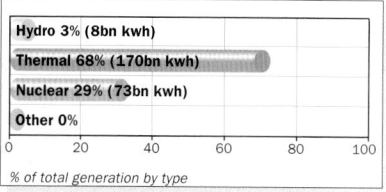

251bn kwh

89,704 b/d

21.6m cattle,
15.3m pigs,
6.1m sheep

Coal, iron, oil, natural
gas, manganese,
lignite, peat, mercury

ELECTRICITY GENERATION

Hydro 3% (8bn kwh)

Thermal 68% (170bn kwh)

Nuclear 29% (73bn kwh)

Other 0%

0   20   40   60   80   100

% of total generation by type

Ukraine's most successfully exploited fuel resource is coal. Most coal is mined in the Donets'k basin or the Donbass, around Donets'k and Luhans'k. There are also smaller reserves in western Ukraine, in the L'vov-Volhynia coal basin. Production has, however, been in decline since the 1970s, and the industry has been hit by a series of strikes since 1989.

Production of natural gas has also been declining since the 1970s. There are some uranium deposits, but Ukraine does not yet have the facilities to produce fuel for its own nuclear reactors. Oil production has not been carried out on a large scale, although there are significant untapped reserves in the Donbass and in the Carpathian Mountains in the west.

UKRAINE : LAND USE

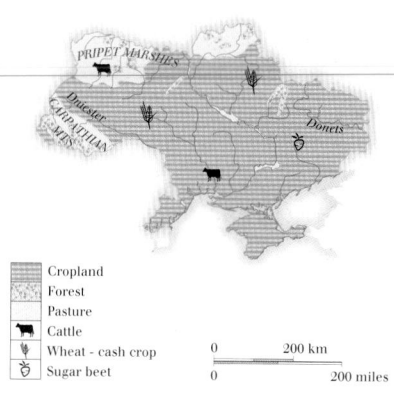

Cropland
Forest
Pasture
Cattle
Wheat - cash crop
Sugar beet

0   200 km
0   200 miles

ENVIRONMENT

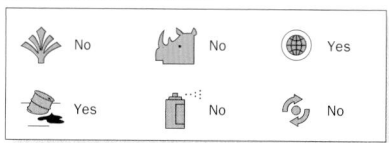

0.9%

Widespread contamination from Chornobyl' incident

ENVIRONMENTAL TREATIES

No	No	Yes
Yes	No	No

As a result of the Chornobyl' nuclear disaster – the worst nuclear accident in history – four million Ukrainians now live in dangerously radioactive areas and 12% of arable land is contaminated.

The government has resumed nuclear production because of the rising cost of Russian oil imports. In 1996, reactors from the Chornobyl' plant were still being used to produce nuclear power, even though they were widely regarded as unsafe. However, under recent agreements concluded with the G7 industrialized countries in 1995–1996, Ukraine is committed to the closure of the Chornobyl' plant by 2000.

Industrial pollution is widespread, especially in the Donbass region.

CRIME

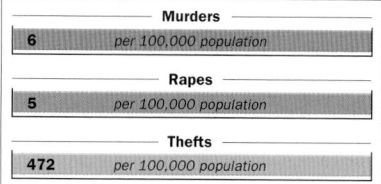

Ukraine does not publish prison figures

Most crime is rising

CRIME RATES

Murders
6   per 100,000 population

Rapes
5   per 100,000 population

Thefts
472   per 100,000 population

The state of the economy, and a breakdown in law and order following the collapse of the Soviet system, have led to an increase in crime. The police are underfunded and are unable to control the increase. Corruption is rampant in all areas of the economy, and the mafia is influential. Foreigners are targets for muggings.

EDUCATION

98%

890,192 students

0   *Education spending as % GNP*   25

6.1%

HEALTH

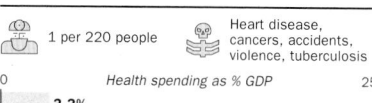

1 per 220 people

Heart disease, cancers, accidents, violence, tuberculosis

0   *Health spending as % GDP*   25

3.3%

There has been a significant decline in health and the health care system in the post-Soviet period. Nevertheless, efforts continue to monitor those affected by the Chornobyl' disaster.

WEALTH

In 1991, 41% of Ukrainians were living below the poverty line

CONSUMER GOODS OWNERSHIP

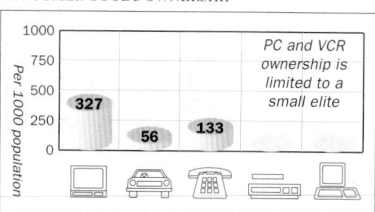

1000
750
500
250
0

Per 1000 population

327

56

133

PC and VCR ownership is limited to a small elite

The division between rich and poor has widened significantly in the post-Soviet period.

MEDIA

There is no tradition of investigative journalism

PUBLISHING AND BROADCAST MEDIA

Pravda Ukrainy has the highest circulation of the daily newspapers	
1 state-run service	1 state-run service
Arabsat 1C	None

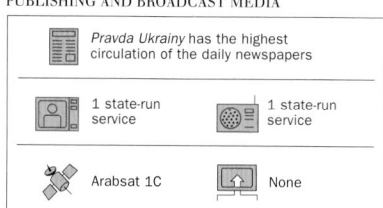

A number of independent, mass-circulation newspapers are now published. Local TV stations reflect regional political differences.

THE EDUCATION SYSTEM

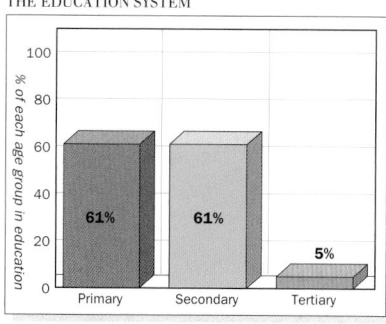

100
80
60
40
20
0

% of each age group in education

61%   61%   5%

Primary   Secondary   Tertiary

In eastern regions, most university teaching is in Russian; in western ones, in Ukrainian. Some schools in the west no longer teach Russian.

WORLD RANKING

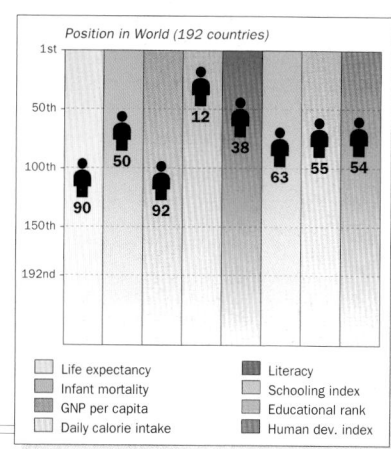

Position in World (192 countries)

1st
50th
100th
150th
192nd

90   50   92   12   38   63   55   54

Life expectancy	Literacy
Infant mortality	Schooling index
GNP per capita	Educational rank
Daily calorie intake	Human dev. index

U

UNITED ARAB EMIRATES

OFFICIAL NAME: United Arab Emirates **CAPITAL:** Abu Dhabi
POPULATION: 1.9 million **CURRENCY:** UAE dirham **OFFICIAL LANGUAGE:** Arabic

THE ARAB WORLD'S only working federation, the United Arab Emirates (UAE) shares borders with Oman, Saudi Arabia and Qatar, as well as a disputed maritime boundary with Iran. The UAE is mostly semi-arid desert relieved by occasional oases. The cities, watered by extensive irrigation systems, have lavish greenery. The UAE's economic prosperity once relied on pearls, but it is now a sizeable gas and oil exporter, and has a growing services sector.

CLIMATE

WEATHER CHART

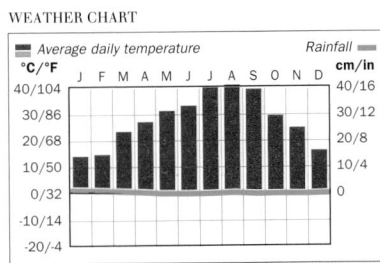

Although rainfall is minimal, summers are humid. Sand-laden *shamal* winds often blow in winter and spring.

TRANSPORTATION

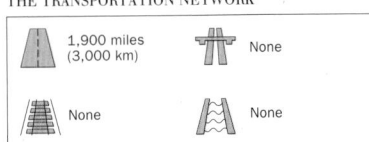

Abu Dhabi International
1.01m passengers

92 ships
1.26m dwt

THE TRANSPORTATION NETWORK

1,900 miles (3,000 km)		None
None		None

The roads are good, though littered with wrecked cars. Five of the seven emirates have international airports.

TOURISM

 1.2m visitors

 Up 1,039% in 1994

MAIN OVERSEAS ARRIVALS

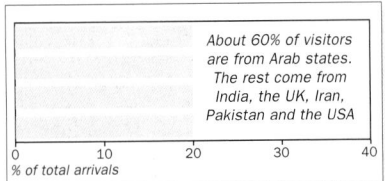

About 60% of visitors are from Arab states. The rest come from India, the UK, Iran, Pakistan and the USA

% of total arrivals

Until the mid-1980s, tourism was minimal. Led by Dubai, the UAE has now launched initiatives to attract visitors during the Western winter for sunshine, heritage, water sports, desert safaris and duty-free shopping.

PEOPLE

Arabic, Persian, Indian and Pakistani languages, English

9 people per sq. mile

THE URBAN/RURAL POPULATION SPLIT

82% 18%

ETHNIC MAKEUP

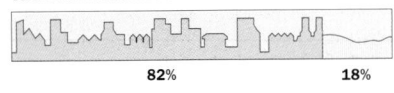

Other 8%
Emirian 19%
South Asian 50%
Other Arab 23%

UAE nationals are largely city dwellers, with Abu Dhabi and Dubai the dominant centers. They are outnumbered by expatriates who flocked to the country in the 1970s during the oil boom; UAE nationals make up one-fifth of the population.

UAE citizens are mostly conservative Sunni Muslims of Bedouin descent. There is a Shi'a community in Dubai with links to Iran. The Western expatriate community is permitted a virtually unrestricted lifestyle. Islamic fundamentalism, however, is a growing force among the young.

Poverty is rare in the UAE. The government remains the biggest employer. Women in theory enjoy equal rights with men.

POLITICS

 Not applicable

President Sheikh Zayed bin Sultan al-Nahyan

THE STATE OF THE PARTIES

Federal National Council 40 members

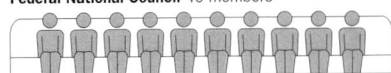

The 40 members are appointed by the emirates. There are no political parties

Supreme Council of Rulers 7 members

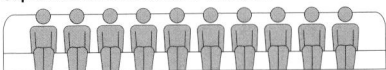

The Supreme Council of Rulers, composed of the rulers of the 7 emirates, has overall authority

The UAE's seven emirates – Abu Dhabi, Dubai, Sharjah, Ras al Khaimah, Ajman, Umm al Qaiwain and Fujairah – are dominated by their ruling families. The main personalities are the ruler of Abu Dhabi and UAE President Sheikh Zayed, and the Maktoum brothers who control Dubai.

President Zayed has relaunched the advisory Federal National Council in response to criticism about the lack of democracy. The growth of Islamic fundamentalism is also a concern. The freedoms granted to Westerners have aroused some anger but, for economic reasons, are unlikely to be withdrawn.

UNITED ARAB EMIRATES

Total Land Area : 83 600 sq. km (32 278 sq. miles)

POPULATION
◎ over 100 000
• under 10 000

LAND HEIGHT
1000m/3281ft
500m/1640ft
Sea Level

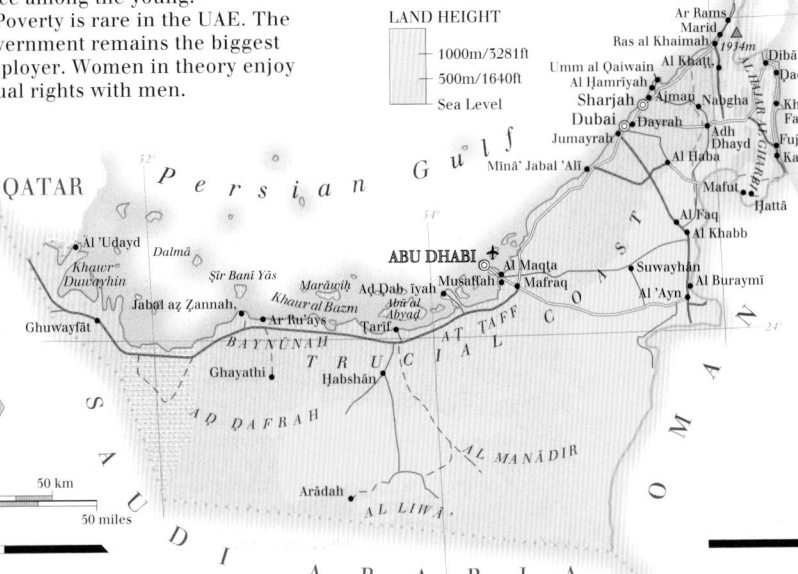

WORLD AFFAIRS

The UAE is well known as an advocate of moderation within the Arab world. It maintains close links with most OECD economies, especially the UK and the USA. In 1992, conflict flared when Iran seized control of three islands in the Strait of Hormuz. Attempts are being made to settle the dispute through diplomacy.

AID

 $236m (donations)   Up 58% in 1993

Once a generous donor to developing countries, the UAE's contributions have fluctuated with varying energy prices.

DEFENSE

 $1.9bn   Down 2% in 1995

At 70,000, the UAE's forces are too small and too scattered among the emirates to pose a threat to the traditional rulers. Although they are well equipped, training is limited and recruits largely drawn from other Arab states and the Indian subcontinent. During the 1991 Gulf crisis, UAE air bases were used by Western forces for strikes against Iraq.

ECONOMICS

 $38.7bn    3.67 UAE dirhams

SCORE CARD

- ❏ WORLD GNP RANKING 52nd
- ❏ GNP PER CAPITA $17,500
- ❏ BALANCE OF PAYMENTS $4bn
- ❏ INFLATION 4.6%
- ❏ UNEMPLOYMENT..................................0.4%

STRENGTHS

Oil and gas reserves are the fourth-biggest in OPEC. Service industries have been developed to support the economy when the wells run dry.

WEAKNESSES

Lack of skilled labor. Most raw materials and foodstuffs have to be imported. Water resources scarce as ground water is depleted.

EXPORTS

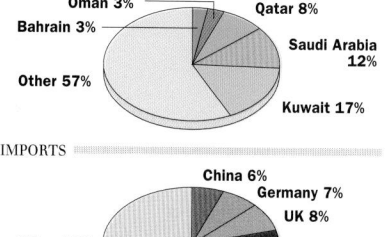

IMPORTS

RESOURCES

 17.5bn kwh (capacity 4.66m kw)

 2.2bn b/d (reserves 98,100,000,000 bbl)

 861,000 goats, 333,000 sheep, 148,000 camels

 Oil, natural gas

The UAE is a major exporter of crude oil and natural gas; Abu Dhabi in particular has abundant reserves. Oil production is the largest economic sector and accounts for 89% of export revenue. Mīnā' Jabal 'Al' in Dubai is the world's largest man-made port and has attracted companies from 58 countries.

ENVIRONMENT

 None    Hunting has made the Arabian oryx extinct in the wild

Despite its harsh desert climate, the UAE has a rich variety of plant and animal life; rare species, however, are threatened by hunting.

MEDIA

 Western print media are censored for taste and political correctness

PUBLISHING AND BROADCAST MEDIA

There are 8 daily newspapers. The leading Arabic newspaper is *Al-Ittihad. Emirates News* is its English-language counterpart

1 state-owned, 2 independent services   2 state-owned, 1 independent service

Radio and TV are state-run; satellite TV is unrestricted. The privately owned press follows censorship guidelines.

CRIME

 The UAE does not publish prison figures   Up 2% in 1992

Street crime and muggings are rare. However, Dubai has a reputation as a transit point for narcotics.

An oasis village, inland from Fujairah, now accessible through a well-developed network of new roads.

EDUCATION

 79%    10,405 students

UAE citizens enjoy free education from nursery to university. The government funds overseas student scholarships.

HEALTH

 1 per 1100 people   Circulatory and respiratory diseases, cancers

A high-standard system of primary health care is in place for all UAE citizens, with hospitals able to perform most operations.

WEALTH

 Poverty is rare in the UAE

CONSUMER GOODS OWNERSHIP

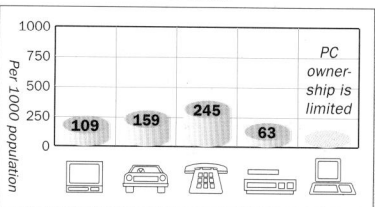

PC ownership is limited

109   159   245   63

UAE nationals have one of the highest incomes per head in the world. There is no income tax and oil revenues subsidize public services. Government policies encourage entrepreneurs.

WORLD RANKING

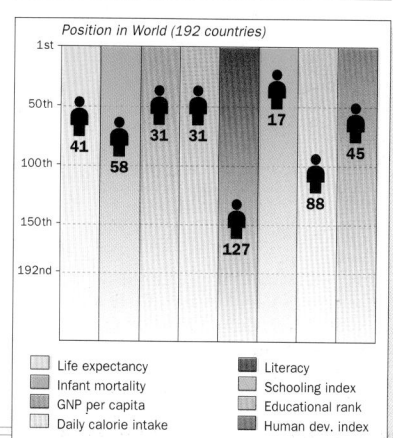

Position in World (192 countries)

- Life expectancy
- Infant mortality
- GNP per capita
- Daily calorie intake
- Literacy
- Schooling index
- Educational rank
- Human dev. index

U

UNITED KINGDOM

OFFICIAL NAME: United Kingdom of Great Britain and Northern Ireland CAPITAL: London
POPULATION: 58.3 million CURRENCY: Pound sterling OFFICIAL LANGUAGE: English OVERSEAS TERRITORIES: 15

LYING IN NORTHWESTERN EUROPE, the United Kingdom (UK) occupies the major portion of the British Isles. It includes the nations of England, Scotland and Wales, the constitutionally distinct region of Northern Ireland and several outlying islands. Its only land border is with the Republic of Ireland. The UK is separated from the European mainland by the English Channel and North Sea. To the west lies the Atlantic Ocean. Most of the population lives in towns and cities and, in England, is fairly well scattered. The most densely populated region is the southeast. Scotland is the wildest region, with the Highlands less populated today than in the 18th century. The UK became a member of the EEC (later the EU) in 1973 and most of its trade is now with its European partners. Membership of the UN Security Council also gives the UK a prominent role in international diplomacy.

PEOPLE

English, Welsh, Scottish, Gaelic

625 people per sq. mile

THE URBAN/RURAL POPULATION SPLIT

89%   11%

RELIGIOUS PERSUASION

Anglican 47%
Methodist 1%
Muslim 3%
Presbyterian 4%
Roman Catholic 9%
Other 36%

ETHNIC MAKEUP

Irish 2%
Welsh 2%
Northern Irish 2%
West Indian, Indian, Pakistani and other 3%
Scottish 10%
English 81%

The UK is the 17th most populous state in the world. The Scottish and Welsh minorities are ethnically and culturally distinct. Both remain recognizable nations and the Scots retain their own legal, religious and educational systems.

Britain's ethnic minorities account for less than 5% of the total population. Over 50% were born in Britain. The ethnic population is concentrated in the inner cities where there are problems of deprivation and social stress. Women in the Bangladeshi community in particular suffer from poor education and isolation from society. However, significant progress has been made in tackling racial disadvantage since the 1970s and there is little support for overt racist politics.

Marriage is in decline in the UK. Over 30% of births now occur outside of wedlock, compared with 12% in 1980. However, most of these births are to cohabiting couples. Around 21% of families with children under the age of 18 are one-parent families.

POPULATION AGE BREAKDOWN

% of population by age group	■ 0–14	□ 15–64	□ 65+		
65+	11.7%	12.9%	15.1%	15.4%	15.2%
15–64	65.1%	62.9%	64%	65.6%	65.2%
0–14	23.2%	24.2%	20.9%	19%	19.6%
	1960	1970	1980	1990	2000

CLIMATE

WEATHER CHART

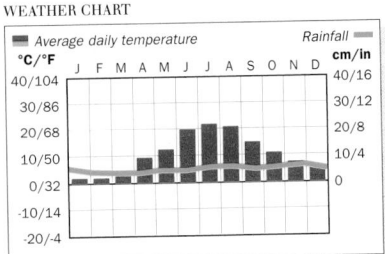

The UK has a generally mild, temperate, and highly changeable climate. Rain, regarded as synonymous with Britain's weather, is fairly well distributed throughout the year. The west is generally wetter than the east, and the south warmer than the north. The most extreme weather conditions occur in the mountains of Scotland, Wales and northern England.

TRANSPORTATION

 Heathrow, London
42.65m passengers

 447 ships
6.62m dwt

THE TRANSPORTATION NETWORK

225,150 miles
(362,330 km)

1,922 miles
(3,093 km)

10,304 miles
(16,583 km)

1,988 miles
(3,200 km)

Since the 1960s, Britain has built an extensive system of expressways, including the world's busiest beltway, the M25. The main link to Scotland is being upgraded to expressway standard. There is concern that British Rail's privatization will result in a fragmented and poorer service. In 1994, the Channel Tunnel opened, though Britain has yet to build a high-speed rail link to London.

TOURISM

 21m visitors
Up 12% in 1995

MAIN OVERSEAS ARRIVALS

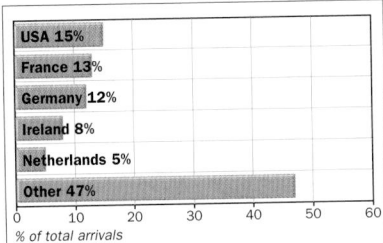

| USA 15% |
| France 13% |
| Germany 12% |
| Ireland 8% |
| Netherlands 5% |
| Other 47% |

% of total arrivals

Tourism is among the UK's most important industries and a growing source of employment. London, with its art galleries, theaters and historical buildings, remains the major destination. However, many visitors choose to bypass the capital and head straight for the Roman splendors of Bath, the Shakespearean theater of Stratford-upon-Avon, medieval York or the Highlands of Scotland. Americans are the main visitors to the UK, although in the early 1990s fear of terrorism, and recession in the USA, dissuaded some from making the trip.

View of Oxford, with the Clarendon Building and Sheldonian Theatre in the foreground. The 17th-century Sheldonian (right) was one of Sir Christopher Wren's first commissions.

U

Black Mount, Rannoch Moor, *in the Scottish Highlands. The Highlands are one of the UK's wildest regions.*

CHRONOLOGY

Great Britain began the 20th century as one of the world's most advanced economies, backed by a massive trading empire.

❑ **1906** Reformist Liberal government.

❑ **1914** World War I begins.

❑ **1918** Armistice signals end of war. Cost to Britain: 750,000 dead.

❑ **1921** Southern Ireland becomes a free state.

❑ **1926** General Strike.

❑ **1929** World stock market crash. Widespread unemployment.

❑ **1931** UK leaves gold standard and devalues pound.

❑ **1934** Arms spending increased in response to Hitler's rise to power.

❑ **1936** Edward VIII abdicates over marriage to Mrs. Simpson.

❑ **1937** Neville Chamberlain prime minister.

❑ **1938** Chamberlain meets Hitler in Munich over Czech crisis and announces that threat of war with Germany has been averted.

❑ **1939** Germany invades Poland. UK declares war on Germany. Start of World War II.

❑ **1940** Winston Churchill becomes prime minister. Battle of Britain. Bombing of London ("Blitz").

❑ **1941** USA joins Allies.

❑ **1942** UK victory at El Alamein. ⇨

UNITED KINGDOM

Total Land Area : 241 600 sq. km
(93 282 sq. miles)

POPULATION

over 5 000 000	▣
over 500 000	◉
over 100 000	⊙
over 50 000	○
over 10 000	●
under 10 000	·

LAND HEIGHT

1000m/3280ft	
500m/1640ft	
200m/656ft	
Sea Level	

U

U

POLITICS

 1992/1997   HM Queen Elizabeth II

THE STATE OF THE PARTIES

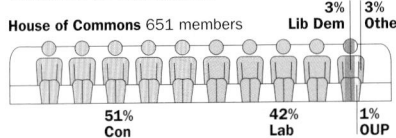

House of Commons 651 members   **3% Lib Dem**   **3% Other**

51% Con   **42% Lab**   **1% OUP**

Con = Conservative and Unionist Party   **Lab** = Labour Party
Lib Dem = Liberal Democratic Party   **OUP** = Ulster Unionist Party   **Other** = Scottish National Party, Plaid Cymru, Democratic Unionist Party, Ulster Popular Unionist Party, Social Democratic and Labour Party

House of Lords 1199 members

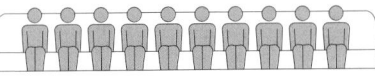

The House of Lords is an unelected body of spiritual, judicial, hereditary and life peers appointed by the monarch. 39% are Conservative peers, 10% Labour peers, 5% Liberal Democratic peers, 23% are independent and 23% have an unspecified allegiance

The UK is a multiparty democracy. The monarch holds no real power.

MAIN POLITICAL ISSUES
Europe
The question of whether the UK should pursue the goal of a federal Europe has split the ruling Conservative Party. The anti-EU "Eurosceptics" are concerned that the EU is eroding British sovereignty. The pro-EU faction believes the UK has no choice but to follow the majority of European states who want integration, if it is to influence the nature of the UK's most important market.

The economy
There is now a broad consensus between the major parties on economic policy. The Labour Party no longer believes in renationalizing privatized industries, and the Conservative Party has toned down the pro-market rhetoric of the Thatcher years. However, the ruling Conservatives have been blamed for the recession and for raising the level of taxation. Opinion polls suggest that both factors have led to a rise in support for Labour.

Health
The creation of an internal market in the National Health Service (NHS) has been opposed by doctors and voters. Many fear that the Conservatives may have plans to privatize the service. Most voters remain attached to the idea of an NHS which is free to all at point of use.

Northern Ireland (Ulster)
The most recent manifestation of sectarian conflict in Northern Ireland began in 1969. The Republican Catholic community backs unification with the Irish Republic. The majority Unionist (predominantly Protestant) community wishes to remain part of the UK. Terrorism by both groups has been

Margaret Thatcher, prime minister 1979–1990; Conservative Party leader 1975–1990.

John Major, leader of the Conservative Party, became prime minister in 1990.

Tony Blair, became Labour Party leader after his predecessor John Smith died suddenly of a heart attack in 1994.

widespread and the Republican Provisional Irish Republican Army (IRA) has also targeted the British mainland. In 1994, both factions declared a ceasefire, pending negotiations with both the UK and Irish governments toward a power-sharing agreement. The process was thrown into doubt in early 1996 when the IRA ended its ceasefire.

PROFILE
Margaret Thatcher's 1979 election victory ushered in 17 years of Conservative rule, and monetarist and privatization policies. The opposition Labour party lost four successive elections, but moved to the political center, abandoning policies of high taxation and renationalization.

In 1990, Thatcher was forced from office and replaced by John Major, who won the elections of 1992. However, Major's popularity soon plummeted. The Conservatives have since lost heavily in local elections, while by-election defeats and defections reduced its parliamentary majority to one by June 1996.

Vauxhall Cross, a postmodern office block by Terry Farrel on the River Thames. Farrel has had more influence on London's skyline than any architect since Wren.

WORLD AFFAIRS

| Comm | EU | G5 | NATO | OECD |

The UK owes much of its prominence in world affairs to its seat on the UN Security Council. However, since 1945, it has followed a largely US line in its foreign policy. It was a founder-member of NATO and maintained front-line troops in West Germany during the Cold War. In 1991, it was a major partner in UN Operation Desert Storm to evict Iraqi forces from Kuwait.

The UK signed the Maastricht Treaty in 1992, although it "opted-out" of the chapter on social policy. However, there is widespread opposition in the UK to participation in economic and monetary union.

Relations with China over the 1997 handover of Hong Kong have been tense.

AID

 $2.9bn (donations)  Up 7% in 1993

Britain gives rather less aid than the European average. Its current donations of 0.3% of GNP are well below the target 0.7% for industrialized nations. Aid fell sharply during the 1980s. In 1996, the emphasis of British policy changed with 85% of bilateral aid directed at 20 countries in sub-Saharan Africa and South Asia. While the general aim of the program is to reduce poverty, other aims are to encourage good government, widen opportunities for women and protect the environment.

Aid is not a highly politicized issue in the UK. However, the country is home to prominent NGOs, including Oxfam. The Voluntary Service Overseas (VSO) organization sends people to share their skills in developing countries.

DEFENSE

 $34.5bn Down 1% in 1995

```
0          Defense spending as % GDP        40
  3.4%
```

BRITISH ARMED FORCES

918 main battle tanks (426 *Challenger*, 472 *Chieftain*, 20 *Challenger 2*)	116,000 personnel
3 carriers, 16 submarines 12 destroyers, 23 frigates and 33 patrol boats	50,500 personnel
559 combat aircraft (315 *Tornado*, 69 *Jaguar*, 93 *Harrier*)	70,400 personnel
48 SLBM in 3 SSBN	

The UK's defense spending as a proportion of GNP is one of the highest in the OECD. However, as a response to the end of the Cold War, the 1990 Options for Change program was implemented in 1993. The army and navy came in for the greatest cuts in personnel and equipment orders. The UK's independent nuclear deterrent was scaled down. The emphasis now is on creating rapid reaction forces and fulfilling the UK's UN commitments.

The UK is one of the world's leading arms exporters. Major buyers include Middle Eastern states and the booming economies of Southeast Asia.

ECONOMICS

 $1069bn 0.64 pounds sterling

SCORE CARD

❑ WORLD GNP RANKING	6th
❑ GNP PER CAPITA	$18,410
❑ BALANCE OF PAYMENTS	$–2.4bn
❑ INFLATION	3.6%
❑ UNEMPLOYMENT	9.6%

EXPORTS

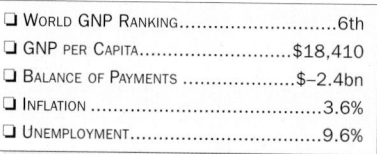

Ireland 5% — Netherlands 7% — France 10% — Germany 13% — USA 14% — Other 51%

IMPORTS

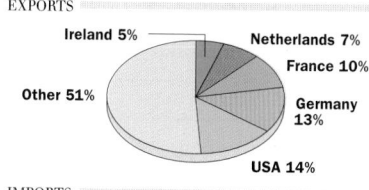

Japan 7% — Netherlands 6% — France 9% — USA 13% — Germany 14% — Other 51%

STRENGTHS

World leader in financial services, pharmaceuticals and defense industries. Successful aerospace sector. Precision engineering and high-tech sectors, including telecommunications. Strong energy sector based on North Sea oil and gas production. Flexible working practices and lower wage rates than France, Germany or Scandinavia. The EU's largest recipient of inward investment. Strong multinational sector, with companies such as Glaxo, ICI, RTZ, BAT and Hanson.

WEAKNESSES

Decline of some key manufacturing sectors since 1970s, particularly the heavy industries. Much of industry still working with outmoded machinery. Past propensity for inflation. High levels of consumer and government debt. Quick-return mentality of many investment decisions does not create the culture to sustain long-term growth.

PROFILE

Manufacturing is still the largest sector of the UK economy, although its

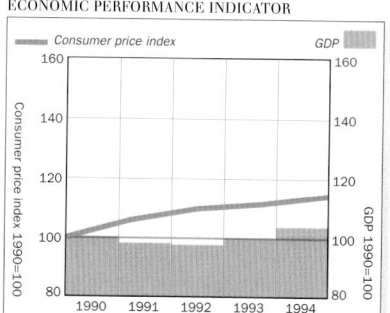

ECONOMIC PERFORMANCE INDICATOR

Consumer price index — GDP
(1990–1994)

importance has declined as the services and energy sectors have grown. During the 1980s, there was a sharp decline in heavy industries such as steel and engineering, located mostly in the Midlands and the North, while sectors like financial services expanded rapidly in the south. A sharp recession led to a 2.5% decline in GDP in 1991. The subsequent revival has been sluggish, with consumer spending hampered by fears of unemployment, and a lack of confidence in John Major's government.

UNITED KINGDOM : MAJOR BUSINESSES

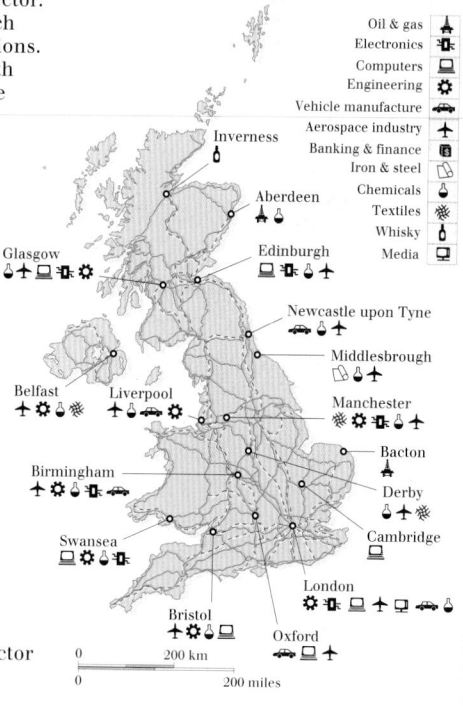

Oil & gas
Electronics
Computers
Engineering
Vehicle manufacture
Aerospace industry
Banking & finance
Iron & steel
Chemicals
Textiles
Whisky
Media

Inverness
Aberdeen
Glasgow
Edinburgh
Newcastle upon Tyne
Middlesbrough
Belfast Liverpool Manchester
Bacton
Birmingham Derby
Swansea Cambridge
London
Bristol
Oxford

```
0          200 km
0                 200 miles
```

U

RESOURCES

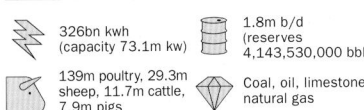

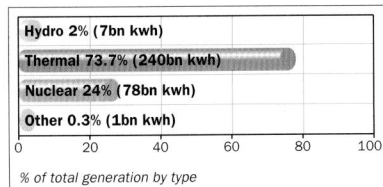

326bn kwh (capacity 73.1m kw)

1.8m b/d (reserves 4,143,530,000 bbl)

139m poultry, 29.3m sheep, 11.7m cattle, 7.9m pigs

Coal, oil, limestone, natural gas

ELECTRICITY GENERATION

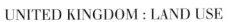

Hydro 2% (7bn kwh)

Thermal 73.7% (240bn kwh)

Nuclear 24% (78bn kwh)

Other 0.3% (1bn kwh)

0   20   40   60   80   100

% of total generation by type

The UK has the largest energy resources of any EU state. The country's energy position is bolstered by substantial oil and gas reserves offshore on the Continental Shelf in the North Sea. Drilled under difficult conditions, the oil is of a high grade. Revenues from taxes on oil companies have been a major contributor to government finances, averaging around $12 billion a year. The oil is expected to last at least until 2010.

Coal reserves are also sizeable, and at current rates could meet Britain's energy needs well into 2400. However, the privatization of the electricity industry resulted in the industry switching from coal to gas-fired power stations. The consequent fall in demand for coal has resulted in the closure of all but a handful of pits.

The UK produces few other minerals in significant quantities. Tin workings in the West Country and gold mines in Wales and Scotland have mostly been mined out.

UNITED KINGDOM : LAND USE

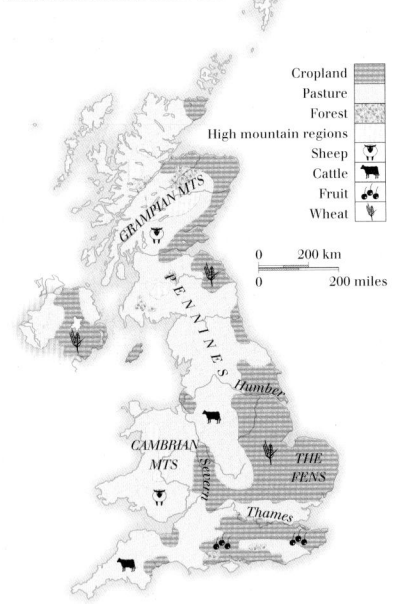

Cropland
Pasture
Forest
High mountain regions
Sheep
Cattle
Fruit
Wheat

0   200 km
0   200 miles

ENVIRONMENT

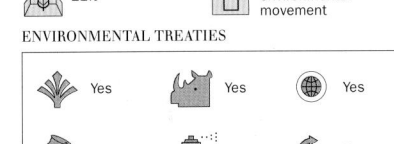

21%

Increasingly active environmental movement

ENVIRONMENTAL TREATIES

Yes   Yes   Yes

Yes   Yes   Yes

Environmental issues have come to the fore and are increasingly a political issue in the UK in the 1990s. Plans for the building of Thorp, a massive new nuclear reprocessing plant, have met with heated opposition. Sellafield, where the plant is due to be built, is already the largest single source of civil radioactive discharge in Europe. The UK's beaches have been condemned by the EU for their high levels of sewage pollution. Meanwhile, several road building projects are the focus of vigorous local opposition campaigns.

MEDIA

 No political restrictions

PUBLISHING AND BROADCAST MEDIA

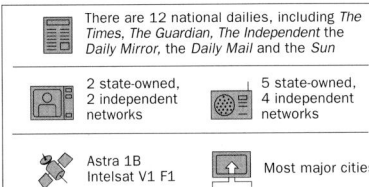

There are 12 national dailies, including *The Times*, *The Guardian*, *The Independent* the *Daily Mirror*, the *Daily Mail* and the *Sun*

2 state-owned, 2 independent networks

5 state-owned, 4 independent networks

Astra 1B Intelsat V1 F1

Most major cities

More newspapers are sold per capita in the UK than in any other European country. Newspapers are owned mostly by large media corporations and often express right-of-center views. Although generally free from censorship, publication of material deemed contrary to "national interests" may be banned. The arrival of satellite TV has increased competition for the highly protected British Broadcasting Corporation (BBC).

The BBC's *World Service* remains an influential international news source.

The Welsh coal industry has virtually disappeared. Wales now has the highest percentage of small business start-ups, relative to the population, of any part of the UK.

CRIME

 53,178 prisoners

 Up 14% in 1991

CRIME RATES

Murders	
4	per 100,000 population

Rapes	
8	per 100,000 population

Thefts	
7752	per 100,000 population

Crime has risen sharply in the UK since the 1970s. The largest increase has been in burglary; car theft rates are the highest in Europe and higher than the USA's. Most crime is opportunistic and committed by young males. In the inner cities there is a growing problem fuelled by drug dependency.

The UK has one of the highest prison populations in Europe. Conservative plans for tougher sentencing will result in a further increase in numbers by 2000.

EDUCATION

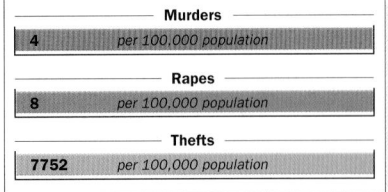

99%

1.4m students

0   *Education spending as % GNP*   25

5.2%

THE EDUCATION SYSTEM

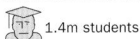
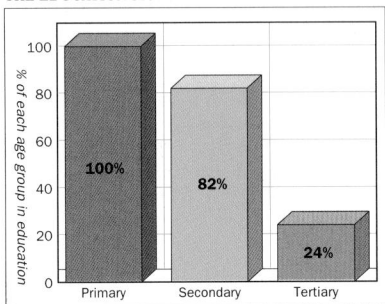

% of each age group in education

100%   82%   24%

Primary   Secondary   Tertiary

Once based on an elitist system of grammar schools, with membership decided by a competitive examination at the age of 11, the British state system underwent extensive reform in the 1970s and 1980s. Standards, however, declined sharply. The 1988 Education Reform Bill attempted to reverse falling standards by introducing a program of required teaching. The state system is used by 94% of children. The rest attend private schools known as public schools. In Northern Ireland, many schools are segregated along religious (Catholic or Protestant) lines.

Compared with its EU partners, relatively few UK students proceed to tertiary education. Entry to university is highly competitive and dependent on grades achieved in the end of school A-level exams. Oxford and Cambridge are the most prestigious universities.

U

REGIONS

SCOTLAND

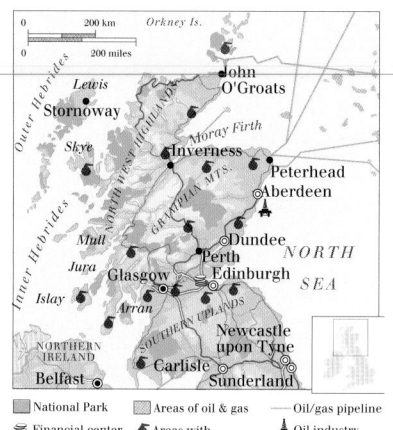

National Park | Areas of oil & gas | Oil/gas pipeline
Financial center | Areas with whiskey distilleries | Oil industry

ALTHOUGH RULED FROM Westminster since 1707, Scotland is still very much a separate nation. It has its own legal and educational systems; its own church and banknotes. It is also one of the most pro-EU parts of the UK, believing closer integration would bring not only economic but also political benefits – notably devolution. Only a minority of Scots want independence, but most would like Scotland to have more control over its affairs. Mining and heavy industry are all but dead. Offshore oil helped fuel growth in the 1980s. New industry is proving hard to attract, a result of Scotland's peripheral positon in Europe.

TYNESIDE

TYNESIDE IN NORTHEAST England is slowly emerging from decades of decline. Like neighboring Wearside and Teesside, it depended on shipbuilding and heavy industry, and on a few large companies which employed successive generations of families. Today, little of that economic base is left, decimated by recession and by competition from cheaper producers. Instead, disused docks and derelict factory sites are being turned into business parks. Foreign investors have included prominent Japanese firms such as Nissan. Inward investment from Scandinavia and the EU has also been significant. A symbol of returning prosperity is Gateshead's huge Metro Centre – the UK's most profitable retail center.

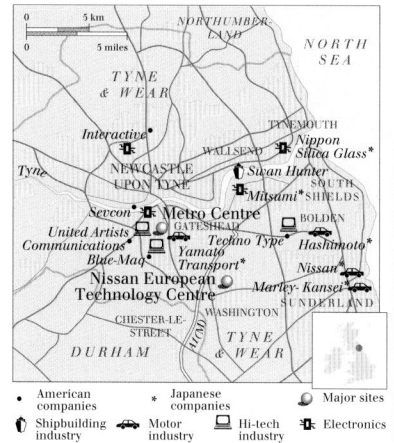

• American companies | * Japanese companies | Major sites
Shipbuilding industry | Motor industry | Hi-tech industry | Electronics

LONDON

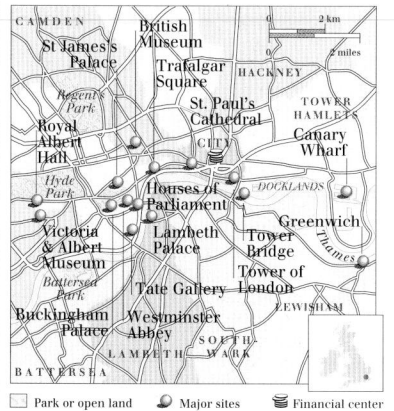

Park or open land | Major sites | Financial center

THE FIRST OF THE WORLD'S mega-cities, the UK's capital today is home to 6.8 million people. London is the seat of government and dominates the country's political, financial and cultural life. The flight of industry to cheaper locations outside the capital means London depends mainly on service industries. Tourism and retail services are important, but the capital's $84 billion economy is underpinned by the financial sector.

Focused on the City of London, the site of the Roman city, this sector carries out 20% of all global banking transactions and is also the location of much international commodity trade. Following the deregulation of the market ("Big Bang") in the 1980s, the City expanded rapidly. Recession in the early 1990s, however, saw many job losses and dented profits.

The 1980s and early 1990s saw considerable redevelopment, including the major Canary Wharf complex. Plans to build the world's largest Ferris wheel to celebrate the Millenium have received a mixed response.

HEALTH

1 per 667 people | Heart, cerebrovascular and respiratory diseases, cancers

0   *Health spending as % GDP*   25
6.6%

The majority of health care is provided by the National Health Service (NHS) which is financed by central government and free to all residents. The system is efficient – the UK spends a smaller proportion of its GNP on health than Germany, France or Italy. However, the pressures of an aging population are reflected in long waiting lists for non-essential operations.

WEALTH

Refuse collector, 221 pounds sterling ($343) per week; accountant, 446 pounds sterling ($692) per week

CONSUMER GOODS OWNERSHIP

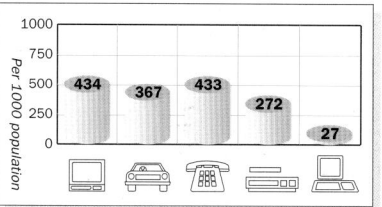

Income inequality in the UK was higher in 1994 than in 1884, when records first began. In part, this is the result of the reductions in taxation for higher earners introduced under the Thatcher administration. The purchasing power of salaries rose sharply during the 1980s and early 1990s. However, in the same period unemployment trebled while the value of state benefits fell. The value of the old age pension has fallen sharply.

Wealth remains well-hidden in the UK. Considerable amounts are invested on the stock market, overseas or in the Lloyds insurance market. A series of disastrous losses at Lloyds between 1991 and 1993 severely dented the fortunes of many investing families.

WORLD RANKING

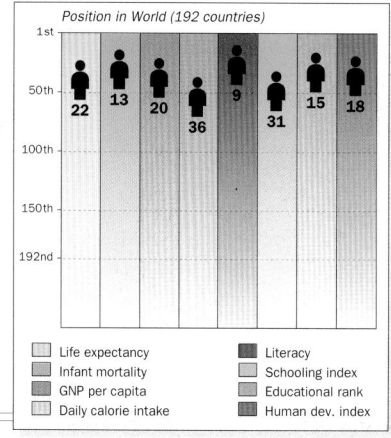

Position in World (192 countries)

22 | 13 | 20 | 36 | 9 | 31 | 15 | 18

Life expectancy | Literacy
Infant mortality | Schooling index
GNP per capita | Educational rank
Daily calorie intake | Human dev. index

U

UNITED STATES

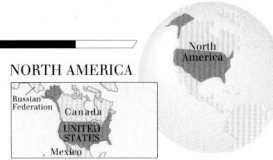

NORTH AMERICA

OFFICIAL NAME: United States of America   **CAPITAL:** Washington, DC
POPULATION: 263.3 million   **CURRENCY:** US dollar   **OFFICIAL LANGUAGE:** English   **OVERSEAS TERRITORIES:** 14

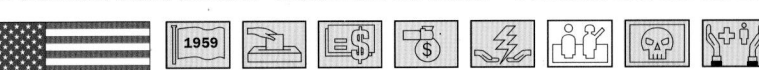

1959

THE UNITED STATES COMPRISES 48 contiguous states, bounded by Canada and Mexico, and the outlying states of Alaska and Hawaii. Alone of the nations that encompass a great landmass, it is neither overpopulated (like China and India), underpopulated (like Australia), nor held hostage to extremes of climate or topography (like Russia and Brazil). The USA also stands apart from most other nations in that it is founded neither on ethnic unity nor within natural geographical boundaries, but instead on the appeal of some powerful ideas. Democracy and liberty, in both a political and an economic sense, continue to be the guiding lights of the USA – as they were for its founders over 200 years ago.

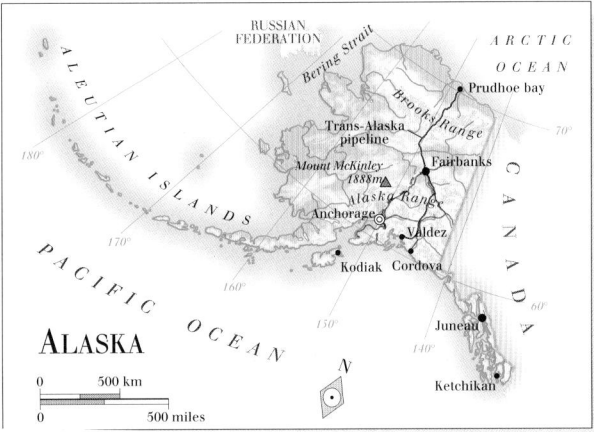

ALASKA

0   500 km

0   500 miles

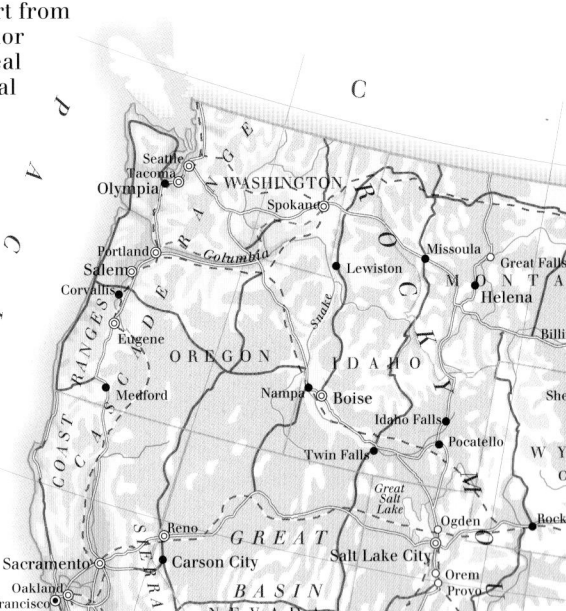

CLIMATE

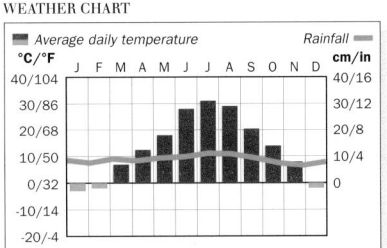

WEATHER CHART

Average daily temperature   Rainfall

Spanning a continent, and extending far into the Pacific Ocean in Alaska and Hawaii, the USA displays a full range of climatic conditions. Mean annual temperatures range from 84°F in Florida to –18°F in Alaska. Except for New England, Alaska and the Pacific North West, summer temperatures are higher than in much of Europe. Southern summers are humid; in the southwest they are dry. Winters are particularly severe in the western mountains and plains and in the Midwest – where the Great Lakes can freeze. The Atlantic northeast can experience heavy snow from November to April. The USA's weather is frequently dramatic. Tornadoes, cyclones, floods, thunderstorms and droughts are common in some areas.

The Chippendale Block, New York, a notable example of postmodern architecture by the influential US architect Philip Johnson.

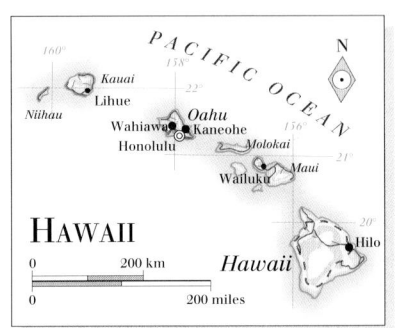

HAWAII

0   200 km

0   200 miles

Hawaii

U

TRANSPORTATION

✈ **John F Kennedy, New York**
29.79m passengers

🚢 502 ships
22.44m dwt

THE TRANSPORTATION NETWORK

🛣	2.28m miles (3.66m km)	🛣	52,419 miles (84,361 km)
🛤	167,964 miles (270,312 km)	〰	25,482 miles (41,009 km)

The Mississippi–Missouri river system provided the USA's first transportation network. Today, the USA has the world's cheapest, most extensive internal air network and also a good system of interstate highways. The rail network is poorly developed, by European standards, and carries mostly freight. Since Henry Ford began mass production in Detroit nearly 90 years ago, Americans have been wedded to the car. In 1919, Ford sold one million cars. Today, there are over 255 million cars in the USA. Many cities, such as Los Angeles, have come to depend on the car; the USA now accounts for more than half of the world's car journeys. Cheap gasoline has underpinned this growth. In the long term, the prospect of dependence on oil imports as domestic supplies run out could force a review of the car's role in society.

The Mittens, Monument Valley, Arizona.
These striking natural rock formations are created by erosion of red sandstone. The Valley is home to the Navajo people.

UNITED STATES

Total Land Area : 9 166 600 sq. km
(3 539 224 sq. miles)

POPULATION

▪	over 5 000 000
◻	over 1 000 000
◉	over 500 000
◎	over 100 000
○	over 50 000
•	over 10 000
·	under 10 000

LAND HEIGHT

3000m/9843ft
2000m/6562ft
1000m/3281ft
500m/1640ft
200m/656ft
Sea Level

U

TOURISM

🧳 45.5m visitors   ⬇ Down 1% in 1994

MAIN OVERSEAS ARRIVALS

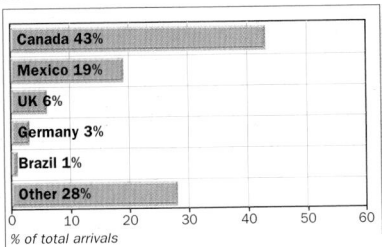

Canada 43%
Mexico 19%
UK 6%
Germany 3%
Brazil 1%
Other 28%

% of total arrivals

Tourism is an important industry, catering to ever-growing demand from both foreign visitors and Americans themselves. The number of overseas visitors has doubled in the past 15 years, reflecting the relative weakness of the dollar and the deregulation of air fares. Domestic tourism has expanded just as rapidly, as real incomes have risen. In 1993, over two billion trips were made within the USA.

The top tourist destinations include Florida's Disney World – with over 20 million visitors a year – Niagara Falls, Las Vegas, New York, San Francisco, LA and Hollywood, the Grand Canyon, New Orleans, Atlantic City and Washington, DC. All the states have their attractions, however, and most court tourists. Tourism is a major generator of jobs, especially in areas of industrial decline, such as the northeast.

Tourism's rapid expansion has also brought some problems. The 367 parks and sites run by the National Parks Service (NPS) have been particular casualties. Visitor numbers have more than doubled since 1970, to a record 275 million in 1992. To try and reduce pressure on the most popular areas, NPS lands have been doubled in area since 1976, to 126,566 square miles. Even so, there is still bumper-to-bumper traffic in Yellowstone Park, and a seven-year waiting list for a raft ride down the Grand Canyon.

PEOPLE

 English, Spanish, Italian, German, French, Polish, Chinese, Tagalog, Greek

 75 people per sq. mile

THE URBAN/RURAL POPULATION SPLIT

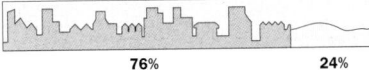

76%   24%

RELIGIOUS PERSUASION

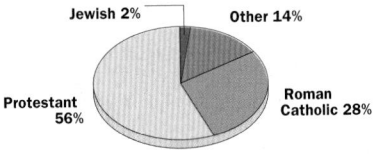

Jewish 2%   Other 14%
Protestant 56%   Roman Catholic 28%

ETHNIC MAKEUP

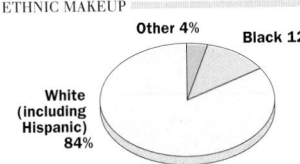

Other 4%   Black 12%
White (including Hispanic) 84%

Unlike Western Europe, the USA is experiencing a population boom, largely as a result of immigration. Since the mid-1960s, and especially since 1980, the USA has undergone an astonishing immigration boom. During the 1980s, probably ten million immigrants (legal and illegal) settled in the country, more than in any other decade. The new immigrants are disproportionately drawn from Asia and Latin America. In the 1980s, more than two million immigrants came from Mexico alone.

There is concern that the growth of immigration will marginalize the position of American blacks, who increasingly find they have to compete both politically and economically with the newer immigrants. In some places, such as Los Angeles, this is already a source of tension. Blacks are exploring new ways of making their voice heard. One group that is gaining popularity is the militant black Muslim organization the Nation Of Islam, led by Louis Farrakhan – its "Million Man March" on Washington D.C. in 1995 was the largest black demonstration since the 1960s.

A Census Bureau report released in 1996 projected that, according to current trends in immigration and birth-rates, only about half of the population of the US would be white by the middle of the 21st century. The Bureau said that by 2050 the non-Hispanic white population of the US would total 53%, compared with the current figure of 74%. The populations with the fastest growth rates (over 2% a year until 2030) would be Hispanics, who were forecast to make up approximately one-quarter of the total population by the middle of the next century, and Asians, who would constitute 8.2%. Currently these groups make up 10.2% and 3.3% of the population.

POPULATION AGE BREAKDOWN

	0–14	15–64		65+
9.2%	9.8%	11.3%	12.6%	12.8%
59.7%	61.9%	66.2%	66%	67%
31.1%	28.3%	22.5%	21.4%	20.2%
1960	1970	1980	1990	2000

% of population by age group

POLITICS

U. House 1994/1996
L. House 1994/1996

President William Jefferson Clinton

THE STATE OF THE PARTIES

House of Representatives 435 members

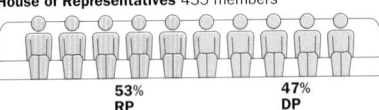

53% RP   47% DP

RP = Republican Party   **DP** = Democratic Party
There are also two independent members of the House of Representatives

Senate 100 members

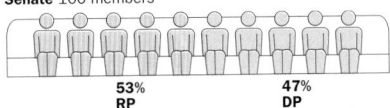

53% RP   47% DP

The USA has a federal democratic government. Under this system, many important issues are dealt with by the states. The federal government, for example, does not have a central role in education or urban development.

MAIN POLITICAL ISSUES
Crime, race and poverty
The USA has seen its crime rates soar for 20 years. At the same time parts of its cities have faced increasing social problems. The black community, which makes up 60% of those living in poor districts, faces particular problems. Both rates of criminality and crime victims are higher in the black community than in any other.

It may be possible to regenerate the cities where the poorest live through a combination of new economic opportunities and programs that give poor people more power over their own lives (for example, by self-management of public housing projects). Whether there is a sufficient political consensus to achieve this remains open to doubt, and there is the real prospect of the country having a permanently disaffected underclass living within its cities.

Health
The USA is wrestling with a health-care system based on private insurance where costs are increasing faster than private or public budgets can tolerate,

President Bill Clinton faces a reelection battle in 1996.

Newt Gingrich, Republican speaker of the House of Representatives.

U

POLITICS *continued*

and which gives a patchy service to clients. In addition to the escalation of costs, some one-third of Americans have no health insurance. President Clinton aimed at a fundamental overhaul of the system, seeking to extend cover to all while forcing employers to bear most of the cost. The plan, for which Hillary Clinton was given prime responsibility, constituted one of the most significant legislative proposals for 50 years and had significant public support. However, although Clinton had characterized the legislation as the defining feature of his domestic agenda, it foundered in Congress in the face of opposition from powerful vested interests and Republican opposition.

Foreign policy

In the post-Cold War world, the USA has to decide how and when to project its unique power abroad. The collapse of the Soviet Union has fueled calls for a return to a more isolationist stance, and has led to a greater examination of the expectation that the USA will automatically play the role of global policeman. While remaining committed to existing military obligations to its allies, the USA has shown a marked reluctance since the Vietnam War to commit troops to unwinnable conflicts.

The Clinton presidency

The Clinton administration has been beset by personal, financial and political scandals. The mid-term elections in November 1994 saw a surge of support for Republican candidates, resulting in Republican majorities in both the House of Representatives and the Senate for the first time in 30 years. However, Clinton is widely expected to gain reelection for a second term in November 1996.

PROFILE

In modern times, the Republican Party has dominated the presidency, and the Democratic Party the Congress. The election of Bill Clinton at the end of 1992 was meant to end the resultant "gridlock" between the executive and legislative branches. This proved not to be the case, however, as the complex

Warren Christopher holds the position of secretary of state.

Richard Holbrooke, the US special envoy, helped secure the Bosnia peace accord.

legislative process and independent power of Congress continued to preclude rapid legislative results. The new Republican majority in the House of Representatives, the first for 30 years, was elected in part on the promise of the enactment of a ten-point "Contract with America." However, most of these measures have faltered in the Senate.

The Supreme Court, which has periodically made some of the country's most momentous decisions, currently has a much less salient position in US politics.

WORLD AFFAIRS

The USA's attitude to international affairs has been colored by two facts. Firstly, it is protected from the rest of the world by two great oceans. Secondly, its immediate neighbors – Canada and Mexico – have historically been benign. As a result, for much of its history the USA has enjoyed the luxury of being able to choose the extent of its involvement in the affairs of others.

For most of the first half of the 20th century it pursued an isolationist policy, becoming only reluctantly involved in World Wars I and II. After 1945, however, it swapped isolationism for involvement. The UN was headquartered in New York, and the USA took its seat on the Security Council. As leader of one side of the struggle between capitalism and communism, the USA helped set up NATO, and subsequently played an active part in the defense of Western Europe. For the USA, the Cold War was most immediate – and costly – in the Korean and Vietnam Wars. The heavy death toll and shock of defeat in Vietnam kept the USA out of military involvement overseas for over a decade. Instead, it concentrated on diplomacy – with particular success in China and the Middle East – and on supporting the opponents of left-wing regimes in the developing world, as in Nicaragua.

The collapse of the eastern bloc after 1989 has led to a renewed debate over foreign policy. In particular, as the only remaining superpower, the USA has to determine the scope of its foreign responsibilities in an era when its own survival is no longer threatened. At times in the early 1990s, it appeared set to take on the role of world policeman, taking a lead in the interventions in Kuwait and Somalia. However, as its subsequent problems in Somalia indicated – and lack of clear policy on Bosnia and Haiti confirmed – the USA is still uncertain about its role in the post-Cold War world.

Manhattan Island, bounded by the Hudson and East Rivers. New York's two main clusters of skyscrapers are found in the financial district and in midtown Manhattan.

AID

 $9.7bn (donations) Up 10% in 1993

The USA gives proportionally little foreign aid, and such aid as it does give is perennially held hostage to special pleading in Congress. The lion's share goes to Israel and Egypt, although of late there has been substantial assistance to the countries of the former USSR and Eastern Europe.

DEFENSE

$270.6bn   Down 3% in 1995

0	Defense spending as % GDP	40

4.3%

AMERICAN ARMED FORCES

	12,245 battle tanks (500 M-48A5, 749 M-60/A1/A2, 3,548 M-60A3, 7,448 M-1)	524,900 personnel
	100 submarines, 12 carriers, 46 destroyers, 49 frigates and 21 patrol boats	441,800 personnel
	2,655 combat aircraft (F-4, F15, F16, F-111, EF111A, A-10A, F-117)	408,700 personnel
	384 SLBM in 16 SSBN, 597 ICBM	

The enormous US military-industrial complex dates from the years since 1945. Before then, the armed forces were small in number, poorly equipped and rapidly dismantled at the end of wars. Defense spending has peaked three times since 1945: at the time of the Korean War in the 1950s, during the 1963–1973 Vietnam War and again in the defense buildup of 1979–1986.

A combination of the end of the Cold War and the need to cut the budget deficit means defense spending has been reduced in the 1990s. In real terms, it is now at its lowest level since 1945. This is having one unanticipated but troubling side effect. The armed forces is the area where blacks have found it easiest to gain top positions. As the military shrinks, so do the opportunities for black American advancement.

U

REGIONS

THE GREAT LAKES

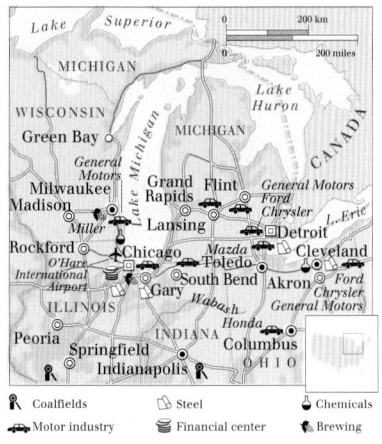

Michigan, Superior and Ontario form the world's largest expanse of fresh water. The Great Lakes provide a natural transportation system, which enabled the adjacent Midwest states to become the USA's leading industrial and agricultural area in the 19th century. Agriculture is still important, especially in Wisconsin and Minnesota; the Minneapolis grain exchange is the USA's largest strictly cash stock market. The region's heavy industries have suffered badly since the early 1980s, hit by overseas competition and the shift toward the high-tech sector. Even so, Detroit, home of Ford, is still the USA's leading vehicle producer. Chicago, once known for its stock markets and the Mob, is now one of the USA's leading cultural centers – and is still its transportation hub.

WITH A TOTAL AREA of 94,500 sq. miles, Lakes Erie, Huron,

SILICON VALLEY

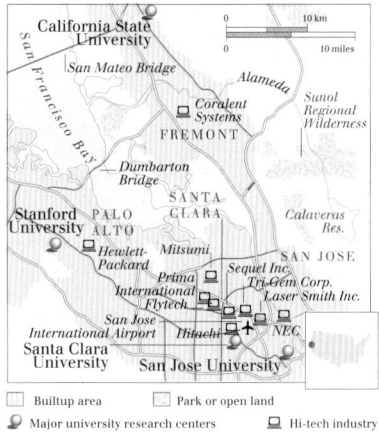

the early 1960s, it had developed into a center of high-tech innovation and entrepreneurialism. Home to scores of established companies – including Hewlett-Packard and Apple – Silicon Valley has lost little of its early spirit. It still generates many imaginative young enterprises. Hewlett-Packard has had recently to face stiff competition from newcomers, such as Sun Microsystems. Apple, too, has had to undertake significant restructuring to meet the demands of the 1990s market. Many Asian, European and Latin American immigrants have been drawn by the region's industry, which has a reputation for extracting the maximum from its work force. Workers often have a stake in their company through share ownership. Local universities, in particular Stanford, have played an important role in developing the new technology on which the Valley thrives.

LOCATED IN NORTHERN CALIFORNIA, Silicon Valley has it origins in the years before World War II. By

HOUSTON

The Enron Building, Houston. *The city is now the headquarters for many top American companies.*

AMERICA'S FOURTH CITY, Houston, has been the center of the oil industry since 1901. However, oil is lessening in importance, as Houston, like the rest of Texas, turns to high-tech industries. In 1980, just 16% of its economy was not dependent on oil; today it is 40%. Houston has two main attractions for investors like computer giant Compaq: the Lyndon B. Johnson Space Center, home to the space shuttle program, and the Texas Medical Center, the world's largest medical complex. The resulting concentration of research facilities, scientists and engineers has enabled Houston to develop as a top applied and bio-technology center.

THE SOUTH

IN THE 1940s, the South almost seemed to be another country. Thanks to abundant cheap labor, its agriculture was still tied to cotton. With a few exceptions, such as Birmingham, Alabama, industry had never taken root. The "Jim Crow" laws epitomized a bitter racial division. World War II started a transformation process. Industry developed along the Gulf Coast, in towns such as Mobile. The cotton harvest was mechanized. Not least, the federal government extended its powers into the South in the battle to end legally sanctioned racial discrimination. Since the 1970s, the South has been one of the USA's fastest-growing areas. Its population has increased by over 33% and many industries have invested there. The core states of the "Confederate" South, however, have done less well. In

NEW YORK

NEW YORK, THE "BIG APPLE," is the largest city in the USA and has been the gateway city for repeated waves of immigrants. During most of the first two centuries of the Republic, New York was its capital for everything but politics. It is a huge and in many ways still vibrant city, partly because it is currently experiencing a new influx of immigrants – this time from Asia and Russia. Its collar of suburbs has a population greater than that of Belgium. However, the extent of the city's decay is evident – more so in the outer boroughs than in Manhattan, where most of its tourist attractions are located. In terms of pop culture, art, sport, finance and recreation, New York has never loomed less large within the USA than it does now.

SEATTLE

THE MOST IMPORTANT CITY of the Pacific North West, Seattle in Washington State has a dramatics location – bounded to the west by the Puget Sound and to the east by Lake Washington. The 1980s boom years saw large numbers of immigrants and new businesses attracted to the region. The latter included Microsoft, the world's leading software manufacturer. Yet, despite the arrival of a different style of industry, Boeing is still the largest employer in the Seattle area. With its newfound wealth, Seattle has swiftly changed from a backwater near America's northwest border with Canada into a cosmopolitan city. Its lively downtown area recently gained international fame as the birthplace of "grunge" rock.

U

National parks/National preserves
National forests   Major sites   Tourism
The Everglades

addition, areas such as West Virginia, already among the poorest in the USA, stagnated and lost population.

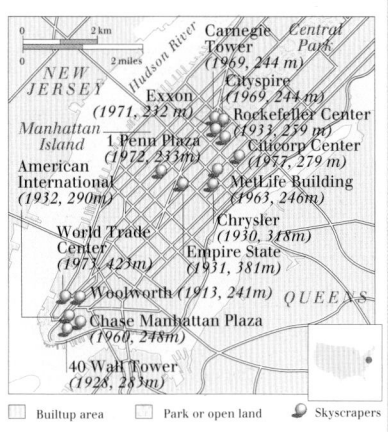

Builtup area   Park or open land   Skyscrapers

ECONOMICS

$6737.4bn   Not applicable

SCORE CARD

❑ WORLD GNP RANKING............................1st
❑ GNP PER CAPITA...........................$25,860
❑ BALANCE OF PAYMENTS ....$–150.9bn
❑ INFLATION 2.6%
❑ UNEMPLOYMENT 6%

EXPORTS

Germany 4%   UK 5%
                  Mexico 9%
Other 49%   Japan 11%
                  Canada 22%

IMPORTS

China 6%   Germany 5%
            Mexico 7%
Other 45%   Japan 18%
            Canada 19%

STRENGTHS

The world's largest economy. Wealth of natural resources, including energy, raw materials and foods. Strong high-tech base and world-leading research and development. Sophisticated service sector, as well as advanced and competitive manufacturing industry. World-class multinationals such as Ford, GM, Exxon. Global leader in computer software. Entrepreneurial business ethic. High quality of post-graduate education, especially related to application of high-tech to business. Global dominance of US culture a major boost to US manufactures.

UNITED STATES : MAJOR BUSINESSES

ECONOMIC PERFORMANCE INDICATOR

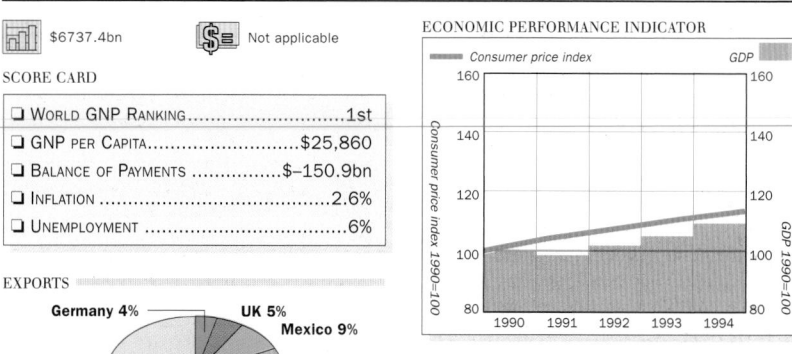

Consumer price index   GDP

WEAKNESSES

Dramatic fall in manufacturing employment over last 20 years; though manufacturing sector has remained constant as a share of GDP. Postwar economic boom was built around low-skilled, high-waged employment in areas such as car industry. Tough competition from Japan, the rest of Asia and EU, particularly in future leading-edge technologies. Lower savings rate than many competitors. World's largest debtor nation.

PROFILE

In 1945, the USA accounted for about 50% of world output, in 1994 this had declined to approximately 25%. That is not, as Americans often think, a sign of failure, but a clear indication that the 1940s and 1950s were unusual years. The current total of 25% is about the same share of the world market that the USA claimed in 1914, when it had already become the world's greatest economy.

The USA is one of the world's great exporters, and continues to have a stable political system and a uniquely strong combination of both skilled labor and natural resources.

U

Seattle

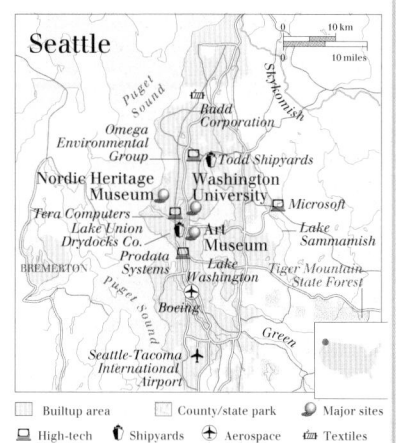

Builtup area   County/state park   Major sites
High-tech industry   Shipyards   Aerospace industry   Textiles

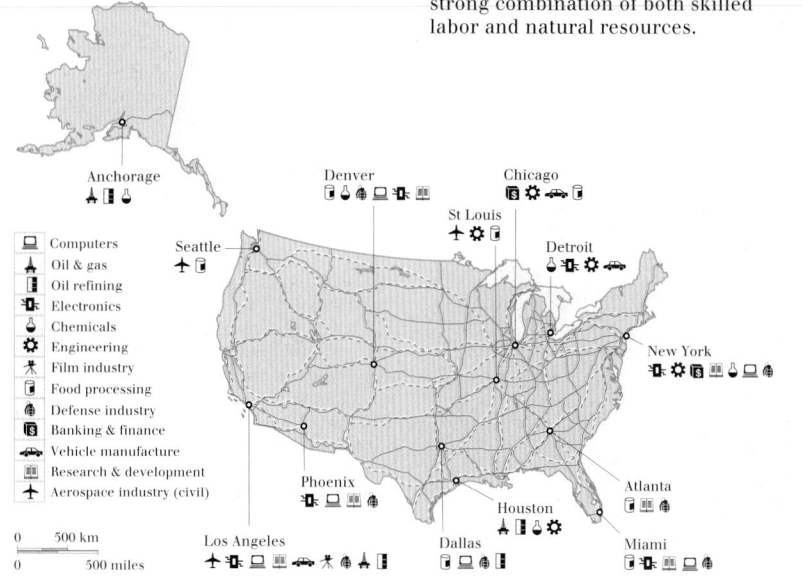

Computers
Oil & gas
Oil refining
Electronics
Chemicals
Engineering
Film industry
Food processing
Defense industry
Banking & finance
Vehicle manufacture
Research & development
Aerospace industry (civil)

CHRONOLOGY

At the beginning of the 17th century, British settlers began to establish colonies on the eastern seaboard. These 13 original colonies waged a war for independence, 1775–1781, which Britain formally recognized in 1783. The Constitution of 1787 joined them together to establish the USA. Following the victory of the northern states in the 1861–1865 Civil War, slavery was abolished throughout the USA. The latter half of the 19th century saw a series of conflicts in which native Americans were dispossessed of their land.

❑ **1917** Enters World War I.
❑ **1929** New York stock market collapse; economic depression.
❑ **1941** Japanese attack on Pearl Harbor. Enters World War II.
❑ **1950–1953** Korean War.
❑ **1954** Supreme Court rules racial segregation in schools is unconstitutional. Blacks, seeking constitutional rights, start campaign of civil disobedience.
❑ **1959** Alaska and Hawaii become 49th and 50th states of the USA.
❑ **1961** John F. Kennedy becomes president. Promises to provide aid to South Vietnamese. Relations with Cuba deteriorate; US-backed invasion defeated at Bay of Pigs.
❑ **1962** Discovery of Soviet missile bases on Cuba; serious threat of war with USSR averted.
❑ **1963** November, Kennedy assassinated. Lyndon Baines Johnson president.
❑ **1964** US involvement in Vietnam stepped up. Civil Rights Act gives blacks constitutional equality.
❑ **1968** Martin Luther King assassinated.
❑ **1969** Republican Richard Nixon takes office as president. Growing public opposition to Vietnam War.
❑ **1972** Nixon reelected. Makes historic visit to China. Relations with USSR also improve.
❑ **1973** Withdrawal of US troops from Vietnam; 58,000 US troops dead by end of war.
❑ **1974** August, Nixon resigns following "Watergate" scandal: revelation that his campaign team had organized breakin to DP headquarters. Replaced by Vice President Gerald Ford.
❑ **1976** Democrat Jimmy Carter elected president.
❑ **1978** Conclusion of US-sponsored "Camp David" agreement between Egypt and Israel.
❑ **1979** Seizure of US hostages in Iran.
❑ **1980** Ronald Reagan wins elections for Republicans. Adopts tough anti-communist foreign policy. ⇨

RESOURCES

3,072bn kwh (capacity 775.4m kw)

7.3m b/d (reserves 24,682,000,000 bbl)

100.9m cattle, 57.9m pigs, 9.6m sheep, 3.9m horses

Phosphate, gypsum, oil, coal, sulfur, lead, zinc, copper, gold

ELECTRICITY GENERATION

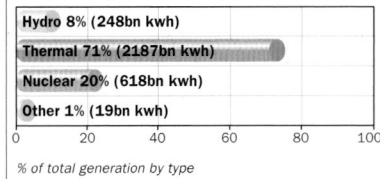

Hydro 8% (248bn kwh)
Thermal 71% (2187bn kwh)
Nuclear 20% (618bn kwh)
Other 1% (19bn kwh)

% of total generation by type

The USA has an abundance of natural resources, including oil, although the country is a net oil importer. There are massive deposits of coal in the western states – where almost all mining is open-pit – and substantial mineral deposits in the mountains and intramontane basins.

Environmental concerns have prevented the development of new sources of nuclear power since the accident at Three Mile Island in 1979. Environmentalism has also forced the

timber industry to retreat from the Pacific North West, especially from Washington State. It has moved to the south, where great stands of pine are harvested as if they were fields of wheat. The USA has harnessed hydroelectric power in the past; today, imports of hydropower from Canada are commonplace.

By comparison with Western Europe, the USA is not intensively farmed. The huge size of farms in the Midwest and West has allowed both arable and livestock farming to be based on a low-input for low-output model.

UNITED STATES : LAND USE

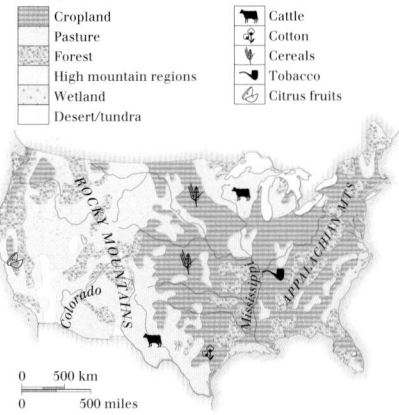

Cropland	Cattle
Pasture	Cotton
Forest	Cereals
High mountain regions	Tobacco
Wetland	Citrus fruits
Desert/tundra	

ENVIRONMENT

11% (6% partially protected)

Political opposition to environmental causes

ENVIRONMENTAL TREATIES

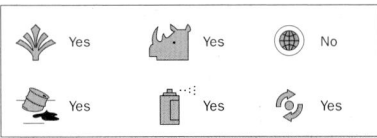

Yes   Yes   No
Yes   Yes   Yes

Although the USA came early to environmentalism, it has in some respects been overtaken by countries such as Germany. Food packaging is astonishingly wasteful and many cars are still "gas-guzzlers." As the suburban sprawl testifies, its wide open spaces have engendered a somewhat cavalier attitude to aspects of the environment.

To an extent which has not been true elsewhere, the ecological movement has been challenged politically. Protection necessarily involves the regulation of market activities; in the USA such a move is always contentious. The intramontane West is a battleground between those who want to maintain its beauty, and those who advocate "wise use" – in practice this often means giving ranchers and miners free rein. Environmental teaching is, however, strong in schools.

MEDIA

Freedom of press guaranteed in constitution

PUBLISHING AND BROADCAST MEDIA

There are 1,700 daily newspapers, including the *New York Times*, the *Washington Post* and the *Wall Street Journal*

3 major independent networks

7 major networks, 10,000 stations

Galaxy 5 Morelos

Available in over 60% of homes

Mass media as a phenomenon was born in the USA. No other society on earth has ever had anything quite like American network TV, and no other society has so easily moved into the world of multichannel TV; homes with 50 or more channels are commonplace. Newspapers, however, are having a difficult time. With a few exceptions, newspapers are local, not national. They also tend to have very low cover prices and to gain most of their revenue from advertising. This business is under increasing threat from cable TV and other outlets. Many companies are exploring multimedia opportunities, investing in ways of providing on-line news, information and other services.

U

Yellowstone National Park, Idaho. The park's ecosystem is under severe strain due to the number of visitors it attracts.

CRIME

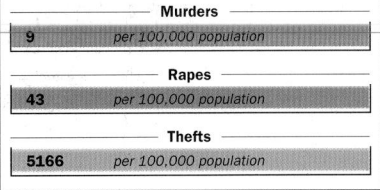

71,998 prisoners   Down 4% in 1992

CRIME RATES

Murders	
9	per 100,000 population

Rapes	
43	per 100,000 population

Thefts	
5166	per 100,000 population

The USA has seen a 20-year long crime wave. Violent crime – especially murder – is much more common than in other developed countries. This is the case even in relatively well-off parts of the country. Seattle, for example, which by US standards is a peaceful city, has a murder rate seven times that of Birmingham, England.

The rate of incarceration for narcotics crimes in the USA is much higher than in most Western countries – and the conditions worse. Capital punishment has made a strong comeback since the 1980s, especially in the South. Texas is the state that carries out most executions; most of the liberal "northern tier" states, by contrast, have abolished the death penalty.

EDUCATION

99%   14.4m students

0   Education spending as % GNP   25
5.3%

THE EDUCATION SYSTEM

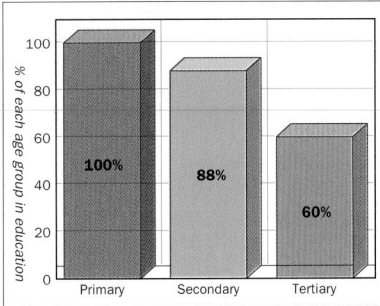

Education in the USA is primarily the responsibility of the state governments. A series of recent reports have been critical of standards in US high schools; yet all accept that US universities are world class.

Private education is a rapidly developing sector. Although the number of pupils in private education does not appear to have increased much in the last generation, this is misleading. While the number of Catholic private schools has shrunk, non-denominational fee-paying schools have been founded to take their place.

HEALTH

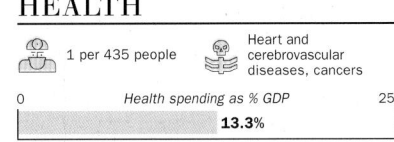

1 per 435 people   Heart and cerebrovascular diseases, cancers

0   Health spending as % GDP   25
13.3%

The US health system is subject to enormous disparities. At one level, sophisticated techniques are available to those with insurance (which they typically receive from their employer). The Texas Medical Center, in Houston, the epitome of high-tech medicine, has a budget equivalent to that of some small countries. On the other hand, infant mortality statistics in some parts of the country are at levels similar to some of the poorer countries in the developing world.

Partly because of these disparities, health-care reform has become a major political issue. It has also been driven by the skyrocketing cost of care, and subsequent cost to employers.

WEALTH

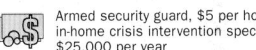

Armed security guard, $5 per hour; in-home crisis intervention specialist, $25,000 per year

CONSUMER GOODS OWNERSHIP

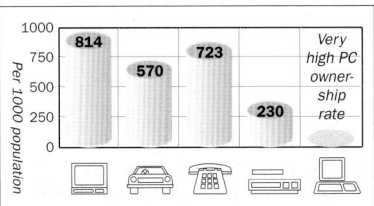

Between 1945 and 1973, all sectors of the population got richer. Since then, however, a new pattern has emerged. Those who finish high school have continued to see their standard of living increase, while those who did not have not seen an improvement for a generation. In a way that has not been seen for more than 50 years, the "education effect" is leading to noticeable class divisions.

WORLD RANKING

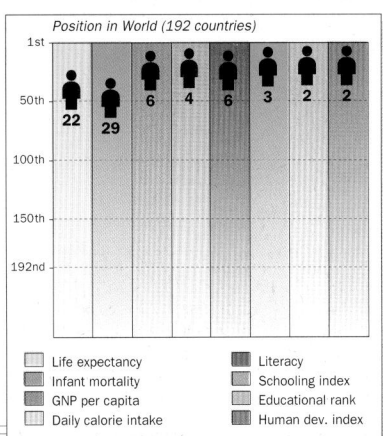

U

See also OVERSEAS TERRITORIES *p.618*

URUGUAY

OFFICIAL NAME: Eastern Republic of Uruguay   **CAPITAL:** Montevideo
POPULATION: 3.2 million   **CURRENCY:** Uruguayan peso   **OFFICIAL LANGUAGE:** Spanish

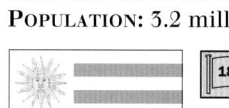

URUGUAY IS SITUATED IN SOUTHEASTERN South America. Its capital, Montevideo, is an Atlantic port on the River Plate, lying across the river from Buenos Aires, Argentina's capital. Uruguay became independent in 1828, after nearly 150 years of Spanish and Portuguese control. Decades of liberal government ended in 1973 with a military coup that was to result in 12 years of dictatorship, during which 400,000 people emigrated. Most have since returned. Almost the entire low-lying landscape is devoted to the rearing of livestock, especially cattle and sheep. Uruguay is the world's second-biggest wool exporter. Tourism and offshore banking now bring in substantial foreign earnings.

Uruguayan grasslands. Rich pasture covers three-quarters of the country, ideal for cattle and sheep. Animals and animal products account for over one-third of export earnings.

CLIMATE

WEATHER CHART

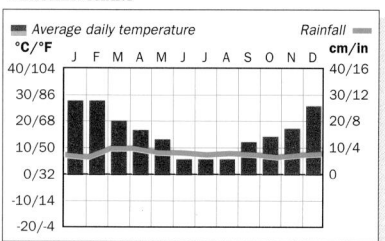

Uruguay has one of the most benign climates in the world. It is uniformly temperate over the whole country. Winters are mild, frost is rare and it never snows. Summers are generally cool for these latitudes and rarely tropically hot. The moderate rainfall tends to fall in heavy showers, leaving most days sunny.

TRANSPORTATION

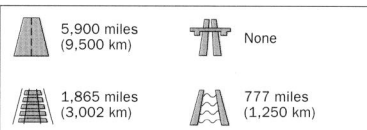

Carrasco, Montevideo
357,000 passengers

16 ships
151,200 dwt

THE TRANSPORTATION NETWORK

5,900 miles (9,500 km)		None	
1,865 miles (3,002 km)		777 miles (1,250 km)	

Uruguay's transportation plans for the 1990s center on privatization. The government has sold off its share in the national coach industry – there are extensive internal and international coach and bus services – and has closed down all passenger railroad services. There is a plan to build a road tunnel from Montevideo to Buenos Aires under the River Plate, but this will take many years to complete.

TOURISM

2.2m visitors

Up 9% in 1994

MAIN OVERSEAS ARRIVALS

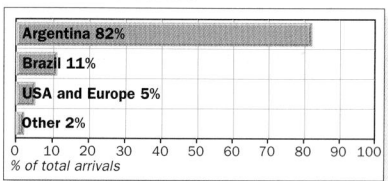

Argentina 82%
Brazil 11%
USA and Europe 5%
Other 2%

% of total arrivals

Most visitors to Uruguay travel through Montevideo to the sandy beaches near the River Plate estuary. Although the old Spanish fortifications of Montevideo have been destroyed, the city retains a colonial atmosphere. Punta del Este, 86 miles east of the capital, Uruguay's major beach resort, is served by direct 737 flights from Buenos Aires.

PEOPLE

Spanish

122 people per sq. mile

THE URBAN/RURAL POPULATION SPLIT

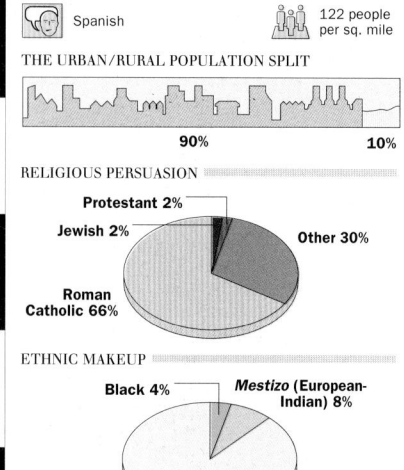

90%   10%

RELIGIOUS PERSUASION

Protestant 2%
Jewish 2%
Other 30%
Roman Catholic 66%

ETHNIC MAKEUP

Black 4%
Mestizo (European-Indian) 8%
European 88%

Most Uruguayans are second or third generation European, mostly of Spanish or Italian descent. There are also some *mestizos* and a small minority of people descended from Africans or immigrants from Brazil, who live in or around the capital Montevideo or near the Brazilian border. All indigenous Indian groups became integrated in the *mestizo* population by the mid-19th century. The population's unusual degree of homogeneity – and the fact that it is small compared with the size of the country – mean that ethnic tensions are few. The birth-rate is low for Latin America.

The considerable prosperity derived from cattle ranching allowed Uruguay to become a welfare state long before any other Latin American country. In spite of Uruguay's serious economic decline since the end of the 1950s, there is still a sizeable, if less prosperous,

middle class. A clear sign of the country's economic and social deterioration during the years of military dictatorship was the unprecedented growth of shanty towns around Montevideo.

Although a Roman Catholic country, Uruguay is liberal in its attitude to religion and all forms are tolerated. Divorce is legal. Women are regarded as equal to men and have the vote. There is no capital punishment.

POPULATION AGE BREAKDOWN

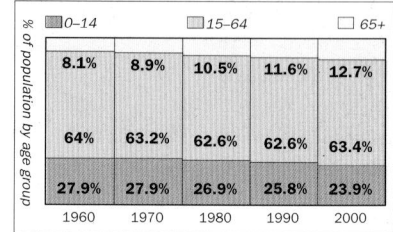

	0–14	15–64	65+		
% of population by age group	8.1%	8.9%	10.5%	11.6%	12.7%
	64%	63.2%	62.6%	62.6%	63.4%
	27.9%	27.9%	26.9%	25.8%	23.9%
	1960	1970	1980	1990	2000

U

POLITICS

U. House 1994/1999
L. House 1994/1999

President Julio
María Sanguinetti

THE STATE OF THE PARTIES

Chamber of Representatives 99 members

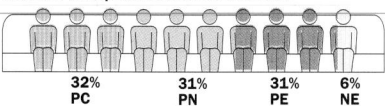

| 32% PC | 31% PN | 31% PE | 6% NE |

PC = Colorado Party **PN** = National Party **PE** = Progressive Encounter **NE** = New Space

Senate 31 members

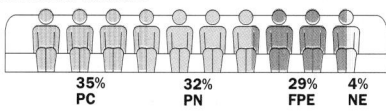

| 35% PC | 32% PN | 29% FPE | 4% NE |

Uruguay is a presidential multiparty democracy.

MAIN POLITICAL ISSUES
Modernization and privatization
After 20 years of military dictatorship and transitional government, Uruguay is seeking the best way of modernizing the state and state-run institutions. The central political question is the slow pace of privatization compared to other regional economies.

The aging population
Uruguay's long-established welfare system is under strain from the increasing proportion of elderly people in the population. The emigration of young workers to Europe and Argentina is exacerbating the problem.

PROFILE
The elections of 1984 marked Uruguay's return to democracy. The winning right-wing Colorado Party addressed some human rights issues, but its attempts to reverse economic recession met with fierce trade-union opposition. The 1989 elections resulted in an uneasy coalition between the *Colorados* and conservative National Party *(Blancos)*. Both parties dominate a broader coalition which took office in 1995. Despite congressional opposition, this allowed the Sanguinetti government to pass the long-delayed reform of the social security system. Reform of the complicated electoral system is a divisive issue.

Luis Alberto Lacalle Herrera, *president from 1990–1994.*

President Julio María Sanguinetti, *who took office in March 1995.*

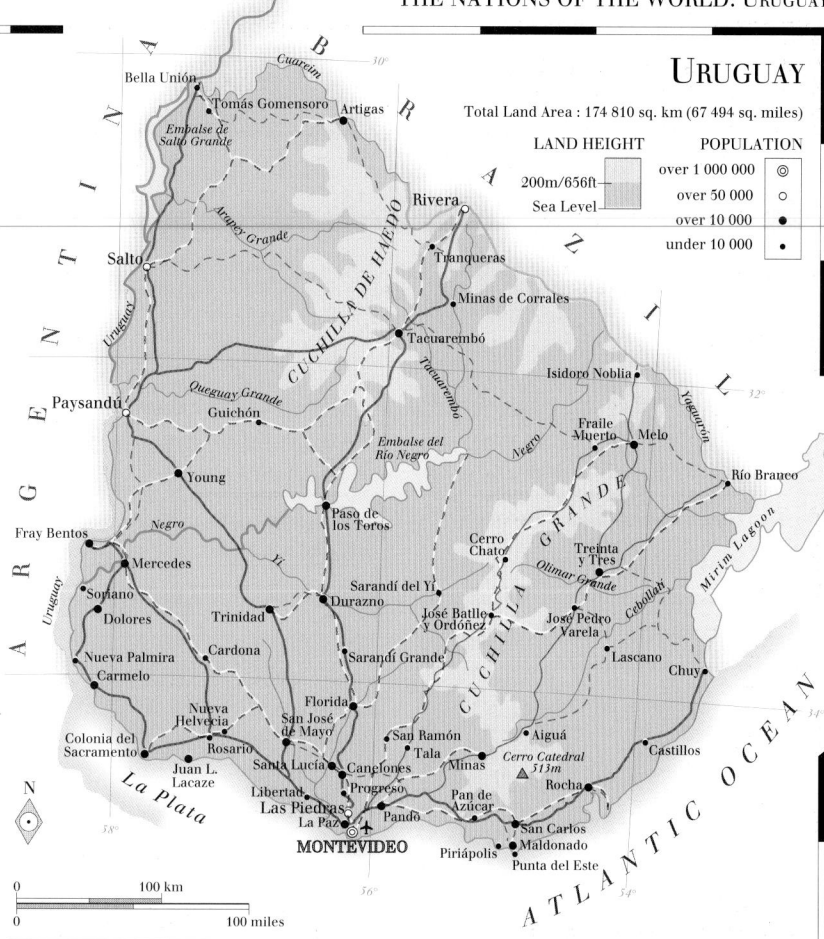

URUGUAY

Total Land Area : 174 810 sq. km (67 494 sq. miles)

LAND HEIGHT	POPULATION
200m/656ft	over 1 000 000 ◎
Sea Level	over 50 000 ○
	over 10 000 ●
	under 10 000 ·

| 0 | 100 km |
| 0 | 100 miles |

WORLD AFFAIRS

 AG   Mercsr   NAM   OAS RG

After many years of political isolation and economic decline, Uruguay's chief foreign policy concern is achieving full regional integration with Argentina, Brazil and Paraguay in MERCOSUR, the common market of southern South America which came into operation in 1995. Uruguay is already part of a continental defense alliance with other Latin American countries and the USA. However, it has some unresolved border problems with Brazil. Uruguay allowed the UK to use its ports during the Falklands conflict.

In 1991, Uruguay and the USA signed a legal-assistance treaty to allow easier access to the bank accounts of those suspected of laundering the proceeds of narcotics-trafficking. This had increasingly been carried out through Montevideo's offshore banking sector.

AID

 $121m (receipts)    Up 66% in 1993

Uruguay received a small but increasing amount of aid in the early 1990s, largely from multilateral sources.

CHRONOLOGY

The Spaniards were the first to colonize the area north of the River Plate. In 1680, the Portuguese also founded a colony there, at Colonia del Sacramento, so starting 150 years of rivalry between the colonial powers for control of the territory.

❑ **1726** Spaniards found Montevideo. By end of century, whole country is divided into large cattle ranches.

❑ **1808** Montevideo declares independence from Buenos Aires.

❑ **1811** Patriotic rancher and local *caudillo* (leader), José Gervasio Artigas, fends off Brazilian attack.

❑ **1812–1820** Uruguayans, known as *Orientales* ("Easterners," from the eastern side of the River Plate), fight wars against Argentinian and Brazilian invaders. Brazil finally takes Montevideo.

❑ **1827** Gen. Lavallejo defeats Brazilians with Argentine help.

❑ **1828** Seeing trade benefits that an independent Uruguay would bring as a buffer state between Argentina and Brazil, Britain mediates and secures Uruguayan independence.

❑ **1836** Start of large-scale European immigration. ⇨

U

CHRONOLOGY *continued*

- **1858–1865** *La Guerra Grande* civil war between *Blancos* (Whites, future conservative party) and *Colorados* (Reds, future liberals).
- **1865–1870** *Colorado* president, Gen. Venancio Flores, takes Uruguay into War of the Triple Alliance against Paraguay.
- **1872** Peace under military rule. *Blancos* strong in country, *Colorados* in city.
- **1890s** Violent strikes by immigrant trade unionists against landed elite enriched by massive European investment in ranching.
- **1903–1907** Reformist *Colorado*, José Batlle y Ordóñez, president.
- **1911–1915** Batllé serves second term in office. *Batllismo* creates the only welfare state in Latin America with pensions, social security and free education and health service; also nationalizations, disestablishment of Church, abolition of death penalty.
- **1933** Military coup. Opposition groups excluded from politics.
- **1942** President Alfredo Baldomir dismisses government and tries to bring back proper representation.
- **1939–1945** Neutrality.
- **1951** New constitution replaces president with nine-member council. Decade of great prosperity follows until world agricultural prices plummet. Sharp drop in foreign investment.
- **1958** *Blanco* party wins elections for first time in 93 years.
- **1962** Tupamaros urban guerrilla group founded. Its campaign of terrorism continues until 1973.
- **1964** Large trade unions unite.
- **1966** Presidency reinstated. *Colorados* back in power.
- **1967** Jorge Pacheco president. Tries to stifle opposition to tough anti-inflation policies.
- **1973** Military coup. Promises to encourage foreign investment counteracted by denial of political freedom and brutal repression of the left; 400,000 emigrate.
- **1974** EEC bans meat imports.
- **1984** Military agrees to step down. Elections held.
- **1985** Dr. Julio Sanguinetti (*Colorado*) president.
- **1986** Those guilty of human rights abuse granted amnesty.
- **1988** Drought: one million cattle die.
- **1989** Referendum endorses amnesty in interests of stability. Fully free elections won by Lacalle Herrera and *Blancos*. Attempt to include *Colorado* ministers fails.
- **1991** Signs MERCOSUR agreement.
- **1994–1995** Sanguinetti reelected, forms coalition government.

DEFENSE

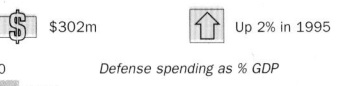

$302m   ⬆ Up 2% in 1995

0	Defense spending as % GDP	40
2.5%		

The military withdrew from power in 1984 and has since respected civilian rule. Four "lodges" operate within the army to promote officers' interests, and in 1995 and 1996 some displayed opposition to the government's replacements and promotions within the military hierarchy. A 1986 law virtually blocked investigations into torture, "disappearances," and killings during the dictatorship, but there is still public pressure to bring guilty officers to justice.

URUGUAYAN ARMED FORCES

68 light tanks (17 M-24, 28 M-3A1, 22 M-41A1)	17,600 personnel
3 frigates and 10 patrol boats	5,000 personnel
36 combat aircraft (12 A37B, 7 T-33A)	3,000 personnel
None	

The defense budget is low; equipment is mostly bought from the USA and less sophisticated weaponry from Brazil.

ECONOMICS

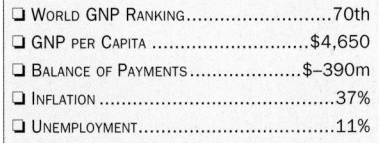

$14.7bn   5.64–7.07 new Uruguayan pesos

SCORE CARD

- ❏ WORLD GNP RANKING..........................70th
- ❏ GNP PER CAPITA $4,650
- ❏ BALANCE OF PAYMENTS....................$–390m
- ❏ INFLATION 37%
- ❏ UNEMPLOYMENT..................................11%

EXPORTS

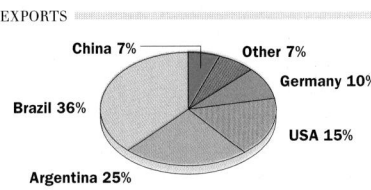

China 7% — Other 7% — Germany 10% — USA 15% — Argentina 25% — Brazil 36%

IMPORTS

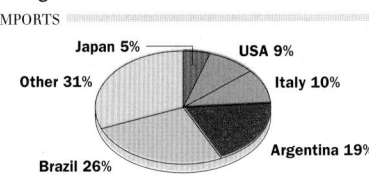

Japan 5% — USA 9% — Italy 10% — Argentina 19% — Brazil 26% — Other 31%

STRENGTHS

Substantial earnings as offshore banking center. Buoyant tourism. Fertile grasslands. World's second-biggest wool exporter.

WEAKNESSES

No oil or minerals except for agate, amethysts, unexploited gold deposits and small quantities of iron ore. Little progress in industrialization. Low world agricultural prices.

PROFILE

Traditionally an agricultural economy, three-quarters of the country is rich pasture, supporting livestock. Much of the rest is given over to crops. Farming still employs about 15% of the labor force, accounting for about 10% of GDP. Livestock and animal products, especially meat and wool, account for over one-third of export earnings. In

ECONOMIC PERFORMANCE INDICATOR

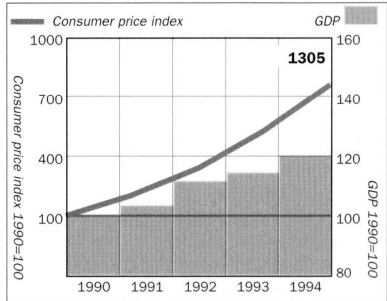

Consumer price index — GDP

1305

(Consumer price index 1990=100; GDP 1990=100; years 1990–1994)

addition, manufacturing, which accounts for 25% of GDP, is farm-based. However, tourism has now overtaken both in terms of economic importance. Most economic activity – and half the population – is in Montevideo and its port. Much of the economy is still state-controlled, including all the largest companies. The Sanguinetti government aims to tighten public sector management in 1996 and to increase private participation in markets once monopolized by the state.

URUGUAY : MAJOR BUSINESSES

Salto
Paysandú
Río Branco
Fray Bentos
Colonia del Sacramento
Durazno
Montevideo

⚙ Heavy engineering
🗄 Food processing
🛢 Oil refining
🧵 Wool spinning
🐄 Meat packing
⬧ Leather
✳ Textiles

0   100 km
0   100 miles

U

RESOURCES

 8bn kwh (capacity 1.68m kw)

 Not an oil producer; refines 28,500 b/cd

 24.4m sheep, 10.3m cattle, 479,000 horses

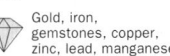 Gold, iron, gemstones, copper, zinc, lead, manganese

Most of Uruguay is farmland, much of it given over to cattle and sheep. Rice is the country's only significant crop on the world market. Mineral resources may be considerable but, despite optimistic geological surveys, are yet to be exploited. Small quantities of building materials and jewelry-quality agate and amethysts are mined.

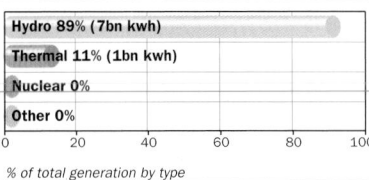

ELECTRICITY GENERATION

Hydro 89% (7bn kwh)
Thermal 11% (1bn kwh)
Nuclear 0%
Other 0%

% of total generation by type

Hydroelectric power generates 89% of the country's electricity. Its export offsets Uruguay's total dependency on imported oil.

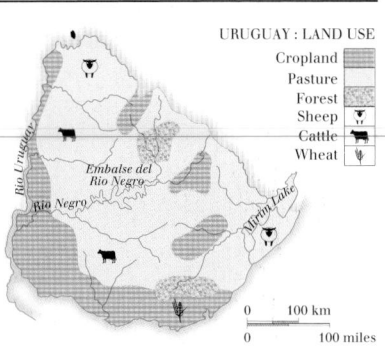

URUGUAY : LAND USE

- Cropland
- Pasture
- Forest
- Sheep
- Cattle
- Wheat

0   100 km
0   100 miles

ENVIRONMENT

 0.2% (0.1% partially protected)

 Rising riverine pollution

ENVIRONMENTAL TREATIES

No	Yes	Yes
No	Yes	Yes

Pollution of the country's two main rivers, the Uruguay and the River Plate, is of increasing concern.

MEDIA

 Full freedom of expression is guaranteed by the constitution

PUBLISHING AND BROADCAST MEDIA

There are 9 daily newspapers, including *El País*, *El Diario* and *La Mañana*

1 state-owned, 25 independent stations

2 state-owned, 160 independent stations

Panamsat 1

None

The press is now relatively free. *El País* supports the *Blancos* (PN), while *La Mañana* backs the *Colorados* (PC).

CRIME

 1,910 prisoners

 Up 29% in 1990

CRIME RATES

Murders
5   per 100,000 population

Rapes
Below Latin American average

Thefts
Below Latin American average

Crime levels in Uruguay are fairly low, particularly when compared with its neighbors Brazil and Argentina. Domestic theft is the main problem. Bribery is not common.

EDUCATION

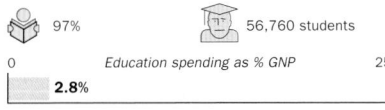 97%   56,760 students

0   Education spending as % GNP   25
2.8%

THE EDUCATION SYSTEM

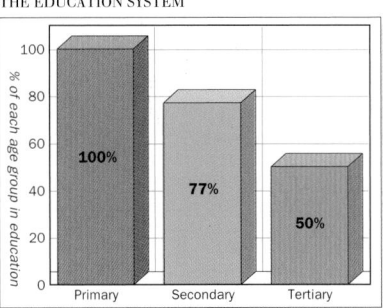

% of each age group in education

- Primary: 100%
- Secondary: 77%
- Tertiary: 50%

Education, inspired by the French *lycée* system, is state-funded up to secondary level (12 years) and compulsory for all children between the ages of six and 14. Comprehensive reform to improve the quality and provision of public education is planned. Both state and private schools follow the same curriculum; private schools are monitored by the government. Facilities are rudimentary in rural areas. Uruguay has two state-funded universities. The children of wealthy Uruguayans tend to complete their studies in the USA.

HEALTH

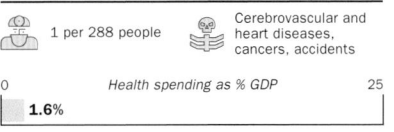 1 per 288 people   Cerebrovascular and heart diseases, cancers, accidents

0   Health spending as % GDP   25
1.6%

Most Uruguayans have easy access to health services. The average life expectancy of 72 years is the highest in South America. Public services cater for 40% of the population and the private sector for the remaining 60%. Despite opposition, the government is determined to privatize some state medical establishments.

WEALTH

 Grain miller, 5 Uruguayan pesos ($ 0.1) per hour; medical general practitioner, 20 Uruguayan pesos ($3) per hour

CONSUMER GOODS OWNERSHIP

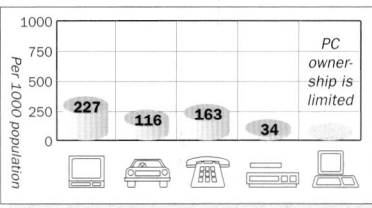

Per 1000 population

- 227
- 116
- 163
- 34

PC ownership is limited

Uruguay possesses the social mobility typical of countries created through decades of large-scale immigration. Many professionals come from modest backgrounds. The wealthy tend either to be landowners or are employed in the financial sector. They still look toward Europe, rather than the USA, for luxury goods and the latest fashions. They travel to Europe for their vacations or visit Uruguay's coastal resorts, such as Punta del Este. The most common status symbol is a Mercedes car.

The most deprived sections of Uruguayan society are the urban poor of Montevideo, a large proportion of whom are of mixed African and European descent, and the rural poor, who have little or no land of their own.

WORLD RANKING

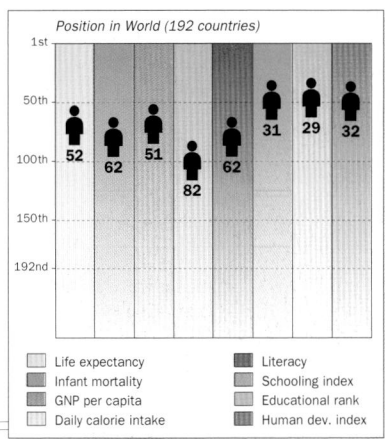

Position in World (192 countries)

- 52
- 62
- 51
- 82
- 62
- 31
- 29
- 32

- Life expectancy
- Infant mortality
- GNP per capita
- Daily calorie intake
- Literacy
- Schooling index
- Educational rank
- Human dev. index

U

UZBEKISTAN

OFFICIAL NAME: Republic of Uzbekistan CAPITAL: Tashkent
POPULATION: 22.8 million CURRENCY: Som OFFICIAL LANGUAGE: Uzbek

SHARING THE ARAL SEA coastline with its northern
neighbor, Kazakhstan, Uzbekistan has common
borders with five countries, including Afghanistan to the south. It is the
most populous Central Asian republic and has considerable natural
resources. Uzbekistan contains the ancient Muslim cities of Samarkand,
Bukhara, Khiva and Tashkent. The dictatorship of President Karimov has
prevented the spread of Islamic fundamentalism.

CLIMATE

WEATHER CHART

Uzbekistan has a harsh continental
climate. Summers can be extremely
hot and dry. Large areas
of the country
are desert.

TRANSPORTATION

 Tashkent Intl	Has no fleet

THE TRANSPORTATION NETWORK

41,700 miles (67,000 km)	None
2,150 miles (3,460 km)	684 miles (1,100 km)

Uzbekistan has a well-developed
transportation system. An extensive
network of buses serves country areas,
while good Soviet-style systems of
trolleybuses and trams operate in
the major cities. Road and rail
networks have, however,
deteriorated since 1991,
and are concentrated in
the south and east. The
national airline is *Uzbek Khavo
Yullari* (Uzbekistan Airways).

TOURISM

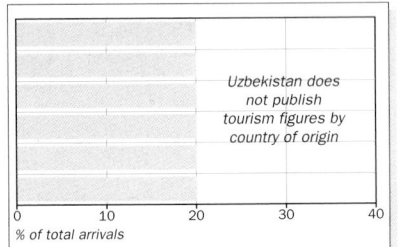

Small numbers of tourists	Little change from previous year

MAIN OVERSEAS ARRIVALS

Uzbekistan does not publish tourism figures by country of origin

Uzbekistan has considerable tourist
potential. Bukhara, once a trading
center on the silk route, is famous
worldwide for its architecture and
carpet-making. To Muslims, it is
second only to Mecca as a religious
centre. Muslims unable to undertake
the *haj* (pilgrimage) to Mecca can
become *hajis* by visiting Bukhara seven
times instead. The city of Samarkand
was built in the 14th century by
Tamburlaine, and is home to the
monumental gateway of the Shir
Dar Madrasa, which vies with
India's Taj Mahal as one of the
most beautiful buildings in Asia.

UZBEKISTAN

Total Land Area : 447 400 sq. km
(172 741 sq. miles)

LAND HEIGHT	POPULATION
3000m/9843ft	⊡ over 1 000 000
2000m/6562ft	◎ over 100 000
1000m/3281ft	○ over 50 000
500m/1640ft	• over 10 000
200m/656ft	
Sea Level	

***Mosque in
Samarkand.***
*The city remained
an Islamic stronghold,
despite communist
attempts at suppression,
when Uzbekistan formed
part of the Soviet Union.*

U

PEOPLE

 Uzbek, Russian   132 people per sq. mile

THE URBAN/RURAL POPULATION SPLIT

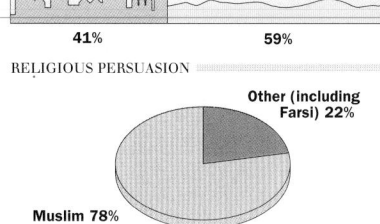

41%   59%

RELIGIOUS PERSUASION

Other (including Farsi) 22%
Muslim 78%

ETHNIC MAKEUP

Kazakh 4% Tajik 5%
Russian 8%
Other 12%
Uzbek 71%

Among ex-Soviet republics, Uzbekistan has a relatively complex makeup. In addition to the Uzbeks, Russians, Tajiks and Kazakhs, there are small minorities of Tatars and Karakalpaks. The proportion of Russians has been declining since the 1970s when net emigration of Russians began. Tensions among ethnic groups have the potential to create regional and racial conflict. The authoritarian nature of the Karimov leadership has so far prevented these antagonisms becoming violent. Incidents such as the 1989 and 1990 clashes between Meskhetian Turks and Uzbeks are rare. The removal of the Communist Party's leadership has meant that Uzbek society has reverted to traditional social patterns based on family, religion, clan and region, rather than on membership of the party. Independence has done little to alter the minor role of women in politics. Arranged marriages are still the custom in the countryside.

POPULATION AGE BREAKDOWN

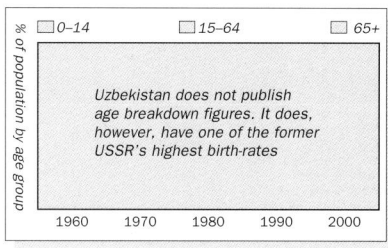

% of population by age group

☐ 0–14   ☐ 15–64   ☐ 65+

Uzbekistan does not publish age breakdown figures. It does, however, have one of the former USSR's highest birth-rates

1960 1970 1980 1990 2000

POLITICS

 1995/1999   President Islam Karimov

THE STATE OF THE PARTIES

Supreme Soviet 250 members

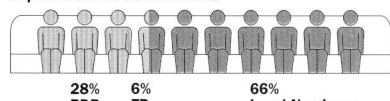

28% 6%   66%
PDP FP   Local Nominees

PDP = People's Democratic Party **FP** = Fatherland Progress Party (the only parties permitted to contest the elections)

Uzbekistan is effectively run by a presidential dictatorship.

MAIN POLITICAL ISSUES
Islamic fundamentalism
The civil war in neighboring Tajikistan has made the Karimov leadership wary of Islamic fundamentalism taking hold in Uzbekistan. The Uzbek constitution stipulates the separation of Islam and the state, and Islam has, up until now, been carefully kept out of politics.

Regionalism
Uzbekistan's high birth-rate is placing pressure on the country's limited agricultural resources. There have been calls for secession from some regions which wish to stop large numbers of people moving from poorer areas. In the Fergana Valley, one of the country's most densely populated regions, there have been a number of violent incidents.

PROFILE
President Islam Karimov's People's Democratic Party of Uzbekistan (PDP) has not been willing to devolve or share power. A constitution adopted in December 1992 appeared to endorse multiparty politics along Western lines. However, Karimov took advantage of greater powers granted to his office by banning a number of opposition parties, including the nationalist movement *Birlik* (Unity), the Islamic Renaissance Party and *Erk* (Will), which was the last to be proscribed in 1993.

Opposition is now entirely underground. The intimidation and arbitrary imprisonment of political dissidents are common. In 1995, *Erk* incurred the wrath of the government when a group of activists received stiff prison sentences after being found guilty of political subversion. President Karimov has won the support of the Russian minority by avoiding nationalist rhetoric.

Islam A. Karimov,
first elected president in 1990; his term has been extended by referendum until 2000

WORLD AFFAIRS

CIS ECO NACC NAM OSCE

Unlike neighboring Turkmenistan, Kyrgyzstan and Tajikistan, Uzbekistan has the resources to allow it to follow a relatively independent foreign policy. The Karimov leadership has used this to promote itself as the leading central Asian state. It has established itself as the CIS powerbase in the region, and was a key player in the formation of a Central Asian common market (with Kazakhstan and Kyrgyzstan) in 1994. In 1995, Karimov called for a common "Turkestan" republic comprising the five former Soviet Central Asian republics, and also endorsed plans for a common central Asian defense council.

Relations with Turkey are also developing. While Western companies have difficulty in sealing contracts in Uzbekistan, Turkish companies have been commissioned to build vital installations such as telecommunications.

The crucial relationship remains that with Russia, which has 100,000 troops stationed in the country. In 1994, a bilateral treaty provided for Uzbekistan's economic integration with Russia. Karimov's anti-nationalist approach to domestic politics has Russian support.

CHRONOLOGY

Part of the great Mongol empire, present-day Uzbekistan was incorporated into the Russian Empire between 1865 and 1876. Russification of the area was superficial, and it was not until Soviet rule that significant Slav immigration occurred. A further influx of Slavs into Uzbekistan occurred during Stalin's programme of forced collectivization.

❑ **1917** Soviet power established in Tashkent.
❑ **1918** Turkestan Autonomous Soviet Socialist Republic (ASSR), incorporating present-day Uzbekistan, proclaimed.
❑ **1923–1941** Language changed four times, from Arabic alphabet to Latin, then based on Iranized Tashkent and finally replaced by Cyrillic.
❑ **1924** Basmachi rebels who resisted Soviet rule crushed. Uzbek SSR founded (which, until 1929, included the Tajik ASSR).
❑ **1925** Anti-Islamic campaign bans schools and closes mosques.
❑ **1936** Karakalpak ASSR (formerly part of the Russian Soviet Federative Socialist Republic) incorporated into the Uzbek SSR. ➪

U

U

CHRONOLOGY *continued*

- ❑ **1937** Stalin purges Uzbek communist leadership.
- ❑ **1941–1945** Industrial boom.
- ❑ **1959** Sharaf Rashidov becomes first secretary of CPUZ. Retains position until 1983.
- ❑ **1983** Yuri Andropov becomes president in Moscow. His anti-corruption purge results in the replacement of 40 party secretaries by a new generation of Central Asian officials. Uzbekistan's managerial elite now the youngest in the USSR.
- ❑ **1989** First non-communist political movement, Unity Party (*Birlik*), formed but not officially registered. June, clashes between Meskhetian Turks and indigenous Uzbek population of Fergana Valley leave more than 100 dead. October, *Birlik* campaign leads to Uzbek being declared the official language.
- ❑ **1990** March, Islam Karimov becomes executive president of the new Uzbek Supreme Soviet. Further inter-ethnic fighting in Fergana Valley; 320 killed.
- ❑ **1991** August, independence proclaimed. September, Republic of Uzbekistan adopted as official name. October, Uzbekistan signs treaty establishing economic community with seven other former Soviet republics. November, Communist Party of Uzbekistan restructured as the People's Democratic Party of Uzbekistan (PDPU). Karimov remains its leader. December, Karimov confirmed in post of president. Uzbekistan joins the CIS.
- ❑ **1992** Price liberalization provokes student riots in Tashkent. New post-Soviet constitution adopted along Western democratic lines. All religious parties banned. September, Uzbekistan sends troops to Tajikistan to suppress violence and strengthens border controls.
- ❑ **1993** Growing harassment of opposition political parties, *Erk* and *Birlik*.
- ❑ **1994** March, signing of economic integration treaty with Russia. July, introduction of new currency, the som, which becomes sole legal tender in October.
- ❑ **1995** January, legislative elections won by Karimov's PDP. March, referendum extends Karimov's presidential term until 2000. April, *Erk* activists receive stiff prison sentences. December, Otkir Sultanov replaces Abdulhashim Mutalov as prime minister.

AID

 $6m (receipts)   Up 500% in 1993

A lack of commitment to economic stabilization or reform and the abuse of human rights have generally deterred bilateral aid donors. However, in 1995 the World Bank announced a package of international loans and grants to Uzbekistan that would total over $900 million.

DEFENSE

💲 $315m ⬇ Down 3% in 1995

0	Defense spending as % GDP	40

2.4%

Uzbekistan has a 700-strong National Guard, which generally acts as the personal army of Karimov. Russian troops are still based on Uzbek territory to protect the Russian minority. In 1995, Uzbekistan approved a joint Central Asian regional defense council with Kazakhstan and Kyrgyzstan.

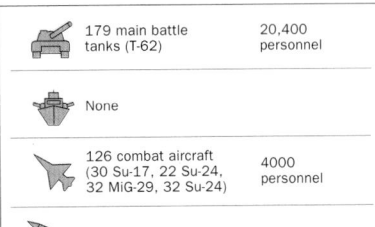

UZBEK ARMED FORCES

🚜	179 main battle tanks (T-62)	20,400 personnel
🚢	None	
✈	126 combat aircraft (30 Su-17, 22 Su-24, 32 MiG-29, 32 Su-24)	4000 personnel
🚀	None	

ECONOMICS

📊 $21.1bn 💲 25.0–35.9 som

SCORE CARD

- ❑ WORLD GNP RANKING 63rd
- ❑ GNP PER CAPITA $950
- ❑ BALANCE OF PAYMENTS ....$–369m
- ❑ INFLATION 1433%
- ❑ UNEMPLOYMENT................................0.2%

ECONOMIC PERFORMANCE INDICATOR

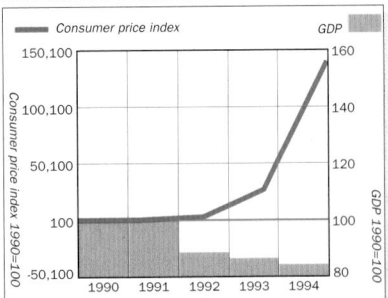

EXPORTS

China 4% — France 6% / Italy 7% / Germany 17% / Other 20% / Russian Federation 46%

IMPORTS

China 3% / Turkey 5% / USA 5% / Other 19% / Germany 20% / Russia 48%

STRENGTHS

Gold. Well-developed cotton market. Large unexploited deposits of oil and natural gas. Current production of natural gas makes significant contribution to electricity generation. Manufacturing tradition includes agricultural machinery and Central Asia's only aviation factory.

WEAKNESSES

Dependent on Russia, Kazakhstan and the US for grain as it produces only 25% of its domestic requirements. Little progress on privatization. Very limited economic reform. High inflation.

PROFILE

Uzbekistan's economy remains predominantly agricultural, with the exception of Tashkent which became an industrial area during World War II. Pro-market reforms have been slow under the former communists. Rocketing food prices have been fueled by inflation running at 1,500%. This led to the reintroduction of food rationing in early 1995. The gold sector has attracted investment by US companies.

UZBEKISTAN : MAJOR BUSINESSES

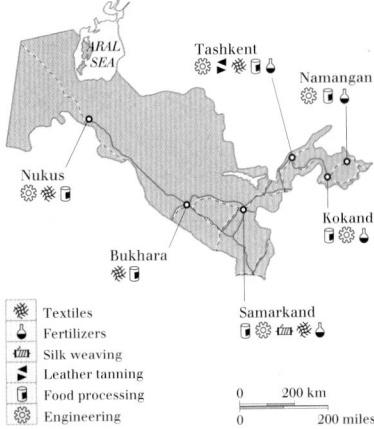

Tashkent, Namangan, Nukus, Kokand, Bukhara, Samarkand, ARAL SEA

- ❋ Textiles
- 🍷 Fertilizers
- 🧵 Silk weaving
- ◢ Leather tanning
- 📋 Food processing
- ⚙ Engineering

0 ——— 200 km
0 ——— 200 miles

RESOURCES

  50bn kwh (capacity 11.9m kw)

  22,055 b/d

5.3m cattle, 8.6m sheep, 968,000 goats

Natural gas, coal, gold, uranium, copper, tungsten, aluminum

ELECTRICITY GENERATION

- Hydro 0%
- Thermal 100% (50bn kwh)
- Nuclear 0%
- Other 0%

0   20   40   60   80   100

% of total generation by type

As well as containing the world's largest single gold mine, at Murantau, Uzbekistan has large deposits of natural gas, petroleum, coal and uranium. An important oilfield was discovered in 1992 in the Namangan region and production will rise with further investment. Most gas production is currently used domestically, but gas could also become a strong export.

Cotton is the main focus of agriculture: Uzbekistan is the world's fourth-largest producer. A post-independence decision to diversify was reversed when the value of cotton as a commodity on the world market became clear. Fruit, silk cocoons and vegetables for Moscow's markets are also of rising importance.

UZBEKISTAN : LAND USE

- Cropland
- Pasture
- Forest
- High mountain regions
- Desert
- Wetlands
- Sheep
- Cotton - cash crop

0 200 km / 0 200 miles

ENVIRONMENT

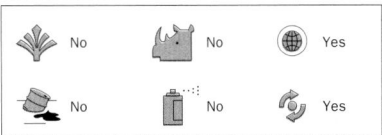 0.5%

No major environmental initiatives underway

ENVIRONMENTAL TREATIES

	No		No		Yes
	No		No		Yes

Under Soviet rule, Uzbekistan's cotton industry became one of the largest in the world. The irrigation schemes required to sustain the crop were ill-conceived and have wreaked considerable environmental damage. Soil salination is now a major problem. The Aral Sea has also been seriously depleted. From an area of 23,875 square miles in 1974, it is expected to have shrunk to only 9,034 square miles by 2000. The almost indiscriminate use of fertilizers and pesticides to raise production has also heavily polluted many rivers.

MEDIA

 The media operate under tight political and religious censorship

PUBLISHING AND BROADCAST MEDIA

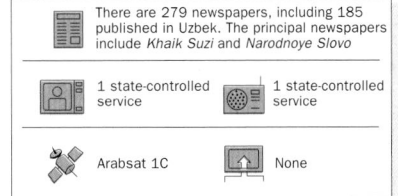

There are 279 newspapers, including 185 published in Uzbek. The principal newspapers include *Khaik Suzi* and *Narodnoye Slovo*

1 state-controlled service | 1 state-controlled service

Arabsat 1C | None

Independent publications were denied registration in 1994, thus permitting the publication only of state organs which promoted the personality cult and policies of Karimov. All opposition press is censored. Expression of Islamic and nationalist opinion is also forbidden. Russian-language newspapers imported from Moscow are censored.

CRIME

Uzbekistan does not publish prison figures | Crime is rising

CRIME RATES

All categories of crime are rising, especially in areas of high unemployment such as the Fergana Valley

A decline in living standards has meant a general increase in crime. Many of the rural population grow drug plants, particularly opium poppies, to supplement their falling incomes. Unofficial Islamic courts set up by disaffected young men in the Fergana Valley are an indication of growing Muslim opposition to the government.

EDUCATION

97% | 340,900 students

0   Education spending as % GNP   25
11%

THE EDUCATION SYSTEM

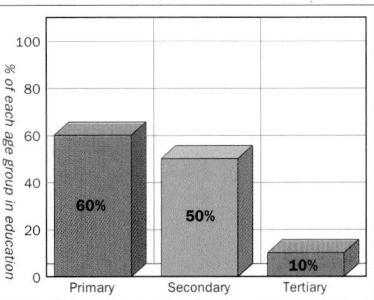

% of each age group in education

- Primary 60%
- Secondary 50%
- Tertiary 10%

The system still follows the Soviet model, though some instruction is in Uzbek. In the late 1980s, a few ethnic Tajik schools appeared in large cities along with a university in Samarkand. They were virtually all closed down in 1992 as a result of a decline in relations between the leaderships of Uzbekistan and Tajikistan.

HEALTH

1 per 280 people | Circulatory and respiratory diseases, accidents, cancers

0   Health spending as % GDP   25
5.9%

The health service has been declining since the dissolution of the USSR. Some rural areas are not served by even the most rudimentary of health services. Serious respiratory diseases among cotton growers are increasing.

WEALTH

There is a very large disparity of wealth between rich and poor

CONSUMER GOODS OWNERSHIP

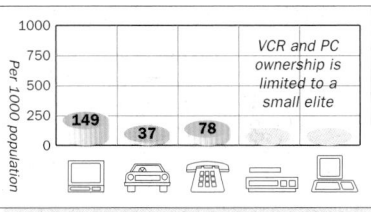

Per 1000 population

VCR and PC ownership is limited to a small elite

149   37   78

Former communists are still the wealthiest group as they retain control of the economy. Many rural poor live below the poverty line.

WORLD RANKING

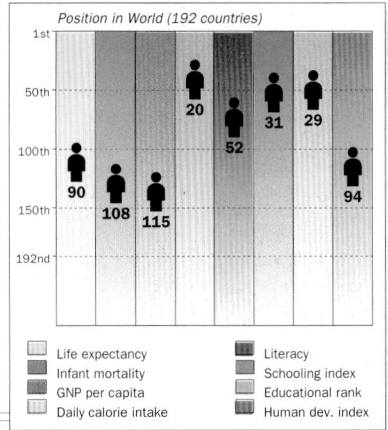

Position in World (192 countries)

- 90, 108, 115
- 20, 52, 31, 29, 94

- Life expectancy
- Infant mortality
- GNP per capita
- Daily calorie intake
- Literacy
- Schooling index
- Educational rank
- Human dev. index

U

VANUATU

OFFICIAL NAME: Republic of Vanuatu   **CAPITAL:** Port-Vila
POPULATION: 200,000   **CURRENCY:** Vatu   **OFFICIAL LANGUAGES:** Bislama, English and French

PACIFIC OCEAN

AN ARCHIPELAGO strung out over 808 miles of the South Pacific, Vanuatu lies 621 miles west of Fiji. Mountainous and volcanic in origin, only 12 of the 82 islands are of significant size – Espiritu Santo and Malekula are the largest. The capital, Port-Vila, is on Éfaté. Formerly the New Hebrides – ruled jointly by France and Britain from 1906 – Vanuatu became independent in 1980. Politics since independence has been democratic but volatile.

CLIMATE

WEATHER CHART

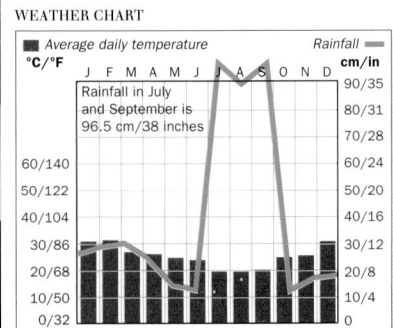

The climate is tropical and hot. Rainfall and temperatures decrease north to south. Cyclones occur November–April.

TRANSPORTATION

 Bauerfield, Port-Vila    119 ships 2.95m dwt

THE TRANSPORTATION NETWORK

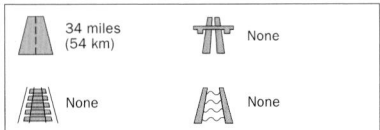

Frequent air and shipping services link the islands. State-owned Air Vanuatu flies to Australia and New Zealand.

TOURISM

 46,000 visitors   Up 2% in 1994

MAIN OVERSEAS ARRIVALS

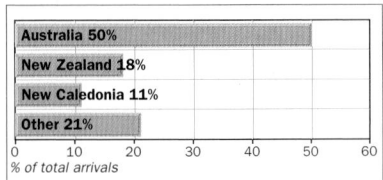

Tourism is the fastest-growing sector of the economy, accounting for 40% of GDP. There are plans to expand hotel capacity and international air links.

PEOPLE

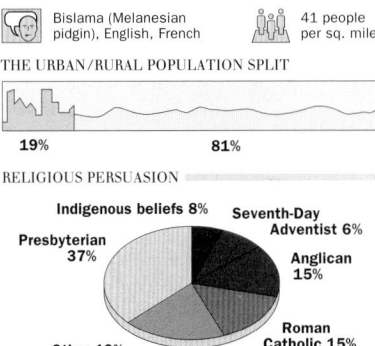 Bislama (Melanesian pidgin), English, French   41 people per sq. mile

THE URBAN/RURAL POPULATION SPLIT

19%   81%

RELIGIOUS PERSUASION

Indigenous beliefs 8%
Seventh-Day Adventist 6%
Presbyterian 37%
Anglican 15%
Roman Catholic 15%
Other 19%

Indigenous Melanesians, ni-Vanuatu, comprise 98% of the population. Of Vanuatu's 82 islands, 67 are inhabited, but 80% of people live on 12 main islands. The population is becoming more urbanized as one in eight ni-Vanuatu now lives in Port-Vila. However, 75% of the population still live by subsistence agriculture.

Vanuatu is home to some of the Pacific's most traditional peoples and local social and religious customs are strong. With 105 indigenous languages, Vanuatu boasts the world's highest per capita density of languages. Bislama pidgin is the *lingua franca*.

Women have lower social status than men and bride price is still commonly paid. Many educated women refuse to marry because of loss of property rights. To boost equality, elementary schools must now take 50% girls.

Vanuatu's *unspoilt beaches are one of the reasons for the upsurge in the tourist industry.*

POLITICS

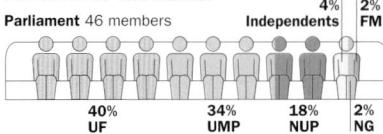
1995/1999   President Jean Marie Leye

THE STATE OF THE PARTIES

Parliament 46 members   Independents 4%   FM 2%

40% UF   34% UMP   18% NUP   2% NG

UF = Unity Front   UMP = Union of Moderate Parties   NUP = National United Party   NG = Na-Griamel   FM = Fren-Melanesian Party

The government of Vanuatu was formerly shared by France and Britain. Political instability in the islands was one of the reasons which contributed to France's reluctance – not shared by the UK – to grant independence in 1980. The anti-French stance of the Vanua'aku Party (Our Land Party – VP), which governed from 1980–1991, was reinforced by French support for the short-lived secession of Espiritu Santo in 1980. Rivalries and splits in the VP ended in a constitutional crisis in 1988, when president Sokomanu backed former VP secretary-general Barak Sope's efforts to oust prime minister Walter Lini. They failed and Fred Timakata became president. Lini's increasingly autocratic stance led to his dismissal by the VP in 1991.

Elections in 1991 saw the victory of the opposition francophone UMP which formed an anti-VP coalition including the NUP set up by Lini. Despite factional fighting, the coalition was returned to power in 1995. Outgoing prime minister, Maxime Carlot Korman, was briefly ousted by coalition members after the election, but regained office in 1996.

WORLD AFFAIRS

 ACP   Comm   NAM   SPC   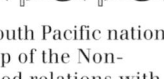 SPF

Vanuatu was the first South Pacific nation to gain full membership of the Non-Aligned Movement. Good relations with Australia; French nuclear testing in the Pacific has strained relations once more.

AID

 $32m (receipts)   Down 29% in 1993

Grant aid is equivalent to 18% of GDP, making Vanuatu Melanesia's most aid-dependent state. Leading donors include Australia, New Zealand, the UK and France. France cut aid twice in the 1980s amid allegations of interference in Vanuatu's internal affairs.

V

DEFENSE

 There are no military forces

 Not applicable

There is a small paramilitary force. Papua New Guinean troops helped to end the 1980 secessionist movement on Espiritu Santo under a defense agreement signed after independence.

ECONOMICS

 $189m

 110.50–114.15 vatu

SCORE CARD

❑ WORLD GNP RANKING	185th
❑ GNP PER CAPITA	$1,150
❑ BALANCE OF PAYMENTS	$–27m
❑ INFLATION	2.3%
❑ UNEMPLOYMENT	Low rate

STRENGTHS

Expanding services sector, including tourism and offshore finance, now accounts for 68% of GDP. Subsistence farming and small-scale cash cropping give majority of population a livelihood. Low foreign debt. GDP increasing.

WEAKNESSES

Large trade and budget deficits. Heavy import–export duties, to compensate for no direct taxes, increase domestic prices and deter exports. Declining prices for two largest exports: copra and cocoa. Limited outlets for new crop exports.

EXPORTS

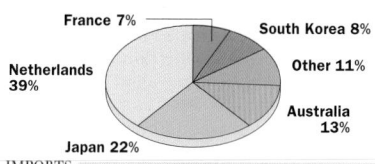

France 7%
South Korea 8%
Netherlands 39%
Other 11%
Australia 13%
Japan 22%

IMPORTS

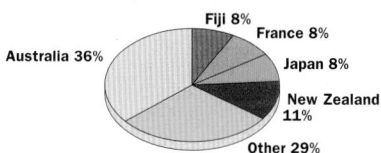

Fiji 8%
France 8%
Australia 36%
Japan 8%
New Zealand 11%
Other 29%

RESOURCES

 29m kwh (capacity 11,000 kw)

 2,925 tons

 132,000 cattle, 59,000 pigs, 11,000 goats

 None

Vanuatu's main resources are its arable land – only 17% is utilized – and its forests and waters. These could be exploited by the tourist, timber and fishing industries. New export crops are being explored to offset declining copra and cocoa exports. Beef is of growing importance. Nuclear-power development was banned under 1983 legislation.

VANUATU

Total Land Area : 12 190 sq. km
(4707 sq. miles)

POPULATION

over 10 000 ●
under 10 000 ·

Hiu TORRES
Tégua ISLANDS
Loh
Toga
Uréparapara
Mota Lava
Vanua Lava
Mota
BANKS ISLANDS
Santa Maria I.
Méré Lava
Big Bay
Espiritu Santo
Maéwo
Tabwémasana 1888m
Aoba
Luganville
Passage Lolvavana
Malo
Pentecost
Norsup
Ambrym
Malekula
Paama
Lopévi
Épi
Tongoa
Émaé
SHEPHERD ISLANDS
Nguna
Émao
Éfaté
Baver Field
PORT-VILA
PACIFIC OCEAN
CORAL SEA
Erromango
Aniwa
Tanna
Isangel
Futuna
Anatom

LAND HEIGHT

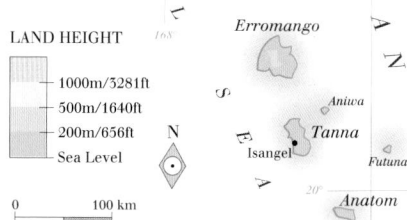

1000m/3281ft
500m/1640ft
200m/656ft
Sea Level

N

0 100 km
0 100 miles

ENVIRONMENT

 None

 No serious environmental imbalances

Logging is growing, but 75% of the rainforest remains. Population growth is high at 3.2% a year, but not yet a major problem. Introduced diseases and the labor trade reduced the population from some 500,000 in 1800 to 40,000 in 1920; it is still recovering.

MEDIA

 There is no censorship

PUBLISHING AND BROADCAST MEDIA

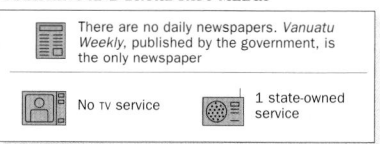

There are no daily newspapers. *Vanuatu Weekly*, published by the government, is the only newspaper

No TV service

1 state-owned service

The dour *Vanuatu Weekly* is published in the three official languages. There is also a monthly, *Pacific Islands Monthly*.

CRIME

 Vanuatu does not publish prison figures

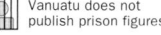 Little change from year to year

Domestic violence is a problem, but otherwise Vanuatu is almost crime-free – unlike other Melanesian states.

EDUCATION

 70%

 Not available

The abolition of fees has helped to boost elementary enrolment to 74%. Secondary enrolment is under 15%.

HEALTH

1 per 7,365 people

Heart diseases, cancers, malaria

A network of rural clinics and village health workers has helped to improve health levels. Nominal fees are charged.

WEALTH

 Wealth disparities are small among the indigenous population

CONSUMER GOODS OWNERSHIP

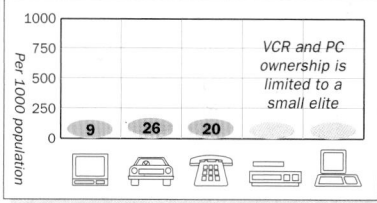

VCR and PC ownership is limited to a small elite

Per 1000 population
1000
750
500
250
0
9 26 20

The dominance of subsistence farming and small-scale cash cropping has helped to prevent extreme poverty. The rich are mainly non-ni-Vanuatu.

WORLD RANKING

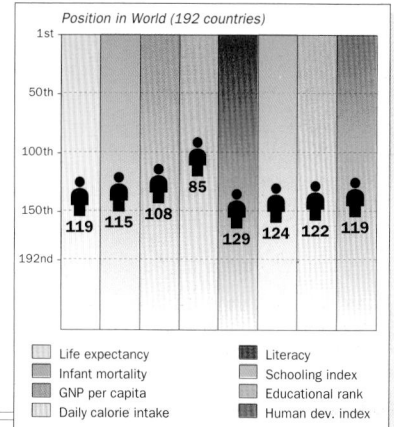

Position in World (192 countries)
1st
50th
100th
150th
192nd

119 115 108 85 129 124 122 119

Life expectancy
Infant mortality
GNP per capita
Daily calorie intake
Literacy
Schooling index
Educational rank
Human dev. index

V

VATICAN CITY

OFFICIAL NAME: State of the Vatican City   **CAPITAL:** *Not applicable*
POPULATION: 1000   **CURRENCY:** Lira   **OFFICIAL LANGUAGES:** Italian and Latin

THE VATICAN CITY lies close to the Tiber in central Rome and is a fully independent state. It also includes ten other buildings in Rome and the Pope's residence at Castel Gandolfo. As the Holy See, it is the seat of the Catholic Church, deriving its income from investments and voluntary contributions known as Peter's Pence.

The buildings and gardens of the Vatican City. St. Peter's Basilica was built from 1506–1626 on the traditional site of St. Peter's tomb.

CLIMATE

WEATHER CHART

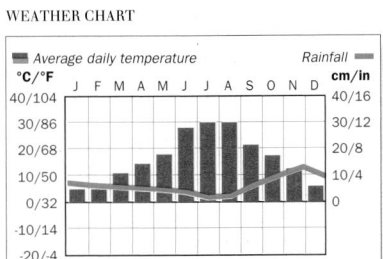

Winters are mild, though November is particularly grey, and summers are hot.

TRANSPORTATION

 Heliport for official visitors

 Has no fleet

THE TRANSPORTATION NETWORK

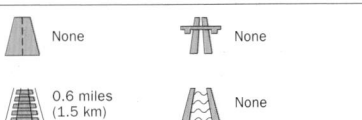

| None | | None |
| 0.6 miles (1.5 km) | | None |

The railroad is only used for carrying freight. Official visitors are transferred from Rome airport by helicopter.

TOURISM

 The Vatican Museums can accommodate 20,000 visitors daily

 Little change from year to year

MAIN OVERSEAS ARRIVALS

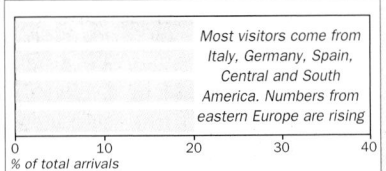

Most visitors come from Italy, Germany, Spain, Central and South America. Numbers from eastern Europe are rising

0   10   20   30   40
% of total arrivals

Almost all tourists who visit Rome visit the Vatican, while others come as pilgrims. Up to 100,000 hear the Pope's annual Easter Message in St. Peter's Square. The Vatican's art collections are among the greatest in the world. Years of restoration work on the Sistine Chapel frescoes were completed in 1994.

PEOPLE

 Italian, Latin

 5,890 people per sq. mile

THE URBAN/RURAL POPULATION SPLIT

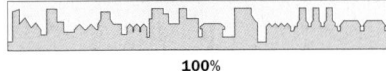

100%

RELIGIOUS PERSUASION

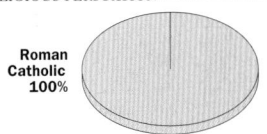

Roman Catholic 100%

The Vatican has about 1,000 permanent inhabitants, including several hundred lay persons, and employs a further 3,400 lay staff. Citizenship can be acquired through stable residence and holding an office or job within the City. A citizen's family can gain residence only by authorization.

The Pope is spiritual head of almost 18% of the world's population. The countries with the largest number of Roman Catholics are Brazil, Mexico, Italy, the USA and the Philippines.

POLITICS

 On death of reigning Pope

 His Holiness Pope John Paul II

THE STATE OF THE PARTIES

Sacred College of Cardinals 162 members

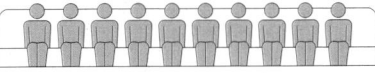

The Cardinals are divided into 3 orders, Bishops, Priests and Deacons

The Vatican City operates in the manner of an elected monarchy, as the reigning Pope has supreme executive, legislative and judicial powers, and holds office for life. He is elected by 120 members of the College of Cardinals, who vote until one candidate for the position of Supreme Pontiff achieves a two-thirds majority.

The administration of the Vatican City State, of which the Pope is temporal head, is conducted by the Pontifical Commission. The Holy See, which is the governing body of the Catholic Church worldwide and of which the Pope is spiritual head, is governed by the Roman Curia, the Church's administrative network. It is the Holy See that maintains diplomatic relations abroad. Pope John Paul II, elected in 1978, is the first non-Italian Pope since 1523.

VATICAN CITY

Total Land Area : 0.44 sq. km (0.17 sq. miles)

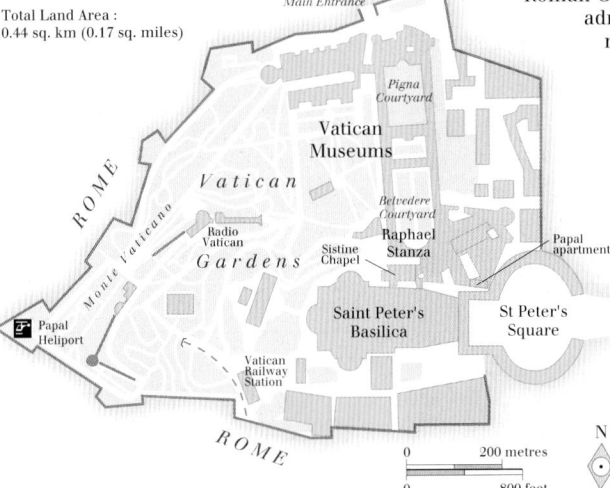

WORLD AFFAIRS

The Vatican maintains a neutral stance in world affairs and has observer status in many international organizations. It has mediated in many conflicts, notably achieving the 1993 peace agreement in Mozambique. Pope John Paul II has traveled more extensively than any other Pope to promote peace and spread Roman Catholicism. His unwavering stance against such issues as abortion, birth-control and homosexuality has received worldwide attention. The Holy See now has diplomatic relations with Russia and other former Soviet-bloc nations, and in 1993 the Pope re-established the Catholic Church in previously atheist Albania.

AID

 Undisclosed   Undisclosed

Aid is donated through the Pope's Charities (The Holy Childhood Association, for example, distributes money for children's causes), through funds donated for use at the Pope's discretion, and through religious orders acting under papal charter.

DEFENSE

 Ceremonial Swiss Guard only    No significant change from year to year

The Vatican is strictly neutral territory. Under the 1954 Hague Convention, it is recognized as "a moral, artistic and cultural patrimony worthy of being respected as a treasure for all mankind."

ECONOMICS

 Not applicable   1,586–1,622 Italian lira

SCORE CARD

❑ WORLD GNP RANKING	....	*The Vatican*
❑ GNP PER CAPITA	....	*does not have*
❑ BALANCE OF PAYMENTS	....	*a national*
❑ INFLATION	....	*economy in the*
❑ UNEMPLOYMENT	....	*usual sense*

STRENGTHS
Istituto per le Opere di Religione has assets of $3–$4 billion. Voluntary contributions from Catholics worldwide (Peter's Pence). Interest on investments. Gold reserves in Fort Knox, USA. Stamp and coin issues.

WEAKNESSES
Growing budgetary deficit (over $90 million): losses incurred by Vatican radio and newspaper, foreign Papal visits, administration and diplomatic missions. Repayment of creditors from Banco Ambrosiano bankruptcy in 1982.

EXPORTS/IMPORTS

The Vatican produces no goods for export. All commodities are imported, mainly from Italy

RESOURCES

 None   None

 None   None

The Vatican imports all its energy. It has no farmland as its area is restricted to buildings and their formal gardens.

ENVIRONMENT

 None   Vatican has set up the St. Francis Prize for the Environment

The Vatican is increasingly concerned about the need to balance development and conservation. In 1993, the Pope urged a gathering of scientists to press colleagues worldwide to inform people on the need to protect the environment.

MEDIA

 The Vatican regards freedom of expression as a fundamental human right. The Vatican's media promote the Catholic Church's beliefs and views

PUBLISHING AND BROADCAST MEDIA

 There is one daily newspaper, *L'Osservatore Romano*, which is also published weekly in 5 European languages, and monthly in Polish

 1 state-owned service   1 state-owned service

The Vatican produces its own religious TV program, but has no transmitter. Its radio broadcasts in 37 languages.

CRIME

 There are no prisons in the Vatican City    Minimal crime levels

The only crime to have rocked the Vatican in recent years was the alleged implication of three of the Vatican Bank's officials in the Italian Banco Ambrosiano's fraudulent bankruptcy. Italy's Supreme Court ruled that Vatican affairs were beyond its jurisdiction.

EDUCATION

100%   12,253 students

The University, founded by Gregory XIII, is renowned for its theological and philosophical learning. There are 79,141 elementary and 31,406 secondary Catholic schools around the world.

CHRONOLOGY

The Vatican is located in Rome because tradition held that St. Peter was buried on the site of the Church of Constantine, which was pulled down in the Renaissance to make way for the building of St. Peter's Basilica. The Vatican has been the Pope's usual residence since 1417, when the pontiffs returned from Avignon in France at the end of the 39 years of Great Schism.

- ❑ **1870** Italy occupies Papal States – 16,019 sq. miles in central Italy.
- ❑ **1929** Lateran Treaty – Italy recognizes Vatican City as independent state.
- ❑ **1978** Cardinal Karol Wojtyła Pope.
- ❑ **1981–1982** Attempts on Pope's life.
- ❑ **1984** Catholicism disestablished as Italian state religion.
- ❑ **1985** Catholic Catechism revised for first time since 1566.
- ❑ **1993** Chinese sanction first official publication of full Bible in Chinese.
- ❑ **1994** Vatican reiterates opposition to contraception and abortion at UN Population Conference in Cairo.
- ❑ **1995** Renewed opposition to birth control and abortion at UN Women's Conference in Beijing.

HEALTH

 Pope's own doctor is in permanent residence at Vatican   Heart and cardiovascular diseases, cancers

The Catholic Church runs 5,617 hospitals, 14,748 dispensaries, 774 leprosariums and 17,519 homes for the sick, the aged and orphans worldwide.

WEALTH

 Vatican employees earn salaries on a par with those in Rome

CONSUMER GOODS OWNERSHIP

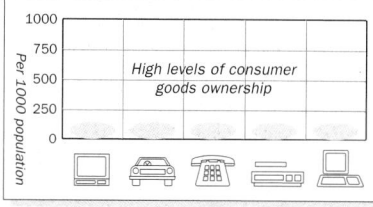

High levels of consumer goods ownership

The wealth of the Vatican is primarily that of the Church. Its art treasures may not be sold. It is not known how much personal wealth its citizens have.

WORLD RANKING

The Pope and his Vatican staff enjoy one of the highest standards of living in the world

V

VENEZUELA

OFFICIAL NAME: Republic of Venezuela **CAPITAL:** Caracas
POPULATION: 21.8 million **CURRENCY:** Bolívar **OFFICIAL LANGUAGE:** Spanish

LOCATED ON THE northern coast of South America, Venezuela's vast central plain is drained by the Orinoco, while the Guiana Highlands dominate the southwest of the country. A Spanish colony until 1811, Venezuela was lauded as Latin America's most stable democracy. Recent political upheavals have, however, led to fears of instability. The country with one of the largest known oil deposits outside the Middle East still has much of its population living in shanty town squalor.

Carlos Andrés Pérez, AD leader, who was deposed from the presidency in 1993.

Dr. Rafael Caldera Rodríguez, who won the presidency for a second time in 1994.

CLIMATE

WEATHER CHART

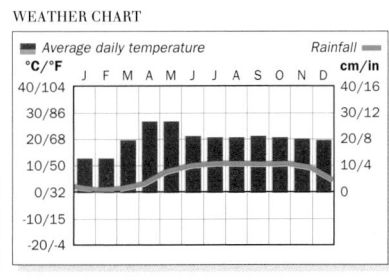

The hot Maracaibo coast is surprisingly dry; the Orinoco *Llanos* are alternately parched or flooded. Uplands are cold.

TRANSPORTATION

Simón Bolívar Intl, Caracas 6.48m passengers

75 ships 1.21m dwt

THE TRANSPORTATION NETWORK

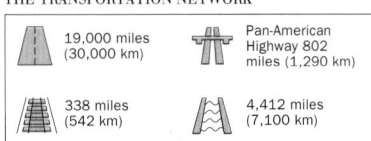

19,000 miles (30,000 km)

Pan-American Highway 802 miles (1,290 km)

338 miles (542 km)

4,412 miles (7,100 km)

Road-building in the 1960s benefited oil and aluminum industries. A new $1 billion, 50-mile railroad and port system on Lake Maracaibo services the oil refining industry. The Caracas subway was completed in 1995. Work on the Centro–Occidental highway and other major roads is ongoing.

The Orinoco. Its huge Llanos (plains) are grazed by five million cattle, which are herded down close to the river in the dry season.

TOURISM

429,000 visitors

Up 8% in 1994

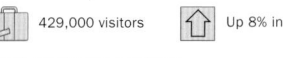

MAIN OVERSEAS ARRIVALS

USA 23%
Netherlands 10%
Trinidad & Tobago 9%
Canada 8%
Germany 8%
Other 42%

% of total arrivals

Tourism is still a relatively minor industry in Venezuela, but one with enormous potential. Venezuela has many beaches that are the equal of any Caribbean island's, and a fascinating jungle interior. For many years, the high value of the bolívar made Venezuela an expensive destination but, after recent devaluations, it has become one of the cheapest in the Caribbean. Now the government is privatizing its state-run hotels and seeking to attract foreign investment.

PEOPLE

Spanish, Indian languages

65 people per sq. mile

THE URBAN/RURAL POPULATION SPLIT

91%   9%

RELIGIOUS PERSUASION

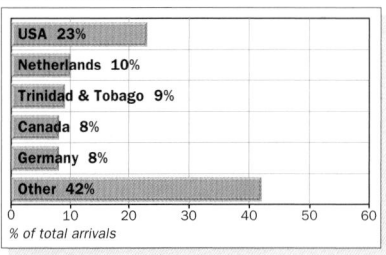

Other 2%   Protestant 2%
Roman Catholic 96%

ETHNIC MAKEUP

Indian 2%   Black 10%
White 21%
Mestizo (European-Indian) 67%

Venezuela is the most highly urbanized society in Latin America, with most of its population living in cities, mainly in the north. Venezuela has traditionally been seen as Latin America's "melting pot," with large-scale immigration from Italy, Portugal, Spain and all over Latin America. There is little of the white Hispanic aristocracy that survives in Colombia and Ecuador. The small number of native Indians, such as the Yanomami, live in remote and inaccessible regions, and are often little touched by modern life. Most of the black population, descended from Africans brought over to work the cacao industry in the 19th century, live along the Caribbean coast.

Oil wealth has brought comparative prosperity, but life in the *barrios* (shanty towns), which sprawl over the hillsides around Caracas, is one of extreme poverty. Discontent peaked in the food riots of 1991, which left scores dead along with the country's reputation for being a model democracy. The oil boom accelerated the pace of emancipation for women, who today find employment in all the professions. Politics, however, remains a masculine preserve. Oil wealth also brought Americanization – boxing and baseball are among the most popular sports.

POPULATION AGE BREAKDOWN

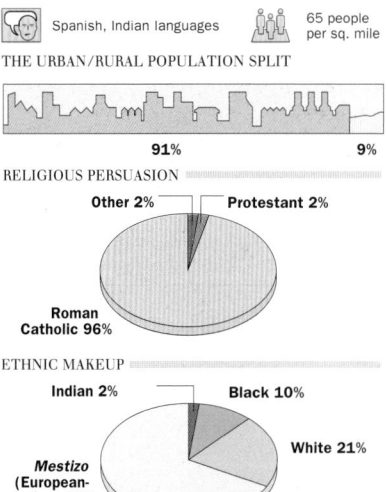

% of population by age group	■ 0–14		□ 15–64		□ 65+
65+	2.4%	2.9%	3.2%	3.7%	4.5%
15–64	51.5%	51.5%	55.7%	58%	63.1%
0–14	46.1%	45.6%	41.1%	38.3%	32.4%
	1960	1970	1980	1990	2000

V

VENEZUELA

Total Land Area : 882 050 sq. km
(340 560 sq. miles)

POPULATION

- ▣ over 1 000 000
- ◉ over 500 000
- ◎ over 100 000
- ○ over 50 000
- ● over 10 000

LAND HEIGHT

- —— 3000m/9843ft
- —— 2000m/6562ft
- —— 1000m/3281ft
- —— 500m/1640ft
- —— Sea Level

- – – Projected Railway

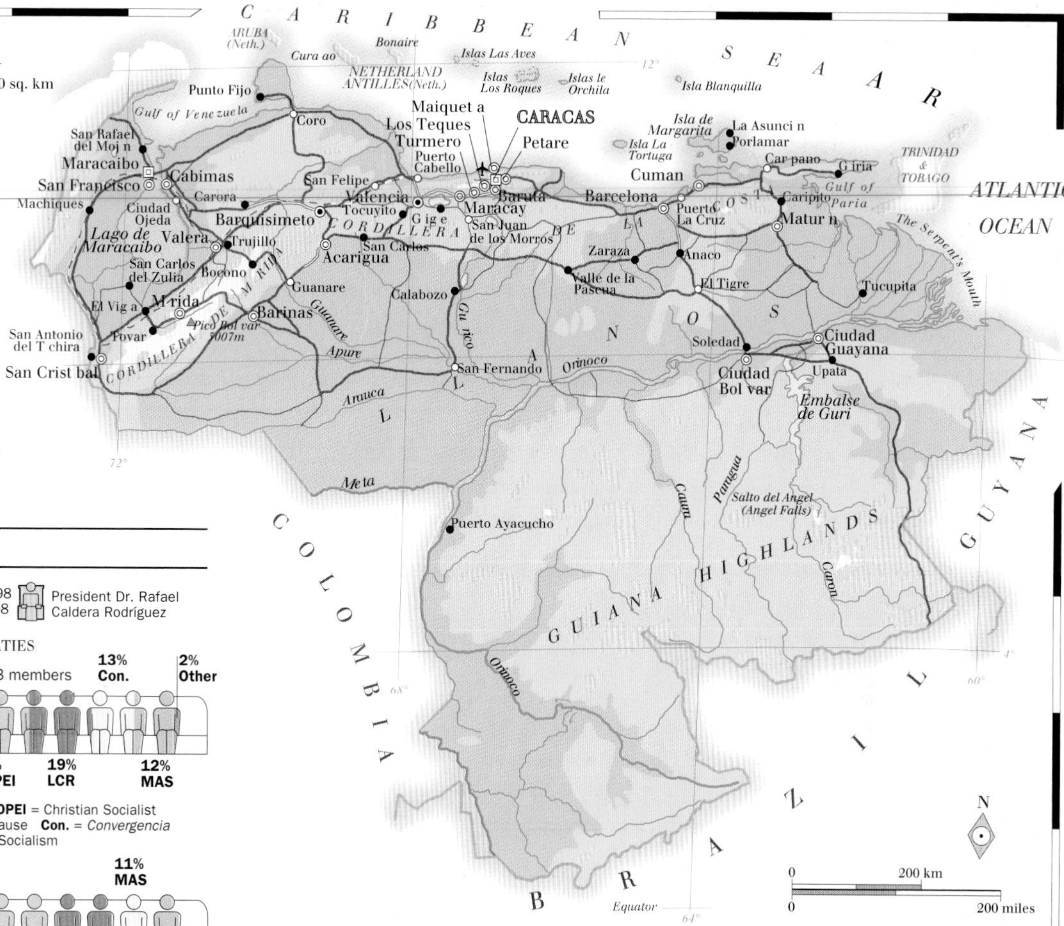

POLITICS

U. House 1993/1998
L. House 1993/1998

President Dr. Rafael
Caldera Rodríguez

THE STATE OF THE PARTIES

Chamber of Deputies 203 members

27% AD	27% COPEI	19% LCR	12% MAS	13% Con.	2% Other

AD = Democratic Action **COPEI** = Christian Socialist
Party **LCR** = The Radical Cause **Con.** = *Convergencia*
MAS = Movement Towards Socialism

Senate 53 members

34% AD	28% COPEI	17% LCR	11% MAS	10% Con.

Venezuela is a democracy, with
multiparty elections.

MAIN POLITICAL ISSUES
Corruption
The Caldera government in 1995
established an anti-corruption
commission to clean up the public
administration. Corruption led to the
ousting of president Carlos Andrés
Pérez in 1993, while Jaime Lusinchi,
another former president and previous
AD leader, reputedly squandered $8.5
billion dollars buying political favors.

Trimming the state sector
For decades, Venezuelan governments
spent on a wasteful scale, assuming
that petro-dollars would keep flowing.
The decline in oil revenue left the state
unable to fulfil its commitments without
cutbacks, which meet fierce resistance
from the large number of state employees.

PROFILE
Official corruption, austerity and rising
poverty led to some 300 deaths in
anti-price-rise riots in Caracas in 1991
and two coup attempts in 1992. In
1993, after president Carlos Andrés

Pérez was deposed on corruption
charges, the incoming Caldera coalition
pledged to restore confidence in
government. However, sustained
protest, the temporary suspension of
civil and economic rights, together
with banking and devaluation crises
have ensured that this pledge remains
unfulfilled. In 1996, MAS deputies
defected to the opposition.

WORLD AFFAIRS

ACS   G3   OAS   OPEC   RG

Venezuela has traditionally been seen
as pro-US, since the USA was the
destination of most of its oil exports
and the source of its imports. It seeks
closer economic integration with the
Caribbean region and Andean
neighbors, and a free trade zone
agreement with MERCOSUR, the South
American Common Market. Oil sector
marketing and technology cooperation
have been agreed with Brazil.

There are ongoing border disputes
with Colombia (fighting almost erupted
in 1987), Guyana (claiming 32,500
square miles of its oil, iron and gold-
rich territory) and Brazil (mainly over
illegal gold prospectors).

CHRONOLOGY

Venezuela was the first of the Spanish
imperial colonies to repudiate Madrid's
authority under the guidance of the
revolutionary, Simón Bolívar, in 1811.

- ❏ **1821** Battle of Carabobo finally
overthrows Spanish rule and leads
to consolidation of independence
within Gran Colombia (Venezuela,
Colombia and Ecuador).
- ❏ **1830** Gran Colombia collapses.
José Antonio Páez rules Venezuela;
coffee planters effectively in control.
- ❏ **1870** Guzmán Blanco in power.
Attracts foreign investment to
build rail system.
- ❏ **1908** General Juan Vicente Gómez
dictator; oversees development of
oil industry.
- ❏ **1935** Gómez falls from power.
Increasing mass participation in
political process.
- ❏ **1945** Military coup overthrows
General Isías Medina Angarita.
Rómulo Betancourt of the Democratic
Action party (AD) takes power as
leader of a civilian-military junta.
- ❏ **1948** February, AD wins elections,
with novelist Rómulo Gallegos as
presidential candidate.

V

CHRONOLOGY *continued*

- ❏ **1948** Gallegos overthrown in military coup. Marcos Pérez Jiménez forms government, with US and military backing.
- ❏ **1958** General strike. Admiral Larrázabal leads military coup deposing Jiménez government.
- ❏ **1958** Free elections. Betancourt, newly returned from exile, wins presidential election as AD candidate. Anti-communist campaign mounted. A few state welfare programs introduced.
- ❏ **1960** Movement of the Revolutionary Left (MIR) splits off from AD and begins anti-government activities.
- ❏ **1961** Venezuela becomes a founder member of OPEC.
- ❏ **1962** Communist-backed guerrilla warfare attempts repetition of Cuban revolution in Venezuela. Fails to gain popular support.
- ❏ **1963** Raúl Leoni (AD) elected president – the first democratic transference of power in Venezuelan history. Anti-guerrilla campaign continues.
- ❏ **1966** Unsuccessful coup attempt by supporters of former president, Pérez Jiménez.
- ❏ **1969** Elections. Dr. Rafael Caldera Rodríguez of the Social Christian Party (COPEI) becomes president. Continues Leoni policies.
- ❏ **1973** Elections. Carlos Andrés Pérez wins back power for AD. Oil and steel industries nationalized. World oil crisis. Venezuelan currency peaks in value against the US dollar.
- ❏ **1978** Elections won by Dr. Luis Herrera Campíns for COPEI. Disastrous economic programs, and failure of huge Workers' Bank.
- ❏ **1983** Elections. AD victory under Jaime Lusinchi. Fall in world oil prices leads to cuts in state welfare schemes. Student and union unrest.
- ❏ **1988** Carlos Andrés Pérez wins elections for AD. Fails to deliver populist election promises.
- ❏ **1991** Caracas food riots; 300 dead.
- ❏ **1993** Andrés Pérez ousted on charges of corruption.
- ❏ **1994–1995** Caldera Rodríguez reelected. Civil and economic rights temporarily suspended.

AID

 $50m (receipts)  Up 61% in 1993

The Inter-American Development Bank and Andean Development Corporation give modest aid.

DEFENSE

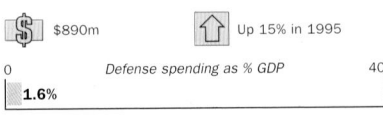

Relatively junior officers, who identified with the austerity squeeze on the middle classes, staged coup attempts in 1992. More recently, the deployment of troops by the Caldera government to quell protests, and the weakness of civil institutions, raised fears about further military intervention in politics.

ECONOMICS

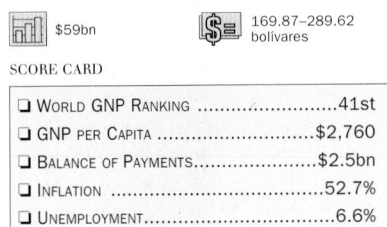

SCORE CARD

- ❏ WORLD GNP RANKING 41st
- ❏ GNP PER CAPITA $2,760
- ❏ BALANCE OF PAYMENTS......................$2.5bn
- ❏ INFLATION 52.7%
- ❏ UNEMPLOYMENT................................6.6%

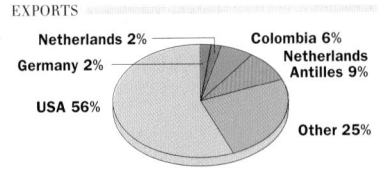

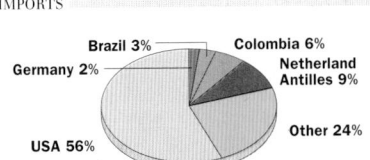

STRENGTHS

The largest proven oil deposits outside the Middle East and CIS. Massive reserves of coal, bauxite, iron and gold. Successful development of new bitumen fuel, Orimulsion, produced in the Orinoco delta. Considerable foreign investment in all these sectors, led by US and giant Japanese concerns such as Mitsubishi. World's most efficient producer of high-grade aluminum.

WEAKNESSES

Huge, cumbersome state sector; despite some privatization, large areas of the state sector are still over-manned and inefficient. Poor public services which, despite Venezuela's wealth during the oil-boom years, have been badly maintained. Major infrastructure renewal is now long overdue. Widespread tax evasion, and lack of political will to reform tax regime (Venezuela, thanks to large subsidies, has the lowest gasoline prices in the world). Weak currency.

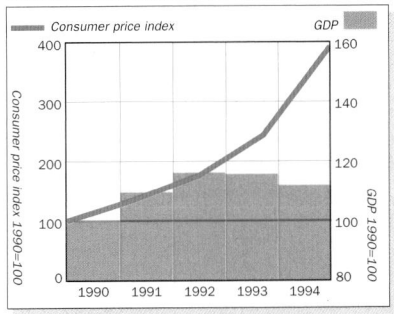

PROFILE

Venezuela is an economic paradox. One of the strongest economies in Latin America, its government finances are in crisis. A culture of non-accountability has been created due to years of politically motivated patronage in state-owned industries and government bureaucracies. To date, privatizations and government cuts have failed to seriously tackle the problem. The oil sector was opened up to private capital in 1996. Conditions for the country's poor have not improved since violent food riots in Caracas in 1991 highlighted their plight. This, along with fears of a military coup, has the effect of deterring future investors.

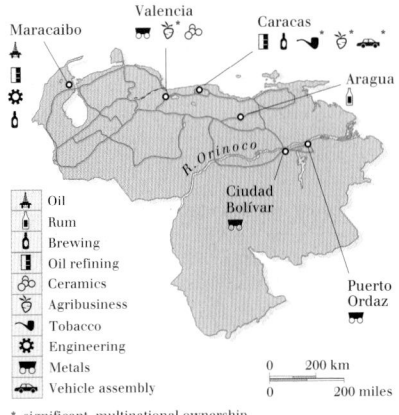

V

RESOURCES

69.5bn kwh (capacity 18.6m kw)

2.71m b/d (reserves 62,650,000,000 bbl)

15m cattle, 2.3m pigs, 1.9m goats, 525,000 sheep

Oil, bauxite, iron, natural gas, coal, gold, aluminum

ELECTRICITY GENERATION

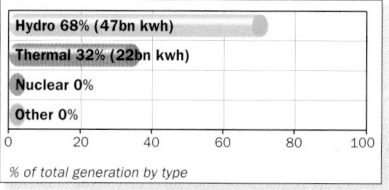

Hydro 68% (47bn kwh)

Thermal 32% (22bn kwh)

Nuclear 0%

Other 0%

% of total generation by type

ENVIRONMENT

29%

Ecology studies are now part of the school curriculum

ENVIRONMENTAL TREATIES

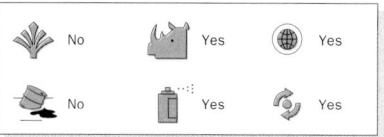

No   Yes   Yes

No   Yes   Yes

Concerns are rainforest destruction, oil pollution of Lake Maracaibo, and illegal gold mining harming soil and lakes.

MEDIA

Attempts have been made to intimidate any press which is critical of the government

PUBLISHING AND BROADCAST MEDIA

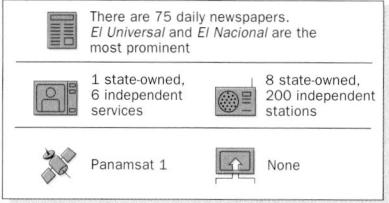

There are 75 daily newspapers. *El Universal* and *El Nacional* are the most prominent

1 state-owned, 6 independent services

8 state-owned, 200 independent stations

Panamsat 1

None

Most of the press is independent of the main political parties. Venezuelan soap operas vie with Mexican rivals for dominance.

CRIME

32,000 prisoners

Up 5% in 1992

CRIME RATES

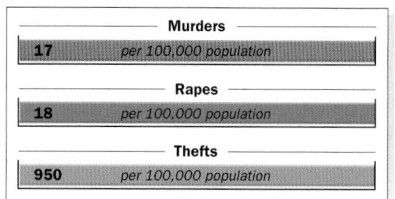

Murders

17   per 100,000 population

Rapes

18   per 100,000 population

Thefts

950   per 100,000 population

Urban robberies and violence involving young delinquents are a major problem as is narcotics-related crime. Cattle smuggling to Colombia is rife.

Venezuela has a remarkable diversity of resources. It has proven oil reserves of 62 billion barrels, vast quantities of coal, iron ore, bauxite and gold, and cheap hydroelectric power. Huge investment programs are currently under way to raise production in all these sectors. Oil companies are also increasing refining capacity. A $10-billion refining expansion program is due for completion in 1996. The state oil company, PDVSA, is also investing in coal, particularly the Guanare fields, to raise annual production from 1.5 to 20 million tons.

Venezuela has begun exploitation of a new bitumen-based fuel from the Orinoco, Orimulsion; commercially exploitable reserves are estimated at 270 billion barrels. The world's most efficient producer of aluminum, Venezuela aims to be the biggest by the year 2000.

EDUCATION

91%   550,783 students

Education spending as % GNP

5.2%

THE EDUCATION SYSTEM

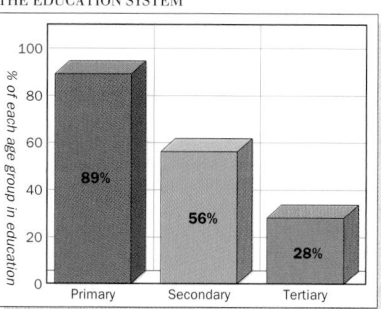

89%   56%   28%

Primary   Secondary   Tertiary

The state education system suffers from a shortage of qualified teachers, and from recent cuts in the state education budget.

HEALTH

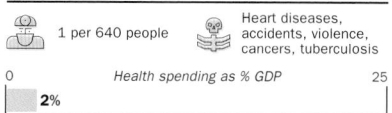

1 per 640 people

Heart diseases, accidents, violence, cancers, tuberculosis

Health spending as % GDP

2%

The health service, although still comparatively good, has suffered along with other public services from poor management in the 1970s and 1980s and the cuts introduced by the Pérez government in the 1990s.

Most health care is concentrated in the towns, and people from indigenous communities often have to travel long distances to receive treatment. Venezuela has a reputation for innovative plastic surgery.

VENEZUELA : LAND USE

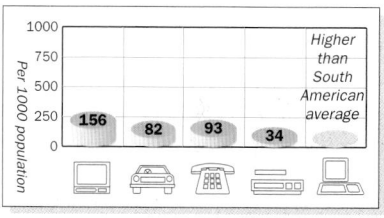

Cropland
Pasture
Forest
Coffee - cash crop
Cattle

0   200 km

0   200 miles

WEALTH

Miner, 276 bolívares ($1) per day; electronics draughtsman, 17,000 bolívares ($59) per month

CONSUMER GOODS OWNERSHIP

156   82   93   34

Higher than South American average

In 1973, when there were just 4.3 bolívares to the US dollar, Venezuela was the world's biggest importer of Chivas Regal whiskey and French champagne, and it was cheaper to spend the weekend in Miami than in Caracas.

Living standards have fallen since the collapse in world oil prices. However, wealth remains concentrated among Venezuelans connected to the government and a few industrialists. The poorest section of society, dependent on the welfare state, has suffered from austerity measures introduced in an attempt to cut the budget deficit. Recent moves to tighten income tax collection (most Venezuelans evade it) have hit the salaried middle classes.

WORLD RANKING

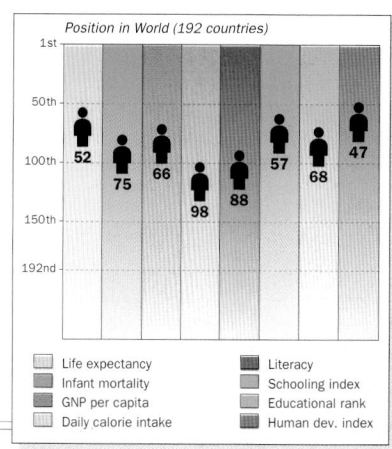

Position in World (192 countries)

52   75   66   98   88   57   68   47

Life expectancy
Infant mortality
GNP per capita
Daily calorie intake
Literacy
Schooling index
Educational rank
Human dev. index

V

VIETNAM

OFFICIAL NAME: Socialist Republic of Viet–Nam   CAPITAL: Hanoi
POPULATION: 74.5 million   CURRENCY: Dông   OFFICIAL LANGUAGE: Vietnamese

LOCATED ON THE EASTERN COAST of the Indochinese peninsula, over half of Vietnam is dominated by the heavily forested mountain range, the Chaîne Annamitique. The most populated areas, which are also the most intensively cultivated, are along the Red and Mekong rivers. Partitioned after the end of World War II, the communist north reunited the country after the world's longest 20th-century conflict, the 1962–1975 Vietnam War. Today, Vietnam is a single-party state ruled by the Communist Party. Since 1986, the regime has followed a liberal economic policy known as *doi moi* (renovation).

PEOPLE

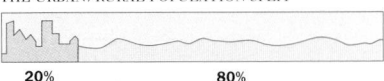

Vietnamese, Chinese, Thai, Khmer, Muong, Nung, Miao, Yao, Jarai

593 people per sq. mile

THE URBAN/RURAL POPULATION SPLIT

20%   80%

RELIGIOUS PERSUASION

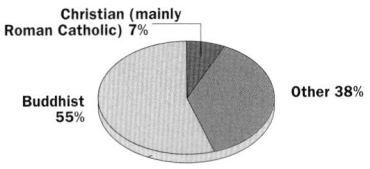

Christian (mainly Roman Catholic) 7%
Other 38%
Buddhist 55%

ETHNIC MAKEUP

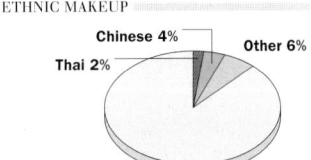

Chinese 4%   Other 6%
Thai 2%
Vietnamese 88%

CLIMATE

WEATHER CHART

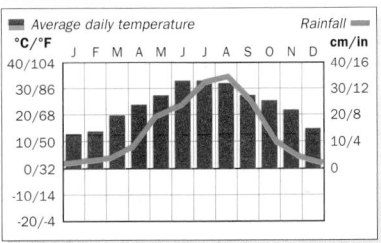

Vietnam has a sharply contrasting climate. The north has cool winters, while the south is tropical with even temperatures all year round. The central provinces are affected by typhoons. The most intensively cultivated areas are the deltas of the Red and Mekong rivers, which are subject to drought and heavy flooding respectively.

TRANSPORTATION

Tan Son Naht Intl, Ho Chi Minh City

184 ships
597,300 dwt

THE TRANSPORTATION NETWORK

6,600 miles (10,500 km)

None

1,616 miles (2,600 km)

11,000 miles (17,702 km)

Rebuilding infrastructure destroyed during the war is still the priority. A key project is likely to be the reconstruction of Highway 1, linking Hanoi and Ho Chi Minh City (formerly Saigon). Ports and railroads will also require rehabilitation, and construction has begun on two new port facilities, at Vung Tau in the south and Cai Lan in the north. Trains travel slowly in Vietnam, with an average speed of around 9 miles an hour. The journey from Hanoi to Ho Chi Minh City takes three days.

TOURISM

750,000 visitors

Up 12% in 1994

MAIN OVERSEAS ARRIVALS

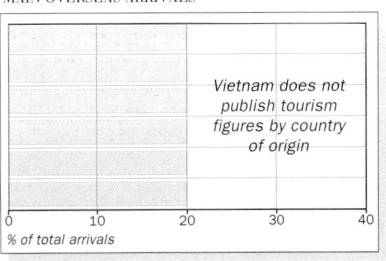

Vietnam does not publish tourism figures by country of origin

% of total arrivals

Russians, Eastern Europeans and backpackers from the West made up the bulk of the 400,000 or so tourists Vietnam received each year during the 1980s. Other travelers were either on business, or overseas Vietnamese, *Viet Kie*, visiting relatives.

Since 1990, the government has opened the way to large-scale tourism – a "master plan" was adopted in 1995. Massive investment is now going into hotels, and an official target of three million tourists a year by 2000 has been set. Poor infrastructure, however, remains a problem. For the moment, Vietnam's appeal rests on its unspoilt Asian way of life and areas of spectacular natural beauty such as Ha Long Bay on the Red river delta.

Boats moored near Nha Trang. *A network connecting Vietnam's main ports provides an important internal communications link.*

Overseas Chinese constitute the largest minority group in Vietnam, and were subject to considerable discrimination in the early years of the communist takeover. The Saigon Chinese, with their Taiwanese links, were viewed as corrupt bourgeoisie, while the northern Mountain Chinese were suspected as a fifth column for China's ambitions in Vietnam. Various other mountain minorities (*Montagnards*), who have a history of collaboration with the French and Americans and who continued armed resistance, were also sidelined by the regime in Hanoi. Today, the main source of tension is the resettling of lowlanders in mountain regions, which is putting pressure on limited farming and forest resources.

Women outnumber men, largely because of war deaths. They form a high proportion of the industrial work force, but have not received any greater political voice. There are still no women in the Politburo, though one, Truong My Hoa, sits on the Secretariat.

Family life is strong and is based on kinship groups within village clans.

POPULATION AGE BREAKDOWN

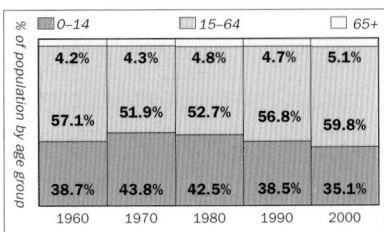

% of population by age group	0–14	15–64	65+		
65+	4.2%	4.3%	4.8%	4.7%	5.1%
15–64	57.1%	51.9%	52.7%	56.8%	59.8%
0–14	38.7%	43.8%	42.5%	38.5%	35.1%
	1960	1970	1980	1990	2000

V

Le Duc Anh, president since 1992.

Vo Van Kiet, prime minister of Vietnam.

POLITICS

 1992/1997

 President
Gen. Le Duc Anh

THE STATE OF THE PARTIES

National Assembly 395 members

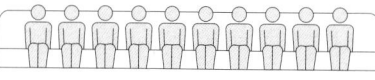

Elections were last held in 1992, following a change in the constitution of the same year.

Vietnam is a one–party communist state.

MAIN POLITICAL ISSUES
Economic reform
Vietnam is seeking to change from a centrally planned to a market economy, without any accompanying political liberalization.

Resisting political reform
The founders of the Communist Party have devolved power to the younger generation, who fought against the French and Americans in the 1950s–1970s. They are unwilling to give up power won by force of arms by democratizing the political process.

PROFILE
Politically, Vietnam operates a traditional communist system. The 17-member Politburo, elected by the 146-strong Central Committee, is the most powerful body. Keeping the Party's legitimacy, when the crux of economic ideology has disappeared, will not be easy. There are signs of multipartyists pressing for reform and criticism that the Party is becoming a "party of power." However, there is resistance to reform from within the Party. Some party members fear that a crucial power base for the communinists will be lost if collective farming and state enterprises are opened up to competition.

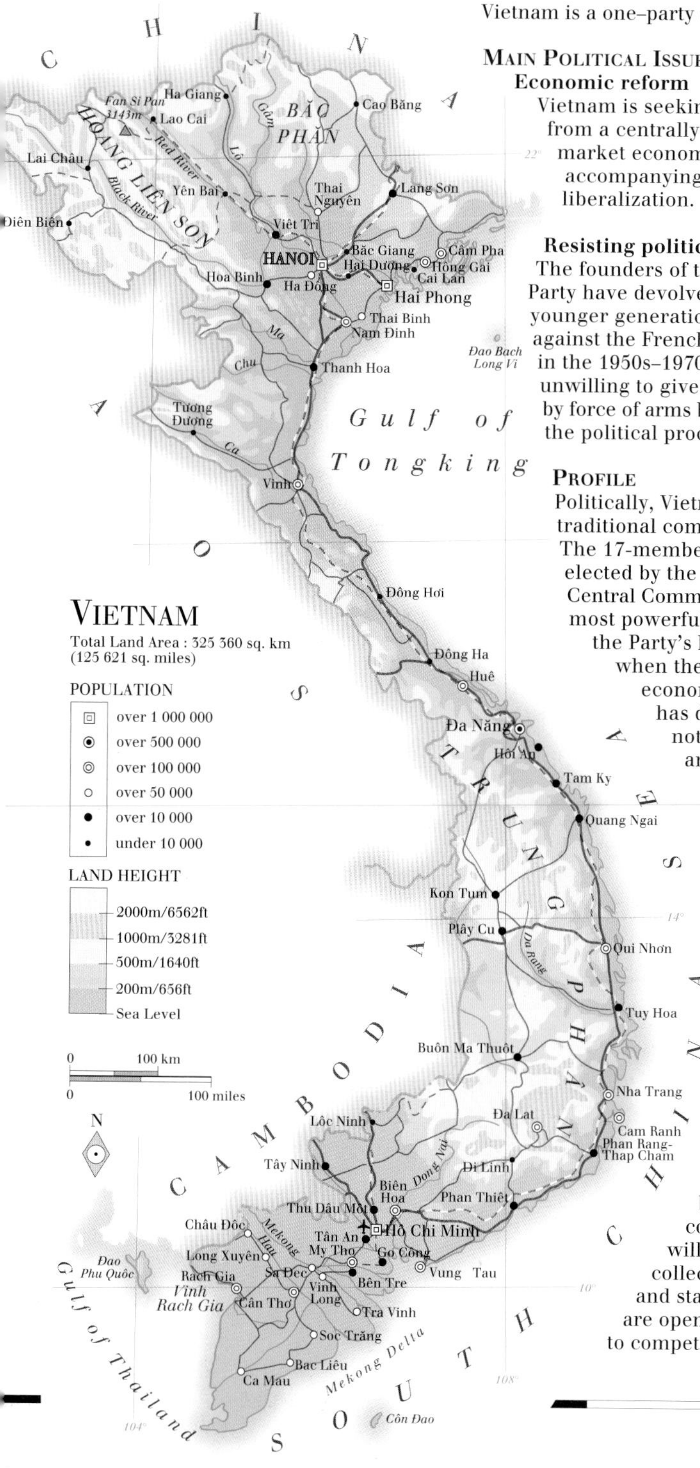

WORLD AFFAIRS

 ASEAN   IAEA   IBRD Mek Riv NAM

Vietnam's economic liberalization has led to improvements in its relationship with the USA. In 1993, Washington finally lifted its aid embargo, allowing the World Bank to start investing in reconstruction, and US companies to bid for contracts. Full diplomatic relations were finally established in mid-1995. The removal of Vietnamese troops from neighboring Cambodia in 1989 led to improved relations with China, although border disputes remain a source of tension. Attacks by Khmer Rouge guerrillas on ethnic Vietnamese in Cambodia have soured Vietnamese–Cambodian relations.

AID

 $319m (receipts)   Down 46% in 1993

The Vietnamese invasion of Cambodia in 1978 halted all aid from China, Japan and the West, with the exception of the Scandinavian countries. Vietnam turned to the Soviet Union, which financed the large trade deficit until 1985. The USA resumed humanitarian aid in 1992 and removed economic restrictions in 1993. Aid now provides for 89% of all capital expenditure.

CHRONOLOGY

From 1825, the brutal persecution of the Catholic community, originally converted by French priests in the 17th century, gave France the excuse to colonize Cochin-China, Annam and Tonkin, and then merge them with Laos and Cambodia.

❏ **1920** *Quoc ngu* (Roman script) replaces Chinese script.
❏ **1930** Ho Chi Minh founds Indochina Communist Party.
❏ **1940** Japanese invade but tolerate Vichy administration until 1945.
❏ **1941** Viet Minh resistance founded in exile in China; aided by USA.
❏ **1945** Viet Minh take Saigon and Hanoi. Emperor abdicates. Republic with Ho Chi Minh as president.
❏ **1946** French (rearmed by UK) re-enter. First Indo–China War.
❏ **1954** French defeated at Dien Bien Phu. Vietnam divided at 17°N. USSR supports North; USA arms South. Communist opposition in South secretly armed by North down Ho Chi Minh Trail.
❏ **1960** Groups opposed to President Diem's repressive regime in South unite as Viet Cong.
❏ **1961** USA pours in "military advisers."

VIETNAM

Total Land Area : 325 360 sq. km
(125 621 sq. miles)

POPULATION

▣ over 1 000 000
◉ over 500 000
◎ over 100 000
○ over 50 000
● over 10 000
• under 10 000

LAND HEIGHT

2000m/6562ft
1000m/3281ft
500m/1640ft
200m/656ft
Sea Level

0   100 km
0   100 miles

V

CHRONOLOGY *continued*

- ❑ **1964** US Congress approves war.
- ❑ **1965** Gen. Nguyen Van Thieu takes over military government of South. First US combat troops arrive; in three years, total 500,000 men.
- ❑ **1965–1968** Operation Rolling Thunder – intense bombing of North by South and USA.
- ❑ **1967** Anti-war protests start in USA and elsewhere.
- ❑ **1968** *Tet* (New Year) Offensive – 105 towns attacked simultaneously in South with infiltrated arms. Viet Cong suffer serious losses. Peace talks begin. USA eases bombing and starts withdrawing troops.
- ❑ **1969** Ho Chi Minh dies. War intensifies again in spite of talks.
- ❑ **1970** USA begins secret attacks in Laos and Cambodia and new mass bombing of North to try to stop arms reaching Viet Cong.
- ❑ **1972** 11-day Christmas Campaign is heaviest US bombing of war.
- ❑ **1973** Paris Peace Agreements signed, but fighting continues.
- ❑ **1975** Fall of Saigon to combined forces of North and Provisional Revolutionary (Viet Cong) Government of South. Further one million flee after end of war.
- ❑ **1976** Vietnam united as Socialist Republic of Vietnam, with Le Duan continuing to hold the real power as General Secretary of Communist Party. Saigon renamed Ho Chi Minh City.
- ❑ **1977** Vietnam begins incursions into Kampuchea (Cambodia).
- ❑ **1978** Thousands of ethnic Chinese flee Vietnam.
- ❑ **1979** Nine-Day War with China. Chinese troops destroy everything for 25 mi. inside Vietnam. Chinese pushed back. Vietnam ousts Pol Pot in full-scale invasion of Kampuchea and installs friendly regime. "Boat-people" (illegal emigrants) now creating crisis of international proportions. At UN conference, Vietnam agrees to allow legal emigration, but exodus continues.
- ❑ **1986** Nguyen Van Linh appointed General Secretary of the Communist Party. Initiates liberal economic *doi moi* (renovation) policy.
- ❑ **1987** Fighting in Thailand as Vietnam pursues Kampuchean resistance fighters across border.
- ❑ **1989** Troops leave Cambodia.
- ❑ **1991** Open anti-communist dissent made a criminal offence.
- ❑ **1992** Revised constitution allows foreign investment, but essential role of Communist Party is unchanged.
- ❑ **1995** US-Vietnamese relations are normalized.

V

DEFENSE

$890m   Up 3% in 1995

0	Defense spending as % GDP	40

5.7%

Since the withdrawal from Cambodia in 1989 (only the Khmer Rouge suggests that the withdrawal has not occurred), the focus of defense spending has moved to the navy, a reflection of growing tensions in the South China Sea. Vietnam's "volunteer force" in Laos has also been much reduced.

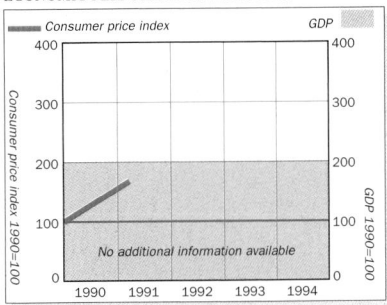

VIETNAMESE ARMED FORCES

🛡	1,300 main battle tanks (T-34/-54/-55, T-62, Ch Type-59, M-48A3)	500,000 personnel
	7 frigates and 57 patrol boats	42,000 personnel
	190 combat aircraft (65 Su-22/-27, 125 MiG-21bis/PF)	15,000 personnel
	None	

ECONOMICS

📊 $13.8bn   💲 11,07–11,011 dông

SCORE CARD

- ❑ WORLD GNP RANKING 74th
- ❑ GNP PER CAPITA $1,904
- ❑ BALANCE OF PAYMENTS ....$–869m
- ❑ INFLATION 13%
- ❑ UNEMPLOYMENT....................................20%

EXPORTS

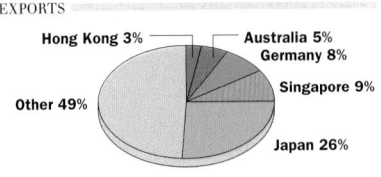

Hong Kong 3% — Australia 5% / Germany 8%
Other 49%
Singapore 9%
Japan 26%

IMPORTS

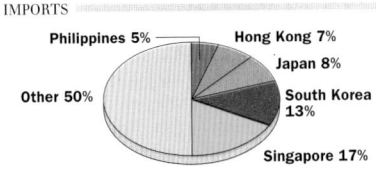

Philippines 5% — Hong Kong 7% / Japan 8%
Other 50%
South Korea 13%
Singapore 17%

STRENGTHS

Diverse resource base. Location in East Asia. Much lower labor costs than second-tier NICS such as Malaysia and Thailand.

WEAKNESSES

Weak economic institutions will make transition to a full market economy difficult. Enormous task of reconstruction after war; dependent on aid from the West, Japan and China.

PROFILE

Vietnam is already being billed by some commentators as the next Asian "tiger." The prospect is still distant, though the potential certainly exists. Mineral resources, located mostly in the north, and a resumption of Western aid to the capital-starved economy, are the foundations on which the adoption of a full market economy will be based. The major concerns are the need to develop the private sector and to maintain inflation at a tolerable level. It is now running at 13%, compared with 600%

ECONOMIC PERFORMANCE INDICATOR

No additional information available

in 1987–1988. The tax net also needs to be widened if government finances are to be set on a proper footing.

Even before the collapse of the Soviet Union, there was a widespread acceptance in Vietnam that the centrally planned economy had problems. The encouragement of private enterprise began in 1988. Between 1988 and mid-1995, foreign investors proposed new projects worth over $16 billion. Most of the money is being put into oil and gas, tourism, property and light industry. In 1995, the economy grew by 9.5%. The government has set a target of doubling Vietnam's GDP in the next decade.

VIETNAM : MAJOR BUSINESSES

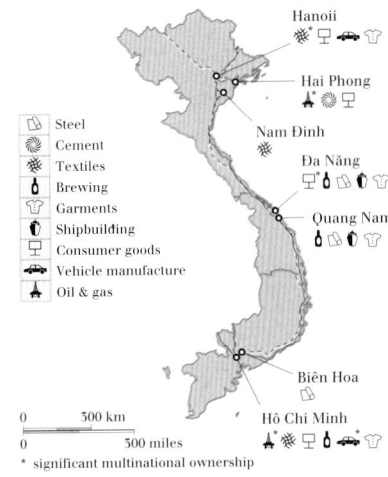

Steel	
Cement	
Textiles	
Brewing	
Garments	
Shipbuilding	
Consumer goods	
Vehicle manufacture	
Oil & gas	

* significant multinational ownership

RESOURCES

 8bn kwh (capacity 1.32m kw)

 110,075 b/d (reserves 500,000,000 bbl)

 15m pigs, 3.4m cattle, 3m buffaloes

Coal, oil, tin, zinc, iron, antimony, apatite, salt, bauxite

ELECTRICITY GENERATION

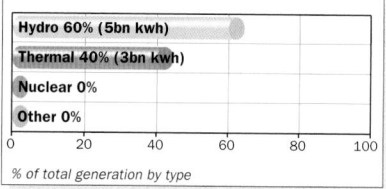

Hydro 60% (5bn kwh)

Thermal 40% (3bn kwh)

Nuclear 0%

Other 0%

% of total generation by type

Vietnam is the world's third-largest exporter of rice, after Thailand and the USA. Oil production at 110,075 b/d is negligible by world standards, but sufficient to make it Vietnam's biggest export earner. Oil and gas exploitation is undertaken by VietSovPetro, a joint venture with Russia. However, Vietnam is linking up with new partners, including the Australian company BHP and British Gas. Mobil Oil is also signing new deals, having abandoned its interests in the face of advancing communist troops in 1975. Vietnam has considerable unexploited gas reserves in the South China Sea; gas from the only producing field currently has to be flared off.

Northern Vietnam has a surplus of electricity. A new power line will make this available to the South.

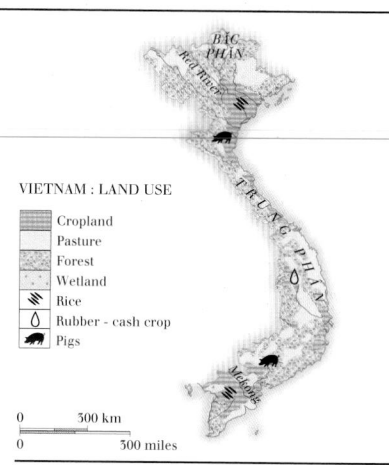

VIETNAM : LAND USE

Cropland
Pasture
Forest
Wetland
Rice
Rubber - cash crop
Pigs

ENVIRONMENT

 4%

Environmental issues are not a priority

ENVIRONMENTAL TREATIES

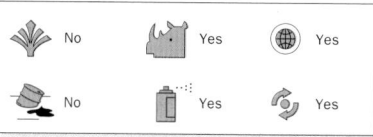

No | Yes | Yes
No | Yes | Yes

Vietnam is still counting the massive environmental cost of the Vietnam War. Seven million tons of bombs were dropped, and the defoliant chemical Agent Orange was sprayed over 4.2 million acres. In addition to the bridges, industrial zones and irrigation works destroyed, 50% of Vietnam's forests were seriously damaged and 5% wiped out. Continuing deforestation is now the major problem. Each year, 494,000 acres are lost, with subsequent soil erosion and flooding.

CRIME

Vietnam does not publish prison figures

Increase in petty theft

CRIME RATES

Rates of murder and rape remain fairly constant. Theft has risen slightly

The judicial system is based on the Soviet model. Although the "education camps" established after liberation have now closed, religious and political dissidents are still held without trial.

Petty theft from foreigners is a problem in the major cities. There has been a sharp rise in corruption since economic liberalization.

Religious tensions have provoked disturbances. In 1995, a number of high-ranking dissident Buddhists were jailed for "sabotaging religious solidarity."

HEALTH

 1 per 2,300 people

Heart disease, cancers, malaria

0 — Health spending as % GDP — 25

1.1%

Vietnam's main medical achievements are the development of a vaccine for Hepatitis B, and the extraction of artemisinin (an anti-malarial drug) from the indigenous Thanh Hao tree.

WEALTH

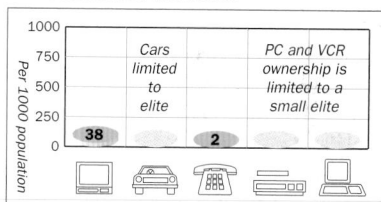

Wealth disparities are small

CONSUMER GOODS OWNERSHIP

Cars limited to elite | PC and VCR ownership is limited to a small elite

Per 1000 population

38 | 2

The Party remains the route to advancement. Ostentatious displays of wealth are still frowned on.

MEDIA

 The media is tightly controlled

PUBLISHING AND BROADCAST MEDIA

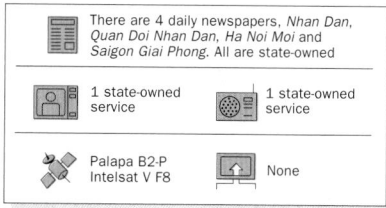

There are 4 daily newspapers, *Nhan Dan*, *Quan Doi Nhan Dan*, *Ha Noi Moi* and *Saigon Giai Phong*. All are state-owned

1 state-owned service | 1 state-owned service

Palapa B2-P Intelsat V F8 | None

Although the media is tightly regulated and all editors have to be Party members, criticism of the authorities is still possible. The weekly *Tuoi Tre* is known for its investigative reporting, and even *Nhan Dan*, the Party newspaper, has been known to expose laxity in the system, especially in the judiciary. The army daily, *Quan Doi Nhan Dan*, is the most hardline paper.

EDUCATION

 94%

157,100 students

0 — Education spending as % GNP — 25

3%

THE EDUCATION SYSTEM

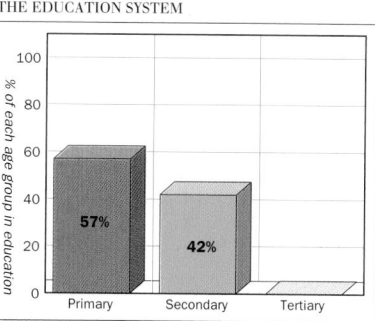

% of each age group in education

57% (Primary)
42% (Secondary)
(Tertiary)

Fees for education have recently been introduced, and enrollment is falling. Vietnamese universities have a strong liberal arts tradition.

WORLD RANKING

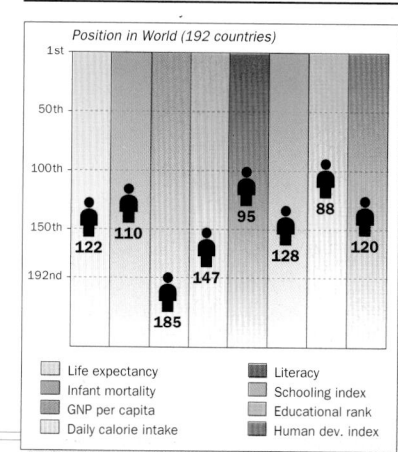

Position in World (192 countries)

1st
50th
100th
150th
192nd

122 | 110 | 95 | 88 | 120
147 | 128
185

Life expectancy | Literacy
Infant mortality | Schooling index
GNP per capita | Educational rank
Daily calorie intake | Human dev. index

V

WESTERN SAMOA

OFFICIAL NAME: Independent State of Western Samoa **CAPITAL:** Apia
POPULATION: 169,000 **CURRENCY:** Tala **OFFICIAL LANGUAGES:** Samoan, English

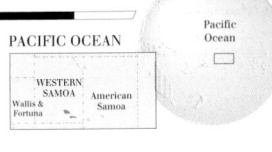

 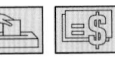

WESTERN SAMOA LIES IN THE HEART of the South Pacific, 1,500 miles north of New Zealand. Four of its nine volcanic islands are inhabited – Apolima, Manono, Sava'ai, the largest, and Upolu, home to 72% of the population. Rainforests cloak the mountains; vegetable gardens and coconut plantations thrive around the coasts. A German protectorate until 1914, Western Samoa was then administered by New Zealand until independence in 1962.

CLIMATE

WEATHER CHART

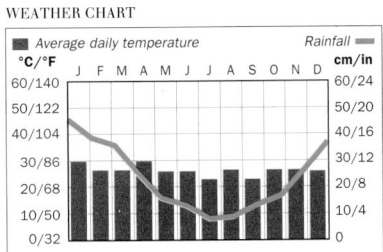

The climate is humid and temperatures rarely drop below 77°F. December to March is the hurricane season.

TRANSPORTATION

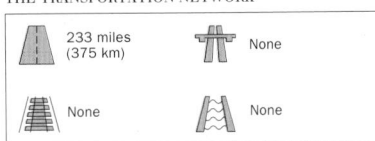

Faleolo Apia
191,727 passengers

3 ships
5800 dwt

THE TRANSPORTATION NETWORK

233 miles (375 km)		None	
None		None	

Apia port has been improved with Japanese aid. International links are mainly by air. Ferries provide inter-island connections.

TOURISM

50,000 visitors

Up 6% in 1994

MAIN OVERSEAS ARRIVALS

American Samoa 37%	
New Zealand 17%	
Australia 11%	
Other 35%	

0   10   20   30   40
% of total arrivals

Concern that the Samoan way of life would be disrupted has limited tourism development until recently. Efforts to improve facilities reflect the need to increase national revenues.

PEOPLE

Samoan, English

155 people per sq. mile

THE URBAN/RURAL POPULATION SPLIT

21%   79%

RELIGIOUS PERSUASION

Christian 100%

Ethnic Samoans – around 93% of the population – are the world's second largest Polynesian group, after the Maoris. The *fa'a Samoa*, Samoan way of life, is communal and formalized. Extended family groups, in which most people live, own 80% of the land, and are not permitted to sell it. Each family is headed by a *matai*, or elected chief, who looks after its political and social interests. Large-scale migration to New Zealand and the USA reflects a lack of jobs and the attractions of Western life. Conflict between the *fa'a Samoa* and modern life is strongest among the young, who have a high suicide rate.

WESTERN SAMOA

Total Land Area : 2830 sq. km (1093 sq. miles)

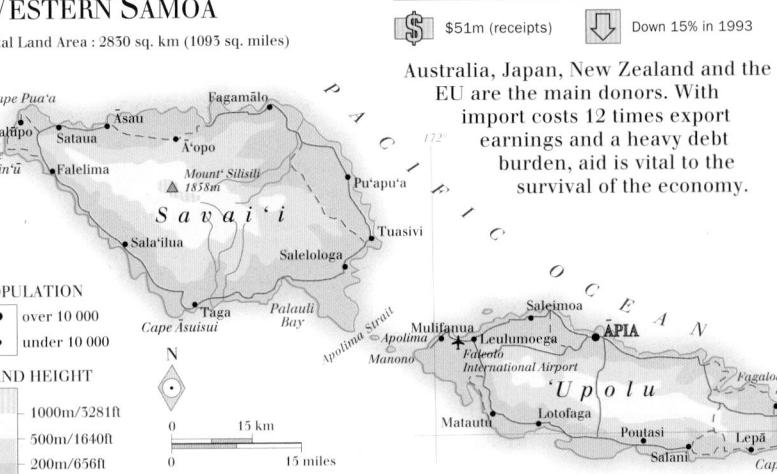

POPULATION

- over 10 000
- under 10 000

LAND HEIGHT

1000m/3281ft
500m/1640ft
200m/656ft
Sea Level

0   15 km
0   15 miles

POLITICS

1991/1996

H.H. Malietoa
Tanumafili II

THE STATE OF THE PARTIES

Legislative Assembly 49 members

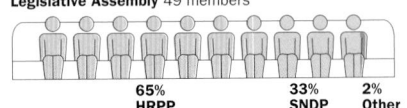

65%	33%	2%
HRPP	SNDP	Other

HRPP = Human Rights Protection Party
SNDP = Samoa National Development Party

The conservatism of the *fa'a Samoa*, reinforced by the Church's influence, has underpinned Western Samoa's political stability. Allegiance to the two main parties is quite fluid, and politics is as much to do with personalities as policies. Until 1990, only the 1,800 elected chiefs, or *matai*, could vote for the 47 ethnic Samoan seats; the other two seats are elected by non-Samoans. Universal suffrage was introduced at the 1991 elections, although only *matai* may stand for the *fono*, or parliament. Following the elections, Fiame Naomi, a woman chief, became the country's first female cabinet minister.

WORLD AFFAIRS

ACP   Comm   IBRD   SPC   SPF

New Zealand is Western Samoa's main trading partner. However, a steady tightening of controls on Samoan immigrants has strained relations with Wellington at times. Australia, the USA and EU are also important trading partners. Ties with Tokyo are growing, linked to Japanese investment.

AID

$51m (receipts)

Down 15% in 1993

Australia, Japan, New Zealand and the EU are the main donors. With import costs 12 times export earnings and a heavy debt burden, aid is vital to the survival of the economy.

W

DEFENSE

 Western Samoa has no army and few police   Not applicable

New Zealand looks after defense under a 1962 treaty. Internal order is mostly maintained by the chiefs, or *matai*.

ECONOMICS

 $163m  2.49–2.52 tala

SCORE CARD

❑ WORLD GNP RANKING	187th
❑ GNP PER CAPITA	$970
❑ BALANCE OF PAYMENTS	$–38m
❑ INFLATION	3.6%
❑ UNEMPLOYMENT	Underemployment

STRENGTHS

Light manufacturing growing; in 1992, it accounted for 75% of export earnings. Attracting foreign, especially Japanese, firms. Services growing rapidly since 1989 launch of offshore banking. Tropical agriculture; taro, coconut cream, cocoa, copra are main exports.

WEAKNESSES

Chronic balance of trade and payments deficits; dependence on aid and expatriate remittances. Declining agricultural exports. Clash between communal *fa'a Samoa* and donor pressure for market-style reforms.

EXPORTS

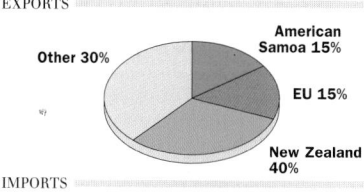

Other 30%
American Samoa 15%
EU 15%
New Zealand 40%

IMPORTS

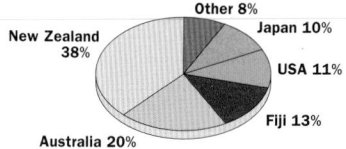

Other 8%
Japan 10%
New Zealand 38%
USA 11%
Fiji 13%
Australia 20%

RESOURCES

 48m kwh (capacity 19,000 kw)   1,608 tons

 179,000 pigs, 26,000 cattle, 7000 asses None

With no minerals, Western Samoa's main resources are its forests and tropical agriculture. The rainforests in lower-lying areas are increasingly exploited for timber. Mahogany and teak plantations are being developed. The volcanic soils, particularly on Upolu, allow a wide range of staple and export crops to be grown. Two-thirds of the population work in agriculture.

Apia, the capital, on Upolu, Western Samoa's second-largest island. It has a central volcanic range of mountains and many rivers.

ENVIRONMENT

 None   Rainforests are increasingly under threat from logging

Efforts to increase revenues are putting the environment under pressure – 80% of lowland rainforest has been replaced by plantations. Overhunting and loss of habitat have endangered rare species of fruit-bat and pigeon. Foreign firms have proposed environmentally damaging projects such as waste disposal plants, but these have so far been rejected.

MEDIA

 Fairly open criticism of the government is possible

PUBLISHING AND BROADCAST MEDIA

	There are no daily newspapers. The *Samoa Times* is published five times a week; the *Samoa Observer*, three times weekly
No TV service	 1 state-owned, 1 independent service

American Samoan TV, linking with the US networks, is widely received. A state-owned service is being set up.

CRIME

 Western Samoa does not publish prison figures   Down 27% in 1992

Alcohol-related violence is a problem at weekends; otherwise, violent crime is almost unknown. Theft is increasing in urban areas.

EDUCATION

 92%  562 students

Education is based on the New Zealand system. School attendance is universal and literacy levels high. A university was established in 1988. Scholarships are available for study abroad.

HEALTH

 1 per 4,075 people 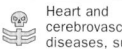 Heart and cerebrovascular diseases, suicide

The Samoan preference for being big went well with traditional diets. Diabetes and heart disease are rising as people change to Western-style foods.

CHRONOLOGY

Polynesians settled Samoa in about 1000 BC. Western rivalry after 1830 led to the 1899 division of the islands into German Western and American Eastern Samoa.

- ❑ **1914** New Zealand occupies Western Samoa. Administers first for League of Nations, then for UN.
- ❑ **1962** Becomes first independent Polynesian nation.
- ❑ **1990** Cyclone Ofa leaves 10,000 homeless. A year later, Cyclone Val causes worse damage, kills 12.
- ❑ **1991** HRPP retains power in first election under universal adult suffrage; follows positive 1990 referendum. Parliamentary term raised from three to five years.

WEALTH

 Many in the private sector earn only the statutory minimum of 1.25 tala ($0.50) per hour

CONSUMER GOODS OWNERSHIP

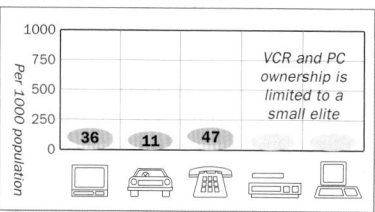

VCR and PC ownership is limited to a small elite

36 11 47

One of the world's least developed nations according to the UN, Western Samoa has the lowest wage and highest unemployment rates in Oceania. As a result, emigration is high. Some 60,000 Samoans live in New Zealand, 50,000 in the USA and 10,000 in neighboring American Samoa, where generous US support makes life much easier. Most people depend on subsistence farming and the remittances of relatives for their livelihood. Two-thirds of those with a job work for the government.

WORLD RANKING

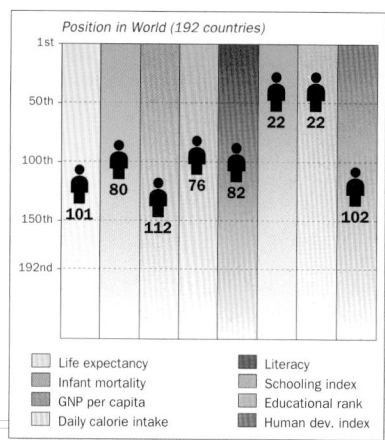

Position in World (192 countries)

101 80 112 76 82 22 22 102

Life expectancy		Literacy
Infant mortality		Schooling index
GNP per capita		Educational rank
Daily calorie intake		Human dev. index

W

YEMEN

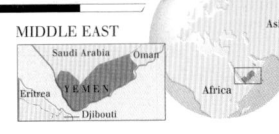

MIDDLE EAST

OFFICIAL NAME: Republic of Yemen   **CAPITAL:** Sana
POPULATION: 14.5 million   **CURRENCY:** Yemeni rial   **OFFICIAL LANGUAGE:** Arabic

YEMEN IS LOCATED in southern Arabia between Saudi Arabia and Oman. The north is mountainous, with a fertile strip along the Red Sea. The south is largely arid mountains and desert. Yemen was formerly two countries, the Yemen Arab Republic in the north and the People's Democratic Republic of Yemen in the south, which united in 1990. The poorer south, with its capital in Adan, was the Arab world's only Marxist state after British rule ended in 1967. The north was run from Sana by successive military regimes, following a coup against the royalist imamate in 1962.

CLIMATE

WEATHER CHART

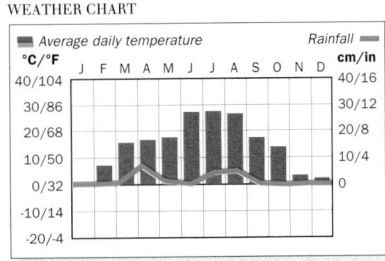

The desert climate is modified by altitude, which affects temperatures by as much as 54°F. Rainfall increases in northwest and central Yemen.

TRANSPORTATION

 Sana International
624,000 passengers

 7 ships
9,700 dwt

THE TRANSPORTATION NETWORK

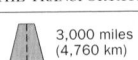 3,000 miles (4,760 km)	None
None	None

Adan's position at the entrance to the Red Sea makes it a key shipping port. The main cities are linked by adequate roads, but many rural areas are inaccessible. Sana and Adan are served by international airlines.

Hilltop village in northern Yemen, showing traditionally decorated, multistorey houses built from mud bricks.

TOURISM

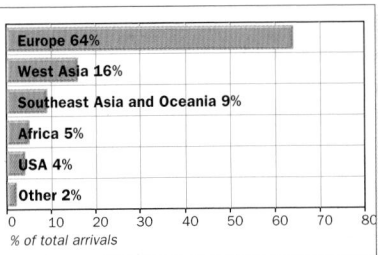

Believed to be the home of the legendary Queen of Sheba, Yemen attracts tourists interested in Arab society, architecture, archaeology and historical remains. The Romans called Yemen *Arabia Felix* because of its fertile farmlands and dominance in the frankincense trade. Yemen was the second country, after Saudi Arabia, to convert to Islam.

Southern Yemen has been open to Western visitors only since 1990. Its run-down infrastructure and lack of hotels, especially on the coast, have hindered tourism. Sana, a walled medieval city, is the more interesting center for tourists. It has impressive architecture, particularly tall stone-and-terracotta Arab houses, and the palaces of the former imamate. Despite being over 600 miles from the capital, the Marib Dam, built in ancient times, is another major attraction.

German and French tourists were among the first to travel in any numbers to North Yemen, when specialist companies began to offer adventure holidays during the 1980s. Tourism declined during the civil war of 1994.

Tourists are subject to a ban on the consumption of alcohol, except in five-star hotels. Whiskey and beer are available on the black market, which operates out of Djibouti.

PEOPLE

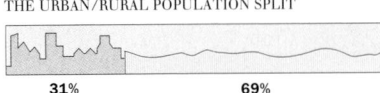

THE URBAN/RURAL POPULATION SPLIT

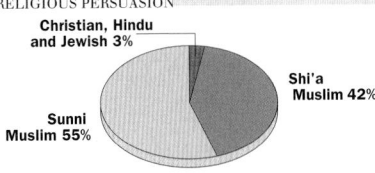

31%   69%

RELIGIOUS PERSUASION

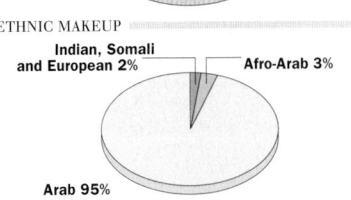

ETHNIC MAKEUP

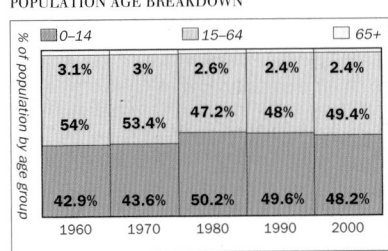

Yemenis are almost entirely of Arab and Bedouin descent, though there is a small, dwindling, Jewish minority. The majority are Sunni Muslims, of the Shafi sect. In the north, many people have close family in Saudi Arabia. Many Yemenis consider Saudi's Asir province to be part of Yemen.

Agriculture employs more than half the population. Many Yemenis sought jobs in Saudi Arabia and the Gulf states during the 1970s oil boom. More than one million worked in Saudi Arabia, most as manual laborers and farmhands. Their expulsion, a result of Yemen's support for Iraq's invasion of Kuwait in 1990, has raised unemployment within Yemen.

In rural areas and in the north, Islamic orthodoxy is strong and most women wear veils. In the south, however, women still claim the freedoms they had under the Marxist regime, especially in urban areas.

Tension continues to exist between the south, led by the cosmopolitan city of Adan, and the more conservative north. Clashes between their former armies escalated into civil war in 1994.

POPULATION AGE BREAKDOWN

% of population by age group	■ 0–14		■ 15–64		□ 65+
65+	3.1%	3%	2.6%	2.4%	2.4%
15–64	54%	53.4%	47.2%	48%	49.4%
0–14	42.9%	43.6%	50.2%	49.6%	48.2%
	1960	1970	1980	1990	2000

Y

YEMEN

Total Land Area : 527 970 sq. km
(203 849 sq. miles)

POPULATION

over 500 000 ◉
over 100 000 ◎
over 10 000 ●
under 10 000 ·

LAND HEIGHT

3000m/9843ft
2000m/6562ft
1000m/3281ft
500m/1640ft
200m/656ft
Sea Level

POLITICS

 1993/1997

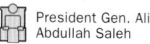 President Gen. Ali
Abdullah Saleh

THE STATE OF THE PARTIES

House of Representatives 301 members

| 40% GPC | 21% YAR | 19% YSP | 20% Other |

GPC = General People's Congress **YAR** = Yemeni Alliance
for Reform **YSP** = Yemeni Socialist Party **Other** = Arab
Socialist Ba'ath Party, Truth Party

Yemen is a multiparty democracy. The
president retains executive power while
the House of Representatives holds
legislative power.

MAIN POLITICAL ISSUES
Instability

Growing animosity between the Yemen
Socialist Party (YSP), which formerly ruled
in Adan, and the conservative hierarchy
in Sana led to the outbreak of full-scale
civil war in 1994. The YSP was defeated
and ousted from the ruling coalition.
Since the war there has also been
growing tension between the ruling GPC
and its junior coalition partner, the YAR.

Saudi interference

The relationship with Saudi Arabia has
long been strained and Sana has often
accused Riyadh of funding dissidents.
Relations appeared to have improved in
early 1995 when the two sides signed a
memorandum of understanding on
border issues.

PROFILE

The merger of North and South Yemen
in 1990 united Yemenis under one ruler
for the first time since 1735. At first,
President Ali Saleh, who had had
difficulty controlling the north even
before the union with the socialist
regime in the south, skilfully maintained
unity. Then, in the spring of 1994,
tensions mounted following an
assassination attempt on a political
supporter of Saleh's, Hassan Makki.
Amid accusations from the South that
President Saleh was attempting to
overthrow Vice-President al-Baidh, the
former leader of South Yemen, civil war
broke out. Most of the fighting was
centered in the South, in particular
around the port of Adan, which became
the scene of mass evacuations by
European workers. By July 1994, the
fighting had died down and the South's
attempted secession had been quashed.

Ali Abdullah Saleh,
*former North Yemen
president, now leader
of the unified Yemen.*

Ali Salem al-Baidh,
*vice-president and
former leader of
South Yemen.*

CHRONOLOGY

From the 9th century AD, the Zaydi
dynasty ruled Yemen, until their
defeat by the Ottoman Turks in
1517. The Turks were expelled by
the Zaydi Imams in 1636.

❏ **1839** Britain occupies Adan.
❏ **1918** Yemen secures independence.
❏ **1937** Adan made a Crown Colony,
the hinterland a Protectorate.
❏ **1962** Army coup. Imam deposed
and Yemen Arab Republic (YAR)
declared in the north.
❏ **1962–1970** Northern civil war
between royalists and republicans.
❏ **1963** Adan and Protectorate united
to form Federation of South Arabia.
❏ **1967** British troops leave Adan.
❏ **1970** South Yemen renamed the
People's Democratic Republic of
Yemen (PDYR). Republicans
victorious in the north.
❏ **1971** Civilian elections in the YAR.
❏ **1972** September, war between YAR
and PDYR. October, peace signed.
❏ **1974** Army coup in YAR.
❏ **1975** Sultan of Oman defeats PDYR-
backed revolt in Dhofar province.
❏ **1978** Lt.-Col. Ali Saleh YAR
president. Coup in PDYR. Radical
Abdalfattah Ismail in power.
❏ **1979** February, war breaks out.
March, peace. October, PDYR signs
20-year treaty with USSR.
❏ **1980** Ismail replaced by
moderate Ali Muhammed. ➡

Y

CHRONOLOGY *continued*

- ❏ **1982** President of PDYR Ali Muhammed signs peace treaty with the Sultan of Oman.
- ❏ **1984** YAR signs 20-year cooperation treaty with USSR.
- ❏ **1986** January, coup attempt against President Muhammed in PDYR develops into civil war. Rebels take control of Adan. February, rebels install Haydar Al Attas as president. July, presidents of PDYR and YAR meet.
- ❏ **1987** Oil production starts in YAR
- ❏ **1988** YAR holds elections for a consultative council, Muslim brotherhood gains influence.
- ❏ **1989** Unification process speeds up dramatically. June, telephone links established. July, PDYR publishes a program of free-market reforms. November, YAR and PDYR sign agreement to unify the two states. December, constitution of unified Yemen published.
- ❏ **1990** January, restrictions on travel between YAR and PDYR end. Growing opposition to unification inside Yemen from fundamentalists against the secular constitution. May, unification of PDYR and YAR. Ali Saleh becomes president of the Republic of Yemen. August, Yemen criticizes Western response to the Iraqi invasion of Kuwait.
- ❏ **1991** Yemeni guest workers expelled by Saudi Arabia in retaliation for Yemen's position over the Iraqi invasion of Kuwait. Arab states boycott independence celebrations.
- ❏ **1992** Assassinations and political unrest delay elections.
- ❏ **1993** April, elections leave the ruling parties still in power.
- ❏ **1994** Southern secessionists defeated in civil war.

WORLD AFFAIRS

AL AMF IBRD NAM OIC

Yemen's links with Saudi Arabia and the West have still not fully recovered from the support Yemen gave to Iraq during the Gulf War. Yemen and Oman's relationship has improved with the signing of a border agreement in 1992.

AID

 $309 (receipts)   Up 18% in 1993

In early 1996, Yemen received some $700 million from the IMF and donor countries in support of its economic reform program.

DEFENSE

 $345m    Up 8% in 1995

0   *Defense spending as % GDP*   40

 5.2%

Following unification, mutual suspicion slowed down the integration of North and South Yemen's defense forces. Sporadic, bitter clashes have taken place, most notably in 1994. In the past, Soviet weapons were bought by both governments, although the North also possesses US arms.

YEMENI ARMED FORCES

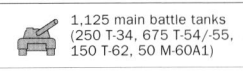
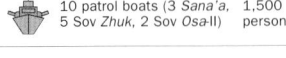

1,125 main battle tanks (250 T-34, 675 T-54/-55, 150 T-62, 50 M-60A1)	37,000 personnel
10 patrol boats (3 *Sana'a*, 5 Sov *Zhuk*, 2 Sov *Osa*-II)	1,500 personnel
69 combat aircraft (11 F-5E, 16 Su-20/-22, 25 MiG-21, 5 MiG-29)	1,000 personnel
None	

ECONOMICS

 $3.9bn    50.00–88.30 Yemeni rials

SCORE CARD

- ❏ WORLD GNP RANKING........................110th
- ❏ GNP PER CAPITA $280
- ❏ BALANCE OF PAYMENTS.....................$–58m
- ❏ INFLATION 71.8%
- ❏ UNEMPLOYMENT..................................30%

EXPORTS

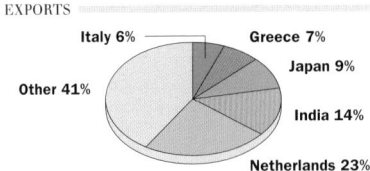

Italy 6% | Greece 7% | Japan 9% | India 14% | Netherlands 23% | Other 41%

IMPORTS

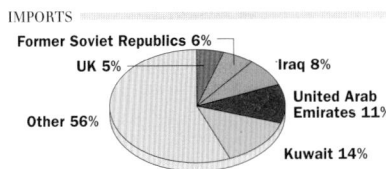

Former Soviet Republics 6% | UK 5% | Iraq 8% | United Arab Emirates 11% | Kuwait 14% | Other 56%

STRENGTHS

Rising oil production. Salt mining. Deposits of copper, gold, lead, zinc and molybdenum. Industries include oil refining, chemicals, food products.

WEAKNESSES

Political instability deters foreign companies from investment. Well-organized black market undermines tax base. Large balance of payments deficit. Overall dependence upon subsistence agriculture.

PROFILE

Yemen's unification in 1990 was designed to transform the economy. High expectations were placed on the exploitation of large oil and natural gas reserves, discovered in 1984. Exports of oil began in 1987. Plans were also made to encourage industrial investment around the port of Adan. Both these policies for regeneration suffered severe setbacks as a result of the 1990–1991 Gulf War. In addition, the expulsion of over one million

ECONOMIC PERFORMANCE INDICATOR

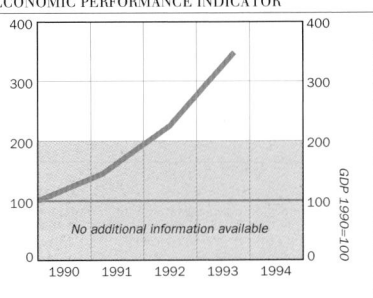

No additional information available

GDP 1990=100

Yemeni guest workers from Saudi Arabia imposed a huge burden on the economy and ended the flow of workers' remittances.

Economic crisis forced the government to reduce expenditure and subsidies on certain staple foods. This provoked widespread civil unrest and encouraged many farmers to switch from food crops, such as wheat, to growing the more profitable narcotic plant qat. As a result, Yemen has increasingly had to import foodstuffs.

The 1994 civil war had a serious impact on the economy – water systems, power stations, oil refineries, airports and communications centers were destroyed throughout the country. In 1995, the government embarked on an IMF-backed reform program aimed at stabilizing the economy.

YEMEN : MAJOR BUSINESSES

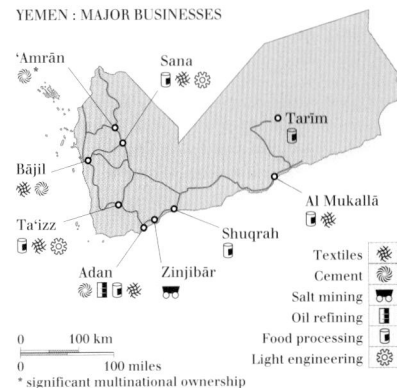

'Amrān | Sana | Tarīm | Bājil | Al Mukallā | Ta'izz | Shuqrah | Adan | Zinjibār

Textiles | Cement | Salt mining | Oil refining | Food processing | Light engineering

0   100 km
0   100 miles
* significant multinational ownership

RESOURCES

2bn kwh (capacity 800,000 kw)

163,267 b/d (reserves 4,000,000,000 bbl)

3.7m sheep, 3.2m goats, 1.1m cattle

Oil, natural gas, salt, marble, gypsum

ELECTRICITY GENERATION

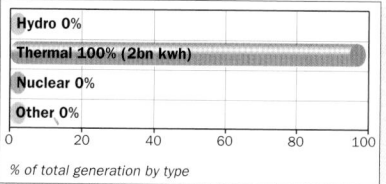

Hydro 0%

Thermal 100% (2bn kwh)

Nuclear 0%

Other 0%

0 20 40 60 80 100

% of total generation by type

There are considerable reserves of oil and gas. Crude oil production has reached 163,267 b/d. It would be more but for Western companies' reluctance to offend Saudi Arabia, whose relations with Yemen are strained. Despite attacks by bandits, exploration is continuing in many areas. Salt is the only other mineral that is commercially exploited at present, and its production continues to grow steadily.

The agricultural sector employs 55% of the working population and accounts for 22% of GDP. Cotton is grown as a cash crop. There is also some forestry and hunting for animal skins. Livestock and livestock products, such as dairy produce and hides, are the economic mainstays of the north.

Yemen's rich fishing grounds in the Arabian Sea have been developed. They now provide a major source of earnings, despite poor equipment.

YEMEN : LAND USE

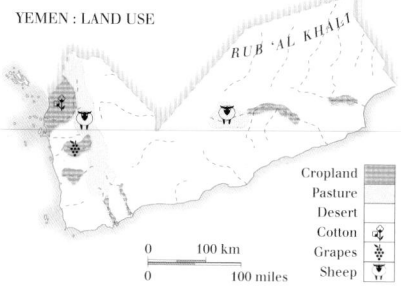

RUB 'AL KHALI

Cropland
Pasture
Desert
Cotton
Grapes
Sheep

0   100 km
0   100 miles

ENVIRONMENT

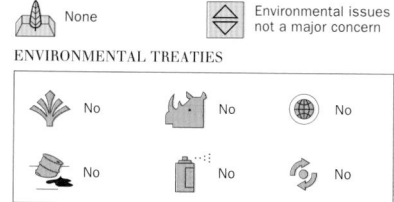

None

Environmental issues not a major concern

ENVIRONMENTAL TREATIES

No   No   No

No   No   No

Yemen's low economic development has resulted in large untouched areas of land. However, game animals are under severe threat from hunters.

MEDIA

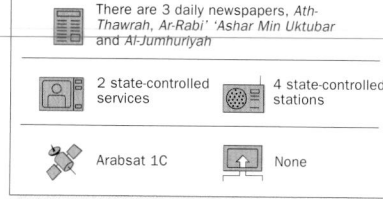

The media is under tight government control

PUBLISHING AND BROADCAST MEDIA

There are 3 daily newspapers, *Ath-Thawrah, Ar-Rabi' 'Ashar Min Uktubar* and *Al-Jumhuriyah*

2 state-controlled services

4 state-controlled stations

Arabsat 1C

None

CRIME

 Yemen does not publish prison figures

 Crime is rising

CRIME RATES

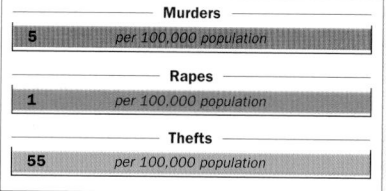

Murders
5   per 100,000 population

Rapes
1   per 100,000 population

Thefts
55   per 100,000 population

Political assassinations have long been a feature of Yemeni life and continue to threaten political stability. Formal law enforcement does not often operate far outside the main cities. As a result of this Western companies face the double risk of their personnel being kidnapped and their equipment being stolen by Bedouin raiding parties.

EDUCATION

 41%

 53,082 students

0   *Education spending as % GNP*   25

4.6%

THE EDUCATION SYSTEM

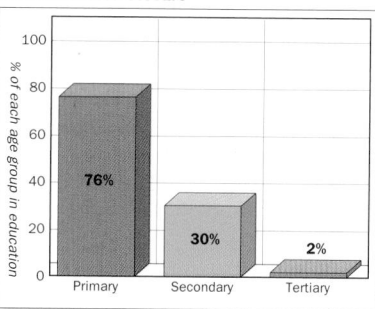

100
80   76%
60
40   30%
20
0   2%
    Primary Secondary Tertiary

% of each age group in education

Some 80% of the population have no formal classroom education. Schooling barely extends into rural areas. Illiteracy is especially high among women: 74% cannot read or write. There are fewer than 10,000 students at Yemen's two universities – Sana and Adan. Yemen also has some technical colleges.

Yemen has a long, distinguished tradition of intellectual debate, but the press is poorly developed. The government keeps a tight control on the media and vets the entry of foreign journalists. TV and radio are state-controlled and have a limited range around the principal cities. Satellite TV is not generally available. The ownership of radio and TV receivers is low; a small minority of the population own a TV.

HEALTH

 1 per 6,700 people

Diarrheal diseases, tuberculosis, malaria, bilharzia

0   *Health spending as % GDP*   25

1.5%

The major cities have an adequate primary health care system. Rural areas are less well served. Yemen has only one doctor for every 6,700 people. Infant mortality is high for the Middle East at 12%. Life expectancy is 52 years for men and 56 for women.

WEALTH

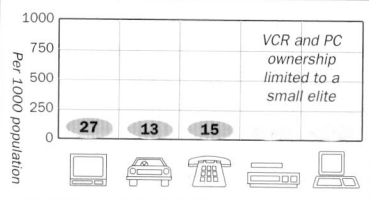

Most Yemenis lead a subsistence existence

CONSUMER GOODS OWNERSHIP

1000
750   VCR and PC
500   ownership
250   limited to a
                   small elite
27   13   15

Per 1000 population

Most Yemenis have experienced a reduced standard of living since Saudi Arabia expelled its Yemeni workers. The lack of jobs in other Gulf states has added to unemployment levels. Except for a small elite, the ownership of consumer goods is low.

WORLD RANKING

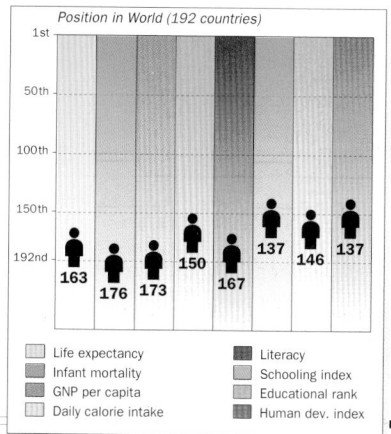

Position in World (192 countries)

1st
50th
100th
150th
192nd

163   176 173   150 167   137 146 137

Life expectancy
Infant mortality
GNP per capita
Daily calorie intake

Literacy
Schooling index
Educational rank
Human dev. index

Y

YUGOSLAVIA (SERBIA & MONTENEGRO)

OFFICIAL NAME: Federal Republic of Yugoslavia **CAPITAL:** Belgrade
POPULATION: 10.8 million **CURRENCY:** Dinar **OFFICIAL LANGUAGE:** Serbian

THE SELF-PROCLAIMED Federal Republic of Yugoslavia (FRY), comprising the republics of Serbia and Montenegro, lays claim to being the successor state to the former Yugoslavia. Serbia was vilified in the international community for its role in the conflict in the region and the FRY has been denied recognition by most countries. UN sanctions imposed in 1992 were lifted in 1995 to coincide with the signing of a Bosnian peace agreement by the Serbs, Croats and Bosnian Muslims. Nationalism among Albanians in Kosovo is a serious source of tension.

CLIMATE

WEATHER CHART

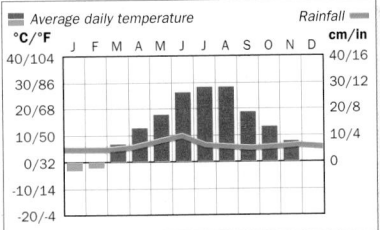

The climate is continental inland and Mediterranean along the Montenegrin coast. Summers are hot and springs rainy. Winters are cold, with heavy snowfalls. In July and August, the average daily maximum in Belgrade is 82°F, while in January it is 37°F.

TRANSPORTATION

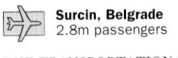

Surcin, Belgrade
2.8m passengers

44 ships
1.5m dwt

THE TRANSPORTATION NETWORK

23,800 miles
(38,300 km)

217 miles
(350 km)

Extensive

River Danube
is the major
waterway

About one-third of railroads in the FRY are electrified. However, the important rail link to Greece, one of Serbia's main trading links, was closed between 1993-1995 as a result of international economic sanctions. Most goods are still available in the stores, but are brought into the country by illegal trade.

Although roads in Serbis were manned by groups of soldiers, now Yugoslavia issues transit visas relatively freely and travel on the main Budapest–Sofia highway through Serbia has resumed. Although Yugoslavia is fairly safe for foreign travelers and harassment by the military is rare, most travelers choose to take longer routes through neighboring countries.

The former Yugoslavia's mountain scenery and beaches attracted over five million tourists a year before 1991.

TOURISM

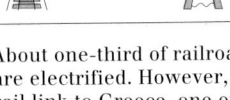
91,000 visitors

Up 18% in 1994

MAIN OVERSEAS ARRIVALS

Yugoslavia does not publish visitor figures by country of origin

% of total arrivals

0   10   20   30   40

Serbia has never been a center of tourism. The Montenegrin coast, however, has renowned beaches. The impact of UN sanctions meant that foreign tourism ceased. Montenegrin tourism is now monopolized by Serbs, particularly by the political and criminal elements of the Serbian elite. The impact of recession and hyperinflation kept the average Yugoslav vacationer away.

YUGOSLAVIA
(SERBIA & MONTENEGRO)

Total Land Area : 102 173 sq. km (39 449 sq. miles)

POPULATION

over 1 000 000
over 100 000
over 50 000

LAND HEIGHT

2000m/6562ft
1000m/3281ft
500m/1640ft
200m/656ft
Sea Level

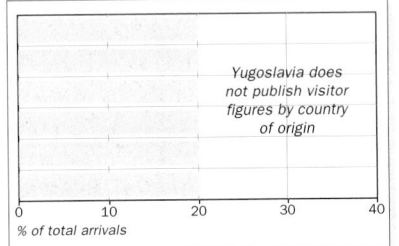

PEOPLE

 Serbian, Croatian

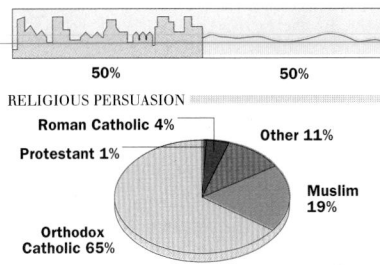 1,088 people per sq. mile

THE URBAN/RURAL POPULATION SPLIT

50%   50%

RELIGIOUS PERSUASION

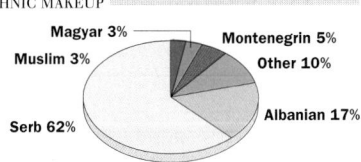

Roman Catholic 4%
Protestant 1%
Other 11%
Muslim 19%
Orthodox Catholic 65%

ETHNIC MAKEUP

Magyar 3%
Muslim 3%
Montenegrin 5%
Other 10%
Serb 62%
Albanian 17%

The social order in the FRY is disintegrating. The professional classes have effectively been driven out of Serbia; At least 100,000 have left since the dissolution of federal Yugoslavia. The absence of a middle class is likely to be most strongly felt now that

sanctions have been lifted; the lack of educated and experienced professionals will undoubtedly affect the prospects for economic recovery.

An estimated two-thirds of the population are currently living below a subsistence level. Many people are suffering from malnutrition and all health problems are aggravated by bitingly cold winters. A modest estimate of a household's basic consumption needs costs roughly two times the average wage. Unsupported pensioners are faring worst. Real monthly pensions are virtually worthless and there is a depressingly high suicide rate among the old living in Belgrade and other towns and cities.

POPULATION AGE BREAKDOWN

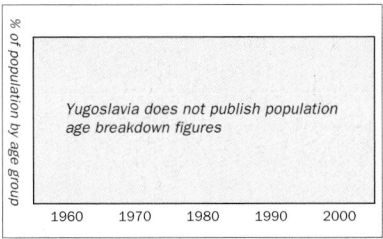

% of population by age group

Yugoslavia does not publish population age breakdown figures

1960   1970   1980   1990   2000

POLITICS

 1993/1996

 Federal President Zoran Lilič

THE STATE OF THE PARTIES

Chamber of Citizens 138 members

4% DP

34% SPS
25% SRP
14% DMS
12% DPS
11% Others

SPS = Socialist Party of Serbia   SRP = Serbian Radical Party
DMS = Democratic Movement of Serbia   DPS = Democratic Party of Socialists   DP = Democratic Party

Chamber of Republics 40 members

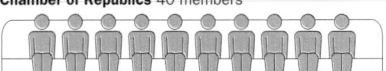

Comprised of 40 members from Serbia and Montenegro selected on a proportional basis to reflect the composition of Serbia's and Montenegro's republican legislatures

Serbia and Montenegro each have a single-chamber, democratically elected parliament and a president. Each also contributes members to the bicameral Federal Assembly.

MAIN POLITICAL ISSUES

Impact of Bosnian peace agreement
Milošević's "delivery" of the Bosnian Serbs to the negotiating table and his signing of the 1995 Bosnian peace agreement appear to have strengthened his grip on power in the FRY. At the international level, the agreement allowed him to be promoted as the guarantor of peace in the Balkans. In the months since the agreement, he has

moved methodically to strengthen his hold on domestic politics. At the Socialist Party convention held in early 1996, he was reelected party chair almost unanimously.

Minority government in Serbia
The Serbian parliament remains unstable. In the 1993 elections, the Socialists increased their share of seats from 101 to 123, which left them still three seats short of an absolute majority.

PROFILE
Serbia is the stronger political player and, as Serbian president, Milošević is at the center of policy making. In Montenegro, the DPS government elected in 1992 formed a coalition with all but one of the other parties, despite having themselves received a clear majority.

Radoje Konić, *who replaced Milan Panić as federal prime minister in 1993.*

Slobodan Milošević, *Serbian president and the FRY's major political influence.*

WORLD AFFAIRS

 G24   IAEA   NAM   OSCE   UN

The Balkans remain in a state of flux after the signing of the 1995 Bosnian peace agreement and the accompanying military, political and diplomatic developments. UN sanctions against the FRY have been suspended, but it will not qualify for the international financing it needs until it demonstrates full cooperation with the international war crimes tribunal. Mutual recognition accords should pave the way for at least a formal normalization of relations among the former Yugoslav states. The FRY has signed such agreements with Bosnia and Macedonia; an accord with Croatia is dependent on the implementation of a 1995 agreement to reintegrate Serb-occupied eastern Slavonia into Croatia. The existence of a strong Hungarian minority in Vojvodina and the more explosive tensions which surround the Albanian minority in Kosovo continue to complicate relations with the neighboring states of Hungary and Albania

AID

 Aid from allies

 Trend upwards after peace settlement

Much needed international assistance is heavily dependent on the FRY complying fully in the implementation of the 1995 Bosnian peace agreement, with particular respect to the issue of war crimes.

CHRONOLOGY
The Serbs were defeated by the Turks at the Battle of Kosovo in 1389. Parts of the region later came under the control of the Austrian Habsburg empire.

❑ **1878** Full independence gained by Serbia and Montenegro at Congress of Berlin.
❑ **1918** Joint Kingdom of Serbs, Croats and Slovenes created.
❑ **1929** King Alexander of Serbia assumes absolute powers over state; changes name to Yugoslavia.
❑ **1941** Germans launch surprise attack. Rival resistance groups: Chetniks (Serb royalist) and Partisans (communist, under Tito).
❑ **1945** Federal People's Republic of Yugoslavia founded with Tito as prime minister. Vojvodina and Kosovo provinces gain autonomy within Serbia.
❑ **1948** Tito breaks with Stalin.
❑ **1950** Workers' councils give employees voice on economy.

Y

CHRONOLOGY *continued*

- ❑ **1951** Farmers permitted to sell produce on free market.
- ❑ **1955** Detente between Yugoslavia and the USSR.
- ❑ **1973** April, economic cooperation agreement signed with West Germany. October, agreement of noninterference signed with Soviet Union. December, Croat nationalists purged from party leadership and government.
- ❑ **1974** New constitution decentralizes the government. Vojvodina and Kosovo are given status within Serbia.
- ❑ **1980** Tito dies. Succeeded by collective presidency.
- ❑ **1981** Unrest among Kosovo Albanians; state of emergency declared.
- ❑ **1985** Serbian intellectuals publish memorandum listing Serb grievances within Yugoslavia.
- ❑ **1986** Slobodan Milošević becomes leader of Communist Party in Serbia (SPS).
- ❑ **1987** Government wage freeze in attempt to combat inflation. Scandals lead to banking system crisis.
- ❑ **1988** Emergency party meeting proposes economic and social reforms. Belgrade protests against economic austerity. Mikulić government brought down over budget failure.
- ❑ **1989** Kosovo Albanians protest at presence of Serb police unit; crackdown leads to loss of autonomy for province. King Nicholas I reburied in Montenegro. 600th anniversary of Battle of Kosovo.
- ❑ **1990** December, Milošević and Socialist Party victorious in elections in Serbia. Communists win presidency and dominate assembly in multiparty elections in Montenegro.
- ❑ **1992** EC recognizes breakaway republics of Croatia, Slovenia and Bosnia-Herzegovina. UN sanctions imposed. Ibrahim Rugova elected president of self-declared republic of Kosovo. Failure of Vance-Owen plan for Bosnia. Milošević defeats Prime Minister Milan Panić and is reelected president, but Socialists lose absolute majority. Momir Bulatović wins Montenegrin presidency.
- ❑ **1993** Socialists improve parliamentary standing in December elections. New EU initiative in Bosnian peace talks.
- ❑ **1995** Milošević and the Croatian and Bosnian Muslim leaders sign a Bosnian peace agreement. UN sanctions are lifted.

DEFENSE

$1.1bn   Up 54% in 1995

0   *Defense spending as % GDP*   40

22.8%

SERBIAN ARMED FORCES

	639 main battle tanks (407 T-54/-55, 232 M-84)	90,000 personnel
	4 submarines, 4 frigates and 41 patrol boats	6,000 personnel
	282 combat aircraft (87 MiG-21F/PF/M/BIS, 10 MiG-21U, 16 MiG-29)	29,000 personnel
	None	

The Serbian desire to reduce Bulatović's influence has resulted in the disestablishment of republican defense and foreign ministries in favor of the Serbian-controlled federal bodies. Montenegro has resisted the initiative.

The Serbian military has been the more visible actor in the conflict in former Yugoslavia. Serbia was traditionally the center of armaments manufacture in the former republic. Its military hardware industry has enabled it to arm itself without being dependent on imports. The need to create money to pay for domestically produced weapons was a major factor in the crippling hyperinflation of 1993.

ECONOMICS

$13.5bn   4.73 dinars

SCORE CARD

- ❑ WORLD GNP RANKING 72nd
- ❑ GNP PER CAPITA $1,298
- ❑ BALANCE OF PAYMENTS ....$–1.2bn
- ❑ INFLATION ....High
- ❑ UNEMPLOYMENT..................................40%

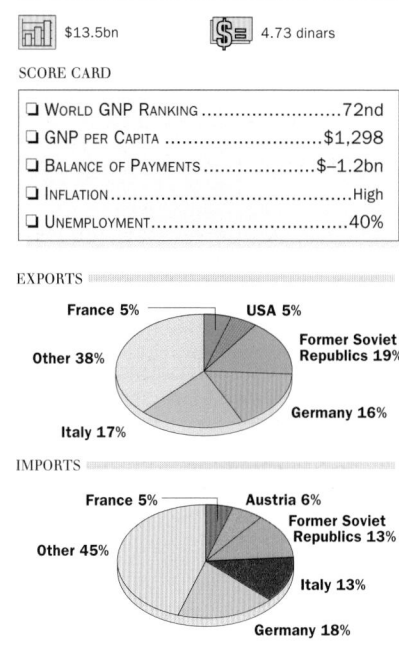

EXPORTS

France 5% — USA 5%
Former Soviet Republics 19%
Other 38%
Germany 16%
Italy 17%

IMPORTS

France 5% — Austria 6%
Former Soviet Republics 13%
Other 45%
Italy 13%
Germany 18%

ECONOMIC PERFORMANCE INDICATOR

Consumer price index   GDP

The breakup of the former Yugoslavia and the extent of current economic collapse in Serbia and Montenegro mean that consistent economic trends between 1988 and 1995 cannot be established

Consumer price index 1990=100

GDP 1990=100

1990 1991 1992 1993 1994

The war in Bosnia devastated these initiatives. Sanctions, which cut off imports and exports, decimated the emerging private sector as well as the state sector. The hyperinflation of 1993–1994 pushed the economy to the verge of complete collapse. Savings were rendered worthless and any incentive to invest in the economy was destroyed. Output levels in 1993 fell to a third of what they were in 1990.

STRENGTHS

The suspension of UN sanctions in 1995 served as a major boost to the economy. Imports, exports and industrial output are rising. The government is negotiating fresh loans.

WEAKNESSES

Virtual economic collapse caused by sanctions. Continued blockage of IMF credits. Dwindling hard currency reserves. Threat of renewed hyperinflation as pressure increases for government to print new money.

PROFILE

Following the transition to a multiparty system, a short-lived reformist government began to implement privatization, fiscal reform and a reorganization of the banking sector.

YUGOSLAVIA : MAJOR BUSINESSES

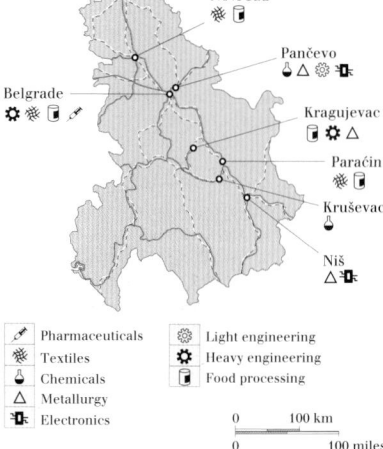

Novi Sad
Pančevo
Belgrade
Kragujevac
Paraćin
Kruševac
Niš

Pharmaceuticals		Light engineering	
Textiles		Heavy engineering	
Chemicals		Food processing	
Metallurgy			
Electronics			

0   100 km
0   100 miles

Y

RESOURCES

36m kwh
(capacity 8.85m kw)

Some oil production

4m pigs, 2.8m
sheep, 1.8m cattle,
82,000 horses

Coal, bauxite, iron,
lead, copper, zinc

ELECTRICITY GENERATION

Hydro 31% (11m kwh)

Thermal 69% (25m kwh)

Nuclear 0%

Other 0%

0	20	40	60	80	100

% of total generation by type

The FRY has attained self-sufficiency in coal and electricity production. The latter comes mainly from hydroelectric or coal-fired plants. Vojvodina caters for one-third of oil needs.

YUGOSLAVIA : LAND USE

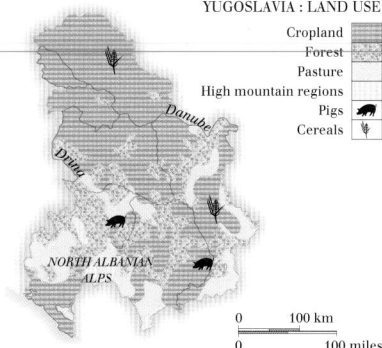

Cropland
Forest
Pasture
High mountain regions
Pigs
Cereals

0	100 km
0	100 miles

ENVIRONMENT

3% (former
Yugoslavia)

Environmental issues
are currently a
low priority

ENVIRONMENTAL TREATIES

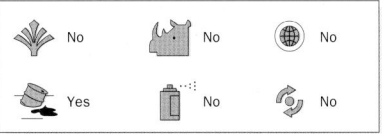

No

No

No

Yes

No

No

In Serbia, ecological awareness peaked in the late 1980s. The Ecological Forum sought to pursue the cross-border implications of pollution. Organized resistance in Montenegro to the Tara River dam project partially succeeded, in that the dam was moved upstream from a scenic canyon. The biosphere reserve at Durmitor National Park preserves unique wetlands.

MEDIA

Independent TV and radio stations have been targets of harassment and police raids

PUBLISHING AND BROADCAST MEDIA

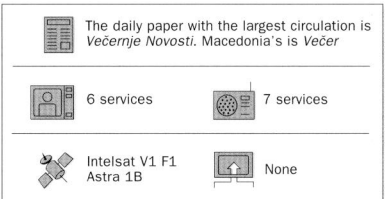

The daily paper with the largest circulation is
Večernje Novosti. Macedonia's is *Večer*

6 services

7 services

Intelsat V1 F1
Astra 1B

None

Public opinion continues to be shaped by the state-regulated media, on which most of the population is dependent for news coverage. The abrupt nationalization in early 1996 of the private TV station Studio B removed the main outlet for opposition news. The main Serbian opposition newspaper *Nasa Borba* is currently under pressure because of government controls over newsprint supplies. *Tanjug*, the official news agency, was purged in 1991 to eliminate criticism of the regime.

CRIME

Serbia does not
publish prison figures

No change in current
high crime levels

CRIME RATES

Civil disorder and the proliferation of weapons have led to a sharp rise in all categories of crime, including extortion

Economic crime, from currency trading to black market goods, is widespread. An estimated 40% of all economic activity takes place in the illegal market. Formerly on the main east-west smuggling route, Montenegro's drugs trade was disrupted by sanctions. Fears exist that the Serbian militia will turn to mafia-type extortion operations.

EDUCATION

93%

143,268 students

0	*Education spending as % GNP* 25
	6.1%

THE EDUCATION SYSTEM

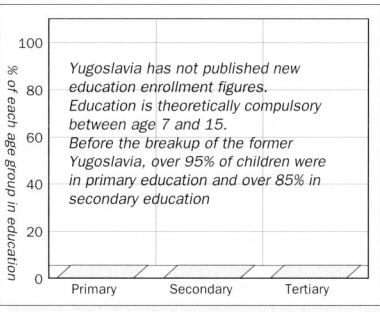

Yugoslavia has not published new education enrollment figures. Education is theoretically compulsory between age 7 and 15. Before the breakup of the former Yugoslavia, over 95% of children were in primary education and over 85% in secondary education

The education system remains in crisis. Since the outbreak of war, some wealthy families have used hard currency earnings to send their children abroad to complete their secondary education. Literacy rates in Kosovo are below average for the FRY, at 82%. There are six universities and 37 colleges.

HEALTH

1 per 530 people

Heart,
cerebrovascular
diseases, cancers

0	*Health spending as % GNP* 25

Yugoslavia does not publish health spending figures

Isolation from former trading partners has affected the quality of the health service, despite the exemption of medicines and medical supplies from sanctions. Most medicines are unaffordable to the general population, and death rates among infants and the elderly have risen dramatically.

WEALTH

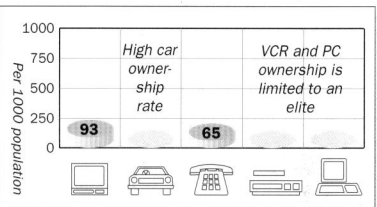

Average wage 640 dinars ($135) per month

CONSUMER GOODS OWNERSHIP

High car ownership rate 93

VCR and PC ownership is limited to an elite 65

The country as a whole has been impoverished as a result of sanctions, but those who have managed to hang on to hard currency savings are at an advantage. With the imposition of sanctions, real incomes fell dramatically, yet food prices remained higher than in much of western Europe. The impact of the suspension of sanctions in 1995 has yet to be seen. Many people were financially destroyed by the loss of their dinar savings in the bank collapses of 1992. Those who have amassed wealth largely did so by exploiting the chaos of war through the black market. One of the few areas of business expansion under sanctions was in exploiting markets for goods which were previously imported. The few rich bought sanctions-busting goods illegally imported from western Europe.

WORLD RANKING

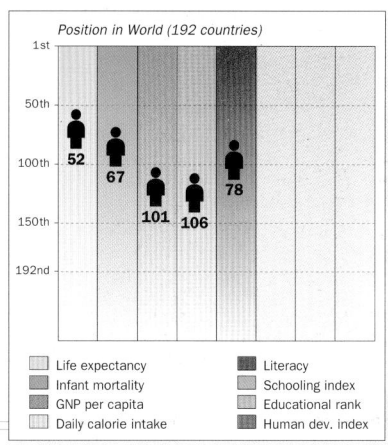

Position in World (192 countries)

52	67
101	106
78	

Life expectancy
Infant mortality
GNP per capita
Daily calorie intake
Literacy
Schooling index
Educational rank
Human dev. index

Y

ZAIRE

OFFICIAL NAME: Republic of Zaire   **CAPITAL:** Kinshasa   **POPULATION:** 43.9 million
CURRENCY: New zaire   **OFFICIAL LANGUAGE:** French

L YING IN EAST-CENTRAL AFRICA, Zaire is one of the continent's largest countries. The rainforested basin of the Congo River occupies 60% of the country; its estuary provides Zaire's only sea access. The former Belgian Congo became independent in 1960; civil war immediately broke out. President Mobutu took power in 1965, renamed the country Zaire, and instituted an increasingly corrupt and unpopular regime. His reluctance to speed the process has hampered the transition to multiparty democracy, begun in 1990. Since 1994, Zaire has been home to one million Rwandan refugees.

***The Zaire River** is navigable for 994 miles and provides one of the most convenient ways of traveling in the country.*

CLIMATE

WEATHER CHART

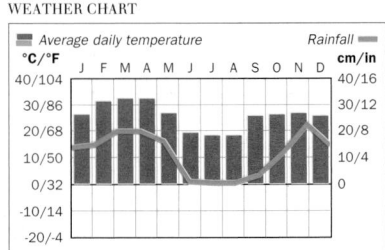

Zaire's climate is tropical and humid. Temperatures average 77°F and vary little through the year. Annual rainfall is around 60–80 inches; mountainous areas are wetter. The equator passes through the north of the country, causing marked regional variations. To its south, well-differentiated wet and dry seasons last from October–May and June–September respectively. North of the equator, a short dry season lasts from December to February; the rest of the year is wet.

TRANSPORTATION

N'Djili, Kinshasa
525,000 passengers

2 ships
15,900 dwt

THE TRANSPORTATION NETWORK

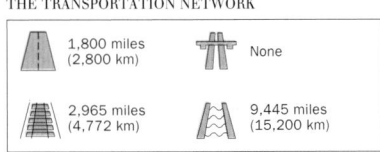

1,800 miles (2,800 km)	None
2,965 miles (4,772 km)	9,445 miles (15,200 km)

The Congo (known locally as the Zaire) and its many tributaries provide the main means of communication. Zaire's size and the fact that most of it is covered by dense rainforest have severely limited the development of road and rail networks. Many forest settlements are inaccessible except by air. Road maintenance, always poor, has virtually ceased outside the main towns since 1990, isolating even more settlements away from the main rivers.

TOURISM

   13,000 visitors   Down 41% in 1994

MAIN OVERSEAS ARRIVALS

- Belgium 12%
- France 9%
- Zambia 8%
- USA 7%
- Italy 5%
- Other 59%

% of total arrivals

Zaire's attractions lie in its scenery, wildlife and the vibrant music of Kinshasa's many bands. Paramount is the Congo, 10 miles wide in places and Africa's longest river after the Nile. President Mobutu's regime, however, has not encouraged tourism. Official restrictions on foreigners traveling around the country, combined with negligible tourism facilities outside the towns, have kept all but a few independent travelers away. Most of these have avoided Zaire since 1990 and the once-large number of business visitors has also collapsed.

PEOPLE

Kiswahili, Tshiluba, Kikongo, Lingala, French   49 people per sq. mile

THE URBAN/RURAL POPULATION SPLIT

29%   71%

RELIGIOUS PERSUASION

- Roman Catholic 50%
- Protestant 20%
- Kimbanguist 10%
- Other 10%
- Muslim 10%

ETHNIC MAKEUP

- Bantu and Hamitic 45%
- Other 55%

Zaire is ethnically diverse, with more than 12 main groups and around 190 smaller ones. The majority are of Bantu origin, but there are also large Hamitic and Nilotic populations, mainly in the north and northeast. Zaire's original inhabitants, the forest Pygmies, today form a tiny and marginalized group. The population is very unevenly distributed. The Shaba mining area and major urban centers are densely populated, while the rainforests have a density of less than 8 people per square mile. Those in remoter areas have always lived on the margins of the cash economy. Since 1990, however, hyperinflation has forced the majority into a subsistence lifestyle.

President Mobutu managed to contain ethnic tensions inherited from the colonial period during most of his rule. Since 1990, however, there have been outbreaks of ethnic violence and "cleansing," notably in Shaba Kivu and Kasai provinces. Over 6,000 people were reported to have been killed in clashes during 1993. Belgium has accused Mobutu of encouraging ethnic strife to delay democratic change.

POPULATION AGE BREAKDOWN

% of population by age group	0–14	15–64	65+

	1960	1970	1980	1990	2000
65+	2.9%	2.8%	2.8%	2.9%	2.8%
15–64	53.1%	52.9%	51.2%	49.8%	49.4%
0–14	44%	44.3%	46%	47.3%	47.8%

ZAIRE

Total Land Area : 2 267 600 sq. km
(875 520 sq. miles)

POPULATION

▣	over 1 000 000
◉	over 500 000
◎	over 100 000
○	over 50 000
●	over 10 000
•	under 10 000

LAND HEIGHT

	2000m/6562ft
	1000m/3281ft
	500m/1640ft
	200m/656ft
	Sea Level

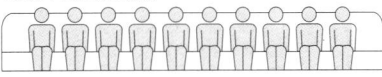

POLITICS

1987/1997

President Marshal
Mobutu Sese Seko

THE STATE OF THE PARTIES

HCR-PT 738 members

A new transitional legislature, the High Council of the
Republic-Parliament of Transition (HCR-PT), which combines the
previous opposition administrations, was formed in 1994
and elected as prime minister Léon Kengo wa Donga, whose
authority has subsequently been accepted by all sides.

President Mobutu Sese Seko has ruled
Zaire since 1965.

MAIN POLITICAL ISSUE
The transition to democracy
The fundamental problem facing Zaire
is how to force President Mobutu to
fulfil his 1990 promise of instituting a
multiparty democracy. All his actions
since have made clear his intention to
hang on to power at all costs. However,
since 1994 he has been effectively
stripped of many powers by the
transitional legislature, and has been
forced to relinquish control of the treasury
and armed forces to the prime minister.
Nevertheless he continues to seek the
delay of multiparty elections. At the same
time, the economy has fallen apart.

PROFILE
From 1965 to 1989, President Mobutu's
absolute rule combined repression with

Kengo wa Donga,
Zaire's prime
minister since 1994.

President Mobutu,
who is under
pressure to resign.

astute political manipulation. In 1990,
growing internal opposition and foreign
pressure led him to announce moves to
multiparty democracy. A High Council,
dominated by the Sacred Union coalition
of opposition parties, was set up to
negotiate a new constitution. The
subsequent stalemate during which the
High Council and Mobutu established
rival governments was ended in 1994
when a mutually acceptable single
transitional legislature was formed and
elected a new prime minister, Kengo
wa Dongo. Kengo appears to have
gained the upper hand in the ensuing
power struggle with Mobutu. However,
elections have been delayed.

WORLD AFFAIRS

| CEPGL | Comesa | Franc | G24 | OAU |

For almost 25 years, President
Mobutu's anticommunism made
Zaire one of the leading African
allies of the West, and of the USA
in particular. Western economic
and military aid – which included
sending troops to help suppress the
1977 and 1978 invasions by exiles
based in Angola – played a critical
role in sustaining his regime. In
return, he guaranteed Western
access to Zaire's mineral wealth and
provided Angola's US-backed UNITA
rebels with bases during the 1980s.
At the same time, however,
Mobutu's political astuteness enabled
him to maintain close ties with several
communist states, notably China.
Relations with African neighbors were
more problematic, complicated by
Mobutu's support for UNITA and for
Morocco's annexation of Western
Sahara. From 1984 to 1986, Zaire
withdrew from the OAU in protest
over its support of Western
Saharan independence.
Since the late 1980s, the
changing political situation in
Eastern Europe, combined with
growing concerns about human rights
abuses and corruption in Zaire, led to
a fundamental shift in attitudes to
Mobutu. Increasingly regarded as an
embarrassment, his former supporters
stopped all but humanitarian aid from
1990 in an effort to force him to
embrace democratic reform. He has
been effectively rehabilitated since
the arrival of the huge flood of
Rwandan refugees in 1994. With Zaire
shouldering the burden of the refugees,
pressure on Mobutu has diminished.

AID

| $191m (receipts) | Down 29% in 1993 |

Zaire's importance to the West during
the Cold War brought it aid revenues
on a large scale. Between 1970 and
1989, it received $8.3 billion in
economic aid – including $1.1 billion
from the USA and $6.9 billion from
other OECD states – as well as large-
scale military assistance. Changing
political priorities led the USA to act
on long-deferred problems of human
rights abuses and misappropriation of
aid by President Mobutu. In 1990, it
suspended all but humanitarian aid;
most other donors quickly followed
suit. In 1992, the IMF declared Zaire
"non cooperative," ending any chances
of rescheduling its $10 billion foreign
debt. Non-humanitarian aid is unlikely
to be resumed until Mobutu goes and a
new democratic government is installed.

Z

CHRONOLOGY

Modern Zaire was the site of the Kongo and other powerful African kingdoms and a focus of the slave trade. Belgium's King Leopold II claimed most of the Congo basin after 1876.

❏ **1885** Congo Free State (CFS) founded as King Leopold's private fief; start of brutal colonization.

❏ **1908** Belgium takes over CFS after international outcry. Renamed Belgian Congo.

❏ **1960** Independence of Republic of Congo. Katanga (Shaba) province secedes. The UN intervenes.

❏ **1963** Katanga secession collapses.

❏ **1964** Belgian troops help crush new revolts in center and east.

❏ **1965** General Joseph-Désiré Mobutu seizes power.

❏ **1970** Mobutu elected president; makes his Popular Revolutionary Movement (MPR) sole legal party.

❏ **1971** Country renamed Zaire.

❏ **1972** Africanization of names. Becomes Mobutu Sese Seko.

❏ **1977–1978** Two invasions by former Katanga separatists repulsed with Western help.

❏ **1982** Opposition parties set up Union for Democracy and Social Progress (UDPS).

❏ **1986–1990** Growing unrest and foreign criticism of human rights abuses.

❏ **1990** Belgium suspends aid after security forces kill democracy demonstrators. April, Mobutu announces transition to multiparty rule. UDPS legalized.

❏ **1991** July, 130 opposition parties form Sacred Union coalition. National Conference (NC) convened. September, UDPS leader Etienne Tshisekedi heads short-lived "crisis government" formed by Mobutu.

❏ **1992** Tshisekedi made prime minister by NC. Mobutu sacks Tshisekedi who refuses to go; NC dissolves itself; elects 435-member High Council of the Republic (HCR).

❏ **1993** HCR endorses Tshisekedi; Mobutu appoints Faustin Birindwa as head of alternative government and reconvenes the National Assembly.

❏ **1994** January, HCR and National Assembly dissolved and reconstituted as the HCR-Transitional Parliament (PT). April, constitutional changes strengthen position of prime minister and Cabinet. June, HCR-PT elects Kengo wa Dongo prime minister.

❏ **1995** Zaire demands international assistance to support million Rwandan refugees and to encourage their return home.

DEFENSE

💲 $112m

⬇ Down 4% in 1995

0   *Defense spending as % GDP*   40

1.9%

Zaire's military has played a key role in keeping President Mobutu in power and has been responsible for widespread human rights abuses. The Israeli-trained presidential guard is the elite force. Ordinary troops, poorly equipped and poorly paid, have taken to rioting, looting and extortion.

ZAIREAN ARMED FORCES

🛡	60 main battle tanks (40 Ch Type-62, 20 Ch Type-59)	25,000 personnel
🚢	4 patrol boats	1,300 personnel
✈	22 combat aircraft (7 *Mirage* 5M, 1 *Mirage* 5DM)	1,800 personnel
🚀	None	

ECONOMICS

📊 $8.1bn

💲 3,179.93–10,624 new zaires

SCORE CARD

❏ WORLD GNP RANKING...........................84th
❏ GNP PER CAPITA $203
❏ BALANCE OF PAYMENTS.....................$–643m
❏ INFLATION 542%
❏ UNEMPLOYMENT.............................Very high

ECONOMIC PERFORMANCE INDICATOR

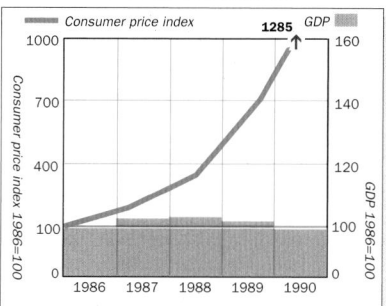

EXPORTS

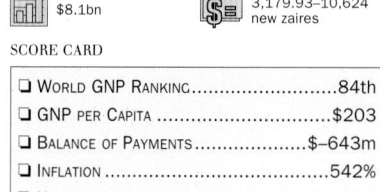

Netherlands 6%   Italy 7%   Germany 8%   Belgium-Luxembourg 21%   USA 29%   Other 29%

IMPORTS

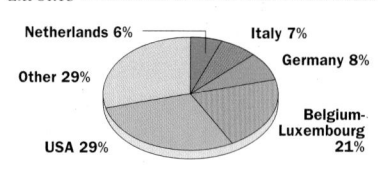

South Africa 7%   USA 8%   Germany 9%   France 10%   Belgium-Luxembourg 18%   Other 48%

STRENGTHS

Rich resource base. Minerals – notably copper, cobalt, diamonds – provide 85% of export earnings. Energy: oil; possibly Africa's largest hydropower potential. Rich soil; much unutilized arable land. Trade surplus in normal years.

WEAKNESSES

Legacy of 25 years of mismanagement and corruption: $10 billion foreign debt; withdrawal of crucial foreign aid; inadequate, disintegrating social and transportation infrastructures; lack of food self-sufficiency. Political instability. Hyperinflation. Loss of export income. Withdrawal of foreign investment.

PROFILE

In the early 1990s, political instability, combined with the legacies of 25 years of mismanagement, brought the economy near to collapse. Real GDP growth in 1990–1993 averaged –8% a year; in 1993 it reached –12%. The budget deficit remains at record levels, despite hyperinflation being reduced

from a maximum of 73,529% in late 1994 to 542% by the end of 1995. Lack of spares and power cuts have closed many mines and halted most other industry. Strikes and riots over plummeting living standards have hastened the flight of foreign capital. Subsistence farming and petty trade keep most people going. But even if political stability is restored, Zaire's immediate outlook is grim. Resumption of large-scale aid and debt relief, essential to rebuild the economy, will depend on difficult reforms and paying off arrears to the IMF and other creditors. In the long term, Zaire's rich resources hold out hope of prosperity.

ZAIRE : MAJOR BUSINESSES

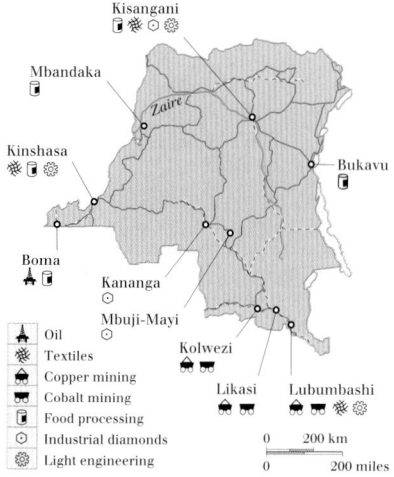

RESOURCES

 6.1bn kwh (capacity 2.83m kw)

 27,569 b/d (reserves 187,000,000 bbl)

 4.3m goats, 1.7m cattle, 1.2m pigs,

Copper, diamonds, oil, cobalt, zinc, uranium, manganese, tin, gold

ELECTRICITY GENERATION

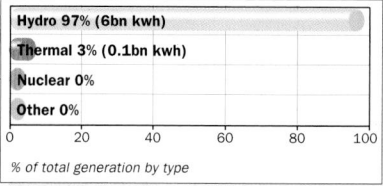

Hydro 97% (6bn kwh)

Thermal 3% (0.1bn kwh)

Nuclear 0%

Other 0%

% of total generation by type

With its huge mineral, agricultural and energy resources, Zaire should be rich. Instead, mismanagement and, since 1990, political instability have reduced it to one of the world's poorest states. Copper, cobalt and diamonds provide almost 80% of export earnings. In the 1980s, Zaire was the world's largest cobalt exporter and second-largest industrial diamond exporter. Since 1990, copper and cobalt output has collapsed and diamond smuggling is booming. Zaire has oil reserves, but its energy wealth lies in its HEP potential, which could supply much of Africa if fully exploited. Lack of maintenance has, instead, shut down many turbines and most urban areas face power cuts. Despite rich soils and the fact that 80% of people are involved in farming, Zaire is not self-sufficient in food.

ZAIRE : LAND USE

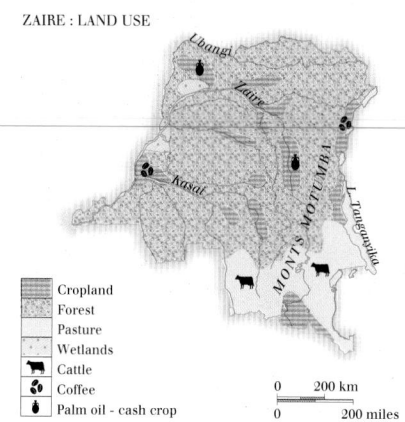

Cropland
Forest
Pasture
Wetlands
Cattle
Coffee
Palm oil - cash crop

0   200 km
0   200 miles

ENVIRONMENT

  4%

Vast size of country means many ecosystems are intact

ENVIRONMENTAL TREATIES

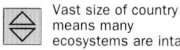

Yes   Yes   Yes

Yes   No   Yes

The predominantly virgin rainforests covering over 60% of Zaire amount to 6% of the world's, and 50% of Africa's remaining woodlands. They are home to important populations of several endangered species, including gorillas. Zaire's poor transportation network has so far prevented large-scale commercial exploitation, but fuelwood clearance is a problem. The collapse since 1990 of many urban refuse and sewage disposal systems has led to major health and pollution problems.

MEDIA

 Press censorship has relaxed since 1990, but journalists critical of Mobutu still face harassment

PUBLISHING AND BROADCAST MEDIA

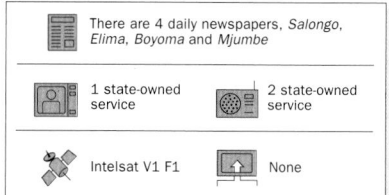

There are 4 daily newspapers, *Salongo*, *Elima*, *Boyoma* and *Mjumbe*

1 state-owned service   2 state-owned service

Intelsat V1 F1   None

In contrast to the broadcast media, the press is privately owned. Coverage of the opposition has widened since 1990, but press criticism of President Mobutu or the security forces is still generally muted. One newspaper's Kinshasa offices were burnt down in 1993 after it published a strongly anti-Mobutu article. Overtly critical journalists risk reprisals.

CRIME

 Zaire does not publish prison figures

 Violence and crime have risen rapidly since 1990

CRIME RATES

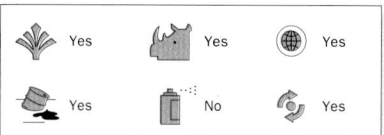

All types of crime are on the increase

Political crisis and economic collapse have exacerbated Zaire's long-standing problems of corruption and human rights abuses. Violence and crime of all kinds, including extortion, robbery, rape and murder, are on the increase. Many murders are attributed to the security forces and politically linked death squads, as are the occasional "disappearances." Ethnic violence, suppressed after 1965, has resurfaced, particularly in the south.

EDUCATION

 77%

 61,422 students

0   Education spending as % GNP   25
1%

THE EDUCATION SYSTEM

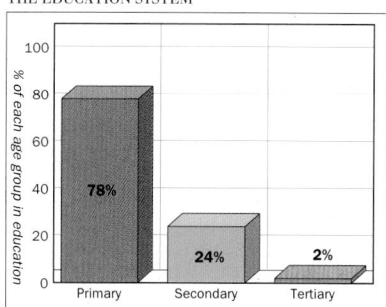

State educational provision, like health care, is patchily distributed and has faced sharp budget cuts since 1980. As a result, about 70% of schooling is now provided by the Catholic Church.

HEALTH

 1 per 13,540 people

Malaria, respiratory and diarrheal diseases

0   Health spending as % GDP   25
0.8%

State services, long underfunded, have virtually collapsed. Disease and death rates are rising, especially in rural areas. HIV/AIDS is a significant problem.

WEALTH

 A large majority of the population lives a subsistence existence

CONSUMER GOODS OWNERSHIP

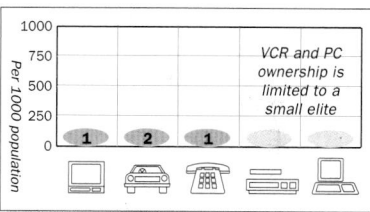

VCR and PC ownership is limited to a small elite

President Mobutu is one of the world's richest men, worth an admitted $50 million and an estimated $5 billion. Most Zaireans live in poverty.

WORLD RANKING

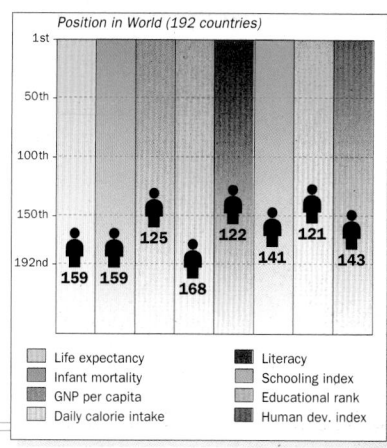

Position in World (192 countries)

Life expectancy
Infant mortality
GNP per capita
Daily calorie intake

Literacy
Schooling index
Educational rank
Human dev. index

Z

ZAMBIA

SOUTHERN AFRICA
Africa
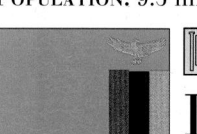

OFFICIAL NAME: Republic of Zambia CAPITAL: Lusaka
POPULATION: 9.5 million CURRENCY: Zambian kwacha OFFICIAL LANGUAGES: English, Bemba and Nyanja

LYING IN THE HEART of southern Africa, Zambia is a country of upland plateaux, bordered to the south by the Zambezi River. Its economic fortunes are tied to the copper industry. Falling copper prices in the late 1970s, and then the growing inaccessibility of remaining reserves, have led to a severe decline in the economy. In 1991, Zambia achieved a peaceful transition from single-party rule to multiparty democracy.

CLIMATE

WEATHER CHART

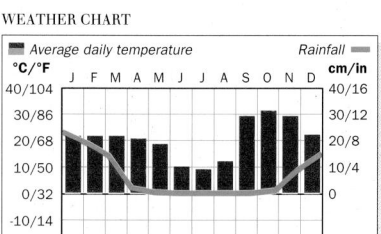

Zambia has a tropical climate, with rains from November to April. The southwest is prone to drought.

TRANSPORTATION

Lusaka International
590,000 passengers

Has no fleet

THE TRANSPORTATION NETWORK

4,090 miles (6,580 km)		None
1,345 miles (2,164 km)		1,398 miles (2,250 km)

Priorities are rehabilitating rail and road networks. The poor state of rural roads hampers harvest collections and undermines food self-sufficiency plans. Zambian Airways was liquidated in 1994.

TOURISM

 172,000 visitors   Up 3% in 1994

MAIN OVERSEAS ARRIVALS

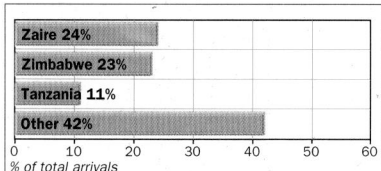

Zaire 24%
Zimbabwe 23%
Tanzania 11%
Other 42%

% of total arrivals

Wildlife, the Victoria Falls and white-water rafting on the Zambezi are Zambia's main attractions. Expansion plans are being hit by funding shortages.

PEOPLE

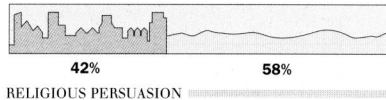
Bemba, Nyanja, Tonga, Kaonde, Lunda, Luvale, Lozi, English

34 people per sq. mile

THE URBAN/RURAL POPULATION SPLIT

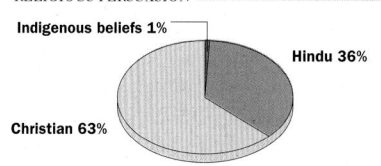
42%   58%

RELIGIOUS PERSUASION

Indigenous beliefs 1%
Hindu 36%
Christian 63%

Although ethnically heterogeneous, with more than 70 different groups, Zambia has been less affected by ethnic tension than many African states. The largest ethnic group, about 18% of the population, is the Bemba, who live in the northeast and predominate in the central Copperbelt. Other major groups are the southern Tonga people, the eastern Nyanja, and the Lozi who live to the west.

Zambia is one of Africa's most urbanized countries with many third- and fourth-generation town-dwellers in the Copperbelt, the main urban area. Urban life has done little to change the traditionally subordinate role of women in the family and politics. They are, however, increasingly involved in business and two women hold cabinet posts. The rural population live mainly by subsistence farming.

***Victoria Falls**, known to Africans as Musi-o-Tunyi (The Smoke That Thunders). Spray from the falls can be seen 19 mi. away.*

POLITICS

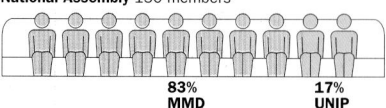
1991/1996
President
Frederick Chiluba

THE STATE OF THE PARTIES

National Assembly 150 members

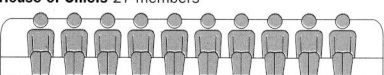

83% MMD   17% UNIP

MMD = Movement for Multiparty Democracy
UNIP = United National Independence Party

House of Chiefs 27 members

Composed of 27 chiefs representing 8 provinces

The 1991 defeat of Dr. Kenneth Kaunda and the UNIP in the first multiparty elections for 19 years expressed popular discontent with the state of the economy and official corruption. President Chiluba and the MMD government have since made little headway in revitalizing the economy, despite socially painful reforms. There have also been renewed allegations of top-level corruption. In 1995, Kaunda staged a dramatic return to politics, resuming leadership of the UNIP in advance of the 1996 elections.

WORLD AFFAIRS

 Comm   G15   NAM   OAU   SADC

Under President Kaunda, Zambia was one of Africa's leading opponents of the South African apartheid regime. The MMD is now forging close links with the new South African government.

AID

 $870m (receipts)   Down 14% in 1993

Aid levels, mainly from the EU and the World Bank, are high. Most is used to support the restructuring of the economy away from the declining mining sector. Donors are concerned at levels of bureaucratic corruption and the need to strengthen democracy.

DEFENSE

 $45m   Up 18% in 1995

Despite the relatively small budget, the 21,600-strong armed forces are well equipped. Security along the Angolan border is a main concern.

Z

ECONOMICS

$3.2bn

694.55–965.96 Zambian kwacha

SCORE CARD

- ❑ WORLD GNP RANKING........................121st
- ❑ GNP PER CAPITA $350
- ❑ BALANCE OF PAYMENTS....................$-306m
- ❑ INFLATION 53.7%
- ❑ UNEMPLOYMENT ....Widespread

STRENGTHS
Potential for self-sufficiency in food; also for export of wide range of crops. Arable land underutilized. Minerals, notably copper, cobalt and coal. Commitment of government to market-oriented reform.

WEAKNESSES
Dependence on copper for 90% of export earnings. Domestic reserves rapidly declining. Poor outlook for world copper prices. Shortage of finance for restructuring due to large deficit in balance of payments. Rescheduling payments on $7.6-billion debt take most export earnings. High inflation. Low productivity.

EXPORTS

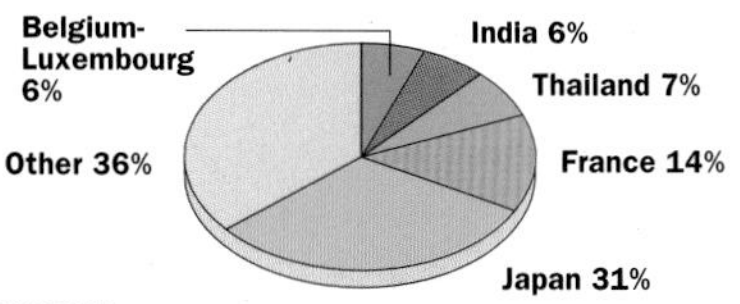
Belgium-Luxembourg 6%
India 6%
Thailand 7%
France 14%
Japan 31%
Other 36%

IMPORTS

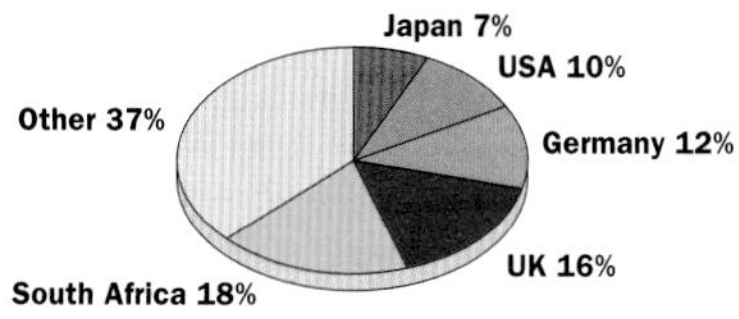
Japan 7%
USA 10%
Germany 12%
UK 16%
South Africa 18%
Other 37%

RESOURCES

7.8bn kwh (capacity 2.44m kw)

Not an oil producer; refines 23,750 b/cd

3.3m cattle, 620,000 goats, 295,000 pigs

Copper, cobalt, coal, zinc, lead, gold, emeralds, amethyst

Despite declining reserves, copper is still the key resource; Zambia is the world's sixth-largest producer. It also has rich hydropower potential.

ENVIRONMENT

9%

Official involvement in conservation projects increasing

Drought is a recurrent hazard. Rhinos are almost extinct as a result of poaching. Revenues from legal hunting are being channeled into villages to encourage support for conservation.

MEDIA

Little press censorship by government

PUBLISHING AND BROADCAST MEDIA

There are 2 daily newspapers, the *Times of Zambia* and the *Daily Mail*

1 state-controlled service

1 state-controlled service

The state-owned *Times* and *Daily Mail* face increasing competition from independents like the *Weekly Standard*.

CRIME

Zambia does not publish prison figures

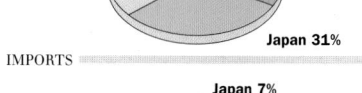

Up 26% in 1992

Cases of violent crime, burglary and rape are rising rapidly, particularly in major towns such as Lusaka and Ndola.

CHRONOLOGY

Former Northern Rhodesia was developed by Britain solely for its copper resources. Dr. Kenneth Kaunda and the UNIP took power at Zambian independence in 1964.

- ❑ **1972** UNIP one-party government.
- ❑ **1980** Attempted coup fails.
- ❑ **1982–1991** Austerity measures introduced. Corruption scandals. Pressure for democracy grows.
- ❑ **1991** Democratically elected MMD government comes to power.

EDUCATION

78%

15,343 students

Elementary education is compulsory. New fees for secondary students will hit the already low attendance rate of 16%.

HEALTH

1 per 11,430 people

Respiratory infections, diarrheal diseases, malaria

Austerity measures have resulted in health service cutbacks. HIV/AIDS is a significant and growing problem.

WEALTH

Copper miner, 8,000 kwacha ($11); per month graduate civil servant 960,000 kwacha ($1,400) per year

CONSUMER GOODS OWNERSHIP

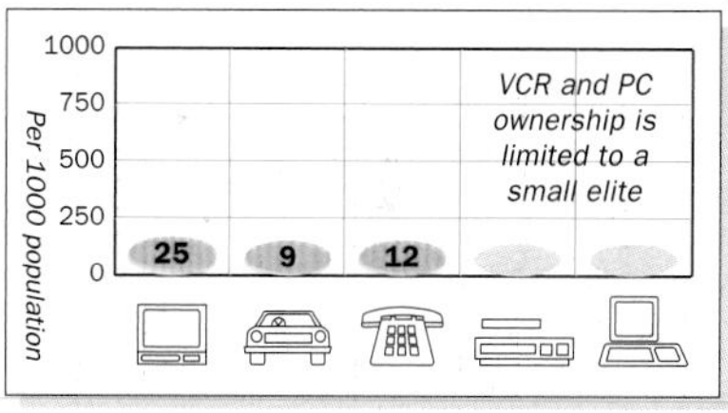
1000
750
500
250
0
Per 1000 population
25
9
12
VCR and PC ownership is limited to a small elite

Declining profits from copper mining mean that per capita GDP is lower now than at independence in 1964.

WORLD RANKING

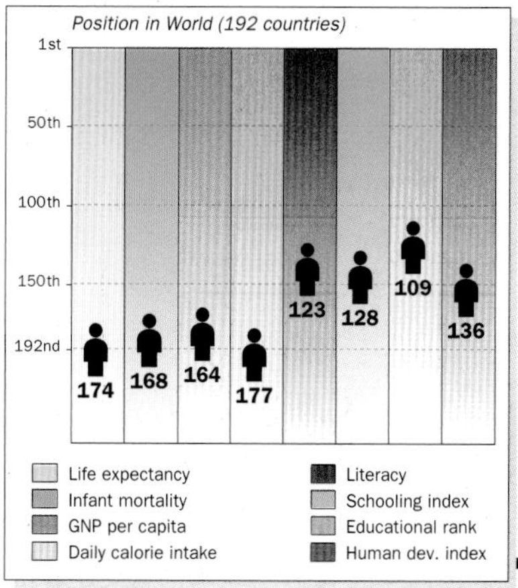
Position in World (192 countries)
1st
50th
100th
150th
192nd
174
168
164
177
123
128
109
136
Life expectancy
Infant mortality
GNP per capita
Daily calorie intake
Literacy
Schooling index
Educational rank
Human dev. index

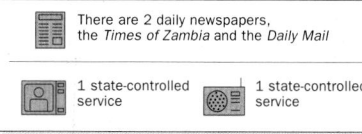

ZAMBIA

Total Land Area : 740 720 sq. km (285 992 sq. miles)

POPULATION

- over 500 000
- over 100 000
- over 50 000
- over 10 000
- under 10 000

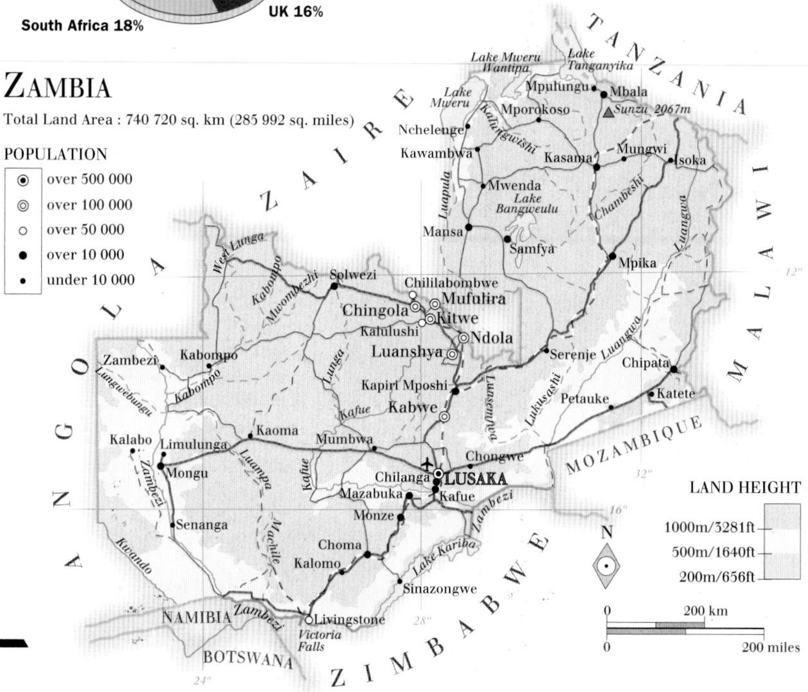
TANZANIA
ZAIRE
MALAWI
MOZAMBIQUE
ZIMBABWE
ANGOLA
NAMIBIA
BOTSWANA
Lake Mweru Wantipa
Lake Tanganyika
Lake Mweru
Lake Bangweulu
Lake Kariba
Mpulungu
Mbala
Sunzu 2067m
Mporokoso
Nchelenge
Kawambwa
Kasama
Mungwi
Isoka
Mwenda
Mansa
Samfya
Mpika
Solwezi
Chililabombwe
Mufulira
Chingola
Kitwe
Kalulushi
Ndola
Luanshya
Serenje
Chipata
Zambezi
Kabompo
Kapiri Mposhi
Kabwe
Petauke
Katete
Kalabo
Limulunga
Kaoma
Mumbwa
Mongu
Chongwe
Chilanga
LUSAKA
Mazabuka
Kafue
Monze
Senanga
Choma
Kalomo
Sinazongwe
Livingstone
Victoria Falls
Luapula
Chambeshi
Luangwa
Kafue
Lunga
Zambezi
Machile
Kwando
LAND HEIGHT
1000m/3281ft
500m/1640ft
200m/656ft
0
200 km
0
200 miles

ZIMBABWE

SOUTHERN AFRICA

Africa

OFFICIAL NAME: Republic of Zimbabwe   **CAPITAL:** Harare   **POPULATION:** 11.3 million
CURRENCY: Zimbabwe dollar   **OFFICIAL LANGUAGE:** English

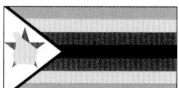

SITUATED IN SOUTHERN AFRICA, Zimbabwe is bordered by South Africa, Botswana, Zambia and Mozambique. The upland center is criss-crossed by rivers, which flow into Lake Kariba and the Zambezi River. The Zambezi possesses Zimbabwe's most spectacular natural feature, the Victoria Falls. Formerly the British colony of Southern Rhodesia, the country achieved independence in 1980 after a struggle between the white minority, led by Prime Minister Ian Smith, and the black majority, represented by Robert Mugabe's and Joshua Nkomo's Patriotic Front (PF).

***The Kariba Dam**, which has created the vast Lake Kariba on the Zambezi River, lies on Zimbabwe's northwest border with Zambia.*

CLIMATE

WEATHER CHART

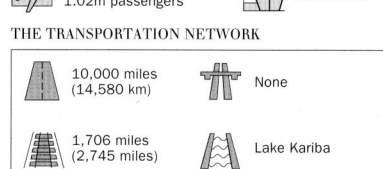

Due to altitude, Zimbabwe is comparatively temperate for a country in the tropics; humidity is also low. The rainy season occurs between November and March. But, with the exception of the eastern highlands, rainfall is erratic and drought is common. Annual rainfall ranges from 55 inches in the Eastern Highlands to 16 inches in the Limpopo valley.

TRANSPORTATION

 Harare International
1.02m passengers

 Has no fleet

THE TRANSPORTATION NETWORK

10,000 miles (14,580 km)		None	
1,706 miles (2,745 miles)		Lake Kariba	

Transportation is a high government priority. Policies include developing and updating railroads, and increasing the number of international air links.

TOURISM

1m visitors

Up 6% in 1994

MAIN OVERSEAS ARRIVALS

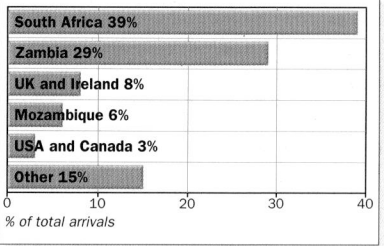

South Africa 39%	
Zambia 29%	
UK and Ireland 8%	
Mozambique 6%	
USA and Canada 3%	
Other 15%	

% of total arrivals

Tourists visit Zimbabwe for both cultural and safari holidays. The country's principal attractions are the Victoria Falls, the Kariba Dam and the many national parks. Great Zimbabwe ruins, near Masvingo, and World's View in the Matopo Hills, are of special interest. Action holidays are being developed, with canoeing trips and white-water rafting on the Zambezi, and trout fishing and climbing in the eastern highlands. Harare and Victoria Falls have conference facilities.

The government does not intend to make Zimbabwe a destination for mass-market tourism owing to fears of serious environmental damage. However, the lure of foreign exchange has encouraged the development of holiday complexes around Victoria Falls, such as Elephant Hills. Import controls relating to the tourist industry have been relaxed and prices deregulated. A two-tier pricing structure now prevails with locals paying less; foreigners must pay in hard currencies.

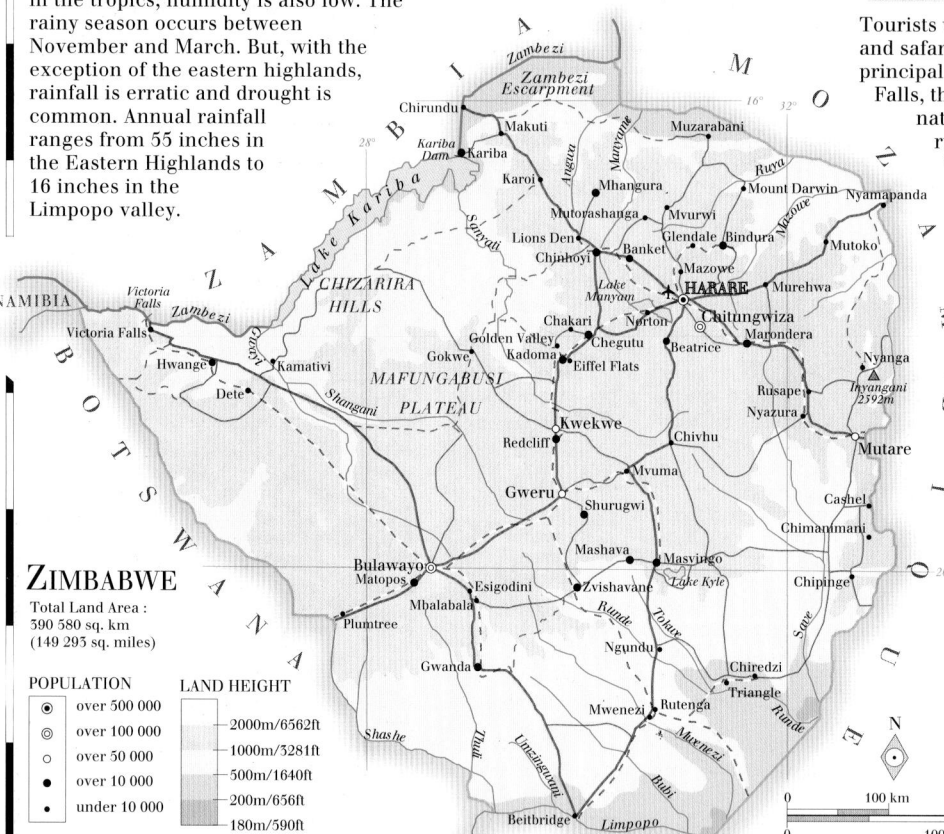

ZIMBABWE

Total Land Area :
390 580 sq. km
(149 293 sq. miles)

POPULATION

- ⊙ over 500 000
- ◎ over 100 000
- ○ over 50 000
- • over 10 000
- · under 10 000

LAND HEIGHT

- 2000m/6562ft
- 1000m/3281ft
- 500m/1640ft
- 200m/656ft
- 180m/590ft

PEOPLE

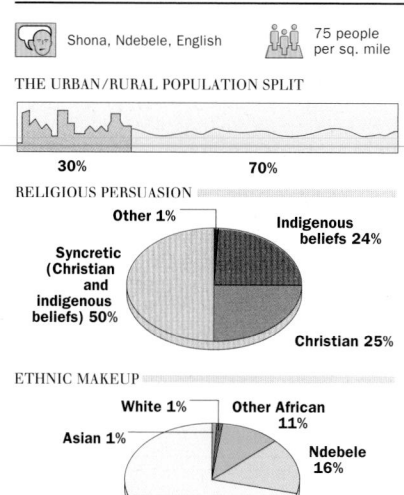

Shona, Ndebele, English

75 people per sq. mile

THE URBAN/RURAL POPULATION SPLIT

30%   70%

RELIGIOUS PERSUASION

Other 1%
Indigenous beliefs 24%
Syncretic (Christian and indigenous beliefs) 50%
Christian 25%

ETHNIC MAKEUP

White 1%
Other African 11%
Asian 1%
Ndebele 16%
Shona 71%

POPULATION AGE BREAKDOWN

%	0–14		15–64		65+
65+	2.9%	2.7%	2.6%	2.7%	2.8%
15–64	50.6%	48.2%	49.6%	52.6%	53.2%
0–14	46.5%	49.1%	47.8%	44.7%	44%
	1960	1970	1980	1990	2000

% of population by age group

There are two main ethnic groups, the Ndebele (popularly known as the Matabele) in the south and the Shona (known as the Mashona) in the north. The Mashona outnumber the Matabele by about four to one. Europeans and Asians comprise 2% of the population.

Tension between the Matabele and the Mashona was rife in the 1980s. This was caused by the attempt of President Mugabe's ruling Zimbabwe African National Union (ZANU–PF), linked to the Mashona, to suppress the leading opposition party, the predominantly Matabele Zimbabwe African People's Union (PF-ZAPU). The conflict was most intense in 1983, when the army killed 1,500 Matabele. Tension abated following the Unity Accord of 1987 and the 1990 appointment of ZAPU leader Joshua Nkomo as vice-president.

As a legacy of colonial rule, whites are still generally far more affluent than blacks. This imbalance has been somewhat redressed by government policies to increase black education and white-collar employment.

Families are large and almost half the population is under 15. Zimbabwean society is traditionally patriarchal, but the number of women managers is growing, and individuals such as Sally Mugabe, late wife of the president, have achieved political prominence.

POLITICS

2000

President Robert Gabriel Mugabe

THE STATE OF THE PARTIES

House of Assembly 150 members

20% Appointed

78% ZANU-PF   2% ZANU-N

ZANU-PF = Zimbabwe African National Union – Patriotic Front
ZANU-N = Zimbabwe African National Union – Ndonga
30 seats are set aside for presidental appointments and traditional chiefs

Zimbabwe is constitutionally a multiparty state; 80% of MPs are elected and serve five-year terms. Every six years, parliament elects the president, who is eligible for reelection.

MAIN POLITICAL ISSUES
Political dominance of ZANU-PF
At independence, the PF was a coalition of ZANU, led by Robert Mugabe, and ZAPU, led by Joshua Nkomo. As ZANU-PF became more powerful, the coalition split and PF-ZAPU supporters resorted to guerrilla activity. This continued until 1987, when a unity agreement was signed with Nkomo, later made vice-president. With the main opposition party absorbed, Mugabe, now president, attempted to assert a one-party, socialist state. These plans were abandoned in 1991 and other parties have since emerged. But repression continues: student dissension has been quashed and the civil service is closed to non-supporters of the ruling party.

Land redistribution
In an attempt to redistribute wealth from the white to the black community, the government introduced the Land Acquisition Act in 1992. This allowed the compulsory purchase of white-owned farmland. The Act provoked a storm of protest, including allegations of corruption.

PROFILE
The ruling ZANU–PF appears to have lost direction following the collapse of the eastern bloc and the end of apartheid in South Africa. The influence of its once-dominant leader, Robert Mugabe, is waning, but he has no clear successor. The only candidate in the 1996 presidential election, Mugabe won the support of less than 30% of the electorate. Political apathy is encouraged by the absence of credible parties able to offer strong opposition.

Robert Mugabe, elected prime minister in 1980 and president in 1987.

Simon Muzenda, senior vice-president. Joint vice-president is Joshua Nkomo.

AID

 $460m (receipts)   Down 37% in 1993

In January 1992, the IMF agreed the equivalent of US$484 million to support an economic and financial reform program. Zimbabwe is also to receive US$117 million in grants, over five years, from the EU. Bilateral donors, including the UK, France, Germany, Denmark and the USA, intend their aid to be used to sustain the local economy and be directed at small farmers. However, the government directs much of it towards large industrial projects. In the 1980s, Zimbabwe sent food to help relieve famine in Ethiopia.

WORLD AFFAIRS

 Comm   G15   NAM   OAU   SADC

Zimbabwe stresses close cooperation with its neighbors, in the context of SADC and the Preferential Trade Area for East and South Africa, and has consistently followed a policy of non-alignment. President Mugabe was chairman of the Non-Aligned Movement from 1985 to 1989. His regime had an activist stance against South Africa and apartheid but, since the 1990 freeing of Nelson Mandela, relations have improved. However, a consistent policy is still evolving.

For ideological reasons and to maintain access to the sea via the Beira corridor, the government began providing military assistance to the socialist Mozambican government against the RENAMO guerrillas in 1982. President Mugabe then played a major mediating role, resulting in a peace accord in August 1992. In 1993, 150 troops were sent to Somalia and training exercises began with the USA.

Z

CHRONOLOGY

In 1953, the British colony of Southern Rhodesia (Zimbabwe) became part of the Federation of Rhodesia and Nyasaland with Northern Rhodesia (Zambia) and Nyasaland (Malawi).

❏ **1959** African National Congress (ANC), led by Joshua Nkomo, banned.
❏ **1961** Nkomo forms ZAPU.
❏ **1962** ZAPU banned. Racial segregationist Rhodesian Front (RF) wins elections. Winston Field prime minister.
❏ **1963** African nationalists in Northern Rhodesia and Nyasaland demand dissolution of Federation. ZANU, offshoot of ZAPU, formed by Rev. Sithole and Robert Mugabe.
❏ **1964** Ian Smith new RF prime minister. British conditions for independence, including majority rule, rejected. ZANU banned.
❏ **1965** May, RF reelected. November, state of emergency declared (renewed every year until 1990). Smith makes unilateral declaration of independence. UK imposes economic sanctions. ANC, ZANU and ZAPU begin guerrilla war.
❏ **1970** Rhodesia declared republic.
❏ **1974** RF regime agrees ceasefire terms with African nationalists.
❏ **1975–1979** Intermittent negotiations between British government, the RF and African nationalists to reach constitutional settlement.
❏ **1976** ZANU and ZAPU unite into Patriotic Front (PF).
❏ **1977** PF backed by "frontline" African states: Mozambique, Tanzania, Botswana and Zambia.
❏ **1979** Internal settlement drafted by Ian Smith and moderate African nationalists. Rejected by PF.
❏ **1979** Constitution agreed.
❏ **1980** Independence. Following violent election campaign, Robert Mugabe becomes prime minister of ZANU-PF/ZAPU-PF coalition. Relations severed with South Africa.
❏ **1983–1984** Unrest in Matabeleland, ZAPU-PF's power base.
❏ **1985** Elections return ZANU-PF, with manifesto to create one-party state. Many ZAPU-PF members arrested.
❏ **1987** Unrest in Matabeleland. June, ban on ZAPU-PF. September, provision for white seats in parliament abolished. November, ban on ZAPU-PF lifted. December, ZANU-PF and ZAPU-PF sign unity agreement (merge in 1989). Mugabe elected president.
❏ **1990** Elections won by ZANU-PF. Mugabe reelected president.
❏ **1991** Mugabe abandons plan for one-party state.

DEFENSE

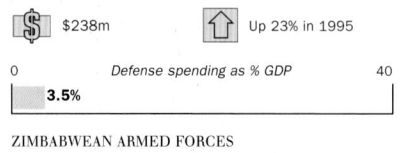

$238m   Up 23% in 1995

0   *Defense spending as % GDP*   40
3.5%

ZIMBABWEAN ARMED FORCES

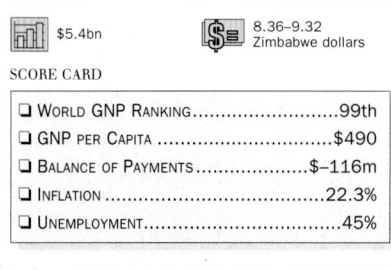

40 main battle tanks (Ch T-59, Ch T-69)	41,000 personnel	
None	None	
52 combat aircraft (12 *Hunter*)	4,000 personnel	
None		

The military appears to be under the complete control of President Mugabe, who is Commander-in-Chief of the armed forces. In the early 1980s, however, some soldiers deserted to fight government forces in the Matabele bush. They provided the nucleus of dissident movements that plagued the regime until the Unity Accord of 1987. Zimbabwe receives military aid and training from the UK and South Korea. Zimbabwe's policy of non-alignment means that it has entered into no formal military alliances. However, it supported the Mozambican regime against RENAMO guerrillas and also backed the US-led operation in Somalia in 1992-1995.

ECONOMICS

$5.4bn   8.36–9.32 Zimbabwe dollars

SCORE CARD

❏ WORLD GNP RANKING 99th
❏ GNP PER CAPITA $490
❏ BALANCE OF PAYMENTS .... $–116m
❏ INFLATION 22.3%
❏ UNEMPLOYMENT 45%

EXPORTS

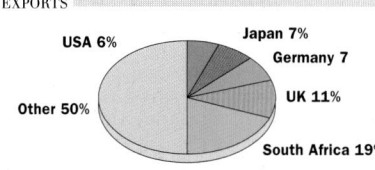

USA 6%
Japan 7%
Germany 7
UK 11%
Other 50%
South Africa 19%

IMPORTS

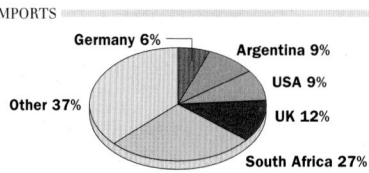

Germany 6%
Argentina 9%
USA 9%
Other 37%
UK 12%
South Africa 27%

STRENGTHS

The most broadly based African economy after South Africa. Sound infrastructure. Unrivalled international credit rating in sub-Saharan Africa, owing to careful policy of debt-servicing in 1980s. Virtual self-sufficiency in food and energy.

WEAKNESSES

Drought has hit agriculture, and also industry, owing to reduction in output of hydroelectric power. Large balance of payments and budgetary deficits. High inflation; unemployment over 40%. Belated moves towards market-oriented economy.

PROFILE

In the 1980s, the government's verbal commitment to socialist policies was in practice tempered by pragmatism. The

ECONOMIC PERFORMANCE INDICATOR

— Consumer price index   GDP

main aim was to correct the imbalance between black and white incomes. In 1991, faced with growing balance of payments problems and a need to create jobs, the government embarked on a five-year structural adjustment program which marked a radical reassessment of priorities. This move to a more market-oriented economy has had heavy social costs, pushing up unemployment and inflation, while leading to cuts in social welfare.

ZIMBABWE : MAJOR BUSINESSES

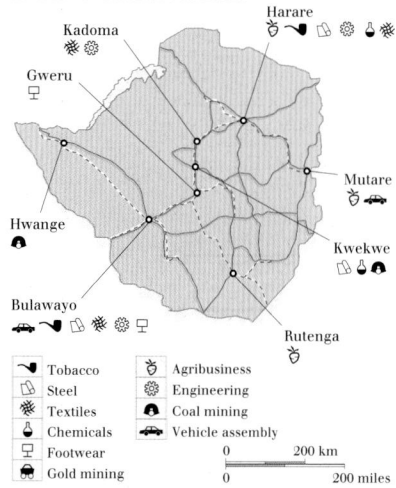

Tobacco		Agribusiness	
Steel		Engineering	
Textiles		Coal mining	
Chemicals		Vehicle assembly	
Footwear			
Gold mining			

0   200 km
0   200 miles

RESOURCES

 8bn kwh (capacity 2.04m kw)

 21,800 tons

 4.5m cattle, 2.5m goats, 550,000 sheep,

 Gold, coal, asbestos, nickel, copper, silver, iron, emeralds, lithium

ELECTRICITY GENERATION

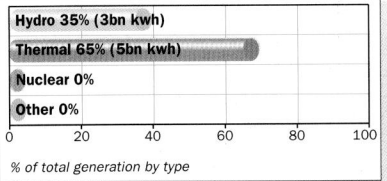

Hydro 35% (3bn kwh)
Thermal 65% (5bn kwh)
Nuclear 0%
Other 0%

% of total generation by type

Almost 40% of Zimbabwe's electricity needs are met by hydropower, notably from the Kariba Dam, jointly owned with Zambia. The state power company is seeking to maximize capacity and to undertake long-term development. In 1991, the government agreed to the construction of an extension facility at Kariba South, and a joint HEP station at Bartoka Gorge with Zambia. An oil pipeline from Beira, Mozambique, to Mutare is being extended to Harare. Coal mining is expanding at Hwange to exploit deposits of 400 million tons.

ENVIRONMENT

 8% (1% partially protected)

 Zimbabwe still suffers the after-effects of drought

ENVIRONMENTAL TREATIES

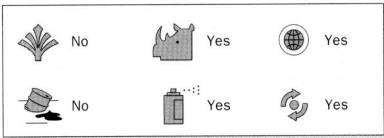

No	Yes	Yes
No	Yes	Yes

The 1991–1992 drought left half the population in need of drought relief, and used up 20% of public spending.

In communal areas, the land is suffering from overpopulation and overstocking. Deforestation, soil erosion and deterioration of wildlife and water resources are widespread.

Measures have been taken to protect the black rhinoceros, including moving animals to safer areas and combating poaching – patrols have killed 150 poachers since 1986. The government also supports a scheme for dehorning rhinos – the horn is the poachers' main target. In 1992, Zimbabwe argued that elephants no longer required special protection. However, the Convention on International Trade in Endangered Species disagreed. It claimed that much poaching still exists, and alleged collusion on the part of the army.

MEDIA

 There is no official censorship

PUBLISHING AND BROADCAST MEDIA

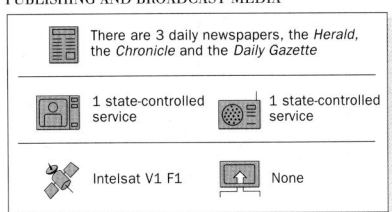

There are 3 daily newspapers, the *Herald*, the *Chronicle* and the *Daily Gazette*	
1 state-controlled service	1 state-controlled service
Intelsat V1 F1	None

The press is free, but the state has a controlling interest in the two main newspapers. There are, however, a great number of politically independent smaller newspapers and periodicals.

CRIME

 21,000 prisoners

Up 9% in 1991

CRIME RATES

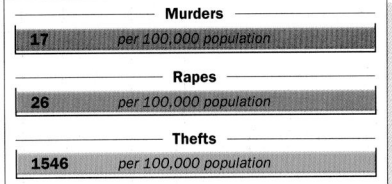

Murders	
17	per 100,000 population
Rapes	
26	per 100,000 population
Thefts	
1546	per 100,000 population

Urban areas have a high incidence of murder and narcotics-related offences. With the worsening economic climate, crime is increasing in rural areas. The secret service, the Central Intelligence Organization, has come in for international criticism for its alleged abuses of human rights.

EDUCATION

 85%

 61,553 students

Education spending as % GNP
0 — 25
7.4%

THE EDUCATION SYSTEM

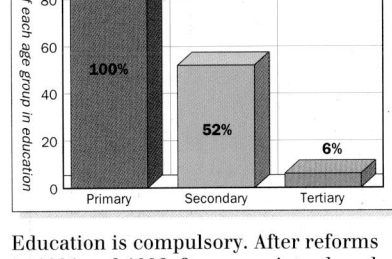

% of each age group in education

- Primary: **100%**
- Secondary: **52%**
- Tertiary: **6%**

Education is compulsory. After reforms in 1991 and 1992, fees were introduced for elementary and secondary education. Schooling is based on the British system and instruction is in English. The emphasis is now on vocational training to create a work force with the skills in agriculture, medicine and engineering that Zimbabwe needs.

ZIMBABWE : LAND USE

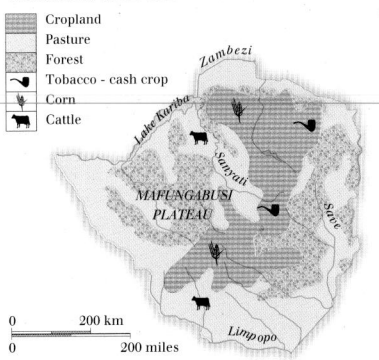

	Cropland
	Pasture
	Forest
	Tobacco - cash crop
	Corn
	Cattle

0 — 200 km
0 — 200 miles

HEALTH

 1 per 7,100 people

Tuberculosis, accidents, malaria, heart disease cancers, typhoid

Health spending as % GDP
0 — 25
3.2%

Free to those on less than a minimum wage, the health system is short of expertise and staff. The government has been slow to react to the spread of AIDS. In 1991, 28.5% of the work force were reported to be HIV positive.

WEALTH

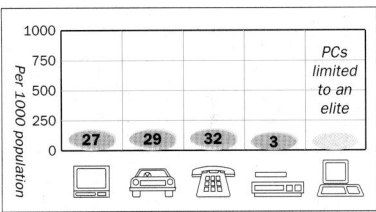

Bus driver, 600 Zimbabwe dollars a month ($67); schoolteacher, 1,500 Zimbabwe dollars a month ($167).

CONSUMER GOODS OWNERSHIP

Per 1000 population

PCs limited to an elite

| 27 | 29 | 32 | 3 | |

In the 1980s, "Growth with Equity" policies lessened the gap between blacks and whites. Growth now has priority over wealth redistribution.

WORLD RANKING

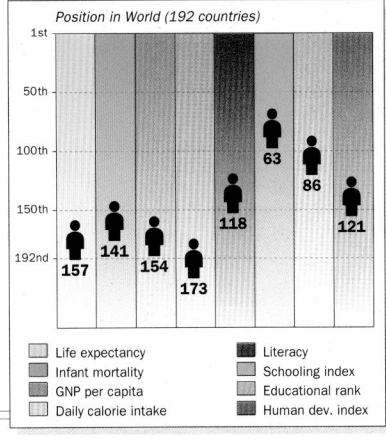

Position in World (192 countries)

| 157 | 141 | 154 | 173 | 118 | 63 | 86 | 121 |

Life expectancy	Literacy
Infant mortality	Schooling index
GNP per capita	Educational rank
Daily calorie intake	Human dev. index

Z

OVERSEAS TERRITORIES & DEPENDENCIES

DESPITE THE RAPID process of decolonization since 1945 (pages 46-49), roughly 13 million people around the world still live in non-sovereign territories under the protection of the UK, USA, France, Portugal, Netherlands, Denmark, Norway, Australia or New Zealand. These remnants of former colonial empires may have persisted for economic, strategic or political reasons.

Hong Kong, the most populous, reverts to Chinese control in 1997. Others await political developments, such as referenda, which will determine their future status. Finally, a large group of territories are considered too small, remote or weak to be able to survive as independent nations.

Svalbard
(to Norway)

*BARENTS
SEA*

Jan Mayen
(to Norway)

UNITED KINGDOM

The UK still has the largest number of overseas territories in the world. They are split into Crown colonies, Crown dependencies and dependent territories. The distinction between each is largely constitutional, since most sustain a large degree of local autonomy. Britain generally operates a policy of non-interference. If a territory expresses a constitutional desire for formal independence then it may have it, as long as it can form a viable independent country.

Faeroe Islands
(to Denmark)

*NORTH
SEA*

Isle of Man
(to UK)

UNITED
KINGDOM

NORWAY

BALTIC SEA

DENMARK

NETHERLANDS

Channel Islands:
Guernsey and Jersey
(to UK)

EUROPE

FRANCE

PORTUGAL

Gibraltar
(to UK)

MEDITERRANEAN SEA

A S I A

*SEA OF
JAPAN*

*YELLOW
SEA*

*EAST
CHINA
SEA*

A F R I C A

*ARABIAN
SEA*

Hong Kong (to UK)
Macao
(to Portugal)
Paracel
Islands
(Disputed)

Northern Mariana
Islands (to US)

Guam (to US)

*SOUTH
CHINA SEA*

Spratly Islands
(Disputed)

JAVA SEA

Ascension
(Administered by
St Helena)

British Indian
Ocean Territory
(to UK)

Cocos (Keeling) Islands
(to Australia)

*ARAFURA
SEA*

Mayotte (to France)

Christmas Island
(to Australia)

Ashmore &
Cartier Islands
(to Australia)

St Helena
(to UK)

*ATLANTIC
OCEAN*

Réunion (to France)

*INDIAN
OCEAN*

Cora
Isla
(to Aus

AUSTRALIA

Europa
(Administered by Réunion)

Bassas da India
(Administered by Réunion)

Tristan da Cunha
(Administered by
St Helena)

Gough Island
(Administered by St Helena)

Amsterdam Island

St. Paul Island

French Southern &
Antarctic Territories
(France)

NEW ZEALAND

New Zealand's government has no desire to retain any overseas territories. However, the economic weakness of its dependent territory Tokelau and its freely-associated states, Niue and the Cook Islands, has forced New Zealand to remain responsible for their foreign policy and defense.

Crozet Islands

Kerguelen

Heard & McDonald Islands
(to Australia)

Bouvet Island
(to Norway)

*French Southern and Antarctic territories
are not included in the following section.
Any territories which involve an Antarctic
claim are not shown.*

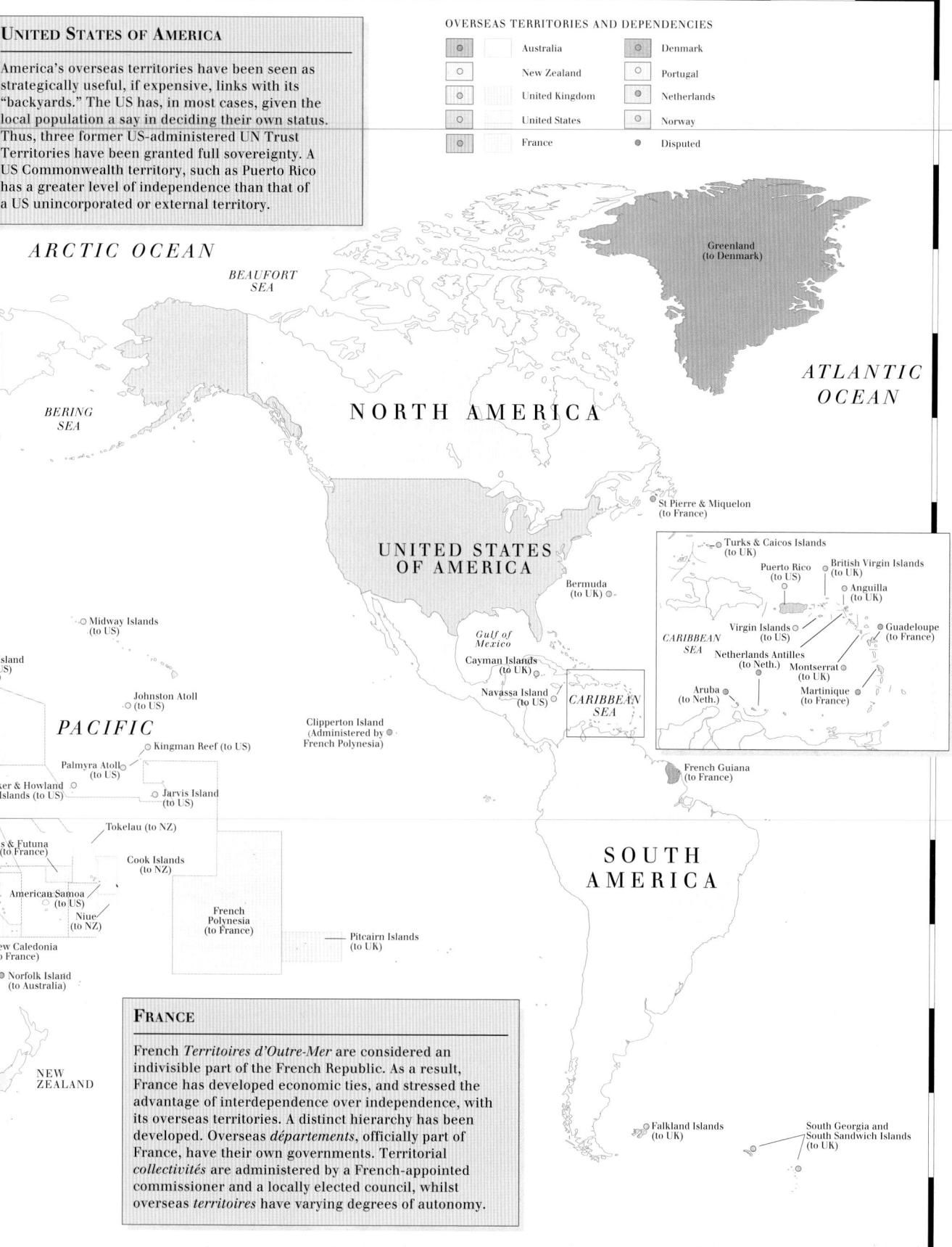

UNITED STATES OF AMERICA

America's overseas territories have been seen as strategically useful, if expensive, links with its "backyards." The US has, in most cases, given the local population a say in deciding their own status. Thus, three former US-administered UN Trust Territories have been granted full sovereignty. A US Commonwealth territory, such as Puerto Rico has a greater level of independence than that of a US unincorporated or external territory.

OVERSEAS TERRITORIES AND DEPENDENCIES

Australia	Denmark
New Zealand	Portugal
United Kingdom	Netherlands
United States	Norway
France	Disputed

ARCTIC OCEAN

BEAUFORT SEA

BERING SEA

NORTH AMERICA

Greenland (to Denmark)

ATLANTIC OCEAN

UNITED STATES OF AMERICA

Bermuda (to UK)

Midway Islands (to US)

Gulf of Mexico

Cayman Islands (to UK)

Navassa Island (to US)

Johnston Atoll (to US)

Island US)

PACIFIC

Clipperton Island (Administered by French Polynesia)

Kingman Reef (to US)

Palmyra Atoll (to US)

ker & Howland Islands (to US)

Jarvis Island (to US)

CARIBBEAN SEA

Turks & Caicos Islands (to UK)

Puerto Rico (to US)

British Virgin Islands (to UK)

Anguilla (to UK)

CARIBBEAN SEA

Virgin Islands (to US)

Netherlands Antilles (to Neth.)

Guadeloupe (to France)

Montserrat (to UK)

Aruba (to Neth.)

Martinique (to France)

French Guiana (to France)

SOUTH AMERICA

Tokelau (to NZ)

s & Futuna (to France)

Cook Islands (to NZ)

American Samoa (to US)

Niue (to NZ)

French Polynesia (to France)

Pitcairn Islands (to UK)

ew Caledonia France)

Norfolk Island (to Australia)

NEW ZEALAND

Falkland Islands (to UK)

South Georgia and South Sandwich Islands (to UK)

FRANCE

French *Territoires d'Outre-Mer* are considered an indivisible part of the French Republic. As a result, France has developed economic ties, and stressed the advantage of interdependence over independence, with its overseas territories. A distinct hierarchy has been developed. Overseas *départements*, officially part of France, have their own governments. Territorial *collectivités* are administered by a French-appointed commissioner and a locally elected council, whilst overseas *territoires* have varying degrees of autonomy.

St Pierre & Miquelon (to France)

AMERICAN SAMOA

STATUS: Unincorporated territory of the USA **CLAIMED:** 1900
CAPITAL: Pago Pago **POPULATION:** 51,000 **DENSITY:** 663 per sq. mile

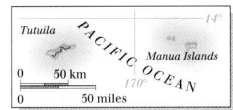
AMERICAN SAMOA CONSISTS of five volcanic islands and two coral atolls in the southern Pacific Ocean. It has a tropical climate with an average annual rainfall of 197 inches. Typhoons and tropical storms are common from December to March.

Samoans are among the last remaining true Polynesians. *Fa'a Samoa*, meaning the Samoan way of life, still directs Samoan society. The extended family, the *aiga*, forms the base of Samoan life, with chiefs still holding a central role in government. This has created tension, however, with a younger generation attracted by the lifestyle of *fa'a America*. As a result, many young Samoans have emigrated to the USA. One-fifth of all tuna consumed in the USA passes through Pago Pago's canneries, so employing 25% of the population. Recently, in an effort to diversify the economy, the American Samoan government has tried to encourage the development of other light industries and tourism.

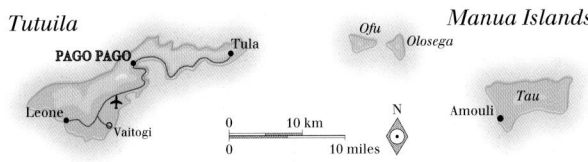

ANGUILLA

STATUS: British dependent territory **CLAIMED:** 1650
CAPITAL: The Valley **POPULATION:** 9,000 **DENSITY:** 249 per sq. mile

ANGUILLA IS SITUATED at the northern end of the Leeward Islands, in the Caribbean. It has a subtropical climate, the heat and humidity being tempered by trade winds. In 1967 Anguillans refused to follow St. Kitts and Nevis into independence, preferring instead to retain the economic stability that came with dependent status. The People's Progressive Party, renamed the Anguilla National Alliance in 1980, dominated politics until ousted by an opposition coalition in 1994. Chief Minister Hubert Hughes continues a policy of developing the tourist sector and attracting foreign investment, particularly in offshore banking. Economic growth in 1994 was due largely to tourism, the expansion of which is controlled in order to preserve Anguilla's natural resources and beauty.

The island of Sombrero, 30 miles north of Anguilla, is also part of the territory

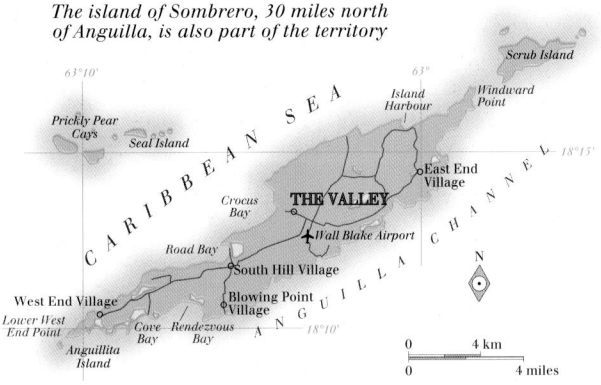

ARUBA

STATUS: Autonomous part of the Netherlands **CLAIMED:** 1643
CAPITAL: Oranjestad **POPULATION:** 69,000 **DENSITY:** 928 per sq. mile

ONE OF THE SMALLEST islands in the Dutch Caribbean, Aruba lies 15 miles off the coast of Venezuela. It has a tropical climate moderated by constant trade winds sweeping in from the Atlantic.

Formerly part of the Netherlands Antilles, Aruba became a separate dependency in 1986. In 1990, a new agreement with the Dutch government ended a transition to full independence. The Netherlands voiced concern over the island's security and the danger of it becoming a base for narcotics-trafficking and the Aruban government, currently led by Hendrik Eman, questioned the desirability of full independence, citing high unemployment and economic instability. The economy, formerly dependent on oil refining, has diversified, with tourism and offshore finance now the most important sectors. The oil refinery, closed in 1985, was reopened in 1991 by Coastal Oil of Texas. Major refining expansion work began in 1994.

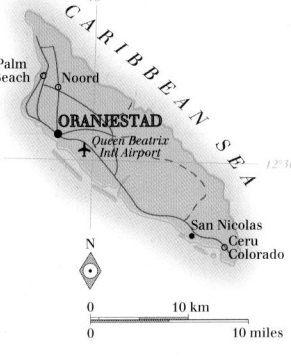

Palm Beach, Aruba, *also known as the Turquoise Coast, lies on the western side of the island. The beach stretches for 6 miles and is the site of a low-rise beach resort.*

ASHMORE & CARTIER IS.

STATUS: Australian external territory **CLAIMED:** 1978
CAPITAL: Not applicable **POPULATION:** None

LYING IN THE Timor Sea, the three Ashmore Islets and Cartier Island are separated by 37 miles of water, and cover a land area of 2 square miles. They are governed from Darwin, capital of the Northern Territories, over 490 miles to the west. Under an agreement with the Australian government, the sand and coral islands' waters are fished by Indonesians. However, reports of overfishing have led the government to monitor their activities. In 1983 Ashmore reef was made a nature reserve.

BAKER & HOWLAND IS.

STATUS: Unincorporated territory of the USA **CLAIMED:** 1856
CAPITAL: Not applicable **POPULATION:** None

THE UNINHABITED BAKER and Howland Islands lie 1,615 miles southwest of Hawaii, in the Pacific Ocean. The USA's interest in the two coral islands centered on rich guano deposits, which were worked out by 1891. The islands were again inhabited between 1936 until 1942, becoming a stop for trans-Pacific flights. They are now a refuge for over a million birds.

LAND HEIGHT ▭ above Sea Level ▭ 200m/656ft ▭ 500m/1640ft ▭ 1000m/3281ft ▭ 1500m/4572ft ▭ above 2000m/6562ft

BERMUDA

STATUS: British Crown colony   CLAIMED: 1612
CAPITAL: Hamilton   POPULATION: 63,000   DENSITY: 3,081 per sq. mile

SITUATED MORE THAN 560 miles off the coast of South Carolina, USA, Bermuda consists of a chain of over 150 coral islands. The Gulf Stream, flowing between Bermuda and America's eastern seaboard,

keeps the climate humid and mild, though hurricanes sometimes occur between June and November. Bermuda is racially mixed; some 60% of the population are black, the remaining 40% are mixed-race and white. Racial tension, which existed in the 1960s and 1970s, has declined in the face of a more representative electoral system which was established after a Royal Commission visited Bermuda in 1978. Despite changes made to the constitution in 1979, all elections have been won by the conservative United Bermuda Party (UBP). Its veteran leader, and the island's premier, Sir John Swan, resigned both posts in 1995 when voters in a referendum decisively rejected his campaign for independence from the UK. David Saul replaced him. Major issues are social and economic challenges posed by the 1995 withdrawal of the US naval base, environmental issues and narcotics-trafficking. A tourist and tax haven, Bermuda has one of the highest per capita incomes in the world. Bermuda is also a leading insurance market and operates one of the world's largest flag-of-convenience shipping fleets.

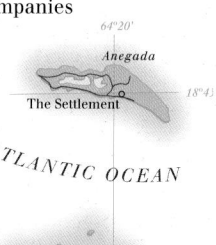

Bermuda has one of the highest densities of golf courses in the world. Eight courses have now been developed.

BOUVET ISLAND

STATUS: Norwegian dependency   CLAIMED: 1927
CAPITAL: Not applicable   POPULATION: None

A VOLCANIC, ICE-COVERED island in the South Atlantic Ocean, Bouvet lies over 990 miles north of Antarctica. Because it lies north of the Antarctic Circle it is not covered by the Antarctic Treaty. A royal decree, issued in 1971, made the whole island a nature reserve. Bouvet Island regularly plays host to scientific expeditions from Norway.

BRITISH INDIAN OCEAN TERRITORY

STATUS: British dependent territory   CLAIMED: 1814
CAPITAL: Diego Garcia   POPULATION: 2,000   DENSITY: 67 per sq. mile

THE BRITISH Indian Ocean Territory, or Chagos Islands, lies in the middle of the Indian Ocean. The coral atolls, previously used for copra production, are now uninhabited, except for the US-UK military base on Diego Garcia – a vital link in US plans to ensure a strategic capability in the Persian Gulf. The UK has undertaken to cede the islands to Mauritius when they are no longer required for military purposes.

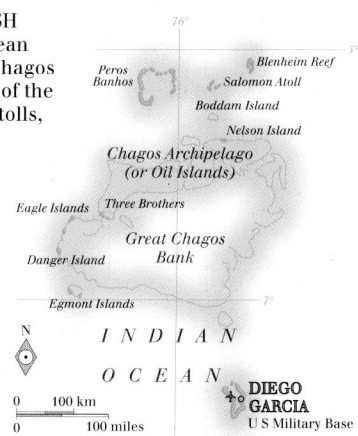

BRITISH VIRGIN ISLANDS

STATUS: British dependent territory   CLAIMED: 1672
CAPITAL: Road Town   POPULATION: 18,000   DENSITY: 305 per sq. mile

AN ARCHIPELAGO OF 40 islands, 15 of them inhabited, the British Virgin Islands lie at the eastern end of the Greater Antilles. The tropical climate suits tourism, a major economic activity along with the offshore finance sector, more tightly regulated since 1990 following scandals involving foreign companies registered in the islands. A British government-sponsored constitutional review, allowing four new Legislative Council members to represent the territory, was strongly opposed. Chief Minister Lavity Stoutt, the dominant political figure for three decades, died in 1995.

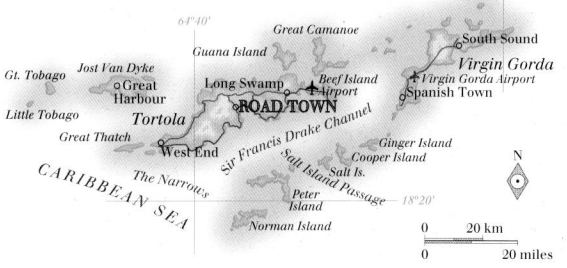

CAYMAN ISLANDS

STATUS: British dependent territory **CLAIMED:** 1670
CAPITAL: George Town **POPULATION:** 29,000 **DENSITY:** 285 per sq. mile

THE LARGEST OF Britain's remaining territories in the Caribbean, the Cayman Islands are situated nearly 190 miles northwest of Jamaica. Convinced that the islands' economic prosperity is directly linked to the stability its dependent territory status gives, the islanders recently shelved plans to rewrite the constitution to give themselves greater autonomy from London. The islands are one of the world's largest offshore financial centers. Absence of tax and foreign-exchange controls currently attracts some 32,000 companies, 560 banks and 361 insurance companies. However, tourism underpins the economy providing 70% of GDP.

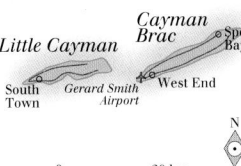

CHRISTMAS ISLAND

STATUS: Australian external territory **CLAIMED:** 1958
CAPITAL: Flying Fish Cove **POPULATION:** 2,871 **DENSITY:** 54 per sq. mile

SO NAMED BECAUSE it was sighted on Christmas Day in 1643, the island lies in the Indian Ocean, some 185 miles south of Java. It was inhabited by labor imported to mine rich phosphate deposits. As a result, the population is mostly Malay and Chinese. Since 1990, the islanders have enjoyed an economic boom. The mine – closed in 1987 – has been reopened and a tourist complex has been built.

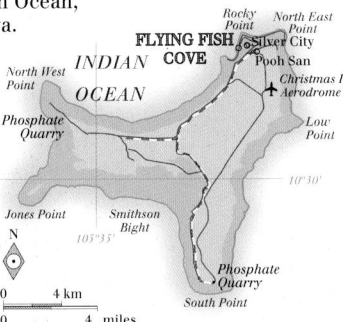

COCOS (KEELING) ISLANDS

STATUS: Australian external territory **CLAIMED:** 1955
CAPITAL: West Island **POPULATION:** 555 **DENSITY:** 101 per sq. mile

IN ALL, 27 coral atolls make up the Cocos (Keeling) Islands. They are situated in the Indian Ocean, roughly half way between Australia and Sri Lanka. The population is split between the European-dominated West Island and the Malays on Home Island. Coconuts are the sole cash crop and are grown throughout the atolls. The sale of postage stamps for foreign currency was stopped in the 1990s.

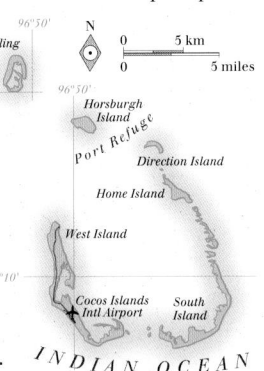

COOK ISLANDS

STATUS: Territory in free association with New Zealand **CLAIMED:** 1901
CAPITAL: Avarua **POPULATION:** 19,000 **DENSITY:** 209 per sq. mile

LYING 2,170 MILES NORTHEAST of New Zealand, the Cook Islands are a combination of 24 coral atolls and volcanic islands. The islands achieved self-government in 1965 and have adopted a diverse approach to their economy. Giant clam and pearl farming, and an ostrich farm, have been developed alongside tourism and banking. With the suspension of the ANZUS alliance in 1986, the Cook Islands declared their neutrality as doubts grew over New Zealand's ability to defend them. In 1991, the territory signed a friendship treaty with France which provided for French surveillance of its territorial waters.

CORAL SEA ISLANDS

STATUS: Australian external territory **CLAIMED:** 1969
CAPITAL: Not applicable **POPULATION:** 8

THE TERRITORY OF THE Coral Sea Islands is a group of reefs and islands, scattered over an area of nearly 400,000 square miles, off the east coast of Queensland, Australia. Uninhabited except for a manned weather station on Willis Island, the islands function as a large nature reserve. They provide sanctuary, in particular, to a number of rare seabirds and turtles.

FAEROE ISLANDS

STATUS: Self-governing territory of Denmark **CLAIMED:** 1380
CAPITAL: Tórshavn **POPULATION:** 47,310 **DENSITY:** 88 per sq. mile

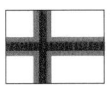

MIDWAY BETWEEN Scotland and Iceland in the North Atlantic, the Faeroe Islands have a moderate climate for their latitude – the result of the warm Gulf Stream current. Home rule since 1948 has given the Faeroese a strong sense of national identity – they voted against joining the EC with Denmark in 1973. In the face of international criticism, they have also continued their traditional cull of pilot whales and bottlenosed dolphins. Sheep farming is common, although fishing has had the strongest influence in shaping Faeroese society. The belief that Denmark's future lies within an integrated Europe has led to a gradual increase in internal pressure for complete independence. However, as the islands' economy depends on Danish subsidies, this appears unlikely in the near future.

LAND HEIGHT   above Sea Level   200m/656ft   500m/1640ft   1000m/3281ft   1500m/4572ft   above 2000m/6562ft

FALKLAND ISLANDS

STATUS: British dependent territory CLAIMED: 1832
CAPITAL: Stanley POPULATION: 2,121 DENSITY: 0.05 per sq. mile

SITUATED IN THE South Atlantic Ocean, more than 7,450 miles from Britain, the Falkland Islands are influenced by the cold Antarctic current. The main islands of East and West Falkland and the hundreds of outlying islands have a cool, temperate climate with frequent strong winds.

The islands gained international renown with the Argentine invasion, and subsequent British recapture, in 1982. Since then, the British government has invested heavily in a "Fortress Falklands" policy. A new runway and military base were built at Mount Pleasant to house an enlarged garrison. Sovereignty over the Falklands, however, continues to exert a negative influence on Anglo-Argentine relations. The islanders, for their part, are determined to maintain the *status quo*.

Since the Falklands war the economy of the islands has prospered. Falklanders invested heavily in schools, roads and tourism in a fresh drive for a strong identity. By 1987 the Falklands had become financially solvent due to the sale of fishing licenses.

However, sales of cheaper, less restrictive licenses by Argentina forced a slump in fishing revenues. In addition, a fall in wool prices began to affect the living standards of the predominantly sheep-farming community. The discovery of oil reserves in their territorial waters now promises to revolutionize the economy. The UK and Argentina in 1995 reached agreement on oil exploration around the Falklands and the islanders indicated a willingness to use oil revenues to offset the cost of their defense.

FRENCH GUIANA

STATUS: French overseas department CLAIMED: 1817
CAPITAL: Cayenne POPULATION: 135,000 DENSITY: 5 per sq. mile

SANDWICHED BETWEEN Brazil and Suriname on the northeast coast of South America, French Guiana is South America's only remaining colony. A belt of coastal marsh, and an interior of equatorial jungle, combine in a location which was, for years, notorious for the offshore penal colony, Devil's Island. The rainforest is particularly rich in flora and fauna. It harbors over 400,000 species, including more different kinds of birds than the whole of Europe.

Concentrated near the coast, the population is ethnically mixed. There are some 5,000 Indians and one of South America's largest group of bush negros, descended from escaped slaves.

A campaign for greater autonomy in the late 1970s and early 1980s led to limited decentralization of power to a regional council. The previous grip on local power by the Guianese Socialist Party (PSG) has been threatened since 1993 by a more unified opposition.

As French Guiana confronts growing economic and social instability, the people have become increasingly vocal in their condemnation of the French government's perceived indifference to their country's problems. Accordingly, the GSP has campaigned for greater autonomy from France in such important areas as transportation, immigration, education and health.

As an overseas *département* of metropolitan France, French Guiana is also a region of the EU. Despite this, the economy is heavily dependent on France for aid, food and manufactured goods. It has a number of valuable natural resources and also considerable tourist potential, but these are yet to be fully exploited, because of a lack of skilled labor and investment and an underdeveloped infrastructure. One asset, however, which has recently made French Guiana strategically important to France is the European Space Agency rocket launch facility for the Ariane rocket at Kourou.

Kourou was selected for the launch of the Ariane rocket because of its equatorial site. The town has grown from 800 to 15,000 people.

FRENCH POLYNESIA

STATUS: French overseas possession   **CLAIMED:** 1843
CAPITAL: Papeete   **Population:** 211,000   **DENSITY:** 137 per sq. mile

A MYRIAD of 130 South Pacific islands and coral atolls combine to form French Polynesia, in an area the size of Europe. The average annual temperature varies between 68°F and 84°F, with annual rainfall of over 59 inches. Nearly 75% of the population live on the main island of Tahiti. The Polynesian majority have seen their simple, self-sufficient economy transformed into one dependent on the French military and tourism. In particular, nuclear testing on Mururoa atoll created many jobs, but the French administration has developed the islands with little regard for local wishes. In response, the Polynesian majority has increased calls for greater autonomy, a reduction in tourism and a program for rebuilding indigenous trade. A final series of nuclear tests was conducted in 1995-1996, despite widespread internal and international protests, before the French government announced an end to further testing. The tests increased calls for independence.

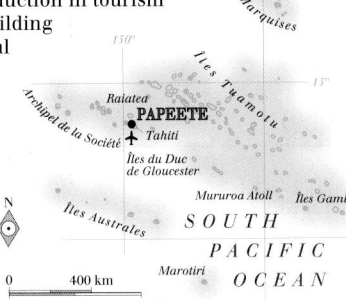

GIBRALTAR

STATUS: British Crown colony   **CLAIMED:** 1713
CAPITAL: Gibraltar   **POPULATION:** 28,074   **DENSITY:** 12,124 per sq. mile

G UARDING THE western entrance to the Mediterranean, Gibraltar has traditionally survived on military and marine revenues. However, as Britain has cut its defense spending so the UK's military presence on the Rock has declined. In response, Gibraltarians have developed a vibrant offshore banking industry. Strict anti-smuggling legislation, in force since 1995, has curbed extensive smuggling into Spain. The critical issue of Gibraltar's relationship with Britain and Spain is under review following the election defeat in 1996 of the pro-independence chief minister Joe Bossano by Peter Caruana of the Gibralter Social Democrats. Meanwhile Spain continues to press for control over the Rock.

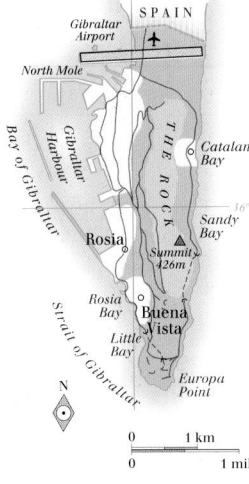

The Rock of Gibraltar. The British built 143 caves, over 30 miles of roads and as many miles of tunnels for defensive purposes.

GREENLAND

STATUS: Self governing territory of Denmark   **CLAIMED:** 1380
CAPITAL: Nuuk   **POPULATION:** 55,385   **DENSITY:** 0.06 per sq. mile

T HE WORLD'S LARGEST island after Australia, Greenland is situated in the North Atlantic and surrounded by seas that are either frozen or cooled by cold Arctic currents. The island has an Arctic climate and much of its land is permanently covered in ice. Granted home rule in 1979, Greenlanders are an independent people – a mix of Inuit and European in origin. Younger islanders are increasingly rejecting the traditional subsistence lifestyle by moving to towns. This move away from self-sufficiency, allied to a decline in the important fishing industry, has placed a heavy burden on Greenland's advanced welfare system.

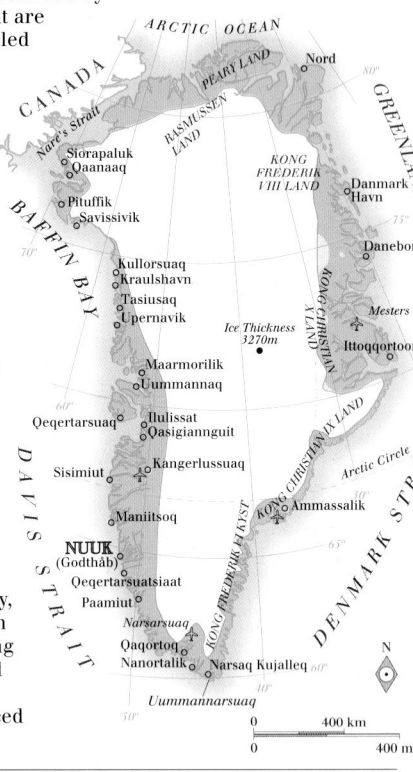

GUADELOUPE

STATUS: French overseas department   **CLAIMED:** 1635
CAPITAL: Basse-Terre   **POPULATION:** 413,000   **DENSITY:** 627 per sq. mile

G UADELOUPE lies at the northern end of the Windward Islands in the Caribbean. The movement for independence from France has been more pronounced here than elsewhere. Demands for more autonomy parallel attempts by local government to play a more interventionist role in the economy which is dependent on large amounts of French and EU aid. In 1995, unemployment was 26%. The local government, given the vulnerability of banana prices on the world market, has sought to expand sugar production and develop tourism.

LAND HEIGHT   above Sea Level   200m/656ft   500m/1640ft   1000m/3281ft   1500m/4572ft   above 2000m/6562ft

GUAM

STATUS: Unincorporated territory of the USA **CLAIMED:** 1898
CAPITAL: Agaña **POPULATION:** 144,000 **DENSITY:** 678 per sq. mile

THE VOLCANIC island of Guam lies at the southern end of the Mariana Archipelago in the Pacific. Its tropical climate has encouraged tourism, although it lies in a region where typhoons are common. Guam's indigenous Chamorro people, who comprise just under half the population, dominate the island's political and social life. They are famous for a set of facial expressions, called "eyebrow," which virtually constitutes a language of its own. The US military base, covering one-third of the island, has made Guam strategically important to the USA. Military spending and tourism revenues have given islanders a high living standard. The influx of American culture and *mores* has, however, threatened to upset Guam's social stability.

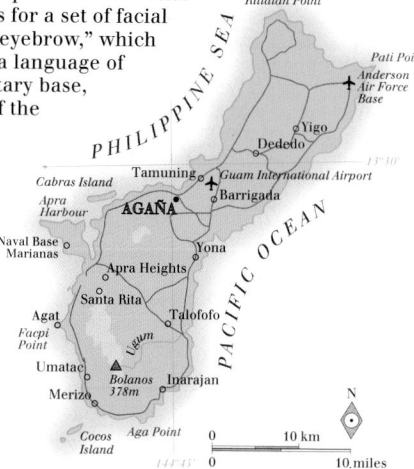

GUERNSEY

STATUS: British Crown dependency **CLAIMED:** 1066
CAPITAL: St. Peter Port **POPULATION:** 58,000 **DENSITY:** 1,928 per sq. mile

LYING 31 MILES off the coast of France, Guernsey and its dependencies form the northwestern part of the Channel Islands. Some of the islands are too small for people to need cars, and life continues in an unhurried manner that has changed little through the centuries. The islanders guard this lifestyle with strict residential laws. Guernsey's mild climate has encouraged the development of tourism and market gardening as major industries.

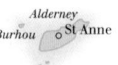

HEARD & MACDONALD IS.

STATUS: Australian external territory **CLAIMED:** 1947
CAPITAL: Not applicable **POPULATION:** None

SITUATED 2,484 MILES southwest of Australia in the Indian Ocean, the Heard and Macdonald Islands are ice-covered, volcanic rock outcrops. Their principal use is for scientific research. In 1991 Heard Island's unique location – it offers direct access to the world's main oceans – led to it being chosen as the site of an experiment to monitor global warming using soundwaves.

ISLE OF MAN

STATUS: British Crown dependency **CLAIMED:** 1765
CAPITAL: Douglas **POPULATION:** 71,000 **DENSITY:** 318 per sq. mile

LYING HALFWAY BETWEEN England and Northern Ireland in the Irish Sea, the Isle of Man has been inhabited for centuries by the Celtic Manx people. Established by the Vikings in the ninth century, the Manx parliament, the Tynwald, has autonomy from the UK in a number of matters, including taxation. The islanders have used this independence to establish a thriving financial and business sector, which has aided employment as the traditional industries of agriculture and fishing decline. The island's culture received a boost in 1993 when Manx, the local language, which was in danger of dying out, began being taught in schools again. The Calf of Man is uninhabited and is administered as a nature reserve.

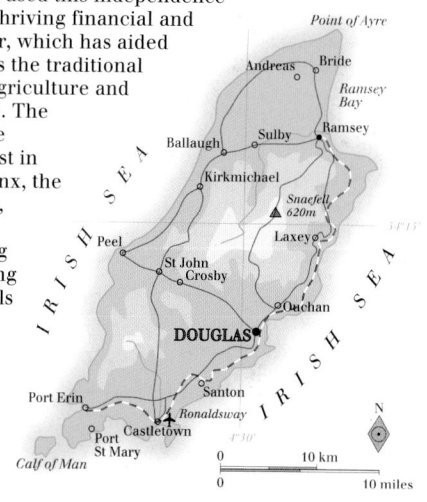

Isle of Man's TT motorbike race. Thousands of bikers come each year to see the island's famous Touring Trophy race. It is run on a 38-mile circuit of the island.

JAN MAYEN

STATUS: Norwegian dependency **CLAIMED:** 1929
CAPITAL: Not applicable **POPULATION:** None

THE MOUNTAINOUS, VOLCANIC island of Jan Mayen lies 560 miles northwest of Norway, in the Arctic Ocean. The island's only resources are its rich fishing grounds. These were the subject of a long dispute with Greenland over fishing rights and possibly also oil and gas deposits. The International Court of Justice helped the two parties reach a compromise in 1993.

JARVIS ISLAND

STATUS: Unincorporated territory of the USA **CLAIMED:** 1856
CAPITAL: Not applicable **POPULATION:** None

A SMALL CORAL ISLAND, only 2 miles long and one-third of a mile wide, Jarvis Island is located 1,240 miles south of Honolulu. It remains uninhabited, although scientists do occasionally visit. The island is managed primarily as a nesting, roosting and foraging site for seabirds and shorebirds.

JERSEY

STATUS: British Crown dependency   CLAIMED: 1066
CAPITAL: St. Helier   POPULATION: 84,082   DENSITY: 1,876 per sq. mile

THE BAILIWICK OF JERSEY, the largest of the Channel Islands, lies some 12 miles from the coast of Normandy in France. The island has a mild climate owing to the Gulf Stream, fine beaches and more sunshine than anywhere in the British Isles.

Jersey has its own legislative and taxation systems which are a blend of the French and British versions. It also has one of the oldest legislative bodies in the world, the Jersey States Assembly. Members stand as independents, rather than for political parties. The islanders have used their autonomy from the UK to develop the economy as an offshore tax haven. Historically, agriculture has been Jersey's most important industry, with dairy cows its most famous export. However, over the past 50 years farming has been eclipsed by the rise of finance and tourism. The growth of these sectors, and rigid controls on the rights of residency, have ensured high living standards for most of the inhabitants. Jersey also plays host to a large Portuguese community who work in the island's tourist industry.

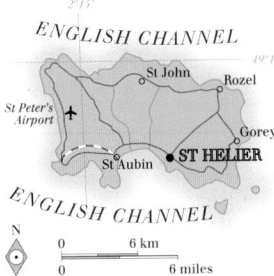

JOHNSTON ATOLL

STATUS: Unincorporated territory of the USA   CLAIMED: 1858
CAPITAL: Not applicable   POPULATION: 327   DENSITY: 282 per sq. mile

JOHNSTON ATOLL LIES 714 miles southwest of Hawaii. The atoll consists of a coral reef, two highly-modified natural islands, Johnston and Sand, and two completely man-made islands, Akau and Hikina. The US military has drastically altered the islands and little of the original habitat remains. They have in the past been used for nuclear-weapons tests and storing nerve gases. However, the atoll is now used for a chemical-weapons disposal scheme by the US government. The islands are inhabited by US government personnel and civilian contractors who support the plant.

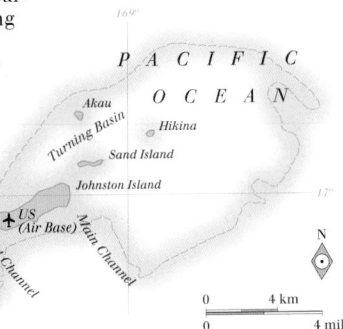

KINGMAN REEF

STATUS: Unincorporated territory of the USA   CLAIMED: 1856
CAPITAL: Not applicable   POPULATION: None

A BARREN, TRIANGULAR reef, only three feet in elevation, Kingman Reef lies 932 miles southwest of Hawaii. The reef is 9 miles long and 5 miles wide. Only the eastern end of it now remains above water. There is no land flora, but it is rich in marine life. The reef is administered by the US Navy.

MACAO

STATUS: Special territory of Portugal   CLAIMED: 1557
CAPITAL: Macao   POPULATION: 388,000   DENSITY: 55,868 per sq. mile

THE PORTUGUESE ENCLAVE of Macao is situated on the South China coast, at the mouth of the Pearl river. It comprises a small area of mainland and two nearby islands, linked to the mainland by bridge and causeway. A subtropical climate brings high humidity and the possibility of typhoons sweeping in from the South China Sea.

Macao is scheduled to become a Special Administrative Region of China in 1999. In contrast to the problems being experienced by the British in Hong Kong, preparations for Chinese sovereignty in historically more compliant Macao have been relatively smooth. Macanese resident before 1981 have been offered Portuguese passports. However, the future status of mixed-blood Macanese is uncertain and tensions exist between the skilled elite and the merchants who support China's takeover. In local legislative elections in 1992, the pro-China candidates secured half of the directly elected seats in the 23-seat assembly.

While Hong Kong, just 17 miles to the east, has built an advanced capitalist economy, Macao has been characterized by stagnation, corruption and bureaucratic inefficiency. It continues to rely on gambling – its casinos luring hundreds of thousands of visitors a year, and the economy is increasingly coming under Chinese control. An early 1990s property boom, fuelled by Chinese capital, collapsed and produced a liquidity crisis. Macao is now a major exporter of cheap, finished goods. Its factories use cheap Chinese labor to produce anything from fire-works to artificial flowers. A new inter-national airport, a joint Sino-Portuguese project, offers the prospect of economic development.

Macao's skyline is dominated by large hotels and casinos which provide the territory with an important source of revenue.

above Sea Level   200m/656ft   500m/1640ft   1000m/3281ft   1500m/4572ft   above 2000m/6562ft

MARTINIQUE

STATUS: French overseas department CLAIMED: 1635
CAPITAL: Fort-de-France POPULATON: 371,000 DENSITY: 873 per sq. mile

CHRISTOPHER COLUMBUS called Martinique "The most beautiful country in the world." It lies in the eastern Caribbean and is dominated by the dormant volcano Montagne Pelée. The island is also situated in the Caribbean's hurricane belt and has therefore suffered an average of one natural disaster every five years. Nearly 90% of the population are of African or mixed ethnicity. However, economic power remains in the hands of the *Bekes* (descendants of white colonial settlers), who own most of the agricultural land. In addition, the bureaucracy is largely staffed by expatriates. This situation has led to outbreaks of violence and increased popular demands for more autonomy.

The French government responded with some measures to increase the island's autonomy. However, the islanders are aware that their high living standards, despite 27% unemployment in 1995, depend on French subsidies. The economy relies on tourism, sugarcane and banana production. EU subsidy reductions have forced the island to diversify its economy.

MAYOTTE

STATUS: French territorial collectivity CLAIMED: 1843
CAPITAL: Mamoudzou POPULATION: 97,088 DENSITY: 668 per sq. mile

PART OF THE Comoros archipelago, Mayotte lies some 4,960 miles from France, between Madagascar and the East African coast. The Mahorais are strongly in favor of maintaining their links with France, despite widespread poverty, endemic unemployment and a cost of living twice that of France. The main political movement has demanded that Mayotte be given the status of a French *département*. They hope that this would bring more aid to develop their largely agricultural economy. The expense involved has led France to oppose the idea. The French have, however, invested in an airport and port. It is hoped these will foster the growth of an upscale tourist sector.

MIDWAY ISLANDS

STATUS: Unincorporated territory of the USA CLAIMED: 1867
CAPITAL: Not applicable POPULATION: 453 DENSITY: 236 per sq. mile

NAMED BECAUSE OF its position on the route between California and Japan, Midway is a coral atoll at the western end of the Hawaiian islands. The scene of a major World War II battle, the atoll comprises two large islands, totaling over 1.5 square miles, and several smaller ones. Midway functions as a naval air base and wildlife refuge. The population is limited to military personnel and civilian contractors.

MONTSERRAT

STATUS: British dependent territory CLAIMED: 1632
CAPITAL: Plymouth POPULATION: 11,000 DENSITY: 279 per sq. mile

MONTSERRAT IS ONE of the Leeward Islands chain in the eastern Caribbean. Luxuriant flora and a tropical climate have made it a tourist destination for the rich and famous – the sector accounts for around one-fifth of GDP. However, the mountainous terrain, and hurricanes such as Hugo in 1989, have impeded its agricultural development. In response, the government has also developed the island as a data-processing and financial center.

The question of independence, which dominated local politics in the late 1980s, fell into abeyance after the hurricane and a financial scandal involving local politicians. Some 4,000 evacuated residents returned in 1996 following renewed volcanic activity.

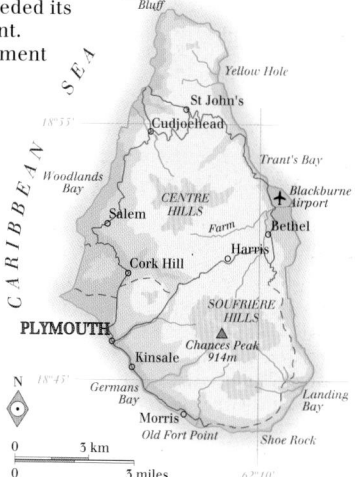

Monserrat. Known as the Caribbean's "emerald isle" because of its luxuriant flora and Irish heritage.

NAVASSA ISLAND

STATUS: Unincorporated territory of the USA CLAIMED: 1856
CAPITAL: Not applicable POPULATION: None

AN UNINHABITED ROCKY outcrop, Navassa Island lies halfway between Cuba and Haiti, in the Caribbean. The island, also claimed by Haiti, is used by Haitians fishing the local waters. They also sometimes hunt the island's goats. Navassa has an automatic lighthouse which is run by the US Coast Guard.

NETHERLANDS ANTILLES

STATUS: Autonomous part of the Netherlands CLAIMED: 1816
CAPITAL: Willemstad POPULATION: 195,000 DENSITY: 632 per sq. mile

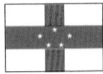

THE NETHERLANDS Antilles comprise two Caribbean island groups. Curaçao – the richest and wealthiest island – and Bonaire lie just off the Venezuelan coast, and Saba and St. Eustatius and the Dutch part of St. Maarten, lie 496 miles to the north. Financial scandals, arguments over the federation's future, political instability – particularly on the four smaller islands – and allegations of narcotics-trafficking have strained relations with the Dutch government, the major aid provider. A structural adjustment program proposed in 1996 to tackle the federal budget deficit and $1.1 billion foreign debt will seriously test the federation.

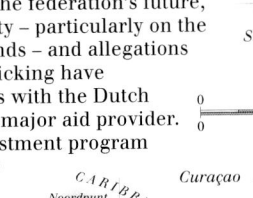

NEW CALEDONIA

STATUS: French overseas territory CLAIMED: 1853
CAPITAL: Nouméa POPULATION: 179,000 DENSITY: 25 per sq. mile

NEW CALEDONIA, or as the indigenous Kanaks call it, Kanaky, is an island group 930 miles off the northeast coast of Australia. Tension between the Kanaks and the *Caldoches*, the francophile expatriate population, over socio-economic inequalities and independence, have resulted in a long history of political violence. Under the 1988 Matignon Accord, the French government imposed a year of direct rule as the prelude to a new constitutional structure which attempted to address Kanak grievances by providing greater provincial autonomy. Economic reforms were initiated and a referendum on independence was promised for 1998. Since then, although there has been some racial violence, this has not reached the pre-1988 level. Nickel mining – the territory produces 25% of world output – tourism and agriculture have greatly enriched the economy. Unemployment remains high among young Kanaks.

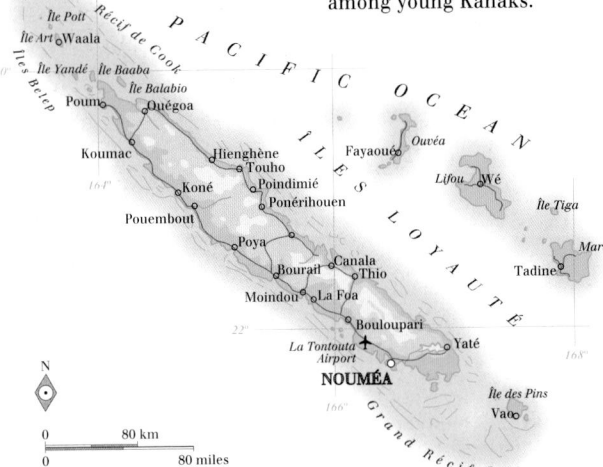

NIUE

STATUS: Territory in free association with New Zealand CLAIMED: 190*
CAPITAL: Alofi POPULATION: 2,000 DENSITY: 20 per sq. mile

THE WORLD'S LARGEST coral island, Niue, lies 1,305 miles northeast of New Zealand. The subsistence economy produces a variety of tropical fruits, while tourism and the sale of postage stamps provide foreign currency. Despite the island's paradise image, nearly 10,000 Niueans, frustrated by the lack of job prospects on Niue, live in New Zealand. In the hope of stopping further emigration, New Zealand has invested heavily in the economy. However, inefficient use of aid and cyclone damage have held back growth.

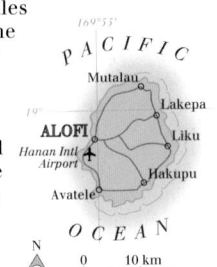

NORFOLK ISLAND

STATUS: Australian external territory CLAIMED: 1774
CAPITAL: Kingston POPULATION: 2,367 DENSITY: 171 per sq. mile

INHABITED by descendants of the *HMS Bounty* mutineers and more recent Australian migrants, Norfolk Island lies 870 miles east of Australia. The islanders speak a hybrid language, mixing West Country English, Gaelic and ancient Tahitian. They enjoy a fair degree of autonomy, and in 1991 rejected a plan to become part of the Australian federal state. Tourists, attracted by the climate and unique flora, have brought islanders a relatively high standard of living.

NORTHERN MARIANA IS.

STATUS: Commonwealth territory of the USA CLAIMED: 1947
CAPITAL: Saipan POPULATION: 47,000 DENSITY: 261 per sq. mile

UNLIKE some UN trust territories in the Western Pacific which opted for independence in 1987, the Northern Marianas preferred to retain links with the USA. However, local politicians have begun to question their new status. While US aid fueled an economic boom during the 1980s, it failed to benefit the local Chamorro population. In addition, tourism has speeded the decline of the traditional subsistence economy.

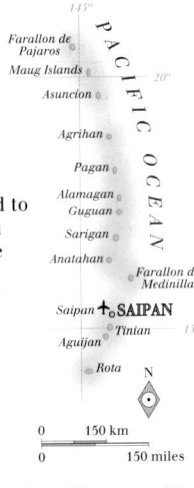

Rota, Northern Marianas. The limestone outcrop of Wedding Cake Mountain overlooks the small village of Songsong.

LAND HEIGHT [ ] above Sea Level [ ] 200m/656ft [ ] 500m/1640ft [ ] 1000m/3281ft [ ] 1500m/4572ft [ ] above 2000m/6562ft

PALMYRA ATOLL

STATUS: Unincorporated territory of the USA **CLAIMED:** 1898
CAPITAL: Not applicable **POPULATION:** None

A PRIVATELY-OWNED, uninhabited collection of 50 islets, Palmyra Atoll is situated some 990 miles southwest of Hawaii. Administered by the USA since 1898, the atoll is covered in dense vegetation, including coconut palms, which have prospered in its hot and humid climate. In 1990, a Hawaiian property developer took out a 75-year lease on Palmyra from its owners, the Fullard-Leo brothers. Plans exist to turn the atoll into a tourist and residential complex, which will promote a "get away from it all" image.

PARACEL ISLANDS

STATUS: Disputed **CLAIMED:** Not applicable
CAPITAL: Woody Island **POPULATION:** Unknown

O CCUPIED BY CHINESE forces, but also claimed by Taiwan and Vietnam, the Paracel Islands are a small collection of coral atolls, situated some 248 miles east of Vietnam, in the South China Sea. Subject to frequent typhoons and with a tropical climate, the Paracels are at the center of a regional dispute over the vast reserves of oil and natural gas, which are believed to lie beneath their territorial waters. China has built port facilities and an airport on Woody Island to support its claim.

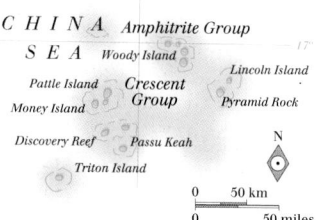

PETER I ISLAND

STATUS: Norwegian dependency **CLAIMED:** 1933
CAPITAL: Not applicable **POPULATION:** None

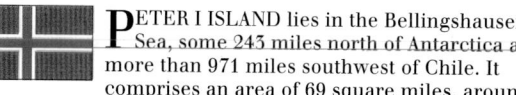

P ETER I ISLAND lies in the Bellingshausen Sea, some 243 miles north of Antarctica and more than 971 miles southwest of Chile. It comprises an area of 69 square miles, around 95% of which is covered by ice. A Norwegian expedition landed on the island in 1929; it was placed under Norwegian sovereignty by royal proclamation in 1931 and declared a dependency in 1933.

PITCAIRN ISLANDS

STATUS: British dependent territory **CLAIMED:** 1887
CAPITAL: Adamstown **POPULATION:** 66 **DENSITY:** 33 per sq. mile

P ITCAIRN, A GROUP of volcanic South Pacific islands with a humid, tropical climate, is Britain's most isolated dependency. Pitcairn Island provided the last refuge for the *HMS Bounty* mutineers. Emigration is a major problem for the Pitcairners, who depend on regular airdrops from New Zealand, and periodic visits by supply vessels. The economy operates by barter, fishing and subsistence farming. Postage stamp sales provide foreign currency earnings. Mineral exploitation could boost the economy in future.

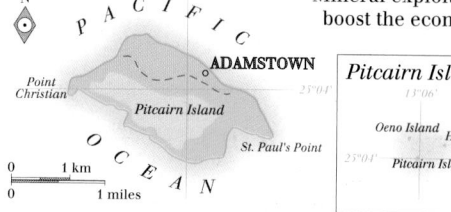

PUERTO RICO

STATUS: Commonwealth territory of the USA **CLAIMED:** 1898
CAPITAL: San Juan **POPULATION:** 3.6 million **DENSITY:** 1,054 per sq. mile

T HE MOST POPULOUS of the US overseas territories, Puerto Rico lies in the Caribbean between the Dominican Republic and the Virgin Islands. The island, which is split by a central mountain range, has a tropical climate which attracts growing numbers of tourists. A US territory since its invasion in 1898, Puerto Rico has an active nationalist movement which has campaigned for independence since the 1920s and which staged an abortive insurrection in 1950. In 1952, the territory was granted its current commonwealth status and in the next decade there was a significant improvement in social conditions as investment and industrialization expanded the economy. A 1967 plebiscite endorsed commonwealth status rather than opting for US statehood, with only a small minority voting for independence. In 1993, the population again voted for the commonwealth, a decision which was a personal blow to governor Pedro Rossello, who had campaigned to make Puerto Rico the USA's 51st state. The population has one of the highest living standards in the region. Tax relief, cheap labor and its role as an export processing zone have encouraged many businesses to the island. As a result, industries – like electronics and petrochemicals – have overtaken agriculture as the major economic activity. Puerto Rico produces nearly 95% of all tranquillizers consumed in the USA.

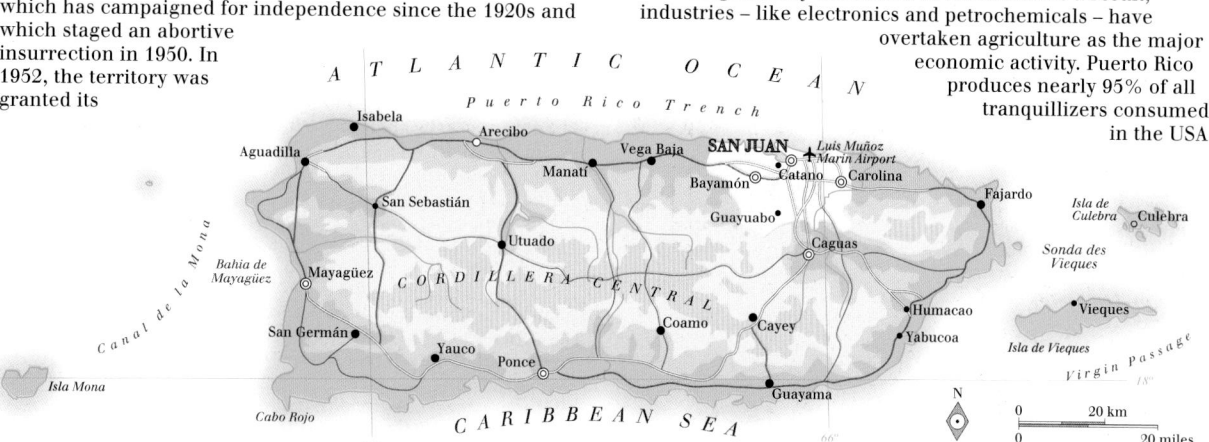

RÉUNION

STATUS: French overseas department **CLAIMED:** 1638
CAPITAL: Saint-Denis **POPULATION:** 632,000 **DENSITY:** 653 per sq. mile

THE LARGE VOLCANIC island of Réunion, 497 miles east of Madagascar, provides France with an important strategic presence – and a large military base – in the Indian Ocean. Its mountainous interior has forced the majority of the population to live along the coast. Socio-economic differences between the poorer black community and the wealthier Indian and European groups raised ethnic tensions. These tensions were the cause of severe rioting in 1991. The French government responded with a series of measures, applicable to all overseas departments, to raise economic and social conditions to the level of those of France itself. Réunion's main crop is sugarcane.

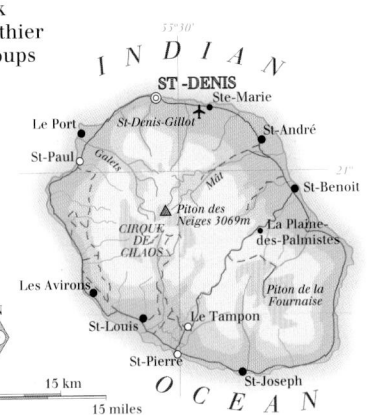

ST. PIERRE & MIQUELON

STATUS: French territorial collectivity **CLAIMED:** 1604
CAPITAL: St Pierre **POPULATION:** 6,000 **DENSITY:** 65 per sq. mile

ST. PIERRE & Miquelon is a group of barren islands, just off the south coast of Newfoundland, Canada. The islands are surrounded by some of the world's richest fishing grounds. Their inhabitants have traditionally earned a living from fishing, and servicing foreign trawler fleets, off the coast. A long-running and sometimes bitter dispute between Canada and France over fishing and mineral rights was settled in 1992. The ruling, which was generally deemed to be in Canada's favor, has led the French authorities to diversify the economy by developing port facilities and encouraging tourism.

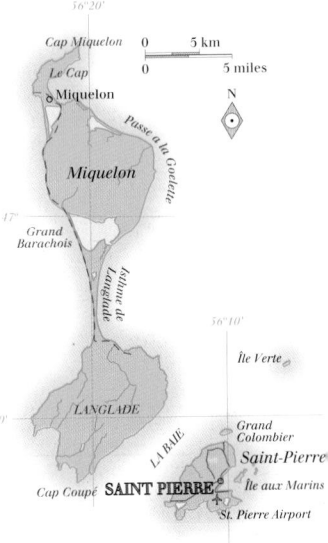

ST. HELENA & DEPENDENCIES

STATUS: British dependent territory **CLAIMED:** 1673
CAPITAL: Jamestown **POPULATION:** 6,000 **DENSITY:** 30 per sq. mile

TOGETHER, the islands of St. Helena, Tristan da Cunha and Ascension form Britain's main dependency in the South Atlantic. St. Helena, the principal island, is the last remaining dependency to need budgetary aid from the UK. The island's main economic activities, fishing, livestock farming and the sale of handicrafts, are unable to support the population. As a result, underemployment is a major problem on St. Helena. Opportunities seem to be better on its dependencies and many St Helenians have been forced to seek work on Ascension Island. Some were also employed building Mount Pleasant airport on the Falklands. No resident population is allowed on Ascension Island, which operates as a military base and communications center. It is an integral part of the air-bridge supplying the Falklands. Tristan da Cunha, a volcanic island 1,242 miles to the south of St. Helena, is inhabited by a small, closely-knit farming

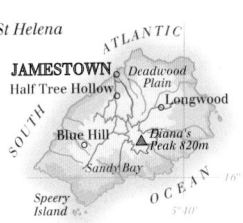

SOUTH GEORGIA & SOUTH SANDWICH ISLANDS

STATUS: British dependent territory **CLAIMED:** 1775
CAPITAL: Grytviken **POPULATION:** No permanent residents

THE SOUTH ATLANTIC island of South Georgia, briefly occupied by Argentine forces during the Falklands War, has a small UK garrison at Grytviken and a British Antarctic Survey base. The volcanic South Sandwich Islands, 446 miles to the southeast, are uninhabited. The territory is increasingly visited by ecotourists, attracted by the abundant wildlife.

SPRATLY ISLANDS

STATUS: Disputed **CLAIMED:** Not applicable
CAPITAL: Not applicable **POPULATION:** Unknown

SCATTERED ACROSS a large area of the South China Sea, the reefs, islands and atolls that make up the Spratly Islands have become one of Southeast Asia's most serious security issues. Claimed, all or in part, by China, Taiwan, Vietnam, Brunei, Malaysia and the Philippines, 44 of the larger islands now have garrisons from some of the claimant nations. The reasons for this interest, and the occasional skirmish, are twofold. Strategically, the islands control some of the world's most important shipping lanes. In addition, surveys suggest that some of the largest oil and gas reserves yet found lie in the Spratlys' territorial waters.

LAND HEIGHT | above Sea Level | 200m/656ft | 500m/1640ft | 1000m/3281ft | 1500m/4572ft | above 2000m/6562ft | Ice Cap

SVALBARD

STATUS: Norwegian dependency **CLAIMED:** 1920
CAPITAL: Longyearbyen **POPULATION:** 3,431 **DENSITY:** 0.15

NINE ICE-COVERED ARCTIC islands, 404 miles north of Norway, make up the territory of Svalbard. In accordance with the 1920 Spitsbergen Treaty, nationals of the treaty powers have equal rights to exploit Svalbard's coal deposits, subject to Norwegian regulation. The only companies still mining are Russian and Norwegian. Falling coal reserves and the end of the Cold War have begun to test Norway's strong attachment to the islands.

TOKELAU

STATUS: New Zealand dependent territory **CLAIMED:** 1926
CAPITAL: Not applicable **POPULATION:** 2,000 **DENSITY:** 433 per sq. mile

ACCORDING TO a 1989 UN report, this island in the South Pacific will disappear under the sea in the 21st century unless action is taken to stop global warming. In 1990, in another blow for the islanders, a cyclone destroyed crops and wrecked Tokelau's infrastructure. The New Zealand government has, however, made efforts to spur development. A tuna cannery and the sale of fishing licences have raised revenue, and a catamaran link between the atolls has increased the islands' tourist potential. However, its small size and continued economic weakness still makes independence unlikely.

TURKS & CAICOS ISLANDS

STATUS: British dependent territory **CLAIMED:** 1766
CAPITAL: Cockburn Town **POPN:** 13,000 **DENSITY:** 77 per sq. mile

SITUATED 25 MILES south of the Bahamas, the Turks and Caicos Islands is a group of 30 low-lying islands, eight of which are inhabited. Services dominate the economy, particularly tourism and offshore banking. There is a committee that seeks political independence. In April 1996 local leaders demanded the replacement of the British governor.

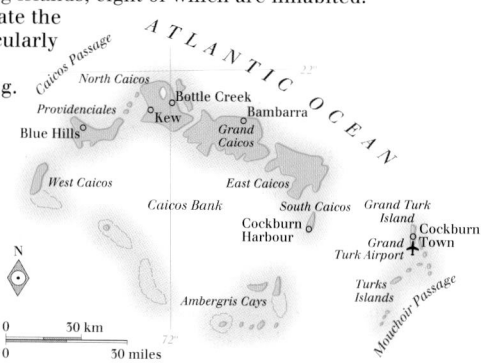

VIRGIN ISLANDS (US)

STATUS: Unincorporated territory of the USA **CLAIMED:** 1917
CAPITAL: Charlotte Amalie **POPN:** 104,000 **DENSITY:** 777 per sq. mile

THE US VIRGIN ISLANDS are a collection of 53 volcanic islands, just to the east of Puerto Rico. Most of the population – a mix of African and European ethnic groups – live on the main islands of St. John, St. Thomas and St. Croix. Tourism is the principal industry, although St. Croix has also used federal aid to develop industry. It has one of the world's largest oil refineries.

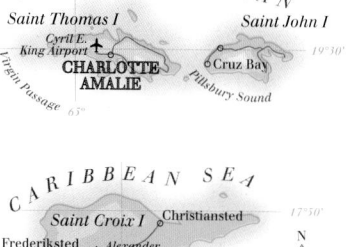

St. Thomas, US Virgin Islands, is a major stop-off for Caribbean cruise ships. Tourists are attracted by the island's duty-free shopping.

WAKE ISLAND

STATUS: Unincorporated territory of the USA **CLAIMED:** 1898
CAPITAL: None **POPULATION:** 302 **DENSITY:** 111 per sq. mile

FORMED BY THE rim of an extinct underwater volcano, Wake Island's strategic importance has declined since the end of the Vietnam War. It is now used as an emergency airstrip for trans-Pacific flights, and as a stopover for cargo planes.

WALLIS & FUTUNA

STATUS: French overseas territory **CLAIMED:** 1842
CAPITAL: Mata Uta **POPULATION:** 14,000 **DENSITY:** 181 per sq. mile

UNLIKE FRANCE'S other overseas territories in the South Pacific, the inhabitants of Wallis and Futuna have little desire for greater autonomy. The islands' subsistence economy produces a variety of tropical crops, while expatriate remittances and the sale of licenses to Japanese and Korean fishing fleets provide foreign exchange. Futuna was hit by an earthquake in 1993.

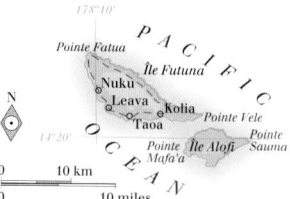

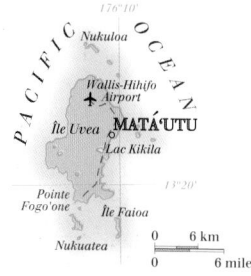

3

GLOBAL ISSUES

WORLD POPULATION

WORLD POPULATION, 5.7 billion people in 1995, is projected to rise to 8-10 billion people by 2025. It is estimated that population will stabilize at around 8-12 billion people after 2050. Despite a decline in total world fertility, population will increase in countries that are in the process of industrialization. There is little indication that fertility is set to decline in the least developed countries, presently comprising some 0.5 billion people. These densely populated regions of the world lack the infrastructure and resources needed to cope with growing populations. On the other hand, birth-rates in the industrialized countries of Europe, in Japan, and in the USA, have fallen to the point where they fail to replace deaths.

WORLD POPULATION DISTRIBUTION

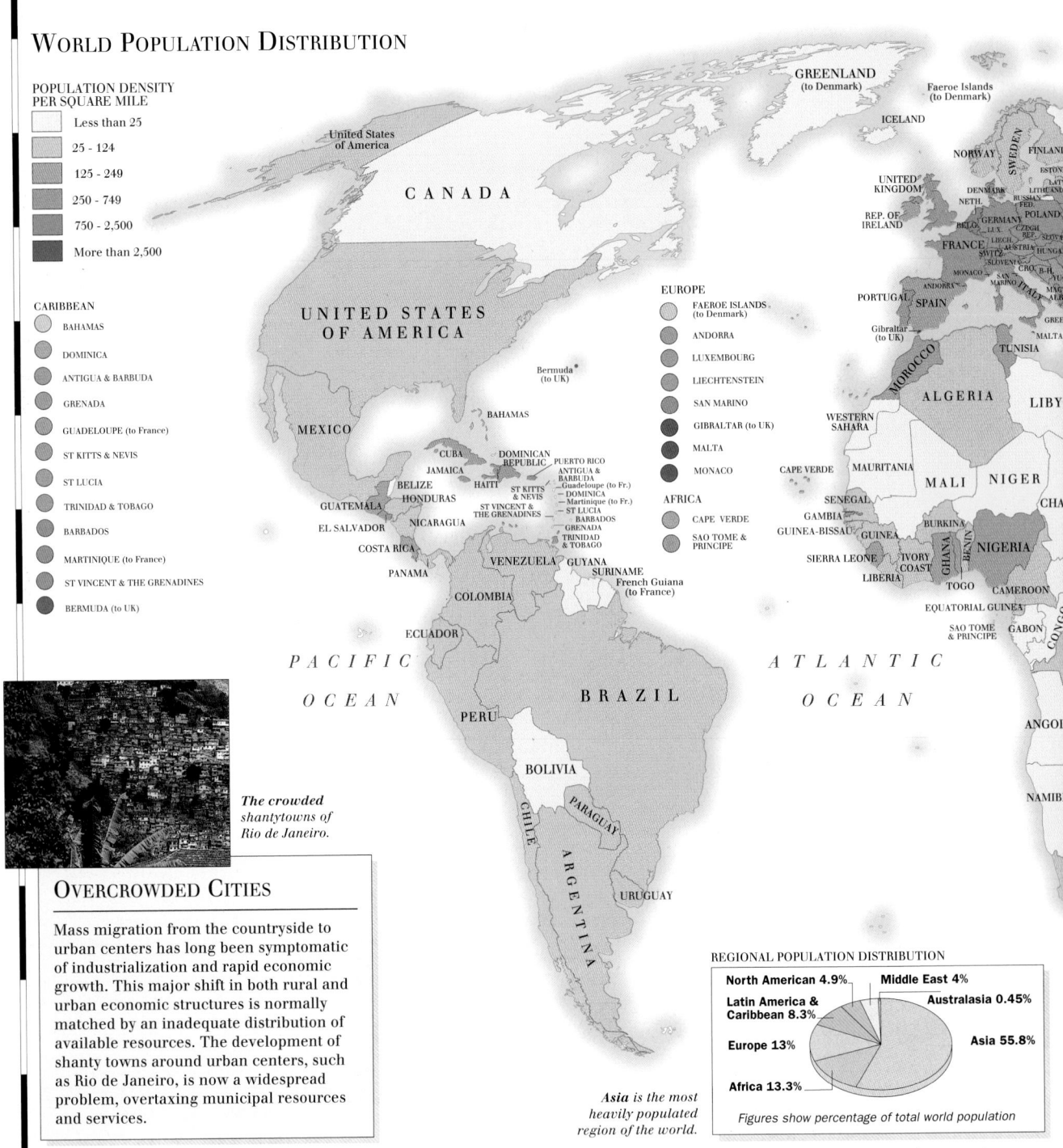

POPULATION DENSITY PER SQUARE MILE

- Less than 25
- 25 - 124
- 125 - 249
- 250 - 749
- 750 - 2,500
- More than 2,500

CARIBBEAN

- BAHAMAS
- DOMINICA
- ANTIGUA & BARBUDA
- GRENADA
- GUADELOUPE (to France)
- ST KITTS & NEVIS
- ST LUCIA
- TRINIDAD & TOBAGO
- BARBADOS
- MARTINIQUE (to France)
- ST VINCENT & THE GRENADINES
- BERMUDA (to UK)

EUROPE

- FAEROE ISLANDS (to Denmark)
- ANDORRA
- LUXEMBOURG
- LIECHTENSTEIN
- SAN MARINO
- GIBRALTAR (to UK)
- MALTA
- MONACO

AFRICA

- CAPE VERDE
- SAO TOME & PRINCIPE

The crowded shantytowns of Rio de Janeiro.

OVERCROWDED CITIES

Mass migration from the countryside to urban centers has long been symptomatic of industrialization and rapid economic growth. This major shift in both rural and urban economic structures is normally matched by an inadequate distribution of available resources. The development of shanty towns around urban centers, such as Rio de Janeiro, is now a widespread problem, overtaxing municipal resources and services.

REGIONAL POPULATION DISTRIBUTION

- North American 4.9%
- Middle East 4%
- Latin America & Caribbean 8.3%
- Australasia 0.45%
- Europe 13%
- Asia 55.8%
- Africa 13.3%

Figures show percentage of total world population

Asia is the most heavily populated region of the world.

The intensively farmed rural landscape of the Netherlands.

THE NETHERLANDS

The most densely populated country of Europe, the Netherlands also remains one of the wealthiest. Over the centuries, a balance between resources and population has been achieved which allows for a sustainable growth of the economy, of individual wealth and of living conditions. The pressure of a large population on very limited quantities of land has led to massive land reclamation projects in the Netherlands. From as early as the 16th century, land has been taken back from the sea – initially for agriculture, but also today for industrial plant and residential development.

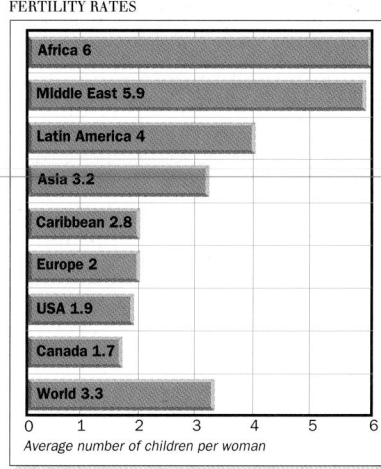

FERTILITY RATES

	Average number of children per woman
Africa 6	
Middle East 5.9	
Latin America 4	
Asia 3.2	
Caribbean 2.8	
Europe 2	
USA 1.9	
Canada 1.7	
World 3.3	

Fertility has declined throughout the industrialized world and is highest in Africa.

RUSSIAN FEDERATION

KAZAKHSTAN · MONGOLIA · GEORGIA · ARM. · AZERB. · UZBEKISTAN · KYRGYZSTAN · RKEY · TURKMENISTAN · TAJIKISTAN · SIA · NE · SYRIA · BANON · IRAQ · IRAN · AFGHANISTAN · CHINA · NORTH KOREA · SOUTH KOREA · JAPAN · ISRAEL · JORDAN · KUWAIT · PAKISTAN · NEPAL · BHUTAN · YPT · BAHRAIN · QATAR · UAE · BANGLADESH · Hong Kong (to UK) · TAIWAN · SAUDI ARABIA · OMAN · INDIA · BURMA · Macao (to Portugal) · ERITREA · YEMEN · LAOS · THAILAND · VIETNAM · DAN · DJIBOUTI · CAMBODIA · PHILIPPINES · ETHIOPIA · SOMALIA · MALDIVES · SRI LANKA · UGANDA · KENYA · BRUNEI · MALAYSIA · A · TANZANIA · SEYCHELLES · SINGAPORE · INDONESIA · PAPUA NEW GUINEA · COMOROS · SOLOMON IS · IA · MALAWI · MOZAMBIQUE · MADAGASCAR · MAURITIUS · ABWE · ANA · AUSTRALIA · New Caledonia (to France) · SWAZILAND · LESOTHO · H · A · NEW ZEALAND

PACIFIC OCEAN

INDIAN OCEAN

PACIFIC OCEAN
- FIJI
- SOLOMON ISLANDS
- VANUATU
- WESTERN SAMOA
- KIRIBATI
- MICRONESIA
- TONGA
- NAURU

MIDDLE EAST
- BAHRAIN

INDIAN OCEAN
- COMOROS
- SEYCHELLES
- MALDIVES
- MAURITIUS

ASIA
- MACAO (to Portugal)
- HONG KONG (to UK)
- SINGAPORE

A nomadic goat-herder in northwest Somalia.

PASTORAL NOMADISM

Traditional ways of life, in which a balance between population numbers and natural resources had achieved equilibrium, are now under threat. Since the mid-1980s a succession of droughts in the Sahel and civil wars in Sudan, Ethiopia, Eritrea and Somalia have disrupted the traditional balance between population and resources in this region.

HUNGER AND DISEASE

T HE RECENT PAST has seen an unparalleled increase in food production and availability. However, underlying global success there is marked regional inequality; drought, conflict and natural catastrophes can have disastrous effects on the ability of people to feed themselves. Current estimates are that nearly 800 million people, almost all in the developing countries, do not have enough food to meet their basic nutritional needs. A third of children in developing countries suffer growth faltering, mainly because of under-nutrition. Undernourished children are handicapped in their intellectual development, fall ill more easily and have lower physical productivity as adults.

WORLD INFANT MORTALITY

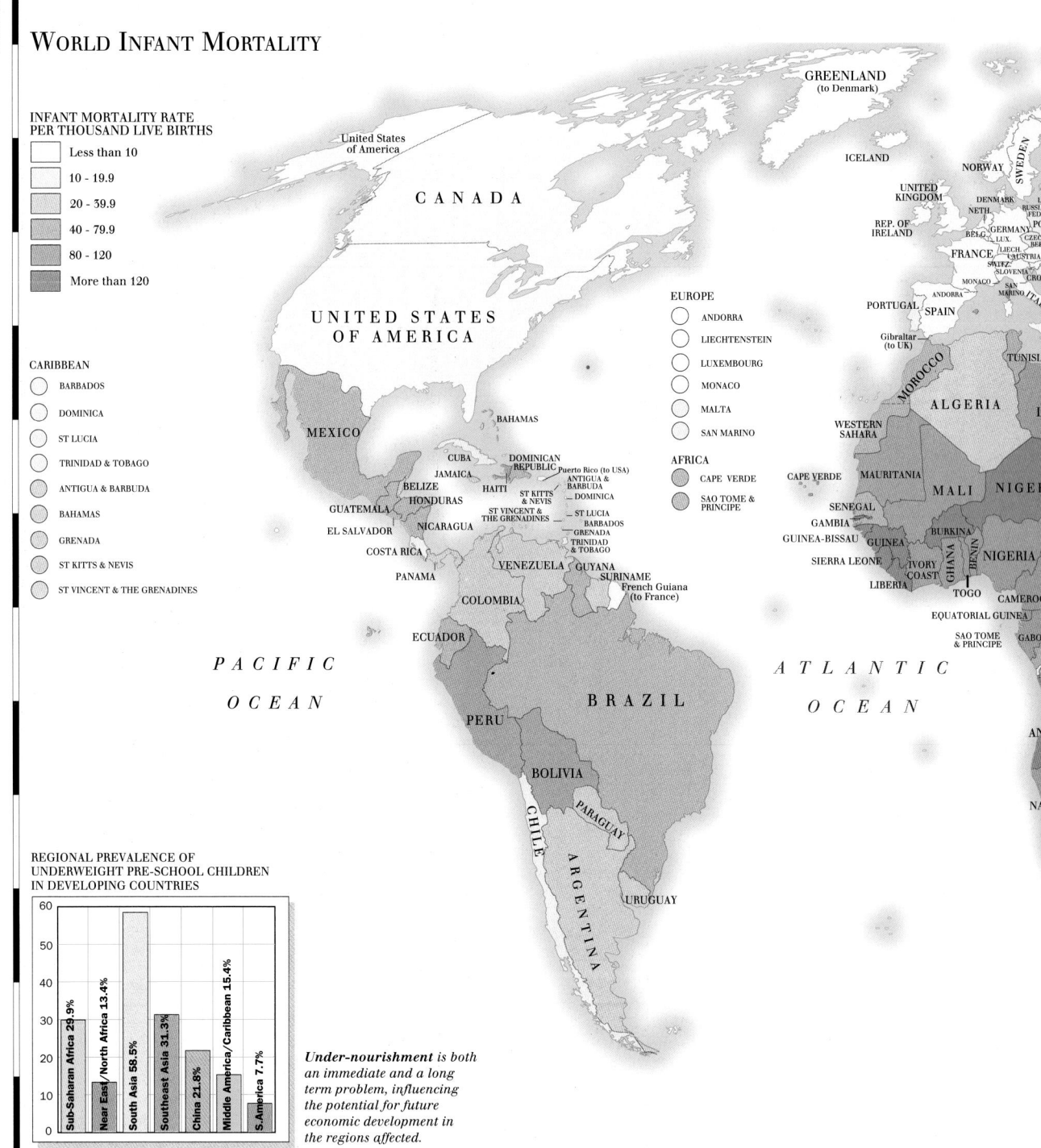

INFANT MORTALITY RATE PER THOUSAND LIVE BIRTHS

- Less than 10
- 10 - 19.9
- 20 - 39.9
- 40 - 79.9
- 80 - 120
- More than 120

CARIBBEAN

- BARBADOS
- DOMINICA
- ST LUCIA
- TRINIDAD & TOBAGO
- ANTIGUA & BARBUDA
- BAHAMAS
- GRENADA
- ST KITTS & NEVIS
- ST VINCENT & THE GRENADINES

EUROPE

- ANDORRA
- LIECHTENSTEIN
- LUXEMBOURG
- MONACO
- MALTA
- SAN MARINO

AFRICA

- CAPE VERDE
- SAO TOME & PRINCIPE

REGIONAL PREVALENCE OF UNDERWEIGHT PRE-SCHOOL CHILDREN IN DEVELOPING COUNTRIES

Bar chart values:
- Sub-Saharan Africa 29.9%
- Near East/North Africa 13.4%
- South Asia 58.5%
- Southeast Asia 31.3%
- China 21.8%
- Middle America/Caribbean 15.4%
- S.America 7.7%

Under-nourishment is both an immediate and a long term problem, influencing the potential for future economic development in the regions affected.

POVERTY

Rural poverty, especially in Asia and Africa, is associated with hunger and malnutrition. People who are reduced to subsistence farming on unproductive land are most at risk. Their children are more likely to be under-nourished, and are prone to infections such as dysentery and respiratory and parasitic diseases. Improving the food supply is not the only solution: better access to health services, improved health education and sanitation, the promotion of breast feeding and immunization are all imporant priorities.

Poor soil, inadequate technology, lack of water control and infestation by pests are all problems afflicting farmers on marginal land in Asia.

CONFLICT

Conflict is increasingly a cause of hunger. In 1993-94, approximately 80% of food aid worldwide was being directed to relieve distress in man-made rather than natural disasters – in Somalia, Angola, Liberia, southern Sudan, Rwanda, Afghanistan and Cambodia. Breakdown of civil order and infrastructure in war zones makes food aid distribution hazardous and inadequate. Refugees are forced to become landless – cultivated land is neglected indefinitely, compounding the difficulties of recovery.

The distribution of food to refugees in war zones is often disrupted by the fighting. Food frequently disappears onto the black market, never reaching the starving.

RUSSIAN FEDERATION

SSIA

INE

A

IA

KAZAKHSTAN

MONGOLIA

GEORGIA
ARM. AZERB.
URKEY
UZBEKISTAN
TURKMENISTAN
KYRGYZSTAN
TAJIKISTAN

NORTH KOREA
SOUTH KOREA
JAPAN

US
LEBANON
SYRIA
ISRAEL
JORDAN
IRAQ
IRAN
AFGHANISTAN
PAKISTAN

CHINA

KUWAIT
BAHRAIN
QATAR
UAE

NEPAL
BHUTAN

GYPT

SAUDI ARABIA

OMAN

BANGLADESH

INDIA

BURMA
LAOS

Hong Kong (to UK)
Macao (to Portugal)
TAIWAN

PACIFIC

OCEAN

ERITREA
YEMEN

THAILAND
VIETNAM
CAMBODIA

PHILIPPINES

UDAN
DJIBOUTI

C

ETHIOPIA

SOMALIA

MALDIVES

SRI LANKA

BRUNEI
MALAYSIA

SINGAPORE

UGANDA
KENYA
RE
A
DI

SEYCHELLES

INDONESIA

PAPUA NEW GUINEA

SOLOMON IS

INDIAN OCEAN

TANZANIA

BIA
MALAWI
COMOROS

MOZAMBIQUE

MADAGASCAR

MAURITIUS

New Caledonia (to France)

ABWE
YANA

AUSTRALIA

SWAZILAND
LESOTHO
TH
CA

NEW ZEALAND

PACIFIC OCEAN
- FIJI
- MICRONESIA
- KIRIBATI
- NAURU
- SOLOMON ISLANDS
- TONGA
- VANUATU
- WESTERN SAMOA

MIDDLE EAST
- BAHRAIN

INDIAN OCEAN
- SEYCHELLES
- MAURITIUS
- MALDIVES
- COMOROS

ASIA
- HONG KONG (U K)
- SINGAPORE

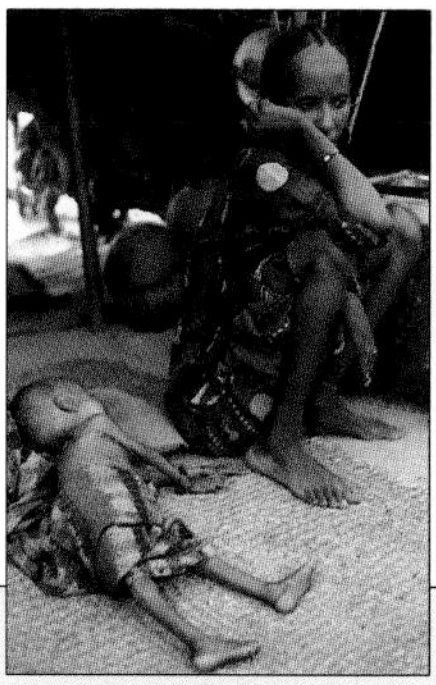

A combination of war and famine in Ethiopia has brought starvation to catastrophic levels.

STARVATION IN AFRICA

Although food production in Africa has actually increased since the 1970s, per capita food production has fallen, and dependence on food imports and foreign aid has increased. In 1994, 204 million Africans (around 35% of the continent's total population) were suffering from chronic hunger and malnutrition.

THE WORLD ECONOMY

THE PATTERN OF THE global economy frequently relates to an underlying equation: the relationship between population and available resources. Japan, for example, had a much "bigger" economy than the former Soviet Union, India or Latin America as a whole. Such imbalances usually occur because countries differ enormously in their living standards, the education and skills of their work forces, the productivity of their agriculture, and in the value of their markets. A country's economic performance can be evaluated by calculating its Gross National Product (GNP). This is the total value of both the goods, and the services (including so-called "invisible exports" – financial services, tourism etc.) that it produces.

NATIONAL ECONOMIC PERFORMANCE

GNP PER CAPITA IN US$
- No data
- $800 or less
- $801 - $5,000
- $3,001 - $9,000
- $9,001 - $20,000
- More than $20,000

CARIBBEAN
- BAHAMAS
- DOMINICA
- ANTIGUA & BARBUDA
- GRENADA
- GUADELOUPE (to France)
- ST KITTS & NEVIS
- ST LUCIA
- TRINIDAD & TOBAGO
- BARBADOS
- MARTINIQUE (to France)
- ST VINCENT & THE GRENADINES
- BERMUDA (to UK)

EUROPE
- FAEROE ISLANDS (to Denmark)
- ANDORRA
- LUXEMBOURG
- LIECHTENSTEIN
- SAN MARINO
- GIBRALTAR (to UK)
- MALTA
- MONACO

AFRICA
- CAPE VERDE
- SAO TOME & PRINCIPE

Mass-market tourism is now an important source of revenue in many countries.

THE SERVICE SECTOR

During the last three decades the most rapidly growing sector of world trade is services – banking, insurance, tourism, accountancy, consultancy, films, music and other cultural services, airlines and shipping. Services account for 21% of world trade, almost equivalent to the volume of trade in food and raw materials.

INTERNATIONAL TRADE

World trade is still dominated by the rich industrialized countries of Northern Europe, Japan and the USA. In 1994 these developed nations accounted for 70% of all imports and exports. Global exports alone accounted for $900 billion. The General Agreement on Tariffs and Trade (GATT), now superseded by the World Trade Organization (WTO), is made up of 130 countries and seeks to liberalize trading worldwide by the harmonization of import tariffs on goods and services.

Baltimore in Maryland is a container port where large quantities of cargo are shipped to worldwide markets. Seaborne trade accounts for more than 80% of the total volume of world trade.

PACIFIC RIM

The "Four Dragons" of the Pacific Rim – South Korea, Taiwan, Hong Kong and Singapore – are high-growth areas, forging ahead with rapid export-led industrialization. Growth rates in the region over the last three decades have consistently been double or treble those of the USA or Western Europe. Low labor costs, stable governments and encouragement of foreign investment have all contributed to this spectacular growth.

South Korea has become a major industrial power, specializing in shipbuilding, car manufacture, and high technology – computers and communications equipment.

THE WORLD'S TOP EXPORTERS 1994

$ bn

(Bar chart, values from 600 to 0, showing exporters: USA, Germany, Japan, France, UK, Italy, Canada, Netherlands, Hong Kong, Belgium/Luxembourg, China, Singapore, South Korea)

Manufactured goods still dominate the export market, but service industries account for an increasingly large sector in the developed world.

PACIFIC OCEAN
- FIJI
- SOLOMON ISLANDS
- VANUATU
- WESTERN SAMOA
- KIRIBATI
- MICRONESIA
- TONGA
- NAURU

MIDDLE EAST
- BAHRAIN

INDIAN OCEAN
- SEYCHELLES
- MALDIVES
- MAURITIUS

ASIA
- HONG KONG (to UK)
- SINGAPORE

ETHNICITY AND THE NATION STATE

WITH THE END OF the Cold War, long-standing alliances and conflicts based on ideological differences – ideas of "left" and "right" – have disappeared into the background. However, others based on some form of cultural identity or ethnicity, whether it is derived from language, religion, color, clan, tribe or cultural tradition, have seemingly proliferated. Very few nation states can claim to have a homogenous identity. Almost all have minorities. In some cases, the alienation between the minority and majority can lead to a threatened breakup of nation states. In others, a sense of cultural identity spans several countries: it is known as "pan-ethnicity."

NATIONS WITHIN NATIONS

NATIONAL & ETHNIC CONFLICT

▦ Countries with active secessionist movements

👑 Intercommunal or ethnic violence

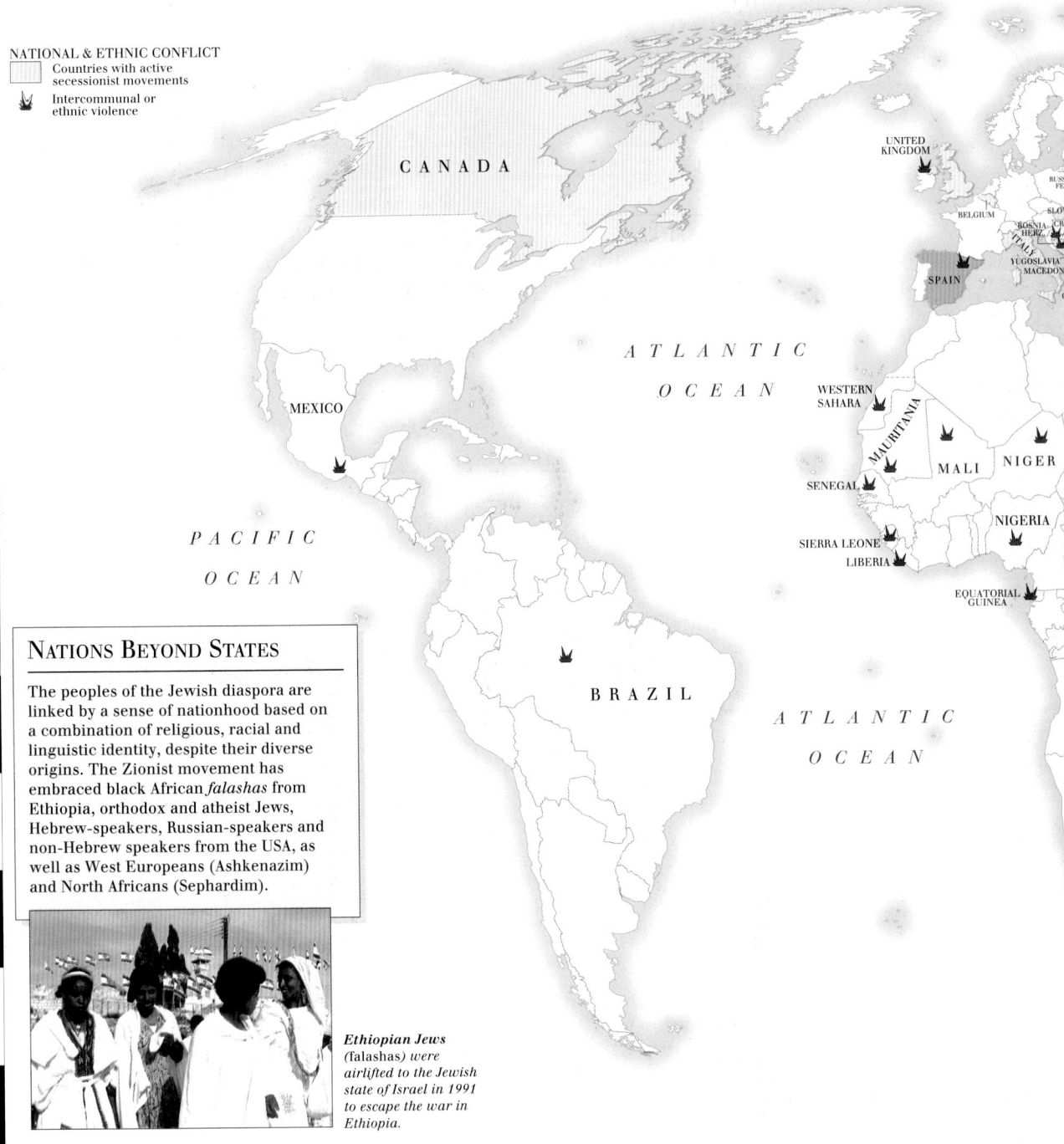

NATIONS BEYOND STATES

The peoples of the Jewish diaspora are linked by a sense of nationhood based on a combination of religious, racial and linguistic identity, despite their diverse origins. The Zionist movement has embraced black African *falashas* from Ethiopia, orthodox and atheist Jews, Hebrew-speakers, Russian-speakers and non-Hebrew speakers from the USA, as well as West Europeans (Ashkenazim) and North Africans (Sephardim).

Ethiopian Jews (falashas) *were airlifted to the Jewish state of Israel in 1991 to escape the war in Ethiopia.*

RELIGIOUS LOYALTIES

Religion can be a politically unifying force, as well as a source of friction with other religions and denominations. In the Irish Republic, Catholics make up the majority of the population, while Protestants dominate in Northern Ireland. More than in any other country in Western Europe, people's daily lives are shaped by their religion, and an acute sense of the roots of their differences has erupted in continuing intercommunal conflict.

Ulster protestants commemorate the English victory against the Irish in 1690. The "marching season" is often a trigger for sectarian violence.

Political posters in northern Spain keep Basque separatism on the political agenda. So far, the Spanish government has failed to deal with the question of Basque devolution.

PAN-ETHNICITY

Sometimes, groups which straddle different countries feel a sense of nationhood which cannot yet be realized in a nation state. There are many examples of ethnic minorities trying to secede, in many cases drawing sustenance from coreligionists or ethnic brethren across borders. In Europe, for example, the Basque people hope for a pan-ethnic Basque state within a federal EU. In West Asia, both the Kurds and the Palestinians aspire to national sovereignty.

RUSSIAN FEDERATION

GEORGIA

AZERBAIJAN

TAJIKISTAN

TURKEY

IRAQ   IRAN   AFGHANISTAN

CHINA

PACIFIC

OCEAN

INDIA   BURMA

LAOS

YEMEN

DJIBOUTI

CAMBODIA

ETHIOPIA

SOMALIA

SRI LANKA

PHILIPPINES

KENYA

TANZANIA

INDONESIA

PAPUA
NEW GUINEA

INDIAN

OCEAN

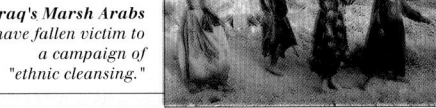

Iraq's Marsh Arabs have fallen victim to a campaign of "ethnic cleansing."

ETHNIC CLEANSING

Minority ethnic groups are frequently at risk because of their religious, cultural or linguistic differences. Extreme forms of persecution, forced relocation or genocide, known as "ethnic cleansing," have recently been witnessed in Iraq, Iran, Bosnia and Rwanda.

THE WORLD ENVIRONMENT

EACH DAY 50 TO 100 species of plant and animal become extinct – it is now internationally recognized that conservation of the world's remaining wildlife and ecosystems is an urgent priority. In many countries, legislation is ensuring that land is protected from urbanization and agriculture – the two greatest threats to the environment. However, environmental protection legislation is much more apparent in the countries of the developed world. In the developing countries, pressure on land and resources creates more urgent priorities: environmental protection is often dependent on grants and aid from the developed world, and foreign currency-earners such as tourism take precedence over conservation.

GLOBAL CONSERVATION

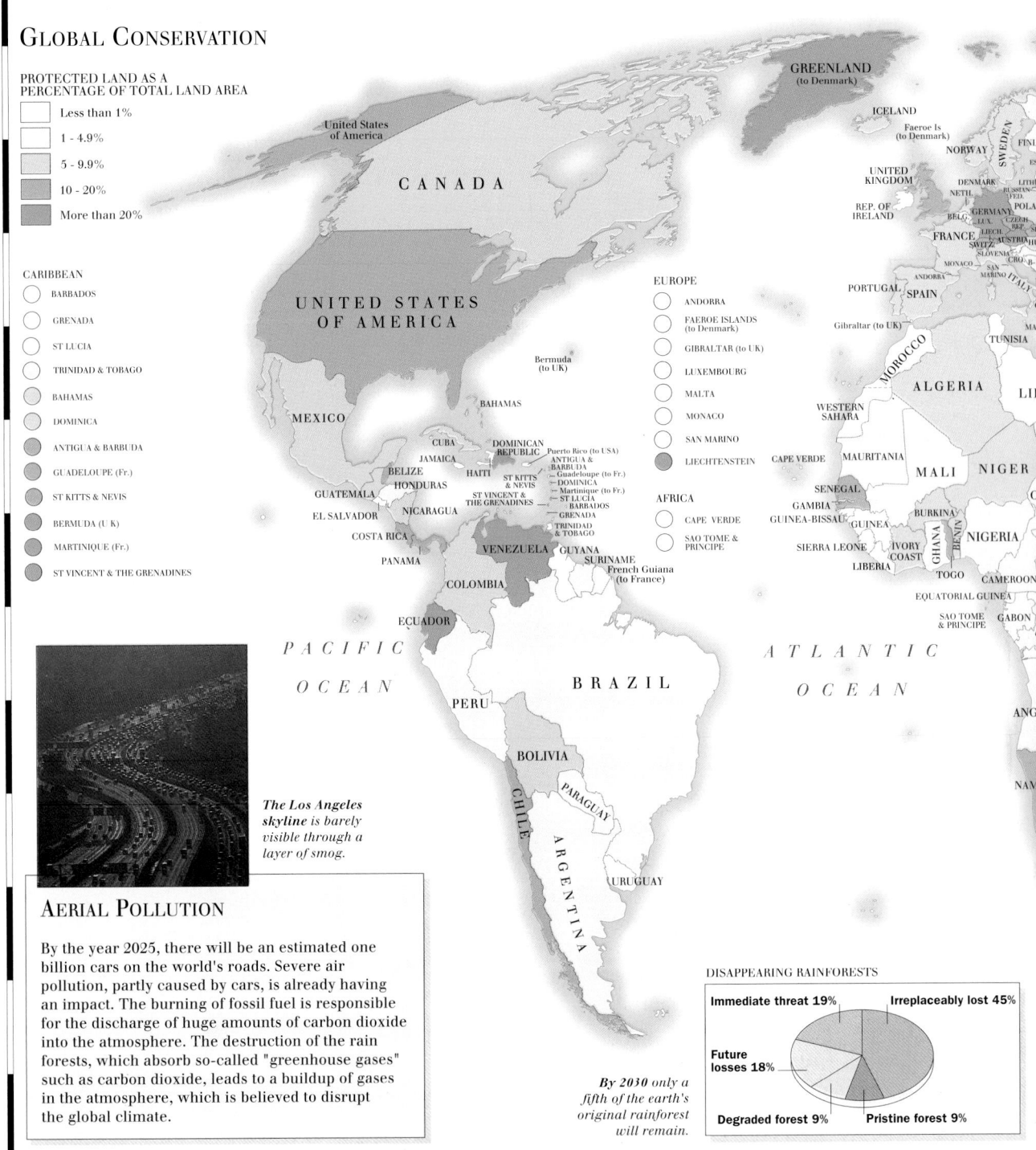

PROTECTED LAND AS A
PERCENTAGE OF TOTAL LAND AREA

- Less than 1%
- 1 - 4.9%
- 5 - 9.9%
- 10 - 20%
- More than 20%

CARIBBEAN
- BARBADOS
- GRENADA
- ST LUCIA
- TRINIDAD & TOBAGO
- BAHAMAS
- DOMINICA
- ANTIGUA & BARBUDA
- GUADELOUPE (Fr.)
- ST KITTS & NEVIS
- BERMUDA (U.K)
- MARTINIQUE (Fr.)
- ST VINCENT & THE GRENADINES

EUROPE
- ANDORRA
- FAEROE ISLANDS (to Denmark)
- GIBRALTAR (to UK)
- LUXEMBOURG
- MALTA
- MONACO
- SAN MARINO
- LIECHTENSTEIN

AFRICA
- CAPE VERDE
- SAO TOME & PRINCIPE

The Los Angeles skyline is barely visible through a layer of smog.

AERIAL POLLUTION

By the year 2025, there will be an estimated one billion cars on the world's roads. Severe air pollution, partly caused by cars, is already having an impact. The burning of fossil fuel is responsible for the discharge of huge amounts of carbon dioxide into the atmosphere. The destruction of the rain forests, which absorb so-called "greenhouse gases" such as carbon dioxide, leads to a buildup of gases in the atmosphere, which is believed to disrupt the global climate.

By 2030 only a fifth of the earth's original rainforest will remain.

DISAPPEARING RAINFORESTS

- Immediate threat 19%
- Irreplaceably lost 45%
- Future losses 18%
- Degraded forest 9%
- Pristine forest 9%

WATER RESOURCES

Global demand for water – for industrial, agricultural, and domestic use – has increased five-fold since 1950. In many parts of the world, water resources are contaminated by industrial waste and pollution, while dams and irrigation schemes transform river and floodplain ecosystems. Localized drought, spread of water-borne diseases, and contaminated drinking water are all major problems.

The Aral Sea has shrunk by 23,000 square miles as a result of schemes to irrigate the cotton fields of Uzbekistan.

The tropical rainforests of Malaysia. Rain forests contain more than 20% of all the known natural species of plants and animals living on Earth.

RAINFOREST

It is thought that there are some 4.5 million plant and animal species, two-thirds of which are to be found in the tropics, with an abundance living in the equatorial rainforests. This diversity of plant and animal life is increasingly threatened by the destruction of the rainforest. Commercial logging and clearing forests for agriculture, ranching and mineral exploitation are destroying the rainforest at the rate of more than 60,000 square miles each year.

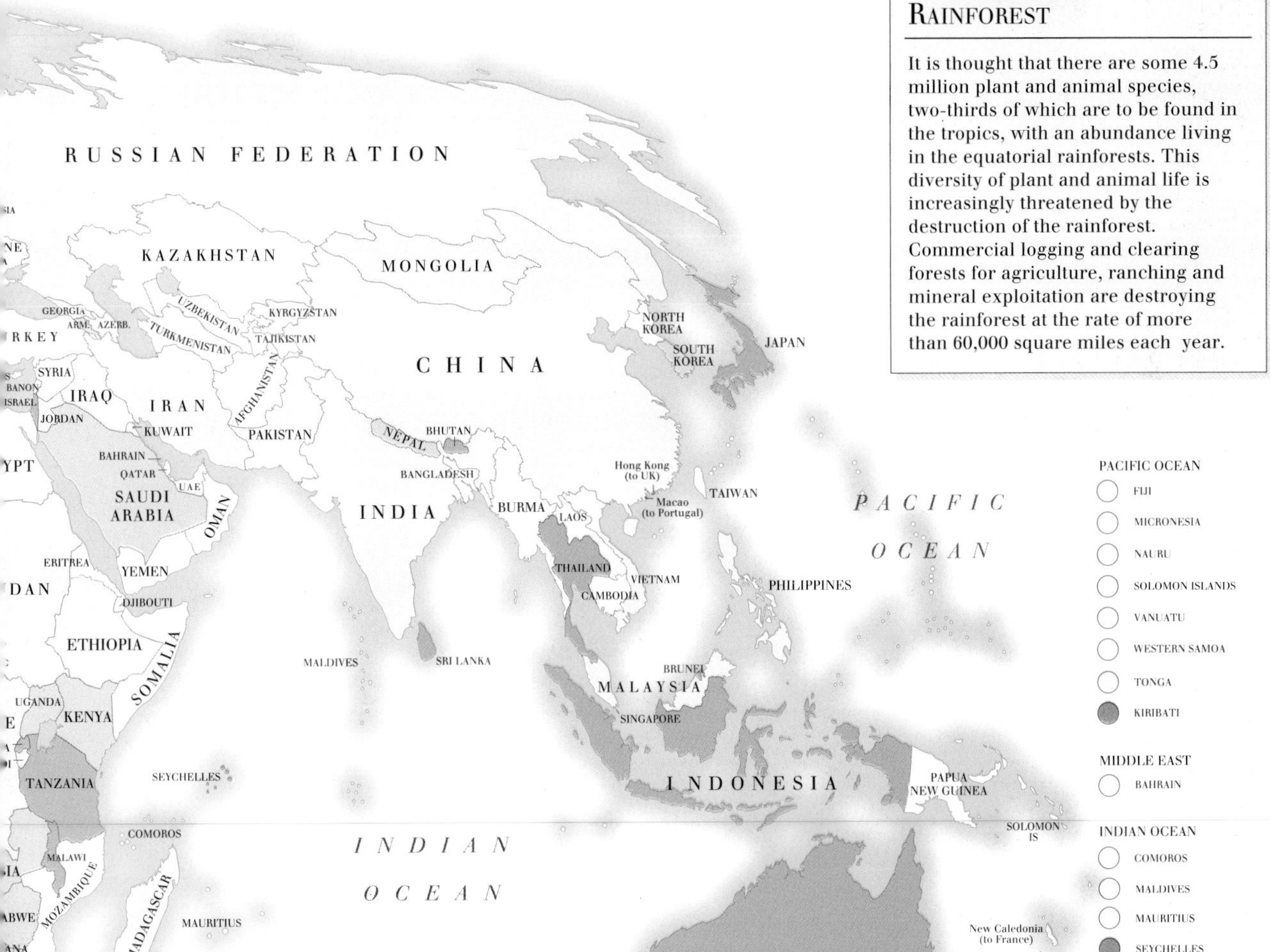

Sand dunes along the edges of the Sahara desert are encroaching on arable land.

MARGINAL LAND

One-third of the world's land area is subject to the risk of soil erosion and desertification – in the absence of other fuels, wood and charcoal burning destroys the forests, removing topsoils and hastening the encroachment of the desert. The onward march of desert can be halted by expensive tree-planting programs and better land management.

Map labels

RUSSIAN FEDERATION

KAZAKHSTAN

MONGOLIA

GEORGIA
ARME. AZERB.
UZBEKISTAN
KYRGYZSTAN
TURKMENISTAN
TAJIKISTAN

TURKEY

SYRIA
LEBANON
ISRAEL
IRAQ
JORDAN
IRAN
AFGHANISTAN
PAKISTAN

KUWAIT
BAHRAIN
QATAR
UAE
OMAN

SAUDI ARABIA

YEMEN

ERITREA

EGYPT
SUDAN

DJIBOUTI

ETHIOPIA

SOMALIA

UGANDA
KENYA

TANZANIA

SEYCHELLES

COMOROS

MALAWI
MOZAMBIQUE
MADAGASCAR
ZIMBABWE
BOTSWANA
MAURITIUS

SWAZILAND
LESOTHO

CHINA

NORTH KOREA
SOUTH KOREA
JAPAN

NEPAL
BHUTAN
BANGLADESH

INDIA
BURMA

Hong Kong (to UK)
Macao (to Portugal)
TAIWAN

LAOS
THAILAND
VIETNAM
CAMBODIA

PHILIPPINES

MALDIVES
SRI LANKA

BRUNEI

MALAYSIA
SINGAPORE

INDONESIA

PAPUA NEW GUINEA

SOLOMON IS

P A C I F I C

O C E A N

New Caledonia (to France)

AUSTRALIA

I N D I A N

O C E A N

NEW ZEALAND

Legend

PACIFIC OCEAN
○ FIJI
○ MICRONESIA
○ NAURU
○ SOLOMON ISLANDS
○ VANUATU
○ WESTERN SAMOA
○ TONGA
● KIRIBATI

MIDDLE EAST
○ BAHRAIN

INDIAN OCEAN
○ COMOROS
○ MALDIVES
○ MAURITIUS
● SEYCHELLES

ASIA
○ HONG KONG (to UK)
○ MACAO (to Portugal)
○ SINGAPORE

GLOBAL COMMUNICATIONS

WHEN ASKED WHAT HAD caused the collapse of communism in eastern Europe, Poland's former president, Lech Wałęsa, pointed to a television set. "It all came from there," he said. Undoubtedly, the globalization of television and printed news has wrought dramatic changes in the world. In addition, a revolution in digital technology has created a truly global village. Television viewers can now receive hundreds of channels by satellite, watch films and the latest news, shop, book tickets and access databanks. With the help of fibre-optic cables, and new software interfaces, the Internet (which links computers all over the world) is rapidly expanding into a global multimedia communications network.

GLOBAL INTERNET HOSTS

COUNTRIES WITH 1
INTERNET HOST PER:

- more than 100,001 inhabitants
- 10,001-100,000 inhabitants
- 1,001-10,000 inhabitants
- 101-1,000 inhabitants
- 1-100 inhabitants
- no data available/ no internet hosts

CARIBBEAN
- BARBADOS
- TRINIDAD & TOBAGO
- BAHAMAS
- ANTIGUA & BARBUDA
- CAYMAN ISLANDS
- BERMUDA (UK)

EUROPE
- ANDORRA
- GIBRALTAR (to UK)
- LUXEMBOURG
- MALTA
- MONACO
- SAN MARINO
- LIECHTENSTEIN

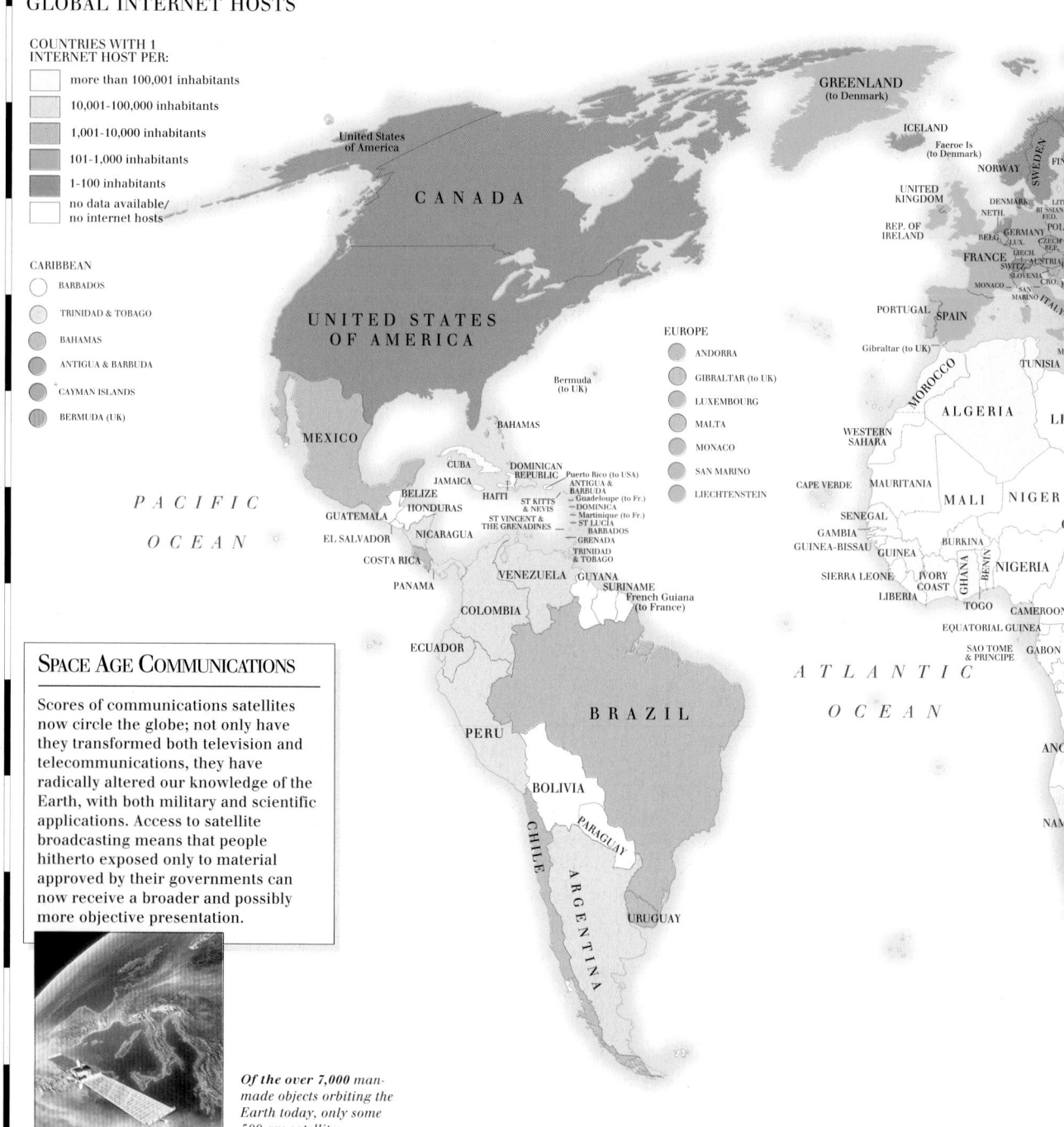

SPACE AGE COMMUNICATIONS

Scores of communications satellites now circle the globe; not only have they transformed both television and telecommunications, they have radically altered our knowledge of the Earth, with both military and scientific applications. Access to satellite broadcasting means that people hitherto exposed only to material approved by their governments can now receive a broader and possibly more objective presentation.

Of the over 7,000 man-made objects orbiting the Earth today, only some 500 are satellites.

GLOBAL COMMUNICATIONS

A bicycle wheel on a Delhi rooftop picks up television signals. Used to makeshift technology, Indians are unwilling to pay for satellite.

GLOBAL VILLAGE

Since 1980, the number of television sets in the world has neary trebled to one billion. Multimedia empires are currently competing for the vast satellite audiences (and lucrative advertising revenues) of the developing world. While there is resistance to the endless diet of Western popular culture broadcast by satellite, which is thought to corrupt traditional values, many governments are powerless to stop the spread of satellites.

Newspapers are still one of the most important means of relaying news. Often even journals in the more developed democracies are subject to state control or impose self-censorship.

FREEDOM OF SPEECH

The basic human right to freedom of speech is one that many countries still do not allow their citizens. While the collapse of communism saw a number of one-party states turn into multiparty democracies, total freedom of expression did not automatically follow. Many governments across the political spectrum still manipulate or suppress the media to further their own ends. In 1995, it was estimated that 182 journalists in 22 countries were being held in prison for printing articles unacceptable to the state.

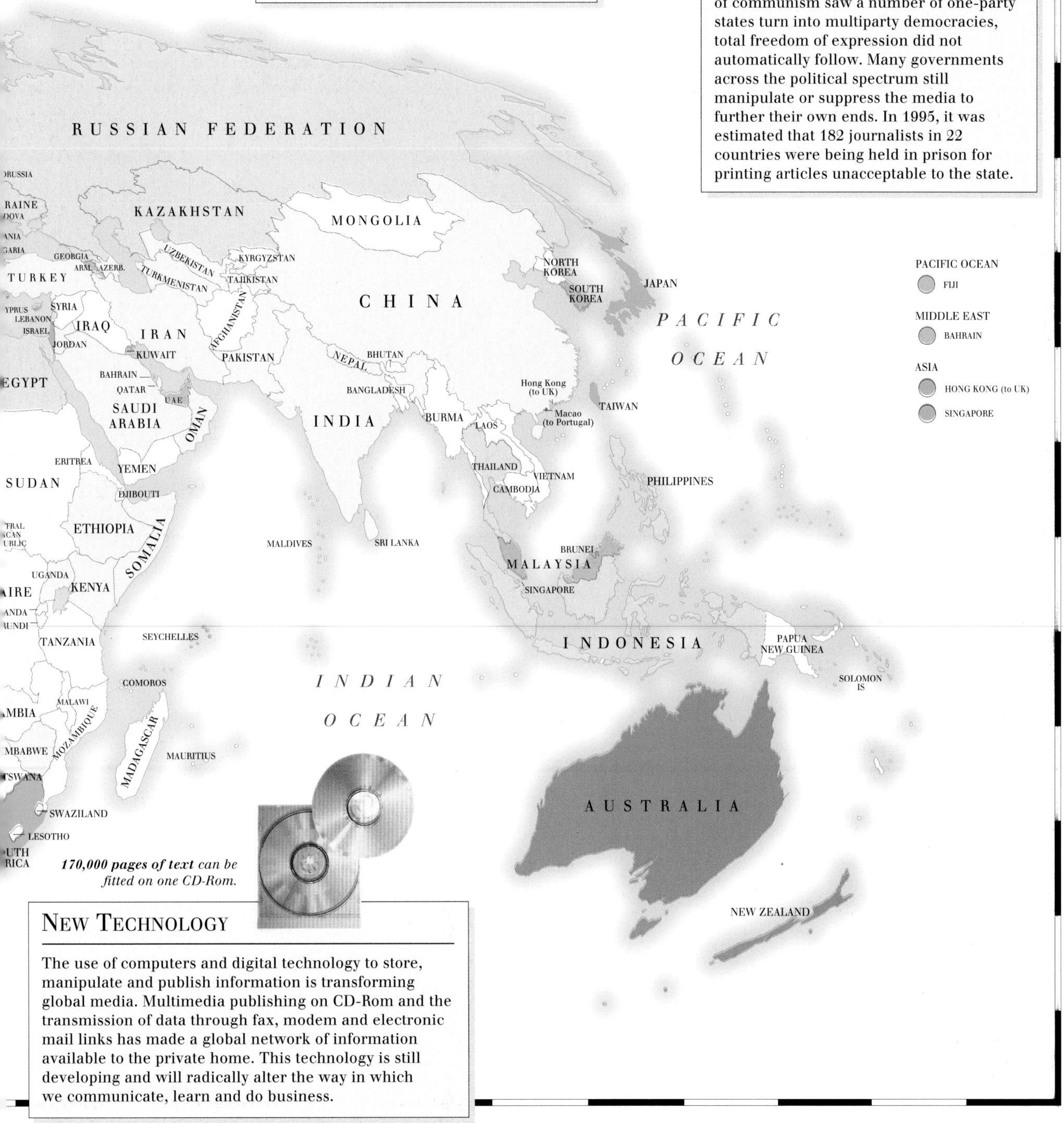

RUSSIAN FEDERATION

PRUSSIA
RAINE
DOVA
ARIA
GEORGIA
TURKEY
YPRUS
LEBANON
ISRAEL
JORDAN
EGYPT
SYRIA
IRAQ
KUWAIT
BAHRAIN
QATAR
SAUDI
ARABIA
UAE
OMAN
YEMEN
SUDAN
ERITREA
DJIBOUTI
CTRAL
CAN
UBLIC
ETHIOPIA
UGANDA
KENYA
ANDA
URUNDI
AIRE
TANZANIA
MBIA
MALAWI
MBABWE
MOZAMBIQUE
TSWANA
SWAZILAND
LESOTHO
UTH
RICA

KAZAKHSTAN
UZBEKISTAN
TURKMENISTAN
TAJIKISTAN
KYRGYZSTAN
AZERB.
ARM.
AFGHANISTAN
IRAN
PAKISTAN
MONGOLIA
CHINA
NEPAL
BHUTAN
BANGLADESH
INDIA
BURMA
LAOS
THAILAND
CAMBODIA
VIETNAM
NORTH KOREA
SOUTH KOREA
JAPAN
Hong Kong (to UK)
Macao (to Portugal)
TAIWAN
PHILIPPINES

PACIFIC OCEAN

SOMALIA
SEYCHELLES
COMOROS
MADAGASCAR
MAURITIUS
MALDIVES
SRI LANKA
MALAYSIA
BRUNEI
SINGAPORE

INDIAN OCEAN

INDONESIA
PAPUA NEW GUINEA
SOLOMON IS

AUSTRALIA

NEW ZEALAND

PACIFIC OCEAN
● FIJI

MIDDLE EAST
● BAHRAIN

ASIA
● HONG KONG (to UK)
● SINGAPORE

170,000 pages of text can be fitted on one CD-Rom.

NEW TECHNOLOGY

The use of computers and digital technology to store, manipulate and publish information is transforming global media. Multimedia publishing on CD-Rom and the transmission of data through fax, modem and electronic mail links has made a global network of information available to the private home. This technology is still developing and will radically alter the way in which we communicate, learn and do business.

SECURITY AND DEFENSE

THE POST-COLD WAR period has produced a range of threats to the principal states of the international community. Ethnic conflict within states, mass migration and environmental hazards provide examples of new insecurities with potential for conflict of a very different sort from its Cold War counterpart. The spectacle of Yugoslavia's collapse into warring factions and the breakup of the Soviet Union were the most dramatic examples of the decline of the state as a source of security for its citizens and as a pillar of world order. Today, while orthodox diplomacy still has its place, recognition of the inability of the state to cope alone makes multi-lateral solutions imperative.

GLOBAL DEFENSE AND CONFLICT

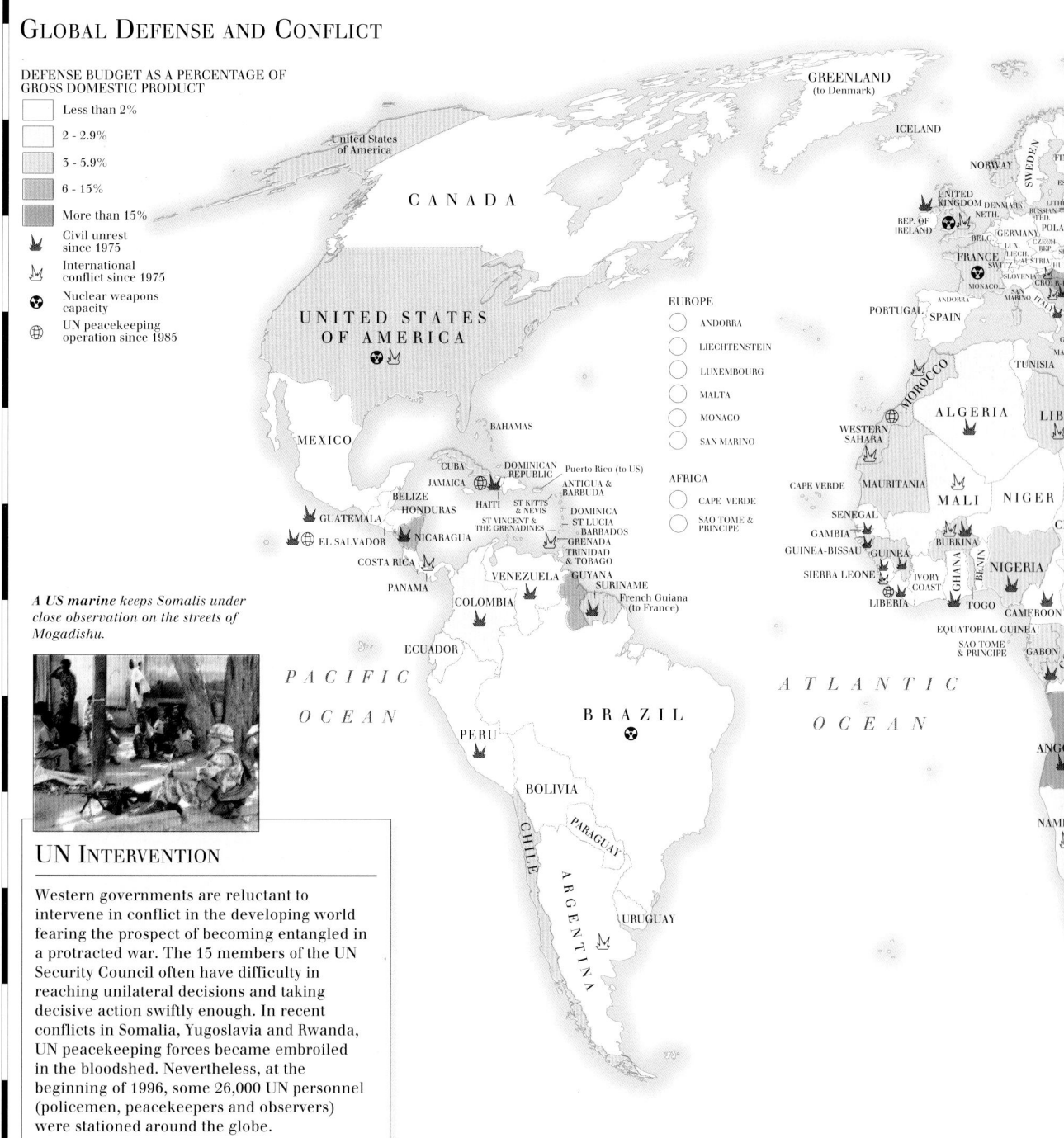

DEFENSE BUDGET AS A PERCENTAGE OF
GROSS DOMESTIC PRODUCT

- Less than 2%
- 2 - 2.9%
- 3 - 5.9%
- 6 - 15%
- More than 15%
- Civil unrest since 1975
- International conflict since 1975
- Nuclear weapons capacity
- UN peacekeeping operation since 1985

A US marine keeps Somalis under close observation on the streets of Mogadishu.

UN INTERVENTION

Western governments are reluctant to intervene in conflict in the developing world fearing the prospect of becoming entangled in a protracted war. The 15 members of the UN Security Council often have difficulty in reaching unilateral decisions and taking decisive action swiftly enough. In recent conflicts in Somalia, Yugoslavia and Rwanda, UN peacekeeping forces became embroiled in the bloodshed. Nevertheless, at the beginning of 1996, some 26,000 UN personnel (policemen, peacekeepers and observers) were stationed around the globe.

THE ARMS RACE

After World War II, international power was
concentrated in the hands of two superpowers,
the USA and USSR, and their military and
economic allies. Potential all-out conflict was
effectively contained by the nuclear deterrent.
Today, the collapse of the Soviet Union and the
diminishing economic and political power of
the USA have led to fundamental changes in
the power balance. The developing economies of Asia
are now acquiring nuclear capability.

An array of weaponry is
paraded through the streets of
Moscow on the anniversary of the
Bolshevik October revolution.

GULF CONFLICT

In 1990, Iraq's President Saddam
Hussein invaded the small oil-rich
nation of Kuwait. This event led to
rare accord amongst members of the
United Nations Security Council, and
troops were sent to the Gulf. The
ensuing war (1990–1991) is a prime
example of successful military
intervention by the UN. However,
the political objective was clear and
limited: to drive the Iraqis out of
Kuwaiti territory – defending one
state against aggression by another.

The oil wells of Kuwait blazed for many
months after the Gulf conflict

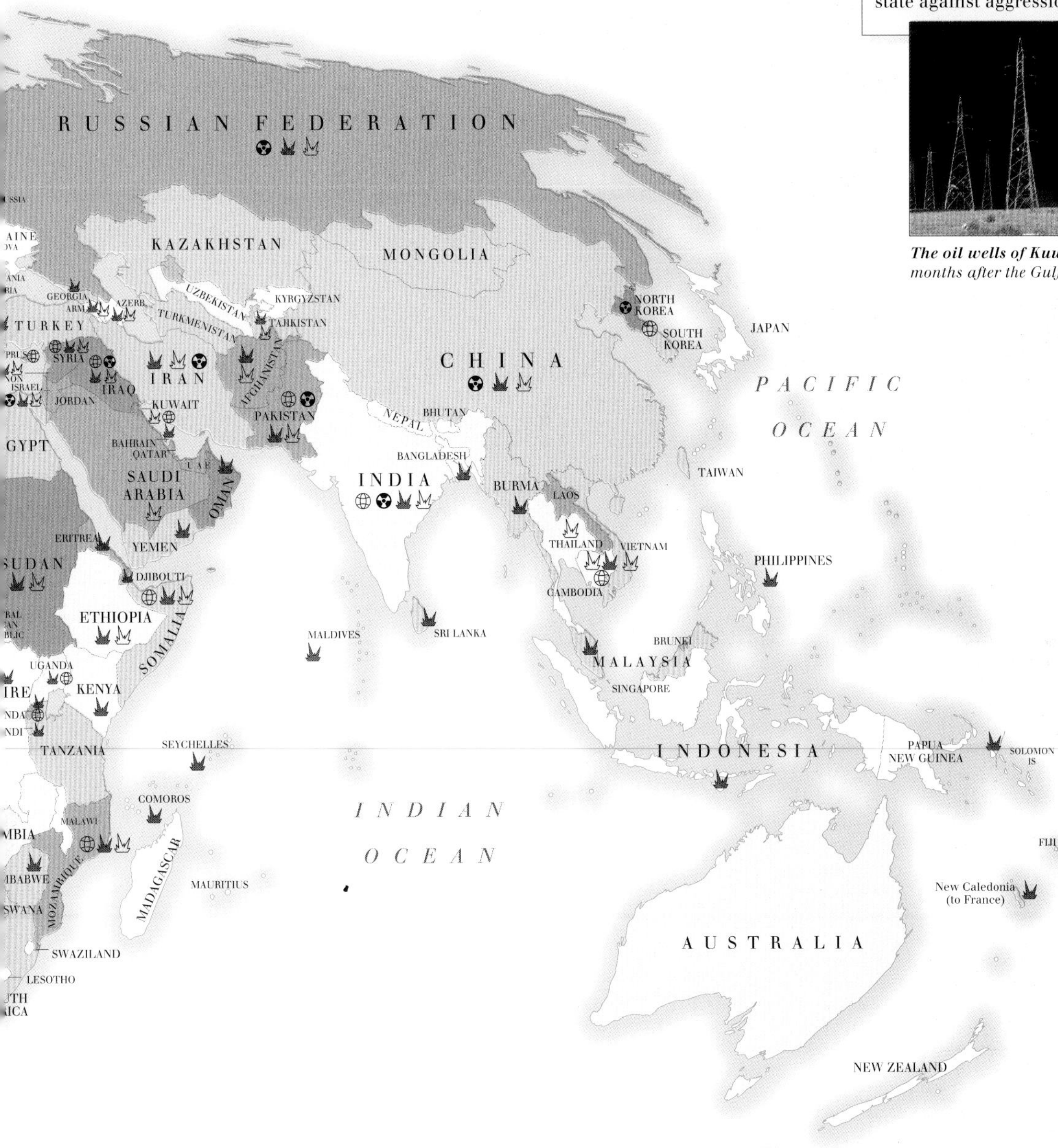

RUSSIAN FEDERATION

KAZAKHSTAN

MONGOLIA

NORTH
KOREA

SOUTH
KOREA

JAPAN

GEORGIA
ARM.   AZERB.
UZBEKISTAN
KYRGYZSTAN

TURKEY   TURKMENISTAN
TAJIKISTAN

PRLS.
SYRIA   IRAN   AFGHANISTAN
ISRAEL
JORDAN   IRAQ   PAKISTAN

CHINA

KUWAIT
NEPAL   BHUTAN

BAHRAIN
QATAR
U.A.E.   BANGLADESH

EGYPT

SAUDI
ARABIA   OMAN   INDIA   BURMA   LAOS

ERITREA   YEMEN   THAILAND   VIETNAM

SUDAN   DJIBOUTI   CAMBODIA

BAL
AN
BLIC
ETHIOPIA   SOMALIA   MALDIVES   SRI LANKA   BRUNEI

PHILIPPINES

UGANDA   MALAYSIA

IRE   KENYA   SINGAPORE

NDA
NDI   TANZANIA   SEYCHELLES   INDONESIA

PAPUA
NEW GUINEA   SOLOMON
IS

COMOROS

MBIA   MALAWI
MADAGASCAR

IBABWE   MOZAMBIQUE   MAURITIUS

SWANA

SWAZILAND

LESOTHO
UTH
ICA

PACIFIC

OCEAN

TAIWAN

INDIAN

OCEAN

AUSTRALIA

FIJI

New Caledonia
(to France)

NEW ZEALAND

PACIFIC OCEAN

○ KIRIBATI
○ MICRONESIA
○ NAURU
○ SOLOMON ISLANDS
○ TONGA
○ VANUATU
○ WESTERN SAMOA
○ FIJI

MIDDLE EAST

◉ BAHRAIN

INDIAN OCEAN

○ COMOROS
○ MALDIVES
○ MAURITIUS
○ SEYCHELLES

ASIA

◉ SINGAPORE

GLOBAL TOURISM

TOURISM IS THE WORLD'S biggest industry. In 1995 there were 567 million tourists worldwide; this number is expected to rise to 937 million by 2010. With improved transportation, cheaper flights and increased leisure time, many of the countries of the developing world are rapidly becoming tourist meccas. Since the 1960s, mass tourism has become increasingly specialized, encompassing sporting and adventure holidays as well as ecological tours. Although the tourist industry employs 127 million people worldwide, the benefits of tourism are not always felt at a local level, where jobs are often low paid and menial. Unregulated growth of tourism is causing both environmental and social damage.

THE GLOBAL TOURIST INDUSTRY

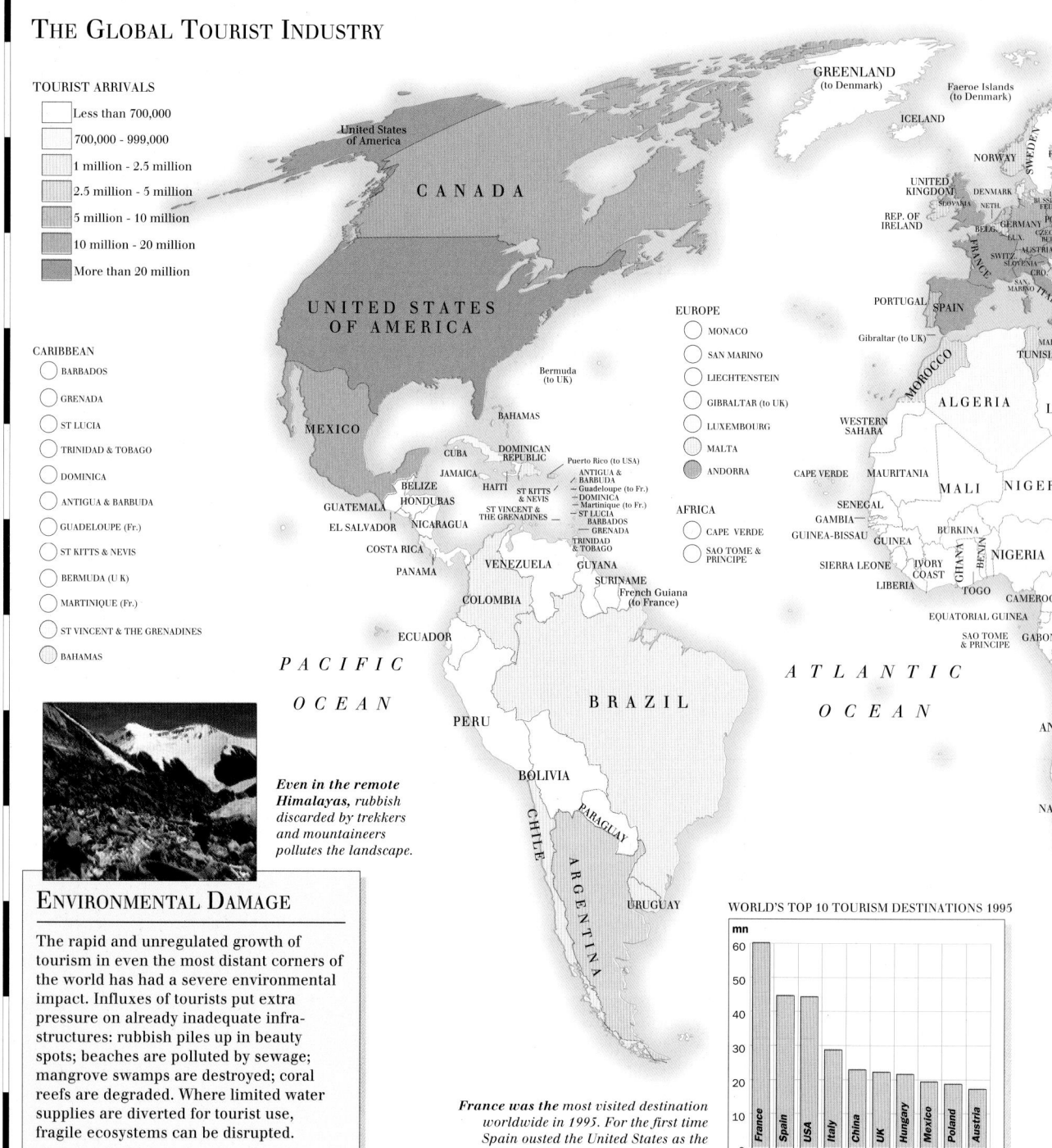

TOURIST ARRIVALS

	Less than 700,000
	700,000 - 999,000
	1 million - 2.5 million
	2.5 million - 5 million
	5 million - 10 million
	10 million - 20 million
	More than 20 million

CARIBBEAN
- BARBADOS
- GRENADA
- ST LUCIA
- TRINIDAD & TOBAGO
- DOMINICA
- ANTIGUA & BARBUDA
- GUADELOUPE (Fr.)
- ST KITTS & NEVIS
- BERMUDA (U K)
- MARTINIQUE (Fr.)
- ST VINCENT & THE GRENADINES
- BAHAMAS

EUROPE
- MONACO
- SAN MARINO
- LIECHTENSTEIN
- GIBRALTAR (to UK)
- LUXEMBOURG
- MALTA
- ANDORRA

AFRICA
- CAPE VERDE
- SAO TOME & PRINCIPE

Even in the remote Himalayas, rubbish discarded by trekkers and mountaineers pollutes the landscape.

ENVIRONMENTAL DAMAGE

The rapid and unregulated growth of tourism in even the most distant corners of the world has had a severe environmental impact. Influxes of tourists put extra pressure on already inadequate infrastructures: rubbish piles up in beauty spots; beaches are polluted by sewage; mangrove swamps are destroyed; coral reefs are degraded. Where limited water supplies are diverted for tourist use, fragile ecosystems can be disrupted.

France was the most visited destination worldwide in 1995. For the first time Spain ousted the United States as the world's number two destination.

WORLD'S TOP 10 TOURISM DESTINATIONS 1995

mn

France	Spain	USA	Italy	China	UK	Hungary	Mexico	Poland	Austria

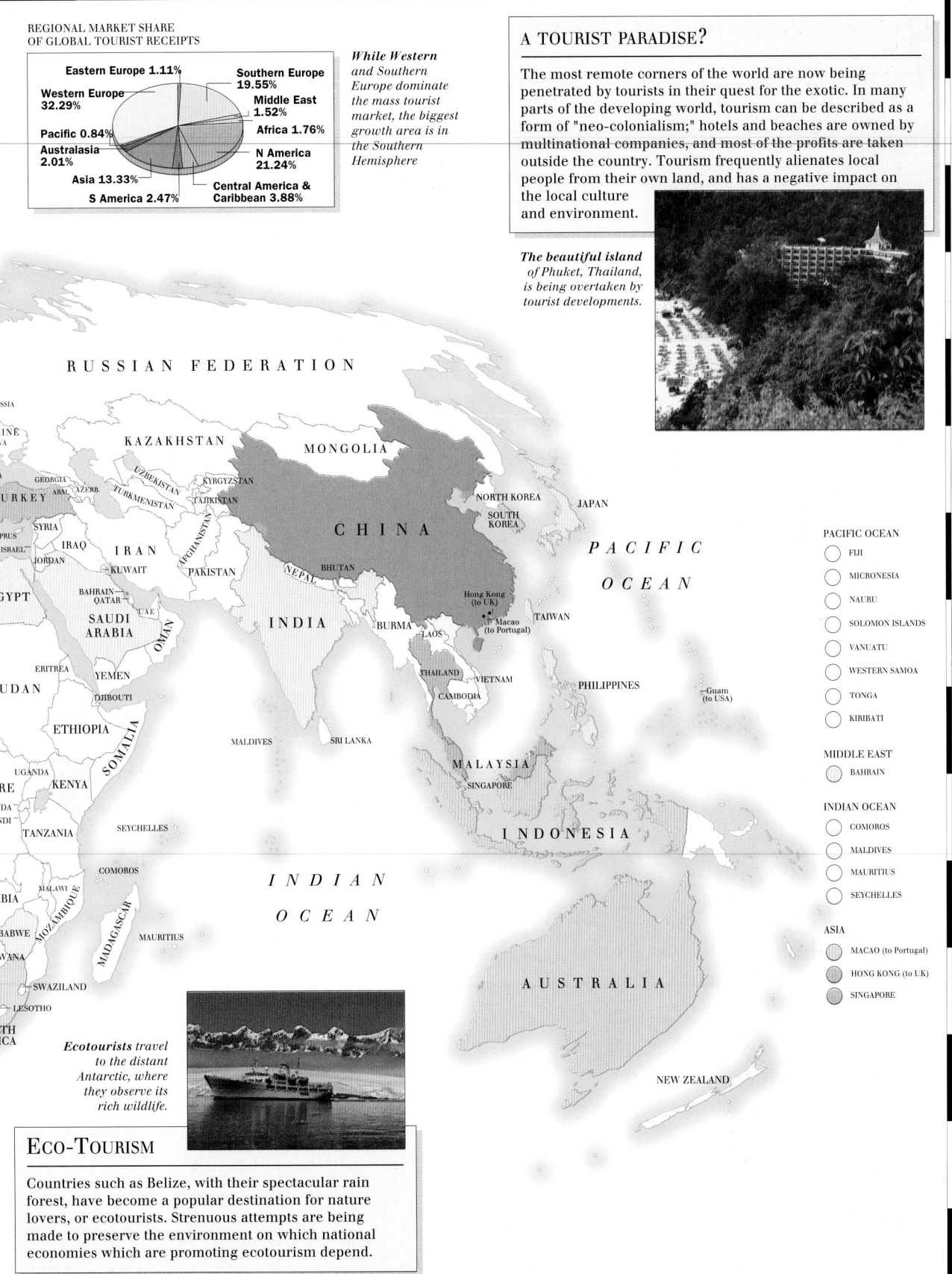

REGIONAL MARKET SHARE
OF GLOBAL TOURIST RECEIPTS

Eastern Europe 1.11%
Western Europe 32.29%
Southern Europe 19.55%
Middle East 1.52%
Pacific 0.84%
Africa 1.76%
Australasia 2.01%
N America 21.24%
Asia 13.33%
S America 2.47%
Central America & Caribbean 3.88%

While Western and Southern Europe dominate the mass tourist market, the biggest growth area is in the Southern Hemisphere

A TOURIST PARADISE?

The most remote corners of the world are now being penetrated by tourists in their quest for the exotic. In many parts of the developing world, tourism can be described as a form of "neo-colonialism;" hotels and beaches are owned by multinational companies, and most of the profits are taken outside the country. Tourism frequently alienates local people from their own land, and has a negative impact on the local culture and environment.

The beautiful island of Phuket, Thailand, is being overtaken by tourist developments.

PACIFIC OCEAN
- FIJI
- MICRONESIA
- NAURU
- SOLOMON ISLANDS
- VANUATU
- WESTERN SAMOA
- TONGA
- KIRIBATI

MIDDLE EAST
- BAHRAIN

INDIAN OCEAN
- COMOROS
- MALDIVES
- MAURITIUS
- SEYCHELLES

ASIA
- MACAO (to Portugal)
- HONG KONG (to UK)
- SINGAPORE

Ecotourists travel to the distant Antarctic, where they observe its rich wildlife.

ECO-TOURISM

Countries such as Belize, with their spectacular rain forest, have become a popular destination for nature lovers, or ecotourists. Strenuous attempts are being made to preserve the environment on which national economies which are promoting ecotourism depend.

THE FINAL FRONTIERS

RESPECT FOR NATIONAL SOVEREIGNTY and the international recognition of national boundaries is a principle central to the United Nations Charter. Nevertheless, there are over 60 disputed borders or territories in the world today; while many of these can be settled by peaceful arbitration, some are sources of international conflict. Ownership of valuable natural resources is a common reason for such disputes, although ethnic concerns provide frequent bloody flashpoints. The legacy of colonial mapmakers, notably in Africa, where inadequate knowledge and political pragmatism led to many arbitrary borders, has caused problems, while territorial acquisitions in long-settled wars can sour international relations.

INTERNATIONAL TERRITORIAL DISPUTES

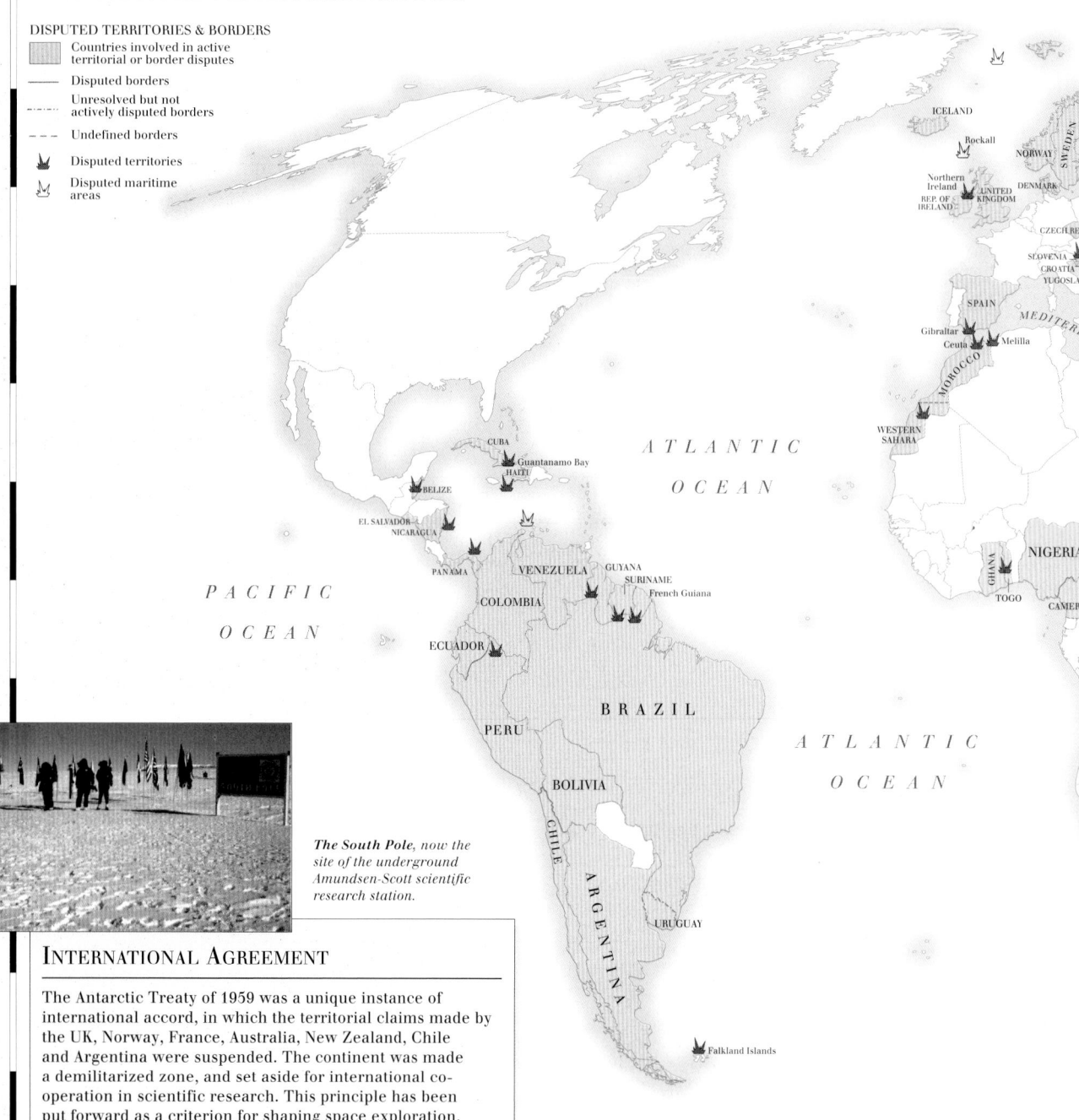

DISPUTED TERRITORIES & BORDERS

- Countries involved in active territorial or border disputes
- —— Disputed borders
- Unresolved but not actively disputed borders
- - - - Undefined borders
- Disputed territories
- Disputed maritime areas

The South Pole, now the site of the underground Amundsen-Scott scientific research station.

INTERNATIONAL AGREEMENT

The Antarctic Treaty of 1959 was a unique instance of international accord, in which the territorial claims made by the UK, Norway, France, Australia, New Zealand, Chile and Argentina were suspended. The continent was made a demilitarized zone, and set aside for international co-operation in scientific research. This principle has been put forward as a criterion for shaping space exploration.

OCCUPIED TERRITORY

During the 1967 Six Day War, Israel captured the Sinai peninsula and Gaza Strip from Egypt, the Old City of Jerusalem and the West Bank from Jordan and the Golan Heights from Syria. Despite international condemnation, successive Israeli governments encouraged the expansion of Jewish settlements in the occupied territories. However, Sinai was returned to Egypt in 1982, and the 1993 Israel-PLO peace accord provided for limited Palestinian control of Gaza and the West Bank.

An Israeli settlement under construction on the West Bank.

MILITARY BORDERS

The border between North and South Korea is the 38th parallel of latitude – the 1945 demarcation line between occupying US and Soviet forces. Since 1953, however, the *de facto* border has been a ceasefire line which straddles the 38th parallel and is designated as a DMZ (demilitarized zone). Beyond this, both countries have formidable fortifications and troop concentrations, making it one of the most militarized frontiers in the world.

The heavily fortified de facto *border between North and South Korea.*

The isolated Chinese occupying force on one of the Spratly Islands.

TERRITORIAL CLAIMS

Ambitious territorial claims are often advanced when the presence of rich mineral deposits is suspected. The Spratly Islands in the South China Sea, the site of potential oil and natural gas reserves, have been claimed by China, Vietnam, Taiwan, Brunei, Malaysia and the Philippines since a wartime claim by the Japanese was relinquished in 1951. Most claimants have even posted small military garrisons to the islands.

Map labels:

RUSSIAN FEDERATION

KAZAKHSTAN

UKRAINE
MOLDOVA
Serpent's Island
ROMANIA
BLACK SEA
GEORGIA
ARMENIA
AZERB.
CASPIAN SEA
TURKEY
Hatay/
Alexandretta
SYRIA
CYPRUS
LEBANON
ISRAEL
Golan Heights
JORDAN
IRAQ
IRAN
TURKMENISTAN
EGYPT
KUWAIT
BAHRAIN
QATAR
UAE
SAUDI ARABIA
RED SEA
Hanish Is.
ERITREA
YEMEN
SUDAN
ETHIOPIA
Ogaden
SOMALIA
KENYA
PAKISTAN
Jammu and Kashmir
Aksai Chin
CHINA
INDIA
BANGLADESH
LAOS
THAILAND
CAMBODIA
VIETNAM
Paracel Islands
Spratly Islands
MALAYSIA
Sipidan and Ligitan
PHILIPPINES
Matsu
Quemoy
TAIWAN
Senkaku Is.
PACIFIC OCEAN
NORTH KOREA
SOUTH KOREA
JAPAN
Liancourt Rocks
Kurile Islands
TANZANIA
ZAMBIA
MALAWI
MADAGASCAR
COMOROS
MAURITIUS
British Indian Ocean Territory
INDIAN OCEAN
INDONESIA
East Timor
VANUATU
New Caledonia (to France)
LESOTHO
SOUTH AFRICA

4

INDEX~ GAZETTEER

INTERNATIONAL ORGANIZATIONS
GEOGRAPHICAL PLACE NAMES
GLOSSARY OF GEOGRAPHICAL TERMS
GLOSSARY OF ABBREVIATIONS
A-Z INDEX~GAZETTEER

INTERNATIONAL ORGANIZATIONS

THIS LISTING GIVES the full names of all international organizations referred to, often by acronym, in the Atlas. (Political parties are to be found under the Politics heading within each national entry.) The full names are followed by the date of establishment or foundation, an indication of membership where appropriate and a summary of the organization's aims and functions.

ACC
Arab Cooperation Council
established 1989
members – Egypt, Iraq, Jordan Yemen; promotes Arab economic cooperation

ACP
African, Caribbean and Pacific Countries
established 1976;
members – 70 developing countries; preferential economic and aid relationship with the EU

ACS
Association of Caribbean States
established 1994
members – 24 Caribbean countries; promotes economic, scientific, and cultural cooperation in the region

ADB
Asian Development Bank
established 1966
members – 39 Asian-Pacific countries and territories, 16 non-regional countries; encourages regional development

AfDB
African Development Bank
established 1963
members – 52 African countries, 24 non-African countries; encourages African economic development

AFESD
Arab Fund for Economic and Social Development
established 1968
members – 20 Arab countries and the PLO; promotes social and economic development in Arab states

AG
Andean Group
(Acuerdo de Cartegena)
established 1969
members – Bolivia, Colombia, Ecuador, Peru and Venezuela; promotes development through integration

AL
Arab League
established 1945
members – 21 Arab countries and the PLO; forum to promote Arabic cooperation on social, political, and military issues

ALADI
Latin American Integration Association
established 1960
members – Argentina, Bolivia, Brazil, Chile, Colombia, Ecuador, Mexico, Paraguay, Peru, Uruguay, Venezuela; promotes trade and regional integration

Amazon Pact
established 1978
members – Bolivia, Brazil, Colombia, Ecuador, Guyana, Peru, Suriname, Venezuela; promotes the harmonious development of the Amazon region

AMF
Arab Monetary Fund
established 1977
members – 19 countries and the PLO; promotes monetary and economic cooperation

AMU
Arab Maghreb Union
established 1989
members – Algeria, Libya, Mauritania, Morocco, Tunisia; promotes integration and economic cooperation among North African Arab states

ANZUS
Australia–New Zealand–United States Security Treaty
established 1951; trilateral security agreement

APEC
Asia-Pacific Economic Cooperation
established 1989
members – 18 Pacific Rim countries; promotes regional economic cooperation

ASEAN
Association of Southeast Asian Nations
established 1967
members – Brunei, Indonesia, Malaysia, Philippines, Singapore, Thailand; promotes economic, social, and cultural cooperation among non-communist states in the region

BADEA
Arab Bank for Economic Development in Africa
established 1974 (as an agency of the Arab League)
members – 21 Arab countries and the PLO; promotes economic development in Africa

BDEAC
Central African States Development Bank
established 1976
members – Cameroon, Central African Republic, Chad, Congo, Equatorial Guinea, France, Gabon, Germany, Kuwait; furthers economic development

Benelux
Benelux Economic Union
established 1958
members – Belgium, Luxembourg, Netherlands; develops economic ties between member countries

BOAD
West African Development Bank
established 1973
members – Benin, Burkina, Ivory Coast, Mali, Niger, Senegal, Togo; promotes economic development and integration

BSEC
Black Sea Economic Cooperation Group
established 1992
members – Albania, Armenia, Azerbaijan, Bulgaria, Georgia, Greece, Moldova, Romania, Russia, Turkey, Ukraine; furthers regional stability through economic cooperation

CACM
Central American Common Market
established 1960
members – Costa Rica, El Salvador, Guatemala, Honduras, Nicaragua; furthers economic ties between members; one of its institutions is the BCIE – Central American Bank for Economic Integration

CAEU
Council of Arab Economic Unity
established 1964
members – 11 Arab countries and the PLO; encourages economic integration

CARICOM
Caribbean Community and Common Market
established 1973
members – 13 Caribbean countries; fosters economic ties in the Caribbean

CBSS
Council of the Baltic Sea States
established 1992
members – Denmark, Estonia, Finland, Germany, Latvia, Lithuania, Norway, Poland, Russia, Sweden; promotes cooperation among Baltic Sea states

CDB
Caribbean Development Bank
established 1969
members – 20 Caribbean countries, 5 non-Caribbean countries; promotes regional development

CE
Council of Europe
established 1949
members – 39 European countries; promotes unity and quality of life in Europe

CEEAC
Economic Community of Central African States
established 1983
members – 11 Central African countries; promotes regional cooperation, and aims to establish a Central African common market

CEFTA
Central European Free
Trade Agreement
established 1992
members – Czech Republic,
Hungary, Poland, Slovakia;
promotes trade and
cooperation

CEI
Central European Initiative
established 1991 (evolved
from Hexagonal Group)
members – Austria, Bosnia &
Herzegovina, Croatia, Czech
Republic, Hungary, Italy,
Poland, Slovakia, Slovenia,
Yugoslavia; promotes
economic and political cooperation, within the OSCE

CEMAC
Economic and Monetary
Community of Central Africa
established 1994
members – 6 Central African
members of the franc zone;
customs union (replaced
UDEAC)

CEPGL
Economic Community of
the Great Lakes Countries
established 1976
members – Burundi, Rwanda,
Zaire; promotes regional
economic cooperation

CERN
European Organization
for Nuclear Research
established 1953
members – 19 European
countries; provides for
collaboration in nuclear
research for peaceful
purposes

CILSS
Permanent Interstate
Committee for Drought
Control in the Sahel
established 1973
members – 11 African
countries in the Sahel
region; promotes prevention
of drought and crop failure
in the region

CIS
Commonwealth of
Independent States
established 1991 (as successor
of the Soviet Union)
members – Armenia,
Azerbaijan, Belorussia,
Georgia, Kazakhstan,
Kyrgyzstan, Moldova,
Russia, Tajikistan,
Turkmenistan, Ukraine,
Uzbekistan; promotes
interstate relationships

COMESA
Common Market for
Eastern and Southern Africa
established 1993
(replacing PTA)
members – 24 African
countries; promotes
economic development
and cooperation

Comm
Commonwealth (evolved
from British Empire)
established 1931
members – 51 countries;
develops relationships and
contacts between members

CP
Colombo Plan
established 1951
members – 26 countries;
encourages economic and
social development in
Asia-Pacific region

Damascus Declaration
established 1991
members – Bahrain, Kuwait,
Oman, Qatar, Saudi Arabia,
UAE, Syria, Egypt; a loose
association, formed after the
Gulf War, which aims to
secure the stablity of
the region

EADB
East African
Development Bank
established 1967
members – Kenya, Tanzania,
Uganda; encourages
economic development

EBRD
European Bank for
Reconstruction and
Development
established 1991
members – 58 countries;
aims to facilitate the
transition of former
communist European states
to market economies

ECO
Economic Cooperation
Organization
established 1985
members – Iran, Pakistan,
Turkey and 7 Central Asian
states; aims at cooperation
in economic, social, and
cultural affairs

ECOWAS
Economic Community of
West African States
established 1975
members – 16 West African
countries; promotes regional
economic cooperation

EEA
European Economic Area
established 1994
members – the 19 members
of the EU and EFTA; aims to
include EFTA members in
the EU single market

EFTA
European Free Trade
Association
established 1960
members – Iceland, Norway,
Liechtenstein, Switzerland;
promotes economic
cooperation

ESA
European Space Agency
established 1973
members – 13 European
countries; promotes co-
operation in space research
for peaceful purposes

EU
European Union
established 1992;
members – 15 countries; aims
to integrate the economies
of member states and
promote cooperation and
coordination of policies

FZ
Franc zone
members – 15 African states,
France and Monaco; aims to
form monetary union among
countries whose currencies
are linked to the French franc

GCC
Gulf Cooperation Council
established 1981
members – Bahrain, Kuwait,
Oman, Qatar, Saudi Arabia,
UAE; promotes cooperation
in economic, political, and
social affairs

G3
Group of 3
established 1987
members – Colombia,
Mexico, Venezuela; aims to
remove trade restrictions

G5
Group of 5
Finance ministers of France,
Germany, Japan, UK, USA,
meeting informally to
establish agenda of G7

G7
Group of 7
established 1975
members – Canada, France,
Germany, Italy, Japan, UK,
USA; the seven major
industrialized countries

G10
Group of 10
established 1962
members – G7 members,
plus Belgium, the
Netherlands, Sweden, and
Switzerland (now 11
members); ministers meet to
discuss monetary issues

G15
Group of 15
established 1989
members – 15 developing
countries; meets annually to
further cooperation among
developing countries

G24
Group of 24
members – the 24 countries
within the IMF which
represent the interests of
developing countries

Geplacea
Latin American and
Caribbean Sugar
Exporting Countries
established 1974
members – 23 countries; a
forum for consultation on the
production and sale of sugar

IAEA
International Atomic
Energy Agency
established 1957
members – 118 countries;
promotes and monitors
peaceful use of atomic energy

IBRD
International Bank for
Reconstruction and
Development (also known
as the World Bank)
established 1945
members – 178 countries; UN
agency providing economic
development loans

IDB
Islamic Development Bank
established 1975 (agency
of the OIC)
members – 45 countries;
promotes economic
development on Islamic
principles among Muslim
communities

IGADD
Inter-Governmental
Authority on Drought
and Development
established 1986
members – Djibouti, Ethiopia,
Kenya, Somalia, Sudan,
Uganda; promotes co-
operation on drought-
related matters

IOC
Indian Ocean Commission
established 1982
members – Comoros, France (representing Réunion), Madagascar, Mauritius, Seychelles; promotes regional cooperation

IWC
International Whaling Commission
established 1946
members – 40 countries; reviews conduct of whaling throughout world; coordinates and funds whale research

LAIA
Latin American Integration Association
established 1960
members – Argentina, Bolivia, Brazil, Chile, Colombia, Ecuador, Mexico, Paraguay, Peru, Uruguay, Venezuela; promotes regional free trade

LCBC
Lake Chad Basin Commission
established 1964
members – Cameroon, CAR, Chad, Niger, Nigeria; encourages economic and environmental development in Lake Chad region

Mekong River Commission
established 1995 (replacing the 1958 interim Mekong Secretariat)
members – Cambodia, Laos, Thailand, Vietnam; accord on the sustainable development of Mekong River basin

MERCOSUR
Southern Common Market
established 1991
members – Argentina, Brazil, Paraguay, Uruguay; promotes economic cooperation

MRU
Mano River Union
established 1973
members – Guinea, Liberia, Sierra Leone; aims to create customs and economic union

NACC
North Atlantic Cooperation Council
established 1991
members – 36 countries (members of NATO and former members of Warsaw Pact); forum for co-operation on political and security issues

NAFTA
North American Free Trade Agreement
established 1994
members – Canada, Mexico, USA; free-trade zone

NAM
Non-Aligned Movement
established 1961
members – 111 countries; fosters political and military cooperation away from traditional Eastern or Western blocs

NATO
North Atlantic Treaty Organization
established 1949
members – 16 countries; promotes mutual defense cooperation. Since January 1994, NATO's **Partnerships for Peace** program has provided a loose framework for cooperation with former members of the Warsaw Pact and the ex-Soviet republics

NC
Nordic Council
established 1952
members – Denmark, Finland, Iceland, Norway, Sweden; promotes cultural and environmental cooperation in the region

OAPEC
Organization of Arab Petroleum Exporting Countries
established 1968
members – Algeria, Bahrain, Egypt, Iraq, Kuwait, Libya, Qatar, Saudi Arabia, Syria, UAE; aims to promote the interests of member countries and increase cooperation in the petroleum industry

OAS
Organization of American States
established 1948
members – 34 American countries; promotes security, as well as economic, and social development in the Americas

OAU
Organization of African Unity
established 1963
members – 53 African countries; promotes unity and cooperation

OECD
Organization for Economic Cooperation and Development
established 1961
members – 26 industrialized democracies; forum for co-ordinating economic policies

OECS
Organization of Eastern Caribbean States
established 1981
members – Antigua & Barbuda, Dominica, Grenada, Montserrat, St. Kitts & Nevis, St. Lucia, St. Vincent & the Grenadines; promotes political, economic, and defense cooperation

OIC
Organization of the Islamic Conference
established 1971
members – 53 Islamic countries; promotes Islamic solidarity and cooperation in social and political affairs

OMVG
Gambia River Development Organization
established 1978
members – The Gambia, Guinea, Guinea-Bissau, Senegal; promotes integrated development of the Gambia River basin

Opanal
Agency for the Prohibition of Nuclear Weapons in Latin America and the Caribbean
established 1969
members – 26 countries; aims to ensure compliance with the Treaty of Tlatelolco (banning nuclear weapons from South America and the Caribbean)

OPEC
Organization of the Petroleum Exporting Countries
established 1960
members – Algeria, Gabon, Indonesia, Iran, Iraq, Kuwait, Libya, Nigeria, Qatar, Saudi Arabia, UAE, Venezuela; aims to coordinate oil policies to ensure fair and stable prices

OSCE
Organization for Security and Cooperation in Europe
established 1972 (as CSCE; renamed 1994)
members – 53 countries; aims to strengthen democracy and human rights, and settle disputes peacefully

Partnerships for Peace (PfP)
see NATO

RG
Rio Group
established 1987 (evolved from Contadora Group, established 1948)
members – Argentina, Bolivia, Brazil, Chile, Colombia, Ecuador, Mexico, Paraguay, Peru, Uruguay, Venezuela; forum for Latin American issues

SAARC
South Asian Association for Regional Cooperation
established 1985
members – Bangladesh, Bhutan, India, Maldives, Nepal, Pakistan, Sri Lanka; encourages economic, social, and cultural cooperation

SACU
Southern African Customs Union
established 1969
members – 5 countries; promotes cooperation in trade and customs matters among southern African states

SADC
Southern African Development Community
established 1992
members – Angola, Botswana, Lesotho, Malawi, Mauritius, Mozambique, Namibia, South Africa, Swaziland, Tanzania, Zambia, Zimbabwe; promotes economic integration

San José Group
established 1988
members – Costa Rica, El Salvador, Guatemala, Honduras, Nicaragua, Panama; a "complementary, voluntary and gradual" economic union

SELA
Latin American Economic System
established 1975
members – 27 countries; promotes economic and social development through regional cooperation

SPC
South Pacific Commission
established 1948
members – 28 countries and territories; a forum for dialogue between Pacific countries and powers administering Pacific territories

SPF
South Pacific Forum
established 1971
members – 15 countries and
territories; develops regional
political cooperation

UEMOA
West African Economic
and Monetary Union
established 1994
members – Benin, Burkina,
Ivory Coast, Mali, Niger,
Senegal, Togo; aims for
convergence of monetary
policies and economic union

UN
United Nations
established 1945
members – 184 countries;
permanent members of
the Security Council –
China, France, Russia,
UK, USA; aims to maintain
international peace and
security and to promote co-
operation over economic,
social, cultural, and
humanitarian problems.
Agencies include the
regional commissions of the
UN's Economic and Social
Council: ECA (Economic
Commission for Africa –
established 1958); ECE
(Economic Commission for
Europe – established 1947);
ECLAC (Economic
Commission for Latin
America and the Caribbean –
established 1948); ESCAP
(Economic and Social
Commission for Asia and the
Pacific – established 1947);
ESCWA (Economic and Social
Commission for Western
Asia – established 1973)

WEU
Western European Union
established 1954
members – 10 countries;
a forum for European
military cooperation

WTO
established 1995 (as the
successor to GATT – General
Agreement on Tariffs
and Trade)
members – 130 countries;
aims to liberalize trade
through multilateral
trade agreements

GEOGRAPHICAL PLACE NAMES

THE CHOICES confronting a map-maker when deciding which place-name style to use on a map are surprisingly varied. The criteria adopted may be affected by a range of factors: the existence of foreign and native language forms of a place name (London, Londres, Londra), variant spellings used within the country itself (Gent, Gand) and the existence of completely different language forms for international features (the English Channel, La Manche).

In addition to these, political expedience, simple clarity and the use to which the published map may be put are all factors that need consideration.

The revision of place-name forms and spellings, which is a continuing administrative activity worldwide, adds a further dimension of complexity to the subject. Since the collapse of Soviet communism, for instance, place names in Russia have been altered to expunge traces of communist ideology (the most famous being the 1991 reversion of Leningrad to its pre-1914 name, St. Petersburg). In many former Soviet republics, Russian names have been replaced with native language forms (notably in Ukraine, Belorussia, Georgia and Armenia).

Standardized Arabic forms and spellings have been instituted throughout most of the Arab world, although in some of the former French North African colonies, such as Algeria, the adoption of standardized Arabic names has been hindered by the persistent use of French forms in practice.

THE MAPS

The maps in the Nations of the World section of the Atlas have used the most up-to-date reference sources available to provide local name forms and spellings, that is to say those used within the country. In an age when international travel, on holiday or on business, is commonplace, this criterion seems the most appropriate.

English conventional forms have been used for all international features (such as sea areas between countries, and cross-border mountain ranges); for all country names (the Index~Gazetteer provides local forms and spellings, while commonly used alternative names, such as Burma/Myanmar are also made clear in the national A-Z entry) and for all capital cities. The Index~Gazetteer provides a fully cross-referenced system that will guide the reader the short distance from the English conventional "Florence" to the local "Firenze," as used on the maps.

English conventional forms also appear on all the maps in The World Today and Global Issues. These maps have not been indexed, as all contemporary places featured are more usefully and accurately identified on the national maps.

THE INDEX~GAZETTEER

The Index~Gazetteer lists all names that appear on the maps in the Nations of the World section of the Atlas. Physical features are defined as such, as are countries and those administrative or regional names included on the maps; all other names are those of population centres. Location is given by page number, then country, and is narrowed down by positional reference as N(orth), S(outh), E(ast), W(est) or C(entral), or combinations of these as appropriate.

Following each main entry name are given: variant spellings of the name most commonly found; its previous name or names; and such foreign-language forms of the name as are pertinent to modern history since 1940. This is the cut-off date generally adopted, permitting the inclusion of all place-name changes made during or after World War II. Exceptionally, name changes made in Russia and other countries of the former Soviet Union before 1940 are given, since many old names in these countries are now being restored.

The following pages provide a glossary of foreign geographical terms (658–659) that occur in the main entry names, and a comprehensive glossary of abbreviations (660) used in the Index~Gazetteer and throughout the Atlas.

GLOSSARY OF GEOGRAPHICAL TERMS

THE GLOSSARY FOLLOWING lists all geographical terms occurring on the maps and in main-entry names in the Index~Gazetteer. These terms may precede, follow or be run together with the proper element of the name; where they precede it the term is reversed for indexing purposes - thus Poluostrov Yamal is indexed as Yamal, Poluostrov.

KEY
Geographical term *Language*, Term

A
Å *Danish, Norwegian*, River
Alpen *German*, Alps
Altiplanicie *Spanish*, Plateau
Älv(en) *Swedish*, River
Anse *French*, Bay
Archipiélago *Spanish*, Archipelago
Arcipelago *Italian*, Archipelago
Arquipélago *Portuguese*, Archipelago
Aukštuma *Lithuanian*, Upland

B
Bahía *Spanish*, Bay
Baía *Portuguese*, Bay
Baḥr *Arabic*, River
Baie *French*, Bay
Bandao *Chinese*, Peninsula
Banjaran *Malay*, Mountain range
Batang *Malay*, Stream
-berg *Afrikaans, Norwegian*, Mountain
Birket *Arabic* , Lake
Boğazı *Turkish*, Lake
Bucht *German*, Bay
Bugten *Danish*, Bay
Buḥayrat *Arabic*, Lake, reservoir
Buheiret *Arabic*, Lake
Bukit *Malay*, Mountain
-bukta *Norwegian*, Bay
bukten *Swedish*, Bay
Burnu *Turkish*, Cape, point
Buuraha *Somali*, Mountains

C
Cabo *Portuguese*, Cape
Cap *French*, Cape
Cascada *Portuguese*, Waterfall
Cerro *Spanish*, Mountain
Chaîne *French*, Mountain range
Chau *Cantonese*, Island
Chäy *Turkish*, River
Chhâk *Cambodian*, Bay
Chhu *Tibetan*, River
-chŏsuji *Korean*, Reservoir
Chott *Arabic*, Salt lake, depression
Ch'ün-tao *Chinese*, Island group
    Cambodian, Mountains
Cordillera *Spanish*, Mountain range
Costa *Spanish*, Coast
Côte *French*, Coast
Cuchilla *Spanish*, Mountains

D
Dağı *Azerbaijani, Turkish*, Mountain
Dağları *Azerbaijani, Turkish*, Mountains
-dake *Japanese*, Peak
Danau *Indonesian*, Lake
Đao *Vietnamese*, Island
Daryā *Persian*, River
Daryācheh *Persian*, Lake
Dasht *Persian*, Plain, desert
Dawḥat *Arabic*, Bay
Dere *Turkish*, Stream

Dili *Azerbaijani*, Spit
-do *Korean*, Island
Dooxo *Somali*, Valley
Düzü *Azerbaijani*, Steppe
-dwīp *Bengali*, Island

E
Embalse *Spanish*, Reservoir
Erg *Arabic*, Dunes
Estany *Catalan*, Lake
Estrecho *Spanish*, Strait
-ey *Icelandic*, Island
Ezero *Bulgarian, Macedonian*, Lake

F
Fjord *Danish*, Fjord
-fjorden *Norwegian*, Fjord
-fjordhur *Faeroese*, Fjord
Fleuve *French*, River
Fliegu *Maltese*, Channel
-fljór *Icelandic*, River

G
-gang *Korean*, River
Ganga *Nepali, Sinhala*, River
Gaoyuan *Chinese*, Plateau
-gawa *Japanese*, River
Gebel *Arabic*, Mountain
-gebirge *German*, Mountains
Ghubbat *Arabic*, Bay
Gjiri *Albanian*, Bay
Gol *Mongolian*, River
Golfe *French*, Gulf
Golfo *Italian, Spanish*, Gulf
Gora *Russian, Serbian*, Mountain
Gory *Russian*, Mountains
Guba *Russian*, Bay
Gunung *Malay*, Mountain

H
Ḥadd *Arabic*, Spit
-haehyŏp *Korean*, Strait
Haff *German*, Lagoon
Hai *Chinese*, Sea, bay
Ḥammādat *Arabic*, Plateau
Hāmūn *Persian*, Lake
Hawr *Arabic*, Lake
Hāyk' *Amharic*, Lake
He *Chinese*, River
Helodrano *Malagasy*, Bay
-hegység *Hungarian*, Mountain range
Hka *Burmese*, River
-ho *Korean*, Lake
Hô *Korean*, Reservoir
Holot *Hebrew*, Dunes
Hora *Belorussian*, Mountain
Hrada *Belorussian*, Mountains, ridge
Hsi *Chinese*, River
Hu *Chinese*, Lake

I
Île(s) *French*, Island(s)
Ilha(s) *Portuguese*, Island(s)
Ilhéu(s) *Portuguese*, Islet(s)

Irmak *Turkish*, River
Isla(s) *Spanish*, Island(s)
Isola (Isole) *Italian*, Island(s)

J
Jabal *Arabic*, Mountain
Jāl *Arabic*, Ridge
-järvi *Finnish*, Lake
Jazīrat *Arabic*, Island
Jazīreh *Persian*, Island
Jebel *Arabic*, Mountain
Jezero *Serbo-Croatian*, Lake
Jiang *Chinese*, River
-joki *Finnish*, River
-jökull *Icelandic*, Glacier
Juzur *Arabic*, Islands

K
Kaikyō *Japanese*, Strait
-kaise *Lappish*, Mountain
Kali *Nepali*, River
Kalnas *Lithuanian*, Mountain
Kalns *Latvian*, Mountain
Kang *Chinese*, Harbor
Kangri *Tibetan*, Mountain(s)
Kaôh *Cambodian*, Island
Kapp *Norwegian*, Cape
Kavīr *Persian*, Desert
K'edi *Georgian*, Mountain range
Kediet *Arabic*, Mountain
Kepulauan *Indonesian, Malay*, Island group
Khalîg, Khalīj *Arabic*, Gulf
Khawr *Arabic*, Inlet
Khola *Nepali*, River
Khrebet *Russian*, Mountain range
Ko *Thai*, Island
Kolpos *Greek*, Bay
-kopf *German*, Peak
Körfäzi *Azerbaijani*, Bay
Körfezi *Turkish*, Bay
Kõrgustik *Estonian*, Upland
Koshi *Nepali*, River
Kowtal *Persian*, Pass
Kūh(hā) *Persian*, Mountain(s)
-kundo *Korean*, Island group
-kysten *Norwegian*, Coast
Kyun *Burmese*, Island

L
Laaq *Somali*, Watercourse
Lac *French*, Lake
Lacul *Romanian*, Lake
Lago *Italian, Portuguese, Spanish*, Lake
Laguna *Spanish*, Lagoon, Lake
Laht *Estonian*, Bay
Laut *Indonesian*, Sea
Lembalemba *Malagasy*, Plateau
Lerr *Armenian*, Mountain
Lerrnashght'a *Armenian*, Mountain range
Les *Czech*, Forest
Lich *Armenian*, Lake
Liqeni *Albanian*, Lake
Lumi *Albanian*, River
Lyman *Ukrainian*, Estuary

M

Mae Nam *Thai*, River
-mägi *Estonian*, Hill
Maja *Albanian*, Mountain
-man *Korean*, Bay
Marios *Lithuanian*, Lake
-meer *Dutch*, Lake
           Russian, Plain
-meri *Estonian*, Sea
Mifraz *Hebrew*, Bay
Monkhafad *Arabic*, Depression
Mont(s) *French*, Mountain(s)
Monte *Italian, Portuguese*, Mountain
More *Russian*, Sea
Mörön *Mongolian*, River

N

Nagor'ye *Russian*, Upland
Nahal *Hebrew*, River
Nahr *Arabic*, River
Nam *Laotian*, River
Nehri *Turkish*, River
Nevado *Spanish*, Mountain (snow-capped)
Nisoi *Greek*, Islands
Nizmennost' *Russian*, Lowland, plain
Nosy *Malagasy*, Island
Nur *Mongolian*, Lake
Nuruu *Mongolian*, Mountains
Nuur *Mongolian*, Lake
Nyzovyna *Ukrainian*, Lowland, plain

O

Ostrov(a) *Russian*, Island(s)
Oued *Arabic*, Watercourse
-oy *Faeroese*, Island
-øy(a) *Norwegian*, Island
Oya *Sinhala*, River
Ozero *Russian, Ukrainian*, Lake

P

Passo *Italian*, Pass
Pegunungan *Indonesian, Malay*, Mountain range
Pelagos *Greek*, Sea
Penisola *Italian*, Peninsula
Peski *Russian*, Sands
Phanom *Thai*, Mountain
Phou *Laotian*, Mountain
Pi *Chinese*, Point
Pic *Catalan*, Peak
Pico *Portuguese, Spanish*, Peak
Pik *Russian*, Peak
Planalto *Portuguese*, Plateau
Planina, Planini *Bulgarian, Macedonian, Serbo-Croatian*, Mountain range
Ploskogor'ye *Russian*, Upland
Poluostrov *Russian*, Peninsula
Potamos *Greek*, River
Proliv *Russian*, Strait
Pulau *Indonesian, Malay*, Island
Pulu *Malay*, Island
Punta *Portuguese, Spanish*, Point

Q

Qā' *Arabic*, Depression
Qolleh *Persian*, Mountain

R

Raas *Somali*, Cape
-rags *Latvian*, Cape
Ramlat *Arabic*, Sands
Ra's *Arabic*, Cape, point, headland
Ravnina *Bulgarian, Russian*, Plain
Récif *French*, Reef
Represa (Rep.) *Spanish, Portuguese*, Reservoir

-rettō *Japanese*, Island chain
Riacho *Spanish*, Stream
Riban' *Malagasy*, Mountains
Rio *Portuguese*, River
Río *Spanish*, River
Riu *Catalan*, River
Rivier *Dutch*, River
Rivière *French*, River
Rowd *Pashtu*, River
Rūd *Persian*, River
Rudohorie *Slovak*, Mountains
Ruisseau *French*, Stream

S

Sabkhat *Arabic*, Salt marsh
Şaḥrā' *Arabic*, Desert
Samudra *Sinhala*, Reservoir
-san *Japanese, Korean*, Mountain
-sanchi *Japanese*, Mountains
-sanmaek *Korean*, Mountains
Sarīr *Arabic*, Desert
Sebkha, Sebkhet *Arabic*, Salt marsh, depression
See *German*, Lake
Selat *Indonesian*, Strait
-selkä *Finnish*, Ridge
Selseleh *Persian*, Mountain range
Serra *Portuguese*, Mountain
Serranía *Spanish*, Mountain
Sha'īb *Arabic*, Watercourse
Shamo *Chinese*, Desert
Shan *Chinese*, Mountain(s)
Shan-mo *Chinese*, Mountain range
Shaṭṭ *Arabic*, Distributary
-shima *Japanese*, Island
Shiqqat *Arabic*, Depression
Shui-tao *Chinese*, Channel
Sierra *Spanish*, Mountains
Sơn *Vietnamese*, Mountain
Sông *Vietnamese*, River
-spitze *German*, Peak
Štít *Slovak*, Peak
Stoeng *Cambodian*, River
Stretto *Italian*, Strait
Su Anbarı *Azerbaijani*, Reservoir
Sungai *Indonesian, Malay*, River
Suu *Turkish*, River

T

Tal *Mongolian*, Plain
Tandavan' *Malagasy*, Mountain range
Tangorombohitr' *Malagasy*, Mountain massif
Tao *Chinese*, Island
Tassili *Berber*, Plateau, mountain
Tau *Russian*, Mountain(s)
Taungdan *Burmese*, Mountain range
Teluk *Indonesian, Malay*, Bay
Terara *Amharic*, Mountain
Tog *Somali*, Valley
Tônlé *Cambodian*, Lake
Top *Dutch*, Peak
-tunturi *Finnish*, Mountain
Tur'at *Arabic*, Channel

V

Väin *Estonian*, Strait
-vatn *Icelandic*, Lake
-vesi *Finnish*, Lake
Vinh *Vietnamese*, Bay
Vodokhranilishche (Vdkhr.) *Russian*, Reservoir
Vodoskhovyshche (Vdskh.) *Ukrainian*, Reservoir
Volcán *Spanish*, Volcano
Vozvyshennost' *Russian*, Upland, plateau
Vrh *Macedonian*, Peak

Vysochyna *Ukrainian*, Upland
Vysočina *Czech*, Upland

W

Waadi *Somali*, Watercourse
Wādī *Arabic*, Watercourse
Wāḥat, Wâhat *Arabic*, Oasis
Wald *German*, Forest
Wan *Chinese*, Bay
Wyżyna *Polish*, Upland

X

Xé *Laotian*, River

Y

Yarımadası *Azerbaijani*, Peninsula
Yazovir *Bulgarian*, Reservoir
Yoma *Burmese*, Mountains
Yü *Chinese*, Island

Z

Zaliv *Bulgarian, Russian*, Bay
Zatoka *Ukrainian*, Bay
Zemlya *Russian*, Bay

GLOSSARY OF ABBREVIATIONS

THIS GLOSSARY provides a comprehensive guide to the abbreviations used in this Atlas, and in the Index~Gazetteer.

A
abbrev. abbreviated
ABM anti-ballistic missile(s)
ACP African, Caribbean and Pacific countries
A.D. Anno Domini
Afr. Afrikaans
Alb. Albanian
ALCM air-launched Cruise missile(s)
Amh. Amharic
ANC African National Congress
anc. ancient
APC armored personnel carrier(s)
approx. approximately
Ar. Arabic
Arm. Armenian
ASSR Autonomous Soviet Socialist Republic
Aust. Australian
Az. Azerbaijani
Azerb. Azerbaijan

B
bbl billion barrels
Basq. Basque
BBC British Broadcasting Corporation
B.C. before Christ
b/cd barrels per calendar day
b/d barrels per day
Bel. Belorussian
Ben. Bengali
Ber. Berber
B-H Bosnia-Herzegovina
bn billion (one thousand million)
BP British Petroleum
Bret. Breton
Brig Brigadier
Brit. British
Bul. Bulgarian
Bur. Burmese

C
C central
C. Cape
°C degrees (Centigrade)
Cam. Cambodian
Cant. Cantonese
Capt Captain
CAR Central African Republic
Cast. Castilian
Cat. Catalan
Chin. Chinese
CIA Central Intelligence Agency
cm centimeter(s)
Cmdr Commander
CNN Cable News Network
Col Colonel
Cro. Croat
Cz. Czech
Czech Rep. Czech Republic

D E
Dan. Danish
dept. department
dev. development
Dom. Rep. Dominican Republic
Dr Doctor
Dut. Dutch
dwt dead weight tonnage
E east
EEC/EC European Community
EEZ Exclusive Economic Zone
ECU European Currency Unit
EMS European Monetary System
Eng. English
est estimated
Est. Estonian
EU European Union

F G
°F degrees (Fahrenheit)
Faer. Faeroese
Fij. Fijian
Fin. Finnish
Fr Father
Fr. French
Franc Francophone – a loose association of French-speaking (mainly African) countries, plus France
Fris. Frisian
ft foot/feet
FYRM Former Yugoslav Republic of Macedonia
FZ Franc Zone
g gram(s)
Gael. Gaelic
Gal. Galician
GDP Gross Domestic Product (the total value of goods and services produced by a country excluding income from foreign countries)
Gen General
Geor. Georgian
Ger. German
Gk Greek
GNP Gross National Product (the total value of goods and services produced by a country)

H I
Heb. Hebrew
HEP hydroelectric power
HH His/Her Highness
Hind. Hindi
hist. historical
HM His/Her Majesty
HMS His/Her Majesty's ship
HRH His/Her Royal Highness
HSH His/Her Serene Highness
Hung. Hungarian
I. Island
ICBM intercontinental ballistic missile(s)
Icel. Icelandic
in inch(es)
In. Inuit (Eskimo)
Ind. Indonesian

Intl International
Ir. Irish
IRBM intermediate-range ballistic missile(s)
Is Islands
It. Italian

J K L
Jap. Japanese
Kaz. Kazakh
kg kilogram(s)
Kir. Kirghiz
km kilometer(s)
km² square kilometer (singular)
Kor. Korean
Kurd. Kurdish
kw kilowatt(s)
kwh kilowatt hour(s)
L. Lake
Lao. Laotian
Lapp. Lappish
Lat. Latin
Latv. Latvian
Liech. Liechtenstein
Lith. Lithuanian
LNG liquefied natural gas
Lt Lieutenant
Lusoph Lusophone – a loose association of Portugeuse-speaking countries, plus Portugal
Lux. Luxembourg

M N
m million/meter(s)
Mac. Macedonian
Maced. Macedonia
Maj Major
Mal. Malay
Malg. Malagasy
Malt. Maltese
mi. mile(s)
Mong. Mongolian
Mt. Mountain
Mts Mountains
N north
NASA National Aeronautics and Space Administration
Nep. Nepali
Neth. Netherlands
NGO Non-Governmental Organization
NIC Newly Industrialized Country
Nic. Nicaraguan
Nor. Norwegian
NZ New Zealand

P Q R
Pash. Pashtu
PC personal computer
Per. Persian
PLO Palestine Liberation Organization
PNG Papua New Guinea
Pol. Polish
Poly. Polynesian
Port. Portuguese
prev. previously
Rep. Represa (Spanish, Portuguese for reservoir)

Rep. Republic
Res. Reservoir
Rev Reverend
Rmsch. Romansch
Rom. Romanian
Rus. Russian
Russ. Fed. Russian Federation

S
S south
SALT Strategic Arms Limitation Treaty
SCr. Serbo-Croatian
Serb. Serbian
Sinh. Sinhala
SLBM submarine-launched ballistic missile(s)
Slvk. Slovak
Slvn. Slovene
Som. Somali
Sp. Spanish
sq. square
SSBN nuclear-fuelled ballistic-missile submarine(s)
SSM surface-to-surface missile(s)
St., St Saint
START Strategic Arms Reduction Treaty
Strs. Straits
Swa. Swahili
Swe. Swedish
Switz. Switzerland

T U
Taj. Tajik
Th. Thai
Thai. Thailand
Tib. Tibetan
Turk. Turkish
Turkm. Turkmenistan
TV television
UAE United Arab Emirates
Uigh. Uighur
UK United Kingdom
Ukr. Ukrainian
UN United Nations
Urd. Urdu
US/USA United States of America
USS United States ship
USSR Union of Soviet Socialist Republics
Uzb. Uzbek

V W X Y
var. variant
VCR videocassette recorder
Vdkhr. Vodokhranilishche (Russian for reservoir)
Vdskh. Vodoskhovyshche (Ukrainian for reservoir)
Vtn. Vietnamese
W west
Wel. Welsh
Yugo. Yugoslavia

INDEX

A

Aa *see* Gauja
Aabenraa *see* Åbenrå
Aachen 236 *Fr.* Aix-la-Chapelle, *Dut.* Aken. W Germany
Aalborg *see* Ålborg
Aalesund *see* Ålesund
Aaley 332 *var.* Ālayh, Aley. C Lebanon
Aalsmeer 397 W Netherlands
Aalst 99 *Fr.* Alost. C Belgium
Aanaarjävri *see* Inarijärvi
Aanjar 332 C Lebanon
Aarau 518 N Switzerland
Aare 518 *var.* Aar. River of W Switzerland
Aarhus *see* Århus
Aarlen *see* Arlon
Aarschot 99 C Belgium
Aassi, Nahr el *see* Orontes
Aba 408 S Nigeria
Abaco Island 88 island of N Bahamas
Ābādān 281 W Iran
Abai *see* Blue Nile
Abaiang 320 island of the Gilbert Is, W Kiribati
Abakan 455 *prev.* Khakassk, Ust'-Abakanskoye. C Russia
Abancay 433 SE Peru
Abariringa *see* Kanton
Ābaya Hāyk' 215 *It.* Abbaia, *Eng.* Lake Margherita. Lake of SW Ethiopia
Abay Wenz *see* Blue Nile
Abbeville 225 N France
'Abd al 'Azīz, Jabal 523 mountains of NE Syria
'Abdalī 322 S Kuwait
Abd-Al-Kuri 601 island of SE Yemen, off the Horn of Africa
Abemama 320 island of the Gilbert Is, W Kiribati
Abengourou 300 E Ivory Coast
Åbenrå 190 *var.* Aabenraa, *Ger.* Apenrade. Jylland, SW Denmark
Abeokuta 408 SW Nigeria
Abercorn *see* Mbala
Aberdeen 262 S Hong Kong
Aberdeen 565 NE Scotland, UK
Aberdeen 571 South Dakota, NC USA
Abergwaun *see* Fishguard
Abersee *see* Wolfgangsee
Abertawe *see* Swansea
Aberystwyth 565 W Wales, UK
Abhā 474 S Saudi Arabia
Abhe, Lake 194, 215 *Amh.* Ābhē Bid Hāyk'. Lake of Djibouti and Ethiopia
Abidjan 300 S Ivory Coast
Åbo *see* Turku
Aboisso 300 SE Ivory Coast
Abo, Massif d' 156 mountain range of N Chad
Abomey 108 S Benin
Abong Mbang 144 SE Cameroon
Abou-Déïa 156 S Chad
Aboumi 230 E Gabon
Abovyan 74 *var.* Abovjan. C Armenia
Abra 437 river of Luzon, N Philippines
Abrād, Wādī 601 seasonal river of NW Yemen
Abraham Bay *see* Carlton, The
Abruzzese, Appennino 295 mountain range of C Italy
'Abs 601 *var.* Sūq 'Abs. W Yemen
Abşeron Yarımadası 86 *Rus.* Apsheronskiy Poluostrov. Oil-rich peninsula of E Azerbaijan
Abū aḍ Ḍuḥūr 523 *Fr.* Aboudouhour. NW Syria
Abū al Abyaḍ 562 island of N United Arab Emirates

Abū al Jirfān, Sha'īb 322 *var.* Sh'ib Abu Jarfan. Dry watercourse of N Kuwait
Abū al Khaşīb 284 *var.* Abul Khasib. SE Iraq
Abu al Mawj, Ra's 91 cape of W Bahrain
Abu Dhabi 562 *Ar.* Abū Ẓaby, *var.* Abū Ẓabī. ❖ of United Arab Emirates
Abuja 408 ❖ of Nigeria, C Nigeria
Abū Jarjūr, Ra's 91 cape of E Bahrain
Abū Kamāl 523 *Fr.* Abou Kémal. E Syria
Abul Khasib *see* Abū al Khaşīb
Abuná 112 river of Bolivia and Brazil
Abū Thaylah 449 NE Qatar
Abū Ẓabī *see* Abu Dhabi
Abū Ẓaby *see* Abu Dhabi
Abyaḍ, Baḥr al *see* White Nile
Ābybro 190 N Denmark
Abyssinia *see* Ethiopia
Acaill *see* Achill Island
Acajutla 207 W El Salvador
Acapulco 370 *var.* Acapulco de Juárez. S Mexico
Acaraí, Serra 120 *Eng.* Acarai Mountains. Mountain range of Brazil and Guyana
Acarigua 591 NW Venezuela
Accra 242 ❖ of Ghana, SE Ghana
Achacachi 112 W Bolivia
Acharnés 245 *prev.* Akharnaí. SE Greece
Acheloos 245 *var.* Aspropotamos, *prev.* Akhelóös. River of W Greece
Achénouma 407 NE Niger
Achill Island 288 *Ir.* Acaill. Island of W Ireland
Achna *see* Athna
Achorstock Point 630 headland of W Tristan da Cunha
Achwa 556 *var.* Aswa. River of N Uganda
Acireale 295 Sicilia, S Italy
Acklins Island 88 island of S Bahamas
Aconcagua, Cerro 71 mountain of W Argentina
Açores *see* Azores
Açores, Arquipélago dos *see* Azores
A Coruña 502 *Cast.* La Coruña. NW Spain
Acoua 627 NW Mayotte
Acquaviva 470 NW San Marino
Acre *see* 'Akko
Acurnam 208 *var.* Acurenan, Akurenan. S Río Muni, Equatorial Guinea
Adalia *see* Antalya
Adalia, Gulf of *see* Antalya Körfezi
Adam 418 N Oman
Adama *see* Nazrēt
Adamaoua, Massif d' 144 *Eng.* Adamawa. Plateau of West Africa
Adam-jo-Tando *see* Tando Ādam
Adam's Bridge 506 chain of shoals to the NW of Sri Lanka
Adamstown 629 ❖ of Pitcairn Islands, NE Pitcairn Island, Pitcairn Islands
'Adan 601 *Eng.* Aden. SW Yemen
Adana 549 *var.* Seyhan. S Turkey
Adapazarı 548 *var.* Sakarya. NW Turkey
Aḍ Ḍab 'īyah 562 C United Arab Emirates
Aḍ Ḍafrah 562 desert region of W United Arab Emirates
Ad Dahnā' 474 N Saudi Arabia
Ad Dakhla 382 W Western Sahara
Ad Dalanj *see* Dilling
Ad Dammām 474 desert region of NE Saudi Arabia
Ad Dawḥah *see* Doha

Ad Dibdibah 322 mountain of W Kuwait
Addīgrat 215 N Ethiopia
Ad Dirāz 91 NW Bahrain
Addis Ababa 215 *Amh.* Ādīs Ābeba. ❖ of Ethiopia, C Ethiopia
Ad Dīwānīyah 284 *var.* Diwaniya. C Iraq
Addu Atoll 358 atoll of S Maldives
Adelaide 77 S Australia
Adelphi 468 E St. Vincent, St. Vincent & the Grenadines
Adelsberg *see* Postojna
Aden *see* 'Adan
Aden, Gulf of 194, 492, 601 *var.* Badyarada 'Admēd. Gulf connecting the Indian Ocean and Red Sea
Adh Dhayd 562 *var.* Deira. NE United Arab Emirates
Adh Dhirā' 310 W Jordan
Ādī Ārk'ay 215 *var.* Addi Arkay. N Ethiopia
Adi Keyih 210 *var.* Adi Keyah. SE Eritrea
Adi Kwala 210 S Eritrea
Ādīs Ābeba *see* Addis Ababa
Ādīs Zemen 215 NW Ethiopia
Adi Tekelezan 210 C Eritrea
Adıyaman 549 SE Turkey
Admiralty Islands 428 island group of N Papua New Guinea
Ado-Ekiti 408 SW Nigeria
Adola *see* Kibre Mengist
Ado-Odo 408 *var.* Ado. SW Nigeria
Adour 225 river of SW France
Adrar des Ifôghas 360 mountainous region of C Sahara, NE Mali
Adriatic Sea 295, 604 *It.* Mare Adriatico, *Slvn.* Jadransko Morje, *SCr.* Jadransko More, *Alb.* Deti Adriatik. Area of the Mediterranean Sea, between Italy and SE Europe
Adriatik, Deti *see* Adriatic Sea
Adventure Sound 623 bay of the South Atlantic Ocean, E Falkland Islands
Ādwa 215 *var.* Adowa, *It.* Adua. N Ethiopia
Adygeya, Respublika 454 autonomous republic of SW Russia
Adzopé 300 SE Ivory Coast
Aeankan District 364 district of Majuro, SE Marshall Islands
Aegean Sea 245, 548 *Gk* Aigaío Pélagos, *Turk.* Ege Denizi. Area of the Mediterranean Sea
Aeolian Islands *see* Eolie, Isole
Ærø 190 *Ger.* Arrö. Island of S Denmark
Afadjado 242 *var.* Afadjato, Afadjoto. Mountain of SE Ghana
'Afak 284 C Iraq
Afar Depression *see* Danakil Desert
Afghanistan 52-55 officially Islamic State of Afghanistan, *prev.* Republic of Afghanistan. Country of C Asia divided into 30 admin. units (velayats). ❖ Kābul
Afgooye 492 *It.* Afgoi. S Somalia
Afikpo 408 SW Nigeria
Afobaka 510 NE Suriname
'Afula 291 N Israel
Afyon 548 *prev.* Afyonkarahisar. W Turkey
Agadez 407 *prev.* Agadès. C Niger
Agadir 382 SW Morocco
Agaña 625 ❖ of Guam, NW Guam
Aga Point 625 headland on the S coast of Guam
Āgaro 215 W Ethiopia
Agat 625 W Guam
Agboville 300 SE Ivory Coast
Ağcabädi 86 *Rus.* Agdzhabedi, *var.* Agdžabedi. C Azerbaijan

Agdam 86 SW Azerbaijan
Agedabia *see* Ajdābiyā
Agen 225 SW France
Agere Hiywet *see* Hāgere Hiywet
Agia Napa *see* Ayia Napa
Agigialousa *see* Yenierenköy
Agona Swedru 242 *var.* Swedru. SE Ghana
Agordat *see* Akordat
Agou Gadzepe 539 SW Togo
Agou, Mont 539 *prev.* Pic Baumann. Mountain of SW Togo
Āgra 270 N India
Agram *see* Zagreb
Agrigento 295 *prev.* Girgenti. Sicilia, S Italy
Agrihan 628 island of N Northern Mariana Islands
Agrínio 245 *prev.* Agrínion. W Greece
Aguachica 171 N Colombia
Aguadilla 629 NW Puerto Rico
Aguadulce 426 S Panama
Aguán 260 river of N Honduras
Aguarico 200 river of Ecuador and Peru
Aguascalientes 370 C Mexico
Aguijan 628 island of S Northern Mariana Islands
Agusan 437 river of Mindanao, S Philippines
Ahaggar 59 *var.* Hoggar. Mountain range of SE Algeria
Ahja 212 *var.* Ahja Jõgi. River of SE Estonia
Ahmadābād 270 *var.* Ahmedabad. W India
Ahmadpur East 421 E Pakistan
Ahuachapán 207 W El Salvador
Ahvāz 281 *var.* Ahwāz. W Iran
Ahvenanmaa *see* Åland
Aḥwar 601 S Yemen
Aibak *see* Āybak
Aigaío Pélagos *see* Aegean Sea
Aiguá 579 S Uruguay
Ai-hun *see* Heihe
Ailigandí 426 E Panama
Ailinginae 364 island of NW Marshall Islands
Ailinglaplap 364 *prev.* Ailinglapalap. Island of S Marshall Islands
Ailuk 364 island of NE Marshall Islands
'Aïn Ben Tili 366 N Mauritania
Aïn Oussera 59 *var.* Aïn Wessara. N Algeria
Aintab *see* Gaziantep
Aïoun el Atroûss *see* 'Ayoûn el 'Atroûs
Aiquile 112 C Bolivia
Airai 425 C Palau
Airdrie 146 SW Canada
Airdrie 565 C Scotland, UK
Airlalang *see* Rokan
Aitape 428 *var.* Eitape. NW Papua New Guinea
Aitos *see* Aytos
Aitutaki 622 island of Southern Cook Islands, S Cook Islands
Aix-en-Provence 225 SE France
Aix-la-Chapelle *see* Aachen
Aizu-Wakamatsu 304 Honshū, N Japan
Ajaccio 225 Corse, SE France
Ajdābiyā 339 *var.* Ajdābiyah, Agedabia. NE Libya
Ajeltake District 364 district of Majuro, SE Marshall Islands
Ajinena *see* Geneina
Ajka 264 W Hungary
Ajman 562 *Ar.* 'Ajmān, *var.* 'Ujmān. NE United Arab Emirates
Ajtos *see* Aytos
Akaba *see* Al 'Aqabah
Akagera 138, 462, 556 *var.* Kagera. River of E Africa

All Saints 68 C Antigua, Antigua &
   Barbuda
Al Lubnān see Lebanon
Al Luḥayyah 601 W Yemen
Al Ma'āmīr 91 NE Bahrain
Alma-Ata see Almaty
Almada 444 W Portugal
Al Madīnah 474 Eng. Medina.
   W Saudi Arabia
Al Mafraq 310 var. Mafraq. N Jordan
Al Mahdīyah see Mahdia
Al Maḥmūdīyah 284 var. Mahmudiya.
   C Iraq
Al Mahrah 601 mountains of E Yemen
Al Majma'ah 474 C Saudi Arabia
Al Mālikīyah 91 W Bahrain
Al Mālikīyah 523 var. Dayrīk. NE Syria
Almalyk see Olmaliq
Al Mamlakah see Morocco
Al Manādir 562 var. Al Manadir.
   Desert region of Oman and United
   Arab Emirates
Al Manāmah see Manama
Al Manāṣif 523 mountains of E Syria
Al Manṣūrah see El Mansûra
Al Maqta' 562 C United Arab Emirates
Al Marj 339 var. Barka. It. Barce.
   NE Libya
Al Marsá see La Marsa
Almaty 312 var. Alma-Ata. ❖ of
   Kazakhstan, SE Kazakhstan
Al Mawṣil 284 Eng. Mosul. N Iraq
Al Mayādīn 523 Fr. Meyadine. E Syria
Al Mazra'ah 310 W Jordan
Almelo 397 E Netherlands
Almendra, Embalse de 503 reservoir
   of NW Spain
Almere 397 C Netherlands
Almería 503 S Spain
Al Mīnā' see El Mina
Al Minyā see El Minya
Al Miqdādīyah see Al Muqdādīyah
Almirante 426 W Panama
Al Mubarraz 474 NE Saudi Arabia
Al Mudawwarah 310 SW Jordan
Al Muḥammadīyah 91
   var. Umm aş Şabbān. Island of
   NW Bahrain
Al Muḥarraq 91 var. Moharek,
   Muharraq, Jazirat al Muharraq.
   Bahrain
Al Mukallā 601 var. Mukalla.
   SE Yemen
Al Mukhā 601 Eng. Mocha. SW Yemen
Al Muknīn see Moknine
Al Munastīr see Monastir
Al Muqdādīyah 284
   var. Al Miqdādīyah. C Iraq
Al Mussayyib 284 C Iraq
Al Obayyid see El Obeid
Alofi 628 ❖ of Niue, W Niue
Alofi, Île 631 island of Île Futuna,
   N Wallis & Futuna
Alohungari 233 E Gambia
Alor, Kepulauan 276 island group of
   E Indonesia
Alor, Pulau 276 island of E Indonesia
Alor Setar 354 var. Alur Setar,
   Alor Star. NW Peninsular Malaysia
Alost see Aalst
Alotau 428 SE Papua New Guinea
Aloupos 187 var. Çiftlik Dere. River of
   NW Cyprus
Alpen see Alps
Alpes see Alps
Alphen aan de Rijn 397
   W Netherlands
Alphonse Group 480 island group of
   C Seychelles
Alpi see Alps
Alps 82, 225, 294, 518 It. Alpi,
   Fr. Alpes, Ger. Alpen. Mountain
   range of C Europe
Al Qābil 418 var. Qabil. NW Oman
Al Qaḍārif see Gedaref
Al Qāhirah see Cairo
Al Qal'ah al Kubrá see Kalaa Kebira
Al Qāmishlī 523 var. Kamishli.
   NE Syria
Al Qaryah 91 NE Bahrain
Al Qaryāt 339 NW Libya
Al Qaṣr 310 W Jordan
Al-Qaṣrayn see Kasserine
Al Qayrawān see Kairouan

Al Qubayyāt see Qoubaïyât
Al Qubbah 339 NE Libya
Al Quds see Jerusalem
Al Qunayṭirah 523 var. El Quneitra,
   Kuneitra. SW Syria
Al Quṣayr 523 var. El Quseir,
   Fr. Kousseir. W Syria
Al Quṭayfah 523 var. Quṭayfah,
   Quteife, Fr. Kouteifé. SW Syria
Al Quwayrah 310 var. Makhfar al
   Quwayrah, El Quweira. SW Jordan
Als 190 Ger. Alsen. Island of
   S Denmark
Alsace 225 cultural region of
   NE France
Alsen see Als
Al Shahaniyah see Ash Shaḥanīyah
Alt see Olt
Alta 414 NE Norway
Altai Mountains 380 mountain range
   of C Asia
Altay 162 Chin. A-le-t'ai,
   prev. Ch'eng-hua, var. Chenghwa,
   Mong. Sharasume. Xinjiang Uygur
   Zizhiqu, NW China
Altay 380 W Mongolia
Alt de la Coma Pedrosa, Pic 62 moun-
   tain of NW Andorra
Altkanischa see Kanjiža
Alto Molócuè 387 C Mozambique
Alto Paraná see Paraná
Alt-Schwanenburg see Gulbene
Altsohl see Zvolen
Altun Shan 162 var. Altyn Tagh.
   Mountain range of Xinjiang Uygur
   Zizhiqu, NW China
Altyn Tagh see Altun Shan
Alu see Shortland Island
Al Ubayyiḍ see El Obeid
Al 'Udayd 562 var. Al Odaid. W United
   Arab Emirates
Alūksne 330 Ger. Marienburg.
   NE Latvia
Al 'Ulā 474 NW Saudi Arabia
Al 'Umarī 310 C Jordan
Al Uqṣur see Luxor
Al Wafrā 322 SE Kuwait
Al Wāḥāt al Khārijah
   see El Wâhât el Khârga
Al Wajh 474 NW Saudi Arabia
Al Wakrah 449 var. Wakra. E Qatar
Al Wukayr 449 var. Al Wukair.
   E Qatar
Alyat see Älät
Alyaty-Pristan' see Älät
Alytus 344 Pol. Olita. S Lithuania
Al Zubair see Az Zubayr
Amadora 444 W Portugal
Amakusa-shotō 304 island group to
   the W of Kyūshū, SW Japan
Amala 316 river of SW Kenya
Amami-Ō-shima 304 island of Amami-
   shotō, SW Japan
Amami-shotō 304 island group of
   Nansei-shotō, SW Japan
Amara see Al 'Amārah
Amarapura 135 C Burma
Amasia 74 Rus. Amasiya,
   var. Amasija. NW Armenia
Amasya 549 N Turkey
Amatique, Bahía de, 250 bay of the
   Gulf of Honduras
Amazon 121, 171, 433 Sp. Amazonas.
   River of South America
Amazonia 120 physical region of
   C South America
Ambalangoda 506 SW Sri Lanka
Ambalavao 350 S Madagascar
Ambam 144 S Cameroon
Ambanja 350 N Madagascar
Ambato 200 C Ecuador
Ambatondrazaka 350 E Madagascar
Ambergris Cay 102 island of
   NE Belize
Ambergris Cays 631 island group of
   S Turks and Caicos Islands
Ambilobe 350 N Madagascar
Amblève 99 river of E Belgium
Ambo see Hägere Hiywet
Amboasary 350 S Madagascar
Ambohidratrimo 350 C Madagascar
Ambon 276 prev. Amboina. Ambon,
   C Indonesia

Ambositra 350 C Madagascar
Ambre, Ile d' 368 Island of
   NE Mauritius
Ambriz 64 NW Angola
Ambrym 587 var. Ambrim. Island of
   E Vanuatu
'Amd 601 C Yemen
Ameland 397 island of
   Waddeneilanden, N Netherlands
American Samoa 620 unincorporated
   territory of the USA, Pacific Ocean.
   ❖ Pago Pago
Amersfoort 397 C Netherlands
Amherst see Kyaikkami
Amiens 225 N France
Amilḥayt, Wādī 418
   var. Wādī Umml Ḥayt. Seasonal
   watercourse of SW Oman
Amīndivi Islands 270 island group of
   Lakshadweep, SW India
Amioun 332 var. Amyūn. N Lebanon
Amirante Islands 480 var. Amirantes
   Group. Island of C Seychelles
Amlamé 539 C Togo
Amman 310 Ar. 'Ammān. ❖ of Jordan,
   NW Jordan
Ammassalik 624 var. Angmagssalik.
   SE Greenland
Ammochostos see Gazimağusa
Ammochostos Bay see Famagusta Bay
Amnok see Yalu
Āmol 281 var. Amul. N Iran
Amorgós 245 island of SE Greece
Amouli 620 var. Tau. Tau,
   E American Samoa
Amourj 366 SE Mauritania
Ampara 506 E Sri Lanka
Amphitrite Group 629 island group
   of N Paracel Islands
'Amrān 601 W Yemen
Amrāvati 270 prev. Amraoti. C India
Amritsar 270 N India
Amstelveen 397 W Netherlands
Amsterdam 397 ❖ of the Netherlands,
   C Netherlands
Amstetten 82 N Austria
Am Timan 156 SE Chad
Amu Darya 53, 530, 552, 582
   Turkm. Amyderya, Uzb. Amudaryo.
   River of C Asia
Amudat 556 E Uganda
Amul see Āmol
Amund Ringnes Island 146 island
   of Sverdrup Islands, N Canada
Amundsen Gulf 146 gulf of the
   Beaufort Sea, on the NW coast
   of Canada
Amundsen-Scott 66 US research
   station at the South Pole, Greater
   Antarctica, Antarctica
Amundsen Sea 66 sea of the Pacific
   Ocean, off Antarctica
Amur 163, 455 Chin. Heilong Jiang.
   River of China and Russia
Amyderya see Amu Darya
Amyūn see Amioun
An Abhainn Mhór see Blackwater
Anaco 591 N Venezuela
Anadolu Dağları see Doğu Karadeniz
   Dağları
Anadyr' 455 NE Russia
Anadyr, Gulf of see Anadyrskiy Zaliv
Anadyrskiy Zaliv 455 Eng. Gulf of
   Anadyr. Gulf of Bering Sea, border-
   ing NE Russia
Anáfi 245 island of SE Greece
Anaiza see 'Unayzah
Analalava 350 N Madagascar
Analamaitsa Plateau 350 plateau
   of NE Madagascar
Anambas, Kepulauan 276 island
   group to the NW of Borneo,
   W Indonesia
Anan 304 Shikoku, SW Japan
Anantapur 270 S India
Anápolis 121 S Brazil
Anarjokka see Inarijoki
Anatahan 628 island of C Northern
   Mariana Islands
Anatolia Plateau 548 plateau of
   C Turkey
Anatom 587 var. Aneityum,
   prev. Kéamu. Island of S Vanuatu
An Bhearú see Barrow

An Bhóinn see Boyne
Anchorage 570 Alaska, USA
Ancona 295 C Italy
Andalucia 502-503 autonomous
   community of S Spain
Andaman Islands 270 island group of
   SE India
Andaman Sea 135, 276, 535 sea of
   Indian Ocean, to the SW of Burma
   and Thailand
'Andām, Wadi 418 seasonal desert
   watercourse of E Oman
Andapa 350 NE Madagascar
Andaung Pech see Bâ Kêv
Andenne 99 SE Belgium
Andersen Air Force Base 625
   NE Guam
Andes 71, 112, 159, 171, 2 mountain
   range of South America, running the
   entire length of the west coast
Andfjorden 414 fjord of NE Norway
Andijon 582 Rus. Andizhan.
   E Uzbekistan
Andizhan see Andijon
Andkhvoy 53 N Afghanistan
Andoany 350 prev. Hell-Ville.
   N Madagascar
Andong 498 Jap. Antō.
   E South Korea
Andong-ho 498 reservoir of E South
   Korea
Andorra 62-63 officially Principality of
   Andorra. Country of SW Europe divid-
   ed into 7 admin. units (parishes).
   ❖ Andorra la Vella
Andorra la Vella 62 ❖ of Andorra,
   W Andorra
Andreas 625 N Isle of Man
Andreas, Cape see Apostolos Andreas,
   Cape
Andria 295 S Italy
Androna, Lembalemba Ambanin' 350
   var. Plateau de l'Androna. Plateau of
   N Madagascar
Ándros 245 island of SE Greece
Andros Island 88 island of
   W Bahamas
Andros Town 88 Andros Island,
   Bahamas
Andújar 503 SW Spain
Anegada 621 island of NE British
   Virgin Islands
Aného 539 var. Anécho,
   prev. Petit-Popo. S Togo
Aneityum see Anatom
Ánew see Annau
An Fheoir see Nore
Anfile Bay 210 bay of the Red Sea
   to the E of Eritrea
Angara 455 river of C Russia
Angarsk 455 C Russia
Angaur 425 island of S Palau
Ånge 515 C Sweden
Angel see Úhlava
Ángel de la Guarda, Isla 370 island of
   NW Mexico
Angeles 437 Luzon, N Philippines
Angers 225 NW France
Ångk Tasaôm 141 prev. Angtassom.
   S Cambodia
Anglesey 565 Wel. Môn. Island of
   NW Wales, UK
Angmagssalik see Ammassalik
Angoche 387 E Mozambique
Angola 64-65 officially Republic of
   Angola, prev. People's Republic of
   Angola. Country of Central Africa
   divided into 18 admin. units
   (provinces). ❖ Luanda
Angora see Ankara
Angoram 428 N Papua New Guinea
Angoulême 225 W France
Angra Pequena see Lüderitz
Angren 582 E Uzbekistan
Angtassom see Ångk Tasaôm
Anguilla 620 British dependent
   territory of the Caribbean Sea.
   ❖ The Valley.
Anguilla Cays 88 islets of W Bahamas
Anguilla Channel 620, 624 channel of
   the Caribbean Sea between Anguilla
   and St-Martin
Anguilles, Rivière des 368 river of S
   Mauritius
Anguillita Island 620 island of
   S Anguilla

Ar Rawḍatayn *322* N Kuwait
Ar Rayyān *449 var.* Al Rayyan.
  E Qatar
Ar Rifā' al Gharbī *91* N Bahrain
Ar Rifā' ash Sharqī *91* NE Bahrain
Ar Riyāḍ *see* Riyadh
Ar Riyān *601* S Yemen
Arrō *see* Ærø
Ar Ru'ays *449 var.* Ar Ruways,
  Al Ruweis, Ruwais. N Qatar
Ar Ru'ays *562 var.* Ruwaisv,
  Ar Ruways. W United Arab Emirates
Ar Rufayq *449 var.* Al Rufaig.
  NW Qatar
Ar Rustāq *418 var.* Rostak. N Oman
Ar Ruwayshid *310* NE Jordan
Ar Safad *see* Ẓefat
'Arta *194* SE Djibouti
Artashat *74 var.* Artašat. S Armenia
Artemisa *182* NW Cuba
Artëm-Ostrov *see* Artyom
Artibonite *258* river of Haiti
Artigas *579 prev.* San Eugenio,
  var. San Eugenio del Cuareim.
  N Uruguay
Art'ik *74* W Armenia
Art, Île *628* island of Îles Belep,
  W New Caledonia
Artois *225* cultural region of N France
Artsvashen *74 var.* Bashkend.
  NE Armenia
Artvin *549* NE Turkey
Artyom *86 Rus.* Artëm-Ostrov.
  E Azerbaijan
Arua *556* NW Uganda
Aruângua *see* Luangwa
Aruba *620* autonomous part of the
  Netherlands, Caribbean Sea. ❖
  Oranjestad
Aru, Kepulauan *276-277*
  prev. Aroe Islands. Island group to
  the SW of Irian Jaya, W Indonesia
Aruliho *490* NW Guadalcanal,
  Solomon Is
Årup *190* Fyn, SW Denmark
Arusha *532* N Tanzania
Aruwimi *609* river of NE Zaire
Arvand Rūd *see* 'Arab, Shaṭṭ al
Arvayheer *380* C Mongolia
Arvika *515* SW Sweden
Aryānah *see* Ariana
Asadābād *53* E Afghanistan
Asad, Buḥayrat al *523* reservoir
  of Syria
Asahi-dake *305* mountain
  of Hokkaidō, N Japan
Asahikawa *305* Hokkaidō,
  N Japan
Asaka *582 Rus.* Assake, *prev.* Leninsk.
  E Uzbekistan
Asamankese *242* SE Ghana
Āsau *598* Savai'i, Western Samoa
Āsbe Teferī *215 var.* Asba Tafari.
  C Ethiopia
Ascension *630* dependent territory
  of St. Helena, South Atlantic Ocean
Ascension *see* Pohnpei
Ascoli Piceno *295* C Italy
Aseb *see* Assab
'As 'Ela *194* SW Djibouti
Āsela *215 var.* Aselle, Asella, Asselle.
  C Ethiopia
Asenovgrad *128* S Bulgaria
Aseri *212 Ger.* Asserin. NE Estonia
Ashburton *401* C South Island, New
  Zealand
Ashdod *291* C Israel
Ashford *565* SE England, UK
Ashgabat *553 prev.* Ashkhabad,
  Poltoratsk. ❖ of Turkmenistan,
  S Turkmenistan
Ashikaga *304* Honshū, SE Japan
Ashkhabad *see* Ashgabat
Ashmyany *104* NW Belorussia
Ashots'k *74 prev.* Ghukasyan,
  Rus. Gukasyan. NW Armenia
Ashqelon *291* C Israel
Ash Shadādah *523*
  var. Ash Shaddādah, Shaddādī,
  Shedadi, Tell Shedadi. NE ria
Ash Shaḥanīyah *449*
  var. Al Shahaniyah. C Qatar
Ash Shāmīyah *284 var.*
Ash Sharāh *310 var.* Esh Sharā.
  Mountains of W Jordan

Ash Shaṭrah *284* SE Iraq
Ash Shawbak *310*
  var. Ash Shawbak an Nijil. W Jordan
Ash Shiḥr *601* SE Yemen
Ash Shiṣar *418* SW Oman
Ash Shuqayq *322 var.* As Shageeg.
  Desert region of S Kuwait
Ashtarak *74 var.* Aštarak. W Armenia
Ashton *468* Union I, St. Vincent
  & the Grenadines
Asidonhopo *510* C Suriname
'Asi, Nahr al *see* Orantes
'Asi Oronte, Nahr al *see* Orantes
Asipovichy *104 Rus.* Osipovichi.
  C Belorussia
'Askar *91* E Bahrain
Asmara *210 Amh.* Asmera.
  ❖ of Eritrea, C Eritrea
Aspinwall *see* Colón
Aspropotamos *see* Acheloos
Assab *210 Amh.* Aseb. SE Eritrea
Aş Ṣabīrīyah *322* NE Kuwait
Aş Ṣabīyah *322 var.* Sabyah.
  NE Kuwait
As Sabkhah *523 var.* Sabkha.
  NE Syria
Aş Ṣafāwī *310* N Jordan
Aş Ṣafi *310 var.* Safi. W Jordan
'Assa Gaïla *194* N Djibouti
As Sahlat al Ḥadrīyah *91* N Bahrain
Aş Ṣaḥrā' *see* Sahara
Aş Ṣaḥrā' al Gharbīyah
  see Sahra el Gharqīya
Aş Ṣaḥrā' al Lībīyah
  see Libyan Desert
Aş Ṣaḥrā' ash Sharqīyah
  see Sahra el Sharqīya
Assake *see* Asaka
As Salimi *322 var.* Salemy. W Kuwait
As Salīmīyah *322* E Kuwait
'Assal, Lac *194* lake of C Djibouti
As Salṭ *310 var.* Salt. NW Jordan
As Salwā *449 var.* Salwah, Salwa.
  SW Qatar
Assamaka *407 var.* Assamakka.
  NW Niger
As Samāwah *284 var.* Samawa. S Iraq
'Assâmo *194* S Djibouti
Aş Ṣarīḥ *310* NW Jordan
Assen *397* NE Netherlands
Asserin *see* Aseri
As Shageeg *see* Ash Shuqayq
As Sīb *418* N Oman
Assiout *see* Asyūt
Assisi *295* C Italy
Assling *see* Jesenice
Assomption *480* island of the Aldabra
  Group, SW Seychelles
Aş Ṣubayḩīyah *322* S Kuwait
As Sufāl *601* S Yemen
As Sukhnah *523 var.* Sukhne,
  Fr. Soukhné. C Syria
As Sulaymānīyah *284 var.*
  Sulaimaniya, *Kurd.* Slēmānī. NE Iraq
As Sulayyil *474* C Saudi Arabia
As Suwaydā' *523 var.* El Suweida,
  Fr. Soueida. SW Syria
As Suwayq *418 var.* Suwaik. N Oman
As Suways *see* Suez
Astara *86* S Azerbaijan
Aštarak *see* Ashtarak
Asti *294* N Italy
Astipálaia *245* island of SE Greece
Astove *480* island of the Aldabra
  Group, SW Seychelles
Astrakhan' *454* SW Russia
Astrakhan-Bazar *see* Cälilabad
Astrida *see* Butare
Asturias *502* autonomous community
  of NW Spain
Āsuisui, Cape *598* cape on the coast of
  Savai'i, Western Samoa
Asuncion *628* island of N Northern
  Mariana Islands
Asunción *430* ❖ of Paraguay,
  S Paraguay
Asunción Mita *250* SE Guatemala
Aswa *see* Achwa
Aswān *202 var.* Aswân. SE Egypt
Aswān High Dam *202* dam of
  SE Egypt
Asyūt *202 var.* Assiout. C Egypt
Ata *540* island of SW Tonga
Atacama Desert *159* desert of N Chile

Atafu Atoll *631* island of NW Tokelau
Atakora, Chaîne de l' *108*
  var. Atakora Mountains. Mountain
  range of N Benin
Atakpamé *539* C Togo
Atâr *366* C Mauritania
Atas, Pulu *see* South Island
Atbara *508 var.* Nahr 'Aṭbarah. River
  of NE Sudan
Atbara *508 var.* 'Aṭbārah. NE Sudan
'Aṭbarah, Nahr *see* Atbara
Atbasar *312* N Kazakhstan
At-Bashy *325 var.* At-Bashi, At-Baši.
  C Kyrgyzstan
Athabasca *146 var.* Athabaska. River
  of W Canada
Athabasca, Lake *146* lake of
  W Canada
Athabaska *see* Athabasca
Athens *245 Gk* Athína, *prev.* Athínai.
  ❖ of Greece, SE mainland Greece
Athi *316* river of S Kenya
Athienou *187* SE Cyprus
Athína *see* Athens
Athínai *see* Athens
Athlone *288 Ir.* Áth Luain. C Ireland
Áth Luain *see* Athlone
Athna *187 var.* Akhna, Akhna,
  Turk. Düzce. E Cyprus
Ati *156* C Chad
Atiak *556* NW Uganda
Atitlán, Lago de *250* lake of
  W Guatemala
Atiu *622* island of Southern Cook
  Islands, S Cook Islands
Atlanta *251* Georgia, SE USA
Atlantic Ocean *66, 268, 565, 621*
  var. Atlantshaf. Ocean bounded to
  the W by the Americas, to the E by
  Europe and Africa and to the S by
  Antarctica
Atlantshaf *see* Atlantic Ocean
Atlas Mountains *382* mountain range
  of C Morocco
Atlas Saharien *59* mountain range of
  N Algeria
Atrak *281, 553 Rus.* Atrek, *Turkm.*
  Etrek. River of Iran and
  Turkmenistan
Atrato *171* river of NW Colombia
Atrek *see* Atrak
Aṭ Ṭaff *562* desert region of
  C United Arab Emirates
Aṭ Ṭafīlah *310* W Jordan
Aṭ Ṭā'if *474* W Saudi Arabia
At Tall al Abyaḍ *523 Fr.* Tell Abaid.
  N Syria
Attapu *327 var.* Attopeu. SE Laos
Attersee *82 var.* Kammersee. Lake of
  N Austria
At Tibnī *523* NE Syria
Attopeu *see* Attapu
At Turbah *601* SW Yemen
Atyrau *312 prev.* Gur'yev.
  W Kazakhstan
Auch *225* SW France
Auckland *401* N North Island,
  New Zealand
Augier *467* S St. Lucia
Augila *see* Awjilah
Augsburg *237* S Germany
Augusta *295* Sicilia, S Italy
Augusta *571* Maine, NE USA
'Aujā et Tahtā *292* E West Bank
Auki *490* NW Malaita, Solomon Is
Auliye-Ata *see* Zhambyl
Aur *364* island of E Marshall Islands
Aurich *236* NW Germany
Aurillac *225* S France
Aurine, Alpi *see* Zillertaler Alpen
Aurora *256* NW Guyana
Aurora *see* Maéwo
Aus *391* SW Namibia
Aussig *see* Ústí nad Labem
Austin *571* Texas, SC USA
Australes, Îles *624* island group of
  SW French Polynesia
Australia *76-81* officially
  Commonwealth of Australia. Country
  situated between the Indian and
  Pacific Oceans, divided into 8 admin.
  units (6 states and 2 territories).
  ❖ Canberra
Australian Alps *77* mountain range of
  SE Australia

Australian Capital Territory *77*
  territory of SE Australia
Austria *82-85* officially Republic of
  Austria, *Ger.* Österreich. Country of
  C Europe divided into 9 admin. units
  (states). ❖ Vienna
Ausuitoq *see* Grise Fiord
Auvergne *225* cultural region of
  SE France
Auxerre *225* N France
Avarua *622* ❖ of Cook Islands,
  Rarotonga, S Cook Islands
Avatele *628* S Niue
Aveiro *444* N Portugal
Avellino *295* S Italy
Aves, Islas les *591* island group of
  N Venezuela
Aveyron *225* river of S France
Avezzano *295* C Italy
Avignon *225* SE France
Avila *503* C Spain
Avilés *502* NW Spain
Avranches *224* NW France
Avuavu *490* SE Guadalcanal,
  Solomon Is
Awaaso *242 var.* Awaso.
  SW Ghana
'Awālī *91* C Bahrain
Awara Plain *316* plain of NE Kenya
Awash *215 var.* Hawash. River of
  C Ethiopia
Awbārī *339* W Libya
Awbārī, Ṣaḥrā *339* desert of W Libya
Awjilah *339 It.* Augila. NE Libya
Awled Djellal *see* Ouled Djellal
Axarfjördhur *see* Öxarfjördhur
Axel Heiberg Island *146*
  var. Axel Heiburg. Island of Sverdrup
  Islands, N Canada
Axim *242* S Ghana
Axios *see* Vadar
Ayabe *304* Honshū, C Japan
Ayacucho *433* S Peru
Ayaguz *312 Kaz.* Ayaköz.
  E Kazakhstan
Ayaköz *see* Ayaguz
Ayamé Reservoir *300* reservoir of
  E Ivory Coast
Ayamiken *208* NW Río Muni,
  Equatorial Guinea
Āybak *53 var.* Aibak, Haibak.
  NE Afghanistan
Aydarkŭl *582 Rus.* Ozero Aydarkuĺ.
  River of E Uzbekistan
Aydın *548* SW Turkey
Ayer Chawan, Pulau *485* island
  of SW Singapore
Ayer Hitam *354* S Peninsular Malaysia
Ayer Merbau, Pulau *485* island of
  SW Singapore
Ayers Rock *see* Uluru
Ayeyarwady *see* Irrawaddy
Ayia Napa *187 var.* Agia Napa.
  E Cyprus
Áyios Amvrosios *see* Esentepe
Áyios Eustratios *245* island of
  E Greece
Ayios Ioannis *187 var.* Agios Ioannis.
  SW Cyprus
Áyios Seryios *see* Yeniboğaziçi
Ayios Theodhoros *see* Çayirova
'Ayn al Ghazāl *339* SE Libya
'Ayn ath Tha'lab *339* C Libya
Aynī *530* W Tajikistan
Ayorou *407* W Niger
'Ayoûn el 'Atroûs *366 var.* Aïoun el
  Atroûss. SE Mauritania
Ayr *565* W Scotland, UK
Ayre, Point of *625* headland on the
  N coast of Isle of Man
Ayrs' *312* S Kazakhstan
Āysha *215* NE Ethiopia
Aytos *128 var.* Aitos, Ajtos. E Bulgaria
Ayutthaya *359 var.* Phra Nakhon
  Si Ayutthaya. C Thailand
Aywat aş Şay'ar, Wādī *601* seasonal
  river of N Yemen
Azaha, Costa del *503* coastal
  region of E Spain
Azaouagh, Vallée de l' *407 var.*
  Azaouak. Seasonal river
  of W Niger
Azaouak *see* Azaouagh, Vallée de l'
Azärbaycan *see* Azerbaijan

A'zāz *523* NW Syria

Azbine *see* Aïr

Azerbaijan *86-87* officially Republic of Azerbaijan, *Az.* Azärbaycan, *prev.* Azerbaijan SSR. Country of SE Caucasus divided into 66 admin. units (rayons). ❖ Baku

Āzezo *215* NW Ethiopia

Azimabad *see* Patna

Azizbekov *see* Vayk'

Azogues *200* S Ecuador

Azores *444 Port.* Arquipélago dos Açores, *var.* Açores. Island group of W Portugal

Azoum *156* river of SE Chad

Azov, Sea of *454, 558 Ukr.* Azovs'ke More, *Rus.* Azovskoye More. Area of Black Sea between Russia and Ukraine

Azovs'ke More *see* Azov, Sea of

Azovskoye More *see* Azov, Sea of

Azraq, Bahr el *see* Blue Nile

Azraq, Wāḥat al *310* oasis of N Jordan

Azrou *382* C Morocco

Azua *198* SE Dominican Republic

Azuero, Península de *426* peninsula of S Panama

Azul *71* E Argentina

Azur, Côte d' *225* coastal region of SE France

'Azza *see* Gaza

Az Zāb al Kabīr *see* Great Zab

Az Zāb aṣ Ṣaghīr *see* Little Zab

Az Zahrān *474 Eng.* Dhahran. NE Saudi Arabia

Az Zallāq *91* W Bahrain

Az Zarqā' *310* NW Jordan

Az Zāwiyah *339* NW Libya

Azzel Matti, Sebkha *59 var.* Sebkra Azz el Matti. Salt flat of C Algeria

Az Zaydīyah *601* W Yemen

Az Zilfī *474* C Saudi Arabia

Az Zubayr *284 var.* Al Zubair. SE Iraq

B

Ba *see* Sông Da Rang

Ba *218 prev.* Mba. Viti Levu, W Fiji

Baa Atoll *see* South Maalhosmadulu Atoll

Baaba, Île *628* island of Îles Belep, W New Caledonia

Baabda *332 var.* B'abdā. C Lebanon

Baalbek *332 var.* Ba'labakk. E Lebanon

Baar *518* N Switzerland

Baardheere *492 var.* Bardere, *It.* Bardera. SW Somalia

Baarle-Hertog *99* exclave of N Belgium

Baba *349 var.* Buševa Planina. Mountain range of Greece and FYR Macedonia

Bababé *366* SW Mauritania

Babahoyo *200 prev.* Bodegas. C Ecuador

Bābā, Kūh-e *53* mountain range of C Afghanistan

Bāb al Mandab *see* Bab el Mandeb

Babatag, Khrebet *see* Bobotogh, Qatorkūhi

Bab el Mandeb *194, 601 Ar.* Bāb al Mändab. Strait connecting the Gulf of Aden and Red Sea, between Djibouti and Yemen

Babelthuap *425* island of E Palau

Babian Jiang *see* Black River

Babonneau *467* N St. Lucia

Babruysk *104 Rus.* Bobruysk. E Belorussia

Babuyan Channel *437* channel connecting South China Sea and Pacific Ocean

Babuyan Islands *437* island of N Philippines

Bacan, Pulau *276 prev.* Batjan. Island of Maluku, E Indonesia

Bacău *450* NE Romania

Bắc Bô, Vinh *see* Tongking, Gulf of

Bắc Giang *595* N Vietnam

Bach Long Vi, Đao *595* island of N Vietnam

Bačka Topola *604 Hung.* Topolya, *prev.* Bácstopolya. N Serbia, Yugoslavia

Bac Liêu *595 var.* Vinh Loi. S Vietnam

Bacolod *437* Negros, C Philippines

Bac Phân *595 var.* Tonkin, Tongking. Cultural region of N Vietnam

Bácstopolya *see* Bačka Topola

Badajoz *502* W Spain

Badalona *503* E Spain

Badas *126* W Brunei

Baden *82 var.* Baden bei Wien. NE AustriaJ678

Baden *518* N Switzerland

Bad Ischl *82* C Austria

Bādiyat ash Badkhyz *553 var.* Badhyz, *Turkm.* Bathyz. Region of S Turkmenistan

Bādiyat ash Shām *see* Syrian Desert

Badkhyz ash Shām *see* Syrian Desert

Badou *539* W Togo

Badulla *506* C Sri Lanka

Badyarada 'Admēd *see* Aden, Gulf of

Baetic Mountains *see* Penibético, Sistema

Bafang *144* W Cameroon

Bafatá *254* C Guinea-Bissau

Baffin Bay *147, 624* bay of the Atlantic Ocean, between Baffin Island, NE Canada and Greenland

Baffin Island *147* island of NE Canada

Bafia *144* C Cameroon

Bafilo *539* NE Togo

Bafing *253, 360* headstream of the Senegal river, Guinea and Mali

Bafoussam *144* W Cameroon

Bafra *549* N Turkey

Baga *409* NE Nigeria

Bagaces *178* NW Costa Rica

Bagamoyo *532* E Tanzania

Baganuur *380* C Mongolia

Baghdad *284 var.* Bagdad, *Ar.* Baghdād. ❖ of Iraq, C Iraq

Bāgherhat *93* SW Bangladesh

Baghlān *53* NE Afghanistan

Baghramyan *74 var.* Bagramyan. W Armenia

Baglung *395* C Nepal

Bago *437 var.* Bago City. Negros, C Philippines

Bago *see* Pegu

Bagoé *360* river of Ivory Coast and Mali

Bagramyan *see* Baghramyan

Baguio *437* Luzon, N Philippines

Bagzane, Monts *407* mountain of N Niger

Bahamas *88-89* officially The Commonwealth of the Bahamas. Island state of the W Atlantic Ocean. ❖ Nassau

Bahāwalpur *421 var.* Bhawalpur. E Pakistan

Bäherden *see* Bakharden

Bahía Blanca *71* E Argentina

Bahía de Caráquez *see* Caráquez

Bahía, Islas de la *260* island group to the N of Honduras

Bahir Dar *215 var.* Bahr Dar. NW Ethiopia

Bahlah *418 var.* Bahla. N Oman

Bahrain *90-91* officially State of Bahrain, *Ar.* Al Baḥrayn, *prev.* Bahrein. Country of the Persian Gulf divided into 9 admin. units (municipalities and regions). ❖ Manama

Bahrain, Gulf of *91, 449 var.* Khalīj al Baḥrayn. Area of the Persian Gulf, off the E coast of Arabian Peninsula

Bahrām Chāh *53* SW Afghanistan

Bahr Dar *see* Bahir Dar

Bahrein *see* Bahrain

Baia Mare *450 Hung.* Nagybánya, *Ger.* Neustadt. N Romania

Baïbokoum *156* S Chad

Baicheng *163 var.* Pai-ch'eng, *prev.* T'aon-an. Jilin. NE China

Baidoa *see* Baydhabo

Baikal, Lake *see* Baykal, Ozero

Baile Átha Cliath *see* Dublin

Bailey's Bay *621* bay of the North Atlantic Ocean, N Bermuda

Bailundo *64 Port.* Vila Teixeira da Silva. C Angola

Bainet *258* S Haiti

Ba'ir *see* Bāyir

Bairiki *320* S Tarawa, Kiribati

Baitadi *395* W Nepal

Baitou Shan *see* Paektu-san

Baiyuda *see* Bayudha Desert

Baja *264* S Hungary

Baja California *370 Eng.* Lower California. Peninsula of NW Mexico

Bajo Boquete *see* Boquete

Bajos de Haina *198* S Dominican Republic

Bājram Curri *57* N Albania

Bajura *see* Martadi

Bakala *155* C Central African Republic

Bakau *233* W Gambia

Bakel *478* E Senegal

Bâ Kêv *141 var.* Bo Kheo, *prev.* Andaung Pech. NE Cambodia

Bakharden *553 prev.* Bakherden, *Turkm.* Bäherden. SW Turkmenistan

Bākhtarān *281 prev.* Kermānshāh, Qahremānshahr. W Iran

Bakı *see* Baku

Bakı Komissarı *86 Rus.* Imeni 26 Bakinskikh Komissarov. SE Azerbaijan

Bakkaflói *268* area of the Norwegian Sea

Bakony *264 Eng.* Bakony Mountains. Mountain range of W Hungary

Bakoumba *230* SE Gabon

Bakoy *360* headstream of the Senegal river, W Mali

Baku *86 Az.* Bakı, *var.* Baky. ❖ of Azerbaijan, E Azerbaijan

Bakwanga *see* Mbuji-Mayi

Balabac Island *437* island of W Philippines

Balabac Strait *355, 437* strait connecting the South China Sea and Sulu Sea

Balabio, Île *628* island of W New Caledonia

Balaka *353* S Malawi

Balakovo *454* W Russia

Bal'amā *310* NW Jordan

Bālā Morghāb *53* NW Afghanistan

Balata *467* N St. Lucia

Balaton *264 var.* Lake Balaton, *Ger.* Plattensee. Lake of W Hungary

Balbina, Represa *120* reservoir of NW Brazil

Balboa *426* C Panama

Balcarce *71* E Argentina

Balclutha *401* S South Island, New Zealand

Bâle *see* Basel

Baleares, Islas *503 Eng.* Balearic Islands. Island group of E Spain

Balearic Islands *see* Islas Baleares

Balḥāf *601* S Yemen

Balho *194* NW Djibouti

Bali *277* island of C Indonesia

Baliceaux *468* island of C St. Vincent & the Grenadines

Balıkesir *548* W Turkey

Balikpapan *276* Borneo, C Indonesia

Balimo *428* SW Papua New Guinea

Balkan Mountains *128 Bul.* Stara Planina. Mountain range of Bulgaria and Yugoslavia

Balkh *53* N Afghanistan

Balkhash *312 Kaz.* Balqash. SE Kazakhstan

Balkhash, Ozero *312 Eng.* Lake Balkhash, *Kaz.* Balqash Köl. Lake of SE Kazakhstan

Balla Balla *see* Mbalabala

Ballarat *77* SE Australia

Ballari *see* Bellary

Ballaugh *625* NW Isle of Man

Balleny Islands *66* island group to the N of Victoria Land, Antarctica

Ballina *288* NW Ireland

Ballymena *565* Northern Ireland, UK

Balqash *see* Balkhash

Balqash Köl *see* Balkhash, Ozero

Balsas *370 var.* Mexcala. River of S Mexico

Balsas *426* river of SE Panama

Bălţi *376 Rus.* Bel'tsy. N Moldova

Baltic Port *see* Paldiski

Baltic Sea *212, 221, 237, 330, 0 Ger.* Ostee. Sea of the Atlantic Ocean between Scandinavia and NE Europe

Baltimore *571* Maryland, E USA

Baltischport *see* Paldiski

Baltiski *see* Paldiski

Baluchistan *420-421* administrative region of SW Pakistan

Balykchy *325 prev.* Issyk-Kul', Rybach'ye, *Kir.* Ysyk-Köl. NE Kyrgyzstan

Balzar *200* W Ecuador

Balzers *342* S Liechtenstein

Bamako *360* ❖ of Mali, SW Mali

Bambadinca *254* C Guinea-Bissau

Bambama *176* SW Congo

Bambari *155* C Central African Republic

Bambarra *631* Grand Caicos, N Turks and Caicos Islands

Bamberg *237* S Germany

Bambey *478* W Senegal

Bamenda *144* W Cameroon

Bāmiān *53* NE Afghanistan

Bamingui *155* river of N Central African Republic

Banaba *320* island of W Kiribati

Banamba *360* W Mali

Banana *320 prev.* Main Camp. Kiritimati, E Kiribati

Banana Islands *482* island group of W Sierra Leone

Bananal, Ilha do *121* island between the two branches of the river Araguaia, C Brazil

Banda, Laut *276 Eng.* Banda Sea. Sea of the Pacific Ocean, E Indonesia

Bandama *300* river of S Ivory Coast

Bandama Blanc *300* river of C Ivory Coast

Bandama Rouge *300 var.* Marahoué. River of C Ivory Coast

Bandar-e 'Abbās *281* SE Iran

Bandar-e Büshehr *281 var.* Büshehr, *Eng.* Bushire. SW Iran

Bandar Maharani *see* Muar

Bandar Penggaram *see* Batu Pahat

Bandar Seri Begawan *126 prev.* Brunei Town. ❖ of Brunei, N Brunei

Bandar Sri Aman *354 prev.* Simanggang. SW Borneo, Malaysia

Banda Sea *see* Banda, Laut

Band-e Torkestān *53* NW Afghanistan

Bandiagara *360* C Mali

Bandırma *548* NW Turkey

Bandoeng *see* Bandung

Bandrélé *627* SE Mayotte

Bandundu *609 prev.* Banningville. W Zaire

Bandung *276 prev.* Bandoeng. Java, C Indonesia

Banes *183* SE Cuba

Baney *208* N Bioko, Equatorial Guinea

Banfora *133* SW Burkina

Bangalore *270, 275* S India

Bangangté *144* W Cameroon

Bangar *126* NE Brunei

Bangassou *155* SE Central African Republic

Bangfai *327* river of S Laos

Banggai, Kepulauan *276* island group to the E of Celebes, C Indonesia

Banggi, Pulau *355 var.* Banggi. Island of NE Borneo, Malaysia

Banghāzī *339 Eng.* Benghazi, *It.* Bengasi. N Libya

Banghiang *327 var.* Bang Hieng. River of S Laos

Bangka, Pulau *276* island to the SE of Sumatra, W Indonesia

Bangkok *327 Th.* Krung Thep. ❖ of Thailand, C Thailand

Bangladesh *92-95* officially People's Republic of Bangladesh, *prev.* East Pakistan. Country of S Asia divided into 4 admin. units (divisions). ❖ Dhaka

Bangor *565* Northern Ireland, UK

Bangor *565* N Wales, UK

Bangor *571* Maine, NE USA

Borgarnes 268 W Iceland
Borgholm 515 Öland, S Sweden
Borgo Maggiore 470 NW San Marino
Borikhan 327 var. Borikhane. C Laos
Borisov see Barysaw
Bor, Lagh 316 var. Lak Bor. Dry watercourse in NE Kenya
Borlänge 515 C Sweden
Borneo 276, 354-355 island of SE Asia divided between Brunei, two Malaysian states and part of Indonesia
Bornholm 190 island of E Denmark
Boromo 133 SW Burkina
Borongo see Black Volta
Borovo 181 NE Croatia
Borujerd 281 var. Burujird. W Iran
Börzsöny 264 mountain range of N Hungary
Bosanska Gradiška 116 N Bosnia & Herzegovina
Bosanski Brod 116 N Bosnia & Herzegovina
Bosanski Šamac 116 N Bosnia & Herzegovina
Boscobelle 97 NE Barbados
Bösing see Pezinok
Boskamp 510 N Suriname
Boskovice 188 SE Czech Republic
Bosna 116 river of N Bosnia & Herzegovina
Bosnia & Herzegovina 116-117 officially The Republic of Bosnia and Herzegovina. Country of SE Europe. ❖ Sarajevo
Bosporus see İstanbul Boğazi
Bossangoa 155 C Central African Republic
Bossembélé 155 C Central African Republic
Boston 571 Massachusetts, NE USA
Boteti 118 var. Botletle. River of C Botswana
Botevgrad 128 prev. Orkhanie, Orkhaniye. W Bulgaria
Bothnia, Gulf of 221, 515 Fin. Pohjanlahti, Swe. Bottniska Viken. Gulf of the Baltic Sea, between Finland and Sweden
Boti-Pasi 510 C Suriname
Botna 376 river of E Moldova
Botoşani 450 NE Romania
Botrange 99 mountain of E Belgium
Botswana 118-119 officially Republic of Botswana. Country of southern Africa divided into 10 admin. units (districts). ❖ Gaborone
Bottle Creek 631 North Caicos, N Turks and Caicos Islands
Bottniska Viken see Bothnia, Gulf of
Bottom, The 628 Saba, N Netherlands Antilles
Bouaflé 300 C Ivory Coast
Bouaké 300 var. Bwake. C Ivory Coast
Bouar 155 W Central African Republic
Bouca 155 C Central African Republic
Bouéni 627 SW Mayotte
Bouéni, Baie de 627 var. Bonéni Bay. Bay of the Mozambique Channel on the SW coast of Mayotte
Bouenza 176 river of S Congo
Boufarik 59 N Algeria
Bougainville Island 428 island of E Papua New Guinea
Bougie see Béjaïa
Bougouni 360 SW Mali
Bougouriba 133 river of SW Burkina
Boujdour 382 W Western Sahara
Boukoumbé 108 var. Boukombé. NW Benin
Boukra 382 C Western Sahara
Boulder 571 Colorado, SW USA
Boulogne-sur-Mer 225 var. Boulogne. N France
Bouloupari 628 S New Caledonia
Bouma 218 Taveuni, N Fiji
Boumango 230 SE Gabon
Boumba 144 river of SE Cameroon
Boumbé II 155 river of Cameroon and Central African Republic
Boûmdeïd 366 S Mauritania
Bouna 300 NE Ivory Coast
Boundiali 300 N Ivory Coast
Boungou 155 river of C Central African Republic

Bourail 628 C New Caledonia
Bourgas see Burgas
Bourg-en-Bresse 225 E France
Bourges 225 C France
Bourgogne 225 Eng. Burgundy. Cultural region of E France
Bourke 77 E Australia
Bournemouth 565 S England, UK
Boussé 133 C Burkina
Boussouma 133 C Burkina
Boutilimit 366 SW Mauritania
Bouton 467 W St. Lucia
Bovec 488 Ger. Flitsch, It. Plezzo. NW Slovenia
Bozen see Bolzano
Bozoum 155 W Central African Republic
Brač 181 var. Brach, It. Brazza. Island of S Croatia
Bradford 565 N England, UK
Braga 444 NW Portugal
Bragado 71 E Argentina
Bragança 444 Eng. Braganza. NE Portugal
Braganza see Bragança
Brahestad see Raahe
Brāhmanbāria 93 E Bangladesh
Brahmaputra 93, 162, 271 var. Tsangpo, Ben. Jamuna. River of S Asia
Brāila 450 E Romania
Braine-l'Alleud 99 C Belgium
Branco 120 river of NW Brazil
Branco, Ilhéu 152 island of N Cape Verde
Brandberg 391 mountain of NW Namibia
Brande 190 Jylland, W Denmark
Brandenburg 237 C Germany
Brandon 146 S Canada
Brani, Pulau 485 island of S Singapore
Brasília 121 ❖ of Brazil, C Brazil
Braslaw 104 N Belorussia
Braşov 450 prev. Stalin, Ger. Kronstadt, Hung. Brassó. C Romania
Brasschaat 99 N Belgium
Brassey, Banjaran 355 var. Brassey Range. Mountain range of E Borneo, Malaysia
Brassey Range see Brassey, Banjaran
Bratislava 487 Ger. Pressburg, Hung. Pozsony. ❖ of Slovakia, SW Slovakia
Bratsk 455 C Russia
Bratskoye Vodokhranilishche 455 Eng. Bratsk Reservoir. C Russia
Braunau am Inn 82 var. Braunau. N Austria
Braunschweig 237 Eng. Brunswick. N Germany
Brava see Baraawe
Brava 152 island of SW Cape Verde
Brava, Costa 503 coastal region of E Spain
Bravo Del Norte see Grande, Río
Bray 288 Ir. Bri Chuallan. E Ireland
Brazil 120-125 officially Federative Republic of Brazil. Country of South America divided into 28 admin. units (26 states, 1 territory, 1 federal district). ❖ Brasília
Brazos 571 river of SW USA
Brazza see Brač
Brazzaville 176 ❖ of Congo, S Congo
Brčko 116 NE Bosnia & Herzegovina
Breda 397 SW Netherlands
Bregalnica 349 river of E FYR Macedonia
Bregenz 82 W Austria
Breidhafjördhur 268 bay of the Denmark Strait, on the coast of W Iceland

Bremen 236 NW Germany
Bremerhaven 236 NW Germany
Bremersdorp see Manzini
Brennero, Passo del see Brenner Pass
Brenner Pass 82, 295 It. Passo del Brennero, Ger. Brennerpass, var. Brenner Sattel. Mountain pass of Austria and Italy
Brerton 97 C Barbados
Brescia 294 N Italy
Breslau see Wrocław
Brest 104 Pol. Brześć nad Bugiem, prev. Brześć Litewski, Rus. Brest-Litovsk. SW Belorussia
Brest 224 NW France
Bretagne 224 Eng. Brittany. Cultural region of NW France
Brewerville 336 W Liberia
Brezhnev see Naberezhnyye
Brežice 488 Ger. Rann. E Slovenia
Brezno 487 prev. Brezno nad Hronom, Ger. Bries, var. Briesen, Hung. Breznóbánya. C Slovakia
Bria 155 C Central African Republic
Bribrí 178 E Costa Rica
Bri Chuallan see Bray
Bride 625 N Isle of Man
Bridgetown 76 SW Australia
Bridgetown 97 ❖ of Barbados, SW Barbados
Bridgwater 565 SW England, UK
Brienzer See 518 lake of SW Switzerland
Brig 518 SW Switzerland
Brighton 565 SE England, UK
Brikama 233 W Gambia
Brindisi 295 S Italy
Brinstone Hill 464 NW St. Kitts, St. Kitts & Nevis
Brisbane 77 E Australia
Bristol 565 SW England, UK
Bristol Channel 565 inlet of the Atlantic Ocean, SW England, UK
British Columbia 146 province of SW Canada
British Guiana see Guyana
British Indian Ocean Territory 621 British dependent territory of the Indian Ocean. ❖ Diego Garcia
British North America see Canada
British Virgin Islands 621 British dependent territory of the Caribbean Sea. ❖ Road Town
Brittany see Bretagne
Brizan 248 W Grenada island, Grenada
Brno 188 Ger. Brünn. SE Czech Republic
Bród see Slavonski Brod
Brodeur Peninsula 146 peninsula of Baffin Island, N Canada
Broken Hill 77 S Australia
Brokopondo 510 NE Suriname
Bromberg see Bydgoszcz
Brønderslev 190 Jylland, N Denmark
Brooks Range 570 mountain range of Alaska, USA
Broome 76 NW Australia
Brorup 190 Jylland, W Denmark
Broughton Bay see Tongjosŏn-man
Brown Hill 464 S Nevis, St. Kitts & Nevis
Browns Town 303 N Jamaica
Brownsweg 510 C Suriname
Bruck an der Mur 82 var. Bruck. C Austria
Brufut 233 W Gambia
Brugge 99 Fr. Bruges. NW Belgium
Bruit, Pulau 354 island of W Borneo, Malaysia
Brunei 126-127, 354 officially Sultanate of Brunei, Mal. Negara Brunei Darussalam. Country on island of Borneo, SE Asia, divided into 4 admin. units (districts). ❖ Bandar Seri Begawan
Brunei Bay 354 var. Teluk Brunei. Bay of the South China Sea
Brunei Town see Bandar Seri Begawan
Brünn see Brno
Brunswick see Braunschweig
Brusa see Bursa
Brussels 99 Fr. Bruxelles, Dut. Brussel, Ger. Brüssel. ❖ of Belgium, C Belgium

Brüx see Most
Bryansk 454 W Russia
Brześć Litewski see Brest
Brześć nad Bugiem see Brest
Bsharri see Bcharré
Bua 353 river of C Malawi
Bu'aale 492 SW Somalia
Buada Lagoon 392 lagoon on the coast of Nauru
Buala 490 SE Santa Isabel, Solomon Is
Bū al Ḩīdān, Wādī 39 dry watercourse of C Libya
Buba 254 S Guinea-Bissau
Bubanza 138 NW Burundi
Bubaque 254 Ilha de Bubaque, Guinea-Bissau
Bubaque, Ilha de 254 island of SW Guinea-Bissau
Bubi 614 var. Bubye. River of S Zimbabwe
Būbīyan, Jazirat 322 island of NE Kuwait
Buca 218 prev. Mbutha. Vanua Levu, N Fiji
Bucaramanga 171 N Colombia
Buchanan 336 prev. Grand Bassa. SW Liberia
Bucharest 450 Rom. Bucureşti. ❖ of Romania, S Romania
Budapest 264 ❖ of Hungary, N Hungary
Búdhardalur 268 W Iceland
Budweis see České Budějovice
Buea 144 SW Cameroon
Buenaventura 171 W Colombia
Buena Vista 102 N Belize
Buena Vista 112 C Bolivia
Buena Vista 624 S Gibraltar
Buenos Aires 71 ❖ of Argentina, E Argentina
Buenos Aires 178 SE Costa Rica
Buenos Aires, Lago 71, 159 Sp. Lago General Carrera. Lake of Argentina and Chile
Buffalo 571 New York, NE USA
Buff Bay 303 E Jamaica
Bug 441, 558 Ukr. Zakhidnyy Buh, Rus. Zapadnyy Bug. River of E Europe
Buga 171 W Colombia
Bugala Island 556 island of Sese Islands, S Uganda
Buganda 138 NW Burundi
Bugarama 462 SW Rwanda
Bughotu see Santa Isabel
Bugibba 363 N Malta
Bugojno 116 C Bosnia & Herzegovina
Bugumya 462 SW Rwanda
Buin 428 Bougainville I, Papua New Guinea
Buitenzorg see Bogor
Bujumbura 138 prev. Usumbura. ❖ of Burundi, W Burundi
Buka Island 428 island of E Papua New Guinea
Bukakata 556 S Uganda
Bukasa Island 556 island of Sese Islands, S Uganda
Bukavu 609 prev. Costermansville. E Zaire
Bukeye 138 var. Bukaye. C Burundi
Bukhoro 582 var. Bokhara, Rus. Bukhara. S Uzbekistan
Bukit Mertajam 354 NW Peninsular Malaysia
Bukit Panjang 485 area of C Singapore
Bukit Timah 485 area of C Singapore
Bükk 264 mountain range of NE Hungary
Bukoba 532 NW Tanzania
Bukum Kechil, Pulau 485 island of SW Singapore
Bukum, Pulau 485 island of S Singapore
Bula 254 W Guinea-Bissau
Bulawayo 614 var. Buluwayo. SW Zimbabwe
Bulembu 512 NW Swaziland
Bulgan 380 N Mongolia
Bulgaria 128-131 officially Republic of Bulgaria, prev. People's Republic of Bulgaria. Country of E Europe divided into 8 admin. units (regions). ❖ Sofia

C

Chad *156-157* officially Republic of Chad, *Fr.* Tchad. Country of Equatorial Africa divided into 14 admin. units (prefectures).
❖ N'Djamena
Chã da Igreja *152* Santo Antão, N Cape Verde
Chad, Lake *144, 156, 407, 409 Fr.* Lac Tchad. Lake of C Africa
Chadyr-Lunga *see* Ciadîr-Lunga
Chaeryŏng *413* SW North Korea
Chāgai Hills *420* mountain range of Afghanistan and Pakistan
Chaghcharān *53* C Afghanistan
Chagos Archipelago *621 var.* Oil Islands. Island group of C British Indian Ocean Territory
Chaguanas *542* W Trinidad, Trinidad & Tobago
Chaguaramas *542* NW Trinidad, Trinidad & Tobago
Chagyl *553* NW Turkmenistan
Chahārborjak *53* SW Afghanistan
Chaillu, Massif du *230* C Gabon
Mongos, Chaîne des *see* Bongo, Massif des
Chainpur *395* W Nepal
Chai Wan *262* S Hong Kong
Chaiyaphum *535* N Thailand
Chakari *614* N Zimbabwe
Chake Chake *532* Pemba, E Tanzania
Chakwāl *421* NE Pakistan
Chalándri *245 prev.* Khalándrion. SE Greece
Chalap Dalam *53* mountain range of W Afghanistan
Chalatenango *207* N El Salvador
Chalbi Desert *316* desert region of N Kenya
Chalchuapa *207* W El Salvador
Chalkída *245 Eng.* Chalcis, *prev.* Khalkís. Evvoia, E Greece
Chalkidikí *245 prev.* Khalkidhikí, *Eng.* Chalcidice. Peninsula of NE Greece
Challapata *112* SW Bolivia
Challengers *464* S St. Kitts, St. Kitts & Nevis
Châlons-en-Champagne *225 prev.* Châlons-sur-Marne. NE France
Chaman *421* NW Pakistan
Chambas *182* C Cuba
Chambéry *225* E France
Chambeshi *613* river of NE Zambia
Chambi, Jebel *545* mountain of W Tunisia
Chamelecón, Río *260* river of NW Honduras
Chamouny *368* S Mauritius
Champagne *225* cultural region of NE France
Champasak *327* S Laos
Chañaral *159* N Chile
Chances Peak *627* mountain peak of S Montserrat
Chan Chen *102* N Belize
Chan-chiang *see* Zhanjiang
Chandīgarh *270* N India
Chandlers Falls *316 var.* Chanlers Falls. Waterfall of C Kenya
Chāndpur *93* E Bangladesh
Changane *387* river of S Mozambique
Changara *387* W Mozambique
Changchun *163 prev.* Hsinking. Jilin, NE China
Changhua *527 var.* Shōka. W Taiwan
Changi *485* area of E Singapore
Chang Jiang *163 var.* Yangtze Kiang. River of C China
Changkiakow *see* Zhangjiakou
Chang, Ko *535* island of C Thailand
Changsha *163* Hunan, S China
Chang-tien *see* Zibo
Changuinola *426* W Panama
Ch'angwŏn *498* S South Korea
Changyŏn *413* SW North Korea
Chaniá *245 Eng.* Canea, *prev.* Khaniá. Crete, S Greece
Channel Islands *224* island group to the NW of France *see* Jersey, Guernsey, Alderney, Sark
Channel, The *see* English Channel
Channel Tunnel *565* tunnel between France and SE England, UK

Chanthaburi *535* C Thailand
Ch'aochou *527 var.* Chaochow, *Jap.* Chōshū. SW Taiwan
Chao Phraya *535* river of C Thailand
Chaouèn *382 var.* Chechaouèn, Chefchaouèn, *Sp.* Xauen. N Morocco
Chapada Diamantina *121* plateau of E Brazil
Chapala, Lago de *370* lake of SW Mexico
Chapelton *303* C Jamaica
Chaplin Bay *621* bay of the North Atlantic Ocean, W Bermuda
Chardonnières *258* SW Haiti
Chardzhev *553 prev.* Chardzhou, *var.* Čardžou, *prev.* Leninsk, *Turkm.* Chärjew. E Turkmenistan
Chardzhou *see* Chardzhev
Ch'arents'avan *74 var.* Čarencaven. C Armenia
Chari *156 var.* Shari. River of C Africa
Chārīkār *53* NE Afghanistan
Charity *256* NE Guyana
Chärjew *see* Chardzhev
Charkhliq *see* Ruoqiang
Charleroi *99* S Belgium
Charleston *571* South Carolina, SE USA
Charleston *571* West Virginia, E USA
Charlestown *464* SW Nevis, St. Kitts & Nevis
Charlestown *468* Canouan, St. Vincent & the Grenadines
Charleville *77* E Australia
Charleville-Mézieres *225* NE France
Charlotte *571* North Carolina, SE USA
Charlotte Amalie *631* ❖ of Virgin Islands (US), S Saint Thomas Island
Charlotte Town *see* Gouyave
Charlottetown *147* Prince Edward Island, SE Canada
Charlotte Ville *196* SW Dominica
Charlotteville *542* N Tobago, Trinidad & Tobago
Charshanga *553 prev.* Charshangy, *Turkm.* Charshangngy. SE Turkmenistan
Charsk *312* E Kazakhstan
Chartres *225* N France
Chartres Settlement *623* West Falkland, W Falkland Islands
Chateaubelair *468* NW St. Vincent, St. Vincent & the Grenadines
Châteauroux *225* C France
Chateaux, Pointe des *624* headland of E Guadeloupe
Châtelet *99* S Belgium
Chatham Island *401* island of Chatham Islands, E New Zealand
Chatham Islands *401* islands of E New Zealand
Chatkal Range *325, 582 Rus.* Chatkal'skiy Khrebet. Mountain range of Kyrgyzstan and Uzbekistan
Chāttagām *see* Chittagong
Chattanooga *571* Tennessee, SE USA
Chatyr-Tash *325* E Kyrgyzstan
Châu Độc *595 var.* Chau Phu. SW Vietnam
Chauk *135* W Burma
Chaumont *224* NE France
Chau Phu *see* Châu Độc
Chautara *395* C Nepal
Chaves *444* N Portugal
Chbar *141* E Cambodia
Cheb *188 Ger.* Eger. W Czech Republic
Chechaouèn *see* Chaouèn
Ch'ech'eng *527* S Taiwan
Che-chiang *see* Zhejiang
Chechnya, Respublika *454, 460* autonomous republic of SW Russia
Chech'ŏn *498 Jap.* Teisen. N South Korea
Checker Hall *97* N Barbados
Cheduba Island *135* island of W Burma
Chefoo *see* Yantai
Chegutu *614 prev.* Hartley. N Zimbabwe
Cheju *498 Jap.* Saishū. Cheju-do, South Korea
Cheju-do *498 prev.* Quelpart, *Jap.* Saishu. Island of S South Korea
Cheju Strait *498 var.* Chejuhaehyop, Cheju-Haehyop. Strait connecting the Korea Strait and Yellow Sea

Chek Chue *262 var.* Stanley. S Hong Kong
Chekiang *see* Zhejiang
Chek Lap Kok *262* W Hong Kong
Chek Mun Hoi Hap *262* NE Hong Kong
Cheleken *553 var.* Čeleken. W Turkmenistan
Chelkar *312* W Kazakhstan
Chelyabinsk *454* C Russia
Chemin Grenier *368* S Mauritius
Chemnitz *237 prev.* Karl-Marx-Stadt. E Germany
Chemulpo *see* Inch'ŏn
Ch'eng-chou *see* Zhengzhou
Chengchow *see* Zhengzhou
Chengdu *163 var.* Chengtu. Sichuan, SW China
Chenghsien *see* Zhengzhou
Ch'eng-hua *see* Altay
Chenghwa *see* Altay
Chenkaladi *506* E Sri Lanka
Cheoc Van, Baía de *626* bay of the South China Sea, S Macao
Cheom Ksan *see* Chŏâm Khsant
Chepo *426* NE Panama
Cher *225* river of C France
Cherbourg *225* NW France
Cheren *see* Keren
Cherepovets *454* W Russia
Chergui, Chott ech *59* salt lake of NW Algeria
Chergui, Île *545 Ar.* Jazirat ash Sharqi. Island of E Tunisia
Cherikaw *104* E Belorussia
Cherkasy *558 Rus.* Cherkassy. C Ukraine
Cherne More *see* Black Sea
Chernivtsi *558 Rus.* Chernovtsy, *Rom.* Cernăuţi, *Ger.* Czernowitz. W Ukraine
Chernobyl' *see* Chornobyl'
Cherno More *see* Black Sea
Cherry Island *see* Anuta
Cherskiy *455* NE Russia
Cherskogo, Khrebet *455* mountain range of NE Russia
Cherso *see* Cres
Cherson *see* Kherson
Cherven-Bryag *128 var.* Červen brjag. NW Bulgaria
Chester *565* NW England, UK
Chetumal, Bahía *102 var.* Chetumal Bay. Bay of the Caribbean Sea
Chetumal Bay *see* Chetumal, Bahía
Cheung Chau *262* SW Hong Kong
Cheviot Hills *565* hills of England and Scotland, UK
Ch'ew Bahir *215 var.* Lake Stefanie. Lake of SW Ethiopia
Cheyenne *571* Wyoming, NW USA
Chhlong *see* Phumĭ Chhlong
Chhuk *see* Phumĭ Chhuk
Chhukha *110* SW Bhutan
Chiai *527 var.* Chiayi, Kiayi, *Jap.* Kagi. W Taiwan
Chiali *527 var.* Kiali, *Jap.* Kari. W Taiwan
Chia-mu-ssu *see* Jiamusi
Chiang-hsi *see* Jiangxi
Chiang Mai *535 var.* Chiengmai. NW Thailand
Chiang-su *see* Jiangsu
Chiat'ura *234* C Georgia
Chiba *304* Honshū, SE Japan
Chibuto *387* S Mozambique
Chicago *571* Illinois, C USA
Chīchāwatni *421* E Pakistan
Chichicastenango *250* W Guatemala
Chichigalpa *404* W Nicaragua
Ch'i-ch'i-ha-erh *see* Qiqihar
Chiclayo *433* NW Peru
Chicoutimi *147* SE Canada
Chicualacuala *387* SW Mozambique
Chiemsee *237* lake of SE Germany
Chiesanuova *470* W San Marino
Chih-fu *see* Yantai
Chihli *see* Hebei
Chihli, Gulf of *see* Bo Hai
Chi-hsi *see* Jixi
Chihuahua *370* NW Mexico
Ch'ikhareshi *234* N Georgia
Chikwawa *353* SW Malawi
Chilanga *613* S Zambia

Chilaw *506* W Sri Lanka
Chile *158-161* officially Republic of Chile. Country of South America divided into 13 admin. units (12 regions and 1 metropolitan area).
❖ Santiago
Chile Chico *159* W Chile
Chilika Lake *270* lake of E India
Chililabombwe *613* C Zambia
Chi-lin *see* Jilin
Chillán *159* C Chile
Chilliwack *146* SW Canada
Chiloé, Isla de *159 var.* Isla Grande de Chiloé. Island of W Chile
Chilumba *353 prev.* Deep Bay. N Malawi
Chilung *527 var.* Keelung, *Jap.* Kirun. N Taiwan
Chilwa, Lake *353 var.* Lake Shirwa, *Port.* Lago Chirua. Lake of SE Malawi
Chimaltenango *250* W Guatemala
Chimanimani *614 prev.* Mandidzudzure, *prev.* Melsetter. E Zimbabwe
Chimbay *see* Chimboy
Chimborazo *200* mountain of C Ecuador
Chimbote *433* W Peru
Chimboy *582 Rus.* Chimbay. NW Uzbekistan
Chimishliya *see* Cimişlia
Chimkent *see* Shymkent
Chimoio *387* C Mozambique
China *162-169* officially People's Republic of China, *Chin.* Zhonghua Renmin Gonghe Guo, *var.* Chunghua Jen-min Kung-ho-kuo, *prev.* Chinese Empire (until January 1912). Country of E Asia divided into 30 admin. units (22 ovinces, 5 autonomous regions, 3 province-level municipalities). ❖ Beijing
Chinan *see* Jinan
Chinandega *404* W Nicaragua
Chincha Alta *433* SW Peru
Chin-chiang *see* Quanzhou
Chin-chou *see* Jinzhou
Chinchow *see* Jinzhou
Chin-do *498 Jap.* Chin-tō, Island of SW South Korea
Chindwin *135* river of NW Burma
Ch'ing Hai *see* Qinghai Hu
Chinghai *see* Qinghai
Chingola *613* C Zambia
Ch'ingshui *527 var.* Tsingshui, *Jap.* Kiyomizu. W Taiwan
Ching-Tao *see* Qingdao
Chinguetti *366* C Mauritania
Chinhae *498 Jap.* Chinkai. S South Korea
Chinhoyi *614 var.* Sinoia. N Zimbabwe
Chinhsien *see* Jinzhou
Chiniot *421* NE Pakistan
Chinit *141 var.* Chinit. River of C Cambodia
Chinju *498 Jap.* Shinshū. S South Korea
Chinkai *see* Chinhae
Chink Kaplankyr *553* ridge of NW Turkmenistan
Chinko *155* river of E Central African Republic
Chintheche *353 var.* Chinteche. N Malawi
Chin-tō *see* Chin-do
Chios *245 prev.* Khíos. Island of E Greece
Chíos *245 prev.* Khíos, *It.* Scio, *Turk.* Sakis-Adasi. Chios, E Greece
Chipata *613 prev.* Fort Jameson. E Zambia
Chipinge *614 prev.* Chipinga. E Zimbabwe
Chiponde *353* SE Malawi
Chiquimula *250* SE Guatemala
Chiquimulilla *250* S Guatemala
Chiradzulu *353* S Malawi
Chirang *110* S Bhutan
Chirchik *582 Rus.* Chirchik. E Uzbekistan
Chire *see* Shire

Chiredzi *614* SE Zimbabwe
Chirilagua *207* SE El Salvador
Chiriquí *426* W Panama
Chiriquí, Golfo de *426* gulf of the Pacific Ocean to the SW of Panama
Chiriquí Grande *426* W Panama
Chiriquí, Laguna de *426* lagoon of W Panama
Chiromo *353* S Malawi
Chirongui *627* S Mayotte
Chirripó Grande, Cerro *178* mountain of E Costa Rica
Chirua, Lago *see* Chilwa, Lake
Chirundu *614* N Zimbabwe
Chisenga *353* NW Malawi
Ch'ishan *527* var. Kishan, Jap. Kizan. SW Taiwan
Chishtiān Mandi *421* E Pakistan
Chisimaio *see* Kismaayo
Chişinău *376* var. Kishinev. ❖ of Moldova, C Moldova
Chissioua Mtsamboro *627* island of NW Mayotte
Chita *455* C Russia
Chitipa *353* prev. Fort Hill. NW Malawi
Chitose *305* Hokkaidō, N Japan
Chitré *426* S Panama
Chittagong *93* Ben. Chāttagām. SE Bangladesh
Chittagong Hills *93* hilly region of S Asia
Chitungwiza *614* prev. Chitangwiza. NE Zimbabwe
Chiuta, Lake *353* lake of SE Malawi
Chivhu *614* prev. Enkeldoorn. C Zimbabwe
Chíxoy *250* var. Río Negro, Salinas. River of Guatemala and Mexico
Chizarira Hills *614* hilly region of NW Zimbabwe
Chizumulu Island *353* var. Chisumulu Island. Island of Lake Nyasa, E Malawi
Chkalov *see* Orenburg
Chlef *59* prev. El Asnam, Orléansville, var. Ech Cheliff, Ech Chleff. NW Algeria
Choa Chu Kang *485* area of W Singapore
Chôăm Khsant *141* prev. Cheom Ksan. N Cambodia
Choiseul *467* SW St. Lucia
Choiseul *490* var. Lauru. Island of the W Solomon Islands
Choiseul Sound *623* area of the South Atlantic Ocean, E Falkland Islands
Cholo *see* Thyolo
Choluteca *260* S Honduras
Choluteca *260* river of S Honduras
Choma *613* S Zambia
Chomo Lhari *110* mountain of NW Bhutan
Chomutov *188* Ger. Komotau. NW Czech Republic
Ch'ŏnan *498* Jap. Tenan. W South Korea
Chon Buri *535* C Thailand
Chone *200* W Ecuador
Ch'ŏngch'ŏn *413* river of W North Korea
Ch'ŏngjin *413* NE North Korea
Chŏngju *413* W North Korea
Chŏngju *498* prev. Chŏngup, Jap. Seiyu. SW South Korea
Ch'ŏngju *498* var. Chŏngju. C South Korea
Chongqing *163* var. Chungking, Ch'ung-ching, Yuzhou. Sichuan, SW China
Chongwe *613* E Zambia
Chŏnju *498* Jap. Zenshū. SW South Korea
Chorne More *see* Black Sea
Chornobyl' *558* Rus. Chernobyl'. N Ukraine
Chorzów *441* Ger. Königshütte. S Poland
Chôsen-kaikyô *see* Korea Strait
Chôshū *see* Ch'aochou
Choshui Hsi *527* river of W and NE Taiwan
Chota Nagpur Plateau *270* plateau of NE India
Choybalsan *380* E Mongolia

Christchurch *401* E South Island, New Zealand
Christiana *303* C Jamaica
Christiania *see* Oslo
Christian, Point *629* headland of Pitcairn Island, S Pitcairn Islands
Christiansand *see* Kristiansand
Christianshåb *see* Qasigiannguit
Christiansted *631* Saint Croix, S Virgin Islands (US)
Christiansund *see* Kristiansund
Christmas Island *622* Australian external territory of the Indian Ocean. ❖ Flying Fish Cove.
Christmas Island *see* Kiritimati
Chrysochou Bay *see* Khrysokhou Bay
Chu *312* Kaz. Shū. SE Kazakhstan
Chu *325* var. Ču, Kir. Chüy. River of Kazakhstan and Kyrgyzstan
Chu *595* river of Laos and Vietnam
Chuādānga *93* W Bangladesh
Ch'uan-chou *see* Quanzhou
Chubek *see* Moskva
Ch'u-chiang *see* Shaoguan
Chucunaque *426* river of E Panama
Chudskoye Ozero *see* Peipus, Lake
Chūgoku-sanchi *304* mountain range of Honshū, W Japan
Chui *see* Chuy
Chukai *354* var. Cukai. E Peninsular Malaysia
Chukchi Sea *455* Rus. Chukotskoye More. Sea of Arctic Ocean between NE Asia and NW N America
Chukotskiy Poluostrov *455* Eng. Chukchi Peninsula. Peninsula of NE Russia
Chulucanas *433* NW Peru
Chumphon *535* S Thailand
Chunan *527* NW Taiwan
Ch'unch'ŏn *498* Jap. Shunsen. N South Korea
Chungyang Shanmo *527* mountain range of C Taiwan
Ch'ung-ching *see* Chongqing
Chungho *527* N Taiwan
Chunghsingsints'un *527* W Taiwan
Chung-hua Jen-min Kung-ho-kuo *see* China
Ch'ungju *498* Jap. Chūshū. C South Korea
Ch'ungju-ho *498* reservoir of C South Korea
Chungking *see* Chongqing
Chungli *527* Jap. Chūreki. N Taiwan
Ch'ungmu *498* S South Korea
Chunya *532* SW Tanzania
Chuquicamata *159* N Chile
Chur *518* It. Coira, Rmsch. Cuera, Fr. Coire. E Switzerland
Church Cay *468* cay of E St. Vincent & the Grenadines
Churchill *147* E Canada
Church Village *97* SE Barbados
Chūreki *see* Chungli
Chūshū *see* Ch'ungju
Chust *582* var. Čust. E Uzbekistan
Chuuk Islands *374* var. Hogoley Islands. Island group of C Micronesia
Chuyashshkiya *454* autonomous republic of W Russia
Chuy *579* var. Chuí. SE Uruguay
Chykotskoye Nagor'ye *455* mountain range of NE Russia
Ciadir-Lunga *376* var. Ceadâr-Lunga, Rus. Chadyr-Lunga. S Moldova
Cibitoke *138* NW Burundi
Ciceron *467* NW St. Lucia
Cicia *218* prev. Thithia. Island of the Lau Group, E Fiji
Cidade Velha *152* Santiago, S Cape Verde
Ciego de Ávila *182* C Cuba
Ciénaga *171* N Colombia
Cienfuegos *182* C Cuba
Cieza *503* SE Spain
Çiftlik Dere *see* Aloupos
Cifuentes *182* C Cuba
Cikobia *218* prev. Thikombia. Island to the N of Vanua Levu, N Fiji
Cilacap *276* prev. Tjilatjap. Java, C Indonesia

Cill Airne *see* Killarney
Cill Choinnigh *see* Kilkenny
Cilli *see* Celje
Cill Mhantáin *see* Wicklow
Cimişlia *376* Rus. Chimishliya. S Moldova
Cina Selatan, Laut *see* South China Sea
Cincinnati *571* Ohio, NE USA
Ciney *99* SE Belgium
Ciotat *225* SE France
Cirebon *276* prev. Tjirebon. Java, C Indonesia
Cirque de Cilaos *630* mountain range of W Réunion
Cirquenizza *see* Crikvenica
Ciskei Bantustan 'self-governing homeland' comprising 2 non-contiguous territories of E Cape Province, South Africa; created in 1981, abolished in 1994
Citlaltépetl *see* Orizaba, Volcán Pico de
Citron *623* NW French Guiana
Citron, River *368* river of NW Mauritius
Ciudad Arce *207* W El Salvador
Ciudad Bolívar *591* E Venezuela
Ciudad de Guatemala *see* Guatemala City
Ciudad del Este *430* prev. Puerto Presidente Stroessner. SE Paraguay
Ciudad de México *see* Mexico City
Ciudad de Panamá *see* Panama City
Ciudad Guayana *591* E Venezuela
Ciudad Juárez *370* NW Mexico
Ciudad Obregón *370* NW Mexico
Ciudad Ojeda *591* NW Venezuela
Ciudad Real *503* C Spain
Ciudad Trujillo *see* Santo Domingo
Ciudad Victoria *370* C Mexico
Civitavecchia *295* C Italy
Clarence *401* river of NE South Island, New Zealand
Clarence Island *66* island of South Shetland Islands, Antarctica
Clarence Town *88* Long Island, Bahamas
Clermont-Ferrand *225* C France
Clervaux *346* N Luxembourg
Cleveland *571* Ohio, NE USA
Clifden *288* W Ireland
Clifton *196* NW Dominica
Clifton *468* Union I, St. Vincent & the Grenadines
Cloncurry *77* NE Australia
Clonmel *288* Ir. Cluain Meala. S Ireland
Cluj-Napoca *450* prev. Cluj, Hung. Kolozsvár, Ger. Klausenburg. NW Romania
Clutha *401* river of SW South Island, New Zealand
Clyde, Firth of *565* estuary of the river Clyde, SW Scotland, UK
Coamo *629* S Puerto Rico
Coast Mountains *146* Fr. Chaîne Côtière. Mountain range of Canada and USA
Coast Ranges *570* mountain range of W USA
Coatepeque *250* W Guatemala
Coatepeque, Lago de *207* lake of W El Salvador
Coatzacoalcos *370* prev. Puerto México. SE Mexico
Cobán *250* C Guatemala
Cobija *112* NW Bolivia
Cochabamba *112* C Bolivia
Cochin *270* var. Kochi. S India
Cocibolca *see* Nicaragua, Lago de
Cockburn Harbour *631* South Caicos, E Turks and Caicos Islands
Cockburn Town *88* Great Exuma I, Bahamas
Cockburn Town *631* ❖ Turks and Caicos Islands, Grand Turk Island, SE Turks and Caicos Islands
Cockpit Country, The *303* physical region of NW Jamaica
Coco *260, 404* var. Wangkí, Segovia. River of Honduras and Nicaragua
Cocobeach *230* NW Gabon
Coco, Isla del *178* island of SW Costa Rica

Cocoli *see* Corubal
Cocos (Keeling) Islands *622* Australian external territory of the Indian Ocean. ❖ West Island
Cocos Island *625* island group of S Guam
Codrington *68* C Barbuda, Antigua & Barbuda
Codrington Lagoon *68* W Barbuda, Antigua & Barbuda
Coeroeni *see* Corantijn
Coëtivy *480* island of E Seychelles
Coffs Harbour *77* E Australia
Cogîlnic *376* var. Cogâlnic, Rus. Kogil'nik. River of SE Moldova
Cognac *225* W France
Cogo *208* var. Kogo, prev. Puerto Iradier. SW Equatorial Guinea
Cohoha *see* Cyohoha-Sud Lac
Coiba, Isla de *426* island of SW Panama
Coihaique *159* var. Coyhaique. S Chile
Coimbatore *270* S India
Coimbra *444* W Portugal
Coin de Mire *see* Gunners Quoin
Coira *see* Chur
Coire *see* Chur
Coi, Sông *see* Red River
Cojutepeque *207* C El Salvador
Colchester *565* E England, UK
Coleraine *565* Northern Ireland, UK
Colesberg *495* Northern Cape, C South Africa
Colihaut *196* var. Kulihao. W Dominica
Collie *76* SW Australia
Collingwood Bay *428* bay of the Solomon Sea to the E of Papua New Guinea
Colmar *225* Ger. Kolmar. NE France
Cöln *see* Köln
Coloane *626* Coloane, S Macao
Coloane *626* island of S Macao
Cologne *see* Köln
Colomb-Béchar *see* Béchar
Colombia *170-173* officially Republic of Colombia. Country of South America divided into 32 admin. units (departments). ❖ Bogotá
Colombo *506* ❖ of Sri Lanka, W Sri Lanka
Colón *182* NW Cuba
Colón *426* prev. Aspinwall. N Panama
Colón, Archipiélago de *see* Galapagos Islands
Colonia *see* Kolonia
Colonia del Sacramento *579* SW Uruguay
Colorado *178* river of NE Costa Rica
Colorado *571* river of Texas, SC USA
Colorado *571* river of SW USA
Colorado *570-571* state of SW USA
Colorados, Archipiélago de los *182* island group of NW Cuba
Colorado Springs *571* Colorado, SW USA
Columbia *570* river of NW USA
Columbia *571* South Carolina, SE USA
Columbia, District of *571* federal district of NE USA
Columbus *571* Georgia, SE USA
Columbus *571* Ohio, NE USA
Columbus Channel *542* channel connecting the Atlantic Ocean and Gulf of Paria
Colville Channel *401* channel linking the Bay of Plenty and Hauraki Gulf, N of North Island, New Zealand
Comarapa *112* C Bolivia
Comas *433* W Peru
Comayagua *260* W Honduras
Comendador *198* prev. Elías Piña. W Dominican Republic
Comer *see* Como, Lago di
Comilla *93* Ben. Kumillā. E Bangladesh
Commissioner's Point *621* headland of Ireland Island North, W Bermuda
Communism Peak *see* Garmo, Qullai
Como *294* N Italy
Comodoro Rivadavia *71* SE Argentina

Como, Lago di *294 var.* Lario, *Eng.* Lake Como, *Ger.* Comer See. Lake of N Italy

Comoros *174-175* officially Federal Islamic Republic of the Comoros. Island group of the Indian Ocean, between Madagascar and the African mainland, divided into 3 admin. units (districts). ❖ Moroni

Comrat *376 Rus.* Komrat. S Moldova

Conakry *253* ❖ of Guinea, SW Guinea

Concepción *112* E Bolivia

Concepción *159* C Chile

Concepción *430 var.* Villa Concepción. C Paraguay

Concepción *see* Riaba

Concepción de La Vega *see* La Vega

Conchos *370* river of NW Mexico

Concord *248* W Grenada island, Grenada

Concord *571* New Hampshire, NE USA

Concordia *71* E Argentina

Condado *182* C Cuba

Côn Dao *595 var.* Con Son. Island of S Vietnam

Condroz *99* physical region of SE Belgium

Congo *64, 176, 609 var.* Zaire, Kongo, Lualaba. River of C Africa

Congo *176-177* officially The Republic of the Congo. Country of C Africa divided into 9 admin. units (regions). ❖ Brazzaville

Congo Basin *609* drainage basin of C Africa

Con, Loch *see* Conn, Lough

Conn, Loch *see* Conn, Lough

Connaught *288* province of W Ireland

Connecticut *571* state of NE USA

Conn, Lough *288 Ir.* Loch Con. Lake of NW Ireland

Consolación del Sur *182* W Cuba

Constance, Lake *82, 236, 518 Ger.* Bodensee. Lake of C Europe

Constanța *450 Ger.* Konstantza, *Turk.* Köstence, *var.* Küstendje, *Eng.* Constanza. SE Romania

Constantine *59 Ar.* Qoussantîna, *var.* Qacentina, NE Algeria

Constantine *248* SW Grenada island, Grenada

Constantinople *see* İstanbul

Constant Spring *303* SE Jamaica

Constanza *198* C Dominican Republic

Contagem *121* SE Brazil

Contuboel *254* N Guinea-Bissau

Cook Islands *622* territory in free association with New Zealand, Pacific Ocean. ❖ Avarua

Cook, Mount *401 prev.* Aorangi. Mountain of W South Island, New Zealand

Cook, Récif de *628* reef of the Pacific Ocean, N New Caledonia

Cook Strait *401 var.* Raukawa. Strait between North and South Islands of New Zealand, connecting the South Pacific Ocean and Tasman Sea

Cooktown *77* NE Australia

Cooper Creek *77 var.* Barcoo, Cooper's Creek. River of C Australia

Cooper Island *621* island of SE British Virgin Islands

Copacabana *112* W Bolivia

Copenhagen *190 Dan.* København. ❖ of Denmark, Sjælland, E Denmark

Copiapó *159* N Chile

Coppename *510 var.* Koppename. River of C Suriname

Coppermine *146 var.* Qurlurtuuq. NW Canada

Coquilhatville *see* Mbandaka

Coquimbo *159* N Chile

Corail *258* SW Haiti

Coral Harbour *147* Southampton Island, NE Canada

Coral Sea *77, 587, 428* sea of the Pacific Ocean between Australia and Papua New Guinea

Corantijn *256, 510 var.* Coeroeni, Corentyne, Courantyne. River of Guyana and Suriname

Córdoba *71* C Argentina

Córdoba *503 var.* Cordoba, *Eng.* Cordova. SW Spain

Cordova *570* Alaska, USA

Corentyne *see* Corantijn

Corfu *see* Kérkyra

Corinth *see* Kórinthos

Corinth *248* SE Grenada island, Grenada

Corinth, Gulf of *see* Korinthiakós Kólpos

Corinth, Isthmus of *see* Korínthou, Isthmós

Corinto *404* W Nicaragua

Coriole *see* Qoryooley

Corisco, Isla de *208* Island of SW Equatorial Guinea

Cork *288 Ir.* Corcaigh. S Ireland

Cork Hill *627* W Montserrat

Corleone *295* Sicilia, S Italy

Corner Brook *147* Newfoundland, E Canada

Corn Exchange *334* NW Lesotho

Corn Islands *see* Maíz, Islas

Cornwallis Island *146* island of Parry Islands, N Canada

Coro *591 var.* Santa Ana de Coro. NW Venezuela

Corocoro *112* W Bolivia

Coromandel Peninsula *401* peninsula of NE North Island, New Zealand

Coronel Bogado *430* S Paraguay

Coronel Oviedo *430* SE Paraguay

Çorovodë *57 var.* Çorovoda, Corovoda. SE Albania

Corozal *102* N Belize

Corrib, Lough *288 Ir.* Loch Corrib. Lake of W Ireland

Corrientes *71* NE Argentina

Corriverton *256* E Guyana

Corriza *see* Korçë

Corse *225 Eng.* Corsica. Island of SE France

Corsica *see* Corse

Cortés *178* SE Costa Rica

Corubal *254 var.* Cocoli, Rio Grande. River of W Africa

Çorum *549* N Turkey

Corvallis *570* Oregon, NW USA

Corvo *444 var.* Ilha do Corvo. Island of the Azores, Portugal

Cosenza *295* S Italy

Cosmolédo Atoll *480* atoll of the Aldabra Group, SW Seychelles

Cospicua *363* E Malta

Costa, Cordillera de la *591 var.* Cordillera de Venezuela. Mountain range of N Venezuela

Costa Rica *178-179* officially Republic of Costa Rica. Country of Central America divided into 7 admin. units (provinces). ❖ San José

Costermansville *see* Bukavu

Cotagaita *112* S Bolivia

Côtière, Chaîne *see* Coast Mountains

Cotonou *108 var.* Kotonu. S Benin

Cotopaxi *200* active volcano of N Ecuador

Cotswold Hills *565* hills of W England, UK

Cottbus *237 prev.* Kottbus. E Germany

Cottica *510* E Suriname

Cotton Ground *464* NW Nevis, St. Kitts & Nevis

Cotuí *198* C Dominican Republic

Coulibistri *196* W Dominica

Coupe, Cap *630* cape of the Atlantic Ocean on the coast of Miquelon, S Saint Pierre and Miquelon

Courantyne *see* Corantijn

Courcelles *99* S Belgium

Courland *see* Kurzeme

Courtrai *see* Kortrijk

Couva *542* W Trinidad, Trinidad & Tobago

Couvin *99* S Belgium

Cova Figueira *152* Fogo, S Cape Verde

Cove Bay *620* bay of the Caribbean Sea on the S coast of Anguilla

Coventry *565* C England, UK

Covilhã *444* E Portugal

Cox's Bāzār *93* S Bangladesh

Coyah *253* SW Guinea

Coyhaique *see* Coihaique

Cozumel, Isla de *370* island of SE Mexico

Cracow *see* Kraków

Cradock *495* Eastern Cape, S South Africa

Craiova *450* SW Romania

Cranbrook *146* SW Canada

Crane, The *97* SE Barbados

Crawley *565* SE England, UK

Créoles, River des *368* river of SE Mauritius

Cres *181 It.* Cherso. Island of W Croatia

Crescent Group *629* island group of C Paracel Islands

Crete *see* Kríti

Créteil *225* N France

Crete, Sea of *245 Gk* Kritikó Pélagos. Area of the Mediterranean Sea, SE Greece

Creuse *225* river of C France

Crikvenica *181 It.* Cirquenizza. NW Croatia

Crimea *see* Krym

Cristóbal *426* N Panama

Cristóbal Colón, Pico *171* peak of N Colombia

Crna Gora *see* Montenegro

Crna reka *349* river of S FYR Macedonia

Crni Drim *see* Drinit të Zi

Črnomelj *488 Ger.* Tschernembl. S Slovenia

Croatia *180-181* officially Republic of Croatia, *SCr.* Hrvatska. Country of S Europe divided into 21 admin. units (provinces). ❖ Zagreb

Crochu *248* SE Grenada island, Grenada

Crocker, Banjaran *355 var.* Crocker Range. Mountain range of C Borneo, Malaysia

Crocodile *see* Limpopo

Crocus Bay *620* bay of the Caribbean Sea on the W coast of Anguilla

Croia *see* Krujë

Cromer *565* E England, UK

Crooked Island *88* island of the E Bahamas

Crooked Island Passage *88* passage of the Atlantic Ocean between Crooked Island and Long Island, Bahamas

Crooked Tree *102* NE Belize

Crosby *625* C Isle of Man

Cross *408* river of Cameroon and Nigeria

Crossroads *288* N Ireland

Crotone *295* S Italy

Cruce Contramaestre *182* S Cuba

Cruz Bay *631* Saint John, E Virgin Islands (US)

Cruz del Eje *71* C Argentina

Csaca *see* Čadca

Csakathurn *see* Čakovec

Csáktornya *see* Čakovec

Csíkszereda *see* Miercurea-Ciuc

Cuamba *387* N Mozambique

Cuan Dhun Dealgan *see* Dundalk Bay

Cuando *64, 613 var.* Kwando. River of southern Africa

Cuango *see* Kwango

Cuan na Gaillimhe *see* Galway Bay

Cuanza *64 var.* Kwanza. River of Angola

Cuareim *579 Port.* Quaraí. River of Brazil and Uruguay

Cuba *182-185* officially Republic of Cuba. Country of the West Indies divided into 15 admin. units (14 provinces and 1 special municipality). ❖ Havana

Cubal *64* W Angola

Cubango *64 var.* Kuvango, *Port.* Vila Artuur de Paiva, Vila da Ponte. C Angola

Cubango *64, 118, 391 var.* Kavango, Kavengo, Kubango, Okavango, Okavanggo. River of Southern Africa

Cúcuta *171 var.* San José de Cúcuta. N Colombia

Cuddapah *270* S India

Cudjoehead *627* NW Montserrat

Cuenca *200* S Ecuador

Cuenca *503* C Spain

Cueno *294* N Italy

Cuera *see* Chur

Cuernavaca *370* S Mexico

Cueto *182* SE Cuba

Cufra *see* Al Kufrah

Cuiabá *121 prev.* Cuyabá. SW Brazil

Cuilapa *250* S Guatemala

Cuito *64 var.* Kwito. River of Angola

Cuito Cuanavale *64* S Angola

Culebra *629* Isla de Culebra, NE Puerto Rico

Culebra, Isla de *629* island of NE Puerto Rico

Culiacán *370* W Mexico

Culion Island *437* island of Calamian Group, W Philippines

Cumaná *591* NE Venezuela

Cumberland *468* river of W St. Vincent, St. Vincent & the Grenadines

Cumberland Peninsula *147* peninsula of Baffin Island, NE Canada

Cumbrian Mountains *565 var.* Lake District. Mountain range of NW England, UK

Cunene *64, 391 var.* Kunene. River of Angola and Namibia

Cunnamulla *77* E Australia

Curaçao *591, 628* island of the Netherland Antilles, Caribbean Sea

Curanilahue *159* C Chile

Curaray *200* river of Ecuador and Peru

Curepe *542* NW Trinidad, Trinidad & Tobago

Curepipe *368* C Mauritius

Curicó *159* C Chile

Curitiba *121 prev.* Curytiba. S Brazil

Curral Velho *152* Boa Vista, Cape Verde

Current *88* Eleuthera Island, Bahamas

Curuguaty *430* E Paraguay

Curzola *see* Korčula

Cusco *433 var.* Cuzco. SE Peru

Čust *see* Chust

Cutch, Gulf of *see* Kachchh, Gulf of

Cuttack *270* E India

Cutting Camp *334* SW Lesotho

Cuxhaven *236* NW Germany

Cuyabá *see* Cuiabá

Cuyo East Passage *437* passage of the Sulu Sea between Cuyo Islands and Panay, Philippines

Cuyo Islands *437* islands of C Philippines

Cuyo West Passage *437* passage of the Sulu Sea between Cuyo Islands and Palawan, Philippines

Cuyuni *256* river of Guyana and Venezuela

Cuzco *see* Cusco

Čvrsnica *116* mountain range of SW Bosnia & Herzegovina

Cyambwe, Lac *462* lake of E Rwanda

Cyangugu *462* SW Rwanda

Cyclades *see* Kyklades

Cymru *see* Wales

Cyohoha Sud, Lac *138, 462 var.* Cohoha, Lac Tshohoha Sud. Lake of Burundi and Rwanda

Cyprus *186-187* officially Republic of Cyprus, *Gk* Kypros, *Turk.* Kıbrıs, Kıbrıs Cumhuriyeti. Country of E Mediterranean divided into 5 admin. units (districts). ❖ Nicosia. Following Turkish invasion of 1974, northern sector became self-proclaimed state, officially Turkish Republic of Northern Cyprus (TRNC). ❖ Nicosia

Cyrenaica *see* Barqah

Czechoslovakia *see* Czech Republic and Slovakia

Czech Republic *188-189 Cz.* Česká Republika, *prev.* constituent republic of Czechoslovakia. Country of C Europe divided into 7 admin. units (regions). ❖ Prague

Czegléd *see* Cegléd

Czernowitz *see* Chernivtsi

Częstochowa *441 Ger.* Tschenstochau. S Poland

D

Dabakala *300* NE Ivory Coast
Dabola *253* C Guinea
Dabou *300* S Ivory Coast
Dąbrowa Górnicza *441* S Poland
Dacca *see* Dhaka
Dachau *237* S Germany
Dadanawa *256* SW Guyana
Dadda 'to *194* N Djibouti
Dadeldhura *395* *var.* Dandeldhura. W Nepal
Ḍaḍnah *562* *var.* Dhadnah. NE United Arab Emirates
Daegu *see* Taegu
Daga *110* S Bhutan
Dagana *478* S Senegal
Dagden *see* Hiiumaa
Dagestan, Respublika *454* autonomous republic of SW Russia
Dagö *see* Hiiumaa
Dagupan *437* Luzon, N Philippines
Dahar *545* physical region of S Tunisia
Da Hinggan Ling *163* *Eng.* Great Khingan Range. Mountain range of Nei Mongol Zizhiqu, NE China
Dahlak Archipelago *210* island group of E Eritrea
Dahlak Island *210* island of Dahlak Archipelago, E Eritrea
Dahm, Ramlat *601* desert region of NW Yemen
Dahomey *see* Benin
Dahra *see* Dara
Dahūk *284* *var.* Dohuk, *Kurd.* Dihōk. N Iraq
Dai Island *490* island of E Solomon Is
Dailekh *395* W Nepal
Daingin, Bá an *see* Dingle Bay
Dajabón *198* NW Dominican Republic
Dakar *478* ❖ of Senegal, W Senegal
Dakoro *407* SW Niger
Ðakovica *604* *var.* Djakovica, *Alb.* Gjakovë. S Serbia, Yugoslavia
Ðakovo *181* *var.* Djakovo, *Hung.* Diakovár. NE Croatia
Dakshin *see* Deccan
Dalaba *253* W Guinea
Dalai Nor *see* Hulun Nur
Dalälven *515* river of SE Sweden
Dalandzadgad *380* S Mongolia
Ða Lat *595* S Vietnam
Dali *see* Dhali
Dalian *163* *var.* Jay Dairen, Ta-lien, *Rus.* Dalny. Liaoning, NE China
Dallas *571* Texas, SC USA
Dallol Bosso *407* seasonal water-course of W Niger
Dalmā *562* island of W United Arab Emirates
Dalmacija *181* *Eng.* Dalmatia. Cultural region of S Croatia
Dalmatia *see* Dalmacija
Dalny *see* Dalian
Daloa *300* C Ivory Coast
Dalvík *268* N Iceland
Damanhûr *202* *var.* Damanhūr. N Egypt
Damar, Kepulauan *276* *var.* Kepulauan Barat Daya. Island group to the E of Nusa Tenggara, C Indonesia
Damara *155* S Central African Republic
Damasak *409* NE Nigeria
Damascus *523* *var.* Esh Sham, *Fr.* Damas, *Ar.* Dimashq. ❖ of Syria, SW Syria
Damāvand, Qolleh-ye *281* mountain of N Iran
Dambulla *506* C Sri Lanka
Dame-Marie *258* SW Haiti
Damêrdjôg *194* E Djibouti
Damietta *see* Dumyât
Damongo *242* NW Ghana
Damoûr *332* *var.* Ad Dāmūr. W Lebanon
Damphu *110* S Bhutan
Damqawt *601* *var.* Damqut. E Yemen
Dâmrei, Chuôr Phmun *141* *Fr.* Chaîne de l'Éléphant. Mountain range of SW Cambodia

Danakil Desert *210, 215* *var.* Danakil Plain, Afar Depression. Desert region of Eritrea and Ethiopia
Danané *300* W Ivory Coast
Ðà Nẵng *595* *prev.* Tourane. C Vietnam
Dandeldhura *see* Dadeldhura
Dandong *163* *var.* Tan-tung, *prev.* An-tung. Liaoning, NE China
Daneborg *624* *var.* Danborg. E Greenland
Dänew *see* Deynau
Dangal *210* SE Eritrea
Dangara *see* Danghara
Danger Island *621* island of W British Indian Ocean Territory
Danghara *530* *Rus.* Dangara. W Tajikistan
Dänglä *215* *var.* Dangila. NW Ethiopia
Dangme *110* river of S Bhutan
Dang Raek, Phanom *141, 535* *var.* Phanom Dong Rak, *Cam.* Chuor Phmum Dângrêk, *Fr.* Chaîne des Dangrek. Mountain range of Cambodia and Thailand
Dangrak, Chaîne des *see* Dang Raek, Phanom
Dângrêk, Chuôr Phmun *see* Dang Raek, Phanom
Dangriga *102* *var.* Stann Creek. SE Belize
Daní *260* S Honduras
Danmark *see* Denmark
Danmark Havn *624* E Greenland
Danmarksstraedet *see* Denmark Strait
Danube *82, 128, 181, 237, 2* *Bul.* Danav, *Hung.* Duna, *Cz.* Dunaj, *Ger.* Donau, *Rom.* Dunărea. River of C Europe
Danube, Mouths of the *450* *Rom.* Delta Dunării. Delta of Romania and Ukraine
Danubian Plain *see* Dunavska Ravnina
Danyi-Apéyémé *539* *prev.* Apéyémé. W Togo
Danzig *see* Gdańsk
Danzig, Gulf of *441* *var.* Gulf of Gdańsk, *Gk* Danziger Bucht, *Pol.* Zatoka Gdańska, *Rus.* Gdan'skaya Bukhta. Gulf of the Baltic Sea, N Pola
Dapaong *539* N Togo
Dara *478* *var.* Dahra. NW Senegal
Dar'ā *523* *var.* Der'a, *Fr.* Déraa. SW Syria
Da Rang *595* *var.* Ba. River of S Vietnam
Dardanelles *see* Canakkale Boğazi
Dar el Beida *see* Casablanca
Dar es Salaam *532* E Tanzania
Darfur *508* *var.* Darfur Massif. Mountain range of W Sudan
Dargan-Ata *553* *var.* Darganata. E Turkmenistan
Dargaville *401* NW North Island, New Zealand
Dargol *407* W Niger
Darhan *380* N Mongolia
Darien, Isthmus of *see* Panamá, Istmo de
Darién, Serranía del *426* mountain range of Colombia and Panama
Darjiling *271* *prev.* Darjeeling. NE India
Darling *77* river of E Australia
Darling Range *76* mountain range of SW Australia
Darlington *565* N England, UK
Darmstadt *236* SW Germany
Darnah *339* *var.* Derna. NE Libya
Daroot-Korgon *325* *var.* Daraut-Kurgan. SW Kyrgyzstan
Darou Mousti *478* NW Senegal
Darrell Island *621* island of W Bermuda
Dartmoor *565* moorland of SW England, UK
Dartmouth *147* SE Canada
Daru *428* SW Papua New Guinea
Daru *482* SE Sierra Leone
Darvaza *553* *Turkm.* Derweze. C Turkmenistan
Darvel Bay *see* Lahad Datu, Telukan

Darvel, Teluk *see* Lahad Datu, Telukan
Darvos, Qatorkûhi *530* *Rus.* Darvazskiy Khrebet. Mountain range of C Tajikistan
Darwin *77* N Australia
Darwin, Isla *200* island of the NW Galapagos Is, Ecuador
Dashkhovuz *553* *prev.* Tashauz, *var.* Tašauz, *Turkm.* Dashhowuz. N Turkmenistan
Dasht Kaur *420* river of SW Pakistan
Daska *421* NE Pakistan
Da, Sông *see* Black River
Dassa *108* *var.* Dassa-Zoumé. S Benin
Datong *163* *var.* Ta-t'ung. Shanxi, N China
Datu, Teluk *354* bay of the South China Sea, on the coast of Borneo, E Malaysia
Daua *316* *Amh.* Dawa Wenz. River of E Africa
Daugava *see* Western Dvina
Daugavpils *330* *Ger.* Dünaburg, *Rus.* Dvinsk. SE Latvia
Daule *200* W Ecuador
Daule *200* river of W Ecuador
Daurada, Costa *502* *var.* Costa Dorada. Coastal region of E Spain
Davao *437* Mindanao, S Philippines
Davao Gulf *437* gulf of the Pacific Ocean
Davenport *571* Iowa, C USA
David *426* W Panama
Davis *66* Australian research station of Greater Antarctica, Antarctica
Davis Strait *147, 624* strait connecting the Atlantic Ocean and Baffin Bay, NE Canada between Baffin Island and Greenland
Davos *518* E Switzerland
Davyd-Haradok *104* *Rus.* David Gorodok, *Pol.* Dawidgródek. S Belorussia
Dawa Wenz *see* Daua
Dawei *see* Tavoy
Dawidgródek *see* Davyd-Haradok
Dawra *382* NW Western Sahara
Dawson *146* NW Canada
Dawwah *418* *var.* Dauwa. E Oman
Dayrah *562* *var.* Deira. NE United Arab Emirates
Dayr az Zawr *523* *var.* Deir ez Zor. E Syria
Dayrik *see* Al Mālikīyah
Dayton *571* Ohio, NE USA
De Aar *495* Northern Cape, C South Africa
Deadman's Bay *630* bay of the South Atlantic Ocean on the SW coast of Tristan da Cunha
Dead Sea *291, 292, 310* *Ar.* Al Baḥr al Mayyit, Baḥrat Lūṭ, *Heb.* Yam HaMelaḥ Salt lake of SW Asia
Deadwood Plain *630* plain of N St. Helena
Debar *349* W FYR Macedonia
Débo, Lac *360* lake of C Mali
Debre Birhan *215* *var.* Debra Birhan. C Ethiopia
Debrecen *264* *prev.* Debreczen, *Ger.* Debreczin. E Hungary
Debre Mark'os *215* NW Ethiopia
Debre Tabor *215* NW Ethiopia
Debre Zebīt *215* N Ethiopia
Debre Zeyit *215* *var.* Debre Zeyt, *prev.* Bishoftu, *It.* Biscoftù. C Ethiopia
Deccan *270* *Hind.* Dakshin. Plateau of C India
Děčín *188* *Ger.* Tetschen. NW Czech Republic
Dedeagach *see* Alexandroúpoli
Dededo *625* N Guam
Dedeaç *see* Alexandroúpoli
Dedoplistsqaro *234* *Rus.* Dedoplis-Tskaro, *prev.* Tsiteli-Tskaro. SE Georgia
Dédougou *133* W Burkina
Deduru Oya *506* C Sri Lanka
Dedza *353* SW Malawi
Dee *565* river of NE Scotland, UK
Dee *565* *Wel.* Dyfrdwy. River of N Wales, UK

Deep Bay *see* Chilumba
Deep Water Bay *see* Hau Hoi Wan
Değirmenlik *187* *var.* Kythrea. N Cyprus
Dehiwala-Mount Lavinia *506* SW Sri Lanka
Deinze *99* W Belgium
Deira *see* Adh Dhayd
Deir el Balah *291, 292* C Gaza Strip
Deir el-Bahri *202* E Egypt
Deir ez Zo *see* Dayr az Zawr
Deirgeirt, Loch *see* Derg, Lough
Dej *450* NW Romania
Dekemhare *210* S Eritrea
Dékoa *155* C Central African Republic
Delagoa Bay *see* Maputo, Baía de
Delap District *364* district of Majuro, SE Marshall Islands
Delārām *53* SW Afghanistan
Delaware *571* state of E USA
Delčevo *349* NE FYR Macedonia
Delcommune, Lac *see* Nzilo, Lac
Delémont *518* *Ger.* Delsberg. NW Switzerland
Delft *397* W Netherlands
Delft *506* island of NW Sri Lanka
Delfzijl *397* NE Netherlands
Delhi *270* *Hind.* Dilli. N India
Délices *196* SE Dominica
Délices *623* C French Guiana
Delsberg *see* Delémont
Delvinë *57* *var.* Delvina, *It.* Delvino. S Albania
Delvino *see* Delvinë
Demba *609* C Zaire
Dembéni *627* E Mayotte
Dembéni *174* S Grande Comore, Comoros
Dembī Dolo *215* *var.* Dembidollo. W Ethiopia
Demerara *256* river of N Guyana
Denau *see* Denow
Dender *99* *Fr.* Dendre. River of W Belgium
Dendre *see* Dender
Den Haag *see* 's-Gravenhage
Den Helder *397* NW Netherlands
Denis, Île *480* island of the Inner Islands, N Seychelles
Denizli *548* SW Turkey
Denmark *190-193* officially Kingdom of Denmark, *Dan.* Danmark. Country of W Europe, divided into 14 admin. units (counties). ❖ Copenhagen
Denmark Strait *268, 624* *var.* Danmarksstraedet. Strait between Greenland and Iceland
Dennery *467* E St. Lucia
Denow *582* *Rus.* Denau. SE Uzbekistan
Denpasar *276* *prev.* Paloe. Bali, C Indonesia
D'Entrecasteaux Islands *428* island group of SE Papua New Guinea
Denver *571* Colorado, SW USA
Der'a *see* Dar'ā
Deraa *see* Dar'ā
Dera Ghāzi Khān *421* C Pakistan
Dera Ismāil Khān *421* N Pakistan
Ðeravica *604* *var.* Durmitor. Mountain of S Yugoslavia
Derby *565* C England, UK
Derg, Lough *288* *Ir.* Loch Deirgeirt. Lake of C Ireland
Dernière Rivière *467* NE St. Lucia
Derrick *463* Bequia, St. Vincent & the Grenadines
Derrière Morne *467* S St. Lucia
Derrubado *152* N Boa Vista, E Cape Verde
Derry *see* Londonderry
Derventa *116* N Bosnia & Herzegovina
Derweze *see* Darvaza
Deryneia *see* Dherinia
Desaguadero *112* river of Bolivia and Peru
Desbarra *467* NE St. Lucia
Desdunes *258* W Haiti
Desē *215* *var.* Desse, *It.* Dessie. N Ethiopia
Desertas, Ilhas *444* island group of the Madeira Is, Portugal
Des Moines *571* Iowa, C USA

Desna *558* river of N Ukraine
Despoto Planina *see* Rhodope Mountains
Desroches, Île *480 var.* Desroches. Island of the Amirante Islands, C Seychelles
Desruisseaux *467* SE St. Lucia
Dessau *237* C Germany
Dessie *see* Desē
Destêrro *see* Florianópolis
Dete *614 prev.* Dett. W Zimbabwe
Detroit *571* Michigan, NC USA
Deutsch-Brod *see* Havlíčkův Brod
Deutsche Bucht *see* German Bight
Deutschendorf *see* Poprad
Deutschland *see* Germany
Deva *450 Ger.* Diemrich, *Hung.* Déva. W Romania
Đevđelija *see* Gevgelija
Deventer *397* E Netherlands
Devil's Island *623* island of N French Guiana
Devollit *57 var.* Devoll. River of SE Albania
Devon Island *146-147 prev.* North Devon Island. Island of Parry Islands, N Canada
Devonport *77* Tasmania, Australia
Deynau *553 var.* Dyanev, *Turkm.* Dänew. E Turkmenistan
Dezfûl *281 var.* Dizful. W Iran
Dhaalu Atoll *see* South Nilandhe Atoll
Dhahran *see* Aẓ Ẓahrān
Dhaka *93 var.* Dacca.
❖ of Bangladesh, C Bangladesh
Dhali *187 var.* Dali. C Cyprus
Dhamar *601* W Yemen
Dhanbād *270* NE India
Dhankuta *395* E Nepal
Dharan *395 var.* Dharan Bazar. E Nepal
Dheere Laaq *492 It.* Lach Dera. Seasonal river of SW Somalia
Dhekelia *187 var.* Dekeleia. UK Air base, SE Cyprus
Dherinia *187 var.* Deryneia. E Cyprus
Dhiarizos *187 var.* Diarizos. River of SW Cyprus
Dhībân *310* NW Jordan
Dhofar *see* Ẓufār
Dhráma *see* Dráma
Dhún na nGall, Bá *see* Donegal Bay
Dhuudo *492 It.* Uadi Dudo. Seasonal river of NE Somalia
Dhuusa Marreeb *492 var.* Dusa Marreb, *It.* Dusa Mareb. C Somalia
Diafarabé *360* C Mali
Diakovár *see* Đakovo
Diamond Island *248* island to the N of Grenada island, Grenada
Diana's Peak *630* mountain of C St. Helena
Diangounté-Kamara *360* W Mali
Diapaga *133* E Burkina
Diarizos *see* Dhiarizos
Dibā *562 var.* Dibā al Ḥiṣn, Dibba. NE United Arab Emirates
Dicle *see* Tigris
Diébougou *133* SW Burkina
Diego Garcia *621* island of S British Indian Ocean Territory
Diego Garcia *621* ❖ of British Indian Ocean Territory, Diego Garcia, S British Indian Ocean Territory
Diégo-Suarez *see* Antsirañana
Diekirch *346* C Luxembourg
Diéma *360* W Mali
Diemrich *see* Deva
Điên Biên *595 var.* Dien Bien Phu. NW Vietnam
Dieppe *225* N France
Dieppe Bay Town *464* N St. Kitts, St. Kitts & Nevis
Diffa *407* SE Niger
Differdange *346* SW Luxembourg
Digne *225* SE France
Digoin *225* C France
Digul *277 prev.* Digoel. River of Irian Jaya, E Indonesia
Dihōk *see* Dahūk
Dijlah *see* Tigris
Dijon *225* NE France

Dikhil *194* SW Djibouti
Dīla *215 var.* Dilla. S Ethiopia
Dilbeek *99* C Belgium
Dilia *407 var.* Dillia. Seasonal river of SE Niger
Dilijan *74 Rus.* Dilizhan, *var.* Diližan. NE Armenia
Di Linh *595* S Vietnam
Dilli *see* Delhi
Dillia *see* Dilia
Dillikot *395* W Nepal
Dilling *508 var.* Ad Dalanj. C Sudan
Dilolo *609* S Zaire
Dimashq *see* Damascus
Dimbokro *300* E Ivory Coast
Dimitrovgrad *128* S Bulgaria
Dimitrovo *see* Pernik
Dimlang *408 var.* Vogel Peak. Mountain of E Nigeria
Dimona *291* S Israel
Dinagat Island *437* island of E Philippines
Dinājpur *93* NW Bangladesh
Dinan *224* NW France
Dinant *99* S Belgium
Dinara *181* mountain of S Croatia
Dinara *116, 181* mountain range of Bosnia & Herzegovina and Croatia
Dinaric Alps *181* mountain range of Bosnia & Herzegovina and Croatia
Dindigal *270* S India
Dingle Bay *288 Ir.* Bá an Daingin. Bay of the Atlantic Ocean, SW Ireland
Dingli *363* SW Malta
Dingli Cliffs *363* cliffs of SW Malta
Dinguiraye *253* C Guinea
Dion *253* river of S Guinea
Diordel *478* W Senegal
Dioro *360 var.* Dyero. SW Mali
Diourbel *478* W Senegal
Dipayal *395* W Nepal
Dipkarpaz *187 var.* Rizokarpaso. NE Cyprus
Direction Island *622 var.* Pulu Tikus. Island of E Cocos Islands
Dirē Dawa *215* E Ethiopia
Diriamba *404* SW Nicaragua
Dirj *339* NW Libya
Dirk Hartog Island *76* island of W Australia
Disappointment, Lake *76* salt lake of W Australia
Discovery Bay *262* W Hong Kong
Discovery Reef *629* reef of the China Sea, W Paracel Islands
Disna *see* Drysa
Disûq *202 var.* Disûq. N Egypt
Diu *270* W India
Diuata Mountains *437* mountain range of Mindanao, S Philippines
Diva *see* Piva
Divinópolis *121* SE Brazil
Divisa *426* S Panama
Divo *300* S Ivory Coast
Diwaniya *see* Ad Dīwanīyah
Diyālá *284 Per.* Rūdkhāneh-ye Sīrvān,irwan. River of Iran and Iraq
Diyarbakır *549* SE Turkey
Dizful *see* Dezfûl
Dja *144* river of SE Cameroon
Djailolo *see* Halmahera
Djakarta *see* Jakarta
Djakovica *see* Đakovica
Djakovo *see* Đakovo
Djamâa *59* NE Algeria
Djambala *176* W Congo
Djambi *see* Hari
Djambi *see* Jambi
Djanet *59 prev.* Fort Charlet. SE Algeria
Djawa *see* Java
Djéblé *see* Jablah
Djelfa *59 var.* El Djelfa. N Algeria
Djéma *155* E Central African Republic
Djember *see* Jember
Djénné *360 var.* Jenné. C Mali
Djérablous *see* Jarābulus
Djerba *see* Jerba, Île de
Djerba *see* Houmt Souk
Djerem *144 var.* Djérem. River of C Cameroon
Djevdjelija *see* Gevgelija
Djibo *133* N Burkina

Djibouti *194 var.* Jibuti. ❖ of Djibouti, E Djibouti
Djibouti *194-195* officially Republic of Djibouti, *var.* Jibuti, *prev.* French Territory of the Afars and Issas 1967-77, French Somaliland -1967. Country of East Africa divided into 5 admin. units (districts). ❖ Djibouti
Djidjel *see* Jijel
Djidjelli *see* Jijel
Djiguéni *366* SE Mauritania
Djirataoua *407* S Niger
Djisr el Choghour *see* Jisr ash Shughūr
Djoua *176* river of Congo and Gabon
Djoué *176* river of S Congo
Djougou *108* W Benin
Djúpivogur *268* SE Iceland
Dmitriyevsk *see* Makiyivka
Dnieper *558 Bel.* Dnyapro, *Ukr.* Dnipro, *Rus.* Dnepr. River of E Europe
Dniester *376, 558 Rom.* Nistru, *Rus.* Dnestr, *Ukr.* Dnister. River of Moldova and Ukraine
Dniprodzerzhyns'k *558 Rus.* Dneprodzerzhinsk, *prev.* Kamenskoye. E Ukraine
Dniprodzerzhyns'ke Vodoskhovyshche *558 Rus.* Dneprodzerzhinskoye Vodokhranilische. Reservoir of C Ukraine
Dnipropetrovs'k *558 Rus.* Dnepropetrovsk, *prev.* Ekaterinoslav. E Ukraine
Dnistrovs'kyy Lyman *558 Rus.* Dnestrovskiy Liman. Inlet of the Black Sea, SW Ukraine
Dnyapro *see* Dnieper
Doba *156* S Chad
Dobele *330 Ger.* Doblen. W Latvia
Doberai, Jazirah *276 Dut.* Vogelkop. Region of Irian Jaya, E Indonesia
Doboj *116* N Bosnia & Herzegovina
Dobrich *128 var.* Dobrič, *prev.* Tolbukhin, *Rom.* Bazargic. NE Bulgaria
Dobrush *104* SE Belorussia
Doctor Pedro P. Peña *430* W Paraguay
Dodekánisos *245 prev.* Dhodhekánisos, *var.* Noties Sporádes, *Eng.* Dodecanese. Island group of SE Greece
Dodoma *532* ❖ of Tanzania, C Tanzania
Dodona *245* site of ancient city, N Greece
Dodwekon *336 var.* Dudwiokahn. SE Liberia
Doetinchem *397* SE Netherlands
Dogana *470* NE San Marino
Dogondoutchi *407* SW Niger
Doğu Karadeniz Dağlari *549 var.* Anadolu Dağları. Mountain range of NE Turkey
Doha *449 Ar.* Ad Dawḥah. ❖ of Qatar, E Qatar
Dohuk *see* Dahuk
Doko *253* NE Guinea
Dolisie *see* Loubomo
Dolobil *336* C Liberia
Dolomites *see* Dolomitiche, Alpi
Dolomitiche, Alpi *295 var.* Dolomiti, *Eng.* Dolomites. Mountain range of N Italy
Dolo Odo *215 var.* Dollo Odo, Dolo. S Ethiopia
Dolores *250* N Guatemala
Dolores *579* S Uruguay
Domagnano *470* NE San Marino
Domel Island *see* Letsok-aw I
Dominica *196-197* officially Commonwealth of Dominica. Country of the West Indies divided into 10 admin. units (parishes). ❖ Roseau
Dominica Channel *see* Martinique Passage
Dominican Republic *198-199* Country of the West Indies divided into 30 admin. units (1 national district and 29 provinces). ❖ Santo Domingo

Dominica Passage *624* passage of the Caribbean Sea, N Guadeloupe
Domoni *174* SE Anjouan, Comoros
Don *454* river of W Russia
Donau *see* Danube
Doncaster *565* S England, UK
Dondo *64* NW Angola
Dondo *387* C Mozambique
Donegal *288* N Ireland
Donegal Bay *288 Ir.* Bá Dhún na nGall. Bay of the Atlantic Ocean, to the N of Ireland
Donets *558 Rus.* Severskiy Donets, *Ukr.* Sivers'kyy Donets'. River of E Ukraine
Donets'k *558 prev.* Stalino, *Rus.* Donetsk. E Ukraine
Donga *144* river of Cameroon and Nigeria
Đông Ha *595* C Vietnam
Đông Hơi *595* C Vietnam
Dong Nai *595 var.* Donnai, Dong-nai, Dong Noi. River of S Vietnam
Dongola *508 var.* Dunqulah, Donqola N Sudan
Dongou *176* NE Congo
Dong Rak, Phanom *see* Dang Rak, Phanom
Dongting Hu *163 var.* Tung-t'ing Hu. Lake of SE China
Donostia-San Sebastián *503* N Spai
Doornik *see* Tournai
Dorada, Costa *see* Daurada, Costa
Dordogne *225* river of SW France
Dordrecht *397* SW Netherlands
Dori *133* N Burkina
Dornbirn *82* W Austria
Dornoch Firth *565* estuary of the river Dornoch, NE Scotland, UK
Dorpat *see* Tartu
Dorra *194* NW Djibouti
Dorsale *545* mountain range of N Tunisia
Dortmund *236* W Germany
Dos D'Âne *196* N Dominica
Dospad Dagh *see* Rhodope Mountains
Dos Puntas, Cabo *208* cape on the W coast of Río Muni, Equatorial Guinea
Dosso *407* SW Niger
Dostuk *325* C Kyrgyzstan
Douai *225* N France
Douala *144 var.* Duala. SW Cameroon
Double Headed Shot Cays *88* islets of W Bahamas
Doubs *518 var.* Le Doubs. River of France and Switzerland
Doudoub Bololé *194* S Djibouti
Doué *478* river of N Senegal
Douglas *623* East Falkland, NE Falkland Islands
Douglas *565, 625* ❖ of Isle of Man, SE Isle of Man
Douma *see* Dūmā
Douro *see* Duero
Dover *565 Fr.* Douvres. SE England, UK
Dover *571* Delaware, E USA
Dover, Strait of *225 var.* Straits of Dover, *Fr.* Pas de Calais. Strait connecting the English Channel and North Sea between England and France
Dovrefjell *414* mountain of SW Norway
Dowa *353* C Malawi
Dōzen *304* island to the N of Honshū, W Japan
Drâa *382* seasonal river of S Morocco
Drac *see* Durrës
Draç *see* Durrës
Dragon's Mouths, The *542 Sp.* Bocas del Dragón. Strait connecting the Caribbean Sea and Gulf of Paria
Dra, Hamada du *59 var.* Haut Plateau du Dra, Hammada du Drâa. Desert region of W Algeria
Drakensberg *334, 495* mountain range of Lesotho and South Africa
Drake Passage *159* passage connecting Pacific Ocean and Atlantic Ocean between South America and Antarctica

Dráma *245 var.* Dhráma. NE Greece

Drammen *414* S Norway

Drangajökull *268* glacier of NW Iceland

Drava *82, 181, 264, 488 Eng.* Drave, *Hung.* Dráva, *Ger.* Drau, *SCr.* Drava. River of C Europe

Dresden *237* E Germany

Drina *116, 604* river of Bosnia & Herzegovina and Yugoslavia

Drin Gulf *see* Drinit, Gjiri i

Drinit *57 var.* Drin. River of NW Albania

Drinit, Gjiri i *57 var.* Pellg i Drinit, Drin Gulf. Gulf of the Adriatic Sea, NW Albania

Drinit të Zi *57, 349 var.* Drin i Zi, *Eng.* Black Drin, *SCr.* Crni Drim. River of Albania and FYR Macedonia

Drin i Zi *see* Drinit të Zi

Drinos *57* river of S Albania

Drissa *104* river of Belorussia and Russia

Drobeta-Turnu Severin *450 prev.* Turnu Severin. SW Romania

Drochia *376 Rus.* Drokiya. N Moldova

Drogheda *288 Ir.* Droichead Átha, E Ireland

Drontheim *see* Trondheim

Druskininkai *344 Pol.* Druskienniki. S Lithuania

Drysa *104 Rus.* Disna. River of Belorussia and Lithuania

Dschang *144* W Cameroon

Duala *see* Douala

Duarte, Pico *198* mountain of C Dominican Republic

Dubai *562 Ar.* Dubayy. NE United Arab Emirates

Dubăsari *376 Rus.* Dubossary. NE Moldova

Dubăsari Reservoir *376* reservoir of NE Moldova

Dubawnt *146* river of C Canada

Dubbo *77* E Australia

Dublanc *196* NW Dominica

Dublin *288 Ir.* Baile Átha Cliath. ❖ of Ireland, E Ireland

Dubnica nad Váhom *487 Hung.* Máriatölgyes, *prev.* Dubnicz. NW Slovakia

Dubnicz *see* Dubnica nad Váhom

Dubossary *see* Dubăsari

Dubréka *253* SW Guinea

Dubrovnik *181 It.* Ragusa. SE Croatia

Duc de Gloucester, Îles du *624* island group of C French Polynesia

Ducie Island *629* island of E Pitcairn Islands

Ducos *627* C Martinique

Dudelange *346* S Luxembourg

Dudo, Uadi *see* Dhuudo

Dudwiokahn *see* Dodwekon

Duékoué *300* W Ivory Coast

Duero *444, 502-503 Port.* Douro. River of Portugal and Spain

Duesseldorf *see* Düsseldorf

Duff Islands *490* small island group within Santa Cruz Is, Solomon Is

Dufourspitze *518* mountain of S Switzerland

Dugi Otok *181 It.* Isola Lunga. Island of W Croatia

Duinkerden *see* Dunkerque

Duisburg *236* W Germany

Duitama *171* C Colombia

Duitse Bocht *see* German Bight

Dukhan *449* W Qatar

Dukhan Heights *see* Dukhān, Jabal

Dukhān, Jabal *449 var.* Dukhan Heights. Hilly region of SW Qatar

Dukhān, Jabal *see* Dukhān, Jabal ad

Dukhān, Jabal ad *91 var.* Dukhan Heights, Jabal Dukhan. Mountain of C Bahrain

Dukou *see* Panzhihua

Dulce, Golfo *see* Izabal, Lago de

Dulce Nombre de Culmí *260* Honduras

Dulit, Banjaran *354 var.* Dulit Range. Mountain range of W Borneo, Malaysia

Duluth *571* Minnesota, NC USA

Dūmā *523 Fr.* Douma. SW Syria

Dumfries *565* SW Scotland, UK

Dumistān *91* NW Bahrain

Dumont d'Urville *66* French research station of Greater Antarctica, Antarctica

Dumyât *202 Eng.* Damietta. N Egypt

Düna *see* Western Dvina

Dünaburg *see* Daugavpils

Dunai *395* W Nepal

Dunaj *see* Danube

Dunaj *see* Vienna

Dunajská Streda *487 Hung.* Dunaszerdahely. SW Slovakia

Dunapentele *see* Dunaújváros

Dunărea *see* Danube

Dunării, Delta *see* Danube, Mouths of the

Dunaszerdahely *see* Dunajská Streda

Dunaújváros *264 prev.* Sztálinváros, *prev.* Dunapentele. C Hungary

Dunav *see* Danube

Dunavska Ravnina *128 Eng.* Danubian Plain. Lowland region of N Bulgaria

Dundalk *288 Ir.* Dún Dealgan. NE Ireland

Dundalk Bay *288 Ir.* Cuan Dhun Dealgan. Bay of the Irish Sea, to the NE of Ireland

Dundas *see* Pituffik

Dundee *495* Kwazulu Natal, E South Africa

Dundee *565* E Scotland, UK

Dunedin *401* S South Island, New Zealand

Dunfermline *565* E Scotland, UK

Dungarvan *288 Ir.* Dun Garbhain. S Ireland

Dunkerque *225 Eng.* Dunkirk, *Dut.* Duinkerken. N France

Dunkirk *see* Dunkerque

Dunkwa *242* SW Ghana

Dún Laoghaire *288 prev.* Kingstown. E Ireland

Dunqulah *see* Dongola

Dupnitsa *128 prev.* Stanke Dimitrov, *prev.* Marek. W Bulgaria

Duqm *418 var.* Daqm. E Oman

Duque de Caxias *121* SE Brazil

Durán *see* Eloy Alfaro

Durance *225* river of SE France

Durango *370* W Mexico

Durazno *579 var.* San Pedro del Durazno. C Uruguay

Durazzo *see* Durrës

Durazzo, Gulf of *see* Durrësit, Gjiri i

Durban *495* Kwazulu Natal, E South Africa

Durbe *330 Ger.* Durben. W Latvia

Durben *see* Durbe

Durdur *492* seasonal river of NW Somalia

Durham *565* NE England, UK

Durmitor *see* Đeravica

Durrës *57 var.* Durrësi, Dursi, *It.* Durazzo, *SCr.* Drač, *Turk.* Draç. W Albania

Durrësit, Gjiri i *57 var.* Gulf of Durazzo. Gulf of the Adriatic Sea, W Albania

Durūz, Jabal ad *523* mountain range of SW Syria

D'Urville Island *401* island to the NE of South Island, New Zealand

Dusa Mareb *see* Dhuusa Marreeb

Dushanbe *530 var.* Dušanbe, Dyushambe, *prev.* Stalinabad. ❖ of Tajikistan, W Tajikistan

Düsseldorf *236 var.* Duesseldorf. W Germany

Düstí *530* SW Tajikistan

Dutch New Guinea *see* Irian Jaya

Dutch East Indies *see* Indonesia

Dutch West Indies *see* Netherlands Antilles

Düzce *see* Athna

Dvinsk *see* Daugavpils

Dyanev *see* Deynau

Dyero *see* Dioro

Dyfrdwy *see* Dee

Dyushambe *see* Dushanbe

Džalilabad *see* Cälilabad

Dzaoudzi *627* Petite-Terre, E Mayotte

Džarkurgan *see* Dzharkurgan

Dzaudzhikau *see* Vladikavkaz

Dzavhan *380* river of W Mongolia

Džebel *see* Dzhebel

Dzerzhinskiy *see* Nar'yan-Mar

Dzhalal-Abad *325 var.* Džalal-Abad, *Kir.* Jalal-Abad. SW Kyrgyzstan

Dzhalilabad *see* Cälilabad

Dzhambul *see* Zhambyl

Džhanak *553* region of W Turkmenistan

Dzharkurgan *see* Jarqürghon

Dzhebel *553 var.* Džebel, *Turkm.* Jebel. W Turkmenistan

Dzhelandy *530* SE Tajikistan

Dzhergalan *325 var.* Džergalan, *Kir.* Jyrgalan. NE Kyrgyzstan

Dzhermuk *see* Jermuk

Dzhetygara *312 Kaz.* Zhetiqara. NW Kazakhstan

Dzhezkazgan *see* Zhezkazgan

Dzhirgatal' *see* Jirgatol

Dzhizak *see* Jizzakh

Dzhugdzhur, Khrebet *455* mountain range of E Russia

Dzhusaly *312* SW Kazakhstan

Dzongsa *110* S Bhutan

Dzunmod *380* C Mongolia

Dzüünharaa *380* N Mongolia

Dzvina *see* Western Dvina

Dzyarzhynskaya, Hora *104* mountain of C Belorussia

E

Eagle Islands *621* island group of W British Indian Ocean Territory

Eagle Passage *623* passage connecting Falkland Sound and Atlantic Ocean, S Falkland Islands

East Caicos *631* island of N Turks and Caicos Islands

East China Sea *527 Chin.* Nan Hai. Sea of Pacific Ocean, off E Asia

East End *622* Grand Cayman, W Cayman Islands

East End Village *620* E Anguilla

Easter Island *159* Pacific island of Chile

Eastern Cape *495* province of SE South Africa

Eastern Desert *see* Sharqîya, Sahara el

Eastern Ghats *270* mountains of SE India

Eastern Sayans *see* Vostochnyy Sayan

Eastern Scheldt *see* Oosterschelde

Eastern Sierra Madre *see* Sierra Madre Oriental

Eastern Transvaal *see* Mpumalanga

East Falkland *623* island of E Falkland Islands

East Fayu Island *374* island of C Micronesia

East Frisian Islands *see* Ostfriesische Inseln

East Lamma Channel *262* channel to the S of Hong Kong

East London *495 Afr.* Oos-Londen. Eastern Cape, S South Africa

East Pakistan *see* Bangladesh

East Malaysia *354-355* eastern part of Malaysia situated on N Borneo

East Siberian Sea *see* Vostochno-Sibirskoye More

East Timor *276* disputed territory, Timor, C Indonesia

Eauripik *374* atoll of C Micronesia

Ebebiyin *208* NE Río Muni, Equatorial Guinea

Ebeltoft *190* Jylland, C Denmark

Ebetsu *305* Hokkaidō, N Japan

Ebeye *364* island of C Marshall Islands

Ebinayon *see* Evinayong

Eblana *see* Dublin

Ebolowa *144* S Cameroon

Ebon *364* island of S Marshall Islands

Ébrié, Lagune *300* lake of SW Ivory Coast

Ebro *503* river of NE Spain

Ech Cheliff *see* Chlef

Echmiadzin *see* Ejmiadzin

Echternach *346* E Luxembourg

Écija *503* SW Spain

Ečmiadzin *see* Ejmiadzin

Ecuador *200-201* officially Republic of Ecuador. Country of NW South America divided into 20 admin. units (provinces). ❖ Quito

Ed *210* SE Eritrea

Ed Damazin *508 var.* Ad Damazîn. E Sudan

Ed Damer *508 var.* Ad Dāmir, Ad Damar. NE Sudan

Ed Dueim *508 var.* Ad Duwaym, Ad Duwêm. C Sudan

Ede *397* C Netherlands

Ede *408* W Nigeria

Edéa *144* SW Cameroon

Eden *565* river of NW England, UK

Edfu *see* Idfu

Edgeøya *631* island of S Svalbard

Edina *336* SW Liberia

Edinburgh *630* N Tristan da Cunha

Edinburgh *565* E Scotland, UK

Edineţ *376 var.* Edineţi, *Rus.* Yedintsy. NW Moldova

Edirne *548* NW Turkey

Edmonton *146* SW Canada

Edward, Lake *556, 609 var.* Lake Rutanzige, Edward Nyanza, Albert Edward Nyanza, Lac Idi Amin. Lake of Uganda and Zaire

Eems *see* Ems

Eesti Vabariik *see* Estonia

Éfaté *587 Fr.* Vaté, *prev.* Sandwich Islands. Island group of C Vanuatu

Egadi, Isole *295* island group to the W of Sicilia, S Italy

Ege Denizi *see* Aegean Sea

Eger *264 Ger.* Erlau. NE Hungary

Eger *see* Cheb

Eger *see* Ohře

Egersund *414* SW Norway

Egilsstadhir *268* E Iceland

Egmont, Cape *401* cape of SW North Island, New Zealand

Egmont Islands *621* island group of W British Indian Ocean Territory

Egmont, Mount *401* mountain of SW North Island, New Zealand

Egypt *202-205* officially Arab Republic of Egypt, *prev.* United Arab Republic. Country of NE Africa divided into 26 admin. units (governorates). ❖ Cairo

Eidsvoll *414* S Norway

Eifel *236* plateau of W Germany

Eiffel Flats *614* C Zimbabwe

Eight Degree Channel *358* channel of the Indian Ocean between N Maldives and Lakshadweep, SW India

Eil *see* Eyl

Eilat *see* Elat

Eil Malk *425* island of S Palau

Eindhoven *397* S Netherlands

Einsiedeln *518* NE Switzerland

Eipel *see* Ipel, Ipoly

Eire *see* Ireland, Republic of

Eisen *see* Yŏngch'ŏn

Eisenstadt *82* E Austria

Eishū *see* Yŏngju

Eitape *see* Aitape

Eivissa *503 Cast.* Ibiza, *var.* Iviza. Island of the Islas Baleares, E Spain

Ejmiadzin *74 Rus.* Echmiadzin, Ečmiadzin, Etchmiadzin. W Armenia

Ekaterinoslav *see* Dnipropetrovs'k

Ekerem *see* Okarem

Ekeren *99* N Belgium

Ekibastuz *312* NE Kazakhstan

El Alto *112* W Bolivia

El Araïche *see* Larache

El 'Arîsh *202 var.* Al Arīsh. NE Egypt

El Asnam *see* Chlef

Elat *291 var.* Elath, Eilat. S Israel

Elat, Gulf of *see* Aqaba, Gulf of,

Elato *374* atoll of C Micronesia

Elâziğ *549 var.* Elâziz, Elâzig̃. E Turkey

Elba, Isola d' *294* island of C Italy

Elbasan *57 var.* Elbasani. C Albania

Elbe *188, 237 Cz.* Labe. River of Czech Republic and Germany

Euxine Sea *see* Black Sea
Evansville *571* Indiana, C USA
Everest, Mount *162, 395*
 Chin. Qomolangma Feng,
 Nep. Sagarmatha. Mountain of China
 and Nepal
Evesham *468* SE St. Vincent,
 St. Vincent & the Grenadines
Evinayong *208 var.* Evinayoung,
 Ebinayon. S Río Muni, Equatorial
 Guinea
Évora *444* C Portugal
Évreux *225* N France
Évry *225* N France
Evrykhou *187 var.* Evrychou.
 W Cyprus
Évvoia *245* Island of E Greece
Ewarton *303* C Jamaica
Ewaso Ngiro *316* river of C Kenya
Ewo *176* W Congo
Exe *565* river of SW England, UK
Exeter *565* SW England, UK
Exuma Cays *88* islets of C Bahamas
Exuma Sound *88* stretch of water
 between Cat I and Exuma Cays,
 Bahamas
Eyasi, Lake *532* lake of N Tanzania
Eyl *492 It.* Eil. E Somalia
Eyre North, Lake *77* salt lake of
 C Australia
Eyre Peninsula *77* peninsula of
 S Australia
Eyre South, Lake *77* salt lake of
 C Australia
Eysturoy *622 var.* Østerø. Island of
 N Faeroe Islands
Extremadura *502* autonomous
 community of W Spain
Ezulwini *512* W Swaziland

F

Faadhippolhu Atoll *358*
 var. Fadiffolu, Lhaviyani Atoll. Atoll
 of N Maldives
Faafu Atoll *see* North Nilandhe Atoll
Fåborg *190* Fyn, S Denmark
Fabriano *295* C Italy
Facpi Point *625* headland on the
 SW coast of Guam
Fada *156* E Chad
Fada-N'gourma *133*
 var. Fadan-Gourma. E Burkina
Fadghāmī *see* Tall Fadghāmī
Fadiffolu *see* Faadhippolhu Atoll
Fadugu *482* N Sierra Leone
Færingehavn *624*
 var. Kangerluarsoruseq, S Greenland
Faeroe Islands *622 Faer.* Føroyar, *Dan.*
 Færøerne. Self-governing territory
 of Denmark, North Atlantic Ocean.
 ❖ Tórshavn
Faetano *470* E San Marino
Fagaloa Bay *598* bay of the Pacific
 Ocean on Upolu, SE Western Samoa
Fagamālo *598* Savai'i, Western Samoa
Făgăraş *450* C Romania
Faguibine, Lac *360*
 var. Lake Fagibina. Lake of NW Mali
Fahaheel *see* Al Fuḩayḩil
Faial *444 var.* Ilha do Faial. Island
 of the Azores, Portugal
Faifo *see* Hôi An
Failaka Island *see* Faylakah
Faioa, Île *631* island of Île Uvea,
 S Wallis & Futuna
Fairbanks *570* Alaska, USA
Fair Isle *565* island of N Scotland, UK
Fairview Park *262* NW Hong Kong
Fais *374* island of W Micronesia
Faisalābād *421 prev.* Lyallpur.
 NE Pakistan
Faizabad *see* Feyzābād
Fajã *152* Brava, S Cape Verde
Fajara *233* W Gambia
Fajardo *178* NE Puerto Rico
Fajãzinha *152* Fogo, S Cape Verde
Fakaofo Atoll *631* island of
 SE Tokelau
Fako *144* active volcano of
 W Cameroon
Falaba *482* N Sierra Leone

Falam *135* NW Burma
Falciano *470* NE San Marino
Fale *555* islet of Nukufetau, Tuvalu
Faleālupo *598* Savai'i, Western Samoa
Falelima *598* Savai'i, Western Samoa
Falémé *360, 478* river of W Africa
Faleshty *see* Fălești
Fălești *376 Rus.* Faleshty.
 NW Moldova
Falkat *210* seasonal river of N Eritrea
Falkirk *565* C Scotland, UK
Falkland Islands *71, 623*
 Sp. Islas Malvinas. British dependent
 territory of the South Atlantic Ocean.
 ❖ Stanley.
Falkland Sound *623* strait of the South
 Atlantic Ocean between East Falkland
 and West Falkland, Falkland Islands
Falluja *see* Al Fallūjah
Falmouth *68* S Antigua, Antigua
 & Barbuda
Falmouth *303* NW Jamaica
Falster *190* island of SE Denmark
Falun *515* C Sweden
Famagusta *see* Gazimağusa
Famagusta Bay *187*
 var. Ammochostos Bay, Gazimağusa
 Körfezi. Bay of the Mediterranean
 Sea, on the E coast of Cyprus
Fandriana *350* C Madagascar
Fangliao *527* SW Taiwan
Fanling *262* N Hong Kong
Fanning Island *see* Tabuaeran
Fano *295* N Italy
Fan Si Pan *595* mountain of
 NW Vietnam
Faradofay *see* Tôlañaro
Farafangana *350* SE Madagascar
Farafenni *233* NW Gambia
Farāh *53* W Afghanistan
Farāh Rūd *53* river of
 W Afghanistan
Farallon de Medinilla *628* island of
 C Northern Mariana Islands
Farallon de Pajaros *628* island of
 N Northern Mariana Islands
Faranah *253* S Guinea
Faraulep *374* atoll of C Micronesia
Farghona *582 Rus.* Fergana, *prev.*
 Novyy Margilan. E Uzbekistan
Fargo *571* North Dakota, NC USA
Farīdābād *270* N India
Farīdpur *93* C Bangladesh
Farim *254* NW Guinea-Bissau
Farkhor *530 Rus.* Parkhar. SW
 Tajikistan
Farm *627* river of E Montserrat
Farmington *570* New Mexico, SW USA
Faro *144* river of Cameroon and
 Nigeria
Faro *444* S Portugal
Farquhar Atoll *480* atoll of the
 Farquhar Group, S Seychelles
Farquhar Group *480* island group of
 S Seychelles
Fars, Khalij-e *see* Persian Gulf
Farvel, Kap *see* Uummannarsuaq
Fass *233* W Gambia
Fastiv *558* NW Ukraine
Fatala *253* river of W Guinea
Fatick *478* W Senegal
Fátima *444* W Portugal
Fatoto *233* E Gambia
Fatua, Pointe *631 var.* Pointe Nord.
 Headland of Île Futuna, N Wallis
 & Futuna
Fatutaka *490 var.* Mitre I. Island of
 E Solomon Islands
Faxaflói *268* bay of North Atlantic
 Ocean, on SW coast of Iceland
Faya *156* N Chad
Fayaoué *628* Ouvéa, Îles Loyauté,
 N New Caledonia
Fayetteville *571* Arkansas, SC USA
Faylakah *322 var.* Failaka Island.
 Island of E Kuwait
Fazao, Monts du *539* mountain range
 of W Togo
Fazzān *339 Eng.* Fezzan. Cultural
 region of W Libya
Fdérik *391 prev.* Fort-Gouraud.
 NW Mauritania
Feabhail, Loch *see* Foyle, Lough
Fédala *see* Mohammedia

Fehmarn *237* island of N Germany
Fehmarnbelt *237* strait connecting
 Kieler Bucht and Mecklenburger
 Bucht, between Denmark and
 Germany
Feira de Santana *121 prev.* Feira.
 E Brazil
Feistritz *82* river of SE Austria
Fejaj, Chott el *545* salt lake of
 C Tunisia
Feldkirch *82* W Austria
Félegyháza *see* Kiskunfélegyháza
Felidhu Atoll *358* atoll of C Maldives
Fénérive *see* Fenoarivo Atsinanana
Fenglin *527 Jap.* Hörin. E Taiwan
Fengshan *527 Jap.* Hōzan.
 SW Taiwan
Fengtien *see* Shenyang
Fengtien *see* Liaoning
Fengyüan *527 var.* Toyohara,
 Jap. Hōgen. W Taiwan
Feni *93* E Bangladesh
Fennern *see* Vändra
Fenoarivo Atsinanana *350*
 prev. Fénérive. NE Madagascar
Fens, The *565* wetlands of E England,
 UK
Ferdinand *see* Montana
Fergana *see* Farghona
Fergana Valley *530* physical region
 of C Asia
Fergusson Island *428 var.* Kaluwawa.
 Island of SE Papua New Guinea
Ferizaj *see* Uroševac
Ferkessédougou *300* N Ivory Coast
Ferlo *see* Vallée du Ferlo
Fernandina, Isla *200* island of
 W Galapagos Is, Ecuador
Fernando de la Mora *430* S Paraguay
Fernando de Noronha *121* island of
 E Brazil
Fernando Po *see* Bioko
Ferrara *295* N Italy
Ferrol *502 prev.* El Ferrol del Caudillo.
 NW Spain
Ferryville *see* Menzel Bourguiba
Ferto-tó *see* Neusiedler See
Fès *382 Eng.* Fez. N Morocco
Fethiye *548* SW Turkey
Feyzābād *53 var.* Faizabad.
 NE Afghanistan
Fezzan *see* Fazzān
Fianarantsoa *350* C Madagascar
Fianga *156* SW Chad
Fichē *215 It.* Ficce. C Ethiopia
Fielding *401* S North Island,
 New Zealand
Fier *57 var.* Fieri. SW Albania
Fierzës, Liqeni i *57* lake of
 N Albania
Fig Tree *464* S Nevis, St. Kitts
 & Nevis
Figueira da Foz *444* W Portugal
Figueres *503* E Spain
Figuig *382 var.* Figig. E Morocco
Fiji *218-219* officially Republic of Fiji,
 Fij. Viti. Country of the Pacific Ocean
 divided into 4 admin. units (divisions).
 ❖ Suva
Filadelfia *178* W Costa Rica
Filingué *407* W Niger
Fimi *609* river of W Zaire
Finike *548* SW Turkey
Finland *220-223* officially Republic of
 Finland, *Fin.* Suomen Tasavalta.
 Country of N Europe divided into
 12 admin. units (11 provinces and
 1 autonomous region). ❖ Helsinki
Finland, Gulf of *212, 221, 454*
 Fin. Suomenlahti, *swe.* Finska Viken,
 Est. Soome Laht, *Rus.* Finskiy Zaliv.
 Gulf of the Baltic Sea, NE Europe
Finnmarksvidda *414* physical region
 of NE Norway
Fins *418* NE Oman
Finskiy Zaliv *see* Finland, Gulf of
Fiorina *470* NE San Marino
Firenze *295 Eng.* Florence. NW Italy
Fischbacher Alpen *82* mountain range
 of E Austria
Fish *391 Afr.* Vis. River of S Namibia
Fishguard *565 Wel.* Abergwaun.
 W Wales, UK
Fiskeræsset *624*
 var. Qeqertarsuatsiaat, S Greenland

Fiume *see* Rijeka
Five Islands Village *68* W Antigua,
 Antigua & Barbuda
Fizuli *see* Füzuli
Fjerritslev *190* Jylland, NW Denmark
Fläming *237* hill region of
 NE Germany
Flanders *99 Dut.* Vlaanderen,
 Fr. Flandres. Cultural region of
 W Belgium
Flat Island *368 var.* Île Plate. Island of
 N Mauritius
Flat Island *630* island of NE Spratly
 Islands
Flatts Village *621* C Bermuda
Flensburg *236* N Germany
Flessingue *see* Vlissingen
Flinders *77* river of N Australia
Flinders Island *77* island of
 SE Australia
Flinders Ranges *77* mountain range
 of S Australia
Flin Flon *146* SW Canada
Flint *571* Michigan, NC USA
Flint Island *320* island of the Line Is,
 E Kiribati
Flitsch *see* Bovec
Floréal *368* C Mauritius
Florence *see* Firenze
Florencia *171* SW Colombia
Flores *250* N Guatemala
Flores *276* island of Nusa Tenggara,
 C Indonesia
Flores *444* island of the Azores,
 Portugal
Flores, Lago de *see* Petén Itza, Lago
Flores, Laut *276 Eng.* Flores Sea.
 Sea of the Pacific Ocean,
 C Indonesia
Floreşti *376 Rus.* Floreshty.
 N Moldova
Florianópolis *121 prev.* Destêrro.
 S Brazil
Florida *182* SE Cuba
Florida *260* W Honduras
Florida *571, 575* state of SE USA
Florida *579* S Uruguay
Floridablanca *171* NE Colombia
Florida Islands *490* group of islands
 of C Solomon Is
Florida, Straits of *88, 182* strait
 connecting the Atlantic Ocean and
 Gulf of Mexico
Flórina *245 var.* Phlórina. N Greece
Flüelapass *518* mountain pass of
 E Switzerland
Flushing *see* Vlissingen
Fly *428* river of Indonesia and Papua
 New Guinea
Flying Fish Cove *622*
 ❖ of Christmas Island
Fnjóská *268* river of C Iceland
Foa *540* island of Ha'apai Group,
 Tonga
Foča *116* SE Bosnia & Herzegovina
Focşani *450* E Romania
Foggia *295* S Italy
Fogo *152* island of SW Cape Verde
Fogo'one, Pointe *631* headland of
 Île Uvea, S Wallis & Futuna
Foix *225* S France
Folkestone *565* SE England, UK
Fomboni *174* N Mohéli, Comoros
Fon *253* mountainous region of
 E Guinea
Fond St. Jean *196* S Dominica
Fongafale *555 var.* Funafuti.
 ❖ of Tuvalu, Funafuti, Tuvalu
Fonseca, Gulf of *207, 260, 404* gulf
 of the Pacific Ocean, on the W coast
 of Central America
Fontvieille *378* SW Monaco
Fonuafo'ou *540* island of Nomuka
 Group, W Tonga
Fonualei *540* island of N Tonga
Foochow *see* Fuzhou
Forécariah *253* SW Guinea
Forestière *467* N St. Lucia
Forlì *295* N Italy
Formentera *503* island of the Islas
 Baleares, E Spain
Formosa *71* NE Argentina
Formosa Bay *see* Ungama Bay
Formosa, Ilha *254* island of
 Arquipélago dos Bijagós, SW Guinea-
 Bissau

Hajdúböszörmény *264* NE Hungary
Ḥājī Ebrāhīm, Kūh-e *24* mountain of Iran and Iraq
Ḥajjah *601* W Yemen
Hakodate *304* Hokkaidō, N Japan
Hakupu *628* E Niue
Ha Kwai Chung *262* W Hong Kong
Ḥalab *523* *Eng.* Aleppo, *Fr.* Alep. NW Syria
Ḥalabja *284* NE Iraq
Ḥalānīyāt, Juzur al *418* *var.* Jazā'iBin Ghalfān, Jazā'ir Khurīyā Murīyā, *Eng.* Kuria Maria Islands. Island group of S Oman
Ḥalānīyāt, Khalīj al *418* *Eng.* Kuria Mur Bay. Bay of the Arabian Sea, S Oman
Halas *see* Kiskunhalas
Haldefjäll *see* Haltiatunturi
Halden *414* *prev.* Fredrikshald. S Norway
Halditjåkko *see* Haltiatunturi
Halfa el Gadida *508* *var.* New Halfa, Halfa Al Jadida. E Sudan
Halfmoon Bay *401* Stewart Island, SW New Zealand
Half Tree Hollow *630* N St. Helena
Halifax *147* SE Canada
Ḥalīl Rūd *281* river of SE Iran
Halla-san *498* *Jap.* Kanra-san. Mountain of Cheju-do, S South Korea
Halle *237* C Germany
Hallein *82* N Austria
Halley *66* UK research station of Greater Antarctica, Antarctica
Hall Islands *374* island group of C Micronesia
Hall Peninsula *147* peninsula of Baffin Island, NE Canada
Halls Creek *77* NW Australia
Halmahera *276* *prev.* Djailolo, Jailolo, Gilolo. Island of Maluku, E Indonesia
Halmahera, Laut *276* sea of the Pacific Ocean, E Indonesia
Halmstad *515* SW Sweden
Ḥalq al Wādī *see* La Goulette
Hälsingborg *see* Helsingborg
Haltiatunturi *221* *Swe.* Haldefjäll, *prev.* Halditjåkko, *Nor.* Reisduoddarhalde. Mountain of Finland and Norway
Ḥamad *see* Madīnat Ḥamad
Hamada *304* Honshū, W Japan
Hamadān *281* NW Iran
Hamada Town *see* Madīnat Ḥamad
Ḥamāh *523* W Syria
Hamamatsu *304* Honshū, C Japan
Hamar *414* S Norway
Hambantota *506* SE Sri Lanka
Hamburg *237* N Germany
Ḥamḍ, Wādī al *474* dry watercourse of W Saudi Arabia
Hämeenlinna *221* *Swe.* Tavastehus. SW Finland
Hamersley Range *76* mountain range to the W of Australia
Ḥamgyŏng-sanmaek *413* mountain range of N North Korea
Hamhŭng *413* C North Korea
Hami *162* *Uigh.* Kumul, *var.* Qomul. Xinjiang Uygur Zizhiqu, NW China
Hamilton *621* ❖ Bermuda, C Bermuda
Hamilton *147* S Canada
Hamilton *401* C North Island, New Zealand
Hamilton *565* C Scotland, UK
Ḥamīm, Wādī al *339* dry watercourse of NE Libya
Hamm *236* W Germany
Hammamet *545* *var.* Ḥammāmāt. N Tunisia
Hammamet, Golfe de *545* gulf of the Mediterranean Sea to the E of Tunisia
Hammam Lif *545* *var.* Ḥammām al Anf. N Tunisia
Ḥammār, Hawr al *284* lake of SE Iraq
Hammerfest *414* NE Norway
Ḥamrīn, Jabal *284* mountain range of N Iraq
Hamriya *see* Al Ḥamrīyah
Hamrun *363* C Malta
Hāmūn, Daryācheh-ye *see* Sīstān, Daryācheh-ye

Han *498* *Jap.* Kan-kō. River of N South Korea
Hanábana *182* river of C Cuba
Hânceşti *see* Hînceşti
Handan *163* *var.* Han-tan. Hebei, NE China
Handeni *532* E Tanzania
Handréma, Baie de *627* *var.* Mandréma Bay. Bay of the Indian Ocean on the N coast of Mayotte
HaNegev *291* *Eng.* Negev. Desert of S Israel
Hanga Roa *159* Easter I, W Chile
Hangayn Nuruu *380* mountain range of W Mongolia
Hangzhou *163* *var.* Hangchow, Hang-chou. Zhejiang, E China
Hanka, Lake *see* Khanka, Lake
Hanko *221* *Swe.* Hangö. SW Finland
Hankow *see* Wuhan
Hannover *236* *Eng.* Hanover. NW Germany
Hanöbukten *515* bay of the Baltic Sea to the S of Sweden
Hanoi *595* *Vtn.* Ha Nôi. ❖ of Vietnam, N Vietnam
Hanover *see* Hannover
Hanstholm *190* Jylland, NW Denmark
Han-tan *see* Handan
Hantu, Pulau *485* island of SW Singapore
Hāora *271* *prev.* Howrah. E India
Haouach, Ouadi *156* dry watercourse of E Chad
Happy Valley-Goose Bay *147* *prev.* Goose Bay. E Canada
Hapsal *see* Haapsalu
Ḥarad *474* *var.* Haradh. E Saudi Arabia
Ḥaraḍ *601* N Yemen
Hara Laht *212* bay of the Gulf of Finland, on the coast of N Estonia
Harare *614* *prev.* Salisbury. ❖ of Zimbabwe, NE Zimbabwe
Haraze-Mangueigne *156* SE Chad
Harbel *336* W Liberia
Harbin *163* *var.* Ha-erh-pin, *prev.* Pinkiang. Heilongjiang, NE China
Harbours, Bay of *623* bay of the South Atlantic Ocean, SE Falkland Islands
Harbour View *303* E Jamaica
Hardangerfjorden *414* fjord of SW Norway
Hardap Dam *391* dam of C Namibia
Haré Meron *291* Mountain of N Israel
Hārer *215* E Ethiopia
Hari *276* *var.* Batang Hari, *prev.* Djambi. River of Sumatra, W Indonesia
Ḥarīb *601* W Yemen
Hari Kurk *212* channel of Baltic Sea, between the island of Hiiumaa and Estonia mainland
Ḥārim *523* NW Syria
Ḥarīma *310* N Jordan
Haringhat *93* river of SW Bangladesh
Harīrūd *53* river of C Asia
Harīrūd *see* Tedzhen
Harlingen *397* *Fris.* Harns. N Netherlands
Harmanli *see* Kharmanli
Harns *see* Harlingen
Harper *336* *var.* Cape Palmas. S Liberia
Ḥarrah *601* SE Yemen
Harrington Sound *621* bay of the North Atlantic Ocean, N Bermuda
Harris *627* E Montserrat
Harrisburg *571* Pennsylvania, NE USA
Harrismith *495* Orange Free State, E South Africa
Harstad *414* NE Norway
Hartford *336* SW Liberia
Hartford *571* Connecticut, NE USA
Hartley *see* Chegutu
Harz *237* *var.* Harz Mountains. Mountain range of C Germany
HaSharon *291* *Eng.* Plain of Sharon. Plain of C Israel
Haskovo *see* Khaskovo
Haspengouw *see* Hesbaye

Hasselt *99* NE Belgium
Hassetché *see* Al Ḥasakah
Hastings *97* SW Barbados
Hastings *401* SE North Island, New Zealand
Hastings *482* W Sierra Leone
Hastings *565* SE England, UK
Hatay *see* Antakya
Hātia *93* river and one of the main mouths of the Ganges, S Bangladesh
Hato Mayor *198* E Dominican Republic
Ḥattā *562* E United Arab Emirates
Hattiesburg *571* Mississippi, SE USA
Hattieville *102* E Belize
Hat Yai *535* *var.* Ban Hat Yai. S Thailand
Haud *215* *var.* Hawd. Plateau of Somalia and Ethiopia.
Haugesund *414* SW Norway
Hau Hoi Wan *262* *Eng.* Deep Water Bay. Bay to the NW of Hong Kong
Haukeligrend *414* S Norway
Haukivesi *221* lake of SE Finland
Hauraki Gulf *401* gulf on the N coast of North Island, New Zealand
Hau *595* river of SW Vietnam
Haut Atlas *382* *Eng.* High Atlas. Mountain range of C Morocco
Haute-Sangha *see* Mambéré-Kadéi
Hautes Fagnes *99* *Ger.* Hohes Venn. Mountain range of Belgium
Haute Sûre, Lac de la *346* reservoir of NW Luxembourg
Haut Plateau du Dra *see* Dra, Hamada du
Hauts Plateaux *59* plateau of NW Algeria
Havana *182* *var.* La Habana. ❖ of Cuba, NW Cuba
Havířov *188* E Czech Republic
Havlíčkův Brod *188* *prev.* Německý Brod, *Ger.* Deutsch-Brod. S CzecRepublic
Hawaii *570* island of Hawaiian group, Hawaii, USA, C Pacific
Hawaii *570* non-contiguous state of USA, C Pacific
Ḥawallī *322* E Kuwait
Hawash *see* Awash
Hawea, Lake *401* W South Island, New Zealand
Hawera *401* SW North Island, New Zealand
Hawick *565* S Scotland, UK
Hawke Bay *401* bay of the South Pacific Ocean, on the SE coast of North Island, New Zealand
Hawlēr *see* Arbīl
Ḥawmat as Sūq *see* Houmt Souk
Ḥawrā' *601* C Yemen
Ḥawrān, Wādī *284* dry watercourse of W Iraq
Hawwārah *310* *var.* Huwwāra. N Jordan
HaYarden *see* Jordan
Hay River *146* N Canada
Ḥayyān, Ra's *91* *var.* Ra's Ḥayyān. Cape of E Bahrain
Hebei *163* *var.* Hopei. Province of NE China
Hebrides, Sea of the *565* sea of the Atlantic Ocean to the NW of UK
Hebron *291, 292* *Ar.* Al Khalil. S West Bank
Heerenveen *397* NE Netherlands
Heerlen *397* S Netherlands
Ḥefa *291* N Israel
Ḥefa, Mifraz *291* *Eng.* Bay of Haifa. Bay of the Mediterranean Sea
Hefei *163* *var.* Hofei, *hist.* Luchow. Anhui, E China
Heichin *see* P'ingchen
Heidelberg *236* SW Germany
Heihe *163* *prev.* Ai-hun. Heilongjiang, NE China
Hei-ho *see* Nagqu
Heilbronn *236* SW Germany
Heiligenkreuz *see* Žiar nad Hronom
Heilong Jiang *see* Amur
Heilongjiang *163* *var.* Heilungkiang, Hei-lung-chiang. Province of NE China
Heimaey Island *268* *var.* Heimaey, Heimaæy. Island of S Iceland

Heitō *see* P'ingtung
Helen *425* island of S Palau
Helena *570* Montana, NW USA
Helgoland *236* *Eng.* Heligoland. Island of NW Germany
Helgoländer Bucht *236* *var.* Helgoland Bay, Heligoland Bight. Bay of the North Sea
Hell-Ville *see* Andoany
Helmand, Daryā-ye *53* river of Afghanistan and Iran
Helmond *397* S Netherlands
Helsingborg *515* *prev.* Hälsingborg. S Sweden
Helsingør *190* *Eng.* Elsinore. Sjælland, E Denmark
Helsinki *221* *Swe.* Helsingfors. ❖ of Finland, S Finland
Helwân *202* *var.* Ḥulwān, Ḥilwān. N Egypt
Henan *163* *var.* Honan. Province of C China
Henderson Island *629* island of N Pitcairn Islands
Hendū Kosh *see* Hindu Kush
Hengduan Shan *162* mountain range of SW China
Hengelo *397* E Netherlands
Hengyang *163* Hunan, S China
Hentiesbaai *391* W Namibia
Henzada *135* SW Burma
Heradhsvötn *268* river of C Iceland
Herāt *53* W Afghanistan
Heredia *178* C Costa Rica
Hereford *565* C England, UK
Herisau *518* *Fr.* Hérisau. NE Switzerland
Héristal *see* Herstal
Herm *625* island of S Guernsey
Hermannstadt *see* Sibiu
Hermansverk *414* SW Norway
Hermel *332* *var.* Hirmil. NE Lebanon
Hermitage *248* C Grenada island, Grenada
Hermon, Mount *523* *Ar.* Jabal ash Shaykh. Mountain of SW Syria
Hermosillo *370* NW Mexico
Hernád *see* Hornád
Hernandarias *430* *prev.* Tacurupucú. SE Paraguay
Herne *236* W Germany
Herning *190* Jylland, W Denmark
Herstal *99* *Fr.* Héristal. E Belgium
Herzliyya *291* C Israel
Herzogenbusch *see* 's-Hertogenbosch
Hesbaye *99* *Dut.* Haspengouw. Physical region of C Belgium
Hesperange *346* SE Luxembourg
Hestur *622* island of C Faeroe Islands
Hetauda *395* C Nepal
Hida-sammyaku *304* mountain range of Honshū, C Japan
Hienghène *628* W New Caledonia
Hierro *503* *var.* Ferro. Island of Islas Canarias, SW Spain
High Atlas *see* Haut Atlas
Highgate *303* NE Jamaica
High Island Reservoir *262* reservoir of E Hong Kong
Highlands, The *68* highlands of Barbuda, Antigua & Barbuda
High Point *621* headland of W Bermuda
High Veld *see* Northern Karoo
Higüey *198* *var.* Salvaleon de Higüey. E Dominican Republic
Hiiumaa *212* *var.* Hiuma, *Ger.* Dagden, Swed. Dagö. Island of W Estonia
Hikina *626* island, NE Johnston Atoll
Hildesheim *236* NW Germany
Hilla *see* Al Ḥillah
Hillaby, Mount *97* mountain of Barbados
Hillerød *190* Sjælland, E Denmark
Hillsborough *248* W Carriacou, Grenada
Hilo *570* Hawaii, USA
Hilversum *397* C Netherlands
Ḥilwan *see* Helwân
Himachal Pradesh *270* state of N India

Himalayas *110, 162, 270, 395* mountain range of S Asia
Himeji *304* Honshū, C Japan
Himora *215 var.* Humera. NW Ethiopia
Ḥimṣ *523 var.* Homs. W Syria
Hînceşti *376 var.* Hânceşti, *prev.* Kotovsk. C Moldova
Hinche *258* C Haiti
Hindenburg *see* Zabrze
Hindiya *see* Al Hindīyah
Hindu Kush *53, 421 Per.* Hendū Kosh. Mountain range of C Asia
Hingol *420* river of SW Pakistan
Hinson Island *621* island of W Bermuda
Hirmil *see* Hermel
Hirosaki *304* Honshū, N Japan
Hiroshima *304* Honshū, W Japan
Hirschberg in Riesengebirge *see* Jelenia Góra
Hirtshals *190* Jylland, N Denmark
Ḥisbān *310* NW Jordan
Ḥisb, Sha'īb *284 var.* Sha'ib Hasb. Dry watercourse of S Iraq
Hisor *530 Rus.* Gissar. W Tajikistan
Hitachi *304* Honshū, SE Japan
Hitra *414 prev.* Hitteren. Island of W Norway
Hitteren *see* Hitra
Hiu *587* Torres Islands, N Vanuatu
Hjälmaren *515 Eng.* Lake Hjalmar. Lake of S Sweden
Hjalmar, Lake *see* Hjälmaren
Hjørring *190* Jylland, N Denmark
Hkakabo Razi *135* mountain of Burma and China
Hlathikulu *512 var.* Hlatikulu. S Swaziland
Hlohovec *487 prev.* Frakštát, *Ger.* Freistadtl, *Hung.* Galgóc. W Slovakia
Hlotse *334 var.* Leribe. NW Lesotho
Hlybokaye *104 Rus.* Glubokoye. N Belorussia
Ho *242* SE Ghana
Hoa Binh *595* N Vietnam
Hoang Liên Sơn *595* mountain range of China and Vietnam
Hoani *174* NW Mohéli, Comoros
Hobart *77* Tasmania, Australia
Hobro *190* Jylland, NW Denmark
Hobyo *492 It.* Obbia. E Somalia
Hô Chi Minh *595 var.* Ho Chi Minh City, *prev.* Saigon. S Vietnam
Hodeida *see* Al Ḥudaydah
Hódmezővásárhely *264* SE Hungary
Hodonín *188 Ger.* Göding. SE Czech Republic
Hoë Karoo *see* Northern Karoo
Hoeryŏng *413* NE North Korea
Höfdhakaupstadhur *see* Skagaströnd
Hofei *see* Hefei
Hofsá *268* river of E Iceland
Hofsjökull *268* glacier of C Iceland
Hofuf *see* Al Hufuf
Hōgen *see* Fengyüan
Hoggar *see* Ahaggar
Hogoley Islands *see* Chuuk Islands
Hohenems *82* W Austria
Hohes Venn *see* Hautes Fagnes
Hohe Tauern *82* mountain range of W Austria
Hohhot *163 var.* Huhehot, *prev.* Kweisui. Nei Mongol Zizhiqu, N China
Hôi An *595 prev.* Faifo. C Vietnam
Hoihow *see* Haikou
Hoima *556* W Uganda
Hojancha *178* NW Costa Rica
Hokitika *401* W South Island, New Zealand
Hokkaidō *305, 309* island of N Japan
Hokkō *see* Peikang
Hokō *see* P'ohang
Hoktemberyan *74 Rus.* Oktemberyan. SW Armenia
Holbæk *190* Sjælland, E Denmark
Holetown *97 prev.* Jamestown. W Barbados
Holguín *182* SE Cuba
Holhol *194* SE Djibouti
Holland *see* Netherlands

Hollandia *see* Jayapura
Hólmavík *268* NW Iceland
Holmsland Klit *190* fjord of Jylland, W Denmark
Holon *291* C Israel
Holonga *540* Uta Vava'u, Tonga
Holot Ḥaluza *291* historic site of S Israel
Holstebro *190* Jylland, W Denmark
Holsteinsborg *see* Sisimiut
Holyhead *565* N Wales, UK
Homa Bay *316* W Kenya
Homāyūnshahr *see* Khomeynīshahr
Hombori Tondo *360* mountain of E Mali
Home Island *622* island of C Cocos Islands
Homenau *see* Humenné
Homonna *see* Humenné
Homs *see* Ḥimṣ
Homs *see* Al Khums
Homyel' *104 Rus.* Gomel'. SE Belorussia
Honan *see* Henan
Hondo *102, 370* river of Central America
Honduras *260-261* officially Republic of Honduras. Country of C America divided into 18 admin. units (departments). ❖ Tegucigalpa
Honduras, Gulf of *102, 250* gulf of the Caribbean Sea to the E of Central America
Hønefoss *414* S Norway
Hông Gai *595 var.* Hongay. N Vietnam
Hong Kong *262-263* dependent territory of UK, due to revert to China in July 1997
Hong Kong Island *262* island of S Hong Kong
Hongwŏn *413* E North Korea
Hongze Hu *163 var.* Hung-tse Hu. Lake of E China
Honiara *490* ❖ of the Solomon Islands, N Guadalcanal, Solomon Islands
Honolulu *570* Oahu, Hawaii, USA
Honshū *304* island of C Japan
Honte *see* Westerschelde
Hoogeveen *397* NE Netherlands
Hoogezand *397* NE Netherlands
Hooker, Cape *495* cape of Marion Island, S South Africa
Hoorn *397* NW Netherlands
Hopei *see* Hebei
Hope Town *88* Great Abaco, Bahamas
Horgen *518* N Switzerland
Hōrin *see* Fenglin
Horki *104 Rus.* Gorki. NE Belorussia
Horlivka *558 Rus.* Gorlovka. E Ukraine
Hormuz, Strait of *281, 419, 562 var.* Strait of Ormuz, *Per.* Tangeh-ye Hormoz. Strait connecting the Persian Gulf and Arabian Sea
Hornád *487 Ger.* Hernad, *Hung.* Hernád. River of Hungary and Slovakia
Horn, Cape *159* cape of S Chile
Horog *see* Khorog
Horoshiri-dake *305* mountain of Hokkaidō, N Japan
Horowupotana *506* NE Sri Lanka
Horqueta *430* C Paraguay
Horsburgh Atoll *358* atoll of N Maldives
Horsburgh Island *622 var.* Pulu Luar. Island of C Cocos Islands
Horsens *190* Jylland, C Denmark
Horseshoe Bay *621* bay of the North Atlantic Ocean, W Bermuda
Horsham *77* SE Australia
Hørsholm *190* Sjælland, E Denmark
Hortabágny-Berettyó *264* river of E Hungary
Horten *414* S Norway
Horug *see* Khorog
Hosa'ina *215 var.* Hosseina, *It.* Hosanna. SW Ethiopia
Hose, Penunungan *354 var.* Hose Mountains. Mountain range of Borneo, E Malaysia
Hotan *162 var.* Khotan, *Chin.* Ho-t'ien. Xinjiang Uygur Zizhiqu. NW China
Hot Springs *571* Arkansas, SC USA

Hotte, Massif de la *258* highlands of SW Haiti
Houaïlou *628* C New Caledonia
Houmt Souk *545 var.* Djerba, Ḥawmat as Sūd, Jerba. Île de Jerba, Tunisia
Houndé *133* SW Burkina
Houston *571* Texas, SC USA
Hovd *380* W Mongolia
Hoverla *558 Rus.* Gora Goverla. Mountain of W Ukraine
Hövsgöl Nuur *380* lake of N Mongolia
Howe, Cape *77* cape on the SE coast of Australia
Howakil Bay *210* bay of the Red Sea to the E of Eritrea
Howrah *see* Hāora
Hōzan *see* Fengshan
Hradec Králové *188 Ger.* Königgrätz. E Czech Republic
Hrazdan *74 Rus.* Razdan. C Armenia
Hrazdan *74 Rus.* Razdan, Zanga. River of C Armenia
Hrodna *104 Rus.* Grodno. W Belorussia
Hron *487 Ger.* Gran, *Hung.* Garam. River of C Slovakia
Hsüeh Shan *527* mountain of N Taiwan
Hsi-an *see* Xi'an
Hsiang-t'an *see* Xiangtan
Hsi Chiang *see* Xi Jiang
Hsinchu *527* NW Taiwan
Hsinchuang *527 var.* Sinchwang, *Jap.* Shinshō. N Taiwan
Hsing-K'ai Hu *see* Khanka, Lake
Hsi-ning *see* Xining
Hsinking *see* Changchun
Hsintien *527 var.* Sintien, *Jap.* Shinten. N Taiwan
Hsin-yang *see* Xinyang
Hsinying *527 var.* Sinying, *Jap.* Shinei. W Taiwan
Hsu-chou *see* Xuzhou
Hsüehshan Shanmo *527* mountain range of N Taiwan
Huacho *433* W Peru
Huainan *163 var.* Hwainan. Anhui, E China
Hualien *527 var.* Hwalien, *Jap.* Karen. E Taiwan
Huallaga *433* river of N Peru
Huambo *64 Port.* Nova Lisboa. C Angola
Huancavelica *433* SW Peru
Huancayo *433* C Peru
Huang Hai *see* Yellow Sea
Huang He *163 Eng.* Yellow River. River of C China
Huánuco *433* C Peru
Huanuni *112* W Bolivia
Huaral *433* W Peru
Huascarán, Nevado *433* mountain of W Peru
Huaraz *433 var.* Huaráz. W Peru
Hubei *163 var.* Hupei. Province of C China
Hubli *270* SW India
Huddersfield *565* N England, UK
Hudson *571* river of NE USA
Hudson Bay *147* bay of the Atlantic Ocean, NE Canada
Hudson Strait *147* strait connecting the Atlantic Ocean and Hudson Bay
Huê *595* C Vietnam
Huehuetenango *250* W Guatemala
Huelva *502* SW Spain
Huesca *503* NE Spain
Hughenden *77* NE Australia
Huhehot *see* Hohhot
Hŭich'ŏn *413* C North Korea
Huizen *397* C Netherlands
Huksan-kundo *498 var.* Huksan-chedo. Island group of SW South Korea
Hull *see* Kingston-upon-Hull
Hull *147* SE Canada
Hullo *212* Vormsi, Estonia
Hulun Nur *163 Chin.* Hu-lun Ch'ih, *prev.* Dalai Nor. Lake of Nei Mongol Zizhiqu, NE China
Ḥulwan *see* Ḥelwân
Humacao *629* E Puerto Rico
Humaitá *430* S Paraguay

Humber *565* river of NE England, UK
Humenné *487 Ger.* Homenau, *Hung.* Homonna. E Slovakia
Humera *see* Himora
Húnaflói *268* bay of the Norwegian Sea on the N coast of Iceland
Hunan *163* province of S China
Hundested *190* Sjælland, E Denmark
Hunga Ha'apai *540* island of the Nomuka Group, W Tonga
Hungary *264-267* officially Republic of Hungary, *Hung.* Magyarország, *prev.* Hungarian People's Republic. Country of C Europe divided into 19 admin. units (counties). ❖ Budapest
Hunga Tonga *540* island of the Nomuka Group, W Tonga
Hŭngnam *413* E North Korea
Hung-tse Hu *see* Hongze Hu
Huntington *571* West Virginia, E USA
Huntsville *571* Alabama, SE USA
Hunyani *see* Manyame
Huon Gulf *428* gulf of the Solomon Sea, to the E of Papua New Guinea
Huo-shao Tao *see* Lan Yü
Hupei *see* Hubei
Hurghada *202* E Egypt
Huron, Lake *147, 571* lake of Canada and USA
Hurunui *401* river of NE South Island, New Zealand
Húsavík *622* Sandoy, C Faeroe Islands
Húsavík *268* NE Iceland
Ḥuşayn, Dawḥat al *449 var.* Dauhat al Husein. Inlet of the Gulf of Bahrain on the NW coast of Qatar
Hūth *601* NW Yemen
Huwār *449* island of SE Bahrain
Huwwāra *see* Hawwārah
Hvammstangi *268* N Iceland
Hvannadalshnúkur *268* mountain of S Iceland
Hvar *181 It.* Lesina. Island of S Croatia
Hvítá *268* river of W Iceland
Hvolsvöllur *268* SW Iceland
Hwach'ŏn-chôsuji *see* P'aro-ho
Hwainan *see* Huainan
Hwang-Hae *see* Yellow Sea
Hwange *614 prev.* Wankie. W Zimbabwe
Hwang-Hae *see* Yellow Sea
Hyargas Nuur *380* lake of W Mongolia
Hyderābād *270 Hind.* Hyderābād. C India
Hyderābād *421 var.* Haidarabad. S Pakistan
Hyères *225* SE France
Hyères, Îles d' *225* island group of SE France
Hyesan *413* NE North Korea
Hyvinge *see* Hyvinkää
Hyvinkää *221 Swe.* Hyvinge. S Finland

I

Ialomiţa *450* river of SE Romania
Ialpug *376 Rus.* Yalpug. River of S Moldova
Iaşi *450 Ger.* Jassy. NE Romania
Ibadan *408* SW Nigeria
Ibagué *171* C Colombia
Ibar *604* river of SW Serbia, Yugoslavia
Ibarra *200 var.* San Miguel de Ibarra. N Ecuador
Ibb *601* W Yemen
Ibbenbüren *236* NW Germany
Ibenga *176* river of N Congo
Ibérico, Sistema *503 var.* Cordillera Ibérica, *Eng.* Iberian Mountains. Mountains of NE Spain
Ibiza *see* Eivissa
Ibo *see* Sassandra
Iboundji *230* C Gabon
Ibrā *418* N Oman
Ibrī *418* NW Oman

Irbīl *see* Arbīl
Ibusuki *304* Kyūshū, SW Japan
Içá *120* river of NW Brazil
Ica *433* SW Peru
Iceflavik *see* Keflavík
İçel *see* Mersin
Iceland *268-269* officially Republic of Iceland, *Icel.* Ísland. Country of the North Atlantic Ocean divided into 8 admin. units (regions). ❖ Reykjavík
Ichinomiya *304* Honshū, C Japan
Ichinoseki *304* Honshū, N Japan
Idah *408* S Nigeria
Idaho *570* state of NW USA
Idaho Falls *570* Idaho, NW USA
Idensalmi *see* Iisalmi
Idfu *202* *var.* Idfū, Edfu. SE Egypt
Idi Amin, Lac *see* Edward, Lake
Idlib *523* NW Syria
Idrija *488* *It.* Idria. W Slovenia
Idzhevan *see* Ijevan
Iecava *330* C Latvia
Ieper *99* *Fr.* Ypres. W Belgium
Ifalik *374* atoll of C Micronesia
Ife *408* SW Nigeria
Iferouâne *407* N Niger
Iferten *see* Yverdon
Iganga *556* SE Uganda
Igarka *455* N Russia
Igatimí *see* Ygatimí
Iglau *see* Jihlava
Iglesias *294* Sardegna, W Italy
Igló *see* Spišská Nová Ves
Ignalina *344* E Lithuania
Iguaçu, Salto do *121* *Sp.* Cataratas del Iguazú, *prev.* Victoria Falls. Waterfall of Argentina and Brazil
Iguetti, Sebkhet *366* salt lake of N Mauritania
Ihavandippolhu Atoll *358* *var.* Ihavandiffulu Atoll. Atoll of N Maldives
Ihema, Lac *462* lake of Burundi and Rwanda
Ihosy *350* S Madagascar
Iida *304* Honshū, C Japan
Iijoki *221* river of C Finland
Irbil *see* Arbīl
Iisalmi *221* *Swe.* Idensalmi. C Finland
Ijebu-Ode *408* SW Nigeria
Ijevan *74* *Rus.* Idzhevan, *var.* Idževan. N Armenia
IJssel *397* *var.* Yssel. River of C Netherlands
IJsselmeer *397* *prev.* Zuider Zee. Lake of N Netherlands
Ikare *408* SW Nigeria
Ikaría *245* island of SE Greece
Ikast *190* Jylland, W Denmark
Ikeja *408* SW Nigeria
Ikerre *408* *var.* Ikerre-Ekiti. SW Nigeria
Iki *304* island to the NW of Kyūshū, SW Japan
Ikom *408* S Nigeria
Ikopa *350* river of N Madagascar
Ila *408* W Nigeria
Ilam *395* W Nepal
Ilan *527* *Jap.* Giran. NE Taiwan
Ile *see* Ili
Ilebo *609* *prev.* Port Francqui. W Zaire
Ilesha *408* SW Nigeria
Ilha Solteira, Represa de *121* reservoir of S Brazil
Ili *312* *Kaz.* Ile. River of China and Kazakhstan
Iligan *437* Mindanao, S Philippines
Ilirska Bistrica *488* SW Slovenia
Il'jaly *see* Ylanly
Illapel *159* C Chile
Illiassa *233* NW Gambia
Illinois *571* state of C USA
Ilobasco *207* C El Salvador
Ilobu *408* W Nigeria
Iloilo *437* Panay, C Philippines
Ilopango, Lago de *207* volcanic lake of C El Salvador
Ilorin *408* W Nigeria
Īluh *see* Batman
Ilulissat *624* *Dan.* Jakobshavn. W Greenland
Il'yaly *see* Ylanly
Imatong Mountains *508* mountains of S Sudan

Imatra *221* SE Finland
Imeni 26 Bakinskikh Komissarov *see* Bakı Komissarı
Imilili *382* W Western Sahara
Īmisli *86* *Rus.* Imishli, Imišli. C Azerbaijan
Imja-do *498* island of SW South Korea
Imola *295* N Italy
Imperatriz *121* NE Brazil
Imperia *294* N Italy
Impfondo *176* NE Congo
Imphāl *271* E India
Ina *304* Honshū, C Japan
Inakona *490* S Guadalcanal, Solomon Is
In Aménas *59* *var.* I-n-Amenas, In Amnas. E Algeria
Inárajan *625* SE Guam
Inarijärvi *221* *Swe.* Enareträsk, *Lapp.* Aanaarjävri. Lake of N Finland
Inarijoki *221* *Nor.* Anarjokka. River of Finland and Norway
Inawashiro-ko *304* lake of Honshū, N Japan
Inbhear Mór *see* Arklow
Inch'ŏn *498* *prev.* Chemiulpo, *Jap.* Jinsen. NW South Korea
Inchope *387* C Mozambique
Incles *62* river of NE Andorra
Independence *102* SE Belize
Inderagiri *see* Indragiri
India *270-275* officially Republic of India, *Hind.* Bharat. Country divided into 32 admin. units (25 states and 7 union territories). ❖ New Delhi
Indiana *571* state of C USA
Indianapolis *571* Indiana, C USA
Indian Desert *see* Thar Desert
Indian Ocean *66, 622* ocean bounded to the W by Africa, to the E by Australia and to the S by Antarctica
Indigirka *455* River of NE Russia
Indonesia *276-279* officially Republic of Indonesia, *Ind.* Republik Indonesia, *prev.* United States of Indonesia, Dutch East Indies, Netherlands East Indies. Country of SE Asia divided into 25 admin. units (24 provinces and 1 autonous district). ❖ Jakarta
Indonesian Borneo *see* Kalimantan
Indore *270* NW India
Indragiri *276* *var.* Inderagiri. River of Sumatra, W Indonesia
Indre *225* river of C France
Indus *270, 421* river of S Asia
Indus, Mouths of the *421* river delta of S Pakistan
Infante Dom Henrique *473* SE Príncipe, Sao Tome & Principe
Ingolstadt *237* S Germany
Inguri *see* Enguri
Ingushetiya, Respublika *454* autonomous republic of SW Russia
Ingwavuma *see* Nggwavuma
Inhambane *387* S Mozambique
I-ning *see* Yining
Inírida *171* river of E Colombia
Inis *see* Ennis
Inland Sea *304* *var.* Seto Naikai. Sea of the Pacific Ocean between Honshū and Shikoku, W Japan
Inn *82, 237* river of C Europe
Inner Channel *102* *var.* Main Channel. Inlet of W Caribbean Sea
Inner Hebrides *565* island group of NW Scotland, UK
Inner Islands *480* *var.* Central Group. Island group of NE Seychelles
Inner Mongolian Autonomous Region *see* Nei Mongol Zizhiqu
Innsbruck *82* W Austria
Inrin *see* Yüanlin
In Salah *59* *var.* I-n-Salah. C Algeria
Insein *135* S Burma
Intelewa *510* S Suriname
Interlaken *518* SW Switzerland
Inthanon, Doi *535* mountain of NW Thailand
Intipucá *207* SE El Salvador
Inuvik *146* NW Canada
Invercargill *401* SW South Island, New Zealand
Inverness *565* N Scotland, UK
Inyanga *see* Nyanga

Inyangani *614* mountain of E Zimbabwe
Inyazura *see* Nyazura
Ioánnina *245* *var.* Janina, Yannina. W Greece
Iolotan' *see* Yëloten
Ionian Islands *see* Iónioi Nísoi
Ionian Sea *57, 245, 295* *Gk* Iónio Pélagos, *It.* Mar Ionio. Area of the Mediterranean Sea, between Italy and SE Europe
Ionio, Mar *see* Ionian Sea
Iónioi Nísoi *245* *Eng.* Ionian Islands. Island group of W Greece
Iori *234* river of Azerbaijan and Georgia
Íos *245* island of SE Greece
Iowa *571* state of C USA
Ipel *see* Ipoly
Ipiales *171* SW Colombia
Ipoh *354* W Peninsular Malaysia
Ipoly *264, 487* *Slvk.* Ipeľ, *Ger.* Eipel. River of Hungary and Slovakia
Ippy *155* C Central African Republic
Ipswich *77* E Australia
Ipswich *565* E England, UK
Iqaluit *147* *prev.* Frobisher Bay. Baffin Island, NE Canada
Iquique *159* N Chile
Iquitos *433* N Peru
Irákleio *245* *Eng.* Candia, *prev.* Iráklion. Crete, S Greece
Iran *280-283* officially Islamic Republic of Iran, *prev.* Persia. Country of SW Asia divided into 24 admin. units (provinces). ❖ Tehrān
Iran, Pegunungan *355* *var.* Iran Mountains. Mountain range of Borneo, Indonesia and Malaysia
Iran, Plateau of *281* plateau of C Iran
Irapuato *370* C Mexico
Iraq *284-287* officially Republic of Iraq, *Ar.* 'Iraq. Country of SW Asia divided into 18 admin. units (governorates). ❖ Baghdad
Irbe Strait *212* *Est.* Kura Kurk, *prev.* Irbe Väin, *Latv.* Irbes Šaurums. Strait connecting the Baltic Sea and Gulf of Riga
Irbid *310* N Jordan
Ireland Island North *621* island of W Bermuda
Ireland Island South *621* island of W Bermuda
Ireland, Northern *see* Northern Ireland
Ireland, Republic of *288-289* officially Republic of Ireland, Éire. Country of W Europe divided into 26 admin. units (counties). ❖ Dublin
Ireng *256* *var.* Maú. River of Brazil and Guyana
Irgalem *see* Yirga 'Alem
Iri *498* *Jap.* Riri. W South Korea
Irian *see* New Guinea
Irian Jaya *276-277* *Eng.* West Irian, *prev.* Dutch New Guinea. Province of W Indonesia
Iringa *532* C Tanzania
Iriomote-jima *304* island of Sakishima-shotō, SW Japan
Iriri *121* river of N Brazil
Irish Sea *288, 565, 625* *Ir.* Muir Eireann. Sea of the Atlantic Ocean between Ireland and UK
Irkeshtam *325* *var.* Irkeštam. SW Kyrgyzstan
Irkutsk *455* C Russia
Irmak *549* river of N Turkey
Iroise *224* area of the Atlantic Ocean to the NW of France
'Irqah *601* SW Yemen
Irrawaddy *135* *var.* Ayeyarwady. River of C Burma
Irrawaddy, Mouths of the *135* delta area of SW Burma
Irrsee *82* lake of N Austria
Irtysh *312, 454* *Kaz.* Ertis. River of Kazakhstan and Russia
Irun *503* N Spain
Iruñea *see* Pamplona
Isabela *629* NW Puerto Rico

Isabela, Isla *200* island of SW Galapagos Is, Ecuador
Isachsen *146* Ellef Ringnes Island, N Canada
Ísafdhardjúp *268* inlet of the Atlantic Ocean, NW Iceland
Isangel *587* Tanna, Vanuatu
Isa Town *see* Madīnat 'Īsā
Isalo, Tangorombohitr' *350* mountains of SW Madagascar
Ischia, Isola d' *295* island of S Italy
Ise *304* Honshū, C Japan
Isefjord *190* fjord of Sjælland, E Denmark
Isére *225* river of SE France
Iseyin *408* W Nigeria
Isfara *530* N Tajikistan
Ísfjördhur *268* NW Iceland
Isha Baydhabo *see* Baydhabo
Isherton *256* S Guyana
Ishigaki-jima *304* island of Sakishima-shotō, SW Japan
Ishikari *305* river of Hokkaidō, N Japan
Ishim *312* *Kaz.* Esil. River of Kazakhstan and Russia
Ishinomaki *304* Honshū, N Japan
Ishkoshim *530* *Rus.* Ishkashim. S Tajikistan
Ishurdi *93* W Bangladesh
Isidoro Noblia *579* NE Uruguay
Isiolo *316* C Kenya
Isiro *609* NE Zaire
İskeçe *see* Xánthi
İskele *187* *var.* Trikomo. E Cyprus
İskenderun *549* *Eng.* Alexandretta. S Turkey
İskenderun Körfezi *549* *Eng.* Gulf of Alexandretta. Gulf of the Mediterranean Sea
Iskŭr *128* river of NW Bulgaria
Iskŭr, Yazovir *128* reservoir of W Bulgaria
Islāmābād *421* ❖ of Pakistan, NE Pakistan
Island Harbour *620* bay of the Caribbean Sea on the N coast of Anguilla
Islay *565* island of Inner Hebrides, W Scotland, UK
Isle *225* river of SW France
Ismâ'īlīya *202* *var.* Al Ismā'īlīyah, *Eng.* Ismaila. N Egypt
Isna *202* *var.* Isnā, Esna. SE Egypt
Isoka *613* NE Zambia
Isonzo *see* Soča.
Ispahan *see* Eşfahān
Īsparta *549* SW Turkey
Israel *290-293* officially State of Israel, *Heb.* Yisra'el. Country of SW Asia divided into 6 admin. units (districts). ❖ Jerusalem
Issano *256* C Guyana
Issia *300* SW Ivory Coast
Issyk-Kul *see* Balykchy
Issyk-Kul', Ozero *325* *var.* Issiq Köl. Lake of NE Kyrgyzstan
İstanbul *549* *prev.* Constantinople, *Bul.* Tsarigrad. NW Turkey
İstanbul Boğazı *549* Karadeniz Boğazi, *Eng.* Bosporus. Strait connecting rmara Denizi and Black Sea
Istra *181* *Eng.* Istria. Peninsula of SE Europe
Istria *see* Istra
Itabuna *121* E Brazil
Itagüí *171* NW Colombia
Itaipú, Represa de *121, 430* reservoir of Brazil and Paraguay
Italy *294-299* officially Italian Republic, *It.* Italia, Repubblica Italiana. Country of S Europe divided into 20 admin. units (regions). ❖ Rome
Itany *see* Litani
Itassi *see* Vieille Case
Iténez *see* Guaporé
Itonamas *112* river of NE Bolivia
Itremo *350* *var.* Massif de l'Itremo. Mountain range of C Madagascar

Itsamia *174* S Mohéli, Comoros
Itsandra *174* W Grande Comore, Comoros
Ittoqqortoormiit *624 Dan.* Scoresbysund. E Greenland
Itu Aba Island *630* island of W Spratly Islands
Ituni *256* C Guyana
Iturup *305* disputed island of Kurile Islands, SE Russia
Ivakoany *350 var.* Massif de l'Ivakoany. Mountain range of SE Madagascar
Ivalojoki *221* river of N Finland
Ivano-Frankivs'k *558 Rus.* Ivano-Frankovsk, *prev.* Stanislav, *Pol.* Stanisławów, *Ger.* Stanislau. W Ukraine
Ivanovo *454* W Russia
Ivatsevichy *104* SW Belorussia
Ivindo *230* river of C Africa
Iviza *see* Eivissa
Ivoire, Côte d' *see* Ivory Coast
Ivory Coast *300 Fr.* Côte d'Ivoire. Coastal region of S Ivory Coast
Ivory Coast *300-301* officially Republic of the Ivory Coast, *Fr.* Côte d'Ivoire. Country of W Africa divided into 34 admin. units (departments). ❖ Yamoussoukro
Ivujivik *147* NE Canada
Iwakuni *304* Honshū, W Japan
Iwaki *304* Honshū, N Japan
Iwo *408* SW Nigeria
Iwŏn *413* E North Korea
Ixcán *250* river of Guatemala and Mexico
Izabal, Lago de *250 prev.* Golfo Dulce. Lake of E Guatemala
Izhevsk *454 prev.* Ustinov. W Russia
Izkī *418* N Oman
İzmir *549 prev.* Smyrna. W Turkey
İzmit *549 var.* Kocaeli. NW Turkey
Izuhara *304* Tsushima, W Japan
Izumo *304* Honshū, W Japan
Izu-shotō *304* island group to the SE of Honshū, SE Japan

J

Jabal aẓ Ẓannah *562 var.* Jebel Dhanna, W United Arab Emirates
Jabāliya *291, 292* NE Gaza Strip
Jabalpur *270 prev.* Jubbulpore. C India
Jabat *364 var.* Jabwot Island. island of S Marshall Islands
Jabbul, Sabkhat al *523* salt-flat of NW Syria
Jablah *523 var.* Jeble, *Fr.* Djéblé. W Syria
Jablanica *57* mountain range of E Albania
Jablonec nad Nisou *188 Ger.* Gablonz an der Neisse. N Czech Republic
Jaboatão *121* E Brazil
Jabwot Island *see* Jabat
Jaceel *492 It.* Uadi Giahel. Seasonal river of NE Somalia
Jackson *571* Mississippi, SE USA
Jacksonville *571* Florida, SE USA
Jacmel *258 var.* Jaquemel. S Haiti
Jacó *178* SW Costa Rica
Jacob *see* Nkayi
Jacobābād *421* SW Pakistan
Jadotville *see* Likasi
Jadransko More *see* Adriatic Sea
Jādū *339* NW Libya
Jaén *503* SW Spain
Jaffna *506* N Sri Lanka
Jaffna Lagoon *506* lagoon of N Sri Lanka
Jafr, Qā' al *310 var.* El Jafr. Salt pan of S Jordan
Jägala *212 var.* Jägala Jõgi. River of N Estonia
Jägerndorf *see* Krnov
Jagodina *see* Svetozarevo
Jaguarão *see* Yaguarón
Jailolo *see* Halmahera

Jaipur *270 prev.* Jeypore. N India
Jaipur Hāt *93* NW Bangladesh
Jajce *116* W Bosnia & Herzegovina
Jakar *110* C Bhutan
Jakarta *276 prev.* Djakarta, *Dut.* Batavia. ❖ of Indonesia, Java, C Indonesia
Jakobshavn *see* Ilulissat
Jakobstad *see* Pietarsaari. W Finland
Jakobstadt *see* Jēkabpils
Jalal-Abad *see* Dzhalal-Abad
Jalālābād *53* E Afghanistan
Jalandhar *270 prev.* Jullundur. N India
Jalapa *370 var.* Jalapa Enríquez, *prev.* Xalapa. SE Mexico
Jalapa *250* C Guatemala
Jalousie *467* SW St. Lucia
Jālū *339* NE Libya
Jaluit *364* island of S Marshall Islands
Jamaame *422 It.* Giamame. S Somalia
Jamaare *408* river of NE Nigeria
Jamaica *302-303* island state of the West Indies, divided in 14 admin. units (parishes). ❖ Kingston
Jamaica Channel *258, 303* channel of the Caribbean Sea between Haiti and Jamaica
Jamālpur *93* N Bangladesh
Jambi *276 prev.* Djambi, *var.* Telanaipura. Sumatra, W Indonesia
Jambol *see* Yambol
Jamdena *see* Yamdena, Pulau
James Bay *147* inlet of Hudson Bay, C Canada
Jamestown *630* ❖ of St. Helena, N St. Helena
Jamestown *see* Holetown
Jammāl *see* Jemmel
Jammerbugten *190* bay to the NW of Denmark
Jammu *270* NW India
Jāmnagar *270 prev.* Navangar. W India
Jämsä *221* S Finland
Jamshedpur *270* E India
Jamuna *93* lower course of the Brahmaputra, N Bangladesh
Jamundá *see* Nhamundá
Janakpur *395* E Nepal
Janela *152* Santo Antão, N Cape Verde
Jangijul *see* Yangiyŭl
Janīn *see* Jenin
Janina *see* Ioánnina
Janow *see* Jonava
Jantra *see* Yambol
Janzūr *339* NW Libya
Japan *304-309* country of E Asia, divided into 47 admin. units (prefectures). ❖ Tokyo
Japan, Sea of *304, 413, 455, 498 Rus.* Yapanskoye More. Sea of Pacific Ocean, between E Asia and Japan
Jappeni *233* C Gambia
Japurá *120 var.* Yapurá. River of Brazil
Jaquemel *see* Jacmel
Jarabacoa *198* C Dominican Republic
Jarābulus *322 var.* Jerablus, *Fr.* Djérablous. N Syria
Jarash *310 var.* Jerash. NW Jordan
Jarbah, Jazīrat *see* Jerba, Île de
Jardines de la Reina, Archipiélago de los *182* island group of S Cuba
Jarej District *364* district of Majuro, SE Marshall Islands
Jari *121 var.* Jary. River of N Brazil
Jarīd, Shaṭṭ al *see* Jerid, Chott el
Jaroměř *188* NE Czech Republic
Jarqŭrghon *582 Rus.* Dzharkurgan. SE Uzbekistan
Jars, Plain of *see* Xiangkhoang, Plateau de
Järvenpää *221 Swe.* Träskända. S Finland
Jason Islands *623* island group of NW Falkland Islands
Jassy *see* Iaşi
Jastrzębie Zdrój *441* S Poland
Jászberény *264* NE Hungary
Jauf *see* Al Jawf
Jaunpiebalga *330* NE Latvia

Java *276 var.* Jawa, *prev.* Djawa. Island of C Indonesia
Javari *120-121 var.* Yavarí. River of Brazil and Peru
Java Sea *see* Jawa, Laut
Jawa *see* Java
Jawa, Laut *276 Eng.* Java Sea. Sea of the Pacific Ocean, C Indonesia
Jawhar *492 var.* Jowhar, *It.* Giohar. S Somalia
Jayapura *277 prev.* Sukarnapura, *Dut.* Hollandia. Irian Jaya, E Indonesia
Jay Dairen *see* Dalian
Jaya, Puncak *277 prev.* Puntjak Sukarno, Puntjak Carstensz. Mountain of Irian Jaya, E Indonesia
Jazā'ir, Ra's al *91* cape of SW Bahrain
Jaz Murian, Hamun-e *281* lake of SE Iran
Jazzin *see* Jezzine
Jbaïl *332 var.* Jubayl. W Lebanon
Jdiriya *382* NE Western Sahara
Jebba *408* river of NW Nigeria
Jebel *see* Dzhebel
Jebel, Bahr el *see* White Nile
Jebel Dhanna *see* Jabal aẓ Ẓannah
Jeble *see* Jablah
Jedda *see* Jiddah
Jeffara Plain *339, 545 var.* Gefara, Al Jifārah. Plain of Libya and Tunisia
Jefferson City *571* Missouri, C USA
Jega *408* NW Nigeria
Jehegnadzor *see* Yeghegnadzor
Jēkabpils *330 Ger.* Jakobstadt. SE Latvia
Jelenia Góra *441 Ger.* Hirschberg in Riesengebirge. SW Poland
Jelgava *330 Ger.* Mitau. C Latvia
Jember *276 prev.* Djember. Java, C Indonesia
Jemmel *545 var.* Jammāl. N Tunisia
Jemo *364* island of C Marshall Islands
Jena *237* C Germany
Jendouba *545 var.* Jundūbah. NW Tunisia
Jenin *291, 292 var.* Janīn, *Ar.* Jinīn. N West Bank
Jenné *see* Djenné
Jennings *68* W Antigua, Antigua & Barbuda
Jenny *510* N Suriname
Jequitinhonha *121* river of E Brazil
Jerablus *see* Jarābulus
Jerada *382* NE Morocco
Jerash *see* Jarash
Jerba *see* Houmt Souk
Jerba, Île de *545 var.* Djerba, Jazīrat Jarbah. Island of E Tunisia
Jérémie *258* SW Haiti
Jerevan *see* Yerevan
Jerez de la Frontera *502* SW Spain
Jericho *291, 292 Heb.* Yeriḥo, *Ar.* Arīḥā. E West Bank
Jerid, Chott el *545 var.* Shaṭṭ al Jarīd. Salt lake of SW Tunisia
Jermuk *74 Rus.* Dzhermuk. SE Armenia
Jersey *224, 626* British Crown dependency of the English Channel. ❖ St. Helier.
Jerusalem *291, 292 Ar.* Al Quds, *Heb.* Yerushalayim. ❖ of Israel, Israel and West Bank
Jesenice *488 Ger.* Assling. NW Slovenia
Jesselton *see* Kota Kinabalu
Jessore *93* W Bangladesh
Jesús Menéndez *182* SE Cuba
Jeta, Ilha de *254* island of W Guinea-Bissau
Jevlah *see* Yevlax
Jeypore *see* Jaipur
Jezercës, Maja e *57 var.* Jezerce. Mountain of N Albania
Jezzine *332 var.* Jazzin. S Lebanon
Jhālakāti *93* S Bangladesh
Jhang *421 var.* Jhang Sadar, Jhang Sadr. NE Pakistan
Jhelum *421* NE Pakistan
Jhelum *421* river of India and Pakistan
Jhenida *93* W Bangladesh
Jiamusi *163 var.* Chia-mu-ssu, Kiamusze. Heilongjiang, NE China

Jiangsu *163 var.* Kiangsu, Chiang-su. Province of E China
Jiangxi *163 var.* Kiangsi, Chiang-hsi. Province of SE China
Jibuti *see* Djibouti
Jičín *188* N Czech Republic
Jiddah *474 Eng.* Jedda. W Saudi Arabia
Jiddah *91* island of NW Bahrain
Jidd Ḥafṣ *91 var.* Judd Ḥafṣ. N Bahrain
Jiftlik Post *292* E West Bank
Jiguaní *182* SE Cuba
Jihlava *188 Ger.* Iglau. S Czech Republic
Jijel *59 var.* Djidjel, *prev.* Djidjelli. NE Algeria
Jijiga *215 It.* Giggiga. E Ethiopia
Jilf al Kabīr, Haḍabat al *see* Gilf Kebir Plateau
Jilib *492 It.* Gelib. S Somalia
Jilin *163 var.* Kirin, Chi-lin, *prev.* Yungki. Jilin, NE China
Jilin *163 var.* Kirin, Chi-lin. Province of NE China
Jima *215 var.* Jimma, Ft. Gimma. SW Ethiopia
Jimaní *198* W Dominican Republic
Jinan *163 var.* Chinan, Tsinan. Shandong, E China
Jinīn *see* Jenin
Jinja *556* S Uganda
Jinotega *404* C Nicaragua
Jinotepe *404* S Nicaragua
Jinsen *see* Inch'ŏn
Jintotlolo Channel *437* channel connecting Mindoro Strait and Visayan Sea
Jinzhou *163 var.* Chin-chou, Chinchow, *prev.* Chinhsien. Liaoning, NE China
Jipijapa *200* W Ecuador
Jiquilisco *207* S El Salvador
Jiquilisco, Bahia de *207* bay of the Pacific Ocean to the S of El Salvador
Jirgatol *530 Rus.* Dzhirgatal'. C Tajikistan
Jirriiban *492 prev.* Ceel Xamurre, *It.* El Hamurre. E Somalia
Jisr ash Shughūr *523 var.* Djisr el Choghour. NW Syria
Jiu *450 Ger.* Schyl, *Hung.* Zsily. River of S Romania
Jiulong *see* Kowloon
Jixi *163 var.* Chi-hsi. Heilongjiang, NE China
Jīzān *474 var.* Qīzān. S Saudi Arabia
Jizuka *304* Kyūshū, SW Japan
Jiz', Wādī al *601* dry watercourse of E Yemen
Jizzakh *582 Rus.* Dzhizak. SE Uzbekistan
Jleeb, Shaqat Al *see* Qalīb, Shiqqat al
Jleeb al Shuyoukh *see* Qalīb ash Shuyūkh
Joal-Fadiout *478 prev.* Joal. W Senegal
João Barrosa *152* Boa Vista, E Cape Verde
João Pessoa *121 prev.* Paraíba. E Brazil
Jo-ch'iang *see* Ruoqiang
Joden Savanne *510* NE Suriname
Jodhpur *270* NW India
Joel's Drift *334* N Lesotho
Joensuu *221* SE Finland
Jõgeva *212 Ger.* Laisholm. C Estonia
Jogjakarta *see* Yogyakarta
Johannesburg *495* Pretoria-Witwatersrand-Vereeniging, NE South Africa
John o'Groats *565* N Scotland, UK
Johnsons Point *68* SW Antigua, Antigua & Barbuda
Johnson, Rapides *609* rapids of Zaire and Zambia
Johnston Atoll *626* unincorporated territory of the USA, Pacific Ocean
Johnston Island *626* island of S Johnston Atoll
Johor Bahru *354* SE Peninsular Malaysia
Johore Strait *485* strait connecting Strait of Malacca and South China Sea

Joinville 121 *var.* Joinvile. S Brazil
Jolo Group 437 island group of Sulu Archipelago, SW Philippines
Jolo Island 437 island of Jolo Group, SW Philippines
Jomsom 395 W Nepal
Jona 518 NE Switzerland
Jonava 344 *Ger.* Janow. C Lithuania
Jones Point 622 headland on the W coast of Christmas Island
Jonglei Canal 508 canal of S Sudan
Jönköping 515 S Sweden
Jonquière 147 SE Canada
Jordan 291, 292, 310 *Ar.* Urdunn, *Heb.* HaYarden. River of SW Asia
Jordan 310-311 officially Hashemite Kingdom of Jordan, *Ar.* Al Urdunn. Country of SW Asia divided into 8 admin. units (governorates). ❖ Amman
Jos 408 C Nigeria
José Batlle y Ordóñez 579 C Uruguay
José E. Bisanó 198 N Dominican Republic
José Pedro Varela 579 SE Uruguay
Joseph Bonaparte Gulf 77 gulf of Timor Sea on the coast of NW Australia
Jos Plateau 408 plateau of C Nigeria
Jos Sudarso *see* Yos Sudarso, Pulau
Jost Van Dyke 621 island of W British Virgin Islands
Jotunheimen 414 mountains of SW Norway
Joûnié 332 *var.* Jūniyah, Juniye. W Lebanon
Jovellanos 182 NW Cuba
Jozini Dam 512 reservoir of South Africa and Swaziland
Jsahaya 304 Kyūshū, SW Japan
Juan Fernández Islands 159 island group of W Chile
Juan L. Lacaze 579 *prev.* Sauce. SW Uruguay
Juarzon 336 *var.* Juazohn. SE Liberia
Juazeiro do Norte 121 E Brazil
Juazohn *see* Juarzon
Juba 215, 492 *Som.* Jubba, *var.* Ganaane, *Amh.* Genale Wenz, *It.* Guiba. River of Ethiopia and Somalia
Juba 508 *var.* Jūbā. S Sudan
Jubba *see* Juba
Jubbulpore *see* Jabalpur
Júcar 503 river of C Spain
Juclà, Estany de 62 lake of NE Andorra
Judd Ḥafṣ *see* Jidd Ḥafṣ
Judenburg 82 C Austria
Juigalpa 404 S Nicaragua
Juishui 527 E Taiwan
Juiz de Fora 121 SE Brazil
Jujuy *see* San Salvador de Jujuy
Juliaca 433 SE Peru
Julian Alps 488 *Ger.* Julische Alpen, *It.* Alpi Giulie, *Slvn.* Julijske Alpe. Mountains of NW Slovenia
Juliana Top 510 mountain of C Suriname
Julianehåb *see* Qaqortoq
Jullundur *see* Jalandhar
Jumayrah 562 *var.* Jumeirah. NE United Arab Emirates
Jumla 395 E Nepal
Jumna *see* Yamuna
Jundūbah *see* Jendouba
Juneau 570 Alaska, USA
Jungbunzlau *see* Mladá Boleslav
Junín 71 E Argentina
Junk Bay *see* Tseung Kwan O
Juntas 178 W Costa Rica
Junten *see* Sunch'ŏn
Juozapinés Kalnas 344 mountain of SE Lithuania
Jupiá, Represa de 121 reservoir of S Brazil
Jura 565 island of Inner Hebrides, W Scotland, UK
Jura 225, 518 *var.* Jura Mountains. Mountain range of France and Switzerland
Juraguá 182 C Cuba
Jura Mountains *see* Jura
Jurbarkas 344 *var.* Jurburg, *var.* Georgenburg. W Lithuania

Jūrmala 330 NW Latvia
Jurong Lake 485 lake of W Singapore
Jurong Town 485 W Singapore
Juruá 120 river of Brazil and Peru
Juruena 120 river of W Brazil
Jutiapa 250 S Guatemala
Juticalpa 260 C Honduras
Jutland *see* Jylland
Juventud, Isla de la 182 *var.* Isla de Pinos, *Eng.* Isle of Pines. Island of W Cuba
Južna Morava 604 river of SE Serbia, Yugoslavia
Jwaneng 118 S Botswana
Jylland 190 *Eng.* Jutland. Island of W Denmark
Jyrgalan *see* Dzhergalan
Jyväskylä 221 S Finland

K

K2 421 *Eng.* Mount Godwin Austen. Mountain of China and Pakistan
Kaabong 556 NE Uganda
Kaafu Atoll *see* Male' Atoll
Kaaimanston 510 NW Suriname
Kaakhka 533 *var.* Kaachka, Kaka. S Turkmenistan
Kaala *see* Caála
Kaapstad *see* Cape Town
Kaba 482 *var.* Little Scarcies. River of Guinea and Sierra Leone
Kabakama 233 E Gambia
Kabala 482 N Sierra Leone
Kabale 556 SW Uganda
Kabalega Falls *see* Murchison Falls
Kabara 218 *prev.* Kambara. Island of the Lau Group, E Fiji
Kabardino-Balkarskaya, Respublika 454 autonomous republic of SW Russia
Kabarnet 316 W Kenya
Kabarole 556 W Uganda
Kabaya 462 NW Rwanda
Kaberamaido 556 C Uganda
Kabinda 609 SE Zaire
Kabinda *see* Cabinda
Kābol *see* Kābul
Kabompo 613 W Zambia
Kabompo 613 river of W Zambia
Kabou 539 N Togo
Kābul 53 *Per.* Kābol. ❖ of Afghanistan, E Afghanistan
Kabul 53, 421 river of Afghanistan and Pakistan
Kabwe 613 C Zambia
Kabye Plateau 539 plateau of E Togo
Kachch, Gulf of 270 *var.* Gulf of Cutch, Gulf of Kutch. Gulf of Arabian Sea to the W of India
Kachhi 421 lowland region of C Pakistan
Kadan Island 135 *prev.* King I. Island of S Burma
Kadavu 218 *prev.* Kandavu. Island to the S of Viti Levu, SW Fiji
Kadavu Passage 218 channel of the Pacific Ocean between Kadavu and Vitu Levu, Fiji
Kadéï 144, 155 river of Cameroon and Central African Republic
Kadoma 614 *prev.* Gatooma. C Zimbabwe
Kadugli 508 *var.* Kāduqlī. S Sudan
Kaduha 462 SW Rwanda
Kaduna 408 C Nigeria
Kaduna 408 river of N Nigeria
Kadzharan *see* K'ajaran
Kadzhi-Say 325 *Kir.* Kajisay. NE Kyrgyzstan
Kaédi 366 S Mauritania
Kaélé 144 N Cameroon
Kaesŏng 413 S North Korea
Kaewieng *see* Kavieng
Kafan *see* Kapan
Kāfar Jar Ghar 53 mountain range of C Afghanistan
Kaffrine 478 C Senegal
Kafr el Dauwâr 202 *var.* Kafr ad Dawwār. N Egypt
Kafr el Sheikh 202 *var.* Kafr ash Shaykh. N Egypt

Kafu 556 *var.* Kafo. River of W Uganda
Kafue 613 river of C Zambia
Kafue 613 SE Zambia
Kaga Bandoro 155 *prev.* Fort-Crampel. C Central African Republic
Kagan *see* Kogon
Kaganovichabad *see* Kolkhozobod
Kagera *see* Akagera
Kagi *see* Chiai
Kâğithane 549 NW Turkey
Kagoshima 304 Kyūshū, SW Japan
Kagul *see* Cahul
Kahama 532 NW Tanzania
Kahayan 276 river of Borneo, C Indonesia
Kahnple 336 NE Liberia
Kahnwia 336 SE Liberia
Ká-Hó, Baía de 626 bay of the South China Sea, SE Macao
Kahramanmaraş 549 *var.* Marash, Maraş. S Turkey
Kaiaf 233 S Gambia
Kaieteur Falls 256 waterfall of C Guyana
Kaifeng 163 Henan, C China
Kai, Kepulauan 276 *prev.* Kei Islands. Island group of Maluku, E Indonesia
Kaikoura 401 NE South Island, New Zealand
Kailahun 482 E Sierra Leone
Kainan 304 Honshū, C Japan
Kainji Reservoir 408 reservoir of W Nigeria
Kaipara Harbour 401 harbour of NW North Island, New Zealand
Kairouan 545 *var.* Al Qayrawān. N Tunisia
Kaiserslautern 236 SW Germany
Kaitaia 401 NW North Island, New Zealand
Kajaani 221 *Swe.* Kajana. C Finland
Kajana *see* Kajaani
Kajang 354 W Peninsular Malaysia
K'ajaran 74 *Rus.* Kadzharan, *var.* Kadžaran. SE Armenia
Kajisay *see* Kadzhi-Say
Kaka *see* Kaakhaa
Kakamega 316 W Kenya
Kakata 336 C Liberia
Kakhovs'ke Vodokhovyshche 558 *Rus.* Kakhovskoye Vodokhranilische. Reservoir of SE Ukraine
Kakia *see* Khakhea
Kakogawa 304 Honshū, C Japan
Kakshaal-Too, Khrebet *see* Kokshaal-Tau
Kalaa Kebira 545 *var.* Al Qal'ah al Kubrá. N Tunisia
Kalabo 613 W Zambia
Kalahari Desert 118, 391, 495 desert region of southern Africa
Kalaikhum *see* Qal'aikhum
Kalai-Mor 553 *Turkm.* Galaymor. SE Turkmenistan
Kalamáki 245 *prev.* Kalmákion. SE Greece
Kalamariá 245 *prev.* Kalamaria. N Greece
Kalámata 245 *prev.* Kalámai. S Greece
Kalandula *see* Calandula
Kalang *see* Kallang
Kalanshiyū, Sarīr 339 *var.* Calanscio Sand Sea. Desert region of E Libya
Kalarash *see* Călăraşi
Kalasin 535 *var.* Muang Kalasin. NE Thailand
Kalāt 53 *var.* Qalāt. S Afghanistan
Kalāt 421 *var.* Kelat. W Pakistan
Kalbā 562 *var.* Kalba, NE United Arab Emirates
Kaldakvísl 268 river of C Iceland
Kalemie 609 *prev.* Albertville. SE Zaire
Kalgan *see* Zhangjiakou
Kalgoorlie 76 SW Australia
Kali Gandaki 395 river of C Nepal
Kalima 609 E Zaire
Kalimantan 276 *Eng.* Indonesian Borneo. Region of Borneo, administered by Indonesia
Kalinin 553 N Turkmenistan

Kalininabad *see* Kalininobod
Kaliningrad 454 W Russia
Kalinino *see* Tashir
Kalininobod 530 *Rus.* Kalininabad. SW Tajikistan
Kalinkavichy 104 *Rus.* Kalinkovichi. SE Belorussia
Kaliro 556 SE Uganda
Kalisz 441 *Ger.* Kalisch. C Poland
Kalixälv 515 river of NE Sweden
Kalkandelen *see* Tetovo
Kalkfeld 391 NW Namibia
Kallang 485 *var.* Kalang. River of C Singapore
Kallaste 212 *Ger.* Krasnogor. E Estonia
Kallavesi 221 lake of SE Finland
Kalmar 515 S Sweden
Kalmykiya, Respublika 454 autonomous republic of SW Russia
Kalomo 613 S Zambia
Kalpeni Island 270 island of Lakshadweep, SW India
Kalsoy 622 *var.* Kalsø. Island of N Faeroe Islands
Kalu Ganga 506 river of S Sri Lanka
Kalulushi 613 C Zambia
Kalundborg 190 Sjælland, C Denmark
Kalungwishi 613 river of N Zambia
Kalutara 506 SW Sri Lanka
Kaluwawa *see* Fergusson Island
Kalyān 270 W India
Kálymnos 245 island of SE Greece
Kama 609 E Zaire
Kamai 156 N Chad
Kamaishi 305 Honshū, N Japan
Kamakwie 482 NW Sierra Leone
Kamālia 421 NE Pakistan
Kamanjab 391 NW Namibia
Kamarān 601 island of W Yemen
Kamarang 256 W Guyana
Kamativi 614 W Zimbabwe
Kambar 421 *var.* Qambar. SW Pakistan
Kambara *see* Kabara
Kamchatka, Poluostrov 455 *Eng.* Kamchatka Peninsula. Peninsula of NE Russia
Kamchiya 128 *var.* Kamčija. River of E Bulgaria
Kamenets-Podol'sk *see* Kam"yanets'-Podil's'kyy
Kamenets-Podol'skiy *see* Kam"yanets'-Podil's'kyy
Kamenica 349 NE FYR Macedonia
Kamenskoye *see* Dniprodzerzhyns'k
Kamina 609 S Zaire
Kamishli *see* Al Qāmishlī
Kamloops 145 SW Canada
Kammersee *see* Attersee
Kamnik 488 *Ger.* Stein. C Slovenia
Kamo 74 C Armenia
Kamp 82 river of N Austria
Kampala 556 ❖ of Uganda, S Uganda
Kampar 354 W Peninsular Malaysia
Kampar 276 river of Sumatra, W Indonesia
Kampo *see* Ntem
Kampong Batang Duri 126 NE Brunei
Kampong Benutan 126 C Brunei
Kampong Bukit Sawat 126 C Brunei
Kampong Bunut 126 N Brunei
Kâmpóng Cham 141 *prev.* Kompong Cham. S Cambodia
Kâmpóng Chhnăng 141 C Cambodia
Kampong Jerudong 126 N Brunei
Kâmpóng Khleăng 141 *prev.* Kompong Kleang. NW Cambodia
Kampong Kuala Abang 126 C Brunei
Kampong Kuala Balai 126 SW Brunei
Kampong Labi 126 S Brunei
Kampong Labu 126 NE Brunei
Kampong Lumut 126 W Brunei
Kampong Paring 126 N Brunei
Kampong Parit 126 N Brunei
Kâmpóng Saôm 141 *var.* Kompong Som, *prev.* Sihanoukville. SW Cambodia
Kâmpóng Saôm, Chhâk 141 *Fr.* Baie de Kompong Som. Bay of the Gulf of Thailand on the SW coast of Cambodia

Kâmpóng Spoe *141*
prev. Kompong Speu. S Cambodia
Kampong Sukang *126* S Brunei
Kampong Tanajor *126* C Brunei
Kampong Teraja *126* S Brunei
Kâmpóng Thum *141*
prev. Kompong Thom. C Cambodia
Kâmpôt *141* S Cambodia
Kampuchea *see* Cambodia
Kamsar *253* W Guinea
Kam"yanets'-Podil's'kyy *558*
Rus. Kamenets-Podol'skiy,
prev. Kamenets-Podol'sk. W Ukraine
Kanacea *218 prev.* Kanathea. Taveuni,
N Fiji
Kanacea *218* island of the Lau Group,
E Fiji
Kananga *609 prev.* Luluabourg.
SW Zaire
Kanazawa *304* Honshū, C Japan
Kanazi *462* SE Rwanda
Kandahār *53 var.* Qandahār.
S Afghanistan
Kandavu *see* Kadavu
Kandé *539* NE Togo
Kandi *108* N Benin
Kandrian *428* New Britain, E Papua
New Guinea
Kandy *506* C Sri Lanka
Kaneohe *570* Oahu, Hawaii, USA
Kanevskoye Vodokhranilische
see Kanivs'ke Vodoskhovyshche
Kang *118* C Botswana
Kangar *354* NW Peninsular Malaysia
Kangaroo Island *77* island of
S Australia
Kangaruma *256* C Guyana
Kangchenjunga *271*
var. Kanchenjunga. Mountain of
NE India
Kangerlussuaq *624 Dan.* Søndre
Strømfjord. SW Greenland
Kanggye *413* N North Korea
Kanghwa-do *498 Jap.* Kōka-tō. Island
of NW South Korea
Kangnŭng *498 Jap.* Kōryō. NE South
Korea
Kango *230* NW Gabon
Kanibadam *530* N Tajikistan
Kani, Baie de *627 var.* Kani Bay. Bay
of the Mozambique Channel on the
SW coast of Mayotte
Kanivs'ke Vodoskhovyshche *558*
Rus. Kanevskoye Vodokhranilische.
Reservoir of C Ukraine
Kanjiža *604 prev.* Stara Kanjiža,
Ger. Altkanischa,
Hung. Magyarkanizsa, Ókanizsa.
N Serbia, Yugoslavia
Kankan *253* E Guinea
Kankesanturai *506* N Sri Lanka
Kan-kô *see* Han
Kankossa *366* S Mauritania
Kanli Dere *see* Pedhieos
Kanmaw Island *135 var.* Kettharin I,
Kisseraing. Island of S Burma
Kano *408* N Nigeria
Kanombe *462* C Rwanda
Kanoya *304* Kyūshū, SW Japan
Kānpur *270 var.* Cawnpore. N India
Kanra-san *see* Halla-san
Kansas *571* state of C USA
Kansas City *571* Kansas, C USA
Kant *325* C Kyrgyzstan
Kantipur *see* Kathmandu
Kanton *320 var.* Abariringa, Canton I,
prev. Mary I. Island of the Phoenix Is,
C Kiribati
Kanyaru *see* Akanyaru
Kanye *118* S Botswana
Kao *540* island of W Tonga
Kao *540* mountain of Kao, Tonga
Kaôh Nhêk *141* E Cambodia
Kaohsiung *527 var.* Kaohiung,
Jap. Takao. SW Taiwan
Kaolack *478 var.* Kaolak. W Senegal
Kaolak *see* Kaolack
Kaolan *see* Lanzhou
Kaoma *613* W Zambia
Kaop'ing Hsi *527* river of C Taiwan
Kapan *74 var.* Ghap'an. *Rus.* Kafan.
SE Armenia
Kapchorwa *556* E Uganda
Kapenguria *316* W Kenya

Kapfenberg *82* C Austria
Kapingamarangi *374* atoll of
S Micronesia
Kapiri Mposhi *613* C Zambia
Kapiti Island *401* island to the
S of North Island, New Zealand
Kapka, Massif du *156* mountains
of E Chad
Kaposvár *264* SW Hungary
Kaproncza *see* Koprivnica
Kapsabet *316* W Kenya
Kapsukas *see* Marijampolė
Kapuas *276 prev.* Kapoeas. River of
Borneo, C Indonesia
Kapuas Mountains *276, 354*
Ind. Pegunungan Kapuas Hulu.
Mountain range of Indonesia and
Malaysia
Kara *539 var.* Lama-Kara.
NE Togo
Karaba *462* SW Rwanda
Kara-Balta *325* NW Kyrgyzstan
Karabil', Vozvyshennost' *553* region
of SE Turkmenistan
Kara-Bogaz-Gol, Zaliv *553*
NW Turkmenistan
Kara-Bogaz-Gol, Proliv *553*
Turkm. Garabogazköl Bogazy. Strait
of the Caspian Sea, on the NW coast
of Turkmenistan
Karabük *549* N Turkey
Karachayevo-Cherkesskaya SSR *454*
autonomous republic of
SW Russia
Karāchi *421* S Pakistan
Karadeniz *see* Black Sea
Karadeniz Boğazı *see* İstanbul Boğazı
Karaferiye *see* Véroia
Karaganda *312 Kaz.* Qaraghandy.
C Kazakhstan
Karaitivu *506* N Sri Lanka
Karaj *281* NW Iran
Karak *see* Al Karak
Kara-Kala *553 var.* Garrygala. SW
Turkmenistan
Karaklin *see* Vanadzar
Karakol *325 var.* Karakolka.
E Kyrgyzstan
Karakol *325 prev.* Przheval'sk,
var. Prževalsk. NE Kyrgyzstan
Karakoram Range *270, 421* mountain
range of C Asia
Karakose *549* NE Turkey
Kara-Kul' *325 Kir.* Kara-Köl.
W Kyrgyzstan
Karakul' *see* Qorakül
Karakul' *see* Qarokül
Karakul', Ozero *see* Qarokül
Karakumskiy Kanal *553*
Turkm. Garagum Kanaly. Canal of
SE Turkmenistan
Karakumy *553 Eng.* Kara Kum,
Turkm. Garagum, *var.* Qara Qum.
Desert region of C Turkmenistan
Karaman *549* S Turkey
Karamay *162 var.* Karamai,
Chin. K'o-la-ma-i. Xinjiang Uygur
Zizhiqu, NW China
Karamea Bight *401* area of the
Tasman Sea, on the NW coast
of South Island, New Zealand
Kara-Say *325* E Kyrgyzstan
Karasburg *391* S Namibia
Kara Sea *see* Karskoye More
Karasjok *411* NE Norway
Kara Su *see* Mesta, Néstos
Karatau *312 Kaz.* Qarataū.
S Kazakhstan
Karatsu *304* Kyūshū, SW Japan
Karavastasë, Laguna e *57*
var. Kënet' e Karavastas, Kravasta
Lagoon. Lagoon of W Albania
Karawang *276 prev.* Krawang. Java,
C Indonesia
Karawanken *82 Slvn.* Karavanke.
Mountain range of C Europe
Karbalā' *284 var.* Kerbala. C Iraq
Kardítsa *245* C Greece
Kärdla *212 Ger.* Kertel. Hiiumaa,
Estonia
Kareliya, Respublika *454*
autonomous republic of NW Russia
Karen *see* Hualien
Kari *see* Chiali

Kariba *614* N Zimbabwe
Kariba Dam *614* dam at NE end of
Lake Kariba, on Zambezi river,
NW Zimbabwe
Kariba, Lake *613, 614* reservoir of
Zambia and Zimbabwe
Karibib *391* C Namibia
Karimama *108* N Benin
Karimata, Selat *276* strait connecting
Laut Jawa and the South China Sea,
E Indonesia
Karisimbi, Volcan *462 var.* Mount
Karisimbi. Mountain of Rwanda and
Zaire
Karkaralinsk *312* E Kazakhstan
Karkar Island *428* island of NE Papua
New Guinea
Karkinits'ka Zatoka *558*
Rus. Karkinitskiy Zaliv. Gulf of the
Black Sea, S Ukraine
Karleby *see* Kokkola
Karl-Marx-Stadt *see* Chemnitz
Karlö *see* Hailuoto
Karlovac *181 Ger.* Karlstadt,
Hung. Károlyváros. N Croatia
Karlovo *128 prev.* Levskigrad.
C Bulgaria
Karlovy Vary *188 Ger.* Karlsbad,
var. Carlsbad. W Czech Republic
Karlsbad *see* Karlovy Vary
Karlskrona *515* S Sweden
Karlsruhe *236 var.* Carlsruhe.
SW Germany
Karlstad *515* SW Sweden
Karlstadt *see* Karlovac
Karmi 'él *291* N Israel
Karnali *395 var.* Kauriala. River of
W Nepal
Karnobat *128* E Bulgaria
Karoi *614* N Zimbabwe
Károlyváros *see* Karlovac
Karonga *353* N Malawi
Karonje, Mount *138* mountain of
W Burundi
Karpasia *187 var.* Karpas Peninsula.
Peninsular of NE Cyprus
Karpaten *see* Carpathian Mountains
Kárpathos *245* island of SE Greece
Karpaty *see* Carpathian Mountains
Karrānah *91* N Bahrain
Kars *549* NE Turkey
Karshi *see* Qarshi
Karskoye More *455 Eng.* Kara Sea. Sea
of Arctic Ocean, bordering
N Russia
Karumba *77* NE Australia
Kartung *233* W Gambia
Kārūn *281* river of W Iran
Karungu Bay *316* bay of Lake Victoria,
to the SW of Kenya
Karuzi *138* C Burundi
Karviná *188 Ger.* Karwin. E Czech
Republic
Karzakkān *91* NW Bahrain
Kas *549* SW Turkey
Kasai *64, 609 var.* Kassai, Cassai. River
of Angola and Zaire
Kasama *613* N Zambia
Kasan *see* Koson
Kasane *118* N Botswana
Kasari *212* river of W Estonia
Kasbegi *see* Qazbegi
Kaschau *see* Košice
Kasese *556* SW Uganda
Kashaf Rūd *281* river of NE Iran
Kāshān *281* NW Iran
Kashgar *see* Kashi
Kashi *162 Uigh.* Kashgar. Xinjiang
Uygur Zizhiqu, NW China
Kashiwa *304* Honshū, SE Japan
Kashiwazaki *304* Honshū, N Japan
Käsmark *see* Kežmarok
Kasongo *609* E Zaire
Kaspi *234* C Georgia
Kaspiyskoye More *see* Caspian Sea
Kaspiy Tengizi *see* Caspian Sea
Kassa *see* Košice
Kassai *see* Kasai
Kassala *508 var.* Kassalā, Kasala.
E Sudan
Kassándra *245* peninsula of
NE Greece
Kassel *236 prev.* Cassel. C Germany

Kasserine *545 var.* Al-Qaṣrayn.
W Tunisia
Kassikaityu *256* river of S Guyana
Kastamonu *549* N Turkey
Kastsyukovichy *104* E Belorussia
Kasugai *304* Honshū, C Japan
Kasulu *532* W Tanzania
Kasumiga-ura *304* lake of Honshū,
SE Japan
Kasungu *353* C Malawi
Kasupe *see* Machinga
Katchang *233* C Gambia
Kateríni *245* N Greece
Katete *613* E Zambia
Katha *135* N Burma
Katherina, Gebel *202*
var. Jabal Katrīnah,
Eng. Mt. Catherine. Mountain
of NE Egypt
Katherine *77* N Australia
Kathmandu *395 prev.* Kāntipur.
❖ of Nepal, C Nepal
Kati *360* SW Mali
Katima Mulilo *391 var.* Ngweze.
NE Namibia
Katiola *300* C Ivory Coast
Kat O Chau *262* NE Hong Kong
Katonga *556* river of SW Uganda
Katowice *441 Ger.* Kattowitz. S Poland
Katrīnah, Jabal *see* Katherina, Gebel
Katsina *408* N Nigeria
Kattaqŭrghon *582 Rus.* Kattakurgan.
SE Uzbekistan
Kattegat *190, 515* strait between
Denmark and Sweden
Katumbi *353* NW Malawi
Katwijk aan Zee *397*
W Netherlands
Kauai *570* island of Hawaii, USA,
C Pacific
Kaufbeuren *237* S Germany
Kaunas *344 Ger.* Kauen, *Pol.* Kowno,
Rus. Kovno. C Lithuania
Kauno Marios *344* reservoir of
S Lithuania
Kauriala *see* Karnali
Kau Sai Chau *262* E Hong Kong
Kaushany *see* Căuşeni
Kau-Ur *233* N Gambia
Kavadarci *349* S FYR Macedonia
Kavajë *57 It.* Cavaia. W Albania
Kavála *245 prev.* Kaválla. NE Greece
Kavango *see* Cubango
Kavaratti Island *270* island of
Lakshadweep, SW India
Kavengo *see* Cubango
Kavieng *428 var.* Kaewieng. New
Ireland I, Papua New Guinea
Kavīr, Dasht-e *281* desert region of
N Iran
Kavirondo Gulf *see* Winam Gulf
Kavkaz *see* Caucasus
Kawagoe *304* Honshū, SE Japan
Kawambwa *613* N Zambia
Kawasaki *304* Honshū, SE Japan
Kaya *133* C Burkina
Kayagangiri, Mont *155* mountain of
W Central African Republic
Kayan *276* river of Borneo,
C Indonesia
Kayan *135* S Burma
Kayangel Islands *425* island group
of N Palau
Kayanza *138* N Burundi
Kayes *360* SW Mali
Kayl *346* S Luxembourg
Kayogoro *138* S Burundi
Kayokwe *138* C Burundi
Kayrakkumskoye Vodokhranilishche
see Qayrokkum, Obanbori
Kayseri *549* C Turkey
Kayts *506* island of N Sri Lanka
Kazakh *see* Qazax
Kazakhskiy Melkosopochnik *312*
Eng. Kazakh Uplands. Uplands of
C Kazakhstan
Kazakhstan *312-315* officially Republic
of Kazakhstan, *Kaz.* Qazaqstan, *prev.*
Kazakh SSR. *Rus.* Kazakhskay SSR.
Country of C Asia divided into 19
admin. units (provinces).
❖ Almaty
Kazakh Uplands
see Kazakhskiy Melkosopochnik

Kazan' *454* W Russia
Kazandzhik *see* Gazandzhyk
Kazanlŭk *128 var.* Kazanlăk, Kazanlik. C Bulgaria
Kazan-rettō *304 Eng.* Volcano Islands. Island group to the SE of Honshū, SE Japan
Kazarman *325* C Kyrgyzstan
Kazbek *234* mountain of N Georgia
Kazi Magomed *see* Qazimämmäd
Kazincbarcika *264* NE Hungary
Kazvin *see* Qazvin
Kéa *245* island of SE Greece
Kéamu *see* Anatom
Kebili *545 var.* Qibilī. C Tunisia
Kebnekaise *515* mountain of N Sweden
Kecskemét *264* C Hungary
Kėdainiai *344* C Lithuania
Kediet ej Jill *366 var.* Kediet Ijill, Kédia d'Idjil. Mountain of NW Mauritania
Kediri *276* Java, C Indonesia
Kédougou *478* SE Senegal
Keeling Islands *see* Cocos Islands
Keelung *see* Chilung
Keetmanshoop *391* S Namibia
Kefallinía *245 Eng.* Cephalonia. Island of W Greece
Kefar Sava *291* C Israel
Kefar Tappuaḥ *292* C West Bank
Keflavík *268 var.* Iceflavik. W Iceland
Kegalla *506 var.* Kegalle. C Sri Lanka
Kegel *see* Keila
Kei Islands *see* Kai, Kepulauan
Keijō *see* Seoul
Keila *212 Ger.* Kegel. NW Estonia
Keila *212 var.* Keila Jõgi. River of NW Estonia
Keishū *see* Kyŏngju
Kéita *156 var.* Doka. River of S Chad
Keïta *407* SW Niger
Keitele *221* lake of C Finland
Këk-Art *325 prev.* Alaykel'. SW Kyrgyzstan
Kékes *264* mountain of N Hungary
Kelang *354 var.* Klang, *prev.* Port Swettenham. W Peninsular Malaysia
Kelantan *354* river of N Peninsular Malaysia
Kelbia, Sebkhet *545 var.* Sabkhat Kalbīyah. Salt flat of NE Tunisia
Këlcyrë *57 var.* Këlcyra. S Albania
Kelifskiy Uzboy *553* region of SE Turkmenistan
Kéllé *176* W Congo
Kelmė *344* NW Lithuania
Kélo *156* SW Chad
Kelowna *146* SW Canada
Keluang *354 var.* Kluang. SE Peninsular Malaysia
Kembolcha *215 var.* Kombolcha. N Ethiopia
Kemerovo *455 prev.* Shcheglovsk. C Russia
Kemi *221* NW Finland
Kemijärvi *221* N Finland
Kemijoki *221* river of NW Finland
Kemin *325 prev.* Bystrovka. N Kyrgyzstan
Kemiö *see* Kimito
Kemmuna *363* island of NW Malta
Kemmunett *363* island of NW Malta
Kempen *99 Fr.* Campine, *Ger.* Kempenland. Heathland of NE Belgium
Kempten *237* S Germany
Kenema *482* SE Sierra Leone
Këneurgench *553 prev.* Kunya-Urgench, Kunja-Urgenč, *Turkm.* Köneür gench. N Turkmenistan
Kénitra *382 prev.* Port Lyautey. NW Morocco
Kenmare *288* SW Ireland
Kentau *312* S Kazakhstan
Kentucky *571* state of C USA
Kenya *316-319* officially Republic of Kenya. Country of E Africa divided into 7 admin. units (provinces). ❖ Nairobi
Kenya, Mount *see* Kirinyaga

Keppel Harbour *485* harbour, S Singapore
Keppel Island *see* Niuatoputapu
Kerava *221 Swe.* Kervo. S Finland
Kerch *558 Rus.* Kerch'. SE Ukraine
Kerema *428* S Papua New Guinea
Keren *210 var.* Cheren. C Eritrea
Kerewan *233* W Gambia
Kericho *316* W Kenya
Kerio *316* river of W Kenya
Kerkenah, Îles *545 var.* Kerkenna Islands, *Ar.* Juzur Qarqannah. Island group of E Tunisia
Kerki *553* SE Turkmenistan
Kerkrade *397* S Netherlands
Kérkyra *245 prev.* Kérkira, *Eng.* Corfu. Island of W Greece
Kérkyra *245 Eng.* Corfu, *prev.* Kérkira. W Greece
Kermān *281 var.* Kirman. SE Iran
Kermānshāh *see* Bākhtarān
Kerora *210* N Eritrea
Kérouané *253* SE Guinea
Kertel *see* Kärdla
Kerulen *380 var.* Herlen Gol. River of China and Mongolia
Kervo *see* Kerava
Keryneia *see* Girne
Kesen'-numa *305* Honshū, N Japan
Késmárk *see* Kežmarok
Kesra *545 var.* Kisrah. NW Tunisia
Keta *242* SE Ghana
Ketchikan *570* Alaska, USA
Kete-Krachi *242 var.* Kete Krakye. E Ghana
Kétou *108* SE Benin
Kettharin Island *see* Kanmaw Island
Keur Massène *366* SW Mauritania
Kévé *539* SW Togo
Kew *631* North Caicos, NW Turks and Caicos Islands
Kežmarok *487 Ger.* Käsmark, *Hung.* Késmárk. NE Slovakia
Khabarovsk *455* SE Russia
Khabura *see* Al Khaburah
Khachmas *see* Xaçmaz
Khairpur *421* S Pakistan
Khakasiya, Respublika *455* autonomous republic of C Russia
Khakassk *see* Abakan
Khakhea *118 var.* Kakia. S Botswana
Khalándrion *see* Chalándri
Khalkidhikí *see* Chalkidikí
Khalkís *see* Chalkída
Khalūf *418 var.* Al Khaluf. S Oman
Khambhat, Gulf of *270 Eng.* Gulf of Cambay. Gulf of Arabian Sea to the W of India
Khamir *601 var.* Khamr. W Yemen
Khamīs Mushayṭ *474* S Saudi Arabia
Khānābād *53* NE Afghanistan
Khānaqīn *284* E Iraq
Khānewāl *421* NE Pakistan
Khanh Hung *see* Soc Trăng
Khanka, Lake *163, 455 var.* Lake Hanka, *Rus.* Ozero Khanka, *Chin.* Xingkai Hu, Hsing-K'ai Hu. Lake of China and Russia
Khanka, Ozero *see* Khanka, Lake
Khanty-Mansiysk *454 prev.* Ostyako-Voguls'k. C Russia
Khānpur *421* SE Pakistan
Khān Yūnis *291, 292 Ar.* Khan Yunus. Gaza Strip
Kharāb, Ghoubbet el *194* bay at the head of Golfe de Tadjoura, E of Djibouti
Kharanah *see* Al Kir'ānah
Khāriān *421* NE Pakistan
Kharīṭ, Wâdi el *202 var.* Wādī al Kharīṭ. Dry watercoursef SE Egypt
Kharkiv *558 Rus.* Khar'kov. NE Ukraine
Kharmanli *128 var.* Harmanli. S Bulgaria
Khartoum *508 var.* Al Khurṭūm. ❖ of C Sudan
Khartoum North *508 var.* Al Khurṭūm al Baḥrī. E Sudan
Khasab *see* Al Khaṣab
Khāsh Rūd *53* river of W Afghanistan
Khashuri *234* C Georgia

Khaskovo *128 var.* Haskovo. S Bulgaria
Khatt *see* Al Khaṭṭ
Khawr al Bazm *562 var.* Khor al Bizm. Inlet of the Persian Gulf, on the coast of United Arab Emirates
Khawr al 'Udayd *449 var.* Khor al Udeid. Inlet of the Persian Gulf on the coast of SE Qatar
Duwayhin, Khawr *562* inlet of the Persian Gulf, on the coast of United Arab Emirates
Khawr Fakkān *562 var.* Khor Fakkan. NE United Arab Emirates
Khaydarkan *325 var.* Khaydarken, Hajdarken. SW Kyrgyzstan
Khazar, Baḩr-e *see* Caspian Sea
Khazar, Daryā-ye *see* Caspian Sea
Khenchela *59 var.* Khenchla. NE Algeria
Khénifra *382* C Morocco
Kherson *558 var.* Cherson. S Ukraine
Khezqazghan *see* Zhezkazgan
Khios *see* Chíos
Khiwa *582 Uzb.* Khiwa. W Uzbekistan
Khmel 'nyts'kyy *558 Rus.* Khmel'nitskiy, *prev.* Proskurov. W Ukraine
Khodzhent *see* Khujand
Khodzheyli *see* Khujayli
Khoi *see* Khvoy
Khojend *see* Khujand
Kholm *53* N Afghanistan
Khomeynīshahr *281 prev.* Homāyūnshahr. W Iran
Khoms *see* Al Khums
Khong Sedone *see* Muang Khôngxédôn
Khon Kaen *535 var.* Muang Khon Kaen. N Thailand
Khor al Udeid *see* Khawr al 'Udayd
Khôr 'Angar *194* NE Djibouti
Khorixas *391* NW Namibia
Khorramābād *281* W Iran
Khorramshahr *281 prev.* Khūnīnshahr. W Iran
Khorugh *530 var.* Horug, *Rus.* Khorog. S Tajikistan
Khotan *see* Hotan
Khouribga *382* C Morocco
Khowst *53* E Afghanistan
Khoyniki *104* SE Belorussia
Khrysokhou Bay *187 var.* Chrysochou Bay. Bay of the Mediterranean Sea, on the NW coast of Cyprus
Khujand *530 prev.* Leninabad, Khodzhent, Khojend. NW Tajikistan
Khujayli *582 Rus.* Khodzheyli. W Uzbekistan
Khulna *93* SW Bangladesh
Khūnīnshahr *see* Khorramshahr
Khurīyā Murīyā, Jazā'ir *see* alānīyāt, Juzur al
Khurramshahr *see* Khorramshahr
Khushāb *421* NE Pakistan
Khvoy *281 var.* Khoi. NW Iran
Khyber Pass *53, 421* mountain pass connecting Afghanistan with Pakistan
Kia *490* SW Santa Isabel, Solomon Is
Kiamusze *see* Jiamusi
Kiangsi *see* Jiangxi
Kiangsu *see* Jiangsu
Kiayi *see* Chiai
Kibondo *532* NW Tanzania
Kibre Mengist *215 var.* Adola. S Ethiopia
Kibungo *462 var.* Kibungu. SE Rwanda
Kibuye *462* W Rwanda
Kičevo *349* W FYR Macedonia
Kidaho *462* NW Rwanda
Kiel *237* N Germany
Kiel Bay *190, 237 Ger.* Kieler Bucht. Bay of the Baltic Sea
Kielce *441* S Poland
Kieler Bucht *see* Kiel Bay
Kieta *428* Bougainville I, Papua New Guinea
Kiev *558 Ukr.* Kyyiv, *Rus.* Kiyev. ❖ of Ukraine, N Ukraine
Kiffa *366* S Mauritania
Kigali *462* ❖ of Rwanda, C Rwanda
Kigembe *462* S Rwanda

Kigoma *532* W Tanzania
Kigwena *138* SW Burundi
Kikila, Lac *138* lake of Île Uvea, S Wallis & Futuna
Kihnu *212* island of SW Estonia
Kikládhes *see* Kyklades
Kikori *428* river of C Papua New Guinea
Kikwit *609* W Zaire
Kilchu *413* NE North Korea
Kili *364* island of S Marshall Islands
Kilien Mountains *see* Qilian Shan
Kilifi *316* SE Kenya
Kilimanjaro *532* mountain of NE Tanzania
Kilingi-Nõmme *212 Ger.* Kurkund. S Estonia
Kilinochchi *506* N Sri Lanka
Kilis *549* S Turkey
Kilkee *288* W Ireland
Kilkenny *288 Ir.* Cill Choinnigh. SE Ireland
Kilkís *245* N Greece
Kilkoch *288* E Ireland
Killarney *288 Ir.* Cill Airne. SW Ireland
Kilmarnock *565* SW Scotland, UK
Kilosa *532* C Tanzania
Kilwa Masoko *532* SE Tanzania
Kimbe *428* New Britain , Papua New Guinea
Kimberley *495* Northern Cape, C South Africa
Kimberley Plateau *76* plateau of NW Australia
Kimch'aek *413 prev.* Sŏngjin. E North Korea
Kimch'ŏn *498* C South Korea
Kimhae *498* SE South Korea
Kimito *221 Swe.* Kemiö. Island of SW Finland
Kimje *498* SW South Korea
Kinabatangan *354* river of NE Borneo, Malaysia
Kinabalu, Gunung *354* mountain of N Borneo, Malaysia
Kindamba *176* S Congo
Kindia *253* SW Guinea
Kindu *609* C Zaire
King George Bay *623* bay of the South Atlantic Ocean, W Falkland Islands
King George Land *66* island of South Shetland Islands, Antarctica
King Island *77* island of SE Australia
King Island *see* Kadan I
Kingissepp *see* Kuressaare
King's Lynn *565* E England, UK
King's Mills *625* SW Guernsey
Kingston *147* SE Canada
Kingston *303* ❖ of Jamaica, E Jamaica
Kingston *628* ❖ of Norfolk Island, S Norfolk Island
Kingston upon Hull *565 var.* Hull. NE England, UK
Kingstown *468* ❖ of St. Vincent & the Grenadines, SW St. Vincent
King William Island *146 var.* King William. Island of N Canada
Kinihira *462* N Rwanda
Kinkala *176* S Congo
Kinneret-Negev Conduit *291* canal of S Israel
Kinsale *627* SW Montserrat
Kinshasa *609 prev.* Léopoldville. ❖ of Zaire, W Zaire
Kintampo *242* C Ghana
Kinyeti *508* mountain of S Sudan
Kinyinya *138* SW Burundi
Kioa *218* island to the E of Vanua Levu, N Fiji
Kipengere Range *532* SW Tanzania
Kipushi *609* SE Zaire
Kirakira *490* San Cristobal I, Solomon Islands
Kirambo *462* N Rwanda
Kirdzhali *see* Kŭrdzhali
Kirehe *462* SE Rwanda
Kirghizia *see* Kyrgyzstan
Kirghiz Range *325 Rus.* Kirgizskiy Khrebet, *prev.* Alexander Range. Mountain range of Kazakhstan and Kyrgyzstan
Kirghiz Steppe *312* plain of W Kazakhstan

Korolevu *218* Viti Levu, W Fiji
Koror *425* ❖ of Palau, C Palau
Kőrös *see* Križevci
Körös *264* river of E Hungary
Koro Sea *218* sea of the Pacific Ocean, C Fiji
Korosten' *558* NW Ukraine
Koro Toro *156* C Chad
Korovou *218* Viti Levu, W Fiji
Korsør *190* Sjælland, S Denmark
Kortrijk *99* *Fr.* Courtrai. W Belgium
Korucam Burnu *see* Kormakiti, Cape
Koryakskoye Nagor'ye *455*
  Eng. Koryak Range. Mountain range of NE Russia
Kŏryŏ *see* Kangnŭng
Kos *245* island of SE Greece
Kosan *413* SE North Korea
Kosciusko, Mount *77* mountain of SE Australia
Koshikijima-rettō *304* island group to the W of Kyūshū, SW Japan
Kōshū *see* Kwangju
Košice *487* *Ger.* Kaschau, *Hung.* Kassa. E Slovakia
Kôsin' i Kelifely *350* *var.* Causse du Kelifely. NW Madagascar
Koson *582* *Rus.* Kasan. S Uzbekistan
Kosŏng *413* SE North Korea
Kosovo *604* *prev.* Autonomous Province of Kosovo and Metohija. Region of S Serbia, Yugoslavia
Kosovska Mitrovica *604*
  prev. Titova Mitrovica,
  prev. Mitrovica, *Alb.* Mitrovicë.
  S Serbia, Yugoslavia
Kosrae *374* *prev.* Kusaie. Island of E Micronesia
Köstence *see* Constanţa
Kosti *508* *var.* Kūstī. C Sudan
Kostroma *454* NW Russia
Koszalin *441* *Ger.* Köslin. NW Poland
Kota *270* *prev.* Kotah. NW India
Kota Bharu *354* N Peninsular Malaysia
Kota Kinabalu *355* *prev.* Jesselton. N Borneo, Malaysia
Kota Kota *see* Nkhotakota
Kotel'nyy, Ostrov *455* island of Novosibirskiye Ostrova, N Russia
Kotido *556* NE Uganda
Kotka *221* S Finland
Kotlas *454* NW Russia
Kotonu *see* Cotonou
Kotovsk *see* Hinceşti
Kottbus *see* Cottbus
Kotte *see* Sri Jayawardenapura
Kotto *155* river of C Africa
Kotu Group *540* island group of W Tonga
Kouandé *108* NW Benin
Kouango *155* S Central African Republic
Koubia *253* NW Guinea
Koudougou *133* C Burkina
Kouffo *108* river of S Benin
K'ouhu *527* W Taiwan
Kouilou *176* river of S Congo
Kouklia *187* *var.* Kophinou, Kofinou. SW Cyprus
Kouklia Reservoir *187*
  var. Köprülü Rezevuar. Reservoir of E Cyprus
Koulamoutou *230* C Gabon
Koulikoro *360* SW Mali
Koulountou *253, 478* river of Guinea and Senegal
Koumac *628* W New Caledonia
Koumandou *253* SE Guinea
Koumra *156* S Chad
Koundâra *253* NW Guinea
Koungheul *478* C Senegal
Koupéla *133* C Burkina
Kouri *187* river of S Cyprus
Kourou *623* N French Guiana
Kouroussa *253* C Guinea
Kousseir *see* Al Quşayr
Kousséri *144* *prev.* Fort-Foureau. NE Cameroon
Koûta Boûyya *194* SW Djibouti
Kouteifé *see* Al Quţayfah
Koutiala *360* S Mali
Kouvola *221* S Finland
Kouyou *176* river of C Congo

Kovel' *558* NW Ukraine
Kovno *see* Kaunas
Kowkcheh *53* seasonal river of NE Afghanistan
Kowloon *262* *Chin.* Jiulong. SW Hong Kong
Kowno *see* Kaunas
Kowŏn *413* E North Korea
Kowtal-e Khaybar *see* Vākhān, Kūh-e
Kowt-e 'Ashrow *53* E Afghanistan
Kōya, Zē-i *see* Little Zab
Koysanjaq *see* Koi Sanjaq
Kozan *549* S Turkey
Kozáni *245* N Greece
Kozara *116* mountain range of NW Bosnia & Herzegovina
Kozhikode *see* Calicut
Kpagouda *see* Pagouda
Kpalimé *539* *var.* Palimé. SW Togo
Kpandu *242* E Ghana
Krâchéh *141* *prev.* Kratie. E Cambodia
Kragujevac *604* C Serbia, Yugoslavia
Krainburg *see* Kranj
Kra, Isthmus of *135, 535* strip of land joining Malay Peninsula to Thailand, and separating the Andaman Sea and Gulf of Thailand
Kraków *441* *Eng.* Cracow, *Ger.* Krakau. S Poland
Králánh *141* NW Cambodia
Kralendijk *628* Bonaire, S Netherlands Antilles
Kraljevo *604* *prev.* Rankovićevo. C Serbia, Yugoslavia
Kranj *488* *Ger.* Krainburg. NW Slovenia
Kranji Reservoir *485* reservoir of W Singapore
Krapina *181* river of N Croatia
Krasnodar *454* *prev.* Yekaterinodar. SW Russia
Krasnogor *see* Kallaste
Krasnogvardeysk *see* Bulunghur
Krasnovodsk *see* Turkmenbashi
Krasnovodskiy Zaliv *553*
  Turkm. Krasnowodsk Aylagy. Gulf of the Caspian Sea, on the W coast of Turkmenistan
Krasnoyarsk *455* C Russia
Krasnoyarsk Kray *459* administrative region of C Russia
Krasnyy Luch *558*
  prev. Krindachevka. E Ukraine
Kraszna *264* river of Hungary and Romania
Kratie *see* Krâchéh
Kratovo *349* NE FYR Macedonia
Kraulshavn *624* *var.* Nuussuaq. NW Greenland
Krâvanh, Chuŏr Phmun *141*
  Eng. Cardamom Mountains,
  Fr. Chaîne des Cardamomes. Mountain range of SW Cambodia
Kravasta Lagoon
  see Karavastaë, Laguna e
Krawang *see* Karawang
Kremenchuk *558* *Rus.* Kremenchug. C Ukraine
Kremenchuts'ke Vodokhovyshche *558*
  Rus. Kremenchugskoye Vodokhranilische. Reservoir of C Ukraine
Krems an der Donau *82* N Austria
Kretinga *344* *Ger.* Krottingen. NW Lithuania
Kreuz *see* Križevci
Kreuzlingen *518* NE Switzerland
Kribi *144* SW Cameroon
Krichev *see* Krychaw
Krindachevka *see* Krasnyy Luch
Krishna *270* *prev.* Kistna. River of C India
Kristiansand *414* *prev.* Christiansand. SW Norway
Kristianstad *515* S Sweden
Kristiansund *414* *prev.* Christiansund. SW Norway
Kríti *245* *Eng.* Crete. Island of S Greece
Kritikó Pélagos *see* Sea of Crete
Kriva Palanka *349* NE FYR Macedonia
Krivoy Rog *see* Kryvyy Rih
Križevci *181* *Ger.* Kreuz, *Hung.* Kőrös. NE Croatia
Krk *181* *It.* Veglia. Island of NW Croatia

Krnov *188* *Ger.* Jägerndorf. E Czech Republic
Krŏng Kaôh Kŏng *141* SW Cambodia
Kronstadt *see* Braşov
Kroonstad *495* Orange Free State, C South Africa
Krottingen *see* Kretinga
Krško *488* *prev.* Videm-Krško, *Ger.* Gurkfeld. E Slovenia
Kruševac *604* C Serbia, Yugoslavia
Krugersdorp *495*
  Pretoria-Witwatersrand-Vereeniging, NE South Africa
Krujë *57* *var.* Kruja, *It.* Croia. C Albania
Krung Thep *see* Bangkok
Krung Thep, Ao *535* bay within Gulf of Thailand
Kruševo *349* SW FYR Macedonia
Krušné Hory *see* Erzgebirge
Krychaw *104* *Rus.* Krichev. E Belorussia
Krym *558* *var.* Crimes. Peninsula and region of SE Ukraine
Kryvyy Rih *558* *Rus.* Krivoy Rog. SE Ukraine
Ksar el Kebir *382* NW Morocco
Kuala Belait *126* N Brunei
Kuala Dungun *354* *var.* Dungun. E Peninsular Malaysia
Kuala Kangsar *354* W Peninsular Malaysia
Kuala Lumpur *354* ❖ of Malaysia, W Peninsular Malaysia
Kuala Pilah *354*
  SW Peninsular Malaysia
Kuala Terengganu *354*
  var. Kuala Trengganu. NE Peninsular Malaysia
Kuang-chou *see* Guangzhou
Kuang-hsi *see* Guangxi
Kuang-tung *see* Guangdong
Kuang-yuan *see* Guangyuan
Kuantan *354* E Peninsular Malaysia
Kuba *see* Quba
Kubango *see* Cubango
Kuching *354* N Borneo, Malaysia
Kŭchnay Darvīshān *53*
  SW Afghanistan
Kuçovë *57* *var.* Kuçova, *prev.* Qyteti Stalin. C Albania
Kudara Ghūdara
Kudat *355* NE Borneo, Malaysia
Kudus *276* *prev.* Koedoes. Java, C Indonesia
Kuei-chou *see* Guizhou
Kuei-Yang *see* Guiyang
K'u-erh-lo *see* Korla
Kufranja *see* Kufrinjah
Kufrinjah *310* *var.* Kufranja. NW Jordan
Kuhmo *221* E Finland
Kuito *64* *Port.* Silva Porto. C Angola
Kuivastu *212* *Ger.* Kuiwast. Muhu, Estonia
Kujang *413* W North Korea
Kujū-san *304* mountain of Kyūshū, SW Japan
Kukës *57* *var.* Kuksi, Kukësi. NE Albania
Kukong *see* Shaoguan
Kulai *354* SW Peninsular Malaysia
Kula Kangri *110* mountain of N Bhutan
Kuldiga *330* *Ger.* Goldingen. W Latvia
Kuldja *see* Yining
Kulihao *see* Colihaut
Kulim *354* NW Peninsular Malaysia
Kullorsuaq *624* NW Greenland
Kŭlyab *530* *Rus.* Kulyab. SW Tajikistan
Kulyab *see* Kŭlob
Kum *see* Qom
Kŭm *498* *Jap.* Kin-kō. River of W South Korea
Kumagaya *304* Honshū, SE Japan
Kumaka *256* SE Guyana
Kumamoto *304* Kyūshū, SW Japan
Kumanovo *349* N FYR Macedonia
Kumasi *242* C Ghana
Kumayri *see* Gyumri
Kumba *144* W Cameroon
Kumbo *144* NW Cameroon
Kŭmch'ŏn *413* S North Korea
Kum-Dag *see* Gumdag

Kumho *498* river of SE South Korea
Kumi *498* C South Korea
Kumillā *see* Comilla
Kumo *408* E Nigeria
Kŭmsong *498* *prev.* Naju *Jap.* Rashū. SW South Korea
Kumul *see* Hami
Kunashir *305* disputed island of Kurile Islands, SE Russia
Kunda *212* N Estonia
Kunda *212* *var.* Kunda Jõgi. River of NE Estonia
Kundiawa *428* C Papua New Guinea
Kunduz *53* *var.* Kondūz, Qondūz, Kondoz. NE Afghanistan
Kuneitra *see* Al Qunayţirah
Kunene *see* Cunene
Kungei Ala-Tau *325*
  Rus. Khrebet Kyungëy Ala-Too,
  Kir. Küngöy Ala-Too. Mountain range of Kazakhstan and Kyrgyzstan
Kungrad Qŭnghirot
Kungsbacka *515* SW Sweden
Kunlun Shan *162* mountain range of W China
Kunming *163* *var.* K'un-ming.Yunnan, SW China
K'un-ming *see* Kunming
Kunoy *622* *var.* Kunøisland. Island of N Faeroe Islands
Kunsan *498* *var.* Gunsan, *Jap.* Gunzan. W South Korea
Kuntaur *233* NE Gambia
Kunu *413* W North Korea
Kunya-Urgench *see* Këneurgench
Kuop *374* atoll of C Micronesia
Kuopio *221* C Finland
Kupa *see* Kolpa
Kupang *276* *prev.* Koepang. Timor, C Indonesia
Kupiano *428* SE Papua New Guinea
Kup'yans'k *558* E Ukraine
Kura *86, 234* *Az.* Kür. River of Azerbaijan and Georgia
Kura Kurk *see* Irbe Strait
Kurama Range *530*
  Rus. Kuraminskiy Khrebet. Mountain range of C Asia
Kurashiki *304* Honshū, W Japan
Kürdämir *86* *Rus.* Kyurdamir. C Azerbaijan
Kŭrdzhali *128* *var.* Kirdzhali. S Bulgaria
Kure *304* Honshū, W Japan
Küre Dağları *548* mountain range of N Turkey
Kuressaare *212* *prev.* Kingissepp, *Ger.* Arensburg. SW Estonia
Kurgan *454* C Russia
Kurgan-Tyube *see* Qŭrghonteppa
Kuria Maria Islands *see* Ḩalānīyāt, Juzur al
Kuria Muria Bay *see* Ḩalānīyāt, Khalī al
Kurīgrām *93* N Bangladesh
Kurile Islands *see* Kuril'skiye Ostrova
Kuril'sk *305* Kurile Islands, SE Russia
Kuril'skiye Ostrova *305, 455*
  Eng. Kurile Islands. Partially disputed island group of E Russia
Kurkund *see* Kilingi-Nõmme
Kurmuk *508* SE Sudan
Kurnool *270* S India
Kurram *421* river of Afghanistan and Pakistan
Kuršénai *344* *var.* Kuršenaj, Kuršenai. NW Lithuania
Kursk *454* W Russia
Kuru *110* river of E Bhutan
Kurubonla *482* NE Sierra Leone
Kurume *304* Kyūshū, SW Japan
Kurunegala *506* C Sri Lanka
Kurupukari *256* C Guyana
Kurzeme *330* *Eng.* Courland. Region of W Latvia
Kusaie *see* Kosrae
Kushiro *305* Hokkaidō, N Japan
Kushiro *305* river of Hokkaidō, N Japan
Kushka *see* Gushgy
Kushmurun *312* N Kazakhstan
Kusho *see* Kwangju
Kushtia *93* W Bangladesh

La Pointe *467* E St. Lucia
Lappeenranta *221* *Swe.* Villmanstrand. SE Finland
Lappland *see* Lapland
Lapta *187* *var.* Lapithos. NW Cyprus
Laptev Sea *see* Laptevykh, More
Laptevykh, More *455* *Eng.* Laptev Sea. Sea of Arctic Ocean, bordering N Russia
L'Aquila *295* *var.* Aquila, Aquila degli Abruzzi. C Italy
Larache *382* *prev.* El Araîche. NW Morocco
La Resource *467* S St. Lucia
La Ressource *467* NE St. Lucia
Large Island *248* island to the S of Carriacou, Grenada
Largo, Cayo *182* island of SW Cuba
L'Ariana *see* Ariana
Larieu *196* N Dominica
Lario *see* Como, Lago di
La Rioja *71* NW Argentina
La Rioja *503* autonomous community of N Spain
Lárisa *245* *var.* Larissa. E Greece
Lārkāna *421* SW Pakistan
Larnaca *187* *var.* Larnaka, Larnax. SE Cyprus
Larnaca Bay *187* *var.* Larnaka Gulf. Bay of the Mediterranean Sea, to the SE of Cyprus
la Rochelle *224* W France
la Roche-sur-Yon *224* W France
La Romana *198* SE Dominican Republic
Larvik *414* S Norway
Larvotto *378* N Monaco
La-sa *see* Lhasa
Lascahobas *258* SE Haiti
Lascano *579* SE Uruguay
Las Cruces *570* New Mexico, SW USA
La Selle *see* Selle, Pic la
La Serena *159* N Chile
la Seyne-sur-Mer *225* SE France
Las Heras *71* W Argentina
Lashio *135* NE Burma
Lashkar Gāh *53* SW Afghanistan
La Sila *295* mountain range of S Italy
Las Minas, Cerro *260* mountain of W Honduras
La Soie *see* Wesley
La Soufrière *468* mountain of N St. Vincent, St. Vincent & the Grenadines
Las Palmas *503* *var.* Las Palmas de Gran Canaria. Islas Canarias, SW Spain
La Spezia *294* N Italy
Las Piedras *579* S Uruguay
Las Tablas *426* S Panama
La Tapoa *407* SW Niger
Lastoursville *230* E Gabon
Las Tunas *182* SE Cuba
Las Vegas *570* Nevada, W USA
Lata *490* E Nendö, Solomon Islands
Latacunga *200* C Ecuador
Latagle *330* *Eng.* Latgalia. Region of SE Latvia
Latakia *see* Al Lādhiqīyah
Late *540* island of the Vava'u Group, Tonga
Latina *295* S Italy
La Tortuga, Isla *591* island of N Venezuela
La Trinité *627* E Martinique
Latvia *330-331* officially Republic of Latvia, *Latv.* Latvija, Latvijas Republika, *Ger.* Lettland, *prev.* Latvian SSR, *Rus.* Latviyskaya SSR. Country of NE Europe divided into 26 admin. units (rajons). ❖ Riga
Laudat *196* S Dominica
Lau Group *218* island group of E Fiji
Lauis *see* Lugano
Launceston *77* Tasmania, SE Australia
La Unión *159* C Chile
La Unión *207* SE El Salvador
Laurentian Highlands *147* highlands of E Canada
Lauru *see* Choiseul

Lausanne *518* SW Switzerland
Lautaro *159* C Chile
Lautoka *218* Viti Levu, W Fiji
Laut, Pulau *276* *var.* Laoet. Island to the SE of Borneo, C Indonesia
Laval *147* SE Canada
Laval *224* NW France
Lava, la *623* river of French Guiana and Suriname
Lavant *82* river of S Austria
La Vega *198* *var.* Concepción de La Vega. C Dominican Republic
Laventure *368* NE Mauritius
Lavumisa *512* *prev.* Gollel. S Swaziland
Lawa *510* river of French Guiana and Suriname
Lawdar *601* SW Yemen
Lawton *571* Oklahoma, SC USA
Laxey *625* E Isle of Man
Layjūn *601* C Yemen
Laylá *474* *var.* Laila. C Saudi Arabia
Layou *196* river of W Dominica
Layou *468* W St. Vincent, St. Vincent & the Grenadines
Lazarus Island *see* Sakijang Pelepah, Pulau
Laz Daua *see* Laas Dawaco
Lazovsk *see* Sîngerei
Leal *see* Lihula
Leamhcán *see* Lucan
Leava *631* Île Futuna, N Wallis & Futuna
Lébamba *230* S Gabon
Lebanon *332-333* officially Republic of Lebanon, *Ar.* Al Lubnān. Country of SW Asia divided into 5 admin. units (governorates). ❖ Beirut
Lebap *553* NE Turkmenistan
Lebombo Mountains *495, 512* mountain range of southern Africa
Le Cap *630* peninsula of N Saint Pierre and Miquelon
Le Cap *see* Cap-Haïtien
Le Carbet *627* NW Martinique
Lecce *295* S Italy
Lecco *294* N Italy
Lech *82* river of Austria and Germany
Leduc *146* SW Canada
Lee *288* *Ir.* An Laoi. River of S Ireland
Leeds *565* N England, UK
Leeuwarden *397* *Fris.* Ljouwert. N Netherlands
Leeuwin, Cape *76* cape on the SW coast of Australia
Léfini *176* river of SE Congo
Lefka *187* *var.* Lefke. W Cyprus
Lefkada *245* *prev.* Levkás, *var.* Leucas, *It.* Santa Maura. Island of W Greece
Lefke *see* Lefka
Lefkoniko *see* Geçitkale
Lefkoşa *see* Nicosia
Lefkosia *see* Nicosia
Le François *627* E Martinique
Leganés *503* C Spain
Legaspi *437* *var.* Legzpi. Luzon, N Philippines
Leghorn *see* Livorno
Legnica *441* *Ger.* Liegnitz. W Poland
le Havre *225* N France
Leiah *421* NE Pakistan
Leicester *565* C England, UK
Leiden *397* *prev.* Leyden. W Netherlands
Leie *99* *Fr.* Lys. River of Belgium and France
Léim an Bhradáin *see* Leixlip
Leinster *288* province of E Ireland
Leipzig *237* *Pol.* Lipsk. C Germany
Leivádia *245* *prev.* Levádhia. SE Greece
Leixlip *288* *Ir.* Léim an Bhradáin. E Ireland
Leizhou Bandao *163* *var.* Luichow Peninsula. Peninsula of S China
Lejone *334* N Lesotho
Lek *397* river of SW Netherlands
Lékana *176* W Congo
Le Kartala *174* mountain of Grande Comore, Comoros

Le Kef *545* *var.* Al Kāf, El Kef. NW Tunisia
Lékéti *176* river of W Congo
Lékéti, Monts de la *176* *var.* Monts de la Leketi, Mont de la Lékéti. Mountain range of W Congo
Lékila *230* E Gabon
Lékoni *230* E Gabon
Le Lamentin *627* C Martinique
Le Lorrain *627* NE Martinique
Lélouma *253* W Guinea
Lelydorp *510* N Suriname
Lelystad *397* C Netherlands
le Mans *225* NW France
Lemberg *see* L'viv
Lemdiyya *see* Médéa
Lemesos *see* Limassol
Le Morne Rouge *627* N Martinique
Le Moule *624* NE Guadeloupe
Lempa *207* river of El Salvador and Honduras
Lemsid *382* NW Western Sahara
Le Murge *295* mountain range of S Italy
Lemvig *190* Jylland, W Denmark
Lena *455* River of E Russia
Lengoué *176* *var.* Bokiba. River of C Congo
Lenin *see* Leninsk
Lenina, Ozero imeni *558* lake of E Ukraine
Leninabad *see* Khujand
Leninakan *see* Gyumri
Leningrad *see* St. Petersburg
Leningradskaya *66* CIS research station of Greater Antarctica, Antarctica
Leninogorsk *312* E Kazakhstan
Leninpol' *325* NW Kyrgyzstan
Leninsk *see* Asaka
Leninsk *553* *Turkm.* Lenin. N Turkmenistan
Leninsk *see* Chardzhev
Lenkoran' *see* Länkäran
Lennox, Isla *159* S Chile
Lens *225* N France
Léo *133* SW Burkina
Leoben *82* C Austria
Léogâne *258* S Haiti
León *370* *var.* León de los Aldamas. C Mexico
León *503* NW Spain
León *404* W Nicaragua
Leonardville *391* E Namibia
Leonarisso *see* Ziyamet
León, Cerro *430* mountain of NW Paraguay
Leonding *82* N Austria
Leone *620* Tutuila, W American Samoa
Léopold II, Lac *see* Mai-Ndombe, Lac
Léopoldville *see* Kinshasa
Leova *376* *Rus.* Leovo. SW Moldova
Lepä *598* Upolu, Western Samoa
Lepel' *see* Lyepyel'
Lépontiennes, Alpes *see* Lepontine Alps
Lepontine, Alpi *see* Lepontine Alps
Lepontine Alps *518* *Fr.* Alpes Lépontiennes, *It.* Alpi Lepontine. Mountain range of SE Switzerland
Le Port *630* NW Réunion
le Puy *225* SE France
Léraba *133, 300* river of Burkina and Ivory Coast
Léré *156* SW Chad
Leribe *see* Hlotse
Lérida *see* Lleida
Le Robert *627* E Martinique
Lerwick *565* Mainland, Shetland Islands, NE Scotland, UK
Les Abymes *624* C Guadeloupe
Les Anses-D'Arlets *627* SW Martinique
Les Avirons *630* W Réunion
Lesbos *see* Lésvos
les Escaldes *62* C Andorra
Les Gonaïves *see* Gonaïves
Lesh *see* Lezhë
Lesina *see* Hvar
Leskovac *604* SE Serbia, Yugoslavia
Lesotho *334-335* officially Kingdom of Lesotho, *prev.* Basutoland. Country

of Africa divided into 10 admin. units (districts). ❖ Maseru
Les Saintes *624* island group of S Guadeloupe
Lesser Antarctica *66* physical region of Antarctica
Lesser Caucasus *86, 234* *Rus.* Malyy Kavkaz. Mountain range of SW Asia
Lesser Khingan Range *see* Xiao Hinggan Ling
Lesser Sunda Islands *see* Nusa Tenggara
Les Tantes *248* islands to the N of Grenada island, Grenada
L'Esterre *248* SW Carriacou, Grenada
Lésvos *245* *var.* Lesbos. Island of E Greece
Le Tampon *630* SW Réunion
Lethbridge *146* SW Canada
Lethem *256* *prev.* Rupununi. SW Guyana
Leticia *171* S Colombia
Leti, Kepulauan *276* island group of Maluku, E Indonesia
Letir Ceanainn *see* Letterkenny
Letpadan *135* SW Burma
Letsok-aw Island *135* *var.* Letsutan Island, *prev.* Domel Island. Island of S Burma
Letsutan Island *see* Letsok-aw Island
Letterkenny *288* *Ir.* Letir Ceanainn. N Ireland
Lettland *see* Latvia
Lëtzebuerg *see* Luxembourg
Leucas *see* Lefkada
Leulumoega *598* Upolu, Western Samoa
Leung Sheun Wan Chau *262* E Hong Kong
Leuven *99* *Fr.* Louvain, *Ger.* Löwen. C Belgium
Léva *see* Levice
Le Vauclin *627* SE Martinique
Levera Island *see* Sugar Loaf
Leverkusen *236* W Germany
Levice *487* *Ger.* Lewenz, *Hung.* Léva. SW Slovakia
Levin *401* S North Island, New Zealand
Levkás *see* Lefkada
Levoča *487* *Ger.* Leutschau, *Hung.* Löcse. NE Slovakia
Levskigrad *see* Karlovo
Levuka *218* Ovalau, C Fiji
Lewenz *see* Levice
Lewis, Isle of *565* island of Outer Hebrides, NW Scotland, UK
Lewiston *570* Idaho, NW USA
Lewiston *571* Maine, NE USA
Lexington *571* Kentucky, C USA
Leyte *437* island of E Philippines
Leyte Gulf *437* gulf of the Pacific Ocean, E Philippines
Lezhë *57* *var.* Lezha, *prev.* Lesh, Leshi. NW Albania
Lhasa *162* *var.* La-sa. Xizang Zizhiqu, W China
Lhaviyani Atoll *see* Faadhippolhu Atoll
Lhuntshi *110* E Bhutan
Lhut, Uadi *see* Luud, Waadi
Liamuiga, Mount *464* *var.* Mount Misery. Mountain of C St. Kitts, St. Kitts & Nevis
Liangyungang *163* *var.* Xinpu, Lien-yun. Jiangsu, E China
Liaodong Bandao *163* *var.* Liaotung Peninsula. Peninsula of NE China
Liaoning *163* *hist.* Shenking, Fengtien. Province of NE China
Lib *364* island of C Marshall Islands
Liban, Jebel *332* *Eng.* Lebanon, Mount Lebanon, *Ar.* Jabal Lubnān. Mountain range of C Lebanon
Libau *see* Liepāja
Liberec *188* *Ger.* Reichenberg. N Czech Republic
Liberia *178* NW Costa Rica
Liberia *336-337* officially The Republic of Liberia. Country of West Africa, divided into 9 admin. units (counties). ❖ Monrovia

Liberta 68 S Antigua, Antigua & Barbuda

Libertad 579 S Uruguay

Libertad 102 prev. Pembroke Hall. N Belize

Librazhd 57 var. Librazhdi. E Albania

Libreville 230 ❖ of Gabon, NW Gabon

Libya 338-341 officially The Great Socialist People's Libyan Arab Jamahiriya, prev. Libyan Arab Republic. Country of N Africa, the current administrative structure is not clear. ❖ Tripoli

Libyan Desert 202, 339, 508 Ar. Aş Şahrā' al Libīyah. Desert of N Africa

Libyan Plateau 202, 339 Ar. Aḍ Ḍiffah. Plateau of Egypt and Libya

Licata 295 Sicilia, S Italy

Lichinga 387 N Mozambique

Lichtenburg 495 North West, N South Africa

Lida 104 W Belorussia

Lido di Ostia 295 C Italy

Liechtenstein 342-343 officially Principality of Liechtenstein. Country of C Europe divided into 11 admin. units (communes). ❖ Vaduz

Liège 99 Dut. Luik, Ger. Lüttich. E Belgium

Liegnitz see Legnica

Lieksa 221 E Finland

Lien-yun see Liangyungang

Lienz 82 W Austria

Liepāja 330 Ger. Libau. W Latvia

Lier 99 Fr. Lierre. N Belgium

Liestal 518 N Switzerland

Lievenhof see Līvāni

Liezen 82 C Austria

Lifford 288 N Ireland

Lifou 628 island, Îles Loyauté, E New Caledonia

Lifuka 540 island of Ha'apai Group, Tonga

Ligatne 330 NE Latvia

Ligure, Appennino 294 mountain range of N Italy

Ligure, Mar see Ligurian Sea

Ligurian Sea 225, 294 It. Mar Ligure, Fr. Mer Ligurienne. Area of the Mediterranean Sea, between France and Italy

Lihue 570 Kauai, Hawaii, USA

Lihula 212 Ger. Leal. W Estonia

Liivi Laht see Riga, Gulf of

Likasi 609 prev. Jadotville. SE Zaire

Likiep 364 island of C Marshall Islands

Likouala 176 river of NW Congo

Likouala aux Herbes 176 river of E Congo

Liku 628 E Niue

Lille 225 Dut. Rijssel. N France

Lillebælt 190 Eng. Little Belt, var. Lille Bælt. Straits between Fyn and Jylland, SW Denmark

Lillehammer 414 S Norway

Lillestrøm 414 S Norway

Lilongwe 353 ❖ of Malawi, W Malawi

Lilongwe 353 river of W Malawi

Lima 433 ❖ of Peru, W Peru

Limassol 187 var. Lemesos. SW Cyprus

Limbe 353 S Malawi

Limbe 144 prev. Victoria. SW Cameroon

Limbé 258 N Haiti

Lim Chu Kang 485 area of NW Singapore

Limerick 288 Ir. Luimneach. SW Ireland

Limfjorden 190 fjord of Jylland, NW Denmark

Límni Megáli Préspa see Prespa, Lake

Limni Prespa see Prespa, Lake

Límnos 245 var. Lemnos. Island of E Greece

Limoges 225 C France

Limón 178 E Costa Rica

Limón 260 NE Honduras

Limon, Mont 368 mountain of Rodrigues, Mauritius

Limousin 225 cultural region of C France

Limpopo 118, 387, 391, 614 var. Crocodile. River of southern Africa

Limulunga 613 W Zambia

Linakeng 334 E Lesotho

Linares 159 C Chile

Linares 503 S Spain

Lincoln 565 E England, UK

Lincoln 571 Nebraska, C USA

Lincoln Island 629 island of E Paracel Islands

Linden 256 E Guyana

Lindi 609 river of NE Zaire

Lindi 332 SE Tanzania

Line Islands 182 island group of E Kiribati

Lingayen Gulf 437 gulf of the South China Sea, N Philippines

Lingga, Kepulauan 276 island group to the E of Sumatra, W Indonesia

Linguère 478 N Senegal

Linköping 515 S Sweden

Linyanti 118 river of Botswana and Namibia

Linz 82 N Austria

Lion, Golfe du 225 Eng. Gulf of Lions. Gulf of the Mediterranean Sea to the S of France

Lions Den 614 N Zimbabwe

Lipa 437 Luzon, N Philippines

Lipari Islands see Eolie, Isole

Lipari, Isola 295 island of S Italy

Lipari, Isole see Eolie, Isole

Lipetsk 454 W Russia

Lippstadt 236 W Germany

Lipsk see Leipzig

Liptovský Mikuláš 487 Ger. Liptau-Sankt-Nikolaus, Hung. Liptószentmiklós. C Slovakia

Lira 556 N Uganda

Liranga 176 E Congo

Liri 295 river of C Italy

Lisala 609 N Zaire

Lisbon 444 Port. Lisboa. ❖ of Portugal, W Portugal

Lisburn 565 Northern Ireland, UK

Lisieux 225 NW France

Lismore 77 E Australia

Lissa see Vis

Litani 510, 623 var. Itany. River of French Guiana and Suriname

Litani 332 river of C Lebanon

Litauen see Lithuania

Litavra see Lithuania

Lithgow 77 SE Australia

Lithuania 344-345 officially Republic of Lithuania, Lith. Lietuva, Ger. Litauen, Pol. Litwa, Rus. Litva, prev. Lithuanian SSR, Rus. Litovskaya SSR. Country of E Europe divided into 44 admin. units (disicts). ❖ Vilnius

Litla Dimun 622 island of S Faeroe Islands

Little Abaco 88 island of N Bahamas

Little Alföld 264 plain of Hungary and Slovakia

Little Andaman 270 island of Andaman Islands to the SE of India

Little Barrier Island 401 island to the N of North Island, New Zealand

Little Belt see Lillebælt

Little Cayman 622 island of C Cayman Islands

Little Coco Island 135 island of SW Burma

Little Inagua 88 island of S Bahamas

Little Minch 565 strait of the Atlantic Ocean, NW Scotland, UK

Little Rock 571 Arkansas, SC USA

Little Scarcies see Kaba

Little Sound 621 bay of the North Atlantic Ocean, W Bermuda

Little Tobago 621 island of W British Virgin Islands

Little Tobago 542 var. Bird of Paradise Island. Island to the E of Tobago, Trinidad & Tobago

Little Zab 284 Ar. Žāb aş Şaghīr, Kurd. Zē-i Kya. River of Iran and Iraq

Litva see Lithuania

Litwa see Lithuania

Liuch'iu Yü 527 island of SW Taiwan

Liukuei 527 S Taiwan

Liuzhou 163 var. Liu-chou, Liuchow. Guangxi, S China

Livadhi 187 var. Leivadi. River of W Cyprus

Līvāni 330 Ger. Lievenhof. SE Latvia

Lively Island 623 island of E Falkland Islands

Lively Sound 623 area of the South Atlantic Ocean, E Falkland Islands

Liverpool 565 NW England, UK

Livingston 250 E Guatemala

Livingstone 613 var. Maramba. S Zambia

Livingstonia 353 N Malawi

Livno 116 SW Bosnia & Herzegovina

Livojoki 221 river of C Finland

Livonia see Vidzeme

Livorno 294 Eng. Leghorn. C Italy

Liwonde 353 S Malawi

Liyāḥ, Jāl al 322 ridge of NW Kuwait

Ljouwert see Leeuwarden

Ljubelj see Loibl Pass

Ljubljana 488 var. Lyublyana, Ger. Laibach, It. Lubiana. ❖ of Slovenia, C Slovenia

Ljubrlj see Loibl Pass

Ljungan 515 river of C Sweden

Ljusnan 515 river of C Sweden

Llallagua 112 SW Bolivia

Lleida 503 Cast. Lérida. NE Spain

Llolleo 159 C Chile

Lloydminster 146 SW Canada

Lô 595 river of China and Vietnam

Loaita Island 630 island of W Spratly Islands

Loangwa see Luangwa

Lobatse 118 var. Lobatsi. S Botswana

Lobaye 155 river of SW Central African Republic

Lobito 64 W Angola

Lob Nor see Lop Nur

Locarno 518 Ger. Luggarus. S Switzerland

Lôc Ninh 595 SW Vietnam

Locri 295 S Italy

Lőcse see Levoča

Lod 291 var. Lydda. C Israel

Lodge 464 NE St. Kitts, St. Kitts & Nevis

Lodja 609 C Zaire

Lodwar 316 NW Kenya

Łódź 441 Rus. Lodz. C Poland

Loei 535 var. Muang Loei. N Thailand

Lofa 336 var. Loffa. River of Guinea and Liberia

Lofoten 414 var. Lofoten Islands. Islands of NE Norway

Loga 407 W Niger

Logan, Mount 146 mountain of NW Canada

Logone 144, 156 var. Lagone. River of Cameroon and Chad

Logroño 503 N Spain

Lögurinn 268 var. Lagarfljót. Lake of E Iceland

Loh 587 Torres Islands, N Vanuatu

Loibl Pass 82 var. Ljubelj, Ger. Loiblpass, Slvn. Ljubrlj. Mountain pass of Austria and Slovenia

Loikaw 135 E Burma

Loir 225 river of NW France

Loire 225 river of C France

Loita Hills 316 hilly region of SW Kenya

Loja 200 S Ecuador

Lokeren 99 NW Belgium

Lokitaung 316 NW Kenya

Lokoja 408 C Nigeria

Lokossa 108 S Benin

Loksa 212 Ger. Loxa. N Estonia

Lol 508 river of S Sudan

Lola 253 SE Guinea

Lolland 190 prev. Laaland. Island of S Denmark

Lolotique 207 SE El Salvador

Lolvavana, Passage 587 strait between Maewo and Pentecost, C Seychelles

Lom 128 prev. Lom-Palanka. NW Bulgaria

Lom 144 river of Cameroon and Central African Republic

Lomahasha 512 NE Swaziland

Lomami 609 river of C Zaire

Lomas de Zamora 71 E Argentina

Lombok 276 island of Nusa Tenggara, C Indonesia

Lomé 539 ❖ of Togo, S Togo

Lomond, Loch 565 lake of C Scotland, UK

Lom Sak 535 var. Muang Lom Sak. N Thailand

Londiani 316 W Kenya

London 565, 569 ❖ of United Kingdom

London 147 S Canada

London 320 Kiritimati, E Kiribati

London Bridge 248 island to the N of Grenada island, Grenada

Londonderry 565 var. Derry. Northern Ireland, UK

Londrina 121 S Brazil

Longa, Proliv 455 Eng. Long Strait. Strait connecting Chukchi Sea and East Siberian Sea, between NE Asia and NW North America

Long Bay 621 bay of the North Atlantic Ocean, E Bermuda

Long Bay 621 bay of the North Atlantic Ocean, W Bermuda

Longford 288 Ir. Longphort. C Ireland

Long Island 621 island of W Bermuda

Long Island 565 Arop Island

Long Island 88 island of C Bahamas

Long Island 68 island to the N of Antigua, Antigua & Barbuda

Longmont 571 Colorado, SW USA

Longoni, Baie de 627 var. Longoni Bay. Bay of the Indian Ocean on the N coast of Mayotte

Longphort see Longford

Longreach 77 E Australia

Long Strait see Longa, Proliv

Long Swamp 621 Tortola, C British Virgin Islands

Longwood 630 E St. Helena

Long Xuyên 595 SW Vietnam

Longyearbyen 631 ❖ of Svalbard, Spitsbergen, W Svalbard

Lonhlupheko 512 E Swaziland

Lons-le-Saunier 225 E France

Loop Head 288 promontory on the W coast of Ireland

Lop Buri 535 C Thailand

Lopévi 587 island of C Vanuatu

Lopez, Cap 230 W Gabon

Lop Nur 162 var. Lop Nor, Lob Nor, Chin. Lo-pu Po. Lake of Xinjiang Uygur Zizhiqu, NW China

Lo-pu Po see Lop Nur

Lora, Hāmūn-i- 420 salt marsh of W Pakistan

Lord Howe Island see Ontong Java Atoll

Lorca 503 S Spain

Lorengau 428 var. Lorungau, Manus I, Papua New Guinea

Lorentz 277 river of Irian Jaya, E Indonesia

Loreto 430 C Paraguay

Lorian Swamp 316 swamp E Kenya

Lorient 224 W France

Lorn, Firth of 565 inlet of Atlantic Ocean, W Scotland, UK

Lorraine 225 cultural region of NE France

Los Amates 250 E Guatemala

Los Andes 159 C Chile

Los Angeles 570 California, W USA

Los Ángeles 159 C Chile

Losap 374 atoll of C Micronesia

Los Chiles 178 NW Costa Rica

Los, Îles de 253 Island group to the SW of Guinea

Lošinj 181 It. Lussino. Island of W Croatia

Loslau see Wodzisław Śląski

Los Mochis 370 W Mexico

Losonc see Lučenec

Losontz see Lučenec

Los Roques, Islas 591 island group of N Venezuela

Los Teques 591 N Venezuela

Lot 225 river of S France

Lotofaga *598* Upolu, Western Samoa
Lo-tung *527* *Jap.* Ratō. NE Taiwan
Louang Namtha *327* *var.* Luong Nam Tha. N Laos
Louangphrabang *327* *var.* Luang Prabang. C Laos
Loubiere *196* SW Dominica
Loubomo *176* *prev.* Dolisie. S Congo
Loudima *176* S Congo
Louéssé *176* river of SW Congo
Louga *478* NW Senegal
Loughrea *288* W Ireland
Louis Gentil *see* Youssoufia
Louisiade Archipelago *428* island group of SE Papua New Guinea
Louisiana *571* state of SC USA
Louis Trichardt *495* Northern Transvaal, NE South Africa
Louisville *571* Kentucky, C USA
Louisville *102* N Belize
Loukoléla *176* E Congo
Loum *144* W Cameroon
Louna *176* river of SE Congo
Louny *188* NW Czech Republic
Lourenço Marques *see* Maputo
Lourenço Marques, Baía de *see* Maputo, Baía de
Louvain *see* Leuven
Lovech *128* *var.* Loveč. NW Bulgaria
Lovell Village *468* Mustique, St. Vincent & the Grenadines
Lóvua *64* N Angola
Lowell *571* Massachusetts, NE USA
Löwen *see* Leuven
Lower Bann *565* river of Northern Ireland, UK
Lower California *see* Baja California
Lower Carlton *97* NW Barbados
Lower Hutt *401* S North Island, New Zealand
Lower Lough Erne *565* lake of Northern Ireland, UK
Lower Mortlocks *374* island group of C Micronesia
Lower Rhine *see* Neder-Rijn
Lower Tunguska *see* Nizhnyaya Tunguska
Lower West End Point *620* headland on the SW coast of Anguilla
Low Point *622* headland on the E coast of Christmas Island
Loyada *194* E Djibouti
l'Oyapok *see* Oiapoque
Loyauté, Îles *628* island group of E New Caledonia
Loyoro *556* NE Uganda
Loznica *604* W Serbia, Yugoslavia
Lualaba *609* *var.* Zaire, *Fr.* Loualaba. River of E Zaire
Luampa *613* river of W Zambia
Luanda *64* ❖ of Angola, NW Angola
Luang Prabang *see* Louangphrabang
Luang Prabang Range *327* mountain range of W Laos
Luangwa *613* *Port.* Aruângua. River of Mozambique and Zambia
Luanshya *613* C Zambia
Luapula *609, 613* river of Zaire and Zambia
Luar, Pulu *see* Horsburgh Island
Luba *208* *prev.* San Carlos. W Bioko, Equatorial Guinea
Lubango *64* *Port.* Sá da Bandeira. SW Angola
Lubao *609* SE Zaire
Lübeck *237* N Germany
Lubelska, Wyżyna *441* plateau of SE Poland
Lubiana *see* Ljubljana
Lublin *441* *Rus.* Lyublin. E Poland
Lubnān, Jabal *see* Liban, Jebel
Lubny *558* C Ukraine
Lubumbashi *609* *prev.* Élisabethville. SE Zaire
Luca *112* SW Bolivia
Lucala *64* NW Angola
Lucan *288* *Ir.* Leamhcán. E Ireland
Lucano, Appennino *295* mountain range of S Italy
Lucapa *64* *var.* Lukapa. NE Angola

Lucea *303* NW Jamaica
Lucena *437* Luzon, N Philippines
Lučenec *487* *Hung.* Losonc, *Ger.* Losontz. C Slovakia
Lucerne *see* Luzern
Lucerne, Lake of *see* Vierwaldstätter See
Luchow *see* Hefei
Lucie *510* river of SW Suriname
Luck *see* Luts'k
Lucknow *270* *Hind.* Lakhnau. N India
Lüderitz *391* *prev.* Angra Pequena. SW Namibia
Ludhiāna *270* N India
Ludwigshafen *236* *var.* Ludwigshafen am Rhein. SW Germany
Luebo *609* SW Zaire
Luena *64* *Port.* Luso. E Angola
Lufira, Lac de Retenue de la *609* *var.* Lac Tshangalele. Lake of SE Zaire
Lugano *518* *Ger.* Lauis. S Switzerland
Luganville *587* Espiritu Santo, Vanuatu
Lugards Falls *316* waterfall of SE Kenya
Lugenda *387* river of N Mozambique
Luggarus *see* Locarno
Lugh Ganana *see* Luuq
Lugo *503* NW Spain
Lugoj *450* W Romania
Lugusi *see* Rugusye
Luhans'k *558* *Rus.* Lugansk, *prev.* Voroshilovgrad. E Ukraine
Luiana *64* river of SE Angola
Luichow Peninsula *see* Leizhou Bandao
Luik *see* Liège
Luimneach *see* Limerick
Luján *71* C Argentina
Lukang *527* *var.* Lu-chiang, *Jap.* Rokkō. W Taiwan
Lukapa *see* Lucapa
Lukenie *609* river of C Zaire
Lukhalweni *512* S Swaziland
Lukusashi *613* river of C Zambia
Luleå *515* NE Sweden
Luleälv *515* river of NE Sweden
Lulonga *609* river of NW Zaire
Lulua *609* river of S Zaire
Luluabourg *see* Kananga
Lumbo *387* NE Mozambique
Lumi *428* NW Papua New Guinea
Lumphāt *141* *prev.* Lomphat. NE Cambodia
Lumpungu *see* Rumpungwe
Lund *515* S Sweden
Lunga *613* river of Zambia
Lunga, Isola *see* Dugi Otok
Lungi *482* W Sierra Leone
Lungkiang *see* Qiqihar
Lungwebungu *613* river of Angola and Zambia
Luninyets *104* *Rus.* Luninets. SW Belorussia
Lunsar *482* W Sierra Leone
Lunsemfwa *613* river C Zambia
Luong Nam Tha *see* Louang Namtha
Luoyang *163* Henan, C China
Luque *430* S Paraguay
Lúrio *387* NE Mozambique
Lúrio *387* river of NE Mozambique
Lusaka *613* ❖ of Zambia, SE Zambia
Lushnjë *57* *var.* Lushnja. C Albania
Luso *see* Luena
Lussino *see* Lošinj
Lustenau *82* W Austria
Lusutfu *512* *var.* Usutu, Great Usutu. River of southern Africa
Lü Tao *527* island of SE Taiwan
Lūt, Baḥrat *see* Dead Sea
Lūt, Dasht-e *281* *var.* Kavīr-e Lūt. Desert region of E Iran
Luton *565* C England, UK
Luts'k *558* *Rus.* Lutsk, *Pol.* Łuck. NW Ukraine
Lüttich *see* Liège
Luud, Waadi *492* *It.* Uadi Lhut. Seasonal river of N Somalia
Luuq *492* *It.* Lugh Ganana. SW Somalia

Luvironza *see* Ruvyironza
Luxembourg *346* ❖ of Luxembourg
Luxembourg *346-347* officially Grand Duchy of Luxembourg, *var.* Lëtzebuerg. Country of W Europe divided into 3 admin. units (districts). ❖ Luxembourg
Luxor *202* *Ar.* Al Uqşur. E Egypt
Luz, Costa de la *503* coastal region of SW Spain
Luzern *518* *Fr.* Lucerne. C Switzerland
Luzon *437* island of N Philippines
L'viv *558* *Rus.* L'vov, *Pol.* Lwów, *Ger.* Lemberg. W Ukraine
Lyallpur *see* Faisalābād
Lyangar *see* Langar
Lyckséle *515* N Sweden
Lydda *see* Lod
Lyepyel' *104* *Rus.* Lepel'. N Belorussia
Lyme Bay *565* bay of S England, UK
Lyon *225* *Eng.* Lyons E France
Lys *see* Leie
Lysi *187* *var.* Akdoğan. C Cyprus
Lyublin *see* Lublin
Lyublyana *see* Ljubljana

M

Ma'ān *310* SW Jordan
Maanselkä *221* mountain range of NE Finland
Maardu *212* *Ger.* Maart. N Estonia
Maarianhamina *see* Mariehamn
Maarmorilik *624* W Greenland
Ma'arrat an Nu'mān *523* NW Syria
Maarssen *397* C Netherlands
Maart *see* Maardu
Maas *see* Meuse
Maasmechelen *99* NE Belgium
Maastricht *397* S Netherlands
Maaza Plateau *202* plateau of NE Egypt
Mabalane *387* S Mozambique
Mabanda *230* S Gabon
Mabayi *138* NW Burundi
Mabouya Island *248* island to the W of Carriacou, Grenada
Macao *626* *var.* Macau. Special territory of Portugal, SE China. ❖ Macao
Macapá *121* N Brazil
Macará *200* S Ecuador
Macarsca *see* Makarska
MacArthur *see* Ormoc
Macas *200* SE Ecuador
Macassar *see* Ujungpandang
Macau - Taipa Bridge *626* bridge between Macao & Taipa islands, C Macao
Macdonnell Ranges *77* mountain range of C Australia
Macedonia *348-349* officially the Former Yugoslav Republic of Macedonia, *abbrev.* FYR Macedonia, FYROM, *Mac.* Makedonija. Country of SE Europe divided into 34 admin. units (opcine). ❖ Skopje
Maceió *121* E Brazil
Macenta *253* SE Guinea
Macgillicuddy's Reeks *288* *var.* Macgillicuddy's Reeks Mountains, *Ir.* Na Cruacha Dubha. Mountain range of SW Ireland
Machakos *316* S Kenya
Machala *200* SW Ecuador
Machaneng *118* SE Botswana
Machanga *387* S Mozambique
Machaze *387* SW Mozambique
Machile *613* *var.* Machili. River of SW Zambia
Machinga *353* *var.* Kasupe, Kasupi. S Malawi
Machiques *591* NW Venezuela
Macia *387* *var.* Vila de Macia. S Mozambique
Macías Nguema Biyogo *see* Bioko
Mackay *77* NE Australia
Mackay, Lake *77* salt lake of C Australia
Mackenzie *146* river of NW Canada
Mackenzie Mountains *146* mountain range of NW Canada

Macleod, Lake *76* lake of W Australia
Macomer *294* Sardegna, S Italy
Macon *571* Georgia, SE USA
Mâcon *225* E France
Macouba *627* N Martinique
MacRitchie Reservoir *485* reservoir of C Singapore
Macroom *288* SW Ireland
Macuelizo *260* W Honduras
Ma'dabā *310* *var.* Mādabā. NW Jordan
Madagascar *350-351* officially Democratic Republic of Madagascar, *Malg.* Madagasikara, *prev.* Malagasy Republic. Country of SE Africa divided into 6 admin. units (provinces). ❖ Antananarivo
Madan *128* S Bulgaria
Madang *428* E Papua New Guinea
Madanīyīn *see* Médenine
Mādārīpur *93* S Bangladesh
Madeira *444* *var.* Ilha de Madeira. Madeira Is, Portugal
Madeira *120* river of Bolivia and Brazil
Madeira, Arquipélago da *see* Madeira Islands
Madeira Islands *444* *Port.* Arquipélago da Madeira. Island group to the SW of Portugal
Madina do Boé *see* Boé
Madīnat al Abyār *339* NE Libya
Madīnat al Ka'bān *449* *var.* Al Ka'aban. N Qatar
Madīnat ash Sha'b *601* *prev.* Al Ittiḩād. SW Yemen
Madīnat ash Shamāl *449* *var.* Madinat el Shamal. N Qatar
Madīnat ath Thawrah *523* N Syria
Madinat el Shamal *see* Madīnat ash Shamāl
Madīnat Ḩamad *91* *var.* Hamada Town, Hamad. W Bahrain
Madīnat 'Isá *91* *var.* Isa Town. N Bahrain
Madīnat Khalīfa *449* E Qatar
Madingo-Kayes *176* S Congo
Madingou *176* S Congo
Madison *571* Wisconsin, NC USA
Madiun *276* *prev.* Madioen. Java, C Indonesia
Madlangampisi *512* N Swaziland
Madona *330* *Ger.* Modohn. E Latvia
Madras *270* S India
Madre de Dios *112, 433* river of Bolivia and Peru
Madrid *503* ❖ of Spain, C Spain
Madriu, Riu *82* river of S Andorra
Madura *276* *prev.* Madoera. Island to NE of Java, C Indonesia
Madurai *270* *prev.* Madura. S India
Maebashi *304* Honshū, SE Japan
Mae Name Khong *see* Mekong
Mae Nam Khong *see* Mekong
Mae Nam Moi *see* Thaungyin
Mae Nam Ping *535* river of NW Thailand
Maéwo *587* *prev.* Aurora. Island of C Vanuatu
Mafa'a, Pointe *631* headland of Île Alofi, N Wallis & Futuna
Mafeteng *334* W Lesotho
Mafia *532* island of E Tanzania
Mafou *253* river of C Guinea
Mafraq *see* Al Mafraq
Mafraq *562* C United Arab Emirates
Mafungabusi Plateau *614* plateau of C Zimbabwe
Mafut *562* NE United Arab Emirates
Magadan *455* NE Russia
Magadi *316* SW Kenya
Magadi, Lake *316* lake of SW Kenya
Magallanes *see* Punta Arenas
Magallanes, Estrecho *see* Magellan, Strait of
Magangué *171* N Colombia
Magaria *407* S Niger
Magat *437* river of Luzon, N Philippines
Magburaka *482* C Sierra Leone
Magdalena *171* river of C Colombia
Magdalena *112* N Bolivia
Magdeburg *237* C Germany
Magelang *276* Java, C Indonesia

Magellan, Strait of *71, 159*
Sp. Estrecho de Magallanes. Strait connecting the S Atlantic and S Pacific Oceans between Tierra del Fuego and mainland South America
Magerøya *414 var.* Magerøy. Island of NE Norway
Maggiore, Lake *294, 518 It.* Lago Maggiore. Lake of Italy and Switzerland
Magh Ealla *see* Mallow
Maglaj *116* N Bosnia & Herzegovina
Magnitogorsk *454* C Russia
Mago *218 prev.* Mango. Island of the Lau Group, E Fiji
Magṭa' Lahjar *366* SW Mauritania
Māgura *93* W Bangladesh
Magwe *135 var.* Magway. W Burma
Magyarkanizsa *see* Kanjiža
Magyarország *see* Hungary
Magyaróvár *see* Mosonmagyaróvár
Mahafaly, Lembalemban' *350 var.* Plateau Mahafaly. Plateau of SW Madagascar
Mahaicony Village *256* E Guyana
Mahajamba *350* seasonal river of N Madagascar
Mahajanga *350 prev.* Majunga. N Madagascar
Mahajilo *350* seasonal river of C Madagascar
Mahakali *395* river of India and Nepal
Mahakam *276 var.* Kutai, Koetai. River of Borneo, C Indonesia
Mahalapye *118 var.* Mahalatswe. SE Botswana
Maḥallah al Kubrá *see* El Mahalla el Kubra
Mahamba *512* SW Swaziland
Mahanādi *270* river of E India
Mahanoro *350* E Madagascar
Maha Sarakham *535* NE Thailand
Mahaut *196* W Dominica
Mahavavy *350* seasonal river of N Madagascar
Mahaweli Ganga *506* river of C Sri Lanka
Mahdia *545 var.* Al Mahdīyah, Mehdia. NE Tunisia
Mahdia *256* C Guyana
Mahé *480* island of NE Seychelles
Mahebourg *368* SE Mauritius
Mahenge *532* SE Tanzania
Mahia Peninsula *401* peninsula of E North Island, New Zealand
Mahilyow *104 Rus.* Mogilëv. E Belorussia
Mahina *360* W Mali
Mahiyangana *506* E Sri Lanka
Maḥmūd-e Rāqī *53* NE Afghanistan
Mahmudiya *see* Al Maḥmūdīyah
Mahou *360* S Mali
Mährisch-Ostrau *see* Ostrava
Mährisch-Schönberg *see* Šumperk
Maiana *320* island of the Gilbert Is, W Kiribati
Maicao *171* N Colombia
Mai Ceu *see* Maych'ew
Mai Chio *see* Maych'ew
Maiduguri *409* NE Nigeria
Mailand *see* Milano
Maimāna *see* Meymaneh
Main *236* river of C Germany
Main Camp *see* Banana
Main Channel *626* channel of the Pacific Ocean, S Johnston Atoll
Main Channel *see* Inner Channel
Mai-Ndombe, Lac *609 prev.* Lac Léopold II. Lake of W Zaire
Maine *571* state of NE USA
Maine *225* cultural region of NW France
Maïné-Soroa *407* SE Niger
Mainland *565* Shetland, NE UK
Mainland *565* Orkney, NE UK
Maintirano *350* W Madagascar
Mainz *236 Fr.* Mayence. SW Germany
Maio *152 var.* Vila de Maio. Maio, S Cape Verde
Maio *152* island of SE Cape Verde
Maiquetía *591* N Venezuela
Maissade *258* C Haiti
Maisur *see* Mysore
Maitland *77* E Australia

Maíz, Islas *404 var.* Corn Islands. Island group of E Nicaragua
Maizuru *304* Honshū, C Japan
Majardah, Wādī *see* Mejerda, Oued
Majimbini, Réserve Forestière de *627* forest reserve of C Mayotte
Majorca *see* Mallorca
Majunga *see* Mahajanga
Majuro *364* atoll of SE Marshall Islands
Majuro District *364* district of Majuro, SE Marshall Islands
Makamba *138* S Burundi
Makarska *181 It.* Macarsca. SE Croatia
Makasar *see* Ujungpandang
Makasar, Selat *276 Eng.* Makassar Strait. Strait connecting the Celebes Sea and Laut Flores, C Indonesia
Makassar Strait *see* Makasar, Selat
Makay, Tangorombohitr' i *350 var.* Massif du Makay. Mountains of SW Madagascar
Makebuko *138* C Burundi
Makeni *482* C Sierra Leone
Makgadikgadi *118 var.* Makarikari Pans. Saltpans of NE Botswana
Makhachkala *454 prev.* Petrovsk-Port. SW Russia
Makharadze *see* Ozurget'i
Makhfar al Quwayrah *see* Al Quwayrah
Makin *320* island of the Gilbert Is, W Kiribati
Makira *see* San Cristobal
Makiyivka *558 Rus.* Makeyevka, *prev.* Dmitriyevsk. E Ukraine
Makkah *474 Eng.* Mecca. W Saudi Arabia
Makō *see* MaKung
Makó *264* SE Hungary
Makogai *218* island to the NE of Viti Levu, C Fiji
Makokou *230* NE Gabon
Makona *253* river of S Guinea
Makoua *176* C Congo
Makran Coast *281* coastal region of SE Iran
MaKung *527 Jap.* Makō. P'eng-hu Tao, W Taiwan
Makunudhoo Atoll *358 var.* Makunudu Atoll. Atoll of N Maldives
Makurazaki *304* Kyūshū, SW Japan
Makurdi *408* C Nigeria
Makuti *614* N Zimbabwe
Makwate *118* SE Botswana
Mala *see* Malaita
Malabo *208 prev.* Santa Isabel. ❖ of Equatorial Guinea, N Bioko
Malacca *see* Melaka
Malacca, Strait of *276* strait connecting the Andaman Sea and South China Sea between Malay Peninsula and Sumatra, SE Asia
Malacka *see* Malacky
Malacky *487 Hung.* Malacka. W Slovakia
Maladzyechna *104 Rus.* Molodechno, *Pol.* Molodeczno. NW Belorussia
Málaga *503* S Spain
Malagasy Republic *see* Madagascar
Malaita *490 var.* Mala, Island of C Solomon Islands
Malakal *508 var.* Malakāl. S Sudan
Malambo *171* N Colombia
Malang *276* SE Java, Indonesia
Malange *see* Malanje
Malanje *64 var.* Malange. NW Angola
Malanville *108* NE Benin
Mälaren *515* lake of SE Sweden
Malatya *548* SE Turkey
Malawi *352-353* officially Republic of Malawi, *prev.* Nyasaland, Nyasaland Protectorate. Country of S Africa divided into 3 admin. units (regions). ❖ Lilongwe
Malawi, Lake *see* Nyasa, Lake
Malaya *see* Peninsular Malaysia
Malāyer *281* NW Iran
Malay Peninsula *535* peninsula of Malaysia and Thailand

Malaysia *354-357* officially Republic of Maldives, *prev.* the separate territories of Federation of Malaya, Singapore (left 1965), Sarawak and Sabah (North Borneo). Country of SE Asia divided into 15 admin. units (13 states, 2 federal territories). ❖ Kuala Lumpur
Maldegem *99* NW Belgium
Malden Island *320* island of the Line Is, E Kiribati
Maldives *358-359* Officially Republic of Maldives, Maldivian Divehi. Country of the Indian Ocean divided into 19 admin. units (districts). ❖ Male'
Maldonado *579* S Uruguay
Male' *358 var.* Male. ❖ of Maldives, Male' Atoll, C Maldives
Male *see* Male'
Male' Atoll *358 var.* Kaafu Atoll. Atoll of C Maldives
Malebo Pool *see* Stanley Pool
Malékoula *see* Malekula
Malekula *587 var.* Malakula, *prev.* Mallicolo. Island of W Vanuatu
Mali *360-361* officially Republic of Mali, *prev.* Sudanese Republic, French Sudan. Country divided into 3 admin. units (7 regions and 1 capital district). ❖ Bamako
Malibamatso *334* river of C Lesotho
Mali Hka *135* river of N Burma forming a headstream of the Irrawaddy river
Malindi *316* SE Kenya
Malines *see* Mechelen
Malinga *230* SE Gabon
Malin Head *288* headland on the N coast of Ireland
Mallâq, Wādī *see* Mellègue, Oued
Mallawi *202 var.* Mallawī. C Egypt
Mallicolo *see* Malekula
Mallorca *503 Eng.* Majorca. Island of the Islas Baleares, E Spain
Mallow *288 Ir.* Magh Ealla. SW Ireland
Malmédy *99* E Belgium
Malmö *515* S Sweden
Malmok *628* headland of Bonaire, S Netherlands Antilles
Malo *587* island of W Vanuatu
Maloelap *364* island of E Marshall Islands
Malolo *218* island of the Mamanuca-i-ra Group, W Fiji
Malolos *437* Luzon, N Philippines
Maloma *512* S Swaziland
Malombe, Lake *353* lake of SE Malawi
Malopolska *441* plateau of S Poland
Maloti Mountains *see* Maluti
Malpasso *198* SW Dominican Republic
Mäls *342* S Liechtenstein
Malta *363* island of the Mediterranean Sea, with Gozo and Kemmuna forms the state of Malta
Malta *362-363* officially Republic of Malta. Country of the Mediterranean Sea. ❖ Valletta
Malta Channel *363 It.* Canale di Malta. Strait of Mediterranean Sea between Malta and Sicily
Maltahöhe *391* S Namibia
Malta, Il-Fliegu ta' *363 Eng.* South Comino Channel. Strait of Mediterranean Sea between Kemmuna and Malta islands, NW Malta
Maluku *276 prev.* Spice Islands, *Eng.* Moluccas. Island group of E Indonesia
Maluku, Laut *276 Eng.* Molucca Sea. Sea of the Pacific Ocean, E Indonesia
Malung *515* C Sweden
Maluti *334 var.* Maluti Mountains, Maloti Mountains, Front Range. Mountain range of C Lesotho
Malvinas, Islas *see* Falkland Islands
Malyy Kavkaz *see* Lesser Caucasus
Mamanuca-i-ra Group *218* islands of W Fiji
Mamates *334* NW Lesotho

Mambéré *155* river of SW Central African Republic
Mambili *176* river of W Congo
Mamer *346* SW Luxembourg
Mamfe *144* W Cameroon
Mamiku *467* E St. Lucia
Mamoré *112* river of Bolivia and Brazil
Mamou *253* W Guinea
Mamoudzou *627* ❖ of Mayotte, N Mayotte
Mampong *242* C Ghana
Mamṭalah, Ra's al *see* Mummaṭalah, Ra's al
Mamuno *118* W Botswana
Man *300* W Ivory Coast
Mana *623* NW French Guiana
Manado *276 prev.* Menado. Celebes, C Indonesia
Managua *404* ❖ of Nicaragua, W Nicaragua
Managua, Lago de *404 var.* Xolotlán. Lake of W Nicaragua
Manaḥ *418 var.* Bilād Manaḥ. N Oman
Manakara *350* SE Madagascar
Mana *623* river of C French Guiana
Manama *91 Ar.* Al Manāmah. ❖ of Bahrain, NE Bahrain
Manambaho *350* seasonal river of NW Madagascar
Manambolo *350* river of W Madagascar
Mananjary *350* SE Madagascar
Manantali, Lac de *360* reservoir of W Mali
Manāqīsh *322 var.* Manageesh. S Kuwait
Manas, Gora *582* mountain of NE Uzbekistan
Manatí *629* N Puerto Rico
Manaus *120 prev.* Manáos. NW Brazil
Manbij *523 Fr.* Membidj. N Syria
Manchester *565* N England, UK
Manchester *571* New Hampshire, NE USA
Man-chou-li *see* Manzhouli
Manda Island *316* island of SE Kenya
Mandal *414* SW Norway
Mandalay *135* N Burma
Mandalgovĭ *380* S Mongolia
Mandali *284* E Iraq
Mandaue *437* Cebu, C Philippines
Mandera *316* NE Kenya
Mandeville *303* SW Jamaica
Mandiana *253* E Guinea
Mandidzudzure *see* Chimanimani
Mandié *387* NW Mozambique
Mandimba *387* N Mozambique
Mandji *230* C Gabon
Mandouri *539* N Togo
Manfredonia *295* S Italy
Manga *133* C Burkina
Mangai *609* W Zaire
Mangaia *622* island of Southern Cook Islands, S Cook Islands
Mangalia *450* SE Romania
Mangalmé *156* SE Chad
Mangalore *270* SW India
Mangde *110* river of S Bhutan
Mange *482* NW Sierra Leone
Mango *see* Sansanné-Mango
Mango *see* Mago
Mangoche *see* Mangochi
Mangochi *353 var.* Mangoche, *prev.* Fort Johnson. SE Malawi
Mangoky *350* river of SW Madagascar
Mangula *see* Mhangura
Mania *350* river of C Madagascar
Mangyshlak *312* W Kazakhstan
Manica *387 var.* Vila de Manica. W Mozambique
Manihiki *622* island of Northern Cook Islands, N Cook Islands
Maniitsoq *624 Dan.* Sukkertoppen. SW Greenland
Manikaraku *490* E Guadalcanal, Solomon Is
Manikganj *93* C Bangladesh
Manila *437 var.* Manila City. ❖ of the Philippines, Luzon, N Philippines

Manisa 548 *prev.* Saruhan. W Turkey
Man, Isle of 565, 625 British Crown dependency of the Irish Sea. ❖ Douglas
Manitoba 146 province of S Canada
Manizales 171 W Colombia
Manjimup 76 SW Australia
Mankayane 512 *var.* Mankaiana. W Swaziland
Mankono 300 C Ivory Coast
Mankulam 506 N Sri Lanka
Mannar 506 *var.* Manar. NW Sri Lanka
Mannar, Gulf of 270, 506 gulf of Indian Ocean, to the S of India
Mannar Island 506 island to the N of Sri Lanka
Mannheim 236 SW Germany
Mano 482 SW Sierra Leone
Mano 482 river of Liberia and Sierra Leone
Manombo Atsimo 350 *var.* Manombo. SW Madagascar
Manono 598 Upolu, Western Samoa
Manono 609 SE Zaire
Manorhamilton 288 N Ireland
Manp'o 413 *var.* Manp'ojin. NW North Korea
Manra 320 *var.* Sydney I. Island of the Phoenix Is, C Kiribati
Mansa 613 *prev.* Fort Rosebery. N Zambia
Mansabá 254 NW Guinea-Bissau
Mansajang Kunda 233 E Gambia
Mansa Konko 233 C Gambia
Mansion 464 NE St. Kitts, St. Kitts & Nevis
Mansôa 254 W Guinea-Bissau
Mansôa 254 river of W Guinea-Bissau
Manta 200 W Ecuador
Mantes-la-Jolie 225 *prev.* Mantes-sur-Seine, Mantes-Gassicourt. N France
Mantova 294 *Eng.* Mantua, *Fr.* Mantoue. N Italy
Mantsonyane 334 C Lesotho
Manuae 622 island of Southern Cook Islands, S Cook Islands
Manua Islands 620 island group of E American Samoa
Manukau Harbour 401 harbour of W North Island, New Zealand
Manurewa 401 N North Island, New Zealand
Manus Island 428 *var.* Great Admiralty I. Island of NE Papua New Guinea
Manyame 614 *var.* Panhame, *prev.* Hunyani. River of Mozambique and Zimbabwe
Manyame, Lake 614 *prev.* Robertson, Lake. Reservoir of N Zimbabwe
Manyara, Lake 532 lake of NE Tanzania
Manyoni 532 C Tanzania
Manzanillo 182 SE Cuba
Manzhouli 163 *var.* Man-chou-li. Nei Mongol Zizhiqu, NE China
Manzil Bū Ruqaybah *see* Menzel Bourguiba
Manzil Tamīm *see* Menzel Temime
Manzini 512 *prev.* Bremersdorp. C Swaziland
Mao 156 W Chad
Mao 198 NW Dominican Republic
Maoke, Pegunungan 277 *Dut.* Sneeuw-gebergte, *Eng.* Snow Mountains. Mountain range of Irian Jaya, E Indonesia
Mapoteng 334 NW Lesotho
Mapou 368 N Mauritius
Maputo 387 *prev.* Lourenço Marques. ❖ of Mozambique, S Mozambique
Maputo, Baía de 387 *var.* Baía de Lourenço Marques, *Eng.* Delagoa Bay. Bay on the coast of Mozambique
Mara 256 E Guyana
Marabá 121 NE Brazil
Maracaibo 591 NW Venezuela
Maracaibo, Lago de 591 inlet of Caribbean Sea, NW Venezuela
Maracay 591 N Venezuela
Marada 339 N Libya
Maradi 407 S Niger
Maragarazi 138, 532 *var.* Muragarazi. River of Burundi and Tanzania
Marāgheh 281 *var.* Maragha. NW Iran

Marahoué *see* Bandama Rouge
Marajó, Baía de 121 N Brazil
Marajó, Ilha de 121 island of N Brazil
Marakabei 334 *var.* Marakabeis. C Lesotho
Marakei 320 island of the Gilbert Is, W Kiribati
Maralal 316 C Kenya
Maralik 74 W Armenia
Maramasike 490 island of E Solomon Is
Maramba *see* Livingstone
Marambio 66 Argentinian research station near Antarctic Peninsula, Antarctica
Maramvya 138 SW Burundi
Marandellas *see* Marondera
Marañón 433 river of N Peru
Marash *see* Kahramanmaraş
Maravovo 490 W Guadalcanal, Solomon Is
Marāwiḥ 562 *var.* Merawwah. Island of W United Arab Emirates
Marbella 503 S Spain
Marburg *see* Maribor
Marburg an der Lahn 236 W Germany
Marcal 264 river of W Hungary
Marche 225 cultural region of C France
Marche-en-Famenne 99 SE Belgium
Marchena, Isla 200 island of N Galapagos Is, Ecuador
Marchfield 97 SE Barbados
Mar Chiquita, Lago 71 lake of C Argentina
Marcounda *see* Markounda
Marcovia 260 S Honduras
Mardān 421 N Pakistan
Mar del Plata 71 E Argentina
Mardin 549 SE Turkey
Maré 264 island, Îles Loyauté, E New Caledonia
Mareeq 492 *var.* Mereeg, *It.* Meregh. E Somalia
Marek *see* Dupnitsa
Marfa Ridge 363 ridge of NW Malta
Margarita, Isla de 591 island of N Venezuela
Margate 495 Kwazulu Natal, SE South Africa
Margherita, Lake *see* Ābaya Hāyk'
Margherita Peak 556, 609 mountain of Uganda and Zaire
Marghilon 582 *var.* Margelan, *Rus.* Margilan. E Uzbekistan
Mārgow, Dasht-e- 53 desert of SW Afghanistan
Mari 187 S Cyprus
Marianao 182 NW Cuba
Marías, Islas 370 island of W Mexico
Maria-Theresiopel *see* Subotica
Máriatölgyes *see* Dubnica nad Váhom
Mar'ib 601 W Yemen
Maribo 190 Lolland, S Denmark
Maribor 488 *Ger.* Marburg. NE Slovenia
Marid 562 NE United Arab Emirates
Marie Byrd Land 66 physical region of Greater Antarctica, Antarctica
Marie-Galante 624 island of SE Guadeloupe
Mariehamn 221 *var.* Maarianhamina. Aland, Finland
Mariel 182 NW Cuba
Marienburg *see* Alūksne
Mariental 391 S Namibia
Marigot 624 St. Martin, N Guadeloupe
Marigot 196 NE Dominica
Marigot de Baïla 478 river of SW Senegal
Mariguana *see* Mayaguana
Marijampolė 344 *prev.* Kapsukas. S Lithuania
Marília 121 S Brazil
Marinduque Island 437 island of C Philippines
Maringá 121 S Brazil
Marins, Île aux 630 island of SE Saint Pierre and Miquelon
Marion Island 495 island of Prince Edward Islands , S South Africa

Maripasoula 623 W French Guiana
Mariscal Estigarribia 430 NW Paraguay
Marisule Estate 467 N St. Lucia
Maritsa 128, 245 *var.* Marica, *Gk* Évros, *Turk.* Meriç. River of SE Europe
Mariupol' 558 *prev.* Zhdanov. SE Ukraine
Mariy El, Respublika 454 autonomous republic of W Russia
Märjamaa 212 *Ger.* Merjama. W Estonia
Marjayoun 332 *var.* Marj 'Uyūn. S Lebanon
Marka 492 *var.* Merca. S Somalia
Marka 353 S Malawi
Market Shop 464 SE Nevis, St. Kitts & Nevis
Markounda 155 *var.* Marcounda. NW Central African Republic
Marlánské Lázně 188 W Czech Republic
Marmara Denizi 548 *Eng.* Sea of Marmara. Sea to the W of Turkey
Marmaris 548 SW Turkey
Marne 225 river of NE France
Marneuli 234 S Georgia
Maro 156 S Chad
Maroantsetra 350 NE Madagascar
Maromokotro 350 mountain of N Madagascar
Marondera 614 *var.* Marandellas. NE Zimbabwe
Maroni 507, 623 *Dut.* Marowijne. River of French Guiana and Suriname
Maros *see* Mureş
Marosvásárhely *see* Târgu Mureş
Marotiri 624 island group of S French Polynesia
Maroua 144 N Cameroon
Marovoay 350 NW Madagascar
Marowijne *see* Maroni
Marqūbān 91 NE Bahrain
Marquises, Îles 624 island group of N French Polynesia
Marrakech 382 *var.* Marakesh, *Eng.* Marrakesh, *prev.* Morocco. W Morocco
Marrupa 387 N Mozambique
Marsa 363 C Malta
Marsá al Burayqah *see* Al Burayqah
Marsabit 316 N Kenya
Marsala 295 Sicilia, S Italy
Marsaxlokk 363 SE Malta
Marsaxlokk Bay 363 inlet on the SW coast of Malta
Marseille 225 *prev. Eng.* Marseilles. SE France
Marshall 336 W Liberia
Marshall Islands 364-365 officially Republic of the Marshall Islands. Country of the Pacific Ocean divided into 33 admin. units (districts). ❖ Majuro
Marsh Harbour 88 Great Abaco, Bahamas
Martaban 135 SE Burma
Martadi 395 *var.* Bajura. W Nepal
Martigny 518 SW Switzerland
Martigues 225 SE France
Martin 487 *prev.* Turčiansky Svätý Martin, *Ger.* Sankt Martin, *Hung.* Turócszentmárton. NW Slovakia
Martinique 627 French overseas department of the Caribbean Sea. ❖ Fort-de-France.
Martinique Passage 196 *var.* Dominica Channel, Martinique Channel. Passage connecting the Atlantic Ocean and Caribbean Sea between Dominica and Martinique
Martuni 74 E Armenia
Marungu 609 mountain range of SE Zaire
Mary 553 *prev.* Merv. SE Turkmenistan
Maryborough 77 E Australia
Mary Island *see* Kanton
Maryland 571 state of E USA
Marzūq *see* Murzuq

Masai Steppe 532 grassland of NW Tanzania
Masaka 556 SW Uganda
Masākin *see* M'saken
Masampo *see* Masan
Masan 498 *prev.* Masampo. S South Korea
Masasi 532 SE Tanzania
Masatepe 404 SW Nicaragua
Masaya 404 S Nicaragua
Masbate 437 island of C Philippines
Mascara 59 *var.* Mouaskar. NW Algeria
Maseru 334 ❖ of Lesotho, W Lesotho
Mas-ha 292 W West Bank
Mashava 614 *prev.* Mashaba. SE Zimbabwe
Mashhad 281 *var.* Meshed. NE Iran
Māshkel 281, 420 *var.* Rūd-i Māshkel, Māshkīd. River of Iran and Pakistan
Māshkel, Hāmūn-i 420 salt marsh of Iran and Pakistan
Māshkīd *see* Māshkel
Mashtagi *see* Maştaği
Masīlah, Wādī al 601 dry watercourse of E Yemen
Masindi 556 W Uganda
Masinga Reservoir 316 reservoir of C Kenya
Masirah, Gulf of *see* Maşīrah, Khalīj
Maşīrah, Jazīrat 418 *var.* Masirah, Masira. Island of E Oman
Maşīrah, Khalīj 418 *var.* Gulf of Masirah. Bay of the Arabian Sea, E Oman
Masis 74 SW Armenia
Masjed Soleymān 281 *var.* Masjed-e Soleymān, Masjid-i Sulaiman. W Iran
Maskall 102 NE Belize
Maskanah 523 *var.* Meskene. N Syria
Maskin 418 *var.* Miskin. N Oman
Mask, Lough 288 *Ir.* Loch Measca. Lake of W Ireland
Ma 595 river of Laos and Vietnam
Massa 294 N Italy
Massachusetts 571 state of NE USA
Massacre 196 W Dominica
Massawa 210 *Amh.* Mits'iwa. E Eritrea
Massawa Channel 210 channel of the Red Sea between Dahlak Archipelago and mainland Eritrea
Massenya 156 SW Chad
Massif Central 225 plateau region of C France
Massih 86 *Rus.* Masally. S Azerbaijan
Massoukou 230 *var.* Masuku, *prev.* Franceville. E Gabon
Maştağa 86 *Rus.* Mastaga, *var.* Maştaga, Mashtagi. E Azerbaijan
Masterton 401 S North Island, New Zealand
Masuda 304 Honshū, W Japan
Masunga 118 NE Botswana
Masvingo 614 *prev.* Nyanda, *prev.* Fort Victoria. SE Zimbabwe
Mât 630 river of NE Réunion
Matacawa Levu 218 island of the Yasawa Group, NW Fiji
Matadi 609 W Zaire
Matagalpa 404 C Nicaragua
Matale 506 C Sri Lanka
Matam 478 NE Senegal
Matamoros 370 E Mexico
Matana 138 C Burundi
Matanzas 182 NW Cuba
Matara 506 S Sri Lanka
Mataró 503 E Spain
Mataura 401 river of SW South Island, New Zealand
Matautu 598 Upolu, Western Samoa
Matá-'Utu 631 *var.* Mata Uta. ❖ of Wallis & Futuna, Île Uvea, S Wallis & Futuna
Matela's 334 W Lesotho
Matelot 542 NE Trinidad, Trinidad & Tobago
Matiguás 404 C Nicaragua
Matina 178 E Costa Rica
Matit 57 *var.* Mat. River of C Albania

Metangula 387 N Mozambique
Metapán 207 NW El Salvador
Metema 215 NW Ethiopia
Meterlam see Mehtarlām
Methariam see Mehtarlām
Metković 181 SE Croatia
Metu 215 var. Mattu, Mettu.
 W Ethiopia
Metz 225 NE France
Meuse 99, 225, 397 var. Maas. River of
 W Europe
Mexcala see Balsas
Mexiana, Ilha 121 island of N Brazil
Mexicali 370 NW Mexico
Mexicana, Altiplanicie 370
 Eng. Plateau of Mexico, Mexican
 Plateau. Plateau of N Mexico
Mexico 370-373 officially United States
 of Mexico, Sp. Estados Unidos
 Mexicanos, Méjico. Country of North
 or Central America divided into 31
 admin. units (states). ❖ Mexico City
Mexico City 370 Sp. Ciudad de México.
 ❖ of Mexico, C Mexico
Mexico, Gulf of 182, 370 Sp. Golfo de
 México. Gulf of the Atlantic Ocean, on
 the SE coast of North America
Mexico, Plateau of see Mexicana,
 Altiplanicie
Meyadine see Al Mayādīn
Meymaneh 53 var. Maimana.
 NW Afghanistan
Mezdra 128 NW Bulgaria
Mfanganu Island 316 var. Mfangano
 Island. Island of Lake Victoria,
 SW Kenya
Mfouati 176 S Congo
Mhangura 614 var. Mangula.
 N Zimbabwe
Mhlambanyatsi 512 W Swaziland
Mhlosheni 512 S Swaziland
Mhlume 512 NE Swaziland
Mhlumeni 512 NE Swaziland
Miami 571 Florida, SE USA
Miānwāli 421 NE Pakistan
Michalovce 487 Ger. Grossmichel,
 Hung. Nagymihály. E Slovakia
Michigan 571 state of NC USA
Michigan, Lake 147, 571 Lake of
 NC USA
Micomeseng see Mikomeseng
Micoud 467 SE St. Lucia
Micronesia 374-375 officially
 Federated States of Micronesia, prev.
 Caroline Islands. Country of the
 Pacific Ocean divided into 4 admin.
 units (states). ❖ Palikir
Middelburg 397 SW Netherlands
Middelburg 495 Eastern Cape,
 S South Africa
Middelburg 495 Eastern Transvaal, NE
 South Africa
Middelfart 190 Fyn, SW Denmark
Middle Andaman 270 island of
 Andaman Islands to the SE of India
Middle Atlas see Moyen Atlas
Middlegate 628 C Norfolk Island
Middle Island 464 W St. Kitts, St. Kitts
 & Nevis
Middlesbrough 565 NE England, UK
Middlesex 102 E Belize
Mīdī 601 var. Maydī. NW Yemen
Miercurea-Ciuc 450
 Hung. Csíkszereda. C Romania
Mieres 503 NW Spain
Mi'eso 215 var. Miesso, Meheso.
 C Ethiopia
Mikhaylovgrad see Montana
Mikhaylovka 454 W Russia
Mikkeli 221 Swe. Sankt Michel.
 S Finland
Mikomeseng 208 var. Micomeseng.
 NE Río Muni, Equatorial Guinea
Mikuni-sammyaku 304 mountain
 range of Honshū, N Japan
Milagro 200 SW Ecuador
Milange 387 N Mozambique
Milano 294, 299 Eng. Milan,
 Ger. Mailand. N Italy
Milas 548 SW Turkey
Mildura 77 SE Australia
Mil Düzü 86 Rus. Mil'skaya Step'.
 Physical region of C Azerbaijan
Milgis 316 var. Malgis. River of
 C Kenya

Mili 364 island of SE Marshall
 Islands
Milḥ, Baḥr al see Razāzah, Buḥayrat ar
Milḥ, Wādī al see Melah, Oued el
Millet 467 C St. Lucia
Millstätter See 82 lake of
 S Austria
Milo 253 river of E Guinea
Milondo, Mont 230 mountain of
 C Gabon
Mílos 245 island of SE Greece
Mil'skaya Step' see Mil Düzü
Milton Keynes 565 C England, UK
Milwaukee 571 Wisconsin,
 NC USA
Milyang see Miryang
Mimongo 230 C Gabon
Mīnā' 'Abd Allāh 322 var. Mina
 Abdulla. E Kuwait
Mīnā' al Aḥmadī 322 var. Mina
 Ahmadi. E Kuwait
Mīnā' Jabal 'Alī 562 NE United Arab
 Emirates
Minas 579 S Uruguay
Mīnā' Sa'ūd 322 var. Mīnā' Su'ūd.
 SE Kuwait
Minas de Corrales 579 N Uruguay
Minas de Matahambre 182 W Cuba
Minatitlán 370 SE Mexico
Minbu 135 W Burma
Minch, The 565 strait of the Atlantic
 Ocean, between Outer Hebrides and
 Scotland
Mincivan 86 Rus. Mindzhivan.
 SW Azerbaijan
Mindanao 437 island of S Philippines
Mindanao Sea see Bohol Sea
Mindelo 152 var. Porto Grande.
 São Vincente, N Cape Verde
Mindoro 437 island of C Philippines
Mindoro Strait 437 strait connecting
 South China Sea and Sulu Sea
Mindouli 176 S Congo
Mindživan see Mincivan
Mingäçevir 86 Rus. Mingechaur
 var. Mingeçaur. C Azerbaijan
Mingäçevir Su Anbarı 86
 Rus. Mingechaurskoye
 Vodokhranilishche. Reservoir
 of NW Azerbaijan
Mingala 155 SE Central African
 Republic
Mingāora 421 var. Mingora, Mongora.
 N Pakistan
Mingechaurskoye Vodokhranilishche
 see Mingäçevir Su Anbarı
Ming-Kush see Min-Kush
Minho see Miño
Minicoy Island 270 island of
 Lakshadweep, SW India
Min-Kush 325 Kir. Ming-Kush.
 C Kyrgyzstan
Minna 408 C Nigeria
Minneapolis 571 Minnesota, NC USA
Minnesota 571 state of NC USA
Miño 444, 502 Port. Minho. River of
 Portugal and Spain
Minorca see Menorca
Minot 571 North Dakota, NC USA
Minsk 104 ❖ of Belorussia,
 C Belorussia
Minto Reef 374 atoll of C Micronesia
Minvoul 230 N Gabon
Minwakh 601 N Yemen
Miquelon 630 N Saint Pierre and
 Miquelon
Miquelon 630 island of N Saint Pierre
 and Miquelon
Miquelon, Cap 630 cape of the Atlantic
 Ocean on the coast of Miquelon, N
 Saint Pierre and Miquelon
Miragoâne 258 SW Haiti
Miranda de Ebro 503 N Spain
Mirbāṭ 418 var. Marbat. SW Oman
Mirebalais 258 C Haiti
Miri 354 NW Borneo, Malaysia
Mirim Lagoon 121, 579 var. Lake
 Mirim. Lagoon of Brazil and
 Uruguay
Mirim, Lake see Mirim Lagoon
Mirnyy 455 C Russia
Mirnyy 66 CIS research station of
 Greater Antarctica, Antarctica
Mīrpur see New Mīrpur

Mirs Bay 262 Cant. Tai Pang Wan.
 Bay to the NE of Hong Kong
Mirtóo Pelagos 245 Eng. Mirtoan
 Sea. Area of the Mediterranean Sea,
 S Greece
Miryang 498 var. Milyang
 Jap. Mitsuō. SE South Korea
Misery, Mount see Liamuiga, Mount
Miskito Coast see Mosquito Coast
Miskitos, Cayos 404 island group of
 NE Nicaragua
Miskolc 264 NE Hungary
Misool, Pulau 276 island of Maluku,
 E Indonesia
Miṣrātah 339 var. Misurata.
 N Libya
Mississippi 571 river of C USA
Mississippi 571 state of SE USA
Missoula 570 Montana, NW USA
Missouri 571 river of NC USA
Missouri 571 state of C USA
Misurata see Miṣrātah
Mitau see Jelgava
Mitèmboni see Mitemele, Río
Mitemele, Río 208 var. Mitèmboni,
 Temboni, Utamboni. River of
 Equatorial Guinea and Gabon
Mitiaro 622 island of Southern Cook
 Islands, S Cook Islands
Mito 304 Honshū, SE Japan
Mitre Island 374 atoll of C Philippines
Mitrovica see Kosovska Mitrovica
Mitrovicë see Kosovska Mitrovica
Mitsamiouli 174 N Grande Comore,
 Comoros
Mits'iwa see Massawa
Mitsoudjé 174 SW Grande Comore,
 Comoros
Mitsuyō see Miryang
Mitú 171 SE Colombia
Mitumba, Monts 609 var. Chaîne des
 Mitumba, Mitumba Range. Mountain
 range of E Zaire
Mitzic 230 N Gabon
Miyako 305 Honshū, N Japan
Miyako-jima 304 island of
 Sakishima-shotō, SW Japan
Miyakonojō 304 Kyūshū,
 SW Japan
Miyazaki 304 Kyūshū,
 SW Japan
Miyoshi 304 Honshū, W Japan
Mizdah 339 var. Mizda. NW Libya
Mjøsa 414 var. Mjøsen. Lake of
 SE Norway
Mkhondvo 512 var. Mkondo.
 River of South Africa and Swaziland
Mladá Boleslav 128
 Ger. Jungbunzlau. N Czech Republic
Mlanje see Mulanje
Mljet 181 It. Meleda. Island of
 S Croatia
Mmabatho 495 North West,
 N South Africa
Mmathethe 118 S Botswana
Mnjoli Dam 512 reservoir of
 NE Swaziland
Mo 414 NE Norway
Moa 482 river of W Africa
Moa 183 SE Cuba
Moabi 230 SW Gabon
Moala 218 island to the SE of Viti Levu,
 S Fiji
Moamba 387 SW Mozambique
Moanda 230 SE Gabon
Moba 609 E Zaire
Mobaye 155 S Central African Republic
Mobile 571 Alabama, SE USA
Moca 198 N Dominican Republic
Moçambique 387 island and
 settlement of NE Mozambique
Moçâmedes see Namibe
Moce 218 island of the Lau Group,
 E Fiji
Mocha see Al Mukhā
Mochudi 118 S Botswana
Mocímboa da Praia 387 var. Vila de
 Mocímboa da Praia. N Mozambique
Môco 64 var. Serra Môco, Morro de
 Môco. Mountain of W Angola
Mocoa 171 SW Colombia
Mocuba 387 E Mozambique
Modena 294 NW Italy
Mödling 82 NE Austria

Modohn see Madona
Modriča 116 N Bosnia & Herzegovina
Moe 77 SE Australia
Moen see Weno
Möen see Møn
Moena see Muna, Pulau
Moengo 510 NE Suriname
Moers 236 W Germany
Moesi see Musi
Moeskroen see Mouscron
Mogadishu 492 Som. Muqdisho,
 It. Mogadiscio. ❖ of Somalia,
 S Somalia
Mogador see Essaouira
Mogilëv see Mahilyow
Mogotón, Pico 404 mountain of
 NW Nicaragua
Mohales Hoek 334 SW Lesotho
Mohammadia 59
 var. El Mohammaidia. NW Algeria
Mohammedia 382 prev. Fédala.
 NW Morocco
Moharek see Al Muḥarraq
Mohéli 174 var. Mwali. Island of
 Comoros
Mohn see Muhu
Moindou 628 C New Caledonia
Mõisaküla 212 Ger. Moisekull.
 S Estonia
Moïssala 156 S Chad
Mokhotlong 334 NE Lesotho
Mokil 374 atoll of E Micronesia
Moknine 545 var. Al Muknīn.
 NE Tunisia
Mokp'o 498 Jap. Moppo. SW South
 Korea
Mokra Gora 604 mountain range
 of SW Serbia, Yugoslavia
Mokwa 408 W Nigeria
Moldau see Vltava
Moldova 376-377 officially Republic of
 Moldova, var. Moldova,
 prev. Moldavian SSR,
 Rus. Moldavskaya SSR. Country of
 E Europe divided into 40 admin.
 units (districts). ❖ Chişinău
Molde 414 SW Norway
Moldo-Too, Khrebet 325 mountain
 range of C Kyrgyzstan
Moldova see Moldova
Molepolole 118 S Botswana
Môle-St-Nicolas 258 NW Haiti
Molineux 464 NE St. Kitts, St. Kitts
 & Nevis
Möll 82 river of S Austria
Mölndal 515 SW Sweden
Molodechno see Maladzyechna
Molodeczno see Maladzyechna
Molodezhnaya 66 CIS research
 station of Greater Antarctica,
 Antarctica
Molokai 570 island of Hawaii, USA,
 C Pacific
Molopo 118, 495 seasonal river
 of southern Africa
Molotov see Severodvinsk
Molotov see Perm'
Moloundou 144 SE Cameroon
Moluccas see Maluku
Molucca Sea see Maluku, Laut
Mombasa 316 SE Kenya
Môn see Anglesey
Møn 190 prev. Möen. Island of
 SE Denmark
Mona, Canal de la 198, 629 channel
 connecting the Atlantic Ocean and
 Caribbean Sea, between Dominican
 Republica and Puerto Rico
Monaco 378-379 officially Principality
 of Monaco. Country of W Europe
 divided into 4 admin. units (quarters).
 ❖ Monaco
Monaco see München
Monaghan 288 Ir. Muineachán.
 NE Ireland
Monagrillo 426 S Panama
Mona, Isla 629 island of SW Puerto
 Rico
Monapo 387 NE Mozambique
Monaragala 506 SE Sri Lanka
Monastir 545 var. Al Munastīr.
 NE Tunisia
Monastir see Bitola
Mönchengladbach 236
 prev. München-Gladbach.
 W Germany

Muir Eireann *see* Irish Sea
Mukacheve *558* W Ukraine
Mukalla *see* Al Mukallā
Mukden *see* Shenyang
Muksu *530* river of NE Tajikistan
Mukungwa *462* river of NW Rwanda
Mulaku Atoll *358* *var.* Meemu Atoll. Atoll of C Maldives
Mulanje *353* *var.* Mlanje. S Malawi
Mulhacén, Cerro de *503* mountain of SE Spain
Mulchén *159* C Chile
Mülheim *236* *var.* Mulheim an der Ruhr. W Germany
Mulhouse *225* *Ger.* Mülhausen. NE France
Mulifanua *598* Upolu, Western Samoa
Mulinu'ū, Cape *598* cape of Savai'i, Western Samoa
Mullaittivu *506* *var.* Mullaitivu. NE Sri Lanka
Muller, Pegunungan *276* *Dut.* Müller-gerbergte. Mountain range of Borneo, C Indonesia
Mullingar *288* C Ireland
Mull, Isle of *565* island of Inner Hebrides, W Scotland, UK
Multān *421* E Pakistan
Mumbai *see* Bombay
Mumbwa *613* C Zambia
Mummatalah, Ra's al *91* *var.* Ra's al Mamtalah. Cape of SW Bahrain
Munamägi *see* Suur Munamägi
Muna, Pulau *276* *prev.* Moena. Island to the SE of Celebes, C Indonesia
München *237, 241* *Eng.* Munich, *It.* Monaco. S Germany
Munch'ŏn *413* SE North Korea
Munda *490* New Georgia, C Solomon Islands
Mundal Lagooon *506* lagoon of W Sri Lanka
Mu Nggava *see* Rennell
Mungla *93* S Bangladesh
Mungwi *613* NE Zambia
Munia *218* island of the Lau Group, E Fiji
Munich *see* München
Munini *462* SW Rwanda
Munshiganj *93* C Bangladesh
Munster *288* province of S Ireland
Münster *236* *var.* Muenster. NW Germany
Muntinlupa *437* Luzon, N Philippines
Muong Sai *see* Muang Xay
Muonioälv *see* Muoniojoki
Muoniojoki *221, 515* *Swe.* Muonioälv. River of Finland and Sweden
Muqdisho *see* Mogadishu
Mur *82, 488* *SCr.* Mura. River of C Europe
Mura *see* Mur
Muragarazi *see* Maragarazi
Murai Reservoir *485* reservoir of NW Singapore
Murambi *462* C Rwanda
Muramvya *138* C Burundi
Murang'a *316* *prev.* Fort Hall. SW Kenya
Murata *470* S San Marino
Murchison Falls *556* *var.* Kabalega Falls. Waterfall of NW Uganda
Murcia *503* autonomous community of SE Spain
Mureş *450* *var.* Mureşul, *Hung.* Maros, *Ger.* Muresch. River of Hungary and Romania
Murehwa *614* *var.* Murewa. NE Zimbabwe
Muresch *see* Mureş
Murgab *553* *prev.* Murgap. SE Turkmenistan
Murgab *553* *var.* Murghab. River of SE Turkmenistan
Murgab *see* Murghob
Murghob *530* *Rus.* Murgab. E Tajikistan
Muri *518* *var.* Muri bei Bern. W Switzerland
Murilo *374* atoll of N Micronesia
Mūrītānīyah *see* Mauritania
Müritz *237* *var.* Müritzee. Lake of NE Germany
Murmansk *454* NW Russia

Muroran *304* Hokkaidō, N Japan
Muroto *304* Shikoku, SW Japan
Murray *77* river of SE Australia
Murray, Lake *428* lake in swamp region of W Papua New Guinea
Murrumbidgee *77* river of SE Australia
Murska Sobota *488* *Ger.* Olsnitz. NE Slovenia
Murua Island *428* *var.* Woodlark I. Island of SE Papua New Guinea
Murupara *401* SE North Island, New Zealand
Mururoa Atoll *624* *var.* Moruroa. Atoll of French Polynesia
Murzuq *339* *var.* Marzūq, Murzuk. W Libya
Murzuq, Ḥammādat *339* plateau of W Libya
Muş *549* E Turkey
Mūša *344* river of N Lithuania
Musaffah *562* C United Arab Emirates
Musā'id *339* NE Libya
Musala *128* *prev.* Stalin Peak. Mountain of W Bulgaria
Musan *413* NE North Korea
Musandam Peninsula *418* *Ar.* Ra's Musandam, *var.* Ras Masandam. Peninsular of N Oman
Musay'id *449* *var.* Umm Sa'īd. SE Qatar
Muscat *418* *Ar.* Masqaṭ. ❖ of Oman, N Oman
Muscat and Oman *see* Oman
Mushin *408* SW Nigeria
Musi *276* *prev.* Moesi. River of Sumatra, W Indonesia
Musoma *532* N Tanzania
Mussau Island *428* island of NE Papua New Guinea
Mustafa-Pasha *see* Svilengrad
Mustique *468* island of C St. Vincent & the Grenadines
Mustvee *212* *Ger.* Tschorna. E Estonia
Mutalau *628* N Niue
Mu-tan-chiang *see* Mudanjiang
Mutare *614* *prev.* Umtali. E Zimbabwe
Mutoko *614* *prev.* Mtoko. NE Zimbabwe
Mutorashanga *614* *prev.* Mtorashanga. N Zimbabwe
Muyaga *138* E Burundi
Muyinga *138* *var.* Muhinga. NE Burundi
Muy Muy *404* C Nicaragua
Mŭynoq *582* *Rus.* Muynak. NW Uzbekistan
Muyunkum, Peski *312* desert region of S Kazakhstan
Muzaffargarh *421* E Pakistan
Muzarabani *614* N Zimbabwe
Mvuma *614* *prev.* Umvuma. C Zimbabwe
Mvurwi *614* *prev.* Umvukwes. N Zimbabwe
Mwali *see* Mohéli
Mwanza *532* NW Tanzania
Mwanza *353* SW Malawi
Mweka *609* C Zaire
Mwenda *613* N Zambia
Mwene-Ditu *609* S Zaire
Mwenezi *614* river of S Zimbabwe
Mwenezi *614* *prev.* Nuanetsi. S Zimbabwe
Mweru, Lake *609, 613* *Fr.* Lac Moero. Lake of Zaire and Zambia
Mweru Wantipa, Lake *613* lake of N Zambia
Mwombezhi *613* river of W Zambia
Myanaung *135* SW Burma
Myanmar *see* Burma
Myaungmya *135* SW Burma
Myingyan *135* C Burma
Myitkyina *135* N Burma
Myitnge *135* river of NE Burma
Mykines *622* island of W Faeroe Islands
Mykolayiv *558* *Rus.* Nikolayev. S Ukraine
Mýkonos *245* island of SE Greece
Mymensingh *93* *prev.* Nasirābād. N Bangladesh
Myŏngch'ŏn *413* NE North Korea

Mýrdalsjökull *268* glacier of S Iceland
Mysore *270* *var.* Maisur. S India
My Tho *595* S Vietnam
Mytilíni *245* Lésvos, E Greece
Mzimba *353* NW Malawi
Mzuzu *353* N Malawi

N

Naas *288* *Ir.* Nás Na Riogh, An Nás. E Ireland
Nabatiyé *332* *var.* Nabatiyet et Tahta, An Nabatīyah at Taḥtā. SW Lebanon
Nabavatu *218* Vanua Levu, N Fiji
Naberezhnyye Chelny *454* *prev.* Brezhnev. W Russia
Nabeul *545* *var.* Nābul. N Tunisia
Nabgha *562* NE United Arab Emirates
Nabīh aş Şaliḥ, Jazīrat an *91* *var.* Nabih Saleh, Nabīh Salīh. Island of NE Bahrain
Nabī Shu'ayb, Jabal an *601* mountain of W Yemen
Nablus *291, 292* *Heb.* Shekhem. N West Bank
Nabouwalu *218* Vanua Levu, N Fiji
Nacala *387* NE Mozambique
Nacaome *260* S Honduras
Na-Chii *see* Nagqu
Nachingwea *532* SE Tanzania
Na Cruacha Dubha *see* Macgillicuddy's Reeks
Nacula *218* *prev.* Nathula. Island of the Yasawa Group, NW Fiji
Nadi *218* *prev.* Nandi. Viti Levu, W Fiji
Nador *382* *prev.* Villa Nador. NE Morocco
Nadur *363* Gozo, Malta
Naduri *218* *prev.* Nanduri. Vanua Levu, N Fiji
Nadym *454* N Russia
Næstved *190* Sjælland, SE Denmark
Nafūsah, Jabal *339* mountain range of NW Libya
Naga *437* *prev.* Nueva Caceres. Luzon, N Philippines
Nagano *304* Honshū, C Japan
Nagaoka *304* Honshū, N Japan
Nagarote *404* SW Nicaragua
Nagasaki *304* Kyūshū, SW Japan
Nāgercoil *270* S India
Nagorno-Karabakh *86* former autonomous region of SW Azerbaijan
Nagoya *304* Honshū, C Japan
Nāgpur *270* C India
Nagqu *162* *Chin.* Na-Ch'ii, *prev.* Hei-ho. Xizang Zizhiqu, W China
Nagua *198* N Dominican Republic
Nagybánya *see* Baia Mare
Nagybecskerek *see* Zrenjanin
Nagykanizsa *264* *Ger.* Grosskanizsa. SW Hungary
Nagykőrös *264* C Hungary
Nagymihály *see* Michalovce
Nagysurány *see* Šurany
Nagyszeben *see* Sibiu
Nagyszombat *see* Trnava
Nagytapolcsány *see* Topolčany
Nagyvárad *see* Oradea
Naha *304* Nansei-shotō, SW Japan
Naḥal Elisha *291* E West Bank
Nahariyya *291* N Israel
Nahičevan' *see* Naxçıvan
Nairai *218* island to the E of Viti Levu, C Fiji
Nairobi *316* ❖ of Kenya, S Kenya
Naitaba *218* *prev.* Naitamba. Island of the Lau Group, E Fiji
Naitamba *see* Naitaba
Naivasha *316* SW Kenya
Naivasha, Lake *316* lake of SW Kenya
Najaf *see* An Najaf
Najafābād *281* W Iran
Najd *474* *var.* Nejd. Region of C Saudi Arabia

Najin *413* NE North Korea
Najrān *474* S Saudi Arabia
Naju *see* Kumsong
Nakadōri-jima *304* island of Gotō-rettō, SW Japan
Nakamura *304* Shikoku, SW Japan
Nakasongola *556* W Uganda
Nakatsu *304* Kyūshū, SW Japan
Nakatsugawa *304* Honshū, C Japan
Nakfa *210* N Eritrea
Nakhichevan' *see* Naxcivan
Nakhodka *455* SE Russia
Nakhon Pathom *535* C Thailand
Nakhon Phanom *535* NE Thailand
Nakhon Ratchasima *535* *var.* Korat. E Thailand
Nakhon Sawan *535* *var.* Muang Nakhon Sawan. W Thailand
Nakhon Si Thammarat *535* S Thailand
Nakskov *190* Lolland, S Denmark
Naktong *498* *var.* Nakdong, *Jap.* Rakutō-kō. River of South Korea
Nakuru *316* W Kenya
Nāl *421* river of W Pakistan
Nalayh *380* C Mongolia
Nal'chik *454* SW Russia
Nālūt *339* NW Libya
Nam *413* river of C North Korea
Nam *498* river of S South Korea
Namaacha *387* S Mozambique
Namacurra *387* E Mozambique
Namak, Daryācheh-ye *281* lake of W Iran
Namak, Kavīr-e *281* desert region of NE Iran
Namanga *316* S Kenya
Namangan *582* E Uzbekistan
Namatanai *428* New Ireland, Papua New Guinea
Nam Đinh *595* N Vietnam
Namen *see* Namur
Namhae-do *498* *Jap.* Nankai-tō. Island of S South Korea
Namib Desert *391* coastal desert region of W Namibia
Namibe *64* *Port.* Moçâmedes, *var.* Mossâmedes. SW Angola
Namibia *390-391* officially The Republic of Namibia, *prev.* South-West Africa, German Southwest Africa. Country of Southern Africa divided into 13 admin. units (districts). ❖ Windhoek
Namoluk *374* island of SE Micronesia
Namonuito *374* atoll of NW Micronesia
Namorik *364* island of S Marshall Islands
Nampa *570* Idaho, NW USA
Namp'o *413* SW North Korea
Nampula *387* NE Mozambique
Namsos *414* C Norway
Namu *364* island of C Marshall Islands
Namuka-i-lau *218* island of the Lau Group, E Fiji
Namunukula *506* SE Sri Lanka
Namur *99* *Dut.* Namen. SE Belgium
Namutoni *391* N Namibia
Namwŏn *498* *Jap.* Nangen. S South Korea
Namyit Island *630* island of S Spratly Islands
Nan *535* *var.* Muang Nan. N Thailand
Nanaimo *146* Vancouver Island, SW Canada
Nanao *304* Honshū, C Japan
Nanchang *163* Jianxi, SE China
Nan-ching *see* Nanjing
Nancy *225* NE France
Nanda Devi *270* mountain of N India
Nandaime *404* S Nicaragua
Nandi *see* Nadi
Nanduri *see* Naduri
Nanga Eboko *144* C Cameroon
Nangbéto, Retenue de *539* reservoir of C Togo
Nangen *see* Namwŏn
Nan Hai *see* East China Sea and South China Sea
Nanhsi *527* SW Taiwan
Nanjing *163* *var.* Nanking, Nan-ching. Jiangsu, E China

Nankai-tō *see* Namhae-do
Nanning *163 prev.* Yung-ning.
Guangxi, S China
Nanortalik *624* S Greenland
Nansei-shotō *304* island group to the
SW of Kyūshū, SW Japan
Nanshan Island *630* island of
E Spratly Islands
Nansio *532* NW Tanzania
Nanterre *225* N France
Nantes *224* W France
Nanthi Kadal Lagoon *506* lagoon of
N Sri Lanka
Nant'ou *527* W Taiwan
Nanuku Passage *218* channel of the
Pacific Ocean between the Lau
Group and Taveuni, NE Fiji
Nanumaga *555 prev.* Nanumanga.
Coral atoll of NW Tuvalu
Nanumea *555* coral atoll of NW Tuvalu
Nan Wan *527* bay of the South China
Sea, S Taiwan
Nanyang *163* Henan, C China
Nanyuki *316* C Kenya
Naogaon *93* NW Bangladesh
Napier *401* SE North Island,
New Zealand
Naples *see* Napoli
Napo *200, 433* river of Ecuador and
Peru
Napoli *295 Eng.* Naples, *Ger.* Neapel.
S Italy
Nāra *421* irrigation canal of S Pakistan
Nara *304* Honshū, C Japan
Narathiwat *535* S Thailand
Narayani *395* river of C Nepal
Narbada *see* Narmada
Narbonne *225* S France
Nare's Strait *624* strait of
NW Greenland
Narew *441* river of E Poland
Narganá *426* NE Panama
Narikrik *364 prev.* Knox Atoll. Atoll of
SE Marshall Islands
Narmada *270 var.* Narbada. River of
C India
Narok *316* SW Kenya
Närpes *221 Swe.* Närpiö. SW Finland
Narrows, The *464* channel
connecting the Atlantic Ocean
and Caribbean Sea, between Nevis
and St. Kitts
Narsaq Kujalleq *624 Dan.*
Frederiksdal. S Greenland
Narsingdi *93* C Bangladesh
Nartës, Gjol i *see* Nartës, Liqeni i
Nartës, Liqeni i *527 var.* Gjol i Nartës.
Lake of SW Albania
Naruto *304* Shikoku, SW Japan
Narva *212 prev.* Narova. River of
Estonia and Russia
Narva *212* NE Estonia
Narva Bay *212 Est.* Narva Laht,
Rus. Narviskiy Zaliv. Bay of the Gulf
of Finland
Narva Reservoir *212 Est.* Narva
Veehoidla. Reservoir of Estonia
and Russia
Narvik *414* NE Norway
Nar'yan-Mar *454 prev.* Dzerzhinskiy,
prev. Beloshchel'ye. NW Russia
Naryn *325* E Kyrgyzstan
Naryn *325* river of Kyrgyzstan
and Uzbekistan
Nasau *218* Koro, C Fiji
Nāshik *270 prev.* Nāsik. W India
Nasho, Lac *462* lake of E Rwanda
Nashville *571* Tennessee, SE USA
Näsijärvi *221* lake of SW Finland
Nasirābād *see* Mymensingh
Nāsir, Buḥeiret *202 var.* Buḥayrat
Nāṣir, *Eng.* Lake Nser. Lake of Egypt
and Sudan
Nasiriya *see* An Nāṣirīyah
Nás Na Riogh *see* Naas
Nassau *88* ❖ of Bahamas,
New Providence, Bahamas
Nassau *622* island of Northern Cook
Islands, N Cook Islands
Nasser, Lake *see* Nāsir, Buheiret
Nata *118* NE Botswana
Natal *121* E Brazil
Nathula *see* Nacula
Natitingou *108* NW Benin

Natl *310 var.* Nitil. NW Jordan
Nator *93* W Bangladesh
Natron, Lake *532* lake of Kenya and
Tanzania
Natuna Besar, Pulau *276* island of
Kepulauan Natuna, W Indonesia
Natuna, Kepulauan *276* island group
to the NW of Borneo, W Indonesia
Nau *see* Nov
Naujoji Akmenė *344* NW Lithuania
Nā'ūr *310* NW Jordan
Nauru *392-393* officially The Republic
of Nauru, *prev.* Pleasant Island. Island
country of the Pacific Ocean divided
into 14 admin. units
(districts)
Naushahra *see* Nowshera
Nausori *218* Viti Levu, Fiji
Navabad *see* Navobod
Navaga *218* W Koro, W Fiji
Navahrudak *104 Rus.* Novogrudok,
Pol. Nowogródek. W Belorussia
Navangar *see* Jāmnagar
Navapolatsk *104 Rus.* Novopolotsk.
N Belorussia
Navarra *503* autonomous community
of N Spain
Naviti *218* island of the Yasawa Group,
NW Fiji
Navoalevu *218* NE Vanua Levu,
N Fiji
Navobod *530 Rus.* Navabad. W
Tajikistan
Navoi *see.* Nawoiy
Navua *218* Viti Levu, W Fiji
Nawābganj *93* NW Bangladesh
Nawābshāh *421* S Pakistan
Nawmah, Ra's *91 var.* Ra's Noma.
Cape of SW Bahrain
Nawoiy *582 Rus.* Navoi. S Uzbekistan
Naxçıvan *86 Rus.* Nakhichevan',
var. Nahičevan'. SW Azerbaijan
Náxos *245* island of SE Greece
Nayau *218* island of the Lau Group,
E Fiji
Nazareth *see* Nazerat
Nazca *433* S Peru
Naze *304* Nansei-shotō, SW Japan
Nazerat *291 Eng.* Nazareth.
N Israel
Nazerat 'Illit *291* N Israel
Nazilli *548* SW Turkey
Nazran' *454* SW Russia
Nazrēt *215 var.* Adama, Hadama.
C Ethiopia
Nazwá *418* N Oman
Nchelenge *613* N Zambia
Ncheu *see* Ntcheu
Nchisi *see* Ntchisi
Ncue *208* N Río Muni, Equatorial
Guinea
Ndaghamcha, Sebkra de
see Te-n-Dghâmcha, Sebkhet
N'Dalatando *64 Port.* Vila Salazar.
NW Angola
Ndali *108* C Benin
Ndélé *155* N Central African Republic
Ndendé *230* S Gabon
Ndeni *see* Nendö
Ndindi *230* S Gabon
N'Djamena *156 var.* Njamena,
prev. Fort-Lamy. ❖ of Chad, W Chad
Ndjolé *230* C Gabon
Ndoki *176* river of N Congo
Ndola *613* C Zambia
Ndora *138* NW Burundi
Ndréméani *174* S Mohéli, Comoros
Ndrhamcha, Sebkha de
see Te-n-Dghâmcha, Sebkhet
Nduindui *490* S Guadalcanal,
Solomon Is
Nduke *see* Kolombangara
Neagh, Lough *565* lake of Northern
Ireland, UK
Neapel *see* Napoli
Nébeck *see* An Nabk
Nebitdag *533* W Turkmenistan
Nebk *see* An Nabk
Neblina, Pico da *120* mountain of
NW Brazil
Nebraska *571* state of C USA
Neckar *236* river of SW Germany
Necochea *71* E Argentina
Nederland *see* Netherlands

Neder-Rijn *397 Eng.* Lower Rhine.
River of C Netherlands
Nefasit *210* C Eritrea
Nefta *545 var.* Naftah. W Tunisia
Neftezavodsk *see* Seydi
Negara Brunei Darussalam
see Brunei
Negēlē *215 var.* Negelli, *It.* Neghelli.
S Ethiopia
Negev *see* HaNegev
Neghelli *see* Negēlē
Negomane *387 var.* Negomano.
N Mozambique
Negombo *506* SW Sri Lanka
Negotino *349* C FYR Macedonia
Negril *303* W Jamaica
Negro, Rio *120, 171* river of N South
America
Negro, Río *see* Sico
Negro, Río *579* river of Brazil and
Uruguay
Negro, Río *see* Chixoy
Negros *437* island of C Philippines
Neiafu *540* Uta Vava'u, Vava'u Group,
Tonga
Neiba *198* SW Dominican Republic
Neiges, Piton des *630* mountain of
C Réunion
Neily *178* SE Costa Rica
Nei Mongol Zizhiqu *163 Eng.* Inner
Mongolian Autonomous Region,
prev. Nei Monggol Zizhiqu.
Autonomous region of N China
Neiva *171* W Colombia
Nek'emtē *215 var.* Nakamti, Lakamti,
Lekemti. W Ethiopia
Nelson *146* river of C Canada
Nelson *401* N South Island,
New Zealand
Nelson Island *521* island of N British
Indian Ocean Territory
Nelspruit *495* Eastern Transvaal,
NE South Africa
Néma *366* SE Mauritania
Neman *104, 344 Bel.* Nyoman,
Lith. Nemunas, *Ger.* Memel,
Pol. Niemen. River of NE Europe
Německý Brod *see* Havlíčkův Brod
Nemunas *see* Neman
Nenagh *288* S Ireland
Nendeln *342* C Liechtenstein
Nendö *490 var.* Ndeni. Santa Cruz Is,
Solomon Islands
Nepal *394-395* officially Kingdom of
Nepal. Country of Asia divided
into 5 admin. units (regions).
❖ kathmandu
Nepalganj *395* W Nepal
Nepean Island *628* island of C Norfolk
Island
Neretva *116* river of S Bosnia
& Herzegovina
Neris *344 Bel.* Viliya, *Pol.* Wilja. River
of Belorussia and Lithuania
Neskaupstadhur *268* E Iceland
Ness, Loch *565* lake of N Scotland, UK
Néstos *128, 245 Turk.* Kara Su,
Bul. Mesta. River of Bulgaria and
Greece
Netanya *291* C Israel
Netherlands *396-399* officially
Kingdom of the Netherlands,
var. Holland, *Dut.* Nederland.
Country of W Europe divided into
12 admin. units (provinces).
❖ Amsterdam, The Hague
Netherlands Antilles *591, 628 prev.*
Dutch West Indies. Autonomous part
of the Netherlands, Caribbean Sea.
❖ Willemstad
Netherlands East Indies *see* Indonesia
Netrakona *93* N Bangladesh
Netze *see* Noteć
Neubrandenburg *237* NE Germany
Neuchâtel *518 Ger.* Neuenburg.
W Switzerland
Neuchâtel, Lac de *518*
Ger. Neuenburger See. Lake
of W Switzerland
Neuenburg *see* Neuchâtel
Neuenburger See *see* Neuchâtel,
Lac de
Neugradiska *see* Nova Gradiška
Neuhäusl *see* Nové Zámky
Neumarkt *see* Târgu Mures
Neumarktl *see* Tržič

Neumünster *237* N Germany
Neunkirchen *82* E Austria
Neuquén *71* SE Argentina
Neusatz *see* Novi Sad
Neusiedler See *82, 264 Hung.* Fertő-tó.
Lake of Austria and Hungary
Neusohl *see* Banská Bystrica
Neustadt *see* Baia Mare
Neustadtl *see* Novo Mesto
Neutra *see* Nitra
Neu-Ulm *237* S Germany
Nevada *570* state of W USA
Nevers *225* C France
Nevis *464* island of the Lesser Antilles
which, with St. Kitts, forms the
independent state of St. Kitts
& Nevis
Nevis Peak *464* mountain peak of
C Nevis, St. Kitts & Nevis
Nevşehir *549* C Turkey
Newala *532* SE Tanzania
New Amsterdam *256* E Guyana
New Britain *428* island of E Papua
New Guinea
New Brunswick *147* province of
SE Canada
New Bussa *408* W Nigeria
New Caledonia *628* French overseas
territory of the Pacific Ocean
❖ Nouméa
Newcastle *77* E Australia
Newcastle *464* N Nevis, St. Kitts
& Nevis
Newcastle upon Tyne *565*
NE England, UK
New Delhi *270* ❖ of India, N India
Newfield *68* SE Antigua, Antigua
& Barbuda
Newfoundland *147 Fr.* Terre-Neuve.
Island of S E Canada
Newfoundland *147* province of
E Canada
New Georgia *490* island of the New
Georgia Is, W Solomon Is
New Georgia Islands *490* island group
of W Solomon Is
New Guinea *277, 428 Dut.* Nieuw
Guinea, *Ind.* Irian. Large island of
W Pacific Ocean, divided
administratively into the Indonesian
state of Irian Jaya and the indepen-
dent country of Papua New Guinea
New Halfa *see* Halfa el Gadida
New Hampshire *571* state of NE USA
New Haven *571* Connecticut, NE USA
New Hebrides *see* Vanuatu
New Ireland *428* island of NE Papua
New Guinea
New Jersey *571* state of E USA
Newman *76* W Australia
New Mexico *570-571* state of
SW USA
New Mîrpur *421 prev.* Mîrpur.
NE Pakistan
New Orleans *571* Louisiana,
SC USA
New Plymouth *401* SW North Island,
New Zealand
Newport *565* S Wales, UK
Newport News *571* Virginia,
E USA
New Providence *88* island of
C Bahamas
New River *256* river of SE Guyana
New River *102* river of N Belize
New Ross *288* SE Ireland
Newry *565* Northern Ireland, UK
New Sandy Bay Village *468*
N St. Vincent, St. Vincent
& the Grenadines
New Siberian Islands
see Novosibirskiye Ostrova
New South Wales *77* state of
SE Australia
Newton Ground *464* NW St. Kitts,
St. Kitts & Nevis
Newtownabbey *565* Northern Ireland,
UK
New Winthorpes *68* N Antigua,
Antigua & Barbuda
New York *571* state of NE USA
New York *571, 575* New York,
NE USA

New Zealand *400-403* officially The Dominion of New Zealand. Country of the Pacific Ocean, divided into 14 admin. units (regions). ❖ Wellington
Nezhyn *558* N Ukraine
Ngabé *176* SE Congo
Ngadda *409* river of NE Nigeria
Ngala *409* NE Nigeria
Ngangerabeli Plain *316* plain of SE Kenya
Ngaoundéré *144* var. N'Gaoundéré, N'Gaundere. N Cameroon
Ngara *532* NW Tanzania
Ngarama *462* N Rwanda
Ngardmau *425* C Palau
Ngaruangl *425* island of N Palau
Ngatik *374* atoll of E Micronesia
Ngau *see* Gau
N'Gaundere *see* Ngaoundéré
Nggamea *see* Qamea
Nggatokae *490* island of the New Georgia Islands, W Solomon Islands
Nggwavuma *512* var. Ingwavuma. River of South Africa and Swaziland
N'Giva *64* var. Ondjiva *Port.* Vila Pereira de Eça. S Angola
Ngo *176* SE Congo
Ngogolo *512* C Swaziland
Ngoko *144, 176* river of Cameroon and Congo
Ngorongoro Crater *532* crater and conservation area of N Tanzania
Ngororero *462* W Rwanda
Ngounié *230* river of Congo and Gabon
Ngouoni *230* E Gabon
Ngourti *407* E Niger
Ngozi *138* N Burundi
Nguigmi *407* SE Niger
Ngulu *374* atoll of W Micronesia
Ngum *327* river of C Laos
Nguna *587* island of C Vanuatu
Ngundu *614* S Zimbabwe
N'Gunza *see* Sumbe
Nguru *408* NE Nigeria
Ngwempisi *512* river of South Africa and Swaziland
Ngweze *see* Katima Mulilo
Nhacra *254* W Guinea-Bissau
Nhamundá *120* var. Yamundá, Jamundá. River of N Brazil
Nha Trang *595* SE Vietnam
Nhlangano *512* prev. Goedgegun. SW Swaziland
Niagara Falls *147* SE Canada
Niagassola *253* var. Nyagassola. NE Guinea
Niamey *407* ❖ of Niger, SW Niger
Niamtougou *539* N Togo
Niandan *253* E Guinea
Niangay, Lac *360* lake of E Mali
Nianija Bolon *233* river of Gambia and Senegal
Niantanina *253* E Guinea
Niari *176* river of S Congo
Nias, Pulau *276* island to the W of Sumatra, W Indonesia
Niassa, Lago *see* Nyasa, Lake
Nicaragua *404-405* officially Republic of Nicaragua. Country of Central America divided into 16 admin. units (departments). ❖ Managua
Nicaragua, Lago de *404* var. Cocibolca, Gran Lago. Lake of S Nicaragua
Nicastro *295* S Italy
Nice *225* *It.* Nizza. SE France
Nicholls Town *88* Andros I, Bahamas
Nickerie *510* river of NW Suriname
Nicobar Islands *270* island group to the SE of India
Nicosia *187* var. Lefkosia, *Turk.* Lefkoşa. ❖ of Cyprus, C Cyprus
Nicoya *178* W Costa Rica
Nicoya, Península de *178* peninsula of W Costa Rica
Nictheroy *see* Niterói
Nidaros *see* Trondheim
Niedere Tauern *82* mountain range of C Austria
Niefang *208* var. Sevilla de Niefang. NW Río Muni, Equatorial Guinea
Niemen *see* Neman
Niéri Ko *478* river of SE Senegal

Nieuw Amsterdam *510* N Suriname
Nieuwegein *397* C Netherlands
Nieuwkoop *397* W Netherlands
Nieuw Nickerie *510* NW Suriname
Niğde *549* C Turkey
Niger *108, 253, 360, 407* river of W Africa
Niger *406-407* officially Republic of Niger. Country of West Africa divided into 7 admin. units (departments). ❖ Niamey
Nigeria *408-411* officially Federal Republic of Nigeria. Country of West Africa divided into 20 admin. units (19 states and 1 federal capital Territory). ❖ Abuja
Niger, Mouths of the *408* delta of the river Niger, on the S coast of Nigeria
Niigata *304* Honshū, N Japan
Niihama *304* Shikoku, SW Japan
Niihau *570* island of Hawaii, USA, C Pacific
Niimi *304* Honshū, W Japan
Nijmegen *397* *Ger.* Nimwegen. SE Netherlands
Nikki *108* E Benin
Nikolainkaupunki *see* Vaasa
Nikolayev *see* Mykolayiv
Nikol'skiy *312* C Kazakhstan
Nikol'sk-Ussuriyskiy *see* Ussuriysk
Nikopol' *558* SE Ukraine
Nikšić *604* N Montenegro, Yugoslavia
Nikumaroro *320* var. Gardner I. Island of the Phoenix Is, C Kiribati
Nikunau *320* island of the Gilbert Is, W Kiribati
Nile *202, 508* *Ar.* Nahr an Nīl. River of N Africa
Nile Delta *202* delta of N Egypt
Nil, Nahr an *see* Nile
Nilphāmāri *93* NW Bangladesh
Nimba, Monts *253* var. Nimba Mountains. Mountain range of W Africa
Nimba, Mount *300, 336* mountain of W Africa
Nimba Mountains *see* Nimba, Monts
Nîmes *225* SE France
Nimwegen *see* Nijmegen
Ningbo *163* var. Ning-po, prev. Ninghsien. Zhejiang, E China
Ning-hsia *see* Ningxia
Ninghsien *see* Ningbo
Ning-po *see* Ningbo
Ningxia *163* *Chin.* Ningxia Huizu Zizhiqu, *Eng.* Ningsia Hui Autonomous Region, *var.* Ning-hsia. Autonomous region of N China
Ninotsminda *234* prev. Bogdanovka. S Georgia
Ninove *99* C Belgium
Niokolo Koba *478* river of SE Senegal
Niono *360* C Mali
Nioro *360* var. Nioro du Sahel. W Mali
Nioro du Rip *478* SW Senegal
Niort *225* W France
Nippon-kai *see* Japan, Sea of
Niquero *182* S Cuba
Nirin *see* Erhlin
Niš *604* *Eng.* Nish. E Serbia, Yugoslavia
Nişāb *601* var. Anşāb. SW Yemen
Nisporeni *376* *Rus.* Nisporeny. W Moldova
Nissan Islands *see* Green Islands
Nissum Bredning *190* inlet of North Sea on the NW coast of Denmark
Nistru *see* Dniester
Niterói *121* prev. Nictheroy. SE Brazil
Nitil *see* Natl
Nitra *487* *Ger.* Neutra, *Hung.* Nyitra. River of SW Slovakia
Nitra *487* *Ger.* Neutra, *Hung.* Nyitra. SW Slovakia
Niuafo'ou *540* var. Niuafoo. Island of NW Tonga
Niuatoputapu *540* var. Niuatobutabu, prev. Keppel Island. Island of N Tonga
Niuatui *555* islet of Nukufetau, Tuvalu
Niue *628* territory in free association with New Zealand, Pacific Ocean. ❖ Alofi

Niulakita *555* var. Nurakita. Coral atoll of S Tuvalu
Niutao *555* coral atoll of NW Tuvalu
Nizāmābād *270* C India
Nizhnevartovsk *454* C Russia
Nizhniy Novgorod *454* prev. Gor'kiy. W Russia
Nizhniy Pyandzh *see* Panji Poyon
Nizhnyaya Tunguska *455* *Eng.* Lower Tunguska. River of C Russia
Nizza *see* Nice
Njaba *see* Nja Kunda
Njaiama *482* E Sierra Leone
Nja Kunda *233* var. Njaba. NW Gambia
Njamena *see* N'Djamena
Njardhvík *268* SW Iceland
Njazidja *see* Grande Comore
Njoeng Jacobkondre *510* C Suriname
Njombe *532* S Tanzania
Njoro *316* W Kenya
Nkanini *512* W Swaziland
Nkata Bay *see* Nkhata Bay
Nkayi *176* var. N'Kayi, prev. Jacob. S Congo
Nkhata Bay *353* var. Nkata Bay. N Malawi
Nkhotakota *353* var. Kota Kota, Nkota Kota. C Malawi
Nkonfap *408* S Nigeria
Nkongsamba *144* var. N'Kongsamba. W Cameroon
Nkumekie *208* C Río Muni, Equatorial Guinea
Nkundla *512* W Swaziland
Nkusi *556* river of W Uganda
Nmai Hka *135* var. Me Hka. River of N Burma forming a headstream of the Irrawaddy river
Noākhāli *93* prev. Sudharam. S Bangladesh
Nobeoka *304* Kyūshū, W Japan
Noboribetsu *304* Hokkaidō, N Japan
Nogal, Uadi *see* Nugaal
Noire, Rivière *368* river of SW Mauritius
Noire, Rivière *see* Black River
Noirmoutier, Île de *224* island of W France
Nokia *221* SW Finland
Nokou *156* W Chad
Nokoué, Lac *108* lake of S Benin
Nola *155* SW Central African Republic
Nólsoy *622* island of E Faeroe Islands
Noma, Ra's *see* Nawmah, Ra's
Nomuka *540* island of the Nomuka Group, Tonga
Nomuka Group *540* island group of W Tonga
Nomwin *374* atoll of C Micronesia
Nông Hèt *327* E Laos
Nong Khai *535* NE Thailand
Nonouti *320* island of the Gilbert Is, W Kiribati
Nonsan *498* *Jap.* Ronzan. W South Korea
Nonsuch Island *621* island of E Bermuda
Noord *620* N Aruba
Noord-Beveland *397* island of SW Netherlands
Noordoewer *391* S Namibia
Noordpunt *628* headland of Curaçao, W Netherlands Antilles
Noordzee *see* North Sea
Nor Achin *see* Nor Hachn
Nor Ačin *see* Nor Hachn
Norak *530* *Rus.* Nurek. W Tajikistan
Nord *624* N Greenland
Nordaustlandet *631* island of NE Svalbard
Norddeutsches Tiefland *236-237* *Eng.* North German Plain. Plain of N Germany
Nordfriesische Inseln *236* *Eng.* North Frisian Islands. Island group of NW Germany
Nordhausen *237* C Germany
Nordishavet *see* Arctic Ocean
Nord, Massif du *258* mountainous region of Haiti
Nord, Mer du *see* North Sea
Nord-Pas de Calais *228* administrative region of N France

Nordsee *see* North Sea
Nordsjøen *see* North Sea
Nordsøen *see* North Sea
Nordtiroler Kalkalpen *82* mountain range of W Austria
Nore *288* *Ir.* An Fheoir. River of SE Ireland
Norfolk *571* Virginia, E USA
Norfolk Island *628* Australian external territory of the South Pacific Ocean. ❖ Kingston
Norge *see* Norway
Nor Hachn *74* var. Nor Hachyn, *Rus.* Nor Achin, var. Nor Ačin. C Armenia
Nor Hachyn *see* Nor Hachn
Noril'sk *455* N Russia
Norman *571* Oklahoma, SC USA
Normanby Island *428* island of SE Papua New Guinea
Normandie *225* *Eng.* Normandy. Cultural region of N France
Normandie, Collines de *225* hilly region of NW France
Norman Island *621* island of S British Virgin Islands
Norrköping *515* S Sweden
Norseman *76* SW Australia
Norskehavet *see* Norwegian Sea
Norsup *587* Malekula, Vanuatu
North Albanian Alps *57, 604* *SCr.* Prokletije, *Alb.* Bjeshkët e Nemuna. Mountain range of Albania and Yugoslavia
Northam *76* SW Australia
Northampton *565* C England, UK
North Andaman *135, 270* island of the Andaman Is, E India
North Battleford *146* SW Canada
North Bay *147* SE Canada
North Caicos *631* island of NW Turks and Caicos Islands
North Carolina *571* state of SE USA
North Channel *565* strait of Atlantic Ocean, between Northern Ireland and Scotland, UK
North Comino Channel *see* Ghawdex, Il-Fliegu ta'
North Dakota *571* state of NC USA
North Devon Island *see* Devon Island
Northern Territory *77* territory of N Australia
North East China *167*
North East Point *622* headland on the NE coast of Christmas Island
Northeast Providence Channel *88* channel between Eleuthera I and Great Abaco I, Bahamas
Northern *495* prev. Northern Transvaal. Province of NE South Africa
Northern Cape *495* province of W South Africa
Northern Cook Islands *622* island group of N Cook Islands
Northern Cyprus, Republic of *see* Cyprus
Northern Dvina *see* Severnaya Dvina
Northern Forest Reserve *196* nature reserve of N Dominica
Northern Ireland *565* var. the Six Counties. Political division of UK
Northern Karoo *495* var. High Veld, *Afr.* Hoë Karoo. Plateau region of W South Africa
Northern Mariana Islands *628* Commonwealth territory of the USA, Pacific Ocean. ❖ Saipan
Northern Rhodesia *see* Zambia
Northern Sporades *see* Vor eioi Sporades
Northern Transvaal *see* Northern
North Frisian Islands *see* Nordfriesische Inseln
North German Plain *see* Norddeutsches Tiefland
North Huvadhu Atoll *358* var. Gaafu Alifu Atoll. Atoll of S Maldives
North Island *401* northernmost of the two main islands that comprise New Zealand
North Keeling Island *622* island of NW Cocos Islands

Oil Islands *see* Chagos Archipelago
Oise *225* river of N France
Oistins *97* S Barbados
Oita *304* Kyūshū, SW Japan
Ojos del Salado, Nevado *159* mountain of N Chile
Okahandja *391* C Namibia
Okakarara *391* N Namibia
Ókanizsa *see* Kanjiža
Okāra *421* E Pakistan
Okarem *553* *Turkm.* Ekerem. W Turkmenistan
Okavango *see* Cubango
Okavango Delta *118* large wetland area of N Botswana
Okaya *304* Honshū, C Japan
Okayama *304* Honshū, W Japan
Okazaki *304* Honshū, C Japan
Okeechobee, Lake *571* lake of Florida, SE USA
Okhotsk, Sea of *455* *Rus.* Okhotskoye More. Sea of Pacific Ocean, bordering E Russia
Oki *304* island to the N of Honshū, W Japan
Okinawa-shotō *304* island group of Nansei-shotō, SW Japan
Oklahoma *571* state of SC USA
Oklahoma City *571* Oklahoma, SC USA
Okondja *230* E Gabon
Okovanggo *see* Cubango
Okoyo *176* W Congo
Okpara *108* river of Benin and Nigeria
Oktemberyan *see* Hoktemberyan
Oktyabr'skoy Revolyutsii, Ostrov *455* *Eng.* October Revolution Island. Island of Severnaya Zemlya, N Russia
Okushiri-tō *304* island to the W of Hokkaidō, N Japan
Ólafsfjördhur *268* N Iceland
Ólafsvík *268* W Iceland
Olaine *330* C Latvia
Olanchito *260* C Honduras
Öland *515* island of S Sweden
Olavarría *71* E Argentina
Olbia *294* Sardegna, W Italy
Oldenburg *236* NW Germany
Old Fort Point *627* headland on the S coast of Montserrat
Old Harbour *303* S Jamaica
Old Road *68* SW Antigua, Antigua & Barbuda
Old Road Town *464* W St. Kitts, St. Kitts & Nevis
Olëkminsk *455* C Russia
Oleksandriya *558* *Rus.* Aleksandriya. C Ukraine
Olenëk *455* *var.* Olenyok. N Russia
Oléron, Île d' *224* island of W France
Ölgiy *380* W Mongolia
Olhão *444* S Portugal
Olimarao *374* atoll of C Micronesia
Olimar Grande *579* *var.* Olimar. River of E Uruguay
Ólimbos *see* Ólympos
Olinda *121* E Brazil
Olita *see* Alytus
Olmaliq *582* *Rus.* Almalyk. E Uzbekistan
Olmütz *see* Olomouc
Olocuilta *207* SW El Salvador
Oloitokitok *316* *var.* Laitokitok. S Kenya
Olomouc *188* *Ger.* Olmütz. SE Czech Republic
Olongapo *437* Luzon, N Philippines
Olosega *620* island of Manua Islands, E American Samoa
Olsnitz *see* Murska Sobota
Olsztyn *441* *Ger.* Allenstein. N Poland
Olt *450* *Ger.* Alt. River of S Romania
Olten *518* NW Switzerland
O-luan Pi *527* *var.* Cape Olwanpi. Cape on the S coast of Taiwan
O-luan-pi *527* S Taiwan
Olympia *570* Washington, NW USA
Ólympos *245* *Eng.* Mount Olympus, *prev.* Ólimbos. Mountain of N Greece
Olympus, Mount *187* *var.* Troodos,

Olympos. Mountain of C Cyprus
Olympus, Mount *see* Ólympos
Omagh *565* Northern Ireland, UK
Omaha *571* Nebraska, C USA
Oman *418-419* officially Sultanate of Oman, *prev.* Muscat & Oman. Country of SW Asia divided into 3 admin. units (governorates). ❖ Muscat
Oman, Gulf of *281, 418, 562* *Ar.* Khalīj 'Umān. Gulf of the Arabian Sea
Omaruru *391* C Namibia
Omba *see* Aoba
Omboué *230* W Gabon
Omdurman *508* *var.* Umm Durmān. C Sudan
Ometepe, Isla de *404* island on Lago de Nicaragua, S Nicaragua
Om Hajer *210* SW Eritrea
Ōmiya *304* Honshū, SE Japan
Omo Wenz *215* river of SW Ethiopia
Omsk *454* C Russia
Ōmuta *304* Kyūshū, SW Japan
Ondangwa *391* *var.* Ondangua. N Namibia
Ondava *487* river of NE Slovakia
Ondjiva *see* N'Giva
Ondo *408* SW Nigeria
Öndörhaan *380* C Mongolia
One and Half Degree Channel *358* channel of the Indian Ocean, S Maldives
Oneata *218* island of the Lau Group, E Fiji
Onega, Lake *see* Onezhskoye Ozero
Onezhskoye Ozero *454* *Eng.* Lake Onega. Lake of NW Russia
Onga *230* E Gabon
Ongjin *413* SW North Korea
Oni *234* N Georgia
Onilahy *350* river of SW Madagascar
Onitsha *408* S Nigeria
Ono *218* island to the S of Viti Levu, SW Fiji
Ono-i-lau *218* island to the S of the Lau Group, SW Fiji
Onomichi *304* Honshū, W Japan
Ononte *see* Orantes
Onotoa *320* island of the Gilbert Is, W Kiribati
Onslow *76* W Australia
Onsŏng *413* NE North Korea
Ontario *146-147* province of S Canada
Ontario, Lake *147, 571* lake of Canada and USA
Ontong Java Atoll *490* *prev.* Lord Howe Island. Atoll of N Solomon Is
Onverwacht *510* N Suriname
Ooma *320* Banaba, W Kiribati
Oos-Londen *see* East London
Oostende *99* *Fr.* Ostende, *Eng.* Ostend. NW Belgium
Oosterhout *397* SW Netherlands
Oosterschelde *397* *Eng.* Eastern Scheldt. Inlet of the North Sea, on the coast of SW Netherlands
Opava *188* *Ger.* Troppau. E Czech Republic
Opole *441* *Ger.* Oppeln. SW Poland
Oporto *see* Porto
Oppdal *414* S Norway
Oppeln *see* Opole
Opuwo *391* NW Namibia
Oqtosh *582* *Rus.* Aktash. S Uzbekistan
Oradea *450* *prev.* Oradea Mare, *Ger.* Grosswardein, *Hung.* Nagyvárad. NW Romania
Oral *see* Ural'sk
Oran *59* *var.* Ouahran, Wahran. NW Algeria
Orange *77* SE Australia
Orange Free State *see* Free State
Orange Mouth *see* Oranjemund
Orangemund *see* Oranjemund
Orange River *334, 391, 495* *Afr.* Oranjerivier. River of southern Africa
Orange Walk *102* N Belize
Orango, Ilha de *254* island of Arquipélago dos Bijagós, SW Guinea-Bissau
Orangozinho, Ilha de *254* island of SW Guinea-Bissau
Oranjemund *391* *var.* Orangemund,

Oranjestad *628* St. Eustatius, N Netherlands Antilles
Oranjestad *620* ❖ of Aruba, W Aruba
Orantes *332, 523* *var.* Ononte, Orontes, *Ar.* Nahr al 'Așī, *var.* Nahr al 'Āsī Oronte, Nr el Aassi. River of SW Asia
Orany *see* Varėna
Orapa *118* C Botswana
Orcadas *66* Argentinian research station of Greater Antarctica, Antarctica
Orchid Island *see* Lan Yü
Orchila, Isla le *591* island of N Venezuela
Ordino *62* NW Andorra
Ordu *549* N Turkey
Ordubad *86* SW Azerbaijan
Ordzhonikidze *see* Yenakiyeve
Ordzhonikidze *see* Vladikavkaz
Ordzhonikidzeabad *see* Kofarnihon
Orealla *256* E Guyana
Örebro *515* S Sweden
Oregon *570* state of NW USA
Orël *454* W Russia
Orem *570* Utah, SW USA
Orenburg *454* *prev.* Chkalov. W Russia
Orense *see* Ourense
Orestiáda *245* *prev.* Orestiás. NE Greece
Öresund *see* Sound, The
Öresund *see* Sound, The
Oreti *401* river of S South Island, New Zealand
Orgeyev *see* Orhei
Orhei *376* *var.* Orheiu, *Rus.* Orgeyev. N Moldova
Orhon Gol *380* river of N Mongolia
Oriental, Cordillera *112* range of the Andes in C Bolivia
Oriental, Cordillera *171* range of the Andes in C Colombia
Oriental, Cordillera *433* range of the Andes of C Peru
Orikum *57* *var.* Oriku. SW Albania
Orinoco *171, 591* river of Colombia and Venezuela
Oristano *294* Sardegna, W Italy
Orizaba, Volcán Pico de *370* *var.* Citlaltépetl. Mountain of SE Mexico
Orkhanie *see* Botevgrad
Orkney *565* islands of NE UK
Orlau *see* Orlová
Orléanais *225* cultural region of N France
Orléans *225* N France
Orléansville *see* Chlef
Orlová *188* *Ger.* Orlau, *Pol.* Orlowa. SE Czech Republic
Ormoc *437* *var.* MacArthur. Leyte, E Philippines
Ormsö *see* Vormsi
Ormuz, Strait of *see* Hormuz, Strait of
Örnsköldsvik *515* NE Sweden
Oro *413* E North Korea
Orodara *133* SW Burkina
Orol Dengizi *see* Aral Sea
Oroluk *374* atoll of C Micronesia
Oron *408* S Nigeria
Orona *320* *var.* Hull I. Island of the Phoenix Is, C Kiribati
Oronoque *256* river of SE Guyana
Orontes *see* Orantes
Orosháza *264* SE Hungary
Orotina *178* W Costa Rica
Orsha *104* NE Belorussia
Orsk *454* C Russia
Ørsta *414* SW Norway
Ortoire *542* river of S Trinidad, Trinidad & Tobago
Orto-Tokoy *325* *var.* Orto Tokoj. N Kyrgyzstan
Orūmīyeh *281* *prev.* Rezāīyeh, Urmia. NW Iran
Orūmīyeh, Daryācheh-ye *281* *prev.* Daryācheh-ye Rezā'īyeh, *Eng.* Lake Urmia. Lake of NW Iran
Oruro *112* W Bolivia
Orvieto *295* C Italy
Oryakhovo *128* *var.* Orjahovo. NW Bulgaria
Oryokko *see* Yalu
Ōsaka *304, 309* Honshū, C Japan
Osa, Península de *178* peninsula of S Costa Rica

Eng. Orange Mouth. S Namibia
Ösel *see* Saaremaa
Osh *325* *var.* Oš. SW Kyrgyzstan
Oshakati *391* N Namibia
Oshawa *147* SE Canada
Oshikango *391* N Namibia
Oshogbo *408* W Nigeria
Osijek *181* *Hung.* Eszék, *Ger.* Esseg. NE Croatia
Osipenko *see* Berdyans'k
Osipovichi *see* Asipovichy
Öskemen *see* Ust'-Kamenogorsk
Ösling *346* physical region of N Luxembourg
Oslo *414* *prev.* Christiania. ❖ of Norway, S Norway
Oslofjorden *414* fjord of S Norway
Osmaniye *549* S Turkey
Osnabrück *236* NW Germany
Osogovski Planini *349* *var.* Osogovske Planine. Mountain range of Bulgaria and FYR Macedonia
Oss *397* S Netherlands
Ossa, Serra de *444* mountain range of SE Portugal
Ostee *see* Baltic Sea
Ostend *see* Oostende
Ostende *see* Oostende
Österbotten *see* Pohjanmaa
Östermyra *see* Seinäjoki
Österreich *see* Austria
Östersund *515* C Sweden
Ostfriesische Inseln *236* *Eng.* East Frisian Islands. Island group of NW Germany
Ostrava *188* *Ger.* Mährisch-Ostrau, *prev.* Moravská Ostrava. E Czech Republic
Ostrobothnia *see* Pohjanmaa
Ostrov *188* NW Czech Republic
Ostrowiec Świętokrzyski *441* E Poland
Ostyako-Voguls'k *see* Khanty-Mansiysk
Ōsumi-shotō *304* island group of Nansei-shotō, SW Japan
Osumit *57* *var.* Osum. River of SE Albania
Otago Peninsula *401* peninsula of SE South Island, New Zealand
Otaru *304* Hokkaidō, N Japan
Otavalo *200* N Ecuador
Otavi *391* N Namibia
Otepää *212* *Ger.* Odenpäh. SE Estonia
Oti *108, 242, 539* river of W Africa
Otjinene *391* NE Namibia
Otjiwarongo *391* N Namibia
Otra *414* river of SW Norway
Otranto, Strait of *57, 295* *It.* Canale d'Otranto. Strait connecting the Adriatic Sea and Ionian Sea, between Albania and Italy
Otrokovice *188* SE Czech Republic
Ōtsu *304* Honshū, C Japan
Ottawa *147* ❖ of Canada, SE Canada
Ottawa *146* *Fr.* Outaouais. River of SE Canada
Otterup *190* Fyn, C Denmark
Otu Tolu Group *540* island group of SE Tonga
Ötztaler Alpen *82* *It.* Alpi Venoste. Mountain range of Austria and Italy
Ou *327* river of N Laos
Ouaddi *194* NE Djibouti
Ouâd Nâga *366* SW Mauritania
Ouagadougou *133* *var.* Wagadugu. ❖ of Burkina, C Burkina
Ouâhayyi *194* river of Djibouti and Somalia
Ouahigouya *133* NW Burkina
Ouahran *see* Oran
Ouaka *155* river of C Central African Republic
Oualâta *366* SE Mauritania
Ouallam *407* *var.* Oualam. W Niger
Ouanary *623* E French Guiana
Ouanda Djallé *155* N Central African Republic
Ouani *174* N Anjouan, Comoros
Ouara *155* river of E Central African Republic
Ouargla *59* *var.* Wargla. NE Algeria

Ouarkziz *382* seasonal river of SW Morocco

Ouarzazate *382* S Morocco

Ouazzane *382* N Morocco

Oubangui *see* Ubangi

Ouchan *625* E Isle of Man

Oued Zem *382* C Morocco

Ouégoa *628* N New Caledonia

Ouéléssébougou *360* *var.* Ouolossébougou. SW Mali

Ouémé *108* river of C Benin

Ouessant, Île d' *224* *Eng.* Ushant. Island of NW France

Ouèssè *108* *var.* Ouéssé. E Benin

Ouésso *176* NW Congo

Ouham *155*, *156* river of Central African Republic and Chad

Ouidah *108* *Eng.* Whydah, *var.* Wida. S Benin

Oujda *382* NE Morocco

Oujeft *366* C Mauritania

Ould Yenjé *366* S Mauritania

Ouled Djellal *59* *var.* Awled Djellal. N Algeria

Oulu *221* *Swe.* Uleåborg. C Finland

Oulujärvi *221* *Swe.* Uleträsk. Lake of C Finland

Oulujoki *221* *Swe.* Uleälv. River of C Finland

Oumé *300* C Ivory Coast

Oum er Rbia *382* river of C Morocco

Oumm ed Droûs Telli, Sebkhet *366* salt lake of N Mauritania

Ounasjoki *221* river of N Finland

Ounianga Kébir *156* NE Chad

Ountivou *539* E Togo

Ouolossébougou *see* Ouéléssébougou

Our *346* river of W Europe

Ourense *502* *Cast.* Orense. NW Spain

Ourthe *99* river of E Belgium

Ouse *see* Great Ouse

Ouse *565* river of N England, UK

Outaouais *see* Ottawa

Outer Hebrides *565* *var.* Western Isles. Island group of NW Scotland, UK

Outer Islands *480* island group of C and SW Seychelles

Outjo *391* N Namibia

Ouvéa *628* island of Îles Loyauté, NE New Caledonia

Ovalau *218* island to the NE of Viti Levu, C Fiji

Ovalle *159* N Chile

Ovan *230* NE Gabon

Overflakkeis *397* island of SW Netherlands

Overhalla *414* C Norway

Ovgos *187* river of NW Cyprus

Oviedo *502* NW Spain

Owando *176* C Congo

Owen Falls Dam *556* dam of S Uganda

Owen Stanley Range *428* mountain range of SE Papua New Guinea

Owerri *408* S Nigeria

Owia *468* N St. Vincent, St. Vincent & the Grenadines

Owo *408* SW Nigeria

Öxarfjördhur *268* *var.* Axarfjördhur. Fjord of NE Iceland

Oxbow *334* N Lesotho

Oxford *565* C England, UK

Oyama *304* Honshū, N Japan

Oyem *230* N Gabon

Oyo *408* W Nigeria

Oyo *176* C Congo

Oyster Island *135* island of W Burma

Ozama *198* river of S Dominican Republic

Ózd *264* NE Hungary

Özgön *see* Uzgen

Ozurget'i *234* *prev.* Makharadze. W Georgia

P

Paama *587* island of C Vanuatu

Paamiut *624* *Dan.* Frederikshåb. SW Greenland

Paarl *495* Western Cape, SW South Africa

Pābna *93* W Bangladesh

Pacaraima, Serra *121*, *256* *var.* Pakaraima Mountains. Mountain range of N South America

Pachao Tao *527* island group of W Taiwan

Pachna *see* Pakhna

Pachuca *370* *var.* Pachuca de Soto. C Mexico

Pacific Ocean *66*, *253*, *304-305*, *620*, *625* world's largest ocean bounded by Asia and Australia to the W, the Americas to the E and Antarctica to the S

Padang *276* Sumatra, W Indonesia

Paderborn *236* NW Germany

Padma *93* name of the Ganges in Bangladesh, *see* Ganges

Padova *295* *Eng.* Padua. N Italy

Paektu-san *413* *Chin.* Baitou Shan. Mountain of China and North Korea

Pafos *see* Paphos

Pag *181* *It.* Pago. Island of C Croatia

Pagan *628* island of C Northern Mariana Islands

Pager *556* river of NE Uganda

Paget Island *621* island of E Bermuda

Pago *see* Pag

Pagon, Bukit *126* mountain of SE Brunei

Pago Pago *620* ❖ of American Samoa, Tutuila, W American Samoa

Pagouda *539* *var.* Kpagouda. NE Togo

Pahang *354* *var.* Syngei Pahang. River of C Peninsular Malaysia

Pai-ch'eng *see* Baicheng

Paide *212* *Ger.* Weissenstein. C Estonia

Päijänne *221* lake of S Finland

Pailĭn *141* W Cambodia

Paine, Cerro *159* mountain of S Chile

Paisance *see* Piacenza

País Valenciano *503* *Cat.* València, *Eng.* Valencia. Autonomous community of NE Spain

País Vasco *503* autonomous community of N Spain

Pakambaru *276* Sumatra, W Indonesia

Pakaraima Mountains *see* Pacaraima, Serra

Pakch'ŏn *413* W North Korea

Pakhna *187* *var.* Pachna. SW Cyprus

Pakin *374* atoll of E Micronesia

Pakistan *420-423* officially Islamic Republic of Pakistan. Country of Asia divided into 4 admin. units (provinces). v Islāmābād

Pak Lay *327* W Laos

Pakokku *135* W Burma

Pākpattan *421* E Pakistan

Pak Sane *see* Muang Pakxan

Pāksey *93* W Bangladesh

Pakwach *556* NW Uganda

Pakxé *327* *var.* Pakse. S Laos

Pal *62* W Andorra

Pala *156* SW Chad

Palapye *118* SE Botswana

Palau *425* *var.* Belau. Country of the Pacific Ocean. ❖ Koror

Palauli Bay *598* bay of Pacific Ocean off Sava'i, SW Western Samoa

Palawan *437* island of W Philippines

Palawan Passage *437* passage of the South China Sea, between Spratly Islands and Palawan, Philippines

Paldiski *212* *prev.* Baltiski, *Eng.* Baltic Port, *Ger.* Baltischport. NW Estonia

Palembang *276* Sumatra, W Indonesia

Palencia *503* NW Spain

Palermo *295* *Fr.* Palerme. Sicilia, S Italy

Palikir *375* ❖ of Micronesia, Pohnpei, Micronesia

Palimé *see* Kpalimé

Palk Strait *270*, *506* strait connecting the Bay of Bengal and Gulf of Mannar, between India and Sri Lanka

Palma *503* *var.* Palma de Mallorca. Mallorca, E Spain

Palma *387* N Mozambique

Palmar Norte *178* SE Costa Rica

Palma Soriano *182* SE Cuba

Palm Beach *620* NW Aruba

Palmeira *152* Sal, NE Cape Verde

Palmer *66* US research station of Antarctic Peninsula, Antarctica

Palmerston *622* island of Southern Cook Islands, S Cook Islands

Palmerston North *401* S North Island, New Zealand

Palmetto Point *68* SW Barbuda, Antigua & Barbuda

Palmira *171* W Colombia

Palmyra *see* Tudmur

Paloe *see* Denpasar

Palu *276* Celebes, C Indonesia

Pamandzi *627* Petite-Terre, E Mayotte

Pamir *530* river of Afghanistan, Pakistan and Tajikistan

Pamirs *530* mountain range of E Tajikistan

Pampa Aullagas, Lago *see* Poopó, Lago

Pampas *71* flatlands of South America

Pampeluna *see* Pamplona

Pamplemousses *368* NW Mauritius

Pamplona *503* *var.* Pampeluna, *Basq.* Iruña. N Spain

Pamplona *171* NE Colombia

Pana *230* S Gabon

Panadura *506* SW Sri Lanka

Panagyurishte *128* *var.* Panagjurište. W Bulgaria

Pānāji *270* SW India

Panama *426-427* officially Republic of Panama. Country of Central America divided into 10 admin. units (9 provinces, and 1 special territory). ❖ Panama City

Panamá, Bahía de *426* bay to the S of Panama

Panama Canal *426* shipping canal linking the Caribbean Sea to the Pacific Ocean, passing through C Panama

Panama City *426* *Sp.* Panamá, *var.* Ciudad de Panama. ❖ of Panama, C Panama

Panamá, Golfo de *426* gulf of the Pacific Ocean to the S of Panama

Panamá, Istmo de *426* *prev.* Isthmus of Darien, *Eng.* Isthmus of Panama. Narrow strip of land, between North America and South America

Panay *437* island of C Philippines

Panay Gulf *437* gulf of the Sulu Sea

Pančevo *604* *Ger.* Pantschowa, *Hung.* Pancsova. N Serbia, Yugoslavia

Panda *387* S Mozambique

Pandan, Selat *485* strait connecting Strait of Malacca and South China Sea

Pandan Reservoir *485* reservoir of SW Singapore

Pandaruan *126* river of NE Brunei

Pan de Azúcar *579* S Uruguay

Pandélys *344* *var.* Pandelis. NE Lithuania

Pandivere Kõrgustik *212* *var.* Pandivere Kõrgendik. Plateau of NW and NE Estonia

Pando *579* S Uruguay

Panevėžys *344* NE Lithuania

Panfilov *312* SE Kazakhstan

Pangai *540* Lifuka, Hai'pai Group, Tonga

Pangani *532* E Tanzania

Pangani *532* river of NE Tanzania

Pangar *144* river of C Cameroon

Pangkalpinang *276* Pulau Bangka, W Indonesia

Panguma *482* E Sierra Leone

Panguna *428* Bougainville I, Papua New Guinea

Pangutaran Group *437* island group of Sulu Archipelago, SW Philippines

Panhame *see* Manyame

Paniai, Danau *276* lake of Irian Jaya, E Indonesia

Panj *530* *Rus.* Pyandzh. SW Tajikistan

Panj *53*, *530* *Rus.* Pyandzh. River of Afghanistan and Tajikistan

Panjakent *530* *Rus.* Pendzhikent. W Tajikistan

Panjang, Pulu *see* West Island

Panji Poyon *530* *Rus.* Nizhniy Pyandzh. SW Tajikistan

Pano Lefkara *187* S Cyprus

Pano Panayia *187* *var.* Pano Panagia. W Cyprus

Pano Platres *187* SW Cyprus

Pantanal *120*, *125* swamp region of SW Brazil

Pantelleria *295* island to the SW of Sicilia, S Italy

Pantschowa *see* Pančevo

Pánuco *370* river of C Mexico

Panzhihua *163* *prev.* Dukou *var.* Tu-k'ou. Sichuan, SW China

Panzós *250* E Guatemala

Pao-chi *see* Baoji

Paoki *see* Baoji

Paola *363* E Malta

Paola *295* S Italy

Pao-shan *see* Baoshan

Pao-ting *see* Baoding

Pao-t'ou *see* Baotou

Paotow *see* Baotou

Pápa *264* W Hungary

Papakura *401* N North Island, New Zealand

Papatoetoe *401* NW North Island, New Zealand

Papayes, River *368* river of W Mauritius

Papeete *624* ❖ of French Polynesia, Tahiti, W French Polynesia

Paphos *187* *var.* Pafos. W Cyprus

Papua, Gulf of *428* gulf of the Coral Sea, to the S of Papua New Guinea

Papua New Guinea *428-429* officially Independent State of Papua New Guinea, *prev.* Territory of Papua and New Guinea. Country of the SW Pacific divided into 19 admin. units (provinces). ❖ Port Moresby

Papuk *181* mountain range of NE Croatia

Paquera *178* W Costa Rica

Pará *see* Belém

Paraburdoo *76* W Australia

Paracel Islands *629* disputed island group of the South China Sea. ❖ Woody Island

Paraćin *604* C Serbia, Yugoslavia

Paradise *248* E Grenada island, Grenada

Paraguá *112* river of NE Bolivia

Paragua *591* river of SE Venezuela

Paraguaçu *121* *var.* Paraguassú. River of E Brazil

Paraguai *see* Paraguay

Paraguarí *430* S Paraguay

Paraguassú *see* Paraguaçu

Paraguay *71*, *120*, *430* *Port.* Paraguai. River of C South America

Paraguay *430-431* officially Republic of Paraguay. Country of South America divided into 20 admin. units (19 departments and 1 province). ❖ Asunción

Paraíba *see* Joao Pessoa

Paraíso *178* C Costa Rica

Parakou *108* C Benin

Paralimni *187* E Cyprus

Paraná *71* E Argentina

Paraná *71*, *121*, *430* *var.* Alto Paraná. River of C South America

Paranam *510* N Suriname

Paraparaumu *401* S North Island, New Zealand

Pardubice *188* *Ger.* Pardubitz, C Czech Republic

Pardubitz *see* Pardubice

Parecis, Chapada dos *120* *var.* Serra dos Parecis. Mountain range of W Brazil

Pares *68* E Antigua, Antigua & Barbuda

Parham *68* NE Antigua, Antigua & Barbuda

Paria, Gulf of *542*, *591* gulf of the Atlantic Ocean, between Trinidad and Venezuela

Parika *256* NE Guyana

Parima, Serra *120* mountain range of Brazil and Venezuela
Paris *225, 228* ❖ of France, N France
Paris *320* Kiritimati, E Kiribati
Parita, Bahía de *426* bay of the Gulf of Panama
Parkan *see* Štúrovo
Párkány *see* Štúrovo
Parkent *582* E Uzbekistan
Parkhar *see* Farkhor
Parma *294* N Italy
Parnaíba *121* river of NE Brazil
Pärnu *212* Rus. Pyarnu, *prev.* Pernov, Ger. Pernau. SW Estonia
Pärnu *212* var. Pärnu Jõgi, Ger. Pernau. River of SW Estonia
Pärnu Laht *212* bay of the Gulf of Riga, on the SW coast of Estonia
Paro *110* W Bhutan
P'aro-ho *498* var. Hwach'ŏn-chŏsuji. Reservoir of N South Korea
Páros *245* island of SE Greece
Parral *159* C Chile
Parrita *178* S Costa Rica
Parry Islands *146* island group of N Canada
Parry's *464* SE St. Kitts, St. Kitts & Nevis
Parson's Ground *464* N St. Kitts, St. Kitts & Nevis
Partizánske *487* prev. Šimonovany, Hung. Simony. W Slovakia
Pasaje *200* SW Ecuador
Pasaquina *207* E El Salvador
Pas de Calais *see* Dover, Strait of
Pa-shih Hai-hsia *see* Bashi Channel
Pashmakli *see* Smolyan
Pasión *250* river of N Guatemala
Pasir Mas *354* N Peninsular Malaysia
Pasir Panjang *485* reservoir of SW Singapore
Paso de los Toros *579* C Uruguay
Passau *237* SE Germany
Passo Fundo *121* S Brazil
Passu Keah *629* island of S Paracel Islands
Pastavy *104* Rus. Postavy, Pol. Postawy. NW Belorussia
Pastaza *200, 433* river of Ecuador and Peru
Pasto *171* SW Colombia
Patagonia *71* semi-arid region of S South America
Patchchacan *102* N Belize
Pate *527* N Taiwan
Pate Island *316* var. Patta Island. Island of SE Kenya
Paterna *503* E Spain
Pathein *see* Bassein
Patía *171* river of SW Colombia
Patience *467* E St. Lucia
Pati Point *625* headland on the NE coast of Guam
Patlong *334* S Lesotho
Patna *270* var. Azimabad. NE India
Patos *57* var. Patosi. SW Albania
Patos, Lagoa dos *121* lagoon of S Brazil
Pátra *245* var. Patras, prev. Pátrai. S Greece
Patta Island *see* Pate Island
Pattani *335* S Thailand
Pattle Island *629* island of W Paracel Islands
Patuākhāli *93* S Bangladesh
Patuca *260* river of E Honduras
Pau *225* SW France
Paungde *135* SW Burma
Pāvilosta *330* W Latvia
Pavlodar *312* NE Kazakhstan
Pavlohrad *558* Rus. Pavlograd. E Ukraine
Pavuvu *490* island of C Solomon Islands
Pawai, Pulau *485* island of SW Singapore
Paysandú *579* NW Uruguay
Paz *207* river of Guatemala and El Salvador
Pazardzhik *128* var. Pazardžik, prev. Tatar Pazardzhik. SW Bulgaria
Pazin *181* NW Croatia
Pčinja *349* river of N FYR Macedonia
Pea *540* Tongatabu, Tongatapu Group, Tonga

Peace *146* river of W Canada
Peak, The *630* mountain of C Ascension Island
Pearl Islands *see* Perlas, Archipiélago de las
Pearl Lagoon *see* Perlas, Laguna de
Pearl River Estuary *626* estuary running into the South China Sea, C Macao
Peary Land *624* physical region of N Greenland
Pebble Island *623* island of N Falkland Islands
Peć *604* S Serbia, Yugoslavia
Pechora *454* River of NW Russia
Pecixe, Ilha de *254* island of W Guinea-Bissau
Pecos *571* river of SW USA
Pécs *264* Ger. Fünfkirchen. SW Hungary
Pedernales *198* SW Dominican Republic
Pedhieos *187* var. Kanli Dere. River of NE Cyprus
Pedhoulas *187* W Cyprus
Pedja *212* var. Pedja Jõgi. River of C Estonia
Pedoulas *see* Pedhoulas
Pedra Lume *152* Sal, NE Cape Verde
Pedro Juan Caballero *430* E Paraguay
Pedro Santana *198* W Dominican Republic
Peel *625* W Isle of Man
Pegasus Bay *401* bay of the South Pacific Ocean, on the E coast of South Island, New Zealand
Pegeia *see* Peyia
Pegu *135* var. Bago. S Burma
Péhonko *108* NW Benin
Pei-ching *see* Beijing
Peikang *527* var. Pei-chiang, Jap. Hokkō. W Taiwan
Peinan Hsi *527* river of C Taiwan
Peineville *196* N Dominica
Peipsi Järv *see* Peipus, Lake
Peipus, Lake *212* Est. Peipsi Järv, Rus. Chudskoye Ozero. Lake of Estonia and Russia
Peiraías *245* prev. Piraiévs, Eng. Piraeus. SE Greece
Peka *334* NW Lesotho
Pekalongan *276* Java, C Indonesia
Pekan Muara *126* N Brunei
Pekan Seria *126* N Brunei
Peking *see* Beijing
Pelée, Montagne *627* mountain of N Martinique
Peleliu *425* island of S Palau
Péligre, Lac de *258* C Haiti
Pelly Bay *146* N Canada
Pelmadulla *506* S Sri Lanka
Pélmonostor *see* Beli Manastir
Pelopónnisos *245* Eng. Peloponnese. Peninsula of S Greece
Pelotas *121* S Brazil
Pemagatsel *110* SE Bhutan
Pematangsiantar *276* Sumatra, W Indonesia
Pemba *532* island of E Tanzania
Pemba *387* prev. Porto Amélia. NE Mozambique
Pembroke *468* SW St. Vincent, St. Vincent & the Grenadines
Pembroke Hall *see* Libertad
Penambo, Banjaran *355* var. Penambo Range, Banjaran Tama Abu. Mountain range of Borneo, Malaysia and Indonesia
Penambo Range *see* Penambo, Banjaran
Penang *see* George Town
Peñas Blancas *404* S Nicaragua
Pen-ch'i *see* Benxi
Pendé *155* river of Central African Republic and Chad
Pendembu *482* E Sierra Leone
Pendjari *108, 133* river of Benin and Burkina
Pendzhikent *see* Panjakent
P'enghu Liehtao *527* Eng. Pescadores Islands. Island group of W Taiwan
P'eng-hu Shui-tao *527* Eng. Pescadores Channel. Channel connecting South China Sea and Taiwan Strait

P'enghu Tao *527* island of W Taiwan
Peng-pu *see* Bengbu
Penibético, Sistema *503* Eng. Baetic Cordillera, Baetic Mountains. Mountain range of S Spain
Peniche *444* W Portugal
Peninsular Malaysia *354* var. Malaya, prev. West Malaysia. Western part of Malaysia situated on S Malay Peninsula
Penki *see* Benxi
Pennine Alps *518* var. Alpes Penninae, Fr. Alpes Pennines, It. Alpi Pennine. Mountain range of SW Switzerland
Pennines *565* var. Pennine Chain. Mountain range of N England, UK
Pennsylvania *571* state of NE USA
Penong *77* S Australia
Penonomé *426* C Panama
Penrhyn *622* island of Northern Cook Islands, N Cook Islands
Penrith *565* NW England, UK
Pentaschoinos *see* Yermasoyia
Pentecost *587* Fr. Pentecôte. Island of C Vanuatu
Penticton *146* SW Canada
Penza *454* W Russia
Penzance *565* SW England, UK
Peoria *571* Illinois, C USA
Pepel *482* W Sierra Leone
Pereira *171* W Colombia
Pergamino *71* E Argentina
Perico *182* NW Cuba
Périgueux *225* SW France
Perim *see* Barīm
Peringat *354* N Peninsular Malaysia
Perkhemahan Berakas *126* N Brunei
Perlas, Archipiélago de las *426* var. Pearl Islands. Island group of SE Panama
Perlas, Laguna de *404* var. Pearl Lagoon. Lagoon of the Caribbean Sea on the E coast of Nicaragua
Perlepe *see* Prilep
Perm' *454* prev. Molotov. W Russia
Përmet *57* var. Permeti, Premet. S Albania
Pernambuco *see* Recife
Pernau *see* Pärnu
Pernik *128* prev. Dimitrovo. W Bulgaria
Pernov *see* Pärnu
Peros Banhos *621* island of N British Indian Ocean Territory
Pérouse *see* Perugia
Perpignan *225* S France
Perquín *207* E El Salvador
Përrenjas *57* var. Prenjasi, Prenjas. E Albania
Persian Gulf *91, 284, 322, 449, 5* var. The Gulf, Ar. Khalij al 'Arabi, Per. Khalīj-e Fars. Gulf of the Arabian Sea between the Arabian Peninsula and Iran
Persia *see* Iran
Perth *76* SW Australia
Perth *565* N Scotland, UK
Peru *432-435* officially Republic of Peru. Country of South America divided into 25 admin. units (24 departments and 1 constitutional province). ❖ Lima
Perugia *295* Fr. Pérouse. C Italy
Perugia, Lake of *see* Trasimeno, Lago
Pesaro *295* N Italy
Pescadores Channel *see* P'enghu Liehtao
Pescadores Islands *see* P'eng-hu Ch'ü-tao
Pescara *295* C Italy
Pesek Kechil, Pulau *485* island of SW Singapore
Pesek, Pulau *485* island of SW Singapore
Peshāwar *421* N Pakistan
Peshkopi *57* var. Peshkopia, Peshkopija. NE Albania
Pessons, Pic dels *62* mountain of SE Andorra
Petaḥ Tiqwa *291* C Israel
Petaling Jaya *354* W Peninsular Malaysia
Pétange *346* SW Luxembourg
Petani *354* var. Patani. NW Peninsular Malaysia

Petare *591* N Venezuela
Petauke *613* E Zambia
Petén Itzá, Lago *523* var. Lago de Flores. Lake of N Guatemala
Peterborough *565* E England, UK
Peterborough *147* SE Canada
Peterhead *565* NE Scotland, UK
Peter Island *621* island of S British Virgin Islands
Peters Mine *256* NW Guyana
Pétionville *258* S Haiti
Petit-Bourg *624* C Guadeloupe
Petit Canouan *468* island of S St. Vincent & the Grenadines
Petite Butte *368* Rodrigues, Mauritius
Petite Côte *478* coastal region of W Senegal
Petite Dominique *248* island to the NE of Carriacou, Grenada
Petite Martinique *248* island to the NE of Carriacou, Grenada
Petite-Rivière-de-l'Artibonite *258* C Haiti
Petite-Rivière Noire, Piton de la *368* mountain range of SW Mauritius
Petite Savane *196* S Dominica
Petite Soufrière *196* E Dominica
Petite-Terre *627* island, E Mayotte
Petit-Goâve *258* S Haiti
Petitjean *see* Sidi Kacem
Petit Mustique *468* island of C St. Vincent & the Grenadines
Petit Piton *467* mountain of SW St. Lucia
Petit-Popo *see* Aného
Petit St. Vincent Island *248* island to the NE of Carriacou, Grenada
Petra *310* archaeological site of W Jordan
Petre Bay *401* bay of the South Pacific Ocean, on the coast of Chatham Island, New Zealand
Petrich *128* var. Petrič. SW Bulgaria
Petrinja *181* N Croatia
Petroaleksandrovsk *see* Tūrtkūl
Petropavlovsk *312* N Kazakhstan
Petropavlovsk-Kamchatskiy *455* NE Russia
Petrópolis *121* SE Brazil
Petrosani *450* N Romania
Petrovgrad *see* Zrenjanin
Petrovsk-Port *see* Makhachkala
Petrozavodsk *454* Fin. Petroskoi. NW Russia
Pettau *see* Ptuj
Pevek *455* NE Russia
Peyia *187* var. Pegeia. SW Cyprus
Pezinok *487* Ger. Bösing, Hung. Bazin. SW Slovakia
Pforzheim *236* SW Germany
Phalaborwa *495* Northern Transvaal, NE South Africa
Phangan, Ko *535* island of S Thailand
Phan Rang-Thap Cham *595* SE Vietnam
Phan Thiêt *595* S Vietnam
Phet Buri *see* Phetchaburi
Phetchaburi *535* var. Phet Buri. C Thailand
Philadelphia *571* Pennsylvania, NE USA
Philip Island *628* island of S Norfolk Island
Philippeville *see* Skikda
Philippines *436-439* officially Republic of the Philippines. Country of SE Asia divided into 14 admin. units (regions). ❖ Manila
Philippine Sea *374, 437* sea of the Pacific Ocean to the E of the Philippines
Philipsburg *628* St. Martin, N Netherlands Antilles
Phillips *464* NE St. Kitts, St. Kitts & Nevis
Phitsanulok *535* var. Muang Phitsanulok. N Thailand
Phlórina *see* Flórina
Phnom Penh *141* Cam. Phnum Pénh. ❖ of Cambodia, S Cambodia
Phnum Aôral *141* prev. Phnom Aural. Mountain of W Cambodia
Phoenix *570* Arizona, SW USA
Phoenix *368* C Mauritius

Port Macquarie 77 E Australia
Port Maria 303 N Jamaica
Port Mathurin 368 Rodrigues,
Mauritius
Port Morant 303 E Jamaica
Portmore 303 SE Jamaica
Port Moresby 428 ❖ of Papua New
Guinea, SE Papua New Guinea
Porto 444 Eng. Oporto. NW Portugal
Porto Alegre 121 prev. Pôrto Alegre.
S Brazil
Porto Alegre 473 S São Tomé, Sao
Tome & Principe
Porto Alexandre see Tombua
Porto Amélia see Pemba
Portobelo 426 var. Porto Bello, Puerto
Bello. N Panama
Porto Edda see Sarandë
Porto Exterior 626 harbour of
NE Macao
Port-of-Spain 542 ❖ of Trinidad
& Tobago, NW Trinidad, Trinidad
& Tobago
Porto Gole 254 C Guinea-Bissau
Porto Grande see Mindelo
Porto Interior 626 harbour of
NW Macao
Porto-Novo 108 ❖ of Benin, S Benin
Porto Santo 444 var. Ilha do Porto
Santo. Island of the Madeira Is,
Portugal
Porto Torres 295 Sardegna, W Italy
Porto Velho 120 prev. Pôrto Velho.
W Brazil
Portoviejo 200 var. Puertoviejo.
W Ecuador
Port Pirie 77 S Australia
Port Refuge 622 strait of the Indian
Ocean between Horsburgh Island and
Direction Island, C Cocos Islands
Port Royal 303 SE Jamaica
Port Said 202 Ar. Bur Sa'īd. N Egypt
Port St. Mary 625 S Isle of Man
Portsmouth 565 S England, UK
Portsmouth 196 var. Grande-Anse.
NW Dominica
Port Stanley see Stanley
Port Stephens 623 West Falkland,
W Falkland Islands
Port Sudan 508 var. Būr Sūdān.
NE Sudan
Port Swettenham see Kelang
Port Talbot 565 S Wales, UK
Portugal 444–447 officially Republic of
Portugal. Country of W Europe
divided into 18 admin. units
(districts). ❖ Lisbon
Portuguese East Africa
see Mozambique
Port-Vila 587 var. Vila. ❖ of Vanuatu,
Éfate, Vanuatu
Porvenir 159 Tierra del Fuego, Chile
Porvenir 112 NW Bolivia
Posadas 71 NE Argentina
Posen see Poznań
Posŏng 498 river of S South Korea
Postojna 488 Ger. Adelsberg,
It. Postumia. SW Slovenia
Pöstyén see Piešťany
Potaro 256 river of C Guyana
Potchefstroom 495 North West,
N South Africa
Potenza 295 S Italy
Potgietersrus 495 Northern Transvaal,
NE South Africa
Pot House 97 E Barbados
P'ot'i 234 W Georgia
Potiskum 408 NE Nigeria
Po Toi Island 262 island of S Hong
Kong
Potoru 482 S Sierra Leone
Potosí 112 S Bolivia
Potsdam 237 NE Germany
Potters Village 68 C Antigua, Antigua
& Barbuda
Pott, Île 628 island of Îles Belep,
W New Caledonia
Pottuvil 506 SE Sri Lanka
Potwar Plateau 420 plateau of
NE Pakistan
Poudre d'Or 368 NE Mauritius
Pouembout 631 W New Caledonia
Poum 628 W New Caledonia
Pout 478 W Senegal
Poutasi 598 Upolu, Western Samoa

Poûthīsăt 141 var. Pursat. River of
W Cambodia
Poûthīsăt 141 prev. Pursat.
W Cambodia
Po Valley 294 valley of N Italy
Považská Bystrica 487
Ger. Waagbistritz,
Hung. Vágbeszterce.
NW Slovakia
Povoaçao de Hác-Sá 626 Coloane,
S Macao
Povoaçao de Ká-Hó 626 Coloane,
S Macao
Povoaçao de Sai Sa 626 Taipa,
C Macao
Povoaçao de Samka 626 Taipa,
C Macao
Póvoa de Varzim 444 NW Portugal
Powell, Lake 570 reservoir of
SW USA
Poya 628 C New Caledonia
Poyang Hu 163 lake of E China
Poyan Reservoir 485 reservoir of
W Singapore
Poza Rica 370 var. Poza Rica de
Hidalgo. C Mexico
Poznań 441 Ger. Posen. W Poland
Pozo Colorado 430 C Paraguay
Pozsega see Slavonska Požega
Pozsony see Bratislava
Prábis 254 W Guinea-Bissau
Præsto 190 Sjælland, SE Denmark
Prague 188 Cz. Praha, Ger. Prag.
❖ of Czech Republic, NW Czech
Republic
Praia 152 ❖ of Cape Verde, Santiago,
S Cape Verde
Praia Grande, Baia da 626 bay of the
South China Sea, N Macao
Praslin 480 island of the Inner Islands,
NE Seychelles
Praslin 467 E St. Lucia
Prato 294 N Italy
Preguiça 152 São Nicolau,
N Cape Verde
Prenjas see Përrenjas
Preparis Island 135 island of
SW Burma
Přerov 188 Ger. Prerau. SE Czech
Republic
Presidente Prudente 121 S Brazil
Prešov 487 Ger. Eperies, var.
Preschau, Hung. Eperjes. NE Slovakia
Prespa, Lake 57, 245, 349 Alb. Liqen i
Prespës, Mac. Prespansko Ezero,
Gk Límni Megáli Préspa, var. Limni
Prespa. Lake of SE Europe
Prespës, Liqen i see Prespa, Lake
Pressburg see Bratislava
Prestea 242 SW Ghana
Preston 565 NW England, UK
Pretoria 495 ❖ of South Africa.
Pretoria-Witwatersrand-Vereeniging,
NE South Africa
Pretoria-Witwatersrand-Vereeniging
495 province of NE South Africa
Préveza 245 W Greece
Prey Vêng 141 S Cambodia
Priboj 604 W Serbia, Yugoslavia
Příbram 188 W Czech Republic
Prickly Pear Cays 620 island group of
NW Anguilla
Prieska 495 Northern Cape, C South
Africa
Prievidza 487 C Slovakia
Prijedor 116 NW Bosnia
& Herzegovina
Prilep 349 Turk. Perlepe.
S FYR Macedonia
Prince Albert 146 SW Canada
Prince Edward Island 147 province
and island of SE Canada
Prince Edward Island 495 island of
the Prince Edward Islands, S South
Africa
Prince Edward Islands 495 island
group of S South Africa
Prince George 146 SW Canada
Prince Island see Príncipe
Prince of Wales Island see Pinang,
Pulau
Prince of Wales Island 146 island of
N Canada
Prince Patrick Island 146 island of
Parry Islands, N Canada

Prince Rupert 146 W Canada
Prince Rupert Bay 196 bay of the
Caribbean Sea, to the NW of
Dominica
Princes Town 542 SW Trinidad,
Trinidad & Tobago
Príncipe 473 var. Príncipe Island,
Eng. Prince Island. Island to the N of
São Tomé, Sao Tome & Principe
Pripet 104 river of S Belorussia
Pripet Marshes 104, 558 forested and
swampy region of Belorussia and
Ukraine
Priština 604 S Serbia, Yugoslavia
Privas 225 SE France
Privigye see Prievidza
Priwitz see Prievidza
Prizren 604 Alb. Prizreni. S Serbia,
Yugoslavia
Probištip 349 N FYR Macedonia
Probolinggo 276 Java, C Indonesia
Progreso 579 S Uruguay
Prome 135 var. Pyè. SW Burma
Promissão, Represa de 121 reservoir
of S Brazil
Proskurov see Khmel 'nyts'kyy
Prostějov 188 Ger. Prossnitz.
SE Czech Republic
Provadiya 128 var. Provadija.
E Bulgaria
Provence 225 cultural region of
SE France
Providence 571 Rhode Island,
NE USA
Providence 97 S Barbados
Providence Atoll 480 var. Providence.
Atoll of the Farquhar Group,
S Seychelles
Providenciales 631 island of
NW Turks and Caicos Islands
Provo 570 Utah, SW USA
Prudhoe Bay 570 Alaska, USA
Prune Island 468 island of
SW St. Vincent & the Grenadines
Prut 376, 450, 558 Ger. Pruth. River of
E Europe
Pruth see Prut
Pruzhany 104 SW Belorussia
Pryazova'ks Vysochyna 558 mountain
range of SE Ukraine
Prychornomors'ka Nyzovyna 558
mountain range of S Ukraine
Prydniprovs'ka Nyzovyna 558
mountain range of NE Ukraine
Prydniprovs'ka Vysochyna 558 moun-
tain range of NW Ukraine
Przemyśl 441 SE Poland
Przheval'sk see Karakol
Pskov 454 Ger. Pleskau. W Russia
Pskov, Lake 212 Est. Pihkva Järv,
Rus. Pskovskoye Ozero. Lake of
Estonia and Russia
Ptsich 104 Rus. Ptich'. River of
C Belorussia
Ptuj 488 Ger. Pettau. NE Slovenia
Pua'a, Cape 598 cape on the coast of
Savai'i, NW Western Samoa
Pu'apu'a 598 Savali'i, Western Samoa
Pucallpa 433 C Peru
Puch'ŏn 498 prev. Punwŏn. NW South
Korea
Pudasjärvi 221 C Finland
Puebla 370 var. Puebla de Zaragoza.
S Mexico
Pueblo 571 Colorado, SW USA
Pueblo Nuevo Tiquisate 250
var. Tiquisate. SW Guatemala
Puente Alto 159 C Chile
Puerto Acosta 112 W Bolivia
Puerto Aisén 159 S Chile
Puerto Armuelles 426 W Panama
Puerto Ayacucho 591 SW Venezuela
Puerto Bahía Negra 430 N Paraguay
Puerto Baquerizo Moreno 200 San
Cristobal I, Galapagos Is.
Puerto Barrios 250 E Guatemala
Puerto Bello see Portobelo
Puerto Berrío 171 N Colombia
Puerto Busch 112 var. Puerto General
Busch. SE Bolivia
Puerto Cabello 591 N Venezuela
Puerto Cabezas 404 var. Bilwi.
NE Nicaragua
Puerto Carreño 171 E Colombia
Puerto Casado 430 C Paraguay

Puerto Cooper 430 C Paraguay
Puerto Cortés 260 NW Honduras
Puerto El Carmen de Putumayo
200 var. Putumayo. NW Ecuador
Puerto el Triunfo 207 S El Salvador
Puerto Inírida 171 var. Obando.
E Colombia
Puerto Iradier see Cogo
Puerto La Cruz 591 NE Venezuela
Puerto Lempira 260 E Honduras
Puertolland 503 SW Spain
Puerto Maldonado 433 E Peru
Puerto México see Coatzacoalcos
Puerto Montt 159 C Chile
Puerto Natales 159 S Chile
Puerto Padre 182 SE Cuba
Puerto Pinasco 430 C Paraguay
Puerto Plata 198 var. San Felipe de
Puerto Plata. N Dominican Republic
Puerto Presidente Stroessner
see Ciudad del Este
Puerto Princesa 437 Palawan,
W Philippines
Puerto Príncipe see Camagüey
Puerto Rico 629 Commonwealth
territory of the USA, Caribbean Sea. ❖
San Juan
Puerto Rico Trench 629 undersea
feature of the Caribbean Sea,
N Puerto Rico
Puerto San José 250 var. San José.
S Guatemala
Puerto Suárez 112 E Bolivia
Puerto Vallarta 370 W Mexico
Puerto Varas 159 C Chile
Puerto Viejo 178 NE Costa Rica
Puertoviejo see Portoviejo
Pujehun 482 S Sierra Leone
Pukaki, Lake 401 lake of C South
Island, New Zealand
Pukapuka 622 island of Northern Cook
Islands, N Cook Islands
Pukch'ŏng 413 E North Korea
Pukë 57 var. Puka. N Albania
Pukekohe 401 NW North Island,
New Zealand
Pukhan 498 river of North Korea and
South Korea
Pula 181 prev. Pulj, It. Pola.
W Croatia
Pulangi 437 river of Mindanao,
S Philippines
Pulap 374 atoll of C Micronesia
Pulau 277 river of Irian Jaya,
E Indonesia
Pulau Tekong Reservoir 485
reservoir of E Singapore
Pul-i-Khumri see Pol-e Khomri
Pully 518 SW Switzerland
Pulusuk 374 island of C Micronesia
Puluwat 374 atoll of C Micronesia
Puná, Isla 200 island to the SW of
Ecuador, in the Gulf of Guayaquil
Punakha 110 C Bhutan
Punata 112 C Bolivia
Pune 270 prev. Poona. W India
Punggol 485 area of NE Singapore
Púngoè 387 var. Pungue, Pungwe.
River of C Mozambique
Punkudutivu 506 island of N Sri Lanka
Puno 433 SE Peru
Punta Arenas 159 prev. Magallanes.
S Chile
Punta Chame 426 C Panama
Punta del Este 579 S Uruguay
Punta Gorda 102 S Belize
Puntarenas 178 W Costa Rica
Punta Santiago 208 S Bioko,
Equatorial Guinea
Punto Fijo 591 NW Venezuela
Punwŏn see Puch'ŏn
Purari 428 river of C Papua New
Guinea
Puri 270 E India
Purmerend 397 NW Netherlands
Pursat see Poûthīsăt
Purus 120 river of Brazil and Peru
Pusan 498 var. Busan, Jap. Fusan.
SE South Korea
Pusat Gayo, Pegunungan 276
mountain range of Sumatra,
W Indonesia
Pushkino see Biläsuvar
Putai 527 W Taiwan

Putorana, Plato 455 mountain range of N Russia
Puttalam 506 W Sri Lanka
Puttalam Lagoon 506 lagoon of W Sri Lanka
Putumayo 171, 433 river of NW South America
Putumayo see Puerto El Carmen de Putumayo
Puyo 200 C Ecuador
Pyandzh see Panj
Pyapon 135 S Burma
Pyarnu see Pärnu
Pyinmana 135 C Burma
Pyltsamaa see Põltsamaa
P'yŏngt'aek 498 NW South Korea
Pyongyang 413 Kor. P'yŏngyang.
❖ of North Korea, SW North Korea
Pyramiden 631 Spitsbergen, W Svalbard
Pyramid Rock 629 island of E Paracel Islands
Pyrenees 62, 224-225, 503 Sp. Pirineos, Fr. Pyrénées. Mountain range of SW Europe
Pyu 135 S Burma
Pyuntaza 135 S Burma
Pyuthan 395 W Nepal

Q

Qaanaaq 624 Dan.Thule. NW Greenland
Qabatiya 292 N West Bank
Qâbis see Gabès
Qafṣah see Gafsa
Qahremānshahr see Bākhtarān
Qala' en Nahl 508 var. Qala' an Naḥl. E Sudan
Qal'aikhum 530 Rus. Kalaikhum. C Tajikistan
Qalali 91 Jazirat al Muharraq, Bahrain
Qalansīyah 601 NW Suqutra, Yemen
Qalāt see Kalāt
Qal 'at Bīshah 474 SW Saudi Arabia
Qal'eh-ye Now 53 var. Qala Nau. NW Afghanistan
Qalīb ash Shuyūkh 322 var. Jleeb al Shuyoukh. C Kuwait
Qalīb, Shiqqat al 322 var. Shagat Al Jleeb. Desert region of NW Kuwait
Qamar, Ghubbat al 601 bay of Arabian Sea, E Yemen
Qamar, Jabal al 418 mountain range of SW Oman
Qambar see Kambar
Qamea 218 prev. Nggamea. Island to the E of Taveuni, N Fiji
Qandahār see Kandahār
Qaqortoq 624 Dan. Julianehåb. S Greenland
Qaraghandy see Karaganda
Qaraoun, Lac de 332 var. Buḥayrat al Qir'awn. Lake of S Lebanon
Qara Qum see Karakumy
Qarataū see Karatau
Qardho 492 It. Gardo. N Somalia
Qareh Chāy 281 river of NW Iran
Qarkilik see Ruoqiang
Qarokŭl 530 Rus. Karakul'. E Tajikistan
Qarokŭl 530 Rus. Ozero Karakul'. Lake of E Tajikistan
Qarshi 582 Rus. Karshi, prev. Bek-Budi. S Uzbekistan
Qartaba 332 var. Qarṭabā. N Lebanon
Qasigiannguit 624 Dan. Christianshåb. W Greenland
Qatar 448-449 officially State of Qatar. Country of SW Asia divided into 9 admin. units (municipalities). ❖ Doha
Qattâra, Monkhafad el 202 var. Munkhafaḍ al Qaṭṭārah, Eng. Qattara Depression. Arid desert bin of NW Egypt
Qayrokkum, Obanbori 530 Rus. Kayrakkumskoye Vodolkhranilishche. Reservoir of NW Tajikistan
Qazaqstan see Kazakhstan
Qazax 86 Rus. Kazakh. W Azerbaijan
Qazbegi 234 Rus. Kazbegi. NE Georgia

Qazimämmäd 86 Rus. Kazi-Magomed. SE Azerbaijan
Qazvīn 281 var. Kazvin. NW Iran
Qena 202 var. Qina. E Egypt
Qena, Wâdi 202 var. Wādī Qinā. Seasonal river of E Egypt
Qeqertarsuaq 624 Dan. Godhavn. W Greenland
Qeqertarsuatsiaat 624 Dan. Fiskenæsset. SW Greenland
Qeshm 281 var. Jazīreh-ye Qeshm, Qeshm Island. Island of S Iran
Qezel Owzan 281 river of NW Iran
Qibili see Kebili
Qilian Shan 162 var. Kilien Mountains. Mountain range of W China
Qingdao 163 var. Tsintao, Ching-Tao, Ch'ing-tao. Shandong, E China
Qinghai 162 var. Chinghai, Tsinghai. Province of W China
Qinghai Hu 162 var. Ch'ing Hai Mong. Koko Nor. Lake of W China
Qing-Zang Gaoyuan 162 Eng. Plateau of Tibet. Plateau of Xizang Zizhiqu, W China
Qiqihar 163 prev. Lungkiang, var. Tsitsihar, Ch'i-ch'i-ha-erh. Heilongjiang, NE China
Qir'awn, Buḥayrat al see Qaraoun, Lac de
Qirba, Khashim Al see Girba, Khashm el
Qiryat Ata 291 N Israel
Qiryat Gat 291 C Israel
Qiryat Motzkin 291 N Israel
Qiryat Shemona 291 N Israel
Qishn 601 SE Yemen
Qishon, Nahal 291 river of N Israel
Qizān see Jīzān
Qizilqum see Kyzyl Kum
Qizilrabot 530 Rus. Kyzylrabot. E Tajikistan
Qom 281 var. Qum, Kum. NW Iran
Qomolangma Feng see Everest, Mount
Qomul see Hami
Qondūz see Kunduz
Qondūz, Daryā-ye 53 seasonal river of NE Afghanistan
Qorakŭl 582 Rus. Karakul'. S Uzbekistan
Qormi 363 C Malta
Qornet es Saouda 332 mountain of NE Lebanon
Qoryooley 492 It. Coriole. SW Somalia
Qoubaïyât 332 var. Al Qubayyāt. NE Lebanon
Qoussantina see Constantine
Quang Ngai 595 E Vietnam
Quan Long see Ca Mau
Quanzhou 163 var. Ch'uan-chou, prev. Chin-chiang, var. Tsinkiang. Fujian, SE China
Quaraí see Cuareim
Quarles, Pegunungan 276 mountain range of Celebes, W Indonesia
Quarnero see Kvarner
Quartier Militaire 368 C Mauritius
Quatre Bornes 368 W Mauritius
Quatre Bornes 480 Mahé, Seychelles
Quatre, Isle à 468 island of C St. Vincent & the Grenadines
Quba 86 Rus. Kuba. N Azerbaijan
Queanbeyan 77 SE Australia
Québec 147 SE Canada
Québec 147, 151 province of SE Canada
Quebo 254 S Guinea-Bissau
Queen Charlotte Bay 623 bay of the South Atlantic Ocean, W Falkland Islands
Queen Charlotte Islands 146 Fr. Îles de la Reine-Charlotte. Island group of SW Canada
Queen Charlotte Sound 146 area of the Pacific Ocean between the Queen Charlotte Islands and Vancouver Island, SW Canada
Queen Elizabeth Islands 146 Fr. Îles de la Reine-Élisabeth. Island group of N Canada
Queen Mary's Peak 630 mountain of C Tristan da Cunha
Queen Maud Gulf 146 gulf of the Arctic Ocean on the coast of N Canada

Queen Maud Land 66 physical region of Greater Antarctica, Antarctica
Queensland 77, 81 state of N Australia
Queenstown 401 S South Island, New Zealand
Queenstown 485 area of S Singapore
Queenstown 495 Eastern Cape, S South Africa
Queguay Grande 579 river of W Uruguay
Quelimane 387 E Mozambique
Quelpart see Cheju-do
Queluz 444 W Portugal
Quepos 178 S Costa Rica
Que Que see Kwekwe
Querétaro 370 C Mexico
Quesada 178 N Costa Rica
Questelles 468 SW St. Vincent, St. Vincent & the Grenadines
Quetta 421 NW Pakistan
Quezaltenango 250 var. Quetzaltenango. W Guatemala
Quezaltepeque 207 C El Salvador
Quibdó 171 W Colombia
Quillacollo 112 C Bolivia
Quilpué 159 C Chile
Quimper 224 W France
Quinhámel 254 W Guinea-Bissau
Quiniluban Group 437 island group of C Philippines
Quissico 387 S Mozambique
Quito 200 ❖ of Ecuador, N Ecuador
Qum see Qom
Qŭnghirot 582 Rus. Kungrad. NW Uzbekistan
Qŭqon 582 var. Khokand, Rus. Kokand. E Uzbekistan
Qurayn, Ra's al 91 cape of SE Bahrain
Qurayyāt 418 var. Qurayat, Quraiyat. NE Oman
Qŭrghonteppa 530 Rus. Kurgan-Tyube. W Tajikistan
Qurlurtuuq see Coppermine
Qus 202 var. Qūṣ. E Egypt
Quthing see Moyeni
Quy Nhơn 595 var. Qui Nhon, Quinhon. SE Vietnam
Qvareli 234 Rus. Kvareli. E Georgia
Qyteti Stalin see Kuçovë
Qyzylorda see Kzyl-Orda

R

Raab see Rába
Raab see Győr
Raahe 221 Swe. Brahestad. W Finland
Ra'ananna 291 C Israel
Raas Xaatuun 492 It. Ras Hafun. NE Somalia
Rába 82, 264 Ger. Raab. River of Austria and Hungary
Rabat 363 W Malta
Rabat 382 ❖ of Morocco, NW Morocco
Rabaul 428 New Britain, NE Papua New Guinea
Rabbit Island 468 island of SE St. Vincent & the Grenadines
Rábca 264 river of NW Hungary
Rabi 218 prev. Rambi. Island to the E of Vanua Levu, N Fiji
Rābigh 474 W Saudi Arabia
Rabinal 250 C Guatemala
Râbniţa see Rîbniţa
Rabyānah, Ramlat 339 var. Ṣaḥrā' Rabyāh. Desert of SE Libya
Rachaïya 332 var. Rāshayyā. S Lebanon
Rach Gia 595 SW Vietnam
Rach Gia, Vinh 595 bay of the Gulf of Thailand on the SW coast of Vietnam
Racine 571 Wisconsin, N USA
Radā 601 var. Ridā. W Yemen
Radom 441 C Poland
Radoviš 349 var. Radovište. E FYR Macedonia
Radviliškis 344 N Lithuania
Rafaela 71 E Argentina
Rafah 291, 292 Heb. Rafiaḥ. SW Gaza Strip
Rafḥā' 474 N Saudi Arabia
Ragged Island Range 88 island group of S Bahamas

Ragusa 295 Sicilia, S Italy
Ragusa see Dubrovnik
Rahachow 104 Rus. Rogachëv. E Belorussia
Rahaeng see Tak
Rahīmyār Khān 421 SE Pakistan
Raiatea 624 island of W French Polynesia
Raipur 270 C India
Rairok District 364 district of Majuro, SE Marshall Islands
Rájahmundry 270 SE India
Rajang 354 river of SW Borneo, Malaysia
Rājbāri 93 C Bangladesh
Rajbiraj 395 E Nepal
Rājkot 270 W India
Rājshāhi 93 prev. Rampur Boalia. W Bangladesh
Rakahanga 622 island of Northern Cook Islands, N Cook Islands
Rakaia 401 river of C South Island, New Zealand
Rakhshān 420 river of W Pakistan
Rakiraki 218 N Viti Levu, W Fiji
Rakka see Ar Raqqah
Rakutō-kō see Naktong
Rakvere 212 Ger. Wesenberg. N Estonia
Raleigh 571 North Carolina, SE USA
Ralik Chain 364 island group of W Marshall Islands
Ramādah 601 W Yemen
Ramallah 291, 292 C West Bank
Ramat Gan 291 C Israel
Ramatlabama 118 S Botswana
Rambi see Rabi
Ramechhap 395 C Nepal
Ramier Island see Glover Island
Ramla 291 C Israel
Ramm, Jabal 310 mountain of SW Jordan
Râmnicu Sarat 450 E Romania
Râmnicu Vâlcea 450 prev. Rîmnicu-Vîlcea. C Romania
Ramotswa 118 S Botswana
Rampur Boalia see Rajshahi
Ramree Island 135 island of W Burma
Ramsey 625 NE Isle of Man
Ramsey Bay 625 bay of the Irish Sea on the NE coast of Isle of Man
Ramsgate 565 SE England, UK
Ramu 428 river of NE Papua New Guinea
Rancagua 159 C Chile
Rānchi 270 E India
Randa 194 C Djibouti
Randers 194 Jylland, N Denmark
Rāngāmāti 93 SE Bangladesh
Rangiora 401 E South Island, New Zealand
Rangitaiki 401 river of E North Island, New Zealand
Rangitata 401 river of C South Island, New Zealand
Rangitikei 401 river of S North Island, New Zealand
Rangoon 135 var. Yangon. ❖ of Burma, S Burma
Rangpur 93 N Bangladesh
Rankin Inlet 146 C Canada
Rankovićevo see Kraljevo
Rann see Brežice
Rann of Kachch 270 var. Rann of Cutch, Rann of Kutch. Salt marsh of India and Pakistan
Ranongga 490 var. Ghanongga. New Georgia Is, Solomon Islands
Rantau, Puala see Tebingtinggi, Pulau
Rapallo 294 C Italy
Rapid City 571 South Dakota, NC USA
Räpina 212 Ger. Rappin. SE Estonia
Rapla 212 Ger. Rappel. NW Estonia
Rapperswil 518 NW Switzerland
Rappin see Räpina
Rarotonga 622 island of Southern Cook Islands, S Cook Islands
Ra's al 'Ayn 523 N Syria
Ras al Hadd see Al Ḥadd
Ras al Khaimah 562 NE United Arab Emirates
Ra's an Naqb 310 SW Jordan
Ras Dashen Terara 215 mountain of N Ethiopia
Rasdu Atoll 358 atoll of C Maldives

Ronde Island *248* island to the N of Grenada island, Grenada
Rongelap *364* island of NW Marshall Islands
Rongerik *364* island of N Marshall Islands
Rong, Kas *see* Rung, Kaôh
Rongrong District *364* district of Majuro, SE Marshall Islands
Rønne *190* Bornholm, E Denmark
Ronne Ice Shelf *66* ice shelf of Antarctica, over Atlantic Ocean
Ronzan *see* Nonsan
Roodepoort-Maraisburg *495* Pretoria-Witwatersrand-Vereeniging, NE South Africa
Rooke Island *see* Umboi
Roosendaal *397* SW Netherlands
Roosevelt *120* river of W Brazil
Roraima, Mount *256* mountain of N South America
Røros *414* S Norway
Rorschach *518* NE Switzerland
Rosa, Lake *88* lake of Great Inagua, Bahamas
Rosalie *196* E Dominica
Rosario *71* E Argentina
Rosario *430* C Paraguay
Rosario *579* SW Uruguay
Roscommon *288* C Ireland
Roscrea *288* C Ireland
Roseau *196* ❖ of Dominica, SW Dominica
Roseau *467* river of NW St. Lucia
Roseaux *258* SW Haiti
Rose Bank *468* NW St. Vincent, St. Vincent & the Grenadines
Rose Belle *368* SE Mauritius
Rose Hall *256* E Guyana
Rose Hill *97* N Barbados
Rose Hill *368* W Mauritius
Rosenau *see* Rožňava
Rosenberg *see* Ružomberok
Rosenheim *237* S Germany
Rosenhof *see* Zilupe
Rosetta *see* Rashīd
Rosh Pinah *391* S Namibia
Rosia *624* W Gibraltar
Rosia Bay *624* bay of the Atlantic Ocean on the SW coast of Gibraltar
Rosignol *256* E Guyana
Rosiori de Vede *450* S Romania
Rosita *404* NE Nicaragua
Rositten *see* Rēzekne
Roskilde *190* Sjælland, E Denmark
Rossano *295* S Italy
Ross Ice Shelf *66* ice shelf of Antarctica, over Pacific Ocean
Rosso *366* SW Mauritania
Ross Sea *66* sea of the Pacific Ocean, off Antarctica
Rostak *see* Ar Rustāq
Rostock *237* N Germany
Rostov-na-Donu *454* var. Rostov, Eng. Rostov-on-Don. SW Russia
Roswell *571* New Mexico, SW USA
Rota *628* island of S Northern Mariana Islands
Rothera *66* UK research station of Antarctic Peninsula, Antarctica
Roti, Pulau *276* island to the SW of Timor, C Indonesia
Rotifunk *482* W Sierra Leone
Rotorua *401* C North Island, New Zealand
Rotorua, Lake *401* lake of C North Island, New Zealand
Rotterdam *397* SW Netherlands
Rotuma *218* island to the W of Vanua Levu, NW Fiji
Rouen *225* N France
Round Island *368* var. Île Ronde. Island of N Mauritius
Roulers *see* Roeselare
Rousselaere *see* Roeselare
Rovaniemi *221* N Finland
Rovigno *see* Rovinj
Rovigo *295* N Italy
Rovinj *181* It. Rovigno. W Croatia
Rovno *see* Rivne
Rovuma *see* Ruvuma
Rowd-e Lūrah *53* river of S Afghanistan

Równe *see* Rivne
Roxa, Ilha *254* island of SW Guinea-Bissau
Roxborough *542* E Tobago, Trinidad & Tobago
Roxo, Cap *478* cape on the SW coast of Senegal
Rozel *626* N Jersey
Rožňava *487* Ger. Rosenau, Hung. Rozsnyó. E Slovakia
Rózsahegy *see* Ružomberok
Rrëshen *57* var. Bresheni, Rrshen. N Albania
Rrogozhinë *57* var. Rrogozhina, Rogozhina, Rogozhinë. W Albania
Ruacana *391* NW Namibia
Ruanda *see* Rwanda
Ruapehu, Mount *401* mountain of C North Island, New Zealand
Ruatoria *401* E North Island, New Zealand
Ruavatu *490* NE Guadalcanal, Solomon Is
Ru'ays, Wādī ar *339* dry watercourse of C Libya
Rub 'al Khali *418, 474, 601* Eng. Great Sandy Desert, Empty Quarter. Desert region of SW Asia
Rubeho Mountains *532* mountain range of C Tanzania
Rubtsovsk *454* C Russia
Rucava *330* SW Latvia
Ruda Śląska *441* S Poland
Rūd-i Māshkel *see* Māshkel
Rudnyy *312* N Kazakhstan
Rudolf, Lake *see* Turkana, Lake
Rudolfswert *see* Novo Mesto
Rufiji *532* river of E Tanzania
Rufisque *478* W Senegal
Ruggell *342* N Liechtenstein
Rugombo *138* NW Burundi
Rugusye *138* var. Lugusi. River of E Burundi
Rugwero, Lac *see* Rweru
Ruhango *462* SW Rwanda
Ruhengeri *462* NW Rwanda
Ruhnu *212* island of SW Estonia
Ruhondo, Lac *462* lake of N Rwanda
Ruhr Valley *236* industrial region of W Germany
Ruhwa *462* river of Burundi and Rwanda
Ruki *609* river of W Zaire
Rukungiri *556* SW Uganda
Rukwa, Lake *532* shallow lake of W Tanzania
Ruma *604* NW Serbia, Yugoslavia
Rumania *see* Romania
Rumbek *508* S Sudan
Rum Cay *88* island of S Bahamas
Rumphi *353* N Malawi
Rumpi, Monts *144* var. Rumpi Hills. Hilly region of W Cameroon
Rumpungwe *138* var. Lumpungu. River of E Burundi
Runde *614* river of SE Zimbabwe
Rundu *391* var. Runtu. N Namibia
Rŭng, Kaôh *141* prev. Kas Kong. Island of SW Cambodia
Rŭng Sâmlœm, Kaôh *141* prev. Kas Rong Sam Lem. Island of SW Cambodia
Rungwa *532* C Tanzania
Runway Bay *303* N Jamaica
Ruo *353* river of S Malawi
Ruoqiang *162* var. Jo-ch'iang, Uigh. Qarkilik, var. Charkhlik, Charkhliq. Xinjiang Uygur Zizhiqu, NW China
Rupat, Pulau *276* prev. Roepat. Island to the E of Sumatra, W Indonesia
Rupel *99* river of N Belgium
Rupununi *256* river of SW Guyana
Rušan *see* Rushon
Rusape *614* E Zimbabwe
Ruse *128* Turk. Rusçuk, var. Ruschuk, Rustchuk. N Bulgaria
Rusengo *138* C Burundi
Rushashi *462* NW Rwanda
Rushon *530* var. Rušan, Rus. Rushan. SE Tajikistan
Rusinga Island *316* island of Lake Victoria, SW Kenya

Rusizi *138* var. Ruzizi. River of E Africa
Russell Islands *490* island group of C Solomon Is
Russia *see* Russian Federation
Russian Federation *454-461* officially Russian Federation, var. Russia. Country of E Europe and N Asia, divided into 77 admin. units (21 autonomous republics, 1 autonomous oblast, 49 oblasts and 6 kraj). ❖ Moscow
Russkaya *66* CIS research station of Lesser Antarctica, Antarctica
Rust'avi *234* SE Georgia
Rustenburg *495* North West, N South Africa
Rusumo *462* E Rwanda
Rutana *138* C Burundi
Rutanzige, Lac *see* Edward, Lake
Rutovu *138* S Burundi
Ru'ūs al Jibāl *418* mountain range of Oman and United Arab Emirates
Ruvubu *138* var. Ruvuvu. River of C Burundi
Ruvuma *387, 532* Port. Rovuma. River of Mozambique and Tanzania
Ruvyironza *138* var. Luvironza. River of C Burundi
Ruwais *see* Ar Ru'ays
Ruwaisv *see* Ar Ru'ays
Ruwenzori *556* mountains of Uganda and Zaire
Ruya *614* river of Mozambique and Zimbabwe
Ruyigi *138* C Burundi
Ružomberok *487* Hung. Rózsahegy, Ger. Rosenberg. N Slovakia
Rwamagana *462* E Rwanda
Rwamatamu *462* W Rwanda
Rwanda *462-463* officially Republic of Rwanda, prev. Ruanda. Country of Central Africa divided into 10 admin. units (prefectures). ❖ Kigali
Rwanyakizinga, Lac *462* lake of NE Rwanda
Rweru *138, 432* var. Lac Rugwero. Lake of Burundi and Rwanda
Rwesero *462* SW Rwanda
Ryazan' *454* W Russia
Rybinskoye Vodokhranilishche *454* Eng. Rybinsk Reservoir. Reservoir of W Russia
Rybnik *441* S Poland
Rybnitsa *see* Rîbniţa
Rykovo *see* Yenakiyeve
Rysy *441* mountain of S Poland
Rzeszów *441* SE Poland

S

Saale *237* river of C Germany
Saarbrücken *236* Fr. Sarrebruck. SW Germany
Sääre *212* Saaremaa, Estonia
Saaremaa *212* var. Saare, Serema, Ger. Ösel, var. Oesel. Island of W Estonia
Saaristomeri *221* sea area of Baltic Sea
Saartuz *530* W Tajikistan
Saati *210* E Eritrea
Saatlı *86* Rus. Saatly. C Azerbaijan
Saatta *210* NW Eritrea
Sab *141* river of S Cambodia
Saba *628* island of N Netherlands Antilles
Šabac *604* NW Serbia, Yugoslavia
Sabadell *503* E Spain
Sabana, Archipiélago de *182* island group of N Cuba
Sabana de la Mar *198* E Dominican Republic
Sabanalarga *171* N Colombia
Sabaneta *198* NW Dominican Republic
Sab'atayn, Ramlat as *601* desert region of C Yemen
Sabaya *112* S Bolivia
Şāberī, Hāmūn-e *53* var. Sīstān, Daryācheh-ye. Lake of Afghanistan and Iran
Sabhā *339* W Libya
Sabi *233* E Gambia
Sabi *see* Save

Sabinal, Cayo *182* island of NE Cuba
Sabirabad *86* C Azerbaijan
Sabkha *see* As Sabkhah
Sabkhat al Mūh *523* river of S Syria
Sabyah *see* Aş Şabyah
Sabzevār *281* NE Iran
Sacavém *444* W Portugal
Sachs Harbour *146* Banks Island, NW Canada
Sacramento *570* California, W USA
Sada *627* W Mayotte
Sá da Bandeira *see* Lubango
Şa'dah *601* NW Yemen
Sadaï *194* river of NE Djibouti
Sa Dec *595* S Vietnam
Sādiqābād *421* SE Pakistan
Sa'dīyah, Hawr as *284* lake of E Iraq
Sadlers *464* N St. Kitts, St. Kitts & Nevis
Sado *304* island to the W of Honshū, N Japan
Safāqis *see* Sfax
Safi *382* W Morocco
Safi *see* Aş Şafī
Safīd Khers, Kūh-e *53* mountain range of NE Afghanistan
Safīd Kūh *53* mountain range of NW Afghanistan
Safīm *254* W Guinea-Bissau
Saga *304* Kyūshū, SW Japan
Sagaing *135* C Burma
Saganthit Island *135* var. Sakanthit, prev. Sellore I. Island of S Burma
Sagarmatha *see* Everest, Mount
Sagay *437* Negros, C Philippines
Sagua la Grande *182* C Cuba
Saguia al Hamra *382* river of N Western Sahara
Saham *310* var. Sahm. N Jordan
Sahara *156, 339, 360, 366, 0* Ar. Aş Şahrā'. Vast desert area of N Africa
Sahara el Gharqiya *202* var. Aş Şahrā' al Gharbīyah, Eng. Western Desert. Desert of C Egypt
Sahara el Sharqiya *202* var. Aş Şahrā' ash Sharqīyah, Eng. Eastern Dest. Desert of E Egypt
Sāhīwal *421* prev. Montgomery. E Pakistan
Saïda *332* var. Şaydā. W Lebanon
Saïda *59* NW Algeria
Saidpur *93* NW Bangladesh
Saigon *see* Hô Chi Minh
Saiki *304* Kyūshū, SW Japan
Sai Kung *262* E Hong Kong
Sail Rock *468* islet of S St. Vincent & the Grenadines
Saimaa *221* lake of SE Finland
Saint Albert *146* SW Canada
St-André *630* NE Réunion
St. Anne *625* Alderney, N Guernsey
St. Ann's Bay *303* N Jamaica
St. Aubin *626* S Jersey
St. Austell *565* SW England, UK
St-Barthélémy *624* island of N Guadeloupe
St-Benoit *630* E Réunion
St-Brieuc *224* NW France
St. Catherine, Mt *248* mountain C Grenada island, Grenada
St. Catherine Point *621* headland of E Bermuda
Saint Catherines *147* SE Canada
St-Chamond *225* E France
Saint Croix *631* island of S Virgin Islands
St. David's *248* SE Grenada island, Grenada
St. David's Island *621* island of E Bermuda
St-Denis *630* ❖ of Réunion, N Réunion
Ste Anne *627* SE Martinique
Ste. Anne *624* E Guadeloupe
Ste. Rose *624* W Guadeloupe
Saintes *225* W France
St-Étienne *225* E France
St. Eustatius *628* island of C Netherlands Antilles
St. François *624* E Guadeloupe
Saint-Gall *see* Sankt Gallen

São Tomé, Pico de *473* mountain of São Tomé, Sao Tome & Principe
São Vicente *121* S Brazil
São Vicente *152* island of N Cape Verde
Sapele *408* S Nigeria
Sapitwa *353* mountain of S Malawi
Saponé *133* C Burkina
Sappemeer *397* NE Netherlands
Sapporo *304* Hokkaidō, N Japan
Sapta Koshi *395* river of India and Nepal
Sār *91* NW Bahrain
Šara *349* mountain range of FYR Macedonia and Yugoslavia
Sara Buri *535* C Thailand
Saragossa *see* Zaragoza
Saragt *553* *prev.* Serakhs, *var.* Serahs. S Turkmenistan
Sarajevo *116* ❖ of Bosnia & Herzegovina, SE Bosnia & Herzegovina
Saran' *312* C Kazakhstan
Sarandë *57* *var.* Saranda, *It.* Porto Edda, *prev.* Santi Quaranta. S Albania
Sarandí del Yí *579* C Uruguay
Sarandí Grande *579* S Uruguay
Sarangani Islands *437* island group of SE Philippines
Saratov *454* W Russia
Saravan *327* *var.* Saravane. SE Laos
Sarbhang *110* S Bhutan
Sardegna *294* *Eng.* Sardinia. Island of W Italy
Sardinia *see* Sardegna
Sargodha *421* NE Pakistan
Sarh *156* *prev.* Fort-Archambault. S Chad
Sārī *281* N Iran
Sarigan *628* island of C Northern Mariana Islands
Sarikol Range *530* *Rus.* Sarykol'skiy Khrebet. Mountain range of China and Tajikistan
Sarimbun Reservoir *485* NW Singapore
Sariwŏn *413* SW North Korea
Sark *625* island of SE Guernsey
Sarpsborg *414* S Norway
Sarrebruck *see* Saarbrücken
Sarstoon *102, 250* *var.* Sarstún. River of Belize and Guatemala
Sarstún *see* Sarstoon
Sarthe *225* river of NW France
Saruhan *see* Manisa
Sarykol'skiy Khrebet *see* Sarikol Range
Sary-Tash *325* *var.* Sary-Ta#. SW Kyrgyzstan
Sasebo *304* Kyūshū, SW Japan
Saseno *see* Sazan
Saskatchewan *146* river of C Canada
Saskatchewan *146* province of C Canada
Saskatoon *146* SW Canada
Sasolburg *495* Orange Free State, C South Africa
Sassandra *300* S Ivory Coast
Sassandra *300* *var.* Ibo. River of S Ivory Coast
Sassari *294* Sardegna, W Italy
Sassnitz *237* NE Germany
Sasstown *336* SE Liberia
Sataua *598* Savai'i, Western Samoa
Satawal *374* island of C Micronesia
Satawan *374* atoll of C Micronesia
Sätkhira *93* SW Bangladesh
Satpura Range *270* mountains of C India
Satu Mare *450* *Hung.* Szatmárnémeti. NW Romania
Satunan-shotō *304* island group of Nansei-shotō, SW Japan
Sau *see* Sava
Sauce *see* Juan L. Lacaze
Saudhárkrókur *268* N Iceland
Saudi Arabia *474-477* officially Kingdom of Saudi Arabia. Country of SW Asia divided into 13 admin. units (provinces). ❖ Riyadh
Saül *623* C French Guiana
Saulkrasti *330* N Latvia
Sault Sainte Marie *147* S Canada
Sauma, Pointe *631* headland of Île Alofi, N Wallis & Futuna

Saûmâtre, Étang *258* lake of SE Haiti
Saurimo *64* *Port.* Vila Henrique de Carvalho. NE Angola
Sauteurs *248* N Grenada island, Grenada
Sava *116, 181, 488, 604* *Eng.* Save, *Hung.* Száva, *Ger.* Sau. River of SE Europe
Savai'i *598* island of NW Western Samoa
Savalou *108* S Benin
Savan Island *468* island of S St. Vincent & the Grenadines
Savannah *571* Georgia, SE USA
Savannakhét *327* S Laos
Savanna-La-Mar *303* W Jamaica
Savave *555* islet of Nukufetau, Tuvalu
Save *387, 614* *var.* Sabi. River of Mozambique and Zimbabwe
Savè *108* SE Benin
Savissivik *624* NW Greenland
Savona *294* N Italy
Savonlinna *221* *Swe.* Nyslott. SE Finland
Savusavu *218* Vanua Levu, N Fiji
Savu Sea *see* Sawu, Laut
Savute *118* river of N Botswana
Sawdā', Jabal *474* mountain of SW Saudi Arabia
Sawdā, Jabal as *339* mountain range of C Libya
Sawdiri *see* Sodiri
Sawhaj *see* Sohâg
Şawqirah *418* SE Oman
Şawqirah, Ghubbat *see* Suqrah Bay
Sawu, Laut *276* *Eng.* Savu Sea. Sea of the Indian Ocean, C Indonesia
Say *407* SW Niger
Sayaboury *see* Muang Xaignabouri
Sayat *553* E Turkmenistan
Sayhūt *601* E Yemen
Saylac *492* *var.* Zeila. NW Somalia
Saynshand *380* S Mongolia
Say'ūn *601* *var.* Saywūn. C Yemen
Sazan *57* *It.* Saseno. Island of SW Albania
Scaldis *see* Scheldt
Scarborough *565* NE England, UK
Scarborough *542* S Tobago, Trinidad & Tobago
Scarborough *97* S Barbados
Scebeli *see* Shebeli
Schaan *342* W Liechtenstein
Schaanwald *342* NE Liechtenstein
Schaffhausen *518* N Switzerland
Schaulen *see* Šiauliai
Schefferville *147* E Canada
Scheldt *99* *Dut.* Schelde, *Fr.* Escaut. River of W Europe
Schellenberg *342* N Liechtenstein
Schiedam *397* SW Netherlands
Schiermonnikoog *397* island of Waddeneilanden, N Netherlands
Schifflange *346* S Luxembourg
Schneekoppe *see* Sněžka
Schneidemühl *see* Piła
Schœlcher *627* W Martinique
Schoten *99* N Belgium
Schouwen *397* island of SW Netherlands
Schwäbische Alb *236* *Eng.* Swabian Jura. Mountain range of SW Germany
Schwarzwald *see* Black Forest
Schwaz *82* W Austria
Schweizer Mittelland *see* Swiss Plateau
Schweizer Reneke *495* North West, N South Africa
Schwerin *237* N Germany
Schweriner See *236* lake of N Germany
Schwyz *518* C Switzerland
Schyl *see* Jiu
Sciacca *295* Sicilia, S Italy
Sciasciamana *see* Shashemenê
Scio *see* Chíos
Scoresbysund *see* Ittoqqortoormiit
Scotland *565, 569* national region of UK divided into 12 admin. units (9 regions, 3 island authorities)
Scott Base *66* New Zealand research station near Ross Shelf, Antarctica

Scott Island *66* island to the N of Ross Ice Shelf, Antarctica
Scotts Head Village *196* *var.* Cachacrou. S Dominica
Scrub Island *620* island of NE Anguilla
Scunthorpe *565* NE England, UK
Scutari *see* Shkodër
Scutari, Lake *57, 604* *Alb.* Liqeni i Shkodrës, *SCr.* Skadarsko Jezero. Lake of Albania and Yugoslavia
Seac Pai Van *626* bay of the South China Sea, SW Macao
Seal Island *620* island of NW Anguilla
Seatons *68* E Antigua, Antigua & Barbuda
Seattle *570, 575* Washington, NW USA
Sébaco *404* C Nicaragua
Sebaiera *382* C Western Sahara
Sebapala *334* SW Lesotho
Sebarok, Pulau *485* island S Singapore
Sebastián Vizcaíno, Bahía *370* bay of the Pacific Ocean, on the NW coast of Mexico
Sebastopol *see* Sevastopol'
Sebenico *see* Šibenik
Sébikhoutane *478* W Senegal
Sebou *382* river of N Morocco
Secos, Ilhéus *see* Rombo, Ilhéus de
Sedberat *210* W Eritrea
Sédhiou *478* SW Senegal
Seeheim Noord *391* S Namibia
Seeland *see* Sjælland
Sefadu *482* E Sierra Leone
Sefrou *382* N Morocco
Segamat *354* S of Peninsular Malaysia
Ségbana *108* NE Benin
Segewold *see* Sigulda
Segna *see* Senj
Ségou *360* *var.* Segu C Mali
Segovia *503* C Spain
Segovia *see* Coco
Segu *see* Ségou
Séguédine *407* NE Niger
Séguéla *300* W Ivory Coast
Séguénéga *133* NW Burkina
Segura *503* river of S Spain
Sehlabathebe *334* E Lesotho
Seinäjoki *221* *Swe.* Östermyra. SW Finland
Seine *225* river of N France
Seine, Baie de la *224-225* bay of the English Channel to the NW of France
Seiyū *see* Chōngju
Sejerø *190* island of C Denmark
Šeki *see* Şäki
Sekoma *118* S Botswana
Sekondi-Takoradi *242* S Ghana
Selânik *see* Thessaloníki
Selemia *see* Salamīyah
Selenge *380* river of Mongolia and Russia
Seletar Reservoir *485* reservoir of C Singapore
Selfoss *268* SW Iceland
Seli *see* Rokel
Sélibabi *366* S Mauritania
Selibi Phikwe *118* E Botswana
Sélingué, Lac de *360* reservoir of S Mali
Selle, Massif de la *258* mountain range of S Haiti
Selle, Pic la *258* *var.* La Selle. Mountain of S Haiti
Sellore Island *see* Saganthit Island
Sellye *see* Skalica
Sellye *see* Šaľa
Sélouma *253* C Guinea
Selukwe *see* Shurugwi
Selvagens, Ilhas *444* island group of the Madeira Is, Portugal
Semakau, Pulau *485* island S Singapore
Semanit *57* *var.* Seman. River of W Albania
Semara *382* N Western Sahara
Semarang *276* Java, C Indonesia
Sembawang *485* area of N Singapore
Sembé *176* NW Congo
Sembehun *482* SW Sierra Leone
Semberong *354* river of SE Peninsular Malaysia

Semendria *see* Smederevo
Semipalatinsk *312* *Kaz.* Semey. E Kazakhstan
Semirara Islands *437* island group of C Philippines
Semliki *556* river of W Uganda
Sên *141* *var.* Sen. River of C Cambodia
Sena *see* Vila de Sena
Senafe *210* SE Eritrea
Senanayake Samudra *506* lake of E Sri Lanka
Senanga *613* SW Zambia
Senang, Pulau *485* island of S Singapore
Sendai *304* Kyūshū, SW Japan
Sendai *304* Honshū, N Japan
Senegal *478-479* officially Republic of Senegal. *Fr.* Sénégal. Country of West Africa divided into 10 admin. units (regions). ❖ Dakar
Senegal *366, 360, 478* *Fr.* Sénégal. River of W Africa
Senica *487* *Ger.* Senitz, *Hung.* Szenice. W Slovakia
Senigallia *295* C Italy
Senj *181* *Ger.* Zengg, Ital. Segna. NW Croatia
Senja *414* *prev.* Senjen. Island of NW Norway
Senkaku-shotō *304* island group of Nansei-shotō, SW Japan
Senmonorom *141* E Cambodia
Sennar *508* *var.* Sannâr. C Sudan
Senne *99* *Dut.* Zenne. River of C Belgium
Senqunyane *334* river of C Lesotho
Senshin-kō *see* Sōmjin
Sensuntepeque *207* NE El Salvador
Sentery *609* SE Zaire
Senye *208* W Río Muni, Equatorial Guinea
Seongnam *see* Sŏngnam
Seoul *498* *Kor.* Sŏul, *prev.* Kyŏngsŏng, *Jap.* Keijō. * of South Korea NW South Korea
Sepik *428* river of Indonesia and Papua New Guinea
Sepone *see* Muang Xéphôn
Sept-Iles *146* E Canada
Serahs *see* Saragt
Seraing *99* E Belgium
Serakhis *see* Serrakhis
Serakhs *see* Saragt
Seram *276* *var.* Serang, *Eng.* Ceram. Island of Maluku, E Indonesia
Seram, Laut *276* *Eng.* Ceram Sea. Sea of the Pacific Ocean, E Indonesia
Serang *276* Java, C Indonesia
Serangoon Harbour *485* harbour, E Singapore
Serasan, Selat *276, 354* strait of the South China Sea between Borneo and Kepulauan Natuna, W Indonesia
Seraya, Pulau *485* island of SW Singapore
Serbia *604* *Serb.* Srbija. Republic of Yugoslavia
Sered *487* *Hung.* Szered. SW Slovakia
Serekunda *233* W Gambia
Seremban *354* W Peninsular Malaysia
Serengeti Plain *532* plain of N Tanzania
Serenje *613* E Zambia
Sereth *see* Siret
Sérifos *245* island of SE Greece
Serov *454* C Russia
Serowe *118* SE Botswana
Serpa Pinto *see* Menongue
Serpent's Mouth, The *542* *Sp.* Boca de la Serpiente. Strait connecting the Colombus Channel and the Gulf of Paria
Serrakhis *187* *var.* Serrachis, Serakhis. River of NW Cyprus
Serravalle *470* N San Marino
Sérres *245* *prev.* Sérrai. NE Greece
Serule *118* E Botswana
Se San *see* Tônlé San
Sesana *see* Sežana
Sese Islands *556* island group of S Uganda
Sesvete *181* N Croatia
Seti *395* river of W Nepal

Simbirsk *see* Ul'yanovsk
Simeto *295* river of Sicilia, S Italy
Simeulue, Pulau *276* island to the NW of Sumatra, W Indonesia
Simferopol *558* S Ukraine
Simikot *395* W Nepal
Siminiout *623* S French Guiana
Šimonovany *see* Partizánske
Simony *see* Partizánske
Simplon Pass *518* mountain pass of S Switzerland
Simplon Tunnel *518* tunnel of Italy and Switzerland
Simpson Desert *77* desert region of C Australia
Simunye *512* NE Swaziland
Sinai *202* *Ar.* Shibh Jazīrat Sīnā'. Desert region of NE Egypt
Sinazongwe *613* S Zambia
Sincelejo *171* NW Colombia
Sinchwang *see* Hsinchuang
Sin Cowe Island *630* island of SW Spratly Islands
Sindh *421* administrative region of SE Pakistan
Sindhulimadi *395* C Nepal
Sindi *212* SW Estonia
Sine *478* river of W Senegal
Sinendé *108* N Benin
Sines *444* S Portugal
Sinfra *300* C Ivory Coast
Singa *508* *var.* Sinjah, Sinja. E Sudan
Singapore *485* river of S Singapore
Singapore *484-485* officially Republic of Singapore. Country of SE Asia divided into 5 admin. units (districts). ❖ Singapore City
Singapore Strait *354, 485* *var.* Strait of Singapore. Strait connecting Strait of Malacca and South China Sea
Singatoka *see* Sigatoka
Singerei *376* *var.* Sângerei, *prev.* Lazovsk. N Moldova
Singida *532* C Tanzania
Singora *see* Songkhla
Sining *see* Xining
Sinj *181* SE Croatia
Sinjavina *604* *var.* Sinjajevina. Mountain range of N Montenegro, Yugoslavia
Sinkiang Uighur Autonomous Region *see* Xinjiang Uygur Zizhiqu
Sinnamary *623* N French Guiana
Sinnûris *202* *var.* Sinnūris. N Egypt
Sino *see* Greenville
Sinoe *see* Greenville
Sinoia *see* Chinhoyi
Sinoie, Lacul *450* *prev.* Lacul Sinoe. Lagoon of E Romania
Sinop *549* N Turkey
Sinp'o *413* E North Korea
Sintien *see* Hsintien
Sint-Niklaas *99* *Fr.* St.-Nicolas. N Belgium
Sintra *444* *prev.* Cintra. W Portugal
Sint-Truiden *99* *Fr.* St.-Trond. E Belgium
Sinŭiju *413* W North Korea
Sinyang *see* Xinyang
Sió *264* river of W Hungary
Sion *518* *Ger.* Sitten. SW Switzerland
Siorapaluk *624* NW Greenland
Sioux City *571* Iowa, C USA
Sioux Falls *571* South Dakota, NC USA
Sipaliwini *510* river of S Suriname
Siparia *542* SW Trinidad, Trinidad & Tobago
Siphofaneni *512* *var.* Sipofaneni. C Swaziland
Siping *163* *var.* Ssu-p'ing, Szeping, *prev.* Ssu-p'ing-chieh. Jilin, NE China
Siple *66* US research station of South Orkney Islands, Antarctica
Siput *354* *var.* Sungei Siput. NW Peninsular Malaysia
Siquirres *178* E Costa Rica
Siracusa *295* *Eng.* Syracuse. Sicilia, S Italy
Sirājganj *93* N Bangladesh
Şir Banī Yās *562* island of W United Arab Emirates

Sirdaryo *see* Syr Darya
Sir Edward Pellew Group *77* island group of N Australia
Siret *450* *var.* Siretul, *Ger.* Sereth. River of Romania and Ukraine
Sir Francis Drake Channel *621* channel connecting the Atlantic Ocean and Caribbean Sea, C British Virgin Islands
Sirte *see* Surt
Sirte, Gulf of *see* Surt, Khalīj
Şirvan Düzü *86* *Rus.* Shirvanskaya Step'. Mountain range of C Azerbaijan
Sirwan *see* Diyālá
Sisak *181* *Hung.* Sziszek, *Ger.* Sissek. N Croatia
Sisian *74* SE Armenia
Sisimiut *624* *var.* Holsteinsborg. SW Greenland
Sisŏphŏn *141* NW Cambodia
Sissek *see* Sisak
Sīstān, Daryācheh-ye *281* *var.* Hāmūṣāberī, Daryācheh-ye Hāmūn. Lake of E Iran
Sisters, The *248* islands N of Grenada island, Grenada
Siteki *512* *var.* Stegi. E Swaziland
Sithoniá *245* peninsula of NE Greece
Sitobela *512* S Swaziland
Sitona *210* SW Eritrea
Sitrah *91* *var.* Sitra. Island of NE Bahrain
Sittang *135* *var.* Sittoung. River of C Burma
Sittard *397* S Netherlands
Sitten *see* Sion
Sittwe *135* *prev.* Akyab. W Burma
Siuna *404* NE Nicaragua
Sivas *549* C Turkey
Sivers'kyy Donets' *see* Donets
Siyäzän *86* *Rus.* Siazan'. NE Azerbaijan
Sjælland *190* *Ger.* Seeland, *Eng.* Zealand. Island of E Denmark
Skadar *see* Shkodër
Skadarsko Jezero *see* Scutari, Lake
Skagaströnd *268* *prev.* Höfdhakaupstadhur. N Iceland
Skagen *190* Jylland, N Denmark
Skagerrak *190, 414, 515* *var.* Skagerak. Area of the Baltic Sea
Skalica *487* *Hung.* Sellye. W Slovakia
Skeleton Coast *391* coastal region of NW Namibia
Skellefteå *515* NE Sweden
Skellefteälv *515* river of N Sweden
Skien *414* S Norway
Skikda *59* *prev.* Philippeville. NE Algeria
Skive *190* Jylland, NW Denmark
Skjálfandafljót *268* river of C Iceland
Skjern *190* Jylland, W Denmark
Skjern Å *190* river of W Denmark
Skon *141* S Cambodia
Skopje *349* *prev.* Skoplje, *Turk.* Üsküb. ❖ of FYR Macedonia, N FYR Macedonia
Skoplje *see* Skopje
Skövde *515* S Sweden
Skrunda *330* W Latvia
Skúvoy *622* island of C Faeroe Islands
Skye, Isle of *565* island of W Scotland, UK
Skýros *245* island of E Greece
Slagelse *190* Sjælland, SE Denmark
Slaney *288* *Ir.* An tSláine. River of SE Ireland
Slatina *see* Podravska Slatina
Slatina *450* S Romania
Slave Coast *539* coastal region of W Africa, Atlantic Ocean
Slavonska Požega *181* *prev.* Požega, *Hung.* Pozsega. NE Croatia
Slavonski Brod *181* *prev.* Brod, *Hung.* Bród. E Croatia
Slavyansk *see* Slov''yans'k
Sléibhte Chill Mhantáin *see* Wicklow Mountains
Slēmānī *see* As Sulaymānīyah
Sliema *363* N Malta
Sligo *288* *Ir.* Sligeach. N Ireland
Sliven *128* *var.* Slivno. E Bulgaria

Slobozia *450* SE Romania
Slobozia *376* *Rus.* Slobodzeya. E Moldova
Slonim *104* *Rus.* Slonin. W Belorussia
Slovakia *486-487* officially Slovak Republika, *prev.* constituent republic of Czechoslovakia. Country of C Europe divided into 4 admin. regions (kraj). ❖ Bratislava
Slovenia *488-489* officially Republic of Slovenia, *Slvn.* Slovenija. Country divided into 62 admin. units (občina). ❖ Ljubljana
Slovenské Rudohorie *487* *Ger.* Slowakisches Erzgebirge, *var.* Ungarisches Erzgebirge. Mountain range of C Slovakia
Slov''yans'k *558* *Rus.* Slavyansk. E Ukraine
Słupsk *441* *Ger.* Stolp. N Poland
Slutsk *104* C Belorussia
Smallwood Reservoir *147* lake of S Canada
Smarhon' *104* NW Belorussia
Smederevo *604* *Ger.* Semendria. N Serbia, Yugoslavia
Smila *558* C Ukraine
Smith's Island *621* island of E Bermuda
Smithson Bight *622* bay of the Indian Ocean on the S coast of Christmas Island
Smolensk *454* W Russia
Smolyan *128* *var.* Smoljan, *prev.* Pashmakli. SW Bulgaria
Smyrna *see* İzmir
Snaefell *625* mountain of C Isle of Man
Snake *570* river of NW USA
Sneeuw-gebergte *see* Maoke, Pegunungan
Sněžka *188* *Ger.* Schneekoppe. Mountain of N Czech Republic
Snow Mountains *see* Maoke, Pegunungan
Snug Corner *248* SW Grenada island, Grenada
Snuŏl *141* E Cambodia
Soacha *171* C Colombia
Sobaek-sanmaek *498* mountain range of S South Korea
Sobat *508* river of Ethiopia and Sudan
Sobradinho, Represa de *121* *var.* Barragem de Sobradinho. Reservoir of E Brazil
Soča *295, 488* *It.* Isonzo. River of Italy and Slovenia
Socabaya *433* SE Peru
Sochi *454* SW Russia
Société, Archipel de la *624* island group of W French Polynesia
Socotra *see* Suquṭrá
Soc Trăng *595* *var.* Khanh, *Hung.* S Vietnam
Sodankylä *221* N Finland
Södertälje *515* SE Sweden
Sodiri *508* *var.* Sawdīrī, Sodari. C Sudan
Sodo *215* *var.* Soddo, Soddu. SW Ethiopia
Soekaboemi *see* Sukabumi
Soela Väin *212* strait of Baltic Sea, between the islands of Hiiumaa and Saaremaa, W Estonia
Soembawa *see* Sumbawa
Soerabaja *see* Surabaya
Soerakarta *see* Surakarta
Sofala, Baía de *387* Bay of Indian Ocean, off Mozambique
Sofia *350* seasonal river of NW Madagascar
Sofia *128* *var.* Sofija, *Bul.* Sofiya. ❖ of Bulgaria, W Bulgaria
Sogamoso *171* C Colombia
Sognefjorden *414* fjord of SW Norway
Sohâg *202* *var.* Sawhaj. C Egypt
Sŏjosŏn-man *413* inlet of Korea Bay, on W coast of N Korea
Sokch'o *498* N South Korea
Söke *549* SW Turkey
Sokhumi *234* *Rus.* Sukhumi. NW Georgia
Sokodé *539* C Togo
Sokolov *188* NW Czech Republic
Sokoto *408* NW Nigeria

Sokoto *408* river of NW Nigeria
Sola *414* SW Norway
Solapur *270* *var.* Sholapur. SW India
Sol, Costa del *503* coastal region of S Spain
Soldeu *62* NE Andorra
Soledad *591* E Venezuela
Soledad *171* N Colombia
Soleure *see* Solothurn
Soligorsk *see* Salihorsk
Solimões *121* local name for a stretch of the Amazon river, NW Brazil
Solin *181* *It.* Salona. S Croatia
Solingen *236* W Germany
Sollum, Gulf of *202* *Ar.* Khalīj as Sallūm. Gulf of the Mediterranean Sea, NW Egypt
Sololá *250* W Guatemala
Solomon Islands *490-491* *prev.* British Solomon Islands Protectorate. Country of the South Pacific Ocean divided into 7 admin. units (provinces). ❖ Honiara
Solomon Sea *428, 490* sea of the Pacific Ocean, to the E of Papua New Guinea
Solothurn *518* *Fr.* Soleure. NW Switzerland
Solun *see* Thessaloníki
Solway Firth *565* arm of the Irish Sea, W UK
Solwezi *613* NW Zambia
Soma *233* C Gambia
Somalia *492-493* officially Somali Democratic Republic, *prev.* Somaliland Protectorate, Italian Somaliland. Country of E Africa divided into 16 admin. units (regions). ❖ Mogadishu
Sombor *604* *Hung.* Zombor. NW Serbia, Yugoslavia
Somerset *621* Somerset Island, W Bermuda
Somerset Island *621* island of W Bermuda
Somerset Island *146* island of N Canada
Somerset Nile *see* Victoria Nile
Someş *264, 450* *Hung.* Szamos, *Ger.* Samosch. River of Hungary and Romania
Sŏmjin *498* *Jap.* Senshin-kō. River of S South Korea
Somme *225* river of N France
Somosomo *218* Taveuni, N Fiji
Somotillo *404* W Nicaragua
Somoto *404* NW Nicaragua
Soná *426* SW Panama
Sonaco *254* NE Guinea-Bissau
Sonda des Vieques *629* bay of the Caribbean Sea, E Puerto Rico
Sønderborg *190* *Ger.* Sonderburg. Als, S Denmark
Søndre Strømfjord *see* Kangerlussuaq
Songea *532* S Tanzania
Songhua Jiang *see* Sungari
Sŏngjin *see* Kimch'aek
Songkhla *535* *Mal.* Singora. S Thailand
Sŏngnam *498* *var.* Seongnam. NW South Korea
Songnim *413* SW North Korea
Songo *387* NW Mozambique
Sŏng Tiên Giang *see* Mekong
Songwe *353* river of Malawi and Tanzania
Sonmiāni Bay *421* bay of the Arabian Sea, on the S coast of Pakistan
Sonsonate *207* W El Salvador
Sonsorol Islands *425* island group of Palau
Soochow *see* Suzhou
Soomaaliya *see* Somalia
Soome Laht *see* Finland, Gulf of
Sop Hao *327* NE Laos
Sopron *264* *Ger.* Ödenburg. NW Hungary
Sôp Xai *327* NE Laos
Sórd Choluim Chille *see* Swords
Soria *503* N Spain
Soriano *579* W Uruguay
Soro *see* Ghazal
Sorø *190* Sjælland, SE Denmark
Soroca *376* *Rus.* Soroki. N Moldova

Suir *288 Ir.* An tSiúir. River of S Ireland

Sukabumi *276 prev.* Soekaboemi. Java, C Indonesia

Sukagawa *304* Honshū, N Japan

Sukarnapura *see* Jayapura

Sukarno, Puntjak *see* Jaya, Puncak

Sukhne *see* As Sukhnah

Sukhumi *see* Sokhumi

Suki *508* E Sudan

Sukkertoppen *see* Maniitsoq

Sukkur *421* S Pakistan

Sukuta *233* W Gambia

Sulaimaniya *see* As Sulaymānīyah

Sulaimān Range *421* mountain range of C Pakistan

Sula, Kepulauan *276 prev.* Xulla Islands, Soela. Island group to the E of Celebes, E Indonesia

Sulawesi *see* Celebes

Sulawesi, Laut *see* Celebes Sea

Sulby *625* N Isle of Man

Sullana *433* NW Peru

Sullivan Island *see* Lanbi Island

Sultan Alonto, Lake *see* Lanao, Lake

Sulu Archipelago *437* island group of SW Philippines

Sulu Sea *355, 437* sea of the Pacific Ocean, to the NE of Borneo, Malaysia

Sulyukta *325 Kir.* Sülüktü. SW Kyrgyzstan

Sumatera *see* Sumatra

Sumatra *276 var.* Sumatera. Island of W Indonesia

Šumava *see* Bohemian Forest

Sumba *622* Sudhuroy, S Faeroe Islands

Sumba *276 prev.* Soemba, *Eng.* Sandalwood Island. Island of Nusa Tenggara, C Indonesia

Sumba, Selat *276* strait of the Indian Ocean between Sumba and Sumbawa, C Indonesia

Sumbawa *276 prev.* Soembawa. Island of Nusa Tenggara, C Indonesia

Sumbawanga *532* W Tanzania

Sumbe *64 Port.* Novo Redondo. W Angola

Sumbuya *482* S Sierra Leone

Šumen *see* Shumen

Sumisu-jima *304* island to the SE of Honshū, SE Japan

Šumperk *188 Ger.* Mährisch-Schönberg. E Czech Republic

Sumpul *207* river of Honduras and El Salvador

Sumqayit *86 Rus.* Sumgait. E Azerbaijan

Sumy *558* NE Ukraine

Sunan *413* SW North Korea

Sunch'ŏn *413* SW North Korea

Sunch'ŏn *498 Jap.* Junten. S South Korea

Sunda, Selat *276* strait connecting Indian Ocean and Laut Jawa between Java and Sumatra, W Indonesia

Sunderland *565* NE England, UK

Sundsvall *515* C Sweden

Sungai Seletar Reservoir *485* reservoir of N Singapore

Sungari *163 Chin.* Songhua Jiang. River of NE China

Sun Koshi *395* river of E Nepal

Suntar-Khayata, Khrebet *455* mountain range of NE Russia

Sunyani *242* W Ghana

Sunzu *613* mountain NE Zambia

Suō *see* Suao

Suomenlahti *see* Finland, Gulf of

Suomenselkä *221* physical region of C Finland

Suŏng *141* SE Cambodia

Superior de Tristaina, Estany *62* lake of NW Andorra

Superior, Lake *147, 371 Fr.* Lac Supérieur. Lake of Canada and USA

Sup'ung-ho *413* reservoir of China and North Korea

Sūq 'Abs *see* 'Abs

Sūq ash Shuyūkh *284* SE Iraq

Suqrah Bay *418* Bay of the Arabian Sea, SE Oman

Suquṭrá *601 Eng.* Socotra. Island of SE Yemen, off the Horn of Africa

Şūr *418* NE Oman

Surabaya *276 prev.* Surabaja, Soerabaja. Java, C Indonesia

Surakarta *276 prev.* Soerakarta. Java, C Indonesia

Šurany *487 Hung.* Nagysurány. SW Slovakia

Sūrat *270* W India

Surat Thani *535* S Thailand

Sûre *346* river of W Europe

Sure, Lagh *316* dry watercourse of NE Kenya

Surin *535* E Thailand

Surinam *368* S Mauritius

Suriname *510-511* officially Republic of Suriname, *var.* Suriname. Country of Central America divided into 8 admin. units (provinces). ❖ Paramaribo

Surinam *97* E Barbados

Surkhet *see* Birendranagar

Surkhob *530* river of C Tajikistan

Şurmān *339* NW Libya

Surt *339 var.* Sidra, Sirte. N Libya

Surt, Khalij *339 var.* Gulf of Sirte, Gulf of Sidra. Gulf of the Mediterranean Sea, off N coast of Libya

Sūsah *see* Sousse

Susana *254* W Guinea-Bissau

Susuman *455* Ostrov Sakhalin, E Russia

Sutlej *421* river of India and Pakistan

Suure-Jaani *212 Ger.* Gross-Sankt-Johannis. C Estonia

Suur Munamägi *212 var.* Munamägi. Mountain of SE Estonia

Suur Väin *212* strait of the Baltic Sea, between the mainland and the island of Muhu, W Estonia

Suva *218* ❖ of Fiji, Viti Levu, W Fiji

Suwa *210* SE Eritrea

Suwarrow *622* island of Northern Cook Islands, N Cook Islands

Suwayhān *562* E United Arab Emirates

Suways, Qanāt as *see* Suez Canal

Suwŏn *498 var.* Suweon, *Jap.* Suigen. NW South Korea

Suzhou *163 var.* Soochow, Su-chou, Suchow, *prev.* Wuhsien. Jiangsu, E China

Suzuka *304* Honshū, C Japan

Svalbard *631* Norwegian dependency of the Greenland Sea

Sväty Kríž nad Hronom *see* Žiar nad Hronom

Svay Chék *141* river of Cambodia and Thailand

Svay Riéng *141* SE Cambodia

Svendborg *190* Fyn, S Denmark

Sverdlovsk *see* Yekaterinburg

Sverdrup Islands *146* island group of N Canada

Sveti Nikole *349 prev.* Sveti Nikola. C FYR Macedonia

Svetlogorsk *see* Svyetlahorsk

Svetozarevo *604 prev.* Jagodina. C Serbia, Yugoslavia

Svilengrad *128 prev.* Mustafa-Pasha. SE Bulgaria

Svínoy *622 var.* Svinø. Island of NE Faeroe Islands

Svishtov *128 var.* Svištov. N Bulgaria

Svitavy *188* E Czech Republic

Svyetlahorsk *104 Rus.* Svetlogorsk. SE Belorussia

Swabian Jura *see* Schwäbische Alb

Swakopmund *391* W Namibia

Swallow Islands *490* small island group within Santa Cruz Is, E Solomon Is

Swan *76* river of SW Australia

Swansea *565 Wel.* Abertawe. S Wales, UK

Swatow *see* Shantou

Swaziland *512-513* officially Kingdom of Swaziland. Country of southern Africa divided into 4 admin. units (districts). ❖ Mbabane

Sweden *514-517* officially Kingdom of Sweden, *Swe.* Sverige. Country of Scandinavia divided into 24 admin. units (läns). ❖ Stockholm

Swedru *see* Agona Swedru

Swellendam *495* Western Cape, S South Africa

Swetes *68* S Antigua, Antigua & Barbuda

Swift Current *146* SW Canada

Swindon *565* C England, UK

Swiss Plateau *518 Ger.* Schweizer Mittelland. Plateau of W Switzerland

Switzerland *518-521* officially Swiss Confederation, *Ger.* Schweiz, *It.* Svizzera. Country of C Europe divided into 26 admin. units (cantons). ❖ Bern

Swords *288 Ir.* Sórd Choluim Chille. E Ireland

Syabrubesi *395 var.* Syabrubensi. C Nepal

Sydney *77, 81* SE Australia

Sydney *147* Cape Breton Island, SE Canada

Sydney Island *see* Manra

Syktyvkar *454 prev.* Ust'-Sisol'sk. NW Russia

Sylhet *93* NE Bangladesh

Syowa *66* Japanese research station of Greater Antarctica, Antarctica

Syracuse *571* New York, NE USA

Syracuse *see* Siracusa

Syr Darya *312, 530, 582 Rus.* Syrdar'ya, *Kaz.* Syrdariya, *Uzb.* Sirdaryo. River of C Asia

Syrdar'ya *582* E Uzbekistan

Syria *522-525* officially Syrian Arab Republic, *var.* Suriyah. Country divided into 13 admin. units (governorates). ❖ Damascus

Syriam *175* S Burma

Syrian Desert *284, 310, 523 Ar.* Bādiyat ash Shām. Desert of SW Asia

Syvash, Zatoka *558* inlet of the Sea of Azov

Szabadka *see* Subotica

Szamos *see* Someş

Szatmárnémeti *see* Satu Mare

Szczecin *441 Ger.* Stettin. NW Poland

Szczeciński, Zalew *see* Oderhaff

Szechuan *see* Sichuan

Szeged *264 Ger.* Szegedin. SE Hungary

Székesfehérvár *264 Ger.* Stuhlweissenburg. W Hungary

Szekszárd *264* S Hungary

Szenice *see* Senica

Szentes *264* SE Hungary

Szeping *see* Siping

Szered *see* Sereď

Sziszek *see* Sisak

Szlatina *see* Podravska Slatina

Szolnok *264* C Hungary

Szombathely *264 Ger.* Steinamanger. W Hungary

Sztálinváros *see* Dunaújváros

T

Tabac, River *368* river of S Mauritius

Ṭabaqah *523* N Syria

Tabaquite *542* C Trinidad, Trinidad & Tobago

Tabarka *345 var.* Ṭabarqah. NW Tunisia

Tabasará, Serranía de *426* mountain range of W Panama

Tabasco *see* Grijalva

Tabernacle *464* NE St. Kitts, St. Kitts & Nevis

Tabiteuea *320* island of the Gilbert Is, W Kiribati

Tablas Island *437* island of C Philippines

Table Hill Gordon *68* SE Antigua, Antigua & Barbuda

Tabligbo *539* SE Togo

Tábor *188* SW Czech Republic

Tabora *532* W Tanzania

Tabou *300 var.* Tabu. S Ivory Coast

Tabrīz *281* NW Iran

Tabuaeran *320 var.* Fanning Island. Island of the Line Is, E Kiribati

Tabūk *474* NW Saudi Arabia

Tabwémasana *587* mountain of Espiritu Santo, W Vanuatu

Täby *515* SE Sweden

Tachia Hsi *527* river of W Taiwan

Tachoshui *527* E Taiwan

Tacloban *437* Leyte, E Philippines

Tacna *433* SE Peru

Tacoma *570* Washington, NW USA

Tacuarembó *579* N Uruguay

Tacuarembó *579* river of C Uruguay

Tacurupucú *see* Hernandarias

Tademaït, Plateau du *59* plateau of C Algeria

Tadine *628* Maré, Îles Loyauté, E New Caledonia

Tadjoura *194* E Djibouti

Tadjoura, Golfe de *194* inlet of the Gulf of Aden, E of Djibouti

T'aebaek-sanmaek *498* mountain range of South Korea

Taedong *413* river of C North Korea

Taegu *498 var.* Daegu, *Jap.* Taikyū. SE South Korea

Taehan-haehyŏp *see* Korea Strait

Taejŏn *498 Jap.* Taiden. C South Korea

Tafahi *540* island of N Tonga

Tafí Viejo *71* NW Argentina

Taftlund *190* Jylland, SW Denmark

Taga *598* Savai'i, Western Samoa

Taganrog, Gulf of *558 Ukr.* Tahanroz'ka Zatoka, *Rus.* Taganrogskiy Zaliv. Gulf of the Sea of Azov, SE Ukraine

Tagarzimat *382* W Western Sahara

Tagiura *see* Tājūrā'

Tagliamento *295* river of N Italy

Tagtabazar *see* Takhta-Bazar

Taguasco *182* C Cuba

Taguatinga *121* C Brazil

Tagula Island *428 prev.* Southeast I. Island of SE Papua New Guinea

Tagum *437* river of Mindanao, S Philippines

Tahanroz'ka Zatoka *see* Taganrog, Gulf of

Tahat *59* mountain of SE Algeria

Tahiti *624* island of W French Polynesia

Tahoua *407* W Niger

Taia *482* river of C Sierra Leone

Taiama *482* C Sierra Leone

T'aichung *527 Jap.* Taichū. W Taiwan

Taiden *see* Taejŏn

Taieri *401* river of S South Island, New Zealand

Taihoku *see* Taipei

T'aihsi *527* W Taiwan

Tai Hu *163* lake of E China

Taikyū *see* Taegu

T'ainan *527 Jap.* Tainan. SW Taiwan

Tai O *262* W Hong Kong

Taipa *626* Taipa, C Macao

Taipa *626* island of C Macao

Taipa - Coloane Causeway *626* bridge between Taipa and Coloane islands, S Macao

Tai Pang Wan *see* Mirs Bay

T'aipei *527 var.* Taipei, *Jap.* Taihoku. ❖ of Taiwan, N Taiwan

Taiping *354* NW Peninsular Malaysia

Tai Po *262* N Hong Kong

T'aitung *527 Jap.* Taitō. SE Taiwan

Tai Van *626* bay of the South China Sea, S Macao

Taiwan *526-531* officially Republic of China (Taiwan). Country of E Asia divided into 16 admin. units (counties). ❖ Taipei

Taiwan Strait *163, 527 var.* Formosa Strait, *Chin.* T'ai-wan Hai-hsia. Strait connecting East China Sea and South China Sea, between Taiwan and China

Taiyuan *163 var.* T'ai-yuan *prev.* Yangku. Shanxi, N China

Ta'izz *601* SW Yemen

Tajarhī *339* SW Libya

Tajikistan *530-531* officially Republic of Tajikistan, *Rus.* Tadzhikistan, *Taj.* Jumhurii Tojikiston *prev.* Tajik S.S.R. Country of C Asia divided into 3 admin. units (2 oblasts, 1 autonomous region). ❖ Dushanbe

Tel Aviv-Yafo *291* C Israel
Teles Piras *see* São Manuel
Telica *404* W Nicaragua
Télimélé *253* W Guinea
Telire *178* river of E Costa Rica
Tell Abaid *see* At Tall al Abyaḍ
Tell Shedadi *see* Ash Shadādah
Tel'mansk *553 Turkm.* Tel'man.
N Turkmenistan
Telok Blangah *485* area of
S Singapore
Telšiai *344 Ger.* Telschen.
NW Lithuania
Teluk Intan *354 prev.* Teluk Anson.
W Peninsular Malaysia
Tema *242* SE Ghana
Tembakul, Pulau *485 prev.* Kusu
Island. S Singapore
Temboni *see* Mitemele, Río
Temburong, Sungai *126* river of
NE Brunei
Temelín *188* SW Czech Republic
Temerluh *354 var.* Temerloh.
SE Peninsular Malaysia
Temes *see* Timiş
Temesch *see* Timiş
Temeschwar *see* Timişoara
Temesvár *see* Timişoara
Temir *312* W Kazakhstan
Temirtau *312 prev.* Samarkandski.
C Kazakhstan
Temotuloto *555* islet of Nukufetau,
Tuvalu
Tempisque *178* river of
NW Costa Rica
Temuco *159* C Chile
Tena *200* C Ecuador
Ténado *133* W Burkina
Téna Kourou *133* mountain of
SW Burkina
Tenan *see* Ch'ŏnan
Tenavatu *490* N Guadalcanal, Solomon
Is
Tendaho *215* NE Ethiopia
Te-n-Dghâmcha, Sebkhet *366*
var. Sebkha de Ndrhamcha, Sebkra
de Ndaghamcha. Salt lake of
W Mauritania
Tendō *304* Honshū, N Japan
Ténenkou *360* C Mali
Tenerife *503* island of Islas Canarias,
SW Spain
Tengeh Reservoir *485* reservoir of
W Singapore
Tengiz, Ozero *312 Kaz.* Tengiz Köl.
Salt lake of C Kazakhstan
Tengréla *300 var.* Tingréla.
N Ivory Coast
Teniente Rodolfo Marsh *66* Chilean
research station of South Shetland
Islands, Antarctica
Tenkodogo *133* S Burkina
Tennant Creek *77* C Australia
Tennessee *571* state of SE USA
Teno *see* Tana
Tenryū *304* river of Honshū, C Japan
Tensift *382* seasonal river of
W Morocco
Tepelenë *57 var.* Tepelena,
It. Tepeleni. S Albania
Tepic *370* W Mexico
Teplice *188 Ger.* Teplitz,
prev. Teplice-Šanov, *Ger.* Teplitz-
Schönau. NW Czech Republic
Téra *407* W Niger
Teracina *295* S Italy
Teraina *320 var.* Washington Island.
Island of the Line Is, E Kiribati
Teramo *295* C Italy
Terceira *444 var.* Ilha Terceira. Island
of the Azores, Portugal
Terek-Say *325 var.* Terek-Saj.
W Kyrgyzstan
Teresina *121 var.* Therezina.
NE Brazil
Terevaka *159* mountain of Easter
Island, W Chile
Terhathum *395* E Nepal
Termiz *582 Rus.* Termez. SE
Uzbekistan
Terneuzen *397* SW Netherlands
Terni *295* C Italy
Ternitz *82* E Austria
Ternopil' *558 Rus.* Ternopol',
Pol. Tarnopol. W Ukraine

Terrassa *503 Cast.* Tarrasa. E Spain
Terre-de-Bas *624* island of
S Guadeloupe
Terre-de-Haut *624* island of
S Guadeloupe
Terre-Neuve *see* Newfoundland
Terschelling *397* island of
Waddeneilanden, N Netherlands
Terter *see* Tärtär
Teruel *503* E Spain
Teseney *210* W Eritrea
Teslić *116* N Bosnia & Herzegovina
Tessalit *360* NE Mali
Tessaoua *407* S Niger
Tete *387* NW Mozambique
Tête Morne *196* S Dominica
Tetepare *490* island of the New
Georgia Is, C Solomon Is
Tétouan *382 Sp.* Tetuán. N Morocco
Tetovo *349 Turk.* Kalkandelen,
Alb. Tetovë, Tetova.
NW FYR Macedonia
Tetschen *see* Děčín
Tetulia *93* river and W outlet
of Ganges, S Bangladesh
Teupasenti *260* S Honduras
Tevere *295* river of C Italy
Teverya *291 Eng.* Tiberias. N Israel
Texas *571* state of SC USA
Texel *397* island of Waddeneilanden,
NW Netherlands
Teyateyaneng *334* NW Lesotho
Tha *327* river of NW Laos
Thaa Atoll *see* Kolhumadulu Atoll
Thabana Ntlenyana *334*
var. Thabantshonyana. Mountain of E
Lesotho
Thaba Tseka *334* C Lesotho
Thai, Ao *see* Thailand, Gulf of
Thai Binh *595* N Vietnam
Thailand *534-537* officially Kingdom of
Thailand, *prev.* Siam. Country
of SE Asia divided into 71 admin.
units (provinces). ❖ Bangkok
Thailand, Gulf of *141, 535, 595*
var. Gulf of Siam, *Th.* Ao Thai,
I'tn. Vinh Thai Lan. Gulf of the South
China Sea on the SW coast of SE Asia
Thai Nguyên *595* N Vietnam
Thakhek *see* Muang Khammouan
Thākurgaon *93* NW Bangladesh
Thamaga *118* S Botswana
Thames *565* river of S England, UK
Thāne *270 prev.* Thana. W India
Thanh Hoa *595* N Vietnam
Thanintari Taungdan
see Bilauktaung Range
Thanlwin *see* Salween
Thar Desert *270, 421 var.* Great Indian
Desert, Indian Desert. Desert region
of India and Pakistan
Tharrawaddy *135* SW Burma
Tharthār, Buḥayrat ath *284* lake of
C Iraq
Thásos *245* island of NE Greece
Thaton *135* SE Burma
Thaungyin *135 Th.* Mae Nam Moi.
River of Burma and Thailand
Thayetmyo *135* W Burma
Thebaide *248* SE Grenada island,
Grenada
Therezina *see* Teresina
Thermaïkós Kólpos *245*
Eng. Thermaic Gulf. Gulf of the
Aegean Sea, N Greece
Thessaloníki *245 Eng.* Salonica,
var. Salonika, *SCr.* Solun, *Turk.*
Selânik. N Greece
Thibaud *196* N Dominica
Thiès *478* W Senegal
Thika *316* S Kenya
Thikombia *see* Cikobia
Thiladhunmathi Atoll *358*
var. Tiladummati Atoll. Atoll of N
Maldives
Thimphu *110* ❖ of Bhutan, W Bhutan
Thio *628* C New Caledonia
Thionville *225* NE France
Thíra *245* island of SE Greece
Thiruvanathapuram *see* Trivandrum
Thisted *190* Jylland, NW Denmark
Thistilfjördhur *268 var.* Thistil Fjord.
Fjord of NE Iceland
Thithia *see* Cicia

Thitu Island *630* island of NW Spratly
Islands
Thjórsá *268* river of C Iceland
Tholen *397* island to the
SW of Netherlands
Thompson *146* C Canada
Thon Buri *535* C Thailand
Thonze *135* SW Burma
Thórisvatn *268* lake of C Iceland
Thorlákshöfn *268* SW Iceland
Thorn *see* Toruń
Thórshöfn *268* NE Iceland
Thoune *see* Thun
Thracian Sea *245*
Gk Thrakikó Pélagos. Area of the
Mediterranean Sea, NE Greece
Three Brothers *621* island group of
C British Indian Ocean Territory
Thu Dâu Môt *595 var.* Phu Cuong.
S Vietnam
Thule *see* Qaanaaq
Thuli *614 var.* Tuli. River of
S Zimbabwe
Thun *518 Fr.* Thoune. W Switzerland
Thunder Bay *147* formed 1970 by
amalgamation of Fort William and
Port Arthur. S Canada
Thuner See *518* lake of C Switzerland
Thüringer Wald *237*
Eng. Thuringian Forest. Forested
mountain range of C Germany
Thurso *565* N Scotland, UK
Thyolo *353 var.* Cholo. S Malawi
Tianjin *163 var.* T'ien-ching, Tientsin.
City and municipality of NE China
Tiaret *59 var.* Tihert. N Algeria
Tiaroye *478* W Senegal
Ti'avea *598* Upolu, Western Samoa
Tibastí, Sarīr *339* desert of Chad and
Libya
Tibati *144* N Cameroon
Tiberias *see* Teverya
Tiberias, Lake *291 var.* Sea of Galilee,
Heb. Yam Kinneret, *Ar.* Bahrat
Tabariya. Lake of N Israel
Tibesti *156, 339 var.* Tibesti Massif.
Mountain range of Chad and Libya
Tibet *167* cultural region of W China
Tibetan Autonomous Region
see Xizang Zizhiqu
Tibet, Plateau of *see* Qing-Zang
Gaoyuan
Tibnine *332 var.* Tibnīn. S Lebanon
Tiburón, Isla del *370 var.* Isla
Tiburón. Island of NW Mexico
Tichau *see* Tychy
Tîchît *366* C Mauritania
Tichla *382* SW Western Sahara
Ticino *294* river of N Italy
Tidjikja *366*
prev. Fort-Cappolani C Mauritania
Tîdra, Et *366* island to the
W of Mauritania
Tiébélé *133* S Burkina
Tiel *397* S Netherlands
T'ien-ching *see* Tianjin
Tienen *99 Fr.* Tirlemont. C Belgium
Tien Shan *162, 325 Chin.* Tian Shan,
Rus. Tyan'-Shan'. Mountain range of
C Asia
Tientsin *see* Tianjin
Tierra del Fuego *71* island of
Argentina and Chile
Tiflis *see* Tbilisi
Tiga, Île *628* island of Îles Loyauté,
W New Caledonia
Tighina *376 prev.* Bendery.
E Moldova
Tigray *215* cultural region of
N Ethiopia
Tigre *433* river of N Peru
Tigris *284, 549 Ar.* Dijlah, *Turk.* Dicle.
River of SW Asia
Tihert *see* Tiaret
Ti-hua *see* Ürümqi
Tijuana *370* NW Mexico
Tikinsso *253* river of C Guinea
Tiko *144* SW Cameroon
Tikopia *490* island of E Solomon Is
Tikus, Pulu *see* Direction Island
Tiladummati Atoll
see Thiladhunmathi Atoll
Tilarán *178* NW Costa Rica
Tilburg *397* S Netherlands
Tilimsen *see* Tlemcen

Tillabéri *407 var.* Tillabéry.
W Niger
Timah, Bukit *485* hill of C Singapore
Timaru *401* C South Island,
New Zealand
Timbedgha *366 var.* Timbédra.
SE Mauritania
Timbuktu *see* Tombouctou
Timiş *450 Hung.* Temes,
Ger. Temesch, *SCr.* Tamiš. River of
Romania and Yugoslavia
Timişoara *450 Hung.* Temesvár,
Ger. Temeschwar. W Romania
Timmins *147* S Canada
Timor *276* island of Nusa Tenggara,
C Indonesia
Timor Sea *76, 276* area of the Indian
Ocean between Australia and
Indonesia
Tindouf *59* W Algeria
Tingréla *see* Tengréla
Tinguilinta *253* river of W Guinea
Tinhosa Grande *473* island to the
S of Príncipe, Sao Tome & Principe
Tinhosa Pequena *473* island to the
S of Príncipe, Sao Tome & Principe
Tinian *628* island of S Northern
Mariana Islands
Tínos *245* island of SE Greece
Tintamarre, Îlot *624* island of
N Guadeloupe
Tîntâne *366* S Mauritania
Tinto *see* Sicó
Tiobraid Árainn *see* Tipperary
Tioman, Pulau *354 var.* Tioman
Island. Island of SE Peninsular
Malaysia
Tipitapa *404* SW Nicaragua
Tipperary *288 Ir.* Tiobraid Árainn.
S Ireland
Tiquisate *see* Pueblo Nuevo Tiquisate
Tiranë *57 Alb.* Tirana. ❖ of Albania,
C Albania
Tiraspol *376 Rus.* Tiraspol'.
E Moldova
Tirlemont *see* Tienen
Tirol *82 var.* Tyrol, *It.* Tirolo. Cultural
region of W Austria
Tirreno, Mare *see* Tyrrhenian Sea
Tirso *294* river of Sardegna, W Italy
Tiruchchirāppalli *270*
prev. Trichinopoly. S India
Tisa *see* Tisza
Tisza *264, 604 Ger.* Theiss,
Cz/Rom/SCr. Tisa. River of E Europe
Titano, Monte *470* mountain of
C San Marino
Titao *133* NW Burkina
Tite *254* SW Guinea-Bissau
Titicaca, Lake *112, 433* lake of Bolivia
and Peru
Titograd *see* Podgorica
Titova Mitrovica *see* Kosovska
Mitrovica
Titovo Užice *see* Užice
Titov Veles *349 prev.* Veles,
Turk. Köprülü. C FYR Macedonia
Titov Vrh *349* mountain of
NW FYR Macedonia
Tivaouane *478* W Senegal
Tivoli *248* NE Grenada island, Grenada
Tivoli *295* C Italy
Ţīwī *418* NE Oman
Tizi Ouzou *59* N Algeria
Tiznit *382* SW Morocco
Tjilatjap *see* Cilacap
Tjirebon *see* Cirebon
Tkibuli *see* Tqibuli
Tkvarcheli *see* Tqvarch'eli
Tlemcen *59 var.* Tilimsen.
NW Algeria
Tlokoeng *334* NE Lesotho
Tlokweng *118* S Botswana
Tmassah *339* C Libya
Toamasina *350 prev.* Tamatave.
E Madagascar
Toba, Danau *276* lake of Sumatra,
W Indonesia
Tobago *542* island of the West Indies
which, with Trinidad, forms Trinidad
& Tobago
Tobago Cays *468* cays of
SW St. Vincent & the Grenadines
Toba Kākar Range *421* mountain
range of NW Pakistan

Tobi *425* island of S Palau
Tobol'sk *454* C Russia
Tobruch *see* Ţubruq
Tobruk *see* Ţubruq
Tocantins *121* river of N Brazil
Tocumen *426* C Panama
Tocuyito *591* NW Venezuela
Todos os Santos, Baía de *121* bay of the Atlantic Ocean, on the E coast of Brazil
Tōen *see* T'aoyüan
Tofua *540* island of Ha'apai Group, Tonga
Toga *587* Torres Islands, N Vanuatu
Togo *538-539* officially Togolese Republic of Togo, *prev.* French Togoland. Country of West Africa divided into 5 admin. units (regions). ❖ Lomé
Tohoun *539* SE Togo
Tokar *508* var. Ţawkar. NE Sudan
Tokat *549* N Turkey
Tŏkchŏk-kundo *498* island group of NW South Korea
Tŏkch'ŏn *413* C North Korea
Tokelau *631* New Zealand dependent territory of the Pacific Ocean
Tŏketerebes *see* Trebišov
Tokmak *325* Kir. Tokmok. N Kyrgyzstan
Tōkō *see* Tungkang
Tokoroa *401* C North Island, New Zealand
Toktogul *325* W Kyrgyzstan
Toku *540* island of N Tonga
Tokuno-shima *304* island of Amami-shotō, SW Japan
Tokushima *304* Shikoku, SW Japan
Tokuyama *304* Honshū, W Japan
Tokwe *614* river of SE Zimbabwe
Tokyo *304, 309* var. Tōkyō. ❖ of Japan, Honshū, SE Japan
Tôlañaro *350* prev. Faradofay, Fort-Dauphin. S Madagascar
Tolbukhin *see* Dobrich
Toledo *112* W Bolivia
Toledo *437* var. Toledo City. Cebu, Philippines
Toledo *503* C Spain
Toledo *571* Ohio, NE USA
Toledo Settlement *102* SE Belize
Toliara *350* var. Toliary, *prev.* Tuléar. SW Madagascar
Tolmin *488* Ger. Tolmein. W Slovenia
Tolo Harbour *262* NE Hong Kong
Tolo, Teluk *276* bay of Laut Banda on the E coast of Celebes, C Indonesia
Tolsan-do *498* island of S South Korea
Toluca *370* var. Toluca de Lerdo. C Mexico
Toluca de Lerdo *see* Toluca
Tol'yatti *454* prev. Stavropol'. W Russia
Toma *133* W Burkina
Tomakomai *305* Hokkaidō, N Japan
Tomar *444* W Portugal
Tomanivi *218* var. Mount Victoria. Mountain of Viti Levu, W Fiji
Tomás Gomensoro *579* N Uruguay
Tombali *254* river of SW Guinea-Bissau
Tombeau, River du *368* river of NW Mauritius
Tombouctou *360* Eng. Timbuktu. N Mali
Tombua *64* Port. Porto Alexandre. SW Angola
Tominé *253* river of W Guinea
Tomini, Teluk *276* prev. Teluk Gorontalo. Bay of Laut Maluku on the E coast of Celebes, C Indonesia
Tomsk *455* C Russia
Tomur Feng *see* Pobedy, Pik
Tönder *190* Jylland, SW Denmark
Tonga *540-541* officially Kingdom of Tonga, Friendly Islands. Country of the Pacific Ocean divided into 5 admin units. ❖ Nuku'Alofa
Tongatapu *540* island of Tongatapu Group, Tonga
Tongatapu Group *540* island group of S Tonga
Tong Fuk *262* SW Hong Kong
Tonghae *498* NE South Korea
Tong-hae *see* Japan, Sea of
Tonghua *163* Jilin, NE China

Tongjosŏn-man *413* prev. Broughton Bay. Bay of the Sea of Japan on the E coast of North Korea
Tongking, Gulf of *163, 595* Chin. Beibu Wan, *Vtn.* Vinh Bắc Bô. Gulf of the South China Sea, SE Asia
Tongsa *110* C Bhutan
Tongue of the Ocean *88* strait between Exuma Cays and Andros I, Bahamas
Tônlé Sap *141* Eng. Great Lake. Lake of W Cambodia
Tonosí *426* S Panama
Tønsberg *414* S Norway
Toowoomba *77* E Australia
Topeka *571* Kansas, C USA
Topła *487* Hung. Toplya. River of NE Slovakia
Toplya *see* Topła
Topol'čany *487* Hung. Nagytapolcsány. W Slovakia
Topolya *see* Bačka Topola
Toraigh *see* Tory Island
Torbeck *258* SW Haiti
Torghay *312* W Kazakhstan
Torino *294* Eng. Turin. N Italy
Tornealv *515* river of NE Sweden
Tornio *221* Swe. Torneå. NW Finland
Tornionjoki *221* Swe. Torneälven. River of Finland and Sweden
Torola *207* river of El Salvador and Honduras
Toronto *147, 151* S Canada
Tororo *556* E Uganda
Toros Dağları *see* Taurus Mountains
Torquay *565* SW England, UK
Torre del Greco *295* S Italy
Torrejón, Embalse de *503* reservoir of W Spain
Torrelavega *503* N Spain
Torrens, Lake *77* salt lake of S Australia
Torreón *370* N Mexico
Torres Islands *587* Fr. Îles Torrès. Island group of N Vanuatu
Torres Strait *77, 428* strait connecting the Arafura Sea and Coral Sea, between Australia and the island of New Guinea
Torsa *110* river of SW Bhutan
Tórshavn *622* var. Thorshavn. ❖ of Faeroe Islands, Streymoy, N Faeroe Islands
Torteval *625* SW Guernsey
Tortoise Islands *see* Galapagos Islands
Tortola *621* island of C British Virgin Islands
Tortosa *503* E Spain
Tortue, Île de la *258* var. Tortuga I. Island of N Haiti
Tortue, Montagne *623* mountain range of C French Guiana
Toruń *441* Ger. Thorn. C Poland
Tõrva *212* Ger. Törwa. S Estonia
Tory Island *288* Ir. Toraigh. Island of N Ireland
Torysa *487* Hung. Tarca. River of NE Slovakia
Toscano, Archipelago *294* var. Tuscan Archipelago. Island group of C Italy
Tosco-Emiliano, Appennino *294* mountain range of C Italy
Tōsei *see* Tungshih
Toshkent *188* Rus. Tashkent. ❖ of Uzbekistan, E Uzbekistan
Toteng *118* C Botswana
Totness *510* N Suriname
Totonicapán *250* W Guatemala
Totota *336* C Liberia
Totoya *218* island to the SE of Viti Levu, S Fiji
Tottori *304* Honshū, W Japan
Touba *300* W Ivory Coast
Touba *478* W Senegal
Touboro *144* NE Cameroon
Toubkal, Jebel *382* mountain of W Morocco
T'ouch'eng *527* NE Taiwan
T'ouch'ien Hsi *527* river of NW Taiwan
T'oufen *527* NW Taiwan
Tougan *133* W Burkina
Tougana *407* SW Niger
Touggourt *59* NE Algeria

Tougué *253* NW Guinea
Touho *628* Île Balabio, E New Caledonia
Toukoto *360* W Mali
Toulon *225* SE France
Toulouse *225* S France
Toumodi *300* C Ivory Coast
Tounan *527* W Taiwan
Toungoo *135* S Burma
Tourane *see* Đà Nâng
Tournai *99* Dut. Doornik. W Belgium
Tours *225* NW France
Tovar *591* W Venezuela
Tovuz *86* Rus. Tauz. W Azerbaijan
Towada *304* Honshū, N Japan
Townsville *77* NE Australia
Towraghondi *53* NW Afghanistan
Towuti, Danau *276* lake of Celebes, C Indonesia
Toyama *304* Honshū, C Japan
Toyohara *see* Fengyüan
Toyohara *see* Yuzhno-Sakhalinsk
Toyohashi *304* Honshū, C Japan
Toyonaka *304* Honshū, C Japan
Toyota *304* Honshū, C Japan
Tozeur *545* var. Tawzar. W Tunisia
Tqibuli *234* Rus. Tkibuli. W Georgia
Tqvarch'eli *234* Rus. Tkvarcheli. NW Georgia
Trabzon *549* Eng. Trebizond. NE Turkey
Trafalgar *196* S Dominica
Tráighlí *see* Tralee
Traiguén *159* C Chile
Traina Garden *see* Mazra'at Turaynā
Traisen *82* river of NE Austria
Trakai *344* SE Lithuania
Tralee *288* Ir. Tráighlí. SW Ireland
Trang *535* S Thailand
Tranqueras *579* N Uruguay
Trans-Alaska pipeline *570* oil pipeline of Alaska, USA
Transantarctic Mountains *66* mountain range of Antarctica
Transkei Bantustan 'self-governing homeland' of E Cape Province, South Africa; created in 1963, abolished in 1994
Transylvania *450* cultural region of NW Romania
Transylvanian Alps *see* Carpaţii Meridionali
Trant's Bay *627* bay of the Caribbean Sea on the E coast of Montserrat
Trapani *295* Sicilia, S Italy
Trâpeăng Vêng *141* C Cambodia
Traralgon *77* SE Australia
Trasimeno, Lago *295* var. Lake of Perugia, Ger. Trasimenischersee. Lake of C Italy
Träskända *see* Järvenpää
Traù *see* Trogir
Traun *82* river of N Austria
Traun *82* N Austria
Traunsee *82* var. Gmundner See, Eng. Lake Traun. Lake of N Austria
Trautenau *see* Trutnov
Tra Vinh *595* var. Phu Vinh. S Vietnam
Travnik *116* C Bosnia & Herzegovina
Trbovlje *488* Ger. Trifail. C Slovenia
Treasury Islands *490* island group of W Solomon Is
Třebíč *188* Ger. Trebitsch. S Czech Republic
Trebinje *116* S Bosnia & Herzegovina
Trebišov *487* Hung. Tŏketerebes. E Slovakia
Trebizond *see* Trabzon
Trebnje *488* SE Slovenia
Treinta y Tres *579* E Uruguay
Trelew *71* SE Argentina
Trenčín *487* Ger. Trentschin, Hung. Trencsén. W Slovakia
Treng *141* prev. Treng. NE Cambodia
Trent *565* river of C England, UK
Trento *294* Eng. Trent, Ger. Trient. N Italy
Trenton *571* New Jersey, E USA
Tres Arroyos *71* E Argentina
Treskavica *116* mountain range of SE Bosnia & Herzegovina
Três Marias, Represa *121* reservoir of SE Brazil

Treviso *295* N Italy
Trial Farm *102* N Belize
Triangle *614* SE Zimbabwe
Tricaorno *see* Triglav
Trichinopoly *see* Tiruchchirāppalli
Trichūr *270* S India
Trient *see* Trento
Trier *236* W Germany
Triesen *342* SW Liechtenstein
Triesenberg *342* SW Liechtenstein
Trieste *295* Slvn. Trst. N Italy
Trieste, Gulf of *488* It. Golfo di Trieste, Slvn. Tržaški Zaliv, Croat. Tršćanski Zaljev. Gulf to the SW of Slonia
Trifail *see* Trbovlje
Triglav *488* It. Tricaorno. Mountain of NW Slovenia
Tríkala *245* prev. Trikkala. C Greece
Trikomo *see* İskele
Trincomalee *506* NE Sri Lanka
Třinec *188* Ger. Trzynietz. SE Czech Republic
Trinidad *112* N Bolivia
Trinidad *542* island of the West Indies which, with Tobago, forms Trinidad & Tobago
Trinidad *579* SW Uruguay
Trinidad and Tobago *542-543* officially Republic of Trinidad and Tobago. Country of the West Indies divided into 6 admin. units (counties). ❖ Port-of-Spain
Trinité, Montagnes de la *623* mountain range of C French Guiana
Triolet *368* NW Mauritius
Trípoli *245* prev. Trípolis. S Greece
Tripoli *332* var. Trâblous, Ţarābulus. N Lebanon
Tripoli *339* Ar. Ţarābulus al-Gharb. ❖ of Libya, NW Libya
Tristan da Cunha *630* dependent territory of St. Helena, South Atlantic Ocean
Tristao, Îles *253* islands to the W of Guinea
Triton Island *629* island of S Paracel Islands
Trivandrum *270* var. Thiruvanathapuram. S India
Trnava *487* Ger. Tyrnau, Hung. Nagyszombat. W Slovakia
Trobriand Islands *see* Kiriwina Islands
Trogir *181* It. Traù. S Croatia
Troía Peninsula *444* peninsula of W Portugal
Trois-Rivières *147* SE Canada
Trojan *see* Troyan
Trollhättan *515* SW Sweden
Tromsø *414* NE Norway
Trondheim *414* prev. Nidaros, Trondhjem, Ger. Drontheim. C Norway
Trondheimsfjorden *414* fjord of SW Norway
Troodos *see* Olympus, Mount
Troodos Mountains *187* var. Troödos. Mountain range of C Cyprus
Troppau *see* Opava
Trou-du-Nord *258* N Haiti
Troumaka *468* NW St. Vincent, St. Vincent & the Grenadines
Troyan *128* var. Trojan. NW Bulgaria
Troyes *225* NE France
Tršćanski Zaljev *see* Trieste, Gulf of
Trst *see* Trieste
Truc Giang *see* Bên Tre
Trucial Coast *562* coastal region of the United Arab Emirates
Trucial States *see* United Arab Emirates
Trujillo *260* N Honduras
Trujillo *433* NW Peru
Trujillo *591* NW Venezuela
Trung Phân *595* prev. Annam. Cultural region of Vietnam
Trunk Island *621* island of C Bermuda
Truro *565* SW England, UK
Trutnov *188* Ger. Trautenau. NE Czech Republic
Tržaški Zaliv *see* Trieste, Gulf of
Tržič *488* Ger. Neumarktl. NW Slovenia
Trzynietz *see* Třinec
Tsabong *see* Tshabong

V

Vaygach, Ostrov *454* island of NW Russia
Vayk' *74 prev.* Azizbekov. SE Armenia
Vedi *74* S Armenia
Vega Baja *629* N Puerto Rico
Veglia *see* Krk
Vejle *190* Jylland, W Denmark
Velasco Ibarra *200* W Ecuador
Velebit *181* mountain range of C Croatia
Velenje *488 Ger.* Wöllan. NE Slovenia
Vele, Pointe *631* headland of Île Futuna, N Wallis & Futuna
Veles *see* Titov Veles
Velika Gorica *181* N Croatia
Velika Morava *604 var.* Morava, Glavn'a Morava, *Ger.* Grosse Morava. River of C Serbia, Yugoslavia
Velika Plana *604* C Serbia, Yugoslavia
Veliki Bečkerek *see* Zrenjanin
Veliko Tŭrnovo *128 prev.* Tŭrnovo. C Bulgaria
Vélingara *478* S Senegal
Velingrad *128* W Bulgaria
Velké Meziříčí *188* SE Czech Republic
Vella Lavella *490 var.* Mbilua. New Georgia Is, Solomon Islands
Vellore *270* S India
Velsen *397* W Netherlands
Venda Bantustan 'self-governing home-land' comprising 2 non-contiguous territories of NE Transvaal, South Africa; created in 1979, abolished in 1994
Venedig *see* Venezia
Vener, Lake *see* Vänern
Venezia *295 Eng.* Venice, *Ger.* Venedig, *Fr.* Venise. N Italy
Venezuela *590-593* officially Republic of Venezuela, *prev.* United States of Venezuela. Country of South America divided into 24 admin. units (20 states and 4 federal entities). ❖ Caracas
Venezuela, Cordillera de *see* Costa, Cordillera de la
Venezuela, Gulf of *591* gulf of the Caribbean Sea, on the N coast of Venezuela
Venice *see* Venezia
Venice, Gulf of *181, 295, 488 It.* Golfo di Venezia, *Slvn.* Beneški Zaliv. Gulf of the Adriatic Sea
Venise *see* Venezia
Venlo *397* SE Netherlands
Vennesla *414* SW Norway
Venoste, Alpi *see* Ötztaler Alpen
Venta *330, 344 Ger.* Windau. River of Latvia and Lithuania
Ventoso *470* N San Marino
Ventspils *330 Ger.* Windau. NW Latvia
Veracruz *370 var.* Veracruz Llave. SE Mexico
Vercelli *294* N Italy
Verdal *414* C Norway
Verde *112* river of Bolivia and Brazil
Verde, Costa *502-503* coastal region of N Spain
Verdun *147* SE Canada
Vereeniging *495* Pretoria-Witwatersrand-Vereeniging, NE South Africa
Verin T'alin *see* T'alin
Verkhneudinsk *see* Ulan-Ude
Verkhoyanskiy Khrebet *455* Mountain range of E Russia
Vermont *571* state of NE USA
Vernon *146* SW Canada
Verőcze *see* Virovitica
Véroia *245 Turk.* Karaferiye. N Greece
Verona *294* N Italy
Versailles *225* N France
Versecz *see* Vršac
Vert, Cap *478* cape of W Senegal
Verte, Île *630* island of E Saint Pierre and Miquelon
Vértes *264* mountain range of NW Hungary
Vertientes *182* S Cuba
Verviers *99* E Belgium
Vesoul *225* NE France
Vesterålen *414 var.* Vesteraalen. Island group of NW Norway

Vestfjorden *414* fjord of NW Norway
Vestmanna *622 var.* Vestmanhavn. Streymoy, N Faeroe Islands
Vestmannaeyjar *268* Heimaey I, S Iceland
Vesuvio *295* volcano of S Italy
Veszprém *264 Ger.* Veszprim. W Hungary
Vetter, Lake *see* Vättern
Vevey *518 Ger.* Vivis. SW Switzerland
Viacha *112* W Bolivia
Viana *64* NW Angola
Viana do Castelo *444* NW Portugal
Vianden *346* NE Luxembourg
Viangchan *see* Vientiane
Viangphoukha *327 var.* Vieng Pou Kha. NW Laos
Viareggio *294* N Italy
Viborg *190* Jylland, NW Denmark
Vicente Noble *198* SW Dominican Republic
Vicenza *295* N Italy
Vichada *171* river of C and E Colombia
Vichy *225* C France
Victoria *77* state of SE Australia
Victoria *146* Vancouver Island, SW Canada
Victoria *159* C Chile
Victoria *248* NW Grenada island, Grenada
Victoria *355 var.* Labuan. Pulau Labuan, NW Malaysia
Victoria *363* Gozo, NW Malta
Victoria *480* ❖ of Seychelles, Mahé Island, Seychelles
Victoria *see* Limbe
Victoria, Mount *see* Tomanivi
Victoria Falls *614* W Zimbabwe
Victoria Falls *613, 614* falls of the Zambezi river, Zambia and Zimbabwe
Victoria Falls *see* Iguaçu, Salto do
Victoria Harbour *262* harbour of S Hong Kong
Victoria Island *146* island of N Canada
Victoria, Lake *316, 532, 556 var.* Victoria Nyanza. Lake of E Africa
Victoria Land *66* physical region of Greater Antarctica, Antarctica
Victoria Nile *556 var.* Somerset Nile. River of C Uganda
Victoria Peak *102* mountain of C Belize
Victoria Peak *262* S Hong Kong
Videm-Krško *see* Krško
Vidin *128* N Bulgaria
Vidoy *622* island of N Faeroe Islands
Vidzeme *330 Eng.* Livonia. Cultural region of NE Latvia
Viedma *71* E Argentina
Vieille Case *196 var.* Itassi. N Dominica
Viekšniai *344* NW Lithuania
Vienna *82 Ger.* Wien, *Hung.* Bécs, *Slvn.* Dunaj. ❖ of Austria, NE Austria
Vienne *225* river of C France
Vientiane *327 Lao.* Viangchan. ❖ of Laos, C Laos
Vieques *629* Isla de Vieques, SE Puerto Rico
Vieques, Isla de *629* island of SE Puerto Rico
Vierwaldstätter See *518 Eng.* Lake of Lucerne, Lake of C Switzerland
Vietnam *594-597* officially Socialist Republic of Viet-nam, *Vtn.* Công Hoa Xa Hôi Chu Nghia Viêt Nam. Country of SE Asia divided into 53 admin. units (50 provinces, 3 municipalities). ❖ Hanoi
Viêt Tri *595* N Vietnam
Vieux Fort *141* S St. Lucia
Vieux-Fort, Pointe du *624* headland of S Guadeloupe
Vigo *502* NW Spain
Vijayawāda *270 prev.* Bezwada. SE India
Vila Artuur de Paiva *see* Cubango
Vila da Ponte *see* Cubango
Vila de Brava *152* São Nicolau, N Cape Verde

Vila de João Belo *see* Xai-Xai
Vila de Macia *see* Macia
Vila de Maio *see* Maio
Vila de Manica *see* Manica
Vila de Mocímboa da Praia *see* Mocímboa da Praia
Vila de Sal Rei *see* Sal Rei
Vila de Sena *387 var.* Sena. C Mozambique
Vila do Conde *444* NW Portugal
Vila do Zumbo *387 prev.* Vila do Zumbu, *var.* Zumbo. NW Mozambique
Vila Henrique de Carvalho *see* Saurimo
Vila Marechal Carmona *see* Uíge
Vila Maria Pia *152* Santo Antão. N Cape Verde
Vila Nova de Gaia *444* NW Portugal
Vila Nova de Portimão *see* Portimão
Vila Pereira de Eça *see* N'Giva
Vila Real *444* N Portugal
Vila Robert Williams *see* Caála
Vila Salazar *see* N'Dalatando
Vila Teixeira da Silva *see* Bailundo
Vil'cheka, Zemlya *455 Eng.* Wilczek Land. Island of Zemlya Frantsa-Iosifa, N Russia
Viliya *see* Neris
Viljandi *212 Ger.* Fellin. S Estonia
Villa Altagracia *198* C Dominican Republic
Villach *82 Slvn.* Beljak. S Austria
Villa Concepción *see* Concepción
Villa del Pilar *see* Pilar
Villa Dolores *71* C Argentina
Villa Hayes *430* S Paraguay
Villahermosa *370* SE Mexico
Villalcampo, Embalse de *503* reservoir of NW Spain
Villa Martín *112* SW Bolivia
Villa Nador *see* Nador
Villa Nueva *71* W Argentina
Villanueva *260* NW Honduras
Villa Rosario *171* NE Colombia
Villarrica *430* SE Paraguay
Villa Sandino *404* S Nicaragua
Villa Sanjurjo *see* Al Hoceima
Villavicencio *171* C Colombia
Villazón *112* S Bolivia
Villmanstrand *see* Lappeenranta
Vilnius *344 Pol.* Wilno, *Ger.* Wilna, *prev. Rus.* Vilna. ❖ of Lithuania, SE Lithuania
Vilvoorde *99 Fr.* Vilvorde. C Belgium
Vilyeyka *104* NW Belorussia
Vina *144* river of Cameroon and Chad
Viña del Mar *159* C Chile
Vincent *628* headland of N Norfolk Island
Vinces *200* C Ecuador
Vindeby *190* S Denmark
Vindhya Range *270 var.* Vindhya Mountains. Mountains of C India
Vinh *595* NE Vietnam
Vinh Loi *see* Bac Liêu
Vinh Long *595* S Vietnam
Vinica *349* NE FYR Macedonia
Vinkovci *181 Ger.* Winkowitz, *Hung.* Vinkovce. NE Croatia
Vinnitsa *see* Vinnytsya
Vinnytsya *558 Rus.* Vinnitsa. W Ukraine
Viranşehir *549* SE Turkey
Virgin Gorda *621* island of E British Virgin Islands
Virginia *495* Orange Free State, C South Africa
Virginia *571* state of E USA
Virgin Islands (US) *631* Unincorporated territory of the USA, Caribbean Sea. ❖ Charlotte Amalie.
Virgin Passage *629, 631* passage of the Caribbean Sea, between Puerto Rico and the Virgin Islands (US)
Virôchey *141* NE Cambodia
Virovitica *181 Ger.* Virovititz, *prev.* Werowitz, *Hung.* Verőcze. NE Croatia
Virtsu *212 Ger.* Werder. W Estonia
Vis *181 It.* Lissa. Island of S Croatia
Vis *see* Fhir
Visākhapatnam *270* SE India
Visale *490* NW Guadalcanal, Solomon Is

Visayan Sea *437* sea of the Pacific Ocean
Visby *515 Ger.* Wisby. SE Sweden
Viscount Melville Sound *146 prev.* Melville Sound. Area of the Arctic Ocean between Melville Island and Victoria Island, N Canada
Viseu *444 prev.* Vizeu. N Portugal
Vistula *see* Wisła
Vistula Lagoon *441 Pol.* Zalew Wiślany, *Rus.* Vislinskiy Zaliv, *Ger.* Frisches Haff. Lagoon of N Poland.
Viterbo *295* C Italy
Vitiaz Strait *428* strait connecting the Bismarck Sea and Solomon Sea
Vitim *455* river of C Russia
Vitória *121* SE Brazil
Vitoria *503 Cast.* Gasteiz, N Spain
Vitória da Conquista *121* E Brazil
Vitsyebsk *104 Rus.* Vitebsk. NE Belorussia
Vittoria *295* Sicilia, S Italy
Vittoriosa *363 Malt.* Birgu. E Malta
Vitu Levu *218* island of W Fiji
Vivis *see* Vevey
Viwa *218* island to the W of Yasawa Group, NW Fiji
Vizcaya, Golfo de *see* Biscay, Bay of
Vjosës *57 var.* Vijosë. River of Albania and Greece
Vlaanderen *see* Flanders
Vlaardingen *397* SW Netherlands
Vladikavkaz *454 prev.* Ordzhonikidze, *prev.* Dzaudzhikau. SW Russia
Vladimir *454* W Russia
Vladimirovka *see* Yuzhno-Sakhalinsk
Vladivostok *455* SE Russia
Vlasenica *116* E Bosnia & Herzegovina
Vlieland *397* island of Waddeneilanden, N Netherlands
Vlissingen *397 Fr.* Flessingue, *Eng.* Flushing. SW Netherlands
Vlorë *57 prev.* Vlonë, *It.* Valona. SW Albania
Vlorës, Gjiri i *57 var.* Bay of Valona. Bay of the Adriatic Sea, SW Albania
Vltava *188 Ger.* Moldau. River of W Czech Republic
Vogan *539* S Togo
Vogelkop *see* Doberai, Jazirah
Vogel Peak *see* Dimlang
Võhandu *212 var.* Võhandu Jõgi. River of SE Estonia
Voi *316* S Kenya
Voinjama *336* N Liberia
Vojvodina *604 Ger.* Wojwodina. Region of N Serbia, Yugoslavia
Volga *454* river of W Russia
Volgograd *454 prev.* Stalingrad, *prev.* Tsaritsyn. SW Russia
Volkovysk *see* Vawkavysk
Volksrust *495* Eastern Transvaal, E South Africa
Vologda *454* W Russia
Vólos *245* E Greece
Volta *242* river of SE Ghana
Volta, Lake *242* reservoir of SE Ghana
Volta Redonda *121* S Brazil
Volta Rouge *see* Red Volta
Volturno *295* river of C Italy
Vopnafjördhur *268* E Iceland
Vorder Grauspitz *342* mountain of Liechtenstein and Switzerland
Vorderrhein *518* river of SE Switzerland
Vordingborg *190* Sjælland, SE Denmark
Vor eioi Sporades *245 prev.* Vórioi Sporádhes, *Eng.* Northern Sporades. Island group of E Greece
Vorkuta *454* NW Russia
Vormsi *212 Ger.* Worms, *Swed.* Ormsö. Island of W Estonia
Voronezh *454* SW Russia
Voroshilov *see* Ussuriysk
Voroshilovgrad *see* Luhans'k
Voroshilovsk *see* Alchevs'k
Voroshilovsk *see* Stavropol'
Vorotan *74* river of Armenia and Azerbaijan

W

Willis 248 SW Grenada island, Grenada
Wilmington 571 Delaware, E USA
Wilna see Vilnius
Wilno see Vilnius
Wiltz 346 NW Luxembourg
Winam Gulf 316 var. Kavirondo Gulf. Gulf of Lake Victoria to the SW of Kenya
Winchester 565 S England, UK
Windau see Ventspils
Windhoek 391 Ger. Windhuk. ❖ of Namibia, C Namibia
Windsor 147 S Canada
Windward 248 N Carriacou, Grenada
Windward Passage 182, 258 channel connecting the Atlantic Ocean and the Caribbean Sea between Cuba and Haiti
Windward Point 620 headland on the NE coast of Anguilla
Winisk 147 C Canada
Winkowitz see Vinkovci
Winneba 242 SE Ghana
Winnipeg 146 S Canada
Winnipeg, Lake 146 lake of S Canada
Winnipegosis, Lake 146 lake of S Canada
Winston-Salem 571 North Carolina, SE USA
Winterthur 518 NE Switzerland
Winton 77 E Australia
Wisby see Visby
Wisconsin 571 state of NC USA
Wisła 441 Ger. Weichsel, Eng. Vistula. River of C Poland
Wiślany, Zalew see Vistula Lagoon
Wismar 236 N Germany
Witbank 495 Eastern Transvaal, NE South Africa
Witten 236 W Germany
Witti, Banjaran 354 var. Witti Range. Mountain range of NE Borneo, Malaysia
W.J. van Blommesteinmeer 510 reservoir of NE Suriname
Włocławek 441 C Poland
Wodzisław Śląski 441 Ger. Loslau. S Poland
Woja District 364 district of Majuro, SE Marshall Islands
Wojwodina see Vojvodina
Woleai 374 atoll of C Micronesia
Woleu see Uolo, Río
Wolfgangsee 82 var. St. Wolfgangsee, Abersee. Lake of N Austria
Wolf, Isla 200 island of NW Galapagos Is, Ecuador
Wolfsberg 82 SE Austria
Wolfsburg 237 N Germany
Wołkowysk see Vawkavysk
Wöllan see Velenje
Wollaston Peninsula 146 peninsula of Victoria Island, NW Canada
Wollongong 77 SE Australia
Wolmar see Valmiera
Wolverhampton 565 C England, UK
Wong Wan Chau 262 NE Hong Kong
Wŏnju 498 Jap. Genshū. N South Korea
Wŏnsan 413 SE North Korea
Woodlands Bay 627 bay of the Caribbean Sea on the W coast of Montserrat
Woodlark Island see Murua Island
Woods, Lake of the 146 Fr. Lac des Bois. Lake of Canada and USA
Woody Island 629 island of Amphitrite Group, N Paracel Islands
Worcester 495 Western Cape, SW South Africa
Worcester 565 C England, UK
Worcester 571 Massachusetts, NE USA
Worms see Vormsi
Worthing 97 SW Barbados
Wotho 364 island of W Marshall Islands
Wotje 364 island of E Marshall Islands
Wrangel Island see Vrangelya, Ostrov
Wrexham 565 N Wales, UK
Wrocław 441 Ger. Breslau. SW Poland
Wu-chou see Wuzhou
Wuday 'ah 474 S Saudi Arabia
Wuhan 163 prev. Hankow, var. Han-k'ou, Hanyang, Wuchang. Hubei, C China

Wu-hsi see Wuxi
Wuhsien see Suzhou
Wuhu 163 var. Wu-na-mu. Anhui, E China
Wukari 408 E Nigeria
Wu-lu-mu-ch'i see Ürümqi
Wum 144 W Cameroon
Wu-na-mu see Wuhu
Wuppertal 236 W Germany
Würzburg 237 SW Germany
Wusih see Wuxi
Wuxi 163 var. Wu-hsi, Wusih. Jiangsu, E China
Wuzhou 163 var. Wu-chou, Wuchow. Guangxi, S China
Wye 565 Wel. Gwy. River of England and Wales, UK
Wyndham 77 N Australia
Wyoming 570-571 state of NW USA
Wysg see Usk

X

Xaçmaz 86 Rus. Khachmas, var. Hačmas. N Azerbaijan
Xaghra 363 Gozo, Malta
Xai-Xai 387 prev. Vila de João Belo, var. João Belo S Mozambique
Xam Nua 327 var. Sam Neua. NE Laos
Xankändi 86 Rus. Khankendy, prev. Stepanakert. SW Azerbaijan
Xánthi 245 var. Eskije, Turk. Iskeçe. NE Greece
Xauen see Chaouèn
Xäzär Dänizi see Caspian Sea
Xi'an 163 var. Hsi-an Sian. Shaanxi, C China
Xiangkhoang 327 var. Xieng Khouang. E Laos
Xiangkhoang, Plateau de 327 var. Plain of Jars. Plateau of C Laos
Xiang Ngeun 327 C Laos
Xiangtan 163 var. Hsiang-t'an, Siangtan. Hunan, S China
Xiao Hinggan Ling 163 Eng. Lesser Khingan Range. Mountain range of NE China
Xieng Khouang see Xiangkhoang
Xi Jiang 163 var. Hsi Chiang. Eng. West River. River of S China
Xilinhot 163 var. Silinhot. Nei Mongol Zizhiqu, N China
Xingkai Hu see Khanka, Lake
Xingu 121 river of C Brazil
Xining 163 var. Sining, Hsi-ning. Qinghai province, W China
Xinjiang Uygur Zizhiqu 162 Eng. Sinkiang Uighur Autonomous Region. Autonomous region of NW China
Xinpu see Liangyungang
Xinyang 163 var. Hsin-yang, Sinyang. Henan, C China
Xitole 254 SE Guinea-Bissau
Xizang Zizhiqu 162 Eng. Tibetan Autonomous Region. Autonomous region of W China
Xolotlán see Managua, Lago de
Xuddur 492 It. Oddur. SW Somalia
Xulla Islands see Sula, Kepulauan
Xuzhou 163 var. Hsu-chou, Suchow, prev. T'ung-shan. Jiangsu, E China
Xylophaghou 187 var. Xylofagou. SE Cyprus

Y

Yabassi 144 W Cameroon
Yabêlo 215 S Ethiopia
Yablonovyy Khrebet 455 mountain range of C Russia
Yabucoa 629 SE Puerto Rico
Yacata 218 island of the Lau Group, E Fiji
Yacuiba 112 S Bolivia
Yadua 218 prev. Yandua. Island to the W of Vanua Levu, NW Fiji
Yafran 371 NW Libya
Yagasa Cluster 218 islands of the Lau Group, E Fiji

Yagoua 144 NE Cameroon
Yaguarón 379 var. Jaguarão. River of Brazil and Uruguay
Yakhegnadzor see Yeghegnadzor
Yako 133 W Burkina
Yakutiya, Respublika see Sakha, Respublika
Yakutsk 455 E Russia
Yala 335 S Thailand
Yalala, Chute 609 waterfall of W Zaire
Yalinga 155 C Central African Republic
Yalova 548 NW Turkey
Yalpug see Ialpug
Yalpuh, Ozero 558 Rus. Ozero Yalpug. Lake of SW Ukraine
Yalta 558 S Ukraine
Yalu 413 var. Yalü, Amnok, Jap. Oryokko. River of China and North Korea
Yamagata 304 Honshū, N Japan
Yamaguchi 304 Honshū, W Japan
Yamal, Poluostrov 454 Peninsula of N Russia
Yaman, Ra's al see Ḥadd al Jamal
Yambio 508 var. Yambiyo. S Sudan
Yambol 128 var. Jambol, Turk. Yanboli. E Bulgaria
Yamdena, Pulau 276 prev. Jamdena. Island of Kepulauan Tanimbar, Indonesia
Yamethin 135 C Burma
Yam HaMelaḥ see Dead Sea
Yamoussoukro 300 ❖ of Ivory Coast, C Ivory Coast
Yamuna 270 prev. Jumna. River of N India
Yamundá see Nhamundá
Yanboli see Yambol
Yanbu' al Baḥr 474 W Saudi Arabia
Yandé, Île 628 island of Îles Belep, N New Caledonia
Yandua see Yadua
Yangambi 609 N Zaire
Yangdŏk 413 S North Korea
Yanggeta see Yaqeta
Yangiyer 582 E Uzbekistan
Yangiyūl 582 var. Jangijul. E Uzbekistan
Yangku see Taiyuan
Yangmei 527 N Taiwan
Yangon see Rangoon
Yangtze Kiang see Chang Jiang
Yannina see Ioánnina
Yan Oya 506 river of N Sri Lanka
Yantai 163 var. Yan-t'ai, prev. Chih-fu, var. Chefoo. Shandong, E China
Yantra 128 var. Jantra. N Bulgaria
Yaoundé 144 var. Yaunde. ❖ of Cameroon, S Cameroon
Yap 374 island of W Micronesia
Yapanskoye More see Japan, Sea of
Yapen, Pulau 277 island to the N of Irian Jaya, E Indonesia
Yapurá see Japurá
Yaqaga 218 island to the W of Vanua Levu, N Fiji
Yaqeta 218 prev. Yanggeta. Island of the Yasawa Group, NW Fiji
Yaque del Norte 198 river of NW Dominican Republic
Yaque del Sur 198 river of SW Dominican Republic
Yaqui 370 river of NW Mexico
Yarīm 601 W Yemen
Yarlung Zangbo Jiang see Brahmaputra
Yarmouth 147 SE Canada
Yaroslavl' 454 W Russia
Yarumal 171 NW Colombia
Yasawa 218 island of the Yasawa Group, NW Fiji
Yasawa Group 218 island group of NW Fiji
Yasyel'da 104 river of SW Belorussia
Yaté 628 S New Caledonia
Yatsushiro 304 Kyūshū, SW Japan
Yatta Plateau 316 plateau of SE Kenya
Yauco 629 SW Puerto Rico
Yaunde see Yaoundé
Yavan see Javan
Yavarí see Javari
Yaviza 426 SE Panama

Yawatahama 304 Shikoku, SW Japan
Yazd 281 var. Yezd. C Iran
Ybbs 82 river of C Austria
Yding Skovhoj 190 hill of Jylland, C Denmark
Ye 135 SE Burma
Yedintsy see Edineţ
Yedseram 409 river of E Nigeria
Yeghegnadzor 74 Rus. Yakhegnadzor, var. Jehegnadzor. SE Armenia
Yégué 539 W Togo
Yekaterinburg 454 prev. Sverdlovsk. C Russia
Yekaterinodar see Krasnodar
Yekepa 336 NE Liberia
Yele 482 C Sierra Leone
Yelisavetpol see Gäncä
Yelizavetgrad see Kirovohrad
Yellow Hole 627 bay of the Caribbean Sea on the NE coast of Montserrat
Yellowknife 146 W Canada
Yellow River see Huang He
Yellow Sea 164 Kor. Hwang-Hae, Chin. Huang Hai. Sea of the Pacific Ocean between China and Korea
Yellowstone 570-571 river of NW USA
Yèloteu 553 prev. Iolotan, Turkm. Yoloten. SE Turkmenistan
Yel'sk 104 SE Belorussia
Yelwa 408 E Nigeria
Yelwa 408 W Nigeria
Yemen 600-603 officially Republic of Yemen, Ar. Al Yaman, Al Jumhuriyah al Yamaniyah, prev. divided into South Yemen and Yemen Arab Republic (North Yemen) prev. Federation of South Arabia, Aden Protectorate. Country dividednto 17 admin. units (governorates). ❖ Sana
Yenakiyeve 558 Rus. Yenakiyevo, prev. Ordzhonikidze, Rykovo. E Ukraine
Yenangyaung 135 W Burma
Yên Bai 595 NW Vietnam
Yendi 242 NE Ghana
Yeniboğaziçi 187 var. Ayios Seryios. E Cyprus
Yenierenköy 187 var. Agigialousa, Yialousa. NE Cyprus
Yenisey 455 river of C Russia
Yenshui 527 W Taiwan
Yeovil 565 S England, UK
Yerevan 74 var. Erevan, Jerevan, Eng. Erivan. ❖ of Armenia, C Armenia
Yeriho see Jericho
Yermak 312 Kaz. Ermak. NE Kazakhstan
Yermasoyia 187 var. Pentaschoinos. River of S Cyprus
Yerushalayim see Jerusalem
Yeu, Île d' 224 island of W France
Yevlax 86 Rus. Yevlakh, var. Jevlah. C Azerbaijan
Yevpatoriya 558 S Ukraine
Yerreyskiya 455 Eng. Jewish Autonomous Oblast. Autonomous region of SE Russia
Yezd see Yazd
Ygatimí 430 var. Igatimí. E Paraguay
Yí 579 river of C Uruguay
Yialias 187 var. Yalyas, Çakilli Dere. River of C Cyprus
Yialousa see Yenierenköy
Yigo 625 NE Guam
Yinchuan 163 var. Yinchwan. Ningxia, C China
Yining 162 var. I-ning, Uigh. Gulja, var. Kuldja. Xinjiang Uygur Zizhiqu, NW China
Yirga 'Alem 215 It. Irgalem. S Ethiopia
Yisra'el see Israel
Yoboki 194 C Djibouti
Yof 478 W Senegal
Yogyakarta 276 prev. Jogjakarta. Java, C Indonesia
Yojoa, Lago de 260 lake of W Honduras
Yokkaichi 304 Honshū, C Japan
Yokohama 304 Honshū, SE Japan
Yokosuka 304 Honshū, SE Japan
Yola 409 E Nigeria

Acknowledgments

DORLING KINDERSLEY would like to express their thanks to the following individuals, companies and institutions for their help in preparing this atlas:

ADDITIONAL CARTOGRAPHY

Advanced Illustration (Congleton, UK)
Andrew Bright
Cosmographics (Watford, UK)
Malcolm Porter
Swanston Publishing (Derby, UK)
Andrew Thompson

DESIGN

Boyd Annison, Icon Solutions (Chesham, UK) *for Macintosh consultancy and chart templates*
Bruno Maag, Dalton Maag (London, UK) *for font consultancy and production*

RESEARCH AND REFERENCE

Dr D Alkhateeb, Organization of Petroleum Exporting Countries (OPEC, Vienna, Austria)
Amnesty International (London, UK)
Caroline Blunden
CNN International (New York, USA)
Dataquest Europe SA (Paris, France)
CSL Davies
Department of Trade and Industry Export Market Information Centre (London, UK)
The Flag Institute (Chester, UK)
Foreign and Commonwealth Office (London, UK)
Alexander Fyges-Walker
Christel Heideloff, Institute of Shipping Economics and Logistics (Bremen, Germany)
International Bank for Reconstruction and Development (World Bank, Washington, DC, USA)
International Committee of the Red Cross (ICRC, Geneva, Switzerland)
International Civil Aviation Organization (ICAO, Montreal, Canada)
International Criminal Police Organization (INTERPOL, Lyon, France)

International Institute for Strategic Studies, for information from *The Military Balance* (London, UK)
International Boundaries Research Unit, University of Durham
Institute of Latin American Studies, University of London (London, UK)
Intermediate Technology Development Group (Rugby, UK)
Chris Joseph, United States Travel and Tourism Administration (USTTA, London, UK)
Latin American Bureau (London, UK)
Patrick Mahaffey, Ohio European Office (Brussels, Belgium)
Peter Mansfield
Robert Minton-Taylor
National Meteorological Library and Archive (Bracknell, UK)
Oil and Gas Journal (Houston, Texas)
Organization for Economic Cooperation and Development (OECD, Paris, France)
Penal Reform International (London, UK)
Matt Ridley
Screen Digest (London, UK)
William Smith, Chicago Sun-Times (Chicago, USA)
Tourism Concern (London, UK)
United Nations Crime Prevention and Criminal Justice Branch (UNCPC, Vienna, Austria)
United Nations Development Program (UNDP, New York, USA)
United Nations Environment Program (UNEP, Nairobi, Kenya)
United Nations Food and Agriculture Organization (UNFAO, Rome, Italy)
United Nations International Labor Organization (UNILO, Geneva, Switzerland)
United Nations Population Fund (UNFPA, New York, USA)
Westminster Reference Library (London, UK)
World Conservation Monitoring Centre (Cambridge, UK)
World Health Organization (WHO, Geneva, Switzerland)
World Tourism Organization (Madrid, Spain)

The many embassies, High Commissions, airports, national information and tourist offices in London and around the world.

PICTURE CREDITS

t=top, b=below, a=above, l=left, r=right, c=centre

Adams Picture Library: 484bl. **Ancient Art & Architecture Collection:** 58bcr, 59cra, 59bl, 41tc, 45br; G. Tortoli 59tr. **G. Andrews:** 428ca. **Aspect Picture Library Ltd:** D. Bayes 538bl; K. Naylor 608tr; F. Nichols 276tr; B. Seed 586ca. **Associated Press:** 215bcr, Peterson 409bcr; 590tr, 605bcl. **Belgian Embassy:** 99bcr. **Bridgeman Art Library:** (artist: J-M Nattier) Hermitage, St. Petersburg 40bcr; ('Bonaparte Crossing The Alps', artist: J.L. David) Lauros-Giraudon, Chateau de Malmaison 42bcr; National Maritime Museum 41br; (artist: G. de Castro) Private Collection 42bcl. **D. Doug Bryant Stock Photos:** 431tc; B. Augustin 404tr. **Camera Press:** 615cr; H. Andrews 601bcr; L. Brook 401tcl; T. Charlier 451cbr, 579bl; F. Goodman 627cbr; A. Pucciano 71cr; S. Smith 215bcl. **J. Allan Cash Ltd.:** 49tl, 82ca, 92bc, 122br, 125tl, 144tr, 147tr, 164tr, 211tr, 261tc, 280tr, 511cra, 516bl, 551tc, 554ca, 406bc, 408tr, 421cb, 422tr, 425bc, 558bc. **Bruce Coleman Ltd.:** 468bl; M. Berge 564tr; B&C Calhoun 150bc; G. Cubitt 64tr, 214bc; P. Davey 186bc; B. Fogden 430ca; J. Fry 477tc; J. Jurka 512bc; Dr. M.P. Kahl 70tr; G. Langesbury 252bc; O. Langrand 358tr; L. Lee Rue 67tl; K. Maj 440ca; L.C. Marigo 251tc; S. Prato 244bc; F. Prenzel 80tc; K. Taylor 481tr. **Colorific!:** J. Howard 505bl; M. Rogers 508tr. **Colorific!/Black Star:** M. Kreiner 48cl; S.Tucci 155bl. **Compix:** 320tr, 335tc, 395bc; J. Leach 490ca; B. McGrath 512ca; J. Thomas 554bc. **Comstock Ltd.:** 170bc, 298tl, 507tc; T.Eigeland 369tc; G.L. Scarfiotti 448bc. **Corbis-Bettmann/Upi:** 185bcr, 409bcl. **Cuban Embassy:** 185bcl. **James Davis Travel Photography:** 62cla, 117bc, 120bl, 121tl, 127tl, 190ca, 302bc, 347tl, 358tr, 569ca, 579tl, 596bc, 400bc, 463tc, 465bl, 466bl, 470tr, 522bc, 530tr, 558tr, 600bl, 621cr, 658cbl; Prisma 198tr; S. Thingeyjar 269tc; World View/Fotothek 153tc. **Embassy of Finland:** 221tcr. **Embassy of the People's Democratic Republic of Laos:** 526bcr, 526br. **Embassy of The Socialist Republic of Vietnam:** 595tl, 595tcl. **Embassy of Peru:** 455tl. **ET Archive:** 58bcl; (artist: N.Dance) 45cr; ("Halt of Boer Family" artist: S. Daniel) 45bl; (artist: D. Gregory) 45tcl. **Finnish Tourist Board:** 220bc. **Mary Evans Picture Library:** 41cra, 41bcl. **Chris Fairclough Colour Library:** 45cr, 543tl, 544br. J. Guest: 140ca, 594bc. **Robert Harding Picture Library:** 156ca, 197tl, 245tc, 252bl, 265tr, 284tr, 308bl, 524bc, 419tc, 424bc, 436tr, 450tr, 454tr, 481tc, 489tc, David Atchison-Jones 571tr, 577bl, 599tc; P. Craven 224tr; F. Dubes 124bl; Explorer 545tc; Explorer/Roy 86tr; R. Frerck/Odyssey 370tr; Rolf Richardson 574bl; Gascoine 582bl; R. Harding/C. Martin 241bl; G. Hellier 189tr, 486tr; D. Hughes 229bc; C. Martin 256bc; Photri 194ca; R. Rainford 565tl; C. Rennie 552ca; G. Roli 414tr; Rosehaven Management Ltd. 651cr; J. Ross 353bc; Sassoon 110cb, 254cl; A. Woolfitt 90bc. 550tr; Jim Zuckerman 573tr. **Paul Harris Photography:** 461bl. **High Commission for India:** 272cb, 272cbr, 272br. **High Commission for The People's Republic of Bangladesh:** 92cla. **Hulton Deutsch Collection:** 44br, 45br, 47br. **Hulton Getty Collections Ltd.** 277bcr, 527tl **Robert Hunt Library:** 47tc. **Hutchison Library:** 112ca, 557tc, 568bc, 614tr; R. Francis 552tr; J.G. Fuller 628br; B. Gerard 251bc; J. Henderson 256ca; A. Hill 612bc; M. Macintyre 540ca; T. Page 492ca; C. Pemberton 182tr; Penn 657tl; L. Taylor 454bl. **The Image Bank:** M. Beebe 181cl; G. Jung 548tr; T. Madison 459tr; M.E. Newman 296tr; C.M. Pasdzior 564br; A. Rippy 162tr; G.A. Rossi 624bl; H. Sund 457tr; P. Trummer 202tr. **Images Colour Library:** 396bl. **Impact Photos Ltd:** P. Cavendish 457c; B. Edwards 420tr, 422tr; A. le Garsmeur 380ca, 651cra; R. Lubbock 206tr; G-J. Norman 522tr; C. Penn 556tr. **David King Collection:** 49cra. **Magnum Photos Ltd.:** H. Cartier-Bresson 47cra; H. Gruyaert 641tr; J. Hillelson Agency 651tc; C. Steele-Perkins 643cbl. **Mexican Embassy:** 371bc, 371bcr. **NASA:** 49br. **Network:** M.

Goldwater 645tl; J. Jordan 647cr. **New Zealand High Commission:** 401tl. **Office of the Leader of the Opposition, Australia:** P. West 78cbr. **PA News:** 415c; AFP 55tr, 587bcl; AFP/M. Clement 545tr; AFP/M. Shoraf 523br. **Panos Pictures:** N. Cooper 102tr, 657cra; M. French 259tc; R. Giling 510tr; J. Hartley 152bc, 657bc; D. Hulcher 526tr; S. Sprague 112bl, 158tr; B. Tobiasson 501bc. **N. Peck:** 182bl and front cover. **Picturepoint Ltd.:** 109tc, 208tr, 472bc, 618c. **Popperfoto:** 45cra, 46br, 49bl, 205bcr; AFP/Armand 48br; EPA, AFP 54br; John Bakers/Reuters 78cr; David Gadd/Sportsphoto 105bcl; EPA 585bcr; 115cr; Official U.S. Air Force Photo 49cr, 281tcl, 296cl; E. Shore/Reuters 445bcr. **Reuters Television:** 105cbl, 122tcl, 272cb, 272bc, 475br, 559tr. **Rex Features Ltd.:** 52tr, 78b, 92cra, 155bcl, 148bc, 158tcr, 164br, 191tc, 221tr, 226cbr, 238cbr, 245tr, 265bcr, 265bcl, 296cbr, 306br, 506bc, 512bcl, 555bcl, 421tr, 425tr, 451cb, 456bcr, 457bcl, 494tr, 494tc, 499bcl, 505tr, 515tr, 556tr, 566cra, 572bl, 573tcl, 585bcr, 601bcl, 609cl, 640bl, 645tr; Action Press 129bc, 226b; M.Hoffmann 258b; Rudy de Mour 148b; Nils Jorgensen 566c; Charles Sykes 572br; Craig Johnston 575br; Albert Facelly 59bl; Filet 92cr; Thierry Charler 99bc, Larry Reider 571bl; Boccon-Gibod 453tc, Sipa-Press 53tc, 59bl, 59bcl, 99bcl, 158tr, 164bcl, 164bcr, 245tcr, 285c, 290br, 506cl, 371br, 587cbl, 397tcl, 415cr, 456br, 457bl, 475br, 555tcr, 605bcr, 623bl, 641tl, 646cbl. **Ann Ronan At Image Select:** 36bc. **Royal Danish Embassy:** 191tr. **Royal Geographical Society:** R. Mear 648cbl. **Royal Thai Embassy:** 555tr. **Science Photo Library:** J. Baum 644bl; Dr. D. Millar 650cbl; Novosti Press Agency 643tc. **Harry Smith Collection:** 40cbl. **South-American Pictures:** J. Berrange 178bcr; P. Dixon 426tr; T. Morrison 578tr. **Spanish Embassy:** 503tcr. **Sovfoto/Eastfoto:** 651clb. **Frank Spooner Pictures:** 47cbl, Chip Hires 517tcr; 579bcl; Amin-Camera Pix 517tr; L. Anticoli 296cbl; Arnaud 129bc; W. Christopher 572bcr; A. Denize 359tr; 281tcr; K.J. Eddy 85cbl; C. Hires 523bcr, 641bcl; P. Perrin 285cr; C. Poulet 625cr; Reglain 141tr; N. Sagansky 609cr; A. Sassaki 122tr, 122cra; Versele-Deville 228bc. **Frank Spooner Pictures/Gamma:** 85cbr, 506b; K. Al Arab 545tc; C. Angel 171tcr, 590tr, 592tr; F. Apesteguy 475cb; J.C. Aunos 290bcr; V. Brynner 421tcr, 423tcr; L. Chaperon 238cbl; R. Gaillarde 445bcl; B. Iverson 205bcl; Iliona-Figaro Magazine 89tc; N. Jallot 376tr; Jasmin 647tc; E. de Keerle 441tcr; Loviny 141tcr; A. Movan 277bcl; Najer 555bcr; Chip Hires 517tcr; Naoto Hosaka 506cr; A. McInnis 148cr; Raphael Woolman 71cr; P. Piel 238bcr; E. Vandeville 171tr; C.H. Vioujard 583bcl; Xinhua 164bl. **Frank Spooner Pictures/Liaison:** Anderson 499bcr; T. Arthur 57br; B. Asoto 437cr; Ferry 452tcl; Halstead 115c; Markel, 615c; B. Stern 213tr. **Tony Stone Images:** 155bc, 174tr, 414br, 500bl; G. Allison 577bl; D. Armand 148tr; O. Benn 69tc, 249tr; K. Biggs 642cbl; M. Brooke 154tr; J. Callahan 262ca; A. Cassidy 274br; P. Chesley 374ca; J. Cornish 289bc; S. Egan 502tr, 518tr; R. Evans 128tr; R. Everts 583tr; D. Hanson 554bl; A. Kearney 158bc, H. Kurihara 240br; G. Pease 639tc; J. Pragen 588tr; F. Prenzel 586bc; S. Rothfeld 361tc; D. Schultz 44bl; A. Smith 330ca; R. Smith 78tr; 201tl; D. Stone 516tr; P. Tweedie 552bc; C. Waite 564bc. **Swiss Embassy:** 519l, 519tr. **Sygma:** Baldev 412tc; R. Reuter 470bl. **Taipei Representative's Office in the UK:** 527tcr. **TASS:** Itar 512bcr. **Telegraph Colour Library:** 76tr; Ford Motor Co. Ltd. 46bcl. **J. Tempest:** 219tc, 565cb. **Topham:** A. Azakir 359tr. **Travel Photo International:** Fotoworld 362bl. Trip: 474bl; M. Barlow 259br, 244tl; T. Goodman 255tc; V. Shuba 104ca; V. Sidoropolev 512tr; G. Spenceley 348tr. **Viva:** M. Franck 74tr. **S. Wheat:** 649cra. **P. Woods:** 271tl, 273br. **World Pictures:** 55ca, 294br, 404ca, 526tr, 635tl. **Zefa:** 56bc, 96bl, 176ca, 494bl, 542bc, 592bl, 649cbl; Damm 639cr; Everts 604ca; F. Lanting 118tr; H. Lutticke 493tc; Smith 626bl; Streichan 238bl, 241c; Sunak 590bl.

JULESBURG HIGH SCHOOL

KEY TO SYMBOLS, ICONS & ABBREVIATIONS

A LL SYMBOLS AND ICONS used in the Atlas are illustrated and defined here. A fuller explanation can be found on pages 9, 10, and 11. Other detailed references include: the list of International Organizations (pages 654–657), the Glossary of Geographical Terms (pages 658–659) and the Glossary of Abbreviations used in the Atlas (page 660).

Abbreviations most regularly used throughout the Atlas are listed below.

bbl	billion barrels
b/cd	barrels per calendar day
b/d	barrels per day
bn	billion (one thousand million)
°C	degrees Celsius (Centigrade)
cm	centimeters

SWITCHES

yellow infill = conditions apply;
grey infill = conditions do not apply

 Date of independence or date current borders established

 Multiparty democracy

 Convertible currency

 Net aid recipient

 Net aid donor

 No significant aid donations or receipts

 Net energy importer

 Net energy exporter

 Compulsory military service

Death penalty currently in use

Unemployment benefits only

Health benefits only

Unemployment and health benefits

TRANSPORTATION

 Main international airport

 Merchant fleet, total tonnage

 Extent of national paved road network (miles/kilometers)

 Extent of expressways or major national highways (miles/kilometers)

 Extent of commercial railroad network (miles/kilometers)

 Extent of inland waterways navigable by commercial craft (miles/kilometers)

TOURISM

 Total number of visitors per year

 Trend indicators: increase/no variation/decrease in tourism over previous year

PEOPLE

 Main languages spoken (including official language)

 Population density (per sq mile)

POLITICS

 Dates of last and next legislative elections

Head of state

WORLD AFFAIRS

 Membership of international organizations

 Nonmembership of the UN

 Nonmembership of additional international organizations

AID

 Total aid given or received in US$

 Trend indicators: increase/no variation/decrease in aid over previous year

DEFENSE

 Annual defense budget in US$

 Trend indicators: increase/no variation/decrease in defense spending over previous year

 Army: equipment and personnel

 Navy: equipment and personnel

 Air force: equipment and personnel

Nuclear capability: armaments

ECONOMICS

Exchange rates against the US$ over the last year

Gross National Product (GNP) in US$